The Penguin Encyclopedia of

PLACES

John Paxton

THIRD EDITION

PENGUIN BOOKS

PENGUIN BOOKS

Published by the Penguin Group
Penguin Books Ltd, 27 Wrights Lane, London W8 5TZ, England
Penguin Putnam Inc., 375 Hudson Street, New York, New York 10014, USA
Penguin Books Australia Ltd, Ringwood, Victoria, Australia
Penguin Books Canada Ltd, 10 Alcorn Avenue, Toronto, Ontario, Canada M4V 3B2
Penguin Books (NZ) Ltd, Private Bag 102902, NSMC, Auckland, New Zealand

Penguin Books Ltd, Registered Offices: Harmondsworth, Middlesex, England

First published 1971
Second edition 1978
Third edition 1999
10 9 8 7 6 5 4 3 2 1

Set in 8/9 pt Monotype Bembo
Typeset by Rowland Phototypesetting Ltd,
Bury St Edmunds, Suffolk
Printed in England by Clays Ltd, St Ives plc

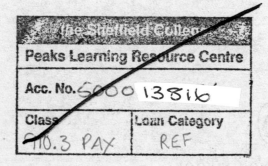

Joan

who has put up with cottages full of paper
throughout our long married life

FOREWORD

It is now over twenty-seven years since the late W. G. Moore compiled the first edition of *The Penguin Encyclopedia of Places* and in that period dramatic changes have taken place in the world. Eastern Europe has completely changed the map with the collapse of the USSR, local authorities have changed dramatically in England, Scotland and Wales, heavy industries have declined and high technology and the service industry have replaced them.

When I agreed to undertake the revision I felt that it would be necessary to completely rethink the structure of the encyclopedia but a year into the project convinced me that Mr Moore's plan had stood the test of time and that I would keep to his ideas. Naturally to reflect the great economic, political and social changes a gigantic revision was necessary and I have given a slightly different emphasis in the articles of sovereign states. I've not attempted to mention *every* place in the world but have taken into consideration such factors as population, history, economic activity.

Place names arouse controversy and I have continued with the method adopted in the first edition by giving the version considered to be most familiar to English-speaking readers: e.g. Florence (not Firenze).

Many institutions have given me tremendous help and these include the London Library, the Royal Geographical Society, Welsh Office, Scottish Office, Department of Trade and Industry, Coal Authority's Licensing Department, most High Commissions and Embassies in London and Local Authorities in England, Scotland and Wales. I must also thank the following for considerable help with the revision: Chris Cook, Dione Daffin, Brian Hunter, Len Jones, Ben Ledger, S. Mukherjee, Heather Reilly and Penny White, who typed and typed and typed.

The encyclopedia will be revised from time to time and the editor will be pleased to receive constructive and informed criticism for future editions.

J. P.
Bruton, Somerset
September 1998

ABBREVIATIONS

Ar.	Arabic	m	metre(s)
b.	born	Mt	Mount
BC	British Columbia	N	North
C	degrees Centigrade	NA	National Area
c.	circa	NE	North-East
cap.	capital	NNE	North-North-East
cent.	century, centuries	NNW	North-North-West
cm	centimetres	NW	North-West
Co.	County	pop.	population
d.	died	R.	River
DC	District of Columbia	rel.	religion(s)
E	East	S	South
e.g.	for example	SE	South-East
ENE	East-North-East	Sp.	Spanish
Eng.	English	sq km	square kilometres
ESE	East-South-East	sq. miles	square miles
esp.	especially	SSE	South-South-East
est.	estimated	SSW	South-South-West
F	degrees Fahrenheit	St	Saint, Street
Fr.	French	stat.	statistical
ft	feet	SW	South-West
Ger.	German	UK	United Kingdom
gm	gramme(s)	UN	United Nations
Gr.	Greek	US	United States
ha	hectare(s)	USA	United States of America
inc.	include(s), including		
ins.	inches	USSR	Union of Soviet Socialist Republics
Is.	Island(s)		
kgm	kilogramme(s)	W	West
km	kilometre(s)	WNW	West-North-West
l.	litre(s)	WWI	World War I
L.	Lake	WWII	World War II
lang.	language(s)	WSW	West-South-West
lat.	latitude	➤	See
long.	longitude	➤➤	See also

A

Aabenraa Denmark. Port on the Aabenraa Fiord (Jutland) 80 km (50 miles) SE of Esbjerg. Pop. (1990) 21,500. Industries inc. fishing and brewing. Part of Germany 1864–1920.

Aachen (Fr. **Aix-la-Chapelle**) Germany. Ancient Aquis Granum. Town in North Rhine-Westphalia 64 km (40 miles) WSW of Cologne, near the Belgian and Dutch borders. Pop. (1990) 243,200.

Industrial town in a coalmining district. Manufactures textiles, glass, chemicals and needles. Important railway centre. Famous for its thermal springs for many centuries.

Has a 14th-cent. Rathaus; the cathedral (begun 796, rebuilt 983) contains the tomb of Charlemagne, who made it his N cap. The Holy Roman Emperors were crowned here 813–1531. Annexed by France 1801; ceded to Prussia 1815. During World War II it was severely damaged by air raids and was the first important German city to fall to the Allies (1944).

Aalborg Denmark. Port on the S side of Lim Fiord (N Jutland) 103 km (64 miles) NNW of Aarhus. Pop. (1991) 155,664.

Industries inc. shipbuilding, cement and textiles. Linked with Nörresundby by a bridge across the fiord.

Aalen Germany. Town in Baden-Württemberg 48 km (30 miles) NNE of Ulm. Pop. (1986) 62,800.

Manufactures textiles and iron.

Aalst ▸ALOST.

Aar (Aare) River Switzerland. The largest river entirely within Switzerland, 290 km (180 miles) long, rising in the Aar glaciers, flowing N past Meiringen (the Aar Gorge), W through L. Brienz, past Interlaken and through L. Thun, then NW past Thun and Berne, entering L. Biel as the Hagneck Canal and leaving it as the Aar Canal, then flowing generally NE past Solothurn, Olten and Aarau and joining the Rhine opposite Waldshut (Germany). Navigable from the Rhine confluence as far as Thun.

Aarau Switzerland. Cap. of the Aargau canton on the Aar R. at the foot of the Jura mountains 39 km (24 miles) SE of Basel. Pop. (1990) 15,900.

Manufactures scientific instruments, textiles and bells.

Cap. of the Helvetic Republic 1798–1803.

Aare River ▸AAR RIVER.

Aargau Switzerland. Canton in the N. Area 1405 sq km (542 sq. miles). Pop. (1992) 496,300 (German-speaking, mainly Protestant). Cap. Aarau. Bounded by the Rhine (N), crossed by the Aar and its tributary the Reuss. Fertile valleys, with cultivation of cereals and fruits. Sulphur springs at Baden and Schinznach and saline springs at Rheinfelden.

Manufactures textiles and metal goods. Chief towns Aarau and Brugg.

The region was the headquarters of the Habsburgs, who lost it to the Swiss Confederates 1415. A dependency of Berne till 1798, it became a separate canton in 1803.

Aarhus Denmark. Second largest city on the E coast of Jutland. Pop. (1991) 264,136.

Seaport. Railway junction. Commercial centre. Oil-refining, iron-founding and brewing.

Aba Nigeria. Town in the SE in Imo state situated 53 km (33 miles) NE of Port Harcourt on the railway to Kaduna. Pop. (1992) 270,500.

Commercial centre. Trade in palm oil and kernels.

Abaco Bahamas. The most northerly of the Bahamian islands consisting of Great Abaco (S), Little Abaco (NW) and many cays. Area 1681 sq km (649 sq. miles). Pop. (1990) 10,061. They are coral limestone and fishing and citrus fruit are the main occupations. A large citrus-processing plant has been recently constructed.

Abadan Iran. Port in Khuzistán (SW) on an island in the Shatt-al-Arab 53 km (33 miles) from the head of the Gulf. Pop. (1985) 294,000.

Major oil-refining and exporting centre; supplied by pipelines from the Khuzistán oilfields.

Abadla ➤BÉCHAR; SAHARA.

Abakan Russia. Cap. of the Khakass Republic, Krasnoyarsk Territory, just N of the confluence of the Abakan and the Yenisei rivers. Pop. (1991) 154,000.

Industrial centre. Sawmilling and metalworking.

Founded 1707.

Abbai River ➤TANA, LAKE.

Abbasia ➤OPATIJA.

Abbeville France. Town in the Somme department on the banks of the Somme 40 km (25 miles) NW of Amiens. Pop. (1990) 24,590.

Manufactures beer, biscuits, sugar and carpets.

Abbotsford Scotland. Home (1812–32) of Sir Walter Scott on the S bank of the Tweed 5 km (3 miles) W of Melrose in Scottish Borders.

Abbots Langley England. Town in SW Hertfordshire 5 km (3 miles) N of Watford. Pop. (1971) 4245. Birthplace of Nicholas Breakspear (Pope Adrian IV, 1080–1159).

Abeokuta Nigeria. Town in the SW on the Ogun R. 77 km (48 miles) N of Lagos on the railway to Kano. Pop. (1992) 386,800. Surrounded by a mud wall. In a fertile valley;

agricultural products yams, palm oil and kernels, cacao, timber.

Main industries cotton-weaving and dyeing.

Founded c. 1830.

Aberavon ➤PORT TALBOT.

Aberconway ➤CONWY.

Aberdare Wales. Town in Rhondda, Cynon, Taff on the R. Cynon 6 km (4 miles) SW of Merthyr Tydfil. Pop. (1991) 29,040.

It was one of the last coalmining areas in Wales, now closed. Industries inc. brewing and the manufacture of cables, radio and television sets.

Aberdare Mountains ➤KENYA; TANA RIVER.

Aberdeen Scotland. City on the bay between the mouths of the Don and the Dee on the E coast. Pop. (1991) 201,099. Aberdeen City created a new Unitary Authority in 1996. The harbour has been continually improved since the completion of the Victoria Dock (1848). There is a ferry service to Bergen.

Important fishing port. Manufactures knitwear, hosiery, paper. Shipbuilding. Known as the 'Granite City' as many of its buildings are constructed of this local stone; granite dressing is an industry. Development of North Sea oil production centred on Aberdeen led to considerable economic activity in the 1970s and 1980s.

An important town as early as the 12th cent.; chartered a royal burgh by William the Lion (1179). In the N part of the city, Old Aberdeen, is King's College (founded 1494), which joined with Marischal College (founded 1593) to form the University of Aberdeen (1860). The granite St Machar's Cathedral (dating in parts from the 14th cent.) and the 13th/14th cent. 'Auld Brig o'Balgownie' are also in Old Aberdeen.

Aberdeenshire Scotland. Former county in the NE becoming part of Grampian Region until 1996 when it became a new Unitary Authority. Pop. (1993) 223,630.

Aberdovey (Welsh, **Aberdyfi**) Wales. Seaside resort on Cardigan Bay in Gwynedd at the mouth of the R. Dovey. Pop. 1300.

Aberfan Wales. Village 6 km (4 miles) SSE of Merthyr Tydfil. Scene of a disaster in 1966; a mass of mine waste and sludge from a coal tip slid down and buried a school and several houses, killing 144 people, inc. 116 children.

Aberfeldy Scotland. Small town in Perth and Kinross on the S bank of the R. Tay 35 km (22 miles) NW of Perth. Pop. (1991) 1748. Salmon and trout fishing resort.

Abergavenny Wales. Market town and tourist centre with some light engineering in Monmouthshire at the confluence of the Usk and Gavenny rivers 26 km (16 miles) N of Newport. Pop. (1991) 14,092.

Abergele Wales. Market town in Conwy 8 km (5 miles) WSW of Rhyl. Pop. (1981) 12,600. Adjoins the seaside resort of Pensarn.

Aberystwyth Wales. Town in Ceredigion at the mouth of the Ystwyth and Rheidol rivers on Cardigan Bay. Pop. (1991) 11,154. University town and seaside resort.

Abidjan Côte d'Ivoire. Cap. on the Ebrié Lagoon and former national cap. Pop. (1990) 2,168,000.

Rail terminal for exports, esp. cacao, cotton, palm oil and kernels, timber. Connected by rail with its outport, Port-Bouet. Industries inc. food-processing and the manufacture of chemicals, soap, beverages and textiles.

Abilene USA. Town in Texas 230 km (145 miles) WSW of Fort Worth. Pop. (1990) 106,654.

Commercial centre. Trade in cotton, wheat, livestock, oil.

Clothing, food-processing and other industries.

Seat of the Hardin-Simmons University (1891).

Abingdon England. Town in Oxfordshire on the R. Thames 10 km (6 miles) S of Oxford. Pop. (1991) 35,234.

Industries inc. tourism, the manufacture of leather goods and brewing. Agricultural trade.

Abitibi, Lake Canada. Lake of very irregular shape covering 900 sq km (350 sq. miles) on the border between Quebec and Ontario provinces. Touching its wooded N banks is the Quebec–Winnipeg railway.

Abitibi River Canada. River in Ontario 540 km (340 miles) long, draining L. Abitibi, flowing N and joining the Moose R. Its power is harnessed at Abitibi Canyon near Fraserdale, used in local gypsum and lignite mines and carried to several other mining centres in Ontario.

Abkhazia Georgia. Autonomous Republic in the NW between the Black Sea and the S slopes of the Greater Caucasus. Area 8600 sq km (3320 sq. miles). Pop. (1990) 538,000 (Georgian 44 per cent, Abkhazian 17 per cent). Cap. Sukhum. Mountainous and well wooded. The majority of the pop. is concentrated in the narrow coastal plain, which has a subtropical climate.

On the plain maize, tobacco, tea, citrus fruits and vines are cultivated. Along the Black Sea coast are a chain of health resorts, inc. Sukhum, Gudauta and Gagra. Hydroelectric power and coal are produced.

Abo ➤TURKU.

Abomey Benin. Cap. of Zou province in the S of the country. Pop. (1992) 65,725.

It is in the centre of a groundnut-growing area. Formerly a base for the slave trade and former cap. of the Kingdom of Dahomey.

Aboukir (**Abu Qir**) Egypt. Village on the bay of the same name 22 km (14 miles) NE of Alexandria, with which it is connected by rail. Nelson defeated the French in Aboukir Bay (the 'Battle of the Nile'; 1798).

Abquaiq Saudi Arabia. Oil town situated SW of Dhahran on the Riyadh railway. It is an important oil centre and terminus.

Abruzzi Italy. S central region. Area 10,794 sq km (4167 sq. miles). Pop. (1990) 306,396. Comprises the provinces of Aquila, Chieti,

Pescara and Teramo. In the highest and most rugged part of the Apennines. Chief town Pescara. In the fertile valleys main occupations are stock-rearing and cultivation of cereals, grapes and sugar-beet.

Abu, Mount India. Isolated mountain (1720 m; 5642 ft) in Rajasthan 96 km (60 miles) W of Udaipur near the Aravalli Range. A well-known place of pilgrimage; two of the Jain temples at Dilwara are of white marble (11th/13th cent.). The nearby small town of Abu is a resort.

Abu Dhabi ➤UNITED ARAB EMIRATES.

Abuja Nigeria. Federal cap. replacing Lagos in 1992. Situated 525 km (325 miles) NE of Lagos in Federal National District. Located in the centre of the country in order to relieve the congestion of Lagos. Pop. (1991) 378,671.

Abu Qir ➤ABOUKIR.

Abu Simbel Egypt. Site of two temples built by Rameses II (1304–1237 BC) hollowed out of the sandstone cliffs on the left bank of the Nile 230 km (145 miles) SW of Aswan near the Sudanese border. The temples were threatened by the rise in water level of the reservoir behind the Aswan High Dam and UNESCO in cooperation with the Egyptian government had them removed (1964–8) in sections and rebuilt 60 m (197 ft) above the original site and 3.6 m (11.8 ft) above the highest expected water level.

Abydos Turkey. Ancient town in Asia Minor on the Hellespont whence Xerxes crossed with his army on a bridge of boats (480 BC). Also scene of the legend of Hero and Leander.

Abymes, Les Guadeloupe. Largest town on Grand-Terre island. Pop. (1990) 62,809.

Abyssinia ➤ETHIOPIA.

Acadia Canada/USA. Name first used in 1603 for all French possessions S of St Lawrence R.; later applied to New Brunswick, Nova Scotia and Maine.

Acapulco de Juárez Mexico. Popular sea-side resort and seaport in Guerrero state 310 km (195 miles) SSW of Mexico City. Pop. (1990) 592,187. Fine sandy beaches and many hotels.

Commercial centre. Trade in fruit and cotton.

Acarnania Greece. District in ancient Greece W of the Aspropotamos R. Now forms a *nome* with Aetolia.

Accra Ghana. Cap., largest city and former 'surf' port on the Gulf of Guinea. Pop. (1984) 867,459. Rail and road terminal from the interior.

Industries inc. food-processing, fishing, engineering, brewing and it exports cacao, timber, gold and fruit.

It grew up round the three fortresses of Fort James, Fort Crèvecoeur (later Fort Ussher) and Christiansborg, built by the English, Dutch and Danes respectively. Replaced Cape Coast as cap. of the Gold Coast in 1876.

Accrington England. Town in Lancashire 8 km (5 miles) E of Blackburn. Pop. (1991) 36,466. Former cotton centre; manufactures textile machinery and bricks.

Achaea Greece. 1. Region of ancient Greece on the N coast of the Peloponnese between the mountains of Erymanthos and the Gulf of Corinth. Its cities combined to form the Achaean League, the main power in Greece (280–146 BC) until the Roman conquest.

2. Region of modern Greece. Area 3209 sq km (1210 sq. miles). Pop. (1990) 297,318. Cap. and chief seaport Patras.

Produces currants and olives. Sheep and goats raised.

Achill Island Ireland. Island off the W coast of Co. Mayo. Area 148 sq km (57 sq. miles). Pop. (1971) 3129. Connected with the mainland by a bridge across the narrow Achill Sound. Mountainous, rising to 671 m (2200 ft) in Slievemore (N).

Main occupations fishing, cultivation of oats and potatoes, raising of livestock. Chief villages and tourist centres Dugort, Keel.

Aconcagua Argentina. Highest peak of the Andes (6960 m; 22,829 ft) in W Argentina near the Chile frontier and the Uspallata Pass.

Aconcagua River Chile. River 190 km (120 miles) long, rising on Aconcagua and entering the Pacific 19 km (12 miles) N of Valparaiso. Irrigates a fertile valley producing fruit and tobacco.

Acre Brazil. State in the W, bounded by Peru, Bolivia and Amazonas state. Area 153,698 sq km (59,343 sq. miles). Pop. (1991) 417,437. Cap. Rio Branco. Named after the Acre R. (tributary of the Purús), which crosses it. Formerly part of Bolivia; passed to Brazil in 1903.

Acre Israel. Port on the Bay of Acre 14 km (9 miles) NNE of Haifa. Pop. (1988) 39,000. It has been a trading port since the days of the Phoenicians (9th cent. BC) although it has, in recent years, lost its importance to Haifa. Taken by the Muslims 638; captured by the Crusaders 1104; fell to Saladin 1187; recaptured (1191) by the Crusaders, who made it their chief port. Finally lost to the Muslims 1291. Taken by the Turks 1517. Successfully defended against Napoleon 1799. Taken by Ibrahim Pasha of Egypt (1832), but recaptured (1840) by combined British, Austrian and Turkish fleets and restored to Turkey. It became part of Israel in 1948.

Actium Greece. Promontory in ancient Greece in NW Arcarnania opposite the modern Preveza. Famous for the naval victory of Octavian over Antony and Cleopatra (31 BC).

Adam, Mount ➤FALKLAND ISLANDS.

Adam's Bridge (Rama's Bridge) Sri Lanka/India. Chain of sandbanks 27 km (17 miles) long between Rameswaram Island (SE India) and Mannar Island (NW Sri Lanka). According to Hindu legend, the remains of a great causeway built by Rama (hero of the *Ramayana*) to take his army from India to Sri Lanka. Evidence suggests that it was once an isthmus.

Adam's Peak Sri Lanka. Mountain 2243 m (7357 ft) high in SW 72 km (45 miles) ESE

of Colombo. Much visited by pilgrims. On the conical summit is a platform with a hollow about 1.5 m (5 ft) long resembling a human footprint; to Buddhists it is that of Buddha, to Hindus that of Siva and to Muslims that of Adam.

Adana Turkey. Cap. of Adana province in SE Asia Minor on the Seyhan R. Pop. (1990) 1,725,950.

Industrial and commercial centre. Manufactures cotton goods, tobacco products. Trade in cereals and cotton.

Adapazari Turkey. Town in the Kocaeli province 210 km (130 miles) WNW of Ankara. Pop. (1985) 171,225.

Manufactures textiles. Trade in rugs and tobacco.

Partly destroyed by an earthquake, with the loss of 83 lives, in July 1967.

Adare, Cape ➤ROSS SEA.

Addis Ababa Ethiopia. Cap. on a plateau 2400 m (7872 ft) above sea level; site chosen (1887) by Emperor Menelek II. Pop. (1989) 1,732,000. Connected with Djibouti by a 778-km (486-mile) railway (1917). It became the cap. of Abyssinia 1896. After the occupation of the country by the Italians (1936), became the cap. of Italian East Africa (inc. Eritrea and Italian Somaliland). Captured (1941) from the Italians during World War II; Ethiopian rule was restored.

Adelaide Australia. Cap. of South Australia on the Torrens R. just W of the Mt Lofty Range near the E shore of Gulf St Vincent. Pop. (1990) 1,049,900. Founded (1836) as the centre of a planned colony for free immigrants.

It is the chief outlet for exports of wheat, wool, fruit, wine, meat, hides and wattle bark. Cultural and commercial centre. Expanding industries inc. the manufacture of agricultural implements, cars, electrical equipment, furniture, paint and textiles.

The Torrens has been dammed and converted into a lake, while water for the city is partly supplied by a 74-km (46-mile) pipeline from a reservoir at Mannum on the Murray

R. Summer droughts are typical of its Mediterranean type of climate; most of its rain, 53 cm (21 ins.) annually, falls in winter; temperatures range from 23°C (73°F) in Jan. to 11°C (52°F) in July. Large airport 8 km (5 miles) W of the city. Ships dock at the outer harbour to Port Adelaide 26 km (16 miles) from the city centre.

Adelboden Switzerland. Resort in the Bern canton 35 km (22 miles) SW of Interlaken in the Bernese Oberland at a height of 1356 m (4448 ft). Pop. (1970) 3326.

Adélie Land ➤TERRE ADÉLIE.

Aden Yemen. Commercial cap. on the SW coast of the Arabian peninsula 160 km (100 miles) E of the S entrance to the Red Sea. Pop. (1995) 562,000 (mostly Arab and Yemeni). Consists of two volcanic peninsulas of barren rock, Aden (E) and Little Aden (W), enclosing Aden Back Bay.

Fuelling station on the route to the E. Entrepôt trade. Activity declined dramatically with closure of Suez Canal (1967), partially revived with its reopening (1975). Produces salt from seawater. There is an underused oil refinery and some industry inc. food-processing, tiles and building materials.

The old Arab town of Crater is on the E side of the main peninsula; Sheikh Othman at the head of the isthmus; the modern port of Steamer Point on the W. Important commercially in very early times, but declined after the discovery of the Cape route to India (1497). Captured by the British 1839. Revived after the opening of the Suez Canal (1869). Scene of many political disturbances in the 1960s. Became part of the Federation of South Arabia (1963), which became the People's Democratic Republic of Yemen (1967) and united with the Republic of Yemen in 1990.

Adige River Italy. The most important river after the Po, rising in small lakes on the Resia Pass, flowing S and E to Merano and then SE to Bolzano (where it is joined by the Isarco), turning SW (receiving the Noce and the Avisio) past Trento and Rovereto, then SE past Verona and Legnago and then E to enter the Adriatic Sea a few miles N of the Po, having flowed for 350 km (200 miles). Used for hydroelectric power and irrigation.

Adirondack Mountains USA. Group of mountains in the N part of New York state, rising from a plateau of 600 m (1968 ft) to a height of 1629 m (5343 ft) in Mt Marcy, structurally a southerly continuation of the Laurentian Shield of Canada. Heavily glaciated during the Great Ice Age. The many lakes, streams and waterfalls make it a popular tourist area. Poor soil has not encouraged settlement; some lumbering, but the greater part of the forest cover remains. Many resorts.

Adiyaman Turkey. Town situated S of Malatya in Malatya province. Pop. (1985) 281,776.

It is the centre of an agricultural area producing wheat, chickpeas, barley, tobacco, lentils and cotton.

Admiralty Islands Australasia. Group of about 40 islands in the Bismarck Archipelago NE of New Guinea; part of Papua New Guinea. Area 2070 sq km (800 sq. miles). Pop. (1973) 22,401. Main island Manus. Chief town Lorengau.

Main occupations coconut-planting, shell-fishing.

Discovered (1616) by the Dutch. Annexed by Germany 1885. Recaptured (1944) from the Japanese in World War II.

Admiralty Range Antarctica. Part of the great mountain range in Victoria Land NW of the Ross Sea. The highest peak is Mt Sabine 3007 m (9859 ft). First seen and named by Sir James Ross (1800–62) in 1841.

Adour River France. River 333 km (208 miles) long, rising in the Hautes-Pyrénées department S of the Pic du Midi de Bigorre, flowing in a wide curve through Gers and Landes and entering the Bay of Biscay below Bayonne.

Adowa ➤ADWA.

Adria Italy. Ancient Atria. Town in Rovigo province, Veneto, between the Po and the Adige rivers 43 km (27 miles) NE of Ferrara.

Pop. (1981) 21,785. A prosperous seaport on the Adriatic (to which it gave its name) in Etruscan and later in Roman times, but now 23 km (14 miles) inland owing to silting.

Manufactures bricks and cement.

Adriatic Sea Europe. Arm of the Mediterranean, extending 770 km (478 miles) NW between Italy and the Balkan Peninsula, from the strait of Otranto (72 km; 45 miles wide) to the Gulf of Trieste. The W coast is low-lying and straight, the E coast steep, rocky and much indented, with many offshore islands. The chief rivers are the Po and the Adige, which continually deposit silt on the coast; Adria (from which the name derives) and other former ports are now inland. Chief ports Ancona, Bari, Brindisi, Dubrovnik, Durrës, Rijeka, Split, Trieste and Venice. Famous for its blue water and fine scenery. There are many tourist resorts on the Italian and Dalmatian coasts.

Aduwa ➤ADWA.

Adwa (**Adowa**, **Aduwa**) Ethiopia. Town in Tigre province 120 km (75 miles) S of Asmara at a height of 1950 m (6396 ft) in an agricultural region. Pop. 16,000. Invading force of Italians repulsed by Ethiopian forces 1896. Bombed and captured by the Italians 1935. Reoccupied by Ethiopian and British troops 1941.

Adygea Russia. Republic within Russia situated N of the Caucasus and S of the Kuban and Laba rivers. Area 7600 sq km (2934 sq. miles). Pop. (1990) 436,000. Cap. Maikop.

Chief industries timber, woodworking, food-processing and engineering.

The people are largely Adygei, Circassians from the mountain valleys who were forced by the Russians to settle in the lowlands (1861). The Region was established in 1922.

Adzharistan Georgia. Autonomous Republic in the SW at the W end of the Lesser Caucasus, bordered on the S by Turkey. Area 8600 sq km (3320 sq. miles). Pop. (1990) 538,000 (mainly Adzhar and Georgian). Cap. Batumi. The mountainous E is thinly popu-lated. Most of the inhabitants live in the narrow coastal plain, which has a subtropical climate with heavy rainfall and where most of the region's tea and citrus fruits are produced. Many seaside resorts, inc. Batumi (also the chief industrial centre). Under the Muslim Turks in the 17th and 18th cent.; annexed by Russia in the 19th cent.

Aegean Sea Europe. Arm of the Mediterranean 640 km (400 miles) long (N–S) and up to 320 km (200 miles) wide (W–E); between Greece and Turkey, linked by the Dardanelles with the Sea of Marmara and the Black Sea. Studded with islands (the great majority belonging to Greece), inc. the Dodecanese, the Cyclades, the N Sporades and Euboea. Leading ports Piraeus, Thessaloniki (Greece); Izmir (Turkey).

Aetolia Greece. Region on the N side of the Gulf of Patras, forming with Acarnania (from which it is separated by the Aspropotamos R.) the *nome* of Aetolia and Acarnania. Combined area 5461 sq km (2108 sq. miles). Pop. (1990) 230,688. Cap. Missolonghi. Largely mountainous.

Cereals, olives and other crops cultivated on the coastal plain.

Aetolia became important with the formation of the Aetolian League (314 BC). Joined Rome to defeat the Macedonians 197 BC. Later opposed the Romans, lost power and was incorporated into Achaea.

Afghanistan. Independent, mountainous, somewhat isolated republic in Central Asia and one of the poorest countries in the world. Bounded by Turkmenistan, Uzbekistan and Tajikistan (N), Pakistan (E and S), Iran (W) and China (NE). Area 652,225 sq km (251,825 sq. miles). Pop. (1995) 18,130,000 (20 per cent urban). Over 3 million are refugees in Pakistan and Iran. Life expectancy, 46 years male, 45 female. Cap. Kabul. Other major towns Kandahar, Herat and Mazar-i-Sharif. Currency: Afghani = 100 puls.

Although most of the country is mountainous, arid and barren, cultivation is successful in the many fertile plains and valleys, generally by means of irrigation. The country is dominated by the Hindu Kush (NE), rising to over 6000 m (19,680 ft) and extending W by the Koh-i-Baba, the Safed Koh and the Paropamisus Range. The central highlands are called the Hazarajat and along part of the N frontier flows the Amu Darya. The longest river, the Helmand, drains SW to the Seistan depression and the Kabul R. E to the Indus. Annual rainfall is less than 25 cm (10 ins.) in many areas. Land use: forested 3 per cent, meadows and pastures 46 per cent, agricultural and permanent cultivation 12 per cent.

The predominant religion is Islam; of the total 74 per cent are Sunni and 25 Shiites. Ethnic groups are Pashtun 52 per cent, Tadzhik 20 per cent, Uzbek 8 per cent and Hazara 8 per cent. Official languages are Pashto and Dari (Persian).

Afghanistan is virtually self-supporting in foodstuffs, apart from wheat and sugar. The castor-oil plant, madder and the asafœtida plant abound. Fruit forms a staple food (with bread) of many people throughout the year, both in the fresh and preserved state and in the latter condition is exported in great quantities. The fat-tailed sheep furnish the principal meat diet and the grease of the tail is substitute for butter. Wool and skins provide material for warm apparel and one of the more important articles of export. Persian lambskins (Karakuls) are one of the chief exports. Mineral resources are scattered and little developed. Coal is mined at Karkar in Pul-i-Khumri, Ishpushta near Doshi, N of Kabul and Dara-i-Suf S of Mazar. Natural gas is found in N Afghanistan around Shiberghan and Sar-i-Pol. Rich, but as yet unexploited, deposits of iron ore exist in the Hajigak hills about 160 km (100 miles) W of Kabul; beryllium has been found in the Kunar valley and barite in Bamian province. Other deposits inc. gold; silver (now unexploited in the Panjshir valley); lapis lazuli (in Badakhshan); asbestos; mica; sulphur (near Maimana); chrome (in the Logar valley and near Herat); and copper (in the N). At Kabul there are factories for the manufacture of cotton and woollen textiles, leather, boots, marble-ware, furniture, glass, bicycles, pre-fabricated houses and plastics. A large machine shop has been constructed and equipped by the Russians, with a capability of manufacturing motor spares. There is a wool factory and a cotton-ginning plant at Kandahar; a small cotton factory at Jabal-us-Seraj and a larger one at Pul-i-Khumri. A cotton-seed oil extraction plant has been built in Lashkargah and there is a large modern cotton textile factory at Gulbahar and another at Bagrami. A large cotton plant has been completed in the N at Balkh.

Afghanistan has been occupied by Persians, Greeks and various Asiatic and Semitic peoples. The Persian monarch Nadir Shah absorbed the entire country in his empire and on his death (1747) one of his Afghan officers, Ahmed Khan, took the royal title and founded modern Afghanistan. His frontiers extended into modern Kashmir and Pakistan, but by 1770 he suffered reversals at the hands of the Sikhs in the Punjab. In the 19th cent. the rivalry between Britain and Russia led to the Afghan Wars; peace was restored when British troops occupied Kabul (1879). Relations with Britain improved, until King Amanuallah's invasion of India (1919) precipitated the 3rd Afghan War, but this ended in a few months and Britain recognized the complete independence of Afghanistan in 1921. Amanuallah abdicated in 1929. The country adopted parliamentary democracy under the new constitution of 1965, but King Zahir Shah was deposed by military *coup* in 1973. A further *coup* in 1978 led to the establishment of a pro-Soviet government. In 1979 Soviet troops invaded Afghanistan and the President was deposed. By 1988 there were some 115,000 Soviet troops in the country but all were withdrawn by 1989. In 1996 Taliban forces captured Kabul and the country was declared an Islamic State under Sharia law. The country is administratively divided into 7 regions.

Africa. The second largest of the world's land masses. Area 29,800,000 sq km (11,506,000 sq. miles). Pop. (1990) 642 million. Cities with populations of over 1 million inc. Alexandria, Addis Ababa, Algiers, Cairo,

Casablanca, Cape Town, El Giza, Johannesburg, Kinshasa and Lagos. Extent N–S 8000 km (5000 miles) from Cape Blanc to Cape Agulhas (South Africa) and E–W 7200 km (4500 miles) from Cape Verde to Cape Guardafui. It falls into two very distinct parts, effectively separated by the Sahara: North Africa, essentially a Mediterranean area, together with the Nile valley, a part of the Old World since antiquity; and a large part S of the Sahara, discovered only slowly by European exploration, where permanent settlement by Europeans is limited to certain parts (e.g. South Africa, Kenya), sparsely inhabited by a great variety of Negro peoples with varying cultures and languages.

The equator runs almost exactly through the centre, but more than two-thirds of Africa lies to the N. The Greenwich meridian passes through North West and West Africa; most of the continent is in E longitudes. Bounded by the Mediterranean Sea (N), the Atlantic Ocean (W) and the Red Sea, the Gulf of Aden and the Indian Ocean (E). Joined to SW Asia by the isthmus of Suez. At the Straits of Gibraltar only 14 km (9 miles) from Europe. Peninsulas and bays are few; the coastline is relatively short (26,000 km; 16,000 miles). Off the SE coast is Madagascar, which is the fourth largest island in the world; it broke away from the continent c. 50 million years ago. Unique plants and animals have evolved there because of its isolation.

Africa is largely a vast plateau and is generally higher in the S and E than in the N and W. Broken in the extreme NW by the folded ranges of the Atlas Mountains. In the extreme SE the Drakensberg forms a high rim. Mean elevation greater than that of Europe but less than that of Asia. A prominent feature is the Great Rift Valley with its many lakes; E of L. Victoria (the largest in the continent) are the highest mountains, the volcanic Mt Kilimanjaro 5895 m (19,340 ft) and Mt Kenya (Kirinyaga) 5200 m (17,058 ft). Other heights are the Ruwenzori Highlands beside the W branch of the Great Rift Valley (NW of L. Victoria) and Ras Dashan in Ethiopia.

The Nile, Africa's longest river, leaves the N side of L. Victoria and enters the N end of L. Albert, as the White Nile; joined at Khartoum by the Blue Nile (fed mainly from L. Tana in the Ethiopian highlands), it flows N to the Mediterranean, receiving no tributaries as it crosses the immense desert region of North West Africa. In spite of its greater length its basin area is much smaller than that of the Congo R., Africa's second great waterway, whose E headstreams rise on the lofty plateau between L. Malawi and L. Tanganyika; fed by many tributaries, it flows N and W to the Atlantic Ocean. The headstreams of the Niger flow from the Futa Jallon plateau NE towards the Sahara; in a roughly semicircular course it turns E and then S entering the Gulf of Guinea. The Zambezi (shortest of Africa's four great waterways, but the largest of those flowing into the Indian Ocean) has many tributaries, including the Shire from L. Malawi, but the basin area is less than half that of the Nile. Other rivers in southern Africa inc. the Orange – which receives the Vaal (both rising on the W slopes of the Drakensberg) and flows into the Atlantic Ocean – and the Limpopo, which follows a roughly semicircular course to the Indian Ocean.

Almost three-quarters of Africa lies within the tropics and experiences the vertical sun. No area extends far into temperate latitudes, but in some regions altitude tempers the heat. Snow and ice are found only on the peaks of the highest mountains. Temperature, humidity and annual rainfall (over 150 cm; 60 ins.) are high throughout the year in equatorial central Africa and on the Guinea coast. In equatorial East Africa temperatures are lower on the plateau, rainfall is lighter, and the cooler climate is more congenial to Europeans. On both sides of the equatorial region temperatures are high but there are marked rainy and dry seasons: despite drought in the cool season, annual rainfall in the coastal areas of Sierra Leone and Liberia is more than 300 cm (120 ins.). N of the equator rainfall decreases northwards and a vast area influenced by the dry NE Trade Winds has a hot desert type of climate and an annual rainfall of less than 25 cm (10 ins.). The Sahara extends virtually from the Atlantic Ocean to the Red Sea, with some of the highest shade temperatures on record, though as the skies are cloudless rapid radiation causes the hot days to be followed by relatively cool nights. In recent years these areas have suffered devastating droughts. In corresponding latitudes S of the equator is the Kalahari Desert: the SE Trade Winds carry rain only to the E part of the plateau, esp. to E Madagascar. Along the North African coast and again around Cape Town the climate is of dry subtropical Mediterranean type: summers are long, dry and hot, and rain falls chiefly in the mild winters.

Tropical rainforest covers most of the Congo basin and the Guinea coast, the belt along the E side of Madagascar and part of the narrow coastal fringe of East Africa; it yields tropical hardwoods, e.g. mahogany. Other products, e.g. palm oil and rubber, now come largely from plantations; the cacao tree has been successfully introduced into forest clearings and bananas grow widely. Savannah extends in a broad belt round these forests and occupies most of the W of Madagascar; the characteristic vegetation is tall, coarse grass with scattered trees, inc. the baobab and varieties of acacia. Cattle are raised, millet and maize cultivated; groundnuts, cotton, sisal, tobacco and coffee are important export crops. Around the drier edge of the savannah the grassland passes gradually to scrub, merging into desert. Scrub and desert together cover a high proportion of the continent. The Sahara contains sandy, rocky and stony areas, but over its greater part there is a sparse vegetation of stunted shrubs. In oases the date palm is important; cotton, cultivated on irrigated land, is an important crop. In the Mediterranean regions of the NW and the S, forests and woodlands contain evergreen trees and shrubs; olives are widely cultivated in the NW and grapes and citrus fruits in both areas.

There is considerable mineral wealth, e.g. uranium, gold, platinum, diamonds (both gemstones and industrial). Rich copper deposits are worked in the Shaba region of the Democratic Republic of Congo and the Copperbelt of Zambia. The Democratic Republic of Congo produces the bulk of the world's cobalt. Chrome ore and phosphates are extensively mined, but Africa is poor in power resources; coal is found only rarely (e.g. in South Africa). Oilfields are found in Algeria, Libya and Nigeria. Hydroelectric power is developed on a relatively small scale, chiefly in Morocco and the Shaba region of the Democratic Republic of Congo; the Owen Falls Dam (Uganda) and the Kariba Dam (Zimbabwe/Zambia) are noteworthy.

Ancient Egypt was one of the earliest civilizations. The Mediterranean littoral was settled and developed first by the Carthaginians, from the 9th cent. BC. After expelling them, the Romans (who gave the name Africa to their new provinces) continued the process. In the 5th cent. BC Herodotus knew something of the Upper Nile and Libya. Later the Arab geographers showed a growing though imprecise knowledge of wider areas. The Arab conquest (7th cent. AD) gave North Africa some unity and a common religion. Later the Portuguese explored the W coast; Diaz rounded the Cape of Good Hope in 1488 and Vasco da Gama reached the E coast by the same route. To the Portuguese (and to the British, the Dutch and the French, who followed them) Africa was a valuable source of slaves, ivory and gold, obtained at various points along the W coast; the interior remained unknown. During the late 18th and the 19th cent. a number of famous explorers gradually penetrated 'the dark continent', esp. Mungo Park in the Niger basin, Bruce in Abyssinia (now Ethiopia), Livingstone in the Zambezi and Upper Congo basins, Burton in Somaliland and round L. Tanganyika, Speke at the source of the Nile and L. Victoria and Stanley in the Congo basin and at L. Tanganyika and L. Albert (Nyasa) and in the Ruwenzori Highlands. In the second half of the 19th cent. and the early 20th cent. various European powers colonized Africa; Abyssinia (Ethiopia) and Liberia alone remained independent. After World War I the German colonies became Mandated Territories of the League of Nations. They became Trust Territories of the United Nations after World War II, when the Italians also lost their colonies. World War II led to increased political consciousness among African peoples and the former colonies and protectorates have now achieved independence. Political progress since independence has taken many forms and few countries have retained the constitutions agreed at independence. At times there have been disputes about borders, about moves to one-party or native self-rule and all this has been complicated by extreme conditions of drought in large areas of the continent.

Agadir Morocco. Port on the Atlantic coast 120 km (75 miles) S of Essaouira. Pop. (1993) 137,000. Serves the fertile Sous region. Linked by road with Essaouira and Marrakesh. There is a fish-canning industry. Devastated by earthquake in 1960, when over 20,000 people were killed. The new town was built 8 km (5 miles) S of the old town and is a popular tourist resort.

Agalega Mauritius. Island situated 950 km (600 miles) N of Mauritius in the Indian Ocean. Pop. (1990) 500. Comprises a N and S island linked by a sandbank. It is a dependency of Mauritius and the main settlement is S island. Occupations are coconut-growing and horse-rearing. There is a meteorological station.

Agaña ►GUAM.

Agen France. Market town on the N side of the Garonne R. (here crossed by a bridge) 93 km (58 miles) NW of Toulouse. Pop. (1990) 33,000. Prefecture of the Lot-et-Garonne department.

In a fruit-growing and market-gardening region, well known for preserved fruits and other food products.

Agincourt (modern **Azincourt**) France. Village in the Pas-de-Calais department 48 km (30 miles) SE of Boulogne-sur-mer. Famous for the victory (1415) of Henry V and English forces over a much larger French army during the Hundred Years War.

Agordat Ethiopia. Town in Eritrea 110 km (70 miles) W of Asmara (with which it is connected by rail) where the Italians defeated the Khalifa and his followers (1893).

Agra India. City in Uttar Pradesh on the Jumna R. 184 km (115 miles) SSE of Delhi. Pop. (1991) 891,800.

Industrial and commercial centre. Manufactures cotton goods, electric lamps, carpets and footwear. Trade in hides and wool. Industries inc. iron-founding, steel, marble and leather goods.

Famous for its buildings, esp. the Taj Mahal (probably the world's most celebrated mausoleum), built 1632–50 in pure white marble by Shah Jahan as a memorial to his wife. In the fortress built by Akbar (1566) are the Moti Masjid (Pearl Mosque) of Shah Jahan and the Jahangiri Mahal of Akbar (whose tomb is 10 km (6 miles) N at Sikandra). Founded (1566) by Akbar; cap. of India for many years, but began to decline when Aurangzeb moved to Delhi (1658). Cap. of the NW Provinces 1835–62.

Agri Turkey. Province in E bounded N by the Aras mountains and E by Iran. Area 11,066 sq km (4273 sq. miles). Pop. (1990) 437,093. Cap. Karakose. The province is mountainous and unproductive; drained by the Murat R. It has a large Kurdish pop.

Agrigento Italy. Ancient Agrigentum. Formerly (until 1927) Girgenti. Cap. of Agrigento province near the S coast of Sicily, 88 km (55 miles) SSE of Palermo. Pop. (1990) 56,661. Trade in sulphur. Harbour at Port Empedocle (SW). Founded 582 BC by Greek colonists from Gela. Plundered by the Carthaginians 406 BC. Occupied by the Romans 210 BC. Greek remains, inc. several temples.

Aguascalientes Mexico. 1. State on the central plateau at a height of 1800 m (5904 ft). Area 5471 sq km (2112 sq. miles). Pop. (1990) 719,650.

Mainly agricultural, producing maize, fruit, vegetables. Cattle ranches provide bulls for Mexican bull rings.

2. Cap. of Aguascalientes state 184 km

(115 miles) NE of Guadalajara. Pop. (1990) 586,384.

Important railway workshops; flour mills, tanneries, potteries. Named after the medicinal hot springs near by.

Agulhas, Cape South Africa. In Portuguese, 'Needles'. The most southerly point of Africa in the Cape Province between the Atlantic and Indian oceans. A rocky headland, with reefs dangerous to shipping.

Ahaggar (Hoggar) Mountains Algeria. Highland region in the central Sahara, rising to 2918 m (9571 ft) in Mt Tahat. Annual rainfall up to 25 cm (10 ins.); many wadis have been formed. Pop. mainly Tuareg. Chief oasis town Tamanrasset.

Ahlen Germany. Town in North Rhine-Westphalia 29 km (18 miles) SSE of Münster. Pop. (1986) 51,900.

Coalmining centre. Manufactures hardware and footwear.

Ahmadabad India. Cap. of the Ahmadabad district in Gujarat on the Sabarmati R. 450 km (280 miles) N of Bombay. Pop. (1991) 2,954,500.

Important railway junction. Cotton-milling. Manufactures pottery, brocades, jewellery and air-conditioners. Industries inc. textiles, chemicals and pharmaceuticals, stainless steel, tubes and ball bearings.

A cultural centre; seat of the University of Gujarat (1950). Many fine buildings, inc. the Jama Masjid and other mosques and the modern Jain temple (1848). Founded (1411) by Ahmad Shah; declined in the 18th cent. but revived with the establishment of the cotton industry in the mid 19th cent.

Ahmadi Kuwait. Town situated SSE of Kuwait City in Ahmadi governorate. Pop. (1980) 24,000. Residential centre for the Burgan oilfields. It is linked with its port and terminal, Mena al Ahmadi 8 km (5 miles) to the ESE, by pipelines.

Ahmadnagar India. Cap. of the Ahmadnagar district in Maharashtra 200 km (125 miles) E of Bombay. Pop. (1991) 181,015.

Commercial and industrial centre. Trade

in cotton and grain. Cotton-milling, tanning and manufactures copper and brass articles.

Founded (1494) by Ahmad Nizam Shah.

Ahuachapán El Salvador. Cap. of the Ahuachapán department, on the W coast. Pop. (1985) 71,846. Centre of an important coffee-producing area. A bridge across the Paz R. carries the Pan-American Highway from Guatemala.

Ahvenanmaa (Swedish **Åland Islands**) Finland. Archipelago of over 6000 granite islands and rocky islets, about 80 of them inhabited, at the entrance to the Gulf of Bothnia. Area 1527 sq km (590 sq. miles). Pop. (1990) 24,604. Cap. Maarianhamina (Mariehamn), a free port, on Ahvenanmaa (Åland), the largest island (area 738 sq km; 285 sq. miles). The inhabitants of Swedish descent and Swedish-speaking are mainly fishermen.

Some cattle-rearing. Rye, barley, flax cultivated. Tourism important.

Swedish almost continuously from the Middle Ages; ceded to Russia 1809. After World War I, despite a plebiscite in favour of secession to Sweden, Finnish sovereignty was confirmed by the League of Nations (1921).

Ahwaz Iran. Cap. of Khuzistán, on the Karun R. 130 km (80 miles) NNE of Abadan. Pop. (1986) 579,826.

Railway junction, commercial centre and river port. Greater industrial activity since the construction of the railway and development of oilfields.

Aigina Greece. Ancient Aegina. Island 29 km (18 miles) SW of Athens. Area 85 sq km (33 sq. miles). Pop. (1971) 9584.

Produces olives, vines and figs. Commercially important in ancient times, but conquered by Athens 457 BC. Its people were exiled (431 BC) and it declined.

Aigues-Mortes France. Town in the Gard department 24 km (15 miles) ESE of Montpellier on the W edge of the Rhône delta. Pop. (1982) 4475. Mainly vineyards.

In the Middle Ages an important seaport,

built by Louis IX (St Louis), who embarked here for his two crusades (1248, 1270); now 5 km (3 miles) from the sea owing to silting. The 13th-cent. walls and the Tour de Constance, built by St Louis, are preserved.

Ailsa Craig Scotland. Rocky granite island in the Firth of Clyde 16 km (10 miles) W of Girvan, rising sharply to 335 m (1100 ft). Area 2.5 sq km (1 sq. mile). Lighthouse. Sanctuary of gannets and other sea-birds.

Ain France. Department in the E between the Rhône and Saône rivers, bounded on the NE by Switzerland. Area 5762 sq km (2225 sq. miles). Pop. (1991) 477,700. Cap. Bourg-en-Bresse. E of the Ain R., which flows SSW through it, are the Jura mountains, where cattle and sheep are grazed and cheese is manufactured; W of the river are the fertile Bresse, where cereals, vines are cultivated and pigs and poultry raised and, to the S, the Dombes region, with its many ponds and its cattle and pig rearing. Important hydroelectric installations on the Rhône (Génissiat) and the Ain. Chief towns Bourg, Belley.

Ain Dar Saudi Arabia. Oilfield established in 1948 in Eastern Province situated 45 km (28 miles) W of Abqaiq and linked to it by pipeline.

Ain River France. River 198 km (124 miles) long rising in the central Jura and flowing SSW through the Jura and Ain departments to join the Rhône 29 km (18 miles) above Lyon. It provides hydroelectric power.

Aintree England. Village in Merseyside just N of Liverpool. Racecourse where the annual Grand National steeplechase has been run since its inception (1839).

Air Highlands Niger. Highlands in the S Sahara region, rising to over 1800 m (5904 ft). Several oases. Chief centre Agadès, a caravan town. There are cave paintings showing human habitation c. 5000 years ago showing a climate wetter and milder than today.

Airdrie Scotland. Industrial town in North Lanarkshire 18 km (11 miles) E of Glasgow. Pop. (1991) 36,998.

Industries inc. engineering, electronics and pharmaceuticals.

Aire River England. River in Yorkshire 110 km (70 miles) long, rising in the Pennines and flowing SE and E past Skipton, Bingley and Leeds to receive the Calder at Castleford and join the Ouse above Goole. The Aire Gap is an important route by rail, road and canal through the Pennines.

Aireborough England. Town in West Yorkshire 8 km (5 miles) NNE of Bradford. Pop. (1971) 29,477 inc. Rawdon, Guiseley and Yeadon. Woollen mills.

Aisne France. Department in the NE comprising parts of the Île-de-France, Picardy and Champagne, taking its name from the Aisne R. Area 7369 sq km (2845 sq. miles). Pop. (1991) 537,600. Cap. Laon. Other towns are St Quentin and Soissons.

Sugar-beet and cereals cultivated. Cattle raised. Manufactures textiles, leather, mirrors and chemicals.

Aisne River France. River 240 km (150 miles) long, rising in the Meuse department, flowing NNW and then W to join the Oise R. near Compiègne. Connected by canals with the Oise and Marne rivers.

Aix-en-Provence France. Ancient Aquae Sextiae. Town in the Bouches-du-Rhône department 25 km (16 miles) NNE of Marseille. Pop. (1990) 126,854. Spa.

Industrial and commercial centre. Trade in olives, almonds and fruits. Manufactures agricultural implements, fertilizers and matches. Famous as a cultural centre.

Seat of the faculties of law and letters of the Aix-Marseille University (founded 1409). Outstanding buildings are the 12th/15th-cent. cathedral and the 17th-cent. baroque town hall. Founded (123 BC) by the Roman consul Sextius Calvinus and named Aquae Sextiae because of the thermal springs. Scene of the defeat of the Teutones by Marius (102 BC). Cap. of Provence during the Middle Ages; lost importance after the union of Provence to the Crown. Birthplace of Cézanne (1839–1906).

Aix-la-Chapelle ➤AACHEN.

Aix-les-Bains France. Ancient Aquae Gratianae. Town in the Savoie department 13 km (8 miles) N of Chambéry near the E side of the Lac du Bourget. Pop. (1990) 22,000. Resort and spa. The mineral springs were known to the Romans; Roman remains in the neighbourhood. Winter sports centre at nearby Mont Révard.

Aiyina ➤AIGINA.

Ajaccio France. Cap. (prefecture) and seaport of Corsica on the W coast near the head of the Gulf of Ajaccio. Pop. (1990) 59,318. Resort and commercial town. Trade in timber. Fishing.

The house where Napoleon was born is now a museum. Occupied by the Germans in World War II; liberated Sept. 1943.

Ajanta India. Small hill town in Maharashtra in the Ajanta Hills 190 km (120 miles) NNE of Ahmadnagar. Famous for the nearby Buddhist cave temples cut into the side of a ravine, consisting of monasteries and meeting halls, many of them decorated with frescoes, constructed between 100 BC and the 7th cent. AD.

Ajman United Arab Emirates. Emirate forming an enclave in Sharjah and the smallest of the seven emirates. Area 250 sq km (100 sq. miles). Pop. (1995) 118,812. Cap. Ajman.

The main occupations are ship repair, pearling, fishing and date-growing.

Ajmer India. City in Rajasthan 350 km (220 miles) SW of Delhi. Pop. (1991) 402,700.

Railway junction. Industrial and commercial centre. Railway engineering. Manufactures cement, cane products, wool, soap and footwear. Trade in grain, oilseeds.

Has the white marble tomb of a Muslim saint and an ancient Jain temple converted into a mosque. Probably founded in the 2nd cent. AD. Formerly cap. of the Ajmer state.

Akershus Norway. County in SE extending N from Oslo fiord to the S end of L. Mjosa.

Area 4917 sq km (1898 sq. miles). Pop. (1992) 421,510. Cap. Oslo, although the city centre is not in the county.

Industry mainly in the suburbs of Oslo inc. shipping and light industry. Tourism is also important.

Akhaia ➤ACHAEA.

Akhtyrka Ukraine. Town situated 102 km (64 miles) WNW of Kharkov. Pop. (1970) 41,000. Agricultural centre. Railway terminus.

Founded by Poles in the 17th cent. Fine 18th-cent. cathedral.

Akimiski Island ➤JAMES BAY.

Akita Japan. Cap. of Akita prefecture on the NW coast of Honshu at the mouth of the Omono R. Pop. (1991) 303,805. Minor seaport.

Exports petroleum products. Railway workshops, oil refinery (supplied from local oilfield). Manufactures fertilizers, woodpulp and foodstuffs.

Aklavik Canada. Village in Eskimo country on the W channel of the Mackenzie delta in the North West Territories. Built (1912) as a Hudson's Bay Company trading-post. Importance diminished when Inuvik 53 km (33 miles) NE was built.

Akmola (Aqmola) Kazakhstan. Cap. since 1997.

Akola India. Industrial and commercial town in Maharashtra 80 km (50 miles) WSW of Amravati. Pop. (1991) 328,000.

Manufactures cotton goods and soap. Important trade in cotton.

Akron USA. City in Ohio 48 km (30 miles) SSE of Cleveland at the highest point on the Erie Canal between the Great Lakes and the Ohio R. Pop. (1990) 223,220. Founded 1825.

Its great growth occurred when its rubber factories expanded to meet the demand for tyres for the automobile industry; it was the leading tyre-manufacturing centre of the USA. Tyres are no longer made, but it manufactures synthetic rubber and plastic products, machinery and chemicals.

Akrotiri Cyprus. Bay on the S of the island. On the shore of the salt lake to the W of the bay is a British naval base.

Aksu (Aqsu) China. Town in Xinkiang Uygur 400 km (250 miles) ENE of Kashi in the Aksu oasis. Pop. 40,000.

Caravan centre. Manufactures textiles, carpets and leather.

Aksum (Axum) Ethiopia. Ancient town in the Tigre province 21 km (13 miles) WSW of Aduwa at a height of 2100 m (6890 ft).

Trade in coffee, cereals.

According to tradition, the Jewish Ark of the Covenant was deposited here.

Aktyubinsk Kazakhstan. Cap. of the Aktyubinsk Region situated 145 km (90 miles) SW of Orsk. Pop. (1991) 266,000.

Important industrial centre. Industries inc. the manufacture of chemicals, ferro-alloys, electrical equipment, engineering and flour-milling.

Akyab ►SITTWE.

Alabama USA. One of the southern states. Area 133,916 sq km (51,705 sq. miles). Pop. (1990) 4,040,587. Cap. Montgomery.

The largest heavy-industry state in the S, with important coal and iron deposits in the region of Birmingham, a busy manufacturing area. Oil and gas are also produced. The rest of the state is largely agricultural. The N boundary reaches the Tennessee R. in a fertile valley now controlled by the Tennessee Valley Authority. Farther S the southern end of the Appalachians (Allegheny and Cumberland ranges) protrudes into the state. Rain falls at all seasons, decreasing from 150 cm (60 ins.) annually on the S coast to 100 cm (40 ins.) inland. The rich fertile soil of central Alabama was once covered with cotton plantations, but now has more diversified agriculture. With increased mechanization, labour requirements were reduced; cotton is increasingly grown in rotation with hay, legumes or grain. The cultivation of fruit, groundnuts, soya beans, vegetables and sugar-cane, and cattle-rearing and dairy-farming are also being developed. The S coastlands of Alabama, low-lying, hot, humid, unhealthy and sparsely populated, are thickly wooded and yield turpentine and resin. Chief towns Birmingham, Mobile, Huntsville, Montgomery.

Explored in the 16th cent. by Spaniards, who named it after an Indian tribe; settled by the French as part of the French province of Louisiana in the 17th cent. and ceded to the British in 1763. Admitted to the Union in 1819 as the 22nd state.

Alabama River USA. River 500 km (312 miles) long formed by the union of the Coosa and Tallapoosa rivers, flowing generally SW to join the Tombigbee R. and form the Mobile R. 70 km (44 miles) above Mobile.

Alagôas Brazil. State in the NE shoulder. Area 27,107 sq km (10,466 sq. miles). Pop. (1990) 2,552,197. Cap. Maceió.

Sugar-cane is grown along the seaboard and cotton inland.

Alai Mountains China/Kirgizia/Tajikistan. Mountain range extending W from the Tian Shan through Kirgizia into Tajikistan, rising to over 4800 m (15,744 ft). To the S is the Trans-Alai range rising to 7134 m (23,400 ft). Between the two ranges is the fertile pastoral Alai Valley, watered by the Kyzyl-Su R.

Alameda USA. Residential town in California on an island in San Francisco Bay. Pop. (1990) 76,460. It has fewer fogs and less chilly winds than the city.

Minor port. Has an important naval air station. Shipbuilding centre for pleasure craft. Seaside resort.

Alamein, El Egypt. Village on the coastal railway in N Egypt 104 km (65 miles) WSW of Alexandria. Scene of the decisive victory (1942) of the British over the Germans during the North African campaign in World War II, which ended the imminent threat of German occupation of Egypt.

Alamo USA. Fort at San Antonio, Texas, heroically defended during the Texan revolt against Mexico (1836) by its 183 guards, who were all killed.

Alaska USA. State in the extreme NW of North America. Area 1,528,110 sq km (590,004 sq. miles). Pop. (1990) 550,043. Cap. Juneau. Largely mountainous, with much volcanic activity; Mt McKinley (6194 m; 20,316 ft) in the Alaska range is the highest peak in North America. Much of Alaska is permanently snow-covered, but the lower mountain slopes are forested. The coast is deeply indented; sinking has reduced the W end of the Pacific mountain system – which inc. the volcano Katmai – to the line of the Aleutian Is. Barren tundra occupies much of the basin of the Yukon R., which flows W to the Bering Sea. N of the Arctic Circle is the Brooks Range, a remote and almost inaccessible Arctic wilderness, the domain of caribou hunters. The state had 988 airports and landing areas (1988). The Eskimos have been encouraged to settle, with the substitution of reindeer for wild caribou. The climate of the W island belt is equable but wet and foggy; the interior has continental extremes with a warm but very short summer. The Arctic region is polar in climate, with long, cold winters and short, cool summers.

Main export formerly fish (esp. salmon), now superseded by oil; others are furs (esp. sealskins), minerals (inc. gold, quartz, silver, lead and zinc), timber. Petroleum and natural gas first produced in 1959. Chief towns Anchorage, on the S coast, Fairbanks and Juneau, which is in the 'panhandle', a coastal strip extending 960 km (600 miles) SE.

Bought from Russia in 1867 for $7,200,000. Admitted to the Union in 1959 as the 49th state.

Alaska Highway Canada/USA. A strategic road from Dawson Creek in N British Columbia to Fairbanks, Alaska. Built by USA (1942) as a defensive precaution against possible Japanese invasion in World War II. Continued by a good road to Edmonton, Alberta, it is used as a military and tourist road, opening up the Canadian Yukon territory and forms the N part of the Inter-American

Highway which extends 26,860 km (16,800 miles) from Alaska to Argentina.

Álava Spain. One of the Basque Provinces in the N, with the Ebro R. on its S boundary. Area 3047 sq km (1176 sq. miles). Pop. (1991) 339,806. Cap. Vitoria.

Cereals, fruit, potatoes cultivated in the fertile valleys. Industries concentrated in Vitoria.

Albacete Spain. 1. Province in the SE. Area 14,858 sq km (5737 sq. miles). Pop. (1991) 339,806. Mainly hilly.

Main occupations agriculture (cereals, vines, olives) and stock-raising (sheep).

2. Cap. of the Albacete province 138 km (86 miles) WSW of Valencia. Pop. (1991) 128,718.

Market town in an irrigated region. Famous for its cutlery and scissors, and also manufactures chemicals and soap.

Alba Longa Italy. Ancient city in Latium, probably on the W shore of L. Albano about 19 km (12 miles) SE of Rome near the modern Castel Gandolfo. Traditionally the oldest Latin city, founded by Ascanius, son of Aeneas. Destroyed by its daughter city Rome in the 7th cent. BC.

Albania. Republic in SE Europe. Bounded by Montenegro (N), Macedonia (E), Greece (S) and the Adriatic Sea (W). Area 28,748 sq km (11,101 sq. miles). Pop. (1995) 3,412,000 (36 per cent urban). Life expectancy: 70 years male, 76 female. Cap. Tiranë. Other important towns Shkodër, Korçë, Vlonë, Durrës and Elbasan. Currency: Lek = 100 qindars.

Rugged, mountainous and difficult of access, rising to nearly 2700 m (8856 ft) in the NE, with marshy but generally fertile coastal lowlands which widen considerably in the centre. Crossed by the Drin, Shkumbi, Seman, Vijosë and other rivers, which are useless for navigation because they almost dry up in the summer and become torrents in the winter. The climate is Mediterranean along the coast and continental in the mountains, where the rainfall is heavier and winters are much cooler. Land use: forested 38 per cent, meadows and pastures 15 per cent, agricultural and under permanent cultivation 26 per cent.

The Albanian language is divided into two dialects, Gheg in the N and Tosk to the S of the Shkumbi R. The official language is based on Tosk. Albania is constitutionally an atheist state but in 1990 the ban on religious activity was lifted and mosques and churches could reopen. Of believers, a small proportion of the pop.: Muslim 65 per cent, Orthodox 20 per cent and Roman Catholic 13 per cent.

Agricultural methods are primitive. Main crops are grain, cotton, potatoes, tobacco and sugar-beet. Olives and citrus fruits are grown near the coast. In the mountains the rearing of sheep and goats is the main occupation, and extensive areas are covered with forests. Mineral wealth is considerable and inc. coal, chromium, copper, nickel and salt, but has only recently been exploited. Oil is produced at Qyteti Stalin (Kuçovë) and sent by pipeline to the port of Vlone. There are hydroelectric power installations at Selitë, at Mt Daita near Tiranë, on the Mati R. and at Shkopeti. The principal industries inc. food-processing, textiles, oil products and the manufacture of cement. Communications infrastructure is inadequate and roads are poor. Many mountain districts are inaccessible to wheeled vehicles; the total length of railways (1988) was only 417 km (261 miles).

The region was nominally under Roman rule in the 1st cent. AD, was overrun by the Goths in the 4th and 5th cent. and was reconquered (535) for the Byzantine Empire by Justinian, but in these and subsequent invasions the mountain tribes were never completely overcome. Turkish rule was imposed in 1478, despite a determined resistance led by Scanderbeg, the national hero, and persisted for more than four centuries. Independence was proclaimed in 1912. The German Prince William of Wied accepted the crown, but left after the outbreak of World War I (1914). It became a republic in 1925. Ahmed Bey Zogu, a former prime minister and president, proclaimed himself King Zog I in 1928. Some economic and educational progress was made but Albania was invaded by the Italians in 1939 and the

king fled. After World War II a Communist single-party government was established under Enver Hoxha. Britain and the USA broke off relations with Albania (1946) and vetoed her admission to the UN, but she was finally admitted in 1955. In recent years Soviet influence has been replaced by that of Communist China and diplomatic relations between Albania and the USSR were broken off in 1961. In 1977 Albania terminated its special relationship with China. In 1990 there were several demonstrations against the government led by students and opposition parties were legalized. A Communist government was elected in 1991 but following a general strike it quickly resigned. It is a multi-party republic with a single legislative house, the People's Assembly.

Albano, Lake Italy. Ancient Albanus Lacus. A crater lake situated SE of Rome in an extinct volcano, drained into a tributary of the Tiber by a tunnel constructed (398–397 BC) because of a pronouncement by the Delphic oracle that Veii could not be conquered until its waters reached the sea. On the E bank is Monte Cavo (ancient Albanus Mons) 949 m (3112 ft) high.

Albany Australia. Seaport and resort in Western Australia on King George Sound 392 km (245 miles) SE of Perth. Pop. (1991) 11,186.

Fish and meat canning. Exports fruit.

Founded as a penal colony and first settled in 1826. It was a coaling station for ships travelling from Europe to Australia and also a whaling station.

Albany (Georgia) USA. Market town on the Flint R. in the SW 120 km (75 miles) SE of Columbus. Pop. (1990) 78,122.

In the centre of a rich agricultural area. Locally grown cotton led to the manufacture of cotton goods. Food-processing (esp. pecans and peanuts) now more important.

Albany (New York) USA. State cap. on the W bank of the Hudson R. 216 km (135 miles) N of New York city. Pop. (1990) 101,082.

Chief industries printing, publishing and

the manufacture of foodstuffs and electrical goods.

Renowned for its fine public buildings. The oldest city in the USA. It was founded in 1614 by the Dutch as a trading post (Fort Nassau); renamed in honour of the Duke of York and Albany (afterwards James II) 1664 and it still operates under its original charter of 1686. The importance of the site, near the confluence of the Mohawk and the Hudson, was realized during the American War of Independence. Became state cap. 1797. Later grew as a railway and commercial centre.

Albany (Oregon) USA. City situated S of Portland at the confluence of the R. Willamette and R. Calapooia. Pop. (1980) 26,546.

Industries inc. retailing, regional banking centre and the manufacture of electrical goods, textiles and chemicals.

Established in 1848.

Albemarle Island ➤GALÁPAGOS ISLANDS.

Albert, Lake Democratic Republic of Congo/Uganda. Lake, also known as L. Nyasa, in the W branch of the Great Rift Valley, 160 km (100 miles) long and up to 35 km (22 miles) wide. Area 5200 sq km (2000 sq. miles). Part of the frontier between Democratic Republic of Congo and Uganda. Fed by the Victoria Nile (NE) and the Semliki R. (S). Drains N through the Albert Nile into the Bahr el Jebel. Discovered (1864) by Sir Samuel Baker.

Alberta Canada. The most W of the three prairie provinces, between British Columbia (W) and Saskatchewan (E), bounded on the S by Montana (USA). Area 661,185 sq km (255,284 sq. miles). Pop. (1990) 2,525,200. Cap. Edmonton; the other important town is Calgary. Consists of a plateau descending E and NE from the Rocky Mountains, which form the S part of its boundary with British Columbia. The N part is drained N by the Peace and Athabaska rivers, and the S is drained E to L. Winnipeg. Climate typically continental.

Mainly agricultural. Chief crops wheat, oats, barley. Cattle-rearing in the S. Largely forest in the N. There are important coalfields

and the discovery (1947) of a major oilfield at Luduc, near Edmonton, led to rapid development: now produces 82 per cent of Canada's oil output. There are considerable reserves of natural gas. Western Alberta is a tourist area.

Albert Canal Belgium. Canal in the NE 129 km (80 miles) long 43 m (140 ft) wide, joining the Scheldt (at Antwerp) to the Meuse (at Liège). Completed 1939. Navigable by barges up to 2000 tonnes.

Albertville ➤KALEMIE.

Albi France. Prefecture of the Tarn department, on the Tarn R. 67 km (42 miles) ENE of Toulouse. Pop. (1990) 48,707.

Textile, glass, dyeing and other industries.

Brick-built cathedral (13th/16th cent.). Musée Toulouse-Lautrec.

Gave its name to the Albigensian heresy (11th-12th cent.) which resulted in the Albigensian Crusade and the creation of the Inquisition.

Albion. Ancient and poetical name for Great Britain, but now usually restricted to England. Possibly a reference to the chalk cliffs of Dover, from Latin *albus* ('white').

Alborz Iran. Mountain range separating the Caspian Sea from the central plateau of Iran and extending in parallel ranges along the S border of the Caspian coastal provinces. Rises to 5669 m (18,600 ft) at Mt Demavand. The N slopes are heavily forested and receive heavy rainfall while the S slopes are dry.

Albula Pass Switzerland. Pass in the Rhaetian Alps in the Graübunden (Grisons) canton reaching a height of 2314 m (7590 ft), leading from the upper Engadine to the valley of the Albula R., a tributary of the upper Rhine (Hinter Rhein). The Albula railway tunnel is about 6 km (4 miles) long and 1800 m (5904 ft) above sea level.

Albuquerque USA. Railway centre and health resort in New Mexico at a height of 1500 m (4920 ft) on the Rio Grande 96 km (60 miles) SW of Santa Fé. Pop. (1990) 384,736.

Pastoral farming in the surrounding

countryside. Railway-engineering, food processing and canning. Tourism is important.

Founded (1706) by the Spaniards. Many distinctively Spanish buildings. Seat of the University of New Mexico (1892).

Albury–Wodonga Australia. Twin cities in New South Wales 216 km (135 miles) WSW of Canberra on the banks of the Murray R. Pop. (1983) 77,970.

Commercial centre. Manufactures furniture and industries inc. engineering. Trade in wool, wheat, wine and fruit.

Alcalá de Guadaira Spain. Market town and resort in Seville province in Andalusia on the Guadaira R. 19 km (12 miles) ESE of Seville. Pop. (1991) 49,099. Well-known for its bread and its olive oil.

Alcalá de Henares Spain. Town in Madrid province in New Castile, on the Henares R. 29 km (18 miles) ENE of Madrid. Pop. (1991) 159,355. Several minor industries.

Famous for its historical associations; birthplace of Cervantes (1547–1616). Noteworthy buildings inc. the old university (founded 1510; removed to Madrid 1836). The Complutensian Polyglot Bible, named after the Roman town Complutum (which stood across the river), was published here (1517).

Alcalá la Real Spain. Town in Jaén province in Andalusia 38 km (24 miles) SSW of Jaén. Pop. (1991) 21,079.

Market town with minor industries. Trade in wine and cereals.

Named la Real ('the royal') to commemorate recapture from the Moors by Alfonso XI (1340).

Alcatraz USA. Rocky island in San Francisco Bay, California, opposite the Golden Gate. From 1933 to 1963, when it was closed, a civil prison used for dangerous long-term criminals.

Alcázar de San Juan Spain. Town in Ciudad Real province in New Castile 80 km (50 miles) NE of Ciudad Real. Pop. (1991) 25,972.

Railway junction. Market town. Trade in wine.

Associated with Cervantes and the story of *Don Quixote*.

Alcoy Spain. Town in the Alicante province in Valencia 40 km (25 miles) N of Alicante. Pop. (1991) 65,514.

Manufactures textiles and paper.

Aldabra Island Indian Ocean. Group of small islands in the form of an atoll, administratively part of the Seychelles until 1965, when they became part of the new colony of the British Indian Ocean Territory. There is no permanent pop. The atoll is regularly visited for the collection of coconuts and turtles.

Aldan Russia. Town in the SE of the Yakut Autonomous Republic 420 km (260 miles) SSW of Yakutsk. Pop. 12,000. Goldmining centre. On the road from Yakutsk to the Trans-Siberian Railway.

Aldan River Russia. River 2700 km (1700 miles) long, rising in the W of the Stanovoi range, flowing generally NE, then N and W and joining the Lena R. near Ust Aldan.

Aldeburgh England. Seaside resort in E Suffolk, 32 km (20 miles) ENE of Ipswich near the estuary of the Alde. Pop. (1991) 2654. Birthplace of the poet George Crabbe (1754–1832). Home of the composer Benjamin Britten (1913–76), who inspired the annual music festival.

Aldermaston England. Village in Berkshire 14 km (9 miles) SW of Reading. Site of the Atomic Weapons Research Establishment. From 1958 to 1963 starting point of the Aldermaston marches organized by the Campaign for Nuclear Disarmament.

Alderney England. Most northerly of the larger Channel Is., a dependency of Guernsey. Area 8 sq km (3 sq. miles). Pop. (1994) 2375. Cap. St Anne (near the centre of the island). Separated from the coast of Normandy by the Race of Alderney 14 km (9 miles) wide. To the W are the Casquets, a group of dangerous rocks (with

Aldershot

a lighthouse) where many ships have been wrecked. Motor vehicles, except tractors, are banned. Alderney cattle reared. Exports early potatoes.

Aldershot England. Town in Hampshire 13 km (8 miles) W of Guildford. Pop. (1991) 51,356. An unimportant village until the permanent military camp was established (1854). Minor industries.

Aldridge-Brownhills England. Town in West Midlands between Walsall and Lichfield, formed in 1966 from the urban districts of Aldridge and Brownhills. Pop. (1971) 88,475.

Engineering and electrical equipment. Manufactures bricks and tiles.

Alegranza Canary Islands. Northernmost islet of the Canaries, situated 232 km (145 miles) NE of Las Palmas. Area 12 sq km (4.5 sq. miles). Uninhabited. Rises to 244 m (800 ft) with extinct volcanoes.

Alençon France. Prefecture of the Orne department, on the Sarthe R. 48 km (30 miles) N of Le Mans. Pop. (1990) 31,139. Market town. Once famous for lace (*point d'Alençon*). Manufactures textiles.

Aleppo (Ar. **Haleb**) Syria. Cap. of the Aleppo province in the NW, Syria's second largest city and the chief industrial and commercial centre of the N. Pop. (1992) 1,445,000.

Manufactures cotton and silk goods, carpets, soap and cement. Trade in cereals, fruit, wool and livestock.

With the ancient citadel on a mount in the centre, it is one of the most picturesque of Eastern cities. Fell to the Hittites *c.* 2000 BC. Taken by the Arabs in AD 638, it flourished as a centre of the caravan trade between Europe and Asia. Under the Turks from 1517; declined with the opening of sea routes to the East. Revived when the railways were constructed early in the 20th cent. and again when Syria achieved independence (1946).

Alès France. Town in the Gard department 40 km (25 miles) NW of Nîmes at the foot of the Cévennes. Pop. (1982) 71,000 (metropolitan area).

Centre of a mining area (coal, iron, zinc). Market for raw silk. Metallurgical, glass, chemical and other industries.

Alessandria Italy. Cap. of Alessandria province in Piedmont, on the right bank of the Tanaro R. 77 km (48 miles) ESE of Turin. Pop. (1990) 93,351.

Railway centre. Engineering, hat manufacture and other industries. It was named in honour of Pope Alexander III.

Aletsch Glacier Switzerland. Glacier in the Bernese Alps, the largest in Europe. Length 26 km (16 miles). Consists of the Great Aletsch (16 km; 10 miles long), Upper Aletsch and Middle Aletsch. To the NW is the Aletschhorn 4195 m (13,763 ft), one of the highest peaks in the Bernese Alps.

Aleutian Islands USA. Chain of over 150 islands, the W continuation of the summits of the Aleutian range of Alaska, extending towards the E Siberian peninsula of Kamchatka. The islands are mountainous, with summits rising to over 5000 m (16,400 ft). Many volcanoes. Owing to the cold Alaska Current and the northerly situation the climate is inhospitable – cold, damp and very foggy. Soil uncultivable. The scanty pop. (of mixed Russian and Eskimo descent) are mainly fur-trappers and fishermen. Though the salmon fisheries are valuable, the main importance of the islands until the end of the Cold War was strategic. Following the Japanese occupation of Kiska and Attu islands (1942) in World War II, the USA has built several air bases here.

Alexander Archipelago USA. Group of over 1000 mountainous islands off the Pacific coast of the Alaskan 'panhandle', the summits of a submerged mountain chain. Main occupation fishing. Chief towns Ketchikan, Sitka.

Alexander Bay ➤ORANGE RIVER.

Alexandria Egypt. Chief seaport and second city on a strip of land separating L. Mareotis (Mariut) from the Mediterranean. Pop. (1990) 3,170,000.

Main export raw cotton. Industries inc. tanneries, cotton-ginning and cottonseed-oil pressing. Manufactures paper, soap, footwear, vehicles, oil and chemicals. Connected by rail with Cairo, Suez and the Nile delta.

Founded (332 BC) by Alexander the Great, partly on the mainland and partly on the island of Pharos ('the lighthouse'), the two being linked by a mole (the Heptastadium), which in time was widened by the accumulation of silt and became an isthmus, forming two harbours, the old (Great) harbour (E) and the present harbour (W). In antiquity Alexandria was a centre of Greek and Jewish culture, with a great university and two famous libraries, a museum, royal palaces and temples; also the most important commercial port of the Mediterranean. The Romans' greatest provincial cap., second city in importance to Rome, with a pop. of 300,000 citizens and a vast number of slaves. Under the later Romans and the Byzantines, a centre of Christian theology. The famous libraries were destroyed or dispersed, largely by the zeal of Theodosius, who destroyed most of the pagan buildings (AD 391). Alexandria fell to the Arabs in the 7th cent. Its commercial importance waned, esp. after the discovery of America and of the Cape route to India; its decline was accelerated when Cairo was chosen as cap. Regained its former splendour in the 19th cent. when Mehemet Ali ordered the construction of the Mahmudiya Canal to the Nile, bringing trade to the city and facilitating irrigation in the neighbourhood. The construction of the Suez Canal (1869) diminished Alexandria's importance, but it has continued to handle the bulk of Egypt's foreign trade. Little of ancient Alexandria remains beyond the granite shaft called Pompey's Pillar, the catacombs and the ruins at Pharos. The two obelisks called Cleopatra's Needles were removed to London and New York in the 19th cent.

Alexandria (Louisiana) USA. Market town on the Red R. 154 km (96 miles) NW of Baton Rouge. Pop. (1970) 41,557.

Centre of a rich cotton-growing area. Engineering, sawmilling, cottonseed-oil pressing, brickmaking.

Alexandria (Virginia) USA. Town on the W bank of the Potomac R. near Washington (DC), of which it is virtually a suburb. Pop. (1990) 111,183. Once a river port of some importance; now mainly residential. Several historic buildings associated with George Washington.

Alexandroupolis Greece. Cap. of the Evros *nome* in Thrace on the Gulf of Ainos, an inlet of the Aegean Sea. Pop. (1971) 22,995. Formerly Turkish; became Greek after World War I.

Alexandrovsk–Grushevsky ►SHAKHTY.

Alfreton England. Town in Derbyshire 21 km (13 miles) NNE of Derby. Pop. (1971) 21,670.

Industrial and former coalmining centre. Ironworks. Manufactures inc. clothing.

Algarve Portugal. S province separated from the rest of the country by mountain ranges ending in Cape St Vincent. Area 5071 sq km (1958 sq. miles). Pop. (1990) 330,000. Cap. Faro.

Produces Mediterranean fruits in the S. Fishing.

Last stronghold of the Moors in Portugal; reconquered 1249. The coastal strip has been overdeveloped for tourism in recent years.

Algeciras Spain. Seaport and resort in the Cádiz province, Andalusia, 88 km (55 miles) SE of Cádiz on Algeciras Bay opposite Gibraltar. Pop. (1991) 101,063.

Exports cork, oranges.

Founded (713) by the Moors. Taken by Alfonso XI of Castile (1344) and destroyed. The modern town was built in 1760.

Algeria. Republic in N Africa, bounded on the W by Morocco and Western Sahara, SW by Mauritania and Mali, SE by Niger, E by Libya and N by the Mediterranean Sea. Area 2,381,741 sq km (919,595 sq. miles). Pop. (1995) 27,939,000 (56 per cent urban). Life expectancy, 67 years male, 69 female. Cap. Algiers. Other major cities Oran, Constantine and Annaba. Currency: Algerian dinar = 100 centimes.

Algeria is divided by elevation and climatic conditions into three unequal parallel zones: The Tell, undulating N region (containing the Little Atlas) of forests and arable land; The Steppe region of herbaceous vegetation and of pasture land diversified by ranges of mountains; The Sahara (S of Sahara Atlas), where agriculture is possible only by irrigation in oases. Coast 1104 km (690 miles), high and rocky. Rivers nothing but torrents (wadis), frequently dried up; some dammed for irrigation; in steppes they form the Shotts of the plains, shallow lakes where snow and rain-water gather in winter. Land use: forested 2 per cent, meadows and pastures 13 per cent, agricultural and under permanent pasture 3 per cent.

The pop. are mainly Berber and Arab Muslims, with some Europeans, principally French. About 83 per cent speak Arabic and 17 per cent Berber. In 1990 Arabic became the sole official language. Virtually the whole pop. are Sunni Muslim.

Much of Algeria has little agricultural value and the chief crops are wheat, barley, dates, potatoes, citrus fruit, grapes, olives and tomatoes. Important oil and natural gas fields are in production in S Algeria. Minerals inc. iron, zinc, lead, mercury, silver, copper and antimony. Principal exports are oil and natural gas (95 per cent by value), wine, iron ore, dates, phosphates, citrus fruits, vegetables and flowers.

The Berbers were the indigenous people of Algeria. It came under Turkish rule in the 16th cent. but the Turks never established total control. They were followed by the Deys, independent rulers who maintained a precarious authority through the Barbary Coast. Annexed by France 1865, it became a department of France. French colonists entered in considerable numbers and with stable government and better communications the pop. grew rapidly. French policy was to integrate Algeria completely into France itself, but the opposition of the colons (established French settlers) to granting equal rights to the Algerians caused an Algerian national movement and the National Liberation Front (FLN, founded 1951) organized open revolt. The colons created the Secret Army Organization (OAS), led by army officers, and both factions opposed the French government's attempts at conciliation during years of violence and terrorism. After a referendum Algeria opted for complete independence (1962), but the nationalization of large estates and the return to France of hundreds of thousands of colons gravely weakened the economy, which France supports by continuing financial help and special trade facilities. Legislative power is held by the 295-member National People's Assembly. Members are elected for 5-year terms as is the President. Following the first round of the 1991 elections the President resigned and the second round was cancelled. A state of emergency was declared and a High Committee of State assumed the power of the President. Algeria is divided, for administrative purposes, into 48 wilayats.

Algiers (El Djezair) Algeria. Cap, chief seaport and largest town on the W side of the Bay of Algiers. Pop. (1987) 1,507,241. Behind the city rises the mountain Bouzaréa (380 m; 1246 ft). The modern French quarter is below the old town and the Kasbah (citadel), which was the residence of the last two native rulers (Deys).

Industries inc. many associated with winemaking, plus chemicals, light engineering and consumer goods. Exports inc. wine, iron ore, fruits, cereals, cork and tobacco.

Muslim city founded in the 10th cent. AD. Flourished under Turkish rule. A base for Barbary pirates from c. 1500 until captured by the French (1830). Supported Vichy France in World War II, until the Allied invasion (1942); then headquarters of General de Gaulle's Free French government. Scene of much violence and bloodshed during the Algerian nationalists' post-war struggle for independence from France.

Alhambra USA. Suburb of Los Angeles, California, with commuter residences. Pop. (1970) 65,125.

Market centre for local fruit and vegetable

farmers. Manufactures oil-refining equipment and plastics.

Alicante Spain. 1. Mediterranean province in the SE formed (1833) from parts of the old provinces of Valencia and Murcia. Area 5863 sq km (2259 sq. miles). Pop. (1991) 1,273,642. Largely barren. Irrigated areas produce wine and fruits.
2. Cap. of Alicante province, seaport 130 km (80 miles) S of Valencia. Pop. (1991) 261,255.

Exports wine, fruits and olive oil. Industries inc. oil-refining and tourism. Manufactures textiles, chemicals, tobacco products and soap.

Alice Springs Australia. Formerly Stuart. Town in the Northern Territory in the Macdonnell ranges at 580 m (1902 ft). Pop. (1991) 24,000. Terminus of the transcontinental railway from the S and of the Stuart Highway from Darwin 1300 km (800 miles) to the NNW. Airport and Flying Doctor base near by. Serves Central Australia, catering for cattlemen, prospectors and tourists.

Aligarh India. Commercial town in the W of Uttar Pradesh, 127 km (78 miles) SE of Delhi. Pop. (1991) 480, 500.

Trade in grain and cotton. Industries inc. cotton-milling, metalworking, food-processing, locks and knives.

Seat of the famous Aligarh Muslim University (1920). Taken from the Mahrattas by the British 1803.

Alima River ➤CONGO.

Al Iskandariya ➤ALEXANDRIA.

Aliwal North South Africa. Town on the Cape Province bank of the Orange R. 180 km (115 miles) SSE of Bloemfontein at a height of 1325 m (4346 ft). Pop. (1970) 12,178. Health resort noted for its hot mineral springs.

Aliwal South ➤MOSSEL BAY

Alkmaar Netherlands. Town in the N Holland province on the N Holland Canal 32 km (20 miles) NNW of Amsterdam. Pop. (1992) 91,817.

Commercial centre with a famous cheese market. Manufactures furniture, clothing and cigars.

Al Kut (Kut al Amara) Iraq. Town on the Tigris R. 160 km (100 miles) SE of Baghdad. Pop. (1970) 59,000.

Trade in grain and dates. The barrage across the Tigris, built to provide irrigation, was opened in 1939.

Allahabad India. City in the SE of Uttar Pradesh, on the Jumna R. near the confluence with the Ganges 560 km (350 miles) SE of Delhi. Pop. (1991) 806,500.

Commercial centre. Trade in grain, cotton and sugar. Industries inc. textiles, cotton-milling, glass, compressors, pumps and telecommunications equipment.

Place of pilgrimage for Hindus because of its position: a religious festival is held annually at the confluence of the sacred Ganges with the Jumna; every 12th year the festival has special significance and is attended by as many as a million pilgrims. Within the fort is the famous pillar (252 BC) with inscriptions of the edicts of Asoka. Nearby are the garden and tomb of Khusru. Ceded to the British in 1801. Cap. of the United Provinces 1901–49.

Allegheny Mountains USA. W part of the Appalachian mountain system, forming the watershed between the Atlantic and the Mississippi R. The mountains contain coal, iron and limestone. Early English colonists coming from the E coast found the plateau difficult to cross and the region was long a frontier zone between the French (in the Mississippi basin) and the English (along the coast). Still heavily wooded, the Alleghenies are of only limited agricultural use.

Allen, Bog of Ireland. Region of peat bogs in central Ireland. Area 958 sq km (370 sq. miles). Drained by the Brosna, Barrow and Boyne rivers. Cultivated in parts. Some of the turf is now cut for use as fuel in power stations.

Allentown USA. Town in Pennsylvania on

the Lehigh R. 80 km (50 miles) NNW of Philadelphia. Pop. (1990) 105,090.

Manufactures textiles, vehicles, steel, industrial gases and high-technology products.

Alleppey India. Seaport and industrial town in Kerala on the Malabar coast 130 km (80 miles) NNW of Trivandrum. Pop. (1981) 169,000.

Exports coir, copra, coconuts. Manufactures coir ropes and matting, coconut oil.

Alliance USA. Town in Ohio 24 km (15 miles) ENE of Canton. Pop. (1990) 24,315.

Iron and steel, engineering and other industries.

Allier France. Department in the centre in the old Bourbonnais province, extending over the upper basins of the Loire, Allier and Cher rivers where they leave the Massif Central. Area 7340 sq km (2834 sq. miles). Pop. (1991) 336,900. Prefecture Moulins.

Cereals and vegetables produced in the Allier basin (Limagne). Pigs and poultry raised. Chief towns are Moulins and Montluçon.

Allier River France. River 430 km (269 miles) long, rising in the Cévennes in the Lozère department, flowing NNW through the fertile Limagne (cereals, vegetables, stock-rearing) and joining the Loire near Nevers.

Alloa Scotland. Industrial town in Clackmannanshire 10 km (6 miles) E of Stirling on the Forth R. Pop. (1991) 18,842.

Industries inc. whisky-distilling, brewing and engineering. Manufactures woollen yarns and glass bottles.

Alloway Scotland. Village in South Ayrshire 3 km (2 miles) S of Ayr. Birthplace of the poet Robert Burns (1759–96).

Alma-Ata ►ALMATY.

Almada Portugal. Town in the Setúbal district on the S bank of the Tagus estuary opposite and S of Lisbon. Pop. (1987) 42,607.

Flour-milling and fish-canning.

Linked with Lisbon by the (Salazar) bridge (opened 1966). Has a huge statue of Christ (total height 109 m; 358 ft) overlooking the Tagus, sculpted (1954–9) by Francisco Franco.

Almadén Spain. Town in the Ciudad Real province in New Castile 83 km (52 miles) WSW of Ciudad Real. Pop. (1991) 7723. Rich mercury mines, which have been worked for centuries.

Almaty Kazakhstan. City and former cap. (as Alma-Ata) situated on the Turksib Railway 680 km (425 miles) ENE of Tashkent. Pop. (1991) 1,156,200. Beautifully situated at 790 m (2591 ft) beneath snow-capped mountains.

Commercial and industrial centre in an agricultural and fruit-growing area. Trade in wheat, sugar-beet, apples, grapes. Manufactures machinery, textiles, food and tobacco products.

Founded by Russians (1854) as a fort on the site of the old Kazakh city of Alma-Ata. Virtually destroyed by earthquakes 1887 and 1911. It developed rapidly after the construction of the Turksib Railway. The Declaration of Alma-Ata was signed in 1991 creating the Commonwealth of Independent States marking the end of the USSR.

Almelo Netherlands. Industrial town in Overijssel province 21 km (13 miles) NW of Enschede. Pop. (1992) 63,383.

Manufactures textiles and furniture.

Almería Spain. 1. Mediterranean province in Andalusia, formed from parts of the ancient kingdom of Granada. Area 8774 sq km (3388 sq. miles). Pop. (1991) 451,649. Mainly mountainous.

Important for minerals (iron, lead). Produces esparto grass and fruits (chiefly grapes).

2. Cap. of Almería province, seaport on the Gulf of Almería 109 km (68 miles) ESE of Granada. Pop. (1991) 153,288.

Exports products of the province, inc. large quantities of grapes.

Flourished under the Moors (8th–15th cent.), when the pop. approached 200,000, but commercial importance declined. The ruins of the San Cristóbal castle overlook the town. Gothic cathedral (16th-cent.).

Alnwick England. Market town in Northumberland on the Aln R. 48 km (30 miles) N of Newcastle upon Tyne. Pop. (1991) 7419.

Industries inc. agricultural engineering, electrical equipment, research and development of pharmaceuticals, opencast mining and the manufacture of fishing rods.

Dominated by Alnwick Castle (14th-cent. in parts). Remains of Alnwick Abbey (12th-cent.).

Alor Star Malaysia. Cap. of Kedah 80 km (50 miles) N of Georgetown on the N–S railway through West Malaysia. Pop. (1980) 71,682.

Commercial centre, esp. for trade in rice.

Alost (Flemish **Aalst**) Belgium. Town in the E Flanders province on the Dender R. 24 km (15 miles) WNW of Brussels. Pop. (1993) 76,514.

Industrial and commercial centre. Manufactures textiles (cotton, linen), clothing. Brewing. Trade in hops.

The Church of St Martin (15th-cent.) has a famous Rubens. Birthplace of Dirk Maartens, who established one of the first printing presses in Europe here (1473).

Alpes-de-Haute-Provence France. Formerly Basses-Alpes: department in the SE, in Provence, bordering on Italy in the NE – renamed on the grounds that the earlier name implied inferiority. Area 6925 sq km (2674 sq. miles). Pop. (1990) 130,900. Prefecture and chief town Digne. Mountainous and infertile in the N and E. Drained by the Durance and its tributaries, inc. the Verdon.

Olives, fruits, vines produced in the valleys.

Alpes-Maritimes France. Department in the SE, in Provence, bounded on the E by Italy, on the S by the Mediterranean Sea and surrounding the principality of Monaco; formed (1860) from the county of Nice and the district of Grasse. Area 4299 sq km (1660 sq. miles) (inc. the 523-sq km (202-sq. mile) frontier strip acquired by the Franco–Italian peace treaty of 1947). Pop. (1991) 963,600. Prefecture Nice. Mountainous, with the Maritime Alps along the N boundary. Principal river the Var.

Flowers, fruits and early vegetables cultivated in the narrow coastal strip. Manufactures perfumes, essences, olive oil.

Along the coast (Côte d'Azur, the W part of the Riviera) are the resorts of Nice, Cannes, Antibes and Menton.

Alphen aan den Rijn (Alfen aan den Rijn) Netherlands. Town situated E of Leiden on the Old Rhine R. in Zuid-Holland. Pop. (1994) 66,143.

It is a railway junction and industries inc. shipbuilding, market-gardening and the manufacture of asphalt, bricks, roofing tiles, ships' machinery, motors, electrical goods, paper, leather products and fruit products.

Alps. The highest and most extensive mountain system of S central Europe curving in a general SW–NE direction from the Mediterranean coast of S France and NW Italy, where they link with the Apennines, through S and central Switzerland and most of Austria, into S Germany, then SE along the Adriatic coast covering in all about 207,200 sq km (80,000 sq. miles). Drained to the North Sea by the Rhine, to the Mediterranean by the Rhône and to the Adriatic by the Po. Usually divided, rather arbitrarily, into Western, Central and Eastern Alps. 1. Western Alps: Maritime, Cottian, Dauphiné and Graian Alps; highest peaks Pic des Écrins (4106 m; 13,467 ft), Gran Paradiso (4064 m; 13,330 ft), Monte Viso (3844 m; 12,608 ft). 2. Central Alps: in the S the Pennine, Lepontine, Rhaetian and Ötztal Alps, in the N the Bernese Alps, Alps of the Four Forest Cantons, Glarus, Allgäu and Bavarian Alps; highest peak is Mont Blanc (4808 m; 15,584 ft), others are: Monte Rosa (4634 m; 15,203 ft), Matterhorn (4477 m; 14,688 ft), Finsteraarhorn (4280 m; 14,038 ft), Jungfrau (4164 m; 13,658 ft), Piz Bernina (4058 m; 13,310 ft). 3. Eastern Alps: Zillertal Alps, Hohe Tauern and Niedere Tauern, flanked to the S by the Dolomites, Carnic Alps, which are continued E by the Karawanken and are linked by the Julian Alps to the Dinaric Alps; highest peaks Gross Glockner (3800 m; 12,464 ft),

Marmolada (3344 m; 10,968 ft). There are numerous passes through the Alps, including the Mont Cenis, Little and Great St Bernard, Simplon, St Gotthard, Maloja, Stelvio, Splügen and Brenner, with railway tunnels at the Mont Cenis, Lötschberg, Simplon and St Gotthard. Altogether there are six tunnels, including one under Mont Blanc. The snow-line varies from about 2400 m (7872 ft) on the N to about 3000 m (9840 ft) on the S side and below this is the zone of characteristic Alpine flora, while the timber line is at 1800 m (5904 ft) to 2100 m (6888 ft) above sea level.

The scenery and the opportunities for mountaineering and winter sports have made tourism an outstanding industry. Dairy-farming is important on the mountain pastures, while vines and other crops are grown in the valleys.

Alps (Australia) ➤AUSTRALIAN ALPS.

Alps (New Zealand) ➤SOUTHERN ALPS.

Alpujarras, Las Spain. Mountainous region in Almería/Granada situated between the Sierra Nevada and the S coast.

Als Denmark. Island off the E coast of S Jutland, separated from the coast by Als Sound but linked with the mainland by a bridge since 1930. Area 313 sq km (121 sq. miles). Chief town Sönderborg. Very fertile and produces grain and fruit. Fishing.

Ceded to Prussia 1864, but returned to Denmark after a plebiscite in 1920.

Alsace (Ger. **Elsass**) France. Ancient Alsatia. Region in the NE between the Vosges and the Rhine, now occupied by the Haut-Rhin and Bas-Rhin departments. Area 8280 sq km (3197 sq. miles). Pop. (1990) 1,624,400.

On the fertile lowlands cereals, hops, tobacco, vegetables, fruit cultivated. Wine produced on the E slopes of the Vosges. Potash mined near Mulhouse. Cotton goods and chemicals manufactured in the Mulhouse–Colmar area. Chief towns Strasbourg (home of the European Parliament), Mulhouse, Colmar and Belfort.

Alsace was for long part of Germany, but in 1648 much of it was ceded to France. More was taken by Louis XIV and the remainder added after the French Revolution (1789). In 1871, after the Franco–Prussian War, all Alsace except the Territory of Belfort was incorporated into Germany to form, with part of Lorraine, the imperial territory of Alsace–Lorraine. By the Treaty of Versailles after World War I, the latter was returned to France and Alsace was divided into its old departments of Haut-Rhin and Bas-Rhin. In addition to preserving their own dialect, the people of Alsace display a strong local patriotism, insisting that they are primarily Alsatian rather than French or German.

Alsace–Lorraine (Ger. **Elsass–Lothringen**). Frontier region between France and Germany, bounded on the E by the Rhine. Incorporated into Germany as an imperial territory (*Reichsland*) after the Franco–Prussian War (1871). Although the inhabitants at that time were mainly Teutonic, since the French Revolution their political sympathies had been with France. They were moving more closely to Germany at the outbreak of World War I, but the region was returned to France by the Treaty of Versailles (1919); Alsace became the departments of Haut-Rhin and Bas-Rhin, and Lorraine the Moselle department. It was again under German rule during World War II, but retaken by French and American forces, and returned to France in 1944.

Altai Mountains Russia. Extensive mountain system in the S of Siberia, continuing SE into Mongolia as the Great Altai. The highest Russian peak is Belukha (4506 m; 14,783 ft). Lead, zinc and silver mined. The principal Russian centre of the atomic industry is at Ust Kamenogorsk. In the NW the lower slopes are thickly forested, in the drier SE there is only semi-desert vegetation.

Altai Territory Russia. Territory in the S of Siberia, bordering on Kazakhstan (W); drained by the upper Ob R. Area 169,100 sq km (65,300 sq. miles). Pop. (1996) 2,690,000. Cap. Barnaul. Includes part of the Altai Mountains and much fertile agricultural land (wheat, sugar-beet, dairy produce). Crossed by the Turksib Railway. Linked by road with Mongolia.

Altamira Cave Spain. Cave 27 km (17 miles) SW of Santander in the Santander province in the N. Palaeolithic wall drawings, discovered in 1879.

Altamura Italy. Town in the Bari province in Apulia 43 km (27 miles) SW of Bari. Pop. (1981) 51,328. Built on the site of a pre-Roman town. Centre of an agricultural district producing wool, cereals, grapes, wine, olives. Manufactures pasta.

Alta River Norway. River flowing 190 km (120 miles) in the Finnmark county in the N, rising near the Finnish border and going generally N to enter the Arctic Ocean by the Alta Fiord. Noted for its salmon.

Altdorf Switzerland. Cap. of the Uri canton near the S end of L. Lucerne. Pop. (1980) 8200. Scene of the adventures of William Tell, with a statue of him where the shooting of the apple from his son's head is supposed to have taken place.

Altenburg Germany. Town in the Gera district in Thuringia 42 km (26 miles) S of Leipzig. Pop. (1981) 55,827.

Commercial and industrial centre in a lignite-mining area. Manufactures sewing-machines, playing cards and hats. Former cap. of the duchy of Saxe-Altenburg.

Altiplano ►ANDES; BOLIVIA.

Alto Adige ►TRENTINO–ALTO ADIGE.

Alton England. Town in Hampshire on the R. Wey 14 km (9 miles) SSE of Basingstoke. Pop. (1991) 16,000.

Industries inc. engineering, brewing and the manufacture of electrical equipment.

Alton USA. Industrial town in Illinois 27 km (17 miles) NNE of St Louis on the E side of the Mississippi. Pop. (1980) 34,171.

Oil-refining, flour-milling. Manufactures glass and paper.

Altona Germany. Industrial town and port on the right bank of the Elbe just below Hamburg (into which it was incorporated 1938).

Industries inc. fish-processing, textiles, tobacco, machine-tool, chemical and other industries.

Became Danish 1640. Burned by the Swedes 1713. Passed to Prussia 1866.

Altoona USA. Industrial town in Pennsylvania 131 km (82 miles) E of Pittsburgh. Pop. (1980) 54,600.

Railway workshops and extensive marshalling yards. Manufactures clothing and electrical equipment.

Developed by the Pennsylvania Railroad (1849), when the line was being constructed across the Alleghenies.

Altötting Germany. Town in Upper Bavaria 83 km (52 miles) E of Munich. Pop. (1985) 12,000. Traditional pilgrimage centre with chapel containing famous image of the Virgin Mary.

Altrincham England. Town in Greater Manchester 13 km (8 miles) SW of the city. Pop. (1991) 40,042.

Industries inc. market gardens supplying the Manchester area and engineering.

Alwar India. Town in the E of Rajasthan 136 km (85 miles) SSW of Delhi. Former cap. of the state of Alwar (which joined the Rajasthan Union 1949). Pop. (1991) 210,010.

Oilseed and flour milling. Trade in millet and cotton goods. Most industries are located in nearby Bhiwadi area and inc. vehicle components, brewing and contact lenses.

Amagasaki Japan. Industrial town in Hyogo prefecture, Honshu, on Osaka Bay just NNW of Osaka. Pop. (1991) 498,038.

Manufactures textiles, chemicals, metal products and glass.

Amager Denmark. Island in The Sound, opposite Copenhagen (part of which is in the N). Area 65 sq km (25 sq. miles). Connected to the mainland by a bridge.

Amalfi Italy. Town in Salerno province in Campania on the Gulf of Salerno 35 km (22 miles) SE of Naples. Pop. (1981) 6000. It is a popular tourist resort. In the 9th cent. an independent republic, becoming a duchy in 953. Taken by the Pisans in the 12th cent. It quickly declined, but its maritime code, the *Tavole Amalfitane*, was recognized in the Mediterranean until 1570.

Amapá Brazil. Federal territory in the NE, N of the Amazon mouth. Area 140,359 sq km (54,193 sq. miles). Pop. (1990) 267,576. Cap. Macapá. Mostly rainforest; coastal mangrove swamps. There are large manganese deposits.

'Amara Iraq. Cap. of the 'Amara province on the Tigris R. 290 km (180 miles) SE of Baghdad. Pop. (1985) 131,800.

Trade in dates, grain and wool. Known for its silverware.

Amarapura Myanmar (Burma). Town in the Mandalay district on the Irrawaddy R. just S of Mandalay. Pop. (1985) 7000. Silk-weaving. Manufactures *lungyis*.

Founded (1783) as the cap.; the pop. rose to 170,000, but the cap. was temporarily moved to Ava 1823. Largely destroyed by earthquake 1839; after Mandalay had become the cap., it was abandoned (1860). Pagodas, the ruins of the old palace and a great statue of Buddha remain.

Amarillo USA. Town in Texas 510 km (320 miles) NW of Fort Worth. Pop. (1990) 157,615.

Commercial and industrial centre in a region producing oil, natural gas and wheat, and raising cattle. Industries inc. oil-refining, meat-packing, flour-milling and synthetic rubber manufacture.

Amaro, Monte ➤APENNINES.

Amasya Turkey. Town and provincial cap. in Amasya province situated SSW of Samsun on Yesil R. Pop. (1985) 63,000.

Industries inc. the manufacture of tiles, and it trades in apples, tobacco, wheat and onions.

Amazonas Brazil. Largest state. In the Amazon basin. Area 1,567,954 sq km (605,390 sq. miles). Pop. (1991) 2,088,682.

Cap. Manáus. One quarter of the pop. live near Manáus, the remainder along the waterways of the vast rainforest.

Amazon River South America. The world's second largest river and largest river system, mainly in Brazil, receiving water from the Andes between 2°N and 20°S, where tributaries in S Bolivia supply the middle Amazon. Its total length is 6515 km (4050 miles). The main river is formed in Peru, only 150 km (95 miles) from the Pacific, by the Marañón–Ucayali confluence (called the Solimoes as far as Manáus). The main north-bank tributary, the Rio Negro, brings water from 5°N in the Guiana Highlands. Other great tributaries, e.g. the Tocantins, Xingu and Tapajos, rise far S in the interior plateaus of Brazil, and on their banks live the few surviving tribes of primitive Indians, under the guardianship of the Indian Protection Service of the Brazilian government. The great silt discharge at the Amazon mouth stains the sea for 300 km (186 miles). Tidal effects are felt 800 km (500 miles) inland and in the lower reaches of the delta there is a bore (*pororoca*) up to 5 m (16 ft) high which travels up the river at the rate of 65 km (41 miles) an hour. Ships of 11,000 tonnes regularly serve Manáus, a distance of 1600 km (1000 miles) upstream, and it is navigable to ocean-going vessels of 6000 tonnes which can reach Iquitos (Peru), 3700 km (2300 miles) from the Atlantic.

The whole system covers 7,050,000 sq km (2,721,000 sq. miles). The lowlands extend for 1300 km (800 miles) N–S; here the rivers have little gradient (the Amazon falls only 11 m (36 ft) in its last 3200 km (2000 miles)) and floods can widen the channels by great distances. There are more than 1000 important tributaries.

The equatorial lowlands have little seasonal or daily temperature variation (monthly averages 27°C (80°F)). Annual rainfall 175–300 cm (70–118 ins.). There are no dry months, but in Sept.-Nov. there is generally less precipitation. Tropical rainforest covers nearly the whole of the Amazon basin, which occupies 40 per cent of the area of Brazil but has less than 7 per cent of its population (which is concentrated around Manáus, Santarém and Belém). Once the tropical forest is cleared, the soil is thin and infertile. The Amazon was discovered in 1500. It was opened to world shipping in 1886.

Ambala India. Town in N Haryana 110 km (70 miles) SE of Ludhiana. Pop. (1991) 139,889.

Railway junction. Industrial and commercial centre. Cotton-ginning, flour-milling, food-processing. Trade in grain and cotton.

Ambato Ecuador. Cap. of Tungurahua province in a hollow near the N base of Mt Chimborazo, at a height of 2500 m (8200 ft), 110 km (70 miles) S of Quito. Pop. (1990) 124,166.

Commercial centre. Resort, the 'garden city of Ecuador', noted for fruit trees and gardens. Manufactures textiles. Industries inc. fruit-canning and tanning.

It suffered severe earthquake damage in 1949.

Amberg Germany. Town in Bavaria on the Vils R. 61 km (38 miles) E of Nuremberg. Pop. (1986) 43,300.

Manufactures enamels, textiles and cement. Iron mines in the neighbourhood.

Cap. of the Upper Palatinate till 1810.

Ambleside England. Town and tourist centre in Cumbria, in the Lake District 1.6 km (1 mile) N of L. Windermere and 19 km (12 miles) NW of Kendal. Pop. (1991) 2905. It has many associations with the poet Wordsworth.

Amboina (**Ambon**) Indonesia. 1. Island in the Moluccas just SW of Ceram in the Maluku province. Area 999 sq km (386 sq. miles). Mountainous, with fertile coastal plains. Main products nutmegs, rice, coconuts and cloves. Chief town Amboina. In 1605 the island was taken from the Portuguese by the Dutch, who in 1623 massacred the inhabitants of a British settlement there – for which Cromwell obtained compensation (1654).

2. Chief town and seaport of Amboina

Island. Pop. (1980) 208,898. Exports copra, spices. Shipbuilding.

Ambon ➤AMBOINA.

America, North and Central. Third largest of the world's six continents. Sometimes considered to comprise Canada, the USA and Mexico, but here taken to include also Greenland, Central America and the West Indies. Total area 24,349,000 sq km (9,785,000 sq. miles). Pop. (1990) 424 million.

In the NW separated from Asia by the Bering Strait (88 km; 55 miles wide) and in the S joined to South America by the Isthmus of Panama. Washed on the N by the Arctic Ocean, on the E by the N Atlantic Ocean, the Gulf of Mexico and the Caribbean, and on the W by the N Pacific Ocean and the Bering Strait. The dominating physical feature is the vast Western Cordillera, extending from Alaska through Canada and the USA and continued by the Sierra Madre ranges of Mexico. The E rim of the Cordillera is formed by the Rocky Mountains; it also inc. the Alaska Range (with Mt McKinley, 6194 m (20,320 ft) the highest peak in North America), the Coast Ranges, the Cascade Range and the Sierra Nevada. Between these W ranges and the Rockies are the Columbia and Colorado Plateaux and the Great Basin in the USA: the central plateau of Mexico lies between the two ranges of Sierra Madre. To the E of the Rockies are the Great Plains, at a height of 600–1500 m (1968–4920 ft). Farther E are the lower central plains, a huge fertile area drained to the Hudson Bay by the Saskatchewan and other rivers, to the Atlantic by the Great Lakes and the St Lawrence, and to the Gulf of Mexico by the great Missouri–Mississippi R. system. Other important rivers are the Mackenzie, the Yukon, the Columbia, the Colorado and the Rio Grande. Large lakes (besides the Great Lakes) inc. (in Canada) Great Bear, Great Slave, Winnipeg and Manitoba; (in the USA) Great Salt; (in Central America) Nicaragua. N of the St Lawrence R. is the Laurentian Plateau; S are the Appalachian Mountains, the principal highlands in the E of the continent, flanked by the Atlantic coastal plain, which widens to the S and continues around the Gulf of Mexico and the Caribbean Sea.

With a N–S length of over 8000 km (5000 miles), the continent has a wide range of climates, from polar in the far N to humid tropical in the S, and a similar variety in the natural vegetation. S of the tundra region (along the Arctic coasts) is a wide belt of coniferous forests, extending along the W mountain slopes as far S as California. In the SW of the USA is an arid desert and semi-desert area; E of the mountains are the vast grass-covered plains. To the E of the grasslands are coniferous (N) and deciduous (S) forests, now widely cleared. Much of the S and SE of the USA is occupied by pine forests. In the more humid parts of tropical Central America and the W Indies there are tropical rainforests; here climate and vegetation are largely dependent on altitude.

North America has great economic resources. The plains produce a high proportion of the world's wheat and maize. The S of the USA is the important cotton-growing area. In Central America and the West Indies coffee, cane sugar and bananas are produced. There is a large output of petroleum, coal and hydroelectric power. The USA produces considerable amounts of copper, lead, sulphur and phosphates, and Canada is rich in nickel, zinc, silver and asbestos. The NE of the USA has become a leading world industrial region and the most densely populated part of the continent.

North America was peopled in prehistoric times from NE Asia, across the Bering Strait, a migration of Mongolian origin which gave rise to the Eskimos and Indians of today. The highest stage of civilization reached in pre-Columbian times was represented by the Aztec and Maya cultures, of which spectacular remains have been found in Mexico and Central America. Farther N the tribes were of a nomadic character. The first Europeans to see North America were Norsemen led by Leif Ericsson, who in the 11th cent. visited a region he called Vinland (probably on the coast of New England), but it was not until after Columbus landed in the Bahamas (1492) that Europe acquired authentic knowledge of the continent. John Cabot discovered the coast of Canada in 1497; Amerigo Vespucci (after whom the continent was named) explored parts of the S Caribbean in 1499. The Spaniards were the first Europeans to conquer and colonize; in the first half of the 16th cent. they established colonies in Mexico and Central America which were to last for 300 years. From the 17th cent. onwards the interior of present-day Canada and the USA was opened up by explorers, fur-traders and missionaries, mainly French and English. The vast majority of immigrants were European; a 10 per cent Negro minority grew in the USA. English became the principal language (though there is a French-speaking minority in Canada). In Mexico and Central America the peoples are largely a mixture of Indian and Spanish; the chief language here and in Cuba is Spanish. In most West Indian islands Negroes are most numerous and the commonest language is English.

America, South. The fourth largest of the six continents. Area 17,611,000 sq km (6,798,000 sq. miles). Pop. (1990) 298 million. Divided politically into the republics of Argentina, Bolivia, Brazil, Chile, Colombia, Ecuador, Paraguay, Peru, Uruguay, Venezuela, Guyana, Suriname and the colony of French Guiana. The chief neighbouring islands, excluding the West Indies, are the Falkland Is., off the SE coast, and the Galápagos Is. (Ecuador).

The Andes, the world's longest mountain system, extends over 6400 km (4000 miles) along the W coast from the Strait of Magellan to the Caribbean Sea, broadening out in Bolivia to a width of about 640 km (400 miles) and enclosing lofty plateaux and the large lakes Titicaca and Poopo, branching out in Colombia (N) into three separate Cordilleras. There are many peaks, exceeding 6000 m (19,680 ft), inc. several volcanoes; Aconcagua 6960 m (22,834 ft) is the highest peak in the Western Hemisphere. The extensive Brazilian plateau (E), rising towards the

Atlantic coast to over 2700 m (8856 ft) and the Guiana Highlands (N) form the ancient core of the continent, being composed of granites, gneisses and schists, overlain in parts by sandstone. Between these highlands are three great river basins: the Orinoco (N), covering the grassy plains (*llanos*) of Venezuela; the Amazon, with a vast network of rivers forming tenuous lines of communication through the *selvas*, the world's largest area of tropical rainforest; the Parana–Paraguay, draining the Gran Chaco (N) and part of the pampas (S), its combined rivers opening out into the estuary of the R. Plate (Río de la Plata).

More than two-thirds of the continent lies within the tropics, but it extends well into the temperate zone (S); as it tapers sharply southwards, however, in its higher latitudes maritime influences are clearly apparent and no region has a high range of temperatures. In the tropical highland areas the climates may be classified according to altitude as *tierra caliente* (hot), *tierra templada* (temperate) and *tierra fría* (cool). The equator crosses the N part of the continent and most of the Amazon basin has an equatorial climate, with constantly high temperatures and abundant rainfall; N and S of the hot, humid rainforest, on the tropical grasslands, the climate shows marked dry and rainy seasons, with summer rainfall maxima, passing S to the warm temperate climate of the pampas, with a moderate, well-distributed rainfall. The climatic pattern W of the Andes is very different from that of the E. In the extreme N the coastal areas are hot and rainy, but the W seaboard of Peru and N Chile, not subject to rain-bearing winds, comprises the arid Atacama desert. S of the desert is the subtropical region of central Chile, with winter rainfall; S Chile, its Andean slopes clothed with forests, has copious all-year rainfall from the prevailing westerlies. Patagonia, on the E side of the Andes and in their rain shadow, consists mainly of steppe and desert.

The importance of agriculture in the South American economy is reflected in the leading exports: coffee from Brazil and Colombia, grains, meat, hides from Argentina and Uruguay, cocoa from Brazil, cotton and sugar from Peru. With certain exceptions, mineral resources are only partially developed. Venezuela is an important producer of petroleum; Bolivia has a significant output of tin and Chile of copper and nitrates. The continent is poor in coal, and hydroelectricity is being developed. Industrial development is still concentrated in the national capitals and seaports. In many countries large areas are served by neither railways nor roads, a result in part of the difficult topography, which in turn has stimulated the development of airlines. Argentina, Brazil and Venezuela are responsible for about three-quarters of the exports of the continent; trade between the republics is very limited.

Vast areas of the interior are practically uninhabited and the only densely populated regions occur as small, isolated pockets, usually near the coast. In many countries *mestizos*, of mixed European and Indian blood, form the majority of the pop., and there are large numbers of blacks and mulattoes in Brazil. In Argentina and Brazil, esp. the former, the peoples are predominantly of European origin; in Bolivia and Peru they are mainly Indian.

South America was probably discovered by Columbus in 1498 and its modern history begins with the agreed division of the continent between Portugal and Spain, the former to receive the E part (later Brazil) and the latter the remainder. The Spanish conquistadors vanquished the Incas of Peru and the Chibchas of Colombia, plundered their mineral wealth, converted them to Christianity and maintained colonial rule by a system of viceroyalties. One colony after another gained independence from Spain in the 1820s under the leadership of Bolívar and San Martín; Brazil became temporarily an Empire in 1822 and a republic in 1889. Only the Guianas remained the colonial possessions of Britain, the Netherlands and France; British Guiana became independent as Guyana (1966) and Dutch Guiana as Suriname (1975). The republics have frequently suffered from political instability and social unrest, at times from disastrous wars.

American Samoa ➤SAMOA, AMERICAN.

Amersfoort Netherlands. Industrial town in the Utrecht province 21 km (13 miles) ENE of Utrecht. Pop. (1992) 104,390.

Manufactures chemicals, bicycles and carpets.

The Koppelpoort is a 14th-cent. watergate.

Amersham England. Town in S Buckinghamshire 11 km (7 miles) ENE of High Wycombe near the Chiltern Hills. Pop. (1991) 17,629.

Manufactures radio isotopes and furniture. Has a 17th-cent. market hall.

Ames USA. Town in Iowa 51 km (32 miles) N of Des Moines. Pop. (1990) 47,196. Centre of a rich maize-growing area. Seat of the Iowa State University (1858).

Amesbury England. Town in Wiltshire, on the R. Avon 11 km (7 miles) N of Salisbury. Pop. (1991) 6300. In a district possessing remains of prehistoric man, inc. Stonehenge.

Amiens France. Prefecture of the Somme department in the N on the Somme R. 118 km (74 miles) N of Paris. Pop. (1990) 136,358. Cap. of Picardy till 1790. Route and industrial centre.

Manufactures cotton, woollen, linen, velvet goods, carpets, clothing and machinery. Market gardens exist to the NE. Trade in grain, beet-sugar and wool.

The Cathedral of Notre Dame (built mainly 1220–88), one of the outstanding French Gothic cathedrals, is the largest church in France. In the Hôtel de Ville (begun 1550) was signed the Treaty of Amiens (1802) between Britain, France, Spain and Holland.

Amirante Islands Indian Ocean. Archipelago 190 km (120 miles) SW of the Seychelles (of which they are a dependency). Pop. about 200. Chief product copra.

Amman Jordan. Cap. 86 km (54 miles) ENE of Jerusalem at a height of 750 m (2394 ft). Pop. (1990) 1,213,300.

Chief industrial centre. Manufactures textiles, cement and tobacco products.

It was established as the cap. in 1921. As Rabbath Ammon, cap. of the Ammonites. Rebuilt by Ptolemy Philadelphus and named Philadelphia in the 3rd cent. BC. Declined after the Arab conquest.

Amoy ➤XIAMEN.

Amravati India. Town in the N of Maharashtra 145 km (90 miles) WSW of Nagpur. Pop. (1991) 421,600.

Commercial centre. Important cotton trade. Industries inc. cotton-ginning.

Amritsar India. Town in the Punjab 51 km (32 miles) E of Lahore (Pakistan). Pop. (1990) 709,456. Railway junction.

Industrial and commercial centre. Manufactures carpets, textiles, agricultural equipment and chemicals. Trade in cotton, wool and hides.

The religious centre of the Sikhs, founded in the 16th cent. around a sacred tank (pool), the Amrita Saras, on a small island on which is the famous Golden Temple. Scene of the Amritsar Massacre (1919), when British troops fired on Indian demonstrators, killing nearly 400.

Amsterdam Netherlands. Cap., seaport and industrial centre, mainly on the S bank of the Ij R. (an arm of the Ijsselmeer) where it is joined by the canalized Amstel R. Pop. (1994) 724,096. It is built on piles; intersected by a network of concentric and radial canals crossed by about 400 bridges. Linked with the sea by the North Holland Canal to the Helder (1825) and the North Sea Canal to Ijmuiden (1876). The Merwede Canal (1892) was widened and deepened 1935–52 and extended from Utrecht to the Waal, accommodating Rhine barges up to 2000 tonnes.

Important centre of diamond cutting and polishing. Shipbuilding, sugar-refining and brewing. Manufactures chemicals and textiles.

Enjoyed its greatest prosperity as a seaport in the 17th cent., when the Treaty of Westphalia (1648) closed the Scheldt to navigation and destroyed the trade of Antwerp. Today overshadowed by Rotterdam. Outstanding buildings inc. the Rijksmuseum, with a priceless collection of Dutch and Flemish paintings, inc. several by Rembrandt; the 13th-cent. Oude Kerk and 15th-cent. Nieuwe Kerk; and the 17th-cent. royal palace (formerly a town hall). The international airport is at Schiphol 8 km (5 miles) to the SW.

Amsterdam USA. Town in New York State on the Mohawk R. 48 km (30 miles) NW of Albany. Pop. (1970) 25,524. Manufactures carpets, textiles and plastics.

Amsterdam Island (Nouvelle Amsterdam) Indian Ocean. Island situated lat. 38°S, long. 78° E, from 1955 part of the French Southern and Antarctic Territories. Area 65 sq km (25 sq. miles). Of volcanic origin; rises to 900 m (2952 ft). Meteorological and research stations. Annexed by France 1843.

Amu Darya Uzbekistan/Afghanistan. Ancient Oxus. River rising in the Pamirs in a headstream called the Pyandzh R. Total length 2400 km (1500 miles). Flows generally W, forming much of the Afghanistan–Russian boundary. It separates the Kara Kum and the Kyzyl Kum deserts and enters the Aral Sea by an extensive delta. Much used for irrigation (e.g. Khiva oasis). Navigable for more than 1450 km (800 miles).

Amur River China/Russia. River in E Asia, formed on the Russia–China frontier by the union of the Shilka and Argun rivers, flowing nearly 2800 km (1800 miles) first SE and then NE, entering the Sea of Okhotsk opposite the N end of Sakhalin. Total length with the Shilka headstream 4300 km (2690 miles). Chief tributaries are the Sungari and the Ussuri, both from the S. Above its confluence with the Ussuri, the Amur with the Argun forms part of the frontier between Russia and China; below the confluence the Ussuri forms another long section of the frontier. It drains 2,072,000 sq km (800,000 sq. miles). The river is ice-free May–Oct. and much of it is navigable. Important towns on its banks are Blagoveshchensk, Khabarovsk, Komso-

molsk and Nikolyevsk. Blagoveshchensk, cap. of the Amur Region of Russia, is the centre of the Amur Railway, linked with the Trans-Siberian Railway.

Anadyr Russia. Small town on the estuary of the Anadyr R. Industries inc. lignite-mining and fish-canning.

Anadyr Range Russia. Mountain range in the extreme NE of Siberia extending SE from the coast of the E Siberian Sea. Rises to over 1500 m (4920 ft).

Anadyr River Russia. River 800 km (500 miles) long, rising at the N end of the Gydan range in NE Siberia, flowing SW and then E, and entering the Gulf of Anadyr on the Bering Sea.

Anaheim USA. City situated S of Los Angeles, California. Pop. (1990) 266,406. It is a manufacturing and tourist centre.

Anáhuac Mexico. 'The land near the waters': pre-Conquest name for the Mexico basin, the densely populated part of the central plateau where Mexico City stands. The name derives from the many former lakes, now mainly dry.

Anambra Nigeria. State comprising the Abakaliki, Enugu and Onitsha provinces of the former East region. Area 17,675 sq km (6824 sq. miles). Cap. Awaka. Pop. (1991) 2,767,903.

Main occupations are mining, car manufacture, cement manufacture, brewing and food-processing. There are considerable reserves of minerals inc. iron ore, salt, coal, zinc, oil and natural gas.

The state is mainly populated by Ibo people and this area formed the centre of the Biafran secession 1967–70.

Anatolia ➤ASIA MINOR.

Anchorage USA. Largest and most important industrial town in Alaska in the S at the head of the Cook Inlet. Pop. (1990) 226,338. On the railway to Fairbanks.

Railway workshops. Salmon canneries. Fur market, airport and seaport. Coal and gold mined near by.

Ancona Italy. Cap. of Ancona province in The Marches; also cap. of The Marches. Pop. (1990) 103,268.

Seaport and industrial centre. Ship-building, sugar-refining.

Founded in the 4th cent. BC by Greeks from Syracuse. Flourished under the Romans and has a white triumphal arch erected in honour of Trajan (AD 115).

Åndalsnes Norway. Town in the Möre og Romsdal county at the head of Romsdal Fiord 170 km (105 miles) WSW of Trondheim. Pop. 1400. Scene of the first British landings in World War II (1940). Severely damaged in the ensuing battle.

Andalusia Spain. Region and former province in the S, bounded S by the Mediterranean and Atlantic. Comprises the modern provinces of Almería, Granada, Málaga, Cadiz, Huelva, Seville, Córdoba and Jaén. Much of it consists of the basin of the R. Guadalquivir and in the SE is the Sierra Nevada, which has Mulhacén (3482 m; 11,420 ft), the highest peak in Spain. Irrigation has made it one of the most fertile parts of Spain, producing olives, vines, cereals, citrus fruits and even sugar-cane. Also rich in minerals, Fishing is important along the coast.

Attained its greatest glory under Moorish rule, which lasted from the 8th to the end of the 15th cent. and left outstanding monuments in such cities as Seville, Córdoba and Granada.

Andaman and Nicobar Islands Indian Ocean. Islands 193 km (120 miles) SSW off Cape Negrai (Myanmar (Burma)); a territory of India. Area 6408 sq km (2503 sq. miles). Pop. (1991) 279,111. Cap. Port Blair (S Andaman). A N–S band; the five large N islands (the Great Andamans, inc. N, Middle and S Andaman) are separated from Little Andaman (S) by the Duncan Passage. Also about 200 islets. Generally hilly; well covered with tropical forests, which yield padouk (Andaman redwood) and other valuable timbers. Coconuts, rice, coffee and rubber cultivated. Copra and timber exported from Port

Blair. The extremely primitive aboriginal Negritos live in the forests and are now few in number (probably less than 100). The islands are accessible by air and sea from Calcutta and Madras.

Andermatt Switzerland. Village in the Uri canton 26 km (16 miles) S of Altdorf in the Urseren valley at a height of 1400 m (4592 ft). Pop. (1970) 1589. Summer resort and winter-sports centre. On the Furka–Oberalp railway and the road to the St Gotthard Pass.

Anderson (Indiana) USA. Industrial town on the White R. 56 km (35 miles) NE of Indianapolis. Pop. (1990) 59,459. Manufactures motor-car parts and machinery.

Anderson (South Carolina) USA. Industrial town 48 km (30 miles) SW of Greenville. Pop. (1970) 27,556. Manufactures cotton goods and chemicals.

Andes South America. Mountain system, raised, folded and faulted in late Tertiary times extending 7200 km (4500 miles) along the W side of South America from the isthmus of Panama to Tierra del Fuego. It is much lower in the S, where it is cut through by glaciated valleys. In Bolivia and S Peru the E and W Cordilleras enclose the Altiplano (3500–4000 m; 11,480–13,120 ft), a high, bleak tableland containing various basins, deep river-cut valleys and the large L. Titicaca 3658 m (11,998 ft). Rivers from the high W Cordillera cut far into the plateaux and through the E foothills and here, only 160 km (100 miles) from the Pacific, the first tributaries of the Amazon start their 4800-km (3000-mile) course to the Atlantic. The N and central Andes enclose many high basins, which are important pockets of pop. North from S Colombia are three parallel Cordilleras, separated by deep valleys containing the Cauca and Magdalena rivers; the E Cordillera has many high basins.

There are many volcanoes still active and Cotopaxi 5996 m (19,457 ft) in Ecuador is the highest in the world. The Andes and foothills are subject to severe earthquakes. The snowline is at 4500 m (14,760 ft) in Ecuador, 6300 m (20,664 ft) in N Chile, and only 700 m (2296 ft) in extreme S Chile, where large permanent icefields and glaciers occur.

Amerindians, e.g. the Chibchas of Colombia, were established in the Andes before the rise of the Inca Empire. From the 13th cent. millions lived under the Inca administration, centred mainly on the Cuzco region of Peru. Gold, silver and copper were worked from early times. Potatoes and maize were first cultivated here. In the 16th cent. the Spanish conquerors destroyed Inca agriculture but intensified the mining of silver.

Many minerals come from the high Andes: manganese, sodium nitrate, borax, quicksilver, copper, tin, silver, lead and zinc. Peru and Bolivia are the richest metal-bearing countries. From the W flanks (where the Andean slopes are separated from the coastal range by debris-filled troughs) come iron ore, nitrates and iodine, and petroleum from the adjoining lowlands E and W. Settlement is concentrated in the high basins. Wool from the sheep, llama and vicuña is the main commodity of exchange. In 1910 the Andes were tunnelled and Argentina and Chile are linked by the Upsallata tunnel which is 3200 m (10,500 ft) above sea level.

Andhra Pradesh India. State in the SE, formed in 1953 from the Telugu-speaking area of N Madras; further boundary adjustments made in 1956 and 1960. Area 275,068 sq km (107,448 sq. miles). Pop. (1991) 66,354,559. Cap. Hyderabad. Chief seaport Visakhapatnam.

Principal crops are rice, sugar-cane, groundnuts, castor and tobacco. Industries inc. machine-tools, pharmaceuticals, heavy electrical machinery, shipbuilding, fertilizers, aeronautical parts, chemicals, asbestos, glass, watches, oil refinery. Important minerals are barytes, copper ore, manganese ore, mica, coal and limestone.

Andizhan Uzbekistan. Cap. of the Andizhan Region in the fertile Fergana valley 260 km (160 miles) ESE of Tashkent. Pop. (1991) 298,300.

Trade in cotton. Produces cotton goods, cottonseed, oil, foodstuffs.

Destroyed by earthquake in 1902 and rebuilt.

Andorra. Independent state in the central Pyrenees on the Franco–Spanish frontier. Area 468 sq km (181 sq. miles). Pop. (1997) 64,479, distributed among seven villages. Life expectancy, 76 years male, 82 female. Cap. Andorra la Vella. Currency: French franc = 100 centimes and Spanish peseta = 100 céntimos. Mountainous, rising to nearly 3000 m (9840 ft) with deep valleys and gorges. Drained by the Valira R. Climate harsh. Land use: forested 24 per cent, meadows and pastures 44 per cent, agricultural and under permanent pasture 4 per cent. The pop. is Catalan in origin, the religion is Roman Catholic and the language Catalan, but Spanish and French also spoken.

The main occupation tourism (12 million visitors annually) and sheep-rearing. Some barley and tobacco is cultivated.

Its independence was instituted by Charlemagne, the first Holy Roman Emperor, in exchange for help against the invading Moors. Until 1993 it was under the joint suzerainty of the President of France and the Spanish Bishop of Urgel, to both of whom nominal tributes were paid. The two 'co-princes' were represented in Andorra by the 'Viguier de France' and the 'Viguiet Episcopal'. A new Constitution came into being in 1993 and Andorra became a sovereign state. It is governed by a 28-member General Council.

Andorra la Vella. Cap. of Andorra situated on the R. Valira at 914 m (c. 3000 ft) above sea level and 4 km (2½ miles) from the Spanish border. Pop. (1997) 21,721. It is mainly modern with good highways but no rail or air services. A centre for duty-free marketing and for tourism, esp. winter sports.

A medieval foundation, the town remained small and served a rustic area until after 1945, since when development has been rapid.

Andover England. Market town in Hampshire 19 km (12 miles) NW of Winchester.

Andria

Pop. (1991) 34,647. Industries inc. flour-milling.

Andria Italy. Town in Bari province in Apulia, 51 km (32 miles) WNW of Bari. Pop. (1981) 83,319.

Produces wine, olive oil and pasta. Founded in the 11th cent.

Andros Bahamas. Largest island in the Bahamas situated W of New Providence Is. Area 5957 sq km (2300 sq. miles). Pop. (1990) 8155. Occupations inc. fishing and forestry (Yellow pine).

Andros Greece. 1. Most northerly island of the Cyclades in the Aegean Sea. Area 303 sq km (117 sq. miles). Mountainous, with many fertile valleys. Famous for wine since ancient times.

2. Chief town of Andros Is. on the E coast. Pop. (1971) 2032.

Andújar Spain. Town in the Jaén province in Andalusia, on the Guadalquivir R. 38 km (24 miles) NW of Jaén. Pop. (1981) 30,875.

Commercial centre. Famous for *alcarrazas* (jars for keeping water cool). Soap, textile and other industries. There is also a uranium plant.

Anécho ▶TOGO.

Aneityum Vanuatu. Island in the southernmost of the New Hebrides group in the SW Pacific. Area 65 sq km (25 sq. miles). Kauri pine is cultivated.

Angara River Russia. River 1840 km (1150 miles) long in SE Siberia, flowing from L. Baikal (SW) NNW past Irkutsk and then W, joining the Yenisei R. at Strelka. In the lower course sometimes called the Upper Tunguska. Navigable for most of the course. Utilized for hydroelectic power.

Angarsk Russia. Industrial town in the Irkutsk Region on the Angara R. 48 km (30 miles) NW of Irkutsk. Pop. (1991) 268,500.

Manufactures building materials, petrochemicals and machinery.

Angel Falls Venezuela. Waterfall in the SE on a tributary of the Caroní R. At 980 m (3214 ft), probably the highest in the world. Named after Jimmy Angel, an airman, who discovered them in 1937.

Ångerman River Sweden. River 448 km (280 miles) long, rising near the Norwegian frontier and flowing SSE to the Gulf of Bothnia near Harnosand. Hydroelectric plants. Used for floating timber down to sawmills on the estuary.

Angers France. Prefecture of the Maine-et-Loire department in the W on the Maine R. 83 km (52 miles) ENE of Nantes. Pop. (1990) 146,163.

Commercial and industrial centre. Produces wine, textiles, footwear, agricultural machinery.

Seat of the Counts of Anjou from the 9th to the 13th cent. Architecturally one of the finest French towns, with the 13th-cent. castle (built by Louis IX), the 12th/13th-cent. cathedral, the Logis Barrault (a 15th-cent. Renaissance house) and various churches and museums.

Angkor Cambodia. Ruins just N of Siemreap N of L. Tonlé Sap. A remnant of the Khmer civilization; dates from the 9th–12th cent. Angkor Thom, the ancient Khmer cap., is enclosed by a wall and contains the royal palace and remarkable Bayon temple. Just S is the great temple of Angkor Wat (or Angkor Vat), the best preserved example of Khmer architecture and one of the world's outstanding buildings. Abandoned in the 15th cent. Discovered in a dense jungle in the 1860s and later cleared.

Anglesey (Ynys Môn) Wales. Ancient Mona. Island and unitary authority of Isle of Anglesey off the NW coast, separated from the mainland (Gwynedd) by the Menai Strait. Area 715 sq km (276 sq. miles). Pop. (1994) 67,800. Chief town Beaumaris. Low-lying, generally flat. Linked with the mainland by road and railway bridges.

Chief occupations agriculture and sheep-rearing. Tourism is important. Other chief towns Holyhead (on Holy Island off the W coast), a ferry port for Ireland (Dun Laoghaire), Amlwch, Menai Bridge.

Angmagssalik Greenland. Small trading post and settlement (mainly of Eskimo) on Angmagssalik Is. in the E about 95 km (60 miles) S of the Arctic Circle. The US base (established 1941) has an important meteorological and radio station.

Angola. Republic of SW Africa bounded on the N by the Republic of Congo and the Democratic Republic of Congo, on the E by the Democratic Republic of Congo and Zambia, on the S by Namibia and on the W by the Atlantic. Area 1,246,700 sq km (481,351 sq. miles), inc. the province of Cabinda, an enclave of territory bounded N by Congo and E and S by Democratic Republic of Congo. Pop. (1995) 11,558,000 (28 per cent urban). Life expectancy, 45 years male, 48 female. Cap. Luanda. Other important towns are Lobito, Benguela, Namibe, Lubango and Huambo. Currency: New kwanza = 100 lwei. Angola consists of a narrow coastal plain (1600-km; 1000-mile coastline) and a broad dissected tableland (at 1200–1800 m; 3936–5904 ft) which descends eastwards to the basins of the Congo and Zambezi. Land use: forested 11 per cent, meadows and pastures 9 per cent, agricultural and under permanent pasture 18 per cent. Ethnic composition, Ovimbundu 37 per cent, Mbundu 22 per cent and 90 per cent are Christian (of which Roman Catholic 69 per cent). The official language is Portuguese but local languages in common use.

There are sugar-cane, cacao and cotton plantations on the hot unhealthy lowlands of the N. Coffee and sisal produced on the plateau. Subsistence crops inc. maize, cassava, rice. Cattle raised on parts of the plateau free from the tsetse fly. Diamonds are mined in the NE. Steel and cement are produced. The Benguela railway runs from Lobito across Angola through Shaba (Democratic Republic of Congo), Zambia and Zimbabwe to Beira in Mozambique. Exports inc. oil, coffee and diamonds. There is considerable unexploited mineral wealth.

The N coast was discovered by the Portuguese in 1491, Luanda was founded in 1575. Portuguese sovereignty over the coastline remained almost continuous. From the 17th to the 19th cent. the colony's prosperity depended on the slave trade; economic development was very slow. There was open rebellion in the N in 1961–2. There was a demand for the end of Portuguese rule, guerrilla warfare broke out and independence was granted in 1975; the liberation groups then fought one another, one faction (eventually successful) being assisted by Soviet arms and equipment and Cuban militiamen, the others by US and South African arms and equipment. Angola is potentially one of Africa's richest countries but several decades of war and an extreme Marxist government have caused considerable poverty and hardship. Moves towards a multi-party state began in 1991.

Angostura ➤CIUDAD BOLÍVAR.

Angoulême France. Prefecture of the Charente department 109 km (68 miles) NNE of Bordeaux on a 90-m (295-ft) high promontory overlooking the Charente R. Pop. (1990) 46,194. Route centre.

Industries inc. paper mills, breweries and distilleries.

It became the seat of the Counts of Angoumois in the 9th cent.

Anguilla West Indies. One of the Leeward Is. situated 96 km (60 miles) NNW of St Kitts and a United Kingdom Overseas Territory. Area 96 sq km (37 sq. miles). Pop. (1990) 7019. Cap. The Valley, where 25 per cent of the pop. live. The agricultural potential is limited because of low rainfall and the main source of income is tourism.

Anguilla was probably given its name by the Spaniards because of its eel-like shape. It was administered by the British in the 17th cent. as part of the Leeward Is. and later was incorporated in the colony of St Kitts–Nevis–Anguilla. In 1967 Anguilla seceded and became a separate dependency of Britain and this was formalized in 1980.

Angus Scotland. New Unitary Authority created in 1996, formerly part of Tayside Region. Area 1937 sq km (748 sq. miles). Pop. (1993) 111,020.

Anhui China. Province in the E on both sides of the Yangtse R. Area 139,900 sq km (54,000 sq. miles). Pop. (1992) 52,290,000. Cap. Hefei.

Chief crops wheat, millets, beans (in the N); rice, tea, cotton (in the hillier S).

Anhwei ➤ANHUI.

Ani Turkey. Ancient Abnikum. Ruined city of medieval Armenia in the Kars province in NE Turkey E of Kars near the Armenian frontier. Remains of cathedral, churches. Cap. of Armenia in the 10th cent. Destroyed by earthquake in the 14th cent.

Aniene (Teverone) River Italy. River 117 km (73 miles) long, rising in the Apennines and joining the Tiber just above Rome. Has supplied Rome with water for centuries. Now a source of hydroelectric power. There is a famous waterfall at Tivoli.

Anjou France. Former province in the Paris Basin, now approximately forming the Maine-et-Loire department. Cap. Angers. Geoffrey Plantagenet, Count of Anjou, was the father of the English king Henry II. Annexed by Louis XI of France 1480.

Anjouan ➤NZWANI.

Ankara Turkey. Cap. of Turkey and of Ankara province on a hill above the Anatolian plateau 320 km (200 miles) ESE of Istanbul at a height of 870 m (2854 ft). Pop. (1990) 2,559,471.

Commercial and industrial centre. Trade in grain, wool and in mohair from Angora goats. Manufactures inc. textiles, cement, leather goods and food.

Architecture reflects all periods of the city's growth from the Roman to the rule of the Ottoman Turks. The modern city dates mainly from post-1923 and is dominated by the mausoleum of Kemal Atatürk; otherwise its main function (government) has dictated its composition. Old Ankara was a trading place at a crossroads of long-distance routes; it retains a 15th-cent. market and a bazaar and caravanserai of the same period. An ancient settlement on an important caravan route, Ankara was taken by Rome in 25 BC. It was finally taken from the Roman (Byzantine) empire by the Seljuq Turks, but it was the Ottoman Turks who restored its prosperity as a trading centre after 1400. Kemal Atatürk made the city his headquarters in 1919; with the success of his republic it replaced Istanbul as the national cap. in 1923.

Anking ➤ANQING.

Annaba Algeria. Formerly Bône. A Mediterranean seaport in the Annaba department 420 km (260 miles) E of Algiers. Pop. (1987) 305,526.

Iron ore was found in the region and industries inc. iron and steel and chemicals. Iron ore, wine, cork and phosphates are exported.

A centre of early Christianity; for 35 years the episcopal see of St Augustine. Taken by the French in 1832.

Annam. Former kingdom and French protectorate in SE Asia. Part of Vietnam since 1946.

Annan Scotland. Market town in Dumfries and Galloway on the Annan R. 24 km (15 miles) ESE of Dumfries. Pop. (1991) 8930.

Flour-milling, whisky-distilling. Manufactures fertilizers.

The first nuclear power station to operate in Scotland was opened nearby in 1959.

Annan River Scotland. River 78 km (49 miles) long, rising in the Moffat Hills and flowing S into the Solway Firth 3 km (2 miles) S of Annan.

Annapolis USA. State cap. of Maryland near the mouth of the Severn R. 37 km (23 miles) S of Baltimore. Pop. (1990) 33,187. Residential town, with historic buildings. Founded 1649, as Providence; renamed (1694) after Princess Anne (later Queen Anne).

Annapolis Royal Canada. Town in Nova Scotia on the Annapolis Basin, an arm of the Bay of Fundy, and at the mouth of the Annapolis R. whose valley is famous for its apple orchards. Founded (1605) by de Monts as Port Royal. Ceded to Britain 1713 and renamed in honour of Queen Anne.

Annapurna Nepal. Mountain in the central Himalayas, part of the mountain massif of Annapurna–Himal, situated about 175 km (110 miles) NW of Kathmandu. It is the ninth highest mountain in the world at 8078 m (26,502 ft).

Ann Arbor USA. Town in Michigan 51 km (32 miles) W of Detroit. Pop. (1990) 109,592.
Manufactures scientific instruments, cameras, motor-car accessories.

Annecy France. Prefecture of the Haute-Savoie department on the N shore of L. Annecy 35 km (22 miles) S of Geneva at a height of 440 m (1443 ft). Pop. (1990) 51,143.
Industrial centre. Manufactures textiles, paper and watches. The arcaded streets, lakeside aspect and pleasant climate have made it a popular resort. Annecy-le-Vieux (3 km (2 miles) NNE) has a famous bell foundry.
At the reconstructed convent of the Visitation is the tomb of St Francis of Sales (1567–1622), bishop of Geneva, who was born nearby.

Annecy, Lake France. Lake in the SE in the Haute-Savoie department. Area 26 sq km (10 sq. miles). A popular tourist area.

Annobón ➤PAGALU.

Annonay ➤ARDÈCHE.

Anqing (Anching/Anking) China. Formerly (1912–49) Hwaining. Commercial town and river port in Anhui province on the N bank of the Yangtse R. 240 km (150 miles) SW of Nanjing. Pop. (1990) 142,170.
Trade in rice and cotton. Once an important regional centre and cap. of Anhui province; declined with the building of the railway to Wuhu and Kiukiang.

Ansbach Germany. Town in Bavaria 42 km (26 miles) WSW of Nuremberg. Pop. (1986) 37,500. Manufactures machinery and textiles.
Residence of the Hohenzollerns 1331–1791. Transferred from Prussia to Bavaria 1806.

Antarctica

Anshan China. Industrial town in Liaoning province in the NE 96 km (60 miles) SW of Shenyang. Pop. (1990) 1,203,986.
A leading metallurgical centre. Important iron and steel plant. Manufactures chemicals and cement.

Anstruther Scotland. Fishing port and seaside resort in Fife on the Firth of Forth 13 km (8 miles) SSE of St Andrews. Pop. (1971) 3000. Consists of Anstruther Easter, Anstruther Wester and Kilrenny.

Antakya ➤ANTIOCH.

Antalya Turkey. Cap. of the Antalya province in the SW on the Gulf of Antalya 375 km (235 miles) W of Adana. Pop. (1990) 353,149.
Freeport. Trade in grain, timber. Industries inc. tourism, flour-milling and canning.

Antananarivo Madagascar. Cap. and chief commercial and industrial centre on the interior plateau at 1460 m (4789 ft) 225 km (140 miles) WSW of Toamasina to which it is linked by rail. Pop. (1990) 802,390.
Manufactures footwear, leather goods, clothing and soap. Other industries inc. tobacco, flour-milling and meat-packing.
It was founded in the 17th cent. by a Hova chief.

Antarctica. Continental land mass surrounding the South Pole with an area of 13,340,000 sq km (5,149,240 sq. miles). Roughly circular, with the Ross Sea indenting the Pacific side and the Weddell Sea the Atlantic side. The central area is an icecap with ice sheet extending over most of the land area at between 1800–3000 m (5904–9840 ft); the movement of ice barriers, glaciers and shelves makes for continual alteration of the coastline. Very severe climate, winter temperatures dropping to −62°C (−80°F) and summer temperatures only rising to −9°C (15°F). Few forms of life survive the cold; birds and animals live mainly on coastline, inc. penguins, whales and seals. Divided between Norway, Australia, France, New Zealand, Great Britain. Chile and Argentina have overlapping claims. Uninhabited, except for visiting survey teams.

Capt. Cook reached 71°10'S on his voyages of 1772–5 and previous to this the search for a 'great south land' had provided a motive for southern exploration, though none survived to describe land S of the Antarctic Circle. In the late 18th and early 19th cent. sealers and whalers began to discover islands off Antarctica. In 1821 a Russian expedition under F. von Bellingshausen reached land within the Antarctic Circle. Whaling and sealing interests brought Weddell, Biscoe and Balleny to make discoveries and scientific investigations and explorations were successfully made in 1839–43 by Wilkes from the USA, Dumont d'Urville from France and Sir James Ross from Great Britain. Investigations of Antarctic waters by Sir John Murray in HMS *Challenger* (1874) and by the Norwegian captains Larsen and Christensen (1892–5) added to knowledge of the continent. Exploration by well-equipped expeditions followed: under Scott (1901–4), Shackleton (1908–9) and Amundsen, who in 1911 first reached the S Pole, a month before Scott, who perished with his companions on the return journey. In 1929 Byrd, who had previously explored in Antarctica, flew to the S Pole. Shortly before his death he directed the 1955–8 expedition, formed to gain scientific information, as a contribution to the International Geophysical Year. Also contributing knowledge was a Commonwealth Trans-Antarctic expedition under Sir Vivian Fuchs, whose tracked vehicles crossed from Shackleton Base on Weddell Sea to Scott Base at McMurdo Sound, Ross Sea, via the Pole. The area S of 60°S is reserved for international peaceful scientific investigation under the International Antarctic Treaty (1959); otherwise various territories are claimed, except in the sector S of the Pacific between 80° and 150° W, where the USA has made much exploration.

Antibes France. Port and resort in the Alpes-Maritimes department on the French Riviera 19 km (12 miles) SW of Nice. Pop. (1990) 70,688.

Exports flowers. Manufactures perfumes, chocolate. The famous resorts of Juan-les-Pins and Cap d'Antibes (on the peninsula of the same name) are nearby. There are Roman remains. The Château Grimaldi, a museum, has works by Picasso.

Anticosti Canada. Large island in Quebec province in the Gulf of St Lawrence 216 km (135 miles) long and up to 48 km (30 miles) wide. Well wooded (mainly conifers); the chief occupation of the small pop. is lumbering. It was discovered (1534) by Cartier.

Antifer France. Oil terminal situated N of Le Havre in Seine-Maritime department. It is equipped to take 500,000-ton oil tankers.

Antigua and Barbuda West Indies. Independent state comprising three islands of the Lesser Antilles situated N of Guadeloupe. Area 442 sq km (171 sq. miles); Antigua 280 sq km (108 sq. miles); Barbuda 161 sq km (62 sq. miles) and uninhabited Redonda 1 sq km (0.38 sq. mile). Pop. (1995) 63,880 (36 per cent urban). Life expectancy, 71 years male, 75 female. Cap. and chief seaport St John's. Currency: East Caribbean dollar = 100 cents. It has a relatively dry climate and occasional hurricanes, but is fertile. Land use: forested 11 per cent, meadows and pastures 9 per cent, agricultural and under permanent cultivation 18 per cent.

English is the official language and the pop. is mainly Christian.

Fruit, sugar-cane for local needs and sea-island cotton are cultivated. Principal products sugar, clothing, rum (from molasses imported from Guyana) and cotton. There is an oil refinery and tourism is of great importance to the economy.

Antigua was discovered in 1493 by Columbus. First colonized by the English 1632; declared a British possession 1667. Became an Associated State of the UK within the Commonwealth 1967 and obtained independence in 1981. There is a bicameral legislature with a 17-member House of Representatives elected for 5-year terms by universal suffrage.

Antigua (Antigua Guatemala) Guatemala. Ancient cap. (hence the name) 26 km (16 miles) W of Guatemala city, whence the cap. was removed when it was virtually destroyed by earthquakes in 1883. Pop. (1989) 27,000.

Now a commercial centre in a coffee-growing region. There is an important tourist industry.

Antilles. A great arc of islands extending more than 3200 km (2000 miles) round the Caribbean Sea and inc. all the W Indies except the Bahamas. The Greater Antilles consist of Cuba, Jamaica, Hispaniola (Haiti and Dominican Republic) and Puerto Rico. The Lesser Antilles consist of the Leeward Is., the Windward Is. and the islands off the coast of Venezuela (inc. the Netherlands Antilles).

Antilles, Netherlands ►NETHERLANDS ANTILLES.

Antioch (Antakya) Turkey. 1. Cap. of the Hatay province in the S 88 km (55 miles) W of Aleppo in Syria on the Orontes R. Pop. (1990) 123,871.

Commercial centre. Trade in grain and cotton. Industries inc. food-processing.

Founded by Seleucus I c. 300 BC. Became a great commercial city. An early centre of Christianity, it fell to the Persians (AD 538), the Arabs (636) and Seljuk Turks (1084), the Mamelukes (1268) and the Ottoman Turks (1516). Thereafter declined. 2. Ancient city of Pisidia near modern Aksehir on the Anatolian plateau. Founded by Seleucus I c. 280 BC. It was visited by St Paul.

Antipodes Islands New Zealand. Small group of uninhabited rocky islands at 49°45'S, 178°40'E, in the S Pacific about 720 km (450 miles) SE of South Island.

Antisana Ecuador. Volcano in the Andes 5704 m (18,714 ft) high 50 km (32 miles) ESE of Quito. Part of a large snow-capped massif, with a village settlement at over 3600 m (11,808 ft) on the W slopes.

Antofagasta Chile. Cap. of the Antofagasta province, largest town on the arid N coast 1040 km (650 miles) N of Valparaiso. Pop. (1991) 221,200. Seaport with an artificial harbour.

Exports nitrates and copper. Ore-refining, brewing and canning. The railway from La Paz carries much of Bolivia's exports and imports. There is a secondary line over the Andes (opened 1953) to Salta in Argentina.

Antrim Northern Ireland. 1. Maritime county in the NE, bounded on the W by the R. Bann and Lough Neagh, and on the S by the R. Lagan. Area 2838 sq km (1096 sq. miles). Pop. (1991) 44,516. County town Belfast. Largely a low basalt plateau, rising to 554 m (1817 ft) in Mt Trostan, reaching the N coast in the columnar basalt of the Giant's Causeway. Famous for picturesque river valleys, the Glens of Antrim.

Chief crops oats, potatoes. Cattle, pigs and sheep reared. Principal industry linen manufacture. Shipbuilding at Belfast. Cotton and woollen manufactures. Chief towns Larne, Lisburn, Ballymena and Portrush.

2. Town in Co. Antrim on the NE shore of Lough Neagh 21 km (13 miles) NW of Belfast. Pop. (1991) 20,878. Linen mills. A famous round tower (10th-cent.).

Antsiranama Madagascar. Seaport at the N end of the island. Pop. (1990) 54,418. It has a good natural harbour but has poor access by road.

It exports coffee, meat (canned and frozen), sisal and soya beans.

Originally named Diégo Suarez, the harbour was discovered in 1500 by the Portuguese and was a French naval base from 1885.

Antwerp (Flemish **Antwerpen**; Fr. **Anvers**) Belgium. 1. Province in the N, bounded on the N by the Netherlands. Area 2867 sq km (1106 sq. miles). Pop. (1991) 1,605,167 (mainly Flemish-speaking). Chief towns Mechelen, Turnhout, Merksem, Lierre.

2. Cap. of Antwerp province on the Scheldt R. 88 km (55 miles) from the open sea and 38 km (24 miles) N of Brussels. Pop. (1991) 467,875. Chief seaport and commercial centre of Belgium. Considerable transit trade with Germany, esp. the Ruhr area.

Important industrial centre. Oil and sugar refineries, flour mills, motor-car assembly plants, textile factories. Diamond-cutting. Of great artistic and historic interest.

The Gothic cathedral (begun 1352) has a spire 120 m (394 ft) high and contains three Rubens masterpieces. It was the home and workplace of Rubens and his tomb is in the Church of St James. The house of the 16th-cent. printer C. Plantin is now a museum. The Stock Exchange (Bourse) was built (1868–72) to replace the 16th-cent. building destroyed by fire. Birthplace of Van Dyck (1599–1641); many fine examples of his work. In the late 15th cent. it became the principal commercial centre of Europe, but declined after being sacked by the Spaniards (1576) and again when the Treaty of Westphalia closed the Scheldt to navigation (1648). After the Scheldt was reopened (1795), the Dutch exercised their right to levy tolls on shipping until 1863, when Belgium redeemed this right by purchase; Antwerp then rapidly regained its commercial prosperity.

Anuradhapura Sri Lanka. Cap. of the North-Central province 177 km (110 miles) NNE of Colombo. Pop. (1981) 35,981. In a rice-growing area (irrigated). Also an ancient ruined city, former cap. of Ceylon, founded in the 5th cent. BC. Remains of shrines, palaces, bathing pools. The famous Bo-tree of Gautama. An important Buddhist place of pilgrimage.

Anzhero Sudzhensk Russia. Coalmining and industrial town in the Kuznetsk basin in the Kemerovo Region 80 km (50 miles) NNW of Kemerovo on the Trans-Siberian Railway. Pop. (1991) 107,000.

Manufactures plastics, dyes and drugs, and machinery.

Anzio Italy. Ancient Antium. Port in the Roma province in Latium on the Tyrrhenian Sea 53 km (33 miles) S of Rome. Pop. (1990) 25,500. Resort. Fishing centre. Birthplace of Nero (AD 37–68), among the ruins of whose villa was found the famous statue of Apollo Belvedere. Severely damaged in World War II; scene of Allied landings (Jan. 1944).

Aomori Japan. Cap. of the Aomori prefec-

ture on Mutsu Bay on the N coast of Honshu. Pop. (1991) 162,477. Seaport; large local trade, esp. with Hokkaido. Exports rice, timber and fish.

Aoraki ➤MOUNT COOK.

Aosta Italy. Cap. of the Valle d'Aosta region on the Dora Baltea R. 83 km (52 miles) NNW of Turin. Pop. (1990) 37,000. Tourist centre for the lovely Valle d'Aosta. Metalworking and other industries.

Many Roman remains. Cathedral (12thcent.). Birthplace of Archbishop Anselm (1033?–1109).

Aoteaoroa. Maori name for New Zealand.

Apeldoorn Netherlands. Town in the Gelderland province 27 km (17 miles) N of Arnhem. Pop. (1992) 148,745. Railway junction.

Industries inc. electronics and tourism. It manufactures paper and blankets.

Het Loo, the summer residence of the Dutch royal family, is nearby.

Apennines Italy. Mountain range extending S from the Alps through Italy and Sicily for 1280 km (800 miles). The average height is 1219 m (4000 ft). The highest point is the Gran Sasso d'Italia rising to 2914 m (9560 ft) in Monte Corno. The S part extends to the Gulf of Taranto and curves SSW into the 'toe' of Italy, with Aspromonte (1956 m; 6416 ft) near the S tip. There are many mineral springs. Near Naples is the still active volcano Vesuvius. The S has long been subject to earthquakes. Forests are now much reduced (though some reforestation has taken place), but well-watered areas have pastures. Marble is found at Carrara. Cereals, vines, olives, fruits and nuts cultivated on the more fertile lower slopes.

Apia Samoa. Cap., seaport on the N coast of Upolu. Pop. (1991) 32,859. Exports bananas, copra and cacao.

Appalachian Mountains USA. A mountain system extending NE–SW more than 2400 km (1500 miles) along the E side of North America from the Gulf of St Lawrence to central Alabama. Three distinct regions are recognized. The Older Appalachians of mainly crystalline rocks form the most easterly belt and inc. such individual ranges as the White Mountains and Green Mountains (N) and the Blue Ridge (S). To the W of this belt is the Great Appalachian Valley and then the Newer Appalachians, consisting of younger strata, with long ridges of folded mountains separated by longitudinal valleys. Still farther W is the third belt, the Appalachian plateau, inc. the extensive Allegheny Mountains. The highest peak in the Appalachians is Mt Mitchell (2037 m; 6684 ft) in the Black Mountains of North Carolina. The mountains contain the richest anthracite and bituminous coalfields in the US, chiefly in the N. Rich deposits of iron ore in the extreme S. There are also reserves of petroleum and natural gas.

Appenzell Switzerland. 1. Canton (founded 1513) in the NE, an enclave of the St Gallen canton. A full canton till 1597, when as a result of the Reformation it broke up into two independent half-cantons: Appenzell Ausser Rhoden (area 241 sq km (93 sq. miles), pop. (1991) 51,570, cap. Herisau (Protestant)); and Appenzell Inner Rhoden (area 186 sq km (72 sq. miles), pop. (1991) 13,573, cap. Appenzell (Roman Catholic)). Appenzell Ausser Rhoden is mainly industrial and manufactures textiles. The principal occupation in Appenzell Inner Rhoden is pastoral farming (dairy produce).

2. Cap. of Appenzell Inner Rhoden on the Sitter R. 11 km (7 miles) S of St Gallen at a height of 790 m (2591 ft). Pop. (1970) 5217. Tourist centre. Manufactures embroidery.

Appleby England. Town in Cumbria on the R. Eden 48 km (30 miles) SE of Carlisle. Pop. (1991) 2570. Has a castle (Norman keep). Traditionally a meeting-place for gypsies at the annual horse fair (June).

Appleton USA. Industrial town in Wisconsin on the Fox R. 145 km (90 miles) NNW of Milwaukee. Pop. (1990) 65,000.

Paper and textile mills, deriving hydro-electric power from the river. Just S is L. Winnebago.

Apulia (Puglia) Italy. Region in the S along the Adriatic Sea, comprising the provinces of Foggia, Bari, Brindisi, Ionio and Lecce. Area 19,348 sq km (7468 sq. miles). Pop. (1990) 4,081,542. Largely hilly, with lowlands in the N and the S (the 'heel' of Italy).

Cereals, vines, olives, almonds, tobacco are cultivated. Much olive oil is produced.

Apuré River Venezuela. River 670 km (420 miles) long, of which over 480 km (300 miles) is navigable, rising in the E Cordillera, flowing NE and E across the W llanos and joining the Orinoco. Cattle raised and some maize and other crops cultivated in the basin.

Apurímac River Peru. River 880 km (550 miles) long, rising in the small L. Villafra in the Andes of S Peru, flowing (deeply entrenched) generally NNW and joining the Urubamba R. to form the Ucayali, one of the main headstreams of the Amazon. In the lower reaches known as the Ene and the Tambo.

Aqaba Jordan. Seaport at the N end of the Gulf of Aqaba, Jordan's only outlet to the sea. Pop. (1983) 40,000. Site of biblical Elath, one of the ports from which Solomon's fleets sailed to Ophir. Was the Roman military post of Aelana. Exports phosphates and imports petroleum. Nearby is the modern port of Eilat in Israel.

Aquila, L' Italy. Town in Abruzzi on the Pescara (Aterno) R. 88 km (55 miles) NE of Rome at a height of 720 m (2561 ft) near the Gran Sasso d'Italia. Pop. (1981) 63,678.

Trade in agricultural produce, livestock. Manufactures textiles and pasta.

Has several notable churches and a famous 13th-cent. fountain with 99 jets. Severely damaged by earthquake in 1703 and in World War II.

Aquitaine France. Ancient Aquitania. Region and ancient province in the SW. Area 42,308 sq km (16,335 sq. miles). Pop. (1991) 2,796,000. Conquered by the Romans in 56 BC. Occupied by the Visigoths in the 5th cent. AD and by the Franks in the 6th cent. Became an independent duchy in the 7th cent. About the 10th cent. the name was corrupted to Guienne and Gascony was joined to it. The two duchies went to the French crown in 1137 and to the English crown in 1152, reverting to France when conquered by Charles VII (1451). The Aquitaine Basin, a fertile plain bounded by the Massif Central (E), the Pyrenees (S) and the Bay of Biscay (W), and drained by the Garonne R. and its tributaries, produces wheat, maize, wine, fruits and vegetables. The region's varied coastline has encouraged the development of tourism. Principal towns Bordeaux, regional cap., and Toulouse.

Arabia SW Asia. Large peninsula bounded N by the Syrian Desert, E by the (Persian) Gulf and Gulf of Oman, S by the Arabian Sea and Gulf of Aden, W by the Red Sea. Area 2,590,000 sq km (1 million sq. miles) divided politically into Saudia Arabia, occupying two-thirds, Yemen, Southern Yemen, Oman, the United Arab Emirates, Qatar and Kuwait. Rocky plateau rising to mountain ridges in the S and W and sloping gradually E to the Persian Gulf. The interior is alternately steppe and desert, inc. the Natud (N), Dahana (E) and Rub' Al Khali (S) deserts. Dissected by deep wadis, but there are now no permanent rivers. The S highlands receive enough rain (50–100 cm (20–40 ins.) annually) for agriculture, mainly coffee and cereals; otherwise cultivation is confined to oases. But by far the most important natural resource is petroleum.

Arabian Desert (Eastern Desert) Egypt. A rocky desert in Egypt, between the Nile (W) and the Gulf of Suez and the Red Sea (E). To the S is the Nubian Desert. Largely mountainous, some peaks rising to over 1829 m (6000 ft).

Arabian Sea. The NW section of the Indian Ocean, between Arabia (W) and India (E). Two arms: the Gulf of Aden leads to the Red Sea, the Gulf of Oman to the (Persian) Gulf.

Aracajú Brazil. Cap. of the Sergipe state in the NE, port 10 km (6 miles) above the mouth of the Cotinguiba R. Pop. (1991) 401,244.

Exports sugar, cotton, rice and hides. Industries inc. sugar-refining, tanning, textiles.

Arad Romania. Industrial town on the Mures R. 48 km (30 miles) NNE of Timişoara, near the Hungarian frontier. Pop. (1989) 191,428.

Railway junction. Railway engineering. Manufactures textiles, spirits, leather, machine tools, electrical goods and rolling-stock. Trade in grain, cattle.

Formerly a Turkish fortress (16th cent.). Passed to Austria, then Hungary and to Romania after World War II.

Arafura Sea. Part of the SW Pacific Ocean, between Australia (S) and New Guinea (N). Adjoins the Timor Sea (W) and the Torres Strait (E).

Aragón Spain. Region and former kingdom in the NE, comprising the modern provinces of Huesca, Teruel and Zaragoza; drained by the Ebro R. and its tributaries. Chief towns Zaragoza, Huesca, Teruel. Thinly populated, apart from some valleys and irrigated areas. Conquered by the Moors in the 8th cent. United with Catalonia in the 12th cent. and with Castile in the 15th cent. through the marriage of Ferdinand of Aragón and Isabella of Castile.

Aragón River Spain. River 130 km (80 miles) long, rising in the Central Pyrenees and flowing generally SW to join the R. Ebro.

Araguaia River Brazil. River 2250 km (1400 miles) long, rising on the Mato Grosso plateau, flowing generally NNE to join the Tocatins R. at São João do Araguaia. Forks in the middle course to enclose the large Bananal Island.

Arak Iran. Formerly Sultanabad. Town on the Trans-Iranian Railway 257 km (160 miles) SW of Tehrán at a height of 1800 m (5904 ft). Pop. (1986) 265,349.

Manufactures rugs and carpets, and matches.

It was cap. of the former province of Iraq (i.e. Persian Iraq), corresponding to ancient Media.

Arakan Myanmar (Burma). A division of Lower Myanmar (Burma), situated on the Bay of Bengal between Pegu and Chittagong. A narrow strip approximately 640 km (400 miles) long and 24−144 km (15−90 miles) wide. Chief town Akyab, situated SSE of Chittagong. A coastal strip growing rice, cotton, fruit and tobacco is bordered by the Arakan Yoma range rising to over 3048 m (10,000 ft) above sea level.

Arakan Yoma Myanmar (Burma). Range of mountains 640 km (400 miles) long, between and parallel to the Irrawaddy R. and the Arakan Coast (Bay of Bengal), extending from the Chin Hills (N) to the Irrawaddy delta (S) and rising to over 3000 m (9840 ft) in the N. A climatic barrier, shielding the 'dry zone' of central Myanmar from the monsoon rains. Tropical rainforest on the W slopes, teak forest on the E slopes.

Aral Sea Kazakhstan. Known as the Sea of Islands, it is separated from the Caspian Sea (W) by the Ust Urt Plateau. Area 61,160 sq km (24,000 sq. miles). In recent years there has been no input from the Syr Darya (NE) and only small quantities from the Amu Darya (S) rivers, and as a result it has shrunk in volume and height. It has no outlet. Fishing is important and magnesium and sodium are mined along the shores.

Aran Islands Ireland. Group of three rocky islands – Aranmore (or Inishmore; the largest, with many antiquities), Inishmaan and Inisheer – 40−50 km (25−30 miles) WSW of Galway. Area 47 sq km (18 sq. miles).
Industries inc. fishing and a little agriculture.

Aranca Venezuela/Colombia. River rising E of Bucaramanga in N central Colombia and flowing 800 km (500 miles) E along Colombia/Venezuela border to enter Venezuela below Arauca and join the Orinoco R. 112 km (70 miles) ESE of San Fernando de Apuré. It is navigable for small boats.

Ararat, Mount (Turkish **Ağri Daği**) Turkey. Volcanic mountain mass in the extreme NE near the border with Armenia and Iran. Consists of two main peaks: Great Ararat, 5165 m (16,945 ft), the traditional resting place of Noah's Ark after the flood; and Little Ararat, 3913 m (12,835 ft).

Aras River. River 960 km (600 miles) long, rising in Turkish Armenia S of Erzurum, flowing generally E, forming parts of the frontier between Turkey and Azerbaijan and between Iran and Azerbaijan. The old course joins the Kura R., but the new course (since 1896) flows direct into the Caspian Sea.

Aravalli Range India. Hills extending 560 km (350 miles) SW−NE through Rajasthan. Generally 450−900 m (1476−2952 ft) high.

Arbil Iraq. Town situated E of Mosul at the head of the Kirkuk railway. Cap. of Arbil province. Trading centre for a farming and oil-producing area, linked by road with Iran, Turkey and Syria. An ancient city continuously inhabited since Assyrian times.

Arbroath Scotland. Town in Angus 26 km (16 miles) ENE of Dundee. Pop. (1991) 23,474. Resort and fishing port.
Manufactures sailcloth, canvas, knitwear and footwear.
Scene of Robert I's Declaration of Independence (1320).

Arcachon France. Fishing port and resort in the Gironde department in the SW on the shore of the Arcachon Basin (a 150-sq km (60-sq. mile) lagoon almost enclosed by sand dunes and pine forests), 51 km (32 miles) WSW of Bordeaux. Pop. (1989) 14,000. Famous for oyster beds.

Arcadia Greece. *Nome* in the central Peloponnese. Area 4419 sq km (1664 sq. miles). Pop. (1990) 103,840. Cap. Tripolis. Mainly mountainous. Largely infertile.
Wheat, tobacco and grapes cultivated. Sheep and goats reared.

Archangel (Arkhangelsk) Russia. Cap. of Archangel Region on the right bank of the

N Dvina R. 32 km (20 miles) from its point of entry into Dvina Bay (White Sea). Pop. (1991) 428,200. Seaport, chief timber-exporting and sawmilling centre of Russia. Centre of White Sea fisheries. Railway terminus. Shipyards, fish canneries and rope mills. Most of the trade is carried on June–Oct., though the port is also kept open in May and November with the help of ice-breakers.

Founded (1553) as a result of the establishment of Anglo–Muscovite trade. Russia's only seaport until 1702, when St Petersburg was founded; after that date it declined. Its importance increased again with the construction of the railway (1897) and it was a leading supply port in both world wars.

Arctic Ocean. Body of water surrounding the North Pole N of the Arctic Circle, connected by the Bering Strait with the Pacific, and by Baffin Bay and Davis Strait (W) and Greenland Sea and Norwegian Sea (E) with the Atlantic. Area 14,055,930 sq km (5,427,000 sq. miles). The greatest depth (5450 m; 17,876 ft) was recorded in 1927 NW of Point Barrow (Alaska). Many rivers, inc. the Lena, Mackenzie, Ob and Yenisei, flow into it. Evaporation is slight and salinity is the lowest of all the oceans. During the winter most of it is covered with ice, which in summer breaks up into masses of pack ice that drift with the outflowing currents. The first surface crossing from Point Barrow (Alaska) via the North Pole to a small island off Spitsbergen, was made by the British Trans-Arctic Expedition 1968–9. Experiments in recent years have shown that the ocean is warming.

Ardebil (Ardabil) Iran. Town in Azerbaijan 185 km (115 miles) E of Tabriz. Pop. (1986) 281,973. Commercial and road centre.

Manufactures carpets and rugs.

Mausoleum of Sheikh Safiuddin (1252–1334), the religious leader.

Ardèche France. Department in the former Languedoc province, crossed in the W by the Monts du Vivarais and in the SE by the Ardèche R., and bounded on the E by the Rhône. Area 5529 sq km (2135 sq. miles). Pop. (1991) 278,800. Prefecture Privas.

Mulberry and chestnut trees, vineyards and orchards in the S. Produces cereals and wines. Coal and iron ore mined. Manufactures silk. Chief towns Annonay, with silk spinning and weaving and paper industries, and Privas famous for marrons glacés.

Ardèche River France. River 120 km (75 miles) long, rising in the Cévennes and flowing generally SE to the Rhône. Near Vallon is the Pont d'Arc, a natural bridge which it has carved in the limestone.

Arden, Forest of England. District in Warwickshire, originally part of a large Midlands forest between the Warwickshire R. Avon and Birmingham. Setting of Shakespeare's *As You Like It*.

Ardennes. A forested plateau, mainly in SE Belgium but extending into Luxembourg and the Ardennes department of France, at a height generally of 350–500 m (1148–1640 ft) but rising to over 650 m (2132 ft) in the NE. Some pastoral farming, but agriculture is poor. The woods still contain much wild game. Much less extensive than were the Arduenna Silva of the Romans.

Ardennes France. Department in the N, containing part of the Ardennes and the Argonne, drained by the Meuse and the Aisne rivers and their tributaries. Area 5229 sq km (2019 sq. miles). Pop. (1991) 295,700. Prefecture Charleville-Mézières.

Lumbering and stock-rearing in the hills. Agriculture in the fertile Aisne valley. Salt quarries. Iron mines.

Ardnacrusha Ireland. Village in SE Co. Clare, on the opposite side of the Shannon R. to Limerick. Pop. (1986) 481. Site of the Shannon hydroelectric scheme.

Ardnamurchan Point Scotland. Rocky headland at the W extremity of the peninsula of the same name, in Highland. The most westerly point on the mainland of Great Britain.

Ardrossan Scotland. Town, seaport and resort in North Ayrshire on the Firth of Clyde 22 km (14 miles) NNW of Ayr. Pop. (1991) 10,750.

Small oil refinery. Exports coal.

Arequipa Peru. Cap. of the Arequipa department in the S at a height of 2290 m (7500 ft) in an irrigated area beneath the volcanic El Misti (5822 m; 10,906 ft). Pop. (1990) 621,700.

Commercial city serving the S Peruvian highlands. Mainly a wool market. Tanning, brewing and flour-milling. Manufactures textiles and soap. Linked by rail with its port, Mollendo, 88 km (55 miles) SW.

An Inca city, refounded by the Spanish (1540).

Arezzo Italy. Cap. of Arezzo province in Tuscany in the upper Arno valley 61 km (38 miles) SE of Florence. Pop. (1981) 90,105.

Commercial centre. Trade in cereals, wine, olive oil. Manufactures textiles, clothing and furniture.

Gothic cathedral (1277–1510), Romanesque Church of Santa Maria della Pieve and the Palazzo della Fraternità (the two last in the famous Piazza Grande). Birthplace of the poet, Petrarch (1304–74) and the painter and art historian, Vasari (1511–74).

Argenteuil France. Town in the Val d'Oise department, a NW suburb of Paris on the right bank of the Seine. Pop. (1990) 94,162.

Manufactures motor-car parts, aircraft engines, electrical equipment and rayon. Market gardens supply Paris with asparagus, beans and peas.

Grew up around a convent (founded 7th cent.) where Héloïse was abbess.

Argentina. Federal republic in the extreme S of South America. Second largest country in South America, but only a third of the size of Brazil. Bounded by Bolivia and Paraguay (N), Brazil, Uruguay and the Atlantic (E) and Chile and the Andes (W). Area 2,780,400 sq km (1,073,518 sq. miles). Pop. (1995) 34,587,000 (87 per cent urban). Life expectancy, 68 years male, 72 female. Cap. Buenos Aires. Other major cities: Córdoba, Rosario, Mendoza and La Plata. Currency: Peso =

100 centavos. Very varied in relief, vegetation and climate, from tropical in the N (the Chaco) through the pleasant climate of the great pampas to the bitter cold of Patagonia in the far S. Four main areas. 1. The Andes, which define the long W frontier with Chile, along which are found 'oases' of cultivable land. 2. The north, with the great forests of the Chaco and the rolling plains between the Paraná and the Paraguay rivers. 3. The pampas, the geographical and economic heart of the country, an area of 648,000 sq km (250,000 sq. miles) covering vast plains, uninterrupted by hills or even trees, suitable for pasture and agriculture. 4. Patagonia, in the far S, an infertile, windswept land where little but sheep can be raised, ending in the cold, barren Tierra del Fuego. Land use: forested 22 per cent, meadows and pastures 52 per cent, agricultural and under permanent cultivation 10 per cent. Religion mainly Roman Catholic. The people are predominantly of European stock. The pop. grew rapidly through immigration (7 million immigrants, mainly Italian and Spanish, 1857–1930). The Indians were virtually exterminated and thus the present pop. is overwhelmingly white. The language is Spanish.

The economic base of the country is mainly agricultural and it has long been a major exporter of meat. Its prosperity depends very largely on the vast grassy plains or pampas around the R. Plate. Export trade is almost wholly in agricultural produce, mainly obtained within 640 km (400 miles) of Buenos Aires (though a third of the sheep are in the far S). Cattle, sheep, wheat, maize and flax are produced on the pampas. Estates are often of immense size, divided by wire fences into fields of several thousand hectares (many thousand acres). Wheat predominates in a great belt from Bahía Blanca towards Rosario; maize and flax to the N of Rosario; dairying and fruit-farming in the milder NW pampas. In the W foothills of the Andes, 'oases' of irrigated land produce fruit and wine; sugar-cane comes from the NW, and cotton-growing is increasing in the E Chaco. Oil is produced by a national undertaking, and there are reserves of copper and uranium.

Buenos Aires has become a large industrial area, with a variety of light manufactures in addition to food-packing enterprises. There are now as many industrial workers as agricultural. Capital (largely British) flowed into the country for the construction of the railways, which transformed the pampas from a primitive pastoral economy to a rich region of intensive cattle-rearing and agriculture. With the advent of refrigeration Argentina became a major meat supplier to the UK.

The first Spanish attempts at settlement on the R. Plate were frustrated by the fierce opposition of the Indians. Having settled in friendlier territory in Asunción, the Spanish later (1580) colonized Buenos Aires. Under the viceroyalty of Peru, the country was neglected. It declared itself independent (1816) with the help of the liberator San Martín; but internal strife and later the tyrannical rule of de Rosas retarded development. Argentina became a federal republic after the expulsion of de Rosas (1852). The political system closely resembles that of the USA. The emergence of a great urban pop. led to a decline in the influence of the land-owning classes, and culminated after World War II in the dictatorship of Perón, who favoured the industrial working class at the expense of other interests. The Perón regime was overturned in 1955, but successor governments continued to face economic difficulties, largely caused by falling exports, increased internal consumption and by past and continued overemphasis on industrialization. Inflation rose in the 1980s to 3084 per cent. In 1982 in an effort to distract attention from domestic failings, it was decided to invade the Falkland Is. (Islas Malvinas). The subsequent military defeat helped to precipitate fall of the junta government later that year. A return to civilian government took place in 1983.

The President is elected for a 6-year term by a 600-member electoral college. There is a National Congress consisting of a 46-member Senate and a 254-member House of Deputies. The country is divided into 22 provinces and 1 federal district and the National Territories of Tierra del Fuego, the Antarctic and the (claimed) South Atlantic Is.

Arges Romania. Province of S central Romania NW of Bucharest. Area 6801 sq km (2626 sq. miles). Pop. (1992) 680,600. Cap. Pitesti. Drained by the Arges R. Mainly agricultural esp. fruit and vine growing.

Argolis Greece. *Nome* in the NE Peloponnese (formerly combined with Corinthia), inc. islands in the Gulf of Argolis. Area 2154 sq km (831 sq. miles). Pop. (1990) 97,250. Cap. Nauplia.

An agricultural region; produces wine, currants, sultanas.

The ancient region of Argolis inc. the important cities Mycenae and Argos.

Argolis, Gulf of Greece. Inlet of the Aegean Sea in the E Peloponnese with the island of Spetsai at the entrance and Nauplia on the NW coast.

Argos Greece. Ancient town, one of the oldest in Greece in the NE Peloponnese 45 km (28 miles) SSW of Corinth. Pop. (1991) 78,884. In the 7th cent. BC it dominated the Peloponnese. A ruined temple, the Heraeum, is 8 km (5 miles) NNE.

Argostólion (Argostoli) Greece. Cap. of Cephalonia in the Ionian Is. on the SW coast. Pop. (1981) 6788. Trade in wine.

Argun River China/Russia. River 1450 km (900 miles) long, rising in the Great Khingan Mountains (NE China) as the Hailar, flowing generally W to the Russian frontier. Here linked with L. Hulun Nor. Turns NNE, forms part of the China–Russia frontier and joins the Shilka to form the Amur R.

Argyll and Bute Scotland. New Unitary Authority created in 1996, formerly part of Strathclyde Region. Area 6754 sq km (2608 sq. miles). Pop. (1993) 90,550.

Arica Chile. Oasis town in the rainless N; the most northerly seaport. Pop. (1991) 194,588. Oil terminal, with a pipeline to Sicasica in Bolivia (completed 1958). A railway climbs 456 km (285 miles) to La Paz and takes about half Bolivia's trade. Much Peruvian trade also passes through Arica.

Ariège France. Department in the S, formed from parts of the provinces of Gascony and Languedoc and the county of Foix, bounded on the S by Spain and Andorra. Area 4890 sq km (1888 sq. miles). Pop. (1991) 136,700. Prefecture Foix. The S is occupied by the N slopes of the Pyrenees, with the Pic de Montcalm rising to 3080 m (10,102 ft), and the N is fertile lowland producing cereals, wine, fruits and potatoes. Iron and lead mined. Chief towns Foix, Tarascon and Pamiers.

Ariège River France. River 160 km (100 miles) long, rising in the E Pyrenees near the Andorra border, flowing generally NNW and joining the Garonne near Toulouse. There are several hydroelectric installations.

Arizona USA. Mountainous state on the Mexican border. Area 193,750 sq km (113,417 sq. miles). Pop. (1990) 3,665,228. Cap. Phoenix. Much of it is desert, with a rainfall varying from 2.5 cm (1 in.) in the extreme W to 90 cm (35 ins.) in the E. The N is part of the Colorado Plateau, in which the Colorado R. has cut the famous Grand Canyon. The high mountain ranges are forested; highest point Humphrey's Peak (3863 m; 12,671 ft). Several enormous irrigation works have been built to store water, notably the Roosevelt, Coolidge, Yuma and Horse Mesa dams, on which depends practically all the agriculture of the state (its main resource). With irrigation good-quality cotton is grown using highly mechanized methods.

Wheat, barley, sugar-beet, citrus fruits and vegetables also cultivated. The mineral resources are valuable, esp. copper and lead. Chief industry smelting and refining metals. Principal towns Phoenix, Tucson.

Largest Indian pop. of any US state, with Hopi, Apache and Navajo reservations. Admitted to the Union in 1912 as the 48th state.

Arkansas USA. Pronounced 'Arkansaw'. State in S central region. Area 137,754 sq km (53,187 sq. miles). Pop. (1990) 2,350,725. Cap. Little Rock. There is a sharp contrast between the NW and SE areas; the former is highland, the latter low-lying and covered by fertile Mississippi alluvium. In the W are the Ozark and Ouachita Mountains, separated by the valley of the Arkansas R. Warm, humid air from the Gulf of Mexico brings considerable rain (up to 150 cm, 60 ins.) and causes high summer temperatures, but precludes winter frost.

Soya beans (soybeans) are the main crop, rice is grown and broilers (poultry) are produced. Minerals inc. bauxite, coal, bromine, diamonds and vanadium. The natural hot mineral water occurring at Hot Springs attracts sufferers from rheumatism. Chief towns Little Rock, Fort Smith, North Little Rock, Pine Bluff.

Secured from France as part of the Louisiana Purchase (1803). Admitted to the Union in 1836 as the 25th state.

Arkansas River USA. River 2400 km (1500 miles) long rising in the Rocky Mountains of central Colorado and flowing generally ESE to the Mississippi. Chief tributary the Canadian R. Wide variations in its volume; though banked by levees, the lower valley is subject to extensive flooding.

Arkhangelsk ➤ARCHANGEL.

Arklow Ireland. Small fishing port and resort in SE Co. Wicklow at the mouth of the Avoca R. 21 km (13 miles) SSW of Wicklow. Pop. (1991) 5847. Manufactures pottery.

Arlberg Austria. Mountain and pass (1800 m; 5904 ft) in the W. The road over the latter and the railway through the Arlberg Tunnel (1884, over 9.5 km (6 miles) long), which was electrified in 1923, link Vorarlberg and Tirol.

Arles France. Market town in the Bouches-du-Rhône department, mainly on the left bank of the Rhône 75 km (47 miles) NW of Marseille. Pop. (1990) 52,593.

Trade in sheep, wine and olives. Industries inc. chemicals, paper, sausages and boat building.

Important in Roman times: cap. of Gaul in the 4th cent. Among the Roman remains are a famous amphitheatre (seating over 20,000) and a theatre.

Arlington (Massachusetts) USA. Town 10 km (6 miles) NW of Boston. Pop. (1970) 53,524.

Commercial centre in a market-gardening and dairy-farming area. Manufactures leather goods.

Arlington (Texas) USA. Town 19 km (12 miles) E of Fort Worth. Pop. (1990) 261,721.

Industrial and commercial centre. Manufactures aircraft and missiles.

Arlington (Virginia) USA. Urban county on the Potomac R. near Washington (DC), with which it is connected by the Arlington Memorial Bridge. Area 62 sq km (24 sq. miles). The military Arlington National Cemetery of 165 ha (407 acres), on what was once the estate of General Robert E. Lee, contains the graves of about 60,000 soldiers killed in the American Civil War, with the tombs of the US Unknown Soldier and of President J. F. Kennedy (as a war hero). Also in Arlington County are Fort Myer, the National Airport (for Washington) and the Pentagon building.

Arlon Belgium. Cap. of Luxembourg province. Pop. (1982) 22,364. Market town for a farming area.

Industries inc. the manufacture of pipes and tobacco products, but many of the pop. work in neighbouring steelworks inc. those in France and Luxembourg.

Armagh Northern Ireland. 1. Inland county in the SE, low-lying in the N and hilly in the S, rising to 577 m (1893 ft) in Slieve Gullion. Area 1327 sq km (489 sq. miles). Pop. (1991) 51,817.

Main crops potatoes and flax. Cattle reared. Main industry linen manufacture. Chief towns Armagh, Portadown and Lurgan.

2. County town of Co. Armagh, created a city in 1994, 53 km (33 miles) SW of Belfast. Pop. (1991) 14,265.

Main industry linen manufacture.

Seat of both Protestant and Roman Catholic archbishops. Outstanding buildings are the Protestant cathedral, built on the site of a church said to have been founded by St Patrick (445), where Brian Boru was buried and the 19th-cent. Roman Catholic cathedral. The ecclesiastic metropolis of Ireland from the 5th to the 9th cent. Suffered much from Danish raids and the English wars; declined, but revived in the 18th and 19th cent.

Armagnac France. Hilly district, formerly a province in Gascony with cap. Auch; now mainly in the Gers department. Famous for its brandy, made from local grapes at Condom and other small towns.

Armavir Russia. Town in Krasnodar Territory on the Kuban R. 168 km (105 miles) E of Krasnodar, on the oil pipeline from Grozny. Pop. (1990) 178,300.

Flour-milling, meat-packing and distilling. Manufactures agricultural machinery and vegetable oils.

Armenia (Armenian **Hayastan**) Asia Minor. Region and former kingdom. The frontiers have varied throughout history, but in general corresponded roughly with the independent Republic of Armenia and nearby areas in Turkey and Iran. Mainly a plateau region of average height 1800–2400 m (5904–7872 ft), with ridges and isolated volcanic peaks, inc. Mt Ararat, 5165 m (16,945 ft); Armenian legend claims that their first king, Haik, was a descendant of Noah. Inc. the lofty L. Van and the sources of the Euphrates and Tigris. By the 6th cent BC the Armenians had become a distinct nation, settled in Asia Minor, governed by a Persian satrap till 330 BC. After brief independence in the 2nd cent. BC they were conquered by the Romans. In AD 66 Nero recognized Tiridates I as king of Armenia. Under Tiridates III it became the first country to adopt Christianity as state religion (303); this led to conflict with Persia and in 387 it was divided into Persian and Roman spheres of influence. For 5 centuries it was repeatedly under Persian, Byzantine or Arab domination. Autonomous under native Bagratid rulers, from the 9th to the 11th cent., it was again conquered by the Byzantines and then by the Seljuks. It was divided between Persia and Turkey from the 16th cent. till Russia obtained what is now the Republic of Armenia in part from Persia (1828) and in part from Turkey (1878). Under the Ottoman Empire, Armenians in Turkey were discriminated against as non-Muslim and frequently persecuted, but they played an important role as bankers and merchants. The ties of religion and language kept alive a sentiment of nationality, which provoked Abdul Hamid to instigate a series of massacres (1894–1915) in which thousands were killed and many fled to other countries. After the Russian Revolution the people of Russian Armenia enjoyed a short-lived independence. The country was proclaimed a Soviet Socialist Republic in 1920. ➤➤ next entry.

Armenia. Independent republic in Trans-caucasia, bounded in the N by Georgia, in the E by Azerbaijan and on the S and W by Turkey and Iran. Area 29,800 sq km (11,490 sq. miles). Pop. (1995) 3,548,000 (68 per cent urban). Life expectancy, 68 years male, 75 female. Cap. Yerevan. Other large towns Kumairi (Leninakan) and Kirovakan. Currency: Dram = 100 lumas. Armenia is mainly high plateaux and mountain ranges. The soil is fertile, but requires irrigation in areas of low rainfall. Land use: forested 14 per cent, pasture 35 per cent, agriculture 22 per cent. In 1989 Armenians accounted for 93 per cent of the pop., Azerbaijanis 3 per cent, Kurds 2 per cent and Russians 2 per cent. The language is Armenian. Believers are mainly Armenian Apostolic.

The Yerevan district and the Arax valley are the chief agricultural regions, where wheat, cotton and vines are cultivated. Stock rearing is important on the plateaux. Copper, zinc and molybdenum exist and mining of minerals is increasing in importance. Hydro-electric power is derived from a series of stations on the Razdan R. between L. Sevan and the Arax R. Industries inc. chemicals, building materials, textiles, carpets, food-processing, wine-making, machine tools and electrical engineering.

For earlier history ➤previous entry. In 1920 it became a Soviet Socialist Republic and was part of the Transcaucasian Soviet Federal Socialist Republic 1922–36. It became a constituent republic of the USSR in 1936. In 1990 it adopted a Declaration of Sovereignty and in 1991 voted with 99 per cent support for fully independent status. There is a 259-seat Supreme Soviet.

Armenia Colombia. Town, founded 1889, in a productive coffee-growing district at 1500 m (4920 ft) in the Central Cordillera. Pop. (1992) 212,310. Railhead for the journey E over the Quindío Pass.

Armentières France. Town in the Nord department on the Lys R. 14 km (9 miles) WNW of Lille. Pop. (1990) 26,240.

Manufactures linen, hosiery.

Entirely destroyed in World War I and again damaged in World War II.

Armidale Australia. Market town and mining centre (gold, antimony) in New South Wales 265 km (165 miles) N of New-castle on the New England plateau at 1000 m (3280 ft). Pop. (1981) 18,922.

Trade in wool, dairy produce and fruit.

Arnhem Netherlands. Cap. of the Gelder-land province on the Rhine R. 56 km (35 miles) ESE of Utrecht. Pop. (1992) 132,928.

Manufactures rayon, textiles, pharmaceutical products and food products.

Scene of an unsuccessful British airborne landing during World War II (Sept. 1944).

Arnhem Land Australia. Region about 155,000 sq km (60,000 sq. miles) in area in the N of the Northern Territory, named after the Dutch vessel *Arnhem* which explored the coast in the 17th cent. Mainly a reserve for aborigines, the majority of whom are semi-nomadic. Plentiful rain Dec.-March, followed by long drought, supports grassland with trees, while mangroves grow along the coasts and estuaries.

Arno River Italy. River 240 km (150 miles) long, rising on Monte Falterona and flowing mainly W past Florence and Pisa to the Ligurian Sea. Barely 32 km (20 miles) are navigable. The valley (Val d'Arno) is fertile and picturesque.

Arnstadt Germany. Town in Erfurt district on the Gera R. 18 km (11 miles) SSW of Erfurt. Pop. (1989) 29,665.

Railway junction and engineering. Manufactures gloves, machinery and footwear. J. S. Bach was organist at the Church of St Boniface 1703–7.

Arran Scotland. Island in North Ayrshire in the Firth of Clyde, separated from Kintyre by Kilbrannan Sound. Area 430 sq km (166 sq. miles). Pop. (1991) 4474. Mountainous, rising to 874 m (2867 ft) in Goat Fell. It is a popular tourist centre.

Arras France. Prefecture of the Pas-de-Calais department on the canalized Scarpe R. 43 km (27 miles) SSW of Lille. Pop. (1990) 42,715.

Trade in cereals. Engineering, textiles, brewing. Manufactures beet-sugar, vegetable oils, agricultural implements. Once famous for tapestry.

In pre-Christian times chief town of the Atrebates. Became cap. of Artois; finally passed to France 1640. Birthplace of Robespierre (1758–94).

Arromanches-les-Bains France. Village in the Calvados department 24 km (15 miles) NW of Caen. Site of the prefabricated Mulberry harbour built by Allied troops to permit landings in German-occupied territory during World War II (D-Day, 6 June 1944).

Arta Greece. 1. *Nome* in Epirus, bounded S by Gulf of Ara, N by Tzoumerka mountains. Area 1662 sq km (642 sq. miles). Pop. (1990) 78,884.

Mainly agricultural, producing cereals, cotton and fruit. There is a fishing industry on the Gulf of Arta.

2. Town situated SSE of Ioannina on Arachthos R. near its mouth. *Nome* cap. Pop. (1981) 18,283.

Trading centre for an agricultural area, handling cotton, cereals, fruit, olives, tobacco and fish. Industries inc. textiles; manufactures leather products.

Seat of Greek Orthodox metropolitan bishop. There are important Byzantine remains.

Artaxata (**Artashat**) Armenia. Ancient cap. of Armenia, S of Yerevan. Founded by Artaxias 189 BC. Destroyed by the Romans, but restored and renamed Neronia.

Artemovsk Ukraine. Town, founded 1571, in the E in the Donbas 69 km (43 miles) NNE of Donetsk. Pop. (1990) 90,600. It has the largest salt mines in the Ukraine.

Iron and glass are manufactured and other industries.

Arthur's Seat. Hill in Edinburgh, Scotland, overlooking the SE area, at 251 m (823 ft).

Artibonite Haiti. Department of W Haiti on the NE shore of the Gulf of Gonaives. Area 4984 sq km (1924 sq. miles). Pop. (1992) 961,447. Cap. Gonaives. Drained by the Artibonite R.

Fertile plain producing coffee, bananas, cotton, sugar-cane and rice.

Artois France. Ancient Artesium. Former province, with cap. Arras; now in the Pas-de-Calais department.

Mainly agricultural. Inc. the W part of the Franco–Belgian coalfield.

Belonged in turn to Flanders, France, Burgundy, Austria and Spain; returned to France 1640. Gave its name to 'artesian' wells: the first European examples were sunk here (1126).

Aru Islands Indonesia. Island group in the S Moluccas (Maluku) between New Guinea and the Tanimbar Is. Area 8500 sq km (3300 sq. miles). Five main islands, separated by narrow channels; about 90 islets. Low-lying and forested.

Chief products pearls, mother-of-pearl, trepang.

Aruba. Island in the West Indies WNW of Curaçao. Area 193 sq km (75 sq. miles). Pop. (1992) 69,100. Chief town Oranjestad.

Gold was discovered in 1825 but is now

found in uneconomic quantities. Tourism is now the main source of income. Oil is refined (from Venezuela) and it manufactures petrochemicals.

In 1986 Aruba was constitutionally separated from the Netherlands Antilles and full independence from the Netherlands was originally promised for 1996.

Arunachal Pradesh India. State, from 1987, formerly the North East Frontier Agency of Assam. Area 83,743 sq km (32,712 sq. miles). Pop. (1991) 858,392. Cap. Itanagar. Wild and mainly mountainous, rising from the Brahmaputra plain in the extreme S to Himalayan peaks over 6000 m (19,680 ft) high in the N, beyond which is Tibet. Heavy rainfall; intersected by many tributaries of the Brahmaputra. More than half the area is forested. Minerals inc. coal, dolomite, limestone and there are oil reserves.

Arundel England. Market town in W Sussex on the Arun R. 13 km (8 miles) WNW of Worthing. Pop. (1991) 3033. Stands below Arundel Castle (seat of the Dukes of Norfolk), built in the 11th cent. and restored in the 18th cent.

Arusha Tanzania. Cap. of the Arusha region in the N just SW of Mt Meru, 4565 m (14,973 ft). Pop. (1986) 57,000. Terminus of the railway from Tanga via Moshi. Market town in a coffee-growing area.

Arvada USA. City immediately SW of Denver in Colorado. Pop. (1990) 89,235. Industries inc. food-processing and chemicals.

Arve River France/Switzerland. River 99 km (62 miles) long, rising in the Savoy Alps, flowing SW past Chamonix and then generally NW, crossing the Swiss frontier to join the Rhône just below L. Geneva.

Arvida Canada. Industrial town in Quebec 8 km (5 miles) W of Chicoutimi. Pop. (1971) 18,488. Electric power harnessed from falls on the Saguenay R. (a tributary of the St Lawrence) is used in one of the world's largest aluminium smelters.

Asahikawa Japan. Town in Hokkaido, on the Ishikari R. 120 km (75 miles) NE of Sapporo. Pop. (1991) 361,631.

Industrial and commercial centre of N Hokkaido. Industries inc. brewing (*sake*) and the manufacture of wood products and textiles.

Asansol India. Town in W Bengal on the Raniganj coalfield 190 km (120 miles) NW of Calcutta. Pop. (1991) 262,200.

It is an important railway junction. Industries inc. railway engineering and the manufacture of pipes, cable, cycles, beer, iron and steel, and railway locomotives and chemicals.

Ascension Island S Atlantic Ocean. United Kingdom Overseas Territory. Of volcanic origin lying 1120 km (700 miles) NW of St Helena. Area 88 sq km (34 sq. miles). Pop. (1993) 1117 (concentrated in Georgetown, an international cable station). Noted breeding place for sea turtles. Discovered by the Portuguese on Ascension Day 1501. Remained uninhabited until the British established a garrison when Napoleon was sent to St Helena (1815). Controlled by the Admiralty until 1922, when it was transferred to the Colonial Office as a dependency of St Helena. The first British civil satellite communications centre began to operate on the island in 1966.

Aschaffenburg Germany. Town in NW Bavaria on the Main R. 37 km (23 miles) ESE of Frankfurt. Pop. (1989) 60,000. River port.

Trade in timber and coal. Manufactures textiles, clothing, scientific and optical instruments.

Originally a Roman fortress.

Aschersleben Germany. Town in Halle district 48 km (30 miles) NW of Halle. Pop. (1989) 41,000.

In a potash- and lignite-mining region. Manufactures chemicals, textiles, beet-sugar and paper.

Ascoli Piceno Italy. Cap. of Ascoli Piceno province in the Marches on the Tronto R.

69 km (43 miles) NW of Pescara. Pop. (1990) 52,624.

Produces pasta, textiles, pottery and glass. Roman remains.

Ascot England. Village in E Berkshire 8 km (5 miles) SW of Windsor. The famous race-course of Ascot Heath was laid out (1711) by order of Queen Anne, who inaugurated the Royal Ascot Meeting (June). Mainly residential with some light industry.

Ashanti Ghana. Administrative region in the S. Area 24,389 sq km (9417 sq. miles). Pop. (1988) 2,308,100. Cap. Kumasi. Hilly, with large areas of tropical rainforest, much of which has been cleared for cacao cultivation.

Also produces kola nuts, tropical hard-woods (e.g. mahogany). Food crops cassava (manioc), yams, maize.

Formerly a British protectorate: at various times in the 19th cent. the Ashanti people were at war with Britain; King Prempeh was deposed and exiled in 1896, but allowed to return in 1924. The Ashanti Confederacy was restored in 1935. Ashanti was virtually part of the Gold Coast colony before the latter became independent as Ghana (1957).

Ashbourne England. Market town in W Derbyshire on the R. Dove 19 km (12 miles) NW of Derby near picturesque Dovedale. Pop. (1991) 6300. Varied light industries.

Ashburton New Zealand. Market and in-dustrial town on the Canterbury Plains, South Island 80 km (50 miles) SW of Christ-church. Pop. (1991) 24,435.

Flour and woollen mills, creameries.

Ashburton River Australia. River in Western Australia rising 240 km (150 miles) S of Nullagine and flowing 480 km (300 miles) WNW to the Indian Ocean near Onslow. The flow, however, is intermittent.

Ashby de la Zouch England. Market town in W Leicestershire 26 km (16 miles) WNW of Leicester in a coalmining area. Pop. (1991) 10,595. Minor industries.

Ashdod Israel. Deep-water seaport situated 31 km (19 miles) SSW of Tel Aviv; of Mediterranean ports second in importance to Haifa.

Ashdown Forest England. Former forest in E Sussex, now heath and woodland. Most of the trees were felled for the furnaces of the one-time iron industry.

Asheville USA. Town in the S Appalachian Mountains of North Carolina 160 km (100 miles) WNW of Charlotte at a height of 690 m (1968 ft). Pop. (1990) 61,607.

Tourist centre. Manufactures textiles, paper and furniture.

Ashford England. Market town in Kent, 27 km (17 miles) ESE of Maidstone. Pop. (1991) 52,002.

There is light industry and it is the site of the Channel Tunnel's passenger terminal.

Ashington England. Town in North-umberland 22 km (14 miles) N of Newcastle-upon-Tyne. Pop. (1991) 27,962. Centre of a declining coalmining area.

Ashkelon Israel. Ancient city in Palestine 22 km (14 miles) NNE of Gaza. Captured by Rameses II in the 13th cent. BC. Later held by the Philistines, the Assyrians and the Persians. Taken by the Crusaders and twice recaptured by Saladin (1187, 1192). De-stroyed by the Sultan Baybars 1270. Roman and Crusader remains. Birthplace of Herod the Great (c. 74–73 BC).

Ashkhabad Turkmenistan. Cap. of Turk-menistan, founded 1881, at the foot of the Kopet Dagh near the Iran frontier in a fertile oasis. Pop. (1991) 412,200.

It manufactures textiles, footwear and glass; other industries inc. meat-packing and food-processing.

On the Trans-Caspian Railway. It was rebuilt after an earthquake in 1948.

Ashland USA. Industrial town and river port in Kentucky on the Ohio R. 160 km (100 miles) ENE of Lexington. Pop. (1970) 29,245.

Oil refineries. Nickel and iron and steel works.

Ashmore and Cartier Islands Indian

Ocean. Islands forming an overseas territory of Australia situated 320 km (200 miles) off the NW coast of Australia. The Ashmore Islands consist of 3 coral islets and are enclosed by a coral reef. Cartier island is sandy and enclosed by a reef. Area 5 sq km (1.9 sq. miles). The islands are uninhabited but Indonesian fishing boats, which have traditionally plied in the area, fish within the Territory and land to collect water.

Ashton-in-Makerfield England. Town in Greater Manchester 8 km (5 miles) S of Wigan. Pop. (1991) 28,105.

Industries inc. general engineering and distribution.

Ashton-under-Lyne England. Town in Greater Manchester 10 km (6 miles) E of the city. Pop. (1991) 43,906.

Industries inc. mechanical, chemical and electrical engineering, clothing, footwear, plastics and textiles.

Ashur (Assur) Iraq. Cap. of ancient Assyria. A site beside the Tigris R. 88 km (55 miles) S of Mosul near modern Sharqat.

Superseded by Nineveh in the 9th cent. BC. Excavations have revealed palaces, temples, etc.

Asia. Occupying nearly a third of the world's land surface, Asia is the largest of the continents. Area 43,608,000 sq km (16,833,000 sq. miles). Pop. (1991) 3113 million (59 per cent of the world's pop.). It is bounded by the Arctic Ocean in the N, the Pacific Ocean to the E and the Indian Ocean S. The W boundary with Europe is generally considered to run along the Ural Mountains, the Caspian Sea, the Caucasus Mountains, the Black Sea, the Bosporus and the Dardanelles. Joined to Africa across the Sinai Peninsula. Features of the E and S coastline are a number of peninsulas, of varied size: Kamchatka, Korea, Indo–China (with its appendage the Malay peninsula) and the peninsulas of India, Arabia and Asia Minor. Off the same coasts are festoons of islands, e.g. Sakhalin and the Kuril Is., the islands of Japan, Taiwan, the Philippines, Indonesia and Sri Lanka.

Asia inc. both the highest point on the earth's surface (Mt Everest, 8848 m (29,028 ft)) and the lowest (the Dead Sea, 395 m (1296 ft) below sea level). It may be divided into a number of major physical units. From the lofty Pamirs to the NW of India radiate several great mountain ranges: the Tien Shan (NE), the Kunlun and Altyn Tagh (E), the Karakoram and the Himalayas (SE), the Sulaiman Range and the Hindu Kush (SW). Between these ranges and others are high plateaux such as those of Tibet and Mongolia. N of the central mountain ranges are the W Siberian plain and the low central Siberian plateau, drained to the Arctic by the Ob, Yenisei and Lena rivers. E Asia inc. the great river basins of the Amur, the Huang He and Chang Jiang, separated and partially closed by mountain spurs. SE and S Asia have the great river plains of the Mekong and the Irrawaddy; the Brahmaputra, the Ganges and the Indus (the extensive Indo–Gangetic Plain); and the Tigris and the Euphrates (Mesopotamia). On the SW margins of the continent are the plateaux of peninsular India, Arabia and Asia Minor. The central mass of mountains and plateaux forms an effective N–S and E–W barrier, encloses regions of inland drainage such as the Tarim and the Furfan basins and is an important climatic divide.

Asia has the coldest known spot on earth (Verkoyansk in Siberia) as well as some of the hottest and the wettest (Cherrapunji in Meghalaya) as well as some of the driest. The climates range from Arctic in the N (where large areas have a permanently frozen subsoil) to equatorial in the S. To the S and E of the central mountains and plateaux is the world's great monsoon region, where changes of temperature and pressure in the interior bring cool, dry out-blowing winds in winter and hot, moisture-laden in-blowing winds in summer. SW Asia, a continuation of the hot desert lands of N Africa, extends E to NW India; a broad belt of mid-latitude desert stretches across the plateaux of central Asia to the Gobi Desert. The coastal fringes of Israel, Syria and Asia Minor have a Mediterranean climate; that of N Asia is cold continental, merging in the far N into Arctic.

There are correspondingly wide variations in the natural vegetation: S of the Arctic tundra is the vast area of coniferous forest called the Siberian taiga and in SW Siberia and Manchuria there are much smaller regions of steppe or mid-latitude grassland, but in E Asia the natural vegetation consists largely of mixed forest, now much depleted. The SE still has considerable areas of evergreen tropical rainforest (esp. in the islands of Indonesia and the Malay peninsula) and of deciduous monsoon forest in Myanmar (Burma), Thailand and NE India.

In the monsoon lands of S and E Asia rice is the principal food crop; wheat and millets are grown in the drier regions. Vegetable oils are obtained from soya beans (China), groundnuts (India, China) and copra (Philippines, Indonesia). Dates are produced in the desert lands (Iraq etc.). Tea is an important export of India and Sri Lanka. Non-food products inc. rubber (Malaysia, Indonesia), cotton (Ukraine) and jute (Bangladesh, India). Many regions produce metallic ores, as well as coal (Russia, China); but the most spectacular mineral development has been the increase in petroleum output from SW Asia (Kuwait, Saudi Arabia, Iran, Iraq). Industrialization has progressed slowly, except in Japan, parts of the Commonwealth of Independent States and latterly China. The majority of Asian peoples are still agriculturists.

The major religions of the world, Buddhism, Christianity, Confucianism, Hinduism, Islam and Judaism began in Asia.

Asia Minor (Anatolia) Turkey. Peninsula in W Asia. Area 569,800 sq km (220,000 sq. miles). Bounded N by the Black Sea, on the E by Iran, on the S by the Mediterranean Sea and Syria, and on the W by the Bosporus, Sea of Marmara, Dardanelles and the Aegean Sea. There is a central tableland at 914–1820 m (3000–6000 ft). The Pontic Mountains (N) and the Aurus Mountains (S) merge in the Armenian Knot (E), which culminates in the peak of Mt Ararat. The dry steppe-like interior has many salt lakes; the W and S coastal regions have a Mediterranean climate.

Passed to the Ottoman Turks in the 13th–14th cent. and was part of the Ottoman Empire until Turkey became a republic after World War I.

Asir Saudi Arabia. Region in the SW, bordering on the Red Sea between Hejaz and Yemen. Area 103,000 sq km (40,000 sq. miles). An arid coastal plain, rising to mountains which exceed 2500 m (8200 ft) and descend E to the desert interior. Resembles East Africa rather than inland Arabia. The highlands have a moderate rainfall and produce coffee, grain and fruits. There are deposits of copper and nickel. Incorporated into Saudi Arabia by Ibn Saud in 1933.

Askja Iceland. Volcano 90 km (56 miles) SE of Akureyri in the Odadahraun lava field. Height 1394 m (4754 ft). Large crater (88 sq km; 34 sq. miles).

Asmara (Asmera) Eritrea. Town on the Hamasen plateau in the central highlands at 2300 m (7544 ft) 61 km (38 miles) SW of Mitsiwa (Masswara), to which it is linked by railway. Pop. (1991) 367,300. Surrounded by rich agricultural land.

Manufactures textiles, matches and soap.

Occupied by the Italians 1889; became cap. of the Italian colony of Eritrea. Captured by the Allies during World War II (1941). Remained under British military rule until Eritrea was federated with Ethiopia by a UN resolution (1952). In the 1980s and 1990s it has been a garrison town during the Eritrean independence war and became cap. when independence was achieved in 1993. Famine and drought have been an aspect during the same period.

Asnières France. Suburb of NW Paris, in the Hauts-de-Seine department on the left bank of the Seine. Pop. (1990) 72,250.

Aircraft, machine-tool, motor-car, perfume and other industries. Leisure and boating centre for Parisians.

Aspromonte Italy. Mountain mass in the Reggio di Calabria province in the 'toe' of Italy, rising to 1956 m (6416 ft). Scene of Garibaldi's defeat and capture (1862).

Aspropotamos River Greece. Ancient Achelous ('White') R. It flows for 208 km (130 miles), rising in the Pindus Mountains and flowing generally S to the Ionian Sea opposite Ithaca.

Assab Eritrea. Port on the Red Sea. Pop. (1989) 36,659.

Salt works and oil refinery.

Purchased by an Italian steamship company as a coaling station after being first settled in 1869. Acquired by the Italian government (1882) as a base for the colonization of Eritrea. Captured by British and Indian forces during World War II (1941). Ethiopia negotiated a right to use the port following the secession of Eritrea in 1993.

Assam India. State in the extreme NE. Area (excluding the NE Frontier Agency) 78,523 sq km (30,300 sq. miles). Pop. (1991) 22,294,562. The majority of the pop. is Hindu but there are considerable numbers of Muslims and Christians plus some Buddhists, Jains and Sikhs. Bounded by Arunachal Pradesh (N), Nagaland (E), Bangladesh (SW) and Bhutan (NW). Almost enclosed by mountains; crossed by the broad fertile valley of the Brahmaputra R. Monsoon climate.

About 77 per cent of the people are engaged in agriculture; rice is extensively grown, but tea accounts for 66 per cent of the country's production. Guwahati is the world's largest tea auction centre. Petroleum is produced and there are 3 refineries located in Digboi, Guwahati and Bongaigaon. Digboi refinery is over a cent. old. A fourth refinery is being located at Numaligarh. Natural gas is available in abundance. Gas-based industries and power-generating stations are being established.

Ceded to Britain after the First Burmese War (1826). Became an autonomous province of British India 1937. On the partition of India (1947), the mainly Muslim district of Sylhet was inc. in E Pakistan (now Bangladesh). The North East Frontier Agency was integrated with Assam (1963) but separated to become Arunachal Pradesh (1972). In the SW the area inc. the Khasi and the Jaintia Hills became the state of Meghalaya (1972)

and in the SE the Mizo Hills area became the Union Territory, now state of Mizoram.

Assen Netherlands. Cap. of the Drenthe province 24 km (15 miles) S of Groningen. Pop. (1992) 50,880. It is a railway and canal junction, and has clothing, food-processing and other light industries.

Nearby there are 4000-year-old standing stones like those at Stonehenge, England.

Assiniboine River Canada. River 940 km (590 miles) long, rising in E Saskatchewan and flowing SE and then E through S Manitoba to join the Red R. at Winnipeg. Its basin is one of Canada's main wheat-growing regions. The name derives from the Assiniboin Indian tribe.

Assisi Italy. Town in the Perugia province in Umbria 21 km (13 miles) ESE of Perugia. Pop. (1990) 24,790. Birthplace of St Francis (1182–1226), founder of the Franciscan religious order, above whose tomb two churches were built (1228–53); they contain frescoes by Cimabue, Giotto and others. Birthplace of St Clare (1194–1253), whose tomb is in the 13th-cent. Church of Santa Chiara.

Assynt, Loch Scotland. Lake 11 km (7 miles) long in Highland, with an outlet to the sea by the R. Inver. Near the E end are the ruins of the 15th-cent. Ardvrech Castle, where Montrose was captured (1650).

Assyria. Ancient empire in SW Asia, around the city of Ashur on the upper Tigris R. in the N of the plain of Mesopotamia. Now part of modern Iraq.

Asti Italy. Cap. of Asti province in Piedmont 45 km (28 miles) ESE of Turin. Pop. (1990) 77,000. Route, industrial and commercial centre.

Noted for sparkling wine (Asti spumante). Distilleries, rayon mills.

Gothic cathedral (14th cent.).

Astrakhan Russia. Cap. of the Astrakhan Region on the delta of the Volga R. 96 km (60 miles) from the Caspian Sea. Pop. (1990)

511,900. Chief Caspian port, though ice-bound for 4 months a year.

Dispatches timber, grain, metals downstream and oil, cotton, fruit and rice upstream. Shipbuilding, fish-processing (esp. the preparation of caviare), sawmilling. Manufactures textiles and footwear.

Standing 20 m (66 ft) below sea level, it is protected from Volga floods by dykes. Consists of the 16th/17th cent. Kreml (citadel) which inc. a cathedral, the White Town (containing offices and shops) and the suburbs (wooden houses). Its name is given to the fur made from the skins of newborn Persian lambs. Formerly cap. of a Tatar khanate. Captured by Ivan the Terrible 1556. Its importance increased with the exploitation of the Baku oilfields in the late 19th cent., but has diminished since the opening of the Volga–Don Canal (1952).

Asturias Spain. Autonomous region and former kingdom in the NW, corresponding to the present Oviedo province. Area 10,567 sq km (4080 sq. miles). Pop. (1991) 1,093,940. During the Moorish invasion it became a Christian stronghold; the reconquest of Spain was started from Asturias and a Christian kingdom founded here. Coal, iron and fluorspar are mined.

Asunción Paraguay. Cap., on the E bank of the Paraguay R. near the confluence with the Pilcomayo. Pop. (1990) 607,706.

Transacts most of Paraguay's business. River transport and a central winding railway to Buenos Aires (1500 km (938 miles)); a ferry link to the Pan-American Highway at Pilcomayo. Flour-milling, food-processing. Manufactures textiles and footwear.

Settled by the Spaniards (1538), who found the Guaraní Indians friendly; became the centre from which Spanish colonization of the S part of the continent proceeded.

Aswan Egypt. Ancient Syene. Town in Upper Egypt on the E bank of the Nile just below the First Cataract. Pop. (1991) 215,000. On the railway to Cairo. Commercial and tourist centre and winter resort. Syenite (granite) quarries in the neigh-bourhood. The new Aswan High Dam was begun in 1960. The project, which was worked out by British engineers but received Soviet financial and technical aid, creates a vast reservoir, stretching 480 km (300 miles). The High Dam is over 100 m (328 ft) high and nearly 5 km (3 miles) long. The first stage was completed in May 1964; the entire structure was completed in July 1970. It greatly increases the irrigation potential of the Nile waters; the flow also serves a large hydroelectric power station, generating about 2000 megawatts. ➤ABU SIMBEL.

Asyût (Assiut) Egypt. Ancient Lycopolis. Chief city in Upper Egypt on the W bank of the Nile. Pop. (1991) 313,000. On the railway to Cairo.

Caravan-trading centre. Cotton-spinning, wood and ivory carving, pottery making. One of the chief centres of the Copts.

The Asyût barrage (1902) across the Nile provides water for irrigation.

Atacama Desert South America. Part of the arid area W of the Andes, stretching from N central Chile to S Ecuador and comprising the barren lands of N Chile and S Peru. One of the driest areas on earth. Between the Andean slopes and the coast (falling steeply to the Pacific) discontinuous basins of dried-up lakes, 60–80 km (40–50 miles) wide, bear caliche deposits yielding nitrates and iodine. Great copper mines in the W Andes. There are iron-ore reserves in desert Chile.

Atbara Sudan. Town on the right bank of the Atbara R. at its confluence with the Nile. Pop. (1983) 73,009.

Important railway junction for Port Sudan. Railway engineering. Manufactures cement. Trade in cotton.

Atbara River Sudan. River over 1120 km (700 miles) long, rising in the Ethiopian highlands, flowing NNW and joining the Nile at Atbara. The only tributary of the Nile between the Blue and the White Nile confluence and the Mediterranean. After the flood season (July–Aug.) becomes a chain of pools.

Atchafalaya River USA. An outlet of the Red R. in Louisiana, leading to the bay of the same name in the Gulf of Mexico. Also carries Mississippi water in flood time. For most of its 350 km (220 miles) it has been strengthened by levees.

Athabaska (Athabasca), Lake Canada. Lake 320 km (200 miles) long and 7800 sq km (3000 sq. miles) in area in NW Saskatchewan and NE Alberta. It receives the Athabaska and Peace rivers in the SW and discharges NW by the Slave R. into the Great Slave L. and thence into the Mackenzie R. The discovery of uranium ores on the N shore led to the growth of Uranium City in the 1950s.

Athabaska (Athabasca) River Canada. River 1225 km (765 miles) long, rising in the Rocky Mountains near Mt Columbia and flowing generally NE to L. Athabaska. Oil-bearing sands extend 190 km (120 miles) along the lower course.

Athelney, Isle of England. Small area near the confluence of the Tone and Parrett rivers in Somerset. Formerly isolated by marshes. Hiding place of Alfred the Great after his defeat by the Danes (878).

Athens (Gr. **Athínai**) Greece. Cap. of Greece and of the Attica *nome* on the chief plain of Attica 8 km (5 miles) from the Saronic Gulf and its port Piraeus (with which it now forms one large city). Total pop. for Greater Athens (1991) 3,096,775; city, 748,110.

Economic and cultural centre of Greece. Manufactures textiles, rugs, chemicals and wine (concentrated mainly in Piraeus). Above the plain rise a number of limestone ridges, two of which, the Lycabettus (280 m; 918 ft) just outside the ancient walls and the Acropolis (156 m; 512 ft), dominate the city. The classical buildings are among the most important in the world. Below its northern face lies the old town with narrow streets and courtyards; the rest of the city is modern, laid out first in the 1830s and greatly expanded since 1920. Expansion since 1950 has been rapid and has produced serious problems from traffic, pollution and overcrowding.

Settled before 3000 BC. Athens grew into a prosperous city 600–500 BC, but was destroyed by the Persians in 480 BC. The present Acropolis buildings date from 447 BC onwards. Athens was a centre of Hellenic thought until the 6th cent. AD. The Turks took it in 1456 and held it until 1833. At independence it had shrunk to a few inhabited streets on the N side of the Acropolis. Its revival began with the German architects of Prince Otho of Bavaria, chosen as first king of Greece.

Athens USA. Town in Georgia on the Oconee R. 93 km (58 miles) ENE of Atlanta. Pop. (1984) 42,500.

In an important cotton-growing area. Commercial and industrial centre. Manufactures textiles, cottonseed oil and fertilizers.

Atherstone England. Town in Warwickshire 6 km (4 miles) NW of Nuneaton. Pop. (1991) 10,677.

Manufactures hats, footwear and knitwear.

On the Roman road Watling Street. In the neighbouring village of Merevale are the remains of the 12th-cent. Merevale Abbey.

Atherton England. Town in Greater Manchester 16 km (10 miles) WNW of the city. Pop. (1985) 22,000.

Industrial centre for light engineering, textiles and soft drinks.

Athlone Ireland. Town in Co. Westmeath on the Shannon R. 113 km (70 miles) W of Dublin. Pop. (1991) 8170. Almost in the geographical centre of Ireland. Main Irish broadcasting station 3 km (2 miles) E. Textile mills. Birthplace of the tenor John McCormack (1884–1945).

Atholl Scotland. Mountainous district in Perth and Kinross on the S slopes of the Grampian Mountains. Area 1165 sq km (450 sq. miles). About one-third deer forest. Chief towns Pitlochry, Dunkeld and Blair Atholl.

Athos, Mount (Gr. **Hagion Oros**, 'Holy Mountain') Greece. Highest point (2033 m; 6668 ft) of the Chalcidice peninsula, in Macedonia, at the SE end of Acte (Akti), the most easterly of the three prongs extending into the Aegean Sea. Connected to the mainland by an isthmus, where there are still traces of a canal cut by Xerxes before 480 BC. Area 336 sq km (131 sq. miles). Pop. (1991) 1560 (mainly Basilian monks). Administrative centre Karyai (pop. 301). A self-governing community of 20 monasteries, formed in the 10th cent. Autonomy was granted by the Greek government in 1927. Foreign visitors are limited to 10 a day and women are banned.

Atitlán Guatemala. Volcano (3524 m; 11,558 ft) just S of L. Atitlán in the S. Active 16th–19th cent.

Atitlán, Lake Guatemala. Lake 38 km (24 miles) long and 16 km (10 miles) wide 64 km (40 miles) W of Guatemala City at a height of 1500 m (4920 ft). Depth 300 m (985 ft). Famed for its beauty. Believed to occupy the crater of an extinct volcano. Near its S shores are inactive volcanoes (inc. Atitlán). There is no visible outlet.

Atlanta USA. State cap. of Georgia, principal state commercial and railway centre. Pop. (1990) 394,017. Railway engineering.
  Manufactures textiles, clothing, furniture, chemicals, cottonseed oil and machinery. It is the home of Coca-Cola and the drink was invented here.
  Partly destroyed by Union troops under Sherman during the American Civil War (1864), but developed rapidly when hostilities were over.

Atlantic City USA. Holiday resort in New Jersey on Absecon Beach, a low sandy island 16 km (10 miles) long 88 km (55 miles) SE of Philadelphia. Luxury and other hotels, amusement piers, recreational facilities. Various industries.

Atlantic Ocean. The world's second largest ocean after the Pacific, lying between Europe and Africa (E) and North and South America (W), named after the Atlas Mountains in North Africa. Area 82,217,000 sq km (31,736,000 sq. miles). Divided by the equator into the North Atlantic and South

Atlantic. Its greatest depth (9220 m; 30,242 ft) is in the Puerto Rico trench, but the average depth is about 3900 m (12,800 ft). A ridge rising some 1800 m (5900 ft) above the ocean floor runs N to S down the middle of the North and South Atlantic, inc. the islands of the Azores in the former and Ascension and Tristan da Cunha in the latter. Other island groups are the Canary Is., Cape Verde Is. and Madeira off Africa; the British Isles and Iceland in Europe; Newfoundland, West Indies and Bermuda off North America; the Falkland Is., South Georgia off South America. It is relatively saltier than other oceans. It provides about one-third of the world's fish catch; the main fishing grounds are the Grand Banks off Newfoundland and the Dogger Bank in the North Sea. The continental shelves of the North Sea and the Gulf of Mexico contain oil reserves. In the North Atlantic the main currents follow a clockwise direction and inc. the Gulf Stream and the North Atlantic Drift, while in the South Atlantic they have an anti-clockwise flow, as exemplified by the Benguela and Brazil Currents.

Atlas Mountains Africa. An irregular series of mountain chains extending WSW–ENE across NW Africa, Cape Ghir in Morocco to Cape Bon in Tunisia. It is a physical and climatic barrier between the Mediterranean region and the Sahara. Among the ranges are the Tell (Maritime) Atlas and the Saharan Atlas; between these are the high plateaux. The highest range is the Great (High) Atlas in Morocco with snow-capped peaks, rising to 4167 m (13,671 ft) in Djebel Toubkal. Some well-watered Atlas slopes are covered with forests of oak, cedar, where cork is the main product. They enclose fertile cultivated valleys.

Atrato River Colombia. River 640 km (400 miles) long, rising in the W Cordillera (the headwaters receive about 1000 cm (395 ins.) of rain annually), flowing N through the forests between the Sierra de Baudo and the W Cordillera and entering the Gulf of Darien. Navigable in the upper course, where there is gold and platinum dredging.

Attleboro USA. Town in SE Massachusetts 19 km (12 miles) NE of Providence (Rhode Island). Pop. (1990) 38,400.

Manufactures jewellery and silverware.

Founded (1669) by immigrants from Attleborough (Norfolk, England).

Atyrau (Guryev) Kazakhstan. Port and cap. of the Atyrau region, on the Ural R. near its mouth on the Caspian Sea (NE). Pop. (1990) 151,400. Terminus of the Orsk–Kandagach railway and of the pipelines from the Emba oilfield. Industries inc. oil-refining, fishing and fish-canning.

Aube France. Department in Champagne SE of Paris on the edge of the Paris Basin. Area 6004 sq km (2318 sq. miles). Pop. (1991) 289,400. Prefecture Troyes. The chalk area of the centre and NW (*Champagne pouilleuse*) is arid and infertile, except along the Aube R. In the wooded and more fertile SE, cereals and vines are cultivated. Manufactures hosiery. Chief towns Troyes, Arcis-sur-Aube, Bar-sur-Aube.

Aube River France. Navigable river 240 km (150 miles) long, rising on the Plateau de Langres and flowing NW through the Haute-Marne and Aube departments to the Seine.

Aubervilliers France. Formerly Notre-Dame-des-Vertus. Industrial suburb NNE of Paris in the Seine–St Denis department.

Manufactures fertilizers, paints, varnishes, perfume and leather goods.

Auburn (Maine) USA. Industrial town on the Androscoggin R. 48 km (30 miles) N of Portland. Pop. (1970) 24,151.

Manufactures plastics, electrical goods and footwear.

Auburn (New York) USA. Town at the N end of L. Owasco 35 km (22 miles) WSW of Syracuse. Pop. (1990) 31,300.

Manufactures agricultural machinery, car spares, plastics, textiles, chemicals, surgical instruments and footwear.

Aubusson France. Town in the Creuse department on the Creuse R. 74 km (46 miles) ENE of Limoges. Pop. (1982) 6153. Famous since the 16th cent. for carpets and tapestries.

Auch France. Ancient Augusta Auscorum. Prefecture of the Gers department in the SW on the Gers R. 72 km (45 miles) W of Toulouse. Pop. (1990) 24,728. Market town.

Trade in Armagnac brandy, wine and cereals. Flour-milling, furniture and hosiery and other industries. Famous for pâté de foie gras.

Gothic cathedral (15th–17th cent.). An important city in Roman Gaul. Cap. of Armagnac and later of Gascony.

Auchinleck Scotland. Town in East Ayrshire 21 km (13 miles) E of Ayr. Pop. (1971) 4883. Former coalmining centre. Nearby is Auchinleck House, seat of the Boswell family. James Boswell (1740–95) is buried in the churchyard.

Auckland New Zealand. Largest city, chief seaport and former cap. (1840–65) of New Zealand, founded 1840, on a narrow isthmus in the N of North Island, between Manukau Harbour (S) and Waitemata Harbour (N). Pop. (1991) 315,925. Most of its trade is handled by Waitemata Harbour, the wharves being reached by a dredged channel.

Exports dairy produce, wool, hides and timber. Imports machinery, petroleum, coal, fertilizers. Manufactures textiles, chemicals, plastics, household appliances and foodstuffs. Shipyards, engineering works, vehicle-assembly plants. The main passenger seaport and trans-Pacific airport.

There are many extinct volcanic cones in the neighbourhood.

Aude France. Department on the Gulf of Lions in Languedoc. Area 6139 sq km (2370 sq. miles). Pop. (1991) 301,000. Prefecture Carcassonne. Largely mountainous, rising to 1231 m (4038 ft) in the Corbières. Crossed W–E by the valley of the Aude R.

Wine, cereals, olives and fruit produced in the fertile N. Salt produced along the lagoon-fringed coast. Chief towns Carcassonne, Narbonne, Castelnaudary and Limoux.

Aude River France. River 224 km (140 miles) long, rising in the Pyrenees near the Pic de Carlitte and flowing N past Carcassonne and then E to the Gulf of Lions.

Aue Germany. Industrial town in the Chemnitz district 19 km (12 miles) SE of Zwickau.

Centre of a uranium-mining region in the Erzgebirge. Manufactures textiles and metal goods.

Aughrables Falls ➤ORANGE RIVER.

Aughrim Ireland. Small village in Co. Galway 6 km (4 miles) WSW of Ballinasloe. Pop. (1991) 756. Scene of the battle (1691) in which the forces of William III (under General Ginkel) utterly defeated those of James II (under the French General St Ruth).

Augsburg Germany. Industrial city in Bavaria on the Lech R. near its confluence with the Wertach 56 km (35 miles) WNW of Munich. Pop. (1991) 256,877. Important railway junction.

Principal textile centre of S Germany (cotton, woollen, linen). Also manufactures diesel engines, agricultural machinery, machine-tools, precision instruments and chemicals.

Noteworthy buildings are the 10th/15th-cent. cathedral, the 17th-cent. Renaissance town hall, the 15th/16th-cent. Church of St Ulrich. Augustus founded a Roman colony here in 14 BC. Became a free imperial city 1276. Birthplace of the painter Holbein (1497–1543). Home of the Fugger merchant-banker family. Important commercial and banking centre in the 15th and 16th cent.

Augusta Italy. Seaport in E Sicily 19 km (12 miles) NNW of Syracuse on a small island connected to the mainland by a bridge. Pop. (1990) 40,000. Fisheries. Salt works. Founded by Emperor Frederick II 1232.

Augusta USA. Town and river port in Georgia on the Savannah R. at the head of navigation 177 km (110 miles) NNW of Savannah. Pop. (1990) 44,640. Connected by bridges with Hamburg (South Carolina). Cotton market with important cotton manufactures. Founded as a trading post 1735. State cap. 1786–95.

Aulnay-sous-Bois France. Residential suburb of NE Paris in the Seine–St Denis department.

Aunis France. Former province on the Bay of Biscay, forming (with part of Saintonge) the department of Charente–Maritime. Inc. the islands of Ré and Oléron. The cap. was La Rochelle.

Aurangabad India. Town in Maharashtra 280 km (175 miles) ENE of Bombay. Pop. (1991) 572,634. Textile manufactures. Trade in grain.

Founded in the early 17th cent. Became the cap. of the Mogul emperor Aurangzeb; has the mausoleum he erected to his wife.

Aurès Mountains ➤TIMGAD.

Aurillac France. Prefecture of the Cantal department in S central France on the Jordanne R. 109 km (68 miles) SSW of Clermont-Ferrand. Pop. (1990) 32,654.

Market town. Trade in cheese and livestock. Manufactures umbrellas and leather goods.

Grew up round the 9th-cent. Abbey of St Géraud, a centre of medieval learning.

Aurora USA. Industrial town in Illinois 54 km (34 miles) W of Chicago. Pop. (1990) 99,581.

Manufactures steel equipment for offices and schools, also pumps and machinery.

Auschwitz (better-known by its Ger. name, but Polish, **Oświęcim**) Poland. Town in the Krakow (Cracow) voivodeship 55 km (34 miles) W of Cracow. Pop. (1989) 45,402.

Manufactures chemicals and metal goods.

During World War II it was the site of a notorious concentration camp where the Germans practised mass extermination; 4 million people, mainly Jews, are estimated to have been murdered here.

Austerlitz (Czech **Slavkov**) Czech Republic. Town in Moravia 21 km (13 miles)

ESE of Brno. Scene of what was probably Napoleon's most brilliant victory (2 Dec. 1805), when he defeated the combined Russian and Austrian armies.

Austin (Minnesota) USA. Town 147 km (92 miles) SSE of Minneapolis. Pop. (1990) 22,000. Railway engineering and meat-packing.

Austin (Texas) USA. State cap. on the Colorado R. 240 km (150 miles) WNW of Houston. Pop. (1990) 465,622.

It is a commercial centre of a ranching and farming region. It undertakes considerable scientific research and is the main campus for the University of Texas.

Austral (Tubuai) Islands S Pacific Ocean. Group of islands S of the Society Is., French Polynesia. Total area 148 sq km (57 sq. miles). Pop. (1988) 6509 (Polynesian). Rurutu and Tubuai are the largest of the 4 main islands; to the S is Rapa-Iti. Discovered by Capt. Cook in 1777 and annexed by France in 1880.

Australasia S Pacific Ocean. Term applied somewhat loosely to the islands of the S Pacific inc. Australia, New Zealand, Papua New Guinea and their adjacent islands, and by some considered to be the whole of Oceania.

Australia. The Commonwealth of Australia is the largest island in the world and the smallest continent, nearly as large as the United States of America. It is bounded on the W by the Indian Ocean and on the E by the Pacific Ocean and is almost bisected by the Tropic of Capricorn. Area 7,682,300 sq km (2,966,200 sq. miles). Pop. (1995) 18,025,000 (85 per cent urban) (257,333 aborigines in 1991). The average pop. density is low (2.3 per sq km; 5.9 per sq. mile). The majority of the pop. live in or near the coastal lands of the E, SE and SW, in the temperate areas. In the occupied interior, agricultural stations and townships are widely dispersed. Two-thirds of the pop. live in a small number of cities, particularly the state caps. The native-born pop. is 78 per cent. Life expect-

ancy, 75 years male, 81 female. Cap. Canberra. State caps: Sydney, Melbourne, Brisbane, Adelaide, Perth and Hobart. Currency: Australian dollar = 100 cents.

The W part of the mainland consists of arid plateau 180–300 m (590–984 ft) high, with dissected tablelands rising above this level. E of this a central plain extends from the Gulf of Carpentaria to the S edge of the Murray R. basin, underlain in the N by the Great Artesian Basin. The Great Dividing Range runs parallel to the E (Pacific) coast, its uplifted blocks generally having steep E faces and sloping more gently inland. The highest point is Mt Kosciusko (2230 m, 7314 ft) in the Australian Alps. The E coastlands, nowhere over 400 km (250 miles) and generally less than 110 km (70 miles) wide, are the most fertile and adequately watered region where the majority of the large towns and pop. are concentrated. Offshore the Great Barrier Reef runs through the Coral Sea to about lat. 24° S. Tasmania, an island of 68,331 sq km (26,383 sq. miles) is separated from the mainland (SE) by the Bass Strait. The dry interior has considerable areas of desert, but there is much semi-arid land with tussock grass and scrub. Between this and the better-watered coastlands a great arc of grass country stretches from the SE to the NW, with eucalyptus forest in the wetter regions and some tropical forest in the NE. In the SW there are forests of jarrah and karri, valuable hardwoods. The N half is tropical, the SE and SW have warm temperate climates, with hot, dry summers and mild, rainy winters, while Tasmania is mild throughout the year. Rainfall diminishes sharply inland from the N and E coasts. Most of the interior has less than 50 cm (20 ins.) annually, much of it below 25 cm (10 ins.) and the rainfall is often unreliable. Many river systems are a maze of wandering channels, filled only after storms. The Murray R. system is the only large perennial one. The L. Eyre basin is the largest area of inland drainage and is usually dry. Artesian water, present in many parts, is often brackish but generally suitable for livestock. Land use: meadows and pastures 55 per cent, agricultural and under permanent cultivation 6 per cent.

The main religion is Christian, Anglican and Roman Catholic, and the lang. English. The people are mainly of British descent, but since 1946 many immigrants ('New Australians') have come from other European countries. At the time of the discovery of Australia various tribes of aborigines with a Stone Age culture were scattered throughout the land. Their numbers declined in the 19th cent. but have since increased, largely in the Northern Territory.

Sheep-rearing is an important occupation, but in spite of the importance of pastoral farming and agriculture there is a large urban pop. and the country is highly industrialized. Since the days of the early settlements, when squatters took up much of the new agricultural lands, farm mechanization, the selective breeding of stock and plants, the use of fertilizers and the development of soil science have established Australia as a major exporter of wool and wheat. Wheat comes mainly from the SE and SW areas receiving 25–65 cm (10–25 ins.) of rain a year. Most of the 162 million (1991) sheep are in the SE and SW where the annual rainfall is 50–75 cm (20–30 ins.) though millions are grazed at low densities in less favourable southern and interior areas, aided by artesian water. Dairy cattle prosper on the moist coastlands of S Queensland, the SE and SW and on irrigated land. Beef cattle are raised on hill country in these regions and on huge ranches in the N, NW and the Great Artesian Basin. Sugarcane, bananas and pineapples come from coastal Queensland and N New South Wales, deciduous fruits from Victoria, Tasmania and the SW. Irrigated lands in the Murray basin and near Adelaide and Perth support citrus and deciduous fruits and vines. In 1990 there were 130,000 farms

Australia has huge mineral wealth. Gold was the first important mineral to be found, but today only 1.5 per cent of the world's gold comes from Australia. Zinc, lead and silver come from New South Wales, Queensland and NW Tasmania, copper from Queensland, tin from the Great Dividing Range and Tasmania, gold from Western Australia and Victoria, and large iron-ore deposits are worked in the NW and in S Australia. Australia is a leading world producer of bauxite (for aluminium), the ore being mined in Queensland, Western Australia and Northern Territory. Coal comes from coastal New South Wales and Queensland, smaller amounts from S and Western Australia, lignite from S Victoria. Oil production started in 1964 in Queensland, but today two-thirds of the country's oil and gas come from the Gippland basin. There are major reserves off the NW coast. Uranium exists in the Northern Territory and N Queensland. Other minerals inc. manganese, gold, diamonds and opals. There is a growing steel industry. Other manufactures inc. industrial metals, machinery, food-processing, chemicals, textiles, paper and petroleum products, mainly for home consumption. The greatest industrial areas are those of Newcastle–Sydney–Port Kembla in E New South Wales, and Melbourne and S Victoria; others are near Adelaide, S of Perth, and inland of Brisbane. Imports are mainly of metals, machinery, crude oil, textiles and chemicals. Exports inc. wool, wheat, meat, metals and metal manufactures, fruits, dairy produce (esp. butter) and sugar. Japan took 30 per cent of exports and was the largest customer in 1991. Trade with Asian countries has increased significantly in recent years.

Hydroelectric power resources are limited except in Tasmania and the SE mountains. The fauna of Australia, like the flora, has certain exclusive features. There are no native cats, pigs or dogs; the destructive dingo or wild dog was introduced long ago and is already doomed. Typical mammals are the marsupials (of which the kangaroo is the largest), the koala bear and the platypus. The rabbit was introduced by settlers and so increased in numbers as to become a threat to sheep and cattle pastures. Its numbers are greatly reduced by the disease myxomatosis.

The first settlers were the Aborigines who migrated from SE Asia and remained isolated for 40,000 years until the N was visited early in the 17th cent. by Dutch navigators and in 1642 Tasman sailed via Tasmania to New Zealand. In 1770 Capt. Cook landed to the S of the present Sydney and this led to the region being claimed and settled by the British as New South Wales. It was at first used largely as a penal settlement (transportation virtually ceased by 1839) and, though the colonies (later states) were founded one by one, it was not until the discovery of gold at Bathurst (1851) that settlers arrived in considerable numbers. The pop. began to increase rapidly: it rose from 405,000 in 1850 to 3,770,000 in 1900 and since 1945 has doubled. The continent was first crossed N–S by J. M. Stuart in 1862. Long before then, however, men had moved in from the early coastal settlements to the lands which have since provided the major part of the country's wealth in wool and wheat. In 1901 the colonies were fused into the Commonwealth and became states; the federal cap. was at Melbourne until 1927, when it was transferred to Canberra. The Northern Territory, annexed to South Australia in 1863, was taken over by the Commonwealth in 1911.

There is a Federal Parliament of two houses: a 76-member Senate and a 148-member House of Representatives. Administration is in the hands of a prime minister and cabinet. Each of the states has its own government, which retains those powers not specifically delegated to the central government. Australia comprises 6 states (New South Wales, Victoria, Queensland, South Australia, Western Australia, Tasmania), the Northern Territory, which obtained responsible self-government in 1979 and the Australian Capital Territory (Canberra). Territories under the administration of the Commonwealth but not inc. in it, comprise Norfolk Is., Ashmore and Cartier Is., Australian Antarctic Territory, Heard Is., McDonald Is., Cocos (Keeling) Is. and Christmas Is.

Australian Alps Australia. Mountain range in the SE extending for about 480 km (300 miles) through Victoria and New South Wales to the S end of the Great Dividing Range. They contain Mt Kosciusko (2234 m; 7328 ft), the highest peak in Australia. Forested and a popular winter sports area.

Australian Antarctic Territory. All islands and territories other than Adelie Land S of 60°S and between 45° and 160°E, under Australian authority since 1933. Scientific bases were established at Mawson in Mac-Robertson Land (1954) and at Davis in Princess Elizabeth Land (1957); in 1959 Australia also took custody of Wilkes station, in Wilkes Land, sharing research with the USA. In 1969 the new Casey station, 1.6 km (1 mile) distant, was opened, taking the place of Wilkes station. By the International Antarctic Treaty (1959), the area S of 60°S is reserved for international peaceful scientific investigation.

Australian Capital Territory
➤CANBERRA.

Austria. Federal Republic in central Europe. Bounded by Germany and the Czech Republic (N), Slovakia and Hungary (E), Slovenia and Italy (S), Switzerland and Liechtenstein (W). Area 83,859 sq km (32,377 sq. miles). Pop. (1995) 8,060,000 (65 per cent urban). Life expectancy, 73 years male, 79 female. Cap. Vienna. Large towns: Graz, Linz, Salzburg, Innsbruck and Klagenfurt. Currency: Schilling = 100 Groschen. Austria is also entirely within the Alps. In the SW the Ötztal Alps rise to 3774 m (12,379 ft) in the Wild Spitze and the Hohe Tauern to 3798 m (12,457 ft) in the Gross Glockner; the latter is continued E towards the centre of Austria by the Niedere Tauern. Drained principally by the Danube (flowing W–E across the N region) and by its tributaries the Lech, the Inn, the Traun, the Raab and the Drave. Austria has no sea frontiers and so the Danube is an important waterway. It has a continental climate, with cold winters, warm summers and a moderate rainfall; temperatures decrease and rainfall increases with altitude. Land use: forested 39 per cent, meadows and pastures 24 per cent, agricultural and under permanent cultivation 19 per cent. Predominantly Christian and mainly Roman Catholic. The lang. is German.

The mountain scenery, esp. in the Tirol, the lakes of Carinthia and the many winter-sports centres and spas, attracts large numbers of visitors; tourism is a major industry. There are about 20,000 hotels and in 1991 there were over 19 million visitors. The mountainous character of the country restricts agriculture and necessitates imports of grain, fats and other foodstuffs. Nearly half of the arable land is in Lower Austria, which occupies less than a quarter of the total area. Forestry is an important occupation and the chief crops are wheat, rye, barley and potatoes. Cattle and pigs are extensively reared. Austria has great mineral wealth and lignite is mined in many districts. The rich iron-ore deposits of Styria form the basis of the steel industry. Since the early 1930s there has been some production of petroleum. Copper, lead, zinc, graphite also mined. There is a wide range of manufactured goods (increasingly using hydroelectric power) and located chiefly in Vienna, Graz and Linz. The other large towns, Salzburg and Innsbruck, are primarily cultural and tourist centres.

In early times inhabited by Celtic tribes. The land S of the Danube was conquered by the Romans (14 BC) and divided into three provinces of the Empire. From the 5th cent. AD the area was overrun by Vandals, Goths, Huns, Lombards and Avars. Conquered by Charlemagne, who established the Eastern mark in the present Upper and Lower Austria at the end of the 8th cent. Otto II presented Austria to the Babenberg family (976), who ruled until 1246 and initiated the long rise to prestige and power. Rudolf of Habsburg, the German king, appointed his son Albert governor of Austria and Styria in 1282 and the house of Habsburg ruled Austria almost continuously from then until 1918. Bohemia and Hungary were united with Austria in the 16th cent. After the second siege of Vienna by the Turks (1683) and the liberation of most of Hungary from the Turks, Bohemia, Moravia and Hungary all underwent thorough Germanization. For a time Prussia was a formidable rival, but Austria gained considerably from the Partitions of Poland (1772, 1793, 1795). With the rise of Napoleon came the end of the Holy Roman Empire and Francis II proclaimed himself Emperor of Austria (1804). Austria played a substantial part in the final defeat of Napoleon and was rewarded with Lombardy, Venetia, Istria and Illyria (abandoning the Netherlands). Internal unrest showed itself in the revolution of 1848, which began in Hungary. Lombardy and Venetia were lost after wars with Sardinia (1859) and Prussia (1866) respectively; nationalist feeling in Hungary was for a time placated by the establishment of the Dual Monarchy (1867), but the disaffection of the Slav minorities remained. The instability of Austria–Hungary helped to bring about World War I, at the end of which the monarchy collapsed and Austria was reduced to an insignificant republic. It was forcibly incorporated into Nazi Germany (1938). After World War II it recovered its independence and 1938 frontiers, following military occupation by the Allies, on the conclusion of the Austrian State Treaty (1955).

The 1920 Constitution was restored in 1955 and Austria is a democratic republic comprising 9 states (Länder): Vienna, Lower Austria, Burgenland, Upper Austria, Salzburg, Styria, Carinthia, Tirol and Vorarlberg. It has a Federal President and a bicameral National Assembly which comprises a 183-member National Council and a 63-member Federal Council.

Auvergne France. Region and former province in the Massif Central, forming the present Cantal and Puy-de-Dome departments and part of the Haute-Loire department. Area 26,103 sq km (10,078 sq. miles). Pop. (1991) 1,321,000. Chief town and regional cap. Clermont-Ferrand. The Auvergne Mountains inc. many volcanic peaks (Plomb du Cantal, Puy de Dome, Mont Dore) and rise to 1886 m (6186 ft) in the Puy de Sancy. Industrial development inc. a tyre factory and some light industry. Tourism is a feature of the area and there are a number of spas. Early inhabitants were the Arverni, a Celtic tribe whose chieftain Vercingetorix was Caesar's chief opponent in the Gallic war.

Auxerre France. Ancient Autissiodurum. Prefecture of the Yonne department on the Yonne R. 69 km (43 miles) SW of Troyes. Pop. (1990) 41,000. Market town.

Trade in wine (from local vineyards). Manufactures metal goods and paints (from locally quarried ochre).

Avalon Canada. The SE peninsula of Newfoundland between Trinity and Placentia Bays, with half the island's pop. At its E tip is the cap., St John's.

Avebury England. Village in Wiltshire on the R. Kennet 14 km (9 miles) SSW of Swindon. Site of a large neolithic structure (discovered by John Aubrey in the 1660s) inc. an outer stone circle 365 m (1197 ft) in diameter and two small circles; the stones are 1.5–6 m (5–20 ft) high and 0.9–3.6 m (3–12 ft) broad. Nearby is the artificial mound of Silbury Hill, the largest prehistoric structure in Britain. The village and site were acquired by the National Trust in 1943.

Avellaneda Argentina. Major industrial suburb of Buenos Aires, where the Riachuelo R. enters the La Plata estuary. Huge *frigoríficos* (meat-packing plants). Pop. (1980) 330,654.

Oil-refining, tanning. Manufactures textiles and matches. Docks for shipping animal products from the pampas.

Avellino Italy. Cap. of Avello province in Campania in the Apennines 45 km (28 miles) ENE of Naples. Pop. (1990) 55,831.

Sulphur mining and refining. Flour-milling. Manufactures hats.

The ruins of ancient Abellinum are 4 km (2½ miles) NE. 6 km (4 miles) NW is the Benedictine convent and shrine of Monte Vergine (founded in the 12th cent.).

Averno Italy. A small crater lake, nearly 3 km (2 miles) in circumference, in Campania 16 km (10 miles) W of Naples. In ancient times the sulphurous fumes were believed to kill passing birds; it was represented as the entrance to hell.

Aveyron France. Department in the SW of the Massif Central, almost corresponding to the ancient county of Rouergue. Area 8736 sq km (3373 sq. miles). Pop. (1991) 269,300. Prefecture Rodez. Mountainous and largely barren, with the Monts d'Aubrac in the NE and the Cévennes in the SE. Inc. much of the limestone Causses region. Cattle and sheep raised.

Cereals and potatoes cultivated and vines, fruits and vegetables in the sheltered valleys. Coal mined at Decazeville and Aubin. The town of Roquefort is famous for cheese. Chief towns Rodez, Millau (glove manufacture).

Aveyron River France. River 240 km (150 miles) long in the Aveyron and Tarn-et-Garonne departments in the S, rising on the Aveyron–Lozère border and flowing generally WSW to join the Tarn R. near Montauban.

Avignon France. Historic town, prefecture of the Vaucluse department on the left bank of the Rhône R. 91 km (57 miles) NNW of Marseille. Pop. (1990) 89,440.

Trade in wines. Manufactures chemicals, soap, cement, paper and rayon. Tourist centre for visitors to Provence. Dominated by the massive papal palace, a 14th-cent. combined castle, fortress and convent, which took 30 years to build. Only 4 arches of the 12th-cent. bridge of St Bénézet (subject of the folk song *Sur le pont d'Avignon*) now extend across the Rhône and among its ruins is the original Romanesque chapel. Almost encircled by enormous crenellated walls built (14th cent.) by the popes when it was the residence of Pope Clement V and his successors during the 'Babylonian exile' (1309–77) and of two antipopes (1378–1408). Remained in the possession of the popes till it was incorporated into France (1791).

Ávila Spain. 1. Province in Old Castile, forming part of the Meseta in the N; mountainous in the S. Area 8048 sq km (3107 sq. miles). Pop. (1991) 174,378. Chiefly agricultural. Cereal cultivation. Livestock (mainly merino sheep) raised.

2. Cap. of Ávila province on the Adaja R. 86 km (54 miles) WNW of Madrid at a height of nearly 1200 m (3936 ft). Pop. (1991) 45,977. Medieval architecture, inc. 12th-cent. granite walls and 11th/14th-cent. cathedral, makes it a popular tourist centre. Has declined in importance since the 17th cent. Birthplace of St Teresa (1515–82).

Avilés Spain. Industrial town and seaport in Oviedo province 24 km (15 miles) NNW of Oviedo on the estuary of the Aviles R. Pop. (1991) 84,787. Chiefly important for steel manufacture.

Avoca (Ovoca) River Ireland. River in Co. Wicklow, formed by the union of the Avonbeg and the Avonmore, flowing SE and entering the Irish Sea at Arklow. The beauty of its valley is celebrated in Thomas Moore's *The Meeting of the Waters* ('Sweet Vale of Avoca . . .').

Avon (Afon) British Isles. In Celtic, 'stream' or 'river'. Applied to several rivers, e.g. East (Hampshire) Avon, Lower Avon, Upper Avon; three in Scotland (tributaries of the Clyde, the Forth and the Spey); the one (the Afon) in S Wales, with the mouth at Aberavon.

Avon England. Former county in the SW, formed in 1974 from SW Gloucestershire and NE Somerset and inc. Bristol and Bath, and abolished in 1996 when four unitary local authorities were formed: Bristol, North Somerset, South Gloucestershire, and Bath and Northeast Somerset.

Avonmouth England. Seaport at the mouth of the Lower Avon in Bristol 10 km (6 miles) NW of and inc. the port of Bristol. Docks, flour mills, chemical works and zinc-smelting.

Avon River, Lower England. The Bristol Avon, 120 km (75 miles) long, rising on the E slope of the Cotswold Hills near Tetbury in Gloucestershire, flowing in a wide curve past Chippenham, Melksham, Bradford-on-Avon, Bath and Bristol, and entering the Severn estuary at Avonmouth. Below Bristol it is an important commercial waterway.

Avon River, Upper England. The Warwickshire Avon 153 km (96 miles) long, rising near Naseby in Northamptonshire, flowing generally SW past Rugby, Warwick, Stratford-upon-Avon and Evesham, and joining the Severn at Tewkesbury.

Avranches France. Town in the Manche department on a hill above the Sée R. 48 km (30 miles) E of St Malo. Pop. (1982) 10,419.
Market town. Trade in grain, fruit, cider and dairy produce. Tanning.
On the site of the former cathedral (destroyed 1790) is a stone to mark the spot where Henry II received absolution for the murder of Thomas à Becket.

Awe, Loch Scotland. Freshwater Lake in Argyll and Bute 35 km (22 miles) long SW–NE and up to 5 km (3 miles) wide at the N end (near which is Ben Cruachan, 1124 m; 3687 ft). Drains into Loch Etive by the R. Awe, 6 km (4 miles) long.

Axminster England. Town in Devon on the R. Axe 38 km (24 miles) E of Exeter. Pop. (1991) 3472.
Noted in the 18th cent. for carpets, now once again a thriving industry and in recent years there has been a growth in the number of small manufacturing companies.

Ayacucho Peru. Cap. of the Ayacucho department, on the Lima–Cuzco highway 240 km (150 miles) WNW of Cuzco. Pop. (1990) 101,600. A historical colonial city, in a basin at 2850 m (9348 ft). Manufactures woollen and leather goods.

Aycliffe (Newton Aycliffe) England. Town in Co. Durham 8 km (5 miles) N of Darlington, designated a 'new town' (1947) to serve the needs of local industries. Pop. (1988) 26,000. Industries inc. the manufacture of washing machines, lawnmowers, pvc resins, electrical and electronic equipment, telephone equipment and vehicle axles.

Aylesbury England. County town of Buck-

Azerbaijan

inghamshire 56 km (35 miles) NW of London. Pop. (1991) 51,497.

Food-processing (esp. dairy products), flour-milling, engineering, printing, hairdressing preparations and a recording company.

Formerly well known for ducks and for lace.

Aylesford England. Town in Kent on the R. Medway 5 km (3 miles) NW of Maidstone. Pop. (1991) 24,085. Paper mills, cement works. About a mile to the NE is a dolmen known as Kit's Coty House.

Ayr Scotland. Town in South Ayrshire on the Firth of Clyde at the mouth of the Ayr 50 km (31 miles) SSW of Glasgow. Pop. (1991) 47,962.

Small port and resort. Engineering, metalworking. Manufactures woollen and leather goods and machinery. In the burgh, 3 km (2 miles) S, is the village of Alloway, birthplace of Robert Burns. Prestwick airport is 3 km (2 miles) NNE of Ayr.

Ayrshire Scotland. Now East, South and North Ayrshire.

Ayrshire, East Scotland. New Unitary Authority created 1996, formerly part of Strathclyde Region. Pop. (1993) 123,820.

Ayrshire, North Scotland. New Unitary Authority created in 1996, formerly part of Strathclyde Region. Pop. (1993) 139,020.

Ayrshire, South Scotland. New Unitary Authority created in 1996, formerly part of Strathclyde Region. Pop. (1993) 113,960.

Aysgarth England. Village in North Yorkshire 45 km (28 miles) NW of Harrogate, with a picturesque waterfall, the Aysgarth Force (on the R. Ure).

Ayutthaya (Ayuthia) Thailand. Ancient cap. (1350–1767) on the Chao Phraya R. 72 km (45 miles) N of Bangkok. Pop. (1990) 62,000.

In a rice-growing region. Commercial and tourist centre.

Azerbaijan Iran. Region in the NW, bounded by the Republic of Azerbaijan and Armenia (N), the Caspian Sea (E) and E Iraq and Turkey (W). Administratively divided into the two provinces of East Azerbaijan (cap. Tabriz) and West Azerbaijan (cap. Rezaiyeh). Mountainous. The extinct volcano Savalan (W of Ardebil) rises to 4810 m (15,777 ft). Main river the Arax (Aras) on the N frontier. Near the W border is the large salt-water L. Urmia. An attempt to achieve autonomy after World War II was suppressed (1946).

Azerbaijan. Independent republic in E Transcaucasia, bounded on the W by Armenia, N by Georgia and Russia, in the E by the Caspian Sea and in the S by Iran. It inc. the Nakhichevan Autonomous Republic (separated from it by Armenia) and the Nagorno–Karabakh Autonomous Region. Area 86,600 sq km (33,400 sq. miles). Pop. (1995) 7,525,000 (53 per cent urban). Life expectancy, 67 years male, 75 female. Cap. Baku. Chief towns Gyandzha (Kirovabad), Sumgait. Nakhichevan is cap. of the Nakhichevan Autonomous Republic, and Stepanakert of the Nagorno–Karabakh Autonomous Region. Currency: Manat = 100 gopik. Across the N part runs the main Caucasus range, rising to over 4000 m (13,120 ft). In the SW is the E part of the Lesser Caucasus. Between these mountainous areas are the hot, dry steppes of the Kura and Arax rivers, which provide water for irrigation and hydroelectric power. The ethnic composition in 1989 was 83 per cent Azerbaijani Turks (Muslims), 6 per cent Russians, 6 per cent Armenians. The official lang. is Azerbaijani. It is a Muslim country: 70 per cent are Shiite and 30 per cent Sunni.

Principal crop cotton; wheat, maize, potatoes also cultivated. Tea, citrus fruits and other subtropical plants cultivated on the humid Caspian lowlands. The most important industry is oil production on the Apsheron peninsula, centred on Baku; the region has associated refining and chemical industries. There is some drilling in the Caspian Sea. Crude and refined petroleum carried by tanker up the Volga and by double pipeline to Batumi on the Black Sea. Other minerals inc. copper, lead, zinc, limestone, salt, iron, aluminium and sulphur. Other industries inc. iron, steel, aluminium, chemicals, food-processing, fisheries, rubber and textiles.

Long a source of dispute between Turkey and Persia, the present Azerbaijan was ceded to Russia in 1828. After the 1917 Revolution, Soviet rule was not established till 1920. Azerbaijan became a member of the Trans-caucasian Soviet Federated Socialist Republic in 1922 and a constituent republic of the USSR in 1936. In 1990 it adopted a declaration of republican sovereignty and in 1991 declared itself formally independent.

There is a 350-member People's Assembly.

Azov, Sea of Russia. Ancient Paus Maeotis. A shallow arm of the Black Sea, with which it is connected by the Strait of Kerch (ancient Bosporus Cimmerius). Area 37,555 sq km (14,500 sq. miles). Low salinity, owing to the discharge into it of several rivers, esp. the Don, which empties into the Gulf of Taganrog, an inlet in the NE. Usually frozen around the shores Nov.–March. Sea currents have created a number of sandspits along the N and E coasts and the Tongue of Arabat, 113 km (70 miles) long, which separates it from the Sivash Lagoon. Important fisheries (the Turkish name means 'Fish Sea'). Principal seaports Rostov-on-Don, Taganrog, Kerch and Zhdanov.

Azul Argentina. Cattle town in the Buenos Aires province 290 km (180 miles) SSW of Buenos Aires in rolling grazing land. Pop. 45,000. Industries inc. flour-milling, meat-packing and tanning.

B

Baalbek Lebanon. Ancient Heliopolis. Town 64 km (40 miles) ENE of Beirut at the foot of the Anti-Lebanon at 1170 m (3838 ft). Pop. (1970) 17,700. A tourist centre, world-famous for its extensive ruins. The early Phoenician city was associated with the worship of the sun-god Baal (hence the name; and also the Greek name Heliopolis ('City of the Sun')). It reached its greatest splendour in Roman times: within the area of the Acropolis (excavated in the early 20th cent.) are the ruins of the great temple of Jupiter, with six enormous columns still standing, and of a smaller but better-preserved temple nearby. Baalbek was sacked by the Saracens and others, and has suffered severely from earthquakes.

Baarle-Hertog Belgium. A small Belgian enclave in the Netherlands within 3 km (2 miles) of the border 43 km (27 miles) NE of Antwerp. Area 7 sq km (2.7 sq. miles). Pop. (1971) 2158.

Bab-el-Mandeb Yemen. In Arabic, 'Gate of Tears'. Strait 24–32 km (15–20 miles) wide connecting the Red Sea with the Gulf of Aden. Separates SW Arabia from Africa. Contains the island of Perim.

Babelthuap ➤PALAU.

Babol (Babul) Iran. Formerly Barfrush. Town in E Mazandaran 153 km (95 miles) NE of Tehran. Pop. (1985) 96,000. Linked by road with its former port, Babol Sar (now a seaside resort) on the Caspian Sea. Commercial centre. Trade in rice and cotton.

Babruysk Belarus. Town on the Berezina R. 137 km (85 miles) SE of Minsk. Pop. (1990) 223,000.
    Commercial centre. Trade esp. in timber and grain. Large paper and cellulose works.

Engineering. Manufactures clothing and footwear.

Babylon Iraq. Ancient city of Babylonia on the R. Euphrates near the town of Hilla 88 km (55 miles) S of Baghdad. Became important when made cap. of Babylonia under Hammurabi. Virtually destroyed by the Assyrians under Sennacherib in the 7th cent. BC. Reached its greatest splendour in the time of Nebuchadnezzar. Captured by Cyrus and by Alexander; declined from the 3rd cent. BC when superseded by Seleucia. The famous Hanging Gardens were one of the Seven Wonders of the World. The ruins revealed by excavations date from the reign of Nabopolassar (Nebuchadnezzar's father) and later. In the N is the mound of Babil, probably the site of a palace of Nebuchadnezzar and possibly of the Hanging Gardens; a central mound, Al Qasr, contained Nebuchadnezzar's chief palace; to the S was the great temple of Marduk, the city's god.

Babylonia. Ancient empire in Mesopotamia, watered by the Euphrates and Tigris rivers; a principal part of Iraq. Strictly, the state created by Hammurabi in the 2nd millennium BC, with Babylon as its cap. Later a subject province of Assyria. Asserted its independence in the 7th cent. BC under Nabopolassar and helped to overthrow the Assyrian empire. Nebuchadnezzar raised it to the peak of its power and prosperity, extended his rule over the whole of Mesopotamia and defeated the Egyptians, taking Jerusalem and carrying many of the people of Judah into captivity. Following Cyrus's capture of Babylon (539 BC), however, Babylonia was a minor province of the Persian empire.

Bacău Romania. Cap. of a district of the

same name in Moldavia on the Bistrita R. 153 km (95 miles) NNW of Galați. Pop. (1992) 204,495.

Industrial town. Manufactures oilfield equipment, textiles and leather goods.

Bacolod Philippines. Commercial town and minor port on the NW coast of Negros island. Pop. (1990) 364,180.

In an important sugar-producing region. Trade in rice, sugar-cane. Sugar-refining and fishing.

Bactria. Ancient country in central Asia between the upper R. Oxus and the Hindu Kush with cap. Bactra. One of the petty kings was Vishtaspa, protector of Zoroaster. It became a satrapy of the Persian empire in the 6th cent. BC. Conquered by Alexander the Great (328 BC) and then part of the Seleucid empire. A powerful independent state (c. 255–139 BC), but conquered by the Scythians. Gave its name to the Bactrian (two-humped) camel.

Bacup England. Town in SE Lancashire 24 km (15 miles) N of Manchester. Pop. (1991) 13,682.

Manufactures cotton goods, felt and footwear.

Badajoz Spain. 1. The largest province in the W, bordering on Portugal. Area 21,657 sq km (8360 sq. miles). Pop. (1991) 645,859. Stock-rearing (chiefly sheep); cereals, olives, vines grown in the more fertile areas. Agriculture much improved from the early 1950s by irrigation schemes. 2. Cap. of Badajoz province on the left bank of the Guadiana R. near the frontier with Portugal, with which it has a considerable trade. Pop. (1991) 121,924.

Flour-milling, distilling, brewing and food-processing.

Because of its strategic position it was frequently attacked by invaders. Birthplace of the artist Luis Morales (1509–86).

Badalona Spain. Town in the Barcelona province in Catalonia, an industrial suburb of NE Barcelona. Pop. (1991) 206,585.

Chemical, textile, glass and other industries.

Bad Ems ➤EMS.

Baden Germany. Former state in the SW. Area 15,074 sq km (5820 sq. miles). Bounded S and W by the Rhine. Mountainous (contains the Black Forest and part of the Swabian Jura) except for the Rhine valley, which is rich agriculturally, producing cereals, fruits and wine. Forestry and woodworking in the Black Forest, a popular tourist area. Manufactures clocks, textiles and chemicals.

Formed (1771) from the Margraviates of Baden-Baden and Baden-Durlach. Became a Grand Duchy 1806. In 1952 in the new arrangement of the *Länder* (States) it became part of Baden-Württemberg.

Baden Switzerland. Resort in Aargau on the Limmat R. 21 km (13 miles) NW of Zürich. Pop. (1986) 14,054.

Famous for hot saline and sulphur springs, suitable for the treatment of gout and rheumatism. Electrical engineering, textile manufacture.

The Confederation Diet sat in the Rathaus from 1424. Thus virtually cap. of Switzerland until 1712.

Baden-Baden Germany. Spa in Baden-Württemberg in the Oos valley 34 km (21 miles) SSW of Karlsruhe. Pop. (1986) 49,300.

The hot springs, known to the Romans, are used for the treatment of rheumatism and gout. Promenades of public gardens are attractively laid out. The old town is dominated by the ruined Old Castle and the restored New Castle.

Baden-bei-Wein Austria. Spa in Lower Austria, beautifully situated at the foot of the Wiener Wald, 24 km (15 miles) SSW of Vienna. Pop. (1991) 23,998. Warm sulphur springs, known since Roman times.

Baden-Württemberg Germany. A *Land* formed (1952), following a plebiscite, from the *Länder* of Baden, Württemberg-Baden and Württemberg-Hohenzollern. Area 35,751 sq km (13,800 sq. miles). Pop. (1992) 10,002,000. Cap. Stuttgart. Other important towns Mannheim, Karlsruhe and Heidelberg.

Bad Godesberg ➤GODESBERG.

Bad Homburg ➤HOMBURG VON DER HOHE.

Bad Kreuznach Germany. Spa and health resort in the Rhineland-Palatinate on the Nahe R. 38 km (24 miles) SW of Wiesbaden. Pop. (1986) 39,700. Saline springs.

Manufactures optical instruments, chemicals. Tanning.

Badlands USA. Dry area in South Dakota *c.* 160 km (100 miles) long and 64 km (40 miles) wide SE of the Black Hills. Eroded by stream action into peaks, pillars and steep-sided gullies. A Badlands National Park was established in 1978. The name is also applied to similar regions elsewhere.

Badminton (Great Badminton) England. Village in the Cotswold hills, South Gloucestershire, 22 km (14 miles) ENE of Bristol. Seat of the dukes of Beaufort. The game of badminton is named after it.

Badrinath India. Village in the Garhwal district in the N of Uttar Pradesh in the central Himalayas. Famous for the temple of Vishnu, an important place of pilgrimage at 3140 m (10,299 ft). The peak of Badinath, 7075 m (23,206 ft) is nearby.

Baeza Spain. Market town in the Jaén province in Andalusia 37 km (23 miles) NE of Jaén. Pop. (1991) 15,064.

Flour-milling, tanning and distilling.

Once cap. of a small Moorish kingdom with a pop. of *c.* 50,000. Sacked by Ferdinand III of Castile (1237); never completely recovered.

Baffin Bay Canada/Greenland. Gulf 1100 km (700 miles) long and up to 640 km (400 miles) wide; part of the Northwest Passage which joins the Atlantic and Arctic Oceans. Linked with the Atlantic by the Davis Strait and with the Arctic by the Smith, Jones and Lancaster Sounds. Navigation dangerous because of icebergs carried by the Labrador Current. Discovered by William Baffin 1616.

Baffin Island Canada. The largest and most easterly island in the Canadian Arctic in the SE Franklin District, Northwest Territories. Area 477,000 sq km (184,000 sq. miles). Resembles N Labrador, from which it is separated by the Hudson Strait; in the E there are mountains rising to *c.* 2400 m (7872 ft) with ice-caps, snowfields and glaciers. Principal occupations whaling, hunting and fur-trapping.

Bagé Brazil. Regional trading centre in the Rio Grande do Sul state 320 km (200 miles) WSW of Pôrto Alegre near the Uruguay frontier. Pop. (1985) 106,300.

Meat-packing. Trade in livestock. It has an experimental agricultural station.

Baghdad Iraq. Cap. of Iraq and of Baghdad province on the R. Tigris. Pop. (1991) 3,910,900.

Commercial and route centre. Manufactures textiles, cigarettes, cement and leather. Connected by rail with Basra and Kirkuk, and with Istanbul by the Baghdad Railway through Mosul (opened in 1940). Focal point of many roads. Airport. University (1926).

Remains of the ancient walls and a few old mosques, but it reflects little of its former glories. A centre of desert routes from Sumerian times, modern Baghdad was founded in AD 762 by the Abbasid caliph Al-Mansur on the site of a Babylonian town. Enlarged by caliph Harun al-Rashid and under him and his successor Mamum acquired fame for learning and commerce, as the 'Abode of Peace' and the fabled city of the *Thousand and One Nights*. Sacked (1258) by the Mongols, who destroyed the irrigation system, the foundation of Mesopotamian prosperity. The caliphate fell and with it the splendour of Baghdad. By 1638, when it was taken by the Turks, it had shrunk to a town of minor significance. When Iraq became an independent state in 1927, Baghdad became the cap. and its fortunes began to revive.

Bagnères-de-Bigorre France. Ancient Vicus Aquensis. Spa in the Hautes-Pyrénées department on the Adour R. 19 km (12 miles) SSE of Tarbes. Pop. (1968) 10,573.

Mineral springs, known since Roman times. Textile and engineering industries.

Bagnolet France. Industrial suburb to the E of Paris in the Seine-St Denis department. Pop. (1982) 32,557.

Manufactures plaster of Paris and furniture.

Bago ➤PEGU.

Baguio Philippines. Mountain resort, summer cap. and goldmining centre in Luzon 210 km (130 miles) N of Manila at a height of 1370 m (4494 ft). Pop. (1990) 183,102.

Bahamas. The Commonwealth of the Bahamas is a democratic sovereign state and consists of an archipelago in the Atlantic Ocean, extending SE over 1100 km (700 miles) from 80 km (50 miles) E of the SE Florida (USA) coast and N of Cuba. Total area 13,939 sq km (5382 sq. miles). Pop. (1995) 276,000 (86 per cent urban). Life expectancy, 68 years male, 76 female. Cap. Nassau on New Providence island. Other towns: Freeport/Lucaya, Marsh Harbour, Bailey Town and Dunmore. Currency: Bahamian dollar = 100 cents. The islands are built of limestone and coral and are low-lying, nowhere exceeding 150 m (492 ft) in height, but only 22 of the hundreds of islands, rocks and cays are inhabited. There are no rivers and freshwater is obtained from desalinization and rainfall. The soil is thin, dry and not favourable to agriculture, though vegetation may obtain moisture from the porous subsoil. The islands are subject to hurricanes, which can cause considerable damage; rainfall can be heavy in summer, when temperatures are high. Land use: forested 32 per cent, meadows and pastures 0.2 per cent, agricultural and under permanent cultivation 1 per cent. The official lang. is English. About 85 per cent of the pop. are black, descendants of liberated slaves from the USA, and white 12 per cent. Of believers non-Anglican protestant 55 per cent, Anglican 20 per cent, Roman Catholic 19 per cent.

A large area is unproductive, but there are forests of yellow pine, and pulpwood is exported. Little more than 1 per cent of the land is arable, producing vegetables and fruit (inc. pineapples, bananas, citrus fruit) for local consumption. The sponge fisheries, once important, are now of very little value, but crayfish are caught and exported to the USA. The many beaches and subtropical climate causes tourism to dominate the economy. It is an offshore banking centre and other exports inc. pharmaceuticals, oil-refining and rum.

San Salvador (Watling's Island) was probably Columbus's first landfall in America (12 October 1492). British settlers arrived in the 17th cent. British possession of the islands was confirmed by the Treaty of Versailles (1783). Navigation is hazardous in waters around the islands and pirates used the Bahamas as a base in the 18th cent., the best-known being Blackbeard. The islands served as a base for blockade runners during the American Civil War (1861–5) and for bootleggers during Prohibition times (1920–33). There was a period when more whisky was in bond in the Bahamas than in the whole of Scotland. In recent years the Bahamas has been used for drug smuggling. Internal self-government was introduced in 1964 and full independence achieved in 1973. The Family (Out) Islands (all islands other than New Providence) are governed by Commissioners appointed by the government. There is a 16-member Senate all appointed by the Governor. The 49-member House of Assembly elected from single-member constituencies.

Bahariya Oasis ➤WESTERN DESERT.

Bahawalpur Pakistan. Town near the Sutlej R. 96 km (60 miles) SSE of Multan. Pop. (1981) 133,956. Former cap. of the Bahawalpur state.

Industrial and commercial centre. Manufactures cotton goods and soap. Trade in rice and cotton.

Bahia (**Baía**) Brazil. Maritime state in the E. Area 561,026 sq km (216,556 sq. miles). Pop. (1990) 11,801,810. Cap. Salvador. A fertile coastal plain up to 80 km (50 miles) wide, backed by a stepped escarpment, with valleys parallel to the coast and a broad N–S mountain range. Inland is the central Brazilian plateau, crossed by the middle São Francisco R. About 90 per cent of Brazil's cacao crop produced in the SE. Sugar-cane, tobacco and cotton grown in the Recôncavo district near Salvador. Principal mineral industrial diamonds.

Bahía Blanca Argentina. Rail centre and seaport in Buenos Aires province, serving the S pampas, at the head of the Bahía Blanca (Blanca Bay). Pop. (1991) 271,467.

Exports grain, wool, meat and hides. Meat-packing, oil-refining, flour-milling and tanning. A fort and trading post since 1828.

Bahrain. The State of Bahrain forms an archipelago of 33 low-lying islands in the (Persian) Gulf, between the Qatar peninsula and the mainland of Saudi Arabia. The main island, Bahrain ('Two Seas'), 48 km (30 miles) long and 16 km (10 miles) wide, is connected by causeway with Muharraq Island, 6.4 km (4 miles) long and 1.6 km (1 mile) wide. Other islands are Sitra and Umm An-Nassan. From Sitra oil pipelines and a causeway, carrying a road, extend out to sea for 4.8 km (3 miles) to a deep-water anchorage. Area 694 sq km (268 sq. miles). Pop. (1995) 579,000 (90 per cent urban). Life expectancy, 71 years male, 76 female. Cap. Manama. Other towns Muharraq, Rifa'a, Jidhafs, Sitra and Isa Town. Currency: Bahrain dinar = 1000 fils. The State consists of a limestone plateau, mainly arid and rising to Jabal Dukhan 137 m (445 ft) from a central depression. The climate is pleasantly warm between December and March, but from June to November the conditions are very hot and humid and it is virtually rainless. Land use: meadows and pastures 6 per cent, agricultural and under permanent cultivation 3 per cent. The official lang. is Arabic and the pop. is mainly Shia and Sunni Muslim. About 64 per cent are Bahraini Arab.

Oil was discovered on Bahrain 1932. The wells are linked by pipeline with a refinery which also processes oil carried by pipeline from Dhahran in Saudi Arabia. Seventy-six per cent of exports are petroleum products. There is also dhow-building and other minor industries. Pearl-fishing has almost disappeared. Aluminium smelting has become an extremely important industry. Irrigation from wells supports agriculture in the N, esp. dates, citrus fruit, alfalfa, wheat and millet.

After being under British protection since 1820, became fully independent in 1971. The form of government is a monarchy with a 30-member advisory consultative council. All members are appointed by the Emir.

Bahr el Ghazal Sudan. In Arabic, 'Gazelle River'. River formed from several streams. It joins the Bahr el Jebel near L. No and forms the Bahr el Abiad (White Nile). Impeded by sudd, but navigable for steamers July–October as far as Wau on the Jur R.

Bahr el Jebel Sudan. In Arabic, 'Mountain River'. A section of the White Nile, between Nimule and the point where it joins the Bahr el Ghazal (near L. No), below which it is called the Bahr el Abiad (White Nile). Flows through sudd swamps, but is navigable between Juba and Nimule, except along rapids.

Baiae (modern **Baia**) Italy. A favourite resort of the ancient Romans on the Gulf of Pozzuoli 14 km (9 miles) WSW of Naples, notorious for luxury and immorality. Julius Caesar and Nero had villas there. A theatre and three sets of baths were discovered 1953. Modern Baia is a small village (pop. c. 1000).

Baia-Mare Romania. Cap. of Maramures district and mountain resort in the NW 55 km (34 miles) ESE of Satu-Mare. Pop. (1992) 148,815.

Industrial centre. Important chemical industry; lead, copper, gold, silver and zinc smelting.

Baikal, Lake Russia. The largest freshwater lake in Asia and the deepest lake in the world, in SE Siberia. Area 32,900 sq km (12,700 sq. miles). Greatest depth 1620 m (5314 ft). Altitude 450 m (1476 ft). Over 300 streams flow into it, mostly mountain torrents, as well as the Selenga, Barguzin and Upper Angara rivers. The only outlet is the Angara

R. Frozen for over 4 months of the year; otherwise navigated by steamers. The Trans-Siberian Railway skirts the S shore. Unusual fauna, inc. a viviparous fish, the *golomyanka*, and the Baikal seal. Well-stocked with edible fish, esp. the *omul*, a member of the salmon family. The largest island is Olkhon. The lake is polluted and is an ecological problem because it contains 2000 unique animal and plant species. The main pollution comes from the Baikalsk cellulose plant, but other factories pump chemicals into the Selenga R., which provides half the water input.

Baja (Lower) California Mexico. A rugged mountainous peninsula in the NW, 1170 km (730 miles) long, extending SE from, and geographically a continuation of, California (USA). Divided into the state of Baja California – area 70,113 sq km (27,064 sq. miles); pop. (1990) 1,657,927; cap. Mexicali – and the territory of Baja California Sur – area 73,677 sq km (28,439 sq. miles); pop. (1990) 317,326; cap. La Paz. From its mountain ranges, rising to 3078 m (10,096 ft) in the Sierra San Pedro Mártir, short unnavigable streams drain W to the Pacific and E to the Gulf of California. The climate is generally hot and arid and the region largely barren, with settlements concentrated mainly near the US border, where irrigation has enabled cotton, fruits, vegetables and vines to be grown. Some minerals are worked, and there is pearl and deep-sea fishing off the S coast.

Bakersfield USA. Town in California on the Kern R. 177 km (110 miles) NNW of Los Angeles. Pop. (1990) 174,820.

In an important oilfield, with refineries. Manufactures refinery equipment and chemicals, and assembles aircraft.

Bakewell England. Market town in Derbyshire 16 km (10 miles) W of Chesterfield. Pop. (1991) 3818. Home of Bakewell tarts. Chatsworth House (Duke of Devonshire) and Haddon Hall (Duke of Rutland) are nearby.

Bakhchisarai Ukraine. In Tatar, 'Garden Palace'. Town in S Crimea 26 km (16 miles) SW of Simferopol. Pop. (1990) 25,700.

Manufactures copper and leather goods. Former cap. of the Crimean khans (princes), whose palace, the Khan Sarai, was destroyed (1736); but restored by the Russian soldier Prince Grigory Potemkin (1787).

Bakhtarán Iran. Formerly Kermanshah. Cap. of province, 400 km (250 miles) WSW of Tehrán at a height of 1480 m (4869 ft), in the Zagros mountains. Pop. (1991) 624,000.

Commercial and route centre in a fertile agricultural region. Sugar-refining and flour-milling. Manufactures footwear, textiles and carpets. Also has an oil refinery linked by pipeline with the Naft-i-Shah oilfield.

Bakony Forest Hungary. Densely forested hill country N of L. Balaton. Chief town Veszprem. Vineyards on the S slopes. Deposits of bauxite and manganese.

Baku Azerbaijan. Cap. on the S coast of the Apsheron peninsula on the Caspian Sea. Pop. (1990) 1,148,700.

Important seaport and oil-producing centre. Oil-refining, shipbuilding. Manufactures oil-drilling equipment, chemicals, cement and textiles. Connected by double pipeline with the Black Sea port of Batumi. Oil is also shipped to Astrakhan. Principal cultural centre of Azerbaijan.

Seat of a state university (1919) and the Azerbaijan Academy of Science (1945). In the old city in the SW are the 12th-cent. Maiden's Tower (now a lighthouse) and the remains of the 15th-cent. Palace of the Khans. The main residential area and public buildings are in the new city. Baku was known to Arab geographers in the 10th cent. Its oil and gas wells (which sometimes burned spontaneously) were revered by Zoroastrian fire-worshippers. From the 16th to the 18th cent. it was under Persian rule and was incorporated in Russia 1806. Rapid growth came with the development of the oil industry in the 1870s. Output has declined since 1940 and has been overtaken by the 'Second Baku' in the Volga–Ural region.

Bala Wales. Market and tourist town in Gwynedd on the R. Dee at the N end of L.

Bala (6 km (4 miles) long, the largest natural lake in Wales). Pop. (1991) 1992.

Balaklava Ukraine. Small port in S Crimea 13 km (8 miles) S of Sevastopol, famous for the battle (1854) during the Crimean War at which the charge of the Light Brigade took place. Pop. 2000.

Balaton, Lake Hungary. The largest lake in Central Europe, SW of Budapest. Area 600 sq km (230 sq. miles). Shallow; frozen in winter. Vineyards and orchards around the shores. Many summer tourist resorts.

Balbi, Mount ►BOUGAINVILLE.

Balboa Panama Canal Zone. Port at the Pacific end of the Panama Canal just W of Panama City. Pop. (1990) 2750. Extensive docks and wharves; ship-repairing. Named after Vasco Nuñez de Balboa, who first crossed the Panama isthmus (1513).

Balbriggan Ireland. Town in Co. Dublin on the Irish Sea 32 km (20 miles) N of Dublin. Pop. (1986) 5680. Manufactures hosiery.

Baldock England. Town in Hertfordshire on the R. Ivel 6 km (4 miles) NE of Hitchin. Pop. (1991) 9232. Manufactures hosiery and there is light engineering.

Bâle ►BASEL.

Balearic Islands Spain. Archipelago off the E coast in the Mediterranean Sea; a province. Area 5014 sq km (1935 sq. miles). Pop. (1991) 702,770. Cap. Palma (Majorca). Consists of four large islands – Majorca (Mallorca); Minorca (Menorca); Iviza (Ibiza); Formentera – and several islets.

Generally undulating, rising to 1445 m (4740 ft) in Puig Mayor near the N coast of Majorca. Vines, almonds, olives and cereals are grown. Fishing is important. The climate has made the islands (esp. Majorca) popular with tourists. The people, who are akin to the Catalans, provided both Carthaginian and Roman armies with regiments of stoneslingers. Later the islands came under Vandal, Byzantine and Moorish rule. Became a dependency of Aragón 1349.

Bali Indonesia. Island just E of Java across the Bali Strait. Area 5400 sq km (2100 sq. miles). Pop. (1993) 2,856,000. Chief town Singaraja. Largely mountainous and volcanic, rising to 3142 m (10,308 ft) in Mt Agung (Holy Mountain). Equable climate, fertile soil and luxuriant vegetation; often called 'the Jewel of the East'. The women are famed for their beauty and graceful dancing. Hinduism, the principal religion, was brought from India in the 7th cent. Rice, copra and coffee are leading products. Trade with the Netherlands began in the 17th cent., but the island did not come wholly under Dutch rule until 1908.

Balikesir Turkey. Cap. of the Balikesir province in the NW 160 km (100 miles) SSW of Istanbul. Pop. (1990) 170,589.

Commercial centre. Trade in cereals and opium. Flour-milling. Manufactures textiles and rugs.

Balikpapan Indonesia. Seaport in SE Borneo on the Strait of Makassar. Pop. (1980) 280,875. Oil refinery. Scene of a naval battle between US and Japanese forces in World War II (1942).

Balkan Mountains (Bulgarian **Stara Planina**) Bulgaria. In Bulgarian, 'Old Mountains'. Mountain range extending across the country from the Yugoslav border to the Black Sea, rising to 2376 m (7793 ft) in Botev Peak and forming the watershed between the Danube and the Maritsa rivers. The most famous pass is the Shipka.

Balkan Peninsula. Extensive peninsula in SE Europe between the Adriatic and the Ionian seas (W) and the Aegean and the Black seas (E). The N boundary is generally considered to lie along the Sava and the lower Danube rivers. Comprises Greece, Turkey-in-Europe, Bulgaria, Albania, Croatia, Bosnia and Hercegovina. Mainly mountainous. Climate continental in the N, Mediterranean in the S. After the fall of the Byzantine Empire, it became one of the most backward areas of Europe, esp. under the Ottoman Empire. The wars of independence against Turkey and subsequent conflicts be-

tween the independent Balkan countries has
made the Balkans a most unstable and disrup-
tive element in Europe in international politics from the late 19th to the late 20th cent.

Balkh (now usually known as **Wazirabad**)
Afghanistan. Town in the N 19 km (12 miles)
WNW of Mazar-i-Sharif. Pop. 10,000. Built
on the site of ancient Bactra and called by
local inhabitants 'the Mother of Cities'.
Sacked (1220) by Genghis Khan; did not
recover its early importance.

Balkhash Kazakhstan. Town on the N shore
of L. Balkhash. Pop. (1970) 76,000. Connected by rail with the copper mines at
Kournradski 24 km (15 miles) N. Copper-
smelting. Vermiculite deposits nearby.

Balkhash, Lake Kazakhstan. Large shallow
salt lake in SE Kazakhstan at a height of
270 m (886 ft). Area 18,000 sq km (7000 sq.
miles). Fed chiefly by the Ili R. No outlet.
Frozen for about 5 months annually. Probably once formed part of a much larger lake.

Ballachulish Scotland. Village in Argyll and
Bute on the S shore of Loch Leven. Pop.
(1991) 557. Large slate quarries, worked since
1760. Glencoe village is just E.

Ballarat Australia. Town in Victoria 108 km
(67 miles) WNW of Melbourne on a plateau
at 433 m (1420 ft). Pop. (1991) 64,980.
Industrial and commercial centre and
railway junction, having risen as a boom
settlement in the 1851 gold rush. It survived
the declining mineral production to become
a market town for the surrounding agricultural area, with textile mills, railway workshops, paper mills and metal works.
The 'Eureka Stockade' incident, involving
bloodshed among the miners, took place here
1854. The Welcome gold nugget, weighing
over 62 kgm, was found 1858.

Ballater Scotland. Town in Aberdeenshire
on the R. Dee 58 km (36 miles) WSW of
Aberdeen and 11 km (7 miles) E of Balmoral
Castle. Pop. (1991) 982. Resort, near picturesque moors and woods.

Ballina Ireland. Market town in Co. Mayo

on the R. Moy near the mouth on Killala
Bay. Pop. (1991) 6714. Salmon fisheries.

Ballinasloe Ireland. Town in Co. Galway
on the R. Suck 56 km (35 miles) E of Galway.
Pop. (1986) 6125. Terminus of the Grand
Canal.
Agricultural centre. Famous annual livestock fair (October). Brewing, flour-milling
and limestone-quarrying.

Ballinrobe Ireland. Market town in Co.
Mayo on the R. Robe near the mouth on
Lough Mask. Pop. (1986) 1270. Noted for
trout fishing. Near by is Lough Mask House,
home of Captain Boycott (1832–97), whose
ostracism (as an absentee landlord's agent)
during the Land League's 'Plan of Campaign'
(1880) is the origin of the word 'boycott'.

Ballybunion Ireland. Fishing village and
popular resort in Co. Kerry at the mouth of
the R. Shannon 14 km (9 miles) WNW of
Listowel. Pop. (1986) 1452.

Ballycastle Northern Ireland. Town and
resort in Co. Antrim on Ballycastle Bay 71 km
(44 miles) NNW of Belfast. Pop. (1971)
2895.

Ballyclare Northern Ireland. Town in Co.
Antrim 16 km (10 miles) SW of Larne. Pop.
(1991) 7108. Linen and bleaching works.

Ballymahon Ireland. Small market town in
Co. Longford on the R. Inny 18 km (11
miles) S of Longford. Pop. 700. Pallas (3 km
(2 miles) E) is the probable birthplace of
Oliver Goldsmith (1728–74); nearby Lissoy
is the 'Sweet Auburn' of his *Deserted Village*.

Ballymena Northern Ireland. Town in Co.
Antrim on the R. Braid 29 km (18 miles) W
of Larne. Pop. (1991) 28,112.
Manufactures linen. Bleaching and dyeing
works.

Ballymoney Northern Ireland. Market
town in Co. Antrim 11 km (7 miles) SE of
Coleraine. Pop. (1991) 7818.
Linen manufacture and milk-processing.

Ballyshannon Ireland. Town in Co. Donegal, at the mouth of the R. Erne on Donegal

Bay 18 km (11 miles) SSW of Donegal town. Pop. (1986) 2573.

Salmon-fishing centre. Seaside resort. Hydroelectric plant on the river.

Balmoral Castle Scotland. In Gaelic, 'Majestic Dwelling'. A private home of British monarchs in Aberdeenshire on the right bank of the R. Dee 11 km (7 miles) W of Ballater. Bought by Prince Albert for Queen Victoria, who built the castle (1854) in white granite in 'Scottish-baronial' style.

Baltic Sea (Ger. **Ostsee**) Europe. Ancient Mare Suevicum. Sea in N Europe, bounded by Denmark, Sweden, Finland, Russia, Estonia, Latvia, Poland and Germany. Connected with the North Sea by the Sound, the Great Belt, the Little Belt, the Kattegat and the Skagerrak. Area 422,000 sq km (163,000 sq. miles) (inc. the Kattegat). Unusually shallow, reaching its greatest depth (463 m; 1519 ft) off Gotland; very small tides. A large number of rivers empty into it, giving low salinity; this and the shallowness cause large areas to become icebound for 3–5 months in winter. Major inlets are the Gulf of Bothnia (N), the Gulf of Finland (E), the Gulf of Riga and the Gulf of Gdańsk. Principal islands are those of Denmark: Fehmarn and Rügen (Germany); Gotland and Öland (Sweden); Ahvenanmaa (Finland); Saaremaa and Hiiumaa (Estonia). Linked with the North Sea by the Kiel Canal and the Gota Canal (through Swedish lakes).

Baltimore USA. Important seaport, also the largest city and chief industrial and commercial centre in Maryland, at the head of a 19-km (12-mile)-long branch of Chesapeake Bay, with a deep natural harbour formed by the estuary of the Patapsco R. Pop. (1990) 736,014.

Chief exports grain, coal, iron and steel. Main imports metallic ores (esp. iron) and petroleum. Manufactures machinery, tractors, railway equipment, aircraft, chemicals, textiles and clothing. Steel mills, copper refineries, printing works, canneries, meat-packing plants, sugar and oil refineries. A great steelworks was built (1916) on a tidewater site at Sparrows Point 16 km (10 miles) away and large shipyards are there. In the 19th cent. 'Baltimore clippers' gained a world reputation.

Despite the disastrous fire of 1904, which destroyed much of the business quarter, it is noted for its public buildings, monuments, squares and parks, and has been nicknamed 'Monumental City'. Seat of the Johns Hopkins University (1876), some schools of the University of Maryland and several colleges. Its Roman Catholic archbishop ranks as Primate of the USA. Founded 1729. Grew rapidly in the 19th cent., shipping goods from the interior to Europe. The defence of Fort McHenry against the British (1814) inspired Francis Scott Key to write *The Star-spangled Banner.* It was the Atlantic port closest to the National Pike Road, the first trans-Appalachian highway, and the Baltimore and Ohio RR (begun 1828) was the first railway in the USA. The world's first nuclear-powered lighthouse, to guide shipping in and out of the harbour, was put into operation 1964.

Baltistan India. Region in the W Ladakh district in Kashmir, inhabited by Balti, a Muslim people of Tibetan origin. Chief town Skardu. Mountainous, containing K2 (8611 m; 28,244 ft) and other peaks of the Karakoram mountains.

Baluchistan Pakistan. Province bounded by Afghanistan (N), the Arabian Sea (S) and Iran (W). Area 347,000 sq km (134,000 sq. miles). Chief town Quetta. The N was formerly under British control; the S comprised the princely states of Kalat, Kharan, Las Bela and Makran. Largely mountainous with lofty ridges, e.g. The Sulaiman, Kirthar and Central Makran ranges, separating arid deserts from fertile valleys. Rainfall scanty; rivers intermittent. Cereals and fruits produced where there is water. Camels, sheep, goats raised. Quetta is reached by the famous Bolan Pass. Natural gas, produced at Sui, is sent by pipeline to Karachi and Multan. A railway runs through the Bolan Pass and via Quetta to the Afghan frontier; a branch line turns

W into Iran. The three main sections of the pop. (predominantly Muslim) are the Baluchi, the Pathans and the Brahui, who speak different lang. (Baluchi, Pushtu, Brahui). Crossed several times by the invaders of India; Alexander the Great passed through the S on his return to Persia from India (325 BC). Much of it was held by the Arabs in the 7th–10th cent. Later ruled by tribal chiefs. British control of the N was secured during the Afghan Wars of the 19th cent. and a military base was established at Quetta. Passed to Pakistan 1947.

Bamako Mali. Cap. on the R. Niger. Pop. (1984) 740,000. Formerly cap. of the French Sudan. Connected by rail with Dakar. Important trading centre for the W Sudan.

Bamberg Germany. Town in N Bavaria on the canalized Regnitz R. near the confluence with the Main 51 km (32 miles) NNW of Nuremberg. Pop. (1986) 69,600.

Engineering and brewing. Manufactures textiles and footwear. Trade in vegetables and fruit.

From 1007 to 1802 the seat of independent prince-bishops. The Romanesque cathedral, founded (1004) by the Emperor Henry II, contains the marble tomb of the founder and his wife.

Bamburgh England. Village and resort in Northumberland on the E coast 26 km (16 miles) SE of Berwick. Pop. (1985) 750. Cap. of the kings of Northumbria in the 6th cent. Birthplace, home and burial-place of the heroic lighthouse-keeper's daughter, Grace Darling (1815–42).

Bamu ►STANLEY POOL.

Banaba ►OCEAN ISLAND.

Bananal Island ►ARAGUAIA RIVER.

Banat Romania. Former administrative region (till 1968), in the W. Area 21,795 sq km (8415 sq. miles). Cap. Timișoara. The name *banat* was originally given to any Hungarian frontier province or territory governed by a *ban* (viceroy), but came to be applied specifically to the Banat of Temesvár (Timișoara),

mainly a fertile plain between the Tisza R. and the Transylvanian Alps. This belonged mainly to Hungary from the the 11th cent. onwards. After World War I it was divided, except for a small district near Szeged, between Romania and Yugoslavia, and the name was then used only of the Romanian region.

Banbridge Northern Ireland. Market town in Co. Down on the R. Bann 35 km (22 miles) SW of Belfast. Pop. (1991) 11,448.

Manufactures linen, rope and fishing nets.

Banbury England. Market town in Oxfordshire on the R. Cherwell 35 km (22 miles) N of Oxford. Pop. (1991) 39,906.

Manufactures aluminium products, electrical goods. Food-processing and printing. Iron ore formerly mined in the neighbourhood. Famous for over 300 years for its cakes.

The Banbury Cross celebrated in nursery rhyme was destroyed by Puritans in the 17th cent. but replaced by another in the 19th cent.

Bandama River ►CÔTE D'IVOIRE.

Bandar ►MASULIPATAM.

Bandar Anzali (Enzeli) Iran. Port in Gilán province on a lagoon of the Caspian Sea 22 km (14 miles) NW of Rasht. Pop. (1982) 80,000.

Exports rice and hides. Fishing.

Bandar Seri Begawan Brunei. Formerly Brunei (town). Cap., on the Brunei R. 20 km (12 miles) from the mouth, partly built on piles. Pop. (1991) 45,867.

Bandjarmasin (Banjermasin) Indonesia. Cap. of the S. Kalimantan province (S Borneo) and port on the Barito R. 39 km (24 miles) from the mouth. Pop. (1980) 381,286.

Exports timber, rattan and rubber. Seat of the Lambung Mangkurat University (1960).

Bandon Ireland. Town in Co. Cork on the R. Bandon 24 km (15 miles) SW of Cork City. Pop. (1986) 1943.

Tanning, brewing, whiskey-distilling. Founded in the early 17th cent. by Richard

Boyle, 1st Earl of Cork, father of the chemist Robert Boyle.

Bandung Indonesia. Cap. of the W Java province 130 km (80 miles) SW of Jakarta at a height of 730 m (2394 ft). Pop. (1990) 2,056,915.

Manufactures textiles, quinine, rubber products. Also a health resort and cultural centre.

Seat of a university (1958) and an Institute of Technology. Beautiful mountain and forest scenery in the neighbourhood.

Banff Canada. Resort in SW Alberta on the Bow R. 101 km (63 miles) WNW of Calgary in the Rocky Mountains at 1384 m (4540 ft). Pop. (1991) 5700. The Canadian Pacific Railway station for the Banff National Park, famous for spectacular scenery (with several peaks over 3000 m; 9840 ft), mountain lakes and glaciers. Hot sulphur springs.

Banff Scotland. Town in Aberdeenshire, a royal burgh, on the Moray Firth at the mouth of the R. Deveron. Pop. (1991) 4110.

Seaside resort. Fishing. Whisky-distilling.

Banffshire Scotland. Former county in the NE on the Moray Firth.

Bangalore India. Cap. of Karnataka 290 km (180 miles) W of Madras at a height of 900 m (2952 ft). Pop. (1991) 3,302,300. Road and railway junction.

Industries inc. textiles and printing and it manufactures electrical apparatus and radio sets, machinery, footwear, generators, aircraft, telephones, automobiles, cement, electronic equipment and earth-moving vehicles.

Founded in the 16th cent. Under British rule, had the largest cantonment in S India (returned to Mysore 1947).

Bangka (Banka) Indonesia. Island separated from the SE coast of Sumatra by the Bangka Strait. Area (with nearby islets) 14,064 sq km (4611 sq. miles). Pop. (1985) 280,000. Chief town Pangkalpinang. One of the world's chief tin-mining centres; also deposits of iron and lead.

Bangkok (Thai **Krung Thep**) Thailand. Cap. and chief seaport on the Chao Phraya R. 24 km (15 miles) from the mouth. Pop. (1993) 5,572,712.

Exports rice, rubber and tin. Industrial centre. Rice-milling, sawmilling, railway engineering, oil-refining and cement manufacture.

At the centre of the city is the 18th-cent. royal town, founded by Rama I as his cap., after the fall of Ayutthaya. The royal temple of Wat Phra Keo (1785) has a remarkable image of Buddha. Numerous government offices and public buildings. Transport through the city was formerly by boat along the many canals (*Klongs*) but since the 1890s modern roads have been constructed. Seat of 5 universities: Chulalongkon (1917), Thammasart (1934) and the Universities of Medical Science, Agriculture and Fine Arts.

Bangladesh. Republic in the NE part of the Indian subcontinent, bounded on the W and N by India, E by India and Myanmar (Burma) and S by the Bay of Bengal. Area 147,570 sq km (56,977 sq. miles). Pop. (1995) 120,093,000 (20 per cent urban). Life expectancy, 57 years male, 57 female. Cap. Dhaka. Other cities Chittagong, Khulna, Rajshahi. Currency: Bangladesh taka = 100 paisa. The country occupies the major part of the great Ganges–Brahmaputra delta and is generally low-lying and flat, with hills only in the SE. Flood plains constitute 80 per cent of the total area. It has a tropical monsoon climate, with high temperatures and a heavy rainfall in the monsoon season from June to October. Land use: forested 15 per cent, meadows and pastures 5 per cent, agricultural and under permanent cultivation 75 per cent. About 88 per cent of believers are Muslim, 11 per cent Hindu, 1 per cent Buddhist. Bengali is the official lang., but English is used for official, legal and commercial purposes.

Bangladesh is one of the poorest countries in the world. About 65 per cent of the people are engaged in agriculture; rice is the main food crop and the country produces much of the world output of jute. In recent years there has been a falling demand for jute, owing to competition from other fibres and the bulk shipment of some commodities, but jute and jute products represent important exports, as does tea and clothing. Other industries inc. textiles, steel and aluminium processing and light engineering.

With the partition of India (1947), Pakistan was divided into Western and Eastern Provinces, separated by about 1400 km (850 miles) of Indian territory, the tenuous link between them being their common Muslim religion. The people of East Pakistan spoke Bengali, like those of West Bengal (India), while those of West Pakistan spoke Urdu. Fundamental differences between the two provinces caused East Pakistan to break with the government, war broke out and East Pakistan, granted military aid by India, succeeded in its struggle, declared itself the independent state of Bangladesh in 1971 and joined the Commonwealth in 1972. Economic and political troubles beset the new state from the beginning; in 1975 Sheikh Mujibur Rahman, 'the father of the nation', was assassinated. The situation had been much worsened by natural calamities, the coastal region in particular being devastated by cyclones and tidal waves, with the loss of thousands of lives. In 1970 a tidal wave from the Bay of Bengal struck the delta and islands, and as many as 500,000 people may have perished; and again in 1974 the country suffered disastrous floods. A bloodless coup took place in 1982 and General Ershad assumed control of the country giving way for elections in 1990. The 1991 Constitution restricts the power of the President and gives more power to the 300-member unicameral Parliament (*Jatiya Sangstad*).

Bangor Northern Ireland. Seaside resort in Co. Down on the S side of Belfast Lough 18 km (11 miles) ENE of Belfast. Pop. (1991) 33,181. Ruins of an abbey founded by St Comgall in the 6th cent.

Bangor USA. Town in Maine on the Penobscot R. 177 km (110 miles) NE of Portland. Pop. (1990) 33,181.
Manufactures wood-pulp, paper and clothing.

A prosperous lumbering and shipbuilding centre in the 19th cent.

Bangor Wales. Town in Gwynedd at the N end of the Menai Strait. Pop. (1991) 12,330. Education centre, seat of the University College of North Wales (founded 1884), a constituent college of the University of Wales since 1893. The 15th/16th-cent. cathedral was restored in the late 19th cent.

Bangui Central African Republic. Cap. of the country, formerly cap. of Ubangi-Shari on the Ubangi R. and on the S border with the Democratic Republic of the Congo. Pop. (1994) 524,000.
Commercial centre. Produces palm oil and soap.

Bangweulu, Lake Zambia. Shallow lake on a plateau at a height of 1130 m (3706 ft) bordered by swamps. Area 9840 sq km (3800 sq. miles). Fed by the Chambezi R. and drained by the Luapula R. Discovered (1868) by David Livingstone, who died on its shore in 1873.

Banias (Baniyas) Syria. Small fishing port on the Mediterranean 145 km (90 miles) SW of Aleppo. Terminal of the oil pipeline from Kirkuk (Iraq).

Banja Luka Bosnia and Hercegovina. Town on the Vrbas R. 145 km (90 miles) NW of Sarajevo. Pop. (1991) 143,000.
Commercial centre. Manufactures textiles. Brewing and flourmilling.
An Orthodox cathedral, a 16th-cent. mosque (and many others) and remains of Roman baths.

Banjermasin ➤BANDJARMASIN.

Banjul Gambia. Formerly Bathurst. Cap. and chief seaport on St Mary's Isle at the mouth of the Gambia R. Pop. (1983) 44,188.
Exports chiefly groundnuts and groundnut oil, also palm kernels. Has two deepwater wharves.

Banka ➤BANGKA.

Banks Island (British Columbia) Canada.

Island 69 km (43 miles) long in the Hecate Strait off the Pacific coast.

Banks Island (Northwest Territories) Canada. The most westerly island of Canada's Arctic Archipelago in the SW Franklin District. Area 67,000 sq km (26,000 sq. miles). Mainly plateau rising to over 600 m (1968 ft) in the S. First explored (1851) by McClure.

Bannockburn Scotland. Town in Stirling 3 km (2 miles) SSE of Stirling on the Bannock Burn, a tributary of the R. Forth. Pop. (1991) 5799. Nearby is the site of the battle (1314) in which Robert Bruce defeated Edward II of England and ensured Scottish independence.

Bann River Northern Ireland. River rising in the Mourne Mountains as the Upper Bann and flowing 64 km (40 miles) NW, past Banbridge and Portadown, into the S end of Lough Neagh. The Lower Bann leaves the N end of Lough Neagh, flows 64 km (40 miles) NNW, through Lough Beg and past Coleraine, to the sea. Famous for salmon fishing.

Banská Bystrica Slovakia. Town on the Hron R. 160 km (100 miles) ENE of Bratislava. Pop. (1990) 87,000.

Formerly an important mining centre (gold, copper); light industries.

Banstead England. Town in Surrey near Epsom 22 km (14 miles) from London, one of its dormitory towns. Pop. (1991) 37,245.

Bantry Ireland. Town at the head of Bantry Bay 72 km (45 miles) WSW of Cork. Pop. (1986) 2811. Manufactures tweed.

Bantry Bay Ireland. Picturesque inlet on the SW coast of Co. Cork 37 km (23 miles) long and 6–10 km (4–6 miles) wide. Fine natural anchorage. Contains Whiddy Island and Bear Island. Scene of the famous attempted landing of a French force under General Hoche, whose 14 warships were scattered by storms (Christmas 1796). Oil storage depot.

Baotow (Paotow) China. Town in the Nei Monggol Autonomous Region just N of the Huang He (Yellow) river and 137 km (85 miles) W of Hohhot. Pop. (1992) 1,200,000. Important route and commercial centre. Connected by rail with Beijing and with Lanzhou, thus linking up the great E–W and N–S trunk lines of China.

Trade in wool, hides, cereals. Important steel industry and it also manufactures rugs and soap.

Bapaume France. Town in the Pas-de-Calais department 116 km (72 miles) SE of Calais. Pop. (1985) 4500. Flour-milling, brickmaking and other industries.

Scene of a French victory over the Prussians (1871).

Baracaldo (Barakaldo) Spain. Industrial town in Vizcaya province just NE of Bilbao on the railway from Bilbao to Portugalete (its outport). Pop. (1991) 104,883.

Manufactures iron and steel, and machinery. A well-planned town, developed during the 20th cent. round its heavy industries. Expanded considerably in the 1960s.

Barbados. Barbados lies to the E of the Windward Islands in the West Indies. Area 430 sq km (166 sq. miles). Pop. (1995) 265,000 (38 per cent urban). Life expectancy, 73 years male, 77 female. Cap. and chief seaport Bridgetown. Other town, Speightown. Currency: Barbados dollar = 100 cents. A low-lying island and the most easterly of the West Indies. The highest point is Mt Hillaby (367 m; 1204 ft) in the centre. Volcanic dust from the neighbouring island of St Vincent has covered the coral limestone and produced a fertile soil which is intensively cultivated. The island is almost encircled by coral reefs. The tropical heat is moderated by the NE Trade Wind December–May; rainfall is heavy and comes mainly during the hot season, June–November. It has suffered many hurricanes. Land use: forested 12 per cent, meadows and pastures 5 per cent, agricultural and under permanent cultivation 37 per cent. The official lang. is English. About 80 per cent are black, mixed race 16 per cent, white 4 per cent. The majority of believers are Christian with Anglican 40 per cent, Protestant 26 per cent, Pentecostalists 13 per cent and Roman Catholic 4 per cent.

Sugar is by far the most important export, followed by molasses, electrical components, chemicals, rum and clothing. There is one oilfield and it is also an offshore banking centre. The fine beaches attract nearly half a million tourists a year.

Barbados was probably first visited by the Portuguese, who named it Los Barbados (Bearded) on account of the many bearded fig trees. The English landed in 1605 and colonization began in 1628; from then Barbados was continuously held by Britain. It achieved independence in 1966. There is a 21-member Senate and a 28-member House of Assembly.

Barbary Coast Africa. The N African coast from Morocco to Tripolitania. Named after the Berber (the principal inhabitants). Notorious from the 16th to the 19th cent. as the haunt of pirates: Moors joined with Algerian and Tunisian corsairs and preyed on shipping in the Mediterranean or levied 'appeasement' tribute from European countries. Several European and US expeditions were sent against the pirates in the 19th cent.: piracy was not wiped out till the French stormed South Algiers (1830).

Barberton South Africa. Town in the SE of Mpumalanga near the Swaziland frontier at a height of 860 m (2821 ft). Pop. (1970) 12,232. Developed 1882–6 as the result of a gold rush, which was over by 1887; declined as a mining town, but became the centre of a prosperous agricultural area producing cotton and citrus fruits.

Barberton USA. Industrial town in Ohio just SW of Akron. Pop. (1985) 30,000.

Manufactures tyres, chemicals and boilers.

Barbican England. District of the City of London with modern housing scheme and cultural amenities.

Barbizon France. Village in the Seine-et-Marne department on the edge of the forest of Fontainebleau. Gave its name to the 'Barbizon School' of painters – Corot, Millet, Rousseau, Daubigny and other 19th-cent. artists who made it their home.

Barbuda ➤ANTIGUA AND BARBUDA.

Barca (Barce, El Merg) Libya. Town in Cyrenaica 80 km (50 miles) ENE of Benghazi, with which it is connected by rail. Pop. 10,000. Founded by the Greeks and Libyans in the 6th cent. BC. Captured by the Persians 512 BC. Later ruled by the Ptolemies. Fell to the Arabs in the 7th cent. AD.

Barcellona Pozzo di Gotto Italy. Market town in the Messina province in Sicily 29 km (18 miles) W of Messina. Pop. (1981) 37,000. Trade in wine and olive oil.

Barcelona Spain. 1. Province in the NE in Catalonia on the Mediterranean Sea. Area 7733 sq km (2985 sq. miles). Pop. (1991) 4,577,396. Mountainous in the N. Narrow coastal plain. Drained by the Llobregat R. and its tributaries. The most densely populated and highly industrialized province in Spain. 2. Ancient Barcino. Cap. of Barcelona province on the Mediterranean. Pop. (1991) 1,623,542. The second largest city in Spain, its main seaport and industrial and commercial centre.

Exports textiles and machinery, which it manufactures along with chemicals, leather goods and plastics. Also exports wine, olive oil and cork from the interior.

Overlooked from the S by the castle on the Montjuich hill (175 m; 574 ft). Bisected by the Ramblas, an avenue constructed over a dry river-bed. In the old city are the 13th/15th-cent. cathedral (damaged in the Civil War, 1937), the 14th-cent. Church of Santa María del Mar, the 16th-cent. Episcopal Palace and the Palacio de la Diputación (seat of the old parliament of Catalonia). Centre of Catalan culture. University (1430). Founded by the Carthaginians, named after Hamilcar Barca. Prospered under the Romans and Visigoths. Captured by the Moors and Franks. Ruled by independent Counts of Barcelona from the 9th to the 12th cent. After the union of Catalonia with Aragón (1137), became one of the leading Mediterranean seaports. Its maritime code, the

Consulado del Mar, was widely recognized. When Catalonia was incorporated into Spain relations with the central government were frequently strained. Barcelona became the centre of Catalan separatism and also of anarcho-syndicalism and socialism. In the Spanish Civil War (1936–9) it was the seat of the government, but after many air attacks finally surrendered to the Franco forces January 1939.

Barcelona Venezuela. Cap. of the Anzoátegui state in the NE on the Neveri R. 5 km (3 miles) from the mouth. Pop. (1990) 106,061.

Commercial centre. Exports cattle, hides and skins, through its port, Guanta.

Barddhaman India. Formerly Burdwan. Cap. of the Barddhaman division of West Bengal 95 km (60 miles) NW of Calcutta. Pop. (1991) 244,800.

Railway and road junction. Rice-milling. Manufactures cutlery, hosiery. Trade in rice, sugar-cane and jute. University (1960).

Bardia Libya. Village and port on the Mediterranean coast of Cyrenaica near the Egyptian frontier. Came into prominence during World War II as the starting-point of the Italian campaign against Egypt (1940). Subsequently captured and recaptured by the British and the Germans alternatively, changing hands five times in 1941–2, until finally held by the British.

Bardsey Wales. Island in Gwynedd 3 km (2 miles) long and 1.6 km (1 mile) wide, separated from the Lleyn peninsula by Bardsey Sound. Ruins of an abbey founded in the 6th cent. A medieval place of pilgrimage.

Bareilly India. Industrial and commercial town and railway junction in Uttar Pradesh 217 km (135 miles) ESE of Delhi. Pop. (1991) 590,700.

Trade in grain and sugar-cane. Produces carpets, furniture, sugar, artificial rubber, timber products and fertilizers.

Barents Sea Arctic Ocean. Shallow part of the Arctic, bounded by Norway, European Russia, Novaya Zemlya, Spitsbergen and Franz Josef Land. Named after Willem

Barents, a 16th-cent. Dutch navigator who made three voyages in search of the NE passage. Navigation in the N part is hampered by pack-ice. The S part is warmed by the N Atlantic Drift and has become an important fishing ground.

Barfleur France. Fishing port in the Manche department 26 km (16 miles) E of Cherbourg. Pop. (1985) 850. An important point of embarkation for England in the Middle Ages. William, only son of Henry I of England, was drowned when the *White Ship* sank off Barfleur (1120); traditionally Henry 'never smiled again'.

Barfrush ►BABOL.

Bari Italy. Ancient Barium. Cap. of Bari province in Apulia, a seaport on the Adriatic Sea 225 km (140 miles) ENE of Naples. Pop. (1992) 342,129.

Iron foundries, oil refinery, canneries, flour mills. Manufactures textiles and soap. Exports wine, olive oil and fruit.

A Roman colony, later governed by Goths, Lombards, Byzantines and Normans. An embarkation port for the Crusades. Cathedral (12th-cent.). University (1924).

Barinas Venezuela. Cap. of Barinas state 225 km (140 miles) SW of Barquismeto in the cattle-rearing and oil-producing llanos. Pop. (1990) 152,853.

Barisal Bangladesh. Town on the Ganges–Brahmaputra delta 113 km (70 miles) S of Dacca. Pop. (1991) 163,481.

Rice and flour milling. Manufactures soap. Trade in rice, jute and oilseeds.

It has suffered severely, with considerable loss of life, from cyclones and tidal waves.

Barking and Dagenham England. London borough (1965) comprising the former municipal borough of Barking (Essex) on the R. Roding (except the part W of Barking Creek) and the former municipal borough of Dagenham (Essex) (except the N part of Chadwell Heath Ward). Pop. (1994) 154,000.

It has a large power station, rubber,

chemical and paint factories, and the huge Ford Motor Works (Dagenham).

Bar-le-Duc France. Prefecture of the Meuse department on the Ornain R. and the Marne–Rhine Canal 72 km (45 miles) W of Nancy. Pop. (1990) 18,577.

Metalworking, brewing. Manufactures textiles and jam.

Cap. of the medieval counts (later dukes) of Bar. Several 15th/17th-cent. houses and remains of the ducal palace.

Barletta Italy. Seaport in the Bari province in Apulia on the Adriatic Sea 56 km (35 miles) WNW of Bari. Pop. (1990) 88,750.

Chemical, soap, cement and other industries. Important trade in wine and fruits.

A 12th/15th-cent. cathedral. During the French siege of Barletta (1503), a famous combat took place between 13 picked knights of Italy and France – the *Disfida di Barletta* of d'Azeglio.

Barmouth Wales. Town in Gwynedd on Cardigan Bay at the mouth of the R. Mawddach 10 km (6 miles) W of Dolgellau. Pop. (1991) 2306. Seaside resort.

Barnard Castle England. Market town in Durham on the R. Tees 24 km (15 miles) W of Darlington. Pop. (1991) 6084. Remains of the 12th-cent. castle, built by Bernard de Baliol, which figures in Scott's *Rokeby*.

Barnaul Russia. Cap. of the Altai Territory on the Ob R. and the Turksib Railway. Pop. (1990) 603,000.

Engineering, sawmilling and food-processing. Manufactures textiles and footwear.

Founded as a mining centre 1739. Expanded rapidly as a manufacturing town in the 1930s.

Barnes England. Former municipal borough in Surrey on the R. Thames 10 km (6 miles) WSW of London: from 1965 part of the London Borough of Richmond-upon-Thames. A dormitory suburb which inc. Mortlake and East Sheen. The famous 17th-cent. Kitcat Club held its meetings in a cottage here. Barnes Bridge is the finishing point of the annual boat race between Oxford and Cambridge universities.

Barnet England. London borough (1965) comprising the former urban districts of Barnet and E Barnet (Hertfordshire), Friern Barnet (Middlesex) and the municipal boroughs of Finchley and Hendon (Middlesex). Pop. (1990) 283,000. Scene of a battle (1471) in the Wars of the Roses in which the Earl of Warwick (the Kingmaker) was killed.

Barnsley England. Town and unitary authority on the R. Dearne 18 km (11 miles) N of Sheffield. Pop. (1991) 75,120.

Coalmining. Engineering, clothing and carpet industries.

Barnstaple England. Market town in Devon on the estuary of the R. Taw 55 km (34 miles) NW of Exeter. Pop. (1991) 27,691.

Holiday resort. Services an agricultural area and was once famous for pottery ('Barum ware').

A 15th-cent. stone bridge of 16 arches across the Taw and a 14th-cent. parish church. Birthplace of John Gay (1685–1732), composer and librettist of *The Beggar's Opera*.

Baroda (Vadodara) India. Former cap. of the princely state of Baroda, now in Gujarat, 385 km (240 miles) N of Bombay. Pop. (1991) 1,115,300.

Industrial and cultural centre. Railway junction. Gas pipeline and oil-refining nearby; heavy water plant. Manufactures textiles, chemicals, matches and metal goods. Trade in cotton.

Distinguished by its handsome public buildings. Seat of the Maharaja Sayajirao University (1949).

Barquisimeto Venezuela. Formerly Nueva Segovia. Cap. of the Lara state in the NW on the Barquisimeto R. in a hilly coffee-growing district on the Pan-American highway. Pop. (1990) 602,622.

Trade in coffee, sugar, cacao and rum. Flour-milling, tanning. Manufactures textiles, cement and leather goods.

Founded (as Nueva Segovia) 1522. Destroyed by earthquake 1812.

Barra Scotland. Island in the Outer Hebrides, Western Isles, separated from S Uist by the Sound of Barra. Area 91 sq km (35 sq. miles). Pop. (1991) 1244 (2250 in 1931). Chief town Castlebay. Mountainous, rising to 384 m (1260 ft). Herring-fishing; but the fishing industry has declined, causing depopulation.

Barrackpore (Barrackpur) India. Town in W Bengal on the Hooghly R. 24 km (15 miles) N of Calcutta. Pop. (1991) 133,265.
Jute and rice-milling and other industries. Formerly an important military station.

Barrancabermeja Colombia. River port on the E bank of the middle Magdalena R. Pop. (1983) 123,000.
A leading oil-drilling and refining centre, with a 560-km (335-mile) pipeline to Cartagena; the refined products are piped to Medellin, Manizales and Bogotá.

Barranqueras ➤RESISTENCIA.

Barranquilla Colombia. Cap. of the Atlántico department, important seaport and international airport, on the Magdalena R. 16 km (10 miles) from the mouth. Pop. (1992) 1,018,763. Now accessible to ocean-going vessels by a dredged channel.
Industrial centre. A wide range of manufactures, e.g. textiles, vegetable oils, chemicals and foodstuffs.

Barreiro Portugal. Town in the Setúbal district on the S bank of the the Tagus estuary opposite and SE of Lisbon. Pop. (1987) 50,863.
Manufactures cork products and fertilizers. Flour-milling. Linked with Lisbon by ferry.

Barren Island, Cape ➤FURNEAUX ISLANDS.

Barrhead Scotland. Town in East Renfrewshire 11 km (7 miles) SW of Glasgow. Pop. (1985) 19,000.
Textile, bleaching and dyeing, sanitaryware and light-engineering industries.

Barrier Reef ➤GREAT BARRIER REEF.

Barrow-in-Furness England. Town in SW Cumbria on the coast of Furness. Pop. (1991) 48,947. Sheltered seawards by Walney Island, to which it is connected by a road bridge. Its growth from a small fishing village of 325 people (1847) to a major industrial centre was due chiefly to the discovery in the area of rich hematite iron ore (1840). Large iron and steel works were established. Shipbuilding followed (both merchant and naval vessels, inc. many submarines; the first British nuclear submarine was launched here (1960)). Engineering. Manufactures paper and chemicals.

Barrow Point USA. The most northerly point of Alaska on the Arctic coast. Meteorological station, with a neighbouring US naval base.

Barrow River Ireland. River 193 km (120 miles) long, rising in the Slieve Bloom Mountains and flowing first E and then S to Waterford Harbour. Navigable to Athy 105 km (65 miles) upriver and then linked to Dublin by a canal.

Barrow Strait Canada. Channel 64 km (40 miles) wide separating the Bathurst, Cornwallis and Devon islands (N) from the Prince of Wales and Somerset islands (S). On the route from Baffin Bay through the Canadian Arctic archipelago to the Beaufort Sea.

Barry Wales. Town in The Vale of Glamorgan on the Bristol Channel 13 km (8 miles) SW of Cardiff. Pop. (1991) 49,887.
Seaport. Exports coal, cement and steel goods. Flour-milling. Barry Island (just S, and joined to the mainland) is a popular holiday resort.

Bartlesville USA. Town in Oklahoma on the Caney R. 66 km (41 miles) N of Tulsa. Pop. (1985) 35,000.
Commercial centre in an oil-producing region. Oil-refining, zinc-smelting.

Barwon River ➤DARLING RIVER.

Barysaw Ukraine. Formerly Borislav. Industrial town situated 80 km (50 miles) SW of Lvov. Pop. (1990) 40,700.

A petroleum and natural gas centre. Oil-refining. Manufactures oilfield equipment.

Passed from Austria to Poland (1919) and under the Potsdam Agreement (1945) to the USSR.

Basel (Fr. **Bâle**, English **Basle**) Switzerland. Ancient Basilia. Town in the NW on the Rhine on the French and German frontiers, forming (with three villages) the half-canton of Basel-Stadt. Pop. (1990) 171,000.

Important commercial, industrial and railway centre. Chemical, metal, silk and printing industries. Divided by the Rhine (navigable downstream) into Greater Basel (left bank) and Lesser Basel.

Founded by the Romans. Became a free imperial city in the 11th cent. Joined the Swiss Confederation 1501. The minster (cathedral) of red sandstone is the burial-place of Erasmus. A 16th-cent. Rathaus and a museum with a fine Holbein collection. Seat of a university (founded 1460 by Pope Pius II), the oldest in Switzerland.

Basel Canton Switzerland. Divided into two half-cantons in 1833. 1. Basel-Land: The countryside surrounding Basel-Stadt on the N slopes of the Jura mountains. Area 428 sq km (165 sq. miles). Pop. (1994) 251,400. Produces cereals. Watchmaking. Textile industry. Salt mines. 2. Basel-Stadt: Practically conterminous with the town of Basel. Area 37 sq km (14 sq. miles). Pop. (1994) 197,700.

Bashkir ➤BASHKORTOSTAN.

Bashkortostan Russia. Republic of the Russian Federation at the S end of and mainly W of the Urals. Area 143,600 sq km (55,430 sq. miles). Pop. (1994) 4,055,300. Cap. Ufa. It has important oilfields, part of the Volga–Ural ('Second Baku') region, with the longest pipeline in the Russian Federation connecting the Tuimazy oilfield with refineries at Omsk. Iron, copper, manganese and other metallic ores also mined. Cereals, potatoes, sugar-beet cultivated. Butter and cheese produced. Chief industrial centres Ufa, Sterlitamak and Beloretsk.

Basildon England. 'New town' in S Essex 16 km (10 miles) S of Chelmsford. Pop. (1991) 100,924. Formed (1955) from the townships of Billericay, Laindon, Pitsea and Wickford.

Engineering, printing. Manufactures tobacco products and aircraft equipment.

Basilicata (Lucania) Italy. Region in the S between the Gulf of Taranto and the Tyrrhenian Sea, comprising the provinces of Potenza and Matera. Area 9992 sq km (3855 sq. miles). Pop. (1992) 610,821. Cereals, olives, vines cultivated. Chief towns Potenza and Matera.

Basingstoke England. Town in Hampshire 43 km (27 miles) NNE of Southampton. Pop. (1991) 77,837.

Road and rail centre. Manufactures agricultural implements, clothing, leather and bricks. Publishing.

Nearby are the ruins of Basing House, burned down (1645) after a two years' siege.

Basle ➤BASEL.

Basque Provinces Spain. The provinces of Álava, Guipúzcoa and Vizcaya in the NE on the Bay of Biscay. Total area 7260 sq km (2803 sq. miles). Total pop. (1991) 2,093,415. Álava is mainly agricultural, producing maize, sugar-beet, vines and fruits. The two maritime provinces, Guipúzcoa and Vizcaya, are highly industrialized, with mining, engineering, shipbuilding and fishing industries.

The Basques are an ancient people; their lang. is distinct from any other European or world tongue. Converted late to Christianity (from the 3rd to the 5th cent.), they have remained fervent Catholics but preserve a strong tradition of being independent of either Spain or France. The Guernica Oak, an ancient tree under which the Council met, remained for cent. a symbol of liberty. Two of their most famous figures were St Ignatius Loyola and St Francis Xavier. They settled in their present region in the 9th cent. and founded the kingdom of Navarre. Later, under the Castilian kings, they enjoyed special democratic rights, but their prosperity diminished after the conquest of Navarre by Ferdinand of Aragón in the 16th cent. The special rights were abolished in 1876. In the Spanish Civil War (1936–9) they supported the government, setting up an autonomous Basque government in Guernica, but were subjugated by Franco's forces (1937) after the bombing of Guernica by air squadrons from Nazi Germany.

Basra Iraq. Chief port and cap. of Basra province on the Shatt-al-Arab 113 km (70 miles) from the (Persian) Gulf, linked by rail with Baghdad. Pop. (1987) 406,296.

Exports chiefly dates, also wool, barley and oil.

Originally founded at Az Zubeir about 13 km (8 miles) distant. Became famous in the time of Harun al-Rashid but later declined and silting sealed it off from the Gulf. It became an important supply base for the USSR in World War II.

Bas-Rhin France. Department in the E, comprising the N part of Alsace, bounded on the E and N by Germany and on the W by the Vosges mountains. Area 4787 sq km (1850 sq. miles). Pop. (1990) 953,100. Prefecture Strasbourg. The lowlands are fertile, growing cereals, hops, fruits, vegetables. Wine produced on the E slopes of the Vosges. The region is highly industrialized. Manufactures machinery, locomotives, leather, textiles. Chief towns Strasbourg and Haguenau.

Bassano del Grappa Italy. Town in Vicenza province in the NE 31 km (19 miles) NNE of Vicenza. Pop. (1981) 64,676.

Manufactures metal goods and pottery. Tanning and printing.

The cathedral, several churches and the museum contain works by the 16th–17th-cent. da Ponte family of artists, surnamed Bassano after their birthplace. Napoleon defeated the Austrians near by in 1796.

Bassein ►PATHEIN.

Bassenthwaite, Lake England. Lake 6 km (4 miles) long and 1 km (¾ mile) wide in the Lake District in Cumbria 5 km (3 miles)

NW of Keswick. Skiddaw (930 m; 3050 ft) is 3 km (2 miles) E.

Basses-Alpes
►ALPES-DE-HAUTE-PROVENCE.

Basses-Pyrénées ►PYRÉNÉES-ATLANTIQUES.

Bass Rock Scotland. Islet in East Lothian 107 m (351 ft) high and 1.6 km (1 mile) in circumference at the entrance to the Firth of Forth. Used as a prison in the 17th cent. Now has a lighthouse. Sea-bird sanctuary (gannets).

Bass Strait S Pacific Ocean. Channel 120–240 km (75–150 miles) wide separating mainland Australia and Tasmania, linking the Indian Ocean (W) with the Tasman Sea (E) and containing King Island and the Furneaux Islands. Identified as a strait (1798) by Surgeon George Bass RN.

Bastia France. Chief town and seaport of Corsica on the NE coast. Pop. (1990) 32,728.

Exports wine, fish and fruits. Fishing. Manufactures tobacco products. Tourism.

Founded by the Genoese in the 14th cent. The *bastiglia* (fortress), built 1383, was later replaced by a citadel, which dominates the port and old town.

Basutoland ►LESOTHO.

Bataan Philippines. Peninsula in S Luzon 48 km (30 miles) long and 24–32 km (15–20 miles) wide on the W side of Manila Bay. Pop. (1990) 425,803. Timber and oil-refining.

Heroically defended during World War II for 3 months (1942) against the Japanese by American and Filipino forces. Recaptured 1945.

Batangas Philippines. Seaport and cap. of Batangas province on SW Luzon. Pop. (1990) 184,790.

Trade in rice, sugar-cane. Oil-refining.

Batavia ►JAKARTA.

Bath England. Ancient Aquae Sulis. Town in Bath and North East Somerset on the R. Avon 16 km (10 miles) ESE of Bristol. Pop.

(1991) 85,202. Tourism, engineering and light industry.

Chiefly known as a spa. The Romans probably discovered the hot springs *c.* AD. 50 and excavations have revealed remains of their watering-place. In the Middle Ages wool-weaving was important. In the 18th cent., through the inspiration of Beau Nash (1674–1761) and the architectural genius of John Wood and his son (also John Wood), such features as Royal Crescent, Lansdown Crescent and the Assembly Rooms were built. The Assembly Rooms were destroyed by bombing in World War II and were re-stored and re-opened in 1963. Bath, one of England's most beautiful cities, also has a 16th-cent. abbey church and old houses built with Bath stone, quarried locally. University (1966). It has given its name to an invalid chair and a bun. Birthplace of the journalist C. P. Scott (1846–1932).

Bath and North East Somerset England. New administrative area created 1996. Formerly part of Avon. Pop. (1994) 158,692.

Bathgate Scotland. Industrial town in West Lothian 26 km (16 miles) WSW of Edinburgh. Pop. (1989) 14,500.

Coal and shale-oil mining. Automobile engineering. Manufactures metal goods and paper.

Bathurst Australia. Town in New South Wales on the Macquarie R. 160 km (100 miles) WNW of Sydney. Pop. (1981) 19,640. One of the first settlements W of the Blue Mountains (1815) and scene of an early gold rush (1851). Still a mining and stock-rearing centre, with tanning and flour-milling industries, in a sheep-farming and wheat-growing region.

Bathurst Canada. Port on the NE coast of New Brunswick in the Gulf of St Lawrence. Pop. (1991) 15,890.

Pulp and paper mill, raw material for which comes from nearby forests of black spruce. Salmon fisheries. Large deposits of lead, zinc and copper were discovered in 1953.

Bathurst ►BANJUL (GAMBIA).

Bathurst, Cape Canada. Promontory on the N coast of the mainland in the Northwest Territories, projecting into the Beaufort Sea. Like several other localities of the same name, it commemorates Earl Bathurst, British Colonial Secretary 1812–28.

Bathurst Inlet Canada. Arm of the Arctic Ocean, extending S nearly 225 km (140 miles) from Coronation Gulf into the Northwest Territories. Also a trading post.

Bathurst Island Canada. One of the Parry Is. in the Arctic Ocean N of the Barrow Strait. Area 18,100 sq km (7300 sq. miles).

Batley England. Town in West Yorkshire 10 km (6 miles) SSW of Leeds. Pop. (1991) 48,030.

Centre of heavy woollen manufacture. Shoddy was first manufactured here.

Baton Rouge USA. State cap., industrial town and river port of Louisiana, at the head of navigation for ocean-going ships on the Mississippi, 113 km (70 miles) WNW of New Orleans. Pop. (1990) 219,531.

Oil refineries and petrochemical industries. Seat of the Louisiana State University (1860).

Battambang Cambodia. Market town in the W 260 km (160 miles) NW of Phnom Penh. Pop. (1981) 551,900 (district). Centre of a rice-growing area.

Belonged to Siam (Thailand) 1894–1907 and 1941–6.

Battersea England. Former metropolitan borough of SW London on the S bank of the R. Thames, here crossed by the Battersea (1890), Albert (1873) and Chelsea (1937) bridges; from 1965 part of the London borough of Wandsworth. Battersea Park (81 ha, 200 acres) beside the river is one of London's playgrounds, has sculptures by Henry Moore and in 1951 accommodated the amusement section of the Festival of Britain. The power station is one of the largest in Europe. The Battersea Dogs' Home is almost equally famous. Formerly (18th cent.) noted for enamel ware.

Battle England. Town in E Sussex 10 km (6 miles) NW of Hastings. Pop. (1991) 5253. Named after the Battle of Hastings, actually fought at Battle in 1066. Ruins of Battle Abbey, founded by William the Conqueror to commemorate his victory.

Battle Creek USA. Town in S Michigan at the confluence of the Kalamazoo R. and Battle Creek 177 km (110 miles) W of Detroit. Pop. (1990) 53,540.

In a maize and wheat growing region. Manufactures cereal foods (Post and Kellogg factories) and agricultural implements.

Batumi Georgia. Cap. of the Adjharia autonomous republic, SW Georgia on the E coast of the Black Sea. Pop. (1990) 137,300.

One of the chief seaports. Naval base. Exports petroleum and manganese. Connected by an oil pipeline with Baku and Alyaty. Main industries oil-refining, marine and railway engineering, fruit and vegetable canning. Manufactures metal cans and clothing. Tea, tobacco and citrus-fruit plantations in the neighbourhood. Resort, with a mild subtropical climate.

Ceded to Russia by Turkey 1878.

Bauchi (Jos) Plateau Nigeria. Highlands in Central Nigeria, rising to over 1500 m (4920 ft). The name 'Land of Slaves' refers to the long practice of slave raiding in the area. Important tin mines had been worked by the Africans; large-scale European exploitation began in 1902 and Jos became the principal mining centre.

Bautzen Germany. Industrial town in Saxony on the Spree R. 51 km (32 miles) ENE of Dresden. Pop. (1989) 50,627.

Manufactures textiles, railway rolling-stock and machinery.

The 15th-cent. cathedral has been used since 1635 by both Protestants and Roman Catholics (kept apart by an iron screen). Scene of the defeat of a combined Russian and Prussian army by Napoleon (1813).

Bavaria (Ger. **Bayern**) Germany. A *Land* in the S, bordered in the E by the Czech Republic, in the SE and S by Austria. Area 70,547 sq km (27,232 sq. miles). Pop. (1992) 11,596,000. Cap. Munich. Bounded on the S by the Alps, on the E by the Bohemian Forest (Böhmerwald) and on the NE by the Fichtelgebirge and the Franconian Forest (Frankenwald); crossed by lower ranges, e.g. the Franconian Jura, between which there are wide plains and fertile valleys. Drained chiefly by the Danube and the Main (linked by the Ludwig Canal) and their tributaries. Predominantly agricultural and pastoral: cereals and potatoes are the main crops; large numbers of cattle and pigs are raised. Valuable forests. Industries are centred on Munich, Nuremberg, Augsburg, Regensburg, Würzburg. Brewing is important. Abounds in beautiful mountain and lake scenery and has many picturesque towns and villages, some of which preserve much of their medieval appearance, e.g. Rothenburg. This, together with the Wagner opera festival at Bayreuth and the Passion Play at Oberammergau, make it a popular tourist area.

The earliest inhabitants were Celts. Conquered by the Romans near the end of the 1st cent. BC. Became a duchy, ruled from 1180 by the House of Wittelsbach, which became the oldest dynasty in Europe. Fought in alliance with Prussia against France 1870. Joined the German Empire 1871. The last Wittelsbach king abdicated in 1918, there was an abortive Communist revolution and Bavaria became a republic. Hitler's first attempt to seize power took place in Bavaria (1923) and the headquarters of the Nazi party were in Munich. After World War II the Rhenish Palatinate (the detached territory on the W bank of the Rhine) and the Lindau district were lost to Bavaria, and it was made a *Land* of the Federal German Republic in 1949.

Since the 18th cent. the largest of the S German states, Bavaria has always preserved a strong sense of individuality. About 67 per cent of the pop. are Roman Catholic, 24 per cent Protestant. The universities at Munich and Würzburg are Catholic, that at Erlangen is Protestant.

Bay City USA. Port in Michigan at the head of Saginaw Bay on L. Huron 160 km (100 miles) NNW of Detroit. Pop. (1990) 38,936.

Manufactures automobile parts, cranes, electronics, prefabricated buildings, lake boats and petrochemicals. Sugar refineries.

Bayeux France. Ancient market town in the Calvados department in the NW 27 km (17 miles) WNW of Caen. Pop. (1982) 15,237. Manufactures lace and pottery.

Noteworthy 12th/13th-cent. cathedral. In the museum is the famous 'Bayeux Tapestry', illustrating William the Conqueror's invasion and conquest of England, possibly made by his wife Queen Matilda.

Bay Islands (Sp. **Islas de la Bahía**) Honduras. Group of islands in the Gulf of Honduras, forming a department. Area 373 sq km (144 sq. miles). Pop. (1988) 22,060. Largest island Roatán 48 km (30 miles) long and 14 km (9 miles) wide. Chief products coconuts, bananas and pineapples.

Discovered by Columbus 1502. Occupied by British settlers in the 17th cent. and made a British colony 1852. Ceded to Honduras 1859.

Bay of Biscay N Atlantic Ocean. Ancient Sinus Aquitanicus. Wide inlet of the Atlantic Ocean, between the W coast of France and the N coast of Spain. The name is a corruption of Basque 'Vizcaya'. Notorious for sudden storms and choppy seas.

Bay of Islands Canada. Bay on the W coast of Newfoundland, studded with many small islands. Several fishing settlements along the shores.

Bay of Plenty New Zealand. Wide inlet into the NE coast of North Island. Contains several small islands (Makatana, Mayor, White). Pop. (1991) 208,000.

Bayonne France. Town in the Pyrénées-Atlantiques department in the SW at the confluence of the Nive and the Adour rivers near the Bay of Biscay. Pop. (1990) 41,846. Chief port of the Basque country.

Exports steel products, timber and brandy.

Distilling, flour-milling. Manufactures fertilizers. Steelworks at Boucau near by.

Gothic cathedral (13th/15th-cent.). Birthplace of the artist Bonnat (1833–1922), whose house is now an art museum. Formerly renowned for the manufacture of cutlery and swords (possibly the origin of the word 'bayonet').

Bayonne USA. Industrial town in New Jersey on a long, narrow peninsula just S of Jersey City between Newark Bay and Upper New York Bay. Pop. (1990) 61,444.

Terminal of the oil pipeline from Texas. Chief industries oil-refining and manufacture of chemicals, cables and boilers.

Bayreuth Germany. Town in Upper Franconia, Bavaria, 64 km (40 miles) NE of Nuremberg. Pop. (1991) 72,780.

Manufactures textiles and pottery. Noted for its connection with Richard Wagner; an annual festival of his works is held in the Festspielhaus.

Burial-place of the composers Franz Liszt, Richter and Wagner. Has an 18th-cent. opera house.

Bayswater England. Residential district in the former metropolitan borough of Paddington, W London (from 1965 in the City of Westminster). Named after Baynard's Water, the former name of the Westbourne, which flowed into the Serpentine. Tyburn Tree, the gallows, stood near Marble Arch.

Baytown USA. Industrial town in Texas founded 1947 on Galveston Bay 37 km (23 miles) E of Houston. Pop. (1990) 63,850.

Centre of an oil-producing region. Oil-refining. Manufactures chemicals and synthetic rubber.

Beachy Head England. Headland 174 m (571 ft) high on the Sussex coast between Eastbourne and Seaford, consisting of chalk cliffs at the E end of the S Downs. Lighthouse. Scene of a naval battle (1690) when combined English and Dutch fleets were defeated by the French.

Beaconsfield England. Town in S Buckinghamshire 35 km (22 miles) WNW of

London. Pop. (1991) 12,282. Home of Edmund Burke, the British politician and writer, who is buried here. Many associations with the British statesman Benjamin Disraeli, who took (1876) the title of Earl of Beaconsfield.

Beardmore Glacier Antarctica. Huge glacier, one of the world's largest, moving from the Queen Alexandra Range to the Ross Ice Shelf. Length 418 km (260 miles). Discovered (1908) by Sir Ernest Shackleton, the explorer.

Béarn France. Former province in the SW, now part of the Pyrénées-Atlantiques department, into which it was incorporated in 1790. The people are partly Basque. Agriculture and stock-rearing. United with France in 1589 when Henry of Navarre (*le Béarnais*) became King of France. Incorporated into the French kingdom 1620.

Bearsden Scotland. Town in East Dunbartonshire 10 km (6 miles) NW of Glasgow, formed in 1958. Pop. (1991) 27,806. Mainly residential.

Beas River India. One of the 5 rivers of the Punjab, rising at 3965 m (13,005 ft) in the Himalayas and flowing 467 km (290 miles) generally W and SW, joining the Sutlej 40 km (25 miles) ENE of Ferozepore. Part of an irrigation scheme.

Beauce France. Natural region (*pays*) in the Paris Basin, a dry, fertile limestone plain, comprising parts of the Eure-et-Loir, Loir-et-Cher, Loiret, Essonne and Yvelines departments. Chief town Chartres. Known as 'the granary of Paris' because of its wheat production.

Beaufort Sea Arctic Ocean. That part of the Arctic between N Alaska and Banks Island. Shallow in the S and E, deepening to 3600 m (11,808 ft) or more in the NW. Usually covered with drifting ice.

Beaujolais France. Region formerly in the Lyonnais province, now forming the N part of the Rhône department and part of the Loire department, on the NE edge of the Massif Central. Famous for Burgundy wines,

produced on the valley slopes. Chief trading centre Villefranche.

Beaulieu England. Pronounced 'Bewly'. Village in S Hampshire on the Beaulieu R. at the edge of the New Forest 10 km (6 miles) SSW of Southampton. Ruins of a Cistercian abbey, founded by King John (1204). The refectory is restored and serves as the parish church. At the Palace House, seat of Lord Montagu, is the Montagu motor museum, a collection of veteran cars.

Beauly Scotland. Pronounced 'Bewly'; a corruption of Beaulieu. Village in Highland at the head of Beauly Firth on the Beauly R. (formed by the confluence of the Farrar and the Glass; the Glass is formed by the confluence of the Cannich and the Affric, the latter flowing through the beautiful Glen Affric). Pop. (1991) 1354. Ruins of the Cistercian Priory of St John, founded in the 13th cent.

Beaumaris Wales. Town in Isle of Anglesey at the N end of the Menai Strait. Pop. (1991) 1561. Seaside resort. Ruins of a 13th/14th-cent. castle built by Edward I. Elizabethan grammar school (1603).

Beaumont USA. Town in Texas 130 km (80 miles) ENE of Houston at the end of the deep-water canal from Port Arthur. Pop. (1990) 114,323.
Commercial and industrial centre. Trade in petroleum, timber, rice and cotton. Oil-refining, synthetic rubber, paper, meat-packing and other industries.

Beaune France. Town in the Côte d'Or department 37 km (23 miles) SSW of Dijon. Pop. (1990) 22,170. Famous for Burgundy wines. Manufactures agricultural implements and casks.
The historic buildings inc. the famous 15th-cent. Hôtel-Dieu, with a polyptych of the Last Judgement by van der Weyden and the 12th/13th-cent. Church of Notre Dame.

Beauvais France. Ancient Caesaromagus and Bellovacum. Prefecture of the Oise department on the Thérain R. 64 km (40 miles) NNW of Paris. Pop. (1990) 56,278.

Market town. Trade in dairy produce, apples and cereals. Manufactures tiles, brushes and rayon.

Formerly noted for Gobelin tapestries; the industry was moved to Paris after the factory was destroyed in World War II. An annual festival, dating from 1472, when Jeanne Hachette defended the town against Charles the Bold. The famous cathedral (begun 1227 and never completed) has the highest of all Gothic choirs (48 m; 157 ft). Scene of the R 101 airship disaster (1930).

Bebington England. Town just S of Birkenhead on the Wirral peninsula in Merseyside. Pop. (1991) 60,148.

Inc. Bromborough (docks and chemicals works), Eastham (at the W end of the Manchester Ship Canal) and Port Sunlight (a model town built in 1888 for the workers of Lever Bros, now Unilever, where soap and margarine are manufactured).

Bec Abbey France. Ruined Benedictine abbey in the village of Le Bec-Hallouin in the Eure department 32 km (20 miles) SW of Rouen. Founded 1034. Became a medieval centre of learning, from which Lanfranc and Anselm went to Canterbury.

Beccles England. Market town in NE Suffolk on the R. Waveney. Pop. (1991) 10,337. Light engineering, printing and agricultural industries. Noted for crayfish.

Has a 14th-cent. church with a detached belfry.

Béchar Algeria. Town in Béchar department near the frontier with Morocco 800 km (500 miles) SW of Algiers. Pop. (1987) 107,311. Oasis town, with many date palms. It is a mining centre for coal, copper, iron and magnesium. Linked by rail with Algeria's only coalmining area, Kenadsa (21 km; 13 miles WSW).

Bechuanaland ➤BOTSWANA.

Beckenham England. Former municipal borough of NW Kent, a dormitory suburb of SE London, inc. W Wickham; from 1965 part of the London borough of Bromley. In Beckenham is the Bethlem Royal Hospital,

the first mental hospital in England, founded 1247 and moved here from London 1930.

Beddgelert Wales. Village and holiday resort in Gwynedd, S of Snowdonia 16 km (10 miles) SE of Caernarvon. Associated with the story of Gelert, the faithful hound of Llewelyn ap Iorweth, which protected Llewelyn's son from a wolf; but Llewelyn, thinking it had slain his child, killed it. The name, however, probably means 'St Kelert's grave'.

Beddington and Wallington England. Former municipal borough in NE Surrey, a dormitory suburb of S London; from 1965 part of the London borough of Sutton.

Bedford England. County town of Bedfordshire on the R. Ouse 72 km (45 miles) NNW of London. Pop. (1991) 73,917.

Manufactures agricultural implements, electrical goods, pumps, beer, confectionery and bricks.

Associated with John Bunyan (born at the nearby village of Elstow), who wrote parts of *The Pilgrim's Progress* during his 12-year imprisonment in Bedford jail. The philanthropist and prison reformer John Howard was High Sheriff of Bedfordshire. The public school (founded 1552) was endowed by Sir William Harper (d. 1573), Lord Mayor of London, a native of Bedford.

Bedfordshire England. County in the S Midlands. Area 1225 sq km (473 sq. miles). Pop. (1994) 543,200. County town Bedford. Generally low-lying, drained by the Great Ouse and its tributary the Ivel. Hilly in the S (Chiltern Hills). Primarily agricultural, with wheat cultivation and market-gardening. Other towns Luton (where industries are largely centred), Dunstable, Leighton Buzzard, Biggleswade. Many associations with John Bunyan (➤BEDFORD).

Bedlington (Bedlintonshire) England. Town in SE Northumberland 18 km (11 miles) N of Newcastle-upon-Tyne. Former coalmining town. Pop. (1991) 15,431. Famous for a breed of terriers.

Bedwas Wales. Town in Caerphilly on the

R. Rhymney 11 km (7 miles) N of Cardiff. Pop. (1991) 8488. Coalmining centre.

Bedworth England. Town in Warwickshire 5 km (3 miles) S of Nuneaton. Pop. (1991) 31,932.

Coalmining, quarry engineering and textiles.

Beersheba Israel. Town 74 km (46 miles) SW of Jerusalem. Pop. (1992) 128,400. In biblical times it was at the S extremity of Palestine, Dan being at the N extremity – hence the phrase 'from Dan to Beersheba'. In World War I it was captured by the British (1917). Has become an important commercial centre for the N Negev. Manufactures pottery and glass.

Beeston and Stapleford England. Town in Nottinghamshire 5 km (3 miles) SW of Nottingham. Pop. (1991) 66,626.

Engineering. Manufactures pharmaceutical products, hosiery, lace and telephones.

Behistun (Bisutun) Iran. Village in the W 29 km (18 miles) E of Kermanshah, with a precipitous rock 520 m (1706 ft) high carrying a cuneiform inscription by Darius I in Old Persian, Susian and Babylonian recording his defeat of the usurper Gaumata. Sir Henry Rawlinson climbed the rock (1835), copied the inscription, deciphered the Persian by 1846 and so made possible the decipherment of the Susian and Babylonian texts.

Beijing (Peking) China. Cap. of the republic in Hebei province 113 km (70 miles) NW of Tianjin. Pop. (1992) 7,050,000. China's political and cultural centre. Seat of the People's University of China (founded 1912 by Sun Yat-sen) and Beijing (Peking) University (founded 1898). Also an important railway junction and airport.

Industries inc. printing and publishing, tanning and food-processing. It is a major industrial centre and manufactures iron and steel machinery, machine-tools, chemicals, textiles and a wide variety of other products.

It consists of the Inner or Tatar City (N) and the adjacent Outer or Chinese City (S), both walled, the former enclosing the Im-perial City, which in turn contains the Purple or Forbidden city (now a museum). Within the Inner City are some of the most famous buildings of China, such as the Hall of Classics and the Temple of Confucius, as well as 7 artificial lakes and several imperial palaces. In the Outer City, which inc. the commercial quarter, is the Temple of Heaven, standing in a large park.

It was founded near the site of a much older city known as Chi; Beijing rose to greatness when Kublai Khan made it his cap. (1267). Known to the Mongols as Khanbalik (Cambaluc) and to the Chinese as Tatu, it was visited and described in all its magnificence by Marco Polo. In 1368 it was replaced by Nanjing (Nanking), but again became cap. in 1421 and was renamed Beijing. In an uprising in 1900 the European Legations were besieged in what became known as the 'Boxer Rebellion'. Remained cap. of China under the Manchu dynasty (1644–1911) and then under the new republic until 1928, when it was renamed Peiping, the government being transferred by the Nationalists to Nanjing (Nanking). During the Sino–Japanese War it was occupied by the Japanese (1937–45). In 1949 it fell to the Chinese Communists, who made it cap. of the new People's Republic of China under its old name of Peking; reverting to Beijing when the *Pinyin* phonetic alphabet was adopted in 1979. In 1989 pro-democracy demonstrations in Tiananmen Square were brutally crushed by government forces.

Beira Mozambique. Seaport on the Mozambique Channel at the mouth of the Pungwe and Busi rivers 756 km (470 miles) NNE of Maputo; cap. of the Manica and Sofala district. Pop. (1990) 299,300. Built on a sandy spit, it has a relatively healthy climate. Linked by rail with the Democratic Republic of the Congo, Malawi, Zimbabwe and Zambia; considerable trade with these, since improvements in harbour accommodation. There is an oil pipeline to Umtali (Zimbabwe).

Beirut Lebanon. Cap. and chief seaport on St George's Bay. Pop. (1991) 1,100,000. Educational centre with four universities – Lebanese (1951), American (1966), French (1881) and Arab (1937), the last a branch of Alexandria University.

Industries inc. food-processing, engineering and textile manufacturing.

It existed in the 15th cent. BC and prospered under Seleucids, Romans and Byzantines, but was severely damaged by earthquakes in the 6th cent. and again suffered from the Arab occupation in the 7th cent. From the 16th cent. it was held by the Turks almost continuously, though in fact dominated by the Druses, till after World War I, when it became cap. of Syria and Lebanon under French mandate; in 1941 it was made cap. of the newly independent state but population has fallen because of loss of life during the civil war, which began in 1975.

Beisan (Hebrew **Beit Shean**) Israel. Ancient Bethshan; Scythopolis. Small town in the NE 58 km (36 miles) SE of Haifa on the site of an ancient fortress, the biblical Bethshan. Excavations from 1921 onwards revealed remains dating back to 1500 BC and beyond, inc. temples mentioned in the Old Testament, Egyptian stelae and the sarcophagus of Antiochus, cousin of Herod the Great. In Roman times the city of Scythopolis, cap. of the Decapolis, stood here.

Béja Tunisia. Ancient Vaga (Vacca). Cap. of the Béja governorate 88 km (55 miles) W of Tunis. Pop. (1985) 20,000. Market town in the fertile Medjerda valley in a district well known for cent. for its wheat. An important centre in Roman times.

Bekescaba (Csaba) Hungary. Chief town of Békés county, 175 km (110 miles) SE of Budapest. Pop. (1993) 68,000.

Commercial centre and railway junction in a fertile agricultural region. Flour mills, brickworks. Manufactures textiles and machinery.

Belarus. The Republic of Belarus is situated along the W Dvina and Dnieper and is bounded W by Poland, N by Latvia and Lithuania, E by Russia and S by Ukraine. Area 207,595 sq km (80,153 sq. miles). Pop. (1995) 10,332,000 (68 per cent urban). Life expectancy, 66 years male, 76 female. Cap. Minsk. Other cities Homel, Vitebsk, Mahilyou, Hrodno. Currency: Belarusian rubel. It is mainly low-lying with the extensive Pripet Marshes in the S. Drained by the Dnieper and its tributaries to the Black Sea, and by the W Dvina and the Neman rivers to the Baltic Sea. All these rivers are used for floating timber from the vast area of forests. There are c. 30,000 lakes. Cultivated land has been considerably increased by draining the marshlands. Land use: forested 34 per cent, meadows and pastures 15 per cent, agricultural and under permanent cultivation 30 per cent. The official lang. is Belarusian. About 80 per cent are Belarusian, 14 per cent Russian and Ukrainian 3 per cent. The majority of believers are Belarusian Orthodox with a Roman Catholic minority.

The peat industry is important and is used in power stations and chemical plants, and provides most of the country's fuel needs. Main crops flax, potatoes, sugar-beet, fodder crops. Large numbers of beef and dairy cattle and pigs are reared. Industries inc. oil-refining, electrical and electronic engineering, and salt extraction. Manufactures inc. vehicles, machine-tools, agricultural machinery, fertilizers and textiles.

From the 14th cent. Belorussia was ruled alternately by Russia and Poland. In the three Partitions of Poland (1772–95) it passed finally to Russia. Suffered severely in the various wars (17th and 18th cent.), during Napoleon's march on Moscow (1812) and in World Wars I and II. The Belorussian Soviet Socialist Republic was formed in 1919; joined the USSR in 1922. Subsequently enlarged and later increased in area by almost two-thirds through the acquisition of a large area of E Poland under the Potsdam Agreement (1945). A declaration of independence was adopted in 1991 and the country was renamed 'Republic of Belarus'. It is a founder-member of the Commonwealth of Independent States (CIS). There is a 260-member Assembly. It is divided administratively into 6 regions: Brest, Homel, Hrodno, Minsk, Mahilyou and Vitebsk.

Belau ➤PELAU.

Belaya River Russia. River 1100 km (700 miles) long in the Bashkortostan Republic, rising in the S Urals and flowing SW past Beloretsk, then N and NW past Sterlitamak and Ufa to join the Kama R. Important for transport and irrigation.

Belaya Tserkov Ukraine. Town situated 80 km (50 miles) SSW of Kiev. Pop. (1990) 200,500.

Commercial centre. Flour mills. Manufactures leather goods and clothing.

Belcher Islands ➤HUDSON BAY.

Belém Brazil. Cap. of the Pará state, seaport and major airport, on the Pará R. 137 km (85 miles) from the open sea and just S of the equator. Pop. (1991) 1,246,435.

Handles the products of the Amazon basin: rubber, Brazil nuts, hardwoods, babassu nuts and jute. Originally a colonial fortified settlement. Developed rapidly with the rubber boom, but its industries are now more varied and inc. steel, textiles and food-processing.

Belfast Northern Ireland. Cap., chief seaport and industrial centre of Ulster; a county borough at the mouth of the R. Lagan on Belfast Lough, a deep navigable inlet from the Irish Sea. Pop. (1991) 279,237. Situated with the hills of Antrim to the N and those of Down to the S. Among its principal buildings are the City Hall and St Anne's Cathedral (Protestant), begun 1899, in Romanesque style. Seat of the Queen's University (founded 1845). Many fine public parks. Nearby, at Stormont, is the classical-style Parliament building of Northern Ireland, built 1928-32.

Industries inc. engineering and shipbuilding. Manufactures tobacco products, aircraft, rope, footwear, clothing, food-processing and whiskey.

The history of Belfast goes back to the building of a castle at a ford over the Lagan in 1177. English and Scottish settlers were brought in during the 16th–17th-cent.

'Plantations' and the 'Old Irish' were expelled. The linen industry was stimulated by the influx of French Huguenots, after the revocation of the Edict of Nantes (1685). Shipbuilding developed with the aid of Scottish coal and iron towards the end of the 18th cent. The major growth came with the Industrial Revolution. It became a city 1888 and has been the cap. of Northern Ireland since 1920. Birthplace of the physicist and mathematician Lord Kelvin (1824–1907) and Sir John Lavery, the portrait painter (1856–1941).

Belfort France. Prefecture of the Territoire de Belfort 40 km (25 miles) WSW of Mulhouse. Pop. (1990) 51,913. Commands the Belfort Gap between the Vosges and the Jura mountains; of strategic importance.

Manufactures textiles, electrical machinery, locomotives and turbines.

The long siege in the Franco–Prussian War (1870–1) is commemorated by a huge carving of a lion (by Batholdi, sculptor of the Statue of Liberty in New York harbour).

Belfort, Territoire de France. Department in the E, the only part of the former province of Alsace left to France after 1871. Area 610 sq km (235 sq. miles). Pop. (1990) 326,000. Prefecture Belfort.

Belgaum India. Town in Karnataka 385 km (240 miles) SSE of Bombay at over 600 m (1968 ft). Pop. (1991) 245,400. Manufactures textiles, leather and furniture. Trade in rice.

Taken by the British 1818.

Belgium. Kingdom in NW Europe bounded by the Netherlands in the N, NW by the North Sea, Germany and Luxembourg in the E and France in the W and S. Area 30,528 sq km (11,787 sq. miles). Pop. (1995) 10,064,000 (97 per cent urban). Life expectancy, 72 years male, 79 female. Cap. Brussels. Other cities Antwerp, Ghent, Charleroi and Liège. Currency: Belgian franc = 100 centimes. It is mainly low-lying and is divided into 3 regions. 1. In the N is the low, sandy area of Flanders and the Campine (in Flemish, Kempen) with an almost straight coast fringed by a narrow belt of dunes 65 km

(40 miles) long, on which stands the port of Ostend, the largest of several popular seaside resorts. Highest point 694 m (2276 ft). 2. The fertile central plain, between the Scheldt and Meuse rivers, both of which are navigable and, with a network of canals, provide an excellent system of inland waterways more than 1600 km (1000 miles) in length. 3. In the SE is the largely forested plateau of the Ardennes, rising to over 600 m (1968 ft). Near the coast the climate is maritime temperate, giving mild winters and cool summers, but in the Ardennes conditions are more continental, with more severe winters and heavier rainfall. Land use: forested 21 per cent, meadows and pastures 21 per cent, agricultural and under permanent cultivation 24 per cent. About 90 per cent of believers are Roman Catholic. The Belgians are divided into two lang. groups by a line running approximately E–W just S of Brussels. To the N are the Flemings, who speak Dutch (Flemish) and to the S the Walloons, whose lang. is French. Brussels is bilingual. Both Dutch and French are official lang., but this has not prevented continuing controversy between the two groups as to their respective status and rights. Some German is spoken in the E.

Belgium is one of the world's most industrialized countries and relies heavily on exports. It has few natural resources and has to import almost all its fuel and raw materials, but has important non-ferrous metal and chemicals industries. The diamond industry is located at Antwerp. Engineering, iron, steel, oil-refining, textiles and plastics are major industries. Light industry is expanding but there is a decline in the older industries such as steel, coal and chemicals.

The country is named after the Belgae, the Celtic peoples who inhabited the area when it was conquered by Julius Caesar. In medieval times it was divided into several counties (Flanders etc.), duchies (Brabant etc.) and the bishopric of Liège; the great textile and commercial cities, e.g. Ghent, Bruges, then achieved virtual independence. In the late Middle Ages and early Renaissance periods the cities of Flanders, Bruges, Ghent and Antwerp became great centres of artistic patronage and this was to the benefit of architecture, sculpture, painting, manuscript illustration and the decorative arts, and the great names of Rubens, van Dyck and van Eyck flourished. In the 15th cent. what is now Belgium passed to the duchy of Burgundy and later to the Habsburgs. From Spain it was transferred to Austria (1713), France (1797) and then the Netherlands (1815). The Roman Catholic Belgians soon quarrelled with the Protestant Dutch, revolted and had their independence recognized (1830). Prince Leopold of Saxe-Coburg became king and his successor, Leopold II, gained wealth and some notoriety through his personal interest in the development of the Congo (annexed 1908). Belgium was invaded and occupied by the Germans in both World War I and II. In 1947 with the Netherlands and Luxembourg it formed a customs union known as Benelux. Belgium is a constitutional, representative and hereditary monarchy. Legislative power rests with the King and the Federal Parliament consists of a 71-member Senate and a 150-member Chamber of Representatives. No act of the King can have effect unless countersigned by one of his ministers. For administrative purposes it is divided into 10 provinces: Antwerp, Brabant, West Flanders, East Flanders, Hainaut, Liège, Limbourg, Luxembourg, Namur and Walloon Brabant.

Belgorod Russia. City situated NNW of Kharkov on the N Donets river. Pop. (1994) 318,000.

Railway junction in an agricultural area. Industries inc. chalk-quarrying, meat-packing, flour-milling and tanning. Nearby are large deposits of iron ore.

Belgrade (Serbo-Croat **Beograd**) Yugoslavia. Cap. of the Federal Republic of Yugoslavia and of Serbia at the confluence of the Danube and the Sava rivers. Pop. (1991) 1,136,786.

River port, railway and road junction. Commercial centre. Manufactures electrical equipment, textiles, pharmaceuticals, vehicles and chemicals; food-processing.

University (1863). In a strategic position between Central Europe and the Balkans, it has been frequently attacked and destroyed. There are few monuments to its past apart from Kalemegdan, the old Turkish fortress. First fortified by the Celts in the 3rd cent. BC. Changed hands several times; became cap. of Serbia 1403, but fell to the Turks 1521. The Turkish garrison finally withdrew in 1867. Again cap. of Serbia from 1878 and became cap. of Yugoslavia 1918.

Belgravia England. Residential district in W London, S of Knightsbridge, mainly in the City of Westminster. Inc. Belgrave, Eaton and Cadogan Squares. Developed (*c.* 1826) on a reclaimed marsh.

Belitung ►BILLITON.

Belize. Independent state situated on the Caribbean coast, forming the SE part of the Yucatán (Mexico) peninsula; bounded on the N by Mexico and on the W and S by Guatemala. Area 22,965 sq km (8867 sq. miles). Pop. (1995) 216,000 (48 per cent urban). Life expectancy, 66 years male, 70 female. Cap. Belmopan. Other cities Belize City (chief seaport) and Orange Walk. Currency: Belize dollar = 100 cents. Inland in the S are the Maya Mountains rising to over 1000 m (3280 ft), but the land is mainly low-lying and flat; along the swampy coast are three atolls and some 300 cays. Climate tropical, but the NE Trade Winds temper the heat; rainfall is heavy, and damage has often been caused by hurricanes. Land use: forested 92 per cent, meadows and pastures 2 per cent, agricultural and under permanent cultivation 3 per cent. The official lang. is English but Spanish is widely spoken. About 30 per cent black, 25 per cent native Indian and Carib, 4 per cent European, the remainder mainly are mixed mulatto and *mestizo*. About 58 per cent are Roman Catholic, 34 per cent Protestant. There is a small group of Bahai.

Manufacturing is mainly confined to processing agricultural products. Sugar-cane and citrus fruits are grown along the coast; sugar, grapefruit and oranges are important exports.

Clothes are also manufactured and garments are exported. Communications in the interior are extremely difficult, being practically confined to the rivers, some of them navigable for short distance by shallow-draught vessels and down which timber is floated. Tourism is expanding and attractions inc. the second largest barrier reef in the world.

Numerous ruins prove that for hundreds of years Belize was heavily populated by the Maya Indians, whose relatively advanced civilization reached its height between AD 300 and 900. Thereafter, for reasons not yet fully known, the civilization collapsed and many of the people migrated. The next regular settlements were established in 1622 by the English (from Jamaica), who exploited the logwood and mahogany. Despite opposition and frequent attacks from the Spaniards, the English remained and their occupation was recognized in 1798. In 1862 British Honduras was formally declared a British colony and became a dependency of Jamaica, and in 1884 an independent colony. It has long been claimed by Guatemala, but it recognized the independence of Belize in 1991. Internal self-government was granted in 1964. In 1974 British Honduras became Belize. Independence was achieved in 1981. There is a 29-member House of Representatives elected by universal suffrage for 5-year terms and an 8-member Senate.

Belize City Belize. Chief seaport and former cap. in a swampy area on both banks and at the mouth of the Belize R.; the harbour is shallow and obstructed with coral reefs and sandbanks. Pop. (1991) 44,087.

Chief exports hardwoods (mahogany), bananas, coconuts, grapefruit.

In 1961 Belize suffered severe damage and loss of life from a hurricane and a 5-m (16-ft) tidal wave; plans were made to move the cap. to an inland site; ►BELMOPAN.

Bellagio Italy. Village and holiday resort on L. Como on a promontory dividing the two southern arms of the lake. Picturesque gardens and villas.

Bellary India. Town and railway junction in Karnataka 320 km (200 miles) N of Mysore. Pop. (1991) 245,400.

Manufactures textiles, iron, steel and alloy steel. Sugar-milling. Trade in cotton. The ancient fort stands on a 135-m (443-ft) granite rock.

Bellegarde-sur-Valserine France. Town in the Ain department at the confluence of the Valserine R. with the Rhône 26 km (16 miles) SW of Geneva. Pop. (1985) 12,000.

Manufacturing centre. Metallurgical, textile and other industries. On the Rhône 6 km (4 miles) S is the Genissiat Dam and hydro-electric plant.

Belle-Île-en-Mer France. Island in the Morbihan department in the Bay of Biscay S of the Quiberon peninsula (Brittany). Area 83 sq km (32 sq. miles). Pop. (1985) 5000. Chief town Le Palais. The impressive cliffs are a tourist attraction.

Main occupations fishing and sardine-canning.

Held by the British 1761–3, then ceded to France in exchange for Nova Scotia.

Belle Isle Canada. Island at the E end of the strait of the same name separating Newfoundland from the coast of Labrador; the first land sighted by ships crossing the Atlantic. The strait, closed by ice November–May, provides the shortest route from Europe to the St Lawrence estuary and seaway.

Belleville Canada. Town in SE Ontario on L. Ontario 64 km (40 miles) W of Kingston. Pop. (1991) 63,000.

Meat-packing, cheese-making. Manufactures cement, plastics and machinery.

Belleville (Illinois) USA. Town 24 km (15 miles) SE of St Louis. Pop. (1980) 41,586.

Industrial centre. Manufactures stoves and clothing. Coal mined in the neighbourhood. US Air Force training school at nearby Scott Field.

Belleville (New Jersey) USA. Industrial town just N of Newark. Pop. (1988) 38,005.

Manufactures machinery and chemicals.

Bellevue USA. City in Washington facing Seattle across L. Washington from the E shore and joined to it by floating-bridge highways. Pop. (1985) 75,000.

Residential and office centre; industries inc. food distribution, advanced medical and aerospace equipment, computer services and software.

Bellingham USA. Seaport in NW Washington on the bay of the same name 130 km (80 miles) N of Seattle. Pop. (1990) 52,000.

Fruit and salmon canning. Processes dairy produce and timber from the surrounding area.

Bellingshausen Sea Southern Ocean. Section of the Southern Ocean W of Graham Land (Palmer Peninsula) (Antarctica). Visited by a Russian expedition under F. von Bellingshausen (1819–21) and named after him.

Bellinzona Switzerland. Cap. of the Ticino canton on the Ticino R. near the N end of L. Maggiore. Pop. (1990) 16,935.

Road, railway and tourist centre. Railway engineering, woodworking, printing and other industries. Three picturesque 15th-cent. castles.

Bell Island Canada. Small island in Conception Bay off SE Newfoundland. Area 28 sq km (11 sq. miles). Pop. 8000.

High-quality hematite iron mines (first worked 1895) extending under the sea.

Bell (Inchcape) Rock Scotland. Reef in the North Sea off the coast of Angus 19 km (12 miles) SE of Arbroath. Lighthouse erected (1807–11) by Robert Stevenson. The legend of the warning bell is told in Southey's *Ballad of the Inchcape Rock*.

Belluno Italy. Cap. of the Belluno province in Veneto, N Italy, on the Piave R. 80 km (50 miles) N of Venice. Pop. (1981) 36,634.

Tourist centre (serves the Dolomites). Manufactures electrical equipment and furniture.

Cathedral (16th-cent.) and a Renaissance palace.

Belmopan Belize. Cap. 80 km (50 miles) WSW of Belize City. Pop. (1991) 3558. Following severe hurricane 'Hattie' in 1961 Belmopan was moved 80 km (50 miles) inland to be away from the hurricane zone. Construction began in 1967 and it became the seat of government in 1970. Many of the public buildings are in the Maya style of architecture.

Belo Horizonte Brazil. Cap. of the Minas Gerais state on the plateau at 750 m (2460 ft) 338 km (210 miles) N of Rio de Janeiro, to which it is linked by motorway and railway; also motorways to Brasilia and São Paulo. Pop. (1991) 2,048,861. Pleasant climate.

Centre of a mining (iron, manganese) and agricultural (cotton, cattle) region. Food-processing, diamond-cutting. Manufactures motor vehicles, iron and steel, textiles and footwear.

University (1927). Brazil's first planned city.

Belomorsk Russia. Formerly Soroka. Seaport in the Karelia Republic on the White Sea at the N end of the Baltic–White Sea Canal and on the Murmansk Railway. Pop. 14,000. Sawmilling, fish-canning. Exports timber.

Beloretsk Russia. Industrial town in the Bashkortostan Republic in the S Urals 88 km (55 miles) NW of Magnitogorsk. Pop. (1970) 67,099.

Metallurgical centre. Manufactures steel, wire, nails from local iron and manganese ores.

Belorussia ➤BELARUS.

Belovo Russia. Industrial town in the Kuznetsk Basin 88 km (55 miles) NW of Novokuznetsk on a branch of the Trans-Siberian Railway. Pop. (1989) 118,000.

Metallurgical and other industries. Coal mined nearby.

Belper England. Town in Derbyshire on the R. Derwent 11 km (7 miles) N of Derby. Pop. (1991) 18,213.

Industrial centre and market town. Cotton and hosiery mills. Chemical works and iron foundries. The cotton industry was founded (1776) by Jedediah Strutt, inventor of a ribbing machine.

Belsen Germany. Village in Lower Saxony near Celle. Site of a notorious concentration camp during the Nazi regime.

Belt, Great ➤GREAT BELT.

Belt, Little ➤LITTLE BELT.

Belterra ➤TAPAJÓS RIVER.

Beltsy Moldova. Town situated 113 km (70 miles) NW of Kishinev. Pop. (1990) 164,800.

Agricultural centre. Sugar-refining, flour-milling and meat-packing.

In Romania (as Balti) between World Wars I and II.

Benares ➤VARANASI.

Benbecula Scotland. Island in the Outer Hebrides in Western Isles between N Uist and S Uist. Area 95 sq km (36 sq. miles). Pop. (1991) 1803. Main occupation fishing.

Bendigo Australia. Formerly Sandhurst. Mining centre in Victoria 137 km (85 miles) NNW of Melbourne. Pop. (1991) 57,427. Developed in the gold rush of 1851; goldfield characterized by deep saddle reefs. Now also a market town.

Flour-milling, egg-producing, tanning, textile manufacture and other industries.

Benevento Italy. Ancient Beneventum. Cap. of the Benevento province in Campania on the Calore R. 51 km (32 miles) NE of Naples. Pop. (1991) 64,700.

Produces confectionery, matches, a liqueur (Strega).

Chief town of the Samnites, but taken by the Romans in the 3rd cent. BC. Became an important town on the Appian Way. Mainly under papal rule from medieval times until 1860, when it was incorporated in the kingdom of Italy. A triumphal arch erected in AD 114 in honour of Trajan.

Benfleet England. Residential town in S Essex 8 km (5 miles) W of Southend. Pop. (1991) 49,701. Inc. S Benfleet (on the

Benfleet Creek which separates Canvey Island from the mainland), Hadleigh and Thundersley.

Bengal India/Bangladesh. 1. Former presidency of British India, in the NE at the head of the Bay of Bengal, approximating to the great Ganges–Brahmaputra delta and bounded on the N by mountainous Sikkim and Bhutan. It has a humid tropical climate, with rainfall varying from 125 cm (50 ins.) to well over 250 cm (100 ins.) annually and is important for the production of rice and jute. Its chief city, Calcutta, was cap. of India from 1833 to 1912, when it was superseded by Delhi. In the 19th cent. Bengal at times included neighbouring regions, e.g. Assam, but the Bengali-speaking core was made a province in 1912 and became autonomous in 1937. With the partition of India (1947), Bengal was divided: the larger, mainly Muslim, area (E) was assigned to Pakistan, and the chiefly Hindu area (W) to India. 2. East Bengal (East Pakistan): now ►BANGLA-DESH. 3. West Bengal: now a state in India.

Bengal, Bay of. Arm of the Indian Ocean between peninsular India and Burma. Receives the combined Ganges and Brahmaputra, Irrawaddy, Mahanadi, Godavari, Krishna and Cauvery rivers. Islands inc. the Andaman, Nicobar and Mergui groups.

Benghazi (Bengasi) Libya. Ancient Hesperides; Berenice. Seaport at the E end of the Gulf of Sidra.Pop. (1984) 485,386. Connected by rail with Barca and Soluk. Founded by the Greeks as Hesperides. Renamed Berenice (in honour of his wife) by Ptolemy III. Important centre of colonization under the Italians 1911–42. Changed hands several times during World War II; finally captured by the British 1942.

Benguela (Benguella) Angola. Seaport 40 km (25 miles) SW of Lobito. Pop. (1983) 155,000. Flourished during the slave-trade period. Has now lost most of its foreign trade to Lobito, ocean terminus of the railway linking it to Angola central plateau, Shaba (Democratic Republic of the Congo), Malawi, Mozambique, Zimbabwe and Zambia.

Benin. Republic on the Gulf of Guinea, bounded by Niger and Burkina Faso in the N, Nigeria in the E and Togo in the W. Area 112,680 sq km (43,500 sq. miles). Pop. (1995) 5,409,000 (40 per cent urban). Life expectancy, 49 years male, 52 female. Cap. Porto Novo. Other cities Cotonou, Djougou, Abomey-Calavi, Parakou. Currency: CFA franc = 100 centimes. The 100-km (60-mile) coastline consists of a sandbar and behind that brackish lagoons. Inland the land rises to a fertile lowland plain which is intensively farmed and in the NW lie the Atakora chain of mountains rising to 500 m (1640 ft). To the NE lies the Alibori river valley which, with the R. Sota, joins the R. Niger which forms part of the border between Benin and Niger. In the coastal parts there is an equatorial climate. The dry season increases in length from the coast. Land use: forested 31 per cent, meadows and pastures 4 per cent, agricultural and under permanent cultivation 17 per cent. The official lang. is French. About 60 per cent follow traditional animist beliefs, 23 per cent are Christians, mainly Roman Catholic. The main ethnic groups are Fon, Yoruba, Goun, Bariba Adjara, Somba and Aizo.

Benin is one of the least developed countries and only recently has abandoned Communism, although some market economy had existed in its trade with Nigeria and Togo. The economy is dependent upon agriculture but productivity is low. Benin is, however, basically self-sufficient in her food supply which is supplemented by fishing and local livestock-farming. Prospecting is taking place for offshore oil, uranium and phosphates. Oil was discovered offshore in 1968 and production began in 1982. Industrial production is on a small scale and mainly concerned with processing primary products, particularly palm oil, for export. Other exports inc. palm kernels, groundnuts. Food crops inc. cassava, maize, millet and yams. Cotton and coffee have been introduced successfully.

Benin was called Dahomey until 1975 after the historical kingdom of Dahomey or Abomey, conquered by the French in 1892–4. The new name came from the Bight of Benin and the former 'French Bight of Benin Settlements'. The kingdom of Dahomey was a powerful, well-organized state from the 17th cent., trading extensively in slaves with the Portuguese, British and French. On the coast an educated African elite grew up in the 19th cent. After the defeat of Dahomey, whose monarchy was abolished, the French occupied territory inland up to the R. Niger and created the colony of Dahomey as part of French West Africa. Subsequently, there were several African revolts, a number occurring during World War I. The African elite protested frequently at French rule. Dahomey achieved independence in 1960. In 1972 it was proclaimed a Marxist–Leninist state, but this was abandoned in 1989. The Benin Party of Popular Revolution held the monopoly of power from 1977, but the constitution was suspended in 1990. Moves to establish a multi-party democracy allowed 34 newly legalized political parties to take part in the 1991 elections. Parliament is an 83-seat national Assembly elected by proportional representation for 4-year terms.

Benin Nigeria. Ancient kingdom of W Africa, with a coastline extending from the Volta R. to the Rio del Rey and inc. the shores of the Bight of Benin, the Niger delta and some of the country E of the delta. Small but powerful. The Bini (Beni) were governed by a theocracy; their ritual involved considerable human sacrifice. The coast came under British protection in 1885; human sacrifice and the slave trade were stopped. Became the Benin Province of S Nigeria 1914.

Benin, Bight of Atlantic Ocean. Bay in the Gulf of Guinea (W Africa), bordered by the coasts of E Ghana, Togo, Benin and W Nigeria as far as the Niger delta. Formerly known as the Slave Coast.

Benin City Nigeria. Town in a forest clearing 249 km (155 miles) E of Lagos. Pop. (1992) 207,200.

Trade in palm oil and kernels, timber. Wood-carving and brassware.

Former cap. of the kingdom of Benin. Formerly a centre of the slave trade.

Beni River ➤MADEIRA RIVER.

Beni Suef Egypt. Cap. of Beni Suef governorate on the W bank of the Nile 113 km (70 miles) SSW of Cairo. Pop. (1991) 174,000. Linked by rail with Cairo and with El Faiyum oasis, for which it is an important trade centre. Cotton-ginning and other industries.

Ben Lomond Scotland. Mountain 973 m (3191 ft) high on the E side of Loch Lomond in Stirling.

Ben Nevis Scotland. Highest mountain in the British Isles (1343 m; 4406 ft) 6 km (4 miles) ESE of Fort William, overlooking the picturesque Glen Nevis. On the NE side is a 450-m (1476-ft) precipice.

Benoni South Africa. Town in the S of the Gauteng on the Witwatersrand 27 km (17 miles) E of Johannesburg at a height of 1700 m (5576 ft). Pop. (1985) 207,000.
Goldmining. Engineering.

Bensberg Germany. Town in North Rhine-Westphalia 14 km (9 miles) ENE of Cologne. Pop. (1970) 41,000. Mainly residential.
Manufactures leather goods. Has an early 18th-cent. castle and ruins of a 13th-cent. castle.

Benue River Cameroon/Nigeria. River 1450 km (900 miles) long, chief tributary of the Niger, rising in the Adamawa Mountains N of Ngaoundéré (Cameroon), flowing N and then generally WSW past Yola and Makurdi (Nigeria) and joining the Niger at Likoja 370 km (230 miles) above the mouth. Navigable to Garoua (Cameroon) in the flood season (July–October).

Beograd ➤BELGRADE.

Berar India. Territory of Madhya Pradesh

consisting largely of the broad, fertile valley of the Purna R. (a tributary of the Tapti), between the Satpura and Ajanta ranges, one of the richest cotton-growing regions in India. It was administered as Hyderabad Assigned Districts 1853–1903 and then became an administrative division of the Central Provinces and Berar; in 1950 the two latter became the state of Madhya Pradesh.

Berbera Somali Republic. Seaport on the Gulf of Aden. Pop. (1987) 65,000.

Exports sheep, goats, skins and gums, mainly to Aden.

Berbice River Guyana. River 480 km (300 miles) long, flowing N from the Guiana Highlands, over falls, to the coastal plain and entering the Atlantic near New Amsterdam.Navigable for 200 km (125 miles). Diamonds are worked in the middle course.

Berchtesgaden Germany. Village in the Bavarian Alps 18 km (11 miles) SSW of Salzburg (Austria) at a height of 520 m (1706 ft) amid fine mountain scenery. Pop. (1990) 24,000.

Popular resort. Salt-mining, potash, wood-carving. Became famous as the site of Adolf Hitler's mountain retreat.

Berdichev Ukraine. Town situated 153 km (95 miles) WSW of Kiev. Pop. (1990) 92,600.

Industrial centre and railway junction. Sugar-refining, tanning and engineering.

Founded 1482. Has belonged to Lithuania, Poland and Russia.

Berezina River Belarus. River 560 km (350 miles) long, rising in the N and flowing S through low-lying wooded country to join the Dnieper R. Linked with the W Dvina R. and the Baltic Sea by the Berezina Canal, thus forming the Baltic–Black Sea waterway. Near Borisov, on the upper course, Napoleon crossed the river with great losses (November 1812) during the retreat from Moscow.

Berezniki Russia. Industrial town situated 153 km (95 miles) N of Perm. Pop. (1989) 201,000.

An important centre of the chemical industry. Manufactures fertilizers, dyes, paper, sulphuric acid and soda, using local common salt, potash and coal.

Bergamo Italy. Cap. of the Bergamo province in Lombardy 45 km (28 miles) NE of Milan, at the foot of the Bergamasque Alps. Pop. (1992) 114,930.

Industrial centre. Engineering, textile manufacture. In the old town, on a 366-m (1200-ft) hill, are a 12th/14th-cent. Romanesque church and the 15th-cent. Colleoni chapel. Birthplace of the composer, Gaetano Donizetti (1797–1848).

Bergen Germany ➤RUGEN.

Bergen Norway. Seaport and second city of Norway in the SW at the head of the Byfjord. Pop. (1990) 187,382. Built round a sheltered and spacious harbour; trade chiefly in fish and fish products.

Shipbuilding and engineering. Manufactures paper, furniture, pottery and rope. Important tourist and cultural centre. University (1948).

Founded (1070) by Olaf III as Bjorgvin. The chief city in medieval times, later surpassed as a trading centre by Oslo. In 1665 an English fleet pursuing a Dutch merchant fleet into Bergen harbour was heavily bombarded: the 'Bergen incident' contributed to the fall of Clarendon and the rise of the Cabal. Suffered severely from fires at various times; the central area was rebuilt 1916. In World War II it was again heavily damaged. Birthplace of Edvard Grieg, the composer (1843–1907).

Bergen-op-Zoom Netherlands. Town in the North Brabant province in the SW on the small Zoom R. near its confluence with the Scheldt. Pop. (1993) 47,546.

Sugar-refining, iron-founding, distilling and other industries.

Strongly fortified (16th cent.) and often besieged.

Bergerac France. Town in the Dordogne department in the SW on the Dordogne R.

76 km (47 miles) E of Bordeaux. Pop. (1990) 28,000.

Famous for wines, truffles and chestnuts. Distilling, tanning. Manufactures footwear.

Bering Sea. A N section of the Pacific Ocean between NE Siberia and Alaska, bounded on the S by the Aleutian Is., connected N through the Bering Strait with the Arctic Ocean. Named after the Danish navigator Vitus Bering (1681–1741), who explored the region for Peter the Great of Russia from 1728. Contains several islands, inc. St Lawrence, St Matthew and the Pribilof Is., in US waters, and the Komandorskiye Is., in Russian waters. Bering died of scurvy on one of the last-named group.

Berkeley England. Small town in SW Gloucestershire 24 km (15 miles) SW of Gloucester. Pop. 790.

The fertile dairy-farming Berkeley Vale is famous for Double Gloucester cheese. Nuclear power station (opened 1963) now de-commissioning.

Edward II was murdered in Berkeley Castle (1327). Birthplace of Dr Edward Jenner, physician and discoverer of vaccination (1749–1823).

Berkeley USA. Residential and university city in California across the Bay from San Francisco, relatively free from the prevailing sea mists. Pop. (1990) 102,724.

Manufactures soap, paint, chemicals. Berkelium, discovered in the university laboratories in 1950, is named after it.

Berkhamsted England. Town in SW Hertfordshire 16 km (10 miles) W of St Albans. Pop. (1991) 18,044. Largely residential. The Foundling Hospital was transferred here in 1935. Birthplace of William Cowper, the poet (1731–1800).

Berkshire England. Former Royal county in the S, bordered partly in the N by the R. Thames. In the rearrangement of county boundaries (1972), lost much of its N area, inc. Abingdon and Didcot, to Oxfordshire, but gained Slough and Eton from Buckinghamshire. In 1998 it ceased to exist as an administrative unit and is now divided into 6 unitary authorities (Bracknell Forest, Newbury, Reading, Slough, Windsor and Maidenhead, Wokingham). Pop. (1991) 716,500. The Berkshire Downs run W–E across the middle of the county, with White Horse Hill reaching 261 m (856 ft); but the highest point is Inkpen Beacon (297 m; 974 ft) in the extreme SW. Sheep, pigs and dairy cattle raised. Wheat and oats cultivated in the fertile valleys, esp. the valley of the R. Kennet.

Berlin Germany. *Land* and city in NE Germany on the R. Spree about 181 km (112 miles) inland from the Baltic coast and 84 km (52 miles) from the Polish frontier. Area 889 sq km (343 sq. miles). Pop. (1994) 3,461,724. Formerly divided by politics, Berlin still appears divided in architectural style and economy. The former East Berlin takes in the Unter den Linden boulevard and its neighbourhood which was the heart of the imperial cap.; the government restored much and rebuilt on the same scale to provide for administration and culture. Dominating all this is a 366 m (1200 ft) TV tower. Restoration of the Cathedral had begun by 1980. West Berlin inc. most of the Tiergarten park and has otherwise dense commercial and housing development. Both districts built high-rise apartment blocks; both have preserved their lake-studded greenbelts. Berlin lies in a flat, watery country and the climate is cool. The city has diverse manufacturing, engineering and processing industries, as well as the strong commercial life of its western half. All this has absorbed many foreign workers as well as incomers from the rest of Germany. The end of the state-supported economy in the E is proving a time of great economic stress for the whole city.

A river-crossing strongpoint, Berlin from c. 1500 was the seat of the Hohenzollern family as rulers of Brandenburg and (from 1701) kings of Prussia. Their building programmes were extensive. Berlin became the cap. of imperial Germany in 1871. After great troubles following World War I it saw the rise and destruction of the 'Third Reich' and was almost destroyed itself. The ruins were partitioned between the occupying forces in 1945; in 1948 the division hardened into East (Soviet-controlled) and West (Western-controlled). The East functioned as cap. of East Germany; the West (BONN) was now only a commercial city, politically in West Germany but physically within East Germany. From June 1948 to May 1949 an attempt by the Soviet Union to force Britain, France and US out of the city was made by blocking road and river access. The Western Powers responded by a round-the-clock airlift supplying food, fuel and mail. Its isolation was completed by a wall and fence encirclement in 1961, preventing all unauthorized movement; this was demolished in 1990 as a prelude to re-unification, when Berlin was reinstated as official cap. of Germany and by the year 2000 most federal ministries will have moved from Bonn to Berlin.

Bermejo River Argentina/Paraguay. River 1046 km (650 miles) long, rising in the extreme NW and flowing SE to join the Paraguay R. near Pilar (Paraguay). In the middle course it divides into two streams (the N one is called the Teuco), which later rejoin.

Bermondsey England. Former metropolitan borough of SE London on the S bank of the Thames, linked with Stepney by Tower Bridge and Rotherhithe Tunnel; from 1965 part of the London borough of Southwark. Name probably derived from 'Beormund's Island', referring to a Saxon overlord and the insular, marshy nature of the district.

Bermuda. United Kingdom Overseas Territory consisting of a group of over 138 islands and islets, about 20 of which are inhabited, situated in the W Atlantic Ocean 1160 km (700 miles) SE of New York City. Area 53.3 sq km (20.59 sq. miles). Pop. (1994) 60,400. Chief town Hamilton. The islands are low-lying and rocky and the highest point is 73 m (239 ft). They have been formed by the growth of coral on the base of a submarine volcanic cone. Coral fragments from the surrounding coral reefs, broken off by wave action, have drifted or been blown to form extensive coral sand dunes. Connected by bridges and causeways, they form an almost continuous arc 32 km (20 miles) long. Owing to the permeability of the soil and rocks there are no surface streams or wells, yet the vegetation is prolific. The subtropical climate ensures a mild winter and summer heat is tempered by the NE Trade Winds. The rainfall is evenly distributed throughout the year and the air is always moist. On the small area of cultivated land (little more than 2.6 sq km (1 sq. mile)) the smallholders grow mainly tropical fruit and vegetables. The chief exports are the sale of fuel to aircraft and ships, and the re-export of pharmaceuticals; the main revenue comes from tourists and its role of an offshore financial centre.

Bermuda derives its name from Juan Bermúdez, a Spaniard, who discovered the islands in 1515. They were first inhabited when a number of colonists under Sir George Somers was shipwrecked here (1609) and were taken over by the Crown 1684. During World War II (1941) sites were leased for 99 years to the USA for naval and air bases. In 1995 at a referendum the majority rejected independence from UK. There is an 11-member Senate and a 40-member House of Assembly.

Bern (Berne) Switzerland. 1. Cap., also cap. of the Bern canton, on the Aar R. at a height of 550 m (1804 ft). Pop. (1994) 129,423.

Manufactures knitwear, furniture, chocolate, musical instruments. Printing and publishing.

University (1834). Headquarters of the Universal Postal Union. Medieval streets with arcades and ornate fountains; the 15th/16th-cent. Gothic cathedral, the 15th-cent. Rathaus and the Federal Palace are outstanding buildings. The name is supposed to refer to bears and a bear-pit is still a tourist attraction. Founded (1191) by Berchtold V of Zahringen. Became a free imperial city 1218. It became cap. of the Swiss Confederation 1848. 2. The second largest canton, between the Bernese Alps and the French frontier. Area 5961 sq km (2302 sq. miles).

Pop. (1994) 956,617. Cap. Bern (Berne). Hydroelectric power.

Manufactures watches, textiles and food products.

Divided geographically into three regions. The Bernese Oberland in the S inc. the Alpine peaks of Finsteraarhorn and Jungfrau, the lakes of Thun and Brienz, and many resorts, e.g. Interlaken, Mürren, Grindelwald, Kandersteg, Meiringen. The Mittelland (central area) inc. the lower valley of the Aar R., the Emmental (Emme valley) – famous for scenery and for cheese – and the city of Bern. The Seeland (lake area) in the N inc. the lakes of Biel and Neuchâtel.

Bernburg Germany. Town in Saxony-Anhalt 42 km (26 miles) NNW of Halle on the Saale R. Pop. (1989) 41,200.

Centre of a potash and rock-salt mining district. Chemical, engineering and other industries.

Formerly cap. of the duchy of Anhalt-Bernburg.

Bernese Oberland ➤BERN, CANTON.

Bernicia England/Scotland. Kingdom in the NE believed to have been founded by Ida in AD 547 and to have extended later from the Tees to the Forth. United with Deira to form the kingdom of Northumbria, 605.

Bernkastel-Kues Germany. Town in Rhineland-Palatinate on the Mosel R. 35 km (22 miles) NE of Trier. Pop. 5500. Famous for wines.

Berre, Étang de France. Lagoon in the Bouches-du-Rhône department in the SE. Area 155 sq km (50 sq. miles). Connected to the Gulf of Fos by the 6-km (4-mile) Étang de Caronte. Eel fisheries. Important oil refineries round its shores, also saltworks.

Berry France. Former province in the S of the Paris Basin, now forming the Indre and Cher departments and parts of other departments. Bought by the French crown 1101. Became a duchy 1360. Divided into the present departments 1790. The cap. was Bourges.

Berwickshire Scotland. Historic county in the SE, bordering in the SE on England, now part of Scottish Borders.

Berwick-upon-Tweed England. Town at the mouth of the R. Tweed on the N bank in NE Northumberland. Pop. (1991) 12,500. Three bridges across the Tweed: an old road bridge (1634), a much larger road bridge (1928) and a railway viaduct (1850).

Engineering. Manufactures fertilizers, hosiery. Salmon fishing.

For cent. involved in English–Scottish border troubles, Berwick changed hands 13 times between 1147 and 1482. Declared neutral territory 1551. Became part of Northumberland 1885.

Berwyn USA. Town in Illinois 14 km (9 miles) WNW of Chicago. Pop. (1970) 520,502.

Residential and industrial centre. Manufactures electrical equipment and machine-tools.

Besançon France. Ancient Vesontio. Prefecture of the Doubs department in the E on the peninsula formed by a loop of the Doubs R. at the foot of the Jura mountains 77 km (48 miles) E of Dijon. Pop. (1990) 119,194.

Chief centre in France of watch and clock making. Manufactures rayon, hosiery and chocolate. Brewing, engineering.

Several Roman remains. Cathedral (founded in the 4th cent.; mainly built in the 11th/13th cent.). Renaissance Palais Granvelle (16th-cent.). Seat of a university (moved from Dôle 1691). Chief town of the Sequani. Taken by Julius Caesar 58 BC. Became an important Roman military post and later a colony. Belonged to Burgundy and then to Franche-Comté. After a period of Austro–Spanish rule, ceded to France in 1678 and replaced Dôle as cap. of the Franche-Comté province. Birthplace of social theorist, François Fourier (1772–1837), journalist, Pierre Proudhon (1809–65) and the poet and author Victor Hugo (1802–85).

Beskids Slovakia/Poland. Two ranges, West and East, of the Carpathian mountains along the Slovak–Polish frontier, rising to

1725 m (5658 ft) in Babia Gora (W Beskids). Well forested. Popular tourist area.

Bessarabia Moldova/Ukraine. Region bounded by the Dniester R. (N and E), the Danube R. (S) and the Prut R. (W); the N and S parts are in Ukraine and the larger central part is in Moldova. Pop. mainly Moldavians, Ukrainians and Russians. Chief town Kishinev.

Principally agricultural. Maize, wheat, sugar-beet, vines cultivated. Sheep, cattle, pigs raised.

Became part of the Roman province of Dacia in the 2nd cent. AD. Afterwards overrun by Goths, Huns, Avars, Bulgars and others, inc. the Thracian Bessi (from whom the name derives) in the 7th cent. Conquered by the ruling prince of Moldavia in the 14th cent. and long disputed between the Turks and the Russians. Ceded to Russia 1812. Annexed by Romania (1918) after World War I. Retaken by the USSR 1940.

Bessemer USA. Industrial town in Alabama just SW of Birmingham. Pop. (1980) 31,729.

Manufactures iron and steel goods, chemicals. Coal and iron mined in the neighbourhood. Named after Sir Henry Bessemer, inventor of the Bessemer process for steel manufacture.

Bethesda Wales. Town in Gwynedd 6 km (4 miles) SE of Bangor. Pop. (1991) 3558. The Penrhyn slate quarries are nearby.

Bethlehem (Ar. **Belt Lahm**) Jordan. Town in the W 8 km (5 miles) SSW of Jerusalem. Pop. (1985) 14,000. The reputed birthplace of Christ. Manufactures souvenirs in olivewood.

The Emperor Constantine built a basilica here (AD 300), subsequently added to and restored, beneath which is the Grotto of the Nativity, where Christ is said to have been born. Latin, Greek and Armenian convents stand near the Church of the Nativity and the cell where St Jerome translated the Bible, as well as his tomb, may be seen.

Bethlehem USA. Industrial town in Pennsylvania on the Lehigh R. 76 km (47 miles)

NNW of Philadelphia. Pop. (1990) 70,419.

Important steel centre (Bethlehem Steel Corporation). Also manufactures textiles and electrical equipment. Seat of the Lehigh University (1866). Famous for an annual music festival and a Bach choir.

Founded (1741) by Moravians and has the Central Moravian Church and a Moravian college.

Bethnal Green England. Former metropolitan borough of E London; from 1965 part of the London borough of Tower Hamlets. Once noted for silk weaving (introduced by Huguenots and spread here from Spitalfields), replaced by cabinet-making and tailoring. Contains part of Victoria Park (88 ha; 217 acres).

Béthune France. Town in the Pas-de-Calais department in the N 34 km (21 miles) WSW of Lille. Pop. (1990) 25,261.

Route centre and market town in a coal-mining and agricultural area. Manufactures beet-sugar and footwear. Severely damaged during German advances in both world wars.

Betsiboka River ➤MAJUNGA.

Betwys-y-Coed Wales. Village in Conwy 26 km (16 miles) S of Llandudno in a picturesque wooded area on the R. Llugwy near its confluence with the R. Conwy. Pop. (1985) 800. Resort. The Swallow Falls are 3 km (2 miles) WNW.

Beuthen ➤BYTOM.

Beveland, North ➤NORTH BEVELAND.

Beveland, South ➤SOUTH BEVELAND.

Beverley England. Town in East Riding of Yorkshire 13 km (8 miles) NNW of Hull. Pop. (1991) 23,632.

Market town. Tanning, brewing, footwear and machinery.

A 13th-cent. minster on the site of a monastery founded by John of Beverley (640–721); a 14th-cent. parish church and a 15th-cent. gateway.

Beverly USA. Industrial town and fishing port on the NE coast of Massachusetts 11 km

(7 miles) NNE of Lynn. Pop. (1980) 37,655.
Manufactures footwear, shoe machinery and clothing.

Beverly Hills USA. Suburb of W Los Angeles, California. Pop. (1980) 32,367. Famous as the home of film stars.

Beverwijk Netherlands. Town in the N Holland province 11 km (7 miles) N of Haarlem. Pop. (1992) 35,185.
Market-gardening. Engineering; jam manufacture, fruit and vegetable canning.

Bewdley England. Market town in Worcestershire on the R. Severn 5 km (3 miles) WSW of Kidderminster. Pop. (1991) 9009.
Manufactures combs.
Ancient Forest of Wyre to the W. Birthplace of Stanley Baldwin, British prime minister (1867–1947).

Bexhill-on-Sea England. Seaside resort in E Sussex 6 km (4 miles) WSW of Hastings. Pop. (1991) 38,905. Inland, in the old town, the Norman church of St Peter.

Bex-les-Bains Switzerland. Spa in the Vaud canton in the SW on the Avançon R. near its confluence with the Rhône. Pop. (1985) 6000. Brine and sulphur baths. Salt mined in the neighbourhood.

Bexley England. London borough (1965) comprising the former municipal boroughs of Bexley and Erith, the urban district of Crayford and the part of the urban districts of Chislehurst and Sidcup N of the A20 road, all in NW Kent. Pop. (1994) 220,400.

Bezhitsa Russia. Formerly (1935–43) Ordzhonikidzegrad. Industrial town on the Dena R. just NW of Bryansk (with which it was incorporated 1956).
Manufactures locomotives, railway rolling-stock, agricultural implements.

Béziers France. Town in the Hérault department on the Orb R. and the Canal du Midi 148 km (92 miles) ESE of Toulouse. Pop. (1990) 72,362.
An important wine-trade centre. Manufactures barrels, corks, insecticides, fertilizers and confectionery.

Scene of a massacre after its capture (1209) by Simon de Montfort (the elder) during the Albigensian crusade. Expanded rapidly after 1850 with the development of viticulture in Languedoc.

Bhadravati India. Industrial town in Karnataka 220 km (137 miles) NW of Bangalore. Pop. (1981) 77,055. Iron and steel manufacture.

Bhagalpur India. Town in Bihar on the Ganges R. 192 km (120 miles) ESE of Patna. Pop. (1991) 253,200.
Trade in rice and oilseeds. Manufactures textiles, esp. silk.

Bhaktapur (Bhadgaon) Nepal. Town 11 km (7 miles) ESE of Katmandu. Pop. (1991) 61,122. Chiefly important as a Hindu religious centre, with many finely carved temples. Founded in the 9th cent.

Bhavnagar (Bhaumagar) India. Port of Gujarat on the Gulf of Cambay 148 km (92 miles) SSW of Ahmadabad. Pop. (1991) 402,300.
Trade in cotton. Manufactures textiles, bricks and tiles, brassware, chemicals, fertilizers, rubber. Other industries inc. cotton-ginning, shipbreaking.

Bhopal India. Cap. of Madhya Pradesh, 169 km (105 miles) ENE of Indore. Pop. (1991) 1,062,800.
Manufactures power generators, steam and hydro-turbines, textiles, plastics, detergents, steel, chemicals, matches and ghee.
Over 2000 killed in the world's worst chemical accident in 1984.

Bhubaneswar India. Cap. of Orissa 29 km (18 miles) S of Cuttack. Pop. (1991) 412,000. Ancient town and place of pilgrimage, famous for its temples, of which the principal example dates from the 11th cent. Utkal University, moved from Cuttack 1962.

Bhutan. State in the East Himalayas bounded by China in the N and on all other sides by India. Area 47,000 sq km (18,150 sq. miles). Pop. (1995) 842,000 (17 per cent urban). Life expectancy, 51 years male, 54 female. Cap. Thimphu. Other town Phuntsholing. Currency: Ngultrum = 100 chetrum. It is entirely mountainous, with some peaks exceeding 6000 m (19,680 ft) and is drained by several tributaries of the Brahmaputra R. Climate varies with altitude and so too does the natural vegetation, with dense forests in the lower valleys and permanent snow on the mountain summits. Land use: forested 66 per cent, meadows and pastures 6 per cent, agricultural and under permanent cultivation 3 per cent. Bhutan was converted to Buddhism in the 8th cent. and there are over 1300 fortress monasteries (*dzongs*). There are also Hindus and Muslims. The dominant people, the Bhotias, are of Tibetan origin, their lang. is a dialect of Tibetan (*Dzongkha*), and their religion, a form of Buddhism, is similar to that of Tibet. Tashi Chho Dzong, the former summer cap., contains the country's principal lamasery with over 1000 priests.

Bhutan is self-sufficient in food; rice, maize and millet are cultivated and ponies are bred. Forestry, metalworking and weaving are among the few minor industries. The small tourist industry is growing.

The original inhabitants were conquered by Tibetan soldiers in the 9th cent. When the Bhotias invaded Cooch Behar (1772), they were driven out by a British force and after further raids part of Southern Bhutan was annexed (1865). By a treaty of 1910 the British government doubled the annual subsidy paid to Bhutan (since 1865), while the latter agreed to be guided by Britain in external affairs; a similar treaty was concluded with India in 1949. From the 16th cent. to 1907 Bhutan was under the dual control of a spiritual ruler (*Dharma*) and a temporal ruler (*Deb Raja*), but since 1907 it has been governed by a hereditary Maharajah of Bhutan (the Dragon King), who has adopted the title of king. Bhutan has no constitution and is an absolute monarchy. Since 1953 there has been a partly elected 150-member National Assembly which exercises some influence on the king and the 9-member Royal Advisory Council and the 6-member

Council of Ministers. There are no legal political parties.

Biafra, Bight of ➤BONNY, BIGHT OF

Bialystok Poland. Cap. of the Bialystok voivodeship in the NE 177 km (110 miles) NE of Warsaw. Pop. (1989) 267,670.

Important industrial centre and railway junction. Manufactures textiles (esp. woollen), agricultural machinery.

Founded 1320. Passed to Prussia (1795) and then to Russia (1807). Returned to Poland 1919.

Biarritz France. Resort in the Pyrénées-Atlantiques department on the Bay of Biscay close to the Spanish frontier. Pop. (1990) 28,890. It has a mild climate and sandy beaches. Developed from a small fishing village into a fashionable resort of international repute under the patronage first of Napoleon III and the Empress Eugénie (France), later of Queen Victoria and Edward VII (Britain).

Bicester England. Market town in Oxfordshire 18 km (11 miles) NNE of Oxford. Pop. (1991) 22,128. Roman remains at nearby Alchester.

Bida ➤DOHA.

Bideford England. Small seaport and holiday resort on the N coast of Devon on the R. Torridge estuary (crossed by an ancient 24-arch bridge). Pop. (1991) 14,328.

Manufactures pottery and other industries inc. boat-building and light engineering.

An active port in the 16th cent., used by Drake, Grenville and Raleigh as starting point of their voyages. Kingsley wrote part of *Westward Ho!* here and the district figures prominently in the novel.

Biel (Bienne) Switzerland. Town in Bern canton at the NE end of L. Biel on the Schuss R. Pop. (1990) 52,736.

Important industrial centre. Noted for watch-making. Also manufactures special steels, machine-tools, cars and paper. Has the Schwab Museum of Archaeology and the West Cantonal Technical Institute. Connected by funicular railway with the resorts of Macolin and Évilard on the Jura slopes.

Biel (Bienne), Lake Switzerland. Lake in the W at a height of 430 m (1410 ft) at the foot of the Jura mountains. Area 41 sq km (16 sq. miles). Drains the Lake of Neuchâtel through the Thièle (Zihl) R. Receives the waters of the Aar R. via the Hagneck Canal and loses them via the Aar Canal to the old bed. Lake dwellings were discovered in the 19th cent.

Bielefeld Germany. Industrial town in North Rhine-Westphalia at the foot of the Teutoburger Wald 93 km (58 miles) WSW of Hanover. Pop. (1990) 320,000. Noted for linen and also manufactures clothing, sewing-machines, bicycles and furniture.

Biella Italy. Industrial town in the Vercelli province in Piedmont 64 km (40 miles) NE of Turin. Pop. (1985) 55,000.

A leading centre of the woollen industry. Also manufactures cotton goods and hats.

Bielsko–Biala Poland. Cap. of the Bielsko-Biala voivodeship in the S 48 km (20 miles) S of Katowice. Pop. (1989) 181,072. Formed (1951) from the towns of Bielsko and Biala Krakowska. An important textile industry since the 16th cent. Also manufactures machinery and paper.

Founded in the 13th cent. Returned to Poland from Austria 1919.

Bienne ➤BIEL.

Bié Plateau ➤NOVA LISBOA; OKAVANGO RIVER.

Biggin Hill ➤ORPINGTON.

Biggleswade England. Town in Bedfordshire on the R. Ivel 14 km (9 miles) ESE of Bedford. Pop. (1991) 12,350. Market-gardening centre.

Bihar India. 1. State in the NE bounded on the N by Nepal. Area 173,877 sq km (67,921 sq. miles). Pop. (1991) 86,338,853. Cap. Patna. The N part is a flat, fertile plain, watered by the Ganges and its tributaries, where rice is by far the most important crop;

the S is hilly and rises in places to over 900 m (2952 ft). Bihar is noted as the main mineral-producing state, yielding principally coal and also iron ore and mica, with two iron and steel works at Jamshedpur and Bokaro. Other important towns are Gaya, Bhagalpur, Darbhanga, Ranchi and Muzaffarpur. Chief lang. Hindi. Formed part of the province of Bihar and Orissa from 1912 to 1936, when Bihar was made a separate province. 2. Town in Bihar state (to which it gave its name) 64 km (40 miles) SE of Patna. Pop. (1991) 200,976.

Trade in rice and oilseeds. Industries inc. oil-refining and the manufacture of fertilizers, automobiles, wire ropes, engineering goods and copper products.

Biisk Russia. Town in Altai Territory near the confluence of the Biya and Katun rivers (which form the Ob R.) 129 km (80 miles) SE of Barnaul. Pop. (1989) 233,000.

Meat-packing, sugar-refining, textiles. Manufactures textiles. Centre of trade between Russia and Mongolia, being the terminus of the railway from Novosibirsk.

Bijagós (Bissagos) Islands Guinea-Bissau. Small archipelago off the Guinea coast. Four large islands (Orango, Formosa, Caravela, Roxa), about 10 smaller islands and many islets; all low-lying and unhealthy. Area 1560 sq km (600 sq. miles). Main products coconuts and rice.

The port of Bolama is on the island of the same name.

Bijapur India. Ancient city in Karnataka 96 km (60 miles) SSW of Sholapur. Pop. (1991) 186,939.

Cotton-ginning, oilseed-milling and other industries. Trade in cotton and grain.

Formerly cap. of the independent kingdom of Bijapur, which fell to Aurangzeb in 1686; never recovered its splendour. Many remains of temples, palaces and mosques, the outstanding building being the Gol Gumbaz, the 17th-cent. tomb of Mohammed Adil Shah, with a large dome 60 m (197 ft) high.

Bikaner India. Industrial and commercial town of Rajasthan on the edge of the Thar

Desert 274 km (170 miles) WNW of Jaipur. Pop. (1991) 416,300.

Manufactures carpets, blankets. Trade in wool and hides. It produces dairy products, gold, clay, sandstone, limestone and has a lignite-based power plant.

Founded (1488) by Bika, a Rajput chief.

Bikini Atoll (Marshall Islands) S Pacific Ocean. Now uninhabited atoll in the Ralik Chain. Scene of US atom-bomb tests (1946) after removal of the pop.

Bilá Hora (White Mountain) Czechoslovakia. Hill (380 m; 1246 ft) in Bohemia 6 km (4 miles) ESE of the centre of Prague. Scene of the defeat of Bohemian forces under Frederick V by a combined Austrian and Bavarian army (1620). Bohemia passed to Austria; independence was not regained till 1918.

Bilaspur India. Town in Madhya Pradesh 105 km (65 miles) NNE of Raipur. Pop. (1991) 192,396.

Railway junction. Trade centre. Rice-milling.

Bilbao Spain. Cap. of the Vizcaya province near the mouth of the Nervión R. (Bay of Biscay). Pop. (1991) 368,710. One of Spain's major seaports. Accessible to large freight steamers via the canalized river; the outer harbour is protected by breakwaters. Noted since the Middle Ages for the manufacture of iron goods, esp. swords; the iron and steel works are still the most important in Spain.

Exports iron ore, lead, wine. Shipbuilding, fishing, oil-refining. Manufactures railway rolling-stock, tyres, machinery, chemicals, paper and cement. The old town, on the right bank of the river, is connected with the new town by several bridges. The Guggenheim Museum, in an exciting modern building, opened in 1997.

Suffered severely in the wars with France. Besieged in the Carlist Wars (1835–6, 1874). Seat of the Basque autonomous government (1936) during the Spanish Civil War. Taken by the Franco forces 1937.

Billingham England. Industrial town 5 km

(3 miles) NNE of Stockton-on-Tees. Pop. (1991) 36,876.

Important centre of the chemical and petrochemical industry, with one of the world's largest plants. Has grown rapidly from a small village. In the town, on the Tees estuary, is Port Clarence.

Billings USA. Town in Montana on the Yellowstone R. 290 km (180 miles) ESE of Helena. Pop. (1990) 85,151. In an irrigated region.

Trade in wool, livestock and beet-sugar. Large sugar refinery. Meat-packing and flour-milling.

Billingsgate England. Formerly chief fish market of London, just below London Bridge on the N bank of the R. Thames, on the site of one of the gates of Roman London's river-wall. Originally a general port, in 1699 it became a free port for fish. The fish market is now at the Isle of Dogs.

Billiton (Belitung) Indonesia. Island between Bangka and SW Borneo. Area 4817 sq km (1860 sq. miles). Pop. (1985) 102,375. Chief town and port Tangjungpandan. Important mainly for its tin mines, worked largely by Chinese.

Bilma (Kawar) Niger. Town in a small Saharan oasis 1290 km (800 sq. miles) S of Tripoli (Libya). Pop. 1200. On caravan routes from Tripoli to L. Chad and to Agadès. Considerable trade in salt, obtained from the salt lakes. Dates also produced in the oasis. Mean annual rainfall 2 cm (¾ in.).

Biloxi USA. Fishing port and seaside resort in SE Mississippi on a peninsula on Mississippi Sound (Gulf of Mexico). Pop. (1984) 48,700.

Fish-canning and boatbuilding.

Bilston England. Industrial town in West Midlands near Wolverhampton.

Manufactures iron and steel products, machinery, enamelled goods and pottery.

Bingen Germany. Town in the Rhineland-Palatinate on the Rhine at the mouth of the

Nahe R. just above the Bingerloch whirl-pool. Pop. (1986) 22,100.

Tourist and commercial centre. Important wine trade. Nearby, on a rock in the Rhine, is the Mauseturm (Mouse-tower), where legend says that Archbishop Hatto II was devoured by mice for ill-treating his subjects.

Binghamton USA. Industrial town in S New York State at the confluence of the Chenango and Susquehanna rivers 124 km (77 miles) SSW of Utica. Pop. (1990) 53,008.

Manufactures aircraft components, cameras, footwear and machinery.

Bingley England. Town in West Yorkshire on the R. Aire 8 km (5 miles) NW of Bradford. Pop. (1991) 19,585.

Manufactures woollens, worsteds, textile machinery and paper.

Bintan ▶RIOUW ARCHIPELAGO.

Bío-Bío River Chile. River 354 km (220 miles) long, rising in the Andes near the Chile–Argentina frontier, flowing NW, and entering the Pacific near Concepción. The upper tributaries provide hydroelectric power.

Bioko Equatorial Guinea. Formerly Fernando Póo and Macías Nguema. Volcanic island in the Gulf of Guinea, divided into Bioko Norte and Bioko Sur, 32 km (20 miles) from the Cameroon coast. Area 2018 sq km (779 sq. miles). Pop. (1987) 77,920. Cap. Malabo. Rises to 2852 m (9355 ft). Hot, humid climate; dense vegetation. Chief product and export cacao. Originally named after Fernãon do Po, the Portuguese discoverer. Ceded by Portugal (with Annobon island) to Spain 1778. Used by the British as a base for suppression of the slave trade 1827–44, and it then reverted to Spain.

Birdum Australia. Small town in the Northern Territory 450 km (280 miles) SE of Darwin, terminus of the railway therefrom, on the Stuart Highway. Centre of an extensive cattle-ranching area.

Birkenhead England. Seaport on the Wirral peninsula in Merseyside on the S bank of the R. Mersey opposite Liverpool, with which it is connected by rail (1886) and road (1934) tunnels and ferry. Pop. (1991) 93,087.

Exports flour, machinery. Imports grain and cattle. The flour mills are among the world's largest. Other industries inc. boiler-making, engineering, food-processing. Its great expansion dates from the opening of the docks (1847).

Birmingham England. City in West Midlands situated near the geographical centre of the country 177 km (110 miles) NW of London. It is the meeting-point of important railways, roads and canals. Pop. (1991) 934,900. A city well-endowed with public parks, gardens and recreation grounds but, owing to the fact that its main expansion was due to the Industrial Revolution, the majority of the leading buildings date only from the 19th cent. The oldest church, for example, is St Martin's, originally erected in the 13th cent. but completely rebuilt in 1873. There is an 18th-cent. Anglican cathedral with stained-glass windows by Burne-Jones and a Roman Catholic cathedral. Birmingham University, main buildings at Edgbaston, dates from 1900; there are now 2 other universities, Aston University (1966) and the University of Central England (1992); the King Edward VI grammar school (1552). Other noteworthy buildings inc. the Town Hall (1834), where Mendelssohn conducted the first performance of *Elijah* (1847), the City Museum and Art Gallery (1855), and the Museum of Science and Industry. Recent developments have been the National Exhibition Centre, the Aston Science Park, the International Convention Centre, the City of Birmingham Symphony Orchestra Centre and the National Indoor Arena.

Although manufacturing has declined it still can claim to manufacture 'everything from a pin to a motor car'. Among its innumerable products are motor vehicles and their components, aerospace components, bicycles, firearms and ammunition, chemicals, electrical and electronic equipment, machine-tools, plastic goods, paint, wire, nails and screws, jewellery and chocolate.

At the end of the 11th cent. Birmingham was a town of no great significance, but two cent. later it had become an important market town, developed around the junction of several roads at the Bull Ring. In the 16th cent. Leland wrote that 'a great parte of the towne is mayntayned by smithes', who (he adds) obtained their iron and coal from Staffordshire and Warwickshire. Standing on the edge of the Black Country, Birmingham grew and prospered with the Industrial Revolution; the Soho ironworks of Watt and Boulton may still be seen. Yet it was not incorporated until the 19th cent. (1838). It became a centre of nonconformism, as exemplified by Joseph Priestley and others, and continued in the late 19th cent. by one of its most distinguished MPs, John Bright. During this period the Chamberlain and the Cadbury families, in their different spheres, contributed much to its development. In 1889 it was made a city; in 1897 its chief magistrate was given the title of Lord Mayor. Its limits were considerably extended in 1911 and again in 1928 and 1931, until the area amounted to 207 sq km (80 sq. miles).

Birmingham USA. Industrial town in Alabama near the S end of the Appalachian mountains. Pop. (1990) 265,968.

Local deposits of coal, iron ore and limestone provide raw materials for the important iron and steel industry. Also manufactures cement, cotton goods and chemicals. Important rail and air route centre.

Birobidzhan Russia. Cap. of the Jewish Autonomous Region in Khabarovsk Territory on the Trans-Siberian Railway 160 km (100 miles) WNW of Khabarovsk. Pop. (1989) 82,000.

Sawmilling and woodworking. Manufactures clothing and footwear.

Birr Ireland. Town in W Co. Offaly on the R. Brosna. Pop. (1986) 3417. Market town. Brewing. In Birr Castle William Parsons, 3rd Earl of Rosse, installed his telescope (1845).

Biscay, Bay of ►BAY OF BISCAY.

Bisceglie Italy. Seaport in the Bari province in Apulia on the Adriatic Sea 35 km (22 miles) WNW of Bari. Pop. (1981) 45,899.

Trade in wine and olives. Engineering and sawmilling. Manufactures furniture. Cathedral (11th-cent.).

Bischoff, Mount (Tasmania) Australia. Tin-mining centre in Tasmania near Waratah 145 km (90 miles) W of Launceston. Production began in 1870.

Bishkek Kyrgyzstan. Formerly Frunze. Cap. of Kyrgyzstan in the Chu R. valley 193 km (120 miles) WSW of Alma-Ata on a branch line of the Turksib Railway. Pop. (1990) 623,000.

Industrial and commercial centre in a fertile, irrigated region. Manufactures agricultural machinery, textiles and other industries inc. meat-packing, flour-milling and tanning.

Founded as a fort (Pishpek) in the 19th cent.; renamed (1925) after M. V. Frunze, the revolutionary leader (1885–1925), who was born here and again renamed in 1990.

Bishop Auckland England. Town in Durham near the confluence of the R. Gaunless with the R. Wear 14 km (9 miles) SSW of Durham. Pop. (1991) 23,154.

Light engineering and ironworks in the neighbourhood.

Seat of the bishops of Durham since the 12th cent.

Bishop's Stortford England. Town in E Hertfordshire on the R. Stort 19 km (12 miles) ENE of Hertford. Pop. (1991) 27,874.

Brewing. Manufactures matches, electrical equipment. Nearby is Stansted airport.

Remains of a Norman castle, formerly belonging to the bishops of London, with a dungeon (the 'Bishop's Hole') long used as an ecclesiastical prison. Birthplace of Cecil Rhodes, the South African statesman (1853–1902).

Biskra Algeria. Town and oasis 193 km (120 miles) SSW of Constantine. Pop. (1987) 128,280.

Vast numbers of date palms; an important

date market. Also olive and pomegranate trees. Connected by rail with Constantine and Touggourt. Hot in summer, but a popular resort owing to the cool, sunny winters and the very light annual rainfall (about 18 cm; 7 ins.). In a small oasis 19 km (12 miles) SE is the mosque with the tomb of Sidi Okbar, the Arab leader who conquered N Africa for Islam and was killed by the Berber in AD 682.

Bisley England. Village in Surrey 5 km (3 miles) WNW of Woking. Venue of the annual meeting of the National Rifle Association since 1890.

Bismarck USA. State cap. of North Dakota on the Missouri R. where it is crossed by the Northern Pacific railway route to the W. Pop. (1990) 49,256.

Market centre for the agricultural produce of the surrounding spring-wheat area.

Bismarck Archipelago SW Pacific Ocean. Volcanic group of islands E of New Guinea in Papua New Guinea. Area 51,800 sq km (20,000 sq. miles). Pop. 218,000 (mostly Melanesians). Largest island New Britain; others inc. New Ireland, Lavongai, Admiralty Islands. Mountainous, with active volcanoes and densely forested. Produces copra, cacao and some copper and gold.

Became a German protectorate (1884) and part of the Australian mandated territory of New Guinea (1921).

Bissagos Islands ►BIJAGÓS ISLANDS.

Bissau (Bissão) Guinea-Bissau. Cap. and chief seaport on the estuary of the Geba R. Pop. (1991) 197,610.

Exports copra, palm oil and rice.

Slave-trade centre from the late 17th to the late 19th cent.

Bisutun ►BEHISTUN.

Bitola (Turkish **Monastir**) Macedonia. Town 113 km (70 miles) S of Skoplje. Pop. (1994) 75,386.

Agricultural centre. Carpet-making and tanning.

Nearby was the ancient Heraclea Lync-

estis. Captured from the Turks by the Serbs and incorporated in Serbia in 1913.

Bitonto Italy. Ancient Butuntum. Town in the Bari province in Apulia 16 km (10 miles) W of Bari. Pop. (1985) 44,000. Market town. Produces wine and olive oil.

Romanesque cathedral (12th/13th-cent.).

Bitter Lakes ►SUEZ CANAL.

Bizerta (Fr. **Bizerte**) Tunisia. Seaport and naval base on the Mediterranean. Pop. (1984) 94,509. On the canalized channel which forms the outlet of the Lake of Bizerta to the sea, with good outer and inner harbours. At the SW corner of the lake is the naval base of Sidi Abdallah. After cent. of neglect, the port was reopened (1895) by the French. Taken by the Germans in World War II, heavily bombed, almost completely destroyed and recaptured by the Allies in 1943. Post-war reconstruction was rapid. After Tunisian independence France retained the naval base; this caused friction between the French and the Tunisians, and fighting in 1961. After UN discussions, Tunisia agreed to temporary French retention of the base. The first steel works in Tunisia were inaugurated at Menzel Bourguiba (formerly Ferryville), near Bizerta, in 1966.

Björneborg ►PORI.

Blackburn England. Town in Lancashire 13 km (8 miles) E of Preston on the Leeds–Liverpool Canal. Pop. (1991) 105,994.

Became a leading centre of cotton-weaving with the invention (1764) of the spinning-jenny by James Hargreaves (a native of the town). Also manufactures textile machinery, chemicals, paint, paper, electrical and leather goods. Brewing and engineering.

Black Country England. Industrialized region in the West Midlands. The name derives from the smoke and soot formerly emitted by the many foundries and furnaces. Towns inc. Wolverhampton, Walsall, West Bromwich and Wednesbury.

Blackdown Hills England. Sandstone hills

in Dorset and Somerset rising to over 300 m (984 ft).

Black Forest (Ger. **Schwarzwald**) Germany. Thickly wooded mountainous district in Baden-Württemberg, separated from Switzerland by the R. Rhine, rising to 1493 m (4897 ft) in the Feldberg. Area 4662 sq km (1800 sq. miles). Source of the Danube, the Neckar and various tributaries of the Rhine.

Manufactures cuckoo-clocks, musical boxes and wooden toys, as an adjunct to the tourist trade.

Blackfriars England. District of the City of London near where the Fleet Ditch enters the Thames. Linked with Southwark by Blackfriars Bridge. The name derives from the Dominican priory (1238) destroyed in the Great Fire (1666).

Blackheath England. Residential district of SE London in the London boroughs of Lewisham and Greenwich, formerly a heath crossed by the Roman road from Dover to London. Wat Tyler, leader of the Peasants' Revolt (1381) and Jack Cade, leader of another peasant rebellion (1450), mustered their forces here. England's first game of golf (brought in by James I and his Scots courtiers) was played on Blackheath (1608). The present open space (108 ha; 266 acres), a remnant of the former heath, is shared by Lewisham and Greenwich.

Black Hills USA. Isolated group of mountains on the borders of SW South Dakota and NE Wyoming, rising in Harney Peak to 2209 m (7246 ft) and generally about 600 m (1968 ft) above the surrounding plains. Much of the area is now a national park. In 1874 gold was discovered and it became the scene of a gold rush. A remarkable feature is a group of gigantic sculptures carved from the granite side of Mt Rushmore.

Black Mountain Wales. Ridge on the border between Carmarthenshire and Powys, rising to 803 m (2634 ft) in Carmarthen.

Black Mountains Wales. Range in SE Powys on the borders with Monmouthshire and Herefordshire, rising to 811 m (2660 ft) in Waun Fach.

Blackpool England. Town and unitary authority on the Irish Sea. Pop. (1991) 146,282. One of Britain's leading holiday resorts. Climate bracing. Sandy beaches, promenades, swimming baths, cinemas, theatres, aquarium, famous illuminations and a tower, 159 m (522 ft) modelled on the Eiffel Tower in Paris. Conferences of various kinds are held here.

Black Sea (Euxine Sea) Europe/Asia. Ancient Pontus Euxinus. Large inland sea between Europe and Asia, bounded by the USSR (N and E), Turkey (S) and Bulgaria and Romania (W). Area 461,000 sq km (178,000 sq. miles) (excluding the Sea of Azov). Connected to the Aegean Sea and the Mediterranean in the SW by the Bosporus, the Sea of Marmara and the Dardanelles, and with the Sea of Azov in the NE by the Kerch Strait. In general the E and S coasts are backed by mountains; the W and N coasts are mostly low-lying, with several extensive *limans* or lagoons at river mouths. The many rivers emptying into it (inc. the Danube, the Dniester, the S Bug and the Dnieper, and the Don and the Kuban into the Sea of Azov) give the surface waters a low salinity. A unique feature is that below about 150 m (492 ft) it is stagnant, charged with sulphuretted hydrogen and without any marine life. Almost tideless, with an outward surface flow through the Bosporus. Principal fisheries in the N and W: the varied catch inc. anchovy, sardine, mackerel and tunny. Virtually a Turkish lake from the 15th to the 19th cent. With the collapse of the Ottoman Empire and the growth of Russian power in the area, it increased in importance as an international trade highway. Turkey's right to fortify the Bosporus and the Dardanelles was removed by the Treaty of Lausanne (1923), but restored by the Montreux Convention (1936).

Blackwater River Ireland. River 167 km (104 miles) long, rising near Castleisland in

Co. Kerry, flowing E through Co. Cork to Co. Waterford, turning S and entering the Atlantic at Youghal. Noted for trout and salmon.

Blackwater River Ireland/Northern Ireland. River 80 km (50 miles) long, rising near Fivemiletown in Tyrone (NI), flowing generally E and N as the SE border with Monaghan (Ireland) and Armagh (NI), and entering the SW end of Lough Neagh.

Blaenau Gwent Wales. County borough created 1996. Pop. (1994) 73,000. An inland valley containing Abertillery and Ebbw Vale.

Blaenavon Wales. Town in Torfaen 10 km (6 miles) NNW of Pontypool. Pop. (1991) 6066. Former coalmining area. Iron and steel works.

Blagoveshchensk Russia. Town and river port in the Amur Region on the Amur R. at the confluence with the Zeya R. on a branch of the Trans-Siberian Railway. Pop. (1989) 206,000.
   Flour-milling and sawmilling. Manufactures machinery, furniture and footwear.

Blair Atholl Scotland. Village and resort in Perth and Kinross at the confluence of the Tilt and the Garry rivers 10 km (6 miles) NW of Pitlochry. Pop. (1985) 1100. Whisky-distilling.
   Blair Castle, seat of the dukes of Atholl, was built in the 13th cent. and restored in the 19th.

Blairgowrie and Rattray Scotland. Two small towns in Perth and Kinross on opposite banks of the R. Ericht, linked by a bridge and amalgamated in 1929. Pop. (1991) 8004.
   Market centre in a fruit-growing region (esp. raspberries).

Blanc (Blanco), Cape Mauritania. Headland at the S end of the frontier between Spanish Sahara and Mauritania. Port Étienne stands on the E coast of the peninsula.

Blanc, Cape Tunisia. Headland on the Mediterranean coast of N Tunisia 8 km (5 miles) NNW of Bizerta. Often considered the northernmost point of Africa (though

the neighbouring coast extends slightly farther N).

Blanc, Mont ►MONT BLANC.

Blanco, Cape ►BLANC, CAPE (MAURITANIA).

Blandford (Blandford Forum) England. Small town in Dorset on the R. Stour 35 km (22 miles) SW of Salisbury. Pop. (1991) 8880.
   Market town in a dairy and sheep farming region.
   Almost completely destroyed by fire in 1731, it was rebuilt in uniform Georgian style.

Blantyre Malawi. Town in the Shire highlands at 1080 m (3542 ft). Pop. (1987) 331,589. On the railway from Beira to L. Malawi. Chief commercial centre. Headquarters of the missionary societies. Founded 1876, when the Church of Scotland Mission building was erected. Named Blantyre after the missionary–explorer, David Livingstone's birthplace.

Blantyre Scotland. Town in North Lanarkshire 13 km (8 miles) SE of Glasgow. Pop. (1991) 18,484. In a coalmining region. Engineering. Inc. the village of Low Blantyre, birthplace of David Livingstone (1813–73), with a Livingstone museum.

Blarney Ireland. Village in Co. Cork 5 km (3 miles) WNW of Cork. Pop. (1986) 1952. Woollen mills.
   Ruins of the 15th-cent. Blarney Castle contain the famous Blarney Stone, kissing which is reputed to endow one with 'blarney', the gift of persuasive speech.

Blasket Islands. Group of rocky islands off Slea Head in Co. Kerry. Pop. (1986) 4. The people used to subsist mainly on fishing.

Blaydon England. Town in Tyne and Wear on the R. Tyne 6 km (4 miles) W of Newcastle-upon-Tyne. Pop. (1991) 15,510.
   Former coalmining centre. Manufactures coal by-products, firebricks, bottle glass. Immortalized in the song *Blaydon Races*.

Bled, Lake Slovenia. Lake in NW. Centre of summer and winter resort.

Blenheim (Ger. **Blindheim**) Germany. Village in W Bavaria 48 km (30 miles) NE of Ulm. Pop. (1985) 1000. Near Blenheim took place an important battle (1704) in the War of the Spanish Succession, when the English and the Austrians, under Marlborough and Prince Eugene, defeated the French and the Bavarians, under Marshals Tallard and Marsin.

Blenheim Palace England. Seat of the dukes of Marlborough, near Woodstock in Oxfordshire. Presented to the 1st Duke of Marlborough, for his many victories in the French wars and named in honour of his greatest victory, the Battle of Blenheim. Designed by Vanbrugh, it was begun in 1705, but Marlborough did not see the work completed. Birthplace of Sir Winston Churchill (1874–1965), who is buried in the nearby village churchyard at Bladon.

Bletchley England. Town in NE Buckinghamshire 16 km (10 miles) E of Buckingham, inc. the small town of Fenny Stratford. Pop. (1991) 41,435.
Railway junction. Market town. Engineering and brickmaking.

Blida (El Djezair) Algeria. Town in the S of the fertile Mitidja plain 48 km (30 miles) SW of Algiers. Pop. (1983) 191,314. On the railway between Algiers and Oran.
Vineyards, citrus orchards and olive groves in the region. Considerable trade in oranges and wine. Flour-milling. Manufactures olive oil and soap.
Almost destroyed by an earthquake in 1825, rebuilt and again damaged by earthquake 1867.

Block Island USA. Island 11 km (7 miles) long off the S coast of Rhode Island, from which it is separated by Block Island Sound. Summer resort, catering esp. for yachtsmen and deep-sea fishermen.

Blocksberg ►BROCKEN.

Bloemfontein South Africa. Cap. of Free State and judicial cap. of the Republic (since 1910), 480 km (300 miles) WNW of Durban at a height of 1400 m (4592 ft). Pop. (1991, urban area) 300,150.
Trading centre for much of the Free State and Lesotho. Railway engineering and meat-canning. Manufactures furniture. Because of its central position it is the venue of agricultural, religious, political and other conferences. Also an educational centre, seat of the Free State University (1855). Because of the altitude and clear air, the US universities of Harvard and Michigan have built observatories nearby. Founded 1846.

Blois France. Prefecture of the Loir-et-Cher department on the Loire R. 53 km (33 miles) SW of Orléans. Pop. (1990) 51,549.
Market town. Trade in wine, brandy and grain. Manufactures furniture and vinegar.
The château, part of which dates from the 13th cent., is one of the most famous in the middle Loire valley.

Bloomfield USA. Formerly Wardsesson. Residential and industrial town in New Jersey just NNW of Newark. Pop. (1990) 45,006.
Manufactures metal and electrical goods, pharmaceutical products.

Bloomington (Illinois) USA. Industrial town 193 km (120 miles) SW of Chicago in the Corn Belt. Pop. (1990) 46,600.
Railway engineering and other industries. Seat of the Illinois Wesleyan University (1850).

Bloomington (Indiana) USA. Industrial town 76 km (47 miles) SSW of Indianapolis. Pop. (1990) 60,333.
Manufactures furniture, gloves and electronic equipment. Seat of Indiana University (1838).

Bloomsbury England. District in central London, from 1965 in the Greater London borough of Camden. Famous for its many squares (Bedford, Brunswick, Gordon, Mecklenburgh, Russell, Tavistock) and for the 'Bloomsbury School' of writers and artists in the 1930s. Seat of the British Museum, much of the University of London, the Royal Academy of Dramatic Art, the headquarters of the YMCA. Home of many famous 19th and early 20th cent. artists and authors. Dickens lived in Doughty Street (now a museum) 1837–9 and Disraeli was born in Theobald's Road (1804). The grounds of the famous 18th-cent. Foundling Hospital are now public gardens named after the founder, Thomas Coram (1668–1751).

Bluefields Nicaragua. Chief Caribbean port near the mouth of the Bluefields (Escondido) R. Pop. (1985) 18,000.
Exports hardwoods and bananas. Outport El Bluff.

Blue Mountains Australia ➤GREAT DIVIDING RANGE.

Blue Mountains Jamaica. Range in the E of average height about 1050 m (3444 ft), but rising to 2256 m (7400 ft) in Blue Mountain Peak. Thickly wooded and picturesque; a popular tourist area. Coffee grown on the slopes.

Blue Ridge Mountains USA. Range of the Appalachian mountains extending SW–NE 1050 km (650 miles) from N Georgia to the Maryland border. Average height 600–1200 m (1968–3936 ft), rising to 2039 m (6688 ft) in Mt Mitchell. Attractive scenery; a popular tourist area with many resorts.

Blumenau Brazil. Market town in Santa Catarina state on the Itajaí R. 177 km (110 miles) S of Curitiba. Pop. (1990) 206,000.

Blyth England. Town in Northumberland at the mouth of the R. Blyth 18 km (11 miles) NNE of Newcastle. Pop. (1991) 35,100.
Seaport. Former coalmining centre. Shipbuilding. Fishing.

Bo Sierra Leone. Cap. of province situated ESE of Freetown. Pop. (1988) 36,000.
Trading centre for palm oil and kernels, cacao and coffee.

Boa Vista ➤RORAIMA.

Bobo-Dioulasso Burkina Faso. Commercial town in the SW 338 km (210 miles)

WSW of Ouagadougou on the railway to the latter from Abidjan (Côte d'Ivoire). Pop. (1985) 231,162.
Goldmining. Trade in groundnuts and shea nuts.

Bobriki ➤NOVMOSKOVSK.

Bobruisk ➤BABRUYSK.

Bocholt Germany. Industrial town in North Rhine-Westphalia 48 km (30 miles) N of Duisburg near the Dutch frontier. Pop. (1986) 66,400.
Manufactures textiles and machinery.

Bochum Germany. Industrial town in North Rhine-Westphalia in the Ruhr district. Pop. (1990) 397,400.
Coalmining. Manufactures steel, mining equipment, chemicals, television sets and textiles.

Bodele Depression ➤CHAD, LAKE.

Bodensee ➤CONSTANCE, LAKE.

Bodmin England. Market town in Cornwall, 43 km (27 miles) WNW of Plymouth. Pop. (1991) 12,553.
China clay and light engineering. To the NE is Bodmin Moor, which rises to 419 m (1374 ft) in Brown Willy.

Bodø Norway. Town near the Lofoten Islands in the N. Pop. (1990) 30,252.
Fish-processing, brewing. N terminus of the railway. The port handles metals, marble and slate.

Bodrum Turkey. Ancient Halicarnassus. Town on the Aegean coast. Resort and fishing. Crusader castle (15th cent.).

Boeotia Greece. *Nome* in the Attica peninsula, bounded on the S by the Gulf of Corinth. Area 3211 sq km (1225 sq. miles). Pop. (1991) 134,034. Cap. Levadia.
Agriculture is important in the fertile valleys. Wheat, wine and olives produced; livestock reared.
The ancient Boeotian League was a confederacy of cities led by Thebes in the 6th cent. BC and inc. Orchomenus and Plataea.

Bofors ➤KARLSKOGA.

Bognor Regis England. Seaside resort in W Sussex·21 km (13 miles) W of Worthing on the English Channel. Pop. (1991) 56,744. Pleasure gardens, promenade. The suffix Regis was added after King George V's convalescence in Bognor (1929).

Bogor Indonesia. Formerly Buitenzorg. Resort 48 km (30 miles) S of Jakarta at a height of 250 m (820 ft). Pop. (1985) 250,000. It was the residence of the governor-general of the Dutch East Indies and has noted botanical gardens (1817). Seat of part of the University of Indonesia.

Bogotá Colombia. Cap. of Colombia and of the Cundinamarca department on the slopes of the fertile Cundinamarca basin in the E Cordillera at a height of 2642 m (8666 ft). Pop. (1992) 4,819,676. Remote from the rest of the country, but served by regular airlines, by highways from Caracas (via Cúcuta) and from the W coast (via Girardot in the Magdalena valley) and by light railways. Mild climate with even temperatures. A suburban sprawl surrounds the old colonial heart of the city and broad avenues cut across narrow colonial streets.

Manufactures texiles, tobacco products, chemicals and food products.

University (1572). Originally a centre of Chibcha culture. Founded (1538) by the Spaniards as Santa Fé de Bogotá; the name derives from Bacatá, the Chibcha name for the district. Became the cap. of the Spanish viceroyalty of New Granada and an important cultural centre.

Bogue Islets ➤MONTEGO BAY.

Bohemia (Ger. **Böhmen**; Czech **Čechy**) Czech Republic. Former kingdom in central Europe, bounded by the Sudeten Mountains, the Moravian Heights, the Böhmerwald and the Erzgebirge. Area 52,064 sq km (20,102 sq. miles). A province of Czechoslovakia 1918–49; then administratively divided into regions. Mainly a plateau cut by the Elbe (Labe) and the Vltava rivers and their tributaries. Many fertile areas, esp. in the river valleys.

Produces cereals, sugar-beet, potatoes, fruit, hops. The chief wealth is mineral: one of Europe's main sources of uranium; also coal, lignite, iron ore, graphite, silver. Metallurgical, textile and other industries in Prague, Plzeň (Pilsen; world-famous for beer), and a number of towns along the S foot of the Erzgebirge, e.g. Ústi nad Labem, Most. The watering-places of Karlovy Vary (Karlsbad) and Mariánske Lazné (Marienbad) are in the NW.

Bohemian Forest ➤BÖHMERWALD.

Böhmerwald (Bohemian Forest; Czech **Český Les)** Czech Republic/Germany. Forested mountain range 240 km (150 miles) long, forming the frontier between Czech Republic and Bavaria (Germany), rising to 1467 m (4812 ft) in Mt Arber. Divided by the Furth pass into a NW portion and a higher SE portion. Little agriculture. Coal, lignite and graphite deposits. Main product timber.

Bois de Boulogne France. A park and fashionable district in W Paris, extending from the former fortifications to the Seine R. Area 851 ha (2102 acres). The name derives from Boulogne-sur-Seine (now Boulogne-Billancourt). Contains the race-courses of Auteuil and Longchamp, and the Jardins d'Acclimatation for plants and animals. Given to the city by Napoleon III when he became emperor (1852).

Boise USA. State cap. of Idaho on the Boise R. in the SW. Pop. (1990) 125,738.

Commercial and financial centre, marketing agricultural produce. Food-processing and other industries.

Bokhara ➤BUKHARA.

Boksburg South Africa. Industrial town in Gauteng 21 km (13 miles) E of Johannesburg at a height of 1630 m (5346 ft). Pop. (1985) 151,000.

Chief centre of the E Rand goldmining industry. Manufactures railway and electrical equipment, soap and pottery.

Bolama ➤BIJAGÓS ISLANDS.

Bolivia

Bolan Pass Pakistan. Pass about 96 km (60 miles) long through the Brahui Range in W Pakistan, used by the railway and the road between Sibi and Quetta. Rises to nearly 1800 m (5904 ft). In the past it was an important route into India from the NW.

Bolivia. Completely land-locked republic of central South America, bounded by Brazil in the N and E, Paraguay and Argentina in the S and Chile and Peru in the W. Area 1,098,581 sq km (424,164 sq. miles). Pop. (1996) 7,592,000 (58 per cent urban). Life expectancy, 61 years male, 66 female. Cap. Sucre (Judicial), La Paz (Administrative). Other cities Santa Cruz, El Atto, Cochabamba, Orura. Currency: Boliviano = 100 centavos. Bolivia is mountainous with difficult communications. The mountain system of the Andes reaches a width of 640 km (400 miles) (W). Between the West Cordillera, studded with large volcanoes along the Chile frontier, and the East Cordillera is the open, wind-swept and treeless Altiplano, a high tableland with large lakes (Titicaca, Poopó), salt flats and loose, dry, porous soil. The high Cordillera Real has forested slopes in the N and drops steeply to the E lowlands. The S slopes are drier and are cut by the tributaries of the Río Grande, Mamoré and Pilcomayo rivers. In the NE are tropical rainforests; in the SE a more open woodland alternates with savannah, swamp and scrub. The low-lying areas in the Amazon basin are warm and damp throughout the year with heavy rainfall from November to March. The Altiplano is dry May–November. Land use: forested 54 per cent, meadows and pastures 24 per cent, agricultural and under permanent cultivation 2 per cent. About 85 per cent of believers are Roman Catholic. Official and commercial lang. is Spanish; the Indians speak Aymará, Quechua and Guaraní. The ethnic composition is mestizo 31 per cent, Quechua 25 per cent, Aymará 17 per cent, white 15 per cent.

Deficient in food production; minerals (esp. tin) are the main resources. The people are divided into widely differing strata, the bulk being illiterate and poor. Handicapped by difficulties of communication and by the fact that most of the pop. live on the Altiplano, where agriculture is unrewarding. The main industry is mining, for which the Indians supply cheap labour and have been long exploited. Tin (the most important mineral), petroleum, antimony, zinc and some decreasing silver are the chief exports. The main manufactures are foodstuffs, tobacco and textiles. About 40 per cent of the pop. is engaged in agriculture. The region E of the Andes produces sugar-cane, rice, coffee and other food crops, but the cost of transporting them to the Altiplano is great and the potentialities of these more fertile areas remain underdeveloped. The Indians of the Altiplano (physically adapted to life at high altitudes by a remarkable lung development) are backward, superstitious and firmly attached to their traditional way of life; efforts to educate them and persuade them to move to more productive areas make slow progress. Their chief crops are potatoes and barley. The illegal production of cocaine probably involves 500,000 people in the drugs trade.

The medieval Tiahuanaco culture around L. Titicaca was followed by small kingdoms of Aymará people, who were conquered by the Incas of Peru after 1450. Quechua, the lang. of the Inca, is still spoken by large minorities in Bolivia today. Spain invaded the empire in 1532 and in 1545 discovered the great silver-ore mountain Cerro Rico that overshadows the city of Potosí. Until about 1700 the wealth extracted was astonishing, matched only by the death rate among Indian miners. Sucre, one of Bolívar's generals, freed the colony from Spain (1825) and named it after the great liberator. But it remained in the grip of rapacious and incompetent rulers and lost land to Chile, Paraguay and Brazil. In the war with Chile (1879–83) it lost its strip of Pacific coast, but in return Chile built the railway from La Paz to Arica, where Bolivia has the use of a free port which has become her main export outlet. Part of the northern territory of Acre was lost to Brazil (1903) and most of the Chaco passed to Paraguay (1938) after a war which left both countries exhausted. World War II brought wealth to the mine-owners, but no general prosperity; social unrest and rebellion grew. The National Revolutionary Movement came to power in 1952 and nationalized the tin mines (both those of the Bolivian millionaire Patiño and those belonging to foreigners) and brought about other social and land reforms, but the country remained dangerously dependent on tin and agricultural production did not rise sufficiently to offset this.

The country is divided administratively into 9 departments: La Paz, Cochabamba, Potosí, Santa Cruz, Chuquisaca, Tarija, Oruro, Beni, Pando. The last period of military rule ended in 1982 and since independence Bolivia has had 189 *coups*. There is a 27-member Senate with 3 members from each department and a 130-member Chamber of Deputies elected for 4 years. Voting is compulsory. The President is elected by universal suffrage.

Bollington England. Town in E Cheshire 5 km (3 miles) NNE of Macclesfield. Pop. (1991) 6767.

Textile printing and finishing, and dyeworks.

Bologna Italy. Ancient Bononia. Cap. of Bologna province in Emilia-Romagna on a fertile plain at the foot of the Apennines on the Aemilian Way 84 km (52 miles) N of Florence. Pop. (1992) 401,308.

Industries inc. engineering, electrical equipment and food-processing. Well known for pasta and salami.

Arcaded streets and historic buildings give it a medieval appearance. The Cathedral of San Pietro (first built in 910 and twice rebuilt) and the 13th-cent. Church of San Francesco were severely damaged in World War II. Many other fine churches (e.g. the great Gothic church of San Petronio), palaces and the early-12th-cent. leaning towers of Asinelli and Garisenda. In the 2nd cent. BC Bononia was made a Roman colony. Became a free city in the 12th cent. In the Middle Ages a leading centre of learning in Europe. The university (founded 1200) was distinguished for the early study of human anatomy. Dante and Petrarch were among the students. Galvani (1737–98), a native of Bologna, lectured here. The civic museum has an excellent collection of local antiquities and the art gallery many fine works of the Bolognese school of painting. Under papal rule almost continuously 1506–1860, then absorbed into the kingdom of Italy. Birthplace of physicist and inventor Guglielmo Marconi (1874–1937).

Bolsover England. Town in NE Derbyshire 10 km (6 miles) E of Chesterfield. Pop. (1991) 11,743. Coalmining. Limestone quarrying.

Grew up round a Norman castle, rebuilt in the 17th cent. The Elizabethan mansion, Hardwick Hall, is 6 km (4 miles) S.

Bolton England. Town and unitary authority 18 km (11 miles) NW of Manchester. Pop. (1991) 139,020.

Important centre of the cotton industry, esp. spinning. Engineering. Manufactures textile machinery and chemicals.

Known from the 14th cent. for its woollen manufactures; with the invention and development of spinning machinery by Arkwright and Crompton in the late 18th cent. it became a leading cotton-manufacturing town. Birthplace of the inventor Samuel Crompton (1753–1827), whose half-timbered house Hall-i'-th'-Wood is now a museum.

Bolzano Italy. Cap. of Bolzano province in Trentino-Alto Adige on the Isarco R. near its confluence with the Adige 60 km (37 miles) S of the Brenner Pass. Pop. (1990) 100,400.

Tourist centre. Industrial and commercial town. Fruit-canning, flour-milling. Manufactures textiles. Trade in fruits and wines.

Passed from Austria to Italy 1919.

Boma Democratic Republic of the Congo. Port on the N bank of the Congo R. 290 km (180 miles) WSW of Kinshasa. Pop. (1994) 135,284.

Exports palm oil and coffee.

Flourishing slave-trade centre from the 16th to the 18th cent. Became the cap. of the Congo Free State 1886. Later cap. of the Belgian Congo; succeeded by Léopoldville (Kinshasa) 1926.

Bombay (Mumbai) India. Cap. of Maharashtra on the Arabian Sea. Pop. (1991) 9,925,900.

The country's leading seaport standing at the S end of Bombay Is., which is about 18 km (11 miles) long and 5 km (3 miles) wide and has a magnificent natural harbour on the sheltered E side. It exports cotton goods, oilseeds, cotton. Important industrial and commercial centre, with the cotton industry pre-eminent; also manufactures chemicals, machinery, paper, carpets, automobiles, pharmaceutical oil-based products, petro-chemicals, plastics and electronic equipment. Shipbuilding is also important. Beside the harbour there are oil refineries, while power for the factories and mills (mainly in the N part of the city) is derived from hydroelectric plants in the Western Ghats on the mainland.

Bombay has many fine public buildings, and almost as imposing are the residences of the wealthier citizens on Malabar Hill and Back Bay, which, despite its name, faces the open sea. The university (founded 1857) has 57 constituent colleges. Bombay Is. was acquired from a Gujarat sultan by the Portuguese in 1534 and was ceded to Charles II of England (1661) as part of the dowry of Catherine of Braganza; from him it passed to the East India Company. Trade gradually increased and the city expanded considerably in the 19th cent. through the building of the railways, the opening of the Suez Canal and the establishment of the textile industry. Under British rule it was cap. of Bombay Presidency; with the partition (1947) it became cap. of Bombay state in the Indian Union and with the re-organization of 1960 cap. of Maharashtra. The pop. is mainly Hindu, but is very cosmopolitan in character.

Bonaire ►NETHERLANDS ANTILLES.

Bonanza Creek ►KLONDIKE RIVER.

Bondy France. Suburb of NE Paris in the Seine-St Denis department on the Ourcq Canal. Pop. (1985) 53,000.

Manufactures chemicals, glass and biscuits.

Bône ►ANNABA.

Bo'ness (Borrowstounness) Scotland. Small industrial town and port in Falkirk on the Firth of Forth 26 km (16 miles) WNW of Edinburgh. Pop. (1991) 14,595.

Manufactures pottery and fertilizers.

To the S are traces of Antoninus's Wall (Graham's Dyke).

Bonin Islands (Japanese **Ogasawaragunto**) Pacific Ocean. Volcanic island group about 960 km (600 miles) S of Tokyo. Area 104 sq km (40 sq. miles). Three main groups: Bailey Is., Beechey Is., Parry Is. The largest island is Chichijima, with the main harbour and a US naval base. Breadfruit and bananas are grown. The Japanese name derives from the reputed 16th-cent. discoverer Ogasawara. Annexed by Japan 1876. Occupied by the US after World War II (1945). Returned to Japan 1968.

Bonn Germany. Cap. (since 1949) in North Rhine-Westphalia on the Rhine 24 km (15 miles) SSE of Cologne. Pop. (1990) 294,300. The city incorporates the towns of Bad Godesberg and Beuel; it was so enlarged in 1969 to enable it to accommodate its function as cap. The government buildings are S of the old city which, despite war damage, still looks like a 19th-cent. residential town for the prosperous. The government and its related institutions are the main employers. Tourism is attracted by the birthplace of the composer Beethoven and by music festivals.

Bonn was a Roman and then a Frankish town, fortifying a river crossing. From the 13th cent. it was the seat of the Archbishop–Elector of Cologne and then a city state. It was attached to Prussia in 1815; in the late 19th cent. it was developed as a fashionable place to live – to the virtual exclusion of industry. Bonn became the cap. of the German Federal Republic in 1949. On reunification (1991) Berlin became the cap. again, Bonn remaining the seat of government.

Bonneville, Lake USA. A large body of water which in the Quaternary era occupied much of present-day Utah; the Great Salt Lake of today is a remnant. The former lake bed is now a dry, flat plain, where shallow *playas* form after heavy rain and soon disappear. In 1935–9 the Bonneville Salt Flats were used for attempts on the motor-car speed record.

Bonny, Bight of Atlantic Ocean. Bay at the E end of the Gulf of Guinea between the Niger delta and Cape Lopez, bordered by the coasts of Cameroon, N Gabon, E Nigeria, Equatorial Guinea. Contains the island of Bioki.

Bonnyrigg and Lasswade Scotland. Small towns in Midlothian 10 km (6 miles) SE of Edinburgh, united in 1929. Pop. (1991) 13,696.

Manufactures carpets and cement.

Boothia Canada. Formerly Boothia Felix. Low-lying peninsula, reaching Murchison Point, 71°55′N, the most northerly limit of the N American mainland. Joined to the mainland by the Boothia Isthmus. Discovered and explored by Sir James Ross (1829–33), who placed the N magnetic pole here. Named after Ross's patron, Sir Felix Booth.

Boothia, Gulf of Canada. Gulf nearly 320 km (200 miles) long, an inlet of the Arctic Ocean between the Boothia Peninsula and Baffin Is.

Bootle England. Town in Merseyside on the R. Mersey adjoining Liverpool, inc. much of the Mersey dock system. Pop. (1991) 65,454.

Seaport and there is extensive timber trade. Industries inc. leather-tanning and there is an automated tannery, engineering, tin-smelting and other industries.

Bophuthatswana South Africa. The main part of this former homeland was integrated (1994) into North West Province and smaller provinces have been inc. in the territory of the Free State.

Boppard Germany. Town in the Rhine-land-Palatinate on the left bank of the Rhine R. 13 km (8 miles) S of Coblenz. Pop. (1990) 16,000.

Tourist centre. Trade in wine.

Borås Sweden. Industrial town in the SW on the Viske R. 56 km (35 miles) E of Göteborg. Pop. (1992) 102,840.

Centre of the textile industry. Manufactures hosiery and clothing.

Founded (1622) by King Gustavus Adolphus.

Bordeaux France. Ancient Burdigala. Prefecture of the Gironde department on the Garonne R. 96 km (60 miles) from the sea. Pop. (1990) 213,274.

Chief port of SW France. Large export trade in wines (known generally as 'Bordeaux'), the produce of four districts of the Gironde department, Graves, Sauternes, Médoc, St Émilion. Also exports petroleum products. Manufactures many of the requisites of the wine trade, e.g. bottles, casks, corks, crates. Shipbuilding, sugar-refining. Oil refineries at Bec d'Ambes, Pauillac on the Gironde. Chemical and food-processing industries.

A well-planned city, with many 18th-cent. buildings. At the centre is the Place des Quinconces, which has imposing statues of Montaigne (1533–92) and Montesquieu (1689–1755), both born in the neighbourhood. Cathedral (12th/15th-cent.), several old churches and an 18th-cent. theatre. University (1441). Important commercial centre in Roman times. In the 4th cent. AD became cap. of Aquitania Secunda, but declined after the collapse of the Roman Empire. Prospered again under the English (1154–1453). Became cap. of the Guienne province under Louis XI. Much improved during the 18th cent. Headquarters of the Girondists during the French Revolution. Temporarily the seat of the French government during the Franco–Prussian War (1870–1) and in both world wars.

Borders Region Scotland. Former region in the SE formed 1975 from the counties of Berwick, Roxburgh, Selkirk, Peebles and the SW part of Midlothian; since 1996 Scottish Borders.

Bordighera Italy. Town and seaport in Imperia province in Liguria on the Gulf of Genoa. Pop. (1985) 12,500.

Popular winter resort; fine coastal scenery and gardens. Exports flowers and large quantities of palm branches for use in churches on Palm Sunday.

Borgholm ➤OLAND ISLAND.

Borislav ➤BARYSAW.

Borku Chad. Region in the L. Chad depression S of the Tibesti highlands. Chief town Faya (Largeau). Mostly sandy desert, with many *khors* (intermittent streams) and oases, where dates and barley are grown and goats raised. Formerly important in the slave trade between N and central Africa.

Borkum Germany. Town at the W end of Borkum Is. Pop. (1989) 5646. Popular holiday resort.

Borkum Island Germany. Island off the estuary of the Ems R.; the westernmost of the E Frisian Islands. Area 36 sq km (14 sq. miles).

Borlänge Sweden. Industrial town in Kopparberg county 193 km (120 miles) NW of Stockholm. Pop. (1992) 47,300.
  Important steelworks. Other industries inc. paper, engineering and chemicals.

Borneo. Largest island of the Malay Archipelago lying E of the Malay peninsula and Sumatra. Area 743,000 sq km (287,000 sq. miles). Pop. (1983) 7,350,000. It is divided politically into four sections, the largest of which forms part of Indonesia, occupies more than two-thirds of the island and is known to the Indonesians as Kalimantan; this section is subdivided into four provinces, W, S, E and Central Kalimantan. The other three sections, all in the N, are the two former British colonies of Sarawak and North Borneo (renamed Sabah), since 1963 part of the Federation of Malaysia, and the State of Brunei. Much of the interior is mountainous, with Mt Kinabalu in Sabah rising to 4101 m (13,451 ft). A central core of ranges extends NE–SW across the island and the many rivers rising therein inc. the Kapuas and Rajang, which flow W, and the Barito, which flows S. The climate is hot and humid throughout

the year, the rainfall exceeding 250 cm (100 ins.) annually, and a large proportion of the island is densely forested.
  Rice and sago are grown as subsistence crops both on the broad coastal lowlands and inland on cleared sections of forest. Rubber and copra are exported. There are important oilfields: in Kalimantan near the port of Balikpapan and on Tarakan Is., in Brunei around Seria and in Sarawak around Miri. In general the island is thinly populated, the various pagan Dyak tribes of the interior living mainly along the banks of the rivers, which form the principal highways; around the coasts there are many Malays (who, like the Dyaks, largely subsist on rice and fish, but are Muslims by religion) and Chinese, who are frequently traders. Apart from those mentioned, the chief towns are Bandjarmasin (Kalimantan), Kota Kinabalu (Sabah), Kuching (Sarawak), Bandar Seri Begawan.
  Borneo has never had political unity and its name is derived from Brunei, once a much more powerful and extensive sultanate than it is at present. The Portuguese and Spaniards established trading relations with the island in the 16th cent. and the Dutch and British in the 17th cent. With European influence removed in the early 19th cent., the coastal natives indulged in large-scale piracy, but British authority was later restored in the N and Dutch in the S, boundaries being defined by treaty in 1891. During World War II Borneo was occupied by the Japanese 1942–5. In 1950 the former Dutch Borneo became part of the republic of Indonesia.

Bornholm Denmark. Island in the Baltic Sea off the SE coast of Sweden. Area 588 sq km (227 sq. miles). Pop. (1990) 45,784. Chief town and seaport Rönne. With 8 small nearby islands it forms the *amt* of Bornholm.
  Principal industries agriculture and fishing. Popular seaside resort.
  Taken by the Hanseatic League 1510. Passed to Denmark 1522 and to Sweden 1645. Returned to Denmark 1660.

Borno Nigeria. A formerly independent Muslim state, dating from the 11th cent. Divided into British, French and German spheres of influence by the end of the 19th cent. The greater part was incorporated into Nigeria as a province in 1902. The German sphere of influence became part of the mandated territory of the British Cameroons in 1922.

Borobudur Indonesia. Ruin of an enormous Buddhist shrine in central Java, near Jogjakarta, consisting of a truncated and terraced pyramid, elaborately carved and a seated Buddha. Probably built in the 9th cent.

Borodino Russia. Village situated 120 km (75 miles) W of Moscow. Scene of a bitter battle between Napoleon's army and the Russians during the march on Moscow (1812).

Boroughbridge England. Market town in North Yorkshire 10 km (6 miles) ESE of Ripon on the R. Ure. Pop. 800. Three prehistoric monoliths, called the Devil's Arrows.

Borromean Islands Italy. Four islands in L. Maggiore. Pop. 300. Named after Count Vitaliano Borromeo, who constructed the famous palace and terraced gardens on Isola Bella in the 17th cent.

Borrowdale England. Picturesque valley in S Cumbria in the Lake District, leading down to the S end of Derwentwater. Graphite mines (now exhausted) formerly supplying the pencil industry at Keswick.

Borrowstounness ➤BO'NESS.

Borsippa Iraq. City of ancient Babylonia 24 km (15 miles) SSW of Babylon near the Euphrates R. The site is marked by two large mounds, one of which may have represented the Tower of Babel.

Borstal England. Village in Kent 3 km (2 miles) SW of Rochester. Seat of the original institution for the rehabilitation of juvenile delinquents (in 1902) from which the Borstal system developed and after which other such institutions are named.

Boscastle England. Fishing port and tourist resort in N Cornwall 24 km (15 miles) N of Bodmin. Pop. 700. Picturesque coastal scenery.

Bosnia–Hercegovina. Republic in SE Europe bounded by Croatia in the N and W and the E and SE by Yugoslavia. Area 51,129 sq km (19,741 sq. miles). Pop. (1996) 32 million (36 per cent urban). Life expectancy, 51 years male, 61 female. Cap. Sarajevo. Other cities Banja Luka, Zenica, Tuzla, Mostar. Currency: Bosnian dinar = 100 paras. It is very mountainous, noted for its limestone gorges, lying mainly in the Dinaric Alps.

Agriculture in the valleys, where cereals, vegetables, fruit (chiefly plums) and tobacco are cultivated. Land use: forested 39 per cent, pasture 24 per cent, agricultural 16 per cent. The official lang. is Serbo-Croat. About 40 per cent of the pop. is Muslim, 31 per cent Serbian Orthodox and 15 per cent Roman Catholic. The ethnic composition is Muslim 50 per cent, Serb 31 per cent and Croat 17 per cent.

From the 10th to the 12th cent. Bosnia was independent. While under Turkish rule 1463–1878 it incorporated Hercegovina. The area then came under Austro–Hungarian rule and was annexed in 1908. Serbian opposition led to the assassination of the Archduke Francis Ferdinand at Sarajevo in 1914, which precipitated World War I. Bosnia and Hercegovina became part of the newly created Yugoslavia 1918. In 1992 it declared its independence and this was recognized by the European Union and USA, but ethnic conflict arose between Muslims, Serbs and Croats, reducing the country to civil war. This caused thousands to flee to neighbouring countries. Up to 1 million citizens may be living abroad (1996). Hostilities ceased with the signing of the Dayton (USA) Peace Agreement in 1995. Under this agreement there will be a Serb Republic containing 49 per cent of Bosnian territory and a Muslim–Croat Federation.

Bosporus (Turkish **Karadeniz Boğazi**) Asia/Europe. Ancient Bosporus Thracius (to distinguish it from Bosporus Cimmerius, the Strait of Kerch). Formerly also known as Bosphorus. Strait 29 km (18 miles) long and

0.8–4 km (½–2½ miles) wide, joining the Black Sea to the Sea of Marmara and separating Asiatic from European Turkey, thus forming part of the boundary between Asia and Europe. The name means 'Ox-ford' and refers to the legend of Io, who crossed it in the form of a heifer. Several inlets along both shores; one of these, the Golden Horn, forms the harbour of Istanbul. The strait was under the control of an international commission from 1918, but in 1936 Turkey was allowed to refortify it. It was bridged 1973 and is polluted by sewage from Istanbul and oil spillage from shipping.

Boston England. Town in SE Lincolnshire on the R. Witham 6 km (4 miles) from the mouth. Pop. (1991) 34,606. Market town and seaport. Fruit and vegetable canning and other industries.

The name (Botolph's Town) derives from St Botolph, founder of a monastery here (654). A leading English port, second only to London, in the 13th cent. The fine parish church of St Botolph is famous for its 83-m (272-ft) tower (the 'Boston Stump'). Some of the Pilgrim Fathers were imprisoned in the 15th-cent. Guildhall in 1607; they later helped to found Boston (Massachusetts) and in memory of this the American city has contributed funds for the restoration of St Botolph's Church. Regained some of its former importance as a port by the deepening of the Witham (1882–4) and the opening of a new quay (1938). Birthplace of John Foxe, the martyrologist (1516–87).

Boston USA. State cap. of Massachusetts, a major seaport and the leading fishing port of the USA, at the head of Massachusetts Bay; an ice-free and almost land-locked harbour 10.4 km (6½ miles) from the open sea. Pop. (1990) 574,283.

The commercial, industrial and financial centre of New England; nicknamed 'the Hub of the Universe' on account of its position of leadership in the 19th cent. Imports are largely raw materials, e.g. wool, cotton, hides, coal and oil, for local industries making textiles, leather goods, footwear, machinery,

food products, soap and chemicals, many of which are exported.

A leading educational centre; seat of Boston University (1869), Northeastern University (1898) and part of Harvard University (the remainder being at neighbouring Cambridge); Boston Latin School, one of the country's first free public schools, was established in 1635. In the second half of the 19th cent. Boston was the literary centre of the USA; Emerson, Hawthorne, Thoreau, Whittier, Longfellow, Oliver Wendell Holmes and Lowell all lived in and around the city. Among its historic buildings are Christ Church (1723), the old State House (1748, restored 1880), near which the Boston Massacre (1770) took place, Faneuil Hall (1762) and the State Capitol (1798). More modern buildings inc. the Boston Museum of Fine Arts and the Symphony Hall, home of the famous Boston Symphony Orchestra.

Founded (1630) by Puritans; named after the town in Lincolnshire from which many of its first citizens had come. Flourished as the principal colony of the Massachusetts Bay Company and played an outstanding part in the struggle for independence. At the Boston Massacre (1770) several people were killed by British soldiers; at the Boston Tea Party (1773) British-taxed tea was thrown in the harbour; the Battle of Bunker Hill was fought in 1775 and in the following year the British withdrew. Incorporated as a city 1822. Again came into prominence with the formation (1831) of the Boston anti-slavery movement. In 1872 it suffered a disastrous fire in which much of the commercial quarter of the city was destroyed.

Bosworth Field ➤MARKET BOSWORTH.

Botany Bay Australia. Inlet on the coast of New South Wales 8 km (5 miles) S of Sydney. Captain Cook and Joseph Banks landed here (1770) and reported favourably on its suitability for colonization and proclaimed British sovereignty over the E Australian coast. Chosen as the site of a penal settlement (1788) and a party of 1030 (inc. 736 convicts) landed, but were later transferred to Port Jackson (Sydney Cove). Modern Sydney has spread S and now there are industries producing chemicals and plastics, and oil refineries, while the outer suburbs of the city lie about the bay.

Bothnia, Gulf of. Arm of the Baltic Sea N of Ahvenanmaa (Åland Is.) between Sweden and Finland, named after the former maritime region of Bothnia (now divided between Sweden and Finland). Shallow and of low salinity, it is closed by ice in winter, but has several important timber ports on its coasts.

Botoşani Romania. Town in Moldavia 96 km (60 miles) NW of Iaşi. Pop. (1993) 127,337. Named after Batu Khan, grandson of Genghis Khan.

Important flour-milling industry. Manufactures textiles and clothing.

Botswana. Republic in southern Africa bounded by Zambia and Zimbabwe in the NE, South Africa in the SE and S and Namibia in the W and N. Area 581,730 sq km (224,607 sq. miles). Pop. (1995) 1,549,000 (26 per cent urban). Life expectancy, 60 years male, 66 female. Cap. Gaborone. Other cities Francistown, Selebe-Pikwe, Molepolole and Kanye. Currency: Pula = 100 thebe. Seventy-eight per cent of Botswana is desert and it is a land-locked country. A dry plateau area, average height over 900 m (2952 ft) with an annual rainfall of about 50 cm (20 ins.) (mainly in summer). In the N large depressions of the Okavango Swamp, the Makarikari Salt Pan and L. Ngami become lakes during the rainy season. In the dry grassland of the Kalahari in the S the mean annual rainfall makes agriculture difficult except with irrigation. Land use: forested 47 per cent, meadows and pastures 45 per cent, agricultural and under permanent cultivation 1 per cent. The official lang. is English but Setswana is the national lang. The most important tribe is the Bamangwato, whose cap. is Serowe. About 50 per cent of the pop. follow traditional beliefs and about 40 per cent are Christians.

Cattle-rearing is the most important industry after diamond-mining. Maize and millets are grown, but unreliability of rainfall makes agriculture precarious except with irrigation. Exports diamonds (79 per cent), beef, hides and skins, and copper-nickel matte. Other industries inc. textiles, food-processing and soap The pop. is chiefly in the E and SE, through which runs the railway from Mafeking (in South Africa) to Bulawayo (Zimbabwe).

There is evidence of human occupation in Botswana dating back some 35,000 years. These were hunter–gatherer Khoisan people and today their descendants are still to be found among the Khoi (Hottentots) and the San (Bushmen). Their occupation of Botswana was unchallenged until the 17th and 18th cent. when the Tswana people migrated westward and gradually displaced or absorbed them. In the early 19th cent. tribal conflicts were rife in Southern Africa, inc. Botswana, and it was not until the latter part of the cent. that peace and stability returned. First taken under British protection in 1885; the area N of the Molopo R. became the Bechuanaland Protectorate, that S of the river a Crown Colony known as British Bechuanaland, which was annexed to Cape Colony (South Africa) 1895. The British government proposed to transfer the Protectorate to the British South Africa Company, but after protests from the Bechuana chiefs agreed to continue the Protectorate, which later became one of the three British High Commission Territories in southern Africa (the others were Basutoland and Swaziland). A new constitution providing for a legislative council with an elected majority and an executive council was introduced in 1961. Bechuanaland achieved independence as the Republic of Botswana in 1966. The 47-member National Assembly (40 elected by universal suffrage and 7 elected by the Assembly) has a 5-year term. There is also a House of Chiefs consisting of the Chiefs of the 8 tribes.

Bottrop Germany. Industrial town in North Rhine-Westphalia, in the Ruhr district just NW of Essen. Pop. (1990) 118,700.

Manufactures steel, machinery, chemicals,

textile and electrical equipment. Developed from the late 19th cent. with the coalmining industry.

Bouaké Côte d'Ivoire. Town 282 km (175 miles) NNW of Abidjan on the railway to the interior. Pop. (1988) 329,850.

Important trade centre for coffee and cacao. Cotton-ginning. Manufactures textiles and sisal products.

Bouches-du-Rhône France. Department in the SE formed (1790) from W Provence. Area 5112 sq km (2026 sq. miles). Pop. (1990) 1,759,400. Prefecture Marseille. The W part (the Camargue) is a marshy plain where livestock are raised. East of this is the arid plain of the Crau and to the E and N are E–W ranges of hills (Maritime Alps). Along the Mediterranean coast are several lagoons (Étang de Berre, Étang de Vaccarès); inland there are many pools.

Produces olive oil, wine and fruit; also lignite and salt. Marseille is the chief commercial and industrial centre. Other towns are Arles and Aix-en-Provence.

Bougainville Papua New Guinea. Mountainous island, largest of the Solomon Is. Area 10,619 sq km (4100 sq. miles). Pop. (1990) 128,000. Rises to 2593 m (8505 ft) in the volcanic Mt Balbi (N). The lowlands are densely forested.

Produces copra, tagua nuts.

Discovered (1768) by Bougainville. Held by Germany from 1884. Occupied by Australia 1914. From 1920 in the Territory of New Guinea, from 1973 in Papua New Guinea. In 1989 Melanesian unilateral independence closed the copper mines. A peace treaty was signed in 1991 but guerrilla activity continues.

Bougie (Bejaia) Algeria. Seaport in the Constantine department 153 km (95 miles) WNW of Constantine. Pop. (1983) 124,122. Favourably situated in abundant subtropical vegetation on the slopes of the Jebel Guraya. Annual rainfall 100 cm (40 ins.).

Chief port of Kabylia. Exports olive oil, fruits, cereals, petroleum, iron ore, phosphates. Connected by a branch line with the main railway from Constantine to Oran. Terminal of the oil pipeline from Hassi Messaoud. Gave its name to the wax candle (Fr. *bougie*), first exported to Europe from here.

An ancient Roman city; became the cap. of the Vandals in the 5th cent. AD. Passed in turn to the Arabs, the Berber, the Barbary pirates, the Spaniards and the Turks. Occupied by the French 1833. Developed rapidly with the exploitation of the nearby mines and improvements to the harbour.

Boulder USA. Town in Colorado 40 km (25 miles) NW of Denver at a height of 1630 m (5346 ft). Pop. (1990) 83,312.

Mining (gold and silver) and ranching centre. Health and skiing resort.

Seat of the University of Colorado (1877). Atomic-energy plant nearby.

Boulder Dam ➤HOOVER DAM.

Boulogne (Boulogne-sur-mer) France. Ancient Gesoriacum, Bononia. Seaport in the Pas-de-Calais department at the mouth of the Liane R. on the English Channel. Pop. (1990) 44,244. Cross-channel services to Folkestone and Dover.

Fish-curing and salting. Manufactures cement, iron and steel, bricks and tiles.

The old upper town contains the 19th-cent. Church of Notre Dame, severely damaged in World War II, the hôtel-de-ville and the castle. The lower town is built round the harbour. Nearby is a column commemorating Napoleon's projected invasion of England (1804). Taken by Philip, Duke of Burgundy 1419. United to the crown by Louis XI 1477. Seized by the English 1544; restored to France 1550.

Boulogne-Billancourt France. Industrial and residential suburb to the SW of Paris in the Hauts-de-Seine department on the Seine. Pop. (1990) 101,971.

Manufactures vehicles, aircraft, rubber, soap, cosmetics and other industries.

Formed (1925) from Boulogne-sur-Seine and Billancourt.

Bounty Islands New Zealand. Group of uninhabited islets in the S Pacific 640 km

(400 miles) ESE of Dunedin (South Island). Discovered (1788) by Captain Bligh in the *Bounty*.

Bourbon ►RÉUNION.

Bourbonnais France. Former province in central France. Cap. Moulins. Divided in 1790 to form the present Allier department and parts of the Cher, Creuse and Puy-de-Dôme departments. Formed the duchy of Bourbon 1327–1527, then united to the French crown. Belonged to the Bourbon-Condé family from 1661 until the Revolution (1789).

Bourg (Bourg-en-Bresse) France. Prefecture of the Ain department on the Reyssouze, a tributary of the Saône 56 km (35 miles) NNE of Lyon. Pop. (1990) 43,955.

Market town and railway junction. Trade in grain, wine and poultry. Manufactures pottery. Flour-milling and cheese-making.

In the suburb of Brou is the remarkable 16th-cent. late Gothic church, built by Marguerite of Austria.

Bourges France. Ancient Avaricum. Prefecture of the Cher department on the Canal du Berry at the confluence of the Auron and the Yèvre rivers. Pop. (1990) 78,770.

Military, route and industrial centre. State ordnance factories. Manufactures inc. aircraft, missiles, woollens, linoleum, hardware, agricultural implements, tyres, brewing and food-processing.

Among important buildings are the beautiful 12th/16th-cent. Gothic cathedral (remarkable for its stained glass and the absence of transepts), the 15th-cent. Hôtel de Jacques Coeur (*c.* 1395–1456; born here) and the Berry museum. In Roman times cap. of Aquitania Prima. Residence of Charles VII (known as 'the King of Bourges'), who proclaimed the Pragmatic Sanction in the 15th cent. The university (1463) was suppressed during the French Revolution. Birthplace of Louis XI (1423–83).

Bourget, Lac du France. Lake 18 km (11 miles) long and up to 3 km (2 miles) wide in the Savoie department. Nearby are the resort of Aix-les-Bains and the Abbey of Hautecombe. Celebrated in Lamartine's poem *Le Lac*.

Bourget, Le France. Town in the Seine-St Denis department 11 km (7 miles) NNE of Paris. Pop. (1985) 10,000. Charles Lindbergh landed here after his historic transatlantic flight (May 1927).

Bourgogne (Burgundy) France. Region and former province, comprising the present departments of Nièvre, Saône-et-Loire, Côte-d'Or and parts of Haute-Marne, Aube and Yonne. Area 31,528 sq km (12,173 sq. miles). Pop. (1991) 1,610,000. Regional cap. Dijon. Long famous for wines. Conquered by Julius Caesar. Settled in the 5th cent. AD by the Burgundii (a Germanic tribe), who established a kingdom of Burgundy. Divided for a time, then reunited in the 10th cent. as a second kingdom (Kingdom of Arles). Fell to the Holy Roman Empire 1032. The imperial dominion inc. the county of Burgundy (later Franche-Comté), between the Jura mountains and the Saône R. The duchy of Burgundy, created from land W of the Saône, became very powerful and ruled most of modern Holland, Belgium and N and E France. With the death of Charles the Bold (1477) the duchy itself passed to France and the remaining territories to the Empire. Franche-Comté was annexed to France (1678) by Louis XIV.

Bourne England. Market town in S Lincolnshire 24 km (15 miles) SE of Grantham. Pop. (1991) 8777. Associated with Hereward the Wake. Birthplace of Lord Burghley, Queen Elizabeth I's favourite minister (1520–98).

Bournemouth England. Popular holiday resort and unitary authority on the Poole Bay. Pop. (1991) 155,488. Long sandy beach, two piers, long drives (Undercliff and Overcliff), winter gardens. It has an equable climate and sheltered position. The sea front is reached by several picturesque dells (the 'chines'). Many parks and open spaces. Museum, art gallery.

Settled in ancient times, but by the mid 19th cent. merely a village of a few hundred houses. Began to develop as a resort in the late 19th cent. Birthplace of the composer, Sir Hubert Parry (1848–1918).

Bournville England. Residential and industrial district in S Birmingham. Founded (1879) by George Cadbury for the workers at his cocoa and chocolate factories. One of the earliest examples of town planning.

Bouvet Island S Atlantic Ocean. Island 2900 km (1800 miles) SSW of Capetown, South Africa. Area 48 sq km (19 sq. miles). Discovered (1739) by a French naval officer, Pierre Bouvet. Claimed for Britain 1825. Norwegian dependency since 1930.

Bovey Tracey England. Market town in Devon 18 km (11 miles) SW of Exeter. Pop. (1991) 3492.
   Manufactures pottery from local china clay.

Bow (Stratford-le-Bow) England. District in the former metropolitan borough of Poplar in E London; from 1965 in the London borough of Tower Hamlets. The name derives from the 12th-cent. bow-arched bridge over the R. Lea. Not to be confused with the Bow of 'Bow bells', the Church of St Mary-le-Bow in Cheapside, within the sound of whose bells every true cockney is supposed to be born.

Bowness England. Village in NW Cumbria on the Solway Firth 19 km (12 miles) WNW of Carlisle. At the W end of Hadrian's Wall, traces of which may still be seen.

Bowness-on-Windermere England. Tourist centre in Cumbria on the E shore of L. Windermere. Part of the town of Windermere since 1905.

Bow River Canada. River 507 km (315 miles) long in Alberta, flowing generally SE from the Rocky Mountains, through the fine scenery of the Banff National Park, past Banff and Calgary to the S Saskatchewan R. From Calgary to the W its course is followed by the Canadian Pacific Railway.

Box Hill England. Picturesque spur of the North Downs in Surrey just NNE of

Dorking 182 m (597 ft) high. Property of the National Trust. Named after the many box trees here.

Boyacá Colombia. Small town in the Boyacá department in the E Cordillera at a height of 2360 m (7741 ft). Scene of Bolívar's defeat of the Spanish (1819), which led to independence for Colombia and Venezuela.

Boyle Ireland. Market town in Co. Roscommon on the R. Boyle 35 km (22 miles) SSE of Sligo. Pop. (1986) 1859. Remains of a Cistercian abbey (founded 1161).

Boyne River Ireland. River 129 km (80 miles) long, rising in the Bog of Allen, flowing generally NE through Co. Meath and entering the Irish Sea 6 km (4 miles) below Drogheda. The Battle of the Boyne (1690), in which James II was defeated by William III, was fought at Oldbridge 5 km (3 miles) W of Drogheda.

Boys' Town USA. Village in E Nebraska 16 km (10 miles) W of Omaha, founded (1917) by Father Edward J. Flanagan as a settlement for homeless boys, occupying 130 ha (320 acres) of farm land. Remarkable for its successful application of the principles of self-rule and self-discipline.

Brabant Belgium/Netherlands. Former province of the Low Countries between the Meuse and the Scheldt rivers. Became a duchy in the Middle Ages and later changed hands several times. When Belgium became independent (1830), it was divided: the S part became two provinces of Belgium and the N part a province of the Netherlands.
   Antwerp (Antwerpen): A province of Belgium; drained by the Scheldt, Dyle, Nèthe and Rupel rivers. Area 2867 sq km (1107 sq. miles). Pop. (1995) 1,628,710. Cap. Antwerp. Largely agricultural. Food-processing and sugar-refining industries.
   Brabant: A province of Belgium; drained by the Dyle, Demer and Senne rivers. Area 3358 sq km (1297 sq. miles). Pop. (1991) 2,245,890. Cap. Brussels. Largely agricultural. Manufactures machinery and textiles. The 1830 revolution began here and the

revolutionary song *La Brabançonne* became the Belgian national anthem.

North Brabant (Noord-Brabant): A province of the Netherlands; drained by the Mark and Dommel rivers. Area 4915 sq km (1903 sq. miles). Pop. (1994) 2,457,329. Cap. 's Hertogenbosch. Textile and electrical industries.

Brač Croatia. The largest of the Dalmatian islands in the Adriatic Sea 16 km (10 miles) SE of Split. Area 394 sq km (152 sq. miles). Tourist and fishing centre. Chief town Supetar, on the N coast.

Brackley England. Town in Northamptonshire 13 km (8 miles) ESE of Banbury on the R. Ouse. Pop. (1991) 9113.

Flour-milling and brewing. Formerly a prosperous trade in wool.

Bracknell England. Town 16 km (10 miles) ESE of Reading. Pop. (1991) 60,894. Headquarters of the Meteorological Office from 1961.

Manufactures clothing and furniture. New town (1949) to meet overspill needs from London.

Bracknell Forest became a unitary authority in 1998.

Bradford England. City and unitary authority 14 km (9 miles) W of Leeds. Pop. (1991) 289,376.

Important centre of worsted and woollen manufacture. Also produces velvet, mohair, silk and rayon goods. Dyeing, electrical and other engineering. Manufactures textile machinery. Probably already associated with the woollen industry in the early 14th cent.

The former parish church of St Peter, dating to the 15th cent., became the cathedral in 1920. Other noteworthy buildings inc. the Cartwright Memorial Hall, with art gallery and Museum (1904), dedicated to the inventor of the power loom; the Town Hall (1873); and the Wool Exchange (1867). Birthplace of the composer, Frederick Delius (1863–1934) and the novelist, J. B. Priestley (1894–1984).

Bradford-on-Avon England. Market town in Wiltshire on the R. Avon 8 km (5 miles) ESE of Bath. Pop. (1991) 9000. Formerly important in the woollen industry. Largely built of lcoal stone. Ancient 9-arched stone bridge with a bridge chapel. Small Saxon church with a nave only 8 m (26 ft) long.

Braemar Scotland. 1. District in SW Aberdeenshire, extending E–W from Ballater to Glen Dee. Deer forests. Several villages up to 300 m (984 ft) above sea level. Tourist centre. Small knitting industry. Inc. Balmoral Castle. 2. Principal village of the Braemar district, a holiday resort on Clunie Water 21 km (13 miles) WSW of Ballater. Scene of the gathering of the clans to the standard of the Earl of Mar in the Jacobite rebellion (1715). Now scene of the annual Highland Games (the Braemar Gathering).

Braga Portugal. Ancient Bracara Augusta. Cap. of the Braga district in the N 45 km (28 miles) NNE of Porto. Pop. (1987) 63,033. Manufactures hats and cutlery.

Important religious centre since the Middle Ages. Seat of the Roman Catholic Primate of Portugal. The Sanctuary of Bom Jesus do Monte, a famous place of pilgrimage, is 5 km (3 miles) SE. Taken by the Suevi and then the Visigoths in the 5th cent. and by the Moors in the 8th; retaken by Ferdinand I of Aragon in 1040.

Brahmaputra River S Asia. Major river 2900 km (1800 miles) long rising in SW Tibet on a Himalayan glacier. As the Tsangpo it flows generally E across S Tibet at a height of about 3700 m (12,136 ft) to the E end of the Himalayas. Here, near the mountain mass of Namcha Barwa (7756 m, 25,440 ft), it turns N, then curves round to flow S through a series of deep gorges and, now known as the Dihang, leaves Tibet and enters NE Assam (India). It flows WSW as the Brahmaputra through the fertile valley of Assam, flanked by tea gardens and rice fields, then turns S into Bangladesh and merges its delta with that of the Ganges before entering the Bay of Bengal. Navigable by steamer for 1300 km (800 miles) to Dibrugarh, but most river traffic ascends only to Gauhati.

Brăila Romania. River port in the Brăila

district on the Danube R. Pop. (1992) 234,706.

Leading centre of the grain trade. Flour mills, railway workshops, timber yards, boat-building. Manufactures paper, cardboard, textiles and footwear.

In Turkish hands 1544–1828.

Braintree England. Town in Essex 24 km (15 miles) W of Colchester. Pop. (1991) 32,229.

Manufactures metal windows, textiles and brushes. The woollen industry introduced by 15th/16th-cent. Flemish refugees was superseded by lace manufacture introduced by 16th/17th-cent. Huguenot refugees.

Brakpan South Africa. Town in Gauteng on the Witwatersrand 32 km (20 miles) E of Johannesburg at a height of 1650 m (5412 ft). Pop. (1985) 85,000. Important goldmining centre.

Brampton England. Market town in NE Cumbria 13 km (8 miles) ENE of Carlisle. Pop. 2600.

Roman remains. Near by are Lanercost Priory (founded 1169) and Naworth Castle (built in the reign of Edward III).

Brandenburg Germany/Poland. 1. *Land* and former Electorate. Area 29,060 sq km (11,224 sq. miles). Pop. (1992) 2,543,000. Cap. Potsdam. Originally inhabited by Slavs (and early a part of the kingdom of Poland); partially conquered by Charlemagne in the 9th cent. and more successfully by the Margrave Albert the Bear in the 12th cent. Passed to Frederick I of Hohenzollern in 1415 and became an Electorate. Expanded considerably in the 17th cent. The elector Frederick III took the title 'King of Prussia' in 1701. At the end of World War II the Potsdam Agreement restored the area E of the Oder (Odra) and Neisse (Nysa) rivers to Poland. The remainder became a *Land* of the German Democratic Republic (East Germany) which was divided into the districts of Frankfurt-an-der-Oder, Cottbus and Potsdam in 1952. In 1994 the *Land* governments of Berlin and Brandenburg agreed to merge the two *Länder* in 1999 or 2002. 2. Industrial town in Ger-

many in the Potsdam district of Brandenburg *Land* on the Havel R. 61 km (38 miles) WSW of Berlin. Pop. (1981) 94,680. Formerly cap. of the Prussian province of Brandenburg.

Manufactures tractors, machinery and textiles.

A 14th-cent. cathedral and a 13th/14th-cent. town hall.

Brandon Canada. Town in SW Manitoba on the Assiniboine R. 209 km (130 miles) W of Winnipeg. Pop. (1991) 38,567.

Commercial centre in a wheat-growing region. Oil-refining and engineering. Manufactures agricultural implements.

Brandywine Creek USA. Stream 32 km (20 miles) long, rising in SE Pennsylvania and flowing SE through N Delaware to join the Christina R. near its confluence with the Delaware R. Famous as the scene of a battle near Chadds Ford, when Washington was defeated by English forces under Howe (1777).

Brantford Canada. Town in S Ontario on the Grand R. 32 km (20 miles) WSW of Hamilton. Pop. (1991) 81,997.

Industrial centre. Manufactures refrigerators, agricultural implements and pottery.

Named after Joseph Brant (1742–1807), a Mohawk Indian chief.

Bras d'Or, Lake Canada. Tidal Lake in NE Nova Scotia, almost dividing Cape Breton Island into two parts. Area 920 sq km (360 sq. miles). At the lakeshore village of Baddeck Dr Alexander Graham Bell founded (1907) the Aerial Experiment Association.

Brasilia Brazil. Cap. (since 1960), in a Federal District within the state of Goiás 960 km (600 miles) NW of Rio de Janeiro at the junction of two small rivers in a bare, rolling upland at 915 m (3001 ft). Pop. (1991) 1,596,274. Built to the plan of the Brazilian architect Lucio Costa, in the shape of an aeroplane, with the government offices and cathedral in the nose, other important buildings along the fuselage and a succession of autonomous community blocks forming the residential area along the wings (11 km (7 miles) long). The transfer of the cap. to this region was provided for in the 1891 Constitution, but it was not until after 1955 (under President Kubitschek) that the scheme, intended to stimulate the development of Brazil's sparsely populated and underdeveloped interior, came into being. The city, which lies roughly at the geographic centre of Brazil, is joined by road to São Paulo and Rio, and by frequent air services to most parts of the country. University (1960).

Braşov Romania. Formerly (1950–61) Stalin (Orasul Stalin). Cap. of the Braşov district in Transylvania on the slopes of the Transylvanian Alps 145 km (90 miles) NNW of Bucharest. Pop. (1992) 323,835.

Important commercial and industrial town. Manufactures aircraft, tractors, machinery, oil-drilling equipment and textiles. Iron and copper smelting. Tourist and winter-sports centre.

A 14th/15th-cent. church, called the Black Church because the walls are smoke-blackened from the fire of 1689. Founded (1211) by the Teutonic Knights. Became an important centre of German pop. Passed from Hungary to Romania 1920.

Bratislava Slovakia. Formerly Pressburg. Cap. of Slovakia and of the administrative region of Zápodoslovenský on the Danube R. near the S end of the Little Carpathian Mountains. Pop. (1990) 440,482.

River port. Railway and industrial centre. Of strategic importance owing to its position on an international waterway and near the frontiers of Austria and Hungary. Large agricultural trade. Important oil refinery. There is an oil pipeline from Brody (Ukraine). Engineering, brewing and printing. Manufactures chemicals, textiles and paper. Flour-milling and sugar-refining.

Seat of the Comenius University (1919). Cap. of Hungary 1526–1784. Many Hungarian kings were crowned in the 13th-cent. Gothic cathedral. Other noteworthy buildings are the 13th-cent. town hall (now a museum) and Franciscan church. Called Pressburg while within the Austro–Hungarian empire. Became the cap. of Slo-

vakia (1918). Cap. of the Slovakian republic 1938–45 and national cap. when Slovakia became a separate state in 1993.

Bratsk Russia. Industrial town in the Irkutsk Region on the Angara R. 460 km (285 miles) NNW of Irkutsk. Pop. (1990) 258,000.

Site of a large hydroelectric power station. Sawmilling and ship repairs. Manufactures wood pulp, cellulose and furniture.

Braunschweig ➤BRUNSWICK.

Bray England. Village on the R. Thames 1.6 km (1 mile) SE of Maidenhead. Made famous by the song *The Vicar of Bray*, which is said to refer to Simon Aleyn (vicar 1540–88), who retained his incumbency through all the religious vicissitudes of the reigns of Henry VIII, Edward VI, Mary I and Elizabeth I.

Bray Ireland. Seaside resort in Co. Wicklow on the Irish Sea near Bray Head 18 km (11 miles) SSE of Dublin. Pop. (1986) 24,686. Became popular in the mid 19th cent.

Brazil. Republic covering nearly half the area of South America. It has frontiers with all the South American republics except Chile and Ecuador and is bounded on the E by the Atlantic Ocean. Area 8,547,404 sq km (3,300,171 sq. miles). Pop. (1996) 157,872,000 (78 per cent urban). Life expectancy, 57 years male, 67 female. Cap. Brasilia. Other cities São Paulo, Rio de Janeiro, Salvador, Belo Horizonte, Recife, Pôrto Alegre, Manaus. Currency: Real = 100 centavos. In the N the tropical rainforests of the Amazon basin, once the centre of a rubber boom, with a hot humid climate, cover one-third of the country. The 'shoulder' of Brazil (NE) is mainly dry and covered with thorn scrub. Central Brazil is a vast tableland; much of it stands at a height of 600–900 m (1968–2952 ft), with higher scarp edges and an even higher series of ridges, with peaks over 2500 m (8200 ft), to the E and SE. Except for the large São Francisco R. and smaller rivers such as the Doce and Paraíba, which flow to the Atlantic, the plateau is drained mostly N to the Amazon or W and S to the

Paraná–Paraguay system and has adequate rainfall for savannah and some woodland. The climate is more invigorating than that of the humid coastal lands, which are wide in the N, narrow to the S and then broaden again in the far S in the more temperate Rio Grande do Sul. This configuration hampers communications between the coastlands and the interior, and has helped to confine economic development to the former, leaving the latter, the immense, thinly peopled *sertão*, largely undeveloped. Land use: forested 58 per cent, meadows and pastures 22 per cent, agricultural and under permanent cultivation 6 per cent. Portuguese is the official lang. and of believers 70 per cent are Roman Catholic. Other churches flourish in the S where there has been mixed European immigration and also some settlement of Asian communities. In the far S, in Rio Grande do Sul, is the Brazilian 'gaucho' country, also accommodating Protestant German farming communities. In the NE, particularly Bahia, the Afro–Brazilian religion called *candomble* is practised. Ethnically Brazil is a mixture of Portuguese, African and American Indian strains. The mixture, however, has been so thorough that the culture of the American Indians has in most regions been absorbed into the other two cultures. The exception is the Amazon basin. There, about 100,000 Indians speaking some 150 lang. survive in isolated villages. As their communities depend on forest resources they are therefore small. Their beliefs and arts are the product of the rainforest.

The great majority of the agriculture, industry, roads and railways are found along the Atlantic coastal belt; the vast basin of the Amazon and the immense interior plateau are scarcely developed at all. There are great resources, but the enormous scale of the country creates formidable problems of transportation. In the past a typical one-crop economy: sugar in early colonial times, replaced by coffee since the 19th cent. Brazilian coffee has long dominated the world market; though its share has fallen, coffee remains an important export, as is cotton. Others are cacao, sugar, oranges, bananas and tobacco.

Brazil has become a major livestock producer, with more cattle, pigs and goats than Argentina. Mineral deposits have been scarcely exploited. There are vast reserves of iron ore, much of the production is exported. Manganese and industrial diamonds are also exported, but Brazil is poor in coal and petroleum. There is a large oilfield in Bahia. There is immense hydroelectric potential; several large generating stations have been built, but demand exceeds supply. Industries are concentrated mainly in the states of Guanabara (Rio), São Paulo and Minas Gerais. The most important is the manufacture of cotton goods. Steel production is located chiefly at Volta Redonda. The country is largely self-sufficient in consumer goods and in a growing variety of engineering, chemical, electrical and other goods. Few manufactured goods except cotton textiles and footwear are exported.

The Treaty of Tordesillas (1494) gave the Portuguese control of territories in South America E of about long. 50° W. Cabral Alvares, the Portuguese navigator, visited Brazil in 1500. By 1537 three settlements existed: São Vicente (near Santos), Olinda (near Recife) and Salvador de Bahia; 15 hereditary 'captaincies' were created along the coastlands, but few flourished. The NE coastland, centred on Salvador, was developed for sugar and Negro slaves were introduced. From Santos the Jesuits founded São Paulo. The French controlled the coastland near Rio de Janeiro 1555–60, and the Dutch held the NE sugar lands from 1630 for nearly 30 years. Mineral finds in Minas Gerais led to the first real settlement of the interior, by Paulistas, towards the end of the 17th cent. Rio de Janeiro became colonial cap. in place of Salvador 1763. Brazil's colonization took a form essentially different from the colonization of the United States of America, Canada and Africa, where the European settlers introduced their own way of life. Though there was a steady inflow of European settlers, mostly of Portuguese origin, there was rapid integration between the White, the Indian and the African slave. This melting pot has produced a society with harmonious race relations and given the Brazilian people a character of their own, further enhanced by the immigration of non-Europeans, mostly Japanese and Arab. As a result of the Napoleonic Wars, the Portuguese royal family lived in Brazil 1808–21; Dom Pedro, son of King João of Portugal, declared Brazil an independent kingdom 1822. Under Dom Pedro II Brazil enjoyed wise and liberal rule: immigration and development went forward rapidly. Slavery was abolished 1888. It became a Federal Republic 1889. A succession of stable and relatively uneventful presidencies followed until 1930, when Getúlio Vargas, Governor of Rio Grande do Sul, deposed the President, assumed power and ruled as dictator 1930–45. He was again elected President 1951, but committed suicide 1954. Kubitschek (President 1956–60) built the new cap. Brasilia and greatly encouraged industrial development. The rapid pace of industrialization has created acute financial, social and political unrest. The Constitution closely resembles that of the USA, but politics depend more upon personalities than upon party programmes. Not immune to revolutions, but those that have occurred have been brief and usually bloodless.

Brazil is a federation of 26 states and 1 federal district. The states are Acre, Amazonas, Pará, Maranhão, Piauí, Ceará, Rio Grande do Norte, Paraíba, Pernambuco, Alagôas, Sergipe, Bahia, Minas Gerais, Espirito Santo, Rio de Janeiro, Guanabara, São Paulo, Paraná, Santa Catarina, Rio Grande do Sul, Mato Grosso, Goiás; the territories are Rondônia, Roraima, Amapá, Fernando de Noronha. State law is autonomous but must agree with the principles of Federal law. Individual states are not allowed to tax inter-state trade. Each state has a governor and a legislature, elected for 4 years. The Federal government is based on a constitution of 1988, the eighth since independence from the Portuguese. The executive president and the vice-president are directly elected to serve a 5-year term. The president is responsible to a two-chamber parliament which has an 81-member Senate (3 Senators per state) and a 513-member Chamber of Deputies. The Senate is part-directly and part-indirectly elected, the Chamber, directly elected. Voting is voluntary from age 16, compulsory from age 18–65, voluntary from age 65 and the parliamentary term is 4 years.

Brazzaville Republic of the Congo. Cap. River port beside Stanley Pool on the Congo R. opposite Kinshasa (Democratic Republic of the Congo). Pop. (1992) 937,579. Formerly cap. of French Equatorial Africa and Middle Congo. Connected by railway with the chief seaport, Pointe Noire. Railway workshops. Manufactures shoes and textiles.

Founded 1883. Became an important base for French colonization.

Brechin Scotland. Market town in Angus on the S Esk R. 16 km (10 miles) NE of Forfar. Pop. (1991) 7655.

Manufactures linen, paper, whisky.

A 13th-cent. parish church (former cathedral) and 11th-cent. round tower.

Brecon (Brecknock) Wales. Town in Powys at the confluence of the R. Honddu with the Usk. Pop. (1991) 7523.

Produces textiles and leather.

The Priory Church of St John became a cathedral (1923) when the new diocese of Swansea and Brecon was formed. Birthplace of the actress Sarah Kemble (Mrs Siddons, 1755–1831).

Breda Netherlands. Industrial town in the N Brabant province at the confluence of the Merk and the Aa rivers. Pop. (1992) 126,709.

Food-canning. Manufactures textiles, textile machinery, matches and footwear.

Having strategic importance, it changed hands many times. The Spanish capture (1625) is the subject of Velásquez's painting, *The Surrender of Breda*. Charles II regained the throne of Britain by signing the Declaration of Breda (1660), guaranteeing indemnity and religious liberty. The colonies of New York and New Jersey were awarded to England by the Peace of Breda (1667).

Bregenz Austria. Ancient Brigantium. Cap. of Vorarlberg at the E end of L. Constance. Pop. (1991) 27,236.

Tourist resort. Textile, electrical and other industries. Cable railway to the summit of Mt Pfänder (1064 m; 3490 ft).

Breisach (Altbreisach) Germany. Town in Baden-Württemberg on the right bank of the Rhine opposite Neuf-Brisach (France) 19 km (12 miles) WNW of Freiburg. Pop. 5000.

Produces sparkling wines.

The surrounding district is named Breisgau. For cent. a German stronghold, frequently besieged by the French. Incorporated into Baden 1805.

Breisgau Germany. District in Baden-Württemberg extending along the right bank of the Rhine, inc. the main peaks of the S Black Forest. Chief town Freiburg. Frequently changed hands from the 17th cent. onwards. Divided between Baden and Württemberg 1805.

Breitenfeld Germany. Village 8 km (5 miles) NW of Leipzig. Scene of two famous battles in the Thirty Years War: the victory of the Swedes (under Gustavus Adolphus) over the imperialists (under Tilly) in 1631; and that of the Swedes (under Torstensson) over the imperialists (under Piccolomini) in 1642.

Bremen Germany. 1. *Freie Hansestadt Bremen*: A *Land* consisting of two enclaves in Lower Saxony centred on the cities of Bremen and Bremerhaven, both on the lower Weser R. Area 404 sq km (156 sq. miles). Pop. (1992) 684,000. 2. Seaport in the Bremen *Land* on the lower Weser R. 80 km (50 miles) from the sea. Pop. (1990) 522,300.

Exports iron and steel and other manufactured goods. Oil-refining, shipbuilding, flour-milling, brewing and sugar-refining. Manufactures chocolate, tobacco products.

The Old Town (Altstadt), on the right bank of the Weser, has the 12th-cent. cathedral and the 15th-cent. Rathaus. Many medieval buildings were destroyed or damaged during World War II. On the left bank of the river, which is spanned by five bridges, is the New Town (Neustadt), founded in the 17th cent. Bremen became a leading member of the Hanseatic League in the 14th cent. and a free imperial city in the 17th. Overseas trade expanded considerably with the establishment of the North German Lloyd shipping line (1857). It became a Republic and Free Hansa City in the German Empire and then in the Weimar Republic and, with Bremerhaven, a *Land* in Germany in 1949.

Bremerhaven Germany. Seaport on the Weser estuary 55 km (34 miles) NNW of Bremen, of which it is the outport. Pop. (1990) 130,800.

Fishing, fish-processing and ship-repairing.

Developed rapidly after the founding of the North German Lloyd shipping line (1857).

Bremerton USA. Town in Washington on a peninsula in Puget Sound 23 km (14 miles) WSW of Seattle. Pop. (1985) 36,000. Naval dockyards and shipbuilding.

Brenner Pass (Italian **Passo Brennero**) Austria/Italy. The lowest of the main Alpine passes (1370 m; 4494 ft) connecting Innsbruck (Austria) with Bolzano (Italy). A road was built over it in 1772 and a railway (with many tunnels and bridges) in 1864–7. Frequent meeting place of Hitler and Mussolini (1940–1).

Brent England. Outer borough of London comprising the former municipal boroughs of Wembley and Willesden (Middlesex). Pop. (1994) 244,500.

Brentford and Chiswick England. Former municipal borough of Middlesex and suburb of W London, the two towns being united in 1927; from 1965 part of the London borough of Hounslow. Brentford stands at the confluence of the R. Brent with the Thames.

Manufactures soap, pharmaceutical products and tyres.

At Brentford Edmund Ironside defeated the Danes (1016) and Prince Rupert defeated the Parliamentarians (1642).

Brentwood

Brentwood England. Town in SW Essex 29 km (18 miles) NE of London of which it is a dormitory town. Pop. (1991) 49,426.

Brescia Italy. Ancient Brixia. Cap. of the Brescia province in Lombardy at the foot of the Alps 82 km (51 miles) E of Milan. Pop. (1992) 192,883.

Industrial centre. Manufactures iron goods, firearms, textiles and hosiery.

A temple erected by Vespasian in AD 73 (now a museum of antiquities); two cathedrals (11th/12th- and 17th-cent.); medieval museum, with many valuable relics. Birthplace of the religious reformer Arnoldo di Brescia (d. 1155).

Breslau ➤WROCLAW.

Bresse France. District in the Ain, Jura and Saône-et-Loire departments between the Saône R. and the Jura mountains. Chief town Bourg. A fertile plain 180–240 m (590–787 ft) above sea level. Noted for pigs and poultry. Ceded to France by the Duke of Savoy in 1601.

Brest France. Fortified seaport and naval station in the Finistère department on the Atlantic coast of Brittany on the N side of Brest Roads, which are entered by Le Goulet, a channel 1.6–3.2 km (1–2 miles) wide. Pop. (1990) 153,099.

Exports fruit, vegetables. Imports wheat, wine, coal, oil and timber. Fishing, flour-milling, engineering and brewing. Manufactures chemicals. Extensive dockyards. Arsenal and naval academy.

Richelieu built a harbour here 1631; Vauban fortified the port 1688. The French fleet was defeated off Brest by the English under Howe 1794. Used as a submarine base by the Germans during World War II and severely damaged by Allied bombing. The siege of 1944 completely destroyed the old town.

Brest (Brest–Litovsk) Belarus. Cap. of Brest Region on the Bug R. (Polish frontier). Pop. (1990) 268,800.

Important agricultural centre, railway junction and river port. Trade in timber,

cereals and cattle. Sawmilling, cotton-spinning, food-processing and engineering.

Founded in the 11th cent. as Brest-Litovsk. Passed to Russia 1795. Reverted to Poland 1921. Restored to the USSR under the Potsdam Agreement 1945. The separate Russo–German peace treaty of World War I was signed here 1918.

Bretagne (Brittany) France. Ancient Armorica. Region and former duchy and province, occupying the peninsula between the English Channel and the Bay of Biscay. Divided administratively into the departments of Finistère, Côtes-du-Nord, Morbihan and Ille-et-Vilaine. Area 27,208 sq km (10,505 sq. miles). Pop. (1990) 2,796,000. Cap. Rennes. The coast is rocky and indented like that of Cornwall (England). The picturesque fishing ports and beaches, the many megalithic monuments (e.g. Carnac) and the observance of local customs have made it popular with holidaymakers. Inland much of the area consists of unproductive moorland. Around Rennes (on the main river, the Vilaine) cider apples and potatoes are cultivated. Market-gardening has developed on the coastal plains and early vegetables are exported to Britain, where the Breton onion-seller is a familiar figure. Main occupations agriculture and fishing. Vehicles are produced in Rennes and there is engineering and electronics in Brest.

Ruled by the Romans from Caesar's invasion (56 BC) till the 5th cent. AD. Then settled by Celtic refugees from Britain, who gave it its name and account for the affinity of the Breton lang. (still spoken in rural areas) with Cornish and Welsh. Became a duchy in the 10th cent. and a province of France in 1532.

Bretton Woods USA. Small resort in New Hampshire in the White Mountains. Scene of an international conference (1944) which led to the establishment of the International Monetary Fund and the World Bank.

Briançon France. Ancient Brigantium. Tourist and winter-sports centre in the Hautes-Alpes department 77 km (48 miles) ESE of Grenoble in the valley of the upper

Durance R. Pop. (1985) 12,000. Consists of the old town at a height of over 1300 m (4264 ft), fortified by Vauban and the lower new town (Sainte-Catherine).

Trade in silk and cheese.

Bridgend Wales. 1. County Borough created in 1996. Pop. (1994) 131,000. 2. Market town on the R. Ogwr 26 km (16 miles) W of Cardiff. Pop. (1991) 38,841.

Manufactures footwear.

Bridge of Allan Scotland. Town and resort in Stirling on the Allan Water 3 km (2 miles) N of Stirling. Pop. (1991) 4864.

Mineral springs. Minor industries.

Bridgeport USA. Industrial town and seaport in SW Connecticut on Long Island Sound. Pop. (1990) 141,686.

Large engineering plants. Manufactures machinery, sewing-machines, electrical equipment, hardware, firearms and plastics.

From 1846, the home of P. T. Barnum, circus showman, who contributed much to the improvement of the town.

Bridgetown Barbados. Cap. and chief seaport on the Carlisle Bay on the SW side of the island, sheltered from the NE Trade Winds. Pop. (1990) 6720.

Principal exports sugar, molasses and rum.

The equable climate and fine beaches have made it a popular tourist resort. Trafalgar Square, in the centre of the town, has public buildings and a monument of Nelson.

Bridgnorth England. Market town in Shropshire on the R. Severn 21 km (13 miles) WSW of Wolverhampton. Pop. (1991) 11,229.

Manufactures carpets, electrical and radio equipment.

Picturesque; divided by the river into the High Town and the Low Town, connected by flights of steps and a funicular railway. Half-timbered 17th-cent. town hall.

Bridgwater England. Town and port in Somerset on the R. Parrett 14 km (9 miles) NNE of Taunton. Pop. (1991) 34,610.

Manufactures bath bricks (from sand and clay deposited by the tides), cement, bricks, tiles, lingerie and cellophane. Hinkley Point nuclear power station is in Bridgwater Bay.

Nearby is the site of the Battle of Sedgemoor (1685), at which the Monmouth rebellion was crushed and after which Judge Jeffreys conducted the Bloody Assize. Birthplace of Admiral Robert Blake (1599–1657).

Bridlington England. Town in East Riding of Yorkshire on Bridlington Bay 8 km (5 miles) WSW of Flamborough Head. Pop. (1991) 31,334. Port. Seaside resort. Remains of a 12th-cent. Augustinian priory in the nave of the parish church. Queen Henrietta Maria landed here in 1643 and, when the town was bombarded, she took refuge in Boynton Hall 5.6 km (3½ miles) W.

Bridport England. Market town in Dorset on the R. Brit 23 km (14 miles) W of Dorchester. Pop. (1991) 11,667.

Manufactures ropes, fishing nets, sailcoth and cordage. The fishing village and seaside resort of West Bay is 2.4 km (1½ miles) S.

Brie France. Agricultural region (*pays*) mainly in the Seine-et-Marne department between the Seine and Marne rivers E of Paris. Chief commercial centre Meaux.

Produces wheat and sugar-beet, but chiefly famous for dairy produce, esp. the soft Brie cheese.

Partly wooded; inc. the Forêt de Sénart.

Brieg ➤BRZEG.

Brienz Switzerland. Town in the Bern canton on the NE side of L. Brienz. Pop. (1985) 3200.

Tourist resort. Wood-carving and violin-making.

Brienz, Lake Switzerland. Lake in the Bern canton in the Bernese Alps at 567 m (1860 ft). Area 28 sq km (11 sq. miles), chief town Brienz. The Aar R. enters at the NE end and leaves at the SW, discharging into L. Thun. On the S shore are the famous Giessbach Falls.

Brierley Hill England. Industrial town in West Midlands 14 km (9 miles) W of Birmingham on the edge of the Black Country.

Manufactures iron and steel, glassware, pottery and bricks.

Brig Switzerland. Town in the Valais canton on the R. Rhône. Pop. (1985) 5500.

Important as a route centre because of its position at the N end of the Simplon Pass and tunnel and at the junction of the Simplon, Lötschberg and Furka railways.

Brighouse England. Industrial town in West Yorkshire on the R. Calder 6 km (4 miles) N of Huddersfield. Pop. (1991) 32,198.

Industries inc. textiles, carpets and textile machinery and engineering.

Brightlingsea England. Town in E Essex on the estuary of the R. Colne. Pop. (1991) 7441.

Yachting and holiday resort. Oyster-fishing.

Brighton England. Popular seaside resort in E Sussex on the Channel coast 77 km (48 miles) S of London. Pop. (1991) 124,851. Situated at the foot of the South Downs, with a sea front over 8 km (5 miles) long. Joins Hove in the W.

Some fishing. Manufactures footwear and food products.

Seat of the University of Sussex (1959). Described as 'a poor fishing town' (then known as Brighthelmstone) in the early 18th cent.; popularized by Dr Russell (who advocated sea bathing) and the Prince Regent (later George IV) who had the Royal Pavilion rebuilt (1817) in oriental style. The opening of the railway (1841) further stimulated its growth as a resort. Birthplace of Aubrey Beardsley, the illustrator (1872–98).

Brindisi Italy. Ancient Brundisium. Cap. of the Brindisi province in Apulia in the 'heel' of Italy on the Adriatic Sea. Pop. (1990) 93,290.

Seaport. Industries inc. petro-chemicals and oil-refining. Exports wine, olive oil. Important as the gateway to Greece. An outer and an inner harbour.

Castle of Frederick II; cathedral (12th-cent., restored in the 18th cent.); a column believed to mark the S end of the Appian

Way. Was a Roman naval station. Declined after the Crusades. Severely damaged by earthquake 1456. Revived with the opening of the Suez Canal (1869).

Brisbane Australia. Cap. of Queensland 23 km (14 miles) up the Brisbane R., which reaches Moreton Bay through much silt and sand; with a dredged channel the city is a major seaport, accommodating vessels of 10-m (33-ft) draught and has a large graving dock. Pop. (1993) 1,421,000.

Railways run N to Cairns, S to Sydney and industrial New South Wales and inland to the growing industrial area round Ipswich and to rural collecting centres. Exports frozen meat, butter, cheese, sugar, wool, hides and canned fruit. Shipbuilding, oil-refining, textiles, food-processing. Manufactures cement, furniture, clothing and footwear.

Seat of the University of Queensland (1911). Fine streets and parks; among outstanding buildings is the City Hall (1930). Its site was selected (1824) by Sir Thomas Brisbane, Governor of New South Wales, as a penal settlement. Opened to free settlement 1842. Became cap. of the colony of Queensland 1859.

Bristol England. Seaport and industrial centre and from 1996 a unitary local authority on the R. Avon 11 km (7 miles) above the mouth on Bristol Channel. Pop. (1991) 407,992.

Important seaport and industrial centre. Port inc. the docks at Avonmouth and Portishead, at the river mouth. Imports grain, fruit (esp. bananas), wine, tobacco, petroleum. Industries inc. aircraft, aerospace equipment, mechanical engineering, packing materials, financial services, tobacco products, chocolate and soap.

The cathedral, dating from the 12th cent. but much restored in later times, is surpassed by the magnificent 14th-cent. Church of St Mary Redcliffe, described by Queen Elizabeth I as 'the fairest, the goodliest, and the most famous parish church in England'. Much of the city (inc. Merchant Venturers' Hall) was destroyed by bombing during World War II, though the Almshouses (1699) have been restored. In front of the 18th-cent. Exchange (designed by John Wood of Bath) are four bronze pillars, the 'Nails', where merchants used to carry out cash transactions, giving rise to the expression 'pay on the nail'. Seat of a university (1909) and a 16th-cent. grammar school. On Brandon Hill is the Cabot tower (1897), commemorating John Cabot's expedition to N America (1497). A replica of his ship the *Matthew* sailed to Newfoundland in 1997. City Art Gallery and Museum; Theatre Royal (1766). Just NW at Clifton the Avon gorge is spanned by Brunel's suspension bridge (1845).

Settled in late Saxon times, Bristol developed primarily through its trade and by the 12th cent. was an important port. Early trade largely with Ireland (wool). Much of its later trade was with the Americas and in the 17th-18th cent. it prospered from the slave trade. Declined somewhat after abolition and the rise of Liverpool. One of the first transatlantic steamships, the *Great Western*, was built and sailed from here in 1838; the *Great Britain* (1843), brought back from the Falkland Islands, is being restored. She was the first ocean-going propeller-driven ironship (designed by I. K. Brunel). As ships increased in size the city docks became inadequate and the docks at Avonmouth and Portishead were taken over (1884). Birthplace of poets Thomas Chatterton (1752–70) and Robert Southey (1774–1843), painter Sir Thomas Lawrence (1769–1830), Samuel Plimsoll (1824–98, the inventor and legislator of the Plimsoll Mark), writer J. A. Symonds (1840–93).

Bristol USA. Industrial town in Connecticut 23 km (14 miles) SW of Hartford. Pop. (1990) 79,000. Noted for clock-making since the end of the 18th cent. Also manufactures springs and sports equipment.

Bristol Channel England/Wales. Inlet of the Atlantic Ocean between Wales and SW England, extending 130 km (80 miles) E to the Severn estuary and narrowing from 80 km (50 miles) to 8 km (5 miles) in width. It has the greatest tidal range in England. On the Welsh side the chief inlets are Milford Haven,

Carmarthen Bay and Swansea Bay; chief ports Cardiff and Swansea; chief rivers the Taff and the Towy. On the English side the chief inlets are Bideford Bay and Bridgwater Bay; chief towns Ilfracombe and Weston-super-Mare; chief rivers the Severn, Parrett, Taw and Torridge.

British Antarctic Territory. United Kingdom Overseas Territory established in 1962 as a consequence of the entry into force of the Antarctic Treaty to separate those areas of the then Falkland Islands Dependencies which lay within the Treaty area from those which did not (i.e. South Georgia and the South Sandwich Islands). The territory encompasses the lands and islands within the area south of 60°S latitude lying between 20°W and 80°W longitude (approximately due S of the Falkland Islands and the Dependencies). It covers an area of some 1,709,400 sq km (660,000 sq. miles) and its principal components are the South Orkney and South Shetland Islands, the Antarctic Peninsula (Palmer Land and Graham Land), the Filchner and Ronne Ice Shelves and Coats Land. There is no indigenous or permanently resident pop. There is however an itinerant pop. of scientists and logistics staff of about 300, manning a number of research stations.

British Columbia Canada. The most westerly province on the Pacific coast. Area 947,800 sq km (365,948 sq. miles). Pop. (1995) 3,766,000. Cap. Victoria on Vancouver Is. Largest city and chief seaport Vancouver, on the mainland. Almost entirely mountainous, 4 distinct ranges running roughly parallel N–S. The most westerly range, invaded by the sea, forms a chain of mountainous islands along the coast; the most easterly, the high, rugged, snow-capped ridge of the Rocky Mountains, towers above the prairies and, until the building of the railroad, discouraged travel farther W. The ranges are cut by the valleys of the main rivers (the Fraser, Kootenay, Thompson and Columbia) and their tributaries. These rivers are fast-flowing and the water-power potential is enormous. The climate varies considerably: maritime temperate along the coast, continental in the interior. At Prince Rupert the mean annual temperature range is 13°C (55°F) and rainfall 245 cm (96 ins.) and at Kamloops they are 32°C (90°F) and 25 cm (10 ins.).

The forests are valuable, with rich stands of Douglas fir, Western hemlock, Sitka spruce and red cedar; lumbering is a major industry. Only about 3 per cent of the land is suitable for agriculture. Dairying and mixed farming are practised in the S; much fruit is grown. The Okanagan valley is famous for apples, grown in irrigated orchards. On the coast there are important salmon and herring fisheries. Mineral deposits are extensive; coal, gold, silver, lead, zinc and copper are mined. Industries, associated with the forestry, farming, fishing and mining which form the basis of the economy, inc. sawmilling, pulp and paper milling, fish and fruit canning, ore smelting and refining. They are aided by abundant hydroelectric power. Chief towns Vancouver, Victoria, New Westminster.

From 1821 British Columbia was the preserve of the Hudson's Bay Company; after the Fraser R. gold rush (1858) the mainland colony was established, to be joined by Vancouver Island in 1886. It joined the Dominion of Canada in 1871, on the understanding that a trans-continental railway would be constructed; in 1885 the Canadian Pacific Railway reached Vancouver.

British Indian Ocean Territory. United Kingdom Overseas Territory established in 1965, consisting then of the Chagos Archipelago (formerly administered from Mauritius) and the islands of Aldabra, Desroches and Farquhar (all formerly administered from Seychelles). The latter islands became part of Seychelles when that country achieved independence in 1976. The group, with a total land area of 60 sq km (23 sq. miles), comprises 5 coral atolls (Diego Garcia, Peros Banhos, Salomon, Eagle and Egmont) of which the largest and southernmost, Diego Garcia, covers 44 sq km (17 sq. miles) and lies 724 km (450 miles) S of the Maldives. The British Indian Ocean Territory was es-

tablished to meet UK and US defence requirements in the Indian Ocean. A US navy support facility has been established on Diego Garcia. There is no permanent pop.

British Isles. The British Isles consist of Great Britain and Ireland surrounded by many smaller islands lying off the NW coast of mainland Europe. Two countries comprise the British Isles: the United Kingdom and Ireland. The United Kingdom, which is often known as Britain, is itself made up of England, Wales, Scotland and Northern Ireland. ➤ENGLAND; GREAT BRITAIN; IRELAND; SCOTLAND; UNITED KINGDOM; WALES.

British Virgin Islands West Indies. Group of 70 islands in the E of the Virgin Is. archipelago. Area 153 sq km (59 sq. miles). Pop. (1991) 16,749. Cap. Road Town (pop. 6330) on Tortola (area 54 sq km (21 sq. miles)), the main island. Other leading islands are Virgin Gorda, Anegada and Jost Van Dyke; altogether only 16 are inhabited. Most of them are hilly and they have a pleasant subtropical climate; their chief products are livestock (cattle), fish, fruit, vegetables. Tourism is the most important economic activity. Offshore financial services are growing and there are over 6000 companies registered.

Became part of the Federation of the Leeward Is. in 1871, but when this came to an end (1956) the Colony of the Virgin Is. was established and became a United Kingdom Overseas Territory in 1998. The territory is administered by a 5-member executive council under the Governor. There is also a 13-member legislative council.

Brittany ➤BRETAGNE.

Brive (Brive-la-Gaillarde) France. Market town in the Corrèze department on the Corrèze R. 84 km (52 miles) SSE of Limoges. Pop. (1990) 52,677.

Trade in fruit and vegetables, cattle, wool and chestnuts. Manufactures food products and paper.

The 12th-cent. Church of St Martin stands in the centre of the old town.

Brixham England. Town in Devon 8 km (5 miles) S of Torquay. Pop. (1991) 15,865.

Fishing port and tourist resort with a picturesque harbour; a new marina with 550 berths recently completed, where there is a replica of Sir Francis Drake's *Golden Hind*.

The landing of William of Orange (1688) is commemorated by a statue on the quay.

Brixton England. District in the London borough of Lambeth S of the Thames. One of London's largest prisons (founded 1820).

Brno Czech Republic. Cap. of the Jihomoravský region just above the confluence of the Svitava and the Svratka rivers 177 km (110 miles) SE of Prague. Pop. (1990) 391,000.

An industrial, commercial and cultural centre. Important textile industry. Manufactures cars, machinery, clothing, furniture, soap and armaments; produced the Bren gun.

The city is dominated by the fortress of Spilberk on a hill 288 m (945 ft) high, an Austrian political prison 1621–1857 (where the Italian poet Silvio Pellico was confined 1822–30). In the old town of narrow, crooked streets, there are many old buildings, e.g. the cathedral (15th-cent.), the old town hall (16th-cent.) and 14th/16th-cent. churches. University (1919). It withstood a long siege by the Swedes under Torstensson 1645.

Broads (Norfolk Broads) England. A region of shallow lakes amid marshland (mainly in Norfolk, with a small part in Suffolk) centred on the R. Bure and its tributaries the Ant and Thurne, partly caused by the widening ('broadening') of rivers. A popular area for holiday-making, yachting, fishing, bird-watching. Wroxham and Barton are among the more picturesque broads.

Broadstairs England. Seaside resort in the Isle of Thanet in NE Kent. Pop. (1991) 22,118. Charles Dickens (1812–70) frequently stayed and wrote many of his novels here.

Brocken (Blocksberg) Germany. Highest peak (1143 m; 3749 ft) of the Harz Mountains in the Magdeburg district. In fog or mist

the 'Spectre of the Brocken' (the magnified shadow of the observer) may be seen. Traditionally the witches' meeting place on Walpurgis Night (1 May). Location of the witch scene in Goethe's *Faust*.

Brockman, Mount ➤HAMERSLEY RANGE.

Brockton USA. Industrial town in Massachusetts 31 km (19 miles) S of Boston. Pop. (1990) 93,000.

Leading centre of shoe manufacture. Also produces footwear machinery and tools, leather.

Broken Hill Australia. Mining and industrial town in W interior of New South Wales 354 km (220 miles) NE of Port Pirie. Pop. (1991) 23,300. Lode 5 km (3 miles) long of metallic sulphides, lead and silver above, zinc below, worked since 1883. Metal concentrates are smelted and refined at Port Pirie and Risdon (Tasmania). The water supply is piped from the Menindee storage on the Darling R.

Broken Hill (Zambia) ➤KABWE.

Bromberg ➤BYDGOSZCZ.

Bromley England. Outer London borough comprising the former municipal boroughs of Beckenham and Bromley and the urban districts of Chislehurst and Sidcup (S of the A20 road), Orpington and Penge, all in NW Kent. Pop. (1994) 293,000. Birthplace of the author, H. G. Wells (1866–1946).

Brompton England. Residential district in S Kensington in SW London. Contains the Roman Catholic Brompton Oratory (built in the Italian Renaissance style); Brompton Chest Hospital; the Victoria and Albert Museum, the Science Museum, the Natural History department of the British Museum and the Geological Museum.

Bromsgrove England. Town in Worcestershire 19 km (12 miles) NNE of Worcester. Pop. (1991) 90,481.

Iron foundries. Manufactures nails and paint brushes.

The grammar school (founded 1553; refounded 1693) was attended by the writers A. E. and Laurence Housman.

Bronx, the ➤NEW YORK.

Brooklyn ➤NEW YORK.

Brownsville USA. Town in S Texas on the Rio Grande 35 km (22 miles) from the mouth opposite Matamoros (Mexico). Pop. (1990) 94,700.

Commercial centre. Trade in petroleum, citrus fruits and cotton. Canning, chemical and other industries.

Bruce, Mount ➤HAMERSLEY RANGE.

Bruges (Flemish **Brugge**) Belgium. Cap. of West Flanders province 40 km (25 miles) WNW of Ghent. Pop. (1991) 117,150.

Market town. Railway and canal junction. Tourist centre. Engineering, flour-milling and brewing. Manufactures lace, electronics and yeast. Linked by ship-canal with Zee-brugge.

Has preserved much of its medieval character. Gothic church of Notre Dame containing Michelangelo's marble *Virgin and Child*. Market hall (13th/15th-cent.) with the famous belfry and 46-bell carillon. Leading market of the Hanseatic League (13th cent.). Reached the peak of its importance in the 15th cent. Repressive measures against the inhabitants after a revolt, religous persecution and the silting up of the Zwin estuary led to a decline. In the late 19th and early 20th cent. some revival of trade was achieved by the construction of new docks and the ship canal to Zeebrugge.

Brugg Switzerland. Small town in Aargau canton on the Aar R. 27 km (17 miles) NW of Zürich. Pop. (1970) 8635. Nearby is the site of Vindonissa, the chief Roman camp in Helvetia, where remains of an amphitheatre were found; also ruins of the 11th-cent. Habsburg castle.

Brühl Germany. Town in North Rhine-Westphalia 11 km (7 miles) S of Cologne. Pop. (1986) 40,700.

In a lignite-mining area. Manufactures briquettes and machinery.

Brunei Darussalam. The State of Brunei, on the coast of Borneo, is bounded on the NW by the South China Sea and on all other sides by Sarawak (Malaysia). Area 5765 sq km (2225 sq. miles). Pop. (1995) 291,000 (90 per cent urban). Life expectancy, 70 years male, 73 female. Cap. Bandar Seri Begawan. Other cities, Kuala Belait, Seria Tutong. Currency: Brunei dollar = 100 cents. Brunei is divided into four districts: Brunei/Muara, Tutong, Seria/Belait and Temburong. The terrain in the W is hilly lowland which rises in the hinterland to about 300 m (984 ft). To the E the wide coastal plain reaches up to the more mountainous regions. The highest point, Bukit Pagon, is 1841 m (6038 ft). The climate is tropical marine, hot and moist, but nights are cool. Humidity is high and rainfall heavy. Land use: forested 85 per cent, meadows and pastures 1 per cent, agricultural and under permanent cultivation 1 per cent. Equatorial rainforests cover much of the country and are inaccessible except by river. The official lang. is Bahasa Melayu (Malay) but English is widely used. Other lang. inc. Chinese, Iban and a number of dialects. Islam is the state religion but about 13 per cent are Buddhists and 10 per cent Christian. Malays constitute 67 per cent of the pop., Chinese 15 per cent.

The finding of oil in the W of the state in 1929 brought in a new economic era and development of offshore discoveries in the 1960s set Brunei on the path to economic prosperity. Brunei also has one of the largest liquified natural gas plants in the world. Most food is imported and most rubber plantations have been abandoned. There are large potential supplies of serviceable timber. Other products are gravel and animal hides. Local industries inc. boatbuilding, cloth weaving and the manufacture of brass and silver ware.

From the 14th to the 16th cent. Brunei had been the centre of an empire which stretched from much of Borneo and parts of the Sulu Islands and the Philippines, but by the end of the 19th cent. much of its territory and almost all its power had been lost in the colonial expansion in SE Asia.

Brunei became a British protectorate in

1888, accepting in 1906 a British resident who advised the Sultan on all matters except the Islamic faith and Malay custom. The Brunei constitution and with it self-government was introduced in 1959, with Britain retaining responsibility for Brunei's foreign affairs, security and defence. In 1962 a rebellion by a section of the community was quickly put down with the aid of British forces. In 1967 the Sultan abdicated in favour of his eldest son, Sultan Hassanal Bolkiah Mu'izzaddin Waddaulah, who became the 29th in line of rulers going back to the 15th cent. In 1979 a treaty signed between Brunei and Britain provided for full independence on 1 January 1984. Supreme power is vested in the Sultan and there is no legislature. A 21-member non-elective Council of Ministers advises the Sultan in legislative matters.

Brunnen Switzerland. Port and tourist resort on L. Lucerne in the Schwyz canton. Pop. (1970) 3000. Linked with Morschach by rack-and-pinion railway. Scene of the re-affirmation by the Forest Cantons (1315) of the Everlasting League (1291), the foundation of Swiss independence.

Brunswick (Braunschweig) Germany. 1. Former duchy in N Germany, comprising 3 larger and 6 smaller enclaves in the Prussian provinces of Hanover and Saxony. Area 3670 sq km (1417 sq. miles). The property of the Guelphs in the 12th cent., becoming later the duchies of Brunswick-Lüneburg (whose Duke became Elector of Hanover 1692) and Brunswick-Wolfenbüttel. Hanover was annexed by Prussia 1866. The last king's grandson was made Duke of Brunswick 1913. Incorporated in the new *Land* of Lower Saxony 1945. 2. City in Lower Saxony on the Oker R., formerly cap. of the duchy of Brunswick. Pop. (1990) 258,500.

Varied industries: fruit and vegetable canning, flour-milling, sugar-refining, publishing; manufactures vehicles, optics, pianos, bicycles and calculating machines.

Brussels Belgium. Cap. of Belgium and of Brabant province on the Senne, a tributary of the Scheldt. Pop. (1991) 960,324. Within the Flemish-speaking region, although most of its people speak French.

Important railway junction. Manufactures textiles, clothing, lace, carpets, chemicals, paper and furniture. The economy is dominated by government and service-sector employment. The city's role in Europe has itself generated employment and has also attracted multinational finance, banking and trading companies.

The inner, old, city is a southward-pointing pentagon with the commercial quarter W of the government quarter. The Grand Place, with its city hall and guild houses, lies between them. Boulevards outline the pentagon and the canalized R. Senne runs beneath it. Industrial development, canals, railway and warehousing, run S and N through Greater Brussels along the Senne valley. Outward growth in all directions has been rapid since 1830 and is continuing. Most of the city's fabric is of the 19th and 20th cent. Brussels was founded as a river crossing on the trade route from the Rhine cities to Bruges.

As a fortified market town it received a charter in 1312. It developed a rich trade in luxury fabrics, making velvets, brocades and lace. Brussels became cap. of the Netherlands in 1531, serving Spanish and Austrian Habsburg emperors in succession. It became the cap. of newly independent Belgium in 1830, headquarters of the European Union in 1959 and of NATO in 1967.

Bryansk Russia. Cap. of the Bryansk Region on the Desna R. 346 km (215 miles) SW of Moscow. Pop. (1989) 452,000.

Railway and industrial centre. Important railway workshops; also sawmills, ironworks and brickworks. Manufactures electrical equipment, chemicals, woollen goods. Oil pipeline from Samara.

Founded (1146) as Debryansk. An independent principality till 1356. Became Russian in the 17th cent.

Brynmawr Wales. Town in Blaenau-Gwent 3 km (2 miles) NE of Ebbw Vale. Pop. (1991) 14,581.

The coalmining and steel industries of the

neighbourhood have been replaced largely by light industries.

Brzeg (Ger. **Brieg**) Poland. Ancient town in the Opole voivodeship on the Odra (Oder) R. 40 km (25 miles) SE of Wroclaw. Pop. (1989) 38,504.

Manufactures textiles, leather goods and chemicals.

Originally part of the medieval Polish state, then in German Silesia (Polish Śląsk). Restored to Poland after World War II under the Potsdam Agreement (1945). Called Brieg during the German administration.

Bucaramanga Colombia. Cap. of the Santander department in the E Cordillera at 900 m (2952 ft). Pop. (1992) 349,403.

Commercial and industrial city in mountainous country growing coffee, tobacco and cotton. Manufactures cement, cigars and cigarettes, textiles, straw hats. Founded 1622.

Bucharest (Romanian **Bucureşti**) Romania. Cap. of Romania in Walachia on the Dambovita R., a tributary of the Danube. Pop. (1992) 2,350,984.

Bucharest has always been a point of transit trade in primary products; it is also an industrial town as well as the centre of government. Oil-refining, tanning, flour-milling. Manufactures aircraft machinery, textiles and chemicals. Considerable trade in petroleum, timber, agricultural produce.

Bucharest has a continental climate of extreme temperatures. The city is mainly modern, having been rebuilt handsomely in the late 19th cent. and redeveloped on an even bigger scale after 1945. The site is mainly flat, spreading from the river banks, sheltered by low hills to the S. Founded in the Middle Ages, the city was a princely seat from *c.* 1400 and a fortress against the Turks; it became the national cap. in 1859. There has been frequent destruction by fire (in the old, wooden city) and earthquakes (the last in 1977). As the centre of the Romanian Orthodox Church it acquired many fine churches and was commanded by its cathedral. After 1866 rebuilding in stone was extensive. Recent rebuilding has produced megalithic structures in uniform style.

Buckfastleigh England. Town in Devon on the R. Dart 18 km (11 miles) W of Torquay. Pop. (1991) 2786. Manufactures woollen goods.

Nearby is Buckfast Abbey, built by Benedictine monks (1907–37) on the site of a medieval Cistercian abbey.

Buckhaven and Methil Scotland. Town in Fife on the Firth of Forth; formed by the union of the two towns (1891). Pop. (1991) 17,069.

Exports coal. Fishing.

Buckie Scotland. Port in Moray situated on Moray Firth coast. Pop. (1991) 8425.

Industries inc. fishing, fish-processing, boat and yacht building, marine engineering and structural engineering.

Buckingham England. Market town in Buckinghamshire on the R. Ouse 24 km (15 miles) NW of Aylesbury. Pop. (1991) 10,168.

Engineering. Manufactures dairy products.

The University of Buckingham (founded as the University College at Buckingham in 1976) was established 1983. Stowe House, former seat of the dukes of Buckingham, since 1923 occupied by the public school, is 5 km (3 miles) NNW.

Buckinghamshire England. County in the S Midlands. Area 1940 sq km (749 sq. miles). Pop. (1994) 658,400. County town Aylesbury. The Thames forms part of the S boundary; drained also by the Thame and the Wye (Thames tributaries) and in the N by the Ouse. The land rises gently N from the Thames to the chalk ridge of the Chiltern Hills and descends more abruptly on their N slopes to the fertile Vale of Aylesbury, where cereals, fruit and vegetables are cultivated and dairy cattle and poultry are raised. The famous woods of the Chilterns were chiefly responsible for their local furniture industry; Aylesbury and High Wycombe are the chief manufacturing centres. Many small towns and villages are notable for their associations with poets or statesmen, e.g. Chalfont St Giles (Milton), Stoke Poges (Gray), Hughenden (Disraeli), Beaconsfield (Burke).

Budapest Hungary. Cap. of Hungary and of Pest county on the R. Danube. Pop. (1993) 2,009,000. The city straddles the Danube at a fordable place and combines Buda, the old city on the W hillside, with Pest, the newer city on the flat E bank. In Buda the central point is castle hill, crowned with fine museums and the medieval Matthias Church, and flanked by two other hills of which Gellért hegy is a steep crag overlooking the river. Pest by contrast has a spacious, level plan with semicircular boulevards around the Inner Town.

Budapest is the dominant city of Hungary in terms of pop., employment, industry, commerce and culture. Industries inc. oil-refining, textiles, pharmaceuticals, food-processing, chemicals, iron and steel. Danube transport and the Danube crossing are central to this role, as is the demonstration of 'market socialism'. Medieval Buda was the Hungarian royal cap., with Pest a small town and trading port. By 1800 Pest was the larger and its growth outstripped that of Buda until the 1950s. The trading community was mainly German, the royal city Magyar and, later, Austrian. Hungarian nationalism flourished in Pest in the 19th cent., but Habsburg power predominated and 'Buda-Pest' was created as one city in 1872. The modern city is ethnically Hungarian and its housing overstretched by regional immigration.

Budaun India. Town in Uttar Pradesh 40 km (25 miles) SW of Bareilly. Pop. (1991) 116,695. Minor industries. Trade in grain and cotton.

Has the 13th-cent. Jama Masjid (Great Mosque), later restored several times.

Buddh Gaya India. Village in Bihar 10 km (6 miles) S of Gaya. Site of a temple (built over the remains of an Asokan temple) and the sacred Bo-tree under which Buddha is said to have received enlightenment.

Bude-Stratton England. Small port and holiday resort on the N coast of Cornwall. Pop. (1991) 5979. Picturesque coastal scenery, esp. to the S.

Budleigh Salterton England. Town in Devon on Lyme Bay (English Channel) 6 km (4 miles) ENE of Exmouth. Pop. (1991) 3759. Fishing port. Holiday resort. East Budleigh, 3 km (2 miles) inland, was the birthplace of the navigator, Sir Walter Raleigh (1552–1618).

Budweis ➤ČESKÉ BUDEJOVICE.

Buea ➤CAMEROON.

Buenaventura Colombia. Chief Pacific seaport in the Valle del Cauca department 64 km (40 miles) NW of Cali. Pop. (1985) 122,500. Outlet for the fertile Cauca valley and the Chocó mining region.

Exports coffee, sugar, hides, gold and platinum. Fish-canning.

Founded 1540. Expanded with the building of the railway to Cali (1914).

Buenos Aires Argentina. Cap. on the W bank of the Río de la Plata estuary. Pop. (1991) 2,965,403.

The country's chief seaport and industrial and commercial centre. Principal exports meat (beef), grain (wheat, maize), wool. Manufactures textiles, paper, paint, chemicals and metal goods. Around the docks there are great meat-packing plants and grain elevators. Power stations use imported coal, and natural gas and petroleum products are piped into the city. Terminal for a network of railways serving the pampas and linking it with Bolivia and Chile. The city has been largely rebuilt in the 20th cent.

University (1821). The main thoroughfare, the Avenida de Mayo, is an imposing tree-lined boulevard extending between the two chief squares, the Plaza de Mayo and the Plaza del Congreso. The cathedral (1804) contains the tomb of the Liberator, San Martín. Founded (1536) by Spaniards, who were driven out by the Indians. Permanently settled 1580. Remained small and relatively unimportant for the next 200 years, though it was made cap. of a viceroyalty (1776) and was freed from the trade restrictions imposed by Spain (1778). Expanded and prospered greatly in the second half of the 19th cent. with the development of the immense hinterland of the pampas. Became cap. of the republic 1880.

Buffalo USA. Industrial city, lake port and commercial centre in New York, at the E end of L. Erie. Pop. (1990) 328,123. At the W end of the easiest route across the Appalachian highlands, the Hudson–Mohawk gap, which is followed by roads, railways and canal to New York City; near the S end of the Welland Canal from L. Ontario. An important gateway to the Middle West. Also linked with Ontario (Canada) by a railway bridge across the Niagara R. and by a road bridge, opened (1927) to commemorate a cent. of peace between Canada and the USA. The lakeside harbour, protected by a break-water 7.2 km (4½ miles) long, handles enormous quantities of iron ore, coal and grain. Manufactures iron and steel, aircraft, plastics, electrical equipment, machinery. Electric power is drawn from Niagara Falls, 32 km (20 miles) distant. Seat of the University of Buffalo (1846) and several colleges. First settled in 1803, under the name of New Amsterdam; renamed *c.* 1810. Almost destroyed in the Anglo–American War (1813). Its rapid development followed the opening of the Erie Canal to New York (1825).

Buganda Uganda. Former powerful kingdom, now part of Uganda. Area 65,500 sq km (25,600 sq. miles). Chief town Kampala (also cap. of Uganda). Chief commercial centre Entebbe. Mainly savannah; dense forests along the rivers. Chief products cotton, coffee and bananas.

Taken under British protection 1894. Granted native self-government 1900. During the preparations for the Independence of Uganda, the people of Buganda (the Baganda) sought autonomy, but have remained within the state. After Uganda had been granted independence (1962), the Kabaka of Buganda became the first President (1963).

Bug River (Southern Bug) Ukraine.

River 853 km (530 miles) long, rising in W Ukraine 120 km (75 miles) ESE of Zolochev, flowing generally SE and entering the Dnieper estuary and the Black Sea below Nikolayev. Navigable for about 95 km (60 miles) of its lower course. The upper reaches are impeded by rapids.

Bug River (Western Bug) Poland/ Ukraine. River 772 km (480 miles) long, rising in W Ukraine near Zolochev, flowing generally NW and joining the Vistula below Warsaw. Navigable below Brest(-Litovsk), where the Mukhanets R. links it to the Dnieper–Bug Canal. Forms the Polish–Ukrainian frontier for over 160 km (100 miles).

Builth Wells Wales. Market town in Powys on the R. Wye 23 km (14 miles) N of Brecon. Pop. (1991) 2474. Resort. Mineral springs.

Buitenzorg ➤BOGOR.

Bujumbura (Usumbura) Burundi. Cap. and chief port at the NE end of L. Tanganyika. Pop. (1994) 300,000.

Exports cotton, coffee and hides. Manufactures pharmaceutical products, canoes and nets.

Formerly cap. of Ruanda-Urundi.

Bukavu Democratic Republic of the Congo. Formerly Costermansville. Cap. of Kivu region at the S end of L. Kivu near the Rwanda frontier at a height of 1450 m (4756 ft). Pop. (1991) 209,556.

Commercial and route centre. Cinchona-processing. Manufactures pharmaceutical products, insecticides, cement and cotton.

Bukhara (Bokhara) Uzbekistan. Cap. of the Bukhara Region 450 km (280 miles) WSW of Tashkent. Pop. (1990) 227,900.

Commercial centre. Manufactures silk, cotton and woollen goods; once famous for its rugs and carpets.

An ancient city in a fertile oasis near the Zeravshan R., surrounded by walls and with many mosques and bazaars. Under Arab rule from the 7th to the 9th cent. and Persian rule from the 9th to the 10th cent., it was a centre of Muslim learning and is still noted for its theological colleges. The early state of Bukhara was conquered and the city destroyed by Genghis Khan (1220). Taken by the Uzbeks in the early 16th cent., became cap. of the emirate of Bukhara. At the Russian revolution the Emir was driven out (1920) and his territory was made a soviet socialist republic, but in 1924 it was divided between the Uzbek, Tadzhik and Turkmen Soviet Socialist Republics. There is a pipeline 2010 km (1250 miles) long from the Bukhars, taking natural gas to Chelyabinsk in the Urals.

Bukovina. Region of SE Europe E of the Carpathians, drained by the Siret and Prut rivers, now divided between the Ukraine and Romania. Passed from Turkey to Austria (1775) and to Romania (1918). N Bukovina was ceded to the USSR 1940, occupied by Romania 1941–4 and returned to the USSR 1947; chief town Chernovtsy (Cernăuti). S Bukovina remained in Romania as a province, abolished 1952. Peopled by a mixture of Romanians, Ruthenians and Ukrainians.

Bulawayo Zimbabwe. Chief commercial and railway centre and second largest town in Matabeleland 386 km (240 miles) SW of Harare at a height of 1360 m (4461 ft). Pop. (1992) 620,936.

Railway workshops, iron foundries, sugar refinery. Manufactures agricultural implements, textiles. Airport.

Founded (1893) on the site of the kraal of Lobengula (chief of the Matabele). About 48 km (30 miles) S, in the Matopo Hills, is the tomb of Cecil Rhodes, the South African statesman.

Bulgaria. Republic in the Balkan Peninsula in SE Europe. Bounded by Romania in the N, the Black Sea in the E, Turkey and Greece in the S and Yugoslavia in the W. Area 110,994 sq km (42,855 sq. miles). Pop. (1996) 8,366,000 (68 per cent urban). Life expectancy, 69 years male, 75 female. Cap. Sofia. Other cities Plovdiv, Varna, Burgas, Ruse. Currency: Lev = 100 stotinki. To the S of the Danube (which forms most of the N frontier) a plain stretches E–W across the country, succeeded farther S by the Balkan Mountains, with several peaks rising to 2300 m (7544 ft). These mountains separate the N lowlands from the plains of the SE, largely the Martisa basin. In the SW are the still higher Rhodope Mountains, rising to 2925 m (9594 ft) in Peak Musala. The Balkan Mountains form an E–W watershed; the N plains are drained by tributaries of the Danube flowing N, and the S part of the country is drained by the Martisa, Mesta and Struma rivers, flowing generally S to the Aegean Sea. The thriving tourist industry is located by the sandy beaches of the Black Sea. On the whole the climate is continental, with warm summers and cold winters. Mediterranean climate in S parts. Land use: forested 35 per cent, meadows and pastures 19 per cent, agricultural and under permanent cultivation 38 per cent. The official lang. is Bulgarian. The great majority of the pop. belongs to the Eastern Orthodox Church, but there are over 1 million Pomaks (Bulgarian Muslims). The ethnic groups are Bulgarians 86 per cent, Turkish 9 per cent, Gypsy 4 per cent.

Primarily agricultural, the principal crops are cereals, sugar-beet, tobacco (an important export), sunflowers (for seed), vines. Attar of roses (from the famous Valley of Roses) is still an important source of revenue. Large numbers of sheep reared. Mineral resources have been little exploited, these inc. manganese ore, iron ore and coal, but there is a considerable output of lignite. Oil is produced near Balchik on the Black Sea and at Pleven. There are refineries at Burgas and Dolni Dubnik. The recognition of the need for economic reform was heeded before political reform took place and management has been decentralized and profit and loss accounting has been introduced. Price subsidies have been removed from many basic goods and small businesses privatized. Emphasis is placed on the development of small high-technology units. The agrarian reforms aim at returning the land to its former owners and agriculture and food-processing is still the core of the economy. The main centres of industry are Sofia, Plovdiv and Pleven.

The chief ports are Varna and Burgas on the Black Sea and Ruse on the Danube.

Invaded in the 7th cent. AD by the Bulgars, who gradually adopted the lang. and culture of the conquered Slavs and acquired considerable power in SE Europe, annexed by the Ottoman Empire 1395, remained under oppressive Turkish rule until 1878. Liberated by Russia during the Russo–Turkish wars, but did not achieve full sovereignty until Ferdinand of Saxe-Coburg-Gotha, the ruling prince, proclaimed himself king (1908). Took part in the Balkan Wars (1912–13) and joined the German side in World War I. Lost S Dobruja to Romania, the Aegean coastline to Greece and some territory to Yugoslavia (1919). Again supported the German cause in World War II. S Dobruja was restored 1945. After a referendum, the monarchy was abolished (1946) and a People's Republic was proclaimed. In 1991 the National Assembly abolished the Communist Party's sole right to govern. A non-Communist government was elected in 1991. There is a 240-member National Assembly directly elected by proportional representation. The President is directly elected for 4-year terms.

Bull Run USA. Small stream in N Virginia. Scene of two Confederate victories (1861, 1862) in the American Civil War. Jackson's stand in the first battle earned him the nickname of 'Stonewall'.

Bunbury Australia. Seaport in SW Western Australia 160 km (100 miles) S of Perth on Geographe Bay. Pop. (1991) 25,657.

Exports timber, wheat, wool. Manufactures superphosphates and textiles. The port has been expanded and an alumina refinery built in recent years.

Buncrana Ireland. Town on the E side of the Lough Swilly in NE Co. Donegal. Pop. (1986) 3106.

Seaside resort, market town and fishing centre.

Bundaberg Australia. Port in SE Queensland 290 km (180 miles) NNW of Brisbane. Pop. (1991) 38,000.

Exports sugar. Sugar-refining, brewing and distilling (rum).

Bundoran Ireland. Fishing port and seaside resort in S Co. Donegal on Donegal Bay. Pop. (1991) 1500.

Bungay England. Market town in NE Suffolk on the R. Waveney 21 km (13 miles) W of Lowestoft. Pop. (1991) 3393.

Industries inc. printing and the manufacture of agricultural implements.

Bunker Hill USA. Small hill in Charlestown, now part of Boston, in Massachusetts; connected by a ridge with Breed's Hill. Scene of the first important battle of the American Revolution (1775); the Bunker Hill Monument marks the battlefield.

Buraida Saudi Arabia. Town and oasis in Nejd 320 km (200 miles) NW of Riyadh. Pop. (1988) 184,000.

Trade in dates and grain.

Burbank USA. Industrial town in California on the outskirts of Los Angeles. Pop. (1990) 93,700.

Film and television studios. Manufactures aircraft.

Burdekin River Australia. River 684 km (425 miles) long, rising 137 km (85 miles) NW of Townsville in E Queensland, flowing generally SE and then N to enter the Pacific through an unnavigable delta at Upstart Bay. The flow varies greatly, but increases to produce widespread flooding in summer.

Burdwan ►BARDDHAMAN.

Burgas Bulgaria. Cap. of the province of Burgas on the Gulf of Burgas on the Black Sea. Pop. (1990) 204,915.

Seaport and industrial centre. Exports tobacco, wool and leather. Manufactures agricultural machinery, textiles and soap. Flour-milling. Fishing. Oil refinery and oil-tanker repair and construction.

Burgdorf Switzerland. Town in the Bern canton on the Emme R. 18 km (11 miles) NE of Bern. Pop. (1985) 18,500.

Manufactures textiles. Trade in Emmenthal cheese.

In the old castle (now a museum) above the modern town, J. H. Pestalozzi, the educationalist (1746–1827), established his first school (1799).

Burgenland Austria. Federal state in the E, bordered in the E by Hungary. Area 3965 sq km (1530 sq. miles). Pop. (1991) 273,541. Cap. Eisenstadt. Mainly low-lying in the N (partly occupied by L. Neusiedler); hilly in the centre and S.

Chief occupations agriculture and stock-rearing.

Ruled by Austria from 1491 and by Hungary from 1647. Restored to Austria after World War I. After a plebiscite, the Sopron salient was returned to Hungary (1921), almost separating the N part of the province from the S.

Burghead Scotland. Town in Moray on the headland at the E end of Burghead Bay in the Moray Firth 11 km (7 miles) NW of Elgin. Pop. (1991) 1495. Fishing port. Resort.

Burgos Spain. 1. Province in Old Castile in the N. Area 14,369 sq km (5531 sq. miles). Pop. (1991) 355,138. Forms part of the Meseta. Largely forested. Drained by the Ebro and the Douro (Duero) rivers. Cereals and other crops cultivated. Sheep reared. 2. Cap. of Burgos province, on the Arlanzón R., a tributary of the Douro, 120 km (75 miles) SW of Bilbao. Pop. (1991) 169,269.

Flour-milling, engineering. Manufactures tyres, paper, woollen and leather goods, and chemicals. Tourist centre.

Famous for its architecture; the magnificent Gothic cathedral (begun 1221, completed 1567) with its 15 chapels, is the burial-place of El Cid. There are several other Gothic churches. The life of the city centres on the arcaded Plaza Mayor. Founded 884. Became cap. of the kingdom of Castile, but declined with the rise of Madrid. Franco's provisional cap. during the Civil War (1936–9). Nearby is the birthplace of the Spanish warrior and hero, El Cid (c. 1043–99).

Burgundy ▸BOURGOGNE.

Burhanpur India. Town in Madhya Pradesh on the Tapti R. 450 km (280 miles) NE of Bombay. Pop. (1991) 172,710.

Manufactures textiles and shellac.

Founded in the early 15th cent. Noted for fine fabrics decorated with gold and silver thread.

Burkina Faso. Republic in W Africa bounded by Mali in the N and W, Niger in the E and Benin, Togo, Ghana and Côte d'Ivoire in the S. Area 274,400 sq km (105,945 sq. miles). Pop. (1995) 10,324,000 (14 per cent urban). Life expectancy, 46 years male, 49 female. Cap. Ouagadougou. Other towns Bobo-Dioulasso, Koudougou. Currency: CFA franc = 100 centimes. The country consists mainly of wooded savannah. Agriculture is the dominant occupation, inc. nomads raising cattle. Irrigation is being extended but most agricultural activity is in river valleys or at oases. It has a tropical climate with a wet season May to November and a dry season December to April. Land use: forested 51 per cent, meadows and pastures 22 per cent, agricultural and under permanent cultivation 13 per cent. The official lang. is French. About 45 per cent follow traditional beliefs, 43 per cent are Muslims and 12 per cent Christians. The principal ethnic groups are Mossi (49 per cent), Fulani, Mandé, Bobo, Gourounsi, Gourmantché.

Millets, beans, sorghum and maize are important subsistence crops; groundnuts and cotton cultivated for export. Cattle, sheep and goats are raised. Manganese, zinc, diamonds and phosphates are found.

Upper Volta was formed in 1919 as a French colony from Upper Senegal and Niger. It was divided up between Ivory Coast (Côte d'Ivoire), Sudan and Niger in 1932 and was formed again in 1947. It became a member state of the French Community in 1958 and gained independence in 1960. The name of the country was changed to Burkina Faso in 1984.

Burlington (Iowa) USA. Industrial town on the Mississippi R. 225 km (140 miles) ESE of Des Moines. Pop. (1990) 27,208.

Manufactures furniture, boilers and electrical equipment.

Burlington (Vermont) USA. Port and largest city of Vermont on L. Champlain. Pop. (1990) 38,633.

Trade by rail and lake. Manufactures food products (inc. maple sugar), furniture and tools.

University of Vermont (1791).

Burma ➤MYANMAR.

Burma Road. Highway about 1290 km (800 miles) long from Lashio, the railway terminus in E Myanmar (Burma), to Kunming and Chongqing in China. Begun by the Chinese 1937; completed 1939. Utilized for the transport of war materials to the Chinese forces in the Sino–Japanese War until closed by the Japanese (1942).

Burnham England. Town in Buckinghamshire just NW of Slough. Nearby is the woodland area (152 ha; 374 acres) of Burnham Beeches, the remains of an ancient forest, purchased (1879) by the City of London.

Burnham-on-Crouch England. Town in SE Essex on the estuary of the R. Crouch. Pop. (1991) 7067.

Noted for yachting and boatbuilding. Oyster culture.

Burnham-on-Sea England. Seaside resort in Somerset on Bridgwater Bay (Bristol Channel). Pop. (1991) 19,588.

Burnley England. Town in E Lancashire at the confluence of the Brun and Calder rivers. Pop. (1991) 47,661.

In a coalmining district. Important textile centre. Cotton-weaving; also spinning and dyeing. Engineering. Manufactures textile machinery, chemicals and car accessories.

Towneley Hall (acquired by the corporation in 1902) is a museum and art gallery. Suffered from the 'cotton famine' during the American Civil War (1861–5), and from the 20th-cent. decline in the Lancashire cotton trade.

Burntisland Scotland. Port, industrial town and resort in S Fife on the Firth of Forth opposite Edinburgh. Pop. (1991) 5951.

Aluminium works. Shipbuilding. Exports coal.

The name may derive from the site having once been an island.

Burren, The Ireland. Region of bare carboniferous limestone in N Co. Clare. Area 259 sq km (100 sq. miles). Noted for its flora and spectacular caves, streams, potholes and seasonal lakes.

Burrinjuck Dam ➤MURRUMBIDGEE RIVER.

Burry Port Wales. Market town and port in Carmarthenshire 6 km (4 miles) W of Llanelli. Pop. (1991) 8508.

Exports coal. Anthracite mining nearby. Manufactures tinplate.

Bursa Turkey. Cap. of Bursa province 88 km (55 miles) S of Istanbul. Pop. (1990) 775,388.

Trade in tobacco, fruit, grain. Manufactures textiles and carpets.

Several imposing mosques and tombs of Ottoman sultans. Probably founded by King Prusias I of Bithynia in the 2nd cent. BC. Taken by the Ottoman Turks (1326), it was their cap. for nearly a cent.

Burslem England. One of the 'Five Towns' of the Potteries in N Staffordshire, since 1910 incorporated in Stoke-on-Trent. Called the 'mother of the Potteries'; the oldest of the pottery towns, the industry having been established here in the 17th cent. Site of the Wedgwood Institute (1863). Birthplace of Josiah Wedgwood (1730–95), who established his first works here in 1759.

Burton-upon-Trent England. Town in E Staffordshire on the R. Trent 16 km (10 miles) SW of Derby. Pop. (1991) 60,525.

Its famous brewing industry (partly due to the presence of sulphate of lime in the local well-water) may date back to the Benedictine abbey founded in 1002; it became important in the 18th cent. Cooperages, engineering works, timber yards. Manufactures tyres and food products.

Burujird Iran. Town in Khuzistán province at a height of 1680 m (5510 ft) 96 km (60 miles) S of Hamadan. Pop. (1991) 201,016.
Commercial centre. Trade in grain and fruit. Manufactures carpets and rugs, and textiles.

Burundi. Republic in Central Africa bounded by Rwanda in the N, Tanzania in the E and S and W by the Democratic Republic of the Congo. Area 27,816 sq km (10,740 sq. miles). Pop. (1996) 5,943,000 (6 per cent urban). Life expectancy, 49 years male, 51 female. Cap. Bujumbura. Other cities Gitega, Bururi, Ngozi and Cibitoke. Currency: Burundi franc = 100 centimes. Burundi is a land-locked upland plateau at 1200–1800 m (3936–5904 ft), rising to over 2400 m (7872 ft) in the S. The Luvironza, the most southerly headstream of the Nile, rises in the S. It has an equatorial climate, modified by altitude. Land use: forested 13 per cent, meadows and pastures 39 per cent, agricultural and under permanent cultivation 46 per cent. The official lang. are Rundi and French. There are 3 ethnic groups: the tall, aristocratic Tutsi; the peasant Hutu of Bantu stock (81 per cent); and a small number of pigmy Twa. Of believers 65 per cent are Roman Catholic, Protestant 14 per cent, Muslim 2 per cent, traditional beliefs 0.3 per cent.

Cattle, sheep, goats raised and maize, cassava and plantains are cultivated. Exports livestock, hides, coffee, cotton. There are some untapped reserves of minerals.

A Tutsi kingdom existed as early as the 16th cent. German military occupation in 1890 incorporated the territory into German East Africa. From 1919 Burundi formed part of Ruanda-Urundi administered by the Belgians, first as a League of Nations mandate and then as a UN trust territory. Internal self-government was granted in January 1962, followed by independence in July 1962. In July 1966 Prince Charles Ndizeye

deposed his father, Mwami Mwambutsa IV, suspended the constitution and in September he was enthroned as Mwami Ntare V. In November while the Mwami was attending a Head of States Conference, the Prime Minister, Michel Micombero, declared Burundi a republic with himself as president. Prince Charles returned to Burundi from Uganda in 1972 and was placed under house arrest. In 1972 President Micombero dissolved the Council of Ministers and took full power; that night heavy fighting broke out between rebels from both Burundi and neighbouring countries and the ruling Tutsi, apparently with the intention of destroying the Tutsi hegemony. Prince Charles was killed during the fighting and it was estimated that up to 120,000 were killed. President Micombero was deposed in 1976 by the army, as was his successor, President Bagaza, in 1987. In 1991 there were attacks by rebels which led to an exodus of Hutu refugees fleeing to Rwanda and the Democratic Republic of the Congo. In 1993 President Ndadaye and 6 ministers were killed in an attempted military *coup*. A wave of Tutsi–Hutu massacres broke out. In 1994 President Ntaryamira was killed, possibly assassinated, together with the President of Rwanda. There is an 81-member National Assembly. Government activities are overseen by a 10-member National Security Council of which the President and Prime Minister are members.

Bury England. Town and unitary authority on the R. Irwell. Pop. (1991) 62,633.
Important in the 14th cent. for the woollen industry, superseded by the cotton industry in the 18th cent. Cotton spinning and weaving, wool-spinning, dyeing. Manufactures textile and paper-making machinery, felts, chemicals and paint.

Birthplace of John Kay (1704–64), co-inventor of the flying shuttle, and the English statesman, Sir Robert Peel (1788–1850).

Buryat (Buryatia) Russia. Republic of the Russian Federation bordering on Mongolia (S) and on L. Baikal (W). Area 351,300 sq km (135,650 sq. miles). Pop. (1994) 1,052,800. Cap. and chief industrial centre Ulan-Ude.

Much of it lies on the Vitim Plateau and forests of larch, fir and cedar cover the slopes of the Barguzin Mountains. Cattle and sheep rearing, engineering, brown coal and lignite are important occupations. Cereals cultivated in the river valleys.

The Buryats, a Mongol people, are Buddhists by religion; they were conquered by the Russians in the 17th cent. and now form about 24 per cent of the pop.

Bury St Edmunds England. Market town in W Suffolk. Pop. (1991) 31,327. Brewing, sugar-refining. Manufactures agricultural machinery.

St Edmund, last king of the East Angles (martyred 870), was buried (903) in the now ruined abbey, which later became a place of pilgrimage; hence the name (originally St Edmund's Bury). Two 15th-cent. churches: St James's (which became a cathedral 1914) and St Mary's, burial-place of Mary Tudor, Duchess of Suffolk (sister of Henry VIII and grandmother of Lady Jane Grey).

Bushey England. Town in SW Hertford-shire 3 km (2 miles) SE of Watford. Pop. (1991) 16,524. Mainly residential.

Bushire (Persian **Bushehr**) Iran. Port on the (Persian) Gulf 177 km (110 miles) WSW of Shiraz, with which it is connected by road. Pop. (1982) 120,000.

Exports wool, rugs and cotton.

Founded in 1736, it superseded the nearby port of Rishire, but has declined in recent years with the development of trade in the Abadan region.

Bussum Netherlands. Town in North Hol-land province 21 km (13 miles) ESE of Amsterdam. Pop. (1992) 31,321. Largely resi-dential: a 'dormitory' town of Amsterdam. Manufactures chocolate. Has noteworthy 20th-cent. churches and other buildings.

Busto Arsizio Italy. Industrial town in Varese province in Lombardy 32 km (20 miles) NW of Milan. Pop. (1985) 81,000.

Important centre of cotton and rayon manufacture. Also produces iron and steel, textile machinery, footwear and dyes.

Noteworthy 16th-cent. church, Santa Maria di Piazza, designed by Bramante.

Bute Scotland. Island in Argyll and Bute in the Firth of Clyde, separated from the Cowal peninsula by the narrow Kyles of Bute. Pop. (1991) 7375. Area (inc. Inchmarnock Island) 122 sq km (47 sq. miles). Chief town Rothesay (on the E coast), a well-known holiday resort. Hilly in the N, rising to 267 m (876 ft). Farming in the centre.

Buteshire Scotland. Former county com-prising several islands in the Firth of Clyde and Kilbrannan Sound. Now part of Argyll and Bute.

Butte USA. Mining town in Montana 76 km (47 miles) SSW of Helena. Pop. (1980) 37,205.

Produces nearly one-third of the copper mined in the USA: also silver, zinc and man-ganese. Manufactures mining machinery and chemicals.

Buttermere, Lake England. Lake in SW Cumbria (in the Lake District), 2 km (1¼ miles) long and 0.5 km (⅓ mile) wide. Con-nected with Crummock Water by a short stream. Popular with tourists for its pictur-esque scenery. Buttermere village is near the N end.

Buxton England. Town in NW Derbyshire on the R. Wye 32 km (20 miles) W of Chesterfield in the Peak District 300 m (984 ft) above sea level; the highest town of its size in England. Pop. (1991) 19,854.

Health resort. Noted for thermal and chal-ybeate springs, used in the treatment of gout, rheumatism. Near by is Poole's Hole, a lime-stone cave with stalactites and stalagmites. Limestone quarried in the neighbourhood.

Buzău Romania. Town in the SE on the Buzău R. 96 km (60 miles) NE of Bucharest. Pop. (1992) 148,247.

Trade in grain, timber, petroleum. Oil-refining, flour-milling, textile and other industries.

Byblos (Jubail) Lebanon. Ancient city and seaport in Phoenicia, its site where the modern town of Jubail stands, 29 km (18 miles) NNE of Beirut. Its export of papyrus gave rise to the Greek word for 'book', hence the word 'Bible'.

Bydgoszcz (Ger. **Bromberg**) Poland. Cap. of the Bydgoszcz voivodeship, on the Brda R. 225 km (140 miles) WNW of Warsaw. Pop. (1989) 380,425.

Industrial town. Manufactures machinery, textiles, clothing, footwear and paper. Trade in timber.

Passed to Prussia 1772. Called Bromberg during the German administration. Returned to Poland (1919) after World War I.

Byelorussia ➤BELARUS.

Bytom (Ger. **Beuthen**) Poland. Industrial town in the Katowice voivodeship (Upper Silesia) 13 km (8 miles) NNW of Katowice. Pop. (1989) 229,991.

Coal, zinc and lead mining centre. Manufactures machinery.

Taken by Prussia 1742. Called Beuthen during the German administration. Returned to Poland under the Potsdam Agreement (1945).

Byzantium. Ancient Greek city on the shore of the Bosporus, on the site of modern Istanbul. Founded *c.* 658 BC by Greeks from Megara and Argos. Prospered on account of the favourable position for trade and the excellent harbour. Taken by the Romans AD 196. Constantine I built the new city of Constantinople (later the cap. of the Byzantine Empire) here in AD 330.

C

Caacupé Paraguay. Departmental cap. situated in La Cordillera province. Pop. (1985) 9200.

Industries inc. sugar-refining and tile-making. Resort in an area growing oranges, sugar-cane and tobacco.

Noted for the Shrine of the Blue Virgin on the central plaza, to which annual pilgrimages are made.

Cabanatuan Philippines. Market town in Luzon 96 km (60 miles) N of Manila. Pop. (1990) 173,000.

Trade in rice and other agricultural produce.

Cabinda (Kabinda) Angola. District on the Atlantic seaboard. Area 7236 sq km (2794 sq. miles). Pop. (1992) 152,100. Chief town and seaport Cabinda. An enclave separated from the rest of Angola by a strip of land belonging to the Democratic Republic of the Congo along the Congo R.

Produces cocoa, coffee, palm oil and timber. Minerals inc. uranium and there is offshore oil production. Angola's main oil-refining base.

Scene of fighting between Africans and Portuguese in the Angola rebellion (1961).

Cáceres Spain. 1. Province bounded on the W by Portugal, forming part of Estremadura. Area 19,945 sq km (7699 sq. miles). Pop. (1991) 404,631. Produces cereals, olive oil. Sheep and pigs raised. 2. Cap. of Cáceres province on the Cáceres R. Pop. (1991) 71,475. Market town.

Trade in grain, olive oil, wool, ham and the red sausages (*embutidos*) for which the province is famous. Manufactures cork and leather goods, textiles, fertilizers and pharmaceuticals.

The upper, old town has medieval walls.

Cadenabbia Italy. Village and resort in Como province in Lombardy on the W side of L. Como. Nearby is the Villa Carlotta (1747) with gardens and art treasures, now the property of the Italian government.

Cader Idris Wales. Mountain ridge in S Gwynedd, rising to 893 m (2929 ft) in the peak of Pen-y-Gader, with a remarkable *cwm* (cirque) in the steep slope down to the tarn of Llyn-y-Cau. Frequently mentioned in Welsh legends.

Cádiz Spain. 1. Province in Andalusia the most southerly of the Iberian peninsula, bounded by the Mediterranean (SE), the Strait of Gibraltar (S) and the Atlantic (SW). Area 7385 sq km (2851 sq. miles). Pop. (1991) 1,072,734. Fertile. Famous for sherry (named after Jerez de la Frontera). Produces olives, vines, oranges, cork. Salt obtained by evaporation of sea water. 2. Cap. of Cádiz province, Atlantic seaport at the end of the spit projecting NW from the Isla de León, commanding the entrance to the Bay of Cádiz. Pop. (1991) 153,550.

Exports of wine, salt, olive oil and cork are chief economic activities together with tourism.

The harbour has been much improved this cent. Within the bay there are shipyards and a naval base. Modern and clean in appearance, with whitewashed houses and fine marine promenades. Medical faculty of the University of Seville. Two cathedrals (13th-cent. and 18th/19th-cent.); the Torre Vigia (watch-tower); art gallery (with paintings by Spanish masters); chapel of the Capuchins, containing Murillo's unfinished picture *The Marriage of St Catherine*, while painting which Murillo fell from the scaffold and was killed (1682). Founded (*c.* 1100 BC) by the Phoenicians. Passed in turn to the Carthaginians, the Romans and the Moors. Recaptured by Alfonso X of Castile 1262. Columbus's port of departure on his second voyage. Rose to wealth and importance during the colonial era, but declined in the 19th cent. Scene of the meeting of the Cortes to promulgate the new liberal constitution (1812). Birthplace of the composer Manuel de Falla (1876–1946).

Caen France. Prefecture of the Calvados department in Normandy on the Orne R. Pop. (1990) 115,624.

Port; industrial, commercial and educational centre. Manufactures steel, pottery, textiles, cement and electronics. Exports iron ore, dairy produce, cement, building stone (several cathedrals and churches of S England were built with Caen limestone). Imports coal, timber and grain.

The university was founded in 1432, its buildings were destroyed in the Normandy campaign of World War II (1944), with most of the city centre; the churches of St Étienne (l'Abbaye aux Hommes), founded by William the Conqueror, and la Trinité (l'Abbaye aux Dames), founded by his wife Queen Matilda, escaped damage. Became important under William. Taken by the English 1346 and 1417. A centre of the Girondist resistance to the Revolutionary Convention 1793. Birthplace of the poet François de Malherbe (1555–1628) and D. F. E. Auber, the composer (1782–1871).

Caerleon Wales. Town in Newport county borough on the R. Usk 3 km (2 miles) NE of Newport. Pop. (1991) 8931. Site of the Roman fortress of Isca Silurum (c. AD 75); considerable remains. Long associated with Arthurian legend.

Caernarvon Wales. Port and resort in Gwynedd, county town, on the Menai Strait. Pop. (1991) 9695. Exports slate. Nearby is the site of the Roman Segontium. The well-preserved castle, built by Edward I (1284), is reputedly the birthplace of Edward II, first Prince of Wales. Here Prince Charles was invested as 21st Prince of Wales in 1969.

Caerphilly Wales. Town and county borough from 1996 11 km (7 miles) N of Cardiff. Pop. (1991) 28,481 (town); (1994) 171,000 (county borough). Former coalmining area. Market town. Originated Caerphilly cheese. The castle (13th/14th-cent.) is the largest in Wales.

Caesarea Israel. Ancient city, formerly Caesarea Palestinae, and seaport 35 km (22 miles) SSW of modern Haifa, founded (13 BC) by Herod the Great as the port to his cap. Sebaste (Samaria). Roman remains. Declined as a port after being occupied by the Muslims (638). Temporarily revived under the Crusaders, but destroyed by the Muslims (1265). Resettled as a kibbutz in 1940.

Caesarea Philippi Syria. City of ancient Palestine, now the village of Banias in the extreme SW of Syria near the Israeli frontier. Site of the Greek Paneas, renamed Caesarea Philippi by the Romans. Nearby are the traditional springs of the Jordan.

Cagliari Italy. Seaport in S Sardinia; chief town of the island and cap. of Cagliari province on the Gulf of Cagliari. Pop. (1992) 180,309. Salt lagoons on both sides.

Exports salt, lead and zinc. Flour-milling, tanning and fishing.

Built at the foot and on the slopes of a long steep hill. Cathedral (13th/14th-cent., later rebuilt); Byzantine churches; Punic necropolis; Roman amphitheatre; two early 14th-cent. Pisan towers, Torre dell' Elefante and Torre di San Pancrazio. University (1626).

Caguas Puerto Rico. Town 29 km (18 miles) S of San Juan. Pop. (1990) 133,450.

Industrial and commercial centre in an agricultural region (tobacco, sugar-cane). Manufactures cigars and leather goods.

Caher (Cahir) Ireland. Market town in Co. Tipperary on the R. Suir. Pop. (1986) 2118. Salmon-fishing centre. Castle (12th-cent.), built by Conor O'Brien, Irish historian and politician, later rebuilt and restored.

Cahors France. Ancient Divona. Prefecture of the Lot department and formerly cap. of

Quercy; in a loop of the Lot R. 92 km (57 miles) N of Toulouse. Pop. (1990) 20,787.

Market town. Food-processing. Trade in wine and truffles.

The 13th/14th-cent. Pont Valentré is the outstanding medieval fortified bridge in France, with three towers. Cathedral (12th/15th-cent.); museum (formerly an episcopal palace). In Roman times famous for linen. A leading banking centre in the 13th cent. Birthplace of Pope John XXII (1249–1334), founder of the university (1331), which united with that of Toulouse in 1751. Also birthplace of Léon Gambetta, French politician (1838–82).

Cairngorm Mountains Scotland. A range of the Grampians in Aberdeenshire, Banffshire and Inverness-shire. Inc. Ben Macdhi (1309 m; 4294 ft), the second highest peak in Scotland, Braeriach (1295 m; 4246 ft), Cairn Toul (1293 m; 4241 ft) and Cairn Gorm (1245 m; 4084 ft, after which the local brown or yellow quartz is named).

Cairns Australia. Seaport in Queensland 290 km (180 miles) NNW of Townsville. Pop. (1991) 64,000.

Exports sugar and timber. An attractively built town in an agricultural (sugar-cane and tropical fruits), lumbering and mining region. Also a tourist centre.

Cairo (Ar. **El Qahira**) Egypt. Cap., the largest city in Africa and the Middle East on the right bank of the Nile at the head of the delta. Pop. (1990) 6,452,000. Connected by rail with Upper Egypt, Alexandria.

The chief commercial centre, with a variety of manufactures: cement, textiles, vegetable oils and beer.

The Mosque and University of El Ashar (founded 972) is the principal theological seminary of Islam; also Cairo University (1908) and the Ein Shamse University (1950). Over 200 mosques, inc. those of Tulun (9th-cent.) and Hasan (14th-cent., near the great citadel); the mosques, representative of different phases of Islamic architecture, make Cairo outstanding among Arab cities. Several museums of Islamic art. Important ancient Egyptian treasures are housed in the Museum of Antiquities.

The Arab city with its mosques and narrow tortuous streets, the Coptic (Egyptian Christian) area and the Jewish quarter are in the E; modern Cairo, with government offices, hotels, opera house, built in more European style, is in the W. To the NE is the modern suburb of Heliopolis. Al Gezireh, an island in the Nile, is the centre for country clubs and horse racing. The river port of Bulag is a NW suburb with a paper and printing industry. The pyramids of Giza are 13 km (8 miles) SW of Cairo.

When the Arabs conquered Egypt they founded El Fustat (AD 641) near the Roman fortress town of Babylon, where 'Old Cairo' now stands. Opposite is the island of Roda, where traditionally Pharaoh's daughter found Moses in the bulrushes. The most important of the later towns, El Qahira (founded c. 968), gave the city its name. After the Crusaders' unsuccessful attack (1176), Saladin built the citadel on the Moqattam Hills but within the city precincts. Under Turkish rule (1517–1798) Cairo declined, but it grew rapidly in size and importance in the 19th and 20th cent.

Caistor England. Market town in N Lincolnshire 18 km (11 miles) SW of Grimsby. Pop. (1991) 2502. Built on the site of a Roman camp and early British fort.

Caistor St Edmunds England. Roman Venta Icenorum. Now a suburb of Norwich (5 km; 3 miles S). Excavations and aerial photography have revealed evidence of a large Roman encampment.

Caithness Scotland. Former county in the extreme NE of the Scottish mainland, *now* Highland.

Cajamarca Peru. Cap. of the Cajamarca department in the W Cordillera (NW) in a basin at a height of over 2700 m (8856 ft). Pop. (1993) 92,447.

Market town in an agricultural (maize, alfalfa, wheat) and mining (gold, copper, silver, zinc) region. Manufactures textiles, leather goods, straw hats.

Here Pizarro ambushed and captured Ata-hualpa, the Inca ruler (1533), executing him 8 months later.

Calabar Nigeria. Seaport in the extreme SE on the estuary of the Cross R. Pop. (1992) 157,800.

Exports palm oil and kernels, cacao, rubber and cement.

Calabria Italy. Region in the S comprising the 'toe' of Italy – provinces of Cosenza, Catanzaro and Reggio di Calabria, between the Ionian and the Tyrrhenian seas. Area 15,080 sq km (5828 sq. miles). Pop. (1992) 2,074,763. Chief town Reggio. Mainly mountainous; still partly forested.

Vines, citrus fruits and olives cultivated. Sheep and goats raised. Has suffered much from earthquakes, droughts, deforestation, erosion and malaria. Economic progress has also been retarded by poor communications. Hydroelectric plants in the La Sila mountains.

In Roman times the 'heel' of Italy was called Calabria; the Byzantines transferred the name to the 'toe' (previously known as Bruttium).

Calais France. Industrial town and seaport in the Pas-de-Calais department on the Strait of Dover 233 km (145 miles) N of Paris and 35 km (22 miles) ESE of Dover. Pop. (1990) 75,836. Owes its importance to its position on the shortest sea crossing between France and England. Nearby is the Sangatte exit of the Channel Tunnel.

Imports raw materials for the NE industrial region (ores, timber). Fishing, boatbuilding. Manufactures lace, tulle, rayon and clothing.

Important since the end of the 10th cent. In English hands 1347–1558. Rodin's group *The Burghers of Calais* commemorates the long, heroic siege of 1346–7. The old town around the harbour was virtually destroyed in World War II.

Calamata (Kalámai) Greece. Cap. of the Messenia *nome* in the SW Peloponnese, port on the Gulf of Messenia. Pop. (1981) 43,235.

Exports citrus fruits, figs, olives and other local produce. Flour-milling. Manufactures cigarettes.

Calapan ►MINDORO.

Calcutta India. Cap. of West Bengal and the largest city in India on the left bank of the Hooghly R. about 129 km (80 miles) by river from the Bay of Bengal. Pop. (1991) 10,916,000, urban agglomeration.

Major seaport. Exports manganese ore, pig iron and jute products, tea, oilseeds. Road and railway junction and industrial city. Centre of jute-milling, railway engineering, shipbuilding, oil-refining and tanning. Manufactures cotton goods, chemicals, paper, soap, fertilizers, acrylic fibre, detergents, refrigerators, sewing-machines, pharmaceuticals, electronic goods, electric lamps and textiles.

Seat of a university (founded 1857). Its life is centred on the Maidan or park (area 5.2 sq km; 2 sq. miles), which contains the later Fort William (1757–73). The outstanding building is the marble Victoria Memorial (opened 1921), erected on the site of the old jail, which houses an enormous collection of pictures and documents, illustrating Indian history. To the N of the Maidan are Government House, until 1912 the residence of the viceroy, and the site of the earlier Fort William (1696) and of the notorious 'Black Hole of Calcutta'. On the E side of the Maidan is Chowringhee Road, which has the Indian Museum, the Bengal School of Art and the Asiatic Society, as well as many imposing hotels, shops and clubs. In the S of the city, beside a canal, is the Kali Ghat, with the famous Kali temple.

Calcutta was virtually founded in 1690 by Job Charnock of the English East India Company with the occupation of the former village of Sutanati, now within the city boundary; the original Fort William was built for its defence. In 1698 the villages of Sutanati, Govindpur and Kalikata were purchased by the English and the settlement was named after the third of these. Because of its defensive position and its excellent anchorage – and in spite of the unhealthy site – Calcutta developed and prospered. In 1756, however, it was captured by Suraj-ud-Dowlah, Nawab of Bengal, who confined 146 prisoners in a small guardroom of Fort William during a torrid June night: there were only 23 survivors from this, the 'Black Hole of Calcutta', on the following morning. Calcutta was recaptured in 1757, a new Fort William was built, the Maidan was formed and the modern city began to arise. It was the cap. of British India from 1773 to 1912, when it was superseded by Delhi, but its commercial importance increased again with the extension of the harbour (1920). The large industrial centre of Howrah, on the opposite side of the Hooghly, is geographically part of Calcutta.

Caldera ➤COPIAPO.

Caledonia Scotland. Roman name, occurring first in the works of Lucan (1st cent. AD) for the part of Britain N of the line traced by the Wall of Antoninus, between the Firth of Forth and the Firth of Clyde. Now used (esp. poetically) for the whole of Scotland.

Caledonian Canal Scotland. Waterway 96 km (60 miles) long, from Loch Linnhe to the Moray Firth along the Great Glen. It comprises Loch Ness, Loch Oich and Loch Lochy, which are linked by canals 35 km (22 miles) long in all. Construction began in 1803; opened in 1823; completed in 1847. The work of Thomas Telford.

Calgary Canada. Town in S Alberta at the confluence of the Bow and the Elbow rivers. Pop. (1991) 710,677.

The largest city of Canada's high plains. Important railway junction in a ranching area, near the Turner Valley oilfields (linked by pipelines). Main industries meat-packing, flour-milling, oil-refining; manufactures explosives.

Founded 1883. Since 1912 the annual Calgary Stampede has been a great tourist attraction.

Cali Colombia. Cap. of the Valle del Cauca department in the Cauca valley, at a height of 1068 m (3503 ft). Pop. (1992) 1,624,401.

Industrial and commercial city in a rich agricultural area growing sugar-cane, rice,

coffee and tobacco and with pastures for livestock. Manufactures textiles, clothing, footwear and soap.

Founded 1536, but developed little until the 20th cent., esp. after the construction of the railway to Buenaventura (1914) and the opening of the Panama Canal.

Calicut ➤KOZHIKODE.

California USA. Third largest state, bordering the Pacific. Area 411,015 sq km (158,693 sq. miles). Pop. (1990) 29,60,021. Cap. Sacramento. The 'Golden' state (because of its gold production). Inland from the Coast Range (N–S, parallel to the coast) is the long Central Valley, in which flow the Sacramento R. from the N and the San Joaquin R. from the S; after joining, they emerge from the valley into San Francisco Bay. Further E is the high range of the Sierra Nevada, along the E border, with many peaks exceeeding 3000 m (9840 ft), rising to 4421 m (14,501 ft) in Mt Whitney. In the extreme SE is Death Valley, a deep depression 85 m (279 ft) below sea level. The climate is as diverse as the topography: the N is cool, wet and often foggy; the S has a typically Mediterranean climate with abundant sunshine, summer drought and rainfall mainly in winter. In the sheltered interior of the SE are the Mojave and Colorado Deserts, containing the Imperial Valley and the Salton Sea. The slopes of the Coast Range and the Sierra Nevada are forested; Californian redwoods are among the world's most magnificent trees. The state is third in lumber production, mainly softwoods.

The leading fruit-producing state; chief crops citrus fruits, grapes. Cotton, cereals, sugar-beet, vegetables also important. About 40 per cent of the country's fish are landed at its ports. One of the main oil-producing states; important output of gold, mercury and other minerals. Famous for the production of films. The processing of farm produce and the manufacture of aircraft, aerospace, machinery, electrical and electronic equipment, and chemicals are of major importance. Leading cities Los Angeles, San Francisco and San Diego.

The Californian coast was first explored by Juan Rodriguez Cabrillo (1542); Drake repaired his ships in one of its bays (1579). But not till 1769 did Spanish settlers arrive in San Francisco Bay; from then till 1823 California was under the control of Franciscans and Dominicans, who established a number of missions. The territory was associated politically with Mexico and was ceded to the USA (1848) after the Mexican War. Admitted to the Union in 1850 as the 31st state.

Callan Ireland. Town in Co. Kilkenny on the Owenree R. 14 km (9 miles) SW of Kilkenny. Pop. (1985) 1700. Market town. Augustinian abbey (15th-cent.).

Callander Scotland. Town and resort in Stirling on the R. Teith. Pop. (1991) 2622. Tourist centre for the Trossachs and Loch Katrine. The region is described in Scott's *The Lady of the Lake*.

Callao Peru. Chief seaport 13 km (8 miles) W of the centre of Lima, to which it is linked by railways and roads. Pop. (1990) 588,600. Large deep harbour on Callao Bay. Handles most of Peru's imports (esp. machinery and metal goods) and one-quarter of the exports. Fishing, fish-processing and canning. Meat-packing, flour-milling and brewing. Connected by railway and road to highland centres via the Rimac valley and to coastal towns by the Pan-American Highway. Founded 1537. Frequently raided by Drake and other adventurers. Destroyed by earthquake and tidal wave (1746) but rebuilt and fortified.

Calne England. Market town in Wiltshire 10 km (6 miles) N of Devizes. Pop. (1991) 11,800. The manufacture of woollen cloth was once important. Site of a palace of the West Saxon kings in the 10th cent.

Calshot England. Promontory on the W side of the entrance to Southampton Water in S Hampshire. Site of a castle built by Henry VIII for coastal defence. Important RAF seaplane base in the 1930s.

Caltagirone Italy. Town in the Catania province in Sicily 61 km (38 miles) SW of Catania at a height of 600 m (1968 ft). Pop. (1981) 35,682. Noted for terracotta and majolica work. To the SE is a Greek necropolis of the 6th and 5th cent. BC.

Caltanissetta Italy. Cap. of Caltanissetta province in Sicily 93 km (58 miles) W of Catania. Pop. (1991) 62,900. Headquarters of the Sicilian sulphur industry. Manufactures cement and soap.

Cathedral (17th-cent.); 17th-cent. baroque palace. School of Mines.

Calvados France. Department in Normandy, bounded on the N by the English Channel. Area 5536 sq km (2197 sq. miles). Pop. (1990) 618,500. Prefecture Caen. Mainly low-lying with the Normandy hills in the SW rising to 365 m (1197 ft). A reef extending about 24 km (15 miles) along the coast, between the Orne and Vire rivers, was named Les Calvados after a Spanish vessel was wrecked there (1588). Extensive stock-rearing and dairy-farming. Produces cider and Calvados (apple brandy). Textile industry also important. Deauville and Trouville are fashionable seaside resorts. Chief towns Caen, Bayeux, Falaise and Lisieux.

Camagüey Cuba. 1. Cap. of the Camagüey province in E Cuba 64 km (40 miles) WSW of its port, Nuevitas, to which it is linked by rail. Pop. (1990) 125,021. Route centre; outlet for a region producing sugar-cane, fruit and timber and raising cattle. Founded in the 16th cent. Cathedral (17th-cent.); many distinguished churches. 2. Archipelago off the N coast of the Camagüey province. Chief islands Romano, Sabinal and Coco.

Camargue, La France. The delta of the Rhône R. in the Bouches-du-Rhône department. Area 777 sq km (300 sq. miles). Lying between the Grand Rhône (E) and the Petit Rhône (W), much of it is marshy and there are several shallow *étangs* (lagoons) in the S, the largest being the Étang de Vaccarès. The marshes are the haunt of flamingoes and other birds.

Fishing and the production of marine salt in salt-pans in the S; the rearing of sheep, cattle and bulls (for the bullring) in the N. In recent years communications have been improved, more land has been reclaimed and rice and other crops (inc. vines) are cultivated.

Cambay India. Town in Gujarat on the Gulf of Cambay 85 km (53 miles) S of Ahmadabad. Pop. (1985) 64,000.

Manufactures textiles and matches. Trade in cotton and grain. It was an important port in the days of Marco Polo and earlier but declined owing to the silting up of the harbour.

Cambay, Gulf of India. Inlet of the Arabian Sea between the S coast of Gujarat and the Kathiawar peninsula. Its ports have lost importance through the silting of their harbours. Offshore oil production in the Gulf began in 1975.

Camberley ►FRIMLEY AND CAMBERLEY.

Camberwell England. From 1965 in the Greater London borough of Southwark. Mainly residential; inc. Dulwich, Peckham and Nunhead. Once the home of George, Prince of Denmark (Queen Anne's consort), after whom Denmark Hill is named. Site of the South London Fine Art Gallery. Birthplace of Robert Browning, the poet (1812–89).

Cambodia. Independent kingdom in SE Asia, bounded by Laos and Thailand in the N, Vietnam in the E and S by the Gulf of Thailand. Area 181,916 sq km (70,238 sq. miles). Pop. (1995) 9,610,000 (21 per cent urban). Life expectancy, 51 years male, 54 female. Cap. Phnom Penh. Other cities Batdambang, Kompong Som. Currency: Riel = 100 sen. The country mainly consists of an alluvial plain drained by the Mekong R. and centred on the extensive L. Tonlé Sap. More than half the cultivated land is devoted to rice production. It has a tropical climate with high temperatures throughout the year. Land use: forested 66 per cent, meadows and pastures 11 per cent, agricultural and under permanent cultivation 14 per cent. About 89 per cent are Khmer (most are Buddhist) and

6 per cent are Vietnamese. The official lang. is Khmer.

Industries inc. rubber-processing, seafood processing, jute-sack making, cigarette manufacture. There are large freshwater fish resources. Considerable areas of forest yield valuable timber. There are phosphates and iron-ore deposits. Some gold and zircon mining is carried out. The majority of the pop. is engaged in agriculture, fishing or forestry. Exports inc. timber and rubber. Phnom Penh, reached by the Mekong R. through Vietnam, is one of the two chief ports, but is accessible only to smaller vessels; ocean-going ships use the port of Kongpong Som (formerly Sihanoukville).

Early in the Christian era Cambodia formed the kingdom of Fu-nan, which extended beyond the present boundaries into Thailand, Cochin China (South Vietnam) and Laos. Absorbed late in the 6th cent. by the Khmers, under whose rulers Angkor was built. Attacked by Siam (Thailand) and Annam (Vietnam), Cambodia was saved by the establishment of a French protectorate (1863). After World War II it joined the French Union (1949), but declared complete independence 1953. The country became involved in the Vietnam War, economic difficulties increased and in 1970 the monarchy was abolished and the Khmer Republic proclaimed. Then followed five years of civil war, which ended with the surrender of Phnom Penh to the communist Khmer Rouge in 1975. Pol Pot became leader, thousands fled into exile and about 2 million were killed. The state was renamed Democratic Kampuchea. Following years of fighting a ceasefire was agreed in 1991 and elections were held in 1993. Prince Sihanouk was elected King and Cambodia became a constitutional monarchy with a 120-member unicameral National Assembly. The Khmer Rouge remained unreconciled to the new government and continued guerrilla warfare, although about 50 per cent defected under an amnesty in 1994.

Camborne–Redruth England. Town in Cornwall 18 km (11 miles) WSW of Truro.

Pop. (1991) 35,915. Industries inc. engineering, textiles and chemicals. School of Metalliferous Mining. The birthplace of the engineer Richard Trevithick (1771–1833), who worked in the neighbourhood, is nearby.

Cambrai France. Ancient Camaracum (of the Nervii). Industrial town in the Nord department at the junction of the Escaut (Scheldt) R. and the St Quentin Canal. Pop. (1990) 34,210.

Famous for fine cambric (named after it). Cloth dyeing and bleaching. Sugar-refining (from locally grown beet), flour-milling.

Scene of the formation of the League of Cambrai against Venice (1508) and of the signing (1529) of the Treaty of Cambrai (Paix des Dames). Burial-place (in the original cathedral destroyed in the French Revolution) of Fénelon, Archbishop of Cambrai 1695–1715. Suffered considerable damage in both world wars. Birthplace of Louis Blériot, French aviator (1872–1936).

Cambridge England. City in Cambridgeshire on the R. Cam (also known as the Granta). Pop. (1991) 95,682.

Radio and electronic, printing and other research-based industries. Famous for its university.

Most of the outstanding features are connected with the colleges: the celebrated stretch of river known as the 'Backs' (along the backs of some of the colleges), such buildings as King's College Chapel (begun 1446, a superb example of the Perpendicular style) and the modern University Library. Noteworthy ecclesiastical buildings inc. the 10th-cent. Saxon Church of St Benedict, the 12th-cent. Church of the Holy Sepulchre (oldest of the four round Norman churches in England) and the 13th-cent. Church of St Edward King and Martyr (where Latimer preached). Evidence of pre-Roman settlement has recently been found and Roman remains indicate the existence of a settlement near a ford over the river. William the Conqueror built a castle to assist his campaign against Hereward the Wake. In the Middle Ages the town grew in importance commer-

cially both as a river port (at the head of navigation) and because of its position on the route between E England and the Midlands. By the 12th cent. there were several schools; early in the 13th cent. the nucleus of the university had been established.

Cambridge USA. City in Massachusetts on the Charles R. opposite Boston. Pop. (1990) 95,800. One of the chief educational centres of the USA; seat of Harvard University (founded 1636, America's first college) and of the Massachusetts Institute of Technology. The earliest printing press in America was set up here (1639); printing and publishing have continued to be leading industries. Manufactures soap and confectionery. Washington established his headquarters (1775–6) at a house which later became the home of Henry Wadsworth Longfellow.

Cambridgeshire England. Inland county in E Anglia inc. since 1974 the Isle of Ely, the former county of Huntingdonshire and the Soke of Peterborough. Area 3408 sq km (1316 sq. miles). Pop. (1994) 687,800. County town Cambridge. Flat, except for low uplands in the S (e.g. the Gog Magog Hills to the SE of Cambridge city); lies largely in the Fens. Soil extremely fertile. Produces cereals, sugar-beet, fruit and vegetables. Chief rivers the Great Ouse (with its main tributaries the Cam, the Lark and the Little Ouse) and the Nene (N); their courses are partly artificial and there are numerous drainage channels. In the S are great earthworks, of which the best-known is Devil's Dyke, 12 km (7½ miles) long, lying over the ancient Icknield Way. Chief towns Cambridge, Peterborough and Wisbech.

Camden England. Inner London borough (1965) comprising the former metropolitan boroughs of Hampstead, Holborn and St Pancras. Pop. (1991) 170,500.

Camden USA. Industrial town and port in New Jersey on the Delaware R. opposite Philadelphia, with which it is connected by bridge. Pop. (1990) 87,992.

Manufactures textiles, canned soups, radio

and television apparatus and pens. Ship-building and oil-refining.

Originally settled by Quakers. Named after Lord Chancellor Camden (1773). Home of Walt Whitman, US poet, from 1873.

Camden Town England. Part of the Inner London borough of Camden from 1965. Built (1791) when Lord Camden allowed his land to be leased for building houses.

Camelford England. Market town in Cornwall on the R. Camel 16 km (10 miles) NNE of Bodmin. One of the places identified with King Arthur's Camelot.

Camelot Britain. Seat of the court of the quasi-legendary British King Arthur. Variously identified with Caerleon, Camelford, Winchester and other places in the S.

Camembert France. Village in the Orne department in Normandy 51 km (32 miles) SE of Caen. The famous Camembert cheese, first made by Marie Harel, is now chiefly produced at Vimoutiers, 5 km (3 miles) to the NNE.

Cameroon. Republic in W Africa bounded W by the Gulf of Guinea, NW by Nigeria, E by Chad and the Central African Republic, S by Congo, Gabon and Equatorial Guinea. Area 475,442 sq km (183,569 sq. miles). Pop. (1995) 13,233,000 (41 per cent urban). Life expectancy, 55 years male, 58 female. Cap. Yaoundé. Other cities Douala, Garoua, Maroua and Bafoussam. Currency: CFA franc = 100 centimes. Mainly plateau, at a height of 600 m (1968 ft). The S is covered with tropical rainforest, with valuable trees, such as mahogany and ebony. The N is largely savannah. It has an equatorial climate with high temperatures and plentiful rainfall. Land use: forested 77 per cent, meadows and pastures 4 per cent, agricultural and under permanent cultivation 15 per cent. About 53 per cent of believers are Christian, about 26 per cent animist and 34 per cent Muslim. The pop. is composed of Sudanic-speaking people in the N and Bantu-speaking groups in the S. The official lang. are French and English.

It is self-sufficient in agricultural products; these are coffee, cocoa, timber, cassava, plantains, millets and durra; there is crude oil and aluminium from a plant at Edéa. Much is exported. Industry is on a small scale and inc. the manufacture of cement, footwear, palm oil, cigarettes, beer and soap. Forestry is important inc. the production of veneer, plywood, paper and board.

Cameroon was a German protectorate 1884–1916 and then trusteeship of the League of Nations and later the United Nations. In 1961 French Cameroons became an independent republic to be joined by part of British Cameroons as the Federal Republic of Cameroon, but in 1972 merged as a united republic and was renamed the Republic of Cameroon in 1984. There is a 180-member National Assembly. It is divided into 10 provinces, each administered by a governor appointed by the President. Cameroon became a member of the Commonwealth in 1995.

Cameroon Mountains Cameroon. Isolated volcanic group SW of the Adamawa Massif. The major peak, Great Cameroon (the highest mountain in W Africa), rises to 4070 m (13,350 ft). Annual rainfall on the W slopes is over 1000 cm (394 ins.). Last eruptions 1909 and 1922.

Camiri ►COCHABAMBA.

Campagna di Roma Italy. Undulating plain in the Roma province in Latium, bounded on the SW by the Tyrrhenian Sea. Drained by the lower Tiber R. and several small intermittent streams. Largely covered with volcanic earth. Once fertile; deteriorated through overgrazing (sheep) and malaria. Long neglected, it has been to a considerable extent restored by drainage and antimalarial measures.

Campania Italy. Region in the S, bordering in the W on the Tyrrhenian Sea; comprises the provinces of Avellino, Benevento, Caserta, Napoli and Salerno, and inc. the islands of Capri, Ischia, Procida and the Pontine Islands. Area 13,595 sq km (5248 sq. miles).

Canada

Pop. (1992) 5,668,895. Chief town Naples. Long famed for its fertility.

Produces fruits, vegetables, hemp and tobacco, as well as vines, olives and cereals. Industries are centred mainly on Naples. Other important towns Salerno, Benevento, Caserta.

Site of the Roman centres of Herculaneum and Pompeii. Many popular modern resorts along the coast. Ancient Campania was much smaller than the modern region. As part of the kingdom of Naples, it was united with Italy in 1861.

Campbeltown Scotland. Fishing port in Argyll and Bute on the SE coast of the Kintyre peninsula. Pop. (1991) 5722. Whisky-distilling and rope-making. Seaside resort.

A 12th-cent. granite cross. Important about the 6th cent. AD as the seat of the Dalriad monarchy.

Campeche Mexico. 1. State in the SE on the Gulf of Campeche, bounded on the S by Guatemala, occupying the SW part of the Yucatán peninsula. Area 56,114 sq km (21,660 sq. miles). Pop. (1990) 528,824. Chief port Ciudad del Carmen, on a sand bar separating the Laguna de Términos from the gulf. Mainly lowlands, with dense forests in the S, from which logwood is obtained. 2. Cap. of Campeche state on the Gulf of Campeche 160 km (100 miles) SW of Mérida, with which it is connected by rail. Pop. (1990) 172,208. Port with shallow roadstead and much diminished trade since Spanish colonial times.

Manufactures cigars, leather, footwear and Panama hats. Picturesque. Founded 1540.

Campinas Brazil. Town in the São Paulo state 80 km (50 miles) NW of São Paulo. Pop. (1991) 846,084.

Considerable trade in coffee. Now a growing industrial area. Sugar-refining. Manufactures sewing-machines, textiles, tyres, wine and cottonseed oil. Experimental agricultural station.

Campobasso Italy. Cap. of Campobasso province in Molise 88 km (55 miles) NNE of Naples. Pop. (1990) 51,300. Market town.

Manufactures cutlery and soap. Restored 15th-cent. castle.

Campo Grande Brazil. Market town in the S of the Mato Grosso state. Pop. (1990) 459,554. On the São Paulo–Corumba railway, serving the high and almost treeless country of the divide between the Paraguay and the Paraná rivers.

Exports livestock, packed and dried meat, hides and skins, and agricultural produce to São Paulo.

Campos Brazil. Industrial town in the Rio de Janeiro state on the Paraíba R. 48 km (30 miles) from the mouth, 240 km (150 miles) NE of Rio de Janeiro. Pop. (1991) 388,640. In a rich agricultural region.

Sugar-refining. Manufactures textiles, leather goods and soap.

Canaan. Name applied to ancient Palestine before being occupied by the Israelites; generally considered to signify the land between the Mediterranean Sea (W) and the R. Jordan and Dead Sea (E); the 'promised land' of the Israelites (Exodus 3: 8).

Canada. An independent federal state, it occupies all the North American continent N of the US apart from the US state of Alaska on the NW and the two small French islands of St Pierre and Miquelon. Bounded in the NW by the Beaufort Sea, N by the Arctic Ocean, NE by Baffin Bay, E by the Davis Strait, Labrador Sea and Atlantic Ocean, S by the USA and W by the Pacific Ocean and USA (Alaska). Area 9,970,610 sq km (3,849,674 sq. miles). Pop. (1995) 29,463,000 (77 per cent urban). Life expectancy, 75 years male, 82 female. Cap. Ottawa. Other cities Toronto, Montreal, Vancouver, Edmonton, Calgary, Winnipeg, Quebec, Hamilton and London. Currency: Canadian dollar = 100 cents. Canada consists of 10 provinces: Newfoundland, Nova Scotia, New Brunswick, Prince Edward Island, Quebec, Ontario, Manitoba, Saskatchewan, Alberta, British Columbia and 2 territories: Northwest Territories and Yukon. In 1993 agreement was reached with Inuit representatives that Nunavut (now part of Northwest

Territories) should become an independent territory in 1999. The majority of the Canadian pop. is concentrated in the SE within 240 km (150 miles) of the US border. Vast areas in the N consist of uninhabited wasteland. Canada stretches from about 42°N latitude in the S, approximately the latitude of Rome, to within 800 km (500 miles) of the North Pole; it extends W–E through about 88° longitude and inc. five different time zones. Its most mountainous region is the Western Cordillera, which occupies the Yukon, most of British Columbia and a narrow strip of SW Alberta. This region is dominated by the Rocky Mountains in the E and the Coast Range in the W, between them a lofty plateau broken by the Selkirk Mountains (N); in the St Elias Mountains of SW Yukon are the country's highest peaks, Mt Logan (6054 m; 19,857 ft) and Mt St Elias (5492 m; 18,014 ft). E of the Cordillera are the Interior Plains, which descend E from the foothills of the Rockies towards the Great Lakes in three great steps. They are an extension of the Great Plains and the central lowlands of the US, their natural vegetation gradually changing from grassland or prairie in the S through coniferous forest to tundra in the far N. To the E of the plains is the Canadian, Laurentian or Pre-Cambrian Shield, a vast region occupying one-third to one-half of the entire country, stretching around Hudson Bay from the Labrador coast to the Arctic. It consists essentially of an enormous mass of ancient rocks, dotted with innumerable lakes and streams, forest-covered in the S and merging into tundra in the N. N of the Canadian Shield are the numerous islands of the Arctic Archipelago, a region of tundra with patches of ice-cap, e.g. on Ellesmere and Baffin islands, and a permanently frozen subsoil. S of the Canadian Shield are the St Lawrence Lowlands, which inc. those lying along the shores of L. Erie and L. Ontario, the most intensively farmed, the most industrialized and the most populous part of Canada. Finally, there is the Appalachian region, an extension of the Appalachians of the US, occupying the Maritime Provinces, the adjacent part of Quebec inc. the Gaspe peninsula, and Newfoundland: a region largely of parallel ridges and valleys, much forested but with considerable areas of good farmland.

In so vast a country there are great variations of climate. Along the coast of British Columbia the climate may be described as maritime temperate. The prevailing westerly winds deposit an abundant and well-distributed rainfall, particularly on the windward slopes of the mountains and winters are mild and summers cool; a drier climate, with more extreme temperatures, is experienced on the plateau of the Western Cordillera, which is shielded from the rain-bearing winds by the coastal mountain ranges. In the Arctic Archipelago and along the Arctic coast the winters are long and very severe, while summers are short and cool. To the S the climate gradually becomes less rigorous, but even on the S prairies it has continental characteristics; the winter is still cold, though the summer is warm and annual precipitation (rainfall and snowfall together) is light. In SE Canada the precipitation increases generally from W to E and along the Atlantic coast is moderately heavy and evenly distributed; here the winters, though fairly cold, are less severe than in the interior. Land use: forested 53 per cent, meadows and pastures 3 per cent, agricultural and under permanent cultivation 5 per cent. Roman Catholics constitute 46 per cent of the pop., well over half of them being in Quebec; the leading Protestant denominations are the United Church, the Anglican Church and the Presbyterian. About 21 per cent of the pop. are of British origin and 23 per cent are French Canadians, the latter being found mainly in Quebec province; the next largest group, those of German origin, 3 per cent. There are American Indians, most of them living in Indian Reserves and Inuktitut (Eskimos) in the far N. Most anthropologists agree that the North American Indian migrated over the Bering Sea from Siberia, 10,000 to 30,000 years ago. The exact origins of the Canadian Inuit (they numbered (1991) 30,085) are unknown. It is generally believed, however, that their ancestors came to North America from Asia, crossing a land bridge formed between the two continents during the last ice age. The official lang. are English and French.

Although only about 5 per cent of the total land area is classified as cultivated land, agriculture occupies an extremely important place in the Canadian economy. Spring wheat is by far the leading single crop.

More than 95 per cent of this enormous output comes from the Prairie Provinces, with Saskatchewan easily first, followed by Alberta and then Manitoba. Between them these provinces also produce most of the oats and barley. Dairy-farming, involving the production of a considerable hay crop, is important in the Great Lakes–St Lawrence lowlands of Quebec and Ontario; fruit (esp. apples) is grown chiefly in Ontario and British Columbia.

In the forests of British Columbia grow the Douglas fir, red cedar and other 'big' trees; E of the Rockies spruce and other species provide the smaller softwood timber used in the manufacture of wood-pulp and paper, and are cut mainly in Ontario, Quebec and Newfoundland. Canada is the world's leading exporter of newsprint, the majority of its great output being taken by the US. Furs, with mink the most important type, are now produced chiefly on fur farms. Fishing, the country's oldest industry, is practised on the Pacific and Atlantic coasts.

Mineral resources are considerable. Coal is mined chiefly in Alberta and Nova Scotia, and large quantities of petroleum and natural gas are produced in Alberta, and are sent by pipeline to refineries both E and W, as far as Montreal (E) and Vancouver (W). Hydro-electric power has also been developed on a tremendous scale and is used, e.g. in the production of aluminium. The principal metallic ores are nickel, copper, gold and uranium; a high proportion of the world's asbestos comes from Quebec. Industries are concentrated in the Great Lakes–St Lawrence area (particularly in Montreal and Toronto, the largest cities) and in Hamilton and Windsor, the leading centre in the W being Vancouver; in the lead are wood-pulp and

paper manufacture, the smelting and refining of metallic ores, and oil-refining.

The railways played an outstanding part in opening up the interior of this vast country and in developing and maintaining trade across the three great physical barriers, the Appalachians, the Canadian Shield and the Rockies. Since the opening of the St Lawrence Seaway (1959) the Great Lakes, now accessible to ocean shipping, have acquired an added importance. In the E, Montreal is the leading seaport, though it suffers the disadvantage, like the Great Lakes, of being closed by ice in winter, when Halifax takes its place. Vancouver handles the major part of the Pacific trade.

Canada's chief exports are machinery and transport equipment, followed by petroleum, then various other minerals – nickel, aluminium, iron ore, asbestos – and the products of the forest (timber, wood pulp, newsprint) and of the prairie (wheat). Imports consist principally of machinery and transport equipment, food, petroleum and forestry products. Of the exports 81 per cent go to the US and about 2 per cent to Britain, while 65 per cent of the imports come from the US and 3 per per cent from Britain.

The Canadian coast was reached by John Cabot, who sailed from Bristol, in 1497, but the first permanent settlement came only in 1608, when Champlain founded Quebec. In 1663 this settlement, known as New France, was made into a royal province of France. French explorers and missionaries journeyed into the interior beyond the Great Lakes and as far as the Mississippi, while fur traders of the Hudson's Bay Company, chartered in England in 1670, concentrated their activities on the immense territories around Hudson Bay. The French and the British inevitably came into conflict: in 1756 the Seven Years War began, Wolfe defeated Montcalm and took Quebec (1759) and by the Peace of Paris (1763) Canada was ceded to Britain. During the American War of Independence the Canadians defeated a revolutionary invasion and thousands of loyalists fled N and played a great part in the development of the country. In 1791 it was divided at the Ottawa

R. into Lower Canada and Upper Canada, the former predominantly French and the latter British. After armed revolts had been quelled in both provinces, the two were united (1841) and then by the British North America Act a confederation of Lower Canada (Quebec), Upper Canada (Ontario), Nova Scotia and New Brunswick was brought about (1867). Two years later the vast territory of Rupert's Land, extending W to the Rockies, was bought from the Hudson's Bay Company. In 1870 the province of Manitoba was created from it, in 1871 British Columbia joined Canada and in 1873 Prince Edward Island. Despite tremendous difficulties, E and W were at last linked in 1885 when the Canadian Pacific Railway was completed; the provinces of Alberta and Saskatchewan were formed from the Northwest Territories in 1905. Economic prosperity increased with the conversion of the prairies into 'the bread-basket of the world', later with the development of hydroelectric power and manufacturing industries and, despite setbacks, e.g. in the years of the great trade depression (1929–35), Canada became one of the world's great trading nations. Inevitably the nation began to demand an increasing degree of autonomy and her equality of status with Britain in the Commonwealth was defined in the Statute of Westminster (1931). In 1949 Newfoundland joined Canada as the tenth province.

In 1982 the Canada Act was adopted by the Parliament of Canada and the UK Parliament. This replaced the British North America Act of 1867 and was the final act of the UK Parliament in Canadian constitutional development.

By the British North America Act (1867) the constitution was required to be 'similar in principle to that of the United Kingdom'. Executive authority is vested in the Queen and is carried on in her name by the Governor-General. In 1977 the Queen of Canada approved the transfer to the Governor-General of functions discharged by the Sovereign. Legislative power is exercised by a Parliament of two Houses, the 104-member Senate and the 295-member House of Commons. Each province has its own government, which deals with matters of local concern, the Queen being represented by a Lieutenant-Governor. Indians are represented in the Assembly of First Nations.

Canary Islands N Atlantic Ocean. Group of Spanish islands 96 km (60 miles) off the NW coast of Africa. Divided into two provinces named after their cap. Las Palmas contain the islands of Lanzarote, Fuerteventura and Grand Canary (Gran Canaria); Santa Cruz de Tenerife contains those of Tenerife, Palma, Gomera and Hierro. Total area 7273 sq km (2807 sq. miles). Total pop. (1991) 1,493,800. Of volcanic origin; mountainous. The mild, healthy climate makes them popular winter resorts. Water is scarce; some areas are almost desert.

Where irrigation is possible, abundant crops are produced. Principal exports bananas, tomatoes, potatoes. Leading industries fishing and canning. The two chief ports, Las Palmas and Santa Cruz de Tenerife, are important fuelling stations.

The Canary Is. were known to the Phoenicians, Greeks, Carthaginians and Romans. The elder Pliny attributed the name Canaria to the large number of dogs; they may have been Plutarch's 'Fortunate Islands'. Came into the possession of Ferdinand and Isabella of Aragón–Castile in 1476; Spanish sovereignty was established (1479) by treaty between Aragón–Castile and Portugal. Became wholly Spanish; the original Guanches (probably of Berber stock) have been assimilated.

Canaveral, Cape USA. For period 1963–73 known as Cape Kennedy after the assassinated US President and the name is still used by NASA. Cape situated on the E coast of Florida 240 km (150 miles) SSE of Jacksonville. Site of the USAF Missile Test Center. US earth satellites and lunar and stellar probes have been launched and men put into orbit round the earth and sent to the moon from the site.

Canberra Australia. Cap. in the Australian Capital Territory on an upland plain dotted with small hills and crossed by the Molonglo R. 240 km (150 miles) SW of Sydney. Pop. (1993) 324,600. The site, consisting of 2432 sq km (911 sq. miles) of grazing land, was adopted in 1909; the new city was planned by W. B. Griffin, a Chicago architect, and the foundation stone was laid in 1913. In 1927 the Commonwealth Parliament was transferred here from Melbourne. Since then, the growth of government departments, the establishment of the Australian National University and of offices controlling research, commerce and manufactures have led to a considerable increase in pop.

Candia ➤IRÁKLION.

Canea (Gr. **Khaniá**) Greece. 1. *Nome* in W Crete. Area 2376 sq km (926 sq. miles). Pop. (1991) 133,774. Mainly agricultural. 2. Cap. of Crete (since 1840) and of Canea *nome* in the NW of the island. Pop. (1981) 47,451. Seaport, probably on the site of ancient Cydonia.

Coastal trade in citrus fruits, carob beans, wine and olive oil.

Flourished in the 13th–17th cent. under Venetian rule; remains of Venetian fortifications. Captured by the Turks 1645. Severely damaged during the German invasion in World War II (1941). The birthplace of the Greek statesman Eleutherios Venizelos (1864–1936) is nearby.

Cannae (modern **Canna**) Italy. Town in ancient Apulia, near the mouth of the Aufidus (Ofanto) R. 10 km (6 miles) NE of Cansium (Canosa). Scene of Hannibal's great victory over the Romans (216 BC).

Cannes France. Resort in the Alpes-Maritimes department on the French Riviera 26 km (16 miles) SW of Nice. Pop. (1990) 69,363.

Fruits and flowers extensively grown in the neighbourhood. Essential oils and candied fruits produced.

Its development as a fashionable resort dates from 1834, when Lord Brougham, attracted by its position and its mild, healthy climate, built himself a villa. Sheltered by low hills. Wide boulevards, many hotels, villas, casinos and sports facilities. On the Mont Chevalier (in the old town), a 17th-cent. church and a medieval watch-tower. Offshore are the Îles de Lerins: on the Île Ste Marguerite the 'Man in the Iron Mask' was imprisoned (1687–98) and the Île St Honorat has the oldest monastery in W Europe. The annual international film festival is held here.

Canning (Desert) Basin Australia. Arid region of NW Western Australia about 1440 km (900 miles) NNE of Perth. Area 400,000 sq km (150,000 sq. miles). Largely unexplored.

Cannock England. Town in Staffordshire 13 km (8 miles) NNE of Wolverhampton. Pop. (1991) 60,106.

Coalmining. Manufactures automotive parts and iron and steel products. Cannock Chase (once a royal preserve) is just to the E.

Canso, Strait (Gut) of Canada. Strait between Cape Breton Island and the mainland of Canada, at its narrowest part 1.6 km (1 mile) wide. Crossed by a causeway carrying a road and a railway, with a lock and drawbridge to allow the passage of shipping.

Cantabrian Mountains Spain. Mountain range in the N extending 480 km (300 miles) E–W from the Pyrenees, parallel to the coast of the Bay of Biscay. Forms a barrier between the central Meseta and the narrow coastal plain. The highest peaks (in the central area) inc. Peña Cerredo (2682 m; 8797 ft) and Peña Vieja (2632 m; 8633 ft). Rich in minerals, esp. coal and iron.

Cantal France. Department in the Auvergne region. Area 5741 sq km (2231 sq. miles). Pop. (1990) 158,700. Prefecture Aurillac. Mountainous (volcanic Monts du Chantal occupying the central area), rising to 1858 m (6094 ft) in the Plomb du Cantal. Drained by the Dordogne R. and its tributaries. It has a harsh climate. Cattle-rearing, dairy-farming. Produces cheese and butter.

Canterbury England. Roman Durovernum; Saxon Cantwaraburh ('Borough of the Men of Kent'). Cathedral city in E Kent on the R. Stour 88 km (55 miles) ESE of London. Pop. (1991) 36,464. Market town and a major tourist centre.

Dominated by the great cathedral; famous chiefly because the archbishop is the Anglican Primate of All England. Situated at a ford over the Stour and a focus of routes across SE England, it flourished and became the cap. of the Saxon kingdom of Kent, the fourth Saxon king of which, Ethelbert, was converted to Christianity and presented St Augustine (who arrived from Rome in AD 597) with land on which to found an abbey; St Augustine became the first Archbishop of Canterbury (597–604) and Canterbury has remained the headquarters of the English Church. The early cathedral occupied by St Augustine was destroyed by fire in 1067; Archbishop Lanfranc (1070–89) began the building of a completely new cathedral, not finished until the 15th cent. Thus the architectural styles range from Norman to Perpendicular; the most striking exterior feature, the 72-m (236-ft) central (Bell Harry) tower, is late 15th-cent. Perpendicular. The two principal periods of building may be distinguished in the two parts in which the interior is divided, the choir being raised in unusual fashion above the nave, with the altar above the choir. When Archbishop Thomas à Becket was murdered in the cathedral (1170) and at once canonized, a magnificent shrine was erected in the Trinity Chapel, which for more than three cent. drew throngs of pilgrims (who provided material for Chaucer's *Canterbury Tales*). Noteworthy features within the cathedral are the fine Norman crypt, the tombs of Edward the Black Prince and Henry IV, the site of Becket's murder and beautiful stained-glass windows illustrating miracles said to have been performed after Becket's martyrdom. The treasure accumulated at Becket's shrine was confiscated by Henry VIII (1535) in the course of the Reformation.

Probably the oldest part of Canterbury is the artificial mound known as the Dane John (now in a public park), with a memorial to Christopher Marlowe, English dramatist (1564–93), who was born in Canterbury.

Nearby is the large Norman keep, sole remnant of the 11th-cent. castle. There are remains of the old city walls, but of the six former gates only the 14th-cent. West Gate has survived. The remains of St Augustine's abbey were converted into a missionary college in 1844. St Martin's Church (restored) was used for Christian worship even before the coming of St Augustine. St Dunstan's Church has in its vault the head of Sir Thomas More (1478–1535). At the King's School (refounded by Henry VIII in 1541, built on the site of the monastery hall) is preserved a superb Norman entry-stair. The University of Kent at Canterbury was established in 1965. Some of the old buildings, inc. parts of the cathedral, were seriously damaged in German air raids during World War II (1942).

Canterbury New Zealand. Region covering the E central part of the S Island. Area 43,432 sq km (16,769 sq. miles). Pop. (1991) 442,392. Chief town Christchurch. It inc. the high mountain country of the Southern Alps, the eastern foothills and the Canterbury Plains, and extends from the Waitaki R. in the S roughly to the Kaikoura Ranges in the N. The central Canterbury Plains, with Christchurch the largest city, form the most closely settled part of the S Island. Formerly used for extensive wheat farming, they now support mixed farms for sheep, fat lambs, dairy cattle and the cultivation of grain and fodder crops, with special areas for horticulture and vegetables. The surface is apt to be dry and tree belts act as windbreaks. S of Christchurch the Rangitata and Rakaia rivers provide irrigation water. Hydroelectric power is developed on several rivers. Inland, hill country supports extensive sheep-farming, as does the Banks Peninsula. Chief seaport Lyttelton.

Canton (China) ►GUANGZHOU.

Canton USA. Industrial town in Ohio 34 km (21 miles) SSE of Akron. Pop. (1990) 84,161.

Outlying centre of the Pittsburgh iron and steel manufacturing district. Steelworks and rolling mills. Manufactures roller bearings, iron and steel pulleys, and hydraulic presses.

Home of President McKinley (1843–1901).

Canton Island ➤KIRIBATI.

Canvey Island England. Residential district in S Essex in the Thames estuary. Pop. (1991) 36,406. Connected by bridge with S Benfleet on the mainland.

Industries inc. iron, wire, bookbinding, oil storage and refining, liquid gas terminal.

Cape Breton Island Canada. Island in NE Nova Scotia (named after a headland on the E coast), separated from the mainland by the Canso Strait which is crossed by a causeway. Area 10,295 sq km (3975 sq. miles). Coastline deeply indented. Almost bisected by the Bras d'Or Lake. Climate cool and damp, the cold Labrador Current reducing the temperature of the coastal water; fogs are common.

Farming is largely dairying, much of it a part-time occupation with fishing and lumbering. Mineral wealth is important, esp. coal, mined in the Sydney–Glace Bay area and used at the Sydney steel works. Gypsum mined in the N.

Much of the NW peninsula, with outstanding coastal scenery, has become the Cape Breton Highlands National Park. Discovered in 1497 by John Cabot (1425–c. 1500). From 1713 the island was a French colony named Île Royale. Not taken by the British until 1758. Joined to Nova Scotia 1820.

Cape Canaveral ➤CANAVERAL, CAPE.

Cape Coast Ghana. Formerly Cape Coast Castle (from the castle built here by the Swedes in 1652). Cap. of the Central Region, seaport 137 km (85 miles) WSW of Accra. Pop. (1984) 51,653. Main export cacao.

Taken from the Swedes by the Dutch. Passed to Britain 1664. Chief city of the Gold Coast till 1876, when Accra became cap.

Cape Girardeau USA. Town in Missouri on the Mississippi R. 160 km (100 miles) SSE of St Louis. Pop. (1980) 34,361.

Industrial centre. Manufactures footwear and clothing.

Cape Province South Africa. Former province. In 1994 it was divided into the provinces of Eastern Cape, Western Cape and Northern Cape.

Capernaum Israel. Modern Tell Hum. Ancient town on the N shore of L. Tiberias (Sea of Galilee), closely associated with Christ's teaching. The remains of a synagogue of the 2nd cent. AD were excavated early in the 20th cent.

Cape Town (Capetown) South Africa. Legislative cap. and also cap. of Western Cape Province on Table Bay in the SW. Pop. (1985) 776,600.

Chief passenger seaport and second largest city. Its harbour has graving docks, oil-storage tanks, cold-storage plants and a large grain elevator. Industries inc. food-processing, wine-making, printing, textiles and tourism.

A city of great scenic beauty, to which much is contributed by Table Mountain (1082 m; 3549 ft), standing just to the S. University (1918). The 17th-cent. castle (now housing the Department of Defence) and Groote Schuur (at Rondebosch on the SE outskirts) are examples of Dutch colonial architecture. Groote Schuur, once the home of Cecil Rhodes, is now the official residence of the Prime Minister and the university buildings are in its grounds. Other important buildings and places of interest are the Houses of Parliament, the National Art Gallery and the Municipal Botanical Gardens; Adderley Street is the principal thoroughfare. The National Botanical Gardens are at Kirstenbosch (S), originally part of the Groote Schuur estate, on the slopes of Table Mountain. Founded (1652) by Jan van Riebeeck, who established a victualling station for ships of the Dutch East India Company; the oldest white settlement in South Africa.

Cape Verde. Republic situated in the Atlantic Ocean 560 km (350 miles) WNW of Cape Verde (Senegal). Area 4033 sq km (1557 sq. miles). Pop. (1995) 392,000 (30 per cent urban). About 600,000 Cape Verdeans live abroad. Life expectancy, 61 years male,

65 female. Cap. Praia, other towns Mindelo and São Filipe. Currency: Cape Verde escudo = 100 centavos. An archipelago consisting of 10 islands and 5 islets, divided into two groups, Barlavento (Windward) and Sotavento (Leeward). The former inc. São Vicente, Santo Antão, São Nicolau, Santa Luzia, Sal and Boa Vista; the latter inc. São Tiago, Maio, Fogo and Brava. The islands are mountainous and of volcanic origin; the highest peak, Pico do Cano (2831 m; 9286 ft), last erupted severely in 1847. The climate is arid, with a cool, dry season from December to June and warm, dry conditions for the rest of the year. Land use: forested 0.2 per cent, meadows and pastures 6 per cent, agricultural and under permanent cultivation 11 per cent. The official lang. is Portuguese but a creole (Criulo) is in general use. The majority of the pop. is Roman Catholic. The ethnic composition is mixed 71 per cent, black 28 per cent and white 1 per cent.

Fishing is an important industry and exports consist of fish, salt and bananas. Industries inc. flour-milling, rum and molasses. Tourism is in the initial stages of development.

The Cape Verde islands were discovered by the Portuguese in 1460, with the first settlers arriving in 1462. It became an overseas province of Portugal in 1951 and achieved independence in 1975. There is a unicameral 79-member National People's Assembly.

Cape Wrath Scotland. Promontory in the NW.

Cape York Peninsula Australia. Peninsula projecting N into Torres Strait between the Gulf of Carpentaria (W) and the Coral Sea (E) with Cape York at the N end. Mainly tropical forest and grassland.

Cap Haïtien (Le Cap) Haiti. Seaport on the N coast. Pop. (1992) 92,122.

Exports coffee, sugar-cane and bananas from the fertile coastal plain.

Under French rule it was cap. of the colony ('the Paris of Haiti'). Largely destroyed by earthquake (1842), but trade later recovered.

Cappadocia. Ancient region of Asia Minor,

of varying extent but occupying a mountainous area of present-day central Turkey. For a time it was an independent kingdom, its cap. at Mazaca (modern Kayseri). Became a Roman province AD 17.

Capri Italy. Ancient Capreae. Rocky island in Napoli province in Campania at the S entrance to the Bay of Naples. Area 10 sq km (4 sq. miles). Pop. (1981) 7489. Popular tourist resort, with picturesque scenery and pleasant climate. Produces white wine.

The two towns (at different levels), Capri (137 m; 449 ft) and Anacapri (299 m; 980 ft), were connected only by a flight of steps until 1874, when a carriage road was constructed. Highest point Monte Solaro (586 m; 1922 ft). Along the precipitous coast there are two landing places, Marina Grande (from which a funicular railway leads to the town) and Marina Piccola. Famous for the Grotta Azzurra (Blue Grotto, rediscovered 1826), accessible only by small boat; Axel Munthe's villa San Michele at Anacapri (with an exquisite garden and magnificent views); and the remains of villas built by the Emperor Tiberius.

Caprivi Zipfel (Caprivi Strip) Namibia. Strip of land in the NE 480 km (300 miles) long and about 48 km (30 miles) wide, giving the Territory access to the Zambezi R. Named after Count Caprivi, the German Chancellor, who negotiated its cession from Britain (1893).

Capua Italy. Ancient Casilinum. Market town in Caserta province in Campania on the Volturno R. 29 km (18 miles) N of Naples. Pop. (1990) 19,520. The 9th-cent. cathedral, severely damaged in World War II, was rebuilt. Ancient Capua (on a site 5 km (3 miles) to the SE), of great strategic importance, was linked with Rome by the Appian Way. Remains of a large amphitheatre. After its destruction by Saracens (840) the inhabitants moved and founded modern Capua.

Caracas Venezuela. Cap. of Venezuela and of the Federal District, in a basin at a height of 900 m (2952 ft). Pop. (1990) 1,824,892.

The centre of economic and cultural life, it derives its wealth mainly from oil and is the headquarters of the oil companies and large business houses. Manufactures textiles, clothing and many other consumer goods.

Climate warm but pleasant; mean annual temperature 20°C (68°F). Stretches 14 km (9 miles) along the valley, beneath deeply gullied hills. Connected with its seaport and the coastal airport by an 18-km (11-mile) tunnelled motorway. Inland a main road leads to the Valencia basin and the W, as part of the Pan-American Highway. Founded 1567. Became the cap. of the captaincy-general of Caracas. Birthplace of Simón Bolívar, Revolutionary leader (1783–1830). Became cap. of independent Venezuela 1829.

Carbonia Italy. Lignite-mining town in Cagliari province in Sardinia 55 km (34 miles) W of Cagliari. Pop. (1989) 33,501. The lignite is used to produce electricity.

Carcassonne France. Prefecture of the Aude department on the Canal du Midi and the Aude R., divided by the Aude into the old town (Cité) and the new Ville Basse. Pop. (1990) 44,991.

Tourist centre. Trade in wine. Tanning, hosiery manufacture and other industries.

The old town, built on a hill, is a medieval fortified city of great architectural interest: a 12th-cent. castle, the 11th/14th-cent. Romanesque and Gothic cathedral of St Nazaire and the massive ramparts and towers. Within the new town (the business and residential area) is the 13th-cent. cathedral (restored). Suffered severely during the Albigensian Crusade; taken by Simon de Montfort (the elder) (1209).

Carchemish. Ancient city on the Euphrates R. in modern S Turkey on the Syrian border. Centre of a neo-Hittite culture. Scene of a battle (605 BC) in which Nebuchadnezzar defeated the Egyptians.

Cárdenas Cuba. Seaport in Matanzas province 37 km (23 miles) E of Matanzas. Pop. (1970) 55,000.

Exports sugar. Sugar-refining, rum-distilling and rice-milling. Manufactures rope and matches.

Cardiff Wales. Cap. of Wales and County Borough on the R. Taff near the mouth of the Severn estuary. Pop. (1994) 307,000.

Seaport. Commercial, financial and administrative centre. Industries inc. high technology, electrical goods, steel production, ship-repairing, engineering, flour-milling, paper-making and chemicals. Port handles timber, fruit, grain, oil and chemical products, steel, coal and coke.

The castle, built in the 11th cent. and partly destroyed by Owen Glendower (1404), was presented to the city by the 3rd Marquis of Bute in 1947. Among outstanding buildings in and around Cathays Park are the Law Courts, the City Hall, the Welsh National Museum, the County Hall, the Cardiff Technical College, the University College and the Temple of Peace and Health. Of modern growth, though it dates from a 1st-cent. AD Roman station.

Cardigan Wales. Market town in Ceredigion on the R. Teifi 5 km (3 miles) above the mouth. Pop. (1991) 3758. Declined as a port through the silting of the river mouth and the advent of steamships. Traces of a 12th-cent. castle.

Caria. Ancient region in SW Asia Minor on the Aegean Sea S of Lydia (the modern SW Turkey). The chief towns were Halicarnassus and Cnidus.

Caribbean Sea W Atlantic Ocean. Part of the W Atlantic, bounded by the Greater and Lesser Antilles (N and E) and the coasts of Venezuela, Colombia and the neighbouring states of Central America (S and W). Linked with the Gulf of Mexico by the Yucatán Channel. Area 2,754,000 sq km (967,000 sq. miles). Maximum depth 7680 m (25,197 ft). Named after the warlike Caribs who formerly inhabited parts of the region.

Cariboo Canada. Mining district in the W foothills of the Cariboo Mountains, British Columbia. Scene of the Cariboo gold rush

(1860). Named after the nearby Cariboo Lake.

Cariboo Mountains Canada. Mountain range 320 km (200 miles) long in E British Columbia, running W of and roughly parallel to the main range of the Rocky Mountains, separated from them by the Fraser R. Mainly above 1500 m (4920 ft).

Carinthia (Ger. **Kärnten**) Austria. Federal state bordering in the S on Italy and Slovenia. Area 9533 sq km (3680 sq. miles). Pop. (1991) 552,421. Cap. Klagenfurt. Mainly mountainous, containing the highest peak in Austria, the Gross Glockner (3798 m; 12,457 ft). Chief river the Drau. Many small lakes, inc. the Weissensee and the Millstattersee, with resorts. Lumbering, stock-rearing and mining (iron, lignite). Principal towns Klagenfurt, Villach. Became Austrian in the 14th cent.

Carisbrooke England. Village in the Isle of Wight just SW of Newport. In the now partly ruined 11th-cent. castle Charles I was imprisoned for 10 months (1647–8) before his trial and execution.

Carlisle England. Ancient Lugavallum (Roman); Caer Luel (British). City in Cumbria at the confluence of the Caldew and the Petteril with the R. Eden. Pop. (1991) 72,439. Railway.

Industrial and commercial centre. Flour-milling. Manufactures textiles, biscuits, agricultural machinery. Liquor trade under state management from 1921.

Castle (11th-cent.) in which Mary Queen of Scots was imprisoned for a time; 12th-cent. cathedral. Destroyed by the Danes 875. Restored by William Rufus 1092. An important fortress in the border wars with the Scots. Withstood a 9-month siege (1644–5) in the Civil Wars.

Carlow Ireland. 1. County in Leinster. Area 896 sq km (346 sq. miles). Pop. (1991) 40,950. Gently undulating with a range of barren mountains in the SE. Highest point Mt Leinster (796 m; 2611 ft). Drained by the Barrow and the Slaney rivers. Stock-rearing, dairy-

farming. Oats and potatoes cultivated. 2. County town of Co. Carlow at the confluence of the R. Burren with the R. Barrow. Pop. (1991) 11,230. Market town. Flour-milling, sugar-refining and brewing. Has an ancient castle (in ruins), a 19th-cent. Roman Catholic cathedral and an 18th-cent. theological college.

Carlsbad USA. Town in SE New Mexico on the Pecos R. 362 km (225 miles) SE of Albuquerque. Pop. (1980) 25,496. Tourist resort for visitors to the Carlsbad Caverns National Park (27 km; 17 miles to the SW), containing limestone caves of which the largest (the Big Room) is more than 0.8 km (½ mile) long. Potash is mined and refined. Commercial centre. Trade in cotton, wool and alfalfa.

Carlton England. Town in Nottinghamshire just E of Nottingham. Pop. (1991) 47,302.

Manufactures bricks, hosiery and furniture.

Carluke Scotland. Industrial town in South Lanarkshire 8 km (5 miles) NNW of Lanark. Pop. (1986) 14,058.

Industries inc. food-processing, general service activities and light engineering.

Carmarthen Wales. Market town in Carmarthenshire on the R. Towy 13 km (8 miles) above the mouth on Carmarthen Bay. Pop. (1991) 13,524.

Railway junction. Flour-milling. Manufactures dairy products.

Remains of a Norman castle; mainly 14th-cent. church.

Carmarthenshire Wales. County in the SW. From 1974 it was part of Dyfed and in 1996 was reinstated as a county. Pop. (1994) 164,000.

Carmel, Mount Israel. Limestone ridge extending 23 km (14 miles) NW from the Samarian Hills to the Mediterranean Sea at Haifa, rising to 528 m (1732 ft). In the Bible, the scene of Elijah's struggle with the priests of Baal. The Order of Carmelites was founded here in the 12th cent.

Carmona Spain. Market town in Andalusia 32 km (20 miles) ENE of Seville. Pop. (1991) 22,660. In a region producing wine and olive oil. Flour-milling, tanning and other industries. A large necropolis and other Roman remains have been excavated. Taken from the Moors (whose influence on the architecture is still apparent) by Ferdinand III of Castile 1247.

Carnac France. Village in the Morbihan department 27 km (17 miles) SE of Lorient. Pop. (1985) 4000. Famous for the standing stones or menhirs, extending about 5 km (3 miles) in parallel rows. A common-burial ground of the Iberians (c. 2000 BC).

Carnforth England. Market town in N Lancashire 10 km (6 miles) N of Lancaster. Pop. (1985) 5000. Railway junction. Gravel pits.

Carniola Slovenia. Former crownland and duchy of Austria; the cap. was Ljubljana (Laibach). Occupied by the Slovenes (6th cent.). Passed to the Habsburg monarchy in the 14th cent. Divided between Yugoslavia and Italy (1919), the former receiving about five-sixths of the 9972 sq km (3850 sq. miles); the whole became part of Slovenia in 1947.

Carnot, Cape ➤GREAT AUSTRALIAN BIGHT.

Carnoustie Scotland. Holiday resort in Angus on the North Sea 16 km (10 miles) ENE of Dundee. Pop. (1991) 10,673. Famous golfing centre.

Caroline Islands Micronesia. Archipelago in the W Pacific W of the Marshall Is.; with the exception of Palau and some lesser islands they form the Federated States of Micronesia. Discovered (1526) by Spaniards. Purchased from Spain by Germany 1899. Occupied by the Japanese in World War I and held under mandate until 1935, when they were claimed by Japan. In 1947 they became part of the US Trust Territory of the Pacific Is. In 1990 the Trusteeship was terminated and Micronesia became an independent country.

Caroní River Venezuela. River 800 km (500 miles) long, rising in the Guiana Highlands (extreme SW) flowing generally W and then N to join the lower Orinoco R. Above the confluence is a large hydroelectric plant, associated with the steelworks at San Torre de Guayana, which first operated in 1962.

Carpathian Mountains. Mountain system of central and E Europe, a connecting link in the great Alpine uplift between the Alps and the Balkan Mountains, extending in a vast arc 1400 km (900 miles) long. From the Czech Republic they form part of the Czech–Polish frontier, crossing the SW of Ukraine into Romania and re-approach the Danube at the Iron Gate. They enclose the Plain of Hungary. The main W–E divisions are the Little Carpathians, the White Carpathians, the W and E Beskids, the High and the Low Tatra, and the Transylvanian Alps. In general considerably lower than the Alps. Crossed by several low passes. The highest peak is Gerlachovka (2665 m; 8711 ft) in the High Tatra, a popular tourist region noted for its beautiful Alpine scenery with jagged peaks, mountain lakes and glacial features. Well wooded to a height of more than 1200 m (3936 ft). Rich in minerals, but of little economic importance and sparsely peopled.

Carpentaria, Gulf of Australia. Large inlet in the N between Arnhem Land and Cape York Peninsula about 480 km (300 miles) W–E and 595 km (370 miles) N–S. Receives many rivers. Contains the islands of Groote Eylandt, the Sir Edward Pellew Group and the Wellesley Is.

Carpentras France. Ancient Carpentoracte. Market town in the Vaucluse department 24 km (15 miles) NE of Avignon. Pop. (1985) 26,000. In a hilly region on the edge of the wide valley of the R. Rhône. Famous for sweetmeats and candied fruits. Cap. of the Meminians and later of the Comtat Venaissin. A 15th/16th-cent. Gothic church (formerly a cathedral); 17th-cent. former bishop's palace; 14th-cent. gateway, the Porte d'Orange.

Carpi Italy. Town in the Modena province in Emilia-Romagna 16 km (10 miles) N of Modena. Pop. (1981) 60,500. Produces wine and food products. Cathedral (16th-cent.).

Carrara Italy. Town in the Massa-Carrara province in Tuscany near the Ligurian Sea 48 km (30 miles) NNW of Pisa. Pop. (1985) 66,000.

Famous for marble, quarried and worked in the neighbourhood and exported throughout the world from its port Marina di Carrara. Cathedral (13th/14th-cent.).

Carrickfergus Northern Ireland. Fishing port in Co. Antrim on the N side of Belfast Lough. Pop. (1991) 22,786.

Manufactures linen, rayon and tobacco products.

Castle (12th-cent.). Scene of William III's landing (1690) before the Battle of the Boyne.

Carrickmacross Ireland. Market town in Co. Monaghan 21 km (13 miles) WSW of Dundalk. Pop. (1986) 1815. Famous for lace. Manufactures alcohol (from potatoes) and shoes.

Carrick-on-Shannon Ireland. County town of Leitrim on the R. Shannon. Pop. (1986) 1984.

Fishing centre. Market for dairy produce, livestock and potatoes.

Carrick-on-Suir Ireland. Market town in Co. Tipperary on the R. Suir. Pop. (1986) 5353.

Slate quarrying. Tanning. Salmon fishing. Castle (14th-cent., restored).

Carron Scotland. Village in Falkirk on the R. Carron 3 km (2 miles) NNW of Falkirk. Famous for the ironworks (established 1760). The carronade gun (first cast here) and carron oil are named after it.

Carshalton England. Former urban district in NE Surrey S of London, for which it acts as a dormitory suburb; from 1965 part of the London borough of Sutton.

Carson City USA. State cap. of Nevada near the Californian border 42 km (26 miles) S of Reno. Pop. (1990) 40,443. In a silver-mining district. Commercial centre. Resort. Named after Kit Carson (1809–68), a famous hunter and scout.

Cartagena Colombia. Cap. of the Bolívar department and principal seaport of the NW on the Caribbean coast. Pop. (1992) 688,306. Linked by canalized waterway to the Magdalena R. and by a highway to southern cities. Terminal of the pipeline from the Barrancabermeja oilfields.

Exports agricultural produce (sugar, rice, maize, tobacco) from an extensive hinterland and gold and platinum from the Atrato valley. Manufactures textiles, footwear, tobacco products, chemicals, soap and fertilizers.

University (1827). Founded and fortified by the Spanish 1533; an export centre for precious metals and stones.

Cartagena Spain. Ancient Carthago Nova. Fortified naval base and seaport in Murcia on the Mediterranean Sea 43 km (27 miles) SSE of Murcia. Pop. (1991) 166,736.

Exports lead and iron mined in the neighbourhood. Lead and iron smelting, metalworking, boatbuilding. Manufactures chemicals, glass and bicycles.

Founded in the 3rd cent. BC by Hasdrubal, it became the Carthaginian headquarters in Spain. Captured (209 BC) by Scipio Africanus (the elder) and thrived under the Romans as a mineral-exporting port (silver, lead). Almost destroyed by the Goths AD 425. Flourished again in the 16th cent. when it was rebuilt and fortified by Philip II of Spain.

Cartago Colombia. Commercial town in the Valle del Cauca department 64 km (40 miles) SW of Manizales. Pop. (1984) 29,564.

Trade in coffee, tobacco and cattle. Founded 1540.

Carthage Tunisia. Ancient city state on the N coast of Africa, near modern Tunis, of which it is now a residential suburb. Founded in the 9th cent. BC by the Phoenicians. From the 6th cent. BC the Carthaginians developed both trade and sea power, controlled the coasts of NW Africa, Sardinia, Malta, the Balearic Is. and much of Sicily, and established colonies in what are now Senegal and

Guinea. They became wealthy by selling Negro slaves, ivory, gold, from tropical Africa, but their rivalry with Rome led to the Punic Wars; in the first (268–241 BC) they were defeated in Sicily but conquered much of Spain; in the second (218–201 BC), largely owing to the insistence of Cato that Carthage must be destroyed (*Delenda est Carthago*), Rome attacked again; in the 3rd Punic War (149–146 BC) Roman armies utterly defeated the Carthaginians and razed the city. More than a cent. later (under Augustus) Carthage was rebuilt; it became one of the greatest cities in the Roman Empire. Later it was of importance in the early history of Christianity. Subsequently taken by the Vandals (AD 439), it became their cap. Recaptured by the Byzantine army 534. Totally destroyed by the Hillali Arabs 698. Almost nothing of Punic Carthage has survived, but extensive Roman ruins testify to its past grandeur. The Bardo museum in Tunis contains a rich collection of Roman art, esp. mosaics.

Carúpano Venezuela. Seaport in the Sucre state (NE). Pop. (1984) 32,000.

Exports coffee, cacao. Manufactures straw hats, pottery and soap.

Casablanca (El Dar-el-Beida) Morocco. Chief seaport and largest city on the Atlantic coast, 80 km (50 miles) SW of Rabat. Pop. (1982) 2,139,204.

Handles more than three-quarters of Morocco's foreign trade. Constant harbour improvements since 1913 have made it one of the world's largest artificial ports. Exports phosphates, manganese ore. Manufactures textiles, glass, cement, soap and superphosphates. Fishing. Founded in the early 16th cent. (on the site of ancient Anfa) by the Portuguese, as Casa Branca ('White House'). Occupied by the French 1907.

Casale Monferrato Italy. Town in the Alessandria province in Piedmont on the Po R. Pop. (1985) 48,000.

Industrial and commercial centre. Important cement works. Manufactures agricultural machinery, silk, rayon and footwear. Trade in fruit and rice.

Romanesque cathedral (11th/12th-cent.). Became the cap. of the marquisate of Montferrat in the 15th cent.

Cascade Range USA. Range of mountains extending from the Fraser R. in British Columbia through W Washington and Oregon practically parallel to the Pacific coast, in general 1200–1500 m (3936–4920 ft) in height but rising to over 3000 m (9840 ft) in several snow-capped extinct volcanoes, inc. Mt Rainier (4394 m; 14,412 ft). Continued S by the Sierra Nevada of California. Named after the cascades of the Columbia R. where this river cuts through the range. The mountain slopes are well forested, with large stands of Douglas fir and other conifers.

Caserta Italy. Cap. of the Caserta province (dissolved in 1927, reconstituted in 1945) in Campania 24 km (15 miles) NNE of Naples. Pop. (1990) 69,350.

Market town. Trade in cereals, citrus fruits, wine and olive oil. Manufactures chemicals and soap.

A 12th-cent. cathedral at Caserta Vecchia 5 km (3 miles) to the NE. A village until 1752, when the magnificent royal palace was begun (completed in 1774). An Allied HQ during World War II; scene of the surrender of the German forces in Italy (29 April 1945).

Cashel Ireland. Town in Co. Tipperary 19 km (12 miles) ENE of Tipperary. Pop. (1991) 2470. Seat of a Protestant bishop. The Rock of Cashel (92 m; 302 ft), 'the holiest spot in Ireland', is crowned by the remains of the 13th-cent. St Patrick's Cathedral, the 12th-cent. Cormac's Chapel and an ancient cross where the kings of Munster were crowned.

Casper USA. Ranching town and route centre on the N Platte R. in central Wyoming. Pop. (1990) 46,742. Airport. An oil well was established nearby in 1890; oil production rose considerably during World War I. The town now has oil refineries and manufactures tents and bricks.

Caspian Sea Iran/Azerbaijan/Russia/Kazakhstan/Turkmenistan. The largest inland

Cassel

sea (salt lake) in the world; 1207 km (750 miles) long N–S and on average 354 km (220 miles) wide. Area 394,000 sq km (152,000 sq. miles). With the Black Sea and the Aral Sea it once formed part of a much greater inland sea. Receiving large volumes of fresh water from the Volga, Ural and other rivers, it has a lower salinity than the Black Sea. There is no outlet and it is tideless. In the N, where it is shallow, it is frozen for 2–3 months annually. Crossed by a submarine ridge extending E from the Apsheron peninsula; the depth increases to the S. The level has fluctuated (partly owing to differential evaporation and partly to varying amounts of water received from the rivers). It fell consistently between the late 1920s and the 1970s. By 1977 it had dropped to almost 30 m (98 ft) below sea level – its lowest point for five cent. In the 1940s Iran and the USSR began to cover the drying sea bed with factories, houses and tourist playgrounds. Now the rising sea is reclaiming this land. Quantities of salt (chiefly Glauber's salt) are deposited through evaporation in Kara Bogaz Gol, an almost land-locked gulf on the E. Principal ports Astrakhan, Makhachkala, Baku, Krasnovodsk. Its fisheries are famous for the finest caviare.

Cassel ➤KASSEL.

Castel Gandolfo Italy. Summer residence of the pope sit. 16 km (10 miles) SE of Rome in the Alban Hills on the W of Lake Albano.

Castellammare di Stabia Italy. Seaport in Napoli province, Campania on the Bay of Naples 26 km (16 miles) SE of Naples. Pop. (1981) 70,317.

Resort with mineral springs. Industrial and commercial centre. Naval dockyard. Pasta factories. Manufactures aircraft equipment, marine engines and textiles.

The nearby Roman resort of Stabiae was buried by the eruption of Vesuvius (AD 79). The ruined castle (which gives the name) was built in the 13th cent. by the Emperor Frederick II.

Castellón de la Plana Spain. 1. Province in Valencia. Area 6679 sq km (2578 sq. miles).

Pop. (1991) 445,065. Mountainous in the N and W with a fertile coastal plain. Mainly agricultural. Produces cereals, vines, fruits, olives in the lowlands. 2. Cap. of the Castellón de la Plana province 5 km (3 miles) from the Mediterranean 68 km (42 miles) NNE of Valencia. Pop. (1991) 133,180.

Manufactures cement, paper, textiles and tiles. Exports oranges and almonds through the harbour of El Gráo de Castellón.

Chiefly modern. Has a 14th-cent. church and a 17th-cent. octagonal bell tower.

Castelvetrano Italy. Market town in the Trapani province in W Sicily. Pop. (1981) 30,577. Railway junction. Produces Marsala wine. Ruins of the ancient Greek colony of Selinus near by.

Castile (Sp. **Castilla**) Spain. Region and former kingdom of central and N Spain, extending from the Bay of Biscay (N) to the Sierra Morena (S), on the central plateau or Meseta at a height of 750–900 m (2460–2952 ft). Generally bare and monotonous. Subject to a harsh continental climate; suffers from frequent droughts. Divided by the Sierra de Guadarrama and the Sierra de Gredos into Old Castile (N) and New Castile (S), the former drained by the Ebro and Duero (Douro) rivers and the latter by the Tagus and the Guadiana. Old Castile (area 50,220 sq km (19,390 sq. miles)) consists of the 6 provinces of Ávila, Burgos, Logroño, Santander, Segovia and Soria (Palencia and Valladolid are also sometimes inc.). New Castile (area 72,346 sq km (27,933 sq. miles)) comprises the 5 provinces of Ciudad Real, Cuenca, Guadalajara, Madrid and Toledo. The name Castile probably derives from the number of castles erected against the Moors. Originally a county of the kingdom of León; became virtually independent in the 10th cent. The kingdoms of Castile and León were united in 1230. The marriage of Ferdinand II of Aragón and Isabella of Castile (1469) united the kingdoms of Aragón and Castile; thereafter the history of Castile is that of Spain.

Castlebar Ireland. County town of Mayo

178

at the E end of Castlebar Lough. Pop. (1991) 6070. Market town. When a mixed French–Irish force landed at Killala (1798) the British garrison fled so precipitately that the incident was named the 'Races of Castlebar'.

Castle Douglas Scotland. Market town in Dumfries and Galloway on Carlingwark Loch 14 km (9 miles) NE of Kirkcudbright. Pop. (1991) 3697. Fishing centre. Livestock market. On an island in the R. Dee 3 km (2 miles) W is the ruined 14th-cent. Threave Castle, stronghold of the Douglas family, presented to the National Trust for Scotland in 1948.

Castleford England. Town in West Yorkshire on the R. Aire near its confluence with the Calder. Pop. (1981) 36,032. Coalmining. Manufactures glass, earthenware and chemicals.

Birthplace of Henry Moore, the sculptor (1898–1986).

Castleton England. Village in the Peak district in N Derbyshire 13 km (8 miles) NE of Buxton. Nearby are several caves and mines (fluorspar) and the ruined Castle of the Peak (Peveril Castle) made famous by Scott's *Peveril of the Peak*.

Castletown (Manx **Bully Cashtel**) Isle of Man. Former cap., port and market town on the S coast 14 km (9 miles) SW of Douglas. Pop. (1991) 3152. Has the 14th-cent. Castle Rushen; near by is the Old House of Keys (where the Manx parliament once sat).

Castres France. Town in the Tarn department on the Agout R. 61 km (38 miles) E of Toulouse. Pop. (1982) 46,877.

Important textile centre since the 14th cent. Manufactures woollen and cotton cloth. Tanning, engineering and metalworking.

Grew up round a 7th-cent. Benedictine abbey. Became a Huguenot stronghold in the 16th cent.

Castries Saint Lucia, Windward Islands. Cap. situated S of Fort de France, Martinique on the NW coast of Saint Lucia. Pop. (1992) 53,883.

The port has a landlocked harbour and coaling station with modern docks. Exports sugar-cane, rum, molasses, cacao, coconuts, copra, lime, limejuice, essential oils, bay rum, fruits and vegetables. Industries inc. processing limes, sugar, bay oil and rum. There is a botanic research station.

It was first settled by the British in 1605. It has many times been destroyed by hurricanes and fire.

Castrop-Rauxel Germany. Town in North Rhine-Westphalia just NW of Dortmund. Pop. (1986) 96,100.

Coalmining. Manufactures chemicals (coal by-products), textiles, cement and bricks.

Formed (1926) by the union of Castrop, Rauxel and other towns.

Catalonia Spain. Region (formerly a principality) in the NE, extending from the Pyrenees along the Mediterranean Sea, comprising the provinces of Barcelona, Gerona, Lérida and Tarragona. Area 32,185 sq km (12,427 sq. miles). Pop. (1991) 6,059,400. Cap. Barcelona. Mainly hilly. Drained by the lower Ebro R., its tributaries and the Llobregat and the Ter rivers.

Wines, olive oil, almonds, citrus and other fruits extensively produced. Lacks raw materials, but is well provided with hydroelectric power and has thus become Spain's most highly industrialized region. Manufactures textiles, metal goods, chemicals. Many bathing resorts.

Under Roman rule the NE of Hispania Tarraconensis. Later fell to the Alani, the Goths and the Moors; the Moors were conquered by Charlemagne 788. United with Aragón in the 12th cent. Both were united with Castile in the 15th cent. The region changed hands several times, between France and Spain, in the succeeding cent. There is a very strong regional patriotism. The Catalan lang. (akin to Provençal) is widely spoken, but its use in broadcasting or in printed publications was virtually forbidden under the Franco regime. An autonomous Catalan government was set up in 1932 and lasted through the Spanish Civil War (1936–9), in which Catalonia played a leading part on the Government side. Fully incorporated into the Spanish state after the victory of the Franco rebellion (1939).

Catamarca Argentina. Old colonial city, cap. of the Catamarca province (NE) 193 km (120 miles) S of Tucumán in a sub-Andean valley at a height of 480 m (1574 ft). Pop. (1991) 110,489.

Agricultural centre producing apricots, cherries, vines and cotton. Famous for hand-woven ponchos. Thermal springs nearby.

Catania Italy. Cap. of the Catania province in Sicily on the Gulf of Catania just S of Mt Etna. Pop. (1992) 329,898.

Seaport and industrial city. Food-processing, sulphur and sugar-refining, ship-building. Manufactures textiles, footwear and paper.

Almost completely destroyed several times by eruptions of Etna (esp. 1669) and by earth-quakes (esp. 1693). An 18th-cent. appear-ance. A former Benedictine monastery, S. Nicolò, with a vast 17th-cent. church. Ca-thedral (11th-cent., restored in the 18th cent.). University (1434). Founded (729 BC) by the Greeks. Conquered by the Romans 263 BC. Remains of a Roman theatre and Roman baths and aqueducts. Birthplace of the composer, Vincenzo Bellini (1801–35).

Catanzaro Italy. Cap. of the Calabria region on a hill near the Gulf of Squillace in a district noted for its orange and lemon groves. Pop. (1990) 103,800. Former centre of the silk industry. Now largely residential. Suffered in several earthquakes, notably in 1783. Dam-aged in World War II (1943).

Caterham and Warlingham England. Town in E Surrey, 11 km (7 miles) S of Croydon. Pop. (1991) 30,177. Pleasantly situated on the N Downs; mainly residential. A military depot. Engineering and cosmetics industries.

Catskill Mountains USA. Group be-longing to the Allegheny Plateau at the N end of the Appalachians; deeply dissected by river gorges ('cloves') into flat-topped, steep-sided mountains. Average height 915 m (3001 ft); the two highest peaks exceed 1200 m (3936 ft). Despite extensive felling and destructive fires, still thickly wooded. The Catskills provide water for New York City. Owing to easy access they are a favourite resort region of New Yorkers in summer and winter. They inc. the area of Washington Irving's Rip Van Winkle story.

Catterick England. Village in North York-shire on the R. Swale 16 km (10 miles) SSW of Darlington. Important military camp. Racecourse near by.

Cauca River Colombia. River 1350 km (840 miles) long, chief tributary of the Mag-dalena R.; flows generally N between the W and central Cordilleras. Partly navigable for small vessels. The valley is extremely fertile, with a great variety of crops, inc. sugar-cane and tobacco.

Caucasus Russia/Georgia/Azerbaijan. Re-gion between Black Sea and Caspian Sea. The N Caucasus is mainly plain, inc. Stav-ropol Plateau and Kuban Steppe. Drained in the N by the Don R. into the Sea of Azov and in the S by the Kuban R. into the same sea, and by the Terek R. into the Caspian Sea. Chief crops are cereals and cotton; industry is concentrated on Armavir, Astrakhan, Kras-nodar, Rostov and Stavropol. The Great Caucasus is mountainous with ranges ex-tending 1200 km (750 miles) WNW to ESE from Taman peninsula in the W to Apsheron peninsula in the E, and rising to Mount El-bruz 5633 m (18,476 ft). Rainfall is up to 254 cm (100 ins.) annually on the S slopes and 25 cm (10 ins.) in the E. There are important deposits of petroleum and man-ganese. Transcaucasia is mountainous with the Surami Range extending N to S between the Great Caucasus and Little Caucasus.

Causses France. Limestone plateau region in the S of the Massif Central. Divided by deeply-cut river channels into a number of smaller plateaux (*causses*: the term derives from *cau*, the local form of *chaux*, 'lime'). Typical limestone (karst) scenery: under-ground streams, caves and swallow-holes (*avens*). Spectacular features like the Tarn gorge are tourist attractions. The E Causses, at a height of 900–1800 m (2952–5904 ft) inc. the famous Causse Méjean, S of the Tarn R. The Causses du Quercy, to the W, chiefly in the Lot department, are lower and less arid. Sparsely populated. Main occupation sheep-rearing. Produces Roquefort (ewes' milk) cheese.

Cauterets France. Fashionable spa and tourist resort in the Hautes-Pyrénées department at a height of 900 m (2952 ft) near the Spanish frontier. Pop. (1985) 900. Well-known for thermal springs and winter sports. Centre for visits to Pyrenean peaks, e.g. the Pic de Chabarrou (2913 m; 9555 ft) and Mont Vignemale (3300 m; 10,824 ft).

Cauvery (Kaveri) River India. River 756 km (470 miles) long rising in the W Ghats and flowing generally ESE through Karnataka and Tamil Nadu to the Bay of Bengal. Here it forms a broad delta, its principal channel being the most northerly, the Coleroon, and the area is irrigated by canals. The river is dammed at Mettur and Krishna-rajasagara and hydroelectric power is developed. It is sacred to the Hindus.

Caux France. Natural region (*pays*) in the Seine Maritime department in Normandy, bordering on the English Channel and extending from Le Havre to Dieppe. A chalk plateau. The fertile loess produces oats, sugar-beet and flax.

Cava de' Tirreni Italy. Holiday resort in Salerno province in Campania 5 km (3 miles) NW of Salerno. Pop. (1981) 50,558. In a beautiful, well-cultivated valley among wooded hills. Manufactures textiles. Nearby is the Benedictine abbey of La Trinità della Cava (founded 1025).

Cavan Ireland. 1. County in the province of Ulster. Area 1891 sq km (730 sq. miles). Pop. (1986) 53,965. Generally hilly, rising to 667 m (2188 ft) in Mt Cuilcagh (NW). Drained by the Annalee and the Erne rivers. Boggy, damp and largely infertile. Many lakes. Cattle and pigs raised. Potatoes cultivated. Becoming depopulated. 2. County

town of Co. Cavan near the E shore of Lough Oughter. Pop. (1986) 3381. Market town. Modern Roman Catholic cathedral; ruined Dominican abbey. The abbey grave-yard is the burial-place of the 17th-cent. hero Eoain Ruagh (Owen Roe) O'Neill, subject of Thomas Davis's famous elegy.

Cawdor Scotland. Village in Highland 8 km (5 miles) SW of Nairn. The castle is traditionally the scene of Macbeth's murder of Duncan (1040).

Cawnpore ➤KANPUR.

Cayenne French Guiana. Cap. and chief seaport on an island at the mouth of the Cayenne R. Pop. (1990) 41,659. A shallow harbour; large vessels discharge into lighters. Imports foodstuffs for the largely undeveloped hinterland. Exports chiefly gold. A French penal settlement 1854–1938. Gave its name to Cayenne pepper, made from a plant of the Capsicum genus common in the vicinity.

Cayman Islands West Indies. Three low-lying coral islands 240 km (150 miles) NW of Jamaica in the Caribbean Sea. The largest is Grand Cayman, the others are Little Cayman and Cayman Brac. Total area 260 sq. km (100 sq. miles). Pop. (1994) 31,930. Chief town and port George Town on Grand Cayman. The climate is tropical maritime. Hurricanes can occur between July and November. Tourism and financial services are the chief industries. Others inc. the transhipment of oil and fish exports.

Discovered in 1503 by Columbus, who named them Las Tortugas because of the many turtles, but they were not colonized until the 17th cent., when they were settled by Britons from Jamaica. A dependency of Jamaica until 1962, when they became a British colony, becoming a United Kingdom Overseas Territory in 1998.

Ceanannus Mór (Kells) Ireland. Town in NW Meath, near the Blackwater R. Pop. (1991) 2187. Grew up round the monastery founded by St Columba in the 6th cent. Many antiquities, esp. the *Book of Kells*, a uniquely and very remarkably illustrated 8th-cent. manuscript of the Gospels in Latin (now in the library of Trinity College, Dublin).

Ceara Brazil. State in the NE 'shoulder'. Area 150,630 sq km (57,134 sq. miles). Pop. (1991) 6,353,346. Cap. Fortaleza.

Exports produce of the dry but irrigated interior: cotton, sugar, hides and skins, and carnauba wax.

Cebu Philippines. 1. Long, narrow, hilly island between Negros (W) and Bohol and Leyte (E), forming, with several smaller islands, Cebu province. Area 5087 sq km (1964 sq. miles). Pop. (1990) 2,645,735. Mainly agricultural, producing maize, sugarcane, abacá, coconuts and tobacco. Maize (not rice) is the chief food crop. Coal and copper mined, limestone quarried. 2. Cap. of Cebu province on the E coast of Cebu island. Pop. (1990) 610,417. An inter-island port.

Exports abacá, copra and cement. Manufactures cement and pottery.

Opposite the city is Mactan Island, where Magellan lost his life (1521).

Cedar Rapids USA. Industrial town in Iowa on the Cedar R. 169 km (105 miles) ENE of Des Moines. Pop. (1990) 108,751.

In a maize-growing and stock-rearing area. Meat-packing. Manufactures food products (esp. cereals), starch, agricultural and road-building machinery.

Celaya Mexico. Town on the central plateau at a height of 1770 m (5806 ft). Pop. (1990) 315,577.

Market town. Railway junction. Manufactures textiles. Trade in grain, cotton and livestock. The town has beautiful parks and squares and some notable examples of Baroque and Classical architecture.

Celebes ➤SULAWESI.

Celle Germany. Town in Lower Saxony on the Aller R. 39 km (24 miles) NE of Hanover. Pop. (1986) 70,200.

Railway junction. Industries inc. oil-refining and the manufacture of machinery, chemicals, textiles and foodstuffs.

Many 16th/18th cent. half-timbered houses in the old quarter of the town. Former residence (1378–1705) of the dukes of Brunswick-Lüneburg.

Central African Republic. Independent republic in the Sahel region of Central Africa, bounded in the N by Chad, in the E by Sudan, the S by the Democratic Republic of the Congo and the Republic of the Congo and W by Cameroon. Area 622,436 sq km (240,324 sq. miles). Pop. (1995) 3,141,000 (48 per cent urban). Life expectancy, 45 years male, 49 female. Cap. Bangui. Other cities Berberati, Bouar, Bamberi and Bossangoa. Currency: CFA franc = 100 centimes. The country is largely savannah with forest belts along the rivers. Drained by the tributaries of the Ubangi R. and by the headstreams of the Shari R. flowing to L. Chad. It has a tropical climate with little variance in temperature. Land use: forested 75 per cent, meadows and pastures 5 per cent, agricultural and under permanent cultivation 3 per cent. Of believers 40 per cent are Protestant, 28 per cent Roman Catholic, traditional beliefs 24 per cent and Muslim 8 per cent. Official lang. are French and Sango. There are about 30 ethnic groups and are divided into river (M'Baka, Yakoma) and savannah (Mandjia, Sara Gbaya) peoples.

Chief products and exports diamonds, wood products, coffee and cotton.

Formerly one of the four countries of French Equatorial Africa under the name of Ubangi-Shari becoming a member state of the French Community in 1958, and independent in 1960. From 1976 to 1979 it became known as the Central African Empire and President Bokassa became Emperor Bokassa I. He was overthrown in 1979 and the empire abolished. Following a bloodless *coup* in 1981 a military government ruled until 1985 and the Constitution of 1992 permitted a multi-party democracy. It has an 85-member National Assembly and the Republic is divided into 16 prefectures.

Central America. Independent states, bounded on the SW by the Pacific Ocean and NE by the Caribbean Sea, situated S of

Mexico and to the N of South America and inc. Belize, Costa Rica, El Salvador, Guatemala, Honduras, Nicaragua and Panama.

Central Lancashire England. Town created from expansion of Preston, Chorley and Leyland. Pop. (1981) 247,224.

Central Region Scotland. Former region formed in 1975 from the county of Clackmannan, most of Stirling, S parts of Perthshire and a small part of W Lothian and in 1996 divided into the unitary authorities of Clackmannan, Falkirk and Stirling.

Centre France. Region of central France comprising the departments of Cher, Eure-et-Loire, Indre, Indre-et-Loire, Loire-et-Cher and Loiret. Area 39,151 sq km (15,122 sq. miles). Pop. (1990) 2,371,000. Regional cap. Orléans.

Agriculture is important and it is a cereal-growing area. Many industries have transferred from Paris, inc. vehicle components, electronics, pharmaceuticals and cosmetics. Its historical heritage attracts many tourists to the Loire châteaux and Chartres cathedral.

Cephalonia (Gr. **Kefallinía**) Greece. The largest of the Ionian Islands, W of the Gulf of Patras, forming, with nearby islands, a *nome*. Area 935 sq km (357 sq. miles). Pop. (1991) 32,474. Cap. Argostolion. Mountainous, rising to 1620 m (5314 ft) in Mt Ainos. Mainly agricultural, producing currants, wine and olive oil. Sided with Athens in the Peloponnesian War (431–404 BC). A member of the Aetolian League in the 4th–3rd cent. BC. Taken by the Romans 189 BC. Held at times by the Byzantines, the Turks and the Venetians.

Ceram (Seram) Indonesia. Island in the S Moluccas W of New Guinea, from which it is separated by the Ceram Sea. Area 17,150 sq km (6622 sq. miles). Chief port Wahai on the N coast. Crossed W–E by a densely forested mountain range which rises to 3357 m (11,011 ft) in Binaja. Exports copra, sago, timber and dried fish.

Cerdaña (Fr. **Cerdagne**) France/Spain.

Valley in the E Pyrenees in the Pyrénées-Orientales department (France) and the Gerona and Lérida provinces (Spain). Divided between the two countries by the Peace of the Pyrenees (1659). Llivia is a Spanish enclave in France.

Ceredigion Wales. County created in 1996, situated on Cardigan Bay. Pop. (1994) 70,000.

Cerignola Italy. Market town in Foggia province in Apulia 37 km (23 miles) SE of Foggia. Pop. (1990) 54,850.

Trade in wine, olive oil and wool. Manufactures cement and footwear.

The Spanish defeated the French nearby (1503) to make the kingdom of Naples a Spanish province.

Cerne Abbas England. Village in Dorset 11 km (7 miles) N of Dorchester. On the face of Trundle Hill is the Cerne Giant (or Long Man), a 55-m (180-ft) representation of a man formed by cutting away the grass from the chalk, of unknown but very ancient date. The hill and Giant are now owned and maintained by the National Trust.

Cerro del Mercado ►DURANGO.

Cerro de Pasco Peru. Cap. of the Pasco department, a mining and smelting town in the Central Andes at a height of 4270 m (14,006 ft); one of the highest towns in the world. Pop. (1991) 62,479.

Silver was formerly the principal mineral; now chiefly copper, also zinc, lead, bismuth. Nearby is the vanadium-mining centre of Minaragra.

Cerro Gordo Mexico. Mountain pass in the foothills of the Sierra Madre Oriental 96 km (60 miles) WNW of Veracruz, on the highway to Mexico City. Scene of a battle in the Mexican War (1847) in which American forces under General Scott decisively defeated the Mexicans under Santa Anna.

Cesena Italy. Town in Forli province in Emilia-Romagna on the Savio R. 21 km (13 miles) SE of Forli. Pop. (1981) 89,640.

Produces pasta, beet sugar and wine.

The Malatesta library (1452) contains many valuable manuscripts. Birthplace of Pius VI (pope 1775–99) and Pius VII (pope 1800–23).

České Budějovice (Ger. **Budweis**) Czechoslovakia. Cap. of the Jihočeský region on the Vltava R. 130 km (80 miles) S of Prague. Pop. (1990) 99,000.

Principal industrial and commercial centre of S Bohemia. Manufactures beer (Budweiser), pencils, enamel goods and furniture. Trade in cereals and timber.

Founded in the 13th cent. by Budivoj Vitkovec. Renaissance town hall (18th-cent.).

Cessnock–Bellbird Australia. Town in New South Wales 39 km (24 miles) WNW of Newcastle. Pop. (1981) 16,916.

In a region noted for fruit and dairy farming. Coalmining and agricultural centre. Produces wine and clothing.

Cetinje Federal Republic of Yugoslavia (Former Yugoslavia). Town in SW Montenegro 29 km (18 miles) WSW of Podgorica (Titograd) at a height of 630 m (2066 ft) in a valley among limestone mountains. Pop. (1985) 12,000. Founded by Ivan the Black in the 15th cent. Cap. of Montenegro until 1918. Gospodija, burial-place of the Montenegrin prince-bishops. Occupied by the Austrians in World War I and by the Italians in World War II. Liberated by Marshal Tito 1944. Subsequently rebuilt.

Cette ➤SÈTE.

Ceuta (Sebta) Morocco. Spanish military station and seaport on a peninsula on the NW coast; an enclave in Morocco opposite Gibraltar, administratively part of the Cádiz province of Spain. Area 18 sq km (6.9 sq. miles). Pop. (1991) 67,615. Captured by Portugal 1415. Fell to Spain (which has held it ever since 1580).

Cévennes France. Mountain range on the SE edge of the Massif Central, extending 240 km (150 miles) generally SW–NE. Average height 900–1200 m (2952–3936 ft).

Highest peaks Mont Mézenc (1755 m; 5756 ft) and Mont Lozère (1702 m; 5583 ft). Watershed between the Loire and the Garonne rivers (W) and the Rhône and the Saône rivers (E); also source of the Allier, Loire, Lot, Tarn and other rivers. Largely barren limestone. A small coalfield N of Alès, Sheep-rearing. Olives, vines and mulberries grown on the S slopes.

Chad. Republic in N central Africa, bounded by Libya in the N, Sudan in the E, Central African Republic in the S, Cameroon, Niger and Nigeria in the W. Area 1,284,000 sq km (495,755 sq. miles). Pop. (1995) 6,361,000 (21 per cent urban). Life expectancy, 46 years male, 49 female. Cap. N'djamena. Other cities Moundou, Sarh, Abéche, Doba. Currency: CFA franc = 100 centimes. Chad is a landlocked country in the N containing the Tibesti highlands and is a desert (Sahara), but the S is mainly dry savannah. The Shari and the Logone rivers overflow in the summer rainy season and create swamps in the SW. It has a tropical climate with adequate rainfall in the S, though November to April are virtually rainless months. Land use: forested 26 per cent, meadows and pastures 36 per cent, agricultural and under permanent cultivation 3 per cent. The official lang. are Arabic and French but there are more than 100 lang. and dialects. The largest ethnic group is the Sara of the S. The N and central parts are predominantly Muslim, making up 54 per cent of believers, Christians 35 per cent and traditional beliefs 11 per cent.

Chief occupations are cotton cultivation and stock-rearing. Chief exports cotton, live cattle and hides. The main caravan routes cross the Sahara to Benghazi and Tripoli.

France proclaimed a protectorate over Chad in 1900 and incorporated it in French Equatorial Africa in 1908. It became a separate colony in 1920 and in 1946 became the northernmost of the four territories of French Equatorial Africa. In 1958 it became an autonomous republic within the French Community and achieved independence in 1960. Since 1965 there have been conflicts between the Government and secessionist groups, particularly from the Muslim N and centre. Economic development has been hampered by damaged infrastructure caused by civil war. There is at present (1996) a transitional regime governing with a 57-member High Transitional Assembly acting as a unicameral legislative house.

Chad, Lake Chad/Nigeria. A shallow lake mainly in the W of Chad, bordering on the NE shoulder of Nigeria. Area variable according to seasons and water supply. A remnant of a former inland sea; now considerably smaller than when discovered in 1823. Many islands and mudbanks; indeterminate marshy shores. Fed chiefly by the Shari R. (S). No apparent outlet, but its waters percolate into the Soro and Bodele depressions.

Chadderton England. Town in Greater Manchester just W of Oldham. Pop. (1991) 34,026.

Manufactures cotton goods and electrical equipment.

Chadileufu River ►SALADO RIVER.

Chagos Archipelago (**Oil Islands**). Group of islands in the Indian Ocean, formerly a dependency of Mauritius, about 1900 km (1200 miles) NE of the latter, belonging to Britain; from 1965 part of the British Indian Ocean Territory. Five main coral atolls, the chief being Diego Garcia. There is no permanent pop. Copra exported.

Chagra River ►GOGRA RIVER.

Chalcedon Turkey. Ancient city in Asia Minor almost opposite Byzantium on a site now occupied by modern Kadikoy. Founded 685 BC. Passed to Rome 74 BC. Scene of the Council of Chalcedon (the fourth ecumenical council of the Catholic Church) AD 451.

Chalchuapa El Salvador. Town in the Santa Ana department at a height of 640 m (2099 ft) 16 km (10 miles) W of Santa Ana in a coffee-growing district. Pop. (1985) 35,000.

Chalcidice (Gr. **Khalkidikí**) Greece. *Nome*

in Macedonia, formed by a peninsula terminating SE in three prongs, Kassandra, Sithonia and Akti. Area 2918 sq km (1227 sq. miles). Pop. (1991) 92,117. Cap. Polygyros. At the tip of the Akti peninsula stands the autonomous Mt Athos. Produces wheat, olive oil and wine. Magnesite mined. The name is derived from Chalcis (Khalkis), from which it was colonized in the 7th–6th cent. BC.

Chalcis (Gr. **Khalkis**) Greece. Cap. of the Euboea *nome* 56 km (35 miles) NNW of Athens at the narrowest point of the Euripus strait. Pop. (1981) 44,800.

Seaport. Trade in wine, citrus fruits, olives, olive oil, cereals and livestock.

Founded many colonies, e.g. Chalcidice (Khalkidikí), from the 8th cent. BC. Called Negropont in the Middle Ages, from the black wooden bridge (built 411 BC) joining it to the mainland, now replaced by a swing bridge.

Chaldaea (Chaldea). Name sometimes applied to Babylonia as a whole, being derived from the people (Chaldaeans) who invaded the region in the 11th cent. BC; more strictly, the lower Tigris–Euphrates basin, in S Babylonia.

Chalfont St Giles England. Village in Buckinghamshire 11 km (7 miles) E of High Wycombe. Pop. (1991) 4987. Milton's Cottage, where he lived during the Great Plague (1665–6) and completed *Paradise Lost*, has been national property since 1887. Near by at Jordans is the grave of William Penn (1644–1718), the Quaker founder of Pennsylvania.

Chalfont St Peter England. Village in Buckinghamshire 13 km (8 miles) ESE of High Wycombe. Mainly residential.

Chalna Bangladesh. Port on the Pussur R. 96 km (60 miles) from the sea and 24 km (15 miles) S of Khulna, developed from 1950 to relieve pressure on Chittagong. Exports jute.

Châlons-sur-Marne France. Ancient Catalaunum. Prefecture of the Marne department on the Marne R. and its lateral canal 43 km (27 miles) SE of Reims. Pop. (1990) 51,533. Important centre of the wine trade of Champagne. Brewing. Manufactures barrels, leather goods and wallpaper.

Has a 13th/17th-cent. cathedral and the 12th/13th-cent. Church of Notre Dame en Vaux. Aetius and Theodoric decisively defeated Attila and the Huns nearby at the Battle of the Catalaunian Plains (451). Famous in the Middle Ages for worsted cloth ('shalloon').

Chalon-sur-Saône France. Ancient Cabillonum. River port in the Saône-et-Loire department at the junction of the Saône R. and the Canal du Centre. Pop. (1990) 56,259.

Leading commercial centre of the Saône valley. Engineering, boat-building, sugar-refining and brewing.

Cap. of the kings of Burgundy in the 6th cent. The 12th/15th-cent. Church of St Vincent was formerly a cathedral.

Chambal River India. River 880 km (550 miles) long rising in the Vindhya Range and flowing N and NE across Madhya Pradesh and Rajasthan to join the Jumna R. below Etawah.

Chambéry France. Prefecture of the Savoie department 47 km (29 miles) NNE of Grenoble. Pop. (1990) 55,603. Market town in a gorge joining the upper Rhône and the Isère valleys, also containing the Lac du Bourget. On the chief route to the Mont Cenis and the Little St Bernard passes. A favourite Alpine tourist centre. Aluminium works. Well-known for vermouth and silk. Cathedral (14th/15th-cent.). A tower of the castle belongs to the original castle of the dukes of Savoy, whose cap. was Chambéry.

Chambord France. Village in the Loir-et-Cher department on the Cosson R. 45 km (28 miles) SW of Orléans. Pop. (1981) 206. Famous for the Renaissance château of Chambord, originally a hunting lodge of the counts of Blois, rebuilt under Francis I from 1526 and extensively altered under Louis XIV in the 17th–18th cent. Its outstanding feature is the double staircase. It was the scene of the first performance of Molière's *Le Bourgeois Gentilhomme* (1671) and was the residence of the kings of France, King Stanislas Poniatowski (the last king of Poland), Marshal de Saxe and Marshal Berthier.

Chamdo China. Chief town of the Chamdo area in E Xizang (Tibet) on the Mekong R. 483 km (370 miles) ENE of Lhasa at a height of 3000 m (10,824 ft). Trading centre on the route between Lhasa and S China.

Chamonix (Chamonix-Mont-Blanc) France. All-year Alpine resort in the Haute-Savoie department 60 km (37 miles) E of Annecy in the Chamonix valley at a height of 1037 m (3401 ft). Pop. (1982) 9255. Through the valley flows the Arve R. The usual base for the ascent of peaks in the Mont Blanc massif to the S. The Brevent and Aiguilles Rouges ranges are to the N.

Champagne–Ardenne France. Region and former province in the NE, now comprising the Ardennes, Marne, Aube and the Haute-Marne departments, with parts of the Aisne, Seine-et-Marne, Yonne and Meuse departments. Area 25,606 sq km (9890 sq. miles). Pop. (1990) 1,347,850. Chief towns: Reims and Châlons-sur-Marne. The name ('Country of Fields') derives from the plains around Reims, Châlons-sur-Marne and Troyes (formerly the cap.). Divided by parallel ridges into sub-regions. In the centre, a dry chalk area (the original *Champagne pouilleuse*); sheep-rearing provides wool for the hosiery industry. To the E the clay dairy-farming *Champagne humide*. To the W (along the slopes between Reims and Épernay) the vine-growing area where the world-famous Champagne wines are produced. The region is traversed by the fertile valleys of the Aisne, Marne, Aube and Seine rivers. The older industries of iron-founding and textiles are being replaced by electronics and agrifoodstuffs. Ruled in the Middle Ages by its own counts, who ensured commercial prosperity by promoting famous fairs. Attached to the French crown 1314. Declined, but flourished again because of its sparkling wines and its textiles. From the defeat of the Huns (451) a frequent battleground for many cent.

Champaign USA. Town in Illinois 77 km (48 miles) SE of Bloomington, forming a single community with Urbana. Pop. (1990) 68,172. Manufactures dairy and soya-bean products and clothing.

Seat of the University of Illinois (1867).

Champigny-sur-Marne France. Town in the Val-de-Marne department on the Marne R., a suburb of Paris. Pop. (1990) 79,778. Largely residential.

Flour-milling. Manufactures furniture and pharmaceutical products. Favourite venue of Parisians for boating and camping.

Champlain, Lake USA. Picturesque narrow lake 172 km (107 miles) long and 1.6–22.5 km (1–14 miles) wide between the Green Mountains (Vermont) and the Adirondacks (New York State). Occupies part of the valley which leads N from New York to Montreal. The shores are lined with summer fishing resorts. Named after the French explorer who discovered it (1609).

Chandernagore India. Former French settlement, now in West Bengal, on the Hooghly R. 35 km (22 miles) N of Calcutta. Pop. (1991) 122,350. Jute-milling. Manufactures cotton goods.

Became a French settlement 1674; flourished commercially for a time but later declined. Ceded to India 1950.

Chandigarh India. Joint cap. of Punjab and Haryana 225 km (140 miles) N of Delhi. Area 114 sq km (56 sq. miles). Pop. (1991) 640,725. Replaced Lahore, which passed to Pakistan with the partition of India (1947). A completely new city, planned in part by the French architect Le Corbusier; divided into residential neighbourhood units each with its bazaar, clinic, police station and cinema.

Manufactures chemicals, pharmaceuticals, electronic goods, plastics, hand tools, synthetic fibres and automotive components. There are 15 large and medium-scale, and over 2700 small-scale industrial units.

University (1947). Inaugurated 1953. Became a Union Territory in 1966.

Changchun China. Formerly Kwangchengtse, Hsinking. Cap. of Jilin province in the NE 240 km (150 miles) SW of Harbin. Pop. (1992) 2,132,000.

Railway junction on the S Manchuria Railway. Industrial centre. Railway engineering, sawmilling and food-processing (soya beans and flour).

Seat of the People's University of NE China (1958). Originally called Kwangchengtse, it developed as the junction of the wide-gauge Chinese Eastern Railway with the standard-gauge S Manchuria Railway (1905). Became cap. of Manchukuo (1934), being greatly enlarged and renamed Hsinking. Made the first major lorry-producing centre in China (1956). Its present name was restored after 1945.

Chang Jiang (Yangtse-kiang) China. Longest river in Asia and third in the world. China's chief commercial river, about 5470 km (3400 miles) long, rising on the N side of the Tanglha Range in SW Qinghai (Tsinghai) province. It flows E and and then SE across S Qinghai into Sichuan (Szechwan) province. As it continues S through a deep gorge, it comes within 64 km (40 miles) of the almost parallel Mekong R. to the W. After taking a series of sharp curves in N Yunnan and receiving the Yalung R. it now flows generally NE through the Red Basin of Sichuan, past Luzhou, Chongqing and Wanhsien. Below Wanhsien it is hemmed in again by mountains, traversing its gorges where navigation is impeded by dangerous rapids. In this section it is joined by a number of tributaries, inc. the Min and Kialing on the left and the Wu on the right bank. From Yichang the head of navigation for ocean-going vessels, it flows alternatively SE and NE until it reaches the sea, crossing fertile basins dotted with numerous lakes. Through two of these lakes, the Tungting and Poyang, which serve as overflow reservoirs for the Chang Jiang during the summer floods, the river receives two of its great tributaries, the Siang and the Kan respectively; at Wuhan it is joined by the Han from the NW. In the lower parts of its course it flows past the city

Changsha

of Nanjing (Nanking) and enters the E China Sea by two main channels separated by Tsungming Is., the port of Shanghai being linked with it by the Hwang-pu R. In contrast to the upper part of its course, where it falls about 4500 m (17,760 ft), below Wuhan its descent is little more than 1.5 cm per km (1 in. per mile). The Chang Jiang is a commercial highway of immense importance, with four of the country's greatest cities, Congqing, Wuhan, Nanjing and Shanghai, on or near its banks. It acquired still greater significance with the completion of the rail and road bridge over the river at Wuhan, on the Beijing–Wangchow route, in 1958. Along its upper course each section has its own local name. The Three Gorges Dam was begun in 1994 and completed in 1997. It is the world's largest hydroelectric project and will generate 8 per cent of China's power output.

Changsha China. Cap. of Hunan province on the Siang R. 298 km (185 miles) SSW of Wuhan. Pop. (1992) 1,330,000.

Important river port and industrial centre. Large trade in rice; also tea and timber. Lead, zinc and antimony smelting. Manufactures textiles, glass, fertilizers. Famous for handicraft industries (porcelain, embroidery and paper umbrellas).

University (1959). A former treaty port and a leading educational and cultural centre.

Channel Islands (Îles Normandes). Group of islands on the S side of the English Channel, W of the Cotentin Peninsula in NW France: British except the Chausey Is. Chief islands Jersey, Guernsey, Alderney, Sark. Others inc. the Casquets, Brechou, Herm and Jethou. Total area 194 sq km (75 sq. miles). Pop. (1985) 130,000. Chief towns St Helier (Jersey) and St Peter Port (Guernsey). The attractive scenery, mild, sunny climate, make them a popular holiday resort. The fertile soil facilitates cultivation of early tomatoes, potatoes and flowers. Jersey, Guernsey and Alderney have also produced famous breeds of dairy cattle. The tax laws have encouraged Jersey and Guernsey to become financial centres. English and French

are the official lang.; a Norman patois is spoken in rural districts. The islands became part of the duchy of Normandy in the 10th cent. and are the only part retained by the English Crown after 1204 but are not part of the United Kingdom. The legislature of Jersey is 'The States of Jersey' and that of Guernsey 'The States of Deliberation'. Sark still has a feudal sovereign. Early in World War II they were demilitarized and many of their inhabitants were evacuated to Britain. They were occupied by the Germans (1940–5). One of the Casquet Is. is the scene of Victor Hugo's *Les Travailleurs de la Mer.*

Channel–Port aux Basques Canada. Town in Newfoundland situated W of St John's on Cabot Strait. Pop. (1986) 5901. It comprises the two towns of Channel and Port aux Basques, united in 1945.

The main industry is cod and halibut fishing and processing.

Chantilly France. Town in the Oise department 39 km (24 miles) N of Paris near the Forest of Chantilly. Pop. (1982) 10,208. Famous horse-racing centre and popular Parisian resort. Formerly noted for lace and porcelain manufacture. The château was destroyed in the French Revolution but rebuilt in the 19th cent. by the Duc d'Aumale, who presented it and its art collections to the Institut de France.

Chao Phraya River Thailand. The chief river 1200 km (750 miles) long, rising in the N highlands near the boundary with Laos and flowing generally S by a winding course past Ayutthaya and Bangkok to the Gulf of Thailand. In its lower course, where it is much used for the transportation of rice and teak, it has a parallel branch, the Tachin, to the W. Navigable for small vessels almost throughout its length. Much fishing.

Chaouèn ▶YAUEN.

Chapala, Lake Mexico. Largest lake in Mexico (113 km (70 miles) long and 24–32 km (15–20 miles) wide) 48 km (30 miles) SE of Guadalajara at a height of 1800 m (5904 ft) on the central plateau. There are many islands and the fine scenery has made it a favourite resort area.

Chapel-en-le-Frith England. Town in Derbyshire 8 km (5 miles) N of Buxton. Pop. (1991) 8715.

Manufactures brake and clutch linings. Limestone quarrying in the neighbourhood. The name derives from the royal forest (frith) of the Peak District.

Chapra India. Town in Bihar 43 km (27 miles) WNW of Patna. Pop. (1991) 136,877. Railway and road junction. Trade in cereals.

Chapultepec Mexico. Rocky hill about 5 km (3 miles) SW of Mexico City, with a beautiful park and a castle (18th-cent.), now the National Museum of History. Scene of the last great battle in the Mexican War (1847). In 1945 the Inter-American Conference of American Republics met here and signed the Act of Chapultepec, which declared 'reciprocal assistance and American solidarity'.

Chard England. Market town in Somerset 18 km (11 miles) SSE of Taunton. Pop. (1991) 10,770.

Manufactures machinery, clothing and lace.

Named after Cerdic, founder of the ancient kingdom of Wessex. Birthplace of Margaret Bondfield (1873–1953), the first British woman cabinet minister.

Chardzhou Turkmenistan. Town situated 480 km (300 miles) ENE of Ashkhabad on the Amu Darya R. and the Trans-Caspian Railway. Pop. (1990) 163,700.

Railway junction. River port. Manufactures textiles (mainly cotton), and has a major oil refinery.

Charente France. Department in the W, comprising the former province of Angoumois and parts of Limousin, Marche, Périgord, Poitou and Saintonge. Area 5953 sq km (2305 sq. miles). Pop. (1990) 342,000. Prefecture Angoulême. In the hilly NE (*Terres Froides*) cattle are raised. The remainder (*Terres Chaudes*), drained by the Charente and Vienne rivers, is rich in agricul-

ture: wheat, oats, barley and potatoes cultivated; the wine of the Cognac district is distilled into brandy. Chief towns Angoulême and Cognac.

Charente-Maritime France. Formerly (till 1941) Charente-Inférieure. Department in the W, bounded on the W by the Bay of Biscay, comprising the former provinces of Saintonge and Aunis, part of Poitou and the Ré, Oléron, Aix and Madame islands. Area 6848 sq km (2792 sq. miles). Pop. (1990) 527,000. Prefecture La Rochelle. Mainly low-lying and flat. Drained by the Charente, Seudre and Sèvre Niortaise rivers. Chiefly agricultural. Cereals, fodder crops cultivated. Dairy-farming. N of the Charente R. the grapes are used for making wine and brandy. Oyster and mussel beds at Marennes. Chief towns La Rochelle, Rochefort (chief port), Saintes.

Charente River France. River 354 km (220 miles) long, rising in the Haute-Vienne department, flowing generally W through the Charente and the Charente-Maritime departments and entering the Bay of Biscay opposite the Île d'Oléron. Navigable for small vessels below Angoulême.

Charenton-le-Pont France. Suburb SE of Paris in the Val-de-Marne department at the confluence of the Marne and the Seine rivers. Wine-bottling, fruit-canning. Manufactures porcelain. The name derives from the 10-arched stone bridge across the Marne, once part of the defences of Paris.

Charleroi Belgium. Town in the Hainaut province on the Sambre R. 48 km (30 miles) S of Brussels. Pop. (1993) 207,045.

Industrial centre in a coalmining and steel-manufacturing area. Manufactures heavy electrical equipment, glass, cement and beer.

Church of St Christophe (17th-cent., rebuilt 1957); modern town hall (1936). Founded (1666) on the site of a village called Charnoy; named after Charles II of Spain by the Spanish governor.

Charleston (South Carolina) USA. Second city, chief commercial centre of South Carolina; seaport on a narrow peninsula at the confluence of the Ashley and the Cooper rivers 11 km (7 miles) from the Atlantic, with a naval station just N on the Cooper R. Pop. (1990) 80,414.

Exports timber, fruit and cotton. Manufactures fertilizers, wood products, pulp and paper, and steel.

Founded 1670. Scene of the first action in the American Civil War, when the Confederates bombarded Fort Sumter (1861). Severely damaged when under siege by Union forces (1863–5) and later by earthquake (1886), but many fine colonial buildings survive. World-famous for its gardens, esp. the magnolias and azaleas.

Charleston (West Virginia) USA. State cap. on the Kanawha R. Pop. (1990) 57,290.

Industrial centre. Oil-refining. Manufactures chemicals, glass, paints (utilizing coal, oil, brine and other natural resources of the region).

First settled 1788. Home of Daniel Boone (1734–1820), American pioneer and backwoodsman.

Charlotte USA. Largest town in North Carolina in the piedmont zone near the South Carolina border. Pop. (1990) 395,934.

Industrial centre. Manufactures textiles (cotton and woollen), machinery and chemicals.

Seat of the Johnson C. Smith University (1867).

Charlottenburg Germany. Residential suburb of W Berlin, incorporated into the city in 1920.

Manufactures glass and paper.

Originally Lietzenburg; renamed (1696) after Sophie Charlotte, wife of the Elector Frederick. Scene of the 1936 Olympic Games.

Charlottesville USA. Town in Virginia 113 km (70 miles) WNW of Richmond. Pop. (1984) 40,600. Manufactures textiles.

Seat of the University of Virginia, founded by Thomas Jefferson (1819).

Charlottetown Canada. Cap. and chief seaport of Prince Edward Island on the S coast. Pop. (1991) 15,396.

Exports dairy produce and potatoes. Canning, meat-packing. Manufactures textiles.

Founded 1768; named after Queen Charlotte, wife of George III. Seat of St Dunstan's University (1855, Roman Catholic).

Charnwood Forest England. Upland area in N Leicestershire SW of Loughborough, rising to 278 m (912 ft) in Bardon Hill. Largely barren, with patches of woodland.

Charters Towers Australia. Town in E Queensland 109 km (68 miles) SW of Townsville. Pop. (1984) 7620. Centre of a cattle-rearing region. Gold was discovered here in 1871 and mined from 1875, but little is now yielded.

Chartres France. Prefecture of the Eure-et-Loir department on the Eure R. 76 km (47 miles) SW of Paris. Pop. (1990) 41,850.

Chief market town of the Beauce region. Considerable trade in cereals, livestock. Sawmilling, brewing and tanning. Manufactures agricultural machinery.

The hill is crowned by the famous 12th/13th-cent. cathedral, Notre Dame, with two lofty spires, the 12th-cent. Clocher Vieux (107 m; 351 ft) and the 16th-cent. Clocher Neuf (115 m; 377 ft), and magnificent portals and 13th-cent. stained glass. Many other noteworthy churches. One of the chief towns of the Carnutes. Became cap. of the county (later duchy) of Chartres.

Chartreuse France. Limestone massif in the Isère department between Grenoble and Chambéry, rising to 2088 m (6849 ft) in Chamechaude, with many cliffs and deep gorges. In a valley 21 km (13 miles) NNE of Grenoble is the Monastery of La Grande Chartreuse. The original Carthusian monastery was founded (1085) by St Bruno near a village then known as Cartusia (hence the name), now St-Pierre-de-Chartreuse. It was destroyed frequently and in 1792 the monks were expelled, returning in 1816, to be expelled again in 1903 and returning again in 1938. They continued to prepare their liqueur, Chartreuse, which they are said to distil from fine brandy and aromatic herbs gathered on the Dauphiné slopes.

Châteauroux France. Prefecture of the Indre department on the Indre R. 68 km (42 miles) SW of Bourges. Pop. (1990) 52,949. Manufactures woollen goods, furniture and tobacco products. Brewing. Trade in grain and livestock. Owes its name (and origin) to castle, founded in the 10th cent. by Raoul, prince of Déols. The present Château-Raoul (14th/15th-cent.) is occupied by the Préfecture. In the suburb of Déols (cap. of lower Berry in the Middle Ages) are the remains of a famous 10th-cent. Benedictine abbey. Birthplace of Count Henry Bertrand (1773–1844), close friend of Napoleon I.

Château-Thierry France. Market town in Brie in the Aisne department on the Marne R. 42 km (26 miles) W of Épernay. Pop. (1982) 14,920.

Manufactures mathematical, precision and musical instruments, and food products.

Scene of many battles throughout history and of much fighting in both world wars. Birthplace of the French poet Jean de La Fontaine (1621–95).

Chatham Canada. Town in Ontario on the Thames R. 74 km (46 miles) ENE of Windsor. Pop. (1989) 42,200.

Industrial and commercial centre in an agricultural region. Sugar-refining, canning, meat-packing.

Chatham England. Town in N Kent on the Medway estuary 48 km (30 miles) ESE of London. Pop. (1991) 71,691. Naval base, established by Henry VIII and Elizabeth I. Dockyard with dry docks, ship-repairing yard; now closed. Forms a conurbation with the other two 'Medway towns', Rochester (W) and Gillingham (E). The naval barracks was opened in 1897 and the naval hospital in 1907.

Chatham (San Cristobal) Island ➤GALÁPAGOS ISLANDS.

Chatham Islands New Zealand. Group consisting of two main islands, Chatham (Whairikauri) (901 sq km; 348 sq. miles) and Pitt (Rangihaute) (62 sq km; 24 sq. miles) and several rocky islets, volcanic in origin, about 640 km (400 miles) ESE of Wellington in the Pacific. Pop. (1990) 760 (mostly Maoris). Chief occupations sheep-rearing and fishing. Discovered (1791) by Lieutenant Broughton; named after the Earl of Chatham. The last of the native Moriorís, almost exterminated in 1831 by Maoris, died here in 1933.

Chatsworth England. Parish in Derbyshire 5 km (3 miles) ENE of Bakewell. Contains Chatsworth House (seat of the dukes of Devonshire), a large Ionic building with gardens and art collections begun by the 1st Duke (1688).

Chattanooga USA. Industrial and commercial town in SE Tennessee in hilly country on the Tennessee R. Pop. (1990) 152,466. Developed rapidly following the provision of cheap electric power by the Tennessee Valley Authority: the Chickamauga Dam is on the N outskirts.

Manufactures machinery, textiles, stoves and boilers, furniture, chemicals and paper.

University (1886). During the American Civil War the city and its neighbourhood were the scene of several important engagements, inc. the battles of Chickamauga, Lookout Mountain ('Battle above the Clouds') and Missionary Ridge (all 1863).

Chaumont (Chaumont-en-Bassigny) France. Prefecture of the Haute-Marne department on high ground above the confluence of the Marne and the Suize rivers. Pop. (1990) 28,900. Tanning. Manufactures gloves and footwear. Scene of the signing of the treaty by which Britain, Austria, Russia and Prussia bound themselves to pursue the war against Napoleon to a successful end (1814).

Chaumont-sur-Loire France. Village in the Loir-et-Cher department on the Loire R. 40 km (25 miles) E of Tours. Famous for the 15th-cent. château, in Gothic and Renaissance styles; residence of both Catherine de Medici and the celebrated mistress of her husband (Henri II), Diane de Poitiers, in the 16th cent.

Chautauqua USA. Village on the W shore of L. Chautauqua, New York. Seat of the Chautauqua Institution (1874), founded to help Sunday-school teachers in their work, which now provides summer lectures and concerts.

Chautauqua, Lake USA. Picturesque lake 27 km (17 miles) long and 1.6–4.8 km (1–3 miles) wide in the extreme W of New York State at a height of 400 m (1312 ft).

Chaux-de-Fonds, La Switzerland. Industrial town in the Neuchâtel canton in the valley of the same name 14 km (9 miles) NW of Neuchâtel at a height of 990 m (3247 ft). Pop. (1990) 36,272.

Important centre of the Jura watch and clock making industry. Has a technical school and a museum (mainly horological).

Cheadle and Gatley England. Town in Greater Manchester 3 km (2 miles) WSW of Stockport. Pop. (1991) 58,457.

Engineering. Manufactures chemical and pharmaceutical products and bricks.

Cheb (Ger. **Eger**) Czech Republic. Town in W Bohemia on the Ohre (Eger) R. 153 km (95 miles) W of Prague near the German frontier. Pop. (1991) 31,800.

Industrial centre. Manufactures agricultural machinery, textiles and beers. Important railway junction.

Its strategic position has meant a stormy history. Wallenstein was murdered (1634) in the 12th-cent. castle. A leading centre of the Sudeten-German movement after World War I. The expulsion of the former large German pop. took place after World War II.

Cheboksary Russia. Cap. of the Chuvash autonomous republic on the right bank of the Volga R. 209 km (130 miles) E of Gorki. Pop. (1989) 420,000. Linked by branch line with the Trans-Siberian Railway.

Manufactures electrical equipment, textiles and matches.

Chechen Republic Russia. Republic on the N slopes of the Great Caucasus, extending N to the plain of the Terek R., bordering in the E on the Dagestan Republic

and in the S on Georgia. Area 19,300 sq km (7350 sq. miles). Pop. (1992) 1,308,000 (chiefly Chechen and Ingush, Muslim herdsmen and farmers). Cap. Grozny. Important oilfield centred on Grozny (opened 1893).

Petrochemical and engineering industries.

A Chechen autonomous region was formed in 1922 and an Ingush autonomous region in 1924; united in 1934, they became an autonomous republic in 1936. Dissolved for alleged collaboration with the Germans (1944); reconstituted 1957. Over 200,000 Chechen and Ingush returned to their homes 1957–9. Independence was declared in 1991. During 1994–6 there was considerable unrest and Grozny was bombed and attacked by Russian ground forces.

Cheddar England. Village in N Somerset just S of the Mendip Hills 11 km (7 miles) NW of Wells. Pop. (1991) 4484.

Agricultural market in a dairy-farming area. Famous for cheese, manufactured since the 17th cent. and strawberries. Nearby is the Cheddar Gorge: tall limestone cliffs and caves containing magnificent stalactites and stalagmites.

Chefoo ➤YANTAI.

Cheju Island South Korea. Island 72 km (45 miles) long and up to 27 km (17 miles) wide 96 km (60 miles) S of the coast of South Korea. Area 1860 sq km (718 sq. miles). Pop. (1990) 515,000 (Korean). Cap. Cheju. Mountainous, rising to over 1800 m (5904 ft). Well wooded. Fishing, cattle-rearing. Chief crops cereals and soya beans.

Chekiang ➤ZHEJIANG.

Chelm Poland. Market town in the Lublin voivodeship 69 km (43 miles) ESE of Lublin. Pop. (1989) 64,683. Flour-milling and brick-making. Founded in the 13th cent.

Chelmsford England. Town in Essex on the R. Chelmer at its confluence with the R. Cann 48 km (30 miles) ENE of London. Pop. (1994) 97,451.

Market town. Manufactures electrical

equipment. Flour-milling, brewing and malting.

Important in the Middle Ages owing to its position on the London–Colchester road. St Mary's parish church, originally completed in 1424 but rebuilt after collapsing in 1800, became a cathedral in 1914.

Chelsea England. Residential area in London on the N bank of the Thames where it is crossed by the Chelsea, Albert and Battersea bridges; from 1965 part of the Royal Borough of Kensington and Chelsea. Long literary and artistic associations, esp. in the 18th and 19th cent. Among those who have lived in Chelsea are Sir Thomas More, Steele, Swift, Carlyle (whose house in Cheyne Row is a public memorial), George Eliot, Turner, Rossetti, Whistler, Oscar Wilde. The 14th-cent. Old Church was destroyed by bombing in World War II (except for the More chapel) and was rebuilt. Chelsea Royal Hospital for old and invalid soldiers (Chelsea Pensioners) founded by Charles II and designed by Wren (completed 1692), was also damaged. Ranelagh Gardens and later Cremorne Gardens were well-known places of entertainment in the late 18th cent. The Chelsea bun is famous; the original bun-house stood till 1839. The Chelsea porcelain works was removed to Derby in 1769.

Chelsea USA. Suburb of NE Boston, Massachusetts, separated from it by the estuary of the Mystic R. Pop. (1980) 25,431. Manufactures shoes, chemicals and paints.

Cheltenham England. Town in Gloucestershire on the R. Chelt (a small tributary of the Severn) 11 km (7 miles) ENE of Gloucester. Pop. (1991) 91,301. Largely residential and noted as an educational centre. Its fame as a spa dates from the discovery of mineral springs in 1716. Several light industries. Centre of hunting and steeplechasing. Birthplace of the composer Gustav Holst (1874–1934).

Chelyabinsk Russia. Cap. of the Chelyabinsk Province (oblast) in the E foothills of the S Urals 720 km (450 miles) ENE of

Samana on the Trans-Siberian Railway. Pop. (1994) 1,125,000.

Major industrial centre. Iron and steel, zinc-refining plants. Manufactures tractors, agricultural machinery and chemicals.

Founded (1658) as a military post. Developed as a commercial centre, trading in grain and coal, with a flour-milling industry. Expanded rapidly with the advent of the Trans-Siberian Railway (1892) and the development of heavy industry in the 1920s. The first reactor of refined plutonium was constructed in 1949 and it was a closed city until 1990.

Chelyuskin, Cape Russia. The most northerly point of Asia and of continental Russia in the Krasnoyarsk Territory at the N end of the Taimyr peninsula.

Chemnitz Germany. Formerly Karl-Marx-Stadt. City in Saxony at the foot of the Erzgebirge 60 km (37 miles) WSW of Dresden. Pop. (1992) 287,551.

An important centre of the textile industry (cotton, wool, rayon). Also manufactures textile machinery, chemicals and glass. Coal and lignite fields nearby. Most of its old buildings were destroyed in World War II.

Chemulpo ➤INCHON.

Chenab River India. One of the 5 rivers of the Punjab, 1130 km (700 miles) long, rising in the Himalayas and flowing first NW and then generally SW. It joins the Jhelum R., later receives the Ravi and then joins the Sutlej E of Alipur. Extensively used for irrigation.

Chengchow ➤ZHENGZHOU.

Chengdu (Chengtu) China. Cap. of Sichuan (Szechwan) province on the fertile Chengdu plain 270 km (170 miles) NW of Chongqing (Chungking). Pop. (1992) 2,840,000.

Commercial centre for trade between the mountain region of NW Sichuan and the Red Basin in an area irrigated by a system created in the 3rd cent. BC. Railway engineering. Manufactures textiles, bricks and tiles.

Important educational centre; seat of

Sichuan University (1931) and a Technical University (1954).

Chennai ➤MADRAS.

Chepstow Wales. Market town in Monmouthshire on the R. Wye 3 km (2 miles) above its mouth in the Severn estuary. Pop. (1991) 9461. River port. Has a ruined castle (mainly 14th-cent.) and a tubular bridge by Brunel (1852). Tintern Abbey is nearby.

Chequers England. Tudor mansion and estate on a historic site in Buckinghamshire 3 km (2 miles) SW of Wendover, presented to the nation (1921) by Lord Lee of Fareham to be used as the official country residence of the Prime Minister.

Cher France. Department comprising parts of the former provinces of Berry, Bourbonnais and Nivernais. Area 7228 sq km (2819 sq. miles). Pop. (1990) 321,000. Prefecture Bourges. Drained by the Cher and the middle Loire rivers. Fertile in the lowlands. Cereals, vines, vegetables, fodder crops cultivated. Extensive pastures for raising sheep and cattle. Many hilly parts are well wooded. Chief towns Bourges and Vierzon.

Cherbourg France. Seaport in the Manche department on the English Channel on the N coast of the Cotentin Peninsula. Pop. (1990) 28,773. The harbour, protected by a breakwater 3 km (2 miles) long, can accommodate the largest transatlantic liners.

Industries inc. shipbuilding and ship-repairing, metals, ropes and fishing.

Probably on the site of Roman Coriallum. Fortified under Louis XIV in the 17th–18th cent. Harbour works were begun under Louis XVI and continued by Napoleon I and Napoleon III. An important naval base before World War II.

Cheremkhovo Russia. Coalmining town of the Irkutsk Region on the Trans-Siberian Railway 130 km (80 miles) NW of Irkutsk. Pop. (1985) 130,000. Manufactures machinery and chemicals.

Cherepovets Russia. Port on the N side of the Rybinsk Reservoir 210 km (130 miles) NW of Yaroslavl. Pop. (1989) 310,000.

Route and industrial centre. Manufactures iron and steel, agricultural machinery, footwear and matches. Shipbuilding and saw-milling. Developed rapidly with the construction of the Rybinsk Reservoir (1941). The integrated iron and steel works (1955) was established to supply steel to the St Petersburg area.

Cheribon ➤TJIREBON.

Cherkasy Ukraine. River port and industrial town on the right bank of the Dnieper R. beside the Kremenchug Reservoir 160 km (100 miles) SE of Kiev. Pop. (1991) 302,000.

Industries inc. sawmilling, metalworking, engineering and food-processing.

Cherkessk Russia. Cap. of the Karachia-Cherkessia Republic on the Kuban R. 88 km (55 miles) S of Stavropol. Pop. (1989) 113,000. N Caucasus railway terminus.

Industrial centre. Metalworking, flour-milling. Manufactures chemicals and electrical equipment.

Founded (as Batalpashinsk) 1825.

Chernihiv (Chernigov) Ukraine. Town on the Desna R. 130 km (80 miles) NNE of Kiev. Pop. (1990) 301,100.

River port and industrial town in a region producing grain, flax, potatoes. Manufactures textiles, knitwear, footwear and chemicals.

An ancient city; Byzantine cathedral (11th-cent.). Cap. of the independent principality of Syeversk in the 11th cent. Destroyed by Tatars 1239. Changed hands several times; fell to Russia in the 17th cent.

Chernivtsi (Chernovtsy) Ukraine. Cap. of the Chernivtsi Region on the Prut R. Pop. (1990) 257,300.

Industries inc. chemicals, sawmilling, engineering and food-processing. Manufactures textiles and rubber products.

Cathedral (19th-cent.). University (1875). Grew in economic importance under Austro–Hungarian rule (1775–1918) as cap.

of Bukovina. In Romania (1918–40) as Cernăuți. Ceded to Russia 1940.

Chernobyl Ukraine. Town N of Kiev and scene of a nuclear accident at a power station in 1986. The fallout covered many thousands of miles and reached parts of Poland, Scandinavia and Britain. Pop. (1985) 244,000, but has been evacuated.

Cherrapunji India. Village in Meghalaya on the S slope of the Khasi Hills at 1314 m (4310 ft) 40 km (25 miles) SSW of Shillong. Pop. (1985) 2000. Famous for world record in mean annual rainfall, 1087 cm (428 ins.). In one year (1861) more than 2286 cm (725 ins.) of rain fell.

Cher River France. River 320 km (199 miles) long, rising in the Massif Central, flowing N and then W, and joining the Loire 16 km (10 miles) WSW of Tours. Navigable in lower course.

Cherry Hill USA. Township in S New Jersey. Pop. (1990) 69,320. Residential, convention and retailing centre; industries inc. telecommunications and engineering.

Cherski Range Russia. Curved mountain system extending NW–SE in NE Siberia over 960 km (600 miles) long, rising to 3147 m (10,322 ft) in Pobeda. The Indigirka R. flows S–N through the range.

Chertsey England. Residential town in Surrey on the Thames 29 km (18 miles) WSW of London. Pop. (1991) 10,016. Market-gardening: the produce is sent to London markets. Has a 7-arch bridge built in 1785. Grew up round a 7th-cent. Benedictine monastery, burial-place of Henry VI.

Cherwell River England. River 48 km (30 miles) long, rising in Northamptonshire, flowing S through Oxfordshire and joining the Thames at Oxford.

Chesapeake Bay USA. Largest inlet in the country's Atlantic coast, nearly 320 km (200 miles) long and up to 48 km (30 miles) wide with the mainland parts of Maryland and Virginia on the W and the Delmarva peninsula on the E; into it flow the Susquehanna,

Potomac, Rappahannock, York and James rivers. Famous for crab and oyster fishing. A 28-km (17½-mile) series of causeways, tunnels and bridges spanning its entrance was opened in 1964.

Chesham England. Town in Buckinghamshire 13 km (8 miles) NE of High Wycombe on the S slopes of the Chiltern Hills. Pop. (1991) 20,290.
  Market town. Manufactures wood products (local beech), pencils, textiles and light engineering.

Cheshire England. County in the NW bounded on the W by Wales and on the NW by Merseyside. Area 2328 sq km (899 sq. miles). Pop. (1994) 975,700. County town Chester. Generally low-lying and flat, or gently undulating. Numerous small lakes or meres; crossed SE–NW by the R. Weaver. Also several canals, inc. most of the Manchester Ship Canal. Dairy-farming important. Long famous for cheese. Salt has been extracted since Roman times (mainly as brine) around the R. Weaver (chiefly at Northwich, Winsford, Middlewich and Sandbach), furnishes raw material for the chemical, petrochemical, pharmaceutical and plastic industries. Food-processing, silk, brewing, vehicle manufacture, high technology are other industries. Principal towns Chester, Crewe, Warrington, Runcorn and Widnes.

Cheshunt England. Residential town in SE Hertfordshire 23 km (14 miles) N of London, for which it is a dormitory suburb. Pop. (1991) 51,998. Market-gardening centre. Horticultural research station. Seat (1792–1905) of the Countess of Huntingdon's College, now Cheshunt College, Cambridge.

Chesil Bank England. Shingle beach 155–180 m (508–590 ft) wide on the coast of Dorset, extending NW from Portland for 14 km (9 miles) to Abbotsbury, where there is a noted swannery; separated from the mainland by the Fleet inlet. It continues along the coast for 11 km (7 miles) more to a point near Bridport. The pebbles increase in size towards the seaward end, as though graded.

Chester England. Ancient Deva (Devana Castra). County town of Cheshire and cathedral city mainly on the right bank of the R. Dee 10 km (6 miles) above its shallow estuary. Pop. (1991) 80,110.

Important railway centre. Cheese market. Brewing. Manufactures clothing, metal windows and aerospace and chemicals.

An ancient and picturesque city: unique in England for its intact surrounding walls (red sandstone) divided into four main sections by the two principal streets, which intersect at right angles; 'the Rows' (covered ways, arcades) are an outstanding feature. The cathedral (the church of St Werburgh's Abbey till 1541) dates from Norman times. The castle (except 'Caesar's Tower') was removed about 1790. Many 16th/17th-cent. timbered houses. Racecourse outside the city walls. The Roman fort, destroyed by Aethelfrith of Northumbria *c.* AD 614, was rebuilt 907. Last English city to fall to William the Conqueror (1066). Taken by the Parliamentarians in the English Civil Wars only after a long siege (1643–6).

Chester USA. Industrial town and port in SE Pennsylvania on the Delaware R. 19 km (12 miles) SW of Philadelphia. Pop. (1980) 45,794. Settled as (Uppland) by Swedes *c.* 1645; renamed by William Penn, who landed here in 1682. Shipbuilding, oil-refining. Manufactures locomotives and textiles.

Chesterfield England. Town in Derbyshire on the R. Rother 16 km (10 miles) S of Sheffield. Pop. (1991) 71,945. Industrial town in a coalmining region. Iron-founding and engineering.

Famous 14th-cent. parish church with a twisted spire. Stephenson Memorial Hall (1879), commemorating George Stephenson the engineer (who died in Chesterfield).

Chester-le-Street England. Town in Durham 10 km (6 miles) N of Durham City. Pop. (1991) 35,123. Manufactures confectionery. Nearby is the 14th-cent. Lumley Castle.

Cheviot Hills England/Scotland. Range of hills extending 56 km (35 miles) SW–NE along the border between England and Scotland. The highest peak is The Cheviot (816 m; 2676 ft) in Northumberland. Sources of the N Tyne and the Coquet rivers. Ample grazing land. The Cheviot breed of sheep is famous.

Cheyenne USA. State cap. of Wyoming in the extreme SE at a height of 1800 m (5904 ft) 153 km (95 miles) N of Denver (Colorado). Pop. (1990) 50,008. Commercial centre in ranching country. Railway workshops, light industries.

Chiana River Italy. Ancient Clanis. River 96 km (60 miles) long, rising in the Apennines near Arezzo, flowing through the flat Val di Chiana and emptying partly into the Arno R. and partly into the Tiber. In the Middle Ages the Val di Chiana was an uninhabitable swamp, but it was reclaimed in the 19th cent. The region is now almost entirely cultivated.

Chiang Mai Thailand. Chief town in the N and cap. of Chiang Mai province on the Ping R. 611 km (380 miles) NNW of Bangkok. Pop. (1991) 161,541. N terminus of the railway from Bangkok. Centre of the teak trade. Founded in the late 13th cent. Long cap. of a Lao or N Thai kingdom. Ruins of several ancient temples.

Chianti, Monti Italy. Small range in the Apennines in Tuscany 24 km (15 miles) long, rising to over 885 m (2903 ft). Grapes for the famous Chianti dry red wine are grown on the slopes.

Chiapas Mexico. Pacific state on the Guatemala frontier. Area 73,887 sq km (28,520 sq. miles). Pop. (1990) 3,203,915. Cap. Tuxtla Gutiérrez. Mountainous, with a narrow coastal plain. Backward agriculture, but exports tropical products (hardwoods, fruit, coffee, cocoa, cotton). Maya ruins in the NE.

Chiatura Georgia. Town on the Kvirila R. Pop. (1985) 28,000. One of the world's leading centres of manganese mining (since 1879). The refined ore is exported through Poti.

Chiba Japan. Cap. of the Chiba prefecture, Honshu, on Tokyo Bay 40 km (25 miles) ESE of Tokyo. Pop. (1990) 829,467. Industries inc. shipbuilding, oil-refining and the manufacture of steel, textiles, paper and chemicals.

Chicago USA. Second city of the USA, hub of the vast Middle West, in Illinois on the lower W shore of L. Michigan. Pop. (1990) 6,070,000. Contains large stockyards and meat-packing plants, and is one of the greatest railway centres and busiest airports in the world. Leading market for grain and one of the greatest industrial regions in the USA, manufacturing iron and steel, agricultural machinery, electrical equipment, railway rolling-stock, chemicals, textiles, food products. Railway development has somewhat reduced the importance of its harbour but large quantities of coal, iron ore and limestone are still imported and grain exported via the Great Lakes. It has the largest airport in the world.

The city (which covers an area of 520 sq km (250 sq. miles)) stretches more than 32 km (20 miles) along L. Michigan; on the lake front are the famous Michigan Boulevard and Grant Park, with the Natural History Museum and the Art institute, while nearby are the Adler Planetarium and Soldier Field, a large sports stadium. Among the educational institutions are the University of Chicago (1892), the Northwestern University (1851), the Loyola University (1870), the De Paul University (1898) and the Oriental Institute, perhaps the world's greatest centre of Oriental studies.

Chicago stands near the site of Fort Dearborn (built 1803). It did not begin to grow until the settling of the Middle West accelerated on the completion of the Erie Canal. It became a city in 1837, but its great expansion came with the construction of the railways. In 1871, the city (then mainly of wood) was devastated by fire. When it was rebuilt, great new industries developed and immigrants poured in, esp. from Germany, Ireland, Poland and Scandinavia. In 1893 the World's Columbian Exposition was held, where

Sullivan the architect made Chicago the leading centre of architectural design and devised the first skyscrapers. In Prohibition times Chicago was notorious for its lawlessness, associated particularly with Al Capone.

Chichén Itzá Mexico. A ruined Maya city in Yucatán 120 km (75 miles) ESE of Mérida. One of the outstanding archaeological sites of the American continent, with pyramids, temples and statues. Founded in the 6th cent. AD by the Itzá, it was abandoned, then re-occupied in the 10th cent., but finally abandoned in the 15th cent.

Chichester England. Ancient cathedral city in W Sussex between the S Downs and the English Channel 21 km (13 miles) ENE of Portsmouth. Pop. (1991) 26,572. Agricultural and livestock markets; little industry but has an important yachting basin. The wool trade for which it was famous in the Middle Ages has declined. The streets show evidence of Roman planning. Features of interest inc. the cathedral (begun in the late 11th cent. and unique in having a detached bell tower, in Perpendicular style), part of the ancient walls (on Roman foundations), a 16th-cent. octagonal market cross and a Roman amphitheatre (discovered 1935). The new 'theatre-in-the-round' under Sir Laurence Olivier was opened in 1962. The Goodwood racecourse ('Glorious Goodwood') is nearby.

Chickamauga USA. Town in Georgia 18 km (11 miles) S of Chattanooga on the small river of the same name, a tributary of the Tennessee R. Pop. (1985) 2000. The Battle of Chickamauga (1863) in the American Civil War took place nearby.

Chickamauga Dam USA. Dam on the Tennessee R. just NE of Chattanooga near the confluence with the Chickamauga R. An important Tennessee Valley Authority dam, designed to provide hydroelectric power and control flooding.

Chiclayo Peru. Cap. of the Lambayeque department on the dry coastal plain of the NW in the Lambayeque valley, irrigated from the Andes. Pop. (1993) 411,536.

Commercial centre of a region growing sugar-cane, rice and cotton. Rice-milling, cotton-ginning, brewing and tanning.

Chicopee USA. Town in S Massachusetts at the confluence of the Chicopee and the Connecticut rivers just N of Springfield. Pop. (1990) 56,630. Manufactures tyres, firearms and textiles.

Chicoutimi Canada. Lumber town and river port in Quebec 180 km (112 miles) N of Quebec at the confluence of the Chicoutimi and the Saguenay rivers. Pop. (1991) 62,670.
Hydroelectric power. Pulp-milling. Manufactures paper and furniture.

Chicoutimi River Canada. River 160 km (100 miles) long in Quebec, a tributary of the Saguenay R. Hydroelectric power station near Chicoutimi.

Chiemsee Germany. The largest lake in Bavaria in the SE at a height of 520 m (1706 ft). Area 85 sq km (33 sq. miles). Fed by the Ache R. Discharges via the Alz R. into the Inn. On Herreninsel (largest of its 3 islands) is a castle built in imitation of Versailles by Ludwig II of Bavaria.

Chieti Italy. Ancient Teate (Theate). Cap. of the Chieti province in Abruzzi 13 km (8 miles) SSW of Pescara. Pop. (1991) 57,540. Manufactures textiles, pasta and bricks, and has Europe's largest glassworks using methane from Abruzzi field.
Cathedral (11th-cent., restored) with a fine Gothic campanile. Remains of Roman temples. The Theatine monastic order was founded in 1524. University (1965).

Chignecto Bay Canada. Inlet of the Bay of Fundy about 56 km (35 miles) long and 16 km (10 miles) wide between SE New Brunswick and Nova Scotia. Exceptionally high tides.

Chignecto Isthmus Canada. Neck of land between Chignecto Bay and the Northumberland Strait 24 km (15 miles) wide at the narrowest point, across which runs the border between Nova Scotia and New Brunswick. The name (of Micmac origin) means 'the great marsh district'.

Chigwell England. Town in Essex 19 km (12 miles) NE of London, of which it is a dormitory suburb and part of Redbridge, Greater London. Pop. (1991) 10,332. The King's Head Inn is the 'Maypole Inn' of Dickens's *Barnaby Rudge*. William Penn, founder of Pennsylvania, was a pupil at the 17th-cent. grammar school.

Chihuahua Mexico. 1. State in the N on the Río Grande R. Area 247,087 sq km (95,376 sq. miles). Pop. (1990) 2,439,954. Climate cool in the mountainous W (Sierra Madre Occidental), mild in the centre and hot in the desert (E). Main industry mining (gold, silver, copper, zinc, lead). Cotton cultivated; cattle reared, esp. in the W and N. The miniature Chihuahua dogs are bred here. 2. Cap. of Chihuahua state and chief town in the N in a valley surrounded by spurs of the Sierra Madre Occidental at a height of 1420 m (4658 ft). Pop. (1990) 530,487. In a mining and cattle-rearing district. Smelting. Manufactures textiles. University (1954). Hidalgo y Costilla, a hero of Mexican independence, was executed here in 1811. Later it was the headquarters of Pancho Villa, who once captured the city (1910) by disguising his men as peasants on their way to market.

Chile. Republic on the W coast of South America. Bounded by Peru in the N, by Bolivia and Argentina in the E and by the Pacific in the S and W. Area 756,626 sq km (292,135 sq. miles) excluding claimed Antarctic territory. Pop. (1995) 14,210,000 (86 per cent urban). Life expectancy, 70 years male, 76 female. Cap. Santiago. Other cities, Viña del Mar, Concepción and Valparaíso. Currency: Peso = 100 centavos. Chile consists of a long, narrow strip of territory, over 4180 km (2600 miles) from 17°30'S to 56°S (Cape Horn). Maximum width about 400 km (250 miles). Many islands to the W and S belong to Chile inc. Islas Juan Fernández and the volcanic island of Isla de Pascua (Easter Island). In 1940 Chile declared, and in each subsequent year has reaffirmed, its ownership of the section of the Antarctic lying between 53° and 90°W long.

Agriculture is deficient, partly because of the unfavourable climate in the N and the S, but largely owing to outmoded patterns of land ownership and production.

In a country of such latitudinal extent there is great diversity of climate and vegetation. Starting from the N (the frontier with Peru), the first 1600 km (1000 miles) comprise the completely rainless hot Atacama desert, without vegetation but containing copper and nitrate deposits, and a semi-desert stretch where some cultivation is possible with irrigation. Then comes the most fertile part of Chile, from Illapel to Concepción, where the farmlands are concentrated in the central valley, an area of abundant winter rains and dry summers, containing the bulk of the pop. and the three largest cities. Crops inc. grain, fruit and vegetables. Next comes a country of lakes and forests and some cultivated land, with frequent rain, extending to Puerto Montt. The final 1600 km (1000 miles) consist of wild and almost uninhabited country, mountainous, with fiords and glaciers, heavy rains and a cold, stormy climate. In the extreme S there is a small region with an Atlantic coastline, less rainy, where sheep-raising, coalmining and oil production are the main occupations. Land use: forested 22 per cent, meadows and pasture 18 per cent, agricultural and under permanent cultivation 6 per cent. About 77 per cent of believers are Roman Catholic and 13 per cent are Protestant. The official lang. is Spanish and about 90 per cent of the pop. is European and mestizo.

Minerals provide the greatest wealth; besides nitrates and iodine, huge copper deposits are worked on the W Andean slopes, at Chuquicamata and Potrerillos (N), and at El Teniente farther S. Iron ore is mined in northern Chile, for export and for the steelworks at Huachipato, near Concepción. Petroleum from Tierra del Fuego is sent to the refinery at Concón, just N of Valparaíso, and provides almost all the petrol requirements. Coal is mined S of Concepción. Large hydroelectric stations are mostly in central Chile; others are planned. Copper contributes three-quarters or more of the exports,

other minerals, esp. iron ore, most of the remainder. Wool (chiefly from the far S) supplies the home textile industries; some is exported. Timber exploitation is increasing. Fishing is important; the production and export of fish-meal have grown rapidly. There are efficient and growing industries, based on indigenous coal, hydroelectric power and iron.

The Spanish conquistadors found central Chile under Inca domination. Valdivia founded Santiago (1541), but the Spanish were turned back by the fierce Araucanian Indians in the S, who remained independent until the 19th cent. (when they made a treaty with the Chileans). The mingling of Spaniards and Indians produced a large mestizo pop.; few of the people are of pure European descent. Colonial Chile became part of the viceroyalty of Peru. Independence was proclaimed in 1810 by General O'Higgins, son of an Irish-born Viceroy of Peru and a Chilean mother; final liberation came in 1818. Chile fought Peru and Bolivia 1879–84 and on victory extended her northern frontier, acquiring nitrates in the northern desert. Formerly governed by a bicameral parliamentary system, broadly similar to that of the USA, but with proportional representation, Chile was ruled 1970–3 by a Marxist coalition under President Salvador Allende Gossens, who expropriated the US-owned copper companies. During the three years the economy declined disastrously, inflation and food shortages led to civil disorders and a military junta assumed control in September 1973; the President committed suicide on the day of the *coup*. The Constitution of 1981 provided for an eventual return to democracy. General Pinochet was rejected as President in a plebiscite in 1988. Chile is a multiparty republic with a 120-member Chamber of Deputies and 47-member Senate and is divided administratively into 13 regions.

Chilkoot Pass Canada/USA. Pass at a height of 1070 m (3510 ft) on the border between the Alaska panhandle and NW British Columbia (Canada), N of Skagway

(Alaska). A route used by many gold prospectors during the Klondike gold rush (1896).

Chillán Chile. Cap. of the Ñuble province in the central valley, 90 km (56 miles) ENE of Concepción. Pop. (1992) 158,731.

Trade in fruit and wine. Manufactures leather goods and footwear. Flour-milling.

Founded 1594. Moved to its present site 1836. Has suffered severely from earthquakes; destroyed by the 1939 earthquake and rebuilt. The original site, Chillán Viejo, was the birthplace of the Chilean liberator, Bernardo O'Higgins (1778–1842).

Chillicothe USA. Commercial and industrial town in Ohio on the Scioto R. 71 km (44 miles) S of Columbus. Pop. (1985) 27,000. Manufactures footwear, paper and furniture. State cap. 1803–10 and 1812–16.

Chillon Switzerland. Castle just S of Montreux at the end of L. Geneva dating mainly from the 13th cent.; now a museum. Formerly a stronghold of Savoie. The state prison where François Bonivard (made famous by Byron's *The Prisoner of Chillon*) was imprisoned 1530–6.

Chiloé Island Chile. Island off the SW coast N of the Chonos Archipelago. Area 8394 sq km (3241 sq. miles). Pop. (1989) 116,000.

Chief town Ancud, an agricultural and timber centre (N). Closely forested, with clearings for potatoes and barley. Many fishing hamlets.

With a section of the mainland, and numerous other sparsely inhabited islands, it forms the province of Chiloé.

Chiltern Hills England. Low range of chalk hills extending 88 km (55 miles) NE from the Goring Gap in the Thames valley, through parts of Oxfordshire, Buckinghamshire, Hertfordshire and Bedfordshire, and continuing as the East Anglian Heights. Highest point Coombe Hill (276 m; 905 ft) 2.4 km (1½ miles) SW of Wendover. A well-defined escarpment, facing NW. Several main railways and roads from London to the Midlands use the gaps in the range. Formerly clothed in dense beech forests, the haunts of robbers, to restrain whom the office of Steward of the Chiltern Hundreds was created; this now nominal post is presented to any member of the House of Commons desiring to retire from Parliament (since an MP may not hold a Crown 'office of profit'). The supplies of beechwood stimulated the furniture industry, esp. at High Wycombe.

Chilung (Keelung) Taiwan. Chief seaport on the N coast 24 km (15 miles) ENE of Taipei, with which it is connected by railway. Pop. (1985) 352,000.

It exports sugar and tea. Industries inc. shipbuilding and flour-milling, and it manufactures cement, chemicals and fertilizers.

Chimborazo Ecuador. Inactive volcano in the N of the Chimborazo province; the highest peak (6272 m; 20,572 ft) in the Ecuadorian Andes, an impressive snow-capped cone, standing out from the massif. The large glaciers are sometimes visible from the Pacific coast.

Chimbote Peru. Seaport with a sheltered natural harbour in the Ancash department 370 km (220 miles) NNW of Lima. Pop. (1990) 297,000. Site of Peru's first iron and steel plant, using ore from S Peru and power from the Santa R. Fishing port. Exports fish products and sugar.

Chimkent Kazakhstan. Industrial town situated 145 km (90 miles) N of Tashkent on the Turksib Railway. Pop. (1990) 400,900.

Important lead–zinc refinery. Manufactures chemicals, cement, cotton goods. Flour-milling and canning.

Taken by the Russians 1864.

China. The Republic of China is bounded N by Russia and Mongolia, E by Korea, the Yellow Sea and the East China Sea, with Macao as an enclave on the SE coast; S by Vietnam, Laos, Myanmar (Burma), India, Bhutan and Nepal; W by India, Pakistan, Afghanistan, Tajikistan, Kyrgyzstan and Kazakhstan. Area 9,572,000 sq km (3,696,100 sq. miles). Pop. (1995) 1,206,600,000 (28 per cent urban). Life expectancy, 69 years male, 72 female. Cap. Beijing (Peking). Other cities: Shanghai, Tientsin, Tianjin, Shenyang, Wuhan, Guangzhou (Canton), Chongqing, Harbin, Chengdu, Zibo, Nanjing, Xian, Changchun, Dalian, Qingdao, Jinan, and there are 11 others with more than 1 million inhabitants. Currency: Renminbi (yuan) = 10 jiao = 100 fen.

China proper falls into three main natural regions which coincide with the basins of the three great rivers. N China is the basin of the Yellow R. inc. the loess plateau of the NW, which merges N into the extensive Mongolian plateau and the Great Plain which is crossed by the lower section of the river; to the NE are the central plain and the E highlands of Manchuria. Central China is drained by the Chang Jiang; it consists of the mountainous region of the far W, which passes into the vast, lofty Tibetan plateau, the Red Basin, occupying much of Sichuan province, and E of the Great Gorge the central lowlands and the delta area. S China, separated from the Chang Jiang basin by the S China Highlands, inc. the plateau of Yunnan in the W, the Xi-Jiang basin and the narrow coastal plains of the SE. The climate of China proper is dominated by the monsoons, with cold, dry winds from the N in winter and warm, rain-bearing winds from the S and SE in summer. In N China the winters are very cold, the strong winds sometimes bringing dust-storms, while summers are hot and the rainfall averages 60–75 cm (24–30 ins.) annually. In Central China the winters are rather less cold and inc. some rain, the annual total amounting to 100–150 cm (40–60 ins.). S China has a subtropical type of monsoon climate, winters being mild and the mean annual rainfall reaching 200 cm (80 ins.) or more. The great plateaux of Tibet and Mongolia have a dry climate with extremes of temperature. Most of the original forest cover of China has long been removed for fuel and the results may be seen in the bare, eroded hills of many areas. Land use: forested 14 per cent, meadows and pastures 43 per cent, agricultural and under permanent cultivation 10 per cent.

The official lang. is Mandarin Chinese. Religions inc. Buddhist, Taoist and Christian. Confucianism has no ecclesiastical organization and acts as a philosophy of ethics and government. Ceremonies of reverence to ancestors are observed by the whole pop. irrespective of philosophical or religious beliefs. About 92 per cent of the pop. is Han (Chinese). In 1958 a phonetic alphabet (Pinjin) was introduced to replace the 30,000 characters of the Chinese script and in 1979 this was officially adopted, replacing the Wade transcription scheme.

Throughout its long history agriculture has been the mainstay of its economy, still employing about 56 per cent of its pop. The three basic food crops are rice, in the S, and wheat and millet farther N. Farming has been of a small-scale subsistence type, practised by millions of peasants on minute plots of land, more accurately described as horticulture rather than agriculture. Only since the establishment of the Communist regime in 1949 has any serious coordinated attempt at mechanization of agriculture or greater industrialization been made.

With so much of the country consisting of infertile mountains and plateaux, its peasant farmers are necessarily confined to the river valleys, deltas and limited plains. Farming is intensive to the utmost degree, every scrap of organic matter, inc. human excrement, being used to enrich the soil. Although in general every available square yard is cultivated, the Chinese villager's traditional veneration for his ancestors often causes him to devote some of the best land to burial grounds. 'Township and village enterprises' in agriculture comprise enterprises previously run by the Communities of the Maoist era. There are about 250,000 such enterprises employing 25,500,000 people. The rural workforce is about 438 million of whom 340,370,000 are employed in agriculture, fishing or land management.

In the S rice occupies about three-quarters of the cultivated land and tea is grown in the hills, but has decreased in importance as an export crop; the warm climate of the S also allows oranges, lichees and other fruits to be grown. Coal is the most important mineral and output is estimated at 1150 million metric

China

tonnes. China is the world's leading producer of tungsten and antimony; iron ore and tin are also produced. Iron and steel are manufactured, and textiles at a number of centres. There are 6 Special Economic Zones at Shanghai and in the provinces of Guangdong and Fujian in which concessions are made to foreign businessmen.

Chinese history may be said to begin in the 3rd millennium BC, the Hsia dynasty (2205–1766 BC) being followed by the better-known Shang (1766–1122 BC) and Chou (1122–249 BC) dynasties; under the Shang the Chinese were already making bronze vases of unsurpassed beauty and under the Chou dynasty lived the great Chinese philosophers, Confucius and Lao Tse. The short-lived Ch'in dynasty, from which the name China may be derived, had one remarkable ruler, Shih Huang Ti (246–210 BC), the 'First Emperor', who united the country, completed the Great Wall against the northern barbarians – and ordered all historic records to be destroyed. Then came the Han dynasty (206 BC–AD 221), which was distinguished for its prosperity and its artistic and other achievements, not the least of which was the invention of paper; the country expanded, contact was made with the Roman Empire and Buddhism was introduced.

The Tang (618–906) and Sung (960–1280) dynasties were separated by a period of decline and disorder and in 1280 the Mongol conquest, begun in 1211 by Genghis Khan, was completed by Kublai Khan, whose court was described by Marco Polo. By 1368 the Mongol Yuan dynasty had been overthrown and replaced by the Ming dynasty, which lasted till 1644 and Chinese rule was again established as far as the Great Wall. In the 16th cent. relations were opened between China and the European nations. The Portuguese reached Kwangchow (Canton) in 1516 and were later allowed to settle in Macao, to be followed by Spaniards, Dutch and English. Meanwhile the Manchu tribes of E Manchuria had invaded the Liaotung peninsula, captured Peking, which had been cap. since 1421 and gradually conquered China, estab-

lishing the last imperial dynasty, the Ch'ing (1644–1912).

Trade with Europe slowly increased, but the Chinese were obstructive and unfriendly; a British embassy was sent to Peking in 1792, but a second embassy was dismissed in 1816 because the ambassador refused to 'kowtow'. War broke out with Britain on the question of opium imports (1839–42) and as a result five ports, Canton, Amoy, Foochow, Ningpo and Shanghai, were opened to foreign trade and Hong Kong was ceded to Britain. The Taiping rebellion (1850–64) destroyed much of S China and a war against Britain and France (1856–60) ended with further concessions, inc. the opening of Tientsin to foreign trade. Chinese power was crumbling. Korea obtained independence, Formosa was ceded to Japan; Russia secured railway rights in Manchuria and the lease of Port Arthur, Britain the lease of Wei-hai-wei and Germany of Kiaochow. The Boxer Rebellion (1900) was a final effort to expel the hated foreigner and exhibited the crying need for reforms. Revolution, led by Sun Yat-sen, broke out in 1911, the last Manchu emperor abdicated (1912) and a republic was established with Yuan Shi-kai as president. The latter died in 1916, however, and China was once more plunged into chaos and civil war. Sun Yat-sen died in 1925 and his successor, Chiang Kai-shek, all but unified the country under Kuomintang rule and removed the cap. from Peking to Nanking (1928). Japan seized Manchuria, setting up the nominally independent state of Manchukuo (1931) and then invaded China proper (1937). China was not liberated from the Japanese till the end of World War II (1945). Kuomintang corruption and incompetence contrasted markedly with the efficiency of the Communists, Chiang Kai-shek and his dwindling Nationalist forces fled to Taiwan (Formosa) before the Red Armies and the People's Republic of China was proclaimed in Peking (1949). China recognized the independence of the Mongolian People's Republic in 1946 but annexed Tibet in 1950. The so-called Cultural Revolution led to considerable internal unrest (1967–8). Mass student demonstrations demanding reform in Beijing in April 1989 culminated in a sit-in in Tiananmen Square. At first peaceful, but on 4 June the army opened fire and many were killed and over 9000 injured. Several demonstrators were executed and a hard-line faction assumed control in the Party Politburo.

The highest organ of state authority is the National People's Congress with 2978 deputies, elected for 5 years by provinces, autonomous regions, municipalities, armed forces and Chinese residents abroad. The highest administrative organ is the State Council, headed by the Prime Minister. The country is divided into 22 provinces, 5 autonomous regions and 3 government-controlled municipalities.

Chinandega Nicaragua. Cap. of the Chinandega department, 113 km (70 miles) WNW of Managua. Pop. (1985) 68,000.

Market town. Sugar-refining, flourmilling. Manufactures cotton goods and furniture.

China Sea. Section of the Pacific Ocean bordering on China and divided by Taiwan into the E China Sea (N) and the S China Sea (S).

Chinchow ➤JINZHOU.

Chindwin River Myanmar (Burma). Chief tributary of the Irrawaddy R., 1046 km (650 miles) long, formed in the extreme N from several headstreams and flowing generally S to join the latter 21 km (13 miles) NE of Pakokku. Navigable for shallow-draught vessels for about 480 km (300 miles).

Chingford England. Part of the London borough of Waltham Forest on the edge of Epping Forest and 16 km (10 miles) NE of London. A half-timbered 16th-cent. house, one of the hunting lodges of Queen Elizabeth I, is now a museum.

Chingola Zambia. Town in the Copperbelt 320 km (200 miles) NNW of Lusaka near the border with the Democratic Republic of the Congo. Pop. (1989) 201,000. Closely associated with the nearby Nchanga copper

mine and linked by road and rail with Lusaka and other Copperbelt towns.

Chinhsien ➤JINZHOU.

Chinkiang ➤ZHENJIANG.

Chinon France. Ancient town in the Indreet-Loire department on the Vienne R. 42 km (26 miles) WSW of Tours. Pop. (1982) 8873.

Produces wine, baskets, ropes and leather.

The ruined castle (3 separate strongholds) on a rock above the town was the death-place of Henry II of England (1189) and the scene of Joan of Arc's first meeting with the Dauphin, later Charles VII of France (1429). Ancient churches: St Mexme (Romanesque), St Étienne, St Maurice. Nearby is the birthplace of the satirist, Rabelais (1494–1553).

Chioggia Italy. Town in Venezia province in Veneto on an island at the S end of the Venetian lagoon 26 km (16 miles) S of the city; connected to the mainland by a bridge. Pop. (1990) 57,000.

Important fishing port. Shipbuilding. Manufactures soap, textiles and cement.

Has the 14th-cent. Church of San Martino and an 11th-cent. cathedral rebuilt in the 17th cent. Scene of naval warfare between Genoa and Venice until Venice triumphed in 1378–81.

Chios (Gr. **Khíos**) Greece. 1. Island in the Aegean Sea off the coast of Asiatic Turkey, forming a *nome* with the neighbouring islands of Psará and Oinousa. Area 904 sq km (336 sq. miles). Pop. (1991) 52,691. Famous for cent. for wine, figs and mastic; also produces olives, almonds and citrus fruits. Sheep and goats raised. Its inhabitants suffered severely in the Turkish massacre of 1822. 2. Cap. of the Chios *nome*, seaport on the E coast. Pop. (1981) 24,070.

Exports wine, mastic and fruits. Boatbuilding, wine-making and tanning.

One of the twelve Ionian city states of antiquity, with a famous school of epic poets. A free city under the Romans. Prospered under Byzantine rule. Passed in turn to the

Venetians, the Genoese, the Turks and finally (1913) the Greeks.

Chippenham England. Market town in Wiltshire on the R. Avon 19 km (12 miles) ENE of Bath. Pop. (1991) 26,100.

In a dairy-farming region. Bacon-curing. Manufactures cheese, condensed milk. Brake and signal engineering. Formerly important for trade in the wool obtained from sheep reared on the Cotswolds.

Chipping Camden England. Picturesque small town in the Cotswold Hills in NE Gloucestershire 11 km (7 miles) ESE of Evesham. Pop. (1991) 1741. Many fine old houses, mainly 15th/16th-cent. and all built of local stone. Tourism. Very important in the wool trade in the later Middle Ages.

Chipping Norton England. Market town in Oxfordshire 18 km (11 miles) SW of Banbury. Pop. (1991) 5386. Manufactures tweeds.

Has the 15th-cent. Church of St Mary the Virgin in Decorated and Perpendicular styles; 17th-cent. almshouses. Churchill, 6 km (4 miles) SW, was the birthplace of Warren Hastings, Indian administrator (1732–1818).

Chiquimula Guatemala. Cap. of the Chiquimula department on the Chiquimula R. 105 km (65 miles) ENE of Guatemala City. Pop. (1985) 42,000.

Market town in a region producing fruit, tobacco, sugar-cane and maize.

Chiquinquirá Colombia. Town in the Boyacá department at a height of 2550 m (8364 ft) in the E Cordillera, 113 km (70 miles) NNE of Bogotá. Pop. (1985) 50,000.

Market for coffee, sugar-cane, cotton, wheat, maize and cattle. The famous Muzo emerald mines to the SW.

It has the shrine of Our Lady of Chiquinquirá, a famous place of pilgrimage.

Chirchik Uzbekistan. Industrial town on the Chirchik R. 32 km (20 miles) NE of Tashkent. Pop. (1990) 156,000.

Manufactures fertilizers, agricultural machinery and footwear.

Chiriqui, Gulf of Panama. Gulf 145 km (90 miles) wide and 24–32 km (15–20 miles) long, on the Pacific coast.

Chiriqui, Mount Panama. Highest peak in Panama (3477 m; 11,405 ft) in the Chiriqui province near the Costa Rica frontier. An inactive volcano.

Chiriqui Lagoon Panama. Lagoon 56 km (35 miles) long and 16–24 km (10–15 miles) wide on the Caribbean coast, enclosed by the Bocas del Toro archipelago.

Chişinău Moldova. Formerly Kishinev. Cap. of Moldova on the Byk R. 160 km (100 miles) WNW of Odessa. Pop. (1991) 753,500.

Commercial centre in a rich agricultural region (grain, fruit and wine). Important food-processing plants. Manufactures leather, footwear and hosiery.

Founded 1436. Annexed to Russia in 1812 and became cap. of Bessarabia. Scene of a notorious pogrom (1903). Ceded to Romania in 1918, but returned to the USSR in 1940.

Chislehurst England. Part of the London borough of Bromley 18 km (11 miles) SE of London, of which it is a dormitory suburb. Camden Place, home of William Camden the antiquary, was the exile residence and death-place of Napoleon III. Ancient manmade cave-dwellings ('dene holes') in the chalk beneath Chislehurst Common.

Chiswick England. Residential district in Middlesex on the N bank of the Thames, formerly a municipal borough with Brentford; from 1965 part of the Greater London borough of Hounslow. Many attractive houses, inc. those of William Morris and Hogarth. Chiswick House (built by Lord Burlington), now national property, was a residence of the dukes of Devonshire. Burial-place of Hogarth and Whistler.

Chita Russia. Cap. of the Chita Province (oblast) on the Trans-Siberian Railway and on the Chita R. near its confluence with the Ingoda R. Pop. (1989) 366,000.

Industrial centre. Railway engineering,

tanning and flour-milling. Developed with the advent of the railway (1897).

Chittagong Bangladesh. Chief seaport on the Karnaphuli R. 16 km (10 miles) from the mouth and 217 km (135 miles) SE of Dhaka. Pop. (1991) 1,363,998.

Exports jute, jute products and tea. Naval base. Industrial centre. Manufactures chemicals, textiles and soap. Has developed greatly as a port since the partition of India (1947), having been overshadowed before by Calcutta.

Suffered severely from cyclones in 1963 and 1965. The first steel mill in the country (as E Pakistan) opened here in 1967.

Chobrum ►K2.

Choisy-le-Roi France. Industrial suburb SSE of Paris in the Val-de-Marne department on the Seine R. Pop. (1982) 35,531.

Manufactures pottery, linoleum and hosiery.

Cholet France. Industrial town in the Maine-et-Loire department 51 km (32 miles) SW of Angers. Pop. (1990) 56,540.

Manufactures textiles and footwear.

Suffered severely in the Vendée rebellion (1793–5).

Cholon Vietnam. Industrial and commercial town 5 km (3 miles) SW of Saigon, since 1932 administered as part of that city.

Rice-milling is a leading industry and is largely in the hands of the Chinese, who form about half the pop. Sawmilling and tanning. Manufactures pottery. Large river trade in rice and dried fish.

Cholula (Cholula de Rivadavia) Mexico. Town on the central plateau 10 km (6 miles) W of Puebla at a height of 2100 m (6888 ft) on the Inter-American Highway. Pop. (1985) 20,000.

Market town. Produces wine.

An old Toltec city, it has the tallest pyramid in Mexico (54 m; 177 ft), built of sundried bricks and earth, of great antiquity. Seat of the University of the Americas.

Choluteca Honduras. Cap. of Choluteca

department on the Choluteca R. 96 km (60 miles) S of Tegucigalpa and on the Inter-American Highway. Pop. (1985) 88,000.

Market town in an area producing maize, beans, coffee and sugar-cane.

Chomutov Czech Republic. Industrial town in NW Bohemia 84 km (52 miles) NW of Prague. Pop. (1984) 57,389.

In a coalmining district. Manufactures steel products, glass and paper.

Chongjin North Korea. Seaport and industrial town on NE coast (Sea of Japan) and cap. of N Hamgyong province 467 km (290 miles) NE of Pyongyang. Pop. (1984) 755,000. Iron and steel manufacture. Port opened 1908.

Chongqing (Chungking) China. Important river port in Sichuan (Szechwan) province on the Yangtse R. at its confluence with the Kiang R. Pop. (1992) 3,010,000.

As the chief outlet for Sichuan, trades in tung oil, hog bristles, tea. Iron and steel plants. Manufactures textiles, paper, chemicals, matches, vehicles and fertilizers. In 1983 it was chosen as a centre for experimental economic reforms.

Linked with Myanmar (Burma) via Kunming and the famous Burma Road, with Chengdu (Chengtu) by rail (1952). Airport. Its history dates back to the Hsia dynasty, in the 3rd millennium BC. Chongqing was the wartime cap. of China (1937–46).

Chorley England. Industrial town in Lancashire 14 km (9 miles) NW of Bolton. Pop. (1981) 33,700.

Cotton spinning and weaving, engineering and other industries.

Birthplace of Sir Henry Tate (1819–99), sugar refiner and founder of the Tate Gallery, London.

Chorzów Poland. Formerly Królewska Huta (Ger. Königshutte). Industrial town in the Katowice voivodeship 6 km (4 miles) NW of Katowice town. Pop. (1990) 131,850. In the Śląsk (Upper Silesia) coal and iron district.

Manufactures steel, railway rolling-stock, chemicals and glass.

Under German administration during the Partition (1794–1921); restored to Poland after World War I.

Chowkowtien China. Village in Hebei province 56 km (35 miles) SW of Beijing where bones of the Peking Man (*Sinanthropus pekinensis*) were discovered in 1929.

Christchurch England. Holiday resort in Dorset just ENE of Bournemouth on Christchurch Harbour and at the confluence of the Avon and the Stour rivers. Pop. (1991) 36,379. Named after the Augustinian priory church, Holy Trinity. Has remains of the 12th-cent. castle and the Norman House.

Christchurch New Zealand. City on an almost flat site in the E of the Canterbury Plains, South Island, just NW of its port, Lyttelton. Pop. (1991) 292,858. Founded 1850. The success of its early planning and development owed much to the Anglican Canterbury Association. Parts of the city have an 'English atmosphere' by virtue of the old buildings, such as the cathedral and the provincial council chambers, schools and colleges and through the use of stone and English trees; spacious suburbs, however, have made it now a large, sprawling city.

Numerous meat works, woollen mills, flour mills, tanneries and canning plants process the produce of the eastern plains. Other factories manufacture chemicals, fertilizers, footwear, and there are railway workshops and various light industries. An electrified railway and a highway pass S through tunnels to Lyttelton.

Christianshaab Greenland. Settlement and meteorological station in the W on Disko Bay. Pop. (1990) 1712. Base for hunting and fishing. Seal-oil refinery. Founded 1734.

Christiansted ➤ ST CROIX.

Christmas Island Indian Ocean. Originally Moni. Island in the Indian Ocean 320 km (200 miles) S of the W end of Java. Area 135 sq km (52 sq. miles). Pop. (1982) 3000. Irregular in shape, with a central plateau, rising in places to over 300 m (984 ft), on which there is large-scale phosphate mining. Annexed by Britain 1888. Administered by Singapore 1900–58, then transferred to Australia.

Christmas Island Pacific Ocean ➤ KIRITMATI.

Chukot Russia. Autonomous area in the extreme NE of Siberia. Area 712,000 sq km (275,000 sq. miles). Pop. (1994) 113,100. Cap. Anadyr. Mainly tundra.

Chief occupations reindeer-herding, fishing, hunting (fur-bearing animals). Also mining for gold, mercury, tin and tungsten in the N.

Chungking ➤ CHONGQING.

Chuquicamata Chile. Mining town in the Antofagasta province on an arid plateau in the Andes at a height of over 3000 m (9840 ft). Pop. (1970) 22,100. One of the world's largest opencast mines (copper). Smelting is carried out by utilizing electric power from Tocopilla, and water is piped from Andean streams.

Chuquisaca ➤ SUCRE.

Chur (Fr. **Coire**) Switzerland. Ancient Curia Rhaetorum. Cap. of the Graubünden (Grisons) canton on the Plessur R. at a height of 595 m (1952 ft), surrounded by mountains. Pop. (1990) 30,975.

Commercial and tourist centre. Trade in wine. The meeting-point of routes from the Splügen and the San Bernardino passes.

Long an episcopal see (5th cent.). Has a 12th/13th-cent. Romanesque and Gothic cathedral and a 15th-cent. Rathaus. Birthplace of the artist Angelica Kauffmann (1741–1807).

Churchill Canada. Seaport and railway terminus in Manitoba at the mouth of the Churchill R. on Hudson Bay. Pop. (1985) 1200. The trading post established (1688) by the Hudson's Bay Company was named after Lord Churchill (later the Duke of Marlborough). Replaced in 1718 by Fort Churchill, which in 1733 was replaced by Fort Prince of Wales; this was destroyed by the

French (1782) and Fort Churchill was re-established. It was reached by the railway in 1929 and grain was shipped (mid August–mid October) from 1931.

Churchill River Canada. 1. River 1490 km (925 miles) long, rising in L. Methy in NW Saskatchewan and flowing generally E through several lakes to Hudson Bay at Churchill. Long known as the English R. (the route to the interior used by English or Hudson's Bay Company fur traders). Hydro-electric power plant at Island Falls. 2. Formerly Hamilton R. River in Labrador 900 km (560 miles) long, rising near the Quebec border in L. Ashuanipi. Flowing N and then SE, through several lakes, at Churchill Falls (formerly Hamilton Falls) just below Lobstick L. it descends over 240 m (787 ft) in 16 km (10 miles), with one spectacular drop of 75 m (246 ft); hydroelectric power is being developed here. Then continues generally E to L. Melville and the Atlantic.

Church Stretton England. Market town in Shropshire. Pop. (1991) 3435. The name Stretton (Street Town) derives from its situation on a Roman road. 3 km (2 miles) NE is the site of an ancient British camp.

Chusan ➤ZHOUSAN.

Chuuk ➤TRUK.

Chuvash Russia. Republic in the middle Volga valley, bordered on the N by the Volga and on the W by the Sura R. Area 18,300 sq km (7064 sq. miles). Pop. (1989) 1,338,000. Cap. Cheboksary.

Agriculture (esp. the cultivation of cereals and fodder crops) and lumbering have long been important occupations, on which the industries developed since the 1917 revolution (e.g. flour-milling, tanning and woodworking) are largely based.

Cicero USA. Industrial town in Illinois just W of Chicago. Pop. (1980) 61,232.

Manufactures radio, telephone and electrical equipment, metal products, building materials and hardware.

Founded 1857.

Ciénaga Colombia. Seaport in the Magdalena department on the Caribbean coast 64 km (40 miles) E of Barranquilla. Pop. (1989) 75,000.

Exports bananas and cotton.

Cienfuegos Cuba. Seaport on the S coast on Cienfuegos (Jagua) Bay 217 km (135 miles) ESE of Havana. Pop. (1990) 123,600.

Exports sugar. Manufactures cigars and soap. Sugar-refining, coffee-processing. Trade in tobacco, coffee and molasses.

One of the most picturesque cities in Cuba. Founded (1819) by the French General Luis d'Clouet, from Louisiana.

Cieszyn (Těšín, Ger. **Teschen)** Poland. Town in the Katowice voivodeship in Silesia. Pop. (1989) 36,682. Former cap. of a principality, long disputed. Passed to the Habsburgs in the 16th cent. Poland occupied the whole area on the dismemberment of Czechoslovakia by Nazi Germany (1938). The division was restored under the Potsdam Agreement (1945).

Cilicia. Ancient region in Asia Minor, now in S Turkey, between the Taurus Mountains and the Mediterranean Sea. The road from Tarsus, one of its chief towns, through the Taurus Mountains by the pass called the Cilician Gates was an important route to the interior. In the 11th cent. a small Armenian (Christian) principality was established here, developed into a kingdom and lasted for almost 3 cent.

Cimarron River USA. River 1046 km (650 miles) long, rising in NE New Mexico and flowing generally E through the Oklahoma Panhandle and SE Colorado, then across SW Kansas and re-entering Oklahoma to join the Arkansas R.

Cincinnati USA. City in Ohio on the Ohio R. Pop. (1990) 364,040.

Route and commercial centre for an extensive region of Ohio, Kentucky and Indiana. Industries inc. meat-packing and the manufacture of chemicals, machine-tools, clothing, paper, motor vehicles, plastics and machinery.

Seat of the Xavier Univeristy (1831) and the University of Cincinnati (1874). Standing largely on two terraces above a bend in the Ohio R., it has spread into the surrounding hills. Founded in 1788, it was named Losantiville (a hybrid word meaning 'the city opposite the mouth of the Licking River'); in 1790 it was renamed Cincinnati in honour of General St Clair, Governor of the North-West Territory and president of the Pennsylvania Society of the Order of Cincinnati. Many German, Irish and British immigrants arrived during the 19th cent., many Italians and Russians in the early 20th cent.

Cinderford England. Town in Gloucestershire 18 km (11 miles) WSW of Gloucester. Pop. (1991) 9566.

In an agricultural area and former coal-mining district in the Forest of Dean; has developed some light industry.

Cinque Ports England. Originally the 5 ports (Hastings, Romney, Hythe, Dover, Sandwich) which in the 11th cent. were given privileges amounting almost to autonomy, in return for furnishing the English Crown with ships in time of war. Later Winchelsea and Rye were added and then subsidiary 'limbs' or 'members', e.g. Deal and Folkestone. Their importance declined in the 17th and 18th cent. The office of Lord Warden formerly carried important civil, military and naval powers; it survives as a title of honour awarded for outstanding service to the Crown.

Cintra ►SINTRA.

Cirencester England. Ancient Corinium. Market town in Gloucestershire on the R. Churn (a headstream of the Thames) 24 km (15 miles) SE of Gloucester. Pop. (1991) 15,221.

Fox-hunting centre. Engineering.

Many Roman remains, inc. an amphitheatre. The parish church is in Perpendicular style. Remains of a 12th-cent. Augustinian abbey. An important wool centre in the Middle Ages, but the trade declined.

Ciskei South Africa. Former 'independent' homeland, now part of Eastern Cape province.

Citlaltépetl ►ORIZABA, PICO DE.

Città di Castello Italy. Walled town in Perugia province in Umbria on the Tiber R. 32 km (20 miles) E of Arezzo. Pop. (1981) 37,242.

Manufactures agricultural machinery and cement. Cathedral. Renaissance palaces.

Città Vecchia (Mdina) Malta. Former cap. 10 km (6 miles) W of Valletta. Roman remains. Cathedral (12th-cent., rebuilt after the destruction of the town by earthquake in 1693).

Ciudad Bolívar Venezuela. Formerly Angostura. Cap. of the Bolívar state, river port on the Orinoco R. 400 km (250 miles) from the delta on narrows: hence the former name (in Spanish, 'Narrows'). Pop. (1990) 225,846. Accessible to ocean-going vessels.

Exports cattle, hides, balata gum, chicle and gold. Angostura bitters were invented here (1824) but the distillery moved (1875) to Port of Spain (Trinidad). Linked by road bridge (1678 m; 5504 ft long) with Soledad on opposite river bank in 1967.

Ciudad Juárez Mexico. Formerly El Paso del Norte. City in the Chihuahua province on the Rio Grande and the US border, opposite El Paso (Texas). Pop. (1990) 797,679.

Commercial centre. Flour-milling and cotton-ginning. Thriving souvenir trade with American tourists. Enclosed by desert, except for the river valley, where maize, cotton and alfalfa are grown and cattle raised.

Originally a base for Spanish colonial expansion northwards. City founded 1681–2. Renamed (1888) in honour of President Benito Juárez who had made it his cap. for a time.

Ciudad Real Spain. 1. Province formed (1833) from parts of New Castile, mostly occupying the La Mancha plain. Area 19,749 sq km (7622 sq. miles). Pop. (1991) 473,899. Agriculture. Mercury and lead mined. 2. Cap. of the Ciudad Real province on the plain between the Guadiana and Jabalón rivers. Pop. (1991) 56,315.

Trade in cereals, olive oil and wine. Flour-milling, brandy-distilling. Textile industry.

Founded in the mid 13th cent. by Alfonso X of Castile.

Ciudad Trujillo ➤SANTO DOMINGO.

Ciudad Victoria Mexico. Cap. of the Tamaulipas province at the E foot of the Sierra Madre Oriental at a height of 335 m (1099 ft); 210 km (130 miles) NNW of Tampico. Pop. (1985) 212,000.

Agricultural and mining centre. Textile and tanning industries.

Civitavecchia Italy. Seaport in Roma province in Latium 60 km (37 miles) WNW of Rome, which it serves. Pop. (1990) 51,240.

Fishing. Manufactures cement and calcium carbide.

Has a citadel designed by Michelangelo. Founded by Trajan in the 1st cent. AD.

Clackmannan Scotland. County town of Clackmannanshire 3 km (2 miles) ESE of Alloa. Pop. (1991) 3420. Woollen manufacture.

Clackmannanshire Scotland. County in Scotland between the Ochil hills (where it rises to 721 m; 2365 ft) and the R. Forth. Area 142 sq km (55 sq. miles). Pop. (1993) 48,660. County town Alloa. Chief towns Alloa, Alva, Clackmannan, Dollar, Tillicoultry and Tullibody. Coalmining. Woollen-milling, brewing and whisky-distilling. Part of Central Region 1975–96.

Clacton-on-Sea England. Town in E Essex 19 km (12 miles) ESE of Colchester. Pop. (1991) 45,085. Popular seaside resort.

Clamart France. Residential suburb in SW Paris. Pop. (1982) 48,678.

Clapham England. Residential district in SW London; from 1965 in the London borough of Wandsworth. Contains Clapham Common (83 ha; 205 acres). Clapham Junction is Britain's busiest railway station. Home of William Wilberforce (1759–1833), slave-trade abolitionist and member of the 'Clapham Sect'.

Clare England. Picturesque market town in SW Suffolk on the R. Stour 21 km (13 miles) SSW of Bury St Edmunds. Pop. (rural district, 1971) 9751. A former stronghold of the E Anglian kingdom. Remains of an ancient castle and of a 13th-cent. priory.

Clare Ireland. County in Munster on the W coast between Galway Bay and the Shannon estuary. Area 3188 sq km (1231 sq. miles). Pop. (1991) 90,800. County town Ennis. Hilly in the E and N, low-lying and more fertile along the Shannon estuary (S), with a rugged Atlantic coastline (Cliffs of Moher). Chief rivers the Shannon (with Lough Derg and the Ardnacrusha power station) and its tributary the Fergus. Salmon-fishing. Dairy-farming. Oats and potatoes cultivated. Many round towers and other historic remains. Chief towns Ennis and Kilrush.

Clarence Australia. City in Tasmania situated on the S shore of the R. Derwent adjacent to Hobart City. Pop. (1989) 48,500. A dormitory residential area of Hobart with commercial and industrial areas.

Clarke Island ➤FURNEAUX ISLANDS.

Clarksburg USA. Industrial town in W Virginia on the West Fork (headstream of the Monongahela R.). Pop. (1980) 22,371.

In a region producing coal and natural gas. Manufactures glass, pottery and clothing.

Birthplace of Thomas J. ('Stonewall') Jackson (1824–63).

Clay Cross England. Town in Derbyshire 8 km (5 miles) S of Chesterfield. Pop. (1991) 24,271 (with North Wingfield).

In a former coalmining district. Iron-founding, engineering and brickmaking.

Clear, Cape Ireland. Headland on Clear Island off the SW coast of Co. Cork; the most southerly point in Ireland.

Clearwater USA. Town in W Florida 32 km (20 miles) W of Tampa. Pop. (1990) 98,784.

Resort. Citrus-fruit packing and market-gardening centre.

Cleator Moor England. Town in Cumbria 5 km (3 miles) SE of Whitehaven. Pop. (1991) 6410. Former coalmining town.

Cleckheaton ➤SPENBOROUGH.

Cleethorpes England. Seaside resort in North East Lincolnshire on the Humber estuary 3 km (2 miles) ESE of Grimsby. Pop. (1994) 32,179.

Clerkenwell England. District in the former metropolitan borough of Finsbury, London and from 1965 in the London borough of Islington. Named after the well, long lost but rediscovered in 1924, where parish clerks used to perform miracle plays. Grew up as two parishes round the nunnery of St Mary and the priory of St John, the latter the headquarters in England of the Knights Hospitallers of the Order of St John of Jerusalem.

Clermont-Ferrand France. Ancient Augustonemetum. Prefecture of the Puy-de-Dôme department at the foot of a volcanic range inc. the Puy de Dôme (1463 m; 4799 ft). Pop. (1990) 140,167.

Chief industrial centre of the Massif Central. Important rubber factories. Manufactures tyres and rubberized clothing, also machinery, chemicals, clothing and footwear.

Gothic cathedral (13th/15th-cent.). University (1808). Founded by the Romans. Cap. of the duchy of Auvergne in the 16th cent. Birthplace of the philosopher, Blaise Pascal (1623–62).

Clevedon England. Seaside resort in North Somerset on the Bristol Channel 19 km (12 miles) W of Bristol. Pop. (1991) 21,670. Clevedon Court (14th-cent.) is 'Castlewood' in Thackeray's *Henry Esmond*.

Cleveland England. 1. Hilly district in North Yorkshire S and SE of Middlesbrough, rising in the S to nearly 460 m (1509 ft). Formerly an important iron-mining district. 2. Former county formed in 1974 round the R. Tees estuary, inc. Tees-side, Hartlepool and (formerly in the N Riding of Yorkshire) Guisborough and Saltburn by the Sea, and abolished in 1996 when four unitary local authorities were formed: Hartlepool, Stockton-on-Tees, Middlesbrough and Redcar, and Cleveland.

Cleveland USA. Largest city in Ohio, tenth largest in the USA, on L. Erie at the mouth of the Cuyahoga R. Pop. (1990) 505,616.

A leading Great Lakes port, ideally placed to manufacture steel from L. Superior iron ore and Ohio coal. The steel mills are among the world's largest; also oil refineries, machine shops, foundries, meat-packing plants and factories manufacturing chemicals, cement, cars and electrical appliances.

Seat of the Western Reserve University (1826) and the Case Institute of Technology (1880). First settled in 1796. Laid out by Moses Cleaveland (1754–1806), agent of the Connecticut Land Company, after whom it was named (the 'a' in Cleaveland was dropped in 1832). Developed rapidly with the coming of the Ohio and Erie Canal (1832) and the railway (1851). The rise of the Rockefeller family began here.

Cleves (Ger. **Kleve**) Germany. Town in North Rhine-Westphalia near the Dutch border. Pop. (1975) 46,000.

Manufactures margarine, biscuits and footwear.

Among buildings damaged in World War II were the Schwanenburg, the 11th-cent. castle of Wagner's *Lohengrin* and the 14th/15th-cent. collegiate church. Birthplace of Anne of Cleves (1515–57), 4th wife of Henry VIII.

Clichy (Clichy-la-Garenne) France. Industrial suburb of NW Paris in the Hauts-de-Seine department. Pop. (1990) 48,000.

Oil-refining. Manufactures motor-vehicle and aircraft parts, chemicals, plastics and electrical equipment.

Clifton USA. Industrial town in NE New Jersey just SSE of Paterson. Pop. (1990) 71,742.

Manufactures aircraft propellers, clothing, machine-tools, textiles and chemicals.

Clinton USA. Town on the Mississippi R. in Iowa 120 km (75 miles) ESE of Cedar Rapids. Pop. (1990) 29,201.

Industrial centre. Manufactures machine-tools, pumps, hardware and cellophane.

Named after De Witt Clinton, former Governor of New York. Grew as a saw-milling centre, but when timber supplies diminished turned to other industries.

Clitheroe England. Market town in E Lancashire on the R. Ribble at the foot of Pendle Hill (558 m; 1830 ft). Pop. (1991) 13,548. Limestone quarried in the neighbourhood. A ruined Norman castle and its grounds serve as a war memorial.

Cloncurry Australia. Town in Queensland 678 km (415 miles) WSW of Townsville to which it is linked by railway. Pop. (1984) 3040.

Once a small goldmining centre; now serves a huge beef-cattle area, sending livestock to the coast. Mineral production now overshadowed by Mt Isa 113 km (70 miles) W. Important airport.

Clonmacnoise Ireland. Village in Co. Offaly on the R. Shannon 16 km (10 miles) E of Ballinasloe, Ireland's most remarkable ecclesiastical ruins, inc. the Seven Churches (the oldest built in 904), two round towers and three Celtic crosses. Site of monastery (founded by St Kieran 541) which became a seat of learning where the medieval works *The Book of the Dun Cow* and *Abbot Tigenach's Annals* were written.

Clonmel Ireland. County town of Co. Tipperary on the R. Suir. Pop. (1991) 12,000.

Market town. Sporting centre (hunting, fishing, horseracing). Flour-milling, ham and bacon curing.

Original starting-point of the 'bians', rapid and regular coaches carrying both goods and passengers, which were Ireland's sole public transport until the railway age, named after Bianconi, who established the service (1815). Birthplace of the humorist Laurence Sterne (1713–68).

Clovelly England. Seaside resort and fishing village in Devonshire on Bideford Bay in the Bristol Channel. Pop. (1989) 500. The steep main street rises 120 m (394 ft) in wide steps, making the use of any wheeled transport impossible.

Cluj Romania. Cap. of the Cluj district and former cap. of Transylvania on the Little Somes R. 338 km (210 miles) NW of Bucharest. Pop. (1992) 328,008.

Has developed from a mainly residential town into an important commercial and industrial centre. Manufactures metal products, hardware, chemicals and textiles. Several educational institutions inc. a university (1945).

Has the 14th/15th-cent. Gothic Church of St Michael. Seat of 4 bishoprics (Eastern Orthodox, Uniate, Reformed, Unitarian).

Cluny France. Town in the Saône-et-Loire department 19 km (12 miles) NW of Mâcon on the Grosne R. Pop. (1985) 5000. Grew up round the famous Benedictine abbey (founded 910), a leading religious and cultural centre in the Middle Ages. Until the erection of St Peter's in Rome the abbey church (a Romanesque building completed in the 12th cent. of which only parts remain) was the largest in Christendom.

Clutha River New Zealand. Longest river in the S Island (240 km; 150 miles) rising in Lakes Wanaka and Hawea and flowing SE through Otago to the delta near Kaitangata. Navigable by small vessels to Roxburgh, where it is dammed for a large hydroelectric station.

Clwyd Wales. Former county in the NE formed in 1974 from the former county of Flintshire, most of Denbighshire and NE Merionethshire, and disbanded in 1996.

Clydebank Scotland. Town in West Dunbartonshire on the R. Clyde 10 km (6 miles) WNW of Glasgow. Pop. (1991) 29,171. Many of the world's largest ships (*Queen Mary* and *Queen Elizabeth*) have been built in the great shipyards.

Manufactures sewing-machines, tyres and biscuits.

Clyde River Scotland. River in Scotland

rising (as the Daer Water) in South Lanarkshire and flowing 171 km (106 miles) N and NW past Lanark, Hamilton, Glasgow, Clydebank and Dumbarton (where it widens into the Firth of Clyde). Near Lanark it descends 70 m (230 ft) in less than 6 km (4 miles) in the four famous Falls of Clyde. Below Lanark it passes through a fertile fruit-growing area, then through the main industrial region of Scotland. Below Glasgow (which is accessible to ocean-going vessels), the banks are lined with shipyards for some 32 km (20 miles). Linked with the R. Forth by a canal.

Cnidus. Ancient Greek city of SW Asia Minor from *c.* 330 BC on Cape Krio. A prosperous port, famous for its educational institutions. Here in one of the temples was the celebrated statue of Aphrodite by Praxiteles. The Athenians defeated the Spartans in a naval battle of Cnidus (394 BC).

Cnossus ➤KNOSSOS.

Coahuila Mexico. State in the N, bounded on the N and NE by Texas (USA), consisting mainly of broken plateau, crossed by the Sierra Madre Oriental and sloping gently down to the Rio Grande. Area 151,571 sq km (58,067 sq. miles). Pop. (1990) 1,971,344. Cap. Saltillo. In the W is Mexico's main cotton-growing area. Coal, silver, lead and copper are mined. First settled by the Spanish (around Saltillo) *c.* 1575.

Coalbanks ➤LETHBRIDGE.

Coalville England. Town in NW Leicestershire 19 km (12 miles) NW of Leicester. Pop. (1991) 30,408.

Coalmining centre. Engineering, brickmaking and other industries.

Coatbridge Scotland. Town in North Lanarkshire 14 km (9 miles) E of Glasgow. Pop. (1991) 43,617.

Manufactures iron and steel, and wire ropes, prefabricated houses and tubes.

Coats Island ➤HUDSON BAY.

Coatzacoalcos (Puerto Mexico) Mexico. Port near the mouth of the Coatzacoalcos

R. on the Gulf of Campeche. Pop. (1990) 232,314. Linked by rail across the Isthmus of Tehuantepec with Salina Cruz on the Pacific. Exports petroleum products and has an oil refinery.

Cobán Guatemala. Cap. of Alta Verapaz department 113 km (70 miles) N of Guatemala City at a height of 1300 m (4264 ft). Pop. (1989) 120,000. Market town in a coffee-growing region.

Cóbh Ireland. Formerly Queenstown. Seaport on the S shore of Great Island in Cork harbour. Pop. (1991) 6200. Port of call for Atlantic liners. Holiday resort. The cathedral (St Colman) is the burial-place of Charles Wolfe (1791–1823), author of *The Burial of Sir John Moore*. Renamed Queenstown after a visit by Queen Victoria (1849); the old name was restored in 1922.

Coblenz (Ger. **Koblenz**) Germany. Ancient Confluentes. City in the Rhineland-Palatinate on the Rhine R. at its confluence with the Mosel R.; the name is a corruption of the Roman name. Pop. (1990) 108,800.

Centre of the wine trade. Manufactures pianos, furniture, footwear and paper.

In the old city are the 13th-cent. castle and a fine 13th/15th-cent. church; in the new city is the 18th-cent. palace of Clement Wenceslaus. Across the Rhine is the fortress of Ehrenbreitstein. Founded *c.* 9 BC as a Roman military post. Held by the archbishop–electors of Trier 1018–1794, was taken by France, passed to Prussia (1815) and was cap. of the Rhine province 1824–1945. In 1946 it became cap. of the new Rhineland-Palatinate *Land*, but was superseded by Mainz (1950). Birthplace of the statesman, Prince Metternich (1773–1859).

Coburg Germany. Town in N Bavaria on the Itz R. 92 km (57 miles) N of Nuremberg. Pop. (1991) 44,700. Manufactures machinery, toys and porcelain.

Has a 16th-cent. ducal palace and a castle (mentioned in the 11th cent.) where Luther lived during the Diet of Augsburg (1530). Former cap. of Saxe-Coburg but united to

Bavaria in 1920. Nearby is the birthplace of Prince Albert (1819–61), consort of Queen Victoria.

Cochabamba Bolivia. Formerly Oropeza. Cap. of the Cochabamba department, the second largest city in Bolivia, in a fertile, closely settled basin, at a height of 2614 m (8574 ft) in the E Andes 129 km (80 miles) ENE of Oruro. Pop. (1992) 404,102.

Centre for Bolivia's main agricultural area, producing grain and fruit. Oil piped from the Camiri oilfield and refined. Manufactures furniture, footwear and tyres. Also a resort with a mild climate. University (1823).

Cochin India. Former state in the SW between the Anaimalai Hills and the Malabar coast; later in Travancore-Cochin state and now part of Kerala.

Cochin ➤KOCHI.

Cochin-China. Former French colony of Indo-China, since 1949 South Vietnam.

Cockatoo Island ➤YAMPI SOUND.

Cockburn Sound ➤KWINANA.

Cockenzie and Port Seton Scotland. Town in East Lothian on the Firth of Forth, comprising two neighbouring fishing ports. Pop. (1991) 4235.

Cockermouth England. Town in W Cumbria at the confluence of the Cocker and the Derwent rivers on the NW edge of the Lake District. Pop. (1991) 7702. Manufactures footwear. Birthplace of the poet William Wordsworth (1770–1850).

Coco River Nicaragua. Formerly Wanks R. River 640 km (400 miles) long, rising in Honduras, flowing generally ENE through Nicaragua, forming the boundary with Honduras for much of its length, and entering the Caribbean Sea by a delta at Cabo Gracias a Díos. Partly navigable; used mainly for floating timber.

Cocos Island (Sp. **Isla del Coco**) Pacific Ocean. Uninhabited island in the E Pacific 320 km (200 miles) SW of the Osa Peninsula in Costa Rica (to which it belongs). Area 23

sq km (9 sq. miles). Famous for stories of buried treasure; searched unsuccessfully by many expeditions.

Cocos (Keeling) Islands Indian Ocean. Two isolated atolls comprising a group of 27 coral islands in the Indian Ocean 2735 km (1700 miles) NW of Perth (Australia); since 1955 forming a Territory of the Commonwealth of Australia. Area 14 sq km (5 sq. miles). Pop. (1994) 670. The main islands, which are low-lying and covered with coconut palms (hence the name), are West, Home and Direction islands. Exports coconuts, copra and coconut oil. The airport on West Island is a refuelling point on the air route between Australia and South Africa. Discovered (1609) by Captain Keeling of the East India Company. Settled (1825) by a Scotsman, John Clunies-Ross. Annexed to the Crown 1857; then attached in turn to Ceylon (1878), Straits Settlements (1882) and Singapore (1903). They passed to Australia in 1955 and the Clunies-Ross rights were bought by the Australian government in 1978.

Cod, Cape USA. Low sandy peninsula 105 km (65 miles) long in SE Massachusetts, curving round to enclose Cape Cod Bay, on the shore of which the Pilgrim Fathers landed in 1620. Produces cranberries. Many summer resorts and fishing villages, inc. Barnstable, Falmouth, Truro and Chatham.

Cognac France. Ancient town in the Charente department on the Charente R. 96 km (60 miles) NNE of Bordeaux. Pop. (1982) 20,995.

The famous brandy is distilled from wine made with local grapes. Subsidiary industries, e.g. making bottles, corks, crates, barrels and hoops.

Birthplace of François I; scene of his alliance against the Emperor Charles V (1526).

Coimbatore India. Industrial town in Tamil Nadu on the Noyil R. 426 km (265 miles) SW of Madras in a pleasant situation at a height of 438 m (1437 ft) in the Nilgiri Hills. Pop. (1991) 816,300.

Rice and flour milling. Manufactures textiles, fertilizers, leather, chemicals, foundry products, textile machinery, vehicle components, hosiery, food products, generators and iron castings. Industries powered by the Pykara hydroelectric scheme.

Coimbra Portugal. Cap. of the Coimbra district on a hill above the Mondego R. 185 km (115 miles) NNE of Lisbon. Pop. (1991) 96,140.

Market for wine, grain and olives. Manufactures pottery. An important cultural centre.

Seat of Portugal's oldest university (founded in Lisbon 1290; permanently transferred here 1537). Two cathedrals. The famous Quinta das Lagrima (House of Tears), where Inés de Castro was murdered (1355). Cap. of Portugal 1139–1260.

Colchester England. Ancient Camulodunum. Market town in NE Essex on the R. Colne. Pop. (1991) 96,083.

Engineering. Market-gardening, rose-growing. Manufactures agricultural implements, chemicals and footwear.

Seat of the University of Essex (1961). Cap. of the British chief Cunobelinus (Cymbeline); sacked in Boadicea's rebellion (AD 62). Many remains, inc. part of the Roman wall. The Norman castle has a museum of Roman and other antiquities. Augustinian priory, St Botolph (12th-cent., built chiefly of Roman brick). An important port in the 13th cent. The oyster fisheries at the mouth of the Colne have been famous for many cent.

Colchis. In ancient times a region on the E coast of the Black Sea along the lower Rion R., now in the Republic of Georgia. Famous in Greek mythology as the home of Medea and the destination of the Argonauts. Now known as Kolkhida; a low-lying, swampy area, much of which has been drained and cultivated (citrus fruits).

Coldstream Scotland. Town in Scottish Borders on the R. Tweed 19 km (12 miles) SW of Berwick-on-Tweed, linked by bridge with Cornhill (England). Pop. (1991) 1746. Once the resort of runaway couples intent on marriage, which was solemnized at the old Toll House. From here General Monck marched into England with the troops he had raised (1660); in commemoration of the event, the pick of his regiments was named the Coldstream Guards.

Colenso South Africa. Village in Natal on the Tugela R. Pop. 2000. Scene of a defeat of the British forces attempting to relieve Ladysmith during the Boer War (1899). Named after the first Anglican bishop of Natal, J. W. Colenso (1814–83), a scholar of the Zulu lang.

Coleraine Northern Ireland. Seaport in Londonderry on the R. Bann estuary. Pop. (1991) 50,438.

Salmon-fishing. Whiskey-distilling. Bacon and ham curing. Manufactures shirts and linen.

Seat of the New University of Ulster (1968).

Coleshill ➤AMERSHAM.

Colima Mexico. 1. Small state in the W on the Pacific, inc. the Revilla Gigedo Is. 800 km (500 miles) offshore. Area 5455 sq km (2016 sq. miles). Pop. (1990) 424,656. Mainly agricultural, producing sugar-cane, rice and maize. 2. Cap. of Colima state on the Colima R. 72 km (45 miles) ENE of Manzanillo, its port. Pop. (1990) 116,155.

Market town processing maize, rice and sugar-cane. Manufactures cigars and shoes.

Colima, Mount Mexico. Volcano (3745 m; 12,284 ft) in the Jalisco state near the Colima border. Erupted, with loss of life, in 1941. Just N is Nevado de Colima (4339 m; 14,232 ft), an inactive volcano.

Colmar France. Prefecture of the Haut-Rhin department on the plain just E of the Vosges 37 km (23 miles) N of Mulhouse. Pop. (1990) 64,889.

Centre of the Alsatian cotton industry. Manufactures woollen, silk and rayon goods, and starch. Brewing and flour-milling. Trade in Alsatian wines.

Typically Alsatian in character. Many notable buildings, e.g. the 16th-cent. Maison

Pfister, the 17th-cent. Maison des Têtes and a 13th/14th-cent. Dominican monastery (now a museum). Became a free imperial city 1226. Annexed to France 1681. Held by Germany 1871–1919 and 1940–5.

Colne England. Industrial town in E Lancashire 10 km (6 miles) NNE of Burnley. Pop. (1991) 18,776.
  Cotton, rayon and woollen industries. Tanning.

Colne River England. 1. River 56 km (35 miles) long, rising in NW Essex, flowing SE past Halstead and Colchester, and entering the North Sea at Mersea Island. 2. River 56 km (35 miles) long, rising near Hatfield (Hertfordshire), flowing SW and S past Watford and Uxbridge, forming part of the boundary between Buckinghamshire and Greater London and joining the Thames at Staines.

Colne Valley England. Town in West Yorkshire 8 km (5 miles) WSW of Huddersfield. Pop. (1971) 21,188.
  Manufactures woollen goods, chemicals and textile machinery.

Cologne (Ger. **Köln**) Germany. Ancient Colonia Agrippinensis. Largest city in North Rhine-Westphalia and third largest city in W Germany on the Rhine R. Pop. (1990) 955,500. River port.
  Industrial city. Banking and insurance centre. Manufactures motor vehicles, railway rolling-stock, machine-tools, cables, chemical and pharmaceutical goods, perfume (inc. *eau de Cologne*, first produced here early in the 18th cent.), chocolate.
  The Gothic cathedral (begun 1248; not completed until 1880) was not seriously damaged in World War II, but many other historic buildings were destroyed. University (founded 1388; suspended from 1798; refounded 1919). Originally the chief town of the Ubii. Made a Roman colony (AD 50) by the Emperor Claudius for his wife Agrippina, who was born here. A bishopric from the 4th cent., it was raised to an archdiocese by Charlemagne in 785 and its archbishops long wielded great political power. In medieval times it prospered commercially, became a leading member of the Hanseatic League (1201) and in 1474 was created a free imperial city. Captured by the French in 1794, the see was secularized (1801) and its territories assigned to Prussia (1815). Once more the city prospered and from 1881 to 1921 its area was considerably increased.

Colombes France. Industrial and residential suburb in NW Paris in the Hauts-de-Seine department. Pop. (1990) 79,058.
  Well-known sports stadium. Engineering, chemical, hosiery, oil-refining, vehicles manufacture and other industries.

Colombey-les-deux-Églises France. Village in the Haute-Marne department 13 km (8 miles) E of Bar-sur-Aube. Private residence of the late President de Gaulle.

Colombia. Republic in the NW of South America, bounded in the N by the Caribbean Sea, NW by Panama, W by the Pacific Ocean, SW by Ecuador and Peru, NE by Venezuela and SE by Brazil. Area 1,141,568 sq km (440,762 sq. miles). Pop. (1995) 35,099,000 (70 per cent urban). Life expectancy, 69 years male, 72 female. Cap. Bogotá. Other cities: Cali, Medellín, Barranquilla and Cartagena. Currency: Peso = 100 centavos. Colombia is the fourth largest country in the continent, and the only one with both Atlantic and Pacific coastlines. Sixty per cent of the country is almost uninhabited tropical lowland. In the SW the Andes divide into parallel Cordilleras, separated by long, deep valleys open to the N. Along the Pacific coast is a relatively low range, inland of which is lowland drained to the Caribbean by the Atrato R. and to the Pacific by the San Juan. The W and central Cordilleras are separated in the S by a high rift valley, with the upper course of the Cauca R. Farther N the Cauca valley is wide and fertile, then narrow and steep-sided, until the river emerges onto flat, marshy lowland and joins the Magdalena R., which rises about 2°N (where the central and E Cordilleras separate) and flows N through a wide, level-floored valley to the N lowlands. The W Cordillera is the lowest, and the central the highest, with Mt Huila rising to

Colombia

5750 m (18,860 ft). The E Cordillera is a broad mountain mass with snowcapped peaks and intermontane basins at 2400–2700 m (7872–8856 ft). SW of L. Maracaibo the system divides, continuing as the Sierra de Perija (N) and the Cordillera de Mérida (E). In the extreme N lies the high isolated Sierra Nevada de Santa Marta, with Cristóbal Colón (5775 m; 18,942 ft) within sight of the coast. The Cauca–Magdalena plains are marshy, with shallow lakes and permanent swamp.

The W hills and lowlands have a high rainfall and hot humid climate throughout the year and are largely clothed with dense rainforests. The NE has long dry seasons and consists mainly of *llanos* (grasslands). There are forests again in the SE. In the mountains climate, vegetation and agricultural products vary with altitude, two wet seasons alternating with two dry. Below 900 m (2952 ft) is the *tierra caliente* with cacao, rice, bananas and tropical lowland products: from 900 to 2000 m (2952–6560 ft) is the *tierra templada*, producing coffee, sugar and maize; from 2000 to 3000 m (6560–9840 ft) is the *tierra fria* with wheat, barley, maize, potatoes and temperate fruits. Above lie the *páramos*, as far as the snowline, with alpine meadow and pastures. The climate therefore inc. equatorial and tropical conditions according to situation and altitude. Land use: forested 48 per cent, meadows and pasture 39 per cent, agricultural and under permanent cultivation 5 per cent.

The official lang. is Spanish. Mestizo make up 58 per cent of the pop., white 20 per cent, mulatto 14 per cent, black 4 per cent, mixed black–Indian 3 per cent and Amerindian 1 per cent. Of believers 93 per cent are Roman Catholic.

Just under a third of the pop. are agriculturalists, the majority growing subsistence crops, e.g. maize, wheat, rice, sugar-cane. Main export crop, coffee and the country is self-supporting in food production. The rubber tree grows wild and fibres are being exploited, notably the *fique* fibre, which provides all the country's requirements for sacks and cordage. It was reported in 1987 that cocaine exports earn Colombia more than its main agricultural export, coffee. The government has made attempts to eradicate production but the cocaine barons are extremely powerful and resort to violence when strong action is taken. Coal, gold, silver, emeralds, iron, lead, zinc, mercury and many other minerals are plentiful, and hydroelectric power is increasingly being developed. Petroleum (from the NW, the Magdalena valley and from the Putumayo R. region) is produced, with a pipeline to Tumaco. Industrial production has expanded: Medellín and Cali, though remote from ports, have many industries, with textiles to the fore; Bogotá, even more remote, is the administrative and cultural centre of the country, and has light industries. Air transport is important in a land of such difficult relief, while the Magdalena R. is a leading artery for passengers and goods.

Before the Spanish conquest, Chibcha Indians practised sedentary farming in the high basins of the E Cordillera; others mined gold and silver in the valleys of the central Cordillera. The Spanish settled first on the Caribbean coast, founding Santa Marta in 1525 and Cartagena in 1533. By 1538 Bogotá had been founded in the Cundinamarca basin. The country formed part of the presidency of New Granada until 1718, then became a viceroyalty independent of that of Peru. Struggles for independence took place 1810–19; Bolívar's forced march through the Andes brought him to Bogotá, and 'Gran Colombia' was proclaimed, but by 1830 Venezuela and Ecuador had become separate states. The name was changed from New Granada to Colombia in 1863. Government was stable 1922–49; there was a civil war 1949–53 and further troubles subsequently made worse by the sale of drugs with its associated violent crime and political corruption.

The government consists of an executive president, directly elected for a 4-year term and his cabinet. The president appoints the governors of the departments, the other units of local government and the mayor of Bogotá. The legislature is a Congress of two houses; the 112-member Senate and 109-

member House of Representatives, both elected for four years. There are two political parties, but there are also powerful insurgent groups. The country is divided into 32 departments and the cap. district of Bogotá and subdivided into 1011 municipalities.

Colombo Sri Lanka. Cap. and chief seaport on the W coast just S of the mouth of the Kelani R. Pop. (1990) 615,000.

Exports tea, rubber, coconut oil, copra, desiccated coconut. With its large artificial harbour, it replaced Galle as the island's leading port when improvements were carried out and the first breakwater was completed (1874–86). Also the principal commercial centre, the business section of the city being still known as the Fort.

Since 1942 seat of the University of Ceylon, formed from Ceylon Medical College (1870) and Ceylon University College (1921). Taken by the Dutch 1656; handed over to Britain 1796.

Colón Panama. Formerly Aspinwall. Cap. of the Colón province, the second largest city in Panama, on Manzanillo Island at the Caribbean end of the Panama Canal. Pop. (1990) 140,908. Divided by the Canal Zone boundary from its twin city and port Cristóbal but the Trans-Isthmian Highway (to Panama City) belongs to Panama. Founded in 1850 as Aspinwall, after one of the builders of the railway, but later renamed (Cristóbal Colón is the Spanish form of Christopher Columbus). Long notorious for yellow fever and malaria, which were overcome by public-health measures at the commencement of work on the Panama Canal (1903).

Colón Archipelago ►GALÁPAGOS ISLANDS.

Colophon. Ancient city in Ionia 24 km (15 miles) N of Ephesus, its port being Notium or New Colophon. One of the places claimed as the birthplace of Homer. The final charge of the Colophon cavalry in action was said to be decisive – hence the use of the word for the finishing touch to a book or manuscript.

Colorado (Argentina) ►RÍO COLORADO.

Colorado USA. State in the W, rectangular in shape. Area 270,000 sq km (104,247 sq. miles). Pop. (1990) 3,294,394. Cap. Denver. A Rocky Mountain state with an average height of 2070 m (6790 ft), the highest state in the USA; more or less bisected by the Continental Divide. Highest peak Mt Elbert (4401 m; 14,435 ft); about 50 others exceed 4250 m (13,940 ft). Climate in general dry, with wide variations in rainfall and temperature. Mainly a stock-raising, farming and mining state.

Dairy-farming has developed round the urban centres and irrigation agriculture is important, esp. for alfalfa; wheat and sugarbeet are also leading crops. Principal minerals bituminous coal, petroleum; main US producer of uranium, radium, molybdenum, vanadium. Gold, silver, zinc and lead also produced. Industries, concentrated mainly in the towns just E of the Rockies, inc. meat-packing, sugar-refining, vegetable-canning, ore-processing. Chief towns Denver, Pueblo (iron and steel industry), Colorado Springs (resort).

The first explorers were Spaniards from Mexico in the 16th cent. Coronado entered the region in 1540; Spanish expeditions continued throughout the 17th and 18th cent. In 1799 Jean de la Maison-neuve arrived at the present site of Denver; in the 19th cent. fur traders helped to explore and develop the territory. Became a state (1876) 100 years after the Declaration of Independence; hence the sobriquet 'Centennial' state. The farmers of Colorado suffered from the droughts of 1932–7, which created dustbowls on the plains. Admitted to the Union in 1876 as the 38th state.

Colorado Desert USA. Arid region in SE California W of the Colorado R.; separated from the Mojave Desert by the San Bernardino and other mountains. It contains the Salton Sea, 76 m (249 ft) below sea level, and the Imperial Valley, which is fertile where irrigated.

Colorado River USA. River 2320 km

(1440 miles) long, rising in the Rocky Mountain National Park in North Colorado, flowing generally SW through Utah and Arizona and then S, and entering the Gulf of California. Forms the state boundaries between Nevada and Arizona, between California and Arizona, and in Mexico between Baja California and Sonora; also a short stretch of the international frontier between Arizona and Baja California. Flowing through a mountainous region, it cuts many deep gorges, while its lower course ends in a large delta which inc. part of the Imperial Valley. Its tributaries inc. the Dolores and the Gunnison rivers in Colorado, the Green and the San Juan rivers in Utah and the Little Colorado and the Gila rivers in Arizona. Below its confluence with the Little Colorado it has carved a path through a great plateau, forming the world-famous Grand Canyon. This enormous gorge, 351 km (218 miles) long and 6–24 km (4–15 miles) wide, reaches a depth of nearly 1800 m (5904 ft). The river has been utilized to a remarkable degree for irrigation and power. Large dams along its course inc. the Hoover Dam (formerly known as Boulder Dam), the Davis Dam, the Parker Dam (with Aqueducts to Los Angeles and San Diego) and the Imperial Dam, which diverts water into the All-American Canal for the irrigation of the Imperial and Coachella Valleys in South California.

Colorado River USA. River 1560 km (970 miles) long, rising on the Llano Estacado and flowing generally SE to Matagorda Bay on the Gulf of Mexico. Used for irrigation and power. Several important dams.

Colorado Springs USA. Health resort and tourist centre just E of Pikes Peak in Colorado at a height of 1800 m (5904 ft). Pop. (1990) 281,140.

Colossae. Ancient city of SW Phrygia (Turkey). St Paul addressed his Epistle to the Colossians to the members of the early Christian Church here.

Columbia (Missouri) USA. Town near the Missouri R. 45 km (28 miles) NNW of Jefferson City. Pop. (1990) 69,101.

Manufactures clothing and furniture. Flour-milling.

Seat of the University of Missouri (1839).

Columbia (South Carolina) USA. Cap. and largest city of South Carolina at the head of navigation on the Congaree R. Pop. (1990) 98,052.

Important textile (cotton) mills. Manufactures fertilizers, cottonseed oil. Cultural and educational centre.

Seat of the University of South Carolina (1801) and the Allen University (1880, black). Founded 1786.

Columbia, District of USA. Federal district on the Potomac R. Area 179 sq km (60 sq. miles). Pop. (1993) 578,448. Co-extensive with the city of Washington. Chosen as the site of the cap. in order to overcome inter-state rivalry and ceded by Maryland. The oldest building, the President's residence, was completed in 1799 and the seat of government was transferred there in 1800. When the British sacked Washington (1814) they set fire to the residence; subsequently painted white to cover the marks, it has remained the 'White House'. Planned by a French engineer, Pierre l'Enfant, the city is laid out in rectangular blocks crossed by diagonal arteries. The skyline is dominated by the Capitol with its great rotunda and dome, where Congress meets and by the Washington Monument (169 m; 554 ft). Other notable buildings are the Lincoln and Jefferson Memorials and the Supreme Court. The District of Columbia has two delegates in Congress who may vote in committees but not on the floor of the House.

Columbia River Canada/USA. River 1850 km (1150 miles) long (740 km; 460 miles in Canada); among US rivers, second in volume only to the Mississippi. Rises in the small L. Columbia in the Rocky Mountains (British Columbia), flows N and doubles round to the N of the Selkirk Range, then S through the Arrow Lakes to the US border, then W, SE and again W, forming the boundary between Washington (N) and Oregon (S), and enters the Pacific by a long estuary.

Has cut many gorges and canyons, e.g. through the Cascade Range. Enormous power potential; important dams along its course inc. the Grand Coulee Dam, the Bonneville Dam and the McNary Dam. Chief tributary the Snake, others being the Kootenay, Spokane and Willamette rivers. Named after the *Columbia*, the ship of Capt. Gray, a Boston trader who explored its mouth (1792).

Columbus (Georgia) USA. Town at the head of navigation of the Chattahoochee R. 154 km (96 miles) SSW of Atlanta. Pop. (1990) 179,278.

Commercial and industrial centre. Textile mills. Manufactures bricks and tiles, fertilizers, agricultural implements, food products. Hydroelectric power from the Chattahoochee.

Founded (1828) as a trading post where the water power and the transport facilities of the river could be used.

Columbus (Ohio) USA. State cap. on the Scioto R. Pop. (1990) 632,900.

Industrial centre. Meat-packing, printing and publishing. Manufactures aircraft and motor-car parts, electrical and electronic equipment, machinery and footwear.

Seat of the Ohio State University (1872).

Colwyn Bay Wales. Seaside resort in Conwy on the Irish Sea; comprises Colwyn Bay, Old Colwyn and Rhos-on-Sea. Pop. (1991) 29,883.

Commander Islands ➤KOKANDORSKI ISLANDS.

Commonwealth of Independent States. Grouping of independent states which is successor to the USSR in some aspects of law and international affairs. The founder members were Russia, Belarus and Ukraine. Other members are Armenia, Azerbaijan, Georgia, Kazakhstan, Kyrgyzstan, Moldova, Tajikistan, Turkmenistan and Uzbekistan. The administrative centre, Minsk (Belarus). Pop. (1991) 276,650,000.

Commonwealth of Nations, The. Voluntary association of 53 (1997) independent states and dependencies consisting of the UK plus states and dependencies that were previously part of the British Empire. In 1995 Cameroon and Mozambique also joined.

Como Italy. Ancient Comum. Cap. of Como province in Lombardy at the SW end of L. Como 39 km (24 miles) N of Milan. Pop. (1981) 95,571.

Tourist centre. Lake port. Railway junction. Important silk industry. Manufactures textile machinery, motor-cycles, furniture and glass.

Marble cathedral (mainly 15th-cent.); several ancient churches; 13th-cent. Gothic town hall. Fell to the Visconti, 1335. Later came under Austrian rule; liberated by Garibaldi 1859. Birthplace of the elder (AD 23–79) and the younger Pliny (61–113), Pope Innocent XI (1611–89), Alessandro Volta, the physicist (1745–1827).

Como, Lake Italy. Third largest lake in Italy in Lombardy at a height of 198 m (649 ft). Area 143 sq km (55 sq. miles) (length 48 km (30 miles) maximum width 4 km (2½ miles)). Formed by the expansion of the Adda R., which enters in the N and leaves in the SE. In the S it is divided by the promontory of Bellagio into two arms, L. Como (W) and the Lake of Lecco (E). Beautifully situated among mountains. Many noted resorts around the shores, inc. Bellagio, Cadenabbia, Como, Lecco and Tremezzo.

Comodoro Rivadavia Argentina. Port on the Gulf of San Jorge 900 km (569 miles) SSW of Bahía Blanca. Pop. (1991) 124,000. Oil wells nearby (discovered 1907), the main source of Argentina's output. Oil-refining. A pipeline 1770 km (1100 miles) long takes natural gas to Buenos Aires.

Comoros. The Federal Islamique Republic of the Comoros consists of three islands (Njazídja, Mwali and Nzwani) in the Indian Ocean between mainland Africa and Madagascar. Area 1862 sq km (719 sq. miles). Pop. (1995) 545,000 (29 per cent urban). Life expectancy, 56 years male, 60 female. Cap. Moroni. Other towns Mutsamudu, Domoni. Currency: Comorian franc = 100 centimes. Njazídja (Grande Comore) is the largest and most westerly island and has the majority of the total pop. The islands are mountainous and the interiors are forested. The small fertile strips are intensively cultivated. The climate is tropical and is affected by the Indian monsoon winds from the N giving a rainy season November–April. Land use: forested 18 per cent, meadows and pastures 7 per cent, agricultural and under permanent cultivation 45 per cent. The indigenous pop. is a mixture of Malagasy, African, Malay and Arab people, and over 99 per cent are Sunni Muslims. The official lang. are Comorian, Arabic and French.

Sugar-cane used to be the main product but now vanilla, cloves, copra and essential oils are important exports, but subsistence farming by 80 per cent of the pop. is the main occupation and over 50 per cent of food has to be imported. Fishing is on an individual basis with no modern equipment. Tourism attracts foreign visitors; about 50 per cent of visitors come from France. Foreign aid is vital for economic survival.

The archipelago was long under Arab influence and it became a French protectorate at the end of the 19th cent. and was proclaimed a colony in 1912. With neighbouring Mayotte they were administratively attached to Madagascar from 1914 until 1947, when the four islands became a French Overseas Territory, achieving internal self-government in 1961. In 1974 the three western islands voted for independence while Mayotte (mainly Christian) voted to remain French, and independence was achieved in 1975. The President who is directly elected appoints ministers to form a Council of Government. There is a 42-member (5 for each island) Senate.

Comotini (Komotini) Greece. Cap. of the Rodhopi *nome* in Thrace. Pop. (1985) 35,000.

Market town. Trade in cereals, tobacco and vegetables.

Formerly under Turkish and Bulgarian rule.

Compiègne France. Ancient Compen-

dium. Town in the Oise department on the Oise R. 69 km (43 miles) NNE of Paris; the forest of Compiègne (148 sq km; 55 sq. miles) is nearby. Pop. (1985) 44,000.

Popular resort. Engineering, sawmilling and other industries.

At the siege of Compiègne Joan of Arc was captured by the English (1430). The 1918 Armistice ending World War I was signed in a railway carriage in the forest and in the same carriage the French capitulation to Germany in World War II was signed in Hitler's presence (1940).

Compton USA. Industrial town in California 18 km (11 miles) S of Los Angeles. Pop. (1980) 81,826.

Oil-refining. Manufactures oil-well equipment, steel and glass products.

Founded 1868. Became a city 1888. Grew rapidly in the 1950s.

Conakry (Konakry) Guinea. Cap. and chief seaport on the offshore island of Tombo, connected with the mainland by a causeway. Pop. (1992) 950,000.

Terminus of the railway from Kankan. Exports alumina, iron ore, bananas and palm kernels. Grew rapidly after iron ore, mined on the nearby Kaloum peninsula, was first exported (1952).

Concarneau France. Sardine-fishing port and seaside resort in the Finistère department on the Bay of Biscay 19 km (12 miles) SE of Quimper. Pop. (1982) 18,225. Fish-canning.

Concepción Chile. Cap. of the Concepción province, the most important city in the S, on the Bio-Bio R. 14 km (9 miles) SE of its port, Talcahuano. Pop. (1992) 330,448.

Manufactures textiles, leather goods, paper, cement and glass. Chile's principal coal mines are nearby.

University (1919). Founded 1550. Destroyed by earthquakes in 1570, 1730 and 1751, then removed to its present site. Again severely damaged in the earthquakes of 1939 and 1960.

Concepción Paraguay. Cap. of the Concepción department; port on the Paraguay R.

217 km (135 miles) NNE of Asunción. Pop. (1984) 25,607.

Commercial centre. Trade in yerba maté, timber, quebracho, hides, livestock. Sawmilling, cotton-ginning and flour-milling.

Concepción del Uruguay Argentina. River port on the Uruguay R. in the Entre Ríos province. Pop. (1985) 40,000. Terminus of the Entre Ríos Railway. Exports grain and beef.

Conchos River ➤MEXICO.

Concord (California) USA. Town 16 km (10 miles) NE of Oakland. Pop. (1990) 111,348. Mainly residential. Expanded rapidly in the 1950s; pop. (1950) 6953.

Concord (Massachusetts) USA. Town on the Concord R. 27 km (17 miles) WNW of Boston. Pop. (1990) 17,000. Largely residential. Famous as scene of the first battle of the Revolution (1775) and home of several American writers: Hawthorne, Emerson, Thoreau and the Alcotts.

Concord (New Hampshire) USA. Cap. of New Hampshire on the Merrimack R. Pop. (1990) 36,000.

Printing and publishing. Manufactures leather goods.

Settled (as Pennycook) 1725. Incorporated (as Rumford) 1733. Renamed Concord 1765. Home of Benjamin Thompson (Count Rumford).

Concordia Argentina. River port on the Uruguay R. in the Entre Ríos province opposite Salto (Uruguay). Pop. (1991) 138,905.

Exports cereals and citrus fruits, trading with Uruguay, Brazil and Paraguay. Manufactures vegetable oils and leather. Tourist centre.

Coney Island USA. Seaside resort in New York, part of Brooklyn (New York City) in the SW of Long Island. A playground for the people of New York City, noted for its amusement parks, sideshows, cafés and dance halls, and for its 8-km (5-mile) beach and promenade.

Congleton England. Industrial town in Cheshire on the R. Dane 18 km (11 miles) ENE of Crewe. Pop. (1991) 24,879.

Manufactures cotton goods, hosiery, cardboard boxes, teleprinters and control gear.

Congo, Democratic Republic of the. Republic (until 1997 Zaïre) in central Africa bounded N by the Central African Republic, NE by Sudan, E by Uganda, Rwanda, Burundi and L. Tanganyika, S by Zambia, SW by Angola and NW by Republic of the Congo. There is a 37-km (23-mile) Atlantic coastline separating Angola's province of Cabinda from the rest of the country. Area 2,344,885 sq km (905,365 sq. miles). Pop. (1995) 43,901,000 (29 per cent urban). Life expectancy, 50 years male, 54 female. Cap. Kinshasa. Other important cities Lubumbashi, Mbuji-Mayi, Kisangani and Kananga. Currency: Congolese franc. The country occupies about two-thirds of the basin of the Congo R., consisting of a vast depression in the African plateau mainly over 300 m (984 ft) above sea level, fringed on the E and S by highlands. The E highlands, on the edge of the W branch of the Great Rift Valley, rise to 5109 m (16,758 ft) in the Ruwenzori range. The N half, lying on both sides of the equator, has a typical equatorial climate, with constant high temperatures and all-year rainfall (150–200 cm (60–80 ins.) annually), and is chiefly covered with tropical rainforest. The S half has a tropical climate, always hot but with a well-marked dry season and is principally savannah country, with belts of forest along the rivers. Lubumbashi (Shaba) is linked by rail with Lobito in Angola and with the Zambian system. The Congo R. is navigable for over 1600 km (1000 miles) above Kinshasa to Kisangani and hundreds of miles of tributaries are also navigable. Matadi, the chief seaport, at the head of the Congo estuary, is linked by rail with Kinshasa. Land use: forested 77 per cent, meadows and pastures 7 per cent, agricultural and under permanent cultivation 4 per cent. The pop. is mainly Bantu, with some Nilotic (in NE), Sudanese (in N) and aboriginal Pygmies and Hamites (in E). French is the only official

Congo

lang. but there are more than 200 langs spoken and 4 are recognized as national langs: Kiswahili, Tshiluba, Kikongo and Lingala. About 41 per cent of the pop. is Roman Catholic, other Christian 30 per cent, Kimbanguist 13 per cent and Muslim 1 per cent.

The principal cash crops are palm oil and kernels, cotton, rubber and coffee; food crops inc. cassava, maize and plantains. About 80 per cent of the pop. is engaged in subsistence farming. Congo is the world's leading producer of industrial diamonds, chiefly from the former Kasai province, and cobalt, from the mineral-rich Shaba (Katanga). Shaba is also an important producer of copper (the main export) and uranium ore; tin, zinc, manganese, cobalt, cassiterite, gold and silver are mined.

The Portuguese discovered the mouth of the Congo R. in 1482, but travel difficulties prevented European exploration until H. M. Stanley's journey down the river (1876–7). He was charged by King Leopold II of Belgium (on behalf of the International Association of the Congo) with continued explorations and the conclusion of agreements with native chiefs. After the Berlin Conference (1884–5) Leopold II was recognized as the head of state founded by the International Association, The Congo Free State. The Arab slave trade and cannibalism were suppressed, but serious charges of illtreatment of natives and the abolition of freedom of trade were made against the administration; Belgium assumed responsibility for government in 1908 and the country became a colony, the Belgian Congo. It became independent in 1960, but disorder followed the withdrawal of the Belgian administrators, doctors and others: tribal violence, attacks on Europeans, army mutiny, famine. Katanga province proclaimed its independence. The UN recognized the Adoula government as the central government of the republic in 1961, UN forces invaded Katanga and fighting with Katangan troops continued into 1963. The secession of Katanga suddenly collapsed, however, and peace and semblance of law and order was imposed. In 1971 the name of the country

was changed from Congo (Kinshasa) to Zaïre, and in 1997 to the Democratic Republic of the Congo. In 1996–8 the country again became unstable and the influx of Rwandan refugees has added to the problems. A successor to the President, who can hold the country together, is doubtful. Shaba has declared autonomy and the diamond-rich province of Kasai uses its own currency.

The country is divided administratively into Kinshasa city and 10 provinces. Congo has a revolutionary military regime.

Congo. Republic of the Congo in W Africa is bounded by Cameroon and the Central African Republic in the N, Democratic Republic of the Congo to the E and S, the Atlantic Ocean to the SW and Gabon to the W. Area 342,000 sq km (132,047 sq. miles). Pop. (1995) 2,590,000 (41 per cent urban). Life expectancy 49 years male, 54 female. Cap. Brazzaville. Other cities: Pointe-Noire, Loubomo, Nkayi, Mossendjo. Currency: CFA franc = 100 centimes. The country largely consists of equatorial forest, interspersed with wooded savannah. It has an equatorial climate with moderate rainfall and a small range of temperature. Land use: forested 62 per cent, meadows and pastures 29 per cent, agricultural and under permanent cultivation 0.5 per cent. The official lang. is French but other national lang. are Lingata and Monokotuba. About 50 per cent of believers are Roman Catholic, Protestant 24 per cent, African Christian 14 per cent. There are some Muslims and traditional animist beliefs are still practised. The ethnic grouping at 52 per cent Kongo, and others inc. Teke, Mboshi, Mbete, Punu, Sango, Maka, Pygmy.

Tropical hardwoods (e.g. mahogany, sapale, okoumé) are exported. Petroleum and natural gas deposits were found in 1969 and petroleum and petroleum products represent 85 per cent of exports. There is a refinery at Pointe-Noire. Other minerals inc. gold, diamonds, potash, phosphates, zinc and lead.

The coast was discovered in the 17th cent. by the Portuguese and was a French trading base from the 17th to the 19th cent. Pierre de Brazza (1852–1905) explored the Alima R., reaching Stanley Pool and claimed the area for France in 1880. Originally named French Congo, later Middle Congo (1903–58). It became a member of the French Community in 1958 and achieved independence in 1960. The first years of independence were turbulent and in 1970 a Marxist–Leninist state was introduced, but in 1992 the country became a multi-party democracy.

There is a 60-member Senate and 125-member National Assembly.

Congo River Africa. River 4667 km (2900 miles) long, the second longest in Africa (formerly Zaïre River); one of the world's great rivers, second only to the Amazon, with its tributaries draining a basin of over 3,700,000 sq km (1,428,000 sq. miles). The E headstream, the Chambezi, rises on the plateau S of L. Tanganyika, passes through L. Bangweulu and continues as the Luapula R., which enters L. Mweru, leaving it as the Luvua R.; the W headstream, the Lualaba R., rises on the Shaba plateau near the Zambia frontier and joins the Luvua; below the confluence the stream is still called the Lualaba R. It receives the Lukuga R., which connects it with L. Tanganyika. Below Stanley Falls it is called the R. Congo; along this middle course, it is very wide, studded with islands and receives several great tributaries, inc. the Ubangi R. from the N and the Kasai R. from the S. The flow in the lower course is regular, because these tributaries are fed during the rainy seasons of both the N and the S hemispheres. Some 560 km (350 miles) above its mouth the river widens into Stanley Pool, then cuts through the Crystal Mountains by a gorge and descends 270 m (886 ft) in 354 km (220 miles), by the Livingstone Falls, widening again into an estuary nearly 160 km (100 miles) long. Matadi, just below the falls, is accessible to ocean-going vessels. Steamers navigate over 1600 km (1000 miles) of the river between Kinshasa and Kisangani, with its tributaries the Congo provides over 12,000 km (7500 miles) of navigable waterways. Some unnavigable stretches are linked by railways, e.g. Matadi–Kinshasa, Kisan-gani–Ponthierville, Kindu–Kabalo. The mouth of the Congo was discovered by the Portuguese in 1482; the middle and upper courses remained virtually unknown until Livingstone reached Nyangwe (on the Lualaba R.) in 1871 and Stanley journeyed down-river from Nyangwe to Boma in 1876–7.

Conisbrough (**Conisborough**) England. Town in South Yorkshire on the R. Don 8 km (5 miles) SW of Doncaster. Pop. (1991) 16,031.

Manufactures bricks and tiles.

Ruins of a 12th-cent. Norman castle with an outstanding circular keep.

Coniston Water England. Lake 8 km (5 miles) long and 0.8 km (½ mile) wide in Cumbria in the Lake District 8 km (5 miles) W of L. Windermere at the foot of the Old Man of Coniston (803 m; 2634 ft). On the E shore is Brantwood, the home of Ruskin, who is buried in Coniston village churchyard (W of the lake). Scene of the establishment of the world water-speed record of Sir Malcolm Campbell (1939) and of his son Donald Campbell (1959).

Connaught (**Connacht**) Ireland. Province in the W, between the R. Shannon and the Atlantic, comprising the counties of Galway, Leitrim, Mayo, Roscommon and Sligo. Area 17,122 sq km (6611 sq. miles). Pop. (1991) 423,000.

Connecticut USA. State in New England. Area 12,592 sq km (4862 sq. miles) (third smallest in the Union). Pop. (1990) 3,287,116. Cap. Hartford. Main rivers the Connecticut, draining the central lowlands, the Thames (E) and the Housatonic with the Naugatuck (W). Highest point Bear Mountain (708 m; 2322 ft) in the extreme NW. Many glacial lakes. The coast, indented by river mouths and bays, has several good harbours. Climate humid continental. Annual rainfall 100–125 cm (40–50 ins.). Agriculture important, esp. tobacco-growing, market-gardening, poultry and dairy farming. Forests of beech, chestnut, birch, maple and poplar. Minerals are of major importance, but granite, limestone, clay and sandstone are quarried. The state is mainly industrial, specializing in precision instruments; its manufactures inc. firearms and ammunition, brassware, textiles, clocks and watches, jewellery, machinery, pins and needles, wire products and precision tools. Chief towns Hartford, Bridgeport, New Haven, Waterbury.

Adriaen Block, a Dutch explorer, discovered the Connecticut R.; a Dutch trading post established in 1633 on the site of Hartford was later abandoned. English colonists from Massachusetts formed the first permanent settlements at Windsor, Wethersfield and Hartford in 1634–5. In the American War of Independence Connecticut strongly supported the colonists; in the American Civil War it was on the side of the Union. One of the original 13 states.

Connemara Ireland. Barren, boggy area in the W of Co. Galway inc. the mountain group called the Twelve Bens, which rise to 730 m (2394 ft) and a great number of small lakes. Wild, picturesque scenery, both coastal and inland, popular with tourists. Fishing.

Consett England. Town in N Durham 19 km (12 miles) SW of Newcastle upon Tyne. Pop. (1991) 20,148. Iron and steel works were closed in 1980. Collieries and engineering.

Constance (Ger. **Konstanz**) Germany. Town in Baden-Württemberg on the Rhine R. at its exit from L. Constance. Pop. (1989) 70,000.

Port. Tourist centre. Railway junction. Manufactures textiles, machinery and chemicals.

Its minster (formerly cathedral) dates from the 11th cent.; an old Dominican monastery is now a hotel. Noted in medieval times for its linen industry. Scene (1414–18) of the Church Council of Constance, which condemned and burned John Huss (1415) and Jerome of Prague (1416). Surrendered to Austria 1548. Ceded to Baden 1805. Birthplace of Count Zeppelin, constructor of the first airship (1838–1917).

Constance, Lake (Ger. **Bodensee**). Ancient Lacus Brigantinus. Lake at a height of 400 m (1312 ft) bordering on Austria, Germany and Switzerland. Area 531 sq km (205 sq. miles) (length 64 km (40 miles), width 13 km (8 miles)). The Rhine enters in the SE near Bregenz and leaves in the NW (from the Untersee) at Stein am Rhein. The greater part of the lake (the Obersee) is in the E and SE. Near Constance in the W it divides into the Untersee (S) and the Uberlingersee (N). Fishing villages and holiday resorts around the shores are linked by steamers. Chief towns Constance, Lindau, Friedrichshafen (Germany), Bregenz (Austria).

Constanţa (Constanza) Romania. Ancient Constantiana. Cap. of the Constanţa district; chief Romanian seaport on the Black Sea. Pop. (1992) 350,476.

Exports petroleum, grain and timber. Oil pipeline from Ploeşti. Seaside resort. Manufactures furniture, bricks, textiles, soap and chemicals.

Founded by Greeks in the 6th cent. BC, rebuilt by Constantine the Great in the 4th cent. AD. Its modern development dates from 1878, when it was ceded to Romania by Turkey.

Constantine Algeria. Ancient Cirta. Cap. of the Constantine department 338 km (210 miles) ESE of Algiers. Pop. (1989) 449,000. On a rocky plateau, cut off on all sides except the W by a deep ravine formed by the Rummel R. Modern suburbs to the SW.

Chief centre for the trade of the High Plateaux and the interior (grain, wool, leather, esparto grass). Flour-milling. Manufactures tractors, diesel engines, woollen and leather goods.

An important town in ancient Numidia. Destroyed AD 311; restored by Constantine the Great 313. Taken by the French 1837.

Constantinople ➤ISTANBUL.

Constanza ➤CONSTANŢA.

Conwy (Conway) Wales. 1. Seaside resort

in Conwy on the estuary of the R. Conwy. Pop. (1991) 3627.

Market town. Light engineering and quarries nearby.

Impressive remains of a 13th-cent. castle and town walls. The river is crossed by a road suspension bridge designed by Telford (1826) and a tubular railway bridge designed by Stephenson (1848).

2. County Borough from 1996. Pop. (1994) 111,000.

Conwy River Wales. River 48 km (30 miles) long in Conwy, flowing generally N and entering the Irish Sea at Conwy.

Cooch Behar (Kuch Bihar) India. Former princely state in the NE; since 1950 part of West Bengal. Area 3421 sq km (1321 sq. miles).

Rice, jute and tobacco grown. Chief town Cooch Behar.

Cook (Aoraki) Mount New Zealand. Highest peak (3764 m; 12,346 ft) in New Zealand in the Southern Alps, South Island. Permanently snow-capped, the surrounding snowfields feeding large glaciers.

Cook Islands S Pacific Ocean. Islands of Polynesia in the S Pacific between 8°S and 23°S lat. and 156°W and 167°W long, roughly in two groups: Northern Group of atolls, inc. Manihiki (Humphrey), Pukapuka (Danger), Penrhyn (Tongareva) and Raka-hanga (Reirson), each of which has several hundred people and produces copra and pearl shell; Southern or Lower Group (Cook Is. proper), inc. Rarotonga and Mangaia, of volcanic origin and Aitutaki, Atiu and 4 others, all coral islands. Total area 392 sq km (113 sq. miles). Pop. (1994) 18,500. Seat of administration is at Avarma on Rarotonga which, with Mangaia, exports copra and fruits. Farming and fishing are the main occupations with tourism, esp. on Rarotonga and Aitutaki, beginning to grow. About 25,000 islanders live and work abroad and money sent back helps the economy. Niue (Savage) Island, W of the other islands, belongs to the group but is under separate administration;

it is a raised coral atoll exporting copra and bananas.

The southern islands were settled by Polynesians about 1500 years ago. Spaniards visited the islands in the 16th cent. as did Capt. Cook in 1773. The Cook Islands were proclaimed a British protectorate in 1888 and in 1901 were annexed and proclaimed part of New Zealand. In 1965 the Cook Islands became a self-governing territory in 'free association' with New Zealand. Internal self-government was achieved in 1965 and the islanders have common citizenship with New Zealand. There is a Premier and 6 other Ministers and a unicameral parliament with 24 elected members. In addition there is also a 15-member Advisory Council composed of hereditary chiefs, House of Ariki, which has no legislative powers.

Cookstown Northern Ireland. Market town in NE Co. Tyrone on the R. Ballinderry 51 km (32 miles) W of Belfast. Pop. (1991) 9842.

Dairy-farming centre. Manufactures linen, hosiery and cement.

Founded (1609) by Allan Cook.

Cook Strait New Zealand. Strait separating the North Island and the South Island 26 km (16 miles) wide at the narrowest point. Well known for its strong, gusty winds.

Coolgardie ➤KALGOORLIE-BOULDER.

Coorg India. Former small state in the W Ghats, now in the extreme S of Karnataka. Area 4121 sq km (1591 sq. miles). Chief town Mercara. Mountainous and wooded, with several peaks, exceeding 1500 m (4920 ft). Heavy rainfall. Rice, coffee and oranges grown.

Copenhagen (Danish **Köbenhavn**) Denmark. In Danish, 'Merchants' Haven'. Cap. and largest city on the E coast of Zealand island near the S end of The Sound (Öresund); linked by bridges with the suburb of Christianshavn on the N coast of Amager island. Pop. (1995) 471,300.

Denmark's chief port and commercial centre. The harbour occupies the channel between Zealand and Amager islands. Exports butter, cheese, eggs and bacon. Shipbuilding, engineering and brewing. Manufactures porcelain, textiles, chocolate and paper.

At the centre is the Kongens Nytorv square, from which the main thoroughfares radiate. Nearby are the 17th-cent. Charlottenborg Palace (now housing the Academy of Arts), the Royal Theatre and the 17th-cent. Thotts palace. Also has a cathedral (rebuilt in the early 19th cent.), Trinity Church, with a remarkable round tower ascended by a spiral incline and the 18th-cent. Christiansborg Palace on the Slottsholm (an island formed by a narrow arm of the harbour), last restored in 1903 and now used as the parliament house. A leading centre of Scandinavian culture. Seat of a university (1479), several learned societies and the Thorvaldsen and other museums. Headquarters of the European Environment Agency.

Only a fishing village until 1167, when the Bishop of Roskilde built a castle on the site of the present Christiansborg Palace. The settlement gradually acquired importance as a trading centre. Became cap. of Denmark 1443. Attacked by the Hanseatic League in the 15th cent. and by the Swedes in the 17th. Bombarded by the English, Dutch and Swedish fleets 1700. Suffered severely from fires in 1728 and 1795. The Danish fleet was destroyed by Nelson at the Battle of Copenhagen (1801). Again bombarded by the English fleet 1807.

Copiapó Chile. Cap. of the Atacama province on the Copiapó R. at a height of 360 m (1181 ft) 64 km (40 miles) ESE of its port, Caldera and 400 km (250 miles) S of Antofagasta. Pop. (1992) 100,946.

Centre of a copper and iron mining region and of an irrigated belt along the river.

Coppermine River Canada. River 845 km (525 miles) long in the Mackenzie District, Northwest Territories, rising in a small lake, flowing S to L. De Gras N of the Great Slave Lake, then flowing generally N and entering the Coronation Gulf.

Coptos (Koptus) Egypt. Ancient Egyptian city near the Nile 32 km (20 miles) NE of Thebes. Trade with India and Arabia via the Red Sea made it a great commercial centre from *c.* 300 BC. After rebelling against Diocletian it was almost destroyed, but recovered and was again important in later Roman times. The village of Kuft (Qift) occupies the site.

Coquimbo Chile. Town in the Coquimbo province on Coquimbo Bay; port for La Serena 14 km (9 miles) NE. Pop. (1992) 122,872.

Market town. Trade in grain, fruit, minerals (chiefly copper). The bay provides winter quarters for the Chilean navy.

Coral Gables USA. Residential town and resort in Florida just SW of Miami. Pop. (1985) 44,000. Seat of the University of Miami (1925).

Coral Sea SW Pacific Ocean. Section of the SW Pacific between Australia (W) and Vanuatu and New Caledonia (E), containing the Great Barrier Reef. In World War II US naval aircraft won a vital battle here with the Japanese fleet (1942).

Corby England. Town in Northamptonshire 10 km (6 miles) N of Kettering. Pop. (1991) 53,044.

Manufactures steel, footwear, tubes and pipes.

Córdoba Argentina. Cap. of the Córdoba province on the Río Primero at a height of 420 m (1378 ft) 676 km (420 miles) NW of Buenos Aires. Pop. (1991) 1,179,067.

Commercial centre. Resort. Manufactures cars, tractors, textiles, cement and glass. Derives hydroelectric power from the great San Roque dam across the Río Primero above the city.

Founded 1573. Has many fine old buildings inc. a cathedral (17th/18th-cent.). Cultural centre; seat of a university (1613), the first in Argentina.

Córdoba Mexico. Market town in the Veracruz state in the Sierra Madre Oriental at a

height of 900 m (2952 ft) 96 km (60 miles)
WSW of Veracruz. Pop. (1990) 150,428.

In a coffee-growing region. Coffee-roasting and sugar-refining.

Córdoba (Cordova) Spain. 1. Province in Andalusia, divided by the Guadalquivir R. into the mountainous N (crossed by the Sierra Morena) and the fertile plain of the S. Area 13,718 sq km (5295 sq. miles). Pop. (1991) 751,699.

Mainly agricultural. Produces olives, fruit, cereals. Silver, lead, copper and coal mined. 2. Cap. of Córdoba province, an ancient typically Moorish city, on the Guadalquivir R. and on the S slopes of the Sierra de Córdoba. Pop. (1991) 300,229.

Industrial, commercial and tourist centre. Engineering, brewing, distilling. Manufactures textiles, pottery, leather and leather goods. Trade in cereals, olives and wine.

Colonized by the Romans 152 BC. In Moorish hands AD 711–1236 (and still has many narrow, twisting streets with fine Moorish houses). Became cap. of Moorish Spain 756; reached the peak of its fame in the 10th cent. The outstanding building is the *mesquita* (mosque), built in the 8th–10th cent., now a cathedral. Declined after conquest by Ferdinand III of Castile (1236). The production of goatskin leather (*cordovan*, cordwain) for which it was long famous has almost disappeared. Birthplace of the two Senecas, Lucan and Maimonides.

Corfe Castle England. Picturesque stone-built village in SE Dorset on the Isle of Purbeck 10 km (6 miles) SSW of Poole. Ruins of an ancient castle (destroyed by Cromwell) where Edward the Martyr was said to have been murdered (978). Edward II after his deposition was imprisoned here.

Corfu (Gr. **Kerkira**) Greece. 1. Ancient Corcyra; probably Homer's Scheria. Second largest and most beautiful of the Ionian Is., forming with small neighbouring islands, a *nome.* Area 641 sq km (246 sq. miles). Pop. (1991) 107,592. The island lies mainly off the coast of Epirus, but at its N end, where the Corfu Channel narrows, comes within

3 km (2 miles) of the Albanian coast. Mountainous in the N. Chief products olive oil, wine, citrus fruits. Settled *c.* 734 BC by Corinth; Corcyra and Corinth became rivals and fought the first recorded naval battle in Greek history (*c.* 664 BC). Under Venetian rule 1386–1797 and British 1815–64, being then ceded to Greece. 2. Cap. of Corfu *nome*, on the E coast of Corfu. Pop. (1985) 29,000.

Seaport. Exports olive oil and fruit. Industries inc. textile and soap manufacture, fishing and tourism.

Seat of Greek and Roman Catholic archbishops. The town, having been built within walls, is a maze of narrow, winding streets.

Corinth (Gr. **Korinthos**) Greece. Cap. of the Korinthia *nome*; port on the Gulf of Corinth near the W end of the 6-km (4-mile)-long Corinth Canal. Pop. (1981) 22,658.

Trade in wine and currants (which are supposed to have been named after it).

Founded 1858, when Old Corinth, 5 km (3 miles) SW, was destroyed by earthquake; itself destroyed by earthquake in 1928 and rebuilt. One of the wealthiest and most powerful of ancient Greek cities, guarded by its citadel or Acrocorinthus (575 m; 1886 ft). Excavations from 1896 onwards have revealed the *agora* (market-place), temple of Apollo, amphitheatre and other Greek and Roman remains. Probably founded *c.* 1350 BC. By the 7th cent. BC it had become a great commercial and industrial centre, famed for its pottery and metalwork and numbering Syracuse and Corfu among its colonies. Athenian help for Corcyra (Corfu) led Corinth to join forces with Sparta against Athens, long a formidable rival, in the Peloponnesian War (431–404 BC), but in the Corinthian War (395–387 BC) it combined with Athens, Thebes and Argos against Sparta. Became a member of the Achaean League 243 BC. In 146 BC it was plundered of its art treasures and destroyed by the Romans. Refounded by Julius Caesar 44 BC; it regained its commercial prosperity and the famous Isthmian Games at nearby Isthmia were restarted. Under the Turks (1458–1687 and 1715–

1822) it declined to an insignificant village and then finally passed to Greece.

Corinth Canal Greece. Ship canal 6 km (4 miles) long, constructed 1881–93, crossing the Isthmus of Corinth and joining the Gulf of Corinth (NW) to the Saronic Gulf (SE), thus separating the Peloponnese from the Greek mainland. Shortens the journey from the Adriatic to the Piraeus by 320 km (200 miles).

Cork (Corcaigh) Ireland. 1. County in the province of Munster in the SW, bordering on the Atlantic in the S; the largest county in Ireland. Area 7485 sq km (2890 sq. miles). Pop. (1986) 412,735. County town Cork. The deeply indented coastline extends from the Kenmare R. (W) to Youghal Harbour (E). Other inlets inc. Bantry Bay (around which is some of Ireland's loveliest scenery), Dunmanus Bay and Cork Harbour. Crossed more or less W–E by mountain ranges rising to over 600 m (1968 ft) in the Boggerah Mountains (W), between which are the fertile valleys of the Blackwater, Lee and Bandon rivers. Dairy farming. Potatoes and root crops grown. Chief towns Cork, Cóbh, Mallow, Youghal. 2. County town of Co. Cork, second largest city in Ireland, built on and around an island at the mouth of the R. Lee and at the head of Cork Harbour. Pop. (1991) 127,000. Seaport (though the largest vessels use Cóbh).

Exports dairy produce and cattle. Distilling, brewing, bacon-curing, motor-vehicle assembly. Manufactures tyres, woollen goods and fertilizers.

Protestant and Roman Catholic cathedrals. Seat of the University College of Cork, part of the National University. An 18th-cent. church, St Ann Shandon, with a parti-coloured steeple. A monastery was founded by St Finbar (Finnbarr) in the 6th or 7th cent. An Anglo–Norman settlement had been established by the 12th cent. Scene of landings by the pretenders Lambert Simnel (1487) and Perkin Warbeck (1497) and their brief acceptance as Yorkist kings of England: hence the cognomen 'the Rebel City'. Part of Spenser's *Faerie Queene* was written

nearby. Taken by Cromwell's forces (1649) and by Marlborough's (1690). Birthplace and burial-place of Francis Mahony (1804–66), author of *The Bells of Shandon*.

Corner Brook Canada. Town in W Newfoundland on the Humber R. near the mouth. Pop. (1991) 22,410.

One of the world's largest paper mills, producing newsprint for export. Iron foundries, cement works and gypsum mill.

Corniche France. Three highways on the Riviera, running S of the Maritime Alps between Nice and Menton. The Grande Corniche (built as a military road by Napoleon I 1806) ascends to over 500 m (1640 ft), the Moyenne Corniche links the intermediate towns; the Petite Corniche runs along the coast through Beaulieu and Monte Carlo.

Cornwall Canada. Industrial town and port in SE Ontario on the St Lawrence R. 85 km (53 miles) ESE of Ottawa. Pop. (1986) 46,425.

Manufactures textiles, paper and chemicals.

Linked by bridge (1934) with Rooseveltown (New York), USA.

Cornwall England. County in the extreme SW, bounded by the Atlantic (N and NW), the English Channel (S and SW) and Devon (E). Area (inc. the Scilly Isles) 3512 sq km (1356 sq. miles). Pop. (1994) 478,900. County town Bodmin. The southernmost point is Lizard Point; the most westerly is Land's End, 40 km (25 miles) WSW of which are the Scilly Isles. Much of the coast is rocky and picturesque; gaunt headlands are interspersed with bays and sheltered coves. Much of the interior consists of hills and moors; Bodmin Moor rises to 419 m (1374 ft) in Brown Willy. Chief rivers the Tamar, the Fowey, the Fal and the Camel. The scenic attractions and mild climate (which in places, e.g. the Scilly Isles, produces almost subtropical vegetation) have made it extremely popular with tourists. Seaside resorts inc. Falmouth, Newquay, Penzance, St Ives.

Fishing is still practised, though on a di-

Corsica

minished scale. Dairy-farming and the production of early vegetables and flowers are
important. Tin and copper mining (for which
the county was long famous) have practically
disappeared. By far the most valuable mineral
is china clay (kaolin). Granite and slate are
quarried. Chief towns Truro (administrative
centre), Camborne-Redruth, St Austell.

Coro Venezuela. Cap. of Falcón state
320 km (200 miles) WNW of Caracas. Pop.
(1990) 124,616. Linked by road and rail with
its port La Vela (11 km (7 miles) ENE).
Industrial and commercial centre. Manufactures cigars and soap. Trade in coffee and
maize.
Founded 1527.

Coromandel Coast India. The SE coast
on the Bay of Bengal between the Krishna
(Kistna) R. delta and Point Calimere (S);
it has no natural harbours and is severely
buffeted during the NE monsoon (October–
April). Site of earliest European settlements.
The name is probably derived from Cholam-
andalam, the land of the ancient Chola
dynasty.

Coronation Gulf Canada. An arm of the
Arctic Ocean, separating Victoria Island from
the mainland. Named (1821) by Franklin in
honour of the coronation of George IV.

Coronel Chile. Port in the Concepción
province 24 km (15 miles) SSW of Concep-
ción. Pop. (1985) 52,000.
In a coalmining area; the chief coaling
station on the Chilean coast. Flour-milling.
Manufactures soap.
Scene of a British naval defeat by the
German Admiral von Spee during World
War I (1914).

Coronel Oviedo Paraguay. Cap. of the
Caaguazú department 130 km (80 miles) E
of Asunción. Pop. (1990) 22,000.
Commercial centre. Sawmilling. Sugar-
refining.

Corpus Christi USA. Port in S Texas on
Corpus Christi Bay, connected by a deep-
water channel to the Gulf of Mexico. Pop.
(1990) 257,453.

Exports cotton, petroleum, sulphur and
fish. Oil-refining, cotton-ginning. Manufactures chemicals, cottonseed oil and cement.
Popular resort with excellent beaches. Industries developed rapidly after the discovery of
natural gas and then oil from 1913 onwards.

Corregidor Philippines. Fortified island at
the entrance to Manila Bay. During World
War II it was defended by the American
garrison against the Japanese (April–May
1942).

Corrèze France. Department formed from
the old province of Limousin in the NW
Massif Central, crossed in the N by the Monts
du Limousin and drained by the Corrèze,
the Vézère and the Dordogne rivers. Area
5860 sq km (2273 sq. miles). Pop. (1990)
238,000. Prefecture Tulle. Largely infertile.
Agriculture in the river valleys. Produces
cereals, fruit, vegetables, wine. Sheep and pig
rearing. Several hydroelectric plants. Chief
towns Brive, Tulle.

Corrèze River France. River 96 km (60
miles) long in the Corrèze department,
flowing SW past Tulle and Brive to the
Vézère R.

Corrib, Lough Ireland. Irregular-shaped
lake, mainly in Co. Galway, with a small part
in Co. Mayo. Area 176 sq km (68 sq. miles).
Drained to Galway Bay by the short R.
Corrib.

Corrientes Argentina. Cap. of the Corri-
entes province, port on the Paraná R. 40 km
(25 miles) below the confluence of the Alto
Paraná with the Paraguay R. Pop. (1991)
267,742. Linked by ferry with Barranqueras
on the opposite bank of the Paraná. Above
Corientes shallow-draught vessels are used.
Trade in agricultural products (cotton, rice).
Manufactures vegetable oils and textiles.
Sawmilling and tanning.
Seat of a college of the National University
of the Litoral (1922). Founded 1588.

Corsica (Fr. **Corse**) France. Island in the
Mediterranean Sea immediately N of Sardinia, from which it is separated by the Strait

of Bonifacio; region of France, it is divided into two departments: Corse-du-Sud with prefecture Ajaccio and Haute-Corse with prefecture Bastia. Area 8681 sq km (3367 sq. miles). Pop. (1993) 253,200. Regional cap. Ajaccio. The interior is mountainous (with plains only along the E coast), rising to 2707 m (8879 ft) in Monte Cinto. The rocky W coast has many headlands and gulfs. Over the lower mountain slopes is spread a tangled undergrowth of shrubs (Fr. *maquis*, Italian *macchio*) which used to provide cover for bandits.

It has practically no industry and farming is primitive. The Region is given special economic status. Sheep and goats raised in large numbers. Produces olives, vines, citrus fruits and chestnuts. Tourism constitutes a substantial source of income to islanders. The seaports Ajaccio and Bastia are the largest towns. Exports olive oil, wine and fruits.

Belongs geographically and historically, more to Italy than to France; outside the towns a dialect akin to Italian is spoken. Held in turn by the Etruscans, the Carthaginians, the Romans, the Vandals and the Saracens. Fell to Pisa in the 11th cent. and to Genoa in the 14th. Ceded to France 1768. Under French rule the long-practised brigandage and the vendetta (blood feud) were gradually suppressed.

Cortona Italy. Town in Arezzo province in Tuscany 23 km (14 miles) SSE of Arezzo, overlooking the Val di Chiana and L. Trasimeno. Pop. (1981) 22,281. Etruscan and Roman remains. Paintings by Luca Signorelli in the cathedral. The 13th-cent. palace houses the museum of the Etruscan Academy (founded 1726).

Corumbá Brazil. Market town and river port in the Mato Grosso state, on the Paraguay R. Pop. (1970) 48,600. Linked by rail with São Paulo and Santa Cruz (Bolivia).

Exports the products of a large area, chiefly dried beef and hides and skins.

Corunna (La Coruña) Spain. 1. Province in Galicia, bounded on the N and W by the Atlantic. Area 7876 sq km (3051 sq. miles).

Pop. (1991) 1,088,505. The rocky coastline has many deep inlets (rías). The heaviest rainfall in Spain. Main occupations fishing, stock-rearing and the cultivation of cereals, vegetables and fruit. 2. Cap. of Corunna province, Atlantic seaport on Corunna Bay. Pop. (1991) 245,549.

Important sardine-fishing and canning centre. Manufactures cigars, cotton goods and glassware.

To the NW is the 47-m (154-ft) Roman Tower of Hercules, now a lighthouse. Scene of the sailing of the Spanish Armada (1588), of Drake's burning of the city (1598) and of the Peninsular War battle in which Sir John Moore was killed (1809). Burial-place of Moore (the old-town San Carlos gardens).

Corwen Wales. Market town and angling resort in Denbighshire on the R. Dee at the foot of the Berwyn Mountains. Pop. (1985) 3000. Headquarters of Owen Glendower before the battle of Shrewsbury (1403).

Cos (Gr. **Kos**) Greece. 1. Island in the Aegean Sea, the second largest of the Dodecanese, separated from the Bodrum peninsula (Turkey) by the narrow Cos Channel. Area 282 sq km (109 sq. miles). Pop. (1981) 21,000. Mainly low-lying and fertile, producing cereals, olive oil, fruits and wine. Cos lettuce originally grown here. It has frequently suffered from earthquakes, being severely damaged in 1933. In ancient times it won fame as a literary and medical centre: birthplace of Hippocrates (c. 460 BC). 2. Cap. of Cos on the NE coast. Pop. (1981) 8000.

Trade in agricultural products.

Castle built by the Knights of St John. In the market square is a famous old plane tree under which Hippocrates is said to have taught.

Coseley England. Industrial town in West Midlands 5 km (3 miles) SSE of Wolverhampton in the Black Country. Metalworking. Manufactures machinery.

Cosenza Italy. Ancient Consentia. Cap. of Cosenza province in Calabria on the Crati R. Pop. (1990) 104,500.

Market town and road junction in a region

producing figs and other fruits. Manufactures furniture and textiles.

Cathedral (12th-cent.).

Costa Brava Spain. Region in Catalonia noted for tourism.

Costa del Sol Spain. Region on the Málaga coast noted for tourism.

Costa Mesa USA. Town in California 51 km (32 miles) SE of Los Angeles. Pop. (1970) 72,660.

Manufactures fibreglass products and electronic equipment.

Costa Rica. Republic of Central America. On an isthmus between the Caribbean Sea and the Pacific Ocean, bounded on the N by Nicaragua and Panama to the SE. Area 50,100 sq km (19,730 sq. miles). Pop. (1995) 3,344,000 (44 per cent urban). Life expectancy, 72 years male, 78 female. Cap. San José. Other cities Desamparados, Limón, Alajuela and Puntarenas. Currency: Costa Rican colón = 100 céntimos. A mountainous country with high volcanoes, now dormant, rising to over 3000 m (9840 ft). It has suffered several severe earthquakes. Two-thirds of the pop. live in the Meseta Central, an upland region with a fertile volcanic soil. The climate is tropical, with a small range of temperature and abundant rains. Land use: forested 32 per cent, meadows and pastures 46 per cent, agricultural and under permanent cultivation 10 per cent. Roman Catholicism is the state religion but there is entire religious liberty. Spanish is the official lang. and about 87 per cent of the pop. is white, mestizo 7 per cent, black/mulatto 3 per cent, East Asian 2 per cent, Amerindian 1 per cent.

Forests yield balsa, sandalwood, mahogany, rosewood and cedar. Agriculture is the principal industry, largely dependent on coffee, the chief crop of the uplands, which is the principal export. Bananas are an important export, and cacao and sugar-cane are also grown in the coastal plains. The manufactured goods are food products, textiles, fertilizers, pharmaceuticals, furniture, cement and tyres.

Columbus discovered the Caribbean coast on his last voyage (1502) and named it the Rich Coast (Costa Rica), possibly because of the gold ornaments of the natives. As part of Guatemala, the country was under Spanish rule until 1821 and a member of the Central American Federation 1823–38. The pop. is well integrated and enjoys stable government. The army was abolished in 1948. There is a 57-member unicameral Legislative Assembly. The country is divided administratively into seven provinces.

Côte d'Argent France. Holiday resort area at the S end of the Bay of Biscay, between Biarritz and the mouth of the Adour R.

Côte d'Azur France. The Mediterranean coast of the French Riviera, so named because of the deep blue of the sea. Inc. the resorts of Antibes, Cannes, Juan-les-Pins, Menton, Monte Carlo (in Monaco), Nice and Villefranche.

Côte d'Ivoire. Republic in W Africa, bounded by Mali and Burkina Faso in the N, Ghana in the E, Guinea and Liberia in the W and the Gulf of Guinea in the S. Area 322,463 sq km (122,470 sq. miles). Pop. (1995) 14,253,000 (42 per cent urban). Life expectancy, 54 years male, 57 female. Cap. Yamoussoukro. Seat of government, Abidjan. Other cities Bouaké, Daloa, Korhogo. Currency: CFA franc = 100 centimes. In the S the dense tropical rainforest, which extends 300 km (240 miles) from W–E and is 100 km (80 miles) wide at its centre, is bordered by a zone of lagoons and sandbars. In the centre the forest gives way to lush savannah interspersed with clumps of trees. In the northern zone the savannah is much sparser and this leads to the great plains of Mali and Burkina Faso. The Bandama, Comoe and Sassandra rivers, impeded by rapids, are of little value for navigation. It has a hot humid climate with heavy rainfall affected by the distance from the sea. Land use: forested 22 per cent, pasture 41 per cent and agricultural 12 per cent. The official lang. is French. There are about 60 ethnic groups, the principal being the Baule (23 per cent), the Bete (18 per cent) and the Senufo (15 per cent). Of believers 38 per cent are Muslim, mainly in the N, and Christian (mainly Roman Catholic) 21 per cent in the S. Traditional animist beliefs are also practised by 17 per cent.

The economic development of the country depends mainly on agriculture, which provides a livelihood for more than 64 per cent of the pop. and provides 53 per cent of the exports. Tropical hardwoods are an important export and a reafforestation programme has been launched, inc. the planting of new species and the protection of existing forests. Deep-sea fishing fleet comprises trawlers and sardine boats, and subsistence fishing is also practised. The offshore oilfields at Grand-Bassam and Jacqueville are beginning to make the country self-sufficient; there are huge reserves of natural gas and a growing petrochemical industry. Food-processing accounts for 30 per cent of all industrial production. There are rice and flour mills, coffee and cocoa processing plants, fish, sardine and pineapple canning plants. In addition textiles, footwear and electrical products are manufactured. Other exports inc. bananas, cacao, coffee and petroleum products. Food crops are cassava, maize, millet, rice and yams. Cotton is cultivated in the savannah (N). Port Bouet (outport of Abidjan) is linked by rail with the interior, esp. Bouaké and with Bobo-Dioulasso and Ouagadougou in Burkina Faso.

Little is known of the early history of the Ivory Coast, although Europeans traded with southern areas for gold, slaves, ivory and palm oil from the 15th cent. Assinie and Grand Bassam, on the coast, were ceded to France in 1842, but the French did not occupy the territory until 1882. It became a colony and was incorporated into French West Africa 1904. It opted to become a member of the French Community in 1958 and became fully independent in 1960.

Côte d'Or France. Department in Burgundy. Area 8765 sq km (3392 sq. miles). Pop. (1990) 493,900. Prefecture Dijon. Crossed by the S part of the Plateau de Langres, which separates the basins of the Saône and Seine

(linked by the Burgundy Canal), and by the Côte d'Or (range of hills), after which the department is named. On the E slopes are the famous vineyards of Beaune, Chambertin, Montrachet, Nuits St Georges. Cereals and vegetables are also cultivated; cattle and sheep raised. A network of railways converges on Dijon. Beaune is an important centre of the wine trade.

Cotentin France. Peninsula forming the N part of the Manche department. Cherbourg, the chief town and only good seaport, is on the N coast. Noted for stock-rearing, dairy-farming and apple-growing. The most northerly points are Cap La Hague (NW) and Barfleur Point (NE).

Côtes d'Armor France. Department in Brittany on the English Channel, with a broken coastline and many small offshore islands. Area 6878 sq km (2786 sq. miles). Pop. (1990) 538,395. Prefecture St Brieuc. Mainly low-lying. Produces cider apples, hemp and cereals. Chief towns St Brieuc, Dinan, Guingamp and Lannion.

Cotonou Benin. Chief seaport and commercial centre 32 km (20 miles) WSW of Porto Novo on a narrow sandy spit between L. Lokoué (a lagoon) and the sea. Pop. (1992) 533,212. Connected by rail with Parakou and Pobé (in the interior). Exports agricultural products, esp. palm oil and kernels, groundnuts. Manufactures vegetable oils and soap.

Cotopaxi Ecuador. World's highest active volcano (5896 m; 19,339 ft) in the Andes 48 km (30 miles) SSE of Quito. An almost symmetrical snow-capped cone. Frequently active, causing devastation in the surrounding settlements. First climbed by Reiss (1872).

Cotswold Hills England. Range of hills, mainly in Gloucestershire, extending SSW–NNE from Bath to Chipping Campden at an average height of 150–180 m (492–590 ft), rising to 330 m (1082 ft) in Cleeve Cloud near Cheltenham. The Severn–Thames watershed. Many sheep are reared. Much visited for the beautiful villages (e.g. Bourton-on-the-Water, Burford, Painswick) built of the local limestone. The fortunes made from wool in the 14th-17th cent. helped to pay for some of the magnificent churches.

Cottbus (Kottbus) Germany. Industrial town in the Cottbus district on the Spree R. 109 km (68 miles) SE of Berlin. Pop. (1990) 124,900.

Manufactures woollen goods, carpets, machinery and soap.

Passed to Brandenburg in 1462 and for a short time (1807–13) belonged to Saxony.

Coulsdon and Purley England. Former residential urban district in NE Surrey 21 km (13 miles) S of London, which it serves as dormitory suburb; from 1965 part of the London borough of Croydon.

Council Bluffs USA. Town in SW Iowa at the foot of the bluffs along the Missouri R. opposite Omaha (Nebraska). Pop. (1990) 54,315. Railway and commercial centre.

Railway workshops. Grain elevators. Manufactures agricultural implements, railway equipment, batteries and paper.

Coupar-Angus Scotland. Market town in Perth and Kinross on the R. Isla 18 km (11 miles) NNE of Perth; to be distinguished from Cupar in Fife. Pop. (1971) 1964. Manufactures linen. Part of it was formerly in Angus.

Courbevoie France. Industrial and residential suburb in NW Paris in the Hauts-de-Seine department on the Seine R. Pop. (1968) 57,998. Manufactures cars, perfumes, cosmetics and soap.

Courland (Ger. **Kurland**, Lettish **Kurzeme**) Latvia. Region and former duchy between the Gulf of Riga and the Lithuanian border. Partly wooded but mainly agricultural, producing cereals, flax and potatoes. Inhabited originally by the Curi, a powerful, warlike people in the 10th–11th cent. Later a duchy under Polish sovereignty 1561–1795. It was then ceded to Russia; became part of independent Latvia in 1920 (except for a small area given to Lithuania), being

divided into two provinces, Kurzeme (W) and Zemgale (E). In 1940 it returned to Russia as part of the Latvian Soviet Socialist Republic.

Courland Lagoon ➤KURISCHES HAFF.

Courtrai (Flemish **Kortrijk**) Belgium. Town in the W Flanders province on the Lys R. 76 km (47 miles) W of Brussels. Pop. (1993) 76,264.

Important textile centre (linen, cotton, rayon, nylon, lace).

In the 12th/13th-cent. Church of Notre Dame is Van Dyck's *Erection of the Cross*. Has a 16th-cent. Gothic town hall and the Broelbrug, an old bridge with 15th-cent. towers. Reached its peak of prosperity in the Middle Ages, when the pop. was probably 200,000. Scene of the defeat of a French army by the burghers of Ghent and Bruges in the 'Battle of the Spurs' (so called because the French fled) in 1302.

Coutances France. Town in the Manche department 68 km (42 miles) S of Cherbourg on the Cotentin peninsula. Pop. (1968) 8599.

Market town. Trade in agricultural produce. Textile and leather industries.

Fine 13th-cent. Gothic cathedral, damaged in World War II.

Coventry England. City in West Midlands 26 km (16 miles) ESE of Birmingham. Pop. (1991) 299,316.

A leading centre of the motor-car industry, which developed from bicycle manufacture. Also produces machinery, aircraft engines, hosiery, electrical equipment.

Grew up round a Benedictine monastery, founded in the 11th cent. by Leofric, husband of Lady Godiva. In the 13th–17th cent. the principal industry was weaving, with important trade in wool and cloth. Suffered severely from air raids during World War II; the cathedral church, St Michael, was destroyed (1940) except for the 90 m (303 ft) spire and some outside walls, and the early 15th-cent. St Mary's Hall (built for the local trade guilds) and the 16th-cent. half-timbered Ford's Hospital were damaged. After the war the devastated city centre was replanned and rebuilt, with a shopping precinct, the Belgrade Theatre, the Hotel Leofric and other noteworthy buildings; the magnificent but highly controversial new cathedral, containing works by Epstein, Graham Sutherland and retaining the ruins of the old cathedral church as a memorial shrine, was consecrated in 1962.

Covington USA. Industrial town in Kentucky on the Ohio R., connected with Cincinnati by a suspension bridge (1866). Pop. (1990) 43,264.

Manufactures X-ray equipment, tobacco products, machine-tools, tiles, bricks and paper.

Cowdenbeath Scotland. Town in S Fife 8 km (5 miles) NE of Dunfermline. Pop. (1991) 12,126.

Cowes England. Town on the N coast of the Isle of Wight on both banks of the estuary of the R. Medina (West Cowes, East Cowes). Pop. (1991) 16,335.

Port. Famous yachting and yacht-building centre. Manufactures hovercraft. Headquarters of the Royal Yacht Squadron (founded 1812), the scene of the annual 'Cowes Week' (August).

In East Cowes is Osborne House, built in Palladian style for Queen Victoria (1845). Scene of the sailing of the founders of Maryland, USA (1633).

Cowley England. Suburb of Oxford where William Morris (later Lord Nuffield) began the manufacture of motor cars on the production-line system. Now an important unit in the UK automobile industry. Headquarters of the Cowley Fathers, an Anglican religious community (1865).

Cox's Bazar Bangladesh. Resort and seaport in Chi Hagung region. Pop. (1985) 30,000. Manufactures cigars.

Cracow (Polish **Kraków**) Poland. Cap. of Kraków voivodeship, Poland's third largest city, on the Vistula R. 257 km (160 miles) SSW of Warsaw. Pop. (1989) 745,568.

Railway junction. Commercial and industrial centre. Trade in salt, timber, cattle, agri-cultural produce. Manufactures iron and steel (at Nova Huta), railway rolling-stock, agricultural machinery, chemicals, clothing, food and tobacco products.

It has long been a leading centre of Polish culture; the famous Jagiellonian University, at which Copernicus was a student, was founded in 1364 – one of the oldest in Europe. Renowned for its many fine buildings and historic monuments. On the Wawel, a hill just SW of the old town, are the 14th-cent. cathedral, which contains the tombs of Polish kings and of Kosciuszko, Mickiewicz and Pilsudski, and the royal castle, begun in the 12th cent. and enlarged in the 16th. The 13th/14th-cent. Church of Our Lady has a magnificent triptych by Veit Stoss; nearby is the 14th-cent. frequently restored Cloth Hall. Probably founded early in the 8th cent. Polish cap. 1305–1609. At the Third Partition (1795) it passed to Austria; became part of the duchy of Warsaw (1809) and the republic of Cracow (1815); was incorporated in Austria (1846) and returned to Poland (1918).

Cradock South Africa. Town in the Cape Province on the Great Fish R. 209 km (130 miles) N of Port Elizabeth. Pop. (1980) 39,160.

Market town in a rich sheep-farming district. 5 km (3 miles) N are hot sulphur springs. The Mountain Zebra National Park is nearby.

Founded 1814. Named after Sir John Cradock, Governor of the Cape (1811–13). Home and burial-place of Olive Schreiner, South African author.

Craigavon Northern Ireland. Town in NE Co. Armagh, formed in 1967 from the rural district of Lurgan. Pop. (1991) 9201.

Crail Scotland. Small town in E Fife near the mouth of the Firth of Forth 3 km (2 miles) W of Fife Ness. Pop. (1991) 1449. Seaside resort. Fishing.

Craiova Romania. Ancient Castra Nova. Cap. of the Dolj district on the Kiu R. in Walachia 193 km (120 miles) W of Bucharest. Pop. (1992) 303,500.

Industrial town. Manufactures textiles, machinery, leather goods and chemicals. Food-processing.

Cramlington England. 'New town' in Northumberland with projected pop. of 60,000. Pop. (1991) 26,238.

Industries inc. pharmaceuticals and toiletries, textiles, industrial rubber hosing, adhesive stickers and razor blades.

Cranbrook England. Market town in Kent 19 km (12 miles) S of Maidstone. Pop. (1991) 3522.

Agricultural centre of the Kent Weald. Trade in hops and fruit.

From the 14th to the 17th cent. had a flourishing broadcloth industry, introduced from Flanders. Has the largest working windmill in England.

Cranston USA. Industrial town in Rhode Island on the Pawtuxet R. just S of Providence. Pop. (1990) 71,992.

Manufactures textiles, machinery, rubber products and chemicals.

Named after Samuel Cranston, Governor of Rhode Island (1698–1727).

Cranwell England. Village in Lincolnshire 18 km (11 miles) NE of Grantham. Site of the Royal Air Force College (1920).

Crawley England. Town in West Sussex 11 km (7 miles) NE of Horsham. Created a 'new town' in 1956. Pop. (1991) 88,203.

Light engineering. Manufactures furniture, electronic equipment, plastics and pharmaceuticals.

Crécy (Crécy-en-Ponthieu) France. Village in the Somme department 16 km (10 miles) NNE of Abbeville. Scene of the victory of Edward III of England over the French (1346).

Crediton England. Market town in Devon 11 km (7 miles) NW of Exeter on the R. Creedy. Pop. (1991) 8142.

Engineering. Manufactures cider and confectionery.

Traditionally the birthplace of St Boniface (680–754).

Crema Italy. Market town in the Cremona province in Lombardy 39 km (24 miles) NW of Cremona. Pop. (1981) 34,610. Manufactures textiles. Cathedral (13th/14th-cent.).

Cremona Italy. Cap. of Cremona province in Lombardy on the Po R. 80 km (50 miles) SE of Milan. Pop. (1990) 81,000.

Industrial and commercial centre for the fertile Po valley. Manufactures confectionery, dairy products (cheese, butter), pasta, silk and musical instruments.

Impressive main square with magnificent cathedral and octagonal baptistery (12th-cent.) and the 13th-cent. Torrazzo (the highest campanile in Italy). Founded by the Romans c. 220 BC. Famous in the 16th–18th cent. for violins, made by the Amati, Guarnieri and Stradivari. Birthplace of the composer Claudio Monteverdi (1567–1643).

Cres Yugoslavia. Island in the Gulf of Kvarner on the Adriatic Sea SSW of Rijeka. Area 337 sq km (130 sq. miles). Pop. (1985) 3500. Chief village and principal port Cres. Main occupations agriculture, sheep-farming and fishing. Belonged to Austria–Hungary till 1919 and to Italy 1919–47.

Crete (Gr. **Kríti**) Greece. Largest island of Greece and fourth largest island in the Mediterranean Sea, to the S of the Aegean Sea. Area 8331 sq km (3217 sq. miles). Pop. (1991) 540,054. Cap. Heraklion. Mostly mountainous, rising to over 2400 m (7872 ft) in Mt Ida (Psiloríti) in the centre. The N coast is deeply indented. The mountain slopes have been almost denuded of forests. In the limited plains and valleys large number of olive trees are grown. Main products olive oil, citrus fruits, wine. Sheep and goats raised.

Divided administratively (with neighbouring small islands) into the four *nomes* of Canea, Iráklion, Lasíthi, Rethymnon. Chief towns Canea (Khanía), Candia (Iráklion). Archaeological discoveries have revealed that Crete was the home of the Minoan civilization, one of the world's oldest: development has been traced c. 3400–1100 BC. The palace at Knossos in particular yields information of immense value. The island played an insignificant part in Greek history. Fell to Rome (67 BC), Byzantium (AD 395), the Muslims (826), the Venetians (1204) and the Turks (1669). After a number of rebellions in the 19th cent. it was finally united with Greece in 1912. Taken by the Germans in the first airborne invasion of World War II (1941).

Creuse France. Department comprising most of the Marche and parts of the Berry and other provinces, in the NW corner of the Massif Central. Area 5559 sq km (2164 sq. miles). Pop. (1990) 131,300. Prefecture Guéret. In the S is the Plateau de Millevaches. Main river the Creuse. The soil is thin and the climate inhospitable. Agriculture (cereals, potatoes) limited to the valleys. Livestock reared on the uplands. Chief towns Guéret and Aubusson.

Creuse River France. River 240 km (150 miles) long, rising in the Plateau de Millevaches, flowing NNW and joining the Vienne R. A famous gorge in the upper course.

Crewe England. Town and important railway junction in Cheshire 32 km (20 miles) ESE of Chester. Pop. (1991) 63,351.
Manufactures cars, chemicals, clothing, pharmaceuticals, electronics and has an eco-business park.

Crewkerne England. Market town in S Somerset 27 km (17 miles) SE of Taunton. Pop. (1991) 7142. Manufactures leather goods and textiles. A 15th-cent. church; 17th-cent. almshouses.

Criccieth Wales. Seaside resort in Gwynedd on the S coast of the Lleyn peninsula (Cardigan Bay). Pop. (1991) 1720. Home and burial-place of David Lloyd George, statesman (1863–1945).

Crieff Scotland. Town on the R. Earn in Perth and Kinross 24 km (15 miles) W of Perth. Pop. (1991) 6023. Health resort. Whisky-distilling and tanning.
An ancient market cross with runic carving. Famous before 1770 for cattle fairs.

Crimea (Krym) Ukraine. Peninsula 338 km (210 miles) long W–E and 193 km (120 miles) N–S on the N side of the Black Sea, joined to the mainland by the narrow Perekop isthmus. Area 25,589 sq km (9880 sq. miles). Pop. (1991) 2,549,800. Cap. Simferopol. To the NE is the shallow Sivash lagoon, separated from the Sea of Azov by the long, sandy Arabat spit or tongue. To the E is the Kerch strait and beyond it the Taman peninsula. Most of the Crimea is arid but generally fertile steppe, drained by the Salgir R. and other intermittent streams, with many small salt lakes. Wheat and cotton cultivated. Mountains extend SW–NE parallel to the S coast and a few miles inland. In contrast to the dusty summers and frosty winters of the steppe, the coastal climate is Mediterranean; the region is called the Russian Riviera and is an important tourist area, centred on Yalta. Here vines, fruits and tobacco are grown. Fisheries around all the coasts. Metallurgical industry is based on the rich iron-ore deposits of Kerch. Sevastopol is the chief seaport and a naval base.

Colonized in turn by the Scythians and the Greeks, it became subject to Rome and later was overrun by the Goths, the Huns and the Khazars. Conquered by the Turks (1475) and under Turkish rule until annexed by Russia (1783). The W Crimea was the scene of the Crimean War (1854–6) in which Britain, France and Turkey were allied against Russia. After the Bolshevik revolution (1917) the Crimean Autonomous Soviet Socialist Republic was formed (within the Russian Soviet Federal Socialist Republic) in 1921. Collaboration of some of the pop. with the Germans during World War II caused subsequent down-grading to the status of a region (1946), transferred to the Ukrainian Soviet Socialist Republic in 1954. In 1995 Parliament adopted a new Constitution defining the Crimea as 'an autonomous republic forming an integral part of Ukraine'. The majority would prefer union with Russia. The Yalta Conference between Roosevelt, Churchill and Stalin took place at Livadia (near Yalta) in 1945.

Crimmitschau Germany. Industrial town

in Saxony 40 km (25 miles) W of Chemnitz. Pop. (1990) 24,000.

Manufactures textiles and textile machinery.

Crna Gora ➤MONTENEGRO.

Croagh Patrick Ireland. Cone-shaped mountain (766 m; 2512 ft) in Co. Mayo on the S shore of Clew Bay. Traditionally the spot where St Patrick first preached. Now a notable place of annual pilgrimage on the last Sunday in July.

Croatia. Republic in SE Europe bounded in the N by Slovenia and Hungary, in the E by Yugoslavia and Bosnia–Hercegovina and SW by the Adriatic. Area 56,691 sq km (21,889 sq. miles). Pop. (1995) 4,495,000 (51 per cent urban). Life expectancy, 66 years male, 75 female. Cap. Zagreb. Other cities Split, Rijeka, Osijek and Zadar. Currency: Kuna = 100 lipa. It has many islands (Krk, Cres, Brač, Korčula) along the coast. Mountainous and barren in the SW (Dinaric Alps). Much lower and more fertile in the NE. Inland Croatia has a central European type of climate with cold winters and hot summers, but the Adriatic coastal region experiences a Mediterranean climate. Land use: forested 37 per cent, pasture 19 per cent, agricultural 23 per cent. The official lang. is Croatian and 77 per cent of the pop. is Roman Catholic, 11 per cent Eastern Orthodox and 1 per cent Muslim. About 81 per cent are Croats, 12 per cent Serbs and 1 per cent Bosnian.

The country is mainly agricultural and produces cereals, fruits and vegetables. It manufactures crude steel, cement, cotton, cloth, woollen yarn, wine and beer. It has important oilfields. Tourism is important. Fifty per cent of Croatia's exports are foodstuffs.

The country was settled by the Croats in the 7th cent. It was conquered by Hungary in 1091 and enjoyed some degree of autonomy until the creation of Yugoslavia in 1918 when it became the province of Croatia–Slavonia. It became the People's Republic of Croatia in 1946. In 1991 in a referendum Croatia voted to become a sovereign independent state. The Serbian area wanted a union with Serbia and there followed a period of conflict; in 1991 a UN peacekeeping mission arrived and a ceasefire was arranged in 1992. There is a bicameral Parliament with a 68-member House of Counties and a 127-member House of Representatives.

Crocodile River ➤LIMPOPO RIVER.

Cromarty ➤ROSS AND CROMARTY.

Cromer England. Seaside resort in Norfolk on the North Sea 34 km (21 miles) N of Norwich. Pop. (1991) 7042. Protected by a sea wall from marine erosion, which encroached on the cliffs for many cent. The 15th-cent. Perpendicular Church of St Peter and St Paul has a 48-m (157-ft) tower.

Crompton England. Industrial town in Greater Manchester, a suburb of Oldham. Pop. (1971) 17,027. Textile mills.

Crook and Willington England. Town in Durham 13 km (8 miles) SW of Durham. Pop. (1991) 8246. Manufactures machinery and firebricks.

Crosby England. Residential suburb of Liverpool in Merseyside, just NW of Bootle. Pop. (1991) 52,869.

Cross Fell England. Highest mountain (894 m; 2932 ft) in the Pennines in E Cumbria 18 km (11 miles) ENE of Penrith.

Crotone Italy. Ancient Crotona. Town in the Catanzaro province in Calabria on the Gulf of Taranto. Pop. (1981) 58,281.

Important chemical works and zinc-smelter, drawing power from hydroelectric plants in the La Sila mountains.

Founded (710 BC) by the Achaeans. Became a wealthy and powerful city. The inhabitants (esp. Milo) won fame at the Olympic Games. Seat of the school established by Pythagoras 540–530 BC.

Croton River USA. River 96 km (60 miles) long in New York, flowing generally SW to join the Hudson R. at Croton Point. An important source of water supply for New

York City since 1842; the water of the Croton R. reservoirs is carried by the two Croton Aqueducts.

Crouch River England. River 39 km (24 miles) long, rising near Brentwood in Essex, flowing E past Burnham-on-Crouch to enter the North Sea at Foulness Point. The estuary is a celebrated yachting centre.

Crowborough England. Market town in NE Sussex 11 km (7 miles) SW of Tunbridge Wells near Crowborough Beacon (242 m, 794 ft, the highest point in Ashdown Forest). Pop. (1971) 11,540.

Crowland (Croyland) England. Market town in S Lincolnshire on the R. Welland 11 km (7 miles) NNE of Peterborough. Pop. (1991) 3172. Ruins of a Benedictine abbey, founded in the 8th cent. by King Aethelbald and restored in the 12th; the restored N aisle is used as the parish church. A 14th-cent. triangular bridge.

Crow's Nest Pass Canada. Pass 1357 m (4451 ft) high in the Rocky Mountains on the border of Alberta and British Columbia, through which runs a branch line of the Canadian Pacific Railway. The name is a translation of the Cree Indian name.

Croydon England. London borough (1965) comprising the former county borough of Croydon and the former urban district of Coulsdon and Purley (Surrey). Pop. (1994) 326,800. Chiefly residential.

Manufactures clocks, pharmaceutical products and foodstuffs. As London's first airport, Croydon was superseded by Northolt.

Site of a palace of the Archbishops of Canterbury from the Conquest till 1780; the hall and chapel are used as a girls' school. The Whitgift Grammar School and 'hospital' (almshouses) were founded in the late 16th cent. by Archbishop Whitgift (1530–1604).

Croyland ➤CROWLAND.

Crozet Islands Indian Ocean. Archipelago in the SW Indian Ocean 2400 km (1500 miles) ESE of Port Elizabeth, consisting of 5 larger and 15 smaller islands in two groups. Area 300 sq km (116 sq. miles). Mountainous and virtually uninhabited. Discovered 1772; annexed for France. A meteorological station was set up on Possession Island in 1964. From 1955 part of the French Southern and Antarctic Territories.

Csongrád Hungary. Market town in the Csongrád county at the confluence of the Tisza and the Körös rivers. Pop. (1984) 22,000. Flour-milling and sawmilling.

Ctesiphon Iraq. Ancient city on the Tigris R. 32 km (20 miles) SE of Baghdad. Famous for the remains of the great vaulted hall of the Sassanian palace. Became cap. of the Sassanian empire in the 2nd cent. but was captured and plundered by the Arabs in 637. Scene of a battle between the British and the Turks in World War I (1915).

Cuba. Island republic, the largest and most W of the West Indies, at the entrance to the Gulf of Mexico about 135 miles S of the tip of Florida, USA. It inc. the Isle of Youth (formerly Pines) and some 1600 small isles (cays). Area 110,861 sq km (42,804 sq. miles). Pop. (1995) 11,068,000 (73 per cent urban). Life expectancy, 74 years male, 78 female. Cap. Havana. Other cities Santiago de Cuba, Camagüey, Holguín and Guantánamo. Currency: Peso = 100 centavos. Cuba is mainly flat or gently undulating; in the Sierra Maestra range (SE) the Pico Turquino rises to 2005 m (6576 ft) and near the centre is the Sierra de Trinidad. The N coast, largely steep and rocky with numerous coral reefs and small islands, is washed by the Atlantic and the S coast, chiefly low and swampy, by the Caribbean. Off the SW coast is the Isle of Youth (area, 3056 sq km; 1180 sq. miles). There are many coastal inlets which provide sheltered harbours. The climate is subtropical, with a small seasonal variation. Hurricanes are likely to occur between June and November. Land use: forested 24 per cent, meadows and pastures 27 per cent, agricultural and under permanent cultivation 30 per cent. Approximately 51 per cent are of mixed race, 57 per cent white and 11 per cent black. About 40 per cent are Roman Catholic, Protestant 3 per cent and non-religious 49 per cent. The official lang. is Spanish.

The main crop is sugar, which with by-products earns 63 per cent of Cuba's foreign exchange. Other exports are metallic ores, tobacco (esp. cigars), pineapples, bananas, citrus fruits. Industries are sugar-refining, rum-distilling, sisal and tobacco processing. All industrial enterprises are state-controlled and a wide mixture of manufactures are produced for home consumption. Tourism is the largest foreign exchange earner. Political events completely changed the direction of Cuban foreign trade: in 1958 about 70 per cent of exports and imports were destined for and came from the USA, but this trade rapidly declined, and by 1964 86 per cent of foreign trade was with the Communist countries, chiefly the USSR and China. In 1994 Russia took 22 per cent of exports, Canada 12 per cent, China 9 per cent, The Netherlands 7 per cent, Spain 6 per cent, Algeria and Japan 5 per cent.

Discovered in 1492 by Columbus and by 1511 it had been settled by Spain. In the 18th cent. it became the haunt of buccaneers. It remained Spanish till the Spanish–American War (1898); after a short occupation by US forces it became independent in 1902, but remained closely linked with the USA. The revolutionary movement against the Batista dictatorship began in 1953 led by Fidel Castro and achieved power in 1959. Under the Castro regime Cuba broke away and developed close ties with the USSR. Emigrés made an unsuccessful invasion at the Bay of Pigs in 1961. The establishment of missile bases (1962) led to a critical confrontation between the USA and the USSR, and for a time Cuba was blockaded by the US navy. In 1990 the USSR provided 66 per cent of imports and took 81 per cent of exports. The loss of this trade has caused economic hardship since 1990. The USA, however, has continued to maintain her naval base at Guantánamo. Cuba is divided administratively into 14 provinces and a special municipality of the Isle of Youth.

Cúcuta (officially **San José de Cúcuta**) Colombia. Cap. of the Norte de Santander department, on the Pan-American Highway (Bogotá–Caracas) 16 km (10 miles) from the Venezuela frontier. Pop. (1992) 450,318.

Commercial centre. Large trade in coffee. Coffee-roasting. Manufactures textiles and soap.

Founded 1734. Used by Bolívar as his base for the march on Caracas. Rebuilt after destruction by earthquake (1875).

Cuddalore India. Seaport on the Coromandel coast in Tamil Nadu 160 km (100 miles) SSW of Madras. Pop. (1991) 144,561.

Exports groundnuts, cotton goods. Weaving and dyeing.

Passed from the French to the British 1785.

Cuenca Ecuador. Cap. of the Azuay province 129 km (80 miles) SE of Guayaquil in a fertile basin at a height of 2590 m (8495 ft). Pop. (1990) 194,981.

Trade in cinchona bark, sugar-cane and cereals. Flour-milling. Manufactures tyres, Panama hats, textiles and leather.

University (1868). Founded 1557. A town of cobbled streets and old colonial buildings.

Cuenca Spain. 1. Province in New Castile. Area 17,061 sq km (6586 sq. miles). Pop. (1991) 204,323. Largely mountainous, part of the Meseta and (S) of La Mancha. Mainly used for rearing sheep and goats. Agriculture in the lower areas. Lumbering on the Serrania de Cuenca. 2. Cap. of Cuenca province on a hill above the Júcar R. at a height of 900 m (2953 ft). Pop. (1991) 42,615.

Market town. Minor flour-milling, sawmilling, tanning and other industries.

Cathedral (13th-cent.). Taken from the Moors by Alfonso VIII of Castile 1177. Became a textile centre in the later Middle Ages; declined from the 17th cent.

Cuiabá Brazil. Cap. of the Mato Grosso state at the head of navigation on the Cuiabá R. Pop. (1985) 283,100. Accessible by river from Corumbá and by road from Campo Grande. Collecting centre for cattle, hides, dried meat and ipecacuanha. Founded (1719) by gold prospectors.

Cuiabá River Brazil. River 480 km (300 miles) long, rising on the divide of the Mato Grosso tableland, flowing generally SSW, joining the São Lourenço R. and then the Paraguay R.

Cuillin Hills Scotland. Mountain group in S Skye in Highland, rising to 1099 m (3310 ft) in Sgurr Alasdair, the highest peak on the island.

Culiacán Mexico. Cap. of Sinaloa state at the foot of the Sierra Madre Occidental 306 km (190 miles) WNW of Durango. Pop. (1990) 602,114.

In an irrigated agricultural region, producing maize, beans, sugar-cane. Manufactures textiles.

Founded 1531.

Cullinan South Africa. Town in Gauteng 32 km (20 miles) ENE of Pretoria. Pop. (1970) 6850. Founded 1903; built up round the Premier diamond mine, where the world's largest diamond (the 'Cullinan') was found (1905).

Culloden Moor (Culloden Muir) Scotland. Moorland area in Inverness-shire 8 km (5 miles) E of Inverness; part of Drummossie Muir. Scene of the defeat (1746) of the Jacobite forces under the Young Pretender ('Bonnie Prince Charlie', grandson of James II) by the Hanoverian forces under the Duke of Cumberland (son of George II) and of the massacres after the battle which earned the victor the title of 'Butcher Cumberland'. Greatly celebrated in songs, poems and novels.

Culross Scotland. Holiday resort in Fife on the Firth of Forth 10 km (6 miles) WSW of Dunfermline. Pop. (1985) 550. Noted for 16th and 17th cent. houses exemplifying Scottish domestic architecture. Remains of a 13th-cent. Cistercian abbey.

Cumae Italy. Ancient city on the W coast of Campania 18 km (11 miles) W of Naples. Said by Strabo to be the earliest Greek settlement in Italy; founded in the 8th cent. BC. Established colonies at Naples, Pozzuoli. Defeated the Etruscan fleet with the help of

Hiero of Syracuse in 474 BC. Conquered by the Samnites before the end of the 5th cent. BC. Pre-Hellenic, Greek, Samnite and Roman graves have been discovered.

Cumaná Venezuela. Formerly Nueva Toledo. Cap. of the Sucre state on the Manzanares R. 1.6 km (1 mile) above the mouth and its port Puerto Sucre. Pop. (1990) 212,492.

Exports coffee, cacao and tobacco. Fishing, fish-canning and cotton-milling.

Founded (as Nueva Toledo) c. 1521; the oldest European settlement in South America. Severely damaged by earthquakes (esp. 1766, 1797 and 1929).

Cumberland England ►CUMBRIA.

Cumberland USA. Industrial town in NW Maryland on the Potomac R. 185 km (115 miles) WNW of Baltimore in the Appalachian Mountains. Pop. (1990) 23,706.

Trade in coal mined in the neighbourhood. Railway engineering. Manufactures tyres and glassware.

Cumberland Peninsula Canada. Peninsula in SE Baffin Island in the Northwest Territories, extending 320 km (200 miles) E into the Davis Strait. Mountainous, rising to over 2400 m (7872 ft). Named in honour of the 3rd Earl of Cumberland (1558–1605).

Cumberland Plateau (Cumberland Mountains) USA. The S part of the westernmost division of the Appalachians mainly in Tennessee. Source of the Cumberland and the Kentucky rivers. The Cumberland Gap, an old settlers' route important in the American Civil War, is a pass in the extreme SW of Virginia. Named in honour of William, Duke of Cumberland, the victor of Culloden.

Cumberland River USA. River 1110 km (690 miles) long, rising on the Cumberland Plateau and flowing generally W to join the Ohio R. at Smithland (Kentucky).

Cumbernauld Scotland. Former village in the detached part of Dunbartonshire 21 km (13 miles) ENE of Glasgow, constituted a 'new town' in 1955 to accommodate people from Glasgow. Pop. (1991) 48,762 (4924 in 1961). Varied industries, inc. computers.

Cumbraes, The Scotland. Two islands in Buteshire in the Firth of Clyde; separated by the 0.8-km (½-mile) wide Tan strait. Area: Great Cumbrae 13 sq km (5 sq. miles); Little Cumbrae 2.6 sq km (1 sq. mile). Pop. (1991) 1393. On Great Cumbrae is the holiday resort of Millport.

Cumbre, La ➤USPALLATA PASS.

Cumbria England. County in the NW formed in 1974 from the former counties of Cumberland and Westmorland, the detached area of N Lancashire known as Furness and an area in the NW of the West Riding of Yorkshire: borders on Scotland (N) and on the Irish Sea and the Solway Firth (W). Area 6886 sq km (2659 sq. miles). Pop. (1994) 475,700. Chief town Carlisle. Picturesque and generally mountainous in the central area, the Lake District, which is drained to the Irish Sea by the Ellen, the Derwent and the Esk rivers: Scafell (979 m; 3311 ft), Helvellyn (951 m; 3119 ft), Skiddaw (931 m; 3054 ft). In the NW is the broad plain of Carlisle, drained into Solway Firth by the R. Eden and its tributaries, the land rising in the E to the Pennines (Cross Fell, 894 m; 2932 ft) and in the NE to the Cheviot Hills. Furness in the S comprises a peninsula bounded by the R. Duddon estuary (W), the Irish Sea (S) and Morecambe Bay (E); its principal town is Barrow-in-Furness.

Dairy farming and the cultivation of oats and root crops in the lowlands, sheep-farming in the hills; granite and limestone quarried. Industries in the small ports of Workington, Whitehaven and Maryport were based on local coal deposits, which have been very largely worked out; new industries have been introduced (e.g. chemicals, plastics). Britain's first atomic energy power station was opened at Calder Hall in 1956.

Cumnock and Holmhead Scotland. Town in East Ayrshire 23 km (14 miles) E of Ayr. Pop. (1991) 9607. The village of New Cumnock is 8 km (5 miles) SE. Burial-place of the Covenanter Alexander Peden, 'the Prophet' (1626–86). Home of the British labour leader Keir Hardie (1856–1915).

Cunaxa. Ancient town in Babylonia near the Euphrates R. Scene of the defeat (401 BC) of Cyrus the Younger (with about 13,000 Greek mercenaries) by his brother Artaxerxes II, which was followed by the famous 'Retreat of the Ten Thousand' under Xenophon.

Cunene River ➤KUNENE RIVER.

Cuneo Italy. Cap. of Cuneo province in Piedmont 76 km (47 miles) S of Turin. Pop. (1981) 55,875.

Important trade in raw silk. Manufactures textiles (silk). Metalworking, food-processing. Important road and rail junction.

Cupar Scotland. County town of Fifeshire 13 km (8 miles) WSW of St Andrews. Pop. (1991) 7545.

Tanning. Manufactures fertilizers. Beet sugar refined nearby.

A school stands on the site of the 12th-cent. castle of the Macduffs.

Curaçao Netherlands Antilles. Largest island of the two Netherlands Antilles groups in the Caribbean Sea between Aruba and Bonaire 64 km (40 miles) N of the coast of Venezuela. Area 444 sq km (183 sq. miles). Pop. (1993) 146,828. Cap. Willemstad.

Agricultural products inc. sisal and citrus fruits. Orange peel is used in the manufacture of the famous Curaçao liqueur. The chief industry was the refining of petroleum from the L. Maracaibo region in Venezuela but production has been much reduced in recent years.

Discovered by the Spaniards 1499. Taken by the Dutch 1634. Apart from a short British occupation, has remained Dutch ever since.

Curicó Chile. Cap. of the Curicó province in the fertile central valley 177 km (110 miles) SSW of Santiago. Pop. (1992) 103,919.

Market town. Trade in cattle. Flour-milling, wine-making and distilling.

Founded 1742. Severely damaged by earthquake 1928.

Curitiba Brazil. Cap. of the Paraná state on a plateau at 900 m (2952 ft) 69 km (43 miles) W of its port, Paranaguá. Pop. (1991) 1,290,142.

Important commercial and industrial centre. Trade in coffee, timber and maté. Manufactures paper and textiles.

Seat of the University of Paraná (1946). A rapidly growing city, esp. since the large-scale immigration of Poles, Germans and Italians from the mid-19th cent. onwards.

Curragh, The Ireland. Plain in Co. Kildare, just E of Kildare, famous for its turf. Area about 2000 ha (5000 acres). Site of a racecourse probably since the 1st cent AD and of a military camp since 1646. The 'revolt' of some British Army officers against the coming into force of the 1913 Home Rule Act, influential in Irish history, is known as 'the Curragh Incident'. The Irish Derby is run on the racecourse (June).

Curzola ►KORČULA.

Cutch, Rann of ►KUTCH, RANN OF.

Cuttack India. River port and commercial town in Orissa at the head of the Mahanadi R. delta. Pop. (1991) 403,400.

Trade in rice and oilseeds. Engineering, tanning, gold and silver filigree work. Manufactures inc. paper, textiles, glass, fertilizers, electronic equipment, beer and handicrafts.

Cuxhaven Germany. Seaport in Lower Saxony at the entrance to the Elbe estuary. Pop. (1986) 56,100. Serves as the outport to Hamburg. Fishing, fish-canning. Shipbuilding. Summer resort.

Cuyaba River ►CUIABÁ RIVER.

Cuyahoga Falls USA. Town in NE Ohio on the Cuyahoga R. Pop. (1990) 48,950.

Manufactures machinery, tools, rubber and paper products, but largely residential.

Cuzco Peru. Ancient city; now cap. of the Cuzco department in the fertile valley of the Vilcanota at a height of 3490 m (11,447 ft). Pop. (1993) 255,568.

Commercial centre. Several small indus-

tries, e.g. brewing, tanning, textile manufacture.

Severely damaged by earthquake 1950. Rich in examples of Spanish colonial architecture and in remains of Inca buildings (inc. the famous Temple of the Sun), of which enough survives to show the massive perfection of the stonework. Cap. (from the 11th cent. until the Spanish conquest early in the 16th cent.) of the Inca empire, a fully planned and regulated state, ruled by a benevolent Inca elite, which gradually extended its rule over the whole area that is now Peru and Bolivia, and over parts of modern Ecuador, Chile and Argentina. The Incas maintained centralized control by an extensive system of roads, over which messengers travelled quickly. They had no writing, but used a mnemonic and reckoning system in the form of *quipus*, cords knotted to record statistical information. Economic security was ensured for all, but at the price of initiative or freedom for the mass of the Indians; the empire crumbled when Pizarro destroyed the ruling class in his conquest (1533). Nearby stands the Inca fortress of Sacsahuamán, remarkable for the enormous and perfectly fitting blocks of rock of which it is built.

Cwmbran Wales. Town in Torfaen 6 km (4 miles) N of Newport, designated a 'new town' in 1949, with an ultimate pop. of 55,000. Pop. (1991) 46,021.

The coalmines closed in 1927. Industries now inc. the manufacture of vehicle parts, wire, electrical goods, bricks, tiles and pipes.

Cyclades (Gr. **Kikládhes**) Greece. Group of over 200 islands in the Aegean Sea, forming a *nome*. Area 2572 sq km (995 sq. miles). Pop. (1991) 94,005. Cap. Hermoupolis on Syros.

Produce wine, tobacco, olives, some minerals (emery, iron ore). Generally rugged but picturesque. Ruled by Turkey from the 16th cent.; passed to Greece 1832.

Cyprus (Kypros). Island republic in the E Mediterranean 80 km (50 miles) S of Turkey, 96 km (60 miles) W of Syria. Area 9251 sq km (3572 sq. miles). Turkish-occupied area, 3335 sq km (1288 sq. miles). Pop. (1992)

714,000; Greek Cypriots 599,000, Turkish Cypriots 95,000 (68 per cent. urban). Life expectancy 75 years male, 79 female. Cap. Nicosia (Lefkosía). Other towns Limassol, Larnaca, Paphos. Currency: Cyprus pound = 100 cents. The greatest length of the whole island is 225 km (140 miles), 74 km (46 miles) of this being the narrow tapering Karpas peninsula (NE). The greatest breadth is 96 km (60 miles). Largely mountainous; the rugged Kyrenia Mountains extend along the N coast, the higher Troödos Mountains in the SW rise to 1953 m (6406 ft) in Mt Olympus. Between the two ranges is the broad fertile Mesaoria plain. The rivers are torrents in winter but run dry in summer. The climate is Mediterranean, with very hot, dry summers and variable winters. About 72 per cent are Cypriot-Orthodox Christians and Maronite 2 per cent. Official lang. are Greek and Turkish, but English is widely spoken.

Large numbers of sheep and goats raised. Wheat, barley, olives, carobs, citrus fruits and wine produced. Celebrated in antiquity for its copper mines ('copper' derives from Kypros). Principal minerals iron, cupreous pyrites. The principal exports are citrus fruits, potatoes, carrots, wine, grapes and clothing. Tourism is a thriving industry.

Cyprus is rich in archaeological remains proving a Bronze Age culture probably before 3000 BC. Settled by the Phoenicians c. 800 BC. Fell to Assyria, Egypt and Persia. Taken by Rome 58 BC. For some cent. it was part of the Byzantine Empire, then changed hands several times until conquered by the Turks 1571. Occupied in 1878 and annexed in 1914 by Britain, it was a Crown Colony 1925–60, then became an independent republic within the Commonwealth. Open violence later demonstrated continuing tension between the Greek and the Turkish communities. In 1974 the military junta in Greece organized a coup to overthrow President Makarios and Turkish troops invaded the island and occupied about 40 per cent of its area in the N, while about 200,000 Greek Cypriots fled to the S to live as refugees. The economy was temporarily ruined and a UN peace-keeping force remained to prevent further hostilities. In 1975 a Turkish Cypriot Federated State was proclaimed and in 1983 the Turkish state unilaterally proclaimed itself 'The Turkish Republic of North Cyprus' (TRNC). Only Turkey recognizes the TRNC and the two ethnic communities have failed to reestablish a single state. Throughout the years 1974–97 strenuous efforts have been made by the United Nations to find a solution and a UN peace-keeping force of 1138 is stationed on the island.

Turkish Republic of North Cyprus. Area 3355 sq km (1295 sq. miles). Pop. (1992) 175,118. Cap. Nicosia (Lefkosía). Other towns: Famagusta (Gazimagusa), Kyrenia (Girne). Currency: Turkish lira = 100 kurush. About 98 per cent of the pop. is Turkish.

Main sources of foreign income inc. tourism, exports of citrus fruit and some industrial products.

There is a 50-member Legislative Assembly.

Cyrenaica Libya. Largest and most easterly province 1951–63. Area 855,000 sq km (330,000 sq. miles). Bounded by Egypt and Sudan (E), Chad (S), Tripolitania and Fezzan (W). The fertile districts in the narrow coastal plain produce barley, wheat, grapes and olives. Dates are grown farther S. Dry farming practised on the Barca plateau, but the raising of livestock (chiefly goats and sheep) is the main occupation. Tunny fishing important. To the S an extensive arid depression gradually rises to the Libyan desert and the Kufra oases. In the extreme SW are the Tibesti highlands. The chief towns are linked by a coastal road running S and W to Tripoli. A short railway joins Benghazi to Barca and Soluk. Caravan routes lead S to Saharan oases. The coastal region was first settled by the Greeks, who founded Cyrene (hence 'Cyrenaica'). Passed to the Ptolemies and then to Rome; became a Roman province 67 BC. Conquered by the Arabs in the 7th cent. Occupied by the Turks in the 16th cent. and part of the Turkish empire until they were driven out by the Italians in 1911, when it became part of the Italian colony of Libya. Scene of many battles in the N African campaigns of World War II. Under British military administration 1942–51. Became one of the three provinces of the new independent federal kingdom 1951; the Amir became King Idris I el-Mahdi el-Senussi.

Cyrene (Ar. **Shahat**) Libya. Original cap. of Cyrenaica on the coast road 80 km (50 miles) W of Derna. Pop. (1985) 500. Founded by Greek colonists from Thera *c.* 630 BC. Passed to the Ptolemies 322 BC and to Rome 96 BC. Anciently famed for its medical school and intellectual life; Callimachus and Eratosthenes were among its outstanding citizens. Many Greek and Roman remains, inc. temples, baths, gymnasium and acropolis.

Cythera (Gr. **Kíthira**) Greece. Island off the SE Peloponnese at the entrance to the Gulf of Laconia. Area 275 sq km (106 sq. miles). Pop. (1985) 6000. Rocky, with some fertile areas. Produces olive oil, wine. Chief town Kíthira. In ancient times it was sacred to Aphrodite, who was supposed to have risen from the sea there.

Czechoslovakia. Former republic in central Europe. ➤CZECH REPUBLIC and SLOVAKIA.

Czech Republic. Republic in central Europe bounded in the W by Germany, N by Poland, E by Slovakia and S by Austria. Area 78,864 sq km (30,450 sq. miles). Pop. (1995) 10,345,644. Life expectancy, 69 years male, 77 female. Cap. Prague. Other cities Brno, Ostrava, Pilsen and Olomouc. Currency: Koruna = 100 halura. The Czech Republic comprises Bohemia and Moravia. Bohemia is a plateau surrounded by mountain ranges and Moravia is mainly lowland

drained to the Danube by the R. Morava and its tributaries. It has a humid continental climate with warm summers and cold winters. Land use: forested 33 per cent, meadows and pasture 11 per cent, agricultural and under permanent cultivation 42 per cent. Czech is the official lang. Czechs make up 95 per cent of the pop., Slovak 3 per cent. The majority are Roman Catholics.

Agriculture uses 6 per cent of the labour force and 31 per cent of agricultural land is state-owned but land seized by the Communist regime, up to 150 hectares (370 acres), was returned to the original owners from 1991. Sugar-beet, cereals and potatoes are the main crops. Forestry important. Privatization of state enterprises began in 1993 and in early 1996 90 per cent had been privatized with 65 per cent of the pop. owning shares. Exports inc. manufactured goods, machinery and transport equipment, chemicals, fuels and lubricants, food and live animals.

In 1992 the Federal Assembly of Czechoslovakia voted for the dissolution of the Czech and Slovak Federal Republic and this came into effect on 1 January 1993. The Czech Republic has a 200-member House of Representatives and an 81-member Senate. There are 8 administrative regions of which one is the cap., Prague.

Częstochowa Poland. Important industrial town and railway junction, cap. of the Częstochowa voivodeship, on the Warta R. 113 km (70 miles) SSW of Lódź. Pop. (1989) 256,578.

Manufactures iron and steel, textiles, chemicals and paper.

In a famous monastery on the hill Jasna Góra (286 m; 938 ft) is an image of the Virgin believed to have been painted by St Luke; reputed to shed tears, it attracts many thousands of pilgrims annually.

D

Dabrowa Górnicza Poland. City in the Katowice voivodeship, 13 km (8 miles) ENE of Katowice. Pop. (1990) 136,000.

It is a recreational centre. Industries inc. mining and steel manufacture.

Coal has been mined since the late 18th cent. and it has one of the thickest coal seams in the world.

Dacca ►DHAKA.

Dachau Germany. Town in Bavaria situated 18 km (11 miles) NNW of Munich. Pop. (1990) 35,000.

Manufactures electrical equipment, paper, beer and textiles.

A concentration camp was established in 1935 by the Nazis and remains as a memorial to the 70,000 who died there.

Dacia. Ancient district in SE Europe comprising the greater part of what is now Romania. It became a Roman province in AD 107 and was abandoned late in the 3rd cent.

Dadra and Nagar Haveli India. Union Territory forming an enclave at the southernmost point of the border between Gujarat and Maharashtra. Area 491 sq km (192 sq. miles). Pop. (1991) 138,477. Capital Silvassa.

Major food crops rice, ragi, but wheat, millet and pulses are also grown. Industries on a small scale inc. textiles, plastics, electronics, chemicals, pharmaceuticals. Bombay is the nearest airport.

A former Portuguese territory attached for administrative purposes to Daman (just NW) and transferred to India in 1961.

Dagenham England. Part of the London borough of Barking and Dagenham on the N bank of the R. Thames. Pop. of borough (1991) 139,000.

In 1921 it had under 10,000 people and owes its expansion to the establishment of the Ford motor works and other industries. Besides the automobile industry, it manufactures knitted goods, chemicals, paints and veneers.

Dagestan Russia. Autonomous Republic within Russia, between the E part of the Great Caucasus and the Caspian Sea. Area 50,287 sq km (19,416 sq. miles). Pop. (1990) 1,823,000 and over 30 nationalities inhabit the republic (Russian 11.6 per cent). Capital Makhachkala. Other important town Derbent. Chiefly mountainous, with a narrow coastal plain.

Agriculture is varied, cattle and sheep are reared; wheat, vines and cotton are cultivated. Some oil and natural gas produced, and industries inc. chemicals, food-processing and textiles.

There was much destruction during the Revolution (1918–20) and, after being made an autonomous republic (1921), it suffered severely from famine.

Dahlak Islands Ethiopia. Archipelago in the SE Red Sea off the Bay of Mitsiwa (Eritrea). Mainly coral. Two large islands (Nora; Dahlak Kebir) and 124 smaller ones; there is no permanent population.

Noted for pearl fisheries; the catch is marketed at Mitsiwa.

Dahomey ►BENIN.

Dairen ►DALIAN.

Dakar Senegal. Capital and seaport at the S end of the Cape Verde peninsula on the Atlantic coast. Pop. (1992) 1,729,823. It was formerly a French naval base and is connected by rail with Kaolack and St Louis, and with Kayes, Bamako and Koulikoro in Mali.

Chief exports are groundnuts, groundnut oil, oil-cake. Industries inc. oil extraction, food-processing, cement manufacture, titanium refining.

The Dutch occupied Gorée Island (opposite Dakar) 1588; it was seized by the French 1677. The slave trade was long the main activity. Became the capital of French West Africa 1902. It supported the Vichy government during World War II and resisted attacks by the British and the Free French (1940), but joined the Allies 1942. It became capital of Senegal in 1958.

Dalian China (**Lüta**). City and port in Liaoning province, situated at the S end of the Liaoning peninsula. Pop. (1992) 2,420,000. It was formed from an amalgamation of Port Arthur and Dairen.

Industries inc. shipbuilding, the manufacture of diesel engines, machine-tools, chemicals, glass and textiles.

The port was built by the Japanese from 1899 and came under the control of the Soviet Union in 1945 until 1954.

Dalkeith Scotland. Market town in Midlothian 13 km (8 miles) SE of Edinburgh between the N and S Esk rivers. Pop. (1991) 11,567.

Important trade in grain. Brewing. Manufactures inc. carpets and brushes.

Dallas USA. City in N Texas, situated on the R. Trinity 51 km (32 miles) E of Fort Worth. Pop. (1990) 1,006,877. It is a financial, commercial and industrial centre. There is an important cotton market, and it is the headquarters of several oil companies.

It manufactures cotton goods, textiles, aircraft, leather goods, oilfield equipment, petroleum products, chemicals and electronic equipment.

It was founded in 1841 and named after Vice-President George Miffin Dallas. It was the scene of the assassination of President J. F. Kennedy in 1963.

Dalmatia. Strip of territory bordering the upper Balkan coast of the Adriatic Sea. It forms part of the republics of Croatia, Bosnia–Hercegovina and Montenegro. The neighbouring Adriatic waters have many islands, inc. Pag, Dugi Otok, Brač, Hvar and Korčula. It is mountainous and largely barren (Dinaric Alps), and has several resorts and ports (inc. Split, Dubrovnik, Šibenik, Zadar).

Settled by Slavs in the 7th and 8th cent. Became part of Yugoslavia (1919) except for Zara (Zadar) and some islands, which remained Italian, but were transferred to former Yugoslavia in 1947.

Daloa Côte d'Ivoire. Town situated NNW of Sassandra in Daloa department. Pop. (1990) 122,000. It is a trading centre in an agricultural area.

It produces rice, coffee, cacao, palm kernels, castor beans, kola nuts, rubber. Gold is mined nearby.

Dalton-in-Furness England. Town in Cumbria 6 km (4 miles) NE of Barrow-in-Furness in the heart of the Lake District. Pop. (1991) 7550.

There is some light industry.

Daly Waters Australia. Village and post station in the Northern Territory about 480 km (300 miles) SSE of Darwin.

Daman and Diu India. Daman is situated on the Gujarat coast 160 km (100 miles) N of Bombay and the island of Diu lies off the SE coast of Kathiawar (Gujarat), and there is a small coastal area. Daman area 72 sq km (28 sq. miles), Diu area 40 sq km (15 sq. miles). Pop. Daman (1991) 61,951; Diu (1991) 39,488. Chief towns Daman (26,895) and Diu (20,443).

Tourism is the main economic activity, also fishing and tapping the toddy palm.

Daman was seized by the Portuguese in 1531 and Diu was captured in 1534. In 1961 the area was occupied by India and incorporated in the Indian Union, and they were administered as one unit, together with Goa. In 1987 Goa became a state.

Damanhûr Egypt. Town in the Nile delta 61 km (39 miles) ESE of Alexandria on the railway to Cairo. Pop. (1991) 216,000.

Market for agricultural products and a cotton-processing centre.

Damao ➤DAMAN.

Damascus (Dimashq) Syria. Capital of the republic at the E foot of the Anti-Lebanon at a height of 690 m (2264 ft) situated on the fringe of an oasis. Pop. (1993) 1,497,000.

Famous for its silks, leather, gold and silver filigree work, brass and copper ware. Other industries are cement manufacturing and sugar-refining.

It is reputedly the oldest city in the world to be continuously inhabited. First mentioned in the Bible in Genesis. In the New Testament of the Bible Damascus and Syria are synonymous. Conquered by the Assyrians in the 8th cent. BC, by Alexander the Great 332 BC and by the Romans 64 BC. Christianized at an early date, but taken by the Arabs (635) and became Muslim. Fell to the Mongols (1260), Tamerlane (1399), the Ottoman Turks (1516). It has few buildings to bear witness to its long history apart from the 13th-cent. citadel and the Great Mosque built in AD 708 but severely damaged in the fire of 1893 and restored. In 1924 it became capital of the French mandate of Syria and in 1941 capital of Syria.

Damietta ➤DUMYAT.

Dammam Saudi Arabia. Town and port on the W shore of the Gulf 13 km (8 miles) N of Dhahran opposite Bahrain. Pop. (1990) 200,000.

Oil was discovered in 1936 and the industry developed from the 1940s. Other industries inc. chemicals, fertilizers and metallurgy.

Damodar River India. River in Bihar and W Bengal rising on the Chota Nagpur plateau and flowing 592 km (370 miles) generally ESE to join the Hooghly R.

Dampier, Mount New Zealand. Peak rising to 3443 m (11,287 ft) in Tasman National Park, Southern Alps, in the South Island.

Dampier Archipelago Indian Ocean. Group of about 20 rocky islands off NW Western Australia, the largest being Enderby Island (54 sq km; 21 sq. miles). Sheep are reared on some islands.

Dan Israel. Biblical town in the extreme N, with which the mound Tell-el-Kadi near the Syrian border is often identified.

Danakil Land (Dankalia). Desert region, mainly in NE Ethiopia but partly in Djibouti, bounded by the Red Sea and an escarpment of the Great Rift Valley. Between the Ethiopian highlands and the mountain ranges parallel to the Red Sea coast is the extensive Danakil Depression, falling to nearly 120 m (366 ft) below sea level.

Da Nang Vietnam. Seaport in central Vietnam 630 km (390 miles) NNE of Saigon. Pop. (1989) 371,000.

During the Vietnamese war it was a US military base.

Danger Island ➤COOK ISLANDS.

Dangs, The India. District in SE Gujarat. Pop. (1981) 113,644.

Forested hilly area produces millet, rice and teak.

Formerly a group of 14 small Indian states.

Dankalia ➤DANAKIL LAND.

Danube River Central/South East Europe. It rises as two head streams, Brigach R. and Brege R., in the Black Forest of Germany and becomes one river near Donaueschingen, Bavaria. It flows 2816 km (1750 miles) NE then SE past Regensburg to join Inn R. near the Austrian frontier; flows past Linz and Vienna, Austria, to enter Slovakia at Bratislava and forms part of the Slovakia Hungarian frontier, until it turns S to Budapest and across the Hungarian plain to enter Former Yugoslavia. It flows past Novi Sad and Belgrade and on to form the Former Yugoslav/Romanian and Romanian/Bulgarian borders, then N below Bucharest, Romania, to Galati and then E to enter the Black Sea by a delta. It is navigable from Ulm, Bavaria. Main tributaries rivers Atlmühl, Inn, Drava, Tisza, Sava, Morava and Prut. It is linked by the Altmühl R. with canals to the rivers Main and Rhine.

The Danube Commission checks that the provisions of the Danube Convention of 1948 are carried out, establishes a uniform buoying system on all the navigable waterways of the Danube and establishes the basic regulations for navigation on the river including customs and sanitation control as well as hydrometeorological services.

Danville (Illinois) USA. City on the Vermilion R. 193 km (120 miles) S of Chicago. Pop. (1990) 41,000. Commercial centre of an agricultural and coalmining region.

Manufactures mining machinery, chemicals, hardware and food products.

Danville (Kentucky) USA. City situated 51 km (32 miles) SSW of Lexington. Pop. (1980) 12,942.

Market for tobacco, hemp and livestock.

Danville (Virginia) USA. City on the Dan R. 92 km (57 miles) SE of Roanoke. Pop. (1990) 53,000.

Important tobacco market. Manufactures textiles, bricks and paints.

The last capital of the Southern Confederacy in the American Civil War, for 7 days in April 1865.

Danzig ➤GDAŃSK.

Daqahilya (Dakahlia) Egypt. Province of NE Lower Egypt bounded W by the Damietta branch of the R. Nile. Area 3471 sq km (1340 sq. miles). Pop. (1990) 3,828,000. Cap. Mansura.

It is an irrigated agricultural area producing cotton and cereals. Industries inc. textiles and fisheries.

Darbhanga India. Commercial town and railway and road junction in N Bihar on the Little Baghmati R. 108 km (67 miles) NE of Patna. Pop. (1991) 218,400.

Trades in rice, wheat, oilseeds and processes sugar.

Dardanelles Turkey. Ancient Hellespont. Narrow strait 72 km (45 miles) long and 1.6–8 km (1–5 miles) wide, connecting the Aegean Sea and the Sea of Marmara and separating European and Asiatic Turkey.

About 580 BC Xerxes I crossed it into Europe and in 334 BC Alexander the Great crossed it into Asia. The name was derived from the Ancient Greek town of Dardanus on the Asiatic shore.

Dardanelles Campaign 1915–16 ➤GALLIPOLI.

Dar-es-Salaam Tanzania. Former cap. and chief seaport on the Indian Ocean 64 km (40 miles) S of Zanzibar. Pop. (1988) 1,360,850. Terminus of the railway crossing Tanzania from Kigoma (on L. Tanganyika).

It handles most of the country's exports, including sisal, cotton, coffee, hides and skins, diamonds, gold. Industries inc. oil-refining, rice-milling, tanning. Manufactures inc. soap, paint, footwear, textiles.

Founded by the Sultan of Zanzibar 1862. It was occupied by the Germans in 1889 and became cap. of German East Africa in 1891. Occupied by British troops in 1916.

Darfur Sudan. Province of West Sudan and bounded by the Central African Republic. Area 196,555 sq km (75,890 sq. miles). Main towns El Fasher (cap.) and Geneina. Extensive plain with bush forest in the S and scrub grassland in the N.

Livestock-raising main occupation. Gum arabic is also produced.

Darién Panama. The E part of the republic between the Gulf of Darién on the Caribbean coast of the isthmus and the Gulf of San Miguel on the Pacific coast, and including the province of Darién; bordering on Colombia. It is the only place where there is a break in the Pan-American Highway. Area (province) 16,671 sq km (6437 sq. miles). Pop. (1990) 43,000. Cap. La Palma.

Mainly agricultural, producing maize, rice, beans.

Settled by the Spaniards in 1510. In 1698–1700 two Scottish expeditions unsuccessfully attempted to colonize the region, which they named 'New Caledonia'.

Darjeeling India. Hill station in West Bengal 507 km (315 miles) N of Calcutta on the S slopes of the Himalayas. Pop. (1991) 79,000. Tea plantations in the neighbourhood. Remarkable views of some of the highest snow-clad peaks of the Himalayas, inc. Kanchenjunga 8598 m (28,170 ft) and on clear days Everest 8848 m (29,028 ft) from Tiger Hill.

Darlaston England. Town in West Midlands situated 6 km (4 miles) ESE of Wolverhampton in the Black Country.

Manufactures inc. nuts and bolts, hardware and castings.

Darling Downs Australia. Undulating plateau in SE Queensland W of the Great Dividing Range, covering 64,750 sq km (25,000 sq. miles). Toowoomba is the chief town.

Main occupation sheep and dairy farming. Wheat, barley, fodder crops are cultivated. There is oil, natural gas and huge reserves of coal.

Darling Range Australia. Ridge 400 km (250 miles) long in the SW of Western Australia, parallel to the coast, generally 240–480 m (800–1500 ft) high and rising to 583 m (1910 ft) in Mt Cooke. Wooded slopes dissected by many streams. Water storages inc. Mundaring and Canning Dam reservoirs.

Darling River Australia. The longest tributary of the Murray R., from the confluence of headstreams near the Queensland–New South Wales border flowing generally SW across New South Wales for about 3057 km (1900 miles) to the Murray R. at Wentworth. Known in the upper course as Macintyre (headstream) and Barwon. Its flow fluctuates considerably, rising at times from a mere trickle to flood large areas.

Darlington England. Borough in Durham on the R. Skerne near its confluence with the R. Tees 21 km (13 miles) WSW of Middlesbrough. Pop. (1991) 96,700.

Industries inc. engineering, bridge-building and newspapers. Manufactures woollen goods.

A market town before the Industrial Revolution, it owes its modern development to the opening of the Stockton–Darlington railway in 1825.

Darmstadt Germany. Industrial town in Hesse 27 km (17 miles) S of Frankfurt. Pop. (1991) 140,000. Cap. of Hesse.

Industries inc. railway engineering and the manufacture of diesel engines, machinery, chemicals, pharmaceutical products, plastics and electronics. It is the centre of a wine-making district.

Dartford England. Town in NW Kent on the R. Darent 11 km (7 miles) W of Gravesend 5 km (3 miles) from the R. Thames. Linked to Essex by the Dartford tunnel. Pop. (1991) 59,411.

Important paper manufacture, site of the first paper mill in England. Industries inc. paper-making, flour-milling, engineering and the manufacture of pharmaceutical products and cement.

Dartmoor England. Upland area in S Devon covering an area of 945 sq km (365 sq. miles) and rising to a height of over 621 m (2039 ft). It is protected by the National Park Authority as an area of outstanding natural beauty. The high peaks on the moor are known as tors and the highest are Willhays Tor 622 m (2041 ft) and Yes Tor 619 m (2031 ft). Bronze Age settlers cleared much of the forest and built hut circles. The Britons circled Dartmoor with hill forts; the Anglo-Saxons built the first long houses. King John retained the heart of the moor as a royal forest until 1204. From the 12th to 20th cent. tin has been extracted from the moor. In the 18th cent. lead, copper, iron and arsenic were also mined. Granite has been quarried and was used in the construction of Nelson's Column in Trafalgar Square, London. Dartmoor ponies have been on the moor since the 10th cent., and cattle and sheep live there. Dartmoor prison near Princetown was founded in 1806 and used for French prisoners of war, and since 1950 it has been used for civilian offenders. Much of the Eastern Moor is used for military training. Many of Devon's rivers originate from the broad peaty flats found over much of Dartmoor.

Dartmouth Canada. Industrial town in Nova Scotia opposite Halifax, with which it is connected by a suspension bridge across Halifax Harbour. Pop. (1991) 68,000.

Industries inc. ship-building, sugar-refining, oil-refining.

First settled in 1750.

Dartmouth England. Seaport in S Devon on the W side of the R. Dart estuary 13 km (8 miles) SSW of Torquay. Pop. (1991) 5676.

Main occupation tourism inc. a yachting marina.

An important seaport in the 11th cent.; in 1190 Richard Coeur de Lion set sail from here on his crusades. The Royal Naval College was established here in 1905.

Darwen England. Industrial town in Lancashire 6 km (4 miles) S of Blackburn. Pop. (1991) 29,864.

Manufactures cotton goods, paper, plastics, chemicals and paints.

Darwin Australia. Cap. and chief seaport of the Northern Territory in the extreme N, overlooking the harbour of Port Darwin. Pop. (1993) 77,900. Connected by 510-km (317-mile) railway to Birdum and by further 1014 km (630 miles) of Stuart Highway to Alice Springs.

It is a commercial and communications centre for the interior. Important as a telegraph and cable terminus.

Founded 1869; named after Charles Darwin. It was almost completely destroyed by a cyclone in 1974 but has been rebuilt.

Darwin Falkland Islands. Small settlement at the head of Choiseul Sound on East Falkland Island.

Dasht-i-Kavir Iran. Salt desert on the central plateau of Iran in W Khurasan. Beneath the salt crust the ground is marshy and treacherous.

Datong (Tatung) China. Town in N Xhanxi province 282 km (175 miles) W of Beijing just S of the Great Wall. Pop. (1990) 798,319.

A coalmining and industrial centre. Industries inc. railway and other engineering, and it manufactures cement, chemicals and mining machinery.

Daugavpils Latvia. Town on the W Dvina R. Pop. (1989) 127,000.

Industries inc. railway engineering, food-processing, textiles and it trades in grain, flax, timber.

Founded by the Livonian Order in the 13th cent. Until 1893 it was the German town of Dünaberg.

Davangere India. Town in E Karnataka in S India 248 km (155 miles) NW of Bangalore. Pop. (1991) 266,100.

Industries inc. the manufacture of automotive components, cement and textiles.

Davao Philippines. City and seaport in SE Mindanao on Davao Gulf. Pop. (1990) 850,000.

The area produces maize, bananas, fish, pineapples and timber. Exports abacá, copra, timber.

Davenport USA. Industrial town in Iowa on the Mississippi R. opposite Rock Island. Pop. (1990) 95,000.

Industries inc. construction equipment, food-processing, the manufacture of agricultural implements and washing-machines.

Daventry England. Town in Northamptonshire 18 km (11 miles) W of Northampton. Pop. (1991) 18,099. Just to the E on Borough Hill is a large prehistoric and Roman camp; a radio transmitting station has been operating since 1925.

Davis ▶AUSTRALIAN ANTARCTIC TERRITORY.

Davis Strait N Atlantic. An arm of the Atlantic, between SE Baffin Island and SW Greenland, 640 km (400 miles) long and 320–640 km (200–400 miles) wide. Usually navigable from late summer and autumn. Named after John Davis, who discovered it (1587) while searching for the Northwest Passage.

Davos Switzerland. Town in the valley of the Landwasser R. 21 km (13 miles) ESE of Chur in Graubünden (Grisons) canton. Pop. (1990) 12,500. Contains two famous health resorts and winter-sports centres: Davos Platz and Davos Dörfli, 5 km (3 miles) apart and both at a height of about 1555 m (5100 ft). At the N end of the valley is L. Davos.

Dawei ►TAVOY.

Dawley ►TELFORD.

Dawlish England. Seaside resort in S Devon near the mouth of the R. Exe 5 km (3 miles) SW of Exmouth. Pop. (1991) 9648.

Tourism and horticulture main occupations.

Dawson Canada. Town in Yukon Territory on the Yukon R. Pop. (1991) 1786. Former cap. of the territory. Trade and communications centre for the Klondike mining region.

Founded (1896) during the Klondike gold rush, when the population rose to about 25,000.

Dawson Creek Canada. City in British Columbia near the Alberta border. Pop. (1990) 10,500. It is the starting point of the Alaska Highway.

A centre of a lumbering and agricultural area. Industries inc. the manufacture of waferboard and chopsticks, coalmining, oil, natural gas and tourism.

Dayton USA. Industrial town in Ohio on the Great Miami R. 108 km (67 miles) WSW of Columbus. Pop. (1990) 182,040.

Manufactures refrigerators, cash registers, air-conditioning equipment, machine-tools, aircraft instruments. The Wright brothers established an aircraft research factory in 1911. Now a centre for military aviation development, with the Wright–Patterson Air Force Base.

Daytona Beach USA. Seaside resort in NE Florida on the Atlantic and on the Halifax R. (a lagoon). Pop. (1990) 70,000.

The main industry is tourism.

Since 1903 the venue of motor speed trials, on the famous hard white beach which is 48 km (30 miles) long.

DC ►COLUMBIA, DISTRICT OF.

De Aar South Africa. Important railway

junction in the Eastern Cape Province 640 km (400 miles) NE of Cape Town. Pop. (1980) 24,000. Large railway workshops.

Dead Sea. Salt lake on the border of Israel and Jordan 74 km (46 miles) long and 5–15 km (3–9 miles) wide, its surface 392 m (1286 ft) below sea level; only 1–10 m (3–33 ft) deep at the S end, up to 390 m (1280 ft) deep in the N; flanked on the E and W shores by steep hills. Occupies part of a rift valley which inc. the Sea of Galilee and the Gulf of Aqaba. At its N end receives the Jordan R. and several intermittent streams, but has no outlet, losing water solely by evaporation. Therefore has a very high salinity, about 25 per cent or 7 times that of the ocean.

From 1947 onwards a number of important manuscripts dating from the 2nd cent. BC–1st cent. AD were discovered in caves near the Dead Sea and are known as the Dead Sea scrolls.

Deal England. Town in E Kent 13 km (8 miles) NNE of Dover opposite the Downs roadstead and Goodwin Sands. Pop. (1991) 27,000. A 'limb' or member of the Cinque Ports.

Industries are mainly tourism and fishing.

It is the probable landing place of Julius Caesar in Britain (55 BC).

Dean, Forest of England. Hilly district and ancient royal forest in W Gloucestershire, area 110 sq km (42 sq. miles), between the Severn and the Wye rivers. Almost completely deforested by the latter half of the 17th cent. but later replanted. There is some private coalmining on a small scale.

Dearborn USA. Town in SE Michigan 14 km (9 miles) W of Detroit on the Rouge R. Pop. (1990) 89,300.

Main industry is the manufacture of vehicles.

Birthplace of Henry Ford (1863–1947), who established the first great mass-production car factory there after World War I. In the city is the Edison Institute of Technology (established by Henry Ford 1933).

Death Valley USA. Arid rift valley in E California and S Nevada, part of the Great Basin region, lying N of the Mojave Desert. Badwater, 86 m (262 ft) below sea level, is the lowest point in the W hemisphere. Telescope Peak, on the W edge of the valley, rises to 3369 m (10,275 ft). The valley contains extensive sand dunes, salt flats and many desert plants. Summers are very hot. Named (1849) by a party of 'forty-niners' seeking gold, some of whom died of thirst and exposure when trying to cross it.

Deauville France. Fashionable resort in the Calvados department, at the mouth of the Touques R. opposite Trouville. Pop. (1990) 4800.

Tourism is the main occupation and there is a racecourse and casino.

Debrecen Hungary. Cap. of Hajdú-Bihar county 193 km (120 miles) E of Budapest. Pop. (1990) 220,000. Railway junction and market town.

Trade in livestock, tobacco. Flour-milling. Industries inc. agricultural machinery, pharmaceutical products and food-processing.

Debryansk ►BRYANSK.

Decatur (Alabama) USA. Industrial town on the Tennessee R. 122 km (76 miles) N of Birmingham. Pop. (1989) 50,078.

Manufactures synthetic fibres, metal goods and pet foods.

Developed industrially after the establishment of the Tennessee Valley Authority (TVA).

Decatur (Illinois) USA. Town on the Sangamon R. 60 km (37 miles) E of Springfield. Pop. (1990) 84,000.

Industries inc. railway engineering, maize and soya-bean processing. Manufactures motor-car accessories, tractors, plastic and metal products.

Deccan India. Peninsula of India S of the Satpura Range and enclosed between the Western Ghats and the Eastern Ghats. Slopes generally E from about 900 m to 450 m (2950–1480 ft); the main rivers Godavari, Krishna and Cauvery flow W–E to the Bay of Bengal.

Some rice is grown and in the wetter areas millet. Cotton is also grown in the S.

Děčín Czech Republic. River port and railway junction near the German border at the confluence of the Polzen (Ploučnice) and Elbe rivers. Pop. (1985) 55,000.

Manufactures chemicals, textiles and paper.

Dedeagach ►ALEXANDROUPOLIS.

Dee River Scotland. 1. River 140 km (87 miles) long rising on Ben Braeriach in the Cairngorms and flowing E past Braemar, Balmoral Castle, Ballater and Aboyne, forming part of the Aberdeenshire–Kincardine border, to the North Sea by an artificial channel at Aberdeen. Good salmon fishing. Has supplied Aberdeen with water since 1864.

2. River 61 km (38 miles) long issuing from Loch Dee, Kirkcudbrightshire and flowing generally S to the Irish Sea at Kirkcudbright. Salmon and trout fishing.

Dee River Wales/England. River 113 km (70 miles) long rising in Bala L., Gwynedd and flowing generally N past Corwen, Llangollen, Chester (which it almost encircles) and Flint to the Irish Sea. The estuary, 21 km (13 miles) long and about 8 km (5 miles) wide, becomes a stretch of sand at low tide.

Dehra Dun India. Town in NW Uttar Pradesh 209 km (130 miles) NNE of Delhi. Pop. (1991) 270,200.

Trade in rice, wheat, oilseeds. Manufactures power generation equipment, watches and opto-electronics.

Noted chiefly for the Indian Military Academy (1932) and the Indian Forest Research Institute and College (1867). Oil and Natural Gas Commission headquarters. Founded in the late 17th cent. by the Sikh guru, Ram Rai.

Deir ez Zor Syria. Town in the E on the Euphrates R. 274 km (170 miles) ESE of Aleppo. Pop. (1970) 66,143. Communication centre for W Syria, S Turkey and Iraq. Industries inc. flour-milling and tanning.

Delagoa Bay Mozambique. Inlet of the Indian Ocean, in the S. Discovered (1502) by António do Campo, commander of a ship on Vasco da Gama's expedition. Maputo (Lourenço Marques) is on the NW shore.

Delaware USA. State on the E seaboard, forming the NE part of the Delmarva peninsula between Chesapeake Bay and Delaware Bay, with Pennsylvania to the N and Maryland to the S. Area 5328 sq km (2057 sq. miles). Pop. (1990) 666,168. Cap. Dover. One of the original 13 states and the first to ratify the Constitution. Generally low-lying, hilly in the extreme N. Climate humid and hot in summer, cool in winter; because of its peninsular location the growing season is long.

Varied agriculture. Wheat, maize, fruit, vegetables cultivated. Substantial poultry-raising and fishing. Manufacturing centred on Wilmington, the one large city (head-quarters of the chemical company Du Pont). Shipbuilding, cotton-dyeing.

Delaware Bay was discovered (1609) by Henry Hudson. In 1610 Lord de la Warr touched there, giving it his name. Although a slave state, Delaware declined to secede from the Union in the American Civil War.

Delaware River USA. River rising in SE New York State and flowing 448 km (280 miles) generally SE to form the NE border between Pennsylvania and New Jersey. It empties into Delaware Bay below Chester, Pennsylvania.

Delémont Switzerland. Cap. of the canton of Jura (which was created in 1979). Pop. (1989) 12,500.

Delft Netherlands. Town in S Holland province 8 km (5 miles) SSE of The Hague on the Schie canal. Pop. (1992) 90,066.

Famous for the pottery and porcelain industry begun in the 16th cent. Also manufactures chemicals, cigars, cables. Among its buildings are the Prinsenhof (formerly a monastery, then a palace, now a museum) where William the Silent was assassinated (1584). An Old Church with the tombs of Leeuwenhoek and van Tromp, and a New Church, with the tombs of William the Silent and Grotius.

Delfzijl Netherlands. Town in NE Groningen on the Eems estuary and canal. Pop. (1992) 31,350.

Industries inc. shipbuilding, sawmilling and the manufacture of salt, soda, polymers, cement.

Delhi India. 1. Union territory in the N, formerly a chief commissioner's state, and a province 1912–50. Area 1483 sq km (579 sq. miles). Pop. (1991) 9,370,475. 2. Cap. of the republic and of Delhi territory on the right bank of the Jumna R. Pop. (1991) 7,206,700. Its importance is largely due to its strategic position on the Indo–Gangetic plain.

Important railway centre. Manufactures textiles, electronics, plastics, sports goods, edible oils, television sets, electronic goods, footwear, automobile parts, pharmaceuticals, hosiery, chemicals, gold and silver filigree articles.

Old Delhi, seventh in the series of cities which have stood in this district, is sometimes locally called Shahjahanabad after the Mogul Emperor Shah Jahan who reconstructed it in the 17th cent. Within its walls are the Fort, which contains the beautiful Imperial Palace (1638–48) of Shah Jahan, the magnificent Jama Masjid or Great Mosque of the same monarch (1648–50) and the once far-famed Chandni Chauk or 'Street of the Silver-smiths'. New Delhi, about 5 km (3 miles) S of the Fort, was chosen as cap. of India in 1912 and became cap. of the republic in 1947. It was designed chiefly by Sir Edwin Lutyens, and among its buildings, which skilfully blend the Eastern and Western styles of architecture, are The President's House and the Secretariat buildings.

Delmarva Peninsula USA. Peninsula lying between Chesapeake Bay (W) and the Delaware R., Delaware Bay and the Atlantic (E). Comprises most of Delaware and parts of Maryland and Virginia, the name deriving from abbreviations of the names of the three states. Main occupations market-gardening, poultry-farming, forestry, fishing.

Delmenhorst Germany. Industrial town in Lower Saxony 14 km (9 miles) WSW of Bremen. Pop. (1991) 76,000.

Manufactures textiles, linoleum, machinery, clothing, soap.

Delos (Gr. **Dhilos**) Greece. One of the smallest islands in the Cyclades in the Aegean Sea, sometimes called Mikra Dhilos (Little Delos) to distinguish it from Rinia or Megali Dhilos (Great Delos), just to the W. Traditionally the centre of the Cyclades, adrift in the Aegean Sea until moored by Zeus as a birthplace for Apollo and Artemis. Served as treasury of the Delian League 478–454 BC until the removal to Athens.

Delphi (Gr. **Delphoi**) Greece. Ancient city of Phocis and seat of the famous Delphic oracle on the slopes of Parnassus high above the Gulf of Corinth. The Pythian Games were held every four years from 582 BC. By the end of the 4th cent. AD the Oracle was no longer consulted. Excavations in the 19th cent. revealed many of the remains of Delphi.

Delta Canada. Suburb of Vancouver, British Columbia situated at the mouth of Fraser R. Pop. (1981) 74,692.

Industries inc. fish and food processing.

Demavend ➤ELBURZ.

Demerara River Guyana. River 346 km (215 miles) long, rising in the central forest area, flowing N and entering the Atlantic at Georgetown. Large quantities of bauxite are shipped from Mackenzie 96 km (60 miles) up river.

Denain France. Town in the Nord department on the Escaut R. 11 km (7 miles) WSW of Valenciennes. Pop. (1989) 21,000.

Industries inc. sugar-refining, brewing, railway engineering.

Denbigh Wales. Town situated in Denbighshire 16 km (10 miles) S of Rhyl. Pop. (1971) 8100. Occupations are agriculture and quarrying.

Remains of a 14th-cent. castle where Charles I took refuge 1645.

Denbighshire Wales. County created in 1996 from part of Clwyd. Pop. (1994) 91,000.

Den Helder ➤HELDER, DEN.

Denizli Turkey. Cap. of Denizli province 177 km (110 miles) ESE of Izmir. Pop. (1990) 190,000. Market town.

Once famous for its gardens. Important in the 14th cent. for its textiles; later declined.

Denmark (Danish **Kongeriget Danmark**). Kingdom of Northern Europe forming part of Scandinavia lying between the North Sea and the entrance to the Baltic Sea. It consists of the N and greater part of the Jutland peninsula, which is bounded on the S by Germany; several islands in the Baltic Sea between this peninsula and Sweden, inc. Zealand, Falster, Laaland and Fünen and, much farther E, Bornholm; some of the North Frisian Is. in the North Sea. In all there are 406 islands. Area 43,075 sq km (16,631 sq. miles). Pop. (1991) 5,146,469; about one-quarter of the total pop. lives in Copenhagen, inc. suburbs. Life expectancy, 72 years male, 78 female. Cap. Copenhagen, also leading seaport. The only other towns with more than 100,000 people (1991) were Aarhus, Odense and Aalborg. Currency: Danish Krone = 100 øre.

Entirely low-lying, the highest point being Ejer Bavnehoj 172 m (525 ft) in East Jutland, but very gently undulating rather than flat; well drained. Along the W coast of Jutland is an almost continuous line of sand dunes, planted with trees and grasses and enclosing lagoons. Other coasts are much indented with fiords; the largest is the Lifjord, which separates the N extremity from the remainder of Jutland. The chief straits leading through the islands from the Kattegat to the Baltic are The Sound (Öresund), the Great Belt and the Little Belt. Owing to maritime influences the climate is relatively mild and damp, only rarely are the straits impassable because of ice. Land use: forested 12 per cent, meadows and pastures 5 per cent, under permanent cultivation 61 per cent.

Denmark is divided into 14 counties in addition to the City of Copenhagen and the borough of Frederiksberg. Ethnically and linguistically the Danes are Scandinavian and 90 per cent belong to the Evangelical Lutheran church.

One of the smaller countries of Europe, its wealth is largely dependent on agriculture; the emphasis is on dairy-farming and much of the land is divided into small-holdings. In 1990 only 6 per cent of the pop. were engaged in agriculture, forestry and fishing. With a favourable climate and fertile soil, especially on the islands, the Danes have become outstanding as dairy farmers, their methods being intensive and highly scientific. They keep a moderate area in permanent pasture, but their crops (esp. barley and root crops) are cultivated mainly to feed to the large numbers of cattle and pigs. Butter, cheese, eggs and bacon are exported to Britain and Germany. Almost half of the farms are less than 10 ha (24 acres) in area, but the proprietors are assisted by an efficient system of cooperative processing and marketing. There are mineral resources, apart from the kaolin on Bornholm, used in porcelain manufacture, and some oil and natural gas. Industries though varied are generally on a small scale and inc. shipbuilding, chemicals, oil-refining, engineering and furniture manufacture. Fishing has become increasingly important since World War II.

The Danes probably migrated to their present home from Southern Sweden in the 5th and 6th cent. Ruled at first by local chieftains, they were united and converted to Christianity in the 10th cent. by Harald Bluetooth. Canute ruled Denmark, Norway and England, but at his death (1035) the kingdoms separated. In 1389, however, Denmark, Norway and Sweden were united and, although Sweden became independent in 1523, Norway remained under Danish rule until 1814. In 1536 Lutheranism was introduced as the national religion. Throughout the 16th and 17th cent. attempts to regain supremacy in the Baltic led to disastrous wars with Sweden; then, having supported Napoleon, Denmark was compelled to cede Norway to Sweden (1814) and lost Schleswig-Holstein to Prussia (1864). Nevertheless, the 19th cent. saw a great cultural renaissance. Denmark was neutral in World War I but recovered North Schleswig after a plebiscite in 1920. In World War II Denmark was occupied by the Germans. Iceland, previously united with Denmark, became independent in 1944.

Denmark is a constitutional monarchy, with a single-chamber *Folketing* elected by proportional representation, the *Landsting* (Senate) having been abolished in 1953. Two members are elected for the Faroe Islands and two for Greenland.

Dent Blanche Switzerland. Alpine peak in Valais situated W of Zermatt and opposite to and N of the Matterhorn at 4405 m (14,318 ft).

Dent du Midi Switzerland. Massif in the Alps in the canton of Valais near the French border comprising several peaks, inc. Haute Cime, the highest, 3262 m (10,700 ft); Cime de l'Est or Dent Noire, 3182 m (10,440 ft); Dent Jaune, 3189 m (10,460 ft); Cathédrale, 3168 m (10,390 ft).

Denton USA. Market town in Texas 55 km (34 miles) NNE of Fort Worth. Pop. (1990) 66,000.

Industries inc. food products, flour-milling and the manufacture of electronic equipment, clothing and machinery.

D'Entrecasteaux Islands Papua New Guinea. Group of volcanic islands off the SE coast of New Guinea. Area 3108 sq km (1200 sq. miles). Three large islands, Goodenough, Fergusson and Normanby, and many islets. Chief product copra.

Denver USA. State cap. of Colorado on the S Platte R. at a height of 1610 m (5282 ft). Pop. (1990) 467,610. The excellent climate makes it a popular health and recreational centre.

Important cattle and sheep markets. Meat-packing. Manufactures agricultural and mining machinery, rubber products.

Founded 1859 and grew as a mining centre for gold and silver.

Deptford England. Former metropolitan borough of SE London on the S bank of the Thames; from 1965 part of the Greater London borough of Lewisham. Industrial and workers' residential district.

Engineering. Manufactures soap, chemicals, furniture.

John Evelyn the diarist lived here and Peter the Great of Russia studied shipbuilding. The royal naval dockyard established by Henry VIII operated 1513–1869.

Dera Ghazi Khan Pakistan. Town 80 km (50 miles) WSW of Multan. Pop. (1981) 103,000.

Trading centre and also manufactures agricultural equipment.

Much of the earlier town was destroyed by the Indus R. floods in 1908–9 and another town was built on the present site W of the river.

Dera Ismail Khan Pakistan. Town on the Indus R. 257 km (160 miles) SSW of Peshawar. Pop. (1981) 68,000.

Trade centre for an agricultural area.

Derbent Russia. Port in the Dagestan Autonomous Republic on the Caspian Sea 120 km (75 miles) SSE of Makhachkala. Pop. (1990) 80,000.

Industries inc. fishing, fish-canning, textiles and wine. Important glassworks at Dagestanskiye Ogni nearby.

Ruins of the 6th-cent. Caucasian Wall, erected by the Persians to defend their frontier. Taken by the Arabs (728) and the Mongols (1220). Finally passed to Russia 1813.

Derby England. Industrial city and unitary authority on the R. Derwent. Pop. (1991) 214,000.

Important railway junction. Railway engineering. Manufactures aircraft engines, lawn mowers, synthetic textiles, electrical equipment, Royal Crown Derby porcelain, paints.

Founded in 880, industrialization began with the introduction of the country's first silk mill in 1719.

Derbyshire England. County in the N Midlands. Area 2631 sq km (1016 sq. miles). Pop. (1991) 914,600. It is divided into the districts of Amber Valley, Bolsover, Chesterfield, Derby, Erewash, High Peak, North-East Derbyshire, South Derbyshire and West Derbyshire. County town Derby. Mountainous and picturesque in the N and NW, rising to 637 m (2086 ft) in the Peak District National Park. Flat or gently undulating in the S and E. Drained by the Derwent, Dove, Wye and Trent rivers. Buxton, the Matlocks and Bakewell are resorts noted for mineral springs. Sheep raised on the uplands and dairy cattle on the lowlands. Coalmining is decreasing in importance but is found in the E of the county. Limestone quarried near Buxton.

Principal industries (centred on Derby, Chesterfield, Ilkeston, Long Eaton, Heanor, Alfreton) iron-smelting, engineering, textile manufacture.

Dereham ➤EAST DEREHAM.

Derg, Lough Ireland. 1. Lake 40 km (25 miles) long and 1.6–4.8 km (1–3 miles) wide at the boundary of Counties Galway, Clare and Tipperary in the lower course of the R. Shannon. On Holy Island or Inishcaltra are a 10th-cent. round tower and the ruins of four ancient churches.

2. Small lake in S Donegal 5 km (3 miles) NNW of Pettigo. Station Island, traditional scene of St Patrick's purgatory.

Derna Libya. Town in Cyrenaica on the coastal road 264 km (165 miles) ENE of Benghazi in an oasis producing dates. Pop. (1989) 38,000.

Occupied by American troops after they had captured it from pirates in 1805. Under Turkish rule 1835–1911, then taken by Italy. Changed hands several times during World War II; finally taken by the British 1942.

Derry ➤LONDONDERRY.

Derwent River Australia. River in Tasmania rising in L. St Clair and flowing 209 km (130 miles) SE to a 4-mile-wide estuary on Storm Bay, Tasman Sea, at Hobart.

Derwent River England. 1. River 56 km (35 miles) long in Cumbria, rising in the Lake District (Borrowdale Fells) and flowing N through Derwentwater and Bassenthwaite, then W to the Irish Sea at Workington.

2. River 96 km (60 miles) long in Derbyshire, rising near The Peak and flowing S to the R. Trent. Supplies water to Derby, Leicester, Nottingham and Sheffield from the Derwent, Howden and Ladybower reservoirs.

3. River 48 km (30 miles) long rising in the Pennines near the Durham–Northumberland border, flowing generally ENE and forming part of their boundary, to the R. Tyne near Newcastle.

4. River 113 km (70 miles) long, rising in the N York Moors and flowing generally SSW to join the R. Ouse 8 km (5 miles) NW of Goole, forming part of the boundary between North Yorkshire and Humberside.

Derwentwater England. Lake just S of Keswick 5 km (3 miles) long and about 1.6 km (1 mile) wide in the Lake District, Cumbria. Surrounded by mountains with several small islands and the Falls of Lodore at the upper (S) end. The R. Derwent enters at the S end and leaves at the N end to connect it with Bassenthwaite L.

Desaguadero River ➤SALADO RIVER.

Désirade, La Guadeloupe. Island situated ENE of Grande-Terre forming a dependency of Guadeloupe. Area 22 sq km (8 sq. miles). Pop. (1990) 1610.

Farming and fishing are the main occupations; sugar, cotton and sisal are grown.

Des Moines USA. State cap. of Iowa on the Des Moines R. at the confluence with the Raccoon R. Pop. (1990) 193,190.

In the heart of the Corn Belt and is a transportation and industrial centre. Manufactures agricultural machinery, tyres, cement and leather goods. Printing and publishing.

Des Moines River USA. River 869 km (540 miles) long rising in SW Minnesota and flowing generally SSE to join the Mississippi R. near Keokuk, in SE Iowa. Used for hydroelectric power.

Desna River Russia. River 1130 km (700 miles) long rising about 80 km (50 miles) ESE of Smolensk and flowing generally SSW past Bryansk to the Dnieper R. above Kiev. Important waterway for timber, agricultural produce. Navigable below Bryansk.

Desroches Seychelles. Island situated NNE of the N tip of Madagascar. It is the S side of a coral atoll reef.

From 1965 it was part of the British Indian Ocean Territory, but returned to Seychelles in 1976.

Dessau Germany. Industrial town in Saxony-Anhalt on the Mulde R. near its confluence with the Elbe. Pop. (1989) 103,200.

Manufactures machinery, chemicals, precision instruments and vehicles.

Dessie Ethiopia. Market town 257 km (160 miles) NNE of Addis Ababa at a height of 2400 m (7874 ft). Pop. (1984) 68,848. Linked by road with Addis Ababa, Asmara, Assab.

Trade in coffee, cereals and hides.

Detmold Germany. Town 27 km (17 miles) ESE of Bielefeld in North Rhine-Westphalia. Pop. (1990) 68,000. Formerly cap. of Lippe.

Industries inc. brewing and coffee-roasting, and the manufacture of furniture and biscuits.

Detroit USA. City in Michigan on the Detroit R. opposite Windsor (Ontario), with which it is linked by tunnel and bridge. Pop. (1990) 1,027,974.

Ford, General Motors and Chrysler operate vast automobile plants which account for a large proportion of its industrial activity. Also manufactures aircraft engines and accessories, electrical and television equipment, adding machines. Oil refineries, shipyards, salt works. It has a large port serving the vast commerce of the Great Lakes.

Founded in 1701 by French settlers under Antoine de la Mothe Cadillac, it became the most important city W of the E seaboard.

Deurne Belgium. Suburb of E Antwerp. Mainly residential with some industries. Antwerp airport.

Deux–Sèvres France. Department in the W in the Poitou-Charentes Region. Area 6004 sq km (2337 sq. miles). Pop. (1990) 345,965. Prefecture Niort.

Mainly agricultural; wheat, oats, potatoes, vegetables widely cultivated. Dairy-farming important.

Name derived from Sèvre-Nantaise and Sèvre-Niortaise, the rivers by which the department is drained. Chief towns Niort, Parthenay.

Deva Romania. Cap. of Hunedoara district situated NW of Bucharest on the Mures R. Pop. (1990) 77,336.

It is a tourist centre and it trades in livestock, fruit and timber. Industries inc. food-processing and engineering.

Deventer Netherlands. Industrial town and railway junction in Overijssel province on the Ijssel R. 14 km (9 miles) ENE of Apeldoorn. Pop. (1992) 68,004.

Manufactures chemicals, textiles, cigars. Flour-milling and engineering. Famous for its honey gingerbread (*Deventer koek*).

In the Middle Ages it was a commercial, educational and religious centre where Erasmus, Thomas à Kempis and Pope Adrian VI were educated.

Devizes England. Town in Wiltshire on the Kennet–Avon canal 26 km (16 miles) ESE of Bath. Pop. (1991) 13,900.

Brewing is the main industry.

It grew round the 12th-cent. castle, destroyed by Cromwell in 1645 and until the 19th cent. was an important cloth market.

Devon England. Maritime county in the SW between the Bristol Channel (N) and the English Channel (S). Area 6765 sq km (2612 sq. miles). Pop. (1991) 998,200. It is divided into the districts of East Devon, Exeter, Mid-Devon, North Devon, Plymouth, South Hams, Teignbridge, Torbay, Torridge and West Devon. County town Exeter. In the NE is Exmoor and in the E the Blackdown Hills, but the highest part of the county is the granitic mass of Dartmoor, which reaches 622 m (2041 ft) in High Willhays and 619 m (2031 ft) in Yes Tor. Chief rivers the Tamar, Exe, Dart, Teign, Taw and Torridge, most of their valleys being wooded. The attractive coastal and inland scenery, coupled with the mild climate, has stimulated tourism, now the main industry, leading resorts being Torquay, Paignton and Ilfracombe. Fishing from Brixham and Plymouth. In the fertile areas beef and dairy cattle are raised, and the county is as well known for its clotted ('Devonshire') cream. On the upland pastures sheep are grazed. Plymouth, with Devonport, is an important seaport and naval station. Other towns are Exeter, Exmouth, Newton Abbot and Barnstaple.

Devonport Australia. Port in Tasmania at the mouth of the Mersey R. 72 km (45 miles) WNW of Launceston; formed (1890) from Torquay and Formby on opposite sides of the river. Pop. (1989) 26,500.

Exports dairy produce, vegetables, timber. Market town. Resort.

Devonport England. Naval and military station in Devon on the R. Tamar estuary, incorporated into Plymouth in 1914.

Devonport New Zealand. Suburb of Auckland, N Island on the NE shore of Waitemata Harbour. Linked to the central commercial area by harbour bridge.

Dewsbury England. Industrial town in West Yorkshire on the R. Calder 11 km (7 miles) SSW of Leeds. Pop. (1991) 50,168.

Important centre of the shoddy trade and dyeworks. Some coalmining in the area. Also manufactures blankets, carpets, heavy woollen goods and leather goods.

Dhahran Saudi Arabia. Town in Hasa (E) near the Gulf. Headquarters of the Saudi Arabian oilfields, to which it is linked by pipelines. Airport. Connected by rail with Riyadh. Developed after 1936, when oil was discovered at nearby Dammam.

Dhaka Bangladesh. Cap. and river port on

the Burhi Ganga R. Pop. (1991) 3,397,187.

It is a commercial centre trading in rice, jute, oilseeds and hides. Manufactures inc. textiles, paper, jute, hosiery, carpets, chemicals and soap; it is a medical radioisotope centre.

Former cap. of Bengal (1608–1704) and of E Bengal and Assam (1905–12). Before the partition of India (1947) it was a small university town and was known as the city of mosques; there are over 1000.

Dhanbad India. Town in SE Bihar in the Damodar valley 240 km (149 miles) SSE of Patna. Pop. (1991) 151,334. Rail and road junction in a coalmining region.

Dharwar ➤HUBLI.

Dhaulagiri Nepal. Mountain peak in Himalaya range first scaled in 1960, situated 224 km (140 miles) NW of Kathmandu at 8172 m (26,810 ft).

Dhule India. Town in Maharashtra on the Panjhra R. 306 km (190 miles) NE of Bombay. Pop. (1991) 278,300.

Manufactures textiles, soap. Oilseed-milling. Trade in groundnuts, linseed, millet, cotton.

Dibrugarh India. River port in Assam on the Dibru R. near its confluence with the Brahmaputra 386 km (240 miles) NE of Shillong. Pop. (1991) 126,000. In a tea-growing district. Trade in tea and rice.

Dickson Island (Ostrov Dikson) Russia. Island off NW coast of Siberia at the mouth of the Yenisei R.

Didcot England. Town and railway junction in Oxfordshire 16 km (10 miles) S of Oxford. Pop. (1991) 17,691. Light industry and a large power station. The atomic research station of Harwell is 3 km (2 miles) WSW.

Diégo-Suarez ➤ANTSIRANAMA.

Dieppe France. Fishing port and resort in the Seine-Maritime department at the mouth of the Arques R. Pop. (1990) 37,000.

Cross-channel ferry service to Newhaven. Shipbuilding, fishing. Manufactures rope,

pharmaceutical goods, ivory and bone articles. Trade in wine, fish and textiles.

With the Revocation of the Edict of Nantes (1685), Dieppe, being Protestant, lost its former position as France's leading port. Suffered considerable damage in World War II; scene of an Allied commando raid (1942), the first landing on the continent after the Dunkirk withdrawal (1940).

Dihang River ➤BRAHMAPUTRA RIVER.

Dijon France. Cap. of the Côte-d'Or department on the Ouche R. and the Burgundy canal. Pop. (1990) 147,000. Important railway and road junction.

Noted for its trade in Burgundy wines. Manufactures motor-cycles, bicycles, chemicals, biscuits, gingerbread, liqueurs, particularly cassis, and mustard.

The 14th/15th-cent. palace of the dukes of Burgundy (almost entirely rebuilt in the 17th and 18th cent.), now the hôtel de ville, houses one of the finest museums in France. Cathedral (13th/14th-cent.); 13th-cent. Gothic Church of Notre Dame; 15th/16th-cent. Church of St Michel. University (1722). Acquired by the dukes of Burgundy early in the 11th cent.; became their cap. in the 13th cent. In 1870 it was twice occupied by the Germans, but gained through the influx of Alsatian immigrants.

Dill (Dilly) Indonesia. Chief port of East Timor on the N coast. Pop. (1980) 60,150.

Exports cotton, coffee, copra.

Former cap. of Portuguese East Timor. ➤➤TIMOR.

Dimitrovgrad Bulgaria. Industrial town on the Maritsa R. 72 km (45 miles) ESE of Plovdiv. Pop. (1990) 133,000.

Important chemical industry (esp. fertilizers). Manufactures cement, earthenware.

Developed rapidly from 1947, when it was named after Georgi Dimitrov, the first Bulgarian Communist leader.

Dimitrovo ➤PERNIK.

Dinan France. Town and holiday resort in the Côtes-du-Nord department on a height above the Rance R. at the head of its estuary

Dinant

24 km (15 miles) S of St Malo. Pop. (1989) 14,157.

Manufactures hosiery, cider, beer.

Dinant Belgium. Town in Namur province on the Meuse R. 26 km (16 miles) S of Namur. Pop. (1990) 12,000.

Main tourist centre for the Belgian Ardennes.

Sacked by Charles the Bold 1466. During World War I (1914) it was almost destroyed and about 600 inhabitants were shot by the Germans.

Dinard France. Fashionable resort in the Ille-et-Vilaine department in Brittany on the Rance estuary opposite St Malo. Pop. (1989) 11,000.

Excellent bathing beach. Noted for its lobster and crayfish dishes.

Dindigul India. Town in Tamil Nadu 53 km (33 miles) NNW of Madurai. Pop. (1991) 182,295.

Manufactures cheroots (from locally grown tobacco).

Dingle Kerry Ireland. Town in the SW on the NW shore of Dingle Bay. Pop. (1980) 1400.

Industries inc. fishing and tourism.

Dingwall Scotland. Town in Highland at the head of Cromarty Firth 18 km (11 miles) NW of Inverness. Pop. (1991) 5224.

Industries associated with tourism, distilling and whisky.

The name derives from the Scandinavian *Thingvöllr* ('Field of the Assembly').

Dinslaken Germany. Industrial town in North Rhine-Westphalia 14 km (9 miles) N of Duisburg. Pop. (1990) 61,000.

Coalmining. Manufactures iron and steel products.

Direction Island Cocos Islands. Island in the Australian Cocos group situated about 1280 km (800 miles) WSW of Singapore.

Main product copra and it has a cable station.

Dire Dawa Ethiopia. Town on the Addis Ababa–Djibouti railway 338 km (210 miles) ENE of Addis Ababa. Main commercial outlet for the Harar province. Pop. (1990) 98,104.

Trade in hides and skins, coffee. Manufactures textiles and cement.

Dismal Swamp (Great Dismal Swamp) USA. Coastal marshland in SE Virginia and NE North Carolina. Now partly reclaimed; once much larger and thickly wooded with cypress, black gum. In the centre is L. Drummond, connected with the Dismal Swamp Canal, which links Chesapeake Bay with Albemarle Sound.

Disneyland USA. Amusement park in a suburb of Los Angeles, S California.

Disney World USA. Amusement park situated 25 km (16 miles) SW of Orlando, Florida.

Dispur India. City in Assam. Built to replace Shillong as cap. of the state.

Diss England. Market town in Norfolk set around a large mere or lake, on the R. Waveney 32 km (20 miles) SSW of Norwich. Pop. (1991) 6301.

Manufactures pottery, brushes, mats.

District of Columbia ➤COLUMBIA, DISTRICT OF.

Diu India ➤DAMAN AND DIU.

Diwaniya Iraq. Cap. of Diwaniya province on the Hilla branch of the Euphrates R. and on the Baghdad–Basra railway 160 km (100 miles) SSE of Baghdad. Pop. (1970) 60,000.

Area producing barley, rice and wheat.

Diyarbakir Turkey. Cap. of Diyarbakir province in Kurdistan on the Tigris R. 169 km (105 miles) ESE of Malatya. Pop. (1990) 388,144.

Trade in grain, wool, mohair. Textile and leather manufacture.

Dizful Iran. Town in Khuzistán 120 km (75 miles) N of Ahwáz on the Díz R., a tributary of the Karun. Pop. (1990) 151,420.

Flour-milling and dyeing.

Djailolo ➤MOLUCCAS.

Dnieper (Dnepr) River

Djajapura ➤NEW GUINEA.

Djakarta ➤JAKARTA.

Djebel Toubkal ➤ATLAS MOUNTAINS.

Djerba (Jerba) Tunisia. Island at the S entrance to the Gulf of Gabès, connected to
the mainland by causeway. Area 510 sq km
(197 sq. miles). Pop. (1984) 92,269.

Produces olives, dates. Manufactures
textiles, pottery. Sponge-diving, fishing.
Tourism is growing.

Djibouti. Republic situated on the strait
of Bab el Mandeb and the Gulf of Aden,
bounded by Ethiopia (N, W and S) and
Somalia (SE). Area 23,200 sq km (8958 sq.
miles). Pop. (1995) 586,000. Life expectancy,
45 years male, 49 female. Cap. and chief
seaport Djibouti. Currency: Djibouti franc =
100 centimes.

It is largely desert and the pop. is Muslim,
47 per cent are Somali (Issa), 37 per cent
Afar, 8 per cent Europeans (mainly French)
and 6 per cent Arab.

The main economic activity is the port.
Gypsum, mica, amethyst and sulphur are supposed to exist.

Occupied by the French in 1881. Formerly
French Somaliland, it became an overseas
territory of the French Union in 1946 and
of the French Community in 1958. At a
referendum in 1967 a majority voted for
continued association with France; the Territory was renamed French Territory of the
Afars and the Issas. In 1977 it became independent and was renamed Djibouti. There
is a National Assembly of 65 members and 4
political parties are permitted by the 1992
Constitution.

Djibouti. Cap. and chief seaport of Djibouti
situated on the Gulf of Aden 240 km (150
miles) SW of Aden. A free port from 1949
and is Ethiopia's main outlet to the sea. Pop.
(1993) 353,000.

Terminus of the railway from Addis Ababa
and its economy depends on its activity as a
transit port.

Founded by the French in 1888 and became cap. in 1892.

Djokjakarta ➤JOGJAKARTA.

Dneprodzerzhinsk Ukraine. Industrial
town on the Dnieper R. 32 km (20 miles)
WNW of Dnepropetrovsk. Pop. (1990)
284,000. Important metallurgical centre.

Manufactures iron and steel, cement and
fertilizers.

Dneproges Ukraine. Suburb of Zaporozhye on the Dnieper R. Site of the largest
dam and power station in Europe. The dam
raised the level of the Dnieper more than
30 m (92 ft) and submerged the rapids below
Dnepropetrovsk; navigation is facilitated by
locks. Partially destroyed by the retreating
Russians during World War II (1941), the
dam was rebuilt by 1947.

Dnepropetrovsk Ukraine. Cap. of the
Dnepropetrovsk Region in Ukraine on the
right bank of the Dnieper R. at its confluence
with the Samara R. Pop. (1990) 1,187,000.

Industries are based on nearby coal, iron
and manganese, and power from the
Dneproges reservoir and inc. iron, steel,
agricultural engineering, chemicals and
machine-tools.

Founded by Potemkin (1786) as Ekat-
erinoslav (after Catherine II). The nearness
of coal, iron and manganese deposits assisted
rapid industrial expansion late in the 19th
cent.

Dnepr River ➤DNIEPER RIVER.

Dnestr River ➤DNIESTER RIVER.

Dnieper (Dnepr) River Russia. River
2250 km (1400 miles) long rising S of the
Valday Hills in the Smolensk Region of
Russia, flowing S through Belarus to form
part of the border with the Ukraine. It passes
Kiev and turns SE, widening to a lake
approximately 123 km (77 miles) long. It
then passes Kremenchug and forms a further
lake and then passes Dnepropetrovsk and
turns S with a further lake before entering
the Black Sea by an estuary below Kherson.
It is navigable in the upper course for eight
months of the year and in the lower for
nine. It forms the Dneproges reservoir for
hydroelectric power. The chief tributaries

Dniester (Dnestr) River

are the Berezina, Pripet, Sozh and Desna rivers.

Dniester (Dnestr) River Ukraine. River 1392 km (870 miles) long, rising in the Carpathian Mountains in the Drogobych Region and following a very meandering course, flowing generally SE through the W of the Ukraine and the E of Moldavia, and entering the Black Sea by an extensive estuary W of Odessa. It is ice-free for ten months.

Döbeln Germany. Industrial town in the Leipzig district of Saxony on the Freiberger Mulde R. 58 km (36 miles) ESE of Leipzig. Pop. (1989) 28,000.

Manufactures steel, agricultural machinery, woollen goods and soap.

Dobrich Bulgaria. Market town in the NE in S Dobruja 42 km (26 miles) NNW of Varna. Pop. (1990) 115,786.

Manufactures textiles and furniture. Flour-milling.

Since being under Turkish rule (until 1878), it has passed between Romania and Bulgaria, belonging to the latter since 1940. Formerly called Bazargic and then Dobrich, it was renamed (1949) after the Soviet Marshal Tolbukhin, who captured it from the Germans during World War II and returned to the name Dobrich in 1991.

Dobruja (Dobrogea) Bulgaria/Romania. Fertile region in SE Romania and NE Bulgaria between the lower R. Danube and the Black Sea; the central part is crossed by the Danube–Black Sea Canal. It covers 23,258 sq km (8980 sq. miles). Cap. Constanța.

Mainly agricultural: cereals, beans and vineyards. The Danube delta is a major wildlife sanctuary and game reserve.

In Roman times part of Moesia. Belonged in turn to the Byzantine, the Bulgarian and the Ottoman empires.

Dodecanese (Gr. **Dhodhekanisos**) Greece. Group of twelve islands and islets in the SE Aegean Sea, forming a *nome*. Area 2714 sq km (1048 sq. miles). Pop. (1990) 162,439. Cap. Rhodes (Ródhos). The largest and most important islands are Rhodes and

Cos (Kos); the others are Astypalaia, Kalymnos, Karpathos, Kasos, Kastellorizon, Khalke, Laros, Lipsos, Nisyros, Patmos, Syme, Telos.

Produce olives, fruits, sponges and there is a thriving tourist industry.

Gained from the Knights Hospitallers by the Turks 1522. Seized by the Italians 1912. Passed to Greece in 1947.

Dodoma Tanzania. City and cap. situated about 400 km (250 miles) W of Dar es Salaam. Pop. (1988) 203,833. It became cap. in 1975 replacing Dar es Salaam.

Doetinchem Netherlands. Town in Gelderland situated E of Arnhem on the Old Ijssel R. Pop. (1992) 42,673.

Industries inc. printing, meat-canning, metal-working and the manufacture of tyres, vehicles and bricks.

Dogger Bank North Sea. Extensive submerged sandbank 160 km (100 miles) E of the Northumberland coast. Depth of water mostly 18–36 m (55–110 ft).

Rich fishing-ground, esp. for cod.

Scene of a naval battle between British and German forces in World War I (1915).

Dogs, Isle of England. District in Poplar (E London) on the N bank of the Thames, bounded on three sides by a horseshoe bend in the river. Opposite Greenwich and connected to it by an under-river tunnel for pedestrians. The origin of the name is unknown.

Doha Qatar. Cap. and chief seaport on the E coast of the peninsula. Pop. (1992) 314,000.

Industries inc. oil-refining, engineering, food-processing and the manufacture of construction material.

Dôle France. Town in the Jura department on the Doubs R. 43 km (27 miles) WSW of Besançon. Pop. (1982) 27,959.

Industrial centre. Manufactures agricultural implements and chemicals. Trade in cheese and wine.

Birthplace of French chemist, Louis Pasteur (1822–95).

Dolgellau Wales. Market town in Gwynedd on the Wnion R. just N of Cader Idris. Pop. (1989) 2261. Tourist centre amid fine mountain scenery. Once famous for cloth manufactured from the wool of Welsh mountain sheep.

Dolhain ►LIMBOURG.

Dollar Scotland. Small market town in Clackmannanshire 10 km (6 miles) NE of Alloa at the foot of the Ochil Hills. Pop. (1991) 2670.

Dolomites Italy. Alpine region in the SE Tirol, rising to 3595 m (10,965 ft) in Marmolada. Impressive scenery, with jagged dolomitic limestone peaks, ridges, scree slopes, etc. A popular tourist area for climbing and skiing. Principal resort Cortina d'Ampezzo.

Dominica West Indies. The Commonwealth of Dominica is an island of the Windward Group in the Lesser Antilles, between the French islands of Martinique and Guadeloupe. Area 751 sq km (290 sq. miles). Pop. (1991) 108,812. Cap. Roseau. Currency: Eastern Caribbean Dollar = 100 cents but the French Franc and £ sterling are also legal tender. The island is crossed N–S by a range of mountains, rising in Morne Diablotin to 1448 m (4747 ft). Solfataras, hot springs and subterranean vapours indicate volcanic activity; Boiling L. in the S gives off gases which are sometimes poisonous. Noteworthy scenery, with spectacular waterfalls, ravines and forests. Land use: forested 41 per cent, meadows and pastures 3 per cent, agricultural 23 per cent.

Eighty per cent of the pop. is Roman Catholic. The pop. is mainly of African descent and mixed origins, with small white and Asian minorities. There is a Carib settlement of about 500.

Cacao, limes, bananas, mangoes, oranges, vanilla, coconuts and avocado pears are cultivated and citrates, copra, limejuice and rum are exported.

Named by Columbus, to commemorate the date of his discovery of the island, Sunday (*Dies Dominica*) 3 Nov. 1493. After changing hands between the French and the British several times, it finally became British during the Napoleonic Wars. It was a presidency of the Leeward Is. 1833–1940; then counted as part of the Windward Is. It became an associated state within the British Commonwealth 1967 and an independent republic as the Commonwealth of Dominica in 1978.

There is a 30-member House of Assembly – 21 members are elected and 9 are nominated.

Dominican Republic West Indies. Republic occupying about two-thirds of the E part of the island of Hispaniola (Haiti occupies the remainder). Area 48,443 sq km (18,704 sq. miles). Pop. (1990) 7,169,846. Cap. Santo Domingo. Other major cities Santiago de los Caballeros and La Romana. It is divided into 26 provinces and a National District, which contains the cap. Currency: Dominican peso = 100 centavos. It has a 1392-km (870-mile) and a 309-km (193-mile) border with Haiti and is mountainous; the Cordillera Central exceeds 3000 m (10,000 ft). It is fertile and well watered. Land use: forested 13 per cent, meadows and pastures 43 per cent, under permanent cultivation 31 per cent.

The pop. is mainly Roman Catholic and partly of Spanish descent, but is mainly composed of a mixed race of European and African blood.

Agriculture and the processing industries are the chief industries. The chief crop and export, sugar; coffee, cacao, bananas, tobacco, also exported. It has few industries apart from sugar-refining, cigars, textiles, cigarettes, food-processing and tourism. Bauxite, gold, ferronickel and rock salt mined.

Hispaniola was discovered (1492) by Columbus. The E part remained Spanish when the W was ceded to France (1697). The Dominican Republic has been independent since 1844, except for a short period of Spanish rule (1861–3) and a US military occupation (1916–24). From 1844 to 1930 the country had 56 revolutions. General Trujillo became President in 1930 and remained in power for 18 of the next 22 years; he was assassinated in 1961. After the end of the Trujillo dictatorship in 1962 the first free elections for 38 years were held, but the government was overthrown by a military coup the following year. Civil war broke out in 1965 and lasted for 4 months. Later there was a significant recovery in the economy, stimulated by government assistance for agriculture.

It is a parliamentary republic with a 27-member Senate and a 120-member Chamber of Deputies, both elected for a 4-year term at the same date as the President.

Donbas ►DONETS RIVER.

Doncaster England. Town and unitary authority on the R. Don 27 km (17 miles) NE of Sheffield. Pop. (1991) 71,595.

Main industries coalmining, railway engineering. Manufactures nylon, machinery, rope and bricks.

Nearby is the racecourse, Town Moor, where the St Leger originated in 1778.

Donegal Ireland. County of Ulster in the NW, bounded on the NW and SW by the Atlantic, on the E and SE by Counties Londonderry, Tyrone and Fermanagh (all in Northern Ireland) and on the SW by Co. Leitrim. Area 4830 sq km (1865 sq. miles). Pop. (1991) 127,994. County town Lifford. The coast is rocky and deeply indented, the main inlets being Loughs Foyle and Swilly, Sheep Haven and Donegal Bay, and there are many offshore islands, inc. Aran and Tory; Malin Head is the northernmost point of Ireland. Inland it is wild, picturesque and mountainous, with the Derryveagh Mountains in the NW rising to 752 m (2294 ft) in Mt Errigal and the Blue Stack Mountains farther S. Chief rivers the Foyle, the Finn and the Erne.

Some fishing. Sheep and cattle raised. Potatoes cultivated and tweed manufactured.

Donetsk Ukraine. Formerly Yuzovka, Stalin, Stalino. Cap. of the Donetsk Region in Ukraine 257 km (160 miles) SSE of Kharkov. Pop. (1990) 1,117,000.

Chief industrial centre of the Donbas. Coalmining. Manufactures iron and steel,

machinery, chemicals, cement and clothing.

The great metallurgical industry here was founded by a British industrialist named Hughes c. 1870 and the town was called Yuzovka (Hughesovka) after him.

Donets River Russia. River 1094 km (680 miles) long rising in SW Russia 129 km (80 miles) NNE of Kharkov and flowing generally S and SE through the Ukraine to join the Don R. 96 km (60 miles) ENE of Rostov. The Donets Basin, or Donbas, is a coalmining and industrial region. It has an area of 25,000 sq km (10,000 sq. miles) and lies N of the Sea of Azov and W of the Donets R. in the Ukraine. Development of the region began in the 1870s, but by the early 1990s there was considerable unrest and an urgent need for modernization.

Dongting Hu (Tung Ting Lake) China. Extensive shallow lake in N Hunan province 185 km (115 miles) SW of Wuhan. Fed by the Siang and Yuan rivers, with an outlet (N) to the Chang Jiang. Area (in winter) 3900 sq km (1500 sq. miles). During the summer it receives the flood waters of the Chang Jiang and more than doubles in size. It is slowly filling up owing to deposition of silt.

Don River England. River 113 km (70 miles) long mainly in South Yorkshire, rising in the Pennines 11 km (7 miles) W of Penistone, flowing SE and then NE through Sheffield, Rotherham and Doncaster, to join the R. Ouse at Goole, Humberside.

Don River Scotland. River 132 km (82 miles) long in Aberdeenshire, rising near the Banffshire border and flowing generally E to enter the North Sea just N of Aberdeen. Important salmon fisheries.

Don River Russia. Ancient Tanais. River in European Russia, 1930 km (1200 miles) long, rising near Tula and flowing generally S and then E within 77 km (48 miles) of the Volga R., to which it is joined by canal near Volgograd; from here it turns SW past Rostov to enter the Sea of Azov by a delta.

It rises at an altitude of only 177 m (540 ft) and has an average fall of about 7.8 cm per km. Navigable to small craft as far upstream as Voronezh. Closed by ice for 3–4 months annually. Important fisheries. Used for transportation of grain, coal, timber. Chief tributaries the Voronezh, the Donets and the Medveditsa.

Doorn Netherlands. Town and health resort, with tourism as the main industry in Utrecht province 18 km (11 miles) SE of Utrecht. Pop. (1992) 10,459. Kaiser Wilhelm II of Germany lived here in exile from 1919 till his death (1941).

Doornik ►TOURNAI.

Dorchester (Dorset) England. Ancient Durnovaria. Market town in Dorset on the R. Frome 39 km (24 miles) W of Bournemouth. Pop. (1991) 15,037. Known chiefly for its associations with Thomas Hardy (1840–1928), being the 'Casterbridge' of his Wessex novels. His birthplace and the house where he spent his last years are both nearby. Many Roman and pre-Roman remains; 3 km (2 miles) SW is the great earthwork of MAIDEN CASTLE nearby at Poundbury is another encampment and at Maumbury Rings are the remains of a Roman amphitheatre. TOLPUDDLE is 11 km (7 miles) ENE. Dorchester is also associated with William Barnes, the Dorset poet (1800–86).

Dorchester (Oxfordshire) England. Village, that was once a city, on the R. Thame near its confluence with the R. Thames 13 km (8 miles) SSE of Oxford. Abbey Church (mainly 13th-cent.) with a remarkable 'Jesse window'. Important in Saxon times, when it was the seat of a bishopric.

Dordogne France. Department formed (1790) mainly from the old district of Périgord. Area 9184 sq km (3561 sq. miles). Pop. (1990) 386,400. Prefecture Périgueux. The E part, on the W slopes of the Massif Central, is rather dry and stony. The W, esp. in the river valleys, is fertile: vines, wheat, tobacco cultivated; chestnuts, walnuts, truffles also

important. Chief towns Périgueux and Bergerac.

Dordogne River France. River 467 km (290 miles) long rising on Mont Dore in the Auvergne Mountains, flowing SW and W to join the Garonne R. and form the Gironde estuary. Famous vineyards (e.g. St Émilion) beside its lower course. Several hydroelectric intallations.

Dordrecht Netherlands. Town and port in S Holland province 19 km (12 miles) SE of Rotterdam, mainly on the S bank of the Oude Maas R. Pop. (1992) 111,791.

Shipbuilding, marine engineering. Manufactures electrical equipment, chemicals and glass.

A 14th-cent. church (Groote Kerk). Chief port of the Netherlands until the 17th cent., then superseded by Rotterdam. First meeting-place of the United Provinces (1572) and scene of the Synod of Dort (1618–19).

Dorking England. Town in Surrey on the R. Mole near the N Downs with Box Hill (182 m; 597 ft) 1.6 km (1 mile) NE. Pop. (1985) 20,000, inc. surrounding villages.

Dornbirn Austria. Town in Vorarlberg province 10 km (6 miles) S of Bregenz near the Swiss frontier. Pop. (1991) 41,000. Manufactures textiles.

Dornoch Scotland. County town of Sutherland on Dornoch Firth in Highland. Pop. (1992) 1200. Seaside resort with well-known golf course. Noted for tourism and particularly fishing.

Scotland's last burning of a witch took place here (1722).

Dorset England. County in the SW, bounded on the S by the English Channel. Area 2688 sq km (1038 sq. miles). Pop. (1991) 645,200. It is divided into the districts of Bournemouth, Christchurch, East Dorset, North Dorset, Poole, Purbeck, West Dorset, Weymouth and Portland. County town Dorchester, other large towns are Bournemouth and Poole. The chalk range of the N Dorset Downs runs across the centre, rising in the E to 275 m (902 ft); in the S are the lower S Dorset Downs and in the N Cranborne Chase, the rest of the country being low-lying. Chief rivers the Frome and the Stour.

Industries inc. computing and computer services, defence and marine electronics and aerospace, together with a number of major research establishments. The tourist industry employs 30,000 people at the resorts of Bournemouth, Weymouth, Swanage and Lyme Regis. Sheep raised on the downs and dairy cattle in the valleys. Portland building stone quarried.

Dorset is immortalized in the novels and poems of Thomas Hardy.

Dortmund Germany. Industrial town and port in North Rhine-Westphalia on the Emscher R. at the head of the Dortmund–Ems Canal 32 km (20 miles) ENE of Essen. Pop. (1990) 599,000.

A major centre of coalmining and steel manufacture. Brewing, engineering. Expanded with the development of the Ruhr coalfield.

A town of importance by the 9th cent., it benefited commercially by joining the Hanseatic League in the 13th. Ceded to Prussia 1815. Among its old buildings are the 13th-cent. Reinoldikirche and the 12th-cent. Marienkirche; many were severely damaged by Allied bombing in World War II.

Dortmund–Ems Canal Germany. Canal, 272 km (170 miles) long, opened in 1899 to link the industrial area of the Ruhr with the North Sea at Emden. It joins the R. Ems 115 km (71 miles) N of Dortmund.

Dorval Canada. Town situated in Quebec 16 km (10 miles) SW of Montreal on the S shore of Montreal Island. Resort and site of airport.

Douai France. Town in the Nord department on the Scarpe R. 29 km (18 miles) S of Lille. On the northern coalfield at the centre of routes by road, rail and canal. Pop. (1990) 44,000.

Manufactures iron and steel, coke, machinery and glass.

Many associations with British Catholics: in 1568 a college for English Catholics was set up here and in 1592 another for Scottish Catholics, and the 'Douai Bible', used by Roman Catholics, was published at the former 1610.

Douala Cameroon. Chief seaport and largest town 200 km (125 miles) W of Yaoundé. Pop. (1991) 810,000. Terminus of the railway from Yaoundé.

Exports tropical hardwoods, cacao, bananas. Brewing, flour-milling. Manufactures textiles and footwear.

Cap. of the German colony of Kamerun (1901–16).

Douarnenez France. Port in the Finistère department on the S shore of Douarnenez Bay 40 km (25 miles) SE of Brest. Pop. (1982) 18,000.

Sardine and tunny fishing. Boatbuilding, fishing-net making, fish-canning.

Doubs France. Department in the E in Franche-Comté Region formed from Montbéliard, bounded on the E by Switzerland and crossed by the Doubs R. Area 5228 sq km (2030 sq. miles). Pop. (1990) 484,800. Prefecture Besançon. Largely mountainous, with four parallel chains of the Jura running NE–SW across it. The NW area is lower and more fertile, producing cereals, vegetables.

Manufactures motor vehicles, bicycles, clocks and watches. Chief towns Besançon, Montbéliard and Pontarlier.

Doubs River France. River 427 km (267 miles) long, rising in the E Jura, flowing first NE through picturesque limestone gorges, forming part of the Franco–Swiss frontier, turning W, N, then SW to join the Saône R. at Verdun-sur-le-Doubs. The source to mouth is only 90 km (56 miles). Towns along its course inc. Pontarlier, Besançon, Dôle.

Douglas Isle of Man. Cap. situated in Douglas Bay on the E coast. Pop. (1991) 22,214. Seaport and resort.

Industries inc. fishing, tourism, banking and financial services, and it is the scene of annual motor-cycle races.

Downs

Dounreay Scotland. Nuclear research establishment on the Pentland Firth in Caithness, Highland W of Thurso.

Douro (Sp. **Duero**) **River** Portugal/Spain. River 895 km (555 miles) long, rising at the W end of the Sierra de Cebollera, flowing S and then swinging W to drain much of the N Meseta; forms part of the Portuguese-Spanish border and enters the Atlantic downstream from Oporto. Navigation impeded by rapids; used chiefly for irrigation and hydroelectric power. Vineyards in its lower valley produce Port wines.

Dover England. Seaport in E Kent on the Strait of Dover 105 km (65 miles) ESE of London. Pop. (1991) 34,179. A Cinque Port, the only one still an important seaport, terminus of the shortest sea route to the continent (to Calais 35 km (22 miles) distant). It has been an important Channel port since Roman times. There are car ferries and hovercraft services. The car-ferry terminal was completed in 1953. In 1992 there was a sailing every 20 minutes and Dover handled 21 per cent of Britain's foreign trade. The opening of the Channel tunnel has caused some unemployment in Dover.

Within the precincts of the Norman castle, which overlooks the town, are a Roman pharos (lighthouse), which guided the legions across the Channel. The castle, successfully defended (1216) against the French by Hubert de Burgh, was long considered to be the key to England. In World War I it was the headquarters of the famous Dover Patrol; in World War II it suffered severely from air raids and long-range bombardments.

Dover, Strait of (Fr. **Pas de Calais**). Strait between England and France, connecting the English Channel with the North Sea and a busy waterway. At its narrowest (between Dover and Cap Gris Nez) 34 km (21 miles) wide. This is the route taken by most Channel swimmers, the first successful one being Capt Matthew Webb (1875, Dover-Calais).

Dove River England. River 64 km (40 miles) long, rising 5 km (3 miles) SW of

Buxton, flowing S and SE and forming much of the Derbyshire-Staffordshire border, joining the R. Trent near Burton-on-Trent. Dovedale, between Dove Holes and Thorpe Cloud, is especially well-known for its scenery.

Dovey River ▶ABERDOVEY.

Dovrefjell Norway. Mountainous plateau in the S, separated from the Jotunheim Mountains (SSW) by the Gudbrandsdal, rising to 2286 m (7500 ft) in Snöhetta. Crossed by the Oslo-Trondheim railway.

Down Northern Ireland. Maritime former county in the E, facing the Irish Sea, bounded by Belfast Lough (N) and Carlingford Lough (S). Area 2466 sq km (952 sq. miles). Pop. (1989) 363,000. County town Downpatrick. Coastline indented, the principal inlet being Strangford Lough, almost enclosed by the low-lying Ards peninsula. Hilly, with Slieve Donard in the Mourne Mountains (SE) rising to 853 m (2729 ft). The fertile valleys of the Lagan, Upper Bann and other rivers produce oats, potatoes and turnips, and cattle are reared.

Main industry linen manufacture. Chief towns Downpatrick, Bangor, Newry and Newtownards.

Downey USA. Suburb 16 km (10 miles) SE of Los Angeles in California. Pop. (1990) 91,400.

Manufactures aircraft, cement and soap.

Downpatrick Northern Ireland. County town of Co. Down, urban district 35 km (22 miles) SSE of Belfast. Pop. (1991) 10,113.

Market town; manufactures textiles, and industries inc. tanning and brewing.

Nearby are the remains of Saul Abbey, where St Patrick died.

Downs England. Chalk hills in the S, the name being generally applied to two roughly parallel ranges running W-E known as the N Downs and the S Downs. The N Downs extend through Surrey and Kent, ending at the white cliffs of Dover, the S Downs through Sussex to Beachy Head, and the scarp slopes of the two ridges face each other across the Weald. Their highest points are Leith Hill 294 m (964 ft) in the N Downs and Butser Hill 264 m (866 ft) in the S Downs. They provide good sheep pasture and have produced the well-known Southdown breed. Farther W are the Hampshire, Berkshire and Marlborough Downs.

Downs, The England. Roadstead off the E coast of Kent opposite Deal, about 13 km (8 miles) by 10 km (6 miles), protected by the Goodwin Sands, except during strong southerly gales.

Drachenfels Germany. Mountain 321 m (1053 ft) in the Siebengebirge on the right bank of the Rhine R. near Honnef, 13 km (8 miles) SE of Bonn. Ruins of a 12th-cent. castle at the summit.

Drakensberg South Africa. Principal mountain range in southern Africa: stretching 1125 km (700 miles) from E Gauteng, through Free State, KwaZulu/Natal and Lesotho to Eastern Cape Province. The highest peaks are in Lesotho: Thaban Ntlenyana 3485 m (10,629 ft) and Mont-aux-Sources 3301 m (10,068 ft) near which is the Natal National Park. An important watershed: the Tugela R. flows to the Indian Ocean, the Orange R. (with its tributaries the Vaal and the Caledon) to the Atlantic.

Drama Greece. 1. *Nome* in Macedonia East and Thrace with Bulgaria on its N border. Area 3468 sq km (1353 sq. miles). Pop. (1990) 96,978. Drained by the Mesta R. Chief crop tobacco.

2. Ancient Drabescus. Cap. of Drama *nome*, 117 km (73 miles) ENE of Salonika. Pop. (1981) 36,000.

Industries inc. processing cotton, tobacco and rice.

Drammen Norway. Port at the mouth of the Drammen R. and the head of Drammen Fiord (Dramsfiord), 37 km (23 miles) SW of Oslo. Pop. (1990) 51,978.

Manufactures and exports paper, wood pulp, cellulose. Engineering.

Drammen (Drams) River Norway. River 306 km (190 miles) long, rising as the Hal-

lingdal R. on the Hallingskarv Mountains, flowing generally E and then SSE to Drammen Fiord (Dramsfiord). Provides hydroelectric power for sawmills.

Drancy France. Suburb of NE Paris in the Seine-St Denis department. Mainly residential, with many large blocks of flats.

Drava (Drave) River Italy/Austria/Croatia. River 724 km (450 miles) long rising in the Carnic Alps near Dobbiaco (Italy) flowing E into Austria and then Croatia, turning ESE to join the Danube R. 19 km (12 miles) E of Osijek, forming part of the Croatian–Hungarian border. Navigable by steamers below Barcs (159 km; 95 miles).

Drenthe (Drente) Netherlands. Province in the NE, bordered on the E by Germany. Area 2655 sq km (1025 sq. miles). Pop. (1991) 443,510. Cap. Assen.

Potatoes, rye are cultivated and cattle reared. Peat digging. Oil and natural gas produced in the SE.

Dresden Germany. City in Saxony on the Elbe R. 101 km (63 miles) ESE of Leipzig. Pop. (1989) 515,900.

Important commercial and industrial centre. Railway and road junction. Manufactures machine-tools, optical and musical instruments, electrical equipment, chemical and pharmaceutical goods, and cigarettes (but the famous Dresden china is made at Meissen).

Once a Slav settlement, Dresden became the cap. of Henry, Margrave of Meissen, in 1270. Later cap. of the electors and kings of Saxony. Became an art centre in the 17th and 18th cent., esp. under the electors Augustus I and II, and was often known as 'the German Florence'. Suffered severely in the Seven Years War (1760) and at the Battle of Dresden (1813), the last of Napoleon's great victories. In World War II it was severely damaged and over 60,000 people may have died. Many of its buildings were destroyed, inc. the baroque Hofkirche and Frauenkirche, the Opera House and the Zainger, with its valuable art collections. There are plans to restore the Frauenkirche. Most of the treasures, however, had been kept in safety outside the city. Among its principal outdoor features are the great public park known as the Grosser Garten (1676) and the Bruhl Terrace, an attractive promenade built (1738) along the S bank of the Elbe. In 1988 it was still a city covered in a crust of soot from industrial pollution, but by 1993 a clean-up had taken place and there is a start on restoring the city's original baroque splendour.

Drin River Albania. River 160 km (100 miles) long, formed by the union of the White Drin R. and the Black Drin R. at Kukës, flowing generally W; divides on the plain of Shkodër, the old course continuing S to the Adriatic, with an arm flowing W to join the Bojana R.

Drina River Montenegro. River 467 km (290 miles) long, formed by the union of the Tara and the Piva rivers on the N border of Montenegro, flowing generally NNE to join the Sava R.

Drogheda Ireland. Pronounced 'Droyeda'. Seaport in Co. Louth on the R. Boyne 6 km (4 miles) above its mouth on Drogheda Bay. Pop. (1991) 24,000.

Exports cattle. Linen and cotton milling, brewing, engineering. Manufactures cement, fertilizers.

Taken by the Danes in the 10th cent., later an Anglo–Norman stronghold. Parliaments were held here until 1494 when 'Poynings' Law' was enacted, by which Irish legislation had to be ratified by the English Privy Council. During the Civil War it was captured by Cromwell (1649) and its inhabitants massacred or transported to the West Indies.

Drogobych (Drohobycz) Ukraine. Town situated 68 km (42 miles) SW of Lvov. Pop. (1990) 78,500.

Centre of petroleum and natural gas production. Oil-refining, metalworking. Manufactures chemicals, soap. Trade in agricultural produce.

Droitwich England. Town in Worcestershire 10 km (6 miles) NNE of Wor-

cester on the R. Salwarpe. Pop. (1990) 24,500.

Spa: salt springs (wyches), among the strongest in Europe and known since Roman times, no longer used for salt manufacture but for treatment of rheumatic ailments. Saltworks at Stoke Prior 6 km (4 miles) to the NE. Conference centre, and industries inc. cold-storage warehousing, metal castings and heating equipment.

Drôme France. Department in the Rhône-Alpes region formed (1790) from parts of Dauphiné and Provence. Area 6530 sq km (2521 sq. miles). Pop. (1990) 414,191. Prefecture Valence. Mountainous in the E, where spurs of the Cottian Alps reach 2406 m (7894 ft) (Dévoluy); slopes W to its W boundary, the Rhône. On the lowlands vines, mulberries, maize, truffles and olives are grown. Chief towns Valence and Montélimar.

Rhône wines are produced and textiles are manufactured.

Drôme River France. River 105 km (65 miles) long, flowing generally WNW across the Drôme department to join the Rhône R. 24 km (15 miles) N of Montélimar.

Dromore Northern Ireland. Market town in Co. Down on the R. Lagan 26 km (16 miles) SW of Belfast. Pop. (1991) 3434.

Linen manufactured.

Droylsden England. Town in Greater Manchester just E of the city. Pop. (1991) 22,666.

Industries textiles and chemicals. Engineering.

Drummondville Canada. Industrial town in Quebec on the St Francis R. 96 km (60 miles) ENE of Montreal. Pop. (1985) 39,000.

Industries publishing and hosiery. It has an important hydroelectric plant.

Drygalski Island Antarctica. Island off the coast of Queen Mary Land in Australian Antarctic Territory. It was discovered (1914) by Sir Douglas Mawson and named after the German explorer Erich von Drygalski.

Duarte Dominican Republic. Province in the centre of the country. Area 2823 sq km (1090 sq. miles). Pop. (1990) 261,725. Cap. San Francisco de Macorís. It is a densely populated farming area producing cacao, coffee, fruit and rice. Iron deposits are found.

Dubai United Arab Emirates. Chief seaport and largest town in the Emirate of Dubai on the Gulf. Pop. (1989) 280,000. ➤ UNITED ARAB EMIRATES.

Dubawnt Lake Canada. Lake in Northwest Territories. Area 4144 sq. km (1600 sq. miles). It is fed by the Dubawnt R. and drains through Baker L. and Chesterfield Inlet into Hudson Bay.

Dubbo Australia. Town in New South Wales on the Macquarie R. 298 km (185 miles) NW of Sydney Pop. (1973) 18,430.

Centre of a wool- and wheat-producing district. Flour-milling. Manufactures clothing.

Dublin Ireland. 1. Maritime county in Leinster, bordering on the Irish Sea (E). Area 922 sq km (356 sq. miles). Pop. (1991) 1,025,304. The N and central parts are low-lying but the S is mountainous, rising to 754 m (2473 ft) at Kippure in the Wicklow Mountains. Chief river the Liffey. Oats and potatoes are cultivated and cattle raised. Dun Laoghaire is a separate borough. 2. Cap. of the republic, seaport and county borough on the E coast of Ireland at the mouth of the R. Liffey where it flows into Dublin Bay, facing the Irish Sea. Irish, Baile Atha Cliath. Pop. (1991) 477,675.

Leading commercial and cultural centre. The main industry is brewing, particularly Guinness; there is also varied light manufacture, inc. food-processing, electrical goods and textiles. The port of Dublin handles cargo and passenger traffic and the principal roads and railways converge on the city.

The axis of Dublin is Grafton Street, a shopping street running S from Parnell Square to St Stephen's Green; the latter is the largest of the city's many squares, built in the 18th cent. and linked by equally fine Georgian terraces. The Liffey has attracted

the Guinness brewery and many public buildings to its banks; twelve bridges cross it and two 18th-cent. canals flow into it. The presidential residence is in Phoenix Park on the N bank; the Park extends over 8 sq km (3 sq. miles). In the library of Trinity College, founded in 1591, is the 8th-cent. *Book of Kells* and the 11th-cent. harp which is used as the trade mark of Guinness. Dublin has many literary connections inc. Edmund Burke, James Joyce, G. B. Shaw, R. B. Sheridan, Jonathan Swift, Oscar Wilde and W. B. Yeats. The first town was built and fortified by the Vikings *c.* 830. It was taken by an Anglo–Norman force in 1170 and subsequently claimed by England. It remained small until 1685 when its official Protestantism attracted Huguenot refugees. From 1700 to 1800 it was the rich and beautiful cap. of an Anglo–Irish establishment, but the Irish parliament was abolished in 1800 and the city declined, only its poor and oppressed Catholic pop. remaining. The scene of much violence until 1927, it only recovered as a cap. city after World War II.

Dubrovnik (Italian **Ragusa**) Croatia. Seaport on the Dalmatian coast 160 km (100 miles) SE of Split. Pop. (1990) 49,000.

Tourist centre with a modern harbour at the suburb of Gruž.

Its medieval ramparts with many towers enclose the 17th-cent. cathedral with altarpiece by Titian, the 15th-cent. rector's palace and cloisters of 14th-cent. Dominican and Franciscan monasteries. Just off Dubrovnik is the small island of Lokrum, where Richard I was said to have been shipwrecked (1190). Founded in the 7th cent. by refugees from Epidaurus (the modern Cavtat). Became a great commercial centre, an independent republic and rival of Venice, but declined from the 16th cent. Passed to Austria (1814), then to Yugoslavia (1918), when it was given its present name. In 1992 the city was shelled by Serbian forces.

Dubuque USA. Town, river port and railway centre in E Iowa 100 km (62 miles) NE of Cedar Rapids on the Mississippi R. Pop. (1990) 57,546.

Ducie Island ➤PITCAIRN ISLAND.

Dudley England. Town and unitary authority 13 km (8 miles) WNW of Birmingham. Pop. (1991) 192,171.

Centre of the wrought-iron industry. Manufactures glass, boilers, chains, welding equipment and other metal goods, as well as bricks and tiles. It has a growing tourist industry.

Dudweiler Germany. Industrial town in Saarland 6 km (4 miles) NE of Saarbrucken. Pop. (1970) 30,078.

Industries inc. coalmining and metalworking. Manufactures inc. electrical equipment.

Duero River ➤DOURO RIVER.

Duff Islands SW Pacific Ocean. Small group of volcanic islands in the Solomon Islands in Melanesia.

Dugi Otok Croatia. Island 45 km (28 miles) long and 5 km (3 miles) wide off the Dalmatian coast. Fishing villages and seaside resorts, the largest being Sali, on the S coast, 23 km (14 miles) S of Zadar.

Duisburg Germany. Industrial town and river port in North Rhine-Westphalia at the confluence of the Rhine and the Ruhr rivers 21 km (13 miles) N of Düsseldorf. Pop. (1990) 537,000.

One of the world's largest and busiest inland ports. It has an important iron and steel industry; also coalmining, shipbuilding, engineering. Manufactures inc. chemicals and textiles.

Dukeries, The England. District in NW Nottinghamshire in Sherwood Forest, between Mansfield and Worksop, consisting of the great parks of a group of former ducal seats: Welbeck, Worksop, Clumber and Thoresby.

Dukhan ➤QATAR.

Dukinfield England. Town in Greater Manchester 10 km (6 miles) E of Manchester. Pop. (1991) 17,917.

Industries inc. engineering and the manufacture of wood and metal products, cotton goods, firebricks and tiles.

Duluth USA. City and port in Minnesota at the mouth of the St Louis R. at the W end of L. Superior. Pop. (1991) 86,000.

It has an excellent harbour but is icebound for 4 months annually. Handles grain, iron ore and coal shipments. Manufactures telephone equipment, cement and steel. There is flour-milling, sawmilling and brewing. An aerial lift bridge spans the ship canal (through Minnesota Point) which forms the harbour entrance.

Dulwich England. Residential suburb in the Inner London borough of Southwark, in S London. Well-known public school, Dulwich College, founded (1619) by Edward Alleyn; large park (29 ha; 71 acres) and famous art gallery (founded 1811).

Dumbarton (Gaelic **Dun Breatann**) Scotland. Town in West Dunbartonshire near the confluence of the R. Leven with the R. Clyde 23 km (14 miles) WNW of Glasgow. Pop. (1991) 21,962.

Main industry shipbuilding; also engineering and whisky-distilling.

Dum-Dum India. Town in W Bengal just NE of Calcutta. Pop. (1991) 382,800.

Manufactures railway wagons, chemicals, pharmaceuticals, textile machinery, boilers, sugar-mill machinery, iron and steel castings and music tapes.

The first soft-nosed 'dum-dum' bullets were made at the arsenal in the late 19th cent. and were used against the tribesmen on the NW frontier. Site of Calcutta international airport.

Dumfries Scotland. Town in Dumfries and Galloway on the R. Nith 47 km (29 miles) WNW of Carlisle. Pop. (1991) 32,136.

Market town. Manufactures tweed, plastics, rubber and hosiery.

Since 1929 inc. Maxwelltown, on the opposite bank of the river. In St Michael's churchyard is the Burns Mausoleum (1815); the house where the poet spent his last five years is now a museum.

Dumfries and Galloway

Dumfries and Galloway Scotland. Local authority of SW Scotland bounded S by the Solway Firth. Area 6475 sq km (2500 sq. miles). Pop. (1993) 147,900. It comprises the counties of Dumfries, Wigtown and Kirkcudbright.

Industries inc. stained glass, woollen, engineering, food-processing, rubber and aluminium.

Dumfriesshire Scotland. Former county in the S, bordering Cumbria, England (SE) and Solway Firth in Dumfries and Galloway.

Dumyat (Damietta) Egypt. City and cap. of governorate situated on the eastern mouth of the R. Nile 13 km (8 miles) from the sea and 153 km (95 miles) NNE of Cairo. Pop. (1991) 113,000.

It is a market centre and manufactures cotton goods, silk and glassware.

Dunajec River Poland. River 209 km (130 miles) long formed by the union of the Czarny (Black) Dunajec and the Bialy (White) Dunajec, rising in the High Tatra and flowing generally E and N to join the Vistula R.

Dunbar Scotland. Fishing port and resort in East Lothian on the North Sea 42 km (26 miles) E of Edinburgh. Pop. (1991) 6518.

Industries inc. tourism, brewing, cement, a nuclear power station and fishing.

Dunbartonshire (Dumbartonshire) Scotland. Former county in the W in Strathclyde Region 1975–96 and now East and West Dunbartonshire.

Dunbartonshire, East Scotland. New unitary authority created in 1996, formerly part of Strathclyde Region. Pop. (1993) 110,220.

Dunbartonshire, West Scotland. New unitary authority created in 1996, formerly part of Strathclyde Region. Pop. (1993) 97,790.

Dunblane Scotland. Market town in Stirling on Allan Water 8 km (5 miles) N of Stirling. Pop. (1991) 7368.

Spa. Woollen mills.

Dundalk Ireland. County town and seaport of Co. Louth near the mouth of the R. Castletown, Dundalk Bay, 32 km (20 miles) N of Drogheda. Pop. (1991) 26,000.

It exports cattle, beef, grain, and industries inc. railway engineering, brewing. Manufactures linen, hosiery, chemicals and electronics.

Here Edward Bruce proclaimed himself king of Ireland (1315) and was killed in battle nearby (1318).

Dundee Scotland. City, in Tayside Region 1975–96, on the N shore of the Firth of Tay 58 km (36 miles) NNE of Edinburgh. Pop. (1990) 176,000.

It has been a Royal burgh since the 12th cent. Seaport, formerly the chief centre of the British jute industry; the last jute mill closed in 1998. Other industries have been developed, particularly engineering and oil-related industries, publishing. Manufactures linen, paper, confectionery, linoleum, jam, marmalade, electrical and electronic equipment, computers, clocks and watches.

Linked with Edinburgh and the S by railway via the Tay Bridge, completed in 1888 to replace the earlier bridge, which was destroyed in a gale (1879); a new road bridge was opened in 1966. Within the city is the residential and resort town of Broughty Ferry on the Firth of Tay 6 km (4 miles) E.

Dunedin New Zealand. Seaport and industrial town on the SE coast of the South Island at the head of Otago Harbour. Pop. (1991) 116,577.

Manufactures woollen goods, clothing, footwear and agricultural machinery. Most of its trade is handled at Port Chalmers 13 km (8 miles) NE along the harbour. Main exports wool, meat, fruit, cheese, condensed milk.

The first shipment of frozen New Zealand meat was dispatched from here 1881.

Dunfermline Scotland. Ancient town in SW Fife. Pop. (1991) 55,083.

Famous from the early 18th cent. for damask and linen; now manufactures silk, rayon, rubber products and electronic equipment. There is also engineering, bleaching and dyeing. The last remaining coalmine in Scotland is in the area.

It is the birthplace of Andrew Carnegie (1835–1919), who presented Pittencrieff Park and Glen, the public library and baths, and other gifts to the town; several of his many endowment trusts are administered from here.

Dungannon Northern Ireland. Market town in Co. Tyrone 56 km (35 miles) WSW of Belfast. Pop. (1991) 9190.

Manufactures linen and bricks.

Dungarvan Ireland. Market town and seaport in Co. Waterford on Dungarvan Harbour 40 km (25 miles) SW of Waterford. Pop. (1991) 7000.

Manufactures pharmaceuticals, leather, dairy products.

Dungeness England. Low shingle headland, the southernmost point of Kent, slowly extending seawards by accumulation of shingle. The Dungeness nuclear power station is nearby.

Dunkeld Scotland. Village in Perth and Kinross on the R. Tay 21 km (13 miles) NNW of Perth. Pop. (1991) 1227. Ruined cathedral partly dating from the 12th cent., presented to the nation by the Duke of Atholl 1918. About 1.6 km (1 mile) S is the probable remnant of Birnam Wood, mentioned in Shakespeare's *Macbeth*.

Dunkirk (Fr. **Dunkerque**) France. Northernmost seaport of France in the Nord department on the North Sea 39 km (24 miles) ENE of Calais. Pop. (1990) 71,071.

Shipbuilding, oil and sugar refining, cotton and jute spinning.

In World War II the harbour was completely destroyed, to be partially reopened in 1946. Scene of the evacuation of over 300,000 Allied troops, hemmed in by German forces, in 1940.

Dun Laoghaire Ireland. Pronounced 'Dunleary'. Formerly Dunleary, Kingstown. Passenger seaport for Dublin, in Co. Dublin on

the S shore of Dublin Bay with steamer service to Holyhead. Pop. (1991) 185,000. Also a seaside resort and yachting centre.

Its original name was changed to Kingstown after George IV had embarked here (1821) and to its present name in 1921.

Dunmow (Great Dunmow) England. Market town in Essex on the R. Chelmer 13 km (8 miles) E of Bishop's Stortford. Pop. (1988) 5705. Here the ancient Dunmow Flitch trial is held annually, a married couple who can testify that they have not quarrelled for one year being awarded a flitch of bacon – the custom having been revived in 1855. The village of Little Dunmow is 3 km (2 miles) ESE.

Dunoon Scotland. Small town in Argyll and Bute on the Firth of Clyde 10 km (6 miles) W of Greenock. Pop. (1991) 9038. Seaside resort; yachting centre.

Traces of an ancient castle. Just N is Holy Loch.

Duns ➤BERWICKSHIRE.

Dunstable England. Town in Bedfordshire at the N end of the Chiltern Hills 6 km (4 miles) W of Luton. Pop. (1991) 49,666.

Noted for printing and engineering. Manufactures lorries and vans, paper, cement, rubber and plastic goods.

In the centre of the town is the intersection of the Roman Watling Street and the ancient Icknield Way.

Dunwich England. Village in E Suffolk 6 km (4 miles) SSW of Southwold. An important port in Roman, Saxon and early medieval times, but it has been destroyed by erosion.

Duque de Caxias Brazil. City on the N outskirts of Rio de Janeiro, an outer suburb of the latter. Pop. (1990) 264,379.

Mainly commercial and residential, but it does manufacture motors and there is some flax and jute spinning.

Durance River France. River 350 km (218 miles) long rising near the Mont Genèvre Pass in the High Alps of the Dauphiné, flowing generally SSW, at first through several deep gorges, then turning W to join the Rhône R. near Avignon.

Durango Mexico. State in the N; a high tableland crossed by the Sierra Madre mountains in the W. Area 123,181 sq km (47,560 sq. miles). Pop. (1990) 1,352,156.

Rich mining areas in the mountains produce silver, gold, iron, copper. Cotton, wheat and other crops are grown, esp. in the Nazas R. valley.

Durazno Uruguay. Cap. of the Durazno department on the Yi R. 177 km (110 miles) NNW of Montevideo. Pop. (1985) 27,602. Road and rail junction.

Market town in a cattle and sheep rearing area. It trades in livestock, hides and grain. Industries inc. meat-packing and flour-milling.

Durazzo ➤DÜRRES.

Durban South Africa. Largest city and major seaport of Natal on the Indian Ocean 485 km (301 miles) SE of Johannesburg. Pop. (1991) 1,137,378. It has a fine harbour and excellent dock and bunkering facilities.

Exports coal, manganese and chrome ore, maize, wool (from the interior), sugar, oranges and pineapples (from the coastal region). Industries inc. car assembly, oil and sugar refining, food-processing and railway engineering. Manufactures machinery, metal goods, furniture and textiles. It is a tourist resort with excellent beaches.

The first European settlers (1824) were British elephant-hunters. Founded 1835; named after the then Governor of Cape Colony, Sir Benjamin D'Urban. There was considerable political unrest in the townships in the 1980s.

Düren Germany. Industrial town in North Rhine-Westphalia on the Ruhr R. 35 km (22 miles) WSW of Cologne. Pop. (1985) 84,100.

Manufactures metal goods, textiles, paper and glass.

Durgapur India. Industrial town in West

Bengal 160 km (100 miles) NW of Calcutta. Pop. (1991) 425,800.

Manufactures fertilizers, alloy steel, cement, carbon black, graphite, mining machinery, glass, oxygen, chemicals, rail and auto wheels.

Durham England. 1. County in the NE bounded on the E by the North Sea. Area 2437 sq km (1015 sq. miles). Pop. (1991) 589,000. It is divided into the districts of Chester-le-Street, Darlington, Derwentside, Durham, Easington, Sedgefield, Teesdale and Wear Valley. Hilly in the W, where it rises to the crest of the Pennines. Descends in the E to a coastal plain. Drained by the upper Wear and Tees rivers. Sheep are grazed on the hill slopes. Oats, wheat and other crops cultivated in the fertile river valleys.

Coalmining ceased in 1993, but it gave rise to the growth in heavy industries; chiefly iron and steel manufacture, shipbuilding and engineering, and chemical manufacture in NE England. 2. Cathedral city in Co. Durham, built round a hill in a loop of the R. Wear 23 km (14 miles) S of Newcastle upon Tyne. Pop. (1991) 85,000. Dominated by its cathedral and castle.

There is limited industry consisting of electrical engineering, the manufacture of carpets, textiles and clothing.

The magnificent Norman cathedral (begun 1093) was built on the site of a shrine erected for the body of St Cuthbert, brought here in 995. Bede is also buried here. Bishop Flambard and Bishop Pudsey, who were largely responsible for the construction of the cathedral, were also concerned in the building of the castle, which was founded by William the Conqueror in 1072 and is now occupied by the University of Durham.

Durham USA. Town in North Carolina 32 km (20 miles) NW of Raleigh. Pop. (1990) 136,611.

Commercial and industrial centre in a tobacco-growing region. Also manufactures hosiery, textiles and clothing. Large business interests here are held by Negroes.

Durrës (Italian **Durazzo**) Albania. Ancient

Epidamnus, Dyrrachium. Country's chief seaport on the Adriatic 31 km (19 miles) W of Tiranë. Pop. (1991) 87,000.

Exports olive oil, tobacco. Industries inc. shipbuilding, flour-milling, tobacco, soap and fertilizers. The majority of the pop. is of Muslim origin.

Founded in the 7th cent. BC. An important port under the Romans. It later changed hands many times and declined under Turkish rule (1501–1913), reviving with the modernization of the port in the 1930s.

D'Urville Island Antarctica. Island off the NE tip of Palmer Peninsula and N of Joinville Island, S Atlantic.

D'Urville Island New Zealand. Island near the N coast of South Island at the E entrance to Tasman Bay. Area 233 sq km (90 sq. miles). Lumbering is the main occupation.

Dushanbe Tajikistan. Formerly Stalinabad. Cap. of the republic 314 km (195 miles) S of Tashkent, with which it is linked by road. Pop. (1990) 602,000.

Meat-packing. Manufactures cotton and silk, textiles and cement; industries inc. engineering and food-processing.

Düsseldorf Germany. City in North Rhine-Westphalia on the Rhine R. 32 km (20 miles) NNW of Cologne. Pop. (1990) 577,000. Important river port and industrial centre.

Manufactures iron and steel, machinery, cars, chemicals, glass, textiles and clothing. Also the leading commercial centre for the Ruhr and Wupper industrial areas.

Dutch Guiana ➤SURINAME.

Dúvida, Rio da ➤ROOSEVELT RIVER.

Dvina River Russia. 1. Northern (Russian Severnaya) Dvina: river 745 km (466 miles) long, formed by the union of the Sukhona and Yug rivers, flowing NW to Dvina Bay, White Sea, below Archangel. It drains an area of 140,000 sq km (54,054 sq. miles). Navigable for most of its course May–November. Linked with the Mariinsk canal

system via the Sukhona R. and the N Dvina canal. Chief tributaries the Vychegda, Pinega and Vaga.

2. Western (Russian Zapadnaya) Dvina: river 1020 km (635 miles) long, rising in the Valdai Hills, Russia, flowing SW and then NW past Riga, Latvia. It drains an area of 32,900 sq km (12,702 sq. miles). Navigable in part May–November. Used for timber floating and hydroelectric power.

Dyfed Wales. Former county in the SW. Area 5768 sq km (2227 sq. miles). Pop. (1991) 341,600. About 43 per cent of the pop. spoke Welsh. In 1996 new unitary authorities were established replacing Dyfed: Carmarthenshire, Ceredigion, Pembrokeshire.

Dzaoudzi Mayotte. Former cap. in W Indian Ocean situated on a small offshore islet. Pop. (1985) 5675.

Dzerzhinsk Russia. Modern industrial town on the Oka R. 32 km (20 miles) W of Nizhny Novgorod. Pop. (1990) 286,000.

Important centre of fertilizer and other chemical manufactures. Sawmilling, engineering, flour-milling.

Dzhambul Kazakhstan. Cap. of the Dzhambul Region situated 459 km (285 miles) W of Alma-Ata on the Turksib Railway. Pop. (1989) 307,000.

Industrial centre; industries inc. manufacture of superphosphates, prefabricated houses, sugar-refining (sugar-beet) and fruit-canning.

Dzierzoniow (Ger. **Reichenbach**) Poland. Industrial town in the Wroclaw voivodeship 48 km (30 miles) SSW of Wroclaw. Pop. (1970) 32,900.

Manufactures textiles and electrical equipment. It became an important textile centre from 1700.

It passed to Prussia in 1742 and became part of Poland again in 1945.

Dzungaria China. Arid plateau region in N Xinjiang Uygur between the Altai Mountains (N) and the Tien Shan (S), bounded by Russia (W) and Mongolia. Most of its rivers drain into inland lakes. As a Mongolian kingdom it extended over a much wider area in the late 17th cent., but was conquered by the Chinese in the mid 18th cent. Chief town Urumqui. The Dzungarian Gate on the border provides an important route between China and Russia.

E

Ealing England. Borough in W London, comprising the former municipal boroughs of Acton, Ealing and Southall (all in Middlesex). Pop. (1991) 280,100. Mainly residential. Birthplace of Thomas Huxley, English biologist (1825–95).

Earby England. Town situated NNE of Burnley in Lancashire. Pop. (1981) 4995.

Industries inc. plastics, textiles, esp. cotton and precision engineering.

Earls Court England. Residential district in the London borough of Kensington and Chelsea. Probably named after the earls of Warwick, who resided here. Since 1884 the venue of many exhibitions in Earls Court Exhibition Building.

Earlston Scotland. Ancient Ercildoune (of which the present name is a corruption). Town in Scottish Borders on Leader Water 8 km (5 miles) ENE of Galashiels. Pop. (1990) 1900.

Market town. Manufactures tweeds.

Has the ruins of 'Rhymer's Tower', the traditional home of Thomas the Rhymer or Thomas of Ercildoune, the 13th-cent. poet and prophet.

Earn River Scotland. River 74 km (46 miles) long flowing E from Loch Earn through Strathearn to the Tay estuary 10 km (6 miles) SE of Perth. Fishing stream.

Easington England. Former coalmining town in E Durham 14 km (9 miles) E of Durham near the North Sea coast. Now part of Peterlee. Pop. (1994) 98,000.

East Anglia England. Region and ancient kingdom in the E, comprising the modern counties of Norfolk and Suffolk, and parts of Cambridgeshire and Essex. Founded by the Angles in the 6th cent. and later con-quered by Mercia and the Danes. The East Anglia of today is known for its agriculture, producing crops of wheat, barley and sugar-beet, and also for its quiet beauty, illustrated in the paintings of Constable and other artists.

East Barnet England. Part of the London borough of Barnet.

East Bengal ➤BANGLADESH.

Eastbourne England. Town in East Sussex on the English Channel at the foot of the South Downs, with Beachy Head 5 km (3 miles) to the SW. Pop. (1991) 94,793. Formerly a group of villages, it developed into a popular seaside resort under the patronage of the 7th Duke of Devonshire (1808–91). Many open spaces and gardens, inc. Hampden Park and Devonshire Park; a terraced marine parade nearly 5 km (3 miles) long. In the Old Town, 1.6 km (1 mile) inland, a fine parish church in Transitional Norman style.

East Chicago USA. Industrial town in NW Indiana on L. Michigan just SE of Chicago. Pop. (1988) 35,990.

Industries inc. oil-refining, railway engin-eering and storage. Manufactures chemicals.

East China Sea Pacific Ocean. Arm of Pa-cific Ocean extending 960 km (600 miles) SSW to NNE between E China coast and Kyushu and Ryukyu Islands. Area 1,243,300 sq km (480,000 sq. miles). Width 480–800 km (300–500 miles), average depth 187 m (615 ft) but reaching 2719 m (8920 ft). Connected SW with South China Sea through Formosa Strait and NE with Sea of Japan through Korea Strait.

East Cleveland USA. City next to Cleve-land in Ohio. Pop. (1990) 33,096.

Mainly residential with some industries, inc. manufacturing metal goods.

East Dereham (Dereham) England. Market town in Norfolk 24 km (15 miles) WNW of Norwich. Pop. (1991) 13,333.

Flour-milling. Manufactures trailers, toys, footwear and there is light engineering.

A 12th-cent. church with the grave of William Cowper, English poet (1731–1800).

Easter Island (Spanish **Isla de Pascua**) Pacific Ocean. An isolated island in the South Pacific 3700 km (2300 miles) W of Chile, to which it belongs. Area 166 sq km (64 sq. miles). Pop. (1989) 1900.

Sheep and cattle are raised on extensive grasslands and tobacco and sugar-cane are cultivated.

Best known for its huge stone statues, carved out of tufa from the volcano Rano Roraku and the wooden tablets carrying an ideographic script, all of unknown origin; these were probably the work of the ancestors of the present Polynesian inhabitants. Discovered by the Dutchman Roggeveen on Easter Day 1722 (hence the name). The pop. was once many times larger than at present, but was much reduced by disease, warfare and emigration. Annexed by Chile 1888.

Eastern Cape South Africa. Province created in 1994. Area 169,600 sq km (65,483 sq. miles). Pop. (1995) 6,481,300. Cap. Bisho.

East Germany ➤GERMANY *formerly* German Democratic Republic.

East Grinstead England. Market town in East Sussex, 18 km (11 miles) SE of Reigate near Ashdown Forest. Pop. (1991) 27,058. It has an almshouse, Sackville College, founded 1608 and many timbered houses. Iron mining and smelting in the neighbourhood from Roman times.

East Ham England. Part of the London borough of Newham. Industrial and residential centre.

East Hartford USA. Industrial town in Connecticut on the Connecticut R. opposite Hartford. Pop. (1985) 53,000.

Manufactures aircraft engines, machinery, paper and furniture.

East Indies. Name formerly applied rather loosely to SE Asia in general, inc. India and the Malay Archipelago, then to the whole Malay Archipelago, inc. the Philippines and Papua New Guinea; then to the Netherlands East Indies now Indonesia.

East Kilbride Scotland. Formerly a small town in South Lanarkshire 11 km (7 miles) SSE of Glasgow, designated a 'new town' in 1947 with a planned pop. of 82,500. Pop. (1991) 72,422 (5136 in 1951).

Manufactures aircraft engines, machinery, knitwear clothing, electronic and electrical appliances and seawater distillation plant.

Birthplace of the brothers John (1728–93) and William (1718–83) Hunter, noted surgeons.

East Lansing USA. Town in Michigan just E of Lansing. Pop. (1990) 50,677. Mainly residential. Seat of the Michigan State University of Agriculture and Applied Science (1855).

Eastleigh England. Town in Hampshire 8 km (5 miles) NNE of Southampton. Pop. (1991) 49,934. Railway engineering and light industry.

East London South Africa. Formerly Port Rex. Seaport in the Eastern Cape Province 240 km (150 miles) ENE of Port Elizabeth at the mouth of the Buffalo R. Pop. (1985) 193,819 inc. King William's Town. Port for the NE of the Eastern Cape Province, the Free State and Lesotho.

Exports maize, wool, hides, fruits. Fishing. Railway engineering. Manufactures soap, furniture, leather goods and clothing. Popular holiday resort.

First called Port Rex when visited by the brig *Kingsna* in 1836; renamed 1847. Railway construction began 1874, harbour improvements 1886.

East Lothian Scotland. Part of Lothian Region 1975–96, when it was reinstated. Pop. (1993) 85,640.

Easton USA. Industrial town in Pennsylvania 82 km (51 miles) N of Philadelphia at the confluence of the Lehigh and the Delaware rivers. Pop. (1980) 26,027.

Manufactures agricultural machinery, textiles, cement and paper.

East Orange USA. Residential and industrial town in New Jersey just NW of Newark, largest of 5 neighbouring municipalities known as 'the Oranges'. Pop. (1990) 73,552.

Manufactures electrical equipment, clothing and paint.

East Pakistan *now* BANGLADESH.

East Point USA. Industrial town in Georgia just SSW of Atlanta. Pop. (1970) 39,315.

Manufactures textiles, fertilizers and furniture.

East Providence USA. Industrial town in Rhode Island on the Seekonk and the Providence rivers opposite Providence. Pop. (1990) 50,380.

Textile dyeing and printing. Manufactures machinery, chemicals, petroleum products, wire and steel goods.

East Prussia. Former province of Prussia on the Baltic Sea SW of Lithuania. From 1919 it was separated from the rest of Germany by the Polish Corridor and the Free City of Danzig. In 1945 it was divided between Poland and the USSR, the former receiving 20,995 sq km (8106 sq. miles) (the S) and the rest about 15,799 sq km (6100 sq. miles) (the N). The cap., Königsberg, was renamed Kaliningrad. Situated between the Vistula and the Neman, the area is low-lying and marshy with many small lakes, inc. the extensive Masurian Lakes region in the E. It was an area of large agricultural estates owned by the Prussian 'Junkers'. The pre-war German pop. has been completely replaced by Russians and Poles.

East Rand South Africa. Part of the Witwatersrand situated E of Johannesburg.

East Riding of Yorkshire England. New administrative area created in 1996. Pop. (1994) 310,000.

East River USA. Tidal strait and navigable waterway of New York City 26 km (16 miles) long, connecting New York Bay with Long Island Sound, and separating the boroughs of Manhattan and the Bronx from Brooklyn and Queens. There are commercial and naval docks, and a waterfront with heavy traffic on the Brooklyn shore.

East St Louis USA. Formerly Illinoistown. Town in SW Illinois on the Mississippi R. opposite St Louis. Pop. (1970) 69,996.

Important industrial and railway centre. Industries inc. meat-packing, oil-refining. Manufactures aluminium, paints, fertilizers, chemicals and glass.

Laid out (1816) as Illinoistown; incorporated as East St Louis in 1865.

East Sussex England. County consisting of the E portion of the former county of Sussex, bounded on the S by the English Channel. Area 1795 sq km (693 sq. miles). Pop. (1974) 685,900. It is divided into the boroughs of Brighton, Eastbourne, Hastings, Hove and the districts of Lewes, Rother and Wealden. An outstanding feature is the chalk ridge of the South Downs (SW), running WNW–ESE and ending in the cliffs of Beachy Head; they descend steeply on the N side to the Vale of Sussex, N of which is the Weald, where the Forest Ridges rise to nearly 240 m (787 ft). Highest point in the county Ditchling Beacon (248 m; 813 ft) in the SW. Chief rivers the Ouse, Rother. Cereals and root crops are grown, as well as fruit and hops, and cattle and sheep are raised. There are extensive woodlands. Industries inc. electronics, pharmaceuticals, furniture, and financial services and tourism are important to the county's economy. Coastal resorts inc. Brighton, Hove, Hastings, Eastbourne and Bexhill-on-Sea. Newhaven is the principal Channel port. Famous for its iron industry from Roman times till the early 19th cent.

Eau Claire USA. Town in Wisconsin at the confluence of the Chippewa and the Eau

Claire rivers 120 km (75 miles) E of St Paul (Minnesota). Pop. (1990) 56,856.

Market town in a dairy-farming and stock-rearing area, having developed first as a lumbering centre. Manufactures plastics, electronic products, rubber and leather goods and paper. Meat-packing and food-processing.

Ebbw Vale Wales. Town in Blaenau Gwent on the R. Ebbw 32 km (20 miles) N of Cardiff. Pop. (1988) 24,100.

Industries inc. the manufacture of tinplate, food-packaging, batteries and vehicle brake systems.

Eberswalde Germany. Town in Brandenburg 48 km (30 miles) NE of Berlin. Pop. (1989) 54,400.

Manufactures iron and steel products (esp. cranes), chemicals and building materials.

Ebro River Spain. Ancient Iberus (Hiberus). River 917 km (570 miles) long rising in the Cantabrian Mountains in Santander province and flowing generally SE to the Mediterranean. Navigable by seagoing vessels only to Tortosa (32 km; 20 miles inland). The delta is canalized. Chief tributaries the Aragón, Gállego, Guadalope, Huerva, Jalón and Segre rivers. Zaragoza and Logroño are the principal towns on its banks. Much used for hydroelectric power. Has been used for irrigation since Moorish times. Gave its name to the Iberii, originally the people living along its banks, and the Iberian peninsula.

Ecclefechan Scotland. Village in Dumfries and Galloway in Annandale 21 km (13 miles) E of Dumfries. Birthplace and burial-place of Thomas Carlyle, Scottish historian (1795–1881).

Eccles England. Town in Greater Manchester on the R. Irwell and the Manchester Ship Canal 8 km (5 miles) W of Manchester. Pop. (1991) 36,000.

Manufactures textiles, machinery, chemicals and pharmaceuticals. Site of Manchester airport. Noted for Eccles cakes, now made in Manchester.

Écija Spain. Ancient Astigis. Town in Seville province, Andalusia on the Genil R. 84 km (52 miles) ENE of Seville. Pop. (1991) 35,566.

Produces olive oil, wine, soap and textiles.

Long noted for its cobblers; according to one story it was the see of St Crispin, patron saint of shoemakers. It has many remnants of Moorish architecture. One of the hottest places in Spain in summer; known as the 'frying-pan of Andalusia'.

Ecuador. Republic on the NW coast of South America, bounded by Colombia in the N, Peru in the E and S and on the W is the Pacific Ocean. Area 270,667 sq km (104,505 sq. miles). Pop. (1995) 11,460,000 (60 per cent urban). Life expectancy, 68 years male, 73 female. Cap. Quito. Other major cities Guayaquil, Cuenca, Machala, Portoviejo. Currency: Sucre = 100 centavos. Ecuador is crossed in the N by the equator. It consists of three distinct regions: the mountainous backbone of the Andes; the coastal plain between the Andes and the Pacific in the W; and part of the basin of the upper Amazon in the E. The Andes extend N–S as two main cordilleras, separated by a long trough in which lies a series of basins 2100–2700 m (6888–8856 ft) high, drained by rivers flowing to the Amazon or the Pacific. Above the Cordilleran crests tower lofty volcanic cones, e.g. Chimborazo (6310 m; 20,702 ft) and Cotopaxi (5896 m; 19,344 ft); several, inc. Cotopaxi, are active. In the W are the broad lowlands of the Guayas R., N and E of Guayaquil and low sandstone and limestone hills farther W and N. E of the Andes are the densely forested foothills and the Amazon plains, with scattered Indian tribes. Resources, mainly agricultural, are largely undeveloped and communications are difficult. Quito, at 2850 m (9348 ft), lies on the Pan-American Highway, which passes from Colombia to Peru via the highland basins. Railways run to Guayaquil, the main seaport and to the small N outlet of San Lorenzo. Esmeraldas (N) is the chief banana port and has become an important oil-exporting port.

The climate varies from equatorial, through warm temperate to mountain conditions, according to altitude which affects temperatures and rainfall. In the NW there are long rainy periods and the land is closely forested, but the hot Guayas lowlands, with a single rainy period (Dec.–June), consist of grassy savannah. In the SW, near the Peruvian frontier, conditions are arid, with xerophytic vegetation; the cold Peruvian current swings W away from the coast about lat. 4°S. On the highlands forests occur up to about 3000 m (9840 ft), vegetation depending on shelter and soil: many of the porous volcanic soils are very dry, supporting tussock grass well below the usual altitude of the *páramos*. Land use: forested 41 per cent, meadows and pastures 18 per cent, agricultural and under permanent cultivation 10 per cent. In 1989 40 per cent of the pop. was Amerindian, mestizo 40 per cent, white 15 per cent, black 5 per cent. About 92 per cent are Roman Catholic and the lang. is Spanish, but many Indian langs. are spoken.

The economy is based on agriculture. The Guayas lowlands produce most of the commercial crops. The hilly districts NW of Guayaquil are renowned for their toquilla straw ('Panama') hats. Ecuador's chief oilfield was formerly the one on the Santa Elena peninsula, petroleum being refined at La Libertad and Salinas. In 1967, however, a new oilfield in the NE province of Napo (Oriente) began to produce and, with the completion of a trans-Andean pipeline in 1972, Ecuador became an oil-exporting country. In 1990 exports of crude oil represented 47 per cent of exports. Other exports are cacao, bananas, coffee and processed fish. Thirty per cent of the pop. work in agriculture cultivating maize, wheat, potatoes, fruit, vegetables and pyrethrum. There is some dairy farming. Sheep, alpacas and llamas are grazed on the *páramos*. Market centres, e.g. Ambato and Riobamba, have textile mills; these towns have frequently suffered from earthquakes. Other industries inc. cement, oil-refining, petrochemicals and food-processing.

The highland basins were well populated in Inca times. Quito, the centre of authority, was occupied by the Spanish in 1534. For nearly three cents. the region formed part of the vice-royalty of Peru. In the 18th cent. Negro slave labour was brought to the coastal plantations. The struggle for independence from Spain was won in 1822; in 1830 Ecuador broke away from 'Gran Colombia' and became an independent republic. Under the 1979 Constitution Ecuador has a directly elected Executive President and a 77-member unicameral National Congress. For administrative purposes the country is divided into 21 provinces.

Edam Netherlands. Town in N Holland province 19 km (12 miles) NNE of Amsterdam. Pop. (1992) 24,968 (with Volendam).

A market for the famous cheese made in the neighbourhood, named after it, and exported in large quantities. Also manufactures earthenware.

Eddystone Rocks England. Dangerous group of rocks in the English Channel 23 km (14 miles) SSW of Plymouth. Its first lighthouse, built by Winstanley (1698), was swept away in a storm; the second (1709) was destroyed by fire (1755); the third, built by Smeaton (1759), was the first lighthouse in which dovetail-jointed stones were used, and was replaced by another in 1882.

Ede Netherlands. Industrial town in Gelderland province 16 km (10 miles) WNW of Arnhem. Pop. (1992) 96,044.

Important rayon industry. Also metalworking.

Edea Cameroon. Town situated W of Yaoundé on the Sanaga R. Communciations centre at the head of navigation. Pop. (1981) 31,016.

Trade in rubber and cacao. Industries inc. aluminium, lumbering, quarrying and palm-oil processing. Hydroelectric dam.

Eden River England. 1. River 109 km (65 miles) long, rising in the Pennines, flowing NW through Cumbria past Appleby and Carlisle and entering the Solway Firth.

2. River 19 km (12 miles) long, rising

in SE Surrey, flowing E and joining the Medway R. at Penshurst (Kent).

Eden River Scotland. River 48 km (30 miles) long, rising in Tayside, flowing ENE across Fife and entering the North Sea near St Andrews.

Eder River Germany. River 137 km (85 miles) long, rising in North Rhine-Westphalia and flowing ENE through Hessen to join the Fulda R. S of Kassel. The Eder Dam, controlling one of Germany's largest reservoirs and providing hydroelectric power, was heavily bombed by RAF planes, in the 'Dambusters' raid, during World War II (1943).

Edessa (Gr. **Edhessa**) Greece. Ancient Aegae. Cap. of Pella *nome* in Macedonia 80 km (50 miles) WNW of Salonika. Pop.(1985) 17,000.

Market town in a picturesque, fertile district. Trade in wine, fruit and tobacco. Manufactures textiles, rugs and carpets.

Scene of the assassination of Philip II (336 BC).

Edfu (Idfu) Egypt. Ancient Apollinopolis Magna. Town on the W bank of the Nile 93 km (58 miles) N of Aswan. Pop. 28,000.

Earthenware manufactured in the district. Trade in cotton, cereals and dates.

Has an almost complete sandstone temple, dedicated to the god Horus, begun by Ptolemy III in 237 BC and completed in the reign of Ptolemy XIII in 57 BC.

Edgehill England. Ridge in S Warwickshire on the border with Oxfordshire, rising to 227 m (745 ft) and forming part of the watershed between the Severn and Thames basins. Here was fought the first large (but indecisive) battle of the English Civil War (1642).

Edgware England. Part of the London borough of Barnet from 1965. On the Edgware Road (the Roman Watling Street), a residential suburb of London.

Edinburgh Scotland. Cap. of Scotland and royal burgh. In Lothian Region 1975–96, near the S shore of the Firth of Forth 66 km

(41 miles) E of Glasgow. Pop. (1991) 439,000. Nicknamed 'Auld Reekie' because of the curtain of smoke that used to hang over the lower parts of the city, Edinburgh has a more dignified and certainly more accurate sobriquet in 'Athens of the North'. It stands on and around a group of hills, with Castle Rock (136 m; 446 ft) at the centre, Calton Hill (106 m; 348 ft) to the E, Arthur's Seat (251 m; 823 ft) to the SE, the Braid Hills to the S and Corstorphine Hill (159 m; 522 ft) to the W; on the N side it slopes gently down to the Firth of Forth. Its principal thoroughfare is Princes Street, one of the finest in Europe, on account of its setting rather than its buildings, dominated by the castle on Castle Rock and flanked by Princes Street Gardens. To the N of Princes Street is the New Town, largely dating from the 18th cent. and to the S the Old Town. In the heart of the Old Town is the 'Royal Mile', the city's second famous thoroughfare, so called because kings and queens so often passed along it on their official duties. It follows the ridge running from the castle to Holyroodhouse; on both sides are tall tenements and narrow wynds (alleys) – for, when the city was enclosed by walls, its people were forced to build upwards. The oldest building in the castle and in Edinburgh is the restored Norman Chapel of St Margaret, dating from 1093, where Queen Margaret, wife of Malcolm Canmore, worshipped. Here, too, is the Old Palace containing the crown room, the royal apartments and the old parliament hall, while nearby is the impressive National War Memorial (1927) for World War I. The Palace of Holyroodhouse, begun *c.* 1500 by James IV, is still the official residence of the monarch when in Scotland; this was the residence of Mary Queen of Scots, scene of her marriage to Bothwell and of the murder of Rizzio (1566). Little remains, however, of the Chapel Royal, once part of the adjoining Abbey. Among the existing ecclesiastical buildings probably the best known are the Church of St Giles, restored 1872–83, with a fine 'crown' steeple, and the 19th-cent. St Mary's Cathedral. Other noteworthy buildings are

the 17th-cent. Parliament House, John Knox's House, the Canongate Tolbooth, Royal Scottish Academy, National Gallery, the unfinished National Monument, the Scott Monument. Register House, containing Scottish national records etc., was designed by Robert Adam, as was much else in the New Town. The University (founded 1583) has long been famous for its medical school, with which the Royal Infirmary is closely associated.

It is an administrative and business centre and leading cultural centre of Scotland. Industries inc. printing and publishing, brewing, whisky-distilling. Manufactures food products, chemicals, machinery, machine tools and electronics. Leith, its port, was incorporated in the city in 1920.

Edinburgh takes its name from Edwin, king of Northumbria, who defeated the Picts and set up a military post here in the 7th cent., and a settlement grew up round the castle on Castle Rock. In 1329 it was made a burgh by Robert the Bruce and in 1437 it replaced Perth, where James I was assassinated, as the national cap.; James II was crowned at Holyrood Abbey instead of at Scone. On the departure of James VI, who was born in the castle, to become James I of Great Britain and Ireland (1603), Edinburgh lost political though not cultural prestige, a change which was emphasized by the Act of Union in 1707. Later in the 18th cent. came a revival, particularly in the literary and academic fields; during the same period the Nor' Loch, N of the castle, was drained, the North Bridge was built and the New Town with its handsome streets and squares was laid out. Since World War II the city has added to its cultural reputation and attracted great numbers of new visitors with the annual Edinburgh Festival, inaugurated 1947. Birthplace of David Hume, Scottish philosopher and historian (1711–76), Allan Ramsay, Scottish portrait painter (1713–84) and Alexander Graham Bell, inventor (1847–1922).

Edirne Turkey. Formerly Adrianople. Cap. of Edirne province in European Turkey at the confluence of the Maritsa and Tundzha rivers near the Greek frontier. Pop. (1990) 102,345.

Manufactures textiles, carpets, soap, leather and perfume.

Oriental in appearance, it has among its buildings the famous 16th-cent. mosque of Sultan Selim II, the ruined palace of the Sultans and the bazaar of Ali Pasha. It was enlarged in the 2nd cent. AD on the site of the ancient Uskadama by the Roman Emperor Hadrian, after whom it was named. Here in 378 the Romans were decisively defeated by the Goths. It was the residence of the Turkish sultans from 1365 (after it had been captured from the Bulgarians) to 1453, when Constantinople fell. In the Russo–Turkish Wars it twice fell to the Russians (1829 and 1878). Taken by the Bulgarians and recovered by the Turks in 1913. After World War I it became Greek, but was returned to Turkey in 1923.

Edjélé Algeria. Oil-producing centre in the Sahara, near the Libyan frontier 217 km (135 miles) S of Ghadames. Oilfield first operated in 1957. There is a pipeline to La Skhirra (Tunisia).

Edmond USA. City situated N of Oklahoma City. Pop. (1989) 50,000.

Trading centre for an agricultural and oil-producing area. Industries inc. manufacture of petroleum products, flour, animal feed, wood products, leather goods, furniture, glass and concrete blocks.

Edmonton Canada. Provincial cap. of Alberta on the N Saskatchewan R. Pop. (1991) 616,741.

Industrial city in an agricultural, coal, oil and fur-trading region. Principal gateway to the Peace R. area and the Mackenzie District. Linked by road with the Alaska Highway, the Mackenzie Highway and the Trans-Canada Highway. Major airport. Oil-refining, meat-packing and tanning. Manufactures chemicals and clothing.

Edmonton England. Part of the London borough of Enfield from 1965. Mainly residential. Keats and Cowper lived here, the Bell Inn having been immortalized in the latter's *John Gilpin*. Charles and Mary Lamb are buried in the graveyard of All Saints' Church.

Edom (Idumaea). District in S Palestine (Israel) between the Dead Sea and the Gulf of Aqaba, presented to Esau.

Edward, Lake (Lake Rutanzige) Democratic Republic of the Congo/Uganda. Lake in the W branch of the Great Rift Valley (N of L. Kivu) at a height of 900 m (2952 ft) on the frontier between Democratic Republic of the Congo and Uganda. Area 2124 sq km (820 sq. miles). One of the W reservoirs of the R. Nile. Connected with L. George (Dweru) (NE), which it drains, by a 40-km (25-mile) channel. Fed also by the Rutshuru R. (S). Empties through the Semliki R. (NW) into L. Albert. Discovered (1888) by H. M. Stanley; named after the then Prince of Wales (later Edward VII). Salt from the surrounding saltpans is sold over a large area. Abundant fish, waterfowl, crocodiles and (S) hippopotami.

Egadi Islands Italy. Island group situated off the W of Sicily. Area 39 sq km (15 sq. miles). Main islands Favignana, Marettimo, Levanzo. The main industry is tunny-fishing.

Eger Hungary. Cap. of Heves county on the Eger R. on the S slopes of the Bükk hills 39 km (24 miles) SW of Miskolc. Pop. (1989) 67,000.

Market town. Produces and trades in wine. Also an ecclesiastical centre with many baroque churches, causing it to be known formerly as 'the Rome of Hungary'.

Egham England. Town in Surrey 29 km (18 miles) WSW of London on the S bank of the R. Thames, containing Runnymede and Virginia Water. Pop. (1971) 30,510. Mainly residential.

Light engineering. Site of the Royal Holloway College, a school of London University. ▶▶RUNNYMEDE.

Egmont (Taranaki), Mount New Zealand. Extinct volcanic peak (2518 m; 8261 ft) in Taranaki, North Island, 24 km (15 miles) S of New Plymouth, in the shape of an almost perfect cone; stands in Egmont National Park. Named by Capt. Cook in 1770.

Egypt. Republic in NE Africa, bounded by the Mediterranean Sea in the N, Israel, the Gulf of Aqaba and the Red Sea in the E, Sudan in the S and Libya in the W. Area 997,739 sq km (385,229 sq. miles). Pop. (1995) 56,690,000 (45 per cent urban). Life expectancy, 65 years male, 69 female. Cap. Cairo. Other large cities Alexandria, Giza, Shubra al Khayma, Port Said and Suez. Currency: Egyptian pound = 100 piastres = 1000 millièmes. Most of Egypt is desert. The delta area is known as Lower Egypt and the region to the S as Upper Egypt. The Nile delta is a broad alluvial plain sloping gently down to the Mediterranean, where the coast is lined with sandhills behind which are a number of extensive lagoons. To reach its delta the Nile flows generally N across the low plateau, irrigating a narrow ribbon of land, in places no more than 1.6 km (1 mile) in width, so creating with the delta an elongated, fertile oasis in what is substantially the E section of the great Sahara. To the E of the Nile valley is the Arabian Desert, which rises to a range of mountains bordering the Red Sea, the highest peak being Shayib el Banat (2187 m; 7173 ft). To the W is the Libyan Desert, the part around the Farafra Oasis being often known as the Western Desert. In the NW the Qattara Depression sinks to about 134 m (440 ft) below sea level. In the NE the Sinai peninsula rises to 2285 m (7495 ft) in Jebel Musa (Mt Sinai). The principal oases of the Libyan Desert are Siwa, Bahariya, Farafra, Dakhla and Kharga; El Faiyum, with its lake Birket Qarun, lies just W of the Nile, with which it is connected by the canalized Bahr Yusef, an old branch of the river. Climate is mainly dry. Along the N coast the climate verges on the Mediterranean type, with Alexandria, for instance, receiving 20 cm (8 ins.) of rain entirely Oct.–April, but even as far N as Cairo the mean annual rainfall is only about 2.5 cm (1 in.), while farther S the country is virtually rainless. A hot, dry southerly wind known as the *khamsin* is sometimes experienced, chiefly in spring.

Land use: pasture 0.6 per cent, agricultural 2.6 per cent. About 90 per cent of the pop. are Sunni Muslims and 7 per cent Coptic Christians who are the descendants of Egyptians who were converted to Christianity in the 1st cent. AD. The official lang. is Arabic.

Home of one of the great civilizations of the past, its economy and the way of life of most of its people have changed little throughout the centuries: agriculture is the mainstay of the economy and it is still as much 'the gift of the Nile' as it was when Herodotus thus described it 2400 years ago. Only about 35,580 sq km (13,737 sq. miles) or 3.6 per cent of its area, comprising the Nile valley and delta and the oases, has been settled and cultivated; the remainder is desert. Agriculture is dependent on the flood waters of the Nile and, while much irrigation is still carried out by primitive methods, these have been displaced by a system of dams and barrages, such as the Aswan High Dam. Cotton, wheat, maize and rice are widely cultivated, and sugar-cane in Upper Egypt. The great majority of the *fellahin*, or peasants, own smallholdings of 0.4 ha (1 acre) or less and even when harvests are good they are unable to rise above a bare subsistence level. Petroleum is drilled around the Gulf of Suez and with petroleum products represents 50 per cent of exports. Phosphates are mined on the Red Sea coast. Other industries, esp. textiles, food-processing, fertilizers and iron and steel, are concentrated in Cairo, Alexandria, Port Said, Tanta and Mahalla el Kubra. Minerals inc. natural gas, iron, phosphates and sea salt. Alexandria handles most of the country's foreign trade, and Port Said and Suez are the chief ports on the Suez Canal. The latter was nationalized in 1956, causing conflict, involving Israel, France and Britain against Egypt. In recent years the country has become increasingly dependent on remittances from Egyptian migrant workers, from oil revenues, from Suez Canal dues and from tourism. The growth in agricultural output has failed to keep pace with dramatic pop. increases and Egypt's industries have been too inefficient to compete in the world markets.

Ancient Egypt, from the foundation of the state until its conquest by Alexander the Great, was ruled over by 30 Dynasties. In 332 BC Alexander the Great defeated the Persians (who then ruled Egypt) and on his death his general Ptolemy founded a new royal line. This was to rule until Cleopatra, who had married the Roman general, Mark Antony, died in 30 BC. Egypt now became part of the Roman Empire. In the third cent. AD the Roman Emperor Diocletian saw Egypt become part of the Christian, Byzantine Empire. Nevertheless, the native Egyptians or 'copts' clung to their own form of religion. After the Arab Muslim conquest in AD 640, most Egyptians accepted Islam, although some 7 per cent have remained Coptic Christians. For over 2 cents. Egypt was nominally ruled by the Muslim Abbasids from Baghdad, although local dynasties functioned virtually independently. Under the Fatamids Egypt enjoyed a golden age. In the 13th cent. the Mamluk (Slave) dynasty was founded but in 1517 nominal authority passed to the Ottomans in Istanbul. Napoleon's conquest in 1798 left a vacuum that was filled by Muhammad Ali, an Albanian officer who modernized Egypt. His dynasty survived until the revolution of 1952 swept away his descendant, King Farouk, and replaced the monarchy with a revolutionary council. Muhammad Ali's grandson, the Khedive Ismail, tried to make Egypt part of Europe and opened the Suez Canal. However, the result was bankruptcy and Egypt became a virtual British colony until the end of World War II.

During that war Egypt was invaded by Axis forces, which were defeated by the British at El Alamein (1942) and driven out of the country. After the war relations with Britain were strained, partly owing to Egypt's claim to the Sudan, but British troops were withdrawn from Cairo and the delta in 1947, from the Canal Zone in 1954. In 1948 Egypt joined other Arab states in the attack on Israel but won only slight initial success; by the truce of 1949 the small Gaza Strip on the Mediterranean coast was occupied. At home discontent over governmental corruption and inefficiency led to a *coup d'état*: King Farouk was compelled to abdicate in 1952. After the 1952 revolution President Nasser's Pan-Arab, socialist ideology gave way to liberalism under Presidents Sadat and Mubarak. Egypt fought four wars with Israel over the rights of the Palestinians but renounced aggression with its neighbour in the peace treaty signed in 1979. It also became more pro-Western, supporting the US-led UN coalition against Iraq in 1990–1. Under the 1971 Constitution there is a 454-member unicameral People's Assembly elected by universal suffrage; the President may appoint 10 further members. In 1980 a 210-member consultative body, the Shura Council, was established. Two-thirds of its members are elected and the rest appointed by the President.

Egypt has been a republic since 1953. It is divided administratively into 26 governorates (with cap. city in brackets): Cairo (Cairo), Alexandria (Alexandria), Port Said (Port Said), Suez (Suez), Damietta (Damietta), Dakahliya (Mansoura), Sharkiya (Zagazig), Qalyoubiya (Benha), Kafr El-Sheikh (Kafr El-Sheikh), Gharbiya (Tanta), Menoufiya (Shebeen El-Kom), Beheira (Damanhour), Ismailia (Ismailia), Giza (Giza), Beni Swif (Beni Swif), Fayyoum (Fayyoum), Menya (Menya), Al-Wadi Al-Gadid (Al-Kharga), Matrouh (Mersa Matrouh), North Sinai (Al-Arish), South Sinai (Al-Tor), Assiut (Assiut), Suhag (Gerga), Qena (Qena), Aswan (Aswan), The Red Sea (Hurghada). Cairo is the smallest governorate and the most populous.

Eider River Germany. River 188 km (117 miles) long in Schleswig-Holstein, rising SW of Kiel and flowing generally WNW to the North Sea at Tonning. Before the opening of the Kiel Canal it connected the Baltic and the North Sea via the Eider Canal.

Eifel Germany. Bleak, desolate plateau of volcanic origin between the Rhine, the Mosel, the Ahr and the Our rivers, in general 450–750 m (1476–2460 ft) above sea level. Many volcanic cones and small crater lakes.

Eiger Switzerland. Mountain peak at 3970 m (12,697 ft) in the Bernese Oberland. The first ascent was made in 1858 and the N face is one of the most difficult climbs in the alps.

Eigg Scotland. Small island in the Inner Hebrides, Highland 11 km (7 miles) from the mainland. Area 28 sq km (11 sq. miles). Rises to 393 m (1289 ft) in the Scuir of Eigg (S). The island was purchased by the Isle of Eigg Heritage Trust in 1997 after 700 years in private ownership.

Eilat Israel. Small port in the S at the head of the Gulf of Aqaba near the Jordanian frontier and 8 km (5 miles) WNW of the Jordanian port of Aqaba. An oil pipeline from Eilat to Ashkelon, entirely within Israel and bypassing the Suez Canal, was opened in 1970.

Eildon Hills Scotland. Range in Scottish Borders 1.6 km (1 mile) S of Melrose, consisting of three conical peaks, the highest rising to 422 m (1384 ft). Associated with many legends, inc. those of Thomas the Rhymer.

Eindhoven Netherlands. Chief industrial centre of North Brabant province. Pop. (1992) 193,966. Owes its rapid growth from a small town of 5700 people (1910) to the great expansion of the radio, television, electrical and electronic industry (founded by Philips in 1891). Also manufactures motor vehicles, textiles, plastics, cigars and matches.

Einsiedeln Switzerland. Town in Schwyz canton 32 km (20 miles) SE of Zürich. Pop. (1985) 9500. Famous for its 10th-cent. Benedictine abbey; in the church is the statue of the 'Black Madonna', much visited by pilgrims. Ulrich Zwingli was parish priest here 1516–18.

Eire ➤IRELAND.

Eisenach Germany. Industrial town in Thuringia 51 km (32 miles) W of Erfurt on the edge of the Thuringian Forest. Pop. (1985) 51,000.

Rock-salt mining. Manufactures motor

vehicles, machine-tools, chemicals. Summer resort.

On a hill overlooking the town is the Wartburg, ancient castle of the landgraves of Thuringia. Birthplace of J. S. Bach (1685–1750).

Eisenhower, Mount Canada. Peak (2864 m; 9393 ft) in SW Alberta in the Banff National Park in the Rocky Mountains. Formerly Castle Mountain but renamed in 1946 in honour of General (later President) Eisenhower.

Eisenhüttenstadt Germany. Industrial town and river port in Brandenburg, on the Oder R. 24 km (15 miles) SSE of Frankfurt-an-der-Oder. Pop. (1971) 45,000. Terminus of the Oder–Spree Canal. Formed (1961) from the towns of Stalinstadt and Furstenberg around blast furnaces and steelworks which use imported fuel and raw materials. Also manufactures glass and dyes.

Eisenstadt ➤BURGENLAND.

Eisleben Germany. Town in Saxony-Anhalt 32 km (20 miles) WNW of Halle. Pop. (1985) 25,000.

Copper smelting, cigar-making. Manufactures textiles, clothing, machinery, tobacco products.

Birthplace of Martin Luther (1483–1546), who was also baptized and died here.

El Aaiún ➤WESTERN SAHARA.

Elam (Susiana). Ancient country in SW Asia E of the Tigris R. and approximating to modern Khuzistán in SW Iran. It warred frequently with Babylonia and was conquered by Assurbanipal in the 7th cent. BC. After the fall of Assyria, towards the close of that cent., it became a Persian province and was known as Susiana, its cap. being Susa.

Elan River Wales. River rising in the Cambrian Mountains of central Wales flowing generally ESE across W Powys to join the R. Wye below Rhayader. On the Elan and its tributary the Claerwen four dams were built between 1904 and 1952, the reservoirs formed supplying water by a 118-km (73½-

mile) aqueduct to Birmingham and surrounding areas. The valley is well-known for its scenery. Trout-fishing in the reservoirs.

El Araish ➤LARACHE.

Elath ➤AQABA.

Elâziğ Turkey. Cap. of Elâziğ province 80 km (50 miles) ENE of Malatya. Pop. (1990) 204,603.

Market town, trading in cereals, cotton and fruit.

Elba Italy. Ancient Aethalia (Gr.), Ilva (Latin). Island off the W coast, the largest in the Tuscan Archipelago, in Lovorno (Leghorn) province. Area 223 sq km (86 sq. miles). Pop. (1971) 26,830. Separated from the mainland by the Strait of Piombino. Steep, rocky coastline; rises to 1019 m (3342 ft) in Monte Capanne. Iron ore has been mined for more than 2000 years and some is smelted at Portoferraio, the chief town and port on the N coast. Produces wine. Anchovy, sardine and tunny fisheries. Expanding tourist industry. Napoleon was exiled here (1814–15), being given full sovereign rights over the island.

Elbasan Albania. Market town on the Shkumbi R. 32 km (20 miles) SW of Tiranë. Pop. (1991) 83,200. Terminus of the railway from Durrës.

Manufactures textiles, leather, soap, olive oil. Trade in olives, tobacco and maize. Nearby is the oil refinery of Çerrik (1957).

Elbe (Czech **Labe) River.** River in Central Europe 1167 km (725 miles) long, rising on the S side of the Riesengebirge in NE Bohemia (Czech Republic). Flowing first S, it turns W below Hradec Králové, then flows generally NW across the Czech–German frontier, past Dresden and Magdeburg to Hamburg, entering the North Sea by a 90-km (56-mile) estuary. At the mouth, which is 14 km (9 miles) wide, is Cuxhaven. Navigable by barges for over 800 km (500 miles). Connected with the Rhine and the Weser via the Mittelland Canal system. By the Treaty of Versailles (1919) it was internationalized below the confluence with the

Vltava, but this was repudiated by Germany in 1938.

Elblag (Ger. **Elbing**) Poland. Cap. of the Elblag voivodeship on the Elblag R. 8 km (5 miles) above the mouth on the Vistula Lagoon (Frishes Haff) 56 km (35 miles) ESE of Gdańsk. Pop. (1992) 126,500.

Industrial centre and seaport. Shipbuilding, engineering. Manufactures textiles. Seaborne trade is now limited, the port having been eclipsed by Gdańsk.

Founded in the 13th cent. Admitted to the Hanseatic League. Belonged to Poland for most of the period 1466–1772 and then passed to Prussia. Returned to Poland 1945.

Elbruz (Elbrus), Mount Russia. Massif in the Caucasus Mountains in the Kabardino-Balkar Republic on the border with the Georgian Republic N of the main range. Consists of two extinct volcanic peaks, the E summit to 5599 m (18,365 ft) and the W summit to 5637 m (18,849 ft) – the highest in the range and in Europe. It has many snowfields and glaciers, from which flow the Kuban and other rivers.

Elburz Iran. Range of mountains in the N, curving round near and more or less parallel to the S shores of the Caspian Sea, rising to 5601 m (18,376 ft) in the extinct volcano Damāvand. Forms a climatic divide, the N slopes being rainy and forested, while the S slopes are arid and cultivable only by irrigation. Tehrán, the cap., stands on the lower S slopes of the central Elburz.

Elche Spain. Town in Alicante province, Valencia 21 km (13 miles) WSW of Alicante. Pop. (1991) 181,658.

Manufactures footwear, textiles, fertilizers, soap, but chiefly noted for its groves of date-palms. The fruit, though inferior to the N African, are exported, and the leaves are sold throughout Spain for Palm Sunday.

Its white, flat-roofed houses and the many date-palms give Elche an oriental appearance: it was held from the 8th to the 13th cent. by the Moors, who provided it with its irrigation system.

El Dar-el-Beida ➤CASABLANCA.

El Djezair ➤ALGIERS.

El Dorado USA. Town in S Arkansas 177 km (110 miles) SSW of Little Rock. Pop. (1970) 25,283.

Important centre of the oil industry. Oil-refining. Manufactures oil-well equipment, petroleum products. Also trade in timber and cotton.

Founded 1843.

Elektrostal Russia. Industrial town in the Moscow Region 51 km (32 miles) E of Moscow. Pop. (1991) 153,000.

Important steel industry. Manufactures machinery, stainless-steel goods. Heavy engineering.

Elephanta India. Island in Bombay harbour 6 km (4 miles) in circumference, famous for the cave temples dedicated to Siva. The Great Temple, in the main cave, probably dating from the 8th or 9th cent., is supported by pillars cut out of the rock and around it are many statues of Hindu deities, the most striking a three-headed bust of Siva.

Eleuthera Bahamas. Island between Great Abaco and Cat Islands, its N point and NE of Nassau. Area 128 km (80 miles) by 10 km (6 miles). Pop. (1990) 9300. Main settlements Governor's Harbour, Palmetto Point and Tarpum Bay.

Main products tomatoes, pineapples and dairy products.

El Ferrol Spain. Chief Atlantic naval base in Coruña province 21 km (13 miles) NE of Corunna. Pop. (1991) 82,371. Strongly fortified, with a deep natural harbour. Besides the arsenal and dockyard, has fishing, fish-processing, boatbuilding and other industries.

Birthplace of General Franco (El Caudillo) (1892–1975).

Elgin Scotland. Market town in Moray on the R. Lossie 58 km (36 miles) ENE of Inverness. Pop. (1991) 19,027.

Industries inc. textiles, structural engineering and whisky-distilling.

Ruins of a 13th-cent. cathedral and a bishop's palace. Gordonstoun School is nearby.

Elgin USA. Town in Illinois, on the Fox R. 56 km (35 miles) WNW of Chicago. Pop. (1990) 77,010.

Noted for watches; also manufactures electrical equipment, radio sets, motor-car accessories and pianos.

First settled in 1832.

Elgon, Mount. Extinct volcano on the Kenya–Uganda border NE of L. Victoria, rising to 4321 m (14,178 ft). The crater is about 8 km (5 miles) in diameter. On the fertile lower slopes coffee and bananas are cultivated. Caves on the S slopes were long used by Africans as dwelling places.

Elis (Gr. **Elia**) Greece. *Nome* of the W Peloponnese. Area 2618 sq km (1011 sq. miles). Pop. (1991) 174,021.

Produces currants, citrus fruits.

Ancient Elis was a district bounded by Achaea (N), Arcadia (E), Messenia (S) and the Ionian Sea (W). Its fertile coastal lowlands were drained by the Alpheus and Peneus rivers. Famed for its horses. The Olympic Games were held at Olympia, but it declined after their abolition (394 BC). The cap. was Elis, now in ruins.

Elisabethville ➤LUBUMBASHI.

Elizabeth USA. Town in NE New Jersey just SSW of Newark. Pop. (1990) 110,002. Long an industrial centre; the Singer sewing-machine factory was established in 1873.

Also manufactures motor-car and aircraft accessories, furniture and printing presses. There is also oil-refining.

First settled 1664. Known as Elizabethtown till 1740.

Elkhart USA. Industrial town in N Indiana 217 km (135 miles) N of Indianapolis at the confluence of the Elkhart and the St Joseph rivers. Pop. (1988) 45,250.

Manufactures electrical equipment, musical instruments (producing nearly three-quarters of all the wind and percussion instruments made in the USA), metal goods and machinery.

Elk Island National Park Canada. The largest fenced animal reserve in Canada; in Alberta 34 km (21 miles) E of Edmonton. Area 194 sq km (75 sq. miles). Since 1906 a sanctuary for elk, moose, buffalo, deer; established as a National Park 1913. Mainly forested, with bathing and camping facilities.

Elland England. Town in West Yorkshire on R. Calder 5 km (3 miles) SE of Halifax. Pop. (1991) 14,232.

Manufactures textiles and clothing.

Ellesmere England. Market town in NW Shropshire 24 km (15 miles) NNW of Shrewsbury on the Ellesmere Canal, linking the R. Severn and the R. Mersey. Pop. (1991) 2967. In a dairy-farming district on the W shore of The Mere (small lake) from which its name is derived.

Ellesmere Island Canada. Arctic island in NE Franklin District, Northwest Territories, off NW Greenland; the northernmost island of Canada, largest of the Queen Elizabeth Is. Area 212,380 sq km (82,000 sq. miles). The coast is indented with fiords, dividing the island into 4 parts (N–S): Grant Land, Grinnell Land, Sverdrup Land, Lincoln Land. Mountainous, rising to over 2700 m (8856 ft). There is sparse vegetation in many areas; the musk-ox is common. Small settlements at Craig Harbour (SE) and Alexandra Fiord (E); a meteorological station on Eureka Sound (NW). Named (after the 1st Earl of Ellesmere) by Sir E. A. Inglefield, who first explored the island in 1852.

Ellesmere Port England. Town and port in NW Cheshire on the S bank of the Manchester Ship Canal 14 km (9 miles) SSE of Liverpool. Pop. (1991) 64,504. Near the town is the important oil refinery of Stanlow.

Besides the manufacture of petroleum products there are vehicle, chemical, paper and engineering industries.

Ellice Islands ➤TUVALU.

Ellis Island USA. Small island, and now a

museum, in Upper New York Bay. All but a small part in New Jersey, the rest in New York. Area 11 ha (27 acres). Used as an immigrant station 1892–1954; over 16 million immigrants entered the US via Ellis Island. Named after Samuel Ellis, a Manhattan merchant who bought it in the 18th cent. It was artificially enlarged from 1.2 ha (2½ acres) to its present size, mainly in 1898 and 1905.

Ellora India. Village in Maharastra 29 km (18 miles) NW of Aurangabad. Famous for the rock temples excavated in the hillside and extending for more than 1.6 km (1 mile). They are in three groups, Buddhist, Hindu and Jain, the outstanding one being the Kailasa temple of the Hindu group, which was carved externally as well as internally out of the rock.

Elmhurst USA. Town in Illinois 26 km (16 miles) W of Chicago. Pop. (1970) 50,547. Mainly residential. Limestone quarried in the neighbourhood.

Elmira USA. Industrial town in New York 137 km (85 miles) SSE of Rochester on the Chemung R. Pop. (1970) 39,945.

Manufactures fire-fighting and office equipment, glass and bottles.

Elmshorn Germany. Industrial town in Schleswig-Holstein 32 km (20 miles) NW of Hamburg. Pop. (1970) 40,883.

Shipbuilding and food-processing. Manufactures textiles and leather goods.

El Paso USA. Town in W Texas on the Rio Grande opposite Ciudad Juarez (Mexico). Pop. (1990) 555,342.

Tourist resort. Industrial centre: copper-smelting, oil-refining and meat-packing. Manufactures textiles, glass, cement and clothing. Considerable trade with Mexico. Mexican handicrafts are practised; there is a large pop. of Mexican descent.

The S (Mexican) bank of the river was originally settled by Spaniards in the 17th cent.; the first settlement on the N (US) bank was made in 1827.

El Salvador. Republic in Central America, bounded in the NE by Guatemala, NE and E by Honduras and S by the Pacific Ocean. Area 21,041 sq km (8124 sq. miles). Pop. (1995) 5,768,000 (45 per cent urban). Life expectancy, 64 years male, 70 female. Cap. San Salvador. Other cities Santa Ana, San Miguel, Mejicanus and Delgado. Currency: colon = 100 centavos. El Salvador comprises three regions: the narrow lowlands on the coast which are banked by two parallel mountain ranges enclosing the fertile inland plateau and this occupies 50 per cent of the land area and is where the majority of the people live. The coastal mountains contain a series of volcanic peaks inc. Santa Ana (2310 m; 7575 ft, the highest) and Izalco (1886 m; 6186 ft, active 1770–1956). Chief river the Lempa, of little navigational value but used since 1954 for hydroelectric power. Land use: forested 5 per cent, meadows and pastures 29 per cent, agricultural and under permanent cultivation 35 per cent. Official lang. is Spanish, but there are many Indian dialects. About 90 per cent of the pop. is Roman Catholic.

Agriculture dominates the economy and the most important export crops are coffee, cotton and sugar, providing 50 per cent of export income; rice and maize are produced for home consumption. It is the world's main source of balsam used in cosmetics and medical drugs. Other exports inc. pharmaceuticals and paper products. Tourism has great potential but the years of civil war have not helped its development. The important industrial sectors are food-processing, textiles, rubber goods, apparel manufacture, petroleum products and footwear.

Conquered by Spain in 1526, it remained under Spanish rule until 1821. It joined the Central American Federation 1824; became an independent republic 1841. A great rise in pop. followed the development of coffee-planting in the late 19th cent. The country's history has been marked by much political violence and a number of enforced changes of rulers. From the late 1970s fighting between government troops and left-wing guerrillas, as well as the activities of death squads apparently organized by the army, guerrilla disruptions of elections, kidnappings, the violation of human rights and many civilian deaths continuing into the 1990s. In 1992 the government and the guerrilla opposition signed a peace agreement and a permanent ceasefire began. Under the 1983 Constitution executive power is invested in a President and legislative power rests with an 84-member Assembly elected by universal suffrage and proportional representation. It is divided for administrative purposes into 14 departments: Ahuachapán, Cabañas, Chalatenango, Cuscatlán, La Libertad, La Paz, La Unión, Morazán, San Miguel, San Salvador, San Vicente, Santa Ana, Sonsonate, Usulután.

Elsinore ►HELSINGØR.

Eltham England. Residential district in the London borough of Greenwich (SE). Remains of 14th-cent. former royal palace. Burial-place of Thomas Doggett (d. 1721), founder of the prize of 'Doggett's Coat and Badge' for Thames watermen.

Eluru (Ellore) India. Town in Andhra Pradesh 290 km (180 miles) ESE of Hyderabad at the junction of the Godavari and Krishna R. canal systems. Pop. (1971) 127,047.
Manufactures textiles, carpets and leather. Rice and jute milling. Trade in rice, oilseeds and tobacco.

Elvas Portugal. Town in the Portalegre district, Alto Alentejo province, near the Spanish border. Pop. (1985) 12,700. Once a strong fortress; a 17th-cent. aqueduct and 15th-cent. cathedral. Now well-known for the preserving of fruit, esp. plums and for jewellery.

Ely England. Cathedral city on the R. Ouse in Cambridgeshire 23 km (14 miles) NNE of Cambridge. Pop. (1991) 10,329.
Market town. Manufactures beet-sugar, baskets, agricultural implements.
Its cathedral, a famous landmark, dates back to the 11th cent., with 7th-cent. Saxon relics; it has a remarkable Norman nave, a Decorated octagon and examples of the Early English and Perpendicular styles. The King's

Grammar School, founded in the 11th cent. and refounded 1541, inc. the Ely Porta, the old monastery gate house and Prior John de Cranden's chapel, both of the 14th cent. Ely grew originally round a 7th-cent. nunnery and here the Saxons under Hereward the Wake offered their final resistance to William the Conqueror. The name is supposed to be derived from the eels in the R. Ouse.

Ely, Isle of England. Slightly elevated land surrounding Ely only capable of being reached by boat or very narrow causeways until The Fens were drained. Area 971 sq km (375 sq. miles).
Mainly agricultural, producing sugarbeet, potatoes, cereals and fruit.

Elyria USA. Town in Ohio on the Black R. 37 km (23 miles) WSW of Cleveland. Pop. (1990) 56,746.
Manufactures foundry products, plastics, pumps, chemicals.
Named after himself by the first settler, Heman Ely, a New Englander, in 1817.

Emba River Kazakhstan. River 611 km (380 miles) long flowing generally SW to the NE part of the Caspian Sea, passing in its lower course through the rich Emba oilfield with centres at Makat, Koschagyl and elsewhere.

Emden Germany. Seaport in Lower Saxony on the R. Ems estuary near the Netherlands border 116 km (72 miles) WNW of Bremen. Pop. (1991) 50,100. Terminus of the Dortmund–Ems Canal.
Exports coal. Imports ores, grain and timber. Shipbuilding, oil-refining, fishing and fish-canning.
Became a free imperial city in 1595. Passed to Prussia 1744, to Hanover 1815 and returned to Prussia 1866.

Emilia-Romagna Italy. Region in the N comprising the provinces of Bologna, Ferrara, Modena, Parma, Piacenza, Reggio nell'Emilia, Forlì and Ravenna. Area 22,124 sq km (8542 sq. miles). Pop. (1991) 3,599,085. Cap. Bologna. The Apennines run WNW–ESE along its S border; N of them are the fertile plains of the R. Po, producing wheat, sugar-beet, tomatoes and other crops. Food-processing is the principal industry. Several popular resorts on the Adriatic coast, e.g. Rimini, Riccione, Cattolica.

Emmen Netherlands. Town in Drenthe province 51 km (32 miles) SSE of Groningen near the German border. Pop. (1992) 93,107. A 'new town' formed since World War II from several separate hamlets. Formerly a centre of peat-digging, a much reduced industry.

Manufactures agricultural machinery, chemicals, nylon and cement.

Emmental (Emmenthal) Switzerland. Valley of the upper Emme R., Bern canton. Noted for its dairy produce, esp. Emmental cheese. Chief market Langnau.

Empoli Italy. Town in Firenze province, Tuscany, on the Arno R. 27 km (17 miles) WSW of Florence. Pop. (1991) 44,000.

Manufactures pasta, hosiery.

Paintings and sculptures by Bartolomeo and the della Robbias in its churches.

Ems (Bad Ems) Germany. Town in the Rhineland-Palatinate on the Lahn R. 11 km (7 miles) ESE of Coblenz. Pop. (1990) 10,000. Well-known spa, famous since Roman times for its hot alkaline springs. At a conference here (1786) four German archbishops made the famous pronouncement against papal interference known as the Punctuation of Ems. The meeting here (1870) between William I of Prussia and the French ambassador, and Bismarck's version of the encounter – the so-called Ems Telegram – led to the Franco–Prussian War.

Ems River Germany. River 370 km (230 miles) long, rising in the Teutoburger Wald and flowing generally NNW to the Dollart and the North Sea. Linked at Meppen to the Ruhr by the Dortmund–Ems Canal.

Encarnación Paraguay. Cap. of the Itapúa department, river port on the Alto Paraná R. opposite Posadas in Argentina and linked with it by train ferry. Pop. (1990) 44,064.

Exports maté, timber, tobacco, cotton and hides. Industries inc. sawmilling and tanning.

Endeavour Strait Australia. The S part of Torres Strait between the N coast of Cape York Peninsula, Queensland and Prince of Wales Island. Named after Capt. Cook's vessel *Endeavour*, which passed through on his return voyage (1770).

Enderbury Island ➤PHOENIX ISLANDS.

Enderby Island ➤DAMPIER ARCHIPELAGO.

Enderby Land Antarctica. The most W part of the Australian Antarctic Territory, extending between 45°E and 55°E long. Discovered (1831) by John Biscoe; visited by Sir Douglas Mawson 1929–31.

Enfield England. London borough. Pop. (1994) 259,800. Once a market town, now a residential and industrial suburb 16 km (10 miles) N of London.

Manufactures metal goods, electrical equipment and cables.

Enfield USA. Town in Connecticut on the Connecticut R. 24 km (15 miles) NNE of Hartford. Pop. (1980) 42,695.

Manufactures hardware and wood products.

Engadine Switzerland. Upper (Swiss) part of the valley of the Inn R. in Graubünden (Grisons) canton, extending from the Maloja Pass about 95 km (60 miles) to the Austrian frontier; divided into Upper Engadine (SW) and Lower Engadine (NE). Villages have whitewashed stone houses. Several resorts and winter sports centres, e.g. St Moritz. The Swiss National Park (158 sq km (61 sq. miles)), founded 1909, famous for its Alpine flora and fauna, is reached from Zernez in the Lower Engadine.

Engelberg Switzerland. Village and resort in the Obwalden half-canton, 29 km (18 miles) SSE of Lucerne at a height of 1020 m (3346 ft) hemmed in by lofty mountains inc. Titlis (3241 m; 10,630 ft). Pop. (1970) 2841. Grew round a Benedictine abbey founded in the 12th cent.

Engels ➤POKROVSK.

England. The S and largest part of Great Britain. Area 130,439 sq km (50,363 sq. miles). Pop. (1991) 46,161,000. Cap. London. Constitutes the largest political division both of Great Britain and of the United Kingdom of Great Britain and Northern Ireland; also the most populous of the four units (England, Scotland, Wales, Northern Ireland). With Scotland to the N and Wales to the W it is separated from the continent of Europe by the North Sea and the English Channel and from Ireland by the Irish Sea. Although rather more than three-quarters of its land surface is classified as agricultural (arable, permanent pasture, rough grazing land), the country depends for its economic wealth on its manufacturing industries.

In 1801 the pop. of England and Wales together was 8,892,536 and within 50 years this number had doubled; by 1901 the pop. of England alone was 30,813,043 and in 1951 it had risen to 41,159,213. In 1985, 75 per cent of the people of England and Wales were living in urban areas. More than one-third of the urban pop. of England were massed in 6 great conurbations; Greater London was by far the largest. The English people are mainly of Anglo–Saxon and Danish origin (although along the Welsh border and in SW England the earlier Celtic strain is more apparent), while over the centuries there has been a continuous intermingling of newcomers: Scots, Welsh and Irish, as well as Normans, Flemings, Dutch, Poles and many others. The influx of coloured immigrants from the Commonwealth, chiefly from the West Indies and Pakistan, followed World War II. The established Church of England is Protestant Episcopal and is divided into the two archiepiscopal provinces of Canterbury and York; in 1990 it had 1.4 million on its electoral rolls. The various Nonconformist bodies, chiefly the Methodist, Baptists and Congregational, number several million, while Roman Catholics are estimated at 4.2 million.

For administrative purposes it is divided into metropolitan counties and non-metropolitan counties. Metropolitan counties: Greater Manchester, Merseyside, South Yorkshire, Tyne and Wear, West Midlands, West Yorkshire. Non-metropolitan counties: Bedfordshire, Buckinghamshire, Cambridgeshire, Cheshire, Cornwall and Isles of Scilly, Cumbria, Derbyshire, Devon, Dorset, Durham, East Sussex, Essex, Gloucestershire, Hampshire, Herefordshire, Hertfordshire, Humberside, Isle of Wight, Kent, Lancashire, Leicestershire, Lincolnshire, Norfolk, Northamptonshire, Northumberland, North Yorkshire, Nottinghamshire, Oxfordshire, Shropshire, Somerset, Staffordshire, Suffolk, Surrey, Warwickshire, West Sussex, Wiltshire, Worcestershire. There are further divisions of unitary authorities and district councils.

Slightly more than half of the agricultural land is arable. The principal crops are wheat, barley – both particularly in the drier, sunnier eastern counties – turnips and similar root crops, sugar-beet – again chiefly in the eastern counties – potatoes – largely in the Fens – hay. Kent is the leading county in the production of hops and fruit, which are also grown in Herefordshire and Worcestershire; some fruits are cultivated in most S counties. Market-gardening is important in the vicinity of the large industrial areas. Permanent pasture occupies about two-thirds as large an area as arable land, emphasizing the importance of livestock in English agriculture. Dairy-farming is located mainly in the western counties which, because of their mild, moist climate, can support rich pastures and Cheshire and Somerset are outstanding. Of the beef cattle, the Hereford, named after its county of origin, has won fame on the ranches of North and South America as well as at home. Sheep are grazed on the poorer upland pastures, e.g. in the Lake district and the Pennines and on the chalk hills of S England, esp. the North and South Downs. The fishing industry, though somewhat less important than formerly, is still substantial, and is centred mainly on the E coast ports of Hull and Grimsby. Coal long formed the basis of the country's leading industries, but the Yorkshire, Notts. and Derby coalfields have contracted dramatically in the 1980s and

1990s. Iron ore is found in the E Midlands and elsewhere, and china clay in Cornwall; salt beds in Cheshire and S Durham supply the nearby chemical industries. Iron and steel are manufactured at various centres in the Midlands and NE. Associated industries are shipbuilding, chiefly in the NE, but generally in decline; the construction and repair of locomotives and railway rolling-stock, at Crewe, Derby and other railway centres; the manufacture of motor vehicles at Coventry, Birmingham, Dagenham, Oxford and Luton. Of the textiles, the cotton industry is concentrated in Lancashire and the woollen industry in West Yorkshire. Boots and shoes are manufactured in the E Midlands (Northants), pottery in N Staffs (Stoke-on-Trent) and glass in S Lancashire (St Helens), while a large number of varied industries are located in Greater London.

Englewood (Colorado) USA. Residential suburb of Denver on the S Platte R. at a height of 1586 m (5202 ft). Pop. (1990) 31,500.

Englewood (New Jersey) USA. Residential town 21 km (13 miles) NNE of Jersey City. Pop. (1980) 23,701.

Manufactures elevators and leather goods.

English Channel (Fr. **La Manche**, 'The Sleeve'). Arm of the Atlantic Ocean between England and France 563 km (350 miles) long and 160 km (100 miles) wide at the W end (between Ushant and the Scilly Isles) and 34 km (21 miles) at the Strait of Dover (E end) where it joins the North Sea. Abounds in fish. Many seaside resorts on both coasts. The principal islands are the Channel Is. and the Isle of Wight. There are several cross-channel ferry services. First crossed by balloon 1785; first swum 1875; first crossed by aircraft 1909 (Blériot), by hovercraft 1959. There have been plans for a tunnel since 1802, a plan was drawn up in 1973 but it was abandoned in 1975. A successful project came to fruition in 1994 when the tunnel was opened for goods and passengers.

Enid USA. Town in N Oklahoma 106 km

(66 miles) NNW of Oklahoma City. Pop. (1990) 45,175.

Commercial centre and wheat market. Industries inc. oil-refining, flour-milling. Manufactures oilfield equipment. The air force base is the main employer.

Enna Italy. Formerly Castrogiovanni. Cap. of Enna province in central Sicily 21 km (13 miles) ENE of Caltanissetta on a plateau at 790 m (2591 ft). Pop. (1981) 27,838. In a sulphur-mining district. Ancient Enna was a centre of the worship of Demeter (Ceres). The town was held by the Saracens 859–1087.

Ennerdale Water England. Lake 4 km (2½ miles) long and up to 0.8 km (½ mile) wide in Cumbria in the Lake District 11 km (7 miles) ESE of Whitehaven, which it supplies with water.

Ennis Ireland. County town of Co. Clare on the R. Fergus 31 km (19 miles) NW of Limerick. Pop. (1991) 13,730.

Brewing, distilling, flour-milling.

Restored 13th-cent. Franciscan abbey.

Enniscorthy Ireland. Market town in Co. Wexford on the R. Slaney 19 km (12 miles) NNW of Wexford, with which it is connected by canal. Pop. (1991) 4127.

Brewing, flour-milling, bacon and ham curing, pottery manufacture.

Roman Catholic cathedral; the keep of a 13th-cent. Norman castle. Taken by Cromwell 1649. Sacked by Irish insurgents 1798.

Enniskillen Northern Ireland. County town of Fermanagh on an island in the R. Erne between Upper and Lower Lough Erne. Pop. (1991) 11,436.

Trade in agricultural produce. Cattle market.

Famous as a Protestant stronghold. James II's forces were defeated here 1689.

Enschede Netherlands. Town in Overijssel province near the German frontier, linked by the Twente Canal with the Ijssel and Rhine rivers. Pop. (1992) 147,199.

Leading centre of the Dutch cotton industry. Also manufactures clothing, paper, chemicals and tyres.

Ensenada Mexico. Port in Baja (Lower) California 96 km (60 miles) SE of Tijuana. Pop. (1990) 260,905.

Tourist resort. Fishing, fish-canning and wine-making.

Entebbe Uganda. Town in the Buganda region on the NW shore of L. Victoria at a height of 1147 m (3762 ft) 33 km (20 miles) SW of Kampala. Pop. (1991) 41,638.

Important international airport. Mainly an administrative centre. Botanical gardens, a virus research institute and a hospital.

Founded in 1893 and was the cap. until 1962.

Entre Minho e Douro Portugal. Popularly known as Minho. Former province between the Minho (N) and the Douro (S) rivers, containing the administrative districts of Braga, Viana do Castelo and Porto divided in 1936 between the new province of Minho and the N part of Douro Litoral province. Intensively cultivated, producing maize, vines, fruit and olives. Chief towns Oporto and Braga.

Entreve Italy. Village in Val d'Aosta at the Italian end of Mont Blanc road tunnel, which links it with Les Pèlerins, France (opened in 1965).

Enugu Nigeria. Cap. of Enugu State 193 km (120 miles) NNE of Port Harcourt, with which it is linked by rail. Pop. (1992) 286,100.

Main coalmining centre in W Africa; supplies the railways, tin mines and shipping. Railway engineering and sawmilling.

Became cap. of the breakaway state of Biafra in 1967 ►►NIGERIA.

Enzeli ►BANDAR ANZALI.

Epe Netherlands. Town in Gelderland situated E of Apeldoorn. Pop. (1992) 33,827.

Market town trading in eggs and wooden shoes.

Épernay France. Town in the Marne department on the Marne R. 26 km (16 miles) SSW of Reims. Pop. (1990) 28,000.

One of the two main headquarters of the Champagne wine industry (the other being Reims). Manufactures corking equipment, corks, bottles and casks; the wine is bottled and stored in vast underground cellars dug in the chalk. Other industries sugar-refining, textile manufacture.

Ephesus. Ancient Ionian city on the W coast of Asia Minor 48 km (30 miles) SSE of the modern Izmir (Turkey). Famous for its wealth and for its temple of Artemis (Diana). Taken by Alexander the Great 333 BC. Passed to the Romans 133 BC, later becoming cap. of Roman Asia. Visited by St Paul, who addressed an epistle to the Christians here; in AD 262 both city and temple were destroyed by the Goths. Never fully recovered and was later abandoned. Excavations in the late 19th and in the 20th cent. revealed ruins of the temple and other buildings.

Epidaurus Greece. Ancient town in Argolis in the NE Peloponnese on the Saronic Gulf. Famous for the sacred precinct of Asclepius; remains of the temple and the theatre, among the finest in Greece, have been excavated. Just NW is the small modern town of Nea Epidhavros ('New Epidaurus'), where Greek independence was proclaimed in 1822.

Épinal France. Prefecture of the Vosges department on the Moselle R. 68 km (42 miles) SSE of Nancy. Pop. (1990) 39,480.

Flourishing cotton industry, introduced by Alsatian immigrants. Also manufactures Kirsch liqueur, cheap engravings, lithographs (*images d'Épinal*).

Grew round a 10th-cent. monastery founded by the Bishop of Metz. Ceded to the duchy of Lorraine 1465. Incorporated into France 1766.

Epirus (Gr. **Ípiros**). 1. Ancient Epeiros. Region in ancient Greece in the NW between the Pindus Mountains and the Ionian Sea; the name means 'the Mainland'. Mountainous and not very fertile. Famous for cattle and horses. One of the tribes, the Molossians, attained their greatest power under Pyrrhus (318–272 BC), whose costly defeats of the Romans were the original 'Pyrrhic victories'.

Passed to the Turks in the 15th cent.; after Greek independence it was ceded to Greece (S part) and Albania (N part).

Region in modern Greece comprising the *nomes* of Árta, Ioánnina, Préveza and Thesprotia. Area 9203 sq km (3494 sq. miles). Pop. (1991) 339,210.

Epping England. Town in W Essex 24 km (15 miles) NNE of London, which it serves as a dormitory suburb. Stands on the N edge of Epping Forest, part of the ancient Waltham Forest which once covered most of Essex; after reduction by enclosures, 22.8 sq km (8.8 sq. miles) were purchased by the Corporation of the City of London and opened to the public in 1882.

Epsom and Ewell England. Residential district of Surrey 21 km (13 miles) SSW of London. Pop. (1991) 64,405. On Epsom Downs just S is the racecourse where several famous races, inc. the Derby (founded 1780) and the Oaks are held. Because of mineral springs containing magnesium sulphate, Epsom became a celebrated 17th-cent. spa and gave its name to Epsom salts. Epsom College was founded 1855. The neighbouring village of Ewell, which was absorbed in 1937, contains part of Nonsuch Park (1 sq km; 0.4 sq. miles), inc. in the Green belt.

Equatorial Guinea. Republic on the Gulf of Guinea. The mainland part of Equatorial Guinea is bounded N by Cameroon, E and S by Gabon and W by the Gulf of Guinea in which lie the islands of Bioko (formerly Macías Nguema, formerly Fernando Póo) and Annobón (called Pagalu from 1973 to 1979). Area 28,051 sq km (10,831 sq. miles) (31 per cent urban). Pop. (1995) 396,000. Life expectancy, 50 years male, 54 female. Cap. Malabo. Other towns Bata, Ela-Nguena, Campo Yaunde and Los Angeles. Currency: CFA franc = 100 centimes. Río Muni, the mainland part of the country, rises quickly from a narrow coastal strip of mangrove swamps towards a plateau of forested mountains. This jungle-plateau has many rivers cutting through it inc. the River Mbini (Beniot) which bisects the country.

The island of Bioko lies 160 km (100 miles) to the NE and is volcanic. The climate is equatorial with alternate wet and dry seasons. Land use: forested 46 per cent, meadows and pastures 4 per cent, agricultural and under permanent cultivation 8 per cent. Spanish is the official lang., but there are several African langs inc. Fang. Fang comprises 83 per cent of the ethnic composition of the country and about 89 per cent is Roman Catholic.

Industry is virtually non-existent. The country produces timber, coffee, cocoa and bananas for export and is just self-sufficient in basic foodstuffs. Minerals, oil and natural gas exist but have yet to be fully exploited, and the lack of adequate infrastructure impedes progress.

Equatorial Guinea was a Spanish colony until 1960 when it became part of Spain and it became two provinces, represented in the *Cortes* in Madeira. It gained independence in 1968. Civil disorders followed and by 1971 almost all of the 7000 Europeans had left; thousands of Nigerian plantation workers also returned home, contributing to the decline in the economy. In 1979 the President was overthrown and under the 1982 Constitution there is an 11-member Council of State and a 60-member House of Representatives. The 1991 Constitution allows multi-party politics.

Erbil (Arbil, Irbil) Iraq. Ancient Arbela. Cap. of Erbil province 80 km (50 miles) E of Mosul. Pop. (1985) 333,903.

Commercial centre. Trade in grain, livestock. Terminus of the railway from Baghdad and Kirkuk.

Important in Assyrian times.

Erciyas Dagi Turkey. Extinct volcano in central Turkey 21 km (13 miles) S of Kayseri, 3916 m (12,850 ft) in height.

Ercolano ➤HERCULANEUM.

Erebus, Mount Antarctica. Active volcano (4024 m; 13,202 ft) on Ross Island in the Ross Sea. Discovered (1841) by Sir James Ross and named after one of his ships.

Erevan ➤YEREVAN.

Erfurt Germany. Cap. of Thuringia on the Gera R. 105 km (65 miles) WSW of Leipzig. Pop. (1991) 208,989. Railway junction.

Industrial and commercial centre. Manufactures machinery, electrical equipment, typewriters and clothing. Trade in flowers, vegetables and seeds. A tourist resort and one of the oldest of German cities, it has a 13th/15th-cent. cathedral, the 13th-cent. Church of St Severus and the buildings of the former university, opened in 1392 and suppressed in 1816, where Luther studied.

Ericht, Loch Scotland. Lake 24 km (15 miles) long and 0.8–1.6 km (½–1 mile) wide in Stirling at a height of 351 m (1151 ft). From the S end water is led by tunnel to a hydroelectric plant on Loch Rannoch.

Erie USA. Port and manufacturing town in NW Pennsylvania on L. Erie. Pop. (1991) 108,718.

Handles coal, petroleum, timber, grain and fish. The harbour is sheltered by the Presque Isle peninsula. Manufactures refrigerators, electrical equipment, metal goods and paper.

Fort Presque Isle was built by the French in 1753 but later abandoned; occupied by the British in 1760 and passed to the USA in 1785.

Erie, Lake Canada/USA. Fourth largest (25,667 sq km; 9910 sq. miles) of the Great Lakes between the USA and Canada at a height of 174 m (571 ft) above sea level; the shallowest of the Great Lakes, with a maximum depth of 64 m (210 ft). It freezes easily and is closed to navigation from mid Dec. to March or April. Through the Detroit R. it receives the waters of the upper lakes; it empties via the Niagara R. into L. Ontario. Chief ports Toledo, Cleveland, Erie, Buffalo and Sandusky in the USA and Port Colborne (at the entrance to the Welland Canal leading to L. Ontario) in Canada. The US–Canadian boundary runs approximately through the lake. Named after the Erie Indians. Discovered by the French in the early 17th cent. In the 18th cent. it became an important fur-trade route, and forts and trading posts were built along its shores.

Erie Canal USA. Waterway 579 km (360 miles) long, from Albany (Hudson R.) to Buffalo (L. Erie); the main canal in the New York State Barge Canal System. Opened 1825. The object (amply fulfilled) was to make eastern markets accessible to farmers of the Great Lakes region and to facilitate the westward movement of settlers; it also enhanced the commercial importance of New York. Tolls were paid until 1882.

Erith England. Part of the London borough of Bexley. Formerly a naval station on the S bank of the R. Thames.

Manufactures chemicals, paints, paper, electrical equipment and cables.

Eritrea. Republic in NE Africa, bounded on the E by the Red Sea, S by Ethiopia and Djibouti, and W by Sudan. Area 117,400 sq km (45,300 sq. miles). Pop. (1995) 3,531,000 (15 per cent urban). Life expectancy, 46 years. Cap. Asmara. Chief seaport Mitsiwa (Massawa). Currency: Ethiopian birr = 100 cents. The narrow coastal strip is hot and arid and inc. part of the desert of Danakil Land. The upland zone, an extension of the Ethiopian highlands, rising to 2989 m (9804 ft) in Mt Soira, is cooler and wetter. Land use: forested 0.5 per cent, woodland and scrubland 5.5 per cent, agricultural and under permanent cultivation 3.5 per cent, meadows and pastures 57.2 per cent, mainly barren 33.3 per cent. Coptic Christians living mainly in the highlands comprise about 50 per cent of pop. and the other 50 per cent are Muslims living in the lowlands.

Principal occupation stock-rearing (cattle, sheep, goats). Coffee is grown in the uplands, gum arabic collected in the lowlands. Salt produced and some pearl fished off the Dahlak Is. Eritrea had considerable industry but the economy has been devastated by the war. There are large reserves of copper, iron, gold and potassium. There has also been considerable famine through drought.

Italy secured various possessions along the Red Sea coast in the late 19th cent. and in

1890 formed the colony of Eritrea, the base for the invasions (1896–1935) of Abyssinia (Ethiopia). Occupied by British forces during World War II (1941) and then was under British military administration. It became an autonomous area, in federation with Ethiopia, by UN decision in 1952. Completely integrated with Ethiopia in 1962 but conflict between Eritrean secessionists and the Ethiopian government continued. A referendum was held in April 1993 and independence was declared 24 May 1993. Ethiopia has the right to use the ports of Mitsiwa (Massawa) and Assab. There is a National Assembly comprising all members of the Eritrean People's Liberation Front Central Committee and 60 others – 11 seats are reserved for women. The Assembly appoints a State Council consisting of 14 Ministers and the governors of the 10 provinces. The 10 provinces are: Akele, Guzai, Asmara, Barker, Den Kel, Gash-Setir, Hamasien, Sahel, Semhar, Senhit and Seraye.

Erivan ➤YEREVAN.

Erlangen Germany. Town in Bavaria at the confluence of the Regnitz and Schwabach rivers 16 km (10 miles) N of Nuremberg. Pop. (1991) 102,500.

Manufactures synthetic fibres, electrical equipment, gloves, cotton goods (first introduced by the Huguenots), and noted for its beer.

Birthplace of Georg Simon Ohm, German physicist (1787–1854).

Ermelo Netherlands. Market town in Gelderland province 26 km (16 miles) WNW of Apeldoorn. Pop. (1992) 26,433. In a poultry and dairy farming region.

Erne, Lough Northern Ireland. Lake in Co. Fermanagh consisting of Upper Lough Erne (18 km; 11 miles long and up to 5 km; 3 miles wide) and Lower Lough Erne (29 km; 18 miles long and up to 9 km; 5½ miles wide), the latter being often known simply as Lough Erne. They are joined by part of R. Erne. Both contain many islands; Devenish island, near the S end of Lower Lough Erne, is famous for its 6th-cent. ruins.

Erne River Ireland. River 103 km (64 miles) long, rising in Lough Gowna on the border of Counties Longford and Cavan and flowing NW through Lough Oughter and Lough Erne past Ballyshannon, near which are hydroelectric plants, to Donegal Bay on the Atlantic.

Erzerum ➤ERZURUM.

Erzgebirge (Czech **Krušné Hory**, 'Ore Mountains'). Mountain range on the border of Bohemia (Czech Republic) and Saxony (Germany), extending about 145 km (90 miles) WSW–ENE and about 40 km (25 miles) wide. Rises to 1245 m (4084 ft) in Klinovec (Czech Republic). Many minerals, inc. silver, copper, lead, were formerly worked, but are now practically exhausted; in recent years uranium ore has been obtained, chiefly at Jachymov (Czech Republic) and Aue (Germany). Several spas and winter-sports centres.

Erzincan Turkey. Cap. of Erzincan province near the Euphrates R. 153 km (95 miles) WSW of Erzurum. Pop. (1990) 91,800.

Manufactures textiles, clothing and copper goods.

Has suffered severely from earthquakes.

Erzurum (Erzerum) Turkey. Cap. of Erzurum province in the E on a fertile plateau at a height of 1922 m (6304 ft). Pop. (1990) 242,391.

Tanning, sugar-refining and other industries. Trade in grain, vegetables.

Seat of Atatürk University (1957). An ancient town, in an important strategic position, it fell to the Turks in 1515 and was taken three times by the Russians (1828, 1878, 1916).

Esbjerg Denmark. North Sea port in Jutland opposite Fanö island 129 km (80 miles) SW of Aarhus. Pop. (1990) 81,500. Grew because of the construction of the railway and harbour in 1874. Denmark's chief fishing port.

Exports dairy produce and bacon. Ferry services to Britain. Manufactures margarine and rope.

Esch-sur-Alzette Luxembourg. Industrial

town and second largest city on the Alzette R. 16 km (10 miles) SW of Luxembourg. Pop. (1991) 24,012.

Iron-mining; centre of the steel industry. Manufactures steel goods and fertilizers.

Eschwege Germany. Town in Hessen on the Werra R. 43 km (27 miles) ESE of Kassel. Pop. (1985) 24,000.

Manufactures soap, textiles and footwear.

Eschweiler Germany. Industrial town in North Rhine-Westphalia 13 km (8 miles) ENE of Aachen. Pop. (1988) 53,516.

Industries inc. open-cast lignite, steel, cables, iron-casting, brewing, tanning and paint.

Escorial (Escurial) Spain. Small town at the foot of the Sierra de Guadarrama 42 km (26 miles) NW of Madrid, near which is one of the most magnificent buildings in Europe, comprising monastery, palace and mausoleum. The monastery, El real monasterio de San Lorenzo del Escorial, was erected by Philip II (1563–84). The famous library and art treasures of El Escorial were added later.

Esdraelon (Jezreel), Plain of Israel. Fertile plain watered by the Kishon R., extending SE–NW from the Jordan valley to the foot of Mt Carmel. Site of the battlefield of Megiddo.

Esfahan (Isfahan) Iran. Ancient Aspadana. Cap. of Isfahan (Esfahan) province and the country's second largest city on the Zayindeh R. 320 km (200 miles) S of Tehrán at 1402 m (4600 ft). Pop. (1991) 1,127,000.

Manufactures textiles, carpets and rugs, brocade and silverwork.

Famous for its inlaid and ornamental work. At the centre of the city is the imposing Maidan-i-Shah, a rectangular space on the S side of which is the famous 17th-cent. Masjid-i-Shah (royal mosque) – an outstanding example of Persian architecture, covered with enamelled tiles. There is also the Lutfullah mosque, with its blue-tiled dome, on the E side; on the W side the Ali Kapu gate leads to the former royal gardens and the throne room of Shah Abbas, the

Chehil Sutun (forty pillars). The city was taken by Timur and its inhabitants massacred 1387. It prospered and became a great cap. under Shah Abbas I, but fell to the Afghans (1722) and never fully recovered the former glory.

Esher England. Town in NE Surrey 24 km (15 miles) SW of London, for which it is a dormitory suburb. Pop. (1991) 46,599. Sandown Park racecourse.

Eskilstuna Sweden. Industrial town in Södermanland on the Hjälmar R., which joins L. Hjälmar and L. Mälar 88 km (55 miles) W of Stockholm. Pop. (1992) 89,584.

Important centre of the iron and steel industry, long noted for the manufacture of cutlery, swords and hardware. Also produces machinery, precision instruments, electrical equipment.

Named after St Eskil, an English missionary martyred here 1181.

Eskişehir Turkey. Cap. of Eskişehir province 217 km (135 miles) W of Ankara. Pop. (1990) 413,082.

Industrial centre noted for sugar-refining. Manufactures textiles, cement and agricultural implements. Trade in grain and other agricultural produce. Centre of the meerschaum industry, now of diminished importance.

Known since the 3rd cent. for its hot sulphur springs. Nearby was the ancient Phrygian city Dorylaeum.

Esk River England. 1. River rising on Scafell, Cumbria and flowing 32 km (20 miles) SW to the Irish Sea near Ravenglass.

2. River in North Yorkshire, rising in the Cleveland Hills and flowing 39 km (24 miles) generally E to enter the North Sea at Whitby.

Esk River England/Scotland. River 58 km (36 miles) long, formed by the union of the Black Esk and the White Esk, flowing SSE through Dumfries and Galloway (Scotland), crossing the border into Cumbria (England) and turning SSW to enter Solway Firth 13 km (8 miles) NNW of Carlisle.

Esk River Scotland. 1. North Esk: river

47 km (29 miles) long, rising in the Grampians and flowing SE to enter the North Sea 6 km (4 miles) NNE of Montrose.

2. South Esk: river in Angus 79 km (49 miles) long, rising in the Grampians and flowing SE and then E to enter the North Sea at Montrose.

3. River in Lothian 6 km (4 miles) long, formed by the union of the North Esk (27 km; 17 miles) and the South Esk (31 km; 19 miles) and flowing N to enter the Firth of Forth at Musselburgh.

Esmeraldas Ecuador. Cap. of Esmeraldas province, at the mouth of the Esmeraldas R. 200 km (125 miles) NW of Quito. Pop. (1990) 98,558.

Chief seaport in the NW. Exports petroleum, bananas and timber.

Esna (Isna) Egypt. Ancient Latapolis. Town on the W bank of the Nile R. 100 km (62 miles) SSW of Qena. Pop. 26,000 (many Copts). Site of an important barrage (rebuilt 1948).

Manufactures pottery.

Ruins of a temple dedicated to Khnum, the ram-headed god.

Esperance Australia. Town in Western Australia situated on Esperance Bay serving a wheat and wood producing area. Pop. (1989) 11,000. Railway terminal, resort and port.

Espirito Santo Brazil. Maritime state in the E; a low coastal strip 370 km (230 miles) long, rising in the W to mountain ranges. Area 45,733 sq km (17,658 sq. miles). Pop. (1991) 2,598,231. Cap. Vitória. Chief river the Rio Doce. The marshy coast has only one good harbour, Vitória.

Produces coffee, sugar-cane and fruits.

Espiritu Santo Island ►VANUATU.

Espoo Finland. Town in Uusimaa situated W of Helsinki. Pop. (1992) 175,806.

Industries inc. granite-quarrying.

Esquimalt (Esquimault) Canada. Port and naval base at the S end of Vancouver Island, British Columbia; a suburb of Victoria. Large dry-dock and other facilities. Taken over by the Canadian government from the British in 1906.

Essaouira Morocco. Formerly Mogador. Seaport and resort on the Atlantic coast 169 km (105 miles) W of Marrakesh, with which it is connected by road. Pop. (1985) 43,000.

Exports wood, olive oil. Fish-canning, sugar-refining and tanning.

Essen Germany. Town in North Rhine-Westphalia between the Ruhr R. and the Rhine–Herne Canal 32 km (20 miles) NNE of Düsseldorf. Pop. (1991) 626,973.

Leading industrial centre of the Ruhr coalfield, owing its impressive growth to the establishment of the Krupp steel works early in the 19th cent. Besides coalmining and steel manufacture, there are chemical, textile, glass and machine-tool, and furniture industries. Railway engineering.

Founded originally round a 9th-cent. convent.

Essendon Australia. Town situated NW of Melbourne, Victoria. Pop. (1990) 55,000.

Retail and commercial centre for a farming area, trading in oats and barley.

Essequibo River Guyana. River 1014 km (630 miles) long, rising in the Guiana highlands on the Brazil frontier, flowing generally N over many falls and rapids and W of Georgetown and at its estuary is nearly 50 km (30 miles) wide. It receives several large tributaries; on one of them, the Potaro, are the famous Kaieteur Falls (226 m; 741 ft).

Essex England. County in the SE, bounded by the North Sea (E) and the Thames estuary (S). Area 3672 sq km (1418 sq. miles). Pop. (1991) 1,495,600. County town Chelmsford. It is divided into the districts of Basildon, Braintree, Brentwood, Castle Point, Chelmsford, Colchester, Epping Forest, Harlow, Maldon, Rochford, Southend on Sea, Tendring, Thurrock and Uttlesford. From the flat coastal plain the county becomes gently undulating inland, particularly in the NW, with several hills 90–120 m

(295–394 ft) in height; the rivers are either affluents of the Thames (e.g. the Lea and the Roding) or flow to the North Sea (the Stour, which forms much of the N boundary with Suffolk, the Colne, Blackwater, Chelmer and Crouch – the estuary of the Colne is noted for its oysters). Along the low but indented coast there are several popular resorts, inc. Southend on Sea and Clacton; Tilbury is a seaport, Harwich has ferry services to the continent and there is a large oil refinery at Shell Haven. The N is mainly agricultural, producing cereals, sugar-beet, fruits and vegetables, while in the S, where Epping Forest is a mere remnant of the former woodlands, dairy-farming is important.

Esslingen am Neckar Germany. Industrial town in Baden-Württemberg on the Neckar R. 10 km (6 miles) ESE of Stuttgart. Pop. (1986) 87,000.

Manufactures machinery, electrical equipment, textiles and gloves.

Old town hall (15th-cent.). Founded in the 8th cent. A free imperial city from 1273. Incorporated into Württemberg 1802. It is now little more than a suburb of Stuttgart.

Essonne France. Department S of Paris formed in 1964, when the former Seine and Seine-et-Oise departments were reorganized. Area 1804 sq km (696 sq. miles). Pop. (1991) 1,096,300. Prefecture Evry.

Estelí Nicaragua. Cap. of Estelí department 96 km (60 miles) NNW of Managua on the Inter-American Highway. Pop. (1971) 34,977.

Market town. Sawmilling and tanning.

Estevan Canada. City situated SE of Regina in Saskatchewan on the Souris R. at the mouth of Long Creek. Pop. (1989) 10,500.

The main industries are crude oil, natural gas and mining lignite-coal, also flour-milling; manufactures mobile homes and coal briquettes.

Esthwaite Water England. Lake in Cumbria in the Lake District 2.5 km (1½ miles) long and 0.4 km (¼ mile) wide between Coniston Water and L. Windermere.

Near the N end is the village of Hawkshead, at whose grammar school the English poet, William Wordsworth (1770–1850) was a pupil (1778–83).

Estonia. The Republic of Estonia is bounded W and N by the Baltic Sea, E by Russia and S by Latvia. Area 45,215 sq km (17,458 sq. miles). Pop. (1993) 1,487,000 (72 per cent urban). Life expectancy, 65 years male, 75 female. Cap. Tallinn. Other principal towns are Tartu, Narva, Khtla-Järve and Pärnu. Currency: kroon = 100 senti. The country is generally low-lying being an extension of the great Russian plain, it has moraine ridges in the S which rise at one point to over 300 m (984 ft). With a maritime location the country has a moderate climate, with cool summers and mild winters. Land use: forested 43 per cent, agricultural and under permanent cultivation 33 per cent. The ethnic composition comprises Estonian 62 per cent, Russian 30 per cent, Ukrainian 3 per cent. Of the believers, Evangelical Lutherans are the religious group in the majority and Estonian is the official lang.

The forests provide raw material for various manufactures such as wood-pulp, paper, textiles, instruments, furniture and matches. Agriculture is based on intensive dairy-farming and grain production. There are valuable oil-shale deposits in the NE producing gas, petrol and asphalt. The manufacturing industries are all centred on Tallinn.

For many cents. the Estonians, a Finno-Ugrian people, were subject to various foreign powers. In the 13th cent. the N part of their territory was conquered by the Danes, who founded Reval (now Tallinn), and the S by the Teutonic Knights. By the 17th cent. (1629) all Estonia had passed to Sweden, but in 1721 it became a province of Russia. It was not until 1920 that Estonia achieved complete independence, after a struggle against both Germans and Russians, but in 1940 it was occupied by Soviet forces and annexed to the USSR. German occupation followed in World War II (1941–4). From 1944 until 1990 it was dominated both politically and economically by the USSR.

In 1990 the Estonian Supreme Soviet proclaimed that Soviet occupation of Estonia in 1940 had not disrupted the continuity of the former republic and adopted by 73 votes to 0, with three abstentions, a declaration calling for the eventual re-establishment of full sovereignty. In a referendum in 1991, 77.8 per cent of those who voted wanted independence. This was conceded by the USSR in 1991. It is now a multiparty republic with a unicameral 101-member Parliament (*Riigikogu*).

Estoril Portugal. Seaside resort on the 'Portuguese Riviera' 21 km (13 miles) W of Lisbon, with which it is connected by electrical railway. Pop. (1991) 24,850. Made popular by its mild climate, beach, casino and many excellent hotels. A magnificent avenue of palm trees leads from the casino to the sea front.

Estremadura (Extremadura) Spain. Autonomous community in the W bordering on the old Portuguese Estremadura, lying between the latter and New Castile. Area 41,602 sq km (16,063 sq. miles). Pop. (1991) 1,050,490. Cap. Mérida. Largely tableland (Meseta), crossed by the Tagus and Guadiana rivers. Agriculture, formerly backward, has been improved by extensive irrigation schemes. Chief products olives, wheat; sheep and pigs raised.

Esztergom (Ger. **Gran**) Hungary. Town in Komárom county on the Danube R. almost opposite its confluence with the Hron R. and near the Czech frontier. Pop. (1993) 30,000.

Resort (thermal springs). Manufactures textiles and machinery.

Famous as the birthplace of St Stephen (979), who in 1001 became the first Christian king of Hungary. The cathedral (1821–70), which is modelled on St Peter's, Rome, stands on a hill overlooking the Danube.

Etawah India. Town in Uttar Pradesh 113 km (70 miles) ESE of Agra. Pop. (1991) 124,072.

Industries inc. oilseed-milling and it manufactures textiles. Trade in cotton, agricultural produce.

Principal building the 16th-cent. Jama Masjid or Great Mosque, originally a Hindu temple.

Ethiopia. State in NE Africa bounded by Eritrea to the N and NE, Djibouti and Somalia to the E, Kenya to the S and Sudan to the N. The secession of Eritrea in 1993 left the country without a coastline but Ethiopia has the right to use the Eritrean ports of Assab and Mitsiwa (Massawa). Area 1,132,882 sq km (437,794 sq. miles). Pop. (1995) 55,053,000 (11.5 per cent urban). Life expectancy, 46 years male, 49 female. Cap. Addis Ababa. Other towns Dire Dawa, Gondar and Nazret. Currency: Ethiopian birr = 100 cents. Ethiopia comprises a plateau divided into a NW region (rising to 4620 m (15,157 ft) in Ras Dashan) and a smaller SE section (rising to 4307 m (14,131 ft) in Mt Bale) by the Great Rift Valley, which cuts across from the Red Sea to L. Rudolf. The largest lake, L. Tana, is the source of the Blue Nile. The Sobat R. (tributary of the White Nile) and the Atbara R. (the Nile's only substantial affluent below Khartoum) also rise in the NW part of the plateau. Land use: forested 25 per cent, meadows and pastures 41 per cent, agricultural and under permanent cultivation 13 per cent. About 45 per cent are Muslim and 40 per cent Christian mainly belonging to the Ethiopian Orthodox Church. The official lang. is Amharic, but there are 286 languages spoken. There are 8 major and some 60 minor ethnic groups. The dominant race, the Amhara, inhabit the central Ethiopian highlands. To the N of them are the Tigreans, akin to the Amhara but speaking a different, though related, lang. Both these races are of mixed Hamitic and Semitic origin, and further mixed by intermarriage with Oromo (Galla) and other races. The Oromos comprise about 40 per cent of the entire pop. and are a pastoral and agricultural people of Hamitic origin. Somalis, another Hamitic race, inhabit the SE of Ethiopia, in particular the Ogaden desert region. The closely related Afar people stretch northwards from the former Wollo region into Eritrea.

The volume of foreign trade is small. The main food crops are maize, barley, teff, sorghum, oilseeds, wheat and pulses. There was severe famine in 1984-5 and again in 1992. Coffee is the most important export, producing over 60 per cent of foreign earnings. There is little industry. Addis Ababa is linked by rail, via Dire Dawa, with Djibouti; this is the principal trade route.

Ancient Ethiopia was an ill-defined territory S of Egypt (which inc. the N of modern Ethiopia). Traditionally, the founder of the Ethiopian royal line (c. 1000 BC) was Menelik, son of Solomon and the Queen of Sheba. Christianity was introduced in the 4th cent. The period of greatest prosperity was after the conquest of Yemen, in the 6th cent. By vanquishing Egypt in the 7th cent. the Arabs isolated the Ethiopians from the civilized world for many cents. A local chief, Lij Kassa, proclaimed himself Emperor Theodore II of Ethiopia 1855. A successor Menelik II (Shoa) defeated the invading Italians at Aduwa in 1896 and preserved Ethiopian independence. The Italians again attacked and occupied (Abyssinia) Ethiopia 1935. After their defeat by British forces during World War II (1941) the Emperor Haile Selassie was restored. The former Italian colony of Eritrea was federated to Ethiopia in 1952 and was integrated into Ethiopia in 1962. After much internal disorder, Haile Selassie was deposed and imprisoned in 1974, and many officials were executed; the former Emperor died during detention in 1975 and the new Military Council took measures to inaugurate 'Ethiopian socialism'. Under the 1987 Constitution a civilian government was installed. Elections held in 1992 caused considerable unrest because it was claimed that they were unfair.

The 1994 Constitution provides for a federated state. For administrative purposes the country is divided into a federation of 9 regions, based mainly on recognized ethnic groups: Afar, Amhara, Benshangi, Gambella, Harar, Oromia, The Peoples of the South, Somali and Tigre.

Etna Italy. Highest volcano in Europe and highest mountain in S Italy 3323 m (10,902 ft) in Catania province, E Sicily 29 km (18 miles) NNW of Catania. An isolated peak, it has the shape of a truncated cone, the uniformity of the slope broken on the E by an immense gully, 600–1200 m (1968–3935 ft) deep and over 5 km (3 miles) wide; on its sides are more than 200 secondary cones. Three distinct zones on its slopes. The lowest, the cultivated zone, extending to about 1200 m (3936 ft) is one of the most densely populated agricultural regions in the world; up to 450 m (1476 ft) it produces citrus fruits, olives and figs and above that height vines and almonds. In the middle, up to 2100 m (6888 ft) is the wooded zone, with pines and chestnuts and above this the desert zone, a desolate area of lava and volcanic ash, almost devoid of vegetation and covered with snow for much of the year. It is one of the world's most active volcanoes and of its many eruptions some of the most noteworthy were those of 475 BC, described by Pindar and Aeschylus; AD 1169, when Catania was destroyed; 1669, the most destructive of all recorded eruptions, when Catania was again destroyed; and 1928, when Mascali was obliterated by lava. On average there have been eruptions about every 6 years during historic times.

Etobicoke Canada. City within Metropolitan Toronto, Ontario. Pop. (1990) 302,973.

Industries inc. electronics and telecommunications. It manufactures tyres and rubber.

Eton England. Town in Berkshire on the R. Thames opposite Windsor. Pop. (1991) 1974. Site of Eton College (public school) founded by Henry VI in 1440–1 simultaneously with King's College, Cambridge.

Etruria Italy. Ancient district in NW Italy, of varying extent but latterly forming what is now Tuscany and part of Umbria. It may once have included all N Italy from the Tiber R. to the Alps, but by the 1st cent. BC it had been reduced to the territory between the Tiber, the Apennines and the Arno. Its people, the Etruscans, were probably immigrants from Asia Minor; they occupied much of Italy, founded many important cities, and reached the peak of their power in the 6th cent. BC. They had succumbed to Rome by the end of the 4th cent. BC. As excavations have shown, they had great artistic skill, particularly in sculpture.

Ettrick Scotland. Village and parish in Scottish Borders on Ettrick Water, a river rising on Capel Fell and flowing 51 km (32 miles) NE to join the R. Tweed. Ettrick Forest formerly covered Selkirkshire and parts of Peeblesshire and Midlothian, was deforested and in the 16th cent. converted into sheep pasturage.

Euboea (Gr. **Evvoia**) Greece. Largest of the Greek islands, forming a *nome* with neighbouring islands and Skyros (N Sporades) with its offshore islands off the E coast of the mainland in the Aegean Sea. Area (*nome*) 4167 sq km (1609 sq. miles). Pop. (1991) 209,132. Cap. Chalcis. The island extends over 160 km (100 miles) NW–SE and is largely mountainous, rising to 1744 m (5720 ft) in Mt Delphi.

Cereals, vines and olives cultivated in the fertile lowlands, sheep and goats raised in the mountains. Chalcis is linked with the mainland by a road bridge at the narrowest part of the Euripus channel.

Taken by the Athenians (506 BC). Fell to the Romans (191 BC), the Venetians (1204) and the Turks (1470), and passed to Greece 1830.

Euclid USA. NE suburb of Cleveland, Ohio, on L. Erie. Pop. (1990) 54,875.

Manufactures electrical equipment, metal goods and tractors.

Settled 1798. Named after the Greek mathematician by the surveyors.

Euganean Hills (Italian **Colli Euganei**) Italy. Range of hills of volcanic origin about 17 km (11 miles) long in Veneto, SW of Padua, rising to nearly 600 m (1968 ft). There are thermal springs and several villas, inc. Petrarch's home at Argua.

Eugene USA. Town in W Oregon on the Willamette R. 177 km (110 miles) SSW of Portland. Pop. (1990) 112,669.

Industries inc. sawmilling and fruit-canning.

Eupen and Malmédy Belgium. Two districts bordering on Germany in the E, ceded to Belgium by the Treaty of Versailles in 1919; in 1925 they were incorporated in Liège province. Chief towns Eupen, Malmédy.

Eupen manufactures woollen goods, domestic appliances and cables. Malmédy manufactures paper and leather.

Euphrates River (Ar. **Al Furat**). River in SW Asia 2815 km (1750 miles) long, rising in two headstreams in the highlands N and NW of L. Van in Turkey: the Murat Su, which flows 640 km (400 miles) WSW and the Kara Su or W Euphrates, which flows 450 km (280 miles) SW to their confluence. The combined river now flows generally SW, turns S into Syria, then SE past Deir ez Zor, to enter Iraq. It continues SE through Iraq, past Haditha, Hit, Falluja and Nasiriya, and joins the Tigris R. just below Al Qurna, to form the Shatt-al-Arab, which flows 182 km (113 miles) to the head of the Gulf. Reaches its highest level in May, lowest in Sept. Navigable for light craft as far as Hit. Many great cities of the past, inc. Babylon, Borsippa and Carchemish, stood on or near its banks. The area between the Euphrates and the Tigris – Mesopotamia ('Between the Rivers') – was in ancient times elaborately irrigated and fertile. Modern irrigation schemes have not yet equalled the ancient systems.

Eure France. Department in the NW in Haute-Normandie. Area 6040 sq km (2332 sq. miles). Pop. (1991) 519,800. Prefecture Évreux. Mainly flat and fertile, but well-wooded. Drained by the lower Seine and Eure rivers. Cereals, apples, flax cultivated. Dairy cattle raised; cheese and cider made. Textile and metalworking industries are important. Chief towns Évreux and Les Andelys.

Eure-et-Loir France. Department in Centre Region. Area 5880 sq km (2270 sq. miles). Pop. (1991) 399,700. Prefecture Chartres. Drained by the Eure and the Loir rivers. Flat in the rich wheat-growing Beauce; in the W are the Perche Hills, a stock-rearing area famous for its Percheron horses. Chief towns Chartres, Châteaudun.

Eureka USA. Fishing port, seaport and commercial centre in NW California on Humboldt Bay 378 km (235 miles) NNW of San Francisco. Pop. (1970) 24,337.

An important sawmilling centre.

Named by the first settler, James Ryan, who in 1850 drove his ship on to mud flats in Humboldt Bay, joyfully shouting 'Eureka!'.

Eure River France. River 225 km (140 miles) long, rising in the Perche Hills (Orne) and flowing ESE and then N through the Eure-et-Loir and Eure departments to the Seine R.

Europe. Continent occupying about 7 per cent of the earth's land surface, with a pop. (1990) 498,371,000. It is a W peninsula of the great land mass of Eurasia. There is no well-marked geographical boundary with Asia, but the line between the two continents is generally considered to run along the low Ural Mountains (Russia) to the Caspian Sea, to inc. the lower Volga, and along the Caucasus, to inc. the Republics of Georgia, Armenia and Azerbaijan. The continent is bounded on the N by the Arctic Ocean; on the S by the Mediterranean Sea, linked through the Dardanelles with the Sea of Marmara and thence, through the Bosporus, with the Black Sea; on the W by the Atlantic Ocean, with its inlets the Bay of Biscay, English Channel, Irish Sea, North Sea and Baltic Sea. From the extreme NE to Cape St Vincent in the SW it has a length of 5470 km (3400 miles), and from Nordkyn, the northernmost point of Norway, to Cape Matapan, the southernmost point of continental Greece, a breadth of 3860 km (2400 miles). A vast number of islands around its

coasts inc. Spitsbergen and Novaya Zemlya (N), the British Isles, Faeroes and Iceland (NW), and the Balearic Is., Corsica, Sardinia, Sicily, Crete and the other Greek islands in the Mediterranean, and with the mainland give it a total area of about 10,498,000 sq km (4,052,000 sq. miles). Its coastline is further lengthened by several extensive peninsulas: Kola, Scandinavia and Jutland in the N and the Iberian peninsula, Italy and the Balkan peninsula, with the Peloponnese, in the S.

A great mountain system stretches W–E across S Europe, with the Pyrenees in the W, the Alps and Apennines in the centre and the Carpathians, Balkan Mountains and Caucasus Mountains in the E. The highest peaks are in the Caucasus, Elbruz (5642 m; 18,510 ft), Dykh Tau (5201 m; 17,059 ft), and Kazbek (5050 m; 16,564 ft) all exceeding the loftiest peak of the Alps, Mont Blanc (4808 m; 15,774 ft). The highest mountain in the Scandinavian peninsula is Galdhöpiggen (2470 m; 8102 ft) in Norway. Between the two mountainous areas of the N and S is the vast N European Plain, which extends from N France through the Low Countries to Poland, broadening out until it occupies the entire N–S width of Russia in Europe; this great plain covers about two-thirds of the continent. Europe has many lakes (esp. in Finland) but they are small compared with the largest of Africa and North America, with the exception of the Caspian Sea, which is a salt lake and in any case belongs to Asia rather than Europe; the greatest European lakes are Ladoga and Onega in Russia, Saimaa in Finland and Väner and Vätter in Sweden. By far the longest river in Europe is the Volga, which rises in the Valdai Hills and flows E and S to the Caspian Sea. The Don, Dnieper and Dniester, also Russian rivers, flow into the Black Sea, as does the Danube, the second longest river, but of greater economic importance is the Rhine, which rises in the Alps, flows generally NNW and enters the North Sea; it is linked by a system of canals with many other rivers of N and W Europe, e.g. the Weser, Elbe, Oder, Danube and Rhône. A ship canal, the Kiel Canal, connects the

Europe

Baltic with the North Sea across Schleswig-Holstein (Germany).

Owing to the influence of the North Atlantic Drift, the NW and W regions of Europe enjoy an exceptionally mild, equable type of climate for their latitudes and such ports as Narvik (Norway) and Murmansk (Russia), well N of the Arctic Circle, are ice-free throughout the year. The influence of the sea diminishes progressively towards the E, with the result that the climate becomes more and more continental: winters are colder, summers are warmer and in general the rainfall is less in the E – but nowhere are conditions so extreme as they are still farther E, in central Siberia. Lands of S Europe around the margins of the Mediterranean Sea experience a climate which is usually classified as Mediterranean or dry subtropical, characterized by hot, dry summers and mild, rainy winters. Away from the coastal areas (as, e.g., on the central plateau or Meseta of Spain and in the central Balkans) the climate is continental.

The regions of natural vegetation correspond closely to the climatic zones. In the extreme N (N Scandinavia, Finland and Russia), with the sub-Arctic climate of long, cold winters, short, cool summers and scanty rainfall, the tundra produces mosses, lichens and dwarf shrubs – a region of reindeer herding. To the S is a broad belt of coniferous forests, occupying much of Scandinavia, Finland and N Russia, which furnishes immense quantities of timber for manufacture into wood-pulp and paper. Much farther S, on the Alps, Carpathians and other mountain ranges, where climate is modified by altitude, there are other forests of pine, spruce, fir and the like. S of the coniferous forests of N Europe is a belt of mixed coniferous and deciduous forest – but it must be added that the natural vegetation of most of this part of the continent, from Britain and France to Russia, has been changed dramatically by agricultural and industrial development. Grasslands cover the Hungarian plain (pusztas) and a much more extensive area in S Russia (steppes), the latter a great wheat-growing region merging into an arid semi-desert zone round the N shores of the Caspian Sea. The Mediterranean region has its own characteristic vegetation, such trees and shrubs as the evergreen oak and myrtle being typical, and among cultivated plants the olive.

The rich coalfields of Britain, Germany, France and Belgium enabled W Europe to take the lead in industrial development from the Industrial Revolution of the 19th cent., and more recently, with abundant coal and iron deposits, the Ukraine has come to the fore. France, Sweden and E England, too, have substantial resources in iron ore and there are important deposits of many other minerals. Industrialization and the growth of great manufacturing centres and conurbations based on mineral wealth were chiefly responsible for the high density of pop. in NW Europe, particularly marked in England and Wales, Germany, Belgium and Holland. Oil sources are richest in Azerbaijan and Russia, notably in the Baku area at first and more recently in the Ural–Volga region. In recent decades oil has been discovered and exploited from the North Sea.

The peoples of Europe may be divided into three main racial types, though mixing is apparent everywhere. In the NW is the Nordic type, with fair hair and skin and blue eyes; around the Mediterranean is the so-called Mediterranean type, with dark hair, eyes and skin and generally of shorter stature. Between them are the Alpine people, who have brown hair, brown to grey eyes and a rather stocky frame, the Slavs of E Europe being similar to them. Although there is some relationship between language and race, these do not always coincide. Most langs. of Europe belong to the Indo–European group. Celtic tongues (Irish, Gaelic, Welsh, Breton) are still spoken in the W parts of the British Isles and Brittany; the Teutonic langs. inc. English, German, Dutch and Flemish and, among the Scandinavians, Norwegian, Swedish, Danish and Icelandic. French, Spanish, Portuguese, Italian and Romanian are among the Romance langs., and Russian, Polish, Serbo-Croatian, Czech, Slovak and Bulgarian among the Slavonic. The langs. of the Basques, Maltese, Finns, Lapps, Estonians, Magyars, Turks, Georgians and Azerbaijanis fall outside the Indo–European group. In religion the vast majority of the peoples of Europe belong, nominally at least, to the various branches of the Christian Church, but there is a considerable number of Muslims in Turkey, Albania and France, and Jews are scattered throughout most parts of Europe.

The Romans imposed some sort of political unity on much of Europe conferring the benefits of the *Pax Romana* – law and order – over a large area; they promoted the development of trade and the langs. of Latin derivation, together with something of Graeco–Roman culture and the Christian religion. But by the end of the 4th cent. the Roman Empire had disintegrated; the W part, with its cap. at Rome, was overrun by barbarians, while the much-weakened E part, the Byzantine Empire, with its cap. at Constantinople (Istanbul), survived till the 15th cent., when it finally succumbed to the Turks. In the W unity was again briefly achieved by Charlemagne, who ruled from the Elbe to the Ebro and in 800 was crowned Emperor by the Pope.

Thereafter the Holy Roman Empire was a pious idea rather than a reality and Europe was divided into a large number of kingdoms and principalities, many of which bore little relationship to either ethnographic or linguistic groupings. However, a sense of nationhood began to emerge in several countries and by the latter Middle Ages England, France and Spain were recognizably nations. The urge for a national identity in fact gradually brought about national states in most of Europe except in Austria, Hungary and the Ottoman Empire.

The nations of Europe have long maintained strict independence in economic matters and each developed its own tariff structure to protect and promote its favoured industries. The German Zollverein (begun in 1833) was a customs union which not only promoted economic progress, but paved the way for the unification of Germany under the leadership of Prussia. It was not till after World War II that any similar effort was made to unite Europe economically. The European Economic Community (Belgium, France, Germany, Italy, Luxembourg and the Netherlands) was established in 1958 and agreement was reached to progress rapidly to internal free trade and a common external tariff. Britain did not initially join this Community and her efforts to do so in 1964 and 1967 were unsuccessful. In 1959 seven of the European countries not members of the EEC (Austria, Denmark, Norway, Portugal, Sweden, Switzerland and the United Kingdom) joined together in a European Free Trade Association (EFTA) which aimed at promoting trade between its members by progressive reduction of tariffs and their eventual elimination. In 1973 Great Britain, Ireland and Denmark joined the EEC, increasing the membership from six to nine; after a referendum in Norway, however, the latter country decided against entry. A further enlargement took place in 1981 when Greece joined, in 1986 Spain and Portugal, followed in 1995 by Austria, Finland and Sweden became part of the European Community (Union). Further countries applied to join in 1994. The European Community (now Union) and EFTA established the European Economic Area in 1994 creating a market of 372 million consumers.

Europoort ➤ROTTERDAM.

Euxine Sea ➤BLACK SEA.

Evanston USA. Residential town in NE Illinois just N of Chicago on L. Michigan. Pop. (1990) 72,233.

Manufactures steel goods, paints and chemicals.

Seat of the Northwestern University (1851) and named after John Evans, one of the university's founders.

Evansville USA. Town in SW Indiana on the Ohio R. Pop. (1990) 126,272.

Manufactures refrigerators, agricultural machinery, furniture, and there is also meat-packing and flour-milling.

Named after Robert M. Evans (1783–1844), one of its founders.

Evenki NA Russia. National Area in the Krasnoyarsk Territory, Eastern Siberia, drained by the Lower Tunguska and Stony Tunguska rivers. Area 767,600 sq km (296,371 sq. miles). Pop. (1991) 25,000 (mainly Evenki). Cap. Tura. Mainly coniferous forest and tundra. Main occupations reindeer breeding, hunting and fishing. Founded 1930.

Everest, Mount (Chinese **Chomolungma**). Peak of the Himalayas, highest on the earth's surface (8848 m; 29,028 ft) on the ill-defined Nepal–Tibet border. Named after Sir George Everest (1790–1866), former surveyor-general of India. Mallory and Irvine, members of the 1924 expedition, reached a height of about 8540 m (28,011 ft) but died there; a Swiss expedition of 1952 attained 8606 m (28,228 ft). Finally, on the British expedition (1953) led by Sir John Hunt, Sir Edmund Hillary of New Zealand and the Sherpa Tensing reached the summit. It has been conquered over 200 times since 1953.

Everett (Massachusetts) USA. Residential and industrial town just N of Boston. Pop. (1980) 37,195.

Manufactures pig-iron, machinery and chemicals.

Named after Edward Everett (1794–1865), an American statesman.

Everett (Washington) USA. Port on Puget Sound at the mouth of the Snohomish R. 42 km (26 miles) N of Seattle. Pop. (1990) 69,961.

Exports timber and paper. Sawmilling. Manufactures wood-pulp and paper.

Everglades USA. Subtropical marshy region in S Florida, a morass of sawgrass prairies extending in the S to mangrove swamps, with scattered clumps of trees (inc. cypress). Occupies most of Florida S of L. Okeechobee, covering over 10,360 sq km (4000 sq. miles). Partly drained and reclaimed. In the Everglades National Park (1947; area 4452 sq km; 1719 sq. miles) the regional fauna and flora are preserved; the birds (inc. the pelican, egret, ibis and spoonbill) are esp. noteworthy.

Evesham England. Market town in Worcestershire on the R. Avon 21 km (13 miles) SE of Worcester. Pop. (1991) 17,823. In the fertile and beautiful Vale of Evesham, famous for fruit-growing and market-gardening. Fruit and vegetable canning and jam-making.

Remains of an 8th-cent. Benedictine abbey. At the Battle of Evesham (1265) Prince Edward defeated Simon de Montfort and the barons.

Évian les Bains France. Town on the S shore of L. Geneva. Pop. (1985) 6300. A health resort and produces bottled mineral water.

Évora Portugal. Ancient Ebora. Cap. of the Évora district in Alto Alentejo 109 km (68 miles) ESE of Lisbon. Pop. (1985) 34,500.

Trade in agricultural produce with some leather, carpet and cork production.

Ancient and picturesque. Ruins of a Roman temple (the so-called temple of Diana). Archiepiscopal cathedral (12th/13th-cent., restored). Taken by the Moors 712; was not recaptured till 1166.

Évreux France. Prefecture of the Eure department in the Iton R. valley 48 km (30 miles) S of Rouen. Pop. (1990) 51,459.

Market town. Manufactures metal goods, chemicals and electrical equipment.

Evritania (Euritania) Greece. Mountainous *nome* in central Greece. Area 1869 sq km (722 sq. miles). Pop. (1991) 23,535. Cap. Karpenision. Sheep and goats reared.

Évros (Hevros) Greece. *Nome* in E Thrace bordering on Bulgaria (N) and Turkey (E) and inc. the island of Samothrace. Area 4242 sq km (1618 sq. miles). Pop. (1991) 143,791. Cap. Alexandroupolis.

Produces wheat, tobacco and cotton. Fishing.

Evry France. Prefecture of Essonne department 39 km (15 miles) S of Paris. Pop. (1991) 45,854. Founded 1970.

Ewell ➤EPSOM AND EWELL.

Exe, River England. River 96 km (60 miles) long, rising on Exmoor and flowing generally SSE past Tiverton and Exeter to enter the English Channel by an estuary at Exmouth, which is noted for its wildlife.

Exeter England. Cathedral city and county town of Devon on the R. Exe 58 km (36 miles) NE of Plymouth. Pop. (1991) 104,800.

Railway junction. Commercial centre. Manufactures agricultural machinery, leather goods and is an important tourist centre.

The cathedral (1270–1369), mainly in Decorated Gothic style but with Norman transeptal towers, was severely damaged, along with other buildings in the city, in air raids of World War II (1942), St James's Chapel being destroyed. Guildhall (14th/ 16th-cent.), one of the oldest municipal buildings in the country. Grammar school, now housed in modern buildings, founded 1332. Seat of Exeter University (1955), founded (1922) as the University College of the Southwest. Birthplace of Sir Thomas Bodley, founder of the Bodleian Library, Oxford (1545–1613) and Archbishop William Temple (1881–1944).

Exmoor England. High moorland in W Somerset and NE Devon, largely forest until the early 19th cent., now covered with heather, bracken and grass, rising to 520 m (1706 ft) in Dunkery Beacon. Wild red deer and Exmoor ponies abound and sheep are grazed. The Exe, Barle and other rivers have picturesque valleys and are well-known for trout-fishing. Immortalized in R. D. Blackmore's *Lorna Doone*. Established as a National Park (area 686 sq km; 265 sq. miles) in 1954. Only 29 per cent of Exmoor is in Devon and there are over 960 km (600 miles) of public footpaths.

Exmouth England. Resort and fishing port in Devon on the estuary of the R. Exe; noted

for wildlife. Pop. (1991) 31,393. In a sheltered position, with a sandy beach and a mild climate. Resort. Fishing port. Sir Walter Raleigh (1552–1618) was born at Hayes Barton (6 km; 4 miles NE).

Exploits River Canada. River 320 km (200 miles) long in Newfoundland, rising in the SW and flowing generally NE through Red Indian L. and past Grand Falls (hydroelectric power station) to Notre Dame Bay on the NE coast.

Extremadura ▶ESTREMADURA SPAIN.

Exuma Bahamas. Islands between Andros (W) and Eleuthera, Cat and Long Islands (E); the N end and ESE of Nassau. Area 259 sq km (100 sq. miles). Pop. (1990) 3539. The group forms Exuma district and extends 224 km (140 miles) NW to SE across the Tropic of Cancer.

Eyre, Lake Australia. Shallow salt lake in South Australia 640 km (400 miles) N of Adelaide 11 m (36 ft) below sea level. Water only occasionally flows through many tributary channels to fill both the large N part (7770 sq km; 3000 sq. miles) and the S part (1165 sq km; 450 sq. miles) and it is dry except during the rainy season. It was completely filled to depths of 2–4 m (6.5–13 ft) after exceptional rains, in 1890–1 and 1949–50. Named after E. J. Eyre (1815–1901), who discovered it (1840).

Eyre (Eyre's) Peninsula Australia. Triangular peninsula in South Australia projecting some 320 km (200 miles) S between Spencer Gulf and the Great Australian Bight. The Middleback Range in the NE is rich in iron ore, mined at Iron Knob, Iron Monarch and Iron Baron. Whyalla, in the E, has become a steel-producing, shipbuilding port, with irrigated dairy-farming land nearby. Crops mainly wheat and barley.

F

Faenza Italy. Ancient Faventia. Town in Ravenna province, Emilia-Romagna 47 km (29 miles) SE of Bologna. Pop. (1989) 54,115. Important road and railway junction on the ancient Aemilian Way. Noted since the Middle Ages for majolica pottery (or *faience*, from the French name of the town).

Also manufactures furniture and textiles.

Cathedral (15th-cent.); museum of ceramics.

Faeroe (Faroe) Islands Denmark. Group of 21 volcanic islands in the North Atlantic between Iceland and the Shetland Is. Area 1399 sq km (540 sq. miles). Pop. (1990) 47,946. Cap. Throshavn (on Stromö). Currency: Faroese krøna interchangeable with the Danish krone. There are 17 inhabited islands, the main ones being Stremoy, Eysturoy, Vágoy, Suduroy, Sandoy and Bordoy. The islands are rugged and have no native trees. The inhabitants speak Faroese, derived from Old Norse, which since 1948 has been the official lang. along with Danish. About 80 per cent are Evangelical Lutheran.

The main occupations are sheep-farming and fishing. Only 2 per cent of the surface is cultivated. Principal exports fresh, frozen, salted and dried fish, especially cod.

A Norwegian province till the peace treaty of 1814, the islands have been represented by 2 members in the Danish parliament since 1851 and in 1852 they obtained an elected assembly of their own, called *løgting*, which in 1948 secured a certain degree of home rule within the Danish realm. The islands are not included in the European Union, but left EFTA together with Denmark in 1972.

Faial ►AZORES.

Fairbanks USA. Town in Alaska 442 km (275 miles) NNE of Anchorage on the Trans-Alaska pipeline. Pop. (1990) 77,720. N terminus of the Alaska Highway and the Alaska Railroad.

Industries inc. tourism, sawmilling and goldmining.

Founded 1902, when gold was discovered in the neighbourhood. The University of Alaska (1922) is at College 5 km (3 miles) NW.

Fairfield USA. Industrial town in SW Connecticut on Long Island Sound near Bridgeport. Pop. (1980) 54,849.

Manufactures chemicals, motor-car accessories.

University (1942). Founded 1639.

Fair Isle Scotland. Isolated rocky island in the Shetlands halfway between the main group and the Orkneys. Area 15.5 sq km (6 sq. miles). Pop. (1991) 67. Noted for multi-coloured handmade knitwear. Bird-migration observatory. Fishing, sheep-rearing. Since 1954 property of the National Trust for Scotland.

Fairmont USA. Industrial town in West Virginia on the Monongahela R. 177 km (110 miles) NE of Charleston. Pop. (1980) 23,863.

Industries inc. coalmining and the manufacture of glass, mining machinery and coal by-products.

Faisalabad Pakistan. (Formerly Lyallpur.) Town 120 km (75 miles) WSW of Lahore. Pop. (1981) 1,104,209.

Flour and oilseed milling, engineering, cotton-ginning. Important trade in grain.

Faiyum, El (Medinet el Faiyum, Medina) Egypt. Cap. of El Faiyum governorate 88 km (55 miles) SW of Cairo. Pop. (1986) 212,523. Chief town in the fertile El

Faiyum oasis, linked by rail and road with the Nile valley.

Cotton-ginning, spinning and weaving (cotton, wool), dyeing and tanning.

Nearby (N) excavations have revealed the site of ancient Crocodilopolis (renamed Arsinoë by Ptolemy Philadelphus) where a sacred crocodile in the Lake of Moeris (Birket Qarun) was worshipped.

Faizabad India. Town in Uttar Pradesh on the Gogra R. 129 km (80 miles) E of Lucknow. Pop. (1991) 125,032. Railway junction.

Sugar-refining. Trade in sugar-cane, grain and oilseeds.

Just E of the historic site of Ajodhya.

Falaise France. Town in the Calvados department on the Ante R. 37 km (23 miles) SSE of Caen. Pop. (1985) 8500.

Livestock trade. Cheese-making.

The ruined castle of the dukes of Normandy, where William the Conqueror was born, stands on a cliff (*falaise*) above the town. Almost destroyed in World War II during the Allied advance from Normandy (1944).

Falkirk Scotland. 1. Industrial and ancient market town in Falkirk on the Forth–Clyde Canal 16 km (10 miles) SE of Stirling. Pop. (1991) 35,610.

Industries inc. iron-casting, chemicals, breweries, printing and coach building.

At the Westerglen (3 km; 2 miles SW) is a BBC radio transmitter. The Wall of Antoninus ran through Falkirk. Scene of Edward I's defeat of Wallace (1298) and Prince Charles Edward's defeat of General Hawley (1746). 2. Falkirk Scotland. New unitary authority created in 1996, formerly in Central Region. Pop. (1993) 142,610.

Falkland Islands (Sp. **Islas Malvinas**) South Atlantic Ocean. United Kingdom Overseas Territory situated 480 km (300 miles) E of the Strait of Magellan, consisting of two main islands, East Falkland and West Falkland and many small islands. Area 12,170 sq km (4700 sq. miles). Pop. (1991) 2121, of whom 1557 live in Stanley, the chief town, on East Falkland. The main islands, separated by Falkland Sound, have many fiords and bays and they consist mainly of rocky moorland with peaty soils and few trees. The highest point being Mt Adam (706 m; 2316 ft) on West Falkland and the open country is called 'The Camp'. It has a cool temperate climate, much affected by strong winds particularly in spring. The Falkland Islands are noted for their outstanding wild life, inc. penguin and seal. Almost all the islanders are of British origin, 67 per cent being born on the islands.

Sheep-farming used to be the only industry, the wool being exported to England. Fishing and associated industries have become the largest source of income. Oil is being explored and tourism and hydroponic market gardens are being developed.

The islands were visited by Capt Davis in 1592 and by Sir John Hawkins in 1594; named in 1690 by Capt Strong. First colonized by the French in 1764; passed to Spain; occupied by the British in 1832–3, after the expulsion of an Argentine garrison. Argentina still does not recognize British occupation, referring to the islands by their old Spanish name, Islas Malvinas, and in 1990 declared the Falkland Islands and other British-held South Atlantic Islands to be part of the province of Tierra del Fuego. On 2 April 1982 Argentine forces invaded the Falkland Islands and the Governor was expelled. At a meeting of the UN Security Council, held on 3 April, the voting was 10 to 1 in favour of the resolution calling for Argentina to withdraw. Britain regained possession on 14–15 June after the Argentine surrender. South Georgia and the South Sandwich Islands ceased to be dependencies of the Falkland Islands in 1985.

Fall River USA. Port, industrial and commercial town in SE Massachusetts at the mouth of the Taunton R. Pop. (1990) 92,703.

Important centre of the cotton industry. Also manufactures rubber products, hats and clothing.

The name derives from the Quequechan or Fall R., which flows through the town.

Falmouth England. Resort and seaport on the W shore of Carrick Roads (the estuary of the Fal and other rivers) in SW Cornwall. Pop. (1991) 20,297.

Important ship-repairing industry with a dry dock. Fishing (pilchards and oysters).

At the entrance to the harbour are the 16th-cent. castles of Pendennis and St Mawes.

Falster Denmark. Island in the Baltic Sea, linked with Zealand (N) by a bridge across Storström Strait and with Lolland (W) by two bridges; with Lolland, forms the county of Maribo. Area 513 sq km (198 sq. miles). Pop. (1985) 46,000. Chief town Nyköbing.

Dairy and pig-farming. Sugar-beet and fruit are cultivated.

Famagusta (Turk. **Gazimağusa** Cyprus. Port in the E on Famagusta Bay 5 km (3 miles) S of ancient Salamis on the site of ancient Arsinoë. Pop. (1994) 22,722.

Before 1974 it was the chief port exporting citrus fruits, carobs, potatoes, and it manufactures footwear and clothing. With its long sandy beaches a popular seaside resort until the invasion in 1974.

Became an important port of call during the Crusades and under Venetian rule. Declined under the Turks; ruined by earthquake 1735.

Fanning Island ➤TABUAERAN.

Fanö Denmark. Island in the North Frisian Is. opposite Esbjerg. Area 57 sq km (22 sq. miles).

Industries fishing and tourism.

Fano Italy. Ancient Fanum Fortunae. Adriatic seaport in Pesaro e Urbino province, The Marches, 11 km (7 miles) SE of Pesaro. Pop. (1989) 34,000.

Industries inc. tourism, fishing, sugar-refining, packaging and brick-making.

Has a triumphal arch of Augustus, the 15th-cent. Malatesta palace, and some noteworthy churches.

Far East. Term used rather loosely of E and SE Asia, but more strictly applied to regions along the Pacific seaboard of E Asia–

E Siberia (Russia), China, Korea and Japan, and possibly to inc. the Philippines, Indonesia and Malaysia.

Fareham England. Market town in S Hampshire on a creek in the NW corner of Portsmouth harbour 10 km (6 miles) NW of Portsmouth. Pop. (1991) 54,866.

Manufactures earthenware, bricks, and there is engineering, boatbuilding and tanning.

At Portchester 5 km (3 miles) ESE is a ruined castle partly of Roman origin.

Farewell, Cape Greenland. Headland at the S tip of Egger Island; the southernmost point of Greenland, reaching a height of over 600 m (1968 ft). Fringed by islets and rocks. Notorious for bad weather and heavy seas.

Farewell, Cape New Zealand. Most northerly point of South Island. Point of departure of Capt Cook (April 1770) on his voyage of discovery along the E coastlands of Australia.

Fargo USA. Town in North Dakota on the Red R. opposite Moorhead (Minnesota). Pop. (1990) 74,111. Largest town in the state.

Manufactures agricultural machinery and food products.

Named after W. G. Fargo (1818–81) of Wells, Fargo and Co., the organizer of the first extensive stagecoach system in North America.

Faridpur Bangladesh. Town 48 km (30 miles) WSW of Dhaka. Pop. (1991) 68,000.

Industries inc. oilseed-milling, and it trades in rice and jute.

Has the shrine of the Muslim saint Farid Shah.

Farmington USA. City in NW corner of state of New Mexico SW of San Juan mountains. Pop. (1990) 33,997.

Farmington Hills USA. City forming part of Detroit industrial area NW of Detroit city centre, Michigan. Pop. (1980) 58,056.

Farnborough England. Town in NE Hampshire 13 km (8 miles) WNW of Guildford. Pop. (1991) 52,535.

Royal Aircraft Establishment, the largest

aeronautical research centre in the UK. Scene of biennial display of civil and military aircraft.

In St Michael's (Roman Catholic) church Napoleon III, the Empress Eugénie (who had it built) and the Prince Imperial are buried.

Farne Islands (The Staples) England. Group of about 30 rocky islets off the coast of Northumberland, separated from it by the Fairway, a channel 2.4 km (1½ miles) wide. Farne Island or Inner Farne, the largest, was the home of St Cuthbert, who died here (687). Longstone Island lighthouse was the scene of Grace Darling's heroic rescue of survivors from the *Forfarshire* (1838).

Farnham England. Town in Surrey on the R. Wey 16 km (10 miles) WSW of Guildford. Pop. (1991) 36,178. Just N is the castle, formerly the palace of the bishops of Winchester. Birthplace and burial-place of politician and controversialist, William Cobbett (1763–1835).

Farnworth England. Town in Greater Manchester 5 km (3 miles) SE of Bolton. Pop. (1991) 25,053.

Cotton and rayon mills, bleaching and dyeing works; engineering.

Faro Portugal. Cap. of the Algarve province on the S coast near Cape Santa Maria. Pop. (1990) 31,970.

Port, sheltered by islands. Exports wine, dried figs, almonds and cork. Fishing (sardine, tunny). Cork-processing, basketmaking. Airport, with developing tourist traffic.

Recovered by the Moors 1249. Burned by the English 1596 and severely damaged by earthquake 1755.

Faroe Islands ➤FAEROE ISLANDS.

Farquhar Islands Seychelles. Atoll situated NE of the northern tip of Madagascar in the Indian Ocean. Length 5 km (3 miles).

Main products copra, fish.

Formerly British Indian Ocean Territory, but returned to Seychelles in 1976.

Farrukhabad India. Town in Uttar Pradesh

near the Ganges R. 129 km (80 miles) NW of Kanpur. Pop. (1991) 193,624. Railway junction.

Trade in grain, sugar-cane and oilseeds. Manufactures cotton and metal goods. Sugar-refining.

Forms a joint municipality with neighbouring Fatehgarh.

Fars Iran. Ancient Persis. Province in the S on the Gulf. Area 125,627 sq km (48,505 sq. miles). Pop. (1986) 3,193,769. Cap. Shiraz. Chief port Bushsire. The coastal lowlands are hot and humid; inland the uplands are drier with cold winters.

Cereals, cotton, opium and dates are cultivated.

Ancient Persis, from which the Persians created their empire, contained the cities of Persepolis and Pasargadae.

Fashoda ➤KODOK.

Fatehgarh ➤FARRUKHABAD.

Fatima Portugal. Village situated 105 km (65 miles) N of Lisbon. Pop. (1991) 5445.

A place of pilgrimage since 1917 when the Virgin Mary is said to have appeared.

Fatshan (Foshan) China. Town in Guangdong province 18 km (11 miles) SW of Kwangchow (Canton). Pop. (1984) 300,000.

Industrial and commercial centre. Manufactures iron and steel, textiles (esp. silk), matches and porcelain.

Faversham England. Town in N Kent on a creek off the Swale 13 km (8 miles) WNW of Canterbury. Pop. (1991) 17,070.

Oyster fisheries. Fruit and vegetable canning, brewing, brickmaking.

An early 'Member' of the Cinque Port of Dover. King Stephen, his wife Matilda and their son are buried in the now ruined Cluniac abbey founded by the king.

Fayetteville USA. Formerly Campbelltown. Industrial town in North Carolina on the Cape Fear R. 80 km (50 miles) SSW of Raleigh. Pop. (1990) 75,695.

Manufactures textiles and furniture. Food-processing and sawmilling. Trade in cotton, tobacco.

Originally called Campbelltown by its Scottish founders (1739). Incorporated 1784 and named after Lafayette (1757–1834).

Fear, Cape USA. The southernmost point of Smith Island and of North Carolina in the Atlantic near the mouth of the Cape Fear R. The dangerous Frying-pan Shoals extend to the S and SE.

Fécamp France. Seaside resort and fishing port in the Seine Maritime department on the English Channel. Pop. (1990) 21,140. Noted for the Bénédictine liqueur, first prepared from local herbs by monks in the 16th cent.

Industries inc. fish-curing, boatbuilding and the manufacture of fishing nets and cod liver oil.

Federal German Republic ➤GERMANY.

Felixstowe England. Seaport and resort in E Suffolk 16 km (10 miles) SE of Ipswich. Pop. (1991) 28,606.

The main industry is tourism and flour-milling is important.

Named after St Felix, first bishop of Dunwich.

Felling England. Town in Tyne and Wear just E of Gateshead. Pop. (1991) 35,053.

Engineering. Manufactures chemicals and paint.

Feltham England. Former urban district in Middlesex 19 km (12 miles) WSW of London; from 1965 part of the Greater London borough of Hounslow. Residential and industrial.

Manufactures aircraft and automobile parts, electronic and electrical equipment.

Kempton Park racecourse is in the district.

Fens England. Flat low-lying area in E England W and S of the Wash in the counties of Lincolnshire, Cambridgeshire and Norfolk; 110–120 km (70–75 miles) N–S and about 56 km (35 miles) E–W at its greatest width. Once formed an extensive bay of the North Sea which was gradually silted up by the Witham, Welland, Nene and Great Ouse rivers, leaving the Wash as the final remnant. From Roman times attempts at reclamation were made, but the Fens remained largely a region of marsh and swamp (apart from 'islands' of higher and firmer ground) until the 17th cent. when Cornelius Vermuyden introduced Dutch methods (1621), with the help of the Earl of Bedford (after whom the tract known as the Bedford Level was named). The work continued in sections until the 19th cent. Today little of the original Fens remains, apart from Wicken Fen, NE of Cambridge. The soil of the area (once known for its wildfowl and freshwater fish), now criss-crossed with watercourses and drainage canals, has proved extraordinarily fertile and produces cereals, sugar-beet, fruit, vegetables and bulbs. The economy is diversifying as agriculture has become increasingly intensive. Less than 15 per cent of the work in Fenland is in fact agriculture, although many other jobs in manufacturing, packing, canning and distribution are agriculture-related. Remains of the monasteries built on the once isolated 'islands' may still be seen, e.g. at Crowland and Kirkstead.

Feodosiya Russia. Ancient Theodosia. Black Sea port and resort in SE Crimea. Pop. (1990) 85,000.

Main export wheat. Industries inc. fishing, flour-milling, brewing and fish-canning. Many sanatoria and rest homes.

Founded in the 6th cent. BC by Greeks from Miletus. Genoese (as Kaffa) from 1265. Passed to the Turks (1475) and to Russia (1774).

Fergana (Ferghana) Uzbekistan/Kirghizia. 1. Valley N of the Pamirs near the Chinese border; also region of Uzbekistan. Almost completely hemmed in by lofty mountains, with the Fergana and Chatkal ranges to the N and the Alai Mountains to the S; easily accessible only from the W. Drained by the Syr Darya and other mountain streams, extensively used for irrigation. In 1939 irrigation was improved by the construction of the Fergana Canal (274 km; 170 miles) and subsequently by other canals; important crops of cotton, alfalfa and grapes are grown. Chief towns Andizhan, Namangan, Kokand. At various periods it has been under Persian, Arab, Mongol and Uzbek domination.

2. Town in the Fergana Region 233 km (145 miles) ESE of Tashkent in Uzbekistan. Pop. (1991) 226,500.

Manufactures cotton goods and clothing.

Founded by the Russians as Novy Margelan in 1876; later called Skobelev and renamed Fergana after the Revolution.

Fermanagh Northern Ireland. County in SW Ulster; hilly in the NE and SW, rising to 667 m (2188 ft) in Cuilcagh on the SW border, the central area being occupied by Upper and Lower Lough Erne and the R. Erne. Area 1852 sq km (715 sq. miles). Pop. (1991) 54,290. County town Enniskillen. Mainly pastoral and agricultural with potatoes cultivated and cattle raised. Tourism is well established.

Fermoy Ireland. Market town in Co. Cork, on the R. Blackwater 31 km (19 miles) NE of Cork. Pop. (1986) 2872. Founded in 1789 by a Scotsman and became a British garrison town.

Fernando de Noronha Brazil. Island in the S Atlantic 370 km (230 miles) NE of Cape São Roque on the 'shoulder' of Brazil; with neighbouring islands forms the federal territory of Fernando de Noronha. Area 26 sq km (10 sq. miles). Pop. (1970) 1241. Served as a penal colony since the 18th cent.

Fernando Póo ➤BIOKO.

Ferozepore India. Town in Punjab 80 km (50 miles) SSW of Amritsar near the Pakistan frontier. Pop. (1985) 55,000.

Cotton-ginning. Trade in grain and cotton.

Strategically important in the mid 19th cent. under British rule.

Ferrara Italy. Cap. of Ferrara province in Emilia-Romagna 43 km (27 miles) NNE of Bologna. Pop. (1990) 140,800.

It manufactures chemicals, fertilizers, plastics, beet-sugar and pasta. Trade in grain, fruit and wine.

The outstanding building is the brick, moated castle of the house of Este (14th/15th-cent.); others inc. the cathedral, dating from the 12th cent., the university (1391) and several palaces, among them the Palazzo dei Diamanti, the Palazzo Schifanoia and the Palazzo di Ludovico il Moro. Became the seat of the Este family in the 13th cent. and flourished as a centre of literature and the arts, with a pop. of 100,000. Declined after 1598 on being incorporated into the Papal States. Birthplace of preacher and reformer, Savonarola (1452–98) and Guarini (1537–1612).

Ferrol, El ➤EL FERROL.

Fertile Crescent Middle East. A historical semicircle of fertile land running from the Nile valley northwards through Palestine, passing through Syria and then SE through Iraq.

Festiniog ➤FFESTINIOG.

Fez (Fès) Morocco. Traditional northern cap. 177 km (110 miles) E of Rabat; chief religious centre. Pop. (1982) 448,823.

Centre of Moroccan handicrafts, particularly carpets, leather goods and musical instruments. Other industries inc. textiles and soap manufacture.

Two important mosques: the Karueein (largest in Africa), which is also a university, and that of Muley Idris, who founded Fez (AD 808). Pilgrimages were made to Fez instead of Mecca in the 10th cent. Reached the peak of its fame in the 14th cent. Gave its name to the man's cap of red felt which became the prevalent head-dress throughout the Ottoman Empire.

Fezzan Libya. Ancient Phazania. Formerly (1951–63) a province in the Sahara, S of Tripolitania. Area 552,000 sq km (213,000 sq. miles). Mainly rocky desert (hammada) and sandy desert (erg); scattered oases. Sebha, Murzuk, Ghadames and other centres of pop. are all oasis towns. In Roman times the area was crossed by several trans-Saharan caravan routes. Lost importance with the decline of the slave trade. Seized by Italy 1911. Captured by French forces during World War II (1943); under French military control until it became part of Libya by UN resolution in 1951.

Ffestiniog (Festiniog, Llan Ffestiniog) Wales. Town in Gwynedd 16 km (10 miles) NE of Harlech in a picturesque valley. Pop. (1991) 4546. Tourist centre. Inc. the former slate-quarrying centre of Blaenau Ffestiniog, which has a pumped storage hydroelectric station. Nearby are the well-known Cynfal Falls.

FGR (Federal German Republic) ►GERMANY.

Fianarantsoa Madagascar. Cap. of Fianarantsoa province 290 km (180 miles) SSW of Antananarivo at a height of 1200 m (3936 ft). Pop. (1990) 124,489.

Market for cattle and agricultural produce. Industries inc. meat-canning and rice-processing.

Fichtelgebirge Czech Republic/Germany. Mountain group on the German–Czech Republic frontier, from which radiate the Erzgebirge (NE), the Bohemian Forest (SE), the Franconian Jura (SW) and the Franconian and Thuringian Forests (NW). Partly covered with spruce forests. Rises to 1052 m (3451 ft) in the Schneeberg.

Fiesole Italy. Ancient Faesulae. Town in Firenze province, Tuscany on a hill (295 m; 968 ft) overlooking the Arno R. Pop. (1971) 44,072. Now mainly a residential suburb 6 km (4 miles) NE of Florence.

Manufactures straw hats.

An Etruscan and then a Roman town; has remains of the Etruscan town wall, a Roman theatre and baths and an 11th-cent. (restored) Romanesque cathedral. Painter, Fra Angelico (1387–1455) lived and worked here.

Fife Scotland. Peninsular area between the Firths of Tay and Forth, bounded on the E by the North Sea. It is conterminous with the former county and kingdom and divided into three districts: Dunfermline, Kirkcaldy and North East Fife. Area 1308 sq km (505 sq. miles). Pop. (1994) 351,200. Chief town Cupar. Hilly in the W, rising to 522 m (1712 ft) in W Lomond. Cultivated valleys and coastal plains. Cereals are grown. Coal is mined and limestone quarried. Various industries in the main towns, Cupar, Kirkcaldy, Dunfermline. Seaside resorts inc. St Andrews and Crail.

Fiji. Melanesian group of 332 islands and islets, about 100 of which are inhabited, in the SW Pacific Ocean. The largest islands are Viti Levu (area 10,429 sq km; 4027 sq. miles) and Vanua Levu (5556 sq km; 2145 sq. miles). Total area 18,274 sq km (7056 sq. miles). Pop. (1995) 791,000 (39 per cent urban). Life expectancy, 61 years male, 65 female. Cap. and chief seaport Suva. Currency: Fiji dollar = 100 cents.

The islands are mountainous rising to about 1350 m (4428 ft). Extinct volcanoes make for vivid skylines. There are dense forests on windward slopes and grass and pandanus in sheltered areas. The soils are fertile and support sugar-cane, taro, rice, coconuts, pineapples, bananas and cotton. Fiji has a tropical climate but oceanic influences prevent extremes of heat or humidity. Land use: forested 55 per cent, agricultural and under permanent cultivation 13 per cent, meadows and pastures 3 per cent. The indigenous Fijians, of Polynesian and Melanesian origin, represent about half of the pop. Descendants of Indian migrants who came to work sugar plantations in the 19th cent. represent an equal number of Fiji's people. There are also Europeans, Part-Europeans, Chinese, Banabans and representatives of the other cultures and communities of the South Pacific. About 50 per cent of the pop. is Christian and Hindu 40 per cent.

Economic growth has come from the sugar industry, tourism, mining, forestry and fisheries. But there has been a major expansion in investment in the manufacturing sector to serve the domestic market. Fiji-made products inc. garments, cement, roofing iron, packaging material, furniture, steel rods, plastics, soap, cooking oil, processed food and flour.

The islands were discovered by Tasman in 1643 and visited by Capt Cook in 1774. From 1874 the islands, with Rotuma (480 km; 300 miles to the NW), were a British Crown Colony, administered from Suva by a governor with an executive council and a legislative council which inc. Fijians and Indians. In 1970 Fiji gained independence.

Filey England. Town in North Yorkshire 11 km (7 miles) SE of Scarborough on Filey Bay. Pop. (1985) 6000. Seaside resort with a sandy beach extending to the rocky headland of Filey Brigg.

Finchley England. Part of the London borough of Barnet. Finchley Common, once a haunt of highwaymen, has virtually disappeared.

Findhorn River Scotland. River 100 km (62 miles) long, rising in the Monadhliath Mountains, flowing NE and entering the Moray Firth near the village of Findhorn.

Findlay USA. Industrial town in Ohio on the Blanchard R. 68 km (42 miles) S of Toledo. Pop. (1985) 36,000.

Manufactures agricultural machinery, tyres and beet-sugar.

Developed after the discovery of natural gas (1836).

Fingal's Cave ➤STAFFA.

Finger Lakes USA. Group of lakes in New York state in the area immediately W and SW of Syracuse; so called because of their length and narrowness. The principal lakes in the group are the following (W–E): Honeoye, Canandaigua, Keuka, Seneca (the largest, 174 sq km; 67 sq. miles), Cayuga (the longest, 61 km; 38 miles), Owasco, Skaneateles, Otisco. There are holiday resorts in the region.

Finistère France. Department formed from the W part of Brittany; bounded by the English Channel (N), the Bay of Biscay (S) and the Atlantic Ocean (W). Area 6733 sq km (2600 sq. miles). Pop. (1991) 839,800. Prefecture Quimper. The coast is rugged and indented. The interior is crossed by the granitic Montagnes d'Arrée (rising to 391 m; 1282 ft) and the Montagnes Noires (326 m; 1180 ft). Much of the land consists of heath, but cereals, cider apples and early vegetables are grown. Fishing (sardines) important along the coast. Many tourists are attracted by such picturesque fishing ports as Douarnenez and Concarneau. Chief towns Quimper, the port and naval base of Brest and Morlaix.

Finisterre, Cabo de Spain. Headland in the Coruña province in the NW. Usually considered the westernmost point of the Spanish mainland.

Finland (Suomi, Suomen Tasavalta). Republic in NE Europe. Bounded by Norway in the N and NE, Russia in the E, the Baltic Sea in the S and the Gulf of Bothnia and Sweden in the W. Area 338,145 sq km (130,559 sq. miles). Pop. (1995) 5,101,000 (64 per cent urban). Life expectancy, 72 years male, 79 female. Cap. Helsinki. Other cities Espoo, Tampere, Turku and Vantaa. Currency: Markka = 100 penniä. Finland is a land of forests and lakes, and inc. in Finland is Ahvenanmaa (Åland Is), with a Swedish-speaking pop. at the entrance to the Gulf of Bothnia. Much of Lapland lies within the Arctic Circle; here Mt Haltia rises to 1325 m (4346 ft). The centre and S are mainly low-lying. There are thousands of lakes in the southern half; the largest are L. Saimaa and L. Paijanne. The reconstructed Saimas Canal links the L. Saimaa region with the Gulf of Finland. L. Oulu and L. Inari are farther N. The chief rivers are the Torne, the Kemi and the Oulu, all flowing into the Gulf of Bothnia. Lakes, rivers and canals, joining the lakes, are widely used for transport, esp. by the lumbering industry. Winters, esp. inland, last for 6 months and are severe; summers are short and warm. Land use: forested 76 per cent, meadows and pastures 0.4 per cent, agricultural and under permanent cultivation 8 per cent. Of the total pop. 87 per cent are Lutheran. Ninety-four per cent Finnish-speaking, 6 per cent Swedish-speaking. In

Finland (Suomi, Suomen Tasavalta)

317

the N the forest gradually merges into tundra, a region where the Lapps, of which there are about 4500, gain a livelihood by reindeer-raising and fishing, and nowadays from tourism. Logs from the mainly coniferous forests are floated down the rivers and canals in summer; the rivers also provide hydroelectric power.

Lumbering is a leading occupation; many workers are employed in the manufacture of wood products, e.g. wood-pulp, cellulose, plywood, paper and furniture. Timber, wood-pulp, paper and cardboard make up about three-quarters of the exports. Agriculture is limited to the more fertile parts of the S; oats, rye, barley and potatoes are grown; dairy-farming is important. Helsinki, chief seaport and cap., is ice-bound in winter, like the other ports, but the harbour is usually kept open by icebreakers. The mining industry is rather small, but Finland is an important producer of certain non-ferrous metals. The basic metal industry inc. high-technology steel and copper production. Key products of mechanical engineering inc. agricultural and forest machinery, forest industry machinery and equipment, cranes and lifts, consumer durables, electrical machinery and equipment, electronic products, land vehicles and various kinds of special ships such as icebreakers, passenger vessels and oil rigs, often designed for operation under difficult conditions.

Finland was occupied by Finno–Ugrian tribes, who drove the Lapps to the N; conquered and converted to Christianity by Eric IX of Sweden in the 12th cent. Disputed for hundreds of years between Sweden and Russia. Became a grand duchy in the 16th cent. The Swedish lang. and culture spread and a Diet was established. Ceded to Russia 1809, but still enjoyed a considerable measure of autonomy, but by the early 20th cent. severe repression had followed. After the Russian Revolution in 1917 independence was proclaimed. In 1939 Soviet troops invaded Finland, for a time the Finns were allied with the Germans. By the peace treaty of 1940 Finland ceded the Karelian Isthmus, Viipuri (Vyborg) and the Finnish shores of

L. Ladoga to the USSR: in 1944 the Petsamo (Pechenga) area was added. The Porkkala headland was also leased to the USSR as a military base; this was returned to Finland in 1956. Finland is governed by a 200-member single-chamber House of Representatives, chosen for 4 years by direct and proportional election; the President is elected for 6 years. Administratively the country is divided into 12 provinces (Swedish names in brackets): Uusimaa (Nyland); Turku-Pori (Åbo-Björneborg); Ahvenanmaa (Åland); Häme (Tavastehus); Kymi (Kymmene); Mikkeli (St Michel); Kuopio; Pohjois-Karjala (Norra Karelen); Keski-Suomi (Mellersta Finland); Vaasa (Vasa); Oulu (Uleåborg); Lapp (Lappland).

Finland, Gulf of. E arm of the Baltic Sea between Finland (N), Russia (E and S) and Estonia (S) 400 km (250 miles) long and 65–130 km (40–80 miles) wide. Shallow and of low salinity. Frozen for 4–6 months annually. On the shores are the seaports of Helsinki, Kota, Vyborg, St Petersburg and Tallinn.

Finnart Scotland. Oil terminal in Dunbarton on the E shore of Loch Long 3 km (2 miles) N of Garelochhead. Linked by 92-km (57-mile) pipeline with Grangemouth oil refinery.

Finnmark Norway. County of N Norway forming most N part of Scandinavian peninsula and bounded S by Finland, E by Russia, N by the Arctic Ocean. Area 48,637 sq km (17,799 sq. miles). Cap. Vadso. Pop. (1992) 75,251. Low-lying with a climate mild enough for crops, but with no sun for 2 winter months and no darkness for 2 summer months. Reindeer-rearing and fishing are the main occupations.

Finsbury England. Part of the London borough of Islington. Residential, commercial and industrial district. In the Bunhill Fields cemetery Bunyan, Defoe and William Blake are buried; Milton died in Bunhill Row. Also contains Sadler's Wells Theatre, John Wesley's Chapel and the Mount Pleasant parcel-sorting postal office.

Finsteraarhorn Switzerland. Highest peak in the Bernese Oberland (4275 m; 14,022 ft) 11 km (7 miles) SSE of Grindelwald on the border of the Bern and Valais cantons.

Firenze ➤FLORENCE.

Firozabad India. Town in Uttar Pradesh 40 km (25 miles) E of Agra. Pop. (1991) 261,600.

Leading centre for the manufacture of glass and glass bangles. Trade in grain and oilseeds.

Fishguard and Goodwick Wales. Town in Pembrokeshire on Fishguard Bay (Irish Sea). Pop. (1991) 2679. Railway terminus; ferry services to Cork and Rosslare (Ireland). Also fishing port.

Fitchburg USA. Industrial town in Massachusetts on the Nashua R. 37 km (23 miles) N of Worcester. Pop. (1985) 39,000.

Manufactures machinery, paper, saws and footwear.

Fitzroy River Australia. 1. River in Queensland 274 km (170 miles) long, formed from the Dawson and Mackenzie rivers and other headstreams and flowing generally E past Rockhampton to Keppel Bay.

2. River in Western Australia 563 km (350 miles) long, rising near the E end of the King Leopold Range and flowing generally SW and NW to King Sound. Swollen after the summer rains; partly dried up in the dry season.

Fiume ➤RIJEKA.

Flamborough Head England. High chalk headland on the coast of Humberside at the N end of Bridlington Bay. Many sea birds breed on the cliffs.

Flanders (Fr. **Flandre**, Flemish **Vlaanderen**) Belgium/France. Former county in the SW of the Low Countries, varying considerably in size throughout its history; now divided between Belgium and France. French Flanders equates approximately to the Nord department. Belgian Flanders comprises the two westernmost provinces: West Flanders (area 3144 sq km (1213 sq. miles): pop. (1991) 1,106,829; cap. Bruges) and East Flanders (area 2982 sq km (1151 sq. miles); pop. (1991) 1,335,793; cap. Ghent). The two provinces form Belgium's chief industrial region, esp. for coalmining and the manufacture of iron and steel and other metals and textiles. Scene of many battles in World War I.

Fleet River England. River formed by the union of two streams rising in Hampstead and Highgate, flowing S and joining the Thames near Blackfriars Bridge, London. Barges used it in the Middle Ages, but it was later choked by mud. It was built over and is now a sewer under Farringdon Street. The Fleet Prison stood on the E Bank.

Fleetwood England. Fishing port and resort in Lancashire at the SW end of Morecambe Bay and at the mouth of the R. Wyre. Pop. (1991) 27,227. Ferry service to the Isle of Man.

Industries inc. chemicals, plastics, electronics, computers and fishing.

Flensburg Germany. Seaport in Schleswig-Holstein near the Danish frontier 71 km (44 miles) NW of Kiel at the head of the Flensburg Fiord. Pop. (1991) 87,240.

Fish-curing, shipbuilding, metalworking.

Probably founded in the 12th cent. Passed from Denmark to Prussia 1864.

Flinders Island Australia. Largest island in the Furneaux Group in the Bass Strait off the NE coast of Tasmania. Area 2077 sq km (802 sq. miles). Pop. 900. Chief settlement Whitemark.

Flinders Range Australia. Mountains in South Australia extending N between L. Torrens and L. Frome, rising to 1188 m (3898 ft) in St Mary Peak. Some copper, lead and other minerals yielded in small quantity; uranium found at Mt Painter and elsewhere, but overshadowed by production in N Australia.

Flinders River Australia. River 837 km (520 miles) long in Queensland, rising in the E highlands 225 km (140 miles) WSW of Townsville, flowing W and N and entering the Gulf of Carpentaria. Named after Matthew Flinders (1774–1814), the English navigator who explored the coasts of Australia.

Flin Flon Canada. Town in Manitoba near the Saskatchewan border 628 km (390 miles) NNW of Winnipeg. Pop. (1991) 7119. Mining began in 1927, producing copper, zinc, gold. Incorporated 1946.

Flint USA. Industrial town in Michigan on the Flint R. 93 km (58 miles) NW of Detroit. Pop. (1990) 140,761. Chiefly important for the motor-car industry; manufactures finished vehicles as well as bodies and parts. Manufacture of carts and carriages was followed by the motor-car industry *c.* 1904, when it was already popularly known as the 'vehicle city'.

Flint Wales. Town in Flintshire on the Dee estuary 18 km (11 miles) WNW of Chester. Pop. (1991) 11,737.
Manufactures rayon and paper.
Ruins of a 13th-cent. castle.

Flintshire Wales. County formerly incorporated in Clwyd, but since 1996 again a separate county. Pop. (1994) 145,000.

Flodden England. Hill in Northumberland 5 km (3 miles) ESE of Coldstream. Famous as the scene of the Battle of Flodden Field (which surrounds it), when James IV of Scotland was defeated and killed by the English under the Earl of Surrey (1513).

Florence (Italian **Firenze**) Italy. Ancient Florentia. Cap. of the Firenze province in Tuscany on both banks of the Arno R. near where it emerges from the Apennines. Pop. (1990) 408,403.
Railway junction, linked with Bologna by a tunnel through the Apennines. Industries inc. engineering, food-processing and the manufacture of chemicals, textiles, pottery, furniture, jewellery and leather goods. It trades in wine and olive oil. There is a considerable tourist industry and it is best known as one of the world's great art centres, rich in works of the Italian Renaissance by such masters as Michelangelo, Leonardo da Vinci, Raphael, Cellini.

Near the great Gothic cathedral of Santa Maria de Fiore (13th/15th cent.) are the campanile by Giotto, possibly the most beautiful in the world and the baptistery of San Giovanni, with its three famous bronze doors. The Church of Santa Croce has frescoes by Giotto; that of San Lorenzo has Michelangelo's tombs of the Medici. Among the many palaces are the Palazzo della Signoria (the city hall), near which is the Loggia, with Cellini's bronze masterpiece, *Perseus*; the Palazzo degli Uffizi, with the Uffizi gallery, housing Italy's most important collection of paintings; the Palazzo Pitti, now an art gallery and the Palazzo Strozzi, both of the 15th cent. Also has the Italian National Library and several learned institutions, inc. the Accademia delle Belle Arti and the Accademia della Crusca. The beautiful Boboli Gardens were designed in the 16th cent. An early Roman colony, as Florentia ('City of Flowers'). In the 13th cent. witnessed the bitter rivalry between the Guelphs and Ghibellines (the papal and imperial factions). Suffered severely from famine and plague in the 14th cent., but became the centre of a powerful republic, largely by waging war on its neighbours and grew commercially prosperous. Its artistic reputation was enhanced by the house of Medici, which ruled, with interruptions, for 3 centuries (1434–1737). Then followed a period under Austria, which lasted (again with breaks) till 1859, when the city was united with Italy. Cap. of Italy 1865–70. Many of the historic buildings were damaged during World War II; much of the medieval section was destroyed by the Germans as they retreated. When the Arno burst its banks and flooded the city in 1966, many buildings and art treasures suffered severely. Birthplace of Dante (1265–1321), the greatest of Italian poets.

Florence USA. Industrial town in Alabama on the Tennessee R. 160 km (100 miles) NNW of Birmingham. Pop. (1984) 36,000.
Meat-packing. Manufactures textiles, aluminium and chemicals. Power derived from the Wilson Dam 6 km (4 miles) upstream. Developed industrially with the establish-

ment of the Tennessee Valley Authority (TVA).

Flores Indonesia. One of the Lesser Sunda Is. with the Flores Sea to the N and the Sawu Sea to the S. Area 14,250 sq km (5500 sq. miles). Chief town and port Ende. Mountainous with several active volcanoes; interior heavily forested and little explored.

Industries inc. fishing, agriculture, and it exports copra.

Flores Portugal. Westernmost island of the Azores in the Atlantic Ocean. Area 142 sq km (55 sq. miles). Pop. (1970) 5302. Chief town Santa Cruz. Rises to over 900 m (2952 ft).

Noted for flowers (hence the name) and hot springs.

The battle took place, off Flores, between a Spanish fleet and Sir Richard Grenville in the *Revenge* (1591).

Florianopolis Brazil. Formerly Desterro. Cap. of the Santa Catarina state 499 km (310 miles) SSW of São Paulo on Santa Catarina island, connected to the mainland by a long suspension bridge. Pop. (1990) 170,000.

Seaport with an excellent harbour. Exports sugar, tobacco and fruit produced in the surrounding region. Tourism is important.

Founded 1700.

Florida USA. State in the extreme SE, mainly along a peninsula, between the Atlantic and the Gulf of Mexico; separated from Cuba by the Florida Strait. Area 151,939 sq km (58,664 sq. miles). Pop. (1990) 12,937,926. Cap. Tallahassee. Largely swampy and low-lying, with many lakes, the largest being L. Okeechobee in the S. Climate humid and subtropical, with hot, rainy summers and occasional hurricanes in the autumn. Pines and cypresses grow in profusion in the Everglades and the Big Cypress Swamp. Contains famous Atlantic resorts, e.g. Palm Beach, Miami, Daytona Beach. Tourist attractions inc. Disney World and the Kennedy Space Center at Cape Canaveral.

Citrus fruits are produced in large quantities. Other crops maize, sugar-cane, tobacco.

Market-gardening and fishing important. Chief mineral phosphates. Industries inc. food-processing and the manufacture of cigars and wood products.

Largest cities Miami, Tampa and Jacksonville. First explored by the Spaniards 1513 and remained a Spanish possession, apart from 20 years under British control (1763–83), until 1821, when it was purchased by the USA. Admitted to the Union in 1845 as the 27th state.

Florida Keys USA. Chain of small islands over 240 km (150 miles) long, extending WSW in a curve from Biscayne Bay, in S Florida, towards the Gulf of Mexico. The largest islands are Key Largo and Key West (the westernmost); the city of Key West is the southernmost in the USA. Others in the group (which is separated from Cuba by the Florida Strait) are Long Key, Big Pine Key, Sugarloaf Key. Mainly covered with small trees and shrubs. Limes are cultivated. Mainly noted as resorts for big-game fishing. The islands are linked with one another and with the mainland by the Overseas Highway, 198 km (124 miles), replacing the railway destroyed in the hurricane of 1935.

Flórina Greece. 1. Sparsely populated mountainous *nome* in Macedonia, bordering on Macedonia (Yugoslavia) (N) and Albania (W). Area 1924 sq km (743 sq. miles). Pop. (1991) 53,147. Main occupations stock-rearing, cultivation of cereals.

2. Cap. of Flórina *nome*, near the frontier of Macedonia (Yugoslavia) (to which it is connected by the Monastir Gap) 134 km (83 miles) WNW of Thessaloniki. Pop. (1985) 12,000.

Trade in cereals, fruit and livestock.

Florissant USA. Formerly (1920–40) St Ferdinand. Residential town in Missouri near the Missouri R. 21 km (13 miles) NNW of St Louis. Pop. (1990) 52,206.

Flushing (Dutch **Vlissingen**) Netherlands. Seaport and resort in Zeeland province on the S coast of Walcheren Island at the mouth of the W Scheldt. Pop. (1993) 44,147.

Oil and coal bunkering. Shipbuilding, engineering and fishing.

Closely associated with the Dutch struggle for independence; the first Dutch city to throw off Spanish rule (1572). Birthplace of Admiral de Ruyter (1607–76).

Fly River Papua New Guinea. River in New Guinea 1287 km (800 miles) long, rising in the centre and flowing generally SE to the Gulf of Papua. Navigable for over 1000 km (620 miles) but commercially unimportant.

Focşani Romania. Cap. of the Vrancea district, Moldavia 169 km (105 miles) NW of Bucharest. Pop. (1992) 101,296.

Trade in cereals, wine. Manufactures soap, metal products, pharmaceuticals and leather.

Scene of the defeat of the Turks by Austrian and Russian armies (1789).

Foggia Italy. Cap. of Foggia province in the middle of the Apulian plain 120 km (75 miles) WNW of Bari. Pop. (1991) 159,541.

Important trade in wheat. Industries inc. food-processing, flour-milling, cheese-making, pasta and olive oil.

Cathedral (12th-cent.); gateway to the palace of the Emperor Frederick II.

Fogo Cape Verde. Island situated ENE of Brava in the Leeward group. Area 476 sq km (184 sq. miles). Pop. (1990) 33,860. Chief town São Filipe. Circular in shape with an active volcano, Cano Peak, 2829 m (9280 ft) above sea level.

Main products beans, coffee, oranges and tobacco.

Foix France. Cap. of department on the Ariège R. Pop. (1982) 10,064. Agricultural and tourist centre.

Foligno Italy. Town in Perugia province in Umbria 32 km (20 miles) SE of Perugia. Pop. (1985) 53,000.

Railway junction. Industries inc. sugar-refining and the manufacture of textiles and paper.

Cathedral (12th/13th-cent.). The first edition of Dante's *Divina Commedia* was printed at the Palazzo Orfini (1472).

Folkestone England. Seaside resort in SE Kent, 11 km (7 miles) WSW of Dover. Pop. (1991) 45,587. At the foot of chalk hills rising to over 150 m (492 ft), with the broad promenade of the Leas along its cliffs. Also a fishing port and connections to Calais and Boulogne by Hoverspeed and Le Shuttle. A 'limb' or member of the Cinque Ports. Birthplace of William Harvey (1578–1657), discoverer of the circulation of the blood.

Fond du Lac USA. Industrial town in Wisconsin at the S end of L. Winnebago (hence the name) 93 km (58 miles) NNW of Milwaukee. Pop. (1990) 37,757.

Manufactures machine-tools, refigerators, textiles. Also a holiday resort with lake boating attractions.

A French trading post in 1785 and first permanently settled in 1836.

Fontainebleau France. Town in the Seine-et-Marne department near the Seine R. 55 km (35 miles) SSE of Paris in the Forest of Fontainebleau. Pop. (1982) 18,750.

A popular resort and has a furniture industry.

A residence of the French kings; the most famous building is the magnificent palace, built largely by Francis I, where Napoleon signed his abdication (1814). The forest (170 sq km; 65 sq. miles), one of the most beautiful in France, has been the inspiration of many artists such as Corot and Millet.

Fontenoy Belgium. Village in the Hainaut province 6 km (4 miles) SE of Tournai. Scene of the defeat (1745) of the British and their Dutch and Austrian allies (under the Duke of Cumberland) by French forces (under Marshal Saxe).

Foochow ►FUZHOU.

Foraker, Mount USA. Mountain situated NNW of Anchorage, Alaska in Mount McKinley National Park at 5267 m (17,280 ft) above sea level.

Foreland Point England. Headland on the N coast of Devon 3 km (2 miles) ENE of Lynmouth. ►►NORTH FORELAND.

Forfar Scotland. Town in Angus 21 km (13 miles) NNE of Dundee. Pop. (1991) 12,961.

Noted for textile industries.

The castle, residence of early Scottish kings, was destroyed (1307) by Robert Bruce; the site is marked by the town cross.

Forlì Italy. Ancient Forum Livii. Cap. of Forlì province in Emilia-Romagna on the Montone R. and the Aemilian Way 61 km (38 miles) SE of Bologna. Pop. (1990) 109,755.

Manufactures textiles, footwear and felt.

Cathedral with 17th-cent. chapel. The church of San Mercuriale has a fine 12th-cent. campanile.

Formby England. Town in Merseyside 18 km (11 miles) NNW of Liverpool. Pop. (1985) 24,000. Mainly residential. Altcar, the venue of the Waterloo Cup (coursing) is 3 km (2 miles) ESE.

Former Yugoslavia ►YUGOSLAVIA.

Formosa Argentina. Cap. of the Formosa province on the Paraguay R. 113 km (70 miles) SSW of Asunción (Paraguay). Pop. (1991) 165,700.

River port. Market town. In an agricultural and stockrearing region. Tanning. Meat-packing.

Formosa (China) ►TAIWAN.

Forres Scotland. Market town in Moray on the R. Findhorn 19 km (12 miles) WSW of Elgin. Pop. (1988) 9180.

Woollen and flour mills. Whisky-distilling, engineering.

An early castle was traditionally the scene of Macbeth's murder of Duncan; the later castle was a residence of Scottish kings in the 12th–14th cent. Swen's stone nearby is an elaborately carved monolith which probably commemorates the victory of Sweno (son of Harold, king of Denmark) over Malcolm II (1008).

Forst Germany. Industrial town in the Cottbus district on the Neisse R. and the Polish frontier 21 km (13 miles) E of Cottbus. Pop. (1989) 26,313.

Manufactures textiles and machinery.

Zasieki, formerly a suburb on the opposite side of the river, was transferred to Poland after World War II (1945).

Fortaleza (Ceará) Brazil. Cap. of the Ceará state (NE), an Atlantic port, with an improved harbour. Pop. (1990) 1,758,334.

Exports cotton, hides, carnauba wax. Sugar-refining, flour-milling. Manufactures textiles and soap.

Fort Augustus Scotland. Village in Highland at the S end of Loch Ness on the Caledonian Canal. A fort erected in 1716 and enlarged in 1730 was later named after William Augustus, Duke of Cumberland (the victor of Culloden); the buildings have been occupied by a Benedictine Abbey since 1876, when the site was presented to the Order by Lord Lovat.

Fort Collins USA. Commercial town in Colorado 93 km (58 miles) N of Denver at a height of 1500 m (4920 ft). Pop. (1990) 87,758.

In a stock-rearing and agricultural region. Industries inc. sugar-refining and flour-milling.

Fort-de-France Martinique. Formerly Fort-Royal. Cap. and chief seaport on the W coast on Fort-de-France Bay with a sheltered deep-water harbour. Pop. (1990) 101,540.

Exports sugar, rum and cacao.

French naval base. Main commercial centre since the destruction of St Pierre by volcanic eruption (1902). Nearby is the birthplace of the Empress Josephine (1763–1814).

Fort Dodge USA. Town in Iowa on the Des Moines R. 116 km (72 miles) NNW of Des Moines. Pop. (1985) 33,000.

Manufactures gypsum products, bricks and tiles. There are gypsum deposits nearby.

Fortescue River Australia. Intermittent river in Western Australia 563 km (350 miles) long, flowing generally WNW through broken country N of the Hamersley Range to the Indian Ocean.

Forth River Scotland. River 106 km (66

miles) long, formed by the union of two headstreams (the Avondhu and Duchray Water) near Aberfoyle, flowing E by a meandering course past Stirling to Alloa at the head of the Firth of Forth, which extends 82 km (51 miles) to the North Sea and is crossed by a road bridge (1936) at Kincardine, the Forth Rail Bridge (1882–90) at Queensferry and the Forth Road Bridge (1964). Islands inc. Bass Rock, Inchcolm and Inchkeith. Principal ports Leith and Grangemouth; just above the Forth Rail Bridge is the naval base of Rosyth. At Grangemouth the river is connected by the Forth and Clyde Canal with Bowling on the Clyde estuary.

Forties Scotland. Oilfield in the North Sea off the NE coast of Scotland. It is linked by pipeline to Cruden Bay and was the first oilfield to pipe oil to the UK.

Fort Knox USA. Military reservation and air base in Kentucky 43 km (27 miles) SSW of Louisville. Pop. (1989) 38,277. Purchased in 1917 by the US government for use as a World War I training camp. The Gold Bullion Depository (built 1936) stores most of the US gold reserves.

Fort Lamy ➤N'DJAMENA.

Fort Lauderdale USA. Seaside resort in SE Florida 40 km (25 miles) N of Miami near the Everglades. Founded as a military camp in 1838. Pop. (1990) 149,377.

Trade in citrus fruits, market-garden produce. Manufactures electronic products and yachts.

Fort McMurray Canada. City situated NE of Edmonton, Alberta. Pop. (1991) 34,706.

Industries inc. timber, fur, fish, sands, petroleum products, oil and tourism. There are large tar sands plants.

Fort Smith USA. Formerly Belle Pointe. Town in Arkansas on the Arkansas R. and the Oklahoma border. Pop. (1990) 72,798.

Chief manufacturing centre in the state. Produces glass, textiles, furniture and metal goods.

Founded (as Belle Pointe) in 1817. Re-

named after General Thomas A. Smith, the commander who ordered its construction.

Fort Wayne USA. Industrial town and railway junction in NE Indiana at the confluence of the St Mary's and the St Joseph rivers. Pop. (1990) 173,072.

Manufactures mining, agricultural and electrical machinery, radio and television equipment, pumps and tanks.

Named after General Anthony Wayne, who built a fort here 1794. Grew as a fur-trading centre.

Fort William (Canada) ➤THUNDER BAY.

Fort William Scotland. Town in Highland near the foot of Ben Nevis at the NE end of Loch Linnhe. Pop. (1991) 10,391.

Tourist centre. Important aluminium works and whisky distilleries.

The fort, built by General Monk (1655), enlarged (1690) and renamed after William III, was dismantled 1866.

Fort Worth USA. Industrial town in Texas 51 km (32 miles) W of Dallas. Pop. (1990) 447,619.

Important grain and livestock market and oil-refining centre. It manufactures aircraft, vehicles, clothing, agricultural machinery and leather goods. Meat-packing and flour-milling.

Seat of the Texas Christian University (1873). Many parks and famous botanical gardens.

Foshan ➤FATSHAN.

Fougères France. Town in the Ille-et-Vilaine department 43 km (27 miles) NE of Rennes. Pop. (1985) 26,000.

Manufactures footwear and clothing. Granite quarried in the neighbourhood.

Famous castle (12th/15th-cent.).

Foumban Cameroon. Town in W province. Pop. (1981) 41,358.

Chief centre of Bamoun area for wood-carving and agricultural products.

Fountains Abbey ➤RIPON.

Fouta Djallon (Futa Jallon). Highland

region in W Africa, mainly in Guinea but extending into Sierra Leone and Liberia. Much dissected; generally at a height of 900 m (2952 ft), but rising to over 1200 m (3936 ft). Source of the Niger, Senegal and Gambia rivers. Chiefly savannah.

Principal occupation cattle-rearing. Main crops rice, bananas.

Foveaux Strait ➤STEWART ISLAND.

Fowey England. Small seaport in Cornwall on the estuary of the R. Fowey 35 km (22 miles) W of Plymouth. Pop. (1991) 1939. Seaside resort.

Exports china clay. Fishing.

Its maritime trade was important in the 14th–15th cent. The 'Troy Town' of Sir Arthur Quiller-Couch (1863–1944), who lived here.

Foxe Channel ➤HUDSON BAY.

Foyers Scotland. Village in Highland on the E shore of Loch Ness at the mouth of the R. Foyers 29 km (18 miles) SW of Inverness. Aluminium works. The first hydroelectric plant in Britain (1896).

Foyle, Lough Ireland. Inlet of the Atlantic 24 km (15 miles) long and 13 km (8 miles) maximum width between Co. Donegal (Irish Republic) and Co. Londonderry (Northern Ireland). Fed by the R. Foyle, on which the town of Londonderry stands.

Framingham USA. Town forming part of the Boston conurbation situated SW of Boston, Massachusetts. Pop. (1985) 65,500.

Framlingham England. Market town in E Suffolk 24 km (15 miles) NNE of Ipswich. Pop. (1991) 2697. Ruined 13th-cent. castle. Well-known public school, founded (1864) as a memorial to the Prince Consort.

Francavilla Fontana Italy. Market town in Brindisi province, Apulia 31 km (19 miles) ENE of Taranto. Pop. (1985) 33,000. Railway junction.

Trade in wine, olive oil and wheat.

Has the former castle of the Imperiali family.

France. Republic in W Europe bounded in the N by the English Channel (*La Manche*), NE by Belgium and Luxembourg, E by Germany, Switzerland and Italy, S by the Mediterranean (with Monaco as a coastal enclave), SW by Spain and Andorra and W by the Atlantic Ocean. Area 543,965 sq km (210,033 sq. miles). Pop. (1995) 58,172,000 (73 per cent urban). Life expectancy, 73 years male, 81 female. Cap. Paris. Other large cities Marseilles, Lyon and Toulouse. Currency: French franc = 100 centimes.

The SE half is mainly mountainous, containing (besides the Pyrenees, Alps and Jura along the frontiers) the Cévennes, the Auvergne and the Vosges. Plains occupy most of the NW half. The great Central Plateau (the Massif Central) takes up nearly one-sixth of the total area; it is a crystalline formation overlaid in parts with lava sheets and volcanic cones (*puys*) and fringed in the SW and S by limestone deposits (*causses*). It rises to 1886 m (6186 ft) in the Puy de Sancy and is largely infertile and sparsely inhabited, the rural pop. gradually moving away to the towns. The Pyrenees, with several peaks exceeding 3000 m (9840 ft) have always proved a considerable barrier between France and Spain. Higher still are the Alps, with the subsidiary ranges of the Maritime, Cottian and Graian Alps lying across the SE frontier; the loftiest point, the Mont Blanc massif (4808 m; 15,774 ft) is on the Italian frontier. To the N are the Jura (1724 m; 5655 ft), and still farther N the Vosges (1418 m; 4651 ft), facing the Black Forest of Germany across the rift valley of the Rhine. Most of the lowland area of France consists of two extensive basins, Aquitaine and the Paris Basin, which, with the Île-de-France as its central area, is the true heartland of France; at its centre is Paris, whence the most important roads and railways radiate in all directions. It is crossed by the Seine (commercially France's principal river) which, with its tributaries the Oise, Marne and Yonne and interconnecting canals, forms a network of busy inland waterways. In the S it inc. the middle course of the Loire, famous for its châteaux. Through the Gate of Poitou the Paris Basin is linked

France

with Aquitaine, which is drained by the Garonne, the third of France's great rivers, joined at the head of its estuary (the Gironde) by the Dordogne. W of the Paris Basin are the low hills, granite moorlands and rocky indented coastline of Brittany and W Normandy. E of the Paris Basin, around the Vosges, are Alsace and Lorraine, linked via the Burgundian Gate with the narrow Rhône–Saône corridor, long the main route between the N and the Mediterranean region. In its lower course the valley of the Rhône, the fourth of France's great rivers, broadens out into the Mediterranean coastlands, with the celebrated resorts of the French Riviera (Côte d'Azur) in the E. The NW has a moderate maritime climate, with small temperature range and abundant rainfall but, inland, rainfall becomes more seasonal, with a summer maximum and the annual range of temperature increases. S France has a Mediterranean climate, with mild, moist winters and hot, dry summers. E France has a continental climate and a rainfall maximum in summer, with thunderstorms prevalent. Land use: forested 27 per cent, meadows and pastures 21 per cent, agricultural and under permanent cultivation 35 per cent. About 76 per cent of the pop. is Roman Catholic, other Christians about 4 per cent. Muslims make up 3 per cent. Seven per cent of the pop. is of foreign origin, mainly from N Africa and Mediterranean countries. The official lang. is French. French culture is Latin in character, but local influences have been preserved: a German dialect is spoken in Alsace, Breton in Brittany, Flemish in the extreme NE, Basque in the extreme SW and an Italian dialect in Corsica.

With its favourable climates and large fertile areas, France is an important agricultural country. Wheat takes up the greatest acreage of arable land, followed by barley and oats; potatoes and sugar-beet are also important crops. The Paris Basin and Aquitaine are the main wheat-growing regions. France is a leading wine producer; only the N lies outside the vine-growing areas and here hops are grown for beer (NE) and apples for cider (NW). The great wine-producing areas are

Champagne, Burgundy, the lower Charente and Garonne valleys (noted for clarets, light Bordeaux wines and brandy), Languedoc (producing large quantities of *vin ordinaire*) and the lower Rhône and Loire valleys. There is a considerable production of apples, pears, plums and peaches. Market-gardening is important, esp. in the Paris Basin and the NW. Large numbers of cattle, sheep and pigs are raised. There are in all just over 1 million agricultural holdings, of which some 300,000 are run part-time by farmers who also have other jobs in tourism and industry. Agriculture is carried on essentially on a family basis, farmers themselves running their farms, of which they are very often the owners, with the help of members of their family and, more seldom, of agricultural workers, whose number is declining. Fishing is a substantial industry, esp. along the Breton coast.

Considerable coal comes from the NE coalfield, which extends across the frontier into Belgium; there are scattered deposits around the edge of the Central Plateau, but coal is also imported (mainly from the Ruhr). In 1990, 12 million tonnes were produced compared with 60 million in 1958. Hydroelectric power has been developed, notably in the Alps, but it represented only 14 per cent of electricity production in 1990 compared with 56 per cent in 1960. Nuclear power produced 75 per cent in 1990.

France became an industrial power in the 19th cent. It was the time when the iron and steel industry and heavy engineering developed near the great coal-mining areas (North, Lorraine, Centre), as well as the chemical and textile industries (wool in the N, cotton in Alsace and Normandy). The 20th cent. saw the birth of new industries which play an important role in the economy, i.e. the motor-vehicle and electrical engineering industries. Today, all types of industrial activities are to be found in France. Side by side with traditional industries, some of which are experiencing difficulties because of competition from recently industrialized countries (footwear, textile, shipbuilding, consumer electronics and electrical goods) are the new high-tech industries: aerospace, computers, telecommunications, chemicals, etc. Steel production is in the hands of a single nationalized group, which is the world's second largest iron and steel company. France also has a large non-ferrous metal industry, of which the main sector is the production of aluminium (326,000 tonnes in 1990) controlled by one (nationalized) company. There are a few non-ferrous ore resources but it has an important ore-refining industry which is supplied by imports of zinc, lead, copper, nickel and uranium. The motor-vehicle industry produced 3,800,000 vehicles in 1990. The factories producing basic chemicals are mainly situated in the former mining areas and near oil refineries. The aerospace industry is based mainly in the Paris region and in the SW of France (Bordeaux and Toulouse); the industry employs about 120,000 people. France has a long tradition in all branches of the textile, clothing and footwear industries. The textile industry uses 600,000 tonnes of fibres per year of which two-thirds are man-made. The rest consists of wool (80 per cent imported) worked in the northern mills and of cotton (all of which is imported), worked mainly in Alsace. Other important industries inc. food-processing, wine production, cement, glass, plastic, paper and rubber.

Ancient Gaul had a common lang. and form of government imposed on it by the Roman conquest of Julius Caesar (57–52 BC) and for some centuries it prospered. The *Pax Romana* was broken by the invasions of Germanic tribes (the Visigoths, Burgundians and Franks) in the 5th cent. AD, but Clovis, King of the Franks, embraced Christianity after his conquests and gained the support of the Church, brought unity again and laid the foundations of the French state. Charlemagne extended the Frankish kingdom over a great part of W Europe and was crowned Emperor of the West (800). After his death the land was again partitioned; feudalism fostered the disintegration and after the Norman conquest of England (1066) much of France fell into the hands of the English. However,

by the end of the Hundred Years War (1337–1454) only Calais remained to England and this too was recovered in 1558 (though England held Dunkirk 1656–62). The commanding position that France now held was due mainly to the House of Capet, founded (987) by Hugh Capet, which had gradually established the authority of the monarch. When the Capetian line became extinct, their successors, the Valois, proved less able, if sometimes equally determined. Louis XI (1461–83) inaugurated the autocratic rule which ultimately became the despotism of Louis XIV (1643–1715). In the 18th cent. France suffered defeat in Louis XIV's War of the Spanish Succession, lost her colonial empire and finally, under Louis XVI, faced bankruptcy. With the French Revolution (1789) and the execution of the king, the *ancien régime* came to an end, to be followed by the dictatorship of Napoleon, who led France through a short period of military glory, abdicated and was defeated at Waterloo (1815). After a period of restored monarchy came the Revolution of 1848 and the Second Republic under Louis Napoleon, which became the Second Empire; this collapsed in the defeat in the Franco–Prussian War (1870–1). Recovery came quickly during the Third Republic and a new colonial empire was built up. World War I took a heavy toll of French life; in World War II France was rapidly overrun by the German army (1940). After liberation (1944) the Fourth Republic was established (1946). In spite of political dissensions, France renewed her economic strength, consolidated her position in W Europe, joined the North Atlantic Treaty Organization (1948), formulated the plan for the highly successful European Coal and Steel community (1950) and worked for a European Economic Community. Her colonial empire began to break up; the use of force, both in Indo-China and in Algeria, could not stifle the demands for independence. The substitution of the French Union (by the constitution of 1946) for the former colonial organization did not satisfy these demands. In 1958 the Fifth Republic was established, under General de Gaulle and with the new constitution which is now in force.

Parliament consists of a 577-member National Assembly (555 from Metropolitan France and 22 from overseas departments and dependencies) and a 321-member Senate. The President is elected for 7-year terms by direct universal suffrage.

For administrative purposes France is divided into 22 Regions: Île de France, Rhône-Alpes, Provence-Alpes-Côte d'Azur, Nord-Pas de Calais, Pays de la Loire, Aquitaine, Bretagne, Midi-Pyrénées, Centre, Lorraine, Languedoc-Roussillon, Picardie, Haute Normandie, Alsace, Bourgogne, Poitou-Charentes, Basse Normandie, Champagne-Ardenne, Auvergne, Franche Comté, Limousin, Corse; and 96 Départements: Ain, Aisne, Allier, Alpes-de-Haute Provence, Alpes-Maritimes, Ardèche, Ardennes, Ariège, Aube, Aude, Aveyron, Bas-Rhin, Belfort (Territoire), Bouches-du-Rhône, Calvados, Cantal, Charente, Charente-Maritime, Cher, Corrèze, Corse-du-Sud, Côte-d'Or, Côtes-du-Nord, Creuse, Deux-Sèvres, Dordogne, Doubs, Drôme, Essonne, Eure, Eure-et-Loir, Finistère, Gard, Gers, Gironde, Haute-Corse, Haute-Garonne, Haute-Loire, Haute-Marne, Hautes-Alpes, Haute-Saône, Haute-Savoie, Hautes-Pyrénées, Haute-Vienne, Haut-Rhin, Hauts-de-Seine, Hérault, Ille-et-Vilaine, Indre, Indre-et-Loire, Isère, Jura, Landes, Loire, Loire-Atlantique, Loiret, Loir-et-Cher, Lot, Lot-et-Garonne, Lozère, Maine-et-Loire, Manche, Marne, Mayenne, Meurthe-et-Moselle, Meuse, Morbihan, Moselle, Nièvre, Nord, Oise, Orne, Paris (Ville), Pas-de-Calais, Puy-de-Dôme, Pyrénées-Atlantiques, Pyrénées-Orientales, Rhône, Saône-et-Loire, Sarthe, Savoie, Seine-et-Marne, Seine-Maritime, Seine-St Denis, Somme, Tarn, Tarn-et-Garonne, Val-de-Marne, Val d'Oise, Var, Vaucluse, Vendée, Vienne, Vosges, Yonne, Yvelines.

Franche-Comté France. Region and former province lying between the Swiss frontier and the Saône R. and consisting of the Jura, Belfort (Territory of), Doubes and Haute-Saône departments. Area 16,189 sq km (6252 sq. miles). Pop. (1990) 1,097,300. Lowland along the upper Saône R., rising to the central Jura (N).

Main occupations farming, lumbering; main industries the manufacture of clocks, machinery and plastics, centred on Besançon, Dôle, Lons-le-Saunier, Vesoul, Belfort and Portarlier.

Franconia (Ger. **Franken**) Germany. Medieval duchy, first inhabited by the Germanic tribe of the Franks, extending along the valley of the Main R. from the Rhine to Bohemia. Later divided into W (Rhenish) Franconia, which disintegrated into free cities and ecclesiastical states and E Franconia, which passed to the bishops of Wurzburg and then to Bavaria. The name fell into disuse but was revived (1837) when Lower, Middle and Upper Franconia were made administrative provinces of Bavaria.

Frankfort USA. City and cap. of Kentucky situated E of Louisville on Kentucky R. Pop. (1990) 25,969.

Commercial centre of a 'Bluegrass' agricultural and stone-quarrying region, trading in tobacco, livestock, dairy products and grain. Industries inc. distilling, sawmilling and the manufacture of vehicles, concrete products, furniture, clothing and hemp twine.

Frankfurt-am-Main (Frankfurt) Germany. Largest city in Hessen on the right bank of the Main R. Pop. (1991) 664,865.

Important commercial, industrial and route centre. Printing and publishing. Banking. Manufactures chemicals, machinery, electrical equipment and textiles. Also an active river port.

The *Altstadt* (old town) with its narrow streets and medieval buildings is in contrast with the more spacious *Neustadt* (new town). The former was severely damaged by bombing in World War II; among buildings destroyed were the 15th-cent. *Romer* (town hall) and the birthplace of Goethe (1749–1832). Became the headquarters of the great I. G. Farbenindustrie (chemicals) and has long been famous for trade fairs, inc. the annual international book fair. In 1993 it became the headquarters of the European Monetary Institute (which has become the European Central Bank of the EU). Probably founded in the 1st cent. AD. Cap. of the E Frankish kingdom in the 9th cent. Already known for its fairs by the 13th cent. Free imperial city 1372–1806. Seat of the Diet of the German Confederation 1815–66, but supported Austria and was seized by Prussia 1866. The treaty ending the Franco–Prussian War was signed here (1871).

Frankfurt-an-der-Oder Germany. Cap. of the Frankfurt-an-der-Oder district on the left bank of the Oder R. 80 km (50 miles) ESE of Berlin. Pop. (1989) 87,300.

Railway and road junction. Sugar-refining, vegetable canning, sausage-making. Manufactures machinery and furniture.

Founded in the mid-13th cent. by Franconian merchants. Belonged to the Hanseatic League in the 14th–15th cent. Its university (founded 1506) was moved to Breslau (Wroclaw) 1811. When the Oder (Odra) R. was made the German–Polish frontier (1945) its suburb on the E bank became the Polish town of Slubice.

Franz-Josef Land (Russian **Zemlya Frantsa Josifa**) Russia. Arctic archipelago of about 85 islands N of Novaya Zemlya. Area 20,720 sq km (8000 sq. miles). Uninhabited save for meteorological observers and migrant fur-trappers. Mostly ice-covered, with mosses and lichens here and there. Animal life consists of bears, foxes, seals and sea birds. Chief islands Aleksandra, George and Wilczek Lands, and Graham Bell Island. Discovered (1873) by von Payer and Weyprecht. Annexed by the USSR 1926.

Frascati Italy. Town and summer resort in Roma province in Latium on the N slopes of the Alban Hills 21 km (13 miles) SE of Rome. Pop. (1985) 18,700. Famed for its villas and gardens (Aldobrandini, Torlonia and Falconieri).

Fraserburgh Scotland. Town and herring-fishing port in Aberdeenshire on the North

Sea near Kinnaird Head. Pop. (1991) 12,843.

Industries inc. fish curing and canning; tourism is important.

Founded in the 16th cent. by Sir Alexander Fraser, after whom it is named.

Fraser River Canada. Chief river of British Columbia 1368 km (850 miles) long, rising near the Yellowhead Pass and flowing NW, S and then W to enter the Strait of Georgia below New Westminster. Main tributary the Thompson. In its lower course the Fraser passes through spectacular canyons; about 160 km (100 miles) from the mouth it becomes navigable. Has the principal salmon spawning grounds along the Pacific coast. The lower valley is an important farming area. The upper valley was the scene of a gold rush in 1858.

Fray Bentos Uruguay. Cap. of the Río Negro department on the Uruguay R. 274 km (170 miles) NW of Montevideo. Pop. (1985) 20,000.

Port accessible to ocean-going ships. Commercial and industrial centre, long important for meat packing and canning. The meat extracts of Justus von Liebig (1803–73) were first produced here in 1861.

Fredericia Denmark. Seaport in E Jutland at the N end of the Little Belt. Pop. (1990) 46,072.

Manufactures cotton and metal goods and fertilizers and has an oil refinery.

Founded 1652.

Frederick USA. City in central Maryland. Pop. (1990) 40,148.

Centre for commerce and retailing; Fort Detrick is here (US Army medical research and defence communications) and associated biomedical and electronics industries. Manufactures dairy products, leather goods, cement, plastics and aluminium.

Fredericton Canada. Cap. of New Brunswick at the head of navigation on the St John R. Pop. (1991) 45,364.

Sawmilling and woodworking. Industries inc. food-processing, tourism, electrical products, footwear, printing and publishing.

Founded (1783) by United Empire Loyalists.

Fredrikstad Norway. Port on the S shore of Oslo Fiord at the mouth of the Glomma R. 77 km (48 miles) S of Oslo. Pop. (1990) 26,546.

Exports timber and chemicals. Industries inc. sawmilling, fishing and fish-canning.

Freeport Bahamas. Chief town of Grand Bahama. Pop. (1985) 30,000. The biggest tourist complex in the West Indies.

Freeport (Illinois) USA. Town 172 km (107 miles) WNW of Chicago. Pop. (1980) 28,500.

Manufactures food products, pharmaceuticals, hardware, electrical equipment and tyres.

Scene of one of the famous Lincoln–Douglas debates (1858).

Free State South Africa. Province reorganized and renamed in 1994, bounded W by Northern Cape, N by North West province, Gauteng and Mpumalanga, E by KwaZulu/Natal and Lesotho and S by Eastern Cape. Area 129,480 sq km (49,992 sq. miles). Pop. (1995) 2,782,500. Cap. Bloemfontein. High, mainly grass-covered plateau, at a height of about 1500 m (4920 ft). The surface is broken by low ridges and isolated hills (kopjes) and drained by the Caledon and Modder rivers, and by other tributaries of the Orange and the Vaal.

Livestock (esp. sheep) raised. Wheat, maize, fruits, cultivated, esp. in the wetter areas (E). Gold production has increased greatly since the exploitation of the Odendaalsrus goldfield began (1946). Diamonds mined in the Jagersfoutein area. Coalmining in the N (chiefly in the Coalbrook district). Industrial development still on a small scale; Kroonstad is an important agricultural and railway centre, Welkom an important gold-mining centre.

Freetown Sierra Leone. Cap., chief seaport and naval base on the estuary of the Sierra Leone R. Pop. (1988) 469,776. Excellent natural harbour.

Chief exports diamonds, palm kernels; iron ore exported from Pepel 19 km (12 miles) ENE. Tuna-fishing. Other industries inc. oil-refining, railway engineering, rice and groundnut milling.

Seat of Fourah Bay College, founded (1827) by the Church Missionary Society and part of the University of Sierra Leone. Hot wet climate, unfavourable to Europeans; formerly called 'the white man's grave'. Health conditions have been much improved by a modern drainage system and anti-malaria measures. Founded (1792) as a home for freed slaves.

Freiberg Germany. Industrial town in Saxony at the N foot of the Erzgebirge 29 km (18 miles) WSW of Dresden. Pop. (1981) 51,377.

Manufactures machinery, textiles, electronics and porcelain.

The 15th-cent. cathedral has a famous Romanesque portal known as the Golden Gate.

Freiburg (Switzerland) ➤FRIBOURG.

Freiburg-im-Breisgau Germany. Town in Baden-Württemberg on the W edge of the Black Forest 53 km (33 miles) NNE of Basel. Pop. (1991) 191,029.

Manufactures textiles, chemicals, paper, furniture, electronics and wine. Also a cultural and tourist centre, with a famous 13th/16th-cent. Gothic cathedral and a university (1457).

Founded in the 12th cent. Under Austrian rule from 1368. Passed to Baden 1805.

Freising Germany. Town in Bavaria on the Isar R. 32 km (20 miles) NNE of Munich. Pop. (1986) 36,200.

Manufactures tractors, hosiery and gloves. It has the oldest brewery in the world.

Cathedral (12th-cent.); bishopric established here by St Korbinian in 724.

Freital Germany. Industrial town in Saxony 8 km (5 miles) SSW of Dresden. Pop. (1989) 413,558.

Manufactures glass, cameras and musical instruments. Processes uranium ore and there are coalmines nearby.

Fréjus France. Ancient Forum Julii. Town in the Var department near the Mediterranean 53 km (33 miles) SW of Nice. Pop. (1985) 51,700. The harbour built by the Romans is now completely silted up and Fréjus is nearly 3 km (2 miles) from the sea. It produces wine, olive oil and cork.

Roman remains inc. an amphitheatre, an aqueduct and the old town walls. Birthplace of Agricola (AD 40–93).

Fremantle Australia. Chief seaport of Western Australia at the mouth of the Swan R. 16 km (10 miles) SW of Perth. Pop. (1991) 23,834. It has a dredged harbour protected by moles and is the terminus of the Trans-Australian Railway.

Exports wheat, wool, timber and fruit. Manufactures fertilizers, ships, clothing, paints, furniture and leather products.

Founded in 1829, it is one of the oldest settlements in Australia.

Fremont (California) USA. City situated S of San Francisco in the San Francisco Bay area. Pop. (1990) 173,339.

Industries inc. micro-technology and data systems, diverse small industry and commerce.

Fremont (Ohio) USA. City situated SE of Toledo on Sandusky R. Pop. (1985) 18,000.

Commercial centre of an agricultural area, trading in cereals, sugar-beet and market-gardening produce. Industries inc. the manufacture of vehicle parts, clothing, cutlery, electrical goods, rubber goods and sugar-refining.

French Guiana. French overseas department on the NE coast of South America, bounded by Suriname to the W, Brazil to the E and S and the Atlantic to the N. Area 83,533 sq km (32,252 sq. miles). Pop. (1990) 114,700. Cap. and chief seaport Cayenne. Rises from the coast to the Tumuc-Humac Mountains in the extreme S. Largely forested. Well watered but little developed. It has a tropical climate with heavy rainfall.

Agriculture, forestry and fishing are the chief occupations and food-processing is being developed. Minerals have been little exploited and inc. iron, copper, silver, lead, mercury, platinum, diamonds and alluvial gold.

First colonized by the French in 1604. A notorious penal settlement was maintained on the Île du Diable (Devil's Island) 43 km (27 miles) NW of Cayenne, 1854–1938. French Guiana became an overseas department of France, with the territory of Inini as a dependency, in 1946.

French Polynesia S Pacific Ocean. Overseas Territory of France comprising 5 main archipelagoes and about 120 islands. Area 4000 sq km (1545 sq. miles). Pop. (1991) 199,031. Cap. Papeete on Tahiti in the Society Is., the most important group; the Marquesas, the Austral (Tubuai), Tuamotu and Gambier Is. are the other main groups. Most of the islands are mountainous. Some are of volcanic origin and coral-fringed, others are atolls.

An important product is copra (coconut trees cover the coastal plains of the mountainous island and the greater part of the low-lying islands). Fruit is grown for local consumption. Tourism is extremely important and earns 50 per cent of visible export earnings.

The Territory is administered by a Council of Ministers and there is a 41-member Territorial Assembly elected every 5 years.

French Shore Canada. Part of the S and E coasts of Newfoundland, in which France had fishing rights from Britain under the terms of various treaties from 1713 to 1904. By the Treaty of Versailles (1783) the limits were Cape St John (N) and Cape Ray (S). The arrangement caused constant friction; in 1904 France sold all her rights.

French Southern and Antarctic Territories Indian Ocean. French Overseas Territory formed in 1955, comprising the Crozel and Kerguelen archipelagoes, the islands of Amsterdam and St Paul and the Antarctic territory of Terre Adélie. Inhabited only by groups of meteorologists and research scientists. In 1992 the French Institute for Polar Research and Technology was established to organize scientific research and expeditions.

French Territory of the Afars and the Issas ➤DJIBOUTI.

Fresh Water Canal ➤ISMAILIA.

Fresnillo Mexico. Officially Fresnillo de González Echeverría. Town in the Zacatecas state on the central plateau at a height of 2250 m (7380 ft). Pop. (1989) 117,000.

Market town in a cereal-growing area. Also a mining centre producing mainly silver.

Fresno USA. Town in California 265 km (165 miles) SE of San Francisco. Pop. (1990) 354,202.

Produces olive oil, agricultural equipment, pottery, and is an important vine-growing area especially for raisins. The drying and packing of fruit is an important industry.

The name (Spanish for 'ash tree') was given by the railroad builders, because of the ash trees in the neighbouring foothills.

Fribourg (Ger. **Freiburg**) Switzerland. 1. Canton in the W lying NW of the Bernese Oberland. Area 1670 sq km (648 sq. miles). Pop. (1991) 207,751 (mainly French-speaking). Mountainous in the S.

Cattle reared; cereals and sugar-beet cultivated. Noted for cheese (esp. Gruyère).

2. Cap. of the Fribourg canton on the Sarine R. 27 km (17 miles) SW of Berne. Pop. (1988) 33,700.

Manufactures chocolate, beer, electrical equipment.

Principal buildings the cathedral of St Nicholas (13th/15th-cent.) and the university (1889). Founded (1157) by a duke of Zahringen. Belonged to the Habsburgs 1277–1452 and joined the Swiss Confederation in 1481.

Friedrichshafen Germany. Town in Baden-Württemberg on the N shore of L. Constance. Pop. (1985) 53,000.

Port, resort and industrial centre. Manufactures cars. Tanning. Formerly the site of the Zeppelin works and a centre of the aircraft and aerospace industry.

Friendly Islands ➤TONGA.

Friesland Netherlands. Ancient Frisia. Province in the N bounded by the Wadden Zee (N) and the Ijsselmeer (W). Area 3353 sq km (1295 sq. miles). Pop. (1990) 599,151. Cap. Leeuwarden, the only large town. Pastoral and agricultural, home of the Friesian breed of cattle.

Frimley and Camberley England. Residential district in W Surrey 10 km (6 miles) N of Aldershot. Pop. (1991) 46,120. Burial-place of the American author Bret Harte (1839–1902).

Frinton and Walton England. The seaside resorts of Frinton-on-Sea and Walton-on-the Naze 24 km (15 miles) ESE of Colchester in Essex. Pop. (1991) 15,043.

Frisia ➤FRIESLAND.

Frisian Islands. Chain of islands off the coasts of the Netherlands, Germany and Denmark, separated from the mainland by shallows 5–30 km (3–20 miles) wide, extending from the Wadden Zee to Jutland. They are low-lying and, despite sand dunes and artificial embankments, are constantly subject to marine erosion. Three groups: the W Frisian Is. belong to the Netherlands and consist of Texel, Vlieland, Terschelling, Ameland, Schiermonnikoog and 4 smaller islands; the E Frisian Is., belonging to Germany, inc. Borkum, Juist, Norderney, Baltrum, Langeoog, Spiekeroog and Wangeroog, all used as seaside resorts, and 4 uninhabited islands; of the separate N Frisian Is., Nordstrand, Pellworm, Amrum, Föhr and Sylt belong to Germany, and Römö, Koresand, Manö and Fanö to Denmark.

Friuli Italy/Slovenia. Ancient Forum Julii. Region between the Carnic Alps and the Gulf of Venice. A Lombard duchy in the 6th cent. and a possession of the Habsburgs after 1500. In 1866 the W part, in 1919 the whole area was inc. in Venezia Giulia (Italy); in 1947 E Friuli, excluding Gorizia, was ceded to Yugoslavia.

Friuli-Venezia Giulia Italy. Region in the

NE formed (1947) from W Friuli and part of E Friuli, retained by Italy after the cession of Istria to Yugoslavia; inc. the provinces of Udine, Gorizia and Trieste. Area 7846 sq km (3030 sq. miles). Pop. (1990) 1,201,027. Cap. Trieste.

Frobisher Bay Canada. Frobisher Bay is an inlet in the extreme SE coastline of Baffin Island, Northwest Territories. The bay is named after Sir Martin Frobisher, who discovered it in 1576. Believing the bay was a strait, it first appeared on maps as Frobisher Strait. The settlement of Iqaluit lies at the head of the bay.

Frome England. Market town in Somerset on the R. Frome 16 km (10 miles) S of Bath. Pop. (1989) 25,000.

Printing, light engineering. Manufactures woollen cloth.

Bishop Thomas Ken (1637–1711) is buried in the 14th-cent. parish church.

Frosinone Italy. Cap. (since 1926) of Frosinone province, in Latium 80 km (50 miles) ESE of Rome on a hill (291 m, 954 ft) in the Apennines. Pop. (1990) 47,826. Market town.

Frunze ➤BISHKEK.

Fthiotis ➤PHTHIOTIS.

Fuenterrabía Spain. Fishing port in Guipuzcoa province on the Bay of Biscay at the mouth of the Bidassoa R. Pop. (1991) 13,454.

Fish-canning, boatbuilding.

The picturesque old town has a ruined castle dating from the 12th cent. The new town has become a popular resort. As a frontier fortress it was often attacked; here Condé was defeated when he invaded Spain (1638).

Fuerteventura ➤CANARY ISLANDS.

Fujairah United Arab Emirates. Sheikdom and part of the federation of UAE bounded on the E by the Gulf of Oman. Area 1150 sq km (440 sq. miles). Pop. (1985) 54,425.

Oil has been produced since 1966, but agriculture is the chief occupation.

Fujian (Fukien) China. Maritime province in the SE on Taiwan Strait. Area 123,100 sq km (47,500 sq. miles). Pop. (1990) 30,048,224. Cap. Fuzhou. Generally mountainous and well wooded. Chief river the Min. Climate humid subtropical with rainfall 150–200 cm (60–80 ins.) annually.

Principal crops rice, tea; timber (pine, fir, camphor) important. Fishing is the chief occupation. Chief towns Fuzhou and Xiamen (Amoy), both seaports.

Fujisawa Japan. Town in Kanagawa prefecture in central Honshu 16 km (10 miles) SW of Yokohama on the N side of Sagami Bay. Pop. (1991) 354,679. An industrial and commercial centre which has expanded rapidly in recent years.

Fujiyama (Fuji, Fuji-san) Japan. Country's highest mountain (3776 m; 12,388 ft) in Shizuoka prefecture in central Honshu 109 km (68 miles) WSW of Tokyo. An isolated extinct volcano, famous for its almost perfect symmetry and its snow-capped summit, it is sacred to the Japanese. Last active 1707.

Fukien ➤FUJIAN.

Fukui Japan. Cap. of Fukui prefecture in central Honshu 126 km (78 miles) NNE of Kyoto. Pop. (1991) 253,470.

Important textile centre (rayon, silk); also manufactures paper, leather goods and food products.

Severely damaged by earthquake in 1948.

Fukuoka Japan. Cap. of Fukuoka prefecture in NW Kyushu. Pop. (inc. port Hakata, 1991) 1,249,320.

Seaport and industrial centre. Exports machinery and porcelain. Shipbuilding. Manufactures chemicals, textiles, metal goods, paper and pottery.

The western terminus of the 'bullet train' from Tokyo.

Fukushima Japan. Cap. of Fukushima prefecture in N Honshu 240 km (150 miles) NNE of Tokyo. Pop. (1991) 279,127.

Important silk-manufacturing centre.

Fukuyama Japan. Industrial town in the

Hiroshima prefecture in SW Honshu 80 km (50 miles) E of Hiroshima. Pop. (1991) 367,322.

Manufactures textiles.

Fulda Germany. Town in Hessen on the Fulda R. 88 km (55 miles) S of Kassel. Pop. (1985) 57,000.

Manufactures textiles, carpets, clothing, tyres and ball-bearings. Trade in agricultural produce.

Grew round a Benedictine abbey founded (744) by St Boniface, who is buried in the cathedral.

Fulda River Germany. River 153 km (95 miles) long, rising in the Rhön and flowing N to join the Werra R., forming the Weser R.

Fulham England. Part of the London borough of Hammersmith. On the N bank of the R. Thames, here crossed by Putney Bridge. Fulham Palace, built from 1506 onwards, is the residence of the Bishop of London.

Fullerton USA. Town in S California 35 km (22 miles) SE of Los Angeles. Pop. (1990) 114,144.

Fruit packing, canning and processing (esp. citrus fruits). Also a centre of petroleum production.

Funabashi Japan. Town in Chiba prefecture in central Honshu 16 km (10 miles) E of Tokyo on the N side of Tokyo Bay. Pop. (1991) 535,572.

Industries inc. fish hatcheries, woodworking, flour-milling and the manufacture of fountain pens.

Funafuti ►TUVALU.

Funchal Madeira. 1. District of Portugal comprising the Madeira archipelago.

2. Cap. of Funchal district on the SE coast of Madeira island. Pop. (1985) 46,000.

Chief seaport and commercial centre. Exports Madeira wines. The mild winter and scenic beauty have made it a popular resort.

Funday, Bay of Canada. An elongated inlet of the N Atlantic between New Brunswick and Nova Scotia 233 km (145 miles) long and 96 km (60 miles) wide at the mouth, narrowing at the head and dividing into Chignecto bay and the Minas Basin. Chief harbour St John. Remarkable for the great rise and fall of the tides (up to 21 m; 69 ft).

Fünen ►FYN.

Furka Pass Switzerland. Alpine pass on the boundary between Valais and Uri cantons through which runs the Furka Road between Andermatt and Gletsch; one of the highest in Europe (2433 m; 7971 ft). Under it is a railway tunnel 1.6 km (1 mile) long.

Furneaux Islands Australia. Group in the Bass Strait off the NE coast of Tasmania, the main islands being Flinders (largest), Cape Barren and Clarke islands. Main occupations sheep-rearing and dairy-farming. Named after their discoverer, Tobias Furneaux (1735–81), commander of one of Capt. Cook's vessels on his second voyage.

Fürstenwalde Germany. Town in the Frankfurt-an-der-Oder district 32 km (20 miles) W of Frankfurt-an-der Oder on the Spree R. Pop. (1989) 35,658.

Manufactures tyres, electrical equipment and footwear.

Seat of the bishops of Lebus from the late 14th to the late 16th cent.

Fürth Germany. Industrial town in Bavaria just NW of Nuremberg, to which it is connected by Germany's first railway (opened 1835). Pop. (1991) 103,362.

Manufactures mirrors, toys, radio and television apparatus, textiles and chemicals.

Founded in the 8th cent. Became prosperous largely because of its tolerance (until the Nazi regime) to the Jews, who found refuge here from persecution in Nuremberg.

Fushun ►FUXIN.

Futa Jallon ►FOUTA DJALLON.

Futuna ►WALLIS AND FUTUNA ISLANDS.

Fuxin (Fushun) China. Industrial town and major coalmining centre in Liaoning province (Manchuria) 40 km (25 miles) ENE of Shenyang. Pop. (1991) 1,202,388.

Manufactures cement and mining equipment. Coalmining began on a large scale in 1902 and the old town stands near a vast opencast mine. Oil-shale mining was developed by the Japanese in about 1930.

Fuzhou (Fuchou/Foochow) China. Formerly Minhow. Cap. of Fujian province and port on the Minkiang 56 km (35 miles) from its mouth. Pop. (1990) 847,809.

An important port exporting timber, bamboo shoots and sugar-cane. Manufactures machinery, chemicals, textiles and paper.

It was made one of the original five treaty ports in 1842 and was linked by two bridges with the foreign settlement on Nantai island. Became important in the tea trade; declined with decreasing tea and lacquerware exports and river silting.

Fylde England. Flat region in Lancashire between the estuaries of the Wyre and the Ribble rivers.

Industries inc. tourism and dairy and poultry farming. Chief towns Blackpool, Fleetwood, Lytham St Anne's.

Fyn (Ger. **Fünen**) Denmark. The second largest island, bounded on the E by the Great Belt and separated from the mainland (W) by the Little Belt. Area 2976 sq km (1148 sq. miles). Pop. (1985) 434,000. Mainly flat and fertile. Dairy-farming; cereals and sugar-beet cultivated. Chief towns Odense, Svendborg, Nyborg. Linked by bridge at Middelfart to the mainland and by train ferry to Zealand (Nyborg-Korsör).

Fyne, Loch Scotland. Sea loch on Argyll and Bute coast 64 km (40 miles) long and 1.5–6 km (1–4 miles) wide, extending N and NE from the Sound of Bute. Inveraray is near the N end. Herring and other fishing.

G

Gabès Tunisia. Seaport on the Gulf of Gabès 320 km (200 miles) S of Tunis. Pop. (1989) 92,500.

It exports large quantities of dates. Fishing. Terminus of the railway from Tunis via Sousse and Sfax. The oasis of Gabès is famous for its orchards (pomegranates and apricots) as well as its date palms.

Gabès, Gulf of Tunisia. Ancient Syrtis Minor. An inlet of the Mediterranean Sea. Fisheries. On the coast are the towns of Sfax and Gabès (linked by coastal railway).

Gabon. Republic of equatorial Africa bounded on the W by the Atlantic Ocean, N by Equatorial Guinea and by Cameroon and on the E and S by Republic of Congo. Area 267,667 sq km (103,374 sq. miles). Pop. (1993) 1,280,000 (46 per cent urban). Life expectancy, 52 years male, 55 female. Cap. Libreville. Other major cities Port-Gentil and Franceville. Currency: CFA franc = 100 centimes. Apart from a narrow coastal strip, low plateaux cover the majority of the country at 1000–1200 m (3280–3936 ft). It is largely tropical rainforest. The climate is equatorial with high temperatures and considerable rainfall. Land use: forested 78 per cent, meadows and pastures 18 per cent, agricultural and under permanent cultivation 2 per cent. The official lang. is French with several spoken dialects inc. Fang, Myene and Bateke. About 71 per cent of the pop. is Roman Catholic and 28 per cent animist; there are about 10,000 Muslims.

The majority are subsistence farmers producing cassava, plantains, bananas and maize. Sugar-cane, palm oil, cocoa and coffee are also grown. Equatorial forests cover 85 per cent of the land area and the timber industry is important. Eighty per cent of exports are from crude petroleum or petroleum prod-ucts. There are two refineries: at Port-Gentil and Pointe Clairette. Minerals exploited inc. manganese, uranium, iron ore, gold, zinc and phosphates. Most manufacturing is based on the processing of food, particularly sugar, timber and mineral resources.

The estuary of the Gabon R. was discovered in 1485 by the Portuguese. The French established a settlement in 1839 and it was known (with Middle Congo) as the French Congo 1888–1908. It became a French colony in 1908, an overseas territory of the French Union in 1946 and achieved independence in 1960. An attempted change of government by *coup d'état* (1964) was prevented by the intervention of French forces. Since independence Gabon has followed pro-Western policies and a multi-party system was established in 1990.

There is a 120-member unicameral National Assembly and there is a directly elected Executive President for 5-year terms and he appoints the Council of Ministers. The country is divided into nine provinces each administered by a governor appointed by the President.

Gaborone Botswana. Cap. in the SE situated WNW of Pretoria (South Africa). Pop. (1991) 133,468. A small village until chosen as the cap. of the new republic, building having commenced in Feb. 1964.

The main occupation is government service. Industries inc. diamonds, textiles, breweries, soap, printing, publishing and construction.

Gabrovo Bulgaria. Industrial town 96 km (60 miles) NNE of Plovdiv on the N slope of the Balkan Mountains. Pop. (1990) 80,694.

Industries inc. textiles, footwear, sawmilling, leather goods and knitwear. Linked with towns to the S by the Shipka Pass.

Gadag-Badigri India. Town in Karnataka 56 km (35 miles) E of Hubli. Pop. (1991) 134,051. Railway junction.

Trade in textiles and grain. Manufactures cotton and leather goods.

Gadsden USA. Industrial town in Alabama on the Coosa R. 93 km (58 miles) NE of Birmingham in a district important for coal and iron. Pop. (1990) 49,000.

Manufactures tyres, textiles, iron and steel goods.

Founded 1840.

Gaeta Italy. Port on a promontory on the Bay of Gaeta in Latina province, Latium 69 km (43 miles) NW of Naples. Pop. (1981) 22,605. Also a resort.

Fishing. Manufactures glass.

The adjoining coast was much admired by the ancient Romans. Scene of the final defeat of Francis II of Naples by Italian troops (1860–1).

Gafsa Tunisia. Ancient Capsa. The largest town in the phosphate-mining area; on the Sfax–Tozeur railway 185 km (115 miles) WSW of Sfax. Pop. (1989) 61,000.

Oasis, producing dates, olives and other fruits.

Famous for hot springs (important in Roman times) and for nearby prehistoric discoveries.

Gainesville USA. Town in Florida 100 km (62 miles) SW of Jacksonville. Pop. (1990) 84,770.

Industries inc. meat-packing and pharmaceuticals. Manufactures electronic equipment and wood products. Trade in market-garden produce.

Gainsborough England. Market town in Lincolnshire on the R. Trent 24 km (15 miles) NW of Lincoln. Pop. (1991) 19,704.

Flour-milling. Manufactures wood products, machinery and clothing.

Founded in the 11th cent. by the Danish king Sweyn I, who died here. Buildings inc. the timbered Old Hall, which was rebuilt in the 15th cent. and an 18th-cent. parish church. Identified with St Ogg's in George Eliot's *The Mill on the Floss*.

Gairdner, Lake Australia. Shallow salt lake N of the Eyre Peninsula, South Australia 160 km (100 miles) long and 48 km (30 miles) wide. Sometimes dry in summer.

Gairloch Scotland. Sea loch in Highland about 8 km (5 miles) long and 5 km (3 miles) wide at its entrance. On its shore stands the fishing village and resort of Gairloch.

Gaithersburg USA. City situated in Maryland N of Washington DC. Pop. (1990) 39,542.

Manufactures electrical and electronic machinery and systems, and photographic supplies.

Galápagos Islands (Colón Archipelago) Ecuador. Group of Pacific islands on the equator 960 km (600 miles) W of Ecuador. There are 13 large islands and many small ones, with extinct volcanic cones. Area 7812 sq km (3016 sq. miles). Pop. (1994) 12,000. The largest, Isabela (Albemarle) (120 km (75 miles) long) and San Cristóbal (Chatham), have most of the pop. The coastal fringes usually have little vegetation, but there is forest at higher levels. Most of the reptiles and half the plants are peculiar to the islands, which have now been made a nature sanctuary. They were originally called Enchanted Islands when discovered accidentally by a Bishop of Panama. The name derives from the Spanish *galápago* (tortoise), after the monster tortoises which were once numerous but are now dying out. They became famous when the English naturalist Charles Darwin (1809–82) visited the Galápagos in 1835 and there gathered valuable evidence to support his theory of the evolution of species.

Galashiels Scotland. Town in Scottish Borders on the Gala Water near its confluence with the R. Tweed. Pop. (1991) 13,753.

Important manufacture of tweeds and knitwear. Technical college associated with the woollen industry.

Galați Romania. Cap. of Galați district and river port in Moldavia on the R. Danube

337

145 km (90 miles) WNW of the mouth at Sulina. Pop. (1992) 325,788.

Exports grain and timber. Shipbuilding. Manufactures textiles, chemicals, hardware and food products. Naval base.

Galatia. Ancient region in Asia Minor around the modern Ankara, so named because Gauls invaded and dominated it (278 BC). They were defeated, however, and their territory was much reduced by Attalus I of Pergamum (c. 230 BC). Became a Roman province 25 BC.

Galesburg USA. Industrial town in Illinois 69 km (43 miles) WNW of Peoria. Pop. (1989) 36,000.

Manufactures agricultural implements, washing-machines and hardware. Railway engineering. Coalmines in the neighbourhood.

Named after the Rev. George Washington Gale, a Presbyterian minister who founded both the town and Knox College in 1836.

Galicia Poland/Ukraine. Region in SE Poland and NW Ukraine extending N from the Carpathians and drained by the Vistula and Dniester and other rivers. The Polish (W) part inc. the towns of Cracow, Tarnow, Rzeszow, Przemyśl and Nowy Sacz, and the Ukrainian part (E) Lvov, Stanislav, Drogobych and Kolomyya. Considerable mineral wealth, particularly oil and natural gas. A Russian principality in the 12th cent. Passed to Poland in the 14th cent. and, with the 1st Partition (1772), to Austria. In 1815 Cracow became an independent republic but, after the unsuccessful Polish rising, it was incorporated in Galicia (1846). Some measure of autonomy was now granted to Galicia, but Polish and Ukrainian (Ruthenian) nationalism continued to grow. In 1919 W Galicia was assigned to Poland and in 1923 E Galicia was also recognized as Polish. After World War II the E part was ceded to the USSR and incorporated in the Ukraine.

Galicia Spain. Autonomous community and former kingdom in the NW, bounded by the Bay of Biscay (N), the Atlantic Ocean (W) and Portugal (S), now comprising the provinces of Corunna, Lugo, Orense and Pontevedra. Area 29,434 sq km (11,364 sq. miles). Pop. (1991) 2,731,669. An area of mountains, plateaux and deep valleys, highest in the E where the land rises to over 1800 m (5904 ft). Rocky coastline with many deep inlets (rías). Chief river is the Miño, forming part of the boundary with Portugal. Cattle and pigs raised. Maize, potatoes grown. Important sardine-fishing. Chief towns Vigo, Corunna, Santiago de Compostela.

Galilee Israel. Region in the N bounded by Lebanon (N), Syria and Jordan (E) and the Plain of Esdraelon (S). Divided into Upper Galilee (N), which is hilly and rises to nearly 1200 m (3936 ft) and Lower Galilee (S), lower and more fertile. Chief towns Tiberias (on the W shore of the Sea of Galilee), Nazareth.

Galilee, Sea of (Lake Tiberias) Israel. Lake 21 km (13 miles) long and up to 11 km (7 miles) wide in the NE on the border with Syria; its surface 212 m (695 ft) below sea level, it occupies part of the Great Rift Valley. The Jordan R. flows through it. In the Old Testament it is also called the Sea of Chinnereth and in the New Testament the Lake of Gennesaret.

Gallarate Italy. Town in Varese province, Lombardy 40 km (25 miles) WNW of Milan. Pop. (1981) 46,915.

Manufactures textiles.

Has a 12th/13th-cent. church.

Galle Sri Lanka. Formerly Point de Galle. Seaport and commercial town on the SW coast 105 km (65 miles) SSE of Colombo. Pop. (1989) 77,000.

Exports coconut oil and coir rope.

Became the island's chief port in the 16th and 17th cent.; declined with the improvement of Colombo harbour in the late 19th cent.

Gallipoli (Turkish **Gelibolu**) Turkey. 1. Peninsula extending 88 km (55 miles) SW between the Dardanelles (S) and the Gulf of Saros (N). Scene of unsuccessful landings by British, Australian and New Zealand troops in an attempt to take the Dardanelles in World War I (1915).

2. Port in Canakkale province on the Dardanelles at the entrance to the Sea of Marmara.

Trade in grain and livestock. Fishing.

The first place in Europe to be conquered by the Turks (c. 1356).

Gällivare Sweden. Town in Norrbotten county 80 km (50 miles) SSE of Kiruna. Pop. (1990) 22,400.

Iron-mining centre linked to Luleå on the Gulf of Bothnia and Narvik (Norway) by railway, the ore being transported thereby for export. Modern working of these rich deposits began in 1893.

Galt now Cambridge, Ontario, Canada.

Galveston USA. Seaport and industrial town in Texas on Galveston Island at the entrance to Galveston Bay, an arm of the Gulf of Mexico, connected to the mainland by two causeways. Pop. (1990) 59,070.

Shipyards and dry docks. Handles large exports of sulphur, cotton and wheat. Flour and rice milling, meat-packing and brewing. Manufactures chemicals, metal goods and hardware. Popular resort ('the Oleander City').

A hurricane destroyed it in 1900, with the loss of about 5000 lives; special precautionary measures were taken when it was rebuilt, inc. the building of a high sea wall.

Galway Ireland. 1. County in Connacht in the W, bounded on the W by the Atlantic Ocean, with Galway Bay to the S. Area 5939 sq km (2293 sq. miles). Pop. (1991) 180,364. Coast deeply indented, with many islands, inc. the Aran Is. The W part is mountainous, with the Twelve Pins (730 m; 2394 ft) and the Maamturk Mountains (704 m; 2309 ft); here is the wild but beautiful Connemara, a region of moors, bogs and lakes. To the E of the large Lough Corrib the land is low-lying and in part fertile, the Suck and the Shannon flowing along the E border. Potatoes grown; sheep raised. Chief towns Galway, Ballinasloe and Tuam.

2. County town of Co. Galway at the mouth of the short R. Corrib, which drains Lough Corrib, on the N shore of Galway Bay. Pop. (1991) 50,853.

Seaport and fishing centre, well-known for its salmon. Manufactures fishing nets, rope and furniture. Flour-milling.

Several old houses ('mansions'); 14th-cent. church; University College (1849), part of the National University of Ireland and a centre of Gaelic studies.

Gambia, The. Republic forming an enclave within Senegal, West Africa, extending along both banks 320 km (200 miles) inland from the estuary of the Gambia R. and never wider than 10 km (6 miles). Bounded by the Atlantic Ocean in the W and on all other sides by Senegal. Area 10,689 sq km (4127 sq. miles). Pop. (1993) 1,033,000 (22 per cent urban). Life expectancy, 43 years male, 47 female. Cap. Banjul. Other cities Serekunda, Brikama, Bakau and Farafenni. Currency: Dalasi = 100 butut. Narrow, low-lying country and does not rise over 43 m (141 ft); mainly savannah. It has a tropical climate with a rainy season June–September. Land use: forested 15 per cent, meadows and pastures 9 per cent, agricultural and under permanent cultivation 18 per cent. English is the official lang. and local langs. such as Madinka, Wolof and Fula are spoken. About 95 per cent of the pop. is Muslim (Sunni) and Arabic is taught in Koranic schools, 4 per cent Christian and 1 per cent traditional beliefs. Ethnic groups inc. Malinke (40 per cent), Fulani (19), Wolof (15), Dyola (10) and Soninke (8).

Tourism is the main foreign currency earner with over 100,000 visitors a year. Nearly 70 per cent of the labour force is engaged in agriculture based on the cultivation of groundnuts which are the most important cash crop.

The Gambia was discovered by the Portuguese in the late 15th cent. Britain became interested in the region in the 17th cent. and it became a British colony 1843; then part of the British West African settlements 1866. It regained its status as a separate colony 1888 and achieved independence in 1965, becoming a republic in 1970. The Gambia together with Senegal formed the Confederation of Senegambia in 1982, but it was officially dissolved in 1989. The unicameral 50-member House of Representatives inc. 5 indirectly elected chiefs and 9 nominated members. The Gambia is divided into 35 districts each traditionally under a Chief.

Gambia River. River 1126 km (700 miles) long, rising in the Fouta Djallon plateau (in Guinea), flowing generally NW and W through Senegal and Gambia and entering the Atlantic Ocean. Navigable to ocean-going vessels for nearly 320 km (200 miles).

Gambier Islands (French Polynesia) S Pacific Ocean. Group of 4 coral islands and several uninhabited islets inside a barrier reef about 64 km (40 miles) long SE of the Tuamotu Is. Total area 31 sq km (12 sq. miles). Pop. (1988) 582. Largest island Mangareva; chief settlement Rikitea.

Produces copra, coffee and mother-of-pearl.

Gander Canada. Town and airport in E Newfoundland just N of Gander L. Pop. (1990) 12,000.

Industries inc. service and communications. Chosen as a transatlantic air base by the British Air Ministry 1935. Flights began in 1939; during World War II it became a leading Allied base and later it became a major N American terminal for flights to Europe.

Ganges Canals India. Irrigation system in Uttar Pradesh comprising the Upper and Lower Ganges Canals. The Upper Ganges Canal (1855–6) leaves the Ganges at Hardwar and divides, one branch continuing to Kanpur and the other to the Jumna; the Lower Ganges Canal (1879–80) leaves the Ganges near Dibai and splits into a number of branches.

Ganges (Ganga) River. Great river of India and Bangladesh 2505 km (1557 miles) long, formed in the Himalayas from the union of the Bhagirathi R., which issues from an ice cave and Aaknanda R. As the Ganges it flows generally SW past Hardwar,

then turns SE past Farrukhabad and Kanpur to Allahabad, where it receives the Jumna. Continues E across the plain, past Varanasi (Benares) and Patna, being joined by the Gogra and Gandak, turns S and SE and begins to divide, about 350 km (220 miles) from the Bay of Bengal, into the many distributaries which cross its great delta. Its main stream, the Padma, enters Bangladesh, is joined by the Jamuna, the main stream of the Brahmaputra and as the Meghna enters the Bay of Bengal on the E side of the delta; on the W side is the Hooghly R., the main channel of navigation. The Ganges, the most sacred of Hindu rivers, is much used for irrigation.

Gangtok India. Cap. and largest town in Sikkim 48 km (30 miles) NE of Darjeeling. Pop. (1991) 25,024.

Commercial trading centre for rice, maize and fruit. Industries inc. brewing and watch-making. Linked by road with Siliguri (India).

Gansu (Kansu) China. Province in the NW between Xizang (Tibet) and Nei Monggol (Inner Mongolia). Area 366,500 sq km (141,500 sq. miles). Pop. (1992) 22,850,000. Cap. Lanzhou. Largely rugged mountain and plateau, containing part of the Nan Shan; also suffers from precarious rainfall. Where irrigation is possible, cereals, opium and melons are grown. Crossed by important caravan routes to Xinjiang Uygur, Nei Monggol and Xizang.

Ganzo Azul ➤PUCALLPA.

Gao Mali. Cap. of region situated NW of Niamey (Niger) on the Niger R. and trans-Saharan road. Pop. (1984) 43,000.

Trading centre for butter, hides, wool and livestock in a farming area. River and airport.

Gap France. Cap. of Hautes-Alpes department on the Luye R. Pop. (1990) 35,647.

Tourist centre. Industries inc. textiles, leather goods and flour-milling.

Gard France. Department in Languedoc-Roussillon Region bordering on the lower Rhône R. and delta (E) and on the Gulf of Lions (S). Area 5853 sq km (2260 sq. miles). Pop. (1992) 598,700. Prefecture Nîmes. Flat in the S with many lagoons and marshes, rising to over 1500 m (4920 ft) in the NW.

Produces olives, mulberries (for silkworms), fruit and wine. Some coal mined. Industries (mainly metallurgy, textiles and paper) concentrated chiefly in Alès and Nîmes.

Near Remoulins the Gard R. is crossed by the Pont du Gard aqueduct, constructed in 19 BC to carry water from springs near Uzès to Nîmes, which has some of the most famous Roman remains in France.

Garda, Lake (Italian **Lago di Garda**) Italy. Ancient Lacus Benacus. The largest lake in Italy (370 sq km; 143 sq. miles), its S end 105 km (65 miles) E of Milan. Fed by the Sarca R. in the N and drained by the Mincio R. in the SE. Well-stocked with fish. Vines, olives, citrus fruits grown around its W and S shores. Sirmione on the S shore was a favourite residence of the Roman poet Catullus and many lakeside villages, linked by ferry services, have long been holiday resorts.

Garden Grove USA. City immediately NW of Santa Ana in South Carolina. Pop. (1990) 143,050.

Residential, commercial and retailing centre.

Garden of the Gods USA. A region of strangely eroded red sandstone just NW of Colorado Springs, Colorado. The rocks resemble animals, gargoyles. Popular tourist attraction. Named by R. E. Cable, a Kansas City lawyer who visited the site in 1859.

Gardéz Afghanistan. Commercial town 88 km (55 miles) S of Kabul on the road to Kandahar at a height of 2250 m (7380 ft) on the central plateau. Pop. (1984) 10,469.

Gardner Island ➤NIKUMARORO.

Garfield USA. Industrial town in New Jersey on the Passaic R. 16 km (10 miles) NNE of Newark. Pop. (1989) 26,000.

Manufactures textiles, chemical and rubber products.

Garfield Heights USA. City immediately SW of Cleveland, Ohio. Pop. (1980) 34,938.

Garibaldi Park Canada. Provincial park in the Coast Mountains of SW British Columbia NE of Vancouver. Area 2520 sq km (973 sq. miles).

Well-known scenic area with mountain lakes, peaks and glaciers. Tourist area with facilities for camping and boating.

Garland USA. City forming a suburb of Dallas, Texas NE of the city centre. Pop. (1990) 180,850.

Industries inc. the manufacture of aircraft, seismic instruments and vehicles.

Garmisch-Partenkirchen Germany. Resort and winter-sports centre in Upper Bavaria 84 km (52 miles) SW of Munich at a height of 690 km (2263 ft). Pop. (1989) 28,000. Rack-and-pinion railway to the Zugspitze. Woodworking.

Garmo, Mount Tajikistan. Formerly Pik Kommunizma and Stalin Peak. Mountain at 7495 m (24,590 ft) in the Akademiya Nauk Range of the Pamirs.

Garonne River France. Ancient Garumna. River 579 km (360 miles) long in the SW, rising in the Val d'Aran in the central Pyrenees, about 48 km (30 miles) of the upper course being in Spain and flowing NE and NW through the Haute-Garonne, Tarn-et-Garonne, Lot-et-Garonne and Gironde departments. About 32 km (20 miles) below Bordeaux it is joined by the Dordogne R. and forms the Gironde estuary, entering the Atlantic at the Pointe de Grave. With its tributaries, the Ariège, Tarn and Lot it drains the Aquitaine basin and at Toulouse it is linked by the Canal du Midi with the Mediterranean. Wheat and maize extensively cultivated in its basin. The lower basin is noted for its wines.

Garoua Cameroon. Cap. of North province situated NNW of Yaoundé on the Benoué R. Pop. (1987) 142,000.

River port and market handling peanuts and cotton.

Gartok China. Main commercial centre in

W Xizang (Tibet) at the W end of the Kailas Range at a height of 4500 m (14,760 ft).

Trade in wool, barley and salt.

Garut Indonesia. Town in W Java 40 km (25 miles) SE of Bandung at a height of 690 m (2263 ft). Pop. (1985) 56,000.

Commercial centre and resort in an agricultural region (tea, rubber and cinchona) amid fine scenery (mountains, lakes and hot springs).

Gary USA. Major industrial city in NW Indiana at the S end of L. Michigan. Pop. (1990) 116,646.

One of the world's leading steel-producing centres. Also manufactures tin-plate, cement and chemicals.

Named after Elbert H. Gary (1846–1927), first chairman of the US Steel Corporation.

Garzan River Turkey. Rises in the Bitlis Mountains 19 km (12 miles) SE of Mus and flows 104 km (65 miles) S past Besiri to join Tigris R. SW of Siirt.

Gascony France. Former province in the SW bounded by the Pyrenees (S) and the Bay of Biscay (W) in the Aquitaine basin, now comprising the departments of Gers, Hautes-Pyrénées and Landes and parts of Haute-Garonne, Lot-et-Garonne and Tarn-et-Garonne. The name is derived from the Vascones (Basques), a Spanish tribe which crossed the Pyrenees and conquered it in the 6th cent., later setting up the duchy of Vasconia (Gascony). In English hands 1154–1453, with Auch as cap. Divided into the present departments 1790.

Gaspé Canada. Peninsula in E Quebec between the St Lawrence R. (N) and Chaleur Bay (S). Area 28,490 sq km (11,000 sq. miles). The interior is mountainous and wooded, with many streams and lakes. The Shickshock Mountains rise to 1269 m (4162 ft) in Mt Jacques Cartier. Chief occupations cod-fishing, lumbering, pulp-milling. The people (largely French Canadians) live mainly in coastal villages and in the town of Gaspé on E end of the Peninsula. Pop. (1989) 17,500. A provincial park (133,230 ha; 329,080 acres) was established 1937.

Gastein (Bad Gastein) Austria. Picturesque valley in Salzburg province near the E end of the Hohe Tauern at a height of about 900 m (2952 ft). Famous for its thermal springs. Principal resorts Bad-Gastein (pop. 5200) and Hof-Gastein (pop. 5500).

Gastonia USA. Town in North Carolina 31 km (19 miles) W of Charlotte. Pop. (1990) 54,732.

Important textile centre, esp. for the manufacture of cotton goods. Also manufactures plastics and non-electrical machinery.

Gateshead England. Town and unitary authority on the S bank of the R. Tyne opposite Newcastle-upon-Tyne, with which linked by tunnel and 5 bridges. Pop. (1991) 83,159.

Engineering, shipbuilding and flour-milling. Manufactures chemicals, pharmaceutical products, glass, rubber and electrical products. Many light industries were established in the 1930s in the Team Valley trading estate to relieve unemployment.

Probably founded in Saxon times. Largely destroyed by fire 1854; the 13th-cent. parish church was rebuilt.

Gatineau River Canada. River 370 km (230 miles) long, rising near Parent (Quebec) and flowing generally SSW to join the Ottawa R. just below Ottawa. Important timber highway and source of hydroelectric power. Named after Nicholas Gatineau, a 17th-cent. fur-trader.

Gatooma ➤KADOMA.

Gatwick England. Village in West Sussex 10 km (6 miles) SSE of Reigate on the London–Brighton road and railway. Site of London's second airport.

Gauhati ➤GUWAHATI.

Gaul. Ancient Gallia. Ancient country of W Europe inhabited by the Gauls and roughly corresponding to modern France. It consisted of Cisalpine Gaul (Gallia Cisalpina), the region of N Italy between the Alps and the Apennines, divided by the Po R. into Cispadane Gaul (Gallia Cispadana) and Transpadane Gaul (Gallia Transpadana); and the larger and more important Transalpine

Gaul (Gallia Transalpina), extending from the Pyrenees as far N and E as the Rhine and the Alps. Its SE part had become a Roman province before 100 BC; Julius Caesar conquered the whole of Transalpine Gaul (58–51 BC). It was divided into 5 administrative areas: Narbonensis, Aquitania, Lugdunensis, Belgica (roughly modern Belgium) and a fifth region comprising two military districts along the Rhine.

Gauteng South Africa. Province created in 1994. Area 18,810 sq km (7263 sq. miles). Pop. (1995) 7,048,300. Cap. Johannesburg.

Gävle Sweden. Formerly Gefle. Cap. of Gävleborg county, seaport on the Gulf of Bothnia at the mouth of the Gävle R. 160 km (100 miles) NNW of Stockholm. Pop. (1992) 89,194.

Exports iron, timber, wood-pulp and paper. Shipbuilding and fish-canning. Manufactures wood-pulp, paper, chemicals, beer and textiles. Ice-free for 9 months of the year.

Gaya India. Town in Bihar 93 km (58 miles) S of Patna. Pop. (1991) 291,700.

Trade in rice, oilseeds, sugar-cane and dairy products.

Important place of Hindu pilgrimage. Buddh Gaya 10 km (6 miles) S is sacred to Buddhists.

Gaza. Ancient city of the Philistines in SW Palestine; biblical history tells how Samson pulled down its temple. Taken by Alexander the Great (332 BC) and later by Maccabees and Romans. Scene of three battles in World War I. The modern town of Gaza 69 km (43 miles) SSW of Tel Aviv (Israel), was occupied by Egypt, along with the Gaza coastal strip, from 1949 until the Israeli–Arab war of June 1967. Israeli troops finally left Gaza strip in May 1993.

Gaziantep Turkey. Cap. of Gaziantep province 177 km (110 miles) E of Adana. Pop. (1990) 603,434.

Important market town. Manufactures textiles and food products. Trade in grain and other agricultural produce.

Strategically important throughout history. Besieged by the French and taken during their conquest of Syria (1921); returned to Turkey 1922.

Gazimağusa ➤FAMAGUSTA.

Gdańsk Poland. Formerly Danzig. Baltic seaport and cap. of the Gdańsk voivodeship near the mouth of the Vistula R. on Gdańsk Bay. Pop. (1992) 466,500.

Exports coal, timber and grain. Industries inc. shipbuilding, food-processing and distilling. Manufactures machinery, wood-pulp and paper. Its outport for ocean-going vessels is Nowy Port 6 km (4 miles) NNW.

At first a Slavonic settlement, it joined the Hanseatic League in the 13th cent. and became an important Baltic port. Remained a free city under Polish sovereignty from 1455 to 1793, when at the 2nd Partition of Poland it passed to Prussia. A free city again 1807–14, it was returned to Prussia and made cap. of the province of West Prussia. After World War I it was made cap. of the territory of the Free City of Danzig under the League of Nations, but in 1939 it was annexed by Germany – an action which was soon followed by the invasion of Poland and the outbreak of World War II. In 1945 it was returned to Poland and with Gdynia and Szczecin handles the majority of the country's seaborne trade. In 1980 it was the birthplace of Solidarity, the independent trade union. Birthplace of German physicist, Gabriel Daniel Fahrenheit (1686–1736) and German philosopher, Artur Schopenhauer (1788–1860).

Gdynia Poland. Seaport in the Gdańsk voivodeship on Gdańsk Bay 19 km (12 miles) NNW of Gdańsk. Pop. (1992) 251,800.

Exports coal and timber. Founded in 1224 and deliberately developed from a small fishing village in 1924 as a purely Polish port to replace Danzig (Gdańsk); within ten years became a major Baltic seaport, handling more of Poland's trade than Danzig. Now shares the majority of Poland's overseas trade with Gdańsk and Szczecin.

Geelong Australia. Port in Victoria on the

flat W shore of Corio Bay, an arm of Port Phillip Bay, 68 km (42 miles) SW of Melbourne. Pop. (1991) 145,323.

Exports wool, wheat and meat. Also railway junction and industrial centre. Manufactures tweeds and other woollen goods, cars, vehicles and agricultural machinery. Oil refinery and cement and chemical works nearby. The first woollen mill in Victoria was established here. Tourism is important.

Founded in 1837 and grew rapidly after the gold rush of 1851.

Geislingen (Geislingen an der Steige) Germany. Town in Baden-Württemberg in the Swabian Jura 51 km (32 miles) ESE of Stuttgart. Pop. (1970) 27,200.

Manufactures metal goods (inc. silverware) and glassware.

Gela Italy. Formerly Terranova di Sicilia. Town and port in Caltanissetta province, Sicily on the S coast. Pop. (1981) 75,000. Founded as a Greek colony *c.* 690 BC; enjoyed its greatest prosperity under Hippocrates at the beginning of the 5th cent. BC. Deserted *c.* 281 BC. Refounded by Frederick II (1233) as Terranova di Sicilia. Scene of one of the first Allied landings in the invasion of Sicily in World War II (1943).

Gelderland Netherlands. Province between Ijsselmeer (NW) and Germany (E and SE). Area 5011 sq km (1935 sq. miles). Pop. (1992) 1,828,800. Cap. Arnhem. Drained by the Ijssel, Waal and Lower Rhine rivers; the fertile region of Betuwe in the SW and the infertile heathland of Veluwe in the N. Main crops wheat, rye, buckwheat and tobacco. Chief towns Arnhem, Nijmegen and Apeldoorn. Formerly duchy. The E part (inc. the town of Geldern, from which the name derives) was ceded to Prussia 1715.

Geleen Netherlands. Industrial town in Limburg province 16 km (10 miles) NE of Maastricht. Pop. (1992) 33,922.

Manufactures chemicals, fertilizers and textiles.

Gelibolu ➤GALLIPOLI.

Gelsenkirchen Germany. Industrial town in North Rhine-Westphalia just NE of Essen. Pop. (1992) 293,839.

Leading coalmining centre of the Ruhr coalfield. Blast furnaces, foundries and steel mills. Manufactures machinery, stoves, chemicals and glass.

Gembloux Belgium. Town situated NW of Namur. Pop. (1992) 19,249.

Railway and roadway junction. The main industry is manufacturing cutlery; also sugar-refining. There is an agricultural college.

Geneva (Fr. **Genève**, Ger. **Genf**) Switzerland. 1. Canton in the SW, almost surrounded by French territory. Area 282 sq km (109 sq. miles). Pop. (1992) 378,849, of whom the majority live in the cap., Geneva and its suburbs, being mainly French-speaking and Protestant. Fruit, vegetables, wine produced in the rural districts.

2. Cap. of the Geneva canton, the third largest city in Switzerland, at the point where the Rhône R. leaves L. Geneva (SW corner). Pop. (1992) 167,679.

Cultural and commercial centre. Manufactures watches, optical and scientific instruments, machinery and confectionery.

Cathedral (12th/13th-cent., restored); town hall (16th/17th-cent.); Museum of Art and History; university (1873), founded (1559) as Calvin's Academy. Also the seat of the International Red Cross (1864) and the International Labour Office and (1920–46) of the League of Nations. Also the home for many United Nations agencies. A town of the Allobroges, taken by the Romans with the rest of S Gaul. Passed with Burgundy to the Holy Roman Empire (1032), its bishops later becoming imperial princes. In the 16th cent. with the advent of Calvin, it became the centre of the Reformation and a refuge for persecuted Protestants. Its fame as a cosmopolitan and cultural centre grew, esp. in the 18th cent. Annexed to France 1798–1814. Became cap. of the 22nd and last canton of the Swiss Confederation 1815. Birthplace of French political philosopher, Jean Jacques Rousseau (1712–78) and French statesman and financier, Jacques Necker (1732–1804).

Geneva, Lake (Fr. **Lac Léman**, Ger. **Gen-fersee**) France/Switzerland. Crescent-shaped lake between SW Switzerland and the Haute-Savoie department of France at a height of 375 m (1230 ft) about 72 km (45 miles) long and up to 13 km (8 miles) wide. Area 578 sq km (233 sq. miles) (363 sq km; 140 sq. miles Swiss, remainder (S) French). The Rhône R. enters it at the E end, making its water muddy, but to the W it becomes deep blue and extraordinarily transparent; the river leaves it at Geneva. Its beauty, with snow-covered mountains to the S and vine-yards and pastures to the N, has been cele-brated by Byron, Voltaire and others, and there are several resorts along its shores, e.g. Montreux, Vevey (Switzerland), Évian-les-Bains (France). Its surface is subject to tem-porary changes of level (*seiches*), similar to tides, both longitudinally and transversely; these are probably caused by variations in atmospheric pressure and wind.

Genf ➤GENEVA.

Genk Belgium. Town in Limbourg prov-ince 37 km (23 miles) N of Liège. Pop. (1992) 61,589.

Manufactures mining machinery and there are reserves of natural gas in the area.

Gennevilliers France. Industrial suburb of NW Paris in the Hauts-de-Seine department in a loop of the Seine R. Pop. (1989) 46,000.

River port. Manufactures aircraft and elec-trical equipment.

Genoa (Italian **Genova**) Italy. Cap. of Lig-uria and of Genoa province on the Gulf of Genoa. Pop. (1991) 701,032.

Italy's chief seaport; exports olive oil, wine and textiles. Industries inc. shipbuilding, engineering, oil-refining, sugar-refining, food-canning, brewing and distilling. Manu-factures iron and steel, aircraft, textiles, soap and paper. Behind the excellent harbour, which is protected by moles, the city rises up the lower slopes of the Ligurian Apennines, setting off to advantage its fine architectural features. Outstanding among them are its many churches, inc. the cathedral of San Lorenzo, consecrated 1118, with campanile and cupola of the 16th cent.; and the churches of Sant'-Ambrogio, reconstructed in the 16th cent. from a 4th-cent. church and Santa Maria di Castello (11th-cent.). The palaces, too, are magnificent, esp. those on the Via Garibaldi, the Palazzo Rosso and Palazzo Bianco, opposite one another and both now museums; in the Palazzo Municipale are let-ters of Columbus and Paganini's violin.

University (1243). In the Middle Ages Genoa became a great maritime republic, at times vanquishing its two chief rivals, Pisa and Venice, but eventually becoming subject to France; its last overseas possession, Corsica, was ceded to France 1768. Birthplace of Christopher Columbus, explorer and dis-coverer of the New World (*c.* 1451–1506), and the Italian leader of the Risorgimento, Giuseppe Mazzini (1805–72).

Gentofte Denmark. Suburb of N Copen-hagen, mainly residential.

George, Lake (Uganda) ➤EDWARD, LAKE.

George, Lake USA. Long narrow lake 51 km (32 miles) long and up to 5 km (3 miles) wide) in NE New York in the foothills of the Adirondack Mountains with an outlet to the N into L. Champlain. Favourite summer resort, noteworthy for mountain scenery and islands. The original Indian name was 'Andiatarocte' ('Place Where the Lake Contracts'); the present name was given by General William Johnson (1755) in honour of George II.

Georgetown Guyana. Cap. and chief sea-port on the right bank of the Demerara R. at the mouth; it is mainly below sea level and is protected by a sea wall. Pop. (1992) 248,000.

Exports sugar, rice and bauxite. Bauxite is loaded at Linden 105 km (65 miles) up R. It manufactures beer, beverages and timber products. Ferry across the river. The botan-ical gardens are noted for their collections of palms and orchids. After disastrous fires (1945 and 1951) many of the old wooden buildings were replaced by concrete structures.

Georgia USA. State in the SE, bordered by

345

Tennessee and North Carolina (N), South Carolina and the Atlantic (E), Florida (S) and Alabama (W). Area 152,576 sq km (58,910 sq. miles). Pop. (1990) 6,917,000. Cap. Atlanta. The land rises gradually from the coast NW to the Appalachians; the highest point is Brasstown Bald (1454 m; 4769 ft) in the NE. On the coastal plain there are swamps and forests of pine, cypress, oak and magnolia, with Okefenokee Swamp in the SE. Climate humid and subtropical, rainfall averaging about 125 cm (50 ins.) annually. Agriculture is of major importance; chief crops maize, cotton, tobacco and groundnuts. The state produces most of the US kaolin output. Principal industries cotton-milling, wood-processing. Chief towns Atlanta, Savannah (chief seaport), Columbus, Augusta and Macon.

Explored by the Spaniards in the 16th cent. Became a British colony 1754, taking its name from George II. In the American Civil War it suffered considerably in Sherman's 'March to the Sea' (1864), commemorated in the song *Marching Through Georgia*. It became one of the original 13 states.

Georgia. Republic in W Transcaucasia, bounded W by the Black Sea, S by Turkey, Armenia and Azerbaijan. Abkhazia and Adjaria are autonomous republics within Georgia. South Ossetia was a separate region, but remains in dispute with Georgia. Area 69,700 sq km (26,900 sq. miles). Pop. (1993) 5,493,000 (56 per cent urban). Life expectancy, 69 years male, 76 female. Cap. Tbilisi. Other cities Kutaisi, Rustavi, Batumi and Sakhumi. Currency: Georgian lari = 100 tetri. The N part lies on the S slopes of the Great Caucasus, the S part is on the Little Caucasus and between the mountainous areas are the valleys of the Kura and Rioni. Land use: forested 0.4 per cent, meadows and pastures, 29 per cent, agricultural and under permanent cultivation 2 per cent. The official lang. is Georgian. About 70 per cent of the pop. are Georgians, 8 per cent Armenians, 6 per cent Russians, 6 per cent Azerbaijanis and 3 per cent Ossetes. Believers are mainly Georgian Orthodox, minorities inc. Russian Orthodox, Muslims and Armenian Orthodox.

The Kura, Rioni and other rivers provide hydroelectric power and there are large irrigation schemes. Although there is very limited cultivable land on the Black Sea lowlands (Colchis), with their humid subtropical climate, tea, citrus fruits, tung oil and tobacco are produced, and wines inland. In the Chiatura district there are manganese deposits, and coal, baryta, oil and other minerals are exploited. Chemicals, food-processing and machine manufacture are major industries.

Georgia was an independent kingdom for more than 2000 years and reached the peak of its power in the 12th and 13th cent. The Golden Age of its culture and political influence came to an end with the Mongol invasion beginning in 1234. At times subject to Turkey and Persia, its principalities were gradually annexed by Russia between 1810 and 1867. After civil war (1917–21) the Georgian Soviet Socialist Republic joined the USSR as a member of the Transcaucasian Soviet Federated Socialist Republic (1922) and in 1936 became a separate constituent republic. In 1991, following a referendum, independence was declared based on the treaty of independence of May 1918. There is a 234-member Parliament elected for a 4-year period, as is the President who appoints the Council of Ministers.

Georgian Bay Canada. The NE part of L. Huron in Ontario. Area 15,022 sq km (5800 sq. miles). Many summer resorts on the shores and islands. The Georgian Bay Islands National Park, comprising 30 small islands, was established in 1929.

Gera Germany. Cap. of Gera district on the White Elster R. 60 km (37 miles) W of Thuringia Chemnitz. Pop. (1990) 128,000.

Railway junction and industrial town. Manufactures textiles, machinery, furniture and carpets. Has a 16th-cent. town hall.

Geraldton Australia. Seaport in Western Australia 370 km (230 miles) NNW of Perth. Pop. (1991) 20,587.

Outlet for the Murchison goldfield and

also for a wide agricultural area. Exports wheat, wood. Manufactures superphosphates. Industries inc. brewing, crayfish-canning, and it is also a tourist centre.

Germantown USA. Residential suburb of NW Philadelphia, Pennsylvania. Noted for 18th-cent. 'colonial' houses. An early centre of printing and publishing. Founded by 13 German families *c.* 1683. Site of the battle of Germantown (1777) in the American War of Independence.

Germany. Country of central Europe bounded on the N by Denmark and the North and Baltic Seas, E by Poland, E and SE by the Czech Republic, SE and S by Austria, S by Switzerland and W by France. Area 356,733 sq km (137,737 sq. miles). Pop. (1993) 81,187,000 (85 per cent urban). Life expectancy, 73 years male, 79 female. Cap. Bonn (Berlin is cap.-designate). Other cities Hamburg, Munich, Cologne, Frankfurt am Main, Essen, Dortmund, Stuttgart, Düsseldorf, Duisburg, Hannover and Leipzig. Currency: Deutschmark = 100 Pfennige. The country may be divided into four main physical regions. In the N a low-lying sandy plain extends W–E from the Netherlands to Poland, forming part of the N European Plain and containing much heath (e.g. Lüneburg Heath) and moorland. S of this plain is the region of plateau and block mountains which comprises Central Germany, inc. the Harz, Thüringerwald and other uplands and the two great industrial regions of Westphalia and Saxony. In the SW is the Rift Valley of the Rhine with its associated highlands (Black Forest etc.) and the ridge of the Swabian and Franconian Jura. In the extreme S the land rises to the Bavarian Alps, which contain Germany's highest peak, the Zugspitze (2963 m; 9719 ft). The principal rivers drain N and NW to the North Sea, outstanding in importance being the Rhine, with its tributaries the Main, Mosel and Ruhr, also the Elbe and Weser; the Oder, on the Polish frontier with E Germany, flows to the Baltic and the Danube through Bavaria to the SE. The commercial value of these rivers has been considerably enhanced by an interconnecting system of canals (Mittelland, Dortmund–Ems), while the Kiel Canal links the Baltic with the North Sea across Schleswig-Holstein. In the NW the climate is maritime temperate and conditions become more continental (i.e. extreme) to the E, while in the S temperatures are somewhat reduced by altitude; rainfall is moderate (50–75 cm; 20–30 ins. annually) and well distributed throughout the year. Land use: forested 30 per cent, pasture 15 per cent, agricultural and under permanent cultivation 34 per cent.

German is the lang. of the country. About 30 million people living mainly in N Germany are Protestants, the 29 million Roman Catholics being strongest in Bavaria and the Rhineland. There are about 38,000 Jews.

Germany is the third industrial power in the world. The rich coal deposits of the Ruhr basin form the basis of the great iron and steel industry of that area, centred on Dortmund, Duisburg and Essen, and much lignite is mined near Cologne; also in North Rhine-Westphalia Düsseldorf is an important commercial centre, Wuppertal is famous for its textiles and Solingen for its cutlery. Germany has the world's greatest output of lignite, mined in Saxony and largely utilized for the generation of electricity; in this area Leipzig is well-known for its printing and publishing, Dresden for its optical and precision instruments, Chemnitz for its textiles, Meissen for its porcelain. Chemicals are manufactured here and along the Rhine at Ludwigshafen and other centres. Frankfurt is one of the world's leading financial centres and banking and finance are foreign-currency earners. Germany has an efficient system of railways and roads. Hamburg, Bremen and Rostock are the chief seaports. Agriculture employs 3 per cent of the labour force. The collective farms of the former German Democratic Republic were privatized in 1990–1. On the poorer soils of the N rye is the main cereal and here and elsewhere potatoes are an important crop. Sugar-beet is widely cultivated in Central Germany and wheat to the S; grapes for the Rhine and Mosel wines are grown along the banks of those rivers and hops for the beers of Munich in Bavaria.

Germany

The ancient Germanic tribes, who originated in Scandinavia, were long held by the Romans between the Rhine, Elbe and Danube, but in the 3rd cent. a group of tribes in the NW, known as Franks, appeared. They gradually extended their power in Belgium and France, and by the time of Charlemagne Germany had become part of their kingdom. After the death of Charlemagne (814) Germany was separated from France and was ruled by its own kings, with the local dukes virtually independent until the establishment of the Saxon dynasty (919). The third of this elected line of kings, Otto I, was crowned Emperor by Pope John XII in 962 and so founded the Holy Roman Empire, which was to last until 1806. He also began the colonization of the Slav territories E of the Elbe and, despite the later conflict between Emperors and Popes, the German people continued to expand, pushing their frontier as far E as the Vistula by the 14th cent., largely through the exploits of the Teutonic Knights. In the 16th cent. Charles V brought to the Empire extensive new possessions in Spain, Italy, the Netherlands and elsewhere. At the same time the Reformation brought disunity to the German people; by the Peace of Augsburg (1555) most of N Germany was Protestant and the ensuing Thirty Years War (1618–48) left the land depopulated, agriculture and commerce in ruin and the imperial power merely nominal. Prussia now appeared as a military power and under Frederick II conquered Silesia and became strong enough to challenge Austria; it was Napoleon, however, who united Germany in the Confederation of the Rhine (1806) and simultaneously brought the Empire to an end. From 1815 Germany was a Confederation of 39 states, in many of which the democratic and nationalistic ideas inspired by the French Revolution expressed themselves in open violence in 1848. Under Bismarck Prussia supplanted Austria as the dominant German power, defeated Austria (1866) and then France (1870–1), and united Germany, with the King of Prussia as the hereditary German Emperor. At home industry developed, abroad a col-

onial empire was founded, but ambitious and aggressive policies led to defeat in World War I (1914–18); the monarchy was overthrown and the democratic Weimar Republic established, while the colonies, chiefly in Africa, were placed under League of Nations mandate. A democratic system of government was short-lived, however, and the extreme right-wing Nazi party, taking advantage of the economic crisis of 1929–33, secured control and established the totalitarian Third Reich. Once more an aggressive foreign policy led to defeat in World War II (1939–45). E Prussia was partitioned between Poland and the USSR. The country was divided into four occupation zones by the US, Britain, France and the USSR; in 1949 the three western zones became the Federal German Republic (West Germany) and the eastern zone became the German Democratic Republic (East Germany), while the former cap. was similarly divided into West Berlin and East Berlin. In 1952, in West Germany, Baden, Württemberg-Baden and Württemberg-Hohenzollern were amalgamated into the new *Land* of Baden-Württemberg-, and in East Germany the five *Länder* were replaced by 15 Districts. A feature of the post-war years in West Germany was the remarkable recovery of the country's leading industries from the devastation of World War II; in East Germany, on the other hand, there was no such revival of economic prosperity. In 1989 there was a large exodus of people from East Germany to the West, travelling via Poland, Czechoslovakia and Hungary. The Berlin Wall was reopened in 1989. Free elections were held in East Germany in March 1990 and saw the collapse of the Communist Party. With the decline in the economy reunification became inevitable and this took place 3 October 1990.

Germany is a Federal state consisting of 16 *Länder.*

	Capital
Baden-Württemberg	Stuttgart
Bavaria	Munich
Berlin	Berlin
Brandenburg	Potsdam
Bremen	Bremen

Hamburg	Hamburg
Hessen	Wiesbaden
Lower Saxony	Hannover
Mecklenburg-West	
Pomerania	Schwerin
North Rhine-Westphalia	Düsseldorf
Rhineland-Palatinate	Mainz
Saarland	Saarbrucken
Saxony	Dresden
Saxony-Anhalt	Magdeburg
Schleswig-Holstein	Kiel
Thuringia	Erfurt

Each *Land* has its own Parliament and Government and is represented in the 79-member Federal Council (*Bundesrat*), the upper house. The 662-member lower house, the Federal Assembly (*Bundestag*) is elected for 4-year terms by universal suffrage.

Germiston South Africa. Town in Gauteng at a height of 1670 m (5478 ft) 14 km (9 miles) ESE of Johannesburg. Pop. (1991) 134,000.

Important railway junction. Site of the world's largest gold refinery, serving the Witwatersrand mines. Railway engineering. Manufactures textiles, furniture, chemicals, steel goods and hardware.

Founded (1887) two years after the discovery of gold in the Witwatersrand.

Gerona Spain. 1. Province in the extreme NE in Catalonia, bounded on the N by the Pyrenees, separating it from France and on the E by the Mediterranean, with the small enclave of Llivia in France. Area 5886 sq km (2272 sq. miles). Pop. (1991) 509,628. Mainly agricultural. Produces wheat, maize and wine. Inc. both the fertile Ampurdán plain and the Costa Brava with its many seaside resorts.

2. Ancient Gerunda. Cap. of the Gerona province on the Ter R. at its confluence with the Oñar R. 88 km (55 miles) NE of Barcelona. Pop. (1989) 87,600.

Flour-milling. Manufactures textiles and chemicals.

Still has remains of the old city walls. Gothic cathedral (13th/16th-cent., 18th-cent. façade) with a remarkable single nave 22 m (72 ft) wide.

Gers France. Department in the SW in Midi-Pyrénées Region at the foot of the Pyrenees, sloping down N towards the Garonne R. and drained by its tributaries (the Save, Gimone, Gers and Baïse rivers) and the Adour R. Area 6257 sq km (2416 sq. miles). Pop. (1992) 175,400. Prefecture Auch.

Chiefly agricultural, famous for Armagnac brandy; also produces cereals, wine, fruit, poultry. Chief towns Auch and Condom.

Gersoppa Falls India. Cataract on the Sharavati R. in Karnataka, renowned for its scenic beauty, 153 km (95 miles) N of Mangalore. There are 4 cascades, the highest 253 m (830 ft). There is a hydroelectric power station near the falls.

Getafe Spain. Town situated S of Madrid on a wide plain near Los Angeles hill, the geographical centre of Spain. Pop. (1991) 138,704.

Industries inc. the manufacture of electrical equipment, pharmaceutical goods, aircraft, radios and telephones, boxes, brushes, alcohol and flour.

Gettysburg USA. Small town (borough) in S Pennsylvania 56 km (35 miles) SW of Harrisburg. Pop. (1989) 8000. Famous as the site of the Battle of Gettysburg (July 1863), the turning-point of the American Civil War, in which the Federal army under Meade defeated the Confederates under Lee. The National Cemetery (dedicated by Lincoln in his famous 'Gettysburg Address') is in the National Military Park, which inc. the battlefield.

Gevelsberg Germany. Industrial town in North Rhine-Westphalia 11 km (7 miles) ENE of Wuppertal. Pop. (1985) 30,700.

Manufactures stoves, locks and bicycles.

Gezira, El Sudan. In Arabic 'The Island'. Plain between the White Nile and the Blue Nile above their confluence at Khartoum, irrigated from the Sennar Dam on the Blue Nile (completed 1925). Chief town Wad Medani. Main crop cotton.

Ghadames (Gadames, Rhadames) Libya. Town in the Sahara in the oasis of the same name 467 km (290 miles) SW of Tripoli. Pop. (1994) 52,247. Near the intersection of the frontiers of Libya, Tunisia and Algeria. Centre of caravan routes, but less important than formerly.

Ghana. Republic in West Africa bounded in the W by the Côte d'Ivoire, N by Burkina Faso, E by Togo and S by the Gulf of Guinea. Area 238,533 sq km (92,098 sq. miles). Pop. (1993) 15,636,000 (33 per cent urban). Life expectancy, 54 years male, 58 female. Cap. Accra. Other cities Kumasi, Tamale, Tema and Sekondi-Takoradi. Currency: Cedi (¢) = 100 pesewas. The majority of the country comprises low-lying plains; on the coast there are sandbars and lagoons. The principal waterway is the Volta R. and the Black Volta which crosses NW–SW. The centre contains Lake Volta. Vegetation consists mainly of tropical rainforests to the S changing gradually to savannah in the N. It has a tropical climate which ranges from a dry, hot savannah in the N to warm, dry coastal belt in the SE and hot and humid in the SW. Land use: forested 35 per cent, meadows and pastures 22 per cent, agricultural and under permanent cultivation 12 per cent. English is the official lang.; other langs inc. Asante, Ewe and Ga. About 62 per cent of the pop. is Christian and 16 per cent Muslim. In the S and centre the people are mainly Akan, Ewe and Ga in the Volta region, and about 20 per cent of those living in the N are Gur people.

About 59 per cent of the labour force is engaged in agriculture. In the S and centre the main food crops are maize, rice, cassava, plantains, groundnuts, yams and cocyams, and in the N groundnuts, rice, maize, sorghum, millet and yams. Cocoa is the main cash crop followed by tobacco and coffee. Forestry and mining for bauxite are important industries. Oil was discovered in commercial quantities in 1978.

The Portuguese, the Dutch and the British established claims along the coast from the late 15th cent. The British Colony of the Gold Coast was created in 1874 and the Northern Territories and Ashanti became a British protectorate in 1901. The Gold Coast became independent in 1957; the Trust Territory of British Togoland was united with the Gold Coast to form the new state, named after the ancient kingdom of Ghana on the Niger R. After much political unrest and treason trials in 1963, President Nkrumah introduced the single-party state in 1964. He was deposed as the result of a military *coup* in 1966. Civilian rule returned in 1969, but again the military took control in 1972. Further *coups* took place in 1979 and 1981. In a referendum in 1992 a new pluralist democratic constitution was opposed. Many opposition parties boycotted the elections for the 200-member House of Parliament in 1992. For local administration the country is divided into 10 Regions each under a Regional Secretary.

Ghats India. Two mountain ranges of peninsular India, the Western and Eastern Ghats, forming the W and E margins respectively to the Deccan. The Western Ghats extend NNW–SSE from the Tapti R. valley to near Cape Comorin in the extreme S, reaching their highest point in Anai Mudi (2697 m; 8846 ft) in Kerala (S); they have a profound climatic influence, for they cause the SW monsoon to deposit abundant moisture on their windward slopes, where the rainfall amounts to 250 cm (100 ins.) or more annually in places, while on the Deccan it averages only 50–100 cm (20–40 ins.). The Eastern Ghats, a much more broken range than the other, has its highest point in Doda Betta (2635 m; 8642 ft) in the Nilgiri Hills, where it meets the Western Ghats; their average height of 450 m (1476 ft), compared with the 900 m (2952 ft) of the Western Ghats.

Ghaziabad India. Town in Uttar Pradesh 20 km (13 miles) E of Delhi. Pop. (1991) 454,200.

Rail and road junction. Industries inc. iron and steel, textiles, distilling sugar, electronics, synthetic fibres, food-processing and vehicle components.

Ghazni Afghanistan. Town 120 km (75 miles) SSW of Kabul on the road to

Kandahar at a height of 2220 m (7282 ft) on the central plateau. Pop. (1984) 33,351.

Trade in livestock, wool and fruit.

It is walled and above it stands the ancient citadel. From the late 10th cent. it flourished under the great Mahmud of Ghazni and was cap. of the Ghaznevid dynasty until destroyed in the mid 12th cent. by the Ghorids.

Ghent (Flemish **Gent**, Fr. **Gand**) Belgium. Cap. of E Flanders province on the Scheldt R. at its confluence with the Lys R. Pop. (1991) 230,446.

Port, linked by canal with Terneuzen, making it accessible to large vessels. It is also an industrial centre manufacturing textiles (cotton, linen, jute), chemicals, fertilizers, glassware and paper. Other industries inc. flour-milling, sugar-refining, brewing and tanning. It has an important flower seed and bulb market.

Cathedral of St Bavon (12th/16th-cent.), which contains the masterpiece of the brothers van Eyck, *Adoration of the Lamb*; Belfry (12th/14th-cent.), with a 90-m (295-ft) tower; Cloth Hall (14th-cent.); castle of the counts of Flanders (12th-cent., restored). Ghent, historic cap. of Flanders, grew up round the 9th-cent. castle of the first count and spread to neighbouring islands which are still connected by numerous bridges. By the 13th cent. it had become an important centre of the textile industry, wealthy and powerful enough to enjoy a considerable measure of independence. Played a leading part in the struggle of the Netherlands against Spain, the Pacification of Ghent (1576) establishing a league in opposition to Spanish rule, but it was taken by the Spaniards in 1584. Freed from Habsburg domination 1794. Its commercial prosperity revived in the 19th cent. Birthplace of the English prince, Count John of Gaunt (Ghent) (1340–99) and the Belgian dramatist, Count Maurice Maeterlinck (1862–1949).

Ghor, El. Depression 3–24 km (2–15 miles) wide in Jordan and Israel between the Sea of Galilee and the Dead Sea, respectively 212 m (695 ft) and 392 m (1286 ft) below sea level, forming part of the Great Rift Valley and continued S to the Gulf of Aqaba as the Araba depression.

Giant's Causeway Northern Ireland. Promontory of columnar basalt on the N coast of Co. Antrim 11 km (7 miles) ENE of Portrush. An important tourist attraction consisting of several thousand pillars, mainly hexagonal, each 35–50 cm (14–20 ins.) across and of varying height.

Gibraltar. United Kingdom Overseas Territory situated off the extreme S of Spain and at the W entrance to the Mediterranean Sea. Area 6.5 sq km (2.5 sq. miles). Pop. (1992) 28,848. Life expectancy, 73 years male, 80 female. Cap. Gibraltar Town. Currency: Gibraltar pound = 100 pence. The Rock of Gibraltar rises abruptly to 426 m (1397 ft) from the low, sandy isthmus which joins it to the Spanish mainland; it consists of limestone and has many caves as well as tunnels excavated for defensive purposes. At its S end is the lighthouse of Europa Point. To the W of the Rock are the town and the harbour, the latter bounded by two long moles and a third detached mole. The climate is warm temperate with westerly winds in winter bringing rain. Summers are warm and rainfall low. The pop. is mainly of Genoese, Portuguese, Maltese and Spanish descent and Roman Catholic in religion, speaking Spanish and English.

Gibraltar is a naval base and much of the town, which is partly built on land reclaimed from the sea, is occupied by barracks and hospitals. In 1991 the Gibraltar Regiment took over responsibility for land defence from the British Army. It is a free port; its trade is chiefly of transit type and the provisioning and fuelling of ships. Tourist industry of increasing importance with over 4 million visitors each year and offshore banking help foreign currency earnings. There are a number of small firms bottling beverages.

The Calpe of the Greeks and Romans, with the ancient Abyla on the African coast it formed the Pillars of Hercules, which for centuries represented the W edge of the Mediterranean world. Its modern name is derived from Jebel-al-Tarik, after its Moorish conqueror, Tarik (711), the remains of whose castle may still be seen. It was regained by the Spaniards 1462 and taken by Admiral Rooke 1704. It has remained in British hands in spite of many Spanish and French attacks, notably the long siege of 1779–83. It was granted a considerable measure of internal self-government in 1964. Spain urged the decolonization of Gibraltar and in accordance with a UN resolution a referendum was held in 1967 and the people of Gibraltar voted by 12,138 to 44 in favour of retaining links with Britain. The border was closed by Spain in 1969, opened to pedestrians in 1982 and fully opened in 1985. There is a 17-member House of Assembly containing 2 non-elected *ex-officio* members.

Gibraltar, Strait of. Ancient Fretum Herculeum. Channel 58 km (36 miles) long connecting the Atlantic and the Mediterranean, between S Spain and NW Africa; 43 km (27 miles) wide at the W end, 13 km (8 miles) at its narrowest, 24 km (15 miles) at the E end between the Rock of Gibraltar and Almina Point, near Ceuta (the ancient Pillars of Hercules). A surface current flows through it E from the Atlantic, while at greater depth another current flows W.

Giessen Germany. Industrial town in Hessen on the Lahn R. 51 km (32 miles) N of Frankfurt-am-Main. Pop. (1989) 75,500.
Manufactures machine-tools, rubber and leather goods, tobacco products and precision instruments.

Gifu Japan. Cap. of Gifu prefecture in central Honshu 32 km (20 miles) NNW of Nagoya. Pop. (1992) 409,928.
Industrial centre. Manufactures textiles, paper goods (lanterns, parasols, fans), cutlery. Centre of fishing with trained cormorants on the Nagara R., a popular tourist attraction.

Gijón Spain. Industrial town and seaport in Oviedo province, Asturias 23 km (14 miles) NE of Oviedo. Pop. (1991) 259,054.
Important iron and steel industry, oil-refining, producing machinery, hardware

and also manufactures chemicals, glass and cement. Exports coal and iron ore.
In the Spanish Civil War it was the last port in N Spain to fall to the Nationalists (1937).

Gila River USA. River 1046 km (650 miles) long rising in SW New Mexico and flowing generally SW across Arizona to join the Colorado R. near Yuma. The Coolidge Dam (built 1928) irrigates large areas for alfalfa, maize and cotton. The river passes several Indian reservations and the Gila Cliff Dwellings National Monument.

Gilbert and Ellice Islands SW Pacific Ocean. Former British colony ►KIRIBATI, ►TUVALU.

Gilbert Islands ►KIRIBATI.

Gilboa Israel. Hilly district in the N on the Jordan border between the Plain of Esdraelon and the Jordan R. In biblical times the scene of Saul's defeat and death.

Gilead Jordan. Mountainous district in ancient Palestine, now in NW Jordan, E of the Jordan R., rising to 1114 m (3654 ft) in Mt Gilead or Jebel Yusha about 5 km (3 miles) N of the modern As Salt.

Gillingham (Dorset) England. Market town on the R. Stour 37 km (23 miles) NNE of Dorchester. Pop. (1971) 3294.

Gillingham (Kent) England. Town on the R. Medway estuary just NE of Chatham, containing much of the dockyard. Pop. (1991) 94,913.
Centre of a fruit-growing district.
Birthplace of William Adams (1564–1620), the first Englishman to enter Japan.

Gippsland Australia. District in SE Victoria. Chief town Sale. Wooded mountains in the N. Fertile plains in the S with numerous dairy farms and butter and cheese factories; maize, oats, hops and vegetables cultivated. Huge lignite deposits in the Latrobe valley, supplying briquettes for Melbourne and fuel for power stations.

Girardot Colombia. River port on the

upper Magdalena R. 88 km (55 miles) WSW of Bogotá. Pop. (1989) 70,000. In a coffee-growing region.

Exports coffee and cattle and hides. Manufactures textiles, leather, tobacco products.

Girgenti ►AGRIGENTO.

Girne ►KYRENIA.

Gironde France. Department in the SW, bounded on the W by the Bay of Biscay and drained by the Garonne and Dordogne rivers, which unite to form the Gironde estuary. Area 10,000 sq km (4140 sq. miles) (largest department in France). Pop. (1968) 1,009,400. Prefecture Bordeaux. Has some of the country's finest vineyards, the districts of Médoc, Graves and Sauternes having given their names to famous wines. Maize, tobacco, fruit also cultivated. The infertile Landes is covered with pine forests. Industry concentrated in Bordeaux. Other towns Arcachon (resort), Libourne (wine trade).

Girvan Scotland. Town in South Ayrshire 29 km (18 miles) SW of Ayr on the Firth of Clyde. Pop. (1991) 7449. Holiday resort and fishing port. The island of Ailsa Craig is 16 km (10 miles) W.

Gisborne New Zealand. Town and port on Poverty Bay on the E coast of the N Island. Pop. (1991) 31,480. Industries inc. engineering, fishing, brewing, canning and food-processing, and exports wool, meat, dairy produce.

Giurgiu Romania. River port and market town in Walachia in the Ilfov district on the left bank of the Danube R. 61 km (38 miles) SSW of Bucharest. Pop. (1992) 74,236. Linked by oil pipelines with Ploeşti.

Exports petroleum, grain, timber. Boat-building, sugar-refining, brewing, flour-milling. Trade with Ruse (Bulgaria) on the opposite bank of the Danube.

Founded (as San Giorgio) by the Genoese.

Giza, El (El Gizeh; Giza) Egypt. Cap. of Giza governorate on the W bank of the Nile opposite Cairo. Pop. (1989) 1,670,000. Manufactures textiles, footwear, etc. 8 km

(5 miles) SW is the Great Pyramid of Cheops (Khufu), covering 5.3 ha (13 acres), one of the Seven Wonders of the ancient world, the pyramids of Khafra and Menkaura and the Sphinx.

Gjirokastër (Argyrocastro) Albania. Town SE of Valona on the Drin R. Pop. (1991) 21,000.

Market centre trading in dairy products, tobacco and wine. Industries inc. tanning, silver-smithing, footwear and chemicals.

Gjøvik Norway. Town in Oppland N of Oslo on the NW shore of L. Mjøsa. Pop. (1990) 15,514.

Industries inc. the manufacture of motors, snowploughs, wallboard, flour, dairy products, furniture and footwear.

Glace Bay Canada. Town in Nova Scotia on the E coast of Cape Breton Island. Pop. (1991) 19,500. Former coalmining centre. Small harbour used by the fishing industry.

Glacier National Park Canada. Park in SE British Columbia in the Selkirk Mountains. Area 1349 sq km (521 sq. miles). Fine mountain scenery, with resorts for climbers, campers. Established 1886.

Glacier National Park USA. Park in NW Montana in the Rocky Mountains, bounded on the N by the Canadian frontier, containing many glaciers and lakes, forests and waterfalls. Area 4040 sq km (1560 sq. miles). Highest peak Mt Cleveland (3187 m; 10,453 ft). Established 1910. Combined with the Waterton Lakes National Park (Alberta, Canada) as the Waterton–Glacier International Peace Park in 1932.

Gladstone Australia. Town in Queensland SE of Rockhampton on Port Curtis inlet. Pop. (1991) 33,447.

Port exporting coal, alumina, aluminium and wheat. The main industries are aluminium and chemicals.

Glåma River ►GLOMMA RIVER.

Glamis Scotland. Village in Angus 8 km (5 miles) WSW of Forfar. Nearby is the 17th-cent. Glamis Castle, birthplace of

Queen Elizabeth the Queen Mother; the earlier structure belonged to Macbeth, thane of Glamis, hero of Shakespeare's play.

Glamorgan ➤SWANSEA, NEATH PORT TALBOT, BRIDGEND, RHONDDA CYNON TAFF, THE VALE OF GLAMORGAN, CARDIFF, MERTHYR TYDFIL.

Glarus Switzerland. 1. Canton comprising the basin of the Linth R., almost enclosed by mountains, esp. in the S, e.g. Tödi (3626 m; 11,893 ft). Area 684 sq km (264 sq. miles). Pop. (1994) 39,300 (chiefly Protestant and almost all German-speaking). Many cattle are raised on the alpine pastures and cheese is made. Some cotton-spinning. 2. Cap. of the Glarus canton on the Linth R. Pop. (1980) 5800.

Industries inc. textiles and woodworking.

Almost completely destroyed (1861) by a fire spread by a violent föhn wind. Zwingli, the Swiss reformer, was parish priest here 1506–16.

Glasgow Scotland. Largest city in Scotland and third largest in the UK, which has had a single-tier council since 1994. It is situated on both banks of the R. Clyde 32 km (20 miles) from its mouth and 68 km (42 miles) W of Edinburgh. Pop. (1993) 623,850.

Although shipbuilding, tobacco and iron and steel began the industrial development of the city, the main industries in 1996 are electronics, chemicals, engineering, finance and printing. Tourism has been much developed and Glasgow is an important conference centre.

Trade and industry created the wealth that built many fine streets and squares, as well as the notorious slums of the Gorbals. The most noteworthy historic building is the Cathedral of St Mungo, dating from the 12th cent. Glasgow University (founded 1451) since 1899 has occupied buildings at Kelvingrove designed by Sir Gilbert Scott. Other buildings are the Royal Exchange, Art Gallery and Museum, Mitchell Library, with a Burns collection, Merchants' Hall, the 17th-cent. Tron steeple (remnant of a church burned down in 1793) and the Crown steeple (the remains of the ancient tolbooth or prison). Cultural attractions inc. the Glasgow School of Art, noted for Charles Rennie Mackintosh (1868–1928), the art nouveau architect and designer and the Burrell Collection. Sauchiehall St and Buchanan St are two of the principal thoroughfares and the Green and Kelvingrove Parks two of the best-known open spaces. Glasgow receives its water supply from Lochs Katrine and Arklet. The name of the city is probably derived from the Celtic Glasghu, meaning 'beloved green spot', a settlement discovered here by St Kentigern (Mungo) in the 6th cent. Little is known of its subsequent history till the 12th cent., when it was made a burgh of barony (1178). Became a royal burgh 1636. In the mid 17th cent. it suffered from plague, famine and fire, but the Treaty of Union (1707) gave it equal status with English ports and it acquired a major share of the American tobacco trade. Its commerce increased with the deepening of the Clyde channel (1768), then the textile, shipbuilding and engineering industries developed, stimulated by the nearness of the Lanarkshire coal and iron mines and Glasgow became one of the leading industrial centres in the UK.

Glastonbury England. Market town in Somerset on the R. Brue 35 km (22 miles) SW of Bath. Pop. (1991) 7747.

Tourism is the dominant industry although some footwear is still manufactured.

According to legend this was where Joseph of Arimathea founded the first Christian church in England and where his staff, planted on Wearyall Hill, took root and blossomed annually at Christmas. Another legend gives it as the burial-place of King Arthur. In the town are the ruins of the famous Benedictine Abbey, founded by the Saxon king Ine in the 8th cent., restored by St Dunstan in the 10th cent., burned down in 1184, rebuilt (by 1303) and suppressed by Henry VIII (1539), finally to be bought by the Church of England (1908). On the nearby Glastonbury Tor (160 m; 529 ft) is a tower, the remains of St Michael's Chapel; NW of the town are the sites of ancient lake villages.

Glauchau Germany. Town in Saxony 11 km (7 miles) NNE of Zwickau on the R. Mulde. Pop. (1989) 26,566.

Manufactures textiles, machinery and dyes.

Birthplace of Georg Agricola (1490–1555), the 'father of mineralogy'.

Glencoe Scotland. Valley ('glen') of the small R. Coe SE of Ballachulish about 11 km (7 miles) long, stretching from Rannoch Moor to Loch Leven, flanked by steep mountains inc. Bidean nam Bian (1149 m; 3769 ft) and Buachaille Etive Mor (954 m; 3129 ft). Legendary birthplace of Ossian. Scene of the massacre of the Macdonalds by the Campbells and English soldiers (1692).

Glendale USA. Residential and industrial suburb of N Los Angeles, California in the San Fernando Valley. Pop. (1990) 180,000.

Manufactures aircraft, optical instruments, furniture, pottery and plastic goods. Contains the Forest Lawn Memorial Park, a cemetery well-known for its reproductions of works of art.

Glendalough, Vale of Ireland. Picturesque valley in Co. Wicklow 24 km (15 miles) SSW of Bray, with two small lakes. Famous for its ecclesiastical ruins, inc. the cathedral, St Kevin's Cross (a granite monolith 3.4 m; 11 ft high), the Round Tower, St Kevin's Kitchen (Church). St Kevin founded a monastery here in the 6th cent.

Gleneagles Scotland. Glen in Perth and Kinross near Auchterarder, site of golf course.

Glenelg Australia. Town and resort in SE South Australia in the metropolitan area SW of Adelaide. Pop. (1989) 14,000. Nearby is the 'Old Gum Tree', beneath which the colony of South Australia was proclaimed (1836).

Glenelg River Australia. River 450 km (280 miles) long, rising in the Grampians, SW Victoria, flowing W and then S to Discovery Bay. Main course often dry, but Rocklands Reservoir in the upper reaches diverts water to supply the Wimmera–Mallee districts.

Glen Fiddich Scotland. Glen in Moray S of Dufftown near the Glenfiddich whisky distillery.

Glenrothes Scotland. 'New town' since 1948 in the centre of Fife 10 km (6 miles) N of Kirkcaldy. Pop. (1991) 38,650.

Gliwice (Ger. **Gleiwitz**) Poland. Industrial town in the Katowice voivodeship, Upper Silesia on the Klodnica R. 27 km (17 miles) W of Katowice. Pop. (1989) 212,481.

Centre of coalmining and steel industries. Manufactures machinery and chemicals. Food-processing.

A city in the 13th cent. Passed to Prussia in 1742. Returned to Poland in 1945.

Glomma (Norwegian **Glåma**) **River** Norway. The longest river in Scandinavia 590 km (365 miles) long, rising in a small lake 93 km (58 miles) SE of Trondheim, flowing generally S past Röros, Elverum and Kongsvinger, through L. Öyeren and past Sarpsborg to the Skagerrak at Fredrikstad. Important waterway for carrying timber to sawmills, paper mills etc. Also supplies power for many hydroelectric installations.

Glossop England. Town in Derbyshire 19 km (12 miles) ESE of Manchester at the NW edge of the peak district of the Pennines. Pop. (1991) 30,771.

Industries inc. textile-finishing and printing, paper manufacturing and food-processing.

Gloucester England. Ancient Glevum. County town of Gloucestershire on the R. Severn 13 km (8 miles) WSW of Cheltenham. Pop. (1991) 91,800. River port connected by the Gloucester–Berkeley Ship Canal (26.5 km; 16½ miles long) with Sharpness at the Severn mouth.

Industries inc. aircraft manufacture and repair, also aerospace components, engineering and textiles. Trade in timber and grain.

Its beautiful cathedral, with a 69-m (226-ft) tower dating from the 15th cent., was the church of an 11th-cent. Benedictine abbey; with Worcester and Hereford cathedrals it is the scene of the annual Three Choirs Festival.

Among the old timbered buildings is the 15th-cent. New Inn and there is also the 12th-cent. church of St Mary-de-Crypt. Founded by the Romans towards the end of the 1st cent. AD. Birthplace of Robert Raikes (1735–1811), who founded one of the first Sunday schools here (1780), Cardinal Vaughan (1832–1903) and the writer, W. E. Henley (1849–1903).

Gloucester USA. Fishing port and summer resort in Massachusetts 43 km (27 miles) NE of Boston. Pop. (1990) 28,000.

For over 200 years fishing for cod, mackerel, haddock and halibut was the main occupation. Now boatbuilding, fish-processing and the making of oilskins, sails and nets are more important.

First settled in 1623.

Gloucestershire England. County in the W Midlands. Area 2642 sq km (1020 sq. miles). Pop. (1991) 520,600. County town Gloucester. Situated around the lower Severn and its estuary, and drained also by the Wye, which forms part of the W boundary, the Warwickshire Avon (N), Bristol Avon (S) and the upper Thames, the county falls into three distinct regions: the Cotswold Hills (E); the lower Severn valley, comprising the Vales of Gloucester and Berkeley (centre); and the Forest of Dean (W). Coal formerly mined in the Forest and near Bristol; sheep raised on the Cotswolds, but it is chiefly known for its dairy (butter, cheese) and fruit (cider apples) farming. The chief towns are Gloucester, Cheltenham and Stroud, where there is still a vestige of the ancient woollen industry.

Gloversville USA. Industrial town in New York 64 km (40 miles) NW of Albany. Pop. (1970) 19,677.

Important centre of tanning and glove manufacture since the early 19th cent. (hence the name). Also manufactures handbags and other leather goods.

Glynde England. Village in East Sussex 3 km (2 miles) ESE of Lewes. Nearby is Glyndebourne mansion, where opera festivals have been held since 1934.

Gmünd (Schwäbisch Gmünd) Germany. Town in Baden-Württemberg on the Rems R. 45 km (28 miles) E of Stuttgart. Pop. (1970) 44,600.

Noted since the Middle Ages for gold and silver working. Also manufactures clocks and watches, and optical instruments.

Gmunden Austria. Summer resort in Upper Austria in the beautiful scenery of the Salzkammergut at a height of 430 m (1410 ft) where the Traun R. issues from L. Traun (Traunsee). Pop. (1971) 12,270.

Brewing and wood-carving. Salt-mining in the neighbourhood.

Gniezno (Ger. **Gnesen**) Poland. Town in the Poznań voivodeship 48 km (30 miles) ENE of Poznań in the region of hills and lakes. Pop. (1990) 70,400. Railway junction.

Industries inc. flour-milling, sugar-refining and brewing.

One of the oldest cities in Poland; in its 10th-cent. cathedral the Polish kings were crowned until 1320 and there St Adalbert was buried.

Goa India. Union state on the W coast, bounded on the N by Maharashtra and on the E and S by Karnataka; formerly a Portuguese overseas territory becoming a state in 1987. Area 3702 sq km (1446 sq. miles). Pop. (1991) 1,168,622. Cap. Panaji.

Rice is the main food crop. Goa has considerable forests and minerals, inc. iron ore and bauxite, which are exported. Industries inc. shipbuilding, footwear, nylon fishing nets and fertilizers. Tourism is of great importance.

Goa was under Portuguese rule from 1510 and with two other Portuguese territories was incorporated into the Indian Union in 1961.

Gobi (Chinese **Shamo**, 'Stony Desert'). In its widest sense the vast area of desert in central Asia extending from the Pamirs through Xinjiang and Mongolia to Manchuria, extending to 1,295,000 sq km (500,000 sq. miles). The Gobi proper, however, the E part of this region (the W being known as the Takla Makan), stretches

1600 km (1000 miles) W–E and 480–960 km (300–600 miles) N–S. It is a plateau of average altitude 900–1500 m (2952–4920 ft) and consists partly of sandy desert, partly of stony desert, with areas of short-grass steppe where sheep, cattle, horses and camels are raised by the Mongolian nomads; its S extension within the great N bend of the Huang He is the Ordos plateau and to the W of this the Ala Shan range. The Gobi is crossed by the Ulan Bator–Tsining railway and several caravan routes.

Godalming England. Town in Surrey on the R. Wey 6 km (4 miles) SSW of Guildford. Pop. (1991) 20,630. Mainly residential. There is some light engineering.

The well-known public school Charterhouse (1611) moved here from London in 1872.

Godavari River India. River 1450 km (900 miles) long rising in the Western Ghats and flowing ESE across the Deccan, penetrating the Eastern Ghats by a gorge and entering the Bay of Bengal by a delta; the extensive irrigation canal system of the delta is linked with that of the Krishna delta. The river is sacred to the Hindus.

Godesberg (Bad Godesberg) Germany. Town and spa in North Rhine-Westphalia on the left bank of the Rhine R. just S of Bonn and now part of the latter. Mineral springs; pharmaceutical industry.

Here in 1938 Neville Chamberlain, prime minister of Britain, and Hitler, the German chancellor, held a meeting in preparation for the later Munich Pact.

Godthaab (Nuuk) Greenland. Chief town in the SW on the Godthaab Fiord at the entrance from Davis Strait. Pop. (1993) 12,181. Small seaport, with a radio station and a hospital. Hans Egede, a missionary, landed in 1721 and later established the first Danish colony in Greenland (1728).

Godwin Austen ➤K2 (CHOBRUM).

Gogra (Chagra) River. River 960 km (600 miles) long rising in the Himalayas SW of Rakas L. in Tibet, flowing SE into Nepal,

turning generally S and then ESE through Uttar Pradesh (India) to join the Ganges R. near Chapra.

Goiânia Brazil. Cap. of Goiás state; on the central Brazilian plateau at a height of 760 m (2493 ft) 209 km (130 miles) WSW of Brasilia. Pop. (1991) 922,222. Market in livestock and coffee. Built on modern lines. Replaced Goiás City as state cap. in 1937. Important as a commercial as well as an administrative centre.

Goiás Brazil. State on the central plateau at an average height of 760 m (2493 ft). Area 341,290 sq km (131,772 sq. miles). Pop. (1991) 4,018,903. Cap. Goiânia. Forested in the N; savannah in the S which is more developed. Main crops coffee, tobacco and rice.

Golcük, Lake Turkey. Lake situated SE of Elazig in E central Turkey. Area 70 sq km (27 sq. miles). Source of the Tigris R.

Gold Coast ➤GHANA.

Gold Coast Australia. District in Queensland extending about 32 km (20 miles) along the coast from Southport to Coolangatta (New South Wales border): a series of seaside resorts. Pop. (1973) 74,500, augmented considerably during the Christmas (summer) holidays.

Golden Gate USA. Strait 8 km (5 miles) long and nearly 3 km (2 miles) wide at the entrance to San Francisco Bay, California. The Golden Gate Bridge, crossing it from San Francisco to Marin county, is the world's longest single-span suspension bridge, measuring 1281 m (4202 ft) between the towers.

Golden Horn ➤ISTANBUL.

Goldsboro USA. Town in North Carolina on the Neuse R. 72 km (45 miles) SE of Raleigh. Pop. (1988) 35,000. Railway junction. Important market for brightleaf tobacco. Manufactures textiles.

Gomal Pass ➤GUMAL PASS.

Gomel ➤HOMEL.

Gomera ➤SANTA CRUZ DE TENERIFE.

Gondar Ethiopia. Town 40 km (25 miles) N of L. Tana at a height of 2290 m (7511 ft). Pop. (1984) 69,000. Linked by road with Asmara and Mitsiwa. Formerly the cap., it suffered considerably in civil wars. The last Italian stronghold in Ethiopia during World War II; captured by the Allies six months after the campaign had officially ended (1941).

Good Hope, Cape of South Africa. Headland in the SW of Western Cape Province at the W entrance to False Bay. Named Cape of Storms by Bartholomew Diaz, who first rounded it (1486); renamed Cape of Good Hope by Prince Henry the Navigator, because it offered hope of finding a sea route to India.

Goodwick ➤FISHGUARD AND GOODWICK.

Goodwin Sands England. Stretch of sandbanks 16 km (10 miles) long separated from the E coast of Kent by The Downs, a roadstead 10 km (6 miles) wide and partly exposed at low water. The sands, whose ends are marked by lightships, shelter The Downs but are a menace to shipping; many vessels have been wrecked here.

Goodwood England. Village in West Sussex 5 km (3 miles) NE of Chichester. Goodwood House, seat of the dukes of Richmond. Racecourse with an annual summer meeting ('Glorious' Goodwood). Motor-racing circuit.

Goole England. Port for containerized traffic in the East Riding of Yorkshire on the R. Ouse at the confluence with the R. Don 76 km (47 miles) from the North Sea through the Humber estuary. Pop. (1991) 18,284.

Exports steel slabs, general scrap metal, cement and timber products. Imports heavy-duty industrial plant, stainless steel scrap, chemicals and fertilizers, timber, cereals and animal feed. Industries inc. food-processing, edible oil refining and flour-milling. Manufactures machinery and chemicals. Linked by canals, rail and road with industrial Yorkshire and the Midlands; developed as a port with the construction of the canal system based on the Aire and Calder Navigation.

Goose Bay Canada. Village in SE Labrador on Goose Bay, L. Melville. The airport was first used in World War II as a ferrying base.

Göppingen Germany. Industrial town in Baden-Württemberg on the Fils R. 35 km (22 miles) ESE of Stuttgart. Pop. (1986) 51,400. Manufactures textiles, machinery, precision instruments, toys and plastics. 5 km (3 miles) N is the ruined Hohenstaufen castle.

Gorakhpur India. Town and railway junction in Uttar Pradesh 169 km (105 miles) NNE of Varanasi. Pop. (1991) 505,600.

Railway engineering. Manufactures inc. fertilizers, textiles and paper. Trade in grain and oilseeds. University (1957).

Gorgonzola Italy. Town in Milano province in Lombardy 18 km (11 miles) ENE of Milan, noted for the famous cheese named after it. Pop. (1990) 16,190.

Gori Georgia. Town on the Kura R. 64 km (40 miles) WNW of Tbilisi (Tiflis). Pop. (1991) 59,000.

Industrial centre in a fruit-growing and market-gardening region. Canning, saw-milling and other industries. Birthplace of Joseph Stalin (1879–1953).

Gorizia Italy. Cap. of Gorizia province in Friuli-Venezia Giulia on the Isonzo R. and on the Yugoslav border, formerly cap. of Austrian Görz-Gradisca. Pop. (1990) 39,000. Almost surrounded by mountains. Winter resort. Industrial town. Manufactures textiles and machinery. Has a cathedral (14th-cent.) and the old castle of the counts of Görz.

Gorky ➤NIZHNY NOVGOROD (named Gorky 1932–91).

Görlitz Germany. Industrial town in Saxony on the Neisse R. and on the Polish border 88 km (55 miles) E of Dresden. Pop. (1991) 70,450. Manufactures textiles, machinery, chemicals and glass. Railway engineering. Gothic church (15th-cent.). Nearby is the Chapel of the Holy Cross with a 15th-cent.

reproduction of the Holy Sepulchre at Jerusalem.

Gorlovka Ukraine. Town in the Donbas 32 km (20 miles) N of Makeyevka. Pop. (1990) 337,900.

Coalmining and industrial centre. Manufactures mining machinery, chemicals and fertilizers.

Gorno-Altai Russia. Republic of the Russian Federation in the Altai Mountains on the Mongolian frontier. Area 92,600 sq km (35,740 sq. miles). Pop. (1989) 192,000. Cap. Gorno-Altaisk. Largely forested. Main occupations cattle-rearing, lumbering, mining for coal, gold and mercury.

Gorno-Altaisk Russia. Cap. of the Republic of Gorno-Altai 225 km (140 miles) SE of Barnaul on the Katun R. Pop. (1990) 39,000. Meat-packing. Manufactures textiles and furniture. Linked with Mongolia by road across the Altai Mountains.

Gorno-Badakhshan Tajikistan. Autonomous Republic in the Pamir massif on the borders of Afghanistan and China. Area 63,700 sq km (24,590 sq. miles). Pop. (1990) 164,300. Cap. Khorog (pop. (1990) 14,800). Mountainous. Main occupation cattle and sheep rearing. Wheat, fruit and fodder crops are grown. Mining for gold, rock-crystal, mica, coal and salt is being developed.

Gorzów Wielkopolski (Ger. **Landsberg-an-der-Warthe**) Poland. Cap. and industrial town of the Gorzów Wielkopolski voivodeship, on the Warta (Warthe) R. 77 km (48 miles) SE of Szczecin (Stettin). Pop. (1990) 124,300. Manufactures textiles, chemicals and wood products. Formerly in the Prussian province of Brandenburg and was returned to Poland in 1945.

Gosforth England. Town in Tyne and Wear 3 km (2 miles) N of Newcastle-upon-Tyne. Pop. (1991) 23,315. Coalmining. Site of a racecourse, near which George Stephenson built his first locomotive (1814).

Goslar Germany. Town in Lower Saxony 40 km (25 miles) S of Brunswick on the NW slope of the Harz Mountains. Pop. (1989) 50,000. Railway junction. Tourist centre. Manufactures inc. furniture, chemicals, clothing and other light industry. Founded c. 920. A free imperial city from the late 13th cent. until 1802. Still medieval in appearance. Among its noteworthy buildings are the imperial palace (Kaiserhaus), the oldest secular building in Germany, built by the Emperor Henry III in the 11th cent. and restored in the 19th and the Zwinger, a 16th-cent. round tower with walls 23 ft thick.

Gosport England. Residential town and former naval base in Hampshire on Portsmouth Harbour opposite Portsmouth. Pop. (1991) 67,802. Has naval barracks and hospital as well as stores. Industries inc. yacht-building, marine engineering. 5 km (3 miles) W is the seaside resort of Lee-on-Solent.

Göta Canal Sweden. Waterway with 87 km (54 miles) of canals, between Göteborg on the Kattegat and the Baltic Sea near Söderköping. Opened in 1832. The W part inc. the Göta R., which avoids the Trollhättan Falls by a series of locks and continues to L. Väner; then a canal extends through several small lakes to L. Vätter, whence another canal leads through L. Rox to the Baltic.

Göteborg (Gothenburg) Sweden. Second largest city in Sweden and cap. of Göteborg och Bohus county at the mouth of the Göta R. on the Kattegat and W terminus of the Göta Canal. Pop. (1992) 433,811. Leading seaport, ice-free all year and fishing port. Shipbuilding, marine engineering. Manufactures ball-bearings, cars and textiles. Here in 1865 was instituted the famous Gothenburg licensing system for spirituous liquors. University (1891). Cathedral (17th/19th-cent., restored); 17th-cent. old town hall. Founded 1619 by Gustavus Adolphus. Became a major European port largely as a result of Napoleon's continental blockade.

Gotha Germany. Town in the Erfurt district of Thuringia 24 km (15 miles) W of Erfurt. Pop. (1991) 59,200. Manufactures railway rolling-stock, machinery, musical instruments, textiles and food products. A village in the time of Charlemagne, it was a town by the close of the 12th cent. It became a famous publishing centre, and here the first *Almanach de Gotha* was published in 1764. Cap. of Saxe-Coburg-Gotha 1826–1918.

Gotham England. Village 10 km (6 miles) SSW of Nottingham. Its inhabitants, the Wise Men of Gotham, won a reputation for stupidity: according to story their foolish behaviour was assumed in order to prevent King John, by no means a popular monarch, from residing in their midst – a ruse which succeeded.

Gothenburg ►GÖTEBORG.

Gotland Sweden. Island in the Baltic Sea comprising, with certain smaller islands, the county of Gotland. Total area 3140 sq km (1225 sq. miles). Pop. (1990) 57,100. Cap. Visby. Main occupations the cultivation of cereals and sugar-beet and sheep-rearing. Tourism also important. Engaged in trade as early as the Stone Age. Settled by German merchants in the 12th cent. Became Swedish in 1280, Danish in 1570 and Swedish again in 1645.

Göttingen Germany. Town in Lower Saxony on the Leine R. 40 km (25 miles) NE of Kassel. Pop. (1991) 124,000. Has a famous university founded (1724) by the Elector of Hanover, later King George II of England; the expulsion of seven professors, inc. the brothers Grimm (1837), because they had protested against the revocation of the liberal constitution of 1833 by King Ernest Augustus of Hanover, led to its decline, but it revived later. In medieval times a centre of cloth manufacture. Headquarters of the Max Planck Institute. Now manufactures optical and scientific instruments and machinery, and has film studios.

Gottwaldov ►ZLÍN.

Gouda Netherlands. Town in South Holland province 19 km (12 miles) NE of Rotterdam. Pop. (1994) 69,917.
Famous cheese market (Gouda cheese). Also manufactures pottery and candles.
Among its buildings are the Groote Kerk,

with a celebrated organ and stained-glass windows and the Gothic town hall.

Gough Island ►TRISTAN DA CUNHA.

Goulburn Australia. Town in New South Wales on the Hawkesbury R. 85 km (53 miles) NE of Canberra. Pop. (1991) 21,450. Railway junction. Wool and livestock markets. Woollen mills. Local granite quarries. Founded 1820.

Goulburn River Australia. River 555 km (345 miles) long, rising in the Great Dividing Range in Central Victoria and flowing generally NW to the Murray R. near Echuca. Irrigates an extensive area of orchards, vineyards, vegetable fields and pastures.

Goulette, La ►HALQ EL OUED.

Gourock Scotland. Small town in Inverclyde on the S shore of the Firth of Clyde 3 km (2 miles) WNW of Greenock. Pop. (1991) 11,743. Seaside resort. Yachting centre. Marine engineering and yachtbuilding.

Gower Wales. Peninsula in Swansea unitary authority between Burry Inlet and Swansea Bay, of considerable geological and archaeological interest. Along the picturesque S and W coasts there are several small holiday resorts.

Gozo (Gozzo) Malta. Island in the Mediterranean off the NW coast of Malta, to which it belongs. Area 67 sq km (26 sq. miles). Pop. (1990) 26,064. Chief town Victoria. More fertile than Malta; fruit and vegetables cultivated.

Graaff-Reinet South Africa. Town in Eastern Cape Province on the Sundays R. 225 km (140 miles) NNW of Port Elizabeth. Pop. (1970) 16,936. Irrigated gardens, orchards and vineyards make it an oasis on the dry Karroo Veld. Wool and mohair produced in the neighbourhood. Founded 1786.

Grafton Australia. Town in New South Wales on the Clarence R. 240 km (150 miles) S of Brisbane. Pop. (1991) 16,640. In a sugarcane and banana-growing and dairy-farming area. Trade in sugar, bananas and timber. Brewing.

Graham Land Antarctica. Barren, mountainous peninsula on the W side of the Weddell Sea, 1046 km (650 miles) S of Cape Horn. Formerly part of the Falkland Is. dependencies. Claimed by Argentina and Chile. Also known as Palmer Peninsula.

Grahamstown South Africa. Town in Eastern Cape Province 116 km (72 miles) NE of Port Elizabeth. Pop. (1970) 41,086. Called the 'most English' town in the province. Important educational and religious centre. Seat of the Rhodes University (1904). Anglican cathedral and Roman Catholic pro-cathedral. Founded as a military post against Kaffir tribesmen by Colonel Graham (1812); settled 1820.

Grain, Isle of England. Island between the R. Thames and the R. Medway in N Kent. Area 13 sq km (5 sq. miles). Connected to the mainland by road and railway across the narrow Yantlet Creek. Site of a large oil refinery.

Grain Coast ➤GUINEA, GULF OF.

Grampian Region Scotland. Former region in the NE formed in 1975 from the counties of Aberdeen, Kincardine, Banff and most of Moray. In 1996 it was again divided into City of Aberdeen, Aberdeenshire and Moray.

Grampians Scotland. Name generally applied to the mountain system of the Scottish Highlands lying between Glenmore and the Central Lowlands. Its S boundary is roughly the line Helensburgh–Stonehaven; it inc. Ben Nevis (1344 m; 4408 ft) and the peaks of the Cairngorm Mountains; Ben Macdhui (1310 m; 4297 ft), Braeriach (1296 m; 4251 ft) and Cairn Gorm (1246 m; 4087 ft). Rivers flowing N from the Grampians inc. the Spey, Don, Dee, Findhorn and tributaries; those flowing S are the Esk, Tay, Forth and tributaries. The name is derived from Mons Graupius, the scene of Agricola's defeat of Galgacus and the northern Picts (AD 84), this having been misread as Grampius.

Granada Nicaragua. Cap. of the Granada department in the SW on L. Nicaragua. Pop. (1985) 89,000.

Manufactures inc. clothing, furniture and soap. Distilling. Trade in coffee and sugar-cane.

Founded in 1524. Raided several times by pirates in the 17th cent. and partly burned in 1856, but some of the old buildings from Spanish colonial times remain.

Granada Spain. 1. Province in the S, in Andalusia, bounded on the S by the Mediterranean. Area 12,531 sq km (4838 sq. miles). Pop. (1991) 806,499. Crossed by the Sierra Nevada, which rises to 3483 m (11,424 ft) in Mulhacén (the highest peak in Spain) and several less formidable ranges. The coastal plain and many of the valleys are fertile and, with irrigation, cereals, sugar-cane and tobacco are produced. 2. Cap. of Granada province on the Genil R. Pop. (1991) 286,688. Trade in agricultural produce. Manufactures inc. sugar, brandy, leather, soap and textiles. Also a famous tourist resort, largely because of the magnificent Alhambra palace, built chiefly in the 13th and 14th cent., the finest example of Moorish art in Spain. On a neighbouring hill is the Generalife, the royal summer residence, with its beautiful gardens. The 16th/18th-cent. cathedral contains in its Chapel Royal the tomb of Ferdinand and Isabella; nearby is the university (founded 1531). With its narrow, tortuous streets and oriental buildings, old Granada preserves many remnants of its long Moorish occupation. The city became cap. of the Moorish kingdom of Granada, which inc. the modern provinces of Granada, Almeria and Málaga, in 1238, flourished as a centre of commerce and learning and fell to the Spaniards in 1492.

Granby Canada. Industrial town in Quebec 68 km (42 miles) E of Montreal. Pop. (1986) 38,508 (mainly French-speaking). Manufactures inc. textiles, rubber and plastic products and furniture.

Gran Chaco South America. An immense plain, about 647,500 sq km (250,000 sq. miles) of lowland between the Andean foothills and the Paraguay and Paraná rivers. Drained to the Paraná by the Pilcomayo and Bermejo rivers. Shared by Bolivia, Paraguay and Argentina. Hot rainy summers; mild, generally dry, winters with sudden cold spells. Huge areas are inundated in the rainy season. Largely scrub forest (where the quebracho is cut down for timber and tannin) and grassland (where there is some ranching). Very sparsely settled, about 1 person per sq km. Over this unpromising area Paraguay and Bolivia fought a costly and exhausting war (1932–5).

Grand Bahama Bahamas, West Indies. Island immediately W of Great Abaco Island and NNW of Nassau. Area 1373 sq km (530 sq. miles). Pop. (1990) 40,898. Chief town West End. Industries inc. tourism, chemicals and oil-refining.

Grand Banks North Atlantic. A section of the continental shelf extending about 800 km (500 miles) SE from Newfoundland, mainly at a depth of 90–180 m (295–590 ft). A fishing-ground, esp. for cod, visited by the trawlers of many nations. Notorious for fogs and icebergs are carried down by the Labrador Current, esp. in spring.

Grand Bassam ➤CÔTE D'IVOIRE.

Grand Canal (Chinese **Yun-ho**) China. The longest canal in China (about 1600 km (1000 miles)), linking Tianjing (N) with Hangzhou (S). The central section, joining the Chang Jiang to the Huang He, is the oldest, probably dating from the 6th cent., the S section having been added in the 7th cent. and the N section in the 13th cent. (by Kublai Khan). Still used in the S, it has lost much of its importance because of silting.

Grand Canal Italy. The main waterway in Venice.

Grand Canary (Gran Canaria) Canary Islands. The most important island in the archipelago, between Tenerife and Fuerteventura. Area 1533 sq km (592 sq. miles). Cap. Las Palmas. Extinct volcanoes rise to over 1800 m (5904 ft). The fine scenery

and pleasant climate have made it a popular resort. Fertile: produces bananas, sugar-cane, tomatoes and potatoes. Exports through Las Palmas and its outport Puerto de la Luz.

Grand Canyon USA. Gorge of the Colorado R. extending E–W from its confluence with the Little Colorado R. to L. Mead; 351 km (218 miles) long, 6–24 km (4–15 miles) wide and in places over 1.6 km (1 mile) deep. Cut into a high plateau, it reveals in its rock strata of varied shape and colour, eroded into 'towers', 'temples' and other bizarre formations, the long geological past; it exhibits vertical river erosion on the grandest scale. A popular tourist region, with excellent facilities. Part of the Canyon, inc. 169 km (105 miles) of gorge, was made into the Grand Canyon National Park in 1919.

Grande Chartreuse ➤CHARTREUSE.

Grande Comore ➤COMOROS ISLANDS.

Grand Falls (Newfoundland) Canada. Town on the Exploits R. Pop. (1991) 14,693 (with Windsor). Manufactures newsprint (since 1909). The nearby falls supply power to an important hydroelectric plant.

Grand Forks USA. Town in North Dakota at the confluence of the Red River of the North and the Red Lake R. Pop. (1970) 39,008. Railway junction. Trade in wheat and livestock. Flour-milling and meat-packing. Seat of the University of North Dakota (1883).

Grand Island USA. Town in Nebraska 200 km (125 miles) WSW of Omaha. Pop. (1970) 31,269. Railway junction. Industries inc. railway engineering, beet-sugar refining and flour-milling. Founded by German settlers in 1857.

Grand Rapids USA. Industrial and commercial town in SW Michigan at the rapids on the Grand R. 160 km (100 miles) W of Flint. Pop. (1990) 189,126.

Leading US centre of furniture manufacture and distribution. Now utilizes imported timber. Also an agricultural market (dairy produce and fruit). Manufactures refrigerators, automobile parts, hardware, paper and chemicals. The town began as a trading-post and lumbering centre in the 1820s; the furniture industry developed from the lumber trade.

Grangemouth Scotland. Port in Falkirk on the S bank of the Firth of Forth and at the E end of the Forth–Clyde Canal 3 km (2 miles) ENE of Falkirk. Pop. (1991) 18,739.

Important oil refinery. Chemical, engineering and shipbuilding industries.

Grange-over-Sands (Grange) England. Town in Cumbria on Morecambe Bay. Pop. (1971) 3627. Seaside resort.

Granite City USA. Industrial town in Illinois 11 km (7 miles) NNE of St Louis. Pop. (1970) 40,440.

Railway junction. Manufactures inc. iron and steel, tinplate, railway equipment and chemicals.

Grantham England. Town in Lincolnshire 35 km (22 miles) SSW of Lincoln. Pop. (1991) 33,243. Railway junction. Engineering. Manufactures agricultural machinery and road rollers. Church of St Wulfram (13th-cent.); medieval Angel Hotel, where Richard III signed the death warrant of the Duke of Buckingham (1483); the grammar school which was attended by Sir Isaac Newton, English scientist and mathematician (1642–1727).

Grasmere England. Village in Cumbria in the Lake District 5 km (3 miles) NW of Ambleside. Pop. (1971) 1173. Tourist centre beside Lake Grasmere amid beautiful scenery. The graves of William and Dorothy Wordsworth, English writers, are in the churchyard; the house where they lived (1799–1808) is a museum.

Grasse France. Town and resort in the Alpes-Maritimes department overlooking the Mediterranean Sea 11 km (7 miles) NNW of Cannes. Pop. (1990) 42,000.

Stands among orange groves and extensive flower gardens (esp. roses) – from the produce of which perfumes and essences are distilled. Demand much reduced by competition from cheap synthetic perfumes; cut flowers, fruit (esp. peaches) and early vegetables now produced.

Birthplace of Jean Honoré Fragonard, painter and engraver (1732–1806).

Graubünden (Grisons) Switzerland. The largest but most sparsely populated canton, in the E. Area 7109 sq km (2744 sq. miles). Pop. (1990) 170,500. Cap. Chur. Mountainous, with many glaciers. Has the upper valleys of the Rhine and Inn; in the latter (the Engadine) and elsewhere are several well-known resorts, inc. Davos, St Moritz, Arosa, Chur. It joined the Swiss Confederation in 1803. German, Romansch and Italian are spoken.

Graves France. Region in the Gironde department in the SW, extending along the left bank of the Garonne R. between Langon and Bordeaux. Produces from its gravel soil (hence the name) the well-known Graves wines.

Gravesend England. Town in N Kent on the S bank of the R. Thames opposite Tilbury. Pop. (1991) 51,435. Port. Customs and pilot station within the Port of London. Yachting centre. Manufactures paper and cement. Industries inc. printing, engineering and market-gardening. Connected by ferry (passengers and vehicles) with Tilbury. In St George's Church is the tomb of the American Indian princess Pocahontas (1617).

Grays (Grays Thurrock) ►THURROCK.

Graz Austria. Second largest city and cap. of Styria province, on the Mur R. where its valley broadens into the fertile plain known as Grazer Feld 145 km (90 miles) SSW of Vienna. Pop. (1991) 232,155.

Cultural, commercial and industrial centre. Also a resort and spa. Industries have expanded with the exploitation of coal and iron deposits and the development of hydroelectric power. Manufactures iron and steel, bicycles, precision instruments, paper, glass, textiles and leather.

The old town is dominated by the Schlossberg, on which there are parks, a famous clock tower and the ruins of a fortress (destroyed 1809). University (1586). Gothic cathedral (15th-cent.); 16th-cent. Landhaus; an opera house (1899).

Great Australian Bight Indian Ocean. Wide bay of the Indian Ocean in the S coast of Australia, extending some 1100 km (700 miles) between Cape Pasley (W) and Cape Carnot (E). Shores generally inhospitable owing to the cliffs of the low semi-arid plateau along much of the perimeter. Surveyed by Matthew Flinders in 1802.

Great Barrier Reef Australia. Greatest coral reef in the world, in the Coral Sea, extending about 1900 km (1200 miles) SSE from Torres Strait to about lat. 24° S off the coast of Queensland. The corals rise from submerged ridges parallel to the Eastern Highlands; in the W the tops of partly submerged folds form islands, separated from the shore by narrow, navigable channels. At low tide some 2500 reefs are exposed. Its natural beauty attracts tourists. Mother-of-pearl and trepang (*bêche de mer*) obtained.

Great Basin USA. Interior region, roughly triangular in shape, nearly 543,900 sq km (210,000 sq. miles) in area, between the Sierra Nevada and the Cascade Range on the W and the Colorado Plateau and the Wasatch Range on the E. Mostly in Nevada and Utah, with a large area in California and small areas in Oregon, Idaho and Wyoming. Not a single basin-shaped depression, but about 100 independent drainage basins, with lofty mountain ranges, deserts (Mohave, Great Salt Lake, Black Rock, Colorado, Death Valley), and salt lakes (Great Salt, Utah, Pyramid, Walker). The entire region is semi-arid and agriculture is possible only with irrigation.

Great Bear Lake Canada. Lake in the Mackenzie District, Northwest Territories. Area 32,260 sq km (12,456 sq. miles). Irregular in shape, with five 'arms' and many small islands. Drained by the Great Bear R. into the Mackenzie R. Owing to surface ice (even in summer), only navigable for four months in the year. Discovered in the late 18th cent. and named after the bears found on its shores.

Great Belt (Danish **Store Bëlt**) Denmark. Strait about 64 km (40 miles) long and between 16 km (10 miles) and 32 km (20 miles) wide between Fyn and Zealand islands and linking the Kattegat with the Baltic Sea.

Great Britain. Largest island of the British Isles, comprising England, Scotland and Wales, and inc. islands governed with the mainland (Isle of Wight, Scillies, Hebrides, Orkneys and Shetlands), but excluding the Channel Is. and the Isle of Man, which are separately governed. With Northern Ireland it is known as the United Kingdom of Great Britain and Northern Ireland and this is often what is meant when the term Britain is used; in this sense the Channel Islands and Isle of Man should also be included. It is bounded on the N, NW and SW by the Atlantic Ocean, on the E by the North Sea, on the S by the English Channel, which separates it from France and on the W by St George's Channel, Irish Sea and North Channel, which separate it from Ireland. Its greatest length N–S (Cape Wrath–Lizard Point) is 960 km (600 miles); greatest width (Land's End–North Foreland) 515 km (320 miles). Like the remainder of the British Isles, it stands on the continental shelf, having once been joined to the mainland of Europe. Its highest land is in the N and W, with the result that most of the principal rivers flow to the E coast, the exceptions being the Severn and the Clyde. ►UNITED KINGDOM.

Great Dividing Range Australia. Name for the E highlands, running roughly parallel to the coast, consisting mainly of a series of tablelands in varying stages of erosion, 600–2235 m (1968–7331 ft) in height, named according to location, e.g. Blue Mountains, New England Ranges, Atherton Plateau. Highest point Mt Kosciusko (2235 m; 7331 ft) in the Australian Alps. The highlands expose rocks of all ages; in Tertiary times there was great volcanic activity so that some highlands have fertile soils weathered from basalt, e.g. parts of the Atherton Plateau. They form the watershed between rivers flowing to the Coral and Tasman Seas and those flowing to the Gulf of Carpentaria and Indian Ocean.

Greater London ►LONDON.

Greater Manchester ►MANCHESTER.

Great Falls USA. Town in Montana on the Missouri R. Pop. (1990) 56,725.

Industrial centre, in a mining and agricultural region. Copper and zinc refineries, oil refinery. Sometimes known as 'electric city'. Manufactures electrical equipment, copper and aluminium wire and cables, and bricks. Named after the falls nearby on the Missouri R. which supply hydroelectric power. Founded 1884.

Great Lake Australia. Shallow lake at a height of 1160 m (3805 ft) on the central plateau of Tasmania. Area 114 sq km (44 sq. miles). Depth increased by Miena Dam on the S shore.

Great Lakes North America. Group of freshwater lakes on the Canadian–US frontier: (W–E) Lakes Superior, Michigan, Huron, Erie, Ontario. Area of water surface 248,640 sq km (96,000 sq. miles). The international frontier passes through all the lakes except L. Michigan, which is entirely within the USA. Their importance as a waterway has been increased by the St Lawrence Seaway. When they are open to navigation (about May-Dec.) vast quantities of iron ore, coal and grain pass through them and through the various ship canals to the St Lawrence R. Also important fisheries, although there is serious pollution. Many lakeside resorts.

Great Marlow ►MARLOW.

Great Oasis ►KHARGA OASIS.

Great Plains North America. Region E of the Rocky Mountains about 610 km (380 miles) wide, inc. parts of Alberta and Saskatchewan (Canada) and extending S to New Mexico and Texas. Height varies from 1800 m (5904 ft) (W) to 450 m (1476 ft) (E). Crossed by broad, shallow river valleys and covered largely with short grass. Main occupations stock-rearing and grain cultivation.

Great Rift Valley Middle East/E Africa. Vast elongated depression extending from the Jordan R. valley (Syria) through the Sea of Galilee, the Dead Sea and the Gulf of Aqaba, along the Red Sea into Ethiopia, then across Kenya, Tanzania and Malawi into Mozambique; in all *c.* 8700 km (5400 miles). In E Africa it is marked by a chain of lakes, mainly long and narrow, inc. (N–S) Rudolf, Natron and Malawi (Nyasa); in its vicinity there are examples of volcanic activity, e.g. Mt Kilimanjaro and Mt Kenya. A W branch extends from the N end of L. Malawi and takes in Lakes Tanganyika, Kivu, Edward and Albert. Between the two branches, on a plateau, is L. Victoria. The altitude of the Great Rift Valley varies from over 1800 m (5904 ft) above sea level in S Kenya to 392 m (1286 ft) below sea level on the floor of the Dead Sea.

Great Salt Lake USA. Inland salt lake in the Great Basin in NW Utah at a height of 1286 m (4218 ft) between the Wasatch Range and the Great Salt Lake Desert, with no outlet. The area has varied in size and depth. It receives the Bear, Jordan and Beaver rivers and has many islands. The salinity increases with a decrease in area and at about 25 per cent is too high for fish. It is the remnant of the much larger prehistoric L. Bonneville.

Great Slave Lake Canada. Lake in the S Mackenzie District of the Northwest Territories. Area 28,490 sq km (11,000 sq. miles). Of irregular shape, it receives the Yellowknife, Slave and Hay rivers and is drained by the Mackenzie R. Navigable July–Oct. Main settlements Yellowknife, Reliance, Fort Resolution, Hay River. Named after the Slave Indians, who once inhabited its shores.

Great Wall China. Defensive wall in N China extending about 2400 km (1500 miles) along the S edge of the Mongolian plateau about 6 m (20 ft) wide at the base and 3.6 m (12 ft) at the top, height 4.5–9 m (15–30 ft) with taller towers at intervals. The E part, built of stone, earth and brick, is well-preserved, but the W part, constructed of earth, is much eroded. Originally built by

Shih Huang Ti of the Ch'in dynasty in the 3rd cent. BC as a defence against the Mongols. Restored by the Ming emperor Hsien-tung in the 15th cent.

Great Yarmouth (Yarmouth) England. Town in E Norfolk on a long, narrow peninsula between the North Sea (E) and the R. Bure, Breydon Water (formed by the R. Yare and the R. Waveney) and the R. Yare (W). Pop. (1991) 47,668. Seaside resort, once famous for its Yarmouth 'bloaters' (cured herring). Industries inc. food-processing and engineering. In the 1960s it became a base for North Sea oil and natural gas exploitation, partially compensating for loss of the herring fishing industry.

The modern town has absorbed Southtown and Gorleston on the opposite (W) side of the estuary. Its Church of St Nicholas, founded in 1101 and one of the largest in England, was destroyed in World War II (1942) and rebuilt; other buildings inc. the 14th-cent. Tollhouse, now a museum, and the 17th-cent. Fishermen's Hospital. Birthplace of Anna Sewell, English author of *Black Beauty* (1820–78).

Greece. Republic in SE Europe occupying the S part of the Balkan Peninsula and many islands in the Aegean and Ionian Seas. It is bounded on the N by Albania, Macedonia and Bulgaria, on the E by Turkey and the Aegean Sea, S by the Mediterranean Sea and W by the Ionian Sea. Area 131,987 sq km (50,943 sq. miles). The islands area 25,042 sq km (9669 sq. miles). Pop. (1995) 10,493,000 (72 per cent urban). Life expectancy, 75 years male, 80 female. Cap. Athens (its port Piraeus). Other cities Thessaloniki, Patras, Heraklion, Larissa and Kallithea. Currency: Drachma = 100 lepta. Greece is a country of mountains, peninsulas and islands. In the N the central backbone of the Pindus Mountains, virtually a continuation of the Dinaric Alps of Yugoslavia and Albania, separates Epirus (W) from Thessaly and Macedonia (E). Branches of this range to the E inc. the Othrys Mountains and Olympus (2911 m; 9550 ft), the country's highest peak and legendary seat of the gods, continuing in the islands of Euboea and Andros, and to the SE Parnassus (2459 m; 8066 ft) and Gióna (2512 m; 8239 ft), reappearing in the more W islands of the Cyclades. The Peloponnese, or Morea, the extensive S peninsula, is joined to central Greece by the narrow Isthmus of Corinth, cut by the Corinth Canal, and rises in the Taygetus Mountains (S) to 2406 m (7892 ft). Crete, the Ionian Is. and many of the numerous Aegean islands are also mountainous. Macedonia and Thrace in the NE have limited plains, crossed by the country's principal rivers – the Vardar (Axios), Struma (Strimon), Mesta (Nestos) and Maritsa (Evros); the last-named separates Thrace from Turkey, while the Rhodope Mountains separate it from Bulgaria. In the coastal regions and the islands the climate is Mediterranean in character, the hot, dry summers making irrigation essential, but continental conditions affect the northern mountainous areas, with severe winters. Land use: forested 20 per cent, meadows and pastures 41 per cent, agricultural and under permanent cultivation 31 per cent. The official lang. is Greek. About 98 per cent of the pop. is Christian, the majority Eastern Orthodox. There are about 100,000 Muslims. The majority of the pop. is Greek but there are small minorities of Macedonians, Turks and Albanians.

It is primarily an agricultural country. About one-third of the land is cultivable, and farming supports about 22 per cent of the pop. The uplands were once well-wooded, but deforestation has caused destruction by soil erosion and they are now used for the grazing of large numbers of sheep and goats. Much of the land is marginal and suffers from lack of fertilizers and yield of some crops is low, but Greece is self-sufficient in barley, maize, wheat, sugar-beet, fruit, cheese and vegetables. On the fertile plains and valleys the tobacco and grapes, chiefly in the form of currants and sultanas, are important exports; other products are olives, olive oil and citrus fruits. The main industries are oil-refining and processing natural gas, lignite, bauxite and uranium, shipbuilding and the manufacture of tobacco products, textiles, steel and cement. They are concentrated chiefly in the districts of Athens, neighbouring Piraeus, its port, which handles most of the foreign trade and Salonika. Greece has an important merchant navy. The highest proportion of its foreign trade is with Germany. Tourism, the merchant fleet, remittances sent back by Greek nationals working abroad and assistance from the European Union are the main sources of foreign currency.

Some of the earliest civilizations in Europe flourished in Greece, notably the Minoan, on Crete, and the Mycenaean, which fell before invasions by Aeolians, Ionians and Dorians, and had disappeared by *c.* 1100 BC. The mountainous nature of the country and the virtual isolation of the various regions led to the development of the city-states, prevented national unity and drove the people into an association with the sea which has lasted to the present day. From the 8th cent. BC the Greeks founded colonies around the coasts of the Black Sea and the Mediterranean, inc. Magna Graecia in S Italy. When the Persians under Darius invaded Greece (490 BC) they were defeated by the Athenians at Marathon; again under Xerxes they were defeated by the Athenians and Spartans together at Salamis (480) and Plataea (479). There now followed the great age of Greek drama, poetry, sculpture, architecture and philosophy, but the attempt at unity through an Athenian empire only led to the Peloponnesian War (431–404), in which Athens was defeated by Sparta, the latter to fall in turn to Thebes (397–371). Strife between the city-states allowed Philip II of Macedon to establish his supremacy (338), paving the way for his son, Alexander the Great, who through his conquests carried Greek culture to Egypt and as far E as India. By 146 BC Greece had been conquered by the Romans and it then remained in the Byzantine Empire (AD 395) until the Turkish conquest (1453). Under Turkish rule parts of Greece were occupied at times by the Venetians and the country was backward and oppressed. Not until 1821, when the War of Independence began, was there a national revival. Recognized as free in 1829, Greece had Prince Otto of Bavaria placed on the throne in 1832, only

to be deposed in 1862 and replaced by Prince George of Denmark. In the Greco–Turkish War (1896–7) Greece was defeated, but turned the tables on the old enemy in the Balkan Wars (1912–13) and gained considerable territory. Led by the Prime Minister, Venizelos and against the wishes of King Constantine, Greece supported the Allied cause in World War I (1917) and was rewarded with a large section of Thrace. Hundreds of thousands of Greek refugees from Turkey were resettled, and many Turks and Bulgarians left the country. A republic was set up in 1923, but the monarchy was restored in 1935. In World War II the Greeks repelled the Italians but were overwhelmed by the Germans and at the end the country, already in a state of political and economic chaos, was torn by civil war. George II returned to the throne in 1946, to be succeeded in the following year by Paul I, who was succeeded in 1964 by Constantine II. Following a military *coup* (1967), the king fled the country and government was taken over by a junta. In 1973 Greece became a republic, the junta was overthrown in a bloodless *coup* and a new Constitution was introduced in 1975. There is a 300-member Chamber of Deputies elected for 4-year terms by proportional representation.

The Monastic Republic of Mount Athos, the easternmost of the three prongs of the peninsula of Chalcidice, is a self-governing community composed of 20 monasteries.

The country is divided for administrative purposes into 13 regions: Attica, Aegean N, Aegean S, Crete, Epirus, Greece Central, Greece West, Ionian Is., Macedonia Central, Macedonia E and Thrace, Macedonia W, Peloponnese and Thessaly; each subdivided into 51 prefectures or *nomes (nomoi)*.

Greeley USA. Town in Colorado 80 km (50 miles) NNE of Denver. Pop. (1990) 60,540. Commercial centre in an irrigated agricultural region. Sugar-refining (beet), vegetable-canning. Founded in 1870 as a cooperative farming and temperance settlement.

Green Bay USA. Port and industrial town

Greenland

in Wisconsin at the head of Green Bay on
L. Michigan. Pop. (1990) 94,466. Excellent
harbour, open April–Dec. Ships large quantities of cheese and other dairy products.
Industries inc. paper mills, engineering
works, furniture and clothing factories.

Greenland. Island off the NE of North
America, lying mainly within the Arctic
Circle, formerly a colony of Denmark; since
1953 an integral part of the Danish kingdom.
Separated in the extreme NW from Ellesmere Island (Canada) by the Kane Basin and
the Kennedy Channel, and in the W and
SW from Baffin Island (Canada) by the Davis
Strait and Baffin Bay; bounded by the Arctic
Ocean in the N, the Greenland Sea in the
E, the Denmark Strait in the SE and the
Atlantic in the S. Area 2,175,600 sq km
(840,000 sq. miles). Pop. (1993) 44,289
(inc. 6559 Danes; most of the remainder are
pure Eskimo or of mixed Eskimo and Danish
descent). Cap. Nuuk (Godthaab). Important
settlements inc. Godhavn, Sukkertoppen and
Angmagssalik (E coast). The greater part of
the surface is covered with an ice cap estimated to be 2100–2400 m (6888–7872 ft)
thick in the form of a basin or depression
surrounded by coastal mountains rising to
3702 m (12,143 ft) in Mt Gunnbjorn in the
SE. Some of the land beneath the ice-cap is
below sea level; so Greenland may be not
one large island but a number of smaller ones.
Peary Land in the extreme N has no ice-cap.
Many glaciers flow from the ice-cap to coastal
fiords, the largest being Humboldt Glacier
in the NW. The polar climate is uncertain
and changeable, with frequent fogs and a
wide range of temperatures and of amounts of
precipitation. Divided into West Greenland,
cap. Nuuk (Godthaab), East Greenland and
North Greenland (Thule). The inhabitants
live mainly on the W coast.

Main occupations are fishing and fish-
processing; whaling and seal hunting have
declined. In 1992 120 whales were caught.
Some sheep raised in the SW. It has large
deposits of uranium. Other minerals inc.
coal, lead, zinc, but the mine was closed
down in 1990. Onshore drilling for oil began

in 1984. There is a US airforce base at Thule.
Discovered (c. 982) by Eric the Red, who
named it Greenland to attract settlers. The
first settlers came from Iceland; by the 14th
cent. there were several thousand inhabitants.
Godthaab dates from 1721, when Hans
Egede, a Danish missionary, began the
'modern' colonization of the country. The
first crossing of the interior was made by
Nansen, who travelled E–W in 1888. Following a referendum in 1979 home rule was
introduced and full internal self-government
was attained in 1981. Greenland left the
European Union in 1984.

Greenland Sea Arctic Ocean. The S part
of the Arctic, between Greenland and Spitsbergen. Largely covered by ice, driven S
through it by the E Greenland Current.

Greenock Scotland. Town and seaport in
Inverclyde on the S bank of the R. Clyde
estuary 34 km (21 miles) WNW of Glasgow.
Pop. (1991) 50,013.

Important shipbuilding, engineering and
sugar-refining industries. Also manufactures
woollen goods, aluminium ware and
chemicals.

Has the reputation of being the wettest
town in Scotland, with a rainfall of 160 cm
(63 ins.) annually. Birthplace of James Watt,
Scottish engineer and inventor (1736–1819).

Greensboro USA. Industrial town in North
Carolina 134 km (83 miles) NE of Charlotte.
Pop. (1990) 183,521. Manufactures textiles,
hosiery, stoves and chemicals. Important
financial and education centre. Named after
General Nathaneal Green, hero of the battle
of Guilford Court House (1781).

Greenville (Mississippi) USA. River port
on the Mississippi R. 160 km (100 miles)
NW of Jackson. Pop. (1970) 39,648. In a
fertile cotton-growing region in the Mississippi–Yazoo delta. Manufactures chemicals,
metal goods and cottonseed oil.

Greenville (South Carolina) USA. Town
on the Reedy R. 160 km (100 miles) NW
of Columbia. Pop. (1990) 58,282. Important
industrial and commercial centre. Manufac-

tures textiles, chemicals and metal goods. Seat of the Furman University (1826).

Greenwich England. Outer borough of SE London on the S bank of the R. Thames. Pop. (1994) 212,200. Connected to Poplar on the N bank by Greenwich Tunnel (pedestrians) and the Blackwall Tunnel (vehicles). In Greenwich Park (75 ha; 185 acres) is the original Royal Observatory, designed by Wren (1675), accepted internationally as being on the prime meridian of longitude (from 1884) and source of Greenwich Mean Time, moved to Herstmonceux in 1950. Greenwich Hospital, also by Wren, stands on the site of a former royal palace, the birthplace of Henry VIII, Elizabeth I and Mary. It became a Royal Naval College in 1873 but is now closed; it may be used by the University of Greenwich. Greenwich is to be the site of a Millennium 2000 exhibition.

Greenwich USA. Town in SW Connecticut 8 km (5 miles) WSW of Stamford. Pop. (1970) 59,755. Picturesque. Largely residential. Boatbuilding Manufactures marine engines and pumps.

Greenwich Village USA. Part of the borough of Manhattan, New York City, bordered on the W by the Hudson R. A popular bohemian quarter, with old houses, winding streets and exotic shops, restaurants and night clubs. Grew up in colonial times as a separate village and soon became a high-class residential quarter much frequented by authors, artists and actors. Thomas Paine, Walt Whitman, Henry James and Mark Twain were all associated with it.

Greifswald Germany. Town in Mecklenburg-West Pomerania on the Ryck R. near its mouth 82 km (51 miles) E of Rostock. Pop. (1981) 61,388. Railway junction. Brewing. Manufactures textiles and has timber industries. Also a cultural centre. University (1456).

Greiz Germany. Town in the Gera district of Thuringia on the White Elster R. 29 km (18 miles) SSE of Gera. Pop. (1971) 39,200.

Engineering. Manufactures textiles, paper and chemicals.

Grenada West Indies. The State of Grenada is the southernmost of the Windward Is. in the Caribbean. Also included in the state are the Grenadines islets, Carriacou and Petit Martinique. Area 344 sq km (133 sq. miles). Pop. (1995) 92,000 (32 per cent urban). Life expectancy, 68 years male, 73 female. Cap. St George's. Other towns Gouyave and Grenville. Currency: East Caribbean dollar = 100 cents. One of the most picturesque of the West Indian islands, it is roughly oblong in shape. Mountainous, rising in Mt St Catherine to 841 m (2758 ft). Grand Étang at a height of 531 m (1742 ft) is a large crater lake. Land use: forested 9 per cent, meadows and pasture 3 per cent, agricultural and other permanent cultivation 32 per cent. About 53 per cent of the pop. is Roman Catholic and 85 per cent are black.

Exports cacao, mace, nutmegs and bananas. Manufactures inc. rum and lime juice.

Grenada, sometimes known as the spice islands, has a thriving tourist industry. For many years, although cruise ships called, there was an inadequate airport; the new Port Salines airport with long runways was built with Cuban help. This was interpreted by the US that it would be used by Communist military aircraft and it indirectly caused the US-led invasion of 1983. It was discovered in 1498 by Columbus. Held by Britain from 1783 and became an associated state within the Commonwealth in 1967, becoming independent in 1974; Queen Elizabeth II is head of state and is represented by a Governor-General. The 1973 constitution was suspended in 1979 following a revolution. US-led forces invaded Grenada at the request of a group of Caribbean countries following the killing of the Prime Minister. The 1973 constitution was later restored. There is a bicameral legislature consisting of a 13-member Senate appointed by the Governor-General and a 15-member House of Representatives elected by universal suffrage.

Grenadines West Indies. Chain of small islands in the Windward Is., extending 96 km

369

(60 miles) between St Vincent and Grenada and divided between them. The largest of the group, Carriacou (area 28 sq km (11 sq. miles), pop. (1985) 7000), belongs to Grenada.

Grenoble France. Prefecture of the Isère department and former cap. of the Dauphiné on the Isère R. 93 km (58 miles) SE of Lyon. Pop. (1990) 153,973. Long noted for the manufacture of kid gloves, now important also for ferro-alloys, turbines, electrical equipment, machine-tools, cement, paper and liqueurs, the metallurgical industries being largely dependent on hydroelectric power. It has a Franco–German nuclear research reactor. Tourism is based on skiing.

Ancient and strongly fortified city. Cathedral (11th/13th-cent.); 16th-cent. Palais de Justice; celebrated university (founded 1339). Beautifully situated; a major tourist centre for the French Alps. Its name is a corruption of Gratianopolis, the town founded here by the Emperor Gratian in the 4th cent. Birthplace of Stendhal, the novelist (1783–1842).

Gretna Green Scotland. Village in Dumfriesshire on the English border 14 km (9 miles) NW of Carlisle. Pop. (1991) 3149. Long famous as the venue of runaway English marriages, usually performed by the local blacksmith. The practice was severely restricted in 1856, when a law was passed requiring 3 weeks' residence in Scotland by one of the parties. The marriages were declared illegal from 1940.

Grevena Greece. *Nome* in Macedonia. Area 2291 sq km (885 sq. miles). Pop. (1991) 36,797. Cereals and tobacco cultivated. Cap. Grevena (Pop. (1981) 7430).

Greymouth New Zealand. Town and port on the W coast of the South Island at the mouth of the Grey R. Pop. (1987) 7530. Exports coal and timber. Linked with Christchurch by rail through the Southern Alps.

Grijalva River ➤MEXICO.

Grimsby (Great Grimsby) England. Town in North East Lincolnshire on the S side and near the mouth of the Humber estuary. Pop. (1991) 88,900. Once claimed to be the world's leading fishing port, with associated industries, e.g. manufacture of fertilizers, nets and ice. Also brewing; manufactures food products and chemicals. Trade in fish, coal, grain and timber.

Its development as a fishing port was chiefly due to extensive harbour improvements from 1846 onwards and provision of fast rail services to distribute the catch. In recent years its prosperity has been threatened by the general decline in the fishing industry.

Grindelwald Switzerland. Resort in Bern canton in a picturesque valley at a height of 1037 m (3401 ft) 14 km (9 miles) ESE of Interlaken; mountain-climbing centre at the foot of the Wetterhorn, Eiger and other peaks. Pop. (1990) 5000.

Gris-Nez, Cap France. In French, 'Grey Nose'. Limestone headland 54 m (177 ft) high in the Pas-de-Calais department at the narrowest part of the Strait of Dover. The nearest point to the English coast.

Grisons ➤GRAUBÜNDEN.

Grodno ➤HRODNA.

Groningen Netherlands. 1. Province in the NE. Area 2157 sq km (832 sq. miles). Pop. (1994) 556,607. Fertile, particularly in the N. Dairy-farming. Potatoes, sugar-beet and vegetables cultivated. It has major natural gas deposits at Slochteren. 2. Cap. of Groningen province 51 km (32 miles) E of Leeuwarden. Pop. (1994) 170,535.

Sugar-refining. Manufactures chemicals, clothing and furniture. Trade in grain and cattle. Railway junction and canal centre.

University (1614). Principal church the 15th-cent. Martinikerk, which has an organ constructed by Rodolphus Agricola (1433–85), who was born near Groningen.

Grønland ➤GREENLAND.

Grosseto Italy. Cap. of Grosseto province in Tuscany 71 km (44 miles) SSW of Siena. Pop. (1990) 71,370. Market town on a reclaimed swamp.

Trade in cereals, wine and olive oil. Manufactures agricultural implements.

Cathedral (12th/13th-cent. restored).

Grozny Russian Federation. Cap. of the Chechenia on the Sunzha R. 200 km (125 miles) NNE of Tbilisi (Tiflis). Pop. (1989) 400,000.

Major centre of the petroleum industry, linked by pipelines with the nearby oilfields and with the oil ports of Makhachkala (Caspian Sea) and Tuapse (Black Sea) and with Rostov. Oil first discovered in 1893. Also manufactures oil-drilling machinery and chemicals. Industries inc. sawmilling and food-processing.

Invaded by Russian forces in 1995.

Grudziaz (Ger. **Graudenz**) Poland. Ancient town and river port on the Vistula R. in the Toruń voivodeship. Pop. (1989) 102,000. Railway junction.

Manufactures agricultural machinery, chemicals, glass and footwear.

Passed from Poland to Prussia in 1772 but was returned in 1919.

Gruyère Switzerland. District in Fribourg canton in the middle Saane valley, famous for the cheese named after it and for its cattle. The small town of Gruyères (pop. (1985) 1300) stands on a hill at 827 m (2713 ft) above the valley.

Gstaad Switzerland. Resort in Bern canton on the Saane R. at 1005 m (3300 ft). Tourist centre for wintersports.

Guadalajara Spain. 1. Sparsely populated province in New Castile, on the Meseta with a harsh continental climate. Area 12,190 sq km (4705 sq. miles). Pop. (1991) 147,868. Cereals, olives and vines grown in the valleys. Salt produced. 2. Cap. of Guadalajara province on the Henares R. 48 km (30 miles) NE of Madrid. Pop. (1987) 59,492.

In an agricultural region producing cereals, vines and olives. Industries inc. flour-milling and tanning.

The noteworthy Infantado Palace (late 15th-cent.) was severely damaged in the civil war (1936–9) and later restored.

Guadalcanal Solomon Islands. Volcanic island in the S Pacific Ocean, the largest of the group. Area 5326 sq km (2060 sq. miles). Pop. (1991) 60,692. Cap. Honiara. Mountainous and closely forested, rising to about 2400 m (7872 ft). Main export copra.

In World War II it was occupied by the Japanese (1942); recaptured by the Americans after heavy fighting (1943).

Guadalquivir River (Ar. **Wadi-el-Kebir**, 'Great River') Spain. River 580 km (360 miles) long, rising in the Sierra de Segura in Jaén province and flowing generally WSW through Córdoba to Seville. Navigable below the city of Seville; divides into several branches as it crosses the swampy region known as Las Marismas; then, reunited, enters the Gulf of Cádiz and the Atlantic. Between Córdoba and Seville it is extensively used for irrigation. Several hydroelectric plants are on its tributaries.

Guadalupe (Spain) ➤SIERRA DE GUADALUPE.

Guadalupe Hidalgo Mexico. Former town; now part of Gustavo A. Madero, Federal District, now a N suburb of Mexico City, the most famous place of pilgrimage in the Americas, containing a great brick basilica with a shrine of Our Lady of Guadalupe. Built after an Indian had described having seen visions on the hill of Tepeyacac in 1531. Scene of the signing of the treaty ending the US–Mexican War (2 Feb. 1848).

Guadeloupe West Indies. An overseas department of France consisting of two neighbouring islands in the Leeward Is. with dependencies. Total area 1702 sq km (583 sq. miles). Pop. (1990) 378,178. Cap. Basse-Terre. The two main islands, Guadeloupe proper or Basse-Terre (W) and Grande-Terre (E), are separated by a narrow strait, the Rivière Salée. The island dependencies inc. Marie-Galante Pop. (1990) 13,463, La Désirade Pop. (1990) 1610, Les Saintes Pop. (1990) 2036, St Barthélemy Pop. (1990) 5038 and the N half of St Martin Pop. (1990) 28,518.

Main occupation agriculture. Chief

products bananas, sugar, rum, coffee and cacao. Tourism is the chief economic activity. Chief commercial centre and seaport Point-à-Pitre (Grande-Terre).

Discovered (1493) by Columbus and named after a monastery in Spain. Continuously under French rule since 1816, it became an overseas department in 1946.

Guadiana River. Ancient Anas River. River 820 km (510 miles) long in Spain and Portugal rising in several headstreams and becoming the Guadiana proper near Ciudad Real, flowing generally W to Badajoz. Here it turns S, forming the Spanish–Portuguese boundary, except for about 160 km (100 miles), where it is flowing through SE Portugal, and enters the Gulf of Cádiz near Ayamonte (Spain). Owing to its lack of volume it has little economic value.

Guainía River ►RIO NEGRO (BRAZIL).

Guaira, La ►LA GUAIRA

Guaíra Falls ►PARANÁ RIVER.

Gualeguay Argentina. Town in the S of the Entre Ríos province 129 km (80 miles) ESE of Rosario. Pop. (1989) 26,000. Has a port, Puerto Ruiz, 8 km (5 miles) S on the Gualeguay R. leading to the Paraná R. Trade in livestock and cereals.

Gualeguaychú Argentina. River port in the SE of the Entre Ríos province, on the Gualeguaychú R. 11 km (7 miles) from the confluence with the Uruguay R. Pop. (1985) 90,000. Opposite Fray Bentos (Uruguay). Industries inc. meat-packing and tanning.

Guam (Marianas Islands) W Pacific Ocean. An unincorporated territory of USA which is the southernmost and largest island of the Marianas archipelago. Area 45 sq km (209 sq. miles). Pop. (1990) 133,152. Cap. Agaña. The native lang. is Chamorro; English is the official lang. and is taught in all schools. It is mountainous and volcanic in the S, rising to 407 m (1335 ft) and is low-lying coral in the N. Climate is tropical maritime with little difference in temperature over the year.

Rice, coconuts and bananas are cultivated.

Cattle and pigs raised. Main export copra, through the only good port, Apra Harbour, in the W. Industries inc. textiles, cement, petroleum distribution, ship repairs. Tourism is important.

It was probably discovered in 1521 by Magellan and was ceded to the USA in 1898 after the Spanish–American War. Occupied by the Japanese in World War II (1941); recaptured by the Americans (1944) and became a major naval and air base occupying about one-third of the usable land.

Guanabara Brazil. State created (1960) when Rio de Janeiro ceased to be federal cap. Area 1356 sq km (523 sq. miles). Pop. (1970) 4,251,918. Inc. the great metropolitan area of Rio de Janeiro on Guanabara Bay.

Guanajuato Mexico. 1. State on the central plateau. Average height 1800 m (5900 ft). Area 30,589 sq km (11,807 sq. miles). Pop. (1990) 3,980,000. One of the main mining states of Mexico, rich in silver; also produces gold, zinc, copper, mercury and lead. 2. Cap. of Guanajuato state in the Sierra Madre Occidental at a height of 2000 m (6560 ft). Pop. (1983) 45,000. Mining centre (principally silver and gold). Manufactures pottery and textiles. Built in a ravine, it has narrow, tortuous streets rising steeply to the hillside mining villages. University (1732).

Guangdong (Kwangtung) China. Maritime province in the S on the South China Sea, inc. the Luichow peninsula, Hainan and many offshore islands. Area 231,400 sq km (89,300 sq. miles). Pop. (1990) 63,210,000. Cap. Guangzhou. Generally hilly. Drained by the lower Sikaing, the Peikiang and the Han rivers. The climate is of the tropical monsoon type and rainfall is everywhere abundant.

Rice, silk, sugar-cane, tobacco and many varieties of fruit are produced; timber is floated down the rivers from the interior. Chief mineral tungsten. Kwangchow (Canton) is the leading industrial centre and Swatow is also an important town. There are two Special Economic Zones to encourage foreign investment.

On the coast is the only remaining foreign enclave in China, Macao (Portuguese). Hong Kong, former British Colony was handed back to China in 1997. This was a former treaty port and it was in Guangdong that Sun Yat-sen began his revolutionary activities (1911).

Guangxi Zhuang (Kwangsi-Chuang) China. Autonomous Region for the Zhuang people in the S bordering on North Vietnam. Area 220,400 sq km (85,100 sq. miles). Pop. (1990) 42,530,000. Cap. Nanning. Generally hilly, it occupies the basin of the upper Si-kiang and in the valleys of this river and its tributaries rice is the main crop; the W is inhabited by aboriginal tribes. Chief towns Nanning and Guilin.

Guangzhou (Canton) China. Cap. of Guangdong province on the Pearl or Canton R. at the head of the delta and 145 km (90 miles) NW of Hong Kong. Pop. (1992) 3,620,000.

Chief seaport, industrial and commercial centre of S China, linked by rail with Beijing and also with Kowloon (Hong Kong). It has a considerable river trade and because of harbour improvements it has become accessible to ocean-going vessels. It has shipyards and a steel complex. It manufactures textiles (cotton and silk), chemicals, machinery, cement, matches and paper.

The walls of the old city were destroyed (1921) and replaced by boulevards, while broad streets were constructed and public parks laid out, and the city was largely modernized. One of its outstanding features was the new Bund or waterfront, lined with offices, restaurants and bazaars, similar to the famous Bund of Shanghai. The European business and residential quarter was on the small island of Shamien in the Pearl R. Seat of the Sun Yat-sen University, founded (1924) by Dr Sun Yat-sen, and Chinan University (1958).

A city of some importance in China from the 3rd cent. BC, Kwangchow was visited by Hindu and Arab traders in the 8th–10th cent. and was the first Chinese seaport to be in regular contact with Europeans – the Portuguese in the 16th and the British in the 17th cent. It was involved in the Opium War between Britain and China (1841–2), as a result of which it became one of the first treaty ports (1842); but its commercial importance was affected by the development of Hong Kong in the later 19th cent. Its former name, Canton, was a European corruption of Kwangtung and no doubt the independent outlook of the Cantonese was largely due to their early association with foreigners; they played a significant part in the revolution of 1911 under the leadership of Sun Yat-sen, whose principles of nationalism, democracy and social reform were accepted first by the Kuomintang and later by the Communists. The city was occupied by the Japanese 1938–45 and was taken over by the Communists in 1949; its foreign treaty-port rights were abolished in 1943.

Guanta ▶BARCELONA (VENEZUELA).

Guantánamo Cuba. Town in the Oriente province 64 km (40 miles) ENE of Santiago de Cuba. Pop. (1970) 130,000.

Commercial and processing centre for an agricultural region. Sugar-milling, coffee-roasting and tanning. Manufactures chocolate and liqueurs.

Founded (1822) by French refugees from Haiti.

Guantánamo Bay Cuba. Inlet in the Oriente province 16 km (10 miles) S of Guantánamo. Site of a US naval and air base, with strong fortifications, ceded to the USA (1901) after the Spanish–American War. Cuba refuses to accept rent from the US for the military base.

Guatemala. The northernmost republic of Central America, lying between the Gulf of Honduras on the Caribbean Sea in the NE and the Pacific Ocean in the S; bordered by Mexico in the N and W, Belize in the NE, Honduras in the E and El Salvador in the SE. Area 108,889 sq km (42,042 sq. miles). Pop. (1995) 10,621,000 (39 per cent urban). Life expectancy, 62 years male, 67 female. Cap. Guatemala City. Other cities Quezaltenango, Puerto Barrios, Mazatenango,

Antigua, Zacapa and Cobán. Currency: Guatemalan quetzal (Q) = 100 centavos. The interior is mountainous, with several volcanoes. Tajamulco 4213 m (13,819 ft) is the highest peak in Central America. Fuego 3838 m (12,589 ft) and Santa Maria 3770 m (12,366 ft) are active volcanoes. W of Guatemala City is the picturesque L. Atitlán, surrounded by volcanic peaks. Chief rivers the Motagua, the Polochik (flowing through L. Izabal, the largest lake) and the Usumacinta. Earthquakes are not uncommon. Climate is hot and humid on the coastal lowlands (*tierra caliente*), but healthy and pleasant in the upland valleys (*tierra templada*); above about 3000 m (9840 ft) is the cool zone (*tierra fria*). Annual rainfall (mainly May–Oct.) 125 cm (50 ins.) on the average but much greater in some areas. Land use: forested 54 per cent, meadows and pastures 24 per cent, agricultural and under permanent cultivation 17 per cent. About 75 per cent are Roman Catholic. It is the only republic in Central America to be predominantly Indian. About 45 per cent of the pop. are Amerindians, who retain their colourful traditional costume and follow a mode of life not essentially changed from Mayan times; few of them speak Spanish and their economy is largely self-contained, with maize and beans as the staple foods. The remainder are of mixed Indian and Spanish descent (*ladinos*). The official lang. is Spanish and there are several Indian dialects.

The economy is chiefly agricultural. Coffee, which provides 21 per cent of the exports, is grown on the upland slopes and sugar, bananas, fish and sea foods and essential oils are also exported. In the extensive tropical forests mahogany, cedar, balsa and cinchona are produced. Prominent in the country's rich bird life is the beautiful quetzal, which has become the national emblem. Guatemala City has textile mills, a cement factory, a chemical plant and a few light consumer industries, such as electrical goods, plastics and metal furniture.

In pre-Columbian times Guatemala was a great centre of the Mayan civilization. The ruins at Quiriguá and elsewhere demonstrate its level of culture. In 1523–4 the Spanish conquered the country and formed the captaincy-general of Guatemala, with the cap. at Antigua. It formed the nucleus of the Central American Federation (1828–38) but in 1839 Rafael Carrera founded the present republic. Its subsequent history was marred by revolutions and dictatorships.

There is an 80-member unicameral Congress, 64 are elected locally and 16 from a national list. The country is divided administratively into 22 departments, each with a governor appointed by the President.

Guatemala City Guatemala. Cap. of the republic and of the Guatemala department in the SE on the Inter-American Highway at a height of 1495 m (4904 ft). Pop. (1995) 1,167,495. The largest city in Central America. Controls most of the country's coffee trade. Manufactures textiles, cement and soap.

Among notable features are the National Palace (completed 1943) in the Parque Central and the cathedral (18th/19th-cent.). Seat of the famous University of San Carlos (1676). Founded (1776) to take the place of the earlier cap., Antigua, which was destroyed by earthquake. Almost entirely destroyed by earthquakes 1917–18 but rebuilt to the original plan.

Guayama Puerto Rico. Town 53 km (33 miles) S of San Juan. Pop. (1970) 20,318. In an agricultural region producing sugar-cane. Sugar-milling, and textile manufacture.

Guayaquil Ecuador. Largest city and chief seaport, also cap. of Guayas province on the Guayas R. 56 km (35 miles) from its mouth on the Gulf of Guayaquil. Pop. (1990) 1,508,444.

Exports bananas, cacao and coffee. Industries inc. sugar-refining, iron-founding, tanning, sawmilling and brewing. Manufactures soap, textiles, pharmaceuticals, vehicles and electrical equipment. Linked by rail and road with Quito.

University (1897). Founded 1537. Suffered frequently from fires and was severely damaged by earthquake in 1942; has been largely rebuilt in recent years.

Gubbio Italy. Ancient Iguvium. Town in Perugia province, Umbria 31 km (19 miles) NE of Perugia. Pop. (1990) 32,000. Long famous for majolica; also manufactures textiles and metal goods.

With its 13th-cent. cathedral and its many palaces, it has a distinctly medieval appearance. In the Palazzo dei Consoli are the famous bronze Tabulae Iguvinae, from which much information about the ancient Umbrians was obtained.

Gudbrandsdal (Gudbrand Valley) Norway. Fertile valley of the Lagen R. running NW–SE between the Rondane Mountains (E) and the Jotunheim Mountains (W). Agriculture, stock-rearing (esp. horses) and dairy-farming. It has a distinctive dialect and folklore and is associated with the Peer Gynt legend. Trade route for many cent.; the Oslo–Trondheim railway (opened 1921) passes through it.

Guelph Canada. Industrial town in S Ontario on the Speed R. 45 km (28 miles) NW of Hamilton. Pop. (1991) 87,976. Manufactures electrical equipment, leather goods and hardware. University (1964). Founded 1827.

Guernica Spain. Town in Vizcaya province 19 km (12 miles) ENE of Bilbao. Pop. (1985) 18,000. Has the old oak tree beneath which the Basque parliament used to meet. Industries inc. metalworking and furniture manufacture. In 1937 a German aircraft supporting the nationalists in the Spanish Civil War bombed and destroyed the town, killing hundreds of civilians and Guernica became the symbol of Fascist ruthlessness, inspiring one of Picasso's most famous paintings.

Guernsey England. Second largest of the Channel Is. 48 km (30 miles) W of the Normandy coast. Area 62 sq km (24 sq. miles). Pop. (1991) 58,867. Cap. St Peter Port.

Tomatoes, grapes and flowers are cultivated, mostly under glass and the island has given its name to a famous breed of dairy cattle. It is a popular holiday resort.

Dependencies are Alderney, Brechou, Great Sark, Little Sark, Herm, Jethou and Lihou.

Guerrero Mexico. A Pacific coast state in the SW. Area 63,794 sq km (24,624 sq. miles). Pop. (1990) 2,622,067. Cap. Chilpancingo. Chief seaport Acapulco. Largely mountainous; crossed by the Sierra Madre del Sur. Mainly agricultural. Crops inc. cereals, cotton, sugar-cane and coffee.

Guienne (Guyenne) France. Former province in the SW, divided (1790) into the present departments of Aveyron, Dordogne, Gironde and Lot and parts of the Tarn-et-Garonne and Lot-et-Garonne departments. In the 12th cent. it formed the duchy of Aquitaine with Gascony. Held by England 1154–1451. Its cap. was Bordeaux.

Guildford England. Dormitory town in Surrey on the R. Wey 42 km (26 miles) SW of London. Pop. (1991) 65,998. Manufactures plastics. Industries inc. engineering and brewing.

Among its buildings are Archbishop Abbot's Hospital, founded 1619; the 17th-cent. guildhall; the grammar school (16th-cent.); the new cathedral (1936); remains of a Norman castle. It was a royal borough in the Middle Ages, when it had an important cloth trade. Seat of the University of Surrey (1966).

Guilin (Kuelin/Kweilin) China. Town in the Guangxi Zhuang (Kwangsi Chuang) Autonomous Region on the Li R. 386 km (240 miles) NW of Guangzhou (Kwangchow/Canton). Pop. (1986) 686,000 with a large Muslim pop. Trade in rice, beans. It is in a limestone region famous for its unusual karst scenery.

Guinea. Republic in West Africa, bounded on the NW by Guinea-Bissau and on the S by Liberia and Sierra Leone. Area 245,857 sq km (94,926 sq. miles). Pop. (1995) 6,700,000 (26 per cent urban). Life expectancy, 44 years male, 45 female. Cap. Conakry. Other cities Kankan, N'zérekoré, Kindia and Kissidougou. Currency: Guinean franc = 100 cauris. A coastal plain is separated from the savanna interior in the N and SE by the Fouta Djallon highland plateau, cut by the valleys of the Niger R. headstreams. Tropical monsoon climate with rainforest in the coastal areas. Land use: forested 59 per cent, pasture 22 per cent, agricultural 3 per cent. About 85 per cent of the pop. is Muslim. Ethnic groups inc. Fulani (40 per cent), Malinka (25 per cent), Susu, Kissi and Kpelle. Besides French there are eight official langs. taught in schools.

The main occupation is cattle-rearing and agricultural exports inc. bananas and palm kernels. Other exports are alumina and bauxite (from the deposits at Boké, the world's second largest producer). Conakry is linked by rail with Kankan on the Milo R. (a tributary of the Niger). Guinea has one-third of the world's proven reserves of bauxite and also reserves of uranium, diamonds, iron and gold.

France established the colony of Rivières du Sud in 1882, renaming it French Guinea 1895. After a referendum in 1958 it declined to join the French Community and became an independent republic. A *coup* in 1984 established a military government. A multi-party system was introduced in 1992 and in 1997 there was a 114-member National Assembly; 38 members are elected by the first-past-the-post system and the remainder from national lists by proportional representation. Local administration is grouped in four regions which correspond to the four geographical and ethnic areas: Guinée-Maritime, Moyenne-Guinée, Haute-Guinée and Guinée-Forestière.

Guinea-Bissau. Republic in West Africa, bounded by the Atlantic Ocean in the W, Senegal in the N and Guinea in the E and SE. Area 36,125 sq km (13,948 sq. miles). Pop. (1995) 1,073,000 (20 per cent urban). Life expectancy 42 years male, 45 female. Cap. and chief seaport Bissau. Other cities Bafatás Gabú, Mansôa and Catió. The coast is fringed with mangrove swamps. Inland the rainforest gradually passes into savanna. It has a tropical monsoon climate. Annual rainfall (mainly May–Nov.) 125–200 cm (50–80 ins.). Land use: forested 38 per cent, meadows and pastures 34 per cent, agricultural and under permanent cultivation 12 per cent.

About 38 per cent of the pop. is Muslim and about 8 per cent are Christian, mainly Roman Catholic. The rest hold animist beliefs. The official lang. is Portuguese.

Main products groundnuts, copra, palm oil and kernels, timber, hides and fish. Exports inc. cashews, groundnuts and frozen fish. Bauxite and phosphate exist but have not been exploited.

Discovered in 1446 by the Portuguese sailor Nuño Tristão. Portuguese Guinea was important in the slave trade in the 17th and 18th cent. The struggle against Portuguese colonial rule began in 1963 and independence was declared 24 Sept. 1973 and it took the name Guinea-Bissau.

There is a National People's Assembly and the 150 Representatives are elected by regional councils for 5-year terms. The country is divided into 8 regions each under a regional council elected for 5 years. Bissau is a separate Region.

Guinea, Gulf of West Africa. Broad Atlantic inlet, from Cape Palmas (Liberia) to Cape Lopez (Gabon). The Niger delta separates two large bays, the Bights of Bonny and Benin. Parts of the Gulf coast are named after the commodities in which Europeans formerly traded, e.g. the Grain Coast ('grains of paradise', i.e. Guinea pepper), the Ivory Coast (Côte d'Ivoire), the Gold Coast (Ghana), the Slave Coast. It receives the waters of the Volta, the Niger and the Ogooué rivers.

Guipúzcoa Spain. One of the Basque Provinces; the smallest in Spain but one of the most densely populated, bounded on the N by the Bay of Biscay and on the NE by France. Area 1997 sq km (771 sq. miles). Pop. (1991) 671,743. Cap. San Sebastian. Largely industrial. Stock-rearing. Fishing.

Guisborough England. Market town in a former iron-mining district in Redcar and Cleveland 13 km (8 miles) ESE of Middlesbrough at the foot of the Cleveland Hills. Pop. (1991) 18,156. Tanning and brewing. Ruins of a 12th/14th-cent. Augustinian priory.

Guiyang (Kueiyang/Kweiyang) China. Cap. of Guizhou province 354 km (220 miles) S of Chongqing (Chungking) at a height of 1040 m (3411 ft). Pop. (1992) 1,560,000.

Important industrial centre, road and rail junction. Manufactures iron and steel, machinery, textiles, glass, paper, matches and chemicals. Trade in grain and hides.

Seat of Guizhou (Kweichow) University (1958).

Guizhou (Kweichow) China. Province in the SW on a lofty plateau between the Yangtse-kiang and the Si-kiang. Area 174,000 sq km (67,200 sq. miles). Pop. (1990) 32,500,000. Cap. Guiyang (Kueiyang/ Kweiyang).

Rice is cultivated in the valleys and maize on the plateau, while tung oil is produced in the forests. Also tobacco and potatoes are grown. There are important deposits of coal, iron, manganese, mercury, alumina and phosphorus.

Miao aborigines form the majority of the rural pop. on the plateau.

Gujarat India. State in the Indian Union, formed (1960) from the N and W part of the former Bombay state and inc. the former states of Saurashtra and Kutch, bordered by Pakistan (NW) and the Arabian Sea (W). Area 196,024 sq km (76,572 sq. miles). Pop. (1991) 41,174,343. Cap. Ahmadabad. Official lang. Gujarati and Hindi. The State consists largely of a fertile plain, but inc. the marshy Rann of Kutch and the partly arid Kathiawar peninsula.

Chief agricultural products are cotton, tobacco, groundnuts, sugar-cane, paddy, wheat, jowar and maize. Industries inc. oil-refining, petrochemicals, cement, fertilizers, dairy products, machine-tools, sugar, diamonds and textiles. The state has deposits of oil and natural gas.

Gujranwala Pakistan. Town 80 km (50 miles) N of Lahore. Pop. (1981) 597,000.

Manufactures textiles, leather and metal goods. Trade in cereals and cotton.

Birthplace of the famous Sikh ruler, Ranjit Singh (1780–1839).

Gujrat Pakistan. Town 48 km (30 miles) N of Gujranwala. Pop. (1981) 154,000.

Trade in grain and cotton. Handicraft industries (textiles and pottery).

Gulbarga India. Town in Karnataka 105 km (65 miles) ESE of Sholapur. Pop. (1991) 304,100.

Cotton manufactures. Flour and oilseed milling. Trade in cereals and cotton.

Cap. of the Bahmani kings in the 14th and 15th cent.; the ruins of their palaces, mosques, remain. The most noteworthy building is a mosque modelled on that at Córdoba, Spain.

Gulfport USA. Seaport and resort in Mississippi on Mississippi Sound 105 km (65 miles) WSW of Mobile. Pop. (1985) 40,000.

Exports wood and cottonseed products. Manufactures textiles and fertilizers.

Gulf States. 1. States bordering on the Gulf of Mexico: Alabama, Florida, Louisiana, Mississippi and Texas. 2. States situated on the (Persian) Gulf inc. Bahrain, Kuwait, Oman, Qatar, Saudi Arabia and the United Arab Emirates; also Iran and Iraq are sometimes included.

Gulf Stream. Warm ocean current in the N Atlantic, originating in the Gulf of Mexico and flowing through the Florida Strait and NE along the US Coast. At the Grand Banks off Newfoundland it fans out, slows down and becomes less clearly defined, so much modified that it is now more correctly termed the N Atlantic Drift. It reaches the coasts of W and NW Europe and considerably influences their climate. First observed in the early 16th cent. but not scientifically studied until the 19th cent.

Gulf, The ►PERSIAN GULF.

Gumal (Gomal) Pass Afghanistan/Pakistan. Pass 6 km (4 miles) long at a height of about 1500 m (4920 ft) on the Afghanistan–Pakistan border 145 km (90 miles) W of Dera Ismail Khan. Traversed by the Gumal R., a tributary of the Indus. Serves as a trade route for Afghan merchants.

Gumati (Gomati) River India. River 800 km (500 miles) long in Uttar Pradesh, rising in the N and flowing generally SE past Lucknow and Jaunpur to join the Ganges R. Navigable for small vessels in its lower course.

Guntur India. Town in Andhra Pradesh 240 km (150 miles) ESE of Hyderabad. Pop. (1991) 471,100.

Trade in cotton and tobacco. Industries inc. oilseed, jute, rice-milling, engineering, cement and pesticides. Grows chillies and turmeric.

Passed from French to British possession in 1788.

Guryev ➤ATYRAU.

Gusau Nigeria. Town in Sokoto situated SSE of Kaura Namoda on the Sokoto R. Pop. (1992) 143,000.

Trading and distribution centre for millet, cattle, skins, timber and cotton. Some gold and diamond deposits nearby.

Güstrow Germany. Town in Mecklenburg-West Pomerania 32 km (20 miles) S of Rostock. Pop. (1989) 38,527. Railway junction. Engineering and woodworking. Cap. of the duchy of Mecklenburg-Güstrow in the 16th–17th cent.

Gütersloh Germany. Industrial town in North Rhine-Westphalia 16 km (10 miles) SW of Bielefeld. Pop. (1986) 79,400. Manufactures machinery, furniture, textiles and food products.

Guwahati (Gauhati) India. Town in Assam on the Brahmaputra R. 69 km (43 miles) N of Shillong. Pop. (1991) 584,342.

Trade in rice, jute and cotton. Industries inc. oil-refining and the manufacture of automobiles, tyres, refrigerators, textiles, plastic containers, weighing-machines, chemicals, electronics, cables, fertilizers and carbon black.

Cap. of the Ahom kingdom in the 18th cent. Later the centre of British adminis-tration in Assam. Nearby are the ruins of two ancient Hindu temples.

Guyana. Republic on the NE coast of South America. Formerly British Guiana. Bounded on the N by the Atlantic Ocean, E by Suriname, W by Venezuela and S and W by Brazil. Area 214,969 sq km (83,000 sq. miles). Pop. (1995) 770,000 (31 per cent urban). Life expectancy, 62 years male, 68 female. Cap. Georgetown. Other towns Linden and New Amsterdam. Currency: Guyana dollar = 100 cents. Mostly covered by jungle and only a narrow coastal belt is cultivable. It is over-populated in relation to the exploitable land. Land use: forested 83 per cent, meadows and pastures 6 per cent, agricultural and under permanent cultivation 2.5 per cent. It has a tropical climate, with a rainy season from April to July and November to January. Humidity is high all the year. About 52 per cent are Christian, 34 per cent Hindu and 9 per cent Muslim. The racial groups are East-Indian 49 per cent, black 36 per cent, mixed 7 per cent, Amerindian 7 per cent.

Chief products are sugar-cane (mainly grown on large estates), bauxite; a consider-able development of rice as a subsistence crop has been promoted. Exports inc. sugar, gold, rice, bauxite, shrimps and rum.

Guyana was first settled by the Dutch West India Company early in the 17th cent. Occu-pied by the British 1796 and finally ceded to Britain 1814. Internal self-government was achieved in 1961, but serious economic difficulties caused rioting and bloodshed; a state of emergency was declared in 1962. Became independent within the Common-wealth (as Guyana) 1966; became a co-operative republic in 1970. There is an executive presidency and a 65-member Na-tional Assembly (53 elected members and 12 appointed by regional authorities).

Guyenne ➤GUIENNE.

Gwadar (Gwadur) Pakistan. Port in Bal-uchistan 483 km (300 miles) W of Karachi, formerly, with adjoining territory (area 777 sq km; 300 sq. miles), a dependency of Oman, but handed over to Pakistan in 1958.

Pop. (1985) 8500. Coastal trade and fishing industry.

Gwalior India. 1. Former princely state in central India consisting of one large area and several detached districts. Area 67,000 sq km (26,000 sq. miles). Its rulers belonged to the Sindhia family of the Mahrattas, by whom it was founded in the 18th cent. Its first cap. was Ujjain. In 1948 it was merged with Madhya Bharat, which became part of Madhya Pradesh in 1956. 2. Former cap. of Gwalior and of Madhya Bharat, now in Madhya Pradesh 105 km (65 miles) SSE of Agra. Pop. (1991) 690,800.

Industrial centre. Flour and oilseed milling. Manufactures cotton goods, pottery, footwear, cast-iron products, toiletries, cement, electrical equipment, transformers, tyres and electronic equipment.

University (1963). An ancient town centred round an imposing fort containing palaces and temples. Now inc. the 19th-cent. town of Lashkar.

Gwelo ➤GWERU.

Gwent Wales. Former county in the extreme SE on the English border, but replaced in 1996 by Monmouthshire, Blaenau Gwent, Newport and Torfaen unitary authorities.

Gweru (Gwelo) Zimbabwe. Town 145 km (90 miles) ENE of Bulawayo at a height of 1418 m (4651 ft). Pop. (1992) 124,735. Chief town of the midland region.

Farming and industrial centre. Engineering. Manufactures footwear, ferrochrome, asbestos products and cement.

Founded 1894.

Gwynedd Wales. County formed in 1974, but reorganized in 1996 to inc. the major part of the former Gwynedd but without Isle

of Anglesey or the area around Conwy. Area 2549 sq km (984 sq. miles). Pop. (1994) 117,000.

Gyandzha (formerly **Kirovabad**) Azerbaijan. The second largest town in Azerbaijan on the Trans-Caspian Railway and the Baku–Batumi oil pipeline 177 km (110 miles) SE of Tiflis. Pop. (1991) 282,000.

Industrial and commercial centre in a fruit-growing district. Manufactures textiles and wine.

An ancient town which changed hands many times, it became Russian in 1804. Birthplace of the Persian poet Nizami (1140–1202).

Gyangtse (Gyantse) China. Town in S Xizang (Tibet) 160 km (100 miles) SW of Lhasa at a height of 3900 m (12,792 ft). Pop. (1985) 10,000.

Trade in wool, barley, salt, borax and tea. Manufactures carpets and woollen cloth.

Gympie Australia. Town in SE Queensland on the Mary R. 145 km (90 miles) NNW of Brisbane. Pop. (1984) 11,380. In a region of dairy-farming and the cultivation of sugar-cane and bananas. Former goldmining centre.

Györ Hungary. Cap. of Györ-Moson-Sopron county on the Rába R. near its confluence with an arm of the Danube 109 km (68 miles) WNW of Budapest. Pop. (1995) 127,000.

Important industrial centre and river port. Flour-milling and distilling. Manufactures machine-tools, chemicals and textiles.

About 18 km (11 miles) SE is the Benedictine abbey of Pannonhalma, founded (1101) by King Stephen.

Gyumri ➤KUMAYRI.

H

Haag, Den ➤HAGUE, THE.

Ha'apai ➤TONGA.

Haarlem Netherlands. Cap. of N Holland province 18 km (11 miles) W of Amsterdam. Pop. (1992) 149,788. Centre of Dutch bulb-growing, with world-wide exports.

Also old-established printing industry. Manufactures textiles, chemicals, cocoa and chocolate.

Typically Dutch in appearance, with many canals and gabled houses. Groote Kerk (15th/16th-cent.); town hall, originally a palace of the counts of Holland, rebuilt in the 17th cent.; Frans Hals museum, with a fine collection of his paintings.

Haarlemmermeer Netherlands. Town, sited on what was formerly a shallow lake in N Holland province between Haarlem, Amsterdam and Leiden. Pop. (1992) 100,659. It was completely drained 1840–52; the polder so formed, mostly fertile, has been used for dairy-farming and the cultivation of wheat and flax.

Habbaniya, Lake Iraq. Lake 31 km (19 miles) long just S of the Euphrates R. 80 km (50 miles) W of Baghdad.

Hachinohe Japan. Industrial town and port in Aomori prefecture, NE Honshu 80 km (50 miles) SE of Aomori. Pop. (1991) 214,009.

Important fishing centre. Industries inc. fish-canning, paper and pulp. Manufactures chemicals, iron and steel, and cement.

Hachioji Japan. Industrial town in Honshu 40 km (25 miles) W of Tokyo. Pop. (1991) 474,698.

Manufactures textiles.

Hackensack USA. Residential and industrial town in New Jersey on the Hackensack R. 19 km (12 miles) N of Jersey City. Pop. (1990) 37,000.

Manufactures furniture, glass, wallpaper, jewellery.

First settled in 1639 by Dutch colonists from Manhattan.

Hackney England. Inner London borough that inc. Shoreditch and Stoke Newington. Pop. (1991) 164,200. Once residential, now largely industrial.

Manufactures furniture, clothing and confectionery.

Hackney Marsh (138 ha; 340 acres), formerly a haunt of highwaymen and robbers, is now the largest playing-field in London.

Haddington Scotland. Town in Lothian Region on the R. Tyne 24 km (15 miles) E of Edinburgh. Pop. (1991) 8140.

Woollen and hosiery manufactures.

A 13th-cent. parish church. Birthplace of Alexander II (1198–1249), John Knox (1505–72), Jane Welsh Carlyle (1801–66) and Samuel Smiles (1812–1904).

Hadhramaut Yemen. Region in Yemen bordered on the N by Saudi Arabia and on the S by the Gulf of Aden and the Indian Ocean. Area 155,376 sq km (55,991 sq. miles). Pop. (1986) 686,000. Roughly co-extensive with the former E Aden Protectorate; consists of the former Qu'aiti State of Shihr and Mukalla and the former Kathiri State of Sai'un. Mainly desert; dates, millet cultivated. Chief ports Mukalla, Shihr.

Hadleigh England. Market town in W Suffolk 14 km (9 miles) W of Ipswich. Pop. (1991) 6595.

Malting, flour-milling. The woollen industry introduced by the Flemings declined after the plagues of 1636 and 1687.

Hadrian's Wall England. Remains of Roman fortifications against the N tribes of Britain, extending for 117 km (73 miles) between Bowness (Solway Firth) and Wallsend (R. Tyne). It is about 4.5 m (15 ft) high and there are 17 forts along its length. Built on the instructions of the Emperor Hadrian *c.* AD 122–6.

Hagen Germany. Industrial town in North Rhine-Westphalia in the Ruhr district 19 km (12 miles) S of Dortmund. Pop. (1991) 214,449.

Important railway junction. Engineering, brewing. Manufactures paper and food products.

Hagerstown USA. Industrial and commercial town in the Cumberland Valley, W Maryland 105 km (65 miles) WNW of Baltimore. Pop. (1990) 35,445.

Manufactures aircraft, dust-control equipment, leather goods and furniture.

Hagion Oros ►ATHOS, MOUNT.

Hague, The (Dutch **Den Haag, 's Gravenhage**) Netherlands. Seat of government of the Netherlands and cap. of S Holland province 51 km (32 miles) SW of Amsterdam and 3 km (2 miles) from the North Sea. Pop. (1992) 445,287.

Chiefly residential, with some industries; distilling, printing, manufacture of clothing.

One of the finest cities in Europe, with handsome streets and buildings; the Binnenhof, founded in the 13th cent., where both chambers of the legislature are housed; the 17th-cent. Mauritshuis, now a famous picture gallery; the Huis ten Bosch ('House in the Wood'), a 17th-cent. royal residence; and the Peace Palace (1913), headquarters of the International Court of Justice. In the 13th cent. it was merely the site of a hunting lodge of the counts of Holland, but before the end of the 16th cent. it had become the meeting place of the States-General and residence of the stadholders. Later it was the scene of many treaties and conferences, inc. the Peace Conferences of 1899 and 1907. The model village of Madurodam is a tourist attraction.

Haguenau France. Industrial town in the Bas-Rhin department in Alsace on the Moder R. 26 km (16 miles) N of Strasbourg. Pop. (1989) 31,993.

Manufactures waterflow meters, clothing, automats, ball-bearings, electric motors and confectionery.

Haifa Israel. Chief seaport and important industrial centre 88 km (55 miles) NNE of Tel Aviv at the foot and on the slopes of Mt Carmel. Pop. (1991) 248,800 (conurbation 680,700).

Manufactures textiles, chemicals, soap, cement, electrical and electronic equipment.

Hail Saudi Arabia. Town and oasis in Jebel Shammar, N Nejd 560 km (350 miles) NW of Riyadh. Pop. (1985) 46,000. On an important pilgrim and caravan route from Iraq to Medina and Mecca. Cap. of the Ibn Rashid dynasty in the 19th cent. Fell to Ibn Saud 1921.

Hailar River ►ARGUN RIVER.

Hainan China. Island off the S coast, in Guangdong province, separated from the Luichow peninsula by Kiungchow Strait. Area 33,670 sq km (13,000 sq. miles). Pop. (1990) 6,420,000. Chief town and port Hoihow (N). Mountainous in the centre and S, rising to 1769 m (5802 ft) in the Wuchih Shan.

Produces timber (mahogany, rosewood), rice, sugar-cane, tobacco and pineapples, also iron ore and other minerals. Oil is found offshore.

Has been under Chinese control since the 2nd cent. BC, but occupied by the Japanese 1939–45.

Hainaut (Hainault) Belgium. Province in the SW, drained by the Scheldt, Dender and Sambre rivers. Area 3787 sq km (1462 sq. miles). Pop. (1991) 1,278,191. Cap. Mons. Low-lying and fertile in the N; the centre and S was formerly an important coalmining and iron and steel manufacturing region centred on Mons and Charleroi, but coalmining finished in the 1970s.

Haines USA. City situated N of Juneau on

the W coast of the Lynn Canal, Alaska. Pop. (1985) 1200.

Industries inc. fishing, timber, sawmilling and seasonal tourism.

Haiphong Vietnam. Chief seaport and third largest city on the Red R. delta 88 km (55 miles) ESE of Hanoi, to which it is linked by railway. Pop. (1989) 456,049.

Exports rice, minerals. Manufactures cement, textiles and plastics.

Developed in the late 19th cent. Badly damaged in the Vietnam war and is being rebuilt.

Haiti West Indies. Republic occupying the western third of the island of Hispaniola in the Greater Antilles. Has an E frontier of 311 km (193 miles) with the Dominican Republic, which occupies the remainder of Hispaniola; on the W it is separated from Cuba by the Windward Passage. Area 27,700 sq km (10,695 sq. miles). Pop. (1995) 6,589,000. Life expectancy, 43 years male, 47 female. Cap. and chief seaport Port-au-Prince, which inc. Carrefour within its metropolitan area; other towns Delmass, Cap Haïtien and Les Cayes. Currency: Gourde = 100 centimes.

It consists mainly of two peninsulas extending into the Windward Passage; also two islands, Île de la Tortue and Île de la Gonâve. Four-fifths of the area is mountainous, rising in the Massif de la Selle to the SE to 2582 m (8469 ft). Other ranges are the Massif du Nord in the N and the Massif de la Hotte to the SW. The remainder consists of fertile plains, where the bulk of the pop. lives. Climate tropical, with little seasonal variation, though somewhat cooler in the mountains. Land use: forested 1.4 per cent, meadows and pastures 18 per cent, agricultural and under permanent cultivation 33 per cent. French and Haitian Creole are the official languages. Blacks form 95 per cent of the pop. and are greatly influenced by the cult of Voodoo, although many are Christians, particularly Roman Catholics.

The economy depends on agriculture; the main commercial crops coffee, sugar-cane, sisal. Forest products inc. mahogany, rose-wood and cedar. Mineral resources are largely unexploited, but bauxite is mined and exported. There are deposits of copper but these have not been exploited. Industry is still on a small scale; there are textile mills producing a cheap denim, a soap factory, a cement factory and a number of food-processing and other plants.

Hispaniola was a Spanish possession from its discovery by Columbus in 1493 until 1697, when the French took possession of the W part of the island (now Haiti, an Indian name meaning 'Mountainous Country'); it became France's most prosperous colony. Large numbers of African slaves were sent to work the cotton and sugar plantations and the present pop. is mainly descended from them. In 1798 Toussaint l'Ouverture, a former slave, led a successful rebellion against the French and became a national hero and symbol of the fight against tyranny, but the real founder of Haitian independence was General Jean-Jacques Dessalines, who proclaimed himself Emperor of Haiti in 1804. From 1822 to 1844 the country was politically united with the Dominican Republic, France recognizing its independence in 1839. There was US occupation 1915–34. Over-population has led Haitians to penetrate into the Dominican Republic, resulting in border incidents and political tension. Under the rule of 'Papa Doc' Duvalier and his son from 1957 to 1986, Haiti became the poorest country in the Americas. Haiti is divided administratively into 9 departments and under its 1987 Constitution has a bicameral legislature comprising a 27-member Senate and a 70-member National Assembly, but there has been constant military intervention so that civilian governments have been unable to function and since 1991 Congress has ceased to operate.

Hakodate Japan. Seaport in Hokkaido on the Tsugaru Strait (S). Pop. (1991) 308,089.

Also an important fishing centre. Exports salted and canned fish, timber. Shipbuilding, woodworking. Manufactures cement, food products, matches. Linked by ferry and rail tunnel with Aomori (Honshu).

Halberstadt Germany. Town in the Magdeburg district N of the Harz Mountains and 51 km (32 miles) SW of Magdeburg. Pop. (1989) 47,600.

Sugar-refining. Manufactures paper, machinery, textiles, rubber and chemicals.

Halesowen England. Industrial town in West Midlands just WSW of Birmingham. Pop. (1991) 64,422.

Industrial centre. Manufactures machine-tools, steel products, chains, nails and rivets.

Halifax Canada. Cap., largest city and chief seaport of Nova Scotia on the W shore of Halifax Harbour, an Atlantic inlet. Pop. (1991) 114,455. Its natural harbour is ice-free at all seasons.

Leading Canadian seaport for transatlantic shipping lines in winter, also E terminus of the Canadian National and E Canadian Pacific railways. Industries inc. shipbuilding, oil-refining, fish-processing and sugar-refining. Manufactures food products, furniture and clothing. Exports fish, fish products and timber.

Canada's first newspaper, the *Halifax Gazette*, was started here (1752). Founded (1749) as a naval base, it was important in this capacity in both world wars. Part of the town was destroyed by the explosion of a munitions ship in the harbour in 1917.

Halifax England. Town in West Yorkshire near the R. Calder 11 km (7 miles) SW of Bradford. Pop. (1991) 91,069.

Worsted, woollen and carpet industries of major importance. Also manufactures clothing, confectionery and textile machinery.

Grammar school (founded in 1585); Piece Hall (1779), the town hall (1863, designed by Sir Charles Barry) and the 15th/17th-cent. Shibden Hall just to the E (containing the West Yorkshire folk museum), are other noteworthy buildings. Its cloth trade dates from the 15th cent. and was later stimulated by the arrival of refugee Flemish merchants.

Halle Germany. Cap. of Halle district on the Saale R. in the *Land* of Saxony-Anhalt 32 km (20 miles) NW of Leipzig. Pop. (1990) 311,400.

Industrial town, river port and railway junction in a lignite-mining region. To the NW Halle Neustadt, a new town, has been built. Manufactures sugar, paper, beer, chemicals and machinery.

University (founded 1694, incorporated in the University of Wittenberg 1817). A member of the Hanseatic League from the 13th to the 15th cent., Halle owed its commercial importance largely to its saline springs, which still produce. Birthplace of Handel (1685–1759).

Hallstatt Austria. Village in the Salzkammergut, Upper Austria, on the SW shore of the Hallstättersee. Salt mines near by. Owing to the discovery of prehistoric remains here in the mid 19th cent., it gave its name to the early Iron Age (Hallstatt period) of Europe.

Halmstad Sweden. Cap. of Halland county on the Kattegat 120 km (75 miles) SSE of Göteborg. Pop. (1991) 80,650.

Seaport. Industrial town. Resort. Exports timber, granite (quarried locally), dairy produce. Industries inc. engineering and the manufacture of textiles, wood-pulp and paper.

Halq el Oued (La Goulette) Tunisia. Town and port 11 km (7 miles) ENE of Tunis on a sand bar between the Lake of Tunis (El Bahira) and the Gulf of Tunis. Pop. 32,000.

Exports iron ore. Fishing. Also a summer resort.

Hälsingborg Sweden. Seaport in Molmöhus county on The Sound 51 km (32 miles) NNW of Malmö with train ferry to Helsingör (Elsinore) in Denmark. Pop. (1992) 109,907.

Industrial centre. Copper-refining. Manufactures machinery, fertilizers, textiles. Exports timber, paper and chemicals.

Changed hands several times between Denmark and Sweden, finally passing to the latter in 1710.

Halstead England. Town in N Essex on

the R. Colne 19 km (12 miles) WNW of Colchester. Pop. (1971) 7621.

Manufactures wood products.

Haltemprice England. Town in Kingston upon Hull; a residential and industrial suburb of NW Hull. Pop. (1971) 52,239.

Boat-building, light engineering and cement manufacture.

Hama Syria. Cap. of the Hama administrative district on the Orontes R. 193 km (120 miles) NNE of Damascus. Pop. (1992) 229,000.

Commercial centre. Trade in cereals and fruit. Tanning and weaving industries.

Famous for its huge wooden water-wheels (*norias*) up to 27 m (89 ft) in diameter used for irrigation. An early Hittite settlement; passed to the Muslims in the 7th cent. AD.

Hamadan Iran. Ancient Ecbatana. Town in Kermanshah province 290 km (180 miles) WSW of Tehrán at a height of 1800 m (5904 ft). Pop. (1986) 272,499.

Trade in hides and skins, and wool. Long famous for its rugs and carpets. Also produces leather goods.

Has the tomb of Avicenna, who died here in 1037. Cap. of Media in the 7th–6th cent. BC and summer cap. of the Achaemenian Persian Empire in the 6th–4th cent. BC. Fell to the Arabs in the 7th cent AD.

Hamamatsu Japan. Industrial town in Shizuoka prefecture, Honshu 88 km (55 miles) SE of Nagoya. Pop. (1991) 549,962.

Manufactures motor-cycles, textiles, musical instruments (esp. pianos, organs), chemicals and tea.

Hamburg Germany. 1. *Land*. Area 755 sq km (292 sq. miles). Pop. (1991) 1,652,400.

2. City on the Elbe R. 88 km (55 miles) from its mouth on the North Sea. Pop. (1991) 1,652,363.

Chief seaport, with an outport at Cuxhaven and meeting place of ocean-going and river traffic. It has a great transit trade, importing raw materials and foodstuffs for the industrial region of Germany and exporting their manufactured goods. Industries inc.

shipbuilding and repair, oil, metalworking, electronics, engineering, packaging, aircraft, vehicles, chemicals, cosmetics, food-processing, brewing and rubber.

There are few old buildings, most of those which survived the disastrous fire of 1842 were destroyed or heavily damaged by bombing in World War II. The site of a fortress of Charlemagne, Hamburg became an archbishopric in 1834 and by the end of the 12th cent. a town had been founded near the old cathedral. In 1241 it formed a defensive alliance with Lübeck which gave rise to the Hanseatic League. Developed considerably as an international seaport in the 19th cent. Joined the German Empire in 1871, became a constituent state of the German Reich and in 1949 a *Land* of the German Federal Republic. Birthplace of Mendelssohn (1809–47) and Brahms (1833–97).

Hamden USA. Residential and industrial town in Connecticut 8 km (5 miles) N of New Haven. Pop. (1970) 49,537.

Manufactures hardware, firearms and metal goods.

Hämeenlinna (Tavastehus) Finland. Cap. of the Häme province 98 km (60 miles) NNW of Helsinki. Pop. (1991) 43,777.

Manufactures textiles and plywood.

Castle dating from the 13th cent. Birthplace of Sibelius, the composer (1865–1957).

Hameln (Hamelin) Germany. Town in Lower Saxony on the Weser R. 49 km (88 miles) SW of Hanover. Pop. (1988) 57,000. Famous for the legend of the Pied Piper of Hamelin, said to have been enacted here in 1284 and illustrated by frescoes at the 17th-cent. Rattenfängerhaus or Ratcatcher's House. Also an industrial centre.

Iron-founding, flour-milling. Manufactures carpets, paper, textiles and chemicals.

Hamersley Range Australia. Mountain range in the W of Western Australia extending W–E about 270 km (170 miles) between the Fortescue and the Ashburton rivers. Highest peaks Mt Bruce (1227 m;

4025 ft) and Mt Brockman (1114 m; 3654 ft). There are rich deposits of iron ore.

Hamhung (Hamheung) North Korea. Industrial and commercial town 185 km (115 miles) NE of Pyongyang. Pop. (1987) 701,000.

Manufactures textiles.

Developed by the Japanese (1910–45) but severely damaged in the Korean War (1950–1). Just SE is the seaport and industrial centre of Hungnam (Heungnam), manufacturing machinery and with chemical and fertilizer plants.

Hamilton Australia. Market town and railway junction in SW Victoria 265 km (165 miles) W of Melbourne in a dairy-farming area. Pop. (1991) 10,500.

Hamilton Bermuda. Cap. and chief port on an inlet of Bermuda Island. Pop. (1992) 3000. A tourist resort, it was founded in 1790, succeeding St George as cap. in 1815; it became a free port in 1956.

Hamilton Canada. Town in Ontario at the W end of L. Ontario. Pop. (1991) 318,499. Lake port.

Railway and industrial centre. Important steelworks. Manufactures heavy machinery, electrical apparatus, typewriters, agricultural machinery, wire, textiles and clothing.

Hamilton New Zealand. Town in the North Island on the Waikato R. 113 km (70 miles) SSE of Auckland. Pop. (1991) 101,276.

Manufactures dairy and wood products, clothing, and industries inc. engineering and brewing.

Hamilton Scotland. Town in South Lanarkshire near the R. Clyde 16 km (10 miles) SE of Glasgow. Pop. (1988) 51,294.

Manufactures metal goods, electrical equipment.

Because of subsidence due to coalmining, many old buildings have been pulled down, inc. Hamilton Palace, seat of the dukes of Hamilton.

Hamilton USA. Industrial town in SW Ohio on the Great Miami R. 32 km (20 miles) N of Cincinnati. Pop. (1991) 61,368.

Manufactures paper, machinery, diesel engines and safes.

Laid out near the site of Fort Hamilton as Fairfield (1794); later renamed.

Hamm Germany. Industrial town in North Rhine-Westphalia on the Lippe R. 31 km (19 miles) ENE of Dortmund. Pop. (1991) 179,639. In a coalmining region.

Manufactures wire and cables, machinery and stoves.

Because of its extensive railway marshalling yards and its factories, it was frequently bombed in World War II and was severely damaged.

Hammamet Tunisia. Town and port in the NE on the Gulf of Hammamet, an inlet of the Mediterranean at S base of the peninsula ending in Cape Bon. Pop. (1985) 30,500. It has good beaches and is an important tourist resort.

Hammerfest Norway. Town in Finnmark, the most northerly in the world, on the W coast of Kvalöy Island some 200 km (125 miles) SW of the North Cape. Pop. (1991) 7100.

Fishing, sealing and whaling station with an ice-free port all the year. It exports fish and furs, and manufactures cod-liver oil.

The sun does not set here between 13 May and 29 July and does not rise between 18 Nov. and 23 Jan.

Hammersmith England. Inner London borough in W London on the N bank of the Thames, here crossed by Hammersmith Bridge, replacing an earlier suspension bridge; from 1965 a borough inc. Fulham. Pop. (1991) 136,500. Largely residential, with varied industries.

Hammond USA. Industrial town in NW Indiana near L. Michigan on the Grand Calumet R. between Chicago and Gary. Pop. (1990) 84,236.

Manufactures railway equipment, agricultural machinery, petroleum products and soap.

Hampshire England. County on the S coast; in the reorganization of local authorities (1974), the Isle of Wight became a separate county, and a small area in the SW (inc. Bournemouth) was transferred to Dorset. Area 3777 sq km (1458 sq. miles). Pop. (1991) 1,511,900. County town Winchester. It is divided into the districts of Basingstoke and Deane, East Hampshire, Eastleigh, Fareham, Gosport, Hart, Havant, New Forest, Portsmouth, Rushmoor, Southampton, Test Valley and Winchester. Crossed by the Hampshire Downs in the N and the South Downs in the SE. Drained by the Itchen, Test and E Avon rivers. The New Forest, noted for its scenic beauty, is in the SW and borders on Southampton Water.

Industries inc. agriculture, sheep, cattle and horse rearing, shipbuilding, oil-refining, chemicals, electrical and electronic equipment, pharmaceuticals, computers and information technology. There are many holiday resorts. Chief towns Basingstoke, Gosport, Portsmouth, Southampton and Winchester.

Hampstead England. Residential suburb of NW London in a hilly district rising in the N to 135 m (443 ft) on Hampstead Hill. Part of the Inner London borough of Camden. Hampstead Heath is one of London's most popular open spaces, famous for its Bank Holiday fairs and for the inns Jack Straw's Castle, the Spaniards and the Bull and Bush. Ken Wood has a fine Adam mansion. Parliament Hill is on the E boundary; in the extreme SE of Primrose Hill. Once a spa, Hampstead has long been favoured by artists and authors, inc. Constable, Romney, Keats, Leigh Hunt, John Galsworthy and H. G. Wells.

Hampton England. Part of the borough of Richmond upon Thames situated 19 km (12 miles) SW of London. It contains Hampton Court Palace, an outstanding example of Tudor architecture, built by Cardinal Wolsey in 1515 and presented by him to Henry VIII in 1526. It remained a royal residence until the reign of George II. In Queen Victoria's reign the state apartments and picture galleries were opened to the public; the palace is also well-known for the Maze and the great vine planted in 1768. The Hampton Court Conference of the clergy was held here in 1604.

Hampton USA. Port in SE Virginia on Hampton Roads just NE of Newport News. Pop. (1990) 133,793.

Fishing is the main industry and it packs and exports fish and oysters.

Hamtramck USA. Town in SE Michigan, completely surrounded by Detroit. Pop. (1970) 27,245 (largely of Polish extraction). Manufactures cars, paints, varnishes.

Named after Colonel J. F. Hamtramck, the first American commander of Detroit fort after its surrender by British troops in 1796.

Hanau Germany. Industrial town in Hessen at the confluence of the Kinzig and the Main rivers 16 km (10 miles) E of Frankfurt. Pop. (1989) 84,300. Centre of the jewellery industry.

Also manufactures rubber products, chemicals. Diamond cutting and polishing.

Birthplace of the brothers Grimm (Jacob, 1785–1863; Wilhelm, 1786–1859) and Paul Hindemith (1895–1963), the composer.

Hangchow ➤HANGZHOU.

Hangchow Bay ➤HANGZHOU BAY.

Hangzhou (Hangchou/Hangchow) China. Cap. of Zhejiang (Chekiang) province on the Fuchun (Tsientang) R. at the head of Hangzhou Bay 160 km (100 miles) SW of Shanghai. Pop. (1991) 1,099,660. S terminus of the Grand Canal which links it with Beijing.

A commercial centre trading in silk, cotton, wheat, bamboo, tea and rice. Industries inc. iron and steel, and the manufacture of textiles and matches.

It is inaccessible to ocean-going ships owing to silting and so waterborne trade is limited to river and canal. It flourished chiefly in the 12th cent. during the later Sung dynasty, when it became cap. of S China. Chiefly because of its picturesque setting, it was considered by Marco Polo, who called it Kinsai

(Chinese Kingshih), to be the world's finest city. It is still a popular resort. Destroyed in the Taiping rebellion (1861) and rebuilt.

Hangzhou Bay China. Funnel-shaped bay in Zhejiang (Chekiang) province, on the E China Sea about 160 km (100 miles) long and 96 km (60 miles) wide (at the mouth); forms the estuary of the Fuchun (Tsientang) R. Notorious for its tidal bore.

Hanley England. Town in the Potteries, N Staffordshire, one of the 'Five Towns'; since 1910 part of Stoke-on-Trent. Birthplace of the author Arnold Bennett (1867–1931).

Hannibal USA. Town on the Mississippi R. in NE Missouri. Pop. (1985) 19,000.

Manufactures shoes, cement, metal goods. Railway engineering. Once an important river port.

Mark Twain (whose home is preserved) spent his boyhood in the town, which provided the setting for *Huckleberry Finn* and *Tom Sawyer*.

Hanoi Vietnam. Cap. of the republic on the Red R. Pop. (1989) 1,088,862.

Industrial centre. Railway junction and river port. Industries inc. engineering, rice-milling, tanning, brewing and the manufacture of textiles, leather goods and matches.

Cap. of French Indo–China 1902–45 and of North Vietnam from 1954.

Hanover (Ger. **Hannover**) Germany. 1. Former province in Prussia in the W part of the N German lowlands, inc. Lüneburg Heath. Area 38,728 sq km (14,953 sq. miles). There is a considerable area of heath and moor, but cereals, potatoes and sugar-beet are cultivated and cattle are raised on the more fertile lowlands; the region is drained by the navigable Ems, Weser, Aller and Elbe rivers. In 1692 Duke Ernest Augustus of Brunswick-Lüneburg was granted the rank of elector, took the city of Hanover as his cap. and was popularly known as the Elector of Hanover. His wife was Sophia, granddaughter of James I of England and their son, the Elector George Louis, succeeded to the English throne in 1714; Britain and

Hanover were thus ruled by the same monarch until the accession of Queen Victoria (1837). Hanover, a kingdom from 1815, was annexed by Prussia as a province in 1866. After World War II it was incorporated into the *Land* of Lower Saxony.

2. Cap. of Lower Saxony and former cap. of Hanover province on the Leine R. and on the Weser–Elbe (Mittelland) Canal. Pop. (1991) 513,010.

Industrial and commercial centre. Manufactures machinery, steel, electrical equipment, textiles, fertilizers, tyres and food products.

Birthplace of Sir William Herschel (1738–1822), the astronomer, who discovered the planet Uranus.

Harar Ethiopia. Cap. of Hararge Region 370 km (230 miles) E of Addis Ababa at a height of over 1500 m (4920 ft). Pop. (1984) 62,160.

Trade in coffee, cotton and hides.

An old walled town; the country's chief Muslim centre, with several mosques. Captured from the Italians by British forces during World War II (1941).

Harare Zimbabwe. Formerly Salisbury. Cap. 370 km (230 miles) NE of Bulawayo at a height of 1472 m (4828 ft). Pop. (1992) 1,184,169. Linked by rail with Bulawayo and Sofala (in Mozambique).

Centre of a gold-mining and agricultural area. Important trade in tobacco. Industries inc. tobacco curing, grading and packing, flour-milling, sugar-refining and brewing. It manufactures clothing, furniture and fertilizers.

Founded in 1890.

Harbin China. Cap. of Heilongjiang province in Manchuria 520 km (325 miles) NNE of Shenyang on the Sungari R. Pop. (1991) 2,443,398.

Important industrial, commercial and route centre. Flour-milling, soya-bean processing, sugar-refining, railway engineering. Manufactures machinery, chemicals, textiles and glass. Its importance is largely due to its position at the junction of the Chinese Eastern and the S Manchurian railways.

It was founded by the Russians in 1897, in fact, during the construction of the Chinese Eastern line and developed rapidly as an industrial town; it is still more Russian than Chinese in character.

Harbour Island Bahamas. Islet situated NE of Nassau. Area 3.9 sq km (1.5 sq. miles). Pop. with Eleuthera and Spanish Wells (1990) 9300.

Tourist centre and the island produces citrus fruit and coconuts.

Hardanger Fiord Norway. Inlet of the North Sea in Hordaland county, penetrating 145 km (90 miles) inland; its mouth, 48 km (30 miles) SSE of Bergen, is fringed by islands. A popular tourist area because of its magnificent scenery, with lofty mountains and waterfalls.

Hardenburg Netherlands. Town situated N of Amelo on the Vecht R. in Overijssel. Pop. (1992) 32,549.

Industries inc. the manufacture of synthetic materials, metal and transport equipment.

Harderwijk Netherlands. Town situated NW of Apeldoorn on Ijsselmeer in Gelderland. Pop. (1992) 36,282.

Industries inc. fishing, fish-processing and the manufacture of soap, furniture, tobacco products and building materials.

Hardwar (Haridwar) India. Town in NW Uttar Pradesh on the Ganges R. 165 km (102 miles) NE of Delhi. Pop. (1991) 148,882. Hindu place of pilgrimage, with the temple of Gangadwara and an adjoining bathing ghat which has the footprint of Vishnu. Here the Upper Ganges Canal leaves the river.

Harfleur France. Town in the Seine-Maritime department on the Seine estuary 6 km (4 miles) E of Le Havre. Pop. (1968) 10,104. During the Middle Ages it was the chief port of NW France, but it declined with the silting up of the Seine estuary and the rise of Le Havre; it was somewhat improved by the cutting of the Tancarville

Canal to Le Havre. Besieged and captured by Henry V of England 1415.

Hargeisa (Hargeysa) Somalia. Town 240 km (150 miles) SSE of Djibouti. Pop. (1989) 80,000. Trading centre for the nomadic herdsmen of the region. Cap. of British Somaliland 1941–60.

Haridwar ➤ HARDWAR.

Haringey England. London borough, comprising the former municipal boroughs of Hornsey, Tottenham and Wood Green, all in Middlesex. Pop. (1991) 187,300.

Hari Rud (Tedzhen River). River 1120 km (700 miles) long in SW Asia, rising in the Koh-i-Baba in central Afghanistan, flowing W past Herat, turning N to form the Afghanistan–Iran border and the former USSR–Iran border, then turning NW as the Tedzhen into Turkmenistan, finally losing itself in the sands of the Kara Kum desert. It irrigates parts of Herat province, Afghanistan and Turkmenistan.

Harlech Wales. Seaside resort in Gwynedd. Former county town of Merionethshire on Cardigan Bay 14 km (9 miles) NNW of Barmouth. Pop. (1989) 1313. The now ruined castle (built by Edward I) surrendered to the Yorkists in 1468 after a bitter struggle, inspiring the song *The March of the Men of Harlech*.

Harlingen USA. Port in S Texas on an offshoot of the Gulf Intracoastal Waterway. Pop, (1985) 44,000. In an intensively cultivated agricultural area.

Exports citrus fruits, vegetables. Industries inc. canning and the manufacture of chemicals.

Harlow England. Town in W Essex 10 km (6 miles) SSW of Bishop's Stortford, with a small part in Hertfordshire. Pop. (1991) 74,629. It was designated a 'new town' in 1947.

Manufactures glass, surgical instruments, scientific equipment and furniture.

Harpenden England. Town in W Hertfordshire 8 km (5 miles) NNW of St Albans.

Pop. (1991) 26,995. Mainly residential. Rothamsted Experimental Station for agricultural research is nearby.

Harpers Ferry USA. Resort and residential town in West Virginia at the confluence of the Potomac and Shenandoah rivers. Pop. 400. Famous for the raid on the US arsenal carried out by John Brown in 1859, which led to his surrender, trial and execution (commemorated in the song *John Brown's Body*). In the American Civil War it was captured by Confederate forces under Jackson 1862.

Harris Scotland. The S and more mountainous part of the island of Lewis-with-Harris in Western Isles, joined to the N part by a narrow isthmus at Tarbert. Famous for hand-woven Harris tweeds.

Harrisburg USA. State cap. of Pennsylvania on the Susquehanna R. Pop. (1991) 52,376. Important railway junction. In a coal-mining region.

Manufactures steel, machinery, bricks, clothing, shoes and food products.

In 1979 a fault at Three Mile Island nuclear power plant nearly caused a disaster, but although some radioactivity escaped no deaths were reported.

Harrogate England. Town in City of York Unitary Authority 23 km (14 miles) N of Leeds. Pop. (1991) 143,300. Spa, famous for the chalybeate, sulphur and saline springs discovered in 1596. The Royal Pump Room is now a museum. Standing at 120–150 m (394–492 ft) in the foothills of the Pennines, it is a tourist centre for the Yorkshire moors and dales and also a popular conference town.

Harrow-on-the-Hill (Harrow) England. London borough in Middlesex 18 km (11 miles) NW of London, for which it is a residential suburb. Pop. (1994) 210,300. The name derives from the isolated hill 124 m (407 ft) high, on the summit of which is the church of St Mary, founded in the 11th cent. Site of one of the country's oldest and most famous public schools, founded by John Lyon in 1571, former pupils having inc.

Byron, Palmerston, Peel, Sheridan, Galsworthy, Cardinal Manning and Winston Churchill.

Hartford USA. State cap. and largest city of Connecticut on the Connecticut R. Pop. (1991) 137,739.

The most important business is insurance. Manufactures typewriters, firearms, electrical equipment, tools, machinery.

Birthplace of Noah Webster, the lexicographer (1758–1843).

Hartlepool England. Unitary authority from 1996 (formerly part of Cleveland) on Hartlepool Bay. Pop. (1996) 92,160.

Industries inc. light engineering, clothing, food-processing, hi-tech and the manufacture of steel tubes and pipes.

Harvey USA. Industrial town in Illinois 31 km (19 miles) S of Chicago. Pop. (1985) 35,000.

Engineering and metalworking.

Harwell England. Village in Oxfordshire 3 km (2 miles) WSW of Didcot. Pop. 700. Atomic research station (established 1947).

Harwich England. Seaport in NE Essex on the estuary of the R. Stour and the R. Orwell, inc. the seaside resort of Dovercourt (SW). Pop. (1991) 18,436.

Industries inc. engineering, electronics and clothing. It is the second largest passenger port in Britain. There is a ferry service to Denmark, Sweden, Germany and the Netherlands.

Haryana India. State formed in 1966 from the Hindi-speaking parts of Punjab. Area 44,056 sq km (17,600 sq. miles). Pop. (1991) 16,317,715. Cap. (shared with Punjab) Chandigarh. There is an oil refinery at Karnal.

Rice, wheat, sugar-cane are the major agricultural products. Industries inc. automobiles, tractors, two-wheelers, automotive tyres, steel tubes, brewery, petrochemicals, refrigerators and chemicals.

The state begins in the Vedic Age and was the home of the Bharata dynasty that gave the name Bharat to India.

Harz Mountains Germany. Wooded range between the Elbe and the Weser rivers, rising to 1143 m (3749 ft) in the Brocken. Formerly well-known for mineral deposits, esp. silver and lead. Now attracts tourists on account of mineral springs, scenery and climate.

Hasa, Al Saudi Arabia. The eastern region of Nejd, on the Gulf, bounded on the N by Kuwait and its neutral zone. Chief town Hofuf.

Dates and cereals grown in the oases of Hofuf and Qatir; sheep, camels and donkeys bred by the Bedouin. It was the country's oil-producing region: petroleum was first discovered here in 1935.

Taken from the Turks by Ibn Saud 1914.

Haslemere England. Town in SW Surrey 19 km (12 miles) SSW of Guildford. Pop. (1991) 12,268. Mainly residential. Nearby, on Blackdown (280 m; 918 ft), is Aldworth, the home of Tennyson, poet (1809–92), who died there.

Hasselt Belgium. Cap. of Limbourg province on the Demer R. and near the Albert Canal 68 km (42 miles) ENE of Brussels. Pop. (1992) 66,865.

Industrial and market town. Industries inc. gin distilleries and the manufacture of laser-optics and agricultural machinery.

Just N is the Campine coalfield. Noted for its septennial Feast of the Assumption pilgrimage. The Belgians were defeated here by the Dutch in their War of Independence (1831).

Hassi Messaoud Algeria. Oil-producing centre in the Sahara 320 km (200 miles) S of Biskra. Oilfield first operated in 1957 with a pipeline to Béjaia. There is a gas pipeline from Hassi Messaoud via Hassi-R'Mel to Mostaganem–Oran–Algiers.

Hastings England. Residential town and seaside resort in East Sussex on the English Channel, inc. St Leonards-on-Sea (W). Pop. (1991) 81,139.

Small fishing industry; main occupation catering for holiday-makers.

Promenade (5 km; 3 miles long), beaches, public gardens; overlooking the town is the ruined Norman castle and there are 14th and 15th cent. churches. Formerly chief of the Cinque Ports. Became popular as a resort in the 18th cent. The Battle of Hastings (1066) was fought at Battle, 10 km (6 miles) NW.

Hastings New Zealand. Town in the North Island 18 km (11 miles) SSW of Napier. Pop. (1990) 57,748. In a region noted for fruit orchards and dairy farms. There are fruit canneries.

Hatfield England. Market and residential town in Hertfordshire 8 km (5 miles) ENE of St Albans. Pop. (1991) 25,468.

It has aircraft and engineering industries. It has Hatfield House (built 1607–11), seat of the Marquess of Salisbury and the remains of Hatfield Palace (1497), where Elizabeth I heard the news of her accession to the throne.

Hatteras, Cape USA. Promontory in North Carolina on Hatteras Island between Pamlico Sound and the Atlantic. Has had a lighthouse since 1798, owing to the frequent storms causing danger to shipping; long known as the 'Graveyard of the Atlantic'. It is designated a 'National Seashore'.

Hattiesburg USA. Town in SE Mississippi 138 km (86 miles) SE of Jackson. Pop. (1985) 41,000.

Sawmilling. Manufactures clothing and fertilizers.

Hattingen Germany. Town in North Rhine-Westphalia on the Ruhr R. 14 km (9 miles) N of Wuppertal. Pop. (1970) 60,500.

Coalmining. Manufactures steel.

Haugesund Norway. North Sea fishing port in Rogaland county 58 km (36 miles) NNW of Stavanger. Pop. (1990) 27,736.

Exports fresh, canned and frozen herring, and has fish canneries and saltworks.

Hauraki Gulf New Zealand. Inlet of the Pacific in the E of the Auckland Peninsula, North Island 61 km (38 miles) E–W and 40 km (25 miles) N–S, with the Great Barrier Island near the entrance and several islands within. In the S is the Firth of Thames and to the SW are Waitemata Harbour and Auckland City.

Haute-Garonne France. Department in the S formed in 1790 from parts of Gascony and Languedoc, bordering S on Spain, from which it is separated by the Pyrenees. Area 6309 sq km (2436 sq. miles). Pop. (1991) 938,500. Prefecture Toulouse. Drained by the Garonne and Ariège rivers; the Canal du Midi crosses the NE. Mainly agricultural; leading crops wheat, maize and vines. Livestock raised. Industries concentrated at Toulouse.

Haute-Loire France. Mountainous department in the Massif Central formed in 1790 from Auvergne, with parts of Languedoc and Lyonnais. Area 4977 sq km (1922 sq. miles). Pop. (1991) 206,800 (slowly decreasing). Prefecture Le Puy. In the SW are the Monts de la Margeride, in the centre the Monts du Velay, separating the Loire and Allier rivers and in the E the Monts du Vivarais. Cereals grown around Le Puy. Livestock raised in the mountains.

Haute-Marne France. Department in the NE formed chiefly from part of Champagne. Area 6211 sq km (2398 sq. miles). Pop. (1991) 203,400. Prefecture Chaumont. Rises in the S to the Plateau de Langres. Drained by the Meuse, Marne and Aube rivers; crossed by the Marne–Saône Canal. Chief towns Chaumont, Langres and St Dizier.

Haute Normandie France. Region in N formerly part of the province of Normandy and comprises the departments of Eure and Seine-Maritime. Area 12,317 sq km (4756 sq. miles). Pop. (1990) 1,737,000. Regional cap. Rouen. There has been considerable development of the lower Seine with its two major ports of Le Havre and Rouen and their industries oil-refining, chemicals and motor vehicles. Agriculture (livestock and cereals), the agri-foodstuffs industry and tourism all contribute to the economic life of the region whose proximity to Paris is a great asset.

Hautes-Alpes France. Mountainous department in the SE formed in 1790 from parts of Dauphiné and Provence, bordering NE on Italy. Area 5549 sq km (2142 sq. miles). Pop. (1991) 114,200. Prefecture Gap. In the N is the Massif du Pelvoux, rising to 4106 m (13,468 ft) and in the E are the Cottian Alps. Occupies the upper basin of the Durance R. Sheep-rearing important. Chief towns Gap, Briançon and Embrun.

Haute-Saône France. Department in the E formed in 1790 from the N part of Franche-Comté, bounded on the NE by the Vosges and drained NE–SW by the Saône R. and its tributary the Ognon R. Area 5360 sq km (2070 sq. miles). Pop. (1991) 229,300. Prefecture Vesoul. Dairy-farming and agriculture, inc. the cultivation of wheat, potatoes and cherries – from which kirsch is distilled.

Haute-Savoie France. Department in the SE formed in 1860 from the N part of Savoie, bounded by L. Geneva (N), Switzerland (E), Italy (SE) and the Rhône (W). Area 4388 sq km (1694 sq. miles). Pop. (1991) 577,600. Prefecture Annecy. Mountainous, occupied by the N part of the French Alps, with the Mont Blanc Massif (4801 m; 15,747 ft) in the SE. Several rivers harnessed for hydroelectric power. Vines and cereals grown in the lower areas; cattle raised and cheese produced in the uplands. Popular tourist resorts inc. Annecy, on the Lake of Annecy, and Chamonix; Évian-les-Bains and Thonon-les-Bains are spas.

Hautes-Pyrénées France. Department in the SW formed in 1790 from part of Gascony, bordering S on Spain, from which it is separated by the Pyrenees. Area 4464 sq km (1724 sq. miles). Pop. (1991) 224,800. Prefecture Tarbes. In the extreme S are Mont Perdu (3353 m; 10,998 ft) and Vignemale (3300 m; 10,824 ft). Several mountain streams provide hydroelectric power, the chief being the Adour. Many resorts and spas. Chief towns Tarbes, Lourdes, Bagnères-de-Bigorre.

Haute-Vienne France. Department in W central France formed in 1790 mainly from Marche and Limousin. Area 5520 sq km

(2131 sq. miles). Pop. (1991) 363,500. Prefecture Limoges. Generally hilly: the Monts de la Marche are separated from the Monts du Limousin by the valley of the Vienne R. The rather harsh climate limits crops in many areas to potatoes, buckwheat and rye; livestock are raised. Kaolin is quarried and used in the porcelain industry of Limoges; other towns St Junion and St Yrieix.

Haut-Rhin France. Department in the NE, in Alsace, bordering E on Germany (Rhine R.) and S on Switzerland. Area 3525 sq km (1361 sq. miles). Pop. (1991) 673,900. Prefecture Colmar. From the Rhine valley it rises W to the Vosges, containing their highest peak, Ballon de Guebwiller (1423 m; 4667 ft) and it is drained by the Ill R. and its tributaries. Crossed by the Rhône–Rhine Canal. Cereals, vines, hops and fruits grown – the cherries for kirsch distilling. Potash mined. Important textile and other industries. Chief towns Colmar, Mulhouse, Guebwiller.

Hauts-de-Seine France. Department just W of Paris, formed in 1964 when the former Seine and Seine-et-Oise departments were reorganized. Area 176 sq km (68 sq. miles). Pop. (1991) 1,393,400. Prefecture Nanterre.

Havana (La Habana) Cuba. Cap., leading seaport, largest city and cap. of the Havana province situated on Havana Bay in the Gulf of Mexico. Pop. (1990) 2,096,054. It has an excellent harbour.

Exports tobacco, sugar-cane, tropical fruit; handles most of the country's imports. The main industry is the manufacture of cigars. Sugar-refining; manufactures textiles, chemicals and perfumes. The tourist trade, chiefly from the USA, declined severely with the advent of the Castro regime (1959).

Buildings are a colourful mixture of the old Spanish 'colonial' and the modern styles, the most noteworthy being the cathedral (built 1656–1724). Founded (1514) as San Cristóbal de la Habana by Diego Velásquez and soon moved to its present location. Cap. since 1552. In 1898 the Spanish–American War was precipitated by the blowing up of the US battleship *Maine* in the harbour; this led to the US occupation (1898–1902).

Havant and Waterloo England. Town in SE Hampshire on Langstone Harbour 10 km (6 miles) NE of Portsmouth. Pop. (1991) 117,000. Connected to Hayling Island by road and railway bridges. Market town.

Manufactures pharmaceutical products, toys and plastic goods.

Havel River Germany. River 343 km (213 miles) long rising in a small lake and flowing generally S to Spandau (Berlin), here receiving the Spree R., which links it with the Oder R. It is linked with the Elbe R. at Plaue by canal.

Haverford USA. Town in Pennsylvania just NE of Philadelphia, of which it is a residential suburb. Pop. (1970) 55,132.

Minor industries.

Haverfordwest Wales. Market town in Pembrokeshire 13 km (8 miles) NNE of Milford Haven at the head of navigation of the W Cleddau R. Pop. (1991) 13,454. Ruins of a 12th-cent. castle and an Augustinian priory. Many Flemish weavers were settled here by Henry I in the 12th cent.

Haverhill England. Town in W Suffolk 18 km (11 miles) S of Newmarket. Pop. (1991) 19,086.

Industries inc. textiles, electrical and electronic equipment and plastics.

Haverhill USA. Important shoe-manufacturing town in NE Massachusetts at the head of navigation on the Merrimack R. Pop. (1991) 54,418. The industry was established in 1795.

Havering England. London borough comprising the former municipal borough of Romford and the urban district of Hornchurch (both in Essex). Pop. (1991) 224,400.

Havre, Le France. Important passenger and cargo transatlantic seaport in the Seine-Maritime department on the English Channel at the mouth of the Seine R. Pop. (1990) 197,219.

A major import centre for coffee, cotton

and wool. Industries inc. oil-refining (pipeline to Paris), flour-milling, sawmilling. Manufactures wire, machinery, chemicals and food-processing.

Founded by Francis I (1516) as Le Havre de Grâce.

Hawaii USA. State in the N Pacific. Area 16,635 sq km (6423 sq. miles). Pop. (1990) 1,108,229 (89 per cent urban). Cap. Honolulu. It comprises about 120 islands but only seven are inhabited: Hawaii, the largest (area 10,451 sq km; 4035 sq. miles; pop. 117,500); Maui (area 1904 sq km; 735 sq. miles; pop. 84,100); Oahu (area 1601 sq km; 618 sq. miles; pop. 762,534), containing the bulk of the pop. and the cap.; Kauai (area 1445 sq km; 558 sq. miles; pop. 49,100); Molokai (area 684 sq km; 264 sq. miles; pop. 6700); Lanai (area 365 sq km; 141 sq. miles; pop. 2200); Niihau (area 184 sq km; 71 sq. miles; pop. 207). The islands contain some of the world's largest volcanoes: on Hawaii are the Kilauea volcano on Mauna Loa (4171 m; 13,681 ft), noteworthy for the size of its crater (3 km; 2 miles across) and still active, and Mauna Kea (4217 m; 13,832 ft), dormant. All the islands have a tropical climate and the fertile soil, formed in the lowlands from disintegrated lava, is excellent for agriculture. Chief crops pineapples and sugar-cane. Tourism is a dominant industry with over 6 million visitors annually. A junction of international shipping and airline routes, the islands are easily accessible from the USA, the Far East and Australia.

The Hawaiian Is. were discovered in 1778 by Capt. Cook; he named them the Sandwich Is., after Lord Sandwich, but the name went out of use. An obelisk at Kaawaloa on Hawaii marks the spot where Cook was killed (1779). Ruled by native monarchs until 1893, when a republic was proclaimed; in 1898 the USA annexed the islands, which officially became US territory in 1900. The Japanese attack on the American naval base at Pearl Harbor (1941) was largely instrumental in bringing the USA into World War II. Admitted to the Union in 1959 as the 50th state.

Hawarden Wales. Market town in Flintshire 10 km (6 miles) W of Chester. Pop. (1971) 42,467. The 18th-cent. castle was residence of W. E. Gladstone for 60 years until his death.

Hawes Water England. Lake in Cumbria in the Lake District 14 km (9 miles) S of Penrith, formerly 4 km (2½ miles) long but extended by damming to 6 km (4 miles) and deepened in order to supply Manchester with water.

Hawick Scotland. Town in Scottish Borders on the R. Teviot 64 km (40 miles) SE of Edinburgh. Pop. (1991) 15,812. Noted for the manufacture of hosiery, knitwear and tweeds of high quality. Also a large sheep market.

In 1514 an English force was defeated at nearby Hornshole, an event commemorated annually by the ceremony 'Riding the Common'. 5 km (3 miles) SW of Branxholm or Branksome Castle, scene of Scott's *The Lay of the Last Minstrel*.

Hawke's Bay New Zealand. Former provincial district in the E of the North Island, consisting of hill country and plain E of the Ruahine Range. Area 11,033 sq km (4260 sq. miles). Pop. (1991) (stat. area) 139,479. The dry eastern hill country supports many sheep and cattle; lowlands noted for orchards, vineyards, fodder crops. Enclosed by the inlet Hawke Bay, on the SW shore of which is Napier.

Haworth England. Moorland village in West Yorkshire, 5 km (3 miles) SW of Keighley. The parsonage, home of the Brontë family, is now a museum and library; Charlotte and Emily Brontë are buried in the church.

Haydock England. Town in Merseyside 5 km (3 miles) ENE of St Helens. Pop. (1991) 16,705. Noted for Haydock Park racecourse.

Hayes and Harlington England. Former urban district in Middlesex 19 km (12 miles) W of London; part of the borough of Hillingdon. Residential and industrial.

Manufactures radio and television sets,

gramophones and records, and food products.

Hayling Island England. Island off the SE coast of Hampshire, connected by road bridge with Havant on the mainland. Area 21 sq km (8 sq. miles). Important mainly as a holiday resort.

Hay-on-Wye Wales. Market town in Powys on the R. Wye. Pop. (1991) 1407. Tourism with 500,000 visitors a year attracted by its 39 secondhand bookshops.

Hay River Canada. River 560 km (350 miles) long rising in NW Alberta, flowing W into British Columbia, turning N and E into Alberta, then NE into Mackenzie District, Northwest Territories, entering the Great Slave Lake at the settlement of Hay River. The Mackenzie Highway runs parallel to it in its lower course.

Hayward USA. Town in W California 24 km (15 miles) SE of Oakland. Pop. (1990) 111,498.
Industries inc. fruit-canning and the manufacture of electrical equipment and metal goods. One of the largest poultry centres in the USA.
Founded 1854.

Haywards Heath England. Residential town in East Sussex situated N of Brighton.

Hazleton USA. Town in Pennsylvania 34 km (21 miles) SSW of Wilkes-Barre. Pop. (1985) 28,000. In an anthracite-mining region.
Manufactures textiles, footwear, clothing and metal goods.

Heanor England. Town in Derbyshire 11 km (7 miles) NE of Derby. Pop. (1991) 22,180. Textile mills.

Heard Island S Indian Ocean. Volcanic island 4000 km (2500 miles) SW of Perth (Australia) 43 km (27 miles) long and 21 km (13 miles) wide, rising to about 3300 m (10,824 ft). Largely under snow and ice. Occasionally used as a meteorological station. Under Australian administration since 1947.

Heathrow England. Site of one of London's airports, 24 km (15 miles) W of the centre of London.

Hebbern England. Industrial town in Tyne and Wear on the S bank of the R. Tyne 6 km (4 miles) E of Newcastle-upon-Tyne. Pop. (1991) 18,183.
Coalmining. Shipbuilding, engineering. Manufactures electrical equipment.

Hebei (Hopei/Hopeh) China. In Chinese 'North of the River' (the Huang He). Province in the NE. Area 202,700 sq km (78,242 sq. miles). Pop. (1990) 61,082,439. Cap. Shijiazhuang. Bounded on the E by the Gulf of Chihli. Mountainous in the N (i.e. N of the Great Wall of China) and in the W. In the S it forms part of the Great Plain of N China, where wheat, maize, groundnuts and soya beans are cultivated. Beijing and Tianjin are within the province but are separate municipalities. It trades in cotton, timber and grain and produces mining equipment, oil, iron and steel.

Hebrides Scotland. Group of about 500 islands off the W coast, about 100 being inhabited, comprising the Inner Hebrides and Outer Hebrides, separated by the North Minch, Little Minch and the Sea of the Hebrides. The principal islands of the Inner Hebrides are Skye, Rhum, Eigg, Coll, Tiree, Mull, Iona, Staffa, Jura and Islay, those of the Outer Hebrides being Lewis-with-Harris, North and South Uist, Benbecula, Barra and St Kilda. Little of the land is arable and the main occupations are stock-rearing, fishing, crofting and the weaving of tweeds. Administratively they are divided between the Western Isles and Highland Regions. From the 6th to the 13th cent. they were under Norwegian rule.

Hebron (Ar. **El Khalil**) Jordan. Town 35 km (21 miles) SSW of Jerusalem at a height of 600 m (1968 ft) in the biblical valley of Eshcol. Pop. (1989) 38,000. Reputed one of the world's oldest towns, at times the home of Abraham and David. Its principal feature is the Haram, built over the Cave of Machpelah, where Abraham, Isaac and Jacob are said to have been buried.

Heckmondwike England. Town in West Yorkshire 10 km (6 miles) NE of Huddersfield. Pop. (1991) 9855.

Manufactures carpets and coach upholstery.

Heemstede Netherlands. Town in N Holland province 5 km (3 miles) S of Haarlem. Pop. (1992) 26,598. Mainly residential.

Bulb-growing is a major occupation.

Heerenveen Netherlands. Town in Friesland province 29 km (18 miles) SSE of Leeuwarden. Pop. (1992) 38,649.

Manufactures bicycles, mopeds, plastics and oscilloscopes.

Heerlen Netherlands. Town in Limburg province 21 km (13 miles) ENE of Maastricht. Pop. (1992) 95,000. Railway junction.

Manufactures fertilizers, chemicals and building materials. It is a computer and tourist centre. Former coal-producing area.

Hefei (Hofei) China. Cap. of Anhui (Anhwei) province 153 km (95 miles) WSW of Nanjing (Nanking). Just S is the large lake Chao Hu. Pop. (1991) 733,278.

Commercial centre in an agricultural region producing rice, tobacco, beans. Industry inc. mining and the manufacture of textiles, chemicals and aluminium and steel.

Heidelberg Germany. Town in Baden-Württemberg on the Neckar R. 18 km (11 miles) SE of Mannheim. Pop. (1991) 136,796. In a picturesque valley with orchards and vineyards. Industries inc. brewing, printing and the manufacture of metal goods, electrical equipment and cigars. There is a flourishing tourist trade.

Chiefly famous for its university (founded 1386) and the ruined castle overlooking the town, begun in the 13th cent. and containing a celebrated wine cask made in 1751 with a capacity of about 223,000 litres (49,000 gallons). Other buildings inc. the 15th-cent. churches of St Peter and the Holy Ghost. Heidelberg was the residence of the Electors Palatine from the 13th to the 18th cent.,

suffered a great deal during the Thirty Years War and was again damaged in World War II. In 1907 the jawbone of the prehistoric Heidelberg man was found near Mauer 10 km (6 miles) SE.

Heidenheim Germany. Industrial town in Baden-Württemberg 34 km (21 miles) NNE of Ulm. Pop. (1991) 136,796.

Manufactures turbines, electrical machinery, textiles, furniture.

Dominated by the ruined castle of Hellenstein on a hill nearly 600 m (1968 ft) high.

Heilbronn Germany. Town in Baden-Württemberg on the Neckar R. 39 km (24 miles) N of Stuttgart. Pop. (1991) 115,843.

Railway junction, river port and industrial centre. Manufactures metal goods, chemicals, textiles, paper and leather goods.

Of commercial importance since the Middle Ages, it was originally called Heiligbronn ('Holy Spring'), owing to the spring at the 11th/12th-cent. Church of St Kilian.

Heilongjiang China. Province in the NE, in Manchuria, bounded on the N across the Amur R. by Russia and called after the Chinese name for this river, the Heilongjiang. Area 463,000 sq km (179,000 sq. miles). Pop. (1990) 35,214,873. Cap. Harbin. Largely mountainous, with the Little Khingan Mountains in the N, extending NW–SE S of the Amur R., and the Changkwansai Mountains in the S, separated from the former by the basin of the Sungari R. Spurs of the Great Khingan Mountains are well forested and on the fertile lowlands crops of soya beans, wheat and flax are grown. Coal and gold are mined. Chief towns Harbin and Qiqihar.

Hejaz (Hedjaz) Saudi Arabia. The W part of Saudi Arabia, extending along the Red Sea from the Gulf of Aqaba and Jordan (N) to Asir (S). Now known as the Western Provinces. Area 347,060 sq km (134,600 sq. miles). Pop. (1985) 3,043,189. Cap. Mecca. Consists of a narrow coastal plain and inland a highland region, both largely barren, cultivation being possible only where water is available for irrigation, near wadis and springs. Principal towns Mecca and Jidda, the chief port. The pop. of both Mecca and Medina is temporarily swollen annually by the influx of pilgrims. Hejaz was under the control of the Turks from 1517 and in 1908 they completed the Hejaz Railway from Damascus to Medina; the section S of Ma'an (Jordan), however, was destroyed in World War I and has not been repaired. In 1925 Ibn Saud occupied the country and in 1932 it was united with Nejd as Saudi Arabia, though each has retained its separate identity and cap.

Hekla Iceland. Active volcano 1491 m (4892 ft) 112 km (75 miles) E of Reykjavik, with several craters. Since the 12th cent. it has erupted 24 times, in 1766 with considerable loss of life, and last in 1970. There are large lava fields covering 420 sq km (162 sq. miles).

Helder, Den Netherlands. Seaport and important naval base in North Holland province on the Marsdiep channel separating it from Texel island. Pop. (1992) 61,225. Naval barracks, arsenal, meteorological station. N terminus of the North Holland Canal.

Industries inc. fishing and shipbuilding.

Fortified by Napoleon 1811.

Helena USA. State cap. of Montana 77 km (48 miles) NNE of Butte in the Prickly Pear valley at a height of 1200 m (3936 ft). Pop. (1990) 24,569.

Commercial centre. Tourist resort in a mining and agricultural region. Manufactures concrete products, bricks and tiles, pottery and it also smelts metal. Goldmines nearby.

Owes its origin to the gold discoveries in Last Chance Gulch (1864).

Helensburgh Scotland. Town in Argyll and Bute on the N bank of the R. Clyde estuary at the entrance to Gare Loch. Pop. (1991) 15,852. Holiday resort.

Helicon (Gr. **Elikón**) Greece. Mountain range in Boeotia rising to 1749 m (5737 ft) known in Greek mythology as the home of the Muses. On its slopes are the springs of Aganippe and Hippocrene, whose waters were believed to give poetic inspiration.

Heligoland (Ger. **Helgoland**) Germany. Small rocky island of Schleswig-Holstein in the North Sea, off the mouths of the Elbe and the Weser rivers. Formed of red sandstone it consists of Unterland ('Lower Town') on a sandy spit and Oberland ('Upper Town') on the cliffs above. Acquired by Britain from Denmark 1807. Ceded to Germany (1890) in exchange for Zanzibar. Its fortifications were destroyed after World War I, but it became an important German submarine base in World War II; the fortifications were again destroyed (1947) and the island was returned to Germany in 1952. It is now a duty-free zone.

Heligoland Bight Germany. Bay between Heligoland and the mouths of the Elbe and the Weser rivers. Scene of an important naval battle between British and German forces (28 Aug. 1914) in World War I.

Heliopolis Egypt. 1. In Greek, 'City of the Sun'. Chief centre of sun-worship in ancient Egypt 10 km (6 miles) NE of Cairo. Its famous schools of philosophy and astronomy were eclipsed by those of Alexandria. Cleopatra's Needle in London (and a similar one in New York) once stood as obelisks before the great temple, where another still marks the site.

2. Residential suburb of modern Cairo near the site of ancient Heliopolis.

3. ➤BAALBEK.

Hellas ➤GREECE.

Hellendoorn Netherlands. Town in Overijssel province 14 km (9 miles) WNW of Almelo. Pop. (1992) 34,833.

Manufactures textiles.

Helmand River Afghanistan. Country's longest river (1100 km; 688 miles) rising W of Kabul and flowing generally SW across the Hazarajat, turning W and then N to empty into a marshy lake known as Hamuni-Helmand, on the border of Iran. Most of its valley is cultivated.

Helmond Netherlands. Industrial town in N Brabant province 16 km (10 miles) ENE of Eindhoven. Pop. (1992) 70,574.

Manufactures textiles, cocoa and chocolate, soap and margarine.

Helmstedt Germany. Town in Lower Saxony 37 km (23 miles) E of Brunswick (Braunschweig). Pop. (1989) 27,900. In a lignite-mining region.

Manufactures machinery and textiles.

The Juleum, where the former university was housed, is a noteworthy building.

Helsingfors ►HELSINKI.

Helsingör (Elsinore) Denmark. Seaport in NE Zealand, separated by The Sound from Hälsingborg, Sweden, with which it is connected by car and train ferry. Pop. (1992) 56,794.

Industries inc. shipbuilding and food-processing.

E of the town is Kronborg, the Elsinore castle of Shakespeare's *Hamlet*.

Helsinki (Helsingfors) Finland. Cap. of Finland and of the Uusimaa province situated on the S coast of Finland on a peninsula jutting into the Gulf of Finland and extending across offshore islands. Pop. (1992) 496,311. The largest city, chief seaport and a cultural centre.

Exports timber, wood-pulp, plywood and paper. Industries inc. shipbuilding, sugar-refining and engineering. Manufactures paper, plywood, textiles, machinery and porcelain.

Helsinki has three main harbours and the central market square has a quay. The old city was timber-built and has not survived, the 'old' quarter was built after the great fire of 1808. There has been more rebuilding and expansion since 1920, with some fine architecture. The grid plan predominates but with an unusual amount of open space in parkland and water. Helsinki is an importing seaport and a light-industrial city as well as the commercial, governmental and intellectual centre of Finland. The industrial quarter lies to the NE, the commercial, NW. The city was founded by the Swedes as Helsingfors in

1550; it was on the Vantaa estuary and moved to its present site in 1640, where it competed with Tallinn for Baltic trade. Helsingfors suffered fires and Russian attacks. It became the cap. of a Russian Grand Duchy in 1812 and the cap. of the independent republic in 1919.

Helston England. Town in Cornwall on the R. Cober 14 km (9 miles) WSW of Falmouth. Pop. (1991) 8505. Well known for its floral Furry Dance (8 May). Soup-canning. The fishing village of Porthleven, 5 km (3 miles) SW on Mount's Bay, was incorporated with it in 1934.

Helvellyn England. Mountain (951 m; 3119 ft) in the Lake District, between Ullswater and Thirlmere, with a sharp ridge known as Striding Edge projecting E.

Helwan Egypt. Town in Giza province 26 km (16 miles) S of Cairo, with which it is linked by rail. Pop. (1986) 352,300. Has a dry, equable climate, warm sulphur springs and is a health resort. Observatory (built 1903).

Manufactures cement, iron and steel.

Hemel Hempstead England. Town in Hertfordshire on the R. Gade 10 km (6 miles) W of St Albans. Pop. (1991) 79,326.

Manufactures fireworks, office equipment and paper.

Henan (Honan) China. In Chinese 'South of the River' (the Huang He). Province in N central China. Area 167,000 sq km (64,479 sq. miles). Pop. 50 million. Cap. Zhengzhou. Mountainous in the W, where outliers of the Tsinling Mountains extend halfway across it. In the E it occupies the SW part of the Great Plain of N China, which yields good crops of wheat, millet, cotton, tobacco, rapeseed and soya beans; in the past, however, until recently there has been constant danger from river floods and drought, but there are now river-control schemes particularly on the Huang-he. Chief towns Zhengzhou, Kaifeng, Luoyang (Loyang).

Henderson Island ►PITCAIRN ISLAND.

Hendon England. Former municipal borough in Middlesex and residential suburb of NW London; from 1965 part of the Greater London borough of Barnet. It inc. the University of London observatory and at Colindale is the newspaper department of the British Museum. Hendon airfield (founded 1909 and closed in 1957) saw the first nonstop flight to Paris in 1911.

Hengelo Netherlands. Industrial town and railway junction in Overijssel province on the Twente Canal 8 km (5 miles) NW of Enschede. Pop. (1992) 76,276.

Manufactures textiles, machinery, electrical equipment; a plant extracts salt from water.

Hengyang China. Town in Hunan province on the Siang R. 153 km (95 miles) SSW of Changsha. Pop. (1990) 487,148. Important route centre on the Beijing–Guangzhu (Canton) railway and at the junction of the line to Kweilin. Has considerable river traffic: at the head of navigation for large junks.

Henley-on-Thames England. Town in Oxfordshire on the left bank of the R. Thames and 11 km (7 miles) NNE of Reading at the foot of the Chiltern Hills. Pop. (1991) 10,558. Famous for its annual rowing festival, Henley Royal Regatta, first held in 1839.

Herakleion ▶IRÁKLION.

Herat Afghanistan. Cap. of Herat province in the NW on the Hari Rud 640 km (400 miles) W of Kabul at a height of 900 m (2952 ft). Pop. (1988) 117,300.

Commercial and road centre. Flourmilling. Manufactures textiles, rugs.

Enclosed by a wall standing on a great earthwork and dominated by by the citadel, the city has 5 gates and partly ruined Jama Masjid or Great Mosque as well as remains of many other buildings testifying to its glory. Fell to the Arabs in the 7th cent. and under them acquired great importance. Sacked by Genghis Khan (1220) and other invaders, to flourish again in the 15th cent. Suffered further attacks, generally declined and was

incorporated into Afghanistan by Dost Mohammed Khan 1863.

Hérault France. Department in the S in Languedoc-Roussillon, named after the chief river, which flows S across it. Area 6101 sq km (2356 sq. miles). Pop. (1991) 805,500. Prefecture Montpellier. Bordering on the Gulf of Lions, where there are three long coastal lagoons, it rises inland to the dry, limestone hills of the Garrigues and then to the S extension of the Cévennes. One of the country's chief wine-producing regions. Also grows olives, mulberries and fruits. Chief towns Montpellier, Béziers and Sète.

Hercegovina ▶BOSNIA-HERCEGOVINA.

Herculaneum (Italian **Ercolano**) Italy. Ancient city in Campania 8 km (5 miles) SE of Naples and just W of Vesuvius. Roman residential city and resort, severely damaged by earthquake in AD 63 and completely buried by semi-liquid lava, which afterwards solidified, in the eruption of Vesuvius along with Pompeii in AD 79. Its site was discovered in 1709 and excavations were begun in 1738 and continued at various times into the 20th cent., yielding relics of greater value than those of Pompeii.

Heredia Costa Rica. Town situated NNW of San José on the Inter-American Highway in Heredia province of which it is the cap. Pop. (1984) 27,117.

A commercial centre of a coffee-growing area. Industries inc. coffee and foodprocessing and the manufacture of soap and matches.

Hereford England. Town in Herefordshire on the R. Wye 39 km (24 miles) NW of Gloucester. Pop. (1984) 54,326.

Important trade in agricultural produce. Manufactures leather, cider and beer.

The cathedral (begun 1079) exhibits every style from Norman to Perpendicular and, with Gloucester and Worcester, is the venue of the Three Choirs Festival; among its treasures is the 14th-cent. *Mappa Mundi*, one of the oldest maps in the world. The Old House, a picturesque half-timbered building now a museum, dates from the 17th cent. The grammar school was founded in 1384. Birthplace of the actor, David Garrick (1717–79) and possibly of Nell Gwynn, Charles II's mistress (1651–87).

Hereford and Worcester England. Former county in the W on the Welsh border, formed in 1974 from the counties of Herefordshire and Worcestershire, with the loss of a small area of NE Worcestershire to West Midlands. In 1998 it reverted to two separate counties.

Herefordshire England. Area 2187 sq km (842 sq miles). Pop. (1996) 167,229. A non-metropolitan unitary authority, Herefordshire consists of broad plains and hills, with the Malvern Hills rising to 425 m (1394 ft) in the E and the Black Mountains in the SW. Chief rivers the Wye, which has salmon and the Teme, Lugg and Monnow; well known for their trout. Hops, apples, plums and pears are grown, cider and perry being produced. Famous for its breed of beef cattle. Principal towns Hereford, Leominster, Ross-on-Wye.

Herford Germany. Industrial town in North Rhine-Westphalia 16 km (10 miles) NE of Bielefeld. Pop. (1989) 62,500.

Manufactures textiles, carpets, machinery, furniture and dairy produce.

Grew up round a Benedictine nunnery of the 9th cent.

Herm ►CHANNEL ISLANDS; GUERNSEY.

Hermon, Mount (Ar. **Jebel esh Sheikh**). A picturesque snow-capped mountain of the Anti-Lebanon 2814 m (9232 ft) high on the Syria–Lebanon border 40 km (25 miles) WSW of Damascus. It is the source of the R. Jordan.

Hermosillo Mexico. Cap. of Sonora state on the Sonora R. Pop. (1990) 449,472.

Commercial centre for an agricultural region (maize, cotton and fruit) and for a mining area (gold, copper and silver). Also a winter resort.

Hermoupolis ►CYCLADES.

Herne Germany. Industrial town in North Rhine-Westphalia in the Ruhr district on the Rhine–Herne Canal. Pop. (1991) 178,132.

Coalmining centre. There are coke ovens, foundries, textiles mills, chemical plant and civil engineering.

Herne Bay England. Town in NE Kent on the Thames estuary. Pop. (1991) 31,861. Seaside resort with a sea front 11 km (7 miles) long. The village of Herne, with an Early English church, is 2.4 km (1½ miles) inland.

Hersham ►WALTON AND WEYBRIDGE.

Herstal Belgium. Industrial town in Liège province on the Meuse R. 5 km (3 miles) NE of Liège. Pop. (1989) 36,343.

Manufactures firearms, precision instruments, electrical equipment, motor-cycles and sporting goods.

Claims to be the birthplace of Charlemagne (747–814).

Herstmonceaux (Hurstmonceux) England. Village in East Sussex 13 km (8 miles) NNE of Eastbourne. Pop. 1800. The castle (1440, restored 1907) has since 1950 housed the Royal Observatory after its transfer from Greenwich. The 249-cm (100 ins.) Sir Isaac Newton telescope came into service in 1967. Wooden garden baskets (trugs) made in the village.

Hertford England. Town in Hertfordshire on the R. Lea 32 km (20 miles) N of London. Pop. (1991) 22,176.

Manufactures brushes. Brewing, flour-milling, printing.

Important in Saxon times. The castle, of which little remains, was built in the 10th cent. and later rebuilt. About 3 km (2 miles) SE of Haileybury College, a public school.

Hertfordshire England. Inland county in the S, bounded on the N by Cambridgeshire, E by Essex, S by London, W by Buckinghamshire and Bedfordshire. It is divided into the districts of North Hertfordshire, Stevenage, East Hertfordshire, Dacorum, St Albans, Welwyn Hatfield, Broxbourne, Three Rivers, Watford and Hertsmere. Area 1637 sq km (633 sq. miles). Pop. (1991) 975,829. County town Hertford. Mainly low-lying, highest in the NW (Chiltern Hills). Drained to the R. Thames by the Lea, Stort and Colne rivers. Much of it is agricultural (cereals, fruit, market-garden and dairy produce) and industries inc. electronic and aerospace equipment, and pharmaceuticals. The S lies on the fringe of the London area and in recent years the 'new towns' of Stevenage and Hemel Hempstead have developed within the county. Other towns Watford, St Albans, East Barnet, Letchworth, Welwyn Garden City and Hertford.

Hertogenbosch, 's ➤HERTOGENBOSCH.

Herzegovina ➤BOSNIA HERCEGOVINA.

Hessen Germany. *Land* of Germany, comprising the territory of the former Hessen grand duchy situated on the right bank of the Rhine with most of the former Prussian province of Hesse-Nassau. Area 21,114 sq km (8152 sq. miles). Pop. (1991) 5,837,330. Cap. Wiesbaden. There are several spas, inc. Wiesbaden, Bad Homburg, Bad Nauheim. Other important towns are Frankfurt, Kassel, Darmstadt and Offenbach. Largely uplands, it inc. parts of the Odenwald, Westerwald, Hohe Rhön and the Taunus, and is well forested.

The Rheingau is famous for its wine, and industries inc. chemicals, vehicle building and electrical engineering.

A former grand duchy, known before 1866 as Hesse-Darmstadt, with çap. Darmstadt; one of several petty states into which Hesse was divided, others inc. Hesse-Kassel, Hesse-Homburg and Hesse-Marburg. After the Austro–Prussian War (1866) they were all absorbed by Prussia or Hesse-Darmstadt, and the latter became known simply as Hesse or Hessen. It was divided into two main areas, the N part (Oberhessen) being separated from the S part (Starkenburg and Rheinhessen) by a strip of Prussian territory; Mainz was the largest town. After World War II (1946) it was divided between the new *Länder* of Hessen and Rhineland-Palatinate.

Hetton-le-Hole (Hetton) England. Town in Tyne and Wear 10 km (6 miles) NE of Durham. Pop. (1991) 13,538. Coalmining centre.

Hexham England. Market town in Northumberland on the R. Tyne 32 km (20 miles) W of Newcastle-upon-Tyne. Pop. (1991) 11,008. The 13th-cent. priory church contains remains of the monastery founded *c.* 674 by St Wilfrid. Also in the town are two towers known as the Moot Hall (15th-cent.) and Manor Office (14th-cent.). In 1464 the Lancastrians were defeated by Edward VI at the Battle of Hexham.

Heysham ➤MORECAMBE AND HEYSHAM.

Heywood England. Town in Greater Manchester 5 km (3 miles) E of Bury. Pop. (1991) 29,286.

Cotton and paper milling, engineering and tanning.

Hialeah USA. Residential suburb of Miami, Florida; merges W with the Everglades. Pop. (1990) 188,004 (20,000 in 1950). Noted for the Hialeah Park racecourse (built 1931), with a vine-covered grandstand seating 10,500; the oval track surrounds a 37-ha (91-acre) area of lawns and flowerbeds, with a 13-ha (32-acre) artificial lake in the centre with pink flamingoes.

Manufactures food products and furniture.

Hidalgo Mexico. Mountainous state in central Mexico, traversed by the Sierra Madre Oriental. Area 20,813 sq km (8036 sq. miles). Pop. (1990) 1,880,636. Cap. Pachuca de Soto.

Produces maize, tobacco, cotton, maguey (from which *pulque,* a drink, is made) and other crops. Silver, gold, copper, iron, lead, zinc and antimony are mined.

Site of the ancient Toltec culture, dating from the 12th cent., with its cap. at Tula.

Hidalgo del Parral Mexico. Important mining town (chiefly silver) in S Chihuahua 193 km (120 miles) SSE of Chihuahua City at a height of 1950 m (6396 ft). Pop. (1990) 73,000. Flour-milling.

Scene of the assassination of Francisco Villa (1923).

Higashi-Osaka Japan. Town in the Osaka prefecture just E of Osaka City and part of its conurbation. Pop. (1991) 517,237.

Higham Ferrers England. Market town in Northamptonshire on the R. Nene 6 km (4 miles) E of Wellingborough. Pop. (1991) 5345.

Industries inc. tanning and the manufacture of footwear.

Highbury England. Residential district in the London borough of Islington, containing the Arsenal football ground.

Highgate England. Residential suburb in N London mainly in the borough of Haringey; so named because of the toll-gate erected by the Bishop of London in the 14th cent. Whittington Stone, at the foot of Highgate Hill, is supposed to be where Dick Whittington sat and heard Bow Bells chime 'Turn again . . .'. Highgate School was founded (1565) by Sir Roger Cholmley, the Lord Chancellor. In Highgate cemetery are the graves of Michael Faraday, Mrs Henry Wood, George Eliot, Karl Marx and Herbert Spencer.

Highland Scotland. Region in the N formed 1975 and reorganized in 1996 from the counties of Caithness, Sutherland, Ross and Cromarty, Nairn, Inverness, with the N part of Argyll. Area 25,391 sq km (9805 sq. miles). Pop. (1993) 206,900. The main sources of employment derive from farming, fishing and forestry, but there is a wide range of manufacturing industries and in particular electronics and light industry. Tourism and service industries are also of increasing importance. Specific industries are the generation of nuclear electricity at Dounreay, Caithness, aluminium-smelting at Fort William and Kinlochleven, oil-platform construction at Nigg and Ardersier, other oil-related industries inc. repair and maintenance of drilling rigs in the Cromarty Firth, timber-processing in Inverness and distilling and winter sports in the Spey Valley. Fish-farming is also a recent growth industry. An Enterprise Zone has been established at Invergordon.

High Peak ➤PEAK DISTRICT.

High Point USA. Town in North Carolina 23 km (11 miles) SW of Greensboro. Pop. (1990) 69,500.

Important centre of the furniture industry, established in the 1880s. Manufactures hosiery, textiles, plywood, crates and chemicals.

High Wycombe England. Town in S Buckinghamshire at the entrance to a gap through the Chiltern Hills and on the R. Wye, a short tributary of the R. Thames. Pop. (1991) 71,718.

Largely residential, but long noted for the manufacture of furniture. The industry originated in chairmaking, using the wood from the beech forests of the Chilterns. Also manufactures paper, metal goods, clothing and precision instruments.

Hildesheim Germany. Industrial town in Lower Saxony on the Innerste R. 29 km (18 miles) SE of Hanover. Pop. (1991) 105,291.

Manufactures machinery, textiles, carpets and cosmetics.

Grew and prospered through the establishment of a bishopric in the 9th cent. Joined the Hanseatic League in the 13th cent. The 11th-cent. cathedral and most of the old churches and timbered houses were either destroyed or severely damaged during World War II.

Hillah (Al Hillah) Iraq. Market town 96 km (60 miles) S of Baghdad on the Hillah branch of the Euphrates R. Pop. (1985) 215,249.

Trade in cereals, dates. Manufactures rugs, leather goods.

Largely built of bricks taken from the nearby ruins of ancient Babylon.

Hillingdon England. London borough comprising the former municipal borough of Uxbridge and the urban districts of Hayes and Harlington, Yiewsley and West Drayton, and Ruislip-Northwood. Pop. (1991) 225,800.

Hilo USA. Seaport and chief town of Hawaii Island, Hawaii on Hilo Bay on the E coast. Pop. (1989) 35,300.

Exports sugar, coffee and fruit. Fruit-canning, rice-milling. Tourist centre for visiting the island volcanoes.

It has suffered severely from tidal waves from time to time.

Hilversum Netherlands. Industrial and residential town, railway junction and summer resort in North Holland province 26 km (16 miles) SE of Amsterdam. Pop. (1992) 84,674.

Manufactures carpets, textiles, dyes, electrical machinery, furniture. Headquarters of Dutch radio and television.

Himachal Pradesh India. State (until 1971 a territory) of the Indian Union in the W Himalayas bounded on the E by Tibet (China). Area 55,673 sq km (21,495 sq. miles). Pop. (1991) 5,111,079 (mainly Hindus). Cap. Simla. Formed (1948) from 30 former Hill States, Bilaspur being added in 1954. Mountainous and forested; an important resource is softwood timber. Rock salt, gypsum, limestone, barytes, dolomite and pyrite are also found. Apples, oranges and potatoes are important crops. Industries inc. brewing, fruit-processing, fertilizers and cement. Tourism is important with Simla, Kulu, Manali, Dharamshala, Kangra Valley the main tourist attractions.

Himalayas, The. In Nepalese 'Home of Snow'. Vast mountain system in central Asia lying along the S edge of the Plateau of Tibet, enclosed by the Indus and Brahmaputra rivers. It extends generally ESE in an immense curve about 2400 km (1500 miles) long from the Pamirs (W) to the deep gorges of the Brahmaputra (E) and is 160–240 km (100–150 miles) in width. Its ranges may be divided into 3 zones, ascending from S to N: the Outer Himalayas, consisting mainly of the Siwalik Range, with an average height of 900–1200 m (2952–3936 ft), the Lesser Himalayas, closely related to and sometimes merging with the Great Himalayas, having an average height of 3600–4500 m (11,808–14,760 ft) and the Great Himalayas, the main range, which have an average height of about 6000 m (19,680 ft) and contain the highest peaks, inc. Everest (8848 m; 29,028 ft, highest in the world), Kanchenjunga (8598 m; 28,170 ft), and Nanga Parba (8126 m; 26,660 ft). All the high peaks are permanently snow-capped, the snowline varying between about 4500 m (14,760 ft) and 5700 m (18,696 ft); glaciers descend to levels about 1200 m (3936 ft) below the snowline. The Himalayas form an effective climatic barrier, shielding the plains of N India from the cold, dry winds from the N in winter and the Tibetan plateau from the moisture-laden winds from the S in summer. At the same time there are great climatic variations within the mountain system, partly due to differences of altitude and partly to the more pronounced influence of the summer monsoon in the E than in the W. In the E, where the rainfall may exceed 250 cm (100 ins.) annually, the land rises from the formerly swampy jungle known as the *terai* through different forest belts to the alpine zone and the snowline; the sal forest of the hills provides valuable timber. In the W, where the rainfall averages 75–100 cm (30–40 ins.) annually, scrub and bamboo give way to temperate forest and then the alpine zone and the snowline. The 'hill stations' of the Himalayas (e.g. Simla, Darjeeling) at altitudes of 2000–2500 m (6560–8200 ft) offer welcome relief from the torrid summer heat of the Indo–Gangetic Plain. The Himalayan ranges are a formidable barrier to N–S communications: railways merely reach the foothills, e.g. Simla and Darjeeling; of the few tracks through the mountains two of the more important are those from Srinagar via the Zoji La pass to Leh and from Kalimpong via the Chumbi Valley to Gyangtse.

Himeji Japan. Industrial town in Hyogo prefecture, Honshu 48 km (30 miles) WNW of Kobe. Pop. (1991) 457,579.

Industries inc. oil-refining and the manufacture of steel, chemicals, cotton and leather goods.

Hinckley England. Town in Leicestershire 19 km (12 miles) SW of Leicester. Pop. (1991) 40,608.

Manufactures hosiery, footwear. Engineering.

Hindu Kush. A westward extension of the Himalayan mountain system, from which it is separated by the Indus valley, extending WSW from the Pamirs for nearly 640 km (400 miles). Hindu Kush means 'Destroyer'. Highest peak Tirich Mir (7690 m; 25,230 ft). The mountain system is crossed by several passes at 3600–3900 m (11,808–12,792 ft), one of which, the Khawak, was negotiated by Alexander the Great. The Salang road-tunnel, 2.4 km (1½ miles) long, between Kabul and Doshi (Afghanistan), was opened in 1964. The slopes of the Hindu Kush are generally barren and treeless.

Hirosaki Japan. Industrial town in Aomori prefecture, N Honshu 34 km (21 miles) SW of Aomori. Pop. (1991) 174,624. Noted for its green lacquer ware.

Other industries textile manufacture, soya-bean processing and woodworking.

To the W is the isolated conical peak of Iwakisan, a place of pilgrimage.

Hiroshima Japan. Cap. of Hiroshima prefecture in SW Honshu 280 km (174 miles) W of Osaka. Pop. (1991) 1,090,048.

Industrial centre and seaport. Manufactures cars and lorries, machinery, textiles, rubber products. Shipbuilding, brewing. Exports canned goods, rayon.

In Hiroshima Bay is the sacred island of Itsukushima. During World War II the city was the target of the first atomic bomb to be dropped in action (6 Aug. 1945): over 78,000 people were killed, about the same number were wounded and most of the buildings were destroyed or severely damaged.

Hisar India. Town in Haryana on a branch of the W Jumna Canal 148 km (92 miles) WNW of Delhi. Pop. (1991) 181,255.

Trade in cattle, cotton and grain.

Founded (1356) by Feroze Shah.

Hispaniola West Indies. Second largest island in the Caribbean E of Cuba. The W third is occupied by Haiti, the E two-thirds by the Dominican Republic. Discovered (1492) by Columbus, who named it 'La Isla Española', later abbreviated to Española and corrupted to Hispaniola. The pre-Columbian Arawak Indians had called it Haiti ('Mountainous Country') or Quisqueya; during the 19th cent. it was called both Haiti and Santo Domingo.

Hitchin England. Town in N Hertfordshire 23 km (14 miles) NW of Hertford. Pop. (1991) 29,742.

Engineering, tanning, cultivation and distilling of lavender.

Hjälmar, Lake Sweden. Lake 64 km (40 miles) long and up to 16 km (10 miles) wide (area 492 sq km (190 sq. miles)). SW of L. Mälar, into which it drains by the Eskilstuna R. The town of Örebro is at its W end.

Hobart Australia. Cap. and chief seaport of Tasmania on the W shore of the Derwent R. estuary. Pop. (1991) 181,838. Excellent natural harbour of 12–15 m (39–49 ft) depth and tidal range of only about 1 m (3.28 ft). The city dominated by Mt Wellington (1271m; 4169 ft) to the W. Founded 1804. The nucleus of the city has old sandstone buildings about the original harbour; new housing has spread outwards with industrial districts to the N and S. Seat of the University of Tasmania (1890).

Hydroelectric power from the hinterland supplies industries, inc. zinc-refining, flour-milling, fruit-canning and chemical, cement and woollen manufactures. Primary exports inc. apples, wool, timber, dairy produce, meat and hops.

Hobbs USA. Market town in SE New Mexico on the Llano Estacado. Pop. (1970) 26,025. In a ranching and agricultural area. Oil-refining.

Founded 1907 and grew rapidly after the discovery of oil in the neighbourhood in 1927.

Hoboken Belgium. Residential suburb of SW Antwerp in Antwerp province on the Scheldt R. Main industry shipbuilding. Also metalworking and refractory metals.

Hoboken USA. Port in New Jersey on the Hudson R. opposite Manhattan (New York City), with which it has tunnel, subway and ferry connections. Pop. (1990) 33,400.

Manufactures electrical equipment, furniture, textiles, chemicals. Shipbuilding.

First settled by Dutch farmers in 1640, in 1658 it was deeded by the Indians to Peter Stuyvesant. The present town was laid out in 1804. The name derives from 'hobocan', an Indian word meaning a tobacco pipe.

Ho Chi Minh City (Saigon) Vietnam. Largest city, formerly cap. and chief port of South Vietnam on the Saigon R. 55 km (34 miles) from the South China Sea. Pop. (1991) 3,450,000.

Exports rice, dried fish, copra and rubber. To the SW it adjoins Cholon, with which it is combined in one administrative unit and the two cities form the country's main industrial region. Rice-milling, brewing and distilling. Manufactures soap, rubber products and textiles.

Formerly cap. of Cochin-China, the French colony which became South Vietnam after World War II. Surrendered to the North Vietnamese army 1975, virtually bringing the Vietnam War to an end. It kept the name Saigon until 1975 when the two Vietnams were unified.

Hoddesdon England. Market town in Hertfordshire 5 km (3 miles) SE of Hertford. Pop. (1991) 19,812.

Glasshouse cultivation of cucumbers, tomatoes and flowers. Manufactures electrical equipment and pharmaceutical goods.

Just NE is Rye House, scene of the plot (1683) against Charles II.

Hodeida (Al Hudaydah) Yemen. Chief seaport, on the Red Sea. Pop. (1986) 155,110.

Exports Mocha coffee, hides and skins. Industries inc. oil-refining, textiles, aluminium, food-processing and an oxygen plant.

Occupied by the Turks in the mid 19th cent. and developed by them. A road has been constructed to San'a.

Hódmezövásárhely Hungary. Cap. of Csongrád county in the S 24 km (15 miles) NE of Szeged near the Tisza R. Protected from its floods by a large dike. Pop. (1984) 54,000.

Centre of a rich agricultural region. Industries inc. flour-milling and distilling, and the manufacture of agricultural implements, pottery and bricks.

Hoek van Holland ➤HOOK OF HOLLAND.

Hof Germany. Industrial town in NE Bavaria on the Saale R. near the frontier with the Czech Republic. Pop. (1992) 53,000.

Manufactures textiles, machinery and chemicals. Brewing, distilling.

Founded in the 13th cent.

Hofei ➤HEFEI.

Hofuf Saudi Arabia. Chief town of Hasa, Nejd 113 km (70 miles) SSW of Dhahran, near the Riyadh–Dammam railway. Pop. (1988) 101,271.

Trading centre in the Hasa oasis (dates, cereals and fruits).

Hohenlimburg Germany. Industrial town in North Rhine-Westphalia 8 km (5 miles) ESE of Hagen. Pop. (1970) 26,300.

There are steel mills, and it manufactures wire and glass.

Hohhot (Huhehot/Huhohaote) China. Cap. of the Inner Mongolian Autonomous Region (Nei Mongol) and formerly cap. of Suiyuan province 434 km (270 miles) WNW of Beijing, with which it is linked by railway. Pop. (1989) 900,000.

Industrial and commercial centre with flour-milling and iron and steel works. It manufactures textiles, rugs, bricks, dairy products and tiles.

It was a Mongolian religious centre and seat of the Grand Lama until the 17th cent. In 1939 the Japanese made it cap. of their puppet state of Mengchiang.

Hokkaido Japan. The most northerly and the second largest of the 4 main islands, separated from Honshu (S) by the Tsugaru Strait. Area (inc. offshore islands) 83,408 sq km (32,204 sq. miles). Pop. (1990) 5,644,000. Cap. Sapporo. Largely mountainous, with some peaks exceeding 1800 m (5904 ft) and several volcanic cones. It has the country's longest river, the Ishikarigawa. The winters are especially long and severe in the N, while the E coast suffers from summer fogs. Well forested.

Soya beans, potatoes, rice are cultivated. The Ishikari district has one of the country's main coalfields. Other industries inc. paper, dairy products and sugar. Main resource fisheries; great quantities of salmon, cod, herring and sardines are caught. Principal seaports Otaru, Muroran, Hakodate.

First settled by the Japanese in the 16th cent. (when it was known as Yezo). Systematically developed from 1871.

Holbeach England. Town in Lincolnshire 11 km (7 miles) E of Spalding. Pop. (1991) 6088.

In a bulb and fruit growing district. Brewing, malting.

Holborn England. Part of the London borough of Camden. Former metropolitan borough of London N of the Thames. In this district are the British Museum, Hatton Garden (centre of the diamond trade), two of the four Inns of Court (Lincoln's Inn and Gray's Inn, severely damaged in World War II) and Lincoln's Inn Fields; Wren's Church of St Andrew (1686) was destroyed in World War II. New office blocks have been erected on the sites of many buildings gutted in air raids. The name is probably derived from Holebourne ('the Stream in the Hollow') referring to the course of the R. Fleet, later crossed by Holborn Viaduct (1869).

Holderness England. Low-lying peninsula and rural district in Humberside between the North Sea and the Humber estuary, forming a fertile agricultural area, with Spurn Head at its S end. Pop. (rural district, 1971) 24,256.

Holguín Cuba. Town in the Oriente province 105 km (65 miles) NNW of Santiago de Cuba. Pop. (1989) 222,794.

Important commercial centre situated on a fertile plateau. Sawmilling, tanning. Manufactures furniture and tiles. Through its port, Gibara, 30 km (19 miles) NNE, it exports tobacco, coffee, maize, sugar and beef.

It has notable Spanish 'colonial' buildings.

Holland ►NETHERLANDS.

Hollywood (California) USA. A suburb of NW Los Angeles. Famous as the leading centre of the film and television industry, though most of the studios are now outside Hollywood itself. Large commercial and shopping districts, and residential areas for film actors reaching up the slopes of the nearby Santa Monica Mountains. A Greek theatre, a planetarium, the Hollywood Bowl for outdoor concerts and many other amenities. Founded in the 1880s. Amalgamated with Los Angeles in 1910.

Hollywood (Florida) USA. Town in SE Florida 26 km (16 miles) N of Miami. Pop. (1990) 121,697. A seaside resort which developed rapidly in the 1950s and 1960s.

Manufactures cement and furniture.

Holyhead Wales. Town in Isle of Anglesey on the N side of Holy Island. Pop. (1991) 11,796.

Railway terminus, seaside resort and packet station for Ireland, with steamer services to Dublin and Dun Laoghaire. The harbour is protected by a breakwater 2.4 km (1½ miles) long.

Holy Island (Lindisfarne) England. Island 5 km (3 miles) long and 1.6 km (1 mile) wide off the coast of Northumberland and 15 km (9½ miles) SE of Berwick-on-Tweed, accessible from the mainland at low water by a causeway (1954). On the W coast is a small village. The church and monastery were founded (635) by St Aidan. St Cuthbert was one of the bishops of Lindisfarne (685–7). In 793 the settlement was destroyed by the Danes. The Lindisfarne Gospels, a 7th-cent. illuminated Latin MS written here, is now in the British Museum. In 1083 a Benedictine priory, of which there are remains, was built on the site of the earlier cathedral.

Holy Island (Inishcaltra) Ireland. Islet in Lough Derg, Co. Clare. Remains of 4 churches dating from the 7th cent.

Holy Island Scotland. Small island off the E coast of Arran in the Firth of Clyde.

Holy (Holyhead) Island Wales. Island off the W coast of Isle of Anglesey separated from it by a narrow strait spanned by an embankment carrying the railway and road. Chief town Holyhead.

Holy Loch ➤DUNOON.

Holyoke USA. Industrial town in S Massachusetts on the Connecticut R. Pop. (1985) 45,000.

Manufactures paper, textiles and electrical equipment.

Holywell Wales. Town in Flintshire near the R. Dee estuary 6 km (4 miles) WNW of Flint. Pop. (1991) 7531. Noted for St Winifred's Well, over which a Gothic chapel was built by Margaret, mother of Henry VII.

Manufactures rayon and paper.

Homberg Germany. Industrial town and river port in North Rhine-Westphalia in the Ruhr district on the left bank of the Rhine nearly opposite Duisburg and now part of the latter.

Coalmining centre. Iron foundries, dyeworks and textile factories.

Homburg von der Hohe (Bad Homburg, Homburg) Germany. Spa in Hessen at the foot of the Taunus Mountains 13 km (8 miles) N of Frankfurt. Pop. (1986) 51,100.

Mineral springs rediscovered in the 19th cent. Manufactures machinery, textiles, leather goods and biscuits.

Home Counties England. Counties surrounding London, particularly those into which Greater London has encroached (Essex, Kent, Surrey and Hertfordshire); with the outward spread of the commuter belt, Buckinghamshire, Berkshire and Sussex have a claim to inclusion.

Homel (Gomel) Belarus. Cap. of the Homel Region on the Sozh R. 290 km (180 miles) SE of Minsk. Pop. (1990) 506,100. Important railway junction and industrial centre.

Industries inc. railway engineering, and it manufactures agricultural implements, electrical goods, footwear, textiles, furniture and matches.

It belonged to Poland and Russia alternately until 1772, when it passed to Russia.

Homs (Hims) Syria. Ancient Emesa. Cap. of Homs province, on the Orontes R. Pop. (1992) 518,000.

Road and rail junction in a fertile region producing cereals and fruit. A tourist centre. Industries inc. sugar-refining, oil-refining and the manufacture of textiles, jewellery and metal goods.

Birthplace of Heliogabalus (Elagabalus, 204–22), the boy priest who became Roman emperor. Taken by the Arabs in the 7th cent. and later by the Turks, who retained it almost continuously till the end of World War II.

Honan ➤HENAN.

Honduras. Republic in Central America bounded N by the Caribbean, by Nicaragua E and SE, Guatemala W, El Salvador to the SW and S by the Pacific Ocean. Area 112,088 sq km (43,277 sq. miles). Pop. (1995) 5,512,000 (42 per cent urban). Life expectancy, 65 years male, 69 female. Cap. Tegucigalpa. Other important cities are San Pedro Sula, La Ceiba, El Progreso and Choluteca. Currency: Honduran lempira = 100 centavos.

It has a N coastline of 560 km (350 miles) on the Caribbean and a S coastline of 64 km (40 miles) on the Pacific. Off the Caribbean coast lie the Bay Is. (Islas de la Bahía), ceded to Honduras by Britain in 1861, forming one of the 18 departments into which the country is divided. The most mountainous country in Central America except for the narrow coastal strips and the undeveloped Mosquito Coast (on the Caribbean) inhabited by Indian tribes. The main cordillera of Central America traverses it, rising to over 2000 m (6560 ft). Chief rivers the Patuca, the Ulúa and the Aguán, flowing to the Pacific. The coastal climate is hot and humid, with heavy rainfall May–Dec.; the higher land of the interior is cooler. Land use: forested 30 per cent, meadows and pastures 23 per cent, agricultural and under permanent cultivation

16 per cent. The main religion is Roman Catholic and the lang. Spanish. Ethnic composition comprises 89 per cent mestizo and Amerindian 7 per cent.

It is chiefly agricultural and the principal exports are bananas (cultivated on large American-owned plantations on the Caribbean coast), coffee, cotton, tobacco and citrus fruits. Extensive forests produce mahogany, rosewood, walnut and pine wood. Complete geological surveys of the country have not yet been undertaken, but zinc, silver, gold, tin, coal and mercury are being mined. Industry comprises small-scale concerns and inc. food-processing, paper, plastic, tobacco products, textiles, sugar and cement.

In pre-Columbian times the area which is now Honduras was part of the Mayan empire. It was discovered by Columbus in 1502 on his fourth voyage. It won independence from Spain 1821 and was a member of the Central American Federation 1823–38. In 1838 the country declared itself an independent sovereign state. Political instability then became the rule; but, following a series of military regimes, civilians took over in 1980 with democratically elected government, but with the military still important. It consists of 23 departments, four intendancies and five commissaries. There is an executive President. The Congress consists of a 102-member Senate and a 161-member House of Representatives.

Honduras, British ►BELIZE.

Hong Kong China. Former British Crown Colony on the coast of Guangdong province in S China, consisting of Hong Kong Island, the ceded territory of Kowloon and the New Territories. Area 1074 sq km (415 sq. miles). Pop. (1991) 5,674,100 (97 per cent Chinese). Life expectancy, 75 years male, 80 female. Cap. Victoria. Currency: Hong Kong dollar = 100 cents. Hong Kong island has an indented coastline and lies across a channel 1½ km (1 mile) from the Kowloon peninsula. To the W of the island Victoria Peak rises to 554 metres (1817 ft). The New Territories are an enclave of the mainland. There are over 230 smaller islands. It has a subtropical climate with hot, humid summers and cold, dry winters. Fresh water is stored in reservoirs and also imported from the mainland. Land use: forested 21 per cent, permanent cultivation 6 per cent, fish ponds 1 per cent, built on scrubland 72 per cent. Ethnically 97 per cent of the pop. is Chinese and the majority belong to the Buddhist and Taoist faiths.

Hong Kong's prosperity is maintained by trading and manufacturing. Agriculture and fisheries account for only about 1 per cent of GDP and most of its foodstuffs have to be imported. Light manufacturing, shipbuilding and banking are important industries and over 5 million tourists visit each year.

Hong Kong Island was ceded by China to Britain after the first and second Anglo–Chinese Wars by the Treaty of Nanking in 1842 and the southern tip of the Kowloon peninsula by the Convention of Peking in 1860. Northern Kowloon was leased to Britain for 99 years by China in 1898. Since then Hong Kong has been under British administration, except from December 1941 to August 1945. In 1984 Britain and China signed a joint declaration whereby China would recover sovereignty over Hong Kong (comprising Hong Kong Island, Kowloon and the New Territories) from 1 July 1997 and establish it as a Special Administrative Region where the existing social and economic systems, and the present life-style, would remain unchanged for another 50 years. Hong Kong also retains a legislature and judiciary. Hong Kong was administered by a UK-appointed Governor who presided over a 14-member Executive Council and there is a partly-elected Legislative Council (Legco).

Honiara ►GUADALCANAL.

Honiton England. Market town in Devon on the R. Otter 26 km (16 miles) ENE of Exeter. Pop. (1991) 8915. Famous since Elizabethan times for the manufacture of pillow-lace, introduced by Flemish refugees.

Honolulu USA. State cap. of Hawaii on the S coast of Oahu. Pop. (1990) 365,272.

An important seaport and centre of communications in the Pacific; airline and shipping connections with the USA, Australia and the Far East. Chief exports sugar, coffee and tropical fruits (esp. pineapples). Sugar-refining, fruit-canning. The tourist trade is considerable, helped by ease of communications and a pleasant, equable climate.

To the W is the US naval base of Pearl Harbor. The Bernice P. Bishop Museum was founded (1889) as a memorial to Princess Bernice Panahi, the last of the Kamechameha family of Hawaiian chiefs.

Honshu Japan. Largest and most important of the Japanese islands, containing most of the principal cities inc. Tokyo, Kyoto, Yokohama, Nagoya and Osaka. Area 230,110 sq km (88,846 sq. miles). Pop. (1990) 99,254,000.

Hoogeveen Netherlands. Town in Drenthe province 51 km (32 miles) S of Groningen. Pop. (1992) 46,456.

Industries inc. food-processing.

Hoogezand–Sappemeer Netherlands. Town in Groningen province 11 km (7 miles) ESE of Groningen. Pop. (1992) 34,210.

Manufactures machinery and tyres.

Hooghly (Hugli) India. Most westerly and most important channel by which the Ganges R. reaches the Bay of Bengal, being thus the W boundary of the great Ganges delta, formed by the union of the Bhagirathi and Jalangi rivers; flows S for 233 km (145 miles) past Chandernagore, Howrah, Calcutta, Garden Reach. Liable to silting, the Hooghly is kept open to ocean-going vessels as far as Calcutta by constant dredging.

Hook of Holland (Hoek van Holland) Netherlands. Seaport in South Holland province 25 km (15 miles) WNW of Rotterdam at the North Sea end of the New Waterway; terminus of cross-channel ferries from Harwich, England.

Hoover Dam USA. Important dam on the Colorado R. in Black Canyon on the Arizona–Nevada border, used for irrigation, hydroelectric power and flood control, built 1931–6; 221 m (725 ft) high and 379 m (1243 ft) long. First named Hoover Dam (after President Hoover), then Boulder Dam (1933–47); renamed Hoover Dam. It forms Lake Mead.

Hopei ➤HEBEI.

Hormuz, Strait of. Passage linking the Gulf to the Arabian Sea, lying between the S coast of Iran and the Musandam Peninsula of Oman. Of great strategic significance for oil supplies.

Horn, Cape (Cabo de Hornos) Chile. Rocky headland 424 m (1391 ft) high at the extreme S end of South America on Horn Island in Tierra del Fuego. Notorious for stormy weather and heavy seas. Discovered (1616) by the Dutch navigator Schouten; named after Hoorn (Netherlands), his birthplace.

Horncastle England. Market town in Lincolnshire on the R. Bain 27 km (17 miles) E of Lincoln. Pop. (1991) 4994. Long famous for its horse fair, described in George Borrow's *Romany Rye*.

Brewing, malting and tanning. Fruit-growing in the neighbourhood.

Somersby, 10 km (6 miles) ENE, was the birthplace of Tennyson (1809–92).

Hornchurch England. Part of the London borough of Havering situated 3 km (2 miles) ESE of Romford. Mainly residential, serving as a dormitory suburb for London.

Engineering. Manufactures office equipment, clothing and chemicals.

Hornsea England. Seaside resort on the North Sea 21 km (13 miles) NE of Hull. Pop. (1991) 7573. Just inland is Hornsea Mere, noted for herons and fish.

Hornsey England. Part of the London borough of Haringey, a N suburb of London.

Horsens Denmark. Port in E Jutland on Horsens Fiord. Pop. (1992) 55,123.

Manufactures textiles, machinery, tobacco products. Trade in dairy produce.

Horsham England. Market town in West Sussex 27 km (17 miles) N of Worthing.

Pop. (1991) 42,552. Railway junction. Engineering and chemicals.

An Early English church and several old houses. Christ's Hospital, the Bluecoat school founded by Edward VI, was moved here from London in 1902. Shelley (1792–1822) was born at nearby Field Place.

Horwich England. Town in Greater Manchester 8 km (5 miles) NE of Wigan. Pop. (1991) 18,017.

Engineering, cotton and paper mills. The railway workshops closed in 1983.

Hoshiarpur India. Town in Punjab 40 km (25 miles) NE of Jullundur. Pop. (1990) 122,705.

Trade in grain and sugar. Manufactures furniture, turpentine and rosin.

Hospitalet Spain. Industrial suburb of Barcelona just SW of the city. Pop. (1991) 269,241.

Industries inc. steel and textile mills, and chemical works.

Hotan (Khotan) China. Town in SW Xinjiang Uygur Autonomous Republic 386 km (240 miles) SE of Kashi on the S edge of the Tarim Basin and on the ancient Silk Road. Pop. (1986) 121,000.

Manufactures cotton and silk goods and carpets. Famous for its jade. The Hotan oasis in which it stands produces cereals, cotton and fruits.

In early times a centre of Buddhist learning. Visited by Marco Polo in 1274.

Hot Springs USA. Health resort in Arkansas in the Ouachita Mountains. Pop. (1990) 32,462. Named after the many thermal springs in the neighbourhood. The Hot Springs National Park was founded in 1921.

Hounslow England. A London borough inc. the municipal borough of Brentford and Chiswick and the urban district of Feltham (both in Middlesex). Pop. (1991) 193,400. Once an important coaching station on the Great West Road. It is adjacent to Heathrow airport. On Hounslow Heath, earlier the haunt of robbers and highwaymen, was marked the baseline of the first trigonometrical survey in England (1784).

Houston USA. Largest city and industrial centre in Texas in the SE. Pop. (1990) 1,630,553.

Noted for the manufacture of chemicals based on the natural resources of the Gulf coast, i.e. sulphur, salt, petroleum, natural gas. Other products are cement, textiles, synthetic rubber, oilfield equipment and pharmaceuticals. An important cargo port, connected to the Gulf of Mexico by the 84-km (52-mile) Houston Ship Channel. Exports petroleum, cotton, chemicals, rice, manufactured goods.

Headquarters of the National Aeronautics and Space Administration (NASA).

Hove England. Residential town in East Sussex adjoining Brighton on the E. Pop. (1991) 67,602. Seaside resort.

Howrah India. Important industrial town and railway junction in West Bengal on the Hooghly R. opposite Calcutta, with which connected formerly by pontoon bridge, now by cantilever bridge. Forms part of Greater Calcutta.

Manufactures jute and cotton goods, hosiery, rope, chemicals and soap.

Howth Ireland. Seaside town in Co. Dublin and residential suburb 13 km (8 miles) ENE of Dublin with which it was incorporated in 1940, on the N side of the peninsula bounding Dublin Bay and at the foot of the Hill of Howth (171 m; 561 ft). Ferry port from England from 1813 until superseded by Dun Laoghaire (Kingstown) in 1833.

Hoxton England. District mainly in the Greater London borough of Hackney. Centre of furniture manufacture.

Hoylake England. Seaside resort in Cheshire at the NW corner of the Wirral peninsula and 11 km (7 miles) W of Birkenhead. Pop. (1991) 25,554. It has an important golf course.

Hradec Králové Czech Republic. Cap. of Východočeský region at the confluence of the Orlice R. with the Elbe (Labe) R. 101 km

(63 miles) ENE of Prague. Pop. (1990) 101,000.

Railway junction. Manufactures machinery, musical instruments, textiles, timber products and photographic equipment.

Hrodna (Grodno) Belarus. Cap. of Hrodna region on the Newman R. near the Polish border. Pop. (1991) 284,000. Railway junction. Manufactures electrical equipment, fertilizers, textiles, leather goods, etc. Sugar-refining. Trade in grain and timber. Important as early as the 12th cent. Cap. of Lithuania in the 14th cent. Changed hands later between Poland and Russia; ceded to the USSR 1945.

Hsinchu Taiwan. Town situated SW of Taipei on the W coast. Pop. (1991) 324,426.

Industries inc. the manufacture of synthetic oil, fertilizers, glass, paper and timber products. A science-based industrial park opened in 1980.

Huacho Peru. Port 113 km (70 miles) NNW of Lima. Pop. (1989) 35,900.

Serves the fertile cotton and sugar growing Huaura R. valley. Cottonseed-oil and soap factories. It is on the Pan-American Highway and is linked by rail with Lima.

Hualien Taiwan. Town situated 120 km (75 miles) S of Taipei on the E coast. Pop. (1996) 410,985. It is the largest port on the Pacific coast and manufactures chemicals, non-ferrous metals, marble, dolomite and is noted for Taiwanese jade.

Huallaga River Peru. River 933 km (580 miles) long, flowing N and NE from the high Andes of central Peru to join the Marañon R. The upper course is a mountain torrent; the lower passes through the forested Amazon lowlands.

Huambo Angola. Formerly Nova Lisboa. Town on the Bié Plateau 520 km (300 miles) E of Luanda at a height of 1650 m (5412 ft). Pop. (1993) 400,000. On the Benguela railway to Shaba (Democratic Republic of the Congo).

Commercial centre. Industries inc. railway workshops, fertilizers, fruit-canning, sugar-refining and cement.

Huancavelica Peru. Town and provincial cap. situated ESE of Lima on the Huancavelica R. Pop. (1988) 25,000.

Industries inc. mining and smelting, silver, mercury and lead. It trades in wool.

Huancayo Peru. Cap. of Junin department 209 km (130 miles) E of Lima. Pop. (1990) 207,600.

In the wheat-growing Mantaro R. valley, at a height of 3260 m (10,693 ft). Market town. Manufactures textiles. Flour-milling. Trade chiefly in wheat, maize and alfalfa.

Huang-he (Yellow River) China. Second longest river in China, 4666 km (2900 miles) long, rising in Tsinghai (Chinghai) province on the plateau at 4200 m (13,780 ft), flowing through two lakes, Tsaring Nor and Ngoring Nor; called 'Yellow River' because of the great amounts of yellow silt (loess) which it carries down from its middle course. It flows generally E and N, but is turned S by the mountains of Shansi, here forming the boundary between this province and Shensi. After about 800 km (500 miles) on this southward course through the loess plateau, it receives the Wei-ho, and turns E and then NE on to the Great Plain of N China. The silt it carries down has extended the delta and provided additional land for crops, but it also raises the river bed, necessitates the construction of embankments and makes the river liable to cause disastrous floods. If the embankments give way, the river may change its course: in the last 4000 years there have been 8 major changes of course. The Huang-he, in fact, has well merited the nickname 'China's sorrow'. Before AD 11 it took a northerly course, emptying into the Bohai Gulf near Tientsin; from 11 to 1194 it flowed further S, and from 1852 it took a direct course E across the plain to the Yellow Sea; since 1947 it has flowed again to the Bohai Gulf.

Huánuco Peru. Cap. of Huánuco department 250 km (155 miles) NNE of Lima. Pop. (1990) 86,300. Centre of a rich agricultural and mining area on the upper Huallaga

R. at a height of 1913 m (6276 ft) in the E Peruvian Andes. Produces sugar, brandy. Founded 1539.

Huascarán Peru. Extinct snow-capped volcano in the Ancash department 240 km (150 miles) N of Huacho. Highest peak in the Peruvian Andes (6768 m; 22,205 ft). An avalanche descending its slopes buried a village and killed over 3000 people in Jan. 1962. Another avalanche, set in motion by a violent earthquake, descended the mountain slopes, buried two towns and killed about 20,000 people, in 1970.

Hubbard, Mount USA/Canada. Mountain in the St Elias range at 4557 m (14,950 ft) situated 224 km (140 miles) W of Whitehorse.

Hubei (Hupeh) China. Province in central China through which flow the Yangtse R. and its tributary the Han R. Area 187,500 sq km (72,394 sq. miles). Pop. (1990) 53,969,210. Cap. Wuhan, the largest town. Mountainous in the W, elsewhere mainly low-lying; along the Yangtse course there are many lakes.

Rice, cotton, wheat cultivated. Iron ore mined. Yichang (Ichang) is an important river port.

Hubli-Dharwad India. Town in Karnataka 19 km (12 miles) SE of Dharwar, with which it was incorporated in 1961. Pop. (1991) 648,300.

Trade in cotton. There are railway workshops, cotton mills, and two-wheelers, automotive components and engineering equipment are manufactured.

Huchow ►HUZHOU.

Hucknall England. Town in Nottinghamshire 10 km (6 miles) NNW of Nottingham. Pop. (1991) 29,160.

Manufactures hosiery.

Byron is buried in the 14th-cent. church.

Huddersfield England. Industrial town in West Yorkshire on the R. Colne. Pop. (1991) 143,726.

Important centre of the woollen and worsted industry with associated manufactures, e.g. dyes, carpets, clothing, textile machinery. Also metalworking and engineering.

Development due to the introduction of the woollen trade in the 17th cent., assisted later by the proximity of coal and transportation facilities by river, canal (to the Calder navigation) and rail.

Hudson Bay Canada. Large gulf (or inland sea) connected to the Atlantic Ocean by the Hudson Strait and to the Arctic Ocean by the Foxe Channel. Area 1,243,000 sq km (480,000 sq. miles). At the N entrance are the Southampton, Coats and Mansel islands. In the E are the Belcher Is. and in James Bay (SE) is Akimiski Island. There are many other islands. Churchill is the chief port on the bay, which is navigable from July to Oct. Salmon and cod fisheries are important. Named after Henry Hudson, the explorer, who discovered it in 1610. The Hudson's Bay Company (chartered 1760) held a monopoly of trading rights in the area until 1869, when its territories were transferred to the Dominion of Canada.

Hudson River USA. River 492 km (306 miles) long, rising in the Adirondacks and flowing S, then E, then mainly S to Upper New York Bay at New York City; the final stretch (part of New York harbour) is called the North R. An important commercial waterway linked to the Great Lakes, the St Lawrence Seaway and L. Champlain by the New York State Barge Canal system. Chief tributary the Mohawk R. (canalized). Named after Henry Hudson, the first European to explore it (1609).

Hué Vietnam. Town on the Hué R. near its mouth. Pop. (1989) 211,085.

Manufactures textiles, cement.

An ancient walled town containing royal palaces and temples. Became cap. of the Annam in the early 19th cent. Taken by the French in 1883, it was cap. of the French protectorate till 1946.

Huelva Spain. 1. Province in the extreme SW in Andalusia, bordered on the W by

Portugal and on the S by the Gulf of Cádiz. Area 10,085 sq km (3893 sq. miles). Pop. (1991) 443,476. The N is mountainous, forming part of the wooded Sierra Morena (here known as the Sierra de Aracena). The S consists of low plains. An important mining region, esp. for copper (Rio Tinto).

2. Cap. of Huelva province, seaport on the peninsula formed by the Odiel and the Tinto river estuaries, 95 km (60 miles) NW of Cádiz. Pop. (1991) 141,041.

Exports copper, manganese, iron and other ores, cork, wine and is also a tuna and sardine fishing centre. Fish-canning and flour-milling are the main industries.

Once a Carthaginian trading centre, later a Roman colony. Near by is La Rábida monastery, where Columbus planned his first voyage, setting sail from Palos de la Frontera (1492).

Huesca Spain. 1. Province in the NE in Aragon, separated from France (N) by the Pyrenees, with the highest point, Pico de Aneto, rising to 3406 m (11,172 ft), descending S to the Ebro R. Area 15,671 sq km (6049 sq. miles). Pop. (1991) 207,810. Mainly agricultural; extensive irrigation. Produces cereals, wine and fruits.

2. Ancient Osca. Cap. of Huesca province, 68 km (42 miles) NE of Zaragoza. Pop. (1991) 44,091.

Trade in agricultural produce. Manufactures agricultural machinery, cement and pottery.

Here Quintus Sertorius founded his school (77 BC) and was assassinated (72 BC). Has a cathedral (13th/16th-cent.) and the Alcázar Real, the ancient palace used by the former university.

Hugli ►HOOGHLY.

Huhehot ►HOHHOT.

Huila Colombia. Snow-capped volcano (5750 m; 18,860 ft) in the Andes 96 km (60 miles) NE of the Popayán. The highest peak in the Central Cordillera.

Hull Canada. Industrial town in SW Quebec on the Ottawa R. at the confluence with the Gatineau R. opposite Ottawa. Pop. (1991) 60,707.

Important timber, pulp and paper centre. Manufactures matches, furniture, clothing and cement.

Founded (1800) by Philemon Wright. Named after Hull, England, former home of Wright's parents.

Hull (officially **Kingston-upon-Hull**) England. City and unitary authority (formerly in Humberside) on the N bank of the Humber at the mouth of the R. Hull. Pop. (1991) 245,300. It has been one of Britain's principal ports since medieval times. Its favourable E coast location encourages short-sea trading connections with N Europe. There is a ferry service to Zeebrugge. The Humber's main tributaries, the R. Ouse and Trent, together with various canals further inland, provide a waterway link for both commercial and leisure craft to an extensive area of northern and central England. The opening of the Humber Bridge and the crossing higher up river by motorway of both the Ouse and Trent together with the completion of a freeway between the bridge and the main Hull docks has cut journey times to the minimum.

Exports manufactured goods from the N and the Midlands and imports dairy produce, timber and wool. Manufactures vegetable oils, paints, chemicals, cement and wood products. Industries inc. fishing, flour-milling and brewing.

Trinity House, an institution for merchant seamen, was founded in 1369. The University College (1929) became a university in 1954. Among the pupils at the grammar school (founded 1485) were Andrew Marvell, the poet, and William Wilberforce (1759–1833), the philanthropist, who was born here and whose home is now a museum. Hull was presented with its charter by Edward I in 1299.

Humber River England. Estuary of the R. Trent and the R. Ouse, flowing E for 29 km (18 miles) and then SE for 31 km (19 miles) to the North Sea, separating N and S Humberside. Chief ports Hull and Grimsby.

Humberside England. Former county created in 1974 around the Humber estuary from the former North Lincolnshire, most of the East Riding of Yorkshire and also the district around Goole, and abolished in 1996 when four unitary local authorities were formed; East Riding of Yorkshire, Kingston upon Hull City, North Lincolnshire and North East Lincolnshire.

Hunan China. Province in S central China, with the Yangtse R. along part of its N border. Area 210,500 sq km (81,274 sq. miles). Pop. (1990) 60,600,000. Cap. Changsha. Mainly hilly, it is crossed by the fertile valleys of the Siang and Yan rivers, which drain into Tung Ting L. Rice, wheat, tea, cotton cultivated. Coal, lead, zinc, antimony are mined. Chief towns Changsha, Hengyang, Changde and Siangtan.

Hunedoara Romania. Town in the Hunedoara district 132 km (82 miles) E of Timişoara. Pop. (1989) 86,000.

Important iron and steel centre, and produces most of the country's pig iron. It also manufactures chemicals.

Hungary (Magyar **Köztársaság**). Republic of SE central Europe. Bounded by Slovakia to the N, the Ukraine NE, Romania E, Croatia and Yugoslavia S and Austria W. Area 93,033 sq km (35,920 sq. miles). Pop. (1995) 10,231,000 (urban 63 per cent). Life expectancy, 65 years male, 74 female. Cap. Budapest. Other major cities Debrecen, Miskolc, Szeged and Pécs. Currency: Forint = 100 filler.

Hungary lies chiefly in the basin of the middle Danube, which crosses it N–S. To the E of the Danube is the Great Hungarian Plain or Alföld, which is drained also by the Tisza R. To the W the area is crossed SW–NE by a spur of the Alps, the main part being the Bakony Forest, S of which is L. Balaton, and this line of hills continues E of the Danube and rises there to over 900 m (2952 ft). The lowland in the NW is known as the Little Hungarian Plain or Little Alföld. Ringed by mountains, the country has a moderate continental climate, with a rainfall

of 50–60 cm (20–24 ins.) annually, temperatures becoming rather more extreme to the E. Land use: forested 18 per cent, meadows and pastures 13 per cent, agricultural and under permanent cultivation 57 per cent. About 88 per cent of the pop. is Christian, of which Roman Catholic 64 per cent. Of the ethnic composition Magyars make up 97 per cent. The lang. is Hungarian.

In 1991 there were about 6,460,000 hectares of agricultural land of which 4,714,000 was arable. The main crops are maize, wheat, sugar-beet, potatoes and barley. Vines are grown in Tokaj and N of L. Balaton. There are deposits of coal, bauxite and iron ore, some oil and natural gas. The main industries are mining coal and bauxite, and it manufactures steel, iron, cement, fertilizers, superphosphates, textiles, vehicles, electrical and electronic equipment and antibiotics.

The Magyars settled in the middle Danube basin in the late 9th cent. under their chieftain, Arpad. In the early 11th cent. they were converted to Christianity under St Stephen, who took the title of king. With the Arpad line extinct (1301), civil war followed and Hungary soon came under the rule of foreign princes. Late in the 14th cent. the country achieved its greatest expansion, inc. the greater part of central Europe within its territory, but it was menaced from the S by the Turks, and in 1526 its army suffered utter defeat at their hands at Mohács. Hungary was now partitioned between Austria and Turkey, and by the end of the 17th cent. the Habsburgs had conquered the whole country. A revolution led by Kossuth (1848–9) was suppressed, but in 1867 the Austro–Hungarian dual monarchy was established, Hungary almost attaining equality with its neighbour. At the end of World War I Hungary was proclaimed a republic and was briefly ruled by a Communist government under Bela Kun (1919), which was followed by the regency of Admiral Horthy with the old monarchical constitution. In the 1930s it came more and more under the influence of Italy and then Germany, entered World War II on their side and was occupied by the Russian army (1944–5). In 1948 the

Communists gained power, a people's republic was proclaimed (1949) and the country was then ruled by a government of the Soviet pattern. The character of Russian domination, in fact, was exemplified in the anti-Stalinist revolution of 1956, which was ruthlessly suppressed by Russian troops and Russian tanks. The Communist party was dissolved in 1989 and reconstituted as the Hungarian Socialist Party and the People's Republic abolished. For administrative purposes the country is divided into 19 counties: Bács-Kiskun, Baranya, Békés, Borsod-Abaúj-Zemplén, Csongrád, Fejér, Györ-Sopron, Hajdú-Bihar, Heves, Komárom, Nógrád, Pest, Somogy, Szabolcs-Szatmár, Szolnok, Tolna, Vas, Veszprém and Zala. There are also 6 county boroughs (Budapest, Miskolc, Debrecen, Pécs, Szeged, Györ). There is a 386-member single-chamber National Assembly.

Hungerford England. Market town in SW Berkshire on the R. Kennet 13 km (8 miles) WNW of Newbury. Pop. (1971) 2784. Noted for trout-fishing. The annual Hocktide festival, on the second Tuesday after Easter, commemorates the granting of manorial rights by John of Gaunt.

Hunstanton England. Town in Norfolk on the E shore of the Wash, consisting of New Hunstanton, the modern seaside resort, and the village of Old Hunstanton 1.6 km (1 mile) N. Pop. (1991) 4736. Hunstanton Hall, at Old Hunstanton, mainly of the 16th cent., belonged to the Le Strange family from the Norman Conquest till 1949.

Hunter River Australia. River 467 km (290 miles) long in New South Wales, rising in the Liverpool Range and flowing SW and then SE to the Pacific Ocean. In the lower valley there are coalfields and industrial development, mostly in the Newcastle area at its mouth.

Huntingdon England. Town in Cambridgeshire on the Great Ouse and on the Roman Ermine Street 24 km (15 miles) NW of Cambridge. Pop. (1991) (with God-

manchester) 15,575. Connected with Godmanchester by a 14th-cent. bridge.

Brewing, hosiery manufacture.

Birthplace of Oliver Cromwell (1599–1658); he and Pepys were both pupils at the grammar school.

Huntington USA. Town in West Virginia on the Ohio R. Pop. (1990) 54,844.

Commercial and industrial centre. Trade in coal. Railway engineering. Manufactures nickel products, electrical equipment, glass and cement.

Named after C. P. Huntington (1821–1900), an American railway builder.

Huntington Beach USA. Coastal town in California 23 km (14 miles) SE of Long Beach. Pop. (1990) 181,519. Has grown rapidly in recent years, largely due to the discovery of oil and natural gas (1920) and the development of oil-refining (pop. 11,492 in 1960).

Huntly Scotland. Market town in Aberdeenshire at the confluence of the R. Deveron and the R. Bogie in Strathbogie. Pop. (1991) 4230.

Holiday and angling resort. Manufactures agricultural implements, woollen goods, prefabricated buildings, stainless-steel products and oil-related engineering.

The ruined Huntly Castle, formerly called Strathbogie Castle, was the seat of the Earls of Huntly. Birthplace of George Macdonald, the novelist (1824–1905).

Huntsville USA. Industrial town in Alabama 137 km (85 miles) N of Birmingham. Pop. (1990) 159,789.

Manufactures textiles, agricultural implements, and rocket and guided-missile centre. The cotton industry began with a mill on the Flint R. in 1818.

Founded (1805) by John Hunt, a Virginian Revolutionary War veteran.

Hupeh ►HUBEI.

Hurlingham England. District in the Greater London borough of Hammersmith, containing Hurlingham Park, part of which has been converted into a housing estate and which also has the headquarters of the Hurlingham polo club, whose committee drew up the first code of rules for the game in 1874.

Huron, Lake. Second largest of the Great Lakes, between the USA and Canada (about 60 per cent in Canada). Area 61,697 sq km (23,860 sq. miles). Bounded on the N, E and SE by Ontario (Canada) and on the W and SW by Michigan (USA). Connected with L. Superior by the St Mary's R. and with L. Michigan by the Straits of Mackinac; it empties into L. Erie by the St Clair R., L. St Clair and the Detroit R. Valuable fisheries. Carries heavy trade in iron ore, coal, grain and limestone. Usually ice-bound from mid Dec. to mid April and subject to violent storms.

Hurstmonceux ▸HERSTMONCEAUX.

Hutchinson USA. Industrial town in Kansas on the Arkansas R. 71 km (44 miles) NW of Wichita. Pop. (1985) 41,000.

Salt-mining, meat-packing, flour-milling and oil-refining. Manufactures oil-well equipment.

Established 1871.

Hutt ▸LOWER HUTT.

Huyton-with-Roby England. Town in Merseyside and residential suburb of Liverpool (E). Pop. (1991) 56,500.

Manufactures cables, metal goods and food products.

Huzhou (Huchou/Huchow) China. Town in Zhejiang province 64 km (40 miles) N of Hangzhou. Pop. (1991) 218,071. Silk manufacture is the main industry. To the S is the famous hill resort of Mokanshan.

Hvar (Italian **Lesina**) Croatia. 1. Island in the Adriatic Sea. Area 290 sq km (112 sq. miles). Pop. (1989) 20,000. Cap and chief port Hvar.

Industries inc. fishing, and grapes, olives and flowers are cultivated. It is a popular tourist centre.

2. Ancient Pharos. Cap. of Hvar island on

the W coast 35 km (22 miles) S of Split. Pop. 2000.

Resort and port. Fishing and boatbuilding. Founded as a Greek colony *c.* 390 BC.

Hwange (Wankie) Zimbabwe. Town situated NW of Bulawayo at a height of 750 m (2460 ft). Pop. (1988) 39,000.

Centre of a chief coalmining area of Zimbabwe with allied trades. The game reserve is one of the finest in Africa and covers 14,651 sq km (5657 sq. miles).

Hwang Ho ▸HUANG-HE.

Hyde England. Town in Greater Manchester 11 km (7 miles) ESE of the city. Pop. (1991) 30,666.

Important textile mills. Engineering. Manufactures rubber products and paper.

Hyderabad India. Cap. of Andhra Pradesh on the Musi R. 628 km (390 miles) ESE of Bombay. Pop. (1991) 3,145,900.

Industrial, commercial and route centre. Railway engineering. Manufactures textiles, building materials, glassware, paper, copper-alloy products, cement, ceiling fans, explosives, lamps and power-generating equipment.

The old city is surrounded by stone walls, entered by 13 gates and contains the Char Minar or Four Minarets, built in 1591, which rise from arches from which 4 of the main highways radiate. Another outstanding building is the Great Mosque, modelled on that at Mecca. Seat of the Osmania University (1918). Hyderabad was formerly cap. of the state of the same name.

Hyderabad Pakistan. City near the Indus R. and 153 km (95 miles) NE of Karachi. Pop. (1981) 751,529.

Industrial and commercial centre. Manufactures textiles, machinery, leather and cement. Trade in cereals, cotton and fruit.

Cap. of Sind province from 1768 to 1843, when it was taken by the British, and again 1947–54.

Hydra (Gr. **Ídhra**) Greece. Island in the Aegean Sea 71 km (41 miles) SW of Piraeus.

Area 47 sq km (18 sq. miles). Pop. (1985) 2800. Chief town Hydra on the N coast.

Industries inc. tourism, fishing and tanning.

Flourished under Turkish rule, when the pop. rose to over 30,000. Its seamen played a prominent part in the Greek War of Independence (1821).

Hymettus (Gr. **Imittos**) Greece. Mountain (1028 m; 3372 ft) in Attica *nome* just E of Athens. Long famous for its honey and formerly for marble.

Hythe England. Seaside resort in SE Kent 6 km (4 miles) W of Folkestone on the English Channel. Pop. (1991) 18,538.

Industries inc. brewing, horticulture and the manufacture of plastics.

One of the Cinque Ports, its harbour long ago silted up. Has a miniature railway to Dymchurch and New Romney. Saltwood Castle, where the plot to murder Thomas à Becket was said to have been planned, is 1.6 km (1 mile) N. 5 km (3 miles) W is the village of Lympne, with remains of the Roman Portus Lemanis.

Hyvinkää (Hyvinge) Finland. Town situated N of Helsinki in Uusimää province. Pop. (1991) 40,351.

Railway junction and tourist centre for winter sports. Industries inc. textiles and woollen goods, granite-quarrying.

I

Ialomita River Romania. Rises in the Transylvanian Alps and flows 320 km (200 miles) S to Targoviste, then E to join the lower Danube R. W of Harsova. The main tributary is the Prahova R. The upper valley has limestone stalactite caverns.

Iaşi (Ger. **Jassy**) Romania. Cap. of Iaşi district in Moldavia about 16 km (10 miles) W of the Prut R. and the Moldavian frontier. Pop. (1989) 330,195. Railway junction and a cultural and commercial centre.

Industries inc. textiles, metal goods, furniture, chemicals, clothing, pharmaceuticals, plastics, food-processing and electronics.

Most of the pop. was Jewish until they were massacred by the Germans in 1941.

Ibadan Nigeria. Cap. of Oyo State on the main railway to N Nigeria 120 km (75 miles) NE of Lagos. Pop. (1991) 1,236,000.

Market for cacao, also palm oil and kernels, and cotton. Industries inc. vehicles, metals, brewing and electronics.

Ibagué Colombia. Cap. of the Tolima department on the E slopes of the Central Cordillera at a height of 1250 m (4100 ft). Pop. (1992) 334,078. Linked by rail and road with Bogotá and by the Quindio Pass (W) with Armenia.

Trade in coffee and cattle. Industries inc. flour-milling, brewing and the manufacture of leather goods.

Founded 1550.

Ibarra Ecuador. Cap. of the Imbabura province 80 km (50 miles) NE of Quito at a height of 2227 m (6792 ft). Pop. (1990) 81,000. It is a tourist centre on the Pan-American Highway.

Trades in coffee, sugar-cane, cotton and manufactures textiles, furniture and 'Panama' hats.

Iberia Georgia. Ancient name for the country between the Greater Caucasus and Armenia.

Iberian Peninsula. Name of area of Europe applied to Spain and Portugal, taken together. Area 593,250 sq km (229,054 sq. miles). It is separated from the rest of Europe by the Pyrenees Mountains. The name is derived from the Iberian people who lived along the R. Ebro (Latin Iberus).

Ibiza ➤BALEARIC ISLANDS.

Ica Peru. Cap. of the Ica department on the Ica R. and the Pan-American Highway 272 km (170 miles) SE of Lima. Pop. (1990) 152,300. Commercial and industrial centre in an irrigated cotton and vine growing region. Cotton-ginning.

Manufactures brandy, soap, textiles.

It was founded in 1563 and twice destroyed by earthquakes.

Içá River (Brazil) ➤PUTUMAYO RIVER.

Ica River Peru. River 192 km (120 miles) long, flowing from the W Andes W and S past Ica entering the Pacific 243 km (152 miles) NW of Atico. It irrigates a rich agricultural valley where cotton and vines are cultivated.

Iceland. An island republic in the North Atlantic Ocean lying close to the Arctic Circle 960 km (600 miles) W of Norway and 800 km (500 miles) NW of Scotland; the most westerly state in Europe. Area 103,000 sq km (39,768 sq. miles). Pop. (1995) 269,000 (91 per cent urban). Life expectancy, 77 years male, 81 female. Cap. Reykjavik. Other towns Kópavogur, Akureyri, Hafnarfjördur and Keflavik. Currency: Króna = 100 aurar.

It is very sparsely inhabited and divided

in 8 regions: the capital area, South West Peninsula, West, Western Peninsula, Northland West, Northland East, East and South. The island consists in the main of a central, virtually uninhabited plateau of volcanic rocks of average height about 600 m (1968 ft). In the S and W of this plateau there are extensive glaciers and snowfields, the largest being Vatnajökull (S), which rises to 2120 m (6954 ft) in Oraefajokull. There are more than 100 volcanoes, one in four of which has been active within historic times, and an area of about 12,044 sq km (4650 sq. miles) is covered with lava fields; Hekla 1559 m (5114 ft), the best-known volcano, has erupted about 20 times since the early 12th cent. Hot springs occur in all parts of the island. There are many lakes, rivers and waterfalls, and hydroelectric power is developed. The coast is rugged and deeply indented with fiords and bays, esp. on the W and N. The climate of Iceland is wet, windy and changeable and, for its rather high latitude, mild, North Atlantic Drift ensuring that the S coasts remain ice-free in winter. Land use: forested 1.2 per cent, meadow and pastures 23 per cent. Eleven per cent of the country is covered with ice and snowfields. The religion is Evangelical and the language Icelandic. Most of the people are almost wholly Icelandic, i.e. Scandinavian in origin.

The economy depends very largely on fishing. Trees are few and consist mainly of small birch trees. Grasses are the commonest form of natural vegetation, providing pasture for large numbers of sheep and some cattle and horses. About 23,000 sq km (8880 sq. miles) of the country is wasteland and on the small area of cultivated land the principal crops are hay, potatoes and turnips. Fishing is by far the most important occupation and fish (chiefly cod and herring) and fish products constitute 76 per cent of exports. Wool and sheepskin products, aluminium and ferrosilicon are also important exports. Tourism has been developed. The USA has the major share of the foreign trade, followed by Germany and the UK.

The first settlers were Norwegians in 874. Iceland had its first general assembly or Al-

thing, which founded the republic, in 930 and Christianity was introduced in 1000. It was under Norwegian rule from 1262, it passed to Denmark in 1380; internal self-government was granted in 1874 and equal status in 1918, and in 1944 the republic was again proclaimed. In 1958 Iceland extended the fishery limits around the coast from 4 to 12 miles; after a prolonged dispute Britain, having gained certain concessions for British fishermen, agreed to the change in 1961. In 1972 Iceland extended the fishery limits from 12 to 50 nautical miles, provoking protests from foreign fishermen, chiefly British, leading to several hostile incidents and a renewal of the 'cod war' of 1958; in 1975 Iceland further extended the fishery limits to 200 miles, despite an adverse judgement by the International Court of Justice. Two new volcanic islands emerged in 1963 just SW of the Vestmann Is. off the S coast. A volcano on Heimaey (Westmann Is.) erupted in 1973, causing the 5300 inhabitants of Vestmannaeyjar to evacuate the town.

The Parliament (*Alpingi*) has 63 members and has Upper and Lower Houses. The President is elected by direct popular vote for a period of 4 years.

Ichalkaranji India. Town in Maharashtra. Pop. (1990) 215,000.

Industries inc. the manufacture of textiles and cotton-ginning.

Ichang China ➤YICHANG.

Ichikawa Japan. Town in Chiba prefecture 16 km (10 miles) ENE of Tokyo on the edge of the conurbation. Pop. (1990) 436,597. Textile mills.

Ichinomiya Japan. Town in Aichi prefecture, Honshu 19 km (12 miles) NNW of Nagoya. Pop. (1990) 262,434. It is an important textile centre esp. for woollen goods.

Ida, Mount ➤CRETE.

Idaho USA. State in the NW, bordered on the N by British Columbia (Canada), on the E by Montana and Wyoming, on the S by Utah and Nevada and on the W by Oregon and Washington. Area 216,431 sq km (83,564 sq. miles). Pop. (1990) 1,006,749. Cap. Boise. Crossed by the Rocky Mountains; mainly mountainous, with Borah Peak 3860 m (12,661 ft) the highest point. Dry continental climate, with cold winters and hot summers.

Agriculture important in the S. Potatoes are a speciality of the Snake valley and wheat, oats, barley, sugar-beet are grown. It is rich in minerals; produces gold, silver and phosphate rock, zinc. Many state parks and national forests, with ample facilities for fishing, hunting, skiing and camping.

The first European explorers were Lewis and Clark (1805), followed by British and American fur traders. The first permanent settlement was at Franklin in 1860, although there had been a mission for Indians in 1836 and a Mormon settlement in 1885. Admitted to the Union in 1890 as the 43rd state.

Idaho Falls USA. Town in SE Idaho on the Snake R. at a height of 1430 m (4590 ft) 346 km (215 miles) E of Boise. Pop. (1980) 40,000.

Industrial and commercial centre in an agricultural region. It manufactures beet-sugar, and there are food-processing plants.

Idfu ➤EDFU.

Ídhra ➤HYDRA.

Idumaea ➤EDOM.

Ife Nigeria. Town in Oyo State 72 km (45 miles) E of Ibadan. Pop. (1991) 262,000.

Centre in the cacao trade, and it processes palm oil and kernels.

Considered to be the oldest settlement and 'holy city' of the Yoruba people.

Ifni. Former Spanish overseas province on the NW African coast. An enclave within Morocco on the edge of the Sahara. Occupied by the Spanish from 1860, it was returned to Morocco in 1969. Arid climate. Irrigation permits the cultivation of grains and vegetables. Nomadic tribes raise sheep and goats.

Igarka Russia. Port on the Yenisei R. N of the Arctic Circle in the Krasnoyarsk Terri-

tory. Sawmilling. Considerable trade in timber and graphite. Founded 1929.

Iglesias Italy. Town in SW Sardinia 55 km (34 miles) WNW of Cagliari. Centre of a mining district (lead, zinc and silver).

Iguassú (Iguaçu) River Brazil/Argentina. River 1207 km (750 miles) long, rising in the Serra do Mar in S Brazil, flowing W and joining the Paraná R. Forms the Brazil–Argentina frontier for the last 120 km (75 miles). The Iguassú Falls (22 km (14 miles) above the confluence) consist of a line of falls over 60 m (197 ft) high, separated by rocky islands.

Ijmuiden ➤VELSEN.

Ijssel (Yssel) Rivers Netherlands. 1. Geldersche Ijssel: river 116 km (73 miles) long, a distributary of the Lower Rhine, branching from it just SE of Arnhem and flowing generally N through Gelderland, forming the boundary with Overijssel province, to the Ijsselmeer 6 km (4 miles) NW of Kampen.
2. Oude Ijssel: a tributary of the Geldersche Ijssel, rising just SW of Borken (Germany) and joining it at Doesburg.
3. Hollandsche Ijssel: a short tributary of the Lek, joining it just E of Rotterdam.

Ijsselmeer (Ysselmeer) Netherlands. Lake formed in N and central Netherlands by damming of the Zuider Zee 30 km (19 miles) from Den Over to 2½ km (1½ miles) SW of Zürich. The lake receives Vecht R., Ijssel R. and Zwartewater. Extensive areas have been reclaimed for agriculture, esp. the Wieringermeer, Beemster and North East Polders.

Ilan Taiwan. Town situated SE of Taipei. Pop. (1985) 84,793.

Market centre for agricultural area, trading in rice, sugar-cane, ramie, citrus fruit. The main industries are food-processing, inc. fish-canning and preserves.

Ilebo Democratic Republic of Congo. Formerly Port Francqui. Town in Kasia-Occidental region, on the right bank of the Kasai R. just above the confluence with the

Sankuru R. 587 km (365 miles) E of Kinshasa. Pop. (1984) 142,000. River port. Terminus of the railway from Shaba.

Île de France France. Region in the Paris Basin, nearly identical to the Paris conurbation, Paris being its cap., so-called because the original boundaries were the Seine, Marne, Aisne, Oise and Ourcq rivers; it is now a region comprising the departments of Essonne, Hauts-de-Seine, Paris, Seine-et-Marne, Seine-St-Denis, Val-de-Marne, Val d'Oise and Yvelines. Area 12,012 sq km (4638 sq. miles). Pop. (1990) 10,660,600. It comprises rich agricultural land as well as the highly industrialized region around Paris and such forests as those of Fontainebleau and Compiègne. It was part of the duchy of France in the 10th cent.

Îles des Saintes ➤SAINTES, LES.

Ilesha Nigeria. Town in Oyo state 96 km (60 miles) ENE of Ibadan. Pop. (1992) 342,400.

Trades in cacao, palm oil and kernels, and industries inc. brewing and cotton-weaving.

Ilford England. Town situated on the R. Roding 11 km (7 miles) ENE of London, for which it is a residential suburb.

Manufactures photographic equipment and materials, electrical equipment.

Ilfracombe England. Town in N Devon on the Bristol Channel. Pop. (1991) 11,991. Seaside resort from Victorian times and former fishing port. There is some light industry.

Ilhéus Brazil. Seaport in Bahía 249 km (155 miles) SSW of Salvador near the mouth of the Cachoeira R. Pop. (1985) 146,100.

Formerly the main export centre for cacao (which is now shipped through Salvador). Now exports piassava and timber.

Ili River. River 1398 km (869 miles) long in central Asia, rising on the N slopes of the Tien Shan, flowing generally W and NW past Kuldja (Sinkiang-Uighur, China) and across Kazakhstan to enter L. Balkhash by a delta. It is used for irrigation.

Ilium ➤TROY.

Ilkeston England. Town in Derbyshire 11 km (7 miles) ENE of Derby. Pop. (1991) 35,000.

Market town in a coalmining area. Manufactures rayon, hosiery, clothing and earthenware.

Ilkley England. Residential town in West Yorkshire on the R. Wharfe 21 km (13 miles) WSW of Harrogate. Pop. (1991) 15,530. Mineral springs. Just S is the Ilkley Moor (632 ha; 1560 acres).

Illampu (Sorata), Mount Bolivia. Highest mountain in the E Cordillera of the Andes. Two peaks: Illampu 6489 m (21,284 ft) and Ancohuma 6554 m (21,497 ft).

Ille-et-Vilaine France. Maritime department in the NW bordering N on the Gulf of St Malo in the province of Bretagne. Area 6775 sq km (2616 sq. miles). Pop. (1990) 798,556. Prefecture Rennes. Drained by the Vilaine and its chief tributary the Ille.

Mainly agricultural, the poor soil having been improved by fertilizers. Cereals, potatoes, apples, pears widely grown. Much cider-making and dairy-farming. Chief towns Rennes, the seaport of St Malo and the resort of Dinard.

Illinois USA. State in the Middle West, bounded by Wisconsin (N), L. Michigan (NE), Indiana (E), Kentucky (S) and Iowa and Missouri (W), and separated from the last two by the Mississippi R. Area 145,934 sq km (56,345 sq. miles). Pop. (1990) 11,430,602. Cap. Springfield. Mainly level prairie. Climate humid continental.

Primarily an agricultural state, with a very large production of maize (about two-thirds of the acreage), oats, hay, soya beans, wheat. Also cattle, pigs, poultry. Chief mineral bituminous coal; petroleum is found in the S. Manufacturing industries are important (with nearly three-quarters of the factories in the Chicago area) and inc. meat-packing, oil-refining and the manufacture of steel, railway and electrical equipment, and agricultural machinery. Chief towns Chicago, Rockford, Peoria.

The first European explorers were the

French (1673). Ceded to the British 1763. Became US territory 1783. Admitted to the Union in 1818 as the 21st state.

Illyria Albania/Croatia. Ancient, vaguely defined region along the E shores of the Adriatic Sea, extending approximately from modern Rijeka to Durrës W of the Dinaric Alps, thus comprising the W coastal strip of Croatia and N Albania.

Ilmen, Lake Russia. Lake situated 160 km (100 miles) SSE of St Petersburg, discharging through the Volkhov R. into L. Ladoga. Area 907 sq km (350 sq. miles).

Fishing, lumbering and agriculture are practised around the shores.

Iloilo Philippines. Seaport and commercial city situated 467 km (290 miles) SSE of Manila. Pop. (1990) 310,000.

Exports sugar, rice and copra.

Imandra, Lake Russia. Lake discharging through the Neva R. into the Kandalaksha Gulf of the White Sea. Area 880 sq km (340 sq. miles). The town of Monchegorsk is on its NW shore and the Murmansk–St Petersburg railway runs along its E shore.

Imathía Greece. *Nome* in Macedonia Central. Area 1701 sq km (656 sq. miles). Pop. (1990) 138,068. Cap. Véroia.

Produces wheat, vegetables and wine.

Imatra Finland. Town in the Kymi province near the Russian frontier. Pop. (1989) 33,566. There is a hydroelectric power station and the metallurgical industry is important.

Imbros (Imroz) Turkey. Island in the Aegean Sea W of the Gallipoli peninsula. Area 280 sq km (108 sq. miles). Pop. 3400. Cap. Imroz.

Cereals, olives and fruits are cultivated.

Occupied by Greece during World War I and it was returned to Turkey in 1923.

Imittos ➤HYMETTUS.

Immingham England. Seaport in North East Lincolnshire on the S bank of the Humber 10 km (6 miles) NW of Grimsby. Pop. (1991) 12,278.

Exports coal. Imports iron ore, timber, sulphur. Development began with the opening of docks in 1912, deeper water being available here than at Grimsby. Further developed by the extension of the oil jetties begun in 1963 and in the 1990s a large new deep-water dry-bulk cargo terminal was constructed.

Imo Nigeria. State comprising the former Owerri and Umuahia provinces of the former East Region. Area 11,850 sq km (4575 sq. miles). Pop., which is almost entirely Obi, (1988) 8,046,500. Chief cities Owerri (cap.), Aba and Umuahia.

Imola Italy. Town in Bologna province in Emilia-Romagna 32 km (20 miles) SE of Bologna on the Aemilian Way.

Industries inc. machinery, pottery and wine.

Imperia Italy. Cap. of Imperia province, Liguria on the Gulf of Genoa 90 km (56 miles) SW of Genoa. Pop. (1990) 41,278.

Port in an olive and vine growing region. Formed in 1923 from the two communities of Porto Maurizio, a holiday resort with olive-oil refineries, and Oneglia, an industrial and commercial centre with iron and steel works, fruit-canning and other industries.

Imphal India. Cap. of Manipur State on the Manipur R. 225 km (140 miles) ESE of Shillong. Pop. (1991) 156,000.

Commercial centre in a fertile agricultural region. Trade in rice, sugar-cane and tobacco.

Imroz ➤IMBROS.

Inaccessible Island ➤TRISTAN DA CUNHA.

Inari, Lake Finland. Lake in Lapland in the extreme N. Area 1386 sq km (535 sq. miles). Hundreds of islets. Drained to Varanger Fiord by the Pasvik R. Visited by tourists mainly for fishing. On the SW shore is the village of Inari, where Lapps evacuated from the Pechenga region (Russia) were resettled after World War II.

Ince-in-Makerfield England. Town in

Greater Manchester just S of Wigan. Pop. (1990) 16,000.

Industries inc. light and heavy engineering and glass-bottle manufacture.

Inchcape Rock ➤BELL ROCK.

Inchon South Korea. Formerly Chemulpo. Seaport and industrial town 40 km (25 miles) WSW of Seoul on the Yellow Sea. Pop. (1990) 1,819,000.

Exports rice, dried fish and soya beans. Manufactures steel, textiles, glass and chemicals.

Independence USA. Industrial town in Missouri 13 km (8 miles) E of Kansas City. Pop. (1990) 112,301.

Manufactures agricultural machinery, cement and stoves.

Headquarters of the Mormon sect known as the Reorganized Church of Jesus Christ of Latter Day Saints. Starting-point for wagon trains travelling W over the Santa Fé, Old Salt Lake and Oregon trails 1831–44.

India (Bharat). Republic in S Asia. Occupies the greater part of the Indian subcontinent, Pakistan and Bangladesh occupying the other part. Besides its frontiers with Pakistan and Bangladesh, it borders N on Tibet (China) and Nepal, and NE on Myanmar (Burma), the shores of its triangular-shaped peninsula being washed by the Bay of Bengal (E) and the Arabian Sea (W). Area 3,166,414 sq km (1,236,880 sq. miles). Pop. (1995) 935,744,000 (excluding the area of Jammu and Kashmir occupied by Pakistan and areas illegally occupied by China). It is 27 per cent urban and it is the second most populous country in the world. Life expectancy, 60 years male, 61 female. Cap. New Delhi. The following cities have a pop. of more than 1 million: Ahmedabad, Bangalore, Bhopal, Bombay, Calcutta, Coimbatore, Delhi, Hyderabad, Indore, Jaipur, Kanpur, Kochi (Cochin), Lucknow, Ludhiana, Madras, Madurai, Nagpur, Patna, Pune (Poona), Vadodara (Baroda), Varanasi (Benares) and Visakhapatnam. Currency: Indian rupee = 100 paise.

India is bounded in the N by the Himalayas, the most formidable mountain barrier in the world and within its boundaries is the great Himalayan peak of Nanda Devi 7817 m (25,640 ft); few passes penetrate this mountain system and on its N side rise the three major rivers of the subcontinent, the Indus, Ganges and Brahmaputra. S of the fertile alluvial plain of the Ganges is the Deccan plateau, fringed by the West and East Ghats. In the NW, on the border with Pakistan, is the Great Indian or Thar Desert, while in the NE is the Chota Nagpur plateau. The two chief W-flowing rivers are the Marmada, between the Vindhya and Satpura Ranges, and the Tapti, between the Satpura and Ajanta Ranges; the three main E-flowing rivers are the Godavari, Krishna and Cauvery, which form wide deltas on the broad coastal plain facing the Bay of Bengal. Generally speaking, the climate of the entire country S of the Himalayas is dominated by the monsoons and may be described as tropical monsoon in character. There are three seasons, determined by the monsoon winds, and varying to some extent with geographical location. From June to September the SW monsoon brings especially heavy rainfall to the W slopes of the West Ghats, but much less to places on the lee side of the mountains as it moves NE across the peninsula; it picks up more moisture during its passage over the Bay of Bengal and again deposits heavy rainfall over Assam, Bengal and the S slopes of the Himalayas. In Cherrapunji, Meghalaya the country has what is reputed to be the world's wettest spot, with 1142 cm (450 ins.) of rain annually: almost 500 cm (195 ins.) fall in June and July, while scarcely 2.5 cm (1 in.) fall in December and January together. This emphasizes the great contrast between the rainy season and the conditions of the NE monsoon which follows and continues from about October to February – a season of dry, cooler weather. Finally there is the season of hot and fairly dry weather, March–May, which precedes the burst of the SW monsoon, with its oppressive heat and torrential rains, once more. Land use: forested 22 per cent, meadows and pastures 4 per cent, agricultural and under permanent cultivation 57 per cent.

Some 1625 languages and dialects are spoken. Under the 1950 Constitution the official language of the Union is Hindi in the Devanagari script. English is used for official purposes. There are 15 recognized languages: Assamese, Bengali, Gujarati, Hindi, Kannada, Kashmiri, Malayalam, Marathi, Oriya, Punjabi, Sanskrit, Sindhi, Tamil, Telugu and Urdu. The decision to adopt Hindi as the official language aroused great controversy. Difficulties are immensely increased by the high illiteracy rate of 48 per cent (1991), but 82 per cent 1951 census. Illiteracy and religious custom together have proved considerable obstacles to social progress in India; Hindus, with their narrow rules of caste, numbered 550 million of the pop. in 1981, Muslims 76 million, Christians 16 million, Sikhs 13 million, Buddhists 5 million and Jains 3 million.

India was once described as a country of villages and, since about 75 per cent of the pop. live in villages, agriculture and allied activities are the mainstay of livelihood of the country's pop. Agricultural and allied products, in some cases processed or manufactured, also form the major part of the country's exports. The output of food crops from the millions of peasant farmers is sufficient for the country's needs in the absence of any natural calamity like drought. Rice and wheat are by far the major foodgrain crops. Rice is the staple food in all the wetter parts of India, the main regions of production being the Ganges valley and the coastal plains. Millet is also of much importance, being the staple food in the drier parts of the Deccan. Area under rice was 42.6 million ha (105.2 million acres) and under wheat 24 million ha (59 million acres) in 1990–1, producing 74.6 million tonnes of rice and 54.5 million tonnes of wheat respectively. Cotton occupies a considerable area, particularly in the W Deccan and oilseeds (inc. groundnuts, sesamum and linseed) almost as large an area; sugar-cane comes from the Upper Ganges region and the Punjab, and jute chiefly from West Bengal. Tea is cultivated in Assam,

West Bengal, Kerala and Tamil Nadu and is an important commodity for export. Crop yields among the peasant farmers are low, the causes inc. primitive agricultural methods, fragmentation of holdings, soil exhaustion and weak economic conditions. India has the enormous total of 192 million cattle (1982), which are used primarily as draught animals, but they are of poor quality and, being regarded as sacred by the Hindus, cannot be slaughtered in most parts of the country and are virtually valueless as a source of food. The necessity for increasing food supplies is probably the country's most difficult economic problem: throughout history India has been subject to famine, but since 1974 has been self-sufficient in food.

Few minerals are produced on a large scale. Coal is produced mainly on the edge of the Chota Nagpur plateau, in West Bengal and Bihar, Orissa, Andhra Pradesh and Madhya Pradesh; output rose from 29 million to 211 millions tons between 1947 and 1991, but is still far short of the country's needs so far as coking coal is concerned. Much of the country's iron and manganese ores is exported and India is also one of the world's leading producers and exporters of mica. Village industries and handicrafts are still important, but there has been a considerable development of factory industries in recent years. Steel was first produced in 1907 and the village of Jamshedpur (Bihar) had become a thriving iron and steel centre of nearly 461,000 inhabitants by 1991, with a number of other manufacturing industries. It was followed by steel plants at Burnpur (West Bengal) in 1919 and Bhadravati (Karnataka) in 1923. Steel plants have been established in Durgapur (West Bengal), Bokaro (Bihar), Bhilai (Madhya Pradesh), after independence. India now manufactures automobiles, aircraft, electric, diesel and steam locomotives, computers, power generators, oceangoing ships, submarines and has launched satellites in space. Textile manufacture, however, is still by far the most significant industry, being the largest single industry accounting for about a quarter of total industrial output, employing 15 million people and contributing 25 per cent of exports. Jute products are manufactured, largely for export, in the Calcutta area, cotton goods in Bombay, Ahmedabad and other large towns.

Before 2000 BC the region was invaded by the dark-skinned Dravidians, ancestors of the principal peoples of the S and later, c. 2400–1500 BC, by waves of Aryans from the NW, the latter spreading over the N and the Deccan and intermarrying with the Dravidians; it was they, the conquerors, who introduced Brahmanism or Hinduism and the caste system, but little is known about the aboriginal inhabitants. In the 6th cent. BC Buddhism and Jainism were introduced as reforming movements, but neither substantially displaced Hinduism. In 327 BC the middle Indus valley was reached by Alexander the Great and in the following cent. all India except the extreme S was first unified under the great Mauryan emperor Asoka, a Buddhist. N India was not again united until the Gupta dynasty (AD 320–480), the 'golden age of Hinduism'. Muslim invasions from the NW began in the early 11th cent. by Mahmud of Ghazni, Muslim rule was then established in the N and the Deccan, and the finest period of Muslim India came with the founding of the Mogul empire by Babur (1526); the empire was consolidated by his grandson Akbar the Great (1556–1605) and reached its furthest extent under Aurangzeb (1658–1707), but declined rapidly after the latter's death. Islam had been imposed on a people who tenaciously clung to the Hindu religion and this led eventually to the partition of the subcontinent into Muslim Pakistan and Hindu India in 1947.

From the early 16th cent. Portuguese, Dutch, French and British were establishing trading posts at various places in India, but after the Battle of Plassey (1757) the British East India Company became dominant; with the mutiny (1857–8) the Company's authority was transferred to the British Crown and Queen Victoria was proclaimed Empress of India in 1877. In 1885 the Indian National Congress was founded to work for representative government. The British Raj maintained peace in India and conferred other benefits such as the construction of great irrigation works and railways; but it was an alien rule and a nationalist movement arose and gained strength, notably under the leadership of Mahatma Gandhi (1869–1948) who, from 1930, led a campaign of civil disobedience for the end of British rule, but little was achieved until World War II. In June 1947 the scheme for partition was announced because Hindus and Muslims found themselves unable to work together in an all-Indian government. The subcontinent was divided into the Dominions of India and Pakistan. In 1950 India declared itself a republic.

The Indian Parliament consists of the President and two houses: the Upper House or Council of States, elected by members of the state legislatures, with not more than 250 members inc. 12 nominated by the President, and the 545-member Lower House or House of the People, directly elected by universal suffrage, with not more than 552 members of which there are 530 to represent the States, 20 to represent the Union territories and 2 Anglo-Indians, nominated. For administrative purposes the country is divided into 25 States and 7 Union territories. The States are: Andhra Pradesh, Arunachal Pradesh, Assam, Bihar, Goa, Gujarat, Haryana, Himachal Pradesh, Jammu and Kashmir, Karnataka, Kerala, Madhya Pradesh, Maharashtra, Manipur, Meghalaya, Mizoram, Nagaland, Orissa, Punjab, Rajasthan, Sikkim, Tamil Nadu, Tripura, Uttar Pradesh, West Bengal. The Union territories are: Andaman and Nicobar Is., Chandigarh, Dadra and Nagar Haveli, Delhi, Daman and Diu, Lakshadweep and Pondicherry.

Indiana USA. State in the Middle West, bounded by L. Michigan (NW), Michigan (N), Ohio (E), Kentucky (S) and Illinois (W). Area 92,903 sq km (35,870 sq. miles). Pop. (1990) 5,544,159. Cap. Indianapolis. It is mainly rolling prairie land, with sand dunes and glacial lakes in the N. Climate humid continental.

Good agricultural land, the main crop is maize, but also wheat, oats, rye, tomatoes (for canning) and hay. Cattle, pigs and sheep raised. Principal mineral bituminous coal. Produces most of the limestone used in the USA for building. The steel industry is the largest in the USA and other industries inc. meat-packing and the manufacture of motor vehicles, agricultural and electrical machinery. Chief towns Indianapolis, Gary, Fort Wayne, Evansville and South Bend.

The first Europeans to explore the territory were the French, who found the Miami Indians the dominant tribe. It was ceded to Britain in 1763 and to the USA in 1783. It was admitted to the Union in 1816 as the 19th state.

Indianapolis USA. State cap. of Indiana on the West Fork of the White R. in the centre of the state. Pop. (1990) 741,952.

It is the centre of important rail, road and air routes. Industrial centre. Meat-packing, flour-milling. Manufactures chemicals, motorcar parts and machinery.

The annual Indianapolis 500 car race is held here.

Indian Ocean. Third largest ocean bounded by Asia (N), Australia (E), Africa (W) and merging S with the Southern Ocean. Area 73.5 million sq km (28.4 million sq. miles). Its greatest depth 8047 m (26,400 ft) is probably in the Sunda Trench (Indonesia); its mean depth is about 3900 m (12,792 ft). S of the equator its currents have a general anti-clockwise circulation, but N of the equator they are determined largely by the SW (summer) and the NE (winter) monsoons. It drains a land area of 13 million sq km (5 million sq. miles). Madagascar and Sri Lanka are the principal continental islands; the Maldive, Chagos and Cocos Is. are of coral formation; Mauritius and the Crozet Is. are of volcanic origin. It is linked with the North Atlantic by the Suez Canal and, when the latter was opened 1869, its N part became the principal shipping route between Europe and the Far East.

Indigirka River Russia. River 1760 km (1100 miles) long in the Yakut Autonomous Republic in NE Siberia, rising in the Verkhoyansk Range and flowing generally N, entering the E Siberian Sea by a broad delta. It is frozen for about 9 months of the year.

Indo-China. Name sometimes applied to the entire peninsula between India and China, inc. Myanmar (Burma), Thailand and the former French Indo-China, but usually restricted to the last, which consisted of the colony of Cochin China and the protectorates of Cambodia, Annam, Laos and Tongking. In 1949 Tongking, Annam and Cochin China formed the republic of Vietnam, which in 1954 was partitioned into North Vietnam, under Communist control, and South Vietnam.

Indonesia. Republic of SE Asia. Comprises the world's largest island group; the territory was formerly known as the Netherlands (Dutch) East Indies. It comprises 5 large islands and 30 smaller archipelagos extending 4800 km (3000 miles) from E of the Malay peninsula to N of Australia. Of the 13,677 islands and islets, about 6000 are inhabited. Area 1,919,317 sq km (741,052 sq. miles). Pop. (1990) 179,323,000; it is the world's fourth most populous nation. Life expectancy, 55 years male, 58 female. Cap. Jakarta; other major towns Surabaya, Medan, Bandung, Semarung. Currency: Indonesian rupiah = 100 sen.

Volcanic mountain ranges cross all the larger islands, with several peaks rising to more than 3000 m (9840 ft) and the slopes are well forested; there are over 100 active volcanoes. Some of the islands lie on the equator; their climate is equatorial, there are almost constant high temperatures throughout the year. The climate is influenced largely by the monsoons. Rainfall everywhere is heavy, increasing seasonally with the onset of the SW and NE monsoons and reaching well over 250 cm (100 ins.) annually in many areas. Land use: forested 63 per cent, meadows and pastures 7 per cent, agricultural and under permanent pasture 12 per cent.

The majority of the pop. are Sunni Muslims (87 per cent), Christians 10 per cent,

Hindu 2 per cent and Buddhist 1 per cent. The official lang. is Bahasa Indonesia (a variant of Malay) but 250 other lang. and dialects are spoken. Dutch is also spoken. The main ethnic groups are the Achinese, Bataks and Menangkabaus of Sumatra, the Javanese and Sudanese of Java, the Madurese of Madura, the Balinese of Bali, the Sasaks of Lombok, the Menadonese and Buginese of Celebes, the Ambonese of the Moluccas and the Dayaks of Borneo. There were 6 million Chinese resident in 1991, the most numerous of the non-indigenous peoples.

It is primarily an agricultural country with 54 per cent of the workforce working on the land. The chief island, Java, has one of the highest densities of pop. in the world and the growing of the main food crop rice is essential. Food crops other than rice inc. maize, cassava, sugar-cane, tea, coffee; rubber is produced both on plantations and on peasant smallholdings. Petroleum is the principal mineral, the oilfields being in Sumatra, Kalimantan (Borneo) and Java and, with natural gas, provide 38 per cent of exports. Other exports are rubber and timber.

In the early times Indonesia came under the influence of the Indian civilization, but by the end of the 16th cent. Islam, introduced earlier by Arab traders, had replaced Hinduism and Buddhism as the dominant religion. The disunited islands fell easily to European colonization and the Dutch became the leading power in the early 17th cent. through the Dutch East India Company. The Company ruled until 1798. The Netherlands government ruled until the Japanese invasion in 1942. There had been virtually no movement towards independence for three centuries, but in 1945 at the end of World War II, Indonesian nationalists proclaimed the new republic; sovereignty was transferred in 1949 and the last region held by the Netherlands, W Irian (W New Guinea), was handed over to Indonesia in 1963. There was a brief period as a federation, but in 1950 Indonesia became a unitary state. Since 1976 it has also included East Timor which was annexed as the 27th Indonesian province after the withdrawal of Portuguese troops.

This act has never been officially recognized by the United Nations.

For administrative purposes the country is divided into 27 provinces, 3 of which, Jakarta, Aceh and Yogyakarta, are special territories. Of the members of the House of People's Representatives 400 are elected every 5 years, and the remaining 100 are appointed by the armed forces. Together with 500 government appointees they make up the People's Consultative Assembly, which meets every 5 years to choose a president.

Indore India. Town in Madhya Pradesh, on the Saraswati R. 338 km (210 miles) ESE of Ahmadabad. Pop. (1991) 1,091,700.

Manufactures cotton goods, hosiery, chemicals, furniture, pharmaceuticals, textiles, vehicles, electronics and generators.

It was founded in the early 18th cent.

Indre France. Department of Centre Region. Area 6791 sq km (2622 sq. miles). Pop. (1990) 237,506. Prefecture Châteauroux. Slopes gently NW from the Massif Central to the Loire valley. Drained by the Indre and Creuse rivers.

Chiefly agricultural. Produces cereals, vegetables, wine. Cattle and sheep raised. Chief towns Châteauroux, Issoudun.

Indre-et-Loire France. Department of Centre Region. Area 6127 sq km (2366 sq. miles). Pop. (1990) 529,416. Prefecture Tours. Crossed by the fertile valleys of the Loire and its tributaries, the Cher, Indre and Vienne.

Produces wine, vegetables, flowers; many market gardens. The area is noted for many Loire chateaux, inc. Amboise, Chenonceaux, and Chinon. Chief towns Tours, Chinon.

Indre River France. River 257 km (160 miles) long, rising in the foothills of the Massif Central just N of Boussac, flowing generally NW through the Indre and Indre-et-Loire departments to join the Loire R. below Tours.

Indus River. One of the important rivers

of the Indian subcontinent, about 3180 km (1985 miles) long, rising in the Kailas Range of the Himalayas at 5182 m (17,000 ft) in SW Tibet. It flows N and W as the Senge Khambab, then NW through Kashmir between the Ladakh and Zaskar Ranges. Continuing through deep gorges and fine mountain scenery, it turns abruptly S and then crosses Pakistan in a general SSW direction, to enter the Arabian Sea by a broad delta. The catchment area is 960,000 sq km (371,000 sq. miles). In its upper course it receives the Shyok and Kabul and lower downstream the Panjnad – the combined waters of the Jhelum, Chenab, Ravi, Beas and Sutlej, the 5 rivers of the Punjab. Below this confluence is the great Sukkur Barrage, whence irrigation water is supplied to the plains of Sind. The river is little used for navigation.

Inglewood USA. Residential and industrial suburb 14 km (9 miles) SW of Los Angeles, California and near Los Angeles International Airport.

Pop. (1990) 110,000.

Manufactures aircraft, metal goods, toys and electronic equipment.

Ingolstadt Germany. Town in Bavaria on the Danube R. 72 km (45 miles) N of Munich. Pop. (1989) 100,100.

Industries inc. the manufacture of vehicles, valves, textiles and oil-refining. It is the terminus of the pipeline for oil supplies from the Mediterranean.

Inishcaltra ►HOLY ISLAND (IRELAND).

Inland Sea Japan. Sea between Honshu (N) and Shikoku and Kyushu (S), opening into the Sea of Japan (W) and the Pacific Ocean (E). In the central area is the Inland Sea National Park (666 sq km; 257 sq. miles).

Inner Mongolia China ►NEI MONGOL.

Innisfree Ireland. Small island in Lough Gill, NE Co. Sligo. Made famous by W. B. Yeats's poem.

Inn River. River 515 km (320 miles) long rising in Switzerland and flowing generally

NE through the Engadine, Tirol (Austria) past Innsbruck and into Bavaria (Germany) to join the Danube R. at Passau; in its lower course it forms the border between Austria and Germany. There are over 20 hydroelectric stations along the course.

Innsbruck Austria. Cap. of Tirol province on the Inn R. at its confluence with the Sill R. and on an important route from Germany via the Brenner Pass to Italy. Pop. (1991) 114,996.

Manufactures textiles and processed foods, but famous chiefly as a tourist centre, largely due to its picturesque situation at a height of 578 m (1896 ft) surrounded by high mountains. Among the notable buildings are the 16th-cent. Franciscan Hofkirche, with the tomb of Maximilian I.

Inowroclaw (Ger. **Hohensalza**) Poland. Town in Bydgoszcz voivodeship 34 km (21 miles) SW of Torún. Pop. (1989) 76,497.

Manufactures machinery, chemicals and glass. Salt and gypsum are mined in the vicinity.

Interlaken Switzerland. Tourist centre in the Bernese Alps in Bern canton on the Aar R. at a height of 569 m (1866 ft) between Lakes Thun and Brienz (hence the name). Pop. (1990) 15,000. Popular as a centre for excursions in the Bernese Oberland.

Inuvik Canada. Town in Mackenzie District, Northwest Territories on the Mackenzie R. delta near Beaufort Sea coast. Pop. (1990) 3500. The first planned town in the Canadian Arctic built on piles above the permanently frozen subsoil. Service centre for oil and gas installations in the Beaufort Sea.

Inveraray Scotland. County town in Argyll and Bute at the mouth of the R. Aray on Loch Fyne 37 km (23 miles) NNW of Greenock. Pop. (1991) 512.

The main industry is fishing.

Invercargill New Zealand. Town in S Otago, South Island on New River Harbour, Foveaux Strait. Pop. (1990) 51,700.

Industries inc. woollen and flour mills, breweries, sawmills and food-processing.

Inverclyde Scotland. New Unitary Authority created in 1996, formerly in Strathclyde Region. Pop. (1993) 89,990.

Invergordon Scotland. Small town and former naval base in Ross and Cromarty on the N shore of Cromarty Firth 24 km (15 miles) N of Inverness. Pop. (1971) 2240. Scene of a mutiny among naval ratings in 1931.

Inverkeithing Scotland. Small town and port in SW Fife near the N shore of the Firth of Forth. Pop. (1991) 6001. Shipyards, paper mills.

Inverness Scotland. City in northern Scotland in Highland at the mouth of the R. Ness and the NE end of Glen More (Great Glen). Pop. (1991) 41,234.

Commercial and tourist centre and seaport. Industries inc. distilling, brewing and the manufacture of woollens.

Inverness–shire Scotland. Former county, now part of Highland.

Inverurie Scotland. Town in Aberdeenshire situated 23 km (14 miles) NW of Aberdeen. Pop. (1991) 9567.

Ioánnina Greece 1. *Nome* in Epirus bordering NW on Albania. Area 4990 sq km (1926 sq. miles). Pop. (1990) 157,214. Mainly stock-rearing (dairy produce).

2. Cap. of Ioánnina *nome*, on L. Ioánnina. Pop. (1971) 40,130. Trade in cereals, wine, fruit.

Iona (Celtic **Icolmkill**, 'Island of Columba's Cell') Scotland. Small island 5 km (3 miles) long and 2.5 km (1½ miles) wide in the Inner Hebrides in Argyll and Bute off the SW coast of Mull. Here in 563 St Columba landed from Ireland, founded a monastery and began the conversion of Scotland and N England. Became the leading centre of Celtic Christianity. The monastery was plundered and burned several times by Norsemen, but was rebuilt by Queen Margaret of Scotland late

in the 11th cent. On the island are the 13th-cent. cathedral church of St Mary, several Celtic crosses and other remains. It has been the centre of the religious brotherhood of the Iona community since 1938.

Ionia. Region on the W coast of Asia Minor, inhabited in ancient times by Ionian Greeks and inc. such cities as Ephesus, Miletus and later Smyrna (Izmir). They came under Persian rule in the 6th cent. BC, were taken by Alexander the Great and retained some importance in the Roman and Byzantine Empires.

Ionian Islands Greece. Group of islands in the Ionian Sea up to 32 km (20 miles) off the W coast, forming 4 *nomes* named after the 4 largest islands – Corfu, Levkas, Cephalonia and Zante. Pop. (1990) 191,003. Mountainous, rising to 1621 m (5316 ft) in Mt Ainos (Cephalonia), but with fertile lowlands producing wine, olive oil and fruit. Tourism and fishing are the other occupations.

Under Venetian rule from the 15th to the end of the 18th cent., the islands temporarily passed to France, became a British protectorate 1815 and were ceded to Greece 1864.

Ioshkar-Ola ➤YOSHKAR-OLA.

Iowa USA. State in the Middle West, bounded by Minnesota (N), Wisconsin and Illinois (E), Missouri (S) and Nebraska and South Dakota (W). Area 146,011 sq km (56,375 sq. miles). Pop. (1990) 2,776,755. Cap. Des Moines. It is mainly rolling plains; the hilliest region is in the NE. Apart from the boundary rivers – the Mississippi (E) and the Missouri and the Big Sioux (W) – the main river is the Des Moines, crossing diagonally NW–SE. The climate is humid continental with cold winters and hot summers.

Agriculture is important and of the whole area 93.5 per cent is arable, but large-scale commercial farming has not developed. Leading state for maize; oats, hay, barley, soya beans also cultivated. Livestock and poultry raised. Principal minerals bituminous coal, gypsum. Main industry is food-processing.

Chief towns Des Moines, Cedar Rapids, Sioux City and Davenport.

The first explorers were French (1673). Became part of the USA through the Louisiana Purchase (1803). It was admitted to the Union in 1846 as the 29th state.

Iowa City USA. Town on the Iowa R. in Iowa 39 km (24 miles) SSE of Cedar Rapids. Pop. (1990) 59,738.

Varied minor industries.

Ipin China ►YIPIN.

Ipoh Malaysia. Cap. and largest town of Perak 177 km (110 miles) NNW of Kuala Lumpur. Pop. (1980) 300,727 (mainly Chinese).

Important tin-mining centre. Rubber plantations in the neighbourhood.

Ipswich England. Saxon Gipeswic. Industrial town and port in E Suffolk at the head of the R. Orwell estuary. Pop. (1991) 130,157.

Manufactures agricultural machinery, fertilizers, electrical and hi-fi equipment, tobacco products, plastics. Brewing, flour-milling and printing. There are many fine medieval buildings.

Iqaluit (formerly **Frobisher Bay**) Northwest Territories, Canada. Town near the NE head of Frobisher Bay on southern Baffin Island. Pop. (1996) 4200. Fifty per cent of the pop. are Inuit. Fishing, trapping, sealing and carving are important occupations. It is the government administrative, communications and transportation centre of the eastern Arctic. Iqaluit means 'the place where the fish are'.

Iquique Chile. Cap. of the Tarapacá province; seaport in the N 200 km (125 miles) S of Arica on the edge of the Atacama Desert. Pop. (1990) 149,000. Practically rainless; water is piped from the Pica oasis 80 km (50 miles) SE. Linked by rail with nitrate fields.

Exports nitrates, iodine and salt. Other industries inc. fish-canning, sugar and oil refining.

Iquitos Peru. Cap. of the Loreto department in the NE on the left bank of the Amazon

R. Pop. (1990) 269,500. Head of navigation for large Amazon steamers; accessible from the Atlantic (3700 km (2300 miles) distant).

Exports rubber, timber and tagua nuts. Industries inc. sawmilling and cotton-ginning.

Iráklion (Candia, Herakleion) Greece. Cap. of the Iráklion *nome* on the N coast of Crete. Pop. (1971) 77,506. The largest city on the island, a seaport, with considerable coastal trade.

Exports raisins, olive oil and wine. Manufactures soap, leather and wine.

The museum contains Minoan antiquities from Knossos, of which it was the ancient port. Taken in the Saracen conquest of Crete *c.* 823. Passed from the Venetians to the Turks in 1669.

Iran. Islamic republic in SW Asia. Bounded by Azerbaijan, Turkmenistan and the Caspian Sea (N), Afghanistan and Pakistan (E), the Gulf of Oman and the (Persian) Gulf (S) and Iraq and Turkey (W). Area 1,638,057 sq km (632,457 sq. miles). Pop. (1991) 57,050,000. Life expectancy, 65 years male, 66 female. Capital Tehrán. Other large cities are Mashhad, Esfahan and Tabriz, each with more than 900,000 inhabitants. Currency: Rial = 100 dinars. Mountain ranges dominate the N and W and the country is somewhat isolated; much of its area is desert. It consists of a central plateau at 1200 m (4000 ft) and is almost surrounded by mountains: in the N the Elburz Mountains, rising to 5771 m (18,933 ft) at the extinct volcano Damavand; in the W and S the Zagros Mountains and their extensions, rising to 4551 m (14,927 ft) in Zard Kuh and in the E a number of ranges close to the country's eastern border. The plateau sinks to about 600 m (1968 ft) in the great saline desert known as the Dasht-i-Kavir and its continuation the Dasht-i-Lut. The largest of the salt lakes is L. Urmia in the NW. There are few perennial streams and on the plateau the climate is arid and continental, with hot summers and cold winters. The humid subtropical conditions along the northern slopes of the Elburz Mountains, which are well-forested, are in marked contrast to the dry desert-like climate experienced S of the range on the plateau, where the rainfall rarely exceeds 33 cm (13 ins.) annually and is practically non-existent in winter; the Gulf coast is hot and humid during the summer. Land use: forested 11 per cent, meadows and pastures 27 per cent, agricultural and under permanent pasture 9 per cent.

The official religion is the Shi'a branch of Islam and 93 per cent of the pop. belong to this branch (5 per cent Sunni). They recognize 12 Imams or spiritual successors of the Prophet Mohammad. The national language is Farsi or Persian which is spoken by 45 per cent of the pop., 23 per cent speak related languages inc. Kurdish and Luri in the W and Baluchi in the SE, while 26 per cent speak Turkic languages.

The Caspian plains have sufficient rainfall for good agriculture. Rice is cultivated along the Caspian coast, wheat and barley in the drier areas. Cotton is the most important cash crop. Sugar-beet and dates are also produced. Large numbers of sheep and goats are raised, much of the wool being used in the making of carpets and rugs. In the limited fertile areas agricultural methods are usually primitive; irrigation is largely by *qanats* or underground channels leading from the mountain slopes. Oil was discovered in Khuzistán in 1908 and this transformed the commercial development of Iran. Pipelines link the oilfields with the great refinery at Abadan and petroleum represents over 90 per cent by value of total exports. The oil industry was disrupted by the revolution of 1978 and during the war with Iraq in 1980. Coal, iron, lead and other minerals are produced on a small scale.

Iran was known as Persia until 1935. Cyrus the Great founded the Persian empire in the 6th cent. BC and during the centuries that followed it was conquered by Alexander the Great in the 4th cent. BC, and in the 7th cent. AD it was overthrown by the Arabs who converted the country to Islam. From 1794 the Qajar dynasty reigned until 1925, when its last member Ahmed was deposed and Riza Khan Pahlevi was proclaimed Shah. It was ruled as an absolute monarchy until in 1906 a Constitution was granted. During World War II Riza Shah showed sympathy with the Axis cause and was forced to abdicate in favour of his son in 1941. In 1951 foreign oil interests were expropriated, but from 1954 the industry was controlled by an international consortium of oil companies. In 1973 a new agreement gave control of the oil industry to the Iranian National Oil Company. Following widespread unrest the Shah left Iran in 1979. Ayatollah Khomeini, spiritual leader of the Shi'a Muslim community, returned to Iran after 15 years of exile and proclaimed an Islamic Republic. In 1988 war broke out with Iraq which caused the destruction of some Iranian towns and damage to oil installations at Abadan. President Saddam Hussein of Iraq offered peace terms in 1990 and Iraqi forces started to withdraw.

Under Iran's Constitution the country is divided for administrative purposes into 24 provinces (*ostan*). Supreme authority is exercised by the spiritual leader (*wali faqih*). There is a State President and a 270-member legislature (*majlis*). In 1982 an 83-member Assembly of Experts was established; its task is to interpret the Constitution and select the Spiritual Leader.

Irapuato Mexico. Town in Guanajuato state on the central plateau at a height of 1795 m (5890 ft). Pop. (1990) 362,471.

Industries inc. flour-milling, iron-founding; it manufactures cigarettes and trades in cereals and fruit. It is probably the largest strawberry-growing centre in the world.

Iraq. Republic of SW Asia bounded on the N by Turkey, E by Iran, SE by the Gulf, S by Kuwait and Saudi Arabia and W by Jordan and Syria. Area 435,052 aq km (167,975 sq. miles). Pop. (1990) 17,856,000. Life expectancy 61 years male, 65 female. Cap. Baghdad. Other large cities inc. Basra and Mosul. Currency: Iraqi dinar = 20 dirhams = 1000 fils. Iraq was formerly known as Mesopotamia, 'the land between the rivers' (i.e. the Tigris and Euphrates). It consists of 3 main regions: the NE highlands, rugged and sparsely wooded, with scattered pastures, home of the Kurds; the desert region of the W and S, part of the vast Syrian Desert; and lower Iraq, the lower basin of the Tigris and Euphrates. The climate is mainly arid with small and unreliable rainfall and a large annual range of temperature. Land use: forested 4 per cent, meadows and pastures 9 per cent, agricultural and under permanent cultivation 13 per cent. Religion is predominantly Muslim (Shi'a 10,760,000 and Sunni 5,940,000). There were (1990) 1 million Christians in 14 sects. The Kurds represent about 19 per cent of the total pop. Arabic is the official language but Kurdish is official in the Kurdish Autonomous Region.

Petroleum, which was discovered in 1927, is the chief source of wealth and economic activity. The oilfields of the N are found at Kirkuk, Jambur and Basi Hassau, and in the S at Rumaila and Zubayr. Oil supply has been disrupted since the outbreak of the war with Iran and the Gulf War. The trans-Syrian pipeline was closed in 1982 and the pipeline of the Mediterranean *via* Turkey was shut down in the Gulf War. Dates, produced in the irrigated belt along the Shatt-al-Arab, were once an important export crop, providing a large proportion of the world's trade in dates, but the war with Iran caused considerable destruction of date palms in the Basra area. Wheat and barley are other leading crops and large numbers of sheep and goats are raised. To extend the area under cultivation there are plans for further irrigation schemes.

Iraq was part of the Ottoman Empire from 1534 until 1916. It became an independent Arab state under British mandate in 1927 and the mandate lapsed in 1932. During World War II a pro-German *coup d'état* was put down by British forces and in 1943 Iraq declared war on the Axis powers. It joined the Arab League in 1945 and took part in the unsuccessful war on Israel in 1948. In 1958 the Hashemite dynasty was overthrown and a Republic declared. In 1968 the Ba'ath Party seized power and established a Revolutionary Command Council as government. Iraq invaded Iran in 1980 in a dispute over territorial rights in the Shatt-al-Arab water-

way which developed into a full-scale war; the war ended in 1990. Also in 1990 Iraq invaded Kuwait and the President announced the annexation of Kuwait in August 1990. The UN authorized military force against Iraq and in January 1991 an attack was made by coalition forces. Iraq agreed to withdraw from Kuwait and to UN inspection of all chemical and biological weapons. Iraq government forces put down insurrection by Shi'ites in the S and Kurds in the N in 1991.

Iraq is divided for administrative purposes into 18 governorates (*liwa*), each administered by an appointed Governor; three of the governorates form a (Kurdish) Autonomous Region with an elected 57-member Kurdish Legislative Council. Political power in Iraq is held by the Revolutionary Command Council which appoints the President. The President appoints the Council of Ministers and legislative authority is shared by the 250-member National Assembly and the Revolutionary Command Council.

Irbid Jordan. Town in the N 71 km (44 miles) N of Amman. Pop. (1989) 167,785. It is a commercial centre and trades in grain.

Nearby is an important Bronze Age archaeological site.

Ireland. Republic occupying the greater part of southern Ireland, *c.* 80 km (50 miles) W of Great Britain across St George's Channel. Ireland is bounded N, W and S by the Irish Sea, NE by Northern Ireland. Area 70,285 sq km (27,137 sq. miles). Pop. (1991) 3,494,000. Life expectancy, 70 years male, 76 female. Cap. Dublin; other cities Cork, Limerick and Waterford. Currency: Irish punt = 100 pence. Low-lying in the centre with mountain ranges around the coast; a deeply indented coastline with many loughs on the W coast. Ireland's insular position on the NW fringe of Europe ensures a mild, equable, humid climate, with about 150 cm (60 ins.) of rain annually in the W, considerably more in the mountains, decreasing to 75 cm (30 ins.) in the E; a climate which favours vegetation, gives a fresh, green appearance to the land and justifies the nickname of the

Ireland

'Emerald Isle'. Land use: forested 5 per cent, pasture 68 per cent, agricultural 14 per cent. Religion predominantly (94 per cent) Roman Catholic. Irish is the first official language and English second.

Agriculture is by far the most important occupation. Main crops are hay and silage, turnips, potatoes, sugar-beet, barley, mangels, wheat, oats. Livestock inc. dairy and beef cattle, sheep, pigs and horses. Industries are concentrated on the E coast and inc. processing dairy products; manufactures tobacco products, milling grain and animal feed, bacon and other meat products, vehicles and metal goods. Noted exports are bloodstock (horses), linen, stout, glassware, and there is a growing tourist trade.

Long before the Christian era Ireland was invaded by Celtic tribes and the island was divided into kingdoms which were nominally subject to a High King at Tara and were frequently at war with one another. Christianity was introduced mainly through the work of St Patrick in the 5th cent. and for the succeeding two centuries Ireland was a centre of culture; settlers and missionaries, of whom the best known was St Columba, were sent to Britain. Towards the end of the 8th cent. Norse raiders began to settle at various places around the coast and founded Dublin and other towns, but they were decisively defeated by Brian Boru, High King of Ireland, at Clontarf (1014). In 1169 the Normans under Richard Strongbow, Earl of Pembroke, invaded Ireland, thus initiating the bitter Anglo–Irish struggles which were to continue for well over 7 centuries. At Drogheda in 1495 was enacted the hated Poynings' Law, which subordinated the Irish legislature to the English. Henry VIII attempted to pacify the Irish chiefs with titles, but only created dissension within the clans. Elizabeth used force to put down rebellions; Irish land was confiscated and settlers were planted in Ireland – notably Scottish Protestants in Ulster, whose arrival was to lead to the long conflict between Northern and Southern Ireland. The confiscation of Ulster was largely responsible for the rebellion of

1641, which lasted for more than 10 years but was ruthlessly crushed by Cromwell. Irish support of James II's cause also ended in failure and defeat at the Battle of the Boyne (1690). Through the penal laws the Catholic majority were now harassed and oppressed at every turn; Irish agriculture was deliberately stifled and the condition of the peasants was made wretched.

Partial independence was granted to the Irish parliament by the Act of Renunciation (1783). Pitt united the British and Irish parliaments (1801), but lost the support he had gained from many Catholics when he failed to redeem his promise of Catholic emancipation. The Catholic Relief Act (1829), however, permitted Catholics to enter parliament; in 1869 the Protestant Church of Ireland was disestablished. Meanwhile, the potato famine (1846–7) had struck the country, causing the deaths of hundreds of thousands from starvation and disease, and the emigration of about 1½ million, mainly to the United States; the final result was that the population was almost halved. In the political sphere such revolutionary movements as the Society of United Irishmen in the 1790s and Young Ireland in the 1840s achieved less for Ireland than the activities of such patriots as Grattan, O'Connell and Parnell. Largely because of Parnell's determination, Gladstone was compelled to introduce the Land Act (1881), which made broad concessions to the Irish tenant, but his Home Rule Bill was rejected twice (1886, 1893). The Third Home Rule Bill was passed in 1914 but did not come into operation owing to the outbreak of World War I. In 1916 an insurrection against British rule took place and a republic was proclaimed. In 1920 an Act was passed by the British parliament, under which separate parliaments were established for 'Southern Ireland' (26 counties) and 'Northern Ireland' (6 counties). The Unionists of the 6 counties accepted this scheme and a Northern parliament was duly elected in 1921. The rest of Ireland, however, ignored the Act.

In 1921 a Treaty was signed between Great Britain and Ireland by which Ireland accepted dominion status subject to the right of Northern Ireland to opt out. This right was exercised and the border between *Saorstát Éireann* (26 counties) and Northern Ireland (6 counties) was fixed in 1925 as the outcome of an agreement between Great Britain, the Irish Free State and Northern Ireland. The agreement was ratified by the three parliaments.

Subsequently the constitutional links between *Saorstát Eireann* and the UK were gradually removed by the *Dáil* (National Parliament). The remaining formal association with the British Commonwealth by virtue of the External Relations Act, 1936, was severed when the Republic of Ireland Act, 1948, came into operation in 1949.

The names of the four historic provinces, Ulster, Leinster, Munster and Connacht (Connaught), are still used, though they have limited significance. For administrative purposes the country is divided into 27 counties and 4 county boroughs: *Ulster* (in part): Cavan, Donegal, Monaghan. *Leinster*: Carlow, Dublin, Kildare, Kilkenny, Laoighis, Longford, Louth, Meath, Offaly, Westmeath, Wexford, Wicklow; Dublin City (county borough). *Munster*: Clare, Cork, Kerry, Limerick, Tipperary (N, S), Waterford; Cork, Limerick and Waterford cities (county boroughs). *Connacht:* Galway, Leitrim, Mayo, Roscommon, Sligo.

Under the 1937 Constitution parliament consists of the President, who is elected for 7 years, the House of Representatives (*Dáil Éireann*), elected by adult suffrage and the Senate (*Seanad Éireann*), partly elected and partly nominated.

Ireland, Northern ➤NORTHERN IRELAND.

Irian Jaya ➤NEW GUINEA.

Irish Sea. Arm of the Atlantic Ocean about 160 km (100 miles) N–S and 190 km (120 miles) W–E, separating England, Wales and Scotland from Ireland. Connected with the Atlantic Ocean by the North Channel on the N and by St George's Channel on the S. It was named Oceanus Hibernicus by the Romans.

Irkutsk Russia. Cap. of the Irkutsk region situated on the Angara R. at its confluence with the Irkut R. 64 km (40 miles) below its exit from the SW end of L. Baikal. Pop. (1991) 641,000.

A major Siberian industrial centre, industries inc. vehicle assembly and other engineering, mica-processing, sawmilling, flour-milling and meat-packing. Power derived from the Cheremkhovo coalfield and the hydroelectric plant on the Angara R.

It was founded in 1652 and increased in importance with the construction of the Trans-Siberian Railway in 1898.

Irlam England. Town in Greater Manchester on the Manchester Ship Canal 13 km (8 miles) WSW of the city. Pop. (1991) 18,504.

Industries inc. the manufacture of margarine and paper.

Iron Gate (Iron Gates) Romania/Yugoslavia. Gorge of the Danube R. about 3 km (2 miles) long on the border between Romania and Yugoslavia between Orşova and Turnu-Severin (Romania). Made navigable in 1896.

Irrawaddy (Ayeyarwady) River Myanmar (Burma). Main river and country's economic artery, rising in two headstreams, the Mali and the Nmai, which unite above Myitkyina and flow about 2150 km (1335 miles) generally SSW through the entire length of Myanmar (Burma). Below the confluence the river continues past Bhamo, the head of navigation, flows through spectacular defiles and reaches Mandalay before receiving its chief tributary, the Chindwin, on the right bank; it then flows between the Arakan Yoma and the Pegu Yoma, past Yenangyaung and Prome and about 290 km (180 miles) from the coast divides across its delta, to enter the Andaman Sea across a broad front of forests and mangrove swamps.

Irtysh River Russia. River 4440 km (2775 miles) long, rising in the Altai Mountains of Xinjiang-Uyghur (China), flowing W and entering L. Zaisan in Kazakhstan. It continues in a general NNW direction past Semipalatinsk, Omsk and Tobolsk, to join the Ob, of which it is the chief tributary. Area drained, 1,643,000 sq km (634,363 sq. miles). Among its own main tributaries are the Ishim and the Tobol. Navigable for small craft below L. Zaisan April–Nov. Its middle course drains the agricultural areas of W Siberia.

Irun Spain. Town in the Basque country of the N situated 16 km (10 miles) E of San Sebastian on the left bank of the R. Bidassoa near the French border. Pop. (1991) 53,570. It is a port and commercial centre and industries inc. foundries, tanneries and the manufacture of paper, porcelain and tools. Iron and lead mining in the vicinity.

Irvine Scotland. Port and industrial town in North Ayrshire on the R. Irvine near its mouth on the Firth of Clyde. Pop. (1991) 33,000.

Iron-founding, sawmilling. Manufactures chemicals and hosiery. Exports tar and cement.

Irvington USA. Town just W of Newark, New Jersey. Pop. (1990) 61,000.

Manufactures tools, machinery and paint.

Isabela Island ➤GALÁPAGOS ISLANDS.

Isar River Austria/Germany. River 262 km (163 miles) long, rising in the Austrian Tirol and flowing generally NNE into Bavaria, past Munich to join the Danube R. just below Deggendorf. Provides power for hydroelectric plants.

Isca ➤CAERLEON.

Ischia Italy. 1. Island of volcanic origin off the coast of Campania at the NW entrance to the Bay of Naples. Area 47 sq km (18 sq. miles). Pop. 14,400. Rises to 790 m (2591 ft) in Monte Epomeo. With its mineral springs and its scenic beauty, an increasingly popular resort. Produces olives, fruits and wine.

2. Chief town of Ischia island on the NE coast. Pop. 7000. Exports wine.

Settled by the Greeks c. 500 BC but later abandoned owing to volcanic eruption.

Iseo, Lake Italy. Lake in Lombardy 26 km (16 miles) long and up to 5 km (3 miles) wide

29 km (18 miles) E of Bergamo. The Oglio R., tributary of the Po, enters at the N end and leaves at the S end. In the centre is an island rising to 559 m (1834 ft) in Monte Isola.

Isère France. Department of Rhône-Alps Region. Area 7431 sq km (2869 sq. miles). Pop. (1990) 1,016,535. Prefecture Grenoble. Mountainous; inc. part of the Massif du Pelvoux (SE) (4106 m; 13,468 ft). Bounded on the W by the Rhône, it comprises most of the upper course of the Isère and is drained also by the latter's tributaries the Drac and Romanche, providing much hydroelectric power.

Wheat, vines, tobacco cultivated in the valley. Cattle, sheep and horses raised. Chief towns Grenoble, Vienne.

Isère River France. River 288 km (179 miles) long, rising in the Graian Alps near the Italian border and flowing generally W and SW to join the Rhône R. near Valence. There are many hydroelectric stations along its upper course.

Iserlohn Germany. Industrial town in North Rhine-Westphalia 24 km (15 miles) SE of Dortmund. Pop. (1985) 90,000.

Manufactures wire, springs, needles, brass and bronze goods.

Isfahan ➤ESFAHAN.

Iskenderun Turkey. Formerly Alexandretta. Cap. of Hatay province 113 km (70 miles) WSW of Gaziantep. Pop. (1990) 176,000. Seaport, naval base. Railway terminus. It was long the port of Aleppo and N Syria.

Islamabad Pakistan. Cap. just NE of Rawalpindi. Pop. (1981) 201,000. National cap. since 1967, formerly at Karachi.

Islay Scotland. Island in Argyll and Bute in the Inner Hebrides off the SW coast of Jura, from which it is separated by the Sound of Islay 1.6 km (1 mile) wide. Area 606 sq km (259 sq. miles). The highest point is Ben Bheigeir 490 m (1609 ft).

Main occupations fishing, stock-rearing,

dairy-farming, whisky-distilling. Chief towns Port Ellen, Bowmore.

Isle of Anglesey ►ANGLESEY.

Isle of Ely ►ELY, ISLE OF.

Isle of Man ►MAN, ISLE OF.

Isle of Pines ►YOUTH, ISLE OF.

Isles of Scilly England. Group of about 140 small granite islands and islets 45 km (28 miles) WSW of Land's End, 5 being inhabited: St Mary's, the largest, with Hugh Town, the only town, Tresco, St Martin's, St Agnes and Bryher. Area 16 sq km (6 sq. miles). Pop. (1994) 2000. With their mild, equable climate, they have become famous for the cultivation of early flowers (esp. daffodils, narcissi) and have a thriving tourist industry. The gardens of Tresco Abbey are subtropical in character and unique in the British Isles. The islands were the scene of many wrecks and on a rock to the SW is the well-known Bishop Rock lighthouse. They were also notorious for smuggling.

Isle of Wight ►WIGHT, ISLE OF.

Islington England. Former metropolitan borough of N London, inc. Holloway, Highbury and Canonbury; from 1965 an Inner London borough inc. Finsbury. Pop. (1991) 155,200. Both residential and industrial.

Ismail ►IZMAIL.

Ismailia Egypt. Town in Lower Egypt halfway along the Suez Canal on the NW shore of L. Timsah 72 km (45 miles) S of Port Said. Pop. (1986) 236,300. On the Ismailia (Fresh Water) Canal. Railway centre, linked with Cairo, Port Said and Suez. Built in 1863 by the Suez Canal Company as a construction camp and market.

Isna ►ESNA.

Isola Bella ►BORROMEAN ISLANDS.

Isparta Turkey. Cap. of Isparta province 298 km (185 miles) ESE of Izmir. Pop. (1985) 112,117.
Manufactures carpets.

Israel. Republic in South West Asia. The modern state of Israel, like Palestine and Canaan before it, occupies a strip of land in South West Asia between the Mediterranean and the Jordan valley, with a triangular wedge of desert, the Negev, extending S to the Gulf of Aqaba. Bounded by Lebanon (N), Syria (NE), Jordan (E) and by Egypt and the Mediterranean (W). Area 20,770 sq km (8017 sq. miles). Pop. (1991) 4,821,000. Pop. of areas under Israeli administration as a result of the 6-day War was 1989: Judaea and Samaria (West Bank) 915,000; Gaza Strip, 612,000. Life expectancy, 74 years male, 78 female. Cap. Jerusalem. Tel Aviv-Jaffa is the largest town and others with more than 100,000 inhabitants are Jerusalem, Haifa, Ramat Gan, Bat-Yam, Holon, Petach-Tikva and Beersheba. Currency: shekel = 100 agorots. The fertile coastal plain rises E to the highlands of Galilee (N) and Judaea (S), the hill country in the region of Nablus and Hebron being now occupied by Jordan; the highest point is Har Meiron at 1209 m (3966 ft) in Upper Galilee in the extreme N. Mt Carmel, rising to 528 m (1732 ft) interrupts the coastal plain in the N. Only a part of the Jordan valley, which is mostly below sea level, lies within Israel, and other streams, inc. the Kishon, are intermittent. On the coastal plain the climate is Mediterranean, with hot, dry summers, the rain falling mainly in winter and increasing S–N; the hill country is cooler and has a moderate winter rainfall, but the Jordan valley and the Negev are arid. L. Tiberias (Sea of Galilee) lies 212 m (695 ft) below sea level entirely within Israel; Tiberias is a popular winter resort because of its mild climate at that season. Only the SW shore of the Dead Sea belongs to Israel and here, at 392 m (1286 ft) below sea level, the climate is hot and oppressive. Land use: forested 6 per cent, meadows and pastures 40 per cent, agricultural and under permanent cultivation 22 per cent.

Israel is a holy land of the Jewish, Muslim and Christian faiths, and there is complete freedom of worship and provision for the observance of days of rest and Holy Days by all faiths. Religious affairs, under the supervision of a special Ministry, are under the control of the different ecclesiastical authorities; the Jewish faith is governed by the Sephardic and Ashkenasic Chief Rabbis, for Eastern and Western Jews respectively (83 per cent of the pop. is Jewish); the Muslim by the Kadi and the Christian by the heads of the various communities; in 1957 the Druses were recognized as an autonomous religious community. Official languages Hebrew and Arabic. In 1947, before the creation of the new state, Muslims numbered more than 1 million, while there were only 615,000 Jews, the great majority of whom had entered as immigrants since 1917. The 'Law of Return 1950' states that 'every Jew shall be entitled to come to Israel as an immigrant'. When Israel was attacked by the neighbouring Arab states (1948–9), about 900,000 Arabs left the country, and from 1948 to 1990 2,028,031 Jewish immigrants entered; 185,000 came from the former USSR in 1990.

On the fertile coastal plain agriculture is intensive and inc. mixed farming, poultry-farming, viticulture and the growing of citrus fruits (grapefruit, oranges), the last providing one of the country's principal exports. Wheat, barley and olives are also cultivated, and farming has been taken into the N Negev with the help of the Yarkon Negev water pipeline. There are several different types of rural settlement in Israel, among them the *kibbutz* and *kvutsa*, communal collective settlements, the *moshav ovdim*, a workers' co-operative smallholders' settlement and *mosha shifufi*, a communal cooperative settlement. The chief mineral resources are the salt deposits of the Dead Sea from which potash and other chemicals are extracted. Among the industries developed are fruit canning and processing, chemicals, textiles, precision instruments, electrical and electronic equipment, diamond-polishing and paper.

The area once designated as Palestine, of which Israel forms part, was formerly part of Turkey's Ottoman Empire. In World War I (1917–18) Palestine was captured from the Turks by the British. By the Balfour Declaration (1917) Britain expressed herself in favour of the establishment of a Jewish na-

tional home in Palestine and under the British mandate (1920) Jewish immigration was encouraged. In spite of conflict between Jews and Arabs, much economic progress was made and tension was reduced with the onset of World War II. After the war, however, Britain refused to allow unlimited Jewish immigration, acts of terrorism were committed and severely countered, the mandate was surrendered and the Jewish state of Israel was proclaimed (1948). Troops from the neighbouring Arab states invaded Israel but were repulsed and in 1950 the cap. was moved from Tel Aviv to Jerusalem. Trouble with the Arab states again came to a head in 1956, when Egypt nationalized the Suez Canal and denied its use to Israeli ships; Israeli troops occupied the Gaza strip and the Sinai peninsula, and inflicted considerable losses on the Egyptian forces, but later withdrew. The continuing influx of immigrants put a severe strain on the country and, although the economy became more viable, economic stability is only maintained by substantial financial help from abroad, mainly from the USA. War with neighbouring Arab states (esp. Egypt, Jordan and Syria) again broke out in June 1967, but ended quickly with complete military victory for Israel. War again broke out in 1973, when Egyptian forces crossed the Suez Canal and Syria attacked on the Golan Heights, but ended in less than three weeks, with Israeli troops advancing towards the Egyptian and Syrian capitals. In 1977 President Sadat of Egypt visited Israel and in 1978 the Camp David conference led to the complete withdrawal of Israel from the Sinai Peninsula by 1982. By 1995 Israeli forces had withdrawn from 6 of the 7 largest Palestinian towns in the West Bank and a Palestinian Council was installed in 1996.

Israel is a parliamentary democracy with a one-chamber parliament (*knesset*) consisting of 120 members elected for 4 years by secret ballot and universal direct suffrage. It is divided into six districts: Central, Haifa, Jerusalem, Northern, Southern and Tel Aviv. Two additional districts, Judaea-Samaria and Gaza, are occupied territories.

Issyk-Kul Kirgizia. Large mountain lake in a deep basin at 1586 m (5202 ft) above sea level, between the Kungei Ala-Tau (N) and Terskei Ala-Tau (S) ranges. Area 6190 sq km (2390 sq. miles). Fed by many streams from the mountain slopes. Its slightly salty waters abound with fish.

Issy-les-Moulineaux France. Suburb of SW Paris in the Hauts-de-Seine department on the left bank of the Seine R. Manufactures cars, aircraft and electrical equipment.

Istanbul Turkey. Cap. of Istanbul province on both sides of the Bosporus at the entrance to the Sea of Marmara. Turkey's largest city. Pop. (1990) 6,293,000.

Chief seaport. Industrial and commercial centre. Its main industries are pottery, textiles, glassware, leather goods, cement, fishing and tobacco. It handles most of the country's imports and a considerable part of the exports.

It was founded by the Greeks in *c.* 600 BC and, like Rome, it is built on seven hills, standing between the Sea of Marmara and its magnificent harbour, the Golden Horn, an inlet of the Bosporus. To the N of the Golden Horn are the suburbs of Galata (commercial quarter) and Pera (European quarter), while on the opposite side of the Bosporus is Uskudar, or Scutari (industrial centre). Istanbul has one of the world's outstanding buildings and the glory of Byzantine art in the Church of St Sophia, which in turn was a church, a mosque and museum. The mosques give the city its remarkable skyline of domes and minarets. The cap. of Turkey was transferred to Ankara in 1923.

Constantinople, the name by which it was known until 1930, was founded (AD 328) by Constantine the Great on the site of Byzantium as the new cap. of the Roman Empire. It was strongly and skilfully fortified by a series of concentric walls, erected at various times from the reign of Constantine, each new wall reflecting the continued growth of the city. Although attacked by Avars in 627, by Saracens in the 7th and 8th cent. and by Bulgarians in the 9th and 10th cent., it did not fall until 1204, when it was taken by the

forces of the 4th Crusade and made the seat of a Latin Empire. Recovered by the Byzantines 1261. Fell to the Turks 1453, to flourish again as cap. of the Ottoman Empire for more than 4 centuries.

Istria Croatia. Peninsula in the N Adriatic Sea, mainly in Croatia; Austrian for most of the period from 1797 to the end of World War I, when it was ceded to Italy. At the end of World War II (1947) it passed to Yugoslavia, except for the Free Territory of Trieste, which in 1954 was divided between Italy and Yugoslavia.

Principal occupations agriculture (cereals, olive oil, wine), fishing. Chief towns Pula, Opatija.

Itabira ►VITORIA (BRAZIL).

Itajaí Brazil. Seaport in the Santa Catarina state (SE) at the mouth of the Itajaí Açu R. Pop. (1985) 105,000. Serves a fertile agricultural region inhabited largely by Germans and Italians.

Exports timber, sugar and tobacco.

Italy. Republic of S Europe. Occupies a long peninsula extending SE from the Alps (N) into the Mediterranean Sea, separating the Tyrrhenian Sea (W) from the Adriatic Sea (E) and inc. the large islands of Sicily, from which it is separated by the narrow Strait of Messina, and Sardinia, as well as many smaller islands. In the N the Alps form the boundary with France, Switzerland, Austria and Slovenia. Area 301,277 sq km (116,324 sq. miles). Pop. (1991) 57,590,000. Life expectancy 73 years male, 79 female. Cap. Rome. Other major cities Milan, Turin, Genoa and Naples. Currency: Lira = 100 centesimi. Along Italy's N frontier the Alps curve round in a vast arc from the Riviera to the Gulf of Trieste and are penetrated by several international railways and roads; their highest peak, Mont Blanc 4808 m (15,774 ft) is on the Franco–Italian frontier, while Monte Rosa 4634 m (15,203 ft) is on the Swiss–Italian frontier. On the S slopes of the Rhaetian Alps are the lakes Maggiore, Lugano, Como and Garda, the first two shared with Switzerland. Within the curve formed by the Alps and the Apennines is a fertile plain, broadening out towards the Adriatic and consisting mainly of the basin of the Po R., which receives numerous tributaries from both mountain systems. The Apennines, continuing from the Maritime Alps, where the mountains come close to the sea, form the backbone of peninsular Italy and extend to the S extremity of Calabria. Of several peninsular volcanic centres the best known are Vesuvius, overlooking the Bay of Naples, Etna in Sicily and Stromboli in the Lipari Is. On both sides of the Apennines the generally narrow coastal plains widen here and there, e.g. in Campania and Apulia, but the majority of the rivers S of the Po basin are necessarily short and of little value for navigation, the most important being the Tiber and the Arno. Climate varies according to position and altitude. In the N the Riviera coast, for example, is famed for its mild winters, but the Po basin has a continental type of climate, with cold winters. Towards the S the climate becomes gradually warmer and more Mediterranean in character; S of Rome winters are mild and summers hot, while the rain falls mainly in the cooler months. At times the *sirocco*, a hot, enervating wind from the Sahara, sweeps over S Italy, while the N Adriatic coast is affected in winter by the cold *bora* from the NE. Land use: forested 23 per cent, meadows and pastures 17 per cent, agricultural and under permanent cultivation 41 per cent. By a treaty between the Holy See and Italy in 1929 Roman Catholicism is the only state religion and the pop. is predominantly Roman Catholic.

Although primarily an agricultural country, there is considerable industry in the N, particularly around Milan, Turin and Genoa. The fertile basin of the Po covers less than one-fifth of the country and economically is the principal region; it produces the bulk of the wheat, maize, rice, hemp, sugarbeet and vines. In the S the land is much less productive, but olives and citrus fruits are cultivated. Sulphur and mercury are exported, but Italy is generally poor in minerals; the lack of coal and oil has been offset by

the development of hydroelectric power, particularly in the N, where the chief industries are concentrated. Main industries are textiles, clothing, leather footwear, foodstuffs, machinery, chemicals and pharmaceuticals. Italy has to import large quantities of foodstuffs and raw materials as well as certain manufactures and normally has an adverse trade balance. This is largely made up by the mercantile marine remittances from Italians abroad and by the millions of tourists who visit the country annually (55 million in 1989) to enjoy such world-renowned resorts as Venice and Capri and the art treasures of Florence, Pisa and many other historic centres.

The history of Italy from the 4th cent. BC to the 5th cent. AD is largely that of Rome. With the fall of the Roman Empire of the W (476), Italy came under the rule of Ostrogoths and then the Lombards, and in 800 Charlemagne was crowned Emperor by the Pope. In 962 it became part of the Holy Roman Empire and for the next three centuries its history reflected the struggle between the Empire and the papacy. At the beginning of the 14th cent. there were five major powers in Italy: the kingdom of Naples, the papal states and the city-republics of Milan, Florence and Venice and, in spite of the constant rivalry and conflict between them, it was in the 14th–16th cent. that Italy made its great contribution to European culture in the Renaissance. Spain and Austria now exercised the dominating influence; by the mid 18th cent. Naples, Sicily and Parma were held by the Spanish Bourbons, Milan and Tuscany by Austria, Sardinia and Piedmont by Savoy, while central Italy was occupied by the papal states and Venice survived as a republic (till 1797). Under the Napoleonic regime Italy was unified, but disintegrated again on the fall of Bonaparte. Democratic and nationalist ideals introduced by the French, however, led to the *Risorgimento* movement. Unification was at last achieved by Victor Emmanuel II of Sardinia, assisted by Cavour and Garibaldi, and in 1861 he became king of united Italy: by the defeat of Austria, Venetia was secured (1866) and then Rome was added (1870). In 1882 Italy concluded the Triple Alliance with Germany and Austria, and embarked on colonial expansion with the annexation of Eritrea and part of Somaliland. The attack on Abyssinia was defeated at Aduwa (1896), but the war with Turkey (1911–12) yielded Libya. In World War I Italy joined the Allies (1915) and received S Tirol, Trieste, Istria, the Dodecanese and other small territories, while Fiume (Rijeka) was seized by d'Annunzio (1921). Political and industrial unrest, seething for some years, paved the way for a Fascist regime, and an aggressive foreign policy expressed itself in the conquest of Abyssinia (1935–6) and Albania (1939) and the entry into World War II (1940) on the side of Germany. Defeat in Africa and the invasion of Sicily (1943) brought about the downfall of Mussolini and the end of his grandiose schemes for a colonial empire, and until 1945 Italy was a battlefield; Victor Emmanuel III abdicated (1946), to be followed later in the same year by his son and successor, Umberto II and a republic was proclaimed. By the peace treaty (1947) Italy lost her colonial possessions; most of Venezia Giulia went to Yugoslavia, small frontier districts to France and Trieste became a Free Territory – to be divided between Yugoslav and Italian administration in 1954. Since World War II, although the economy has thrived, politically there has been a multi-party political stalemate with many changes of government and the Christian Democrats and Communists polling most of the votes.

The Italian parliament comprises a 630-member Chamber of Deputies, elected for 5 years by universal suffrage and a 315-member Senate elected for 5 years, while the President holds office for 7 years. For administrative purposes the country is divided into 15 autonomous regions (Piedmont, Liguria, Lombardy, Veneto, Emilia-Romagna, Marches, Tuscany, Umbria, Latium, Campania, Abruzzi, Molise, Apulia, Basilicata and Calabria), and 5 autonomous regions with special statute (Valle d'Aosta, Trentino-Alto Adige, Friuli-Venezia Giulia, Sicily and Sardinia). Enclaves in Italy are the republic of San Marino, near Rimini and the Vatican City, in Rome.

Ithaca (Gr. **Itháki**) Greece. One of the Ionian Is. off NE Cephalonia, reputed to have been the home of Homer's Odysseus (Ulysses). Area 85 sq km (33 sq. miles). Pop. (1971) 6466. Chief town Itháki.

Produces olive oil, wine, currants.

Ithaca USA. Town in New York at the S end of Cayuga L. Pop. (1970) 24,800.

Manufactures adding machines, firearms.

Situated in the beautiful scenery of the Finger Lakes region, with gorges and waterfalls. Seat of Cornell University (1865).

Itzehoe Germany. Ancient town in Schleswig-Holstein on the Stor R. 51 km (32 miles) NW of Hamburg. Pop. (1986) 32,000.

Manufactures cement, machinery, fishing and nets.

The oldest town in the *Land*; grew up round a 9th-cent. castle.

Ivano-Frankovsk Ukraine. Formerly Stanisławów, Stanislav. Town situated 113 km (70 miles) SSE of Lvov. Pop. (1991) 226,000.

Railway engineering, oil-refining. Manufactures machinery, textiles.

An old Polish town, it reverted to Poland after World War I (as Stanisławów) but was ceded to the USSR in 1945.

Ivanovo Russia. Cap. of the Ivanovo Region on the Uvod R. 257 km (160 miles) NE of Moscow. Pop. (1991) 482,000.

The earliest and still the major centre of the cotton industry; also manufactures textile and other machinery and chemicals.

Founded in the 14th cent. A commercial centre by the 17th cent.

Iviza ➤BALEARIC ISLANDS.

Ivory Coast ➤CÔTE D'IVOIRE.

Ivry-sur-Seine (Evry) France. Suburb of SE Paris in the Essonne department on the left bank of the Seine R. Pop. (1968) 60,342.

Industries inc. engineering, chemicals, cement and earthenware.

Iwakisan ➤HIROSAKI.

Iwakuni Japan. City situated SW of Hiroshima on Nishiki R. Pop. (1990) 109,534.

It is a railway junction and industries inc. the manufacture of petro-chemicals, textiles, flour and sauces.

Iwo Jima ➤VOLCANO ISLANDS.

Ixtaccihuatl Mexico. In Nahuatl (the language of the Aztecs), 'White Woman'. Snow-capped dormant volcano 5288 m (16,128 ft) 61 km (38 miles) SE of Mexico City. Three separate summits, giving it the appearance of a hooded figure (hence the name).

Izabal, Lake Guatemala. Formerly Golfo Dulce. Country's largest lake, in the E, draining into the Caribbean Sea by the Rio Dulce 48 km (30 miles) long and up to 19 km (12 miles) wide.

Izhevsk Russia. Cap. of the Udmurt Autonomous Republic on the Izh R. 563 km (350 miles) ENE of Nizhny Novgorod. Pop. (1990) 613,000.

Railway junction. Important metallurgical centre. Manufactures agricultural machinery, firearms (inc. the Kalashnikov rifles), lathes. Sawmilling, brickmaking, flour-milling.

Founded 1760.

Izmail (Ismail) Ukraine. Cap. of the Izmail Region in Bessarabia on the Kiliya (Chilia) branch of the Danube R. 193 km (120 miles) SW of Odessa. Pop. (1990) 94,000.

Port. Commercial centre. Flour-milling, tanning. Trade in cereals and hides.

After being taken by Russia (1770), was twice transferred to Romania (1856, 1918); became part of the USSR in 1944.

Izmir Turkey. Formerly Smyrna. Cap. of Izmir province and country's third largest city, at the head of the Gulf of Izmir on the Aegean Sea. Pop. (1990) 2,319,188.

Seaport and naval base. Important exports of tobacco, figs and cotton. Also an industrial centre. It manufactures textiles, soap, tobacco products, leather goods, pharmaceuticals and silk.

Founded by Greeks and later conquered by the Romans. An early centre of Christianity. In 1424 it was taken by the Turks, who held it till 1919, when it was occupied by Greek forces. It was restored to Turkey in 1923.

Izmit Turkey. Cap. and minor port of Kocaeli province at the head of the Gulf of Izmit on the Sea of Marmara. Pop. (1990) 257,000.

In a tobacco-growing region. Manufactures cement and chemicals.

J

Jabalpur (Jubbulpore) India. Industrial town and important railway junction in Madhya Pradesh 240 km (150 miles) NNE of Nagpur. Pop. (1991) 764,600.

Manufactures cement, glass, textiles, vehicles, ammunition, cement and cast-iron products.

Jablonec (Ger. **Gablonz**) Czech Republic. Town in N Bohemia on the Nisa (Neisse) R. 88 km (55 miles) NE of Prague. Pop. (1984) 44,742.

Important centre of the glass industry. Also well known for imitation jewellery. Manufactures textiles.

Jachymov (Ger. **Joachimsthal**) Czech Republic. Town in W Bohemia in the Erzgebirge 19 km (12 miles) N of Karlovy Vary. Pop. (1985) 3500.

Important centre of pitchblende-mining, producing uranium, radium and other metals.

From 1516 it was noted for its silver mines and a silver coin struck here was known as the Joachimsthaler, the name being abbreviated to *thaler*, which was later modified to dollar.

Jackson (Michigan) USA. Industrial town and railway centre in the S on the Grand R. Pop. (1990) 37,450.

Manufactures motor-car and aircraft parts, clothing, lawn mowers. Railway engineering.

The Republican Party was founded here in 1854.

Jackson (Mississippi) USA. State cap., on the Pearl R. Pop. (1990) 196,637.

Chief industrial and commercial centre of the state. Manufactures glass, textiles and cottonseed oil.

Noteworthy buildings are the old Capitol (1839) and the Governor's mansion (1842). Named after Andrew Jackson, the 7th US President.

Jackson (Tennessee) USA. Town in the W on the S Fork of the Forked Deer R. Pop. (1990) 48,949.

Manufactures textiles, furniture and toys. Trade in timber, cotton and maize.

Jacksonville USA. One of the chief commercial towns on the S Atlantic coast on the St John's R. in NE Florida. Pop. (1990) 672,971.

Deep-water port. Exports timber and fruit. Boatbuilding, fishing and canning. Manufactures wood products, glassware, cigars and paper. A tourist resort.

Named after Andrew Jackson (1767–1845), the 7th US President.

Jadida, El (Mazagan) Morocco. Atlantic seaport 96 km (60 miles) WSW of Casablanca. Pop. (1982) 81,455.

Exports cereals, and eggs from the fertile Doukkala.

Founded (1502) by the Portuguese. It lost some of its importance with the development of Casablanca.

Jadotville ▶LIKASI.

Jaén Spain. 1. Province in Andalusia. Area 13,498 sq km (5210 sq. miles). Pop. (1991) 637,633. Mountainous, bounded by the Sierra Morena (N) and the Sierra de Segura (E). Drained by the Guadalquivir R. and its tributaries.

Occupations mining (chiefly lead) and agriculture, with large production of olive oil. Principal towns Jaén and Linares.

2. Capital of Jaén province 69 km (43 miles) NNW of Granada. Pop. (1991) 101,938.

Trade in olive oil. Manufactures chemicals, brandy and leather goods.

Renaissance cathedral (16th/18th-cent.). Liberated from the Moors by Ferdinand III of Castile 1246.

Jaffa Israel. Ancient Joppa. Port on the Mediterranean coast just S of Tel Aviv (with which it was incorporated in 1949), now largely superseded by Haifa; formerly exported the Jaffa oranges. Destroyed by Vespasian AD 68. Twice changed hands between Crusaders and Muslims in the 12th cent. Most of its predominantly Arab pop. left the town in 1948.

Jaffna Sri Lanka. 1. Peninsula at the N extremity of the island, separated from the rest of Sri Lanka by the Jaffna Lagoon and from India by Palk Strait. Intensively cultivated and densely populated, chiefly by Sri Lanka Tamils.

2. Town and minor port in the Northern province on the Jaffna peninsula and Jaffna Lagoon. Pop. (1990) 129,000.

Trade in small vessels, chiefly with S India.

Has a 17th-cent. Dutch fort. Tamil guerillas seek an independent Tamil state and in untroubled time this is a popular tourist resort.

Jagannath ►PURI.

Jagersfontein South Africa. Small diamond-mining town in Free State 105 km (65 miles) SW of Bloemfontein at a height of 1400 m (4592 ft). Pop. (1970) 4040. Two important diamonds, the 'Excelsior' (971 carats) and the 'Jubilee' (634 carats) were found in the mine which was opened in 1870.

Jaipur India. Cap. of Rajasthan and formerly of the princely state of Jaipu 240 km (150 miles) SW of Delhi. Pop. (1991) 1,458,200.

Trade in grain, wool and cotton. Manufactures carpets, blankets, metal goods, plastic tanks, gem products, pottery, dairy products, handicrafts and textile printing.

Jakarta (Djakarta) Indonesia. Formerly Batavia. Cap. of the republic on the coast of NW Java facing the Java Sea, its port at nearby Tanjungpriok. Pop. (1990) 8,222,500.

Exports rubber and tea. Railway engineering, tanning and sawmilling. Manufactures textiles and soap.

Has an old town (founded 1619), with a few Dutch colonial buildings still surviving and a modern residential area. Seat of the University of Indonesia (1947).

Jalgaon India. Town in Maharashtra 354 km (220 miles) W of Nagpur on the main road from Bombay and at the junction of railways from Bombay and Surat. Pop. (1991) 242,200.

It is in a cotton-growing district and the industries are related to cotton. It trades in grain, bananas and banana products.

Jalalabad Afghanistan. Cap. of Nangrahar province 120 km (75 miles) E of Kabul on the Kabul R. at a height of 600 m (1968 ft). Pop. (1985) 55,000.

Trading centre for an agricultural region producing dried fruits, grain and almonds.

Seat of Nangrahar University (1963). Defended for 5 months by British troops in the 1st Afghan War (1841–2).

Jalandhar India. City situated NNW of Delhi in Punjab. Pop. (1990) 509,500.

Industries inc. the manufacture of steel castings, steel ingots, rolled steel, engineering goods, textiles, electronics and chemicals.

Jalapa (Jalapa Enríquez) Mexico. Cap. of Veracruz state in the Sierra Madre Oriental 80 km (50 miles) NW of Veracruz at a height of 1427 m (4680 ft). Pop. (1990) 288,331.

Health resort in a picturesque setting, well-known for its flowers. Sugar-refining, flour-milling and coffee-roasting.

Gave its name to jalap, a drug formerly produced here from the roots of a climbing plant.

Jalisco Mexico. Maritime state in the W. Area 80,836 sq km (31,211 sq. miles). Pop. (1990) 5,302,689. Cap. Guadalajara. Mainly mountainous, crossed NW–SE by the Sierra Madre Occidental. Sugar-cane, cotton and tobacco are cultivated in the hot coastal regions, cereals and beans on the uplands. Mercury, gold, silver, lead, zinc and copper are mined. Industries inc. the manufacture of textiles, leather goods, chemicals, tobacco products, glass, pottery, cement and beverages. The L. Chapala area is a tourist attraction.

Jamaica. Republic and island in the Caribbean in the Greater Antilles situated 145 km (90 miles) S of Cuba. Area 10,991 sq km (4244 sq. miles). Pop. (1995) 2,520,000 (50 per cent urban). Life expectancy, 71 years male, 76 female. Cap. Kingston. Other towns, Spanish Town, Montego Bay and Portmore. Currency: Jamaica dollar = 100 cents. The third largest island in the Caribbean, it is predominantly mountainous; the main range running W–E across the island ends in the Blue Mountains, with the Blue Mountain Peak (2309 m; 7574 ft) the highest point. The climate is tropical along the coast (the temperature often exceeds 30°C (86°F) in the daytime, but falls considerably at night; humidity is high); the mountains are cooler. Rainfall varies widely from place to place. The island falls in the hurricane zone and these cause great damage; particularly severe ones occurred in 1944, 1979 and 1980. There were destructive earthquakes in 1692 and 1907. Land use: forested 17 per cent, meadows and pastures 18 per cent, agricultural and under permanent cultivation 25 per cent. About 75 per cent of the pop. is black, 13 per cent mixed-black and 1–2 per cent East Indian. Sixty per cent is Protestant of which the Church of God is the largest church. Rastafarians and Bahai followers are about 5 per cent.

The economy depends largely on agriculture. Principal crop sugar-cane, bananas taking second place; coffee, cacao, coconuts, citrus fruits and tobacco also important. A leading exporter of bauxite, some of which is processed into alumina; gypsum is also mined. Industrial output consists largely of products made from the crops, e.g. rum and molasses from sugar; copra, cigars and fruit juices also exported. It also manufactures textiles, foodstuffs and chemicals. The tourist industry is important and this is aided by the pleasant climate and attractive landscape. Growth has been threatened by internal disorders and a high crime rate.

Discovered in 1494 by Columbus, who named it St Jago, but the native Arawak name Xaymaca (anglicized to Jamaica) was adopted. Occupied by the Spaniards from 1509 to 1655, when it was captured by the English; formally ceded to England in 1670 at the Treaty of Madrid. Slavery was abolished in 1833 and the violence that followed culminated in the insurrection of 1865, after which representative government was suspended for 20 years. In 1944 self-government was introduced and in 1958 the West Indies Federation was established, but in 1962 Jamaica opted out and achieved complete independence.

Parliament consists of two chambers. There is a 21-member Senate consisting of 13 nominated by the Prime Minister and 8 on the advice of the Leader of the Opposition. The 60-member House of Representatives is elected by universal adult suffrage.

Jambi ➤TELANAIPURA.

James Bay Canada. S extension of Hudson Bay. Shallow, containing many islands, notably Akimiski. Discovered (1610) by Henry Hudson; named after Thomas James, who explored it.

James River USA. River in Virginia 547 km (340 miles) long, formed by the union of the Jackson and the Cowpasture rivers, flowing generally ESE past Richmond, the head of navigation, to Newport News on the estuary. Along its lower course is the region where the first permanent English settlement in the Western Hemisphere was established.

Jamestown (New York) USA. Industrial town on L. Chautauqua. Pop. (1990) 34,681 (predominantly of Swedish extraction).

Manufactures furniture, washing and milking machines, textiles, toys.

Named after James Prendergast, an early settler.

Jamestown (Virginia) USA. Ruined village on Jamestown Island (632 ha; 1561 acres) in the James R. Famous as the site of the first permanent English settlement in the New World, established 14 May 1607. Named after King James I. Incorporated in the Colonial National Historical Park 1936.

Jammu India. Cap. of Jammu province and winter cap. of the state of Jammu and Kashmir 153 km (95 miles) S of Srinagar on the Tavi R. Pop. (1990) 206,135. Terminus of a railway from Sialkot (Pakistan), now disused. The railway to Pathankot (Punjab) was opened in 1972, linking with the rest of the Indian rail system.

Manufactures rubber products, leather and pottery. Trade in grain and cotton.

Jammu and Kashmir India. State in the extreme NW; Kashmir has been disputed by India and Pakistan since partition in 1947. Area 222,236 sq km (85,783 sq. miles), but India only occupies about 50 per cent and is bounded in the N by a line of control separating areas claimed by both India and Pakistan; a further area is claimed by India but administered by China as part of the Xianjiang autonomous region. Pop. (1991) 7,718,700 (Indian side of the line). Caps Jammu (winter), Srinagar (summer). Mountainous, except for a narrow strip along the S edge of Jammu province.

About three-quarters of the pop. live by agriculture; cattle and sheep are raised, grains cultivated. The major crops are paddy, wheat, maize. The state is noted for its traditional handicrafts industry, which inc. carpets, shawl-making and wood-carving, also for its lakes, mountains and scenic beauty, making it an important tourist centre. The forests provide valuable timber.

Jamnagar India. Town in Gujarat on the Kathiawar peninsula. Pop. (1991) 350,500.

Trade in oilseeds, cotton, millet and vegetables. Manufactures textiles, leather, cement, metal goods, plastics, mineral products. An oil refinery was being planned in 1993.

Founded 1540.

Jamshedpur India. Industrial town in SE Bihar 225 km (140 miles) WNW of Calcutta. Pop. (1991) 479,000.

Has the country's chief iron and steel works, founded (1909) by the Tata family near the coal and iron fields of the Bihar-West Bengal region. This was responsible for the rapid growth of the former village and Jamshedpur now manufactures tinplate, steel wire, agricultural implements, automobiles, cable, steel tubes, wire ropes and springs. There is a copper smelter at Ghatsila nearby and the largest iron and steel plant in the private sector is located here.

Janesville USA. Commercial town in S Wisconsin on the Rock R. 93 km (58 miles) SW of Milwaukee. Pop. (1990) 52,133.

In a dairy-farming and tobacco-growing region. Manufactures cars, textiles and fountain pens.

Jan Mayen Norway. Island in the Arctic Ocean between Iceland and Spitsbergen, belonging to Norway. Area 380 sq km (147 sq. miles). Mountainous; the ice-covered dormant volcano Beerenberg, which rises to 2278 m (7472 ft), temporarily became active again in 1970. Named after one of its discoverers, the Dutch captain Jan May, who established a whaling station here (1614). The Norwegians have maintained a meteorological station on the island since 1921. Officially annexed to Norway 1929.

Japan. State of E Asia. A crescent-shaped archipelago off the E coast of Asia consisting of 4 main islands, Hokkaido, Honshu, Shikoku and Kyushu, and many smaller islands. In the N it is separated from Sakhalin by La Pérouse Strait and in the SW from Korea by the Korea Strait. Area 377,835 sq km (145,883 sq. miles). Pop. (1995) 125,362,000 (77 per cent urban). Life expectancy, 77 years male, 83 female. Cap. Tokyo. Other cities Yokohama, Osaka, Nagoya, Sapporo, Kobe, Kyoto, Fukuoka, Kawasaki, Hiroshima and Kitakyushu, each with a pop. over 1 million. Currency: Yen = 100 sen. Mountain ranges run through the 4 main islands, sending out lateral branches and rising at Mount Fujiyama on Honshu to 3776 m (12,388 ft); the latter, a sacred peak, is volcanic, like many others, inc. 77 which are classified as still active. Japan is subject to earthquakes, an average of 4 shocks daily being experienced in some parts of the country. The earthquakes are esp. prevalent along the Pacific seaboard, where the mountains shelve steeply down to the Japan Trench which reaches a depth of 9984 m (32,748 ft); some of the earthquakes have reached the magnitude of national disasters. This is an area where two plates of the earth's crust meet. Rivers are generally short, the longest being the Ishikari-gawa on Hokkaido (365 km; 227 miles), but they are extensively used for hydroelectric power development. The climate is dominated by the monsoons: the SE monsoon brings heavy summer rains, while the NW monsoon makes the winters relatively cold in the centre and N. Temperatures vary considerably from N to S, particularly in winter; rainfall is plentiful everywhere, and exceeds 200 cm (80 ins.) annually in many areas in the S. Typhoons occur in the late summer and autumn and are a great hazard to crops. Land use: forested 67 per cent, meadows and pastures 2 per cent, agricultural and under permanent cultivation 12 per cent. The Japanese give the appearance today of a homogeneous people, but stem from a mixture of Malay, Manchu and Korean stocks, the original inhabitants, the Ainu, having survived only in small numbers on Hokkaido. Shinto is the oldest religion and claims 109 million adherents, but there are about 96 million Buddhists and about 1,464,000 Christians.

All arable land is intensively cultivated; the Japanese fishing catch is the second largest in the world, but the outstanding feature of the country's economy is the high degree of industrialization; in manufacture of both iron and steel and textiles the Japanese have become one of the world's leading nations, and the recovery of their basic industries after the destruction of World War II has been remarkable. Agriculture is practised mainly in the coastal plains and valleys, though the hill slopes are terraced wherever practicable. Farming is based on the smallholding, the average area of which is barely 1 ha (2 acres); after World War II land hunger was appeased to some small extent by distributing over 2 million ha (4 million acres) from large estates to tenant farmers. Rice is the staple food crop, occupying more than half the cultivated area, and wheat, barley, sweet potatoes, sugar-beet, soya beans, apples and mandarins are important; mulberry trees are grown for the raising of silkworms. The forests are exploited and, in a country with little stock-rearing, a considerable quantity of fish is caught. Japan has few mineral resources and the economy is a thriving complex of industry, commerce, finance, agriculture and all the other elements of a modern economic structure. Japan is in an advanced stage of industrialization and one feature of the economy is the major contribution of manufacturing and services, such as transport, wholesale and retail commerce, and banking, to the country's wealth, in which such primary industries as agriculture and fisheries now have a minor share. Another feature is the relative importance of international trade in the economy. Despite the devastation of its manufacturing base during World War II, Japan has managed not only to rebuild its economy but to become one of the leading industrial nations in the world. Manufactures inc. vehicles, electrical equipment, television sets, radios, cameras, computers and automation equipment.

Little is known of early Japan until the 6th cent. AD, when Buddhism was introduced and Chinese culture was generally adopted. A feudal system developed, real power being held by rulers known as shoguns, the first to take this title being Yoritomo of the Minamoto family (1192). The first Europeans to make contact with Japan were the Portuguese (1542), followed by Spaniards, Dutch and English, but within a century only the Dutch were allowed to trade and no Japanese were permitted to leave the islands. For about two centuries Japan remained in isolation till in 1853 the United States insisted on opening up trade and the last shogun was compelled to abdicate (1867). Feudalism was abolished, executive power was restored to the Emperor and a parliament was established (1889). Modern industries were developed, trade expanded and a policy of aggression was pursued – through wars with China (1894–5) and Russia (1904–5), both of which brought territorial gains. Having supported the Allied cause in World War I, Japan received the German Pacific islands as mandates. Extreme nationalist elements gained control in Japan and the puppet state of Manchukuo was set up in Manchuria (1931); then the war with China was renewed (1937); Japan entered World War II by attacking Pearl Harbor (1941). Most of SE Asia was occupied by the Japanese but gradually lost, and surrender came after the dropping of atomic bombs on Hiroshima and Nagasaki (1945). A new and democratic constitution was put into effect in 1947 and Japan was admitted to the United Nations in 1956. The Bonin Is. and the Volcano Is. were restored to Japan in 1968, Okinawa in 1972.

Before World War II Japan was governed according to the constitution of 1889, modelled on that of Prussia, but the constitution of 1947 deprived the Emperor of his 'divine' attributes as well as all political power, abolished the peerage and extended the franchise to women. Legislative power rests with the 512-member House of Representatives, elected by all over the age of 20 years and the 254-member House of Councillors, and executive power with the Prime Minister and the Cabinet. For administrative purposes the country is divided into 8 regions and 47 prefectures: Hokkaido (Hokkaido); Tohoku (Aomori, Akita, Iwate, Yamagata, Miyagi, Fukushima); Kanto (Ibaraki, Tochigi, Gunma, Saitama, Tokyo, Chiba, Kanagawa); Chubu (Yamanashi, Nagano, Niigata, Toyama, Ishikawa, Fukui, Gifu, Aichi, Shizuoka); Kinki (Mie, Nara, Osaka, Wakayama, Shiga, Kyoto, Hyogo); Chugoku (Tottori, Okayama, Hiroshima, Shimane, Yamaguchi); Shikoku (Tokushima, Kagawa, Kochi, Ehime); Kyushu (Fukuoka, Saga, Nagasaki, Oita, Miyazaki, Kumamoto, Kagoshima, Okinawa).

Japan, Sea of. Arm of the Pacific Ocean between the islands of Japan and the mainland of Asia (Russia, Korea). Area 1,007,500 sq km (389,000 sq. miles). Maximum depth 3743 m (12,277 ft). Important fishing region.

Jarrow England. Industrial town in Tyne and Wear on the R. Tyne estuary 8 km (5 miles) E of Newcastle-upon-Tyne. Pop. (1991) 25,983.

There is a variety of light industries and it manufactures electrical and electronic components, food products, chemicals, windows and doors.

In 681 Benedict Biscop founded a monastery in which the Venerable Bede lived, worked and died. The town suffered severely from unemployment after World War I and was starting point of 'hunger marches' when the shipyards closed down, but they revived when they were reopened in World War II.

Jasper National Park Canada. The second largest of the country's scenic National Parks in W Alberta, bordering the Banff National Park. Area 10,878 sq km (4200 sq. miles). Noted for wild life, some of the highest peaks in the Canadian Rockies, waterfalls and glaciers inc. the famous Columbia icefield. Established 1907. Well provided with camping sites and other facilities. Jasper is the chief tourist centre.

Jassy ➤IAŞI.

Játiva (Játiba) Spain. Ancient Saetabis. Town in Valencia province 55 km (34 miles) SSW of Valencia. Pop. (1970) 21,578.

Produces brandy, leather and cement.

Home of several of the Borgia family in the 15th and 16th cent. Birthplace of Pope Alexander VI (1431–1503) and Ribera, the painter (1588–1652).

Jaunpur India. Town in Uttar Pradesh on the Gumti R. 56 km (35 miles) NW of Varanasi (Benares). Pop. (1990) 136,062.

Manufactures perfumes.

Noted for its ancient buildings, inc. the 15th-cent. Jama Masjid and other mosques, the 15th-cent. baths of Ibrahim Shah and the 16th-cent. bridge over the Gumti R.

Java Indonesia. The country's most productive and most populous island, also the most important politically and culturally; lies SE of Sumatra. Area (with Madura) 134,045 sq km (51,740 sq. miles). Pop. (1989) 107,513,798. The narrow island is traversed by a volcanic mountain chain inc. Semeru 3675 m (12,057 ft) and 112 volcanoes, inc. the constantly steaming Mt Bromo; the coastal plain is wider in the N than the S, and the numerous rivers are short. Its climate is equatorial, the mean monthly temperatures at Jakarta, e.g., varying only between 25° and 27°C (77° and 80°F) but the heat is much reduced by altitude. The N coast receives its rain mainly from the NW monsoon (Dec.–Mar.), the S coast from the SE monsoon (April–Oct.); the humidity is high, thunderstorms are frequent and the annual rainfall is moderate to heavy. There is a rich tropical vegetation, though much of the forest on the plains and lower mountain slopes has been cleared for cultivation; teak is one of the most valuable timbers and forest exploitation is carefully controlled to prevent soil erosion and flooding.

Rice is the principal food crop and maize, cassava, sweet potatoes and coconuts are also grown on smallholdings; rubber, coffee, tea, sugar-cane and cinchona (quinine) are chiefly plantation crops. Despite the fact that a great part of its surface is mountainous, Java is one of the most densely populated agricultural regions in the world. The difficulty of producing sufficient food for the rapidly increasing pop., in fact, has led to the settlement of tens of thousands of Javanese elsewhere in Indonesia in recent years. Oil is produced in N central Java near Rembang. Jakarta, the national cap., Surabaya and Semarang, all on the N coast, are the chief seaports and Bandung and Jogjakarta are important inland towns.

Java Sea. Section of the Pacific Ocean between Borneo (N) and Java (S), connnected with the Celebes Sea by the Strait of Macassar, with the Indian Ocean by Sunda Strait and with the South China Sea by Karimata Strait. Area about 310,800 sq km (120,000 sq. miles). Scene of a Japanese naval victory in World War II (1942).

Jebel Aulia Sudan. Village on the White Nile 45 km (28 miles) S of Khartoum near a hill of the same name. Site of a storage dam (completed 1937) which makes possible the irrigation of 200,000 ha (400,000 acres) of the Nile valley.

Jedburgh Scotland. Royal burgh on the Jed Water, tributary of the R. Tweed, 66 km (41 miles) SE of Edinburgh in Scottish Borders. Pop. (1991) 4118.

Manufactures tweeds, woollen and rayon goods.

Remains of a 12th-cent. Augustinian abbey. Became notorious (somewhat unjustly) for 'Jeddart [Jedburgh] justice', by which a prisoner was hanged first and tried later.

Jedda ►JIDDA.

Jefferson City USA. State cap. of Missouri on the Missouri R. 219 km (136 miles) ESE of Kansas City. Pop. (1990) 35,480.

Manufactures electrical goods, shoes and clothing. Printing.

Seat of Lincoln University, founded (1866) for Negroes by two regiments of Negro infantry.

Jelenia Góra (Ger. **Hirschberg**) Poland. Cap. of the Jelenia Góra voivodeship on the Bobrawa R. 96 km (60 miles) WSW of Wroclaw. Pop. (1970) 55,700.

Manufactures textiles, paper, machinery and glass.

Returned to Poland from Germany after World War II.

Jelgava (Yelgava, Mitau) Latvia. Industrial town 48 km (30 miles) SW of Riga. Pop. (1991) 74,500.

Manufactures linen and woollen goods, rope, bricks and tiles, and soap. Sugar-refining.

Founded in the 13th cent. Became cap. of Kurland (Courland) 1561. Later passed to Russia (1795).

Jena Germany. Town in the Gera district

37 km (23 miles) WNW of Gera on the Saale R. Pop. (1990) 102,700. Home of the famous Zeiss optical and precision instrument factories, founded in 1846 and partly removed by the Russians after World War II.

Also manufactures machinery, chemicals and pharmaceuticals.

Seat of a university (1558) at which Hegel and Schiller taught. Napoleon defeated the Prussians on the N outskirts of the city in 1806.

Jenolan Caves Australia. Series of limestone caves in New South Wales 115 km (72 miles) W of Sydney in the Blue Mountains. A tourist attraction, with magnificent stalactites and stalagmites and a natural tunnel 90 m (295 ft) high. Made national property 1866.

Jerada Morocco. Town situated SSW of Oujda, an important coalmining centre, esp. for anthracite.

Jerba ►DJERBA.

Jerez de la Frontera (Jerez) Spain. Town in Cádiz province, Andalusia 24 km (15 miles) NE of Cádiz. Pop. (1991) 182,939.

In a fertile agricultural region producing vines, cereals and olives. A world-famous centre of the wine industry, having given its name to sherry. Also manufactures bottles and casks.

A picturesque town of white buildings, with many *bodegas* (wine-lodges) where the sherry is made and stored, and many fine churches. Taken by the Moors 711; recaptured by Alphonso X of Castile 1264.

Jericho Israel-occupied W bank of Jordan. Oasis town in the Jordan valley 24 km (15 miles) ENE of Jerusalem at 251 m (825 ft) below sea level and 11 km (7 miles) from the N end of the Dead Sea. The first Canaanite city to be captured by the Israelites; later destroyed and rebuilt several times, as recent excavations have shown. Herod the Great made it his winter residence and died here.

Jersey Channel Islands. Largest of the islands situated 24 km (15 miles) W of the French coast. Area 117 sq km (45 sq. miles). Pop. (1991) 84,082. Cap. St Helier (S coast). The island has a southward slope, with some fine cliff scenery in the N and a mild climate, and has become very popular with holidaymakers. The original home of Jersey cattle and woollen 'jerseys'; the knitting of the latter is no longer important. French and English are official lang.

Exports early potatoes and tomatoes, and flowers. Light industry inc. the manufacture of electrical goods, textiles and clothing.

Jersey City USA. Industrial town in New Jersey on the peninsula between the Hackensack and the Hudson rivers opposite Manhattan, with which it is connected by ferry, tunnel and subway. Pop. (1990) 228,537.

Meat-packing, oil-refining. Manufactures foundry and paper products, metal goods, ink, chemicals and cigarettes.

Jerusalem Israel. Ancient city in central Palestine in hill country at a height of 750 m (2460 ft); formerly cap. of the British mandated territory of Palestine, but since 1948 divided into the new city (Israel) and the old city (Jordan). Pop. (1991) 535,000. Holy to both Jews and Christians; contains several Muslim shrines. Most of the sacred places of the three religions are in the old city, which is enclosed by walls built in the 16th cent. by Selim I and contains the 7th-cent. Mosque of Omar (on the site of Solomon's temple) near which is the Wailing Wall, sacred to the Jews. Other places of religious interest are the Church of the Holy Sepulchre, around which are monasteries and chapels of various Christian denominations, the Garden of Gethsemane and the Mt of Olives. In the new city (W), built mainly since the mid 19th cent., are the 14th-cent. citadel, the former buildings of the Israeli parliament, the Archaeological Museum and many churches and synagogues. Here, too, are the city's modern industries, which inc. printing, metalworking and the manufacture of pharmaceutical and food products and leather goods.

The history of Jerusalem probably extends through more than 4000 years; David made it his cap., Solomon developed it and built the Temple. In 586 BC it was taken by Nebuchadnezzar and many of its inhabitants were deported to Babylon, but its walls were rebuilt by Nehemiah (*c.* 444 BC). It was again captured by Alexander the Great (332 BC), by Ptolemy I of Egypt (320 BC) and by Antiochus Epiphanes (168 BC), who destroyed the city and the Temple. Under Herod the Great the Temple was rebuilt, the fortifications restored and a new city was created, only to be destroyed yet again by Titus in AD 70; sixty years later Hadrian established the city of Aelia Capitolina on the site, with a temple to Jupiter in the place of the earlier Jewish Temple. In the 4th cent. under Constantine the Church of the Holy Sepulchre was built where the present church stands, but in the 7th cent. the Muslims took Jerusalem, made it one of their most sacred cities after Mecca and erected the Mosque of Omar. Apart from the period after its capture by the Crusaders (1099–1187), the city remained almost continuously in Muslim hands, from 1517 under the Turks, until taken by the British in 1917. After the partition of Palestine the new city was made cap. of Israel (1950), but this has not been accepted by international law. The new building of the Knesset (the Israeli Legislative Assembly) was inaugurated in 1966. After the Israeli–Arab war (1967), the entire city was occupied by Israeli forces.

Jervis Bay Australia. Inlet on the coast of New South Wales with two small peninsulas to the N and S of the entrance. Part of the S peninsula and harbour was transferred to the Commonwealth as an outlet port (1915) 137 km (85 miles) ENE of the Australian Capital Territory (►CANBERRA); area 73 sq km (28 sq. miles).

Jesselton ►KOTA KINABALU.

Jessore Bangladesh. Chief town of Jessore district situated 20 km (12 miles) from the Indian border. Pop. (1991) 160,198.

It trades in rice, jute, tamarind, tobacco and sugar-cane. It has rice and linseed mills and manufactures plastics.

Jethou ►CHANNEL ISLANDS; GUERNSEY.

Jewish Republic Russia. Part of the Khabarovsk Territory bordered (S) across the Amur R. by Heilongjiang (China). Area 36,000 sq km (13,895 sq. miles). Pop. (1991) 220,000 (84 per cent Russians). Cap. Birobijan.

Agriculture (cereals, soya beans) is important. Also some lumbering and mining.

Established as a Jewish National District 1928. Became an Autonomous Region 1934, declaring itself an Autonomous Republic in 1991.

Jhang-Maghiana Pakistan. Town 193 km (120 miles) WSW of Lahore. Pop. (1981) 195,558.

Manufactures textiles, pottery, leather and metal goods. Trade in cereals and wool.

Jhansi India. Market town and railway junction in Uttar Pradesh 209 km (130 miles) SW of Kanpur. Pop. (1991) 313,500.

Trade in grain, oilseeds. Manufactures brassware and Ayurvedic medicines.

Founded in the 17th cent.

Jhelum Pakistan. Town on the Jhelum R. 166 km (109 miles) NNW of Lahore. Pop. (1981) 106,462.

Trade in timber. Manufactures textiles.

Jhelum River. The most westerly of the 5 rivers of the Punjab 720 km (450 miles) long, rising in Kashmir and flowing first NW past Srinagar, then W and generally SSW across the plains of the Punjab to join the Chenab R. Much used for irrigation. Near its banks Alexander the Great defeated Porus (326 BC). The Mangla Dam (Pakistan), the world's largest earth-filled dam, built to store water for hydroelectric power and irrigation, was inaugurated 1967.

Jiangsu (Kiangsu) China. Maritime province in the E. Area 102,600 sq km (39,600 sq. miles). Pop. (1990) 67,056,519. Cap. Nanjing. Consists mainly of a flat alluvial plain which inc. the Yangtse delta and is crossed N–S by the Grand Canal, linking the Kaoyu and Tai lakes.

Rice, cotton and mulberry trees, for silk production, are grown. Several large cities: Shanghai, Nanjing, Wusih and Chinkiang.

Jiangxi (Kiangsi)

Jiangxi (Kiangsi) China. Province in the S situated on the Gan Jiang R. Area 164,800 sq km (63,600 sq. miles). Pop. (1990) 37,710,281. Cap. Nanchang. Mountainous in the S, it consists essentially of the basin of the Kan R., which flows NNE to the extensive Poyang L.

It is a leading rice producer and cotton, tea and tobacco are grown. Coal and tungsten are important minerals. Principal towns Nanchang and Kiukiang.

Jibuti ➤DJIBOUTI.

Jidda (Jiddah, Jedda) Saudi Arabia. Chief seaport of Hejaz on the Red Sea 70 km (44 miles) W of Mecca. Pop. (1988) 1,400,000. Principal port of entry for pilgrims to Mecca, said to exceed 100,000 annually, and connected by a good motor road with the city.

Also imports manufactured goods for Saudi Arabia. Walled town with a large *souk* (bazaar).

Jihlava Czech Republic. Town in W Moravia on the Jihlava R. 80 km (50 miles) WNW of Brno. Pop. (1984) 52,828.

Once important for silver-mining, now an industrial and commercial centre. Manufactures textiles, leather goods and furniture. Trade in cereals and timber.

Jilin (Chilin) China. 1. Province in E central Manchuria (NE). Area 187,000 sq km (72,200 sq. miles). Pop. (1990) 24,658,721. Cap. Changchun. Mountainous in the SE, where it borders on Korea and the USSR. In the NW it forms part of the Manchurian plain.

Wheat, millet, and soya beans grown on the plains. Timber and coal and other minerals are obtained from the highlands. Chief towns Changchun and Jilin.

2. Town and river port in Jilin province on the Sungari R. 96 km (60 miles) E of Changchun. Pop. (1991) 1,036,858.

Sawmilling. Manufactures chemicals, paper, matches and cement, power being derived from the hydroelectric plant at Fengman. Trade in timber, grain and tobacco.

Founded 1673. Developed industrially with the advent of the railway from Changchun (1912).

Jinan (Chinan) China. Cap. of Shandong province just S of the Hwang-ho and 362 km (225 miles) S of Beijing. Pop. (1991) 1,480,915.

It is a railway junction and industrial centre. Industries inc. railway engineering, flour-milling and food-processing. It manufactures machinery, textiles, paper and cement.

Ancient city, probably inhabited for over 3000 years. Opened to foreign trade in 1904. Occupied by the Japanese 1937–45.

Jinja Uganda. Lake port on the N shore of L. Victoria at the outlet of the Victoria Nile near the Owen Falls and dam. Pop. (1991) 60,979. Linked by rail with Kampala (72 km; 45 miles NE). Has expanded rapidly owing to industrial development resulting from the Owen Falls hydroelectric scheme (opened 1954).

Copper-smelting, sugar-refining and brewing. Manufactures textiles, tobacco products and engineering products.

Jinotepe Nicaragua. Town situated SSE of Managua on the Inter-American Highway. Cap. of Carazo Department. Pop. (1985) 23,538.

Trading centre of an agricultural area. Industries inc. processing coffee, rice, sugarcane, salt, limestone and timber.

Jinzhou (Chinchou/Chinchow) China. Industrial town in Liaoning province 217 km (135 miles) WSW of Shenyang on the railway to Beijing. Pop. (1991) 569,518.

Manufactures chemicals, synthetic fuels, textiles, paper and food products. It was developed by the Japanese in the 1930s.

Joachimsthal ➤JACHYMOV.

João Pessôa Brazil. Formerly Paraíba. Cap. of Paraíba state 18 km (11 miles) above the mouth of the Paraíba R. (NE). Pop. (1991) 497,214.

Exports (through its outport Cabedelo) sugar, cotton. Manufactures plastics, paper and textiles.

Renamed (1930) in honour of a patriot killed in the Vargas revolution.

Jodhpur India. Commercial town and railway junction in Rajasthan 282 km (175 miles) WSW of Jaipur. Pop. (1991) 666,300. Formerly cap. of the princely state of Jodhpur.

Trade in cotton, wool, hides. Manufactures textiles, tools, cutlery, engineering products, cement, rotary kiln products, transformers and furniture.

Dominated by a red sandstone fort containing the handsome Maharajah's palace. University (1962). Gave its name to a type of riding breeches, introduced into Britain in the late 19th cent. Founded in the mid 15th cent.

Joensuu Finland. Town situated ESE of Kuopio on a lake in the Saimaa R. system. Pop. (1990) 47,100.

Railway junction and lake port handling most of the trade of N Karelia, esp. timber. Lumbering and sawmilling are the main industries.

Jogjakarta (Yogyakarta) Indonesia. Town near the S coast of Java 274 km (170 miles) WSW of Surabaya. Pop. (1992) 398,727. In an intensively cultivated region producing rice, sugar-cane, rubber and tobacco.

Manufactures textiles, tobacco products and leather; also famous for batik work.

Seat of the Gadjah Mada University (1949) and the State Institute of Islam (1960). Provisional cap. of Indonesia 1945–50.

Johannesburg South Africa. Largest city in the republic, in Gauteng province on the Witwatersrand 1290 km (800 miles) NE of Cape Town at a height of 1750 m (5740 ft). Pop. (1991) 1,916,063.

Centre of the world's richest goldmining area. A conurbation of large mining towns stretches from Krugersdorp (W) to Springs (E). Mainly modern; many skyscrapers and notable buildings, e.g. City Hall, Municipal Art Gallery, Public Library, South African Institute of Medical Research. Anglican and Roman Catholic cathedrals. Seat of the University of Witwatersrand (1922), formerly the School of Mines and Technology (1903).

Engineering, diamond-cutting. Manufactures textiles, foodstuffs, furniture. Important rail, road and air transport centre.

Founded (1886) after the discovery of gold and then grew rapidly and became South Africa's chief commercial and industrial centre.

Johnson City. Town in Tennessee 137 km (85 miles) ENE of Knoxville. Pop. (1970) 35,199.

Manufactures hardwood flooring, textiles and plastics.

Johnstone Scotland. Town in Renfrewshire 5 km (3 miles) WSW of Paisley. Pop. (1991) 18,635.

Industrial centre. Manufactures machine-tools and textiles.

Johnstown USA. Industrial town in Pennsylvania at the confluence of the Conemaugh R. and Stony Creek 85 km (53 miles) E of Pittsburgh. Pop. (1984) 33,100.

Manufactures machinery, iron and steel goods and chemicals. There is coalmining in the neighbourhood.

Johor Malaysia. The most southerly state of Peninsular Malaysia (Malaya), separated from Singapore island by the narrow Johor Strait. Area 18,986 sq km (7331 sq. miles). Pop. (1990) 2,106,500. Cap. Johor Baharu. Generally low-lying and forest-covered.

Produces rubber, copra, pineapples, iron ore and bauxite.

First came under British protection in 1885.

Johor Baharu Malaysia. Cap. of Johor state (West Malaysia): port on Johor Strait, linked with Singapore by causeway (road and rail). Pop. (1980) 246,395. Textile industry.

Joinville (Jonville) Brazil. Industrial town in Santa Catarina state (SE). Pop. (1991) 346,095.

Brewing, maté-processing. Manufactures textiles, plastics and furniture. Exports (through its port, São Francisco do Sul) timber, maté tea.

Founded by German settlers in the mid 19th cent.

Joliet USA. Railway centre and industrial town in NE Illinois on the Des Plaines R. Pop. (1990) 76,836.

Manufactures machinery, chemicals and paper. Railway engineering, oil-refining. Bituminous coalmines and limestone quarries in the neighbourhood.

Named after Louis Joliet, a French-Canadian explorer.

Jonesboro USA. Town situated NW of Memphis (Tennessee) in Arkansas. Pop. (1990) 41,248.

Distribution centre for a farming area. Industries inc. printing, rice-milling, and manufactures flour, footwear, electric motors, agricultural machinery.

Jönköping Sweden. Cap. of Jönköping county at the S end of L. Vätter. Pop. (1992) 112,277.

Industrial town; the chief centre of Swedish match manufacture. Also manufactures paper, textiles, machinery and footwear.

Jonquière Canada. Town in Quebec 14 km (9 miles) W of Chicoutimi. Pop. (1989) 58,467.

Industries inc. aluminium and timber, and it manufactures pulp, food products, furniture, metal products and paper.

Named after the Marquis de la Jonquière.

Joplin USA. Industrial town in SW Missouri 225 km (140 miles) S of Kansas City. Pop. (1990) 41,000.

Industries inc. health services, truck haulage and the manufacture of power units, chemicals, explosives, food products, pet foods and batteries.

Joppa ➤JAFFA.

Jordan. Independent kingdom of SW Asia, bounded by Syria in the N, Iraq in the NE, Saudi Arabia in the E and S, and Israel and the 'West Bank' in the W. Area 88,946 sq km (34,342 sq. miles). Pop. (1995) 4,187,000 (72 per cent urban). Life expectancy, 70 years

male, 73 female. Cap. Amman. Other towns Zarqa, Irbid and Balqa. Currency: Jordan dinar = 1000 fils. To the W of the country the deep Jordan valley, El Ghor, leads S to the Dead Sea, 392 m (1286 ft) below sea level and then via the Wadi Araba to the Gulf of Aqaba, where Jordan has its only port, Aqaba: the entire depression forms part of the Great Rift Valley which extends into E Africa. To the E of the Jordan valley the country becomes a barren plateau which merges with the Syrian Desert. It has a predominantly Mediterranean climate but in hilly parts the summers are cooler and the winters colder. Land use: forested 0.8 per cent, meadow and pastures 9 per cent, agricultural and under permanent cultivation 5 per cent. The majority of the people are Sunni Muslims but there are several thousand Christians. Arabic is the lang., but English is understood.

Wheat and barley are grown and vines in the extreme N, and there is usually a surplus of fruit and vegetables for export, while numbers of sheep and goats are raised. Chief mineral resources phosphates and potash from the Dead Sea; phosphates are an important export. Manufactures account for 14.8 per cent of National income, and industries inc. petroleum production, light manufacturing, fertilizers and chemicals.

Part of the Ottoman Empire from the 16th cent. In 1923 Transjordan became a semi-independent emirate under Abdullah ibn Hussein whilst remaining a British mandated territory. In 1946, after supporting the Allies in World War II, the mandate was terminated and Abdullah took the title of King of the Hashemite Kingdom of Jordan. In 1950, after its troops had occupied much of E central Palestine, designated by the UN as Arab territory, that area was formally annexed; lying W of the Jordan, it has since been known as W Jordan, the former emirate being E Jordan. Suffered complete military defeat by Israel in the short Arab–Israeli war of June 1967; after the war all Jordanian territory W of the Jordan R. was occupied by Israeli forces. An acute political problem was the presence in Jordan of Palestinian guerrillas, whose militancy led to a brief civil war in 1970. In 1988 Jordan abandoned its efforts to administer the Israeli-occupied West Bank and surrendered its claims to the Palestine Liberation Organization.

For administrative purposes Jordan is divided into 8 governorates. It is a constitutional monarchy and the legislature consists of an 80-member lower house elected by male suffrage and a 30-member Senate nominated by the King.

Jordan River. Principal and only perennial river of Israel and Jordan, about 320 km (200 miles) long, rising in several headstreams in Syria and Lebanon and flowing through the marshy L. Hula to the Sea of Galilee (L. Tiberias). It then meanders S through the depression known as El Ghor to the Dead Sea 392 m (1286 ft) below sea level, both lying in a great rift valley. It thus descends about 900 m (2952 ft) in its short course and is unnavigable; in its lower reaches it is muddy and foul. Hydroelectric power station at Naharayim. It forms part of the Israel–Jordan and Israel–Syria borders. The main crossing point is the Allenby Bridge on the Jerusalem–Amman road (Jordan).

Jos Nigeria. Town on the Bauchi (Jos) Plateau at a height of 1250 m (4100 ft) 233 km (145 miles) SSE of Kano. Pop. (1992) 185,600.

Industries inc. tourism, food products, chemicals, textiles, tin, bricks and brewing. Linked by rail with the main line from Port Harcourt to Kaduna.

Jostedalsbreen Norway. Largest snowfield on the mainland of Europe about 880 sq km (340 sq. miles) in area W of the Jotunheim Mountains, rising to 2084 m (6835 ft). Many glaciers descend from it into neighbouring valleys. At the E foot is the village of Jostedal.

Jotunheimen (Jotunheim Mountains) Norway. In Norwegian, 'Home of the Giants'. Highest mountain range in Scandinavia, between Jostedalsbreen and Gudbrandsdal, the loftiest peaks being Galdhöpiggen (2474 m; 8115 ft) and Glittertind (2454 m; 8049 ft).

Juan de Fuca Strait Canada/USA. Channel 130 km (80 miles) long and 24 km (15 miles) wide, separating Vancouver Island (Canada) from the state of Washington (USA). Named after a Greek sailor, Apostolos Valerianos, reputed to have discovered it (1592) while serving Spain as Juan de Fuca. Rediscovered by Capt. Charles Barkley 1787.

Juan Fernández Islands S Pacific Ocean. Group of 3 volcanic islands belonging to Chile 640 km (400 miles) W of Valparaiso. The largest is Más-a-Tierra (in Spanish, 'Nearer Land'; area 93 sq km (36 sq. miles); pop. about 500; main occupation lobster-fishing). Más-a-Fuera ('Farther Out') is 160 km (100 miles) W; it is well-wooded. The Santa Clara islet lies SW of Más-a-Tierra. Alexander Selkirk's stay on Más-a-Tierra (1704–9) is supposed to have inspired Defoe's *Robinson Crusoe*.

Juan-les-Pins France. Fashionable resort in the Alpes-Maritimes department on the French Riviera just SSW of Antibes, of which it forms part.

Jubaland Somalia. Former province of Kenya; ceded to Italy in 1925, incorporated into Italian Somaliland in 1926. Semi-arid except for the fertile Juba valley. Main occupation cattle and camel rearing.

Juba River Somalia. River over 1600 km (1000 miles) long formed by the union of the Ganale and the Dawa rivers, rising in the Ethiopian Highlands, leaving Ethiopia near Dolo, flowing S across Somalia and entering the Indian Ocean 16 km (10 miles) NE of Kismayu. Navigable for dhows as far upstream as Bardera. Cotton, maize and rice cultivated in the valley.

Júcar River Spain. River 505 km (314 miles) long in the E, rising in the Montes Universales, flowing S past Cuenca and then turning E to enter the Mediterranean at Cullera. Used for irrigation and hydroelectric power.

Judea Israel and Israel-occupied West Bank of Jordan. S part of ancient Palestine. Mount

Hebron rises to 1013 m (3323 ft) situated 30 km (19 miles) SW of Jerusalem.

Juiz de Fora Brazil. Industrial town in Minas Gerais on the Rio de Janeiro—Belo Horizonte road and railway, and on the Paraibuna R. Pop. (1990) 383,200.

Manufactures textiles, esp. knitted goods. Other industries inc. steel, sugar-refining and brewing. Trade in coffee and tobacco.

Jujuy Argentina. Cap. of Jujuy province in the NW at a height of 1260 m (4133 ft) on the Río Grande de Jujuy. Pop. (1991) 180,102.

Industries inc. flour-milling, sawmilling, and there is mining of copper, iron, tin, lead and zinc. Trade in wheat, maize and livestock.

Founded 1593.

Julian Alps Slovenia. Mountain range extending into NE Italy and rising to 2866 m (9396 ft) at Triglav.

Jumet Belgium. Town in Hainaut province 5 km (3 miles) N of Charleroi. Pop. (1974) 28,062.

Coalmining. Manufactures glass.

Jumna (Jumuna, Yamuna) River India. Chief tributary of the Ganges R., 1384 km (860 miles) long, rising in the Himalayas in the Tehri-Garhwal district (Uttar Pradesh) and flowing generally SW and then S along the Punjab—Uttar Pradesh border, past Delhi, turning SE past Agra and Etawah to join the Ganges just below Allahabad. It feeds the E and W Jumna Canals, which irrigate large areas, near the point where it leaves the Siwalik Hills for the plains.

Junagadh (Junagarh) India. Town in Gujarat 93 km (58 miles) SSW of Rajkot. Pop. (1990) 151,207.

Trade in cotton, millet and sugar-cane. Manufactures pharmaceutical products, metal goods.

Was cap. of the former princely state of Junagadh.

Jundiaí Brazil. Industrial town in São Paulo state 53 km (33 miles) NW of São Paulo. Pop. (1988) 210,000.

Manufactures cotton goods, steel, matches and pottery. Trade in grapes, coffee and grain.

Juneau USA. State cap. of Alaska in the SE on the Gastineau Channel. Pop. (1990) 26,751. An ice-free port.

Salmon-canning and sawmilling.

Founded (1880) after the discovery of gold in the district. Named after Joe Juneau, who helped to start the gold rush.

Jungfrau Switzerland. Mountain (4164 m; 13,658 ft) in the Bernese Oberland 18 km (11 miles) SSE of Interlaken. First ascended (1811) by the Meyer brothers. A rack railway, the highest in Europe, was built (1896–1912) from Kleine Scheidegg to the Jungfraujoch, the col between the Jungfrau and the Mönch, whence there are magnificent views.

Junín Argentina. Market town and railway junction 233 km (145 miles) W of Buenos Aires. Pop. (1990) 60,000.

Trade in grain and cattle. Railway engineering. Manufactures pottery and furniture.

Jura France. Department in the E in Franche-Comté, bordered on the E by Switzerland. Area 5008 sq km (1934 sq. miles). Pop. (1990) 248,760. Prefecture Lons-le-Saunier. Largely occupied by the Jura (Mountains) and drained by the Doubs and Ain rivers, it is an agricultural department; cereals grown (W); wines and cheeses (Gruyère) produced. Chief towns Lons-le-Saunier, Dôle.

Jura France/Switzerland. System of parallel mountain ranges about 240 km (150 miles) long and 64 km (40 miles) wide along the Franco—Swiss border on average 600–750 m (1968–2460 ft) in height but rising to 1724 m (5655 ft) in Crêt de la Neige and 1721 m (5645 ft) in Reculet. Extends through the French departments of Dura, Doubs and Ain and the Swiss cantons of Basel, Solothurn, Neuchâtel and Vaud, and continues NE beyond the Rhine R. as the Swabian Jura and the Franconian Jura. Belonging geologically to the Alpine system, the limestone formations of the Jura gave the Jurassic period its name. The Doubs and Ain rivers rise here, draining longitudinal valleys on the French side and there are many transverse gorges (*cluses*); the waterfalls, limestone caves and forested slopes attract many tourists. An important region for the manufacture of watches and clocks, esp. at La Chaux-de-fonds and Le Locle, both in Switzerland.

Jura Scotland. Island in Argyll and Bute in the Inner Hebrides, separated from the mainland by the Sound of Jura. Area 381 sq km (147 sq. miles). Pop. (1991) 196. Crossed by a range of hills rising to 784 m (2572 ft) in the Paps of Jura. Main occupations fishing and crofting. Off the N coast, between Jura and Scarba, is the whirlpool of Corrievreckan.

Jura Switzerland. Canton created 1979 from part of the canton of Bern. Area 836 sq km (323 sq. miles). Cap. Delémont. Pop. (1996) 69,188.

Juruá River Brazil/Peru. River 1900 km (1200 miles) long, rising in E Peru near the Brazil frontier, flowing generally NE through dense forests and joining the Amazon (Solimões) below Fonte Boa.

Jutland (Danish **Jylland**). Peninsula of N Europe bounded by the Skagerrak (N), the Kattegat and Little Belt (E) and the North Sea (W), comprising the continental part of Denmark and most of the German *Land* of Schleswig-Holstein; at the N end separated by Lim Fiord from Mors, Vendsyssel and Thy islands. Area (Danish Jutland) 29,526 sq km (11,400 sq. miles). The peninsula is low-lying, rising to only 172 m (564 ft), with sand dunes on the W coast and fiords on the E coast. Principal occupation dairy-farming, esp. in the more fertile E half. The biggest naval engagement of World War I, the Battle of Jutland, was fought off NW Jutland (1916).

Jyväskylä Finland. Town in the Vaasa province near the N end of L. Päijänne 130 km (80 miles) NNE of Tampere. Pop. (1991) 67,026.

Railway junction. Centre of a wood-pulp, paper and plywood industry, and it also manufactures matches and margarine.

K

K2 (Chubrum) India. World's second highest peak (8611 m; 28,250 ft) in the Karakoram range in N Kashmir; it was originally named after Lt-Col. Godwin-Austen of the Survey of India. Discovered in 1856 and first climbed by two members of an Italian expedition in 1954.

Kabardino–Balkar Russia. Autonomous Republic on the N slopes of the Caucasus. Area 12,500 sq km (4825 sq. miles). Pop. (1992) 784,000. Cap. Nalchik. Contains Mt Elbruz (5642 m; 18,510 ft), the highest peak in the Caucasus and in Europe. Cereals cultivated. Cattle and horses raised. Important molybdenum and tungsten mining at Tyrny Auz.

Kabinda ►CABINDA.

Kabul Afghanistan. Cap. and largest city of Afghanistan and of Kabul province on the Kabul R. 225 km (140 miles) WNW of Peshawar (Pakistan), with which it is linked through the Khyber Pass. Pop. (1993) 700,000. In a valley at a height of 1800 m (5904 ft) just below the Kabul R. gorge.

The commercial and cultural centre of Afghanistan. Manufactures textiles, leather, footwear, matches, furniture and vehicle components.

Just W of the city is the tomb of Baber, who made it the cap. of the Mogul Empire (1504). Long of strategic importance; the major invasions of India by Alexander the Great, Genghis Khan, Baber and others passed through it.

Kabul River Afghanistan. River 507 km (315 miles) long, rising in the Paghman Mountains W of Kabul and flowing generally E to join the Indus R. near Attock (Pakistan). With its tributaries it waters Kabul province. Hydroelectric plant at Sarobi.

Kabwe Zambia. Formerly Broken Hill. Administrative headquarters of the Central Province 113 km (70 miles) N of Lusaka on the railway. Pop. (1990) 166,519.

The oldest mining town in Zambia producing lead, zinc and vanadium. Supplied with power from the Mulungushi and Lunsemfwa hydroelectric stations.

A skull of prehistoric man, *Homo rhodesiensis*, was discovered here 1921.

Kabylia Algeria. Highland coastal region between Algiers and Annaba (Bône). Divided into two areas, Great Kabylia (W) and Little Kabylia (E). Produces olives, figs, wheat, wine and cork. The Kabyles are a Berber people, who long resisted the French; though Muslim, they are monogamous and the women are unveiled. Poverty is widespread and male emigration has been considerable, chiefly to Algerian and French towns.

Kadiyevka Ukraine. Town in the Donets basin 45 km (28 miles) W of Lugansk. Pop. (1990) 112,300.

A major coalmining centre. Metallurgical and chemical industries.

Kadoma (Gatooma) Zimbabwe. Town situated SW of Harare in a farming and cotton-growing area. Pop. (1992) 45,000.

Industries inc. nickel-refining, cotton-milling, processing agricultural products; manufactures glass, paper, bricks, timber products. There is a cotton research station.

Kaduna Nigeria. Town in central Nigeria 72 km (45 miles) SSW of Zaria. Pop. (1993) 317,400.

Railway junction. Manufactures cotton goods, furniture, footwear, ammunition and bicycles. Trade in cotton and grain.

Kaesong North Korea. Town 48 km (30

miles) NW of Seoul, near the South Korean border. Pop. (1988) 120,000.

Famous for its porcelain. Trade in ginseng.

Cap. of Korea in the 10th–14th cent. Many temples and other ancient buildings were destroyed in the Korean War (1950–1).

Kaffa ➤KEFA.

Kafue River Zambia. River 960 km (600 miles) long, rising on the Congo (Democratic Republic) frontier W of Lubumbashi (Elisabethville), flowing generally S and E and joining the Zambezi R. just below Chirundu (Zimbabwe). In its lower course it flows through the Kafue Gorge, site of a hydroelectric power station. Navigation is restricted by rapids.

Kagera River Rwanda/Tanzania/Uganda. River 480 km (300 miles) long in central Africa formed by the union of the Ruvuvu and the Nyavarongo rivers, flowing N along the Rwanda–Tanzania frontier, turning E and forming part of the Tanzania–Uganda frontier and entering L. Victoria near the frontier.

Kagoshima Japan. Cap. of Kagoshima prefecture in S Kyushu on the W coast of Kagoshima Bay. Pop. (1992) 537,775. Minor seaport. Nearby is the volcanic peak Sakurajima.

Manufactures textiles and metal goods. Important in feudal times.

Kahoolawe USA. Island SW of Manui across the Alalakeiki Channel in Hawaii. Rocky, rising to 440 m (1444 ft) above sea level. Infertile and uninhabited. Military target-practice zone.

Kaifeng China. Ancient city in Honan province near the Hwang-ho R. 650 km (400 miles) S of Beijing. Pop. (1990) 507,763.

Commercial centre. Trade in wheat, groundnuts and fruits. Manufactures chemicals and agricultural machinery.

It was an important route centre in early times and in the 10th–12th cent. was the Imperial cap.

Kaikoura Ranges New Zealand. Two mountain ranges in the NE of South Island: the Inland and the Seaward Kaikouras, running SW–NE and separated by the lower valley of the Clarence R. Highest peak Tapuaenuku (2887 m; 9469 ft).

Kailas Range Tibet. Mountain range in the SW containing the sources of the Indus and the Brahmaputra rivers; N of L. Manasarowar is one of its highest peaks, Kailas (6719 m; 22,038 ft), while at the E end of the range is Lombo Kangra (7065 m; 23,173 ft). Kailas is sacred to both Buddhists and Hindus.

Kaimanawa Mountains New Zealand. Range extending 96 km (60 miles) E and S of L. Taupo in the centre of North Island. Rises to 1728 m; 5668 ft.

Kainji Dam ➤NIGER RIVER.

Kairouan (Kairwan, Qairwan) Tunisia. Muslim holy city 113 km (70 miles) S of Tunis. Pop. (1985) 72,300. Founded (671) by the Arab conqueror Sidi Okba. A major place of pilgrimage. Several outstanding mosques (open to non-Muslim visitors), esp. the Great Mosque or Mosque of Sidi Okba.

Manufactures carpets, rugs and leather goods. Trade in cereals, olives and wool.

Kaiserslautern Germany. Industrial town in the Rhineland-Palatinate on the Lauter R. 48 km (30 miles) W of Ludwigshafen. Pop. (1992) 100,541.

Road and rail junction. Manufactures vehicles, textiles, tobacco products and furniture.

Name derived from the Emperor (Kaiser) Frederick I, who built a castle here in the 12th cent.

Kakinada India. Seaport in Andhra Pradesh 400 km (250 miles) ESE of Hyderabad. Pop. (1991) 280,000.

Exports cotton and groundnuts. Industries inc. cotton, sugar, flour-milling and the manufacture of marine products and fertilizers. Natural gas has been discovered.

Kalahari (Kalahari Desert). Semi-desert region at a height of 900–1200 m (2952–3936 ft) mainly in Botswana. Area 520,000 sq km (200,800 sq. miles). Mean annual rainfall 12.5–25 cm (5–10 ins.). The Molopo R. and other streams dry up as they cross the region. Vegetation principally short grass; scattered acacias and thorn bushes. Home of the nomadic Bushmen; some cattle and sheep are reared. The Kalahari National Park (SW) has gemsbok, springbok, ostriches and other native fauna.

Kalámai ➤CALAMATA.

Kalamazoo USA. Industrial town in Michigan on the Kalamazoo R. 77 km (48 miles) S of Grand Rapids. Pop. (1990) 80,277.

Chief industry paper-making. Manufactures pharmaceutical products, aircraft, missile components and medical equipment.

The name is a shortened form of 'Kee-Kalamazoo' ('Where the Water Boils in the Pot'), applied to the river by local Indian tribes.

Kalemie Democratic Republic of Congo. Formerly Albertville (renamed 1966).Town and port in the E on the W shore of L. Tanganyika. Pop. (1985) 195,000. Linked by rail with the interior via Kabalo (on the Lualaba R.) and by lake steamer with Kigoma (Tanzania) – terminus of the railway from Dar-es-Salaam.

Manufactures cotton goods and cement.

Kalgan China ➤ZHANGJAKOU.

Kalgoorlie-Boulder Australia. Gold-mining town in Western Australia 547 km (340 miles) ENE of Perth. Pop. (1992) 26,079. First proclaimed a town in 1895 following the Coolgardie gold rush of 1892, mining having begun in 1893. Water is piped here nearly 563 km (350 miles) from Mundaring Weir in the Darling Range and power is generated by a local plant with coal from Collie (Western Australia). Junction on the Trans-Australian Railway. Airport. Flying Doctor centre. Combined with Boulder in 1947.

Kalimantan Indonesia. The Indonesian part of the island of Borneo. Area 539,460 sq km (208,286 sq. miles). Pop. (1989) 8,677,459.

Oil and natural gas are the important industries.

Kalinin ➤TVER.

Kaliningrad Russia. Formerly Königsberg. Cap. of the Kaliningrad Region on the Pregel R. near its mouth in the Frisches Haff. Pop. (1992) 411,000. Ice-free Baltic seaport linked by deep-water channel 47 km (29 miles) long with the outport of Baltisk.

Exports grain, flax, lentils and timber. Also an important industrial centre. Paper and flour milling. Manufactures machinery, chemicals and food products.

Many of its old buildings, inc. the 14th-cent. Gothic cathedral, were damaged in World War II. Immanuel Kant, German philosopher (1724–1894), was born here and taught at the university, which was founded (1544) as a Lutheran institution and was housed in new buildings in 1865. The city itself grew up (as Königsberg) around the castle built (1255) by the Teutonic Knights, consisting at first of three separate towns, Altstadt, Löbenicht and Kneiphof (united 1724). Joined the Hanseatic League 1340. Residence of the grand masters of the Teutonic Knights from 1457 and of the dukes of Prussia 1525–1618. Became cap. of the province of E Prussia. Renamed when the latter passed to the USSR (1946).

Kalisz Poland. Ancient Calissia. Cap. of the Kalisz voivodeship on the Prosna R. 96 km (60 miles) W of Lodz. Pop. (1992) 106,500.

Industrial centre. Manufactures textiles, pianos, foodstuffs and leather and food products.

One of the oldest towns in Poland, having been identified with the Calissia of Ptolemy; many archaeological remains have been found here.

Kalmar Sweden. Cap. of Kalmar county in the SE, partly on the mainland and partly on a small island in Kalmar Sound, opposite Öland. Pop. (1992) 56,862.

Seaport. Shipbuilding. Manufactures matches and paper.

The Kalmar Union (1397), by which Sweden, Norway and Denmark were united in one kingdom, was signed in the great 12th-cent. castle (rebuilt in the 16th and 17th cent.).

Kalmykia Russia. Autonomous Republic bounded by the lower Volga R., the Caspian Sea and the Manych R. Area 76,100 sq km (29,400 sq. miles). Pop. (1992) 327,000. Cap. Elista. Largely barren steppe. Main occupation sheep-rearing. Some fishing. Its people, the Kalmyks, are the Mongols of Buddhist faith, descendants of 17th-cent. immigrants; originally nomadic, many have now been settled.

Kaluga Russia. Cap. of the Kaluga Region on the Oka R. 160 km (100 miles) SSW of Moscow. Pop. (1992) 347,000.

Industrial and commercial centre. Saw-milling, brewing, railway engineering. Manufactures iron and steel goods, bricks, matches and glass.

Founded in the 14th cent.

Kalyan India. Town and port for coastal trade situated NE of Bombay in Maharashtra. Pop. (1991) 1,014,600.

Manufactures engineering and electronic products, chemicals, pharmaceuticals, textiles and paint. Also rice-milling.

Kalymnos (Kalimnos) Greece. Island in the Dodecanese. Area 106 sq km (41 sq. miles). Pop. (1985) 26,900. Chief town Kalymnos, near the SE coast.

Produces olive oil and citrus fruits.

Kamakura Japan. Town in the Kanagawa prefecture in central Honshu 19 km (12 miles) S of Yokohama. Pop. (1992) 173,492. Mainly a residential dormitory town for Tokyo. Famous for its Daibutsu (Great Buddha), a 13th-cent. bronze figure 13 m (43 ft) high. Founded in the 7th cent. Cap. of the Minamoto and Hojo shoguns 1192–1333; declined later with the expansion of Tokyo.

Kamaran Islands Yemen. Group of islands in the Red Sea off the coast of Yemen, until 1963 a dependency of Aden; formerly a Turkish possession, occupied by the British in 1915. Opted to remain with the Southern Yemen Republic in 1967. Area 57 sq km (22 sq. miles). Pop. (1985) 1500. The main island, Kamaran, has an airfield and a quarantine station for pilgrims to Mecca.

Kama River Russia. River 1900 km (1200 miles) long in European Russia, rising in the N of the Udmurt Autonomous Republic, flowing first N and turning E and then S to Perm (Molotov); from here it flows generally SW to join the Volga R. below Kazan. Since the construction of the dam near Perm it has provided hydroelectric power. Navigable for about half the year. Carries a considerable volume of traffic, esp. timber (by ship and raft).

Kamchatka Russia. Region in the Khabarovsk Territory in the extreme NE of Russia, inc. Kamchatka peninsula, the Komandorski Is. and the Chukot and Koryak National Areas. Area of Kamchatka region 472,300 sq km (182,400 sq. miles). Pop. (1992) 472,000. Chief town Petropavlovsk-Kamchatski. Mountainous, with several volcanoes of which 22 are active, the highest being Klyuchevskaya Sopka (5483 m; 17,984 ft). Agriculture possible only in the S. Main occupations hunting and fishing. Some of the people are still nomadic.

Kamensk-Uralski Russia. Industrial town in the Sverdlovsk Region 130 km (80 miles) ESE of Sverdlovsk. Pop. (1992) 209,000.

Important centre of bauxite-mining and aluminium-refining. Manufactures machine-tools and pipes.

Founded 1682. Developed chiefly in the late 1930s.

Kamet India. Himalayan peak (7756 m; 25,446 ft) in the SE of the Zaskar Range in NW Uttar Pradesh near the Tibet border.

Kamloops Canada. Town in British Columbia at the confluence of the N and S Thompson rivers and the junction of the Canadian Pacific and Canadian National railways. Pop. (1991) 75,950.

Industries inc. mining, lumbering and the marketing of livestock, fruit and vegetables.

The name is a corruption of the Indian word 'cumcloups' ('meeting of the waters').

Kampala Uganda. Cap. and chief commercial centre on the railway from Mombasa (Kenya) 32 km (20 miles) NNE of Entebbe at a height of 1190 m (3903 ft). Pop. (1991) 773,463. The former headquarters of the Kabaka (king) of Buganda are at Mengo 10 km (6 miles) SW. On the NW outskirts is the Makerere University College (1961), centre of higher education for E Africa.

Industries inc. coffee and tobacco processing, and goods for local consumption.

Kampen Netherlands. Town in Overijssel province on the Ijssel R. near the Ijsselmeer. Pop. (1992) 32,643.

Manufactures cigars, enamelware and photographic equipment.

Gothic church (14th-cent.). Member of the Hanseatic League in the 15th cent.

Kampot Cambodia. Town situated SSW of Phnom Penh at the foot of the Elephant Mountains on the Gulf of Siam. Pop. (1981) 337,879.

The main product is pepper, with some local limestone and phosphates. Shallow water port.

Kamyshin Russia. Town and river port in the Volgograd Region on the Volga R. opposite Nikolayevski. Pop. (1992) 125,000.

In an agricultural area noted for water melons. Trade in melons, grain and timber. The Volga is dammed here to irrigate a large area and supply hydroelectric power for the lumber and flour mills.

Kananga Democratic Republic of the Congo. Formerly Luluabourg. Town on the Lulua R., a tributary of the Kasai R., 800 km (500 miles) ESE of Kinshasa. Pop. (1991) 371,862.

Commercial and route centre on the Lubumbashi–Ilebo railway. One of the chief strongholds of the Baluba tribe.

Kanazawa Japan. Cap. of the Ishikawa prefecture, Honshu 160 km (100 miles) NNW of Nagoya. Pop. (1992) 445,522.

Industrial centre. Manufactures textiles, machinery, porcelain and lacquer ware. Outstanding landscape garden.

Kanchenjunga (Kinchinjunga) India/Nepal. Third highest mountain in the world (8598 m; 28,250 ft) in the Himalayas on the Nepal–Sikkim border, visible in all its majestic beauty from Darjeeling. First climbed (1955) by an English expedition.

Kanchipuram India. Formerly (until 1949) Conjeeveram. Sacred Hindu town in Tamil Nadu 64 km (40 miles) WSW of Madras, known as 'the Benares of the South'. Pop. (1991) 144,955.

Manufactures silk and cotton fabrics and saris.

Remarkable for its many temples, among them those to Vishnu and Siva dating from the Pallava kings of the 7th and 8th cent. AD, whose cap. it was.

Kandahar Afghanistan. Cap. of Kandahar province and the country's second largest city 475 km (295 miles) SW of Kabul at a height of 1020 m (3346 ft). Pop. (1988) 225,000.

Chief commercial centre in the S in a fertile region. Textile and fruit-canning industries.

The citadel and the tomb of Ahmed Shah are the only noteworthy buildings; about 6 km (4 miles) W are the ruins of old Kandahar, destroyed by Nadir Shah (1738). It had a violent history, changing hands many times. The first cap. of modern Afghanistan in the 18th cent. Occupied by the British 1839–42 and 1879–81.

Kandersteg Switzerland. Village in the Bern canton at a height of 1190 m (3903 ft), the highest station on the railway from Bern to Brig at the N end of the Lötschberg tunnel. Pop. (1989) 960. Resort and winter-sports centre.

Kandi Benin. Town in Bourgou in the N in the centre of an iron-rich area. Pop. (1992) 74,169.

Kandla India. Port in Gujarat situated SE of Anjar. Pop. (1991) 19,778.

Railway terminus and port on the Gulf of

Cutch, trading in grain, textiles and timber. Some salt extraction.

Kandy Sri Lanka. Town in Central Province on the Mahaweli Ganga at a height of 480 m (1574 ft) 96 km (60 miles) ENE of Colombo. Pop. (1990) 104,000.

Important centre of the tea trade in a scenically beautiful district.

Famous for a Buddhist temple where a reputed tooth of Buddha is preserved. Formerly cap. of the kingdom of Kandy.

Kangaroo Island Australia. Island 145 km (90 miles) long and 48 km (30 miles) wide in South Australia in the Indian Ocean 40 km (25 miles) S of Yorke Peninsula. Chief settlement Kingscote.

Has a large reserve in W (Flinders Chase) for native flora and fauna. Barley is cultivated and sheep raised. Salt and gypsum are produced.

Kankakee River USA. River 370 km (230 miles) long, rising near South Bend in Indiana, flowing SW and then NW and joining the Des Plaines R. to form the Illinois R. Used by early settlers as a connecting link between the Mississippi and the Great Lakes.

Kankan Guinea. Market town 480 km (300 miles) ENE of Conakry, with which it is linked by railway. Pop. (1983) 88,760.

Trade in rice and other agricultural produce.

Kanniyakumari India. Southernmost tip of India in Tamil Nadu, meeting point of the Bay of Bengal, the Arabian Sea and the Indian Ocean, a place of pilgrimage for the Hindus. Pop. (1991) 17,206.

Kano Nigeria. Chief town in Kano state 880 km (550 miles) NE of Lagos. Pop. (1993) 625,500.

Trade in cotton, groundnuts, hides and skins. Manufactures cotton goods, leather, furniture and soap. For cent. an important centre of caravan routes; now also an international airport.

The new town has developed outside the mud wall 21 km (13 miles) long surrounding

the old town. Occupied by the British (to suppress the slave trade) 1903.

Kanpur (Cawnpore) India. City in Uttar Pradesh on the Ganges R. 71 km (44 miles) SW of Lucknow. Pop. (1991) 1,958,282.

Important railway and road junction. Leading industrial centre. Manufactures textiles (chiefly cotton goods), leather goods, chemicals, soap, fertilizers, paper and scooters. Other industries inc. engineering, flour-milling, sugar-refining, and there is an ordnance factory. Trade in grain, oilseeds, cotton and sugar.

Developed quickly after being ceded to the British (1801) and again after World War I. Scene of one of the worst episodes of the Indian Mutiny (1857), when hundreds of women and children were massacred on the river bank after a promise of safe conduct; a memorial church and memorial gardens now stand there.

Kansas USA. Central state bounded by Nebraska (N), Missouri (E), Oklahoma (S) and Colorado (W). Area 213,096 sq km (82,277 sq. miles). Pop. (1990) 2,531,000. Cap. Topeka. Mostly consists of gently undulating prairie land; the highest point is 1261 m (4136 ft) near the W border. Climate continental with extremes of summer heat and winter cold.

Mainly agricultural with over 90 per cent of the area devoted to crops and livestock. Main crop wheat; sorghums and maize also important. Chief minerals petroleum, natural gas, coal. Oil refineries. Manufactures machinery, transportation equipment, food and dairy products.

Chief towns Wichita, Kansas City and Topeka. First explored by the Spaniards during Coronado's expedition (1540–1). French explorers came in the 17th cent. Ceded to Spain 1762; transferred to France 1800. Acquired by the USA through the Louisiana Purchase (1803). Admitted to the Union in 1861 as the 34th state.

Kansas City (Kansas) USA. Industrial city at the confluence of the Kansas and the Missouri

Kansas City

rivers opposite Kansas City (Missouri). Pop. (1990) 149,767.

Oil-refining, food-processing. Manufactures chemicals, vehicles, steel and foundry products, cement, soap and paper.

Kansas City (Missouri) USA. Industrial city on the Missouri R. at the confluence with the Kansas R. Pop. (1990) 435,146.

Important market and distribution centre for agricultural produce. Headquarters of the livestock industry. Meat-packing, flour-milling. Manufactures agricultural machinery, cars, refrigerators and food products.

Kansas River USA. River 274 km (170 miles) long in NE Kansas, formed by the union of the Smoky Hill and the Republican rivers, flowing E to join the Missouri R. between Kansas City (Kansas) and Kansas City (Missouri).

Kansk Russia. Industrial town in the Krasnoyarsk Territory on the Kan R. and the Trans-Siberian Railway 177 km (110 miles) E of Krasnoyarsk. Pop. (1992) 110,000.

In a lignite-mining region. Manufactures textiles and there is sawmilling and food-processing.

Kansu ➤GANSU.

Kanye Botswana. Town in the SE 113 km (70 miles) NNE of Mafeking (South Africa). Pop. (1991) 31,354. Cap. of the Bangwaketse tribe.

Kaohsiung Taiwan. Seaport on the SW coast 48 km (30 miles) S of Tainan. Pop. (1992) 1,396,425.

Exports sugar, rice, salt. Also an industrial centre. Oil-refining. Manufactures textiles, chemicals, cement, fertilizers, plastics and toys.

Developed under Japanese rule (1895–1945).

Kaolack Senegal. River port 137 km (85 miles) ESE of Dakar on the Saloum R. Pop. (1992) 179,894. Linked by rail with the line from Dakar to Bamako (Mali).

Market centre. Considerable exports of groundnuts and there are saltworks.

Kapfenberg Austria. Town in Styria on the Murz R. 40 km (25 miles) NNW of Graz. Pop. (1991) 23,380.

Important iron and steel works and paper mills.

Kaposvár Hungary. Cap. of Somogy county on the Kapos R. 47 km (29 miles) NW of Pecs. Pop. (1993) 71,000.

In a wine and tobacco producing region. Sugar-refining and flour-milling.

Kara Bogaz Gol Turkmenistan. Shallow gulf on the E side of the Caspian Sea about 20,720 sq km (8000 sq. miles) in area, enclosed except for a narrow strait. As a result of rapid evaporation, there are extensive deposits of chemical salts (esp. Glauber's salt), which are exploited.

Karachai–Cherkess Republic Russia. Republic in S European Russia, part of Stavropol Territory. Area 14,100 sq km (5442 sq. miles). Pop. (1992) 431,000. Cap. Cherkessk. The region declared itself a republic in 1990. There are ore-mining, engineering, chemical and woodworking industries.

Karachi Pakistan. Chief seaport and former cap., now cap. of Sind province, on the Arabian Sea NW of the Indus delta. Pop. (1991) 6,700,000.

Exports grain, cotton, oilseeds, hides and wool. Also a naval base. Manufactures textiles, chemicals, cement and metal goods.

University (1951). Important international airport. Developed rapidly as a port from the mid 19th cent. after harbour improvements and the construction of the railway and again expanded on becoming cap. of Pakistan in 1947. In 1948 the city with a surrounding area and some neighbouring islands (total area 2103 sq km; 812 sq. miles) was made federal territory, but in 1962 this was again incorporated in Pakistan.

Karaganda Kazakhstan. Cap. of the Karaganda Region 788 km (490 miles) NNW of Alma-Ata. Pop. (1991) 608,600.

Centre of the important Karaganda coal basin, which supplies coking coal to the Ural metallurgical industry. Manufactures iron and steel, cement.

Founded 1928. Developed rapidly after the construction of the railway (1931).

Karaj Iran. Town situated WNW of Tehrán on Karaj R. Pop. (1991) 442,000.

Industries inc. manufacture of chemical products and beet-sugar. There is an agricultural college.

Karakalpak Autonomous Republic Uzbekistan. Autonomous Republic in NW Uzbekistan. Area 164,900 sq km (63,920 sq. miles). Pop. (1990) 1,244,700. Cap. Nukus. Contains parts of the Ust Urt and Kyzyl Kum deserts and the lower basin of the Amu Darya and its delta on the Aral Sea.

Cereals, fruits and cotton cultivated by irrigation along the Amu Darya. Fisheries in the Aral Sea.

Became an autonomous region in the Kazakh Autonomous Republic in 1925 and an autonomous republic in 1932, joining the Uzbek Soviet Socialist Republic in 1936.

Karakoram (Karakorum). Mountain system in N Kashmir extending about 480 km (300 miles) NW–SE. Contains some of the world's highest peaks, inc. Godwin-Austen or K2 (8611 m; 28,250 ft) and several others over 7000 m (22,960 ft) and many great glaciers. Separated from the W Himalayas by the Indus R. The principal pass is the Karakoram Pass (5578 m; 18,296 ft) on the main trade route between Kashmir and China.

Karakorum Mongolia. Ruins of the cap. of Genghis Khan on the Orkhon R. 320 km (200 miles) WSW of Ulan Bator. Established in the early 13th cent. When the cap. was moved to Peking (Beijing) by Kublai Khan (1267), the town declined and was later abandoned. About 40 km (25 miles) NW there had been another Karakorum, cap. of the Uighur kingdom in the 8th–10th cent.

Kara-Kul Tajikistan. Mountain lake with no outlet on the plateau between the Pamirs and the Alai Mountains at a height of nearly 3900 m (12,792 ft), one of the highest in the world. Area 363 sq km (140 sq. miles).

Kara-Kum Turkmenistan. Desert in Turkmenistan S and SE of the Ust Urt plateau and between the Caspian Sea and the Amu Darya. Area 285,000 sq km (110,000 sq. miles). Much of it is covered with shifting sands (the name means 'black sands'), but it contains the Tedzhen and Urgab oases. The Kara-Kum Canal from the Amu Darya, extending 800 km (500 miles) through the oases to Ashikhabad, was constructed 1954–62 and is used for irrigating an extensive area.

Kara Sea. Part of the Arctic Ocean off the N coast of the Russian Federation between Novaya Zemlya and Severnaya Zemlya. Navigable when ice-free, usually for a few weeks in late summer. Receives the Ob and Yenisei rivers. Chief port Novy Port.

Karbala (Kerbela) Iraq. Cap. of the Karbala province 88 km (55 miles) SSW of Baghdad. Pop. (1985) 184,574.

Commercial town and pilgrimage centre for Shia Muslims, with the tomb of Husain, martyr and grandson of Mohammed, who was killed here in 680. Trade in dates, wool and hides.

Kardítsa Greece. 1. *Nome* in SW Thessaly. Area 2576 sq km (936 sq. miles). Pop. (1991) 124,498. Mainly agricultural. Cereals cultivated. Livestock raised.

2. Cap. of the Kardítsa *nome*. Pop. (1985) 28,000.

Trade in cereals, vegetables and livestock.

Karelian Isthmus Russia. Strip of land between the Gulf of Finland and L. Ladoga, under Soviet control since the Russo–Finnish War (1939–40), having been incorporated into the Leningrad (now St Petersburg) Region. Of great strategic importance for the defence of its chief city, St Petersburg; other important town Vyborg.

Karelian Republic Russia. Republic between the White Sea and Lakes Ladoga and Onega, bounded on the W by Finland. Area 172,400 sq km (66,560 sq. miles). Pop. (1992) 800,000. Cap. Petrozavodsk. It is linked geologically with Finland and on its surface there are many marshes and over 2000 lakes; its boundary with the St Petersburg region

(Russia) in the S passes through the largest of these, Ladoga and Onega.

Almost 70 per cent of the land consists of coniferous forests and lumbering, sawmilling and the manufacture of wood-pulp, paper and other wood products (furniture, plywood, veneers) are the main industries, while hydroelectric power is developed from its rivers. Iron and lead–zinc ores are mined, and mica and various building stones are quarried. Petrozavodsk and other industrial centres are linked by the White Sea–Baltic Canal and the Murmansk Railway. There is considerable fishing both on the White Sea coast and in the lakes and rivers.

The Karelians, who are closely related to the Finns, have been known since the 9th cent. Their territory came under Russian rule, and under the Tsars was backward and ill-developed. Before the Revolution of 1917 it was known as Olonetz province. In 1917 it became part of the Russian Soviet Federal Socialist Republic and in 1923 the Karelian Autonomous Soviet Socialist Republic. After the Russo–Finnish War (1940) it was increased by nearly all the land ceded by Finland and was made the Karelo-Finnish Soviet Socialist Republic. In 1946, however, the S part was transferred to the Russian Soviet Federal Socialist Republic and in 1956 its status was altered to that of an Autonomous Republic within the Russian Soviet Federal Socialist Republic once more. In 1991 it declared itself the Republic of Karelia.

Kariba, Lake Zimbabwe/Zambia. Lake along the Zambezi R. on the Zimbabwe–Zambia frontier 282 km (175 miles) long and 19 km (12 miles) wide. Created by the building of the Kariba Dam across the Zambezi for hydroelectric power development (begun 1955, first power available 1959). The Kariba Dam scheme involved the evacuation of 40,000 Africans from the inundation area (known as Operation Noah) and also large numbers of wild animals (marooned on temporary islands). The installation is linked with Harare and Bulawayo (Zimbabwe) and with Lusaka and the Copperbelt (Zambia). It is being developed for tourism.

Karkar Papua New Guinea. Island situated NE of New Guinea. Area 363 sq km (140 sq. miles). Volcanic and active, rising to 1494 m (4900 ft) above sea level. Chief products coconuts and cacao.

Karl-Marx-Stadt ►CHEMNITZ.

Karlovac Croatia. Town 48 km (30 miles) SW of Zagreb. Pop. (1971) 47,532.

Manufactures textiles and footwear. Trade in grain, wine, honey and timber.

Karlovy Vary (Ger. **Karlsbad, Carlsbad**) Czech Republic. Famous spa in W Bohemia on the Ohře R. 109 km (68 miles) WNW of Prague. Pop. (1991) 56,300.

Many warm springs, the waters being taken for their medicinal properties; also exported. Manufactures porcelain, glass and footwear.

Here were framed the Karlsbad Decrees (1819) limiting the freedom of German and Austrian universities after the murder of Kotzebue.

Karlskoga Sweden. Industrial town in Örebro county 40 km (25 miles) W of Örebro. Pop. (1988) 59,300.

Manufactures steel, chemicals. In its suburb Bofors, which gave its name to the Bofors gun, there is an important armament works.

Karlskrona Sweden. Cap. of Biekinge county in the SE on the Baltic coast 177 km (110 miles) ENE of Malmö. Pop. (1992) 59,390.

Seaport with a fine harbour, inc. dry docks cut out of granite. Exports granite, timber, dairy produce. Air base. Since 1680 the main Swedish naval base. Metalworking, brewing, sawmilling, granite quarrying. Manufactures naval equipment.

Karlsruhe Germany. Industrial town in Baden-Württemberg 6 km (4 miles) E of the Rhine R. and 64 km (40 miles) WNW of Stuttgart. Pop. (1992) 278,579. Former cap. of Baden.

Railway engineering. Manufactures machinery, cement, furniture, cosmetics, electrical and electronic equipment, pharmaceuticals and food products. There is also oil-refining and nuclear research laboratories. Linked by canal with the Rhine, it has an important river trade.

Severely damaged in World War II. Birthplace of Karl Benz, the engineer (1844–1929).

Karlstad Sweden. Cap. of Värmland county on the N shore of L. Väner and on Tingvalla island at the mouth of the Klar R. Pop. (1992) 77,290.

Industrial town and port. Timber, pulp and textile mills. Manufactures machinery, leather goods and matches.

Here the union of Norway and Sweden was dissolved (1905).

Karnak Egypt. Village on the E bank of the Nile in the Qena governorate in Upper Egypt. On the N part of the site of ancient Thebes.

Karnal India. Town in Haryana near the Jumna R. and S of Simla. Pop. (1991) 176,131.

Manufactures inc. cotton goods.

Karnataka India. Constituent state of the Indian Union, mainly on the S Deccan plateau, with a narrow plain along the Malabar Coast. Area 191,791 sq km (74,918 sq. miles). Pop. (1991) 44,806,468. Cap. Bangalore. The average height of the plateau region is about 740 m (2457 ft), but in the Baba Budan Hills the land rises to over 1800 m (5904 ft). The principal rivers, e.g. the Krishna and Cauvery, flow E from the Western Ghats to the Bay of Bengal. Rainfall is heavy in the hill country, where there are dense forests, producing sandalwood. More than three-quarters of the pop., however, are engaged in agriculture.

Main crops rice, groundnuts, cotton, sugar-cane, coffee, cardamom, chillies, castorseed and tobacco. Industries inc. aeronautics, telephones, electronics, chemicals, fertilizers, textiles, silk, cement, machine-tools, electronic items, printing and oil-refining. All India's gold is produced in Karnataka, as well as iron and manganese ore. Other important minerals are copper ore,

chromite, china clay, limestone. Kolar goldfield is in this state.

Kárpathos Greece. Island in the Dodecanese in the Aegean Sea about 48 km (30 miles) SW of Rhodes. Area 290 sq km (112 sq. miles). Pop. (1985) 8500. Chief town Pigádhia.

Cereals, olives, grapes cultivated. Sheep and goats are raised.

Karroo South Africa. Two semi-desert plateaux in the S of the West Cape Province. The Little (Southern) Karroo, at a height of 300–600 m (984–1968 ft) is separated from the coastal plain by the Langeberg range and from the Great (Central) Karroo (N) by the Zwarteberg range. The Great Karroo at a height of 600–900 m (1968–2952 ft) extends as far N as the Nieuwveld range and like the Little Karroo is crossed by ranges of hills. Mainly dry grassland. Sheep and goats reared. Irrigation makes the cultivation of cereals and citrus fruits possible. The dry, healthy climate has made some of the towns, e.g. Beaufort West, Graaff Reinet, popular resorts. The High Veld of South Africa, N of the Great Karroo, mainly at a height of 1200–1800 m (3936–5904 ft) is sometimes called the Northern Karroo.

Kars Turkey. Cap. of Kars province 169 km (105 miles) ENE of Erzurum. Pop. (1990) 78,450.

Manufactures woollen goods, carpets and food products.

Ceded to Russia 1878 and returned to Turkey 1921.

Karst Former Yugoslavia. Arid limestone plateau in the Dinaric Alps (NW), with an uneven topography of ridges and closed hollows, sinks, underground streams and little surface drainage, and caves containing stalactites and stalagmites, these last being well exemplified at Postojna. The term, derived from the Serbo-Croat *kras*, has been applied to limestone areas of similar topography in other parts of the world.

Karum River Iran. River 848 km (527 miles) long in the SW, rising in the Zardeh

Kuh of the Zagros Mountains and flowing generally W, at first through deep gorges, then turning S and entering the plain near Shushtar; divides into two channels which reunite further S and flows past Ahwaz to enter the Shatt-al-Arab at Khorramshahr. Navigable to Ahwaz.

Karviná (Karvinná) Czech Republic. Coalmining town in the Severomoravský region, in the Ostrava–Karviná coal basin 13 km (8 miles) E of Ostrava. Pop. (1990) 70,000. Associated gas, coke, iron and chemical industries.

Karyai ➤ATHOS, MOUNT.

Kasai Democratic Republic of the Congo. Former province from 1967 divided into W and E Kasai in the SW, bordering on Shaba. Area 321,160 sq km (124,000 sq. miles). Cap. Kananga. An agricultural region, but with some mineral resources, esp. most of the world supplies of industrial diamonds, washed from the many rivers. Food crops cassava, yams and maize. Cotton and coffee also cultivated. Cattle raised. After Zaire (now Democratic Republic of the Congo) became independent, it attempted secession (like Katanga (now Shaba)); a Baluba chief was proclaimed king of South Kasai in 1960, but the regime was dissolved in 1961. There were further revolts against the central government in 1962 and 1963.

Kasai River Angola/Democratic Republic of the Congo. River 2150 km (1350 miles) long, rising in Angola, flowing N as part of the frontier with Congo and joining the Congo R., of which it is a main tributary. Navigable for 772 km (479 miles) above the confluence; a main trade artery, joined by many navigable streams, rich in alluvial diamonds.

Kashan Iran. Town 177 km (110 miles) S of Tehrán at a height of 960 m (3148 ft). Pop. (1985) 84,600.

In an oasis where wheat, melons and figs are grown. Famous for rugs and carpets. Also manufactures cotton and silk goods and copperware.

Kashgar ➤KASHI.

Kashi (Kashgar) China. Town in an oasis of W Xinjiang Uygur Autonomous Republic at the W end of the Tarim Basin 720 km (450 miles) SW of Kuldja. Pop. (1990) 174,570. A caravan centre linked with Kyrgyzstan by the Torugart Pass.

Manufactures textiles and rugs. Trade in wool, cotton and tea.

Visited c. 1725 by Marco Polo. Taken by the Chinese in 1759, it has remained almost continuously in their hands.

Kashmir India. A province of the state of Jammu and Kashmir, since partition (1947) disputed by India and Pakistan. Almost entirely mountainous, with the Karakoram system separated by the Indus R. from the Himalayas, both extending NW–SE across Kashmir; the former inc. such peaks as K2 (8611 m; 28,250 ft) and Rakaposhi (7788 m; 25,550 ft), while at the W end of the latter is Nanga Parbat (8126 m; 26,660 ft). It is also crossed by the valley of the Upper Jhelum, the beautiful Vale of Kashmir. About 5 per cent of the land is cultivated, and here rice, maize and wheat are grown; cattle, sheep and goats are raised. Kashmir is famous for a fine wool (Cashmere) obtained from the undercoat of its goats.

Kashmir became part of the Mogul Empire 1586. Ceded to the Afghans 1756. Taken by the Sikhs under Ranjit Singh 1819. Later rulers were Hindu Maharajahs, while the people were predominantly Muslim, so that both India and Pakistan claimed the territory at the partition (1947). The Maharajah acceded to India, fighting broke out, the dispute was brought before the UN and a cease-fire agreement took effect (1949); attempts to arrange a plebiscite, however, failed. In 1956 the constituent assembly of Indian Kashmir declared Jammu and Kashmir to be an integral part of India; meanwhile, the area occupied by Pakistan, known as Azad Kashmir (Free Kashmir), in the NW, was administered by a provisional government at Muzaffarabad.

Kassala Sudan. Cap. of Kassala province

on the Gash R. 410 km (255 miles) E of Khartoum and 24 km (15 miles) from the Ethiopian frontier. Pop. (1985) 143,000. On the Sennar–Port Sudan railway. Centre of an important cotton-growing area. Founded (1840) by the Egyptians as a military post. Captured by the dervishes 1885; recovered by the Italians 1894; ceded to Egypt 1897. Briefly in Italian hands during World War II (1940–1).

Kassel (Cassel) Germany. Industrial town in Hessen on the Fulda R. 148 km (92 miles) NNE of Frankfurt. Pop. (1992) 196,828.

Manufactures locomotives and railway rolling-stock, machinery, scientific and optical instruments, chemicals and textiles.

As a centre of aircraft and tank production in World War II it was heavily bombed and suffered severe damage, many of its historic buildings being destroyed. Cap. of the former electorate of Hesse-Kassel and of the Prussian province of Hesse-Nassau (1866–1945).

Kassérine Tunisia. Town and district cap. situated SW of Tunis at the foot of the Djebel Chambi Mountain. Pop. (1984) 47,606. Route junction in an irrigated agricultural area.

Kastoría Greece. 1. *Nome* in Macedonia bounded on the NW by Albania. Area 1720 sq km (664 sq. miles). Pop. (1991) 52,721. Wheat and tobacco cultivated.

2. Cap. of Kastoría *nome* on a peninsula of L. Kastoría 145 km (90 miles) W of Thessaloníki. Pop. (1985) 20,700.

Trade in wheat and wine.

Kateríni Greece. Cap. of Pieria *nome* in Macedonia 56 km (35 miles) SW of Thessaloníki. Pop. (1985) 40,000.

Agricultural centre. Trade in wheat, vegetables and wine.

Kathiawar India. Peninsula in the W between the Gulfs of Cambay and Kutch. Now part of Gujarat.

Kathmandu (Katmandu) Nepal. Cap. of the kingdom on the Baghmati R. in the Nepal Valley at a height of 1300 m (4624 ft). Pop. (1991) 419,073. Royal palaces and many temples, inc. a 16th-cent. wooden temple from which its name (which means 'Wooden Temple') is derived. Founded in the 8th cent. Taken by Gurkhas 1768; has since remained the cap. A new 110-km (70-mile) highway to the Tibet (Chinese) frontier was opened in 1967. Favourite destination of young people trekking there in the 1960s.

Katmai, Mount USA. Active volcano (2100 m; 6888 ft) in S Alaska in the Aleutian Range, with a crater 1110 m (3641 ft) deep and 4 km (2½ miles) across. Erupted violently in 1912; Kodiak Island was blanketed with ash and the Valley of Ten Thousand Smokes, a region of 186 sq km (72 sq. miles) punctured by thousands of fumaroles, was formed. The Katmai National Monument (10,917 sq km; 4215 sq. miles) was established in 1918.

Katowice Poland. Formerly (1953–6) Stalinogrod. Cap. of the Katowice voivodeship 71 km (44 miles) WNW of Cracow. Pop. (1992) 366,900.

Important industrial centre and railway junction in a coal and iron mining district. Manufactures iron and steel, machinery, chemicals and bricks.

Became a town 1867; passed from Germany to Poland (1921) with the partition of Upper Silesia.

Katrine, Loch Scotland. Freshwater lake 13 km (8 miles) long and 1.6 km (1 mile) wide in Stirling, projecting SE into the Trossachs, and drained by the R. Teith. Made famous by Scott's *Lady of the Lake*. Main source of Glasgow's water supply since 1859, its level having been raised considerably for this purpose.

Katsina Nigeria. Town in the N 145 km (90 miles) NW of Kano. Pop. (1993) 191,600.

Commercial centre and a Hausa cultural centre. Enclosed by a partly ruined mud wall. Trade in groundnuts and cotton. Crafts inc. metal and leather working, pottery manufacture.

Kattegat Strait 240 km (150 miles) long and 65–130 km (40–80 miles) wide between Sweden and Jutland (Denmark), connected on the N to the Skagerrak at the Skaw and on the S to the Baltic Sea.

Katwijk Aan Zee Netherlands. Seaside resort in South Holland province at the mouth of the Old Rhine (Oude Rijn) 8 km (5 miles) NW of Leiden. Pop. (1992) 40,498.

Kaufbeuren Germany. Town in Bavaria on the Wertach R. 77 km (48 miles) WSW of Munich. Pop. (1990) 41,500.

Manufactures textiles. Dyeing, printing and brewing.

Kaunas Lithuania. Town on the Neman R. at its confluence with the Viliya R. Pop. (1993) 429,000.

Manufactures agricultural implements, metal goods, chemicals, textiles, food products, electrical goods and paper.

Since its foundation in the 11th cent. it has often been partly or completely destroyed in war; it was an important commercial centre even in medieval times. Between the two world wars (1918–40) it served as provisional cap. of Lithuania (Vilnius (Vilna) being then in the hands of Poland).

Kaválla (Cavalla) Greece. 1. *Nome* in Macedonia on the Aegean Sea, inc. the off-shore island of Thásos, ceded to Greece after the Balkan War of 1912–13. Area 2111 sq km (815 sq. miles). Pop. (1991) 135,747. Noted for tobacco cultivation.

2. Ancient Neapolis. Cap. of Kaválla *nome*, port on the Gulf of Kaválla. Pop. (1990) 56,700.

Exports tobacco, clothing, furniture and plastics. There are offshore oil wells at Prinos.

Ruled by the Turks until 1912, then three times occupied by Bulgarians. Birthplace of Mehemet Ali (1769–1849), who founded a Turkish school here.

Kavirondo Kenya. 1. Shallow gulf in the NE of L. Victoria. Connected to the lake by a strait 5 km (3 miles) wide. The port of Kisumu stands on the shore.

2. Area round the Kavirondo gulf. The name derives from the Kavirondo, a local tribe.

Kawaguchi Japan. Town in Saitama prefec-

ture, Honshu just N of Tokyo. Pop. (1990) 438,700.

Metallurgical and textile industries.

Kawasaki Japan. Industrial town in Kanagawa prefecture, Honshu between Tokyo and Yokohama. Pop. (1992) 1,195,464.

Shipbuilding, engineering. Manufactures steel, textiles and chemicals.

Kayseri Turkey. Ancient Caesarea Mazaca. Cap. of Kayseri province just N of Erciyas Daği (3916 m; 12,884 ft) at a height of 1020 m (3356 ft). Pop. (1990) 421,362.

Manufactures textiles, carpets and rugs, tiles. Trade in grain, fruit, vegetables.

Ancient cap. of Cappadocia.

Kazakhstan. Republic in central Asia bounded in the W by the Caspian Sea, Russia W and N, China in the E and by Uzbekistan and Kyrgystan in the S. Area 2,717,300 sq km (1,049,150 sq. miles). Pop. (1995) 16,669,000 (57 per cent urban). Life expectancy, 63 years male, 73 female. Cap. Akmola. Other cities Karaganda, Chimkent, Pavlodar and Semipalatinsk. Currency: Tenge = 500 rubles. Essentially a dry-steppe region, with the Caspian lowlands, the Ust Urt plateau and the Turanian basin in the W half, and rising in the E and S to the Altai Mountains, the Tarbagatai Range and other highlands of Central Asia. Extends round part of the Caspian and Aral Seas. Contains L. Balkhash. Longest river the Syr Darya, 2240 km (1400 miles) which flows into the Aral Sea. Climate continental, with extremes of summer heat and winter cold; over much of the area the rainfall is 25 cm (10 ins.) annually or less, rising to about 50 cm (20 ins.) only in the mountains. Land use; forested 6 per cent, meadows and pastures 69 per cent, agricultural and under permanent cultivation 13 per cent. The pop. is predominantly Sunni Muslim with a Christian minority mainly Russian Orthodox or Baptist. The official lang. is Kazakh. Other lang. Russian, German and Ukrainian. The ethnic composition: Kazakh 40 per cent, Russian 38 per cent, German 6 per cent, Ukrainian 5 per cent.

Kazakh agriculture has changed from nomadic cattle-rearing and is still noted for the large numbers of sheep, cattle and pigs raised, but it now also produces important crops of wheat and other cereals, sugar-beet and cotton. Much virgin land has been brought under cultivation and a considerable area is irrigated. Tobacco, rubber plants and mustard are also cultivated. Rich in mineral resources; coal is mined in the Karaganda basin, oil along the Emba (W), copper at Younradski and Dzherzkazgan; lead, zinc, nickel and manganese, molybdenum and tungsten also produced. Many new industries have been opened up in recent years; principal manufacturing centres Almaty, Karaganda, Semipalatinsk, Chimkent and Petropavlovsk. These industries inc. non-ferrous metallurgy, heavy engineering and chemicals.

The region became part of Russian Turkestan in the 19th cent., the Kirghiz Autonomous Soviet Socialist Republic (1920), Kazakh Autonomous Soviet Socialist Republic (1925) – within the Russian Federation. It became a constituent republic of the USSR in 1936. Kazakhstan declared its independence in 1961 and joined the Commonwealth of Independent States. There is a 150-member legislature and the President is elected for a 4-year term by universal suffrage.

Kazan Russia. Cap. of the Tatarstan Republic on the Kazanka R. at the confluence with the middle Volga R. Pop. (1992) 1,104,000.

Industries inc. railway and automobile engineering, oil-refining. Manufactures typewriters, musical instruments, chemicals, textiles and tools.

It is a city where western and eastern influences have mingled and there are Muslim mosques as well as Orthodox churches; its famous Kremlin has the Suyumbeka Tower (75 m; 247 ft). Became cap. of the Kazan khanate in the 15th cent. Taken by Ivan the Terrible 1552; commercial importance increased thereafter. Suffered severely during the revolution of 1917 and again in the ensuing famine (1921).

Kazerun Iran. Town in Fars province 88 km (55 miles) W of Shiraz at a height of 840 m (2764 ft). Pop. (1986) 70,000.

In a region producing tobacco, rice, opium and cotton.

Nearby are the ruins of ancient Shapur.

Kazvin (Qazvin) Iran. Town in Gilan province 145 km (90 miles) WNW of Tehrán at the S foot of the Elburz Mountains at a height of 1265 m (4162 ft). Pop. (1986) 248,591.

Manufactures carpets and rugs, textiles and soap. Trade in silk and rice.

Founded in the 4th cent. by Shapur II; made the national cap. in the 16th cent. by Tahmasp I. It has been frequently damaged by earthquakes.

Kearny USA. Industrial town in New Jersey on the Passaic R. just E of Newark. Pop. (1970) 37,585.

Manufactures metal goods, chemicals, and has shipyards and docks.

Kecskemét Hungary. Cap. of Bács-Kiskun county 80 km (50 miles) SE of Budapest. Pop. (1992) 104,563.

In a fertile fruit-growing region. Trade in fruit, cereals and cattle. Manufactures agricultural implements, wine, brandy, fruit and vegetable preserves, textiles and leather.

Kedah Malaysia. State in NW Peninsular Malaysia bordering NE on Thailand. Area 9426 sq km (3639 sq. miles). Pop. (1991) 1,304,800. Cap. Alor Star.

Rice and rubber cultivated. Tin and tungsten mined.

Under British protection from 1909, when it was transferred from Thailand; it was one of the unfederated Malay States until 1947.

Kediri Indonesia. Town in E Java 80 km (50 miles) SW of Surabaya. Pop. (1990) 235,602.

Commercial centre in a region producing sugar, rice, rubber and coffee.

Keele ➤NEWCASTLE-UNDER-LYME.

Keelung ➤CHILUNG.

Keewatin Canada. The E mainland District of the Northwest Territories (except the

Melville and Boothia peninsulas), inc. the islands of Hudson Bay. Area 530,930 sq km (228,160 sq. miles).

Chief occupation fur-trapping by Indians and Eskimos, who make up the greater part of the scattered pop. The name is a Cree Indian word meaning 'the north wind'.

Kefa (Kaffa) Ethiopia. Forested highland province in the SW bordering on Sudan at a height of 2400 m (7896 ft) with peaks rising to over 3000 m (9870 ft). Cap. Jimma. Main waterway the Omo R. (E) emptying into L. Rudolf.

Home of the coffee plant, growing wild on the mountain slopes ('coffee' probably derives from 'Kaffa'). Produces coffee, cereals and beeswax.

Formerly an independent kingdom. Conquered by Menelik and incorporated into Ethiopia 1897.

Kefallinía ➤CEPHALONIA.

Keflavik Iceland. Fishing port in Suderland SW of Reykjavik. Pop. (1992) 7508.

Important for fish-processing and the second export town in Iceland.

Keighley England. Town in West Yorkshire on the R. Aire 13 km (8 miles) NW of Bradford. Pop. (1991) 49,567.

Important centre of the woollen and worsted industry. Also manufactures machine-tools, and textile machinery.

Keith Scotland. Town in Moray on the R. Isla 27 km (17 miles) WSW of Banff, with Fife Keith on the opposite bank. Pop. (1991) 4793.

Manufactures woollen goods. Whisky-distilling.

The Roman Catholic church has an altar-piece *The Incredulity of St Thomas*, presented by Charles X of France.

Kelantan Malaysia. State in NE Peninsular Malaysia bordering (NW) on Thailand. Area 14,943 sq km (5769 sq. miles). Pop. (1991) 1,181,680. Cap. Kota Baharu.

Produces rice, rubber and copra.

Transferred from Thailand to Britain 1909; one of the unfederated states until 1947.

Kells ➤CEANANNUS MÓR.

Kelowna Canada. City in British Columbia on the E shore of the Okanagan lake midway between Penticton and Vernon. Pop. (1991) 75,950.

There are large manufacturing and processing plants, and other industries inc. forestry, agriculture, wine manufacture, fruit-processing and tourism.

Kelso Scotland. Market town in Scottish Borders at the confluence of the R. Tweed and the R. Teviot. Pop. (1991) 5989.

Manufactures agricultural implements, oilcake, electrical and electronic equipment, plastics, printed-board circuits and fertilizers.

Ruins of the 12th-cent. abbey founded by David I.

Kemerovo Russia. Formerly Shcheglovsk. Cap. of the Kemerovo Region on the Tom R. Pop. (1992) 520,000.

Important coalmining centre in the Kuznetsk basin. Manufactures chemicals, fertilizers, plastics and agricultural machinery.

Kemi Finland. Town and port in the Lappi province near the mouth of the Kemi R. 96 km (60 miles) NNW of Oulu. Pop. (1992) 25,121.

Exports timber. Sawmilling.

Kempten Germany. Town in SW Bavaria on the Iller R. 85 km (53 miles) SSW of Augsburg. Pop. (1990) 60,000.

Chief commercial centre of the Allgäu. Trade in dairy produce and timber. Industries inc. engineering and the manufacture of textiles and paper.

Kendal England. Town in Cumbria on the R. Kent 34 km (21 miles) N of Lancaster. Pop. (1991) 25,461.

Manufactures footwear and textiles.

Has a church dating in part from the 13th cent. and the ruins of a Norman castle where Catherine Parr, Henry VIII's last queen, was born. The woollen industry was introduced by Flemish immigrants in the 14th cent. and later the town was noted for a coarse cloth known as 'Kendal green'. Birthplace of Sir

Arthur Eddington, the astronomer (1882–1944).

Kenema Sierra Leone. Cap. of Eastern Province. Pop. (1988) 13,000.

Centre for diamond-mining, cocoa, wood carvings and timber.

Kenilworth England. Market town in Warwickshire 8 km (5 miles) SW of Coventry. Pop. (1990) 21,000.

Light engineering.

Its ruined castle (founded in the 12th cent.) was presented by Queen Elizabeth I to Robert Dudley, Earl of Leicester, who entertained her here; it is described in Scott's *Kenilworth*.

Kenitra (Mina Hassan Tani) Morocco. Formerly Port Lyautey. Seaport on the Sebou R. 16 km (10 miles) above the mouth, 40 km (25 miles) NE of Rabat on the Rabat–Meknès railway. Pop. (1989) 190,000.

Exports grain and cork.

Kennedy, Cape USA. Also Cape Canaveral. Cape on the E coast of Florida 240 km (150 miles) SSE of Jacksonville. Site of the USAF Missile Test Center. US earth satellites and lunar and stellar probes have been launched and men put into orbit round the earth and sent to the moon from the site. Renamed after the assassination of President J. F. Kennedy (1963) but returned to the name of Cape Canaveral in 1973 as the inhabitants complained that Canaveral was the oldest named place on the E seaboard; however NASA still use the name Cape Kennedy.

Kennington England. District in the London borough of Lambeth which has the cricket ground, The Oval. Birthplace of Viscount Montgomery of Alamein, British soldier (1887–1976).

Kenosha USA. Industrial town and port in SE Wisconsin on L. Michigan. Pop. (1990) 80,352.

Manufactures cars, furniture and hosiery.

First settled in 1832 as Pike Creek. Named Southport in 1837; incorporated in 1850 as Kenosha, an Indian word meaning 'pike' (probably the source of the 1832 name).

Kensal Green England. District in W London, partly in Hammersmith and partly in Kensington, with a cemetery (laid out 1832) containing the graves of many famous people, inc. Thackeray, Trollope, Leigh Hunt, Hood, Wilkie Collins, Michael Balfe and Cardinal Manning.

Kensington and Chelsea England. Royal borough of W London (from 1965), mainly residential, comprising the former metropolitan boroughs of Chelsea and Kensington. Pop. (1991) 141,300. Kensington Palace, originally Nottingham House, was purchased by William III, and later Queen Anne, George II and Queen Victoria, who was born here, resided in it. Its grounds are now Kensington Gardens (111 ha; 273 acres), a public park adjoining Hyde Park, in which are the Round Pond, the Orangery and the famous Peter Pan statue by Frampton; just S of them are the Albert Memorial and Albert Hall. South Kensington is a centre of museums and colleges, inc. the Victoria and Albert, Natural History and Science Museums, the Royal College of Art, the Imperial College of Science and Technology, and the Royal Geographical Society.

Kent England. County in the SE lying between the Thames estuary (N) and the English Channel (S). Area 3950 sq km (1525 sq. miles). Pop. (1991) 1,538,800. The chalk ridge of the N Downs curves round from the NW near Westerham, where it exceeds 240 m (790 ft), to the white cliffs of Dover, and in the SW is part of the once-forested Weald; otherwise, the county is mostly low-lying and in the S is the almost flat, fertile Romney Marsh, famous for its sheep. Apart from the Thames, the principal rivers are the Medway, Stour, Darent and Cray. Off the N coast are the Isle of Thanet, Isle of Sheppey and Isle of Grain, all separated from the mainland by narrow channels or rivers and linked with the mainland by rail and road. Often termed 'the Garden of England', it is well-known for its orchards (apples, cherries), hop gardens and oast-houses; but there is also considerable cereal cultivation and market-gardening. Inland from Deal was the E Kent coalfield, which is now closed. Chalk, sand and gravel are quarried. In the Medway area there are important cement and paper industries. Chatham has a naval dockyard, Rochester engineering works, Gravesend is a river port and Dover and Folkestone are linked with the continent by cross-Channel services, and from 1994 the Channel tunnel has operated from Cheriton to Sargette, near Calais (France). Margate, Ramsgate and other coastal towns are popular resorts, while Canterbury is much visited for its famous cathedral, the mission of St Augustine here (597) making it the centre of the English Church. Maidstone is the historic county town. Kent, the first part of the country to be colonized by the Romans, became a kingdom of Anglo–Saxon Britain in the 5th cent. with approximately its present boundaries.

Kentish Town England. District in the London borough of Camden, residential but also industrialized, a considerable area being occupied by railway sidings and marshalling yards.

Kentucky USA. State in S central USA, bounded by Ohio and Indiana (N), by West Virginia and Virginia (E), Tennessee (S) and by Missouri and Illinois (W). The N boundary is formed by the Ohio R. and the W boundary by the Ohio and Mississippi rivers. Area 104,693 sq km (40,410 sq. miles). Pop. (1990) 3,789,000. Cap. Frankfort. Drained by the Licking, Kentucky, Green and other rivers to the Ohio and Mississippi. The highest area is in the SE, with Big Black Mountain rising to 1264 m (4159 ft). Well-known for its limestone caves, the most famous being the Mammoth Cave. The climate is marked by hot summers and short, cold winters when heavy snowfalls may occur. Rainfall moderate and well distributed. Largely agricultural. Chief crops tobacco (by far the most important), maize, wheat, soya beans, apples and bluegrass seed. Agriculture has suffered considerably from soil erosion. The state has long been famous for its horses. Principal mineral coal; petroleum, natural gas and fluorspar also important. Leading manufacturing centres Louisville (where the Kentucky Derby is run), Lexington and Covington.

Among the principal industries are lumbering, clothing and cigars, and the manufacture of machinery and electrical equipment.

The territory was first explored by the English in 1750. After Daniel Boone's expeditions (beginning 1769), Boonesborough was founded (1775) and many new settlers came in from the E. From 1776 to 1792 it was part of Virginia and then became a separate state. During the American Civil War, Kentucky's loyalties were sharply divided between North and South. Admitted to the Union in 1792 as the 15th state.

Kentucky River USA. River 418 km (260 miles) long, formed by the union of the North Fork and Middle Fork rivers (both rising in the Cumberland Mountains), flowing NW through Kentucky and joining the Ohio R. at Corrollton.

Kenya. Republic in E Africa bounded by Ethiopia and Sudan in the N, Uganda in the W, Tanzania in the S and by the Indian Ocean and Somalia in the E. Area 582,646 sq km (224,961 sq. miles). Pop. (1995) 28,626,000 (57 per cent urban). Life expectancy, 63 years male, 73 female. Cap. Nairobi. Other cities Kisumu, Kakuru and Machakos. Currency: Kenya shilling = 100 cents. A coastal strip 16 km (10 miles) wide, the former Protectorate, extends from the Tanzania frontier to Kipini at the mouth of the Tana R. The N, about 60 per cent of the total area, is arid and sparsely peopled, largely by nomads. The S has a low, marshy coastal belt, rising to a high plateau dominated by the great volcanic cones of Mt Kenya (Kirinyaga) and Mt Elgon. The equator crosses the country. The W is crossed N–S by the Great Rift Valley, with a chain of lakes inc. lakes Kurana, the largest, Baringo, Nakuru, Naivashi and Magadi. Along the E flanks of the Great Rift Valley are the steep Kikuyu and Laikipia escarpments; farther E are the

Aberdare Mountains, rising to 3900 m (12,792 ft). The SW upland climate is favourable to Europeans and the region was the principal area of white settlement (the 'white highlands'). The climate is tropical, with wet and dry seasons, but considerable differences in altitude make for varied conditions between the hot, coastal lowlands and the plateau, where temperatures are very much cooler. Land use: forested 4 per cent, meadows and pastures 67 per cent, agricultural and under permanent cultivation 4 per cent. Kenyans make up 98 per cent of the pop. Most of the people belong to various tribes: Kikuyu, Luo, Kavirondo, Nandi, Suk, Turkana, Masai, Somali and Galla. The official lang. is Swahili. Other lang. English, Kikuyu, Nakuru, Luo and Kamba. About 73 per cent Christian, traditional beliefs 19 per cent, Muslim 6 per cent.

Because of the range of altitudes, Kenya produces a wide variety of crops, esp. wheat and mazie for domestic use and for export, coffee, pyrethrum, sisal, tea in the highlands (SW), and in the lowlands cotton and sugarcane. Cattle-raising is also important. The forests are mainly in the highlands, at 1800–3000 m (5904–9840 ft) with bamboos at the higher levels, camphor trees and cedar trees below. Little mineral exploitation except the production of carbonate of soda from L. Magadi. Industries inc. cement manufacture, meat-packing, flour-milling, coffee and sisal preparation. Principal exports coffee, hides and skins, meat and meat preparations, pyrethrum extract, sisal and tea. Tourism is important to the economy and it is famous for big game, e.g. large herds of antelope and zebra, also the giraffe, elephant, rhinoceros, lion, leopard and many other species. Hunting is strictly regulated. The Tsavo National Park and the Nairobi National Park help to preserve wildlife.

The coastal strip was long under the influence of Arab traders. Through the Imperial British East Africa Company, Britain leased the N from the Sultan of Zanzibar and began to open up the hinterlands towards the end of the 19th cent. The frontier between British East Africa and German East Africa (later Tanganyika, now Tanzania) was fixed in 1890; Kenya became a British Crown Colony (except the leased coastal strip, which became the Kenya Protectorate) in 1920. Jubaland was ceded to Italy in 1925. White settlers entered in considerable numbers from the early years of the 20th cent. Their interests frequently conflicted with those of the Africans, largely because of their occupation of extensive areas of land; Kikuyu discontent led to campaigns of violence by the secret Mau Mau organization (1952–4), but these were gradually suppressed. The first elections of African representatives to the Legislative Council took place in 1957 and the state of emergency came to an end in 1960. African leaders played an increasing part in preparations for independence; among political difficulties was a desire for secession on the part of the Arabs in the Protectorate and the Somali in the Northern Province. The former Protectorate was ceded to Kenya in 1963. Kenya became independent in 1963 and a republic in 1964 under the President, Jomo Kenyatta (1893–1978). There was an attempted military *coup* in 1982. Multiparty elections were held in 1993. There is a 202-member National Assembly elected by universal suffrage every 5 years.

Kenya (Kirinyaga), Mount Kenya. The second highest mountain in Africa after Kilimanjaro, rising to 5200 m (17,058 ft), it is an extinct volcano situated 129 km (80 miles) NNE of Nairobi, just S of the equator, and consists of 3 peaks. The crater is much eroded and within the area there are 32 lakes and 15 glaciers, most of which end at about 4500 m (14,760 ft). Thick forest extends to 3300 m (10,824 ft).

Kerala India. State in the SW, bounded on the W by the Arabian Sea (Malabar Coast), created in 1956 and consisting of most of the former state of Travancore-Cochin together with parts of the Malabar district and S Kanara, previously in Madras. Area 38,863 sq km (15,181 sq. miles). Pop. (1991) 29,032,828 (the highest pop. density of any state). Cap. Thiruvananthapuram. Hilly in the E, it rises to 2697 m (8873 ft) in Anai Mudi and inc.

the Cardamom Hills, but most of its area consists of plains where the chief crops are cashew, coffee, tea, coconuts, rubber, and it supplies 40 per cent of the world's pepper. Industries inc. shipbuilding, tyres, machine-tools, cables, electronics, paper, newsprint, oil-refining. Important minerals inc. ilmenite, rutile, monazite, zircon, sillimanite, clay and quartz sand. Chief towns Kochi (chief port), Kozhikode, Alleppey. Claims the highest literacy rate of all states, 91 per cent (1991).

Kerch Ukraine. Seaport on a small bay in Kerch Strait at the E end of the Kerch Peninsula. Pop. (1991) 178,000.

Main industrial centre of the Crimea. Manufactures iron and steel from iron ore mined just S; also ships iron ore to the mainland. Ship-repairing, fishing and fish-canning, railway engineering.

Founded by the Greeks from Miletus in the 6th cent. BC; has many features of archaeological interest.

Kerch Peninsula Ukraine. Peninsula 96 km (60 miles) long and up to 48 km (30 miles) wide in E Crimea, between the Sea of Azov (N) and the Black Sea (S); separated from the mainland by Kerch Strait and joined to the rest of the Crimea by an isthmus 16 km (10 miles) wide. Important iron-ore deposits. Chief town Kerch.

Kerch Strait Ukraine. Ancient Bosporus Cimmerius. Shallow strait 40 km (25 miles) long and up to 14 km (9 miles) wide, connecting the Black Sea with the Sea of Azov and separating E Crimea from the mainland.

Kerguelen Islands Indian Ocean. Archipelago consisting of one large volcanic island (Kerguelen or Desolation Island) and about 300 small islands, at 48°–50°S lat., 68°–70°E long. in the Indian Ocean. Total area 6675 sq km (2577 sq. miles). Pop. 67 (scientists). Forms part of the French Southern and Antarctic Territories. The main island rises to over 1800 m (5922 ft) and is partly covered with snowfields and glaciers; famous for its unique Kerguelen cabbage. Reindeer, trout and sheep have been acclimatized. Dis-

covered by Yves D. Kerguelen (1772) but only effectively occupied by France in 1949.

Kerkira ►CORFU.

Kerkrade Netherlands. Town in Limburg province 24 km (15 miles) E of Maastricht on the German frontier. Pop. (1992) 53,364.

Kermadec Islands SW Pacific Ocean. Group of volcanic islands belonging to New Zealand 960 km (600 miles) NE of Auckland. Area 34 sq km (13 sq. miles). Mountainous and fertile, but only Raoul (Sunday) Island, the largest (28 sq km; 11 sq. miles), is inhabited, serving as a meteorological station. Annexed by New Zealand in 1887.

Kerman Iran. Cap. of Kerman province 434 km (270 miles) ENE of Shiraz at a height of 1700 m (5593 ft). Pop. (1986) 257,284.

Commercial centre and road junction. Manufactures carpets, shawls and brass-ware.

Surrounded by walls of sun-baked clay. Has an 11th-cent. mosque (restored).

Kermanshah ►BAKHTARÁN.

Kerry Ireland. County in Munster province in the SW. Area 4701 sq km (1815 sq. miles). Pop. (1991) 121,719. Cap. Tralee. The coastline is much indented, the main inlets being Tralee Bay, Dingle Bay and Kenmare R.; there are many offshore islands. Inland is the range Macgillicuddy's Reeks, rising to 1041 m (3425 ft) in Carrantuohill, the highest point in Ireland.

Fishing, farming and catering for holidaymakers are important occupations. Noted for its beautiful scenery, particularly in the district round the lakes of Killarney; among the resorts are Tralee, Ballybunion, Killarney and Listowel. Manufactures inc. engineering products, footwear, woollen goods and cutlery.

Keswick England. Town in Cumbria on the R. Greta near the N end of Derwentwater. Pop. (1991) 4836.

Tourist centre and market town; it manufactures pencils.

Ketchikan USA. City in Alaska on the SE

coast of Revillagigedo Island in the SE of Alaska. Pop. (1990) 13,828. Noted for heavy rainfall.

Trade and service centre for a mining, lumbering and fishing area, with associated manufactures.

Kettering England. Town in Northamptonshire 21 km (13 miles) NNE of Northampton. Pop. (1991) 76,150.

Important centre of leather and footwear manufacture. Also manufactures machine-tools, clothing and computer software.

Baptist Missionary Society founded here in 1792.

Kettering USA. City situated S of Dayton, Ohio and forming a suburb. Pop. (1990) 60,569.

Residential, service and professional economy; other industries inc. automobiles, health services and electronics.

Kew England. Residential district in the London borough of Richmond-upon-Thames on the S bank of the R. Thames. The world-famous Kew Gardens (officially the Royal Botanic Gardens) (117 ha; 288 acres), containing hothouses, conservatories and museums, were founded in 1759 and presented to the nation in 1840. Here is Kew Palace, home of George IV when Prince of Wales. Just SW of the Gardens is Kew Observatory.

Keweenaw Peninsula USA. Peninsula in Michigan, curving NE into L. Superior and tapering off to Keweenaw Point. Formerly well-known for its copper; rich deposits of the metal were worked by the Indians before the arrival of European explorers. It is now mainly a resort area.

Key West USA. Southernmost city of the USA in S Florida on the island of Key West, the most westerly of the Florida Keys. Pop. (1990) 30,000. A naval and air station and a coastguard base. It is a popular tourist resort and fishing is an important occupation. Terminus of the highway spanning the Florida Keys from the mainland. Discovered by Spanish sailors in the early 16th cent. The

haunt of pirates and smugglers in the 17th and 18th cent.

Khabarovsk Russia. Cap. of Khabarovsk Territory on the Amur R. at the point where the river is crossed by the Trans-Siberian Railway. Pop. (1992) 615,000.

Chief industrial centre in E Siberia. Oil-refining, tanning, brewing, flour-milling. Manufactures machinery and chemicals. Trade in furs.

Named after the Russian explorer Khabarov, who built a fort here (1652). Became the administrative centre of the Russian Far East 1880; increased in importance after being reached by the railway (1937).

Khakassia Russia. Republic on the upper Yenisei R. Area 61,900 sq km (23,855 sq. miles). Pop. (1992) 581,000. Cap. Abakan. Dairy-farming and lumbering are important occupations; coal and other minerals are produced. Formed in 1930 and granted republican status in 1991.

Khanka, Lake Russia/China. Lake N of Vladivostok on the China/Russia frontier. Area 4400 sq km (1700 sq. miles). Fed by the Mo and Lefu rivers, drained by the Sungacha river into the Ussuri river.

Khanty-Mansi Russia. Autonomous district in W Siberia in the Tyumen Region. Area 523,100 sq km (202,000 sq. miles). Pop. (1992) 1,305,000. Cap. Khanty-Mansiisk at the confluence of the Ob and Irtysh rivers. Fishing and lumbering.

Kharagpur India. Town in West Bengal 113 km (70 miles) WSW of Calcutta. Pop. (1991) 264,800.

Industrial centre. Railway junction. Industries inc. railway and other engineering, rice-milling and scooter and car manufacture.

Kharga Oasis (Great Oasis) Egypt. Largest and southernmost of the Egyptian oases, occupying a depression in the Libyan Desert 160 km (100 miles) long N–S and up to 80 km (50 miles) wide E–W. Pop. 11,000 (mainly Berber). Chief town El Kharga 177 km (110 miles) WSW of Nag Hammadi on the Nile, with which it is linked by rail.

Chief products dates, cereals, rice, vines and bananas.

Kharkov (Kharkiv) Ukraine. Cap. of the Kharkov Region at the confluence of two small tributaries of the N Donets R. 418 km (260 miles) ESE of Kiev. Pop. (1992) 1,623,000. The second largest city in the Ukraine after Kiev and an important railway and road junction and major industrial centre, specializing in heavy engineering. Manufactures tractors and other agricultural machinery, food products, coalmining, oil-drilling and electrical equipment, locomotives and machine-tools, chemicals and textiles.

Seat of a university (1804), with many technological and other educational institutions. Founded in the mid 17th cent. Became cap. of the Ukraine 1765. Grew rapidly in the latter half of the 19th cent. with the development of the Donets coalfield and the Krivoi Rog iron deposits, which fed its metallurgical industries. Cap. of the Ukrainian Soviet Socialist Republic 1920–34, being superseded by Kiev.

Khartoum Sudan. Cap. of Sudan and of Khartoum province on the left bank of the Blue Nile just above the confluence with the White Nile. Pop. (1983) 476,218.

The largest trade centre, esp. for cotton. Connected with Khartoum North by a rail and road bridge across the Blue Nile and with Omdurman by a bridge across the White Nile. Terminus of railways from Port Sudan and El Obeid (via Sennar) and from Wadi Halfa. Steamer services up the White Nile to Kosti and thence to Juba. There is an oil pipeline running NE to Port Sudan. The Gordon Memorial College and Kitchener School of Medicine were amalgamated into the University College of Khartoum in 1951. Founded (1822) by the Egyptians after their conquest of the Sudan. Developed quickly as a general and slave market. Destroyed by the Mahdists in 1885 (when General Gordon was killed), but recaptured by Anglo–Egyptian forces under Lord Kitchener in 1898; Kitchener drafted the new layout in the form of a Union Jack.

Khartoum North Sudan. Town in Khartoum province on the right bank of the Blue Nile opposite Khartoum, with which it is linked by bridge. Pop. (1983) 341,146.

River dockyards and workshops. Trade in cotton and cereals; industries inc. food-processing, weaving and tanning.

Khasi Hills India. Range of hills in Meghalaya extending over 160 km (100 miles) W–E and rising to 1893 m (6228 ft). Cherrapunji, on the S slope, is said to have the world's heaviest rainfall, 1087 cm (428 ins.) annually.

Khaskovo (Haskovo) Bulgaria. Cap. of Khaskovo province 72 km (45 miles) ESE of Plovdiv. Pop. (1992) 95,807.

Centre of the tobacco trade. Manufactures cigarettes, carpets, woollen goods and food products.

Khatanga River Russia. River 659 km (412 miles) long in NE Krasnoyarsk Territory, formed by the union of the Kotui and Moiero rivers and flowing N and NE to enter the Laptev Sea by a long estuary. It is well-stocked with fish.

Kherson Ukraine. Cap. of the Kherson Region and port on the Dnieper R. 29 km (18 miles) from the mouth. Pop. (1991) 365,000.

Exports grain and timber. Industries inc. flour-milling, brewing and shipbuilding. Manufactures machinery, textiles, food products.

So named because it was believed to be the site of the Greek colony of Chersonesus Heracleotica, but the present city was founded in 1778 by Potemkin as a naval base and seaport.

Khingan Mountains China. Two mountain ranges, the Great Khingan and Little Khingan Mountains. The former extend NNE for about 1100 km (700 miles) along the E edge of the Mongolian plateau to the Amur R., rising to 2034 m (6692 ft); from their extension, the Ilkhuri Shan, the latter extend SE parallel to and S of the Amur R. rising to 1421 m (4675 ft). The Great Khingan

Mountains are well-forested and lumbering is important.

Khios ➤CHIOS.

Khiva Uzbekistan. Town in the fertile Khiva oasis 40 km (25 miles) from the left bank of the Amu Darya (Oxus), by which it is irrigated. Pop. (1986) 24,500.

Manufactures carpets and textiles.

Remains of the former khan's palace and mosques. Khiva was a powerful kingdom in the 10th–13th cent., but was conquered by Genghis Khan (1220), Timur (1379) and the Uzbeks (1512). In the late 16th cent. the town of Khiva became cap. of the khanate of Khiva, which was taken by the Russians in 1873; in 1920 the khan was deposed and the Khorezm Soviet People's Republic was established. In 1924 the territory was divided between the Uzbek and Turkmen Soviet Socialist Republics.

Khmelnitsky Ukraine. Formerly Pro-skurov. Cap. of the Khmelnitsky Region (formerly Kamenets Podolsk) on the Southern Bug R. 274 km (170 miles) WSW of Kiev. Pop. (1991) 245,000.

Railway junction. Engineering, furniture and food-processing industries.

Khmer Republic ➤CAMBODIA.

Khodzhent ➤KHUDZHAND.

Khoper River Russia. River 960 km (600 miles) long, rising 42 km (26 miles) WSW of Penza and flowing generally SSW to join the Don R. Unnavigable. Ice-bound for about 3 months annually.

Khorramshahr (Khurramshahr) Iran. Port in Khuzistán province on the Shatt-al-Arab at the confluence with the Karun R. Pop. (1986) 104,647.

Handles the major part of the country's overseas trade. Exports dates, cotton, hides and skins. Linked by pipeline with the oil-fields and by rail and road with Ahwáz and Tehrán. The port was modernized during World War II, being on one of the lend-lease routes to the USSR.

Khotan ➤HOTAN.

Khouribga Morocco. Town situated SE of Casablanca. Pop. (1986) 128,000.

Important phosphate-mining centre with associated industries.

Khudzhand Tajikistan. Formerly Leninabad. Town on the Syr Darya 200 km (125 miles) NNE of Dushanbe. Pop. (1991) 164,500.

Manufactures textiles, clothing, embroideries, silks and footwear.

Khulna Bangladesh. Cap. of division. Situated on the Ganges delta SW of Dacca. Pop. (1991) 601,051. Subject to cyclones causing high tidal waves.

It exports timber and builds ships.

Khurramabad Iran. Town in Khuzistán 240 km (150 miles) N of Ahwáz. Pop. (1986) 208,592.

Commercial centre. Trade in wool and fruit.

Khuzistán Iran. Province of Iran in SW at the head of the (Persian) Gulf. Area 66,532 sq km (25,688 sq. miles). Cap. Ahwáz. Pop. (1986) 2,681,978.

Main source of oil, and produces vegetables, dates, melons, cotton and rice.

Khyber Pass Afghanistan/Pakistan. Defile 53 km (33 miles) long through the Safed Koh range between Afghanistan and Pakistan, joining the valley of the Kabul R. with the Peshawar plains and the Indus valley. Flanked by high, barren cliffs, narrowing to 4.5 m (15 ft) at one point, it carries a railway and a road. Important strategically and as a trade route. The surrounding country is inhabited by Afridis.

Kiangsi ➤JIANGXI.

Kiangsu ➤JIANGSU.

Kicking Horse Pass Canada. Pass in the Rocky Mountains on the border of Alberta and British Columbia 56 km (35 miles) NW of Banff at a height of 1627 m (5339 ft). On the route followed by the Canadian Pacific Railway. Discovered (1859) by Sir James Hector, geologist of the Palliser expedition;

so named because he was kicked by his horse when crossing the mountains at this point.

Kidderminster England. Town in Worcestershire on the R. Stour 21 km (13 miles) N of Worcester. Pop. (1991) 56,644. Noted since 1735 for the carpet industry, introduced from Flanders.

Also manufactures textile machinery, woollen goods, electrical equipment, drop forging and chemicals.

Birthplace of Sir Rowland Hill (1795–1879), who introduced the penny post (1840).

Kidwelly Wales. Small town in Carmarthenshire on Carmarthen Bay 8 km (5 miles) NW of Llanelli. Pop. (1991) 2664. A silted-up harbour. Castle (13th-cent.). Limestone quarrying.

Kiel Germany. Cap. of Schleswig-Holstein on the Kieler Förde at the E end of the Kiel Canal. Pop. (1992) 247,107.

Chief industries shipbuilding, engineering; also flour-milling, brewing and fishing.

University (1665). It entered the Hanseatic League 1284. The naval base was established in 1871.

Kiel (North Sea–Baltic) Canal Germany. Formerly the Kaiser Wilhelm Canal. Waterway 98 km (61 miles) long connecting the Elbe estuary on the North Sea with the Kieler Förde on the Baltic Sea. Built 1887–95 to permit movement of the German fleet between the two seas and later widened. Given international status by the Treaty of Versailles (1919), but this was repudiated by Hitler in 1936.

Kielce (Kelsty) Poland. Cap. of the Kielce voivodeship 151 km (94 miles) S of Warsaw in the low hills of Gory Swietokrzyskie. Pop. (1992) 215,000.

Railway junction. Industries inc. brewing, tanning, flour-milling, sawmilling, and it manufactures textiles, cement, electrical goods and food products. There are copper mines and marble quarries.

Founded in 1173.

Kiev (Kyyiv) Ukraine. Cap. of Ukraine (since 1934) and of the Kiev Region on the right bank of the Dnieper R. Pop. (1991) 2,635,000.

River port. Important railway and road junction. Industrial centre. Flour-milling, sugar-refining, tanning. Manufactures machinery, chemicals, textiles, clothing and footwear. Also a leading cultural centre, with a university, transferred here in 1833, the Ukrainian Academy of Sciences and many other educational institutions.

Among its historic buildings are the Byzantine Cathedral of St Sophia and the Pechersky monastery, with its caves and catacombs, which in pre-revolution times was visited by over 20,000 pilgrims annually and has since been adapted to secular uses; both date from the 11th cent. Kiev is built mainly on bluffs overlooking the river, but the ancient Podol, where the famous 'contract fair' was held, stands on lower ground. Known as 'the mother of Russian cities', it was founded some time before the 9th cent. and in 988 its ruler, Prince Vladimir became a Christian and made it the first home of the Greek Church in Russia. With its considerable transit trade along the Dnieper, on the route between Scandinavia and Byzantium, the city and its principality flourished, but after its capture by Bogolyubsk (1169) and its destruction by the Tatars (1240) it declined. Held by Lithuania (1320–1569) and Poland (1569–1654) and was then annexed to Russia. Its commercial prosperity revived in the 19th cent. and sugar-refining and other industries developed, but it suffered cruelly in the revolution and again in World War II. Chernobyl, scene of the nuclear accident is about 90 km (55 miles) to the N.

Kigali Rwanda. Cap. of the republic 177 km (110 miles) NNE of Usumbura (Burundi). Pop. (1991) 232,733.

Commercial centre. Trade in coffee, hides and cattle.

Kikinda Serbia. Town 84 km (52 miles) NE of Novi Sad in Vojvodina near the Romanian border. Pop. (1981) 70,000.

Railway junction. Trade in wheat and flour.

Kildare (Cill Dara) Ireland. 1. County in Leinster province. Area 1694 sq km (654 sq. miles). Pop. (1991) 122,156. County town Naas. Generally low-lying and fertile, it has part of the Bog of Allen in the N and the Curragh (noted for its racehorses) in the centre. Drained by the Liffey and Barrow rivers. Cattle and horses raised. Potatoes and cereals grown.

2. Market town in Co. Kildare 50 km (29 miles) WSW of Dublin. Pop. (1991) 4196. Grew up round a monastery founded (490) by St Brigid. The 13th-cent. cathedral, destroyed in 1641 by Cromwell, was rebuilt 1683–6 and again in 1875.

Kilimanjaro, Mount Tanzania. Extinct volcano in the NE near the Kenya frontier 467 km (290 miles) NNW of Dar-es-Salaam. Two peaks: Mt Kibo (5895 m; 19,340 ft), the highest peak in Africa, permanently snow-capped, and Mt Mawanzi (5277 m; 16,896 ft). From 1200 m (3948 ft) to 1800 m (5922 ft) the slopes are planted with coffee, sisal, bananas and maize. From 1800 to 3000 m (5922 to 9870 ft) there are forests; above this level there are grasslands to about 3600 m (11,844 ft).

Kilkenny (Cill Chainnish) Ireland. 1. Inland county in Leinster in the SE. Area 2062 sq km (796 sq. miles). Pop. (1991) 73,613. Mainly hilly, rising to 517 m (1701 ft) in Mt Brandon (SE). Drained by the Nore, Barrow and Suir rivers. Oats, barley and potatoes cultivated and cattle reared in the fertile valleys.

2. County town of Co. Kilkenny on the R. Nore 103 km (64 miles) SW of Dublin. Pop. (1991) 9154.

Industries inc. textiles, footwear manufacture. There is limestone quarrying in the neighbourhood.

One of Ireland's oldest towns, once cap. of the ancient kingdom of Ossory. It has the 13th-cent. Protestant cathedral (restored) of St Canice after whom the town is named (*Cill Chainnish* 'Church of St Canice'), the

19th-cent. Roman Catholic Cathedral of St Mary, a 12th-cent. castle rebuilt in the 19th cent. and 13th-cent. Dominican and Franciscan abbeys.

Killarney (Cill Airne) Ireland. Market town and tourist centre in Co. Kerry in a district renowned for its scenic beauty. Pop. (1990) 7963. Has a 19th-cent. Roman Catholic cathedral and bishop's palace.

Manufactures footwear.

Near the town are the three famous Lakes of Killarney, Upper, Middle and Lower, the last also known as Lough Leane, being by far the largest. Also in the neighbourhood are the Gap of Dunloe, between Carrantuohill (1041 m; 3425 ft) and Purple Mountain (835 m; 2747 ft) and the ruins of the 14th-cent. Muckross Abbey.

Killiecrankie Pass Scotland. Wooded pass 5 km (3 miles) NW of Pitlochry, through which the R. Garry flows, used by road and railway. At its N end was fought the Battle of Killiecrankie (1689) in which Claverhouse (Bonnie Dundee) defeated William III's forces under Mackay but was himself killed.

Kilmarnock Scotland. Industrial town in East Ayrshire on Kilmarnock Water near its confluence with the R. Irvine. Pop. (1990) 48,000.

Industries inc. railway and other engineering. Manufactures carpets, knitwear and whisky.

Here the first edition of Robert Burns's poems was published (1786); in Kay Park is the Burns Memorial museum, which has many of his manuscripts and relics.

Kilrush Ireland. Small port and seaside resort in Co. Clare on the Shannon estuary. Pop. (1991) 2740. Scattery Island offshore has remains of ancient churches.

Kilsyth Scotland. Town in North Lanarkshire 21 km (13 miles) NNE of Glasgow. Pop. (1991) 9918.

Industrial centre in a coalmining region. Manufactures hosiery.

In 1645 Montrose defeated the Covenanters nearby.

Kilwinning Scotland. Town in North Ayrshire on the R. Garnock 14 km (9 miles) WNW of Kilmarnock. Pop. (1991) 15,479.

Industries inc. engineering, electronics and worsted spinning.

The reputed birthplace of Scottish freemasonry. Ruins of a 12th-cent. abbey dedicated to St Winnin – hence the name.

Kimberley Australia. District in the N of Western Australia consisting of rugged mountains surrounded by a grassland belt of potentially fertile country, drained by the Fitzroy, Ord and other rivers; often referred to as the Kimberleys (W and E). Gold, discovered 1882, mined at Hall's Creek. The first great cattle drive from New South Wales to the Kimberleys was made by the MacDonald brothers (1883); in recent years the Air Beef project, whereby livestock and carcases are flown, has made such long drives unnecessary.

Kimberley South Africa. Town in Northern Cape Province 869 km (540 miles) NE of Cape Town at a height of 1220 m (4014 ft). Pop. (1989) 154,000.

One of the world's chief diamond-mining centres. Also metalworking. Manufactures cement, furniture and clothing.

Founded 1870. The three main mining camps developed into the town, incorporated into Cape Colony in 1880. The two financial groups controlling the mines amalgamated and the entire diamond production came into the hands of De Beers Consolidated Mines Ltd (1899). It became an important railway centre; linked with Cape Town 1885, Johannesburg 1906 and Bloemfontein 1908. It was besieged for 5 months during the Boer War (1899–1900).

Kindia Guinea. Cap. of Kindia region. Pop. (1986) 80,000.

Trading centre for locally grown fruit. There is a branch of the Pasteur Institute, researching into apes. There are rich bauxite deposits in the area but they have not been exploited because of the difficulty of transport.

Kineshma Russia. Industrial town in the Ivanovo Region on the Volga R. 80 km (50 miles) ENE of Ivanovo, for which it is the river port. Pop. (1992) 104,000.

Textile centre. Also paper, sawmilling and other industries.

King Edward VII Land ➤ROSS DEPENDENCY.

King Faisal Port Saudi Arabia. Deep-water port at Jidda between Suez and Aden was commissioned in January 1973 and serves as the main port of entry for pilgrims to Mecca.

Kinghorn Scotland. Town in S Fife on the Firth of Forth 5 km (3 miles) S of Kirkcaldy. Pop. (1991) 2931. Monument nearby to Alexander III, thrown from his horse and killed here in 1286.

Kingsbridge England. Market town in S Devon at the head of Kingsbridge Estuary 16 km (10 miles) WSW of Dartmouth. Pop. (1991) 5258.

Flour-milling and brewing.

Kings Canyon National Park USA. Region of peaks, canyons and corries on the W slopes of the Sierra Nevada in California. Area 1834 sq km (708 sq. miles). Traversed by the Middle and South Forks of the Kings R., from which it takes its name. In the SW are stands of giant sequoia trees. Established 1940.

King's Lynn (Lynn Regis, Lynn) England. Market town in Norfolk on the Great Ouse R. just S of the Wash. Pop. (1991) 34,943.

Beet-sugar refining, canning, brewing, engineering. Manufactures food products. It is unusual in that it has two market places and two medieval guildhalls.

Among its buildings are the 12th-cent. Church of St Margaret, the 13th-cent. Greyfriars Tower, the 15th-cent. Red Mount Chapel and the 17th-cent. Custom House. Important from Saxon times; in medieval times a leading port.

King's Peak USA. Mountain peak in Utah situated E of Salt Lake City in the Uinta range at 4114 m (13,498 ft) above sea level, the highest point in Utah.

Kingsport USA. Industrial town in Tennessee on the Holston R. 140 km (87 miles) ENE of Knoxville. Pop. (1990) 36,365.

Manufactures paper, chemicals and textiles.

Kingston Canada. Port in Ontario at the NE end of L. Ontario. Pop. (1991) 56,597.

Manufactures locomotives, mining machinery, aluminium goods, man-made fibres and chemicals.

Seat of the Queen's University (1841) and the Royal Military College (1875). Cap. of United Canada 1841–4. Originally settled by the French in 1673, as Fort Frontenac. Destroyed by the English in 1758, it was refounded in 1782 by United Empire Loyalists and given its present name (after King George III).

Kingston Jamaica. Cap. and largest city on the SE coast; one of the chief ports of the West Indies with a deep, land-locked harbour. Pop. (1991) 103,771.

Headquarters of the coffee trade. Industries largely concerned with the processing of the island's agricultural produce. Manufactures cigars and cigarettes, matches, jam and clothing. Also brewing and fruit-canning.

The University of the West Indies is at Mona 6 km (4 miles) NE. The city was founded 1692, after the destruction of Port Royal by earthquake. Superseded Spanish Town as the official cap. 1872. Hurricanes have caused great damage at times. The earthquake of 1907 caused much destruction. There were serious fires in 1780, 1843, 1862 and 1882.

Kingston (New York) USA. Industrial town on the Hudson R. 142 km (88 miles) N of New York City. Pop. (1970) 25,544.

Manufactures clothing, bricks and tiles, and cement.

Originally settled in 1652 by the Dutch. The Senate House, built in 1676, was the meeting-place of the first state legislature.

Kingston (Pennsylvania) USA. Town on the Susquehanna R. opposite Wilkes-Barre. Pop. (1970) 18,325.

Anthracite-mining. Railway engineering. Manufactures cigars and hosiery.

Kingston-upon-Hull ➤HULL.

Kingston-upon-Thames England. Royal borough of London on the S bank of the R. Thames inc. Malden and Coombe and Surbiton. Pop. (1991) 136,800. Mainly residential with varied industries. Saxon kings were crowned here and the Coronation Stone is near the Guildhall (opened 1935).

Kingstown ➤ST VINCENT.

Kingswood England. Town in South Gloucestershire on the E outskirts of Bristol. Pop. (1971) 30,269 (19,000 in 1951).

Industries inc. engineering and the manufacture of footwear and brushes.

Kingussie Scotland. Town and tourist resort in Highland on the R. Spey 47 km (29 miles) SSE of Inverness. Pop. (1971) 1076.

Tourist centre in a sheep-farming district.

Ruthven on the opposite bank of the Spey was the birthplace of James 'Ossian' Macpherson, Scottish poet (1736–96).

Kinlochleven Scotland. Town in Highland at the head of Loch Leven and at the mouth of the R. Leven 14 km (9 miles) SE of Fort William. Pop. (1990) 1100.

Important hydroelectric plant and aluminium works.

Kinross Scotland. Town in Perth and Kinross on the W shore of Loch Leven. Pop. (1991) 4552. Textile mills and holiday resort.

Kinross-shire Scotland. Former county now part of Perth and Kinross.

Kinsale Ireland. Small fishing port and holiday resort in Co. Cork on the R. Bandon estuary. Pop. (1991) 1759. The liner *Lusitania* was torpedoed off the Old Head of Kinsale (S) in 1915.

Kinshasa Democratic Republic of the Congo. Formerly Léopoldville. Cap. on the left bank of the Congo R. just below Stanley

Pool. Pop. (1991) 3,804,000. A centre of air, river and rail routes. Connected by rail with Matadi 145 km (90 miles) down the river.

The largest city and chief commercial centre. Manufactures textiles and footwear.

One of the most modern cities in Africa, with wide avenues lined with tropical trees and plants. Founded (1887) by Stanley; named after Leopold II of Belgium. Replaced Boma as cap. of the Belgian Congo in 1929. Renamed Kinshasa in 1966.

Kintyre Scotland. Peninsula in Argyll and Bute extending 68 km (42 miles) SSW from Tarbert. Mainly hilly, rising to 446 m (1462 ft); the Mull of Kintyre, a headland 21 km (13 miles) across the North Channel from Northern Ireland in the S. Chief town Campbeltown.

Kioga (Kyoga), Lake Uganda. Shallow, swampy lake 129 km (80 miles) long with several long arms in the middle course on the Victoria Nile. Area 4400 sq km (1700 sq. miles). Navigable by vessels of shallow draught. Steamer services.

Kirghizia ➤KYRGYZSTAN.

Kiribati. Republic situated in the SW Pacific Ocean comprising 3 groups of coral atolls and one isolated volcanic island scattered over more than 4,180,000 sq km (2 million sq. miles) of ocean. Area 811 sq km (313 sq. miles). Pop. (1995) 80,400 (36 per cent urban). Life expectancy, 53 years male, 56 female. Cap. and main port Bairiki on Tarawa. Currency: Australian dollar = 100 cents. The 3 groups of coral islands are the Gilbert group inc. 16 islands, the Phoenix group 8 and the Line group 8. The highest point is 81 m (265 ft). The most important island is Tawara in the Gilbert group. The islands N of the equator have a plentiful rainfall, but many of those in the S suffer droughts. Temperatures uniformly high. Land use: forested 3 per cent, agricultural and under permanent cultivation 52 per cent. The official lang. is English but away from the cap. people are more likely to speak Gilbertese (I-Kiribati). The majority of the pop. belong to the Roman Catholic or

Congregational church. The pop. is almost entirely Micronesian.

Fish, together with copra, is Kiribati's major export. The sale of fishing rights brings in valuable foreign currency. Kiribati has granted licences to Russian fleets to fish for tuna in its waters. It imports most manufactured goods. However, there is a thriving handicraft industry, which is an important earner of foreign currency. Banaba was once rich in phosphate ores. These have now been almost mined to exhaustion. Phosphate production was discontinued in 1979.

The group was inc. in the British colony of the Gilbert and Ellice Islands in 1915. Several of them were occupied by the Japanese during World War II (1941), but were retaken by US forces in 1943. In 1975 the former Ellice Islands severed its constitutional link with the Gilbert Islands and took the name Tuvalu. Internal self-government was achieved in 1976 and independence in 1979 as the Republic of Kiribati (pronounced Kiribass). There is a 41-member unicameral House of Assembly elected for 4-year terms.

Kirin ➤JIRIN.

Kiritimati Kiribati (formerly Christmas Island). One of the Line Is. in the central Pacific. The largest atoll in the Pacific, it has an area of 359 sq km (139 sq. miles). Pop. (1990) 2537.

There are coconut plantations, producing copra.

Discovered (1777) by Capt. Cook. It was annexed by Britain and inc. in the Gilbert and Ellice Is. colony in 1919.

Kirkby-in-Ashfield England. Town in Nottinghamshire 18 km (11 miles) NNW of Nottingham. Pop. (1991) 27,014.

Industries inc. textiles and engineering.

Kirkcaldy Scotland. Port and industrial town in S Fife on the Firth of Forth. Pop. (1991) 50,000. Sometimes known as the 'Lang Toun' because of its main street, which runs nearly 6 km (4 miles) along the coast.

Important centre of linoleum manufacture. Textile and engineering industries. Coalmining in the neighbourhood.

Birthplace of Adam Smith, the economist (1723–90).

Kirkcudbright Scotland. Town in Dumfries and Galloway 40 km (25 miles) SW of Dumfries. Pop. (1989) 3500. Market town. Ruins of a 16th-cent. castle and of the 12th-cent. Dundrennan Abbey (7.2 km; 4½ miles SE).

Kirkcudbrightshire Scotland. Former county, now part of Dumfries and Galloway.

Kirkenes Norway. Port in Finnmark county in the extreme NE on an arm of Vaanger Fiord near the Russian border. Pop. (1997) 6500.

Formerly iron ore was exported from the nearby mines, which were closed in 1996.

It was a German submarine base in World War II and was largely destroyed by bombing, but has been rebuilt.

Kirkintilloch Scotland. Industrial town in East Dunbartonshire 10 km (6 miles) NE of Glasgow. Pop. (1991) 20,780.

Industrial centre. Iron-founding, engineering (esp. switchgear). Its Gaelic name means 'the Fort at the End of the Ridge', referring to the fort here on the Wall of Antoninus.

Kirkuk Iraq. Cap. of Tamim governorate in the NE 240 km (150 miles) N of Baghdad. Pop. (1981) 570,000.

Important chiefly as the centre of a rich oilfield (discovered 1927) with pipelines leading to Tripoli (Lebanon) and Banias (Syria), as well as a third, out of use since the Arab–Israeli War in 1948, to Haifa (Israel). Also a market town. Trade in sheep, grain and fruit.

Kirkwall Scotland. Port and county town of Orkney on Mainland. Pop. (1991) 6469. Largest town in the Orkneys.

Fishing. Distilling. Exports agricultural produce and whisky.

Its outstanding building is the Cathedral of St Magnus (founded 1137) and there are ruins of the bishop's palace.

Kirov Russia. Formerly Khlynov (till 1780),

Vyatka (1780–1934). Cap. of Kirov Region on the Vyatka R. 434 km (270 miles) NE of Nizhny Novgorod. Pop. (1992) 493,000.

Important railway junction. Railway engineering. Manufactures machine-tools, agricultural implements, textiles, matches, chemicals and footwear.

Founded by Novgorod merchants in the 12th cent. Annexed by Moscow 1489.

Kirovabad ➤GYANDZHA.

Kirovograd Ukraine. Formerly Elisavetgrad (till 1924), Zinovievsk (1924–36), Kirovo (1936–9). Cap. of the Kirovograd Region 257 km (160 miles) SE of Kiev. Pop. (1991) 278,000.

Manufactures agricultural machinery, soap and clothing. Sawmilling and brewing. Trades in grain.

Kirriemuir Scotland. Market town in Angus 8 km (5 miles) WNW of Forfar. Pop. (1989) 5000. There are grain and jute mills.

Birthplace of Sir J. M. Barrie, Scottish novelist and dramatist (1860–1937), and the 'Thrums' of his stories.

Kiruna Sweden. Town in Norrbotten county in the N. Pop. (1990) 26,500.

Important iron-mining centre, famous for the purity of its ore, sent by rail to Luleå 265 km (165 miles) to the ESE and Narvik (Norway) 143 km (89 miles) to the WNW for export. Stands between the two great ore-bearing mountains of Kiirunavaara and Luossavaara.

Kiryu Japan. Town in central Honshu in Gumma prefecture 96 km (60 miles) NNW of Tokyo. Pop. (1992) 124,556.

Manufactures textiles, esp. rayon and silk.

Kisangani Democratic Republic of the Congo. Formerly (till 1966) Stanleyville, situated on the upper Congo R. below Stanley Falls. Pop. (1991) 373,397.

Route centre with an important airport; the river port at the head of steam navigation (from Kinshasa) and terminus of the railway from Ponthierville circumventing Stanley Falls. Commercial and tourist centre.

Kiselevsk Russia. Town in the Kemerovo Region 40 km (25 miles) NW of Prokopyevsk. Pop. (1992) 126,000.

A coalmining centre in the Kuznetsk basin.

Kish Iraq. Ancient Sumerian city near the Euphrates R. 16 km (10 miles) E of Hilla, which flourished in the 4th millennium BC and was last mentioned in the 6th cent. BC. Among finds revealed by 20th-cent. excavations was an extensive collection of pottery dating from the early Sumerian.

Kishinev ➤CHIŞINĂU.

Kislovodsk Russia. Town and health resort in the Stavropol Territory in a deep valley of the N Caucasus at a height of 820 m (2690 ft) 29 km (18 miles) WSW of Pyatigorsk. Pop. (1992) 118,000.

Famous for mineral waters, bottled and sold throughout Russia. Sanatoria, convalescent homes and baths.

Kisumu (Port Florence) Kenya. Cap. of Nyanza province, port at the head of the Kavirondo gulf on the NE shore of L. Victoria 265 km (165 miles) WNW of Nairobi. Pop. (1986) 198,000.

Fishing. Once the terminus of the railway from Mombasa; the Nakuru–Kisumu section is now a branch line off the main route through Uganda.

Kitakyushu Japan. City in N Kyushu formed in 1963 by the union of the five towns Moji, Kokura, Tobata, Yawata and Wakamatsu, and given special autonomous rights. Pop. (1992) 1,020,877. All except Kokura are modern industrial cities and have little charm. Seat of the Kyushu Institute of Technology (1909).

Kitchener Canada. Industrial town in S Ontario 55 km (34 miles) WNW of Hamilton, Pop. (1991) 168,282.

Tanning, brewing and meat-packing. Manufactures lorries, trailers, textiles and furniture.

Originally settled in 1800 by Mennonites from Pennsylvania; first called Sand Hills, later Ebytown. In 1824, because of the large influx of German immigrants, renamed

Berlin. In 1916 the name was changed in honour of Lord Kitchener (drowned at sea in that year).

Kithira Greece. Island at the entrance to the Gulf of Laconia off the SE coast of Peloponnessos. Area 274 sq km (106 sq. miles). Chief town Kithira.

Main occupation growing vines and olives.

Kitimat Canada. Port in British Columbia at the head of the Douglas Channel 113 km (70 miles) ESE of Prince Rupert. Pop. (1986) 11,196.

An aluminium smelter, the largest in the world, receives power from the Kemano hydroelectric station 77 km (48 miles) away.

Kitwe Zambia. Town in the Western Province 48 km (30 miles) WNW of Ndola on a branch railway. Pop. (1990) 338,207.

Commercial centre for the nearby coppermining centre Nkana; the two together form the largest town in the Copperbelt. Minor industries.

Kitzbühel Austria. Former coppermining town in E Tirol 80 km (50 miles) ENE of Innsbruck. Pop. (1991) 8233. Now a resort and winter-sports centre.

Kivu, Lake Democratic Republic of the Congo/Rwanda. Lake in the W branch of the Great Rift Valley between L. Tanganyika and L. Edward 88 km (55 miles) long and up to 48 km (30 miles) wide at a height of 1473 m (4846 ft) (the highest lake in Africa). Drains S into L. Tanganyika through the Ruzizi R. Steamer services. Main ports Bukavu and Goma in Congo and Kisenyi in Rwanda.

Kizil Irmak River Turkey. River 1130 km (700 miles) long rising in the Kizil Dagh and flowing in a wide curve across the Anatolian plateau first SW, then NW and finally NE to the Black Sea.

Kladno Czech Republic. Industrial town in the Středočeský region, Bohemia 24 km (15 miles) WNW of Prague. Pop. (1990) 73,000.

Coalmining and metallurgical centre. Important iron and steel industry.

Knoxville

Klagenfurt Austria. Cap. of Carinthia province on the Glan R. near the E end of the Wörthersee. Pop. (1991) 89,415.

Resort in beautiful mountain scenery. Manufactures metal and leather goods and chemicals. A well-planned town, it has lost many of its old buildings in various fires, but still has the 16th-cent. Landhaus and Lindwurmbrunnen.

Klaipėda Lithuania. Formerly Memel. Baltic seaport at the entrance to the Kurisches Haff (Courland Lagoon). Pop. (1993) 206,400.

Industries inc. shipbuilding, fish-canning, flour-milling and the manufacture of wood-pulp, paper, plywood, textiles and soap. Trade in timber, grain and fish.

Founded (1252) by the Teutonic Knights; passed to Prussia (as Memel) and came under Lithuanian rule in 1924.

Klerksdorp South Africa. Town in Gauteng 160 km (100 miles) WSW of Johannesburg at a height of 1300 m (4264 ft) on the left bank of the Schoonspruit 16 km (10 miles) above the confluence with the Vaal R. Pop. (1980) 238,680.

Goldmining and agricultural centre. Railway junction.

The first Boer settlement in the Transvaal, founded here in 1839.

Klondike River Canada. River 160 km (100 miles) long in Yukon Territory, flowing W to join the Yukon R. at Dawson; it gives its name to the gold-producing region to the S. Gold was discovered on Bonanza Creek, a tributary, in 1896 and the Klondike gold rush began. Dawson rapidly grew from a few houses to a town of over 20,000 people; but gold production reached its maximum in 1900 and has steadily declined since.

Klosterneuburg Austria. Town on the Danube R. on the N outskirts of Vienna. Pop. (1991) 24,591. Wine-making.

Has a magnificent Augustinian monastery, the oldest and one of the wealthiest in Austria, founded by Leopold the Holy in 1106, with the Leopold Chapel containing the 12th-cent. altar by Nicholas of Verdun.

Klyuchevskaya Sopka Russia. Highest active volcano on the mainland of Asia (4750 m; 15,627 ft) in the Kamchatka peninsula 354 km (220 miles) NNE of Petropavlovsk.

Knaresborough England. Market town in North Yorkshire on the R. Nidd 5 km (3 miles) ENE of Harrogate. Pop. (1991) 13,380.

Industries inc. tourism and electronics. Limestone-quarrying in the neighbourhood.

Has a ruined castle (mainly 14th-cent.) and the Dropping Well, with petrifying properties, near which is Mother Shipton's Cave, where the 15th/16th-cent. prophetess was supposed to have been born.

Knock (Cnoc) Ireland. Village 60 km (37 miles) NE of Galway city on the W coast. Over 2 million pilgrims visit each year to see where a vision of the Virgin Mary was seen in 1879. An international airport (Horan) was constructed in the 1980s.

Knockmealdown Mountains Ireland. Range extending 29 km (18 miles) E–W along the border between Co. Tipperary and Co. Waterford and rising to 796 m (2619 ft).

Knokke-Heist Belgium. Resort situated 18 km (11 miles) N of Bruges. Pop. (1992) 31,965. Its beach is 12 km (7 miles) long, one-fifth of the Belgian coastline.

Knossos (Cnossus) Crete. Ancient city near the N coast 6 km (4 miles) SE of Iráklion, its port. Centre of a Bronze Age civilization, occupied well before 3000 BC. Excavations, esp. by Sir Arthur Evans (1851–1941), revealed many archaeological treasures, inc. the great palace (2000–1400 BC), from which a great deal of information about the Minoan civilization has been obtained. Destroyed by fire c. 1400 BC, but its ruins were inhabited till Roman times.

Knoxville USA. Industrial town and river port in E Tennessee on the Tennessee R. Pop. (1990) 165,121.

In a region of coal, iron and zinc mines, and marble quarries. Trade in tobacco. Manufactures textiles, cement and furniture.

Seat of the University of Tennessee

(1794). Headquarters of the Tennessee Valley Authority (TVA). First settled 1786. State cap. 1796–1812 and 1817–19.

Knutsford England. Town in Cheshire 23 km (14 miles) SSW of Manchester, for which it is a residential suburb. Pop. (1991) 13,352.

Manufactures textiles and paper.

The name is supposed to be derived from 'Canute's Ford' (though there is no evidence that it was inhabited before the Norman Conquest).

Kobarid Slovenia. Village in the NW on the Isonzo R. near the Italian frontier. Formerly in Italy; ceded to Yugoslavia in 1947. Scene of the disastrous defeat of the Italians by the Austro–German army in World War I (1917).

Kobe Japan. Cap. of Hyogo prefecture in SW Honshu 31 km (19 miles) W of Osaka on Osaka Bay. Pop. (1992) 1,499,195.

Important seaport and industrial centre extending 14 km (9 miles) along the coast. One of the world's largest container terminals. Exports textiles, ships and metal goods. Industries inc. shipbuilding (esp. important), engineering, sugar-refining and it manufactures iron and steel, chemicals, textiles and rubber products.

In the rapid growth of the city the old port of Hyogo was absorbed in 1878.

Köbenhaven ➤COPENHAGEN.

Koblenz ➤COBLENZ.

Kochi (Cochin) India. Major port in Kerala on the Malabar coast 177 km (110 miles) NNW of Trivandrum. Pop. (1991) 564,038.

Industries inc. oil-refining, shipbuilding, fertilizers, petrochemicals and tyres.

This was the earliest European settlement in India (1503).

Kochi Japan. Cap. of Kochi prefecture in S Shikoku. Pop. (1992) 318,009.

Seaport. Exports dried fish (bonito), coral and paper.

Kodiak Island USA. Island 160 km (100 miles) long in Alaska in the Gulf of Alaska.

Pop. (1984) 6469 (city), 13,389 (island). Hilly with a deeply indented coastline. The first European settlement in Alaska was that of the Russians under Shelekhov at Three Saints Bay (1784); this was moved to Kodiak on the NE coast (1792), which was the head-quarters of the Russian–American Company until it moved to Sitka. Kodiak town is a fishing port with salmon canneries.

Kodok Sudan. Formerly Fashoda. Town on the left bank of the White Nile 628 km (390 miles) S of Khartoum. Pop. (1989) 3000. Its temporary occupation by Marchand, a French officer, caused a diplomatic crisis between England and France ('the Fashoda incident') in 1898.

Koforidua Ghana. Town in Eastern Province situated N of Accra. Pop. (1984) 58,731.

Distribution centre for cacao.

Kofu Japan. Cap. of Yamanashi prefecture in central Honshu 109 km (68 miles) W of Tokyo. Pop. (1992) 200,611.

Industrial centre. Manufactures silk goods, glassware, saké and food products.

Kohat Pakistan. Town 48 km (30 miles) S of Peshawar. Pop. (1985) 78,000.

Trade in grain and salt. Minor industries. Linked with Peshawar by road through the Kohat Pass.

Kokand Uzbekistan. Town in the fertile Fergana Valley. Pop. (1991) 175,000.

Sugar-refining, flour-milling. Manufactures textiles, fertilizers and silk. Trade in cotton.

Has the former khan's palace. An ancient town, it was cap. of the powerful khanate of Kokand in the 18th cent. Taken by the Russians 1876.

Kokkola Finland. Town situated in Kaarlela NNE of Vaasa on the Gulf of Bothnia. Pop. (1992) 34,942.

There is heavy industry and also textiles and leather.

Kokomo USA. Industrial town in Indiana 80 km (50 miles) N of Indianapolis. Pop. (1984) 45,400.

Manufactures iron, steel and brass products, motor-car and tractor parts and plastics.

Named after a Miami Indian chief, Kokomoko.

Koko Nor China. Salt lake in NE Qinqhai province about 80 km (50 miles) WNW of Sining at a height of over 3000 m (9870 ft). Area 4144 sq km (1600 sq. miles). Shallow and variable in extent.

Kokura Japan. Industrial town and seaport in Fukuoka prefecture, N Kyushu 64 km (40 miles) NE of Fukuoka.

Manufactures steel, chemicals, textiles and porcelain.

Merged (1963) with the neighbouring towns of Moji, Tobata, Yawata and Wakamatsu to form the new city of Kitakyushu.

Kola Peninsula Russia. Peninsula in the Murmansk Region between the Barents Sea (N) and the White Sea (S), and mainly N of the Arctic Circle. Area 129,500 sq km (50,000 sq. miles). A low plateau mainly of granite and gneiss, with tundra in the N and thin forests in the S and with many lakes, the largest being L. Imandra. In recent years it has become an important mining region, producing apatite, nepheline in the Kirovsk area, the minerals being exported from Kandalaksha. Chief town and seaport Murmansk on Kola Bay (N).

Kolarovgrad ➤SHUMEN.

Kolding Denmark. Town and port in E Jutland on Kolding Fiord (Little Belt). Pop. (1993) 58,493.

Manufactures machinery, cement and food products.

Ruins of the 13th-cent. castle, Koldinghus, lie NW.

Kolhapur India. Town in Maharashtra 290 km (180 miles) SSE of Bombay. Pop. (1991) 406,400.

Manufactures textiles, pottery, matches, leather, sugar and silverware. Also cotton-ginning.

Köln ➤COLOGNE.

Kolobrzeg (Ger. **Kolberg**) Poland. Baltic

seaport and seaside resort in the Koszalin voivodeship. Pop. (1989) 40,200.

Manufactures machinery, and tourism is important.

An ancient town; has a 14th-cent. red-brick church.

Kolomna Russia. Industrial town in the Moscow Region on the Moskva R. near the confluence with the Oka R. 105 km (65 miles) SE of Moscow. Pop. (1992) 164,000.

Important railway engineering centre; manufactures locomotives, wagons, diesel engines and textile machinery.

Founded in the 12th cent., it suffered repeatedly from the Tatar invasions.

Kolomyya (Polish **Kolomyja**) Ukraine. Town on the Prut R. Pop. (1970) 41,000. Formerly in Poland (from 1919) but ceded to the USSR in 1945.

Railway junction. Trade in agricultural produce. Metalworking and oil-refining. Manufactures textiles and chemicals.

Kolonia Micronesia. Town in Pohnpei state. Pop. (1989) 6160.

Kolonjë Albania. Town situated S of Koritsa at the foot of the Grammos mountains, a lignite-mining centre.

Kolwezi Democratic Republic of the Congo. Town in the S of Shaba 145 km (90 miles) W of Likasi. Pop. (1991) 544,497.

Commercial, tourist and transport centre for an important mining region producing copper and cobalt.

Kolyma Range Russia. Mountain range in the N Khabarovsk Territory extending 800 km (500 miles) NE between the Kolyma R. and the Sea of Okhotsk.

Kolyma River Russia. River 2575 km (1600 miles) long in N Khabarovsk Territory and the Sakha Republic rising in the Cherski Range and flowing generally N and NE to the East Siberian Sea, passing in its upper course through the Kolyma goldfields. Navigable for about 1600 km (1000 miles) in summer.

Komandorski (Commander Islands)

Russia. Group of islands in the Khabarovsk Territory between the Kamchatka peninsula and the Aleutian Is., the largest being Bering and Medny. Main settlement Nikolskoye. Home of fur seals.

Komárom Hungary. Town on the right bank of the Danube R. opposite Komarno, Czech Republic. Pop. (1985) 36,000.

Railway centre and river port. Industries inc. textiles and sawmilling.

Komati River Mozambique/South Africa. River 800 km (500 miles) long rising in SE Gauteng, flowing generally E through N Swaziland, crossing into Mozambique at Komatipoort (on the railway from Johannesburg to Maputo), taking a wide curve N, E and then S and entering the Indian Ocean at Delagoa Bay. Navigable from the mouth to Komatipoort.

Komi Republic Russia. Autonomous republic. Area 415,900 sq km (160,540 sq. miles). Pop. (1992) 1,225,000. Cap. Syktyvkar. Consisting mainly of the basins of the Pechora, Vychegda and upper Mezen rivers, it is generally low-lying but rises to over 1500 m (4935 ft) along the E border in the Ural Mountains. Most of it is forested, there is a considerable stretch of tundra in the N and the relatively small farming area is devoted chiefly to stock-rearing, with reindeer-raising and fishing in the tundra. Coal is produced in the Pechora basin (Vorkuta) and oil at Ukhta, both industries having been stimulated by the construction of the railway across the republic. Timber is floated down the rivers to the coast.

Komi-Permyak Autonomous Area Russia. National area in the Perm Region. Area 32,900 sq km (12,700 sq. miles). Pop. (1992) 160,000. Cap. Kudymkar (153 km; 95 miles NW of Perm). Largely forested: provides timber for cellulose and paper mills.

Kommunizma Pik ►GARMO, MOUNT.

Komotini ►COMOTINI.

Kompong Cham Cambodia. Town situ-

ated NE of Phnom Penh on the Mekong R. Provincial cap. Pop. (1990) 33,000.

Centre of a rubber-growing area. Industries inc. the manufacture of rubber and beverages.

Kompong Chhnang Cambodia. Town situated NNW of Phnom Penh on the Tonle Sap R. at the head of navigation. Pop. (1987) 15,000.

Trading centre for livestock, and industries inc. the manufacture of bricks and pottery.

Komsomolsk (Komsomolsk-na-Amur) Russia. Industrial town in the S Khabarovsk Territory on the Amur R. 282 km (175 miles) NE of Khabarovsk, with which it is linked by rail. Pop. (1992) 319,000. Founded (1932) by the Komsomol or Communist Youth League; developed rapidly as a centre of heavy industry.

Shipbuilding and sawmilling. Manufactures steel, wood-pulp, paper and chemicals.

Kong Karls Land Norway. Island group E of Spitsbergen, Svalbard in the Barents Sea. Area 332 sq km (128 sq. miles). The main island is Kongsoya, rising to 320 m (1050 ft) above sea level.

Königsberg ►KALININGRAD.

Konstantinovka (Kostyantynovka) Ukraine. Town in the Donbas 58 km (36 miles) N of Donetsk. Pop. (1991) 108,000.

Important metallurgical centre. Manufacures iron and steel, chemicals and glass.

Konstanz ►CONSTANCE.

Konya Turkey. Ancient Iconium. Cap. of Konya province 233 km (145 miles) S of Ankara at a height of 990 m (3257 ft) on the edge of the central plateau. Pop. (1990) 513,346.

Manufactures textiles, carpets and leather goods. Trade in grain, wool and mohair.

Ancient cap. of Lycaonia; visited by St Paul. Conquered by the Seljuk Turks in the 11th cent.; under them it became cap. of the sultanate of Iconium or Rum and reached the peak of its fame in the 13th cent.

Kootenay River Canada/USA. River

655 km (407 miles) long, rising in SE British Columbia (Canada), flowing S through Montana and Idaho (USA), where it is known as the Kootenai and then turning NW to form the Kootenay L. in British Columbia, by which it is connected with the Columbia R. Around the upper reaches is the Kootenay National Park (1380 sq km; 533 sq. miles), established in 1920 to preserve the wildlife and beautiful scenery of the area. The headquarters is the small town and resort of Radium Hot Springs.

Kopelsk Russia. Formerly Ugolnye Kopi, Goskopi, Kopi. Town in the Chelyabinsk Region just S of Chelyabinsk. Pop. (1974) 156,000.

Important lignite-mining centre.

Koptus ►COPTUS.

Kórcë Albania. Cap. of the Kórcë region and district in the SE. Pop. (1991) 67,100.

Market town in a cereal-growing area. Industries inc. knitwear, flour-milling, brewing and sugar-refining.

It was an important Orthodox and Muslim religious centre. The fifth largest town in Albania.

Korčula Croatia. Island in the Adriatic Sea 43 km (27 miles) long and 8 km (5 miles) wide. Area 277 sq km (107 sq. miles). Pop. (1985) 30,000. Chief town Korčula on the E coast, a port and seaside resort.

Main occupations fishing, cultivation of vines and olives. There is also marble-quarrying.

Korea, North. State situated on a peninsula in E Asia bounded on the N by China, E by the Sea of Japan, W by the Yellow Sea and S by South Korea, from which it is separated by the demilitarized zone of 1262 sq km (487 sq. miles). Area 122,762 sq km (47,400 sq. miles). Pop. (1995) 23,487,000 (61 per cent urban). Life expectancy, 67 years male, 73 female. Cap. Pyongyang. Other cities Chongjin, Nampo, Sinuiju and Wonsan. Currency: Won = 100 chŏn. About 75 per cent of the country is mountainous; its highest peak is Paek-tu 2744 m (9003 ft).

There is a warm temperate climate, with hot, rainy summers and dry, cold winters. Land use: forested 75 per cent, meadows and pastures 0.4 per cent, agricultural and under permanent cultivation 17 per cent. Confucianism was introduced as the official religion of the Yi dynasty which came to power in 1392, but was subsequently mixed with Buddhism. There are about 3 million Chindoists, 400,000 Buddhists and 200,000 Christians. The Korean people are distinct from both the Chinese and Japanese and the Korean lang. is not related to any other; they developed a phonic alphabet in c. 1400.

In 1946 all estates exceeding 5 ha (12 acres) were divided among smallholders and landless peasants, and agriculture has been largely mechanized. Oil wells went into production in 1957. There are 3 thermal power stations and 4 hydroelectric plants. Earlier its economy was supported by loans from China and the former USSR. About 40 per cent of the pop. are engaged in agriculture working on collective farms. Main food crop rice; barley, wheat, soya beans, tobacco and cotton are also cultivated. Minerals inc. coal, zinc, iron ore, lead and gold. Industrial development has inc. machine and metallurgical production, textiles, chemicals and cement. The economy has declined with the collapse of the USSR.

Korea has a very ancient history, with traditions and a culture of its own although subject to Chinese and Japanese influence. It was subject to attacks by the Chinese, Manchus and Japanese and was for long a vassal of Manchu China and kept so segregated as to be known as the Hermit Kingdom. After the Sino–Japanese War (1894–5) Japan compelled China to give up control of Korea and, after the Russo–Japanese War (1904–05), annexed the country (1910) and brought to an end the Yi dynasty which had ruled since 1392. At the end of World War II US troops occupied the S and Russian troops the N (1945), the peninsula being divided along the 38th parallel. In 1948 two separate regimes were established, the Republic of Korea in the S and the People's Republic of Korea in the N. In 1950 North Korean troops invaded the S without warning, but were driven back by UN forces to the Manchurian border; Chinese troops now supported the N and advanced far into the S, only to be driven back to the 38th parallel again. In June 1951 a ceasefire was called and two years later an armistice was signed, the boundary running across the 38th parallel. In 1991 both North and South Korea signed a declaration of non-aggression, but further progress in normalization has been slow. There is a 687-member Supreme People's Assembly elected every 5 years by universal suffrage. In practice the country is governed by the Korean Workers' (i.e. Communist) Party.

Korea, South. State (generally known as Korea) situated on a peninsula in E Asia bounded on the N by the demilitarized zone (separating it from North Korea), E by the Sea of Japan, S by the Korea Strait (separating it from Japan) and W by the Yellow Sea. Area 99,263 sq km (38,326 sq. miles). Pop. (1995) 44,834,000 (81 per cent urban). Life expectancy, 68 years male, 76 female. Cap. Seoul. Other important towns Pusan, Taegu, Inchon and Kwangju. Currency: Won = 100 chon. Most of the country is mountainous apart from the limited coastal lowlands and the areas around the river basins where the majority of the pop. live. It has a continental temperate climate, while the extreme S has a humid warm temperate climate. Land use: forested 65 per cent, meadows and pastures 0.8 per cent, agricultural and under permanent cultivation 21 per cent. Confucianism was introduced as the official religion of the Yi dynasty which came to power in 1392, but was subsequently mixed with Buddhism; about 24 per cent are Buddhist, 16 per cent Protestants, 5 per cent Roman Catholic, 2 per cent Confucians. The official lang. is Korean.

Industrial development has been made difficult by lack of raw materials and power resources, formerly supplied from the N. About 16 per cent of the pop. is engaged in farming. Main crops rice, barley, wheat, soya beans; tobacco and cotton are also cultivated. There is a strong manufacturing base that

started with the textile industry and has now expanded to shipbuilding, footwear, electrical and electronic equipment, steel, vehicles, toys and petrochemicals.

For history of Korea to 1951 ►KOREA, NORTH. Talks in recent years on reunification have failed. There is a 299-member National Assembly directly elected for 4-year terms. The President is directly elected for a single 5-year term. For local government the country is divided into 15 provinces.

Korinthos ►CORINTH.

Koriyama Japan. Industrial town in the Fukushima prefecture, Honshu 43 km (27 miles) S of Fukushima. Pop. (1992) 320,209.

Manufactures textiles, chemicals and machinery.

Kortrijk ►COURTRAI.

Koryak Autonomous Area Russia. National Area in NE Siberia, inc. the isthmus and the N part of the Kamchatka peninsula. Area 301,500 sq km (116,400 sq. miles). Pop. (1992) 39,000. Cap. Palana. Its people are mainly Koryaks who gain a livelihood by reindeer-breeding, fishing and hunting.

Kos ►COS.

Kosciusko, Mount Australia. Highest peak in Australia (2230 m; 7316 ft) on a high plateau of the Australian Alps, New South Wales 145 km (90 miles) SSW of Canberra. Winter-sports centre. Named after the Polish patriot and statesman Tadeusz Kosciuszko (1746–1817).

Košice Slovakia. Cap. of the Východoslovenský region on the Hernád R. Pop. (1991) 234,840.

Manufactures textiles, machinery, fertilizers and food products.

The inner old town was built round the 14th/15th-cent. Gothic cathedral. Transferred from Hungary to Czechoslovakia in 1920.

Koso Gol (Höbsögöl) Mongolia. Lake in the extreme N at a height of 1708 m (5620 ft) its N end near the Russian frontier. Area 3108 sq km (1200 sq. miles). It is well stocked with fish. Frozen for 4–5 months annually. Drains S to the Selenga R.

Kosovo-Metohija Serbia. Former autonomous region in the SW, bordering SW on Albania. Area 10,887 sq km (4203 sq. miles). Pop. (1991) 1,956,196 (1,596,072 Albanians). Cap. Priština. A plateau drained by the S Morava, Ibar and White Drin rivers; in the fertile valleys it produces cereals, tobacco and fruits, and sheep are raised.

Under the Turks until 1913, it was then divided between Serbia and Montenegro. It became an autonomous region in 1946. In 1990 its National Assembly voted for republican status but this was opposed by the Serbian National Assembly and direct Serbian rule was imposed. In 1998–9 'ethnic cleansing' of Kosovo by Serbia began. NATO forces bombed Serbia and Kosovo.

Kostroma Russia. Cap. of the Kostroma Region at the confluence of the Volga R. with the Kostroma 72 km (45 miles) ENE of Yaroslavl. Pop. (1992) 282,000.

Famous since the 16th cent. for linen. Also manufactures clothing, footwear, paper and excavators. Flour-milling, sawmilling.

Kostroma River Russia. River 400 km (250 miles) long flowing generally SW across the Kostroma Region to join the Volga R. at Kostroma.

Koszalin (Ger. **Köslin**) Poland. Cap. of the Koszalin voivodeship 145 km (90 miles) NE of Szczecin. Pop. (1992) 109,800.

Manufactures agricultural machinery, cement and bricks.

Formerly in Pomerania (Germany); passed to Poland after World War II.

Kotah India. Town in Rajasthan on the Chambal R. 257 km (160 miles) SW of Gwalior. Pop. (1991) 537,400.

Manufactures textiles, synthetic fibres, nylon tyre cord, cement, fertilizers, chemicals, electronic equipment, non-ferrous metals, oxygen and instruments. Trade in grain, cotton and oilseeds.

It was cap. of the former Rajput state of Kotah.

Kota Kinabalu Malaysia. Formerly Jesselton. Cap. and chief seaport of Sabah on the W coast facing the South China Sea. Pop. (1990) 55,997.

Exports timber, rubber. Industries inc. rice-milling and fishing.

Replaced Sandakan as cap. of British North Borneo in 1947.

Köthen Germany. Industrial town and railway junction in the Halle district 32 km (20 miles) N of Halle. Pop. (1971) 36,600.

Engineering and sugar-refining. Manufactures textiles.

Cap. of the duchy of Anhalt-Köthen 1603–1847.

Kotka Finland. Seaport and cap. of the Kymi province in the SE, built on an island in the Gulf of Finland. Pop. (1992) 56,462.

Exports timber, wood-pulp and paper. Flour-milling, sugar-refining. Manufactures wood-pulp and paper.

It was founded in 1879.

Kotlas Russia. Town in the Archangel Region on the N Dvina R. near the confluence with the Vychegda R. Pop. (1989) 57,201.

Minor port. Industries inc. shipbuilding and repairing, cellulose and wood-processing.

Kotor Gulf Montenegro, Yugoslavia. Picturesque inlet of the Adriatic Sea, surrounded by mountains and forming a sheltered harbour, with Kotor and other small towns on its shores.

Kottbus ►COTTBUS.

Koudougou Burkina Faso. Centre for an agricultural area producing cotton, tobacco and groundnuts. Textile manufacture. Pop. (1985) 51,670.

Kovno ►KAUNAS.

Kovrov Russia. Industrial town and railway junction on the Moscow–Gorki railway and the Klyazma R. 64 km (40 miles) ENE of Vladimir. Pop. (1992) 162,000.

Railway engineering. Manufactures metal goods, textiles and excavators.

Kowloon China. Town on Kowloon peninsula in SE China opposite Victoria on Hong Kong island and forming part of the former British Crown Colony of Hong Kong. The former colony's main industrial area.

Manufactures cotton goods, rubber footwear, cement and ropes. Important commercial centre with accommodation for ocean-going ships and a railway link with Guangzhou (Canton). On its NE outskirts is Kai Tak airport.

Kozáni Greece. 1. *Nome* in Macedonia with the Pindus Mountains on the W and drained by the Aliákmon R. Area 3516 sq km (1375 sq. miles). Pop. (1991) 105,159. Mainly agricultural. Produces wheat, tobacco and cheese.

2. Cap. of Kozáni *nome* at a height of 705 m (2319 ft) on the Aliákmon R. Pop. (1971) 23,240.

Market town. Hydroelectric plant on the river.

Kozhikode India. Formerly Calicut. Seaport in Kerala on the Malabar coast 274 km (170 miles) SW of Bangalore. Pop. (1991) 456,600.

Exports copra, coconuts, coffee and tea. Manufactures coir rope and mats, soap and hosiery. Industries inc. timber, rayon and boatbuilding. Sawmilling. The manufacture of calico (called after its earlier name) is now almost extinct.

Visited by Vasco da Gama 1498; later trading posts were established here by the Portuguese (1511), English (1664), French (1698) and Danes (1752). Taken in 1765 by Hyder Ali, who expelled the merchants and destroyed coconut palms, pepper vines, in order to keep away Europeans.

Kpalimé Togo. Town situated in Plateaux NW of Lomé. Pop. (1987) 31,000. Railway terminus serving an agricultural area handling cacao, palm products and cotton. The main industry is cotton-ginning.

Kra Isthmus Thailand. The narrowest part of the isthmus which joins the Malay peninsula to the mainland of Asia 50–80 km (30–50 miles) wide in S. Thailand. A ship canal across it has been twice planned and abandoned.

Kragujevac Serbia, Yugoslavia. Town in Serbia 96 km (60 miles) SSE of Belgrade. Pop. (1991) 146,607.

Industrial centre. Manufactures munitions, vehicles and metallurgical products. Also vegetable-canning and flour-milling.

Cap. of Serbia 1818–29.

Krakatao (Krakatau) Indonesia. Small volcanic island in Sundra Strait between Java and Sumatra. Its volcano erupted with great violence in 1883, blowing away the entire N part of the island; the noise of the explosion was heard nearly 5000 km (3000 miles) away; volcanic dust spread round the world and gave brilliant sunsets; more than 36,000 people were drowned in tidal waves. There have been minor eruptions in the present cent. (1927–9).

Kraków ➤ CRACOW.

Kraljevo Serbia, Yugoslavia. City situated near the junction of the Ibar and Morava. Pop. (1985) 121,700.

Industries inc. machinery, locomotives, railway equipment and metal goods.

Nearby are several monasteries inc. Kalenic, noted for its 15th-cent. frescoes.

Kramatorsk Ukraine. Industrial town in the Donbas 177 km (110 miles) SSE of Kharkov. Pop. (1991) 201,000.

Important centre for the manufacture of iron and steel, mining and other machinery, excavators, machine-tools and cement. Railway engineering.

Krasnodar Russia. Formerly (till 1920) Ekaterinodar (Yekaterinodar). Cap. of the Krasnodar Territory on the lower Kuban R. 257 km (160 miles) SSW of Rostov. Pop. (1992) 635,000.

Important industrial centre, mainly engaged in food-processing. There is oil-refining (connected by pipeline with the Maikop oilfields) and railway engineering. Manufactures chemicals, machinery, textiles and machine-tools. Railway junction.

Founded (1794) as a fort under Catherine II.

Krasnovodsk Turkmenistan. Port on the SE coast of the Caspian Sea. Pop. (1990) 59,200.

Trade in oil, cotton, grain and timber. Oil-refining (connected by pipeline with the Nebit–Dag oilfield), ship-repairing and fish-canning. Terminus of the Trans-Caspian Railway.

Founded (1717) as a fort under Peter the Great.

Krasnoyarsk Russia. 1. Large territory in central Siberia inc. the Taimyr and Evenki National Areas and the Khakass Autonomous Republic. Area 2,339,700 sq km (903,400 sq. miles). Pop. (1992) 3,051,000. Extends from the Taimyr peninsula in the N through tundra, coniferous forests and wooded steppes to the Sayan Mountains in the S and contains the vast Yenisei basin. Wheat and sugar-beet are grown and dairy cattle are reared in the S. Produces gold. Crossed by the Trans-Siberian Railway. Principal towns Krasnoyarsk, Kansk and Igarka (chief port).

2. Cap. of Krasnoyarsk Territory on the Yenisei R. and the Trans-Siberian Railway. Pop. (1992) 925,000.

Industrial centre. Manufactures agricultural and other machinery, locomotives, cranes, cement, textiles and paper. Railway engineering, sawmilling and flour-milling. Also the centre of gold production and has a gold-refining plant.

Founded 1628. Expanded rapidly with the construction of the railway.

Krefeld Germany. Industrial town in North Rhine-Westphalia 6 km (4 miles) W of the Rhine R. and 21 km (13 miles) NW of Düsseldorf. Pop. (1990) 245,000.

Manufactures textiles, clothing, steel, machinery, chemicals and hosiery. Dyeing and printing.

In the Middle Ages it was already a flourishing town; developed with the establishment of the textile industry by Huguenots. First it specialized in linen weaving, then this was superseded by silk and in more recent times rayon has taken the place of the latter. In 1929 Ürdingen on the Rhine was incorporated with it.

Kremenchuk Ukraine. Industrial town, river port and railway junction on the Dnieper R. 265 km (165 miles) ESE of Kiev. Pop. (1991) 241,000.

Industries inc. metalworking, sawmilling and food-processing. Manufactures agricultural machinery and textiles. A hydroelectric power station was completed in 1960 and the canal also constructed made the Dnieper navigable for large vessels from Kanev (105 km (65 miles) SE of Kiev) to the Black Sea.

Founded 1571.

Krems (Krems-an-der-Donau) Austria. Town in Lower Austria on the Danube R. 56 km (35 miles) WNW of Vienna. Pop. (1991) 22,766.

Manufactures leather goods, jam, and trades in wine and fruit.

Kreuznach ➤BAD KREUZNACH.

Krishna (Kistna) River India. River 1285 km (800 miles) long, rising in the W Ghats in SW Maharashtra and flowing generally ESE across India to the Bay of Bengal, which it enters by a broad delta. Irrigation canals of the delta are linked with those of the Godavari delta. Only a short length of the river is navigable, but is an important source of irrigation water and power.

Kristiansand Norway. Cap. of Vest-Agder county at the mouth of the Otra R. on the Skagerrak. Pop. (1990) 65,543.

Seaport. Industrial town. Exports timber, metals and fish. Copper and nickel smelting, woollen-milling and brewing.

Founded 1641. Rebuilt in stone after disastrous fire in 1892.

Kristianstad Sweden. Cap. of Kristianstad county on the Helge R. 88 km (55 miles) E of Hälsingborg. Pop. (1992) 72,789.

Manufactures textiles. Engineering, flour-milling and sugar-refining.

Founded (1614) as a Danish fortress, it

changed hands twice and was finally acquired by Sweden (1678).

Kristiansund Norway. Cap. of the Möre og Romsdal county on four small North Sea islands connected by bridges and ferries 137 km (85 miles) WSW of Trondheim. Pop. (1990) 18,000.

Fishing port. Fish canning and processing. Severely damaged in World War II when occupied by the Germans; rebuilt later.

Krivoi Rog ►KRYIV RIH.

Krk Croatia. Island in the N Adriatic Sea SSE of Rijeka. Area 427 sq km (165 sq. miles). Pop. (1989) 14,500. Chief town and port Krk (pop. (1985) 1500).

Vineyards and olive groves. Several bathing resorts.

From the early 19th cent. it was successively ruled by Italy, France and Austria; passed to Yugoslavia 1918.

Kronstadt Russia. Naval base and port on Kotlin Island in the Gulf of Finland 23 km (14 miles) W of St Petersburg. Pop. (1989) 45,000.

Fortifications, arsenal, docks and shipyards. Industries inc. sawmills and the manufacture of footwear and clothing. Icebound for about 5 months annually.

Kotlin was taken from Sweden by Peter the Great in 1703 and he constructed docks and a fortress on it; for a time Kronstadt functioned as a commercial port for St Petersburg, but the construction of a deep-sea canal to the latter (1875–85) reduced its importance in this respect. Naval mutinies took place at Kronstadt in 1905, 1906, 1917 and 1921, the last being against the Soviet government.

Kroonstad South Africa. Town in the Free State 190 km (120 miles) NNE of Bloemfontein on the Vale R. (a tributary of the Orange R.) at a height of 1370 m (4507 ft). Pop. (1970) 50,898 (16,500 Europeans).

Railway junction. Agricultural and educational centre. Resort. Engineering, flour-milling. Manufactures clothing.

Kropotkin Russia. Town in the Krasnodar Territory on the Kuban R. 129 km (80 miles) ENE of Krasnodar. Pop. (1970) 68,000.

Railway engineering. Trade in agricultural produce (cereals, vegetable oils and meat).

Kruger National Park South Africa. Wildlife sanctuary along the NE Gauteng frontier with Mozambique 320 km (200 miles) long and 50–100 km (30–60 miles) wide.

Founded (1898) by President Kruger as the Sabi game reserve. Later enlarged and renamed. Contains almost every species of game native to South Africa and is a great tourist attraction.

Krugersdorp South Africa. Town on the Witwatersrand 32 km (20 miles) WNW of Johannesburg at a height of 1704 m (5589 ft). Pop. (1990) 103,000.

A gold, uranium and manganese mining centre. Railway junction. Metalworking. Chemical industry.

Named after President Kruger.

Krung Thep ►BANGKOK.

Kryiv Rih Ukraine. Town on the Ingulets R. 145 km (90 miles) WSW of Dnepropetrovsk. Pop. (1991) 724,000.

Important iron-mining centre; still produces about half the country's iron ore. Manufactures iron and steel, machine-tools and chemicals.

Kuala Lumpur Malaysia. Federal Cap. of Malaysia on the Klang R. Pop. (1989) 1,209,800 (largely Chinese).

Commercial centre in a tin-mining and rubber-growing area. Linked by rail and road with Port Kelang.

Well-planned and modern with fine public buildings. Became cap. of the Federated Malay States (1896), of the Federation of Malaya (1948) and of the Federation of Malaysia (1963).

Kuban River Russia. The ancient Hypanis of Herodotus and Strabo. River 900 km (560 miles) long rising in glaciers W of Mt Elbruz in the Greater Caucasus. A mountain torrent in its upper course, it flows N past Armavir, becomes a sluggish, meandering stream as it crosses the steppes in its lower course, turns W past Kropotkin and Krasnodar and enters the Sea of Azov and the Black Sea by a broad, swampy delta. Its valley is a fertile agricultural region producing cereals, sunflowers and cotton.

Kubena, Lake Russia. Lake in the Vologda Region with an outlet via the Sukhona R. to the North Dvina R. Area 363 sq km (140 sq. miles). Linked by canal with the Sheksna R. and thus with the Mariinsk canal system.

Kuching Malaysia. Cap. of Sarawak, port on the Sarawak R. 34 km (21 miles) above the mouth. Pop. (1989) 157,000 (inc. many Chinese).

Exports rubber, pepper and sago flour.

Kudymkar ►KOMI-PERMYAK NA.

Kuenlun ►KUNLUN.

Kufra (Kufara) Oases Libya. Group of 5 oases in the Libyan Desert (S Cyrenaica), an important centre of the Senussi. Produces dates, barley. Camel-rearing. Junction of caravan routes from the Mediterranean coast, Egypt and Chad.

Kuh-e-Sahand ►TABRIZ.

Kuibyshev ►SAMARA.

Kuldja (Chinese **Ining**) China. Town in NW Xinjiang-Uygur Autonomous Region on the Ili R. 63 km (40 miles) from the Russian border.

Trade in tea and livestock. Tanning. Stands on the caravan route to Alma-Ata (Kazakhstan).

Kumamoto Japan. Cap. of Kumamoto prefecture in W Kyushu. Pop. (1992) 663,144.

Industries inc. food-processing and the manufacture of textiles. It grew up round the 16th-cent. castle.

Kumasi Ghana. Second largest city, cap. of Ashanti 200 km (125 miles) NW of Accra. Pop. (1988) 365,192.

Important road and rail junction connected by main lines to Accra and Takoradi. Weaving, metalworking and other crafts. Important trade in cocoa.

Sometimes known as the 'City of the Golden Stool'. The old town was almost destroyed by the British in 1874. Modern development dates from the building of the railway from Sekondi (1903).

Kumayri (Gyumri) Armenia. Formerly Leninakan. Town in the NW 88 km (55 miles) NW of Yerevan. Pop. (1990) 123,000.

Manufactures textiles and carpets. Sugar-refining.

Founded in 1837 as the fortress Aleksandropol.

Kumbakonam (Combaconum) India. Ancient town in Tamil Nadu on the Cauvery R. delta 257 km (160 miles) SSW of Madras. Pop. (1991) 139,483.

Manufactures textiles and metal goods. Cultural centre with a Sanskrit library; also many temples.

Cap. of the Chola kingdom in the 7th cent.

Kunene (Cunene) River Angola. River 960 km (600 miles) long, rising near Huambo, flowing generally S and then W, in its lower course forming the frontier between Angola and Namibia and entering the Atlantic. Descending to the coastal plain by a number of falls, it diminishes in volume as it crosses an arid region; the mouth is closed at low water.

Kungur Russia. Town in the Perm Region 77 km (48 miles) SSE of Perm. Pop. (1985) 85,000.

Long famous for leather goods. Gypsum-quarrying nearby.

Founded c. 1640.

Kunlun (Kuenlun). Great mountain system in central Asia lying between the plateau of Tibet (S) and the Tarim Basin (N) and extending well over 1600 km (1000 miles) E from the Pamirs. Highest peak Ulugh Muztagh (7723 m; 25,331 ft). The most northerly range, the Altyn Tagh, passes E into the Nanshan; farther S the system is continued in the complex ranges of E Tibet and W China.

Kunming China. Formerly Yunnan (Yunnanfu). Cap. of Yunnan province 628 km (390 miles) SW of Chongqing just N of L. Tien Chih at a height of 1920 m (6198 ft). Pop. (1990) 1,127,411.

Commercial, cultural and route centre; terminus of the Burma Road. Manufactures textiles, chemicals, cement and machinery.

Developed rapidly with the construction of the railway to Hanoi (1910) and during World War II was an important supply base.

Kuopio Finland. Cap. of the Kuopio province on L. Kallavesi 338 km (210 miles) NE of Helsinki. Pop. (1992) 82,340.

Commercial and tourist centre. Wood-working industry. Manufactures plywood, doors, bobbins and clothing.

Kurashiki Japan. Town in Okayama prefecture in SW Honshu 16 km (10 miles) WSW of Okayama. Pop. (1992) 416,703.

Industries inc. oil-refining, petrochemicals, iron and steel, and rayon.

Kurdistan Central Asia. The land inhabited by the Kurds comprising the mountain and plateau region of SE Turkey and the adjoining parts of Iran, Iraq and Syria. The Kurds are a semi-nomadic pastoral people, well-known for their fiercely independent spirit; they are mainly Sunni Muslims and speak Kurdish, an Indo-European lang. somewhat similar to Persian. They probably number 5 million, of whom nearly half live in Turkey. Their claims for autonomy after World War I were never realized. Iran has a province of Kurdistan, its cap. Sanandaj.

Kure Japan. Seaport and naval base in Hiroshima prefecture, SW Honshu 24 km (15 miles) SSE of Hiroshima. Pop. (1992) 213,474.

Noted for its shipbuilding (esp. oil tankers), engineering. Manufactures iron and steel, and machinery.

Kurgan Russia. Cap. of the Kurgan Region on the Tobol R. and the Trans-Siberian Railway 257 km (160 miles) E of Chelyabinsk. Pop. (1992) 365,000.

Meat-packing, flour-milling and tanning.

Manufactures agricultural machinery. Trade in agricultural produce.

Founded in the 17th cent.

Kurgan–Tyube Tajikistan. Town situated S of Dushanbe. Pop. (1989) 58,400.

The main industries are cotton and food processing.

Kuria Kiribati. Island formerly called Woodle atoll in the N Gilbert group, West Pacific. Area 16 sq km (6 sq. miles). Pop. (1990) 985.

Kuria Maria Islands. Group of 5 islands in the Arabian Sea off the S coast of Oman, the largest and only inhabited one being Hallaniya. Area 73 sq km (28 sq. miles). Pop. 85.

Ceded to Britain by the Sultan of Oman (1854) for a cable station; administered through Aden. Returned to the Sultan of Muscat and Oman 1967.

Kuril (Kurile) Islands Russia. Chain of 32 small islands extending from the S end of the Kamchatka peninsula to Hokkaido (Japan) in the Sakhalin Region. Area 10,200 sq km (3938 sq. miles). Of volcanic origin, with several active volcanoes; the two southernmost are forested. Climate characterized by cool, foggy summers.

Main occupations fishing, hunting, market-gardening, lumbering and sulphur-mining. Other minerals inc. iron and copper.

Discovered (1634) by the Dutch navigator Martin de Vries, passed to Japan in 1875; surrendered to the USSR after World War II (1945), but still claimed by Japan.

Kurisches Haff (Courland Lagoon, Russian **Kurskiy Zaliv**) Russia. Large coastal lagoon formerly in E Prussia but since World War II in Lithuania and Russia; separated from the Baltic Sea, except for a narrow outlet, by the Kurische Nehrung (Courland Spit, Kurskaya Kosa), a sandy spit 116 km (72 miles) long and 1.5–3 km (1–2 miles) wide. On the low E shore of the lagoon is the delta of the Neman R.

Kurland ►COURLAND.

Kurnool India. Town in Andhra Pradesh

on the Tungabhadra R. 177 km (110 miles) SSW of Hyderabad. Pop. (1991) 236,800.

Commercial centre in an agricultural region. Manufactures textiles, carpets, leather, chemicals, sugar, distillery products, paper and edible oils.

Kuroshio (Kuro Siwo, Japan Current). In Japanese, 'Black Stream' (because of its dark blue colour). Warm ocean current in the Pacific Ocean flowing N and NE past the S and E coasts of Japan, to which it gives heat. Similar to the Gulf Stream of the Atlantic.

Kurow ►WAITAKI RIVER.

Kursk Russia. Cap. of the Kursk Region on the Seim R. 200 km (125 miles) W of Voronezh. Pop. (1992) 435,000.

Railway junction. Manufactures machinery, electrical equipment, clothing, flour, sugar, alcohol and chemicals. Nearby is one of the largest iron-ore deposits in the world. Also a market town in a rich agricultural region. Trade in cereals and sugar-beet.

An ancient town, founded in the 9th cent.

Kurskiy Zaliv ►KURISCHES HAFF.

Kurzeme ►COURLAND.

Kusaie Island ►CAROLINE ISLANDS.

Kushtia Bangladesh. District cap. on the Ganges delta. Situated W of Dacca. Pop. (1984) 120,000.

Sugar-milling, cotton cloth weaving and textile manufacture. Trade in rice, jute, linseed, cane and wheat.

Kustanay Kazakhstan. Cap. of the Kustanay Region on the Tobol R. 240 km (150 miles) SE of Chelyabinsk. Pop. (1991) 233,900.

Industrial and commercial centre in an agricultural region. Flour-milling, tanning and meat-packing. Trade in grain and cattle.

Founded in 1871.

Kutaisi Georgia. Industrial town on the Rion R. 190 km (120 miles) WNW of Tbilisi. Pop. (1991) 238,200.

In a region of citrus-fruit and vine growing and market-gardening. Manufactures chemicals and textiles. Other industries inc. food-processing and vehicle assembly.

Ancient cap. of Imeritia (W Georgia).

Kut-al-Amara ►AL KUT.

Kutch (Cutch), Rann of India. Extensive waste of mud and salt flats in NW Gujarat, consisting of the larger area of Great Rann just S of the Pakistan border and the smaller area or Little Rann to the SE. During the rainy season it becomes a saltmarsh and in the dry season a salt-encrusted desert. It was probably once a shallow arm of the Arabian Sea. The extensive salt deposits are exploited. It is an area of dispute between India and Pakistan.

Kuwait. Independent Arab state on the NW coast of the (Persian) Gulf and bounded on the N and W by Iraq and on the S by Saudi Arabia. There are 9 offshore islands and a neutral zone jointly owned by Kuwait and Saudi Arabia. Area 17,818 sq km (6880 sq. miles). Pop. (1995) 1,691,000 (97 per cent urban). Life expectancy, 73 years male, 77 female. Cap: Kuwait City. Other cities Hawalli, as-Salimya, Jahra and Farawaniya. Currency: Kuwaiti dinar = 1000 fils. It is mainly desert and has a dry desert climate; cool in winter but very hot and humid in summer. Rainfall is slight. Land use: forested 0.1 per cent, meadows and pastures 8 per cent, agricultural and under permanent cultivation 0.3 per cent, wasteland 92 per cent. The official lang. is Arabic. Only about 43 per cent of the pop. is Kuwaiti. Muslim 90 per cent (of which Sunni 63 per cent), Christian 8 per cent, Hindu 2 per cent.

Kuwait's economy was transformed by the discovery of Burgan oilfield, where production began in 1946 and rapidly expanded. The oilfields are connected by pipelines to the port of Mina al Ahmadi, where some of the petroleum is refined. Just S of Mina al Ahmadi there are 3 small oil ports. In the period 1990–1 Iraqi forces fired 732 of the 950 oil wells – all were extinguished by 1991. Other industries inc. boatbuilding, fishing, food production, petrochemicals, gases and construction. Pearl-fishing has declined and is now on a small scale.

Kuwait was under British protection from 1914 but the independence of the sheikhdom was recognized by Britain in 1961. In August 1990 Iraq overran the country. The Kuwaiti government established itself in exile in Saudi Arabia. The UN called for Iraq's withdrawal and in February 1991 coalition forces entered Kuwait and Iraq withdrew all its forces from Kuwait on 26 February. Kuwait is a Constitutional Monarchy with a 75-member National Assembly (50 elected and 25 appointed by the Amir). The franchise is limited to men over 21 whose families have been of Kuwaiti nationality for at least one generation.

Kuwait City Kuwait. Cap. of Kuwait on the Gulf 120 km (75 miles) S of Basra (Iraq). Pop. (1993) 31,241 (with suburbs 400,000).

Port with a good natural harbour. Its entrepôt trade has declined with the development of the oil industry. Boatbuilding (Arab dhows).

Kuznetsk Russia. Town in the Penza Region 105 km (65 miles) E of Penza. Pop. (1992) 101,000.

Tanning, brickmaking. Manufactures agricultural machinery and rope. Trade in cereals and salt.

Kuznetsk Basin Russia. Important coal-mining area in the Kemerovo Region E and SE of Novosibirsk, with enormous reserves. Principal mines around Anzhero-Sudzhensk and Kemerovo. Considerable industrial development has also taken place here, Kuzbas coal being exchanged for iron ore from Magnitogorsk, through the Ural–Kuznetsk Combine, and more recently iron ore from Temir Tau has been utilized. Non-ferrous metallurgy draws on local supplies of copper, manganese. Chief industrial centre Novokuznetsk.

Kwangchow ►GUANGZHOU.

Kwangsi-Chuang ►GUANGXI ZHUANG.

Kwangtung ►GUANGDONG.

KwaZulu South Africa. The NE part of KwaZulu/Natal, bounded by Mozambique (N), Swaziland (NW) and the Tugela R. (S). Area 26,871 sq km (10,375 sq. miles). Cap. Eshowe. From the coastal plain, where sugarcane and cotton are cultivated, the land rises to the plateau, on which cattle are raised. Inc. several game reserves. Early in the 19th cent. the Zulu were transformed from a small and insignificant tribe into a powerful nation by the military prowess of their chief, Chaka. For a time they repulsed both Boers and British, but in 1879 the latter defeated them at Ulundi and Chief Cetewayo was captured. It became a British protectorate in 1887 and was annexed to Natal in 1897. Formerly known as Zululand, created as a national state in 1971 but was reunited with Natal in 1994.

Kweichow ►GUIZHOU.

Kweilin ►GUILIN.

Kweiyang ►GUIYANG.

Kwekwe Zimbabwe. City in central region. Pop. (1982) 48,000.

Industries inc. steel and chrome processing and gold-roasting. Distribution centre for agricultural products inc. tobacco.

Kwinana Australia. Town in Western Australia 27 km (17 miles) S of Fremantle.

Large oil refinery, steel mill and cement works. Cockburn Sound was dredged to form a deep-water harbour.

Kyle of Lochalsh Scotland. Small fishing port and railway terminus in Highland at the entrance to Loch Alsh. Pop. (1990) 500. Car ferry to Kyleakin, Skye.

Kyoga, Lake ►KIOGA, LAKE.

Kyoto Japan. Cap. of Kyoto prefecture, Honshu 370 km (230 miles) WSW of Tokyo and near L. Biwa, with which it is connected by canal. Pop. (1992) 1,456,527.

Important manufacturing centre famous for its craft industries – porcelain, lacquer ware, dolls, fans, silk goods and brocades. Also manufactures textiles, chemicals and machinery.

The chief Buddhist centre, it has many temples and shrines as well as the former imperial palace. An important tourist centre often known as 'the Florence of the East'. Founded 793 and was the Japanese cap. until 1868.

Kyrenia 'Turkish Republic of Northern Cyprus'. Port situated N of Nicosia. Pop. (1989) 7000.
Tourism is the main industry.

Kyrgyzstan. Republic in Central Asia, bounded on the E by China, W by Kazakhstan and Uzbekistan, N by Kazakhstan and S by Tajikistan. Area 198,500 sq km (76,600 sq. miles). Pop. (1995) 4,483,000 (37 per cent urban). Life expectancy, 64 years male, 73 female. Cap. Bishkek. Other cities Osh, Dzhalal-Abad, Tokmak and Przhevalsk. Currency: Som = 100 tyiyn. Mountainous, lying at the W end of the great Tien Shan system and rising in the E, near the Chinese border, to 7439 m (24,406 ft) in Pobedy (Tomur Feng) and in the NE is the extensive L. Issyk-Kul, surrounded by mountains. Climate and natural vegetation vary considerably with altitude.

The official lang. is Kyrgyz. The Kyrgyz are of Turkic origin and form 52 per cent of the pop., Russians 21 per cent, Uzbeks 13 per cent, Ukrainian 2 per cent, German 2 per cent and Tatars 2 per cent. They are predominantly Sunni Muslims.

Stock-rearing has long been the main occupation, sheep being by far the most numerous, with cattle, pigs, goats, horses and yaks; the last in the higher districts unsuitable for other animals. Agriculture has been developed in the valleys in recent years and is largely mechanized. Chief crops wheat, maize, sugar-beet and cotton. Minerals inc.

coal, lead and zinc. Industries inc. sugar-refining, tanning, cotton and wool cleaning, textiles, sericulture and food-processing.

Kyrgyzstan, then known as Kirghizia, became an autonomous region of Russia 1924, an autonomous republic 1926 and a constituent republic of the USSR 1936. The republic adopted a declaration of sovereignty in 1990. In 1991 declared itself an independent, sovereign and democratic state and became a member of the Commonwealth of Independent States. There is a 350-member Grand Council which is the sole legislative body, elected for 4-year terms by universal adult suffrage.

Kyushu Japan. Southernmost of the 4 main islands, inc. about 370 small islands and divided into 7 prefectures. Area 42,080 sq km (16,247 sq. miles). Pop. (1990) 13,500,000. Much of it is mountainous and it rises to 1690 m (5543 ft) in the volcanic Mt Aso; there are many hot springs. In the Chikuho Basin it has the country's chief coalfield, while nearby is the important region of heavy industry centred on Kitakyushu.

Kyzyl Russia. Formerly (until 1917) Byelotsarsk. Cap. of the Tuva Republic 499 km (310 miles) SSE of Krasnoyarsk at the confluence of the two main headstreams of the Yenisei R. Pop. (1993) 80,000. Linked by road and by steamer service along the Yenisei R. with Minusinsk, by air with Krasnoyarsk.
Sawmilling.

Kyzyl Kum Kazakhstan/Uzbekistan. Means 'Red Sand'. Desert situated SE of the Aral Sea between the Amu Darya and the Syr Darya, consisting largely of sand dunes, with patches of bare rock.

L

Laaland (Lolland) Denmark. Island in the Baltic Sea S of Zealand, with the German Fehmarn Is. to the SW. Area 1243 sq km (480 sq. miles). Low-lying, rising to only 30 m (98 ft). Cereals and sugar-beet cultivated. Chief towns Maribo and Nakskov.

Labé Guinea. Town and cap. of Labé region situated NE of Conakry in the Fouta Djallon mountains. Pop. (1986) 110,000.

Industries inc. slate-quarrying and the manufacture of essential oils, honey, beeswax and food products.

Labrador Canada. The most northerly district of the Newfoundland province. Area 285,800 sq km (112,826 sq. miles). The coast extends NW from Blanc Sablon (at the entrance to the Straits of Belle Isle) to Cape Chidley (at the entrance to Hudson Strait); it is deeply indented, cold and bleak, and swept by the cold Labrador Current. Of the rivers the Churchill (Hamilton) is the most important. Large hydroelectric plants have been developed at Twin Falls and Churchill Falls. Labrador and Wabush are important mining towns and Goose Bay is the airport. The climate is harsh, with long winters and short, cool summers; heavy snowfalls occur in the interior.

Main occupation cod-fishing; herring and salmon fisheries also important. Some trapping of fur-bearing animals. Forests cover considerable areas and there are vast iron-ore deposits.

The Labrador coast was probably the first part of the American continent to be sighted by Europeans (a party of Norsemen c. 986). Rediscovered by John Cabot 1498. It became British in 1763 and has been under the jurisdiction of Newfoundland continuously since 1809. The boundary with Quebec was finally settled in 1927.

Labuan Malaysia. Island off the SW coast of Sabah, Malaysia. Area 98 sq km (38 sq. miles). Chief town Victoria.

Produces copra, rubber and sago.

Ceded to Britain by the Sultan of Brunei in 1846. Became part of the new colony of North Borneo (renamed Sabah 1963) in 1946 and is a free port. It became a federal territory in 1984. ➤FEDERATION OF MALAYSIA.

Laccadive Islands India. Group of 14 coral islands and several reefs in the Arabian Sea about 320 km (200 miles) W of the Malabar Coast, forming a Union Territory with the Amindivi Is. and Minicoy. Area (Territory) 32 sq km (12 sq. miles). Chief lang. Malayalam.

Main products copra and coir.

The Union Territory was renamed Lakshadweep in 1973.

La Ceiba Honduras. Caribbean port. Pop. (1988) 68,200.

Exports coconuts, bananas and pineapples. Flour-milling and tanning. Manufactures footwear and soap.

Lachine Canada. Industrial town, port and resort in Quebec on the S coast of Montreal Island. Pop. (1986) 35,000. At the SW end of the Lachine Canal.

Manufactures iron and steel, wire, tyres, chemicals.

First settled 1675. The name is said to refer ironically to La Salle's dream of finding a westward route to China (La Chine).

Lachlan River Australia. River 1480 km (920 miles) long in New South Wales, rising in the Great Dividing Range near Gunning, flowing NW and then SW to join the Murrumbidgee R. Wyangala Dam and Reservoir above Cowra is used to irrigate an extensive area.

Lacq France. Village situated NW of Pau in Pyrénées-Atlantiques. Pop. (1985) 700. Noted for its petroleum and natural gas deposits. Sulphur is extracted from the gas and a new town (Moureux) was built nearby for the oil industry workers.

La Crosse USA. Town in Wisconsin on the Mississippi R. at its confluence with the Black and La Crosse rivers. Pop. (1990) 51,003.

Commercial centre in a dairy-farming region. Manufactures agricultural equipment, motor-car parts and footwear.

Named by early French fur traders after a game played by the Winnebago Indians resembling the French game 'la crosse'.

Ladakh (Ladak) India. District in NE Kashmir bounded on the N by Xinjiang-Uyghur (China) and E by Tibet (Xizang). Area 118,524 sq km (45,762 sq. miles). Cap. Leh. The upper Indus valley which traverses it stands at a height of 3300 m (10,824 ft) near Leh and surrounding mountain ranges rise on average to 5700 m (18,696 ft). The W part, known as Baltistan, contains the highest peaks of the Karakoram, inc. K2 (8611 m; 28,250 ft). The Balti, who represent about four-fifths of the total pop., are Muslims; the Ladakhi are Buddhists. Chief town Leh, Skardu.

Wheat and other cereals cultivated. Sheep and goats raised.

Ladakh Range India. Mountain range in E Kashmir, extending 320 km (200 miles) SE just N of and parallel to the upper Indus R. on the S side of which are the Zaskar Mountains. Inc. peaks exceeding 6000 m (19,680 ft).

Ladoga, Lake Russia. Lake in the NW, the largest in Europe, 200 km (125 miles) long and up to 130 km (80 miles) wide. Area 18,390 sq km (7100 sq. miles). Lakes Onega, Ilmen (Russia) and Saimaa (Finland) drain into it. Discharges by the Neva R. into the Gulf of Finland. Frozen from about December to March; navigation also impeded by storms and fogs. Canals along the S shore carry considerable traffic between the Volga

R. and the Baltic Sea. Fishing important. A species of seal provides evidence of its former association with the Arctic Ocean. During the siege of Leningrad (St Petersburg) (1941–3) such provisions as reached the city were transported over the frozen lake.

Ladysmith South Africa. Town in Kwa-Zulu/Natal on the Klip R. 190 km (120 miles) NW of Durban at a height of 1080 m (3542 ft). Pop. (1985) 22,000. A railway junction on the main line from Durban, which divides here to Gauteng and the Free State.

Industries inc. railway engineering and the manufacture of textiles and clothing.

During the South African War it was besieged by the Boers Nov. 1899–Feb. 1900, and was relieved by Sir Redvers Buller's force.

Lae Papua New Guinea. Industrial city and port situated N of Port Moresby on Huon Gulf. Pop. (1990) 80,655.

It exports gold, timber, cattle, coffee, cocoa and has considerable light industry.

Lafayette (Indiana) USA. Town on the Wabash R. 96 km (60 miles) NW of Indianapolis. Pop. (1970) 44,955.

Market for grain, cattle, pigs. Industries inc. meat-packing and the manufacture of electrical equipment, machinery and pharmaceutical products.

Lafayette (Louisiana) USA. Formerly Vermilionville. Town on the Vermilion R. 84 km (52 miles) WSW of Baton Rouge. Pop. (1990) 94,440.

Commercial centre for an agricultural and mining region. Sugar-refining, cotton and cottonseed processing. Also a centre of the oil industry.

French is widely spoken. Founded (as Vermilionville) 1824; renamed (1884) after the Marquis de la Fayette (1757–1834).

Lagan River Northern Ireland. River 72 km (45 miles) long, rising near Ballynahinch, Co. Down and flowing NW and then NE past Lisburn to Belfast Lough at Belfast. Linked by canal with Lough Neagh.

Lågen River (Gudbrandsdalslågen)

Norway. River 190 km (120 miles) long, rising N of the Jotunheim Mountains and flowing generally SSE through the Gudbrandsdal to L. Mjosa.

Lågen River (Numedalslågen) Norway. River 320 km (200 miles) long, rising in the Hardangervidda and flowing generally SSE through the Numedal to the Skagerrak at Larvik.

Lagos Nigeria. Former cap. and chief seaport on an island in a lagoon on the coast of the Gulf of Guinea. Pop. (1992) 1,347,000. Reached from the Bight of Benin by a channel dredged through the sand bar at the entrance to the lagoon; linked by a 793-m (2600 ft) bridge with Iddo Island, in turn linked with the mainland by bridge.

It is a tanker terminal and industries inc. tourism, fishing, brewing and the manufacture of metal products, chemicals, textiles and food products.

La Grande USA. City situated SE of Pendleton in Oregon on the Grande Ronde R. at the foot of Blue Mountains at 849 m (2786 ft) above sea level. Pop. (1985) 13,500.

Industries inc. railways and sawmilling. Manufactures particle board, trailers and chemical products.

La Guaira Venezuela. Chief seaport on the Caribbean Sea 11 km (7 miles) N of Caracas in the Federal District. Pop. (1985) 21,000.

It has an excellent harbour, accommodating the largest ships. Exports coffee, cacao and tobacco.

Linked by motorway with Caracas. Founded 1577.

Lahore Pakistan. Cap. of Punjab province and the country's second largest city near the Ravi R. 1046 km (650 miles) NE of Karachi. Pop. (1991) 3 million.

Important industrial, commercial and route centre. Industries inc. railway engineering and the manufacture of textiles, carpets, metal goods, footwear and chemicals.

Much of its architecture is undistinguished, but the Badshahi Masjid of Aurangzeb and the tomb of Ranjit Singh are notable, and to the E of the city are the famous Shalamar gardens, created by Shah Jahan in 1637. Probably founded before the 7th cent., Lahore became cap. of the Ghaznevid and Ghori lands in India in the 11th and 12th cent. and of the Sikh empire of Ranjit Singh in the 18th cent. Came under British rule 1846; was cap. of the former larger province of Punjab before the partition of India in 1947.

Lahti Finland. Town and winter sports resort in the Häme province at the S end of the L. Päijänne waterway 92 km (57 miles) NE of Helsinki. Pop. (1991) 93,414.

Industries inc. sawmilling and the manufacture of furniture, plywood, spools, matches and glass.

Laillahue Mountain Peru. Mountain peak in extreme SE Peru on the Bolivian frontier at 5180 m (16,995 ft).

Lake Charles USA. Town in SW Louisiana on the Calcasieu R. (widened into L. Charles with an 11-m (36-ft) channel to the Gulf of Mexico). Pop. (1990) 70,580.

Exports petroleum, timber, rice and cotton. Oil-refining, sawmilling and cotton-ginning.

Lake District England. Scenic area of lakes and mountains (Cumbrian Mountains) in the NW, now entirely in Cumbria about 48 km (30 miles) N–S and 40 km (25 miles) W–E. The principal lakes are: in the centre Derwentwater, Thirlmere, Grasmere and Tydal Water; in the N Bassenthwaite; in the E Ullswater and Hawes Water; in the S Windermere, Esthwaite Water and Coniston Water; in the W Wast Water, Ennerdale Water, Crummock Water and Buttermere. Scafell (979 m; 3211 ft), Helvellyn (951 m; 3119 ft) and Skiddaw (931 m; 3053 ft) are the highest mountains. Waterfalls and dales add beauty to the scenery and in spite of the rather heavy rainfall it is a popular tourist region. There are many literary associations, esp. with Wordsworth, Southey and Coleridge – the so-called Lake Poets.

Lake Edward ➤EDWARD, LAKE.

Lakeland USA. Town and resort in Florida 56 km (35 miles) ENE of Tampa. Pop. (1990) 70,576. In a region of many small lakes and centre of the citrus-fruit industry. Packing plants and canneries.

Lake of the Woods Canada/USA. Lake on the Canada–USA frontier in Minnesota (USA) and Manitoba and Ontario (Canada). Area 3846 sq km (1485 sq. miles). In a beautiful pine-forest region, with thousands of islands. Fed from L. Rainy by the Rainy R. and drained into L. Winnipeg by the Winnipeg R. A popular tourist region.

Lakewood USA. Town in Ohio on L. Erie just W of Cleveland, of which it is a residential suburb. Pop. (1990) 59,718.
Manufactures tools, hardware and plastics.

Lakonia (Laconia) Greece. *Nome* in the SE Peloponnese. Area 3636 sq km (1453 sq. miles). Pop. (1990) 94,916. Cap. Sparta.
Mainly agricultural. Produces citrus fruits, wheat, olives. Sheep and goats raised.

Lakshadweep India. Union Territory formed in 1956 from the Laccadive Is. and the Amindivi Is. and Minicoy (largest island) and renamed in 1973. Consists of 36 islands, of which 10 are inhabited. Area 32 sq km (12 sq. miles). Pop. (1991) 51,707 (almost entirely Muslim). Chief lang. Malayalam.
Main product coconuts, but coir and fish also produced.

La Línea Spain. Town situated ESE of Cádiz on the isthmus of Algeciras Bay immediately N of frontier zone with Gibraltar.
Trading centre for fruit and vegetables. Industries inc. the manufacture of cement, fish products, wines and foodstuffs.

Lambeth England. London borough inc. the E part of Wandsworth. Pop. (1994) 260,700. Here the Thames is crossed by the Vauxhall, Lambeth, Westminster and Waterloo road bridges and the Charing Cross railway bridge. Also has London's largest railway station, Waterloo; nearby is the Old Vic theatre, famous in the past for its Shakespearian productions. At the end of Westminster Bridge stand the former London County Hall on one side and St Thomas's Hospital on the other; downstream is the Royal Festival Hall, a modern concert hall (1951), the National Theatre (1976), and upstream Lambeth Palace, London residence of the Archbishop of Canterbury, which has the 15th-cent. Lollards' Tower, once a prison for heretics and since 1867 has been the scene of the periodic Lambeth Conferences, assemblies of Anglican bishops. Lambeth was formerly the site of Vauxhall Gardens, the Regency amusement centre and inc. the Oval cricket ground.

Lamía Greece. Cap. of Phthiotis *nome* 160 km (100 miles) NW of Athens. Pop. (1985) 43,000.
Market town. Trade in wheat and olive oil.
Gave its name to the Lamian War (Antipater took refuge and was besieged here 323 BC).

Lampedusa Italy. Largest of the Pelagian Islands in the Mediterranean Sea between Malta and Tunisia. Area 21 sq km (8 sq. miles). Pop. (1985) 4400.
Industries inc. fishing and sardine-canning.

Lampeter Wales. Market town in Ceredigion on the R. Teifi 39 km (24 miles) E of Cardigan. Pop. (1991) 1989. Seat of St David's College (1822), founded as a centre for training students for holy orders, now a constituent college of the University of Wales.

Lanark Scotland. Town in South Lanarkshire near the R. Clyde 35 km (22 miles) SE of Glasgow. Pop. (1991) 8877.
Market town. Textile mills.
New Lanark, 1.6 km (1 mile) S, was built by the socialist reformer Robert Owen (1784). The Falls of Clyde are 3.2 km (2 miles) S.

Lanarkshire Scotland. Inland county in the W; was in the Strathclyde Region under reorganization 1975. In 1996 it was divided into two counties: North Lanarkshire and South Lanarkshire.

Lanarkshire, North Scotland. New unitary authority created in 1996, formerly in Strathclyde Region. Pop. (1993) 326,750.

Lanarkshire, South Scotland. New unitary authority created in 1996, formerly in Strathclyde Region. Pop. (1993) 307,100.

Lancashire England. County in the NW bounded on the W by the Irish Sea. Area 3070 sq km (1185 sq. miles). Pop. (1991) 1,365,100. It comprises North Lancashire (districts of Fylde, Lancaster and Wyre); Central Lancashire (districts of Chorley, Preston, South Ribble and West Lancashire); North East Lancashire (districts of Blackburn, Burnley, Hyndburn, Pendle, Ribble Valley and Rossendale). Hilly in the E; in the N, Furness, which contains the S part of the Lake District, was transferred to Cumbria (1974). Chief rivers the Ribble and Lune. The Pennine moorlands are of little value agriculturally, but in the more fertile lowlands of the W oats and potatoes are cultivated, and dairy-farming and pig and poultry rearing are important, esp. on the Fylde peninsula. Lancashire is famous chiefly for its manufactures, however, based on the coalfield, which has a declining output. S Lancashire became the world's leading cotton spinning and weaving region, but the loss of overseas markets has led to a considerably reduced production and reorganization of the industry. Engineering, shipbuilding and the manufacture of rayon and other textiles, paper, chemicals, glass and hosiery are also of great significance. Much of this industrial area since 1974 has formed the metropolitan counties of Merseyside and Greater Manchester. Nowadays the chief industries are electronics, aerospace and hi-tech. Chief industrial centres Blackpool (better known as a seaside resort), Preston and Blackburn. In 1351 Lancashire became a county palatine; the Duchy of Lancaster is vested in the Crown and its Chancellor holds Cabinet rank in the British government.

Lancaster England. Town in Lancashire on the R. Lune 32 km (20 miles) N of Preston. Pop. (1991) 125,600.

Manufactures paper, chemicals, furniture and plastic products.

Castle (partly 13th-cent.) on the site of a Roman camp.

Lancaster (Ohio) USA. Town on the Hocking R. 42 km (26 miles) SE of Columbus. Pop. (1990) 34,507.

Manufactures machinery, footwear and glass.

Birthplace of General William T. Sherman (1820–91).

Lancaster (Pennsylvania) USA. Town 96 km (60 miles) W of Philadelphia. Pop. (1990) 55,551.

Important market town in a fertile agricultural district. Manufactures linoleum, electrical goods and watches.

State cap. 1799–1812.

Lanchow ►LANZHOU.

Landau Germany. Town in the Rhineland-Palatinate 29 km (18 miles) NW of Karlsruhe. Pop. (1986) 35,300

Trade in wine and grain. Brewing. Manufactures tobacco products and furniture. Carriages called Landaus were first made here.

Landes France. 1. Department in the SW formed (1790) from parts of Guienne, Gascony and Béarn, occupying most of the Landes region. Area 9243 sq km (3569 sq. miles). Pop. (1990) 306,000. Prefecture Mont-de-Marsan. Drained by the Adour R. and its tributaries. Soil generally infertile; only the hilly Chalosse region is intensively cultivated; sheep-rearing is important.

Industries sawmilling and the manufacture of turpentine and resin. Chief towns Mont-de-Marsan and Dax.

2. Region in the SW extending along the Bay of Biscay, mainly the Landes department, but also occupying parts of the Gironde and Lot-et-Garonne departments. Formerly a waste of marsh and moorland, with a strip of sand dunes, many over 45 m (148 ft) high, along the coast, separating a number of lagoons (the largest being the Arcachon Basin) from the sea. The dunes were fixed by

the planting of pine forests, yielding timber, turpentine and resin.

Land's End England. Ancient Bolerium. Granite headland 18 m (59 ft) high on the coast of W Cornwall, the westernmost extremity of England.

Landshut Germany. Town in Bavaria on the Isar R. 61 km (38 miles) NE of Munich. Pop. (1991) 60,000.

Industrial centre. Manufactures metal goods, dyestuffs, chemicals and soap. Industries inc. engineering, brewing and tanning.

Above the town is the 13th-cent. castle of Trausnitz.

Landskrona Sweden. Seaport in Malmöhus county on The Sound 34 km (21 miles) NNW of Malmö. Pop. (1990) 36,340.

Industries inc. tanning, flour-milling, sugar-refining, and it manufactures fertilizers.

Landale Pikes England. Two peaks in the Cumbrian Mountains, Lake District 5 km (3 miles) W of Grasmere: Harrison Stickle (733 m, 2404 ft) and Pike-o'-Stickle (709 m, 2326 ft).

Langeland Denmark. Island in the Baltic Sea between Fyn and Laaland islands 51 km (32 miles) long and up to 11 km (7 miles) wide. Area 285 sq km (110 sq. miles). Pop. (1985) 17,800. Chief town Rudköbing. It is fertile and cereals are cultivated.

Langholm Scotland. Market town in Dumfries and Galloway Region on the R. Esk 39 km (24 miles) ENE of Dumfries. Pop. (1990) 2600.

Manufactures tweeds, sheepskin products and ceramics.

Languedoc-Roussillon France. Region and former province in the S, bounded approximately by the Massif Central, the Rhône R., the Gulf of Lions and the foothills of the Pyrenees, now divided into the departments of Ardèche, Gard, Hérault, Lozère, Aude and Tarn and parts of Haute-Garonne, Haute-Loire, Pyrénées-Orientales

and Ariège. Area 23,376 sq km (9025 sq. miles) Pop. (1991) 2,115,000.

Important wine-producing, farming and tourist region. Chief towns Toulouse (historical cap.), Montpellier (regional cap.), Nîmes, Béziers and Carcassonne. The name derives from *Langue d'oc*, referring to the Provençal tongue (*langue*) in which *oc* meant 'yes' – as distinct from the *Langue d'oïl* (present-day *oui*) of the centre and north.

Lansing USA. State cap. of Michigan (since 1847) on the Grand R. 129 km (80 miles) WNW of Detroit. Pop. (1990) 122,899.

Important centre of the car industry and also manufactures engines, fire-fighting equipment and tools.

First settled 1837. Industrial development came with the railways; the manufacture of railway carriages was the leading industry until 1901, when the automobile industry superseded it.

Lanzarote Spain. Island situated NE of Las Palmas between Fuerteventura (S) and Graciosa in the Canary Islands. Area 795 sq km (307 sq. miles). Chief town Arrecife. Volcanic and rocky, rising to 675 m (2215 ft) above sea level. The Montaña de Fuego volcano is active.

Agricultural areas produce onions, cereals, peas, potatoes and fruit. Fisheries are important.

Lanzhou (Lanchou/Lanchow) China. Cap. of Gansu province on the Huang-he 1120 km (700 miles) WSW of Beijing at a height of 1560 m (5117 ft). Pop. (1991) 1,510,000. Important route, commercial and cultural centre. The Silk Road to Xinjiang starts here and it is the centre of caravan trade with Tibet (Xizang), India and Russia. It is the terminus of the Paotow railway, linking NW China with Nei Monggol.

Industries inc. tobacco-processing, oil-refining and metallurgy, and it manufactures oilfield equipment, chemicals, cement, textiles, soap and matches.

Laoag Philippines. Port in NW Luzon on the Laoag R. 8 km (5 miles) from the mouth.

In a region producing rice, maize and sugar, which it exports.

Manufactures cotton goods.

Laoighis (Leix) Ireland. Formerly Queen's County. Inland county in Leinster province. Area 1720 sq km (664 sq. miles). Pop. (1991) 52,325. County town Port Laoighise (Maryborough). Generally flat and boggy; hilly in the SE and NW, where it rises to 518 m (1700 ft) in the Slieve Bloom Mountains.

Main occupations agriculture and dairy-farming.

Laon France. Prefecture of the Aisne department 47 km (29 miles) NW of Reims on an isolated hill 99 m (325 ft) above the surrounding plain. Pop. (1990) 28,670.

Manufactures metal goods and sugar.

Fortified by the Romans. From the end of the 5th cent., when it became a bishopric, it was one of the chief towns of the Franks. In the Hundred Years War it passed from Burgundian to English to French hands.

Laos. Republic in SE Asia. Bounded by China in the N, Vietnam in the E, Cambodia in the S and Thailand and Burma in the W. Area 236,800 sq km (91,400 sq. miles). Pop. (1995) 4,882,000 (22 per cent urban). Life expectancy, 51 years male, 54 female. Cap. Vientiane. Other cities Savannakhét, Louangphrabang and Pakxé. Currency: kip = 100 at. Apart from the valley of the Mekong (which forms much of the W boundary with Thailand) and its tributaries, the landlocked country is mountainous and in places densely forested. A tropical monsoon climate with high temperatures throughout the year and very heavy rains from May to October. Lao is the official lang. and most of the people belong to the Lao and other Thai ethnic groups. About 58 per cent are Buddhist and about 30 per cent follow tribal religions.

About 80 per cent of the pop. is engaged in agriculture. Rice, maize, tobacco, seed cotton, coffee and sugar-cane are the main crops and some opium is also produced. The forests produce much valuable timber such as teak. Industry is not highly developed and

is limited; wood-processing, textiles and light industry.

Laos became a French protectorate in 1893 and an independent sovereign state within the French Union 1949. In 1953 Communist Vietminh forces from Vietnam, aided by Pathet Lao rebels, invaded Laos, but in the following year both Vietminh and French Union troops withdrew from the country. Disorders continued, but in 1960 civil war broke out; a ceasefire was arranged in 1961, however, and a government of National Union was formed in 1962. There was again civil war from 1967, government forces engaging the Pathet Lao and both sides receiving foreign support; the Pathet Lao gradually assumed control and in 1975 the monarchy was abolished and a People's Democratic Republic (Communist) was proclaimed. It is a one-party state and the Supreme People's Assembly was replaced by an elected 80-member National Assembly in 1992.

La Paz Bolivia. Cap. of La Paz department in the steep-sided valley of the La Paz R. at a height of 3600 m (11,808 ft) (360 m; 1181 ft below the bleak Altiplano). Pop. (1990) 1,126,000. Seat of government; *de facto* cap. of Bolivia since 1898 (although Sucre is still the nominal cap.). The highest large city in the world. Its airport on the Altiplano at over 3900 m (12,792 ft) is the world's highest commercial airfield.

Commercial centre. Trade in the products of the Andean valleys and the Altiplano. Tanning, brewing, flour-milling. Manufactures textiles and chemicals.

Founded (1548) by the Spaniards. Named La Paz de Ayacucho (1827) after the battle for independence.

Lapland Norway/Sweden/Finland/Russia. Extensive region in N Europe inhabited by the Lapps, covering the N parts of Norway, Sweden and Finland and the extreme NW of the USSR, mainly within the Arctic Circle but of undefined limit in the political sense. In the W it is mountainous, rising to 2124 m (6967 ft) in Kebnekaise and 2091 m (6858 ft) in Sarektjåkko, both in

Sweden. The N is mainly tundra, while the S is densely forested and there are many lakes and rivers. Many of the Lapps, who are of Mongolian stock, are nomadic, making seasonal migrations with their reindeer herds between the lowlands and the mountains; others, who gain a livelihood by fishing or hunting, are settled in villages. They were frequently the prey of their more powerful neighbours and were largely absorbed, and their pop. declined long before the legislation of a more tolerant age gave them protection. In Swedish Lapland are some of the richest deposits of iron ore in the world, chiefly at Kiruna and Gällivare and other minerals such as copper, pyrites, nickel, apatite and gold.

La Plata Argentina. Cap. of the Buenos Aires province, near the Río de la Plata 56 km (35 miles) SE of Buenos Aires. Pop. (1991) 542,567.

Exports products of the pampas (meat, grain, wool and oil) through its port Ensenada. Meat-packing, oil-refining and flour-milling. Manufactures cement and textiles.

Founded 1882.

Lappeenranta Finland. Industrial town and lake port in Kymi province, picturesquely situated at the S end of L. Saimaa 96 km (60 miles) NE of Kotka. Pop. (1991) 55,358.

Industries inc. sawmilling and it manufactures sulphuric acid, cement, cellulose and machinery.

In Russian hands 1743–1812.

Larache (El Araish) Morocco. Port in the NW on the Atlantic coast 69 km (43 miles) SSW of Tangier. Pop. (1985) 65,000.

Exports cork and wool, wax, fruit and vegetables. Fishing. Orchards and market gardens in the neighbourhood.

Under Spanish protection 1912–56.

Laramie USA Town in Wyoming on the Laramie R. 69 km (43 miles) WNW of Cheyenne at a height of 2180 m (7150 ft). Pop. (1990) 26,687.

Commercial and route centre in a stock-rearing area. Railway engineering. Manufactures cement, bricks and tiles.

Laramie Mountains USA. A range of the Rocky Mountains in SE Wyoming, extending into North Colorado. Highest point Laramie Peak (3133 m, 10,276 ft).

Laramie River USA. River 338 km (210 miles) long rising in the Front Range, Colorado, flowing N and NE past Laramie (Wyoming) and joining the N Platte R. at Fort Laramie.

Laredo USA. Town in SW Texas on the Rio Grande opposite Nuevo Laredo (Mexico), with which it is connected by two international bridges. Pop. (1990) 122,899.

Commercial centre for an agricultural and oil-producing region. Oil-refining, meat packing and canning. Also a tourist resort on the Inter-American Highway.

Founded (1751) by the Spanish. Captured by Texas Rangers 1846.

Largo Scotland. Fishing village and resort in SE Fife on the Firth of Forth. Pop. (1971) 3215. Birthplace of Alexander Selkirk, Scottish sailor and the original of Daniel Defoe's *Robinson Crusoe* (1676–1721).

Largs Scotland. Town and port in North Ayrshire on the Firth of Clyde 18 km (11 miles) SSW of Greenock. Pop. (1991) 10,925. Seaside resort. Alexander III of Scotland defeated Haakon IV of Norway (1263).

Larisa (Larissa) Greece. 1. *Nome* in E Thessaly. Area 5381 sq km (2078 sq. miles). Pop. (1991) 269,300. Contains the fertile basin of the Peneus R.; produces wheat, citrus fruits and olives.

2. Cap. of Larisa *nome* on the Peneus R. 56 km (35 miles) NW of its port, Volós. Pop. (1991) 113,426.

Trade in agricultural produce. Railway junction. Manufactures textiles.

Important city in ancient Thessaly from the 6th cent. BC. Taken by the Turks 1393; passed to Greece 1881.

Larkana Pakistan. Town 240 km (150 miles) N of Hyderabad. Pop. (1985) 48,000. Manufactures metal goods and textiles.

Larnaca Cyprus. Port in the SE 39 km (24 miles) SE of Nicosia. Pop. (1991) 59,600.

Trade in barley, wine, fruit and livestock. Industries inc. petroleum-refining, clothing, textiles, food-processing, furniture and plastics.

Larne Northern Ireland. Municipal borough in Co. Antrim at the entrance to Lough Larne 29 km (18 miles) NNE of Belfast. Pop. (1991) 17,525.

Seaport, tourist centre. Ferry connection to Stranraer (Scotland) and transport ferry service to Preston (England). Industries inc. engineering, bauxite-refining and manufactures clothing, cement and paper.

La Rochelle France. Prefecture of the Charente-Maritime department on the Bay of Biscay. Pop. (1990) 73,744.

Fishing and commercial port. Tourist centre. Manufactures fertilizers, plastics and cement. Industries inc. shipbuilding, fish processing and canning and sawmilling. Exports brandy and wine.

Among its buildings are the 14th-cent. Tower of St Nicholas, the 15th-cent. Lantern Tower (once used as a lighthouse) and the 18th-cent. cathedral. From the 14th to the 16th cent. it was a leading French seaport; it became a Huguenot stronghold, but fell to Richelieu after a long siege (1627–8). Its trade declined when France lost Canada and never fully recovered despite the construction of its outport, La Pallice, for accommodation of the larger ocean-going vessels.

La Romana Dominican Republic. Seaport in La Altagracia province 103 km (64 miles) E of Santo Domingo. Pop. (1986) 101,360.

Exports sugar. Sugar-refining, flour-milling, coffee and tobacco processing.

La Salle Canada. City, S suburb of Montreal, Quebec. Primarily residential with a variety of industries.

Las Alpujarras Spain. Mountainous region in Andalusia in the Granada and Almería provinces between the Sierra Nevada and the coast. Fertile valleys. Scene of strong resistance by the Moors after the fall of Granada (1492); they were not subdued till 1571.

Las Cruces USA. Market town in S New Mexico on the Rio Grande. Pop. (1990) 62,126. It is a stock-rearing and agricultural region.

La Serena Chile. Cap. of the Coquimbo province 362 km (225 miles) N of Valparaiso. Pop. (1992) 120,336.

Resort. Market town. Trade in fruit, flowers. Picturesque, with old-world charm; beach and casino nearby at Peñuelas.

Founded 1543. Severely damaged by earthquake 1922.

Lashio Myanmar (Burma). Town in Shan State 209 km (130 miles) NE of Mandalay, with which it is connected by rail. Pop. (1985) 5000. Also terminus of the Burma Road to Chungking (China).

Las Palmas Spain. 1. Spanish province in the Canary Is. Area 4065 sq km (1569 sq. miles). Pop. (1991) 749,527. Consists of the islands of Gran Canaria, Lanzarote and Fuerteventura and the small barren islands of Alegranza, Roque del Este, Roque del Oeste, Graciosa and Montãna Clara y Lobos.

2. Cap. of Las Palmas province, on the island of Grán Canaria. Pop. (1991) 342,030. Largest city in the Canary Is. Its fertile valley is famous for palms (hence the name). Mild subtropical climate; a popular resort, esp. during winter (mean temp. Jan. 17°C; 62°F.) Its port, La Luz, is an important fuelling station.

Exports fruit, vegetables and wine.

La Spezia Italy. Cap. of La Spezia province, Liguria 80 km (50 miles) ESE of Genoa on the Gulf of Spezia. Pop. (1991) 103,008. Since 1861 Italy's chief naval base, with shipyards and arsenal.

Manufactures electrical equipment, textiles and porcelain. Other industries inc. oil-refining.

At nearby Lerici Percy Bysshe Shelley, English poet (1792–1822), spent his last months before being drowned off the coast.

Lassithi Greece. *Nome* in E Crete, with Mt

Dhikti or Lassithi (2148 m, 7048 ft) in the extreme W. Area 1823 sq km (704 sq. miles). Pop. (1991) 70,762. Cap. Ayios Nikolaos.

Olives, carobs and wheat are cultivated. Sheep and goats raised. Tourism is important.

Las Vegas USA. Town in SE Nevada at a height of 620 m (2034 ft). Pop. (1990) 258,295.

Commercial centre for a mining and agricultural region. More famous as a resort, esp. for the gambling casinos.

First settled (1855) by Mormons. Later abandoned, it was permanently settled in 1905, with the arrival of the railway.

Latakia (Ar. **El Ladhiqiya**) Syria. Ancient Laodicea ad Mare. Cap. of Latakia province 137 km (85 miles) WSW of Aleppo. Pop. (1992) 284,000. The chief seaport.

Exports Latakia tobacco, also grain and cotton.

Flourished under the Romans and under the Crusaders. Declined in the 16th cent., but revived later with the development of the tobacco trade. Since 1950 improvements have been made in its harbour in order to divert Syrian trade to it from Beirut (Lebanon).

Latin America. A convenient term for all countries S of the US–Mexico frontier (except the West Indies). Inc. Mexico (part of the North American subcontinent), Central America and South America. The majority of the pop. are Spanish-speaking, but the lang. of the largest country, Brazil, is Portuguese. Dutch, English and French are spoken in Suriname, Belize and Guyana and French Guiana respectively. Various Indian lang. survive in much of the area.

Latium Italy. Region of ancient Italy S of the Tiber R. Originally the home of the Latini, but after conquest by the Romans it inc. also lands of neighbouring tribes, the Rutuli, Hernici, Volsci and Aurunci.

Latium (Italian **Lazio**) Italy. Region of modern Italy more extensive than ancient Latium, comprising the provinces of Frosinone, Latina, Rieti, Roma and Viterbo. Area

17,227 sq km (6651 sq. miles). Pop. (1991) 4,970,681. Cap. Rome. Inc. the coastal plain between the Fiora R (N) and the Garigliano R. (S) and the W slopes of the Apennines. Land has been reclaimed in Campagna di Roma and the Pontine Marshes.

Cereals, vines and olives are cultivated.

Latvia. Republic on the Baltic Sea and the Gulf of Riga, bounded by Estonia in the N, Russia in the E, Lithuania and Belorussia in the S. Area 64,610 sq km (24,946 sq. miles). Pop. (1995) 2,515,000. (69 per cent urban). Life expectancy, 64 years male, 75 female. Cap. and chief seaport Riga. Other cities are Liepaja, Ventspils, Daugavpils (Dvinsk) and Jelgava. Currency: Lat = 100 santims. Mostly low-lying and flat, with a small area in the extreme E rising to 300 m (984 ft). Chief river the Western Dvina (Daugava). About 40 per cent of the land is forested and yields a considerable output of timber; about 25 per cent is cultivated. The official lang. is Latvian and the ethnic groups are 52 per cent Latvian and 34 per cent Russian. The main religions are Evangelical Lutheran, Russian Orthodox and Roman Catholic.

Until after World War II agriculture dominated the economy but since then industrialization has been rapid. Crops are oats, barley, rye, potatoes and flax. Leading agricultural occupations are dairy-farming, cattle and pig rearing; in addition forestry and fishing. Industries inc. dairy produce, timber, paper, textiles, footwear, electrical, fertilizers, electric railway passenger coaches and telecommunications equipment.

Inhabited by the Letts from about the 10th cent., but were a disunited people and, until the 20th cent., remained subject to foreign domination: in the 13th and 14th cent. to the Teutonic Knights and thereafter to Russia, Poland and Sweden, to be incorporated in Russia in 1721. Although the Letts were long in a condition of serfdom, under Russian rule their economy developed and by the end of the 19th cent. nearly one-quarter of the country's exports passed through Latvian ports. Independence came in 1918, but with it the decline of much of its industrial and

Lauder

commercial prosperity, even though agriculture still flourished. In 1940 Latvia was annexed by the USSR and it became a constituent republic. In World War II the country was devastated, as it had been in World War I. In 1990 the Latvian Supreme Soviet declared that the Soviet occupation of 1940 was illegal and that the Constitution of 1922 should be reinstated. Full independence was conceded by the USSR in 1991. There is a 100-member parliament (*Saeima*).

Lauder Scotland. Town in Scottish Borders on Leader Water in Lauderdale 14 km (9 miles) N of Melrose. Pop. (1985) 620. Scene of the hanging (at Lauder Bridge) of James III's favourites (1482).

Launceston Australia. Second largest city in Tasmania in the N at the confluence of the N Esk and S Esk rivers where they form the Tamar R. 64 km (40 miles) from the open sea. Pop. (1991) 93,520.
   Commercial centre with a mainland trade, esp. through Melbourne. It exports agricultural produce and industries inc. sawmilling, brewing and flour-milling. Manufactures inc. woollen goods.
   Founded 1805.

Launceston England. Market town in E Cornwall on the R. Kensey. Pop. (1990) 6500.
   Industries inc. light engineering.
   Formerly (till 1837) the county town. George Fox the Quaker was imprisoned here (1656) for 'disturbing the peace' in St Ives.

Laurel USA. Town in Mississippi on Tallahala Creek 45 km (28 miles) NNE of Hattiesburg. Pop. (1970) 24,145.
   Commercial centre. Trade in timber. Manufactures fibre-board, furniture. Oil-refining.

Laurentides Park Canada. Provincial park in Quebec situated N of Quebec city. Area 10,360 sq km (4000 sq. miles). Rises to 1173 m (3847 ft). Over 1500 lakes, many streams. A game reserve for moose and deer. Hunting forbidden, but fishing for speckled trout is a popular sport. Hotels and fishing camps. Established 1895.

Laurium Greece. Ancient town in Attica 42 km (26 miles) SE of Athens. Site of the small modern seaport of Lávrion.

Lausanne Switzerland. Cap. of Vaud canton on the N shore of L. Geneva. Pop. (1991) 123,159.
   Tourist resort. Industrial and commercial centre. Printing, woodworking. Manufactures leather goods, clothing, chocolate and biscuits. Trade in wine.
   A hilly city, divided by two short rivers into three sections, the old Cité, the Bourg (the commercial quarter) and St Laurent; the upper part is connected by funicular railway with Ouchy, its port on the lake. Educational centre. The university (founded 1891 but existing as a college since 1537) has a valuable library and art museum; there is also a School of Technology. The principal building is the cathedral (12th/13th-cent., restored), standing 150 m (492 ft) above the lake. Headquarters of the Swiss Federal Supreme Court and of the International Olympic Committee. It originally stood on the shore of the lake, SW of its present situation, but when it was destroyed in the 4th cent. the inhabitants founded a new town on the hill of the Cité. The bishopric was established in the 6th cent. Protestantism was introduced in 1536. It became cap. of the new canton of Vaud in 1803.

Lauterbrunnen Switzerland. Summer resort in the Bern canton on the White Lütschine R. in the Bernese Alps 10 km (6 miles) S of Interlaken. Pop. (1970) 3431. The walls of the valley, the Lauterbrunnental, are steep-sided and deep, and the floor is often in shadow; there are 72 waterfalls, inc. the Staubbach and Trümmelbach.

Laval Canada. City in Quebec province. It is separated from Montreal by the Rivière des Prairies. Pop. (1991) 314,398. Established in 1965.

Laval France. Cap. of Mayenne department

on the Mayenne R. 69 km (43 miles) E of Rennes. Pop. (1990) 53,479.

Textile centre, well-known for linen since the 14th cent. Manufactures cotton goods, hosiery, leather goods and furniture. Cheese-making.

Its 'old' castle dates from the 11th and 12th cent. Cathedral partly of the 12th cent.

Lawrence (Kansas) USA. Town on the Kansas R. 53 km (33 miles) WSW of Kansas City. Pop. (1990) 65,608. Mainly a residential and cultural centre in a rich agricultural region.

Flour-milling. Manufactures pipe organs, agricultural chemicals, greeting cards, plastics and paper products.

Lawrence (Massachusetts) USA. Industrial town on the Merrimack R., which provides hydroelectric power. Pop. (1990) 70,207.

Important woollen and worsted manufacturing centre. Also manufactures clothing, plastic, cotton and leather goods.

Lawton USA. Town in Oklahoma 129 km (80 miles) SW of Oklahoma City. Pop. (1990) 80,561.

Industrial centre in an agricultural region. Manufactures cottonseed oil, leather goods. Flour-milling, meat-packing. Granite and limestone quarries nearby.

The Fort Sill military reservation is 6 km (4 miles) N.

Lea (Lee) River England. River 74 km (46 miles) long, rising near Dunstable (Beds) and flowing SE and S past Hertford and Ware, along the Greater London–Essex boundary to the R. Thames at Blackwall. A source of water supply for London. The Lea valley is well-known for the cultivation of tomatoes and flowers in glasshouses.

Leamington Spa England. Health resort in Warwickshire on the R. Leam 13 km (8 miles) S of Coventry, conveniently near Warwick, Kenilworth and Stratford-upon-Avon. Pop. (1991) 55,396.

Engineering. Manufactures gas cookers and automobile parts.

It has saline springs, the waters being taken at the Royal Pump Room. Of little importance till the end of the 18th cent., when the first baths were built, it was visited by Queen Victoria in 1838 and was thereafter officially known as Royal Leamington Spa.

Leatherhead England. Town in Surrey on the R. Mole at the foot of the North Downs. Pop. (1991) 42,903. Largely residential but there is some light industry.

A 14th-cent. church.

Lebanon. Republic in SW Asia. Bounded by Syria in the N and E, Israel in the S and the Mediterranean Sea to the W. Area 10,230 sq km (3950 sq. miles). Pop. (1995) 3,009,000 (87 per cent urban). Life expectancy, 73 years male, 78 female. Cap. Beirut. Other towns Tripoli, Zahlé, Saida (Sidon) and Tyre. Currency: Lebanese pound = 100 piastres. Lebanon is mountainous: the Lebanon Mountains extend through the country near and parallel to the coast; the fertile Bekaa valley lies between this range and the Anti-Lebanon. About 50 per cent of the country is at an altitude of 915 m (3000 ft). The climate is Mediterranean, with long, hot, rainless summers and short, warm winters with high humidity in coastal areas. Land use: forested 8 per cent, meadows and pastures 1 per cent, agricultural and under permanent cultivation 29 per cent. Christianity has been established in Lebanon since early times and it is probable that nearly 50 per cent of the pop. are Christians, the majority are Maronites, the remainder Eastern Orthodox, Greek and Roman Catholics and Armenians. Over 50 per cent of the people are Muslims, divided between Sunnis and Shiites, and there are many Druses. The official lang. is Arabic and other lang. are French, Kurdish and Armenian. It is primarily an agricultural country, although only about one-third of its area is cultivated. Before the wars the considerable adverse balance of trade was normally offset by receipts from foreign tourists and Lebanese living abroad. In the Bekaa valley cereals (esp. wheat), wines, oranges, lemons and other fruits are cultivated. The forests, inc. the famous Cedars of Lebanon, have been much depleted by reckless exploitation. Industry was growing fast before the civil war but has suffered badly since. The oil refineries have not been fully active since the 1970s and the country depends on imports.

After World War I Lebanon was put under French mandate and its independence was proclaimed in 1941, but this did not become effective until 1944. In 1958 a Muslim revolt broke out but was suppressed after American forces had been landed at the President's request. The activities of Palestinian guerrillas based in S Lebanon led to Israeli reprisals, but the conflict between Lebanese Christians and Muslims (1975–6) caused far more destruction and loss of life, notably in Beirut, numerous ceasefires being declared and broken, and was ended mainly through Syrian intervention. In 1992 Syrian forces still remained in Lebanon, being wary of pulling out while Israeli forces remained in the S of the country.

The Legislature consists of a 128-member House of Assembly, with equal numbers of Muslims and Christians, elected for four years by universal adult suffrage. The Executive inc. the President (a Maronite Christian) and the Prime Minister (a Sunni Muslim), while the Speaker is a Shia Muslim.

Lebanon USA. Town in Pennsylvania 113 km (70 miles) WNW of Philadelphia. Pop. (1985) 29,000.

Manufactures iron and steel goods, textiles and electrical equipment. Developed largely because of local iron deposits.

Lecce Italy. Cap. of Lecce province in Apulia 40 km (25 miles) SSE of Brindisi. Pop. (1991) 102,344.

Market town. Trade in olive oil, wine, tobacco and other products of the region. Manufactures papier-mâché toys and pottery.

Has many buildings in rococo style, built of the local yellow stone, inc. the 17th-cent. cathedral. There is also a Roman amphitheatre.

Lecco Italy. Town in Como province in Lombardy on the SE branch of L. Como (L. Lecco). Pop. (1971) 53,583.

Industrial and tourist centre. Iron and brass founding. Manufactures textiles. Important cheese market; exports esp. Gorgonzola cheese.

Lech River. River 285 km (177 miles) long, rising in the Vorarlberg Alps (Austria), flowing generally NE to the German border, then N past Fussen and Augsburg to join the Danube below Donauwörth.

Le Creusot France. Industrial town in the Saône-et-Loire department 77 km (48 miles) SW of Dijon. Pop. (1985) 32,000.

Situated on a coalfield, it has important iron and steel works. Manufactures locomotives, armaments and machinery.

Ledbury England. Market town in Herefordshire on the R. Leadon 19 km (12 miles) ESE of Hereford. Pop. (1991) 6,216.

Trade in cider and perry. Limestone quarried in the neighbourhood.

Many timbered buildings, inc. the 17th-cent. market house. Birthplace of John Masefield, English poet (1878–1967).

Leeds England. City and unitary authority on the R. Aire. Pop. (1991) 451,841.

Important commercial and industrial centre and a junction for rail, road, canal and air services. From the 14th cent. it had a prosperous woollen industry which in more recent times developed into the manufacture of ready-made clothing, now the largest single industry. With the Industrial Revolution engineering assumed great importance and today textile and printing machinery, agricultural implements and electrical equipment are produced. Other industries inc. printing, tanning and the manufacture of footwear, clothing, furniture, chemicals and glass.

Leeds was incorporated by Charles I in 1626. The university (1904) was formerly the Yorkshire College of Science. St John's Church exemplifies the 17th-cent. Gothic style, but the majority of the city's notable buildings are modern. The remains of the 12th-cent. Kirkstall Abbey beside the R. Aire to the NW and the park and fine mansion of Temple Newsam, which dates from the 17th cent. and is 5 km (3 miles) E, both belong to the city of Leeds.

Leek England. Town in N Staffordshire 13 km (8 miles) NE of Stoke-on-Trent. Pop. (1990) 20,000.

Manufactures textiles and clothing.

Nearby are the ruins of the 13th-cent. Cistercian abbey of Dieulacresse.

Lee River ➤LEA RIVER.

Leeuwarden Netherlands. Cap. of Friesland province 55 km (34 miles) W of Groningen. Pop. (1992) 86,405. Railway and canal junction.

Important cattle market. Trade in dairy and agricultural produce. Industries inc. boatbuilding, iron-founding and tourism, and it manufactures clothing, footwear and furniture.

It has the museum of the Frisian Society.

Leeuwin, Cape Australia. Cape in the extreme SW of Western Australia at the W end of Flinders Bay. Notorious for stormy weather and dangerous currents.

Leeward Islands (Pacific) ➤SOCIETY ISLANDS, FRENCH POLYNESIA.

Leeward Islands West Indies. Chain of islands in the lesser Antilles, extending SE from Puerto Rico to the Windward Islands. 1. Anguilla, Antigua and Barbuda, British Virgin Islands, Montserrat, St Kitts (St Christopher)-Nevis. 2. The US Virgin Islands. 3. Guadeloupe and dependencies (French). 4. The Dutch islands of St Eustatius, Saba and part of St Martin (divided with France). The islands are generally fertile, producing sea-island cotton, sugar, molasses, tropical fruits; also salt. Discovered (1493) by Columbus. Long in dispute between England and France. The present disposition was made in 1815. Dominica was transferred from the Leeward Is. colony to the Windward Is. in 1940.

Lefkas ➤LEVFÁS.

Lefkosia ➤NICOSIA.

Legaspi Philippines. Cap. and chief seaport of Albay province in SE Luzon. Pop. (1990) 121,000.

Exports copra and abacá (Manila hemp).

Leghorn (Italian **Livorno**) Italy. Cap. of Livorno province, Tuscany on the Ligurian Sea 21 km (13 miles) SSW of Pisa. Pop. (1991) 171,265.

Resort. Seaport. Exports wine, olive oil, coral goods, straw hats and marble. Industries inc. shipbuilding, flour-milling, engineering, and it manufactures soap and cement.

Birthplace of Pietro Mascagni, the composer (1863–1945).

Legnano Italy. Industrial town in Milano province, Lombardy on the Olona R. 26 km (16 miles) NW of Milan. Pop. (1985) 49,500.

Manufactures textiles, shoes and soap. Engineering.

Nearby Frederick Barbarossa was defeated by the Lombard League (1176).

Legnica (Ger. **Liegnitz**) Poland. Cap. of the Legnica voivodeship 64 km (40 miles) WNW of Wroclaw. Pop. (1992) 105,500.

Manufactures copper, textiles, chemicals, paints, machinery, electronic equipment and pianos.

Cap. of the duchy of Liegnitz from the 12th to the 17th cent. Passed to Prussia 1742 and ceded to Poland in 1945.

Leh India. Cap. of the Ladakh district, Kashmir just N of the Indus R. and 257 km (160 miles) E of Srinagar at a height of 3500 m (11,480 ft) in the Ladakh Range. Pop. (1991) 9000. Commercial centre on a trade route between India and Tibet. Has a Buddhist monastery.

Le Havre ➤HAVRE, LE.

Leicester England. County town of Leicestershire on the R. Soar. Pop. (1991) 328,835.

Industrial centre. Manufactures chiefly hosiery and footwear. Industries inc. engineering and brewing.

A charter was granted to the city by Queen Elizabeth I in 1589. Standing on the ancient Fosse Way, it has among its Roman remains the Jewry Wall, parts of the Forum and baths.

Among the old churches are those of
St Nicholas, which has Roman building materials, St Mary de Castro and St Martin,
which has been the cathedral since 1926. The
Great Hall of the 12th-cent. Norman castle
is preserved as part of an 18th-cent. brick
building and is used now as an assize court.
The Guildhall and Trinity Hospital date from
the 14th cent. Thomas Cook organized the
first rail excursion, from Leicester to Loughborough and back, in 1841.

Leicestershire England. A midland county.
Area 2159 sq km (834 sq. miles). Pop. (1991)
860,500. It is divided into the districts of
Blaby, Charnwood, Harborough, Hinckley
and Bosworth, Leicester, Melton, North
West Leicestershire, Oadby and Wigston.
Rutland became a separate county in 1997.
County town Leicester. Generally low and
undulating, it is bisected S–N by the R. Soar,
which separates Charnwood Forest (278 m;
912 ft) from the E uplands (230 m; 754 ft).
Much of the land is devoted to dairy-farming,
Stilton cheese being produced near Melton
Mowbray, and to cattle and sheep rearing.
Cereals (wheat and barley) cultivated in the
W. Well-known for fox-hunting, the famous
Quorn hunt being located at the village of
that name. Main industrial centres Leicester,
Hinckley and Loughborough.

Textiles, footwear, clothing and engineering are important industries. High technology industries have grown in recent years
and there is a Bioscience park.

Leiden (Leyden) Netherlands. City in
South Holland province on the Oude Rijn
(Old Rhine) R. 16 km (10 miles) NE of the
Hague. Pop. (1992) 112,976.

Educational and industrial centre. Industries inc. printing and publishing. Manufactures cloth, blankets and cigars.

University founded (1575) by William of
Orange as a reward for the heroic defence
of the city against the Spaniards (1574). In
this siege Leiden was saved by the piercing
of the dikes, which flooded the surrounding
area and enabled the ships of the Beggars of
the Sea to bring relief. The Leyden jar was
invented at the university (1745); among its

celebrated scholars were Grotius and Goldsmith. Important for its weaving from the
14th cent. but the industry had declined by
the 18th cent. For 11 years it was the home
of the Pilgrim Fathers before they sailed for
America (1620). Birthplace of the painters
Rembrandt (1606–69), Jan van Goyen
(1596–1658) and Jan Steen (1626–79).

Leigh England. Town in Greater Manchester 18 km (11 miles) W of the city. Pop.
(1991) 43,150.

In a coalmining district. Industries also inc.
cotton and rayon, and the manufacture of
machinery.

Leighton Buzzard England. Market town
in SW Bedfordshire 18 km (11 miles) WNW
of Luton. Pop. (1991) 32,610 (inc. Linslade).

Sand-quarrying and engineering. Manufactures bricks and cement.

A 14th-cent. market cross.

Leinster Ireland. Province comprising the
whole E and SE part of the republic and inc.
the counties of Carlow, Dublin, Kildare, Kilkenny, Laoighis, Longford, Louth,
Meath, Offaly, Westmeath, Exford and
Wicklow. Area 19,633 sq km (7580 sq. miles).
Pop. (1991) 1,860,037 (about 60 per cent in
the city of Dublin). Mainly agricultural.

Leipzig Germany. City in Saxony at the
confluence of the Elster, Pleisse and Parther
rivers 145 km (90 miles) SSW of Berlin.
Pop. (1991) 511,079.

Industrial, commercial and cultural centre.
Manufactures textiles, machinery, chemicals,
electrical equipment, musical instruments,
leather goods and glass. Noted for its industrial fairs, its trade in furs and its book
publishing.

Its old or inner city, with narrow streets
and 16th- and 17th-cent. houses, surrounded
by inner and outer suburbs, was severely
damaged by bombing in World War II.
Among its ancient buildings are the 15th-
cent. Thomaskirche, where J. S. Bach was
organist, the 13th-cent. Paulinerkirche (restored), the 17th-cent. Johanneskirche, the
16th-cent Gothic Rathaus and Auerbach's
Keller immortalized in Goethe's *Faust*; the

new Gewandhaus, famed for its concerts, dates from 1884. The university was founded (1409) by a secession of German students from Prague. First mentioned as a town in the 11th cent. Rapidly became important as a commercial centre. Suffered severely in the Thirty Years War. Scene of the Battle of the Nations (1813), in which Napoleon was defeated. Birthplace of Wagner (1813–83) and Leibniz (1646–1716), and home for a time of Mendelssohn and Schumann.

Leiria Portugal. Town situated SSW of Coimbra in the Beira Litoral on Liz R. Pop. (1991) 27,530.

Trading centre of an agricultural area and district cap. Industries inc. tanning, woodworking and it manufactures cement.

Batalha Abbey has the tomb of Henry the Navigator.

Leith Scotland. Port on the S shore of the Firth of Forth, incorporated in Edinburgh in 1920.

Industries inc. flour-milling, brewing and whisky-distilling. It manufactures paper and chemicals.

Trinity House was founded in 1558 as a home for sailors, but later became the licensing authority for pilots.

Leitha River Austria/Hungary. River 177 km (110 miles) long rising in E Austria and flowing generally E into NW Hungary to join the Danube. Formerly part of the boundary between Austria and Hungary.

Leitrim Ireland. County in Connacht extending SE from Donegal Bay. Area 1525 sq km (581 sq. miles). Pop. (1991) 25,300. County town Carrick-on-Shannon. Hilly and barren in the N (rising to 644 m; 2112 ft in Truskmore), lower in the S. Many lakes, the largest Lough Allen. Main occupations dairy-farming, cattle-rearing and potato cultivation.

Leix ➤LAOIGHIS.

Le Kef Tunisia. Town situated SW of Tunis near the Algerian border. It is a railway terminus and trading centre.

Léman, Lake ➤GENEVA, LAKE.

Le Mans ➤MANS, LE.

Lemnos (Limnos) Greece. Island in the N Aegean Sea. Area 453 sq km (175 sq. miles). Chief town Kastron. Mountainous, with fertile valleys where fruits and cereals are cultivated.

Lena River Russia. Country's longest river (4400 km; 2730 miles), the most easterly of the three great Siberian rivers, rising just W of L. Baikal. Flows generally NE past Kirensk, Olekminsk and Yakutsk, then turns N and enters the Laptev Sea by an extensive delta, draining an area of over 2,420,000 sq km (934,000 sq. miles). Chief tributaries the Vitim, Olekma, Aldan and Vilyui. Navigable for more than 3860 km (2400 miles) but at the delta completely icebound for all but three months (July–Oct.). Gold has long been produced along the river and its tributaries.

Leninabad ➤KHUDZHAND.

Leninakan ➤KUMAYRI.

Leningrad ➤ST PETERSBURG.

Leninsk-Kuznetsi Russia. Industrial town in the Kemerovo Region of the Kuznetsk basin 32 km (20 miles) S of Kemerovo. Pop. (1991) 134,400.

Coal and iron mining centre. Industries inc. railway engineering, brickmaking and sawmilling.

Lenkoran Azerbaijan. Town situated SSW of Baku on the Caspian Sea near the Iranian frontier.

Industries inc. sawmilling, food-canning and fishing.

Lennoxville Canada. Town just SE of Sherbrooke at the mouth of Massawippi R. on St Francis R. in Quebec. Pop. (1987) 8200.

Industries inc. paper, bronze and steel and hosiery. Centre of a farming and lumbering area.

Lens France. Town in the Pas-de-Calais department 27 km (17 miles) SW of Lille. Pop. (1990) 35,278.

Mining centre on the important coalfield. Manufactures chemicals and metal goods.

Leoben Austria. Town in Styria on the Mur R. 42 km (26 miles) NW of Graz. Pop. (1991) 28,504.

Lignite-mining centre. Iron-founding and brewing.

Leominster England. Market town in Herefordshire on the R. Lugg 19 km (12 miles) N of Hereford. Pop. (1991) 9453.

Manufactures agricultural machinery, plastics and cider. Tourism is important.

Leominster USA. Industrial town in N Massachusetts 10 km (6 miles) SSE of Fitchburg. Pop. (1970) 32,939.

Manufactures plastics, furniture and toys.

León (officially **León de los Aldamas**) Mexico. City in Guanajuato state in the Río Turbio valley at a height of 1884 m (6181 ft). Pop. (1990) 872,453.

Important commercial and industrial centre in a mining and agricultural region. Manufactures footwear and leather goods (saddles), textiles, cement and steel products. Flour-milling and tanning.

Founded 1576. Has frequently suffered from floods, but now protected by a dam.

León Nicaragua. Cap. of the León department 80 km (50 miles) NW of Managua. Pop. (1985) 100,982. The country's cultural centre and the second largest city.

Manufactures leather goods, footwear, fertilizers, insecticides and soap.

Founded (1524) 32 km (20 miles) away at the foot of the volcano Momotombo; destroyed by earthquake and moved to its present site 1610. Has the appearance of an old 'colonial' city. Seat of a university (1812), which became part of the National University in 1952. Cap. of the republic until 1857.

León Spain. 1. Region and former kingdom in the NW, comprising the present-day provinces of León, Palencia, Salamanca, Valladolid and Zamora. One of the earliest Christian kingdoms of Spain following the liberation from the Moors, having been es-

tablished early in the 10th cent. Finally united with Castile 1230.

2. Province in the NW, mountainous in the N (Cantabrian Mountains) and W (Montañas de León); the remainder is on the central plateau. Area 15,468 sq km (5972 sq. miles). Pop. (1991) 524,139. Mainly agricultural. There are coal mines in the N.

3. Cap. of León province 129 km (80 miles) NW of Valladolid. Pop. (1991) 144,137.

Manufactures textiles, leather and pottery. Trade in agricultural produce.

Cathedral (12th/14th-cent.), an outstanding example of Spanish Gothic. Cap. of the kingdom of León early in the 10th cent. It declined after the union with Castile (1230).

Léopold II, Lake ➤MAI-NDOMDE, LAKE.

Léopoldville ➤KINSHASA.

Leptis Magna Libya. Ancient port, now known as Lebda, just E of Homs, in Tripolitania. Founded by Phoenicians from Sidon, it paid tribute to Carthage. Its Roman remains are among the most important in North Africa and have been excavated since 1911, chiefly by Italian archaeologists.

Le Puy ➤PUY, LE.

Lérida Spain. 1. Province in the NE in Catalonia, bounded on the N by France and Andorra. Area 12,028 sq km (4659 sq. miles). Pop. (1991) 353,455. Drained by the Segre R. and its tributaries.

Mainly agricultural. Produces wine, olive oil.

2. Cap. of Lérida province on the Segre R. 34 km (83 miles) WNW of Barcelona. Pop. (1991) 111,880.

Manufactures textiles and paper. Tanning.

Old cathedral (13th-cent.), last used for public worship in 1707 and a new 18th-cent. cathedral. Captured by the Romans (49 BC), the Moors (714), the French (1707, 1810). By reason of its strategic position frequently attacked and besieged.

Lérins, Îles de France. Two islands and two islets 5 km (3 miles) SE of Cannes. On Ste-Marguerite is the fort in which the 'Man

Lesotho

in the Iron Mask' and Marshal Bazaine were imprisoned. On St-Honorat is a monastery founded at the beginning of the 5th cent.

Lerwick Scotland. Chief town of the Shetland Is. on the E coast of Mainland. Pop. (1991) 7336.

Fishing centre and chief port for the islands. Hand-knitting is an important industry.

Lesbos (Lesvos) Greece. 1. Island in the Aegean Sea off the coast of Turkey. Area 1632 sq km (630 sq. miles). On the fertile lowlands wheat, olives, citrus fruits and wines are produced. Reached the peak of its prosperity in the early 6th cent. BC, esp. under Pittacus, of whom the lyric poets Alcaeus and Sappho were contemporaries. Became a member of the Delian League. Passed from Byzantium to a Genoese family (1354) and then to the Turks (1462); regained by Greece 1913. Sometimes known by the name of its chief town, Mytilene (Mitilíni).

2. *Nome* comprising the islands of Lesbos, Lemnos and Hagios Eustratios. Area 2154 sq km (836 sq. miles) Pop. (1991) 103,700. Cap. Mytilene.

Lesina ►HVAR.

Leskovac Yugoslavia. Industrial town in S Serbia 37 km (23 miles) S of Niš on the S Morava R. Pop. (1991) 61,963.

Manufactures textiles, soap and furniture.

Lesotho. Kingdom in southern Africa, an enclave within South Africa, bounded W by Free State, E by Natal and S by Transkei and Cape Province. Area 30,355 sq km (11,720 sq. miles). Pop. (1995) 2,057,000 (21 per cent urban). Life expectancy, 58 years male, 63 female. Cap. Maseru. Other towns Maputsoe, Teyateyaneng and Mafeteng. Currency: loti = 100 lisente. Mainly a high dissected volcanic plateau; the Maluti Mountains in the N rise to over 2700 m (8856 ft) and another great escarpment, the Drakensberg, forms the E frontier and rises to over 3000 m (9840 ft) in Mont-aux-Sources (3301 m; 10,827 ft). In the W is a belt of lower land (1500–1800 m; 4925–5904 ft), the most

accessible part of the country. The Orange R. rises in the NE, flows to the SW and with its tributaries drains almost the whole country. The climate is dry and bracing and the rainfall variable, averaging about 75 cm (30 ins.) annually, mainly in the summer months. Land use: meadows and pastures 66 per cent, agricultural and under permanent cultivation 11 per cent. About 99 per cent of the pop. is Basuto, a branch of the Bechuana family of Bantu. The official lang. Sesotho and English. About 93 per cent of the pop. is Christian of which a large proportion is Roman Catholic.

Lesotho has few natural resources and most of the country's income comes from male contract labour employed in South Africa, and wool and mohair. On the grasslands sheep and goats are raised. Principal crops are maize, corn and wheat. It has suffered from soil erosion, combated by reforestation, terracing and construction of irrigation dams. The land is the common property of the nation, held in trust by the chiefs and no European settlement is permitted.

In the early 19th cent. the Basuto constantly quarrelled with the Boers and the British. After defeat by the Boers they came under British protection (1868) at the request of Moshesh, the paramount chief. The territory was annexed to Cape Colony in 1871 but restored to direct British control in 1884. It became one of the three British High Commission Territories, as Basutoland, in Southern Africa (the others were the Bechuanaland Protectorate and Swaziland). Constitutional reforms creating an executive council and a partly elected national council were introduced in 1960. Internal self-government was granted in 1965 and the paramount chief Moshoeshoe II took the title of king. It became independent as the Kingdom of Lesotho in 1966. However, the Constitution was suspended in 1970. In 1973 a National Assembly with nominated members was introduced but dissolved in 1985. Chief Jonathan was deposed in a military *coup* in 1986, subsequently the King ruled with the assistance of a Military Council. In 1990 King Moshoeshoe II went into exile and his eldest son Letsie III was elected King by the Assembly of Chiefs. In 1992 Mosh-oeshoe II returned to Lesotho as chief of the royal family, but not as monarch. He died in 1996 and was succeeded by Letsie III. Multi-party elections took place in 1993. There is a 65-member National Assembly and a Senate comprising 22 principal chiefs and 11 members nominated by the King.

Lesvos ►LESBOS.

Leszno (Lissa) Poland. Cap. of the Leszno voivodeship 68 km (42 miles) SSW of Poznań. Pop. (1989) 57,673.

Industries inc. flour-milling and the manufacture of machinery and footwear.

Returned by Prussia to Poland in 1919.

Letchworth England. Town in Hertford-shire 23 km (14 miles) NNW of Hertford. Pop. (1991) 32,099.

Engineering, printing. Manufactures cor-sets and rubber products. The first 'garden city' in England, founded 1903.

Lethbridge Canada. City in Alberta on the Oldman R. 177 km (110 miles) SSE of Cal-gary. Pop. (1991) 60,974.

Coalmining and market centre in an irrigated agricultural and ranching region. Industries inc. vegetable-canning and food-processing, oil and natural gas.

Founded in the 1870s as Coalbanks but renamed in 1885.

Leticia Colombia. Town situated SE of Bogotá on the upper Amazon R. in Amazonas Department, where it forms the border with Peru and Brazil. River port and airfield in a tropical forest. Pop. (1992) 32,694.

Drug trafficking has replaced tourism as a major industry.

Leuven ►LOUVAIN.

Levant. Name of the coastlands of the E Mediterranean, in Turkey, Syria, Lebanon and Israel, or, in a wider sense, for all the countries around the coasts of this region from Greece to Egypt inclusive. The Levant States were the lands in the original French mandate over Syria (1920).

Leven Scotland. Town in E Fife at the mouth of the R. Leven on the Firth of Forth. Pop. (1971) 9454.

Seaside resort. Manufactures golf clubs. Sawmilling and engineering.

Leven, Loch Scotland. 1. Sea loch in High-land extending about 14 km (9 miles) E from Loch Linnhe, with Kinlochleven at its head.

2. Inland lake in E Perth and Kinross 5.5 km (3½ miles) long and 3.2 km (2 miles) wide. Noted for trout fishing. On Castle Island is the ruined castle where Mary Queen of Scots was imprisoned (1567–8).

Leven River Scotland. 1. River 11 km (7 miles) long, flowing S from Loch Lomond at Balloch to the R. Clyde at Dumbarton. The Vale of Leven has an important textile printing and dyeing industry.

2. River 24 km (15 miles) long in Fife flowing E from Loch Leven to the Firth of Forth at Leven.

Leverkusen Germany. Industrial town and river port in North Rhine-Westphalia on the right bank of the Rhine R. 8 km (5 miles) N of Cologne. Pop. (1991) 160,919.

Important centre of the chemical industry. Also manufactures machinery and textiles.

Levittown USA. Residential town in New York on Long Island 51 km (32 miles) E of New York City. A large planned suburb of New York, developed (1947–51) by the firm of Levitt and Sons Inc.

Levkás (Leucas) Greece. 1. One of the Ionian Islands off the coast of Acarnania, forming a *nome* with the islands of Ithaca and Meganesi. Area (*nome*) 356 sq km (125 sq. miles). Pop. (1991) 20,900.

Chief products currants, olive oil and wine.

2. Cap. of Levkás *nome* on the NE coast of Levkás island. Pop. (1971) 6818.

Lewes England. County town of East Sussex on the R. Ouse 13 km (8 miles) ENE of

Brighton in the South Downs. Pop. (1991) 15,376.

Market town. Manufactures agricultural machinery.

Remains of a Norman castle which once guarded the gap through the Downs and of an 11th-cent. Cluniac priory; house of Anne of Cleves, now a museum. At the Battle of Lewes (1264) Simon de Montfort and the rebel barons defeated Henry III.

Lewisham England. Inner London borough which inc. Deptford. Pop. (1991) 215,300. It is mainly residential and inc., among open spaces, part of Blackheath.

Lewiston USA. Town in SW Maine on the Androscoggin R. (from which hydroelectric power is derived) opposite Auburn. Pop. (1989) 41,500. Long important in the textile industry.

Also manufactures clothing and footwear.

Lewis–with–Harris Scotland. Largest and northernmost of the Outer Hebrides (or Western Isles), separated from the mainland by the Minch. Area 2137 sq km (825 sq. miles). Pop. (1986) Lewis 21,400, Harris 2400. Chief town Stornoway. Divided by Loch Resort (W), an isthmus and Loch Seaforth (E) into a larger N part, Lewis (1637 sq km; 632 sq. miles), and a smaller S part, Harris (500 sq km; 193 sq. miles). The island is hilly, esp. in Harris, which rises to 800 m (2624 ft); much of the land consists of peat bog and bleak moorland. Among the crofters the main occupations are fishing, sheep and cattle rearing, and the spinning and weaving of the famous Harris tweed. Stornoway on the E coast is a herring port.

Lexington (Kentucky) USA. Town in the heart of the Bluegrass region 113 km (70 miles) ESE of Louisville. Pop. (1990) 225,366.

Chief US centre for breeding thoroughbred horses. Important market for tobacco, livestock, bluegrass seed. Manufactures electrical and electronic equipment and furniture.

Two race tracks (running and trotting). Among many outstanding racehorses bred in the neighbourhood was the stallion Man o' War.

Lexington (Massachusetts) USA. Residential town 16 km (10 miles) NW of Boston. Pop. (1990) 29,479. Famous as the scene of the Battle of Lexington (1775), the first armed conflict in the American War of Independence.

Leyden ►LEIDEN.

Leyland England. Industrial town in Lancashire 8 km (5 miles) S of Preston. Pop. (1991) 37,381.

Industrial town, manufactures inc. tyres, textiles and paint.

Leyte Philippines. Island between Luzon and Mindanao. Area 7213 sq km (2785 sq. miles). Pop. (1990) 1,368,510. Chief town Tacloban.

Main products rice, copra and abacá.

During World War II the Japanese suffered a severe defeat in the Battle of Leyte Gulf (1944).

Lhasa Xizang (Tibet). Cap. of Xizang on the Kyichu R. 400 km (250 miles) NE of Darjeeling (India) at a height of 3600 m (11,808 ft). Pop. (1990) 106,885. Chief centre of Lamaism. Main commercial centre of Xizang (Tibet). Trade in grain, wool, furs, tea and salt. Minor weaving and other industries.

Dominated by the great Potala, formerly the official residence of the Dalai Lama. In the centre of the city is the Jokang temple, an important centre of Buddhist pilgrimage built originally in the 7th cent. In the neighbourhood are the three leading lamaseries of Xizang: Drepung, Sera and Ganden. Became cap. of Tibet in the 7th cent. Under Chinese rule with the rest of Tibet, 1720–1912. Owing to its inaccessibility and its hostility to foreigners, it was long known as the 'Forbidden City'. It again came under Chinese control in 1951 becoming an autonomous region of China in 1965. The Chinese have several projects for modernizing Xizang, inc. light industry. There have been several anti-Chinese demonstrations. Martial law was imposed in 1989 and lifted in 1990.

Liaoning China. Province in the NE (Manchuria) bordering SE on North Korea. Area 151,000 sq km (58,300 sq. miles). Pop. (1990) 39,459,697. Cap. Shenyang (Mukden). With highlands in the W and E it is crossed in the centre by the broad plains formed by the Liao R., where cereals and soya beans are cultivated; in the SE is the Liaotung peninsula. Contains the principal mining and industrial region of Manchuria, with the great coalmining centre of Fushun and the steel centre of Anshan. Leading seaport Lü-ta (Port Arthur-Dairen).

Liaoyang China. Town in Liaoning province 64 km (40 miles) SSW of Shenyang on the S Manchuria Railway. Pop. (1990) 492,559.

Trade in cotton. Textile manufactures, flour-milling.

Scene of an important Japanese victory in the Russo–Japanese War (1904).

Liard River Canada. Rises E of White Horse in the Yukon and flows 912 km (570 miles) ESE to British Columbia and N from Nelson Forks past Fort Liard in Mackenzie District, Northwest Territories, to enter Mackenzie R. at Fort Simpson.

Liberec (Ger. **Reichenberg**) Czech Republic. Town in Bohemia on the Neisse R. 88 km (55 miles) NE of Prague. Pop. (1991) 101,934.

Leading centre of the textile industry and there is food-processing. Manufactures textile machinery and footwear.

Cloth manufacture was introduced in the 16th cent. and the town's prosperity is shown in such buildings as the 17th-cent. castle and the Renaissance town hall. Before World War II it was a centre of the Sudeten German movement.

Liberia. Republic on the W coast of Africa bounded by Sierra Leone in the NW, Guinea in the N, the Côte d'Ivoire in the E and SW by the Atlantic Ocean. Area 99,067 sq km (33,250 sq. miles). Pop. (1995) 2,380,000. Life expectancy, 54 years male, 57 female. Cap. Monrovia. Other cities Buchanan, Congo Town and Yekepa. Currency: Liberian dollar = 100 cents. There is a 570-km (354-mile) coastline behind which there is a coastal plain that rises inland, reaching a height of 1768 m (5799 ft) at Mount Nimba. It is largely covered with tropical rainforest. The climate is equatorial, with constant high temperatures and rainfall exceeding 250 cm (100 ins.) annually along the coast, decreasing inland. Land use: forested 18 per cent, meadows and pastures 59 per cent, agricultural and under permanent cultivation 4 per cent. The majority of the pop. is of indigenous origin and the remaining 5 per cent are descendants of repatriated slaves from America, known as Americo-Liberians. English is the official lang., but over 20 dialects are spoken. About 75 per cent of the pop. follow tribal religions, Muslims are about 15 per cent and Christians 10 per cent.

The extraction and export of iron ore dominates industry (55 per cent of exports in 1988, much of which goes to the USA). Sixty-eight per cent of the pop. rely on subsistence farming and the main cash crops are rubber, timber and palm oil. Main exports are iron ore, rubber, timber, diamonds, gold and coffee. It has a large mercantile fleet sailing under 'flags of convenience'. The political unrest slowed foreign investment and there has been a decline in economic growth.

Liberia is Africa's oldest independent state and originated in 1822 when the American Colonization Society settled freed American slaves near Monrovia. The descendants of these settlers, known as Americo–Liberians, remained the governing group for many years. Liberia was established as a republic in 1847. The rule of the Americo-Liberians often discriminated against the native tribes and investigations into charges of forced labour and slavery led to the resignation of the President and Vice-President in 1931. More enlightened policies were followed and tribal representatives played an increasing part in government; the franchise was granted to men and women of the tribes by 1947. Samuel Doe seized power in 1980 and from 1989 there have been a series of civil wars. Peace-keeping forces from five West African countries entered the country in 1991. Liberia has always maintained close ties with the USA. The Constitution is based on that of the USA.

Libreville Gabon. Cap., near the equator on the N shore of the estuary of the Gabon R. Pop. (1992) 352,000.

A major port exporting hardwood, palm oil and kernels. There is sawmilling and plywood manufacture.

Founded in 1849 as a settlement for freed slaves.

Libya. Republic of N Africa bounded by the Mediterranean Sea to the N, by Egypt and Sudan to the E, Niger and Chad to the S and Tunisia and Algeria to the W. Area 1,759,540 sq km (679,358 sq. miles). Pop. (1995) 5,407,000 (86 per cent urban). Life expectancy: 62 years male, 67 female. Cap. Tripoli. Other cities Benghazi and Misurata. Currency: Libyan dinar = 1000 dirhams. Libya is almost entirely desert. The Sahara reaches the Mediterranean along the Gulf of Sirte. Only in narrow coastal fringes round Tripoli and Benghazi does the rainfall exceed 20 cm (8 ins.) annually and agriculture is limited to these areas and scattered oases. Land use: meadow and pastures 8 per cent, agricultural and under permanent cultivation 1 per cent, desert and built-up areas 90 per cent. About 98 per cent belong to the Sunni Muslim sect and the lang. is Arabic. The majority of the pop. is of Arab and Berber origin with a small number of nomads of the Tebou and Touareg tribes in the S.

The main agricultural products are wheat, barley, olives and oranges along the coast with dates cultivated in the oases. In the semi-desert zone esparto grass is grown and goats and sheep are grazed. S of this belt of scrub is an enormous expanse of rocky, stony and sandy desert, with oases such as Ghadames, Ghat, Murzuk, Kurfra. Since 1984 a major project has been under way to bring water from wells in S Libya to the coast. The scheme is named 'Great Man-made River' and on completion will irrigate 74,000 ha (185,000 acres) of land. Libya's economy was transformed when an important oilfield was

discovered at Zelten in 1959 and the oil and natural gas terminal at Marsa el Brega, at the head of the 167-km (104-mile) pipeline, was opened in 1961. Oil has also been discovered in other parts of Tripolitania and Cyrenaica. Oil represents 97 per cent of export earnings. Sponge and tunny fishing are important on the coast.

Libya has been governed by the Phoenicians, Carthaginians, Greeks, Vandals and Byzantines and Arabs, but Turkish domination began in the 16th cent.; Libya was annexed by Italy in 1912. A period of colonization followed and about 90,000 Italian peasants had been settled by 1938. When the Italians and Germans were driven out in World War II, Tripolitania and Cyrenaica came under British and the Fezzan under French military government. Libya became an independent federal kingdom in 1951, with the Amir of Cyrenaica as its first king. The monarchy was overthrown by military *coup* in 1969, and the king left the country. A group of officers formed the Revolutionary Command Council which was chaired by Colonel Muammar Qadhafi; proclaimed the Libyan Arab Republic. In 1977 a new form of direct democracy, the 'Jamahiriya' (state of the masses) was promulgated and the official name of the country was changed to Great Socialist People's Libyan Arab Jamahiriya. Under this system, every adult is supposed to be able to share in policy-making through the Basic People's Congresses of which there are some 2000 throughout Libya. The Congresses have some control over the General People's Committee (Council of Ministers). Qadhafi favoured Arab unity, but his efforts in that direction have been abortive. The Federation of the Arab Republics formed in 1972 with Libya, Egypt and Syria as members; an agreement to merge Libya and Egypt in 1973; a proposed union with Tunisia in 1974; and a union with Syria in 1980, all proved unsuccessful. Throughout the 1980s Libya has had constant disagreements with her neighbours and her relations with the USA and other Western countries have deteriorated, culminating in the American bombing of the capital in 1987, in an attempt to punish

Qadhafi for his alleged support of international terrorism.

Libyan Desert. The most easterly part of the Sahara, extending over E Libya, W Egypt and NW Sudan to the Nile valley. Largely a sandy waste, rainless for years at a time. Principal oases Siwa, Bahariya, Farafra, Dakhla, Kharga (Egypt) and Kufra (Libya). The N part, where there was much fighting in World War II (1940–4) is sometimes known as the Western Desert.

Licata Italy. Seaport at the mouth of the Salso R. in Agrigento province, S Sicily. Pop. (1985) 41,000.

Refines and exports sulphur.

Off its coast the Romans defeated the Carthaginian fleet in 256 BC.

Lichfield England. Town in Staffordshire 19 km (12 miles) SW of Burton-on-Trent. Pop. (1991) 28,861.

Industries inc. the manufacture of pneumatic controls, ball-bearings, bathroom fittings, cutlery, motor cycles and tyres.

The famous cathedral with its three spires, dating from the 13th and 14th cent., suffered severely at the hands of the Parliamentary forces in the Civil War, but was restored in the 19th cent. Also celebrated for its associations with Dr Johnson (1709–84), who was born here and whose house is now a museum.

Liddel Water Scotland. River 34 km (21 miles) long, rising on Peel Fell (602 m; 1975 ft) in Dumfries and Galloway and flowing SW to join the R. Esk 3 km (2 miles) S of Canonbie. Its valley is known as Liddesdale or Liddisdale.

Lidice Czech Republic. Village 6 km (4 miles) E of Kladno in Bohemia, whose name became world known when (June 1942) the occupying German forces announced that, as a reprisal for the assassination of Gauleiter Heydrich, all the men and many women had been shot, the remaining women sent to concentration camps and children to 'correction schools'; the village itself was completely destroyed and rebuilt on a nearby site in 1947.

Lidingö Sweden. Town on Lidingö Island in the Baltic Sea NE of Stockholm city. Pop. (1990) 38,400.

Industries inc. the manufacture of electrical equipment and shipbuilding.

Lidköping Sweden. Town situated ENE of Trollhattan at the mouth of Lida R. on L. Vänern in Skaraborg county. Pop. (1988) 35,168.

Railway junction. Industries inc. sugar-refining, sawmilling, metalworking, stone-quarrying and the manufacture of porcelain, matches. It is also a resort.

Liechtenstein. Independent principality in central Europe, bounded in the E by Austria and in the W by Switzerland. Area 160 sq km (62 sq. miles). Pop. (1995) 30,900. Life expectancy, 67 years male, 80 female. Cap. Vaduz. Other main town Schaan. Currency: Swiss franc = 100 (rappen) centimes. Much of the country is mountainous, with the Rhätikon Alps in the S, rising to 2572 m (8436 ft) in Naafkopf. The plains are intensively cultivated. Land use: forested 35 per cent, meadows and pastures 16 per cent, agricultural and under permanent cultivation 24 per cent. The official lang. is German and Roman Catholicism is the predominant faith.

Cattle-rearing and the cultivation of cereals and vines are important occupations. Tourism and international banking have grown in importance in recent years. Industries inc. vacuum engineering and the manufacture of semi-conductors, bearings, heat equipment, synthetic fibres and woollen fabrics.

The history of Liechtenstein dates back to 1342, but the Principality was founded in 1719 by the union of the Vaduz and Schellenberg countships. It later belonged to the German Confederation and became independent in 1866. Since 1868 it has had no army and remained neutral in World War II. It is a constitutional monarchy and is ruled by the Princes of the House of Liechtenstein. There is an elected 15-member unicameral parliament (*Landtag*) elected every 4 years by proportional representation.

Liège (Flemish **Luik**) Belgium. 1. Province in the E, bounded on the E by Germany. Area 3862 sq km (1491 sq. miles). Pop. (1991) 999,646. The N is a fertile agricultural region; in the S at the foot of the Ardennes dairy-farming is important; the centre, along the Meuse and Vesdre rivers, is a coalmining and industrial area. Formerly ruled by prince-bishops; became part of Belgium in 1830. Chief towns Liège and Verviers.

2. Cap. of Liège province on the Meuse R. at the confluence with the Ourthe R. 95 km (60 miles) E of Brussels. Pop. (1991) 195,201.

Formerly the centre of coalmining, but this has now ceased, although iron, steel and armament manufacture continues. Also produces machinery, machine-tools, chemicals, glass and tyres.

Cultural centre of French-speaking Belgium. Among its noteworthy buildings are the Cathedral of St Paul (partly 13th-cent.) and the 16th-cent. Palais de Justice. Birthplace of César Franck, composer (1822–90).

Liepaja (Lepaya, Ger. **Libau)** Latvia. Baltic seaport 203 km (126 miles) WSW of Riga. Pop. (1991) 114,900.

Exports timber and grain and manufactures steel and steel products, agricultural machinery and linoleum. Industries inc. flour-milling and brewing.

Passed to Russia 1795; developed rapidly as one of her main ice-free ports after the arrival of the railway (1871). In independent Latvia 1920–40.

Lierre (Flemish **Lier**) Belgium. Industrial town in Antwerp province at the confluence of the Grande Nèthe and Petite Nèthe rivers 14 km (9 miles) SE of Antwerp. Pop. (1992) 31,393.

Manufactures cutlery and tools.

Liffey River Ireland. River 80 km (50 miles) long rising in the Wicklow Mountains and flowing generally W into Co. Kildare, then NE and E through Dublin to Dublin Bay. Important hydroelectric plant at Poulaphouca Falls.

Lifu ►LOYALTY ISLANDS.

Liguria Italy. Region in the NW between the Ligurian Alps and the Ligurian Apennines on the N and the Gulf of Genoa on the S, comprising the provinces of Genoa, Imperia, La Spezia and Savona, and inc. the Italian Riviera. Area 5418 sq km (2092 sq. miles). Pop. (1991) 1,701,788.

Produces olives, vines, fruits and flowers. Industries inc. shipbuilding, iron and steel and chemical manufactures.

The ancient Ligures occupied a much larger area than the present region, even in Roman times.

Ligurian Sea Italy. Arm of the Mediterranean Sea lying between Liguria, Tuscany and Corsica and inc. the Gulf of Genoa (N); separated from the Tyrrhenian Sea by the Tuscan Archipelago. It is becoming heavily polluted.

Lihou ►GUERNSEY.

Likasi Democratic Republic of the Congo. Town 115 km (70 miles) NW of Lubumbashi, with which it is connected by rail. Pop. (1991) 279,839.

Chiefly important as a centre of copper and cobalt production, with plants for refining these metals; the country's first electrolytic copper refinery was opened here in 1929. Other industries inc. chemical manufacture, railway engineering and brewing.

Lille France. Prefecture of the Nord department on the canalized Deule R. Pop. (1990) 178,301.

Major industrial and commercial centre, particularly important for the manufacture of textiles (cotton, woollen, linen and rayon goods). Also large metallurgical and engineering industries (locomotives and machinery). Brewing, sugar-refining. Manufactures chemicals and biscuits. Obtains coal for its industries from the coalfield just S.

Among its notable buildings are the citadel, built by Sébastian Vauban, French military enginer (1633–1707) and the Bourse (both of the 17th cent.). In the 14th cent. Charles V of France handed Lille to the dukes of Burgundy, under whom it prospered, and from them it passed in turn to Austria, Spain and to France (1668). Birthplace of General Charles de Gaulle (1890–1970).

Lillehammer Norway. Town in Oppland county situated N of Oslo on Lagen R. at its mouth on L. Mjoesa. Pop. (1990) 22,850. Resort and trading centre for a mountain farming area.

Lilongwe Malawi. Cap. (since 1975) 230 km (143 miles) NNW of Blantyre in the Central Region. Pop. (1987) 223,973.

A trading centre serving a fertile agricultural area producing maize, groundnuts and tobacco.

Lima Peru. Cap. of Peru and of the Lima department on the Rimac R. on a wide, gently sloping plain W of the Andean foothills 13 km (8 miles) E of Callao, its port. Pop. (1990) 421,570, the metropolitan area Lima–Callao, 6,115,700. Largest city and chief commercial centre, with four-fifths of the country's industry.

Manufactures textiles, furniture, pharmaceuticals and soap. There is oil-refining, tanning, brewing, flour-milling and food-processing. Climate dry, with mild winters.

Founded (1535) by Pizarro, who named it the 'City of the Kings' and laid the cornerstone of the cathedral. In colonial times it was the chief city of Spanish South America. Seat of the San Marcos university (1551), the oldest in the continent. The Central Railway climbs spectacularly to the highland mining centres; the Pan-American Highway links it with coastal towns. Several resorts nearby. In the city's vicinity are many Incan and pre-Incan remains of which the best known are Pachacámac to the SE and Cajamarquilla to the ENE.

Lima USA. Industrial town in Ohio on the Ottawa R. 126 km (78 miles) NW of Columbus. Pop. (1990) 45,549.

Oil-refining. Manufactures machine-tools, diesel engines, chemicals and electrical equipment.

Limassol Cyprus. Ancient Lemessus. Sea-port on Akrotiri Bay on the S coast. Pop. (1990) 132,100.

It exports wine, carobs, and manufactures brandy, perfumes and cigarettes. A tourist centre and second largest town.

Here Richard I of England married Berengaria of Navarre (1191).

Limavady Northern Ireland. Market town in Co. Londonderry on the R. Roe 24 km (15 miles) ENE of Londonderry. Pop. (1991) 10,350. Here the song, *Londonderry Air* was first noted down from a travelling fiddler (1851).

Limbourg (Flemish **Limburg**) Belgium. 1. Province in the NE, bounded on the N and E by the Netherlands. Area 2422 sq km (935 sq. miles). Pop. (1991) 750,435. Cap. Hasselt. Agricultural with coalmining in the Campine (Kempen) region. In 1839 the old duchy of Limburg was divided between Belgium and the Netherlands, Belgium taking the part W of the Meuse R. except for a small area around the town of Limbourg which passed to Liège province.

2. Old town in Liège province on the Vesdre R. 6 km (4 miles) ENE of Verviers. Pop. (1985) 5000. Until 1648 the cap. of the duchy of Limburg. The new town, with spinning and wool weaving, is known as Dolhain.

Limburg Netherlands. Province in the SE, bounded by Belgium (W and S) and Germany (E). Area 2170 sq km (838 sq. miles). Pop. (1990) 1,103,960. Cap. Maastricht.

Cereals, sugar-beet, fruit cultivated. In the S are the country's chief coalmines.

In 1839 the old duchy of Limburg was divided between Belgium and the Netherlands, the latter taking the part lying E of the Meuse R.

Limehouse England. District in the London borough of Tower Hamlets. The name probably derives from the limekilns that once stood in the district.

Limeira Brazil. Industrial town in São Paulo state 51 km (32 miles) NW of Campinas. Pop. (1980) 137,812.

Lincoln

In an orange-growing region. Industries inc. fruit-packing and the manufacture of coffee-processing machinery, matches and hats.

Limerick Ireland. 1. County in Munster in the SW, bounded on the N by the R. Shannon estuary. Area 2686 sq km (1037 sq. miles). Pop. (1991) 161,856. Mainly an undulating plain, containing most of the fertile Golden Vale, but mountainous in the S; in the SE rises to 919 m (3015 ft) in Galtymore (Galty Mountains). Dairy-farming, stock-rearing and salmon-fishing.

2. County town of Co. Limerick on both banks of the R. Shannon at the head of the estuary. Pop. (1991) 52,000. Seaport.

Tanning, bacon-curing, brewing and flour-milling. Manufactures butter, tobacco products.

Divided into English Town, Irish Town and Newton Pery. Outstanding buildings are the 12th-cent. Protestant cathedral, 19th-cent. Roman Catholic cathedral and the remains of the Norman King John's castle. At Ardnacrusha, 3 km (2 miles) N on the R. Shannon, is the country's major hydroelectric power station. Originally a Danish settlement; taken by Brian Boru and became cap. of the kingdom of Munster. Captured by the English 1174. William III besieged the city and resistance was ended by the Treaty of Limerick (1691), subsequently broken, granting political and religious freedom.

Limoges France. Ancient Augustoritum, Lemovices. Prefecture of the Haute-Vienne department on the Vienne R. 180 km (110 miles) NE of Bordeaux. Pop. (1990) 136,407.

Important centre of the porcelain industry, using local kaolin. Also manufactures footwear, paper and textiles.

Cathedral (13th/16th-cent.), two 13th-cent. bridges over the Vienne and a museum with a fine ceramics collection. Converted to Christianity by St Martial in the 3rd cent. In 1370 it was burned and its pop. massacred by the Black Prince, and it frequently suffered in religious wars. Turgot (1727–81), intendant of Limoges for 13 years (1761–74),

did much to aid its recovery, inc. the introduction of porcelain manufacture. Birthplace of the painter, Pierre Auguste Renoir (1841–1919).

Limón (Puerto Limón) Costa Rica. Cap. of the Limón province on the Caribbean Sea 113 km (70 miles) E of San José. Pop. (1985) 43,500.

Second largest city and chief Caribbean seaport. Exports coffee, bananas and coconuts. It is also a popular resort.

Limousin France. Region and former province in the W of the Massif Central, now forming the department of Corrèze and part of Haute-Vienne. Area 16,942 sq km (6541 sq. miles). Pop. (1991) 723,000. Limoges is the regional cap. Largely occupied by the infertile Monts du Limousin. Annexed to the crown by Henri IV (1589) but remained economically backward until the introduction of reforms by Turgot, intendant of Limoges. It produces fruit and vegetables, and minerals inc. kaolin.

Limpopo (Crocodile) River Mozambique/Zimbabwe/South Africa. River 1600 km (1000 miles) long, rising in Gauteng, flowing N and then SE in a wide curve through southern Africa; forms the frontier between South Africa and Zimbabwe, flows generally SE through Mozambique and enters the Indian Ocean 137 km (85 miles) NE of Maputo. Navigable for about 160 km (100 miles) above the mouth. The region of its lower course is well-watered and fertile.

Linares Spain. Town in Jaén province in Andalusia in the foothills of the Sierra Morena 40 km (25 miles) NNE of Jaén. Pop. (1991) 58,039.

Important lead-mining centre. Industries inc. lead-smelting and the manufacture of metal goods and chemicals.

Lincoln England. Ancient Lindum Colonia. City in Lincolnshire on the R. Witham at the confluence with the R. Till. Pop. (1991) 83,600.

Manufactures agricultural implements,

excavating machinery, pumps, feed cakes, food products and vehicle parts.

Famous chiefly for its cathedral, originally built 1075–90 and restored 1922–32, one of the finest in the country, with its 83-m (272-ft) central tower containing the bell 'Great Tom of Lincoln' and one of the original copies of Magna Carta (1215). Also has a castle begun by William the Conqueror, the Jew's House and other Norman remains. Was a British fortress, then the Roman settlement of Lindum Colonia.

Lincoln USA. State cap. of Nebraska in the SE. Pop. (1990) 191,972.

Railway, commercial, financial and industrial centre for an agricultural region. Industries inc. food-processing and flour-milling. It manufactures agricultural machinery.

Lincolnshire England. County bounded on the E by the North Sea. The northern part was transferred to Humberside (1974). Area 5915 sq km (2284 sq. miles). Pop. (1991) 573,900. It is divided into the districts of Boston, East Lindsey, Lincoln, North Kesteven, South Holland, South Kesteven and West Lindsey. Apart from the chalk escarpment of the Lincoln Wolds in the E, it is mostly low-lying and fertile; in the SE around the Wash is a considerable area of the Fens, drained by the Witham, Welland and Nene rivers and many canals. Sandy shores have given rise to such seaside resorts as Skegness and Mablethorpe. Sheep and cattle reared. Cereals, potatoes, sugar-beet cultivated. In the S the Spalding district is noted for its bulbs.

Linden USA. Town in New Jersey 29 km (18 miles) SW of Newark. Pop. (1970) 41,409.

Oil-refining. Manufactures chemicals, clothing, beverages and paint.

Lindisfarne ➤HOLY ISLAND (ENGLAND).

Line Islands Kiribati. Group in the Pacific Ocean extending across the equator. Pop. (1985) 2500. The group inc. Flint, Vostock, Caroline, Starbuck, Malden, Jarvis, Palmyra, Kingman Reef, Kiritimati, Tabuaeran and Teraina. Jarvis, Palmyra and Kingman Reef are US-owned.

Línea, La (La Línea de la Concepción) Spain. Town and port in Cádiz province just N of Gibraltar, from which it is separated by a neutral strip and which it supplies with fruit and vegetables. Pop. (1991) 57,918.

Lingga Archipelago Indonesia. Group of islands off the E coast of Sumatra. Area 2176 sq km (840 sq. miles). Pop. 31,000. Largest islands Lingga and Singkep. Main products sago, copra and tin.

Linköping Sweden. Cap. of Östergötland county 160 km (100 miles) SW of Stockholm. Pop. (1990) 122,270.

Railway junction. Industrial centre. Railway engineering and brewing. Manufactures aircraft, cars, textiles and tobacco products.

Romanesque cathedral (12th/15th-cent.).

Linlithgow Scotland. Town in West Lothian 26 km (16 miles) W of Edinburgh. Pop. (1989) 11,800.

Manufactures computer components. Whisky-distilling.

Mary Queen of Scots (1542–87) was born in the now ruined Linlithgow Palace.

Linnhe, Loch Scotland. Sea loch on the W coast in Argyll and Bute at the SW end of Glenmore, with Fort William near its head. At its mouth is Lismore Island.

Linz Austria. Cap. of Upper Austria (Oberösterreich) on the Danube R. 160 km (100 miles) W of Vienna. Pop. (1991) 202,855.

Busy river port and industrial centre. Manufactures steel, machinery, chemicals, textiles, fertilizers and paper.

Connected by bridges with the left-bank suburb of Urfahr.

Lions (Lion), Gulf of France. Ancient Sinus Gallicus. Wide bay of the Mediterranean extending from the Franco–Spanish border (W) to Toulon (E). Chief port Marseille.

Lipa Philippines. Town in Batangas province, Luzon 64 km (40 miles) SSE of Manila. Pop. (1990) 160,000.

Trade in sugar, abacá, maize and tobacco. Manufactures textiles.

Lipari Islands Italy. Ancient Aeoliae Insulae (Aeolian Islands). Volcanic group off the N coast of Sicily comprises 7 islands and many islets. Area 114 sq km (44 sq. miles). Pop. (1985) 10,700. Chief town Lipari, on the island of Lipari. Stromboli and Vulcano are active volcanoes and the highest peak (961 m; 3152 ft) is on Salina.

Exports pumice stone, wine and fruit.

Lipetsk Russia. Town in the Lipetsk Region on the Voronezh R. 113 km (70 miles) NNE of Voronezh. Pop. (1991) 460,000.

Important iron-mining centre. Manufactures pig iron, tractors, chemicals, building materials and food products.

Founded in the 18th cent., it has long been famous for its chalybeate springs and is a health resort.

Lippe Germany. Former principality between Hanover and Westphalia, with cap. Detmold; since 1945 part of North Rhine-Westphalia. Area 1215 sq km (469 sq. miles). A region of small but prosperous farms, and also has valuable deciduous forests.

Lippe River Germany. River 237 km (147 miles) long in North Rhine-Westphalia rising in the Teutoburgerwald and flowing generally W past Lippestadt and Hamm to join the Rhine R. at Wesel. Declined in importance with the construction (1930) of the parallel Lippe Canal (Hamm–Wesel).

Lippstadt Germany. Town in North Rhine-Westphalia on the Lippe R. 37 km (23 miles) E of Hamm. Pop. (1986) 60,100.

Iron-founding, metalworking. Manufactures wire and textiles.

It was founded in 1168.

Lisbon (Lisboa) Portugal. Cap. of Portugal and of the Lisbon district on the right bank of the Tagus R. 13 km (18 miles) upstream from its mouth. Pop. (1991) 677,790. The port is accessible to large vessels although there is a bar at the river mouth where it becomes the Mar da Palha (Sea of Straw, from its colour). The Ponte 25 Abril (formerly Salazar) bridge over the Tagus, linking Lisbon with Almada, was inaugurated in 1966 and has the seventh longest suspension span in the world. It is the country's chief industrial and commercial centre and manufactures inc. chemicals, cement, electronics, diamond-cutting, food-processing, paper, pottery and textiles. Tourism and banking are of growing importance. Exports inc. cork, olive oil and wine.

An ancient settlement and Roman town, Lisbon was taken by the Moors who held it for more than 400 years, losing it to Portuguese attacks in 1147. The medieval hill town had already begun to spread towards the river. Lisbon is built largely in white stone, rising in terraces from its shores. The finest street is the Avenida da Liberdade, running from the Rossio square to the Edward II Park. The Alfama, or old town, lies to the E, with its narrow alleys and its cathedral, founded in the 12th cent. and twice rebuilt. S of Praça Dom Pedro IV, but generally known as Rossio, is the Cidade Baixa or lower town, reconstructed by the Marquis de Pombal after the earthquake of 1755. In the W is the Hieronymite monastery and nearby the Tower of Belém, a white tower built 1512–21, near the place from which Vasco da Gama sailed on his voyage to India. Lisbon was recaptured from the Moors in 1147 and became the cap. in 1256. The establishment of Portuguese colonies in Africa and India in the 16th cent. created great wealth for the city.

Lisburn Northern Ireland. Town in Co. Antrim on the R. Lagan 13 km (8 miles) SW of Belfast. Pop. (1991) 42,110. A centre of the linen industry, developed in the late 17th cent. by Huguenots.

Other industries inc. textiles, engineering and furniture manufacture.

Jeremy Taylor, English theologian (1613–67) was bishop at the 17th-cent. Protestant cathedral, and died here in 1667.

Lisdoonvarna Ireland. Town and spa situated NW of Ennis in Co. Clare, with sulphur and chalybeate springs. Pop. (1991) 842.

Lisieux France. Town in the Calvados department on the Touques R. 43 km (27 miles) E of Caen. Pop. (1985) 26,000.

Manufactures textiles. Brewing and tanning. Large trade in dairy produce, esp. Camembert cheese.

The shrine of St Thérèse (canonized 1925) is a place of pilgrimage.

Liskeard England. Market town in Cornwall 18 km (11 miles) ESE of Bodmin. Pop. (1971) 5255. Formerly a tin-mining centre.

Lismore Australia. Market town and river port in New South Wales on the Richmond R. 153 km (95 miles) S of Brisbane. Pop. (1991) 27,250.

Centre of a dairy-farming region. Manufactures butter. Exports dairy produce and sugar-cane.

Lismore Ireland. Market town in Co. Waterford on the R. Blackwater 56 km (35 miles) WSW of Waterford. Pop. (1991) 715. Protestant cathedral of St Carthagh (17th-cent.) and a 19th-cent. Roman Catholic cathedral. Despite repeated Danish raids in the 9th and 10th cent., the 7th-cent. monastery founded by St Carthagh became a famous cultural and religious centre. Birthplace of Irish physicist and chemist Robert Boyle (1627–91).

Lismore Island Scotland. Island in Argyll and Bute at the entrance to Loch Linnhe 15 km (9½ miles) long and up to 2.5 km (1½ miles) wide. Several ruined castles; the 13th-cent. cathedral (restored) is now used as the parish church. A collection of Gaelic poetry was made by a 16th-cent. Dean of Lismore.

Listowel Ireland. Market town in Co. Kerry on the R. Feale 64 km (40 miles) WSW of Limerick. Pop. (1991) 3347. Remains of a castle of the Desmonds.

Lithgow Australia. Town in New South Wales in the Blue Mountains 113 km (70 miles) WNW of Sydney. Pop. (1973) 12,800.

Coalmining centre. Manufactures small-arms and woollen goods. Sawmilling and brickmaking.

Lithuania. Bounded N by Latvia, E and S by Belorussia and W by Poland, the Kaliningrad area of Russia and the Baltic Sea. Area 65,301 sq km (25,213 sq. miles). Pop. (1995) 3,700,000 (68 per cent urban). Life expectancy, 63 years male, 75 female. Cap. Vilnius. Other important cities, Kaunas, Klaipéda, Siauliai and Paneveẑys. Currency: Litas = 100 Centai. Lithuania is mainly low-lying and flat, rising to about 300 m (984 ft) in the moranic hills in the SE with many small lakes and marshes. It is drained by the Neman R. and its tributaries, and has a moderate continental climate, approaching the maritime along the coast, with an annual rainfall of 50–60 cm (20–24 ins.). Land use: forested 28 per cent, pasture 17 per cent and agricultural 35 per cent. Eighty per cent of the pop. is Lithuanian, 9 per cent Russian and 7 per cent Polish. The official lang. is Lithuanian, which is the oldest Indo-European lang. still extant and resembles ancient Sanskrit, and believers are mainly Roman Catholic.

Main agricultural products are rye, oats, potatoes, sugar-beet, dairy produce; pigs and poultry are raised. Chief industries shipbuilding and engineering; manufactures electronic and computer equipment, machine-tools, textiles, footwear and paper. Oil production started in 1990.

A grand duchy in the 13th cent., Lithuania extended from the Baltic to the Black Sea in the 15th cent. and was united to Poland 1385–1795. By the partitions of Poland most of Lithuania passed to Russia, but oppression led to a strong nationalist movement and in 1918 Lithuania was proclaimed a republic. Its area was reduced when Poland seized Vilnius (1920) and increased when Lithuania occupied Memel (now Klaipéda) in 1923. In 1940 it was made a constituent republic of the USSR, but during World War II it was occupied by German forces (1941–4). In 1990 a newly-elected Soviet, by 120 to nil, proclaimed independence based on the continued validity of the act of independence of 1918. This was not accepted by the USSR. Demonstrations in 1991 saw Soviet army units firing on demonstrators and there were fatalities. In Feb. 1991 a referendum resulted in 90.5 per cent voting in favour of independence and in Sept. 1991 the USSR conceded independent status for the country. Parliament is a 141-member *Seimas* and is elected on a partly proportional and partly constituency-based system.

Little Belt (Danish **Lille Baelt**) Denmark. Strait about 48 km (30 miles) long and up to 29 km (18 miles) wide between Jutland and Fyn island and connecting the Kattegat with the Baltic Sea.

Little Cayman West Indies. The smallest of the Cayman Islands situated ENE of Grand Cayman and E of Cayman Brac. Area 24 sq km (9¼ sq. miles). Pop. (1989) 33.

Main products turtle shell and coconuts.

Littlehampton England. Seaside resort in West Sussex at the mouth of the R. Arun. Pop. (1991) 50,408.

It is a minor port and there is boatbuilding, food-processing and engineering.

Little Rock USA. State cap. of Arkansas on the Arkansas R. Pop. (1990) 175,795. Largest city in the state.

Important commercial centre for an agricultural and mining region. Trade in cotton, bauxite and coal, and industries inc. food-processing and the manufacture of clothing, wood and cotton-seed products, and building materials.

The name derives from the smaller of two rocky formations on the banks of the Arkansas R., called La Petite Roche by the French explorer Bernard de la Harpe (1722).

Liuchow ➤LIUZHOU.

Liuzhou (Liuchou/Liuchow) China. Town in the Guangxi Zhuang Autonomous Region on the Liukiang R. 209 km (130 miles) NE of Nanning. Pop. (1990) 609,320. A road and railway junction and river port situated in a picturesque mountainous region.

It developed into an important industrial centre in the 1960s and manufactures machinery, chemicals, textiles and food products.

It has a 9th-cent. temple (restored).

Liverpool England. City and unitary authority on the right bank of the Mersey estuary 48 km (30 miles) W of Manchester. Pop. (1991) 544,661. Once one of the greatest trading centres of the world, it is the second most important seaport in Great Britain and a major industrial centre.

Flour-milling, sugar-refining and electrical engineering. Manufactures chemicals, soap and margarine. Merseyside generally is important for the tanning of leather. It exports an immense variety of manufactured goods from the North and Midlands, esp. textiles and machinery. Both its own docks and those of Birkenhead, with which it is linked by road tunnels, are administered by the Mersey Docks and Harbour Board (established 1858).

Liverpool is not a city of historic buildings, possessing scarcely anything earlier than the 18th cent.; outstanding are the Anglican cathedral (designed by Sir G. G. Scott; begun 1904 and completed in 1980), the Roman Catholic cathedral (designed by Sir E. Lutyens; begun 1933 and opened in 1967), the Town Hall (1754), St George's Hall (1854), the Royal Liver Building, the Cunard Building and the Walker Art Gallery. Probably founded by Norsemen in the 8th cent., but not mentioned by name until late in the 12th cent., Liverpool was granted its first charter by King John (1207). Its development as a seaport was at first slow, but in 1709 the first wet dock in Britain was built here and later the growth of trade with the American colonies and the West Indies gave a great impetus to its expansion; the slave trade was especially lucrative until its abolition (1807). The industrialization of S Lancashire assisted its export trade; it became the main importing centre for raw cotton and superseded Bristol as the leading seaport on the W coast of Britain.

Livingston Scotland. Former village in West Lothian 24 km (15 miles) WSW of Edinburgh. Pop. (1990) 40,600. It was designated a 'new town' in 1962 and has seen a Japanese-led growth in electronics and hi-tech, and has been nicknamed the 'Capital of Scotland's Silicon Glen'.

Livingstone (Maramba) Zambia. Chief town of the Southern Province near the N bank of the Zambezi R. Pop. (1989) 102,000. Only 11 km (7 miles) from the Victoria Falls, it has become a tourist centre. Rhodes-Livingstone Museum, which contains relics of the explorer. It was cap. of Northern Rhodesia 1907–35, then replaced by Lusaka.

Livorno ►LEGHORN.

Lizard Point England. Southernmost point of Great Britain in SW Cornwall. Noted for its fine coastal scenery and serpentine rock. Nearby is the village of Lizard Town.

Ljubljana (Ger. **Laibach**) Slovenia. Cap. on the Ljubljanica R. near the confluence with the Sava R. some 80 km (50 miles) from the Austrian border. Pop. (1991) 286,681. The old city, crowned by its medieval fortress, runs down to the winding course of the river; modern districts beyond inc. the extensive Tivoli Park. Ljubljana is an educational centre and a commercial city. It also has diverse manufacturing industries producing turbines, textiles, paper and consumer goods. The city came under Habsburg rule in 1277, as Laibach. In 1849 the Austrians built a railway to it and growth followed at once, but only stimulated nationalism. In 1895 an earthquake destroyed much and little Austrian baroque building remains. Ljubljana became a state cap. in 1918 and the Slovene national cap. in 1992.

Llanberis Wales. Town in Gwynedd 13 km (8 miles) ESE of Caernarvon at the W end of Llanberis Pass. In a slate-quarrying district. Chief base for the ascent of Snowdon, with a mountain railway to the summit.

Llandaff Wales. Town in the county borough of Cardiff 5 km (3 miles) NW of Cardiff (of which a suburb since 1922) on the R. Taff. The bishopric was created in the 6th cent., the oldest in Wales.

Llandrindod Wells Wales. Town in Powys.

Pop. (1989) 5020. Spa, famous since the late 17th cent. for its mineral springs.

Llandudno Wales. Town in Conwy on a peninsula just E of the R. Conwy mouth. Pop. (1991) 14,576. Seaside resort on a bay between Great Orme's Head (NW) and Little Orme's Head, having developed from a fishing village from the mid 19th cent.

Llanelli Wales. Town in Carmarthenshire on Burry Inlet of Carmarthen Bay 16 km (10 miles) WNW of Swansea. Pop. (1991) 44,953.
Seaport. Important centre of tinplate manufacture; other industries inc. chemicals, engineering and lens manufacture.

Llanfairfechan Wales. Seaside resort in Conwy on Conwy Bay 13 km (8 miles) SW of Llandudno. Pop. (1991) 3380.

Llanfairpwll Wales. Village in SE Isle of Anglesey 3 km (2 miles) W of Menai Bridge, made famous by an 18th-cent. poet-cobbler who lengthened its name to Llanfairpwllgwyngyllgogerychwyrndrobwllllantysiliogogogoch ('St Mary's Church in the hollow of the white hazel near to the rapid whirlpool of Llandysilio of the red cave').

Llangollen Wales. Market town in Wrexham County Borough on the R. Dee 14 km (9 miles) SW of Wrexham in the picturesque Vale of Llangollen. Pop. (1991) 3267. Summer resort. Manufactures flannel.
The ruined 13th-cent. Cistercian Valle Crucis Abbey is just NW and there is a 14th-cent. bridge over the river.

Llanidloes Wales. Town in Powys on the R. Severn. Pop. (1991) 2616. Formerly a centre of lead-mining and flannel-weaving. Tanning. Scene of Chartist riots in 1839.

Llanquihue, Lake Chile. Lake in the Llanquihue and Osorno provinces (S) 24 km (15 miles) N of Puerto Montt. Area 852 sq km (329 sq. miles); the largest lake in Chile. Drains to the Pacific through the Maullin R. A picturesque resort area, with wooded hills. The volcano Osorno (2681 m; 8794 ft) lies to the E.

Llanrwst Wales. Town in Conwy on the R. Conwy 16 km (10 miles) S of Conwy. Pop. (1991) 3012. A 15th-cent. church.

Llantrisant Wales. Town in Rhondda, Cynon, Taff. Pop. (1991) 9136 (with Pontyclun). From 1968 site of the Royal Mint.

Lleyn Peninsula Wales. Hilly peninsula in Conwy between Carnarvon Bay and Cardigan Bay, rising to 564 m (1850 ft). Pwllheli is on the S coast.

Lloyd (Sukkur) Barrage Pakistan. Irrigation dam across the Indus R. just below Sukkur, completed in 1932; water supplied to 7 canals. It has greatly increased the production of cotton, wheat and other crops in Sind, where agriculture used to depend on inundation canals.

Lloydminster Canada. Town NW of North Battleford on the border betwen Alberta and Saskatchewan and situated in both. Pop. (1989) 16,254 (Alberta 9457; Saskatchewan 6797).

Commercial and distribution centre for a grain-growing and lumbering area. Industries inc. agricultural products, oil and oil by-products, natural gas, salt, gravel and coal. Deposits of oil and natural gas.

Llullailaco, Mountain Argentina/Chile. Peak situated WSW of San Antonio de los Cobres on the Argentina/Chile frontier; height 6710 m (22,015 ft) above sea level, an extinct volcano.

Lobatse Botswana. Town situated N of Mafeking near the border of South Africa in a dairy-farming area. Headquarters of the Baralong tribe. Pop. (1989) 26,841.

Lobito Angola. Chief seaport. Pop. (1983) 150,000. One of the best harbours on the African Atlantic coast, with a protective sandspit; built mainly on reclaimed land. It has bulk-loading facilities and is connected by rail with Beira (Mozambique), Shaba (Democratic Republic of the Congo), Malawi, Zimbabwe and Zambia; the Atlantic terminus for the trans-Africa railway, to the building of which (1929) it owes its rapid commercial development. Exports coffee, cotton, maize, ores, salt, sisal and sugar. Handles exports for Democratic Republic of the Congo and Zambia. Founded in 1834.

Lobos (Seal) Islands Peru. Two groups of small islands off the N coast. Rich guano deposits, accumulated in the dry climate.

Locarno Switzerland. Resort in Ticino canton at the N end of L. Maggiore 19 km (12 miles) W of Bellinzona. Pop. (1989) 15,000. Taken from the Milanese by the Swiss (1512) but built in Italian style. Scene of the Locarno Conference (1925).

Lochaber Scotland. District in Highland around Ben Nevis. Pop. of district (1991) 20,803. It consists of mountains, moors and glens and is well-known for its wild and picturesque scenery. The lochs provide water for the Lochaber hydroelectric scheme.

Lochgelly Scotland. Town in Fife 10 km (6 miles) WNW of Kirkcaldy. Pop. (1971) 7982. It is in an opencast coalmining district. Loch Gelly is just to the SE.

Lockerbie Scotland. Market town in Dumfries and Galloway in Annandale 16 km (10 miles) ENE of Dumfries. Pop. (1991) 3982. Noted for its sheep sales.

Lockport USA. Industrial town in New York on the Erie Canal 34 km (21 miles) NNE of Buffalo. Pop. (1985) 25,000.

Manufactures paper, wallboard.

Named after the series of locks which take the canal through a deep limestone gorge.

Locle, Le Switzerland. Town in Neuchâtel canton 14 km (9 miles) WNW of Neuchâtel near the French border. Pop. (1970) 14,452.

Important watch-making centre, the industry having been established in 1705.

Lod (Lydda) Israel. Town and railway junction 18 km (11 miles) SE of Tel Aviv. Pop. (1989) 42,000.

The country's chief international airport. Manufactures inc. electronic and aircraft equipment.

Traditional birthplace of St George. Destroyed by Vespasian (AD 68) and rebuilt by

Hadrian. Destroyed again by Saladin (1191) and rebuilt by Richard Cœur de Lion.

Lodi Italy. Town in Milano province in Lombardy on the Adda R. 29 km (18 miles) SE of Milan. Pop. (1985) 43,000.

In a rich dairy-farming district. Large trade in cheese, esp. Parmesan. Manufactures linen, silk and majolica.

Founded (1162) by Frederick Barbarossa. Here Napoleon defeated the Austrians (1796).

Lódź Poland. Second largest city in Poland 124 km (77 miles) WSW of Warsaw. Pop. (1992) 846,500.

Leading centre of the textile industry. Also manufactures clothing, electrical and metal goods.

With its satellite towns, Łęczyca, Pabianice and Zgierz, it is a province in its own right. University (1945). The city is laid out in blocks about the main street, which is nearly 11 km (7 miles) long. It developed rapidly in the early 19th cent. with the introduction of German weavers and became known as the 'Manchester of Poland'.

Lofoten Islands Norway. Group of islands off the NW coast forming part of Nordland county, separated from the mainland by Vest Fiord and entirely within the Arctic Circle. Chief islands Austvågöy, Vestvågöy, Moskenesöy, Flakstadöy, chief town Svolvaer (Austvågöy). A partly submerged mountain range, rising to 1162 m (3811 ft) on Austvågöy, they enjoy mild winters owing to the influence of the North Atlantic Drift. To the E and N is the Vesterålen group, often inc. with the Lofoten Is.; chief island Hinnöy. The waters off the two groups form one of the world's richest cod and herring fisheries, and in the spring thousands of fishermen from all parts of Norway come here. Fish-curing and the preparation of cod-liver oil are important occupations in the fishing villages.

Logan, Mount Canada. Peak in SW Yukon in the St Elias Mountains (6050 m; 19,849 ft). The highest in Canada and the second highest in North America. Named after Sir William

E. Logan (1798–1875), Director of the Geological Survey of Canada 1842–69.

Logar River Afghanistan. Rises in the SW Hindu Kush mountains and flows 240 km (150 miles) E past Shaikhabad and Baraki Rajan, then N to join Kabul R. The middle course is known as the Wardak R. Used for logging.

Logroño Spain. 1. Province in Old Castile, mountainous in the SW rising to 2306 m (7566 ft) in the Sierra de la Demanda and descending to the fertile plain of La Rioja along the Ebro R. Area 5034 sq km (1985 sq. miles). Pop. (1991) 263,434. Mainly agricultural. Produces wine, olive oil and cereals.

2. Cap. of Logroño province on the right bank of the Ebro R. 160 km (100 miles) NW of Zaragoza. Pop. (1991) 112,066.

Fruit-canning, flour-milling. Important trade in wine.

An ancient walled town, it has a bridge spanning the Ebro which dates back to the 12th cent.

Loire France. Department on the E margin of the Massif Central, formed from the old province of Lyonnais. Area 4781 sq km (1846 sq. miles). Pop. (1991) 747,100. Prefecture St Étienne. Drained S–N by the Loire R. Rises to the Monts du Forez in the W and the Monts du Beaujolais and the Monts du Lyonnais in the E. Cereals and vines cultivated in the lowlands. Chief towns St Étienne and Roanne.

Loire–Atlantique France. Formerly Loire-Inférieure. Department in S Brittany, crossed E–W by the Loire R. estuary and by its tributaries the Erdre and the Sèvre-Nantaise. Area 6815 sq km (2631 sq. miles). Pop. (1991) 1,058,100. Prefecture Nantes. Many salt marshes along the coast; France's largest lake, Grand-Lieu (54 sq km; 21 sq. miles), lies S of the Loire estuary. Wheat, vines, sugar-beet and potatoes widely cultivated. Industry concentrated in Nantes and St Nazaire.

Loire River France. Ancient Liger. Longest river in France (1012 km; 629 miles), rising on the volcanic Mont Gerbier de Jonc in the Massif Central. From its source it flows generally NNW to Orléans, where it turns SW to Tours and then W to enter the Bay of Biscay by an estuary. Along its course are the fertile regions of Sologne, Berry and Beauce, and the towns of Roanne, Nevers, Orléans, Tours, Nantes and the estuary port of St Nazaire. With its tributaries, the chief of which are the Allier, Cher, Indre, Vienne and Maine, it drains an area of over 119,140 sq km (46,000 sq. miles), more than one-fifth of France. Except for the lower reaches it is only seasonally navigable; in summer it becomes shallow and thin, but since the Middle Ages several of the towns on its banks have had to be protected from the sudden and treacherous floods to which it is subject.

Loiret France. Department formed from Orléanais province, drained E–W by the Loire R. Area 6775 sq km (2616 sq. miles). Pop. (1991) 585,900. Prefecture Orléans. Mainly agricultural, producing wheat, sugar-beet, apples and vines, and containing parts of Beauce, Gâtinais and Sologne. Chief towns Orléans, Montargis.

Loir-et-Cher France. Department formed from Orléanais, drained by the Loire R. and also by the Loir (N) and the Cher (S). Area 6343 sq km (2449 sq. miles). Pop. (1991) 307,100. Prefecture Blois. In the N is part of the fertile Beauce, where wheat is grown and in the S is the less productive Sologne region. Many famous châteaux, inc. those of Chaumont, Cheverny and Montrichard. Chief towns Blois, Vendôme.

Loir River France. River 306 km (190 miles) long rising in the Collines du Perche (Eure-et-Loir department) and flowing generally S and W to join the Sarthe R. near Angers.

Lokeren Belgium. Town in E Flanders province 19 km (12 miles) ENE of Ghent. Pop. (1992) 35,132.
Industrial centre. Manufactures textiles and lace.

Lolland ►LAALAND.

Lombardy (Italian **Lombardia**) Italy. Region in the N bordering N on Switzerland

and extending N–S from the Alps to the Po R. Area 23,857 sq km (9211 sq. miles). Pop. (1991) 8,940,594. Comprises the provinces of Bergamo, Brescia, Como, Cremona, Mantua, Milan, Pavia, Sondrio and Varese. The mountainous N half, with Lakes Como and Iseo and parts of Garda, Lugano and Maggiore, attracts large numbers of tourists and has many hydroelectric plants, while the S half is the Lombard plain. The region is drained by the Po and its tributaries, the Adda, Oglio, Chiese, Lambro, Serio and Mella. Agriculture is important and is assisted by irrigation; maize, wheat, rice, wine and cheese are produced and mulberries are grown for sericulture. Lombardy is also Italy's chief industrial region manufacturing textiles, iron and steel, chemicals. Trade is encouraged by the convergence of such important Alpine passes as Simplon, St Gotthard, Bernina and Splügen on to the Lombard plain, and particularly on to Milan. In the 12th cent. the cities of the Lombard plain formed the Lombard League and defeated Frederick I at Legnano (1176). Later the region was ruled successively by Spain, Austria, France and Austria again, to become part of Italy in 1859.

Lombok Indonesia. Island of the Lesser Sundas between Bali and Sumbawa. Area 4727 sq km (1825 sq. miles). Mountainous, rising to 3728 m (12,228 ft) in Mt Rindjani. Main products are rice and coffee. Chief town Mataram, cap. of the province of W Nusa Tenggara. The flora and fauna of Lombok are transitional between Asiatic and Australian.

Lomé Togo. Cap. and chief seaport on the Bight of Benin 169 km (105 miles) ENE of Accra (Ghana). Pop. (1990) 450,000.
Exports cocoa, coffee, palm kernels and copra. It handles much of the trade of Burkina, Mali and Niger. Important economic conferences between the EC and Third World Countries were held in the city in 1975 and 1979.

Lomond, Loch Scotland. Largest lake in West Central Scotland 35 km (22 miles) long

N–S, 8 km (5 miles) wide in the S narrowing to 1.6 km (1 mile) in the N; several inlets, the outlet being the short R. Leven emptying into the Clyde estuary at Dumbarton. Receives the outfall of the Loch Sloy hydroelectric scheme. Well-known for its scenic beauty, it has many mountains around its banks and wooded islands in its waters; one of the mountains is Ben Lomond (973 m; 3192 ft).

London Canada. Town in SW Ontario on the Thames R. Pop. (1991) 303,165.

Important commercial and industrial centre, described as a 'microcosm of Canadian life'. There are over 500 diversified industries inc. tanning, printing and brewing. It manufactures textiles, electrical equipment, food products, leather goods, refrigerators and paper.

Named after London, England. Chosen (1792) as the site of the future cap. of Upper Canada.

London England. Ancient Londinium. Cap. of England and the United Kingdom situated in the SE of England on a meander of the R. Thames some 65 km (40 miles) W of its estuary on the North Sea coast. Pop. of Greater London, 32 boroughs and the City of London (1991) 6,803,100. London occupies a shallow oval basin across which Greater London extends for some 40 km (30 miles) E to W and for slightly less N to S. The centre is divided into the City of London (known as the 'square mile' pop. (1991) 4100) and the City of Westminster. The former is the oldest quarter; it has St Paul's Cathedral and the medieval Tower. It is now the financial centre and most of its fabric is modern. In 1994 the area of the City of London was increased and the population (1994) was 5443. The latter has the parliament, royal palace and Westminster Abbey. Here also are the larger parks, once royal gardens and the main shopping areas of Regent Street and Oxford Street, Knightsbridge and Piccadilly. E of the City of London, the former dock and industrial area is undergoing great changes with the decline of the port. New industries have developed to the W and around the edge of Greater London on sites convenient for airports and road networks. Government property, finance, services and retailing are all important, as are transport and distribution. Publishing, printing, broadcasting and varied manufacture continue in the central area; old heavy industry has largely moved to cheaper sites. The city is the national centre for the arts and a tourist centre. Employment in the cap. draws in thousands of commuters daily, while resident pop. shrinks.

The 32 boroughs of Greater London are Barking and Dagenham, Barnet, Bexley, Brent, Bromley, Camden, Croydon, Ealing, Enfield, Greenwich, Hackney, Hammersmith and Fulham, Haringey, Harrow, Havering, Hillingdon, Hounslow, Islington, Kensington and Chelsea, Kingston upon Thames, Lambeth, Lewisham, Merton, Newham, Redbridge, Richmond-on-Thames, Southwark, Sutton, Tower Hamlets, Waltham Forest, Wandsworth and Westminster.

London was a Roman fort and river port, but its real importance was only established after 1066 by Norman kings. The medieval merchants and shippers achieved many freedoms and the right of self-government. After 1500 swift expansion spilled outside the walls, especially into Westminster and across the Thames. During the Civil War the city's armies defied the king and its wealth financed the great reconstruction after the fire of 1666. Expansion after that was disorganized. By 1821 the pop. was 1.2 million and by 1901 it was 6.6 million; railway building had stimulated the spread of suburbs and the central districts had received heavy Continental immigration. Vigorous programmes of public health were necessary and central authorities were formed to coordinate them.

After 1945 immigration was from the former colonies. The port declined and moved its docks downstream. The City of London and the eastern districts had been heavily bombed in World War II; reconstruction was on a massive scale and entirely modern in style.

Londonderry (Derry) Northern Ireland. 1.

County in the NW bounded on the N by the Atlantic Ocean and on the W by Co. Donegal. Area 2108 sq km (814 sq. miles). Pop. (1991) 94,721. County town Londonderry (Derry city). The surface is generally hilly, rising to 683 m (2240 ft) in Mt Sawel in the Sperrin Mountains in the S. Drained by the Foyle (W), the Bann (E) and the Roe (S–N) rivers. The NW boundary passes through Lough Foyle, the SE through Lough Neagh. Oats, potatoes and flax cultivated. Industries are concentrated on Derry city and Coleraine. The English name derives from the grant of land around the two towns to the Corporation of the City of London in 1613.

2. County town of Co. Derry, county borough on the W bank of the R. Foyle 6 km (4 miles) from the mouth (Lough Foyle). Pop. (1989) 62,500.

Seaport. Industrial centre. Manufactures food products, alcoholic beverages, shirts, collars, other clothing and linen.

The city walls (completed 1618) and the Protestant cathedral of St Columba (1633) are memorials to the work of the Irish Society, representing the Corporation of London, which was granted lands at Derry (afterwards called Londonderry) in 1613. Other buildings are the Roman Catholic cathedral, St Eugene (1873), the Guildhall (1912) and Magee University College (since 1951 affiliated to Queen's University, Belfast). Derry originated with an abbey founded (546) by St Columba. The name derives from the Irish *doire* ('Oak Wood'). From the 9th to the 11th cent. it was frequently raided and taken by the Danes. 'Planted' with Scottish Presbyterians in the 17th cent., it underwent a long siege (1688–9) by the army of James II, but held out (under the leadership of Reverend George Walker), earning the cognomen of the 'Maiden City'.

Londrina Brazil. Town in the N of the Paraná state. Pop. (1991) 540,982.

In a region of rapid development since the introduction of coffee to Paraná. Trade also in cotton and oranges.

Founded 1932.

Long Beach USA. Tourist resort and industrial town in California 29 km (18 miles) S of Los Angeles. Pop. (1990) 429,433. Excellent recreational amenities.

Varied industries: oil-refining, fish and fruit canning; manufactures aircraft, tyres, chemicals and soap. It has a large fishing fleet and a fine deep-water harbour protected by Catalina Island. Exports petroleum and cement.

Named because of the 11-km (7-mile) bathing beach.

Long Branch USA. Seaside resort in New Jersey 64 km (40 miles) ENE of Trenton, one of the oldest in the USA. Pop. (1990) 90,000.

Manufactures clothing and rubber products. Fishing is important.

First settled 1740.

Longchamp France. Fashionable racecourse SW of Bois de Boulogne, Paris where the race for the Grand Prix is run in June.

Long Eaton England. Town in SE Derbyshire near the R. Trent 10 km (6 miles) SW of Nottingham. Pop. (1991) 44,826.

Formerly important in the lace industry. Now manufactures electrical equipment, hosiery, upholstery, furniture and food products.

Longford Ireland. 1. County in Leinster bounded on the SW by Lough Ree. Area 1044 sq km (403 sq. miles). Pop. (1991) 30,293. Generally low-lying except in the N, where it rises to 278 m. (912 ft) Contains much bog, with pastures for cattle-rearing in the S. Oats and potatoes cultivated. Drained by the Shannon and its tributaries.

2. County town of Co. Longford on the R. Camlin 96 km (60 miles) W of Drogheda. Pop. (1991) 6393.

Manufactures textiles.

It has a 17th-cent. castle and a 19th-cent. Roman Catholic cathedral.

Long Island USA. Island in New York state 190 km (118 miles) long and 19–37 km (12–23 miles) wide, extending ENE from the mouth of the Hudson R.; separated from the mainland by Long Island Sound. Many resorts and residential towns, esp. in the E. The W part (comprising the boroughs of Brooklyn and Queens) is essentially part of New York City. Famous resorts inc. Coney Island (Brooklyn), Fire Island and Long Beach.

Longleat ➤ WARMINSTER.

Longton England. Town in NW Staffordshire in the Potteries district; since 1910 part of Stoke-on-Trent. Porcelain was first made here in the mid 18th cent. at Longton Hall by William Littler.

Longview USA. Town in Texas 200 km (125 miles) E of Dallas. Pop. (1990) 70,311.

On an oilfield. Oil-refining. Manufactures chemicals, oilfield equipment.

Grew rapidly after the discovery of oil in 1930.

Lons-le Saunier France. Cap. of Jura department. Pop. (1990) 20,140.

Manufactures optical goods and produces wines.

Looe England. Town in Cornwall at the mouth of the R. Looe 21 km (13 miles) W of Plymouth. Pop. (1991) 5022. Consists of W and E Looe, on opposite banks of the river, both fishing ports and resorts.

Lop Nur (Lob Nor) China. Depression in E Xinjiang–Uygur Autonomous Region at the E end of the Tarim Basin, once filled by a large lake but now largely dried, consisting of small temporary lakes which move their location owing to the changes in the course of the Tarim R. This apparent movement of the lake was observed by the explorers Przhevalski in 1876 and Sven Hedin in 1928.

Lorain USA. Industrial town in Ohio at the mouth of the Black R. on L. Erie. Pop. (1990) 71,245. Excellent harbour.

Trades largely in coal and iron ore. Shipbuilding. Manufactures iron and steel goods, machinery, cranes and clothing.

Lorca Spain. Ancient Eliocroca. Town in Murcia province 60 km (37 miles) SW of Murcia. Pop. (1991) 65,832.

Industrial centre. Manufactures fertilizers, woollen goods and footwear. Tanning, flour-milling and brandy-distilling. Trade in agricultural produce.

Built on a hill crowned by a medieval castle and has several baroque churches.

Lord Howe Island Australia. Small volcanic island in SW Pacific c. 860 km (534 miles) ENE of Sydney, a dependency of New South Wales. Area 17 sq km (7 sq. miles). Pop. (1989) 320. Hilly; reaches 866 m (2840 ft). It produces Kentia palm-seeds, and was discovered by the British in 1788. It is also a popular resort.

Lord Howe Islands ➤ SOLOMON ISLANDS.

Loreto Italy. Town in Ancona province in The Marches 21 km (13 miles) SSE of Ancona. Pop. (1990) 10,700. Famous place of pilgrimage because of the Santa Casa (Holy House), believed to be the home of the Virgin Mary miraculously transported here from Nazareth late in the 13th cent. A church, begun in 1468, was built round it.

Lorient France. Fishing port in the Morbihan department on an inlet of the Bay of Biscay 113 km (70 miles) SE of Brest. Pop. (1990) 61,630.

Fish-canning. Manufactures nets and rope.

Founded by the Compagnie des Indes Orientales (1664) for trade with the Orient and named L'Orient. Taken over by the French government (1782) and became an important naval base. During World War II it was a German submarine base and was almost completely destroyed by Allied bombing, but was subsequently rebuilt.

Lorraine (Ger. **Lothringen**) France. Region and former province in the E, bounded on the N by Belgium and Luxembourg and on the NE by Germany, now divided into the departments of Moselle, Meurthe-et-Moselle, Meuse and Vosges. Area 23,547 sq km (9092 sq. miles). Pop. (1991) 2,306,700. Consists in the main of a low plateau rising in the E to the Vosges and cut S–N by the valleys of the Meuse and Moselle. Varied agriculture; coal mined in the NE on the extension of the Saar coal basin; but the extremely rich iron-ore deposits around Longwy, Thionville, Briey and Nancy are by far the most important resource.

Prior to the 9th cent. a part of the kingdom of Lotharingia. Divided (960) into the duchies of Upper and Lower Lorraine. The latter became Brabant (now in Belgium and the Netherlands) and the former, from the 11th cent. known simply as Lorraine, was united to France in 1766 as a province, with Nancy as cap. In 1871 the present Moselle department (largely German-speaking) was united with Alsace to form the German imperial territory of Elsass-Lothringen; it reverted to France in 1919, but was again annexed to Germany (1940–4) and returned to France after World War II.

Los Alamos USA. Town in New Mexico 39 km (24 miles) NW of Santa Fé at a height of 2230 m (7314 ft). Pop. (1980) 11,039. Famous for US government atomic-energy laboratories, where the first atom bomb was made during World War II; later the first H-bomb was made here.

Los Andes Chile. Town in the Aconcagua province 77 km (48 miles) N of Santiago. Pop. (1989) 30,500. On the Trans-Andean Railway. In a district producing cereals, wine and fruit.

Los Angeles USA. City in South California on the Pacific coast and 200 km (125 miles) from the Mexican border. It is the largest in the state and third largest in the USA. Pop. (1990) 3,485,398; area 1171 sq km (452 sq. miles). It is a major seaport and has several airports. The favourable 'Mediterranean' climate attracts residents and tourists in large numbers. The long hours of sunshine, dry dependable weather and beautiful scenery have helped to promote its major industry, the production of films. Oil-refining and aircraft manufacture rank next in importance.

Other industries inc. tourism and there are several universities.

Some early 19th-cent. buildings survive, inc. the old Plaza church (1818) and the Avila

Adobe (1818), the oldest house in the city. Within the city boundaries there are many districts which have retained a separate identity, e.g. Hollywood, Beverly Hills, Burbank, Pasadena, Santa Ana, Santa Monica. There are several foreign communities – e.g. Chinese, Japanese, Mexican have their own districts. Founded (1781) by Franciscan fathers; the full name is El Pueblo Nuestra Señora la Reina de los Angeles de Porciuncula. Became cap. of the Mexican state of California in 1845, but was captured by US forces in 1846 during the Mexican War. The advent of the railways and the discovery of oil in the late 19th cent. stimulated its growth. Then came the film industry in the early 1900s and the aircraft industry after 1920.

Los Islands Guinea. Group of islands near Conakry, the five most important being Tamara, Factory, Crawford, White and Coral. Chief products bauxite, palm kernels. They were British possessions from 1818 to 1904, when they were ceded to France.

Los Santos Panama. Town situated NW of Tablas on a branch of the Inter-American Highway in Los Santos Province. Pop. (1989) 14,000.

Commercial centre of an agricultural area. Industries inc. distilling and salt extracting.

Lossiemouth and Branderburgh Scotland. Small town in Moray at the mouth of the R. Lossie on Moray Firth. Pop. (1991) 7184.

Fishing port and resort. Birthplace of J. Ramsay MacDonald, British Prime Minister (1866–1937).

Lostwithiel England. Market town in Cornwall on the R. Fowey 8 km (5 miles) SSE of Bodmin. Pop. (1990) 2700. Fishing port. One of the four Cornish 'Stannary towns', with the monopoly of minting tin coinage.

Lot France. Department in the SW, formed (1790) from the Quercy district of the Old Guyenne province, sloping NE–SW from the Massif Central to the Garonne valley, with the limestone Causses in the centre.

Area 5217 sq km (2014 sq. miles). Pop. (1991) 156,100. Prefecture Cahors. Drained by the Lot and Dordogne rivers. Cereals, vines and fruits are cultivated; sheep and cattle raised. Chief towns Cahors and Figeac.

Lota Chile. Seaport in the Concepción province 32 km (20 miles) SSW of Concepción. Pop. (1989) 52,000.

Important coalmining centre and bunkering port for coastal vessels. Copper smelters. Ceramics factory.

Lot-et-Garonne France. Department in the SW formed (1790) from parts of Gascony and Guyenne provinces. Area 5361 sq km (2070 sq. miles). Pop. (1991) 306,900. Prefecture Agen. Drained by the Garonne and its tributaries the Lot, Gers and Baïse, in whose fertile valleys wheat, maize, tobacco, vines, plums and vegetables are grown and cattle and poultry are raised. Chief towns Agen, Villeneuve-sur-Lot and Marmande.

Lothian Region Scotland. Former region in the SE. Since 1996 divided between East Lothian, City of Edinburgh, Midlothian and West Lothian.

Lothian, East Scotland. New unitary authority created in 1996, formerly in Lothian Region. Pop. (1993) 85,640.

Lothian, West Scotland. New unitary authority created in 1996, formerly in Lothian Region. Pop. (1993) 146,730.

Lot River France. River 479 km (298 miles) long, rising in the Lozère department and flowing W, crossing the limestone Causses by a deep gorge and joining the Garonne R.

Lötschberg Tunnel Switzerland. Railway tunnel 14 km (9 miles) long in the Alps, linking Thun (Bern canton) and Brig (Valais canton) and reaching 1244 m (4080 ft). Lies beneath the Lötschen Pass (2693 m; 8833 ft). It was built 1906–12.

Loughborough England. Town in Leicestershire on the R. Soar 16 km (10 miles) NNW of Leicester. Pop. (1989) 53,000.

Industries inc. printing, high technology and engineering. Manufactures hosiery, shoes, electrical equipment and pharmaceutical products. There is also a bellfounding industry; the great bell of St Paul's, London, was cast here (1881).

Loughrea Ireland. Town in Co. Galway on the N shore of Lough Rea 34 km (21 miles) ESE of Galway. Pop. (1986) 3360. Industries inc. cotton manufacturing.

Louisbourg Canada. Town situated SE of Sydney on the E coast of Cape Breton Island in Nova Scotia. Formerly an important French fortress. Pop. (1990) 1450.

The main industry is fishing and tourism.

Louisiade Archipelago Papua New Guinea. Chain of volcanic islands and coral reefs in the SW Pacific SE of New Guinea. Gold obtained on many islands. Named (1768) by de Bougainville after Louis XV. During World War II the Americans won an important naval and air battle over the Japanese in the Coral Sea off Misima island (1942).

Louisiana USA. State on the Gulf of Mexico (S) and bordered by Arkansas (N), Mississippi (E) and Texas (W). Area 125,836 sq km (48,566 sq. miles). Pop. (1990) 4,219,973. Cap. Baton Rouge. Part of the Gulf coastal plain; the highest point is only 163 m (534 ft) above sea level and the average elevation is about 30 m (98 ft) above sea level. Floods from the Mississippi (whose delta is within Louisiana) present a serious problem; hundreds of miles of levees have been constructed. Along the Red R. (which bisects the state) there are several lakes. The Gulf coast is indented with numerous bays and lagoons. Climate humid subtropical; summers are hot and long, winters mild and short. Rainfall averages 125–140 cm (50–55 ins.) annually. Forests cover 56 per cent. of the state, but farming is the main occupation. Leading crop cotton; sugar-cane, rice and maize also important. The manufacturing industries are chiefly those associated with the petroleum, lumber, chemicals, food-processing and paper, mainly in the Gulf region. There are also rich sulphur and salt mines. Largest town New Orleans, followed by Baton Rouge, Shreveport and Lake Charles.

Named Louisiana after Louis XIV; the French originally gave the name to the entire Mississippi basin. The first settlement in the present state was made at New Orleans (1718). The region E of the Mississippi was ceded to Britain in 1763 and became US territory in 1783. The region W of the Mississippi (a territory of 2,292,000 sq km (885,000 sq. miles)) was sold by France to the USA in 1803 (the Louisiana Purchase) for $15 million. Out of this area the Territory of Orleans was organized in 1804; it became the state of Louisiana in 1812 when it was admitted to the Union.

Louisville USA. Industrial and commercial town in N Kentucky on the Ohio R., whose falls provide hydroelectric power. Pop. (1990) 269,063.

Important trade in tobacco. Whiskey-distilling, meat-packing and flour-milling. Manufactures tobacco products, textiles and chemicals.

Nearby is the Churchill Downs race-course, scene of the Kentucky Derby since 1875. The city is named after King Louis XVI of France, in recognition of the French help given to the American colonies during the American War of Independence. The city has at times suffered severely from the flooding of the Ohio R.

Lourdes France. Town in the Hautes-Pyrénées department at the foot of the Pyrenees 130 km (80 miles) SW of Toulouse. Pop. (1989) 17,800. Here in 1858 an illiterate peasant girl, Bernadette Soubirous, had visions in a grotto of the Virgin Mary. A church was built near the spot (1862) and the fame of Lourdes as a place of miraculous cures rapidly grew. It is today a leading place of Catholic pilgrimage and annually attracts thousands of pilgrims, invalids and tourists.

Lourenzo Marques ➤MAPUTO.

Louth England. Town in Lincolnshire on the R. Lud 39 km (24 miles) ENE of Lincoln. Pop. (1991) 14,248.

Malting and brewing. Manufactures agri-cultural machinery, plastic bags and cartons.

About 1.6 km (1 mile) E are the ruins of the 12th-cent. Cistercian Louth Park Abbey.

Louth Ireland. County in Leinster, the smallest in Ireland, bounded on the E by the Irish Sea and extending from Carlingford Lough (N) to the R. Boyne (S). Area 821 sq km (317 sq. miles). Pop. (1991) 91,800. County town Dundalk. Generally low-lying and flat but rising to over 570 m (1870 ft) in the N. Drained by the Fane, Lagan and Dee rivers. Main occupations fishing, cereal and potato cultivation and cattle-rearing. Industrial centres Dundalk and Drogheda.

Louvain (Flemish **Leuven**) Belgium. Town in Brabant province on the Dyle R. 24 km (15 miles) E of Brussels. Pop. (1993) 85,592.

Railway junction. Industries inc. brewing, distilling, engineering and flour-milling.

Its university was founded in 1426; the university library was destroyed by the Germans (1914), rebuilt with the aid of international donations, chiefly from the USA (1921–8) and again destroyed by the Germans in 1940. Prior to being a seat of learning, Louvain was a centre of the wool trade and from the 11th to the 15th cent. was cap. of the duchy of Brabant, being then replaced by Brussels.

Lowell USA. Industrial town in Massachusetts on the Merrimack R. Pop. (1990) 103,439.

A textile centre; the first mills were established in 1822. Also manufactures electrical equipment, chemicals and plastics.

Birthplace of the artist J. A. M. Whistler (1834–1903).

Lower Austria (Niederösterreich) Austria. Largest federal state in the NE bordering on the Czech Republic. Area 19,174 sq km (7403 sq. miles). Pop. (1994) 115,555. Drained W–E by R. Danube. Low-lying in the Danube basin, largely hilly elsewhere, rising to 2075 m (6806 ft) in Schneeberg (S), an outlier of the Alps. Farming important (cereals, root crops, vines in the Weinviertel (NE)); much land forested, esp. in the

Waldviertel (NW). Towns inc. St Pölten (State cap.), Wiener Neustadt.

Lower Egypt Egypt. Egypt N of Cairo inc. the R. Nile delta and the Mediterranean coast. ➤EGYPT.

Lower Hutt New Zealand. Town in the SW of the North Island 11 km (7 miles) NE of Wellington. Pop. (1986) 63,860.

Important industrial centre. Meat-freezing, vehicle assembly, engineering. Manufactures textiles, clothing and furniture. Industries mainly located in the lower valley of the R. Hutt near the N shore of Port Nicholson.

Lower Saxony (Ger. **Niedersachsen**) Germany. *Land* bordering N on the North Sea and W on the Netherlands, and inc. the East Frisian Is. Area 47,364 sq km (18,262 sq. miles). Pop. (1991) 7,475,790. Cap. Hanover. Chief towns Hanover, Brunswick, Osnabrück, Oldenburg, Saltzgitter and Wilhelmshaven. The *Land* is part of the N European plain and the central area comprises much heath and moor, inc. Lüneburg Heath. The region is drained by the Ems, Weser, Aller and Elbe rivers. Farming is the main occupation except in the wooded Harz Mountains in the extreme SE. It produces rye, wheat, fodder crops and potatoes. The *Land* was formed in 1946 from the former Prussian province of Hanover and the *Länder* of Oldenburg, Schaumburg-Lippe and most of Brunswick. Lower Saxony has 7 seats in the *Bundesrat*.

Lowestoft England. Fishing port and Britain's most easterly town in E Suffolk 14 km (9 miles) S of Yarmouth. Pop. (1991) 62,907.

Resort and yachting centre. Lowestoft Ness, on the North Sea, is England's most easterly point. Shipbuilding. Manufactures electrical equipment.

In the 18th cent. a type of china was made here and was named after it. Birthplace of Benjamin Britten, the composer (1913–76).

Loyalty Islands New Caledonia. Group of coral islands 100 km (60 miles) E of New Caledonia in the SW Pacific Ocean, of which they are a dependency. Area 2072 sq km (800 sq. miles). Pop. (1989) 17,912 (chiefly Melanesians, except on Uvéa which is partly Polynesian). Three main islands, Maré, Lifu and Uvéa, and many small islands. Chief export copra.

Loyang ➤LUOYANG.

Lozère France. Department in the S of the Massif Central, formed from part of the Languedoc province. Area 5167 sq km (1995 sq. miles). Pop. (1991) 72,700; one of the most sparsely populated regions of France. Prefecture Mende. Mountainous, rising to over 1500 m (4920 ft) in the Monts de la Margeride (N). Drained by the Allier, Lot and Tarn rivers, the last-named cutting a remarkable gorge in the limestone Causses. Sheep and dairy cattle are raised, and cereals and fruit grown. Chief towns Mende and Marvejols.

Lualaba River Democratic Republic of the Congo. The W headstream of the Congo R. rising in Shaba region near the Zambia border and flowing generally N. After passing through a region of marshes and lakes, it is joined by the Luvua R., the E headstream of the Congo R. Known as the Lualaba as far as Kisangani, 1770 km (1106 miles) from its source, below which it becomes the Congo. Navigable downstream from Bukama. Livingstone thought it was the source of the Nile but Stanley proved it to be the source of the Congo.

Luanda (São Paulo de Luanda) Angola. Cap. and seaport 338 km (210 miles) SSW of Matadi. Pop. (1990) 1,544,000. Terminus of a railway to the interior (Malange).

Exports coffee and cotton. Industries inc. oil-refining, food-processing, paper, textiles and woodworking.

Founded 1576, it was the centre of the slave trade to Brazil in the 17th and 18th cent. Declined in the late 19th cent.

Luang Prabang Laos. Royal cap. and river port on the Mekong R. 217 km (135 miles)

NNW of Vientiane, with which it is also linked by road. Pop. (1985) 68,399.

Trade in rice and timber.

Formerly cap. of a kingdom of the same name.

Lubango Angola. Formerly Sa da Bandeira. Town situated 260 km (162 miles) S of Benguela at the W edge of the central plateau. Pop. (1985) 106,000. The surrounding area produces coffee and cattle. Civil war has disrupted production.

Lubbock USA. Town in NW Texas 362 km (225 miles) WNW of Fort Worth. Pop. (1990) 182,206.

Commercial centre for the S Plains area. Important market for cotton; also trade in cattle, poultry and grain.

Founded 1891. The first citizens were ranchers, buffalo hunters and trail drivers.

Lübeck Germany. Seaport in Schleswig-Holstein on the Trave R. 16 km (10 miles) from its mouth on the Baltic Sea. Pop. (1991) 214,758. Linked by canal with the Elbe R.

Exports fertilizers, machinery. Shipbuilding, engineering. Manufactures steel, machinery, textiles and wool products.

Cathedral (founded 1173); 13th-cent. Marienkirche; 13th/16th-cent. town hall; two 15th-cent. gates. Founded 1143. Became the chief city of the Hanseatic League; the last diet was held here in 1630. Remained a free Hanseatic city until 1937, when it was incorporated in Schleswig-Holstein. Birthplace of writer, Thomas Mann (1875–1955).

Lublin Poland. Cap. of the Lublin voivodeship on the Bystrzyca R. 160 km (100 miles) SE of Warsaw. Pop. (1992) 262,200.

Railway junction. Industrial and commercial centre. Manufactures agricultural machinery, electrical equipment, textiles, glass and vehicles. Other industries inc. flour-milling and sugar-refining.

Temporary seat of the Polish government in 1918 and again in 1944.

Lubumbashi Democratic Republic of the Congo. Formerly Elisabethville. The second largest city; cap. of the Shaba region at a height of 1200 m (3936 ft). Pop. (1991) 739,082. Connected by rail with Zambia and Angola. Founded 1910. Grew rapidly with the development of copper-mining by the Union Minière du Haut Katanga.

Industries inc. cobalt and copper-refining, food-processing, brewing, printing and flour-milling.

Lucca Italy. Cap. of Lucca province in Tuscany in the valley of the Serchio R. 16 km (10 miles) NE of Pisa. Pop. (1990) 86,437.

Noted for olive-oil production. Also manufactures silk, pasta, wine and woollen goods.

In its cathedral, which was begun in the 11th cent., is a cedar crucifix believed to have been brought miraculously to Lucca in 782. Several old churches and palaces. Scene of Julius Caesar's conference with Pompey and Crassus (56 BC). Birthplace of Giacomo Puccini, composer (1858–1924).

Lucena Spain. Town in Córdoba province in Andalusia 58 km (36 miles) SSE of Córdoba. Pop. (1991) 32,054.

Manufactures earthenware jars for oil and wine storage, furniture, copper and zinc products, and produces wine, brandy and olive oil.

Lucerne (Ger. **Luzern**) Switzerland. Canton in central Switzerland lying to the NW of the Lake of Lucerne. Area 1492 sq km (576 sq. miles). Pop. (1991) 319,525 (mainly Roman Catholic and German-speaking). Mountainous in the S. Agricultural and pastoral with a large area of forests. Drained by the Reuss and the Kleine Emme rivers. One of the Four Forest Cantons; joined the Swiss Confederation in 1332.

2. Cap. of Lucerne canton on the Reuss R. at the point where it leaves the Lake of Lucerne. Pop. (1990) 60,600. One of the country's largest and most popular resorts.

Manufactures aluminium goods, sewing-machines, chemicals. Fine views of the mountains with the Rigi and Pilatus nearby. In the town are the 17th-cent. Hofkirche and town hall. It grew round an 8th-cent. Benedictine monastery and developed with the opening of the St Gotthard Pass in the 13th cent.

Lucerne, Lake (Ger. **Vierwaldstättersee**) Switzerland. In German, 'Lake of the Four Forest Cantons'. An irregular-shaped lake at a height of 437 m (1433 ft) bordering on the Four Forest Cantons – Unterwalden, Uri, Schwyz and Lucerne. Area 111 sq km (43 sq. miles). Fed from the S and drained from the NW by the Reuss R. With its picturesque scenery it is a popular tourist area, the resorts on its shores inc. Lucerne, the principal town, Weggis, Brunnen and Fluelen. The best-known of the neighbouring mountains are the Rigi (N) and Pilatus (SW).

Luchow ►LUZHOU.

Luck ►LUTSK.

Luckenwalde Germany. Town in the Brandenburg *Land* 37 km (23 miles) SSE of Potsdam. Pop. (1989) 26,552.

Manufactures textiles, paper, metal goods, chemicals, footwear and beer.

During the Nazi regime it was the site of a concentration camp.

Lucknow India. Cap. of Uttar Pradesh on the Gumti R. 418 km (260 miles) SE of Delhi. Pop. (1991) 1,619,700.

Industries inc. railway engineering and the manufacture of paper, chemicals, carpets, copper and brass articles, aeronautical and electronic equipment, automobiles, scooters, chikon work (textiles), synthetic fibres and plastics. Trade in grain and oilseeds. It is also an education centre.

University (1920). Cap. of the Nawabs of Oudh 1775–1856. One of its outstanding buildings is the great Imambara or mausoleum of Asuf-ud-Daula. The defence and relief of the residency were dramatic episodes of the Indian Mutiny (1857).

Lüdenscheid Germany. Town in North Rhine-Westphalia 32 km (20 miles) ESE of Wuppertal. Pop. (1986) 73,400.

Industrial centre. Manufactures aluminium, hardware and plastics.

Ludhiana India. Industrial and commercial town in Punjab 120 km (75 miles) SE of Amritsar. Pop. (1991) 1,042,700.

Manufactures inc. sewing-machines, cycles, sports goods, clothing, iron and steel items, hosiery, textiles, furniture, machinery and agricultural implements. Trade in grain and cotton.

Seat of an agricultural university (1962).

Ludlow England. Market town in Shropshire on the R. Teme near the confluence with the R. Corve 37 km (23 miles) S of Shrewsbury. Pop. (1989) 7500.

Important in medieval times on account of its position on the Welsh border and among its buildings are the remains of the 11th/16th-cent. castle and the 13th/15th-cent. parish church. The poet A. E. Housman (1859–1936), author of *A Shropshire Lad*, is buried here.

Ludvika Sweden. Town situated SW of Falun on L. Vasman in Kopparberg. Pop. (1989) 29,324.

Railway junction and industrial centre. Industries inc. the manufacture of electrical equipment, copper-smelting, metalworking, sawmilling, bricks.

Ludwigsburg Germany. Town in Baden-Württemberg near the Neckar R. 11 km (7 miles) N of Stuttgart. Pop. (1986) 76,900.

Manufactures metal goods, pianos and organs, also textiles.

Founded in the early 18th cent. by the Duke of Württemberg.

Ludwigshafen Germany. Town and river port in Rhineland-Palatinate on the left bank of the Rhine R. opposite Mannheim. Pop. (1990) 161,100.

A major centre of the German chemical industry. Manufactures dyes, plastics, fertilizers, pharmaceutical products, machinery and vehicle bodies. There is brewing and flour-milling.

Lugano Switzerland. Town in Ticino canton on the N shore of L. Lugano near the Italian border. Pop. (1990) 26,000. Italian in appearance and character, it is a popular resort amid beautiful lake and mountain scenery, with Monte San Salvatore (916 m; 3004 ft) and Monte Brè (934 m; 3064 ft) nearby. From 1848 to 1866 it was Mazzini's base in his struggle to expel the Austrians from Lombardy.

Lugansk ►LUHANSK.

Lugo Spain. 1. Province in Galicia in the NW, bordering N on the Bay of Biscay. Area 9803 sq km (3785 sq. miles). Pop. (1991) 381,888. Mountainous, with broken, rocky coastline; drained by the Miño R. and its tributaries. Agriculture, fishing and lumbering.

2. Cap. of Lugo province on the Miño R. 80 km (50 miles) SE of Corunna. Pop. (1991) 82,658.

Market town. Industries inc. tanning, flour-milling and the manufacture of textiles.

Has Roman walls; 12th-cent. bridge across the Miño and a 12th-cent. Gothic cathedral.

Luhansk Ukraine. Formerly Voroshilovgrad. Cap. of region in the Donbas mining area. Pop. (1991) 504,000.

Industrial centre. Manufactures locomotives, steel pipes, coalmining machinery, ball-bearings, television sets, chemicals, textiles and foodstuffs. Brewing and flour-milling.

Founded in 1795 when an iron foundry was established by an Englishman, Gascoyne, using local coal.

Luik ►LIÈGE.

Luleå Sweden. Cap. of Norrbotten county on the Gulf of Bothnia at the mouth of the Lule R. Pop. (1991) 68,523. Seaport, icebound Dec.-April.

Exports iron ore from Gällivare and Kiruna, timber floated down the Lule, wood-pulp. Manufactures iron and steel, and wood-pulp.

Lule River Norway/Sweden. River 450 km (280 miles) long rising just inside the Norwigian border and flowing SE through Stora Lule L. across Norrbotten to the Gulf of Bothnia at Luleå. Important hydroelectric plants derive power from falls at Porjus and Harspranget. Much timber floated downstream to Luleå.

Lulworth England. Two villages, E and W Lulworth, Dorset situated SW of Wareham in Dorset. The seaside resort of W Lulworth stands near Lulworth Cove, a circular land-locked inlet surrounded by high cliffs of great beauty.

Lund Sweden. Town in Malmöhus county 16 km (10 miles) NE of Malmö. Pop. (1991) 89,598. Cultural centre with a university founded in 1668.

Industries inc. printing and publishing, sugar-refining. It manufactures paper and furniture.

Cathedral (11th-cent.) with an exceptionally large crypt and a medieval astronomical clock.

Lundy England. Rocky island 5 km (3 miles) long and about 0.8 km (½ mile) wide off the N Devon coast 18 km (11 miles) NNW of Hartland Point at the entrance to the Bristol Channel. It has a ruined castle and is a sanctuary for gannets, guillemots, puffins and razorbills.

Lüneburg Germany. Town in Lower Saxony on the Ilmenau R. 40 km (25 miles) SE of Hamburg. Pop. (1986) 59,500.

Manufactures chemicals, ironware, clothing and cement. Also a resort with saline springs.

The churches of St John, St Michael and St Nicolas and the great 13th/18th cent. town hall are outstanding. A leading member of the Hanseatic League. Cap. of the duchy of Brunswick-Lüneburg 1235-1369.

Lüneburg Heath (Ger. **Lüneburger Heide**) Germany. Sandy region in Lower Saxony between the Elbe and the Aller rivers, largely covered with heather and scrub. Sheep raised and potatoes and honey produced. In 1945 the German troops surrendered to Gen. Montgomery here, ending World War II in Europe.

Lünen Germany. Industrial town in North Rhine-Westphalia on the Lippe R. just NE of Dortmund. Pop. (1986) 84,400.

Coalmining centre. Iron-founding. Manufactures glass and aluminium.

Lunéville France. Town in the Meurthe-et-Moselle department 31 km (19 miles) ESE of Nancy. Pop. (1968) 22,961.

Manufactures porcelain and textiles. Railway engineering.

The treaty of Lunéville between France and Austria was signed here (1801).

Lunghai Railway China. Chief E–W railway of central China, running from Lianyungang on the Yellow Sea to Luzhou, where it links up with the Luzhou–Xinjiang Railway. At Zhengzhou it crosses the Beijing–Guangzhou (Canton) Railway and at Paoki the new N–S trunk line (to Chongqing).

Luoyang (Loyang) China. Town in Henan province 113 km (70 miles) W of Zhengzhou on the Ho-ho, a tributary of the Hwang-ho. Pop. (1990) 759,752.

Commercial and industrial centre. Trade in cereals and cotton. Manufactures tractors, machinery and ball-bearings.

The city dates from 2100 BC and from 770 to 221 BC it was cap. of the Eastern Zhou Kingdom.

Lurgan Northern Ireland. Town in Co. Armagh just S of Lough Neagh 31 km (19 miles) WSW of Belfast. Pop. (1991) 21,905.

Centre of the linen industry since the early 17th cent. Also manufactures nylon fabrics and handkerchiefs.

Lusaka Zambia. Cap. 48 km (30 miles) N of the Kafue R. at a height of 1260 m (4133 ft). Pop. (1989) 921,000. Linked by road across the Zambezi with Harare (Zimbabwe) and by rail with Bulawayo (Zimbabwe).

Commercial centre in an agricultural region. Manufactures cement, tobacco products, vehicles and textiles.

Became cap. of Northern Rhodesia 1935.

Lushnjë Albania. Town situated NW of Berat at the N edge of the Myzeqe plain. Pop. (1991) 24,000. Centre of an agricultural area.

Lü-ta ➤DALIAN.

Luton England. Industrial town and unitary authority on the R. Lea 29 km (18 miles) S of Bedford. Pop. (1991) 164,743.

Important motor-vehicle works. Also manufactures ball-bearings, refrigerators and vacuum cleaners. Industries inc. engineering, brewing. The centre of the straw-plaiting industry, introduced in the reign of James I; still manufactures hats (inc. straw 'boaters'), but on a much reduced scale. Airport caters largely for 'package' holidays.

Lutsk (Polish **Luck**) Ukraine. Town on the Styr R. 137 km (85 miles) NE of Lvov. Pop. (1991) 210,000.

Manufactures agricultural machinery. Industries inc. flour-milling and tanning.

Has a cathedral and a ruined 16th-cent. castle. Passed from Poland to Russia 1791, returned to Poland after World War I and again passed to Russia after World War II.

Lutterworth England. Town in S Leicestershire 10 km (6 miles) NNE of Rugby. Pop. (1991) 7380.

Hosiery and engineering industries.

The Church of St Mary has relics of John Wycliffe, English religious reformer, who was rector here 1374–84.

Luxembourg. 1. Grand duchy and independent state in W Europe, bounded E by Germany, S by France and W by Belgium. Area 2586 sq km (999 sq. miles). Pop. (1995) 409,000 (88 per cent urban). Life expectancy, 73 years male, 79 female. Cap. Luxembourg. Other towns Esch-sur-Alzette, Differdange and Dudelange. Currency: Luxembourg franc = 100 centimes. In the N it is crossed by the Ardennes and rises to over 540 m (1771 ft). The S is gently undulating. Drained by the tributaries of the Moselle, which forms part of its E boundary. Land use: forested 34 per cent, meadows and pastures 27 per cent, agricultural and under permanent cultivation 22 per cent. About 94 per cent. of the pop. is Roman Catholic and most speak Luxembourgish which, since 1985, has been the official lang. with French and German.

There is mainly mixed farming and the chief crops are oats, potatoes, wheat, some

Lvov (Lviv)

wine being also produced. The principal resource is the iron ore which is mined in the SW on the extension of the Lorraine fields; this forms the basis of the important iron and steel industry, centred on Esch-sur-Alzette. Industries are concentrated in the cap. and the small towns and inc. food-processing, iron and steel products, tyre manufacture, chemicals and engineering.

Luxembourg is a constitutional monarchy under a Grand Duke or Duchess. A country in the 11th cent., when it inc. the present Luxembourg province of Belgium. Became a duchy 1354. From the 15th cent. it was held by the House of Habsburg, apart from brief intervals, until the Congress of Vienna (1815), when it was made a grand duchy and passed to William I of the Netherlands; in 1839 it lost the present Luxembourg province of Belgium. Personal union with the Netherlands ended in 1890 on the death of William III and a collateral branch of the House of Nassau became the ruling line. In both world wars the country was occupied by the Germans. In 1922 it entered into a customs union with Belgium and in 1948 the two countries with the Netherlands formed the Benelux Customs Union. There is a 21-member Council of State nominated by the Grand Duke and a 60-member Chamber of Deputies elected every five years.

2. Cap. in the S of Luxembourg, equidistant from the German, French and Belgian frontiers. Pop. (1991) 75,377. The old town is on a rocky height within a loop of the Alzette R; later suburbs spread westward into the valley. The original massive fortifications separating the two have been replaced by parks.

The city has diverse industries in the suburbs, notably iron to the N. It is also a centre of banking and of transport. The European Parliament and Court of Justice are here.

Founded as a Roman fortress, the city was an important strongpoint of great strategic value until 1867, when its fortifications were taken down. It retained its commercial importance and began its present role in the European Community as the seat of the

European Coal and Steel Community in 1952.

Luxembourg Belgium. Province in the SE in the Ardennes. Area 4440 sq km (1714 sq. miles). Pop. (1991) 238,813. Cap. Arlon. Largely wooded with some agriculture. Iron ore mined in the extreme S.

Luxor (Uqsur) Egypt. Town situated SSW of Qena on the E bank of the Nile R. Pop. (1986) 125,404.

Centre of an agricultural area; industries inc. pottery and sugar-refining.

Noted for the ruins of ancient Thebes inc. the temple built by Amenhotep III. ➤➤THEBES, EGYPT.

Luzern ➤LUCERNE.

Luzhou (Luchou/Luchow) China. Formerly Luhsien. River port and commercial town in Sichuan province at the confluence of the Chang Jiang and the To-kiang 137 km (85 miles) WSW of Chongqing. Pop. (1990) 262,892. It trades in sugar, salt and tung oil.

Luzon Philippines. Largest and most important island of the archipelago in the N. Area 104,688 sq km (40,320 sq. miles). Pop. (1989) 29,500,000. Largely mountainous, it rises to 2932 m (9617 ft) in Mt Pulog. In the fertile Cagayan valley rich crops of rice, abacá, sugar-cane and tobacco are produced. Chief mineral chrome ore. Has the old cap. Manila and the new cap. Quezon City.

Lviv ➤LVOV.

Lvov (Lviv) Ukraine. City and cap. of the Lvov Region 480 km (300 miles) WSW of Kiev. Pop. (1991) 802,000.

Communications and industrial centre. Oil-refining, motor-vehicle assembly. Manufactures agricultural machinery, railway equipment, textiles, chemicals, glass and clothing.

Roman Catholic, Armenian and Greek cathedrals. University (1661). Founded in the 13th cent. Became cap. of the Austrian province of Galicia 1772. Returned to Poland 1919. Ceded to the USSR 1945.

Lyallpur ➤FAISALABAD.

Lydd England. Town in S Kent 11 km (7 miles) E of Rye (Sussex) and a 'member' of the Cinque Port of New Romney, though now 5 km (3 miles) from the sea. Pop. (1990) 5000. Gave its name to the explosive lyddite, first tested here.

Lydda ➤LOD.

Lydia. Ancient country on the W coast of Asia Minor which became a wealthy kingdom in the 7th cent. BC, its cap. at Sardis. Its last king was Croesus, who was conquered by Cyrus the Great of Persia (546 BC).

Lyme Regis. England. Seaside resort in W Dorset on Lyme Bay. Pop. (1991) 3,851. Small port. Has a picturesque harbour and curved breakwater, known as the Cobb, the scene of Monmouth's landing (1685). Here was discovered the first ichthyosaurus (1811).

Lymington England. Town in SW Hampshire at the mouth of the R. Lymington on the Solent. Pop. (1991) 13,508.

Holiday resort. Yacht-building. Ferry service to the Isle of Wight.

Lynchburg USA. Town in Virginia on the James R. 71 km (44 miles) ENE of Roanoke. Pop. (1990) 66,049. In a picturesque location in the foothills of the Blue Ridge. An important market for tobacco.

Manufactures footwear, textiles, clothing and metal goods.

Named after John Lynch, Quaker of Irish origin, who established a ferry (1757) and built a tobacco warehouse on the hill.

Lynmouth ➤LYNTON.

Lynn USA. Industrial town and port in E Massachusetts on an arm of Massachusetts Bay. Pop. (1990) 81,245.

Noted as a centre of footwear manufacture dating from 1636. Also manufactures electrical equipment and shoemakers' tools.

First settled in 1629 as Saugus. Renamed in 1637, after Lynn Regis (King's Lynn), England, the home of the town's pastor.

Lynton England. Village and resort in N Devon 19 km (12 miles) E of Ilfracombe near the Bristol Channel. Pop. (1989) 2000. Lynton is on a cliff 131 m (430 ft) above Lynmouth which has a harbour and is at the mouth of the E and W Lyn rivers. Near by is the Doone Valley, described in R. D. Blackmore's *Lorna Doone*. In 1952 31 people were killed and much damage was caused in Lynmouth when the R. Lyn flooded.

Lyonnais France. Former province bounded on the E by the Saône and Rhône rivers and on the W by the Monts du Forez. United to the crown 1307. Became the Rhône-et-Loire department 1790 and the present departments of Rhône and Loire 1793.

Lyon (Eng. **Lyons**) France. Ancient Lugdunum. Cap. of the Rhône department and the third largest city in France at the confluence of the Rhône and Saône rivers. Pop. (1990) 424,444.

A leading textile centre from the 15th cent., specializing in silk manufacture, largely replaced in recent years by rayon, nylon and other synthetic fibres. Engineering. Also manufactures cars, cables, chemicals (esp. those used in the textile industry), hosiery, clothing and pharmaceuticals.

Divided by the two rivers into the central area, the commercial and shopping quarter on the tongue of land between them; the old town, on the W bank of the Saône; and the new town, E of the Rhône, with residential and industrial suburbs. Within the central district are the 17th-cent. hôtel de ville and Palais des Arts, the 11th-cent. Church of St Martin d'Ainay (restored) and the 15th-cent. Church of St Nizier, and in the old town the 12th/15th-cent. Cathedral of St Jean and the Church of Notre Dame de Fourvière, perched on the hill of that name (293 m; 961 ft). Lyon is an important road and rail centre, a financial centre, with the headquarters of the Crédit Lyonnais, one of France's leading banks and a cultural centre. Founded (43 BC) as a Roman colony. The first place in Gaul to be converted to Christianity, in the 2nd cent. The silk industry was introduced by Italians. During the Revolution (1793) it was partly destroyed after an insurrection. Birthplace of Claudius (10 BC–AD 54), Ampère (1775–1836), Jacquard (1752–1834), inventor of the loom named after him, and the artist, Puvis de Chavannes (1824–98).

Lytham St Anne's England. Seaside resort in W Lancashire, consisting of Lytham, on the estuary of the R. Ribble and St Anne's, just WNW on the Irish Sea. Pop. (1991) 40,866.

Manufactures pharmaceutical products and footwear. Has a championship golf-course.

Lyubertsy Russia. Industrial town situated 19 km (12 miles) SE of Moscow. Pop. (1991) 164,900.

Manufactures machinery, electrical equipment and plastics.

M

Maas River ➤MEUSE RIVER.

Maastricht Netherlands. Cap. of Limburg province 24 km (15 miles) NNE of Liège (Belgium) on the Maas R. Pop. (1992) 118,152.

Railway and canal junction and industrial centre, of considerable strategic importance because of its proximity to the Belgian and German borders. Manufactures cement, textiles, glass, china and paper. Industries inc. brewing and tanning.

The Church of St Servatius, founded in the 6th cent., is the oldest in the country. It also has a town hall of the 15th cent. (now a museum) and a new town hall (17th-cent.). The Treaty on European Union was negotiated and signed here in 1992.

Mablethorpe England. Seaside resort in Lincolnshire 34 km (21 miles) SE of Grimsby. Pop. (1991) 9719.

McAllen USA. Town in S Texas 87 km (54 miles) WNW of Brownsville near the Rio Grande and the Mexican frontier. Pop. (1990) 84,000.

Commercial centre. Winter resort. Trade in citrus fruits and vegetables. Industries inc. oil-refining and food-processing.

Macao China. Portuguese overseas province in SE China 64 km (40 miles) W of Hong Kong, from which it is separated by the estuary of the Pearl or Canton R. Area 16 sq km (6 sq. miles). Pop. (1991) 467,000. Consists of the town of Macao and the small islands of Taipa and Colôane.

Considerable transit trade with China. Exports salted and fresh fish. Manufactures cement and metal goods. There is a considerable tourist trade.

Leased from China by the Portuguese 1557; recognized as Portuguese territory by China 1887. Declined in the late 19th cent. with the rapid development of Hong Kong. It is scheduled to be handed back to China in 1999.

Macapá Brazil. Cap. of the Amapá territory (NE) on the N channel of the Amazon delta. Pop. (1991) 175,000. On the Equator.

Trade in rubber and cattle.

Modern town with old fortifications. Manganese and iron mining to the NW.

Macassar (Makassar) ➤UJANG PANDANG.

Macclesfield England. Town in Cheshire on the R. Bollin 26 km (16 miles) SSE of Manchester. Pop. (1991) 50,270.

Important centre of the silk industry since the mid 18th cent. Also manufactures rayon, nylon and cotton goods, textile machinery, paper, pharmaceuticals and plastics.

To the E is the bleak moorland area of Macclesfield Forest.

Macdonnell Ranges Australia. System of mountain ranges in the S of the Northern Territory rising to nearly 1500 m (4920 ft) at the highest point. Alice Springs stands near a gap through the mountains.

Macduff Scotland. Small fishing port in Aberdeenshire on the Moray Firth at the mouth of the R. Deveron. Pop. (1991) 3894. Seaside resort.

Macedonia. Region in SE Europe to the NW of the Aegean Sea. Mainly mountainous, rising in several parts to over 2400 m (7872 ft).

Economy primarily pastoral (sheep and goats) and agricultural (tobacco and wheat).

An ancient kingdom, under Philip II it ruled the whole of Greece through his victory at Chaeronea (338 BC). By military conquest his son, Alexander the Great, extended the Macedonian Empire over Egypt, Asia Minor and Persia to India. After Alexander's death, however, the Empire disintegrated and in the 2nd cent. BC Macedonia itself was conquered by the Romans. In the 6th cent. AD it was permanently settled by Slavs. Passed to the Bulgarians and Serbs, and was held by the Turks from the 15th to the 20th cent. (1912).

Macedonia Greece. Division of N Greece and divided into the Regions of Macedonia Central, Macedonia East and Thrace, and Macedonia West, comprising the *nomes* of Chalcidice, Imathia, Kilkis, Mount Athos, Pella, Pieria, Serres, Thessaloniki, Cavalla, Drama, Evros, Rhodope, Xanthi, Florina, Grevena, Kastoria and Kozani. Area 42,755 sq km (16,507 sq. miles). Pop. (1991) 2,236,019.

Macedonia. Republic in SE Europe bounded in the N by Yugoslavia, E by Bulgaria, S by Greece and W by Albania. Area 25,713 sq km (9928 sq. miles). Pop. (1994) 1,936,877 (59 per cent urban). Life expectancy, 70 years male, 74 female. Cap. Skopje. Other cities Bitolj, Prilep and Kumanovo. Currency: Denar. Macedonia is mainly mountainous and practically comprises the basin of the upper Vardar river. It has a mixed Mediterranean–continental type climate, with cold, moist winters and hot, dry summers. Land use: forested 39 per cent, meadows and pastures 25 per cent, agricultural and under permanent cultivation 26 per cent. Most believers are Christian, mainly Eastern Orthodox Church and there is a considerable Muslim community. About 66 per cent are Macedonian, other groupings inc. Albanian, Turkish, Serb and Gypsy.

Chromium is mined near Skopje; other minerals mined are lead-zinc ore, copper and silver. Manufactures inc. ferro-alloys, refrigerators, buses, sulphuric acid, pharmaceuticals, cotton yarn, wood-pulp and detergents.

Slavs settled in Macedonia in the 6th cent. It became part of 'South Serbia' in 1918, later becoming a republic of the Socialist Federal Republic of Yugoslavia. Macedonia de-

clared its independence from Yugoslavia in 1992. Claims to the historical Macedonian territory have long been a source of contention with Bulgaria and Greece but in 1993 Macedonia became a member of the UN as 'Former Yugoslav Republic of Macedonia', a decision acceptable to Greece. There is a 120-member unicameral Parliament elected by universal suffrage and local government is administered by 34 communes.

Maceió Brazil. Cap. of the Alagôas state (NE) 193 km (120 miles) SSW of Recife. Pop. (1991) 628,209.

Exports cotton and sugar through Jaraguá harbour (just E). Sugar-refining, distilling and sawmilling. Manufactures textiles, soap and tobacco products.

Has many well-preserved colonial buildings and a lighthouse on a low hill near the middle of the town.

Macerata Italy. Cap. of Macerata province in The Marches 35 km (22 miles) S of Ancona. Pop. (1991) 44,000.

Market town. Manufactures musical instruments, agricultural machinery and textiles.

Stands on a hill over 300 m (984 ft) above sea level. Surrounded by medieval walls. University (1290).

Macgillicuddy's Reeks Ireland. Mountain range in Co. Kerry rising to 1041 m (3414 ft) in Carrantuohill, the highest peak in Ireland. Extends 11 km (7 miles) W from the Gap of Dunloe just W of the Lakes of Killarney.

Machala Ecuador. Town in El Oro situated S of Guayaquil and just NE of its port, Port Bolívar. Pop. (1990) 159,600.

Trading centre for an agricultural area handling cacao, coffee and hides.

Machilipatnam India. Port in Andhra Pradesh ESE of Hyderabad situated on the N side of Krishna R. delta. Pop. (1991) 159,007.

Industries inc. carpet-weaving, rice and cotton-milling. Groundnuts and castor seeds are exported.

Machu Picchu Peru. Ruined Inca city in the Cuzco department 88 km (55 miles) NW of Cuzco on a mountain saddle at a height of 2040 m (6691 ft). Terraced slopes descend to the Urubamba R. One of Peru's great tourist attractions. Discovered (1911) by Dr Hiram Bingham of Yale University.

Machynlleth Wales. Market town in Powys 11 km (8 miles) ENE of Aberdovey. Pop. (1991) 2033. Tourist centre. Owen Glendower summoned a parliament here in 1403.

Macías Nguema ➤BIOKO.

Mackay Australia. Port on the coast of Queensland 290 km (180 miles) NW of Rockhampton. Pop. (1991) 53,200.

Exports sugar and some copper and gold from nearby workings. Industries inc. sugar-refining and sawmilling.

Mackenzie Canada. The W mainland District of the Northwest Territories. Area 1,366,199 sq km (527,490 sq. miles). In the W are the Mackenzie Mountains, rising to over 2700 m (8856 ft). E of them is the valley of the Mackenzie R. Main lakes the Great Bear Lake and the Great Slave Lake. Oil produced and refined at Norman Wells. Gold mined in the Yellowknife district. Main occupation of the Indian and Eskimo inhabitants fur-trapping. The fisheries of the Great Slave Lake are also commercially important. Over 6000 reindeer are maintained in the Mackenzie delta region and 10,000 buffalo are protected in the Wood Buffalo National Park. Important trading posts inc. Fort Smith, Aklavik, Coppermine. Formed 1895; named after the Mackenzie R.

Mackenzie Guyana. Mining centre, collectively known as Linden, 108 km (67 miles) up the Demerara R. Pop. (1990) 35,000 together with Wismar and Christianburg situated on the bank of the river. In forest country near large deposits of bauxite, which is loaded on to ocean-going vessels for export.

Mackenzie River Canada. River 1770 km (1100 miles) long in the Northwest Territories, flowing from the Great Slave Lake generally NW to the Beaufort Sea of the Arctic Ocean, with a delta over 177 km (110 miles) long. Chief tributaries the Liard,

Peace, Athabaska and Slave rivers. The Mackenzie–Slave–Peace–Finlay rivers form a continuous waterway of more than 4000 km (2500 miles), the longest river system in Canada, of which over 3060 km (1900 miles) are navigable. The navigation season is from early June to mid October. Named after Sir Alexander Mackenzie (1764–1820), who explored the river to its mouth in 1789.

McKinley, Mount USA. Peak in central Alaska in the Alaska Range and the Mt McKinley National Park, the highest in N America (6182 m; 20,277 ft). Named (1896, by W. A. Dickey, a prospector) first Denali and then McKinley after President McKinley (1843–1901). First climbed (1913) by Hudson Stuck and his party.

McMurdo Sound ➤ROSS DEPENDENCY.

Mâcon France. Prefecture of the Saône-et-Loire department on the Saône R. 64 km (40 miles) N of Lyon. Pop. (1990) 35,500.

Commercial centre. Trade in Burgundy wine. Manufactures cognac, casks and hardware.

Birthplace of Lamartine (1790–1869).

Macon USA. Town in Georgia at the head of navigation on the Ocmulgee R. 120 km (75 miles) SE of Atlanta. Pop. (1990) 160,610. River port.

Manufactures clothing, chemicals and metal goods.

Seat of Mercer University (1833). Named after Nathaniel Macon (1758–1837), an American politician.

Macquarie Island Australia. Volcanic island 1290 km (800 miles) SE of Tasmania, to which it belongs, with a meteorological and scientific station established 1948, but otherwise uninhabited.

Macquarie River Australia. River 950 km (590 miles) long, rising in the Blue Mountains, New South Wales and flowing NW to the Darling R. through sheep-rearing and grain-growing country.

Macroom Ireland. Market town in Co.

Madeira

Cork on the Sullane R. 32 km (20 miles) W of Cork. Pop. (1986) 2500.

Trade in dairy produce, potatoes. Salmon and trout fishing centre.

Madagascar. Republic, and the fourth largest island in the world. It is situated in the Indian Ocean and separated from SE Africa by the Mozambique Channel. Area 587,041 sq km (226,658 sq. miles). Pop. (1995) 14,764,000 (24 per cent urban). Life expectancy, 55 years male, 58 female. Cap. Antananarivo. Other cities Toamasina, Antsirabe, Mahajanga, Fianarantsoa. Currency: Malagasy franc = 100 centimes. A plateau at a height of 900–1200 m (2952–3936 ft) extends NNE–SSW through the island and descends fairly steeply to the E coast and more gradually to the W. The volcanic massifs Tsaratanana and Ankaratra rise to nearly 3000 m (9840 ft). A chain of lagoons off the E coast is linked by the Canal des Pangalanes, forming an important trade route. Owing to the prevailing SE Trade Wind the E has a hot, wet climate; there are large areas of dense forest with valuable hardwoods. The plateau is mainly savannah. The distinctive flora (e.g. the remarkable traveller's palm) and fauna (esp. the lemurs) demonstrate the long separation from the African mainland. Zebu cattle are raised on the grasslands. It has a tropical climate, but the mountains cause large variations in rainfall which are heavy in the E and very light in the W. Land use: forested 40 per cent, meadows and pastures 41 per cent, agricultural and under permanent cultivation 5 per cent. The people are predominantly Malayo–Polynesian; the Hova (Merina) form over one-quarter of the pop. and the Nova lang. is spoken throughout the island. Of believers 51 per cent are Christian, traditional beliefs 47 per cent, Muslim 2 per cent.

Agriculture employs 80–85 per cent of the work force. Principal food crops are cassava, maize and rice. Cash crops are coffee, sugar-cane, tobacco, vanilla; these and surplus rice are the major exports. Chief mineral graphite. The few industries are based on agricultural products, e.g. meat-packing; processing sugar, rice and tapioca.

The Arabs had established settlements and profoundly influenced the native peoples cent. before the Portuguese explorer, Diego Diaz, discovered the island in 1500. Both France and Britain sought to influence the Hova monarchy in the 19th cent. Opposition to France's demands led to French occupation and Madagascar and its dependencies were declared a French colony in 1896. It became an overseas territory of the French Union in 1946, a member of the French Community in 1958 and (as the Malagasy Republic) achieved full independence in 1960. A Third Republic was instituted in 1993 with a 138-member National Assembly. There are six provinces each governed by an elected council.

Maddalena Island Italy. Island 21 sq km (8 sq. miles) in area, largest of the archipelago off the NE coast of Sardinia. Pop. (1985) 11,000. Chief town and port La Maddalena, formerly an important naval base. Fishing. Maddalena is linked by causeway with the neighbouring island of Caprera, which attracts visitors to see Garibaldi's home and tomb.

Madeira N Atlantic Ocean. Ancient Insulas Purpurariae ('Purple Islands'). Volcanic archipelago 640 km (400 miles) W of the coast of Morocco, forming the Madeira Antonomous Region of Portugal. Total area 794 sq km (306 sq. miles). Pop. (1993) 253,800. Cap. Funchal. Two inhabited islands: Madeira, Porto Santo. Two uninhabited groups: the Deserta Is., the Selvagen Is. Madeira (the largest island and by far the most important) is mountainous, rising in the Pico Ruivo to 1862 m (6107 ft). Luxuriant vegetation. The picturesque rugged basalt peaks, deep wooded ravines and precipitous sea cliffs, with the exceptionally mild climate, have made it a world-renowned health and tourist resort. The lower slopes are carefully terraced and irrigated.

Principal crops vines (for Madeira wine), sugar-cane, early vegetables for the European market; also bananas, pineapples and other

551

fruit. Dairy cattle raised. Oxen are widely used as draught animals. Abundant fish, esp. tunny and mackerel. Embroidery work is done by the women and wickerwork by the men.

The islands were probably known to the Romans. Rediscovered (uninhabited) by João Gonçalvez Zarco, who sighted Porto Santo in 1418, brought settlers on the orders of Prince Henry the Navigator and discovered Madeira in 1420. Portuguese colonization proceeded rapidly; Funchal was founded in 1421. Madeira was twice occupied by the British (1801, 1807–14).

Madeira River Brazil. River 3200 km (2000 miles) long (with the Mamoré) in the NW, formed by the union of the Mamoré and the Beni rivers near the Bolivia–Brazil frontier, flowing NE and joining the Amazon R. 137 km (85 miles) E of Manaus.

Madeleine, La France. Site of archaeological importance in the Dordogne department on the Vézère R., giving its name to the Magdalenian culture. Near by are other sites, inc. the Cro-Magnon and Le Moustier caves.

Madhya Pradesh India. Largest state of the Indian Union, mainly on the N Deccan plateau, bounded on the N by Uttar Pradesh. Area 443,446 sq km (173,221 sq. miles). Pop. (1991) 66,135,862 (mainly Hindi-speaking). Cap. Bhopal. In the W it is crossed by the Vindhya and Satpura ranges; most of the state is at an altitude of more than 300 m (984 ft). Drained to the W by the Narmada R. and to the E by the Mahanadi. Monsoon climate with 100–125 cm (40–50 ins.) of rain annually. About 80 per cent of the pop. is dependent on agriculture.

Principal crops rice, pulses, wheat, oilseeds and cotton. More than one-quarter of the state is covered by forests, which are the chief source of teak in India. Madhya Pradesh supplies the greater part of India's manganese ore; coal, bauxite, limestone and iron ore also mined. Industries inc. aluminium, steel, paper, newsprint, cables, fertilizers and electronic goods.

Chief towns Indore, Gwalior, Jabalpur,

Ujjain, Raipur. Formed originally from the Central Provinces and Berar, Madhya Pradesh became a constituent state under its present name in 1950 and was much enlarged, absorbing most of the former state of Madhya Bharat in 1956.

Madison USA. State cap. of Wisconsin on the isthmus between L. Mendota and L. Monona 121 km (75 miles) W of Milwaukee. Pop. (1990) 191,262.

Commercial centre for a rich dairy-farming region. Manufactures electrical equipment, machinery and footwear.

Seat of the University of Wisconsin (1848) on the wooded shores of L. Mendota. Named after US President Madison (1751–1836).

Madiun Indonesia. Town in Java 145 km (90 miles) WSW of Surabaya. Pop. (1990) 165,999.

Commercial centre in a region producing sugar-cane, rice and coffee. Industries inc. railway engineering.

Madras ▶TAMIL NADU. Cap. of Tamil Nadu, the fourth largest city of India on the Coromandel Coast. Also known as Chennai. Pop. (1991) 3,841,400. Chief seaport of Tamil Nadu and the third leading seaport of India.

Exports hides and skins, groundnuts and cotton. It is also an industrial centre with engineering works. It manufactures cement, chemicals, textiles, clothing, petrochemicals, fertilizers, automobiles, plastics, brake systems, tyres and sugar.

University (1857). The main commercial section, George Town, lies W of the harbour, while the residential districts are largely in the S, where, too, is the Roman Catholic cathedral of S Thomé, traditional burialplace of St Thomas. Founded by the British East India Company (1640) as Fort St George.

Madre de Dios River Bolivia/Peru. River 960 km (600 miles) long rising in the Cordillera de Carabaya in SE Peru, flowing N and NE and joining the Beni R. in N Bolivia.

Madrid Spain. 1. Province in central Spain in New Castile. Area 7995 sq km (3089 sq.

miles). Pop. (1991) 4,845,851. Lies on the dry central plateau or Meseta, with the Sierra de Guadarrama rising to 2470 m (8102 ft) on its NW boundary and the Tagus (Tajo) R. in the extreme S.

2. Cap. and largest city of Spain and of Madrid province near the centre of the peninsula at a height of about 640 m (2099 ft) on the small Manzanares R. Pop. (1991) 2,909,792. Spain's chief centre of communications by road, rail and air. Also an industrial centre.

Industries inc. flour-milling and printing. It manufactures aircraft, electrical equipment, agricultural machinery and leather goods.

Because of its altitude and its exposed situation, the city has a rigorous continental climate, with hot summers and cold winters. Situated on the E bank of the river, the palace marks the centre of the old city, much cleared and expanded since. Eastward lies the banking, shopping and business district, its broad avenues crossing the main N–S boulevard; the latter is four miles long and generously planted with trees, the Prado museum lying at its S end. There is parkland E of the Prado and more along the river round University City in the NW quarter. The main northward expansion (1872) is the smart Salamanca district. The city first extended W of the river in 1948; modern expansion has been rapid. The traditional working-class district S of the Plaza Mayor has stretched southwards, with large housing estates on reclaimed marshes. As well as government, Madrid is active in banking and finance, in tourism and in industries of which manufacturing is the most recent. The city has always been a centre of transport and is the hub of Spanish railways.

A Moorish fort, Madrid was taken by a Christian Spanish force in 1083, a Moorish quarter surviving. The tiny city expanded eastward under a succession of kings for whom it proved a convenient central headquarters. It remained the Castilian royal seat until Philip III made it the national cap. in 1607. The first big expansion followed, notably the Plaza Mayor; this eastward push

had reached the Plaza de la Independencía by 1788. The Gran Via of the city centre (Avenida José Antonio) was created in 1910. The city suffered in the Civil War (1936–9) but all damage has been repaired. It withstood the Nationalist siege for 2½ years.

Madura Indonesia. Island off the NE coast of Java. Area 4564 sq km (1762 sq. miles). Pop. (1990) 2 million. It has an undulating surface rising to over 450 m (1475 ft).

Salt, rice, maize and cassava are produced. Cattle-rearing is important.

Madurai India. Formerly Madura. Industrial town in Tamil Nadu on the Vaigai R. 426 km (265 miles) SW of Madras. Pop. (1991) 941,000.

Manufactures textiles, brassware, tyres, automotive components and clothing.

It has a mainly 16th-cent. temple noted for its elaborate carving and ancient palaces. Cap. of the Pandya dynasty from the 5th cent. BC to the 14th cent. AD.

Maeander ➤MENDERES.

Maebashi Japan. Cap. of the Gumma prefecture 105 km (65 miles) NW of Tokyo. Pop. (1990) 286,261. Centre of sericulture and the silk industry. University (1949).

Maelström Norway. Name originally applied to the strong tidal current, Moskenstraumen, in the Lofoten Is. between Moskenesöy and Mosken, its danger having been considerably exaggerated. Later applied to strong whirlpools elsewhere.

Maesteg Wales. Town in Bridgend County Borough 8 km (5 miles) E of Port Talbot. Pop. (1991) 21,966. In a former coalmining district; last coal mine in the area closed in 1985. Dormitory town for steel works at Port Talbot. Manufactures cosmetics, porcelain, vehicle parts and clothing.

Mafeking (Mafikeng) South Africa. Town near the frontier of Botswana. Formerly the Bechuanaland Protectorate's extra-territorial administrative headquarters. Pop. (1990) 7000. Commercial centre. Railway engineering.

During the Boer War a British force (under Baden Powell) was besieged for seven months (1899–1900); the rejoicings when the siege was raised gave the English lang. the verb 'to maffick'.

Mafikeng ➤MAFEKING.

Magadan Russia. Seaport and airport in the Khabarovsk Territory on the N side of the Sea of Okhotsk. Pop. (1989) 152,000. Industries inc. ship-repairing and fishing. Founded 1932.

Magadi, Lake Kenya. Lake 48 km (30 miles) long in the Great Rift Valley 80 km (50 miles) SW of Nairobi near the Tanzania frontier. Carbonate of soda is extracted. Magadi town is on the E shore.

Magallanes ➤TIERRA DEL FUEGO.

Magdalena River Colombia. The most important river in Colombia 1530 km (950 miles) long, rising in the Central Cordillera in the Cauca department, flowing N and entering the Caribbean. The upper river soon descends, to follow a wide level-floored rift valley between the Central and the E Cordilleras, emerges to wind sluggishly across a marshy plain and falls only 60 m (197 ft) in the last 160 km (100 miles). Ships travel 920 km (570 miles) to the rapids near Honda, above which the river is navigable to Neiva. Carries a large proportion of Colombia's trade. Oilfield in the lower middle valley. Coffee-growing is important on the slopes of the upper middle valley.

Magdalen Islands Canada. Group of 16 islands in the Gulf of St Lawrence in Quebec. Area 264 sq km (102 sq. miles). Pop. (1971) 13,305 (largely French-Canadian stock). Main occupation fishing (lobsters, herring, cod and mackerel).

Magdeburg Germany. Cap. of Saxony-Anhalt on the Elbe R. 129 km (80 miles) WSW of Berlin. Pop. (1990) 277,200. Railway and industrial centre in an important sugar-beet growing region.

Industries inc. sugar-refining. Manufactures machinery, paper, textiles, chemicals and glass.

Stands at the E end of the Weser–Elbe Canal, which opened in 1938, completed the Mittelland Canal across Germany and increased the commercial importance of Magdeburg. The cathedral (13th/16th-cent.) is a mixture of Romanesque and Gothic architecture. Magdeburg was a leading member of the Hanseatic League and its local laws, the Magdeburger Recht, were long the model for other European cities. During the Thirty Years War it was almost completely destroyed (1631).

Magelang Indonesia. Town in central Java 37 km (23 miles) NNW of Jogjakarta. Pop. (1980) 123,500.

Commercial centre in a region producing rice, sugar-cane and tobacco.

Magellan Strait Chile. Winding strait 595 km (370 miles) long and 3–32 km (2–20 miles) wide between the mainland of South America and Tierra del Fuego, connecting the S Pacific with the S Atlantic. Discovered in 1520 by Magellan. Punta Arenas is the only important town.

Magenta Italy. Town in Lombardy. Pop. (1990) 23,800. Battle in 1859 in which the Austrians defeated the French and Sardinian armies. The colour magenta was given as an honour to the town after the victory.

Maggiore, Lake Italy. Ancient Verbanus Lacus. Lake in Lombardy, with the N end in Ticino canton, Switzerland. Area 212 sq km (82 sq. miles). Through it flows the Ticino R. and in the SW are the Borromean Is. Surrounded by mountains, on whose terraced slopes vines and olives are grown. Around its shores are the resorts of Locarno, Pallanza and Stresa.

Maghreb Africa. The states of Algeria, Morocco, Tunisia, Libya and Mauritania.

Magnesia Greece. *Nome* of SE Thessaly bounded SW by the Orthrys mountains and inc. the Northern Sporades Is. except Skyros. Area 2636 sq km (1018 sq. miles). Cap. Volos. Pop. (1991) 198,434.

Farming area producing olives, citrus fruit, cereals, tobacco, almonds and livestock. Fisheries are important on the Gulf of Volos.

Magnitnaya, Mount Russia. Mountain 600 m (1968 ft) high in the S Urals. Rich deposits of magnetite iron ore, supplied to Magnitogorsk.

Magnitogorsk Russia. Industrial town in the Chelyabinsk Region 209 km (130 miles) SW of Chelyabinsk on the upper Ural R., here dammed to supply water. Pop. (1989) 440,000.

A major metallurgical centre using magnetite iron ore from nearby Mt Magnitnaya, coal from the Kuznetsk and Karaganda basins and other raw materials from the Urals and elsewhere. It was first developed in 1929 and now has a massive complex of blast furnaces, open-hearth furnaces, steel mills and coke batteries. Also manufactures machinery, fertilizers, cement and clothing.

Mahaila el Kubra Egypt. Town on the Nile delta 105 km (65 miles) N of Cairo. Pop. (1990) 358,844.

Important cotton-manufacturing centre. Cotton, cereals and rice are cultivated in the region.

Mahajanga (Majunga) Madagascar. Town and second seaport on the NW coast at the mouth of the Betsiboka R. 370 km (230 miles) NNW of Antananarivo. Pop. (1990) 121,967.

Industries inc. meat-packing, rice preparation. Manufactures cement, soap. Exports coffee, raffia, sugar, rice and vanilla.

Mahanadi River India. River 880 km (550 miles) long, rising in S Madhya Pradesh 120 km (75 miles) S of Raipur, flowing generally NNE and then ESE, crossing Orissa and entering the Bay of Bengal by a broad delta below Cuttack. Used for irrigation mainly in the delta area.

Maharashtra India. Constituent state of the Indian Union, formed in 1960 from the S and E parts of the former Bombay state; mainly on the Deccan plateau, with a narrow coastal plain W of the Western Ghats facing the Arabian Sea. Area 311,295 sq km (120,191 sq. miles). Pop. (1991) 78,748,215 (60 per cent Marathi-speaking). Cap. Bombay. Chief rivers the Godavari and the Krishna, which flow SE to the Bay of Bengal.

Most of the people are engaged in agriculture; chief crops millets, rice, cotton, sugarcane, oranges, groundnuts, and the state has significant oil and gas reserves. The main industrial centres are Bombay, Pune, Nashik, Thane, Aurangabad, Nagpur, Sholapur and Kolhapur. Industries inc. aeronautics, automobiles, shipbuilding, oil-refining, petrochemicals, fertilizers, chemicals, pharmaceuticals, electronic goods, plastic-processing, paper, heavy engineering and textiles.

Maiden Castle England. Prehistoric hill fortress in S Dorset 3 km (2 miles) SW of Dorchester, occupying about 49 ha (121 acres), the finest ancient earthwork in Britain. Excavations in 1934 showed that it was occupied in the Neolithic period, c. 2000 BC. Later there was a fortified Iron Age village, taken by the Romans in AD 43.

Maidenhead England. Town in Windsor and Maidenhead on the R. Thames 40 km (25 miles) W of London. Pop. (1991) 59,605.

A boating centre, mainly residential. Industries inc. brewing, boatbuilding, publishing and chemicals.

Maidstone England. Town in Kent on the R. Medway 48 km (30 miles) ESE of London. Pop. (1991) 90,878.

Manufactures paper, confectionery and cement.

Has the 14th-cent. All Saint's Church, a 15th-cent. former archbishop's palace and a 16th-cent. mansion (museum), Cobtree Manor, the 'Dingley Dell' of Dickens's *Pickwick Papers* is 3 km (2 miles) N. Birthplace of William Hazlitt, English essayist (1778–1830).

Maiduguri Nigeria. Town in the NE 500 km (310 miles) E of Kano. Pop. (1992) 289,100 (inc. the nearby town of Yerwa).

Market town. Trade in groundnuts, cotton and gum arabic.

Maikop Russia. Cap. of the Adygei Republic in the Krasnodar Territory on the Belaya R. 96 km (60 miles) SE of Krasnodar. Pop. (1990) 149,000.

Industrial centre. Manufactures food and tobacco products, furniture and leather. To the SW are the Maikop oilfields. Founded 1858.

Main–Danube Canal. Canal of 171 km (107 miles) linking the rivers Main and the Danube, opened in 1992, part of the 3500-km (2188-mile) continuous navigable waterway from Rotterdam in the Netherlands to Constanza on the Black Sea in Romania.

Mai-Ndomde, Lake Democratic Republic of the Congo. Lake in the W 129 km (80 miles) long N–S and 48 km (30 miles) wide at its N end, shallow and irregular in shape. Fed chiefly by the Lokoro and the Lukenye rivers. Drains into the Kasaï R. via the Fimi R. Discovered in 1882 by H. M. Stanley, Welsh explorer and journalist.

Maine France. Former province, divided in 1790 to form the present departments of Mayenne and Sarthe and parts of Eure-et-Loir and Orne; the cap. was Le Mans. Passed to the crown 1481.

Maine USA. State in the extreme NE, the largest of the New England states. Area 86,027 sq km (33,215 sq. miles). Pop. (1990) 1,227,928. Cap. Augusta. Hilly in the W, it rises to 1607 m (5271 ft) in Mt Katahdin. Features resulting from glaciation inc. many beautiful lakes, e.g. Moosehead Lake (303 sq km; 117 sq. miles). Chief rivers the Penobscot, the Kennebec, the Androscoggin and the St John. Climate humid continental, with cold winters, short, warm summers. Annual rainfall 100–110 cm (40–42 ins.). Forestry important. Many sawmills and pulp mills. Leading state for potatoes, grown chiefly in the Aroostook valley. Other crops oats, hay, apples, blueberries. Herring 'sardines' and lobsters are caught. There are many flourishing tourist resorts in the lake and woodland regions. Main cities Portland, Lewiston, Bangor. After abortive attempts at settlement by the French, an English settlement was established (1607) near Phippsburg. Annexed by Massachusetts in 1652, Maine was part of it until 1820. The boundary with Canada was finally settled by the Webster–Ashburton Treaty (1842). Admitted to the Union in 1820 as the 23rd state.

Maine-et-Loire France. Department formed in 1790 from S Anjou. Area 7131 sq km (2787 sq. miles). Pop. (1990) 705,900. Prefecture Angers. Generally low-lying and extremely fertile. Drained by the Loire and its tributaries, the Mayenne, Sarthe and Loir. Produces vines, fruits and cereals. Chief towns Angers, Saumur and Cholet.

Main River Germany. River 515 km (320 miles) long formed by the union of the White Main and the Red Main near Kulmbach, flowing generally W, but with wide bends, past Würzburg, Aschaffenburg and Frankfurt to join the Rhine R. just above Mainz. Navigable for about 354 km (220 miles). Linked with the Danube R. via the Ludwig Canal.

Mainz Germany. Cap. of Rhineland-Palatinate on the left bank of the Rhine R. opposite the confluence with the Main R. Pop. (1990) 180,800.

River port. Industrial and commercial centre. Manufactures chemicals, machinery, furniture, textiles, optical glass and food products. Trade in wine, timber and grain.

Seat of a university, founded 1477, suppressed 1798 and revived 1946. The cathedral, founded in the 10th cent. but frequently burned and rebuilt, was finally restored in the 19th cent.; this and the 17th-cent. electoral palace were severely damaged in World War II. The town grew round a Roman camp and by the Middle Ages was an important commercial centre. An archbishopric from the 8th cent. until the early 19th cent. Birthplace of Johann Gutenberg (1398–1468), the printer.

Maison-Alfort France. Suburb of SE Paris, the Val-de-Marne department. Pop. (1990) 54,065. Manufactures cement, soap and furniture.

Maitland Australia. Town in New South

Wales on the Hunter R. 24 km (15 miles) NW of Newcastle. Pop. (1991) 41,600. Industrial centre with a declining coalmining industry. Railway junction. Manufactures textiles and clothing.

Majorca (Sp. **Mallorca**) Spain. Ancient Balearis Major. Largest of the Balearic Is. in the W Mediterranean between Minorca and Ibiza (Iviza). Area 3639 sq km (1405 sq. miles). Cap. and chief seaport Palma. A range of mountains along the NW coast, rising to 1446 m (4743 ft) in Puig Mayor, shelters the island from northerly winds and its mild climate and luxurious vegetation have made it popular with holiday-makers. Main occupation agriculture. Olives, vines, almonds, wheat, citrus fruits cultivated. Limestone caves.

Majuba (Amajuba) Hill South Africa. In Zulu, 'Hill of Doves'. Mountain 1950 m (6396 ft) high in the Drakensburg situated 14 km (9 miles) S of Volksrust, overlooking the Laing's Nek pass. During the Boer War of 1880–1 it was the scene of the defeat of the British by a Boer force under Piet Joubert (1881).

Majunga ➤MAHAJANGA.

Makassar ➤MACASSAR.

Makeyevka Ukraine. Formerly Dmitriyevsk. Industrial city in the Donbas. Pop. (1991) 424,000. Once a suburb of Donetsk (formerly Stalino), now a major coalmining and metallurgical centre. Iron and steel works, coking plants. Manufactures machinery and footwear.

Makhachkala Russia. Formerly Petrovsk. Cap. of the Dagestan Republic. Port on the Caspian Sea. Pop. (1989) 315,000. Linked by pipeline with the Grozny oilfield.

Industries inc. oil-refining, shipbuilding, railway engineering and food-processing. Manufactures textiles and footwear. Crude oil and petroleum products are shipped to the Volga. Founded 1844.

Makran. Coastal region of Baluchistan on the Arabian Sea, mostly in Pakistan, but ex-

tending into Iran. Apart from the Kej valley (dates), a barren area with the Makran Coast Range and the Central Makran Range inland. Chief port Gwadar. The former princely state of Makran acceded to Pakistan in 1948.

Malabar (Malabar Coast) India. Coastal region in the SW extending roughly from Goa SSE to Cape Comorin and inland to the Western Ghats, now mainly in Kerala. Chief ports Cochin, Kozhikode (Calicut). Chief products rice, coconuts, spices. The first part of India to be visited by Europeans inc. Vasco da Gama.

Malacca ➤MELAKA.

Malacca, Strait of. Channel between the Malay Peninsula and Sumatra, connecting the Indian Ocean with the South China Sea, with Singapore at its S end; narrows to 40 km (25 miles) just NW of Melaka.

Málaga Spain. 1. Province in Andalusia bordering S on the Mediterranean Sea. Area 7276 sq km (2813 sq. miles). Pop. (1991) 1,140,717. Largely mountainous, rising to about 2100 m (6888 ft). Drained chiefly by the Guadalhorce R. Olives, grapes, almonds and figs grown on fertile lowlands.

2. Ancient Malaca. Cap. of Málaga province on the coastal plain 109 km (68 miles) NE of Gibraltar. Pop. (1991) 512,136.

Seaport and industrial centre. Exports wine, raisins and fruit. Industries inc. sugar-refining, wine-making, inc. the sweet wine Malaga, distilling and brewing. Manufactures textiles and cement. On account of its mild winter climate it is also a popular resort. There are ferry links with Genoa, Italy and N Africa.

Among its old buildings are the ruined Alcázaba and Gibralfaro citadels and the Renaissance cathedral (16th/18th-cent.). Founded by the Phoenicians and held in turn by Carthaginians, Greeks, Romans, Visigoths and Moors to be taken in 1487 by Ferdinand and Isabella. Birthplace of Pablo Picasso, the painter (1881–1973).

Malagasy Republic ➤MADAGASCAR.

Malahide Ireland. Seaside resort in Co. Dublin. Pop. (1991) 700. Has a 12th-cent. castle.

Malakoff France. Suburb of S Paris in the Hauts-de-Seine department. Pop. (1985) 36,000.

Manufactures electrical equipment, pharmaceutical products and musical instruments.

Named after a fort captured by the French in the Crimean War.

Malang Indonesia. Town in E Java province 80 km (50 miles) S of Surabaya on a low plateau surrounded by volcanoes. Pop. (1990) 695,000.

Commercial centre. Trade in coffee, rice and sugar. Manufactures textiles.

Mälar, Lake (Swedish **Mälaren**) Sweden. Lake extending 117 km (73 miles) W from Stockholm, which stands on a narrow strait connecting it with the Baltic; very irregular in shape, with over 1200 islands. Its shores are a favourite residential area for Stockholm businessmen. Many old castles and palaces, inc. Gripsholm and Drottningholm.

Malatya Turkey. Ancient Melitene. Cap. of Malatya province just W of the Euphrates R. at a height of 870 m (2854 ft) 300 km (185 miles) NE of Adana. Pop. (1990) 304,760.

Commercial centre for a rich agricultural region. Trade in opium and grain. Mainly of military importance in Roman times.

Malaŵi. Republic in central Africa bounded by the W and S shores of L. Malaŵi (Nyasa), by Tanzania in the N and NE, Mozambique in the SE, S and SW and Zambia in the N. Area 94,276 sq km (36,400 sq. miles). Pop. (1995) 9,940,000 (11 per cent urban). Life expectancy, 45 years male, 46 female. Cap. Lilongwe. Other cities Blantyre and Mzuzu. Currency: Malaŵi kwacha = 100 tambala. Part of the Great Rift Valley is occupied by L. Malaŵi, the third largest lake in Africa and the Shiré R., its S outlet, which flows through the wedge-shaped S part of the country to the Zambezi R. The W highlands (average 1200 m (3936 ft)) rise to over 2400 m

(7782 ft) in the Nyika Plateau. The Shiré Highlands (SE) (average 750 m (2460 ft)), rise to 3048 m (10,000 ft) in Mt Mulanje. In the lower and marshy SE area bordering on Mozambique are L. Chiuta and L. Shirwa. Land use: forested 39 per cent, meadows and pastures 20 per cent, agricultural and under permanent cultivation 18 per cent. It is entirely within the tropics, but temperatures are considerably modified by the altitude. The rains, which are esp. abundant in the highlands, fall mainly Oct.–May. Of believers 64 per cent are Christian, those following traditional beliefs 19 per cent, Muslim 16 per cent. Of the ethnic composition over 58 per cent are Maravi and the official lang. is Chichewa, spoken by 50 per cent of the pop., and English.

Malaŵi is predominantly an agricultural country. Major export crops are tea, tobacco; also cotton, groundnuts, tung oil. Agricultural products account for 90 per cent of exports. Food crops beans, cassava, maize, millet, sugar, rice; also cotton. Coal has been mined since 1985. A railway runs from just N of Chipoka (on L. Malaŵi) through Blantyre–Limbe (chief commercial centre) to Beira in Mozambique.

Although visited by the Portuguese at a much earlier date, the country was not opened up to Europeans until David Livingstone, Scottish missionary (1813–73) had discovered L. Malaŵi in 1859. Missions were founded 1875–6; the first European settlements were established (in the Blantyre–Limbe area) a few years later. Britain intervened to suppress Arab slave trading and prevent a Portuguese attempt to annex the S highlands. The territory became the British Central Africa Protectorate in 1891; renamed the Nyasaland Protectorate in 1907. It joined Northern Rhodesia (now Zambia) and Southern Rhodesia (now Zimbabwe) in 1953 in the Federation of Rhodesia and Nyasaland. African nationalists demanded universal suffrage and majority rule; there were outbreaks of violence in 1959, followed by demands for independence in 1961. The Federation broke up in 1962. Nyasaland became a self-governing member of the British

Commonwealth in 1963 and (as Malaŵi) an independent member of the UN in 1964, becoming a republic in 1966. It was a one-party state until 1994 when a new Constitution came into force. There is a single chamber 177-member Parliament (National Assembly) and there are three Regions (Northern, Central and Southern) for local government.

Malaŵi, Lake. Formerly Lake Nyasa. Southernmost and third largest of Africa's great lakes, 560 km (350 miles) long N–S and 16–80 km (10–50 miles) wide W–E, in the S of the Great Rift Valley on the frontiers of Malaŵi (W and S), Mozambique (E) and Tanzania (NE and N), at a height of 475 m (1558 ft). Fed by the Songwe R. and other short streams (W) and by the Ruhuhu R. (NE). Drained periodically by the Shiré R. into the Zambezi R. Explored by David Livingstone, Scottish missionary and traveller in 1859.

Malaysia, Federation of. The federal state of Malaysia comprises the 11 states and 1 federal territory of peninsular Malaysia on the Malay peninsula, SE Asia, bounded in the N by Thailand and with the island of Singapore as an enclave on its S tip; and on the island of Borneo to the E, the state of Sabah (which inc. the federal territory of the island of Labuan) and the state of Sarawak, with Brunei as an enclave, both bounded in the S by Indonesia and in the NW and NE by the South China and Sulu Seas.

East Malaysia	Capital
Sabah	Kota Kinabalu
Sarawak	Kuching

Peninsular Malaysia	
Johor	Johor Baharu
Kedah	Alor Setar
Kelantan	Kota Baharu
Melaka	Melaka
Negeri Sembilan	Seremban
Pahang	Kuantan
Penang	Penang (Georgetown)
Perak	Ipoh
Perlis	Kangar
Selangor	Shah Alam
Terengganu	Kuala Terengganu

Federal Territories	
Kuala Lumpur	–
Labuan	–

Total area 329,748 sq km (127,316 sq. miles). Pop. (1995) 19,948,000 (54 per cent urban). Life expectancy 69 years male, 73 female. Cap. Kuala Lumpur. Other cities Ipoh, Johor Baharu, Melaka, Petaling Jaya. Currency: Ringgit (Malaysian dollar) = 100 cents. The dominating physical feature is a central range of mountains which rises to over 2100 m (6888 ft), but the highest peak in West Malaysia, Gunong Tahan 2192 m (7190 ft), is in another range farther E. These mountains are flanked by hills and coastal plains which are drained by innumerable rivers and streams; more than three-quarters of the land is covered with jungle. East Malaysia is covered with extensive jungle and swamp. The entire country lies within a few degrees of the equator and its climate is equatorial. It is affected by the monsoon climate, hot and humid throughout the year with abundant rainfall. Land use: 68 per cent forested, agricultural and under permanent cultivation 15 per cent. The official lang. is Malay and about 60 per cent of the pop. is Malay, 30 per cent Chinese and 10 per cent Indian. Malays who are of Mongolian origin are Muslims and the official religion is Islam; the large Chinese minority are mainly Buddhist, Confucian and Taoist, and the Indians are mainly Hindu by religion. In the heart of the jungle live small numbers of such aboriginal tribes as the Senoi.

A relatively prosperous country, largely dependent for its wealth on rubber, palm oil, tin and oil. The Malays are essentially peasant farmers who cultivate rice, vegetables and coconuts, but the most important agricultural product is rubber. Main exports are rubber, palm oil, timber, crude oil and tin.

From the 9th to the 14th cent. Malay was the centre of the Buddhist empire of Sri Vijaya, which was overthrown by the Hindu Javanese. The Muslim religion was introduced by traders from India, who found

Malacca an ideal entrepôt for the spice trade, in which, by the early 16th cent., they had almost gained a monopoly. In 1511 Malacca was taken by the Portuguese who were followed by the Dutch (1641) and the British (1824). Meanwhile Penang (1786) and Singapore (1819) were founded by the British and in 1826 the three territories became the Straits Settlements, which were ruled from India until 1867, when they were made a Crown Colony. British influence was extended over the native states, four of which were ceded by Siam (1909), and Malaya was divided into the Federated and Unfederated Malay States and the Straits Settlements. During World War II Malaya was occupied by the Japanese (1942–5) and afterwards the Federation of Malaya was created (1948), with Singapore a Colony; in 1965 Singapore seceded from Malaysia. Internal disorder, fomented particularly by Communist guerrillas operating in the jungle, continued for some years, but did not seriously impair the country's economic recovery. In 1963 the Federation of Malaysia was established, despite opposition from neighbouring Indonesia. By the constitution of 1956 (amended 1983) the hereditary rulers of the Malay states elect the *Yang di-Pertuan Agong,* Supreme Head of the Federation, from among themselves for a period of five years. The special interests of Sabah and Sarawak are recognized in the constitution. There is a 69-member Senate (*Dewan Negara*) and and 180-member House of Representatives (*Dewan Rakyat*).

Maldan USA. Residential suburb of N Boston, Massachusetts. Pop. (1985) 54,000.

Manufactures paint, radio and electronic equipment, rubber footwear, hosiery and furniture.

First settled 1640. Incorporated in 1649 as Mauldon, after Maldon (Essex, England), the home of many of the early settlers.

Malden and Coombe England. Former municipal borough in N Surrey 16 km (10 miles) SW of London, consisting of Old and New Malden and Coombe. Mainly residential. Merton College was founded here (1264) before being transferred to Oxford. Birth-

place (Coombe) of John Galsworthy, English novelist and playwright (1867–1933).

Maldives. The republic consists of about 1200 islands, of which 199 are inhabited, situated in the Indian Ocean 640 km (400 miles) SW of Sri Lanka. Area 298 sq km (115 sq. miles). Pop. (1995) 253,000 (30 per cent urban). Life expectancy, 65 years male, 62 female. Cap. Malé. Currency: Maldivian rufiyaa = 100 laari. They consist of 26 clusters of coral atolls, all low-lying, the highest point is 1.8 m (6 ft) above sea level. The islands are hot and humid and affected by monsoons. Land use: forested 3 per cent, meadows and pastures 3 per cent, agricultural and under permanent cultivation 10 per cent. The State religion is Sunni Muslim and the majority of the pop. is Sinhalese or Dravidian. The official and spoken lang. is Divehi.

The principal crops are coconuts, maize, cassava, sweet potatoes, onions and chillies, and the islanders are famed as fishermen and sailors. The chief export is Bonito (Maldive fish). Tourism is a major foreign currency earner.

Formerly a dependency of Ceylon (Sri Lanka), it became a British protected sultanate in 1948 and then an independent republic in 1968. The Gan air base was handed over to the republic by Britain in 1976. There is a 48-member Citizens' *Majlis* (Parliament), 8 members are nominated by the President and 40 directly elected. There are no political parties.

Maldon England. Market town in Essex on the R. Blackwater estuary at the mouth of the R. Chelmer 13 km (8 miles) E of Chelmsford. Pop. (1991) 15,841. Port. Resort.

Industries inc. flour-milling. Manufactures machinery, steel window frames and wood products.

Has a church with a 13th-cent. triangular tower. Beeleigh Abbey, with its remarkable chapter house, is 1.6 km (1 mile) W. Scene of a battle (991) in which Danish invaders defeated the Saxons.

Malé ►MALDIVES.

Malegaon India. Commercial town in Maharashtra on the Girna R. 250 km (155 miles) NE of Bombay. Pop. (1991) 342,400.

It trades in fabrics and grain, and manufactures textiles.

Mali. A land-locked republic in West Africa, bounded by Algeria in the NE, Niger in the E, Burkina Faso and Côte d'Ivoire in the S, Guinea in the SW, Senegal in the W and Mauritania in the NW. Area 1,248,574 sq km (482,077 sq. miles). Pop. (1995) 9,008,000 (26 per cent urban). Life expectancy, 45 years male, 48 female. Cap. Bamako. Other cities Ségou, Mopti, Sikasso and Gao. Currency: CFA franc = 100 centimes. The N comprises an extensive, almost uninhabited section of the Sahara. The S, mainly savannah, with a moderate rainfall, occupies much of the Upper and Middle Niger basin and the Upper Senegal basin. Over 90 per cent of the pop. are in the S. It has a tropical climate, with adequate rain in the S and W but conditions become increasingly arid to the N and E. Land use: forested 6 per cent, meadows and pastures 25 per cent, agricultural and under permanent cultivation 2 per cent. The official lang. is French and Bambara is spoken by about 80 per cent of the pop. About 90 per cent. are Muslim. The majority belong to tribes of the Mande group.

Chief crops cotton, groundnuts, maize, millet and rice. Chief exports cotton, groundnuts, dried fish, livestock (mainly sheep) and gold. Manufactures inc. food products, textiles and clothes, cement and pharmaceuticals. Mineral resources have not been exploited. A railway from Dakar in Senegal runs through Kayes and Bamako to Koulikoro. Steamers ply from Koulikoro to Timbuktu and Gao, and from Bamako to Kouroussa for seven months of the year.

It was occupied by the French at the end of the 19th cent. The Senegambia and Niger French Overseas Territories were established in 1902 and the Upper Senegal and Niger colony created from them in 1904 was renamed French Soudan in 1920. It became a member of the French Community in 1958 and a partner with Senegal in the Federation of Mali (1959–60). The Federation achieved independence in 1960 but Senegal seceded later that year and Mali declared itself an independent republic. It is a multiparty republic with a unicameral 116-seat National Assembly. For local government purposes the country is divided into the Capital district of Bamako and 8 regions.

Malines ➤MECHELEN.

Malin Head Ireland. Headland 69 m (226 ft) high in NE Co. Donegal at the N extremity of Inishowen peninsula; the northernmost point in Ireland.

Mallaig Scotland. Village, fishing port and railway terminus in Highland on the Sound of Sleat. Ferry services to Skye and the Hebrides.

Mallorca ➤MAJORCA.

Mallow Ireland. Market town and resort in Co. Cork on the R. Blackwater 29 km (18 miles) NNW of Cork. Pop. (1986) 6488.

Industries inc. sugar-refining, tanning, food-processing and salmon-fishing.

Malmédy ➤EUPEN AND MALMÉDY.

Malmesbury England. Market town in Wiltshire on the R. Avon 23 km (14 miles) WNW of Swindon. Pop. (1991) 4300.

Once famous for its silk and wood industries; now manufactures electronic and electrical equipment and vacuum cleaners.

The nave, now used as the parish church, is all that remains of the magnificent 12th-cent. Benedictine abbey church where Athelstan is buried. Birthplace of Thomas Hobbes, the philosopher (1588–1679).

Malmö Sweden. Cap. of Malmöhus county on The Sound 240 km (150 miles) SSE of Göteborg opposite Copenhagen (Denmark). Pop. (1992) 236,684.

Important seaport. Exports grain, timber and dairy produce. Linked by train ferry with Copenhagen. Industrial centre. Industries inc. shipbuilding, sugar-refining, engineering, brewing, textile and chemical manufactures.

Has a 14th-cent. church, a 16th-cent. town hall and the 15th/16th-cent. Malmöhus

Castle. Founded in the 12th cent. Part of Denmark until 1658.

Malta. Republic in the Mediterranean Sea about 96 km (60 miles) S of Sicily, comprising the islands of Malta (246 sq km; 95 sq. miles), Gozo (67 sq km; 26 sq. miles) and Comino (2.6 sq km; 1 sq. mile) and some inhabited islets. Area 316 sq km (122 sq. miles). Pop. (1995) 370,000 (89 per cent urban). Life expectancy, 73 years male, 78 female. Cap. Valletta. Currency: Maltese lira = 100 cents = 1000 mils. The island of Malta is oval in shape and generally hilly, rising to over 240 m (787 ft) in the S. Land use: agricultural and under permanent cultivation 41 per cent. English and Maltese are the official lang. and Italian is also commonly spoken. Of believers 98 per cent are Roman Catholic and 96 per cent of the pop. is Maltese.

A wide range of cereals and vegetables are cultivated despite the dry climate and shallow soil. Fishing is an important industry. Malta was for many years important as a British naval base, strategically placed about halfway between Gibraltar and Suez. Valletta stands on a peninsula which separates Grand Harbour and Marsamxett (Marsamuscetto) Harbour. The decline of Malta as a naval base has been partly offset by a considerable expansion of the tourist industry which, together with ship repair and shipbuilding, are the mainstays of the economy. Manufacturing on a small scale inc. food products, chemicals, clothing, electrical and electronic parts.

Malta has numerous megalithic remains, notably at Tarxien and was held in turn by Phoenicians, Greeks, Carthaginians and Romans; in 870 it was conquered by the Arabs, from whom it was taken by the Sicilian Normans in 1091. Charles V granted it in 1530 to the Knights of St John, afterwards known as the Knights of Malta, but the French gained possession in 1798. Following an appeal by the Maltese people, the island was annexed to Britain in 1814. During World War II Malta was ceaselessly bombed by enemy aircraft (1940–3) and for its gallantry was awarded the George Cross (1942). After World War II it was granted a measure of self-government and in 1964 it achieved independence, becoming a republic within the Commonwealth in 1974. There is a unicameral 65-member House of Representatives.

Maltby England. Town in Rotherham unitary area 10 km (6 miles) E of Rotherham. Pop. (1991) 18,158. Coalmining centre.

Malton England. Market town in North Yorkshire on the R. Derwent 27 km (17 miles) NE of York, consisting of Old and New Malton. Pop. (1991) 4294.

Industries inc. tanning, brewing and flour-milling. Limestone quarrying in the neighbourhood.

In Old Malton are the ruins of a 12th-cent. Gilbertine priory and there is a 16th-cent. grammar school.

Malvern England. Town in Worcestershire on the E slope of the Malvern Hills, consisting of Great Malvern, 11 km (7 miles) SSW of Worcester and the villages of Malvern Wells, Little Malvern, Malvern Link and W and N Malvern. Pop. (1991) 31,537. Spa and resort with medicinal springs. Ruins of an 11th-cent. Benedictine priory church; a public school (founded 1863). The annual dramatic festival (established 1928) is associated especially with the plays of G. B. Shaw, the Irish dramatist (1856–1950).

Malvern Hills England. Range about 13 km (8 miles) long extending N–S along the Herefordshire–Worcestershire border, rising to 425 m (1394 ft) in Worcestershire Beacon.

Malvinas, Islas ➤FALKLAND ISLANDS.

Mammoth Cave USA. A vast natural cavern, formed by the solution of limestone, in the Mammoth Cave National Park, S Kentucky. A series of subterranean caves on five levels, with high domes, underground lakes, stalactites and stalagmites, and many remarkable limestone formations. The principal cave is 38 m (125 ft) high and 12–90 m (39–295 ft) wide; 240 km (150 miles) of underground passages have been explored. There are blind fish 108 m (354 ft) below the surface in the Echo R., which empties into the Green R.

Mamoré River ►MADEIRA RIVER.

Man, Isle of. Island in the Irish Sea between Cumbria and Northern Ireland. Area 572 sq km (221 sq. miles). Pop. (1991) 69,788. Cap. Douglas. Generally hilly, with Snaefell reaching 620 m (2036 ft); off the SW coast is a small, detached island, the Calf of Man. Its equable climate and attractive scenery have made it popular with tourists, on whom the economy now largely depends. Chief towns Douglas, Ramsey, Peel, Castletown.

The Manx government controls direct taxation and the island has become a financial centre. Agriculture contributes 2 per cent of the island's GNP. Oats, barley, turnips and potatoes are the chief crops, and a large area is under grass, mainly for sheep and cattle.

The island has its own parliament, the Court of Tynwald, consisting of the Governor, with an Executive Council, the Legislative Council and the elected House of Keys; it is not bound by Acts of the Westminster Parliament unless specially mentioned in them. Ample evidence of prehistoric settlement on the island. Long a dependency of Norway until, with the Hebrides, it was ceded to Scotland (1266). Granted to the Stanley family (the earls of Derby) 1406; from them passed to the dukes of Atholl (1736) and then to the British Crown (1828). The Manx lang., akin to Gaelic, is now used only on ceremonial occasions.

Manaar, Gulf of ►MANNAR, GULF OF.

Manado (Menado) Indonesia. Cap. of N Sulawesi (Celebes) province near the E end of the NE peninsula. Pop. (1990) 275,374. Principal seaport of N Celebes.

Exports copra, coffee and nutmegs.

Managua Nicaragua. Cap. of the republic and of the Managua department on the SE shore of L. Managua. Pop. (1985) 682,211.

The country's largest city and administrative, trade and industrial centre. Manufactures textiles, cement, cigarettes and matches.

Seat of a Roman Catholic university

(1961). Became cap. in 1855. Largely destroyed by an earthquake in 1931 and badly damaged by fire in 1936, it was completely rebuilt. The city was again devastated by earthquake in 1972, with the loss of about 6000 lives.

Managua, Lake Nicaragua. Second largest lake in the republic 61 km (38 miles) long and 16–26 km (10–16 miles) wide, draining into L. Nicaragua by the Tipitapa R. Managua is on the SE shore.

Manama Bahrain. Cap., at the N end of the largest island, Bahrain. Pop. (1991) 136,999.

It is a banking and commercial centre and free transit port (since 1958). Oil-refining and also the centre of the much reduced pearl-fishing industry. There is boatbuilding and fishing.

Manasarowar Lake Tibet. Lake at a height of 4500 m (14,760 ft) in the W Himalayas in SW Tibet NNE of Gurla Mandhata (7733 m; 25,364 ft). Area 51 sq km (20 sq. miles). A Hindu place of pilgrimage.

Manáus Brazil. Cap. of the Amazonas state and chief inland trading port of the Amazon basin on the left bank of the Negro R. 19 km (12 miles) above the confluence with the Amazon, 1385 km (860 miles) WSW of Belém. Pop. (1990) 1,010,558. Accessible to ocean-going steamers.

Exports timber, rubber, Brazil nuts and other forest products. Jute-milling, oil-refining.

Founded 1660. Grew with the early 20th-cent. rubber boom and has recently established a free zone to encourage development in Amazonas and this inc. steelworks and an oil refinery. It has a famous botanical garden and has a tourist industry.

Mancha, La Spain. Former province in the S part of New Castile, now comprising Ciudad Real and parts of Albacete, Cuenca and Toledo provinces. An extensive, arid plateau of average altitude about 600 m (1967 ft) experiencing a harsh climate. Sparsely peopled. Some esparto grass, cereals and wine are produced. Because of its aridity, many windmills are used to supply water from underground sources. Made famous by Cervantes as the setting of adventures of Don Quixote de la Mancha.

Manche France. Department in Normandy bordering W, N and NE on the English Channel ('La Manche'). Area 6410 sq km (2296 sq. miles). Pop. (1990) 479,600. Prefecture St Lô. The Cotentin peninsula forms the N part and the W end of the Normandy Hills extends into the S. Dairy-farming is important. Apples and other fruits, cereals, vegetables are cultivated. The island of Mont St Michel attracts tourists. Chief towns Cherbourg and St Lô.

Manchester England. City in the NW 48 km (30 miles) E of Liverpool situated on the R. Irwell and the terminus of the Manchester Ship Canal, but in 1997 only one dock out of 8 left open. Now part of the metropolitan county of Greater Manchester. Area (Greater Manchester) 1289 sq km (498 sq. miles). Besides the city, Greater Manchester inc. a cluster of industrial centres, from Bolton to Stockport, Rochdale to Altrincham. The city itself, is a great commercial centre, at the heart of a vast conurbation. Pop. (Greater Manchester) (1994) 2,578,000; city, 431,200.

Important as the centre of the Lancashire cotton industry, it is concerned mainly with the business and warehousing aspects of the latter; some of its industries, e.g. the manufacture of textile machinery, dyestuffs and chemicals, are directly connected with textile milling. Also manufactures electrical equipment, rubber products, pharmaceuticals and paper. The construction of the Manchester Ship Canal (1887–94), giving it direct access to the sea, transformed it from an inland city into one of the country's leading seaports, importing raw cotton and exporting finished textiles.

Probably the site of the Roman fort of Mancunium (whence the name Mancunians for its inhabitants), Manchester was mentioned in the Domesday Book and received its first charter in 1301. It had a woollen industry as early as the 13th cent. and later became well-known for its linen and cotton

manufactures. In the mid 18th-cent., with the Industrial Revolution, came the immense growth of the cotton industry, for which Manchester had the advantages of nearness to the coalfields, a humid climate and abundant labour supply, and it became the hub of a network of roads, railways and canals. The first passenger railway in England was opened (1830) between Manchester and Liverpool with Stephenson's *Rocket*. Meanwhile, discontent largely caused by its non-representation in parliament led to political agitation, culminating in the 'Peterloo Massacre' at St Peter's Fields (1819). With the Reform Bill of 1832 it was given two MPs; it continued to be a centre of liberalism and was the headquarters of the Anti-Corn Law League. There are several noted libraries and art galleries and it is the home of the Hallé Orchestra (founded 1857). Birthplace of David Lloyd George, British statesman (1863–1945).

Manchester (Connecticut) USA. Industrial town on the Hockanum R. 13 km (8 miles) E of Hartford. Pop. (1970) 47,994.

Manufactures textiles (since the late 18th cent.), also electrical equipment and clothing.

First settled (1672) as part of Hartford; separated from the parent town in 1823.

Manchester (New Hampshire) USA. Largest town in the state on the Merrimack R. 26 km (16 miles) SSE of Concord. Pop. (1970) 87,754.

Industrial centre. Manufactures textiles, leather goods, electrical equipment.

The first cotton mill was established in 1805. Named after Manchester, England (1810). Remained the leading US cotton-manufacturing centre for about 100 years.

Manchester (New York) USA ➤NIAGARA FALLS USA.

Manchester Ship Canal England. Artificial waterway running 57 km (35½ miles) generally WSW from Manchester to the Mersey estuary at Eastham. Depth 8.5–9 m (28–30 ft). Bottom width 36 m (118 ft). Construction began in 1887 and it was opened in

1894, enabling ocean-going vessels to reach Manchester.

Manchukuo ➤MANCHURIA.

Manchuria China. Extensive region in the NE, now partly in the Autonomous Region of Nei Monggol and partly forming the provinces of Heilongjiang, Jilin and Liaoning. Consists of the great central Manchurian plain, watered by the Sungari and the Liao rivers, and flanked on the W and N by the Great Khingan, Ilkhuri and Little Khingan Mountains and on the E by the complex E Manchurian Mountains.

The central plain is extremely fertile, producing soya beans, kaoliang, millet, wheat, maize and rice. Large numbers of sheep, goats and other livestock are raised in the W. Valuable forests on the mountain slopes. Also rich in minerals, esp. coal and iron ore, which have led to the development of an important metallurgical industry in the S.

The Manchus, originally of nomadic Mongol–Tungus stock, conquered China in the 17th cent. and established the last imperial dynasty (1644), which persisted until 1911. In the late 18th cent. Chinese colonization of Manchuria began and by the end of the 19th cent. the Chinese formed 80 per cent of the pop.; today they form 90 per cent of the pop. and the Manchus are virtually absorbed. In 1898 Russia obtained the lease of Kwantung, at the tip of the Liaotung peninsula, but this passed to Japan after the Russo–Japanese War (1904–05). The Japanese, tempted by the agricultural and mineral wealth, occupied the whole of Manchuria in 1931 and in the following year set up the puppet state of Manchukuo. After the defeat of Japan in World War II, Manchuria was returned to China.

Mandalay Myanmar (Burma). The second largest city on the Irrawaddy R. 563 km (350 miles) N of Yangôn (Rangoon), with which it is linked by rail and river. Pop. (1983) 532,985.

Manufactures silk goods, gold and silver ware and matches.

Fort Dufferin, the old Burmese walled and moated city at its centre, contained the wooden royal palace, which was destroyed by fire during the Japanese occupation (1942–5). Many pagodas. University (1958). Founded 1857. Last cap. of the Burmese kingdom (1860–85) before annexation to British Burma.

Manfredonia Italy. Seaport in Foggia province, Apulia on the Gulf of Manfredonia 37 km (23 miles) NE of Foggia. Pop. (1985) 53,000.

Fishing. Manufactures leather goods and cement. Founded by King Manfred of Sicily c. 1263.

Mangalore India. Seaport in Karnataka on the Malabar coast 209 km (130 miles) WNW of Mysore. Pop. (1991) 281,200.

Exports coffee, cashew nuts, spices and iron ore. Manufactures tiles, textiles and hosiery. An oil refinery and steel plant are under construction.

Scene of a gallant defence by the English garrison against the army of Tippoo Sultan (1784).

Mangotsfield England. Town in South Gloucestershire just NE of Bristol. Pop. (1971) 23,268.

Manufactures clothing, footwear and confectionery.

Manhattan USA. Island in New York state, a borough of New York City. Area 57 sq km (22 sq. miles). Pop. (1990) 1,487,536. Bounded by the Harlem R. and Spuyten Duyvil Creek separating it from the Bronx (N), by the East R. separating it from the Queens and Brooklyn boroughs (E), by New York Bay (S) and by the Hudson R. separating it from New Jersey (W). Business and cultural centre of New York. The most notable educational institution is Columbia University (1745). Famous for its skyscrapers, inc. the Empire State Building (381 m, 1250 ft). Named after the Manhattan Indians, who sold it to the Dutch in 1626. It contained the whole of New York City till 1874 and became one of the boroughs of greater New York 1898.

Manila Philippines. Former cap. and chief seaport on Manila Bay in SW Luzon. Pop. (1990) 7,928,867.

Exports sugar, abacá (Manila hemp). Coconut-oil milling, sugar-refining. Manufactures textiles and cigars.

Seat of the University of Santo Tomas (1611), maintained by the Dominican Order and of the University of the Philippines (1908). The short Pasig R. divides the city into the old walled city of Intramuros (S) and the modern part (N). Founded 1571. Taken by the USA during the Spanish American War (1898). Occupied by the Japanese during World War II (1942-5) and in its defence and recapture much of the city was destroyed.

Manipur India. State in the Indian Union in the NE, bounded on the E by Myanmar (Burma). Area 22,326 sq km (8721 sq. miles). Pop. (1991) 1,826,714 (the majority Hindus, chiefly inhabiting the central valley, with Animist Naga and Kuki tribes in the hills). Cap. Imphal. Apart from the central valley, through which the Manipur R. flows, it is mainly mountainous, rising to over 2700 m (8856 ft) in the N.

Rice is cultivated and teak is obtained from the hill forests. There are over 5000 small-scale industrial units. Other industries inc. cement, steel re-rolling mill, plywood and vegetable oil. It is noted for its handicrafts.

Manisa Turkey. Ancient Magnesia ad Sipylum. Cap. of the Manisa province 32 km (20 miles) NE of Izmir. Pop. (1990) 158,426.

Commercial centre. Trade in grain, raisins, tobacco and olives.

Scene of the defeat of Antiochus the Great by the Romans (190 BC).

Manitoba Canada. Easternmost of the Prairie Provinces. Area 649,947 sq km (211,721 sq. miles). Pop. (1991) 1,091,942. Cap. Winnipeg. Mainly low-lying, rising to the W. Highest point Duck Mountain (832 m; 2729 ft). Many lakes of glacial origin; the largest are L. Winnipeg (25,651 sq km; 9904 sq. miles), L. Winnipegosis (5403 sq km; 2086 sq. miles), and L. Manitoba (4706 sq km; 1817 sq. miles). In the N part, in the Laurentian Shield, 45 per cent of the land is forested, one-third of commercial importance.

The rich soils of the SW prairie zone produce wheat, oats and barley. Mineral products inc. nickel, copper, gold, zinc, silver and petroleum. Main industries meatpacking and flour-milling.

The first explorer was Sir Thomas Button, who discovered the mouth of the Nelson R. in 1612. British claims to the territory were recognized by the Treaty of Paris (1763). The Hudson's Bay Company formed a colony on the Red R. in 1812, which was part of territory annexed to Canada in 1870. The Metis colonists (part-Indian, mostly French-speaking, Catholic) objected to the arrangements for the purchase of the Company territory by Canada and the province of Manitoba was created to accommodate them. It was extended northwards and westwards in 1881 and to Hudson Bay in 1912. The majority of the people are of British extraction, but there is a French community centred on St Boniface and there are many immigrants from the Ukraine, Poland and Germany.

Manitoba, Lake Canada. Elongated lake in S Manitoba 200 km (125 miles) long and up to 43 km (27 miles) wide at a height of 248 m (813 ft). Receives the outflow from L. Winnipegosis and drains into L. Winnipeg by the Dauphin R.

Manitoulin Islands Canada/USA. Chain of islands in L. Huron, mostly in S Ontario (Canada). The largest is Manitoulin (Great Manitoulin), 130 km (80 miles) long and up to 48 km (30 miles) wide, the largest freshwater-lake island in the world. Others inc. Cockburn (in Ontario) and Drummond (in Michigan). Farming, lumbering and fishing are important. Many summer resorts.

Manitowoc USA. Port in Wisconsin on L. Michigan at the mouth of the Manitowoc R. Pop. (1990) 34,000.

Shipbuilding. Manufactures aluminium

goods and furniture. The name is an Indian word meaning 'Land of Spirits'.

Manizales Colombia. Cap. of the Caldas department on the W flank of the Central Cordillera at a height of 2100 m (6888 ft). Pop. (1992) 327,115.

Route and commercial centre in a rich coffee-growing district. Linked by railway (W) with Buenaventura. Manufactures textiles and leather goods.

Mannar (Manaar), Gulf of. Gulf of the Indian Ocean between the coast of Tamil Nadu (India) and Sri Lanka, lying S of Adam's Bridge; 320 km (200 miles) across at its widest. Famous for pearl fisheries.

Mannheim Germany. Town in Baden-Württemberg on the right bank of the Rhine R. at the confluence with the Neckar R. opposite Ludwigshafen. Pop. (1990) 312,000.

River port. Considerable trade in grain and coal. Also a road and rail and industrial centre. Railway engineering. Manufactures agricultural and other machinery, electrical equipment, chemicals, textiles and tobacco products.

The inner old town is laid out in rectangular pattern with numbered streets; many of its old buildings, however, were destroyed or severely damaged in World War II. A settlement in the 8th cent. Residence of the Electors Palatine 1720–78.

Manora Pakistan. Headland protecting the S entrance to Karachi harbour.

Manresa Spain. Town in Barcelona province, Catalonia on the Cardoner R. 45 km (28 miles) NNW of Barcelona. Pop. (1991) 63,274.

Industrial centre. Manufactures textiles, paper and leather goods.

Beneath one of its churches is a cave which served as a spiritual retreat for St Ignatius Loyola.

Mans, Le France. Prefecture of the Sarthe department on the Sarthe R. at the confluence with the Huisne R. Pop. (1990) 148,465.

Important railway junction. Manufactures railway rolling-stock, agricultural machinery, tobacco products, textiles and paper. Flour-milling and tanning. Trade in livestock and agricultural produce. The annual 24-hour sports-car race is held at Le Mans.

Traces of the Roman wall are still apparent and in the cathedral (11th/13th-cent.) is the tomb of Queen Berengaria, wife of Richard Cœur de Lion. Here the French were finally defeated in the Franco–Prussian War (1871). Birthplace of Henry II of England (1133–89).

Mansfield England. Town in Nottinghamshire on the R. Maun 21 km (13 miles) N of Nottingham. Pop. (1991) 71,853.

Industrial centre in a coalmining district. Manufactures hosiery and footwear.

Has a 16th-cent. grammar school. Mansfield Woodhouse (pop. 24,787), mainly residential, is 2.4 km (1½ miles) N.

Mansfield USA. Industrial town in Ohio 87 km (54 miles) WSW of Akron. Pop. (1990) 50,627.

Manufactures electrical equipment, metal goods, tyres and rubber goods. Named after Lieutenant-Colonel Jared Mansfield, US surveyor general.

Mansûra Egypt. Cap. of the Daqahliya governorate on the Damietta branch of the Nile. Pop. (1986) 316,870. Important railway junction. Cotton-manufacturing centre. Founded 1221. Scene of the defeat of the Crusaders under Louis IX of France (St Louis) by the Mamelukes (1250).

Mantua (Italian **Mantova**) Italy. Cap. of Mantova province in Lombardy 37 km (23 miles) SSW of Verona, almost enclosed by lakes formed by the Mincio R. Pop. (1990) 54,200.

Industries inc. tanning, brewing, sugar-refining and tourism.

Among its buildings are the 14th-cent. ducal palace, with paintings by Rubens, El Greco; the castle; the Church of St Andrea, which has the tomb of Mantegna; and, just outside the town, the Palazzo del Tè. Governed by the Gonzaga family 1328–1708; under them attained fame as a centre of culture. Ruled by Austria for most of the 18th cent. and again 1814–66, and then passed to Italy. Birthplace of Virgil (70–19 BC) nearby.

Manych Depression Russia. A broad trough 560 km (350 miles) long between the Lower Don R. and the Caspian Sea, extending ESE through the Rostov Region (Russia) and Kalmykia. For most of the year it is dry or contains a series of salt lakes. In spring a stream, the W Manych R., flows WNW to join the Don and another, the E Manych R., flows ESE and disappears in the arid steppe.

Manzala (Menzala, Menzhaleh), Lake Egypt. Coastal lagoon in Lower Egypt, from the Damietta branch of the Nile to the Suez Canal. Area 2072 sq km (800 sq. miles). Separated from the Mediterranean Sea by a narrow spit, at the E end of which is Port Said. Abundant fish and waterfowl.

Manzanillo Cuba. Seaport on the SE coast at the head of the Gulf of Guacanayabo. Pop. (1991) 107,650.
    Exports sugar, molasses, coffee and hides. Sugar-refining, sawmilling and fish-canning. Founded 1784.

Maputo Mozambique. Formerly Lourenzo Marques. Cap., chief seaport and largest city. Pop. (1991) 1,098,000.
    Excellent harbour. Connected by rail with Gauteng, Zimbabwe and Swaziland. Mozambique's chief industrial centre manufacturing furniture, footwear and cement. Oil refinery and ore terminal and there is much transit trade. Also a popular holiday resort with a pleasant winter climate.
    Originally named after a Portuguese trader who explored the area (1544). Superseded Mozambique as cap. 1907.

Maracaibo Venezuela. Cap. of the Zulia state on the hot humid NW shores of L. Maracaibo. Pop. (1990) 1,207,513.
    With oil exploitation (from 1917) it grew from a small coffee-exporting port to an important commercial centre. The port is accessible to ocean-going vessels, since the dredging of a channel from L. Maracaibo to the Caribbean in 1956. Main export oil. Founded 1571.

Maracaibo, Lake Venezuela. Lake in the NW 210 km (130 miles) long and up to 110 km (70 miles) wide. Area 13,200 sq km (5097 sq. miles). Connected with the Gulf of Venezuela by a 55-km (34-mile) waterway, with a dredged channel through the bar, completed in 1956. The rich oilfields beneath the lake and its margins (discovered 1917) are Venezuela's main source of revenue with over 70 per cent of the country's oil ouput coming from the lake area; thousands of derricks stand in the waters of the lake.

Maracay Venezuela. Cap. of the Aragua state 80 km (50 miles) WSW of Caracas just NE of L. Valencia. Pop. (1990) 354,428. Modernized under the Gómez dictatorship 1909–35. Military training centre. Manufactures textiles.

Marágheh (Marágha) Iran. Town in E Azerbaijan province 80 km (50 miles) S of Tabriz. Pop. (1982) 70,000. Commercial centre in a fruit-growing district. Cap. of Hulagu (grandson of Genghis Khan) in the 13th cent. Has bridge and towers dating from the 12th–14th cent.

Marajó Island Brazil. Large island in the Amazon delta 290 km (180 miles) long and 190 km (120 miles) wide. The W is low, swampy and covered with rainforest, producing timber and rubber. The E is higher grassland, used for cattle-rearing. Source of handsome prehistoric pottery.

Maramba ➤LIVINGSTONE.

Maranhão Brazil. State in the NE, bounded on the N by the Atlantic. Area 328,663 sq km (126,897 sq. miles). Pop. (1991) 4,922,339. Cap. São Luis. The low coastal plain, with a hot humid climate, is covered with rainforest and tall-grass savannah. In the S there is some cattle-rearing on the short-grass plateaux. Agriculture (cotton, sugar-cane) in the valleys. Copper, gold and oil are also found.

Marañón River Peru. Headstream of the

Amazon R. 1450 km (900 miles) long, rising in small Andean lakes in central Peru, flowing N and NE, leaving the highlands by the Pongo de Manseriche Gorge and joining the Ucayali R. in the lowlands to form the Amazon.

Maraş Turkey. Cap. of Maraş province 153 km (95 miles) ENE of Adana on the S slope of the Taurus Mountains. Pop. (1985) 210,500.

Commercial centre. Trade in wheat, cotton. In ancient times a Hittite town.

Marathon Greece. Village in Attica 32 km (20 miles) NE of Athens. On the plain of Marathon to the SE the Athenians under Miltiades defeated the Persians under Darius I (490 BC). The feat of the soldier who carried the news of the victory from Marathon to Athens has been commemorated in the marathon race of the Olympic Games since 1896.

Marazion England. Fishing village and holiday resort in Cornwall on Mount's Bay 5 km (3 miles) E of Penzance. Pop. (1991) 1381. At low tide it is connected by a natural causeway to the small island of St Michael's Mount, formerly a place of pilgrimage.

Marburg Germany. Town in Hessen on the Lahn R. 80 km (50 miles) N of Frankfurt. Pop. (1986) 77,100.

Manufactures metal goods, precision and optical instruments, pottery and soap.

University (1527). The 13th-cent. Church of St Elizabeth was built by the Teutonic Knights to hold the saint's tomb. In the 13th/14th-cent. castle the famous religious debate between Luther and Zwingli took place (1529).

March England. Market town in the Isle of Ely, Cambridgeshire on the Nene R. 21 km (13 miles) NW of Ely. Pop. (1985) 14,500. Railway junction. Beet-sugar refining. The 14th-cent. Church of St Wendreda has an outstanding timber roof.

Marches, The Italy. Central region bordering E on the Adriatic Sea and comprising the provinces of Ancona, Ascoli-Piceno, Macerata and Pesaro-Urbino. Area 9692 sq km (3742 sq. miles). Pop. (1992) 1,433,994. Cap. Ancona. Mountainous in the W (Apennines). Many river valleys and a coastal plain on which agriculture (cereals, vines, olives) and stock-rearing are the main occupations.

Mar del Plata Argentina. Large resort on the Atlantic coast in Buenos Aires province about midway between Buenos Aires and Bahía Blanca. Pop. (1991) 407,024.

More than a million visitors annually. Extensive beaches, casino, night clubs and other tourist attractions. Industries inc. fish-canning, meat-packing and flour-milling.

Mardin Turkey. Cap. of Mardin province 282 km (175 miles) E of Gaziantep. Pop. (1970) 118,466.

Market town in an agricultural region producing cereals and wool. Manufactures textiles.

Maré ►LOYALTY ISLANDS.

Maree, Loch Scotland. Lake 21 km (13 miles) long and up to 3 km (2 miles) wide in Highland E and SE of Gairloch noted for its fine scenery. Almost surrounded by mountains, inc. Ben Slioch (981 m; 3218 ft). Contains many small islands. Its sea outlet is the short R. Ewe.

Maremma Italy. Marshy region in S Tuscany bordering on the Tyrrhenian Sea from the Cecina R. southwards. It was fertile and well-populated in Etruscan and Roman times, being drained by underground canals, but in the Middle Ages it was largely abandoned owing to malaria. From the early 19th cent. reclamation has continued with success and large areas of malarial swamp have been converted into fertile agricultural land.

Mareotis (Mariut), Lake Egypt. Salt lake in the Nile delta, separated from the sea by the narrow strip of land on which Alexandria stands.

Margarita Island Venezuela. Island off the NE coast, forming the major part of the Nueva Esparta state. Area 1150 sq km (440 sq. miles). Pop. (1985) 33,000. Cap.

La Asunción. Chief port and commercial centre Porlamar. Resort area; pleasant climate. Deep-sea fishing important. Formerly a pearl-fishing centre. Discovered in 1498 by Columbus.

Margate England. Town on the coast of the Isle of Thanet, Kent 24 km (15 miles) ENE of Canterbury. Pop. (1991) 56,734. Seaside resort with good beach and piers; noted for its sea bathing since 1750. Inc. the resorts of Westgate-on-Sea (W) and Cliftonville (E).

Mari Republic Russia. Republic situated between Gorki and Kazan on the left bank of the Volga R. Area 23,200 sq km (8955 sq. miles). Pop. (1994) 764,700. Cap. Yoshkar Ola. More than half forested.

Principal industries sawmilling, woodworking and the manufacture of paper, cellulose, furniture and food-processing.

The Mari people, of Finnish origin, were conquered by Ivan the Terrible and annexed to Russia in 1552.

Mariana Islands ➤NORTHERN MARIANA ISLANDS.

Mariánské Lázně (Ger. **Marienbad**) Czech Republic. Spa town in W Bohemia 53 km (33 miles) WNW of Pilsen. Pop. (1991) 15,380. There are mineral springs, known for many cent., but first achieving popularity about the end of the 18th cent.

Maribor (Ger. **Marburg**) Slovenia. Town on the Drava R. 90 km (56 miles) NNW of Zagreb. Pop. (1991) 104,000.

Manufactures textiles, leather, footwear, chemicals and armaments. Trade in grain, wine and timber.

Its chief buildings are the cathedral (begun in the 12th cent.) and the 15th-cent. castle.

Marienbad ➤MARIÁNSKÉ LÁZNĚ.

Mariinsk Canals Russia. Canal system 1094 km (680 miles) long dating from the early 19th cent., constructed and repeatedly improved to link St Petersburg with the Volga R. via the Neva, Svir, Vytegra, Kovzha and Sheksna rivers and the Rybinsk Reservoir.

Marion (Indiana) USA. Town on the Mississinewa R. 72 km (45 miles) SW of Fort Wayne. Pop. (1990) 35,000.

Commercial centre in an agricultural region. Manufactures oilfield machinery, electrical equipment and paper.

Named after General Francis Marion, a soldier in the American War of Independence.

Marion (Ohio) USA. Town 69 km (43 miles) N of Columbus. Pop. (1990) 34,075.

Commercial centre in a rich farming area. Manufactures excavating and road-construction machinery and metal goods.

Maritime Provinces Canada. Three provinces on the Atlantic seaboard; New Brunswick, Nova Scotia and Prince Edward Island. Known as Acadia (Acadie) during the French administration. Chief cities and ports Halifax (Nova Scotia), St John (New Brunswick).

Maritime Territory ➤PRIMORYE TERRITORY.

Maritsa (Evros) River. River 480 km (300 miles) long rising in the Rila Mountains in Bulgaria, flowing E and ESE through Bulgaria past Plovdiv, then past Edirne in Turkey, then forming parts of the Greco–Bulgarian and the Greco–Turkish frontiers, turning S and SSW and entering the Aegean Sea. Unnavigable, but used for irrigation and hydroelectric power.

Maritzburg ➤PIETERMARITZBURG.

Mariupol (Zhdanov) Ukraine. Seaport and industrial town in the Donetsk region 96 km (60 miles) SSW of Donetsk on the Sea of Azov. Pop. (1991) 522,000.

Industries inc. fishing, fish-processing and the manufacture of iron and steel, machinery, chemicals and clothing. Exports grain, coal and salt from the nearby harbour.

Mariut, Lake ➤MAREOTIS, LAKE.

Market Bosworth England. Town in Leicestershire 18 km (11 miles) W of Leicester. Pop. (1991) 900. 3 km (2 miles) S is Bosworth Field, scene of the battle (1485) in which Richard III was defeated and killed, to be succeeded by his conqueror the Earl of Richmond as Henry VII.

Market Drayton England. Market town in Shropshire on the R. Tern 27 km (17 miles) NE of Shrewsbury. Pop. (1991) 9482. Has a 16th-cent. grammar school. Styche, nearby, was the birthplace of Lord Clive, English soldier (1727–74).

Market Harborough England. Market town in Leicestershire on the R. Welland 19 km (12 miles) SE of Leicester. Pop. (1991) 16,563.

Manufactures electrical equipment, textiles, corsetry and foodstuffs. A famous fox-hunting centre. Has a 13th-cent. church.

Market Rasen England. Market town in Lincolnshire on the R. Rasen 23 km (14 miles) NE of Lincoln. Pop. (1991) 2948. Racecourse.

Markinch Scotland. Small town in Fife on the R. Leven 10 km (6 miles) NNE of Kirkcaldy. Pop. (1991) 2176.

Manufactures paper, but the distillery closed in 1983.

Marlborough England. Small town in Wiltshire on the R. Kennet 14 km (9 miles) SSE of Swindon near Savernake Forest. Pop. (1991) 6429. Town in a dairy-farming region. Engineering. Marlborough College, the public school, was founded 1843.

Marlborough New Zealand. Former provincial district in the NE of South Island. Area 10,930 sq km (4220 sq. miles). Pop. (1991) 36,765. Principal town Blenheim. Chief port Picton, with regular services to Wellington. Sheep-rearing. Grain and fruit-growing.

Marlow (Great Marlow) England. Market town in S Buckinghamshire on the R. Thames 6 km (4 miles) S of High Wycombe. Pop. (1991) 17,771. Mainly residential. Brewing. Popular boating centre. The village of Little Marlow is 3 km (2 miles) ENE.

Marmara (Marmora), Sea of Turkey. Ancient Propontis. Sea between European and Asiatic Turkey, linked with the Black Sea by the Bosporus and with the Aegean

Sea by the Dardanelles. Area 11,400 sq km (4400 sq. miles). Takes its name from its largest island, Marmara, in the W.

Marne France. Department in the NE in the former Champagne province. Area 8205 sq km (3168 sq. miles). Pop. (1990) 558,200. Prefecture Châlons-sur-Marne. Drained chiefly by the Marne R. and its tributaries, it is crossed by the infertile dry Champagne (*Champagne pouilleuse*) and the humid Champagne (*Champagne humide*); the vineyards on its hill slopes produce some of the finest champagne. Reims, Épernay and Châlons-sur-Marne are important centres of the Champagne wine trade.

Marne River France. River 525 km (326 miles) long rising on the Plateau de Langres in the Haute-Marne department, flowing N and then W in a wide curve, past Chaumont, St Dizier, Vitry-le-François, Châlons-sur-Marne, Épernay and Meaux, joining the Seine R. at Charenton-le-Pont just above Paris. Linked by canal with the Aisne, Rhine and Rhône rivers; an important waterway. Two vital battles of World War I (1914, 1918) were fought on its banks and were named after it.

Maroni (Marowijne) River French Guiana. River 720 km (450 miles) long rising in the Tumuc-Humac Mountains and flowing generally N through tropical rain-forests to the Atlantic. Forms most of the frontier between French Guiana and Suriname.

Marple England. Town in Greater Manchester 6 km (4 miles) ESE of Stockport. Pop. (1991) 19,829. Industries inc. engineering.

Marquesas Islands (Îles Marquises) S Pacific Ocean. Group of volcanic islands 1200 km (750 miles) NE of Tahiti, forming part of French Polynesia. Area 1274 sq km (492 sq. miles). Pop. (1988) 7540. Largest island Nukuhiva, second largest Hivaoa, with cap. Atuona. The S group (Mendana Is.) was discovered by Mendana (1595), the N group (Washington Is.) by Ingraham (1791). Passed to France in 1842, when the pop. was about

20,000. European diseases were largely responsible for the subsequent decrease.

Marrakesh Morocco. Traditionally the southern cap.; second largest city 225 km (140 miles) SSW of Casablanca at the foot of the High Atlas Mountains. Pop. (1993) 602,000.

Chief commercial centre of a fertile irrigated region. Connected with Casablanca by rail. Manufactures carpets and leather goods. Tourist centre.

Hot summers, mild winters; annual rainfall (mainly Nov.–April) 23 cm (8½ ins.). Founded 1062. The mosque and tower of Koutoubiya (still the outstanding landmark) were built by the Sultan Yakout-el-Mansour 1184–98. Became a N terminus of trans-Saharan caravan routes. Occupied by the French in 1912, since when the modern town has developed.

Marsala Italy. Ancient Lilybaeum. Town and port in Trapani province in W Sicily. Pop. (1990) 81,000.

Considerable trade in Marsala wine. Manufactures bottles. Industries inc. fishing.

Founded in the 4th cent. BC. The chief Carthaginian fortress in Sicily; later a Roman base for expeditions against Carthage. Named by the Saracens Marsa Ali ('the Port of Ali'). Garibaldi landed here at the opening of his campaign in Sicily (1860).

Marseille (English **Marseilles**) France. Ancient Massilia. Country's second largest city and principal seaport, cap. of the Bouches-du-Rhône department on the Gulf of Lions of the Mediterranean Sea. Pop. (1990) 807,736.

Exports wines, liqueurs, olive oil, soap and sugar. Manufactures soap and margarine, using imports of vegetable oils. Also oil-refining, flour-milling, sugar-refining, ore-smelting, ship-repairing, chemical and glass manufactures. The harbour accommodates the largest vessels and is linked inland by the Rhône–Marseille Canal through the Rove tunnel and the Étang-de-Berre. Stands on a bay and is flanked on three sides by limestone hills. Offshore is the islet with the Château d'If.

In spite of its long history it has few old buildings. The pilgrim Church of Notre Dame de la Garde (1864) has a gilded statue of the Virgin and replaces a 13th-cent. building on the same site; The Church of St Victor, however, dates from the 13th cent. Founded by Greeks from Phocaea c. 600 BC. A free city under the Romans. Several times besieged and captured, it passed to France in 1481. Its modern development as a great seaport dates from the opening of the Suez Canal in 1869. Birthplace of Louis Adolphe Thiers, statesman and historian (1797–1877), Honoré Daumier, painter (1808–79) and Edmond Rostand, poet and dramatist (1868–1918).

Marshall Islands. Republic in the W Pacific Ocean situated N of Kiribati and E of Micronesia. Area 181 sq km (70 sq. miles). Pop. (1995) 56,200 (65 per cent urban). Life expectancy, 62 years male, 65 female. Cap. Dalap-Uliga-Darrit; only other town Ebeye. Currency: US dollar = 100 cents. Group of coral islands and atolls in two roughly parallel NW–SE chains, Ralik and Ratak, Kwajalein in the Ralik Chain is the largest atoll. Rainfall is heavy, esp. in the S atolls and temperatures are uniformly high. Land use: forested 23 per cent, meadows and pastures 14 per cent, agricultural and under permanent cultivation 33 per cent. About 90 per cent are Protestant Christians and 97 per cent are Marshallese. The official lang. are Marshallese and English.

Tourism and copra production are the main occupations. Main export copra and others inc. tomatoes and melons. High-grade phosphate deposits are mined.

Discovered in 1526 by the Spaniards. It was a German protectorate 1885–1914. Occupied by the Japanese until 1944. From 1947 inc. in the US Territory of the Pacific Is. under UN trusteeship. US atom and hydrogen bomb tests were conducted on Bikini Atoll 1946–62 and in 1982 a missile range was built. The UN trusteeship was terminated in 1990 and the islands became a full member of the United Nations in 1991.

There is a 33-member elected House of Assembly (*Nitijela*) and an appointed 12-member Council of Chiefs (*Iroij*).

Martaban, Gulf of Myanmar (Burma). Inlet of the Indian Ocean receiving the Salween and Sittang rivers, with the Irrawaddy delta to the W. The village of Martaban, at the mouth of the Salween, opposite Moulmein, probably founded in the 6th cent., was once cap. of an independent kingdom; it is the terminus of a railway to Pegu.

Martha's Vineyard USA. Island off the Massachusetts coast 32 km (20 miles) long and 3–16 km (2–10 miles) wide. Pop. (1985) 6000. Formerly a whaling and fishing centre. Now mainly a summer resort. First visited and named by Bartholomew Gosnold (1602). Administered by New York until 1692.

Martina Franca Italy. Town in Taranto province, Apulia 27 km (17 miles) NNE of Taranto. Summer resort. Pop. (1985) 41,000.
Produces wine and olive oil.

Martinique West Indies. Overseas department of France since 1946. Island in the Windward Is. of the Lesser Antilles, between Dominica (N) and St Lucia (S). Area 1079 sq km (417 sq. miles). Pop. (1990) 359,600. Cap. Fort-de-France. Of volcanic origin and extremely mountainous. Highest point Mont Pelée (1351 m; 4431 ft), a volcano which erupted in 1902 and destroyed the town of St Pierre, killing about 40,000 people. Also suffers from hurricanes, earthquakes and tidal waves.
Principal crops sugar-cane, bananas, cacao, coffee and fruits.
Main exports, crude petroleum, bananas and rum. Tourism is important.
Probably discovered by Columbus in 1502. Colonized by the French 1635 and apart from brief intervals it has remained French.

Marton ►MIDDLESBROUGH.

Martos Spain. Town in Jaén province, Andalusia 16 km (10 miles) WSW of Jaén. Pop. (1991) 20,900.
Manufactures cement, textiles, soap and pottery. Trade in olive oil and wine. Mineral springs nearby.

Mary (Merv) Turkmenistan. Town in an oasis in the Kar-dum desert 354 km (220 miles) ESE of Ashkhabad. Pop. (1990) 93,000. On the Trans-Caspian Railway, with a branch line to Kushka.
Textile manufacturing using cotton grown by irrigation on the oasis; also carpet manufacture, brewing and food-processing.
The old city of Merv, 32 km (20 miles) E, according to Hindu and Arab tradition, was the source of the Aryan race; in medieval times it was a centre of Muslim culture.

Maryborough Australia. Town and port in SE Queensland on the Mary R. 217 km (135 miles) NNW of Brisbane. Pop. (1991) 23,286.
In a sugar-growing and dairy-farming region. Iron and steel manufacture, railway engineering, sawmilling. Exports sugar, pineapples, citrus fruits, timber and coal.

Maryland USA. A middle Atlantic state. Area 31,865 sq km (12,303 sq. miles). Pop. (1990) 4,781,468. Cap. Annapolis. Extremely irregular in shape; Chesapeake Bay almost separates the two parts of the Atlantic coastal plain, known as the Eastern Shore (on Delmarva Peninsula) and the Western Shore. The shores of the bay, too, are much indented, with many river estuaries. Inland there are rolling uplands; highest point Mt Backbone (1019 m; 3342 ft) in the Alleghenies in the extreme W. Climate humid continental; temperatures are much lower in the W than in the S and E. Annual rainfall 100–120 cm (40–48 ins.).
Tomatoes, maize, soya beans and tobacco are important crops, and oysters, crabs and clams are fished in Chesapeake Bay. Leading industrial city Baltimore.
The history of Maryland began with the granting by Charles I (1632) of a charter to George Calvert, 1st Baron Baltimore. The first settlement was established at St Mary's (1634). The boundary with Pennsylvania, long in dispute, was settled in 1763 by the drawing of the Mason–Dixon Line. In

1790–1 Maryland ceded the 177 sq km (69 sq. miles) on the Potomac R. which form the District of Columbia. Named after Henrietta Maria, wife of Charles I. One of the original 13 states.

Maryport England. Town in Cumbria at the mouth of the R. Ellen on Solway Firth 42 km (26 miles) SW of Carlisle. Pop. (1991) 9797. Former port. Modern light industries.

Masaya Nicaragua. Cap. of the Masaya department in the SW. Pop. (1995) 88,971.

Commercial centre for a fertile agricultural region (coffee and tobacco). Railway junction. Crater lake nearby. Indian handicrafts, esp. hammocks, rope and straw hats. Manufactures footwear and cigars.

Masbate Philippines. Island between Negros and the SE tip of Luzon. Area 3269 sq km (1262 sq. miles). Pop. (1990) 599,915. Cap. Masbate (pop. 32,000). Formerly one of the country's chief goldmining areas. Rice, coconuts and abacá cultivated.

Maseru Lesotho. Cap. 1.6 km (1 mile) inside the W border 130 km (80 miles) E of Bloemfontein (South Africa) near the Caledon R. at a height of 1510 m (4953 ft). Pop. (1992) 367,000.

Mashaba ➤ZIMBABWE.

Mashhad (Meshed) Iran. Cap. of Khurasan province 708 km (440 miles) ENE of Tehrán, close to the Turkmenistan border, at a height of 960 m (3149 ft). Pop. (1991) 1,800,000.

Important commercial and industrial centre. Trade in carpets, cotton goods. Manufactures rugs. Industries inc. tanning, flour-milling and is linked by oil pipeline to Esfahan and by railway to Turkmenistan.

The most sacred city in Iran, for it contains the golden-domed tomb of the Imam Riza and is a place of pilgrimage for Muslims of the Shia sect – to which most Iranians belong. University founded in 1955. About 24 km (15 miles) NW are the ruins of Tus, birthplace and burial place of Firdausi, the Persian poet of the 10th-11th cent.

Mashonaland Zimbabwe. NE region, inhabited by the Mashona, a Bantu tribe. Pop. (1992) 857,315. Chief town Salisbury. Administered by the British South Africa Company 1889–1923, then part of Southern Rhodesia. Other towns Umtali, Gatooma.

Mason City (USA). Industrial town in Iowa 177 km (110 miles) N of Des Moines. Pop. (1990) 29,040.

Manufactures cement, bricks and tiles. Named after the first settlers, who were Freemasons.

Mason–Dixon Line USA. State boundary between Pennsylvania (N) and Maryland (S). Surveyed (1763–7) by two English astronomers, Charles Mason and Jeremiah Dixon, it settled the long-standing dispute between Pennsylvania and Maryland. In 1779 it was extended to mark the S boundary between Pennsylvania and Virginia (now West Virginia). Total length about 386 km (240 miles). Before the American Civil War it divided the slave states from the 'free' states. Later it came to distinguish the 'South' from the 'North'.

Massachusetts USA. State in New England on the Atlantic. Area 21,386 sq km (8257 sq. miles). Pop. (1990) 6,016,425. On the coast is Massachusetts Bay, with its two arms Boston Bay (N) and Cape Cod Bay (S). The E part belongs to the Atlantic coastal plain, the W to the New England uplands, cut by the N–S Connecticut R. valley. Highest point Mt Greylock (1065 m; 3493 ft), in the extreme NW. Climate humid continental, the long severe winter passing quickly into a hot summer. Annual rainfall 100–120 cm (40–48 ins.).

Potatoes, tobacco, cranberries and apples widely grown. Fishing is still important, but manufacturing is the main activity. Principal products textiles, footwear, electrical machinery, paper.

Chief towns Boston, Worcester, Springfield, Cambridge and New Bedford. Distinguished for its centres of higher education. First permanently settled by the Pilgrim Fathers, who landed from the *Mayflower* at

Plymouth (1620). Prominent in resistance to the English colonial policy which led to the American Revolution. United with Maine in 1691, but the union was terminated in 1820. One of the original 13 states.

Massawa ►MITSIWA.

Massillon USA. Industrial town in Ohio 11 km (7 miles) W of Canton. Pop. (1985) 33,000. Manufactures special steels and hardware. Founded in 1826.

Masterton New Zealand. Town in North Island 80 km (50 miles) ENE of Wellington. Pop. (1991) 22,947.
    Dairy factories, meatworks and woollen mills.

Masulipatam (Bandar, Machilipatnam) India. Seaport in Andhra Pradesh on the N side of the Krishna delta 314 km (195 miles) ESE of Hyderabad. Pop. (1991) 159,007.
    Exports groundnuts, castor seeds. Rice-milling. Manufactures cotton goods.
    Site of the first British settlement on the Coromandel coast (established 1611).

Matabeleland Zimbabwe. Region in the SW inhabited by the Matabele, a Bantu tribe of Zulu origin. Pop. (1992) 640,937. Chief town Bulawayo. The Matabele were driven out of Natal and the Transvaal, and settled N of the Limpopo R., absorbing the Mashona and other tribes. Administered by the British South Africa Company 1889–1923. Cecil Rhodes obtained from the Matabele chief, Lobengula, the right to exploit its rich gold deposits. Became part of Southern Rhodesia 1923.

Matadi Democratic Republic of the Congo. Chief seaport on the left bank of the Congo R. just below the Livingstone Falls 160 km (100 miles) from the coast. Pop. (1990) 172,926. Head of navigation for ocean-going vessels. Linked by rail with Kinshasa.
    Principal exports cacao, coffee, cotton, palm oil and minerals.

Matagalpa Nicaragua. Cap. of the Matagalpa department, the country's second largest town, 96 km (60 miles) NNE of Managua. Pop. (1985) 37,000.
    Coffee-processing and flour-milling.

Matamoros Mexico. Town in the Tamaulipas state on the Río Grande near the mouth, opposite Brownsville (Texas). Pop. (1990) 404,000.
    Cotton-ginning, vegetable-oil processing, tanning and distilling. Important largely as a point of entry for US tourists.
    Founded 1824. Named after the Mexican patriot Mariano Matamoros (1770–1814).

Matanzas Cuba. Cap. of the Matanzas province on the N coast 80 km (50 miles) E of Havana. Pop. (1990) 113,724.
    Seaport. Commercial centre in a rich agricultural region producing sugar-cane, sisal. Exports sugar. Industries inc. sugar-refining and tanning. Manufactures rayons and footwear. Excellent beaches, wide avenues, handsome plazas; second only to Havana as a tourist centre.

Matapan (Tainaron), Cape Greece. Southernmost point of the Peloponnese at the extremity of the Matapan peninsula, between the Gulfs of Messenia and Laconia. During World War II a British naval force defeated the Italians nearby (1941).

Matarani ►MOLLENDO.

Mataró Spain. Mediterranean seaport in Barcelona province, Catalonia 32 km (20 miles) NE of Barcelona. Pop. (1991) 101,501.
    Manufactures textiles, knitwear, paper and soap. Trade in wine.
    The Barcelona–Mataró railway was the first in Spain (1848).

Matera Italy. Cap. of Matera province, Basilicata 58 km (36 miles) WNW of Taranto. Pop. (1981) 50,712.
    Trade in cereals and olive oil. Manufactures pasta and pottery.
    Cathedral (13th-cent.). In the neighbourhood there are many caves and rock dwellings.

Mathura India. Town in W Uttar Pradesh

on the Jumna R. 48 km (30 miles) NW of Agra. Pop. (1991) 235,900.

Trade in grain, cotton, oilseeds and oil-refinery products. Manufactures chemicals, paper and textiles.

Also an important Hindu religious centre; the river bank is lined with bathing ghats and temples. An early Buddhist stronghold, it was sacked by Mahmud of Ghazni (1017), Aurangzeb (1669) and the Afghans (1756).

Matlock England. Town in Derbyshire on the R. Derwent 24 km (15 miles) N of Derby, comprising Matlock and Matlock Bath. Pop. (1991) 14,680.

Resort with mineral springs. In the vicinity are limestone cliffs and caves and petrifying springs. Richard Arkwright, English inventor (1732–92) established the first cotton mill in Derbyshire here (1771).

Mato Grosso Brazil. Inland state on the SW plateau. Area 906,807 sq km (350,119 sq. miles). Pop. (1990) 2,023,000. Cap. Cuiabá. In the N, in a vast tropical rainforest part of the Amazon basin, live many Indian tribes (not inc. in the census), largely untouched by western influence, under the care of the Indian Protection Service. SW lies the *pantanal*, a region near the Paraguay R. where cattle thrive in the dry season. Main occupation cattle-raising. Manganese mined near Corumbá. Many other unexploited mineral resources.

Mato Grosso do Sul Brazil. State created in 1979 from part of Mato Grosso. Area 350,548 sq km (135,347 sq. miles). Pop. (1991) 1,780,373. Cap. Campo Grande.

Matopo Hills Zimbabwe. Range S of Bulawayo 80 km (50 miles) long, rising to over 1500 m (4920 ft). At the point called World's View is the tomb of Cecil Rhodes, South African statesman (1853–1902).

Matozinhos Portugal. Fishing port and seaside resort in the Pôrto district at the mouth of the Leça R. 8 km (5 miles) NW of Oporto. Pop. (1985) 43,500. Fish-canning.

Matsue Japan. Seaport in Honshu, cap. of Shimane prefecture on a lagoon of the Sea of Japan 137 km (85 miles) NNE of Hiroshima. Pop. (1990) 142,956. An ancient castle town, relatively little modernized. Manufactures textiles.

Matsumoto Japan. Industrial town in Nagano prefecture, Honshu 169 km (105 miles) WNW of Tokyo. Pop. (1990) 200,723.

Formerly an important centre of the silk industry; now manufactures machinery and paper.

Matsuyama Japan. Cap. of Ehime prefecture, NW Shikoku. Pop. (1990) 443,317.

Industrial centre and seaport. Oil-refining, fruit-canning. Manufactures chemicals, rayon, textiles and agricultural machinery.

Seat of Ehime University (1949).

Matterhorn (Fr. **Mont Cervin**, Italian **Monte Cervino**) Switzerland. Peak 4484 m (14,708 ft) high in the Pennine Alps on the Swiss–Italian border 10 km (6 miles) SW of Zermatt. First climbed (1865) by a party of five, all but Edward Whymper, English climber (1840–1911) being killed on the descent.

Maturín Venezuela. Cap. of the Monagas state (NE). Pop. (1990) 207,382.

Commercial centre near the oilfields. Trade in cacao and cotton.

Mauchline Scotland. Market town in Ayrshire 16 km (10 miles) ENE of Ayr. Pop. (1991) 3931. Famous for its association with Robert Burns, Scottish poet (1759–96). Nearby is the farm of Mossgiel, where the poet lived (1784–8).

Mauretania Africa. Ancient region in the NW consisting roughly of modern Morocco and W Algeria, inhabited by the Mauri (Moors), a Berber people. In the 1st cent. BC there were two kingdoms, but Juba II of Numidia became ruler of the whole area (25 BC). Claudius annexed it to the Roman Empire (AD 42) and divided it into two provinces, Mauretania Tingitana (W) and Mauretania Caesariensis (E). The area prospered until the Vandal invasion in the 5th cent. AD.

Mauritania. Republic in NW Africa, bounded by Western Sahara in the N, by Algeria in the NE, Mali E and SE, Senegal S and the Atlantic Ocean in the W. Area 1,030,700 sq. km (398,000 sq. miles). Pop. (1993) 2,170,000 (39 per cent urban). Life expectancy, 44 years male, 50 female. Cap. Nouakchott. Other cities Nouadhibou, Kaédi, Kiffa and Rosso. Currency: Ouguiya = 5 khoums. Mainly desert broken by mountain ridges running NE to SW with some large oases. The highest point is Kediet Ijill 915 m (3050 ft). It has a tropical climate but conditions are generally arid with a little rain near the coast. Land use: forested 4 per cent, meadows and pasture 38 per cent, agricultural and under permanent cultivation 0.2 per cent, desert 57 per cent. About 99 per cent of the pop. is Muslim. Arabic is the official lang. and Fulani Soninke and Wolof together with Arabic are natural lang. About 70 per cent of the people are of Arab/Berber (Moor) origin, or of mixed black and Moorish descent.

Agriculture is mainly confined to the Senegal river valley in the S where millet, dates, maize, sweet potatoes, rice and groundnuts are grown. The wild acacias growing in the S produce gum arabic. Minerals inc. iron ore (the second most important export after fish) and copper. Other industries inc. food-processing and fishing.

Originally a Berber kingdom, Mauritania became a French protectorate in 1903, a colony in 1920 and an overseas territory in 1946. It became a member of the French Community in 1958 and achieved independence in 1960. It became a one-party state in 1964 but under the 1991 Constitution multi-parties were restored although parties specifically Islamic are not permitted. There is a 56-member Senate and a 79-seat National Assembly. In 1976 part of the former colony of Spanish Sahara was integrated into Mauritania but in 1979 Mauritania withdrew from the territory.

Mauritius. Republic in the Indian Ocean comprising a volcanic island almost completely encircled with coral reefs about 805 km (550 miles) E of Madagascar, the island of Rodrigues about 560 km (350 miles) E and the outer islands of Agalega and the St Brandon Group. Area 2040 sq km (788 sq. miles). Pop. (1993) 1,105,739 (41 per cent urban). Life expectancy, 66 years male, 73 female. Cap. Port Louis. Other towns Beau Bassin-Rose Hill, Vacoas-Phoenix. Currency: Mauritian rupee = 100 cents. A plateau rising to mountains around its edges and then descending abruptly to coastal lowlands. There are numerous unnavigable rivers and true crater lakes. The subtropical climate is humid and has rainfall to 500 cm (200 ins.) with frequent cyclones between November and April. Land use: forested 28 per cent, meadows and pastures 3 per cent, agricultural and under permanent cultivation 52 per cent. The official lang. is English, but French is more widely spoken. About 52 per cent are Hindus, 32 per cent Christian, 17 per cent Muslim. The composition is Indo–Pakistani 68 per cent, Creole 27 per cent, Chinese 3 per cent, white 2 per cent.

Industry inc. sugar-cane production (there were (1993) 19 sugar factories). Tea, tobacco and potatoes are also grown. Manufactures inc. textiles, footwear, diamond-cutting, jewellery, furniture, watches, plastics, chemicals, electrical appliances and pharmaceuticals. Sugar and clothing, and tea are major exports. Tourism is important.

With its dependencies it was formerly a British Crown Colony. Discovered (1505) by the Portuguese and held by the Dutch (who named it Mauritius) 1598–1710 and by the French. It became independent in 1968 and a republic in 1992. There is a unicameral Legislative Assembly consisting of 62 directly elected members and 8 'best losers' appointed to redress any imbalance of representation between ethnic communities without distorting the balance between political parties.

Mawlamyine ►MOULMEIN.

May, Isle of Scotland. Island at the mouth of the Firth of Forth 8 km (5 miles) from the Fife coast. Lighthouse. Ruins of a priory dedicated to St Adrian, martyred by the Danes in the 9th cent.

Mayagüez (Puerto Rico) USA. Seaport on the W coast. Pop. (1990) 100,371.

In an agricultural region producing sugar-cane, coffee and tobacco. Famous for embroidery and needlework. Sugar-refining. Manufactures beer, rum and cigars.

Founded 1760.

Maybole Scotland. Market town in South Ayrshire 13 km (8 miles) S of Ayr. Pop. (1991) 4737.

Manufactures agricultural machinery and footwear.

Once cap. of the district of Carrick. The ruins of Crossraguel Abbey are 2.4 km (1½ miles) SW.

Mayenne France. Department in the NW, formed chiefly from Maine. Area 5146 sq km (1987 sq. miles). Pop. (1990) 278,000. Prefecture Laval. General low-lying but hilly in the NE, where it rises to over 390 m (1279 ft). Drained by the Mayenne R. and its tributaries. Cereals, sugar-beet, cider apples grown. Cattle reared. Chief towns Laval, Mayenne.

Mayenne River France. River 196 km (122 miles) long, rising in the Orne department and flowing W and then S past Mayenne and Laval to join the Sarthe R. above Angers, forming the Main R. Tributaries the Varenne and the Oudon.

Mayfair England. Fashionable residential district in the City of Westminster, London, bounded approximately by Oxford Street (N), Bond Street (E), Piccadilly (S) and Park Lane (W). Named after the annual fair held here in May from the 16th cent. to 1809.

Maynooth Ireland. Small market town in Co. Kildare 23 km (14 miles) WNW of Dublin. Pop. (1985) 1350. Seat of St Patrick's College (1795), the chief Roman Catholic training centre for the clergy. Near the college are the remains of Maynooth Castle, built in the 12th cent., dismantled after being besieged in 1647.

Mayo Ireland. County in Connacht bounded in the W and N by the Atlantic. Area 5398 sq km (2085 sq. miles). Pop. (1991) 110,700. County town Castlebar. Its coastline is rugged and deeply indented, with Killala, Blacksod and Clew bays. Achill and Clare are the largest offshore islands. The W is largely mountainous and barren, rising in the NW to 806 m (2644 ft) in Nephin and in the SW to 820 m (2690 ft) in Muilrea and 766 m (2512 ft) in Croagh Patrick. The E is lower and more fertile; potatoes and oats are grown and cattle, pigs and poultry are raised. Lough Conn is wholly and Loughs Corrib and Mask are partly within the county. Chief towns Castlebar, Ballina, Ballinrobe and Westport.

Mayotte Indian Ocean. French dependency. Island with offshore islets, easternmost of the Comoro group and NW of Madagascar. Area 374 sq km (144 sq. miles). Pop. (1994) 109,600. It is fertile, producing sugar, rum, sisal, spices and oils. In 1979 it became a *collectivité particulière*, an intermediate status prior to becoming an Overseas Department.

Mazar-i-Sharif Afghanistan. Cap. of Mazar-i-Sharif province 306 km (190 miles) NW of Kabul. Pop. (1988) 131,000.

Industries inc. chemicals, fertilizers from natural gas, textiles and bricks. Flour-milling. Trade in karakul skins and carpets.

Has a 15th-cent. mosque, said to be the tomb of Ali, son-in-law of Mohammed, and therefore greatly venerated by Shia Muslims.

Mazatenango Guatemala. Cap. of the Suchitepéquez department 29 km (18 miles) S of Quezaltenango. Pop. (1989) 38,000.

Commercial centre in a district producing coffee, sugar-cane and cotton.

Mazatlán Mexico. Chief Pacific seaport in the Sinaloa state at the S extremity of the Gulf of California. Pop. (1990) 314,249.

Exports tobacco, bananas and minerals. Industries inc. sugar-refining, textile manufacture, flour-milling, distilling and shrimp-packing. Tourist resort with facilities for game-fishing.

Mbabane Swaziland. Cap. 153 km (95 miles) WSW of Maputo at a height of 1144 m (3752 ft). Pop. (1986) 38,300. Some tin-mining in the neighbourhood.

Mbandaka Democratic Republic of the Congo. Formerly Coquilhatville. Town in Équateur region on the Congo R. at its confluence with the Ruki R. 595 km (370 miles) NE of Kinshasa. Pop. (1991) 165,623. Centre of river trade. Founded 1883 by H. M. Stanley, Welsh explorer (1841–1904).

Mdina ➤CITTÀ VECCHIA.

Meath Ireland. County in Leinster, bordering E on the Irish Sea. Area 2339 sq km (903 sq. miles). Pop. (1991) 105,500. County town Trim. In general gently undulating and fertile. Drained by the Boyne and Blackwater rivers. Potatoes and oats cultivated. Cattle and horses raised. Chief towns Trim, An Uaimh (Navan), Ceanannus Mór (Kells). Meath was once a kingdom which inc. Westmeath, Longford and parts of Cavan, Kildare and Offaly as well as the present county, and there are many tumuli, round towers and other antiquities. By the early 17th cent. it had become established as a county.

Meaux France. Town in the Seine-et-Marne department on the Marne R. and the Ourcq Canal 39 km (24 miles) ENE of Paris. Pop. (1985) 46,000.

Commercial and industrial centre in the Brie region, supplying the Paris markets with agricultural produce. Sugar-refining, flour-milling. Manufactures starch, mustard and cheese.

The cathedral (13th/14th cent.) contains the tomb of Bossuet, bishop from 1681 to 1704.

Mecca Saudi Arabia. Joint cap. (with Riyadh) of Saudi Arabia and Cap. of the Hejaz 64 km (40 miles) E of Jidda, its port on the Red Sea. Pop. (1991) 630,000. The holiest city of Islam, being the birthplace of Mohammed (c. 569–632). Lies in a hollow surrounded by barren hills. In early times it was the hub of desert caravan routes and

long before the time of Mohammed it had a reputation as a holy place; in modern times its prosperity depends very largely on visiting pilgrims (about a million annually). The only notable building is the Great Mosque, which consists of a large courtyard enclosed by cloisters. At its centre is the Kaaba, a small stone building without windows, almost cubical in shape, which was a pre-Islamic temple and has been twice rebuilt. Part of the ceremonial duty of the pilgrim is to kiss the sacred black stone embedded in the SE corner of the Kaaba as he circumambulates the building seven times; this stone, probably a meteorite, is believed to have been given to Abraham by Gabriel. In the courtyard, too, are the well Zamzam, associated with Hagar and Ishmael, the reputed tombs of Hagar and Ishmael, and the Maqam Ibrahim, a sacred stone said to bear the imprint of Abraham's foot. Mecca was under the rule of the Turks from 1517 (though at times only nominally) until 1916, when they were expelled by Husain ibn Ali; the city was taken by Ibn Saud in 1924.

Mechelen (Mechlin, Fr. **Malines)** Belgium. Town in Antwerp province on the Dyle R. 23 km (14 miles) NNE of Brussels. Pop. (1993) 75,740. Once famous for its lace; now a railway junction and industrial centre.

Railway engineering and motor-car assembly. Manufactures furniture, machinery, textiles and paper.

The cathedral (12th/14th-cent.) contains Van Dyck's *Crucifixion*; two other churches have Rubens masterpieces.

Mecklenburg-West Pomerania Germany. *Land* divided into six urban districts, 12 rural districts and 1079 communes. Area 22,947 sq km (8860 sq. miles). Pop. (1996) 1,817,196. Bounded on the N by the Baltic. Cap. Schwerin. Rostock and Warnemünde are leading ports. Flat, forming part of the N German lowlands with many lakes. Chief occupation agriculture. Principal crops rye, potatoes, sugar-beet. Occupied in the 6th cent. by Slavonic tribes. Created a duchy 1348. By 1701 its lands had been divided into two duchies, Mecklenburg-Schwerin and

Medan

Mecklenburg-Strelitz, later elevated to grand duchies, which joined the German Empire 1871. At the end of World War I the grand dukes were deposed and in 1934 the two states were reunited as the state of Mecklenburg. Later Pomerania was inc. with it.

Medan Indonesia. Cap. of N Sumatra province on the Deli R. in NE Sumatra; its port, Belawan is 24 km (15 miles) N. Pop. (1990) 1,730,000. Commercial centre. Trade in tobacco and rubber. Seat of the University of North Sumatra (1952).

Medellín Colombia. Cap. of the Antioquia department in the NW in an enclosed valley of the Central Cordillera on a tributary of the Cauca R. at a height of 1500 m (4920 ft). Pop. (1992) 1,581,364. Despite its remoteness, it has Colombia's main textile industries.

Also manufactures steel, cement, leather goods. Centre of a coffee-growing, cattle-rearing and goldmining area. Also centre for the drugs trade.

Seat of the University of Antioquia (1871). Founded 1675.

Medford (Massachusetts) USA. Industrial town and residential suburb of NW Boston. Pop. (1990) 57,400.

Manufactures machinery, chemicals and soap.

Developed in the 18th and 19th cent. as a centre of shipbuilding and rum production.

Medford (Oregon) USA. Town on Bear Creek 190 km (120 miles) S of Eugene. Pop. (1987) 45,290.

Commercial centre for an agricultural region, esp. noted for pears. Fruit canneries, lumber and flour mills.

Media. Ancient country in SW Asia inhabited by the Medes in the area now NW Iran between the Zagros and the Elburz Mountains. With its cap. Ecbatana (modern Hamadan), it became powerful in the 8th cent. BC. and helped to overthrow the Assyrian Empire in the following cent. Conquered by Cyrus of Persia 550 BC; thereafter part of the Persian Empire.

Medicine Hat Canada. Industrial town in SE Alberta on the S Saskatchewan R. Pop. (1991) 43,265. In a region producing natural gas and coal. Railway engineering.

Medina (Ar. **Al Madinah**) Saudi Arabia. Town in the Hejaz 354 km (220 miles) N of Mecca in a basin of the plateau at a height of 600 m (1968 ft). Pop. (1991) 400,000. Sacred city of the Muslims, second only to Mecca, situated in an oasis well-known for its dates and also producing cereals and fruits. Here Mohammed lived after his flight from Mecca (622) and here he died. The most important building is the Mosque of the Prophet, which is supposed to contain the tombs of Mohammed and Omar. The Hejaz Railway, built to it from Damascus (1908), is now disused, but it still receives many pilgrims. Taken by Ibn Saud 1925.

Medina (Egypt) ➤FAIYUM, EL.

Mediterranean Sea. Ancient Mare Internum. Extensive inland sea lying between Europe, Africa and SW Asia. Area (excluding the Black Sea) 2,512,300 sq km (970,000 sq. miles). Length W–E 3700 km (2300 miles). Greatest width 1290 km (800 miles). Divided by a ridge from Cap Bon (Tunisia) to Sicily into a W and an E basin. Its major subdivisions, formed by various large islands and peninsulas, inc. the Tyrrhenian Sea, Adriatic Sea, Ionian Sea, Aegean Sea and the Black Sea with the Sea of Azov. Connected with the Atlantic (W) by the narrow Strait of Gibraltar; with the Black Sea (NE) by the Aegean Sea, Dardanelles, Sea of Marmara and Bosporus; and with the Red Sea (SE) by the Suez Canal and the Gulf of Suez. Among its many islands are the Balearic Is., Corsica, Sardinia and Sicily in the W section and Malta, Crete, Cyprus, Rhodes, the Ionian Is., the Dodecanese and the Aegean Is. in the E.

Evaporation exceeds precipitation and inflow from rivers, so that the Mediterranean has a higher salinity than the Atlantic; a current from the Atlantic therefore enters through the Strait of Gibraltar near the surface, while a return current at greater depth flows from the Mediterranean into the Atlantic. Similar opposing currents flow between the Mediterranean and the Black Sea. A further characteristic of the Mediterranean is that it is almost tideless. It experiences such a distinctive type of climate that the term 'Mediterranean climate' has been applied to similar regions in other parts of the world. In the winter it enjoys mild weather and moderate rainfall, received from depressions driven along by the prevailing westerly winds; in summer the winds have a more northerly trend and the weather is hot, dry and sunny. Thus there are many popular resorts along its shores, e.g. on the Riviera, while the natural vegetation of the surrounding lands consists of drought-resistant, evergreen trees and shrubs, and olives, citrus fruits and flowers are characteristically cultivated. Among the local winds are the hot sirocco from N Africa and the cold mistral down the Rhône valley. Important tunny and anchovy fisheries.

Encouraged by its relative calmness, the Phoenicians, Greeks, Romans, Venetians and Genoese made the Mediterranean a commercial highway; to the Romans it was *mare nostrum*. Declined in importance in the late 15th cent. with the opening of the route to India by the Cape of Good Hope, but revived with the construction of the Suez Canal (1869). Britain sought to safeguard the route by establishing naval bases at Gibraltar and Malta.

Medjerda River Algeria/Tunisia. Ancient Bagradas. Principal river of Tunisia 418 km (260 miles) long, rising near Souk Ahras in NE Algeria and flowing ENE to the Gulf of Tunis 32 km (20 miles) N of Tunis. The extremely fertile valley produces olives, cereals, fruits and vegetables, and provides the main route by rail and road from Algeria to Tunis.

Médoc France. District in the Gironde department in the SW, consisting of a strip of land extending about 80 km (50 miles) along the left bank of the Gironde. Contains such famous vineyards as those of Château Mar-

gaux and Château Latour and produces some of France's finest wines (mainly red).

Medway River England. River 113 km (70 miles) long, rising in three headstreams in Surrey and Sussex and flowing N and E through Kent past Tonbridge, Maidstone (head of navigation) and the Medway Towns (Rochester, Chatham and Gillingham) to enter the Thames estuary at Sheerness.

Meerut India. Town in Uttar Pradesh 60 km (37 miles) NE of Delhi. Pop. (1991) 753,000.

Industries inc. iron and steel, flour and oilseed milling, Manufactures cotton goods, chemicals, soap, pottery, plastics, sports goods, transformers and electronic equipment. Trade in cereals, sugar-cane, oilseeds and cotton.

Owes its modern importance to the establishment of the former British military cantonment (1806). Here the Indian Mutiny began (1857).

Megara Greece. Town in the Attica *nome* 32 km (20 miles) W of Athens. Pop. (1985) 18,000. Trade in wine, olive oil. The ancient Megara was an influential city from the 8th cent. BC, declined in the 5th cent., revived somewhat in the 4th cent. Founded Chalcedon, Byzantium and other colonies.

Meghalaya India. State in the NE, formed in 1972 from the Garo Hills district and the Khasi Hills and Jaintia Hills districts of Assam. Area 22,429 sq km (8761 sq. miles). Pop. (1991) 1,760,626, mainly of various hill tribes. Cap. Shillong.

Rice and maize are the major food crops. Commercial cultivation of tea has started and forests on the hill slopes provide abundant timber. Minerals inc. coal, limestone, dolomite, fire-clay, felspar and quartz. Industries inc. the manufacture of cement, tantalum capacitors, electronic goods and watches.

Megiddo Israel. Town in ancient Palestine at the S edge of the Plain of Esdraelon 29 km (18 miles) SE of Haifa. Scene of several battles (possibly the biblical Armageddon): Thothmes III defeated the Canaanites (c. 1500 BC); King Josiah was defeated and killed by Pharaoh Necho II (609 BC); the British under Gen. E. H. H. Allenby (1861–1936) defeated the Turks (1918).

Meissen Germany. Town in Saxony in the Dresden district on the Elbe R. 23 km (14 miles) NW of Dresden. Pop. (1989) 37,100. Since 1710 the centre of manufacture of Dresden china, made from local kaolin. Also manufactures matches, glass, textiles. Industries inc. sugar-refining and brewing.

Founded in the 10th cent. Cathedral (13th/15th-cent.); castle (15th-cent.).

Meknès (Mequinez) Morocco. Former cap. 56 km (35 miles) WNW of Fès at a height of 510 m (1673 ft) on a spur N of the Middle Atlas range. Pop. (1985) 325,000. Linked by rail and road with Fez, Rabat and Casablanca.

In a fertile region producing olives, cereals and vines. Manufactures pottery, leather and carpets.

Became famous when the Sultan Muley Ismail built its 17th-cent. palace, for which it was called the 'Moroccan Versailles'. Occupied by the French 1911.

Mekong River. Great river in SE Asia 4000 km (2500 miles) long, rising in the Tanghla Range of Qinghai province (China) and flowing SE and S through deep gorges at about 3000 m (9840 ft) across E Tibet parallel to the Chang Jiang (E) and Salween (W) rivers in W Yunnan province. It then forms the boundary of Laos with Myanmar (Burma) and part of that with Thailand, continuing past Luang Prabang and Vientiane, crosses Cambodia and in South Vietnam enters the Nan Hai (South China Sea) by an extensive delta. At Phnom Penh (Cambodia) the river is linked with L. Tonlé Sap, which pours water into it during the dry season and acts as a flood reservoir in the rainy season. For about 483 km (300 miles) of its lower course the Mekong is navigable by vessels of moderate size. The delta is a great rice-growing region.

Melaka (Malacca) Malaysia. 1. State in West Malaysia. Area 1658 sq km (640 sq. miles). Pop. (1990) 627,400. Consists of a low coastal plain rising to low hills inland. Chief products rubber, coconuts, rice. Came into British hands as one of the Straits Settlements 1824. Joined the Federation of Malaya after World War II.

2. Cap. of Melaka on the Strait of Malacca 200 km (125 miles) NW of Singapore. Pop. (1980) 88,000. Seaport. Exports rubber and copra.

Probably founded in the 14th cent. Held by the Portuguese from 1511, the Dutch from 1641 and the British from 1824. Later overshadowed by Singapore and trade much reduced by harbour silting.

Melanesia W Pacific Ocean. One of the three principal divisions of the Pacific islands, the others being Micronesia and Polynesia. Inhabited by Melanesians, a dark-skinned people with frizzy hair, thick lips and flattened noses, in general of negroid stock but often showing traces of Polynesian admixture. Melanesia inc. Fiji, New Caledonia, Vanuatu, Loyalty Is., Solomon Is., Santa Cruz Is., Admiralty Is. and the Louisiade and Bismarck archipelagoes.

Melbourne Australia. Cap. of Victoria on the Yarra R. near the outlet into Hobson's Bay, Port Phillip Bay. Pop. (1993) 3,189,200.

Second city of Australia and chief seaport of the state; inc. Port Melbourne and Williamstown, together handling about one-quarter of the Commonwealth shipping. Most of the industries of the state are located in the city and its suburbs. Engineering, oil-refining, meat-processing and fruit-canning. Manufactures agricultural machinery, vehicles, aircraft, electrical equipment, woollen textiles, fertilizers and soap. Exports wool, flour, dairy produce, meat, fruit and canned produce.

Among its notable buildings are the Anglican and Roman Catholic cathedrals and the State Parliament House; has a famous cricket ground, the Flemington racecourse and spacious botanical gardens. Founded 1835; soon became a commercial centre and, like the state, developed rapidly after the gold rush of 1851. University (1854). First cap. of the Commonwealth 1901–27.

Melcombe Regis ➤WEYMOUTH AND MELCOMBE REGIS.

Melilla Spanish N Africa. Seaport and garrison town on the Mediterranean coast of N Africa 257 km (160 miles) ESE of Tangier; an enclave in Morocco. Pop. (1991) 56,497. Important fishing port. Exports iron ore from the Beni bu Ifrur mines (16 km; 10 miles SW). Founded by the Phoenicians; later occupied by the Carthaginians and the Romans.

Taken by Spain 1470; has remained Spanish despite many sieges, inc. that during the revolt led by Abdel Krim (1921–6); Spanish troops withdrew from Morocco to the enclaves of Melilla and Ceuta in 1961.

Melitopol Ukraine. Town on the Molochnaya R. 113 km (70 miles) S of Zaporozhye. Pop. (1990) 175,800.

Manufactures agricultural machinery, diesel engines, clothing and food products.

Melksham England. Market town in Wiltshire on the R. Avon 14 km (9 miles) E of Bath. Pop., urban area (1991), 16,900.

Manufactures tyres and rubber products, rope and matting, flour.

Melos (Milos) Greece. Island of volcanic origin in the Cyclades 23 km (14 miles) long and 13 km (8 miles) wide in the Aegean Sea. Pop. (1985) 4500. Here the statue known as the Venus de Milo, now in the Louvre, was discovered (1820).

Melrose Scotland. Market town in Scottish Borders on the R. Tweed 10 km (6 miles) NE of Selkirk. Pop. (1991) 2270. Resort favoured by tourists wishing to explore the 'Scott country'. The ruins of the 12th-cent. Cistercian abbey, which was destroyed and rebuilt several times and in which Robert Bruce's heart is buried, became national property in 1918; it was described in Walter Scott's *The Lay of the Last Minstrel*, while the town appears as Kennaquhair in his *The Abbot* and *The Monastery*.

Melrose USA. Town in Massachusetts 11 km (7 miles) N of Boston. Pop. (1985) 31,000. Mainly residential. First settled c. 1630.

Melton Mowbray England. Market town in Leicestershire 23 km (14 miles) NE of Leicester. Pop. (1991) 23,348.

Produces pork pies, Stilton cheese, pet foods and footwear. Also a well-known fox-hunting centre.

Memel ➤KLAIPÉDA.

Memel River ➤NEMAN RIVER.

Memmingen Germany. Industrial town and railway junction in Bavaria 51 km (32 miles) SSE of Ulm. Pop. (1986) 37,300. Manufactures textiles, machinery and soap.

Memphis Egypt. Ancient city on the left bank of the Nile 23 km (14 miles) S of Cairo. The first cap. of united ancient Egypt; probably founded by Menes, the first Pharaoh. Pyramids of the Old and Middle Kingdoms extend for 32 km (20 miles) along the Nile to Giza. Under the Ptolemies, second in importance to Alexandria; finally declined when the Arabs founded El Fustat (to the N) and used its stones to build the new city (later Cairo).

Memphis USA. Commercial and industrial city in SW Tennessee on the Chickasaw bluffs above the Mississippi R. Pop. (1990) 610,337. River port. Railway centre.

Important market for cotton and timber. Manufactures agricultural machinery, tyres and other rubber products, glass and textiles. Well-provided with parks, museums and art galleries.

The name was suggested by the similarity of its location on the Mississippi to that of the ancient Egyptian city of Memphis on the Nile. Martin Luther King, US civil rights campaigner (1929–68) was assassinated here.

Menai Strait Wales. Channel 24 km (15 miles) long separating Anglesey from the mainland, crossed by Thomas Telford's suspension bridge (road, 1825) and a tubular bridge (railway, 1850) near the small town of Menai Bridge (Isle of Anglesey).

Menderes River Turkey. Name of several rivers, the most important being the Büyük Menderes ('Great Menderes'), in the SW 400 km (250 miles) long, flowing generally WSW through a valley where figs and olives are cultivated to the Aegean Sea. Has a winding course: the term 'meander' derives from its ancient name (Maeander).

Mendip England. 1. Range of hills in Somerset extending 37 km (23 miles) ESE from Axbridge and rising to 326 m (1069 ft) in Blackdown. Composed mainly of carboniferous limestone; inc. the famous Cheddar Gorge and numerous caves, some of which have yielded human and animal prehistoric remains. 2. District of Somerset inc. Frome, Wells, Shepton Mallet, Glastonbury and Street. Pop. (1994) 98,000.

Mendoza Argentina. Cap. of Mendoza province in the valley of the Mendoza R. in the Andean foothills at a height of 750 m (2460 ft). Pop. (1991) 121,696. Commercial centre in an irrigated region known as 'the garden of the Andes', dealing chiefly in wine. University (1939). Largely destroyed by earthquake 1861. The new planned city is characterized by broad avenues, squares and attractive public parks.

Mendoza River Argentina. River 320 km (200 miles) long, rising on the slopes of Mt Aconcagua, flowing E and N across the Mendoza province and entering L. Guanacache. Followed by the Transandine Railway to Mendoza. Used for hydroelectric power and irrigation.

Menindee ►BROKEN HILL AUSTRALIA.

Menorca ►MINORCA.

Menton (Italian **Mentone**) France. Town in the Alpes-Maritimes department 21 km (13 miles) ENE of Nice on the Mediterranean coast near the Italian border. Pop. (1982) 25,449. Resort with a backcloth of mountains and subtropical vegetation inc. orange, lemon and olive tres. Belonged to Monaco 1815–48, proclaimed its independence and in 1860 was ceded to France.

Menzala (Menzaleh), Lake ►MANZALA, LAKE.

Mequinez ►MEKNÈS.

Merano Italy. Town in Bolzano province, Trentino-Alto Adige 26 km (16 miles) NW of Bolzano. Pop. (1985) 42,000.
Tourist centre and winter resort. Fruit-canning and pottery manufacture.
Gothic church (14th/15th-cent.); 15th-cent. palace.

Mercedes (Buenos Aires) Argentina. Industrial town and railway junction in Buenos Aires province 96 km (60 miles) W of Buenos Aires. Pop. (1984) 40,000.
Manufactures metal goods and footwear.

Mercedes (Villa Mercedes) (San Luis) Argentina. Railway junction and commercial town in San Luis province 96 km (60 miles) ESE of San Luis. Pop. (1984) 20,000.
Trade in wheat, maize and alfalfa.

Mercedes Uruguay. Cap. of the Soriano department in the SW on the Río Negro 257 km (160 miles) NW of Montevideo. Pop. (1985) 37,110.
Resort. River port. Livestock centre. Trade in cereals and wool.

Mercia England. Former kingdom of central England.

Mer de Glace France. Glacier 7 km (4½ miles) long on the N slope of Mont Blanc, formed from 3 confluent glaciers: Talèfre, Leschaux, Tacul. Much visited by tourists. The Arveyron R., tributary of the Arve R. flows from it.

Mergui Archipelago Myanmar (Burma). Group of several hundred islands off the Tenasserim coast in the Andaman Sea. Mountainous, largely covered with forest, picturesque and sparsely populated. Products inc. edible birds' nests, bêche-de-mer and pearls.

Mérida Mexico. Cap. of the Yucatán state in the SE. Pop. (1990) 557,340.
Industrial, commercial and tourist centre. Manufactures rope, twine and sacks from

the locally produced henequen sisal. Exports indigo, sugar, henequen, hides and timber through its port Progreso. Founded (1542) on the site of a Mayan city. Some fine 16th-cent. buildings remain, inc. the cathedral and a Franciscan convent. In the Park of the Americas there is an open-air theatre.

Mérida Spain. Ancient Emerita Augusta. Town in Badajoz province on the Guadiana R. 56 km (35 miles) E of Badajoz. Pop. (1991) 47,982. Rail and road junction. Market town. Famous chiefly for its Roman remains, inc. bridge over the Guadiana, theatre, amphitheatre and circus, a triumphal arch of Trajan, two aqueducts and a fort which was converted into a Moorish alcázar or citadel. Founded 25 BC. As cap. of Lusitania it was one of the finest cities in Iberia and it still prospered under the Visigoths and Moors. Taken from the latter by Alfonso IX of León (1228) and soon declined.

Mérida Venezuela. Cap. of the Mérida state (W) at the foot of the Sierra Nevada de Mérida at a height of 1640 m (5379 ft). Pop. (1990) 167,922. Manufactures textiles and furniture.

Seat of the University of Los Andes (1785). Founded 1558. Often damaged by earthquakes, esp. in 1812 and 1894.

Meriden USA. Industrial town in Connecticut 27 km (17 miles) NNE of New Haven. Pop. (1980) 57,118.

Varied industries, inc. the manufacture of silverware, ball-bearings, glass, equipment for offshore gas wells and electrical equipment.

Meridian USA. Town in Mississippi 140 km (87 miles) E of Jackson. Pop. (1980) 46,577.

Manufactures textiles, clothing, cotton-seed oil.

Merksem Belgium. Town in Antwerp province 3 km (2 miles) NE of Antwerp. Pop. (1982) 41,782. Manufactures glassware.

Meroë Sudan. Ancient city on the right bank of the Nile near Kabushiya (193 km (120 miles) NE of Khartoum). Formerly a cap. of the Ethiopian kingdom (700–300 BC) and

later of the Meroitic kingdom (till AD 350). The latter inc. the Meroë Insula ('Isle of Meroë'), the region bounded by the Nile, the Blue Nile and the Atbara R. Excavations (chiefly 1909–14 and 1921–3) revealed the ruins of palaces and temples, with groups of pyramids nearby.

Merrimack River USA. River 177 km (110 miles) long, formed by the union of the Pemigewasset and Winnipesaukee rivers, flowing SE through New Hampshire, then ENE across NE Massachusetts and entering the Atlantic near Newburyport.

Merseburg Germany. Town in Saxony-Anhalt in the Halle district 16 km (10 miles) S of Halle on the Saale R. Pop. (1991) 46,500.

Industries inc. tanning and brewing. Manufactures paper and machinery.

Cathedral (11th/16th-cent.); 15th-cent. bishop's palace.

Mersey River England. River 113 km (70 miles) long formed by the union of the Goyt and the Etherow rivers, flowing W along the Lancashire–Cheshire border to enter the Irish Sea by a 26-km (16-mile) estuary. Tributaries the Irwell and the Weaver; also joined by the Manchester Ship Canal at Eastham. Warrington, Widnes, Runcorn, Liverpool and Birkenhead stand on its banks and make it commercially the second most important river in the country. Liverpool and Birkenhead are connected across it by railway (1856) and road (1934) tunnels.

Merseyside England. Metropolitan county formed in 1974 around Liverpool and the Mersey estuary from SW Lancashire and part of the Wirral peninsula of Cheshire; inc. also Southport, St Helens and Birkenhead. The S districts are Knowsley, Liverpool, St Helens, Sefton and Wirral. Area 648 sq km (250 sq. miles). Pop. (1994) 1,434,400.

Mersin Turkey. Cap. of İçel province 56 km (35 miles) WSW of Adana. Pop. (1990) 422,360. Chief seaport on the S coast.

Exports cotton, wool, chrome. Large oil refinery (opened 1962).

Merthyr Tydfil Wales. County Borough

on the R. Taff 32 km (20 miles) NNW of Cardiff. Pop. (1990) 59,300.

Industries inc. engineering. Manufactures washing-machines, chemicals and toys. Iron-works were established in the 18th cent. and the town became one of the leading iron and steel centres in Britain. Following the decline in coalmining the town is now largely dependent on light industries.

The name is supposed to be derived from St Tydfil, a Welsh princess martyred by the Saxons in the 5th cent.

Merton England. From 1965 a Greater London borough in the SW, comprising the former urban district of Merton and Morden and the municipal boroughs of Mitcham and Wimbledon, all in Surrey. Pop. (1994) 177,200. Mainly residential. Manufactures toys.

Remains of a 12th-cent. Augustinian priory where Thomas à Becket and Walter de Merton were educated.

Meru, Mount ►TANZANIA.

Mesa USA. Town in Arizona on the Salt R. 21 km (13 miles) E of Phoenix. Pop. (1990) 288,091.

Commercial centre. Cotton-ginning, citrus-fruit packing. Manufactures helicopters.

Founded (1878) by Mormons.

Mesa Verde USA. High plateau in SW Colorado, of great archaeological interest. Occupied for many cent. till AD 1300, it has well-preserved pueblos and cliff dwellings. The Mesa Verde National Park (207 sq km; 80 sq. miles) was established (1906) in order to preserve these settlements.

Meshed Iran ►MASHHAD.

Mesolóngion ►MISSOLONGHI.

Mesopotamia. Name applied rather loosely to a region of SW Asia between the Armenian mountains (N) and the Persian Gulf (S) and between the Syrian Desert (W) and the plateau of Iran (E), and sometimes held to correspond to modern Iraq. It belongs more strictly, however, to the N part of this area between the Tigris and the Euphrates rivers, i.e. about as far S as Baghdad. The name, derived from Greek, means 'Between the Rivers'.

Messenia Greece. *Nome* in the SW Peloponnese, bordering W and S on the Ionian Sea. Area 2991 sq km (1315 sq. miles). Pop. (1991) 116,964. Cap. Kalamáta.

Mainly agricultural. Produces citrus fruits, vines, olives and wheat.

Messina Italy. Ancient Zancle. Cap. of Messina province in Sicily on the W shore of the Strait of Messina 87 km (54 miles) NNE of Catania. Pop. (1992) 232,911.

Seaport. Industrial centre. Exports olive oil, wine, citrus fruit. Manufactures pasta, chemicals and soap.

Twice severely damaged by earthquakes, in 1783 and 1908, the latter being particularly disastrous; the city has few old buildings and modern structures are generally low as a precaution against further possible shocks. The cathedral was rebuilt in the original 11th-cent. style, but again suffered damage in World War II. University (1549). Colonized by Greeks in the 8th cent. BC. Held in turn by Carthaginians, Mamertines, Romans, Saracens, Normans and Spaniards. The last city in Sicily to be liberated by Garibaldi (1860).

Messina, Strait of Italy. Strait between Italy and Sicily 32 km (20 miles) long, 13 km (8 miles) wide in the S but only 3 km (2 miles) in the N. Feared by sailors in ancient times for its currents and whirlpools, the latter giving rise to the legend of Scylla and Charybdis.

Meta River Colombia/Venezuela. River 998 km (620 miles) long, rising S of Bogotá, flowing NE and E across the grassy plains (*llanos*) and joining the Orinoco R. Forms part of the Colombia–Venezuela frontier. Floods extensively in the rainy season (May–October).

Metohija ►KOSOVO-METOHIJA.

Metz France. Ancient Divodurum, Mediomatrica. Prefecture of the Moselle department on the Moselle R. at the confluence with the Seille R. 43 km (27 miles) N of Nancy. Pop. (1990) 123,920.

Centre of the Lorraine iron-mining region. Tanning, brewing, flour-milling, fruit and vegetable preserving. Manufactures footwear, cement, metal goods.

In the old town are the 13th/16th-cent. cathedral and the castellated 15th-cent. Porte des Allemands. Chief town of the ancient Mediomatrici. Became a free imperial city in the 13th cent. Annexed to France 1552. Ceded to Germany after the Franco–Prussian War (1871), but returned to France after World War I (1918). Birthplace of poet Paul Verlaine (1844–96).

Meudon France. Suburb of SW Paris on the Seine R. in the Hauts-de-Seine department. Pop. (1982) 49,004. Manufactures munitions and electrical equipment.

Observatory. The Forest of Meudon to the SW is a favourite resort for Parisians.

Meurthe-et-Moselle France. Department in Lorraine formed (1871) from parts of the old Meurthe and Moselle departments left to France after the Franco–Prussian War; bounded on the N by Belgium and Luxembourg. Area 5235 sq km (2036 sq. miles). Pop. (1990) 711,800. Prefecture Nancy. In the main a plateau drained by the Moselle and its tributary the Meurthe, it is less important for its agriculture than for its rich iron deposits and its metallurgical industry, centred on Nancy, Longwy and Briey. Other towns Lunéville, Toul.

Meuse France. Department in the NE formed mainly from Lorraine and drained by the Meuse R. Area 6220 sq km (2402 sq. miles). Pop. (1990) 196,300. Prefecture Bar-le-Duc. Along the banks of the Meuse SSE–NNW run two ridges, the Argonne (W) and the Côtes de Meuse (E). Cereals, potatoes and fruits cultivated in the valleys. Chief towns Bar-le-Duc, Commercy and Verdun.

Meuse (Dutch **Maas**) **River**. River 933 km (580 miles) long, rising on the Plateau de Langres in the Haute-Marne department, France, flowing generally NNW between the Argonne and the Côtes de Meuse past Sedan and Mézières-Charleville. It turns N through the Ardennes, NE past Namur and Liège (Belgium) and Maastricht (Netherlands), then W to join the Waal, a distributary of the Rhine. Picturesque in the upper course. Carries a great deal of traffic in the lower reaches.

Mexborough England. Town in South Yorkshire on the R. Don 18 km (11 miles) NE of Sheffield. Pop. (1991) 15,282. Potteries.

Mexicali Mexico. Cap. of the Baja (Lower) California state, in the NW on the US frontier adjoining Calexico (California). Pop. (1990) 602,390.

Tourist resort. Commercial centre for an irrigated agricultural area producing cotton, alfalfa, dates, grapefruit and vines. Cotton-ginning. Manufactures cottonseed oil and soap.

Mexico. Federal republic bordered on the N by the USA, W and S by the Pacific Ocean, SE by Guatemala and Belize and the Caribbean Sea and NE by the Gulf of Mexico. Area 1,958,201 sq km (756,066 sq. miles). Pop. (1993) 89,955,000 (71 per cent urban). Life expectancy, 67 years male, 73 female. Cap. Mexico City. Other major cities are Guadalajara, Ciudad Netzahualcóyotl, Monterrey, Mexicali, Puebla, Ciudad Juárez and León. Currency: Peso = 100 centavos. Mexico is extremely mountainous; the dominating physical feature is the Sierra Madre (consisting of two separate ranges, the Sierra Madre Oriental along the Gulf of Mexico and the Sierra Madre Occidental along the Pacific), covering about three-quarters of the country. The highest peaks, which are in the Anáhuac region in the interior, are the three magnificent snow-capped volcanoes, Pico de Orizaba (Volcán Citlaltépetl, 5699 m; 18,697 ft), Popocatépetl, and Ixtaccihuatl (the two latter both over 5200 m (17,030 ft)). The volcano Paricutin erupted in 1943 on the site of the former village, now 2264 m (7451 ft). Mexico is prone to earthquakes. Apart from the Río Bravo de Norte (Rio

Mexico

Grande), the chief rivers are the Río de Las Balsas and the Pánuco, Grijalva, Santiago and Conchos rivers. The largest lake is L. Chapala (1080 sq km; 417 sq. miles). There are two large peninsulas: in the extreme NW the 1223-km (760-mile) mountainous peninsula of Lower Californa (Baja California), separated from the mainland (except in the N) by the Gulf of California; and in the SE is the broad limestone lowland Yucatán peninsula, extending N from the mainland and dividing the Gulf of Mexico from the Caribbean Sea. The broad Gulf of Campeche washes the SE coast and forms an arm of the Gulf of Mexico. The Tropic of Cancer crosses the centre of Mexico, but altitude determines climate. There is a hot zone (*tierra caliente*) along the coast, at up to 900 m (2961 ft); a temperate zone (*tierra templada*) at 900–1800 m (2961–5922 ft); and a cold zone (*tierra fria*) at above 1800 m (5922 ft). Annual rainfall (mainly June–Sept.) varies from about 5 cm (2 ins.) in Sonora (NW) to over 300 cm (120 ins.) in the jungles of Tabasco (SE). Land use: forested 22 per cent, meadows and pastures 39 per cent, agricultural and under permanent cultivation 13 per cent. About 89 per cent of the pop. is Roman Catholic. The official lang. is Spanish but about 25 per cent speak only an Indian lang. There were at least 130 such lang.; today about 80 with about 270 different dialects. The ethnic composition is mestizo 60 per cent, Amerindian 30 per cent. Spanish influence is strong, but Mexican culture and outlook is a distinctive amalgam of Spanish and Indian; in many towns buildings are designed in the Spanish–Moorish or Spanish-colonial style, though in recent years modern architecture has been introduced in the main cities and particularly in Mexico City.

Because of limitations imposed by climate and topography, only a small proportion of the land is under cultivation, but on the plateau the soil is fertile and two crops a year can be grown. About 58 per cent of cultivated land is devoted to grains and of this 43 per cent is maize and 5 per cent wheat. About 26 per cent of the working pop. is engaged in agriculture. Export crops inc. cotton, fruit, vegetables, sugar and coffee. Half the world supply of henequen sisal is grown in the Yucatán peninsula. Mexico is exceptionally rich in minerals and is the world's largest supplier of silver. Other minerals inc. lead, zinc, copper, sulphur, phosphates, coal, iron and uranium. There are large reserves of oil and natural gas and these have been exploited in recent decades. Also industrial production has increased and manufactures inc. textiles, iron and steel, petrochemicals, vehicles, cement and food-processing. Tourism is important and there were more than 6 million foreign tourists (mainly from the USA) in 1991.

A number of ancient civilizations have flourished in the lands occupied by modern Mexico, which takes its name from the central valley ruled by the Aztecs at the time of the coming of the Spaniards. In Yucatán farther S was the last centre of the Mayan civilization, then already in decline. The Aztecs, although they had neither metal tools nor the wheel, had evolved a highly sophisticated culture, marred by their obsession with the need for human sacrifice to propitiate their gods; their cap., Tenochtitlán, aroused the admiration and the cupidity of the Spanish invaders, who by 1521 destroyed both the cap. and the Aztec rulers. A 300-year period of Spanish rule began. Mexican independence was regained, in 1821, when General Itúrbide established his empire; when he died (1824), a republic was set up. At that time Mexico possessed large areas in what is now the USA; in 1836 Texas rebelled and formed an independent republic, joining the USA in 1845. This led to the Mexican War (1846–8), as a result of which Mexico ceded to the US all territories N of the Rio Grande. The country thus acquired its present boundaries and, except for the brief French occupation (1864–7) under the Emperor Maximilian, it has remained a republic. After a half-century of political disorder Porfirio Díaz assumed power in 1876 and was installed as president, remaining in office (except 1880–4) until 1910. He imposed stability, encouraged foreign investment, and developed the railways and mining industries, but also ruthlessly suppressed opposition and ignored the grinding poverty of the masses. A spontaneous rebellion against his dictatorship (1910) became a revolution inaugurating the modern period of Mexican history, marking the beginning of an era of reform which has included the new constitution of 1917 and has been amended from time to time. There is a General Congress of two chambers: a 500-seat Chamber of Deputies directly chosen for 3 years and a 64-member Senate directly elected for 6 years; 2 from each state and 2 from the Federal District.

Mexico is administratively divided into 31 states and a Federal District: (cap. in brackets) –

Distrito Federal (México City)
Aguascalientes (Aguascalientes)
Baja California (Mexicali)
Baja California Sur (La Paz)
Campeche (Campeche)
Chiapas (Tuxtla Gutiérrez)
Chihuahua (Chihuahua)
Coahuila (Saltillo)
Colima (Colima)
Durango (Victoria de Durango)
Guanajuato (Guanajuato)
Guerrero (Chilpancingo)
Hidalgo (Pachuco de Soto)
Jalisco (Guadalajara)
México (Toluca de Lerdo)
Michoacán de Ocampo (Morelia)
Morelos (Cuernavaca)
Nayarit (Tepic)
Nuevo León (Monterrey)
Oaxaca (Oaxaca de Juárez)
Puebla (Puebla de Zaragoza)
Querétaro (Querétaro)
Quintana Roo (Chetumal)
San Luis Potosí (San Luis Potosí)
Sinaloa (Culiacán Rosales)
Sonora (Hermosillo)
Tabasco (Villahermosa)
Tamaulipas (Ciudad Victoria)
Tlaxcala (Tlaxcala)
Veracruz (Jalapa Enríquez)
Yucatán (Mérida)
Zacatecas (Zacatecas)

Mexico Mexico. State on the central plateau,

comprising part of the valley of Mexico, and the Toluca Valley, encircling the federal district. Area 21,461 sq km (8284 sq. miles). Pop. (1990) 9,815,901. Cap. Toluca. The volcanoes Popocatépetl (5456 m; 18,191 ft) and Ixtaccihuatl (5289 m; 17,348 ft) are on the SE border. The Federal District, containing Mexico City, the national cap. is administratively separate.

Main occupations agriculture, dairy-farming, mining (silver, gold, copper, lead and zinc). Bulls for the bullrings bred in the Toluca Valley.

The most notable of Aztec and pre-Aztec remains is the Pyramid of the Sun at Teotihuacán.

Mexico, Gulf of. Arm of the Atlantic Ocean, bounded by the USA (N and NE) and Mexico (W and SW). Linked with the Atlantic by the Florida Strait and with the Caribbean Sea by the Yucatán Channel. Area 1,813,000 sq km (700,000 sq. miles). The most important rivers flowing into it are the Mississippi and the Rio Grande. Shores generally low and sandy, with many lagoons; few harbours. Has considerable influence on the climate of N America; a branch of the Equatorial Current enters it via the Yucatán Channel and originates the Gulf Stream. There is submarine oil drilling.

Mexico City Mexico. Cap. of Mexico and of the Federal District, near the S end of the central plateau at a height of 2260 m (7413 ft). Pop. (1990) 8,236,960 (Federal District). Dominated by the snow-capped Sierra Nevada, with the lofty volcanoes Popocatépetl and Ixtaccihuatl to the SE. Mild, healthy climate; rainfall 50–60 cm (20–25 ins.) annually. The administrative, commercial, industrial and cultural centre. Roads, railways and airways radiate from it.

Manufactures textiles, glass, tyres, tobacco products. Motor-vehicle assembly, gold and silver refining, brewing.

Architecture ranges from Spanish-Baroque to modern skyscrapers; there has been much demolition and rebuilding in recent years. The cathedral, begun in 1573, stands with other public buildings (inc. the

National Palace) on the Plaza Mayor (Zócalet), the central square into which many of the main streets lead. Seat of the National University (founded 1551). It also has a mint, a large bullring and many interesting churches. Built on the site of the Aztec cap. Tenochtitlán, captured and destroyed by Cortés 1521. An earthquake in 1985 killed some 2000 people.

Mezzogiorno Italy. Area of southern Italy S of Naples, which is economically undeveloped. Mezzogiorno is Italian for 'noon' and refers to the heat at that time of the day.

Miami USA. City in Florida and famous holiday resort on Biscayne Bay at the mouth of the short Miami R. Pop. (1990) 358,548. Warm climate and magnificent beaches. Greater Miami inc. Miami Beach, Coral Gables and Hialeah. Important airport and harbour where many cruise ships call. Varied industries. The main development came with the Florida land boom of the 1920s. University (1925), at Coral Gables. Landing place for Caribbean immigrants.

Miami Beach Florida. Holiday resort on an island in SE Florida, separated from Miami by Biscayne Bay. Pop. (1990) 92,640. Connected with Miami by causeways and bridges.

Miass Russia. Town in the Chelyabinsk Region 80 km (50 miles) WSW of Chelyabinsk. Pop. (1989) 168,000. Manufactures motor cars and is a gold-mining centre.

Michigan USA. State on the Great Lakes. Area 150,779 sq km (58,216 sq. miles). Pop. (1990) 9,295,300. The Lower Peninsula (S) and the Upper Peninsula (N) are separated by the narrow Straits of Mackinac. Generally low-lying; rises to 617 m (2024 ft) in the Porcupine Mountains of the Upper Peninsula. The generally continental climate is much modified by the Great Lakes. Annual rainfall 60–90 cm (25–35 ins.). About 40 per cent of the land is cultivated. Main crops maize, oats, hay, wheat, sugar-beet, potatoes, fruits. The best farmlands are in the S part of the Lower Peninsula. Cattle and pig rearing also important. Principal mineral iron ore (from the Upper Peninsula), followed by petroleum. Leading industry automobile manufacture; produces about half the USA's motor vehicles. Chief towns Detroit, Flint, Grand Rapids, Dearborn, Lansing. First explored by the French in the early 17th cent. The first permanent settlement was established (1668) by Marquette at Sault Ste Marie. Ceded to England in 1763 and to the USA in 1783 (as part of the NW Territory). Became a separate territory in 1805, comprising only the Lower Peninsula; the Upper Peninsula was added on the attainment of statehood (1837). Admitted to the Union in 1837 as the 26th state.

Michigan, Lake USA. Third largest of the Great Lakes, the only one wholly within the USA, at a height of 177 m (581 ft). Area 58,016 sq km (22,400 sq. miles). Linked with L. Huron by the Straits of Mackinac (NE). Carries an immense amount of shipping. Leading ports Chicago, Milwaukee. Main cargoes coal, iron ore and grain.

Michigan City USA. Industrial town, port and resort in Indiana on L. Michigan 37 km (23 miles) ENE of Gary. Pop. (1988) 35,330. Manufactures furniture and machinery.

Michoacán Mexico. Mountainous state on the Pacific seaboard with a narrow coastal plain. Area 59,864 sq km (23,202 sq. miles). Pop. (1990) 3,534,042 (largely Tarascan Indians). Cap. Morelia. Several volcanoes inc. Paricutin. Many large lakes. Cereals, sugar-cane, rice, tobacco cultivated. Minerals inc. silver, lead and copper.

Michurinsk Russia. Town on the Voronezh R. 68 km (42 miles) WNW of Tambov. Pop. (1989) 109,000. Railway junction. Industrial centre. Railway and other engineering. Founded 1636. Became an important horticultural centre, with an experimental institute founded by the botanist Michurin and was named after him in the 1930s.

Micronesia, Federated States of. Comprising 607 islands in the W Pacific Ocean. It inc. 4 states: Yap, Kosrae, Chuuk and Pohnpei. Area 701 sq km (271 sq. miles).

Pop. (1995) 105,000 (26 per cent urban). Life expectancy, 71 years male, 77 female. Cap. Palikir. Other towns Weno, Tol and Kolonia. Currency: US dollar = 100 cents. Yap consists of 4 islands and 13 coral atolls, Kosrae is a single island, Pohnpei a single island and 8 scattered atolls, Chuuk consists of 14 islands within a large reef-fringed lagoon. Land use: forested 23 per cent, meadows and pastures 14 per cent, agricultural and under permanent cultivation 34 per cent.

Mainly subsistence farming but some cash crops are exports: copra, bananas, citrus fruits, taro and peppers. Tourism is an important industry, as is fishing.

There are 8 indigenous lang. spoken but English is the official lang. and is used in schools. The US administered the islands as part of the Pacific Islands Trust Territory 1947 to 1986 when it became an independent state in association with the US. There is an executive presidency with a 14-member National Congress.

Middelburg Netherlands. Cap. of Zeeland province on Walcheren island 6 km (4 miles) NNE of Flushing. Pop. (1994) 40,118.

Market town, linked by canal with Flushing. Railway engineering. Manufactures furniture. An important commercial centre in medieval times.

Has a 12th-cent. abbey. Suffered severely in World War II.

Middleback Range Australia. Sandstone range in South Australia 64 km (40 miles) long N–S in the Eyre Peninsula. Rich deposits of iron ore, exported via Whyalla, mining being mainly in open workings at Iron Knob, Iron Monarch and Iron Baron.

Middle East. Area of the E Mediterranean esp. Israel and the Arab countries from Turkey to N Africa and E to Iran.

Middlesbrough England. Industrial town and now a unitary authority from 1996 on the S bank of the Tees estuary, spanned by transporter (1911) and lift (1934) bridges. Pop. (1991) 147,430.

Important iron and steel centre. Also manufactures chemicals and fertilizers. Har-

bour protected by two large breakwaters. Exports iron and steel, machinery and chemicals. Imports iron ore and timber.

Its rapid development in the 19th cent. was due to the discovery of iron ore in the neighbouring Cleveland Hills and the opening of the Stockton–Darlington railway. Marton, 5 km (3 miles) SSW, was the birthplace of Captain James Cook, English explorer (1728–79).

Middlesex England. Former county in the SE, bounded by Hertfordshire (N), Essex (E), the County of London (SE), Surrey (S) and Buckinghamshire (W), but the name still used by the Royal Mail and cricketers. Generally low-lying, rising from the R. Thames (S) to hills on the N boundary which reach 150 m (492 ft). Mainly residential and industrial. Chief municipal boroughs were Harrow, Ealing, Willesden, Hendon, Wembley. Historic buildings Hampton Court Palace, Syon House. In 1965 almost the entire county was absorbed into Greater London.

Middleton England. Town in Greater Manchester on the R. Irk 8 km (5 miles) NNE of Manchester. Pop. (1991) 45,621.

Manufactures textiles, textile machinery and foam rubber.

Middletown (Ohio) USA. Industrial town on the Great Miami R. 35 km (22 miles) SW of Dayton. Pop. (1990) 46,022. Steel and paper mills.

Middle West, The (Midwest) USA. Loosely, the N part of central USA: Illinois, Indiana, Iowa, Michigan, Minnesota, Ohio and Wisconsin. Sometimes understood to inc. other peripheral states. One of the world's chief grain-producing areas (mainly maize and wheat). Many important industrial centres in the area of the Great Lakes.

Middlewich England. Town in Cheshire 11 km (7 miles) N of Crewe. Pop. (1991) 101,000. The middle of the three 'wiches' or salt towns – the others being Northwich and Nantwich. Salt-refining. Manufactures chemicals and clothing.

Mid Glamorgan Wales. Former county established in 1974 but reorganized in 1996.

Midhurst England. Town in W Sussex on the R. Rother 16 km (10 miles) N of Chichester. Pop. (1991) 6451. Has a 17th-cent. grammar school and the ruins of the 16th-cent. Cowdray House.

Midi-Pyrénées France. Region in the S. The largest region centred on Toulouse situated between the Pyrénées and the Massif Central. Area 45,348 sq. km (17,516 sq. miles). Pop. (1990) 2,431,000. Regional cap. Toulouse. It comprises the departments of Ariège, Aveyron, Haute-Garonne, Gers, Lot, Hautes-Pyrénées, Tarn and Tarn-et-Garonne.

Midland (Michigan) USA. Industrial town 31 km (19 miles) NW of Saginaw. Pop. (1985) 38,500.

Important chemical industry. Oil-refining. Manufactures cement products and toys.

Midland (Texas) USA. Industrial town 450 km (280 miles) WSW of Fort Worth. Pop. (1990) 89,500.

In an oil-producing and cattle-ranching region. Oil-refining. Manufactures oilfield equipment and chemicals.

Midlands England. The central counties, corresponding roughly to the Anglo-Saxon kingdom of Mercia, which originally comprised Staffordshire, Derbyshire and Nottinghamshire and the N parts of Warwickshire and Leicestershire. Mercia expanded far beyond this area, however, and the term is often assumed to inc. also parts of Northants, Bedfordshire, Oxfordshire and Buckinghamshire.

Midlothian Scotland. New Unitary Authority created in 1996, formerly in Lothian Region. Pop. (1993) 79,910.

Midway Islands N Pacific Ocean. Atoll and two small islands 2100 km (1300 miles) WNW of Honolulu. Area 5 sq km (2 sq. miles). Pop. (1981) 453 (excluding military personnel). The outer reef is 24 km (15 miles)

in circumference; the lagoon is entered on the S side, between the two islands. Discovered (1859) by Captain Brooks. Annexed by the USA 1867. A naval air base was established in 1941. The Americans decisively defeated the Japanese nearby in an air–sea battle in 1942, the first serious reverse for the Japanese in the Pacific in World War II.

Mieres Spain. Town in Oviedo province, Asturias, 14 km (9 miles) SSE of Oviedo. Pop. (1981) 58,000.

Industrial centre in a coal and iron mining region. Steel and chemical manufactures.

Milan (Italian **Milano**) Italy. Ancient Mediolanum. Cap. of Milano province and the country's second largest city on the Olona R. and on the Plain of Lombardy. Pop. (1992) 1,358,627.

Important railway, road and canal junction. The country's chief industrial, commercial and banking centre. Centre for printing and publishing. Manufactures textiles, locomotives, cars, chemicals, machinery and there is a large trade in cereals and cheese.

In the heart of the city is the Piazza del Duomo, at one end of which is the great Gothic cathedral, with its many turrets and pinnacles and over 4000 statues, the third largest church in Europe, begun in 1386 and not completed until the 19th cent. Among the oldest churches are S Ambrogio, founded by St Ambrose in 386, the present Romanesque building dating from the 12th cent., and S Lorenzo, several times restored since the 6th cent.; in the former refectory near the 15th-cent. S María delle Grazie is Leonardo da Vinci's painting of *The Last Supper*. There are notable art galleries and museums in the Palazzo di Brera, the Palazzo dell'Ambrosiana and the Castello Sforzesco. La Scala theatre (1778) was severely damaged in World War II, like many other historic buildings, and was rebuilt. Both the universities were founded in the 1920s. Important in Roman times. Destroyed by the Huns and later the Goths; passed to the Lombards 569. Ruled by the Visconti family 1277–1447 and by the Sforza family 1450–1535. Napoleon made it cap. of the Cisalpine Republic (1797) and of the kingdom of Italy 1805–14. United with Italy 1861 and rapidly developed into an industrial city.

Mildenhall England. Market town in NW Suffolk on the Lark R. 31 km (19 miles) NE of Cambridge. Pop. (1991) 10,468. Important RAF station.

Mildura Australia. Town in Victoria on the Murray R. 480 km (300 miles) NW of Melbourne. Pop. (1986) 18,382.

Centre of an irrigated region, built on gridiron pattern, grew with irrigation of vineyards and orchards of citrus fruits, apricots and peaches. Fruit and vegetables canned and packed; dried fruits, wool and wheat are handled.

Miletus Turkey. Ancient city and seaport in Asia Minor near the mouth of the Maeander R. Leading commercial centre of Ionia with an extensive trade in the Black Sea area, where it had founded more than 60 cities by the mid 7th cent. BC. Also a centre of learning. Birthplace of such famous Greeks as Thales (c. 640–546 BC) and Anaximander (611–547 BC). Its harbour was gradually silted up by the Maeander, however, and it declined.

Milford USA. Town in SW Connecticut on Long Island Sound. Pop. (1987) 52,100. Resort.

Oyster fisheries. Manufactures metal goods and hardware.

A typical old-fashioned New England town. Founded 1639.

Milford Haven Wales. Town in Pembrokeshire on the N side of the inlet of the same name and 10 km (6 miles) WNW of Pembroke. Pop. (1991) 13,194.

Fishing port. Owing to its development as an oil terminal (with refineries), capable of accommodating the largest tankers.

Millwall England. District in the London borough of Tower Hamlets on the Isle of Dogs. Contains Millwall Docks. Known as Marshwall until the 18th cent., when several windmills were set up in the area.

Milngavie Scotland. Town in East Dunbartonshire 8 km (5 miles) NNW of Glasgow. Pop. (1991) 12,592.

Mainly residential. Paper-milling, bleaching and dyeing.

Milos ►MELOS.

Milton ►SITTINGBOURNE AND MILTON.

Milton Keynes England. Town, designated a 'new town' in 1967, in N Buckinghamshire. Pop. (1989) 142,900. About 230 international companies have been attracted to the town, ranging from French perfumes to Japanese electronic components. Over 12 million trees and bushes have been planted since the town began. Headquarters of the Open University (1969).

Milwaukee USA. In Indian 'Good Lands'. The largest city in Wisconsin and an important port on L. Michigan. Pop. (1990) 628,088.

Large brewing and meat-packing industries. Manufactures heavy machinery, electrical equipment and leather goods. Many canals and parks.

Seat of the Marquette University (1881, Roman Catholic). Much of its development was due to German immigrants.

Minaragra ►CERRO DE PASCO.

Minas Uruguay. Cap. of the Lavalleja department (SE) 105 km (65 miles) ENE of Montevideo. Pop. (1985) 26,000.

Granite and marble quarrying in the neighbourhood. Industries inc. brewing. Founded 1783.

Minas Gerais Brazil. In Portuguese 'general mines'. State in the E. Area 587,172 sq km (224,701 sq. miles). Pop. (1991) 746,200. Cap. Belo Horizonte. Mainly plateau. Dry and usually pleasant climate. The first part of the interior to be settled as a result of the discovery of gold and diamonds in the 18th cent. For 100 years the richest part of Brazil, centred on the earlier cap., Ouro Prêto.

The gold is now largely exhausted, but the state is rich in minerals, esp. iron ore. Also diamonds, manganese, uranium and aluminium. Agriculture now well developed: maize, beans, coffee, cotton, tobacco and fruit are grown; dairy-farming, cattle-rearing. Belo Horizonte is a fast-growing industrial centre.

Minch (North Minch) Scotland. Arm of the Atlantic separating Lewis in the Outer Hebrides from the mainland, 32–74 km (20–46 miles) wide. Continued SW by the Little Minch, 23–40 km (14–25 miles) wide, separating Harris and N Uist from Skye.

Mindanao Philippines. Second largest island at the S end of the group and NE of Borneo. Area 101,919 sq km (39,351 sq. miles). Pop. (1990) 14,297,462. Chief towns Davao, Zamboanga. Irregular in shape, with several peninsulas. Densely forested. Mountainous, rising to 2898 m (9505 ft) in Mt Apo, an active volcano. Abacá (Manila hemp), coconuts, rice and maize cultivated. Gold is mined.

Minden Germany. Town in North Rhine-Westphalia on the Weser R. where it is crossed by the Mittelland Canal 42 km (26 miles) NE of Bielefeld. Pop. (1986) 75,400.

Manufactures soap, chemicals and glass. Industries inc. brewing.

The 11th/13th-cent. cathedral was destroyed in World War II. In 1759 the English and Hanoverians under Ferdinand, Duke of Brunswick, defeated the French here.

Mindoro Philippines. Island S of Luzon. Area 10,236 sq km (3952 sq. miles). Pop. (1990) 832,642. Chief town Calapan (pop. 27,000). Interior mountainous, rising to over 2400 m (7872 ft). Rice, maize, coconuts cultivated.

Minehead England. Town in Somerset on the Bristol Channel 34 km (21 miles) NW of Taunton. Pop. (1991) 9158. Seaside resort. A port of some importance from the 16th to the 18th cent., but later declined.

Minho ►ENTRE MINHO E DOURO.

Minho River. River 338 km (210 miles) long rising in the Sierra de Meira in Galicia (Spain), flowing generally SSW, then turning WSW past Orense and forming part of the Spanish–Portuguese border, entering the Atlantic near Caminha (Portugal).

Minneapolis USA. The largest city in Minnesota on the Mississippi R. at the Falls of St Anthony (an important source of water power in the early development) and adjacent to St Paul; the 'Twin Cities' form the financial, commercial and industrial centre of a large agricultural area. Pop. (1990) 368,383.

One of the world's great wheat markets. Principal industry flour-milling. Also manufactures other food products, agricultural machinery and clothing. The silhouette of flour mills and creameries along the Mississippi has been called the 'bread-and-butter skyline'. In one of the parks are the Minnehaha Falls celebrated in Longfellow's *Hiawatha*. L. Minnetonka is 19 km (12 miles) W. Seat of the University of Minnesota (1851).

Minnesota USA. State in the N on the Canadian frontier (N) and L. Superior (NE). Area 217,736 sq km (84,068 sq. miles). Pop. (1990) 4,375,100. Cap. St Paul. Inc. a small detached area on the W side of the Lake of the Woods N of the 49th parallel, the most northerly part of continental USA (excluding Alaska). Mostly prairie, at a height of 300–450 m (984–1476 ft). In the N it forms the watershed of three great drainage systems, Hudson Bay, the St Lawrence and the Mississippi. Thousands of lakes, formed by glacial action. Climate continental. Annual rainfall 50–75 cm (20–30 ins.). Primarily agricultural. Main crops oats, maize, barley and rye. Leading state in butter production. Also produces (chiefly in the Mesabi Range) iron ore. Principal towns Minneapolis, St Paul, Duluth. Early explorers were French missionaries and fur traders. The territory passed to Britain in 1763; the land E of the Mississippi was acquired by the USA in 1783 (from the British) and that W of the river in 1803 (from the French). Admitted to the Union in 1858 as the 32nd state.

Minorca (Sp. **Menorca**) Spain. Second largest and most westerly of the Balearic Is. in the W Mediterranean 40 km (25 miles)

ENE of Majorca. Area 702 sq km (271 sq. miles). Pop. (1985) 59,200. Chief town and seaport Mahón. Generally low-lying, rising to only 338 m (1109 ft) in El Toro, it is exposed to north winds in winter, and has a less equable climate and less fertile soil than Majorca.

Produces cereals, wine, olives. Livestock raised. Tourist industry, though much less developed than in Majorca.

Minot USA. Town in North Dakota on the Souris R. 185 km (115 miles) NNW of Bismarck. Pop. (1985) 33,000. Railway and commercial centre in an agricultural and lignite-mining region.

Minsk Belarus. Cap. of the Belarus (White Russia) on the Svisloch R. Pop. (1990) 1,612,800.

Important railway junction and industrial and cultural centre. Manufactures motor vehicles, tractors, machinery, bicycles, electronics and television sets, textiles and furniture.

Seat of a university (1921) and the Byelorussian Academy of Sciences (1929). Conquered by Lithuania in the 14th cent. and Poland in the 15th cent.; annexed by Russia 1793. During World War II it was almost completely destroyed and its Jewish pop., formerly 40 per cent of the total, fell to 2 per cent.

Minya, El Egypt. Cap. of Minya governorate on the left bank of the Nile 217 km (135 miles) S of Cairo. Pop. (1990) 179,136. River port. Trade in cotton and cereals. Sugar-refining and cotton-ginning.

Mirfield England. Industrial town in West Yorkshire on the R. Calder 6 km (4 miles) NE of Huddersfield. Pop. (1991) 18,459.

Railway and other engineering. Manufactures woollen goods. Seat of a theological college (Community of the Resurrection).

Mirzapur India. Town in SE Uttar Pradesh on the Ganges R. 48 km (30 miles) WSW of Varanasi (Benares). Pop. (1991) 169,336.

Trade in grain, oilseeds, sugar-cane. Manufactures shellac, carpets and brass-ware. Its river banks are lined with bathing ghats and temples; within the municipality is Bindhachal, an important place of pilgrimage.

Miskolc Hungary. Cap. of Borsod-Abaúj-Zemplén county in the NE on the Sajo R. 145 km (90 miles) ENE of Budapest. Pop. (1993) 191,000.

Industrial centre, second in importance only to Budapest. Manufactures iron and steel (using local iron ore and lignite), railway rolling-stock, textiles, leather goods and furniture. Industries inc. food-processing, flour-milling and wine-making. Considerable trade in cattle, wine and tobacco.

Seat of a technical university (1949). A 13th-cent. church and other ancient buildings.

Mississippi USA. State in the S bordering SE on the Gulf of Mexico. Area 123,584 sq km (47,716 sq. miles). Pop. (1990) 2,573,216. Cap. Jackson. Mainly within the Gulf coastal plain. Highest point Woodall Mountain (246 m; 807 ft) in the NE. Drained (in the W) by the Yazoo R. system and the Big Black R., flowing into the Mississippi and (in the E and S) by the Pearl, Pascagoula and Tombigbee river systems, flowing into the Gulf of Mexico. Extensive swamps in the Mississippi flood plain. Climate humid subtropical, with long, hot summers, short, mild winters and an annual rainfall of 120–140 cm (50–55 ins.). Over half the state is forest; lumbering important.

Main occupation agriculture. Leading crop cotton, esp. in the Yazoo basin. Principal mineral products petroleum, natural gas. Chief towns Jackson and Meridian. First settled (1699) by the French at Biloxi Bay. Part of Louisiana till 1763, when France yielded her lands E of the Mississippi to Britain. On the side of the Confederacy in the American Civil War. Coast devastated by hurricane Camille, with much loss of life, esp. between Gulfport and Biloxi (1969). Admitted to the Union in 1817 as the 20th state.

Mississippi River USA. River in central

USA, second in length among N American rivers only to the Missouri, its chief tributary; 3778 km (2348 miles) long, rising in streams draining into L. Itasca at a height of 450 m (1476 ft) in N Minnesota, flowing generally S and entering the Gulf of Mexico. The Missouri R. and the lower Mississippi (from the confluence) are sometimes considered as one river, the Mississipppi–Missouri, a continuous waterway 6050 km (3760 miles) long, whose drainage basin covers 3,222,000 sq km (1,244,000 sq. miles). The lower Mississippi meanders freely in a wide flood plain and constantly changes course.

In its upper course the Mississippi descends over 18 m (60 ft) in less than 1.6 km (1 mile) at the Falls of St Anthony near Minneapolis and St Paul (as against an average descent of little more than 0.3 m (1 ft) in every 3.2 km (2 miles)). It is joined by the Missouri R. 27 km (17 miles) above St Louis, the largest city on the river. At Cairo (Illinois) it is joined by the Ohio R. and continues past Memphis to the Red R. confluence in Louisiana, then flows SE past Baton Rouge and New Orleans, through the delta, to the Gulf of Mexico. Along the lower Mississippi flooding is a serious problem; the river is lined by artificial levees rising 6–8 m (20–26 ft) above the natural banks. Even so, floods occasionally (e.g. 1927, 1937) inundate large areas of 'protected' land.

In Algonquin Indian, Mississippi means 'Great River'. Discovered (1541) by the Spaniard de Soto. The upper reaches were explored by Marquette and Jolliet (1673) and the lower course by La Salle (1682). Navigated by steamboats from c. 1820, ushering in the most colourful period in its history, richly celebrated in American literature. The development of the railways gradually diminished its navigational importance. Today its main value lies in irrigation and urban water supply.

Missolonghi (Gr. **Mesolóngion**) Greece. Cap. of the *nome* of Aetolia and Acarnania on the N side of the Gulf of Patras and 32 km (20 miles) WNW of Patras. Pop. (1985) 10,000. Trade in agricultural produce. Noted for its defence against the Turks in 1822, 1823 and again in 1825–6. Has a monument to Byron, English poet, who died here (1824).

Missoula USA. Town in W Montana 153 km (95 miles) WNW of Helena. Pop. (1985) 34,000.
Industries inc. flour-milling and sugar-refining. Tourist industry. Seat of Montana State University (1895).

Missouri USA. State in central USA, bordered on the E by the Mississippi R. Area 180,456 sq km (69,674 sq. miles). Pop. (1990) 5,117,073. Cap. Jefferson City. The N consists of rolling prairies, crossed W–E by the Missouri R., which also forms part of the W boundary. The S is largely occupied by the Ozark Mountains, with an average height of c. 330 m (1080 ft). The SE corner comes within the Mississippi flood plain. Climate generally humid continental. Annual rainfall 75–125 cm (30–50 ins.). Tall prairie grass abounds in the N and W, and helps in the raising of livestock (chiefly cattle and pigs). Leading crops maize, winter wheat, oats, soya beans. Leading state in lead production. St Louis and Kansas City, by far the largest cities, are the main industrial centres. The first European explorers were the Frenchmen Marquette and Jolliet (1673) and La Salle (1682). Belonged to Spain 1752–1800 and was then returned to France; ceded to the USA by the Louisiana Purchase (1803). In the American Civil War Confederate sympathizers were at first dominant, but the Union forces gradually gained control. Admitted to the Union in 1821 as the 24th state.

Missouri River USA. Chief tributary of the Mississippi R., 4367 km (2714 miles) long (the longest river in N America), rising near Three Forks in the Rocky Mountains in SW Montana at a height of 1200 m (3936 ft), formed by the union of the Jefferson, Gallatin and Madison rivers; flowing N and E through Montana, it turns S and SE, traverses North Dakota and South Dakota, forms several state boundaries and finally crosses Missouri, flowing E to its confluence with the Mississippi 27 km (17 miles) above St Louis. Tributaries inc. the Yellowstone, the Cheyenne, the White, the Niobrara, the Big Sioux, the Little Sioux, the Platte and the Kansas rivers. The most important towns on its banks are Kansas City (Missouri), Kansas City (Kansas), Omaha (Nebraska). Its discharge fluctuates widely, for example increasing in the flood season at Kansas City to more than 20 times the minimum flow. Flood-control, power and irrigation projects are now amalgamated into one overall scheme for the river basin; several dams have been constructed, e.g. Fort Peck Dam (Montana). High water is in April (from spring rain and snow melting on the plains) and June (from snow melting in the Rockies). Long used as a waterway by the Indians, it was first explored by European fur traders in the 18th cent. Steam-boats were introduced in 1819, but river traffic declined with the advent of the railways. Today it is more important for irrigation and water supply than as a trade route.

Misurata Libya. Cap. of Misurata division in Tripolitania 193 km (120 miles) ESE of Tripoli on the coast road to Benghazi. Pop. (1984) 178,300. Oasis. Trade in dates and cereals. Manufactures carpets and mats. The port is Misurata Marina 11 km (7 miles) E. Cap. of the short-lived Republic of Tripolitania during World War I.

Mitau ➤JELGAVA.

Mitcham England. Former municipal borough in NE Surrey 11 km (7 miles) S of London, for which it is a dormitory suburb; from 1965 part of the London borough of Merton. Mainly residential.

Manufactures paints, varnishes and pharmaceutical products. Formerly noted for the cultivation of lavender and other aromatic herbs.

Mito Japan. Cap. of the Ibaraki prefecture 96 km (60 miles) NE of Tokyo. Pop. (1990) 234,970. Ancient castle town and commercial centre. Site of two nuclear power plants nearby. In the early 17th cent. it became the seat of one of the main branches of the Tokugawa family.

Mitsiwa Eritrea. Formerly Massawa. Chief seaport on the Red Sea, partly on Mitsiwa Is. Pop. (1989) 19,404. Exports hides and coffee. Occupied by the Italians 1885. Cap. of Eritrea until 1900, then superseded by Asmara. Used by the Italians as a base for the expedition against Abyssinia (Ethiopia) in 1935. Since 1993 Ethiopia has rights to use the port.

Mittelland Canal Germany. Canal 439 km (273 miles) long consisting of the Ems–Weser and Weser–Elbe canals, linking the Rhine R. through the Rhine–Herne and Dortmund–Ems canals with the Elbe R. E of the Elbe the W–E inland waterway across Germany is completed by the Havel R. and canals to the Oder R.

Miyazaki Japan. Cap. of the Miyazaki prefecture in SE Kyushu 105 km (65 miles) ENE of Kagoshima. Pop. (1990) 287,367. Market town. Manufactures porcelain. Has an important Shinto shrine. University (1949).

Mizoram India. Union Territory in the NE formed from the Mizo or Lushai Hills district of Assam (1972), bounded on the E and S by Myanmar (Burma). Area 21,081 sq km (8235 sq. miles). Pop. (1991) 686,217. Hills, rising to over 1500 m (4920 ft). Largely covered with forest and bamboo, and the scattered inhabitants cultivate rice, tobacco, in clearings. There are over 2500 small-scale industries. Cap. Aizwal.

Mjösa, Lake Norway. Long narrow lake in the SE, the largest in Norway (365 sq km; 141 sq. miles), fed by the Lågen R. from the Gudbrandsdal and drained by the Vorma R. to the Glomma R. On its shores are the towns of Lillehammer, Gjövik and Hamar.

Moab. Ancient country situated in the plateau area E of the Dead Sea, now in W Jordan. The inhabitants were akin to the Hebrews, though often at war with them. The Moabite Stone from the 9th cent. BC, found at Dibon (Dhiban) in 1868, records the successful revolt of the Moabite king, Mesha, against Israel.

Mobile USA. The only seaport in Alabama on Mobile Bay in the Gulf of Mexico. Pop. (1990) 196,278.

Exports cotton, timber, steel products and coal. Industries inc. shipbuilding and meat-packing. Manufactures paper, textiles, clothing, food products and petroleum products.

Successively in French, British and Spanish hands from 1702 to 1813, when it was seized for the USA.

Mobutu Sese Soko, Lake Africa. Lake situated on the Uganda/Democratic Republic of the Congo border within the W branch of the Great Rift Valley. Area 5346 sq km (2064 sq. miles), *c.* 160 km (100 miles) N to S. Formerly named L. Albert.

Moçambique ➤MOZAMBIQUE.

Moçambique Channel ➤MOZAMBIQUE CHANNEL.

Moçâmedes ➤NAMIBE.

Mocha (Mokha) Yemen. Small town and seaport on the Red Sea 160 km (100 miles) S of Hodeida. Pop. (1985) 35,000. Formerly exported the Arabian coffee named after it, but declined in the 19th cent. with the rise of Hodeida and Aden. Also gave its name to Mocha stones, agates used for jewellery.

Modder River (Free State) South Africa. River 306 km (190 miles) long, a tributary of the Vaal R., flowing NW and W and joining the Riet R. near the small town of Modder River.

Modena Italy. Ancient Mutina. Cap. of Modena province in Emilia-Romagna, on the Aemilian Way 37 km (23 miles) WNW of Bologna. Pop. (1992) 176,072. Industrial centre. Manufactures agricultural implements, motor vehicles, glass, pasta and balsamic vinegar. Romanesque cathedral (11th/14th-cent.); 17th-cent. ducal palace. University (1678). Taken by the Romans in the 3rd cent. BC. Ruled by the Este family from the 13th to the 19th cent.

Modica Italy. Market town in Ragusa province, Sicily 6 km (4 miles) SSE of Ragusa. Pop. (1981) 45,769. Trade in olive oil, wine, cheese. 10 km (6 miles) SE of the Cava d'Ispica, a limestone gorge with many early Christian and Byzantine tombs and cave dwellings.

Moers (Mörs) Germany. Town in North Rhine-Westphalia in the Ruhr region 10 km (6 miles) WNW of Duisburg. Pop. (1990) 105,000. Coalmining centre. Manufactures machinery.

Moeskroen ➤MOUSCRON.

Moffat Scotland. Town and resort in Dumfries and Galloway on the R. Annan 29 km (18 miles) NNE of Dumfries. Pop. (1991) 2342. Medicinal springs. Dumcrieff House, 3 km (2 miles) SW, was the home of John L. McAdam, the road builder.

Mogadishu (Mogadiscio) Somalia. Cap. and chief seaport, which has been modernized, serving the irrigated Webi Shebeli valley. Pop. (1987) 1 million. Taken by the Sultan of Zanzibar 1871. Sold to Italy 1905. During the civil war (1990–4) it was badly devastated.

Mogador ➤ESSAOUIRA.

Mogilev Belarus. Town on the Dnieper R. 177 km (110 miles) E. of Minsk. Pop. (1990) 362,600.

Railway junction. Industrial centre. Manufactures machinery, rayon, clothing and leather.

Has Eastern Orthodox and Roman Catholic cathedrals. Long ruled by the Poles; annexed to Russia 1772.

Mojave (Mohave) Desert USA. Arid region in S Californa forming part of the Great Basin S of the Sierra Nevada. Area 38,850 sq km (15,000 sq. miles). Average height 600 m (1968 ft). Roughly parallel mountain ranges with intervening wide basins. The only stream is the Mojave R., flowing generally N and mainly underground for about 160 km (100 miles). Centre of aerospace technology at Edwards Air Base.

Moji Japan. Seaport in the Fukuoka prefecture, N Kyushu on Shimonoseki Strait opposite Shimonoseki (Honshu), with which it is connected by bridge, railway and road tunnel.

Exports coal, cement and sugar. Manufactures steel. Industries inc. sugar-refining and brewing.

Joined (1963) with neighbouring Kokura, Tobata, Yawata and Wakamatsu to form the new city of Kitakyushu.

Mokha ►MOCHA.

Mokpo South Korea. Seaport in the SW. Pop. (1990) 253,420. Industrial centre. Cotton-ginning and rice-milling.

Mold Wales. Market town in Flintshire on the R. Alyn 16 km (10 miles) WSW of Chester. Pop. (1991) 8745. About 1.6 km (1 mile) W is the reputed site of the battlefield of Germanus.

Moldau River ►VLTAVA RIVER.

Moldavia (Romanian **Moldova**) Romania. Former principality of SE Europe in NE Romania mainly between the Prut and the Siret rivers. Founded in the 14th cent., then inc. Bukovina and Bessarabia. Under the Turks from 1504; lost Bukovina to Austria (1775), Bessarabia to Russia (1812) and came more and more under the influence of Russia. After the Crimean War it united with Walachia to form Romania (1859).

Moldova. Republic in E Europe bounded on the E and S by the Ukraine and on the W by Romania, from which it is separated by the Prut R. Area 33,700 sq km (13,010 sq. miles). Pop. (1995) 4,350,000 (47 per cent urban). Life expectancy: 68 years male, 72 female. Cap. Chisinau. Principal towns Tiraspol, Beltsy and Tighina. Currency Moldovan leu = 100 bani. It is mainly low-lying and covered largely with fertile black-earth soil. Drained by the navigable Dniester R. Its climate is warm and dry with mild winters. Land use: forested 13 per cent, meadows and pastures 13 per cent, agricultural and under permanent cultivation 65 per cent. Most believers are Moldovan Orthodox. About 65 per cent of the pop. are Moldovan, 14 per cent Ukrainian, 13 per cent Russian and 4

per cent Gagauz. The official Moldovan lang. (i.e. Romanian) was written in Cyrillic prior to the restoration of the Roman alphabet in 1989. It is spoken by 75 per cent of the pop.

Moldova is well-known for its wine and also produces maize, wheat, sugar-beet, sunflower seeds. Industries inc. canning, flour-milling, sugar-refining, tobacco-processing. There are sturgeon fisheries in the S.

After Romania had annexed Bessarabia in 1919, the Moldavian Autonomous Soviet Socialist Republic was formed E of the Dniester R. as part of the Ukrainian Soviet Socialist Republic. In 1940 Bessarabia was ceded to the USSR and the part with a predominantly Moldavian pop. was united with most of the former Moldavian Autonomous Soviet Socialist Republic. It was a former constituent republic of the USSR, but a declaration of republican sovereignty was adopted in 1990 and in 1991 the republic declared itself independent and joined the Commonwealth of Independent States (CIS). There is a 104-member unicameral Parliament.

Molfetta Italy. Seaport and industrial town in Bari province, Apulia 24 km (15 miles) WNW of Bari on the Adriatic. Pop. (1981 65,951.

Manufactures soap, pottery and cement. Exports wine, olive oil.

Romanesque cathedral (12th/13th-cent.) and 18th-cent. baroque cathedral.

Moline USA. Industrial town, river port and railway centre in NW Illinois on the Mississippi R. Pop. (1980) 46,278.

Manufactures agricultural machinery, an industry brought in by John Deere (inventor of a steel plough) in 1847. Also manufactures tools and furniture.

Molise Italy. Region in the S central area, co-extensive with Campobasso province, formerly part of the Abruzzi e Molise region. Area 4438 sq km (1714 sq. miles). Pop. (1992) 331,494. No large towns; mainly agricultural (cereals and vines).

Mollendo Peru. Port in the Arequipa department. Pop. (1985) 14,700. Long the outlet for S Peru and Bolivia but now replaced by Matarani (14 km; 9 miles NW) which has a sheltered harbour.

Industries inc. brickmaking. Fishing and fish-canning. Tourism has grown considerably in recent years.

Mölndal Sweden. Industrial town in Göteborg and Bohus county 5 km (3 miles) SE of Göteborg. Pop. (1992) 52,423.

Manufactures textiles, paper and margarine.

Has the famous 18th-cent. mansion of Gunnebo.

Moluccas (Spice Islands) Indonesia. Large group of islands between Celebes (W) and New Guinea (E) forming the province of Maluku. Area 86,286 sq km (33,315 sq. miles). Pop. (1990) 1,857,790. Cap. Amboina (Ambon) on the island of the same name. The N Moluccas inc. Halmahera, the largest of the Moluccas, Morotai and the Obi and Sula Islands; the S Moluccas inc. Ceram, Buru, the Aru and Tanimbar Islands, and Wetar. Most of them are mountainous and some have active volcanoes; others are low-lying coral islands. Many are uninhabited. The inhabitants are of mixed Malay and other stock, the majority being Muslims.

Coconut and sago palms and pepper vines are widely grown and copra and spices are important exports.

The Portuguese visited the Moluccas early in the 16th cent. They were followed by the Dutch, who conquered the islands and remained in possession almost continuously from 1667 to World War II, when the group was seized by the Japanese (1942). With the end of the Netherlands East Indies, after World War II, the islands became a province of Indonesia; for a short time in 1950 an independent republic of the S Moluccas was formed on Amboina (Ambon) and Ceram.

Mombasa Kenya. Chief seaport on the E side of the coral island of the same name within an inlet of the Indian Ocean and also on the neighbouring mainland. Pop. (1989) 465,000. Old Mombasa harbour is used mainly by dhows, but at Kilindini in the SW of the island there is the finest modern deep-water harbour in E Africa, an important entrepôt handling the major part of the trade of Kenya, Uganda and NE Tanzania, with all of which it is linked by rail.

Exports coffee, cotton, hides and skins, pyrethrum, sisal, soda, tea. Coffee-curing and brewing. Manufactures cement, glass and soap.

Largely oriental in character, with mosques as well as Anglican and Roman Catholic cathedrals, Arab and Indian bazaars, and the Mombasa Institute for Muslim technical education. An Arab and Persian settlement from the 11th cent. Already a busy port when visited by Vasco da Gama (1498, on his first voyage to India). Remained in Portuguese hands in the 16th–17th cent. Recaptured by the Arabs in 1698 and, after changes of rulers, ceded to the British by the Sultan of Zanzibar in 1887. Cap. of the British East Africa protectorate till 1907. The first oil refinery in E Africa was opened here in 1964.

Mona ►ISLE OF ANGLESEY.

Monaco. Independent principality in Europe on the Mediterranean Sea, an enclave within the Alpes-Maritimes department of France 14 km (9 miles) ENE of Nice. Area 1.05 sq km (0.75 sq. miles). Pop. (1990) 29,972. Monaco is divided into four districts: Monaco-Ville, the cap., on a rocky headland; La Condamine, the business quarter; Monte Carlo, famous for its gambling casino and as a resort; and Fontvieille. Ninety per cent of the resident pop. are Roman Catholic.

Gambling in the casino used to be the main source of income for the principality but now only about 4 per cent of its income comes from that source. Monégasques are not admitted to the gambling tables, but are exempt from taxation. Tourism is the main source of revenue inc. a thriving business conference activity, some income being derived from postage stamps. Perfumes are manufactured and Mediterranean fruits are grown, and in the exceptionally mild climate the vegetation is luxuriant. There are some

700 small businesses inc. engineering and the manufacture of chemicals, plastics, electronics and paper.

In the town of Monaco are a Romanesque–Byzantine cathedral, a 13th/16th-cent. palace and the oceanographical museum founded in 1910 by Prince Albert I. Monaco was settled by Phoenicians and later by Greeks. From 1297 it was ruled by the Genoese Grimaldi family, but was annexed to France 1793–1814 and was a Sardinian protectorate 1815–61. In 1911, by the introduction of a constitution providing for a National Council, Monaco changed from an absolute to a constitutional monarchy. Prince Rainier III suspended this constitution in 1959 but restored it in 1962. The 18-member National Council elected for 5-year terms. The Principality has a customs union with France and an interchangeable currency,

Monadnock, Mount USA. Isolated mountain (965 m; 3165 ft) in SW New Hampshire 53 km (33 miles) WNW of Nashua. Gave its name to a geological feature (a hill of hard rock which has successfully resisted erosion).

Monaghan Ireland. 1. Inland county in Ulster province lying E of Co. Fermanagh (Northern Ireland). Area 1290 sq km (498 sq. miles). Pop. (1991) 56,260. Generally undulating and rising to over 360 m (1181 ft) in Slieve Beagh (NW), with a central valley, it is drained chiefly by the Blackwater and the Finn rivers; it has a number of small lakes and bogs. Oats and potatoes cultivated. Livestock reared. Chief towns Monaghan, Clones, Carrickmacross and Castleblaney.

2. County town of Co. Monaghan on the Ulster Canal 45 km (28 miles) NW of Dundalk. Pop. (1991) 5750. Bacon and ham curing. Manufactures footwear. Has a 19th-cent. Roman Catholic cathedral.

Monastir ➤BITOLJ.

Monchegorsk Russia. Town on the NW shore of L. Imandra 105 km (65 miles) S of Murmansk. Pop. (1985) 48,000. Copper and nickel are smelted from ores mined in the neighbourhood. Founded in the 1930s.

Mönchengladbach ➤MÜNCHEN GLADBACH.

Moncton Canada. Originally The Bend. Industrial town in SE New Brunswick on the Petitcodiac R. Pop. (1991) 80,744.

Railway engineering. Manufactures clothing and hardware.

Renamed after General Robert Monckton, British commander, who captured Fort Beauséjour in 1855.

Monfalcone Italy. Industrial town in Gorizia province, Friuli-Venezia Giulia 26 km (16 miles) NW of Trieste. Pop. (1981) 30,277.

Important shipbuilding industry. Oil-refining. Manufactures chemicals.

Monghyr India. Town in Bihar on the Ganges R. 51 km (32 miles) WNW of Bhagalpur. Pop. (1971) 102,462.

Commercial centre. Manufactures cigarettes.

Walls and ramparts of a 16th-cent. fort.

Mongolia. Independent republic in E central Asia, formerly called Outer Mongolia. It is bounded by the Russian Federation in the N and by China in the E, S and W. Area 1,565,000 sq km (604,250 sq. miles). Pop. (1995) 2,307,000 (59 per cent urban). Life expectancy, 60 years male, 64 female. Cap. Ulan Bator. Other cities Darkhan, Erdenet and Choybalsan. Currency: Tugrik (Tug) = 100 möngö. Its vast grazing lands have made it a country of herdsmen and it has the highest number of livestock per head of pop. in the world. On the whole an extensive plateau at 900–1200 m (2952–3936 ft), with the lofty Altai and Khangai Mountains in the W and the Gobi desert in the S. Chief rivers are the Selenga, which drains to L. Baikal, and the Kerulen, which drains to the Amur R. Large numbers of sheep and goats, as well as horses, cattle and camels are raised on cooperative and state farms. Wheat is the chief crop but oats, barley and potatoes are also grown. Some copper and coal are produced. About 25 per cent of the foreign trade is with Russia and 20 per cent with China. There are rail links with both the USSR and China.

Mongolia has a very extreme climate, with six months of mean temperature below freezing but much higher temperatures prevail for a month or so in summer. Land use: forested 9 per cent, meadow and pastures 80 per cent, agricultural and under permanent cultivation 1 per cent. The religion is Lamaistic Buddhism with the Dalai Lama as it spiritual head. About 79 per cent of the pop. are Khalkma Mongol and the lang. is Khalkma Mongolian.

The Mongols were fierce nomadic raiders, attaining their greatest power under Genghis Khan (c. 1162–1227). His great empire extended across Asia and far into Europe. In the 13th cent. his grandson, Kublai Khan, became the first Mongol emperor of China. But the Mongol empire was short-lived; with the overthrow of the Mongol dynasty of China by the Mings, Mongolia became separated into Outer Mongolia (N) and Inner Mongolia (S). The former was a Chinese province from 1686 to 1911, when it became autonomous under the rule of the Living Buddha of Urga (Ulan Bator). When he died in 1924 the Mongolian People's Republic, on the Soviet pattern, was proclaimed. Its independence was recognized by China in 1946 and the republic was admitted to the UN in 1961. Under the 1992 Constitution democratic institutions, a market economy and freedom of speech were introduced. The Legislature consists of a 76-member unicameral State Great Hural (Parliament). For administrative purposes it is divided into 18 provinces and three cities (Ulan Bator, Darkhan and Erdenet).

Monmouth Wales. Market town in Monmouthshire at the confluence of the R. Wye and the R. Monnow 31 km (19 miles) NE of Newport. Pop. (1991) 7246. Remains of the ancient walls and the 12th-cent. castle where Henry V was born. Also has a 13th-cent. gateway on the bridge over the R. Monnow.

Monmouthshire Wales. County in SE. Disbanded in 1974 and the major portion incorporated into Gwent. Reinstated in 1996. Pop. (1994) 84,000.

Monongahela River USA. River 206 km (128 miles) long, formed in W Virginia by the union of the Tygart R. and the W Fork, flowing generally N into Pennsylvania and joining the Allegheny R. at Pittsburgh to form the Ohio R. An important waterway.

Monopoli Italy. Adriatic seaport in Bari province, Apulia 42 km (26 miles) ESE of Bari. Pop. (1981) 43,424.

Exports olive oil, wine, fruit. Flour-milling and food-canning. Manufactures textiles and pasta.

Monroe USA. Industrial town in NE Louisiana on the Ouachita R. Pop. (1990) 54,900.

Manufactures carbon black, chemicals, wood-pulp and paper, and furniture. Extensive natural-gas fields nearby.

Monrovia Liberia. Cap. and chief seaport near the mouth of the St Paul R. Pop. (1984) 425,000.

Exports mainly rubber and iron ore; also diamonds, palm oil and kernels.

Named after the US President James Monroe, during whose term it was founded (1822) as a settlement for former slaves from America.

Mons (Flemish **Bergen**) Belgium. Cap. of Hainaut province 53 km (33 miles) SW of Brussels. Pop. (1993) 92,533.

Industrial centre in the Borinage coal-mining region. Sugar-refining. Manufactures chemicals, textiles, soap and cement.

Cathedral of St Waudru (15th/16th-cent.); 15th-cent. town hall. Scene of the first engagement between British and German forces in August 1914.

Montana USA. Mountain state in the NW, bordering in the N on Canada, along the 49th parallel. Area 381,087 sq km (147,138 sq. miles). Pop. (1990) 799,065. Cap. Helena. In the W are the Rocky Mountains (about two-fifths of the state), rising to 3919 m (12,854 ft) in Granite Peak in the Absaroka Range (S). In the E are the Great Plains, interspersed with hills and river valleys, at an altitude of 600–1200 m (1968–3936 ft). The winters are severe, with fierce snowstorms, though modified by warm chinook winds. Annual rainfall 25–40 cm (10–15 ins.). Several important irrigation projects (e.g. Fort Peck Reservoir on the Missouri R.). Dry farming is practised. Leading crops spring wheat, barley and sugar-beet. Noted for minerals; the most valuable are petroleum, copper, silver and gold. Chief towns Great Falls, Billings, Helena. White settlement began with the Louisiana Purchase (1803), by which the territory passed from France to the USA, and increased with the discovery of gold in 1858. Admitted to the Union in 1889 as the 41st state.

Montauban France. Prefecture of the Tarn-et-Garonne department in the SW on the Tarn R. 48 km (30 miles) N of Toulouse. Pop. (1990) 52,278.

Market town. Trade in fruit, poultry. Food-processing. Manufactures textiles, furniture, vehicles and typewriters.

Early 14th-cent. brick-built bridge; 18th-cent. cathedral; fine collection of paintings by Ingres (1780–1867), who was born here. An ancient fortress, founded 1144. A stronghold of the Huguenots in the 16th and 17th cent.

Mont Blanc France. Highest mountain (4813 m, 15,787 ft) in the Alps in the Haute-Savoie department in the massif of the same name extending into Switzerland and Italy. The Massif is nearly 48 km (30 miles) long, its greatest width 16 km (10 miles). There are several sharp peaks (*aiguilles*) and glaciers; the best-known glacier is the Mer de Glace. The mountain was first ascended (1786) by Dr Michel Paccard and Jacques Balmat, of Chamonix; may now be climbed with guides from the terminus of the Aiguille du Midi overhead cable-way. A 12-km (7½-mile) road tunnel linking Courmayeur (Italy) with Chamonix (France) opened to traffic in 1965. Closed in 1999 because of fire.

Mont Cenis France. Alpine pass (2083 m, 6832 ft) in the Savoie department between the Cottian and Graian Alps on the road between Lanslebourg (France) and Susa (Italy), built (1803–10) by Napoleon. The Mont Cenis (Fréjus) railway tunnel (14 km; 8¼ miles long, opened 1871) is 27 km (17 miles) SW.

Montclair USA. Residential town in New Jersey 10 km (6 miles) NNW of Newark. Pop. (1990) 37,792.

Manufactures chemicals, paints and metal goods. Founded 1666.

Monte Bello Islands (Australia) S Pacific Ocean. Group of uninhabited coral islands off the NW coast of Western Australia NNE of Onslow, the largest being Barrow Island 19 km (12 miles) long and up to 8 km (5 miles) wide. First British atomic weapon tested here in 1952.

Monte Carlo Monaco. Resort on the Riviera 16 km (10 miles) ENE of Nice. Pop. (1985) 12,000. Famous for its gambling casino and various artistic and sports events (chiefly in the winter season), inc. an annual motor rally.

Monte Cassino Italy. Hill 519 m (1702 ft) high overlooking the town of Cassino in Frosenone province, Latium 120 km (75 miles) SE of Rome. On it the famous monastery was founded (*c.* 529) by St Benedict, who established the Benedictine Order, and this was long an important centre of learning and religion. Its buildings were three times destroyed, by the Lombards (581), Saracens (884) and by earthquake (1349). Then in World War II the Germans used the abbey as a stronghold and the buildings were destroyed a fourth time by Allied air attacks; some of the manuscripts and art treasures, however, were saved. The abbey was completely restored and was rededicated by Pope Paul VI in 1964.

Monte Gargano Italy. Mountainous peninsula in N Apulia projecting about 56 km (35 miles) E into the Adriatic, rising to 1056 m (3464 ft) in Monte Calvo (or Gargano). Sheep-rearing. Olives and grapes cultivated. Chief town Monte Sant' Angelo.

Montego Bay Jamaica. Second largest town

and second seaport (after Kingston) on the NW coast. Pop. (1991) 83,446.

Exports bananas and sugar. Most famous as a tourist resort, largely because of the exceptionally fine bathing beach. In the bay is a cluster of coral atolls, the Bogue Islets.

Montélimar France. Town in the Drôme department in the SE on the Roubion R. near the confluence with the Rhône 69 km (43 miles) N of Avignon. Pop. (1990) 31,390.

Famous for its nougat. Food-processing, silk-spinning, sawmilling and tanning.

Once belonged to the Adhémar family and was called Monteil d'Adhémar.

Montenegro Federal Republic of Yugoslavia. The smaller of the two Yugoslav constituent republics, bounded in the W by Croatia, NW by Bosnia-Hercegovina, NE by Serbia, SE by Albania and the Adriatic Sea in the SW. Area 13,812 sq km (5333 sq. miles). Pop. (1994) 631,000. Cap. Podgorica (formerly Titograd). Entirely mountainous, except in the extreme S around L. Shkoder (Scutari), with a few fertile river valleys; rises to over 2400 m (7842 ft) in Mt Durmitor (NW) and Mt Komovi (SE).

Principal occupation is rearing of sheep and goats. Cereals, potatoes, tobacco, cotton and fruits are cultivated; but agriculture is primitive. Some lignite, bauxite and pig-iron is produced. Cetinje is the cap. of the former kingdom.

Its history is closely linked with that of Serbia, of which it was a semi-independent province (as Zeta) in the Middle Ages. In Serbo-Croat, Crna Gora 'Black Mountain'. After the Turks defeated the Serbs at Kosovo (1389), it retained its independence and continually resisted Turkish aggression. It became a kingdom in 1910 and fought against Turkey in the Balkan Wars and against Austria–Hungary in World War I, becoming a province of Yugoslavia in 1918 and a people's republic after World War II (1946). In a referendum held in 1992, to determine whether Montenegro should remain within a common state, Yugoslavia, as a sovereign republic, 66 per cent voted in favour. There

is a unicameral 85-member National Assembly.

Monte Rosa Italy/Switzerland. Mountain group in the Pennine Alps on the Italo–Swiss border, consisting of 10 peaks. Highest peak Dufourspitze (4641 m; 15,222 ft), first climbed (1855) by a party led by Charles Hudson, who was killed 10 years later on the Matterhorn.

Monterrey Mexico. City and cap. of the Nuevo León state in the fertile valley of the Santa Catarina R. at a height of 538 m (1765 ft). Pop. (1990) 1,064,197.

Important industrial centre. Large iron and steel works and lead smelters. Manufactures textiles, glass, chemicals and cigarettes.

Founded 1579. Much excellent architecture, both Spanish-colonial and modern. The 18th-cent. cathedral is specially noteworthy.

Montevideo Uruguay. Cap. of Uruguay and of the small Montevideo department (663 sq km; 256 sq. miles) on a wide bay backed by hills on the N shore of the Río de la Plata. Pop. (1992) 1,383,660.

Major seaport, handling most of Uruguay's trade. Chief exports wool, hides and skins, and meat. Uruguay's only important industrial centre. Meat-packing, tanning, flour-milling. Manufactures textiles, footwear, soap and matches. An attractive city, with fine avenues, parks, gardens and beaches which make it a favoured summer resort.

Among outstanding buildings are the cathedral (1804) and the Cabildo (town hall, 1810). Seat of the University of the Republic (1849). Founded 1726; named after the conical hill (148 m; 485 ft) the Cerro, on which stands an old Spanish fort. Became cap. of the republic 1828.

Montgomery USA. State cap. of Alabama on the Alabama R. Pop. (1990) 187,106.

Manufactures fertilizers, cotton goods. Trade in livestock, cotton and dairy produce.

First settled 1817. Cap. of the Confederate States during the American Civil War (1861).

Montgomery Wales. Market town in Powys near the R. Severn 31 km (19 miles)

SW of Shrewsbury. Pop. (1990) 1000. Ruins of a 13th-cent. castle. Just E is a well-preserved section of Offa's Dyke.

Montluçon France. Town in the Allier department on the Cher R. 76 km (47 miles) NNW of Clermont-Ferrand. Pop. (1982) 51,765.

Industrial centre. Manufactures steel, chemicals, tyres and glass.

Became important through the discovery of coal in the Commentry area to the SE in the early 19th cent. In the upper old town are narrow streets with many 15th/16th-cent. houses.

Montmartre France. District in N Paris on the hill Butte de Montmartre (99 m; 325 ft), the highest point of the city. Frequented by artists; noted for its night clubs and cafés. Dominated by the basilica of Sacré-Cœur.

Montparnasse France. District in Paris on the left bank of the Seine R. Famous cafés frequented by artists and writers. Seat of the Pasteur Institute. The cemetery contains the tombs of the writers Guy de Maupassant (1850–93) and Charles Baudelaire (1821–67), also the composers César Franck (1822–90) and Camille Saint-Saëns (1835–1921).

Mont Pelée Martinique. Volcano 1351 m (4431 ft) high 24 km (15 miles) NW of Fort-de-France, which erupted violently in 1902, completely destroying the town of St Pierre (then the chief commercial centre). All but one of the 28,000 inhabitants, and many thousands of others in the district, were killed. The name means 'bald mountain' and refers to the absence of vegetation.

Montpelier ➤VERMONT.

Montpellier France. Prefecture of the Hérault department in the S on the Lez R. 129 km (80 miles) WNW of Marseille. Pop. (1990) 210,866. Chief town of Languedoc; commercial and cultural centre.

Trade in wine, brandy. Manufactures soap, chemicals, perfumes and confectionery.

Seat of a famous university (founded 1289). Picturesque narrow streets with 17th/18th-cent. buildings. Amongs its features are the

Musée Fabre, and botanical garden founded in 1593, and the 14th-cent. Gothic cathedral. Purchased by Philip VI of France from Aragón 1349. Suffered much during the religious wars; supported the Huguenot cause; besieged and captured by Louis XIII 1622.

Montreal (Fr. **Montréal**) Canada. In French, 'Royal Mountain'. Largest city in Canada in S Quebec on Montreal Island at the confluence of the Ottawa and St Lawrence rivers. Pop. (1991) 1,017,666 (metropolitan area 2,921,357). The second largest French-speaking city in the world (after Paris).

A major seaport; the world's largest grain-shipping port. Also exports other agricultural produce, timber and paper. The harbour has 16 km (10 miles) of piers and wharves, large grain elevators, cold-storage warehouses and a floating dry dock. Closed by ice December-April. Many industries. Manufactures aircraft, railway equipment, cement, plastics, clothing and footwear. Canada's banking and insurance centre.

Built on the slopes of the extinct volcano Mt Royal (270 m; 886 ft) from which the name derives and on which is Mt Royal Park, the largest of many. Seat of the McGill University (1821, English-speaking) and the University of Montreal (1876, French-speaking, Roman Catholic). Foremost among the buildings is the Cathedral of St James (1870), copied from St Peter's, Rome. The Victoria Bridge across the St Lawrence was opened in 1860, the Jacques Cartier Bridge in 1930. Montreal Island was discovered (1535) by Jacques Cartier. A permanent settlement was founded in 1642 by Maisonneuve.

Montreuil-sous-Bois France. Suburb of E Paris in the Seine-St Denis department. Pop. (1990) 95,038. Famous for peaches. Manufactures metal containers, chemicals, paints and glass.

Montreux Switzerland. Town in the Vaud canton at the E end of L. Geneva, extending nearly 6 km (4 miles) along the lakeside. Pop. (1990) 19,850. Tourist centre. Woodworking and printing. Inc. the smaller resorts of Clarens, Caux, Les Avants, Glion, Territet and Veytaux. A mountain railway runs almost to the summit of Rochers de Naye (2046 m; 6711 ft). Nearby is Chillon castle.

Montrose Scotland. Town in Angus at the mouth of the South Esk R. 42 km (26 miles) NE of Dundee on a sandy peninsula between the North Sea and Montrose Basin, a tidal lagoon. Pop. (1991) 11,440. Fishing port. Seaside resort. Flax and jute spinning, and sawmilling.

Birthplace of Andrew Melville (1545–1622), James Graham, 5th Marquess of Montrose (1612–50) and Joseph Hume (1777–1855).

Mont St Michel France. Conical, rocky islet in the Manche department about 1.2 ha (3 acres) in area and 78 m (256 ft) high in the Bay of St Michel 13 km (8 miles) WSW of Avranches. Rises abruptly above the level sands and is accessible from the mainland by a causeway. Famous for its Benedictine monastery (founded 966), whose buildings were used as a prison from the Revolution until 1863. The medieval walls may be entered by a single gateway, from which the only street leads up to the abbey, and above all other buildings is the church.

Montserrat West Indies. Island in the Caribbean Sea 40 km (25 miles) SW of Antigua. Area 102 sq km (39½ sq. miles). Pop. (1991) 11,957. Cap. Plymouth. It is volcanic and rugged, rising to 915 m (3002 ft) in Soufrière and is often subject to earth tremors. In 1996 the cap. and the S part of the island was evacuated because of volcanic activity and by 1999 the pop. was only 2500. It has a tropical climate with no well-defined rainy season.

Crops inc. sea-island cotton, potatoes, tomatoes, bananas, mangoes and limes. Chief exports are cotton clothing, electronic parts and lighting fittings. Tourism was important and contributed about 30 per cent of gross domestic product.

Discovered (1493) by Columbus, who probably named it after the Spanish monastery. Colonized by the British 1632. Montserrat formed part of the federal colony of the Leeward Islands 1871–1956 when it became a separate British colony; in 1998 becoming a United Kingdom Overseas Territory. It is governed by a Governor who presides over a 6-member Executive Council and 11-member Legislative Council.

Montserrat Spain. Ancient Mons Serratus. Mountain 1236 m (4054 ft) high in Catalonia 48 km (30 miles) NW of Barcelona, above the valley of the Llobregat R. The Roman name probably derives from its jagged pinnacles, precipices and ravines. On a ledge about 720 m (2362 ft) high is the Benedictine monastery, reached by funicular railway and motor road. The church contains a small black image of the Virgin, Nuestra Señora de Montserrat, said to have been carved by St Luke and brought to Spain by St Peter; for cent. it has been one of the outstanding religious shrines in Spain, attracting thousands of pilgrims annually.

Monza Italy. Industrial town in Milano province, Lombardy on the Lambro R. 13 km (8 miles) NNE of Milan. Pop. (1992) 120,054.

Manufactures textiles, hats, carpets and machinery.

The 13th-cent. cathedral, built on the site of a church founded (590) by the Lombard queen Theodelinda, contains relics of her reign and also the celebrated iron crown of Lombardy, said to have been beaten out of one of the nails used in the Crucifixion. An expiatory chapel was built (1910) after the assassination here of King Umberto I (1900). Noted motor-racing circuit.

Mooltan ➤MULTAN.

Moorea ➤SOCIETY ISLANDS.

Moose Jaw Canada. Industrial town in Saskatchewan 64 km (40 miles) W of Regina. Pop. (1991) 33,593.

Flour-milling, meat-packing and oil-refining.

Moosonee ➤JAMES BAY.

Moradabad India. Industrial town in Uttar Pradesh on the Ramganga R. 160 km (100 miles) ENE of Delhi. Pop. (1991) 429,200.

Manufactures ornamental brassware, cotton goods and carpets.

Founded 1625. Has a Jama Masjid (Great Mosque), built (1631) by Rustam Khan.

Morar, Loch Scotland. Lake in Highland 18 km (11 miles) long and up to 2.4 km (1½ miles) wide; with a depth of 301 m (987 ft), the deepest lake in Scotland. At the W end is the village of Morar.

Morava (Ger. **March**) **River** Czech Republic. River 370 km (230 miles) long rising in the Sudeten Mountains and flowing generally S through Moravia, then forming part of the Austro–Czech border and joining the Danube 11 km (7 miles) above Bratislava. Navigable for 129 km (80 miles) of the lower course.

Morava River Yugoslavia. Chief river of Serbia, 209 km (130 miles) long, formed by the union of the S Morava and the W Morava near Stalac and flowing generally N to join the Danube R. 48 km (30 miles) ESE of Belgrade.

Moravia Czech Republic. Region between Bohemia and Slovakia and bordering S on Austria. An extension of the Bohemian plateau, drained by the Morava R. and its tributaries and in the NE by the Oder (Odra) R. To the N are the Sudeten Mountains, to the E the Carpathians, separated by the Moravian Gate; to the W are the Moravian Heights. The centre and S are fertile agricultural areas, there are considerable mineral resources and industries are well developed. By the late 8th cent. the region was peopled by Slavs, who took the name of Moravians from the Morava R. Incorporated in Bohemia 1029, but became a separate Austrian crownland in 1849. In 1918 it formed a province of the new republic of Czechoslovakia, combining with Silesia in 1927. In 1949 the three former provinces of Czechoslovakia were abolished and Moravia and Silesia no longer formed a political unit.

Moravská Ostrava ▶OSTRAVA.

Moray Scotland. Former county, new local authority formed 1996, in the NE on Moray Firth. Area 2230 sq km (861 sq. miles). Pop. (1993) 86,250.

Moray Firth Scotland. Inlet of the North Sea in the NE, sometimes considered to extend seawards to a line from Duncansbay Head (Caithness) to Kinnaird's Head (Aberdeen), sometimes only to a line from Tarbat Ness to Lossiemouth. At its head is Inverness.

Morbihan France. Department in Brittany in the NW on the Bay of Biscay. Area 7094 sq km (2739 sq. miles). Pop. (1990) 619,800. Prefecture Vannes. Its coastline is very broken, with many picturesque bays and estuaries, inc. the Gulf of Morbihan E of the Quiberon peninsula and many offshore islands. Much of the area is unproductive, inc. the barren Landes de Lanvaux. Chief crops cereals, potatoes, cider apples. Sardine and tunny fisheries important. Chief towns Vannes and Lorient. Carnac and Locmariaquer are famous for their megalithic monuments.

Mordovia Russia. Autonomous Republic situated in the great bend of the Volga R. ESE of Moscow. Area 26,200 sq km (10,116 sq. miles). Pop. (1989) 963,500. Cap. Saransk.

Agriculture and dairy-farming are important; many of the industries are concerned with the processing of produce.

Morecambe and Heysham England. Town in NW Lancashire on Morecambe Bay. Pop. (1991) 46,657. Consists of Morecambe, a seaside resort, and Heysham, a seaport with a ferry service to Belfast (Northern Ireland), an oil refinery, and has 2 advanced gas-cooled reactor nuclear power stations.

Morecambe Bay England. Inlet of the Irish Sea into NW Lancashire and S Cumbria, separating the Furness peninsula from Lancashire. Natural gas has been found.

Morelia Mexico. Formerly Valladolid. Cap. of the Michoacán state 209 km (130 miles)

WNW of Mexico City near the S edge of the central plateau at a height of 1890 m (6199 ft). Pop. (1990) 489,758.

Flour-milling, sugar-refining and tanning. Manufactures textiles and tobacco products.

A noteworthy cathedral (17th/18th-cent.) and many fine colonial houses. Birthplace of the Mexican patriots Itúrbide (1783–1824) and Morelos (1765–1815); named after the latter.

Morelos Mexico. State just S of the Federal District, mainly on the S slopes of the central plateau. Area 4962 sq km (1916 sq. miles). Pop. (1990) 1,195,381. Cap. Cuernavaca. Mainly agricultural. Produces maize, rice, sugar-cane, coffee and wheat. Named after the Mexican patriot Morelos (1765–1815).

Moreton Bay Australia. Bay in SE Queensland into which the Brisbane R. empties; the penal settlement here (1824–39) led to the development of Queensland.

Morioka Japan. Cap. of Iwate prefecture in NE Honshu 169 km (105 miles) N of Sendai. Pop. (1990) 235,440. Commercial centre. Manufactures iron goods and toys.

Morlaix France. Port in the Finistère department in the NW on a tidal estuary 55 km (34 miles) ENE of Brest. Pop. (1982) 19,541.

Exports fruit, vegetables and dairy produce. Manufactures tobacco products. Tanning, brewing and flour-milling.

Several 15th/17th-cent. wooden houses.

Morley England. Town in West Yorkshire 6 km (4 miles) SSW of Leeds. Pop. (1991) 47,579.

Manufactures woollen goods, textile machinery and glass.

Birthplace of H. H. Asquith, British statesman (1852–1928).

Morocco. Independent kingdom in NW Africa, bounded by the Mediterranean Sea to the N, Algeria to the E and SE, Mauritania to the S, Western Sahara to the SW and the Atlantic Ocean to the W. Area 458,730 sq km (177,116 sq. miles). Pop. (1995) 26,980,000. (48 per cent urban). Life expectancy, 67 years male, 71 female. Cap. Rabat.

Other cities Casablanca, Fès, Marrakesh and Meknès. Currency: Moroccan dirham = 100 Moroccan francs. Along the Mediterranean coast is the mountainous region, the Rif. The dominating physical feature is the Atlas Mountains forming three distinct ranges, the High Atlas, the Middle Atlas and the Anti Atlas, which separate the Atlantic coastlands from the Sahara. The High Atlas rise to 4165 m (13,661 ft) in Djebel Tubkal (the highest peak in N Africa). The S and SE fringe lies within the Sahara. The climate ranges from semi-arid in the S to warm temperate Mediterranean in the N, but cooler temperatures occur in the mountains. Land use: forested 20 per cent, meadows 47 per cent, agricultural and under permanent cultivation 22 per cent. About 98 per cent of Moroccans are Sunni Muslims. The official lang. is Arabic, spoken by 75 per cent of the pop.; the remainder speak Berber. French and Spanish are considered subsidiary lang. Ethnically 70 per cent are Arab and 30 per cent Berber.

Agriculture is by far the most important occupation and principal crops are cereals (chiefly wheat and barley), vines, olives, almonds, citrus fruits, dates and early vegetables for the European market. Livestock (mainly sheep and goats) are raised. The forests yield cork and fishing is an important coastal occupation; sardines are canned at Safi. Tourism is important. Chief agricultural exports citrus fruits, barley, wheat, wine and tomatoes. Other exports inc. phosphates, mined at Khouribga and Youssoufia (formerly Louis Gentil), and also iron, manganese, lead ores. Dams have been constructed on several Atlantic streams (e.g. the Oum er Rbia and its tributaries) for the storage of irrigation water and the development of hydroelectric power. Casablanca, the largest city and leading seaport, handles most of the foreign trade.

The N and W of present-day Morocco formed part of the Roman province of Mauretania. The region fell to the Vandals in the 5th cent. AD and was conquered in the 7th cent. by the Arabs, who imposed the Muslim religion on the native Berber; it achieved its greatest power under the Berber dynasties of the Almoravides and the Almohades in the 11th-13th cent. The Portuguese led the European penetration of Morocco by the capture of Ceuta in 1415, but were dislodged from their final stronghold, Mazagan in 1769. French and Spanish influence conflicted with German aspirations in the late 19th and early 20th cent. The Algeciras Conference of 1906 and the Agadir incident in 1911 were followed by the establishment of the French and Spanish protectorates in 1912. The Tangier international zone was created in 1923. Considerable economic progress was made under the first French resident general, Marshal Lyautey (1912–25), but the Berber of the Rif mountains revolted under Abdel-al-Krim (1921), evicted the Spanish from most of Spanish Morocco and were subjugated only by a joint Franco–Spanish expedition (1926). The Moroccan nationalist movement continued to grow; Sultan Mohammed V was deposed and exiled in 1953 but after much internal disorder was restored in 1955, changing his title to King in 1957. France and Spain relinquished their protectorates in 1956; the international status of the Tangier zone was abolished. Morocco became an independent member of the UN. Spain retained the Ceuta, Melilla, Alhucemas and Peñon de Veloz enclaves; Ifni was returned to Morocco in 1969. Reached tacit agreement with Mauritania (1975) on the division of the former Spanish Sahara between the two countries, despite opposition from Algeria, the rich phosphate deposits being the main interest. This was achieved in 1976 but in 1979 Mauritania renounced its claim to the territory and it was incorporated into Morocco. Morocco is a constitutional monarchy with a unicameral 333-member legislature. ➤➤WESTERN SAHARA.

Morón de la Frontera Spain. Town in Seville province, Andalusia 56 km (35 miles) SE of Seville. Pop. (1991) 27,207.

Manufactures cement, ceramics and soap. Trade in cereals, olive oil and wine.

Moroni Comoros. Cap. and port on the W coast of Njazidja (Grande Comore). Pop. (1994) 24,000. It is a trading centre for vanilla, cacao, coffee and is noted for its numerous mosques.

Morpeth England. Market town in Northumberland on the R. Wansbeck 21 km (13 miles) N of Newcastle-upon-Tyne. Pop. (1991) 14,300. Iron-founding, brewing and tanning. Remains of its ancient castle and the 12th-cent. Newminster Abbey.

Mortlake England. District in the London borough of Richmond-upon-Thames on the S bank of the Thames 11 km (7 miles) WSW of London. Finishing point of the annual Oxford and Cambridge boat race. Famous in the 17th cent. for tapestry. Brewing.

Moscow (Russian **Moskva**) Russia. Cap. and largest city of Russia on the Moskva R. Pop. (1994) 8,793,000.

The country's chief industrial, cultural and political centre, and the hub of routes by road, rail, air and waterway. Principal industries are the manufacture of textiles and metal goods, inc. steel, locomotives, cars, aircraft, machinery and machine-tools; also produces chemicals, rubber and leather goods, paper and cigarettes.

At the centre of the city is the Kremlin or citadel, triangular in shape and surrounded by a wall with 18 towers and 5 gates, one side extending along the left bank of the Moskva R. Inside the Kremlin there are many ecclesiastical buildings: the 15th-cent. Uspenski (Assumption) Cathedral, where the Tsars were crowned; the 15th-cent. Blagoveshchenski (Annunciation) Cathedral with its 9 cupolas; and the 16th-cent. Arkhangelski (Archangel) Cathedral, where many of the Tsars were buried. Other buildings in the Kremlin are the Great Palace and the Oruzheinaya Palata (Armoury), now a museum containing a vast collection of armour, costumes and crowns, both of the 19th cent.; the 15th-cent. Granovitaya Palata; the lofty bell-tower of Ivan the Great, with nearby the great broken Tsar Bell (cast 1735), the largest in the world; the former arsenal; and the 18th-cent. building of the Presidium of the Supreme Soviet of the Russian Federation. Just outside the Kremlin (E) is the enormous Red Square, traditional site of parades and demonstrations; here are the Lenin Mausoleum and the tombs of other Revolutionary leaders, the fantastic 16th-cent. Cathedral of St Basil with its coloured towers and domes, and the historical museum. This part of the city, the Kitai Gorod, formerly the commercial and banking quarter, is now occupied chiefly by government offices. Among the many museums in Moscow perhaps the most famous is the Tretyakov Gallery, which was enriched by thousands of works from private collections; the city also has the Bolshoi Opera House, the Moscow Art Theatre and other theatres. The Russian Academy of Sciences is in Moscow and there are two state universities, the older founded 1755. Passenger transport is served by an underground railway system, first opened in 1935, while the main streets radiate from the central Kremlin and Kitai Gorod to the suburbs, cutting across the boulevards which mark the positions of the former walls. Moscow has a central and outer airports, and traffic by waterway is served by three ports, two on the Moskva R. and the third on the Moscow–Volga Canal (opened 1937), which transformed the city into an important inland port.

Founded in the 12th cent. Cap. of a small principality by the end of the 13th cent. The Kremlin was enclosed by an earth and timber wall in 1300 and in 1367 by a stone wall. In spite of destruction by Tatar invasions and fires, it expanded until in the 16th cent. it became the national cap. and Ivan IV, Prince of Moscow, took the title of Tsar. In 1703, however, Peter the Great transferred the cap. to St Petersburg and the city declined. It was again burned following the Napoleonic invasion (1812), but was rebuilt and later in the 19th cent. grew rapidly as an industrial and railway centre. During World War II the German army was halted about 32 km (20 miles) from the city centre; further rapid expansion came after the end of hostilities.

Moselle France. Department in the NE in Lorraine, bordering N on Luxembourg and NE on Germany. Area 6214 sq km (2399 sq miles). Pop. (1990) 1,011,030. Prefecture Metz. Contains part of the Lorraine iron field. Coal mined.

The important metallurgical industry is concentrated in the Metz–Thionville area. Cereals, vines, hops and fruits cultivated. Chief towns Metz and Thionville.

Moselle (Ger. **Mosel**) **River**. River 547 km (340 miles) long, rising in the Vosges and flowing generally NW past Épinal, Toul, Metz and Thionville (France), forming part of the Luxembourg–German frontier then turning NE past Trier (Germany) to join the Rhine R. at Coblenz. In its lower course, between Trier and Coblenz, it meanders considerably and here on the valley slopes are grown the grapes from which the famous Moselle wines are made. Navigable to small vessels below Frouard (near Nancy). Chief tributaries the Meurthe and the Saar (Sarre). Canalization of the 270-km (168-mile) stretch between Thionville (France) and Coblenz (Germany) was completed in 1964.

Moshi ➤TANGA.

Moskenstraumen ➤MAELSTROM.

Moskva River Russia. River 499 km (312 miles) long, flowing generally E past Moscow and Kolomna, joining the Oka R. near the latter. Linked with the Volga R. by the Moscow Canal; canalized below the junction.

Mosquito (Miskito) Coast Nicaragua. Strip of land about 64 km (40 miles) wide along the Caribbean coast, named after the former Mosquito (Miskito) Indian inhabitants, who now have a pronounced Negro admixture. The Mosquito Reserve forms part of the departments of Zelaya and Río San Juan; chief town Bluefield. Sparsely populated.

Main occupation lumbering (mahogany), banana cultivation.

Discovered (1502) by Columbus. Under British protection as an autonomous 'kingdom' 1655–1860. Incorporated into Nicaragua 1893. The name is also sometimes understood to inc. the neighbouring coastal strip of Honduras as far as Cape Camarón, formerly claimed by Nicaragua; the present boundary was fixed (1961) by a commission of the Organization of American States.

Mossamedes ►MOÇÂMEDES.

Mossel Bay South Africa. Formerly Aliwal South. Seaport and holiday resort in the Western Cape Province midway between Cape Town and Port Elizabeth. Pop. (1970) 17,359. Serves the Little Karroo region. Important oyster and other fisheries.

The bay was visited by Bartholomew Diaz (1487) and by Vasco da Gama (1497). The modern town was founded in 1848.

Mossley England. Town in Greater Manchester on the R. Tame 14 km (9 miles) ENE of Manchester. Pop. (1990) 10,569. Textile and metal working industries.

Most (Ger. **Brüx**) Czech Republic. Town in NW Bohemia 76 km (47 miles) NW of Prague. Pop. (1990) 71,000.

In a lignite-mining region. Metallurgical and chemical industries. Manufactures ceramics and glass.

Mostaganem Algeria. Seaport on the Gulf of Arzew 80 km (50 miles) ENE of Oran, with which it is linked by rail. Pop. (1982) 169,526.

Exports wine and fruits (from the neighbouring lowlands) and wool (from the Tell Atlas).

Founded in the 11th cent. Enjoyed considerable prosperity under the Turks in the 16th cent. Later declined, but revived after the French occupation in 1833. A gas pipeline runs to it from Hassi Messaoud.

Mostar Bosnia-Hercegovina. Market town on the Neretva R. 77 km (48 miles) SW of Sarajevo. Pop. (1981) 110,377.

In a fruit-growing and wine-producing region. Manufactures textiles and tobacco products.

Has a fine 16th-cent. bridge, possibly built on Roman foundations (hence the name);

Turkish mosques; Orthodox cathedral. Devastated in civil war (1993).

Mosul Iraq. Cap. of Mosul province and Iraq's second largest city, on the Tigris R. 354 km (220 miles) NNW of Baghdad. Pop. (1987) 664,221.

Important commercial centre, near rich oilfields. Trade in grain, fruit, livestock and wool. Tanning, flour-milling. Manufactures cotton goods and cement.

Across the river are the ruins of Nineveh. Mosul was not handed over to Iraq by Turkey till 1925, four years after the foundation of the new country. Its importance increased with the completion of the Baghdad Railway through Mosul to Syria and Turkey.

Motala Sweden. Town in Östergötland county, where the Motala R. leaves L. Vätter. Pop. (1992) 42,264.

Manufactures locomotives and railway rolling-stock, machinery, radio sets. Site of a hydroelectric power plant and a radio station.

Motala River Sweden. River 96 km (60 miles) long leaving L. Vätter to flow generally E through Lakes Bor, Rox and Gla, past Norrköping and entering Bråviken (Bra Bay) and the Baltic Sea. Between lakes Vätter and Rox the Gota Canal follows its course.

Motherwell Scotland. Town in North Lanarkshire 18 km (11 miles) ESE of Glasgow. Pop. (1991) 30,717. Industries inc. engineering and textiles. Manufactures iron and steel, machinery and bricks.

Moulins France. Prefecture of the Allier department on the Allier R. 90 km (56 miles) NNE of Clermont-Ferrand. Pop. (1990) 23,353.

Railway junction. Industries inc. brewing and tanning. Manufactures hosiery and furniture.

Cap. of the duchy of Bourbonnais in the late 15th cent. Birthplace of Marshal Villars (1653–1734).

Moulmein (Mawlamyine) Myanmar (Burma). Chief town and seaport of Tenasserim on the estuary of the Salween R.

160 km (100 miles) ESE of Rangoon. Pop. (1983) 219,991.

Exports rice and teak. Industries inc. saw-milling and rice-milling.

Mountain Ash Wales. Town in Rhondda, Cynon, Taff on the R. Cynon 26 km (16 miles) NNW of Cardiff. Pop. (1991) 21,301. Former coalmining area with new light industries.

Mount Gambier Australia. Town in the extreme SE of South Australia 362 km (225 miles) SSE of Adelaide. Pop. (1991) 21,156.

Railway junction. Market town. Trade in timber, agricultural produce. Named after the nearby Mt Gambier, an extinct volcano with crater lakes.

Mount Isa Australia. Mining town in W Queensland 105 km (65 miles) W of Cloncurry. Pop. (1991) 23,935. Terminus of the railway from Townsville on the E coast.

Zinc, lead and silver ores are mined from a long lode, copper from a lower level. Smelters produce metallic lead, blister copper and zinc concentrates.

Mount Lyell Australia. Copper-mining centre in Tasmania 153 km (95 miles) WSW of Launceston, near Queenstown. Electrolytic refinery.

Mount Morgan Australia. Mining town in E Queensland 35 km (22 miles) SSW of Rockhampton. Pop. (1971) 3733. Considerable gold production in the late 19th cent.; output is now small, but copper ore is mined from beneath the goldbearing quartz.

Mount Rushmore National Memorial USA. Massive sculptures carved in the granite side of Mt Rushmore in the Black Hills of W South Dakota 27 km (17 miles) SW of Rapid City. A national memorial (494 ha; 1220 acres) was established in 1929. The sculptures represent the heads of four US presidents (Washington, Jefferson, Lincoln, Theodore Roosevelt); each face is 18–20 m (59–66 ft) high. They are the work of Gutzon Borglum, who began in 1927 and continued till his death in 1941; they were completed by his son Lincoln Borglum.

Mount Vernon (New York) USA. Residential and industrial suburb of New York City, New York, just N of the Bronx. Pop. (1990) 67,153.

Manufactures electrical equipment, metal goods and chemicals.

Mount Vernon (Virginia) USA. National shrine on the Potomac R. 24 km (15 miles) S of Washington (DC); the estate and mansion where George Washington lived from 1747 till his death (1799). In the grounds is the tomb of George and Martha Washington and several other members of the family.

Mourne Mountains Northern Ireland. Range 23 km (14 miles) long in Co. Down extending NE–SW between Dundrum Bay and Carlingford Lough, rising to 853 m (2739 ft) in Slieve Donard. Reputedly the most picturesque mountains in Northern Ireland.

Mouscron (Flemish **Moeskroen**) Belgium. Town in W Flanders province 51 km (32 miles) SW of Ghent near the French border. Pop. (1993) 53,606. Manufactures cotton goods and carpets.

Mousehole England. Fishing village and seaside resort in SW Cornwall on Mount's Bay 5 km (3 miles) S of Penzance. Pop. (1985) 1300.

Mozambique (Moçambique). Republic in SE Africa on the coast of the Mozambique Channel opposite Madagascar. It is bounded by Tanzania to the N, Malawi and Zambia to the NW, Zimbabwe W and South Africa and Swaziland to the SW and S. Area 799,379 sq km (308,642 sq. miles). Pop. (1995) 17,889,000 (28 per cent urban). Life expectancy, 45 years male, 48 female. Cap. Maputo. Other cities Beira and Nampula. Currency: Metrical = 100 centavos. The coastal plain, which is much wider in the S than in the N, is fringed with mangrove swamps and rises gradually to a plateau 300–600 m (984–1968 ft) high, with heights of over 2000 m (6560 ft) near the Malawi frontier. In the centre is the extensive delta of the Zambezi R. It has a tropical climate, but the mountains cause large variations in rainfall, which is very heavy in the E and very light in the W. Land use: forested 18 per cent, meadows and pastures 56 per cent, agricultural and under permanent cultivation 4 per cent. About 48 per cent of the pop. follow traditional animist religions, Christians are about 39 per cent of which Roman Catholic 31 per cent. The official lang. is Portuguese but local dialects and Swahili are widely spoken. The majority of the pop. belong to local tribal groupings: Makua 47 per cent, Thonga 23 per cent, Shona 10 per cent.

Principal exports petroleum, sugar, cashew nuts, cotton and shrimps. Food crops inc. beans, maize, millet and rice. There is a considerable amount of industry in the Maputo area inc. engineering and the manufacture of steel and textiles. There are deposits of tin, iron ore, bauxite, coal, salt, marble and gold.

Discovered by Vasco da Gama in 1498, settlements were established by the Portuguese from 1505 onwards. The present boundaries were settled 1886–94. The Moçambique Company was granted a charter to administer the area (which later became the Manica and Sofala province, inc. Beira) in 1891. In 1951 Mozambique became a Portuguese Overseas Province. Independence was achieved in 1975 after a decade of guerrilla activity. Fighting continued between rival factions until 1992 when the civil war ended. There is a 250-member unicameral Assembly of the Republic. Mozambique became a member of the Commonwealth in 1995.

Mozambique Channel Indian Ocean. Strait between the SE coast of Africa and Madagascar over 1600 km (1000 miles) long and 400–960 km (250–600 miles) wide. At the N end is the Comoro. Chief ports Mozambique and Beira on the mainland, Mahajanga and Toliary in Madagascar.

Mpumalanga South Africa. Province created in 1994. Area 78,370 sq km (30,258 sq. miles). Pop. (1995) 3,007,100. Cap. Pietermaritzburg.

Muchinga Mountains ➤ZAMBIA.

Mufulira ➤NDOLA.

Muharraq ➤BAHRAIN.

Mühlhausen Germany. Town in Thuringia on the Unstrut R. 50 km (31 miles) NW of Erfurt. Pop. (1981) 43,348. Industrial centre. Manufactures textiles, machinery and furniture. An ancient town, fortified in the 10th cent., with 14th-cent. churches and a 17th-cent. town hall.

Mukden ➤WHENYANG.

Mülhausen ➤MULHOUSE.

Mülheim-an-der-Ruhr Germany. Industrial town in North Rhine-Westphalia on the Ruhr R. 8 km (5 miles) WSW of Essen. Pop. (1990) 170,200.

Coalmining centre. Max Planck Institute for coal research. Manufactures iron and steel, machinery and textiles. Brewing and tanning.

Mulhouse (Ger. **Mülhausen**) France. Industrial town in the Haut-Rhin department on the Ill R. and the Rhône–Rhine Canal. Pop. (1990) 109,905.

Important textile centre. Manufactures cotton, silk and rayon goods, also hosiery, chemicals from the potash deposits to the N, paper and machinery. Engineering.

Had planned residential districts for workers from the mid 19th cent. A 16th-cent. town hall. Became a free imperial city in the 14th cent. Remained a member of the Swiss Confederation 1515–1798 and then joined France. Held by Germany, with the rest of Alsace, 1871–1918.

Mull Scotland. Island in the Inner Hebrides in Argyll and Bute, separated from the mainland by the Sound of Mull and the Firth of Lorne. Area 909 sq km (351 sq. miles). Pop. (1991) 2708. Chief town Tobermory (NE). Mountainous, rising to 967 m (3171 ft) in Ben More. Picturesque broken coastline. Main occupations crofting and fishing. Tobermory attracts tourists in the summer. Duart and Aros are the principal ancient castles; near the former is a lighthouse commemorating the novelist William Black (1841–98), who described the island.

Mullingar Ireland. County town of Co. Westmeath on the R. Brosna and the Royal Canal 72 km (45 miles) WNW of Dublin. Pop. (1986) 8077. Market town. Trade in cattle, horses and dairy produce. Modern Roman Catholic cathedral. Loughs Ennell, Owel and Derravaragh nearby are well-known for their trout-fishing.

Multan (Mooltan) Pakistan. City near the Chenab R. Pop. (1981) 730,000.

Trade in wheat, cotton and sugar. Manufactures textiles, hosiery and carpets. Natural gas for its industries is supplied by pipeline from Sui.

Has the tombs of two Muslim saints and the ruins of an ancient Hindu temple.

Mulungushi ➤KABWE.

Mumbai ➤BOMBAY.

München ➤MUNICH.

München Gladbach Germany. Industrial town in North Rhine-Westphalia on the Niers R. 24 km (15 miles) W of Düsseldorf. Pop. (1990) 260,700.

Centre of the cotton industry. Also manufactures textile machinery, clothing, paper and chemicals.

Grew up round a Benedictine monastery founded in the 10th cent.

Muncie USA. Industrial town in Indiana on the White R. 80 km (50 miles) NE of Indianapolis. Pop. (1990) 71,035.

Manufactures glassware, electrical equipment and furniture.

Mundaring ➤KALGOORLIE; PERTH AUSTRALIA.

Munich (Ger. **München**) Germany. Cap. of Bavaria and the third largest city of Germany on the Isar R. Pop. (1995) 1,240,600.

Industrial, commercial, cultural and route centre. Brewing, printing and publishing. Manufactures precision instruments, chemicals, machinery, clothing and food products.

Picturesque with fine parks, inc. the En-

glischer Garten; many of its famous buildings were destroyed or severely damaged in World War II, inc. the Alte and Neue Pinakothek (though most of their art collections were preserved); the 15th-cent. Frauenkirche; the Renaissance church of St Michael; the Glyptothek, another art museum; and the 15th-cent. old town hall. The Hofbrauhaus, scene of the Hitler Putsch of 1923, however, survived and the Bavarian National Museum was only slightly damaged. The university was transferred here from Landshut in 1826. Became the home of the Wittelsbach family (1255) and later the cap. of Bavaria (1508). Under Ludwig I (1786–1868) developed into a great art centre. Headquarters of the Nazi movement from 1919. Scene of the Munich Agreement (1938).

Münster Germany. Industrial town in North Rhine-Westphalia on the Dortmund–Ems Canal 61 km (38 miles) W of Bielefeld. Pop. (1990) 261,400.

Manufactures agricultural and mining machinery, hardware and furniture. Brewing, flour-milling and printing.

Formerly well-known for its medieval character; many of its buildings were severely damaged in World War II, inc. the 13th/14th-cent. cathedral, the 14th-cent. Gothic town hall and the university (1773). A prominent member of the Hanseatic League in the 13th and 14th cent.

Munster Ireland. Largest of the four provinces, comprising counties Clare, Cork, Kerry, Limerick, Tipperary and Waterford. Area 24,126 sq km (9315 sq. miles). Pop. (1991) 1,008,440. One of the ancient kingdoms of Ireland, its cap. being Cashel.

Murano Italy. Suburb of Venice, built on several islets in the lagoon, famous since the 13th cent. for its Venetian glass industry. This industry had declined by the 18th cent., but has since been revived by the manufacture of cheaper types of glass. The 9th/12th-cent. Church of SS Maria e Donato has some outstanding mosaics.

Murren

Murchison Falls ➤NILE RIVER; SHIRÉ RIVER.

Murcia Spain. 1. Region and former kingdom in the SE, comprising the present provinces of Albacete and Murcia. Taken from the Moors 1242. Annexed to Castile 1269. 2. Province in the SE on the Mediterranean Sea. Area 11,317 sq km (4369 sq. miles). Pop. (1991) 1,032,275. Cap. Murcia. Generally mountainous. Hot, dry climate; agriculture (oranges, mulberries, cereals) is largely dependent on irrigation. Lead, zinc and other minerals produced. Chief towns Murcia, Cartagena (seaport), Lorca. 3. Cap. of Murcia province on the Segura R. 69 km (43 miles) SW of Alicante, in the low-lying fertile huerta or garden of Murcia. Pop. (1991) 318,838. Industrial centre. Has a silk industry dating from Moorish times; manufactures other textiles. Tanning, distilling, flour-milling. Largely modern; 14th/15th-cent. cathedral. University (1915). Under the Moors it was twice made cap. of the independent kingdom of Murcia.

Mureş (Hungarian **Maros**) **River** Hungary/Romania. River 880 km (550 miles) long chiefly in Romania, rising in the Carpathians and flowing generally WSW past Tîrgu-Mureş and Arad to join the Tisza R. at Szeged (Hungary).

Murghab (Murgab) River. River 720 km (450 miles) long in Central Asia rising in the W of the Hindu Kush and flowing W and NW across NW Afghanistan; it enters SE Turkmenistan, turns N across the Kara Kum desert, waters the Mary oasis and then loses itself in the desert.

Murmansk Russia. Cap. of the Murmansk Region on the E shore of Kola Bay, Barents Sea, in the NW of the Kola Peninsula. Pop. (1990) 472,000. Being an ice-free port and linked by rail with Leningrad, it developed rapidly after its foundation (1915).

Exports timber and apatite. Important fishing centre. Shipyards, fish canneries, sawmills and refrigeration plants. Had great strategic importance in World War II as the port to which US and British supplies for the USSR were shipped by the Arctic route.

Murom Russia. Industrial town and railway junction in the Vladimir Region on the Oka R. near the confluence with the Tesha R. 290 km (180 miles) E of Moscow. Pop. (1990) 125,000.

Railway engineering, flax-spinning, tanning. One of the oldest Russian towns, founded in the 10th cent.

Muroran Japan. Industrial town and seaport in S Hokkaido 72 km (45 miles) NNE of Hakodate. Pop. (1990) 136,209.

Important iron and steel industry. Oil-refining. Manufactures cement. Exports iron and steel, coal and timber.

Murray River Australia. The chief river of Australia, 2574 km (1600 miles) long, rising in the Australian Alps near Mt Kosciusko, New South Wales, flowing W through a level basin and then S through L. Alexandrina to reach the Indian Ocean at Encounter Bay, South Australia. For some 1920 km (1200 miles) it forms the boundary between New South Wales and Victoria, though its shallow, winding, braided course scarcely makes it ideal for this purpose. Its major tributaries are the Lachlan-Murrumbidgee from the E, the Goulburn from the S and the lengthy but very erratic Darling from the far NE. The upper waters, snow-fed in spring, now benefit from the Snowy R. diversion scheme. About two-thirds of Australia's irrigated area lies in the Murray R. basin: water is retained in major storages such as the Hume Reservoir, raised in level by barrages, weirs and locks at various points, and distributed by diversion of pumping into and through channels. Besides grain and pastoral products (esp. wool) there is a large output of dried and canned fruits from the river basin. Hydroelectric power comes from stations on the upper river, its tributaries and the Snowy Mountains project.

Mürren Switzerland. Health resort and winter-sports centre at a height of 1650 m (5412 ft) in the Bernese Oberland, above the Lauterbrunnen valley and near the Jungfrau.

Pop. (1990) 320. Fine mountain views. Reached by mountain railway.

Mur (Mura) River. River 480 km (300 miles) long rising in Austria at the W end of the Niedere Tauern and flowing generally E, then SE past Graz, forming parts of the Austro–Yugoslav and Yugoslav–Hungarian borders and joining the Drava R. at Legrad. Navigable below Graz.

Murrumbidgee River Australia. River 1690 km (1050 miles) long in New South Wales, rising in the Great Dividing Range and flowing N and then W to join the Murray R. Its chief tributary is the Lachlan R. from the N. Water impounded by the Burrinjuck Dam aids irrigation in the basin, where sheep and dairy cattle graze on sown pastures, and cereals, fruits and vines, and vegetables flourish.

Murviedro ➤SAGUNTO.

Murzuk ➤FEZZAN.

Musala, Mount ➤RHODOPE MOUNTAINS.

Muscat and Oman ➤OMAN.

Musgrave Ranges Australia. Much-eroded mountain ranges in the NW of South Australia extending about 320 km (200 miles) along the border with the Northern Territory, rising to 1516 m (4972 ft) in Mt Woodroffe.

Muskegon USA. Industrial town in Michigan on L. Michigan at the mouth of the Muskegon R. Pop. (1985) 41,000.
Manufactures motor-car parts, aircraft engines, metal goods and furniture.

Muskegon River USA. River 370 km (230 miles) long in Michigan, rising in L. Houghton and flowing generally SW to L. Michigan. Widens to form L. Muskegon at the mouth.

Muskogee USA. Town in Oklahoma near the Arkansas R. 74 km (46 miles) SE of Tulsa. Pop. (1985) 41,000.
Railway and commercial centre for an agricultural and oil-producing region. Oil-refining, meat-packing. Manufactures glassware and clothing.

Musselburgh Scotland. Town in East Lothian on the Firth of Forth at the mouth of the R. Esk 10 km (6 miles) E of Edinburgh. Pop. (1991) 20,630.
Brewing. Manufactures paper, wire rope and nets. Seat of Loretto School, a leading Scottish public school.
Has the Jacobean mansion Pinkie House. The Battle of Pinkie (1547) took place just SE.

Mutare (Umtali) Zimbabwe. Town 209 km (130 miles) SE of Harare near the Mozambique frontier at a height of 1080 m (3542 ft). Pop. (1991) 131,808. Market town on the Beira–Harare railway.
Industries inc. engineering and the manufacture of textiles and clothing. There is gold-mining in the neighbourhood.

Muzzaffarabad Kashmir. Cap. of the Pakistani-occupied part of Kashmir (Azad Kashmir) on the Upper Jhelum R. Commercial centre.

Muzaffarnagar India. Town in Uttar Pradesh 56 km (35 miles) N of Meerut. Pop. (1991) 240,600.
Commercial centre, with trade in cereals and sugar-cane. Industries inc. textiles, sugar, steel products and distilling.

Muzaffarpur India. Town in Bihar on the Burhi Gandak R. 64 km (40 miles) NNE of Patna. Pop. (1991) 241,100.
Trade in grain, tobacco and sugar-cane. Rice and sugar-milling. University (1952).

Mweru, Lake Democratic Republic of the Congo/Zambia. Lake 120 km (75 miles) long and 48 km (30 miles) wide on the frontier between the Democratic Republic of the Congo and Zambia, at a height of 930 m (3050 ft). Receives the Luapula R. (a headstream of the Congo R.) in the S. Drained by the Luvua R. in the N. Discovered by Dr Lacerda (Portuguese) 1798; rediscovered by David Livingstone 1867. Sir Alfred Sharpe explored the W shore 1890.

Myanmar (Burma). Independent republic of SE Asia. Bounded on the E by China, Laos and Thailand, and on the W by the Bay of Bengal, Bangladesh and India. Area 676,577 sq km (261,228 sq. miles). Pop. (1993) 44,613,000 (25 per cent urban). Life expectancy, 56 years male, 60 female. Cap. Yangôn (Rangoon). Other cities, Mandalay, Moulmein, Pegu and Bassein. Currency: Myanmar kyat = 100 pyas. Separated from India and Bangladesh by a succession of ranges known N–S as the Patkai, Naga and Chin Hills and continued as the Arakan Yoma that divides the coastal strip of Arakan from the rest of the country. The Irrawaddy and Chindwin flow S from the mountainous N (the valley of the former being separated in its lower course from the Sittang basin by the Pegu Yoma range) to enter the sea by a broad delta. E of the central plain of Myanmar is a plateau averaging 900 m (2953 ft) in altitude and cut by the deep N–S gorges of the Salween R. To the S of the plateau is the long narrow coastal strip of Tenasserim, extending as far as the Isthmus of Kra and fringed by the chain of islands known as the Mergui Archipelago. The climate is equatorial in coastal areas, changing to tropical monsoon over most of the interior, but humid temperature in the N. The natural vegetation varies with the rainfall: where the latter exceeds about 200 cm (80 ins.) annually the lower lands are clothed with tropical rainforests, while the somewhat drier regions (100–200 cm; 40–80 ins.) support deciduous monsoon forests, home of the teak; the dry belt has only scrub and semi-desert vegetation. Land use: forested 49 per cent, meadows and pastures 0.5 per cent, agricultural and under permanent cultivation 15 per cent. Religion is chiefly Buddhist. Inhabited by a number of different races speaking different lang. The official lang. is Burmese, but English is in use. The Burmese, who are of Mongolian stock and Buddhist by religion, represent the most advanced section of the pop. and live mainly in the fertile lowlands.

It is primarily an agricultural country, its heart the basin of the great Irrawaddy R. and the main tributary, the Chindwin. About two-thirds of the cultivated area is sown with rice, which is concentrated in the wet alluvial lands of the Irrawaddy delta and the valleys of the lower Chindwin and Sittang rivers. In the dry belt, where about 1.6 million ha (4 million acres) are irrigated, the principal crops are jute, cotton, groundnuts, millet and sesamum. Teak is floated down the rivers from the monsoon forests to sawmills at Yangôn and elsewhere and is exported. There is oil production at Yenangyaung and Chauk. Jade and rubies are mined in the N, silver and lead in the E, and tin and tungsten in the S. Industrial manufactures inc. cement, fertilizers, sugar, paper, cotton yarn, vehicles and tractors, and bicycles.

The inhabitants of Myanmar are the descendants of various Mongolian tribes which moved into the country from W China and Tibet, probably in the 7th cent. Unity was achieved in 1054 with the founding of the Pagan dynasty by Anawrahta, who introduced Buddhism, and lasted till 1287, when Burma fell to the Mongols under Kublai Khan. For much of the following five cent. the land was split into petty states, but in 1752 Alangpaya (Alompra) controlled the whole country. His successors came into conflict with the British, however, and as a result of the Burmese Wars (1823–6, 1852, 1885–6) the country was gradually annexed by Britain; in 1886 it was made a province of India. Burma was separated from India in 1937. During World War II it was occupied by the Japanese (1942–5), and the destruction and demoralization of these years left the country disorganized and difficult to govern. In 1948 the Union of Burma became an independent republic. In 1958 and again in 1962, however, government was taken over by a Revolutionary Council. In 1974 military government ended and the Union of Burma became the Socialist Republic of the Union of Burma. In 1988 the armed forces seized power and in 1989 changed the country's name to Union of Myanmar. There were elections for the 492-seat National Assembly in 1990 and the National League for Democracy won a majority of the seats, but the military government refused to hand over power, placing the League's leader, Aung San Suu Kyi, under house arrest. Myanmar is divided into seven states and seven administrative districts.

Mycenae Greece. Ancient city in the NE Peloponnese 27 km (17 miles) SW of Corinth near the modern village of Mikinai. Ruled over by Atreus and Agamemnon, it flourished *c.* 1400 BC. Destroyed by the people of Argos in the 5th cent. BC and never recovered. The excavations of Schliemann and others (begun 1874) revealed a palace, the city walls with the famous Lion Gate, and tombs.

Myitkyina Myanmar (Burma). Cap. of Kachin State on the Irrawaddy R. 400 km (250 miles) NNE of Mandalay. Pop. (1985) 15,000. Market town. Linked by rail and waterway with Mandalay and Yangôn and by road with Yunnan province (China).

Mykolayiv (Nikolayev) Ukraine. Black Sea port on the southern Bug R. at its confluence with the Ingul R. Pop. (1991) 512,000.

Exports grain, sugar, metallic ores (iron, manganese) and timber. A naval base and the main shipbuilding centre on the Black Sea. Flour-milling also an important industry and has some of the largest grain elevators in Europe. Manufactures machinery, footwear, knitwear, food products and furniture.

Mysore India. 1. ►KARNATAKA. 2. City in Karnataka 129 km (80 miles) SW of Bangalore. Pop. (1991) 606,800.

Manufactures silk and cotton goods, paints, fertilizers, automobiles, brake systems, paper, tyres, sandalwood products, lamps and railway coaches.

Seat of a university (1916), with Bangalore. Within the fort is the former Maharajah's palace.

Mytilene (Mitilíni) Greece. Cap. of Lesbos *nome*, seaport on the SE coast of Lesbos island, in the Aegean Sea. Pop. (1981) 24,991.

Trade in olive oil, citrus fruits, cereals. Built first on an offshore island, it was later linked to Lesbos by a causeway and spread along the coast.

Mytishchi Russia. Industrial town in the Moscow Region 23 km (14 miles) NNE of Moscow. Pop. (1974) 127,000.

Manufactures railway rolling-stock and textiles.

N

Naaf River Myanmar (Burma)/Bangladesh. Tidal inlet of the Bay of Bengal extending 48 km (30 miles) from Taungbro past Maungdaw.

Naaldwijk Netherlands. Town situated SW of The Hague in Zuid Holland. Pop. (1992) 28,100.

Centre of an agricultural area, trading in fruit and potatoes.

Naantali Finland. Town situated W of Turku on the Gulf of Bothnia in Turku-Pori province. Pop. (1990) 11,335.

Railway terminus and seaside resort with some industry inc. paper-making.

Naas Ireland. County town of Co. Kildare 29 km (18 miles) WSW of Dublin. Pop. (1991) 11,141. Once the residence of the kings of Leinster. Hunting centre. Punchestown racecourse is 4 km (2½ miles) S.

Naberejnye-Chelny Russia. Town situated ESE of Yelabuga in Tatarstan Republic on the Kama R. Pop. (1991) 513,100.

Grain trading and distribution centre. Industries inc. flour-milling, sawmilling, metalworking, and it manufactures bricks, railway sleepers and wine.

Nablus (Nabulus) Israeli-occupied West Bank. Town in the NW in Samaria between Mt Ebal (942 m; 2889 ft) and Mt Gerizim (881 m; 3090 ft) 50 km (31 miles) N of Jerusalem. Pop. (1984) 80,000.

Manufactures soap.

Built on the site of ancient Shechem; nearby are the reputed Jacob's well and Joseph's tomb.

Nacka Sweden. Suburb of SE Stockholm. Pop. (1989) 63,145.

Industries inc. the manufacture of steam turbines and diesel motors, and drills.

Nafud (Nefud) Saudi Arabia. Large desert area consisting of sand dunes and bare rock. The main part, S of the Syrian Desert, is known as the Great Nafud and the SE extension, which joins the Rub al Khali, as the Little Nafud or Dahna.

Naga Hills India. Ranges of hills in the extreme NE on the Burmese border, which gave their name to a former district of Assam. Height rises to 3826 m (12,553 ft). Much forested but little developed.

Nagaland India. State of the Indian Union in the extreme NE, bordered on the E by Myanmar (Burma), formed in 1962 from the former Naga Hills district of Assam and the former Tuensang Frontier division of the North-East Frontier Tract. Area 16,579 sq km (6476 sq. miles). Pop. (1991) 1,215,573. Cap. Kohima. Inhabited by the Nagas, a Tibeto–Burmese group of tribes who speak a variety of dialects; more than 50 per cent are Christians (mainly Naga Baptists).

Agriculture is the main occupation for 80 per cent of the people. They practise shifting agriculture, growing rice, maize and vegetables, and were formerly notorious headhunters. Industries inc. pulp and paper, sugar and the manufacture of plywood and electronic equipment. There are about 2000 small-scale industrial units in the state.

For some years before the formation of the state they sought independence and the Indian government was forced to take military action against rebels.

Nagano Japan. Cap. of Nagano prefecture in central Honshu 177 km (110 miles) NW of Tokyo. Pop. (1991) 348,791.

Manufactures machinery, textiles and electrical equipment. Food-processing.

Trade in silk. Also a religious centre, with a 7th-cent. Buddhist temple.

Nagaoka Japan. Industrial town in Niigata prefecture, Honshu 50 km (31 miles) SSW of Niigata. Pop. (1991) 186,536.

Oil-refining, engineering. Manufactures chemicals and textiles.

Nagar Haveli ➤DADRA HAVELI.

Nagasaki Japan. Cap. of Nagasaki prefecture in W Kyushu 80 km (50 miles) W of Kumamoto. Pop. (1991) 443,823.

Seaport. Exports coal, cement, canned fish. Important shipbuilding and engineering industry (Mitsubishi). Fishing. Picturesque, in an amphitheatre facing a narrow bay.

In the 16th cent. it was the only Japanese port with foreign trade, being visited first by the Portuguese and Dutch. During World War II it was largely destroyed by the second atomic bomb, which killed and injured over 75,000 people (9 August 1945).

Nagercoil India. Town in S Tamil Nadu 64 km (40 miles) SE of Trivandrum. Pop. (1990) 190,084.

Manufactures coir rope, mats.

Cape Comorin, the southernmost point of India, is 16 km (10 miles) SE.

Nagorno–Karabakh Azerbaijan. Autonomous region on the E slopes of the Lesser Caucasus. Area 4400 sq km (1700 sq miles). Pop. (1990) 192,000. Cap. Stepanakert. Mountainous.

Main products wine, silk and dairy produce.

Once a separate khanate. Became an autonomous region in 1923.

Nagoya Japan. Cap. of Aichi prefecture, central Honshu on Ise Bay 109 km (68 miles) E of Kyoto. Pop. (1991) 2,158,784.

Seaport, industrial centre and Japan's fourth largest city. First opened to foreign trade in 1907. Engineering, metalworking. Manufactures machinery, porcelain, textiles, chemicals and vehicles.

University (1939). The 17th-cent. castle was severely damaged by bombing in World War II. Also has the Buddhist temple of Higashi Honganji.

Nagpur India. Commercial city and railway junction in N Maharashtra 708 km (440 miles) ENE of Bombay. Pop. (1991) 1,624,800.

Manufactures cotton goods, hosiery, dyes, springs, polyester, staple fibre and explosives. Cotton-ginning is carried on as is manganese ore mining.

Became cap. of the Mahratta kingdom of Nagpur (1743), of the Central Provinces (1861) and for a short time of Madhya Pradesh (1956).

Nagykanizsa Hungary. Town in Zala county in the SW 105 km (65 miles) WNW of Pécs. Pop. (1984) 56,000.

Manufactures footwear, glass, heavy equipment. Brewing, distilling and flour-milling. Trade in grain and livestock.

Nagykörös Hungary. Market town in Szolnok county 77 km (48 miles) SE of Budapest. Pop. (1984) 27,000.

Trade in fruit and wine. Flour-milling, distilling and canning.

Naha Japan. Seaport and largest city of Okinawa on the SW coast. Pop. (1991) 303,480.

Exports sugar and dried fish. Manufactures textiles and pottery.

Nahuel Huapí, Lake Argentina. Andean lake (area 531 sq km; 205 sq. miles) at a height of 767 m (2516 ft) near the Chilean border in Neuquén and Río Negro provinces. Resort area with a National Park established 1903. Picturesque with many islands; the largest, Victoria, has a forestry research station.

Nairn Scotland. Town and port in Highland at the mouth of the Nairn R. on Moray Firth. Pop. (1991) 7892.

Fishing port. Holiday resort. Golf courses.

Nairn River Scotland. River 61 km (38 miles) long rising NE of Fort Augustus and flowing NE through Highland to the Moray Firth at Nairn.

Nairnshire Scotland. Now part of Highland Region.

Nairobi Kenya. Cap., 442 km (275 miles) NW of Mombasa at a height of 1662 m (5451 ft). Pop. (1990) 1,504,900. Situated near the equator, but has a pleasant climate on account of the altitude. Views of Mt Kenya and Mt Kilimanjaro.

In a fertile area producing mainly coffee, sisal, pyrethrum. Railway and other engineering, meat-packing, flour-milling and brewing. Manufactures pottery and chemicals. Outside the city is the Nairobi National Park, a game reserve.

Founded in 1899 as the headquarters of the Mombasa–Uganda railway. With the influx of white settlers it rapidly became important. Replaced Mombasa as administrative centre in 1907.

Naivasha, Lake Kenya. Lake 16 km (10 miles) long and 14 km (9 miles) wide in the Great Rift Valley at a height of 1887 m (6189 ft). There is no known outlet. On its NE shore is the small town and resort of Vaivasha, centre of a dairy-farming and sheep-rearing area.

Najaf (Nejef) Iraq. Town near the Euphrates R. 145 km (90 miles) S of Baghdad. Pop. (1985) 243,603. Founded by Haroun al Rashid in the 8th cent. Centre of pilgrimage for the Shia Muslims, as the burial place of Ali, Mohammed's son-in-law.

Nakhichevan Azerbaijan. Ancient Naxuana. Cap. of Nakhichevan Autonomous Republic 129 km (80 miles) SE of Yerevan at a height of 885 m (2903 ft). Pop. (1990) 37,000.

Flour-milling, tanning.

Long disputed by Armenians, Turks and Persians.

Nakhichevan Autonomous Republic Azerbaijan. Situated on the Iranian and Turkish borders, an enclave within Armenia. Area 5500 sq km (2124 sq. miles). Pop. (1990) 300,000 (mainly Azerbaijanis). Cap. Nakhichevan.

Mainly agricultural. Chief crops cotton and tobacco.

Annexed by Russia 1828. Became an autonomous republic within Azerbaijan in 1924.

Nakhodka Russia. Seaport in the Primorye Territory on the Pacific coast 88 km (55 miles) ESE of Vladivostok. Pop. (1991) 164,500. Acts as outpost for and has largely superseded Vladivostok, owing to greater freedom from ice in winter.

Ship repairing, sawmilling and food-processing. Manufactures plywood and matches.

Nakhon Ratchasima (Korat) Thailand. Cap. of Nakhon Ratchasima province on the Mun R. 225 km (140 miles) NE of Bangkok. Pop. (1989) 206,605.

Railway junction. Chief commercial and engineering centre of E Thailand. Trade in rice and livestock.

Increased in importance with the construction of the railway from Bangkok (1892) and its later extension to the N and E.

Nakhon Sawan Thailand. Cap. of Nakhon Sawan province on the Chao Phraya just below the confluence of the Nan and Ping rivers 217 km (135 miles) N of Bangkok. Pop. (1989) 107,907.

River port. Important trade in teak, floated down river.

Nakhon Sithammarat Thailand. Cap. of Nakhon Sithammarat province near the E coast of the Malay peninsula 595 km (370 miles) S of Bangkok. Pop. (1989) 63,162.

Market town. Trade in rice, coconuts and fruits.

One of the oldest towns in Thailand; cap. of a kingdom until the 13th cent.

Nakuru Kenya. Cap. of the Rift Valley province on the N shore of L. Nakuru 137 km (85 miles) NW of Nairobi at a height of 1800 m (5904 ft). Pop. (1986) 112,000.

Commercial centre in a district important for coffee, maize, pyrethrum, sisal, wheat, dairy produce and food-processing.

Nakuru, Lake Kenya. Salt lake 13 km (8 miles) long and 6 km (4 miles) wide in the Great Rift Valley, with the town of Nakuru on its N shore. Famous for its bird life, esp. the flamingo.

Nalchik Russia. Cap. of the Kabardino-Balkar Republic on the N slopes of the Greater Caucasus 169 km (105 miles) W of Grozny. Pop. (1990) 235,000.

Industrial centre with flour-milling and meat-packing. Manufactures oilfield equipment, furniture, textiles, clothing and footwear.

Founded (1818) as a Russian fortress.

Namangan Uzbekistan. Town in the fertile Fergana valley 193 km (120 miles) E of Tashkent. Pop. (1991) 319,200.

Industries inc. cotton manufactures and food-processing, wine. Trades in livestock and fruit.

Namaqualand South Africa/Namibia. Arid coastal region with little vegetation. Pop. 30,000 (mainly Namaquas (Namas), consisting of Hottentot tribes). Divided into two parts by the Orange R. Great Namaqualand is in the N (in Namibia) and Little Namaqualand in the S (in South Africa). Produces copper, diamonds and tungsten.

Namen ➤NAMUR.

Namib Desert Namibia. Desert region 1290 km (800 miles) long and 96 km (60 miles) wide between the plateau and the Atlantic Ocean. The coastal strip receives less than 2.5 cm (1 in.) of rain annually and is practically barren, and moisture comes from sea mists.

Namibe Angola. Formerly Moçâmedes. Seaport in the SW 320 km (200 miles) SSW of Benguela. Pop. (1985) 100,000.

Industries inc. fishing and fish-canning. Linked by rail with Ghivemba in the interior. Exports cotton, fish (canned, dried and salted), hides and skins.

Namibia. Independent republic bounded in the N by Angola and Zambia, W by the Atlantic Ocean, S and SE by South Africa and E by Botswana. The Caprivi Strip about 300 km (188 miles) long extends E up to the Zambezi R., projecting into Zambia and Botswana and touching Zimbabwe. Area 825,580 sq km (318,580 sq. miles). Pop. (1995) 1,596,000 (33 per cent urban). Life expectancy, 58 years male, 60 female. Cap. Windhoek. Currency: Namibian dollar = 100 cents. Namibia is part of the plateau of southern Africa, rising sharply from the arid coastal plain of the Namib Desert to an average height of 1050 m (3444 ft). No permanent streams of importance; many saltwater depressions, the largest of which is the Etosha Pan in the N and E. Chief seaport is Walvis Bay and in 1992 joint administration with South Africa was agreed. Other ports are Swakopmund and Luderitz. All three are linked by rail with Windhoek and the South African railway system. Rainfall increased E from the coast (Swakopmund 1.8 cm; 0.7 ins.) to the plateau (Windhoek 35 cm; 14 ins.); it reaches 50 cm (20 ins.) in the N but decreases again on the Kalahari plateau. Mostly poor grassland and scrub. Land use: forested 22 per cent, meadows and pastures 46 per cent, agricultural and under permanent cultivation 0.8 per cent. Most of the inhabitants are Bantu, chiefly Ovambo (665,000), Damaras (100,000) and Herero (100,000). There are about 85,000 whites. About 90 per cent of the pop. is Christian (50 per cent Lutheran) and the official lang. is English.

The main occupation is stock-rearing; cattle in the N and centre, sheep and goats in the drier S. Noted for karakul sheep, from which 'Persian lamb' skins are exported. After independence a 200-mile exclusive economic zone was declared for fishing, which is a growing industry. Other industries inc. food-processing and the manufacture of mining equipment, footwear, textiles and steel goods. The chief minerals found are diamonds, uranium, copper, lead, zinc, tin, silver and gold. Minerals represent 76 per cent of exports of which diamonds 31 per cent. The tourist industry is expanding.

The first European to visit the territory was Bartholomew Diaz, who landed at Lüderitz (Angra Pequena) in 1486. Britain annexed Walvis Bay in 1878. Germany established a settlement at Lüderitz in 1883 and created the colony of German South West Africa in 1892; after World War I the League of Nations mandated the territory and it was administered by the then Union of South Africa. After World War II South Africa passed a South West Africa Affairs Amendment Act; in 1950; however, the International Court of Justice ruled that South West Africa was still under international mandate from the UN and that South Africa was not competent to modify the international status of the territory without UN consent. South Africa left the British Commonwealth in 1961 and the status of the South West Africa territory was reviewed by the International Court of Justice, which announced in 1966 that it could not give a decision. In 1971 in a further statement the International Court of Justice ruled that South Africa's presence in Namibia was illegal and independence was eventually agreed in 1990. Under the 1990 Constitution Namibia is a multi-party republic. There is a bicameral legislature consisting of a 78-member National Assembly and a 26-member National Council.

Nampula Mozambique. Cap. of Nampula province situated W of Mozambique town. Pop. (1991) 250,473. An agricultural trading centre.

Namur (Flemish **Namen**) Belgium. 1. Province in the SW, bordering S on France. Area 3666 sq km (1415 sq. miles). Pop. (1991) 423,317.

Fruit-growing in the fertile N, lumbering in the wooded S. Much quarrying. Drained by the Meuse and Sambre rivers. Chief towns Namur and Dinant.

2. Cap. of Namur province at the confluence of the Meuse and Sambre rivers 56 km (35 miles) SE of Brussels. Pop. (1991) 103,443.

Manufactures cutlery, glass. Tanning, flour-milling.

Cathedral (18th-cent.). The fortifications built in the late 19th cent. were reduced by the Germans in World War I (1914) and the town was severely damaged in World War II.

Nanaimo Canada. City situated W of Vancouver on the Vancouver Island, British Columbia. Pop. (1991) 60,129.

Port exporting lumber and pulp. Industries inc. pulp, lumber, fishing and tourism.

Nanchang China. Cap. of Jiangxi province on the Kan R. 274 km (170 miles) SE of Wuhan. Pop. (1990) 1,086,124.

Commercial and industrial centre. Trade in tea, rice, cotton, hemp and tobacco. Manufactures machinery, aircraft, trucks, chemicals, textiles, glass, pottery and paper.

In the Sino–Japanese War it was occupied by the Japanese (1939–45).

Nancy France. Prefecture of the Meurthe-et-Moselle department in the NE on the Meurthe R. and the Marne–Rhine Canal. Pop. (1990) 102,410. Formerly cap. of Lorraine. Situated near the ironfield, it has become a centre of iron and steel manufacture.

Engineering. Manufactures textiles, glass, footwear and tobacco products.

Extraordinarily well planned; outstanding features are the Place Stanislas, with impressive 18th-cent. buildings, a triumphal arch leading from it to the Place Carrière and the 18th-cent. cathedral. Became cap. of the dukes of Lorraine in the 12th cent. and developed culturally and architecturally under the last of them, Stanislas Leszczynski of Poland in the 18th cent. Finally became French in 1766.

Nanda Devi India. Himalayan peak (7817 m; 25,646 ft) in the Garhwal district, N Uttar Pradesh. First climbed (1936) by an Anglo-American expedition (Tilman and Odell).

Nanga Parbat India. Himalayan peak (8126 m; 26,660 ft) in W Kashmir 96 km (60 miles) W of Skardu. Several climbers, particularly on the German expeditions of 1934 and 1937, lost their lives in trying to reach the summit; it was finally scaled in 1953 by Buhl, an Austrian.

Nanjing (Nanking) China. Cap. of Jiangsu province and river port on the Chang Jiang 265 km (165 miles) WNW of Shanghai. Pop. (1990) 2,090,204.

Industrial centre manufacturing textiles, paper and fertilizers; it gave its name to the cloth 'nankeen'.

Once one of the leading literary centres of China, it was founded in 1368 on the site of a more ancient city. It was made the 'southern capital' by the first Ming emperor but was deserted for Beijing in 1421. During the Taiping rebellion the city was taken by the rebels in 1853, who destroyed its ancient walls and the famous 15th-cent. porcelain tower. In 1928 it was made the cap. of China by the Nationalist government, but in 1937 it fell to the Japanese. In 1945 the Japanese surrender in China was signed here and in 1946 it became cap., but in 1949 under the Communist regime the cap. was again moved to Beijing. A road–rail bridge (double-decker construction) about 6 km (4 miles) long over the Chang Jiang, the longest in China, was opened 1968; previously trains had to be ferried across the river.

Nanking ►NANJING.

Nanning China. Formerly (1913–45) Yungning. Cap. of the Guangxi-Zhuang Autonomous Region from 1958 on the Siang R. 169 km (105 miles) SW of Liuzhou. Pop. (1990) 721,877.

River port. Trade in rice, hides and tobacco. Industries inc. the manufacture of textiles, sugar-refining and flour-milling.

Nanterre France. Suburb of NW Paris in the Hauts-de-Seine department near the left bank of the Seine R. at the foot of Mont Valérien. Pop. (1990) 86,627.

Industries inc. metalworking and the manufacture of electrical equipment, hosiery, chemicals and paints.

Nantes France. Prefecture of the Loire-Atlantique department on the Loire R. at its confluence with the Erdre and Sèvre Nantaise rivers. Pop. (1990) 251,133.

Important seaport, with outport St Nazaire. Exports petroleum products. Also an industrial centre. Oil-refining, flour-milling, sugar-refining, tobacco-processing and vegetable-canning. Manufactures chocolate, vegetable oils. Harbour accessible to ocean-going ships owing to post-war improvements.

Castle founded in the 10th cent., once residence of the dukes of Brittany; 15th-cent. cathedral, not completed till the 19th cent. Before the Roman conquest of Gaul Nantes was the chief town of the Namnetes. Here Henry IV signed the famous Edict of Nantes (1598), which deprived the Huguenots of religious and civil liberty until it was revoked by Louis XIV in 1685. Birthplace of Jules Verne (1828–1905).

Nantucket USA. Low-lying island 24 km (15 miles) long, situated off the coast of SE Massachusetts 40 km (25 miles) S of Cape Cod. Formerly an important whaling centre but now chiefly a summer resort.

Nantwich England. Town in Cheshire on the R. Weaver 6 km (4 miles) SW of Crewe. Pop. (1991) 11,695.

Formerly important in the salt industry; now has brine baths. Tanning. Manufactures footwear and clothing.

Has a 14th-cent. church.

Nanyuki Kenya. Town situated NNE of Nairobi in Central Province at 2743 m (9000 ft) at the foot of Mount Kenya. Pop. (1984) 27,000. Rail terminus, resort and centre of a farming area.

Napier New Zealand. Former cap. of the Hawke's Bay provincial district, North Island on the SW shore of Hawke Bay. Pop. (1990) 52,468.

Serves an intensively farmed region. Wool, frozen lamb, hides and skins are exported from its port, Port Ahuriri 3 km (2 miles) distant.

In 1931 it suffered considerable earthquake damage, with loss of life, the coastal area being raised 2.4 m (7.9 ft); the town was largely rebuilt.

Naples (Italian **Napoli**) Italy. Ancient Neapolis. Cap. of Napoli province in Campania, the second seaport and third largest city of Italy, 193 km (120 miles) SE of Rome. Pop. (1991) 1,206,013.

Important for industry and commerce. Industries inc. shipbuilding, railway and other engineering, oil-refining, tomato-canning and other food-processing. Manufactures pasta, textiles, chemicals, coral and tortoiseshell articles. Exports wine, olive oil and fruits. Tourism is important and Naples is a base for nearby attractions of Sorrento, Capri and Ischia.

Situated on a beautiful site at the base and on the slopes of a volcanic ridge on the N shore of the Bay of Naples and best viewed from the sea. Divided into two crescents by a hill surmounted by a fortress (Sant' Elmo) and the promontory of Pizzofalcone; the W part is a residential district, while the E is the much larger, more crowded and older section of the city. On the small Isola del Salvatore, joined by a causeway to the foot of the Pizzofalcone, is the Castel dell' Ovo, while near the harbour are another medieval castle, the Castel Nuovo, the Royal Palace and the San Carlo Opera House. Among the many churches is the 13th/14th-cent. Cathedral of San Gennaro, and the city is celebrated for the Museo Nazionale, which contains most of the objects excavated at Pompeii and Herculaneum. Probably founded by Greeks in the 6th cent. BC, the city surrendered to the Romans in the 4th cent. BC and became a fashionable resort; Virgil often stayed here and is buried nearby. Neapolis long retained its Greek culture, but in the 6th cent. AD it was under Byzantine rule, in the 8th cent. an independent duchy. Later it became cap. of the kingdom of Naples, the latter sometimes a separate kingdom and sometimes united with Sicily, and from the end of the 15th cent. it was held for varying periods by France, Spain and Austria, till it was taken by Garibaldi in 1860 and incorporated in Italy in 1861.

Nara Japan. Cap. of Nara prefecture, S Honshu 29 km (18 miles) E of Osaka. Pop. (1991) 351,985. In a picturesque setting, in wooded hills.

Manufactures textiles, dolls, fans and brushes and ink for calligraphy. Chiefly important as a religious and tourist centre.

The first permanent cap. of Japan 709–84. Many ancient Buddhist temples (one with a massive bronze image of Buddha) and Shinto shrines.

Narbonne France. Ancient Narbo Martius. Market town in the Aude department 8 km (5 miles) from the Gulf of Lions and 39 km (24 miles) N of Perpignan. Pop. (1990) 47,000.

Industries inc. sulphur-refining, brandy-distilling, flour-milling, and it manufactures barrels, bricks and tiles, and pottery. Trade in wine and brandy.

The first Roman colony in Gaul; later cap. of Gallia Narbonensis. The harbour, improved by the Romans, silted up in the 14th cent. Part of the former archiepiscopal palace of the 13th/14th cent. now serves as town hall.

Narew River Poland/Belorussia. River 434 km (270 miles) long rising in W Belorussia and flowing first WNW into NE Poland, then turning SSW to join the W Bug N of Warsaw.

Narmada River India. River 1287 km (800 miles) long rising in the Maikala Range 80 km (50 miles) NW of Bilaspur (Madhya Pradesh) and flowing generally W and then WSW through a depression between the Vindhya and Satpura Ranges, entering the Gulf of Cambay by a broad estuary. Sacred to Hindus. Used for navigation only in the lowest section.

Narragansett Bay USA. Inlet of the Atlantic in the Rhode Island coast, enclosing Rhode Island, Prudence Island, Conanicut Island and others. Mainly fishing centres and resorts around its shores. Providence stands at its head.

Narva Estonia. Port and industrial town in the NE on the Narva (Narova) R. 13 km (8 miles) from the mouth on the Gulf of Finland. Pop. (1991) 87,900.

Important textile manufacturing centre; the mills derive power from the falls on the Narva R.

Founded (1223) by the Danes. Scene of the defeat of Peter the Great of Russia by the Swedes (1700); he captured the town in 1704.

Narvik Norway. Ice-free port on Ofot Fiord 150 km (93 miles) SSW of Tromsö. Pop. (1990) 18,500. Also a railway terminus.

Exports iron ore from Sweden.

Scene of an important naval battle in World War II (1940).

Naryan-Mar ►NENETS A.A.

Naseby England. Village in Northampton-shire 18 km (11 miles) W of Kettering, where the Royalists under Charles I and Prince Rupert were decisively defeated by the Parliamentarians under Cromwell and Fairfax (1645).

Nashik India. Town situated NE of Bombay on upper Godavari R. in Mahar-ashtra. A holy place for Hindus, with many temples and shrines. Pop. (1990) 646,896.

Agricultural products inc. grapes and onions. Manufactures inc. brass and copper goods and soap. There is an aeronautics in-dustry in the vicinity.

Nashua USA. Industrial town in New Hampshire 24 km (15 miles) S of Manchester at the confluence of the Merrimack and Nashua rivers. Pop. (1990) 77,662.

Manufactures shoes, plastics and paper.

Nashville USA. State cap. of Tennessee on the Cumberland R. Pop. (1990) 448,374.

Important road and rail junction, industrial and commercial centre. Industries inc. railway engineering, printing and publishing. Manufactures rayon, cellophane, footwear, hosiery, glass and aircraft components.

The Hermitage, formerly the plantation home of President Andrew Jackson, is 18 km (11 miles) E.

Nasik India. Town in Maharashtra on the upper Godavari R. 145 km (90 miles) NE of Bombay. Pop. (1991) 657,000.

Manufactures copper and brassware, soap, aircraft, paper, sugar and foodstuffs.

Many temples and shrines. An important centre of Hindu pilgrimage. Nearby are

ancient Buddhist caves dating from the 3rd cent BC and later.

Nasirabad Bangladesh ►MYMENSINGH.

Nassau Bahamas. Cap. and chief seaport on the NE coast of New Providence Island. Pop. (1990) 172,196.

Exports pulpwood, salt, crawfish, cucum-bers. Mild climate with fine beaches. Tourism is the most important industry with over 1,250,000 visitors a year, mainly from USA. Finance and banking also important.

Laid out 1729. Named after King William III (of the House of Orange-Nassau).

Nassau Germany. Former duchy in Ger-many with cap. Wiesbaden. The family of Orange-Nassau provided the present ruling houses of the Netherlands and Luxembourg. Well wooded and fertile; famous for wines and for mineral springs, esp. at Wiesbaden and Bad Ems. In 1866 it was incorporated in the Prussian province of Hesse-Nassau and in 1945 was incorporated into Hessen.

Nässjö Sweden. Town situated ESE of Jön-köping. Pop. (1990) 30,749.

Railway junction. Industries inc. metal-working, woodworking, textiles, paper-making; manufactures clothing.

Natal Brazil. Cap of Rio Grande do Norte state in the NE on the Potengi R. near the mouth. Pop. (1991) 606,541.

Seaport. Exports sugar, cotton, salt, hides and carnauba wax. Manufactures textiles, ce-ment and furniture, and there is salt-refining. A large international airport (Parnamirim) 13 km (8 miles) SSW.

Natal South Africa ►KWAZULU/NATAL.

Natick USA. Town in Massachusetts 26 km (16 miles) WSW of Boston. Pop. (1970) 31,057.

Manufactures footwear and metal goods.

On the site of land granted to John Eliot for his 'praying Indians' (converts) in 1650.

Natron, Lake Tanzania. Lake in the Great Rift Valley on the Kenya frontier 58 km (36 miles) long and 24 km (15 miles) wide. There are deposits of salt and soda.

Natural Bridge USA. Village in Virginia 42 km (26 miles) NW of Lynchburg. Nearby is the 'natural bridge' from which the name derives, an arch of limestone 66 m (216 ft) high, with a span of 27 m (89 ft) over Cedar Creek; a road crosses the arch.

Naucratis (Naukratis) Egypt. Ancient city in Egypt 72 km (45 miles) SE of Alexandria. Founded by the Greeks *c.* 615 BC as a trading centre, the first Greek settlement in Egypt. The site was discovered (1884) by Flinders Petrie. Excavations have revealed much Greek pottery and the remains of temples.

Naumburg Germany. Town in the Halle district on the Saale R. 40 km (25 miles) SSW of Halle. Pop. (1990) 30,000.
Industrial centre. Manufactures textiles, leather goods and toys.
Founded in the 10th cent. by the margraves of Meissen. The 13th-cent. cathedral has an unusually large crypt.

Nauplia (Gr. **Návplion, Nauplion**) Greece. Cap. of Argolis *nome* in the E Peloponnese, a seaport on the Gulf of Argolis. Pop. (1985) 11,000.
Trade in tobacco, citrus fruits and vegetables.
Cap. of Greece 1822–34 during the War of Independence.

Nauru. Republic situated in the SW Pacific Ocean. An oval-shaped raised atoll situated W of Kiribati forming an independent Commonwealth Republic. Area 21 sq km (8 sq. miles). Pop. (1990) 8100. A thick phosphate layer covering the central plateau is worked, treated and shipped by Nauruans and Chinese, but the deposits will be exhausted by 2000. The plateau has little top soil and has been mined out, and this prevents regeneration of fruit-bearing trees and crops, but there is fertile land at lower levels where coconuts and some vegetables are grown. It has a tropical climate tempered by sea breezes, but with a high and irregular rainfall.
Discovered in 1798 by Capt. Fearn and annexed by Germany 1888. It was occupied by Australia 1914 and held under League of Nations Mandate 1920–47. From 1947 Nauru was jointly held by Australia, Great Britain and New Zealand, though administered in fact by Australia. It became independent in 1968 and took over the ownership of the phosphate industry in 1969, since when over half the revenue from phosphates has been invested in long-term trust funds to help the bleak future when phosphate products cease.
An 18-member Legislative Assembly was established in 1966.

Navarino ➤PYLOS.

Navarra Spain. A Basque province extending from the W Pyrenees along the French border in the N and to the Ebro R. in the S. Area 10,421 sq km (4023 sq. miles). Pop. (1991) 516,333. Cap. Pamplona. Largely mountainous, with fertile valleys. Drained by the Ebro and its tributaries. Sugar-beet, cereals and vines cultivated.

Navarre France/Spain. Former kingdom of N Spain and SW France, co-extensive with the modern Spanish province of Navarra and the French department of Basses-Pyrénées. Founded in the 9th cent. from lands inhabited by the Vascones. The Spanish section, S of the Pyrenees, was annexed to Spain (1515) by Ferdinand the Catholic. The N part was incorporated in France by Henry IV (1589).

Navasari India. Town situated SSE of Surat in Gujarat in W central India. Pop. (1990) 144,249.
Manufactures inc. copper and brass goods and textiles. Trades in millet and cotton.

Naxos Greece. Largest island in the Cyclades in the Aegean Sea. Area 438 sq km (169 sq. miles). Pop. (1985) 14,500. Known since ancient times for its wine. Also produces fruits, olive oil, emery.
Associated with the worship of Dionysus; taken by Athens in the 5th cent. BC.

Nayarit Mexico. State on the Pacific seaboard. Area 26,979 sq km (10,417 sq. miles). Pop. (1990) 824,623. Cap. Petic. Largely mountainous. The narrow coastal plain is crossed by the Santiago and other rivers.

Maize, cotton, tobacco, sugar-cane, coffee and beans are cultivated. Timber is produced and tourism has grown in recent years.

Nazareth Israel. Town in Lower Galilee 31 km (19 miles) ESE of Haifa. Pop. (1970) 34,000. Famous for its associations with the early life of Jesus. Main building the church on the traditional site of the annunciation. A dormitory town in Haifa and also produces textiles and tobacco products.

Nchanga ►ZAMBIA.

N'djamena Chad. Formerly Fort Lamy. Cap., at the confluence of the Shari and Logone rivers S of L. Chad, near the Cameroon frontier. Pop. (1992) 687,800.

Communications and caravan centre. Groundnuts are grown in the surrounding area and it trades in salt, dates, millet and livestock. Chilled meat is exported to the Democratic Republic of the Congo and cattle to Nigeria.

It was founded in 1900 by the French.

Ndola Zambia. Cap. of the Copperbelt province near the frontier with the Democratic Republic of the Congo 265 km (165 miles) N of Lusaka. Pop. (1990) 376,311.

Commercial, industrial and railway centre, linked with the mining centres of Mufulira, Nchanga, Nkana and Roan Antelope, and on the railway to Lubumbashi in the Democratic Republic of the Congo.

Industries inc. copper and cobalt refining, brewing and sugar-refining.

Settled in 1902 and became a municipality 1932.

Neagh, Lough Northern Ireland. Largest lake in the British Isles 29 km (18 miles) long, 18 km (11 miles) wide, bordering on counties Antrim, Down, Armagh, Tyrone and Londonderry. Fed by the Upper Bann, Blackwater and other rivers. Drained by the Lower Bann. Its shores are generally low and in places marshy.

Neanderthal Germany. Valley in North Rhine-Westphalia 11 km (7 miles) E of Düsseldorf where parts of the skeleton of Neanderthal man were discovered in a limestone cave (1856).

Neath Wales. Town in Neath Port Talbot on the R. Neath 11 km (7 miles) ENE of Swansea. Pop. (1991) 66,000.

Industrial centre. Manufactures vehicles, metal boxes, chemicals and oil.

Remains of a 12th cent. castle and abbey. Its port, Briton Ferry, is within the borough.

Neath Port Talbot Wales. County Borough created 1996, formerly part of West Glamorgan. Pop. (1994) 140,000.

Nebit-Dag Turkmenistan. Town situated ESE of Krasnovodsk on the Trans-Caspian railway. Pop. (1991) 89,100. It has an oil refinery serving the Yshka oilfield.

Nebraska USA. State in central USA, bounded on the E and NE by the Missouri R. Area 200,349 sq km (77,355 sq. miles). Pop. (1990) 1,606,000. Much prairie land; slopes gradually from the W, where it reaches 1654 m (5425 ft), to the SE. Drained by the Niobrara and Platte rivers (tributaries of the Missouri). Climate continental; hot summers, cold winters. Annual rainfall 50–75 cm (20–30 ins.) (decreasing to the W).

Primarily agricultural with (1991) 56,000 farms. Principal crops maize, wheat and oats. Large numbers of cattle and pigs raised. Main industry the processing of agricultural produce. Chief towns Omaha and Lincoln.

First explored (1541) by a Spanish party under Coronado, followed by the French in the 18th cent. Passed to the USA as part of the Louisiana Purchase (1803). Admitted to the Union in 1867 as the 37th state.

Nechako River Canada. River 462 km (287 miles) long in British Columbia, rising in the Coast Mountains, flowing NE and E, and joining the Fraser R. at Prince George. The waters have been harnessed for hydroelecric power.

Neckar River Germany. River 370 km (230 miles) long, rising in the Black Forest and flowing generally N past Tübingen and Heilbronn, turning W past Heidelberg and joining the Rhine R. at Mannheim. It is picturesque throughout its course and meanders in its lower reaches.

Necochea Argentina. Seaport at the mouth of the Quequén Grande R. 320 km (200 miles) E of Bahía Blanca. Pop. (1989) 60,000. It has a large Danish pop.

It exports grain and is also a popular resort.

Needles, The England. Three isolated chalk rocks off the W extremity of the Isle of Wight near the entrance to the Solent. Lighthouse on the most westerly rock.

Negev (Negeb) Israel. Desert and semi-desert region in the S, mainly limestone plateau and hill country, triangular in outline, bordering on Egypt (W) and Jordan (E).

There has been considerable development of agriculture by irrigation (e.g. the Yarkon Negev water pipeline) and cereals, sunflowers, sugar-beet are grown. Oil is produced at Heletz and the port of Eilat (Elath) has been developed on the Gulf of Aqaba.

Scene of much fighting between Israeli and Egyptian forces in 1948 and again in 1967.

Negombo Sri Lanka. Town and fishing port on the W coast 32 km (20 miles) N of Colombo. Pop. (1981) 60,762.

Manufactures brassware.

Negri Sembilan Malaysia. State in West Malaysia on the Strait of Malacca. Area 6643 sq km (2565 sq. miles). Pop. (1990) 1,054,800. Cap. Seremban. Chief seaport Port Dickson.

Main products rice, rubber, palm oil and tin.

Formed by the union of 9 small states (1889). Joined the Federated Malay States (1896), the Federation of Malaya (1947) and the Federation of Malaysia in 1963.

Negro, Río ►RÍO NEGRO.

Negropont ►CHALCIS.

Negros Philippines. Fourth largest island NW of Mindanao and between Panay and Cebu. Area 12,710 sq km (4907 sq. miles). Pop. (1985) 2,750,000. Chief town Bacolod. Largely mountainous.

Produces sugar-cane and rice on the rich volcanic soils of the coastal plains.

Nei Mongol (Inner Mongolia) China. Autonomous Region in the NE, bounded on the N and NW by Mongolian People's Republic and Russia. The Great Wall of China forms part of the S border. Area 1,177,500 sq km (454,600 sq. miles). Pop. (1990) 21,456,798. Cap. Hohhot. It lies mainly on the Mongolian plateau, but rises in the E to the Great Khingan Mountains and in the SW to the Ala Shan; in the S it inc. the N part of the great loop of the Juang He and in the extreme E reaches the valleys of the Nun and the Upper Liao.

Nomadic stock-rearing, chiefly horses, sheep, goats and camels, is the traditional occupation of the Mongolian people, but under Chinese influence agriculture is being introduced. The leading crops are millet, kaoliang and wheat; wool, hides and skins are exported. There are considerable reserves of coal, asbestos, talc, mica and iron. Mining is being developed at Bayan Obo.

Neisse (Nysa) River (Glatzer/Silesian Neisse) Poland. River 193 km (120 miles) long in SW Poland, rising near the Czech frontier and flowing generally N and E past Bystrzyca Klodzka and Klodzko (Glatz) to join the Oder R. near Brzeg.

Neisse (Nysa) River (Görlitzer/Lusatian Neisse) Czech Republic/Germany/Poland. River 225 km (140 miles) long rising in N Bohemia, Czech Republic, in the Isergebirge, flowing generally N and after leaving the Czech Republic forming the boundary between Germany and Poland, past Görlitz and Forst to join the Oder R. near Gubin.

Neiva Colombia. Cap. of Huila department on the upper Magdalena R. 240 km (150 miles) SSW of Bogotá. Pop. (1985) 178,130.

Trade in coffee, tobacco and cattle. Manufactures Panama hats. Founded 1539. Destroyed by Indians but refounded 1612.

Nejd (Central Province) Saudi Arabia. Central area consisting of an extensive plateau sloping gradually E from 1500 m (4,920 ft) to 450 m (1,476 ft) and bordered on the E by Kuwait and Hasa. Area 1,087,800 sq km (420,000 sq. miles). Pop. (1985) 4 million. Cap. Riyadh. Largely desert with many oases in the N and E, where dates form the staple product. Ibn Saud, after his conquest of Hejaz (1925), united it with Nejd to form the Kingdom of Saudi Arabia (1932).

Nellore India. Commercial town in Andhra Pradesh on the Penner R. 153 km (95 miles) NNW of Madras. Pop. (1991) 316,600.

Trade in rice and oilseeds. Industries inc. rice and oilseed milling, stone for flooring, glazed stones.

Nelson England. Town in Lancashire 6 km (4 miles) NNE of Burnley. Pop. (1991) 29,120.

Industries inc. engineering and the manufacture of cotton and rayon goods, food products, furniture and hospital disposables.

Nelson New Zealand. Port on the N coast of the S Island at the head of Tasman Bay. Pop. (1990) 47,391.

Seaport, dealing mainly with inter-island passenger and freight traffic. Exports fruit, vegetables, tobacco and timber, from a hinterland with intensive horticulture and market-gardening. Fruit-canning and saw-milling.

Birthplace of the physicist Lord Rutherford (1871–1937).

Nelson River Canada. River 640 km (400 miles) long in Manitoba flowing generally NE through L. Cross and L. Split and entering Hudson Bay. Port Nelson is a minor port at its mouth. Discovered (1612) by Sir Thomas Button.

Neman River ➤NEMUNAS RIVER.

Nemi, Lake Italy. Crater lake in Latium in the Alban Hills 26 km (16 miles) SE of Rome. After draining (1930–1), two pleasure barges probably built for the Roman emperor Caligula were raised, but these were burned by the retreating Germans in World War II (1944).

Nemunas River. River 880 km (550 miles) long rising in Belarus 48 km (30 miles) S of Minsk. It flows generally W through the former NE Poland past Grodno, then turns N into Lithuania; it turns W again past Kaunas and Sovetsk and enters the Kurisches Haff (Courland Lagoon) by a delta. Navigable for about 480 km (300 miles). Much used for floating timber.

Nenagh Ireland. Market town in Co. Tipperary on the R. Nenagh 35 km (22 miles) NE of Limerick. Pop. (1991) 5525.

Trade in dairy produce, potatoes.

The circular keep of the 12th-cent. castle survives.

Nene (Nen) River England. River 145 km (90 miles) long, rising near Daventry, Northamptonshire, flowing generally E and NE past Northampton, Wellingborough, Peterborough and Wisbech, and entering The Wash near Sutton Bridge. Below Peterborough it flows by a straightened artificial channel, while the old Nene takes a longer, more southerly course, rejoining the other at Wisbech.

Nenets Autonomous Area Russia. Situated in the Arkhangelsk (Archangel) Region. Area 176,700 sq km (68,224 sq. miles). Pop. (1990) 55,000 (mainly Nentsy). Cap. Naryan-Mar (676 km (420 miles) NE of Archangel), a small port at the head of the Pechora R. delta. Principally tundra; chief occupations reindeer-herding, fishing and hunting.

Nepal. Independent kingdom in S Asia on the S slopes of the Himalayas, bounded by China (Tibet) in the N, E, S and W by India. Area 147,181 sq km (56,827 sq. miles). Pop. (1995) 19,525,000 (10 per cent urban). Life expectancy, 54 years male, 53 female. Cap. Kathmandu; other chief towns Morang (Biratnagar), Patan (Lalitpur) and Bhatgaon (Bhaktapur). Currency: Nepalese rupee = 100 paisa. Himalayan ranges traverse the country across the N, with spurs running out SSW and gradually descending to the Terai swamps and jungles, and some cultivated land. Towards the Tibetan border the mountains rise to high peaks and inc. Everest,

Kanchenjunga and Dhaulagiri. The range of temperature is moderate and it is very dry Nov.–Jan., but rainfall is high for the rest of the year; maximum amounts May–Sept. Land use: forested 18 per cent, meadows and pastures 15 per cent, agricultural and under permanent cultivation 19 per cent. About 90 per cent of the pop. is Hindu, 5 per cent Buddhist and 3 per cent Muslim. Lang. mainly Nepali. The people are of Mongolian stock with a strong admixture of Hindu blood and since 1769 the Gurkhas have been the dominant race.

Minerals inc. bismuth, antimony, cobalt, sapphire, rubies, corundum, iron ore, bauxite and sulphur. Industries recently developed inc. jute and sugar milling, lumbering and associated manufacturing, chemicals, matches, cigarettes, footwear, leatherworking and tourism. Leading crops inc. rice, wheat, maize, barley, sugar-cane, millet, and medicinal herbs are collected from mountain slopes for export.

The Gurkhas, a Mongol–Rajput people originally driven out of India by the Muslims, conquered the Newars of the Nepal Valley (1769) and invaded Tibet (1790), but were defeated by the Chinese; their activities along the Indian frontier brought them into conflict with Britain and they were again defeated in 1816. From then the Gurkhas formed a noteworthy section of the British Indian army and still figure in several serving battalions of the British army. Ostensibly ruled by a hereditary king, but from 1846 actual power was in the hands of a hereditary prime minister of the Rana family. After political disturbances in 1950–1, a more democratic form of government was promised; in 1962 the King proclaimed a new constitution based on an indirectly elected legislature and in 1963 formed a National Guidance Council, but this was abolished in 1990 and under a new Constitution Nepal became a Constitutional Monarchy based on a multiparty democracy. There is a bicameral Parliament consisting of a 205-member House of Representatives (*Pratinidhi Sabha*) and a 60-member House of Estates (*Rashtriya Sabha*) of which 10 members are nominated

by the King. The country is administratively divided into 14 zones.

Ness, Loch Scotland. Long narrow lake in Highland extending 39 km (24 miles) NE from Fort Augustus along the Great Glen. Outlet the R. Ness, flowing 11 km (7 miles) NE past Inverness to the Moray Firth. Home of the fabled 'Loch Ness monster', first 'discovered' in 1933.

Netanya Israel. Town and seaside resort in the Plain of Sharon 31 km (19 miles) NNE of Tel Aviv. Pop. (1991) 136,100.

Industries inc. diamond-cutting and food-processing, and manufactures textiles and chemicals.

Netherlands. Kingdom of NW Europe. Bounded N and W by the North Sea, E by Germany and S by Belgium. Area inc. inland water 41,863 sq km (16,163 sq. miles). Pop. (1995) 15,401,000 (89 per cent urban). Life expectancy, 74 years male, 80 female. Cap. Amsterdam, Seat of Government The Hague. Other large cities Rotterdam, Utrecht and Eindhoven. Currency: Netherlands Guilder = 100 cents. Forms the lowest part of the N European Plain, about 25 per cent of the land being below sea level. Consists substantially of the delta formed by the Rhine and Maas (Meuse) and their various arms, inc. the Lek, Waal and Ijssel. Many islands in the SW (Zeeland), inc. Walcheren, and the N coast is fringed by the W Frisian Is. For centuries large areas of land have been reclaimed from the sea, these so-called polders being protected from inundation by dykes, and the work is still continuing. The greatest reclamation scheme which began in 1920 has taken place in the former Zuider Zee, now the Ijsselmeer, and was made possible by the construction of a long dam, the Afsluitdijk, across its entrance. The first phase of the Delta Plan, to seal off the estuaries of Zeeland and S Holland provinces from the sea by dykes, was completed in 1961; and was completed in 1986. Three main regions may thus be distinguished in the Netherlands: the strip of sand dunes along the coast, the adjoining intensively farmed polders, and the

E, formerly sandy and infertile but made productive by the use of fertilizers. Almost the only relief to the monotonous flatness of the surface is in the extreme SE (Limburg), where the hills rise to 300 m (984 ft). The climate, which is maritime temperate, is marked by mild winters and cool summers, but with occasional continental influences. Rainfall amounts to 60–75 cm (24–30 ins.) annually. Land use: forested 9 per cent, meadows and pastures 32 per cent, agricultural and under permanent cultivation 38 per cent. Religion 36 per cent Roman Catholic, 31 per cent Protestant (various denominations). The largest denomination of the Protestants is the Dutch Reformed Church, to which the royal family belongs.

Much of the country is intensively farmed, the raising of dairy cattle being esp. important, but industrial and commercial activities also play a leading part in the economy. From the large numbers of Friesian cattle cheese (esp. the Edam and Gouda varieties), butter and condensed milk are produced for export. Wheat, oats, rye, potatoes and sugar-beet are cultivated; in the Haarlem neighbourhood bulbs are produced, and these, along with flowers and fresh vegetables, are also significant exports. Holland has few mineral resources. Since 1950 the rich fields of natural gas in Groningen and Overijssel provinces, however, have continually increased production, and the gas is distributed by pipeline through the Netherlands and is also exported; it accounts for about 50 per cent of demand for energy. Manufacturing industries are varied and inc. the manufacture of steel at Utrecht and Velsen; shipbuilding, which has declined in recent years, at Rotterdam, now the world's leading seaport; diamond-cutting at Amsterdam, the largest city and also a seaport, accessible to ocean-going vessels by the North Sea Canal; electrical and electronic equipment at Eindhoven; textiles at Tilburg, Arnhem and elsewhere. Margarine, spirits (gin, liqueurs), chemicals, machinery and china (Delft) are also manufactured, and vast quantities of petroleum are refined (Rotterdam); The Hague is the seat of government, Scheveningen nearby is the

leading seaside resort and Ijmuiden is the main fishing port. Transport is facilitated by the intricate system of inland waterways, the length of navigable rivers and canals exceeding that of either roads or railways. Foreign trade is chiefly with Germany, Belgium, France, UK and Italy.

Until the 16th cent. the Netherlands were known as the Low Countries, i.e. modern Holland and Belgium. In Roman times the areas were divided along the Rhine: S of the river were Belgic tribes, who were conquered by Julius Caesar, while N of the river lived the Teutonic Frisians. The whole region became part of the empire of Charlemagne, then passed to Lotharingia and so to the Holy Roman Empire. In the 15th cent. it was acquired by the dukes of Burgundy and from them by the Habsburgs. When Philip II of Spain succeeded his father, Charles V (1555), he attempted to crush the Protestant faith, but met with determined opposition which culminated in the Union of Utrecht (1579); this united the seven N provinces againt Spain, and they declared their independence in 1581, unrecognized by Spain until 1648, and so laid the foundation of the modern Dutch state. The S Netherlands remained under Spanish rule, and from this time its history is that of Belgium. In the first half of the 17th cent. the Dutch enjoyed great prosperity, took the major share of the world's carrying trade, founded colonies in North America, West Indies, East Indies and India, and led the world in art; in 1689 William of Orange became William III of England. But the wars with England and then France exhausted the country, and the 18th cent. was a period of decline. In 1814 the former United Provinces (Holland) and the former Austrian Netherlands (Belgium) were united under the House of Orange, but in 1830 Belgium declared its independence. During World War I the Netherlands was occupied by the Germans, while the Dutch government took refuge in England. After the war (1945) the Dutch East Indies declared its independence as the Republic of Indonesia, but the former empire Suriname (Dutch Guiana) and the Netherlands Antilles in 1954 became constituent parts of the Kingdom of the Netherlands, with full autonomy. Suriname gained independence in 1975. Aruba separated from the Netherlands Antilles in 1986 and independence was promised for 1996. However at Aruba's request, in 1990, references to independence have been dropped. The Netherlands is a constitutional monarchy under the House of Orange-Nassau. There is a two-chamber legislature, a 75-member First Chamber elected by members of the Provincial States and the 150-member Second Chamber, who are elected directly with proportional representation. The country is divided into 12 provinces: Groningen, Friesland, Drenthe, Overijssel, Flevoland, Gelderland, Utrecht, Noord-Holland, Zuid-Holland, Zeeland, Noord-Brabant and Limburg.

Netherlands Antilles. Island group in the Caribbean Sea, an autonomous region of the Kingdom of the Netherlands. Area 800 sq km (308 sq. miles). The Leeward group, off the coast of Venezuela: Curaçao 444 sq km (171 sq. miles); Bonaire 288 sq km (111 sq. miles). The Windward group: Saba 13 sq km (5 sq. miles); St Eustatius 21 sq km (8 sq. miles); Sint Maarten 34 sq km (13 sq. miles), the N half of which (St Martin) belongs to France. Pop. (1992) 191,000; Curaçao 143,816; Bonaire 11,139; Saba 1116; St Eustatius 1781; Sint Maarten 33,459 (92 per cent urban). Life expectancy (Curaçao only) 71 years male, 76 female. Cap. Willemstad (on Curaçao). Currency: Netherlands Antillean guilder = 100 cents. All the islands are rocky and infertile, and only about 10 per cent of the land is under permanent cultivation. All the islands have a tropical marine climate with very little difference in temperatures over the year. There is a short rainy season Oct.–Jan. Dutch is the official lang. in the islands; in the Leeward group Papiamento, a lang. derived from Dutch, Spanish and Portuguese, is the lang. usually spoken. The ethnic composition is 84 per cent Creole and the pop. is Christian (mainly Roman Catholic).

The Leeward group is by far the more

important, the economy depending on the refining of oil imported from Venezuela to Curaçao, and employs 20 per cent of the workforce. There are also petrochemical, textile, electronic and tobacco factories. The Windward group is of small economic importance, with subsistence agriculture the main activity; rum is distilled on Sint Maarten.

The Windward Islands, inhabited by Caribs, were discovered in 1499 and claimed for Spain. The Netherlands Antilles has been a Dutch possession since the 17th cent. It was made an integral part of the Netherlands in 1922, the islands were known as Curaçao until 1949, when they were officially renamed the Netherlands Antilles and were granted full autonomy in internal affairs in 1954 and became an integral part of the Kingdom of the Netherlands. There is a 22-member unicameral legislature (*Staten*).

Netherlands East Indies ➤Indonesia.

Nettilling, Lake Canada. Lake in SW Baffin Island, Northwest Territories in NE Canada, within the Arctic Circle. Area 112 km (70 miles) by 104 km (65 miles). Drains W into Foxe Basin.

Neubrandenburg Germany. Cap. of Neubrandenburg district on the Tollensee R. near the N end of the Tollensee 120 km (75 miles) N of Berlin. Pop. (1988) 90,000.
Manufactures machinery, paper and chemicals.
Has 14th-cent. walls and gates and a 13th-cent. church. Founded 1248.

Neuchâtel (Ger. **Neuenburg**) Switzerland. 1. Canton in the Jura, bordering NW on France. Area 797 sq km (308 sq. miles). Pop. (1991) 160,609. Consists chiefly of the typical longitudinal ridges and valleys of the Jura, rising to 1443 m (4733 ft) in Mont Racine. Asphalt produced in the Val de Travers. Dairy-farming. Vines cultivated. Principally famous for its watch-making industry, centred on the towns of La Chaux-de-fonds and Le Locle. Virtually independent from the 13th cent. Joined the Swiss confederation 1815.

Cap. of Neuchâtel canton on the N shore of the Lake of Neuchâtel at a height of 439 m (1440 ft). Pop. (1988) 32,600.

Manufactures chocolate, condensed milk, watches, paper and tobacco products.

Outstanding buildings are the 15th/17th-cent. castle and the Musée des Beaux Arts. The university was originally founded (as an academy) in 1838.

Neuchâtel, Lake of Switzerland. The largest lake wholly in Switzerland (215 sq km; 83 sq. miles), extending 39 km (24 miles) SW–NE along the S foot of the Jura. The Thièle (Zihl) R. enters at the SW and leaves at the NE end. There are extensive vineyards along the NW shore.

Neuilly-sur-Seine France. Residential and industrial suburb of NW Paris on the right bank of the Seine R. in the Hauts-de-Seine department. Pop. (1990). 62,000.

Manufactures cars, machine-tools and perfumes.

The first level bridge in France was constructed here across the Seine in the 18th cent.

Neumünster Germany. Industrial town in Schleswig-Holstein 32 km (20 miles) SSW of Kiel. Pop.(1985) 79,500.

Railway junction. Manufactures textiles, machinery and paper. It grew up round a 12th-cent. monastery.

Neunkirchen Germany. Town in Saarland 19 km (12 miles) NE of Saarbrücken. Pop. (1986) 49,500. Commercial and shopping centre.

Neuquén River Argentina. River 480 km (300 miles) long rising in the Andes in Neuquén province near the Chilean frontier, flowing S and SE and joining the Limay R. to form the Río Negro. Near the confluence is Neuquén, cap. of the province.

Neuruppin Germany. Industrial town and tourist resort in the Potsdam district on L. Ruppin 64 km (40 miles) NW of Berlin. Pop. (1985) 27,000.

Industries inc. printing and the manufacture of dyes, starch and chemicals.

Neuss Germany. Ancient Novaesium. Industrial town in North Rhine-Westphalia near the left bank of the Rhine R. opposite Düsseldorf. Pop. (1991) 147,019.

Food-processing and paper-milling. Manufactures agricultural machinery and tractors.

A Roman camp was founded and a bridge built across the Rhine here by Drusus, brother of the Emperor Tiberius. Has the 13th-cent. Church of St Quirinus and a 17th/18th-cent. town hall.

Neustadt-an-der-Weinstrasse Germany. Town in the Rhineland-Palatinate at the E foot of the Hardt Mountains 26 km (16 miles) SW of Ludwigshafen. Pop. (1990) 54,000.

Important centre of the wine trade. Manufactures agricultural and viticultural implements and textiles.

Neustrelitz Germany. Residential town and resort in the Neubrandenburg district between two small lakes, Zierker See and Glambecker See, 100 km (62 miles) NNW of Berlin. Pop. (1990) 27,000.

Industries inc. food-processing, woodworking and engineering. Former cap. of the grand duchy of Mecklenburg-Strelitz.

Nevada USA. State in the W almost wholly within the Great Basin. Area 286,352 sq km (110,561 sq. miles). Pop. (1992) 1,327,000. Cap. Carson City. A vast plateau, but with several mountain ranges rising well above the general level of 1200–1500 m (3936–4920 ft) reaching 4009 m (13,150 ft) in Boundary Peak in the White Mountains (W) and 3983 m (13,064 ft) in Wheeler Peak in the Snake Range (E). Also many buttes and mesas. Apart from the Colorado R. in the extreme SE corner, most of the rivers are small and flow only in the rainy months. Climate dry continental. Annual rainfall 10–25 cm (4–10 ins.). Sheep and cattle raised. Mining has dominated the economy since the discovery (1859) of the rich Comstock lode of silver and gold. Chief minerals copper, gypsum, iron ore, gold. Leading towns Las Vegas, Reno, Carson City. Ceded to the USA by Mexico 1848. Separated from

Utah Territory 1861. Admitted to the Union in 1864 as the 36th state.

Neva River Russia. River 74 km (46 miles) long issuing from the SW corner of L. Ladoga and flowing W to enter the Gulf of Finland by a delta on which St Petersburg stands. At the delta it branches into 5 arms, the Great and Little Neva and the Great, Middle and Little Nevka, and is impeded by reefs and sandbanks, but a sea channel 29 km (18 miles) long to Kronstadt allows large vessels to reach St Petersburg; it is frozen usually from late Nov. to late April. Carries a large volume of water and with its low banks is subject to floods; particularly disastrous floods took place in 1777, 1824, 1879, 1903 and 1924. Forms part of the inland waterway system connecting the Baltic Sea with the Volga R. and the White Sea.

Nevers France. Ancient Noviodunum. Prefecture of the Nièvre department, on the Loire R. at its confluence with the Nièvre R. 60 km (37 miles) ESE of Bourges. Pop. (1989) 47,611.

Light engineering. Manufactures pottery, metal goods, pharmaceutical products and aircraft parts.

Among its buildings are the 11th-cent. Romanesque Church of St Étienne, the mainly 13th-cent. cathedral and the 15th/16th-cent. former ducal palace. Has yielded many Roman remains.

Nevis St Christopher (St Kitts) and Nevis. Island in the Lesser Antilles in E Caribbean 3 km (2 miles) SE of St Christopher (St Kitts). Area 93.2 sq km (36 sq. miles). Pop. (1989) 10,080. Cap. and chief seaport Charlestown. Roughly circular; rises to Nevis Peak (1097 m; 3598 ft) in the centre.

Chief products cotton and sugar-cane.

Discovered (1493) by Columbus. An English colony was established 1628. St Kitts and Nevis became independent in 1983. Nevis has its own Island Assembly and the right of secession from St Kitts. Birthplace of Alexander Hamilton (1757–1804). ►ST CHRISTOPHER (ST KITTS)-NEVIS.

Nevis, Ben ►BEN NEVIS.

New Albany USA. Industrial town in Indiana on the Ohio R. opposite Louisville (Kentucky). Pop. (1988) 37,540.

Manufactures plywood, veneers, furniture and refrigerated bakery products.

New Amsterdam Guyana. Seaport at the mouth of the Berbice R. 88 km (55 miles) SE of Georgetown. Pop. (1989) 25,000.

Centre of a district producing rice and sugar-cane.

Founded by the Dutch, as Fort St Andries, 1740.

New Amsterdam (USA) ►BUFFALO; NEW YORK.

Newark (New Jersey) USA. Largest city in the state on the Passaic R. and Newark Bay 13 km (8 miles) W of lower Manhattan (New York City). Pop. (1990) 275,221.

Road, rail and air centre. Varied industries inc. insurance and banking, and the manufacture of electrical equipment, metal goods, fountain pens, cutlery, chemicals and food products.

Founded by Puritans from Connecticut 1666. Photographic film was first made here (1887). Birthplace of the novelist Stephen Crane (1871–1900).

Newark (Ohio) USA. Town on the Licking R. 48 km (30 miles) ENE of Columbus. Pop. (1990) 42,000.

Railway engineering. Manufactures lawn mowers, fibreglass and plastics.

Newark-upon-Trent England. Town in Nottinghamshire on the R. Devon at its confluence with an arm of the R. Trent 26 km (16 miles) NE of Nottingham. Pop. (1988) 24,365.

Industries inc. engineering, textiles, food-processing and vehicles, and the manufacture of building materials from local gypsum and limestone.

Has a 14th/15th-cent. parish church with a spire 77 m (253 ft) high; ruined castle dating from the 12th cent. where King John died (1216), besieged three times in the Civil War; 16th-cent. grammar school. Owes its early development to its position on the Roman

Fosse Way. Birthplace of Sir William Nicholson, painter (1872–1949).

New Bedford USA. Seaport, resort and industrial town in Massachusetts on Buzzards Bay. Pop. (1990) 99,922.

Industries inc. fishing and the manufacture of cotton goods, clothing, electrical equipment and metal goods.

First settled in 1652. A leading whaling port from the mid 18th to the mid 19th cent.

New Brighton England. Holiday resort in Merseyside on the Wirral peninsula, part of the county borough of Wallasey.

New Britain Papua New Guinea. Volcanic island, largest in the Bismarck Archipelago, to the E of New Guinea. Area 36,519 sq km (14,100 sq. miles). Pop. (1990) 311,955. Chief town Rabaul in the NE. Mountainous, rising to 2288 m (7505 ft).

Exports copra and cacao.

Rabaul was a vital Japanese base in World War II. It was discovered and named by William Dampier 1700.

New Britain USA. Industrial town in Connecticut 14 km (9 miles) SSW of Hartford. Pop. (1990) 75,491.

Manufactures builders' hardware and electronic and electrical equipment, ball-bearings and clothing.

New Brunswick Canada. One of the Maritime Provinces on the Gulf of St Lawrence and the Bay of Fundy, bounded on the W by Maine (USA). Area 73,440 sq km (28,355 sq. miles). Pop. (1991) 723,900. Cap. Fredericton. Generally low-lying, but rises to 820 m (2690 ft) in Mt Carleton. The St John is the most important of the many rivers. It has a continental climate; annual rainfall 100–120 cm (40–47 ins.) Heavy snowfalls (250 cm (100 ins.) or more in the N). Despite the severe winters, the port of St John is kept ice-free by the strong tides of the Bay of Fundy. Extensive forests; lumbering and wood-pulp and paper manufacture are leading industries. Fisheries also important. Potatoes, cereals and fruits cultivated. Tourism is an important contributor to the economy and important minerals inc. zinc, silver, lead and peat. Chief towns St John, Moncton, Fredericton. Chaleur Bay was explored by Jacques Cartier 1534. First settlement established by the French 1604. Later formed part of the British province of Nova Scotia. The United Empire Loyalists came in force in 1783. New Brunswick left Nova Scotia to become a separate province in 1784.

New Brunswick USA. Industrial town in New Jersey at the head of navigation on the Raritan R. 37 km (23 miles) SW of Newark. Pop. (1989) 41,500.

Manufactures machinery, medical, surgical, pharmaceutical products and dairy products.

Seat of Rutgers Unviersity, founded, as Queen's College, 1766. First settled 1681.

Newburgh Scotland. Town in Fife on the Firth of Tay 14 km (9 miles) ESE of Perth. Pop. (1991) 1401.

Fishing port. Linoleum and oilskin manufacture.

The ruins of Lindores Abbey (Benedictine), founded (1178) by David, Earl of Huntingdon, are 1.6 km (1 mile) E.

Newburgh USA. Port and industrial town in New York on the Hudson R. 85 km (53 miles) N of New York City. Pop. (1990) 26,686.

Manufactures textiles, clothing and leather goods.

Hasbrouck House, Washington's headquarters 1782–3, is now a museum.

Newbury England. Market town on the R. Kennet 24 km (15 miles) WSW of Reading. Pop. (1991) 33,273.

Engineering, brewing and flour-milling.

Formerly a centre of the woollen industry; its 16th-cent. Cloth Hall is now a museum. Well-known racecourse. Two battles were fought here in the Civil War (1643, 1644).

Newbury became a unitary authority in 1998.

New Caledonia (Fr. **Nouvelle Calédonie**) SW Pacific Ocean. Volcanic island 1600 km (1000 miles) E of Queensland (Australia), forming with its island dependencies a French overseas territory. Area 18,576 sq km (7172 sq. miles). Pop. (1989) 164,173 (73,589 Melanesians, 55,085 Europeans). Cap. Nouméa.

It has great mineral resources, esp. nickel, chromium and iron. Industries inc. chlorine and oxygen plants, cement, soft drinks, boat construction, nails and confectionery. Chief exports metallic ores, copra. The native Melanesians raise livestock and grow vegetables, maize, fruits and coffee.

Discovered in 1774 by Capt. Cook and annexed by France in 1853 as a penal settlement.

Newcastle Australia. Industrial city and seaport in New South Wales 120 km (75 miles) NNE of Sydney at the mouth of the Hunter R. Pop. (1991) 427,703.

Centre of Australia's chief coalfield, which supplies its important iron and steel works. Among the products of its heavy industries are locomotives and railway rolling-stock, girders, corrugated iron, ships; manufactures textiles, fertilizers, chemicals and cement. Exports coal, wool, wheat and dairy produce.

Newcastle Northern Ireland. Town in Co. Down on Dundrum Bay 45 km (28 miles) S of Belfast. Pop. (1991) 7214. Seaside resort at the foot of Slieve Donard (853 m; 2798 ft) in the Mourne Mountains.

Newcastle South Africa. Town in Kwa-Zulu/Natal at the foot of the Drakensberg at a height of 1190 m (3903 ft) 265 km (165 miles) NNW of Durban. Pop. (1985) 55,700. On the railway to Johannesburg.

Industries inc. coalmining and the manufacture of iron and steel, bricks, tiles and stoves. Noted for butter-making.

New Castle USA. Industrial town in Pennsylvania 71 km (44 miles) NNW of Pittsburg. Pop. (1985) 34,000. In a coal and limestone region.

Manufactures tinplate, metal goods, pottery, cement.

Settled 1798 and named after Newcastle-upon-Tyne, England, by John Stewart, who built a charcoal furnace here to make pig-iron from local ore.

Newcastle-under-Lyme England. Town in N Staffordshire in the Potteries 3 km (2 miles) W of Stoke-on-Trent. Pop. (1991) 73,731.

Industrial centre. Manufactures bricks and tiles, textiles. Last coal mine closed in 1998.

Its name is due to the fact that a castle was built here in the 12th cent. to take the place of an older fortress and that it was situated under or near the former forest of Lyme. In 1932 the borough was extended to inc. Wolstanton, Chesterton and Silverdale. District pop. (1995) 123,100. At Keele nearby the University College of N Staffordshire was opened in 1950 and became Keele University in 1962.

Newcastle-upon-Tyne England. City, port and unitary authority on the N bank of the R. Tyne about 14 km (9 miles) from the mouth. Pop. (1991) 189,500.

A cathedral and university city and an administrative, commercial and cultural centre. It is also an important manufacturing centre for a wide variety of industries.

Stands opposite Gateshead, with which it is linked by tunnel and 5 bridges, inc. the old high-level bridge (1849) and the new Tyne bridge (1928). In all 9 bridges span the Tyne at Newcastle. Remains of the 12th-cent. castle from which its name was taken and of the 13th-cent. town wall; the Cathedral of St Nicholas dates mainly from the 14th cent. The handsome appearance of the city centre is largely due to the enterprise of a local builder, Richard Grainger (1798–1861). Best-known of the many open spaces is the Town Moor (area nearly 400 ha; 1000 acres). On the site of the Roman Pons Aelii, on Hadrian's Wall. First engaged in the coal trade in the 13th cent. George Stephenson's ironworks were established in 1823 and here the first locomotives for the Stockton–Darlington railway were made. Ferry service to Hamburg, Amsterdam, Stavanger and Bergen.

New Delhi ➤DELHI.

New England USA. Region made up of 6 states in the extreme NE: Maine,

New Hampshire, Vermont, Massachusetts, Rhode Island and Connecticut. The name was given by Capt. John Smith (1614). The first English settlement was established at Plymouth (Massachusetts) in 1620 and the New England Confederation (formed by the colonies of Plymouth, Massachusetts Bay, Connecticut and New Haven) lasted from 1643 to 1684. Later New England played an important part in the American Revolution. It took the Union side in the American Civil War.

New England Range ➤GREAT DIVIDING RANGE.

New Forest England. Area of ancient woodland and heath 376 sq km (145 sq. miles) in area in SW Hampshire, bounded by the Solent, Southampton Water and the R. Avon. Managed as a national park by the Court of Verderers, a remnant of the former forest administration. One-quarter of the area is cultivated; pigs, cattle and half-wild ponies bred. A popular tourist area and within it are the towns of Lyndhurst and Ringwood. A royal hunting ground under the West Saxon kings; received its name in 1079 owing to afforestation by William I. A stone marks the spot in the forest where William Rufus was killed by an arrow (1100).

Newfoundland Canada. Province in the extreme E, consisting of the island of Newfoundland and Labrador. Area 405,649 sq km (156,649 sq. miles). Pop. (1991) 568,474. Cap. St John's. Newfoundland island, separated from Labrador by the Strait of Belle Isle, has a much indented coastline and many offshore islands; in the NW and SE respectively are the large Great Northern and Avalon peninsulas. The Long Range Mountains, along the Great Northern peninsula rise to 813 m (2667 ft) in Mt Gros Morne. The maritime climate is modified by the cold Labrador Current. Annual rainfall 75–150 cm (30–60 ins.). In the centre of the island the snowfall amounts to 300 cm (120 ins.). Fishing (esp. haddock, lobsters; cod fishing has closed down (1995)) and fish-processing are traditionally the leading occu-

pations, largely owing to the nearness of the Grand Banks fishing grounds. Of greater economic importance are the extensive forests; newsprint manufacture is a leading industry. Iron ore is mined, chiefly on Bell Island; other minerals are worked. Chief towns St John's, Corner Brook and Grand Falls.

Newfoundland was discovered (1497) by John Cabot. Annexed for England by Sir Humphrey Gilbert 1583. Formal recognition of English rule was made by the Treaty of Utrecht (1713); Newfoundland was granted jurisdiction over the coast of Labrador 1809. A larger area was awarded 1927. Responsible government was maintained 1855–1934, but the Dominion was then in serious financial difficulties and for a time Newfoundland was governed by commission. After a referendum (1949) it joined Canada (the 10th province). ➤LABRADOR.

New Guinea. Second largest island (after Greenland) in the world, lying N of Australia, from which it is separated by the Arafura Sea and Torres Strait. Area 808,510 sq km (312,085 sq. miles). It is divided politically into two areas; to the W as Irian Jaya, Indonesia, and to the E Papua New Guinea.

Newham England. London borough formed (1965) from the former county boroughs of East Ham and West Ham, that part of the former municipal borough of Barking W of Barking Creek, and that part of the former metropolitan borough of Woolwich N of the Thames. Pop. (1991) 217,000.

New Hampshire USA. State in New England, bordering on Canada, with a short Atlantic coastline in the SE. Area 24,032 sq km (9279 sq. miles). Pop. (1990) 1,111,000. Cap. Concord. Generally hilly with many lakes. The White Mountains in the N rise to 1918 m (6291 ft) in Mt Washington. The winters are long and rather severe. Annual rainfall 75–125 cm (30–50 ins.). There are annual snowfalls of 250 cm (100 ins.) or more in the mountains. Main crops hay, potatoes, market-garden produce. Manufacturing industries, mainly textiles and the manufacture of machinery, are concentrated chiefly in the S; leading centres Manchester, Nashua, Concord. Land granted to John Mason (1586–1635) of King's Lynn (England) in 1629 was called by him New Hampshire. The early English settlements came under the jurisdiction of Massachusetts in 1641. New Hampshire became a separate province in 1679. One of the original 13 states and the 9th to ratify the Constitution in 1788.

Newhaven England. Seaport in East Sussex on the English Channel at the mouth of the R. Ouse. Pop. (1991) 11,208. Ferry service (summer only) to Dieppe (France).

Industries inc. the manufacture of fountain pens and lighting fittings.

New Haven USA. Seaport and industrial city in Connecticut on Long Island Sound. Pop. (1990) 130,474. Famous chiefly as the seat of Yale University (1701), named after Elihu Yale (1648–1721), one of its principal benefactors.

Manufactures hardware, clocks and watches, sewing machines, firearms and cutlery.

Many of the streets are broad and lined with elms. The 6.5 ha (16 acres) Green with its three churches is an outstanding feature. Birthplace of Charles Goodyear (1800–1960), inventor of the vulcanization of rubber.

New Hebrides ►VANUATU.

New Iberia USA. Town in Louisiana 79 km (49 miles) SW of Baton Rouge. Pop. (1970) 30,147.

In a fertile agricultural region producing sugar-cane and rice. Manufactures wood products and paper.

New Ireland Papua New Guinea. Volcanic island, second largest in the Bismarck Archipelago, N of New Britain, from which it is separated by St George's Channel. Area 9600 sq km (3707 sq. miles). Pop. (1990) 87,194. Mountainous in the central area. Chief town Kavieng at the NW extremity, amid numerous coconut plantations. Produces

copra, cocoa and there is a thriving tuna-fishing industry.

New Jersey USA. State in NE on Atlantic coast, with the Delaware R. as its W boundary. Area 20,168 sq km (7787 sq. miles). Pop. (1990) 7,789,000. Cap. Trenton. More than half the state lies on the Atlantic coastal plain. The coastline is characterized by sand-spits, dunes, lagoons and marshes with no good harbours. In the extreme NW are the Kittatinny Mountains, an Appalachian ridge rising to 550 m (1804 ft) in High Point. Climate humid continental; annual rainfall 100–125 cm (40–50 ins.). Market-gardening and fruit and poultry farming are important. Primarily an industrial state: copper smelting and refining, oil-refining. Manufactures chemicals, paints and varnishes. Chief industrial centres Newark, Jersey City, Paterson, Camden, Trenton and Elizabeth. First settled by the Dutch; became English in 1664. Named in honour of Sir George Carteret (1610–80), a former governor of Jersey (Channel Is.). One of the original 13 states and the 3rd to ratify the Constitution in 1787.

New London USA. Seaport and summer resort in Connecticut on the Thames R. estuary near Long Island Sound, opposite the submarine base at Groton. Pop. (1970) 35,714.

Industries inc. shipbuilding and repair and the manufacture of metal goods, machinery, clothing, collapsible tubes, dentifrice, floor coverings, doors and windows.

The annual Harvard and Yale boat races are held on the Thames.

Newlyn England. Fishing village in Cornwall on Mount's Bay just SW of Penzance. Much frequented by artists and gave its name to a late 19th-cent. school of painting.

Newmarket England. Town in W Suffolk 19 km (12 miles) ENE of Cambridge. Pop. (1991) 16,498. A racing centre since the reign of James I, many racehorses being trained here and is known as the 'racing capital of the world'. Its racecourse on Newmarket Heath is crossed by the Devil's Ditch, an ancient earthwork; here several important racing events take place, inc. the Two Thousand Guineas, One Thousand Guineas, Cesarewitch and Cambridgeshire. As the headquarters of British horse-racing, Newmarket is the home of the Jockey Club.

New Mexico USA. State in the SW, bordering in the S on Texas and Mexico. Area 314,924 sq km (121,593 sq. miles). Pop. (1990) 1,581,000. Cap. Santa Fé (the largest city). A region of high plateaux and mountains with an average height of 1740 m (5707 ft). Several peaks in the Sangre de Cristo Mountains (N) exceed 3600 m (11,808 ft). Crossed N–S by the Rio Grande; the E is drained by its tributary the Pecos. Generally dry and sunny. Annual rainfall varies from 15 cm (6 ins.) in the deserts (S) to 65–75 cm (25–30 ins.) in the mountains (N). Chief crops cotton, wheat, grain, sorghums, largely dependent on dry farming or irrigation. Many cattle and sheep raised. Mining important, esp. perlite, potassium salts, petroleum, natural gas, copper, zinc and there are large reserves of uranium. Largest city Albuquerque. Ceded to the USA after the Mexican War (1846–8). Admitted to the Union in 1912 as the 47th state.

New Orleans USA. Largest city in Louisiana on the E bank of the Mississippi R. 172 km (107 miles) from the mouth with L. Pontchartrain to the N. Pop. (1990) 496,938.

A major seaport. Exports petroleum, cotton, iron and steel, timber. The chief commercial and financial centre in the South. Industries inc. sugar and oil refining, textiles, chemicals and ship-repairing.

Low-lying, the altitude ranging from 1.2 m (4 ft) below sea level to 4.5 m (15 ft) above; entirely below the river high-watermark and protected by levees. The nucleus and most interesting quarter is the Vieux Carré (French Quarter), divided from the modern American section by Canal Street; here are the historic buildings, the Cabildo (1795), now a museum, the St Louis Cathedral (1794), the Pontalba buildings (1849) and many fine 'colonial' houses. A gay and colourful city, New Orleans annually stages

the most noteworthy carnival in the USA, the Mardi Gras, which takes place just before Lent. Also the home of jazz music. Named in honour of the Duc d'Orléans. Became cap. of the vast French colonial region of Louisiana. Transferred to Spain 1763. Returned to France 1803, but passed to the USA in the same year with the Louisiana Purchase. A section of the present-day pop., the Creoles, are descended from French and Spanish settlers.

New Plymouth New Zealand. Chief town and port in the Taranaki district in the W of the North Island just N of Mt Egmont. Pop. (1990) 48,519.

Industries inc. oil and gas and tourism. It trades in and exports dairy products.

Founded 1841.

Newport (Isle of Wight) England. Market town on the R. Medina 8 km (5 miles) above its mouth. Pop. (1988) 25,700. Has a 17th-cent grammar school and a 19th-cent. town hall designed by John Nash. Within the borough (N) is Parkhurst prison. Carisbrooke Castle is 1.6 km (1 mile) SW.

Newport (Shropshire) England. Town 26 km (16 miles) ENE of Shrewsbury. Pop. (1991) 10,964.

Market town. It manufactures valves and garden furniture.

The ruins of the 12th-cent Lilleshall Abbey are 5 km (3 miles) SSW.

Newport (Kentucky) USA. Industrial town on the Ohio R. opposite Cincinnati (Ohio) at the confluence with the Licking R. Pop. (1970) 25,998.

Manufactures metal goods, clothing and food products, and there is also a printing industry.

Newport (Rhode Island) USA. Fashionable resort and naval base on Narragansett Bay. Pop. (1980) 29,259.

Manufactures precision instruments, jewellery and electrical equipment. It is an important tourist resort and major yachting centre.

Has many historic buildings and fine 'colonial' homes. Founded 1639. Joint state cap. with Providence until 1900.

Newport Wales. 1. County Borough created 1996. Formerly part of Gwent. Pop. (1994) 137,000.

2. Town in Newport on the R. Usk 8 km (5 miles) above its entry into the Severn estuary. Pop. (1991) 115,522. Seaport with extensive docks. Manufactures iron and steel, plastics, confectionery, boilers and electronic products.

The old parish church of St Woollos became the cathedral 1921. Owes its rapid development in the late 19th and early 20th cent. to its favourable position on a tidal river.

Newport News USA. Seaport in SE Virginia on the N side of the James R. estuary and the Hampton Roads. Pop. (1990) 170,045.

Exports coal, petroleum, tobacco, and has important shipyards. Manufactures wood-pulp and paper and machinery.

Settled by Irish colonists 1621. Named after Captain Christopher Newport, commander of the first ship to reach Jamestown (1607) and Sir William Newce, who chose the site.

Newport Pagnell England. Market town in N Buckinghamshire on the R. Ouse at its confluence with the R. Ouzel 18 km (11 miles) WSW of Bedford. Pop. (1991) 12,285.

Industries inc. motor-car assembly.

New Providence ▶NASSAU BAHAMAS.

Newquay England. Town and seaside resort in Cornwall 16 km (10 miles) N of Truro. Pop. (1991) 17,390. Sheltered from the W by Towan Head.

New Rochelle USA. Suburb of New York City on Long Island Sound. Pop. (1990) 67,265. Largely residential.

Manufactures heating equipment, medical supplies.

Founded (1688) by Huguenot refugees, who named it after their place of origin, La Rochelle (France). Once the home of

Thomas Paine (1737–1809), philosopher; contains Paine Cottage (where he lived) and the Paine Memorial House (1925).

New Romney England. Market town in Kent on Romney Marsh 19 km (12 miles) SW of Folkestone. Pop. (1991) 8340. One of the Cinque Ports; declined since the sea receded and now more than a mile inland.

New Ross Ireland. Market town in Co. Wexford on the R. Barrow just below the confluence with the R. Nore. Pop. (1991) 5018. Industries inc. brewing and tanning.

Newry Northern Ireland. Town and port in Co. Down on the border with Co. Armagh on the R. Newry and the Newry Canal at the head of Carlingford Lough. Pop. (1985) 11,500. Industries inc. linen, clothing and food-processing. Birthplace of Lord Russell of Killowen, distinguished judge (1832–1900).

New Siberian Islands (Novosibirskiye Ostrova) Russia. Archipelago in the Arctic Ocean between the Laptev Sea and the E Siberian Sea, separated from the mainland by the Dimitri Laptev Strait, and in the Sakha Republic (Yakutia). Area 28,490 sq km (11,000 sq. miles). The largest islands of the central group are Kotelny, Faddeyev and New Siberia. The De Long Is. (NE) and Lyakhov Is. (S) are often inc. in the archipelago. Discovered 1770. Uninhabited apart from research stations. The islands have yielded much fossil ivory.

New South Wales Australia. State in the SE, bounded by Queensland (N), the Pacific (E), the Murray R. and Victoria (S) and South Australia (W). Area 801,600 sq km (309,433 sq. miles) (inc. Lord Howe Island in the SW Pacific with 320 residents). Pop. (1991) 5,731,926 (excluding Canberra). Cap. Sydney. In the E the uplifted and dissected plateaux of the Great Dividing Range (e.g. the New England Range, Liverpool Range and Blue Mountains) are flanked by a narrow coastal plain. In the SE are the higher Snowy Mountains and part of the Australian Alps. The W slopes of the Great Dividing Range are crossed by tributaries of the Murray and Darling rivers. The forested E hills and coastlands experience occasional heavy storms and droughts, but otherwise have a well-distributed, adequate rainfall with mild winters and hot summers, suitable for dairying, market-gardening and horticulture. In the N sugar-cane, bananas and citrus fruits are grown. New South Wales is the leading pastoral and agricultural state, and the inner slopes of the Murray basin, with 50–75 cm (20–30 ins.) rainfall, are the chief wool and wheat producing areas. Dams on the Murray, Murrumbidgee and Lachlan rivers provide irrigation for stock, grain and fruit growing districts in the W lands of low rainfall. In the NW, with under 25 cm (10 ins.) annually, grasslands give way to saltbush and other shrubs, which support only low-density grazing.

About 64 per cent of the pop. live in Sydney and in the large industrial and coal-mining areas centred on Newcastle and Port Kembla–Wollongong. Power comes mainly from thermal stations, but the Snowy Mountains scheme is increasing the hydroelectric output. Chief exports wool, wheat, dairy produce, fruits and meat. Discovered and named by Capt. Cook 1770. The first penal settlement was made at Sydney in 1788 and it became the first colony. Since federation (1901) it has ceded to the Commonwealth the Australian Capital Territory (1911) and Jervis Bay (1915).

New Territories Hong Kong. Part of the former British Crown Colony extending from the peninsula of Kowloon to the Shun Chun R., Lantan Is. and other islands. Area 1075 sq.km (415 sq. miles) leased from China for 99 years and returned to China in 1997. A large part is steep and unproductive hillside. Eight new towns, pop. (1992) 2,300,000, have been established since 1974.

Newton USA. Town in Massachusetts on the Charles R. just W of Boston; divided into 14 villages. Pop. (1990) 82,585. Mainly residential.

Manufactures electrical equipment, plastics and knitwear.

Newtonabbey Northern Ireland. Urban district in Co. Antrim just N of Belfast, formed (1958) from Belfast rural district. Pop. (1991) 56,811.

Newton Abbot England. Market town in Devon at the head of the R. Teign estuary 23 km (14 miles) SSW of Exeter. Pop. (1991) 23,801.

Malting, tanning. Racecourse (National Hunt).

William III was proclaimed king here (1688) at St Leonard's Tower.

Newton and Llanllwchaiarn Wales. Market town in Powys on the R. Severn 19 km (12 miles) SW of Welshpool. Pop. (1991) 10,548. Formerly a centre of the flannel industry. Birthplace of Robert Owen, social and educational reformer (1771–1858).

Newton Aycliffe England ➤AYCLIFFE.

Newton-le-Willows England. Town in Merseyside 8 km (5 miles) E of St Helens. Pop. (1991) 19,416.

Railway engineering. Manufactures machinery, paper and glassware.

Newton Stewart Scotland. Small market town in Dumfries and Galloway on the R. Cree 10 km (6 miles) NNW of Wigtown. Pop. (1991) 3673.

Newtownards Northern Ireland. Town in Co. Down near the N end of Strangford Lough 16 km (10 miles) E of Belfast. Pop. (1991) 23,869.

Manufactures linen, hosiery.

Grew up round a Dominican monastery (founded 1244).

New Westminster Canada. Seaport in British Columbia on the Fraser R. 14 km (9 miles) E of Vancouver. Pop. (1986) 39,972.

Exports timber and grain. Oil-refining. Salmon, fruit and vegetable canning, paper and flour milling.

Founded 1859. Cap. of British Columbia till 1866.

New York USA. State in the NE on the Atlantic seaboard extending to the Great

Lakes and the Canadian border in the W and N, and inc. Long Island close to the SE shore. Area 136,583 sq. km (52,735 sq. miles). Pop (1990) 18,119,000 (second largest in the USA). Cap. Albany. Popularly known as the 'Empire' state. Along the N border is the St Lawrence valley and in the E the Hudson R. valley. The Mohawk R. cuts across the state W–E, providing a route for the New York State Barge Canal. N of the Mohawk are the Adirondack Mountains, rising to 1630 m (5346 ft) in Mt Marcy; S is a plateau 300–600 m (984–1968 ft) high. Climate humid continental; cold winters (often with heavy snowfalls), hot summers. Annual rainfall 100–120 cm (40–48 ins.). Dairy-farming is the main agricultural activity. Cereal cultivation, fruit-growing (esp. around the shores of L. Ontario and L. Erie) and market-gardening are important. In manufactures New York ranks first in the USA, the industries being concentrated chiefly around New York City. Other leading centres are Buffalo, Rochester, Syracuse, Yonkers, Albany, Niagara Falls (which supplies hydroelectric power), Utica. Despite its many large urban centres, the state has several regions of scenic beauty, e.g. L. Champlain, Finger Lakes, Niagara Falls, the Adirondacks and the Catskills.

Explored in 1609 by Champlain (who discovered L. Champlain) and Henry Hudson (who sailed up the Hudson R.). The first permanent settlers were the Dutch, who established Albany as a fur-trading post (1623) and founded New Amsterdam (1625) on Manhattan Island. Prominent in the Anglo-French struggles and again in the American War of Independence. One of the original 13 states and the 11th to ratify the Constitution in 1788. The rapid commercial expansion in the 19th cent. was largely due to the completion of the Erie Canal (1825).

New York City (New York) USA. Largest city in the USA (known as 'The Big Apple') and the commercial, financial and cultural centre of the USA, on New York Bay (Atlantic coast) at the mouth of the Hudson R. Land area 774 sq km (299 sq. miles). Pop. (1990) 7,322,564. Five boroughs: Manhattan;

the Bronx; Queens (Long Island); Brooklyn (Long Island); Richmond (Staten Island). The leading seaport of the USA importing petroleum, sugar, coffee, rubber, copper, fruit.

Exports machinery, grain, meat, textiles, clothing, metal goods. The chief industry is the manufacture of clothing; also furs, hats, jewellery and leather goods. Printing and publishing, sugar-refining, food-processing, brewing also important. Most of these industries are concentrated in Manhattan.

Manhattan (area 57 sq km; 22 sq. miles pop. (1990) 1,487,536) inc. a few small islands, e.g. Ellis Island (formerly an important immigration station) and Bedloe's Island, renamed Liberty Island in 1960 (site of the Statue of Liberty); it is famous for its skyline of skyscrapers, esp. the Empire State Building (1931; 381 m; 1250 ft), and the Chrysler Building (1929; 320 m; 1050 ft). There are many world-renowned streets and districts, e.g. Wall Street, the financial hub; Broadway, the world's longest street (26 km; 16 miles), with many theatres and other places of entertainment; Greenwich Village, the Bohemian quarter; Chinatown; Harlem, the Negro quarter; Times Square; the fashionable shopping and residential thoroughfares of Fifth Avenue, Madison Avenue and Park Avenue; Central Park, with attractive walks and children's playgrounds; Riverside Drive, a beautifully situated residential thoroughfare extending over 10 km (6 miles) along the Hudson R. embankment.

Brooklyn (area 184 sq km; 71 sq. miles, pop. (1990) 2,291,664), primarily residential, inc. the amusement centre of Coney Island and is connected with Manhattan by 3 bridges and several tunnels. Queens (area 280 sq km; 108 sq. miles, pop. (1990) 1,951,598) contains New York's two airports and Flushing Meadow (site of the New York World's Fair 1939–40 and 1964–5) and is connected with Manhattan and the Bronx by 4 bridges and many tunnels. The Bronx (area 111 sq km; 43 sq. miles, pop. (1990) 1,203,789) has Bronx Park (with botanical and zoological gardens) and the Hall of Fame, inc. a high proportion of Jews amongst its inhabitants, and is connected with Manhattan and Queens by 3 bridges and tunnels. Staten Island, which is co-extensive with Richmond County (area 148 sq km; 57 sq. miles, pop. (1990) 378,977), across the Narrows from Brooklyn, is linked by ferry with Manhattan.

New York is well served by its transport system; all the boroughs except Richmond are interconnected by railways, tunnels, subways and bridges (e.g. the George Washington, the Brooklyn, the Henry Hudson, the Manhattan, the Triborough and the Queensborough). The Verrazano-Narrows Bridge, between Brooklyn and Richmond (Staten Island), was opened in 1964; with a total length of 4179 m (4569 yards) it was the longest in the world. Twelve railway systems serve the city. There are two airports, La Guardia and the International Airport, Kennedy. Seat of the Columbia University (1754), the New York University (1831), the Fordham University (1846, Roman Catholic), the City of New York University (1847) and the St John's University (1871, Roman Catholic). Many museums, libraries and other cultural institutions. The new Metropolitan Opera House was opened in 1966. Protestant and Roman Catholic cathedrals. The United Nations headquarters is in Manhattan on East R. (1951). New York has an extremely cosmopolitan pop., with more Irish than in Dublin, as many Jews as in Israel and more Negroes than in any other city in the world, as well as many Scandinavians, Germans, Italians, Puerto Ricans, Chinese and others. It cannot therefore be considered a typical American city.

The Dutch bought Manhattan Island from the local Indians for 24 dollars' worth of beads and ribbons in 1624. Today it is the most valuable piece of land in the world; the massive phalanx of skyscrapers is a manifestation of its value. The Dutch settlement on Manhattan, New Amsterdam, was seized by the English in 1664 and renamed New York (after the Duke of York, later James II). Cap. of New York state (1788–97) and Union cap. (1789–90); it lost these distinctions but was already the largest city in the USA.

From the early 19th cent. its financial and commercial leadership was undisputed.

New Zealand. Independent member of the Commonwealth lying SE of Australia in the S Pacific Ocean. Area 270,534 sq km (104,454 sq. miles) Pop. (1995) 3,525,000., inc. 321,399 Maoris, (69 per cent urban). Life expectancy, 72 years male, 78 female. Cap. Wellington. Other major cities Auckland, Christchurch, Manukau and North Shore. Currency: New Zealand dollar = 100 cents.

New Zealand proper consists of the North Island, 115,777 sq km (44,702 sq. miles), the South Island 151,215 sq km (58,384 sq. miles), Stewart Island, 1746 sq km (674 sq. miles), Chatham Island 903 sq km (372 sq. miles) and several minor islands 854 sq km (322 sq. miles). The Cook Is. and the Ross dependency in the Antarctic are also under New Zealand administration. Extends for over 1600 km (1000 miles) N–S with a maximum width E–W of 450 km (280 miles). Its main islands and their mountain chains lie roughly SW–NE. In the South Island the Southern Alps and the Fiordland Plateau give a high relief to the W; mountain crests rise well above the snowline (about 1800 m; 5904 ft), with many peaks above 3000 m (9840 ft). Mt Cook (3764 m; 12,349 ft) is the highest; nearby is the Tasman Glacier, the longest (29 km; 18 miles) of many in the Southern Alps. Ice-cut, moraine-blocked valleys and ribbon lakes drain E through deeply cut river courses. S of the Otago plateau are alluvial plains. N of the Waitaki R. soft Tertiary rocks lie E of the Alps, with rivers which have carried alluvial material to build the Canterbury Plains. E of these Banks Peninsula is of volcanic origin, though the South Island is almost free from volcanic activity. W of the Southern Alps there are discontinuous lowlands and in the N and NE the Nelson and Blenheim lowlands. In the North Island the lower fold mountains continue N to East Cape. To the W is a central plateau of volcanic material, with three large active volcanoes, inc. Ruapehu (2798 m; 9177 ft), S of the shallow L. Taupo. Many hot springs and geysers esp. near Rotorua. From L.

Taupo the Waikato R. flows across the plateau and the lowlands in the NW, beyond which extends the Auckland Peninsula. Flanking the fold mountains and the central volcanic plateau are hill lands of soft Tertiary rocks; coastal and valley lowlands contain most of the area utilizable for agriculture and pasture. Most of the North Island and the W of the South Island supported dense, mixed evergreen temperate forest, with broad-leafed and coniferous species, tree ferns and many creepers. Extensive beech forests grew in the mountains of the South Island, while the E foothills and plains were mostly tussock grassland. The isolation of New Zealand from other land masses has led to the development of many plant species not found elsewhere; tree ferns up to 15 m (49 ft) high are a striking feature of the dense evergreen forest. Indigenous species inc. the kauri, valued for its gum. No native mammals except bats, so that wingless birds like the kiwi and weka could survive, but the introduction of stoats, cats, rabbits and deer has upset the original ecological relationships. The prevailing winds are westerly and the climate is broadly similar to that of Britain but with much more sunshine. The extreme N is affected by subtropical anticyclones and occasional summer storms from the tropics. Contrasts in relief cause marked rainfall and temperature differences, but on the whole the mean annual temperature ranges are everywhere small. Land use: forested 27 per cent, meadows and pastures 50 per cent, agricultural and under permanent cultivation 2 per cent. The lang. are English and Maori. The religion is mainly Protestant and about 74 per cent are New Zealand European, 10 per cent New Zealand Maori.

New Zealand's economy is heavily dependent on overseas trade. Traditionally, a large proportion of exports, mainly agricultural products, went to the UK. In recent years, however, New Zealand has been forced to diversify its markets and products. At present, Australia is the largest export market, followed by Japan, the US and the UK. Over the decades, New Zealand has moved away from dependence on dairy, meat and wool exports as forestry, horticulture, fishing and manufacturing have become more significant. Tourism is also an increasingly important sector of the economy. A large proportion of forest has been transformed into grazing and with refrigeration, which was introduced in 1882, it became possible to export meat and butter as well as wool and cheese. Wool, dairy produce and meat constitute 50 per cent of the country's exports by value. The majority of the dairy cattle are in the North Island, mostly in W and NW coastal and valley lowlands where grazing on sown pastures is controlled in small paddocks and by electric fencing. Cooperative organizations run dairy factories and other aspects of farming. The Canterbury plains and downlands support mixed farming and produce a large proportion of the country's grain. Few minerals of value. Coal is mined in Westland, S Auckland and S Otago. Natural gas is found in Taranaki. Thermal power is exploited near L. Taupo. There has been considerable hydroelectric development: in the North Island, with greater demand, the chief source is the Waikato R., and in the South Island, which has the larger potential, the principal power station is the Clutha R. The main industries are those processing farm products. Other industries are expanding, esp. in the Auckland and Hutt valley districts, and inc. engineering, vehicle assembly and the manufacture of chemicals and textiles. Road and rail communications are difficult but coastal shipping is well developed and air transport important.

Polynesian settlers, ancestors of present-day Maoris, arrived in the 10th cent. and in greater number in the 14th cent. Earlier Maoris were few and had retreated to the Chatham Is., where the last died in 1933. Tasman discovered New Zealand (1642) and Cook circumnavigated the islands 1769–70 and were the first Europeans to set foot on New Zealand soil. Later came sealers, whalers and kauri seekers, who lived in a state of lawlessness. It was not till 1840 that Queen Victoria assumed sovereignty, and the first Lieutenant-Governor negotiated the Treaty of Waitangi, guaranteeing Maori tribes undisturbed possession of their lands and protection under the British Crown. Permanent settlements were made at Wellington (1840), New Plymouth (1841) and Nelson (1842). In spite of difficulties over the purchase of land from the Maoris further settlements followed in various parts of the islands. In 1853 provincial councils were set up, with a central governor, legislative council and general assembly, but aggravated land disputes caused fighting between the British colonists and the Maoris; peace was permanently established in 1871. In the 1860s gold rushes to Otago, Westland and Central Auckland further accelerated settlement. It became a dominion in 1907. Parliament comprises a 99-member House of Representatives who provide an Executive Council to advise the Governor General, who represents the Crown. The Maoris, who have 4 representatives are more than 7 times as numerous as they were in 1896 and now take an increasing part in the life of the country.

Ngami, Lake Botswana. Former lake S of the Okavango swamp; now a marsh. It originally covered about 52,000 sq km (20,000 sq. miles). Discovered by David Livingstone in 1849, who described it as a large lake.

Ngaoundéré Cameroon. Cap. of Adamaoua province situated NE of Yaoundé. Pop. (1987) 112,000. Important agricultural market and has experimental farms.

Niagara Falls Canada. Town in S Ontario on the W bank of the Niagara R. opposite Niagara Falls (USA). Pop. (1991) 75,399.

Important tourist centre. Hydroelectric power installation. Manufactures wood-pulp and paper, fertilizers and machinery.

Niagara Falls USA. Industrial town and tourist centre in New York on the E bank of the Niagara R. opposite Niagara Falls (Canada), with which it is connected by bridges. Pop. (1990) 61,840.

Important hydroelectric plants, supplying power to the city and the state. Manufactures chemicals, electrical equipment, machinery and paper.

Seat of the Niagara University (1856,

Roman Catholic). Founded as the village of Manchester 1806. Amalgamated with the village of Suspension Bridge 1892.

Niagara River and Falls Canada/USA. River 56 km (35 miles) long, flowing generally N from L. Erie to L. Ontario, forming part of the frontier between New York state (USA) and Ontario (Canada). The Niagara Falls are rather more than halfway down the river; they have gradually receded upstream, at a decreasing rate. In two sections, the American (51 m; 167 ft high; 305 m; 1000 ft wide) and the Canadian or Horseshoe (48 m; 157 ft high; 793 m; 2601 ft wide); they are separated by Goat Island. Thousands of tourists visit the Falls every summer. The most favourable place to view them is Rainbow Bridge, a suspension bridge opened to traffic in 1941. They are even more impressive in winter, in the grip of frost and snow. Also an important source of hydroelectric power. Shipping between L. Erie and L. Ontario circumvents the Falls by using the Welland Canal (Canada).

Niamey Niger. Cap. since 1926, on the left bank of the Niger R. about 100 km (60 miles) E of the Burkino Faso border. Pop. (1988) 398,265. Terminus of a Trans-Saharan motor route from N Algeria and of the railway which runs from the Gulf of Guinea through Benin and Niger. It is a commercial centre.

Industries inc. textiles, food-processing, plastics, ceramics and chemicals.

Nicaragua. The largest of the Central American republics, it is bounded N by Honduras, E by the Caribbean Sea, S by Costa Rica and W by the Pacific Ocean. Area 130,700 sq km (50,464 sq. miles). Pop. (1994) 4,210,000. (62 per cent urban). Life expectancy, 61 years male, 66 female. Cap. Managua. Other towns are León, Granada, Massaya and Chinandega. Currency: Córdoba ora = 100 centavos. Swampy and lowlying (E), the land rises to mountains of which the main ranges run NW to SE with spurs running W to E. The lowlands (E) are drained by Río Grande, Escondido, Coco and San Juan rivers, the last forming the Caribbean outlet for a wide depression W of the mountains which encloses L. Nicaragua and L. Managua. The lakes are separated from the Pacific by a 19-km (12-mile) wide isthmus with a chain of volcanic peaks, some active. Managua was almot completely destroyed in 1972. The climate is tropical with a wet season May–Jan., annual rainfall 375 cm (148 ins.) or more in the Caribbean lowlands, but much less to the W of the mountains. Land use: forested 30 per cent, meadows and pastures 45 per cent, agricultural and under permanent cultivation 11 per cent. Ninety-one per cent of the pop. is Roman Catholic and the official lang. is Spanish. Ethnic composition: 77 per cent mestizo, 10 per cent white, 9 per cent Black, 4 per cent Amerindian.

Agriculture is the chief source of the country's wealth; chief crops are coffee, cotton, cacao, bananas, rice, wheat, tobacco, sesame seed and sugar-cane. Many cattle raised. In the forests mahogany, cedar and other timbers are obtained for export. Principal mineral gold; copper, tungsten and silver are also found. Industrial production consists of textiles, chemicals, construction materials, petroleum and food-processing.

Nicaragua was under Spanish rule 1523–1821 and then independent. Part of the Central American Federation 1824–38, it then became a separate republic. Between 1910 and 1930 it was under almost continuous US military occupation. The Somoza family held political domination of Nicaragua from 1933 to 1979. Through a brutal dictatorship imposed through the National Guard, they secured for themselves a large share of the national wealth. In 1962 the radical Sandinista National Liberation Front was formed with the object of overthrowing the Somozas. After 17 years of civil war the Sandinistas triumphed. On 17 July 1979 President Somoza was overthrown and fled into exile. Under the Constitution of 1987 there is a unicameral directly elected 90-member National Assembly. Executive power is vested in the President who governs with the assistance of a Vice President and an appointed Cabinet.

Nicaragua, Lake Nicaragua. Largest freshwater lake in Central America, 160 km (100 miles) long and up to 68 km (42 miles) wide. Separated from the Pacific by an isthmus 19 km (12 miles) wide. Fed by the Tipitapa R. from L. Managua. Discharges into the Caribbean via the San Juan R. There are many islands and fish is abundant.

Nice France. Ancient Nicaea. Prefecture of the Alpes-Maritimes department in the SE, at the mouth of the Paillon R. on the Baie des Anges of the Mediterranean Sea; fashionable resort on the French Riviera. Pop. (1990) 345,625. In a beautiful position on a small coastal plain sheltered by the N by hills rising to the mountains of the Maritime Alps; noted for its mild, sunny climate. Among its many festivals the 'battle of flowers' is the most famous.

Considerable trade in Mediterranean fruits, flowers and essential oils. Manufactures perfumes, soap, olive oil, textiles and furniture.

One of the outstanding features is the Promenade des Anglais, built by the English colony in the 19th cent. Has a cathedral and on Mont Gros (372 m; 1220 ft) an observatory. Founded by the Phocaeans (a colony of Greek mariners) from Massilia (Marseille) in the 3rd or 4th cent. BC. Its prosperity dates from 1388, when it came under the rule of the counts of Savoy. Ceded by Sardinia to France 1860. Birthplace of Giuseppe Garibaldi (1807–82) and Masséna (1756–1817).

Nickerie River Suriname. Rises in the Guiana Highlands in S Suriname and flows 320 km (200 miles) N then WNW to enter the Atlantic below Nieuw Nickerie. Navigable for 96 km (60 miles). Linked to Coppename R. It has fertile rice lands on its lower course.

Nicobar Islands Indian Ocean. Group of 19 islands S of the Andaman Is., forming with the latter a centrally administered territory of India. Area 1841 sq km (719 sq. miles). Pop. (with Andaman Is.) (1991) 279,111.

The main islands, 12 of which are inhabited, are Great Nicobar, Camotra,

Nancowrie and Car Nicobar. There is a good landlocked harbour between Camotra and Nancowrie. Coconut palms are numerous and the coconuts provide both the main foodstuff and the leading item of trade. The people are of Mongoloid stock, akin to the Malays and are animists. Occupied by Denmark for a considerable period, they were gradually abandoned after 1848 and were annexed by Britain 1869. During World War II they were occupied by the Japanese 1942–5.

Nicosia Cyprus. Cap. and largest city of the republic in the N central part of the island on the Mesaoria plain and 15 km (10 miles) from the N coast. Pop. (1990) 168,800 (excludes Turkish-occupied area). The central walled city has a 5-km (3-mile) circumference and is divided by the 'Green Line' between Turkish-controlled areas (N) and government-controlled Greek Cypriot districts (S). The suburbs extend over at least four times the area of the old town, which has itself been rebuilt, so that overall, Nicosia is modern, but the walled centre much neglected.

Manufactures inc. clothing, footwear, cotton, tobacco products and foods, all mainly for local consumption. The city is the market for the surrounding agricultural region.

The walls were built by the Venetians in the 16th cent., replacing earlier walls enclosing a larger area. The Turks took Nicosia in 1570, converting the 14th cent. St Sophia Cathedral into a mosque. The city did not spread beyond the walls until after 1900.

Nidd River England. River 80 km (50 miles) long in Yorkshire, rising on Great Whernside and flowing generally SE and E through Nidderdale and past Knaresborough to join the R. Ouse 10 km (6 miles) NW of York.

Niederösterreich ➤LOWER AUSTRIA.

Niedersachsen ➤LOWER SAXONY.

Niederwald Germany. Hill at the SW end of the Taunus Hills in Hessen 329 m (1089 ft)

high. The S and W slopes are covered with vineyards.

Niemen River ➤NEMAN RIVER.

Nieuport (Flemish **Nieuwpoort**) Belgium. Fishing port in W Flanders province on the Yser R. 16 km (10 miles) SW of Ostend. Pop. (1971) 7230.

Manufactures chemicals.

Rebuilt after destruction during World War I. To the NW is Nieuport-Bains (Nieuwpoort Bad), a seaside resort.

Nieuwveld Mountains ➤SOUTH AFRICA.

Nièvre France. Department formed mainly from the old province of Nivernais. Area 6817 sq km (2632 sq. miles). Pop. (1991) 232,600. Prefecture Nevers. Rises in the E to nearly 900 m (2952 ft) in the barren but picturesque Monts du Morvan. Drained chiefly by the Loire and Yonne rivers. Cereals and potatoes are grown, and vines cultivated. There are extensive forests. Some minerals inc. coal in the Decize area. Chief towns Nevers, Fourchambault.

Niger. Republic in NW Africa, bounded by Algeria and Libya in the N, Chad in the E, Nigeria in the S, Benin and Burkina Faso in the SW and Mali in the W. Area 1,186,408 sq km (458,075 sq. miles). Pop. (1995) 8,813,000 (20 per cent urban). Life expectancy, 50 years male, 48 female. Cap. Niamey; other cities Zinder, Maradi, Tahoua and Agadez. Currency: CFA franc = 100 cents. Niger is an arid country except for the wooded savannah along the Niger R. and the Nigerian frontier (extreme SW and S). The vast northern area is part of the Sahara. There are a number of oases in the Aïr highlands, e.g. Agadès, Niamey and Zinder (formerly caravan posts) are termini of trans-Saharan motor routes. Rainfall determines the geographical division into a southern zone of agriculture, a central zone of pasturage and a desert-like northern zone. The country lacks water, with the exception of the south-western districts, which are watered by the Niger and its tributaries, and the southern zone, where there are a number of wells. Land use: forested 2 per cent, meadows and pastures 7 per cent, agricultural and under permanent cultivation 3 per cent. There are about 6 million Sunni Muslims, the rest of the pop. has traditional (animist) belief, and there are some Christians. The official lang. is French and about 53 per cent are Hausa, 21 per cent Zerma-Songhai, 11 per cent Tuareg and 10 per cent Fulani.

Cattle, sheep and goats raised. Cotton, groundnuts, cassava, sugar-cane, natron, tin and iron ore. There are some small manufacturing industries, mainly in the cap. producing textiles, food products, chemicals and furniture.

Niger was occupied by France 1883–99, becoming a military territory in 1901 and part of French West Africa in 1904. From 1958 it became an autonomous republic within the French Community, achieving independence in 1960. From 1974 the country was ruled by a Military Council and the Constitution was suspended. In 1992 under a new Constitution an 83-member National Assembly was established.

Niger River. River 4030 km (2505 miles) long, an ancient highway for trade, rising in the S highlands of Guinea, near the Sierra Leone frontier 274 km (170 miles) from the Atlantic and flowing N, NE, SE and S in a broad semicircular course through Mali, Niger and Nigeria to the Gulf of Guinea. Divides into several channels below the irrigation dam of Sansanding, passing through a region of marshes and lakes extending to Kabara (port of Timbuktu), then for 800 km (500 miles) flanked along the left bank by the Sahara. In various stretches impeded by rapids. The Kainji Dam, reservoir and hydro-electric scheme, 96 km (60 miles) N of Jebba, is one of the largest in Africa; it provides power and irrigation water. Joined at Lokoja by its principal tributary, the Benue, navigable in the rainy season (as are the Niger's upper and lower reaches). The great delta of the Niger enters the sea through a belt of mangrove swamps, begins S of Onitsha and covers some 20,000 sq km (7720 sq. miles). First explored (1795–6, 1805) by Mungo

Park. The course, long a subject of controversy, was not completely known until almost the end of the 19th cent.

Nigeria. Federal republic in W Africa, bounded N by Niger, NE by Chad, E by Cameroon, W by Benin and the Atlantic Ocean to the S. The republic consists of the Federal Capital Territory (Abuja) and 30 states (caps. in brackets): Abia (Umuahia), Adamawa, formerly Gongola (Yola), Akwa Ibom (Uyo), Anambra (Awaka), Bauchi (Bauchi), Benue (Makurdi), Borno (Maiduguri), Cross River (Calabar), Delta (Asaba), Edo, formerly Bendel (Benin), Enugu (Enugu), Imo (Owerri), Jigawa (Dutse), Kaduna (Kaduna), Kano (Kano), Katsina (Katsina), Kebbi (Birnin-Kebbi), Kogi (Lokoja), Kwara (Ilorin), Lagos (Ikeja), Niger (Minna), Ogun (Abeokuta), Ondo (Akure), Oson (Oshogbe), Oyo (Ibadan), Plateau (Jos), Rivers (Port Harcourt), Sokoto (Sokoto), Taraba (Jalingo), Yobe (Damaturu). Six new states were created in 1996, 3 in the north and 3 in the south. In the north, Zamfara State was created from Sokoto, with its headquarters at Gusau; Nassarawa State was created from Plateau, with its headquarters at Lafia; and Gombe State was created from Bauchi, with its headquarters at Gombe. In the south, Ekiti State was created from Ondo, with its cap. at Ado-Ekiti; Bayelsa State was created from Rivers, with its headquarters at Yenagoa; and Ebonyi State was created by merging Abia and Enugu, with its headquarters at Abakaliki. Area 923,768 sq km (356,669 sq. miles). Pop. (1995) 93,472,000. (37 per cent urban). Life expectancy, 54 years male, 60 female. Cap. Abuja. Other important cities Lagos, Ibadan, Kano, Ogbomosho, Oshogbo and Ilorin. Currency: Nigerian naira = 100 kobo. The extreme N is a semi-desert thorn-and-scrub region. The highest land is on the Bauchi plateau and along the Cameroon frontier, with some heights above 1500 m (4920 ft). The hot, dust-laden harmattan blows from the Sahara during the dry season. Along the 800-km (500-mile) coast there are sand dunes behind which are mangrove swamps which reach 100 km (60 miles) across in the Niger delta. North of this is a zone of tropical rainforest, 80–160 km (50–100 miles) wide. The land then rises to an undulating plateau of savannah country, dissected by the Niger and Benue rivers. Lying wholly within the tropics, temperatures everywhere are high. Rainfall varies very much, but decreases from the coast to the interior. The main rains occur from April to Oct. Land use: forested 13 per cent, pasture 44 per cent, agricultural 36 per cent. English is the official lang. but it is estimated that there are as many as 250 langs. spoken and there are also as many ethnic groups, chief among which are the Hausa, Yoruba, Igbo, Fulani, Ibibio, Kanuri, Edo, Tiv, Ijaw, Bura and Nupe. The N is mainly Muslim, the S predominantly Christian and the W evenly divided between Muslim, Christian and animists.

About 80 per cent of the land mass is suitable for agriculture and it employs 43 per cent of the labour force. The N produces groundnuts, tobacco, cotton, soybeans, hides, and the S palm products, cocoa, timber and rubber. Minerals inc. tin, coal, columbite, gold and tantalite. Manufactures are mainly for local consumption, such as ply-wood, soap, cigarettes, groundnut oil, fertilizers, petrochemicals, assembly of vehicles and food-processing. Export income from petroleum and natural gas has been falling since the early 1980s and production is now limited to OPEC's quotas, but represents 96 per cent (1991) of value of exports, and economic policy is to encourage non-oil exports and the use of local rather than imported raw materials.

Farming communities settled in the area of present-day Nigeria 4000 years ago, which was previously occupied by hunter-gatherers. They developed the large centralized state of Kanem-Bornu in the 8th cent., based on control of trans-Saharan trade. Adjacent states, notably the Hausa, Oyo and Benin empires arose later, and became caught up in the slave trade by the 18th cent. British occupation aimed at enforcing the abolition of the trade. Lagos was captured by Britain in 1851 and annexed in 1861 to check the traffic in slaves. The slave trade was abolished and palm oil (for the manufacture of soap) became the main commercial commodity; the streams draining the Niger delta became known as the 'oil rivers', and the Oil Rivers Protectorate was formed in 1885. (Renamed the Niger Coast Protectorate 1893). The Royal Niger Company was granted a charter in 1886, giving it control of the delta area and the land bordering the Niger upstream to the confluence with the Benue. On the termination of the charter the Protectorate of Southern Nigeria was formed in 1900. Amalgamated with the colony of Lagos as the Colony and Protectorate of Nigeria 1914, it became a federation, under a Governor-General in 1954 and full independence was achieved in 1960. It became a republic in 1963. The territory of the Cameroons (formerly a German colony) was inc. in Nigeria for administrative purposes (under British trusteeship) from 1923; in 1961 the South voted to unite with the Republic of Cameroon, the North to join Nigeria. The Federal Prime Minister was assassinated and military government established in 1966. Eastern Nigeria seceded as the independent republic of Biafra in 1967 and war broke out between Federal Nigeria and the breakaway state, but Federal forces re-established control in 1970. Civilian rule returned in 1979 but again the Military took over in 1983. Attempts to return to civilian rule in 1992 were unsuccessful and a Transitional Council was installed in 1993.

Nightingale Island ►TRISTAN DA CUNHA.

Niigata Japan. Cap. of Niigata prefecture, N Honshu 260 km (160 miles) NNW of Tokyo. Pop. (1991) 487,856. Chief seaport on the W coast of Honshu; harbour handicapped by silting and lack of shelter.

Exports oil from nearby oilfield and fertilizers. Industries inc. oil-refining and the manufacture of chemicals, machinery and textiles.

Niihau USA. Island SW of Kauai across Kaulakahi Channel, Hawaii. Area 186 sq km (72 sq. miles). Pop. (1980) 226. It is privately owned and is arid lowland with a rocky E coast.

Main occupations cattle-raising, making rush matting.

Nijmegen (Nymegen) Netherlands. Industrial town in Gelderland province on the Waal R. 16 km (10 miles) SSW of Arnhem. Pop. (1992) 146,344. Linked with the Maas R. by the Maas–Waal Canal.

Industries inc. engineering, brickmaking, sugar-refining and the manufacture of rayon, electrical equipment, chemicals and food-processing.

In the beautiful Valkhof park is the site of the palace built by Charlemagne (777). Seat of a Roman Catholic University (1923). The Treaty of Nijmegen between Louis XIV (France) and the Netherlands, Spain and the Holy Roman Empire was signed here (1678).

Nikolayev ➤MYKOLAYIV.

Nikopol Ukraine. Town on the right bank of the Dnieper R. 88 km (55 miles) ESE of Krivoi Rog. Pop. (1991) 159,000.

Important manganese-mining centre, supplying the steel plants of the Donbas and Dnepropetrovsk. Iron-founding, flour-milling. Manufactures machinery.

Nikumaroro Kiribati. Formerly Gardner Island. Atoll in the Phoenix group S of Canton. Area 4 sq km (1.5 sq. miles). No permanent pop. (1993).

The only product is copra.

Nile River (Ar. **El Bahr ('the River') En Nîl**). Longest river in Africa; 5607 km (3485 miles) from L. Victoria. With its farthest headstream, the longest river in the world, 6695 km (4160 miles). The remotest headstream is the Luvironza R. (a tributary of the Ruvuvu R.); the Ruvuvu joins the Kagera R. (the main headstream), which enters the W of L. Victoria (a vast natural reservoir, in a region of equatorial rains). At Jinja the river leaves the N side of L. Victoria, at a height of 1129 m (3703 ft) by the Ripon Falls (submerged behind the Owen Falls dam farther downstream); now called the Victoria Nile, it passes through the marshy L. Kioga, descends

by the Murchison Falls and at a height of 619 m (2030 ft) enters L. Albert, which drains the Ruwenzori highlands through L. Edward and the Semliki R. Leaving L. Albert as the Albert Nile and after Nimule called the Bahr el Jebel, below Juba it meanders through and spreads over the *sudd* region; here much water is lost by evaporation and dispersal, and navigation is seriously impeded. Joined at L. No by the Bahr el Ghazal, it is then called the White Nile. Receiving the Sobat R., it flows generally N until at Khartoum it meets its most important tributary, the Blue Nile (which after rising in the Ethiopian Highlands and flowing through L. Tana has swept round in a wide SE-to-NW curve and descended over rapids and through gorges, receiving many tributaries, into Sudan). The combined river is joined by its last tributary, the Atbara R., 320 km (200 miles) below the confluence of the White Nile and the Blue Nile. Crossing the Sahara in a vast S-bend, between Khartoum in Sudan and Aswan in Egypt, it passes through a narrow valley and over a series of 6 cataracts alternating with almost level stretches. It then descends by a gentler slope, through a much wider valley, to the head of the delta just below Cairo, where it divides into two main channels each 240 km (150 miles) long, the Rosetta (W) and the Damietta (E). The Nile drains some 1,900,000 sq km (733,000 sq. miles).

The prosperity of Egypt, and of the N of Sudan, depends on irrigation water from the Nile; the flood waters (swollen by heavy monsoon rains in the Ethiopian Highlands during the summer) were first used, by basin irrigation, c. 4000 BC, and the height of the annual flood has been recorded since c. 3600 BC. The Blue Nile contributes 68 per cent of the volume of the main river at the height of the flood (late Aug. and early Sept.) but only 17 per cent at low water; the White Nile, however, is fed chiefly from the great lakes and maintains a regular flow throughout the year, so that it contributes 83 per cent of the volume of the main river at low water but only 10 per cent at the peak of the Blue Nile flood. In modern times perennial irrigation has been made possible by the construction of huge dams at Aswan and Jebel Aulia (White Nile) and Sennar (Blue Nile). There are also several regulating barrages across the river, e.g. Asyût, Esna. The need for more land under irrigation has led to further projects, e.g. the Aswan High Dam which has created L. Nasser. At high water the river provides a continuous waterway from the delta up to Juba on the White Nile, though in the sudd region it is sometimes obstructed; the Blue Nile is navigable from Khartoum to Roseires (640 km; 400 miles). At low water it is unnavigable (owing to the Cataracts) from Khartoum to Aswan, except in the Kareima–Khartoum section between the Third and Fourth Cataracts.

The Nile Valley saw the beginning of the earliest civilizations. The river's course was almost certainly known to the ancient Egyptians (who held it sacred) as far upstream as the junction with the Blue Nile. Herodotus followed the river as far as the First Cataract (460 BC) but failed to obtain reliable information on the source, which remained a matter of speculation and legend until after the explorations of Speke and Stanley in the late 19th cent.

Nilgiri Hills India. Plateau mainly in W Tamil Nadu rising steeply from the plain on all but the N side. Average height 1980 m (6494 ft); rises to 2637 m (8649 ft) in Doda Betta. Much is forested, but tea, coffee, rubber and medicinal herbs are cultivated.

Nîmes France. Ancient Nemausus. Prefecture of the Gard department 105 km (65 miles) NW of Marseille. Pop. (1990) 133,607. Tourist, commercial and industrial centre. Trade in wine, brandy, grain. Manufactures textiles (the word 'denim' gets its name from *serge de Nîmes*), clothing, footwear and agricultural machinery. Best known, however, for its many Roman remains, the finest in France, among them the famous arena of the 1st or 2nd cent. AD, the Maison Carrée (a temple), the temple of Diana and the Tour Magne (Turris Magna), on the summit of Mont Cavalier, one of the barren limestone hills near the city. To the NE is the Pont du Gard. Founded by Augustus; an

important city in Roman times. Flourished as a Protestant stronghold in the 16th and 17th cent. but declined after the revocation of the Edict of Nantes (1685).

Nimule ➤BAHR EL JEBEL; NILE RIVER.

Nineveh. Ancient cap. of the Assyrian Empire on the Tigris R. opposite modern Mosul (Iraq). Attained its greatest glory in the 8th and 7th cent. BC under Sennacherib and Assurbanipal. Destroyed by the Medes 612 BC. Excavations of the mount Kouyunjik have revealed palaces and temples.

Ningbo (Ningpo) China. Commercial town and port in NE Zhejiang province on the Yuyao R. 145 km (90 miles) ESE of Hangzhou (Hangchou/Hangchow). Pop. (1991) 552,540.

Exports tea, cotton, fish products, bamboo shoots. Industries inc. fishing, shipbuilding, fish-processing and textiles.

There was a Portuguese trading post in the 16th cent. and it became one of the original treaty ports in 1842.

Ningpo ➤NINGBO.

Ningsia-Hui ➤NINGXIA HUI.

Ningxia Hui (Ningsia-Hui) Autonomous Region China. Autonomous region in the N, S of Nei Monggol (Inner Mongolia). Area 66,400 sq km (25,640 sq. miles). Pop. (1990) 4,655,451. Cap. Yinchuan. The region consists of lofty plateaux and mountain ridges, with the Huang He (Yellow R.) crossing it in the N. The river valley is irrigated and crops of wheat, kaoliang, beans are grown. Rugs are woven from the wool of local sheep.

Niort France. Prefecture of the Deux-Sèvres department on the Sèvre Niortaise R. 58 km (36 miles) ENE of La Rochelle. Pop. (1990) 58,660.

Market town. Industries inc. tanning, leather-dressing and glove-making.

Nipigon, Lake Canada. Lake in S Ontario. Area 4840 sq km (1870 sq. miles). Contains about 1000 islands and islets. Drains S into

L. Superior via the Nipigon R. (48 km; 30 miles long).

Nipissing, Lake Canada. Lake in Ontario between the Ottawa R. and Georgian Bay (L. Huron), into which it is drained by the French R. Area 855 sq km (330 sq. miles).

Niš (Serbia) Yugoslavia. Ancient Naissus. Town on the Nišava R. 204 km (127 miles) SSE of Belgrade. Pop. (1991) 247,533. Important railway junction, with the country's largest railway workshops.

It also manufactures tobacco products and textiles. Trade in wine and grain.

The Emperor Claudius defeated the Goths here in AD 269. Birthplace of Constantine the Great (c. 280–337). Nearby is the famous Tower of Skulls (Čele Kula), built by the Turks after the Serbian revolt of 1809, in which they embedded more than 900 Serbian skulls placed there as a warning to others who thought of rebelling.

Nishapur Iran. Town in Khurasan province 64 km (40 miles) W of Meshed at a height of 1200 m (3936 ft). Pop. (1985) 63,000. In a fertile region producing cereals and cotton.

Manufactures pottery.

Birthplace and burial-place of Omar Khayyam (1050?–1122). About 30 km (20 miles) NW are the famous Iranian turquoise mines.

Nishinomiya Japan. Industrial town in Hyogo prefecture, central Honshu just NW of Osaka. Pop. (1991) 426,711.

Industries inc. brewing, particularly saké (rice wine) and manufactures machinery, chemicals and soap.

Niterói Brazil. Cap. of Rio de Janeiro state on the E shore of Guanabara Bay opposite Rio de Janeiro, to which it is linked by frequent ferry services. Pop. (1991) 416,123. Largely residential and is a suburb of Rio.

Shipbuilding. Manufactures textiles, metal goods and matches. Also a popular resort with excellent beaches.

Nith River Scotland. River 113 km (70 miles) long, rising near Dalmellington and flowing generally E and then SE through Nithsdale in Dumfries to the Solway Firth. The Afton Water joins it at New Cumnock.

Nitra Slovakia. Town situated ENE of Bratislava on the Nitra R. Pop. (1990) 91,000.

Centre of a farming area. Industries inc. processing agricultural produce.

Noted as a centre of Christianity, seat of a 9th cent. bishopric.

Niue (Savage) Island S Pacific Ocean. Coral island belonging to New Zealand 930 km (580 miles) WNW of Rarotonga. Area 258 sq km (100 sq. miles). Pop. (1991) 2239. Chief town and port Alofi.

Produces coconuts, honey, limes and root crops.

Annexed 1901 and granted internal self-government 1974.

Nivernais France. Former region and province with cap. Nevers, becoming a duchy in 1559 and passing to the French crown in 1669. Practically co-extensive with the modern Nièvre department.

Nizhny Novgorod Russia. River port and cap. of Nizhny Novgorod *oblast* at the confluence of the Volga and Oka rivers 418 km (260 miles) ENE of Moscow. Pop. (1991) 1,445,000.

A railway junction and an important industrial centre, it manufactures locomotives, cars, aircraft, machine-tools, generators, radio sets, chemicals, textiles. Other industries inc. oil-refining, shipbuilding (inc. hydrofoils), sawmilling and woodworking.

Founded in 1221 as the frontier fortress of Nizhni Novgorod by Yuri, Prince of Suzdal-Vladimir. It has a 13th-cent. kremlin (citadel) and two 13th-cent. cathedrals. Sacked by Tatars 1377–8, it was annexed to Moscow 1417. Its great fairs gained a European reputation from 1817. Birthplace of Balakirev (1836–1910), the composer and Maxim Gorki (1868–1936), the novelist.

Nizhni Tagil Russia. Industrial town in the Sverdlovsk region 129 km (80 miles) NNW of Sverdlovsk near the Tagil R. Pop. (1991) 439,200.

Important metallurgical centre, in an

iron-mining region. Manufactures railway rolling-stock, aircraft, agricultural machinery, machine-tools and chemicals.

Founded 1725 with the building of the Visokaya ironworks.

Nizké Tatry ➤TATRA MOUNTAINS.

Njazídia ➤COMOROS.

Nkongsamba Cameroon. Town situated NW of Yaoundé. Pop. (1987) 112,000. Railway terminus and airport; trading centre. Industries inc. sawmilling, palm-oil production, railway repair shops.

Nocera Inferiore Italy. Town in Salerno province, Campania 34 km (21 miles) ESE of Naples. Pop. (1985) 48,000.

Tomato-canning. Manufactures cotton goods.

To the E is the village of Nocera Superiore, near which is a circular domed church dating from the 4th cent.

Nogales Mexico. Town in Sonora 257 km (160 miles) N of Hermosillo at a height of 1179 m (3868 ft) on the US frontier. Pop. (1990) 107,119.

Market town. Trade in livestock, agricultural produce. Also a mining centre for silver and gold. Across the border is Nogales, Arizona (USA) which is also a commercial centre.

Noginsk Russia. Industrial town in the Moscow region on the Klyazma R. 51 km (32 miles) E of Moscow. Pop. (1991) 122,700.

Important textile-manufacturing centre. Also chemical and metalworking industries. Power station supplying electricity to Moscow.

Nome USA. Seaport in W Alaska on the S coast of the Seward Peninsula. Pop. (1990) 8288. Open June–Nov.

Fishing. Tourist centre.

Owes its origin to the discovery of gold nearby (1898). The pop. rose to about 20,000 in 1900.

Nomo Peninsula Japan. Peninsula extending 27 km (17 miles) S from the Hizen Peninsula in Kyushu, between the Amakusa

Sea (E) and the East China Sea. Chief town Nagasaki, at the base, on the W coast.

Noord-Holland ➤NORTH HOLLAND.

Nord France. Department in the N, bounded by the North Sea (N) and by Belgium (NE and E). Area 5742 sq km (2217 sq. miles). Pop. (1991) 2,533,000. Prefecture Lille. Generally low-lying. Drained by the Scheldt (Escaut) and its tributaries and the Sambre; served by many canals. Cereals, flax, sugar-beet and hops cultivated. Contains much of the Franco–Belgian coalfield. Besides coalmining there are important textile and metallurgical industries. Chief towns Lille, Cambrai, Douai, Dunkirk, Valenciennes, Armentières, Roubaix, Tourcoing. Much fighting took place here in World War II prior to the Allied evacuation from Dunkirk.

Nordenham Germany. Fishing port in Lower Saxony on the Weser R. 11 km (7 miles) SW of Bremerhaven. Pop. (1986) 29,000.

Lead and zinc smelting.

Nordhausen Germany. Town in the Erfurt district at the S foot of the Harz Mountains 63 km (39 miles) NNW of Erfurt. Pop. (1971) 44,600.

In a potash-mining district. Distilling, printing and textile manufacture.

Roman Catholic cathedral. Founded in the 10th cent. Became a free imperial city 1253. Passed to Prussia 1815.

Nord-Pas de Calais France. Region in N comprising Nord and Pas de Calais. Area 12,412 sq km (4792 sq. miles). Pop. (1990) 3,965,100. Chief towns Lille (regional cap.), Valenciennes, Lens, Douai, Béthune, Dunkirk, Maubeuge, Calais, Boulogne-sur-Mer and Arras. Major industrial region in the 19th cent. and the most heavily populated. In recent years mines have closed, the steel industry has declined and there have been problems with the textile industry. In spite of this, the region, which has long been an area of vast economic potential, is developing modern industries and will take advantage of the new opportunities offered by the building of the Channel tunnel.

Nore England. Sandbank in the Thames estuary off Sheerness, marked by a lightship and buoys. The name is also applied to the anchorage around it, much used by the Royal Navy in the 17th and 18th cent. A naval mutiny took place here in 1797.

Norfolk England. Eastern county bounded by the North Sea (N and E) and by The Wash (NW). Area 5356 sq km (2068 sq. miles). Pop. (1991) 745,613. It is divided into the districts of Beckland, Broadland, Great Yarmouth, King's Lynn and West Norfolk, North Norfolk, Norwich, South Norfolk. County town Norwich. Generally low-lying and flat, with fens in the extreme W and mudbanks around The Wash. The coast has suffered considerably from marine encroachment. Drained by the Yare, Bure, Waveney and Great Ouse rivers. In the E are the famous Norfolk Broads, a region of lakes popular with yachtsmen. Soils are fertile and agriculture is highly developed. Barley, wheat, sugar-beet and turnips are important crops. Livestock, inc. many turkeys intensively reared. Industries inc. tourism, food-processing, biotechnology, footwear, vehicles, insurance, publishing and oil. Norwich, King's Lynn, Cromer, East Dereham and Yarmouth are important towns.

Norfolk USA. Seaport in SE Virginia on the Hampton Roads and the Elizabeth R. Pop. (1990) 261,229.

Exports coal, tobacco, cotton, timber. Headquarters of the US Atlantic Fleet. Extensive shipyards, foundries. Manufactures chemicals, fertilizers, textiles and cars. Also a popular seaside resort.

Suffered severely in the American Revolution and the American Civil War, but several buildings from the colonial period remain, inc. St Paul's Church (1739), which still has a British cannon-ball embedded in its walls.

Norfolk Island (Australia) S Pacific Ocean. Small volcanic island, 1450 km (900 miles) ENE of Sydney, belonging to Australia. Area

35 sq km (14 sq. miles). Pop. (1992) 2000. Has an equable climate, fertile soil and luxuriant vegetation. Exports citrus and other fruits. Tourism provides most of the public revenue.

Discovered (1774) by Capt. Cook. Was a penal settlement 1788–1813 and 1826–55. Received *Bounty* mutineers from Pitcairn Island 1856. Transferred from New South Wales to the Commonwealth in 1913.

Norilsk Russia. Mining town in the Krasnoyarsk Territory 80 km (50 miles) ESE of the Yenisei port of Dudinka, with which it is linked by rail. Pop. (1991) 169,000.

Important nickel-mining centre. Nickel, gold, cobalt, platinum and copper are refined.

Founded in 1935 as part of a chain of penal settlements known as the Gulag Archipelago.

Norman USA. Town in Oklahoma 29 km (18 miles) SSE of Oklahoma City. Pop. (1990) 80,070. Market town. Seat of the University of Oklahoma (1899).

Normandy ➤BASSE NORMANDIE.

Normanton England. Town in West Yorkshire 5 km (3 miles) ENE of Wakefield. Pop. (1991) 18,775. Railway junction. Coal-mining centre.

Norristown USA. Industrial town in Pennsylvania on the Schuylkill R. 23 km (14 miles) NW of Philadelphia. Pop. (1970) 38,169.

Manufactures textiles, metal goods and drugs.

Norrköping Sweden. Industrial town and seaport in Östergötland county on the Motala R. near its mouth on the Bravik, an inlet of the Baltic Sea. Pop. (1992) 120,756.

Important textile centre (cotton, woollen, rayon goods). Manufactures plastics, paper and carpets. Exports wood-pulp and paper. Power for its industries is derived from the river.

Norrtälje Sweden. Town situated NE of Stockhom at the head of Norrtälje Bay on the Baltic Sea. Pop. (1990) 45,000.

Industries inc. fishing, farming and the manufacture of printing paper, giant television screens, rotosign systems, medals, precision engineering tools, boats and electronics.

Northallerton England. Market town in North Yorkshire, 23 km (14 miles) NNE of Ripon. Pop. (1991) 13,774.

Industries inc. tanning and flour-milling.

Has a 12th/13th-cent. church with a Perpendicular tower. The English defeated the Scots at the Battle of the Standard (1138) about 5 km (3 miles) N.

North America ►AMERICA.

Northampton England. County town of Northamptonshire on the R. Nene 97 km (60 miles) NW of London. Pop. (1991) 180,567.

Important centre for the manufacture of footwear, shoe machinery, leather goods and vehicle accessories.

The 12th-cent. Church of St Sepulchre is one of the 4 round churches in England; St Peter's church also dates from the 12th cent. Many old buildings were destroyed in the fire of 1675.

Northampton USA. Town in Massachusetts on the Connecticut R. 26 km (16 miles) N of Springfield. Pop. (1970) 29,664.

Manufactures cutlery, brushes, plastics, hosiery.

Seat of Smith College for women (1871). Founded 1654.

Northamptonshire England. County in the E Midlands. Area 2369 sq km (914 sq. miles). Pop. (1991) 578,807. It is divided into the districts of Corby, Daventry, East Northamptonshire, Kettering, Northampton, South Northamptonshire and Wellingborough. Generally undulating, rising to 214 m (701 ft) near Daventry. Drained to The Wash by the Welland and the Nene rivers. Farming is the main occupation on its fertile soil; 80 per cent is used for agriculture. Famous as a fox-hunting county. Large numbers of cattle and sheep are raised. Chief crop wheat. Iron ore mined, and other industries inc. brewing, food-processing and distribution. Principal industrial towns

Northampton, Kettering, Corby and Wellingborough.

North Berwick Scotland. Holiday resort and golfing centre in East Lothian on the S shore of the Firth of Forth 31 km (19 miles) ENE of Edinburgh. Pop. (1991) 5687. Fishing port.

The ruins of the 14th-cent. Tantallon Castle are 5 km (3 miles) E on the cliffs.

North Beveland Netherlands. Island in the Zeeland province in the Scheldt estuary. Area 91 sq km (35 sq. miles). Produces sugar-beet and wheat.

North Borneo ►SABAH.

North Cape (Norwegian **Nordkapp**) Norway. Promontory on the island of Mageröy, Finnmark county about 300 m (984 ft) high. Popularly supposed to be the most northerly point of Europe, but Knivskjärodden, to the W, is actually about 1.6 km (1 mile) nearer the North Pole.

North Carolina USA. State on the SE Atlantic seaboard. Area 136,412 sq km (52,669 sq. miles). Pop. (1990) 6,843,000. Cap. Raleigh. The coast is much indented, particularly by the Pamlico and Albemarle Sounds, and fringed with a chain of sandy islands. The E half is in the Atlantic coastal plain. To the W are the Piedmont plateau and the Appalachian Mountains, rising to 2039 m (6688 ft) in Mt Mitchell (the highest point E of the Mississippi). Climate humid subtropical in the SE; cooler and more continental in the mountains. Annual rainfall 110–140 cm (43–55 ins.). Agriculture important. Chief crops flue-cured tobacco, wheat, sweet potatoes and apples, peanuts and maize. Manufactures textiles, furniture, electrical equipment and machinery, and food products. Chief towns Charlotte, Raleigh, Greensboro and Winston-Salem.

Supported the Confederate cause in the American Civil War and was one of the original 13 states.

North Channel ►IRISH SEA.

North Dakota USA. State in the N,

bounded on the N by Saskatchewan and Manitoba (Canada). Area 183,117 sq km (70,702 sq. miles), Pop. (1990) 638,000. Cap. Bismarck. Generally flat; rises E–W in three plains, from the Red R. basin in the E to the Missouri plateau in the W. Highest point Black Butte (1058 m; 3470 ft) in the SW. In the extreme W are the much eroded and infertile Badlands. Drained by the Missouri R. and its tributaries, with the extensive Garrison Reservoir (flood control, irrigation, hydroelectric power) on the Missouri. Climate dry continental, with extremes of heat and cold and an annual rainfall of 35–50 cm (14–20 ins.). Mainly agricultural. Chief crops barley (leading state), sunflowers, flaxseed, spring wheat and pinto beans. Oil was discovered in 1951. Largest towns Fargo, Grand Forks and Bismarck.

The first permanent settlement was made at Pembina (1851). Dakota was organized as a separate territory in 1861 and the two states of North Dakota and South Dakota were formed in 1889. Admitted to the Union in 1889 as the 39th state.

North East Frontier Agency ➤ARUNA-CHAL PRADESH.

North East Lincolnshire England. New administrative area created in 1996, formerly Humberside. Pop. (1994) 164,000.

Northern Cape South Africa. Province created in 1994. Area 361,800 sq km (139,691 sq. miles). Pop. (1995) 742,000. Cap. Nelspruit.

Northern Ireland. The 6 counties of NE Ireland (Antrim, Armagh, Down, Fermanagh, Londonderry and Tyrone) form part of the United Kingdom of Great Britain and Northern Ireland. Area 13,409 sq km (5238 sq. miles). Pop. (1991) 1,569,971. Mainly plateau with hills around it and an indented coastline, containing few natural resources. Chief city Belfast. Other important cities Londonderry, Lisburn, Ballymena and Armagh.

It is primarily agricultural. Principal crops barley, oats, potatoes. Pigs, poultry, sheep and cattle raised in large numbers; dairy pro-duce and other goods are exported mainly to Britain. Little coal and few other mineral resources. Industries are centred chiefly on Belfast and Londonderry. There is ship-building and engineering in Belfast. Lignite is found on the E shores of L. Neagh in County Antrim.

Northern Ireland consists of 6 of the 9 counties of Ulster, the N province of ancient Ireland. Home Rule was opposed in Northern Ireland by the majority Protestant pop. who feared becoming a minor part of a mainly Roman Catholic independent country. In 1920 separate parliaments were set up for 'Southern Ireland' and 'Northern Ireland'. Only the Protestant Ulster Unionists accepted the scheme and a Northern Parliament was duly elected in 1921. The Roman Catholic minority in Northern Ireland (about 28 per cent) has never been content with these arrangements. What began as a Civil Rights campaign in 1968 escalated into a full-scale terrorist campaign designed to overthrow the State. This campaign was originally mounted by an illegal organization, the Irish Republican Army (the IRA, and not to be confused with the legitimate Army of the Republic of Ireland). At times counter-measures have required the services of over 20,000 regular troops, in addition to the Royal Ulster Constabulary, the RUC Reserve and the part-time Ulster Defence Regiment. The devolved Parliament at Stormont was prorogued and direct rule imposed from Westminster in 1974. Subsequent attempts to create a new administrative structure failed. The Anglo–Irish agreement, signed in 1985, allows the Irish government the right of consultation on Northern Ireland's affairs. It is opposed by Unionists. In 1993 the Prime Ministers of the UK and the Republic of Ireland issued the declaration calling on the IRA to renounce violence and join discussions to solve the political problems.

In 1994 the IRA announced 'a complete cessation of military operations', and in 1995 the British and Irish prime ministers announced new proposals for a settlement. Preliminary talks with the main political parties started, supervised by a 3-member international body chaired by US senator George Mitchell. It reported in 1996. The IRA exploded a bomb in London in 1996 and this ended the ceasefire which was resumed in 1997. A planned settlement was reached in 1998 which included that the Irish government would move to eliminate its territorial claim to Northern Ireland. Elections to the New Northern Ireland Assembly took place in June 1998 for 108 seats. The decommissioning of weapons was still a stumbling block in 1999 and Northern Ireland was still governed from London.

Northern Mariana Islands, Commonwealth of. Group of a single chain of 16 volcanic islands N of New Guinea and E of the Philippines in the W Pacific Ocean. The chain runs almost N–S. The three most populated islands are Saipan, Rota and Tinian. Area 5054 sq km (1950 sq. miles) of which 464 sq km (179 sq. miles) are dry land. The largest town is Chalan Kanoa on Saipan; it is on this island where the majority of the pop. (39,000) live. Pop. (1995) 47,200 (26 per cent urban).

Tourism is important and the main products are copra, sugar-cane and phosphates.

To the E and S is the Mariana (Marianas) Trench (11,033 m; 36,188 ft). Its bottom was reached in 1960 by the US bathyscope *Trieste*. Visited by Magellan in 1521, who called them the Islas de los Ladrones ('Thieves' Islands'); under Spanish rule 1668–1898. Guam was ceded to the USA 1899; the others were sold to Germany, but were occupied by Japan from 1914 until captured by the USA in 1944 and became a UN Trusteeship in 1947. In 1978 a Commonwealth, in association with the US government, was established and in 1986 islanders were granted US citizenship. The UN trusteeship status terminated in 1990. The Commonwealth is administered by an elected Governor and Lieut.-Governor. There is a 9-member Senate and an 18-member House of Representatives.

Northern Province South Africa. Province created in 1994. Area 123,280 sq km (47,598

sq. miles). Pop. (1995) 5,397,200. Cap. Pietersburg.

Northern Rhodesia ►ZAMBIA.

Northern Territory Australia. Territory bounded N by the Timor and Arafura Seas, E by Queensland, S by South Australia and W by Western Australia. Area 1,346,200 sq km (519,770 sq. miles). Pop. (1991) 175,253 (inc. 37,698 aborigines). Cap. Darwin. Arnhem Land in the N contains the largest aboriginal reservation in Australia; the people are semi-nomadic, wandering from the N mangrove swamps and river forests across areas of tall grass and open woodland according to the season – the monsoon rains of 100–150 cm (40–60 ins.) being followed by a long drought. To the S the rainfall decreases on the low tableland but a broad belt of grassland across the central N parts of the territory, with a rainfall of about 50 cm (20 ins.) annually, provides pasture for cattle and buffalo, herded largely by aborigines, which roam over the vast areas of widely scattered stations. Farther inland the rainfall decreases to under 25 cm (10 ins.) a year; desert and semi-desert occur, but there is enough pasture for roaming livestock. Road transport by trains of trailers facilitates the carriage of cattle to terminal points. The Stuart Highway runs N from Alice Springs to the pastoral zone and Darwin; the Barkly Highway from Tennant Creek to Mt Isa links up with the Queensland transport system. Other activities are the uranium works at Rum Jungle, gold and copper mines at Tennant Creek, tungsten at Hatches Creek and Wauchope. Oil and gas reserves have been discovered and developed offshore in the Joseph Bonaparte Gulf and Timor Sea areas and onshore in the Amadeus Basin. Chief towns Darwin and Alice Springs. Tourism is important to the Territory's economy.

The N coast was discovered by the Dutch (1623) but was not settled by the British until 1824. The territory was under New South Wales 1825–63 and under South Australia 1863–1911, being then transferred to the Commonwealth. Between 1926 and 1931 it was divided administratively into Northern Australia and Central Australia. Self-government was granted in 1978.

Northfleet England. Town in Kent on the Thames estuary 1.6 km (1 mile) W of Gravesend. Pop. (1971) 26,679.
Manufactures cement, paper, chemicals and cables.

North Foreland England. Chalk headland on the E coast of Kent, just N of Broadstairs.

North Holland (Dutch **Noordholland**) Netherlands. Province in the NW inc. the W Frisian islands of Texel, Vlieland and Terschelling. Area 2665 sq km (1029 sq. miles). Pop. (1990) 2,376,015. Cap. Haarlem.
Dairy-farming and cheese production are important occupations. Leading commercial centre Amsterdam. Other towns Ijmuiden, Alkmaar, Hilversum.

North Island ➤NEW ZEALAND.

North Lincolnshire England. New administrative area created in 1996, formerly Humberside. Pop. (1994) 153,000.

North Little Rock USA. Industrial town in Arkansas on the Arkansas R. opposite Little Rock. Pop. (1990) 513,117.
Industries inc. railway engineering, sawmilling and cottonseed oil processing.

North Miami USA. Town in Florida 11 km (7 miles) N of Miami. Pop. (1970) 34,767. Mainly residential with some light industries.

North Ossetian Republic Russia. Autonomous republic on the N slopes of the Caucasus. Area 8000 sq km (3088 sq. miles). Pop. (1991) 643,000. Cap. Ordzhonikidze. Agriculture inc. the cultivation of maize, wheat, cotton and fruits. Lead, zinc and silver mined. North Ossetia became an autonomous *oblast* (region) 1924 and an autonomous republic in 1936.

North Platte USA. City in W Nebraska situated NE of Denver, Colorado on the North Platte R. Pop. (1990) 22,490. Main employers Union Pacific railway, local services, packing, construction.

North Platte River USA. River 1094 km (680 miles) long, rising in the Rocky Mountains in North Colorado, flowing generally N and then E and SE, through Wyoming and Nebraska and joining the South Platte R. at North Platte city, forming the Platte R. Important in hydroelectric and irrigation projects, with the Pathfinder, Seminoe and other reservoirs along its course.

North Rhine-Westphalia (Ger. **Nordrhein-Westfalen**) Germany. Area 34,070 sq km (13,155 sq. miles). The most densely populated *Land*, drained by the R. Rhine and its tributaries and formed after World War II from the former Prussian province of Westphalia, the state of Lippe and the N part of the former Prussian Rhine Province, inc. the districts of Aachen, Cologne and Düsseldorf. In 1949 a small area about 93 sq km (36 sq. miles) was lost by frontier adjustments to the Netherlands and Belgium. Contains the districts of Armsberg, Detmold, Cologne, Düsseldorf and Münster. Pop. (1991) 17,349,700. Cap. Düsseldorf. A highly industrialized region with coal-mining, manufacturing machines, chemicals and textiles.

North Sea Europe. Sea lying between Great Britain in the W and the continent of Europe in the E, about 960 km (600 miles) long N–S and up to 640 km (400 miles) wide. Generally shallow, resting on the continental shelf which extends around the British Isles and reaching its maximum depth (over 500 m; 1640 ft) in the Skagerrak. In its central area there are a number of banks, the principal one being the Dogger Bank; the shallow waters here have become important fishing grounds. Many busy shipping lanes cross the North Sea and some of the world's leading seaports, notably London, Rotterdam, Antwerp and Hamburg, stand on its shores. Site of important oil and gas fields.

North Solomons Papua New Guinea. Province (formerly Bougainville) comprising Bougainville and Buka islands with several atolls. Area 9300 sq km (3600 sq. miles). Pop. (1990) 159,500. Mountainous, rising to 2591 m (8500 ft) in Mount Balbi (volcanic) and heavily forested. Main products copra and tagua nuts.

North Somerset England. New administrative area created 1996. Formerly part of Avon. Pop. (1994) 177,000.

North Tonawanda USA. Industrial town and port in New York on the State Barge Canal at its junction with the Niagara R. 16 km (10 miles) N of Buffalo. Pop. (1990) 34,988.

Trade in timber and manufactures chemicals, paper, plastics and metal goods.

Northumberland England. The most northerly county, bounded on the N by Scotland, across the Cheviot Hills and the R. Tweed, on the E by the North Sea. Area 5032 sq km (1943 sq. miles). Pop. (1991) 300,600. It is divided into the districts of Alnwick, Berwick-on-Tweed, Blyth Valley, Castle Morpeth, Tynedale and Wansbeck. Hilly, chiefly in the N, where it rises to 816 m (2676 ft) in the Cheviot Hills, and in the W, where it reaches 519 m (1702 ft) in the Pennines. Drained by the Tyne, Blyth and Coquet rivers. Much sheep-rearing. Other industries inc. electronics, textiles, pharmaceuticals and engineering. Chief town Morpeth; other towns Ashington, Alnwick, Blyth and Berwick-on-Tweed. The most famous of the many Roman remains is Hadrian's Wall, which crosses the county from near Haltwhistle to Wallsend (Tyne and Wear).

Northumbria Britain. Anglo-Saxon kingdom extending from the Forth to the Humber, formed in the early 7th cent. by Aethelfrith by uniting two older kingdoms, Bernicia (N) and Deira (S). Christianity was introduced in the 8th and early 9th cent.; the kingdom gained fame as a centre of learning and it was extended to inc. Strathclyde and Dalriada. In 827, however, it accepted the supremacy of Wessex and in the late 9th cent. was conquered by the Danes.

North Walsham England. Market town in Norfolk 23 km (14 miles) NNE of Norwich.

Pop. (1991) 9534. The 16th-cent. grammar school was attended by Horatio Nelson.

Important wool-weaving centre in medieval times: Worstead, 5 km (3 miles) SSE, gave its name to the cloth known as 'worsted'.

Northwest Passage North America. Sea route from the Atlantic Ocean to the Pacific, round the N coast of America, sought by navigators and explorers for more than three centuries before being successfully navigated. Frobisher (1576) and Davis (1585–8) reached Baffin Island and Henry Hudson (1610) discovered Hudson Bay; further progress to the W was made by Ross and Parry in the early 19th cent., but Sir John Franklin's ill-fated expedition (1845–7) was unsuccessful, though rescue expeditions made important discoveries. It was not until Amundsen's voyage (1903–6) that the Passage was actually traversed. Owing to the prevalence of ice it can be used only when conditions are esp. favourable. It was first navigated by a commercial vessel in 1969, when the American SS *Manhattan*, an adapted oil tanker, sailed through to Point Barrow (Alaska).

Northwest Territories Canada. Vast administrative region in the N, consisting of the mainland N of 60° lat. (except those parts in the Yukon Territory, Quebec and Newfoundland) and the islands of the Arctic Archipelago and the Hudson and Ungava Bays and Hudson Strait. Area 3,379,700 sq km (1,304,903 sq. miles). Pop. (1992) 57,649 (37 per cent Inuit (Eskimos) and 16 per cent Indians). Seat of government Yellowknife. Subdivided into 5 administrative regions: Fort Smith, Inuvik, Kitimeot, Keewatin and Baffin. Mainly low-lying. In the W are the Mackenzie Mountains, rising to 2700 m (8856 ft). The W is drained by Canada's longest river, the Mackenzie. Innumerable lakes, the largest being the Great Bear Lake and the Great Slave Lake. The winters are very cold, the summers short but warm. On the mainland the annual precipitation is 25–40 cm (10–15 ins.), but it is less on the Arctic islands; it falls mostly as snow. Zinc, lead and gold mined. Oil produced and refined at

Norman Wells. Fur trapping still important; pelts with highest values are of polar bears, black and brown bear, wolf, wolverine and lynx. Aircraft and caterpillar tractors are widely used for transport. The region formerly inc. the Prairie Provinces and the N parts of Quebec and Ontario. Passed from the Hudson's Bay Company to the Dominion of Canada 1869. ➤NUNAVUT.

North-West South Africa. Province created in 1994. Area 116,190 sq km (44,861 sq. miles). Pop. (1995) 3,351,800. Cap. Mmabatho.

Northwich England. Town in Cheshire at the confluence of the R. Weaver and the R. Dane 26 km (16 miles) ENE of Chester. Pop. (1991) 34,520.

Centre of the salt industry. Manufactures chemicals, food products, and other industries inc. printing and construction. Has suffered from subsidence owing to brine-pumping.

North Yorkshire England. County formed in the main from the former North Riding of Yorkshire (1974). Area 8309 sq km (3208 sq. miles). Pop. (1991) 698,700. It is divided into the districts of Craven, Hambleton, Harrogate, Richmondshire, Ryedale, Scarborough, Selby and York. In the W are some of the higher Pennine peaks, inc. Ingleborough (723 m; 2371 ft) and Pen-y-Ghent (693 m; 2273 ft). E of the central Vale of York are the North York Moors; the Cleveland Hills (NE) are separated from the Yorkshire Wolds (SE) by the Vale of Pickering. In the fertile Vale of York cereals, sugar-beet and potatoes are produced. Scarborough and Whitby are popular coastal resorts; Harrogate is an inland spa and tourist centre; York is an important route, industrial and tourist centre. Other industries inc. the manufacture of plastics, footwear, clothing, vehicles and foodstuffs.

Norwalk USA. Industrial town in Connecticut on Long Island Sound 21 km (13 miles) WSW of Bridgeport. Pop. (1989) 81,770.

Manufactures hats, textiles, clothing and rubber products.

Norway. Kingdom in NW Europe, bounded by the Skagerrak (S), the North Sea and the Norwegian Sea (W), the Arctic Ocean (N) and Sweden, Finland and Russia (E). Area 323,878 sq km (125,050 sq. miles). Pop. (1994) 4,325,000 (75 per cent urban). Life expectancy, 74 years male, 80 female. Cap. Oslo. Other important cities Bergen, Trondheim and Stavanger. Currency: Norwegian krone = 100 øre. Mountainous country occupying the W part of the Scandinavian peninsula. The coast is deeply indented by many fiords, some of which penetrate far into the country, the largest and best-known being the Oslo, Hardanger, Sogne and Trondheim fiords. It is also fringed by thousands of islands, the so-called Skärgård or 'skerry fence', of which the most important are the Lofoten Is. and the Vesteralen group. From the coast the land rises steeply to plateaux and mountain ranges; in the Jotunheim Mountains is Norway's highest peak, Galdhöpiggen (2469 m; 8098 ft), and immediately W is the Jostedalsbre, the largest icefield in Europe, over 777 sq km (300 sq. miles) in area and feeding several glaciers. Between the plateaux and mountain ranges are such deep valleys as the Gudbrandsdal, Hallingdal and Romsdal; along many of them flow swift rivers which provide hydroelectric power, the longest being the Glomma.

The distinguishing feature of the climate is the unusual mildness of the winters for, although the country extends well beyond 70°N lat., its coast is icefree throughout the year because of the heating effects of the SW winds from the Atlantic and North Atlantic Drift, which washes its shores. At the same time the winds bring considerable rainfall to the W coastal regions, with frequent snow in the N. A well-known phenomenon N of the Arctic Circle is the Midnight Sun. At North Cape, for example, at least part of the sun is visible continuously from the second week in May till the end of July, but in winter the sun does not rise above the horizon for over two months. Land use: forested 27 per cent, meadows and pastures 0.4 per cent, agricultural and under permanent cultivation 3 per cent.

The religion is Evangelical Lutheran. The Norwegian lang., which is derived from the Danish, exists in two official forms: the Bokmål or Rigsmål, the literary lang., and the Landsmål or Nynorsk, the more popular variant. With an average of 13 per sq km, Norway has the lowest density of pop. in Europe apart from Iceland. Besides the Norwegians themselves, who are typically Nordic, there are Lapps, living mainly in Finnmark, part of Lapland, and some Finns.

Because of the high proportion of unproductive land, Norway has been compelled to rely largely on the sea for its wealth and fishing and the activities of its merchant navy figure prominently in the economy, while many foreign tourists are attracted by its picturesque coastal scenery. Agriculture is confined to the sheltered lowlands of the SE, the valleys and the narrow ledges beside the fiords. Main crops hay, barley, oats, potatoes. Dairy-farming is important and much use is made of mountain pastures in the summer. Reindeer are raised by the partly nomadic Lapps of the far N. The most valuable stands of timber, consisting chiefly of conifers, are in the S and provide raw material for the manufacture of wood-pulp and paper. Iron, copper and pyrites are mined, and there has been much expansion of the electro-metallurgical (aluminium etc.) and electro-chemical industries. Most of the large quantity of hydroelectric power produced is used in industry, but domestic consumption is also high. Cod and mackerel form the major part of the catch from the North Sea fishing grounds. The mercantile marine has a substantial share of the international carrying trade. Leading exports crude petroleum, natural gas, metals and metal products, wood-pulp and paper, fish and fish products. Foreign trade is chiefly with Germany, Britain and Sweden. Overseas possessions inc. Svalbard (Spitsbergen), Jan Mayen, Bouvet Island (in the S Atlantic), Peter I Island and Queen Maud Land (in the Antarctic).

In early times Norway was divided into *fylker*, each with its own king, and unity was first achieved by Harald Haarfager (872), who imposed his rule also on the Orkneys and Shetlands. After his death, however, the country was again divided, until, after much civil strife, the power of the crown was established by Haakon IV in the 13th cent.; during this latter period Iceland came under Norwegian rule. By the Union of Kalmar (1397) Norway, Sweden and Denmark were united under a single monarch. For Norway this union continued even after Sweden achieved independence (1523) and the country became little more than a Danish province. In 1814 Norway was ceded to Sweden, but the national movement grew in strength and in 1905 the union was dissolved and Prince Charles of Denmark was elected king as Haakon VII of Norway. A cultural revival had also developed and was represented by the works of Ibsen, Björnson, Grieg, etc. Early in World War II the country was invaded and occupied by German troops (1940) and the King and the government took refuge in Britain. Norway is a constitutional and hereditary monarchy. The parliament, the *Storting*, is divided into a 38-member upper house (*Lagting*) and a 112-member lower house (*Odelsting*). For administrative purposes the country is divided into the following 19 counties or *fylker*: Oslo (city), Akershus, Østfold, Hedmark, Oppland, Buskerud, Vestfold, Telemark, Aust-Agder, Vest-Agder, Rogaland, Hordaland, Sogn og Fjordane, Møre og Romsdal, Sør-Trøndelag, Norf-Trøndelag, Nordland, Troms and Finnmark.

Norwich England. County town of Norfolk on the R. Wensum near the confluence with the R. Yare 160 km (100 miles) NE of London. Pop. (1991) 173,286.

Industrial centre. Manufactures footwear and other leather goods, mustard, starch, vinegar and electrical and electronic products. Other industries inc. insurance, bookbinding and printing.

The cathedral (founded 1096) is one of the finest examples of Norman work in the country. Of the castle only the Norman keep remains and now houses the museum and art gallery. Also has several old churches, the 15th-cent. Guildhall and the Maddermarket Theatre. Seat of the University of East Anglia (1963). Many buildings were damaged or destroyed in air raids during World War II. Birthplace of Elizabeth Fry, Quaker prison reformer (1780–1845) and Harriet Martineau, writer (1802–76).

Norwich USA. Industrial town in SE Connecticut at the confluence of the Yantic and Shetucket rivers (forming the Thames). Pop. (1985) 39,000.
Manufactures textiles, clothing and leather goods.

Norwood USA. Industrial and residential town in Ohio, within but independent of Cincinnati.
Manufactures motor vehicles, electrical equipment and footwear.

Nossi-Bé Madagascar. Fertile volcanic island off the NW coast. Area 337 sq km (129 sq. miles). Pop. 26,000. Chief town and seaport Hellville.
Main products bananas, coffee, essential oils, sugar, vanilla.
Ceded to France 1840. Became a dependency of the French colony of Madagascar in 1896.

Nottingham England. City and unitary authority (from 1998) on the R. Trent. Pop. (1991) 277,203.
Industrial centre, once famous for lace-making but now more important for the manufacture of hosiery, also bicycles, tobacco products, pharmaceutical products and leather goods. Other industries inc. brewing, engineering and printing.
Roman Catholic cathedral; 16th-cent. grammar school; castle (rebuilt 1674–9, burned down 1831, restored 1875–8). The University College (opened 1881) became a full university 1948. In the 9th cent. it was one of the 5 Danish boroughs. Parliaments were held here 1334, 1337 and 1357. Charles

I raised his standard here (1642) at the start of the Civil War. Birthplace of William Booth (1829–1912), founder of the Salvation Army.

Nottinghamshire England. Inland county, largely in the valley of the R. Trent. Area 2164 sq km (836 sq. miles). Pop. (1991) 980,600. It is divided into the districts of Ashfield, Bassetlaw, Broxtowe, Gedling, Mansfield, Newark and Sherwood, Nottingham and Rushcliffe. Mainly low-lying, but hilly in the SW between Nottingham and Mansfield. Parts of Sherwood Forest remain. Wheat, oats, root crops cultivated. Cattle reared. Coal mined in the W. Chief towns Nottingham, Newark and Mansfield. Industries inc. chemicals, electronics, bicycles, tobacco products and knitwear.

Nouakchott Mauritania. Cap. of the republic in the W near the Atlantic coast 400 km (250 miles) NNE of Dakar (Senegal). Pop. (1988) 393,325, inc. about 200 refugees from drought.
Commercial centre on caravan routes. Trade in grain and gums.

Nouméa New Caledonia. Formerly Port de France. Cap. and chief seaport, with fine land-locked harbour on the SW coast. Pop. (1989) 65,110.
Exports nickel, chrome, iron and manganese ores, and nickel matte from local smelters.

Nouvelle Amsterdam ➤AMSTERDAM ISLAND.

Nova Goa ➤PANAJI.

Nova Lisboa ➤HUAMBO.

Novara Italy. Cap. of Novara province, Piedmont 47 km (29 miles) W of Milan. Pop. (1991) 103,349.
Manufactures cotton and silk goods, and chemicals. There is rice-milling, map-making and printing.
Cathedral (rebuilt in the 19th cent.) with a 10th-cent. baptistery; mainly 16th-cent. Church of S Gaudenzio. Here the Austrians defeated the Piedmontese under Charles

Albert, King of Sardinia (1849) and the latter abdicated.

Nova Scotia Canada. One of the Maritime Provinces, consisting of a peninsula joined to New Brunswick by the Chignecto isthmus and Cape Breton Island. Area 55,490 sq km (21,425 sq. miles). Pop. (1991) 899,942. Cap. and chief seaport Halifax. The indented coastline provides many harbours. Mainly low-lying, rising to 533 m (1748 ft) in the Cape Breton Island uplands. Drained by many small rivers and streams. Bras d'Or Lake (on Cape Breton Island) is the largest of the numerous lakes. The influence of the sea prevents temperatures from reaching the extremes experienced farther inland in the same latitudes. Precipitation is abundant, about 100–140 cm (40–55 ins.) annually. Dairy-farming and fruit-growing important; the Annapolis valley is noted for apple orchards. The development of the wood-pulp and paper industry has increased the value of the extensive forests. Around the coasts are fishing and fish canning and processing industries. Coal, supplying the iron and steel industry, is mined in the Sydney and Inverness fields on Cape Breton Island.

The French were the first settlers, calling the region Acadia. In 1621 James I of England granted the whole peninsula to Sir William Alexander, who wished to found a 'New Scotland' (the Nova Scotia of his charter). Separated from New Brunswick 1784. Cape Breton Island was incorporated 1820. Entered the Confederation, as one of the original provinces of Canada, 1867.

Novaya Zemlya (Nova Zembla) Russia. In Russian, 'New Land'. Arctic land in the Archangel region between the Barents Sea and the Kara Sea. Area 90,650 sq km (35,000 sq. miles). Consists of two large islands separated by a narrow strait, Matochkin Shar and several smaller islands. The two main islands are about 1050 km (650 miles) long and 48–113 km (30–70 miles) wide. Typical Arctic climate, with tundra vegetation in the S. The few inhabitants live by fishing, sealing and hunting.

Novgorod Russia. Cap. of Novgorod region on the Volkhov R. near the point where it leaves L. Ilmen and 169 km (105 miles) SSE of Leningrad. Pop. (1991) 233,800.

Industries inc. fish-canning, sawmilling, flour-milling and brewing. Manufactures clothing, footwear and pottery.

Famous chiefly as one of the country's oldest towns. Within the kremlin or citadel is the 11th-cent Cathedral of St Sophia, modelled on the cathedral of the same name in Constantinople (Istanbul). Many other ancient churches and monasteries, inc. the 14th-cent. Znamenski cathedral. Several museums. In 862 the inhabitants invited the Varangians under Rurik to Novgorod and Rurik became the first Prince of Novgorod; this date is thus regarded as marking the foundation of the Russian state and a monument commemorating the 1000th anniversary was erected in 1862. In the 12th cent. Novgorod became the chief trading centre of a vast region and was known as Novgorod Veliki ('Novgorod the Great'). In 1478 it was taken by Ivan III of Moscow and in 1570 it was destroyed by Ivan IV ('the Terrible') and thousands of its inhabitants were slaughtered.

Novi Sad Yugoslavia. Cap. of Vojvodina, Serbia; a river port on the Danube 72 km (45 miles) NW of Belgrade. Pop. (1991) 264,533. Before World War I the Serbian cultural and religious centre; now an industrial and commercial centre.

Manufactures textiles, agricultural machinery, electrical equipment, pottery and foodstuffs.

Novocherkassk Russia. Town 40 km (25 miles) ENE of Rostov. Pop. (1991) 188,500.

Industrial centre. Manufactures locomotives, machinery, textiles. Trade in wine, grain, timber.

Founded 1805 as the cap. and cultural centre of the Don Cossacks, succeeding Old Cherkassk, on the Don, which had suffered from frequent floods from the river.

Novokuznetsk Russia. Industrial city in Kemerovo region on the Tom R. 185 km

(115 miles) SSE of Kemerovo. Pop. (1991) 601,900.

A leading metallurgical centre in the Kuznetsk basin. Manufactures iron and steel, aluminium, locomotives, machinery, chemicals and cement. Coalmining in the neighbourhood.

Formed from the old city of Kuznetsk (founded 1618) and the new industrial town of Novo Kuznetsk (founded 1929) across the river, the two uniting as Stalinsk in 1932. In the 1930s it expanded rapidly with the development of the Kuznetsk basin.

Novomosksovsk Russia. Formerly Bobriki (1930–4), Stalinogorsk (1934–61). Industrial town in the Moscow region 193 km (120 miles) SSE of Moscow. Pop. (1991) 145,800.

Lignite-mining centre. Manufactures chemicals, machinery. Large coal-fed power station. Founded 1930.

Novorossiisk Russia. Seaport and industrial town in the Krasnodar Territory on the Black Sea 96 km (60 miles) WSW of Krasnodar. Pop. (1991) 188,600.

Exports grain, cement, petroleum. An important centre of the cement industry. Oil-refining. Manufactures machine-tools, agricultural machinery and bicycles.

Developed rapidly after the construction of the railway from Rostov (1888).

Novoshakhtinsk Russia. Formerly Komintern. Town 51 km (32 miles) NNE of Rostov. Pop. (1991) 107,300.

Important anthracite-mining centre in the Donets basin.

Novosibirsk Russia. Cap. of the Novosibirsk region and the largest city in Siberia on the Ob R. and the Trans-Siberian Railway. Pop. (1991) 1,446,300.

Important industrial and route centre. Manufactures agricultural and mining machinery, machine-tools, lorries, bicycles, textiles, electrical goods and plastics. Sawmilling, flour-milling, brewing. Trade in grain, meat and butter. Also a cultural centre. Linked by the Turksib Railway with Central Asia and by another direct line with the Kuznetsk basin.

Novosibirskiye Ostrova ►NEW SIBERIAN ISLANDS.

Novotroitsk Russia. Town situated W of Orsk in Orsk-Khalilovo industrial centre on the Ural R. Pop. (1991) 107,600.

The main industry is manufacturing steel, also mining nickel, cobalt and chromium.

Nowa Huta Poland. In Polish 'New Foundry'. Industrial town, now a suburb of Cracow on the Vistula R. 10 km (6 miles) E of Cracow. Pop. (1989) 224,386.

Important steel centre: blast furnaces, rolling mills and coke ovens.

Nowy Sącz Poland. Cap. of the Nowy Sącz voivodeship 72 km (45 miles) SE of Cracow in the picturesque valley of the Dunajec R. Pop. (1989) 77,000.

Railway engineering. Manufactures agricultural implements, textiles, chemicals.

Nubia Sudan/Egypt. Ancient state in NE Africa; region on both sides of the Nile from Aswan to Khartoum. Divided between the S of Egypt and the N of Sudan. Inc. part of the Nubian Desert and the Libyan Desert; no clearly defined boundaries. The only fertile area is the narrow irrigable strip along the Nile. Known under the Pharaohs as Cush. Incorporated in Egypt during the 18th dynasty; later formed part of Ethiopia.

Nubian Desert Sudan. A rocky barren waste in the NE between the Nile valley and the Red Sea. Mainly sandstone plateau, rising in the coastal range to over 2100 m (6888 ft). The surface is scored by many wadis.

Nuevo Laredo Mexico. Town in Tamaulipas state on the Rio Bravo opposite Laredo (Texas). Pop. (1990) 217,914. Point of entry for American tourists; starting point of the road via Monterrey to Mexico City.

Manufactures textiles. Flour-milling. Trade in agricultural produce.

Nuevo León Mexico. State in the NE with a narrow corridor bordering N on the Rio Bravo and the USA. Area 64,924 sq km (25,067 sq. miles). Pop. (1990) 3,086,466. Cap. and chief industrial centre Monterrey.

Largely mountainous; crossed by the Sierra Madre Oriental.

Sugar-cane is grown (in the N irrigated areas), also cotton, citrus fruit, tobacco, cereals cultivated. Gold, silver, lead and copper are among the leading minerals. Tourism is important and steel, plastics, glass, textiles and ceramics are manufactured.

Nuku'alofa ➤TONGA.

Nukuhiva ➤MARQUESAS ISLANDS.

Nukus Uzbekistan. Cap. of the Karakalpak Autonomous Republic at the head of the Amu Darya delta 800 km (500 miles) WNW of Tashkent. Pop. (1989) 169,000.

Manufactures cotton goods, clothing and footwear.

Nullarbor Plain Australia. Arid plain in SW South Australia and SE Western Australia, between the Great Victoria Desert and the Great Australian Bight, without trees (hence the name) or rivers. Extensive limestone areas with karst features. Vegetation consists largely of saltbush and supports only a few sheep. Crossed by the Trans-Australian Railway.

Numidia N Africa. Ancient kingdom, corresponding approximately to the NE of modern Algeria. After the 2nd Punic War it was united under Masinissa (previously ruler of E Numidia), who had supported Rome. His grandson Jugurtha fought the Romans and was defeated; the E then became a Roman province (Africa Nova) and the W was added to Mauretania. Prosperous under the Romans, with chief towns Cirta (➤CONSTANTINE) and Hippo Regius (modern Annaba). Invaded by the Vandals in the 5th cent. AD and by the Arabs in the 8th. Suffered decay and misgovernment until the French conquest of Algeria in the 19th cent.

Nunavut Canada. Territory established for Inuit (Eskimos) from Northwest Territories in 1999.

Nuneaton England. Town in Warwickshire on the R. Anker 13 km (8 miles) NNE of Coventry. Pop. (1986) 71,300.

Industries inc. light engineering, electronics, distribution services and the manufacture of textiles.

Has the remains of a 12th-cent. nunnery after which the town was named. Arbury, just SW, was the birthplace of George Eliot, the writer (1819–80).

Nuremberg (Ger. **Nürnberg**) Germany. City in Bavaria on the Pegnitz R. in the district of Middle Franconia. Pop. (1991) 493,692.

Industrial and commercial centre. Centre of the toy industry. Manufactures machinery, electrical equipment, precision instruments, office equipment, pencils. Brewing, distilling.

Before World War II it was famous for its medieval appearance, esp. its Gothic architecture, but many of its finest buildings were destroyed by bombing; among those badly damaged were the partly 14th-cent. town hall and the Albrecht Dürer house. The principal buildings have since been restored. Grew up round the 11th-cent. castle, and in the 15th and 16th cent. was a centre of art and culture; here the first pocket watches, known as 'Nuremberg eggs', were made. Under the Hitler regime the annual Nazi rallies were held here, the anti-Semitic 'Nuremberg laws' being decreed at the 1935 congress. In 1945–6 the Nazi leaders were tried here for their war crimes.

Nutley USA. Town in New Jersey 11 km (7 miles) N of Newark. Pop. (1970) 32,099. Mainly residential.

Manufactures textiles, chemicals and paper.

Nuuk ➤GODTHAAB.

Nuwara Eliya Sri Lanka. Hill station in Central Province at 1890 m (6199 ft) 40 km (25 miles) SSE of Kandy. Pop. 15,000. Established as a resort by the British in the 1820s.

Nyasa, Lake ➤MALAWI, LAKE.

Nyasaland ➤MALAWI.

Nyika Plateau ➤MALAWI.

Nyiregyháza Hungary. Cap. of Szabolcs-Szatmár county 72 km (45 miles) ESE of Miskolc. Pop. (1991) 114,594.

Market town in a district producing tobacco, wine and fruits. Manufactures furniture, soap and cement; it is a tourist centre.

Nyköping Sweden. Cap. of Södermanland county on the Baltic coast 51 km (32 miles) ENE of Norrköping. Pop. (1992) 68,093.

Seaport and industrial centre. Manufactures textiles, furniture and machinery. Timber, wood-pulp, iron and zinc are exported.

Nymegen ➤NIJMEGEN.

Nysa River ➤NEISSE RIVER.

Nzwani Comoros. Formerly Anjouan. Island in the Mozambique Channel off NW Madagascar between Mayotte and Njazídja in the Indian Ocean. Area 424 sq km (164 sq. miles). Pop. (1991) 197,900. Chief town Mutsamuda. The island is hilly, rising to Mount Tingue.

The main products are coffee, vanilla, copra, essential oils, sweet potatoes and peanuts. Industries inc. sisal-processing and sugar-milling.

O

Oahu Hawaii. Island in the Hawaiian group NW of Molokai across the Kaiwi Channel and SE of Kauai across the Kauai Channel. Area 1601 sq km (618 sq. miles). Pop. (1990) 836,231. Chief towns Honolulu (Hawaiian cap.), Waipahu, Wahiawa, Kaneohe, Kailua and Lanikai. Mountains rise to Kaala, 1233 m (4066 ft) with fertile valleys. The most developed and commercially important island. Army and navy bases, esp. at Pearl Harbor.

Industries inc. sugar planting and processing, pineapple-growing and tourism.

Oakengates ▶TELFORD.

Oakham England. Market town in Rutland 27 km (17 miles) E of Leicester. Pop. (1991) 8691.

Industries inc. engineering and the manufacture of plastics, hosiery and footwear.

Ruins of a 12th-cent. castle. Birthplace of Titus Oates (1648–1705).

Oakland USA. Seaport and industrial centre in California, founded 1852 on the E shore of San Francisco Bay. Pop. (1990) 372,242. Connected with San Francisco by the San Francisco–Oakland Bay Bridge (over 13 km; 8 miles long, opened 1936). Naval air station and airport.

Industries inc. oil-refining, shipbuilding, sawmilling, food-processing, motor-car assembly and the manufacture of electrical equipment, glass, chemicals and computers. The residential district extends over the slopes of the Berkeley Hills, facing the Golden Gate and giving views of the bay.

Oak Park USA. Town in Illinois just W of Chicago. Pop. (1990) 55,006. Mainly residential. Some light industries. Birthplace of Ernest Hemingway (1899–1961).

Oak Ridge USA. Town in Tennessee 27 km (17 miles) WNW of Knoxville. Pop. (1990) 27,310. Site of the US Atomic Energy Commission: has the Oak Ridge National Laboratory and two uranium-processing plants. Established 1943. Its pop. exceeded 70,000 before the end of World War II, but afterwards declined.

Oakville Canada. Town in Ontario situated SW of Toronto. Pop. (1991) 114,700.

Industries inc. the manufacture of automobiles.

Oamaru New Zealand. Chief town and seaport of N Otago, South Island 96 km (60 miles) NNE of Dunedin. Pop. (1990) 12,500.

Exports grain, flour, limestone. Woollen and flour milling, engineering.

Oaxaca (Oaxaca de Juárez) Mexico. 1. State in the S on the Pacific coast. Area 93,952 sq km (36,375 sq. miles). Pop. (1990) 3,019,560. Mainly mountainous, rising to 3399 m (11,149 ft) in Zempoaltépetl. Fertile valleys. Rice, maize, cotton, coffee, tobacco cultivated. Stock-rearing important.

2. Cap. of Oaxaca state in the Atoyac R. valley, at a height of 1640 m (5000 ft). Pop. (1990) 212,943 (mainly Mixtec and Zapotec Indians). Industries inc. textile manufacture and Indian handicrafts, esp. pottery, leather goods.

Founded by the Aztecs in 1486. Noteworthy Spanish-colonial architecture.

Oban Scotland. Tourist resort in Argyll and Bute on the Firth of Lorne. Pop. (1991) 8203. Port. Built around Oban Bay, sheltered by Kerrera island. Roman Catholic cathedral. Ruins of Dunollie Castle; 5 km (3 miles) NE are those of Dunstaffnage Castle.

Obeid, El Sudan. Cap. of the Kordofan

province 354 km (220 miles) SW of Khartoum. Pop. (1983) 140,024. Linked by railway (via Wad Medani, Sennar Junction and Er Rahad) with Khartoum.

Trading centre for gum arabic, cereals and cattle.

Scene of the defeat of the Egyptian forces by the Mahdi (1883); largely destroyed but later rebuilt.

Oberammergau Germany. Village in Bavaria on the Ammer R. in the foothills of the Bavarian Alps 74 km (43 miles) SSW of Munich. Pop. (1989) 4980.

Resort and winter-sports centre. Sawmilling and wood-carving.

Chiefly famous for the Passion play performed by the inhabitants every 10 years; this was instituted in 1634 as a thanksgiving for the ending of the plague known as the Black Death.

Obergurgl Austria. Winter sports and tourist centre in the Tyrol situated 50 km (31 miles) SW of Innsbruck, at 1927 m (6322 ft). Pop. (1990) 400.

Oberhausen Germany. Industrial town in North Rhine-Westphalia in the Ruhr district just NE of Duisburg on the Rhine–Herne Canal. Pop. (1991) 223,840.

Former important coalmining centre. Zinc-smelting and oil-refining. Manufactures iron and steel, chemicals, glass, soap and new media technology.

It was founded in 1862. A vast new complex *Die Neue Mitte* on a 100-ha (247-acre) site is being built on industrial wasteland in the heart of the city.

Oberösterreich ►UPPER AUSTRIA.

Ob River Russia. River of W Siberia. The river system is 5570 km (3460 miles) long, formed by the union of the Biya and Katun rivers, both rising in the Altai Mountains and joining near Biisk. It flows generally NW and N across the W Siberian Plain to the vast Gulf of Ob, about 800 km (500 miles) long, to enter the Arctic Ocean; its drainage basin covers well over 2,430,000 sq km (938,000 sq. miles). It is navigable for most of its length,

as also are its chief tributaries, the Irtysh, Chulym and Tom. The principal towns on its banks are Barnaul and Novosibirsk. It is a major source of hydroelectricity. In the spring its upper reaches thaw while the lower reaches are still frozen, so that large areas of coniferous forest land are flooded.

Obwalden Switzerland. Half canton comprising the W part of Unterwalden canton. Area 491 sq km (189 sq. miles). Pop. (1991) 21,813. ►UNTERWALDEN.

Oceania. A rather ambiguous term generally applied to the islands of the Pacific Ocean which are inc. in Polynesia, Melanesia, Micronesia and Australasia. Sometimes held to inc. also the Philippines and Indonesia, sometimes to be simply equivalent to Australasia.

Ocean (Banaba) Island Kiribati. Small island W of the Gilbert Islands in the SW Pacific Ocean. Area 5 sq km (2 sq. miles). Pop. (1990) 284.

Exports phosphates. Spoilation caused by phosphate mining and general overcrowding led to the resettlement of many of the inhabitants in Fiji, Teraina, Tabuaeran and Kiritmati.

Ochil Hills Scotland. Range of volcanic origin 45 km (28 miles) long extending WSW–ENE from just NE of Stirling to the Firth of Tay. Highest peaks Ben Cleuch (721 m; 2365 ft), King's Seat (644 m; 2112 ft).

Oda Ghana. Town situated NNW of Winneba in Eastern Region. Pop. (1985) 42,000. Diamond-mining centre.

Odense Denmark. Cap. of Odense county on the Odense R. in the N of Fyn island. Pop. (1990) 138,996. Port, with a ship canal to Odense Fiord.

Exports dairy produce, bacon. Industries inc. sugar-refining, shipbuilding, flour-milling and brewing. Manufactures machinery, textiles and glass.

Founded in the 10th cent. Cathedral (rebuilt in the 13th cent.). Birthplace of Hans Christian Andersen (1805–75).

Odenwald Germany. Wooded range of

hills S of the Main R. extending about 80 km (50 miles) W–E, mainly in Hessen. Highest point Katzenbuckel (626 m; 2053 ft).

Oder (Czech and Polish **Odra**) **River.** River 901 km (560 miles) long, rising near the SE end of the Sudeten Mountains in Moravia, Czech Republic, flowing generally NE through the Moravian Gate into Poland. It turns NW past Wroclaw, then N, to enter the Baltic Sea by the Stettiner Haff; N of its confluence with the lusatian Neisse it forms part of the boundary between Germany and Poland. Connected by canals with the Katowice industrial region and with the Havel, Spree and Vistula rivers. Chief tributaries the two Neisse rivers and the Warthe. An important commercial waterway, esp. below Wroclaw.

Odessa USA. Town in W Texas 480 km (300 miles) WSW of Fort Worth. Pop. (1990) 89,699.

Important centre of the oil industry. Oil-refining. Manufactures oilfield equipment, chemicals, synthetic rubber and carbon black. Trade in livestock.

Expanded rapidly after the discovery of oil in the 1920s.

Odessa (Odesa) Ukraine. Cap. of the Odessa region and Black Sea port. Pop. (1991) 1,101,000.

Exports grain, timber, wood and sugar. Also an industrial centre. Industries inc. sugar and oil refining, flour-milling, and it manufactures agricultural machinery, machine-tools, chemicals and bricks.

Situated on a low plateau facing the sea and has broad, tree-lined streets. Along the coast nearby there are several health resorts. Founded on the site of a Greek colony, Odessos, after which it was named. Became Russian 1795. Developed rapidly in the 19th cent. as the chief Russian grain-exporting port. Its inhabitants, along with the mutineers of the battleship *Potemkin*, were involved in the 1905 revolution. In World War II it was besieged and taken by German and Romanian forces (1941) and suffered severely during the occupation.

Odra River ➤ODER RIVER.

Oeno Island ➤PITCAIRN ISLAND.

Offaly Ireland. Formerly King's County. Inland county in Leinster province. Area 1998 sq km (771 sq. miles). Pop. (1991) 54,448. County town Tullamore. Generally low-lying, with part of the Bog of Allen in the NE and the Slieve Bloom Mountains in the SE. Drained by the Shannon (on the W boundary), Barrow, Nore and Brosna rivers. Crossed by the Grand Canal.

Cattle raised. Potatoes, barley, turnips cultivated. Chief towns Tullamore, Birr, Portarlington. In the NW is Clonmacnoise.

Offa's Dyke England. Earth and stone rampart extending from the mouth of the R. Dee to the R. Severn near Chepstow, believed to have been built by Offa, King of Mercia, in the 8th cent. as a boundary between the English and Welsh. Parts still form the border between the two countries.

Offenbach am Main Germany. Industrial town in Hessen on the Main R. on the outskirts of Frankfurt. Pop. (1991) 114,992.

Chief centre of the leather industry (footwear, luggage and handbags). Manufactures machinery, metal goods and chemicals. Has a unique leather museum and an annual leather fair.

Its development was largely due to the influx of Huguenots in the late 17th cent.

Ogaden Ethiopia. Area in SE bounded E and S by Somalia. It is an arid plateau at 457–914 m (1500–3000 ft). It is watered by intermittent rivers and nomadic farming is the main occupation.

Ogbomosho Nigeria. Town and state capital in the W 209 km (130 miles) NE of Lagos in Oyo state. Pop. (1992) 660,600.

In an agricultural district producing yams, cassava and cotton. Cotton-weaving.

Founded in the 17th cent., it is a traditional Yoruba tribal town.

Ogden USA. Town and railway junction in N Utah 53 km (33 miles) N of Salt Lake City. Pop. (1990) 63,909.

Industries inc. meat-packing and food-processing. Manufactures clothing and cement.

Settled by the Mormons 1847. Developed after the completion of the Union Pacific Railway (1869).

Ogooué (Ogowé) River. River 1094 km (680 miles) long, rising on the Baleke plateau in Congo, flowing generally NW and W through a densely forested region in Gabon, draining a number of lakes in the lower course and entering the Atlantic Ocean by a delta near Cape Lopez and Port Gentil. Chief tributaries the Lolo and the Ivindo. Navigable throughout the year below Lambaréné. Important timber trade along the lower course.

Ogun Nigeria. State formed from the Abeokuta and Ijebu provinces of the former W region. Area 16,762 sq km (6472 sq. miles). Pop. (1991) 2,338,570. Inhabitants primarily of the Egba, Egbado and Ijebu sub-divisions of the Yoruba people. Main towns Abeokuta (cap.), Ijebu-Ode and Shagamu.

Ohio USA. State bordering on L. Erie in the N. Area 115,998 sq km (44,787 sq. miles). Pop. (1992) 11,016,000. Cap. Columbus. Along the S boundary is the Ohio R.; a range of hills running WSW from the NE corner forms a watershed between the Allegheny Mountains to the E and the prairies to the W. Climate humid continental (cold winters, warm summers) but less extreme round the shores of L. Erie. Annual rainfall 75–100 cm (30–40 ins.).

Agriculture important. Chief crops maize, wheat, oats, soya beans (largely fed to livestock; cattle, pigs and wool-bearing sheep). Coal is the outstanding mineral. A leading industrial state. Manufactures iron and steel, machinery, rubber products (tyres, inner tubes), motor vehicles and parts, paper. Industries centred on Cleveland, Cincinnati, Columbus, Toledo, Akron, Dayton, Youngstown, Canton.

Ceded to Britain in 1763 and to the USA in 1783. Became part of the Northwest Territory 1787. Admitted to the Union in 1803 as the 17th state.

Ohio River USA. River 1577 km (980 miles) long, principal E tributary of the Mississippi, formed by the union of the Allegheny and Monongahela rivers at Pittsburgh (Pennsylvania), flowing generally SW, and joining the Mississippi at Cairo (Illinois). Navigable from 160 km (100 miles) below Pittsburgh. The tributaries from the N inc. the Miami, Scioto, Beaver, Muskingum and Wabash, and from the S the Big Sandy, Licking, Kentucky, Salt, Green, Cumberland and Tennessee. Lost much trade to the railways, but still carries considerable cargoes of coal, coke, cement and sand. Dams, reservoirs and levees have been constructed as a protection against floods, which were especially destructive in 1913, 1936, 1937 and 1993.

Ohrid Macedonia. Town on the NE shore of L. Ohrid. Pop. (1985) 65,000.

Commercial and fishing centre. Important tourist resort.

Turkish in appearance. Originally a Greek colony; settled by Slavs in the 9th cent. The most famous building is the 11th-cent Church of St Sophia.

Ohrid, Lake Albania/Macedonia. Lake on the Macedonian/Albanian border at a height of 695 m (2280 ft) and exceptionally deep (maximum 286 m; 938 ft); 31 km (19 miles) long and 13 km (8 miles) wide. Famed for the unusual clarity of its water (sometimes down to 20 m; 66 ft), its scenic beauty, its fishing and the many historic churches and monasteries on its shores. On its NE shore is the town of Ohrid.

Oil Islands ➤CHAGOS ARCHIPELAGO.

Oise France. Department in the N forming parts of the Île-de-France and Picardy. Area 5860 sq km (2263 sq. miles). Pop. (1991) 548,300. Prefecture Beauvais. Mostly low-lying; large areas of woodland inc. the Forest of Compiègne. Forms much of the lower basin of the Oise R.

Wheat, sugar-beet, fodder crops, fruits cultivated. Cattle-rearing and dairy-farming important. Racing stables in the Chantilly district. Chief towns Beauvais, Compiègne.

Oise River France. River 302 km (188 miles) long, rising in the Belgian Ardennes and flowing generally SW into France, past Compiègne, joining the Seine R. just below Pontoise. Navigable upstream to Noyon, thence paralleled by a lateral canal. Also linked by canals with the Somme, Scheldt (Escaut) and Sambre rivers. Chief tributary the Aisne R.

Oita Japan. Cap. of Oita prefecture on the NE coast of Kyushu. Pop. (1991) 412,860.
Industrial town and minor seaport. Manufactures metal goods and paper.

Ojos del Salado Chile/Argentina. Mountain peak in the Andes situated WSW of Cerro Incahuasi at 6908 m (22,664 ft) above sea level. The second highest peak in the W hemisphere, after Aconcagua, situated on the Chile/Argentina frontier.

Okanagan, Lake Canada. Long (113 km; 70 miles), narrow lake in S British Columbia, drained S by the Okanagan R., a tributary of the Columbia R. The Okanagan valley is famous for fruit-growing (esp. apples), the chief town being Penticton.

Oka River (Irkutsk) Russia. River 800 km (500 miles) long in the Irkutsk region, rising in the E Sayan Mountains and flowing generally N to join the Angara R.

Oka River (Kursk) Russia. River 1450 km (900 miles) long, rising in the Kursk region and flowing N past Orel, then E and NE past Kaluga, Serpukhov, Komomna and Ryazan to join the Volga R., of which it is the chief right-bank tributary. Main tributaries the Moskva and the Klyazma. Although frozen for 5 months or more annually, it is an important waterway, esp. for wheat and timber.

Okavango (Okovango) River. River 1600 km (1000 miles) long, rising on the Bié Plateau in Angola as the Cubango R., flowing generally SE to the Namibian border and across the Caprivi strip, and entering the Okavango Swamp N of L. Ngami in Botswana.

Okayama Japan Cap. of Okayama prefecture, SW Honshu on the Inland Sea 113 km (70 miles) W of Kobe. Pop. (1991) 597,238. Port. Industrial town.
Manufactures agricultural implements, cotton goods, porcelain and chemicals.

Okazaki Japan. Town in Aichi prefecture, Honshu 32 km (20 miles) SE of Nagoya. Pop. (1991) 311,906.
Manufactures textiles, chemicals, machinery.
Grew up around the 15th-cent. castle.

Okeechobee, Lake USA. Lake 56 km (35 miles) long and 51 km (32 miles) wide in S Florida; the second largest freshwater lake entirely in the USA. Receives the Kissimmee R. from the N. Drains to the Atlantic through the Everglades.

Okefenokee Swamp USA. Swamp mainly in SE Georgia but partly in NE Florida. Area about 1550 sq km (600 sq. miles). Much of it is in the Okefenokee National Wildlife Refuge (established 1937). Alligators, deer, bears, raccoons, snakes and many species of birds (inc. the ibis).

Okehampton England. Market town in Devon on the N side of Dartmoor 34 km (21 miles) W of Exeter. Pop. (1991) 4688. 7 km (4½ miles) S is High Willhays, the highest point on Dartmoor (621 m; 2037 ft).

Okhida, Okhrida ►OHRID.

Okhotsk, Sea of. Arm of the NW Pacific Ocean on the E coast of Siberia and almost enclosed by the Kamchatka peninsula, the Kuril Is. and Sakhalin. Area 1,554,000 sq km (600,000 sq. miles). Icebound in the N Nov.–May.

Okinawa Japan. Largest of the Ryukyu Is. 531 km (330 miles) SSW of Kyushu. Area 2264 sq km (874 sq. miles). Pop. (1990) 1,229,000. Cap. Naha City.
Sugar-cane, rice and sweet potatoes cultivated.
During World War II it was the scene of

bitter fighting between American and Japanese forces (1945). Reverted to Japan 1972.

Oklahoma USA. State in the S, with the Red R. along the S boundary and the 'panhandle' in the NW. Area 181,185 sq km (69,956 sq. miles). Pop. (1990) 3,212,000. Cap. Oklahoma City. Mainly plains, sloping downwards from the NW (where the Black Mesa rises to 1518 m; 4979 ft) to the SE. Parts of the Boston and Ouachita Mountains in the E. Drained chiefly by the Arkansas R. and its tributaries the Cimarron, the North Canadian and the Canadian. Climate continental; cool winters, hot summers and a generally light rainfall, increasing W–E. Originally cattle country.

The main occupation is now agriculture, though cattle-rearing is still important. Chief crops winter wheat, sorghum, cotton. Rich in minerals, esp. petroleum and natural gas. Principal industry oil-refining. Largest cities Oklahoma City and Tulsa.

First explored by the Spaniards. Passed from France to the USA under the Louisiana Purchase (1803). Before the American Civil War most of Oklahoma was known as 'the Indian Territory'; a large area was opened to white settlers in 1889, some of whom, having illegally entered ahead of time, were called 'Sooners' (hence the popular name). Admitted to the Union in 1907 as the 46th state.

Oklahoma City USA. State cap. of Oklahoma on the N Canadian R. at a height of 360 m (1180 ft). Pop. (1990) 444,719.

Industrial and commercial centre in an agricultural and oil-producing region. Oil-refining, flour-milling, meat-packing, printing, publishing, food-processing and the manufacture of petrochemicals, oilfield equipment and aircraft.

Founded 1889 as a pioneer city, acquiring a pop. of about 10,000 (under tents) in a single day.

Olafsjordur Iceland. Town situated NE of Reykjavik on a SW arm of Eyja Fjord. Pop. (1988) 1179. Fishing port.

Öland Island Sweden. Long, narrow island in Kalmar county in the Baltic Sea, separated from the mainland by Kalmar Sound (5–29 km; 3–18 miles wide). Area 1347 sq km (520 sq. miles). Pop. (1985) 22,500. Chief town Borgholm.

Farming and limestone-quarrying are important occupations. Popular with tourists in the summer.

Borgholm has the ruins of a 13th-cent. castle.

Oldbury England. Town situated WNW of Birmingham in West Midlands. Pop. (1981) 46,450.

Manufactures iron, steel, aluminium, machinery, chemicals and glass.

Oldenburg Germany. 1. Former *Land*, since World War II part of Lower Saxony. Area 5398 sq km (2084 sq. miles). Before 1937 it consisted of three parts: Oldenburg proper, an enclave on the North Sea in Hanover province; Birkenfeld, an enclave in Rhine province, Lübeck district. Birkenfeld and Lübeck districts became part of Prussia 1937. A county in the 11th cent. In 1448 Count Christian became king of Denmark. Became a grand duchy 1815. Joined the German Empire 1871. Its cap. was Oldenburg.

2. Former cap. of the Oldenburg *Land*, in Lower Saxony on the Hunte R. 42 km (26 miles) WNW of Bremen. Pop. (1991) 143,131.

Market town. Railway junction. Manufactures textiles, dyes, ceramics and glass, and there is food-processing.

Oldham England. Town and unitary authority 10 km (6 miles) NE of Manchester. Pop. (1991) 103,931.

Important centre of the cotton industry, esp. spinning. Also manufactures textile and other machinery, electrical equipment, plastics, clothing. Linen-weaving was introduced in the early 17th cent. to be followed by cotton in the 18th cent. and the town prospered with mechanization. With the decline of the cotton trade in the present cent., the earlier specialization proved a liability.

Olekma River Russia. River 1130 km (700 miles) long, rising in the Yablonovy Range and flowing generally N through the N Chita region and the Yakut Autononomos Region and joining the Lena R. below Olekminsk. The basin is important for goldmining.

Oléron France. Island in the Bay of Biscay in the Charente-Maritime department opposite the mouth of the Charente R., separated from the mainland by the narrow Pertuis de Maumusson. Area 176 sq km (68 sq. miles). Pop. (1985) 16,000.

Oyster beds. Produces early vegetables. Chief towns Le Chateau d'Oléron and St Pierre.

Olímbos ➤OLYMPUS.

Olives, Mount of (Olivet) Jordan. Ridge 817 m (2680 ft) high just E of the Old City of Jerusalem, separated from it by the valley of Kidron. At its foot is the Garden of Gethsemane.

Olmütz ➤OLOMOUC.

Olney England. Market town in Buckinghamshire on the R. Ouse 16 km (10 miles) WNW of Bedford. Pop. (1991) 4484.

William Cowper, the poet, lived here (1767–86) and assisted John Newton, the curate, in writing the *Olney Hymns*.

Olomouc (Ger. **Olmütz**) Czech Republic. Industrial town in Moravia on the Morava R. 66 km (41 miles) NE of Brno. Pop. (1991) 105,690.

Manufactures malt, sugar, beer, confectionery, agricultural machinery and cement.

Among historic buildings are the 14th-cent. Gothic cathedral (restored) and the 15th-cent. town hall with its astronomical clock.

Olsztyn (Ger. **Allenstein**) Poland. Cap. of the Olsztyn voivodeship in the NE 142 km (88 miles) ESE of Gdańsk. Pop. (1992) 163,900. Before 1945 in E Prussia.

Manufactures machinery, leather.

Founded by the Teutonic Knights in the 14th cent.

Olt River Romania. Rises E of Georgheni and flows 557 km (348 miles) S past Sfgntu-Gheorghe, then W past Fagaros and S

through the Turnu-Rosu Pass in the Transylvanian Alps to enter Danube R. S of Turnu-Magurele and opposite Nikpol (Bulgaria). Used for logging.

Olympia Greece. Ancient city in Elis in the W Peloponnese at the confluence of the Cladeus R. with the Alpheus R. 68 km (42 miles) S of Patras. Site of the ruined temple of Zeus, with the statue of Zeus by Pheidias (destroyed), one of the Seven Wonders of the World. Founded *c.* 1000 BC, scene of the Olympic Games, held every 4 years from 776 BC. Nearby is the modern village of Olympia, with a museum containing many famous sculptures, inc. the Hermes of Praxiteles.

Olympia USA. State cap. of Washington, founded 1850, at the S end of Puget Sound. Pop. (1989) 30,000. Seaport.

Exports timber and fish (esp. oysters).

Olympus (Gr. **Olímbos**) Greece. Mountain ridge near the Aegean coast on the border between Thessaly and Macedonia, rising to 2913 m (9555 ft), the country's highest summit. Snow-capped for much of the year. Traditional home of the gods, esp. of Zeus.

Olympus, Mount ➤CYPRUS AND GREECE.

Omagh Northern Ireland. Market town in Co. Tyrone on the R. Strule 43 km (27 miles) S of Londonderry. Pop. (1991) 17,280.

Trade in cattle, potatoes and oats. Manufactures milk products.

Omaha USA. Largest city in Nebraska on the Missouri R., founded 1854. Pop. (1990) 335,795.

Railway junction. Lead-smelting, oil-refining, meat-packing. Manufactures agricultural machinery, paints and beverages.

It was named after the Omaha Indians. Originally developed as a river port, but trade now depends much more on the railways.

Oman. Independent sultanate in E Arabia, bounded NE by the Gulf of Oman, SE by the Arabian Sea, SW by Yemen and NW by Saudi Arabia and the United Arab Emirates. It is divided into 7 planning regions,

Nuscat, Janubiah, Dakhiliah, Sharqihay, Batinah, Dhahirah and Musandam. Area 306,000 sq km (118,150 sq. miles). Pop. (1995) 2,163,000 (13 per cent urban). Life expectancy, 68 years males, 72 females. Cap. Muscat. Other towns Nizwa, Samail and Salalah. Currency: Omani rial = 1000 baizas.

There is a fertile coastal plain NW of Muscat town. The interior, which is generally arid, consists of a plateau and a mountain range extending NW–SE and rising in some peaks to over 2700 m (8856 ft). It has a desert climate with exceptionally hot and humid months from April to October. Land use: meadows and pastures 5 per cent, agricultural and under permanent cultivation 0.3 per cent. Omani Arabs comprise 74 per cent of the pop., Pakistani (mainly Baluchi) 21 per cent. The religion is Muslim.

The dominant industry is oil. Production began in 1967 and provides over 80 per cent of the government revenue. Other industries inc. refining copper. The largest non-oil export is fish.

Oman was dominated by Portugal from 1507 to 1649. The Al-Busaid family assumed power in 1744 and are still in power. In 1970 the then Sultan was deposed by his son Qaboos who has brought about many reforms and social developments. Oman is an absolute monarchy and there is no formal Constitution. The Sultan legislates by decree and appoints a Cabinet to assist him.

Oman, Gulf of. Arm of the Arabian Sea in the NW 480 km (300 miles) long, between Oman and Iran, leading through the Strait of Hormuz to the Persian Gulf.

Omdurman Sudan. Town 8 km (5 miles) NW of Khartoum, with which it is connected by a bridge across the White Nile. Pop. (1983) 528,287. Famous for native markets.

Trade in hides, gum arabic, livestock.

The Mahdi made Omdurman (then a village) his cap. in 1884; his successor the Khalifa was utterly defeated by Anglo–Egyptian forces (under Lord Kitchener) at the Battle of Omdurman (1898). The Mahdi's tomb was destroyed, but rebuilt in 1947.

Omsk Russia. Cap. of the Omsk region at the confluence of the Irtysh R. and the Om R. and on the Trans-Siberian Railway 600 km (375 miles) W of Novosibirsk. Pop. (1991) 1,166,000. In a flat treeless steppe.

Industrial and route centre. Manufactures agricultural and other machinery, locomotives, synthetic rubber, tyres, motor vehicles and other industries inc. food-processing and brewing. Also an important oil-refining centre, being the terminus of one of the country's longest pipelines from Tuimazy, completed in 1955.

Founded (1716) as a fortress. Expanded rapidly with the advent of the railway and again in World War II.

Omuta Japan. Port and industrial town in Fukuoka prefecture, W Kyushu 56 km (35 miles) S of Fukuoka. Pop. (1991) 149,214.

In a coalmining region. Exports coal. Zinc-refining. Manufactures chemicals, machinery, cotton goods and dyes.

Ondo Nigeria. State, formerly the Ondo province of West Region. Area 20,959 sq km (8092 sq. miles). Pop. (1991) 3,884,485. Cap. Akure, other towns Ado-Ekiti, Ikerre-Ekiti, Owo, Ondo, Effon-Alaiye, Oka-Akoko and Ikare.

Onega, Lake Russia. Second largest lake in Europe mainly in the Karelia Republic. Area 9600 sq km (3705 sq. miles). The N coast is much broken. Many islands. Drains into L. Ladoga via the Svir R. Connected to canals with the Volga R. and the White Sea. Frozen from about mid Dec. to mid May. Greatest depth 124 m (407 ft). Principal town on the shores Petrozovodsk (W). Large quantities of fish are caught.

Onega Bay (Onega Gulf) Russia. Inlet of the White Sea (SW) 177 km (110 miles) long and up to 80 km (50 miles) wide. At its head (SE), at the mouth of the Onega R. (not connected with L. Onega), is the small seaport of Onega.

It exports timber, and has a sawmilling industry.

Onitsha Nigeria. Town in the S on the left

bank of the Niger R. 72 km (45 miles) WSW of Enugu. Pop. (1992) 336,600.

Commercial centre. Trades in cassava, maize, palm oil and kernels, yams.

Onotoa Kiribati. (Formerly Clark Is.). Atoll in S Gilbert Group, W Pacific Ocean. Pop. (1990) 2112. Chief product copra.

Ontario Canada. Province in central Canada lying between Hudson Bay and James Bay (N) and the Great Lakes (S). Area 1,068,590 sq km (412,582 sq. miles). Pop. (1991) 9,906,400. Cap. Toronto (second largest city in Canada). The province extends 1690 km (1050 miles) N–S and 1600 km (1000 miles) W–E, with the great majority of the pop. concentrated in the SE between the Great Lakes, the St Lawrence R. and the Ottawa R. To the N it slopes down to the sparsely inhabited lowlands around Hudson Bay and James Bay. Numerous rivers and lakes. Apart from the Great Lakes (none of which lies wholly in Ontario), the largest are L. Nipigon, the Lake of the Woods (shared with Manitoba and Minnesota (USA)), L. Seul, L. Nipissing and L. Abitibi. Owing to the great range of lat., the climate is extremely varied, but in general it is continental, with quite severe winters and warm or hot summers, though in the S it is tempered by proximity to the Great Lakes. Annual rainfall 50–100 cm (20–40 ins.) (with considerable depths of snow in winter). About two-thirds of the province is covered by forests; both softwood and hardwood timber are produced, and wood-pulp and paper manufacture are important.

Principal crops in the S are cereals, fruit, vegetables, tobacco. Dairying and stock-rearing important. In mineral production Ontario is Canada's leading province: nickel, copper, uranium, gold and zinc. Mining employs 24,000. Ontario is Canada's most highly industrialized province with abundant hydroelectric power. Highly diversified industries. Meat-packing, flour-milling, and cheese and butter making depend on agriculture. Also manufactures cars, machinery, railway equipment and textiles. Toronto, Hamilton, London and Windsor (the main

industrial centres) are all in the tapering peninsula between L. Ontario, L. Erie and L. Huron; Hamilton and Toronto are important lake ports. On the Ottawa R. is Ottawa, the federal cap.

The interior was first explored in 1613 by Champlain; fur traders and missionaries followed. The territory was ceded by France to Britain in 1763. By the constitution of 1791 Canada was divided into Upper Canada (Ontario) and Lower Canada (Quebec); the two were united 1840–67, but Ontario then became one of the four original provinces of the confederation. The boundaries were extended to Hudson Bay in 1912.

Ontario USA. Town in South Carolina 53 km (33 miles) E of Los Angeles. Pop. (1990) 113,179.

Commercial centre in a region producing vines, citrus fruits. Manufactures aircraft parts and electrical equipment.

Ontario, Lake Canada/USA. The smallest and most easterly of the Great Lakes, elliptical in shape, at a height of 75 m (246 ft) above mean sea level. Area 19,230 sq km (7425 sq. miles). Connected (SW) with L. Erie through the Niagara R., by which it receives water from the other Great Lakes; the Niagara Falls are circumvented by the Welland Canal. Discharges (NE) into the St Lawrence R. and so to the Atlantic. Main ports Hamilton, Toronto, Cobourg and Kingston in Ontario (Canada), Rochester and Oswego in New York (USA). Main cargoes coal, grain and timber. The lake freezes only near the shore, but harbours are closed from mid Dec. to mid April. Its greatest depth is 237 m (778 ft.). Along the SW shore there is a noted fruit-growing district. Discovered (1615) by Étienne Brûlé.

Oostende ►OSTEND.

Oosterhout Netherlands. Town in N Brabant province 10 km (6 miles) NNE of Breda. Pop. (1992) 49,036.

Manufactures footwear and tobacco products.

Ootacamund India. Hill station in Tamil

Nadu in the Nilgiri Hills at a height of 2200 m (7216 ft). Pop. (1971) 63,003. Has a mean annual temperature of 15°C (59°F). Also noted for hunting and fishing. Cinchona and tea plantations near by. Popularly known as Ooty.

Opatija (Abbazia) Croatia. Town on the Kvarner Gulf 11 km (7 miles) W of Rijeka. Pop. (1971) 27,118. Popular seaside resort, picturesquely situated at the foot of Mt Učka (1350 m; 4430 ft). Belonged to Austria; ceded to Italy (1924), then to Yugoslavia (1947).

Opava (Ger. **Troppau**) Czech Republic. Industrial town in the Severomoravsky region on the Opava R. 29 km (18 miles) WNW of Ostrava. Pop. (1974) 52,000.

Manufactures textiles and knitwear, and there is sugar-refining and brewing.

Founded in the 13th cent. It was formerly cap. of Austrian Silesia.

Opole (Ger. **Oppeln**) Poland. Cap. of the Opole voivodeship in the S on the Oder R. 85 km (53 miles) SE of Wroclaw. Pop. (1992) 128,900.

Industrial and commercial town. Manufactures cement, lime, chemicals and soap. Industries inc. brewing and flour-milling. Trade in grain and livestock.

Cap. of the duchy of Oppeln 1163–1532; passed to Austria and then to Prussia (1742). Cap. of the German province of Upper Silesia 1919–45.

Oporto (Portuguese **Pôrto**) Portugal. Second largest city in Portugal and port on the Douro R. 5 km (3 miles) above the mouth. Pop. (1991) 310,640. Artificial harbour for large vessels at Leixões 8 km (5 miles) NW on the Atlantic.

Famous for port wine, shipped largely to Britain; also exports fruits, olive oil and cork. Industries inc. chemicals, metals, silk, electrical and electronic equipment, tyres, leather goods, soap and footwear.

Built above the Douro gorge, largely in granite and is connected by the double-deck Dom Luis I bridge (1881–5) with its S suburb, Vila Nova de Gaia, where vast quantities of wine are stored. An outstanding landmark is

the Torre dos Clerigos, a granite tower 74 m (243 ft) high; other buildings inc. the 14th-cent. cathedral (much modernized) and the 12th-cent. São Martinho church.

Orádea Romania. Cap. of the Bihor district in the NW on the Crişul Repede R. near the Hungarian frontier. Pop. (1992) 220,848. Railway junction.

Manufactures machinery, textiles, glass and pottery. Trade in livestock, fruit and wine.

An old town with a bishopric dating from 1080. Ceded to Romania by Hungary 1919.

Oran (Wahran) Algeria. Cap. of the Oran department, seaport and Algeria's second largest city on the Gulf of Oran (an inlet of the Mediterranean Sea). Pop. (1989) 664,000.

Chief exports wine, wheat, early vegetables (from the Tell Atlas), wool, esparto grass (from the High Plateaux). Industries inc. chemicals and cement, iron-smelting, food-processing, textiles, footwear, glass and cigarettes. Receives natural gas by pipeline from the Hassi R'Mel field. Linked by railway with Algiers and (via Tlemcen and Oujda) with Morocco.

Founded early in the 10th cent. A prosperous commercial centre in the 15th cent. Fell to the Spaniards 1509; except for a period in Turkish hands (1708–32), held by Spain till shortly after much of the town had been destroyed by earthquake (1790). In Turkish hands again, it was occupied by the French 1831. Expanded rapidly; the port was developed in the late 19th cent.

Orange Australia. Town on the Central Tableland of New South Wales 200 km (125 miles) WNW of Sydney. Pop. (1991) 29,640. Railway junction. Market town in sheep-farming and fruit-growing country.

Manufactures woollen goods.

Orange France. Town in the Vaucluse department 23 km (14 miles) N of Avignon. Pop. (1985) 25,000.

Minor industries.

Notable Roman remains, inc. a triumphal arch, a theatre and an amphitheatre. Once cap. of the small principality of Orange, to which was added through marriage the countship of Nassau in the 16th cent.; the descendants of the union became the Dutch royal family, the House of Orange.

Orange (California) USA. Town in the S 5 km (3 miles) N of Santa Ana. Pop. (1990) 110,658. In an orange-growing region (hence the name). Citrus-fruit packing.

Orange (New Jersey) USA. Industrial town 6 km (4 miles) NW of Newark. Pop. (1990) 30,000.
Manufactures chemicals, clothing and aircraft parts. With its neighbours East, West and South Orange and Maplewood, it is known as the Oranges.

Orange (Texas) USA. Port and industrial town 37 km (23 miles) E of Beaumont at the head of the Sabine R. waterway to the Gulf of Mexico. Pop. (1985) 25,000.
Boatbuilding. Manufactures chemicals and paper.

Orange Free State South Africa ➤FREE STATE.

Orange River. River 2092 km (1300 miles) long, the longest in South Africa, rising in the Drakensberg at Mont-aux-Sources, flowing SW through Lesotho, continuing generally W and NW and entering the Atlantic Ocean at Alexander Bay (where the mouth is obstructed by a sand bar). Principal tributaries the Vaal and the Caledon. In the winding lower course, passing through an arid region, it loses much water by evaporation. Below Upington it plunges 146 m (479 ft) over the Aughrabies Falls.

Oranjestad Aruba. Cap. and seaport. Pop. (1990) 20,000.
Oil-refining was the dominating industry, but tourism now the main economic sector.
It grew round a fort built by the Dutch to protect against British and Spanish invasion.

Oranjestad Netherlands Antilles. Port and cap. of the island of St Eustatius. Pop. (1990) 1250.

Orapa Botswana. Town and site of the world's second industrial diamond mine.

Pop. (1989) 5000. An important proportion of government income comes from this mine, which was discovered in 1967 and began production in 1971.

Ord River Australia. River 480 km (300 miles) long in the NE of Western Australia, flowing E and then N through rugged cattle country to Cambridge Gulf, near Wyndham.

Ordzhonikidze ➤VLADIKAVKAZ.

Örebro Sweden. Cap. of the Örebro county at the W end of L. Hjälmar. Pop. (1992) 122,756.
Railway junction. Centre of the country's shoe industry. Also manufactures paper and soap.
The town was established in the 11th cent. Its castle on an island in the Svarta R. has been the scene of many diets.

Oregon USA. State in the NW on the Pacific Ocean. Area 251,418 sq km (97,073 sq. miles). Pop. (1990) 2,842,321 (70.5 per cent urban). Cap. Salem. The Cascade Range, running N–S parallel to the coast divides it into two contrasting climatic zones. The W has a maritime temperate climate; the E is a larger dry upland region. Annual rainfall varies from 175 cm (70 ins.) or more in the coastal zone to 25–50 cm (10–20 ins.) in the dry zone. Famed for its mountain and lake scenery, the Cascade Range averages 1500–2100 m (4920–6888 ft) and inc. Mt Hood (3427 m; 11,241 ft) and Mt Jefferson (3200 m; 10,496 ft). Also running parallel to the coast is the Coast Range, which links up with the Cascades in the Klamath Mountains (S). In the NE are the Blue Mountains. The leading timber state, over 50 per cent of which is forested.
Agriculture important. E of the Cascades wheat-growing and stock-rearing predominate. To the W cereals, fruit and vegetables are the main crop; the Willamette valley is particularly noted for its orchards and market gardens. Industries are based on the processing of farm and forest produce. High technology is the second most important industry. Chief towns Portland, Eugene and Salem.

The Oregon country was jointly held by Britain and the USA 1818–46. Became a territory 1848. The pop. rapidly increased in the 1840s with the influx of settlers arriving by the Oregon Trail. Admitted to the Union in 1859 as the 33rd state.

Orekhovo-Zuyevo Russia. Town on the Klyazma R. 88 km (55 miles) E of Moscow. Pop. (1991) 136,800.

Railway junction. Important centre of the cotton industry. Also sawmilling and flour-milling.

Orel (Oryol) Russia. Cap. of the Orel region on the Oka R. 330 km (205 miles) SSW of Moscow. Pop. (1990) 342,000.

Road, railway and industrial centre. Iron-founding, flour-milling, meat-packing. Manufactures textile machinery. On the Moscow–Kharkov railway.

Founded 1564.

Orenburg Russia. Cap. of the Orenburg region on the Ural R. 338 km (210 miles) ESE of Samara. Pop. (1991) 556,500. Much increased in importance since the opening of the railway to Tashkent (1905).

A major agricultural and flour-milling centre. Trade in grain, hides, meat, wool, textiles and livestock. Industries inc. railway engineering, sawmilling, brewing and food-processing. Manufactures inc. metal goods and clothing.

Founded (1743) as a fortress.

Orense (Ourense) Spain. 1. Province in Galicia (NW) on the Portuguese border. Area 7278 sq km (2694 sq. miles). Pop. (1991) 350,458. Generally mountainous. Drained by the Miño R. and its tributaries.

Agriculture in the valleys: cereals, potatoes and flax cultivated; cattle reared.

2. Cap. of Orense province on the Miño R. 71 km (44 miles) ENE of Vigo. Pop. (1991) 101,623.

Sawmilling, tanning, flour-milling.

Has warm springs, known from Roman times and a remarkable 13th-cent. bridge over the river. Destroyed by the Moors in the 8th cent. Restored by Alfonso III of Asturias in the 9th cent.

Oresund ➤SOUND, THE.

Orihuela Spain. Town in Alicante province on the Segura R. in a fertile irrigated region 48 km (30 miles) SW of Alicante. Pop. (1991) 48,013.

Trade in fruit, olive oil, wine, cereals. Manufactures textiles, leather goods, and furniture.

Orinoco River Venezuela. One of the great rivers of South America, 2200 km (1370 miles) long, rising in the Serra Parima in the SE, following a C-shaped course, W, N and E, and entering the Atlantic by a wide delta through many banks and channels. In its middle course are the Atures and Maipures rapids. Linked by the 320-km (200-mile) Casiquiare with the Río Negro and Amazon. Navigable for small vessels to the Maipures rapids, about 1450 km (900 miles) from the mouth. Ciudad Bolívar is the main commercial centre for the Orinoco basin, but the flow is sometimes so reduced through seasonal variation that goods have to be transhipped at San Felix. Industrial development is taking place in the lower course near the Caroní R. junction. The Angostura suspension bridge linking Ciudad Bolívar and Soledad, the first across the river, was opened in 1967.

Orissa India. State in the E on the Bay of Bengal. Area 155,707 sq km (60,823 sq. miles). Pop. (1991) 31,592,070. Cap. Bhubaneswar. Partly hilly, with a coastal plain and the valley and delta of the Mahanadi R.

Chief occupations agriculture, about four-fifths of the pop. being engaged in rice cultivation. Other major crops are oil seeds, groundnut and soyabean. The state has taken massive plantation programmes. Extensive sal forests. Iron and manganese ores and coal mined. Bhubaneswar, Konarak and Puri are places of tourist interest. Industries inc. steel plant, fertilizers, paper, sponge iron and electronics. An oil refinery and a second steel plant are being established. Principal towns Cuttack and Bhubaneswar.

Fell in the Mogul conquest 1568. From the 14th cent. until 1592 Orissa was ruled by Muslim kings. Later passed to the Mahrattas

(1742) and the British (1803). In 1912 the province of Bihar and Orissa was created, but in 1936, owing to the intense nationalism of the Oriyas, Orissa became a separate province. Acceded to India 1947; enlarged by the addition of several native states (1949).

Orizaba Mexico. Town in Veracruz state 96 km (60 miles) WSW of Veracruz at a height of 1280 m (4198 ft). Pop. (1990) 113,516.

Chief centre of the textile industry. Also manufactures paper, tobacco products. Railway engineering, brewing. Trade in sugar, tobacco, coffee and maize. In magnificent scenery with the Pico de Orizaba (Citlaltépetl) 29 km (18 miles) N. A resort, with a mild healthy climate.

Orizaba, Pico de (Citlaltépetl) Mexico. In Nahuatl, 'Star Mountain'. Extinct snow-capped volcano 29 km (18 miles) N of Orizaba town; the highest peak in Mexico (5699 m, 18,697 ft). Last erupted in the 16th cent. First climbed 1848.

Orkney Islands Scotland. Group of about 15 main and many smaller islands, designated an Island Authority Area, separated from the mainland by Pentland Firth. Total area 976 sq km (377 sq. miles). Pop. (1991) 19,612. About 20 of the islands are inhabited. County town Kirkwall, only other burgh Stromness, both on Mainland. Principal islands Mainland (pop. 15,128), Westray (704), Sanday (533), Stronsay (382), South Ronaldsay (943) and Hoy (450). Generally low-lying and fertile. Hoy contains the only mountainous area (highest point 477 m; 1455 ft). Bleak and treeless, but the climate is relatively mild.

Agriculture (mainly beef cattle), fishing and aquaculture, food-processing, whisky-distilling and traditional crafts are the main occupations. Base for the exploitation of North Sea oil, with the Piper, Claymore, Saltire, Chanter and four other fields linked to the Flotta island terminal. Piper B platform was installed in 1992.

There are prehistoric remains inc. the standing stones at Stenness (Mainland). The islands were conquered by the Viking Harold

Haarfager (875) and remained under Norse rule until 1468, when they were pledged to James III of Scotland by Christian I of Denmark. Scapa Flow was a naval base in both World Wars, closing in 1957. The German fleet was scuppered here in 1919 rather than fall into British hands. The Orkney Islands Council of 24 elected members is responsible for all local government functions within the islands.

Orlando USA. Town in Florida 124 km (77 miles) ENE of Tampa. Pop. (1990) 164, 693.

Commercial centre for the surrounding citrus-fruit growing and market-gardening region. Fruit packing and canning. Manufactures machinery and clothing. Also a tourist resort and base for Cape Canaveral and Disney World.

Orléanais France. Region and former province on both sides of the Loire R., now forming Loiret and Loir-et-Cher and parts of Eure-et-Loir and Yonne departments. Included Beauce, Sologne and part of Gâtinais. The cap. was Orléans.

Orléans France. Ancient Genabum, Cenabum. Prefecture of the Loiret department on the Loire R. 113 km (70 miles) SSW of Paris. Pop. (1990) 107,965.

Important railway and road junction. Industries inc. food-processing, and it manufactures blankets, knitwear, machinery, tobacco products, vehicle parts and chemicals. Trade in wine and cereals from the surrounding agricultural region.

The old city lies along the right bank of the river and is surrounded by boulevards, beyond which are the modern suburbs. The Cathedral of Ste Croix, destroyed by Huguenots in 1567, rebuilt in the 17th-19th cent., was severely damaged in World War II; among the old houses are those of Diane de Poitiers and Joan of Arc. In the 7th cent. it became the chief residence, after Paris, of the French kings. In 1428-9 it was besieged by the English and Burgundians and was relieved by Joan of Arc – an event celebrated annually in the city. Became the Huguenot headquarters and was again besieged (1563) by the Catholics under Francis, Duke of Guise, who was assassinated here.

Orly France. Suburb of Paris in Val-de-Marne department containing a Paris international airport.

Ormskirk England. Town in SW Lancashire 19 km (12 miles) NNE of Liverpool. Pop. (1991) 23,425.

In a potato-growing district. Metalworking, flour-milling.

Nearby are the remains of the 12th-cent. Burscough Priory.

Orne France. Inland department in Basse-Normandie region, named after the Orne R. Area 6103 sq km (2356 sq. miles). Pop. (1991) 292,900. Prefecture Alençon. Undulating, crossed by the Normandy and Perche Hills, rising to 417 m (1368 ft) in the Forest of Écouves. Noted for the powerful Percheron horses, bred here; products inc. cereals, cider apples, Camembert cheese. Chief towns Alençon, Flers, Bagnoles (spa).

Orontes River. River in SW Asia 370 km (230 miles) long, rising near Baalbek (Lebanon) and flowing generally N past Homs and Hama (Syria), turning SW past Antioch (Antakya) in Turkey to the Mediterranean Sea. Unnavigable, but used for irrigation, esp. in Syria, where large wooden water-wheels (*norias*) driven by the current are used to raise and distribute the river water.

Oroya (La Oroya) Peru. Town in Junín department in the Andes at a height of 3720 m (12,202 ft) at the confluence of the Mantaro and Yauli rivers 120 km (75 miles) ENE of Lima, to which it is connected by rail and road. Pop. (1972) 25,900.

Important metallurgical centre (copper, zinc, lead, silver); smelting, copper-refining. Ores brought from Cerro de Pasco and other mining centres.

Orpington England. Former urban district in NW Kent; from 1965 part of the Greater London borough of Bromley. Mainly residential.

Orsha Belarus. Town in the Vitebsk region on the Dnieper R. 80 km (50 miles) S of Vitebsk. Pop. (1991) 125,300.

Railway junction. Industrial centre. Industries inc. meat-packing, flour-milling, brewing and textiles.

Orsk Russia. Industrial town in the Orenburg region on the Ural R. 282 km (175 miles) ESE of Orenburg. Pop. (1991) 275,600.

Manufactures locomotives, agricultural machinery. Meat-packing, flour-milling. Terminus of a pipeline from the Emba oilfield, and oil-refining is an important industry; nickel and other metals are also refined.

Orta, Lake Italy. The most westerly of the Italian Alpine lakes, draining into L. Maggiore. Area 18 sq km (7 sq. miles). On the island of San Giulio is a church dating from the 4th cent.

Orumiyeh Iran. Formerly Rizaiyeh. Cap. of W Azerbaijan province just W of L. Urmia and 113 km (70 miles) WSW of Tabriz. Pop. (1996) 435,200.

Commercial centre in an agricultural region producing cereals, fruits and tobacco.

Oruro Bolivia. Cap. of the Oruro department in the Altiplano at a height of 3710 m (12,169 ft), 200 km (125 miles) SE of La Paz. Pop. (1989) 176,700.

Commercial and railway centre in a mining district (tin, silver, copper, tungsten). Industries inc. tin-smelting, flour-milling and brewing.

Founded in 1606 and first important as a silver-mining centre. It declined as the output of silver decreased in the 19th cent., but revived with the development of tin-mining.

Orvieto Italy. Town in Terni province, Umbria on an isolated rock at a height of 310 m (1017 ft) near the Paglia R. 96 km (60 miles) NNW of Rome. Pop. (1985) 22,000.

Market town. Well-known for its wine and pottery. Tourism is an important industry.

Has an outstandingly beautiful cathedral, begun in the late 13th cent., the exterior in black and white marble, with frescoes by Fra Angelico and Luca Signorelli. Nearby is the 13th/14th-cent. Palazzo Papale containing a museum with Etruscan relics.

Osage River USA. River 800 km (500 miles) long, rising in E Kansas, flowing generally E on a meandering course into Missouri and joining the Missouri R. below Jefferson City. The Bagnell Dam (1931) in Missouri forms the artificial Lake of the Ozarks, 209 km (130 miles) long; its power station supplies electricity to St Louis.

Osaka Japan. Cap. of Osaka prefecture and Japan's second largest city in S Honshu 400 km (250 miles) WSW of Tokyo. Pop. (1991) 2,613,199.

Important seaport on Osaka Bay. Great industrial and commercial centre. Exports textiles, machinery, metal goods. Sometimes called the 'Manchester of Japan' because of its many cotton mills. Also manufactures steel, machinery, chemicals, electrical equipment and cement. There is considerable air pollution, urban congestion and land subsidence.

Osh Kirghizia. Cap. of the Osh region 298 km (185 miles) SW of Frunze. Pop. (1990) 213,000. On the Uzbek border and at the E end of the fertile Fergana valley.

Silk manufacturing, food-processing.

In the neighbourhood is a peculiarly shaped rock called Takht-i-Suleiman (Solomon's Throne), well known in Muslim legend.

Oshawa Canada. Port and industrial town in Ontario on L. Ontario 43 km (27 miles) ENE of Toronto. Pop. (1991) 129,344.

Manufactures motor vehicles, glass, plastics, furniture, pharmaceuticals, textiles, metal and leather goods.

Oshkosh USA. Town in Wisconsin on the W shore of L. Winnebago 120 km (75 miles) NNW of Milwaukee. Pop. (1990) 55,006.

Manufactures machinery, leather goods

and clothing. Formerly important in the lumber industry.

Oshogbo Nigeria. Town in the SW 200 km (125 miles) NE of Lagos. Pop. (1992) 441,600. On the railway to the N.

Commercial centre. Trade in cacao, palm oil and kernels. Cotton weaving.

Osijek Croatia. Ancient Mursa. Town in NE and port on the Drava R. 169 km (105 miles) NW of Belgrade. Pop. (1991) 164,589.

Tanning, sugar-refining, flour-milling. Manufactures textiles and furniture. Trade in grain, fruit, timber, plum brandy and matches.

Oslo Norway. Cap. of Norway, chief industrial centre and ice-free seaport at the head of Oslo Fiord, an inlet of the Skagerrak. Pop. (1992) 467,090.

Exports timber, wood-pulp, paper and fish. Manufactures electrical equipment, machinery, chemicals, machine-tools and textiles.

The city was founded E of the R. Aker c. 1050; the Akershus fortress was built c. 1300. In 1624 a fire destroyed the old town. Christian IV rebuilt it further W (below the fortress) as Christiania; it grew rapidly in the 19th cent., absorbing nearby townships and was renamed Oslo in 1925.

Osnabrück Germany. Industrial town in Lower Saxony 93 km (58 miles) NE of Dortmund. Pop. (1991) 163,168.

Manufactures iron and steel, machinery, turbines, motor-vehicle bodies, textiles, paper and food products.

It was a member of the Hanseatic League; reaching the peak of its prosperity in the 15th cent.

Osorno Chile. Cap. of Osorno province in the Chilean lake district 80 km (50 miles) SSE of Valdivia. Pop. (1991) 136,223.

Market town. Flour-milling, meat-packing, sawmilling. Trade in grain and livestock.

Founded 1558. Destroyed by Araucanian

Indians; refounded 1776. Received many German immigrants in the late 19th cent.

Osorno, Mount Chile. Volcanic peak 2680 m (8790 ft) high on the E shore of L. Llanquihue in the Chilean lake district.

Oss Netherlands. Town in N Brabant province 40 km (25 miles) NE of Tilburg. Pop. (1992) 52,132.

Industrial centre. Manufactures margarine, pharmaceutical products and electrical equipment.

Ossetia ➤NORTH OSSETIAN REPUBLIC; SOUTH OSSETIAN AUTONOMOUS REGION.

Ossett England. Town in West Yorkshire 5 km (3 miles) W of Wakefield. Pop. (1991) 20,405.

Woollen and leather industries. Coalmining in the neighbourhood.

Ostend (Fr. **Ostende**, Flemish **Oostende**) Belgium. Naval base, seaport and holiday resort in W Flanders province on the North Sea 21 km (13 miles) W of Bruges. Pop. (1992) 68,947.

Exports cement, chemicals, fish. Belgium's chief fishing centre. Important railway terminus. Fish curing and canning, shipbuilding. Manufactures fertilizers. Linked by ferry service to Ramsgate (England). Among its attractions as a resort are the casino and the racecourse.

Östersund Sweden. Cap. of Jämtland county on the E shore of L. Storsjö 160 km (100 miles) NW of Sundsvall. Pop. (1991) 58,700.

Industrial centre on the railway from Sundsvall to Trondheim (Norway). Manufactures machinery and furniture.

Ostia Italy. Port of ancient Rome on the S mouth of the Tiber R. Probably the first Roman colony, dating from the 4th cent. BC. Claudius and Trajan built new harbours and it flourished in the 2nd and 3rd cent. AD but then declined. Fortified by Gregory IV 830. The castle was built (1483–6) by Julius II, whilst Cardinal, but it never regained its former importance. Since 1854 its ruins have been systematically excavated and it provides an excellent example of a Roman town. Lido di Roma, the modern seaside resort, stands 3 km (2 miles) from the ruins.

Ostrava Czech Republic. 1. *Moravská Ostrava:* Cap. of the Severomoravský region, on the Moravian bank of the Ostravice R. near it confluence with the Oder R.

Important iron and steel industry; also manufactures railway rolling-stock, tinplate, cranes, boilers and chemicals.

2. *Slezska Ostrava*: Coalmining town on the Silesian side of the Ostravice R. opposite Moravská Ostrava. Combined pop. (1991) 327,553.

Ostrov Dikson ➤DICKSON ISLAND.

Ostrów Wielkopolski Poland. Town in the Poznań voivodeship 108 km (67 miles) SE of Poznań. Pop. (1989) 72,085.

Railway junction. Manufactures agricultural machinery and chemicals. Trade in agricultural produce.

Oswestry England. Market town in Shropshire 26 km (16 miles) NW of Shrewsbury. Pop. (1991) 15,612.

Light engineering, malting and tanning.

Named after St Oswald, Christian king of Northumbria, killed here (642) whilst warring with Penda, King of Mercia.

Oświęcim ➤AUSCHWITZ.

Otago New Zealand. Former provincial district in the S of the South Island. Area (stat. area) 36,441 sq km (14,070 sq. miles). Pop. (1991) 186,067. In addition, the stat. area Southland (S) has area 29,681 sq km (11,460 sq. miles). Inc. the high country of the Southern Alps in the NW, Fiordland in the SW. Long glacial lakes. The rivers drain E across dissected central plateaux and fertile lowlands. Gold was discovered in the 1860s. Chief towns Dunedin, with Port Chalmers and Invercargill, served by Bluff.

Produces wool, fruits, dairy produce.

Otaru Japan. Seaport on the W coast of Hokkaido 40 km (25 miles) WNW of Sapporo. Pop. (1991) 163,475.

Exports coal, timber and fertilizers. Fishing, fish-processing, engineering. Manufactures rubber products.

Otley England. Town in West Yorkshire on the R. Wharfe 14 km (9 miles) NW of Leeds. Pop. (1991) 13,596.

Manufactures woollen goods, leather, printing machinery.

Birthplace of Thomas Chippendale, the cabinet-maker (1718–79).

Otranto Italy. Ancient Hydruntum. Fishing port in Lecce province, Apulia on the Otranto Strait. Pop. (1970) 4240. Has a cathedral (11th-cent.) and the ruined castle which provided the title for Horace Walpole's novel *The Castle of Otranto*. Important port in Roman times. Destroyed by the Turks (1480) and never recovered its former importance.

Otranto Strait Italy. Strait 72 km (45 miles) wide connecting the Ionian Sea with the Adriatic, between the 'heel' of Italy (Cape Otranto) and S Albania.

Otsu Japan. Cap. of Shiga prefecture, Honshu at the S end of L. Biewa just E of Kyoto. Pop. (1991) 262,953. A historic town and tourist centre in a picturesque region.

Trade in rice. Manufactures chemicals and textiles.

Ottawa Canada. Cap. of Canada in SE Ontario on the Ottawa R. opposite Hull (Quebec). Pop. (1991) 313,987. Impressively situated on hills overlooking the river. Canada's political, social and cultural centre. River port and important centre of the lumber industry; the output of the sawmills is enormous.

Other leading industries pulp and paper milling, woodworking, flour-milling and watchmaking. Manufactures leather goods, matches, metal products. Hydroelectric power for factories and mills comes from the Chaudière and Rideau Falls. It is dominated from Parliament Hill by the group of Gothic-style Parliament buildings; the originals (1859–65), burned down in 1916, were rebuilt in the same style. Other notable buildings inc. Rideau Hall (the Governor General's residence), the Anglican and Roman Catholic cathedrals, the National Victoria Museum and the National Art Gallery; also the government offices, Ottawa University (1866) and Carleton University (1942).

The site was discovered (1613) by Champlain, but the city's origin dates from 1826, when a town grew up round the headquarters of the British army engineers who were constructing the Rideau Canal and was named Bytown after Colonel By, the commanding officer. Became a city in 1854 and was renamed Ottawa after the river. Chosen as cap. of Canada by Queen Victoria in 1857.

Ottawa River Canada. River 1120 km (696 miles) long, chief tributary of the St Lawrence R., rising on the Laurentian Plateau in Quebec and flowing W to L. Timiskaming, then generally SE and E past Pembroke and Ottawa and joining the St Lawrence W of Montreal. For most of its course it forms the boundary between Ontario and Quebec. It expands into a large number of lakes, inc. the Grand Lake Victoria, L. Simard, L. Quinze, L. Timiskaming, L. Allumette, L. Chats, L. Deschênes and Two Mountains Lake. Many rapids, but it is navigable up to Ottawa and is connected with L. Ontario by the Rideau Canal. Its chief importance today is for the transportation of lumber and the production of hydroelectric power; the valley has become a region of considerable industrial activity. Named after the Ottawa Indians. A major factor in Canada's early development, as the highway for fur traders, missionaries and explorers. First explored by Étienne Brûlé (1610) and Champlain (1613). The canoe, the first recognized means of transport, was succeeded by the steamboat, which gave way to the railways in the 1870s.

Ottery St Mary England. Market town in Devon on the R. Otter 18 km (11 miles) E of Exeter. Pop. (1991) 3253. Has a church begun in 1260 and built on the lines of Exeter cathedral. Birthplace of S. T. Coleridge, the poet (1772–1834).

Ottumwa USA. Town in Iowa on the Des Moines R. 126 km (78 miles) SW of Cedar Rapids. Pop. (1990) 24,488.

Manufactures agricultural machinery, furniture and dairy products. Meat-packing.

Ötztal Alps. Alpine range on the Austro–Italian border but mainly in the Austrian Tirol. Highest peak Wildspitze (3777 m; 12,389 ft).

Ouachita River USA. River 960 km (600 miles) long, rising in the Ouachita Mountains of W Arkansas, flowing generally SE and then S to join the Red R. in E Louisiana.

Ouagadougou Burkina Faso. Cap. and terminus of the railway from Abidjan in Côte d'Ivoire (840 km; 520 miles SSW). Pop. (1985) 441,514.

Commercial centre in an agricultural region. Trade in groundnuts, millet, shea nuts, livestock. Vegetable-oil extraction, cotton-ginning. Manufactures soap and textiles.

It has been the cap. of the Mossi people since the 15th cent.

Ouarzazate Morocco. Town situated 130 km (82 miles) SE of Marrakesh on the S slopes of the Atlas mountains. Pop. (1985) 29,000. Oasis and former fortress town of French North Africa, now a thriving tourist centre.

Oudenarde (Flemish **Oudenaarde**) Belgium. Town in E Flanders province on the Scheldt R. 24 km (15 miles) SSW of Ghent. Pop. (1985) 28,000.

Brewing. Manufactures textiles. Has a 16th-cent. town hall.

Here in 1708 the English and Austrians under Marlborough and Prince Eugene defeated the French under Vendôme.

Oudh India. Region in central Uttar Pradesh, associated historically with the ancient kingdom of Kosala. Annexed by Britain (1856). One of the centres of the Indian Mutiny (1857–8). Joined with Agra 1877; renamed the United Provinces of Agra and Oudh 1902. The name United Provinces was changed to Uttar Pradesh in 1950.

Oudtshoorn South Africa. Town in Western Cape Province 360 km (225 miles) ENE of Cape Town on the Little Karroo. Pop. (1970) 26,525.

In an ostrich-farming district. Manufactures furniture, footwear and tobacco products. It is a tourism area and ostrich feathers and meat are sold. Near by there are the limestone Cango Caves, with remarkable stalactites and stalagmites, 27 km (17 miles) N at the foot of the Swartberg Range.

Oujda (Ujda) Morocco. Cap. of Oujda province 360 km (225 miles) ESE of Tangier near the Algerian frontier. Pop. (1982) 260,082. On the main Casablanca–Tunis railway, with a branch line to the S serving the coalmines of Jerada and the manganese mines of Bou Arfa.

Important commercial centre. Trade in wine, citrus fruits, early vegetables, cereals, sheep and wool.

Oulu (Uleåborg) Finland. Cap. and seaport of the Oulu province at the mouth of the Oulu R. on the Gulf of Bothnia. Pop. (1992) 102,032. It is a railway junction and exports timber, tar and wood products.

Industries inc. shipbuilding, sawmilling, tanning, and it manufactures fertilizers.

Oulu River Finland. River 105 km (65 miles) long issuing from the NW end of L. Oulu (area 1002 sq km; 387 sq. miles) and flowing NW to the Gulf of Bothnia at Oulu. Used for lumber transportation. At Pyhä Falls, 32 km (20 miles) SE of Oulu, is a hydroelectric plant.

Oundle England. Market town in Northamptonshire on the R. Nene 14 km (9 miles) E of Corby. Pop. (1991) 3996. Has a 14th-cent. church and a well-known public school (founded 1556).

Ouro Prêto Brazil. In Portuguese, 'Black Gold'. Town in the Minas Gerais state (of which it was cap. 1823–97) 68 km (42 miles) SE of Belo Horizonte at a height of 1070 m (3510 ft). Pop. (1985) 30,000. Founded c. 1700 on the discovery of gold. Declined from the mid 18th cent. Some goldmining continues in the neighbourhood, also iron and manganese mining.

Manufactures textiles. Has retained its colonial architecture virtually intact, with many splendid baroque churches, was decreed a national monument in 1933 and UNESCO has declared it part of the world's cultural heritage.

Ouse River (Sussex) England. River 48 km (30 miles) long, rising 10 km (6 miles) SSW of Crawley, flowing E and then S past Lewes, cutting through the South Downs and entering the English Channel at Newhaven.

Ouse River (Yorkshire) England. River 98 km (61 miles) long, formed by the union of the Ure and the Swale rivers near Boroughbridge, flowing generally SE past York, Selby and Goole, joining the R. Trent and forming the Humber estuary. Chief right-bank tributaries the Nidd, the Wharfe, the Aire and the Don rivers (all, like the Ure and the Swale, rising in the Pennines). Chief left-bank tributary the Derwent.

Ouse River, Great England. River 251 km (156 miles) long, rising near Brackley in Northamptonshire, flowing generally E, NE and then N, past Buckingham, Bedford, Huntingdon, Ely and King's Lynn, and entering the Wash 5 km (3 miles) NNW of King's Lynn. As it crosses the Fens it follows its natural course and also two straight artificial channels, the 'Bedford Rivers'.

Ouse River, Little England. River 39 km (24 miles) long, rising in Suffolk, flowing mainly WNW along the Norfolk–Suffolk border and joining the Great Ouse.

Outer Mongolia ➤MONGOLIA.

Ovalle Chile. Town in Coquimbo province on the Limarí R. 282 km (175 miles) N of Valparaiso. Pop. (1985) 72,770. In a fruit-growing, sheep-rearing and mining district.

Founded (1831) by President Ovalle.

Ovamboland Namibia. Area in the N bordered N by Angola; the most densely populated part of the country. The Etosha Pan (a marshy salt lake) is in the S. The main

indigenous peoples are the Ovambos, who number (1991) 665,000.

Main occupations cattle-rearing and the cultivation of maize, kaffir corn.

Overijssel Netherlands. Province in the E, bordering E on Germany and NW on the Ijsselmeer. Area 3339 sq km (1289 sq. miles). Pop. (1990) 1,015,515. Cap. Zwolle. Drained by the Ijssel and Vecht rivers. Largely agricultural, with dairy-farming predominating. Important textile industry. Chief towns Enschede, Zwolle, Hengelo, Deventer and Almelo.

Oviedo Spain. Cap. of Oviedo province, Asturias 24 km (15 miles) SW of the port of Gijón. Pop. (1991) 194,919.

Industrial centre. Manufactures iron and steel, armaments, metal goods, chemicals, cement and glass.

University (1604). Has a 14th-cent. Gothic cathedral and the 9th-cent. Cámara Santa, which contains valuable relics. Founded in the 8th cent. Became cap. of the Asturian kingdom during the time of Alfonso II (789–842). Declined in the 10th cent.

Owensboro USA. Town and river port in Kentucky on the Ohio R. 124 km (77 miles) WSW of Louisville. Pop. (1990) 53,549.

In a region producing oil and natural gas. Trade in tobacco, maize, oil, sand and gravel. Manufactures electric lamps, furniture and building materials.

Oxford England. County town of Oxfordshire on the R. Thames (or Isis) at the confluence with the R. Cherwell 80 km (50 miles) WNW of London. Pop. (1991) 109,000.

Famous chiefly for its university, but in recent years with considerable industrial development in the suburbs. Industries inc. publishing, the manufacture of vehicles, steel products, paper and electrical equipment. There is a considerable tourist industry.

Almost all the colleges of the university have some architectural distinction, in their hall, chapel or lawned quadrangle. As academic institutions, University (1249), Balliol (1263) and Merton (1264) are the oldest, though the last-named claims to be the oldest college, as it was the first to be organized on collegiate lines and it is the oldest architecturally. St Edmund Hall, also dating from the 13th cent. is the only survivor of the early academic halls. The first women's college, Lady Margaret Hall, was founded in 1878. Among the non-collegiate buildings are the Bodleian Library (1602), the Ashmolean Museum (1682, the first public museum in England), the Sheldonian Theatre (1668, designed by Wren and used for university ceremonies) and the Radcliffe Camera (1737). Ecclesiastical buildings inc. the 11th-cent. St Michael's church and the 13th-cent. St Mary the Virgin Church.

Mentioned in the 10th cent., Oxford became prominent in the 13th cent., when the first colleges of the university were founded and several parliaments met here – notably that of 1258 which forced the Provisions of Oxford on Henry III. In the Civil War it was the Royalist headquarters and surrendered only in 1646. Modern industrial development began when William Morris, later Viscount Nuffield, set up his automobile factory in the suburb of Cowley (1912).

Oxfordshire England. County in the S Midlands. Area 2583 sq km (997 sq. miles). Acquired part of Berkshire (inc. Abingdon and Didcot) 1974. Pop. (1991) 547,584. County town Oxford. It is divided into the districts of Cherwell, Oxford City, South Oxfordshire, Vale of the White Horse, West Oxfordshire. Bounded on the SW by the Berkshire Downs, it is drained by the R. Thames and tributaries – the Windrush, Evenlode, Cherwell and Thame. In the W are the Cotswolds, in the SE the Chilterns, rising to over 240 m (787 ft), and between is the broad and gently undulating Oxfordshire clay vale. On the fertile soil cereals are grown and dairy and beef cattle and sheep raised. Mainly rural. Principal towns Oxford, Banbury, Abingdon, Didcot, Witney and Henley-on-Thames.

Oxnard USA. Market town in S California 85 km (53 miles) WNW of Los Angeles. Pop. (1990) 142,216.
In a fertile agricultural region producing sugar-beet, citrus fruits and vegetables. Sugar-refining and vegetable-canning.

Oxus River ►AMU DARYA.

Oyapock (Oiapoque) River French Guiana/Brazil. River about 480 km (300 miles) long, rising in the Tumuc Humac Mountains in SW French Guiana, flowing generally NNE and forming most of the boundary with Brazil, entering the Atlantic near Cape Orange.

Oyo Nigeria. 1. State comprising the Ibadan and Oyo provinces of the former West Region. Pop. (1991) 3,448,789, almost entirely Yoruba. Cap. Ibadan.
2. Town in Oyo state in the SW 169 km (105 miles) NNE of Lagos. Pop. (1992) 237,400.
Commercial centre. Trade in cacao, palm oil and kernels. Cotton-weaving.

Ozark Mountains (Plateau) USA. A dissected plateau, mainly in Missouri but reaching its greatest altitude in Arkansas, where the Boston Mountains rise to over 600 m (1968 ft). Important deposits of lead, barytes and other minerals. Development has been slow, chiefly owing to poor soil and inadequate communications.

P

Paarl South Africa. Town in Western Cape Province 55 km (34 miles) ENE of Cape Town on the Great Berg R. Pop. (1985) 59,000.

An important wine-making centre; has the world's largest wine cellars. Fruit farms, vineyards, tobacco plantations in the neighbourhood. Jam-making, fruit-canning and flour-milling. Manufactures tobacco products and textiles.

Founded (1687) by Huguenots, who introduced the vine from France.

Pabna Bangladesh. Cap. of Rajshahi district situated WNW of Dakha on the N bank of the Ganges R. Pop. (1991) 113,146.

Industries inc. rice-milling and engineering, and the manufacture of hosiery.

Pachuca de Soto Mexico. Cap. of Hidalgo state on the central plateau at a height of 2400 m (7872 ft) 88 km (55 miles) NNE of Mexico City. Pop. (1990) 174,013.

Important silver-mining and silver-refining centre. Also manufactures woollen and leather goods.

The silver mines, known to the Indians in pre-Columbian times, were worked by the Spaniards for some years before the town was founded (1534).

Pacific Ocean. World's largest ocean, lying between Asia and Australia (W) and N and S America (E). Area, with peripheral seas 165,384,000 sq km (63,838,000 sq. miles). In the N it is almost landlocked, being connected with the Arctic Ocean only by the Bering Strait, but in the S its boundary is indeterminate. At its greatest width, approximately along the parallel of latitude 5°N, it measures about 17,700 km (11,000 miles), and it is about 16,000 km (10,000 miles) N–S. With an average depth of just over 4200 m (13,776 ft) it is also the world's deepest ocean. Around its edge are a number of exceptionally deep trenches, of which the outstanding example is the Marianas Trench, which reaches a depth of 11,524 m (37,799 ft). There is a considerable number of islands of volcanic and coral origin, esp. in the S and W, the majority of them comprising Oceania – in the region frequently termed the South Seas. N of the equator the main ocean currents of the Pacific circulate in a clockwise direction and inc. the Kuroshio and California Currents; S of the equator the circulation is anticlockwise, and here the currents inc. the Peruvian or Humboldt and the E Australian currents. The commercial importance of the Pacific increased considerably with the opening of the Panama Canal (1914). Regular air services began to operate across the Pacific in 1935.

Padang Indonesia. Seaport on the W coast of Sumatra 64 km (40 miles) S of Bukit Tinggi. Pop. (1990) 447,344.

Exports coal, coffee, copra and rubber. Trading post established here by the Dutch in 1667.

Paddington England. Part of the London borough City of Westminster, mainly residential, inc. Bayswater and Maida Vale. Contains Paddington Station. Tyburn Tree, the gallows which once stood near Marble Arch, was demolished 1759. Alexander Fleming discovered penicillin (1928) in St Mary's Hospital here.

Paderborn Germany. Town in North Rhine-Westphalia 37 km (23 miles) SSE of Bielefeld. Pop. (1992) 125,730.

Manufactures agricultural machinery, textiles and cement.

Charlemagne held a diet here (777) and

later made it a bishopric. Seat of a university 1614–1819.

Padiham England. Town in Lancashire 5 km (3 miles) WNW of Burnley. Pop. (1991) 12,570.

Industries inc. engineering, including gas-appliances and textiles.

Padova ➤PADUA.

Padstow England. Market town in N Cornwall on the estuary of the R. Camel, which has silted, thus causing its decline as a port. Pop. (1991) 2460. Seaside resort.

Padua (Italian **Padova**) Italy. Ancient Patavium. Cap of Padova province, Veneto 37 km (23 miles) W of Venice. Pop. (1992) 213,656.

Manufactures machinery, electrical goods, chemicals, food products and textiles.

A picturesque city, with fine squares, arcaded streets and several bridges crossing the branches of the Bacchiglione R. The university, at which Galileo taught (1593–1610), was founded in 1222. Has the oldest botanical gardens in Europe (1545). The outstanding church is the 13th/14th-cent. basilica of St Anthony, near which is the famous equestrian statue of Gattamelata by Donatello. Other historic buildings inc. the Palazzo della Ragione with its great hall and the Palazzo del Capitanio, residence of the Venetian governors. A wealthy city in Roman times. Independent from the 12th to the 14th cent. Held by the Carrara family 1318–1405 and was then ruled by Venice until 1797. Birthplace of the historian, Livy (59 BC–AD 17).

Paducah USA. River port in SW Kentucky on the Ohio R. at the confluence with the Tennessee R. Pop. (1990) 27,256.

Important trade in tobacco. Manufactures hosiery, textile machinery. Site of an atomic energy plant.

Paestum Italy. Originally Poseidonia. Ancient Greek city in Campania 35 km (22 miles) SE of Salerno, founded c. 600 BC as a Sybarite colony and called Poseidonia. Flourished as an independent city for about 200 years, then fell to the Lucanians. Came under Roman rule 273 BC, being renamed Paestum; praised by Latin poets for its roses. Sacked by the Saracens 871. By the 16th cent. it was deserted. Among Greek remains are three Doric temples and most of the city wall; the forum and an amphitheatre date from Roman times.

Pagalu Equatorial Guinea. Formerly Annobón: island in the Gulf of Guinea. Area 17 sq km (6½ sq. miles). Discovered by the Portuguese (1473) on New Year's Day: the former name means 'Happy New Year'. Ceded (with Fernando Póo) to Spain 1778. The inhabitants are probably descendants of Africans shipwrecked in the 16th cent.

Pago Pago Samoa. Chief port in American Samoa, pronounced 'Pango Pango', in the SE of Tutuila Island, ceded to the USA (1872) as a naval base and coaling station. The naval base closed in 1951. Pop. (1990) 46,773.

The chief industry is tuna fish canning.

Pahang Malaysia. Largest state in West Malaysia on the South China Sea. Area 35,965 sq km (13,886 sq. miles). Pop. (1991) 1,036,724. Cap. Kuantan. Consists largely of the basin of the 434-km (270-mile) long Pahang R. Chief products rubber and tin.

Paignton England. Seaside resort in Devon on Tor Bay 3 km (2 miles) SSW of Torquay, from 1968 in the county borough of Torbay. Has the Bible Tower, part of the ancient palace of the Bishops of Exeter; so called because it was believed (wrongly) that Miles Coverdale (1488–1569), a Bishop of Exeter, made his translation of the Bible here.

Painter, Mount ➤FLINDERS RANGE.

Paisley Scotland. Industrial town in Renfrewshire on the White Cart R. near its confluence with the R. Clyde 10 km (6 miles) WSW of Glasgow. Pop. (1991) 75,526.

Noted for the manufacture of cotton thread, also for bleaching, dyeing and engineering. Manufactures textiles, starch, cornflour and preserves.

Once famous for Paisley shawls and for its

Paita

linen and silk gauze, but these are no longer
produced. Among noteworthy buildings are
the Coats memorial church and the observatory. The abbey was founded in 1163, destroyed by the English in 1307 and rebuilt
later by the Stuart kings.

Paita Peru. Town in the Piura department
in the NW 64 km (40 miles) W of Piura.
Pop. (1988) 51,500.

A small but important port, being the
outlet for a cotton-growing region. Exports
chiefly cotton, also hides, wool and Panama
hats.

Pakistan. Federal republic of S Asia.
Bounded by Afghanistan in the NW, by
China in the N, Kashmir in the NE, India
in the E, the Arabian Sea in the S and Iran
in the W. Area 796,095 sq km (307,374 sq.
miles), excludes the area of Jammu and
Kashmir occupied by Pakistan. Pop. (1995)
140,497,000 if Afghan refugees and residents
of Pakistani-occupied Jammu and Kashmir
are inc. (urban 32 per cent). Life expectancy,
62 years male, 64 female. Cap. Islamabad.
Other cities are Karachi, the chief seaport
(formerly the federal cap.), Lahore,
Faisalabad and Rawalpindi. Currency: Pakistan rupee = 100 paisa. Pakistan is mountainous in the N, where the E Hindu Kush
rise to 7690 m (25,230 ft) in Tirich Mir, and
the W, where are the Sulaiman, Kirthar and
other ranges; the remainder consists of fertile
plains watered by the Indus and its tributaries,
with the Thar Desert in the E.There is also
considerable desert in the SW. A weak form
of tropical monsoon climate occurs over
much of the country, with arid conditions
in the N and W, where the wet season is
only from Dec. to March. Elsewhere, rain
comes mainly in the summer. Summer temperatures are high everywhere, but winters
can be cold in the mountainous N. Land use:
forested 5 per cent, meadows and pastures
7 per cent, agricultural and under permanent cultivation 27 per cent. Religion 95
per cent Muslim. Urdu is the national lang.,
while English is used for official purposes.
Other langs Punjabi, Sindhi, Pushto and
Baluchi.

Agriculture occupies 44 per cent of the
pop., and is almost completely dependent on
irrigation by the great rivers; wheat is the
principal crop, followed by cotton and rice.
There are considerable mineral reserves
of coal, graphite, copper, gold, manganese,
but these have been little developed. The
manufacturing industries are mainly food-
processing, textiles and consumer goods.

The name Pakistan originated in the 1930s
based on first letters of the western provinces
in former British India with Muslim majority, *P*unjab, *A*fghania (North West Frontier) and *K*ashmir, with suffix taken from
Baluch*istan*.

For history prior to 1947 ▸INDIA.

When the former India was partitioned in
1947 Pakistan was created from the areas
where Muslims formed the majority of the
pop. and, as a result, it comprised the two
widely separated regions of W and E Pakistan. As in India, one of the most difficult
problems facing the new country was the
rehabilitation of millions of refugees from
across the border; externally, the outstanding
problem has been the continuing dispute
with India over Kashmir. At first a Dominion
of the British Commonwealth, Pakistan was
proclaimed an Islamic republic 1956. In 1958
martial law was declared, the central and
provincial governments were dismissed and
all political parties were abolished. In 1962 a
new Constitution was proclaimed. In 1969
the army assumed control and martial law was
again proclaimed. Disaffection in E Pakistan
developed into civil war in 1971 and the
province declared itself the independent state
of Bangladesh. A new Constitution was adopted in 1973, providing for a federal parliamentary system and a bicameral Parliament
comprising an 87-member Senate and a 217-
member National Assembly directly elected
but with 10 religious minority representatives. It is divided administratively into 6
provinces: Punjab, Sind, Baluchistan, North-
West Frontier Province, the Federally administered tribal areas and the Federal Capital
Territory, Islamabad. In addition there are
Azid Kashmir (that part of Jammu and
Kashmir occupied by Pakistan) and Northern

690

Areas of Baltistan, Diamir and Gilgit (administered by Pakistan but disputed by India).

Pakse Laos. Town situated SE of Savannakhet in Champassac on the Mekong R. at the mouth of the Se Done R. Pop. (1985) 441,244.

Provincial cap., communications and trading centre for the Boloven Plateau, handling cardamom, cotton, hemp, tobacco and cattle.

Palau (Belau) W Pacific Ocean. The Republic of Palau is an archipelago with a land area of 497 sq km (192 sq. miles). It comprises 26 islands and over 300 islets, the largest being Babelthuap which will be the future cap. Pop. (1995) 17,225 (40 per cent urban). Life expectancy 69 years male, 73 female. Cap. Koror. Currency US dollar = 100 cents.

Exports copra, tapioca, dried fish.

A Japanese stronghold in World War II, taken by the USA 1944. It was administered by the USA as part of the Trust Territory of the Pacific Islands, but in 1978 the islanders voted against joining the Federated States of Micronesia and in 1981 it became an autonomous republic; it became an independent republic on 1 October 1994. The republic has a bicameral legislature with a 16-member Senate and 18-member House of Delegates.

Palawan Philippines. The most westerly of the country's large islands, between the South China Sea (W) and the Sulu Sea (E). Area 11,785 sq km (4550 sq. miles). Pop. (1990) 528,287. Cap. Puerto Princesa. A mountain range runs through the island, rising to 2085 m (6839 ft) in Mt Mantalingajan. Largely forested. Produces coconuts, rice and rubber.

Palembang Indonesia. Cap. of S Sumatra province on the Musi R. 80 km (50 miles) from the mouth. Pop. (1981) 903,000.

Port. Commercial centre. Important oil refineries nearby. Exports petroleum products and rubber.

Palencia Spain. 1. Inland province in Old Castile (though sometimes considered part

of León). Area 8029 sq km (3096 sq. miles). Pop. (1991) 185,479. Crossed by the Cantabrian Mountains in the N, the remainder being dry, barren plateau, drained by the Pisuerga and Carrión rivers, with fertile valleys where cereals, fruits and vegetables are cultivated.

2. Cap. of Palencia province on the Carrión R. 45 km (28 miles) NNE of Valladolid. Pop. (1991) 77,752.

Railway engineering, tanning and flour-milling. Manufactures soap and textiles.

The Gothic cathedral (14th/16th cent.) has paintings by El Greco and Zurbarán. The university, believed to be the oldest in Spain, was founded in 1208 and removed to Salamanca in 1239.

Palermo Italy. Ancient Panormus. Cap. of Palermo province and of the region of Sicily on the NW coast and on the edge of the Conca d'Oro plain. Pop. (1991) 734,238.

Seaport. Industrial centre. Exports fruit, olive oil, wine. Shipbuilding. Manufactures steel, glass, chemicals and furniture.

The earliest buildings date from the time of the Norman kings, many of whose tombs are in the 12th-cent. cathedral, founded by an Englishman, Archbishop Walter of the Mill and built in mixed Norman and Saracen styles. Nearby are Monte Pellegrino (600 m; 1968 ft) and the resort of the Mondello beach. Belonged to Carthaginians, Romans, Byzantines, Saracens and then Normans, who made it cap. of the kingdom of Sicily. Liberated from the Bourbons by Garibaldi 1860.

Palestine ➤ISRAEL.

Palestinian-Administered Territories ➤ISRAEL.

Palk Strait. Channel between SE India and N Sri Lanka 53 km (33 miles) wide at its narrowest. Named after Sir Robert Palk, Governor of Madras 1763–6.

Palma (Canary Islands) ➤SANTA CRUZ DE TENERIFE.

Palma (Palma de Mallorca) Spain. Cap. of Majorca and of the Baleares (Balearic Is.) province at the head of the Bay of Palma in the SW of Majorca. Pop. (1991) 296,754.

Seaport exporting almonds, fruits and wine. Manufactures cement, paper, textiles, shoes and glass.

Mild climate and attractive situation on the bay; best known as a tourist resort. Noteworthy buildings are the Gothic cathedral (13th/17th-cent.), the adjacent Almudaina castle (a former Moorish palace) and the 15th-cent. Lonja or old exchange. Founded as a Roman colony. Liberated from the Moors (1229) by James I of Aragón.

Palm Beach USA. Expensive and luxurious winter resort in SE Florida on the E shore of L. Worth, a sea lagoon and 108 km (67 miles) N of Miami. Connected by bridges to West Palm Beach, on the opposite shore of the lagoon, a winter resort and commercial town. Pop. West Palm Beach (1990) 67,643.

Palmerston Cook Islands, South Pacific. Atoll in the N situated W of Rarotonga. Area 2 sq km (0.8 sq. miles). Pop. (1986) 66.
Produces copra.

Palmerston North New Zealand. Chief town on the Manawatu R. plains in North Island on the Manawatu R. 129 km (80 miles) NNE of Wellington. Pop. (1992) 72,900.
Railway junction in dairying and sheep-farming country. Manufactures clothing and furniture.

Palmira Colombia. Town in the Valle del Cauca department 32 km (20 miles) NE of Cali at a height of 1070 m (3510 ft). Pop. (1985) 185,244.
Commercial centre. Trade in tobacco, coffee, sugar-cane, cereals and rice.

Palm Springs USA. Exclusive winter resort in S California 122 km (76 miles) E of Santa Ana. Pop. (1990) 40,180. Sulphur springs in the neighbourhood. Developed in the 1930s when the mild climate and picturesque situation attracted Hollywood actors.

Palmyra Syria. Ancient city and oasis 209 km (130 miles) NE of Damascus, known as early as the 12th cent. BC: the biblical Tadmor ('City of Palms'). Reached the height of its power and commercial importance in the 3rd cent. AD until the ambitions of Queen Zenobia provoked Rome: in 272 it fell to and was partly destroyed by Aurelian. Later, when under the Arabs, it was sacked by Tamerlane. Near the remains of the great Temple of the Sun, which testify to its former splendour, today lies the insignificant village of Tadmor, through which passes the Kirkuk–Tripoli oil pipeline.

Palo Alto USA. Attractive residential town in California 43 km (27 miles) SE of San Francisco near the S end of San Francisco Bay. Pop. (1990) 55,900. Name derived from a nearby fallen tree. Seat of Stanford University (1891).

Palomar, Mount USA. Mountain 1868 m (6127 ft) high in S California 72 km (45 miles) NNE of San Diego. Site of the Mt Palomar Observatory (at 1708 m; 5602 ft), famous for its 500-cm (200-ins.) reflecting telescope.

Palos de la Frontera Spain. Small town in Huelva province on the Río Tinto estuary. Pop. (1991) 6753. Former port (now silted up), from which Columbus sailed to discover America (1492) and to which he returned (1493); also where Cortés landed (1528) after his conquest of Mexico.

Pamir (Pamirs). Dissected plateau in Central Asia, mainly in the Gorno-Badakhshan Autonomous Region of Tajikistan, but extending into Afghanistan and Xinjiang Uygur (China). Consists of a series of high mountain valleys (the true 'Pamirs') at 3600–4200 m (11,808–13,776 ft) largely covered with grass on which the nomadic Kirghiz pasture their sheep, goats and other livestock, flanked by lofty mountain ranges. The highest peaks are in the Akademia Nauk Range.

Pamphylia. Ancient region in Asia Minor to the S of Pisidia, now in Turkey. Among its cities were Perga and Olbia. Under the Romans it was held to inc. Pisidia.

Pamplona Colombia. Town in the Norte de Santander department in the E Cordillera 58 km (36 miles) S of Cúcuta at a height of 2200 m (7216 ft). Pop. (1985) 23,200.
Commercial centre. Trade in coffee, cacao

and cereals. Textile industry, brewing and distilling.

Founded 1548. Suffered severely from earthquakes 1644, 1875.

Pamplona (Pampeluna) Spain. Ancient Pompaelo, Cap. of Navarra province on the Arga R. 145 km (90 miles) NNW of Zaragoza. Pop. (1991) 179,251.

Flour-milling and tanning. Manufactures textiles, soap and paper.

The mainly 14th/15th-cent. Gothic cathedral is remarkable for the 18th-cent. façade and the fine cloisters. On the feast of St Fermin a bull fight is held for which the bulls run through the streets to the ring and young men run ahead of the animals. An old Basque town, rebuilt (68 BC) by Pompey the Great and named Pompaelo after him. Later became cap. of the kingdom of Navarre and was fortified and improved by Charles III (1361–1425). Under Philip II (1556–98) it became the best fortified city in Spain.

Panaji India. Cap. of the state of Goa. Pop. (1991) 85,515.

Commercial centre and port. It is a tourist centre and trades in rice, fish and salt; it also exports manganese ore.

Velha Goa (Old Goa), the former cap. of all Portuguese possessions in India, is now mainly in ruins. Has the church of Bom Jesus (1594–1603), with the tomb of St Francis Xavier, and the convent of St Francis, a converted mosque. Founded 1440. Taken by Albuquerque 1510. Declined after the removal of the cap. to Panjim (formerly a suburb) in 1759.

Panama. Republic in Central America lying between the Caribbean Sea (N) and Pacific Ocean (S), bordered by Costa Rica in the W and Colombia E. Area (inc. the former Canal Zone) 77,082 sq km (29,762 sq. miles). Pop. (1995) 2,631,000 (53 per cent urban). Life expectancy, 71 years male, 75 female. Cap. Panama. Other cities San Miguelito, Colón and David. Currency: Balboa = 100 cents. The Caribbean coast is indented by the Mosquito Gulf; on the Pacific coast are the Gulf of Panama, the Azuero Peninsula

and the Gulf of Chiriqui (in which is the largest island, Coiba). There are narrow coastal lowlands, but the interior is mountainous; the highest peak is the inactive volcano Chiqui (3480 m, 11,414 ft). Climate in the lowlands tropical, temperature averaging 28°C (82°F), with little seasonal variation; much cooler in the mountains. Annual rainfall varies from about 175 cm (70 ins.) on the Pacific coast to 400 cm (160 ins.) on the Caribbean coast. Land use: forested 43 per cent, meadows and pastures 21 per cent, agricultural and under permanent cultivation 9 per cent. Eighty-four per cent of the pop. is Roman Catholic and Spanish is the official lang. Ethnic groups: mestizo 60 per cent, black and mulatto 20 per cent, white 10 per cent, Amerindian 8 per cent, Asian 2 per cent.

Income from the Canal is the major source of income. Timber (chiefly mahogany) produced from the extensive forests. Leading export bananas and rice, maize and coffee grown for domestic consumption. Sea fisheries are important, with shrimps the second most valuable export.

Panama was first explored by the Spaniards (1501); Columbus claimed the region for Spain (1502). Buccaneers (inc. Drake in the 16th cent. and Morgan in the 17th) raided and looted the ports and coastal settlements. It was placed under the Viceroyalty of New Granada 1739. After Spain had relinquished control (1821) it joined the federation of Colombia, Venezuela and Ecuador, which was dissolved in 1830. It then became a province of Colombia until Colombia refused to allow the USA to construct the canal across the isthmus and Panama declared its independence (1903). In 1979 Panama assumed sovereignty over what was previously called the Panama Canal Zone and now called the Canal area, and complete control will be handed over in 2000. From 1983 to 1989 political control of the country was in the hands of General Manuel Noriega, but the US invaded Panama in 1989 and Noriega was deposed. Under the amended 1972 Constitution there is a 67-seat Legislative Assembly and it provides for a president and two vice presidents elected by popular vote for 5-year terms. The country is divided into 9 provinces and a Special Territory.

Panama, Gulf of. Inlet of the Pacific in SE Panama 193 km (120 miles) wide. At the head is the Bay of Panama, with Panama City and Balboa. It contains the Pearl Islands.

Panama, Isthmus of. Narrow neck of land between the Caribbean Sea and the Pacific Ocean (Gulf of Panama), crossed by the Panama Canal. The term is sometimes applied to the entire territory of the Republic of Panama.

Panama Canal Central America. Ship canal across the Isthmus of Panama connecting the Atlantic Ocean with the Pacific, 64 km (40 miles) long from coast to coast; runs generally NW–SE (the Pacific entrance is farther E than the Caribbean entrance). Vessels move in both directions, as all the locks are double. A ship entering from the Caribbean is raised to 26 m (85 ft) above sea level by the three sets of the Gatun Locks, crosses the artificial L.Gatun (about 39 km; 24 miles) goes through the Gaillard Cut and finally passes through the Pedro Miguel Locks and the two sets of the Miraflores Locks to the short sea-level canal leading to the Pacific. The average time of a vessel in Canal waters is 24 hours, 8–12 hours of which is transit through the Canal proper. Constructed 1904–14. The first ship passed through in Aug. 1914. The idea of a canal dates from the Spanish explorers of the 16th cent. The USA became increasingly interested in the 19th cent. as settlers moved to the far W. After an abortive attempt by a French company (1880–9), the USA secured (1903) from the new republic of Panama the lease in perpetuity of the Panama Canal Zone but this was relinquished in 1979. Work began in 1904. A fixed bridge 1.6 km (1 mile) long over the Pacific entrance was opened at Balboa in 1962; it links the two parts of the Republic of Panama and the N and S American sections of the Pan-American Highway.

Panama Canal Area. Formerly Panama Canal Zone; an administrative region of the USA, a strip of land about 16 km (10 miles) wide along the Panama Canal, bordered on each side by the Republic of Panama. It included the canal ports of Cristóbal (Caribbean) and Balboa (Pacific); Panama City and Colón were geographically within the Zone but were Panamanian. In 1979 the area was formally transferred to Panama.

Panama City Panama. Cap. of Panama and of the Panama province. Pop. (1990) 411,549.

Industrial and route centre. Its port is Balboa. Manufactures clothing, plastics, footwear and food products.

The ruins of the old city (founded in 1519 and destroyed by Henry Morgan, the buccaneer, in 1671) are 8 km (5 miles) NE. The city was rebuilt on its present site in 1673. Became cap. of Panama 1903.

Panama City USA. Port and resort in NW Florida on St Andrew Bay, Gulf of Mexico. Pop. (1984) 34,100.

Sawmilling. Manufactures paper. Fishing.

Panay Philippines. Island between Mindoro and Negros. Area 12,287 sq km (4744 sq. miles). Pop. (1990) 8,031,271. Chief town Iloilo. Mountainous in the W, rising there to 2051 m (6727 ft). Lower and more fertile in the E. Chief products rice, sugar and copra.

Pančevo Serbia, Yugoslavia. Town in the former autonomous province of Vojvodina 18 km (11 miles) ENE of Belgrade. Pop. (1991) 72,793.

Railway junction. Flour-milling.

Pantelleria (Pantellaria) Italy. Ancient Cossyra. Mediterranean island 101 km (63 miles) SW of the SW coast of Sicily. Area 83 sq km (32 sq. miles). Pop. (1985) 10,000. Chief town and port Pantelleria on the NW coast. Volcanic with fumaroles and hot springs. Fertile but lacking fresh water.

Produces wine and cereals.

Paotow China ➤BAOTOU.

Papal States Italy. Territories of central Italy formerly ruled by the Pope, constituting an area of 40,663 sq km (15,700 sq. miles) in the mid 19th cent. In 1860 parts and in 1870 the remainder were incorporated into Italy. By the Lateran Treaty (1929) the Pope was recognized as sovereign of the Vatican City.

Papeete ►TAHITI.

Paphos Cyprus. Town situated WSW of Nicosia on the SW coast. District cap. Pop. (1991) 30,900.

Trades in nuts, wine, olives, bananas, citrus fruits and vegetables. Tourism is important.

Papua New Guinea. Independent state situated off the N coast of Queensland, Australia. It forms the E portion of the main island of New Guinea, together with over 600 SW Pacific islands inc. New Britain, New Ireland and Bougainville. Area 462,840 sq km (178,704 sq. miles). Pop. (1995) 4,302,000 (16 per cent urban). Life expectancy, 56 years male, 58 female. Cap. Port Moresby. Other towns Lae, Madang and Wewak. Currency: Papua New Guinea Kina = 100 toea. Mainland mostly central high mountain chain broken into ranges by wide valley: extensive foothills and swamp in the N and S. It has a monsoon climate with high temperatures and humidity all the year. Land use: forested 84 per cent, agricultural and under permanent cultivation 1 per cent. The principal local langs are Neo-Melanesia (Pidgin, a creole of English) and Aira Motu but there are over 800 spoken langs (many have several dialects). There are about 2 million Protestants and 1 million Roman Catholics. New Guinea Papuan 84 per cent and New Guinea Melanesian 15 per cent.

Leading exports oil, timber and copra, coconut oil, cocoa and coffee.

Papua came under Australian control in 1906 with adjacent islands. New Guinea became an Australian mandate in 1921 and a trust territory in 1946 (inc. Bismarck Archipelago, NW Solomon Is.). It gained self-government 1973 and became independent in 1975 as Papua New Guinea. There is a 109-seat unicameral National Parliament.

Pará Brazil. State in the N lying in the Amazon basin and consisting mainly of tropical rainforest. Area 1,246,833 sq km (481,405 sq. miles). Pop. (1991) 5,084,726. Cap. Belém.

Produces rubber, Brazil nuts, medicinal plants, tropical hardwoods, jute and skins. Transportation chiefly by water.

Paracel Islands Vietnam. Group in the South China Sea 240 km (150 miles) SE of Hainan Island (China) claimed by both Vietnam and China. Inc. numerous coral islands and reefs, mainly the Amphitrite and Crescent groups, Lincoln and Triton Islands. The main product is phosphates.

Paraguay. Paraguay is an inland republic of South America bounded by Bolivia in the N and NW, Brazil NE and E and Argentina in the SE, S and SW. Area 406,752 sq km (157,048 sq. miles). Pop. (1995) 4,828,000 (51 per cent urban). Life expectancy, 65 years male, 70 female. Cap. Asunción. Other cities Ciudad de Este, San Lorenzo, Lambaré and Fernando de la Mora. Currency: Paraguayan Guaraní = 100 céntimos. The Paraguay R. receives water from the interior of Brazil and flows S through Paraguay, dividing the country into two contrasting parts. To the W lies the sparsely inhabited scrub forest of the Gran Chaco, while to the E is a richer area containing most of the pop., with gently rolling hills, flat moist plains and the edge of the Paraná plateau, where the forests yield yeraba maté and timber. It has a tropical climate with abundant rainfall, with hot summers and mild winters. Rainfall generally plentiful ranging from 75 cm (30 ins.) annually in the W to 200 cm (80 ins.) in the E. Land use: forested 33 per cent, meadows and pastures 54 per cent, agricultural and under permanent cultivation 6 per cent. Religion Roman Catholic. Langs Spanish, Guaraní. Most Paraguayans are bilingual, but a majority speak Guaraní in preference to Spanish. The pop. is remarkably homogeneous, the original Spanish minority having been absorbed by the indigenous Indians. There are also Mennonite, Korean and Japanese settlers.

Quebracho trees from the E Chaco are used mainly for tanning, hides being the chief product from the rough grazing areas of these

Paraguay River

plains. The only well-organized agricultural lands are E of the Paraguay R., esp. near Asunción. Maize is the principal subsistence crop; rice, cotton, sugar-cane, tobacco, oranges and other fruits also grown. S of the cap. the grasslands support cattle for the production of leather and dried meat, and small areas produce cotton and oranges. SE of Asunción, near Villarrica, tobacco, vines, cotton, oranges and sugar-cane are cultivated. Other industries inc. food-processing, cement, vegetable-oil refining, textiles and forestry. Industry is helped by cheap hydro-electricity. Manganese and iron ore exist but have not been fully exploited. Main exports cotton, soya, timber, hides, meat and quebracho extract. Road and rail communications are poor, and access to the sea is principally by rivers draining into the Río de la Plata system. Asunción, the leading port and commercial centre and only large city, on the Paraguay R., is 1529 km (950 miles) from the ocean. It is linked by rail with Encarnación, on the Alto Paraná R., where a ferry connects with the Argentine system.

The Guaraní Indians, unlike the warlike tribes farther S, did not oppose the Spaniards who founded Asunción (1537), which they used as a springboard for further colonization of Buenos Aires (Argentina) in 1580. Paraguay subsequently came under the viceroyalty of Peru and then of La Plata (1776); the Jesuits, who had established many well-organized settlements in which the Indians lived free from exploitation by the Spanish landowners, were expelled in 1767. Independence from Spain was achieved in 1811, but the third dictator Solano López led the country into a war against Brazil, Argentina and Uruguay (1865–70) in which more than half the pop. and nearly all able-bodied males were killed. In a later war with Bolivia, ended in 1935, over rival claims in the Chaco, Paraguay was victorious and gained possession of a considerable area – but at the price of exhaustion. An authoritarian regime followed, civil war broke out in 1947 and subsequent political stability has been precarious. From 1959 to 1989 there was a military dictatorship but in 1989 Gen. Stroessner was

deposed. In 1992 the Constituent Assembly approved a new Constitution. There is an 80-member Chamber of Deputies and a 45-member Senate. The country is divided into two parts, the 'Oriental', E of the Paraguay R., comprising 15 departments, and the 'Occidental' W of the river, with 5 departments.

Paraguay River. River 2092 km (1300 miles) long, rising in the central Mato Grosso (Brazil), near Diamantino, descending to wooded, swampy lowlands and flowing generally S, joining the Alto Paraná in the SW corner of Paraguay to form the Paraná R. Navigable by small craft as far upstream as Cáceres (Brazil) and by larger vessels to Concepción, though it winds greatly; an important means of communication, esp. to Paraguay. Divides the Paraguayan Chaco to the W from the richer pastoral and agricultural lands to the E, and forms part of the boundary of Paraguay with both Brazil and Argentina.

Paraíba Brazil. State in the NE consisting of a narrow coastal plain backed by a hilly region of uncertain rainfall, partly irrigated, with much *sertão* ('backwoods'). Area 53,958 sq km (20,833 sq. miles). Pop. (1991) 3,200,620. Cap. João Pessoa.

It is an important cotton-growing state and also produces sugar-cane, tobacco and pineapples.

Paraíba do Norte River Brazil. River 320 km (200 miles) long, rising near the Paraíba–Pernambuco border and flowing generally ENE to the Atlantic below João Pessoa.

Paraíba do Sul River Brazil. River 960 km (600 miles) long, rising in the Serra do Mar near São Paulo and flowing NE to the Atlantic below Campos. Its valley carries the road and railway between São Paulo and Rio de Janeiro and contains the Volta Redonda steelworks.

Parakou Benin. Cap of Borgou department situated N of Porto-Novo. Pop. (1992) 106,708.

Rail terminus serving an agricultural area, handling cotton, nuts, beans, kapok, butter, rice and soya. Industries inc. cotton and kapok ginning.

Paramaribo Suriname. Cap. and chief seaport on the Suriname R. 27 km (17 miles) from the mouth. Pop. (1993) 200,970.

Exports coffee, citrus fruits, timber and bauxite. Dutch in appearance with many canals.

Paraná Argentina. Formerly Bajada de Santa Fé. Cap. of Entre Ríos province and port on the left bank of the Paraná R. opposite Santa Fé, to which it is linked by ferry. Pop. (1991) 277,338.

Commercial centre for an extensive grain and cattle area.

Has the famous Urquiza Park and a noteworthy cathedral. Cap. of Argentina 1853–62.

Paraná Brazil. State in the S to the E of the Paraná R., consisting of a narrow coastal lowland and an interior dissected plateau. Area 199,324 sq km (76,959 sq. miles). Pop. (1991) 8,415,659. Cap. Curitiba. Well-wooded, with extensive stands of Paraná pines.

Coffee grown on the fertile *terra roxa* in the N; cotton, citrus fruits, maté and timber are also important products.

Paraná River. River 2882 km (1800 miles) long formed by the union of the Rio Grande and the Paranaibá R. on the plateau of SE Brazil, being known in its upper course as the Alto Paraná. It flows generally S, receives several long tributaries that cross the tablelands of Paraná and São Paulo from the E, descends the Guaíra Falls (known in Brazil as Sete Quedas) and forms the Brazil–Paraguay boundary. It then turns W, in this section forming the Paraguay–Argentina boundary and below the confluence with the Paraguay is called the Paraná. Two main navigable channels pass through the delta and meet the Uruguay R. in the La Plata estuary. River ports, serving as outlets for the pampas and industrial centres, lie along the lower Paraná, among the most important being Santa Fé, Paraná and Rosario.

Pará River Brazil. Navigable arm of the Amazon R. delta S and E of Marajó island about 320 km (200 miles) long and 64 km (40 miles) wide at the mouth. Joined by the Tocantins R. from the S.

Parbhani India. Town in Maharashtra situated NW of Hyderabad (Andhra Pradesh). Pop. (1991) 190,225. District cap.

Railway centre for an agricultural area. Industries inc. cotton-ginning.

Pardubice (Ger. **Pardubitz**) Czech Republic. Town in NE Bohemia on the Elbe R. 96 km (60 miles) E of Prague. Pop. (1990) 96,000.

Railway junction. Industrial centre. Oil-refining and brewing.

Cathedral (13th-cent., restored).

Paricutín, Mount Mexico. Volcano in Michoacán state, formed in a cultivated field on 20 Feb. 1943 after a week of earth tremors. Steam forced its way out of the ground and by the evening black smoke was belching from a hole, while stones and cinders were thrown up. By the next morning a cinder cone 7.5 m (25 ft) high had built up round the vent and grey ash covered the countryside for miles around; the village of Paricutín was later buried under lava. At the end of a year the volcano had risen, from its base at 2250 m (7380 ft) above sea level, to a height of 2500 m (8200 ft). Activity ceased in 1952.

Paris France. Ancient Lutetia. Cap.of France and from 1964 a department, and the country's largest city, built on both sides of a meander in the Seine R. just below its confluence with the Marne R., at the centre of the Paris Basin; the only French city with more than 1 million inhabitants. Pop. (1990) 2,175,000. Greater Paris (1990) 9,318,821 inc. the towns of Boulogne-Billancourt (101,971), Montreuil (95,038), Argenteuil (94,162), Versailles (91,029), Saint-Denis (90,806), Nanterre (86,627), Vitry-sur-Seine (82,280), Aulnay-sous-Bois (82,537) and Créteil (82,390). Paris is the centre of its principal railways, roads and airways, with 7 main railway termini and three airports (Orly, Le Bourget, Charles de Gaulle), and is the junction of many important routes between N, W and S Europe. The Seine carries a considerable volume of barge traffic, making it the country's leading inland port; and it is linked by canals with all the main rivers of France. Of the 33 bridges spanning the Seine (three for pedestrians only) the oldest and most famous is the 16th/17th-cent. Pont Neuf, which connects the Île de la Cité with both banks of the river. Communications inc. an underground railway system, the Métropolitain (Métro). In addition to being the administrative, business and financial centre of France, Paris has many industries, being esp. famed for luxury goods, e.g. jewellery, cosmetics, perfume, *haute couture* – which form a significant part of French exports. A major part of the French motor-car industry is in the Greater Paris region and this, together with factories for aircraft, metal goods and chemicals, is located in the suburbs – e.g. Boulogne-Billancourt, Issy-les-Moulineaux, Suresnes. Paris is also a mainstay of another of France's chief sources of income, the tourist trade.

A characteristic of Paris is the combination of spaciousness and compactness in which the old mingles with the modern in a remarkably integrated way, partly due to the planning of Haussmann, partly a result of the expansion of the city in concentric rings from the early Gallo–Roman town on the Île de la Cité. Most of the old Paris lies within the Grands Boulevards, which roughly occupy the site of the 14th–17th-cent. ramparts. Beyond these are the first suburbs, the *faubourgs*, around which is another ring, the *boulevards extérieurs*, built over the 18th-cent. ramparts; beyond these are the more recent suburbs, incorporated into the city in 1860 as *arrondissements XII–XX*, extending to the boulevards which mark the line of fortifications erected after 1860 and demolished in 1919 to provide for housing developments, open spaces and, in the S, for the Cité Universitaire. The Île de la Cité is the true heart of Paris; on it stands the cathedral of Notre-Dame (1163–1240),

with its magnificent façade and two great towers. Most of the island is occupied by massive buildings of the Palais de Justice, among which stand the 13th-cent. Sainte-Chapelle, a gem of Gothic architecture and the Conciergerie, where Marie Antoinette was imprisoned. The Île de la Cité is connected by bridge with the Île St-Louis, which has several fine 17th-and 18th-cent. buildings. Nearby on the right bank of the Seine is the Louvre, certainly the supreme art gallery and museum in France, and possibly in the world. The Musée d'Orsay opened in 1986. W of the Louvre are the beautiful Tuileries gardens; the Place de la Concorde, the greatest of the Parisian squares, with the 23-m (75-ft) Luxor obelisk; then the Avenue des Champs-Élysées, leading to the Place de l'Étoile, on which 12 avenues converge, and the Arc de Triomphe, with the tomb of the Unknown Soldier. The Pompidou Centre opened in 1977. To the W and E of the city lie the Bois de Boulogne and the Bois de Vincennes. Just N of the Louvre is the Palais-Royal, in the SW wing of which is the Comédie-Française, linked by the Avenue de l'Opéra; also on the right bank is the Place de la Bastille, site of the prison destroyed in the Revolution. N of the Grands Boulevards is Montmartre, the highest part of Paris (128 m; 420 ft), crowned by the church of Sacré-Cœur. On the left bank the Boulevard St Michel or Boul' Mich leads S from the Île de la Cité to the Latin Quarter, with the Sorbonne or University of Paris, one of the oldest in the world (founded 1150). S of the river, too, are the Panthéon, the Chamber of Deputies, the Eiffel Tower, the principal landmark of Paris (300 m; 984 ft), and the district of Montparnasse, SW of the Luxembourg Palace.

The city is named after its early inhabitants, the Parisii, the Gallic tribe whose original village on the Île de la Cité spread to the left bank after the Roman conquest, when it was called Lutetia. The town was captured by the Franks and in the 6th cent. became the residence of the Merovingian king Clovis. It was later repeatedly attacked and destroyed by the Norsemen, who were finally beaten off, and Capet chose Paris as the cap. of his kingdom in AD 987. It grew rapidly in the 12th and 13th cent. and from then on remained the focus of the life and history of France. Notre-Dame and the fortress of the Louvre were built and the university was founded. The city came under attack in the Hundred Years War and was for a time occupied by the English. A period of great development came in the Renaissance period under Francis I and Marie de Medici when the Louvre was rebuilt, and the Tuileries, Luxembourg and Hôtel de Ville constructed. It suffered tragedy in the massacre of the Huguenots (1572) and allowed Henry IV to enter the city only after a public declaration of his conversion to Roman Catholicism ('Paris is well worth a Mass'). In the 17th and 18th cent. Paris grew in size and amenities, its cultural life flourished and the splendour of the court increased until Louis XIV moved to Versailles. The storming of the Bastille in Paris signalled the beginning of the French Revolution, followed by the execution of Louis XVI, the Reign of Terror and the meteoric career of Napoleon Bonaparte. After 1800 industrialization brought overcrowding in the unimproved districts, to the point of revolt. The revolutions of 1830 and 1848 caused no damage to the city and from 1855 Baron Georges Haussmann (1809–91), Prefect of the Seine, carried out the bold planning which characterizes modern Paris. In the Franco–Prussian War (1870–1) Paris was besieged for 4 months and after capitulation was further damaged during the suppression of the Commune. In World War I the German advance was halted a few miles from Paris. It was occupied by the Germans 1940–4, suffering only minor damage.

Paris Basin France. Saucer-shaped depression in the N, drained by the Seine R. and its tributaries, the Somme R., and the middle course of the Loire R. At the heart of the central area, the Île de France, is Paris. It covers 120,000 sq km (46,000 sq. miles). Surrounding this area are concentric chalk and limestone escarpments, most apparent to the E, where the Champagne wine country

is situated. Much of the Paris Basin is very fertile and esp. productive of wheat and dairy produce.

Paris-Plage ➤TOUQUET, LE.

Parkersburg USA. Industrial town in West Virginia on the Ohio R. at the confluence with the Little Kanawha R. Pop. (1990) 33,882.
In a region producing oil and natural gas. Manufactures oilfield equipment, metal and metal products and glass.
First settled 1785. Chartered 1820.

Park Ridge USA. City and suburb of NW Chicago in Illinois near the international airport at O'Hare Field. Pop. (1980) 38,704. Residential community.

Parma Italy. Cap. of Parma province in Emilia-Romagna on the Parma R. and the Aemilian Way. Pop. (1991) 173,991.
Manufactures machinery, glass and food products. Trade in grain, livestock, Parmesan cheese and other dairy produce.
The 11th-cent. Romanesque cathedral has Correggio's fresco of the Assumption decorating the dome. Other outstanding buildings are the octagonal 12th/13th-cent. baptistery, the 16th/17th-cent. Church of San Giovanni Evangelista with more frescoes by Correggio and the wooden Teatro Farnese. A Roman colony from 183 BC. A cultural centre in medieval times; the university was founded 1502. Birthplace of Arturo Toscanini, the conductor (1867–1957).

Parma USA. Town in N Ohio just S of Cleveland. Pop. (1990) 87,876. Mainly residential.
Manufactures motor-vehicle parts and machine-tools.

Parnaíba Brazil. Town in Piauí state near the mouth of the Parnaíba R. Pop. (1985) 79,000.
Commercial centre for the entire state. Exports cotton, sugar, carnauba wax and cattle.

Parnaíba River Brazil. River 1200 km (750 miles) long, rising in the Serra das Mangabeiras and flowing generally NNE, forming the boundary between the Maranhão and Paiuí states.

Parnassus, Mount Greece. Mountain 2457 m (8061 ft) high in the NW of Boeotia *nome* 72 km (45 miles) NE of Corinth. One of the holiest mountains of ancient Greece, sacred to Dionysus, Apollo and the Muses, with Delphi and the Castalian spring on its S slopes.

Pärnu (Pyärnu) Estonia. Seaport at the mouth of the Pärnu R. on Pärnu Bay, Gulf of Riga 117 km (73 miles) S of Tallinn. Pop. (1991) 58,600.

Exports timber and flax. Sawmilling. Manufactures textiles, leather goods.

Founded 1255.

Páros Greece. Aegean island in the Cyclades. Area 166 sq km (64 sq. miles). Pop. (1985) 7000. Rises to a central peak 748 m (2453 ft) high, on the N side of which are the quarries of white Parian marble, used by sculptors from the 6th cent. BC.

Parthia. Ancient kingdom in SW Asia, roughly co-extensive with the modern Khurasan in NE Iran, founded by Arsaces in 248 BC and reaching its greatest power under Mithridates I and II in the following two cent. Its rule was extended over the whole of Persia and present-day Iraq to the Euphrates, and its mounted bowmen, formidable in battle, were frequently successful against the Romans. The Parthian kingdom fell in AD 226 to the Sassanids and was annexed to Persia. Among the caps of Parthia were Hecatompylos and Ctesiphon.

Pasadena USA. Mainly residential town in California just NE of Los Angeles. Pop. (1990) 131,591.

Some light industries.

Seat of the California Institute of Technology (1891). The Henry E. Huntington Library and Art Gallery and the pine-clad Mt Wilson and Mt Lowe, each with an observatory, are nearby. Pageants, football matches and similar events are held in the famous Rose Bowl, an amphitheatre seating 85,000

people. The Tournament of Roses, a fiesta dating to 1890, is held every New Year's Day.

Pasargadae Iran. Ancient city in Persia 96 km (60 miles) NE of the modern Shiraz, built by Cyrus the Great after his victory over Astyages and made his cap. Among the remains are the tomb and palace of Cyrus. Later replaced as cap. by Persepolis.

Pascagoula USA. City and port in Mississippi at the mouth of the Pascagoula R. on the Gulf of Mexico. Pop. (1990) 25,899.

Industries inc. fishing, paper, chemicals and shipbuilding.

Pascua, Isla de ➤EASTER ISLAND.

Pas-de-Calais France. Department in the N bounded to the N by the Straits of Dover (in French, *Pas de Calais*), formed (1790) from Artois and part of Picardy. Area 6671 sq km (2576 sq. miles). Pop. (1992) 1,436,400. Prefecture Arras.

Cereals, sugar-beet, flax and hops cultivated, but it is mainly industrial, with the emphasis on coalmining, metallurgy and textile manufactures.

Chief towns Calais and Boulogne, both seaports, Arras, Béthune, St Omer, Lens. Le Touquet is a seaside resort.

Passaic USA. Industrial town in New Jersey on the Passaic R. 14 km (9 miles) N of Newark. Pop. (1990) 58,041.

Manufactures textiles, rubber and leather products, radio and television equipment.

Settled by the Dutch 1678.

Passau Germany. Town in Bavaria at the confluence of the Danube with the Inn and Ilz rivers 113 km (70 miles) SE of Regensburg near the Austrian frontier. Pop. (1991) 50,670.

River port and tourist centre. Manufactures agricultural machinery, tobacco products, paper and lenses. Industries inc. brewing and tanning.

The cathedral stands in the old town, on the tongue of land between the Danube and the Inn. Colonized by the Romans. The bishopric was founded 738.

Passchendaele Belgium. Village 60 km (35 miles) W of Ghent. Over 500,000 Allies and Germans died here in heavy fighting in 1917.

Pasto Colombia. Cap. of Nariño department 265 km (165 miles) SSW of Cali at a height of 2590 m (8495 ft). Pop. (1992) 303,400.

Commercial centre of an agricultural and cattle-rearing region. Food-processing. Manufactures hats, wooden bowls (decorated with locally made varnish).

Founded 1539. Has lost its former colonial character.

Paston England. Village in Norfolk 27 km (17 miles) NNE of Norwich. Here lived the Paston family, whose correspondence (1422–1509) became known as the Paston Letters, documents of great historical importance (now mainly in the British Library).

Patagonia Argentina/Chile. Originally the most southerly part of South America – S of about 39° S lat. – inc. Argentine and Chilean territory, but now applied usually to the E or Argentine part. This consists mainly of a semi-arid tableland extending for 1600 km (1000 miles) S of the Limay and Negro rivers to the Strait of Magellan. The plateau rises from the coast by low terraces to the base of the Andes. In the S the W part overlooks a depression, interrupted by Andean spurs and containing volcanic debris and glacial material. Large lakes extend from the Andes into this trough; several drain W, and rivers such as the Chico, Chubut and Deseado flow in deep trenches across the plateau.

Patagonia is shielded from the prevailing westerly winds by the Andes and is affected by the cold Falkland Current to the E, so that little rain falls in the cool winters or warm summers. Vegetation consists largely of tussock grass and small shrubs; extensive sheep-farming is the main occupation, cattle being raised in the moister W parts. Many settlers came from Britain, inc. the Welsh who founded Trelew, Puerto Madryn; others came from the pampas and from S. Chile. Comodoro Rivadavia is Argentina's chief source of petroleum, sending oil to La Plata and piping gas to Buenos Aires; coal in the S (Río Turbio) is sent by rail to Río Gallegos for dispatch to the pampas ports.

Chilean Patagonia has good grassland and supports large numbers of sheep, with cattle in the piedmont area. Punta Arenas exports wool, skins and frozen meat and was a point of entry for early colonists. Oil is obtained from Chilean Tierra del Fuego. The boundary between Chile and Argentina was fixed by treaty in 1881, but the demarcation was not completed till 1907.

Paternò Italy. Town and resort in Catania province, E Sicily just to the S of Mt Etna. Pop. (1981) 45,000.

In a region producing citrus fruits and wine.

Has a 14th-cent. castle and cathedral.

Paterson USA. Industrial town in NE New Jersey on the Passaic R., deriving hydroelectric power from the falls. Pop. (1990) 140,891.

A leading centre for silk weaving and dyeing, which have declined somewhat in recent years. Manufactures textile machinery, plastics, clothing and rubber products.

One of the first American factory strikes took place in a cotton mill here (1828); workers left their looms to demand a reduction of daily hours of work from 13½ to 12.

Pathein (Bassein) Myanmar (Burma). Port in Lower Myanmar (Burma) on the Pathein R. (the westernmost distributary of the Irrawaddy R.) 113 km (70 miles) from the mouth. Pop. (1983) 144,000.

Centre of the rice trade. Rice-milling. Pottery manufacture.

Patiala India. Town in Punjab 209 km (130 miles) NNW of Delhi. Pop. (1991) 253,700.

Trade in cotton and grain. Manufactures metal goods, textiles, footwear, sports goods and chemicals.

Seat of the Punjabi University (1962). Formerly cap. of Patiala state and of the Patiala and E Punjab States Union.

Patmos Greece. Aegean island in the N

Dodecanese. Area 33 sq km (13 sq. miles). Chief town Patmos on the SE coast. Here St John the Divine wrote the Revelation whilst in exile. The monastery of St John was founded in the 11th cent. to commemorate his stay on the island.

Patna India. Cap. of Bihar on the Ganges R. 467 km (290 miles) NW of Calcutta. Pop. (1991) 917,200.

Railway junction. Manufactures brassware, carpets, furniture, steel tubes, plastics and footwear. Trade in rice and oilseeds.

Contains the mosques of Husain Shah and Sher Shah and a Sikh temple.

Patras (Gr. **Pátrai**) Greece. Cap. of Achaea *nome* on the Gulf of Patras in the NW Peloponnese. Pop. (1991) 155,180.

Seaport. Exports chiefly currants, also olive oil, wine and tobacco. Flour-milling. Manufactures textiles.

The Greek War of Independence began here (1821).

Patras (Gr. **Pátrai**), **Gulf of** Greece. Inlet of the Ionian Sea on the W coast, linked by a narrow strait to the Gulf of Corinth (E). Patras is on the SE shore.

Pau France. Prefecture of the Basses-Pyrénées department on the Gave de Pau R., tributary of the Adour, 153 km (95 miles) WSW of Toulouse. Pop. (1990) 83,928.

Tourist resort. Engineering, tanning, brewing and flour-milling. Manufactures textiles and footwear. Trade in wine and foodstuffs.

Was the cap. of Béarn and from 1512 residence of the French kings of Navarre.

Paulo Afonso Falls Brazil. Falls on the lower São Francisco R. 314 km (195 miles) from the mouth, consisting of rapids and three cascades together 82 m (269 ft) high. The large hydroelectric power station supplies much of NE Brazil. The surrounding area has been made a National Park.

Pavia Italy. Ancient Ticinum. Cap. of Pavia province in Lombardy on the Ticino R. 32 km (20 miles) S of Milan. Pop. (1990) 80,070.

Railway and road junction. Market for the agricultural produce of the Po valley (cereals and wine). Manufactures textiles, sewing-machines, agricultural machinery, furniture and electrical goods. Cathedral (15th-cent.); among the many famous churches that of San Michele dates from the 11th and 12th cent. An early centre of learning; its law school was probably founded in the 9th cent. and became the university in 1361. The 14th-cent. covered bridge across the Ticino was severely damaged in World War II (1944). The magnificent Carthusian monastery of Certosa di Pavia is 8 km (5 miles) N. Francis I of France was defeated and captured here by the Emperor Charles V (1525). Under Spanish, French and Austrian rule in turn in the 18th cent.; passed to Italy 1859.

Pavlodar Kazakhstan. Cap. of the Pavlodar region on the Irtysh R. 400 km (250 miles) ENE of Tselinograd. Pop. (1991) 342,500.

Industries inc. meat-packing, milk-canning and flour-milling.

Pawtucket USA. Industrial town in NE Rhode Island on the Blackstone R. at a 15-m (49-ft) waterfall. Pop. (1990) 72,644.

Manufactures textiles, textile machinery and machine-tools.

The first water-power cotton mill in the USA was built here (1790).

Paysandú Uruguay. Cap. of the Paysandú department on the Uruguay R. 338 km (210 miles) NW of Montevideo. Pop. (1985) 75,081.

Important port and meat-packing centre. Manufactures soap, leather, footwear and textiles.

Pays de la Loire France. Region in the W comprising the departments of Loire-Atlantique, Maine-et-Loire, Mayenne, Sarthe and Vendée. Area 32,082 sq km (12,387 sq. miles). Pop. (1990) 3,059,100. Originally the region's economy was based essentially on the agri-foodstuffs industry but it has become gradually more diversified and now inc. electronics, engineering, clothing and footwear. The hub of its activity is the

Nantes–Saint Nazaire port complex. A high-speed train service (TGV) links Nantes with Paris in 2 hours, thus furthering development of the economy and of tourism to the Atlantic beaches.

Pazardzhik Bulgaria. Town situated W of Plovdiv on the Martisa R. Pop. (1990) 87,277.

Railway junction and processing centre serving a fertile agricultural and vine-growing area. Manufactures textiles, rubber and leather goods.

Peace River Canada. River 1920 km (1195 miles) long, formed by the union at Finlay Forks of two headstreams, the Finlay and the Parsnip, both rising in the Rocky Mountains; flowing generally E and N through British Columbia and Alberta by a fertile valley, it joins the Slave R.

Peak District England. Hilly district in the Pennines in N Derbyshire, rising to 637 m (2089 ft) in Kinder Scout 16 km (10 miles) N of Buxton. The N part is known as the High Peak. Many limestone caves, the best known being Peak Cavern, near Castleton.

Pearl Harbor USA. Major US naval and air base in the Pacific on the S coast of Oahu, Hawaii. On 7 Dec. 1941 the Japanese made a surprise attack without previous declaration of war (repeating the pattern of their attack on Russia in 1905), using aircraft and submarines which sank or put out of action a great part of the US fleet. This precipitated US entry into World War II.

Pearl Islands (Sp. **Archipiélago de las Perlas**) Panama. Group of about 180 islands in the Gulf of Panama. Pearl-fishing. Sea angling. Chief islands San Miguel (Isla del Rey), San José, Pedro González.

Pearl River ►XI JIANG.

Peć Serbia. Town in Kosovo-Metohija 124 km (77 miles) NW of Skoplje. Pop. (1971) 42,100. Much of the town is oriental in appearance with narrow, winding streets, mosques and Turkish houses. Seat of the Serbian patriarchs for over 300 years between

the 14th and the 18th cent.; their 13th-cent. monastery stands above the town. Freed from Turkish rule 1913.

Pechora River Russia. River 1770 km (1100 miles) long, rising in the N Urals and flowing generally N and W through coniferous forest and tundra, entering the Gulf of Pechora on the Barents Sea by a delta. When ice-free (June–Sept.) it carries cargoes of timber, coal, furs and fish.

Peckham England. District in the metropolitan borough of Camberwell, SE London; from 1965 in the London borough of Southwark. Inc. Peckham Rye Common and Park (46 ha; 113 acres).

Pecos River USA. River 1191 km (740 miles) long, rising in N New Mexico in the Sangre de Cristo Range, flowing generally SSE through New Mexico and Texas and joining the Rio Grande. Important dams provide irrigation water for a large agricultural region.

Pécs (Ger. **Fünfkirchen**, 'Five Churches') Hungary. Cap. of Baranya county in the S on the S slopes of the Meczek Hills. Pop. (1992) 170,542.

Industrial town in a coalmining area. Manufactures clothing, leather goods, porcelain, tobacco products and soap. Trade in wine.

Has a magnificent 11th-cent cathedral, rebuilt in the 19th cent. The university, founded 1367, lapsed in 1526 and was revived in 1921. Under Turkish rule 1543–1686.

Peebles Scotland. Market town in Scottish Borders on the R. Tweed 34 km (21 miles) S of Edinburgh. Pop. (1991) 7065.

Resort. Manufactures woollen goods and has a photography processing laboratory.

Has the remains of the 13th-cent. Cross Kirk, which was supposed to have contained a fragment of the Cross. Became a royal burgh 1367. Birthplace of William (1800–83) and Robert Chambers (1802–71), the publishers.

Peeblesshire (Tweeddale) Scotland.

Former county in the Southern Uplands now in Scottish Borders.

Peel Isle of Man. Port and seaside resort on the W coast 16 km (10 miles) WNW of Douglas. Pop. (1991) 3829.

Industries fishing and tourism.

Remains of a 13th/14th-cent. cathedral. Just offshore, and connected with the mainland by causeway, is St Patrick's Isle, almost entirely occupied by the ruins of Peel Castle; here St Patrick is believed to have founded the first church on Man.

Peenemünde Germany. Village in Rostock district on the NW of Usedom island at the entrance to the Peene R. estuary from the Baltic Sea. Site of a research station for rockets and guided missiles in World War II, captured by Russian forces in 1945.

Pegu (Bago) Myanmar (Burma). Ancient town on the Pegu R. 72 km (45 miles) NE of Rangoon. Pop. 47,000.

Manufactures pottery.

The outstanding building is the Shwemawdaw pagoda, 99 m (325 ft) high, and there is a large recumbent figure of Buddha. Founded in the 6th cent. Became cap. of a united Burma in the early 16th cent. Destroyed in the mid 18th cent., but was rebuilt and became the cap. of Pegu province.

Pegu Yoma Myanmar (Burma). Range of hills 400 km (250 miles) long extending N–S parallel to and E of the lower Irrawaddy R. Generally below 300 m (984 ft) but rising to 1520 m (4986 ft) in Mt Popa, an extinct volcano. Teak forests.

Peipus, Lake Estonia/Russia. Lake between Estonia and Russia, consisting of two basins: L. Peipus proper (L. Chudskoye), the larger (N) and L. Pskov (S), connected by a strait 24 km (15 miles) long. Total area 3512 sq km (1346 sq. miles). Empties by the Narova (Narva) R. into the Gulf of Finland. The shores are flat and marshy or sandy. Frozen Dec.–March.

Pekalongan Indonesia. Seaport in Central Java province on the Java Sea 88 km (55 miles) W of Semarang. Pop. (1990) 227,535.

In a district producing rice, sugar-cane. Exports sugar.

Pekin USA. River port and industrial town in Illinois 14 km (9 miles) S of Peoria. Pop. (1970) 31,375.

Trade in grain, livestock. Manufactures food products and metal goods.

Peking ▸BEIJING.

Pella Greece. 1. *Nome* in Macedonia bordering N on Yugoslavia. Area 2506 sq km (1082 sq. miles). Pop. (1991) 138,261. Cap. Edessa. Largely mountainous. Produces cotton, wheat and tobacco.

2. Ancient town 11 km (7 miles) ESE of the modern Giannitsa (Yiannitsa) and near the modern village of Pella. Cap. of Macedonia under Philip II. Birthplace of Alexander the Great (356–323 BC).

Peloponnese (Gr. **Peloponnisos**, 'the Island of Pelops') Greece. Formerly Morea, probably from its resemblance in shape to a mulberry leaf. The S peninsula of the country, joined to central Greece by the Isthmus of Corinth. Area 21,439 sq km (8354 sq. miles). Pop. (1991) 1,077,002. Largely mountainous with deeply indented S and E coasts.

Vines, citrus fruits and olives cultivated. Sheep and goats raised.

Pelotas Brazil. Seaport in Rio Grande do Sul state, on the São Gonçalo Canal near the entrance to the lagoon Lagôa dos Patos. Pop. (1985) 278,400.

Exports meat products, wool and hides. Meat-packing, flour-milling and tanning. Manufactures food products, soap, footwear and furniture.

Pemba Tanzania. Coral island in the Indian Ocean 40 km (25 miles) NNE of Zanzibar. Area 984 sq km (380 sq. miles). Pop. (1988) 265,039. Cap. Chake.

Produces most of the world's cloves. Also exports copra. ▸▸ZANZIBAR AND PEMBA.

Pembroke Wales. Market town in Pembrokeshire on Milford Haven 14 km (9 miles) W of Tenby. Pop. (1991) 6773.

Engineering.

Dominated by the 11th-cent. castle. Nearby are the remains of the 11th-cent. Monkton Priory. A government dockyard was established in 1814 and closed in 1926, the new town that grew around it being called Pembroke Dock (1.6 km (1 mile) NW); it was used as a naval base in World War II. Pop. (1991) 8651. Birthplace of Henry VII (1457–1509).

Pembroke Dock ➤PEMBROKE.

Pembrokeshire Wales. County in SW disbanded in 1974 when it became part of Dyfed, but reinstated in 1996. Pop. (1994) 114,000.

Penang ➤PULAU PINANG.

Penarth Wales. Town in the Vale of Glamorgan 5 km (3 miles) S of Cardiff on the Bristol Channel at the mouth of the R. Taff. Pop. (1971) 23,965. Seaside resort. Port.

Pendlebury ➤SWINTON AND PENDLEBURY.

Penge England. Part of the London borough of Bromley. Mainly residential: a dormitory suburb of SE London.

Manufactures electrical equipment.

Site of the Crystal Palace (1854) until its destruction by fire (1936). Now site of the Crystal Palace National Recreation Centre.

Peninsular Malaysia Malaysia. The S end of the Malay Peninsula formerly named Western Malaysia and bounded N by Thailand. Area 131,588 sq km (50,806 sq. miles). ➤➤FEDERATION OF MALAYSIA.

Penistone England. Town in South Yorkshire on the R. Don 19 km (12 miles) NW of Sheffield. Pop. (1991) 8627.

Steel mills.

Penmaenmawr Wales. Town in Conwy on Conwy Bay 10 km (6 miles) SW of Llandudno. Pop. (1990) 4000. Seaside resort. At the foot of Penmaenmawr headland (450 m; 1476 ft) on which stood the ancient British fortress of Dinas Penmaen.

Pennine Range (Pennines, Pennine Chala) England. System of hills extending from the Cheviot Hills in the N to the valley of the R. Trent in the S, separated from the former by the Tyne Gap. Forms the watershed of the main rivers of N England and is sometimes termed 'the backbone of England'. Separated from the mountains of the Lake District by the Eden and Lune rivers, cut by the Yorkshire dales and farther S by the Aire Gap, and ends in the S with the Peak District of Derbyshire. Highest peak is Cross Fell (893 m; 2929 ft) in the loftier N section; other heights are Mickle Fell (790 m; 2591 ft), Whernside (737 m; 2417 ft), Ingleborough (723 m; 2371 ft); in the lower S part is The Peak (636 m; 2086 ft). Moorland and rough pasture, where sheep are grazed, occupy most of the upper region, and the wild scenery here, the picturesque dales, the limestone caves and underground streams attract many tourists. Reservoirs in the upland valleys provide a water supply for industrial areas on both sides of the Pennines. A 400-km (250-mile) footpath along the Pennines, the Pennine Way, was opened in 1965; it extends from Edale (Derbyshire) to Kirk Yetholm (Roxburghshire) and passes through three National Parks, the Peak District, the Yorkshire Dales and Northumberland.

Pennsylvania USA. State in the NE, bordered on the NW by L. Erie. Area 119,251 sq km (46,043 sq. miles). Pop. (1993) 12,048,000. Cap. Harrisburg. Almost entirely within the Appalachian Mountains system; contains the Allegheny Plateau and parts of the Allegheny Mountains, inc. the highest point, Mt Davis (980 m; 3214 ft). Principal rivers the Delaware (on the E boundary), the Susquehanna and the Ohio (formed by the union of the Allegheny and the Monongahela, in the W). Climate humid continental. Annual rainfall 85–125 cm (34–50 ins.). Extensive forests yield a variety of hardwoods. Main crop hay; vegetables and fruit important. Rich in coal, both anthracite (of which it is the main US source) and bituminous coal. Natural gas and petroleum also obtained. Second in value of manufactures only to New York; the great iron and steel industry centred on Pittsburgh produces 30 per cent of the total US steel output. Philadelphia, the largest city, is a great textile centre. Other important industrial towns are Erie, Scranton and Allentown. Originally settled by the Swedes (1643), who were dispossessed by the Dutch (1655). William Penn (1644–1718), English Quaker, received a grant of land, which inc. most of the present state, in 1681; he named it Pennsylvania (Penn's woods). One of the original 13 states and the second to ratify the constitution (1787).

Penrith England. Town in Cumbria 27 km (17 miles) SSE of Carlisle. Pop. (1990) 12,500.

Tourist centre for the Lake District. Brewing, tanning and engineering.

Has a ruined 14th-cent. castle. In St Andrew's churchyard are two monuments, probably dating from the 10th cent., 'Giant's Grave' and 'Giant's Thumb'. Just NE is Penrith Beacon (286 m; 938 ft) and 8 km (5 miles) SW is Ullswater.

Penryn England. Market town in Cornwall at the head of the R. Penryn estuary 3 km (2 miles) NW of Falmouth. Pop. (1991) 7027.

Port. A centre of the granite-quarrying industry.

Pensacola USA. Seaport and naval air base in NW Florida 85 km (53 miles) ESE of Mobile (Alabama). Pop. (1990) 58,165.

Fishing, fish-canning. Manufactures furniture and paper.

First settled (1559) by the Spaniards. Changed hands several times between Spain, France and Britain. Finally acquired by the USA 1821.

Penticton Canada. Town in S British Columbia on the Okanagan R. near the S end of Okanagan Lake. Pop. (1991) 27,258.

Commercial centre in a fruit-growing region. Fruit packing and canning.

Pentland Firth Scotland. Channel 32 km (20 miles) long and up to 13 km (8 miles) wide between Caithness on the mainland and the Orkney Is. Notorious for its rough seas. Contains the islands of Stroma, Swona and the Pentland Skerries.

Pentland Hills Scotland. Range extending 26 km (16 miles) SW from just S of Edinburgh. Highest point Scald Law (579 m; 1899 ft).

Pentonville England. District in the London borough of Islington. Pentonville prison is in Caledonian Road. Birthplace of John Stuart Mill, English philosopher (1807–73).

Penza Russia. Cap. of the Penza region on the Sura R. 209 km (130 miles) NNW of Saratov. Pop. (1992) 552,000.

Railway junction. Industrial centre. Sawmilling, engineering. Manufactures watches, paper, matches and cement. Trade in grain and timber.

Founded in the 17th cent.

Penzance England. Town in SW Cornwall on Mount's Bay. Pop. (1985) 20,000.

Fishing port. Resort. Sends locally grown early vegetables and flowers (inc. those from the Scilly Is.) by train to London and elsewhere.

Birthplace of Sir Humphry Davy, English chemist (1778–1829).

Peoria USA. Town in Illinois on the Illinois R. where it widens to form L. Peoria 101 km (63 miles) N of Springfield. Pop. (1990) 113,504.

Manufactures agricultural machinery, food products, washing-machines, radio equipment and electrical goods. Trade in grain and livestock.

Perak Malaysia. The second most populous state in West Malaysia; borders N on Thailand and W on the Strait of Malacca. Area 21,005 sq km (8110 sq. miles). Pop. (1990) 1,880,016. Cap. Ipoh. Consists mainly of the basin of the Perak R. Rises to over 2100 m (6999 ft) in the interior. The chief tin-mining state. Also produces rice, rubber and copra. Chief towns Ipoh and Taiping.

Pereira Colombia. Cap. of Risaralda department 40 km (25 miles) SW of Manizales at a height of 1400 m (4723 ft). Pop. (1992) 335,960.

Commercial centre. Trade chiefly in coffee and cattle. Coffee-processing, brewing. Manufactures clothing, paper and foodstuffs.

Founded 1863.

Perekop Isthmus. Isthmus 6 km (4 miles) wide at its narrowest, joining the Crimea to the mainland of the Ukraine. Scene of heavy fighting between German and Russian forces in World War II. On it is situated a strategically important village of the same name.

Pergamum (Pergamus). Ancient Greek city in W Asia Minor, now occupied by the modern town of Bergama 80 km (50 miles) N of Izmir in Turkey. Among the ruins excavated here were the great altar of Zeus, the temple of Athena and the famous library. Attained its highest splendour in the 3rd and 2nd cent. BC as cap. of the kingdom of Pergamum, which was bequeathed to the Romans in 133 BC by Attalus III and part of which became the Roman province of Asia.

Périgord France. Area in the old Guienne province in the SW now mostly in the Dordogne department, consisting of dry limestone plateaux with the fertile valleys of the Dordogne and Isle rivers. Famous for truffles. Has yielded many important prehistoric remains.

Périgueux France. Prefecture of the Dordogne department on the Isle R. 80 km (50 miles) SW of Limoges. Pop. (1990) 32,848.

Famous for *pâté de foie gras* and truffles. Trade in grain, wine and poultry. Manufactures hardware, cutlery and chemicals.

Besides the modern town there are two old districts – the old Roman town and the medieval town known as Le Puy-St Front. In the last-named are the 12th-cent. cathedral of St Front, restored in the 19th cent. and the remains of a 6th-cent. basilica. In the Roman town is the 11th/12th-cent. Church of St Étienne, once the cathedral. Among the Roman remains are the amphitheatre and the tower of Vésone, the latter probably part

of a temple in the Roman town (Vesunna). Taken by the English 1356; returned to France in the reign of Charles V.

Perim Yemen. Island in the strait of Bab-el-Mandeb off the SW coast of the Arabian peninsula. Area 13 sq km (5 sq. miles). Rocky, barren and crescent-shaped. Formerly important as a coaling station (1883–1936), but its operations were transferred to Aden. Occupied by the British in 1799, abandoned, then re-occupied in 1857 and became part of Aden. From 1963 it was administered by the Commissioner for Kamaran and Perim. In 1967 it became part of the republic of Southern Yemen.

Perlis Malaysia. The smallest and most north-westerly state of West Malaysia, bounded on the NE and NW by Thailand. Area 795 sq km (307 sq. miles). Pop. (1991) 184,070. Cap. Kangar. Main products rice, rubber, tin and sugar. Transferred by Siam to Britain 1909. Became one of the nonfederated Malay States. Joined the Federation of Malaya 1948.

Perm Russia. Formerly (1940–62) Molotov. Cap. of the Perm region on the Kama R. Pop. (1992) 1,099,000.

Important railway junction. River port. Railway engineering, sawmilling and tanning. Manufactures agricultural equipment, excavators, aircraft and tractor parts, fertilizers, paper and matches.

The town developed industrially with the building of copper works (1723) but its greatest expansion came in the 20th cent., after World War I and again after World War II. In geology the Permian System of rocks was named after the Perm region because of their great development there.

Pernambuco Brazil. State in the NE with a narrow humid coastal zone, a drier intermediate zone and a dry interior (the *sertão*) which suffers periodic droughts. Area 101,023 sq km (39,005 sq. miles). Pop. (1991) 7,109,626. Cap. Recife. Produces sugar, tropical fruits and cotton.

Pernik Bulgaria. Formerly (1949–62)

Dimitrovo. Town in Sofia province on the Struma R. 27 km (17 miles) WSW of Sofia. Pop. (1990) 99,643.

Coalmining and industrial centre. Manufactures iron and steel, cement and glass. Other industries inc. engineering.

Perpignan France. Prefecture of the Pyrénées-Orientales department, near the Gulf of Lions and the Spanish border on the Têt R. and on the Paris–Barcelona railway. Pop. (1990) 108,049.

Tourist and commercial centre. Trade in wine, fruits and olives.

Cathedral (14th/16th-cent.); large citadel enclosing the castle (13th-cent.). Founded in the 10th cent. Cap. of the kingdom of Majorca (1278–1344) and in the 17th cent. of the province of Roussillon.

Persepolis Iran. Ancient city of Persia 48 km (30 miles) NE of modern Shiraz. Cap. of the Persian Empire, founded by Darius. The ruins of many of its great buildings still stand on a large terrace approached by a remarkable flight of steps. Among the remains are the hall of the 'Hundred Columns' and the palaces of Darius and his successors, built in marble from the neighbouring mountains. In the mountains themselves are the tombs of ancient Persian kings, inc. Darius. Persepolis was attacked and partly destroyed by Alexander the Great (330 BC) and thereafter declined. Extensively excavated in the 1930s and is today a tourist attraction.

Pershore England. Market town in Worcestershire on the R. Avon 13 km (8 miles) SE of Worcester. Pop. (1991) 7087.

Centre of a soft fruit-growing (chiefly plums) and market-gardening area.

Persia ➤IRAN.

Persian Gulf. Usually called 'The Gulf', extensive but shallow arm of the Arabian Sea between Iran and Arabia, linked with the Arabian Sea by the Strait of Hormuz and the Gulf of Oman. Area 238,790 sq km (92,200 sq. miles). Notorious for its extremely hot, humid summers. The only significant river that it receives is the Shatt-al-Arab, which

brings it the waters of the Tigris, Euphrates and Karun. Its once-famous pearl fisheries are now in decline and it is far more important for the vast oilfields around its shores.

Perth and Kinross Scotland. New Unitary Authority created in 1996, formerly Tayside Region. Pop. (1993) 130,470.

Perth Australia. Cap. of Western Australia on the N bank of the Swan R. 19 km (12 miles) from the mouth of a shallow tidal estuary. Pop. (1991) 1,143,249.

Administrative, commercial and industrial centre serving a vast territory, from its immediate agricultural hinterland to the huge NW cattle stations and inland goldfields. Manufactures textiles, clothing, furniture, cars, fertilizers, flour and cement.

The city and its suburbs are well spaced, with numerous parks, about a wide stretch of the river. Its port, Fremantle, at the river mouth, and Kwinana, to the S, are expanding industrial centres. The water supply comes chiefly from the Canning Dam and Mundaring Reservoir on short rivers to the W and SW. Terminus of the Trans-Australian Railway. Founded 1829.

Perth Scotland. Formerly St Johnstoun. Town in Perth and Kinross on the R. Tay. Pop. (1991) 41,453.

Important dyeing industry. Whisky distilling and bottling. Manufactures textiles and carpets.

One of its few architectural links with the past is the 15th-cent. Church of St John, where John Knox, Scottish Protestant reformer (c. 1513–72) preached his sermon against idolatry (1559). Cap. of Scotland from the early 12th cent. till 1437, when James I was assassinated here.

Perth Amboy USA. Seaport and industrial town in New Jersey at the mouth of the Raritan R. 27 km (17 miles) SSW of Newark. Pop. (1990) 45,000.

Industries inc. copper-smelting and oil-refining. Manufactures metal products, chemicals and plastics.

Founded 1683.

Perthshire Scotland. Former county in central Scotland now Perth and Kinross.

Peru. Republic in the W of South America. Bounded on the N by Ecuador and Colombia, E by Brazil, SE by Bolivia, S by Chile and W by the Pacific Ocean. Area 1,285,216 sq km (496,225 sq. miles). Pop. (1995) 23,489,000 (72 per cent urban). Life expectancy, 63 years male, 67 female. Cap. Lima. Other cities Arequipa, Callao, Trujillo and Chiclayo. Currency: Nuevo sol = 100 centimos. A country of great contrasts in relief, climate, vegetation and pop. Much of it is unsuitable for agriculture, and transport between regions is difficult. Consists of a dry coastal plain which quickly rises to the Sierra (average height 3900 m, 12,792 ft), covering about half the area of the country, beyond which is the *montāna*, the forested part of the Andes, an area of potential riches which has scarcely been tapped. The narrow coastal plain 2250 km (1400 miles) long occupies about one-ninth of the total area of Peru. It is desert, being shielded from the rain-bearing Trade Winds by the Andes. The cold Peruvian sea current causes low cloud and mist but scarcely any rain. Few of the short streams are perennial, but there are productive irrigated regions at intervals. E of this strip rise the Andean Cordilleras, where the rivers traverse broad valleys at 3000−4500 m (9840−14,760 ft) and plunge through great canyons to the E lowlands. The W Cordillera is the highest, with Huascarán rising to 6770 m (22,211 ft). In the S are volcanic peaks such as the perfect snow-capped cone of El Misti (5822 m, 19,096 ft). In this region the boundary with Bolivia crosses the deep freshwater L. Titicaca, at a height of 3814 m (12,510 ft). There are great climatic differences between the high, bleak Andean plateaux, the milder sheltered basins and the deep tropical valleys farther E. A gigantic river system drains N through the lowland forests, the Apurimac and Urubamba join to form the Ucayali, which in turn joins the Marañón to form the Amazon in the NE. Land use: forested 53 per cent, pasture 21 per cent, agricultural 3 per cent. Religion about 92 per cent Roman Catholic. Official langs are Spanish, Quechua and Aymará (Indian). Ethnic groups Quechua 47 per cent, mestizo 32 per cent, white 12 per cent.

A large proportion of the pop. live by subsistence farming. Staple foods are maize and potatoes, and coca leaves are chewed to alleviate hardships. Many highland Indians migrate to the coast, and as a result the suburbs of Lima are overcrowded. Wool of the sheep, alpaca and llama flocks is sent to highland markets. Arequipa and Lima have textile industries. Cotton and sugar-cane are important crops, being grown mainly on irrigated land; rice and coffee are also produced. There has been a great expansion in the fishing industry in recent years, largely for the production of fishmeal; in 1972 the anchovy catch diminished seriously owing to the cool Peruvian ocean current being temporarily replaced by the warm El Niño current, and fishmeal exports were much reduced, but the industry later recovered. On offshore islands guano has accumulated in the dry climate from multitudes of seabirds; this is now worked by a government monopoly and the birds are protected. Mineral resources are considerable in the highlands; Cerro de Pasco is important for copper, lead, zinc and silver; bismuth, gold and vanadium are also mined. Coal is sent to the Oroya smelting centre; petroleum is found in the far N, near the coast, and in the E *montaña*. Coal and iron deposits in the Santa R. valley supply the steelworks of Chimbote (opened 1958). Other industries inc. food-processing, textiles, smelting, fishing and forestry. Callao is the leading seaport; Iquitos, a port on the upper Amazon, is the principal outlet to the E. The main exports copper, petroleum and petroleum products, lead, zinc, coffee and fish products.

The coastal area of Peru produced some of the earliest cultures of South America, and from the end of the 11th cent. the Inca civilization was based on Cuzco. This planned society controlled extensive territories with the help of a common religion, centrally organized production and consumption, and an efficient road system.

Pizarro reached Peru in 1532 and seized Cuzco, executing the Inca monarch Atahualpa at Cajamarca; in 1535 Lima was founded and with Callao became a focal point for Spanish settlement and political power. Wheat and barley were added to maize and potatoes as highland crops; horses, sheep and cattle were introduced. Huge estates were granted to individual Spaniards, to be worked by Indian labour; other Indians worked communally, paying rent to Spanish landlords, and others provided forced labour in the mines. The hard conditions and diseases greatly reduced the pop.; meanwhile, the lowland irrigated areas suffered neglect. In 1820 San Martín landed in S Peru and in the following year proclaimed Peruvian independence, but much of the country remained under Spanish control until Bolívar and Sucre won decisive battles (1824). From 1864 to 1879 Peru was nominally at war with Spain. In the War of the Pacific (1879–83) Peru and Bolivia were defeated by Chile, losing the S nitrate fields, but Peru regained the S oasis of Tacna in 1929. Boundary disputes with Colombia and Ecuador were settled in 1934 and 1942 respectively. From 1968 following a *coup* Peru had a reformist military government but a civilian government was restored in 1980. In 1992 an economic crisis and the activities of the 'Shining Path', a left-wing guerrilla movement, caused the President to suspend the Constitution. Congress comprises a 180-member House of Congress and a 60-member Senate.

Perugia Italy. Ancient Perusia. Cap. of Perugia province in Umbria E of L. Trasimeno on a group of hills above the Tiber valley. Pop. (1991) 150,576.

Manufactures chocolate, woollen goods and furniture. Trade in grain, wine and olive oil. The medieval city attracts tourists.

It has a Gothic cathedral (14th/ 15th-cent.); the Palazzo Comunale, with its valuable art collection, dates from the 13th cent. University (1276). Was an important Etruscan city and has Etruscan, Roman and medieval remains. Taken by the Romans 40 BC. Later ruled by the Popes (9th cent. AD).

Became the centre of the Umbrian school of painting, whose outstanding figure was Perugino (1450–1524), born nearby.

Perugia, Lake ►TRASIMENO, LAKE.

Pervouralsk Russia. Industrial town 45 km (28 miles) WNW of Sverdlovsk on the railway to Perm. Pop. (1992) 140,000.

Industries inc. metalworking, brickmaking and sawmilling. Iron ore mined in the neighbourhood.

Pesaro Italy. Cap. of Pesaro e Urbino province in The Marches 35 km (22 miles) SE of Rimini on the Adriatic coast. Pop. (1971) 86,239.

Port and seaside resort. Manufactures majolica, agricultural machinery and soap.

Has a 15th-cent. ducal palace and fortress, and a school of music endowed by Gioacchino Rossini, Italian composer (1792–1868), who was born here.

Pescadores Taiwan. Group of about 60 islands (only 24 inhabited) off the W coast of Formosa (Taiwan), the largest and most important being Penghu. Area 127 sq km (49 sq. miles). Pop. (1990) 120,000.

Main occupations fishing, fish-processing.

With Formosa they were ceded to Japan by China 1895. Since World War II they have been controlled by Taiwan.

Pescara Italy. Cap. of Pescara province in Abruzzi at the mouth of the Pescara R. on the Adriatic coast. Pop. (1991) 128,563.

Port. Seaside resort. Manufactures furniture, soap, glass and textiles.

Birthplace of Gabriele d'Annunzio (1863–1938).

Peshawar Pakistan. Cap. of the NW Frontier Province 370 km (230 miles) NW of Lahore. Pop. (1981) 566,248.

Important commercial centre, particularly for trade between Pakistan and Afghanistan, being 18 km (11 miles) E of Jamrud, at the entrance to the Khyber Pass. Rice-milling. Handicraft manufacture of textiles, pottery, leather goods and copperware.

Pest Hungary. City on the left bank of the

Danube R. opposite Buda. Together they form Budapest. Pop. (1993) 965,000.

Commercial centre; almost completely rebuilt after flooding in 1838. Traditionally the business centre of the city, Buda being the residential sector.

Petach Tikuah Israel. Town on the Plain of Sharon 11 km (7 miles) E of Tel Aviv. Pop. (1991) 146,700.

Industrial centre. Manufactures textiles, chemicals and furniture.

Pétange Luxembourg. Town situated NW of Esch-sur-Alzette on the Chiers R. Pop. (1993) 12,345.

Iron-mining centre.

Peterborough Canada. Industrial town and railway junction in S Ontario on the Otonabee R. 113 km (70 miles) NE of Toronto. Pop. (1991) 68,371.

Manufactures clocks and watches, knitwear, electrical machinery, dairy equipment and hardware.

Peterborough England. Originally Medehamstede. City in Cambridgeshire on the R. Nene 58 km (36 miles) NE of Northampton. Pop. (1991) 114,733.

Railway junction and industrial centre at the W edge of the Fens. Industries inc. electronics, textiles, domestic appliances, engineering, beet-sugar refining and brickmaking (at Fletton).

The cathedral, the third church on the same site, was begun in the 12th cent. and has been much restored; it contains the tomb of Catherine of Aragon, and Mary Queen of Scots (1587–1612) was buried here. Also has a 15th-cent. church (St John's) and a market hall dating from 1671. A Saxon village before the abbey was founded here (655).

Peterborough, Soke of England. Flat, low-lying region (area 218 sq km; 84 sq. miles) between the Welland and the Nene rivers, part of the Bedford Level. The former area of jurisdiction ('soke') of the Benedictine abbey founded here in 655.

Peter I Island (Peter I Øy) Norway. Island in the Bellingshausen Sea off Thurston Peninsula, Antarctica, sighted in 1821 by the Russian explorer, Admiral von Bellingshausen. The first landing was made in 1929 by a Norwegian expedition which hoisted the Norwegian flag. Area 178 sq km (69 sq. miles). Dependency of Norway. Uninhabited.

Peterhead Scotland. Town in Aberdeenshire on the North Sea 45 km (28 miles) NNE of Aberdeen. Pop. (1991) 18,674.

Largest fishing port in the European Community and also white-fish market. The main industry is food-processing, also woollen cloth manufacture, light engineering and oil-rig repairs.

Founded 1587. Landing place of the Old Pretender (1715).

Peterlee England. Town in Co. Durham 16 km (10 miles) E of Durham City. Pop. (1990) 23,500. Founded as a 'new' town in 1948 in the rural district of Easington. The Development Corporation was wound up in 1988.

Industries inc. engineering and the manufacture of textiles and transport equipment.

Petersburg USA. Industrial town in Virginia on the Appomattox R. 37 km (23 miles) S of Richmond. Pop. (1970) 35,610.

Manufactures tobacco products, luggage, textiles and optical goods.

Withstood a long siege by Federal troops (1864–5) in the American Civil War.

Petersfield England. Town in Hampshire 24 km (15 miles) NNE of Portsmouth. Pop. (1991) 12,177.

Once engaged in the woollen industry. Now a market town for a farming area.

Petra Jordan. Ancient city in a basin on the E side of the Wadi el Araba in the SW. Cap. of the Nabataéans and an important centre of caravan trade. Flourished from the 1st cent. BC to the 3rd cent. AD Annexed to the Roman Empire AD 106. Declined as Palmyra grew in importance and was forgotten until its ruins were discovered by Burckhardt (1812). These ruins inc. temples, houses and a great theatre, carved out of the multi-coloured, largely red rock. An important tourist centre.

Petrograd ➤ST PETERSBURG.

Petropavlovsk Kazakhstan. City on the Ishim R. and at the junction of the Trans-Siberian Railway and the Transkazakh Trunk Line. Pop. (1991). 248,300.

Commercial centre. Trade in grain, furs and textiles. Industries inc. meat-packing, flour-milling and tanning.

Petropavlovsk-Kamchatsky Russia. Cap. of the Kamchatka region, Khabarovsk Territory on the SE coast of the Kamchatka peninsula. Pop. (1992) 273,000.

Naval base and chief seaport of the peninsula. Industries inc. shipbuilding, fish-canning and sawmilling.

Petrópolis Brazil. Town in Rio de Janeiro state 43 km (27 miles) NNE of Rio de Janeiro at a height of 810 m (2657 ft). Pop. (1985) 275,100.

Fashionable summer resort with pictur-esque mountain scenery. Brewing. Manufactures textiles and chemicals.

Has a cathedral in Gothic style and an imperial museum which has many relics of the Brazilian emperors Dom Pedro I and Dom Pedro II; it was named after the latter.

Petrozavodsk Russia. Formerly Kalininsk (1930s). Cap. of the Karelian Republic on the W shore of L. Onega 298 km (185 miles) NE of St Petersburg. Pop. (1992) 280,000.

Industrial centre. Sawmilling and mica-processing. Manufactures machinery, furniture, cement and skis.

Named Petrozavodsk ('Peter's Works') in 1777 after the ironworks founded here (1703) by Peter the Great.

Pevensey England. Village in East Sussex 6 km (4 miles) NE of Eastbourne. Landing place of William the Conqueror (1066). Once a port and member of the Cinque Port of Hastings, but declined on the recession of the sea. The ruined, mainly 13th-cent. castle stands within an outer wall of Roman origin.

Pforzheim Germany. Town in Baden-Württemberg on the Enz R. at its confluence with the Nagold R. at the N edge of the Black Forest. Pop. (1992) 115,547.

Leading centre of the jewellery and watchmaking industry. Also manufactures precision instruments, machinery and tools.

Phenix City USA. Residential and industrial town in E Alabama on the Chattahoochee R. opposite Columbus (Georgia), of which it is a suburb. Pop. (1970) 25,281.

Manufactures wood products.

Phet Buri Thailand. Cap. of Phet Buri province 113 km (70 miles) SW of Bangkok. Pop. 12,000. Remains of ancient Brahman and Buddhist temples in the neighbourhood.

Philadelphia USA. Largest city in Pennsylvania and 5th largest in the USA on the Delaware R. at the confluence with the Schuylkill R. in the extreme SE of the state. Pop. (1990) 1,586,577.

A leading seaport with 60 km (37 miles) of waterfront along the two rivers. Exports petroleum products, coal, grain, timber, flour and manufactured goods. It has a large US Navy yard, a mint and arsenals.

Industries inc. financial services, chemicals, printing, electrical and electronic products, textiles and publishing.

Laid out in gridiron pattern: the great N–S and E–W axes are Broad Street and Market Street. A famous thoroughfare is the wide, tree-lined Benjamin Franklin Parkway; halfway along this is Logan Circle, the 'Piccadilly Circus' of Philadelphia. Many famous and historic buildings. The City Hall, topped by a statue of William Penn, rises to 167 m (548 ft); its predecessor, the old City Hall (1791), still stands. The most famous building, however, is Independence Hall (1732–41), the old State House of Pennsylvania, where the Declaration of Independence was adopted and signed (1776) and the US Constitution was drawn up. Seat of the University of Pennsylvania (1740), the Temple University (1884) and the Drexel Institute of Technology (1891).

Founded (1682) by William Penn, who

named his city Philadelphia ('City of Brotherly Love') to emphasize the religious and political tolerance he intended to promote. As many European Protestant religious sects were suffering persecution, settlers were attracted to the new city; it rapidly became the leading commercial and cultural centre in the American colonies and was the federal cap. 1790–1800.

Philippi Greece. Ancient city in Macedonia 16 km (10 miles) NW of the modern Kavalla. Here Brutus and Cassius were defeated by Octavius and Antony (42 BC), and St Paul first preached in Europe (AD 53); he addressed his Epistle to the Philippians to converts here.

Philippines, Republic of the. A republic of SE Asia comprising a group of over 7100 islands and islets (nearly 3000 are named) of the Malay Archipelago in the SW Pacific, the largest and most important being Luzon in the N, and Mindanao in the S, followed by Samar, Negros, Palawan, Panay, Mindoro, Leyte, Cebu, Bohol and Masbate. Taiwan lies to the N and Indonesia to the S. Area 300,076 sq km (115,860 sq. miles). Pop. (1995) 70,011,000 (54 per cent urban). Life expectancy, 66 years male, 69 female. Cap. Manila. Other important cities Quezon City, Caloocan (a city within metropolitan Manila), Cebu and Davao. Currency: Philippine peso = 100 centavos. The republic lies entirely within the tropical zone, the islands have extensive forests, but the economy depends chiefly on agriculture. The Philippine Is. are the upper portions of partly submerged mountain chains, mostly volcanic in origin but sometimes overlaid with coral. Ranges of mountains traverse the larger islands, and volcanoes are conspicuous features of the landscape; Mt Apo (2955 m; 9692 ft), an active volcano in SE Mindanao, is the highest point in the Philippines. There are several lakes, inc. Laguna de Bay on Luzon and L. Manao on Mindanao. The longest river is the Cagayan, 354 km (220 miles) in length, on Luzon. The climate, which is hot and humid on the plains but cooler in the mountains, is determined mainly by the NE and SW monsoons, which bring abundant

rainfall to the windward sides of the islands; in general, then, the year is divided into a rainy and a 'dry' season. Typhoons are most frequent in the N islands and earthquakes are common. Land use: forested 34 per cent, meadows and pastures 4 per cent, agricultural and under permanent cultivation 27 per cent. The official langs are Philipino and English. Spanish is also important and many native langs and dialects are spoken. Religion: 84 per cent are Roman Catholic and 4 per cent Philippine Independent Church (Aglipayen). The majority of the pop. known as Filipinos, belong to the Malay racial group, but in places reveal an admixture of Chinese and Spanish blood; in the mountains there are still small numbers of aboriginal Negritos.

The forests contain constructional and cabinet hardwoods, as well as rattans, bamboos, tan and dye barks, and dye woods. Rice and maize are the principal food crops, though more rice has to be imported; the leading cash crops are coconuts, from which copra, coconut oil and desiccated coconut are obtained, sugar-cane and abacá, and these along with certain minerals, inc. gold, iron, nickel and silver, are the important exports. The economy depends chiefly on agriculture, the principal products being rice, Manila hemp (abacá), copra, sugar-cane, maize and tobacco. In recent years manufacturing has become a major source of economic development; this has inc. foodprocessing, footwear, clothing, machinery, chemicals, and wood and cork products. Water buffaloes or carabaos are widely employed in the rice fields and large numbers of pigs are raised. Fishing and mining are also important.

The Philippines were discovered (1521) by Magellan, who was killed here. From 1565 the Spaniards gradually conquered the islands, converting the people to Roman Catholicism and ruled them almost continuously until 1898. Then, following the Spanish American War, the Philippines were ceded to the USA: in 1934 they were granted commonwealth status and in 1946 complete independence. During World War II they were invaded by the Japanese (1941) and occupied until 1944. The republic is divided for administrative purposes into 15 regions and 76 provinces. The head of government is the President, who is elected for 4 years, and the legislature consists of a 24-member Senate and a 200-member House of Representatives.

Philistia. Ancient region in SW Palestine comprising fertile lowlands along the Mediterranean coast, inhabited in Old Testament times by Philistines, now in Israel. The chief towns, Gaza, Ashkelon, Ashdod, Ekron and Gath, formed a confederacy. In its Greek form, Palaestina, it gave its name to Palestine.

Phnom Penh Cambodia. Cap. at the confluence of the Mekong and Tonlé Sap rivers and at the head of the Mekong delta. Pop. (1991) 900,000, before the civil war the pop. was 2,500,000. Once the commercial and road centre and river port. Accessible to smaller ocean-going ships via the Mekong (through South Vietnam). Linked by road with the Cambodian seaport of Kompong Som. In 1975 the pop. of the city was sent to undertake agricultural work by order of Pol Pot, the communist leader.

Phocis (Phokis, Fokis) Greece. *Nome* in central Greece bordering on the Gulf of Corinth (S). Area 2120 sq km (806 sq. miles). Pop. (1991) 43,889. Cap. Amphissa. Mountainous. Main occupation stock-rearing. Ancient Phocis (larger than the present *nome*) included Delphi, but the Phocians were defeated by Philip II of Macedon and finally lost the sanctuary in the 4th cent. BC.

Phoenicia. Ancient region of the E Mediterranean roughly constituting the coastlands of modern Syria and Lebanon and lying N of Mt Carmel. Its Semitic inhabitants, the Phoenicians, were organized in city states ruled by hereditary kings and by the 13th cent. BC they had become the outstanding navigators and merchants of the Mediterranean area. Their chief cities were Tyre and Sidon (Saida) and others included the present-day Beirut and Acre. They established colonies on many Mediterranean islands, e.g. Cyprus, Rhodes, Crete, Sicily,

as well as in Spain and N Africa, e.g. Carthage, traded as far afield as the British Isles and the Baltic, and may even have sailed their small ships round the coasts of Africa. They became famous for their glassware and metal goods and for the Tyrian purple with which they dyed cloth, but probably their greatest legacy to mankind was their development of an alphabet. The Phoenicians were long independent and survived the attacks of Assyrians and Babylonians, but in the 6th cent. BC they were incorporated into the Persian empire. From that time until they finally came under Roman rule (64 BC) the cities retained much of their commercial importance, but the Phoenician civilization was gradually waning and becoming superseded by that of Greece.

Phoenix USA. State cap. and largest city in Arizona on the Salt R. at a height of 330 m (1082 ft). Pop. (1990) 983,403.

Commercial centre for an irrigated agricultural region producing citrus fruits, cotton, alfalfa and other crops. There is flour-milling, brewing and fruit-canning. Manufactures steel and aluminium products, leather goods; and Indian handicrafts. The warm, dry climate has promoted the tourist industry.

Within the city limits is La Ciudad, a collection of prehistoric Indian pit-dwellings excavated in 1927.

Phoenix Islands Kiribati. Group of 8 coral islands in the S Pacific Ocean. Area 55 sq km (21 sq. miles). Formerly an important trans-Pacific airline base and before that they had little commercial use except for guano deposits. Until 1976 they formed part of the Gilbert and Ellice Islands.

Phrygia. Ancient region in central Asia Minor, now Turkey, inhabited by people speaking an Indo-European lang. and probably coming from Thrace or Macedonia before 1200 BC. Flourished in the 8th cent. BC under kings named alternatively Gordius and Midas. Later superseded by Lydia.

Phthiotis (Fthiotis) Greece. *Nome* in central Greece bordering E on the Gulf of Euboea. Area 4441 sq km (1715 sq. miles).

Pop. (1991) 168,291. Cap. Lamia. Mainly mountainous. Wheat and cotton cultivated in the Sperkhios R. valley.

Piacenza Italy. Ancient Placentia. Cap. of Piacenza province in Emilia-Romagna, on the Po R. 64 km (40 miles) SE of Milan. Pop. (1992) 102,161.

Manufactures pasta, agricultural machinery and leather goods.

Has a 12th/13th-cent. cathedral (restored) with a campanile 67 m (220ft) high, the 11th-cent. San Antonio church and the massive Palazzo Farnese, begun 1558 and never completed. One of the first Roman colonies in N Italy (218 BC) and the Roman influence may be seen in the rectangular pattern of streets in the centre, through which passes the Aemilian Way. United with Parma to form the duchy of Parma and Piacenza 1545.

Piatra Neamţ Romania. Cap. of Neamţ county; resort in a wooded part of Moldavia on the Bistriţa R. Pop. (1992) 123,175.

Industries inc. woodworking, food-processing and it manufactures textiles and pharmaceutical products. Trade in wine and timber.

Piauí Brazil. State in the NE with a very short coastline, lying E and S of the Parnaíba R., rising inland gradually to a plateau with open grasslands. Area 251,273 sq km (97,017 sq. miles). Pop. (1991) 2,581,054. Cap. Teresina.

Stock-raising important. Cotton and tobacco cultivated. Exports babassu nuts, carnauba wax and oiticica oil.

Piave River Italy. River 225 km (140 miles) long, rising in the Carnic Alps and flowing generally SW past Belluno, then SE to the Adriatic 32 km (20 miles) ENE of Venice.

Pica ►IQUIQUE.

Picardie France. Region in the N now forming the Somme and parts of the Pas-de-Calais, Aisne and Oise departments. Area 19,399 sq km (7490 sq. miles). Pop. (1991) 1,811,000.

Fertile agricultural region. Its textile industry is centred on Amiens. Set half-way between Île de France and the North Region it has also been able to develop its chemical, tyre-manufacturing and other industries.

Annexed to France 1477.

Pichincha Ecuador. Volcano (4784 m; 15,696 ft) 10 km (6 miles) NW of Quito, with a large crater. Last eruption 1988. In the battle of Pichincha fought nearby (1822) Sucre defeated the Spanish and won independence for Ecuador.

Pickering England. Market town in North Yorkshire 37 km (23 miles) NE of York. Pop. (1991) 5914. Tourist centre for the Yorkshire moors. Has a ruined mainly 14th-cent. castle where Richard II was imprisoned.

Piedmont (Italian **Piemonte**) Italy. Region in the N bounded on the NE by Switzerland and on the W by France, consisting of the upper basin of the Po R. Area 25,399 sq km (9817 sq. miles). Pop. (1992) 4,303,830. Mainly agricultural. Industries are centred largely on Turin, the chief city. From early in the 11th cent. it was associated with the house of Savoy.

Piedras Negras Mexico. Town in Coahuila state on the Río Bravo and on the US frontier opposite Eagle Pass (Texas) at 220 m (722 ft). Pop. (1985) 150,000.

Commercial centre in an agricultural and stock-rearing region on a busy route from the USA into Mexico. Coal, silver, zinc and copper mined in the neighbourhood.

Piemonte ►PIEDMONT.

Pieria Greece. *Nome* in Macedonia on the Aegean Sea. Area 1516 sq km (585 sq. miles). Pop. (1991) 116,820. Cap. Katerini. A narrow coastal plain; mountainous inland, with Mt Olympus (2917 m; 9568 ft) in the S.

Pierre USA. State cap. of South Dakota on the E bank of the Missouri R. opposite Fort Pierre at a height of 440 m (1443 ft). Pop. (1990) 12,906.

Commercial centre for an agricultural region producing grain and livestock.

Pietermaritzburg (Maritzburg) South Africa. Cap. of Natal province 71 km (44 miles) WNW of Durban at a height of 675 m (2214 ft). Pop. (1990) 133,809.

Important railway centre and fine mountain scenery. Manufactures wattle extract, furniture, footwear and metal goods.

Anglican and Roman Catholic cathedrals, the Voortrekker and Natal museums, and a campus of the University of Natal. Founded (1838) by Voortrekker Boers; named after their leaders Pieter Retief and Gert Maritz.

Pietersburg South Africa. Town in the N of Northern Province 249 km (155 miles) NE of Pretoria at a height of 1300 m (4264 ft). Pop. (1990) 35,000.

Mining centre (gold, asbestos) in a district also important for dairy-farming and the cultivation of fruit, cotton and tobacco.

Piet Retief South Africa. Town in Mpumalanga situated SE of Ermelo near the Kwa-Zulu/Natal and Swaziland borders. Pop. (1985) 12,000.

Centre of an agricultural area with gold deposits nearby.

Pigs, Bay of (Bahía de Cochinos) Cuba. Bay on the S coast 175 km (110 miles) SE of Havana. Scene of an attempted invasion in 1961 by exiled anti-Castro Cubans; within 4 days the 1600 invaders were killed or captured.

Pikes Peak USA. Mountain (4301 m; 14,107 ft) in central Colorado, in the Front Range of the Rocky Mountains. Named after Zebulon Pike, who discovered it (1806). Somewhat lower than many other peaks in Colorado, but well-known chiefly because of its isolated position; it commands extensive views from the summit. A popular tourist attraction. Ascended by a cog railway and a road.

Pila (Ger. **Schneidemühl**) Poland. Industrial town and railway junction, cap. of the Pila voivodeship 84 km (52 miles) N of Poznań. Pop. (1989) 71,109.

Manufactures agricultural machinery, textiles. Lignite mines nearby.

Formerly a German border town; after 1945 in Poland.

Pilatus, Mount Switzerland. Mountain 8 km (5 miles) SSW of Lucerne, rising to 2133 m (6996 ft). Ascended by rack-and-pinion railway. Owes its name to the legend that the body of Pontius Pilate lay in a lake (now dry) on the mountain.

Pilcomayo River. River 1600 km (1000 miles) long, rising in the Bolivian Andes near L. Poopó, flowing generally SE and forming part of the Argentina–Paraguay boundary, joining the Paraguay R. near Asunción.

Pilgrims' Way England. Track from Winchester, in Hampshire, to Canterbury, in Kent, by which medieval pilgrims journeyed from S and W England to see the shrine of Thomas à Becket in Canterbury Cathedral. The route had been in use in much earlier times. Much of it has been preserved or can be traced.

Pillars of Hercules ►GIBRALTAR.

Pilsen (Czech **Plzeň**) Czech Republic. Cap. of the Západočeský region in W Bohemia at the confluence of the Radbuza and Mze rivers. Pop. (1991) 173,129.

Famous for its beer and for the great metallurgical works, producing armaments, machinery, locomotives and cars. Also manufactures clothing, pottery, leather goods and paper. Commercial centre for a fertile agricultural region with cereal and cattle markets.

Largely modern; 13th-cent. Gothic church with a 99-m (325-ft) tower and a 16th-cent. town hall.

Piltdown (Pilt Down) England. Common 3 km (2 miles) W of Uckfield, East Sussex, where parts of the skull of the 'Piltdown man' (Eoanthropus) were found in 1911. In 1953, however, the discovery was proved to be a hoax, the jawbone being that of a modern ape.

Pimlico England. District in the City of Westminster, London, on the N bank of the

Thames. Mainly residential. Contains Victoria railway station.

Pinar del Río Cuba. Cap. of the Pinar del Río province (W) 160 km (100 miles) WSW of Havana. Pop. (1990) 121,774.

Famous for cigars and cigarettes, made from tobacco grown in the Vuelta Abajo region. Also manufactures furniture and pharmaceutical products.

Pindus (Gr. **Píndhos**) **Mountains** Greece. Range of mountains about 160 km (100 miles) long, running NNW–SSE along the border between Epirus and Thessaly, rising to 2637 m (8649 ft) in Smolikas in the N.

Pine Bluff USA. Town in Arkansas on the Arkansas R. 63 km (39 miles) SSE of Little Rock. Pop. (1990) 57,140.

In a cotton-growing region. Industries inc. railway engineering, cotton and timber processing. Manufactures chemicals, paper, radiator caps and steel radial cord for tyres.

Pines, Isle of ➤YOUTH, ISLE OF.

Pingtung Taiwan. Town situated ENE of Kaohsiung. Pop. (1992) 212,335.

Produces rice, sugar, sisal and bananas, and has food-processing industries.

Pinkie ➤MUSSELBURGH.

Pinner England. Residential district in the London borough of Harrow. Has a 14th-cent. church.

Pinsk Belorus. Town SSW of Minsk situated in the Pripet Marshes. Pop. (1991) 123,800.

Industries inc. manufacture of paper, furniture, soap, matches and leather.

Piotrków Trybunalski Poland. Cap. of Piotryków Trybunalski voivodeship 43 km (27 miles) SSE of Lódź. Pop. (1989) 80,598.

Flour-milling, sawmilling, tanning, brewing. Manufactures textiles, agricultural machinery.

One of the oldest towns in Poland, founded in the 12th cent. Was the meeting-place of several diets in the 15th and 16th cent.

Piraeus (Gr. **Piraiévs**) Greece. Seaport 8 km (5 miles) SW of Athens and within the metropolitan area. Pop. (1991) 169,622.

The country's leading port and industrial centre. Exports wine, olive oil. Shipbuilding, oil-refining and flour-milling. Manufactures fertilizers and textiles.

Founded in the 5th cent. BC as the port of Athens, it was linked with that city by the famous Long Walls, which were destroyed along with Piraeus by Sulla 86 BC. It then declined, but was refounded as the port of modern Athens in 1834 and grew rapidly with the cap. in the 19th cent.

Pirmasens Germany. Town in Rhineland-Palatinate 68 km (42 miles) SW of Ludwigshafen. Pop. (1991) 47,800.

Important for the manufacture of footwear and leather goods. Reputedly founded by St Pirmin in the 8th cent.

Pirna Germany. Industrial town in the Dresden district on the Elbe R. 21 km (13 miles) SE of Dresden. Pop. (1989) 46,000.

Manufactures rayon, paper, electrical equipment, glass and pottery.

Has a 16th-cent. church, town hall and castle (Sonnenstein).

Pisa Italy. Cap. of Pisa province in Tuscany on the Arno R. 11 km (7 miles) from the mouth and 72 km (45 miles) WSW of Florence (Firenze). Pop. (1991) 101,500.

Manufactures textiles, bicycles and pottery, but is better known for its historic monuments. Four of the most famous of these are grouped round the Piazza del Duomo: the 11th/12th-cent. cathedral, with its three bronze doors; the 12th/13th-cent. baptistery, with its tall dome and hexagonal pulpit by Niccolò Pisano; the Campo Santo, or cemetery, created in the 12th cent. with earth from the Holy Land, and surrounded by galleries containing priceless frescoes; and the Leaning Tower, a campanile, begun in 1173, 55 m (180 ft) high and about 5 m (16 ft) out of the perpendicular. Galileo (1564–1642), who was born here, was a student and a lecturer at the university (founded 1338). A flourishing maritime republic in the 11th and 12th cent. Defeated by Genoa at the Battle of Meloria (1284) and its final decline from greatness came when it fell to the Florentines (1509). It declined as a port when the river silted and its trade was transferred to Leghorn (Livorno). The Campo Santo and many ancient churches and other buildings were severely damaged by bombing in World War II.

Pisco Peru. The chief seaport between Callao and Mollendo in the Ica department 225 km (140 miles) SSE of Lima. Pop. (1985) 82,250.

Serves the irrigated agricultural lands and the mines of the interior. Exports cotton, copper and lead concentrates. Manufactures cotton goods and cottonseed oil.

Gave its name to Pisco brandy.

Pistoia Italy. Cap. of Pistoia province, Tuscany at the foot of the Apennines 34 km (21 miles) NW of Florence. Pop. (1990) 89,990.

Manufactures pasta, agricultural machinery, textiles and musical instruments.

Cathedral (13th-cent.) with a fine silver altar and a 66-m (216-ft) campanile, an octagonal baptistery in black and white marble and several noteworthy churches and palaces. The site of the Roman Pistoriae, it was here that Catiline was defeated and killed (62 BC).

Pitcairn Island S Pacific Ocean. United Kingdom Overseas Territory, a volcanic island about midway between Australia and South America. Area 5 sq km (2 sq. miles). Pop. (1992) 67. Adamstown is the only settlement.

Fruit and vegetables are sold to passing ships.

Discovered (1767) by Carteret; occupied in 1790 by mutineers from HMS *Bounty* with women from Tahiti. By 1856 the island was overpopulated and the inhabitants were transferred to Norfolk Island, but many returned. The uninhabited neighbouring islands of Henderson, Ducie and Oeno were annexed in 1902 and included in the Pitcairn group. The island is administered by a Governor, who is also British High Commissioner in New Zealand.

Piteşti Romania. Cap. of the Argeş district in Walachia on the Argeş R. 109 km (68 miles) WNW of Bucharest. Pop. (1992) 179,479.

A former market town and has expanded since oil was discovered in the 1960s. Industries inc. vehicle and electric-motor manufacture, chemicals, footwear and textiles.

Pitlochry Scotland. Town in Perth and Kinross on the R. Tummel 39 km (24 miles) NNW of Perth. Pop. (1991) 2541.

Highland resort for trout and salmon fishing. Industries inc. distilling.

Pitsea ►BASILDON.

Pitt Island ►CHATHAM ISLANDS.

Pittsburgh USA. City in SW Pennsylvania at the confluence of the Allegheny and the Monongahela rivers (which form the Ohio R.). Pop. (1996) 350,363.

Important industrial centre, second largest city in the state. With adjacent industrial towns, it produced a large proportion of the US output of iron and steel but now manufactures a vast range of goods, e.g. electrical and electronic equipment, petroleum products, machinery, railway equipment, glassware and tinplate. A centre for scientific and technological research.

Once the dirtiest and most disagreeable of US cities, named 'Smoky City'; a vigorous smoke-abatement campaign and a growth of civic spirit have completely transformed it. The French Fort Duquesne was captured and renamed Fort Pitt by the British (1758). The settlement which grew around the fort in the modern business district (the 'Golden Triangle') was called Pittsburgh. River trade and later the railways promoted rapid expansion.

Pittsfield USA. Industrial town in W Massachusetts between the headstreams of the Housatonic R. 68 km (43 miles) NW of Springfield. Pop. (1970) 57,020.

Manufactures electrical equipment, textiles, paper and chemicals. Also a tourist centre for the Berkshire Hills.

Named after the elder Pitt.

Piura Peru. Cap. of the Piura department in the NW 209 km (130 miles) NNW of Chiclayo. Pop. (1990) 153,000.

Commercial centre for a large oasis irrigated by the Piura R. where long-staple cotton, rice and sugar-cane are grown. Trade in cotton. Cotton-ginning. Manufactures cottonseed oil.

Founded 1532, the oldest Spanish city in Peru; many colonial buildings.

Plainfield USA. Industrial and residential town in New Jersey 26 km (16 miles) SW of Newark. Pop. (1990) 46,567.

Manufactures printing and other machinery, tools, concrete products and clothing.

Plassey India. Village in West Bengal on the Bhagirathi R. 51 km (32 miles) NNW of Krishnanagar. Scene of the victory (1757) of English soldier Robert Clive (1725–74) over Suraja-Dowlah, the Nawab of Bengal, which led to the passing of Bengal to Britain.

Plata, Río de la ➤RÍO DE LA PLATA.

Plataea Greece. Ancient city in S Boeotia near Mt Cithaeron, whose inhabitants fought with the Athenians at Marathon (490 BC). They incurred the enmity of Thebes, however, and their city was twice destroyed (427 and 373 BC) but was rebuilt by Philip and Alexander of Macedon and was inhabited till the 6th cent. AD.

Plate, River ➤RÍO DE LA PLATA.

Plateau Nigeria. State, formerly Plateau province and the N part of Benue province of the N region. Area 58,030 sq km (22,405 sq. miles). Pop. (1991) 3,488,789. Main towns Jos (cap.), Lafia and Keffi.

Important mining area with major deposits of tin and columbite.

Platte River USA. River 499 km (310 miles) long in Nebraska, formed by the union of the N Platte and S Platte rivers at North Platte, flowing generally E through an agricultural region and joining the Missouri R. at Plattsmouth 24 km (15 miles) S of Omaha. Total length with the N Platte, 1480 km (920

miles). Unnavigable owing to shallowness. Used for irrigation and hydroelectric power.

Plauen Germany. Industrial town in Saxony on the Elster R. 96 km (60 miles) SSW of Leipzig. Pop. (1990) 70,860.

Manufactures textiles (curtain, embroidery and lace), textile machinery, machine-tools and paper. The textile industry dates from the 15th cent. Formerly cap. of the region known as Vogtland.

Plenty, Bay of New Zealand. A wide inlet on the NE coast of North Island, containing several small islands. Named by Captain Cook in 1769.

Pleskau ➤PSKOV.

Pleven (Plevna) Bulgaria. Cap. of Pleven province in the N 137 km (85 miles) NE of Sofia. Pop. (1992) 137,466.

Manufactures textiles, agricultural machinery, cement, leather and ceramics. Trade in wine and cattle.

In 1877, during the Russo–Turkish War, it was the scene of two battles and a siege in which Osman Pasha, the Turkish general, was engaged.

Plock Poland. Cap. of the Plock voivodeship on the Vistula R. 96 km (60 miles) WNW of Warsaw. Pop. (1992) 125,300.

Industries inc. flour-milling and fruit-canning. Manufactures agricultural implements. Oil-refining. Trade in cereals.

The cathedral (12th-cent., restored) has tombs of the Polish kings.

Ploeşti Romania. Cap. of the Prahova district in Walachia 56 km (35 miles) N of Bucharest. Pop. (1992) 252,073.

Leading centre of the Romanian petroleum industry since 1856. Oil refineries; pipelines to Giurgiu, Bucharest and Constanţa. Also manufactures chemicals, textiles, hardware, cardboard and leather. Frequently bombed by the Allies during World War II.

Plovdiv Bulgaria. Ancient Philippopolis. Cap. of Plovdiv province on the Maritsa R. 135 km (84 miles) ESE of Sofia. Pop. (1992) 379,112.

Bulgaria's second largest city, industrial and commercial centre. Manufactures chemicals, textiles, soap, furniture and cigarettes. Other industries inc. flour-milling and tanning. Trade in wheat, tobacco and attar of roses.

Taken by Philip II of Macedon in the 4th cent. BC (hence its ancient name). Formerly cap. of Eastern Rumelia; ceded to Bulgaria 1885.

Plymouth (West Indies) ➤MONTSERRAT (WEST INDIES).

Plymouth England. City in S Devon at the head of Plymouth Sound, since 1914 comprising the Three Towns of Plymouth, Stonehouse and Devonport. Pop. (1991) 254,500.

Long important as a naval base but now much reduced in size, second only to Portsmouth, and a seaport. Manufactures chemicals and food products. Engineering, brewing and boatbuilding. There is a ferry service to Roscoff and Santander.

Stands on the broad tongue of land between the estuaries of the Plym and the Tamar, the latter known as the Hamoaze. The old town extends N from the ridge of Plymouth Hoe, where Drake played his legendary game of bowls as the Armada approached. On the Hoe is Smeaton's tower, the upper part of the earlier Eddystone Lighthouse, and nearby are the Marine Biological Laboratory and Sutton Pool, whence the *Mayflower* left on its voyage to America. At Devonport are large naval dockyards and barracks and at Stonehouse the Royal William Victualling Yard. A noteworthy building in Plymouth is the 19th-cent. Roman Catholic cathedral in Early English style. Known as Sutton in the Middle Ages, Plymouth was given its present name in the 15th cent. Associated with the seafaring adventures of Drake, Hawkins, Raleigh, Grenville and others, in Elizabethan times it became the country's leading port. The community known as the Plymouth Brethren was so called in 1830 when the Rev. J. N. Darby converted many Plymouth people to his beliefs. Became a city 1928; the title of Lord Mayor was granted 1935. During World War II the city was severely damaged in air raids (1941) and the centre was replanned and rebuilt. Devonport was the birthplace of Capt. R. F. Scott (1868–1912), the Antarctic explorer.

Plymouth USA. Town in Massachusetts on Plymouth Bay 56 km (35 miles) SE of Boston. Pop. (1990) 44,000.

Fishing. Manufactures rope and textiles.

A popular resort, famous as the place where the Pilgrim Fathers landed from the *Mayflower* (21 Dec. 1620). The first permanent colonist settlement in New England. Plymouth Rock (the granite boulder on which according to legend the Pilgrims stepped ashore) was replaced (1880) on the spot it had originally occupied.

Plymouth Sound England. Inlet of the English Channel between Cornwall and Devon 5 km (3 miles) wide at the entrance into which flow the Tamar and the Plym rivers. Plymouth is at its head. In it is Drake's or St Nicholas' Island. An important roadstead, it is sheltered from SW gales by a breakwater 1.6 km (1 mile) long with a lighthouse at its E end.

Plynlimmon Wales. Mountain 752 m (2466 ft) high on the borders of Ceredigion and Powys, on which the Severn, Wye and other rivers rise.

Plzeň ➤PILSEN.

Po, River Italy. River in N Italy rising in the Cottian Alps near the French frontier and flowing 652 km (405 miles) past Turin and Chivasso and discharging at its delta just S of Venice. Its discharge basin covers 69,000 sq km (27,000 sq. miles). Italy's longest river, it has been an important trade route since Roman times.

Pobeda Peak Kyrgyzstan. Highest peak of the Tien Shan mountain system (7438 m; 24,406 ft). Discovered 1943.

Pocatello USA. Town in SE Idaho on the Portneuf R. at a height of 1360 m (4461 ft). Pop. (1990) 46,117.

Railway junction. Industries inc. railway engineering, microchips and natural gas. Trade in dairy produce.

Founded (1882) as a tent colony.

Pocklington England. Market town in Humberside 19 km (12 miles) ESE of York. Pop. (1991) 5908. The 16th-cent. grammar school was attended by William Wilberforce, English philanthropist (1759–1833).

Podgorica Montenegro. Cap of Montenegro (Crna Gora) on the Morača R. 290 km (180 miles) SSW of Belgrade. Pop. (1991) 118,059.

Manufactures tobacco products and aluminium.

Although largely destroyed in World War II and later rebuilt, it retains the old Ljubić mosque and other Turkish buildings. Renamed Titograd (1948–92) in honour of Marshal Tito, Yugoslav statesman.

Podolia Ukraine. Region between the Dniester and S Bug rivers. Chief towns Vinnitsa, Kamenets-Podolski. From the 13th cent. ruled mainly by Lithuania and Poland. Became Russian 1793.

Podolsk Russia. Industrial town in the Moscow region 42 km (26 miles) S of Moscow on the Pakhra R. Pop. (1992) 208,000.

Railway engineering. Manufactures oil-refining machinery, sewing-machines, cables, lime and cement.

Podor Senegal. Town situated ENE of Saint Louis on the Senegal R. River port serving an agricultural area with some fishing.

Podrinje Bosnia. Plain extending 48 km (30 miles) N to S from Loznica and partly bounded E by Drina R.

Cattle-raising and fruit-growing area, with lead-mining near Krupanj.

Pogradec Albania. Town situated NNW of Koritsa on the SW shore of L. Ochrida.

Trading centre in a fruit-growing area. Industries inc. fishing.

Point Barrow USA. The most northerly point on the Arctic coast of Alaska. US

meteorological station (established 1882–3). US naval base 10 km (6 miles) S (1944).

Pointe-à-Pitre Guadeloupe. Chief seaport and largest town in the SW of Grande Terre island. Pop. (1988) 25,312.

Exports bananas, sugar-cane, rum and coffee. Sugar-milling and rum-distilling.

Pointe-Noire Republic of Congo. Chief seaport 386 km (240 miles) WSW of Brazzaville. Pop. (1992) 576,602. Connected by rail with Brazzaville.

Important airport. Exports palm oil and kernels, cotton, rubber, timber (mahogany, okoumé). Also handles much of the foreign trade of Gabon. Manufactures aluminium goods.

Poitiers France. Ancient Limonum. Prefecture of the Vienne department at the confluence of the Clain and Boivre rivers 160 km (100 miles) ESE of Nantes. Pop. (1990) 82,507.

Market town. Trade in wine, wool and honey. Manufactures chemicals, brushes and hosiery.

A picturesque town with a 12th/14th-cent. cathedral; the baptistery of St John, built in the 4th cent. and enlarged in the 7th cent. – probably the oldest religious building in France; and the 11th/12th-cent. Notre-Dame-la-Grande church. University (1431). Named after its Gallic founders, the Pictavi or Pictones. In 732 Charles Martel defeated the advancing Muslims at Moussais-la-Bataille to the NE. At Poitiers in 1356 the English under the Black Prince defeated and captured John II of France. Cap. of the old province of Poitou till 1790.

Poitou-Charentes France. Region and former province in the W, now forming the departments of Vendée, Deux-Sèvres and Vienne, with cap. Poitiers; part of Aquitaine. Area 25,809 sq km (9965 sq. miles). Pop. (1991) 1,595,000.

A mainly rural region; beef cattle and vineyards for the production of Cognac. Poitou-Charentes has been undergoing growing industrialization during the last few decades, with the creation of agri-foodstuffs industries and light industries (engineering and tyres). The seaport of La Rochelle and the beaches along the Atlantic also contribute to the region's economic life.

The name was derived from the Pictavi or Pictones, the Gallic tribe living here in pre-Roman times.

Pokrovsk Russia. Formerly Engels. Town on the Volga R. opposite Saratov. Pop. (1991) 183,600.

Industries inc. railway engineering, meatpacking and flour-milling. Manufactures textiles and leather goods.

Poland. Republic in E central Europe, bounded in the N by the Baltic Sea and Russia, E by Lithuania, Belorus and the Ukraine, S by the Czech Republic and Slovakia and the W by Germany. Area 312,683 sq km (120,727 sq. miles). Pop. (1995) 38,641,000 (62 per cent urban). Life expectancy, 67 years male, 76 female. Cap. Warsaw. Other cities Lódź, Cracow, Wrocław, Poznań, Gdańsk, Szczecin and Katowice. Currency: złoty = 100 groszy. Consists in the main of a low, undulating plain dotted in the N with lakes of glacial origin. In the S is a low plateau, and the Sudetic Mountains and the Carpathians form a mountain barrier rising to over 2400 m (7872 ft) in the High Tatra. The chief river, the Vistula, which rises in the West Beskids (Carpathians) and flows S–N, passes through Cracow and Warsaw. The Oder and Neisse rivers form most of the boundary with Germany and the West Bug, a tributary of the Vistula, part of the boundary with the Ukraine. Both the Vistula and the Oder, and chief waterways, are usually frozen for about 2 months each year. Climate continental, with long and severe winters and warm summers, extremes of temperatures becoming more marked from N–S and from W–E. A moderate rainfall of 50–65 cm (20–25 ins.) annually is well distributed through the year. Land use: forested 28 per cent, meadows 13 per cent, agricultural 47 per cent. Religion 93 per cent Roman Catholic. Lang. Polish (Slavonic, but written in the Roman alphabet). About 98 per cent Polish and Ukrainian 0.6 per cent.

Forestry and agriculture are still of great importance, but the agricultural labour force has been reduced by 50 per cent since 1945. The principal crops are rye, potatoes, oats, wheat, barley and sugarbeet. Large numbers of cattle, pigs and sheep raised. The leading manufactures are iron and steel, railway rolling-stock, machinery, glass and chemicals, largely centred on the Silesian coalfield, while the textile industry is concentrated here and in the Lódź region. Much of the industrial base needs re-equipping and steel and shipbuilding industries make large losses. It has large resources of raw materials esp. coal. Other minerals inc. iron ore, lead and zinc. The changes brought about by political change in the 1990s and a move towards a full market economy and the restructuring of industry, should see an improvement in living standards in the next decade.

Polish history begins with the introduction of Christianity to this W Slavonic people in the latter part of the 10th cent. The dominating factor throughout its history has been the vulnerability of its borders. In 1025 one of their princes, Boleslaus I, became the first king, ruling an area extending from the Baltic Sea to the Carpathians and from the Elbe R. to the Bug R. With the death of Boleslaus III (1138) the kingdom was partitioned into independent principalities, lost power and was raided by Tatars and threatened by the Teutonic Order. Poland was saved, however, by Wladislaus I, who reunited Great and Little Poland, and by his son, Casimir the Great (1333–70); the threat from the Teutonic Order was removed when they were utterly defeated at Tannenberg (1410). By the Union of Lublin (1569) Poland absorbed Lithuania and at this time reached its widest limits, extending from the Baltic to the Black Sea. In 1573 the monarchy became elective, and the period of glory, with Poland's prestige high and arts and sciences flourishing, was followed by two cent. of conflict and finally humiliation. The Ukrainian Cossacks under Chmielnicki rebelled and the country was attacked by Sweden and Russia and lost considerable territory. Taking advantage of the ensuing chaos, Frederick II of Prussia and Catherine II of Russia arranged the First Partition of Poland (1772), by which Prussia gained West Prussia, Russia much of Lithuania and Austria most of Galicia. A new Constitution making the monarchy hereditary only led to the Second Partition (1793), by which Russia took all the eastern provinces and Prussia further territory in the W, so that Poland was now reduced to one-third of her former area. Kosciuszko heroically led an insurrection and won early successes, but was defeated by overwhelming Russian forces and taken prisoner at Maciejowice. The Third Partition followed (1795): Prussia received West Masovia with Warsaw, Austria West Galicia and South Masovia and Russia the rest of the country. Thus Poland was effaced from the map of Europe for more than a cent.

By the Peace of Tilsit (1807) Napoleon created the grand duchy of Warsaw under the King of Saxony as a buffer state, but with his defeat it disappeared. The Congress of Vienna (1815) established a nominally independent state in personal union with Russia, the W went to Prussia and Galicia to Austria, while Cracow, at first a city republic, was annexed by Austria (1848). After the insurrections of 1830 and 1863 had been crushed, Russian Poland became virtually a province of Russia, and the history of each section of the Polish people followed that of the country into which each had been incorporated.

During World War I Polish troops under Pilsudski fought with Germany and Austria against Russia, and Polish independence, promised by all three countries, was established by the peace treaties. Poland gained access to the Baltic by the Polish Corridor and regained Prussian Poland and part of Silesia. Dissatisfied with the placing of the Polish–Russian border along the Curzon Line, however, Poland made war on Russia and by the Treaty of Riga (1921) secured most of its claims, having also seized the Vilna region from Lithuania (1920). More than one-third of the pop. now consisted of minorities – Germans, Ukrainians, Byelorussians, Jews and Lithuanians. In 1926 Pilsudski over-

threw the government by a military *coup d'état* which made him a virtual dictator. World War II was precipitated by the German invasion of Poland (1 Sept. 1939) when the Poles rejected Hitler's demands concerning Danzig and 16 days later Russian troops invaded from the E. Polish resistance was soon crushed and the country was partitioned between Germany and the USSR. In 1941 Germany attacked Russia and occupied the whole of Poland. Meanwhile, a Polish government in exile was set up in London; an underground movement operated in Poland; many Poles escaped and formed substantial contingents which fought in North Africa and France. By the Potsdam Conference (1945) Poland ceded 175,954 sq km (67,936 sq. miles) in the E to the USSR and received 102,836 sq km (39,705 sq. miles) in the W from Germany, the Polish–East German border running along the Oder and Neisse rivers. In 1939 the pop. was 35 million inc. more than 3 million Jews, but that of post-war Poland (1946), reduced by about 72,500 sq km (28,000 sq. miles), was only 24 million. During the German occupation the Jews were systematically exterminated, the death camp at Oświęcim (Auschwitz) being especially notorious; only about 100,000 survived. In 1947 'free' parliamentary elections were held in the familiar atmosphere of Communist coercion, a government was formed largely from members of the 1944 provisional Lublin government and Poland became a Soviet satellite; large numbers of Poles still abroad refused to return to their native land. A new Constitution was promulgated in 1952 and, after the Poznań riots (1956) and the 'bloodless revolution' against Stalinism, Wladyslaw Gomulka took control of the Communist Party, and Poland succeeded in regaining a measure of freedom greater than that in any of the other 'people's democracies'. The church retained considerable anti-Communist influence, and agriculture remained largely under individual ownership modified by peasant cooperatives and many large state farms. Industrial unrest in 1980 led to the formation of Solidarity, an independent trade union. In 1981 martial law was declared, Solidarity was banned and its leaders arrested. In 1989 Solidarity was legalized and political reform started. By constitutional amendments in 1989 the country adopted the name of the Polish Republic, dropping the word 'People's' and created a new bicameral National Assembly comprising a lower house, the 460-seat *Sejm* and a 100-seat Senate.

Polotsk Belarus. Town on the W Dvina R. 96 km (60 miles) WNW of Vitebsk. Pop. (1990) 77,800.

Railway junction. Industrial centre. Sawmilling, oil-refining and flour-milling.

Probably founded in the 9th cent.; was a large and important commercial centre under Poland in the 16th cent. Declined, chiefly because of fires and plagues and passed to Russia 1772.

Polperro England. Fishing village and resort in E Cornwall on the S coast 8 km (5 miles) E of Fowey. Pop. (1990) 1675. Popular with artists.

Poltava Ukraine. Town on the Vorskla R. 306 km (190 miles) ESE of Kiev. Pop. (1991) 320,000.

Commercial centre in a fertile region producing sugar-beet, wheat and fruits. Flourmilling, tanning, meat-packing and brewing. Manufactures textiles.

In a battle nearby Peter the Great of Russia defeated Charles XII of Sweden (1709).

Polynesia. Pacific Ocean. One of the three main divisions of the Pacific islands, in the central and SE Pacific, the others being Melanesia and Micronesia. Inhabited by Polynesians, a tall, well-built people with a light brown skin and straight or wavy hair, who probably colonized the islands from Asia, though their origins are still not conclusively established. The island groups lie within the New Zealand–Hawaii–Easter Island triangle and inc. the groups of Hawaii, Samoa, Tonga and Tokelau, and also Tubuai, Tuamotu, Society, Marquesas, Cook, Tuvalu and Easter islands. Ethnologically the New Zealand Maoris are of Polynesian stock. A great number of the islands are volcanic summits,

surrounded by coral reefs, while some are low coral atolls.

Pomerania ►POMORZE.

Pomfret ►PONTEFRACT.

Pomona USA. Town in California 42 km (26 miles) E of Los Angeles. Pop. (1990) 131,723.

Commercial centre for a fruit-growing and agricultural region, and in recent years an outer residential suburb of Los Angeles. Industries inc. the manufacture of water pumps and paper products.

Pomorze (Pomerania, Ger. **Pommern)** Germany/Poland. Region in N central Europe bordering N on the Baltic Sea and extending W from the lower Vistula R. beyond the lower Oder R. to inc. Rügen Island and Stralsund; now mainly in Poland, with a small area in the NE of Germany. A mainly flat, low-lying agricultural region. Chief crops rye, potatoes and oats. In 1919, after World War I, part of it formed the Polish Corridor and was in the Pomorze voivodeship (province), separating the German E Pomerania (Hinterpommern) from E Prussia. In 1945, after World War II, E Pomerania passed to Poland and W Pomerania (Vorpommern), i.e. Pomerania W of the Oder R., to the German Democratic Republic, except for the district round Szczecin (Stettin) which also became Polish. By 1950 the larger Polish Pomerania was divided into the four voivodeships Gdańsk, Bydgoszcz, Szczecin and Koszalin.

Pompeii (Italian **Pompei)** Italy. Ancient city in Campania, near the Bay of Naples and the foot of Vesuvius and 23 km (14 miles) SE of Naples. A military colony was settled here by Sulla (80 BC) and the pop. had been Romanized by AD 63, when a violent earthquake caused damage. In AD 79 the city was buried under a mass of cinders and ash thrown out in the great eruption of Vesuvius; judging by the number of bodies found during subsequent excavations, about 2000 people must have perished – probably about 10 per cent of the pop. Pompeii was rediscovered in 1748 and the excavations began in 1763, revealing a wealth of information about Roman life in the 1st cent. AD. The city was roughly oval, about 3 km (2 miles) in circumference, with 8 gates and well-paved streets. There were fine public buildings and villas ornamented with remarkable murals and mosaics; many of the works of art were removed after excavation to museums. The much smaller Herculaneum was buried by the same eruption of Vesuvius.

Ponce Puerto Rico. Seaport and third largest city on the S coast 80 km (50 miles) WSW of San Juan. Pop. (1990) 159,151.

Exports sugar, tobacco, textiles and rum. Industries inc. sugar-refining, rum-distilling, brewing and fruit-canning. Manufactures textiles, shoes and cement.

A picturesque city, with attractive squares, avenues, parks and 'colonial' mansions. Named after Juan Ponce de León (1460–1521), the Spanish explorer who conquered Puerto Rico (1509) and was appointed governor.

Pondicherry India. 1. Territory of the Indian Union on the Coromandel Coast of the SE, inc. Karikal, Mahé and Yanaon. Area 492 sq km (192 sq. miles). Pop. (1991) 807,045.

Main food crop rice; groundnuts and sugar-cane also cultivated.

Founded (1674) by the French, it was the chief French settlement in India until 1954, when it was transferred to India. Became a Union Territory in 1962.

2. Cap. of Pondicherry territory and formerly of French India on the Coromandel Coast 137 km (85 miles) SSW of Madras. Pop. (1991) 203,100.

Seaport and commercial centre. Manufactures cotton goods, textiles, sugar, automotive components, chemicals, tin containers, glass, disposable syringes, nylon filaments, polymers and diesel power generators.

Ponta Delgada ➤AZORES.

Ponta Grossa Brazil. Town in Paraná state 105 km (65 miles) WNW of Curitiba at a height of 870 m (2854 ft). Pop. (1985) 224,000.

Commercial centre in a region important for rice and tobacco cultivation, pig-rearing, lumbering. Trade in timber and maté. Industries inc. meat-packing and sawmilling.

Pontchartrain, Lake USA. Shallow lake 64 km (40 miles) long and 40 km (25 miles) wide in SE Louisiana just N of New Orleans. Linked by navigable canal with the Mississippi R. and via L. Borgne with the Gulf of Mexico by the deltaic channels Rigolets and Chef Menteur.

Pontefract (Pomfret) England. Market town in West Yorkshire 18 km (11 miles) SE of Leeds. Pop. (1991) 28,358.

Well known for its liquorice sweetmeats known as Pontefract or Pomfret cakes. Industries inc. tanning, brewing, furniture and engineering. Market-gardening in the neighbourhood.

An 11th-cent. castle, now in ruins, where Richard II was imprisoned and murdered (1400).

Pontevedra Spain. 1. Province in the NW on the Atlantic Ocean in Galicia, bordering S on Portugal along the Miño R. Area 4477 sq km (1729 sq. miles). Pop. (1991) 888,892. Largely mountainous with a deeply indented coastline. Main occupations agriculture, fishing. Chief port Vigo.

2. Cap. of Pontevedra province, seaport at the head of the Ría de Pontevedra. Pop. (1991) 71,182.

Fishing and boatbuilding. Manufactures pottery, leather. Trade in livestock, fruit, cereals and wine.

A Roman bridge of 12 arches, the Pons Vetus (from which it takes its name), spans the Lerez R., on which it stands. Medieval fortifications; a 16th-cent. church.

Pontiac USA. Industrial town in Michigan on the Clinton R. 39 km (24 miles) NW of Detroit. Pop. (1990) 71,166.

An important centre of the motor-car industry. Manufactures lorries, buses, rubber products and paint.

Founded 1818. Carriage-making in the

Pontianak

late 19th cent. led to the modern automobile industry.

Pontianak Indonesia. Cap. of W Kalimantan province (W Borneo) at the mouth of a distributary of the Kapuas R. Pop. (1990) 387,112.

A seaport with shipbuilding, rubber and food-processing.

Pontine Marshes Italy. Low-lying coastal region along the Tyrrhenian Sea in Latium, extending NW–SE from Cisterna di Latina to Terracina. Fertile and well-peopled in early Roman times; later abandoned owing to the unhealthy marshes. Several attempts at reclamation were made, but a drainage system was not completed until the Fascist regime, when large estates were divided into smallholdings and the rural town of Littoria (now Latina) was established (1932), to be followed by Sabaudia (1934) and others. Cereals, sugar-beet, vines, fruits and vegetables cultivated.

Pontoise France. Cap. of Val-d'Oise department, situated NW of Paris. Pop. (1990) 28,500.

Pontresina Switzerland. Town in Graubünden (Grisons) canton at a height of 1802 m (5915 ft) in the Upper Engadine 8 km (5 miles) E of St Moritz. Pop. (1970) 1646. Summer resort and winter sports centre.

Pontus. Ancient region in NE Asia Minor bordering the Black Sea, now in Turkey. Became a kingdom c. 300 BC and was an important power under Mithridates the Great, who was defeated by Pompey (65 BC). His son Pharnaces was defeated by Julius Caesar (47 BC) and Pontus gradually lost its identity.

Pontypool Wales. Town in Torfaen 13 km (8 miles) NNW of Newport. Pop. (1991) 35,564.

Manufactures glass, nylon, pharmaceuticals, brake and suspension components. Tinplate was first made here in the late 17th cent.

Pontypridd Wales. Town in Rhondda,

Cynon, Taff on the R. Taff at the confluence with the R. Rhondda 18 km (11 miles) NW of Cardiff. Pop. (1991) 28,487.

Coalmining. Iron and brass founding. Industries inc. engineering, electronics and chemicals. Varied light industries at the Treforest trading estate, established in the 1930s to relieve unemployment.

There is a single-arch bridge (built 1755) across the R. Taff.

Poole England. Town in Dorset on Poole Harbour, an inlet of the English Channel 8 km (5 miles) W of Bournemouth. Pop. (1991) 138,479.

Seaport. Holiday resort. Boatbuilding, engineering. Manufactures pottery (from local clay), chemicals. Considerable tourist trade in the neighbourhood and there is a passenger and freight ferry service to Cherbourg.

There are town cellars of the 15th cent. and, on one of the islands in Poole Harbour, a Tudor castle.

Poona ➤PUNE.

Poopó, Lake Bolivia. Shallow lake at a height of 3690 m (12,103 ft) on the Altiplano about 56 km (35 miles) S of Oruro. Fed by the Desaguadero R. from L. Titicaca 108 m (354 ft) higher. Area 2538 sq km (980 sq. miles).

Popayán Colombia. Cap. of the Cauca department at the foot of the volcano Puracé (4914 m; 16,118 ft) 129 km (80 miles) S of Cali at a height of 1536 m (5039 ft). Pop. (1992) 203,800.

Cultural and commercial centre in a coffee-growing region. Flour-milling and tanning.

A picturesque city with fine colonial buildings, distinguished old monasteries. University (1640). Founded (1536) by Benalcázar. Birthplace of Francisco José de Caldas (1771–1815), the Colombian scientist.

Poplar England. Part of the London borough of Tower Hamlets. Linked with Greenwich by the Blackwall Tunnel under the R. Thames. Largely industrial.

Popocatépetl, Mount Mexico. In Nahnatl,

'Smoking Mountain'. Dormant volcano 68 km (42 miles) SE of Mexico City, the second highest peak in Mexico (5432 m; 17,887 ft). A snow-capped cone, with a large crater. The lower slopes are green with conifers. There was a minor eruption in 1920 and sulphur (which has never been fully exploited) is continually deposited from the vapour which still rises from the crater. Probably first ascended by one of Cortés' soldiers (1519); frequently climbed since.

Porbandar India. Seaport in Gujarat on the Kathiawar peninsula 145 km (90 miles) SW of Rajkot. Pop. (1991) 134,139.

Exports cotton and salt. Manufactures textiles and cement.

Birthplace of Mahatma Gandhi, Indian statesman (1869–1948).

Pori (Swedish **Björneborg**) Finland. Industrial town and seaport in Turku-Pori province in the SW on the Kokemäki R. near the mouth on the Gulf of Bothnia. Pop. (1992) 76,331.

Exports timber, wood products. Copper-refining. Manufactures wood-pulp, paper, textiles and matches.

Porjus Sweden. Village in Norrbotten county on the Lule R. 193 km (120 miles) NW of Luleå. Site of a great hydroelectric power station supplying power to the Luleå–Narvik railway and the iron mines of Kiruna and Gällivare.

Porsgrunn Norway. Industrial town and seaport in Telemark county 109 km (68 miles) SW of Oslo. Pop. (1990) 31,268.

Manufactures fertilizers and electrical equipment.

Port Adelaide Australia. Chief seaport of South Australia 11 km (7 miles) NW of Adelaide on Gulf St Vincent. Pop. (1985) 37,000.

Has inner and outer harbours. Exports wheat, flour, wool, fruit. Iron-smelting. Manufactures chemicals and cement.

Portadown Northern Ireland. Town now part of Craigavon on the R. Bann 39 km (24 miles) WSW of Belfast. Pop. (1991) 21,299.

Railway junction. Fruit-canning, bacon-curing. Manufactures linen, electronics, clothing, carpets and furniture. Has famous rose nurseries.

Portage la Prairie Canada. Town in Manitoba on the Assiniboine R. 82 km (51 miles) W of Winnipeg. Pop. (1991) 13,186.

Industries inc. food-processing.

Formerly the starting point of a portage route for fur traders to L. Manitoba.

Port Ahuriri ►NAPIER.

Port Alberni Canada. Port in British Columbia on Vancouver Island 142 km (88 miles) NW of Victoria. Pop. (1991) 18,403.

Lumbering, fishing. Exports timber.

Portalegre Portugal. Cap. of Portalegre district situated ENE of Lisbon on the W slopes of the Serra de São Mamede near the Spanish frontier.

Trading centre for agricultural produce. Industries inc. textiles, and cork-processing.

Portarlington Ireland. Town in Co. Laoighis on the R. Barrow and on the boundary with Co. Offaly. Pop. (1991) 3618.

Market town in a cereal and potato growing region. The first Irish power plant to use peat for fuel was built here (1948).

Port Arthur (Canada) ►THUNDER BAY.

Port Arthur (China) ►LUSHAN.

Port Arthur USA. Port in SE Texas on the W shore of L. Sabine. Pop. (1990) 58,724. Connected with the Gulf of Mexico by the Sabine–Neches Waterway.

Exports petroleum, grain, timber. Oil-refining. Manufactures chemicals and rubber products.

Port Augusta Australia. Port and railway junction in South Australia at the head of Spencer Gulf 274 km (170 miles) NNW of Adelaide. Pop. (1991) 14,966.

Exports wool and wheat. Large thermal power station. Engineering.

Port-au-Prince Haiti. Cap. and chief seaport on the Gulf of Gonaïves on the W coast. Pop. (1990) 752,600.

727

Good natural harbour. Rum-distilling, sugar-milling and brewing. Manufactures textiles.

Cathedral (18th-cent.). Has often been damaged by earthquakes and fires.

Port Blair ➤ANDAMAN ISLANDS.

Port-Bouet ➤ABIDJAN.

Portchester ➤FAREHAM.

Port Dickson Peninsular Malaysia. Town in Negri Sembilan situated SW of Seremban on the Strait of Malacca. Pop. (1980) 24,000.

Port shipping rubber, copra and tin. Resort.

Port de France ➤NOUMEA.

Port Elizabeth South Africa. Seaport in the Eastern Cape Province on the W shore of Algoa Bay 684 km (425 miles) E of Cape Town. Pop. (1985) 585,400.

Exports fruits, hides and skins, mohair and wool. Motor-car assembly. Manufactures tyres, leather, furniture and clothing. Fruit and jam canning, flour-milling.

The Addo Elephant National Park is 48 km (30 miles) N. Fort Frederick was built in 1790; the town was founded by British settlers in 1820. The port developed rapidly with the construction of the modern harbour and the railway to Kimberley.

Port Glasgow Scotland. Town in Inverclyde on the R. Clyde estuary 5 km (3 miles) ESE of Greenock. Pop. (1991) 19,693.

The former outport of Glasgow, but its trade declined after the improvement of the river channel. Now important for shipbuilding and engineering. Manufactures rope, twine and canvas.

Port Harcourt Nigeria. Seaport in the SE in Rivers State on the Bonny R. arm of the Niger R. delta 434 km (270 miles) ESE of Lagos. Pop. (1993) 380,300.

Exports palm oil and kernels, groundnuts, cacao, tin (from Bauchi), coal (from Enugu, Udi). Also a centre for the nearby oilfield, from which natural gas is piped to an industrial estate. Manufactures cement, tyres and cigarettes.

Built in 1914 and named after the then Colonial Secretary, Sir William Harcourt.

Porthcawl Wales. Town in Bridgend on the Bristol Channel 23 km (14 miles) SE of Swansea. Pop. (1991) 15,922.

Seaport. Seaside resort.

Porthmadog ➤PORTMADOC.

Port Huron USA. Lake port and industrial town in SE Michigan on the St Clair R., which connects L. Huron with L. Erie via L. St Clair and the Detroit R.; opposite Sarnia (Canada), with which it is connected by road bridge and railway tunnel. Pop. (1985) 34,000.

Manufactures metal goods, vehicle components, paper and cement. A summer lake resort.

Portici Italy. Town in Napoli province, Campania on the Bay of Naples 6 km (4 miles) SE of Naples. Pop. (1981) 79,300.

Fishing, silk-weaving and tanning.

Has a former royal palace (built 1738). Destroyed in the eruption of Vesuvius 1631. Terminus of the first railway in Italy (1839), from Naples to Portici.

Portimão Portugal. Town in Faro situated WNW of Faro at the mouth of the Arade R. estuary on the S coast. Pop. (1980) 19,600.

Important fishing and fish-canning centre, esp. sardine and tuna.

Portishead England. Seaport in North Somerset on the Severn estuary 13 km (8 miles) WNW of Bristol. Pop. (1991). 14,721.

Resort. The docks form part of the Port of Bristol.

Port Jackson Australia. A deep, silt-free drowned valley in New South Wales forming an excellent land-locked harbour for Sydney. The many inlets allow long wharves with deep water alongside. Spanned by Sydney Harbour Bridge (1932) 503 m (1650 ft) long, linking the city with its N suburbs.

Port Kelang Malaysia. Formerly Port Swettenham. Port situated on the Strait of Malacca, Selangor SW of Kuala Lumpur, mainly handling rubber. Pop. (1980) 192,080.

Port Kembla Australia. Industrial town and port, centre of heavy industry in New South Wales 72 km (45 miles) SSW of Sydney, forming part of Greater Wollongong. Pop. (1985) 8000.

Important iron and steel industry. Also copper-refining, tinplate, wire and cable, fertilizer manufacture.

Chief residential area Wollongong 8 km (5 miles) N.

Portland (Maine) USA. Largest city and chief seaport of the state, on a peninsula on Casco Bay. Pop. (1990) 64,358.

Excellent harbour. Exports timber, grain. Manufactures paper, footwear, furniture and textiles. Fishing.

Founded by the English (1632) as Falmouth. Destroyed by Indians and French, and later by a British fleet. State cap. 1820–31. Birthplace of Henry Wadsworth Longfellow (1807–82).

Portland (Oregon) USA. Largest city in the state in the NW on the Willamette R. near the confluence with the Columbia R. Pop. (1990) 437,319.

Port; excellent freshwater harbour, served by ocean-going vessels. Exports timber, grain and flour. Manufactures wood products, paper and furniture, electrical equipment and clothing.

Named after Portland, Maine. Grew rapidly during the California and Alaska gold rushes.

Portland, Isle of England. Rocky peninsula on the coast of Dorset connected with the mainland by the ridge of shingle known as Chesil Bank (Beach). Area 12 sq km (4½ sq. miles). At the S end is Portland Bill, with a lighthouse. The highest point is the Verne (N). Also on the island are Portland Castle, built by Henry VIII in 1520, and the former convict prison, since 1921 a Borstal institution. Portland Harbour, on the NE side, is a naval base protected by great breakwaters. The island consists largely of a mass of lime-

stone, which has been long quarried for building stone and was used in the construction of St Paul's Cathedral and many other London buildings.

Portlaoighise Ireland. County town of Co. Laoighis 77 km (48 miles) WSW of Dublin. Pop. (1990) 9500.

Has remains of a fort erected in the reign of Mary Tudor.

Port Lincoln Australia. City in South Australia and port S of Port Augusta situated at the S tip of the Eyre Peninsula on Boston Bay. Pop. (1986) 13,100.

Port exports cereal grain, inc. wheat, barley and oats. Industries inc. fishing and tourism.

Port Louis Mauritius. Cap. and chief seaport on the NW coast. Pop. (1991) 142,087.

Small but excellent harbour. Large exports of sugar. Industries inc. railway engineering and tourism. Manufactures cigarettes, matches, soap, clothing, footwear, jewellery and food products.

Dominated by the Citadel (1830). Founded by Mahé de la Bourdonnais c. 1735. Achieved city status in 1966.

Portmadoc (Porthmadog) Wales. Market town in Gwynedd on Tremadoc Bay 26 km (16 miles) SSE of Caernarvon. Pop. (1981) 4000.

Seaport and tourism is an important industry.

Port Moresby Papua New Guinea. Cap., in the SE. Pop. (1990) 193,242.

Chief seaport. Exports copra and rubber. Important Allied base in World War II.

Pôrto ➤OPORTO.

Pôrto Alegre Brazil. Cap. of Rio Grande do Sul state at the N end of the Lagôa dos Patos 240 km (150 miles) NNE of Rio Grande, its outport. Pop. (1991) 1,262,631.

A modern city of rapid growth. Seaport. Important commercial centre. Exports meat products, hides and wool. Meat-packing, tanning and brewing. Manufactures textiles and chemicals. An attractive city amid picturesque scenery.

Founded 1742.

Portofino ➤RAPALLO.

Port of Spain Trinidad and Tobago. Cap., chief seaport and largest city on the Gulf of Paria in the NW of Trinidad. Pop. (1990) 50,878.

A sheltered but shallow harbour. Exports petroleum products, sugar, rum and cacao. Rum-distilling, brewing and sawmilling. Manufactures cement, cigarettes, electrical equipment and also assembly of vehicles.

One of the finest cities in the West Indies, in a beautiful setting, with many parks and squares, attractive streets and noteworthy public buildings. Government House is in the famous Botanical Gardens, near the Queen's Park Savannah, a large recreation ground. Replaced St Joseph as cap. 1783.

Porto Novo Benin. Cap. and seaport on the N shore of a coastal lagoon 80 km (50 miles) W of Lagos (Nigeria). Pop. (1992) 177,660.

Linked by rail with the seaport of Cotonou and with Pobé in the interior. Exports palm oil and kernels, cotton and kapok.

Porto Rico ➤PUERTO RICO.

Pôrto Velho Brazil. Cap. of the remote forested Amazonian territory of Rondônia 800 km (500 miles) SSW of Manáus at the head of navigation on the Madeira R. Pop. (1991) 286,000.

Terminus of the railway bypassing the Madeira R. rapids. Trade in rubber, timber and medicinal plants. Mining of gold, manganese, iron and casseterite.

Portoviejo Ecuador. Cap. of Manabí province on the coastal plain 129 km (80 miles) NNW of Guayaquil. Pop. (1990) 132,937.

Market town; trade in coffee and cacao. Manufactures baskets, vegetable oil, cotton and Panama hats.

Port Phillip Bay (Port Phillip) Australia. Large inlet off Bass Strait in S Victoria, 56 km (35 miles) N–S and 64 km (40 miles) W–E, with Melbourne at its head and Geelong on Corio Bay (W).

Port Pirie Australia. Seaport in South Australia on Germein Bay leading to Spencer Gulf 200 km (125 miles) NNW of Adelaide. Pop. (1987) 15,160.

Receives metal concentrates from Broken Hill; its smelters produce lead bullion and extract silver, zinc and gold. Also exports wheat and wool. Manufactures chemicals.

Portree Scotland. Chief town of the Isle of Skye in Highland on the Sound of Raasay 32 km (20 miles) NW of Kyle of Lochalsh. Pop. (1991) 2126.

Fishing port. Resort.

Portrush Northern Ireland. Town in Co. Antrim 48 km (30 miles) ENE of Londonderry. Pop. (1991) 5598. Seaside resort and centre for the Giant's Causeway 11 km (7 miles) ENE. The ruins of the 14th-cent. Dunluce Castle are 3 km (2 miles) E.

Port Said Egypt. Seaport and important fuelling station (coal, oil) at the Mediterranean entrance to the Suez Canal 160 km (100 miles) NE of Cairo on a narrow strip of land between L. Manzala and the sea. Pop. (1991) 449,000.

Linked by rail with Suez and Cairo (via Ismailia). Large entrepôt trade. Exports cotton. Manufactures chemicals and cigarettes. Salt panning.

Founded 1859 when the Suez Canal was begun. Named after Said Pasha (then Khedive of Egypt). On the opposite bank is Port Fuad (opened 1926).

Portslade-by-Sea England. Minor port in East Sussex on the English Channel just W of Hove. Pop. (1991) 17,762.

Manufactures electrical equipment.

Portsmouth England. City in SE Hampshire on Portsea Island at the entrance to Portsmouth Harbour opposite Gosport. Pop. (1991) 177,905. The country's chief naval base, with Nelson's flagship, HMS *Victory* in dry dock near the entrance to the Royal Dockyard. The Tudor warship *Mary Rose* is also here. Consists of Landport, Portsea,

Cosham and Southsea, the last a residential district and popular seaside resort. There is a ferry service to France. Engineering and general manufacturing.

Since 1927 the Church of St Thomas, dating from the 12th cent. (restored), has been the cathedral; also a modern Roman Catholic cathedral. Portsmouth nicknamed 'Pompey', became important as a naval base in the reign of Henry VIII. Birthplace of Charles Dickens, English writer (1812–70), George Meredith, English novelist (1828–1909), Sir Walter Besant, English social reformer and novelist (1836–1901) and Isambard Brunel, English engineer and inventor (1806–59).

Portsmouth (New Hampshire) USA. The only seaport in the state, in the SE, at the mouth of the Piscataqua R. Pop. (1992) 25,342.

Summer resort. Manufactures clothing, machinery and instruments.

Several 18th-cent. and early 19th-cent. houses. Naval base, with a submarine-building and repair yard, on an island in the Piscataqua R. (on the Maine side), where the Treaty of Portsmouth ending the Russo–Japanese War was signed (1905). State cap. 1679–1775.

Portsmouth (Ohio) USA. Industrial town on the Ohio R. at the confluence with the Scioto R. Pop. (1980) 25,943.

Railway engineering. Manufactures iron and steel, footwear and furniture.

Portsmouth (Virginia) USA. Seaport and industrial town on the Elizabeth R. opposite Norfolk. Pop. (1990) 103,907.

Exports cotton, tobacco. Food-processing and railway engineering. Manufactures cottonseed oil, chemicals, fertilizers and hosiery.

The Norfolk Navy Yard on the E waterfront is one of the most important in the USA; in the American Civil War it was evacuated by Federal troops (1861) but was retaken in 1862.

Portstewart Northern Ireland. Town in Co. Londonderry 45 km (28 miles) NE of

Londonderry. Pop. (1991) 6459. Seaside resort.

Port Sudan Sudan. Chief seaport, a fuelling station (coal, oil) on the Red Sea. Pop. (1983) 206,727.

Terminus of the railway from the Nile valley and Khartoum (via Haiya Junction). Handles almost all Sudan's foreign trade. Exports cotton, cotton and sesame seeds, gum arabic, hides and skins. Cotton-ginning. Salt-panning.

Founded 1906, superseding Suakin.

Port Sunlight ➤BEBINGTON.

Port Swettenham ➤PORT KELANG.

Port Talbot Wales. Town in Neath Port Talbot on Swansea Bay 11 km (7 miles) ESE of Swansea, formed in 1921 from the town of Aberavon and the urban district of Margam. Pop. (1991) 36,647.

Seaport with large imports of iron ore. Important steelworks, one of the largest in Europe. New harbour to accommodate large ore vessels opened in 1970. Other industries inc. steel, electronics, engineering and chemicals.

Portugal. Republic in SW Europe occupying the W part of the Iberian peninsula. Bounded by Spain to the N and E and the Atlantic to the S and W. Area (inc. Madeira and the Azores) 92,389 sq km (35,672 sq. miles). Pop. (1995) 9,906,000 (35 per cent urban). Life expectancy, 71 years male, 78 female. Cap. Lisbon. Other major cities Oporto and Amadora. Currency: escudo = 100 centavos. Portugal is divided into two zones by the R. Tagus with mountain ranges running generally NE–SW across the country, rising to a height of 1993 m (6540 ft) in the Serra de Estrela. The four main rivers are the Douro, Guadiana, Minho and the Tagus, and for much of their lengths flow first through Spain. The climate is generally equable, temperate with moderately heavy rainfall. The country is well forested, but the soil generally poor and droughts occur. In the Algarve to the S climate and vegetation are subtropical. Land use: forested 32 per cent, meadows and pastures 9 per cent, permanent cultivation 35 per cent. The Portuguese people are basically of Iberian descent and about 95 per cent are Roman Catholics.

The country is primarily agricultural, with important forests and fisheries. Traditionally the economy has relied heavily on two products, cork (from the cork oak) and port wine, but in recent years textiles and clothing have assumed importance. Industries given state help after the revolution of 1974, such as shipbuilding, steel and oil-refining, are stagnant. Membership of the European Union has brought more competition. On the plains and in the valleys of the W the leading crops are wheat, maize, vines and olives. Port from the Douro valley is the most important wine, but many others are produced. The wooded slopes of the interior produce cork; resin from the pine forests is another significant export. Around the coasts many men are employed in the fishing industry, and the sardines which represent the chief part of the catch are canned. It is indicative of Portuguese maritime interests that the two largest cities are Lisbon, the cap., and Oporto, both seaports; they are also the main industrial centres chiefly manufacturing textiles. Minerals are little exploited, owing to poor communications and lack of fuel. Development of the thriving tourist industry is most apparent in the Algarve in the S and on the so-called Portuguese Riviera, W of Lisbon, where Estoril is the leading centre.

The early history of Portugal was that of the Iberian peninsula as a whole, most of the country being incorporated with part of W Spain in the Roman province of Lusitania. The Moors defeated the Visigoths, who had later overrun the peninsula and they in turn were vanquished in 1139 by Alfonso I; he proclaimed himself king, though the last of the Moors did not leave for another cent. In 1386, after English archers had assisted in the defeat of Castile, the alliance between Portugal and England was confirmed, and John I married the daughter of John of Gaunt. Now began the most illustrious period of Portuguese history, initiated by Prince Henry the Navigator, son of John I: the Azores, Madeira and the Cape Verde Is. were colonized and the Cape of Good Hope was rounded by Bartholomew Diaz in 1488, and the route to India was discovered by Vasco da Gama in 1498, Brazil was acquired in 1550, the Portuguese Empire was founded. But in 1580 Philip II of Spain seized the throne and Portuguese independence was not again recognized by the Spaniards until 1668. The country suffered severely in the Wars of the Spanish Succession and the Peninsular War, later from civil war and dictatorships, and Brazil was lost in 1822. In 1908 King Carlos was assassinated and with the revolution of 1910 a republic was established, the Roman Catholic Church was disestablished and religious orders were expelled. The Constitution of 1933 established a corporative state and Salazar, the Prime Minister, became virtually a dictator. He relinquished office only in 1968 and died in 1970. After a period of relative political stability, but economic uncertainty at home, the government was overthrown by military *coup* in 1974 brought about by the lack of political liberalization and the cost of the war in the African colonies. Anti-Portuguese movements gained strength in the colonies especially in Angola and Mozambique, and the Portuguese gradually withdrew and the colonies became independent. Macau is the last remaining territory, which will be returned to China in 1999. Executive power is held by the President who is elected for 5-year terms. He appoints the Prime Minister and, on the latter's nomination, other members of the Council of Ministers. The 250-member Assembly of the Republic is elected for 4-year terms. The administrative districts of Portugal are: Aveiro, Beja, Braga, Bragança, Castelo Branco, Coimbra, Évora, Faro, Guarda, Leiria, Lisboa, Portalegre, Pôrto, Santarém, Setúbal, Viana do Castelo, Vila Real, Viseu. The islands of the Azores and Madeira are politically an integral part of the country; the Azores are divided into the three districts of Angra do Heroismo, Horta and Ponta Delgada, and Madeira is known as the district of Funchal.

Posadas Argentina. Cap. of Misiones province on the Alto Paraná R. 298 km (185 miles) E of Corrientes. Pop. (1991) 219,824.

Linked by ferry with Encarnación (Paraguay). River port. Trade in rice, tobacco and maté. Meat-packing and flour-milling.

Poseidonia ►PAESTUM.

Posen ►POZNAŃ.

Posillipo (Posilipo) Italy. Ridge in Campania extending SW from Naples, penetrated by a tunnel (the Grotto of Posillipo) through which passes the road from Naples to Pozzuoli. The village of Posillipo, which has remains of Roman villas, is still a fashionable residential area.

Postojna Slovenia. Small town 40 km (25 miles) SW of Ljubljana. Pop. (1985) 5000. The largest caves in Europe, containing stalactites and stalagmites of fantastic shapes, in the limestone Karst region. Here was first discovered the remarkable amphibious creature *Proteus anguinus*.

Potchefstroom South Africa. Town in North West Province on the Mooi R. above the confluence with the Vaal R. 113 km (70 miles) WSW of Johannesburg, at a height of 1353 m (4438 ft). Pop. (1985) 57,000.

In an agricultural district where wheat, maize and alfalfa are cultivated and dairy cattle raised. Educational centre.

Seat of a university (1951) and of an agricultural college and government experimental farm. Founded 1838 and is the oldest town and first cap. of the Transvaal (now Gauteng province).

Potenza Italy. Cap. of Potenza province in Basilicata on a hill above the Basento R. at a height of 820 m (2690 ft) 88 km (55 miles) E of Salerno. Pop. (1991) 68,500.

Market town. New industries inc. food-processing, clothing and construction.

Largely destroyed by the earthquake of 1857 and again damaged by earthquake in 1910.

Poti Georgia. Seaport on the Black Sea at the mouth of the Rion R. 64 km (40 miles) N of Batumi. Pop. (1990) 54,000.

Exports chiefly manganese from the Chiatura mines. Industries inc. fish-canning and ship-repairing. The neighbouring marshes (Colchis) have been largely drained.

Potidaea Greece. Ancient city in Macedonia on the Kassandra isthmus of the Chalcidice Peninsula. Founded from Corinth; its opposition to the Athenian League led to the Peloponnesian War. Captured by the Athenians 429 BC. Destroyed by Philip II of Macedon 356 BC; later rebuilt by Cassander.

Potomac River USA. River in the E 462 km (287 miles) long, formed by the union of the N and S branches (from the Allegheny Mountains), flowing NE and then generally SE and entering Chesapeake Bay. In the upper course it forms the boundary between Maryland and West Virginia and in the lower course that between Maryland and the District of Columbia on one side and Virginia on the other. Cuts a gorge through the Blue Ridge Mountains at Harper's Ferry, where it receives it main tributary, the Shenandoah. Washington (DC), 185 km (115 miles) upstream from the mouth, stands at the head of navigation for shipping; the Great Falls of the Potomac R., a series of cascades and rapids in a 60-m (197-ft) gorge, are 24 km (15 miles) above the city. The river has many historical associations: on the right bank below Washington (DC) is George Washington's estate of Mount Vernon (Virginia).

Potosí Bolivia. Cap. of the Potosí department in the Andes at a height of 4070 m (13,350 ft) 88 km (55 miles) SW of Sucre. Pop. (1992) 112,291. One of the highest towns in the world. Founded 1545; became famous for its rich silver mines. As the lodes deteriorated, the pop. declined (from 150,000 in the mid 17th cent. to 8000 by 1825). Revived with the development of tin-mining in the Cerro de Potosí.

Also manufactures footwear and furniture.

University (1571). Has many colonial buildings, inc. the famous Casa Real de

Moneda or Mint (1572), and a 19th-cent. cathedral.

Potsdam Germany. Cap. of Potsdam district and Brandenburg on the Havel R. 26 km (16 miles) SW of the centre of Berlin. Pop. (1990) 139,500.

Residential and industrial. Manufactures chemicals, precision instruments, soap, furniture and there is railway and other engineering.

Formerly the residence of Prussian kings and German emperors, it became the centre of Prussian militarism, reflected even in the uniformity of its streets. Frederick the Great left his mark in the palace and park of Sans Souci (1745–7) and most of the noteworthy buildings date from the 18th cent. Scene of the Potsdam Conference of Truman, Stalin and Attlee (1945). Later became the headquarters of the Soviet army in Germany.

Potteries England. District in N Staffordshire in the upper Trent valley 14 km (9 miles) long (NW–SE) and about 5 km (3 miles) wide, inc. Stoke-on-Trent, Hanley, Burslem, Tunstall, Longton and Fenton, amalgamated in 1910 as Stoke-on-Trent. The country's leading area for china and earthenware manufacture. Newcastle-under-Lyme, though not a pottery-manufacturing town, lies on its W edge. The modern pottery industry dates from c. 1769, when Josiah Wedgwood founded his works at Etruria (now in Hanley); Wedgwood and Minton are the outstanding family names associated with it. Local coal and coarse clay were long important raw materials, but fine china clay is imported from Cornwall and Dorset.

Potters Bar England. Former urban district in N Middlesex, transferred to Hertfordshire in 1965 when most of Middlesex was absorbed into the Greater London Council area. Pop. (1991) 32,099. Mainly residential.

Pottstown USA. Industrial town in Pennsylvania on the Schuylkill R. 51 km (32 miles) NW of Philadelphia. Pop. (1970) 25,355.

Manufactures iron and steel goods and tyres.

The first ironworks in Pennsylvania were established here c. 1720.

Poughkeepsie USA. Industrial town in New York on the Hudson R. 109 km (68 miles) N of New York City. Pop. (1990) 28,844.

Manufactures dairy machinery, ball-bearings, business machines and precision instruments.

Settled by the Dutch 1687.

Poverty Bay New Zealand. Inlet on the E coast of North Island where Capt. Cook first landed in New Zealand (1769); so named because he could not obtain provisions there. Gisborne is on its N coast.

Powell USA. City in Wyoming situated NE of Cody at 1338 m (4390 ft) above sea level. Pop. (1980) 5310.

Trading centre for an irrigated agricultural area, handling sugar-beet, sweet clover seed, alfalfa and potatoes. Industries inc. seed-processing.

Powys Wales. County in Central Wales formed (1974) from Montgomeryshire, Radnorshire and Breconshire, except for small areas in the last-named which passed to the former counties of Mid Glamorgan and Gwent. Area 5072 sq km (1958 sq. miles). Pop. (1990) 118,600. County town: Llandrindod Wells. Mainly mountainous, inc. the S slopes of the Berwyn Mountains (N), Radnor Forest (E) and the Black Mountains and Brecon Beacons (S), which rise to 886 m (2906 ft). Sheep-rearing on the uplands. Drained by the Severn, Vyrnwy, Dovey, Wye and Usk rivers. L. Vyrnwy supplies Liverpool, reservoirs in the Elan valley supply Birmingham with water. Sparsely inhabited, with scattered small towns (e.g. Welshpool, Brecon) and villages.

Poyang Lake China. Shallow lake in N Jiangxi province connected by canal with the Chang Jiang R. In summer it receives the latter's flood waters and reaches its maximum dimensions (129 by 64 km; 80 by 40 miles); in winter considerably diminished. Gradually decreasing in area owing to deposition of sediment.

Poznań (Ger. **Posen**) Poland. Cap. of the Poznań voivodeship on the Warta R. 290 km (180 miles) W of Warsaw. Pop. (1992) 589,700.

Important railway junction, industrial and commercial centre. Manufactures machinery, railway rolling-stock, boilers, bicycles, tyres, glass, chemicals, machine-tools, rubber and paper. Brewing and distilling.

One of the oldest cities in Poland and an archiepiscopal see since the 10th cent. The 16th-cent. town hall and the 18th-cent. cathedral were severely damaged in World War II and rebuilt. University (1919). Founded before Poland was Christianized. Its later history was largely a reflection of the Polish struggle against the Germans. Birthplace of Field Marshal von Hindenburg (1847–1934).

Pozzuoli Italy. Ancient Puteoli. Port in Napoli province, Campania 11 km (7 miles) WSW of Naples. Pop. (1985) 71,100. Iron and steel works. A Roman seaport, having been colonized in the 2nd cent. BC; its remains inc. an amphitheatre and the so-called Temple of Serapis (a market-place). Gave its name to *pozzuolana*, the volcanic ash found here and used, as in Roman times, for making cement. Nearby is the crater Solfatara, which emits sulphurous jets and has given its name to this type of volcanic feature. Pozzuoli was twice severely damaged by earthquake (1198, 1538).

Prague (Praha) Czech Republic. Cap. situated on the Vltava R. in the NW of the Czech Republic and some 90 km (60 miles) from the German border. Pop. (1990) 1,215,076. Prague occupies a hilly site surrounding the winding course of the R. Vltava; the suburbs spread out into the tributary valleys. The centre is largely baroque and carefully preserved. It is dominated, however, by the medieval Hradčany Castle and St Vitus Cathedral, twin-spired, on a hill above the left bank of the river. The oldest part of the city contains an important Jewish quarter.

Heavy industry has been encouraged since the early 19th cent.; manufactures inc. food products, machinery, textiles and consumer goods. Brewing and printing are significant; also tourism.

A 9th-cent. settlement, Prague became the centre of Bohemia. The city flourished esp. in the 14th cent. under Charles IV, king of Bohemia and Holy Roman Emperor. After 1400 Protestantism was a strong but divisive force, as was the influence of a rich merchant class. The Catholic Habsburg dynasty succeeded in 1526, producing further religious upheaval but artistic and architectural splendour. Industrial suburbs were built from 1817, fostering an expanded pop. that was artisan, nationalistic and anti-Habsburg. Prague became the cap. of independent Czechoslovakia in 1918 and further expansion was rapid. When the Czech and Slovak states divided in 1993 it remained the Czech cap.

Prahova River Romania. Rises SW of the Predeal Pass in the Transylvanian Alps and flows 128 km (80 miles) S past Sinaia then SE past Campina to enter the Ialomita R. SE of Ploesti. Its valley is an important corridor between the Transylvanian Alps and Moldavian Carpathians.

Praia ►CAPE VERDE ISLANDS.

Prato Italy. Town in Firenze province, Tuscany, on the Bisenzio R. 14 km (9 miles) WNW of Florence. Pop. (1991) 166,688.

Centre of the woollen industry. Manufactures textile machinery and furniture.

The 12th/15th-cent. cathedral has frescoes by Filippo Lippi and an open-air pulpit by Donatello and Michelozzo; several other noteworthy churches.

Přerov Czech Republic. Town in Moravia on the Bečva R. 23 km (14 miles) SE of Olomouc. Pop. (1984) 54,000.

Manufactures machinery and textiles.

Prescot England. Town in Merseyside

13 km (8 miles) E of Liverpool. Pop. (1991) 37,486.

Manufactures electric cables, watch movements and tools.

Prešov Slovakia. Town on the Torysa R. 32 km (20 miles) N of Košice. Pop. (1990) 89,000.

Railway junction. Market town. Distilling. Manufactures linen.

Founded by Germans in the 12th cent. Almost completely rebuilt since a disastrous fire in 1887.

Prespa, Lake. Lake mainly in Macedonia, former Yugoslavia, with the SW part in Albania and the SE part in Greece; at a height of 850 m (2788 ft). Area 285 sq km (110 sq. miles). Drained by underground channels to L. Ohrid 10 km (6 miles) W.

Pressburg ►BRATISLAVA.

Prestatyn Wales. Market town in Denbighshire 6 km (4 miles) ENE of Rhyl. Pop. (1985) 16,000. Seaside resort. The Point of Ayr coalmine 8 km (5 miles) to the E, closed in 1996; the last mine in N Wales.

Presteigne Wales. Market town in Powys on the R. Lugg 31 km (19 miles) NW of Hereford. Pop. (1985) 1300. Has a 15th-cent. parish church.

Preston England. Town in Lancashire on the R. Ribble 43 km (27 miles) NW of Manchester. Pop. (1991) 129,000.

Engineering. Manufactures textiles (cotton, rayon), machinery, electrical equipment, motor vehicles, footwear, chemicals and plastics. Trade in agricultural produce and livestock.

The epithet 'proud Preston' dates from the 18th cent., when it acquired a reputation for its fashionable society. Birthplace of Richard Arkwright (1732–92), inventor of the spinning frame and Francis Thompson (1859–1907), the poet.

Prestonpans Scotland. Small town in East Lothian on the Firth of Forth 13 km (8 miles) E of Edinburgh. Pop. (1991) 7014.

Coalmining, brewing. Industries inc. oil-skin manufacture; specialist fabrication and precision engineering.

At the Battle of Prestonpans (1745) Prince Charles Edward defeated the English forces under Sir John Cope. The name derives from the pans, or ponds, in which salt was formerly obtained from seawater by evaporation.

Prestwich England. Town in Greater Manchester 6 km (4 miles) NNW of the city. Pop. (1991) 31,810. Mainly residential.

Manufactures textiles (cotton, rayon).

Prestwick Scotland. Town in South Ayrshire on the Firth of Clyde 3 km (2 miles) NNE of Ayr. Pop. (1991) 13,705.

Seaside resort. Well-known golf course. International airport and freeport developed during World War II as a transatlantic terminal.

Pretoria South Africa. Administrative cap. in Gauteng 51 km (32 miles) NNE of Johannesburg at a height of 1402 m (4600 ft). Pop. (1991) 1,080,187 (urban area).

Important railway centre. Railway engineering. Manufactures cement, leather, chemicals. South Africa's largest steelworks is 8 km (5 miles) W.

Seat of the University of Pretoria (1930) and the Radcliffe Observatory (1937). President Kruger's house is a national monument. Has jacaranda-lined streets. Founded 1855. Named after the Boer leader Andries Pretorius (1799–1853). Became the administrative cap. of the new Union of South Africa 1910. Voortrekker Monument (1949), commemorating the South African *voortrekkers* (pioneers) of 1834–8, is 6 km (4 miles) S.

Préveza Greece. 1. *Nome* in Epirus on the Ionian Sea. Area 1036 sq km (400 sq. miles). Pop. (1991) 58,910. Mainly mountainous. Produces olive oil, citrus fruits and cereals. Fishing. 2. Cap. and chief port of Préveza *nome* at the entrance to the Gulf of Arta. Pop. (1985) 13,000. Exports olives and olive oil, citrus fruits.

Pribilof Islands USA. Group of 4 islands in the Bering Sea off SW Alaska. Area 168 sq km (65 sq. miles). Pop. about 600 (entirely

Aleuts and government officials, no others being permitted to reside on the islands). Only St Paul and St George are inhabited. Important for trade in seal furs; a major breeding ground for the Alaskan fur seal, recognized as an international seal reserve. Until the Pacific Sealing Convention (1911) the seal was threatened with extermination. Named after Gerasim Pribilof, the Russian who discovered them (1786).

Prijedor Bosnia. Town situated NW of Banja Luka on the Sana R. and railway. Pop. (1990) 112,470.

Distribution centre for iron ore from Ljubija. The main industry is the manufacture of wood-pulp.

Prilep Macedonia. Market town 72 km (45 miles) S of Skoplje. Pop. (1991) 70,152.

In an agricultural region. Important trade in tobacco.

Birthplace of the 14th-cent. Serbian national hero, Marko Kralyević, the ruins of whose fortress lie just NE.

Primorye (Maritime) Territory Russia. Territory in SE Siberia on the Sea of Japan opposite S Sakhalin and Hokkaido (Japan). Area 165,900 sq km (64,100 sq. miles). Pop. (1992) 2,309,000. Cap. Vladivostok. Inc. part of the Sikhote Alin Range (E) and the lowlands beside the Ussuri R. and L. Khanka (W) along the border with Manchuria. Produces coal and other minerals, timber. In 1993 it was considering proclaiming itself a republic.

Prince Albert Canada. Town in Saskatchewan on the North Saskatchewan R. 134 km (83 miles) NNE of Saskatoon. Pop. (1991) 34,181.

Commercial centre for N Saskatchewan. Woodworking, tanning.

Founded (1866) as a mission station.

Prince Edward Island Canada. Province of Canada in the Gulf of St Lawrence. Area 5660 sq km (2185 sq. miles). Pop. (1993) 131,600.

Cap. Charlottetown. Generally low-lying. The coastline is deeply indented, with sandy beaches in the N and low cliffs of red sandstone in the S. Maritime climate, milder than that of the neighbouring mainland. Annual rainfall 100 cm (40 ins.).

Dairy-farming, cattle-rearing, agriculture and fishing (esp. lobsters). The railways closed in 1989; there is a twice-daily bus service to the mainland and there are modern car ferries.

Discovered by Jacques Cartier in 1534. Annexed by France 1603 (as Île St Jean). Ceded to Britain 1763. Remained part of Nova Scotia until it became a separate colony (1769). Many Scottish and Irish immigrants settled here in the early 19th cent. Joined the Confederation of Canada 1873.

Prince George Canada. Town in British Columbia on the Fraser R. at its confluence with the Nechako R. 523 km (325 miles) N of Vancouver. Pop. (1991) 69,653.

Commercial centre for a mining and lumbering region.

Founded as a fur-trading post in the early 19th cent.

Prince of Wales Island ➤ENDEAVOUR STRAIT.

Prince Rupert Canada. Seaport in British Columbia near the mouth of the Skeena R., on an island connected to the mainland by a bridge. Pop. (1991) 16,620.

Exports grain. Serves mining, lumbering and farming communities. Important halibut and salmon fisheries. Fish-canning and pulp-milling.

Princess Elizabeth Land ➤AUSTRALIAN ANTARCTIC TERRITORY.

Princeton USA. Residential town in New Jersey on the Millstone R. 18 km (11 miles) NE of Trenton. Pop. (1990) 12,020. Famous as the seat of Princeton University, opened at Elizabeth (1747), moved to Newark (1748) and then to Princeton (1756), and known as the College of New Jersey until 1896. Settled by Quakers 1696. Incorporated 1813.

Prince William Sound USA. Sound of the Gulf of Alaska lying N of Middleton Island, extending c. 190 km (120 miles) NW from Kayak Island.

Príncipe ►SÃO TOMÉ and PRÍNCIPE.

Pripet (Russian **Pripyat**) **River** Ukraine. River 800 km (500 miles) long rising in NW Ukraine just E of the Bug R., flowing generally ENE into Belarus, then turning E and SE to join the Dnieper R. Navigable for much of its course and linked by canals with the Bug and the Neman rivers. Around the upper course of the river and its tributaries are the Pripet Marshes, a wooded, swampy area in which flax and potatoes are cultivated near scattered villages; before World War II it was in Poland. The chief town here is Pinsk.

Priština Serbia. Cap. of Kosovo 80 km (50 miles) NNW of Skoplje. Pop. (1985) 216,000.

Market town in an agricultural district. Oriental in character and appearance; under Turkish rule until 1912. The remarkable 14th-cent. monastery of Gračanica is 6 km (4 miles) SW.

Privas France. Cap. of Ardèche department situated NNW of Marseille. Pop. (1990) 10,490.

Prokopyevsk Russia. Coalmining town in the Kemerovo region in the Kuznetsk Basin 27 km (17 miles) WNW of Novokuznetsk. Pop. (1992) 272,000. Linked by rail with Novokuznetsk and also with the Trans-Siberian Railway.

Prome Myanmar (Burma). River port on the Irrawaddy R. 240 km (150 miles) NNW of Yangôn (Rangoon) with which it is connected by rail. Pop. 37,000. An ancient town with the famous Shwe Tsandaw pagoda on a nearby hill.

Prostějov (Ger. **Prossnitz**) Czech Republic. Town in Moravia 16 km (10 miles) SW of Olomouc. Pop. (1984) 51,100.

Brewing. Manufactures textiles, clothing and footwear.

Provence–Alpes–Côte d'Azur France. Region and former province in the SE, bounded by Italy (E), the Mediterranean Sea (S) and the Rhône R. (W); now forms the Bouches-du-Rhône, Var and Alpes-de-Haute Provence, and parts of the Alpes-Maritimes and Vaucluse departments. The region owes its wealth to its Mediterranean coastline, its excellent climate and its natural sites. Marseilles, France's largest port, shapes the region's economic life and there are oil refineries, iron and steel production, chemicals and food-processing. To the E, Nice and the Côte d'Azur are tourist resorts. The French perfume industry has its base in and around Grasse. The region also attracts high technology. Regional cap. Marseilles.

Became a kingdom in the 9th cent. United to the French crown 1486. The Provençal lang. was used from the early Middle Ages until the 16th cent., but the literature never completely died out and was vigorously revived in the 19th cent.

Providence USA. State cap., largest city and seaport of Rhode Island on the Providence R. at the head of Narragansett Bay. Pop. (1990) 160,728.

Oil-refining. Manufactures jewellery, textiles, textile machinery, machine-tools and rubber products. Education centre.

Founded (1636) by Roger Williams; named in recognition of 'God's merciful providence'. Many noteworthy 18th-cent. buildings. Joint state cap. with Newport until 1900.

Provo USA. Town in Utah on the Provo R. 63 km (39 miles) SSE of Salt Lake City at a height of 1390 m (4559 ft). Pop. (1990) 86,835.

Commercial centre for an agricultural and mining region. Manufactures iron and steel, bricks and tiles, food products.

Seat of the Brigham Young University (1875, Mormon). Settled by the Mormons (1849). Developed considerably after the arrival of the railway from Salt Lake City (1873).

Prudhoe Bay USA. Bay of N coast in the Beaufort Sea, Alaska, with important arctic oilfield; small town with oil pipeline terminal opposite Jones Island.

Prussia (Ger. **Preussen**). Former German

state in N and Central Europe extending from France, Belgium and the Netherlands to Poland and the Baltic Sea. Cap. was Berlin. It was the chief military power in Europe and led the North German Confederation when the German Empire was established. After World War II it was dissolved; most of E Prussia and the lands E of the Oder–Neisse (Odra–Nysa) line were restored to Poland and the N part of E Prussia was ceded to the USSR; the remainder of Prussia was broken up into various *Länder* in East and West Germany.

Prut River Romania/Moldavia. River 853 km (530 miles) long, rising in the Carpathians in the SW Ukraine, flowing generally N and then E past Kolomyya and Chernovtsy, then generally SSE, forming the Romania–Moldavia border and joining the Danube R. 13 km (8 miles) E of Galaţi (Romania).

Przemyśl Poland. Cap. of the Przemyśl voivodeship in the SE on the San R. near the Ukrainian frontier. Pop. (1989) 68,121.

Flour-milling, sawmilling and tanning. Manufactures machinery.

An ancient town, probably dating from the 8th cent. Occupied by Austria 1773–1915. Ceded to Poland 1919.

Pskov (Pleskau) Russia. Cap. of the Pskov region on the Velikaya R. near its mouth in L. Pskov 265 km (165 miles) SW of St Petersburg. Pop. (1992) 209,000.

Railway junction. Industrial centre in an important flax-growing region. Manufactures linen, rope, agricultural machinery and leather.

One of the oldest Russian cities. Has many churches and monasteries dating from the 14th and 15th cent. A prosperous and commercially important city in the Middle Ages. Annexed to Moscow 1510; thereafter declined.

Pskov, Lake ➤PEIPUS, LAKE.

Pucallpa Peru. Town in the Loreto department on the Ucayali R. 480 km (300 miles) NE of Lima. Pop. (1990) 153,000. Accessible from Iquitos by river steamer. Linked with Lima by the Andean Highway since 1944.

Sawmilling. Trade in agricultural produce. Reached by pipeline from the Ganzo Azul oilfield to the SSW.

Pudsey England. Town in West Yorkshire 5 km (3 miles) E of Bradford. Pop. (1991) 31,636

Important woollen industry; also engineering and tanning.

Puebla Mexico. 1. State on the central plateau. Area 33,902 sq km (13,090 sq. miles). Pop. (1990) 4,126,101. Largely mountainous; Mexico's 3 highest peaks, Pico de Orizaba, Popocatépetl and Ixtaccihuatl, are on its borders. Mainly agricultural. Produces maize, wheat, sugar-cane and tobacco. Minerals inc. gold, silver and copper.

2. Formerly Puebla de los Angeles, later Puebla de Zaragoza. Cap. of Puebla state on the central plateau at a height of 2170 m (7118 ft) 105 km (65 miles) ESE of Mexico City. Pop. (1990) 1,007,170.

Manufactures textiles, cement, glazed tiles, pottery and articles in onyx (quarried locally). Picturesque; known as 'the City of Churches'.

The 16th/17th-cent. cathedral is one of the finest ecclesiastical buildings in Latin America, noteworthy for its work in marble and onyx. Has the Teatro Principal, one of the oldest theatres on the continent (built 1790). University (1537).

Pueblo USA. Industrial town in Colorado on the Arkansas R. at a height of 1430 m (4690 ft) 169 km (105 miles) SSE of Denver. Pop. (1990) 98,640.

Known as 'the Pittsburgh of the West' because of the large iron and steel industry. Also oil-refining and meat-packing, and high technology.

Puerto Ayacucho Venezuela. Town and cap. of the Amazonas territory situated S of Caracas on the Orinoco R. where it forms the Colombia border. Pop. (1985) 15,000.

Trading centre for a forest region, handling balata and rubber.

Puerto Barrios Guatemala. Cap. of the Izabal department on the Caribbean coast 240 km (150 miles) NE of Guatemala City. Pop. (1989) 338,000.

The country's chief seaport. Exports coffee and bananas. Oil-refining.

Puerto Cabello Venezuela. Seaport in Carabobo state on the Caribbean coast 32 km (20 miles) N of Valencia. Pop. (1985) 71,200.

Exports coffee, cacao and hides. Manufactures soap and candles. Flour-milling.

Puerto de Santa María (commonly **El Puerto**) Spain. Seaport in Cádiz province, Andalusia, at the mouth of the Guadalete R. on the Gulf of Cádiz. Pop. (1991) 65,517.

Important trade in sherry. Manufactures alcohol, liqueurs and soap. Tanning, fish-canning. Has many sherry bodegas.

Puerto Deseado Argentina. Town in Patagonia situated SE of Comodoro Rivadavia at the mouth of the Deseado R. on the Atlantic. Pop. (1985) 3750.

Railway terminus and port serving a sheep-farming area. Exports wool and skin. Industries inc. meat-packing; manufactures furniture.

Puerto la Cruz Venezuela. Town and oil-exporting port in Anzoátegui state in the NE 10 km (6 miles) NNE of Barcelona. Pop. (1985) 180,000.

Terminus of oil pipelines from the E llanos. Large oil refineries.

Puerto Montt Chile. Cap. of Llanquihue province and seaport on Reloncaví Sound 185 km (115 miles) SSE of Valdivia. Pop. (1992) 130,737.

The S terminus of the country's railway system. Serves a sheep-farming area and Chiloé Island. Resort, with access to fine mountain scenery and the Chilean lake district. Founded (1853) by German immigrants.

Puerto Plata Dominican Republic. Town situated N of Santiago. Officially called San Felipe de Puerto Plata. Pop. (1986) 96,500.

Seaport serving an agricultural area. Processing and shipping centre for tobacco,

coffee, cacao, rice, sugar-cane, bananas, hides and timber. Manufactures dairy products, matches, lard, pasta and essential oils.

Puerto Rico (West Indies) USA. The smallest and most E island of the Greater Antilles lying between the Dominican Republic and the US Virgin Islands. The Puerto Rican island of Vieques has a pop. of 8602 and the island of Culebra 1542. Area 9104 sq km (3515 sq. miles). Pop. (1995) 3,725,000 (71 per cent urban). Life expectancy, 70 years male, 79 female. Cap. San Juan. Other cities Ponce, Caguas, Mayagüez and Arecibo. Currency: US dollar = 100 cents. It is mostly mountainous, rising to over 1200 m (3936 ft) in the Cordillera Central. It has a tropical climate but pleasant, with little seasonal variation. Annual rainfall 150–175 cm (60–70 ins.). Land use: forested 20 per cent, meadows and pastures 38 per cent, agricultural and under permanent cultivation 14 per cent. The official langs. are Spanish and English. About 80 per cent are white, 20 per cent black. Over 85 per cent of the pop. is Roman Catholic.

The main agricultural product sugar-cane (at one time virtually the only crop); pineapples, citrus fruits, coffee, tobacco also grown. Industries (sugar and tobacco processing) are chiefly concentrated in San Juan, Ponce and Mayagüez.

Discovered (1493) by Columbus on his second voyage; settled (1508) by one of his companions, Juan Ponce de León, the first governor. Ceded by Spain to the USA (1898) after the Spanish–American War and was known as Porto Rico (1898–1932). The present Constitution of the Commonwealth of Puerto Rico was proclaimed in 1952. It is a self-governing Commonwealth in association with the US and it has a 29-member Senate and 53-member House of Representatives. A referendum held in 1998 about the future status of the Commonwealth (*status quo*, 51st state or independence) showed 50 per cent in favour of *status quo*.

Puerto Varas Chile. Town in the Chilean lake district in Llanquihue province 19 km (12 miles) N of Puerto Montt on the shore of

L. Llanquihue. Pop. (1985) 24,000. Tourist centre.

Puget Sound USA. Inlet of the Pacific Ocean in NW Washington, extending 160 km (100 miles) S of the Juan de Fuca Strait (by which it is connected with the Pacific, through the Admiralty Inlet) to Olympia. Several islands, the largest being Whidbey Island. Chief ports Seattle and Tacoma.

Puglia ►APULIA.

Pula (Italian **Pola**) Croatia. Ancient Pietas Julia. Seaport in the NW near the S end of the peninsula of Istria; also a modern tourist resort. Pop. (1991) 62,300. Taken by the Romans 178 BC; has many Roman remains, inc. a fine amphitheatre. Captured by the Venetians 1148. An Austrian naval base 1856–1918, then became cap. of the Italian province of Pola and later of Istria. Passed to Yugoslavia 1947.

Pulau Pinang (Penang) Malaysia. State in West Malaysia consisting of the island of Pinang off the NW coast in the Strait of Malacca, and a mainland strip formerly known as Province Wellesley. Area 1031 sq km (398 sq. miles). Pop. (1991) 1,065,075. Largely forested and rising to 810 m (2657 ft), the island has rubber and coconut plantations on its lower ground. On the island is the cap., officially George Town but always known as Penang, the chief seaport of N Malaya. Formerly one of the Straits Settlements; joined the Federation of Malaya 1948.

Pune (Poona) India. City in Maharashtra in the Western Ghats at a height of 560 m (1837 ft) 126 km (78 miles) SE of Bombay. Pop. (1991) 1,566,700.

Military station. Commercial centre. Trade in grain, cotton. Manufactures cotton goods, paper, chemicals, commercial vehicles and components, electronic goods, steel castings, cables and forgings.

Has a pleasant, healthy situation and during British rule in India was made the hot-weather cap. of the Bombay Presidency. Seat of the Mahratta rulers in the 18th cent.

Punjab India. In Sanskrit, 'Five Waters'. 1. Former province of NW India divided in 1947 between India and Pakistan, the E part to the former and the W part to the latter. The Sanskrit name refers to the five tributaries of the Indus R. – Jhelum, Chenab, Ravi, Beas and Sutlej – which flow through it. On the irrigated lands (*doabs*) between the rivers, wheat is the outstanding crop, and cotton, maize, rice and sugar-cane are also grown. About two-thirds of the people are dependent on agriculture. After the break-up of the Mogul Empire the Sikhs became the dominant power in the Punjab, but after the death of Ranjit Singh (1839) the Sikh Wars (1845–9) led to the annexation of the region to British India and the Punjab became a province. In 1901 the NW Frontier Province and in 1912 Delhi were detached from it. Constituted an autonomous province 1937.
2. Constituent state of the Indian Union bounded on the W by Pakistan. Area 50,362 sq km (19,673 sq. miles). Pop. (1991) 20,190,795. Cap. Chandigarh. Principal towns Chandigarh, Amritsar, Ludhiana, Jalandhar and Patiala. Amritsar has the golden temple, a holy place for the Sikh community. With the creation of the new state of Haryana and the reorganization of Punjab as a Punjabi-speaking state (1966), Punjab lost about 46,620 sq km (18,000 sq. miles) of territory and 8,500,000 people, mainly to Haryana.

Important industries are the manufacture of machine-tools, textiles, sewing-machines, hand tools, leather and hosiery goods, sports equipment, automotive parts, electronic items, railway coaches, fertilizers, chemicals, pharmaceuticals, woollen textiles and sugar.

Punjab Pakistan. Province of Pakistan, before 1947 part of the province of NW India, bounded NE by Kashmir and E by Punjab, India. Area 205,344 sq km (54,407 sq. miles). Pop. (1985) 53,840,000. Cap. Lahore. Other cities Rawalpindi and Islamabad.

The main products, from irrigated lands, are wheat, cotton, maize, rice and sugar-cane.

Puno Peru. Town situated ENE of

Arequipa on the NW shore of L. Titicaca. Department cap., communication and commercial centre for SE Peru. Pop. (1993) 89,745.

Lake port, railway terminus and customs point. Trade in wool and fur.

Punta Arenas Chile. Cap. of Magallanes province and seaport on Magellan Strait. Pop. (1992) 113,661.

Port of call for ships passing between the Atlantic and the Pacific. Centre of a sheep-farming area. Exports wool and meat. Coal mined nearby. Known as the most southerly city in the world.

Puntarenas Costa Rica. Cap. of the Puntarenas province on the Pacific coast 80 km (50 miles) W of San José. Pop. (1984) 37,390.

The country's chief Pacific seaport. Exports coffee and bananas. Tuna fishing and processing. Manufactures soap.

Puracé, Mount ➤POPAYÁN.

Purbeck, Isle of England. Peninsula in S Dorset 19 km (12 miles) long and 11 km (7 miles) wide, S of Poole Harbour. St Alban's Head is at the S end. Purbeck marble (limestone) is quarried. Principal towns Swanage and Corfe Castle.

Purfleet ➤THURROCK.

Puri (Jagannath) India. Commercial town and seaside resort in E Orissa 72 km (45 miles) S of Cuttack. Pop. (1991) 125,199.

Handicraft industries.

Sometimes known as Jagannath (Juggernaut); famous chiefly for its temple of Jagannath (meaning 'lord of the world'), built in the 12th cent. During an annual Hindu festival the image of the god is dragged through the town on a large cart by pilgrims.

Purmerend Netherlands. Town in Nord-Holland situated N of Amsterdam on the S edge of Beemster Polder. Pop. (1992) 62,504.

Market for a farming and agricultural area. Industries inc. the manufacture of refrigerators, wood products, food products and tiles.

Purús River Brazil/Peru. River 3200 km (2000 miles) long, rising in the Peruvian Andes, flowing NE through the tropical rainforest of NW Brazil and joining the Amazon R. 177 km (110 miles) WSW of Manáus.

Pusan South Korea. Country's chief seaport and second largest city on the SE coast. Pop. (1990) 3,798,113.

Exports rice, fish and soya beans. Also a railway and industrial centre. Railway engineering, shipbuilding, rice-milling and salt-refining. Manufactures textiles.

A centre of Japanese influence from the end of the 16th cent. During the Korean War (1950–2) it was the chief supply base for the UN troops.

Puteaux France. Industrial suburb in W Paris on the left bank of the Seine R. in the Hauts-de-Seine department. Pop (1982) 36,000.

Industries inc. engineering and printing. Manufactures perfumes.

Putney England. Residential district in the London borough of Wandsworth in SW London on the S bank of the R. Thames. Putney Bridge across the Thames is the starting point of the Oxford and Cambridge annual boat race. Putney Heath, once a haunt of highwaymen, adjoins Wimbledon Common. Birthplace of Thomas Cromwell, English statesman (1485–1540) and Edward Gibbon, English historian (1737–94).

Putumayo River. River 1577 km (980 miles) long, rising in the Colombian Andes and flowing generally ESE, forming most of the Colombia–Peru boundary. It then enters Brazil (where it is called the Içá R.) and joins the Amazon R. Its basin consists of dense, sparsely populated tropical rainforest.

Puy, Le (Le Puy en Velay) France. Prefecture of the Haute-Loire department near the Loire R. 58 km (36 miles) SW of St Étienne. Pop. (1968) 29,549.

Famous for its lace; also produces liqueurs.

Has a 12th-cent. Romanesque cathedral and, on the summit of a tall slender rock, the Church of St Michel d'Aiguilhe.

Puy-de-Dôme France. Department in central France, mainly in Auvergne and partly in Bourbonnais, in the N part of the Massif Central. Area 7970 sq km (3077 sq. miles). Pop. (1992) 597,700. Prefecture Clermont-Ferrand. In the W are the Auvergne Mountains, with the volcanic Puy de Sancy (1866 m; 6186 ft) and Puy de Dôme (1463 m; 4799 ft), on the summit of which are the meteorological observatory and the ruins of a Roman temple. In the E are the Forez Mountains rising to 1641 m (5382 ft). Between these highlands is the fertile plain of the Limagne, watered by the Allier and Dore rivers, where vines, fruits and cereals are cultivated, and cattle and sheep are raised. There are spas with mineral springs in the Auvergne Mountains. Coal mined. Industries are concentrated mainly in Clermont-Ferrand and Thiers.

Puy de Sancy ►PUY-DE-DÔME.

Pwllheli Wales. Town in Gwynedd on Cardigan Bay 31 km (19 miles) SSW of Caernarvon. Pop. (1971) 3832. Port and seaside resort.

Pyatigorsk Russia. In Russian, 'Five Mountains'. Town in the Stavropol Territory in the N Caucasus 145 km (90 miles) SE of Stavropol. Pop. (1992) 132,000. There are five peaks around it (hence its name). Spa, with sanatoria and sulphur springs.
. Metalworking. Manufactures furniture and clothing.
The poet, Mikhail Lermontov (1814–41) was killed here in a duel.

Pylos Greece. Ancient town in the SW Peloponnese at the N entrance to Pylos Bay, where the Athenians defeated the Spartans in 425 BC. In the Middle Ages it was renamed Old Navarino. A new town, now known as Pilos, grew up on the S shore of the bay. At the Battle of Navarino (1827) in Pylos Bay, a British, French and Russian fleet defeated a Turkish and Egyptian fleet.

Pyongyang North Korea. Cap. of North Korea on the Taedong R. 200 km (125 miles) NW of Seoul in South Pyongan province. Pop. (1987) 2,355,000.
Industrial centre in an anthracite-mining area. Sugar-refining. Manufactures textiles, chemicals, paper and matches. Hydroelectric power is derived from plants on the Yalu R.
Reputedly founded in the 12th cent BC; has remains of the ancient walls. Suffered severely during the Japanese invasion (1592), the Sino–Japanese War (1894), the Russo–Japanese War (1904) and again in the Korean War (1950–2).

Pyrenees (Fr. **Pyrénées**, Sp. **Pirineos**) France/Spain. Mountain range in SW Europe extending about 440 km (275 miles) W–E from the Bay of Biscay to the Mediterranean Sea, separating the Iberian peninsula from France. The central Pyrenees, in the E of which is the small state of Andorra, form the widest and highest part of the range, with such peaks as the Pico de Aneto (3404 m, 11,165 ft) and Monte Perdido (3355 m; 11,004 ft). The W Pyrenees are much lower, in general 900–1350 m (2952–4428 ft), descending gradually W, while the E Pyrenees fall abruptly from 2700 m (8856 ft) to the Mediterranean coast. Outstanding features of the Pyrenees are the mountain torrents (*gaves*) on the French side, where most of the resorts and spas are situated; the natural amphitheatres (*cirques*), caused by glacial action, at the upper ends of many valleys; and the small number of passes, among them Perthus (279 m; 915 ft), the lowest, Roncesvalles (1058 m; 3470 ft) and Somport (1633 m; 5356 ft). There has been considerable development of hydroelectric power on both sides of the range.

Pyrénées-Atlantiques France. Department in the SW, formed from Béarn and part of Gascony, bordering on Spain, and bounded by the Bay of Biscay (W) and the crest of the Pyrenees (S). Area 7645 sq km (2952 sq. miles). Pop. (1992) 585,000 (largely Basque). Prefecture Pau. Drained by the Adour R. and tributaries.
Hydroelectric power developed from the mountain streams. Maize, wheat, fruits and wine produced in the lowlands. Many

Pyrénées-Orientales

popular spas and resorts: Biarritz, St-Jean-de-Luz, Hendaye on the coast; Pau and several smaller towns such as Salies and Cambo inland. Chief towns Pau and Bayonne.

Pyrénées-Orientales France. Department in the S, bordered by the Gulf of Lions (E) and Spain (S), formed in 1790 mainly from Roussillon. Area 4116 sq km (1589 sq. miles). Pop. (1992) 371,400. Prefecture Perpignan. The W part is occupied by the E Pyrenees, with Pic Carlitte rising to 2923 m (9587 ft), the E part by a coastal plain crossed by the

Agly, Têt and Tech rivers. Vineyards, orchards, olive groves and market gardens abound in the valleys and lowlands; wine is a particularly important product. Several spas.

Pyrgos Greece. Town in Elia situated SSW of Patras near the mouth of the Alpheus R. Pop. (1981) 21,958.

Commercial centre. Industries inc. the manufacture of beverages, and tobacco products. Exports fruit and wine through the port of Katokolon.

Q

Qatar. Independent emirate which inc. the whole of the Qatar peninsula, extends on the landward side from Khor al Odeid to the boundaries of the Saudi Arabian province of Hasa. It also inc. a number of small islands in the coastal waters. Area 11,427 sq km (4412 sq. miles). Pop. (1995) 579,100 (90 per cent urban). Life expectancy, 71 years male, 76 female. Cap. Doha. Other towns Dukham, the centre of oil production; Umm Said, the oil terminal. Currency: Riyal = 100 dirhams. An arid country consisting largely of stony desert. The climate is hot and humid but mild in winter. Land use: meadows and pastures 5 per cent, agricultural and under permanent cultivation 0.5 per cent, desert and built-up 94 per cent. The pop. is almost entirely Muslim, mostly Sunni. Only about 20 per cent of the pop. is Qatari. The official lang. is Arabic.

The oil industry dominates the economy but there is heavy industry, inc. cement, steel, fertilizers and petrochemicals. Many of the Arab tribesmen are camel breeders and the fishing industry is important. Dates are exported.

Qatar became part of the Ottoman Empire in 1872 but was evacuated by Turkey in 1914. By a treaty of 1916 Qatar became a British protectorate ruled by Shaikh Abdullah-Al-Thani, with internal self-government. A further treaty was signed in 1934. Having failed to form a federation of states, Britain withdrew its forces from Qatar in 1971 and later that year the State of Qatar declared itself independent from Britain, the ruler taking the title of emir. A treaty of friendship was also signed between the two countries. The emir rules as an absolute monarch with neither a legislative body nor political parties. There is a Council of Ministers assisted by a 30-member nominated Advisory Council.

Qattara Depression Egypt. Arid depression in the Libyan Desert 48 km (30 miles) S of El Alamein, about 290 km (180 miles) long (NE–SW) and 120 km (75 miles) wide, 133 m (436 ft) below sea level at the lowest point. Contains an extensive area of salt marsh. During World War II it was the S flank of the Allied defence line at El Alamein, the soft sand making it an impassable obstacle to military vehicles. ➤➤WESTERN DESERT.

Qazvin ➤KAZVIN.

Qena Egypt. Cap. of Qena governorate on the E bank of the Nile on the railway 193 km (120 miles) SE of Asyut. Pop. (1986) 119,794.

Market town. Trade in cereals and dates. Famous for porous pottery, made into water jars and bottles. Terminal of the road from Port Safaga on the Red Sea.

Qeshm (Qishm) Iran. Island in the Strait of Hormuz in the Gulf 105 km (65 miles) long and up to 32 km (20 miles) wide. Pop. (1985) 15,500. Chief Town Qishm. The largest island in the Gulf.

Industries inc. fishing and salt-mining. Cereals and dates are cultivated.

Qingdao China. Seaport and industrial town in Shandong province on the peninsula on the Yellow Sea (Huang Hai) 440 km (225 miles) SE of Beijing. Pop. (1992) 2,060,000.

Has a deep-water harbour and an oil jetty for Shengli oilfield. Exports soya beans, groundnuts. Manufactures textiles, machinery, cement and soap. Railway engineering and flour-milling.

Passed to Germany (1898) as part of the Kiaochow lease and was quickly developed. Returned to China in 1922.

Qinghai (Tsinghai/Chinghai) China.

Province on the NE border of Xizang (Tibet), inc. much of the former NE Xizang. Area 721,000 sq km (278,400 sq. miles). Pop. (1990) 4,456,946. Cap. Xining. Consists largely of a lofty, barren plateau crossed by the Nan Shan, which rises to over 6000 m (19,680 ft) and the Bayan Khara Shan. In the N is the Tsaidam, a desolate swampy depression and in the NE another basin occupied by the lake Koko Nor or Qinghai, after which the province is named. Main occupation nomadic livestock-farming, mainly sheep.

Qiqihar (Tsitsihar) China. Formerly (1913–47) Lungkiang. Town in Heiliongjiang province on the Nun-kiang 282 km (175 miles) NW of Harbin. Pop. (1992) 1,380,000.

Industries inc. flour-milling and soya-bean processing. It manufactures chemicals and matches, and trades in grain.

Cap. of Lungkiang province in Manchukuo 1934–46.

Qishn ➤SOCOTRA.

Quantock Hills England. Range in Somerset 14 km (9 miles) long, extending SE from near Watchet, rising to 385 m (1263 ft) in Will's Neck.

Quebec Canada. Largest province in the E, bounded on the S by the US states of Maine, New Hampshire, Vermont and New York. Area 1,540,687 sq km (594,860 sq. miles). Pop. (1991) 6,895,963. Cap. Quebec. Inc. Anticosti and the Magdalen Is. in the Gulf of St Lawrence and several islands in the St Lawrence R. The greater part lies within the Canadian Shield. S of the St Lawrence R. are the Notre Dame Mountains (an extension of the Appalachian system) continued into the Gaspé Peninsula, which has the highest point in the province, Mt Jacques Cartier (1310 m, 4297 ft). Innumerable lakes, inc. L. Mistassini (2176 sq km; 840 sq. miles) and L. Minto (1256 sq km; 485 sq. miles). Climate very varied, but generally continental. Annual rainfall 100 cm (40 ins.) in the S, 35–40 cm (14–16 ins.) in the N (inc. abundant snowfalls). Immense areas of forest, the basis of the leading industry, the manufacture of wood-pulp and paper. Agriculture (cereals and hay) and stock-rearing are important in the S. Mineral resources inc. the vast iron-ore deposits of Ungava (NE), gold, copper and asbestos. Hydroelectric power is extensively developed. A large proportion of the industrial capacity is located in Montreal; other chief centres Quebec, Sherbrooke, Trois Rivières. Most of the pop. are of French descent and French-speaking. Known under French rule as New France (or Canada). Passed to Britain 1763. Became a province of the Dominion of Canada 1867.

Quebec City Canada. Cap. and Canada's oldest city, of Quebec province, on the St Lawrence R. at the confluence with the St Charles 225 km (140 miles) NE of Montreal. Pop. (1991) 167,517.

Important port, but closed by ice Dec.–April. Exports timber, grain. Industrial centre. Manufactures wood-pulp and paper, newsprint and paper products, clothing and food products.

Built around Cape Diamond, a cliff rising 100 m (328 ft) above the St Lawrence R., on the summit of which is the Citadel (built 1823–32). Now divided into the upper town and the lower town. Below the Citadel are the Château Frontenac (a hotel) and the Dufferin Terrace (a well-known promenade). Many of the notable buildings date from the 17th cent., among them the Hôtel-Dieu hospital (1639) and the Chapel of Notre Dame des Victoires (1688). Like Montreal, a leading French Canadian cultural centre; seat of the Laval University (Roman Catholic, 1852). More than 80 per cent of the pop. are French-speaking.

Jacques Cartier visited the site (1535) but the real founder was Samuel Champlain, who in 1608 built a fort where the lower town now stands. The British under General Wolfe defeated the French under Montcalm on the nearby Plains of Abraham (1759). Quebec (cap. of New France since 1663) became cap. of the new British colony of Quebec in 1763 and of Lower Canada in 1791. On the founding here of the Confederation of

Canada (1867) it was made cap. of the newly constituted province of Quebec.

Quedlinburg Germany. Town in Saxony-Anhalt on the Bode R. 72 km (45 miles) NW of Halle near the Harz Mountains. Pop. (1990) 30,000.

A market town. Horticulture. Minor industries.

Fortified in 922 by Henry I, whose tomb is in the 11th/12th-cent. Church of St Servatius.

Queenborough in Sheppey England. Queenborough is a small port on the W coast of the Isle of Sheppey. Founded by Edward III; named after Queen Philippa.

Queen Charlotte Islands Canada. Archipelago of about 150 islands off the coast of British Columbia, separated from the mainland by Hecate Strait. Area 9790 sq km (3780 sq. miles). Pop. (1985) 3000. Chief islands Graham, Moresby. Haida Indians are the main inhabitants. Main occupations fishing and lumbering.

Queen Charlotte Sound Canada. Stretch of water in the Pacific between the Queen Charlotte Is. (NW) and Vancouver Island (SE) in British Columbia; leads SE into Queen Charlotte Strait, which separates Vancouver Island from the mainland.

Queen Elizabeth Islands Canada. Northernmost islands of the Canadian Arctic archipelago, lying N of 74°N lat. A separate group since 1953, part of the Franklin District of the Northwest Territories; 19 main islands. The largest are Ellesmere, Devon, Melville and Axel Heiberg.

Queen Maud Land Norwegian Antarctica. Area of the Antarctic continent between 20° W and 45° E, forming a dependency of Norway, acquired in 1939, hitherto it had been ownerless.

Queens USA. Borough of New York City forming E district. Pop. (1990) 1,951,598.

Queensferry (South Queensferry) Scotland. Town within the City of Edinburgh on the Firth of Forth 13 km (8 miles) WNW of Edinburgh. Pop. (1991) 8887. Here are the Forth railway bridge and the Forth road bridge. On the opposite side is N Queensferry.

Queensland. Second largest state of Australia bounded by the Torres Strait to the N, the Pacific Ocean to the E, New South Wales to the S and the Northern Territory to the W; situated off the Pacific coast is the Great Barrier Reef. Area 1,728,000 sq km (667,000 sq. miles). Pop. (1993) 3,155,400. Aboriginals and the islanders of the Torres Strait make up 2 per cent of the pop. Cap. Brisbane, which has 43 per cent of the State's pop.

The Great Dividing Range runs N to S separating the coastal strip from the dry plains to the W. Drained E by tributaries of the Burdekin and Fitzroy rivers, N to the Gulf of Carpentaria by the Mitchell, Flinders and others, and SW to the L. Eyre basin or the Darling R. by rivers of intermittent flow. Two important plateau areas are the fertile, basalt-capped Darling Downs in the S and the higher Atherton Plateau in the N. The western plains have been tapped for artesian wells. There are great varieties of climate ranging from tropical to subtropical and the rainy season is from December to March. Queensland is mainly a primary producer and only a small proportion of the state is cultivated because of arid conditions. Eucalyptus forests cover the coastal hills but rainforests cover the wetter slopes and deltas in the N. In the E sugar-cane is a major export crop and bananas, pineapples and pawpaws flourish. In the drier valleys cotton is grown, while groundnuts and tobacco are widely cultivated. Dairying is important on the southern lowlands and on the cooler, moist Atherton Plateau, dairying and wheat growing on the Darling Downs. Inland, on grasslands with scattered eucalyptus trees, artesian water helps to maintain cattle in the N and sheep and cattle farther S. There are considerable reserves of timber and mineral centres are Mount Isa-Cloncurry, with copper, lead, nickel, zinc and silver; Mount Morgan, near Rockhampton, with copper and gold; tin is found in the N parts of the

Great Divide and bauxite at Weipa. The Ipswich–Toowoomba area, with its coal, is an expanding industrial zone; the first commercial oilfield in Australia was discovered at Moonie in 1961. Food-processing is the main industry and the ports of Rockhampton and Brisbane have large meat-processing plants. Leading exports are sugar, meat, dairy produce, wool and minerals.

Capt. Cook sailed along the E coast in 1770 but little was known of Queensland until Flinders visited Moreton Bay in 1802 and Oxley ascended the Brisbane R. in 1823. A penal settlement was established at Moreton Bay in 1826 and from 1842 free settlers were granted permission to live in Queensland. It was part of the New South Wales colony from 1788 until it became a separate colony in 1859. It became a state of the Commonwealth of Australia in 1901. There is a unicameral parliament consisting of one house, the 89-member Legislative Assembly; the Legislative Council was abolished in 1922.

Queenstown Ireland ►CÓBH.

Queenstown New Zealand ►WAKATIPU, LAKE.

Queenstown South Africa. Town in the Eastern Cape Province 160 km (100 miles) NW of East London at a height of 1080 m (3542 ft). Pop. (1980) 49,000

Centre of a wheat-growing, cattle-rearing and wool-producing region. Founded 1853.

Que Que ►KWEKWE.

Quercy France. Region in the SW, now forming the Lot and part of the Tarn-et-Garonne departments, divided in the Middle Ages into Upper Quercy, with cap. Cahors, and Lower Quercy, with cap. Montauban; mainly in the Causses, crossed by the fertile Lot valley. Sheep are reared and it produces wine and fruits.

A Protestant stronghold in the 16th cent.

Querétaro Mexico. 1. State mainly on the central plateau, lying almost exactly in the centre of Mexico. Area 11,449 sq km (4420 sq. miles). Pop. (1990) 1,051,235. Climate generally dry and subtropical. Crops inc. maize, wheat, fruits. Opals, mercury are mined. Home of the Otomi Indians numbering about 300,000, who speak a lang. of their own.

2. Cap. of Querétaro state 193 km (120 miles) NW of Mexico City at a height of 1860 m (3562 ft). Pop. (1990) 456,458.

Manufactures cotton goods, pottery.

Founded by the Otomi Indians and incorporated in the Aztec empire in the mid-15th cent. Outstanding buildings are the 16th-cent. cathedral (much restored) and the federal palace. Receives water by an 18th-cent. aqueduct. Centre of the movement for independence: here Hidalgo y Costilla's rising against the Spaniards was plotted (1810). The Emperor Maximilian was shot here (1867).

Quetta Pakistan. Cap. of Baluchistan 426 km (265 miles) W of Multan in a mountainous region at a height of 1650 m (5412 ft). Pop. (1991) 350,000.

Military station and commercial centre on the route through the Bolan Pass to Afghanistan. Trade in carpets and wool. There is engineering and flour-milling. Fruits are grown and coal mined in the neighbourhood.

It came under British administration in 1876. The Indian Army Staff College was established here in 1907. Almost destroyed in 1935 by an earthquake, but has since been rebuilt.

Quezaltenango Guatemala. Cap. of the Quezaltenango department, the second largest city, 113 km (70 miles) WNW of Guatemala City at a height of 2335 m (7659 ft). Pop. (1989) 246,000.

Industries inc. textiles, flour-milling and brewing.

Largely destroyed by an eruption of the nearby volcano Santa María in 1902.

Quezon City Philippines. Major suburb of the cap., Manila. Pop. (1990) 1,632,000. Chiefly residential. Named after Manuel Luis Quezon (1878–1944), first president of the Commonwealth of the Philippines. Seat of the University of the Philippines (1908).

Quibdó Colombia. Cap. of Choco department on the Atrato R. 320 km (200 miles) WNW of Bogotá. Pop. (1992) 119,027.

Centre of platinum and gold mining. In the tropical rainforest.

Quilon India. Seaport in Kerala on the Malabar coast 56 km (35 miles) NW of Trivandum. Pop. (1991) 139,717.

Exports copra and coir. Manufactures textiles, coir rope and mats.

Quimper France. Prefecture of the Finistère department on the Odet R. 51 km (32 miles) SSE of Brest. Pop. (1990) 62,541.

Industrial, commercial and tourist centre. Famous for its Breton pottery. Also manufactures hardware and cider.

Quincy (Illinois) USA. Town on the Mississippi R. 153 km (95 miles) W of Springfield. Pop. (1985) 50,000.

Manufactures agricultural machinery, footwear, clothing and chemicals. Once an important river port; declined with the passing of the steamboat.

Quincy (Massachusetts) USA. Industrial town on Massachusetts Bay 13 km (8 miles) SSE of Boston. Pop. (1990) 84,985.

Shipbuilding and granite-quarrying. Manufactures machinery, hardware and food products.

Birthplace of John Adams (1735–1826) and John Quincy Adams (1767–1848).

Quintana Roo Mexico. State in the SE in the E of the Yucatán peninsula. Area 50,212 sq km (19,387 sq. miles). Pop. (1990) 493,277.

Cap. Chetumal. Low-lying, largely tropical jungle and swamp. The resort of Cancún is to the N. Main products chicle, copra and henequen.

Quito Ecuador. Cap. of the republic and of Pichincha province at the foot of Pichincha volcano at a height of 2850 m (9438 ft). Pop. (1990) 1,100,847. In an Andean basin dominated by snow-capped peaks. Although only 24 km (15 miles) from the equator, because of its altitude it has a pleasant, temperate climate with warm days and cool nights and a mean annual temperature of 13°C (55°F). The country's chief textile centre. Other industries inc. brewing, flour-milling and tanning, and the manufacture of clothing, footwear, soap and pharmaceuticals. Many attractive parks and gardens and much old-world charm.

Outstanding buildings are the cathedral, the archbishop's palace, the Jesuit church (La Compañía), the great church and monastery of San Francisco and the Central University of Ecuador (founded 1787). The Pan-American Highway passes through it from Colombia to Peru. Once inhabited by Quitu Indians, after whom it is named; captured by the Incas and later by the Spaniards (1533) to become cap. of the presidency of Quito under the viceroyalty of Peru.

Qum (Qom) Iran. Holy city and route centre 120 km (75 miles) SSW of Tehrán. Pop. (1986) 543,139.

Manufactures footwear and pottery.

Sacred to Shia Muslims, it has the golden-domed shrine of Fatima, sister of the Imam Riza, and the tombs of many other saints.

R

Raasay Scotland. Island in the Inner Hebrides in Highland, separated from the E coast of Skye by the Sound of Raasay and from the mainland by the Inner Sound. Area 73 sq km (28 sq. miles). Pop. (1985) 170. Rises to 444 m (1456 ft) in the SE.

Rabat Morocco. Cap., chief residence of the King of Morocco, on the Atlantic at the mouth of the Bou Regreg R. on the main railway from Casablanca (through Oujda) to Algiers. Pop. (1993) 1,220,000.

Flour-milling. Manufactures textiles, bricks and hand-made Moroccan rugs. Overshadowed in trade and industry by Casablanca, but a city of considerable charm. The harbour is obstructed by a bar; a bridge (1957) now prevents seaborne trade.

The walled old town dominated by the 12th-cent. Hassan tower, a minaret 55 m (180 ft) high, near a ruined mosque. Became important with the establishment of the French protectorate (1912).

Rabaul Papua New Guinea. Seaport and tourist town in the NE of New Britain in the Bismarck Archipelago. Pop. (1994) 30,000.

Exports copra and cacao.

Set amid active volcanoes, it was severely damaged by eruptions in 1937 and again in 1994 when Vulcan and Tavurur volcanoes erupted. It also suffered from bombardments during World War II, when it was occupied by the Japanese (1942–5).

Racibórz (Ger. **Ratibor**) Poland. Town in the Opole voivodeship in the S on the Oder R. 68 km (42 miles) SSE of Opole. Pop. (1989) 62,733. River port. Railway junction.

Manufactures machinery, electrical equipment, soap and foodstuffs.

Cap. of an independent principality 1288–1532. Later in the Prussian province of Silesia.

Racine USA. Industrial town and port in Wisconsin on L. Michigan 37 km (23 miles) SSE of Milwaukee. Pop. (1990) 84,928.

Manufactures agricultural machinery, electrical equipment, hardware, paints and varnishes. Developed chiefly in the mid 19th cent. with the coming of the railway and improvement of the harbour.

Radcliffe England. Town in Greater Manchester 11 km (7 miles) NNW of the city. Pop. (1991) 32,587.

Manufactures textiles (cotton, rayon), chemicals and paper.

Radium Hill Australia. Small mining settlement in South Australia 96 km (60 miles) SW of Broken Hill. Mine worked in the 1920s for radium, abandoned 1930, reopened 1952 for uranium but closed in 1961.

Radnor Wales. Market town (New Radnor) and village (Old Radnor, 3 km (2 miles) ESE) in Powys 38 km (22 miles) NW of Hereford. Pop. (rural district, 1971) 1748.

Radom Poland. Industrial town and cap. of the Radom voivodeship 96 km (60 miles) S of Warsaw. Pop. (1992) 229,300.

Manufactures agricultural machinery, leather, glass, wire and nails.

One of the oldest towns in Poland. New Radom was founded (1340) by Casimir the Great, King of Poland. Held by Austria from 1795 and by Russia from 1815; returned to Poland 1918.

Ragged Islands Bahamas. Archipelago situated SE of Nassau and N of Cuba. A chain of cays extending c. 112 km (70 miles) N, main islands Great Ragged Island, Little Ragged Island. Area 13 sq km (5 sq. miles). Pop. (1990) 89.

Ragusa Italy. Cap. of Ragusa province in

Rajshahi

Sicily on the Irminio R. 55 km (34 miles) WSW of Syracuse. Pop. (1985) 65,000.

Important oil-producing and asphalt-mining centre. Oil-refining. Manufactures cement, textiles and chemicals.

In the lower town was the ancient Hybla Heraea, where Hippocrates of Gela fell (491 BC).

Ragusa (Croatia) ➤DUBROVNIK.

Rahway USA. Industrial and residential town in New Jersey 18 km (11 miles) SSW of Newark. Pop. (1985) 27,000.

Manufactures machinery, chemicals, rubber products and drugs.

Raichur India. Town in Karnataka 257 km (160 miles) ENE of Hubli. Pop. (1991) 157,551.

Commercial centre. Trade in cereals and cotton. Cotton-ginning.

Rainier, Mount USA. Highest mountain in the Cascade Range (4392 m; 14,410 ft) in Washington 64 km (40 miles) SE of Tacoma. Famous for 26 great glaciers and many permanent icefields. The Mt Rainier Naional Park (976 sq km; 377 sq. miles) was established in 1899.

Rainy Lake Canada/USA. Lake on the boundary between Ontario (Canada) and Minnesota (USA). Area 894 sq km (345 sq. miles). The Rainy R. 137 km (85 miles) long, flows from it, generally W, forming part of the Canada–USA frontier and enters the Lake of the Woods.

Raipur India. Commercial town and railway junction in E Madhya Pradesh 265 km (165 miles) E of Nagpur. Pop. (1991) 438,600.

Trade in rice and oilseeds. Engineering, rice and oilseed-milling. Manufactures iron and steel, cement, engineering goods and plastics. A pig-iron plant is under construction.

Has the ruins of a 15th-cent. fort and several ancient temples.

Rajahmundry India. Town in Andhra Pradesh at the head of the Godavari R. delta 346 km (215 miles) ESE of Hyderabad. Pop. (1991) 324,900.

Trade in rice and salt. Manufactures cotton goods, paper, tiles, fertilizers, machine-tools, boats, food products, alcoholic beverages, crude oil and natural gas.

Passed to the French in 1753 and the British in 1758.

Rajasthan India. Constituent state in the Indian Union in the NW bordering W on Pakistan. Area 342,239 sq km (133,687 sq. miles). Pop. (1991) 43,880,640. Cap. Jaipur. Other important towns Ajmer, Jodhpur, Bikaner, Kotah and Udaipur. Its W part occupies much of the Thar Desert and is separated from the more fertile E by the Aravalli Range, which rises to 1723 m (5651 ft) in the extreme S. Rainfall varies from 12.5–25 cm (5–10 ins.) (W) to 125 cm (50 ins.) or more (S). Most of the pop. are engaged in agriculture.

Wheat, maize, pulses, tobacco, mustard, red chillies, millets and cotton are cultivated. Major industries inc. textiles, sugar, cement, zinc, fertilizers, railway wagons, synthetic yarn, tyres, electronic equipment, nylon and tyre cords. Minerals inc. zinc ore, gypsum, silver ore, asbestos, felspar, marble and red stone.

Formed in 1948 and 1949 from a number of former princely states of Rajputana. The Rajputs, although a minority, are the dominant race.

Rajkot India. Commercial town and railway junction in Gujarat in the Kathiawar peninsula 200 km (125 miles) WSW of Ahmadabad. Pop. (1991) 612,500.

Trade in cotton and grain. Industries inc. oilseed and flour milling, and tanning. Manufactures chemicals, diesel-gas engines, compressors, oil engines, metals, food products and textiles.

Was cap. of the former princely state of Rajkot (730 sq km; 282 sq. miles).

Rajputana ➤RAJASTHAN.

Rajshahi Bangladesh. Town on the Ganges R. 200 km (125 miles) WNW of Dacca. Pop. (1991) 299,671. Commercial centre. Trade in rice.

Raleigh USA. State cap. of North Carolina 290 km (180 miles) ENE of Charlotte. Pop. (1990) 207,951.

Printing and publishing. Manufactures textiles, cottonseed oil. Important trade in tobacco.

Rama's Bridge ➤ADAM'S BRIDGE.

Ramat Gan Israel. Industrial town on the Plain of Sharon just E of Tel Aviv. Pop. (1991) 121,300.

Manufactures textiles, food products and furniture.

Seat of the religious Bar-Ilan University (1955). Founded 1921.

Rameswaram India. Island in Palk Straits at the extreme SE limit of the Indian peninsula, Tamil Nadu. Pop. (1981) 27,938. An important centre of pilgrimage for the Hindus, associated with Lord Rama.

Rampur India. Commercial town in Uttar Pradesh 177 km (110 miles) E of Delhi. Pop. (1991) 243,700.

Trade in grain, cotton and sugar-cane. Industries inc. sugar-refining and metal-working, and it manufactures chemicals, pottery, paper, fertilizers, metal knives, alcoholic beverages, electronic items, computers and photocopying machinery.

Was cap. of the former princely state of Rampur.

Ramsbottom England. Town in Greater Manchester on the R. Irwell 11 km (7 miles) NE of Bolton. Pop. (1991) 17,318. Industries inc. engineering and the manufacture of textiles, paper and soap.

Ramsey England. Market town in Cambridgeshire 14 km (9 miles) NNE of Huntingdon. Pop. (1991) 7577. Has the remains of the 10th-cent. Benedictine abbey and the partly Norman Church of St Thomas à Becket.

Ramsey Isle of Man. Port and seaside resort on the NE coast 19 km (12 miles) NNE of Douglas. Pop. (1991) 6491. Mooragh Park has a marine lake and other attractions.

Ramsgate England. Town in E Kent in the Isle of Thanet. Pop. (1991) 37,895. Fishing and yachting port and popular seaside resort, its harbour protected by stone piers. There is a ferry service to Ostend and Dunkirk. Its development as a resort dates from the late 18th cent. Nearby at Ebbsfleet, on Pegwell Bay, the Saxons under Hengist and Horsa are supposed to have landed in 449 and St Augustine in 597.

Rancagua Chile. Cap. of O'Higgins province in the central valley 80 km (50 miles) S of Santiago. Pop. (1991) 200,361.

Commercial and industrial centre in an agricultural region. Manufactures tractors. Flour-milling, fruit and vegetable canning. Also a railway junction, linked with the large El Teniente copper mine.

Rance River France. River 100 km (62 miles) long in the Côtes-du-Nord department, flowing E and N and entering the Gulf of St Malo by an estuary 19 km (12 miles) long. The world's first marine power station using the energy of the tides was opened on the estuary just above St Malo in 1966.

Ranchi India. Commercial town in Bihar on the Chota Nagpur plateau at a height of 600 m (1968 ft) 113 km (70 miles) NW of Jamshedpur. Pop. (1991) 598,498.

Trade in rice, maize, oilseeds and cotton. Manufactures heavy engineering equipment, wire ropes, mining machinery and insulators.

University. Hot-weather seat of the State government.

Rand ➤WITWATERSRAND.

Randers Denmark. Cap. of Randers county in E Jutland at the mouth of the Gudenaa R. and at the head of Randers Fiord. Pop. (1992) 61,440.

Port and industrial town. Manufactures gloves, railway rolling-stock. Brewing and distilling.

Although dating from the 11th cent., it has a modern appearance. Has a 15th-cent. church.

Randfontein South Africa. Goldmining town in Gauteng on the Witwatersrand 32 km (20 miles) W of Johannesburg at a height of 1700 m (5576 ft). Pop. (1985) 28,000.

Rangoon ►YANGÔN.

Rannoch, Loch Scotland. Lake in Perth and Kinross extending W from Kinloch Rannoch about 14 km (9 miles) long and 1.6 km (1 mile) wide, fed by the R. Ericht and other streams and drained by the R. Tummel. The surrounding district is known as Rannoch. S and W is the wild, bleak Rannoch Moor.

Rapallo Italy. Port and resort in Genova province, Liguria on the Gulf of Rapallo 27 km (17 miles) ESE of Genoa. Pop. (1990) 30,000. Beautifully situated on the Riviera di Levante, in a region producing vines, olives, flowers.

Manufactures olive oil, wine and cement.

Two treaties were signed here: between Italy and Yugoslavia (1920) and between Russia and Germany (1922). Nearby is the small and now fashionable resort of Portofino.

Rapid City USA. Town in South Dakota in the Black Hills 233 km (145 miles) WSW of Pierre. Pop. (1990) 54,523.

Commercial centre in an agricultural and mining region. Manufactures cement, bricks and tiles; other industries inc. flour-milling and sawmilling.

Rappahannock River USA. River 338 km (210 miles) long in Virginia, rising in the Blue Ridge and flowing generally SE to Chesapeake Bay. Chief tributary the Rapidan R. Scene of severe fighting during the American Civil War.

Rarotonga ►COOK ISLANDS.

Ras al Khaimah United Arab Emirates. Former Trucial State joining the UAE in 1971. It produces much of the fresh food for the UAE. Area 1700 sq km (660 sq miles). Pop. (1985) 116,470. ►UNITED ARAB EMIRATES.

Ras Tanura Saudi Arabia. Oil port on the Gulf 40 km (25 miles) N of Dhahran. Oil brought by pipelines from the Dhahran, Abqaiq and Qatif oilfields is refined here and also shipped from the marine terminal.

Rathenow Germany. Town in Brandenburg on the Havel R. 72 km (45 miles) WNW of Berlin. Pop. (1989) 30,935.

Important centre for optical and precision instruments. Also manufactures agricultural machinery and chemicals.

Rathlin Island Northern Ireland. Island off the N coast of Co. Antrim 10 km (6 miles) long and L-shaped. St Columba founded a church here in the 6th cent. Refuge of Robert Bruce (1274–1329) King of Scotland in 1306: traditionally the scene of his encounter with the persevering spider.

Ratlam India. Town in Madhya Pradesh 113 km (70 miles) NW of Indore. Pop. (1991) 183,370.

Railway junction. Commercial centre. Trade in cotton, grain and manufactures textiles.

Was the cap. of the former princely state of Ratlam.

Ravenna Italy. Cap. of Ravenna province in Emilia-Romagna 68 km (42 miles) ESE of Bologna and 8 km (5 miles) from the Adriatic Sea, with which it is connected by canal. Pop. (1991) 132,724.

Varied industries; trade in agricultural produce.

Rich in Byzantine art, esp. famous for its mosaics. Among its outstanding buildings are the 5th-cent. mausoleum of Galla Placidia, the 5th/6th-cent. churches of S. Giovanni Evangelista, S. Apollinare Nuovo and S. Vitale - the last-named with fine mosaic - and the 18th-cent. cathedral. Here, too, is the tomb of Dante. Just outside the city is the mausoleum of Theodoric the Ostrogoth (454–526), with its massive dome cut from a single block of stone. In Roman times a seaport and naval base, it was made cap. by Honorius early in the 5th cent. Became the seat of the exarchs from Constantinople 553–752. Ceded to the Papal States 1509 and passed to Italy 1860.

Ravensburg Germany. Industrial town in Baden-Württemberg 76 km (47 miles) SSW of Ulm. Pop. (1986) 43,200.

Industries inc. engineering and the manufacture of textiles and pharmaceutical products.

Founded in the 11th cent.

Ravi River. River 720 km (450 miles) long in NW India and Pakistan; one of the 5 rivers of the Punjab, rising in the Pir Panjal Range of the Himalayas, flowing generally W and SW past Lahore and joining the Chenab R. Feeds the Upper Bari Doab irrigation canal. Navigable below Lahore.

Rawalpindi Pakistan. Formerly the provisional federal cap. 257 km (160 miles) NNW of Lahore. Pop. (1981) 794,843. A military station and commercial centre.

Trade in grain, wool and timber. Oil-refining, railway engineering. Manufactures chemicals, furniture.

Became temporary cap. (in place of Karachi) in 1959, pending the move to Islamabad nearby.

Rawson Argentina. Cap. of Chubut province (Patagonia), near the Atlantic coast 555 km (345 miles) SSW of Bahía Blanca. Pop. (1985) 13,000.

Market town. Trade in grain and sheep. Named after one of its Welsh founders (1865).

Rawtenstall England. Town in Lancashire on the R. Irwell 10 km (6 miles) SSW of Burnley. Pop. (1991) 21,933.

Manufactures cotton and woollen goods, carpets and footwear.

Rayleigh England. Town in Essex 10 km (6 miles) NW of Southend-on-Sea. Pop. (1991) 28,912. Dormitory town for London. Remains of a Norman castle.

Ré, Île de France. Island in the Charente-Maritime department in the Bay of Biscay W of La Rochelle, separated from the mainland by the Pertuis Breton. Area 78 sq km (30 sq. miles). Pop. (1985) 9700.

Fishing (particularly oysters) salt-panning. Vines and early vegetables cultivated.

Reading England. Town at the confluence of the R. Thames and the R. Kennet 61 km

(38 miles) W of London. Pop. (1991) 122,600.

Industries inc. engineering, electronics, brewing and computing.

Here the imprisoned playwright Oscar Wilde (1854–1900) wrote the *Ballad of Reading Gaol*. A 13th-cent. Reading monk is said to have composed *Sumer is icumen in* here. Occupied by Danes in the 9th cent., it was burned in 1006. From the 12th to the 16th cent. it was the scene of a protracted struggle between the abbey and the merchant guild. Birthplace of Archbishop Laud (1573–1645).

Reading became a unitary authority in 1998.

Reading USA. Town in Pennsylvania on the Schuylkill R. 74 km (46 miles) NW of Philadelphia. Pop. (1990) 78,380.

Railway engineering. Manufactures metal goods, machinery, optical goods and hosiery.

Recife (Pernambuco) Brazil. Cap. of Pernambuco state in the NE, of which it is the chief seaport, tourist resort and largest city. Pop. (1991) 1,290,149.

Exports sugar, grown on the neighbouring coastlands, rum and molasses, cotton, timber, fruit and coconuts. Industries inc. sugar-refining, cotton-milling and pineapple-canning. Manufactures textiles and cement.

Built in three parts, on the mainland, on a peninsula and on an island, with waterways bridged by modern roads running through the city; hence sometimes called the 'Venice of Brazil'. First settled (*c.* 1535) by the Portuguese.

Recklinghausen Germany. Industrial town in North Rhine-Westphalia in the Ruhr district 19 km (12 miles) NW of Dortmund. Pop. (1991) 125,060.

Coalmining, iron founding and brewing. Manufactures coal-tar products, mining machinery, soap and cement.

Redbridge England. London borough (1965) comprising the former municipal boroughs of Ilford and Wanstead and Woodford and parts of Chigwell (the Hainault Estate area) and Dagenham (the N part of Chadwell

Heath ward), all in Essex. Pop. (1991) 229,800.

Redcar England. Seaside resort in Redcar and Cleveland 11 km (7 miles) NE of Middlesbrough, of which it is a growing residential satellite. Pop. (1990) 40,000.

Manufactures steel, chemicals. Racecourse.

Redcar and Cleveland England. New administrative area created in 1996. Area 242 sq km (93 sq. miles). Pop. (1994) 144,000. Industry includes chemicals steel, ports and oil-servicing facilities.

Red Deer Canada. Market town in Alberta on the Red Deer R. 132 km (82 miles) N of Calgary. Pop. (1991) 58,134. Railway junction.

Redditch England. Town in Worcestershire 19 km (12 miles) S of Birmingham. Pop. (1991) 77,304.

Manufactures needles, springs, clips, washers, aircraft components and machine-tools.

Rede River England. River 34 km (21 miles) long in Northumberland rising on Carter Fell in the Cheviot Hills and flowing SE and S through the picturesque Redesdale, joining the R. Tyne at Redesmouth.

Redhill England. Residential town in Surrey forming the E part of Reigate. Developed after the construction of the London–Brighton railway.

Redlands USA. Town in California 96 km (60 miles) E of Los Angeles. Pop. (1990) 60,394. Largely residential.

Packing and trade centre for the citrus fruit (chiefly oranges) cultivated in the region.

Redondo Beach USA. Town in California 26 km (16 miles) SW of Los Angeles on the Pacific Ocean. Pop. (1990) 60,167. Originally developed as a commercial port in the late 19th cent. but now mainly a residential and tourist centre.

Red River USA. Tributary of the Mississippi R. 1600 km (1000 miles) long, rising on the Llano Estacado and flowing generally E across NW Texas, forming the Texas–Oklahoma boundary, then turning SE across SW Arkansas and Louisiana to join the Atchafalaya and the Mississippi rivers. On the Texas–Oklahoma border is Denison Dam (completed 1943) for flood control and hydroelectric power, which impounds L. Texoma (578 sq km; 223 sq. miles), one of the country's largest reservoirs. In its lower course the river is sluggish and meandering; silt and falling trees have always impeded navigation.

Red River USA/Canada. River 560 km (350 miles) long, formed by the union of the Otter Tail and the Bois de Sioux rivers (in North Dakota), flowing generally N, forming the border between North Dakota and Minnesota, entering Manitoba (Canada) and emptying into L. Winnipeg. The valley inc. some of the best farming land in North America; wheat is cultivated on a large scale.

Redruth England. Market town in Cornwall 24 km (15 miles) ENE of Penzance, now part of Camborne-Redruth. Pop. (1991) 35,915, including Camborne. Formerly a centre of Cornish tin-mining. Industries inc. brewing and tanning.

Here William Murdock first used coal gas for lighting purposes (1792).

Red Sea. Sea 2400 km (1500 miles) long and up to 340 km (210 miles) wide between NE Africa and SW Asia, extending SSE from Suez to the Strait of Bab el Mandeb. It covers 438,000 sq km (169,000 sq. miles). Divides in the N into the Gulf of Aqaba and the Gulf of Suez, which are separated by the Sinai peninsula. Linked by the Gulf of Suez via the Suez Canal with the Mediterranean Sea, and by the Strait of Bab el Mandeb with the Gulf of Aden and the Indian Ocean. Forms part of the Great Rift Valley. Both coasts fringed by coral reefs; few indentations. In the S are the Dahlak Archipelago and the Farasan Is. Receives few rivers, rainfall is scanty and evaporation considerable; the salinity is high. Chief ports Suez (Egypt), Port Sudan (Sudan), Mitsiwa (Ethiopia), Jidda

(Saudi Arabia). An important trade route from early times, it declined after the discovery of the route to India via the Cape of Good Hope (1497), but became one of the world's busiest shipping lanes after the opening of the Suez Canal (1869).

Redwood City USA. Port and residential and industrial town in California 39 km (24 miles) SSE of San Francisco. Pop. (1990) 66,072.

Exports oil and salt. Manufactures cement, leather, electronic equipment.

Named for its connection with the redwood timber trade.

Ree, Lough Ireland. Lake 27 km (17 miles) long and up to 11 km (7 miles) wide on the R. Shannon between Counties Roscommon, Longford and Westmeath. Many small islands, and noted for trout-fishing.

Regensburg (Ratisbon) Germany. Ancient Castra Regina. Town in Bavaria on the Danube R. at the confluence with the Regen R. 105 km (65 miles) NNE of Munich. Pop. (1991) 121,691.

River port. Railway junction. Manufactures machinery, pencils, soap, furniture. Brewing and sugar-refining.

Noteworthy buildings are the Gothic cathedral (founded 1275), the Romanesque churches of St James and St Emmeran, and the partly 14th-cent. town hall, where the Imperial Diet met 1663–1806; there are also Roman remains. An important stronghold of the Romans. Seat of the dukes of Bavaria in the Middle Ages and a free imperial city from 1245, but declined in commercial importance in the 15th cent. and suffered severely in the Thirty Years War.

Reggio di Calabria Italy. Ancient Rhegium. Seaport and tourist resort in Calabria region on the Strait of Messina. Pop. (1991) 178,496.

Exports citrus fruits, olive oil, wine and figs. Fruit-canning. Manufactures olive oil, pasta and furniture.

It suffered severely, with great loss of life, from the earthquakes of 1783 and 1908. Serious riots occurred 1970–1 over the proposal to make the smaller town of Catanzaro the cap. of Calabria; a compromise was reached – Catanzaro became the cap., Reggio the permanent seat of the regional assembly.

Reggio nell'Emilia Italy. Cap. of Reggio nell'Emilia province in Emilia-Romagna on the Aemilian Way 61 km (38 miles) WNW of Bologna. Pop. (1991) 131,880.

Manufactures locomotives, aircraft engines, agricultural machinery, cement and wine.

Cathedral (13th-cent., restored in the 15th and 16th cent.); Renaissance palaces. Birthplace of Lodovico Ariosto (1474–1533), the poet.

Regina Canada. Cap. of Saskatchewan province in the S. Pop. (1991) 179,178.

In the heart of a large wheat-growing area. The major commercial centre for Saskatchewan and one of the world's largest distribution centres for farm implements. Also distributes cars, hardware, chemicals. Oil-refining. Manufactures cement, paints and varnishes, furniture and footwear.

The W headquarters of the Royal Canadian Mounted Police.

Regnitz River Germany. River 64 km (40 miles) long in Bavaria formed by the union of the Pegnitz and Rednitz rivers at Fürth, flowing N to join the Main R. near Bamberg.

Rehoboth Gebiet Namibia. Area of central SW Africa immediately S of Windhoek district. Area c. 32,168 sq km (c. 12,420 sq. miles). Chief town Rehoboth. Occupied by the Basters, a race of mixed European–Nama descent.

Rehovoth Israel. Town situated SSE of Tel Aviv on the Judaean plain.

Centre of an area growing citrus fruit. Manufactures dairy products, metal products, glass, pharmaceutical goods and fruit juice. Weizmann Institute of Science.

Reichenbach Germany. Industrial town 18 km (11 miles) SW of Zwickau. Pop. (1989) 26,000.

Textile centre; manufactures cotton,

woollen, rayon goods, also machinery. Other industries inc. printing and dyeing.

Reigate England. Town in Surrey 32 km (20 miles) S of London at the foot of the North Downs, inc. the newer town of Redhill. Pop. (1991) 47,602. Mainly residential. The Priory is on the site of a 13th-cent. Augustinian foundation.

Reims (Rheims) France. Ancient Durocortorum. Town in the Marne department on the Vesle R. 132 km (82 miles) ENE of Paris. Pop. (1990) 185,164.

Leading centre of the country's champagne industry. Manufactures wine-growing equipment, wine bottles, woollen goods and biscuits. Flour-milling, sugar-refining, engineering. There are vineyards on the nearby hills; the wine is stored in great caves cut in the chalk.

The famous 13th/14th-cent. Gothic cathedral was seriously damaged in World War I but was completely restored by 1938. University (1547). Was cap. of the Remi, after whom it was named, before the Roman conquest. In 496 Clovis I was crowned king of the Franks in the earlier cathedral and the coronation of later French kings took place here. Birthplace of Jean Baptiste Colbert, French statesman (1619–83).

Reindeer Lake Canada. Lake in NE Saskatchewan and NW Manitoba 233 km (145 miles) long and up to 64 km (40 miles) wide, draining S to the Churchill R. by the Reindeer R. Many small islands.

Remscheid Germany. Industrial town in North Rhine-Westphalia on the Wupper R. 10 km (6 miles) S of Wuppertal. Pop. (1991) 123,155.

Important steel centre. Manufactures machine-tools, cutlery, tools, drills and agricultural implements.

Linked with Solingen by bridge across the Wupper R. The suburb of Lennep was the birthplace of the physicist, W. K. Röntgen (1845–1923).

Rendsburg Germany. Industrial town and railway junction in Schleswig-Holstein on the Kiel Canal 29 km (18 miles) W of Kiel. Pop. (1986) 30,600.

Iron-founding, shipbuilding. Manufactures machinery and fertilizers.

Founded in the 13th cent. Passed to Prussia 1866.

Renfrew Scotland. Town in Renfrewshire on the R. Clyde 8 km (5 miles) WNW of and virtually a suburb of Glasgow. Pop. (1991) 20,764.

Shipbuilding and engineering. Manufactures tyres.

Renfrewshire Scotland. County reinstated in 1996, having been part of Strathclyde Region 1975–96. Pop. (1993) 176,970.

Renkum Netherlands. Town in Gelderland province 11 km (7 miles) W of Arnhem. Pop. (1992) 33,039.

Manufactures rubber and paper products.

Has the memorial to the British airborne forces involved in the Battle of Arnhem in World War II.

Rennes France. Ancient Condate. Prefecture of the Ille-et-Vilaine department at the confluence of the Ille and the Vilaine rivers. Pop. (1990) 203,533.

Important route and commercial centre. Industries inc. printing, engineering and tanning. Manufactures electronics, footwear, hosiery and chemicals. Trade in agricultural produce.

Also the cultural centre of Brittany, with a university (1735). The outstanding building is the 17th-cent. parliament house, now the law courts, where the famous Dreyfus case was conducted; this is one of the few important buildings to survive the great 7-day fire of 1720. The cathedral was rebuilt 1787–1844.

Reno USA. Town and resort in W Nevada on the Truckee R. at a height of 1350 m (4428 ft). Pop. (1990) 133,850.

Meat-packing, flour-milling. Manufactures bricks and tiles, metal products.

Seat of the University of Nevada (1874). Perhaps best known as a centre for gambling, which is legalized and for divorce, which the state law makes easily obtainable.

Renton USA. City immediately SSE of Seattle on Cedar R., Washington. Pop. (1980) 30,612.

Industries inc. aircraft and heavy manufacture.

Repton England. Town in Derbyshire 6 km (4 miles) NE of Burton-upon-Trent. Pop. (1991) 2012.

Has a public school (founded 1557), which incorporates parts of a 12th-cent. Augustinian priory. Once the cap. of Mercia and seat of a bishop.

Republican River USA. River 724 km (450 miles) long, rising in NE Colorado, flowing generally ESE through Nebraska and Kansas, joining the Smoky Hill R. at Junction City and forming the Kansas R.

Resht (Rasht) Iran. Cap. of Gilán province 240 km (150 miles) NW of Tehrán near the Caspian Sea. Pop. (1986) 293,881.

Trade in agricultural produce, esp. rice, grown in the district. Manufactures textiles, hosiery and carpets.

Resistencia Argentina. Cap. of Chaco province 16 km (10 miles) W of Corrientes, served by the port of Barranqueras (on the Paraná R.). Pop. (1991) 218,438.

Trade in cotton, timber, livestock and hides. Industries inc. meat-packing and sawmilling.

Reşiţa Romania. Cap. of Caraş-Severin district 76 km (47 miles) SE of Timişoara. Pop. (1989) 110,519.

Important iron and steel industry. Also manufactures machinery and electrical equipment.

Restigouche River Canada. River 209 km (130 miles) long in N New Brunswick, flowing generally NE, forming part of the New Brunswick–Quebec border and emptying into Chaleur Bay. Salmon-fishing.

Retalhuleu Guatemala. Cap. of Retalhuleu department 129 km (80 miles) W of Guate-

mala City. Generally known as Reu. Pop. (1988) 42,000.

Commercial centre in a region producing coffee and sugar-cane.

Retford (East Retford) England. Market town in Nottinghamshire 13 km (8 miles) E of Worksop on the R. Idle. Pop. (1991) 20,697.

Engineering, and manufactures wire ropes and rubber. Has a grammar school founded in the 16th cent.

Rethimnon Greece. 1. *Nome* in W central Crete. Area 1496 sq km (570 sq. miles). Pop. (1991) 69,290. Cap. Rethimnon.

Mainly agricultural. Cereals, vines and olives cultivated. Sheep and goats reared.

2. Cap. and chief port of Rethimnon *nome*, Crete on the N coast 47 km (29 miles) ESE of Canea (Khanía). Pop. (1985) 18,000.

Trade in cereals, wine and olive oil.

Réunion. Formerly Bourbon. Island in the Indian Ocean 177 km (110 miles) SW of Mauritius, an overseas department of France. Area 2512 sq km (969 sq. miles). Pop. (1990) 596,693. Cap. St Denis. Of volcanic origin, rising to 3071 m (10,073 ft) in the Piton des Neiges, and Piton de la Fournaise (2692 m, 8830 ft) is a still active volcanco and an eruption in 1986 sent lava flowing into the ocean, creating extra land. Subject to the SE Trade Wind and at times to destructive cyclonic storms, it has a much heavier rainfall on the windward than on the leeward side. Sugarcane is by far the most important crop; chief exports sugar and rum. Chief towns St Denis (pop. 121,671), St Paul (72,000), St Pierre (50,000) and St Louis (35,000). Discovered by the Portuguese in the early 16th cent. Annexed by France 1643. Renamed 1848. It became an overseas department 1947 and in 1974 it also became an administrative region.

Reus Spain. Town in Tarragona province, Catalonia 92 km (57 miles) WSW of Barcelona. Pop. (1991) 86,864.

Manufactures textiles, agricultural machinery and leather goods. Trade in wine and fruit.

Its commercial prosperity dates from the

arrival of an English colony in the mid 18th cent.

Reuss Germany. Two former small principalities, Reuss-Greiz and Reuss-Schleiz-Gera, both incorporated in Thuringia in 1920. The house of Reuss dates from the 12th cent. By custom all the male members of the two branches of the family (which survived till the present cent.) were named Heinrich and were distinguished by numbers.

Reutlingen Germany. Industrial town in Baden-Württemberg 29 km (18 miles) S of Stuttgart on the N edge of the Swabian Jura. Pop. (1991) 103,687.
Manufactures textiles, textile machinery, leather and paper.

Revel ➤TALLINN.

Revelstoke Canada. Town in British Columbia on the Columbia R. and on the Trans-Canada Highway 153 km (95 miles) ENE of Kamloops. Pop. (1990) 8500.
A supply centre for a lumbering and mining region. Tourist centre for the Mt Revelstoke National Park.

Revere USA. Town in Massachusetts 8 km (5 miles) NE of Boston. Pop. (1970) 43,159. A coastal resort, sometimes termed 'the Coney Island of Boston', with the popular Revere Beach.
Manufactures electrical equipment and chemicals.

Rewa India. Town situated SSW of Allahabad in Madhya Pradesh. Pop. (1991) 128,981.
District cap. and trading centre for grain, timber and building stone.

Reykjavik Iceland. Cap. of the republic on a small peninsula on Faxa Fiord on the SW coast. Pop. (1991) 99,623.
Chief seaport; a commercial and fishing centre. Exports fish and fish products. Fish processing and canning, shipbuilding. Manufactures textiles and rope.
Reykjavik is mainly built of concrete to withstand earth tremors. There are extensive

areas of water, with modern highway bridges. Most of the public buildings date from after 1850. Said to have been founded by Norse seamen in 874, Reykjavik was a fishing village until it became the seat of a Danish administrator in 1786. With rising national feeling in the 19th cent. it grew in size and importance until it became the cap. of self-governing Iceland (1918) and of the fully independent republic (1944). The hot springs in the vicinity provide a natural hot-water supply for the city.

Reynosa Mexico. Town in Tamaulipas state on the Rio Grande (Río Bravo) 209 km (130 miles) ENE of Monterrey, opposite McAllen (Texas). Pop. (1990) 325,000. Market town on one of the main routes from the USA into NE Mexico.

Rezaiyeh ➤RIZAIYEH.

Rhadames ➤GHADAMES.

Rhayader Wales. Town in Powys on the R. Wye 42 km (26 miles) ESE of Aberystwyth. Pop. (1985) 1800. To the SW are the reservoirs of the Elan valley, which provide Birmingham with water.

Rheims ➤REIMS.

Rheingau Germany. District extending about 24 km (15 miles) along the right bank of the Rhine R. from Biebrich (near Wiesbaden) to Assmannshausen. Famous for its wines, inc. Johannisberger and Steinberger.

Rheinhausen Germany. Industrial town in North Rhine-Westphalia in the Ruhr on the Rhine R. opposite Duisburg. Pop. (1970) 71,700.
Coalmining. Manufactures iron and steel, briquettes, mining machinery, armatures, concrete products and barrels.

Rheinland-Pfalz
➤RHINELAND-PALATINATE.

Rhein River ➤RHINE RIVER.

Rheydt Germany. Industrial town in North Rhine-Westphalia 24 km (15 miles) WSW of Düsseldorf. Pop. (1974) 100,939.

Manufactures textiles, machinery, cables, chemicals and soap.

From 1929 to 1933 it was incorporated with München-Gladbach, just N, and known as Gladbach-Rheydt.

Rhine–Herne Canal Germany. Important Ruhr waterway 39 km (24 miles) long, from Duisburg to Herne, forming part of the Mittelland Canal. Completed 1914.

Rhineland Germany. The region on both banks of the Rhine R. in Germany, comprising parts of the *Länder* of North Rhine-Westphalia, Rhineland-Palatinate, Hessen and Baden-Württemberg. Sometimes the name refers only to the former Prussian Rhine Province.

Rhineland-Palatinate (Ger. **Rheinland-Pfalz**) Germany. *Land* formed in 1945 from Rhenish Palatinate and parts of Hessen and the former Prussian provinces of the Rhine and Hesse-Nassau. Area 19,849 sq km (7664 sq. miles). Pop. (1991) 3,763,500. Cap. Mainz.

Chief occupations farming and wine-making in the lower Moselle.

Rhine Province Germany. Formerly the most westerly province of Prussia, constituted in 1824 from a large number of independent principalities. Cap. Coblenz. It was divided into 5 administrative districts: Aachen, Düsseldorf, Cologne, Coblenz and Trier, the first three of which were incorporated into North Rhine-Westphalia in 1945, and the last two into Rhineland-Palatinate.

Rhine–Rhône Canal France/Germany. Waterway leading from the Rhine R. via the Ill R. to Strasbourg, thence by artificial channel parallel to the Ill via Mulhouse to the Doubs, Saône and Rhône. Constructed 1784–1833. Of limited use to modern canal transport.

Rhine (Ger. **Rhein**, Fr. **Rhin**, Dutch **Rijn**) **River**. River 1320 km (820 miles) long in central and W Europe, flowing from the Alps generally NNW to the North Sea, through one of the continent's most highly industrialized and densely populated regions; commercially Europe's most important waterway, with a drainage basin of 225,000 sq km (86,900 sq. miles). Formed from two principal headstreams: the Inter Rhein issues from glaciers of the Rheinwaldhorn at a height of 2217 m (7272 ft), the Vorder Rhein rises in L. Toma at a height of 2345 m (7692 ft). The two unite 10 km (6 miles) WSW of Chur and the Rhine proper then flows N between Switzerland (W) and Liechtenstein and Austria (E) into L. Constance; then it passes Schaffhausen, descends 21 m (69 ft) at the famous Rhine Falls and continues W along the Swiss–German border to Basle (head of navigation). It turns N through the rift valley and forms part of the Franco–German border (receiving the Ill, the Neckar and the Main), enters Germany, at Mainz turns W to Bingen. From here to Bonn it travels 129 km (80 miles) NW (receiving the Moselle at Coblenz) through the picturesque Rhine gorge, with such legendary landmarks as the Lorelei, its high banks in places covered with vineyards and crowned with ancient castles. Beyond Bonn it passes Cologne and Düsseldorf, receives the Ruhr at Duisburg and below Emmerich enters the Netherlands; it then turns W and crosses extraordinarily complex delta which it shares with the Meuse (Maas). From the Lower Rhine (the more northerly of its two principal arms) the Ijssel branches N to the Ijsselmeer; the Lower Rhine itself becomes the Lek, passes Rotterdam as the New Maas and enters the North Sea at Hook of Holland. The Waal (the southerly principal arm) takes about two-thirds of the water and with the Maas enters the North Sea by the Hollandsch Diep.

In Roman times the Rhine formed the E frontier of Gaul. For centuries it has had great strategic importance, esp. to France and Germany; to the Germans 'Father Rhine' is a national symbol. Declared free to international shipping 1868. Linked by canals with many other European rivers, it carries an immense volume of traffic, esp. between the Rhine–Ruhr industrial region and Rotterdam. Principal cargoes oil, motor vehicles, coal, iron ore, grain and stone.

Rhode Island USA. State in New England bordering S on the Atlantic Ocean. Area 3139 sq km (1212 sq. miles). Pop. (1990) 1,005,000. Cap. and chief seaport Providence. Mainly low-lying. Its outstanding feature is Narragansett Bay, which penetrates 48 km (30 miles) inland to Providence, where it receives the Blackstone R. The chief island in the bay is Rhode, on which is the town of Newport. Climate humid continental. Annual rainfall about 100 cm (40 ins.). Famous for poultry (esp. the Rhode Island Red) but primarily industrial, chiefly in the manufacture of textiles. Leading industrial centres Providence, Pawtucket, Warwick and Cranston. The coast was explored by Verrazano in 1524, but the first permanent white settlement was made in 1636 by Roger Williams at Providence. The first colony to declare its independence and one of the original 13 states, the 13th to ratify the Constitution (1790).

Rhodes (Gr. **Ródhos**) Greece. 1. *Nome* and largest island in the Dodecanese and the most easterly in the Aegean Sea 16 km (10 miles) from the Turkish coast. Area 1399 sq km (540 sq. miles). Pop. (1985) 88,500. Crossed N–S by mountains rising to nearly 1200 m (3936 ft) at the highest point. Well-watered and fertile. Produces cereals, fruits and wine.

2. Cap. of Rhodes and of the Dodecanese *nome*, at the NE extremity of the island. Pop. (1985) 45,000.

Manufactures tobacco products, brandy, and there is considerable tourism. Trade in fruit, tobacco and grain.

Surrounded by walls and towers, it rises from the main harbour in the form of an amphitheatre and has a medieval appearance, the Street of the Knights with its old houses being especially picturesque. Founded 408 BC. In the following cent. it attained great commercial prosperity, but in 227 BC suffered severely from an earthquake which destroyed the Colossus of Rhodes, a statue 32 m (105 ft) high of the god Helios, one of the Seven Wonders of the ancient world. It declined, was taken by the Knights of St John

1309, by the Turks 1523 and by the Italians 1912. Ceded to Greece 1946.

Rhodesia ►ZIMBABWE.

Rhodesia, Northern ►ZAMBIA.

Rhodesia, Southern ►ZIMBABWE.

Rhodope (Rodhópi) Greece. *Nome* in Thrace, bounded on the N by Bulgaria and on the S by the Aegean Sea. Area, 2543 sq km (984 sq. miles). Pop. (1991) 103,295. Cap. Komotíni. The N is occupied by part of the Rhodope Mountains, the S by a coastal plain on which tobacco and other crops are grown.

Rhodope Mountains. Mountain system in the Balkan Peninsula extending SE from SW Bulgaria along the Bulgarian–Greek border. Highest peak Mt Musala (2925 m, 9594 ft) in the Rila Mountains (Bulgaria).

Rhondda Wales. Borough in Rhondda, Cynon, Taff extending along the valleys of the Rhondda Fawr and Rhondda Fach rivers in the E of the S Wales former coalfield. Pop. (1991) 79,300 (141,346 in 1931). The district suffered severely from the depression of the 1930s, when nearly half the male insured workers were unemployed. The closure of coal mines brought further unemployment but the Welsh Development Agency has been successful in attracting new industry inc. Japanese companies, manufacturing vehicles and electronic equipment.

Rhondda, Cynon, Taff Wales. County Borough created in 1996, formerly part of Mid Glamorgan. Pop. (1994) 239,000.

Rhône France. Department in Lyonnais, bounded on the E by the Saône and Rhône rivers. Area 3249 sq km (1254 sq. miles). Pop. (1991) 1,516,500. Prefecture Lyon. Largely mountainous; the Monts du Beaujolais rise to over 900 m (2952 ft). Vines and fruits grown in the Saône–Rhône valley. Industries concentrated in Lyon and Villefranche-sur-Saône.

Rhône-Alps France. Region in the E. Comprises the departments of Ain, Ardèche, Drôme, Isère, Loire, Rhône, Savoie and

Haute-Savoie. Area 43,698 sq km (16,872 sq. miles). Pop. (1990) 5,350,700. Cap. Lyon. The region ranks second in importance among the 22 regions.

Important wine-making area. The Lyon conurbation constitutes France's second most important manufacturing and services centre, inc. electrical and mechanical engineering, chemicals and clothing.

Lyon is also renowned for its universities; besides, it is the second largest financial centre. The region is one of France's major tourist areas.

Rhône River France/Switzerland. River 811 km (504 miles) long, one of the most important in Europe, rising in the Rhône glacier at the foot of the Furka Pass in the E of Valais canton (Switzerland), flowing WSW and then NW to L. Geneva, which it leaves at Geneva to enter France, cutting through several narrow gorges (*cluses*) between the Jura and the Alps. At Lyon it receives its chief tributary, the Saône and turns S along a valley between the Massif Central (W) and the French Alps (E); receiving the Isère, Durance and other tributaries, it flows past Vienne, Valence and Avignon to Arles, where it divides into the Grand Rhône and the Petit Rhône, which enclose the delta of the Camargue and enter the Gulf of Lions. Navigation is limited, but the river is now much utilized for hydroelectric power. The great dam and power station at Génissiat was opened in 1948; a group of 20 power stations was then planned for the lower valley and the first – at Donzère-Mondragon, with a 27-km (17-mile) canal for navigation – was opened in 1952 and 11 others since then. For centuries the Rhône–Saône valley has been the principal route between the Mediterranean and N France.

Rhum ➤RUM.

Rhyl Wales. Seaside resort in Denbighshire, at the mouth of the R. Clwyd 42 km (26 miles) WNW of Chester. Pop. (1991) 24,909. Developed in the 19th cent. from a small fishing village.

Rhymney Wales. Town in Caerphilly on the R. Rhymney 6 km (4 miles) ENE of Merthyr Tydfil. Pop. (1991) 7991. Light engineering.

Riau Archipelago ➤RIOUW ARCHIPELAGO.

Ribble River England. River 120 km (75 miles) long, rising in the Pennines in the W of North Yorkshire, flowing generally S past Settle and then SW through Lancashire, past Preston, entering the Irish Sea by an estuary between St Anne's and Southport.

Ribe Denmark. Town situated SE of Esbjerg in SW Jutland. Flourishing medieval port now 6 km (4 miles) from the sea. Pop. (1990) 17,872.

Industries inc. plastics and iron.

Ribeirão Prêto Brazil. Town in São Paulo state 306 km (190 miles) NNW of São Paulo at a height of 570 m (1870 ft). Pop. (1991) 430,805.

In a rich coffee-growing region. Commercial centre serving São Paulo and the neighbouring states. Trade in coffee, cotton, sugar and grain. Cotton-milling, distilling and brewing. Manufactures steel and agricultural machinery.

Richborough England. Ancient Rutupiae. Small port in Kent on the R. Stour about 1.6 km (1 mile) N of Sandwich, of which it is a suburb. Was Caesar's chief port and a military base. Several Roman remains.

Richland USA. City situated WNW of Pasco in Washington on a government reservation on the Colombia R. next to the US Centre for atomic energy research plant and plutonium production plant. Pop. (1990) 33,300.

Richmond England. Market town in North Yorkshire on the R. Swale 18 km (11 miles) SW of Darlington. Pop. (1991) 7862.

Trade in agricultural produce.

Has the ruins of an 11th-cent. Norman castle, the tower of a 13th-cent. Franciscan abbey, a grammar school dating from the 14th cent. and refounded in 1567 and the

Georgian Theatre (1788), one of the oldest in the country.

Richmond (California) USA. Industrial town and seaport 16 km (10 miles) NNW of Oakland on San Francisco Bay. Pop. (1990) 74,676.

Oil refining, motor-car assembly, railway engineering. Manufactures chemicals, electronic equipment and metal goods.

Richmond (Indiana) USA. Industrial town 109 km (68 miles) E of Indianapolis. Pop. (1988) 39,200.

Manufactures machine-tools, agricultural implements and vehicle parts.

Richmond (Virginia) USA. State cap., at the head of navigation of the James R. Pop. (1990) 203,056.

Seaport, commercial and cultural centre. Exports tobacco, grain and coal. Major tobacco market. Tobacco-processing. Manufactures chemicals, food products, textiles and paper.

Among the famous buildings are the state Capitol (1785–92), St John's Church (1741) and the White House of the Confederacy, now a Confederate museum. It is an important education centre and became cap. of the Confederate states 1861; in 1865 it was evacuated and set on fire by the Confederates, about one-third of the city being destroyed.

Richmond-upon-Thames (Richmond) England. London borough inc. the former municipal boroughs of Barnes (Surrey) and Twickenham (Middlesex) on the R. Thames 13 km (8 miles) WSW of London. Pop. (1991) 163,400. Mainly residential, also a popular resort for Londoners; the attractions, besides the river, inc. Richmond Park (951 ha; 2342 acres), the Royal Botanic Gardens (Kew) and Ham Common and Ham House (Ham). The present Richmond Park was added to the Old Deer Park by Charles I (1637). White Lodge, in the park, built for George II, was the birthplace of Edward VIII. Renamed (1500) by Henry VII after his earldom in Yorkshire, and the Palace of Sheen was the residence of several monarchs from Edward III onwards.

Rickmansworth England. Town in SW Hertfordshire 6 km (4 miles) WSW of Watford at the confluence of the R. Chess and the R. Gade with the R. Colne. Pop. (1991) 10,263. Mainly residential. Basing House was the home of William Penn, English Quaker and founder of Pennsylvania (1672–6).

Ridderkerk Netherlands. Town situated SE of Rotterdam on Ijsselmonde island, Zuid-Holland. Pop. (1992) 45,834.

Industries inc. shipbuilding. Fruit and vegetable market for Rotterdam.

Riesa Germany. Town in Saxony on the Elbe R. 40 km (25 miles) NW of Dresden. Pop. (1985) 52,000.

River port, railway junction and industrial centre. Sawmilling, brewing. Manufactures iron and steel, glass, soap and furniture. Trade in petroleum and grain.

Rieti Italy. Ancient Reate. Cap. of Rieti province in Latium on the Velino R. 26 km (16 miles) SE of Terni. Pop. (1990) 44,500.

Manufactures textiles, olive oil and pasta.

Roman remains; 13th-cent. cathedral and episcopal palace.

Rif, Er Morocco. Mountain range near the Mediterranean coast, rising to over 2400 m (7872 ft), extending 320 km (200 miles) S and then E from Ceuta on the Strait of Gibraltar to the lower Moulouya valley near the Algerian border. Inhabited by the Riffs, Berbers who (under the leadership of Abdel-al-Krim) successfully rebelled against French and Spanish rule from 1921 until defeated in 1926.

Riga Latvia. Cap. and chief seaport on the West Dvina R. 15 km (9 miles) above the mouth (on the Gulf of Riga). Pop. (1991) 910,200.

Industries inc. engineering, chemicals, textiles and shipbuilding. The port is the biggest Baltic port after St Petersburg; it operates May–Nov. when the Gulf is ice-free.

The old city on the river banks has been destroyed more than once, but the 13th-cent. cathedral survives together with merchants' houses on the quay and the castle which protected them. The old city is surrounded by a canal, once a defensive moat. The industrial areas are mainly beyond it and there is a resort area in the coastal suburb of Rigas Jūrmala. Riga was founded by a German bishop in 1201; it became the headquarters of a German knightly order and a Hansa League port. It passed to Poland in 1581, Sweden in 1621 and Russia in 1721, always increasing its importance as a trading port. It was a national cap. from 1918 until recapture by Russia in 1940, after which many of its Latvian citizens were deported and replaced by Russians. Riga became a national cap. again in 1991.

Riga, Gulf of of Estonia/Latvia. Inlet of the Baltic Sea into the coasts of Estonia and Latvia about 160 km (100 miles) long and 96 km (60 miles) wide, with the Estonian islands of Saaremaa, Hiiumaa and others across its entrance. Icebound Jan.–April. Chief port Riga.

Rigi Switzerland. Mountain ridge in the Alps, between the lakes of Lucerne, Zug and Lauerz, reaching 1802 m (5911 ft) at the highest point (Kulm). Ascended by rack-and-pinion railway. A popular excursion for tourists from Lucerne.

Rijeka (Italian **Fiume**) Croatia. Important seaport on the Adriatic Sea 129 km (80 miles) SW of Zagreb. Pop. (Rijeka-Sušak, 1991) 205,842.

Also an industrial centre. Shipbuilding, oil-refining. Manufactures machinery, chemicals, tobacco products, food products and paper.

Now inc. the E suburb of Sušak, whence the medieval castle and church of Trsat can be reached, the latter a place of pilgrimage. It has become a tourist centre for the islands of the Adriatic. It became a free port 1723. Annexed to Hungary 1779. Claimed by Yugoslavia and Italy in 1919, it was seized by d'Annunzio, and again by the Fascists in 1922, and was annexed to Italy in 1924. Sušak was developed as a Yugoslav port, but in 1947 Fiume (now Rijeka) was transferred to Yugoslavia and the two towns were re-united.

Rijn River ➤RHINE RIVER.

Rijswijk (Ryswick) Netherlands. Town in S Holland province just SE of The Hague. Pop. (1992) 47,456. Largely residential. Manufactures furniture.

The Treaty of Ryswick (1697) was signed here.

Rimac River Peru. River 129 km (80 miles) long, rising in the W Cordillera of the Andes, flowing WSW to the Pacific near Lima. Lower course used for irrigation. With its tributary the Santa Eulalia it supplies power for hydroelectric plants.

Rimini Italy. Ancient Ariminum. Town in Forlì province, Emilia-Romagna, on the Adriatic 105 km (65 miles) SW of Bologna. Pop. (1991) 130,896.

Popular seaside resort, port and railway junction. Manufactures textiles, shoes and pasta. Popularity as a summer resort largely due to its extensive beaches.

Has a triumphal arch built by Augustus, but its finest building was the Renaissance Church of S Francesco or Tempio Malatestiano (completed 1450), severely damaged, like much of the rest of the town in World War II. An important route centre in Roman times, being a seaport and standing at the junction of the Aemilian Way to Piacenza and the Flaminian Way to Rome. Passed to the Malatesta family 1237 and was ruled by them until 1509, when it became a papal possession.

Riobamba Ecuador. Cap. of Chimborazo province at a height of 2700 m (8856 ft) in a high Andean basin SE of Mt Chimborazo and 169 km (105 miles) S of Quito. Pop. (1990) 94,505.

Manufactures textiles, carpets and footwear. Has a picturesque weekly fair, held in the main plazas, made colourful by Indians from the surrounding agricultural region.

Rio Branco Brazil. River 640 km (400 miles) long formed from several headstreams, inc. the Uraricuera and the Tacutu, rising in the Sierra Pacaraima and flowing S to join the Rio Negro.

Río Bravo ➤RIO GRANDE (MEXICO/USA).

Río Colorado Argentina. River 853 km (530 miles) long formed on the Mendoza–Neuquén border by the union of the Río Grande and the Barrancas. Flows SE to the Atlantic Ocean. Often regarded as dividing the pampas (N) from Patagonia (S).

Río Cuarto Argentina. Town in Córdoba province on the Río Cuarto 209 km (130 miles) S of Córdoba. Pop. (1991) 217,717.

Commercial and industrial centre and garrison town. Trade in cereals and other agricultural produce. Manufactures cement and textiles.

Rio de Janeiro Brazil. 1. Usually known as Rio. Chief seaport and former cap. of Brazil on the SW shore of Guanabara Bay. Pop. (1991) 5,336,179.

Exports coffee, sugar and iron ore. Manufactures clothing, furniture, chemicals and tobacco products. Industries inc. flour-milling, sugar-refining and railway engineering.

The city, in an outstandingly beautiful setting, first occupied only the narrow alluvial plain along the coast, but it has now spread farther inland. Stands against a background of towering mountains, extending about 10 km (6 miles) around the bay; its best-known strip of coastline is the famous Copacabana beach facing the Atlantic. The highest peak, the Corcovado (690 m; 2263 ft), surmounted by a giant figure of Christ, dominates the whole; the entrance to the great landlocked harbour is overshadowed by the Conical Sugar Loaf Mountain or Pão de Açúcar (396 m; 1299 ft). Many buildings remain from the colonial period, inc. a number of fine churches, and there are also tall modern structures, many of considerable architectural merit. Numerous distinguished squares, parks and gardens, inc. the Botanical Gardens (founded 1808), with their avenues of lofty Royal Palms. Seat of the University of Brazil (1920) and the Catholic University of Rio de Janeiro (1940). Discovered by the Portuguese (Jan. 1502) and mistakenly thought to be at the mouth of a river; hence

the name, 'River of January'. First settled (1555) by the French, but they were driven out by the Portuguese 1567 and Rio became the cap. of the southern province of Brazil. Replaced Salvador (Bahia) as the colonial cap. of all Brazil, and remained cap. under the Empire and the Republic till Brasilia was inaugurated in 1960.

2. State on the Atlantic coast. Area 43,653 sq km (16,855 sq. miles). Pop. (1991) 14,133,300. Cap. Rio de Janeiro. Largely mountainous; crossed by the Serra do Mar and drained by the Paraiba R. and its tributaries. Produces coffee, citrus fruits and sugarcane. Much recent industrial development, inc. steel manufacture at Volta Redonda.

Río de la Plata (River Plate) Argentina/Uruguay. Estuary of the Paraná and Uruguay rivers between Uruguay (N) and Argentina (S), extending about 257 km (160 miles) SE to the Atlantic, 32 km (20 miles) in width at its head broadening to 96 km (60 miles) between Montevideo and the Argentine shore and 225 km (140 miles) at the E end. Much silt is brought down by the rivers and deposited on the banks, esp. in the S; the water is relatively shallow and continuous dredging of channels is necessary. Discovered by Diaz de Solis 1516. Explored by Magellan 1520. During World War II (Dec. 1939) a naval action took place off its mouth after which the German pocket battleship *Graf Spee*, unable to leave the river, was scuttled. Main seaports Buenos Aires (Argentina), Montevideo (Uruguay).

Río de las Balsas ➤MEXICO.

Rio Grande Brazil. Seaport in Rio Grande do Sul state at the entrance to the Lagôa dos Patos 240 km (150 miles) SSW of Pôrto Alegre, whose outport it is. Pop. (1989) 125,000.

Exports meat products and hides. Industries inc. meat-packing, fish and vegetable canning, oil-refining. It manufactures textiles and footwear.

Founded 1737.

Rio Grande (Río Bravo) Mexico/USA. Known in Mexico as the Río Bravo (Río

Bravo del Norte). River 2870 km (1785 miles) long, rising in the San Juan Mountains in SW Colorado, flowing SE across Colorado and then almost due S through New Mexico, generally SE, forming the USA–Mexico frontier and ultimately discharging into the Gulf of Mexico. The Big Bend National Park (2802 sq km (1082 sq. miles)) in Texas is a wild region of desert and mountains in the wide angle formed along the lower course. Not used for navigation, but has been dammed for irrigation, flood control and hydroelectric power. The largest dam is the Elephant Butte Dam in New Mexico, which impounds a lake 518 sq km (200 sq. miles) in area, irrigating over 200,000 ha (494,000 acres). Chief tributary the Pecos R., which joins it below the Big Bend.

Rio Grande do Norte Brazil. State in the NE 'shoulder'. Area 53,167 sq km (20,528 sq. miles). Pop. (1990) 2,318,900. Cap. Natal. Consists mainly of plateau with a semi-arid climate and a more humid sandy coastal plain. Important saltworks. Also produces sugarcane, cotton, carnauba wax and hides.

Rio Grande do Sul Brazil. The southernmost state, bounded on the W by Argentina and on the S by Uruguay. Area 280,674 sq km (108,369 sq. miles). Pop. (1991) 9,127,611. Cap. Pôrto Alegre.

Main occupation stock-rearing, but cereals, fruit and wine production are of growing importance. In the N lumbering and maté gathering.

Río Muni ►EQUATORIAL GUINEA.

Río Negro Argentina. River in Patagonia 640 km (400 miles) long formed by the union of the Neuquén and Limay rivers, flowing E and SE through irrigated fruit-growing lands to the Atlantic N of the Gulf of San Matías. Irrigation is made possible by the great Río Negro dam near the town of Neuquén.

Rio Negro Brazil. River 2092 km (1300 miles) long rising in E Colombia (where it is known as the Guainía), flowing generally E and SE, a major tributary of the Amazon.

Forms part of the Colombia–Venezuela border and enters Brazil in the densely forested Amazon basin. Joins the Amazon about 16 km (10 miles) below Manáus, where its blue-black waters mingle with the light, silt-choked flow of the main river. Its system is linked with that of the Orinoco R. by the Casiquiare.

Río Negro Uruguay. River 800 km (500 miles) long rising in Brazil 24 km (15 miles) E of Bagé and flowing generally WSW across Uruguay to join the Uruguay R. A dam in the middle course (with hydroelectric installation) creates an artificial lake 140 km (87 miles) long and 29 km (18 miles) wide.

Rion (Georgian **Rioni**) **River** Georgia. River 290 km (180 miles) long in W Georgia rising in the Caucasus and flowing generally WSW past Kutaisi (near which is a hydroelectric plant) to enter the Black Sea at Poti. In its lower course it flows through the Colchis marshes.

Río Tinto Spain. River 96 km (60 miles) long in Huelva province in the SW near the source of which is the famous copper-mining town of Río Tinto.

Riou (**Riau**) Indonesia. Province on Sumatra. Area 94,561 sq km (36,510 sq. miles). Cap. Pakanbaru.

Riouw (**Riau**) **Archipelago** Indonesia. Group of islands off the E coast of Sumatra at the S entrance to the Strait of Malacca. Area 5905 sq km (2280 sq. miles).

Tin and bauxite are mined on Bintan, the largest and most important island, which has the chief town, Tandjungpinang.

Ripley England. Town in Derbyshire 14 km (9 miles) NNE of Derby. Pop. (1991) 18,310.

Industries inc. ironworking, engineering and knitwear manufacture.

Ripon England. Cathedral city and resort in North Yorkshire on the R. Ure 34 km (21 miles) NW of York. Pop. (1991) 13,806.

Industries inc. tanning and brewing. Manufactures paints and varnishes.

Its cathedral or minster, in various architectural styles and with a Saxon crypt, was built between the mid 12th and early 16th cent. The ruins of the famous 12th-cent. Fountains Abbey are 5 km (3 miles) SW.

Risca Wales. Town in Caerphilly on the R. Ebbw 8 km (5 miles) WNW of Newport. Pop. (1991) 15,124.

Risdon Australia. Oldest settlement in Tasmania (1803) on the left bank of the Derwent R. estuary opposite Hobart.

Rivera Uruguay. Cap. of Rivera department 418 km (260 miles) N of Montevideo on the Brazilian frontier. Pop. (1985) 56,335.
Trade in grain, cattle, fruit, vegetables. Manufactures textiles.

Riverina Australia. Region in New South Wales between the Lachlan-Murrumbidgee (N) and the Murray R. (S). Consists of flat, fertile, grassy plains, important for sheep-rearing and wheat cultivation. Much of the arable land is irrigated.

Rivers Nigeria. State formed from the Degema, Port Harcourt and Yenagoa provinces of the former E region. Area 21,850 sq km (8436 sq. miles). Pop. (1991) 3,983,857. The cap. and major port is Port Harcourt. The inhabitants are mainly Ijaw.
Major oilfields providing 96 per cent of Nigeria's exports.

Riverside USA. Residential town and resort in California on the Santa Ana R. 77 km (48 miles) E of Los Angeles. Pop. (1990) 226,505.
Important centre for the packing and distribution of citrus fruits. Also manufactures aircraft engines and paints.
Seat of the citrus experiment station of the University of California (1907). Founded 1870. The cultivation of the navel orange was introduced from Brazil (1873); the parent tree is still preserved.

Riviera France/Italy. Narrow strip of coast between the mountains and the sea around the Gulf of Genoa, generally considered to extend from Hyères, at the W end of the French Riviera (Côte d'Azur), to La Spezia,

at the E end of the Italian Riviera. Renowned for its scenery, its mild winter climate and its subtropical vegetation; has become one of the leading playgrounds of Europe, with numerous resorts. On the French Riviera are Nice, Cannes, Menton, Antibes, Juan-les-Pins, Monte Carto (Monaco). Genoa divides the Italian Riviera into the Riviera di Ponente (W), which has San Remo, Bordighera, Imperia and Ventimiglia, and the Riviera di Levante (E), with Rapallo, Portofino and Sestri Levante. From Nice to Genoa runs the road built by Napoleon, the Corniche or Grande Corniche; between Nice and Menton are two parallel roads, the Moyenne and Petite Corniche. Throughout the Riviera vines, olives and citrus fruits are cultivated, and flowers are grown, partly for the preparation of perfumes.

Rivne ➤ROVNO.

Riyadh Saudi Arabia. Cap. of Nejd and joint cap. (with Mecca) of Saudi Arabia in an oasis in the centre of the country 800 km (500 miles) ENE of Mecca. Pop. (1988) 2 million. Formerly a walled city surrounded by groves of date palms, it has been greatly modernized and enlarged in recent years.
Industries inc. oil-processing.
Grew to importance early in the 19th cent. when it became the headquarters of the Wahhabi movement. Linked by railway (completed 1951) with Dammam on the Persian Gulf. Birthplace of Ibn Saud (1880–1953).

Rizaiyeh ➤ORUMIYEH.

Road Town British Virgin Islands. Cap. and port on the island of Tortola. Pop. (1991) 6330.
Tourism is important with cruise ships calling.

Roan Antelope ➤NDOLA.

Roanne France. Industrial town in the Loire department on the Loire R. 69 km (43 miles) WNW of Lyon. Pop. (1990) 42,848.
Important textile industry; also manufactures paper, leather goods and tiles. Terminus of the Roanne–Digoin Canal, which runs parallel to the Loire.

Roanoke USA. Formerly Big Lick. Town in SW Virginia on the Roanoke R. Pop. (1990) 96,397.

Industrial centre and railway junction in the natural amphitheatre formed by the Blue Ridge and the Allegheny Mountains. Railway engineering. Manufactures textiles and chemicals.

Founded 1834 and named because of its salt deposits. Renamed 1882.

Roanoke Island USA. Island 19 km (12 miles) long and 5 km (3 miles) wide off the coast of North Carolina, to which Raleigh sent unsuccessful expeditions (1585, 1587), attempting to establish an English colony. The disappearance of the would-be colonists is annually commemorated by performances of *The Lost Colony*, a historical drama by Paul Green (1937).

Roanoke River USA. River 660 km (410 miles) long rising in SW Virginia, flowing generally ESE into North Carolina and entering Albemarle Sound.

Robben Island South Africa. Island in Table Bay, Western Cape. Used as a prison for political prisoners inc. Nelson Mandela; formerly a leper colony.

Robin Hood's Bay England. Fishing and tourist village in North Yorkshire 8 km (5 miles) SE of Whitby on an inlet of the same name which is fringed by high cliffs.

Robson, Mount Canada. Highest peak in the Canadian Rocky Mountains (3954 m; 12,969 ft) in E British Columbia near the Alberta border. Surrounded by the Mt Robson Provincial Park 105 km (65 miles) long and up to 32 km (20 miles) wide.

Rochdale England. Town in Greater Manchester on the R. Roch 16 km (10 miles) NNE of Manchester. Pop. (1991) 94,313.

Formerly an important centre of the cotton industry, esp. spinning. It manufactures woollen, rayon and asbestos goods. Other industries inc. engineering.

Here the Equitable Pioneers Society (Rochdale Pioneers) founded the co-operative movement of Great Britain (1844).

Birthplace of John Bright, British statesman and orator (1811–89).

Rochefort-sur-Mer (Rochefort) France, Port in the Charente-Maritime department on the Charente R. 16 km (10 miles) above the mouth on the Bay of Biscay. Pop. (1990) 26,900.

Industries inc. fish-processing and saw-milling.

Developed by Colbert in the 17th cent. but later superseded as a naval base by Brest.

Rochelle, La France. Cap. of Charente-Maritime department. Pop. (1982) 78,231.

Fishing and international leisure port situated on the Bay of Biscay.

Rochester England. Ancient Durobrivae. Town in N Kent on the S side of the Medway estuary adjoining Chatham. Pop. (1991) 23,971.

Industrial centre. Manufactures agricultural machinery, air-conditioning equipment and cement.

In the 11th cent. Bishop Gundulf built a cathedral on the site of one founded (604) by St Augustine; part of his work survives in the present building. Also remains of the 12th-cent. Norman castle. Charles Dickens lived at Gad's Hill, just NW. A Roman stronghold, important as the site of the bridge carrying Watling Street over the Medway.

Rochester (Minnesota) USA. Town 113 km (70 miles) SSE of St Paul. Pop. (1990) 70,745.

Commercial centre in an agricultural region. Manufactures dairy products, medical and electrical equipment.

Chiefly famous for the Mayo clinic, founded in 1889 and now internationally known.

Rochester (New York) USA. Industrial town and port on L. Ontario at the mouth of the Genesee R., whose falls provide hydroelectric power. Pop. (1990) 231,636.

Manufactures cameras, photographic equipment, optical appliances, thermometers, office equipment and machine-tools.

In a fruit-growing and market-gardening region.

Roche-sur-Yon, La France. Prefecture of the Vendée department on the Yon R. 61 km (38 miles) S of Nantes. Pop. (1990) 48,568.

Market town. Railway junction. Industries inc. flour-milling and tanning.

After being almost destroyed (1794), it was rebuilt by Napoleon (1805) and for a time was known as Napoléon-Vendée.

Rockall N Atlantic Ocean. Rocky uninhabited islet 380 km (240 miles) W of the Outer Hebrides. Annexed by Britain in 1955 and incorporated into Scotland to ensure control of oil and natural gas deposits. Also claimed by Denmark, Ireland and Iceland.

Rockford USA. Industrial town in Illinois on the Rock R. 129 km (80 miles) WNW of Chicago. Pop. (1990) 136,426.

Manufactures machine-tools, agricultural machinery, hardware, hosiery, furniture and paints. Hydroelectric power is derived from a dam on the Rock R.

Founded (1834) as a stage-coach ford; hence the name.

Rockhampton Australia. Seaport and commercial town in E Queensland 64 km (40 miles) up the Fitzroy R. from Keppel Bay. Pop. (1990) 62,475.

Exports meat, hides, copper, gold, coal from an extensive hinterland. Large meat-processing plants downstream.

Founded 1858 after an unsuccessful gold rush.

Rock Hill USA. Town in South Carolina 124 km (77 miles) N of Columbia. Pop. (1970) 33,846.

Manufactures textiles and paper.

Rock Island USA. Town in Illinois on the Mississippi R. near the confluence with the Rock R., adjoining Moline and opposite Davenport (Iowa). Pop. (1985) 47,000.

Railway engineering. Manufactures electrical and agricultural equipment, hardware, clothing and footwear.

On the island of the same name in the Mississippi is the main US arsenal (established

1862). With Moline, East Moline and Davenport (Iowa) the town forms the group known as the Quad Cities.

Rocky Mount USA. Town in North Carolina on the Tar R. 80 km (50 miles) ENE of Raleigh. Pop. (1970) 37,400.

Railway engineering, tobacco-processing and cotton-milling. Manufactures pharmaceuticals, textiles, clothing and chemicals. Important trade in tobacco and cotton.

Rocky Mountains (Rockies) N America. Vast mountain system in W Canada and USA, extending from the Yukon to New Mexico; the backbone of the Continent, divisible into four sections: the Canadian Rockies and the N, Central and S Rockies of the USA.

The Canadian Rockies (the boundary between British Columbia and Alberta for about half of their 1450 km; 900 miles) contain many glaciers, lakes and icefields, now preserved for sport and recreation in National and Provincial Parks (e.g. Jasper, Banff). Passes inc. the Vermilion (1640 m, 5380 ft), Kicking Horse (1628 m, 5340 ft) and Crow's Nest (1357 m, 4451 ft).

In the US Rockies there are 20 or more principal ranges of complex structure, the N, Central and S sections corresponding approximately with the states of Montana (N), Wyoming (Central) and Colorado, Utah, New Mexico (S). The Glacier National Park in the N contains magnificent glacier and lake scenery and has 26 peaks over 2700 m (8856 ft). In the Central Rockies, the rugged Teton Range has probably the finest scenery in the entire mountain system; the Grand Teton rises to 4193 m (13,753 ft). The Sawatch Range of the S Rockies contains the highest peak of all, Mt Elbert (4398 m, 14,431 ft), and several others over 4200 m (13,776 ft). Some geographers consider the ranges of Yukon and Alaska as part of the Rockies; in this case Mt Logan (6050 m, 19,849 ft) is the highest peak.

Rodrigues (Rodriguez) Mauritius. Island in the Indian Ocean 563 km (350 miles) ENE of Mauritius island, of which it is a dependency. Area 104 sq km (40 sq. miles). Pop. (1993) 35,536. Chief town Port Mathurin. Volcanic in origin; rises to 396 m (1299 ft) in Mt Limon. Frequently subject to tropical cyclones.

Chief products maize, fruit, tobacco and salted fish.

Taken by the British in 1810.

Roermond Netherlands. Industrial town in Limburg province on the Maas R. at the confluence with the Roer R. 45 km (28 miles) NNE of Maastricht. Pop. (1993) 42,744.

Manufactures textiles, food products, bicycles, paper, and there is flour-milling and brewing. Trade in agricultural produce.

Has a 13th-cent. Romanesque church.

Roggeveld Mountains ➤SOUTH AFRICA.

Rohtak India. Town in Haryana 64 km (40 miles) NW of Delhi. Pop. (1991) 215,844.

Commercial centre. Trade in grain, cotton and oilseeds. There is cotton-ginning and it manufactures fasteners, vehicle components, sugar, textiles, glass, chemicals, confectionery and sanitary ware.

Roma Australia. Town situated WNW of Brisbane in Queensland serving an agricultural area. Pop. (1988) 7000.

The largest industries are connected with food-processing. Natural gas was found in the 1960s and is used locally and is also piped to Brisbane. Oil wells are found in the vicinity.

Roma, Campagna di Italy. Plain in Rome province, Lazio, bounded SW by the Tyrrhenian Sea. Drained by the Tiber R. Neglected land much restored by drainage.

Romagna Italy. Region of N Italy, now the E part of the Emilia-Romagna region, comprising the provinces of Forlì and Ravenna and part of Bologna. Long formed part of the Papal States.

Roman Romania. Town in the Neamt district (Moldavia) on the Moldava R. near its confluence with the Siret R. 56 km (35 miles) WSW of Iaşi. Pop. (1985) 68,000.

Railway junction. Industrial centre for flour-milling and sugar-refining.

Romana, La Dominican Republic. Port situated E of Santo Domingo in La Altagracia province. Pop. (1986) 101,350.

Industries inc. sugar-refining and coffee and tobacco processing.

Romania. Republic in SE Europe. Bounded N and NE by Russia, E by the Black Sea, S by Bulgaria, SW by Serbia and NW by Hungary. Area 237,500 sq km (91,699 sq. miles). Pop. (1995) 22,693,000 (55 per cent urban). Life expectancy, 69 years male, 75 female. Cap. Bucharest. Major cities Constanţa, Iaşi, Timişoara and Cluj-Napoca. Currency: Leu = 100 bani. The country is crossed N–S by the Carpathians and E–W by the Transylvanian Alps; the two ranges form a great arc which encloses the Bihor Mountains and the plateau of Transylvania. The Carpathians rise to over 2000m (6888 ft); several peaks in the Transylvanian Alps exceed 2400 m (7872 ft). To the E and S of the mountains are the plains of Moldavia and Walachia and the low plateau of the Dobrogea (Dobruja); to the W the lowlands merge with the adjoining plains of former Yugoslavia and Hungary. The Danube empties into the Black Sea by a broad delta and is an important artery of trade. Of the other rivers, the Prut and Siret are tributaries of the Danube: the Mureş flows W to join the Tisza. It has a continental climate, with hot summers and cold winters. Annual rainfall 50–75 cm (20–30 ins.) on the plains, substantially more in the mountains. Land use: forested 28 per cent, pasture 21 per cent, agricultural 44 per cent. The pop. inc. a number of minorities, with over 1,714,000 Hungarians, 359,000 Germans and many Ukrainians, Yugoslavs, Russians and Tatars, and 227,000 gypsies. Religion mainly Eastern Orthodox. In 1948 the Uniate (Greek Catholic) Church, with more than 1 million members, broke with the Vatican and was reincorporated in and increased the predominance of the Eastern Orthodox Church. The official lang. is Romanian.

The fertile Moldavian and Walachian

Rome

plains form one of Europe's leading granaries. Principal crops maize, wheat, sugarbeet, flax, hemp, vines and deciduous fruits. Large numbers of sheep, cattle, pigs and poultry raised, chiefly in Transylvania. Privatization of small plots of land began in 1991. Extensive forests in Transylvania supply an important timber industry. Chief minerals natural gas and petroleum, produced mainly from wells around Ploeşti. Industries inc. iron and steel manufacture and flour-milling, but production has been falling for some years. Chief exports cereals, oil, timber, cattle and industrial equipment.

Modern Romania corresponds roughly to the Roman province of Dacia (AD 107–275) and from the Romans are derived the country's present name and to a considerable extent the major Romanian element in the pop. and their lang. After the withdrawal of the Romans the area was overrun by Goths, Huns, Bulgars, Slavs. The principalities of Walachia and Moldavia were founded in the late 13th and early 14th cent. Walachia became subject to the Turks in the 15th cent. and Moldavia in the 16th. The two principalities were united as Romania (1859) with Alexander Cuza as prince, but he was deposed (1866) and Prince Charles of Hohenzollern-Sigmaringen elected as Carol I. Romania's independence was recognized 1878. Romania supported the Allied cause in World War I and was rewarded with Bessarabia and Transylvania. The 1930s saw the rise of fascism. Carol II established a dictatorship in 1938 but was forced to abdicate (1940) after Bessarabia, Transylvania and southern Dobrogea had been lost to the USSR, Hungary and Bulgaria respectively. After World War II Transylvania was restored. King Michael returned to the country and held elections but in 1947 he was compelled to abdicate and the republic was established. The former political parties were abolished and the Communists took control. From 1963 Romania began to take a more independent line on Soviet policy, increasing trade with non-communist countries as well as the USSR. A popular uprising in Timişoara in 1989 spread to other areas. A state

of emergency was declared but the army went over to the uprising. The President and his wife were captured, received a 2-hour trial and were executed. A new Constitution was adopted in 1991. The National Assembly consists of a 341-member Chamber of Deputies and a 143-member Senate, both are elected for 4-year terms. It is divided administratively into 41 counties (judet).

Rome (Italian **Roma**) Italy. Cap. of Italy and of the Latium region and Roma province, on both banks of the Tiber R. 24 km (15 miles) from the mouth in the Campagna di Roma. Pop. (1991) 2,791,354. Port Civitavecchia. Called 'the Eternal City'; one of the world's outstanding historical, religious, cultural and art centres.

There is a large tourist trade. Industries inc. film production, printing and publishing. Manufactures inc. machinery, furniture, cement, glass and silverware.

The old walls enclose the classical city on its seven hills, but this is now only 4 per cent of the area of the metropolis. There are 35 urban quarters outside it and 6 suburbs beyond them; the municipality covers 1507 sq km (582 sq. miles). The walled city lies E of the Tiber; on the W bank is Trastevere, the traditional foreign-trade quarter. Also on the W bank, farther N, is St Peter's basilica and the Vatican City, approached from the Castel Sant'Angelo on the riverbank. From the N wall the ancient Via del Corso runs to the city centre – the Forum beside the Capitoline Hill. The other six hills are the Palatine and (peripherally from the S) the Aventine, Caelian, Esquiline, Viminal and Quirinal. There was permanent settlement from c. 1000 BC but no unified state until after 600 BC. As cap. of the republic the city was walled and improved, but overcrowded. As an imperial cap. from 27 BC it became magnificent in palaces, aqueducts, fountains, theatres and baths. In AD 330 it lost its power to Constantinople, suffering decline and frequent attack. The city of the medieval Popes was small, with the old city lying waste beside it. From 1420 Rome was rebuilt (much early fabric being destroyed) in increasing grandeur, but it declined as a power until taken by Napoleon in 1798. In 1870 it became cap. of united Italy; the territorial claims of the Papacy were finally settled in 1929 when the Vatican City was recognized as a sovereign state.

Rome (Georgia) USA. Industrial town at the confluence of the Etowah and Oostanaula rivers 88 km (55 miles) NW of Atlanta. Pop. (1970) 20,759.

Manufactures cotton and rayon goods, hosiery, paper, agricultural machinery and clothing.

Founded 1834.

Rome (New York) USA. Industrial town on the Mohawk R. 23 km (14 miles) WNW of Utica. Pop. (1990) 44,350.

Important copper and brass-working industry. Manufactures cables, wire, machinery and vacuum cleaners.

Romford England. Part of the London borough of Havering. Largely residential.

Industries inc. brewing, engineering. Manufactures pharmaceutical and plastic products.

Romney ►NEW ROMNEY.

Romney Marsh England. Level stretch of drained marshland mainly in S Kent, between Winchelsea (Sussex) and Hythe, now used as sheep pasture. Much of it was once covered by the estuary of the R. Rother, but a great storm (1287) diverted the river from New Romney to Rye, and the subsequent recession of the sea led to the deline of New Romney, Rye and Winchelsea as seaports. Part of Romney Marsh was reclaimed in Roman times.

Romsdal Norway. Valley of the Rauma R. in the SW mainly in Möre og Romsdal county about 96 km (60 miles) long with several waterfalls and flanked by the lofty mountains inc. Romsdalshorn (1556 m; 5104 ft). The Rauma R. enters the sea by Romsdal Fiord.

Romsey England. Market town in Hampshire on the R. Test 13 km (8 miles) NW of Southampton. Pop. (1990) 14,773.

It has a 12th-cent. Norman church built over the church of a 10th-cent. Benedictine nunnery. Birthplace of Sir William Petty, English economist (1623–87).

Roncesvalles (Fr. **Roncevaux**) Spain. Village in Navarra province 35 km (22 miles) NE of Pamplona and 8 km (5 miles) from the French frontier, at a height of 980 m (3214 ft) in the Pyrenees. Pop. (1985) 90. Its pass is famous as the scene of the defeat of Charlemagne and the death of Roland.

Ronda Spain. Town in Málaga province, Andalusia on the Guadiaro R. 64 km (40 miles) W of Málaga. Pop. (1991) 33,730.

Industries inc. flour-milling and tanning. Trade in olives, wine and leather. Tourists are attracted to this picturesque town, divided into two parts by the Tajo de Ronda, a deep gorge crossed by an 18th-cent. bridge. The old town, S of the Tajo, is Moorish in character and has the alcazaba or fortress; the new town, to the N, dates from the 15th cent. and possesses the oldest bullring in Spain.

Rondônia Brazil. Formerly Guaporé. Federal state in the W, bounded on the W and S by Bolivia. Area 238,379 sq km (92,039 sq. miles). Pop. (1991) 1,130,400. Cap. Pôrto Velho. Largely tropical rainforest.

Chief products rubber, Brazil nuts. Some Bolivian trade passes along the Madeira–Mamoré railway, which bypasses the Madeira R. rapids, through Pôrto Velho.

Established 1943. Renamed 1956.

Ronse (Fr. **Renaix**) Belgium. Town in E Flanders province 56 km (35 miles) WSW of Brussels. Pop. (1992) 24,152.

Industries inc. textiles.

Roodepoort-Maraisburg South Africa. Town in Gauteng on the Witwatersrand 14 km (9 miles) W of Johannesburg at a height of 1750 m (5740 ft). Pop. (1985) 141,764.

Goldmining and residential centre. Inc. the towns of Roodepoort, Florida and Maraisburg.

Roosendaal en Nispen Netherlands. Industrial town and railway junction in North

Brabant province 19 km (12 miles) WSW of Breda. Pop. (1992) 61,354.

Railway engineering, sugar-refining, chemicals and food-processing are the main industries. It manufactures cigars and furniture.

Roosevelt (Teodoro) River Brazil. Formerly Rio da Dúvida. River 800 km (500 miles) long rising in the Serra dos Parecis (Rondônia) and flowing N to join the Aripuana R. Explored in 1914 by Theodore Roosevelt (1914) and named after him.

Roquefort-sur-Soulzon (Roquefort) France. Village in the Aveyron department 14 km (9 miles) SSW of Millau. Pop. (1985) 875. Long famous for its cheese, made principally from ewes' milk and ripened in limestone caves nearby.

Roraima Brazil. Formerly Rio Branco. Federal state in the N in the basin of the Rio Branco. Area 225,017 sq km (88,880 sq. miles). Pop. (1991) 215,790. Cap. Boa Vista. Formed 1943 from part of Amazonas. Chiefly undeveloped tropical rainforest. Some stock-rearing on the higher savannah round Boa Vista. Became a state in 1990.

Rosa, Monte Italy/Switzerland. The highest mountain group in the Pennine Alps, situated SSW of Brig, Switzerland and inc. 10 peaks of which the highest is Dufourspitze 4638 m (15,217 ft) above sea level.

Rosario Argentina. River port in Santa Fé province on the Paraná R. 274 km (170 miles) NW of Buenos Aires. Pop. (1991) 875,664.

Railway, industrial and commercial centre. Industries inc. sugar-refining, meat-packing, flour-milling and brewing. Manufactures steel, agricultural machinery, bricks and furniture. Terminus for the pampas railways. Exports wheat, meat and hides.

Roscoff France. Fishing and ferry port and resort in the Finistère department 19 km (12 miles) NW of Morlaix. Pop. (1985) 4000.

Trade in market-garden produce, esp. onions.

Roscommon Ireland. 1. Inland county in

Connacht, bounded on the E by the R. Shannon and on the SW by the R. Suck. Area 2463 sq km (951 sq. miles). Pop. (1991) 51,876. Partly hilly, rising to 330 m (1082 ft) in the Bralieve Mountains in the extreme N. Many lakes, inc. Lough Key and parts of Loughs Gara, Allen, Boderg and Ree. Most of it lies within the limestone plain of central Ireland and is largely devoted to pasture for cattle and sheep.

2. County town of Co. Roscommon 27 km (17 miles) NW of Athlone. Pop. (1991) 1314.

Market in livestock and agricultural produce.

Ruins of the large 13th-cent. castle and the Dominican priory.

Roscrea Ireland. Market town in the extreme N of Co. Tipperary on the Little Brosna R. Pop. (1991) 4231.

Malting, bacon and ham curing.

Has a ruined 12th-cent. Augustinian priory. To the W is the modern Cistercian Abbey of Mt St Joseph.

Roseau Dominica. Cap. and port. Pop. (1991) 20,755. Formerly Charlottetown.

Exports tropical products.

Rosenheim Germany. Industrial town and railway junction in Bavaria on the Inn R. 51 km (32 miles) SE of Munich. Pop. (1991) 56,700.

Manufactures chemicals, textiles. Salt works.

Roskilde Denmark. Port in Zealand at the S end of Roskilde Fiord 31 km (19 miles) WSW of Copenhagen. Pop. (1990) 49,100.

Industries inc. tanning, meat-canning. Manufactures agricultural machinery and paper.

Cap. of Denmark till 1443; in its 13th-cent. cathedral (later restored and enlarged) are the tombs of most of the Danish kings. The Peace of Roskilde (1658) between Denmark and Sweden was signed here.

Ross and Cromarty Scotland. Former county now in Highland and Western Isles.

Ross Dependency Antarctica. The New

Zealand sector of Antarctica, from 160° E to 150° W long. and S of 60° S lat., inc. the snow and ice covered mainland area, the Ross Sea and various islands, also the coastal regions of Victoria Land and King Edward VII Land. Area about 450,000 sq km (175,000 sq. miles). The huge inlet of the Ross Sea gives a relatively short approach to the South Pole, hence the use of the coast for such bases as Little America for the Byrd 1929 expedition and the McMurdo Sound bases for the Commonwealth Trans-Antarctic Expedition of 1957–8. Placed under New Zealand jurisdiction in 1923.

Rossendale England. District in SE Lancashire comprising Bacup, Haslingden and Rawtenstall.

Ross Island Antarctica. Island in the Ross Sea off Victoria Land, containing the active volcano Mt Erebus (3744 m; 12,447 ft) and Mt Terror (3279 m; 10,775 ft). Named after Sir James Ross (1800–62), explorer.

Rosslare Ireland. Small resort in Co. Wexford 8 km (5 miles) SE of Wexford. Rosslare Harbour, 5 km (3 miles) SE, is the port for ferry services to Fishguard (Wales).

Ross-on-Wye England. Market town in Herefordshire on the R. Wye 18 km (11 miles) SSE of Hereford. Pop. (1991) 9606.
Manufactures cider and leather goods.

Ross Sea Antarctica. Large inlet in the coast of the Ross Dependency between Cape Adare and Cape Colbeck, containing Ross Island.

Rostock Germany. City and port in Mecklenburg at the head of the estuary of the Warnow R. 13 km (8 miles) from the Baltic. Pop. (1995) 231,300. Outport at Warnemünde.
Railway junction. Commercial centre. Shipbuilding, fishing, fish-processing, brewing. Manufactures agricultural machinery, chemicals, textiles and electrical equipment.
Has a 14th-cent. Gothic town hall and several old churches. Birthplace of Marshal Blücher, Prussian soldier (1742–1819).

Rostov-on-Don   (Rostov-on-Donu) Russia. Cap. of the Rostov region on the Don R. 40 km (25 miles) from the mouth on the Sea of Azov. Pop. (1991) 1,027,600. Port. Railway junction.
Major industrial and commercial centre. Overseas trade handled mainly by Taganrog. Linked via the Volga–Don Canal with Volgograd. Shipbuilding. Manufactures agricultural machinery, aircraft, locomotives, chemicals, tobacco products, textiles, leather goods, food products and wire.
Inc. the former Armenian suburb of Nakhichevan. Founded 1761. Important for grain exports in the 19th cent.

Roswell USA. Town in New Mexico on the Rio Hondo 274 km (170 miles) SE of Albuquerque. Pop. (1988) 59,300.
Commercial centre in a district irrigated by artesian water. Industries inc. oil-refining and food-processing.

Rosyth Scotland. Naval base and dockyard in Fife on the Firth of Forth 3 km (2 miles) S of Dunfermline, with which it was incorporated in 1911. Pop. (1990) 12,000.

Rothamsted England. Estate 6 km (4 miles) NW of St Albans, Herts where Sir John Bennet Lawes (1816–1900) carried out his soil researches and founded (1843) the experimental station.

Rotherham England. Industrial town in South Yorkshire on the R. Don at the confluence with the R. Rother 8 km (5 miles) NE of Sheffield. Pop. (1991) 123,312.
Has important iron foundries and steel mills. Manufactures machinery, brassware and glass. Coalmining in the neighbourhood.
The 15th-cent. Chantry Bridge over the Don was rebuilt in 1930.

Rotherhithe England. District in the London borough of Southwark on the S bank of the R. Thames.

Rother River (Derbyshire–Yorkshire) England. River 34 km (21 miles) long, flowing generally N through Derbyshire and South Yorkshire and joining the R. Don at Rotherham.

Rother River (Hampshire–Sussex) England. River 39 km (24 miles) long, rising 8 km (5 miles) NNE of Petersfield in Hampshire, flowing S and then E past Midhurst in Sussex and joining the R. Arun 11 km (7 miles) N of Arundel.

Rother River (Kent–Sussex) England. River 50 km (31 miles) long, rising just W of Mayfield, flowing E and the S, forming part of the Kent–Sussex boundary and entering the English Channel near Rye. Before its diversion by the great storm of 1287, it flowed through Romney Marsh and entered the sea at New Romney.

Rothesay Scotland. Town in Argyll and Bute on the E coast of Bute island. Pop. (1991) 5264.
Fishing port and resort.
Ruins of an 11th-cent. castle.

Rothwell (Northamptonshire) England. Town in Northamptonshire 5 km (3 miles) WNW of Kettering. Pop. (1991) 7070.
Manufactures footwear, clothing, welding equipment and plastics.

Rothwell (Yorkshire) England. Town in West Yorkshire 6 km (4 miles) SE of Leeds. Pop. (1991) 7070.
Industries inc. coalmining headquarters and chemicals.

Rotorua New Zealand. Health resort and tourist centre S of L. Rotorua, North Island 193 km (120 miles) SE of Auckland. Pop. (1991) 65,096. In a district of hot springs and geysers, the water being used medicinally and for bathing; sanatorium on the S shore of the lake. Also renowned for its scenic beauty and nearby there are Maori showplace villages.

Rotterdam Netherlands. Country's chief seaport in South Holland province on the New Maas R. Pop. (1992) 589,707.
Also handles considerable overseas trade for Germany, exporting Ruhr coal as well as margarine, dairy produce from the Netherlands. Industrial centre. It has important oil refineries and shipyards. Industries inc. petrochemicals, engineering, brewing, distilling.

Manufactures margarine and other food products, soap, chemicals, bicycles, clothing and electronic equipment.
Chartered 1328. Expanded most in the 19th cent. after the construction of the New Waterway in 1872 made it accessible to the largest ocean-going vessels. It became the leading European seaport and the approach channel was enlarged in 1984. Its importance as a seaport was much increased by the development of Europoort, near the North Sea entrance to the New Waterway, in the 1960s, enabling it to secure a still greater share of the overseas trade of western Europe. Rotterdam handled 291 million tonnes of goods in 1991.
Birthplace of Erasmus, Dutch philosopher and theologian (1466–1536) and Pieter de Hooch (?1629–?84), the painter.

Rotuma ➤FIJI ISLANDS.

Roubaix France. Industrial town in the Nord department near the Belgian frontier 10 km (6 miles) NE of Lille. Pop. (1990) 90,806.
With its twin town Tourcoing, just NNW, it is the chief centre of the woollen industry. Also manufactures other textiles, clothing, carpets, textile machinery, rubber and plastic products.

Rouen France. Ancient Rotomagus. Prefecture of the Seine-Maritime department on the Seine R. 113 km (70 miles) NW of Paris. Pop. (1990) 105,470. Port.
Industrial centre. Exports mainly manufactured goods. Imports coal and oil. There is oil-refining and it manufactures textiles (esp. cotton goods), paper and chemicals. A considerable trade in wines and spirits.
Great historical interest; many of its finest buildings were damaged in World War II, inc. the 13th/16th-cent. cathedral, the 15th/16th-cent. Church of St Maclou and the Gothic Palais de Justice; the 14th/16th-cent. Church of St Ouen and the 14th-cent. Tour de la Grosse Horloge (clock tower) were unharmed. Became cap. of Normandy in the 10th cent.; here William the Conqueror died (1087). Held by the English 1419–49; Joan of Arc was tried and burned here 1431.

An important British military base in World War II. Birthplace of Corneille (1606–84) and Flaubert (1821–80).

Roulers (Flemish **Roeselare**) Belgium. Industrial town in West Flanders province 45 km (28 miles) WSW of Ghent. Pop. (1992) 53,180.

Manufactures textiles (chiefly linen) and carpets.

Rourkela (Raurkela) India. Industrial town in Orissa near the West Bengal border and 153 km (95 miles) WSW of Jamshedpur. Pop. (1991) 398,900.

Industries inc. the manufacture of iron, steel, fertilizers, cement, paper, aluminium and engineering products.

Roussillon France. Region and former province in the S, roughly corresponding to the modern department of Pyrénées-Orientales. Area 2000 sq km (770 sq. miles). Cap. Perpignan. Long in the possession of Aragón; passed to France (1659) by the Treaty of the Pyrenees.

Rouyn-Noranda Canada. Mining centre in W Quebec near the Ontario border on L. Osisko. Pop. (1985) 29,000.

Produces chiefly copper, but also gold, silver and zinc.

Founded in 1922.

Rovaniemi Finland. Town in the Lappi province on the Kemi R. 169 km (105 miles) N of Oulu, just S of the Arctic Circle. Pop. (1990) 33,500.

Commercial and winter-sports centre. Trade in timber and furs.

Destroyed in World War II but rebuilt by the Finnish architect, Alvar Aalto (1898–1976).

Rovereto Italy. Industrial town in Trento province, Trentino-Alto Adige 23 km (14 miles) SSW of Trento. Pop. (1985) 31,000.

Manufactures textiles, paper and leather goods.

Rovigo Italy. Cap. of Rovigo province, Veneto 60 km (37 miles) SW of Venice. Pop. (1985) 53,000.

Manufactures rope and furniture. Sugar-refining.

Rovno (Rivne) Ukraine. Cap. of the Rovno region 177 km (110 miles) ENE of Lvov. Pop. (1990) 239,000.

Railway junction. Industrial centre. Manufactures machinery, textiles, food products.

Passed from Poland to Russia 1793; returned to Poland 1921; ceded to the USSR 1945.

Roxburghshire Scotland. Former county now in Scottish Borders.

Royal Oak USA. Town in Michigan 19 km (12 miles) NNW of Detroit. Pop. (1990) 65,410.

Mainly residential. Manufactures tools and paint.

Royston (Hertfordshire) England. Market town in Hertfordshire 29 km (18 miles) N of Hertford. Pop. (1991) 14,087.

Ruanda-Urundi ➤RWANDA; BURUNDI.

Ruapehu New Zealand. Highest mountain in the North Island (2791 m, 9176 ft), an intermittently active volcanic peak in Tongariro National Park SSW of L. Taupo, with a crater lake at the summit.

Rub' al Khali. In Arabic 'Empty Quarter'. Desert of the Arabian peninsula, mainly in Saudi Arabia. Area about 582,750 sq km (225,000 sq. miles). Consists partly of stony desert, partly of sandy desert, with large dunes in the E. First crossed in 1931 by Bertram Thomas.

Rubicon (Italian **Rubicone**) **River** Italy. Short river in ancient Italy flowing NE to the Adriatic 13 km (8 miles) NW of Rimini. It formed the S boundary of Cisalpine Gaul and when Julius Caesar crossed it with his troops (49 BC) his action was tantamount to a declaration of war against Pompey and the Senate – hence the phrase 'crossing the Rubicon' for taking an irrevocable step.

Rubtsovsk Russia. Industrial town in the Altai Territory near the Kazakhstan border

129 km (80 miles) NNE of Semipalatinsk. Pop. (1991) 172,500.

Manufactures tractors, farm implements, and there is also flour-milling.

Ruda Śląska Poland. Town in the Katowice voivodeship just SE of Zabrze. Pop. (1992) 171,400.

There is coalmining. Manufactures chemicals.

Inc. the industrial town of Nowy Bytom.

Rudolf, Lake ►TURKANA, LAKE

Rudolstadt Germany. Town in Thuringia on the Saale R. 56 km (35 miles) WSW of Gera. Pop. (1990) 32,500.

Tourist and industrial centre. Manufactures porcelain and chemicals.

Rueil-Malmaison France. Suburb 13 km (8 miles) WNW of Paris in the Hauts-de-Seine department. Pop. (1990) 67,323.

Manufactures photographic equipment, pharmaceutical products and cement.

In a church rebuilt by Napoleon III is the tomb of the Empress Josephine; nearby is the Château Malmaison, once a favourite residence of Napoleon I and later of Josephine.

Rufiji River Tanzania. River 603 km (375 miles) long, flowing generally NE and E and entering the Indian Ocean by a delta 145 km (90 miles) S of Dar-es-Salaam. Navigable by small craft for most of its course. Chief tributary the Great Ruaha R. Rice is grown in the lower valley.

Rugby England. Town in Warwickshire near the R. Avon 18 km (11 miles) E of Coventry. Pop. (1991) 61,106.

Important railway junction. Industries inc. electronic, electrical and mechanical engineering.

Probably best known for its famous public school (founded 1567), which gained renown under the headmastership of Dr Thomas Arnold (1795–1842) and inspired Thomas Hughes's *Tom Brown's Schooldays*; here William Webb Ellis initiated the game of Rugby football (1823) when a player of normal football picked up the ball and ran

with it. Rupert Brooke, the poet (1887–1915), was born at Rugby.

Rugeley England. Market town in Staffordshire on the R. Trent 13 km (8 miles) ESE of Stafford. Pop. (1991) 22,975.

Industries inc. electronics, coalmining, engineering and there is a power station.

Rügen Germany. Island in Mecklenburg-West Pomerania in the Baltic Sea opposite Stralsund, separated from the mainland by the narrow Strelasund (Bodden). Area 927 sq km (358 sq. miles). Pop. (1985) 85,000. Chief town Bergen. Irregular in shape with a deeply indented coastline. Main occupations fishing and agriculture. Several seaside resorts. Connected to the mainland by a causeway (1936). Arkona, in the extreme N, has the remains of ancient fortifications and a temple, destroyed by the Danes in 1168. Passed to Pomerania 1325, to Sweden 1648 and to Prussia 1815.

Ruhr Germany. Leading industrial region of Germany in North Rhine-Westphalia, substantially in the valley of the Ruhr R. and based on its rich coalfields but in fact extending N to the Lippe R. and S to the Wupper R. It stretches W–E from Duisburg to Dortmund and inc. Oberhausen, Essen, Gelsenkirchen and Bochum, forming one great conurbation intersected by numerous railways, roads and waterways (inc. the Rhine–Herne and Dortmund–Ems canals). Industrial development came in the 19th cent. with large-scale coalmining and iron and steel manufacture, and much of the post-war prosperity of Germany has been due to the revival of these industries after the widespread destruction of World War II.

Ruhr River Germany. River 233 km (145 miles) long, rising in the Sauerland, flowing N and then generally W past Witten and Mülheim, and joining the Rhine R. at Duisburg.

Ruislip-Northwood England. Part of the London borough of Hillingdon. Mainly residential. Some light industries in Ruislip.

Rukwa, Lake Tanzania. Shallow lake in the

777

Rum (Rhum)

SW 129 km (80 miles) long and up to 32 km (20 miles) wide at a height of 794 m (2604 ft). Fed by the Songwe and the Momba rivers. There is no outlet.

Rum (Rhum) Scotland. Island in the Inner Hebrides (Highland) S of Skye. Area 109 sq km (42 sq. miles). Mountainous, rising to 811 m (2660 ft) in the SE.

Rumelia (Roumelia) Bulgaria/Turkey. Name formerly used for Turkish possessions in the Balkan Peninsula, inc. Thrace and Macedonia. Eastern Rumelia, an autonomous province of the Turkish Empire 1878–85, is now S Bulgaria.

Rum Jungle Australia. Uranium-mining centre in the Northern Territory about 80 km (50 miles) S of Darwin. Discovered in 1949. There are also deposits of copper, lead and silver.

Runcorn England. Industrial town in Cheshire on the R. Mersey and the Manchester Ship Canal 18 km (11 miles) ESE of Liverpool. Pop. (1991) 64,154.

Industries inc. chemicals, brewing and light engineering. Has a pipeline carrying petrochemicals from Teesside. Linked by railway bridge and high-level bridge (1961) with Widnes. Its importance dates from the construction of the Bridgewater Canal (1773).

Rungwe, Mount Tanzania. Volcanic peak 32 km (20 miles) SE of Mbeya in the S Highlands province. Height 2961 m (9713 ft) above sea level.

Runnymede England. Meadow on the S bank of the R. Thames in Egham, Surrey. Either here or on Magna Carta island, in the river, King John granted Magna Carta (1215). Presented to the nation in 1929. Nearby are the war memorial to the Commonwealth Air Forces (1953) and the national memorial to US President J. F. Kennedy (1965).

Ruse (Russe, Turkish **Ruschuk)** Bulgaria. Cap. of Ruse province on the right bank of the Danube R. opposite Giurgiu (Romania). Pop. (1991) 192,365.

Port. Industrial and commercial centre. Exports cereals. Sugar-refining, tanning, flour-milling and brewing. Manufactures textiles, soap and tobacco products.

A fortified town in Roman times. Developed as a port in the 17th cent. under Turkish rule. Ceded to Bulgaria in 1877.

Rushden England. Town in Northamptonshire 6 km (4 miles) E of Wellingborough. Pop. (1991) 23,854.

Manufactures footwear, and there is light engineering.

Russe ➤RUSE.

Russia. The Russian Federation is bounded on the W by Norway, Finland, Estonia, Latvia, Belarus and Ukraine, on the S by Georgia, Azerbaijan, the Black and Caspian Seas, Kazakhstan, China, Mongolia and North Korea, on the E by the North Pacific and Bering Strait and N by the Arctic Ocean and Barents Sea. Area 17,075,400 sq km (6,592,800 sq. miles). Pop. (1995) 147,168,000 (73 per cent urban). Life expectancy, 64 years male, 71 years female. Cap. Moscow, other important cities: St Petersburg, Novosibirsk, Nizhny Novgorod, Yekaterinburg, Samara, Omsk, Chelyabinsk, Ufa, Perm and Rostov on Don. Currency: Ruble = 100 kopecks.

Russia stretches 8000 km (5000 miles) W–E from the Gulf of Finland to the Pacific Ocean, and up to 4000 km (2500 miles) N–S from the Arctic Ocean to the Caucasus, the Caspian Sea and the Altai and Sayan Mountains and the Amur R., which form the Russian border with China and Mongolia. It covers 10 per cent of the world's land area. The W belongs to the vast plain of E Europe, separated by the Urals from the W Siberian Plain, E of which is the Central Siberian Plateau. To the E, beyond the Lena R., is a great system of fold mountains in E Siberia, inc. the Verkhoyansk and Anadyr Ranges (N) and the Yablonovy and Sikhote Alin Ranges (S). In Europe the principal rivers are the Volga, the Don and the North Dvina, and in Asia the Ob, Yenisei, Lena and Amur. L. Baikal (deepest freshwater lake in the world) lies S of the Central Siberian Plateau. A land of such enormous extent exhibits much variety in climate and natural vegetation. In the extreme N, along the Arctic coast, is a belt of tundra; S of this is a far wider belt of coniferous forests (taiga) extending W–E across the entire republic. S of the forests, in the European part and in W Siberia, is a zone of mid-latitude grasslands (steppes) inc. the N portion of the fertile black-earth region. In the extreme S there are patches of arid semi-desert and desert. The Moscow region has coniferous forests (N) and fertile steppes (S) where wheat, sugar-beet and sunflowers are cultivated. Land use: forested 45 per cent, meadows and pastures 6 per cent, agricultural and under permanent cultivation 8 per cent.

Density of pop. is highest in the W, S and central areas of European Russia. About 82 per cent of the pop. are Russians, but Russia has a great mixture of nationalities. There are 38 national minorities, inc. Tatars, Jews, Poles, Bashkirs, Udmurts, Yakuts, Ossetians, most of them living in their own Autonomous Republics or Regions. Russian is spoken by 83 per cent of the pop., Tatar by 4 per cent, Ukrainian by 3 per cent and Chuvash by 1 per cent. Believers are mainly Russian Orthodox and there are Roman Catholic, Protestant, Muslim, Jewish and Buddhist minorities.

Russia contains great mineral resources and is one of the largest producers: iron ore in the Urals, the Kerch Peninsula and Siberia; coal in the Kuznets Basin, Eastern Siberia, Urals and the sub-Moscow Basin; oil in the Urals, Azov–Black Sea area, Bashkiria and West Siberia. It also has abundant deposits of gold, platinum, copper, zinc, lead, tin and rare metals. Until 1985 the country was run as a highly centrally-planned economy dominated by bureaucratic inefficiency. Since 1991 economic reform has been accelerated and private enterprise and market prices have been introduced but the immense difficulty of restructuring plus the loss of trading patterns with former USSR partners, makes progress slow. Because of poor distribution and an unmotivated labour force acute short-

ages and high inflation have resulted. In agriculture relaxation of rules on private ownership has been introduced but because of poor harvests, transportation difficulties and lack of investment, self-sufficiency in foodstuffs has not been achieved and much grain is imported. Petroleum and oil products, machinery and transport equipment and textiles are the main exports.

Peter the Great (1682–1725) was responsible for transforming the Principality of Muscovy into Russia and for much of the early territorial expansion which continued until the 19th cent. World War I saw the collapse of the Tsarist regime and the establishment of Communism. Following the establishment of the USSR and the death of Lenin, Stalin ruled by terror aided by show trials and purges. After his death there was less repression but it was not until 1985 when Gorbachev was elected President and introduced *glasnost* (openness in public affairs) and *perestroika* (restructuring of society and the State) that profound change came about. Hardline Communists attempted a *coup* in 1991 and Gorbachev fell and the USSR broke up; the Commonwealth of Independent States was established. Yeltsin became the first-ever elected President in 1991. There is a 1068-seat Congress of Deputies which elects the 2-chamber Parliament, the Supreme Soviet, from amongst its members.

The Russian Federation consists of:

Republics (21): Adygeya, Altai, Bashkortostan, Buryatia, Chechenia, Chuvashia, Dagestan, Ingushetia, Kabardino-Balkaria, Kalmykia, Karachai-Cherkessia, Karelia, Khakassia, Komi, Mari El, Mordovia, North Ossetia (Alania), Sakha, Tatarstan, Tuva, Udmurtia.

Territories (*krai*) (6): Altai, Khabarovsk, Krasnodar, Krasnoyarsk, Primorye, Stavropol.

Provinces (*oblast*) (49): Amur, Arkhangel, Astrakhan, Belgorod, Bryansk, Chelyabinsk, Chita, Irkutsk, Ivanovo, Kaluga, Kaliningrad, Kamchatka, Kemerovo, Kirov, Kostroma, Kurgan, Kursk, Lipetsk, Magadan, Moscow, Murmansk, Nizhni Novgorod, Novgorod, Novosibirsk, Omsk, Orel, Orenburg, Penz, Perm, Pskov, Rostov, Ryazan, St Petersburg, Sakhalin, Samara, Saratov, Smolensk, Sverdlovsk, Tambov, Tomsk, Tula, Tver, Tyumen, Ulyanovsk, Vladimir, Volgograd, Vologda, Voronezh, Yaroslavl.

Autonomous Areas (*avtonomny okrug*): Agin-Buryat, Chukot, Evenki, Khanty-Mansi, Komi-Permyak, Koryak, Nenets, Taimyr (Dolgano-Nenets), Ust-Ordyn-Buryat, Yamalo-Nents.

Cities of federal status: Moscow, St Petersburg.

The Jewish Autonomous Region (Birobijan).

Rustavi Georgia. Town situated SSE of Tiflis on Kura R. Pop. (1991) 161,900.

The main industries are iron and steel milling and the manufacture of metal products. Industry is based on coal from Tkibuli and Tkvarcheli, ore from Dashkesan.

Rustenburg South Africa. Town in North West Province 96 km (60 miles) W of Pretoria near the foot of the Magaliesberg Range. Pop. (1990) 46,000.

Commercial centre in a region where citrus fruits, tobacco and cotton are grown and chrome, platinum and nickel mined. Other industries citrus-packing and tobacco-processing.

Rutba (Rutbah, Rutba Wells) Iraq. Frontier post (military, customs) with hotel on the trans-desert routes from Baghdad to Damascus and Jerusalem 378 km (235 miles) W of Baghdad in the Syrian desert. The most westerly permanently inhabited place in Iraq, with well water sufficient only for a small community.

Ruthenia Slovakia/Ukraine. Ethnological region in central Europe, mostly now incorporated in the Zakarpatskaya (Transcarpathia) region in the Ukraine. At the E extremity of Slovakia on the S flanks of the Carpathians. Inc. the small towns of Uzhgorod and Mukachevo. The mountain slopes are forested.

Cereals, potatoes cultivated on the plains. Lumbering and agriculture, the main occu-

pations, have always been notoriously primitive.

Belonged to Hungary from the late 14th cent. to 1918 and to Czechoslovakia 1918–39; during the latter period many improvements in the economy were made. Again occupied by Hungary in 1939 but was ceded to the USSR in 1945. The majority of the people are Ruthenians, closely related to the Ukrainians.

Rutherglen Scotland. Industrial town on the R. Clyde, now part of Glasgow.

Industries inc. engineering and the manufacture of chemicals, tubes, wire ropes, bolts and paper.

Here was signed the treaty between the Scots and the English (1297) which led to the betrayal of Wallace.

Ruthin Wales. Town in Denbighshire on the R. Clwyd 11 km (7 miles) SSE of Denbigh. Pop. (1991) 5029. Ruined 13th/14th-cent. castle and a 14th-cent. church.

Ruthven ➤KINGUSSIE.

Ruthwell Scotland. Village in Dumfries and Galloway near the Solway Firth 14 km (9 miles) SE of Dumfries. Well-known for the runic cross, probably of the 8th cent., now in the parish church.

Rutland England. Historic county in the Midlands E of Leicestershire abolished in 1974 when it became part of Leicestershire, re-instated as a county in 1997. Area 394 sq km (152 sq. miles). Pop. (1995) 34,600. County town Oakham. Industries inc. breweries, cement, plastics, tourism, agriculture and clothing.

Rutland USA. City situted N of Bennington on Otter Creek, Vermont. Pop. (1990) 20,000.

Railway centre and winter sports resort situated between the Green and Taconic Mountains. Industries inc. marble-cutting, food-processing, and the manufacture of machinery, aircraft parts, tools, scales, cement products and timber products.

Ruvuma (Rovuma) River Mozambique/

Tanzania. River 800 km (500 miles) long rising in S Tanzania E of L. Malawi (Nyasa), flowing generally E (forming most of the Mozambique–Tanzania frontier) and entering the Indian Ocean just NW of Cape Delgado.

Ruwenzori Democratic Republic of the Congo/Uganda. Mountain massif 113 km (70 miles) long and up to 48 km (30 miles) wide on the Democratic Republic of the Congo/Uganda frontier between L. Albert and L. Edward, rising in Mt Stanley (Margherita) to 5110 m (16,763 ft). By day the higher parts are almost completely enveloped in cloud; the climate is extremely humid. Clearly marked zones of natural vegetation, from dense equatorial forests at the foot to snowfields and glaciers in the upper regions. Discovered (1889) by Sir Henry Stanley. The main peaks were scaled by the Duke of Abruzzi's expedition (1906). Generally identified with the 'Mountains of the Moon' which were once believed to be the source of the Nile.

Rwanda. Republic in central Africa, bounded by Uganda in the N, Tanzania in the E, Burundi in the S and the Democratic Republic of the Congo in the W. Area 25,271 sq km (9757 sq. miles). Pop. (1995) 6,700,000 (5 per cent urban). Life expectancy, 46 years male, 49 years female. Cap. Kigali. Other towns Ruhengeri, Butare, Gisenyi. Currency: Rwanda franc. A mountainous state at a height of 1200–1800 m (3936–5904 ft) with most of the W boundary formed by L. Kivu. Land use: forested 23 per cent, meadows and pastures 19 per cent, agricultural and under permanent cultivation 47 per cent. Kinyarwanda, the lang. of the whole pop., and French are the official lang. and Kiswahili is spoken in commercial centres. Hutus are 90 per cent of the pop., with Tutsis 9 and the Twa (pygmy) 1 per cent. About 65 per cent of the pop. is Roman Catholic, animists 17 per cent, Protestant 9 per cent and Muslim 9 per cent.

Subsistence farming dominates the economy. Chief crops are maize, manioc and beans; long-horned cattle are raised. The main cash crops are coffee, tea and pyrethrum and there is an experimental rice-growing project. Minerals inc. tin, cassiterite and wolframite that are mined E of L. Kivu; natural gas is found under the lake and is being exploited.

From the 16th cent. Rwanda was part of the wider Tutsi kingdom and inc. present-day Burundi. It was part of German East Africa from 1899 to 1917 and then Belgian-administered, as part of Ruanda–Urundi, under a League of Nations mandate (1923) and as a UN Trust Territory (1946–62). A referendum (1961) declared against the retention of the monarchy and a republic was proclaimed. Full independence was achieved in 1962. The invasion of the country by Tutsi émigrés (1963–4) caused panic which resulted in the massacre of thousands of Tutsi. Again in 1990–1 Tutsi refugees invaded and occupied part of the N. Fighting continued in 1992–9. About 1 million Rwandans were killed in 1994 through genocide and civil war and about 2 million fled to neighbouring countries. A new Constitution was promulgated in 1991 which allows for a multi-party political system. The President appoints a Council of Ministers. Legislative power is exercised by a 70-member National Development Council elected for 5 years by a compulsory universal adult suffrage.

Ryazan Russia. Formerly (till 1778) Pereyaslavl-Ryazanski. Cap. of the Ryazan region near the Oka R. 185 km (115 miles) SE of Moscow. Pop. (1991) 527,200.

Industries inc. flour-milling and tanning. Manufactures agricultural machinery, footwear, clothing and chemicals.

Originally founded in the 11th cent. about 48 km (30 miles) SE, cap. of the Ryazan principality; moved to its present site in the 13th cent.

Rybinsk Russia. River port and industrial town in the Yaroslavl region on the Volga R. near the point where it issues from the Rybinsk Reservoir. Pop. (1991) 252,000.

Site of dam and hydroelectric station. Industries inc. shipbuilding, flour-milling, tanning and sawmilling. Manufactures matches and wire. Trade in grain, petroleum and timber. Linked with St Petersburg by the Mariinsk canal system.

Rybinsk Reservoir Russia. Large artificial reservoir 113 km (70 miles) long and up to 48 km (30 miles) wide, formed (1941) by the damming of the upper Volga R. at the confluence with the Suda and the Sheksna rivers.

Rydal England. Village in Cumbria just NW of Ambleside on the small lake Rydal Water. Has Rydal Mount, English poet, William Wordsworth's home from 1813 till his death.

Ryde England. Seaside resort on the NE coast of the Isle of Wight overlooking Spithead 8 km (5 miles) SW of Portsmouth. Pop. (1991) 20,502. On the site of the old village of La Rye or La Riche. Nearby are the ruins of Quarr Abbey (founded 1132).

Rye England. Town in East Sussex on the R. Rother 16 km (10 miles) NE of Hastings. Pop. (1991) 3708. Market town and tourist centre, built on a hill. Has the 12th-cent. Ypres Tower, the remains of a 14th-cent. Augustinian friary, old timbered houses and

steep cobbled streets. Was a member of the Cinque Port of Hastings, but declined in the 16th cent. as the sea began to recede. Birthplace of John Fletcher (1579–1625), the dramatist.

Ryukyu Islands Japan. Archipelago SW of Japan between Kyushu and Taiwan in a chain 1130 km (700 miles) long. Area 2255 sq km (871 sq. miles). Pop. (1991) 1,229,000. Larger islands mountainous and volcanic.

Principal crops sweet potatoes and sugarcane. Main island Okinawa.

Japanese from 1879. After World War II they came under US jurisdiction. The Amami–Oshima group (N) was returned to Japan in 1953, Okinawa in 1972.

Rzeszów Poland. Industrial town, cap. of the Rzeszów voivodeship, on the Wislok R. 148 km (92 miles) E of Cracow. Pop. (1992) 153,900.

Manufactures aircraft engines, agricultural machinery and bricks.

Rzhev Russia. Town and river port in the Tver region on the Volga R. 120 km (75 miles) SW of Tver. Pop. (1970) 61,000.

Railway junction. Sawmilling and distilling. Manufactures agricultural machinery, paper and linen.

S

Saale River Germany. River 426 km (265 miles) long, sometimes known as the Saxonian (Thuringian) Saale to distinguish it from the much shorter Franconian Saale; rises in the Fichtelgebirge and flows generally N past Hof, Saalfeld, Rudolstadt, Jena and Halle to join the Elbe R. 21 km (13 miles) NE of Bernburg. Navigable for 193 km (120 miles) to Naumburg.

Saalfeld Germany. Town in the Gera district on the Saale R. Pop. (1989) 32,300.

In an iron-mining region. Manufactures machine-tools, textiles and electrical equipment.

An ancient town, it has a 13th-cent. Gothic church and a 16th-cent. Gothic town hall.

Saarbrücken Germany. Cap. of Saarland on the Saar R. Pop. (1991) 191,694.

Industrial centre in an important coal-mining region. Manufactures inc. iron and steel, machinery, cement, clothing, paper and soap. There is also brewing and printing.

The bridge across the Saar was here in Roman times – hence its name. Passed from France to Prussia 1815. Became cap. of Saarland 1919.

Saaremaa Estonia. Island in the Baltic Sea at the entrance to the Gulf of Riga. Area 2720 sq km (1050 sq. miles). Chief town Kuressaare on the S coast, a port and resort. Low-lying. Main occupations farming and fishing. Passed to Denmark (1561), Sweden (1645), Russia (1721) and Estonia (1918).

Saarland Germany. *Land* bordering on France (S and SW) and Luxembourg (W). Area 2570 sq km (992 sq. miles). Pop. (1991) 1,073,000. Cap. Saarbrücken.

Chiefly important for its rich coalfield, on which an important iron and steel industry is dependent, iron ore being imported from Lorraine. Other industries inc. the manufacture of vehicles, electrical products, vehicle components.

Drained by the Saar R. Chief towns Saarbrücken and Saarlouis. In 1919 the Saar Territory was placed under League of Nations control, France being accorded the right to exploit the coalmines for 15 years. As the result of a plebiscite it was returned to Germany in 1935. After World War II it was in the French occupation zone, in 1947 gained independence (inc. economic union with France) and in 1957 was returned to Germany.

Saarlauten ➤ SAARLOUIS.

Saarlouis Germany. Formerly Sarrelouis and (1936–45) Saarlauten. Industrial town in Saarland on the Saar R. 21 km (13 miles) NW of Saarbrücken. Pop. (1970) 36,350.

Manufactures steel, glass and pottery. Coalmining in the neighbourhood.

Founded (1681) by Louis XIV and named after him Sarrelouis. It was ceded to Prussia 1815. Birthplace of the French soldier Marshal Ney (1769–1815).

Saar (Fr. **Sarre**) **River** France/Germany. River 240 km (149 miles) long, rising in the Vosges and flowing generally N through the Moselle and Bas-Rhin departments (France) past Sarreguemines (head of navigation): then crosses the German border past Saarbrücken and turns NW through Saarland to join the Moselle R. 10 km (6 miles) SW of Trier.

Saba Arabia. Ancient kingdom in SW Arabia, the biblical Sheba, corresponding to the modern Yemen, Asir. The Sabaeans were known in the 8th cent. BC; their cap. was Marib and another important city was Sana. In the 4th cent. AD they were conquered by the Ethiopians. The last native king was killed AD 525.

Saba (Netherlands Antilles) ➤NETHERLANDS ANTILLES.

Sabadell Spain. Industrial town in Barcelona province, Catalonia 18 km (11 miles) N of Barcelona. Pop. (1991) 184,460.

Important textile industry. Also manufactures textile machinery, dyes, paper and fertilizers. Other industries inc. wine-making, flour-milling, distilling and sawmilling.

Sabah Malaysia. Until 1963 known as North Borneo. Most E state of Malaysia, comprising the N part of Borneo with offshore islands, inc. Labuan. Area 73,620 sq km (24,425 sq. miles). Pop. (1990) 1,669,000. Cap. Kota Kinabalu. Largely mountainous, rising to 4094 m (13,431 ft) in Mt Kinabalu, the highest peak in Borneo. Climate hot and humid, with a heavy rainfall. Chief products and exports timber and crude oil. Principal towns Kota Kinabalu, Tawau and Sandakan. ➤➤FEDERATION OF MALAYSIA.

Sabará Brazil. Once an important goldmining centre in Minas Gerais 13 km (8 miles) ENE of Belo Horizonte. Pop. (1985) 42,000. Remains a picturesque relic of an 18th-cent. mining town with interesting old churches and a museum. Rich iron deposits exist nearby.

Sabine Hills (Italian **Monti Sabini**) Italy. Range in the Apennines NE of Rome, rising to 1369 m (4490 ft) in Monte Pellecchia.

Sabine River USA. River 800 km (500 miles) long, rising in NE Texas, flowing generally SE and S, forming the boundary between Texas and Louisiana below Logansport (Louisiana) and discharging through the Sabine Lake into the Gulf of Mexico. A canal system links it with the Mississippi R. at New Orleans.

Sable Island Canada. Crescent-shaped sandy island in the Atlantic 32 km (20 miles) long and 1.6 km (1 mile) wide 290 km (180 miles) ESE of Halifax in Nova Scotia. Scene of many shipwrecks; long called 'the grave-yard of the Atlantic'. It is the exposed part of a large sandbank or shoal and is gradually shrinking.

Sache ➤YARKAND.

Sachsen ➤SAXONY.

Sackville Canada. Town situated SE of Moncton, New Brunswick in an area of reclaimed coastal marshes. Pop. (1990) 6000.

Industries inc. woodworking, printing, and the manufacture of leather, paper and plastic products, stoves and machinery.

Sacramento USA. State cap. of California (since 1854) and river port on the Sacramento R. 120 km (75 miles) NE of San Francisco. Pop. (1990) 369,365.

Food-processing plants: large packing and canning factories for fruit, vegetables, dairy products. Industries inc. food-processing, weapons, defence systems and high technology.

Chief building the State Capitol (1874). First settled 1839. Suffered disastrous floods three times and a great fire between 1849 and 1853. Terminus of the Pony Express (1860) and the first transcontinental railway (1869).

Sacramento River USA. Longest and most important river in California 628 km (390 miles) long, rising in the Klamath Mountains, flowing generally S and emptying into San Francisco Bay. The Sacramento valley (N) and the San Joaquin valley (S) form California's great Central Valley, irrigated by the Shasta Dam (on the upper Sacramento) and the Keswick Dam (below the Shasta). The two dams also play a vital part in supplying the Central Valley with hydroelectric power and in flood control. Chief tributaries the McCloud and the Pit, from the Cascade Range, the Feather and the American, from the Sierra Nevada.

Saffron Walden England. Market town in Essex 23 km (14 miles) SSE of Cambridge. Pop. (1990) 14,500.

Industries inc. the manufacture of scientific instruments and engineering.

Noted for saffron culture from Edward

III's reign till *c.* 1770. The 15th-cent. church contains the tomb of Lord Audley, chancellor to Henry VIII. Remains of a 12th-cent. castle. Audley End, a Jacobean mansion built by the 1st Earl of Suffolk on the ruins of an ancient abbey, is 1.6 km (1 mile) SW.

Safi Morocco. Atlantic seaport 129 km (80 miles) WNW of Marrakesh. Pop. (1982) 197,309. Linked by rail with Youssoufia (phosphate mining) and the Ben Guérir junction on the main Marrakesh–Casablanca line.

Exports large quantities of phosphates. Important fishing port. Industries inc. sardine-canning, boatbuilding, pottery manufacture, chemicals and fertilizers.

Sagamihara Japan. Town situated NW of Yokohama, Honshu. Pop. (1991) 542,000.

Industries inc. machinery, agriculture and electronics.

Sagar India. Town in N Madhya Pradesh 145 km (90 miles) NW of Jubbulpore, picturesquely situated in the Vindhya Hills at a height of 510 m (1673 ft) beside a small lake. Pop. (1991) 220,000.

Trade in wheat, cotton, oilseeds. Manufactures steel utensils, engineering products, and processes tendu leaf and beedi.

Saginaw USA. Town in Michigan on the Saginaw R. 24 km (15 miles) above the mouth (on L. Huron). Pop. (1985) 73,081.

Commercial and industrial centre in an agricultural region. Oil wells, salt and coal deposits nearby. Manufactures machinery, tools, vehicle components, furniture, paper and food products.

Saginaw River USA. River 35 km (22 miles) long in Michigan, flowing generally NNE past Saginaw and Bay City and entering Saginaw Bay (a SW arm of L. Huron).

Sagres Portugal. Port situated SE of Cape St Vincent in Faro district. Henry the Navigator (1394–1460) founded a school of navigation here in 1416 and the voyages of the Portuguese navigator, Vasco da Gama (1469–1525), were planned here.

Saguenay River Canada. River 764 km (475 miles) long in Quebec, its farthest headstream the Peribonca R., leaving L. St John by the Grande Décharge and the Petite Décharge (which later unite), flowing ESE and entering the St Lawrence R. near Tadoussac. Important hydroelectric power stations at Isle Maligne and Chute à Caron (above Chicoutimi), on the Grande Décharge. Widens to as much as 3 km (2 miles) below Chicoutimi, flowing between banks rising to over 480 m (1574 ft) in Cape Trinity and Cape Eternity.

Sagunto Spain. Ancient Saguntum. Formerly Murviedro. Town in Valencia 26 km (16 miles) NNE of Valencia. Pop. (1991) 55,416.

Manufactures iron and steel, hardware, textiles, brandy and tiles. Exports iron ore.

Was allied to Rome and was taken by the Carthaginians under Hannibal (219–218 BC) at the start of the 2nd Punic War. Nearby are the remains of a large Roman theatre.

Sahara N Africa. The largest desert in the world. Area over 9,065,000 sq km (3,500,000 sq. miles). Extends across N Africa from the Atlantic to the Red Sea 5000 km (3000 miles); the E part inc. the Libyan Desert (W of the Nile) and the Arabian Desert and the Nubian Desert (E of the Nile). Bounded by the Atlas Mountains in Morocco, Algeria, Tunisia and by the Mediterranean Sea in Libya, Egypt (N) and merging into Sudan and the basin of the Niger R. (S). Mainly plateau, at a height of 300 m (984 ft), surmounted by the Ahaggar Mountains, the Aïr Highlands and the Tibesti Highlands, descending in NE Algeria and Tunisia to a depression (partly below sea level) containing the salt lakes Chott Melrhir and Chott Djerid. Annual rainfall (irregular, in short violent thunderstorms) less than 25 cm. (10 ins.) Daily range of temperature extreme, sometimes from well over 35°C (95°F) by day to near freezing at night. Hot dust-laden winds (e.g. sirocco, khamsin) originate in the desert. Three types of surface: *erg* (shifting sand dunes), *hammada* (rock), *reg* (boulders and stones). Wind erosion is considerable. No permanent streams (apart from the Nile and the Niger, near the E and the S flanks respectively). In the oases (which derive water from wadis or from subterranean sources) date palms abound and cereals, Mediterranean fruits and vegetables are grown; chief export dates. Elsewhere vegetation is meagre or absent. Mining and exploring for oil and natural gas has taken place in recent years.

About 2 million live in the Sahara, mainly farmers in the oases and a smaller number of nomadic herdsmen. Along the S margins the inhabitants are mainly Sudanese Negroes; elsewhere Arabs and Berber predominate. Among the nomadic peoples, the Berber Tuareg ('people of the veil') of the Ahaggar and Aïr highlands are noteworthy. The Tibesti region (inhabited by the Tibbu) is one of the few parts where Blacks form the majority.

Saharanpur India. Commercial town and railway junction in NW Uttar Pradesh 153 km (95 miles) NNE of Delhi. Pop. (1991) 374,000.

Trade in grain and sugar-cane. Industries inc. railway engineering, paper-milling, wood-carving. Manufactures cigarettes and hosiery.

Sahel ►SAHARA.

Saida (Sidon) Lebanon. Small seaport on the Mediterranean 40 km (25 miles) SSW of Beirut. Pop. (1990) 100,000.

Exports citrus fruits and apricots. Has an oil refinery, handling petroleum received by pipeline from Saudi Arabia.

Sidon was once the chief city of Phoenicia, older than Tyre, which it colonized. Excavations from the mid 19th cent. onwards revealed many valuable sarcophagi in a Phoenician necropolis. In ancient times the city was an important commercial centre, but it had a stormy history, being taken by Assyrians, Babylonians, Persians, Romans, Crusaders and Muslims. In recent times it has been superseded by Beirut.

Saigon ►HO CHI MINH CITY.

St Agnes ►ISLES OF SCILLY.

St Albans England. Cathedral city and market town in Hertfordshire 31 km (19 miles) NNW of London. Pop. (1991) 61,528.

Printing. Manufactures hosiery, electrical and electronic equipment and rubber products.

Just W, across the R. Ver, is the site of the Roman city of Verulamium. The Benedictine abbey was founded (793) by Offa, King of Mercia, in honour of St Alban (after whom the town was named), martyred here c. 303. The church (built partly with bricks and stone taken from Verulamium), consecrated 1116, is still largely early Norman; much restored 1871–85, it became a cathedral in 1877. The 10th-cent. Church of St Michael has the tomb of Francis Bacon, Viscount St Albans. The school (also originally founded in the 10th cent.) was refounded under Edward VI. Scene of a Yorkist victory (1455) and a Lancastrian victory (1461) in the Wars of the Roses.

St Andrews Scotland. Market town in Fife on the North Sea 16 km (10 miles) SE of Dundee. Pop. (1989) 14,000. Resort. Has the Royal and Ancient Golf Club (founded 1754), headquarters of the game.

The economy depends on tourism and the manufacture of textiles.

The university (founded 1411) is the oldest in Scotland. The town church was originally founded in the 12th cent. There are ruins of a cathedral (founded 1159) and a 13th-cent. castle. Created a royal burgh 1124.

St Asaph Wales. Cathedral city in Denbighshire 8 km (5 miles) SSE of Rhyl. Pop. (1991) 3399. The cathedral, largely destroyed by Owen Glendower (1402) was restored in the 19th cent. It was dedicated to a 6th-cent. bishop here.

St Augustine USA. Holiday resort in Florida 60 km (37 miles) SSE of Jacksonville. Pop. (1985) 11,985. Oldest town in the USA; founded 1565, by Pedro Menéndez de Avilés.

St Austell England. Market town in Cornwall 19 km (12 miles) ENE of Truro and NW of St Austell Bay. Pop. (1991) 21,622.

Chiefly important as the centre of the

china clay industry; large white refuse heaps in the neighbourhood. Other industries inc. brewing.

St Barthélemy West Indies. Island situated NW of Guadeloupe of which it is a dependency. Area 21 sq km (8 sq. miles). Pop. (1990) 5038. Chief town Gustavia. Hilly, rising to 302 m (990 ft) above sea level.

Produces cotton, fruit, livestock, fish and salt, all in small quantities.

St Bernard Passes. 1. Great St Bernard: Alpine pass (2473 m; 8113 ft) on the Swiss–Italian border, on the road between Martigny and Aosta over the SW Pennine Alps. The hospice here, founded c. 1050 by St Bernard of Menthon, was run by Augustinian monks who became famous for their rescue of travellers, assisted by the St Bernard dogs which were reared for this work. The pass was crossed by Napoleon I and his army (1800). The Great St Bernard road tunnel, 5.6 km (3½ miles) long, was completed in 1962, opened to traffic 1964.

2. Little St Bernard: Alpine pass (2188 m; 7178 ft) on the Franco–Italian border S of the Mont Blanc massif on the road between Bourg St Maurice and Aosta. Less frequented than the Great St Bernard Pass. The hospice here was also founded by St Bernard of Menthon. This was probably the pass crossed by Hannibal when he invaded Italy.

St Boniface Canada. Industrial town in Manitoba on the Red R. opposite Winnipeg. Pop. (1971) 46,714.

Meat-packing, flour-milling, oil-refining. Manufactures paint and soap.

Centre of French Canadian culture in Manitoba. Roman Catholic cathedral. Founded by missionaries 1818.

St Brieuc France. Prefecture of the Côtes-du-Nord department near the English Channel 93 km (58 miles) NW of Rennes. Pop. (1968) 49,305.

Manufactures brushes, hosiery and furniture. Fishing from its port, Le Légué.

Cathedral (13th-cent., restored). Founded by and named after St Briocus, a Welsh missionary who came here in the 5th cent.

St Catharines Canada. Industrial town in S Ontario on the Welland Canal 53 km (33 miles) ESE of Hamilton. Pop. (1991) 129,300.

Centre of a fruit-growing region; popularly called 'the Garden City'. Industries inc. shipbuilding, vehicle components, food-processing, engineering, fruit and vegetable canning.

St Charles USA. Town situated NW of St Louis, Missouri on the N bank of the Missouri R. Pop. (1990) 54,555.

Centre of an agricultural area. Industries inc. sawmilling, and it manufactures steel dies, railway stock, diesel engines, metal products and footwear. Deposits of sand, coal and gravel nearby.

Noted as the first permanent white settlement on the Missouri R., made by French traders in 1769.

St Christopher ➤ST KITTS.

St Clair, Lake Canada/USA. Lake on the border between S Ontario (Canada) and SE Michigan (USA). Area 1119 sq km (432 sq. miles). Fed by the St Clair R. from L. Huron, drained by the Detroit R. to L. Erie. The St Clair R. has a deepened channel for shipping.

St Clair Shores USA. Town in Michigan on the W shore of L. St Clair 19 km (12 miles) NE of Detroit. Pop. (1990) 68,107. Mainly residential. Boating centre.

St Cloud France. Suburb of W Paris, in the Hauts-de-Seine department on a hill overlooking the Seine R. Pop. (1968) 28,016. Has the Sèvres porcelain factory, but is largely residential. The famous 17th-cent. palace was destroyed in the siege of Paris (1870). Named after St Clodvald (Cloud), who built a monastery here in the 6th cent.

St Cloud USA. Commercial and industrial town in Minnesota on the Mississippi R. 96 km (60 miles) NW of Minneapolis. Pop. (1970) 36,691.

Centre of an agricultural region. Produces canned vegetables and beverages. Railway engineering. Granite quarried nearby for buildings and monuments.

St Croix West Indies. Largest of the US Virgin Is. Area 212 sq km (82 sq. miles). Pop. (1990) 50,139. Cap. Christiansted.

Tourist centre. Chief occupations cattle-rearing, cultivation of sugar-cane, vegetables and rum-distilling.

St Cyr-l'École (St Cyr) France. Small town in the Yvelines department 5 km (3 miles) W of Versailles. Once famous for the military school, founded (1808) by Napoleon.

St David's Wales. Village and cathedral city in Pembrokeshire 21 km (13 miles) WNW of Haverfordwest. Pop. (1991) 1627. Famous for its cathedral, built from *c.* 1180 onwards partly from local sandstone; in medieval times an important place of pilgrimage. Nearby are the ruins of the 14th-cent. Bishop Gower's palace.

St Denis France. Industrial suburb N of Paris on the Seine R. in the Seine-St Denis department. Pop. (1990) 90,806.

Manufactures railway rolling-stock, barges, boilers, diesel engines, chemicals, glass, pottery and liqueurs.

The 12th/13th-cent. Gothic abbey church contains the tombs of many French kings, inc. Louis XII, Francis I and Henry II. The 7th-cent. Benedictine abbey was founded by Dagobert at the place where St Denis was buried.

St Denis (Réunion) ➤RÉUNION.

St Dizier France. Town in the Haute-Marne department on the Marne R. and the Marne–Saône Canal 100 km (62 miles) SE of Reims. Pop. (1968) 35,742.

Manufactures nails, wire, tools and hardware.

St Elias Mountains USA. Mountains in SE Alaska and SW Yukon, continued NW by the Wrangell Mountains. Highest peaks Mt Logan (6050 m; 19,849 ft, the second highest mountain in North America) and Mt St Elias (5489 m; 18,008 ft). The flow of ice from the Mt St Elias area forms the world's largest icefield outside polar regions, and inc. the great Malaspina glacier (area 3885 sq km; 1500 sq. miles) extending 80 km (50 miles) along the seaward base.

Saintes, Les (Îles des Saintes) West Indies. Archipelago of islets, between Dominica and Guadeloupe, a dependency of Guadeloupe (French). Area 14 sq km (5½ sq. miles). Pop. (1990) 2036. Of volcanic origin.

Main occupations stock-rearing and fishing. The two principal islands are Terre-de-Bas and Terre-de-Haut.

St Étienne France. Prefecture of the Loire department on the Furens R. 50 km (31 miles) SW of Lyon. Pop. (1990) 201,695.

Industries inc. precision engineering, plastics and textiles.

Has a School of Mines founded in 1816. The manufacture of firearms dates from the 16th cent. and that of ribbons, trimmings, etc. from the early 17th cent.

St Eustatius ➤NETHERLANDS ANTILLES.

St Francis River USA. River 756 km (470 miles) long, flowing generally S through SE Missouri and NE Arkansas, forming part of the boundary between the two states and joining the Mississippi R. 80 km (50 miles) SW of Memphis (Tennessee).

St Gall (Ger. **Sankt Gallen**) Switzerland. 1. Canton in the NE bordering N (in part) on L. Constance and E. on Austria and Liechtenstein. Area 2014 sq km (778 sq. miles). Pop. (1991) 420,268. Mountainous in the S.

Largely industrial in the centre and N, producing glass and metal products.

The people are almost all German-speaking and the majority are Catholics.

2. Cap. of St Gall canton in the N. Pop. (1988) 72,600.

Industrial town. Important cotton industry. Also manufactures chemicals, chocolate and biscuits.

Its abbey has a famous library with valuable incunabula and early manuscripts. The town grew up round the Benedictine abbey, which was founded in the 8th cent. on the site of the cell of the 7th-cent. Irish hermit, St Gall. In 1805 the abbey was secularized.

St George's ▸GRENADA.

St George's Channel (Bismarck Archipelago) ▸NEW IRELAND.

St George's Channel British Isles. Channel linking the Irish Sea and the Atlantic Ocean, separating SE Ireland from Wales, at its narrowest only 74 km (46 miles) wide.

St Germain-en-Laye (St Germain) France. Town in the Yvelines department, an outer suburb 19 km (12 miles) WNW of Paris on the Seine R. Pop. (1968) 36,251. Largely residential and a favourite resort for Parisians.

Manufactures musical instruments, hosiery and chocolate.

Just N is the Forest of St Germain (area 39 sq km; 15 sq. miles) with the famous terrace overlooking the Seine. The Treaty of St Germain (1919) between the Allied powers and Austria was signed here. Birthplace of the composer, Claude Debussy (1862–1918).

St Gotthard Pass Switzerland. Important pass (2109 m, 6917 ft) over the Lepontine Alps on the road from Andermatt to Airolo which was constructed 1820–30. Below the pass is the St Gotthard railway tunnel (constructed 1872–80), at 15 km (9¼ miles) the second longest in the Alps and reaching a maximum height of 1155 m (6917 ft) on the main Lucerne–Milan line. In 1980 a new road tunnel was opened.

St Helena South Atlantic Ocean. Volcanic island and United Kingdom Overseas Territory 1930 km (1200 miles) W of the coast of Angola. Area 122 sq km (47 sq. miles). Pop. (1992) 5700. Cap. and port Jamestown. Mountainous, rising to 825 m (2709 ft) in Diana's Peak; deep gorges are cut into the slopes by rapidly flowing streams. Climate tempered by the SE Trade Wind. Dependencies are Ascension Island (1922) and Tristan da Cunha, Gough Island, Nightingale Island and Inaccessible Island (1938). Fishing and tourism are the main industries.

Discovered (1502) by the Portuguese. Became famous as the place of exile of Napoleon from 1815 till his death (1821). Declined as a port of call with the opening of the Suez Canal (1869), but is an important cable station.

St Helens England. Industrial town and unitary authority 16 km (10 miles) ENE of Liverpool. Pop. (1991) 106,293.

The chief centre in England for the manufacture of crown, plate and sheet glass. Also produces chemicals, pharmaceutical products and soap. Iron-founding; coal-mining in the neighbourhood.

St Helier Channel Islands. Chief town of Jersey on the S coast and on the E side of St Aubin's Bay. Pop. (1971) 26,418.

Important tourist resort. Market town. Trade in early potatoes, vegetables and cattle.

On a rocky islet W of the harbour is the 16th-cent. Elizabeth Castle, in which Prince Charles, later Charles II, took refuge in 1646 and 1649. In the town is the house where the French poet and author, Victor Hugo (1802–85) lived (1852–5). Near the castle is the Hermitage, with the remains of the reputed cell of St Helier.

St Hyacinthe Canada. Industrial town in Quebec on the Yamaska R. 51 km (32 miles) ENE of Montreal. Pop. (1986) 38,603.

Manufactures woollen goods, footwear, furniture and organs.

Roman Catholic cathedral.

St Ives (Cambridgeshire) England. Market town on the Great Ouse 8 km (5 miles) E of Huntingdon. Pop. (1991) 16,510.

Industries inc. food-processing, plastics and engineering.

A picturesque 15th-cent. bridge across the river carries a chapel, restored in 1689.

St Ives (Cornwall) England. Holiday resort on St Ives Bay 11 km (7 miles) NNE of Penzance. Pop. (1991) 10,092. Fishing port. Has long been a haunt of artists. Believed to take its name from St Ia, an Irish martyr who came to Cornwall in the 5th cent.

St Jean (St Johns) Canada. Town in

Quebec on the Richelieu R. 32 km (20 miles) SE of Montreal. Pop. (1986) 34,745.

Manufactures textiles, paper and sewing-machines.

Terminus of the first Canadian railway, to Montreal (1836).

St Jean de Luz France. Fishing port and seaside resort in the Pyrénées-Atlantiques department on the Bay of Biscay 19 km (12 miles) SW of Bayonne. Pop. (1968) 10,206.

Its fishing vessels were the first to sail to the Newfoundland cod-fishing grounds (1520).

St John Canada. Largest city in New Brunswick at the mouth of the St John R. on the Bay of Fundy. Pop. (1991) 74,969.

Important seaport, esp. in winter, when it remains ice-free. One of the world's largest dry docks, which can accommodate the largest ships. Exports timber as well as grain and minerals. Manufactures cotton goods, bricks and tiles, wood-pulp and paper. Oil and sugar refining. Terminus of the Canadian Pacific Railway and the Canadian National Railway.

Named after the river. After a fire in 1877, when over half the city was destroyed, the wooden buildings were then replaced by stone and brick.

St John, Lake Canada. Lake in SE Quebec, fed by the Peribonca and other rivers. Area 971 sq km (375 sq. miles). Only outlet the Saguenay R., by two channels (Grande Décharge, Petite Décharge). The district has many paper mills and is a popular tourist region.

St John Island ➤VIRGIN ISLANDS OF THE USA.

St John River Canada/USA. River 673 km (418 miles) long, rising in several branches in Maine (USA) and Quebec, flowing NE and then E, forming part of the international frontier between Maine and New Brunswick, then turning generally SE through New Brunswick, past Fredericton, to enter the Bay of Fundy at St John. Navigable for small vessels as far as Fredericton. Near St John are the famous Reversing Falls, where the strong tides of the Bay of Fundy cause the river to reverse its flow at high tide. Discovered (1604) by Champlain and de Monts.

St John's (Newfoundland) Canada. Provincial cap. of Newfoundland on the E coast of the Avalon Peninsula in the SE. Pop. (1991) 95,770. The island's largest city and chief seaport. The harbour is approached through The Narrows, flanked by cliffs 150–180 m (492–590 ft) high.

Centre of the Newfoundland fishing fleet; principal catch cod and herring. Fish-processing. Manufactures fishing equipment, marine engines, textiles, footwear and paper. Industries inc. retail services, construction, transport and government services.

First settled by Devonshire fishermen in the 16th cent. Sir Humphrey Gilbert landed here and claimed Newfoundland for Queen Elizabeth I in 1583. The city was devastated by fires in 1816, 1846 and 1892; stone buildings then replaced wooden.

St Johns (Quebec, Canada) ➤ST JEAN.

St John's (West Indies) ➤ANTIGUA.

St John's Wood England. Residential district in the London borough of the City of Westminister just W of Regent's Park. Contains Lord's cricket ground, headquarters of the MCC, authority for the game.

St Joseph (Missouri) USA. River port on the Missouri R. 77 km (48 miles) NNW of Kansas City. Pop. (1990) 71,852.

Trade in livestock. Industries inc. meat-packing, flour-milling. The E terminus of the Pony Express (1860) and later became an important railway centre.

St Joseph River USA. River 338 km (210 miles) long, rising in the S of Michigan, flowing generally W, with a southward curve into the N of Indiana and discharging into L. Michigan at St Joseph.

St Just (St Just-in-Penwith) England. Market town in Cornwall 11 km (7 miles) W of Penzance. Pop. (1989) 4072. Has an amphitheatre called St Just Round where medieval Cornish miracle plays were performed.

St Kilda Scotland. Largest of a group of small islands in the Outer Hebrides, Western Isles 64 km (40 miles) WSW of North Uist, 5 km (3 miles) long and 3 km (2 miles) wide. Now uninhabited, the pop. of 36 having been evacuated at their own request in 1930. Bird sanctuary (gannets and puffins).

St Kitts (St Christopher) and Nevis. State consisting of 2 islands forming part of the Lesser Antilles in the Eastern Caribbean. Area 269 sq km (104 sq. miles). Pop. (1995) 39,400 (43 per cent urban). Life expectancy, 63 years male, 69 female. Cap. Basseterre. Other important town Charlestown. Currency: Eastern Caribbean dollar = 100 cents. St Kitts and Nevis are two islands 3 km (2 miles) apart and are of volcanic origin. St Kitts is crossed by mountains which rise to 1157 m (3795 ft) in Mt Misery. The climate is tropical. Land use: forested 17 per cent, meadows and pasture 3 per cent, agricultural and under permanent cultivation 39 per cent. The lang. is English and the citizens are descendants of African slaves. About 75 per cent of the pop. is Christian, mainly Anglican and Methodist.

Important crops are sugar and cotton, and the main export is cane sugar, shipped through Basseterre. Main industries are the assembly of electronic equipment, footwear, and food and drink processing. Tourism is important to the economy.

First discovered by Columbus in 1493 and by the British in 1623. Three times seized by the French but finally ceded to Britain 1783. St Kitts-Nevis-Anguilla became an associated state within the Commonwealth in 1967. Anguilla became a separate dependency of Britain in 1969. St Kitts and Nevis became fully independent in 1983.

Under the 1983 Constitution there is a unicameral Parliament consisting of 11 elected members (8 from St Kitts and 3 from Nevis) and 3 appointed Senators.

St Laurent Canada. Industrial and residential town in Quebec on Montreal island

10 km (6 miles) W of Montreal city. Pop. (1991) 72,402.

Industries inc. engineering. Manufactures chemicals and textiles. Founded in 1845.

St Lawrence River and Seaway Canada/ USA. One of the greatest rivers and waterways in North America and the world. The river issues from the NE end of L. Ontario and flows generally NE for 1200 km (750 miles) to the Gulf of St Lawrence; it forms the easternmost link in the St Lawrence Seaway, 3990 km (2480 miles) long, which enables ocean-going vessels to reach the W end of L. Superior. The first 183 km (114 miles) of its course form the Canada–USA frontier; entering Canada, for a short distance it forms the Ontario–Quebec boundary, but most of its course is in Quebec. On leaving L. Ontario it passes through the Thousand Islands, a well-known tourist region; narrowing, it enters the turbulent International Rapids and passes 7 other rapids, inc. the Coteau, the Cedars, the Cascades and Lachine (circumvented by canals), before reaching Montreal. It widens to form L. St Francis and then L. St Louis. Near Montreal it is joined by the main tributary, the Ottawa R.; thereafter the course is gentler and more winding. Widening again, it forms L. St Peter (Lac St Pierre) and below Quebec widens considerably into a tidal estuary 640 km (400 miles) long and from 5 to 110 km (3 to 70 miles) wide. Main tributaries the Ottawa, the St Maurice, the Saguenay, the Chaudière and the Richelieu rivers. The islands inc. Montreal Island (on which Montreal stands) and Anticosti Island (at the mouth). Near Quebec is the famous Quebec Bridge (1917); other bridges are the Victoria Bridge (1898) and the Jacques Cartier Harbour Bridge (1930) at Montreal, the Roosevelt Bridge (1934) and the Thousand Island Bridge (1938). Main cities Quebec, Montreal, Trois Rivières, Sorel (Quebec); Kingston, Brockville, Cornwall (Ontario); Ogdensburg (New York). The heavily wooded valley contains many lumbering centres and paper mills; the river provides abundant hydroelectric power.

St Lô

Jacques Cartier first ascended the St Lawrence in 1535. Colonization began with the founding of Quebec by Champlain (1608). The French used the river as a fur-trade route; explorers and missionaries also made use of it. French possession of the valley ended when Canada was surrendered to the British (1763). Since the early 19th cent. all disputes between Canada and the USA regarding the use and navigation of the river have been settled by arbitration. Improvements on the waterway have been continuous. The work has consisted in dredging the natural channel between Quebec and Montreal and in making and improving the canals which circumvent the rapids. These improvements culminated in the St Lawrence Seaway, opened in 1959 by Queen Elizabeth II and President Eisenhower.

St Lô France. Cap. of Manche department on the Vire R. Pop. (1982) 24,792.

Centre for an agricultural district and noted for breeding stallions.

St Louis (Réunion) ►RÉUNION.

St Louis Senegal. Seaport on the small island of St Louis in the Senegal R. estuary 177 km (110 miles) NE of Dakar, with which it is connected by rail. Pop. (1992) 125,717.

Exports groundnuts, hides and skins. Manufactures textiles.

Founded 1659. First cap. of French West Africa (1895–1902). Cap. of Senegal until replaced by Dakar in 1958.

St Louis USA. City in Missouri on the right bank of the Mississippi R. 16 km (10 miles) downstream from the confluence with the Missouri opposite East St Louis (Illinois). Pop. (1990) 396,685.

Major centre of communications and trade (rail, road, river and air), with 31 km (19 miles) of river frontage, inc. the harbour. Important international trade in fur pelts. Also handles grain, timber, wool and livestock. Industries inc. oil-refining, meat-packing, brewing and distilling. Manufactures motor vehicles, aircraft, spacecraft, electrical equipment, machinery, chemicals and food products.

Founded as a French fur-trading post 1764. Named after Louis IX of France (St Louis). Retained its French character till the 19th cent. Prosperity came with the Mississippi steamboats (1817); tobacco and other industries soon began to operate. A cent. of growth and progress was celebrated in 1904 with the St Louis Fair (officially, the Louisiana Purchase Exposition).

St Louis Park USA. Town in Minnesota just SW of Minneapolis. Pop. (1970) 48,883. Largely residential.

Manufactures metal goods.

First settled 1854.

St Lucia. Island in the E Caribbean situated between Martinique and St Vincent. Area 617 sq km (238 sq. miles). Pop. (1994) 133,308 (46 per cent urban). Life expectancy, 69 years male, 74 female. Cap. Castries. Currency: East Caribbean dollar = 100 cents. The island is of volcanic origin, but all are now extinct; mountainous, rising to 959 m (3146 ft) in Mt Gimie. More spectacular are the forest-clad cones of the Gros Piton and Petit Piton, rising to nearly 800 m (2624 ft), sheer from the sea in the SW. Famous for hot sulphur springs and solfataras. The climate is tropical. Land use: forested 13 per cent, meadows and pastures 5 per cent, agricultural and under permanent cultivation 30 per cent. Over 82 per cent of the pop. are Roman Catholics and are mainly descendants of African slaves; many speaking a French patois, although English is the official lang.

Industries inc. food-processing, clothing, rum manufacture, electrical equipment, petroleum products, fishing and tourism. Chief exports bananas, packaging material, sugar and coconut products.

St Lucia was discovered about 1500. Attempts to colonize the island by the English took place in 1605 and 1638. The French settled in 1650 and St Lucia was ceded to Britain in 1814. Self-government was achieved in 1967 and independence in 1979.

St Malo France. Seaport on the English Channel at the mouth of the Rance R. in the Ille-et-Vilaine department. Pop. (1990) 49,300.

Exports early vegetables, fruit and dairy produce. Fishing is important and there is a considerable tourist industry here and in neighbouring St Servan and Paramé.

Stands on a rocky island connected with the mainland by a causeway, the Sillon. Many of the old buildings within its ramparts were destroyed or severely damaged in World War II. Flourished from the 15th to the 18th cent. largely owing to the activities of its privateers. Birthplace of Jacques Cartier (1491–1557) and Chateaubriand (1768–1848).

St Martin (Sint Maarten) West Indies. Island in the Leeward Is., since 1648 divided between France and the Netherlands. The N belongs to France and is a dependency of Guadeloupe: area 54 sq km (21 sq. miles), pop. (1990) 28,518. The S is part of the Netherlands Antilles: area 34 sq km (13 sq. miles), pop. (1991) 33,459. Little cultivable land. Chief export salt, from the coastal lagoons. Principal settlements Marigot (French), Philipsburg (Dutch).

St Martin's ➤ISLES OF SCILLY.

St Marylebone England. Part of the London borough of the City of Westminster, bounded on the S by Oxford Street and W by the Edgware Road. Within it lie most of Regent's Park, with the Zoological Gardens, Lord's cricket ground (in St John's Wood) and Harley Street and Wimpole Street, famous for their doctors. The name is derived from that of the church, St Mary at Bourne, the latter referring to the Tyburn, a stream which flowed S through the borough to the Thames.

St Mary Peak ➤FLINDERS RANGE.

St Mary's ➤ISLES OF SCILLY.

St Maur-des-Fossés (St Maur) France. Suburb of SE Paris within a loop of the Marne R. in the Val-de-Marne department. Pop. (1990) 77,429.

Manufactures hosiery, toys, furniture, electrical equipment and food products.

St Maurice River Canada. River in Quebec 523 km (325 miles) long, flowing generally SE and S, through the Gouin Reservoir and smaller lakes and joining the St Lawrence R. at Trois Rivières. Logs are floated down it to the many pulp and paper mills along the banks. Important hydroelectric power stations at Shawingan Falls, Grand'mère. The power resources have attracted plastics, chemical and aluminium industries.

St Mawes England. Small fishing port and resort in Cornwall on St Mawes Harbour 3 km (2 miles) E of Falmouth. Pop. (1985) 1500. Has a castle built by Henry VIII standing opposite Pendennis Castle, Falmouth.

St Michael's Mount England. Rocky island off the shore of Mount's Bay, Cornwall, connected at low tide with Marazion, on the mainland, by a natural causeway. Surmounted by a castle, now used as a residence, and there is also the 15th-cent. Chapel of St Michael, in the battlemented tower of which is 'St Michael's Chair' (actually the stone frame of an old lantern). In Edward the Confessor's reign the priory was granted to the Benedictine abbey of Mont St Michel, but in Henry V's time, with the dissolution of the alien houses, it was transferred to the abbey of Sion. Since 1659 the island has belonged to the St Aubyn family.

St Michel, Mont ➤MONT ST MICHEL.

St Moritz Switzerland. Resort in Graubünden (Grisons) canton in the upper Engadine on the Inn R. Pop. (1989) 6000. Esp. famous as a winter-sports centre, originally known (16th cent.) for its mineral springs. Consists of the village of St Moritz-Dorf (1854 m; 6081 ft) and the spa St Moritz-Bad (1776 m; 5825 ft) on the N and SW shores respectively of the small L. of St Moritz.

St Nazaire France. Seaport in the Loire-Atlantique department at the mouth of the Loire R. 51 km (32 miles) WNW of Nantes. Pop. (1990) 66,087. The outport of Nantes, accommodating the largest vessels. Here is the country's main shipyard.

It also manufactures steel and fertilizers. Other industries inc. marine engineering, brewing and vegetable-canning.

During World War II it was used by the Germans as a submarine base and as such was repeatedly bombed and almost completely destroyed; the shipyards were again in operation by 1948. Here the liners *Normandie* (1935) and *France* (1961) were built.

St Neots England. Market town in Cambridgeshire on the R. Ouse 13 km (8 miles) SSW of Huntingdon. Pop. (1991) 13,471.

Industries inc. paper manufacture and brewing.

It has a 15th/16th cent. Perpendicular church and a 16th-cent. stone bridge.

St Niklaas (Fr. **St Nicolas**) Belgium. Town in E Flanders province 19 km (12 miles) WSW of Antwerp. Pop. (1992) 68,253.

Textile industry (cotton, linen, rayon); manufactures carpets, bricks and pottery. Also a market for the fertile Waasland.

St Omer France. Town in the Pas-de-Calais department on the Aa R. 37 km (23 miles) SW of Calais. Pop. (1982) 53,800 (metropolitan area).

In a market-gardening area. Manufactures hosiery, soap and electrical equipment. Other industries inc. sugar-refining, brewing.

Its outstanding building is the 13th/15th-cent. Gothic basilica of Notre Dame, a cathedral 1559–1801.

St Ouen France. Suburb of N Paris in the Seine-St Denis department. Pop. (1982) 43,743.

Railway engineering. Manufactures machine-tools, glue and chemicals.

Here Louis XVIII signed the Declaration of St Ouen (1814), promising the nation a constitution.

St Pancras England. Part of the London borough of Camden. It inc. Camden Town, Kentish Town and parts of Highgate (N) and Bloomsbury (S), also the great railway termini of Euston, St Pancras and King's Cross. Among open spaces are Parliament Hill and Fields, Ken Wood and part of Regent's Park.

St Paul (Réunion) ►RÉUNION.

St Paul USA. State cap. of Minnesota on the Mississippi R. at the confluence with the Minnesota R. adjoining Minneapolis. Pop. (1990) 272,235.

The 'Twin Cities' are the commercial and industrial centre of an extensive agricultural region. St Paul has a large trade in livestock. Motor-car assembly, oil-refining, meat-packing, food-processing, brewing, printing and publishing. Manufactures refrigerators, electronic equipment and chemicals.

St Paul Island Indian Ocean. Island situated lat. 39°S, long. 78°E, from 1955 part of the French Southern and Antarctic Territories. Area 7 sq km (2¾ sq. miles). Of volcanic origin and uninhabited. Annexed by France 1843.

St Peter Port Channel Islands. Chief town and seaport of Guernsey on the E coast. Pop. (1986) 16,100. The harbour is protected by breakwaters.

Exports tomatoes, vegetables.

Castle Cornet, defending the harbour, dates partly from the 12th cent. and the Church of St Peter partly from the 14th cent. Elizabeth College was founded in 1563. Hauteville House, home (1856–70) of Victor Hugo, the French poet and author, is now a museum.

St Petersburg Russia. St Petersburg (1703–1914), Petrograd (1914–24), Leningrad (1924–91). Cap. of the St Petersburg Region at the mouth of the Neva R. on the Gulf of Finland. Pop. (1991) 4,466,800.

The second largest city of Russia, an important seaport, railway, industrial and tourist centre. Shipbuilding (inc. hydrofoils). Manufactures machinery, chemicals, textiles, food products, clothing and cigarettes. Considerable fur trade.

Became important as a seaport through the construction of a ship canal (1888) linking it with the outport and naval base of Kronstadt and, except when icebound (Dec.–

March), exports timber, phosphates. Connected by the Neva R. and canal with the Volga. The city is built mainly on the left bank of the Neva and on the islands formed by the various channels of the delta. Renowned for its wide boulevards and many fine buildings of the 18th and early 19th cent., esp. the Admiralty buildings, the baroque Winter Palace, the Peter and Paul fortress and the three cathedrals. It has long rivalled Moscow as a cultural centre, with a university (1819), many other educational institutions and the famous Hermitage, with its outstanding collection of European painting and sculpture, as well as many museums. Also the traditional home of the Russian ballet.

Founded (1703) by Peter the Great on a marshy, low-lying site: so many workers died in erecting the city on piles that it was said to have been 'built on bones'. At various times it has suffered from floods. The site was chosen as a 'window looking on Europe' and an outlet to the Baltic, and under Peter the Great and his successors the city was developed as an up-to-date western cap. and a centre of art and culture. It succeeded Moscow as Russian cap. and remained so for over two cent. (1703–1917). In the late 19th cent. it developed as an industrial centre and the wretched condition of the factory workers, in sharp contrast to the splendours of the court, led to the revolutions of 1905 and 1917. During World War II the city was virtually isolated from the rest of the USSR and withstood continual shelling and bombing from Aug. 1941 to Jan. 1944.

St Petersburg USA. Winter resort in W Florida on Tampa Bay 26 km (16 miles) SW of Tampa. Pop. (1990) 238,629. Known as the 'Sunshine City'; numerous recreational amenities.

Manufactures electronic equipment, air conditioners, cement and holiday equipment.

St Pierre Martinique. Town on the coast at the foot of the volcano Mont Pelée.

Chief industry rum-distilling.

Founded 1635. Formerly the chief town; its pop. was 28,000 in 1900, but it was suddenly destroyed by an eruption of Mont Pelée (1902); only one citizen is believed to have survived. Now of minor importance. Birthplace of the Empress Josephine (1763–1814), consort of Napoleon I.

St Pierre (Réunion) ►RÉUNION.

St Pierre and Miquelon North America. Since 1985 a French territorial collectivity. An island group off the S coast of Newfoundland. Total area 242 sq km (93 sq. miles). Total pop. (1990) 6392. Cap. St Pierre (on St Pierre Island), with a permanently ice-free harbour. Some sparsely inhabited rocky islets (inc. the Île aux Marins) and two main islands: St Pierre group (area 26 sq km; 10 sq. miles, pop. 5683); Miquelon group (area 216 sq km; 83 sq. miles, pop. 709). Miquelon's two parts, Grande Miquelon (N) and Petite Miquelon (S), are now joined by a mudbank (Isthme de Langlade). Often shrouded in fog. Thin soil, scanty vegetation, but some vegetables are grown and livestock kept. Main occupation cod-fishing. In 1992 an international tribunal awarded France a 24-mile fishing and economic zone around the islands. A French possession almost continuously since 1660.

St Pölten Austria. Industrial town and railway junction in Lower Austria 53 km (33 miles) W of Vienna. Pop. (1985) 50,419.

Manufactures textiles, machinery.

Grew up round an abbey founded in the 9th cent. and dedicated to St Hippolytus (of which the name is a corrupted version).

St Quentin France. Ancient Augusta Veromanduorum. Industrial town in the Aisne department on the Somme R. 129 km (80 miles) NE of Paris. Pop. (1990) 62,085.

Important textile industry, specializing in the manufacture of curtains and muslin. Also manufactures chemicals and machinery.

Grew from the 7th cent. as a place of pilgrimage round the tomb of St Quentin. Here the French were defeated by the Spaniards (1557) and the Prussians (1871); the Battle of St Quentin in World War I (March 1918) saw the beginning of the great German counter-offensive.

St Thomas Island ➤VIRGIN ISLANDS OF THE USA.

St Tropez France. Fishing port and seaside resort in the Var department on the French Riviera 45 km (28 miles) SW of Cannes. Pop. (1985) 6300.

St Vincent and the Grenadines. Island with dependencies in the Grenadines in the E Caribbean situated between St Lucia and Grenada. Area 389 sq km (150 sq. miles). Pop. (1995) 112,000 (25 per cent urban). Life expectancy, 71 years male, 74 female. Cap. and chief port Kingstown. Currency: East Caribbean dollar = 100 cents. A wooded mountainous country of volcanic origin, it is crossed by a mountain range rising to 1234 m (4048 ft) in Mont Soufrière, an active volcano. Land use: forested 36 per cent, meadows and pastures 5 per cent, agricultural and under permanent cultivation 28 per cent. The pop. is mainly of black (82 per cent) and mixed origin (14 per cent). Anglican, Methodist and Roman Catholic are the main religious denominations.

Agriculture dominates the economy and chief exports are bananas, arrowroot starch. Sea-island cotton is cultivated. Electronic and electrical equipment is assembled and garments are manufactured.

Discovered in 1498, it was ceded to Britain in 1763. It became an associated state within the Commonwealth in 1969 and gained independence in 1979. There is a unicameral House of Assembly consisting of 15 elected members and 6 Senators.

St Vincent, Cape Portugal. Headland at the SW extremity of Portugal. Lighthouse, on a cliff 53 m (174 ft) high. Scene of the defeat of the Spanish fleet by Admiral Sir John Jervis (later Earl St Vincent) in 1797.

St Vincent, Gulf Australia. Inlet of the Indian Ocean just E of Yorke Peninsula, South Australia about 153 km (95 miles) long and up to 64 km (40 miles) wide. Adelaide is near the E shore.

Saipan Mariana Islands. Island situated NNE of Guam in the W Pacific. Area 122 sq km (47 sq. miles). Pop. (1990) 38,896. Cap. of Commonwealth of N Mariana Islands. Volcanic limestone, rising to extinct Mount Tapotchan, 474 m (1554 ft) above sea level.

Main products sugar, coffee, copra, manganese and phosphates.

Sais Egypt. Ancient city site 88 km (55 miles) SE of Alexandria on the Rosetta branch of the Nile. Cap. of lower Egypt in the 7th and 6th cent. BC.

Sakal Japan. Industrial town in Osaka prefecture on Osaka Bay just S of Osaka. Pop. (1991) 808,072.

Manufactures chemicals, fertilizers, machinery, aluminium products and hosiery. Formerly an important port; declined when its harbour became silted up.

Sakarya River Turkey. Rises NNE of Afyonkarahisar in W Turkey and flows 784 km (490 miles) in great curves E, NW and N past Osmaneli Geyve and Adapazari to enter the Black Sea at Karasu.

Sakha Republic Russia. (Formerly Yakutia) in NE Siberia, bounded on the N by the Arctic Ocean and on the S by the Stanovoi Range. Area 3,103,200 sq km (1,197,760 sq. miles). Pop. (1991) 1,109,000. Cap. Yakutsk. Other important towns Verkhoyansk, Vilyuisk, Olekminsk and Sredne Kolymsk. A thinly populated republic entirely in the tundra and coniferous forest regions. Consists largely of the basins of the Lena, Yana, Indigirka and Kolyma rivers, but in the E half there are the Verkhoyansk and Cherski Ranges, the latter rising to over 3000 m (9940 ft). It has an extreme continental climate, with exceptionally cold winters and relatively warm summers; near Verkhoyansk in the so-called 'cold pole' of the earth. The people, who are 37 per cent Yakuts and 50 per cent Russians, are mainly settled in the river valleys.

Principal occupations are mining (coal, gold, mica and tin) and the trapping and breeding of fur-bearing animals, fishing, the raising of reindeer and cattle. It produces most of Russia's diamonds. Chief products furs, gold, mammoth ivory. Some agriculture on collective and state farms. The severity of the climate and the lack of railways impede economic development, though roads and airways are established; Yakutsk is linked by air with Irkutsk.

The region was taken by the Russians in the 17th cent. The Yakut Autonomous Republic was formed in 1922. The Supreme Soviet has 205 deputies.

Sakhalin Russia. Island off the E coast of Siberia in the sea of Okhotsk, forming a region of the Khabarovsk Territory, separated from Hokkaido (Japan) by La Pérouse Strait. Area 76,923 sq km (29,700 sq. miles). Pop. (1985) 660,000. Has a central N–S valley flanked by parallel mountain ranges, that in the E rising to 2014 m (6606 ft) in Mt Nevelski. Climate cold and inhospitable, with frequent fogs; much of the island is covered with tundra and forest. Main occupation fishing. Rye, oats, potatoes and vegetables are grown in the S. Some coal and oil produced.

Settled by the Russians in the mid 19th cent.; became a place of exile for Tsarist prisoners. After the Russo–Japanese War (1905) the S part of the island was occupied by Japan and was known as Karafuto, but it was returned to the USSR after World War II (1945).

Sakkara (Saqqara) Egypt. Village in the Giza governorate 24 km (15 miles) SW of Cairo. Pop. (1985) 8000. Principal necropolis (with Giza) of ancient Memphis. Famous for its step pyramids.

Sal Cape Verde. Island in the E of the archipelago containing Amilcar Cabral International Airport. Area 216 sq km (83 sq. miles). Pop. (1990) 8150. Cap. Santa Maria.

Salaberry de Valleyfield ➤VALLEYFIELD.

Salado River Argentina. River 668 km (415 miles) long, flowing generally SE along a shallow course through the Buenos Aires province and entering the Río de la Plata.

Salado (Chadileufú, Desaguadero) River Argentina. River 1370 km (850 miles) long, rising in the Andes, flowing SSE (as the Desaguadero R.) and forming the boundary between the Mendoza and San Luis provinces, disappearing in the marshes of La Pampa. Later (as the Chadileufú R.) reaches the Colorado R. and the Atlantic in times of high water.

Salado (Juramento) River Argentina. River 2010 km (1250 miles) long, rising in the Andes (as the Juramento R.), flowing SE through the Salta, Santiago del Estero and Santa Fé provinces, and joining the Paraná R. at Santa Fé.

Salamanca Spain. 1. Province in León, bordering W and NW on Portugal. Area 12,336 sq km (4754 sq. miles). Pop. (1991) 356,845. Consists of plateaux and mountains, rising to 1720 m (5642 ft) in the S; within the basin of the Duero (Douro) R. Mainly agricultural.

2. Cap. of Salamanca province on the Tormes R., a tributary of the Duero (Douro). Pop. (1991) 162,544.

Important railway and road centre. Manufactures chemicals, and other industries inc. tanning, brewing and flour-milling.

A city of outstanding historic and artistic interest, centred on the great arcaded Plaza Mayor. Has a Roman bridge retaining many of the original arches, an old 12th-cent. Romanesque cathedral and a new 16th/18th cent. cathedral, the 16th-cent. Casa de la Conchas – its façade decorated with shells – and many other fine old buildings. Taken by Hannibal (222 BC) and later by Romans, Visigoths and Moors. The university was founded c. 1230 by Alfonso IX of León. In the Battle of Salamanca (1812) Wellington decisively defeated the French under Marmont.

Salamís Cyprus. In the N Turkish-dominated area on the E coast. Site of a ruined Greek city founded 1180 BC. It has the remains of an amphitheatre and a temple to Zeus.

Salamís Greece. Island in the Aegean Sea off the coast of Attica just W of Piraeus. Area 93 sq km (36 sq. miles). Off the NE coast the Greeks under Themistocles won a naval victory over the Persians under Xerxes (480 BC).

Salcombe England. Market town, fishing port, seaside resort in Devon on the W side of Salcombe Harbour 27 km (17 miles) SW of Dartmouth. Pop. (1991) 1921.

Saldanha Bay South Africa. Sheltered inlet of the Atlantic Ocean 96 km (60 miles) NNW of Cape Town. Arid hinterland. Formerly used by whalers; now a naval training base. Fish-canning.

Sale Australia. Chief market town of Gippsland, Victoria 185 km (115 miles) E of Melbourne. Pop. (1986) 13,559.

In dairy-farming country. Linked by canal with the Gippsland lakes. Trade in grain, livestock. Flour and woollen mills; dairy and bacon factories.

Sale England. Town in Greater Manchester 8 km (5 miles) SW of the city, of which it is a residential suburb. Pop. (1991) 56,052.

Salé Morocco. Seaport on the Atlantic coast just NE of Rabat. Pop. (1982) 289,391.

Fish-canning. Manufactures carpets and pottery.

Home of pirates, the celebrated Sallee Rovers, in the 17th cent.

Salem India. Industrial town and railway junction in Tamil Nadu in a picturesque valley SW of the Shevaroy Hills and 274 km (170 miles) SW of Madras. Pop. (1991) 366,700.

Manufactures cotton goods and stainless steel.

Salem (Massachusetts) USA. Industrial town on Massachusetts Bay 24 km (15 miles) NE of Boston. Pop. (1985) 38,600.

Manufactures textiles, electric lamps and footwear.

One of the oldest towns in New England. Among the buildings are the Custom House (1819) and the 17th-cent. birthplace of Nathaniel Hawthorne, American novelist (1804–64). Founded 1626. Became notorious for the witchcraft trials in 1692, when 19 people were hanged.

Salem (Oregon) USA. State cap. on the Willamette R. 69 km (43 miles) SSW of Portland. Pop. (1990) 107,786.

Flour-milling, fruit and vegetable canning, meat-packing. Manufactures metal goods and paper.

Seat of the Willamette University (1842).

Salerno Italy. Cap. of Salerno province in Campania on the Gulf of Salerno 48 km (30 miles) ESE of Naples. Pop. (1991) 151,374.

Port. Industrial centre. Electrical engineering, tomato-canning, flour-milling, tanning. Manufactures textiles.

The university (founded in the 9th cent., the earliest in Europe), with a famous medical school, was overshadowed by Naples University from the 13th cent.; it was closed in 1811 but refounded in 1944. The 11th-cent. cathedral was restored in the 18th cent. Scene of the Allied landings in World War II (1943).

Salford England. City and unitary authority on the R. Irwell opposite Manchester. Pop. (1991) 79,755. Has the principal docks of the Manchester Ship Canal.

Important industrial centre. Electrical engineering. Manufactures textiles, textile machinery, chemicals, clothing, electrical equipment and tyres.

Roman Catholic cathedral (1848). Birthplace of James Joule (1818–89), the physicist.

Salgótarján Hungary. Cap. of Nógrád county 88 km (55 miles) NE of Budapest near the Slovakian border. Pop. (1989) 49,000.

Industrial and mining centre. Manufactures iron and steel and machinery. Coal and lignite mined in the neighbourhood.

Salina USA. Town in Kansas on the Smoky Hill R. 137 km (85 miles) NNW of Wichita. Pop. (1970) 39,013.

Commercial centre in an agricultural region. Important flour-milling industry. Manufactures agricultural machinery, cement, bricks and tiles.

Salinas USA. Town in California 74 km (46 miles) SSE of San José. Pop. (1990) 108,777.

Centre of a cattle-rearing and market-gardening area (lettuces, celery). Beet-sugar refining.

Salisbury England. City and market town in Wiltshire on the R. Avon at the confluence with the R. Wylye 32 km (20 miles) NW of Southampton. Pop. (1991) 39,200.

Market town. Industries inc. light engineering, brewing, carpet manufacture at Wilton and tourism.

Famous chiefly for the magnificent mainly 13th-cent. cathedral, in Early English style, with the highest spire in England (123 m, 403 ft). The library has valuable Anglo–Saxon manuscripts. Three ancient parish churches, St Martin, St Thomas, St Edmund; 15th-cent. banqueting hall of John Halle. Audley House (16th-cent). 3 km (2 miles) NNW is Old Sarum, site of an important early fortress and settlement known to the Romans as Sorbiodunum. All that now remains is a bare conical mound; the site, abandoned in the 13th cent. when New Sarum (Salisbury) was built, was in ruins by the 16th cent.

Salisbury (Zimbabwe) ➤HARARE.

Salisbury Plain England. Region of open chalk downs about 32 km (20 miles) long and 16 km (10 miles) wide in Wiltshire. Largely used as a military training ground. It inc. Stonehenge.

Salonika ➤THESSALONÍKI.

Salop ➤SHROPSHIRE.

Salta Argentina. Cap. of Salta province in the NW in the irrigated Lerma valley at a height of 1190 m (3903 ft). Pop. (1990) 373,857.

Commercial centre trading in tobacco, livestock and agricultural produce. Industries inc. meat-packing, flour-milling, tanning and tourism.

Founded 1582. Several old colonial buildings. Stands on the narrow-gauge Trans-Andean Railway to Antofagasta (Chile), opened 1948.

Saltaire ➤SHIPLEY.

Saltash England. Market town in Cornwall

on the estuary of the R. Tamar 6 km (4 miles) NW of Plymouth. Pop. (1989) 17,000. Port. The estuary is crossed here by Brunel's Royal Albert railway bridge (1859) and the Tamar suspension bridge (1961); the latter replaces the ancient Saltash ferry.

Saltburn England. Town in Saltburn and Cleveland 16 km (10 miles) E of Middlesbrough. Pop. (1991) 6145. Consists of the small town and seaside resort of Saltburn-by-the-Sea.

Saltcoats Scotland. Seaside resort in Highland on the Firth of Clyde 21 km (13 miles) NNW of Ayr. Pop. (1991) 11,865. Formerly important for saltworks.

Saltillo Mexico. Cap. of Coahuila state at a height of 1600 m (5248 ft) 77 km (48 miles) WSW of Monterrey. Pop. (1990) 440,845.

Commercial, industrial and mining centre. Manufactures textiles, clothing and ceramics.

Famous for woollen shawls (*sarapes*). Cathedral (18th-cent.). Founded 1586.

Salt Lake City USA. State cap. of Utah on the Jordan R. 14 km (9 miles) SE of the Great Salt Lake at a height of 1280 m (4198 ft). Pop. (1990) 159,936.

Important route centre. Leading commercial and industrial centre of Utah. Oil-refining, copper-smelting and refining. Manufactures textiles, metal goods and food products.

A city of wide avenues in a splendid setting of mountain scenery, with the Wasatch Range to the E and SE rising to 3600 m (11,808 ft). Founded (1847) by the Mormon leader Brigham Young as the Mormon cap. He came with 143 followers and within 2 hours of arriving the first fields were being ploughed. Notable buildings inc. the Mormon Temple (1893) and the Mormon Tabernacle (1867).

Salto Uruguay. Cap. of the Salto department and river port at the head of navigation on the Uruguay R. opposite Concordia (Argentina). Pop. (1985) 88,787.

Commercial and industrial centre in a stock-rearing and fruit-growing district.

Salvador

Trade in agricultural produce. Industries inc. meat-packing, flour-milling and wine-making.

Salvador ➤EL SALVADOR.

Salvador Brazil. Formerly Bahia. Cap. of Bahia state, on a peninsula separating Todos Santos Bay from the Atlantic Ocean 1290 km (800 miles) NNE of Rio de Janeiro. Pop. (1990) 1,506,602.

Seaport exporting cocoa, sugar, tobacco. Sugar-refining, flour-milling. Manufactures cigars and cigarettes, textiles and cement.

Consists of a lower town, built round the harbour and a modern residential upper town. Has several 17th and 18th-cent. churches and other buildings. Founded 1549. Cap. of Brazil until 1763.

Salween River. Great river of SE Asia, 2816 km (1750 miles) long, rising in the Tanglha Range in E Tibet, flowing generally SE in a deep gorge, for a time parallel to the gorges of the upper Mekong and Chang Jiang rivers. Then turns S through Yunnan province (China) and enters Myanmar (Burma), cutting another gorge through the Shan plateau and reaching the Gulf of Martaban near Moulmein. Frequently impeded by rapids; navigable for only about 113 km (70 miles) above its mouth.

Salzach River Austria. River 209 km (130 miles) long, rising in the Hohe Tauern, flowing E and then N through Salzburg province past Salzburg to join the Inn R. 50 km (31 miles) NNW of Salzburg.

Salzburg Austria. 1. Federal state bordering NW on Germany. Area 7154 sq km (2762 sq. miles). Pop. (1991) 483,880. Chiefly mountainous, containing the Hohe Tauern and part of the Niedere Tauern in the S, with glaciers and snowfields, rising to well over 3000 m (9840 ft). Drained by the Salzach R. and its tributaries. Cattle reared on the Alpine pastures. Produces timber. Salt-mining. Industries centred on Salzburg. Thriving tourist trade.

2. Cap. of Salzburg state, on both banks

of the Salzach R. 249 km (155 miles) WSW of Vienna. Pop. (1991) 143,971.

Tourist centre. Brewing. Manufactures metal goods and textiles.

Dominated by the Hohensalzburg (11th/16th-cent. castle). Among other noteworthy buildings are the 17th-cent. cathedral, the old and new residences of the archbishops, a 13th-cent. Franciscan church, the 8th-cent. Benedictine monastery (round which the city grew up) and a Mozart house and museum. Birthplace of Mozart (1756–91). The university (founded 1623) was reduced to a theological seminary in 1810.

Salzgitter Germany. Industrial town in Lower Saxony 24 km (15 miles) SSW of Brunswick. Pop. (1991) 114,355.

Iron and potash mining. Manufactures iron and steel, coke, chemicals, textiles and machinery.

Incorporated in 1942 chiefly to exploit the rich iron deposit of the district.

Salzkammergut Austria. Mountain and lake area in the E Alps in Upper Austria, Styria and Salzburg, crossed by the Traun R. Among its lakes are Attersee and Traunsee. Highest peak Dachstein (2998 m; 9836 ft). Once important for salt production. Now a tourist region with Bad Ischl its chief centre. Other leading occupations stock-rearing and forestry.

Samar Philippines. Third largest island, separated from S Luzon by the San Bernardino Strait. Area 13,080 sq km (5050 sq. miles). Pop. (1985) 1.1 million. Cap. Catbalogan. Pop. (1990) 115,000. Mountainous and forested, rising to 840 m (2755 ft). Frequently subject to typhoons. Little developed. Produces abacá, copra and rice.

Samara Russia. Formerly Kuibyshev. Cap. of the Samara Region on a large loop of the Volga R. at the confluence with the Samara R. Pop. (1992) 1,239,000.

Important industrial and commercial centre. Oil-refining and flour-milling. Manufactures aircraft, locomotives, tractors, cables, chemicals and textiles. Considerable trade in cereals. Also a river port, airport and railway junction. Site of an important hydroelectric power station.

Founded 1586; fortified chiefly to protect traffic along the Volga. During World War II it expanded greatly in the main because of the transference here of the Soviet government owing to the German assault on Moscow. Industrial expansion continued after the war.

Samaria Jordan. Ancient city in Palestine on the site of the modern village of Sabastiya 10 km (6 miles) NW of Nablus. Founded in the 9th cent. BC by Omri, who made it cap. of his N kingdom of Israel.

Captured and colonized by Assyria (722 BC). Fell to Alexander the Great (331 BC). Later destroyed by John Hyrcanus, rebuilt by Herod the Great; according to tradition here were the tombs of Elisha and John the Baptist. Excavations begun in 1908 revealed the palace of Omri and other valuable remains.

Samarinda Indonesia. Town situated NE of Banjermasin, Kalimantan on the Mahakam R. delta. Pop. (1980) 264,718.

Port handling coal, timber, rattan, skins, rubber and guttapercha.

Samarkand Uzbekistan. Cap. of the Samarkand region in the fertile valley of the Zeravshan R. at a height of 720 m (2362 ft) and on the Trans-Caspian Railway 274 km (170 miles) SW of Tashkent. Pop. (1991) 370,500.

Industries inc. brewing, distilling, flour-milling and tobacco-processing. Manufactures textiles, clothing, chemicals and footwear. Trade in grain, fruits and karakul lambskins.

Divided into an old quarter, which has many historic buildings and a new Russian town. Among the famous buildings are the mausoleum of Tamerlane, the *madrassa* or Muslim college of Bibi-Khanum, both dating from the early 15th cent., and other *madrassas*, all centred round the Rigistan or main square. Ancient cap. of Sogdiana; stands in a strategic position among the W spurs of the Tien Shan. Destroyed by Alexander the Great 329 BC. As Samarkand it was taken by

the Arabs (AD 712) and became a centre of Arab culture, but was destroyed by Genghis Khan in 1220; it again flourished under Tamerlane, who made it his cap. and constructed mosques, palaces and gardens within its walls. Later ruled by the Chinese and the emirs of Bukhara, and fell to the Russians in 1868; its pop., about 500,000 in 1220, was only 60,000 in 1990.

Samarra Iraq. Holy city of the Shia Muslims on the Tigris R. 113 km (70 miles) NNW of Baghdad. Has a golden-domed mosque of the 17th cent. and the remains of a much earlier mosque. Also extensive ruins of ancient Samarra, cap. of the Abbasid dynasty 836–76.

Samarska Luka Russia. Region within the ox-bow of the Volga R. W of Samara. Area 1010 sq km (390 sq. miles). Agricultural lowland on the river rises to forested mountains in the centre. Chief product petroleum, with extracting centre at Zhigulevsk; also asphalt, dolomite and limestone.

Sambre River Belgium/France. River 190 km (118 miles) long, rising in the Aisne department (France), flowing generally ENE past Maubeuge, entering Belgium, continuing past Charleroi and joining the Meuse R. at Namur. Navigable from Landrecies and linked by canal with the Oise R.; also joins the Charleroi–Brussels Canal.

Samoa S Pacific Ocean. Group of islands 720 km (450 miles) ENE of Fiji. Mainly mountainous and of volcanic origin. Climate tropical, with heavy rainfall. Samoans are Polynesian, akin to the New Zealand Maoris. Chief occupations agriculture (taro, breadfruit and yams), fishing. Discovered (1722) by the Dutch. Divided politically into American Samoa and Samoa.

1. American Samoa: US territory (since 1899) consisting of the principal island Tutuila and several smaller islands about 1040 km (650 miles) ENE of Fiji. Area 197 sq km (76 sq. miles). Pop. (1990) 46,773 (34 per cent urban). About 85,000 American Samoans live in the USA. Cap. and chief

seaport Pago Pago. Fatatogo is the seat of government. Currency: US dollar = 100 cents. The main islands are of volcanic origin and are hilly and forested. The climate is tropical marine with a small range of temperature and plentiful rainfall. Fish-canning is an important occupation. Many of the islanders are small farmers growing breadfruit, yams, bananas and coconuts. Exports inc. canned fish (mainly tuna), pet food, watches and handicrafts. American Samoa is an unorganized unincorporated territory of the US administered by the Department of the Interior. There is a 20-member lower house, or House of Representatives and an 18-member Senate.

2. Samoa: Independent state consisting of the two principal islands, Savai'i and Upolu, two smaller islands, Manono and Apolima, and several uninhabited islets situated in the SW Pacific Ocean. Until 1997 known as Western Samoa. Total area 2831 sq km (1093 sq. miles). Pop. (1991) 161,298 (21 per cent urban). Life expectancy, 67 years male, 71 female. Cap. and chief seaport Apia, on Upolu. Currency: Tala = 100 sene. The islands are of volcanic origin and are surrounded by coral reefs. Savai'i (area 1707 sq km; 659 sq. miles, pop. 44,930) rises to 1859 m (6098 ft) and Upolu (area 1119 sq km; 432 sq. miles, pop. 112,228) to 1100 m (3608 ft). It has a tropical marine climate. Land use: forested 47 per cent, meadows and pastures 0.4 per cent, agricultural and under permanent cultivation 43 per cent. The official langs. are Samoan and English and about 88 per cent of the pop. is Samoan (Polynesian). Congregationalists make up the largest Christian denomination. Subsistence farming is the main occupation and copra, bananas and cocoa are the main exports. There is some industrial activity associated with food-processing and forestry. Western Samoa was a German protectorate 1899–1914 and administered by New Zealand under League of Nations mandate 1920–47 and under UN Trusteeship Agreement 1947–62. It became independent in 1962. It is a constitutional monarchy. The king is executive head of state and appoints the prime minister. The 47-member Legislative Assembly is elected by *matai* (customary family heads).

Samos Greece. Island in the Aegean Sea separated from the W coast of Turkey by a strait about 3 km (2 miles) wide, forming a *nome* with neighbouring islands. Area 778 sq km (300 sq. miles) (Samos alone 492 sq km (190 sq. miles)). Pop. (1991) 41,850. Cap. Samos. Largely mountainous but fertile. Produces wine, olive oil, tobacco and citrus fruits. Attained its greatest prosperity under the tyrant Polycrates in the 6th cent. BC Birthplace of the Greek philosopher and mathematician, Pythagoras.

Samothrace (Gr. **Samothráki**) Greece. Island in the NE Aegean Sea 43 km (27 miles) SSW of Alexandroúpolis in the Évros *nome*. Area 181 sq km (70 sq. miles). Mountainous, rising to 1601 m (5251 ft) in Fengári.

Chief occupations goat-rearing, sponge-fishing.

It was early an important centre of worship of the Cabeiri. The famous statue, the Winged Victory of Samothrace (discovered 1863), is now in the Louvre, Paris.

Samsö Island Denmark. Island in the Kattegat between Jutland and Zealand. Area 111 sq km (43 sq. miles). Mainly agricultural.

Samsun Turkey. Ancient Amisus. Cap. of Samsun province, a Black Sea port 330 km (205 miles) ENE of Ankara. Pop. (1990) 277,222.

In the chief tobacco-growing region. Exports tobacco and cereals. Tobacco-processing.

At first overshadowed by Sinope, it superseded the latter in the 13th cent.

Sana (San'a) Yemen. Cap., on a plateau at a height of 2288 m (7505 ft) 145 km (90 miles) ENE of its port Hodeida, with which it is connected by a mountain road. Pop. (1990) 500,000.

Handicraft industries inc. weaving and the manufacture of jewellery.

Contains the palace of the former Imam, the citadel, the Great Mosque (with a model of the Kaaba of Mecca) and several other mosques. A cap. at various times from the 4th cent. AD; became cap. of Yemen when Turkish rule ended after World War I (1918). A large, but backward, Jewish community had lived in Sana for cents. until the creation of Israel led to their expulsion or withdrawal (1948).

San Andrés y Providencia (St Andrew's and Old Providence) Islands Colombia. Two islands in the Caribbean off the Mosquito Coast of Nicaragua, with several coral reefs; an intendancy of Colombia. Area 44 sq km (17 sq. miles). Pop. (1992) 41,581. Cap. San Andrés. Exports coconuts, copra and oranges.

San Angelo USA. Town in W Texas on the Concho R. 298 km (185 miles) NW of San Antonio. Pop. (1990) 84,474.

Important wool and mohair market in a ranching and farming area. Industries inc. cotton-ginning, oil-refining and meat-packing.

San Antonio Chile. Seaport and holiday resort in Santiago province 60 km (37 miles) S of Valparaiso. Exports copper, agricultural products of the central valley (cereals and wine). Tourism is important.

San Antonio USA. Third largest city in Texas on the San Antonio R. 314 km (195 miles) W of Houston. Pop. (1990) 935,933.

Route, commercial and industrial centre. Trade in cattle, wool and cotton. Industries inc. electronics, general manufacturing and biotechnology, meat-packing, oil-refining, food-processing and brewing. There are military and air force bases in the neighbourhood.

Founded (1718) by the Spaniards. Named after the original mission of San Antonio de Valero, whose chapel is the historic Alamo. Part of the city is Mexican in character and Spanish is widely spoken.

San Bernardino USA. Town in California 80 km (50 miles) E of Los Angeles in the fertile San Bernardino valley. Pop. (1990) 164,164.

Important packing and marketing centre

for citrus fruits. Railway engineering. Manufactures cement and food products.

San Bruno USA. Town in California 16 km (10 miles) S of San Francisco. Pop. (1970) 36,254. Largely residential. Printing.

Site of San Francisco international airport and Tanforan racecourse.

San Buenaventura (Ventura) USA. Coastal town in California 100 km (62 miles) WNW of Los Angeles. Pop. (1970) 57,964.

In an agricultural (citrus fruits, lima beans) and oil-producing district. Exports oil, and tourism is important.

San Carlos River Costa Rica. River rising NW of Ramón in the Aguacate mountains and flowing 112 km (70 miles) NNE past Muelle de San Carlos to enter San Juan R. ENE of San Juan del Norte. Navigable in the lower and middle course.

San Carlos Philippines. Town situated ESE of Bacolod on Tañon Strait opposite Refugio Island in the Negros Occidental. Pop. (1990) 106,000. Ferry port for Toledo, Cebu Island.

Industries inc. sugar-milling and saw-milling. Exports sugar and tobacco.

San Carlos Venezuela. Town situated WSW of Caracas on the Tirgua R., sometimes called San Carlos R., in Cojedes. Pop. (1971) 21,029. State cap. and trading and processing centre for an agricultural area.

Industries inc. the manufacture of dairy products, rice-milling and sawmilling.

San Cristóbal Venezuela. Cap. of Táchira state near the Colombian border 320 km (200 miles) S of Maracaibo at a height of 810 m (2657 ft). Pop. (1990) 220,697.

Commercial and route centre in a coffee-growing region, serving the W llanos. Tanning, distilling. Manufactures cement.

Has a cathedral partly rebuilt in colonial style (1961). Founded 1561.

San Cristóbal Island ➤GALÁPAGOS ISLANDS.

Sancti Spiritus Cuba. Town in Las Villas

province 80 km (50 miles) SE of Santa Clara. Pop. (1986) 75,600.

Commercial centre in an agricultural region. Trade in sugar-cane, tobacco and cattle. Manufactures cigars, dairy products and other industries inc. tanning.

Many narrow, winding streets, with 16th/17th cent. churches and houses. Founded 1516.

Sancy, Puy de ➤PUY-DE-DÔME.

Sandakan Malaysia. Seaport in Sabah on the E coast. Pop. (1990) 223,432.

Exports rubber and timber. Sawmilling, fishing.

Sandbach England. Town in Cheshire 8 km (5 miles) NE of Crewe. Pop. (1991) 15,839.

A picturesque market town best known for its production of salt. Manufactures vehicles, chemicals and clothing.

Two Saxon crosses in the market place were reconstructed (1816) after being demolished.

Sandefjord Norway. Town situated SSW of Oslo at the head of a small fjord near the mouth of Oslo Fjord in Vestfold. Pop. (1990) 36,095.

The main industries are shipping and paint and varnish manufacture.

Sandhurst (Australia) ➤BENDIGO.

Sandhurst England. Village 16 km (10 miles) SE of Reading. Seat of the Royal Military Academy, founded (1799) as the Royal Military College and combined (1946) with the Royal Military Academy, Woolwich; has the National Army Museum.

San Diego USA. Seaport in California on San Diego Bay 177 km (110 miles) SSE of Los Angeles. Pop. (1990) 1,110,549. Excellent natural harbour.

Exports canned fish, cotton and other agricultural produce. Important tuna fishing and canning; other industries inc. electronics, aerospace, biomedical, fruit and vegetable processing and shipbuilding. A leading US naval base. With its mild, equable climate and gamefishing and bathing facilities, it has become a popular resort.

The first Californian mission, San Diego de Alcalá, was founded here in 1769 and the city was named after it.

Sandnes Norway. Town situated S of Stavanger at the head of Gands Fjord, Rogaland. Pop. (1990) 44,798.

Industrial town manufacturing metal products, bicycles, marine equipment, bricks, furniture, clothing and ceramics.

Sandown–Shanklin England. Urban district on the E coast of the Isle of Wight. Pop. (1991) 17,305. Consists of the towns and seaside resorts of Sandown and Shanklin. Both have sandy beaches. Shanklin, with the Chine, a wooded cleft in the sandstone and some thatched cottages, is the more picturesque.

Sandringham England. Village in Norfolk 11 km (7 miles) NE of King's Lynn. Sandringham Hall is a residence of the royal family, the estate having been acquired by Edward VII when Prince of Wales (1863). George VI (1895–1952) was born and died here.

Sandviken Sweden. Town in Gävleborg county 21 km (13 miles) WSW of Gävle. Pop. (1989) 39,940.

Important speciality steel industry. Manufactures cemented-carbide products.

Sandwich England. Town in E Kent on the R. Stour 18 km (11 miles) E of Canterbury. Pop. (1991) 4164.

Resort, golfing centre. One of the Cinque Ports, in the Middle Ages it was a leading port for trade with the continent, but by the end of the 16th cent. the harbour was silted up and practically useless; it was saved from complete decline by the settlement of wool weavers from Flanders. Buildings inc. the 14th-cent. Fisher Gate and the 13th-cent. chapel of St Bartholomew's Hospital.

San Felipe Chile. Cap. of Aconcagua province at a height of 637 m (2089 ft) 72 km (45 miles) N of Santiago. Pop. (1970) 26,000.

Agricultural and mining centre.

San Fernando Argentina. Seaport and NW suburb of Buenos Aires on the Río de la Plata. Pop. (1991) 144,761.

Industrial centre. Manufactures footwear and furniture. Fish-canning.

San Fernando Chile. Cap. of Colchagua province at a height of 336 m (1102 ft) in the central valley 129 km (80 miles) S of Santiago. Pop. (1970) 27,600.

Market town. Trade in cereals, wine and fruit.

Founded 1742.

San Fernando Spain. Seaport in Cádiz province, Andalusia on the Isla de León 13 km (8 miles) SE of Cádiz. Pop. (1991) 85,191. An arsenal founded 1790.

Industries inc. distilling, tourism and tanning. Salt produced in the neighbourhood.

San Fernando Trinidad. Seaport on the Gulf of Paria (SW). Pop. (1980) 34,200. Second largest town in Trinidad.

Exports petroleum products and sugar. Main industry sugar-refining.

San Francisco USA. Seaport, with land-locked harbour, and second largest city in California, on the Pacific coast 563 km (350 miles) NW of Los Angeles. Pop. (1990) 723,959. At the end of a peninsula, bounded by the Pacific (W), the Golden Gate (N) and San Francisco Bay (E). A great cosmopolitan city and a commercial and financial centre, the hub of a group of cities round San Francisco Bay.

Exports iron and steel products, oil, canned fruit and fish, and cereals. Ship-building, oil-refining, food-processing and canning, sugar-refining, printing and publishing. Manufactures clothing and furniture.

Seat of the University of San Francisco (Roman Catholic, 1930) and of schools of the University of California. Within the city are the 'Latin Quarter', with French, Spanish, Italian and Portuguese colonies, and Chinatown, the largest Chinese settlement outside the Far East. The city's cable-cars, a unique form of public transport necessitated by its hilly location, are a source of pride to the natives and entertainment to visitors.

Transportation to and from the city has been greatly facilitated by the bridges to Oakland and across the Golden Gate. Founded 1776, when the Spanish mission of San Francisco de Asis was established. A disastrous earthquake and fire (1906) destroyed much of the city, but within three years it was rebuilt in brick, steel and concrete.

Sangli India. Town situated SSE of Bombay on the Kistna R. in Maharashtra. Pop. (1990) 226,500.

Railway terminus and market for agricultural produce. Industries inc. cotton and oilseed milling, processing coffee, peanuts, dairy produce, brewing, and it manufactures agricultural implements.

Sangre de Cristo Mountains USA. In Spanish, 'Blood of Christ'. Range of the Rocky Mountains, extending 340 km (210 miles) N–S through South Colorado and N New Mexico, so named because of the reddish colour of the snow-capped peaks seen at sunrise. Highest mountain Blanca Peak (4364 m, 14,317 ft).

San Joaquin River USA. River 515 km (320 miles) long in California, much used for irrigation, in the S part of the Central Valley, rising in the Sierra Nevada, flowing SW and then NNW to join the Sacramento R. just E of Suisun Bay. The fertile irrigated valley is one of the USA's richest farming regions.

San José Costa Rica. Cap. of Costa Rica and of San José province on the central plateau at a height of 1160 m (3805 ft). Pop. (1991) 299,456.

Costa Rica's chief industrial and commercial centre. Industries inc. coffee and cacao processing, flour-milling, fruit and vegetable canning, and the manufacture of clothing, textiles and pharmaceuticals.

Laid out on a rectangular pattern; the architecture is a mixture of Spanish-colonial and modern American, and the buildings inc. a cathedral and a national museum. Founded 1738.

San José USA. Town in California in the fertile fruit-growing Santa Clara Valley

64 km (40 miles) SE of San Francisco. Pop. (1990) 782,248.

A leading world fruit-canning and dried-fruit-packing centre. Meat-packing and brewing. Centre of the Silicon Valley high technology complex. Manufactures electrical and electronic equipment, semiconductors, computers and guided missiles.

Founded 1777. Prospered rapidly with the California Gold Rush (1849). State cap. 1849–51.

San José de Cúcuta ➤CÚCUTA.

San Juan Argentina. Cap. of San Juan province 160 km (100 miles) N of Mendoza at a height of 640 m (2099 ft). Pop. (1991) 119,399.

Commercial centre in a wine-growing region where the water of the San Juan R. is used for irrigation. Trade in wine, frozen meat, dried fruit and dairy produce.

Founded 1562.

San Juan Puerto Rico. Cap. and chief seaport on the NE coast. Pop. (1990) 437,745.

Exports coffee, sugar and tobacco to the USA. The main industry is tourism but there is also sugar-refining, rum-distilling and brewing. Manufactures cigars and cigarettes.

The older part of the city is situated on an island, connected by two bridges to the mainland, where the residential quarters are now located. La Fortaleza, the governor's residence, was built c. 1530; Casa Blanca (1523); cathedral (begun 1512). The School of Tropical Medicine, part of the University of Puerto Rico is located here. Named after Juan Ponce de León, who founded the city (1521) and is buried in the cathedral.

San Juan River Nicaragua. River 193 km (120 miles) long, flowing generally ESE from L. Nicaragua to the Caribbean Sea, forming part of the Nicaragua–Costa Rica frontier.

San Juan River USA. River 640 km (400 miles) long, rising in the San Juan Mountains of SW Colorado, flowing generally W and joining the Colorado R. in S central Utah. On the Colorado Plateau it passes through a series of spectacular twisting canyons (incised meanders) known as the Goosenecks. Unnavigable but used for irrigation.

Sankt Gallen ➤ST GALL.

San Leandro USA. Town in California immediately SE of Oakland. Pop. (1990) 68,223.

Main industries food-processing and the manufacture of tractors and electrical equipment. Noted for the annual cherry and flower festival, exhibiting the produce of the surrounding district.

Sanlúcar de Barrameda Spain. Seaport and resort in Cádiz province, Andalusia on the estuary of the Guadalquivir R. 27 km (17 miles) N of Cádiz. Pop. (1991) 55,934.

Exports wine (manzanilla). Industries inc. flour-milling and distilling.

Site of a Roman settlement. Became important in the late 15th cent. A 16th-cent. hospital founded by Henry VIII for English sailors. Here Columbus embarked on his third voyage (1498) and Magellan on his circumnavigation of the world (1519).

San Luis Argentina. Cap. of San Luis province just S of the Sierra de San Luis at a height of 750 m (2460 ft) 260 km (160 miles) ESE of Mendoza. Pop. (1991) 121,146.

Trade in grain, wine and livestock. Hydroelectric station and irrigation dam nearby. Onyx-quarrying.

Founded (1596) by Martín de Loyola, governor of the captaincy general of Chile.

San Luis Potosí Mexico. 1. A central state. Area 63,068 sq km (24,351 sq. miles). Pop. (1990) 2,001,966. Mountainous; crossed by the Sierra Madre Oriental. The N part is arid, the SE fertile and irrigated. Chiefly a mining state (silver). Coffee and tobacco grown in the SE.

2. Cap. of San Luis Potosí state on the plateau at a height of 1880 m (6166 ft) 362 km (225 miles) NW of Mexico City. Pop. (1990) 525,819.

Railway and commercial centre. Smelting and metal-refining (silver, arsenic). Manufactures textiles, clothing, footwear, brushes and ropes.

Has a noteworthy cathedral and government palace. Famous for the multi-coloured glazed tiles in many of the old buildings.

San Marcos Guatemala. State of SW Guatemala on the Mexican border. Area 3792 sq km (1464 sq. miles). Pop. (1992) 723,075. Chief towns San Marcos, San Pedro. Coastal plain on a short Pacific coastline rises to highlands inc. Tacaná and Tajumulco volcanoes. Drained by the Suchiate and Naranjo Rs. Agricultural area with stock-farming in the highlands. Main industries textiles and salt-working.

San Marino. 1. A land-locked independent republic in central Italy near the Adriatic coast 14 km (9 miles) SSW of Rimini. Area 61 sq km (24 sq. miles). Pop. (1995) 24,900 (90 per cent urban). Life expectancy 77 years male, 85 female. Cap. San Marino. Other towns Serravalle/ Dogano, Borgo Maggiore. Currency: Italian lira = 100 centesimi, but it issues its own coins. A mountainous country reaching 743 m (2438 ft) in Monte Titano with a Mediterranean climate. Land use: agricultural and under permanent cultivation 74 per cent, meadows and pastures 22 per cent. The majority of the pop. is Roman Catholic and Sanmarinesi, about 19 per cent are Italian. The official lang. is Italian.

Main occupations are tourism (over 3.5 million visitors per annum), agriculture, stock-rearing. Industries also inc. textiles and the manufacture of bricks and tiles. Exports wine, textiles, postage stamps, building stone, quarried on Monte Titano.

The smallest republic in Europe and claims to be the oldest in the world, having been founded, according to tradition, by St Marinus, a Christian stone-cutter, in the 4th cent. There were several unsuccessful attempts to annex the republic to the papal states in the 18th cent. When Napoleon invaded Italy in 1797 he respected the rights of the republic and in 1815 the Congress of Vienna recognized its independence. San Marino is governed by a 60-member Grand Council elected every 5 years by popular vote, 2 of whom are appointed every 6 months to act as regents.

2. Cap. of San Marino republic on Monte Titano. Pop. (1991) 2339. It is linked by road with Rimini. In its principal church is the tomb of St Marinus.

San Mateo USA. Residential town in California on San Francisco Bay 24 km (15 miles) S of San Francisco, Pop. (1970) 78,991. In a horticultural and market-gardening district. First settled (1851) by John B. Cooper, a deserter from the British Navy.

San Miguel El Salvador. Cap. of the San Miguel department, at the foot of the volcano San Miguel 2130 m (6990 ft) 113 km (70 miles) ESE of San Salvador. Pop. (1971) 110,966.

Industries inc. flour-milling. Manufactures cotton goods and rope. Trade in cereals, cotton and sisal.

Founded (1530) by Spanish settlers.

San Miguel (Panama) ➤PEARL ISLANDS.

San Nicolás Argentina. River port and industrial town in Buenos Aires province on the Paraná R. 61 km (38 miles) SE of Rosario. Pop. (1970) 55,353.

Trade in meat, hides, wool and grain. Has a large steel plant and power station.

Founded 1748.

San Pablo Philippines. Town in Luzon 76 km (47 miles) SSE of Manila. Pop. (1990) 161,000.

Commercial centre. Trade in copra and rice.

San Pedro de Macorís Dominican Republic. Cap. of the San Pedro de Macorís province 64 km (40 miles) E of Santo Domingo. Pop. (1982) 115,000.

Caribbean seaport. Exports sugar and molasses. Sugar and flour milling and tanning. Manufactures clothing and soap.

San Pedro Sula Honduras. Cap. of the Cortés department and second largest town in Honduras 169 km (105 miles) NW of Tegucigalpa. Pop. (1989) 300,400.

Industrial and commercial centre in a region producing bananas and sugar-cane.

Industries inc. flour-milling, tanning and brewing.

Manufactures soap, cigarettes, food products, zinc roofing and furniture.

Founded 1536.

Sanquhar Scotland. Town in Dumfries and Galloway on the R. Nith 39 km (24 miles) NW of Dumfries. Pop. (1991) 2095. The 'Declarations of Sanquhar' were affixed to the market cross by Covenanters (1680, 1685) renouncing allegiance to Charles II and James II respectively.

San Rafael Argentina. Town in Mendoza province 200 km (125 miles) SSE of Mendoza. Pop. (1989) 46,000.

In an area irrigated for vines, fruit and cereals. A commercial centre. Industries inc. meat-packing, fruit drying and canning, wine-making.

San Remo Italy. Port and resort in Imperia province, Liguria on the Italian Riviera (Riviera de Ponente) 113 km (70 miles) SW of Genoa. Pop. (1989) 60,000.

Trade in flowers, olives and fruit.

The old town with its narrow streets stands above the modern town of hotels, villas and gardens, which was severely damaged in World War II.

San Salvador (Watling Island) Bahamas. Island in the central Bahamas. Area 163 sq km (63 sq. miles). Pop. (1990) 539 with Rum Cay.

Chief occupation farming.

Scene of Columbus's first sight of land on the American continent (1492).

San Salvador El Salvador. Cap., also cap. of the San Salvador department, at a height of 680 m (2230 ft) at the foot of the dormant volcano San Salvador. Pop. (1987) 481,397.

The country's largest city and chief commercial and industrial centre. Manufactures textiles, clothing, cigars and cigarettes, and soap. Meat-packing and flour-milling.

Has repeatedly suffered from earthquakes (esp. 1854); the frequent rebuilding has given it a modern appearance. Founded 1525. Cap. from 1841.

San Sebastián Spain. Cap. of Guipúzcoa province on the Bay of Biscay at the mouth of the Urumea R. Pop. (1991) 169,933.

Port and seaside resort. Industries inc. fishing and the manufacture of soap, cement, glass, electronics and paper.

Situated on a narrow peninsula at the foot of Monte Urgull, which is topped by a fortress; the old town is separated from the new town by the Alameda (avenue) crossing the peninsula. The municipal museum has paintings by Goya and El Greco.

San Severo Italy. Town in Foggia province, Apulia 29 km (18 miles) NNW of Foggia. Pop. (1971) 49,011.

Produces wine, olive oil and pasta. Brick-making.

Santa Ana El Salvador. Cap. of the Santa Ana department 51 km (32 miles) NW of San Salvador at a height of 650 m (2132 ft). Pop. (1987) 232,210. El Salvador's second largest city.

Chief industry coffee-processing; also sugar-milling and brewing. Manufactures textiles, leather goods, cigars and food products. Claims to have the world's largest coffee mill (El Molino).

Cathedral (Spanish Gothic).

Santa Ana USA. Town in California at the foot of the Santa Ana Mountains 45 km (28 miles) SE of Los Angeles. Pop. (1990) 293,742.

Main industry fruit packing and canning (citrus and deciduous fruits). Beet-sugar refining.

Santa Barbara USA. Residential town and resort in California on the Pacific coast 140 km (87 miles) WNW of Los Angeles. Pop. (1990) 85,571.

In a district noted for citrus fruits and flowers. Fine beach and a beautiful setting, with a mild climate, luxuriant subtropical vegetation and picturesque buildings in the Spanish style. Industries inc. space research.

The principal historic building is the Santa Barbara Mission, completed in 1820 to replace an earlier one destroyed by earthquake in 1812. Founded 1782.

Santa Barbara Islands USA. Group of 8 main islands and several uninhabited islets off the Pacific coast of S California. The N group. inc. San Miguel, Santa Rosa, Santa Cruz, Anacapa; the S group has Santa Catalina, San Clemente, San Nicolas, Santa Barbara. Santa Catalina, the largest, is a well-known resort with fine bathing beaches and deep-sea fishing.

Santa Catarina Brazil. Maritime state in the S. Area 95,318 sq km (36,803 sq. miles). Pop. (1991) 4,536,433. Cap. Florianopolis. Narrow coastal lowlands with lagoons and offshore islands; to the W the Serra do Mar and the plateau. Forested in the N; grassy areas in the S. Economy largely based on maize cultivation and pig-rearing. Coal mined in the SE.

Santa Clara Cuba. Cap. of Villa Clara province on the plateau 257 km (160 miles) ESE of Havana. Pop. (1989) 190,735.

Important route and commercial centre in an agricultural region. Trade in coffee, sugar-cane and tobacco. Manufactures cigars and leather.

Some fine old 'colonial' buildings. Founded 1689.

Santa Clara USA. Town in California immediately NW of San José. Pop. (1990) 93,613.

Main industry fruit packing and canning. Manufactures machinery and chemicals.

Santa Clara Island ➤JUAN FERNANDEZ ISLANDS.

Santa Cruz Bolivia. Cap. of Santa Cruz department 306 km (190 miles) ESE of Cochabamba at a height of 480 m (1574 ft). Pop. (1989) 529,200.

Commercial centre. Trade in rice, sugar-cane. Sugar-milling, tanning and distilling. Since 1953 linked by road with Cochabamba, by rail with Corumbá (Brazil) and with Aguaray (Argentina), leading to much expansion. In the SE there are large deposits of iron ore and manganese. Oil and natural gas are also exploited.

Founded (1560) in the uplands; removed to its present site in 1595.

Santa Cruz USA. Town in California on Monterey Bay 96 km (60 miles) SSE of San Francisco. Pop. (1989) 50,050.

Holiday resort: bathing beaches, deep-sea fishing and yachting. Industries inc. fishing, fish-canning and electronics.

Santa Cruz de Tenerife Canary Islands. 1. One of the two Spanish provinces; the four main W islands (Tenerife, Gomera, Palma, Hierro). Area 3208 sq km (1238 sq. miles). Pop. (1991) 1,456,474.

2. Cap. of Santa Cruz de Tenerife province on the island of Tenerife. Pop. (1991) 189,317.

Important tourist centre and fuelling station (oil and coal) for ships travelling from Europe to South Africa and S America. Excellent harbour. Oil refinery. Exports bananas, tomatoes and potatoes.

Santa Cruz Islands ➤SOLOMON ISLANDS.

Santa Cruz River Argentina. River 320 km (200 miles) long in Santa Cruz province in Patagonia, rising in L. Argentino and flowing E to the Atlantic.

Santa Fé Argentina. Cap. of Santa Fé province and river port on the Salado R. 160 km (100 miles) N of Rosario. Pop. (1991) 442,214.

Serves a grain-growing and stock-rearing area. Flour-milling and tanning. Manufactures dairy produce.

Founded 1573.

Santa Fé USA. State cap. of New Mexico at a height of 2100 m (6888 ft) 88 km (55 miles) NE of Albuquerque. Pop. (1990) 55,859.

Tourist and commercial centre of great historical interest. The first atomic bomb was developed near here at the nuclear weapons research centre.

Among notable buildings are the 17th-cent. adobe Palace of the Governors and the Cathedral of St Francis (1869). Founded (1609) by the Spaniards. Headquarters of Spanish, Indian, Mexican, Confederate and

US governors in turn. W terminus of the Santa Fé Trail in the 19th cent. Developed with the coming of the railway (1880).

Santa Maria (Azores) ►AZORES.

Santa Maria Brazil. Town in Rio Grande do Sul state 257 km (160 miles) W of Pôrto Alegre. Pop. (1990) 151,202.

Railway junction. Trade in agricultural produce. Railway engineering, brewing and tanning.

Santa Marta Colombia. Cap. of the Magdalena department on a deep bay NW of the Sierra Nevada de Santa Marta in the N. Pop. (1985) 177,922. Terminus of the Atlantic railroad from Bogotá.

Important tourist centre and banana port. Also exports coffee and hides.

Founded 1525. Sacked many times in the early colonial period. Simón Bolívar died at an hacienda nearby (1830).

Santa Monica USA. Residential town and resort in Californa 24 km (15 miles) W of Los Angeles. Pop. (1990) 88,905. Beautifully situated on Santa Monica Bay near the picturesque Santa Monica Mountains. Bathing beaches, yachting, fishing facilities.

Manufactures aircraft, plastics and cosmetics.

Santander Spain. 1. Province in Old Castile on the Bay of Biscay. Area 5289 sq km (2042 sq. miles). Pop. (1991) 526,866. Crossed W–E by the Cantabrian Mountains, which rise to over 2600 m (8528 ft) in the Picos de Europa (W). Main occupations mining (iron, zinc, lead), fishing and stock-rearing.

2. Cap. of Santander province on an inlet of the Bay of Biscay. Pop. (1991) 189,069.

Important seaport and resort. Exports minerals, wine and wheat. Shipbuilding, oil-refining, tanning. Manufactures chemicals, cables, nuclear equipment and machinery.

Santarém Portugal. Town situated NE of Lisbon on Lower Tagus R. in Ribatejo. Pop. (1985) 24,733.

Commercial centre of an agricultural area, noted for raising horses and fighting bulls, corn, viticulture, rice and tomato pro-

duction, trading in olive oil, wine, fruit, grain and cork. Industries inc. the manufacture of alcohol and fertilizers.

Santa Rosa USA. Town in California 80 km (50 miles) NNW of San Francisco. Pop. (1990) 113,313.

In a fruit-growing region. Fruit canning and drying, wine-making.

Scene of the plant-breeding experiments of Luther Burbank (1849–1926).

Santa Tecla (Nueva San Salvador) El Salvador. Cap. of La Libertad department 11 km (7 miles) W of San Salvador at a height of 900 m (2952 ft). Pop. (1971) 55,718.

An attractive residential and commercial centre in a coffee-growing and stock-rearing region.

Founded (1854) to replace San Salvador as cap. when the latter was destroyed by earthquake; San Salvador was rebuilt by 1859, however, and became cap. again.

Santee River USA. River 230 km (143 miles) long in South Carolina, formed by the union of the Congaree and the Wateree rivers, flowing SE to the Atlantic. Part of a large hydroelectric and waterway development (1939–42): the Santee Dam forms L. Marion 64 km (40 miles) long and up to 19 km (12 miles) wide.

Santiago Chile. Cap. of the republic and of Santiago province on the Mapocho R. at a height of 595 m (1952 ft). Pop. (1991) 3,604,056. Situated on a wide plain at the foot of the Andes, it has a colonial nucleus, but is essentially a modern city.

Its industries (textiles, clothing, footwear, chemicals, metal goods and food products) produce more than half the national output. Linked by rail through the central valley with the N and S, with its port Valparaiso 96 km (60 miles) to the WNW and by the Trans-Andean Railway with Argentina.

Cathedral, originally built in 1619 and several times reconstructed; many fine parks and squares. Its principal thoroughfare is the Avenida Bernardo O'Higgins (The Alameda), over 3 km (2 miles) long. Founded (1541) by Pédro de Valdivia.

Santiago de Compostela (Santiago)
Spain. Ancient Campus Stellae. City in Corunna province, Galicia 56 km (35 miles) SSW of Corunna. Pop. (1991) 87,472.

Trade in cereals, fruit and wool. Caters for tourists. Industries inc. brewing and distilling. It manufactures linen, soap, paper and matches.

The most famous place of pilgrimage in Spain since medieval times; the 11th/13th cent. Romanesque cathedral contains the tomb of St James, patron saint of Spain, and noted for the processions swinging the huge censer known as the *Botafumeiro*. Besides the cathedral, with its finely sculptured 12th-cent. Pórtico de la Gloria, there is a noteworthy archbishop's palace. University (1501).

Santiago de Cuba Cuba. Cap. of the Oriente province on the S coast 770 km (480 miles) ESE of Havana. Pop. (1989) 397,024.

Major seaport and industrial centre. Exports tobacco and cigars, sugar, rum and mineral ores. Industries inc. sugar-milling, tanning, rum-distilling, brewing and oil-refining. It manufactures cigars, soap, perfumes and textiles. Picturesquely situated in a natural amphitheatre, approached from the sea by a narrow channel 8 km (5 miles) long.

Founded (1514) by Diego Velázquez, who is buried in the cathedral.

Santiago del Estero Argentina. Cap. of Santiago del Estero province on the Río Dulce 145 km (90 miles) SE of Tucumán. Pop. (1991) 201,709.

Commercial centre. Trade in cotton, cereals and livestock. Flour-milling, tanning and textile manufacture.

Founded 1553 by settlers moving S from Peru.

Santiago de los Caballeros (Santiago)
Dominican Republic. Cap. of Santiago province 145 km (90 miles) NW of Santo Domingo. Pop. (1986) 308,400.

Important commercial centre, in a fertile agricultural region producing coffee, rice and tobacco. Coffee and rice milling. Manufac-tures cigars and cigarettes, furniture and pottery.

Founded (*c.* 1500) by Bartholomew Columbus. Rebuilt after the earthquake of 1564.

Santiago River ➤MEXICO.

Santo Domingo Dominican Republic. Cap. and chief seaport on the S coast. Pop. (1989) 2,200,000.

Exports sugar, cacao and coffee. Distilling, brewing and tanning. Manufactures soap.

In the 16th-cent. Renaissance cathedral is the reputed tomb of Columbus. In many ways a typical Spanish colonial town. Founded (1496) by Bartholomew Columbus. Suffered severely in a hurricane (1930) and was largely rebuilt. Renamed after President Rafael Trujillo Molina 1936; when he was assassinated (1961) the old name was restored.

Santos Brazil. Seaport in São Paulo state 53 km (33 miles) SE of São Paulo. Pop. (1991) 428,526. Serves São Paulo city and is linked with it by rail and road over the steep Serra do Mar. The world's leading coffee port.

Other exports sugar, bananas, citrus fruits and cotton. Has a modern well-equipped harbour and is served by the Cubatão hydro-electric power station 10 km (6 miles) to the NW.

San Vicente El Salvador. Cap. of the San Vicente department at the foot of the volcano San Vicente (2175 m; 7134 ft) 43 km (27 miles) ESE of San Salvador. Pop. (1971) 46,844.

In an agricultural region producing coffee, sugar-cane, tobacco. Manufactures textiles, leather goods and hats.

Founded in 1634 on the site of Tehuacan, an ancient Aztec city. Cap. 1832–9.

São Francisco River Brazil. River 2900 km (1800 miles) long rising in the Serra da Canastra in SW Minas Gerais, flowing generally NNE and then E, forming the Bahia–Pernambuco and Alagôas–Sergipe boundaries, to enter the Atlantic 88 km (55 miles) NE of Aracajú. Navigable by small vessels in much of the middle course; in the lower course impeded by rapids and the Paulo Afonso Falls.

São Jorge ➤AZORES.

São Luís Brazil. Cap. and chief seaport of Maranhão state on São Luís island 480 km (300 miles) ESE of Belém. Pop. (1991) 695,780.

Exports cotton, babassu oil, hides and skins. Cotton-milling, sugar-refining and distilling.

Founded (1612) by the French; named after Louis XIII.

São Miguel ➤AZORES.

Saône-et-Loire France. Department in E central France in Burgundy. Area 8575 sq km (3311 sq. miles). Pop. (1991) 558,500. Prefecture Mâcon. Bordered on the W by the Loire and extending E beyond the Saône into Bresse, it is crossed by the Canal du Centre, which links the two rivers. Rises to 902 m (2959 ft) in the Monts du Morvan in the extreme NW. Varied and prosperous agriculture; well-known for its red wines. The wine trade is centred on Mâcon; Chalon-sur-Saône is an important agricultural centre.

Saône River France. River 450 km (280 miles) long, rising in the Monts Faucilles in the Vosges department. The chief tributary of the Rhône, it flows generally SSW past Chalon-sur-Saône, Mâcon and Villefranche to join the Rhône R. at Lyon. Its own principal tributaries are the Doubs and the Ognon. Its valley forms part of the important route to Marseille and it is connected by canals with the Moselle, Marne, Loire, Seine, Meuse and Rhine rivers.

São Paulo Brazil. 1. State in the SE with an outlet to the sea at Santos; in size about equal to the UK. Area 248,256 sq km (95,852 sq. miles). Pop. (1991) 31,192,818. Apart from the small coastal strip, which has the advantage of a practicable approach to the interior plateau traversed by rail and road, it consists of a tableland drained W to the Paraná R., with an equable climate and rainfall ad-

equate for all crops. The most populous and highly developed state in Brazil; bears comparison in standards of living and productivity with many advanced countries. Much of its soil is the fertile *terra roxa* so well suited for coffee-growing and its development as the main coffee-producing area led to massive immigration, mainly from S Europe and Germany, in the 19th cent. Remains the leading coffee-producing state, but cotton, oranges, bananas and other agricultural crops are of importance.

2. Cap. of São Paulo state on the plateau at a height of 810 m (2657 ft) in a small basin W of the escarpment (Serra do Mar) and 53 km (33 miles) NW of its port Santos. S America's leading industrial centre and one of the world's most rapidly growing cities: pop. (1874) 25,000; (1920) 579,000; (1960) 3,825,351; (1991) 9,480,427. A city of modern buildings, with a highway network and two airports, served by power from the Cubatão and Tietê valley hydroelectric plants.

Manufactures textiles, clothing, paper, chemicals, metal goods, cars, machinery and pharmaceuticals. Has two excellent collections of pictures both modern and old masters, and the famous Butanta Institute where snake serums are produced.

Founded in 1554 by Jesuits on the site of an Indian village. The original settlers came from S Portugal and were ambitious, energetic people, bands of whom (*bandeirantes*) pressed on into the interior; the 'Paulistas' have remained the most enterprising of all Brazilians.

São Paulo de Luanda ➤LUANDA.

São Tomé São Tomé e Príncipe. Cap. and main port on the NE coast of São Tomé island. Pop. (1984) 34,997.

Exports coffee and cocoa. Tourism is being developed.

São Tomé e Príncipe. Independent republic comprising the islands of São Tomé, Príncipe, Pedras Tinhosas and Rolas, lying about 200 km (125 miles) off the W coast of Gabon in the Gulf of Guinea. Area 1001 sq km (386 sq. miles). Pop. (1995) 131,000 (44 per cent urban). Life expectancy, 62 years male, 65 female. Cap. São Tomé on São Tomé island. Currency: Dobra = 100 centimos. The republic consists of 2 volcanic mountainous islands with Pico de São Tomé at 2024 m (6640 ft) the highest point. These are roughly 144 km (90 miles) apart. It has a tropical climate which is modified by altitude and the effect of the cool Benguela current. The inhabitants comprise descendants of Angolan slaves, descendants of freed slaves, contract labour from Angola, Mozambique and Cape Verde, children born on the islands (*Tongas*) and Europeans, and are mainly Roman Catholic. Portuguese is the official lang.

Agriculture is the chief occupation and accounts for all exports which inc. cacao, copra and coconuts.

The islands of São Tomé and Príncipe were discovered in 1471 by Pedro Escobar and João Gomes, and from 1522 constituted a Portuguese colony. In 1951 it became an overseas province of Portugal. Independence was gained in 1975. There is a 55-member People's Assembly elected for a 4-year term.

Sapele ➤NIGERIA.

Sapporo Japan. Cap. of Hokkaido prefecture in the SW of the island 153 km (95 miles) NNE of Hakodate. Pop. (1991) 1,696,056.

Industrial and cultural centre. Industries inc. winter sports, flour-milling, brewing and sawmilling. Manufactures agricultural machinery. Founded 1871.

Saqqara ➤SAKKARA.

Saragossa ➤ZARAGOZA.

Sarajevo Bosnia and Hercegovina. Cap. situated 200 km (125 miles) SW of Belgrade on the Valley of the Miljacka R. Pop. (1991) 525,980.

It is a busy transport and commercial centre. It manufactures chemicals, carpets, pottery, tobacco products, and there is flour-milling, brewing and engineering. Lignite is found in the vicinity.

The old city centre is Muslim-influenced, with mosques, bazaars and public baths, and streets devoted to particular trades. Among extensive modern building are structures dating from the Winter Olympics of 1984. There has been great destruction during the civil war and it was besieged during 1993–4. The finest mosque is the Begova Džamia (1530), built by Husref Bey and containing an early copy of the Koran. The Austrians drove out the Turks in 1878. The assassination of the Archduke Francis Ferdinand in Sarajevo (1914) led to World War I.

Sarandë Albania. Town situated SE of Valona on the Ionian Sea. Port and commercial centre. Naval base.

Saransk Russia. Cap. of the Mordovian Republic 250 km (155 miles) SSE of Nizhni Novgorod. Pop. (1991) 319,600.

Industries mainly concerned with the processing of agricultural produce (grain, sugarbeet, hemp and dairy produce). Also manufactures agricultural machinery, electrical equipment and clothing.

Founded 1641.

Sarapul Russia. River port in the Udmurt Republic on the Kama R. 53 km (33 miles) SE of Izhevsk. Pop. (1991) 110,600.

Manufactures leather, footwear and rope. Trade in grain and timber.

Sarasota USA. Winter resort on Sarasota Bay, SW Florida 72 km (45 miles) S of Tampa. Pop. (1970) 40,237.

Exports citrus fruit and vegetables. Has the famous Ringling museums.

Saratoga Springs USA. Resort in New York state 48 km (30 miles) N of Albany. Pop. (1970) 18,845. State-owned mineral springs; the water is bottled and distributed to other parts of the USA. A favourite retreat for authors and artists. Well-known for its summer race meetings.

Saratov Russia. Cap. of the Saratov Region on the Volga R. 346 km (215 miles) SW of Samara. Pop. (1990) 911,100.

Important industrial centre. Manufactures tractors and combine harvesters, diesel engines, railway rolling-stock, ball-bearings and processed food. It has an oil refinery and produces natural gas, and is linked by pipeline with Moscow. Flour-milling and sawmilling.

Founded in 1590 on the left bank of the Volga R.; moved to its present site on the higher right bank in the 17th cent.

Sarawak Malaysia. State in Eastern Malaysia bounded N and S by the China Sea, NE by Brunei and Sabah and E and S by Kalimantan (Indonesia). Area 124,449 sq km (48,050 sq. miles). Pop. (1990) 1,669,000. Cap. Kuching. Low-lying around the coast; mountainous and forested inland. Mainly agricultural, chief products rubber, timber, pepper and sago. Principal towns Kuching and Sibu. In 1841 the territory was granted to Sir James Brooke by the Sultan of Brunei in return for help in quelling a revolt and the former became rajah. It was gradually enlarged and in 1888 became a British protectorate. During World War II it was occupied by the Japanese (1941–5). In 1946 Sarawak was ceded by the last rajah to Britain and became a Crown Colony. Joined the Federation of Malaysia in 1963. ➤FEDERATION OF MALAYSIA.

Sarcelles France. N suburb of Paris in the Val-d'Oise department. Pop. (1982) 53,732.
Manufactures plastics and paints.

Sardes (Sardis) Asia Minor. Ancient city in W Asia Minor, cap. of Lydia; a small village in modern Turkey 56 km (35 miles) ENE of Izmir. Captured by Persians, Athenians and Romans. An early centre of Christianity, it was one of the Seven Churches of Asia. Destroyed by Tamerlane (1402).

Sardinia (Italian **Sardegna**) Italy. The second largest island in the Mediterranean, separated from Corsica (N) by the Strait of Bonifacio, 12 km (7½ miles) wide. Area 24,090 sq km (9301 sq. miles). Pop. (1991) 1,645,192. Cap. and chief seaport Cagliari. With some neighbouring small islands, an autonomous region; divided into 4 provinces. Largely mountainous and wild, rising to 1834 m (6016 ft) in the Monti del Gennargentu, near the centre. Hot, dry summers

follow mild winters. Annual rainfall 35–65 cm (14–25 ins.) in the lowlands, higher in the mountains.

Agriculture is most successful in the fertile Campidano plain (SW), where cereals, grapes (for wine) and olives are grown and sheep and goats raised. One of Italy's chief mining areas, esp. for zinc and lead; chief centres Cagliari, Sassari, Iglesias.

Evidence of the earliest inhabitants of the island is seen in the strange stone dwellings called *nuraghi*. Fell to the Carthaginians (c. 500 BC) and to the Romans (238 BC). Invaded by Saracens in the 8th–11th cent. AD. Disputed by Pisa and Genoa in the 11th–14th cent. Passed to the House of Savoy as part of the Kingdom of Sardinia 1720. Incorporated into the newly united Italy 1861.

Sardis ➤SARDES.

Sarema ➤SAAREMAA.

Sargasso Sea. Calm region in the North Atlantic Ocean lying between 20° and 40°N and bounded on the W and N by the swift NE flowing Gulf Stream, on the E by the Canary current and on the S by the North Equatorial current. Under the influence of the earth's rotation, this clockwise (anti-cyclonic) gyre causes the water to pile up towards the centre of the Sargasso Sea, which is about 1 m (3.28 ft) higher than the sea-level on the E coast of the USA. The Sargasso derives its name from a floating brown sea-weed, *Sargassum natans*, which was first observed there by Christopher Columbus in 1492. It is a breeding-ground for eels which migrate to Europe.

Sari Iran. Town situated E of Babul on Tajan R. near the Caspian Sea. Pop. (1983) 125,000.
Centre of an agricultural area growing rice, sugar-cane and oranges.

Sark (Fr. **Sercq**) England. Smallest of the four main Channel Is. 10 km (6 miles) E of Guernsey. Area 5 sq km (2 sq. miles). Pop. (1986) 550. Consists of Great Sark (N) and Little Sark (S), connected by an isthmus, the Coupée. The interior is reached by tunnels from the harbour at Creux (E).

Main occupations farming, fishing and tourism. Much natural beauty within a small compass. Motor traffic, except tractors, not allowed.

The island, which has a semi-feudal constitution, is governed by a hereditary seigneur. There is no income tax.

Sarnath India. Site in Uttar Pradesh 6 km (4 miles) N of Varanasi (Benares) of the Deer Park where Buddha preached his first sermon after the enlightenment. The ruins inc. an Asokan pillar.

Sarnia Canada. Industrial town and port in Ontario on the St Clair R. opposite Port Huron in Michigan. Pop. (1991) 74,167.

Trade in coal, grain and timber. A major oil-refining centre. Much of the petroleum from the Alberta oilfields is refined here; a pipeline was completed in 1953. A natural-gas pipeline has been laid to Toronto and Montreal. A great concentration of petro-chemical industries has developed. Manufactures synthetic rubber.

Sarrelouis ➤SAARLOUIS.

Sarre River ➤SAAR RIVER.

Sarthe France. Department in the W in Maine, drained by the Sarthe R. and its tributaries the Huisne and the Loir. Area 6206 sq km (2396 sq. miles). Pop. (1991) 514,600. Prefecture Le Mans.

Mainly low-lying and agricultural. Produces cereals, hemp, cider apples and pears. The famous Percheron horses are raised. Chief towns Le Mans and La Flèche.

Sarthe River France. River 285 km (177 miles) long, rising in the Perche Hills and flowing SW and S past Alençon and Le Mans to join the Mayenne R. above Angers and form the Maine R.

Sarum ➤SALISBURY (ENGLAND).

Sasebo Japan. Seaport and naval station in NW Kyushu in the Nagasaki prefecture 53 km (33 miles) NNW of Nagasaki. Pop. (1991) 243,960.

Exports coal and there is shipbuilding and engineering.

Saskatchewan Canada. Central province of the three Prairie Provinces, bounded on the S by Montana and North Dakota in the USA. Area 652,330 sq km (251,866 sq. miles). Pop. (1991) 988,928. Cap. Regina. The N half (a region of coniferous forest, lake and swamp, containing most of L. Athabasca and Reindeer L.) is drained by the Churchill R. and its tributaries. To the S the forests give way to open prairie and the land gradually rises, reaching 1387 m (4549 ft) in the SW. Climate continental; long, cold winters, short, hot, sunny summers. Annual rainfall only 25–40 cm (10–15 ins.). Wheat is the mainstay of the agriculture; the province produces about two-thirds of Canada's output. Principal minerals petroleum (SW), uranium (NW), copper. Chief towns Regina, Saskatoon. First explored by white fur traders in the late 17th cent. The District of Saskatchewan was formed (1882) as part of the Northwest Territories. It became a separate province in 1905.

Saskatchewan River Canada. River formed by the union of the N and the S Saskatchewan rivers. The N Saskatchewan, 1223 km (760 miles) long, rises near Mt Saskatchewan in the Rocky Mountains in SW Alberta and flows generally E in a winding course past Edmonton and Prince Albert. The S Saskatchewan, 1392 km (865 miles) long (from the farthest headstream), is formed from the Bow and the Oldman rivers in S Alberta and flows generally E and NE past Saskatoon. After their junction 48 km (30 miles) E of Prince Albert, the Saskatchewan R. proper flows 595 km (370 miles) E to the NW end of L. Winnipeg.

Saskatoon Canada. Second largest city in Saskatchewan on the S Saskatchewan R. 233 km (145 miles) NW of Regina. Pop. (1991) 186,058 (113 in 1900; 12,440 in 1911).

Distribution centre for a large agricultural region. Industries inc. flour-milling, meat-packing, brewing, oil-refining and oil-related products.

Sassari Italy. Second largest city in Sardinia

18 km (11 miles) SE of Porto Torres, its port. Pop. (1991) 120,011.

Olive-growing in the district. Produces cheese, pasta and olive oil.

In the modern town there is a cathedral and a university founded by the Jesuits in 1667.

Satpura Range India. Range of hills of average height 600–900 m (1968–2952 ft) rising to over 1200 m (3936 ft) between the Narmada and Tapti rivers. Extends about 960 km (600 miles) partly along the boundary between Madhya Pradesh and Maharashtra.

Satu Mare Romania. Town in the extreme NW on the Someş R. near the Hungarian frontier. Pop. (1992) 131,859.

Manufactures textiles, electric motors, machinery, funiture and toys. Trade in agricultural produce.

Saudi Arabia. Kingdom in SW Asia bounded W by the Red Sea, E by the Gulf and the United Arab Emirates, N by Jordan, Iraq and Kuwait and S by Yemen and Oman. Area 2,240,000 sq km (865,000 sq. miles). Pop. (1995) 17,880,000 (80 per cent urban). Life expectancy, 67 years male, 70 female. Political cap. Riyadh and the religious cap. Mecca. Important towns are Medina, Taif, Hofuf and Buraida. Chief seaports Jidda and Damman. Currency: Saudi riyal = 100 lalalah. Saudi Arabia occupies 70 per cent of the peninsula of Arabia. A large proportion of the country consists of desert, agriculture being possible only in the upland regions of Asia in the SW and in the oases. It is divided into 14 provinces, the Eastern province being the largest. It has a desert climate with very little rain and none between June and December. Land use: forested 0.6 per cent, meadows and pastures 40 per cent, agricultural and under permanent cultivation 1 per cent. About 92 per cent are Sunni Muslims and the official lang. is Arabic.

Oil production began in 1938 and proven reserves, in 1995, represented 25.7 per cent of the world's resources. Production comes from 14 major oilfields, the most important are Ghawar, the world's largest oilfield in

operation, Abqaiq, Safaniyah, the largest offshore field and Berri. There are 5 domestic oil refineries. Natural gas production is also important, originally this was flared as a waste product but is now being used for the petrochemical industry which is being developed along with other manufacturing industries. In the oases dates form the main crop; wheat, barley, coffee and limes are also produced. The chief products of the nomadic Bedouin tribes are hides, wool and clarified butter, obtained from their camels, sheep and goats. Formerly much of the national income was derived from visitors to Mecca and Medina.

The Kingdom of Saudi Arabia is the union of two regions, Hejaz and Nejd in 1926. They were united by Abdul Aziz Ibn Saud who founded the kingdom of Saudi Arabia in 1932. The King is also Prime Minister and the religious leader; there is no legislative body and no political parties. King Ibn Saud was succeeded by his sons Saud, Faisal, Khalid and Fahd. In 1992 the King decreed that a 60-member Consultative Council of royal nominees should be established.

Sault Sainte Marie Canada. Port in Ontario on the St Mary's R. connecting L. Superior (W) and L. Huron (E), opposite the twin city of Sault Sainte Marie in Michigan. Pop. (1991) 81,476.

Holiday resort. Industrial centre. Railway engineering. Manufactures steel, wood-pulp and paper. The rapids are circumvented by a canal; this canal and the canal on the US side are known as the Soo Canals. 'Sault' is Old French for waterfall or rapids.

Sault Sainte Marie USA. Port in Michigan on the St Mary's R. connecting L. Superior (W) and L. Huron (E), opposite the twin city of Sault Sainte Marie in Ontario. Pop. (1989) 17,842.

Manufactures carbide, leather goods, textiles, plastics, vehicle components and veneers. A resort with hunting and fishing facilities.

The rapids were circumvented by a canal in 1919.

Saumur France. Town in the Maine-et-

Loire department 43 km (27 miles) SE of Angers at the confluence of the Loire and the Thouet rivers and on an island in the former. Pop. (1989) 35,000.

Industrial and market town, famous for the sparkling white wines made in the district. Also manufactures brandy, liqueurs, leather and rosaries.

As a centre of Protestantism it suffered severely from the revocation of the Edict of Nantes, losing more than half its pop.

Sauternes France. Village in the Gironde department 39 km (24 miles) SSE of Bordeaux. Has given its name to the sweet white wines of the district, which inc. the vineyards of the world-famous Château d'Yquem.

Savannah USA. River port in Georgia on the Savannah R. 29 km (18 miles) from the mouth. Pop. (1990) 137,560.

Exports naval stores, raw cotton. Shipbuilding. Sugar-refining. Pulp and paper milling. Manufactures cottonseed oil, fertilizers and chemicals. Mild climate, subtropical vegetation. It is a popular resort.

Many historic buildings. Port of departure (1819) of the *Savannah*, the first steamship to cross the Atlantic (25 days to Liverpool).

Savannah River USA. River 502 km (314 miles) long, formed by the union of the Tugaloo and the Seneca rivers, forming the Georgia–South Carolina boundary, flowing generally SE past Augusta and Savannah (both in Georgia) and entering the Atlantic. Navigable for barges below Augusta and used for hydroelectric power.

Sava (Save) River Slovenia/Croatia/Bosnia/Serbia. River 928 km (580 miles) long rising in two headstreams in the Karawanken Alps, flowing generally ESE through Slovenia and Croatia, forming part of the boundary of Croatia with Bosnia and joining the Danube R. at Belgrade. Chief tributaries the Una, Vrbas, Bosna, Drina. Navigable below Sisak.

Savoie (Italian **Savoia**, English **Savoy**) France. 1. Former duchy in the SE, now divided into two departments, Haute-Savoie

(N) and Savoie (S); bounded by L. Geneva (N), Switzerland (NE) and Italy (E). Mainly in the Savoy Alps, with the Mont Blanc massif in the E and the Graian Alps in the SE. Cap. Chambéry. Cattle-rearing and dairy-farming important; many tourist centres and hydroelectric stations. Lost much of its area to Switzerland and France after 1472. Became part of the Kingdom of Sardinia 1720 and again in 1815; finally returned to France in 1860, when the present departments were created.

2. Department forming the S part of the former duchy of Savoie. Area 6028 sq km (2327 sq. miles). Pop. (1991) 351,400. Prefecture Chambéry. Bounded by Italy on the E and SE, it is mountainous, lying almost entirely in the Savoy Alps and rising to 3787 m (12,421 ft) in Mont Pourri. Drained by the Isère R. Linked with Piedmont (Italy) by the Mont Cenis and Little St Bernard passes. Dairy produce and wine are important products; hydroelectric plants supply power for metallurgical and chemical industries. Chief towns Chambéry and the spa of Aix-les-Bains.

Savona Italy. Cap. of Savona province in Liguria on the Gulf of Genoa 39 km (24 miles) WSW of Genoa. Pop. (1990) 68,997.

Seaport. Exports pottery, glassware. Also the main industrial centre of the Riviera di Ponente. Manufactures iron and steel, pottery (important since the 16th cent.), glass and bricks.

Long a rival of Genoa, it had lost the struggle by the 16th cent.

Savu (Sawu) Islands Indonesia. Group of islands in the Lesser Sundas between Sumba and Timor. Area 598 sq km (231 sq. miles). Chief island Savu (area 414 sq km; 160 sq. miles, pop. 29,000).

Main products copra, rice and tobacco.

Saxe-Altenburg Germany. Former duchy (1603–72 and again 1825–1918); incorporated into the province of Thuringia 1918.

Saxe-Coburg-Gotha Germany. Former duchy, formed (1826) when Ernest III of Saxe-Coburg received the duchy of Gotha

Saxe-Meiningen

and became Ernest I, Duke of Saxe-Coburg-Gotha. In 1918 his successor abdicated and in 1920 Coburg was incorporated into Bavaria, Gotha into Thuringia.

Saxe-Meiningen Germany. Former duchy founded (1681) by a son of the Duke of Saxe-Gotha, comprising the district round Meiningen. In 1826 it acquired the duchy of Saxe-Saalfeld and other territory, but in 1920 was incorporated into Thuringia.

Saxe-Weimar-Eisenach Germany. Former grand duchy, formed (1728) by the union of the duchies of Saxe-Weimar and Saxe-Eisenach. In the late 18th cent. under Duke Charles Augustus, its cap., Weimar, became one of the leading intellectual centres of Europe, with Goethe and Schiller among its scholars. At the Congress of Vienna (1815) it was raised to the status of a grand duchy and was incorporated into Thuringia in 1920.

Saxony (Ger. **Sachsen**) Germany. *Land* bordered S by the Czech Republic. Area 18,341 sq km (7081 sq. miles). Pop. (1991) 4,784,300. Cap. Dresden. In the S it inc. much of the Erzgebirge and its foothills; descends in the N to the N European plain. Historically the name has been used of two distinct areas. It was originally applied to a region in the NW, roughly corresponding to the present *Land* of Lower Saxony between the North Sea, the Rhine and the Elbe. The Saxons who inhabited this area were conquered by Charlemagne. The first duchy of Saxony was created in the 9th cent. Duke Henry I the Fowler was elected German king in 919; he and his successors ruled until 1002. The duchy was broken up in 1180 and the title passed to Bernard, a son of Albert the Bear of Brandenburg, along with the small regions of Lauenburg and Wittenberg. From 1260 the territories were divided into the duchies of Saxe-Lauenburg and Saxe-Wittenberg; in 1356 the duke of the latter was made Elector. When the line became extinct (1423) Frederick, Margrave of Meissen, added Saxe-Wittenberg to Meissen and Thuringia and became the Elector Frederick I of Saxony. Many changes

took place in the succeeding cent. The Electors of Saxony were kings of part of Poland 1697–1763. The Elector Frederick Augustus III assumed the title of King (1806), but lost the N part of his kingdom, which became a province of Prussia. Subsequently Saxony was a member of the Confederation of the Rhine (1815), the North German Confederation (1866) and the German Empire (1871). At the end of World War I King Frederick Augustus III abdicated and a republic was proclaimed. After World War II the republic, with part of the Prussian province of Lower Silesia, became the *Land* of Saxony; the former Prussian province of Saxony, with the state of Anhalt, became the *Land* of Saxony-Anhalt, both in the former German Democratic Republic (1946). In 1952 Saxony was replaced by the administrative districts of Leipzig, Dresden and Karl-Marx-Stadt, and Saxony-Anhalt by Halle and Magdeburg. The *Land* was reconstituted as the Free State of Saxony in 1990.

Saxony-Anhalt (Ger. **Sachsen-Anhalt**) Germany. *Land* of Federal Germany, created 1990. Area 20,446 sq km (7894 sq. miles). Pop. (1994) 2,778,000. Cap. Magdeburg. Historically part of the former kingdom of Saxony and the former duchy of Anhalt.

Sayan Mountains Russia. Mountain system in the extreme S of Russia, consisting of the Eastern Sayan Mountains, which extend SE from the Yenisei R. to the Russia–Mongolia border and rise to 3491 m (11,457 ft) in Munku Sardyk; and the Western Sayan Mountains, extending ENE from the Altai Mountains to the E Sayan Mountains and rising to over 2700 m (8856 ft). The region yields timber as well as gold, silver, lead and coal.

Scafell (Scaw Fell) England. Mountain mass in Cumbria in the Lake District 16 km (10 miles) WNW of Ambleside. Comprises Scafell Pike (978 m; 3210 ft), the highest peak in England, and Scafell (964 m; 3162 ft), joined by the narrow ridge of Mickledore, together with Great End (910 m; 2985 ft)

818

and Lingmell (808 m; 2650 ft). Belongs to the National Trust.

Scandinavia. Scandinavia is a peninsula in NW Europe comprising the four countries of Denmark, Finland, Norway and Sweden, plus Iceland and the Faeroes.

Scapa Flow Scotland. Stretch of sea in the Orkneys bounded on the N by Mainland, on the E and SE by Burray and S Ronaldsay, on the W and SW by Hoy. Area 129 sq km (50 sq. miles). In the early part of World War I it was the chief base of the British Grand Fleet; here most of the ships of the interned German High Sea Fleet were scuttled by their crews (1919). Again a naval base in World War II.

Scarborough England, Town in North Yorkshire on the North Sea 64 km (40 miles) N of Hull. Pop. (1989) 50,908.

Seaside resort, conference centre and fishing port on the peninsula between North Bay and South Bay and extending inland and along both bays. Minor industries.

Crowning the peninsula are the remains of the 12th-cent. castle, built on the site of a 4th-cent. Roman signal station. The spa contains gardens, theatre, concert hall. Bombarded by German warships in World War I. Birthplace of the painter, Frederic Leighton (1830–96) and the poet, Edith Sitwell (1887–1964).

Scaw Fell ➤SCAFELL.

Schaffhausen Switzerland. 1. Small canton in the N, N of the Rhine R. and almost surrounded by territory of Germany. Area 298 sq km (115 sq. miles). Pop. (1991) 71,697 (German-speaking, mainly Protestant). Its forests are an important source of revenue. Hydroelectric power is derived from the Rhine falls. Industry is concentrated in Schaffhausen. It joined the Swiss Confederation in 1501.

2. Cap. of the Schaffhausen canton on the right bank of the Rhine R. Pop. (1988) 33,800.

Industrial centre, obtaining hydroelectric power from the Rhine falls. Industries inc.

aluminium smelting, railway engineering, iron and steel, and it manufactures metal goods, textiles and watches.

Medieval and modern buildings are intermingled, among the former being the 11th/12th-cent. Romanesque minster, formerly a Benedictine monastery.

Schaumburg-Lippe Germany. Former state between Westphalia and Hanover, now incorporated in Lower Saxony. Area 339 sq km (131 sq. miles). Mainly agricultural; coalmining around Bückeburg, the cap.

Schefferville Canada. Formerly Knob Lake. Town in E Quebec near the Labrador border. Pop. (1971) 3277. The settlement developed in the early 1950s to mine the rich local iron-ore deposits. The railway for transporting the ore to the seaport of Sept Îles was opened in 1954.

Scheldt (Fr. **Escaut**; Flemish, Dutch **Schelde**) **River.** River 434 km (270 miles) long rising in the Aisne department (France), flowing generally NNE past Valenciennes, then crossing Belgium past Tournai, Ghent and Antwerp. Below Antwerp its estuary, the Western Scheldt, enters Dutch territory, separating S Beveland and Walcheren islands from the mainland; the Eastern Scheldt, once a N branch of the estuary, is linked with the Western Scheldt by the S Beveland Canal. In 1648 the Dutch reserved the right to close the Scheldt, but in 1863 navigation was declared free. Chief tributary the Lys. A bridge 5 km (3 miles) long across the Eastern Scheldt, linking the islands of N Beveland and Schouwen-Duiveland, was opened in 1965.

Schenectady USA. Industrial town in New York state on the Mohawk R. 24 km (15 miles) NW of Albany. Pop. (1990) 65,566. Largely dependent on the manufacture of electrical equipment and locomotives. Originally settled by the Dutch (1661). Grew rapidly after the coming of the railways in the 1830s.

Scheveningen Netherlands. Popular seaside resort and fishing port in South Holland province 3 km (2 miles) NW of The Hague, of which it is a suburb.

Schiedam Netherlands. Town and river port in South Holland province 5 km (3 miles) W of Rotterdam. Pop. (1992) 71,117.

Famous for its gin industry, connected with which are manufactures of glass, bottles, crates and corks. Also has shipyards and chemical works.

Schiphol ►AMSTERDAM.

Schleswig Germany. Fishing port, residential and industrial town in Schleswig-Holstein, at the W end of the Schei, an inlet of the Baltic 43 km (27 miles) NW of Kiel. Pop. (1989) 26,817.

Manufactures leather goods, chemicals. Tanning, flour-milling.

Cap. of Schleswig-Holstein 1879–1917. Birthplace of A. J. Carstens (1754–98), the German painter.

Schleswig-Holstein Germany. *Land* bounded on the N by Denmark and mainly occupying the S part of the Jutland peninsula, fringed by the N Frisian Is. (W) and Fehmarn Island (E). Area 15,731 sq km (6074 sq. miles). Pop. (1991) 2,611,300. Cap. Kiel. Low-lying and drained by the Elbe R. (which forms much of the S border) and the Eider R. Crossed by the Kiel Canal linking the Elbe estuary with the Baltic Sea. Main occupation agriculture. Rye, wheat and potatoes cultivated. Many cattle and pigs reared.

The irregular Baltic coastline provides excellent natural harbours; the three chief towns (Kiel, Lübeck, Flensburg) are all seaports. For cent. the duchies of Schleswig and Holstein were associated with the Danish Crown. The Danish–German dispute (the 'Schleswig-Holstein Question') came to a head with the death of Frederick VII of Denmark (1863); the duchies were occupied by Prussian and Austrian troops (1864) and, after the Austro–Prussian War (1866), annexed to Prussia. After World War I a plebiscite restored N Schleswig to Denmark (1920). The present Schleswig-Holstein became a *Land* in 1949.

Schönbrunn Austria. District of Vienna noted for the palace, designed in the 18th cent. for Empress Maria-Theresa, which was the summer residence of the Habsburgs.

Schönebeck Germany. Industrial town and river port in the Magdeburg district 14 km (9 miles) SSE of Magdeburg. Pop. (1989) 45,000.

Salt works. Manufactures chemicals, explosives and machinery.

Schuylkill River USA. River 209 km (130 miles) long in Pennsylvania, flowing generally SE, through an anthracite-mining region, past Reading and joining the Delaware R. at Philadelphia. Navigable by barges for nearly 160 km (100 miles) upstream.

Schwaben ►SWABIA.

Schwäbisch Gmund ►GMUND.

Schwarzwald ►BLACK FOREST.

Schweinfurt Germany. Industrial town in NW Bavaria on the Main R. 37 km (23 miles) NE of Würzburg. Pop. (1984) 51,500.

Manufactures paints and dyes, machinery, ball-bearings.

Founded in the late 8th cent. Became a free imperial city in the late 13th cent.

Schwerin Germany. Cap. of the Schwerin district on the SW shore of L. Schwerin 72 km (45 miles) SW of Rostock. Pop. (1991) 127,447.

Manufactures furniture, soap, pharmaceutical products and tobacco products.

Has a mainly 15th-cent. brick-built cathedral. Founded in 1161, it was cap. of the county of Schwerin, of the duchy (later republic) of Mecklenburg-Schwerin and then of the *Land* of Mecklenburg.

Schwyz Switzerland. 1. Canton in central Switzerland bordering the Lakes of Zürich, Lucerne and Zug. Area 908 sq km (351 sq. miles). Pop. (1991) 110,526 (German-speaking and Catholic). Mountainous, esp. in the S; much of its area consists of pastures, on which cattle are raised, and forests. In 1291 it created the league with Uri and Unterwalden which formed the basis of

Scotland

Swiss independence and gave its name (in the form of Schweiz) to that of the whole confederation.

2. Cap. of the Schwyz canton 24 km (15 miles) E of Lucerne. Pop. (1970) 12,914. Tourist centre at the foot of the Gross Mythen (1903 m; 6242 ft).

Sciacca Italy. Seaport in Agrigento province, Sicily, 72 km (45 miles) SSW of Palermo. Pop. (1971) 30,876. An ancient town surrounded by 16th-cent. walls. Sulphur springs 5 km (3 miles) E.

Scilly Isles ►ISLES OF SCILLY.

Scone Scotland. Parish in Perth and Kinross consisting of the villages of Old Scone and New Scone, the latter 3 km (2 miles) NE of Perth. Old Scone was the Pictish and later the Scottish cap., where the kings of Scotland were crowned 1157–1488 and Charles II in 1651. The Coronation Stone ('Stone of Destiny') on which they were crowned was taken by Edward I of England to Westminster Abbey (1297) and placed beneath the Coronation chair; it was removed from there by Scottish nationalists in 1950 but recovered later; restored to Scotland in 1997.

Scoresby Sound Greenland. Deep inlet into the E coast about 320 km (200 miles) long. Many fiords, which receive glaciers from the interior ice-cap. At the entrance (N side) is the small settlement of Scoresbysund founded in 1925. Named after William Scoresby (1789–1857), the English Arctic explorer.

Scotland. The N part of Great Britain, inc. many islands, e.g. the Inner and Outer Hebrides, the Orkneys, the Shetland (Zetland) Is. Bounded by the Atlantic (W and N), the North Sea (E) and England (S). The structure of local government in Scotland from 1996 consists of 29 single-tier councils responsible for the majority of local government services. The 9 Regional Councils established in 1975 are now abolished, but the 3 Island Councils remain unchanged. The new local authorities are: Aberdeen City,

Aberdeenshire, Angus, Argyll and Bute, East Ayrshire, North Ayrshire, South Ayrshire, Clackmannanshire, Dumfries and Galloway, East Dunbartonshire, West Dunbartonshire, Dundee City, City of Edinburgh, Falkirk, Fife, City of Glasgow, Highland, Inverclyde, North Lanarkshire, South Lanarkshire, East Lothian, West Lothian, Midlothian, Moray, Orkney, Perth and Kinross, Renfrewshire, East Renfrewshire, Scottish Borders, Shetland, Stirling and Western Isles. Area 78,762 sq km (30,410 sq. miles). Pop. (1991) 4,957,000. Cap. Edinburgh. Other cities Glasgow, Aberdeen and Dundee. The highland area rises to the Cairngorm mountains and Ben Nevis (W), 1343 m (4606 ft) above sea level. Mountain ranges rise from high moorland, used for rough grazing and watered by many short, fast-flowing rivers which provide hydroelectric power. The area is bisected by a chain of lakes, along the Great Glen fault which extends SW to NE across the country from Loch Linnhe to Moray Firth. Central Scotland is agricultural, and the industrial lowland is situated mainly in the Forth and Clyde river basins, with extensive coalfields and supporting c. 80 per cent of the pop. S of it is a hilly region with stock-farming predominant and agricultural in the river valleys, esp. the Tweed R. The agricultural areas cover c. 24 per cent of the land.

Religion is mainly Presbyterian and the principal church is the Church of Scotland which is Protestant in theology and Presbyterian in organization. About 1.4 per cent of the pop., mainly in the Highlands, speak the Scottish form of Gaelic.

Nearly 66 per cent of the land surface is classified as rough grazing land. Main crops oats, potatoes and turnips. Stock-rearing is important; Scottish breeds of cattle, notably the Aberdeen Angus beef cattle and the Ayrshire dairy cattle, have won a world reputation. Large numbers of sheep, bred for meat as well as wool, in the E of the Southern Uplands (e.g. Scottish Borders). In the Highlands and the islands the poverty of resources led to crofting, a type of subsistence farming and the consequent low standard of living

821

has caused a gradual drain of pop. The fishing industry has declined in recent years but the economy of the NE (esp. Aberdeen) has benefited enormously, however, from the development of the North Sea oil industry. The coalfields of Ayrshire, Lanarkshire, Fifeshire, Midlothian and Clackmannan (now nearly extinct) formed the basis of the industrial development in the Central Lowlands, exemplified esp. in the great shipbuilding industry along the Clyde estuary, engineering and textile manufacture in the Glasgow area, woollens and tweeds in the Tweed basin, jute in Dundee, beer in Edinburgh. Whisky-distilling is a leading industry. Hydroelectric power has been developed in the Highlands and is utilized in part for aluminium production. The railway network is relatively sparse, esp. in the Highlands; N of the Caledonian Canal the W coast is reached at only two points, Mallaig and Kyle of Lochalsh. The roads are good; the route from Edinburgh to the NE has been much improved by the opening of a road bridge near the famous railway bridge across the Forth (1964).

The Romans, who invaded England under Julius Caesar in 55 BC, were unable to penetrate Scotland until AD 80, when Agricola began his campaign against the northern tribes. Neither the victory at Mons Graupius nor the building of Antoninus's Wall between the Firths of Clyde and Forth (AD 142) was sufficient to hold the Caledonians permanently; by the end of the 2nd cent. the Romans had withdrawn to Hadrian's Wall in the N of England. In the 6th cent. Scotland was occupied by Picts (N), Scots from Ireland (W), Britons (SW) and Angles (SE). The first unifying influence came in 563, with the spread of Christianity by the Irishman St Columba (who had been preceded by St Ninian and St Kentigern); his missionaries travelled far and wide from the settlement on Iona. An army from Northumbria marched as far as the Firth of Forth but was defeated by the Picts (685). Kenneth MacAlpine, King of the Scots, united his people with the Picts in 844. Malcolm II inflicted a further defeat on the Northum-

brians (1018) and occupied the SE; his grandson Duncan succeeded to Strathclyde in the SW, uniting the Picts, the Scots, the Britons and the Angles of mainland Scotland. The islands were still held by the Norsemen: the Hebrides were not recovered till the 13th cent. and the Orkneys and the Shetlands till the 15th.

With Malcolm III's marriage to the English princess Margaret (sister of Edgar Atheling; later St Margaret) the kingdom began to lose its purely Celtic character: English was spoken at court, the Church was Anglicized, Anglo–Norman nobles settled in the S and sometimes married Celtic ladies, and a form of feudalism was established. Under David I (1124–53, a son of Malcolm and Margaret) Scotland was united, a central government was organized and trade developed, esp. with England. By the end of the 13th cent. the English lang. was spoken over most of Scotland S of the Highlands. Anglicization of the Scots, however, did not win their friendship. When Edward I of England claimed overlordship of Scotland and gave the crown to John Balliol, the latter made an alliance with France: the Scots rose under William Wallace, who was captured and executed (1305). Robert Bruce continued the struggle for independence, was crowned at Scone (1306) and utterly defeated the English at Bannockburn (1314). Scottish independence was recognized by England in 1328; the first Stewart, Robert II, came to the throne in 1371. James IV married Margaret Tudor, daughter of Henry VII of England, but the ensuing peace was short-lived; he was killed at the disastrous defeat at Flodden (1513), as was his son, James V, at Solway Moss (1542). French Catholic influence grew under the regency of Mary of Guise (mother of Mary Queen of Scots) but aroused the opposition of people and nobles. The Reformation gained ground and Protestantism was established as the national religion in 1560. After civil war in the reign of Mary (and of Elizabeth I of England), James VI of Scotland became James I of England (1603). There was a temporary union under Cromwell (1651–60) and much civil dissension throughout the Restoration period. Under Queen Anne of England the two Parliaments were united (1707). Opposition to the Act of Union was largely responsible for the Jacobite risings in 1715 and 1745 against the Hanoverian Protestant succession in favour of the exiled Stewarts. The economic benefits of the union ultimately became apparent in a great expansion of commerce; with the Industrial Revolution came the development of the coal, iron, shipbuilding and textile industries in the Central Lowlands. Scotland's justifiable grievance over ther poor political representation at Westminster was rectified by successive Reform Acts in the 19th cent.

Divided administratively into 29 single-tier councils and 3 Islands Councils: Orkney, Shetland and Western Isles. Scotland is represented at Westminster by 72 members in the House of Commons. The Secretary of State for Scotland has a seat in the Cabinet and is assisted at the Scottish Office by a Minister of State. A referendum was held in 1997 to consider whether there should be a Scottish Parliament and whether the Parliament should have tax powers; 74.3 per cent voted for a Parliament and 63.5 per cent for tax powers.

Scottish Borders Scotland. New Unitary Authority created in 1996, formerly Borders Region. Pop. (1993) 105,300.

Scottsdale USA. City immediately NE of Phoenix, Arizona. Pop. (1990) 130,069.

Employment is in services, wholesale and retail trade and some manufacture.

Scranton USA. Industrial town in Pennsylvania on the Lackawanna R. 169 km (105 miles) NNW of Philadelphia. Pop. (1990) 81,805.

Important centre in an anthracite-mining region. Manufactures textiles, clothing, metal goods and plastics.

Scunthorpe England. Town in North Lincolnshire 37 km (23 miles) W of Grimsby, inc. Frodingham. Pop. (1987) 61,500.

An important iron and steel, and engineering centre, it expanded rapidly owing to

exploitation of the iron-ore deposits in the neighbourhood; has blast furnaces and rolling mills. It manufactures clothing, furniture, electronics and foodstuffs.

Scutari (Albania) ➤SHKODËR.

Scutari (Turkey) ➤ISTANBUL.

Scutari, Lake ➤SHKODËR, LAKE.

Scythia. Ancient region in SE Europe on the steppes N of the Black Sea between the Carpathians and the Don R. Its people, the Scythians, flourished between the 7th and 3rd cent. BC and were superseded by the Sarmatians.

Seaford England. Seaside resort in East Sussex 13 km (8 miles) W of Eastbourne. Pop. (1991) 19,622. Formerly at the mouth of the R. Ouse and was a member of the Cinque Port of Hastings, but the river changed course to Newhaven in the 16th cent. and the decline of Seaford as a port, already begun two cent. earlier, was hastened. Its revival as a resort began in the early 19th cent.

Seaforth, Loch Scotland. Inlet into the SE coast of Lewis with Harris, Outer Hebrides, Western Isles, forming part of the boundary between them and extending 24 km (15 miles) inland.

Sea Islands USA. Chain of islands off the coasts of South Carolina, Georgia and N Florida, between the mouths of the Santee and the St John's rivers. Low-lying and sandy on the seaward side. The long-stapled 'Sea Island' cotton was formerly grown, but its cultivation was replaced by mixed farming after destruction by the boll weevil in the 1920s.

Seal Islands ➤LOBOS ISLANDS.

Seaton Carew ➤WEST HARTLEPOOL.

Seattle USA. Largest city in Washington on the isthmus between Puget Sound and L. Washington. Pop. (1990) 516,259.

Important seaport, trading esp. with Alaska and the Far East. Exports timber, canned and fresh fish and fruit. The industrial, commercial and financial cap. of the Pacific NW. Industries inc. tourism, shipbuilding, aircraft manufacture and food-canning.

It became a boom town with the Alaska gold rush (1897). Expanded again with the opening of the Panama Canal (1914). Fine views of the Olympic Mountains (W) and the Cascade Ranges (E).

Sebastopol ➤SEVASTOPOL.

Sebha ➤FEZZAN.

Sebta ➤CEUTA.

Secunderabad India. Former town and cantonment in Andhra Pradesh just N of Hyderabad, in which it is now incorporated. Commercial centre and railway junction. Founded 1806.

Sedan France. Town in the Ardennes department on the Meuse R. 85 km (53 miles) NE of Reims near the Belgian frontier. Pop. (1968) 22,998.

Industries inc. transport and tourism and it manufactures woollen goods, machinery, chemicals and mirrors.

For some time an independent principality; passed to the French crown 1642. A Protestant stronghold in the 16th and 17th cent.; Huguenot weavers laid the foundations of its prosperity. During the Franco–Prussian War (1870) the French were decisively defeated at the Battle of Sedan. In World War II the Germans broke through the French lines here (1940).

Sedbergh England. Town in Cumbria 13 km (8 miles) E of Kendal. Pop. (1991) 1670.

Market town for agriculture and tourism.

Sedgemoor England. Former marshy area, now drained, in Somerset 5 km (3 miles) ESE of Bridgwater, where the forces of James II defeated the Duke of Monmouth (1685).

Segovia Spain. 1. Province in Old Castile on the Meseta, with the Sierra de Guadarrama, rising to 2471 m (8105 ft) in the SE separating Old from New Castile. Area 6949 sq km (2683 sq. miles). Pop. (1991) 146,443. Mainly

agricultural: cereal cultivation, sheep-rearing.

2. Cap. of Segovia province 68 km (42 miles) NW of Madrid. Pop. (1991) 54,142. A town of great historical and architectural interest.

Flour-milling and tanning. Manufactures pottery.

Stands on a rocky ridge above the Eresma R. and a tributary at a height of 999 m (3277 ft), dominated by the mainly 15th-cent. Alcázar (restored) and the 16th-cent. Gothic cathedral. Another noteworthy feature is the Roman aqueduct, which still supplies the city with water.

Seine-et-Marne France. Department in the Paris Basin formed (1790) mainly from Île-de-France and Champagne. Area 5915 sq km (2284 sq. miles). Pop. (1991) 1,102,100. Prefecture Melun. Drained by the Seine and Marne and their tributaries. Between these two important rivers is the fertile Brie region, famous for its wheat and other crops and its cheese, the department supplies many food products to the Paris markets. Principal forest that of Fontainebleau. Chief towns Melun, Fontainebleau.

Seine-Maritime France. Formerly Seine-Inférieure. Department in E Normandy bounded on the NW and N by the English Channel and on the S by the Seine R. and its estuary. Area 6278 sq km (2424 sq. miles). Pop. (1991) 1,226,200. Prefecture Rouen. Flax and other crops are cultivated on the chalky Caux plateau (W), dairy cattle are raised in the Bray district (E) and the valley of the meandering Seine R. is well wooded. Industry and trade concentrated in Rouen, Le Havre and Dieppe.

Seine River France. One of the chief rivers 761 km (473 miles) long, rising on the Plateau de Langres, flowing generally NW across the Paris Basin, crossing Champagne, turning WSW below Troyes, then NW again meandering through Paris and the Île-de-France to Normandy past Rouen and entering the English Channel by an estuary between the ports of Le Havre (N) and Honfleur (S).

Tributaries inc. the Aube, the Marne and the Oise on the right bank and the Yonne on the left, forming an important network of waterways. Linked by canals with the Scheldt (Escaut), the Meuse, the Rhine, the Rhône and the Loire. Navigable for ocean-going vessels as far as Rouen and for barges (partly by lateral canal) as far as Bar-sur-Seine.

Seine-St Denis France. Department just NE of Paris, formed in 1964 when the former Seine and Seine-et-Oise departments were reorganized. Area 236 sq km (91 sq. miles). Pop. (1991) 1,388,000. Prefecture Bobigny.

Sekondi Ghana. Cap. of the Western Region, seaport 8 km (5 miles) NE of Takoradi, with which it is linked by rail. Pop. (Sekondi-Takoradi) (1988) 103,600. It was the Gold Coast colony's chief port after the construction of the railway to the interior, but was superseded by Takoradi in 1928. The two became a single municipality in 1946.

Selangor Malaysia. State in West Malaysia on the Strait of Malacca. Area 7956 sq km (3072 sq. miles). Pop. (1991) 1,978,000. Cap Shah Alam.

Chief products rubber and tin. It produces nearly 50 per cent of Malaysia's industrial output. Main port Port Swettenham.

Selborne England. Village 6 km (4 miles) SSE of Alton, Hampshire, where Gilbert White (1720–93), author of *The Natural History and Antiquities of Selborne*, was born, lived for much of his life and is buried.

Selby England. Town in the City of York unitary area on the R. Ouse 19 km (12 miles) S of York. Pop. (1991) 15,292.

Industries inc. flour-milling, beet-sugar refining and the development of a major coalfield since 1983 linked to the building of a power station in the Aire valley. It manufactures oilcake, chemicals and paper.

The Church of St Mary and St German, which belonged to a Benedictine abbey founded (1069) by William the Conqueror, which was damaged by fire in 1906 and later restored. Reputed to be the birthplace of Henry I (1068–1135).

Selenga River. River 1207 km (750 miles) long, rising in the N Mongolian People's Republic and flowing generally ENE to the Russian frontier, then turning N through the Buryat Republic past Ulan Ude to L. Baikal. Navigable in summer along the Russian section.

Seleucia. Name of several ancient cities founded in the 4th and 3rd cent. BC and called after Seleucus Nicator.

1. Seleucia on the Tigris. City founded 312 BC by Seleucus Nicator, 32 km (20 miles) SE of modern Baghdad (Iraq), as his cap. An important river port with a pop. of about 600,000. Ctesiphon, on the opposite bank of the river, was made cap. by the Parthians, and in AD 164 Seleucia was destroyed by the Romans.

2. Seleucia Pieria. City just N of the mouth of the Orontes R. in modern Turkey, founded 300 BC. Port of Antioch. Was largely destroyed by earthquake (AD 526); the remains of walls, temples and other buildings have been excavated.

Selkirk Scotland. Market town in Scottish Borders on Ettrick Water. Pop. (1991) 5922.

Manufactures tweeds, woollen goods and electronics. Once famous for its 'souters' (shoemakers).

The Common Riding (June), when the bounds are ridden by horsemen, commemorates the Battle of Flodden, where the 'souters' fought valiantly. Andrew Lang, the author (1844–1912) was born here, and both he and the explorer Mungo Park (1771–1806) were educated at the grammar school.

Selkirk Mountains Canada. Mountain range 320 km (200 miles) long in SE British Columbia, extending NNW into the great bend of the Columbia R. W of the Rocky Mountains. Highest peak Mt Sir Sandford (3535 m; 11,595 ft). Several others exceed 3000 m (9840 ft).

Selkirkshire Scotland. Former county now part of Scottish Borders.

Selma USA. Town in Alabama on the

Alabama R. 64 km (40 miles) W of Montgomery. Pop. (1970) 27,379.

In a fertile agricultural region (cotton, pecan nuts). Industries inc. clothing, switches, food-processing, aircraft, wood-pulp and tobacco products.

Seat of the Selma University (1878). Scene of anti-segregation demonstrations in 1965.

Selsey England. Seaside resort in West Sussex 11 km (7 miles) S of Chichester. Pop. (1988) 8555. Site of an abbey founded by St Wilfrid in the 7th cent. Just S at the tip of the Selsey peninsula is the headland of Selsey Bill.

Semarang Indonesia. Cap. of Jawa Tengah province and seaport on the Java Sea 420 km (260 miles) ESE of Jakarta. Pop. (1985) 1,269,000.

Exports sugar, copra, kapok, tobacco. Shipbuilding, railway engineering. Manufactures textiles and electrical equipment.

Semipalatinsk Kazakhstan. Cap. of the Semipalatinsk region on the Irtysh R. and the Turksib Railway 840 km (520 miles) NNE of Alma Ata. Pop. (1991) 344,700.

Industrial and route centre. Industries inc. meat-packing, flour-milling, tanning and textiles.

Founded 1718.

Semliki River ➤ALBERT, LAKE; EDWARD, LAKE; NILE RIVER.

Semmering Pass Austria. Alpine pass (980 m; 3214 ft) 19 km (12 miles) WSW of Neunkirchen, in Lower Austria, leading into Styria. In a tourist district popular as a winter-sports resort.

Semnan Iran. Town in the Semnan Province 169 km (105 miles) E of Tehrán at a height of 1110 m (3641 ft) at the foot of the Elburz Mountains. Pop. 40,000.

Commercial centre in a tobacco-growing region. Manufactures rugs.

Sendai Japan. Cap. of Miyagi prefecture and chief city in N Honshu 306 km (190 miles) NNE of Tokyo. Pop. (1991) 930,520.

Food-processing. It manufactures metal goods, textiles and pottery.

Senegal. Republic in West Africa. Bounded by Mauritania to the N and NE, Mali to the E, Guinea and Guinea-Bissau to the S and the Atlantic to the W with The Gambia forming an enclave along the shore. Area 196,712 sq km (75,951 sq. miles). Pop. (1995) 8,312,000 (41 per cent urban). Life expectancy, 48 years male, 50 female. Cap. Dakar. Other cities Thiès, Kaolack, Ziguinchor and St Louis. Currency: CFA franc = 100 centimes. Senegal has a generally flat terrain and is mainly dry savannah of the Sahara and Sahel. The volcanic peninsula of Cape Verde is the most westerly point in Africa. It has a tropical climate and has rain June–Oct., with high humidity. Land use: forested 55 per cent, meadows and pastures 16 per cent, agricultural and under permanent cultivation 12 per cent. The majority of the pop. is Sunni Muslim, the remainder Christian, mainly Roman Catholic. The official lang. is French. The largest ethnic group is the Wolof people, about 43 per cent, who speak Wolof.

Agriculture is the most important industry employing 80 per cent of the pop. Food crops inc. maize and millet. Other industries inc. fishing, forestry, food-processing, salt extraction, footwear, textiles and fertilizers. Mining for phosphate, zirconium, iron, gold and titanium. Oil and natural gas are found offshore.

France established a fort at St Louis in 1659 and later acquired other coastal settlements from the Dutch; the interior was occupied in 1854–65. Senegal became a territory of French West Africa in 1902 and an autonomous state within the French Community in 1958. In 1959 Senegal joined with French Sudan to form the Federation of Mali, which achieved independence in 1960, but in the same year withdrew from the Federation and became a separate independent republic. Senegal was a one-party state from 1966 until 1974, when a pluralist system was established. The Senegambia Confederation with The Gambia was established in 1982 and dissolved in 1989.

Senegal River. River in W Africa 1430 km (893 miles) long, formed by the union of the Bafing and the Bakhoy rivers. Rises in the Fouta Djallon highlands, flows generally NW and is joined by the Falémé R., forms the Mauritania–Senegal frontier, turns W and enters the Atlantic below St Louis. Navigable July–Oct. as far as Kayes (in Mali) which is linked by rail with Bamako on the Niger R.

Senge Khambab ➤INDUS RIVER.

Senigallia Italy. Ancient Sena Gallica, later Sinigaglia. Town in Ancona province, Marches 27 km (17 miles) WNW of Ancona.

Port and seaside resort. Manufactures pasta.

Senlis France. Town in the Oise department 43 km (27 miles) NNE of Paris. Pop. (1982) 15,280.

A market town and resort surrounded by forests (Hallatte, Chantilly, Ermenonville). Manufactures furniture and rubber products.

Has Gallo–Roman walls and the 12th/16th cent. early Gothic Church of Notre Dame, formerly a cathedral.

Sennar Sudan. Town on the left bank of the Blue Nile 257 km (160 miles) SSE of Khartoum. Pop. 8000. Linked by rail (through Sennar Junction) with Khartoum, El Obeid and Kassala. The Sennar Dam is part of the Gezira irrigation scheme. Old Sennar (10 km; 6 miles NNW) was the cap. of the ancient kingdom of Sennar in the 16th–19th cent.

Sens France. Ancient Agedincum. Market town in the Yonne dpartment on the Yonne R. 61 km (38 miles) WSW of Troyes. Pop. (1982) 26,691.

Industries inc. electrical and mechanical engineering, and the manufacture of footwear and brushes. Trade in wine, grain and timber.

Its 12th/16th-cent. cathedral is one of the earliest Gothic buildings in France. An important road centre in Roman times. United to the French crown in 1055.

Senta (Hungarian **Zenta**) Former Yugoslavia. Town in Vojvodina on the Tisza R. 39 km (24 miles) SE of Subotica. Pop. (1971) 24,714.

A railway junction with the chief industry flour-milling.

Here the Austrians under Prince Eugene defeated the Turks (1697).

Seoul South Korea. Formerly (1910–45) Keijo. Cap. in the Han R. valley 40 km (25 miles) ENE of Inchon, its seaport. Pop. (1990) 10,627,790.

Industrial centre. Tanning, flour-milling and railway engineering. Manufactures textiles. Also a cultural centre.

Has remnants of the ancient walls and has been much modernized in the 20th cent. Became cap. of Korea in the late 14th cent. As Keijo, seat of Japanese government 1910–45. Became cap. of South Korea 1948. Suffered severely in the Korean War (1950–1), but expansion and reconstruction since 1953 has been dynamic.

Sept Îles (Seven Islands) Canada. Port in E Quebec on the N shore of the St Lawrence R. estuary. Pop. (1987) 29,300. Terminus of the railway from the Schefferville (Knob Lake) iron mines.

Main industry shipping.

Sequoia National Park USA. Park on the W slopes of the Sierra Nevada, California, from the upper Kings R. (N) to the upper Tule R. (S). Area 1559 sq km (602 sq. miles). Established in 1890 to preserve remarkable groves of sequoia trees, which are found in the W half, W of the N–S granite ridge known as the Great Western Divide, at heights of 1200–1400 m (3936–7872 ft). The largest trees are about 90 m (295 ft) tall and are probably 1500 to 3000 years old.

Seraing Belgium. Industrial town in Liège province on the Meuse R. 5 km (3 miles) SW of Liège. Pop. (1992) 61,182.

Coalmining. Manufactures steel, locomotives, machinery and glass.

Its industrial expansion was due to John Cockerill, an Englishman, who founded the iron and steel works (1817); the first Belgian locomotive was built at these works in 1835.

Serampur India. Industrial town in West Bengal on the Hooghly R. 19 km (12 miles) NNW of Calcutta. Pop. (1991) 131,719.

Important for jute and cotton milling.

It was a Danish settlement from 1755 and purchased by Britain in 1845.

Serbia. State of Federal Republic of Yugoslavia (Former Yugoslavia) inc. the autonomous region of Kosovo-Metohija. Area 88,361 sq km (34,107 sq. miles). Pop. (1991) 9,721,177. Cap. Belgrade. Bounded on the N by Hungary, on the E by Romania and Bulgaria and on the SW by Albania. Although generally mountainous, it is in the main agricultural, producing wheat, maize and vines. Minerals inc. copper and antimony.

Chief towns Belgrade, Niš, Kragujeva, Leskovac. The Serbs settled here in the 7th cent., were converted to Christianity in the 9th cent. and founded an independent kingdom; but after their defeat at Kosovo (1389) they were subject to the Turks. They regained their independence in 1878, forming a kingdom in 1882, but friction with Austria led to World War I, after which they became the nucleus of the new Kingdom of the Serbs, Croats and Slovenes, or Yugoslavia (1918). Under the 1990 Constitution Serbia is defined as a 'democratic' instead of a 'socialist' republic and as 'united and sovereign on all its territory', thus Kosovo and Vojvodina lost the autonomy granted under the 1974 federal Constitution. There is a 250-member unicameral National Assembly.

Sercq ➤SARK.

Seremban Malaysia. Cap. of the state of Negri Sembilan in West Malaysia 72 km (45 miles) SE of Kuala Lumpur. Pop. (1980) 132,911. Linked by rail with Port Dickson.

Centre of a region producing rubber and a declining tin-mining industry.

Seret River ➤SIRET RIVER.

Sergipe Brazil. State in the NE. Area 21,863 sq km (8441 sq. miles). Pop. (1991) 1,492,400. Cap. Aracajú. A low coastal plain rising to a low plateau inland.

Produces sugar-cane, coconuts, cotton and rice in the lowlands. Cattle raised on the plateau.

Sergiyev Posad Russia. Formerly Zagorsk. Town in the Moscow region 60 km (37 miles) NE of Moscow. Pop. (1991) 115,600. Famous for the monastery (*lavra*) of Troitsko-Sergiyevskaya, the Trinity Monastery of St Sergius, founded in 1340 and still visited by large numbers of pilgrims, being converted into a museum at the revolution in 1917. The traditional craft of the monks was toy-making. Within the monastery were 15th and 16th cent. cathedrals, several churches, a bell tower 96 m (315 ft) high and the tomb of Boris Godunov, as well as ecclesiastical treasures.

Seria Brunei. Town on the coast 88 km (55 miles) SW of Brunei. Pop. (1988) 23,415.

Centre of an oilfield discovered in 1929. Much oil exported; remainder sent by pipeline to the refinery at Lutong (Sarawak).

Seringapatam (Srirangapatnam) India. Former cap. of Mysore state (1610–1799) on an island in the Cauvery R. 11 km (7 miles) NNE of Mysore. Famous for its fortress, taken by the British in 1799, and for the tombs of Tippoo Sultan and his father, Hyder Ali.

Serov Russia. Industrial town in the Sverdlovsk region 306 km (190 miles) N of Sverdlovsk. Pop. (1991) 106,800.

Important metallurgical centre, manufacturing special steels.

Serowe Botswana. Town in the E 414 km (160 miles) NNE of Gaberone. Pop. (1989) 95,041. Cap. of the Bamangwato tribe. A market town founded in 1902.

Serpukhov Russia. Industrial town on the Oka R. at the confluence with the Nara R. 96 km (60 miles) S of Moscow. Pop. (1989) 144,000.

Important textile centre (cotton, wool, flax). Sawmilling, metal working. Trade in grain and timber.

From the 14th to the 16th cent. its fortress protected Moscow from the S.

Sérrai (Serres, Seres) Greece. 1. *Nome* in Macedonia bounded on the N by Bulgaria. Area 3926 sq km (1516 sq. miles). Pop. (1991) 191,890. Drained by the Struma R. Produces cotton, tobacco and cereals.

2. Ancient Sirrhae. Cap. of Sérrai *nome* 69 km (43 miles) NE of Thessaloniki Pop. (1971) 39,897.

Commercial centre in a fertile region known to the Turks as the Golden Plain. Trade in tobacco, cotton and cereals. Manufactures cotton goods and cigarettes.

Sète (Cette) France. Seaport in the Hérault department 29 km (18 miles) SW of Montpellier, on a narrow strip of land separating the Étang de Thau from the Gulf of Lions. Pop. (1968) 40,220. Chief French Mediterranean seaport after Marseille.

Exports wine, petroleum products. Fishing. Oil-refining and distilling. Manufactures chemicals, cement and wine casks.

Founded (1666) by Colbert and developed as the terminus of the Canal du Midi, which, with the Rhône–Sète Canal, links it with the interior. Birthplace of Paul Valéry (1871–1945), the poet.

Sete Quedas ►PARANÁ RIVER.

Sétif Algeria. Town in the NE at a height of 1050 m (3445 ft), 32 km (20 miles) S of Djebel Bator (2005 m; 6576 ft) and 113 km (70 miles) WSW of Constantine. Pop. (1987) 170,182. On the railway from Algiers to Constantine and Tunis.

Grain and livestock market. Flour-milling.

Settle England. Town in North Yorkshire on the R. Ribble 21 km (13 miles) NW of Skipton. Pop. (1991) 3082. At the foot of Castleberg cliff in a picturesque limestone region.

Market town. Tanning, cotton-milling. An excellent centre for seeing the limestone country of the Pennines: Ingleborough, Penyghent, Ribblesdale and Malham Cove.

Setúbal Portugal. Cap. of the Setúbal district on the N side of the Bay of Setúbal (the estuary of the Sado, Marateca and São Martinho rivers) 29 km (18 miles) SE of Lisbon. Pop. (1987) 77,885.

Seaport. Exports oranges, grapes, wine and salt. Industries inc. fishing, sardine-canning and boatbuilding. Manufactures fertilizers and cement.

Has a 16th-cent. castle built by Philip III of Spain, but most of its old buildings were destroyed in the earthquake of 1755.

Sevastopol (Sebastopol) Ukraine. Seaport on the SW coast of Crimea. Pop. (1991) 366,000.

An excellent natural harbour; leading naval base and shipbuilding centre. Fish-processing, tanning and flour-milling. Has a famous marine biological station. Popular seaside resort.

On the peninsula just W are the ruins of an ancient Greek colony founded in the 5th cent. BC. During the Crimean War it was captured and destroyed by British, French and Turkish forces after an 11-month siege (1854–5) and scarcely a dozen buildings escaped unharmed.

Seven Islands ►SEPT ÎLES.

Sevenoaks England. Market town in Kent 32 km (20 miles) SE of London. Pop. (1991) 24,489. Pleasantly situated in the North Downs. Has a school founded (1432) by Sir William Sevenoke and the 'Vine', said to be the oldest cricket ground in England. To the E is Knole, a mansion built partly in the 15th cent. by Archbishop Bourchier.

Severn River England/Wales. River 354 km (220 miles) long rising on the NE slope of Plynlimmon, in Powys, Wales, flowing generally NE at first and then following a roughly semicircular course and entering the Bristol Channel. The chief towns on its course are Welshpool (Wales) and Shrewsbury, Worcester, Tewkesbury and Gloucester (England). Its main tributaries are the Vyrnwy, Stour, Teme and Warwickshire Avon; it is joined by the Wye and Bristol Avon at about the point where its estuary enters the Bristol Channel. The canals which link it with the Thames, Trent and other rivers are little used, but the Gloucester and Berkeley Canal (from Sharpness) allows small vessels to reach Gloucester. Owing to its funnel-shaped estuary, the Severn is subject to a high bore which may travel as far upstream as Tewkesbury. The road suspension bridge over the river between Aust (Avon) and Beachley (Glos.) was opened in 1966, replacing the old ferry service for cars and passengers and a further bridge was opened in 1996.

Severodvinsk Russia. Formerly Molotovsk. Seaport in the Archangel region on Dvina Bay (White Sea) 40 km (25 miles) W of Archangel. Pop. (1991) 254,100.

Exports timber.

Seville (Sp. **Sevilla**) Spain. 1. Inland province in Andalusia. Area 14,001 sq km (5408 sq. miles). Pop. (1991) 1,585,099. Drained by the Guadalquivir R. Mainly agricultural; produces olive oil, wine and cereals.

2. Ancient Hispalis. Cap. of Seville province, the chief city of Andalusia, on the Guadalquivir R. 87 km (54 miles) from the Atlantic Ocean. Pop. (1991) 659,126.

A major port and industrial centre. Exports wine, olives and olive oil, citrus fruits and cork. Manufactures textiles, pottery, pharmaceutical goods and soap.

It has a 15th/16th-cent. Gothic cathedral, one of the largest churches in the world which has a campanile of Moorish origin, the Giralda, 90 m (295 ft) high, and is decorated with works by Murillo and other great Spanish painters. Nearby are the 12th-cent. Alcázar, probably the outstanding monument to the Moorish occupation; the Lonja or exchange, containing the priceless Archives of the Indies; and the 17th-cent. archbishop's palace. There are paintings by the Spanish masters in many of the churches as well as in the museum. University (1502). Captured by Julius Caesar 45 BC. Prospered under the Moors (712–1248), declined, flourished in the 16th and 17th cent., again declined, but has again revived in the 20th cent. Birthplace of the painters, Velázquez (1599–1660) and Murillo (1617–82).

Sèvres France. Suburb WSW of Paris in the Hauts-de-Seine department on the Seine R. Pop. (1987) 20,300.

Famous for the manufacture of porcelain, established here in 1756, the factory being in the park of St Cloud. A ceramics museum and school.

Seward USA. Town and port in Alaska at the head of Resurrection Bay 120 km (75 miles) S of Anchorage. Pop. (1989) 3149. Terminus of the Alaska Railway from Fairbanks. Supply centre for the interior and for visiting hunters and fishermen.

Seychelles Indian Ocean. The Republic of Seychelles comprises a group of 115 islands and islets situated 960 km (600 miles) NE of Madagascar. The principal island is Mahé; the other inhabited islands are Praslin, La Digue, Silhouette, Frégate and North. Area 455 sq km (176 sq. miles). Pop. (1995) 75,000 (59 per cent urban). Life expectancy, 66 years male, 73 female. Cap. Victoria on Mahé. Currency: Seychelles rupee = 100 cents. The islands are mainly of granite and the highest point is Morne Seychellois at 906 m (2972 ft). The climate is tropical. Land use: forested 19 per cent, agricultural and under permanent cultivation 22 per cent. Roman Catholicism is the dominant religion and Creole, English and French are spoken.

It exports copra and cinnamon. Fishing is important but the major industry is tourism employing 33 per cent of the labour force.

It was first occupied by the French in 1756 and then taken by the British in 1794. A dependency of Mauritius 1814–1903, it then became a separate Crown Colony, becoming an independent republic in 1976. There is a 43-member unicameral People's Assembly elected for 5 years.

Sfax Tunisia. Seaport and second largest city on the N shore of the Gulf of Gabès 217 km (135 miles) SSE of Tunis. Pop. (1989) 221,770. Linked by rail with Tunis and Gafsa (phosphate mines).

Exports phosphates, olive oil and sponges. Fishing (octopuses, sponges). Manufactures olive oil and soap.

It consists of a modern quarter built in

European style and an Arab town enclosed by the ancient walls.

's Gravenhage ➤HAGUE, THE.

Shaanxi (Shensi) China. Province in the NW, with the Great Wall running near its N boundary with Nei Monggol (Inner Mongolia). Area 195,800 sq km (75,600 sq. miles). Pop. (1992) 33,630,000. Cap. Xian. Largely mountainous, esp. in the S, where it is crossed W–E by the Tsinling Shan; N of the latter is the valley of the Wei-ho (also extending W–E), where Xian and Paoki are situated.

Wheat, millet, cotton and fruits are cultivated. There are large coal deposits and also molybdenum and mercury.

Shaba Democratic Republic of the Congo. Formerly Katanga. Region in the SE bordered by Zambia (E, S), Angola (SW). Area 496,877 sq km (191,845 sq. miles). Pop. (1991) 5,207,000. Cap. Lubumbashi. Mainly comprises the Shaba plateau, at a height of 900–1800 m (2952–5904 ft). Wooded savannah drained by the Lualaba R. (W headstream of the Congo R.), the Luvua and the Lukuga rivers, and other affluents of Upper Congo. Food crops cassava, plantains, yams. Cattle raised. Important chiefly for its great mineral wealth, esp. cobalt, copper and uranium. Also produces coal, manganese, silver, zinc. Mining is now mainly state-owned. Main industry the smelting of copper and other metallic ores. Manufactures chemicals. Chief industrial centres Lubumbashi, Likasi. Linked by rail with Angola and Zambia. After Congo became independent (1960), Katanga seceded; Katangan troops fought against the Congolese army and then against UN forces, which invaded Katanga in 1962. The Katangan government accepted proposals for reunification and the region was reconstituted a province in 1967.

Shadwell England. District in the London borough of Tower Hamlets (E) on the N bank of the R. Thames adjoining Wapping.

Shaftesbury England. Market town in Dorset on a hill 29 km (18 miles) WSW of Salisbury. Pop. (1991) 6203. Remains of an

abbey founded (880) by Alfred the Great, whose daughter was the first abbess. Known locally by its old name, Shaston.

Shahjahanpur India. Town in Uttar Pradesh 69 km (43 miles) SE of Bareilly. Pop. (1991) 260,400.

Industries inc. sugar-milling, carpet manufacture and fertilizers. Trade in grain and sugar-cane.

Named after Shah Jahan, in whose reign it was founded in 1647.

Shaker Heights USA. Residential town in NE Ohio just SE and virtually a suburb of Cleveland. Pop. (1985) 33,000.

Shakhty Russia. Formerly Aleksandrovsk-Grushevky. Industrial town in the Rostov region 64 km (40 miles) NE of Rostov. Pop. (1992) 228,000.

Important coalmining centre in the E of the Donets Basin. Manufactures machinery, clothing and furniture.

Shandong (Shantung) China. Maritime province in the E, inc. the Shandong peninsula jutting E into the Yellow Sea. Area 153,300 sq km (59,174 sq. miles). Pop. (1992) 85,700,000. Cap. Jinan. Much of the province consists of the fertile alluvial plain of the lower Hwangho, but there are mountains in the central area and the peninsula where deforestation has led to serious soil erosion.

Wheat, millet, kaoliang and groundnuts cultivated on the lowlands.

The province has long been known for soft undressed silk cloth known as shantung. Considerable deposits of iron ore and coal. Chief towns Tsingtao and Jinan.

Shanghai China. The largest city in China in SE Jiangsu; stands on the Huangpu R. 23 km (14 miles) from its junction with the Chang Jiang R. estuary and 265 km (165 miles) ESE of Nanjing. Pop. (1990) 7,496,509. Its importance as a seaport is due largely to the vast, populous hinterland of the Chang Jiang valley and its favourable position for trans-Pacific and coastal trade.

Exports raw silk, hog bristles, tea and tung oil. Also a major industrial centre. Important textile manufactures (cotton, wool and silk). Also shipbuilding, engineering, tanning, rice-milling; manufactures chemicals, matches and paper. Important publishing industry.

Most of the city is on a tidal flat on the left bank of the Huangpu at the mouth of Soochow Creek and its commercial life is centred around the confluence in the former International Settlement, where banks, business houses, hotels and large stores line the boulevards and streets; here is its best-known thoroughfare, the Bund or waterfront.

A mere fishing village in the 11th cent., walled only in the 14th cent., Shanghai was still of small significance till the mid 19th cent. Then the Treaty of Nanking (1842) opened it to foreign trade and the British (1843) and US (1862) Concessions were consolidated into the International Settlement (1863), which, with the French Concession (1849), enjoyed autonomy and extraterritorial rights. In 1941 the city was taken by the Japanese and the International Settlement (1943) and the French Concession (1946) were relinquished.

Shanklin ➤SANDOWN-SHANKLIN.

Shannon River Ireland. Chief river of Ireland 386 km (240 miles) long, rising on Cuilcagh Mountain, Co. Cavan and flowing generally S through Loughs Allen, Boderg, Forbes, Ree, Derg to Limerick. Here it turns W into a wide estuary, nearly 96 km (60 miles) long, entering the Atlantic Ocean between Co. Clare (N) and Counties Limerick and Kerry (S). Chief tributaries the Suck, Brosna, Little Brosna, Deel. Principal towns on the banks Carrick-on-Shannon, Athlone, Limerick. At Ardnacrusha, 5 km (3 miles) N of Limerick, is Ireland's main hydroelectric power station. At Rineanna 21 km (13 miles) W of Limerick is Shannon airport.

Shansi ➤SHANXI.

Shan State Myanmar (Burma). Constituent part of the Union in the E, bounded on the E by China and on the SE by Laos and Thailand. Area 155,801 sq km (60,155 sq.

miles). Pop. (1983) 3,716,841 (largely Shans, a Thai people who are migrants from SW China). Consists essentially of the Shan plateau, with an average height of 600–1200 m (1968–3936 ft) cut N–S by the gorge of the Salween R. Formerly divided into 6 Northern and 36 Southern Shan States, which were semi-independent, but in 1922 these were united into the Federation of Shan States. When Burma became independent (1947) they were combined with the Wa States of the extreme NE to form the Shan State.

Shantou China. Formerly Swatow. Seaport, industrial and commercial town in Guangdong province at the mouth of the Han R. 350 km (220 miles) E of Guangzhou (Canton). Pop. (1990) 578,630.

Exports sugar, tobacco and fruit. Manufactures pharmaceutical products, matches, cigarettes, pottery, electronic goods, textiles, clothing, plastic goods and cellophane, and in 1980 became a special economic zone.

Opened to foreign trade in 1858; became an important emigration port.

Shantung ➤SHANDONG.

Shanxi (Shansi) China. Inland province in the N bounded on the N by Nei Monggol (Inner Mongolia). Area 157,100 sq km (60,700 sq. miles). Pop. (1992) 24,420,000. Cap. Taiyuan. Generally mountainous; bordered on the W and S by the Hwang-he and crossed by the Fen-he. Rainfall is somewhat uncertain, but wheat, millet and other crops are cultivated. China's leading coal producer with important mines at Datong.

Shap England. Village in Cumbria 16 km (10 miles) SSE of Penrith. Pop. (1985) 250. Granite-quarrying. Remains of the 13th-cent. Shap Abbey.

Shari (Chari) River Central African Republic/Chad. River 2250 km (1400 miles) long rising in the N of the Central African Republic, flowing generally NW, passing through Chad, forming part of the Chad–Cameroon border and entering L. Chad (of which it is the principal feeder) by a broad delta.

Sharjah (Sharja) United Arab Emirates. Seaport on the (Persian) Gulf 13 km (8 miles) NE of Dubai and chief town of the sheikhdom of Sharjah and Kalba. Pop. (1980) 125,123.

Manufactures plastic goods, paint, pipes and cement, but has little oil.

Sharon Israel. Plain in the W between the Mediterranean Sea (W) and the hills of Samaria (E), extending from Haifa in the N to Tel Aviv in the S. Generally fertile. Important occupations the cultivation of citrus fruits and vines, mixed farming and poultry-rearing.

Sharon USA. Industrial town in Pennsylvania on the Shenango R. near the Ohio border. Pop. (1970) 22,653.

Manufactures steel, textiles and chemicals.

Shashi China. River port in Hubei province on the Yangtze R. 193 km (120 miles) WSW of Wuhan. Pop. (1990) 281,352.

Textile manufactures, flour-milling. Trade in cotton and grain.

Shatt-al-Arab Iraq. River 193 km (120 miles) long in the SE formed by the union of the Euphrates and Tigris rivers, flowing SE past Basra (Iraq), Khorramshahr and Abadan (Iran) to the (Persian) Gulf. Flanked by marshes and date groves. The lower part forms the Iraq–Iran border and disagreements over this disputed waterway led to the Iran–Iraq War in 1980.

Shawinigan Canada. Industrial town in Quebec on the St Maurice R. 29 km (18 miles) NW of Trois Rivières. Pop. (1971) 27,792.

Manufactures wood-pulp and paper, aluminium, chemicals and textiles. Power is derived from the large hydroelectric plants at the falls.

Shcherbakov ➤RYBINSK.

Sheba ➤SABA.

Sheboygan USA. Port and industrial town in Wisconsin on L. Michigan at the mouth of the Sheboygan R. 80 km (50 miles) N of Milwaukee. Pop. (1990) 49,676.

Centre of a dairy-farming region. Trade in cheese. Manufactures furniture, footwear and knitwear.

Sheerness England. Town in Kent in the NW of the Isle of Sheppey. Port formerly with a naval dockyard in the old section known as Blue Town, founded (17th cent.) and fortified to protect the entrance to the R. Thames and the R. Medway. The modern part of the town, which functions as a holiday resort, is divided into Banks Town, Marine Town and Mile Town. From 1968 part of the municipal borough of Queenborough in Sheppey.

Sheffield England. City and unitary authority on the R. Don at the confluence with the Sheaf 53 km (33 miles) ESE of Manchester. Pop. (1991) 501,202. In the 19th cent. 45,000 worked in the iron and steel industry, in 1993 c. 4000, but as much steel is still produced esp. special steels.

Produces cutlery, tools, machinery, bicycles, rails, armour plate. Manufactures silverware, glassware, optical instruments and food products.

The 14th/15th-cent. cruciform parish church of St Peter and St Paul became the cathedral in 1914. Many other notable public buildings inc. the City Hall (1932), the Ruskin Museum and the Graves Art Gallery. The university (1905) began as Firth College, founded (1879) by a steel manufacturer. Iron was already being smelted here at the time of the Norman Conquest, the essential raw materials being available nearby. Celebrated for its cutlery by the 14th cent. With the industrial revolution the steel industry expanded rapidly; an outstanding development was Bessemer's establishment of a steelworks (1860) to manufacture cheap steel by his own process.

Sheksna River Russia. River 160 km (100 miles) long, rising in L. Beloye and flowing generally S to the Rybinsk Reservoir, forming part of the Mariinsk canal system. Before the filling of the Rybinsk Reservoir (1941) it joined the Volga R. at Rybinsk.

Shellharbour Australia. Town in a coal-mining district of New South Wales 24 km (15 miles) S of Wollongong. Pop. (1990) 50,000.

Shenandoah National Park USA. Park in N Virginia in the Blue Ridge Mountains. Area 785 sq km (302 sq. miles). Established 1935. Heavily forested, renowned for its scenery. Highest point Hawksbill Mountain (1235 m; 4051 ft). The Skyline Drive runs its entire length 169 km (105 miles).

Shenandoah River USA. River 88 km (55 miles) long, formed by the union of the North Fork and the South Fork, flowing generally NE through Virginia and W Virginia to join the Potomac R. near Harper's Ferry. The picturesque Shenandoah Valley is noted for orchards and pastures. Scene of much fighting in the American Civil War.

Shensi ➤SHAANXI.

Shenyang China. Formerly Mukden. Cap. of Liaoning province in the NE (Manchuria) on the Hun-he, tributary of the Liao-he, 630 km (390 miles) ENE of Beijing. Pop. (1990) 3,603,712.

Chief commercial centre in the NE. Important railway junction. Trade in grain, soya beans. Manufactures textiles, chemicals, matches, paper and aircraft.

In the 17th cent. the Manchu cap. and at times known as Fengtien, it expanded rapidly after Manchukuo was founded by the Japanese (1932).

Shenzhen China. Special economic zone near to Guangzhou (Canton) and Hong Kong in Guangdong. Created in 1980 to encourage foreign investment. Manufactures cement, electronic equipment, petrochemicals and toys (60 per cent of world production in 1998). Pop. (1984) 337,000.

Shepparton Australia. Town and railway junction in Victoria on the Goulburn R. 160 km (100 miles) NNE of Melbourne. Pop. (1986) with Mooroopna, 37,086.

In a rich, irrigated agricultural and stock-rearing district which produces wheat, wool, dairy produce and wine. Fruit-canning and meat-packing.

Sheppey, Isle of England. Island 16 km (10 miles) long and up to 6 km (4 miles) wide off the N coast of Kent in the Thames estuary, separated from the mainland by a narrow channel, the Swale. Low-lying and fertile. Produces cereals, vegetables. The large flocks of sheep justify the name, which means 'Island of Sheep'. Chief towns Sheerness, Queenborough. In 1968 the rural district of Sheppey became part of the municipal borough of Queenborough in Sheppey.

Shepshed England. Town in Leicestershire 6 km (4 miles) W of Loughborough. Pop. (1989) 11,500.

Manufactures hosiery. Other industries inc. engineering and quarrying.

Shepton Mallet England. Town in Somerset 26 km (16 miles) SSW of Bath at the foot of the Mendip Hills. Pop. (1990) 7000.

Industries inc. perry and cider-making, agricultural machinery and footwear manufacture.

Has a market cross dating from 1500 and a church with a 13th-cent. oak roof.

Sherborne England. Town in Dorset on the R. Yeo 8 km (5 miles) E of Yeovil. Pop. (1991) 7606.

Industries inc. tourism and engineering.

Once cap. of Wessex, it became the seat of a bishopric under St Aldhelm (705); the see was transferred to Old Sarum 1075. The Abbey church is a magnificent example of the Perpendicular style; some of the other Abbey buildings are now occupied by Sherborne School, founded in the 16th cent.

Sherbrooke Canada. Industrial town in Quebec on the St Francis R. 129 km (80 miles) E of Montreal. Pop. (1991) 76,429.

Manufactures hosiery, textiles, clothing,

leather goods, mining machinery, and is a commercial centre of a dairy-farming region.

Sheringham England. Seaside resort in Norfolk on the North Sea coast 6 km (4 miles) WNW of Cromer. Pop. (1991) 7620. Small fishing port noted for lobsters.

's Hertogenbosch (Den Bosch) Netherlands. Cap. of North Brabant province at the confluence of the Dommel and Aa rivers 48 km (30 miles) SSE of Utrecht. Pop. (1992) 93,171.

Railway junction and industrial centre. Manufactures bicycles, beer, compressors, refrigerating equipment, tools and tobacco products.

There is a 14th/16th-cent. Gothic cathedral. Birthplace of Hieronymus Bosch (1450–1516), the painter.

Sherwood Forest England. Ancient forest in Nottinghamshire stretching between Nottingham and Worksop, a royal hunting ground and well-known as the traditional home of Robin Hood and his men. Most of the original forest has long since been cleared, but portions remain – principally in the Dukeries.

Shetland Islands (Shetlands, Zetland) Scotland. Archipelago of over 100 islands and islets NE of the Orkneys, the largest being Mainland, Yell and Unst, forming the county of Zetland and the Shetland Islands Area. Area 1427 sq km (551 sq. miles). Pop. (1991) 22,017. County town Lerwick. The islands are bleak, almost treeless and largely infertile.

Shetland ponies, sheep and cattle raised. Important occupations tourism, fishing, fish-curing and knitting; Fair Isle is famous for its characteristically patterned knitted goods. Base for exploitation of North Sea oil, with pipeline from the Brent field (ENE) and for serving the platforms from Sullom Voe terminal.

Under Scandinavian rule 875–1468 (►ORKNEY ISLANDS); the people still show evidence of their Norse origin in custom and speech.

Shibin el Kôm Egypt. Cap. of the Menûfiya

governorate on the Nile delta 56 km (35 miles) NW of Cairo. Pop. (1991) 153,000.

Rail centre in an agricultural area producing cereals, cotton. Manufactures cigarettes and textiles.

Shifnal England. Market town in Shropshire 26 km (16 miles) ESE of Shrewsbury. Pop. (rural district, 1971) 15,859. Has a 12th-cent church. In the neighbourhood is the 18th-cent. Haughton Hall.

Shigatse China. Commercial town in Xizang (Tibet) in the SE near the Tsangpo (Brahmaputra) R. 217 km (135 miles) WSW of Lhasa, to which it is second only in importance. Just SW is the famous monastery of Tashi Lumpo.

Shihkiachwang ►SHIJIAZHUANG.

Shijiazhuang (Shihchiachuang/Shihkiachwang) China. Cap. of Hebei province 265 km (165 miles) SW of Beijing. Pop. (1990) 1,068,439.

A major railway junction having grown rapidly with the building of a railway in 1905. Industrial and commercial centre. There is railway engineering and mining. It manufactures textiles, machinery and pharmaceuticals.

Shikarpur Pakistan. Town in N Sind 32 km (20 miles) NW of Sukkur. Pop. (1972) 66,100. Commands the trade route through the Bolan Pass.

Trade in grain, precious stones. Engineering, rice and flour milling. Manufactures cotton goods and carpets.

Shikoku Japan. Smallest of the country's 4 main islands, S of Honshu and E of Kyushu. Area (with offshore islands) 18,772 sq km (7248 sq. miles). Interior mountainous and heavily forested.

Rice, tobacco, tomatoes, cucumbers and soya beans grown on the lowlands.

Divided into 4 prefectures: Kagawa, Tokushima, Kochi, Ehime. Chief towns Matsuyama, Takamatsu.

Shildon England. Town in Durham 3 km

(2 miles) SSE of Bishop Auckland. Pop. (1987) 11,379. Railway engineering.

Shillelagh Ireland. Village in Co. Wicklow on the R. Shillelagh 68 km (42 miles) SSW of Dublin. An ancient oak forest. Gave its name to an Irish cudgel, originally oak and later blackthorn.

Shillong India. Cap. of Meghalaya at a height of 1518 m (4963 ft) in the Khasi Hills 499 km (310 miles) NE of Calcutta. Pop. (1991) 130,691.

Commercial centre. Trade in rice, cotton and fruit.

Became cap. of the Khasi States in 1864 and of Assam in 1874.

Shimla ➤SIMLA.

Shimoga India. Town in Karnataka on the Tunga R. 249 km (155 miles) NW of Bangalore. Pop. (1991) 178,882.

Cotton-ginning and rice-milling.

Shimonoseki Japan. Seaport and industrial town in the extreme SW of Honshu in Yamaguchi prefecture. Pop. (1992) 260,692. Connected with Kitakyushu (Kyushu) by rail and road tunnels beneath Shimonoseki (Kammon) Strait.

Industries inc. shipbuilding, engineering, metalworking, fishing and fish-processing. Manufactures textiles and chemicals.

The treaty ending the Sino–Japanese War was signed here (1895).

Shipka Pass Bulgaria. Pass (1271 m; 4169 ft) through the Balkan Mountains on the road between Kazanluk and Gabrovo. Scene of fierce battles in the Russo–Turkish War (1877–8).

Shipley England. Town in West Yorkshire on the R. Aire 5 km (3 miles) NNW of Bradford. Pop. (1991) 28,165.

Manufactures woollen and worsted goods. Engineering.

Inc. the model town of Saltaire, built (1853) by Sir Titus Salt for his mill workers.

Shiraz Iran. Cap. of Fars province at a height of 1500 m (4920 ft) on a plain surrounded by mountains 177 km (110 miles) ENE of Bushire. Pop. (1986) 848,289.

Commercial centre in an agricultural region producing cereals, sugar-beet and vines. Manufactures textiles, rugs, carpets and cement.

At times the cap. of Persia. Birthplace of two great Persian poets, Sadi (1184–1291) and Hafiz (1300–88), whose tombs are features of the town.

Shiré Highlands Malawi. Uplands in the S to the E of the Shiré R. at a height of about 900 m (2952 ft), rising in parts to 1768 m (5800 ft). The main area of tea and tobacco cultivation.

Shiré River Malawi/Mozambique. River 595 km (370 miles) long, a tributary of the Zambezi. The only outlet of L. Malawi (Nyasa), from which it flows generally S. In the middle course it forms cataracts and rapids; the most famous are the Murchison Falls. Leaving Malawi near Port Herald, it enters Mozambique and joins the Zambezi near Vila Fontes 160 km (100 miles) from the Indian Ocean.

Shizuoka Japan. Cap. of Shizuoka prefecture SE Honshu 145 km (90 miles) SW of Tokyo. Pop. (1992) 474,388.

Commercial and industrial centre in a tea-growing region. Trade in tea, oranges. Tea processing and packing. Manufactures machinery and chemicals.

Shkodër (Italian **Scutari**) Albania. Cap. of the Shkodër region in the NW at the SE end of L. Shkodër where the Boiana R. leaves the lake. Pop. (1991) 83,700.

Manufactures textiles and cement. Trade in wool, grain and tobacco.

Has an ancient Venetian citadel and a Roman Catholic cathedral. Once cap. of Illyria; taken by the Romans 168 BC, later held by Serbs, Venetians and Turks.

Shkodër, Lake Albania/Montenegro. Largest lake in the Balkan peninsula on the Montenegro–Albanian border, but mainly within Montenegro. Area 391 sq. km (143 sq. miles). Average depth normally 6–8 m

(20–26 ft) but deeper and more extensive after winter rains. Picturesque, well-stocked with fish. Fed by the Morača R. Formerly an inlet of the Adriatic, but now separated from the latter by an alluvial isthmus and drained by the Bojana (Buenë) R.

Shoeburyness England. Former urban district in Essex, since 1933 incorporated in Southend-on-Sea (5 km; 3 miles W) on the N side of the Thames estuary and near the promontory of Shoeburyness.

Sholapur (Solapur) India. Industrial town and railway junction in Maharashtra 360 km (225 miles) SE of Bombay. Pop. (1990) 603,870.

Important cotton industry. Also manufactures carpets, glass and leather goods. Trade in grain, cotton and oilseeds.

Shoreditch England. Part of the London borough of Hackney in E London N of the R. Thames. Residential and industrial; furniture-making and printing important. The Geffrye Museum has an interesting collection of furniture and woodwork. The first theatre in London was built here by James Burbage in 1576.

Shoreham-by-Sea England. Town in West Sussex near the mouth of the R. Adur 10 km (6 miles) W of Brighton. Pop. (1991) 17,322. Seaport. Old Shoreham was an important port in medieval times, but its harbour was silted up and it was superseded by New Shoreham and is now 1.6 km (1 mile) inland. Nearby is Lancing College, the public school. Charles II escaped to France from Shoreham in 1651.

Shotton Wales. Town in Flintshire. Pop. (1985) 24,000 (with Hawarden). Manufactures steel.

Shreveport USA. Industrial town in Louisiana on the Red R. 338 km (210 miles) NW of Baton Rouge. Pop. (1990) 198,525.

Centre of an oil and natural-gas region. Important oil refineries and railway workshops. Manufactures cotton goods and timber products.

Shrewsbury England. County town of Shropshire on the R. Severn, partly within a southward loop of the river. Pop. (1991) 64,219. Picturesque and historic market town.

Industries inc. engineering, tanning, brewing and agricultural products.

Outstanding among its buildings is the 11th-cent. red sandstone castle, restored by Telford and belonging to the local authority, and there are many fine half-timbered houses and two ancient bridges, the English and the Welsh. Its early importance was due to its commanding position with respect to routes into Wales and along the border; in the more peaceful days of the late Middle Ages and Tudor and Elizabethan times, when commerce took the place of conflict with the Welsh, it prospered and in the late 16th cent. were erected such buildings as the Market Hall and Ireland's and Owen's mansions.

Shropshire England. County in the Midlands, bounded on the W and NW by Powys and Wrexham (Wales). Area 3455 sq km (1347 sq. miles). Pop. (1991) 412,600. It is divided into the districts of Bridgnorth, North Shropshire, Oswestry, Shrewsbury and Atcham, South Shropshire and Wrekin. County town Shrewsbury. To the N and E of the Severn, which crosses the county, it is generally low-lying and level apart from the isolated Wrekin (407 m; 1335 ft) but to the S and W of the river it is hilly, rising to 547 m (1794 ft) in the Clee Hills and 517 m (1696 ft) in Long Mynd. Mainly agricultural, with dairy-farming in the lowlands (N) and cattle and sheep rearing on the uplands (S). The coal measures around Coalbrookdale are virtually exhausted, but there are still vestiges of the former iron industry. High-technology industries at Telford. Here also is the world's first iron bridge built in 1778 and now the centre of an industrial museum complex. Castles at Ludlow, Shrewsbury, Bridgnorth and elsewhere, in varying stages of preservation, testify to the stormy border history of the region. Chief towns Shrewsbury, Telford, Wenlock, Wellington, Oakengates and Oswestry.

Shumen (Kolarovgrad) Bulgaria. Cap. of Shumen province 84 km (52 miles) W of Varna. Pop. (1992) 112,091.

Manufactures metal and leather goods. Trade in cereals and wine.

Founded in the 10th cent. Taken by the Turks 1387. Fell to the Russians (1878) and was ceded to Bulgaria.

Sialkot Pakistan. Town in Punjab 105 km (65 miles) NNE of Lahore. Pop. (1981) 302,009.

Manufactures sports goods, textiles, carpets, leather and rubber goods, surgical instruments, cutlery and ceramics. Trade in grain and sugar-cane.

The shrine of Guru Nanak is a Sikh place of pilgrimage.

Siam ➤THAILAND.

Sian ➤XIAN.

Šibenik Croatia. Adriatic seaport 50 km (31 miles) NW of Split. Pop. (1989) 30,000.

Exports timber, bauxite. Manufactures textiles, chemicals.

An ancient town, once the residence of the Croatian kings. Has a remarkable cathedral, begun in the 15th cent., built entirely in the local stone.

Siberia Russia. Region extending W and E from the Ural Mountains to the Pacific Ocean, and N and S from the Arctic Ocean to the Central Asian mountain ranges. Area 13,500,000 sq km (5,200,000 sq. miles). Plains in W drained by R. Ob and Yenisei, and bounded S by the Altai and Sanai mountain ranges. The central area is a plateau bounded E by the Lena R. The E is mountainous. All rivers except the Amur flow into the Arctic Ocean and are frozen for most of the year. The climate is continental. Verkhoyansk in E Siberia has a mean Jan. temperature of −50°C (−59°F).

Chief occupations of the N are timber-felling, fur-trapping and fishing. In the S and SW, where agriculture is concentrated, cereal-growing, cattle and sheep farming occur. Coal, oil, gold and iron ore exist in large quantities. Important industries are concentrated in the Kuznetsk coal basin and adjoining industrial region centred on Sverdlovsk and Chelyabinsk in the Ural Mountains. Other chief towns are Novosibirsk, Omsk and Vladivostok on the Trans-Siberian railway.

Sibiu (Ger. **Hermannstadt**, Hungarian **Nagyszeben**) Romania. Cap. of the Sibiu district, Transylvania 217 km (135 miles) NW of Bucharest. Pop. (1992) 169,696.

Manufactures machinery, textiles, electrical equipment and paper. Industries inc. tanning, brewing, distilling. Picturesquely situated in a fertile valley and an important tourist area.

A Roman colony, resettled in the 12th cent. by colonists from Nuremberg, it has retained a medieval German appearance. Has a 14th/16th-cent. Gothic Protestant church, a 15th-cent town hall and a large Orthodox cathedral.

Sibu Malaysia. Town in Sarawak on the Rajang R. 185 km (115 miles) NE of Kuching. Pop. (1970) 50,635.

Commercial centre. Accessible to large steamers. Trade in rubber, rice and sago.

Sichuan (Szechwan) China. Province in the SW; the most populous of all provinces and regions. Area 569,000 sq km (219,700 sq. miles). Pop. 107,218,172. Cap. Chengdu. Mainly mountainous, rising in the W to the lofty Xizang plateau. Crossed SW–NE by the Yangtze R.; the heart of the province is the Red Basin. In this fertile region rice, maize, sugar-cane, beans and tobacco are cultivated, and tung oil is an important export product. Chengdu is now linked by railway with the chief port Congqing on the Yangtse R.

Sicily (Italian **Sicilia**) Italy. The largest and most populous island in the Mediterranean; with the small Lipari and Egadi Islands, Pantelleria and Ustica, an autonomous region of Italy. Area (region) 25,709 sq km (9926 sq. miles). Pop. (1991) 4,989,871. Cap. Palermo. Divided into 9 provinces. Separated from mainland Italy by the narrow Strait of Messina. Ranges of mountains rising to over

1800 m (5904 ft) run W–E across the N. The highest point is Mt Etna (3323 m, 10,902 ft), N of Catania, the only extensive plain. The coast is generally rocky and steep in the N and NE, flat in the S and SE. Summers are hot and dry and occasionally subject to the sirocco; winters are mild and rainy.

Citrus and other fruits, vines, olives, cereals and vegetables are cultivated on the coastal plains, but agriculture is backward and there is much poverty. Important tunny fisheries. Long one of the world's main sources of sulphur, but output has declined. A productive oilfield has been opened up in the SE. Industries are centred mainly on Palermo, Catania and Messina.

Among the earliest inhabitants were the Siculi, after whom the island is named. The Phoenicians established trading posts along the coast, notably on the site of modern Palermo. They were followed from the 8th cent. BC by the Greeks, who founded settlements in the E and SE at Syracuse, Catania, Messina. In the 5th cent. BC the Carthaginians crossed from Africa and occupied the W; after their defeat Sicily became a Roman colony (241 BC). After the fall of the Roman Empire it was conquered by Vandals (AD 440), Byzantines (535), Saracens (9th cent.) and, in the 11th cent., by the Normans, under whom it was for the first time both united and independent. Ruled by the Aragonese from the early 14th cent. and by Spain from the early 16th cent. and again 1738–1806. Formed, with Naples, the Kingdom of the Two Sicilies (1815). Garibaldi liberated it from the Bourbons (1860) and it was incorporated into Italy. During the early years of the 20th cent. there was considerble emigration. The notorious Mafia, a secret society dating from the 15th cent., has had its influence reduced by the Italian authorities in recent years.

Sidcup England. Residential district divided between the London boroughs of Bexley (N of the A20 road) and Bromley (S of the A20 road).

Manufactures electrical, radio and television equipment.

Sidi-Bel-Abbès Algeria. Town in the NW 48 km (30 miles) S of Oran. Pop. (1987) 152,778.

Commercial centre. Trade in cereals, wine, olives and livestock. Industries inc. flour-milling and the manufacture of cement and furniture.

Ancient walled town; became famous as the headquarters of the French Foreign Legion.

Sidlaw Hills Scotland. Range extending SW–NE through E Perthshire and SW Angus, rising to 455 m (1492 ft).

Sidmouth England. Town in Devon on Lyme Bay at the mouth of the R. Sid 21 km (13 miles) ESE of Exeter. Pop. (1991) 13,181.

Market town and popular seaside resort in a sheltered position between red sandstone cliffs.

Sidra (Sirte), Gulf of Libya. Ancient Syrtis Major. An inlet of the Mediterranean Sea stretching 480 km (300 miles) from Benghazi (Cyrenaica) to Misurata (Tripolitania). Tunny and sponge fisheries. The coast is mainly desert.

Siebengebirge Germany. In German, 'Seven Mountains'. Range of hills of volcanic origin extending along the right bank of the Rhine R. S of Bonn. Rises to 464 m (1522 ft) in Ölberg. Drachenfels (325 m; 1066 ft) is the best-known peak.

Siedlce Poland. Cap. of the Siedlce voivodeship 88 km (55 miles) E of Warsaw. Pop. (1989) 61,500.

Manufactures cement, glass, soap and leather.

Under Austrian and then Russian administration during the Partitions of Poland; restored to the newly re-formed Poland 1921. Before the Nazi occupation (1939–44) about half the pop. were Jews.

Siegburg Germany. Industrial town and railway junction in North Rhine-Westphalia on the Sieg R. 10 km (6 miles) ENE of Bonn. Pop. (1970) 34,586.

Manufactures machinery, chemicals and furniture.

Founded in the 11th cent. Flourished in the 15th and 16th cent. because of its pottery. Has a Benedictine abbey founded in the 11th cent.

Siegen Germany. Industrial town in North Rhine-Westphalia 72 km (45 miles) ENE of Bonn on the Sieg R. Pop. (1992) 110,374.

In an iron-mining region. Manufactures iron and steel.

Birthplace of the painter, Rubens (1577–1640).

Siena Italy. Cap. of Siena province in Tuscany 51 km (32 miles) S of Florence. Pop. (1989) 60,500. In a beautiful setting on three hills. Much of the ancient walls and gates is preserved. Famous for its art treasures, esp. the many examples of medieval architecture: the 13th/14th-cent. cathedral, an outstanding example of Italian Gothic; the 13th/14th-cent. Gothic Palazzo Pubblico; San Domenico, San Francesco and other churches. In the Piccolomini Library adjoining the cathedral are Pinturicchio's celebrated 16th-cent. frescoes. Many paintings of the Sienese school. University (1300). A historic horse race is held annually in the Piazza del Campo in which horses from the 17 districts compete for the *palio* (Banner). An Etruscan city, Siena was a Roman colony in the time of Augustus. The chief banking and trading centre in Italy in the early 13th cent., it came into conflict with Florence and gradually lost political power through military defeat and internal dissension. Birthplace of St Catherine of Siena (1347–80).

Sierra de Guadalupe Spain. Mountain range in Cáceres province in the W about 48 km (30 miles) long and rising to 1444 m (4736 ft) between the Tagus and Guadiana rivers. The small town of Guadalupe in the range has a 14th-cent monastery, built to contain the shrine of Our Lady of Guadalupe. Guadalupe Hidalgo (Mexico) was named after it.

Sierra de Guadarrama Spain. Mountain range NW and N of Madrid extending about 177 km (110 miles) NE along the border of Madrid and Segovia provinces, rising to 2471 m (8104 ft) in the Peñalara. Well forested and yields much timber. Several winter-sports centres and sanatoria on its slopes.

Sierra Leone. Republic in West Africa bounded by Guinea to the N and NE, Liberia to the SE and the Atlantic Ocean to the SW. Area 71,740 sq km (27,699 sq. miles). Pop. (1995) 4,509,000 (35 per cent urban). Life expectancy, 41 years male, 45 years female. Cap. Freetown. Other cities Koidu-New Sembehun and Bo. Currency: Leone = 100 cents. Much of the coastline is flat and lined with mangrove swamps, but inland the country rises to a plateau, an extension of the Guinea Highlands, with peaks exceeding 1800 m (5904 ft). The climate is hot and humid. In the dry season the dust-laden harmattan blows from the Sahara. Land use: forested 29 per cent, meadows and pasture 31 per cent, agricultural and under permanent cultivation 9 per cent. English is the official lang. but Krio Mende and Temne are other langs. in use. Muslims represent about 39 per cent of the pop. and about 52 per cent follow traditionalist religions; Christians about 8 per cent.

Timber is obtained from the tropical rainforests and fishing is important along the coast. Principal food crop rice, which is grown on the swamplands. Exports inc. diamonds, bauxite, coffee, iron ore, palm kernels and some cocoa.

The colony of Sierra Leone originated in 1787 with the sale by native chiefs to English settlers of a piece of land intended as a home for natives of Africa who were waifs in London. The land was later used as a settlement for Africans rescued from slave-ships. The hinterland was declared a British protectorate in 1896. Sierra Leone became independent in 1961 and a republic in 1971. From 1978 to 1991 it was a one-party state. There is a 124-member Parliament; 105 members are directly elected, there are 12 Paramount Chiefs representing the 12 districts and 7 members are appointed by the President.

Sierra Madre Mexico. Principal mountain system of Mexico, dominating the country and profoundly influencing many aspects of Mexican life; extends 2400 km (1500 miles) SE from the N border. Three main ranges: the Sierra Madre Oriental (E) parallel to the coast of the Gulf of Mexico; the Sierra Madre Occidental (W), wider and more spectacular, parallel to the Gulf of California and the Pacific coast; the Sierra Madre del Sur (S). The three enclose the great central plateau. Highest peak is the Pico de Orizaba (Citlaltépetl) at 5699 m; 18,697 ft.

Sierra Morena Spain. Broad mountain range in the S, forming the watershed between the Guadiana and the Guadalquivir rivers. It is a considerable barrier between Andalusia and the N, with a mean height of about 750 m (2460 ft). Important mineral deposits, chiefly of copper, lead, silver and mercury.

Sierra Nevada Spain. In Spanish, 'Snowy Range'. High mountain range in the S in Andalusia, extending about 95 km (60 miles) W–E and rising to 3482 m (11,424 ft) in Mulhacén, the highest peak in Spain and to 3392 m (11,125 ft) in the Picacho de Veleta. Many summits permanently snow-capped, hence the name.

Sierra Nevada USA. Mountain range extending 640 km (400 miles) NW–SE through E California between the Central Valley (W) and the Great Basin (E). A massive block of the earth's crust with a steep escarpment along the E edge. Inc. Mt Whitney (4418 m; 14,495 ft) the highest peak in the USA outside Alaska. Several other peaks exceed 4200 m (13,776 ft). Also contains three of the USA's most famous National Parks, the Yosemite, Sequoia and King's Canyon.

Sierra Pacaraima Brazil/Venezuela. Mountain range forming part of the Venezuela–Brazil frontier, rising to 2810 m (9217 ft) in Mt Roraima at the E end. Forms the watershed between the Orinoco and Amazon basins.

Sikhote Alin Range Russia. Mountain range in the Primorye and Khabarovsk Terri-

tories, extending 1200 km (750 miles) parallel to and near the Pacific coast from Vladivostok to Nikolayevsk near the mouth of the Amur R. Rises to over 1800 m (5904 ft). Largely forested. Mineral resources inc. coal, iron, lead and zinc.

Si-kiang ➤XI JIANG.

Sikkim India. State and former protectorate of India on the S slopes of the E Himalayas between Nepal and Bhutan, bounded on the N and NE by Tibet (China). Area 7096 sq km (2772 sq. miles). Pop. (1991) 405,505 (75 per cent Nepalese). Cap. Gangtok. Entirely mountainous, rising to 8598 m (28,170 ft) in Kangchenjunga on the W border. Several other peaks exceed 6000 m (19,680 ft). Much forested, rich in flora, particularly orchids.

Chief crops rice, maize, fruits, cardamom, oranges and potatoes. Industries inc. fruit-processing, brewing and the manufacture of watches, electric cables and industrial gems.

Passed from British to Indian protection 1950, becoming a State in 1975.

Silchester England. Village in Hampshire 10 km (6 miles) N of Basingstoke on the site of the Roman town of Calleva Atrebatum. Excavated 1889–1909.

Silesia (Polish **Śląsk**, Ger. **Schlesien**, Czech **Slezsko**). Region of E central Europe in the basin of the upper Odra (Oder) R., bordering on the Sudeten and W Beskid Mountains (S). Mainly in SW Poland. The wealth of the region is based on the rich coalfield in the SE of Polish Silesia; iron, lead and zinc are also mined. Important metallurgical industries are centred on Wroclaw, Katowice, Zabrze, Bytom, Chorzów, Gliwice, Sosnowiec (all Polish). Chief towns in Czech Silesia are Opava and Ostrava.

Simbirsk Russia. Formerly Ulyanovsk. Cap. of Simbirsk region on Volga R. Pop. (1991) 667,700. ➤ULYANOVSK

Simferopol Ukraine. Cap. of the Crimea region on the Salgir R. 56 km (35 miles) NE of Sevastopol. Pop. (1991) 353,000.

Industrial centre in a district famous for

fruits, vines, vegetables and tobacco. Industries inc. fruit and vegetable canning, flour-milling and tanning.

The Tatar settlement of Akmechet: renamed after the Russian conquest of the Crimea (1784).

Simla (Shimla) India. Cap. of Himachal Pradesh 274 km (170 miles) N of Delhi. Pop. (1990) 102,186. A hill station in a beautiful position on a ridge of the lower Himalayas at heights of 2000–2430 m (6600–8000 ft).

Industries inc. machinery, tools, tobacco products, perfume and food-processing.

Under British rule it was the summer residence of the Viceroy and government.

Simonstown South Africa. Town and naval base on False Bay 32 km (20 miles) S of Cape Town. Pop. (1985) 6500. Headquarters of the South African Navy.

Industries inc. fishing, gemstone-polishing, food-processing and the manufacture of animal feeds, soap and margarine. Seaside resort on the S outskirts.

Named after Simon van der Stel, governor of the Cape 1679–99; established as a naval base 1814. Ceded to Britain by the Cape Province 1898. Transferred to South Africa 1957.

Simplon Pass Switzerland. Alpine pass between the Pennine and Lepontine Alps followed by the road from Brig to Domodossola (Italy), built (1800–07) by Napoleon. The hospice is at a height of 2001 m (6565 ft). The road passes through a tunnel and the wild Gondo gorge. To the NE is the Simplon Tunnel, the longest railway tunnel in the world (19.7 km; 12¼ miles) and the lowest Alpine tunnel (705 m; 2312 ft) through Monte Leone opened in 1906.

Sinai Egypt. Two governorates N and S formng a triangular peninsula in the extreme NE, separated from the rest by the Gulf of Suez and the Suez Canal. Area 60,714 sq km (23,442 sq. miles). Pop. (1991) 264,000. Chief towns Al Arish (S) and At Tur (N) on the railway and the coast. Bounded on the E by the Gulf of Aqaba and by Israel. Politically

part of Egypt but geographically in Asia rather than Africa. A belt of sand dunes runs along the N coast; the central area consists of the plateau of El Tih and the S is a mountainous region rising to 2639 m (8656 ft) in Jebel Katrin, just N of which is Jebel Musa (2287 m; 7501 ft), the 'Mount of Moses' often identified with Mt Sinai, mentioned in the Old Testament as the site of the Giving of the Law to Moses, though Jebel Serbal (2053 m; 6734 ft) has also been identified as Mt Sinai. The N coastal strip is crossed by the railway built during World War I from El Qantara to Jerusalem. The peninsula as a whole is barren; waterless apart from a number of wadis, it is inhabited mainly by nomads. Turquoise and copper were mined by the ancient Egyptians. Some manganese, iron and oil are now produced in the W. Occupied by Israeli forces after the 1967 war and returned to Egypt in 1979.

Sinaloa Mexico. State in the NW extending NW–SE between the Pacific Ocean (W) and the Sierra Madre Occidental (E). Area 58,328 sq km (22,521 sq. miles). Pop. (1990) 2,204,054. Cap. Culiacán. Principal seaport Mazatlán. The 5 rivers flowing from the mountains have been dammed to provide irrigation systems. Chief occupations mining (silver, gold), agriculture. Cereals cultivated on the uplands and sugar-cane and cotton on the lowlands.

Sind (Sindh) Pakistan. Province in the SE mainly comprising the lower Indus R. valley. Area 140,914 sq km (54,407 sq. miles). Pop. (1983) 20,312,000. Cap. Karachi. The central plain, irrigated through the Lloyd (Sukkur) Barrage and the Ghulam Muhammad (Kotri) Barrage, produces wheat, rice and cotton. Rainfall is very light and except for the irrigated lands the region is arid. The W is hilly and the E reaches the edge of the Thar Desert. Karachi stands on the coast; Hyderabad, Sukkur and Shikarpur are the chief inland towns.

Singapore. Republic, island and city at the southern extremity of the Malay peninsula, from which it is separated by the narrow

Johore Strait, crossed by a 1056-m (1155-yard) causeway carrying a road, a railway and a water pipeline. Area 639 sq km (24 sq. miles), inc. some 58 adjacent islets, 20 of which are inhabited. Pop. (1991) 2,762,700 (2,146,000 Chinese, 391,200 Malays, 195,000 Indians). Life expectancy, 70 years male, 76 female. Currency: Singapore dollar = 100 cents. On the S side of the island is the city of Singapore. The latter is a seaport of outstanding importance on the route from Europe and India to the Far East and possesses a fine, almost landlocked harbour. It is the world's third largest oil-refining centre. Most of the swamps and jungles have been reclaimed for urban development. The climate is equatorial with uniformly high temperatures and rain plentiful throughout the year. Land use: forested 5 per cent, agricultural 2 per cent. Malay, Mandarin Chinese, Tamil and English are the official lang. Malay is the natural lang. and English is the lang. of administration. Religious affiliation: Buddhists and Taoists 54 per cent, Muslims 15 per cent, Christians 13 per cent and Hindus 4 per cent.

Industries inc. tin-smelting on the offshore island of Pulau Brani, ship-repairing, electronics, chemicals, petroleum, paper, printing, food-processing, clothing and rubber-processing. Agriculture employs 1 per cent of the work force, but most food is imported. Tourism is important.

Singapore was destroyed by the Javanese in the 14th cent., it was inhabited by only a few fishing people when Sir Stamford Raffles secured the island from the Sultan of Johore in 1824. It became one of the Straits Settlements in 1826 and rapidly superseded Penang and Malacca in commercial importance. In World War II (1942) it was taken by the Japanese and became a British Crown Colony in 1946, and then a self-governing state in 1957, joining the Federation of Malaysia in 1963. Singapore seceded from the Federation and became a independent republic in 1965. There is a unicameral 87-member Parliament, inc. 6 non-elected members and at elections voting is compulsory.

Sining ►XINING.

Sinkiang-Uighur ►XINJIANG–UYGUR.

Sint Maarten ►ST MARTIN.

Sint Niklaas Belgium. Town situated WSW of Antwerp in East Flanders province. Pop. (1992) 68,253.

Market town for agricultural district of Waasland. Industry textiles; manufactures carpets, bricks and pottery.

Sintra (Cintra) Portugal. Town in the Lisboa district 23 km (14 miles) WNW of Lisbon. Pop. (1989) 20,200. On the Serra da Sintra, which rises to 540 m (1771 ft) in Cruz Alta and is largely covered with pines, cork oaks and other trees. Its beauty has been celebrated by many poets and authors, inc. Camões and Byron. The outstanding building in the town is the 14th/15th-cent. royal palace, in Moorish and Gothic styles, with two great conical chimneys. On a nearby height is the fantastically designed 19th-cent. Pena palace and on another the remains of the Moorish castle.

Sinuiju North Korea. Cap. of N Pyongan province on the Yalu R. opposite Antung (China). Pop. (1987) 289,000.

Industrial and commercial centre. Industries inc. sawmilling and the manufacture of paper and rayon.

Sion Switzerland. Ancient Sedunum. Cap. of the Valais canton on the Rhône R. 68 km (42 miles) SE of Lausanne at a height of 510 m (1673 ft). Pop. (1988) 23,700. Built around two low hills; on one are the remains of the castle of Tourbillon, on the other those of the castle of Valère (Valeria).

Woodworking and printing. Trade in wine, fruit and vegetables.

An ancient town and seat of a bishopric in the 7th cent.

Sioux City USA. Town in Iowa on the Missouri R. 240 km (150 miles) WNW of Des Moines. Pop. (1990) 80,505.

Large trade in livestock and grain. Meat-packing and flour-milling. Manufactures dairy products, clothing, fertilizers and electric tools.

Sioux Falls USA. Largest town in South Dakota on the Big Sioux R. near the Minnesota and Iowa borders. Pop. (1990) 100,814. Named after a series of cascades, which provide hydroelectric power.

Meat-packing. Manufactures biscuits and soap.

Siret (Russian **Seret**) **River** Romania/Ukraine. River 450 km (280 miles) long, mainly in Romania; rises on the E slopes of the Carpathians in the Ukraine and flows generally SSE to join the Danube R. just above Galaţi.

Sitka USA. Port in Alaska on the W coast of Baranof Island in the Alexander Archipelago. Pop. (1985) 7000. Excellent harbour.

Main industries tourism, fishing, fish-canning and sawmilling. Manufactures wood-pulp.

Cap. of Russian America until 1867. The original Russian settlement (New Archangel), built in 1799, was moved to the present site (1804) by Alexander Baranof. Scene of the formal transfer of Alaska from Russia to the USA in 1867 and remained cap. of Alaska until 1906, then replaced by Juneau. An important US naval base in World War II.

Sittard Netherlands. Market town in Limburg province 23 km (14 miles) NE of Maastricht. Pop. (1992) 46,314.

Tanning. Coalmining in the neighbourhood.

Sittingbourne England. Town in Kent 16 km (10 miles) ENE of Maidstone. Pop. (1991) 38,771.

Market town in a fruit-growing district. Industries inc. engineering and the manufacture of paper, cement and bricks.

Sittwe (Akyat) Myanmar (Burma). Cap. of Rakhine state, a seaport on the Bay of Bengal. Pop. (1983) 107,621.

Exports rice and has a rice-milling industry. It was developed in the 19th cent. from a small fishing village.

Sivas Turkey. Ancient Sebasteia. Cap. of Sivas province in the valley of the Kizil Irmak at a height of 1340 m (4395 ft) 354 km (220 miles) E of Ankara. Pop. (1990) 221,512.

Trade in agricultural produce. Manufactures carpets and textiles.

Has outstanding buildings erected by the Seljuk sultans in the 13th cent.

Siwa (Siwah) Egypt. Oasis in the Libyan Desert 475 km (295 miles) WSW of Alexandria, near the Libya–Egypt frontier. In a depression about 30 m (98 ft) below sea level; many salt lakes and ponds. Dates and olives are cultivated.

Once famous for the oracle temple of Jupiter Ammon, visited by Alexander the Great (331 BC).

Siwalik Range India/Nepal. Range of hills extending 1600 km (1000 miles) WNW–ESE parallel to and S of the Himalayan system, from Kashmir through Punjab, Uttar Pradesh and Nepal. Average height 610–1067 m (2000–3000 ft).

Sjaelland ➤ZEALAND.

Skagerrak Denmark/Norway. Strait about 128 km (80 miles) wide between Norway and Denmark (Jutland), continuing to the SE as the Kattegat.

Skagway USA. Port in SE Alaska at the head of the Chilkoot Inlet on the Lynn Canal. Pop. (1990) 712. Terminus of the railway from Whitehorse, Yukon (Canada). During the Klondike gold rush (1897–8) it had a floating pop. of 10,000–20,000.

Skara Brae Scotland. Prehistoric village on the W coast of Mainland, in the Orkneys, revealed after a storm in 1851, subsequent excavations discovering several stone huts and a section of street. Coarse pottery was found, but there was no evidence that the people had possessed textiles, metals or grain.

Skeena River Canada. River 580 km (360 miles) long in British Columbia rising in the Stikine Mountains, flowing S and SW, and entering the Hecate Strait on the Pacific Ocean 24 km (15 miles) SE of Prince Rupert.

Skegness England. Town in Lincolnshire 60 km (37 miles) ESE of Lincoln on the North Sea coast. Pop. (1991) 15,149.

Popular seaside resort with extensive sands, a pier and a holiday camp nearby.

Skellefteå Sweden. Town and port in Västerbotten county on the Skellefte R. near the mouth. Pop. (1988) 74,127.

Exports metallic ores, timber, tar. Copper and lead smelting, using ores from the nearby Boliden mines.

Skellefte River Sweden. River in the N 400 km (250 miles) long, rising near the Norwegian frontier and flowing SE through Lakes Hornavan, Uddjazur and Storavan to the Gulf of Bothnia. Much used for transporting logs. Near its mouth is the port of Skellefteå, which exports timber, tar and metallic ores.

Skelmersdale England. Town in Lancashire 10 km (6 miles) W of Wigan, formed in 1968 from the urban districts of Skelmersdale and Up Holland and parts of Ormskirk urban district and Wigan rural district. Pop. (1991) 37,184. Designated for development (1961) primarily to relieve overcrowding on Merseyside.

Industries inc. engineering producing turbo chargers, gas and electronic control equipment and electronics.

Skibbereen Ireland. Market town in Co. Cork on the R. Ilen 66 km (41 miles) SW of Cork. Pop. (1991) 1892.

Trade in agricultural produce.

The district suffered severely in the famine of 1847.

Skiddaw England. Mountain 931 m (3054 ft) high in Cumbria in the Lake District 5 km (3 miles) N of Keswick. Bassenthwaite Lake is 3 km (2 miles) W.

Skien Norway. Cap. of Telemark county on the Skien R. 101 km (63 miles) SW of Oslo. Pop. (1990) 47,870.

River port. Industrial centre. Sawmilling and tanning. Manufactures wood-pulp and paper. The gateway to the beautiful mountain and lake scenery of Telemark.

Birthplace of Henrik Ibsen, Norwegian dramatist (1828–1906).

Skikda Algeria. Port 56 km (35 miles) NNE of Constantine, with which it is connected by rail. Pop. (1988) 128,747.

Exports wine, citrus fruits, early vegetables, dates from the Saharan oases, iron ore and marble.

Built on the site of the Roman Rusicada. Founded 1838.

Skipton England. Town in North Yorkshire 26 km (16 miles) NW of Bradford. Pop. (1991) 13,583.

The chief market town of the Craven district. Industries inc. tourism and general manufacture. Limestone-quarrying nearby.

Part of the castle dates from the 11th cent.

Skíros ➤SKYROS.

Skoplje (Skopje) Macedonia. Cap. in N near the Serbian border on the Vardar R. Pop. (1991) 563,301.

The city serves a farming area, trading in and processing local produce as well as being the centre of distribution. Heavy industry inc. steel and chemicals. It manufactures cement, carpets and tobacco products.

The city, nearly all rebuilt after an earthquake in 1963, is planned in zones (industrial, residential) and with satellite units. Survivals from the older town are on the terraces above the river bank, where an early fortress remains at the top. Roman Skopje was destroyed by earthquake in 518. The medieval town recovered and the conquering Turks made it the cap. of their Macedonian province. The city was Serbian from 1913; it became the Macedonian cap. once more in 1945.

Skövde Sweden. Town in Skaraborg county 72 km (45 miles) NNW of Jönköping. Pop. (1974) 45,416.

Manufactures chemicals and cement.

Skye Scotland. Largest island in the Inner Hebrides in Highland, reached from the mainland by car ferry from Kyle of Lochalsh and connected by bridge since 1995. Area 1665 sq km (643 sq. miles). Pop. Skye and Lachalsh district (1991) 8868. Chief town

Portree on the E coast. Coast deeply indented with sea lochs. In the S are the gaunt Cuillin Hills, rising to 1009 m (3310 ft) in Sgurr Alasdair; in the N the Storr reaches 720 m (2362 ft).

Sheep and cattle reared, but both crofting and fishing are declining as the tourist industry increases in importance.

In the NW is Dunvegan Castle, home of the Macleods for well over 7 cent.

Skyros (Skíros) Greece. Island in the N Sporades in the Aegean Sea and in Euboea *nome*. Area 205 sq km (79 sq. miles).

Mainly agricultural, producing wheat and olive oil.

Burial-place of Rupert Brooke, English poet (1887–1915).

Slave (Great Slave) River Canada. River 418 km (260 miles) long in the Northwest Territories, leaving the NW end of L. Athabaska, flowing NNW, receiving the Peace R. and entering the Great Slave Lake.

Slavonia Croatia. Region in Croatia mainly between the Drava R. (N) and the Sava R. (S). Chief town Osijek. Mostly low-lying and fertile. Its history has closely followed that of Croatia: in 1699 it was returned to Hungary by the Turks; became an Austrian crownland 1848–9; restored to Hungary 1868; became part of Yugoslavia 1918.

Slavyansk ➤SLOYANSK.

Sleaford England. Market town in Lincolnshire on the R. Slea 27 km (17 miles) SSE of Lincoln. Pop. (1991) 10,388.

Manufactures agricultural machinery.

The Church of St Denis, with an early 15th-cent. carved oak rood screen, is noteworthy.

Sligo Ireland. 1. County in Connacht, bounded on the N by the Atlantic Ocean. Area 1796 sq km (693 sq. miles). Pop. (1991) 54,736. The chief inlets into the low, sandy coast are Sligo and Killala Bays. In the W the Slieve Gamph or Ox Mountains rise to 542 m (1778 ft) in Knockalongy and in the NE is Benbulbin (525 m; 1722 ft). Cattle raised.

Potatoes cultivated. On Inishmurray island are the remains of 6th-cent. buildings.

2. County town of Co. Sligo and port at the mouth of the R. Garavogue. Pop. (1991) 17,302.

Industries inc. tourism, toolmaking, light manufacture and medical supplies.

Its ruined abbey was founded in the 13th cent., rebuilt in the 15th cent. and burned in 1641. The Roman Catholic cathedral was built 1869–74. Nearby, on the hill Carrowmore, are megalithic remains inc. three dolmens and a stone circle.

Sliven Bulgaria. Cap. of Sliven province at the S foot of the Balkan Mountains 100 km (62 miles) WNW of Burgas. Pop. (1992) 114,596.

Industrial centre. Manufactures woollen goods, carpets and wine. Picturesquely situated, it stands in an important strategic position and was frequently involved in Balkan conflicts.

Slobozia Romania. Town situated N of Calarasi on Ialomita R. Pop. (1989) 52,189.

Railway junction and cattle market. Industries inc. flour-milling and the manufacture of candles.

Slough England. Industrial town and unitary authority (from 1998) 31 km (19 miles) W of London. Pop. (1991) 110,708.

Manufactures paints, plastics, food products, pharmaceutical goods, aircraft and automobile parts, radio and television sets. Its rapid growth dates from the 1920s, when an industrial estate was established here.

Home of the Herschel family, the astronomers; birthplace of Sir John Herschel (1792–1871).

Slovak Republic ➤SLOVAKIA.

Slovakia. Republic in E Europe bounded W by the Czech Republic, N by Poland, E by the Ukraine and S by Hungary. Area 49,036 sq km (18,933 sq. miles). Pop. (1991) 5,268,935 (57 per cent urban). Life expectancy, 69 years male, 75 female. Cap. Bratislava. Other cities Kosice, Nitra, Zilina. Currency: Slovak koruna = 100 halura. It is largely mountainous rising to 2665 m (8741 ft) at Gerlachovka in the High Tatra in the N. It slopes S towards the Danube valley. The climate is humid continental with warm summers and cold winters. The official lang. is Slovak but Hungarian is spoken by about 12 per cent of the pop.; there is a 500,000 minority of Hungarians. About 60 per cent of pop. is Roman Catholic.

The principal occupation is farming. Wheat, maize, barley and potatoes are important crops. Sheep and cattle are reared. It has some brown coal and iron ore. Industrialization is very limited but there is chemical and steel production.

Slovakia was part of Hungary before 1918 and then became a province of Czechoslovakia. During World War II it was nominally independent, but was reincorporated into Czechoslovakia in 1945. In the 1989 velvet revolution Communism faded and in 1990 Soviet troops withdrew. Separatists gained their objectives in 1993 when Slovakia became an independent State. There is a 150-member National Council elected by universal adult suffrage with proportional representation for 5-year periods.

Slovenia. Mountainous republic bounded by Austria in the N, Hungary in the NE, Croatia in the SE and Italy in the W. Area 20,256 sq km (7796 sq. miles). Pop. (1995) 1,971,000 (49 per cent urban). Life expectancy, 69 years male, 77 female. Cap. Ljubljana; other towns Maribor, Kranj, Ptuj and Celje. Currency: Slóvene tolar = 100 stotin. Slovenia is mostly mountainous with the Karawanken Mountains in the N and the Julian Alps in the NW, with the highest peak Triglav (2863 m; 9391 ft). Principal rivers the Sava and Drava. Land use: forested 50 per cent, pasture 32 per cent, agricultural 12 per cent. The official lang. is Slovene and 91 per cent of the pop. is Slovene. Roman Catholicism is the main religion.

Sugar-beet, potatoes, maize and vegetables are grown. Cattle are raised and forestry is important. Coal, lead and mercury are mined. Manufactures inc. cotton and woollen goods, vehicles and steel.

The area of Slovenia came under the control of the Habsburgs from the 15th cent. until 1918 when it became a province of Yugoslavia. After World War II it was divided between Germany, Italy and Hungary. It was restored to Yugoslavia, being made a people's republic in 1946, and land on the Adriatic was returned to Slovenia in 1954; Italy retaining Trieste. In 1989 because of the fear of Serb dominance the Constitution was altered, giving the right to secede from the Yugoslav Federation. In 1991 Slovenia declared its independence, which was agreed and was suspended for three months. Federal troops moved in to secure Yugoslavian external borders in June 1991 but after some fighting they withdrew in late July. Slovenia finally became independent on 8 Oct. 1991. Parliament consists of a 90-member National Assembly and a 40-member State Council.

Sloyansk (Slavyansk) Ukraine. Industrial town in the Donbas 96 km (60 miles) NNW of Donetsk. Pop. (1991) 137,000.

Manufactures chemicals, glass, porcelain and salt. Mineral springs nearby.

Founded 1676.

Slupsk (Ger. **Stolp**) Poland. Cap. of Slupsk voivodeship on the Slupia R. 113 km (70 miles) WNW of Gdańsk (Danzig). Pop. (1992) 102,400.

Manufactures chemicals and agricultural machinery.

Smethwick England. Industrial town in West Midlands just W of Birmingham in the county borough of Warley.

Manufactures glass, car components, screws and other metal goods. At the Soho ironworks nearby James Watt and Matthew Boulton worked together to produce the first steam engines.

Smolensk Russia. Cap. of the Smolensk region on the Dnieper R. 370 km (230 miles) WSW of Moscow. Pop. (1992) 352,000.

Important railway junction and industrial centre. Manufactures linen, textile and other machinery, clothing, footwear and furniture. Flour-milling, brewing, sawmilling.

Within the city are the remains of an old kremlin and it also has a 17th/18th-cent. cathedral. Founded in the 9th cent.; soon became an important commercial centre. Napoleon defeated the Russians here (1812) and there was heavy fighting again in World War II. In each conflict the city was all but destroyed. Birthplace of K. D. Glinka (1867–1927), the soil scientist.

Smyrna ➤IZMIR.

Snaefellsjökull Iceland. Volcanic peak 1446 m (4744 ft) in the W of the island on a peninsula of the same name. The setting of *Journey to the Centre of the Earth* by Jules Verne.

Snake River USA. Chief tributary of the Columbia R. 1670 km (1038 miles) long, rising in the Yellowstone National Park in NW Wyoming, flowing S then W, crossing S Idaho in a gigantic arc, turning N to form part of the borders between Idaho and Oregon and Washington, and discharging into the Columbia R. The largest and deepest of its many gorges is the Grand Canyon (Hell's Canyon), more than 160 km (100 miles) long and in places over 1.6 km (1 mile) deep. At, e.g. American Falls and Twin Falls, dams have been constructed for hydroelectric power and irrigation.

Snowdon Wales. Mountain in northern Gwynedd broken up into 5 peaks, one of which at 1085 m (3559 ft) is the highest in Wales and England. At its foot are the passes of Llanberis, Aberglaslyn and Rnyd-ddu. There is a magnificent view from the summit and it offers slopes of varying difficulty to the climber. Ascended by rack-and-pinion railway from Llanberis (the only mountain railway in Britain). The National Park of Snowdonia (established 1951) inc. a wide area around Snowdon.

Snowy Mountains Australia. Part of the Australian Alps in the SE, mainly in SE New South Wales near the Victoria border. In no sense 'alpine', they consist of a much dissected tableland with a general elevation of 900–1800 m (2952–5904 ft) with Mt Koscuisko, summit of a block, rising to 2230 m

(7316 ft). Snow-covered in winter; the melt water increases the volume of the rivers in spring. The Snowy Mountains hydroelectric scheme conserves much of this water and diverts the Snowy River headwaters. The Talbingo Dam, on the Tumut R. (a tributary of the Murrumbidgee R.), the last and largest dam in the scheme, was completed in 1970.

Snowy River Australia. River 418 km (260 miles) long, rising in the Snowy Mountains in the SE and flowing generally S to Bass Strait. Its waters were long unused in a region with a severe water shortage. Now, under the Snowy Mountains scheme, its upper waters are diverted from large new storages W to the Murray R. and N to the Murrumbidgee via its tributary, the Tumut. When the full scheme was completed (1972) the capacity of the associated power stations was greater than all the hydroelectric stations previously installed in the Australian Commonwealth. The first hydroelectric power from the Snowy Mountains scheme was fed into the New South Wales grid in 1957. The last mountain tunnel carrying water from the E to the W side of the Snowy Mountains was completed in 1967.

Sobat River Ethiopia/Sudan. Tributary of the Nile, formed by the union of the Pibor and the Baro rivers and several smaller streams, 740 km (460 miles) long from the source of the Baro to the confluence with the Nile. Joins the White Nile just above Malakal. Navigable during flood time (June–Dec.) as far as Gambela in Ethiopia (on the Baro). Flow retarded by swamps; makes its main contributuion to the Nile flood water late in the season (Nov.–Dec.).

Soche ➤YARKAND.

Sochi Russia. Resort on the Black Sea in the Krasnodar Territory 177 km (110 miles) SSE of Krasnodar Pop. (1992) 344,000.
One of the leading Russian seaside resorts, with many hotels and sanatoria. Manufactures food and tobacco products.

Society Islands French Polynesia. Two groups of islands, some volcanic and some coral, the Windward Is. (Îles du Vent) and the Leeward Is. (Îles sous le Vent), in the South Pacific. 1. Windward Islands: Area 1042 sq km (455 sq miles). Pop. (1988) 140,341. Main island Tahiti, its chief town Papeete (pop. 78,814); other islands Moorea, Makatea.

2. Leeward Islands: Area 404 sq km (160 sq. miles). Pop. (1988) 22,232. Main islands Huahine, Raiatea.

The group was discovered in 1767 and visited by Capt. Cook (1769) with a member of the Royal Society – hence the name. Became a French protectorate in 1843 and a colony in 1880. Now part of the overseas territory of French Polynesia. Chief products phosphates, copra and vanilla.

Socotra (Soqotra, Sokotra) Indian Ocean. Island in Yemen 240 km (150 miles) ENE of Cape Guardafui (Somalia). Area 2250 sq km (1400 sq. miles). Chief town Tamrida (Hadibo). A barren plateau with a ridge rising to nearly 1410 m (4625 ft). Along the coast and in the fertile valleys dates and gums are produced and livestock raised. Held briefly by the Portuguese (16th cent.). Placed under British protection 1886.

Södertälje Sweden. Town in Stockholm county 29 km (18 miles) WSW of Stockholm. Pop. (1989) 80,660. On the Södertälje Canal, linking L. Mälar with the Baltic.

Manufactures textiles, chemicals and matches.

Soest Germany. Industrial town and railway junction in North Rhine-Westphalia 45 km (28 miles) E of Dortmund. Pop. (1985) 40,298.

Manufactures machinery, electrical equipment, soap.

In the Middle Ages an important Hanseatic town.

Soest Netherlands. Town in Utrecht province 14 km (9 miles) NE of Utrecht. Pop. (1992) 41,639.

Manufactures dairy products.

Birthplace of Sir Peter Lely (Pieter van der Faes, 1618–80), the artist.

Sofia Bulgaria. Ancient Serdica. Cap. and largest city in the valley of the R. Iskür below the Ljulin Mountains which lie between the city and the Serbian border. Pop. (1992) 1,140,795. Important railway junction on the route from Belgrade to Istanbul. Within the usual residential and industrial suburbs the central city is mainly as planned in the 1880s.

Industrial centre. Industries inc. engineering, food-processing, manufacturing chemicals and printing.

Among its older buildings are the Chapel of St George, originally a Roman bath, the 6th-cent. Church of St Sophia, the Black Mosque, now an Orthodox church and the Banyabashi mosque. A Thracian and then a Roman town, Sofia was contested between Bulgar and Byzantine empires in the Middle Ages. The Turks took it in 1382 and it was the Turkish governor's seat until 1878. It became the cap. of independent Bulgaria in 1879.

Sogne Fiord Norway. The country's longest (177 km; 110 miles) and deepest fiord, its mouth 74 km (46 miles) N of Bergen. Penetrates almost to the Jotunheim Mountains, with many long arms extending N and S. Its magnificent scenery attracts many summer tourists.

Sohag Egypt. Cap. of Sohag governorate on the W bank of the Nile and on the railway 80 km (50 miles) SE of Asyût. Pop. (1990) 132,965. Industries inc. cotton-ginning and pottery manufacture.

Ruins of ancient Coptic churches.

Soho England. District in the City of Westminster, London, between Regent Street and Charing Cross Road, well known for its foreign restaurants, with theatres (Shaftesbury Avenue) and film company offices (Wardour Street). Many French Protestants settled here in the late 17th cent. and it still has a sufficiently high proportion of foreign residents to be called London's 'Latin Quarter'.

Soissonnais France. Region in the Paris Basin NE of Paris, traversed by the Aisne R. Chief town Soissons.

Dairy produce, grain and sugar-beet are important products.

Soissons France. Ancient Noviodunum, later Augusta Suessionum. Town in the Aisne department on the Aisne R. 92 km (57 miles) NE of Paris. Pop. (1968) 25,409.

Market town. Trade in agricultural produce from Soissonnais. Manufactures boilers, agricultural implements and rubber products.

Cathedral (12th/13th-cent.) and the ruined abbey of St Jean-des-Vignes, both damaged in the world wars and the ruined abbey of St Médard, where Merovingian kings were buried. Under the Romans became the second cap. of Gallia Belgica. In the Middle Ages and subsequently it suffered often in time of war.

Sokode Togo. Cap. of Centrale region and chief town of N. Pop. (1990) 55,000.

Sokoto Nigeria. 1. State primarily formed from the Sokoto province of the former N region, comprising the emirates of Sokoto, Argungu, Gwandu and Yauri. Area 102,535 sq km (39,589 sq. miles). Pop. (1991) 4,392,391. Main cities Sokoto (cap.), Gusuau, Kaura Namoda, Birnin Kebbi and Argungu.

2. Cap. of Sokoto state in the NW on the Kebbi R. (a tributary of the Sokoto) 370 km (230 miles) WNW of Kano. Pop. (1993) 190,100.

Commercial centre. Trade in cotton and rice.

In the 19th cent. Cap. of Sokoto (Fulah) empire.

Solent, The England. Channel about 24 km (15 miles) long between the Isle of Wight and the mainland of Hampshire; the main route from the W English Channel to Southampton and Portsmouth.

Solihull England. Town and unitary authority 11 km (7 miles) SE of Birmingham. Pop. (1991) 94,531.

Important manufactures of cars and machinery.

Has a 13th/15th-cent church.

Solikamsk Russia. Town in the Perm region 185 km (115 miles) N of Perm. Pop. (1992) 110,000.

A mining and industrial centre. Manufactures chemicals from locally mined potash and common salt, also magnesium. Founded as a salt-mining centre in the 15th cent.

Solingen Germany. Industrial town in North Rhine-Westphalia 21 km (13 miles) ESE of Düsseldorf. Pop. (1992) 165,924.

Noted for its cutlery industry (knives, scissors and razor blades) since early medieval times, when the manufacture of sword blades is supposed to have been introduced from Damascus. Also manufactures agricultural machinery and bicycles.

Solna Sweden. Town situated NW of Stockholm. Pop. (1990) 52,402.

Industries inc. film-making, paper-milling and the manufacture of machinery, electrical and electronic goods, graphics and chocolate.

Sologne France. Region in the SSW of the Paris Basin between the Loire and Cher rivers. A gently undulating plain with many marshes and a large area of forest. Cereals and vegetables cultivated. Small market towns with minor industries.

Solomon Islands. Independent state comprising an archipelago of volcanic islands situated between Bougainville (Papua New Guinea) in the NW and Vanuatu in the SE in the SW Pacific Ocean. Area 28,370 sq km (10,954 sq. miles). Pop. (1995) 382,000 (17 per cent urban). Life expectancy, 69 years male, 73 female. Cap. Honiara on Guadalcanal. Other towns Gizo, Auki, Kira Kira and Buala. Currency: Solomon Islands dollar = 100 cents. The group inc. the main islands of Guadalcanal, Malaita, New Georgia, San Cristobal (now Makira), Santa Isabel and Choiseul; the smaller Florida and Russell groups; the Shortland, Mono (or Treasury), Vella la Vella, Kolombangara, Ranongga, Gizo and Rendova Islands; to the E, Santa Cruz, Tikopia, the Reef and Duff groups; Rennell and Bellona in the S; Ontong Java or Lord Howe to the N; and innumerable smaller islands. The larger islands are mountainous and forest-clad with flood-prone rivers of considerable energy potential. Guadalcanal has the largest land area and the greatest amount of flat coastal plain. The islands have an equatorial climate with only small seasonal variations. Land use: forested 92 per cent, meadows and pastures 1.4 per cent, agricultural and under permanent cultivation 2 per cent.

About 90 per cent of the pop. is engaged in agriculture, and coconuts, sweet potatoes, bananas, taro, rice and yams are grown. Exports inc. copra, timber, palm oil, cocoa and rice. Industries inc. palm oil milling, forestry, canning and freezing food products. Bauxite and phosphate exist and gold and silver are exploited.

The Solomon Islands were discovered in 1568 by the Spanish explorer Alvaro de Mendaña. Two hundred years went by before contact was made again. A British protectorate was established over most of the islands in 1893 and further islands were added in 1898 and 1899. Santa Isabel and other islands were ceded to Germany in 1900 and in 1920 they were mandated to Australia. Full internal self-government was achieved in 1976 and independence in 1978 as a constitutional monarchy. There is a 36-member National Parliament.

Solothurn (Fr. **Soleure**) Switzerland. 1. Canton in the NW, crossed by the Jura and containing part of the fertile Aar R. valley. Area 791 sq km (306 sq. miles). Pop. (1988) 220,300 (mainly Roman Catholic and German-speaking). Agricultural and industrial. Chief towns Solothurn, Olten and Grenchen. Joined the Swiss Confederation in 1481.

2. Cap. of Solothurn canton on the Aar R. 29 km (18 miles) NNE of Bern. Pop. (1988) 15,400.

Industrial centre. Manufactures watches, precision instruments and textiles.

One of the oldest towns in Switzerland.

Solway Firth England/Scotland. Inlet of the Irish Sea separating Cumbria (England) from Dumfries and Galloway (Scotland). At its head it receives the Esk and Eden rivers, and it broadens out to a width of 35 km (22 miles). Being funnel-shaped, it has strong tides. Salmon-fishing important.

Somalia. Republic in the NE occupying the 'Horn' of Africa. It is bounded N by the Gulf of Aden, E and S by the Indian Ocean and W by Kenya, Ethiopia and Djibouti. Area 637,657 sq km (246,201 sq. miles). Pop. (1995) 6,734,000 (37 per cent urban). Life expectancy, 45 years male, 49 female. Cap. and chief seaport Mogadishu. Other cities Hargeysa, Kismaayo, Berbera and Marko. Currency: Somali shilling = 100 cents. In the N the coastal plain is narrow, rising abruptly to a plateau which reaches 2410 m (7901 ft); in the S it is much wider and the land generally lower. The climate is hot and arid but rainfall increases towards the S. Land use: forested 14 per cent, meadows and pastures 69 per cent, agricultural and under permanent cultivation 2 per cent. About 98 per cent of the pop. are Somalis, who are Sunni. The official lang. is Somali but Arabic, Italian and Swahili are also spoken.

The main occupation nomadic stock-rearing. Along the Webi Shebeli and the Juba rivers in the S there are plantation crops, grown by irrigation, such as sugar-cane, bananas, durra and maize. Industries inc. textiles, tobacco and food processing.

The region became an Italian sphere of influence in the late 19th cent. and the colony of Italian Somaliland after World War I. Jubaland was ceded, from Kenya, by the British in 1925. Taken by Britain during World War II (1941); returned to Italian trusteeship 1950. In 1960 the Republic of Somalia was formed by the unification of the British Somaliland Protectorate and the UN Trust Territory of Somalia. There have been continuing frontier disputes with Ethiopia and in 1977 Somalia invaded Ethiopia seeking to capture the Ogaden desert, but it lost the ensuing war. The Somali National Movement, the main insurgent group in the N, claimed independence as 'Somaliland Republic' in 1991. The area constituted the former British Somaliland Protectorate. The declaration was rejected by the Somalian government. Civil war, starvation and the collapse of government caused US-led military intervention in 1992 in an effort to restore order; this operation had UN backing.

Somaliland, French ▶DJIBOUTI.

Sombor Serbia. Market town in Vojvodina region 56 km (35 miles) SW of Subotica. Pop. (1971) 43,971.

Trade in grain and cattle. There is flour-milling and dairy products are manufactured.

Somerset England. County in the SW bounded on the N by the Bristol Channel and Avon, E by Wiltshire, S by Dorset and W by Devon. Area 3458 sq km (1335 sq. miles). Pop. (1991) 469,400. It is divided into the districts of Mendip, Sedgemoor, South Somerset, Taunton Dean and West Somerset. County town Taunton. In the W and SW are the moorland stretch of Exmoor (with Dunkery Beacon rising to 520 m; 1705 ft), the Quantock Hills and the Blackdown Hills; between these uplands and the Mendip Hills to the NE is the formerly marshy plain crossed by the Parret, Tone and Brue rivers now drained by numerous ditches. It is a dairy-farming county and Cheddar cheese is esp. well-known. Sheep reared. Cider apples grown. Industries inc. agricultural engineering and the manufacture of leather products, footwear, aircraft, paper and beverages. Tourists are attracted by the coastal resorts (e.g. Burnham-on-Sea, Minehead), by the natural beauties of Cheddar Gorge and Wookey Hole in the Mendips, and by the ancient towns of Wells and Glastonbury. Other important towns are Taunton, Street and Bridgwater.

Somerville USA. Town in Massachusetts on the Mystic R. just NW of Boston. Pop. (1990) 76,210. Mainly residential.

Industries inc. meat-packing and the manufacture of paper products, textiles and furniture.

Somme France. Department in the N in Picardy on the English Channel, crossed by the Somme R. Area 6170 sq km (2382 sq. miles). Pop. (1992) 548,900. Prefecture Amiens. Low-lying, flat and fertile. Produces wheat, sugar-beet, cider apples, vegetables. Industries inc. textiles and fertilizers. Chief towns Amiens, Abbeville.

Somme River France. River 245 km (152 miles) long rising in the Aisne department and flowing generally W past St Quentin, Amiens and Abbeville to enter the English Channel by an estuary. Linked by canals with other waterways in the N. The scene of an extended engagement of World War I (1916).

Songkhla Thailand. Town situated S of Bangkok on the E coast of the Malay peninsula in Songkhla province. Pop. (1989) 67,945. Provincial cap. and port trading in rubber and copra.

Industries inc. fishing, tin-mining.

Sonora Mexico. Second largest state in the NW, bordered by Arizona, USA (N) and the Gulf of California (W). Area 182,052 sq km (70,291 sq. miles). Pop. (1990) 1,823,606. Cap. Hermosillo. Chief seaport Guaymas. Off the coast lies Mexico's largest island the Isla del Tiburón. Mountainous except for the narrow coastal plain; traversed by the Sierra Madre Occidental. Drained and irrigated by the Magdalena, Sonora, Yaqui and Mayo rivers. Mainly arid; subtropical conditions near the coast and a more temperate climate at higher altitudes. Rich in minerals, esp. copper (at Cananea, N), silver, gold, lead and zinc. Crops grown in the irrigated valleys inc. sugar-cane, rice, alfalfa and wheat. There has been a steady increase in tourism in recent years.

Son River India. River 756 km (470 miles) long rising in Madhya Pradesh, flowing generally ENE and joining the Ganges above Patna. Used for irrigation in its lower course (NW Bihar).

Sonsonate El Salvador. Cap. of the Sonsonate department in the SW 58 km (36 miles) W of San Salvador. Pop. (1992) 76,200.

Commercial centre. Trade in hides, livestock and agricultural produce. Manufactures cotton goods and cigars.

Has a cathedral with many cupolas.

6

Founded in 1524 and was cap. of Salvador 1833–4.

Soo Canals ➤SAULT SAINTE MARIE (CANADA).

Soochow ➤SUZHOU.

Sopot Poland. Seaport on the Gulf of Gdańsk 11 km (7 miles) NNW of Gdańsk. Formerly a seaside resort; now part of the developing industrial and commercial conurbation of Gdańsk-Gdynia-Sopot.

Sopron Hungary. Industrial town and railway junction in Györ-Sopron county 80 km (50 miles) W of Györ near the Austrian frontier. Pop. (1970) 44,950.

Manufactures chemicals and textiles. Sugar-refining.

Has several old churches. Occupied since pre-Roman times. Assigned to Austria after World War I but returned to Hungary (1921) after a plebiscite.

Soria Spain. 1. Province in Old Castile in the N part of the Meseta. Area 10,287 sq km (3977 sq. miles). Pop. (1991) 94,280. Crossed by the Duero (Douro) R., it is a dry, infertile, sparsely inhabited region. Sheep-rearing important.

2. Cap. of Soria province on the Duero (Douro) R. at a height of 1050 m (3444 ft). Pop. (1991) 32,175. Industries inc. flour-milling and tanning, and the manufacture of tiles. Has 12th/13th-cent. Romanesque churches.

Sorocaba Brazil. Town in São Paulo state 88 km (55 miles) W of São Paolo. Pop. (1980) 255,000. In a rich cotton, coffee and orange growing region. Orange-packing, railway engineering. Manufactures textiles, fertilizers and cement.

Sorrento Italy. Town in Napoli province, Campania, on the S shore of the Bay of Naples. Pop. (1991) 17,500. Picturesquely situated on a cliff-lined peninsula separating the Bay of Naples from the Gulf of Salerno. A popular resort because of its climate and its position. Well-known since Roman times

for its wine. Birthplace of Torquato Tasso (1544–95), the poet.

Sorsogon Philippines. Seaport and cap. of Sorsogon province, SE Luzon on Sorsogon Bay. Pop. 48,000.

Exports Manila hemp and copra.

Sosnowiec Poland. Industrial town in the Katowice voivodeship 10 km (6 miles) ENE of Katowice. Pop. (1992) 259,000.

Iron-founding. Manufactures machinery, chemicals, textiles and bricks. Developed in the late 19th cent. with the exploitation of the nearby coalmines.

Sound, The (Öresund) Denmark/ Sweden. The most E of the straits linking the Kattegat with the Baltic Sea, between Zealand (Denmark) and Sweden; about 113 km (70 miles) long and 5 km (3 miles) wide at its narrowest. Tolls were collected at Helsingör (Denmark) from ships passing through 1429–1857.

Souris River Canada/USA. River 720 km (450 miles) long rising 23 km (14 miles) N of Weyburn, Saskatchewan, flowing generally SE into North Dakota (USA) then turning N and NE and joining the Assiniboine R. 34 km (21 miles) SE of Brandon, Manitoba.

Sousse (Susa) Tunisia. Ancient Hadrumetum. Seaport on the Gulf of Hammamet 101 km (63 miles) SSE of Tunis. Pop. (1984) 83,509.

Exports olive oil, phosphates. Main industry olive-oil production. Seaside resort.

In the old town are the Great Mosque and the Ksar er Ribat, a square fortress, both dating from the 9th cent. Founded by the Phoenicians in the 9th cent. BC. Later a Carthaginian and then a Roman colony. Rebuilt by Justinian and named Justinianopolis. Restored and fortified by the Aghlabid rulers of Kairouan in the 9th cent.

South Africa. Republic in the southernmost part of Africa between the Atlantic and Indian Oceans. Bounded on the N by Namibia, Botswana and Zimbabwe, NE by Mozambique and Swaziland. Area 1,219,090

South Africa

sq km (470,693 sq. miles). Pop. (1996) 37,859,000 (55 per cent urban). Life expectancy, 56 years male, 60 female. Capitals: Pretoria (executive), Bloemfontein (judicial), Cape Town (legislative). Other cities: Johannesburg, Durban, Port Elizabeth. Currency: Rand = 100 cents. In 1994 the Republic was divided into 9 provinces: Eastern Cape, Free State, Gauteng, KwaZulu/Natal, Mpumalanga, Northern Cape, Northern Province, North-West and Western Cape. The former homelands of Transkei and Ciskei were integrated into Eastern Cape, Venda into Northern Province and Bophuthatswana into Free State, Mpumalanga and North-West. Walvis Bay was ceded to Namibia in 1994.

Narrow plains on the coast rise to mountain ranges which surround the extensive high plateaux covering most of the area. Plateau areas are separated by ranges running roughly parallel to the coast, so that the land appears to rise in steps; the coastal range is at 152–183 m (500–600 ft), the plateau beyond at 457 m (1500 ft); the inner range is at 1829–2134 m (6000–7000 ft) and the plateau beyond at 610–914 m (2000–3000 ft). Beyond that is the range inc. the Nieuwveld, Sneeubergen and Drakensberg mountains, and the N is sit. on the High Veld plateau at 914–1829 m (3000–6000 ft). The climate is healthy and invigorating, with abundant sunshine and relatively low rainfall. The factors controlling this inc. the latitudinal position, the oceanic location of much of the country, and the existence of high plateaux. The SW has a Mediterranean climate, with rain mainly in winter, but most of the country has a summer maximum, though quantities show a clear decrease from E to W. Temperatures are remarkably uniform over the whole country. Land use: forested 7 per cent, meadows and pasture 67 per cent, agricultural and under permanent cultivation 11 per cent. About 68 per cent of the believers are Christian inc. 22 per cent black independent churches, Afrikaans Reformed 12 per cent, Roman Catholic 8 per cent, Methodist 6 per cent, Anglicans 4 per cent, Lutheran 3 per cent and Muslim, Hindu and Jews. The

official lang. are: Afrikaans, English, Ndebele, Pedi, Sothno, Swazi, Tsonga, Tswana, Venda, Xhosa and Zulu. Ethnic composition comprises 76 per cent Black, White 13 per cent, Coloured 9 per cent.

A Reconstruction and Development Programme was instituted in 1994. It aims to redistribute 30 per cent of agricultural land, build annually 300,000 houses, provide safe drinking water for 12 million people, provide sanitation for 21 million and create 300,000 non-agricultural jobs. The programme was to run until 1999. Agricultural areas produce tropical plants, cereals, sheep, dairy cattle, maize, citrus fruit, some cotton and tobacco, vines. The most important minerals are gold, silver, iron ore, iron pyrites, manganese, chrome, coal, copper, diamonds, phosphates, lime and limestone. The main mining centres are the Witwatersrand (gold), Kimberley (diamonds). Industries inc. food processing, canning and packing; manufactures machinery, vehicles, paper, basic metals, metal products, chemicals, textiles. The fishing industry is important off Natal. Main exports are gold, base metals and metal products, coal, food products, diamonds, chemicals, machinery and transport equipment, and textiles.

The Colony of the Cape of Good Hope was founded by the Dutch in 1652; Britain took possession in 1795 until 1803. It was under Dutch rule 1803–6, British 1806–14, when it was finally ceded to the British by the Dutch. Descendants of the Dutch settlers (Boers) went NE and founded the republics of Orange Free State and Transvaal. After the Boers' defeat in the Second Boer War (1899–1902), they became British colonies. The Union of South Africa was established in 1910 and became a republic in 1961 and embarked on a formal policy of political and social racial segregation (*apartheid*). Restrictions of apartheid were reduced in 1989 and in 1990 the 30-year ban on the African National Congress was removed and its leader, Nelson Mandela, released from prison. Constitutional equality for all races was granted in 1992. South Africa is a multi-party republic with two legislative houses; a 90-member

Senate and 400-member National Assembly directly elected for 4-year terms.

Southall England. Part of the London borough of Ealing situated 18 km (11 miles) W of London.

Industrial and residential. Manufactures heavy commercial vehicles, food products and pharmaceutical goods.

South America ►AMERICA.

Southampton England. City in Hampshire at the head of Southampton Water on the peninsula between the estuaries of the R. Test and the R. Itchen. Pop. (1991) 214,802.

Leading British deep-sea port. Passenger traffic has decreased owing to competition from the airlines, but container traffic has greatly increased. The double tides caused by its position opposite the Isle of Wight (S) are advantageous. Imports fruit, vegetables, meat and wool. Industries inc. flour-milling, yacht-building. Manufactures marine engines, electrical equipment, cables and petrochemicals. Large oil refinery at Fawley on Southampton Water.

Evidence of its long history may still be seen in part of the medieval walls, the 14th-cent. Bar Gate, the 12th-cent. house known as King John's Palace and other old buildings. The Pilgrim Fathers sailed from here (1620) for Plymouth on the first stage of their voyage to America. Raised to city status 1964. Birthplace of Sir John Millais, English painter (1829–96) and George Saintsbury, English literary critic (1845–1933).

Southampton Island Canada. Island in the E Keewatin District, Northwest Territories at the entrance to Hudson Bay. Area 43,864 km (16,936 sq. miles). Pop. about 200.

South Australia Australia. State in the central S part of the continent, bounded by the Northern Territory (N), Queensland, New South Wales and Victoria (E), the Indian Ocean (S) and Western Australia (W). Area 984,377 sq km (379,000 sq. miles). Pop. (1993) 1,460,100 (inc. 16,020 aboriginals and Torres Strait Islanders). Cap. Adelaide. The W is part of the old western plateau, overlain by flat sediments of the arid Nullarbor Plain. In the S and centre considerable faulting in late Tertiary times has given a series of peninsulas, low mountain blocks and drowned gulfs. Inland of Spencer Gulf are lakes, swamps and salt flats, while farther inland L. Eyre, 12 m (39 ft) below sea level, intermittently receives water from a vast inland drainage area. E of the Mt Lofty Range is the W part of the Murray basin, with the river flowing S to Encounter Bay. Kangaroo Island is a S extension of the Mt Lofty Range.

The arid interior carries coarse spinifex and low acacias, the Nullarbor Plain saltbush and small shrubs. These are empty lands, crossed by the Trans-Australian Railway and the road and railway to Alice Springs; between the two is Woomera, on a missile range. Bordering the moister SE is a zone of grassland with acacias (mulga); the SE highlands bear mainly open eucalypt woodland.

The 'Mediterranean' region is the chief agricultural area, growing wheat, barley, fruit and vines. There are numerous sheep, though away from the SE their density is low. Along the Murray R. is much irrigated land with fruit and vine growing and dairy-farming; wheat is cultivated on improved soils S of the Murray R. 'bend'. The extreme S is cooler and moister and has timber plantations and sawmills, and near Mt Gambier specializes in potatoes and vegetables.

The Middleback Range is a major source of iron ore and Whyalla consequently has become an iron-smelting centre with shipyards. Port Pirie, across Spencer Gulf, has metal and chemical works. Low-grade coal is mined 320 km (200 miles) N at Leigh Creek. Other minerals inc. opals, natural gas, uranium, copper and crude oil. The most industrially developed part, however, is in and near Adelaide, E of Gulf St Vincent, with Elizabeth. Adelaide contains over 70 per cent of the state pop. Port Adelaide is the principal port. The chief agricultural exports are wool, wheat, fruit, wine, the mineral exports iron, pyrites, salt and limestone.

The S coast of South Australia was explored (1802) by Flinders. In 1836 the territory was proclaimed a British Crown Colony, to become a state of the Commonwealth in 1901.

South Bend USA. Town in Indiana on the south bend of the St Joseph R. (hence the name) 120 km (75 miles) ESE of Chicago. Pop. (1990) 105,511.

Manufactures cars, aircraft equipment, agricultural machinery, clothing and toys.

South Beveland Netherlands. Peninsula in the Zeeland province in the Scheldt estuary. Area 350 sq km (135 sq. miles). Chief town Goes.

Vegetables, red currants and raspberries cultivated. Crossed by a ship canal and linked by railway with the mainland and Walcheren.

South Carolina USA. State in the SE, bordered on the E by the Atlantic. Area 80,582 sq km (31,113 sq. miles). Pop. (1990) 3,643,000. Cap. Columbia. About two-thirds of the area is the low-lying coastal plain. Highest point Sassafras Mountain (1085 m, 3559 ft) in the Blue Ridge. Chief rivers the Savannah, the Santee, the Pee Dee, the Edisto. Offshore lie the Sea Is. (shared with Georgia and Florida). Climate humid subtropical, with hot summers and mild winters. Annual rainfall 115–125 cm (45–50 ins.). Agriculture important. Main crops tobacco, cotton, maize, soya beans. Stock-rearing is a major occupation. The forests produce oak, poplar, pine. Industries (principally cotton-milling and wood-processing) centred on Columbia, Charleston (chief seaport), Greenville. Settled first by the Spaniards (1526), then by the English (1670). Played a leading part in the American Civil War, on the side of the Confederates, as a large slave-owning state; the first to secede from the Union (1860).

South Dakota USA. N central state. Area 199,730 sq km (77,116 sq. miles). Pop. (1990) 715,000. Cap. Pierre. Mostly in the Great Plains; largely treeless short-grass prairie. Highest point Harney Peak (2207 m; 7239 ft) in the Black Hills (SW); also in the SW are the heavily eroded Badlands. Roughly bisected by the Missouri R. Climate conti-

nental; hot summers and bitterly cold winters with heavy snowfalls. Annual rainfall 40–60 cm (15–24 ins.). Primarily agricultural. Chief crop maize, followed by oats and wheat. Large numbers of cattle, sheep and pigs reared. Leading state in gold production (Black Hills). Other industries inc. timber products and printing. Largest towns Sioux Falls, Rapid City. Explored by the French (1742); first settlement a fur-trading post (1817), later known as Fort Pierre. The Dakota Territory was created in 1861; this was divided into the states of North Dakota and South Dakota in 1889. Admitted to the Union in 1889 as the 40th state.

Southend-on-Sea England. Town and unitary authority (from 1998) in SE Essex on the N side of the Thames estuary 56 km (35 miles) E of London. Pop. (1988) 165,400. Residential town and seaside resort, popular with Londoners. Inc. Leigh-on-Sea, Westcliff, Thorpe Bay and Shoeburyness. The tide recedes for nearly a mile, but the pier, over 2 km (1¼ miles) long, accommodates ferries at all tides; there is an airport nearby.

Manufactures radio and television sets, electrical equipment, pharmaceutical goods, and is a financial centre for credit cards.

Southern Alps New Zealand. Mountainous 'backbone' in the W of South Island, running NE–SW about 320 km (200 miles). Average crest height over 2400 m (7872 ft); many peaks exceed 3000 m. The central snowfields near Mt Cook (3764 m, 12,349 ft) feed great glaciers such as the Tasman Glacier, 29 km (18 miles) long and 1.6 km (1 mile) wide; ice-cut, moraine-blocked valleys and long ribbon lakes lie along the E flanks.

South Foreland England. Chalk headland on the E coast of Kent 5 km (3 miles) ENE of Dover. Lighthouse.

Southgate England. Part of the London borough of Enfield 14 km (9 miles) N of London. Mainly residential.

South Gate USA. Industrial town in California 10 km (6 miles) S of Los Angeles. Pop. (1990) 86,284.

Manufactures chemicals, tyres, furniture and building materials.

South Georgia S Atlantic Ocean. Island situated about 1290 km (800 miles) E of the Falkland Is. and a dependency of this United Kingdom Overseas Territory. Area 3750 sq km (1450 sq. miles). Formerly an important whaling base. There is a small military garrison. Mountainous, snow-covered most of the year, with glaciers. Claimed for Britain by Capt. Cook in 1775. Argentine forces invaded South Georgia in April 1982; a British naval task force recovered the island later that month.

South Glamorgan Wales. Former county; since 1966 reorganized. ➤VALE OF GLAMORGAN.

South Gloucestershire England. New administrative area created 1996. Formerly part of Avon. Pop. (1994) 220,000.

South Holland (Zuid-Holland) Netherlands. Province bounded on the W by the North Sea. Area 2908 sq km (1123 sq. miles). Pop. (1992) 3,271,500. Cap. The Hague. Mainly below sea level, being protected along the coast by dunes. Drained by distributaries of the Rhine delta. The most densely populated province in the country. Chief towns The Hague, Rotterdam, Dordrecht, Leiden and Delft. Dairy-farming and market-gardening are important.

South Ijssellakepolders Netherlands. Polder lands reclaimed from the former Zuider Zee (now Ijsselmeer) and drained in 1957. Area 664 sq km (256 sq. miles). Pop. (1985) 27,000.

South Island ➤NEW ZEALAND.

South Molton England. Market town in Devonshire 39 km (24 miles) NW of Exeter. Pop. (1987) 3804. Centre for Exmoor. Flour-milling.

South Orkney Islands S Atlantic Ocean. Island group in the S Atlantic 720 km (450 miles) SW of South Georgia. Area 622 sq km (240 sq. miles). Formerly a dependency of the Falklands colony; since 1962 part of British Antarctic Territory administered from London. Discovered in 1821. Claimed by Argentina.

South Ossetia Georgia. Autonomous region on the S slopes of the Great Caucasus. Area 3909 sq km (1505 sq. miles). Pop. (1990) 99,000 (mainly Ossetian). Cap. Tskinvali. Mountainous. Main occupations stock-rearing (sheep, goats), lumbering, mining and electrical engineering. Established in 1922.

Southport England. Town in Merseyside on the Irish Sea 26 km (16 miles) N of Liverpool. Pop. (1991) 90,959. Seaside resort with an extensive promenade and a long pier; famous golf-course (Royal Birkdale).

Industries inc. engineering and the manufacture of hosiery, knitwear and confectionery.

South Sandwich Islands S Atlantic Ocean. Group of small volcanic islands in the S Atlantic 720 km (450 miles) ESE of South Georgia; formerly a dependency of the Falkland Islands, but since 1985 administered by a Commissioner. Area 340 sq km (130 sq. miles). Discovered (1775) by Capt. Cook. Claimed by Argentina.

South San Francisco USA. Industrial town in California 14 km (9 miles) S of San Francisco on San Francisco Bay. Pop. (1990) 54,312.

Meat-packing. Manufactures steel, chemicals and paint.

South Shetland Islands S Atlantic Ocean. Group of islands in the S Atlantic off the NW coast of Graham Land; Deception is volcanic. Area 4660 sq km (1800 sq. miles). Formerly a dependency of the Falkland Islands; since 1962 part of British Antarctic Territory. Discovered in 1819 and claimed for Britain by Capt. William Smith.

South Shields England. Seaport and resort in Tyne and Wear on the S side of the Tyne estuary, opposite North Shields (in Tynemouth), with which it is connected by ferry. Pop. (1991) 83,704.

Industries inc. coalmining, printing, plastics, and it also manufactures clothing, furniture, electrical equipment, circuit boards, alloy castings.

The first lifeboat was launched here (1790).

Southwark England. London borough on the S bank of the R. Thames comprising the former metropolitan boroughs of Bermondsey, Camberwell and Southwark. Pop. (1991) 222,200. Connected with the City of London by Blackfriars, Southwark and London Bridges. Has a 13th-cent. cathedral containing the tombs of John Fletcher and Philip Massinger, the dramatists; 19th-cent. Roman Catholic cathedral; Guy's Hospital (1721). Inc. Bankside, site of the Globe Theatre, with which Shakespeare was associated (a reconstructed Globe Theatre was opened in 1997 near the original site); nearby was the Clink Prison for heretics, which gave rise to the expression 'in the clink' (in prison). From medieval times Southwark was famous for its inns and the 17th-cent. The George, the last galleried inn in London, still survives.

Southwell England. Town in Nottinghamshire 19 km (12 miles) NE of Nottingham. Pop. (1986) 6560.

Flour-milling. Industries inc. general light engineering and garden centres.

The minster (built 12th/14th cent.) was elevated to a cathedral in 1884. The remains of the 15th-cent. palace of the Archbishops of York were incorporated into a residence for the Bishop of Southwell.

South-West Africa ➤NAMIBIA.

Southwold England. Seaside resort in E Suffolk 18 km (11 miles) SSW of Lowestoft. Pop. (1991) 3905. Has a Perpendicular 15th-cent. church.

South Yemen ➤YEMEN.

South Yorkshire England. Metropolitan county E of the Peak and the S end of the Pennines, drained E by the R. Don. Area 1560 sq km (602 sq. miles). Pop. (1991) 1,292,700. It is divided into the boroughs of Barnsley, Doncaster, Rotherham and Sheffield.

Largely industrial, esp. in the Don valley. Industries inc. coalmining, iron and steel manufacture, and engineering.

Sovetsk Russia. Formerly Tilsit. Industrial town in the Kaliningrad region on the Neman R. 96 km (60 miles) ENE of Kaliningrad. Pop. (1970) 38,000.

Manufactures cheese, wood-pulp, leather, soap. Trade in dairy produce.

Founded in the 13th cent.; later in the German province of E Prussia (as Tilsit). By the Treaty of Tilsit (1807), signed by Russia, France and Prussia, the last-named lost almost half her territory. After World War II it passed to the USSR and was renamed.

Soviet Central Asia ➤CENTRAL ASIA, SOVIET.

Sowerby Bridge England. Town in West Yorkshire on the R. Calder 5 km (3 miles) SW of Halifax. Pop. (1971) 16,260.

Manufactures textiles, carpets and chemicals.

Soweto South Africa. Black African township in Gauteng; its name being a contraction of South-West Townships. Pop. (1989) 850,000. A residential area for blacks who travel to white areas for work.

Spa Belgium. Tourist and health resort famous for its mineral springs (discovered in the 14th cent.) in Liège province 11 km (7 miles) S of Verviers in wooded hills. Pop. (1989) 10,000. Esp. fashionable in the 18th cent. Has given its name to all such resorts.

Spain. Kingdom in SW Europe bounded N by the Bay of Biscay and the Pyrenees (which form the frontier with France and Andorra), E and S by the Mediterranean and the Straits of Gibraltar, SW by the Atlantic and W by Portugal and the Atlantic. Area (inc. the Balearic and Canary Is., and the towns of Ceuta and Melilla in N Africa) 504,750 sq km (194,884 sq. miles). Pop. (1995) 39,188,000 (78 per cent urban). Life expectancy, 73 years male, 81 female. Cap. Madrid. Other large cities Barcelona, Valencia, Seville and Saragossa. Currency: Peseta = 100 céntimos. The interior consists of a vast plateau, the Meseta, at an average height of 600 m (1968 ft), crossed by several lofty mountain ranges. To the N of the Meseta are the fold mountain ranges of the Pyrenees, rising to 3404 m (11,165 ft) in the Pico de Aneto and the rather lower Cantabrian Mountains, which at few points exceed 2400 m (7872 ft). S of the Meseta, near the Mediterranean coast of Andalusia, is another fold range, the Sierra Nevada; here Mulhacén (3482 m; 11,424 ft) is the highest peak in mainland Spain. Between the Pyrenees and the Meseta are the plains of Aragón, drained by the Ebro R. Between the Sierra Nevada and the southern edge of the Meseta (the Sierra Morena) are the fertile plains of Andalusia, drained by the Guadalquivir R. Narrow plains extend along the E and SE coasts, broadening somewhat around Valencia, Alicante, Almería and Málaga. Across the Meseta itself the Douro, Tagus and Guadiana rivers have cut deep valleys; between the Douro (Duero) and the Tagus (Tajo) are the ridges of the Sierra de Gredos and the Sierra de Guadarrama, both rising to over 2400 m (7872 ft), and between the Tagus and the Guadiana the lower Sierra de Guadalupe and the Montes de Toledo. Much of the coastline is steep and rocky; the best natural harbours are the narrow inlets (*rías*) of the NW, where the ports of Vigo and Corunna are situated.

Most of Spain has a form of Mediterranean climate with mild, moist winters and hot, dry summers, but the northern coastal region has a moist, equable climate, with rainfall well-distributed throughout the year, mild winters and warm summers, though having less sunshine than the rest of Spain. Land use: forested 31 per cent, meadows and pastures 20 per cent, agricultural and under permanent cultivation 41 per cent. About 97 per cent of the pop. is Roman Catholic. Castilian Spanish is the lang. of literature and of most of the people. Catalan (NE, allied to Provençal), Galician (NW, akin to Portuguese) and Basque (unlike any other lang.) are spoken in their respective regions.

Productive agricultural land is about equally divided between crops and pasture.

Of the cereals the most important is wheat (grown esp. in Old Castile and Andalusia), followed by barley. Rice is produced in the irrigated S and SE where cotton and sugarcane are also cultivated and Elche has the only groves of date palms in Europe. Spain is a leading world producer of olives, grown mainly in Andalusia. There are vineyards in all regions; Jerez is famous for sherry, Almería for table grapes and Valencia for raisins. Oranges come largely from the irrigated *huertas* of the Mediterranean coastlands. Esparto grass is a product of the plateau. Sheep are numerous and Spain is the original home of the famous wool-producing merino breed. Oranges, olive oil and wine are the leading export items. Spain has a wide range of minerals; iron ore (mined in the Cantabrian Mountains) is exported and coal, copper, mercury, zinc and lead are also produced, mainly in the Cantabrians and the Sierra Morena. Agriculture, once the dominant industry, is still important, but the aim in recent years is to high-quality products for export. Main exports are transport equipment, agricultural and food products, chemicals, chemical products and the main market is the European Union. The older industries of shipbuilding, chemicals and steel are declining but there is growth in the electronic and electrical machinery and transport equipment industries. Other industries inc. food-processing, textiles, petroleum-refining, engineering, forestry, fishing and cement. Spain is dependent on imported oil, although this fell in the 1980s because of the rise in energy production. The tourist trade has expanded considerably, esp. along the Mediterranean coast (Costa Brava) and in the Balearic Is. (Majorca). Sixty-two million foreign tourists visited Spain in 1996, producing US$15,000 million in foreign currency.

Palaeolithic Man has left his mark in the famous rock paintings of Altamira, 29 km (18 miles) WSW of Santander. Much later the S and E were inhabited by Iberians (from N Africa) and the N and W by Celtic tribes from beyond the Pyrenees; Greek writers of the 3rd cent. BC described the mingled peoples of the Meseta as Celtiberians. Colonies were established by the Phoenicians (notably at Cádiz), the Greeks and the Carthaginians, who conquered most of the peninsula in the 3rd cent. BC. The end of the 2nd Punic War (201 BC) was followed by the Romanization of the peninsula, which was divided into the provinces of Tarraconensis (N, E and SE), Lusitania (roughly modern Portugal) and Baetica (roughly Andalusia). After the collapse of the Roman Empire it was invaded by the Suevi, the Vandals and the Visigoths in the 5th cent. AD. A Muslim army under Tarik crossed from N Africa and defeated Roderick, the last Visigoth king (711); the Moors soon conquered most of the peninsula and established a separate Caliphate, with Córdoba as cap. Charlemagne also gained a temporary foothold in the Spanish March (NE) in the 8th cent. Under Moorish rule agricultural methods were improved, new industries introduced and the arts encouraged, but the Christians advanced S and by the mid 13th cent. had assumed control of the entire country apart from the kingdom of Granada. Two powerful Christian states, Aragón and Castile, emerged from the conflict; they were united by the marriage of Ferdinand II of Aragón to Isabella of Castile (1474). Granada was conquered in 1492 and in the same year Columbus's voyage led to the acquisition of most of Central and South America. Charles V was elected Emperor (of the Holy Roman Empire) in 1519; Naples and Milan were annexed, Burgundy and the Netherlands became Spanish provinces, and Spain was the foremost country in Europe. Under Philip II the union with Portugal (independent since the 12th cent.) added the Portuguese overseas possessions to the Spanish Empire (1581). But the Netherlands continued permanently in revolt, the Armada was defeated (1588), the constant wars brought on economic exhaustion (worsened by the expulsion of the Moors and the Jews) and by the 17th cent. the power of Spain was declining. Portugal became independent again in 1640. Spain lost the Netherlands, Milan, Naples, Sardinia and Sicily in the early 18th cent. A

cent. later it was occupied by French troops and Napoleon ejected the Bourbon monarchy, declaring his brother Joseph King of Spain. The French were evicted by the Peninsular War, with British assistance. The remaining American colonies rebelled (1821–4); most of Latin America was independent by 1825. Spain suffered severely from civil wars, revolutions and dictatorships during the 19th cent. Puerto Rico, Cuba and the Philippines were lost in the Spanish American War (1898). Primo de Rivera's dictatorship (1923–30) could not save the monarchy; Alfonso XIII abdicated and a republic was established in 1931. A liberal government was elected in 1936 but a military revolt (headed by General Franco) broke out in Spanish Morocco and was followed by a rebel invasion. In the ensuing civil war (1936–9) the rebels were aided by Germany and Italy and the republicans by the USSR and an International Brigade. The rebels were victorious and a totalitarian regime was established with the quasi-fascist Falange the only political party and General Franco as *El Caudillo*; in 1947 he announced that Spain was to become a monarchy again, the succession after his death (by king or regent) to be determined by a Regency Council. Franco died in 1975; Prince Juan Carlos was proclaimed king and under the 1978 Constitution is a parliamentary monarch with a bicameral Parliament (*Cortes Generales*) comprising a 350-member Congress of Deputies elected by proportional representation and a 280-member directly elected Senate.

Spain is divided into 17 autonomous regions each with its own elected legislative assembly (capitals in brackets): Andalusia (Seville), Aragón (Saragossa), Asturias (Oviedo), Balearic Islands (Palma de Mallorca), The Basque Country (Vitoria), Canary Islands (dual and alternative cap., Las Palmas and Santa Cruz de Tenerife), Cantabria (Santander), Castilla-La Mancha (Toledo), Castilla-León (Valladolid), Catalonia (Barcelona), Extremadura (Mérida), Galicia (Santiago de Compostela), Madrid (Madrid), Murcia (Murcia has regional parliament in Cartagena), Navarra (Pamplona), La Rioja (Logroño), Valencian Community (Valencia).

Spalato ➤SPLIT.

Spalding England. Town in Lincolnshire on the R. Welland 23 km (14 miles) SSW of Boston. Pop. (1991) 18,731.

Market town in a region growing potatoes, sugar-beet and bulbs. Sugar-refining, fruit and vegetable canning and engineering. Much visited in spring for the nearby tulip fields.

Spandau Germany. Suburb of W Berlin situated at the confluence of the rivers Havel and Spree.

Industry engineering.

Spanish Guinea ➤EQUATORIAL GUINEA.

Spanish Sahara ➤MOROCCO; WESTERN SAHARA.

Sparks USA. Town immediately E of Reno in Nevada. Pop. (1990) 53,367.

Railway centre with repair shops. There is a gold and silver mining area nearby.

Sparta (Gr. **Spárti**) Greece. Cap. of Lakonia *nome* on the Eurotas R. 145 km (90 miles) SSE of Patras. Pop. (1971) 10,549.

Commercial centre. Trade in citrus fruits, olive oil.

Just S are the ruins of ancient Sparta (Lacedaemon), which was founded by the Dorians. Sparta was ruled by two hereditary kings; under the constitution, attributed to Lycurgus, citizens were trained for war from an early age and were taught indifference to pain or death; they distinguished themselves in battle but contributed little to Greek literature and art. Reached the height of its power in the Persian Wars (500–449 BC) and the Peloponnesian War (431–404 BC, when it defeated Athens and became the most powerful city-state in Greece). Defeated by Thebes at Leuctra (371 BC) and later compelled to submit to Philip II of Macedon, after which it declined. The modern town was founded in 1834.

Spartanburg USA. Town in South Caro-

lina 142 km (88 miles) NW of Columbia. Pop. (1988) 45,550.

A leading textile centre and railway junction. Manufactures clothing, food products and electrical equipment.

Spencer Gulf Australia. Inlet of the Indian Ocean in the coast of South Australia between Eyre Peninsula and Yorke Peninsula 320 km (200 miles) long and up to 120 km (75 miles) wide, with Port Augusta, Port Pirie and Whyalla on its shores.

Speyer Germany. Town in Rhineland-Palatinate on the left bank of the Rhine R. 19 km (12 miles) S of Ludwigshafen. Pop. (1989) 45,089.

Manufactures tobacco products, paper, footwear, bricks, sugar and alcoholic beverages.

Romanesque cathedral of sandstone, originally built 1030–61, and many times restored, with the tombs of 8 German emperors. Was a bishopric by the 7th cent. Became a free imperial city 1294. Many imperial diets were held here and it was the seat of the imperial supreme court 1527–1689, but it did not recover altogether from the destruction wrought by the French in 1689.

Spey River Scotland. River 172 km (107 miles) long, rising in Highland 16 km (10 miles) SSE of Fort Augustus and flowing generally NE, through Strathspey and past Kingussie, Aviemore and Fochabers to Moray Firth. Swiftly flowing and noted for its salmon.

Spezia, La ➤LA SPEZIA.

Spice Islands ➤MOLUCCAS.

Spion Kop South Africa. Hill near the Tugela R. 39 km (24 miles) WSW of Ladysmith. Scene of a battle (1900) in which the British were defeated by the Boers while trying to raise the siege of Ladysmith.

Spitalfields England. District in the London borough of Tower Hamlets, E London. Named after the priory and hospital or 'spital' of St Mary (founded 1197).

Manufactures footwear, furniture.

Formerly noted for the silk industry, introduced by Huguenot refugees in the 17th cent.

Spithead England. Anchorage in the Solent, off Portsmouth. Scene of many naval pageants and of a historic mutiny (1797). The name is sometimes wrongly applied to the E half of the Solent.

Spitsbergen ➤SVALBARD.

Split (Italian **Spalato**) Croatia. Chief seaport on the Dalmatian coast 257 km (160 miles) SE of Rijeka. Pop. (1991) 200,249. Stands on a small peninsula; has an excellent harbour.

Tourist centre. Shipbuilding, fish-canning. Manufactures cement and carpets.

It grew up in and around the great palace built (AD 295–305) by Diocletian, who was born in a nearby village. Many parts of this massive structure, which covers about 3.8 ha (9.3 acres) and is an outstanding example of Roman architecture, are still well preserved. In the 7th cent. the palace was occupied by refugees from neighbouring Salona, who thus established the modern Split. The city passed to Venice (1420–1797), Austria (1815–1919) and then to Yugoslavia.

Splügen Pass Switzerland. Alpine pass (2118 m; 6944 ft) in Graubünden (Grisons) canton on the Swiss–Italian border, linking the village of Splügen (Switzerland) with Chiavenna (Italy).

Spokane USA. Industrial town in Washington on the Spokane R. 380 km (235 miles) E of Seattle. Pop. (1989) 172,100.

Commercial centre for a large agricultural, lumbering and mining region. Aluminium works and plants for processing meat, wheat, dairy produce and timber.

Spoleto Italy. Ancient Spoletium. Town in Perugia province, Umbria 53 km (33 miles) SSE of Perugia. Pop. (1989) 38,000.

Manufactures textiles and leather.

Has a Roman bridge and remains of a theatre and amphitheatre, a 12th-cent. cathedral and frescoes by Filippo Lippi and medieval churches. An important town in Roman times: repulsed Hannibal (217 BC).

Became cap. of an independent duchy in the 6th cent. AD.

Sporades Greece. Scattered islands of the Aegean Sea outside the Cyclades, generally divided into two groups. 1. North Sporades: NE of Euboea, inc. Skiathos, Skopelos and Skíros.

2. South Sporades: now generally known as the Dodecanese, off the SW coast of Asia Minor, with Samos, Icaria.

Spree River Germany. River 397 km (247 miles) long, rising in the Dresden district and flowing generally N and NW past Bautzen and Cottbus, and through Berlin to join the Havel at Spandau. Below Cottbus is the Spreewald, a popular resort area for Berliners.

Springfield (Illinois) USA. State cap., on the Sangamon R. 290 km (180 miles) SW of Chicago. Pop. (1990) 105,227.

Manufactures agricultural machinery, electrical equipment, food products and footwear.

Home (1837–61) and burial-place of Abraham Lincoln.

Springfield (Massachusetts) USA. Industrial town on the Connecticut R. 126 km (78 miles) WSW of Boston. Pop. (1990) 156,983.

Manufactures electrical machinery, machine-tools and firearms. Industries inc. plastics, chemicals, printing and publishing.

Founded 1636. Seat of an armoury dating from 1794. Home of the Springfield rifle.

Springfield (Missouri) USA. Town in the SW in the Ozark Mountains 240 km (150 miles) SSE of Kansas City. Pop. (1990) 140,494.

Commercial and industrial centre in a poultry-farming, dairying and stock-rearing agricultural region. Railway engineering. Manufactures typewriters, furniture, clothing, television sets and electronic components.

Springfield (Ohio) USA. Industrial town on the Mad R. 71 km (44 miles) W of Columbus. Pop. (1990) 70,487.

Manufactures motor vehicles, agricultural machinery and electrical appliances.

Springs South Africa. Industrial town in Gauteng in E Witwatersrand (Rand) at a height of 1615 m (5300 ft) 40 km (25 miles) ESE of Johannesburg. Pop. (1985) 78,700.

Important goldmining centre, with uranium extraction; coal also mined in the neighbourhood. Manufactures mining machinery, electrical equipment, glass and paper.

Spurn Head England. Headland of sand and shingle at the S end of Holderness in Humberside across the entrance to the Humber estuary; narrow but about 6 km (4 miles) long (from Kilnsea). Has 2 lighthouses and a bird-migration observatory.

Sri Lanka. Republic situated in the Indian Ocean. A pear-shaped island off the SE coast of India, from which it is separated by Palk Strait and the Gulf of Mannar. Area 65,616 sq km (25,332 sq. miles). Pop. (1995) 18,090,000 (22 per cent urban). Life expectancy 70 years male, 75 female. Cap. Colombo. Other important towns Dehiwala-Mount Lavinia, Moratuwa and Jaffna. Currency: Sri Lanka rupee = 100 cents. Although tropical, it exhibits considerable variety in climate and vegetation and has some delightful scenery. Primarily agricultural, tea being by far the most important cash crop, followed by rubber and coconut products. Consists of a S central mountainous area surrounded by broad coastal plains; the highest peak is Pidurutalagala (2524 m; 8279 ft), but more famous is Adam's Peak (2243 m; 7357 ft). Rivers radiating from the mountain mass are generally short and of limited value, the most important being the Mahaweli Ganga (331 km; 206 miles), which flows NNE to Koddiyar Bay. Much of the coast is fringed with coconut palms and lined with sandbanks and lagoons: in the NW Mannar Island is almost joined to Rameswaram Island (India) by the line of sandbanks known as Adam's Bridge. Sri Lanka has an equatorial climate with low annual temperature variations. At Colombo, on the SW coast, the mean

monthly temperature varies little from 27°C (80°F), but at the hill station and health resort of Nuwara Eliya (1890 m; 6199 ft), overlooked by Pidurutalagala, it fluctuates between 14°C (57°F) and 17°C (62°F). Most of the island has abundant rainfall, distributed by the two monsoons: the W and S coasts and mountains receive rain mainly from the SW monsoon (May–Oct.) and the NE and E mainly from the NE monsoon (Nov.–Dec.), the annual total varying from 100 cm (40 ins.) to well over 250 cm (100 ins.); the N plain is a relatively dry region. A great deal of the original tropical forest has been cleared for rubber plantations and tea gardens. Land use: forested 32 per cent, meadows and pastures 7 per cent, agricultural and under permanent cultivation 29 per cent. Buddhism was introduced from India in the 3rd cent. BC and is the majority religion. Sinhala and Tamil are the official langs; English is in use. About 74 per cent are Sinhalese and 18 per cent Tamil. The two groups of Sinhalese people, lowland and Kandyan, are descendants of the colonists from NE India who came to Sri Lanka in the 6th cent. BC; they are Buddhists, the centre of their religion being the old cap., Kandy. Tamils from S India, divided now into Sri Lanka Tamils and Indian Tamils, and Hindus by religion, form the next largest group; others are the Moors, who came from Arabia and are Muslims, the Burghers, who are descendants of Portuguese and Dutch settlers, with much mixed Sinhalese blood, and a small and diminishing number of primitive aboriginal Veddas.

Rice, the main food crop, occupies about one-third of the cultivated land, but more has to be imported. Coconuts are grown chiefly along the W and SW coasts, tea in the hills, esp. between Kandy and Nuwara Eliya, and rubber in the SW. Coffee was the earliest cash crop, but it all but disappeared from the island after being attacked by a fungus disease c. 1870; the economy was saved by the introduction of tea and rubber. Graphite is the principal mineral and certain precious and semi-precious stones, inc. sapphires and rubies, are found. The great majority of the foreign trade passes through Colombo. Tea represents about 25 per cent of the total exports, rubber, coconut products (copra, coconut oil, desiccated coconut) and semi-precious stones most of the remainder. The main industries are food-processing, beverages, tobacco, clothing, chemicals, petroleum, plastics and rubber.

The aborigines of Sri Lanka were first conquered by Vijaya, an Aryan prince from NE India, in the 6th cent. BC. Buddhism was introduced about three cents. later and a branch of the sacred Bo-tree was planted at Anuradhapura. Sri Lanka was often invaded by Tamils, but in the 12th cent. AD a despotic monarch, Prakrama Bahu I, inaugurated a native dynasty and the so-called 'golden age of Lanka'. The Portuguese established trading settlements in the 16th cent., to be driven out by the Dutch, who in turn were expelled by the British. The whole island was annexed by Britain in 1815. Ceylon achieved independence in 1948 and became a republic as Sri Lanka in 1972. War between N Tamil separatists and government forces began in 1983. The State of Emergency ended in 1989 but violence has continued. Under the 1978 Constitution the republic has a presidential form of government. The President is elected for a 6-year term. Parliament consists of a 225-member single chamber elected by proportional representation. For purposes of general administration the country is divided into 25 districts.

Srinagar India. Summer cap. of Jammu and Kashmir on the Jhelum R. at a height of 1600 m (5248 ft) 600 km (400 miles) NNW of Delhi. Pop. (1991) 594,775.

Manufactures carpets, leather goods, copperware, wool, silk, handicrafts and telecommunication equipment. Timber and fruit-based industries are important. Picturesque, with the river, spanned by 9 wooden bridges, winding through; centre of houseboat excursions through the beautiful Vale of Kashmir.

Stade Germany. Town in Lower Saxony on the Schwinge R. near the Elbe estuary 37 km (23 miles) WNW of Hamburg. Pop. (1984) 43,000.

River port. Manufactures chemicals, leather goods. Formerly an important commercial centre.

Staffa Scotland. Uninhabited island in the Inner Hebrides, Argyll and Bute 13 km (8 miles) W of Mull. Well-known for its basalt caves, esp. the remarkable Fingal's Cave, 69 m (227 ft) long and with an entrance 20 m (66 ft) high.

Stafford England. Town in Staffordshire on the R. Sow (tributary of the R. Trent). Pop. (1991) 120,300.

Important footwear industry; also manufactures chemicals, electrical goods. Engineering.

Richard Brinsley Sheridan, the dramatist, was its MP 1780–1806; of the already important boot and shoe industry he said, 'May its trade be trod underfoot by all the world.' The unfinished 19th-cent. castle was intended to replace a Norman predecessor. Birthplace of Izaak Walton, English writer (1593–1683).

Staffordshire England. County in the Midlands. Area 2716 sq km (1049 sq. miles). Pop. (1991) 1,047,000. It is divided into the districts of Cannock Chase, East Staffordshire, Lichfield, Newcastle-under-Lyme, South Staffordshire, Stafford, Staffordshire Moorlands, Stoke-on-Trent and Tamworth. County town Stafford. Hilly in the N rising to 536 m (1758 ft) in Axe Edge with Cannock Chase in the centre, in the main it is a gently undulating plain drained by the R. Trent and its tributaries. Mainly industrial, with the N Staffordshire coalfield and the Potteries in the N. Chief manufacturing centres Stoke-on-Trent, Stafford, Newcastle-under-Lyme, Burton-upon-Trent.

Staines England. Town in Surrey at the confluence of the R. Colne with the R. Thames; inc. Ashford, Stanwell and Laleham. Pop. (1991) 51,167.

Largely residential. Industries inc. engineering and the manufacture of paint.

Has reservoirs for the London water

supply. An important bridging point since Roman times.

Stalybridge England. Town in Greater Manchester on the R. Tame 11 km (7 miles) E of the city. Pop. (1987) 21,932.

Engineering. Manufactures cotton goods and metal products.

Stamford England. Market town in Lincolnshire on the R. Welland 18 km (11 miles) WNW of Peterborough. Pop. (1990) 17,000.

Manufactures agricultural machinery, electrical and marine equipment.

Has several old buildings, inc. Brasenose Gateway, which recalls the Oxford students who seceded in 1333 and set up their headquarters here. The 15th-cent. Browne's Hospital is one of the almshouses or 'Callises', named after the wool merchants of Calais. Nearby is Burghley House, built by Lord Burghley in the 16th cent.

Stamford USA. Town in SW Connecticut on Long Island Sound 32 km (20 miles) WSW of Bridgeport. Pop. (1990) 108,056.

Industrial, commercial and residential centre. Manufactures chemicals, ball-bearings and machinery.

Founded in 1641.

Stamford Bridge England. Village in Humberside on the R. Derwent 11 km (7 miles) ENE of York, where Harold II of England defeated his brother Tostig and Harald Hardrada, king of Norway, in 1066, prior to being himself defeated by William of Normandy at the Battle of Hastings three weeks later.

Standerton South Africa. Market town in Mpumalanga on the Vaal R. at a height of 1500 m (4920 ft) 148 km (92 miles) SE of Johannesburg. Pop. (1985) 40,200.

In an agricultural region. Coalmining in the neighbourhood.

Stanley England. Town in Durham 13 km (8 miles) NNW of Durham. Pop. (1991) 18,905. In a former coalmining region.

Stanley Falkland Islands. Town in East Falk-

land on Port William inlet of the NE coast. Pop. (1991) 557. Cap. of the Falkland Islands, main port and commercial centre.

Exports wool and skins; imports food, coal, oil and timber.

Also called Port Stanley. A new airport at nearby Mount Pleasant was completed in 1986.

Stanley Falls Democratic Republic of the Congo. Series of 7 cataracts on the Lualaba (Congo) R. between Kisangani and Ponthierville. The total fall is only 60 m (197 ft) in 90 km (56 miles), but they render this part of the river unnavigable; a railway therefore links the two towns. Below the falls the Lualaba is known as the Congo R.

Stanley Pool Republic of the Congo/Democratic Republic of the Congo. Lake formed by the widening of the Congo R. 560 km (350 miles) above the mouth 29 km (18 miles) long (E–W) and 24 km (15 miles) wide (N–S). Kinshasa in Democratic Republic of the Congo is on the SW shore and Brazzaville in Republic of the Congo on the W. The large swampy island of Bamu (area 181 sq km; 70 sq. miles) divides the Congo into N and S branches, of which the latter is always navigable. The lake was discovered in 1877 by Henry Morton Stanley, Welsh explorer (1841–1904).

Stanleyville ➤KISANGANI.

Stanmore (Great Stanmore) England. Town within the London borough of Harrow. Largely residential.

Stanovoi Range Russia. Mountain range in the SE extending 800 km (500 miles) E from the Olekma R. and continued NNE by the Dzhugdzhur Range. Rises to 2484 m (8147 ft) in Skalisty Mt and forms part of the watershed between rivers flowing to the Arctic and the Pacific.

Staples, The ➤FARNE ISLANDS.

Stara Planina ➤BALKAN MOUNTAINS.

Stara Zagora Bulgaria. Ancient Augusta Trajana. Formerly Eski-Zagra. Cap. of Stara

Zagora province 80 km (50 miles) ENE of Plovdiv. Pop. (1992) 162,368.

Manufactures fertilizers and textiles. Flour-milling, brewing, distilling and tanning. Trade in wheat, wine and attar of roses.

Called by the Turks Eski-Zagra until it was ceded to Bulgaria (1877).

Stassfurt Germany. Town in the Magdeburg district 32 km (20 miles) SSW of Magdeburg. Pop. (1989) 24,666.

Important centre of potash and rock-salt mining. It also manufactures chemicals.

Staten Island USA. Island in SE New York, co-extensive with Richmond borough of New York City. Area 148 sq km (57 sq. miles). Pop. (1970) 295,443. Separated from New Jersey by the Kill van Kull and the Arthur Kill channels, both spanned by bridges, and from Long Island (NY) by the Narrows. Largely residential. Resorts and bathing beaches on the E shore.

Several industries inc. shipbuilding, oil-refining, printing and paper manufacture.

Stavanger Norway. Cap. of Rogaland county in the extreme SW and a seaport on Bökn Fiord. Pop. (1990) 98,109.

Centre for the construction of drilling rigs and tankers, and is the headquarters of Norwegian Oil Board. It is also a fishing centre with an important fish-canning industry and there is shipbuilding and woodworking.

Staveley England. Town in Derbyshire 6 km (4 miles) NE of Chesterfield Pop. (1971) 17,644.

Coalmining centre. Manufactures iron and chemicals.

Stavropol Russia. 1. Formerly N Caucasus Territory (1924–37), Ordzhonikidze (1937–43). Territory N of the Caucasus. Area 66,500 sq km (25,700 sq. miles). Pop. (1992) 2,536,000. Drained by the Kuma, Kuban and other rivers. Has a dry climate but is irrigated. Main occupations agriculture (wheat, maize), sheep-rearing. Formed 1924. Chief towns Stavropol and Pyatigorsk.

2. Formerly (1930s–1943) Voroshilovsk.

Cap. of the Stavropol Territory 306 km (190 miles) SE of Rostov. Pop. (1992) 332,000.

Flour-milling, tanning. Manufactures agricultural machinery and textiles. Trade in grain and livestock. Natural gas produced in the neighbourhood.

Founded 1777.

Steiermark ▶STYRIA.

Stellenbosch South Africa. Town in Western Cape Province 40 km (25 miles) E of Cape Town. Pop. (1989) 55,914. In a picturesque region of vineyards and orchards. Mainly residential.

Wine-making, sawmilling. Manufactures bricks and tiles.

Educational centre; seat of the University of Stellenbosch (1918). Famous for its oak-lined avenues. The oldest settlement in South Africa after Cape Town; founded in 1679.

Stelvio Pass Italy. Pass between the Italian–Swiss frontier and the Ortler group (3902 m; 12,799 ft); third highest Alpine road pass (2761 m; 9056 ft), linking Merano with Tirano (both in Italy).

Stendal Germany. Industrial town and important railway junction in the Magdeburg district 56 km (35 miles) NNE of Magdeburg. Pop. (1989) 48,700.

Railway engineering, metalworking and sugar-refining.

Founded in the 12th cent.

Stenness Scotland. Parish in Mainland in the Orkneys 14 km (9 miles) W of Kirkwall. Has two groups of standing stones in circles, the Ring of Brogar and the Ring of Stenness.

Stepney England. Part of the London borough of Tower Hamlets. Industrial and residential. Contains the Tower of London, St Katharine and London Docks (closed); along its W boundary runs Middlesex Street (Petticoat Lane), famous for its Sunday morning market. Severely damaged by bombing in World War II. Probable birthplace of Edmund Spenser, English poet (c. 1552–99), in E Smithfield.

Sterling Heights USA. City situated W of

L. St Clair on the Clinton R., Michigan. Pop. (1990) 117,810.

Industrial and commercial, inc. vehicle assembly.

Sterlitamak Russia. Industrial town and river port in the Bashkir Republic on the Belaya R. 137 km (85 miles) S of Ufa. Pop. (1991) 252,200.

Heavy engineering. Manufactures synthetic rubber, chemicals, cement, clothing and food products.

Stettin ►SZCZECIN.

Stettiner Haff Germany/Poland. Lagoon 55 km (34 miles) long (W–E) separated from the Baltic Sea by Usedom and Wolin islands; divided between Poland and Germany. The Oder R. flows into it below Szczecin (Stettin).

Stevenage England. Town in Hertfordshire 45 km (28 miles) N of London. Pop. (1991) 75,026 (7168 in 1951). Formerly a small market town, but developed after 1946 as a satellite town to London.

Manufactures school furniture and equipment.

Stewart Island (Rakiura) New Zealand. Volcanic island S of South Island, separated from the mainland by the Foveaux Strait. Area 1746 sq km (674 sq. miles). Pop. (1985) 600. Mountainous, rising to over 900 m (2952 ft). The small settlement of Oban is in the NE. Purchased (1864) from the Maoris, who call it Rakiura.

Stewarton Scotland. Small town in East Ayrshire 8 km (5 miles) N of Kilmarnock. Pop. (1971) 4490.

Hosiery and dyeing indstries and light engineering.

Steyning England. Small picturesque market town in West Sussex 16 km (10 miles) WNW of Brighton. Pop. (1985) 4500. In the 11th cent. it was a flourishing port, but it declined when the sea receded. Chanctonbury Ring (239 m; 784 ft) is 3 km (2 miles) W.

Steyr Austria. Town in Upper Austria at the confluence of the Enns and the Steyr rivers 29 km (18 miles) SSE of Linz. Pop. (1991) 39,542.

Centre of the iron and steel industry; manufactures motor vehicles, bicycles, ball-bearings, machinery and sporting guns.

Stilton England. Village in Cambridgeshire 10 km (6 miles) SSW of Peterborough. Gave its name to the famous Stilton cheese, which is made principally in Leicestershire.

Stirling Scotland. 1. New unitary authority (1996) replacing former Central Region, bounded on the W by Loch Lomond. Area 2162 sq km (835 sq. miles). Pop. (1993) 81,630.

2. Town on the R. Forth 48 km (30 miles) WNW of Edinburgh. Pop. (1985) 39,000.

Manufactures agricultural machinery and carpets.

Once the gateway to the Highlands by its 15th-cent. Old Bridge, it is dominated by the ancient castle where Alexander I of Scotland died and where Mary Queen of Scots and James VI were crowned. Other notable buildings are the unfinished 16th-cent. Mar's Work and the 17th-cent. Argyll's Lodging, now a hospital. The 66-m (216-ft) Wallace Monument (1869) is 2.4 km (1½ miles) NE.

Stockholm Sweden. Cap. and an important seaport on the E Coast. Pop. (1993) 684,576.

The main industrial, commercial and cultural centre. Shipbuilding, flour-milling and brewing. Manufactures iron and steel, machinery, cables, telephones, textiles and chemicals. Exports timber and paper.

Beautifully situated between L. Mälar and its outlet to the Baltic Sea, the Saltsjö, partly on a group of islands and partly on the adjacent mainland; has been called the Venice of the North. The oldest part is on the island of Staden, with the Royal Palace (1754), the 17th-cent. House of the Nobles and the 13th-cent. Church of St Nicholas (Storkyrka). On the nearby Riddarholm island is the 13th-cent. Franciscan church where the Swedish kings are buried. Mainly a modern city; among the outstanding buildings are the City Hall (1911–23), the Houses of

Parliament (1905) and the Stadium (1912). Founded 1255. Already an important commercial centre in the Middle Ages. Birthplace of Alfred Nobel, Swedish chemist (1833–96) and August Strindberg, Swedish dramatist and novelist (1849–1912).

Stockport England. Industrial town and unitary authority at the point where the R. Tame and the R. Goyt join to form the R. Mersey. Pop. (1991) 136,792.

Industries inc. engineering, electrical machinery, chemicals, plastics and paper.

A high railway viaduct (543 m; 1781 ft long) crosses the valley which was the site of the old town.

Stockton USA. Inland port in California 113 km (70 miles) SSE of Sacramento at the head of navigation of the San Joaquin R. Pop. (1990) 210,943. A deep-water channel, navigable for most ocean-going vessels, extends E from the river to the town centre.

Exports the agricultural produce of the San Joaquin valley. Manufactures agricultural machinery, motor-boats and food products.

Stockton-on-Tees England. New unitary authority from 1996, formerly in Cleveland; industrial town on the R. Tees 5 km (3 miles) WSW of Middlesbrough. Pop. (1991) 83,576.

Engineering, ship-repairing, chemicals and the manufacture of steel tubes and pipes.

Expanded after the opening of the Stockton–Darlington railway (1825), the first passenger line in the country. Birthplace of Thomas Sheraton (1751–1806), the furniture designer.

Stoke Newington England. Part of the London borough of Hackney. Contains Clissold Park and the 18th-cent. Clissold Mansion; large waterworks.

Stoke-on-Trent England. City and unitary authority on the R. Trent, formed (1910) by amalgamation with Burslem, Fenton, Hanley, Longton and Tunstall – the 'Five Towns' immortalized by Arnold Bennett – becoming a city in 1925. Pop. (1991) 275,168.

Centre of the pottery industry and practically co-extensive with the Potteries; associated with such famous manufacturers as Wedgwood, Spode and Minton. Also engineering, tyre and cable works. Coalmining in the neighbourhood.

Josiah Wedgwood, English potter (1730–95) was born at Burslem and Arnold Bennet, English novelist (1867–1931) at Hanley.

Stoke Poges England. Village in Buckinghamshire 3 km (2 miles) N of Slough. Its churchyard was probably the scene of Thomas Gray's *Elegy*, and in it the poet is buried.

Stolberg Germany. Industrial town in North Rhine-Westphalia 11 km (7 miles) E of Aachen. Pop. (1989) 58,900.

Metalworking and chemical manufacture.

Stone England. Market town in Staffordshire on the R. Trent 11 km (7 miles) S of Stoke-on-Trent. Pop. (1991) 12,305.

Manufactures pottery.

Has the remains of a 7th-cent. abbey. Birthplace of Peter de Wint (1784–1849), the painter.

Stonecutters Island Hong Kong. Small island off W coast of Kowloon peninsula and N of Victoria. Area 1.6 km (1 mile) by 0.4 km (¼ mile).

Stonehaven Scotland. Small town in Aberdeenshire 23 km (14 miles) SSW of Aberdeen. Pop. (1988) 9040.

Fishing port. Holiday resort. Manufactures fishing nets and leather.

The ruined Dunnottar Castle is 1.6 km (1 mile) S on a rocky cliff above the sea.

Stonehenge England. Chief prehistoric monument in the British Isles on Salisbury Plain 5 km (3 miles) W of Amesbury in Wiltshire. A circular earthwork over 90 m (295 ft) in diameter, enclosing the remains of 4 series of stones: 2 outer circles, a horseshoe and an inner oval. The outermost circle (30 m; 98 ft in diameter) originally had 30 upright stones, of an average height of over 3.9 m (13 ft); the 16 which are still standing are secured by stone lintels, each dovetailed with its neighbour. The second circle (over

23 m; 75 ft in diameter) originally had more than 40 stones; 9 upright and 11 fallen remain. The horseshoe-shaped group comprises 5 large trilithons, only two of them standing, 6.6 m (22 ft) high. Within the inner oval is the 'Altar Stone'. From the NE, Stonehenge is approached by a track called 'the Avenue', first completely revealed by aerial photography (1921), flanked by ditches 22 m (72 ft) apart at the Stonehenge end. The existing monument probably dates from the Bronze Age, in the 2nd millennium BC, and was religious in purpose. New evidence published suggests that the trilithons were erected about 3670 years ago. Stonehenge was presented to the nation in 1918.

Stonehouse Scotland. Town in North Lanarkshire 11 km (7 miles) S of Motherwell, designated a 'new town' in 1973 and inc. the villages of Blackwood and Kirkmuirhill, mainly to attract and serve local industries.

Stony Stratford ➤WOLVERTON.

Stormberg Mountains ➤SOUTH AFRICA.

Stornoway Scotland. Chief town on the E coast of Lewis with Harris in the Outer Hebrides (Ross and Cromarty). Pop. (1989) 8400.

Fishing port. Manufactures Harris tweeds.

Stourbridge England. Industrial town in West Midlands on the R. Stour 16 km (10 miles) WSW of Birmingham. Pop. (1991) 82,610.

Centre for steel-based industries and manufactures glass (first made in 1556) and firebricks.

Stourport-on-Severn England. Town in Worcestershire at the confluence of the Worcestershire Stour with the R. Severn 16 km (10 miles) N of Worcester. Pop. (1991) 18,283. A river port, but less important in this respect than formerly.

Industries inc. tourism and the manufacture of iron goods, vinegar, carpets and plastics.

Stour River (Essex–Suffolk) England. River 76 km (47 miles) long, formed from several headstreams, flowing E along the Essex–Suffolk border and entering the North Sea at Harwich.

Stour River (Oxfordshire–Warwickshire) England. River 32 km (20 miles) long, flowing generally NW and joining the Upper Avon R.

Stour River (West Midlands/Worcestershire) England. River 32 km (20 miles) long, flowing W and SW past Stourbridge and joining the R. Severn at Stourport-on-Severn.

Stour River (Wiltshire/Dorset) England. Rises in SW Wiltshire 6 km (4 miles) NW of Mere, enters Dorset and flows SE for 88 km (55 miles) past Sturminster Newton and Blandford Forum to enter the Avon R. at Christchurch.

Stour River, Great England. River in Kent 64 km (40 miles) long, formed by the union of two headstreams at Ashford, then flowing NE past Canterbury, and dividing, one branch flowing into Pegwell Bay and the other reaching the sea near Reculver.

Stowmarket England. Market town in Suffolk on the R. Gipping 18 km (11 miles) NW of Ipswich. Pop. (1991) 13,229.

Manufactures chemicals and agricultural implements.

Strabane Northern Ireland. Market town in Co. Tyrone at the confluence of the R. Finn and the R. Mourne, which form the R. Foyle. Pop. (1991) 11,670.

Manufactures shirts and collars. Trade in oats and potatoes. A salmon-fishing centre.

Stralsund Germany. Seaport and railway centre in the Rostock district on an arm of the Baltic Sea opposite Rügen Island, with which it is connected by a causeway carrying railway and road. Pop. (1990) 76,000.

Shipbuilding, fish-curing, metalworking and sugar-refining. Manufactures machinery.

Among its many old and picturesque buildings are the 14th-cent. town hall and several Gothic churches. Founded 1209. An important member of the Hanseatic League. Passed to Sweden (1648), France (1807), Denmark (1814) and Prussia (1815).

Stranraer Scotland. Seaport in Dumfries and Galloway at the head of Loch Ryan. Pop. (1991) 11,348. Has a ferry service to Larne (Northern Ireland). Also a market town. Fishing. Ruins of a 15th-cent. castle.

Strasbourg (Ger. **Strassburg**) France. Ancient Argentoratum. Prefecture of the Bas-Rhin department on the Ill R. and the Rhine R. Pop. (1990) 255,937.

Industrial, commercial and cultural centre of Alsace. Also an important river port and railway junction. Brewing, tanning, fruit and vegetable canning, flour and paper milling, printing. Manufactures metal goods, electrical equipment, chemicals, soap and foodstuffs. Famous for its *pâté de foie gras*. Trade in Alsatian wines, vegetables, iron ore and potash. Its position on the Rhine and on the Marne–Rhine and Rhône–Rhine canals has made it one of France's leading inland ports.

Notable buildings are the 11th/15th-cent. cathedral, with a remarkable spire 142 m (466 ft) high and the famous astronomical clock, and the university (founded 1567). Became a free imperial city in the 13th cent. Taken by Louis XIV 1681. Surrendered to the Germans, after siege, in 1871; returned to France 1919. Headquarters of the Council of Europe, and the European Parliament holds sessions here.

Stratford Canada. Town in Ontario on the Avon R. 90 km (56 miles) WNW of Hamilton. Pop. (1986) 26,000.

Industries inc. railway engineering and flour-milling. Manufactures textiles, furniture and agricultural machinery.

Has an annual Shakespearian festival.

Stratford USA. Resort in SW Connecticut on Long Island Sound at the mouth of the Housatonic R. Pop.(1989) 56,625.

Boatbuilding. Manufactures chemicals and hardware.

Stratford-upon-Avon England. Market town in Warwickshire on the R. Avon. Pop. (1991) 22,231.

Brewing and a few light industries.

Celebrated chiefly as the birthplace of William Shakespeare (1564–1616), visited by thousands of tourists each year. Among the many buildings closely associated with the poet is the half-timbered house where he was born, containing a museum. New Place, which he bought in 1597 and to which he retired (1610), was destroyed (1759), but its garden remains, and adjoining the latter is Nash's House, where his granddaughter, Elizabeth Hall, lived. The beautiful Holy Trinity Church has the graves of Shakespeare and his wife, Anne Hathaway. About 1.6 km (1 mile) W is Anne Hathaway's Cottage. The Memorial Theatre (built 1877) was destroyed by fire (1926), but a new theatre was opened in 1932 and regularly presents seasons of Shakespeare's plays. In addition to its Shakespearian connections, Stratford, an ancient town; has a fine 16th-cent. stone bridge of 14 arches crossing the river, and is set in picturesque countryside.

Strathclyde Scotland. Ancient kingdom in the SW, mainly in the Clyde basin, its cap. being Dumbarton. Finally incorporated in Scotland in the 11th cent.

Strathclyde Region Scotland. Former Region of SW Scotland created under the Local Government (Scotland) Act 1973 and came into effect 16 May 1975. A new Act of 1994 coming into effect on 1 April 1996 abolished the Strathclyde Region.

Strathmore Scotland. Broad vale extending SW–NE between the Grampians (N) and the Sidlaw Hills (S). Well-known for its fertile soil and its scenery.

Straubing Germany. Ancient town in Bavaria on the Danube R. 37 km (23 miles) ESE of Regensburg. Pop. (1990) 41,000.

Manufactures machinery, chemicals and textiles. Industries inc. brewing and tanning. Trade in grain, wine and cattle.

Streatham England. Residential district in

SW London in the London borough of Lambeth.

Street England. Company town in Somerset 18 km (11 miles) E of Bridgwater. Pop. (1991) 10,539.

Manufactures footwear and leather goods, and is also known for Clark's shopping village and Millfield School.

Stresa Italy. Port and resort in Novara province, Piedmont, on the W shore of L. Maggiore. Pop. (1971) 5422. Famous for its beautiful scenery. The Conference of Stresa (1935) between Italy, France and Britain was held on Isola Bella, in the Borromean Is. (in L. Maggiore).

Stretford England. Town in Greater Manchester 6 km (4 miles) W of the city on the Bridgewater Canal. Pop. (1991) 43,953.

Varied industries, inc. those on the Trafford Park industrial estate. Has the Lancashire County cricket ground, Old Trafford.

Stromboli Italy. The most N of the Aeolian or Lipari Is., N of Sicily in the Tyrrhenian Sea. Area 13 sq km (5 sq. miles). Pop. 470. Famous for its active volcano (927 m; 3041 ft), the stream of incandescent lava being an impressive sight at night.

Stromness Scotland. Small fishing port on the SW coast of Mainland in the Orkneys. Pop. (1991) 1890. 8 km (5 miles) E are the standing stones of Stenness.

Stroud England. Market town in Gloucestershire on the R. Frome 13 km (8 miles) S of Gloucester. Pop.(1991) 38,835.

Formerly an important centre of the West of England cloth industry, famous for its scarlet dyes; still specializes in the manufacture of uniform cloth. Also produces plastics, food products and oil-drilling equipment.

Stuttgart Germany. Cap. of Baden-Württemberg on the Neckar R. Pop. (1992) 591,946.

Railway junction. Industrial and commercial centre. Important publishing trade. Manufactures machinery, scientific and optical instruments, clocks and watches, musical instruments, chemicals, leather goods, textiles and paper.

Two of its three medieval churches and the Akademie, where Schiller studied, were destroyed by bombing in World War II. Became a town in the mid 13th cent., having originated in a stud farm (*Stuten Garten*) of the counts of Württemberg and was cap. of Württemberg from 1482. Birthplace of Georg Wilhelm Friedrich Hegel, German philosopher (1770–1831).

Styria (Ger. **Steiermark**) Austria. Federal state in the SE, bordering S on Slovenia. Area 16,388 sq km (6327 sq. miles). Pop. (1991) 1,184,720. Cap. Graz. Mainly mountainous, esp. in the N, it inc. the E part of the Niedere Tauern, and slopes generally to the SE. Drained by the Mur, Enns, Murz and Raab rivers.

Forestry, lignite and iron mining important. Agriculture in the SE. Industry concentrated mainly in Graz.

Part of the duchy of Carinthia under Charlemagne; in the 13th cent. it passed to the Habsburgs. Its S part was ceded to Yugoslavia in 1919.

Subic Bay Philippines. Inlet in the South China Sea. It was a major US naval base until 1992 and is now a free port with new hotels and the US airstrip is now an airport.

Subotica Serbia. Market town and railway junction in N Vojvodina region near the Hungarian frontier. Pop. (1991) 100,219.

Flour-milling, meat-packing. Manufactures chemicals, furniture and footwear.

Suceava Romania. Cap. of the Suceava district on the Suceava R. 116 km (72 miles) WNW of Iaşi. Pop. (1992) 114,355.

Market town. Flour-milling and tanning.

A historic town; cap. of Moldavia 1388–1565.

Suchow ➤SUZHOU.

Sucre Bolivia. Formerly Chuquisaca. Judicial cap. of Bolivia and cap. of the Chuquisaca department 434 km (270 miles) SE of La Paz (the actual seat of government) at a height of 2700 m (8856 ft) in the E Andes.

Pop. (1992) 130,952. Long isolated, now linked to Potosí by rail and road. Commercial centre for agricultural produce. Seat of the Supreme Court, a university (1624) and an archbishopric. Has a fine 17th-cent. cathedral. Founded 1538. Renamed (1839) after Bolivia's first president, Antonio José de Sucre (1795–1830).

Sudan. Republic in NE Africa, bounded by Egypt in the N, the Red Sea in the NE, Eritrea and Ethiopia in the E, Kenya, Uganda and the Democratic Republic of the Congo in the S, the Central African Republic and Chad in the W, and Libya in the NW. Area 2,503,890 sq km (966,757 sq. miles). Pop. (1995) 28,098,000 (22 per cent urban). Life expectancy, 53 years male, 55 female. Cap. Khartoum. Other cities Omdurman, Khartoum North, Port Sudan and Wad Madani. Currency: Sudanese dinar. Mainly plateaux, descending from over 450 m (1475 ft) where the Nile leaves for Egypt (N). The highest parts are the Lolebai Mountains, rising to 3189 m (10,460 ft) in the extreme S, and the Etbai Mountains on the Red Sea coast, with Jebel Erba reaching 2218 m (7275 ft). The Nile R. system provides the chief physical features and trade routes. In the S the Bahr el Jebel is joined by the Bahr el Ghazal to form the White Nile in the S which joins the Blue Nile at Khartoum. The Sibat and Atbara rivers, the other two important right-bank tributaries of the Nile, also join the main river in Sudan. The climate everywhere is tropical; annual rainfall increases southwards, from negligible amounts in the N to 100–125 cm (40–50 ins.) in the S. Vegetation ranges from xerophytic desert plants and scrub (N) to wooded savannah (S). Agriculture is practised on irrigated land, esp. on the Gezira plain beside the Blue Nile (watered from the Sennar dam). Land use: forested 19 per cent, meadows and pastures 46 per cent, agricultural and under permanent cultivation 5 per cent. Sunni Muslims are concentrated in the N and constitute the majority religion. Christians and animists are found in the S. Arabic is the official lang. but English and Nubian are also important langs. The ethnic composition comprises about 50 per cent Sudanese Arabs, Dinka 12 per cent, Nuba 8 per cent.

Sudan is predominantly agricultural with cotton by far the most important export crop. Durra (millet) is the staple food crop. Other crops inc. sorghum, sugar-cane, groundnuts, wheat, citrus and sesame. Gum arabic from the *Acacia senegal* tree growing in the Kordofan province is the sole forest product exported on a major scale; 80 per cent of world production. The government aims at self-sufficiency but years of drought have resulted in acute food shortages. There are reserves of minerals inc. iron ore, copper, gold and salt, but little has been exploited.

Sudan was conquered and unified by Mehemet Ali of Egypt in 1820–2. The successful Mahdist revolt (1881–98) caused the withdrawal of Egyptian forces after the defeat of Mahdi's successor near Omdurman in 1898, but the Anglo–Egyptian condominium in Sudan was established in 1899. It was reaffirmed in 1936, but abrogated by Egypt in 1951. A new constitution was agreed by Britain and Egypt in 1952 and it became an independent republic in 1956. A military *coup* in 1969 established a one-party state. A further *coup* in 1985 allowed for transfer to civilian rule in 1986. A series of coalition governments led to a further military *coup* in 1989 and a 12-man Revolutionary Council took control.

Sudbury Canada. Town in Ontario 338 km (210 miles) NNW of Toronto. Pop. (1991) 92,884.

In a rich mining region, producing most of the world's nickel, also lead, zinc, copper, silver, gold and platinum. One of the world's leading nickel smelting and refining centres. There is also engineering and sawmilling.

Sudbury England. Market town in W Suffolk on the R. Stour 23 km (14 miles) S of Bury St Edmunds. Pop. (1991) 19,512.

Manufactures textiles and diesel injectors.

Has three 15th-cent. Perpendicular churches and many old half-timbered houses. Birthplace of Thomas Gainsborough, English landscape and portrait painter (1727–88).

Sudetenland ►SUDETIC MOUNTAINS.

Sudetic Mountains Czech Republic. Mountain system along the NE frontier consisting of several ranges, rising to its highest point in the Schneekoppe (1604 m, 5261 ft) in the Riesengebirge. Rich in mineral resources, esp. coal. Sudetenland, named after the mountains, was the area on the fringes of Bohemia and Moravia that was formerly inhabited mainly by Germans; it was annexed by Hitler in 1938 but returned to Czechoslovakia in 1945 when the Germans were expelled.

Suez Egypt. Port at the head of the Gulf of Suez and at the S end of the Suez Canal 113 km (70 miles) ESE of Cairo. Pop. (1991) 376,000. Linked by rail with Cairo and Port Said.

An important oil-fuelling station; two oil refineries. Manufactures fertilizers.

The water supply formerly came from a nearby oasis (the 'Springs of Moses') whose water Moses is said to have miraculously sweetened; it now comes from the Fresh Water Canal. Suffered considerably during and after the Israeli–Arab war, inc. partial destruction of the oil refineries.

Suez Canal Egypt. Ship canal 173 km (108 miles) long, excluding 11 km (7 miles) of approach canals to the harbours, in NE Egypt connecting the Mediterranean with the Gulf of Suez (Red Sea): Port Said to the N end and Suez to the S. Built by the French engineer Ferdinand de Lesseps; opened 1869. Passes through L. Timsah and the Bitter Lakes; without locks. Minimum width 60 m (197 ft); average time of transit just over 11 hours. It has been deepened to take vessels of 22 m (72 ft) draught and also widened from 365 m (1197 ft) to 415 m (1361 ft) to take oil tankers of 250,000 tonnes. By the Convention of Constantinople (1888), open to the vessels of all nations and free from blockade, but Egypt did not allow Israeli ships to use the canal until 1979. Formerly owned by the Suez Canal Company, in which Britain held, from 1875, the controlling interest. The Canal Zone was occupied by British troops till 1954, then evacuated, under an Anglo–Egyptian agreement; the Canal was nationalized by the Egyptian government in 1956 and a Franco–British military expedition was sent against Egypt in Oct. but withdrawn in Dec. Israeli troops invaded the frontier lands but withdrew in 1957. In 1958 Egypt agreed to pay compensation to the shareholders of the Suez Canal Company, whose concession was to have ended in 1968. The canal was closed, several vessels having been sunk, after the Israeli–Arab war of June 1967 and was not reopened until 1975. In 1990 17,664 vessels went through the canal.

Suez, Gulf of Egypt. The NW arm of the Red Sea 274 km (170 miles) long and up to 40 km (25 miles) wide. Linked with the Mediterranean by the Suez Canal.

Suffolk England. County in the E, bordering E on the North Sea. Area 3807 sq km (1470 sq. miles). Pop. (1991) 636,266. It is divided into the districts of Babergh, Forest Heath, Ipswich, Mid Suffolk, St Edmundsbury, Suffolk Coastal and Waveney. Generally low and undulating, it rises in the SW to 128 m (420 ft) in the chalk hills of the East Anglian Heights. Coastline flat and marshy. Separated from Norfolk (N) by the Little Ouse and Waveney rivers and from Essex (S) by the Stour; other rivers are the Deben, Orwell and Alde. Primarily agricultural. Chief crops wheat, barley, sugar-beet. Suffolk punch horses are still raised and Newmarket is an important centre for the breeding and training of racehorses. The country has a broad economic base apart from agriculture. Industries inc. agricultural machinery, electronics, telecommunications research and development, insurance, port activities, printing, motor-vehicle components, food-processing and North Sea oil and gas exploration. Chief towns Bury St Edmunds, Felixstowe, Ipswich and Lowestoft.

Suhl Germany. Cap. of the Suhl district in the Thuringian Forest 48 km (30 miles) SW of Erfurt. Pop. (1990) 57,400.

Manufactures sports equipment, motor

cycles and bicyles, and pottery. Once famous for the manufacture of firearms.

Suir River Ireland. River 137 km (85 miles) long rising in N Tipperary and flowing S and then E past Clonmel to Waterford Harbour, where it joins the R. Barrow.

Suita Japan. Town situated N of Osaka in Honshu. Pop. (1992) 342,020.

The main industry is brewing.

Sukhum Georgia. Ancient Dioscurias. Formerly Sukhum-Kaleh. Cap. of the Abkhazian Autonomous Republic on the Black Sea 160 km (100 miles) NNW of Batumi. Pop. (1990) 122,000.

Seaport and health resort. Industries inc. metalworking, processing of fruit, tobacco and fish. Has a famous botanical garden.

An ancient Greek colony; later the Turkish fortress of Sukhum-Kaleh. Passed to Russia in 1810.

Sukkur Pakistan. Town in N Sind on the Indus R. 370 km (230 miles) NE of Karachi. Pop. (1981) 190,551.

Trade in grain, oilseeds. Manufactures textiles, leather goods and cement. Just below it is the Lloyd (Sukkur) Barrage across the Indus.

Sulaimaniya Iraq. Cap. of Sulaimaniya province 217 km (135 miles) ESE of Mosul near the Iranian frontier. Pop. (1985) 279,424. Market town. On trade routes with Iran.

Sulaiman Range Pakistan. Barren mountain range extending 290 km (180 miles) N–S parallel with and about 60 km (38 miles) W of the Indus R., rising to 3383 m (11,096 ft) in Takht-i-Sulaiman (N).

Sulawesi (Celebes) Indonesia. Island E of Borneo. Area 229,108 sq km (88,459 sq. miles). Divided into 4 provinces: Sulawesi Utara, Sulawesi Tengah, Sulawesi Selatan and Sulawesi Tenggara. Cap. and chief port Ujang Padang. Pop. (1989) 12,507,650.

Products inc. copra, coffee and spices.

Sullum Voe Scotland. Situated N of Lerwick on the N part of Mainland in the Shetland Islands. Pop. (1989) 1100. It is a deep coastal inlet and the site of Europe's largest oil and liquefied gas terminal.

Sumatra Indonesia. Island separated from Malay Peninsula by the Strait of Malacca, and from Java to SE by the Sunda Strait. Area 473,606 sq km (182,859 sq. miles). Pop. (1989) 36,881,990. Divided into the provinces of Atjeh, North Sumatra, West Sumatra, Djambi and South Sumatra. The island lies across the equator and has a hot climate with heavy rain in the SW and NE monsoons. Mainly forest with mountains along the W coast, chiefly volcanic and rising to Kerintji, 3805 m (12,484 ft) above sea level.

Chief occupation growing rice, rubber, tobacco, tea, coffee and coconuts. It is the centre of Indonesia's petroleum industry and there are deposits of coal.

Chief towns Palemban, Telanaipura, Bukit Tinggi, Medan and Bedan Atjeh.

Sumba Indonesia. Formerly Sandalwood Island. Island in the Lesser Sunda Is., separated from Flores and Sumbawa (N) by Sumba Strait. Area 11,153 sq km (4306 sq. miles). Chief town Waingapu.

Formerly an important source of sandalwood. Rice, tobacco, maize and fruit cultivated; copra exported. Livestock raised.

Sumbawa Indonesia. Island in the Lesser Sunda Is., between Lombok and Flores. Area 14,750 sq km (5695 sq. miles). Cap. Raba. Generally mountainous, rising to 2853 m (9358 ft) in Mt Tambora (N).

Tropical products are grown inc. rice, soya beans and sweet potatoes. Cattle raised.

Chief towns Raba, Bima and Sumbawa.

Sumer. Region of Mesopotamia (modern Iraq) occupying the S part of Babylonia, where a civilization developed in the 5th millennium BC. Its people, the Sumerians, who were non-Semitic, invented the cuneiform system of writing.

Sumgait Azerbaijan. Industrial town situated 24 km (15 miles) NW of Baku. Pop. (1991) 236,200.

Manufactures chemicals, synthetic rubber, using the products of the Baku oilfields.

Summerside Canada. Town situated WNW of Charlottetown on Bedeque Bay, Prince Edward Island. Pop. (1989) 12,000.

Port shipping dairy products and seed potatoes. Main industries farming, fishing and tourism.

Sumy Ukraine. Cap. of the Sumy region situated 314 km (195 miles) ENE of Kiev. Pop. (1991) 301,000.

Sugar-refining, sawmilling, and tanning. Manufactures agricultural machinery, fertilizers, textiles and food products. In a fertile farming region where wheat and sugar-beet are the chief crops.

Founded in 1658.

Sunbury-on-Thames England. Town 24 km (15 miles) WSW of London in Surrey. Pop. (1991) 27,392. Largely residential with some industrial estates.

Sunda Islands Indonesia. Island group comprising the W part of the Malay Archipelago, between the South China Sea and the Indian Ocean.

1. Greater Sunda Is.: Borneo, Java, Sumatra and Celebes, with adjacent islands.

2. Lesser Sunda Is.: Islands E of Java, the most important being Bali, Lombok, Sumbawa, Sumba, Flores and Timor.

Sundarbans. Region in the S of the Ganges delta in Bangladesh and adjoining W Bengal (India), extending 240 km (150 miles) inland. Swampy, with a network of tidal rivers and creeks, much of it covered with mangroves and other trees. It is gradually being reclaimed and brought under cultivation, but much has been designated a wildlife sanctuary.

Sundyberg Sweden. Town in Stockholm county 8 km (5 miles) NW of Stockholm. Pop. (1989) 31,600.

Industries inc. banking and high technology.

Sunderland England. City (since 1992) and unitary authority Seaport at the mouth of the R. Wear. Pop. (1991) 289,000.

Industries inc. car assembly and components, heavy and light engineering, glass products, clothing, printing and brewing.

In the suburb of Monkwearmouth (N of the Wear) are remains of the Benedictine monastery founded (674) by St Benedict Biscop, incorporated in St Peter's Church. The Venerable Bede (672–735) was born nearby.

Sundsvall Sweden. Seaport in Västernoorland county on the Gulf of Bothnia 338 km (210 miles) NNW of Stockholm. Pop. (1990) 93,808.

Important exports of timber and woodpulp, but is icebound in winter. Industries inc. sawmilling and it manufactures woodpulp and paper.

Founded in 1621 by Gustavus II.

Sungari River China. River 1850 km (1150 miles) long in the NE (Manchuria), rising in the Changpai Shan in SE Jilin province and flowing first NW past the Fengman Dam and hydroelectric power station, with the large Sungari Reservoir, just above Jilin. At the confluence with the Nun R. it turns sharply ENE past Harbin and Kiamusze to join the Amur R. near Tungkiang. Ice-free May–Oct.

Suomi ➤FINLAND.

Superior USA. Port in NW Wisconsin at the W end of L. Superior. Pop. (1970) 32,237. With the nearby port of Duluth, the W terminus of the St Lawrence Seaway.

Ships vast quantities of iron ore from Minnesota and grain from the Middle West. Shipbuilding, oil-refining, railway engineering, flour-milling and brewing.

Superior, Lake Canada/USA. The most westerly and the largest of the Great Lakes and the largest freshwater lake in the world; in central N America, 180 m (590 ft) above sea level (at the surface). Area 83,270 sq km (32,140 sq. miles). Bounded by Ontario (N and E), Michigan and Wisconsin (S) and Minnesota (W). The water is deep and clear; greatest depth 407 m (1335 ft). Never freezes completely, but its temperature does not rise much above freezing point even in summer, though it tempers the winter cold and summer heat of the districts around the shores. The navigation season is mid April to mid Dec.

Fed by about 200 rivers, inc. the Nipigon and the St Louis. Drains into L. Huron and L. Michigan at the SE end via the St Mary's R.; canals constructed around the rapids at Sault Ste Marie enable ships to enter and leave it. Isle Royale (USA) is the largest of the many islands. The N shore has deep bays and high cliffs rising to 450 m (1476 ft); the low and sandy S shore has the famous red-sandstone Pictured Rocks, 90 m (295 ft) high, so called from the effects of wave action. The main Canadian port is Thunder Bay; main US ports Duluth, Superior, Ashland, Marquette. Grain, timber and iron ore and copper ore are the principal eastbound cargoes, and coal the chief westbound cargo. Discovered (1623) by the French explorer Étienne Brûlé.

Surabaya Indonesia. Cap. of E Java province on the Mandura Strait near the mouth of the Kali Mas R. Pop. (1990) 2,421,016.

Important seaport and naval base. Handles nearly half of Java's exports. Exports sugar, tobacco and coffee. Also an industrial and commercial centre. Shipbuilding and ship-repairing, railway engineering, oil-refining. Manufactures textiles, glass, chemicals and tobacco products.

Surakarta (Solo) Indonesia. Town in central Java on the Solo R. 48 km (30 miles) ENE of Jogjakarta. Pop. (1990) 540,176.

Trade in rice, sugar and tobacco. Textile manufacture, tanning.

Has the former Sultan's palace.

Surat India. Industrial city in Gujarat on the Tapti R. 23 km (14 miles) from the mouth. Pop. (1991) 1,504,007.

Industries inc. engineering, steel and sugar. Manufactures cotton and silk goods, paper, soap, fertilizers, chemicals and synthetic yarn. Trade in cotton and grain.

During the reigns of Akbar, Jahangir and Shah Jahan it was an important seaport and chief commercial centre in India. Here the English established their first trading post in India (1612), but the city declined when the headquarters of the East India Company was transferred to Bombay (1687). Has revived somewhat in the 20th cent.

Surbiton England. Part of the Royal Borough of Kingston-upon-Thames.

There is light engineering, but it is mainly a dormitory suburb of London.

Suresnes France. Industrial suburb of W Paris in the Hauts-de-Seine department on the Seine R. Pop. (1982) 35,744.

Manufactures cars, bicycles, chemicals and perfumes.

Suriname. Republic on the NE coast of South America, bounded in the N by the Atlantic Ocean, by French Guiana in the E, Brazil in the S and Guyana in the W. Area 163,820 sq km (63,251 sq. miles), excluding 17,635 sq km (6809 sq. miles) disputed with Guyana. Pop. (1995) 430,000 (49 per cent urban). Life expectancy, 67 years male, 72 female. Cap. and chief seaport Paramaribo. Other towns Nieuw Nickerie, Meerszorg, Marienburg. Currency: Suriname guilder = 100 cents. There are three main regions: the N coastal lowlands, where sugar-cane, rice and citrus fruits are produced; an intermediate savannah region and densely forested highlands in the S. Climate is equatorial with uniformly high temperature and rainfall. Land use: forested 95 per cent, meadows and pastures 0.1 per cent, agricultural and under permanent cultivation 0.4 per cent. The official lang. is Dutch: other langs Sranang Tongo, Hindi and Javanese. There is complete religious liberty and main religions are Hindu, Christian (Roman Catholic), Muslim and Moravian Brethren. The ethnic composition comprises Indo–Pakistani 37 per cent, Suriname Creole 31 per cent, Javanese 14 per cent, Bush negro 9 per cent, Amerindian 3 per cent, Chinese 3 per cent, Dutch 1 per cent.

Alumina, bauxite and aluminium, produced near the Cottica and Para rivers, represent 74 per cent of exports. Other industries inc. food-processing and timber-using products. Agricultural crops inc. rice, sugar, citrus fruits, bananas and coconuts.

Dutch Guiana was ceded by Britain to the Netherlands by the Peace of Breda in 1667. Twice subsequently it was in British hands, but returned to the Netherlands in 1815. It became a self-governing part of the kingdom of the Netherlands in 1950 and gained independence in 1975 as Suriname. The government was overthrown in a *coup* in 1980 and a National Military Council was established, but in 1988 returned to democracy. A further military *coup* took place in 1990. The country is divided administratively into 9 districts.

Surrey England. County in the SE bounded on the N by Greater London. Area 1679 sq km (648 sq. miles). Pop. (1991) 1,035,500. It is divided into the boroughs of Elmbridge, Epsom and Ewell, Guildford, Reigate and Banstead, Runnymede, Spelthorne, Surrey Heath, Waverley and Woking, and the districts of Mole Valley and Tandridge. County town Guildford. The NE is almost entirely urban, being an extension of Greater London, but the county is crossed E–W by the chalk ridge of the North Downs, which has such well-known heights as the Hog's Back and Box Hill. Highest point Leith Hill (294 m; 964 ft), farther S. The two chief rivers cut through the North Downs, the Wey near Guildford and the Mole between Dorking and Leatherhead, to join the Thames. Although the county is mainly residential, market-gardening and dairy-farming are important, sheep are grazed on the Downs and fuller's earth is obtained at Nutfield.

Susa Iran. Cap. of ancient Elam 26 km (16 miles) SSW of the modern Dizful near the Karcheh R. Destroyed by the Assyrians 645 BC; was restored and became cap. of Persia. Excavations begun in the mid 19th cent. yielded remains of the palace of Darius I and considerable pottery and coins. The modern village of Shush is nearby.

Susquehanna River USA. River 714 km (444 miles) long, rising in Otsego Lake (NY), flowing generally S through New York and Pennsylvania, and entering the head of Chesapeake Bay. Not navigable. There are several hydroelectric power stations.

Sussex ►EAST SUSSEX; WEST SUSSEX.

Sutherland Scotland. Former county now in Highland.

Sutlej River China/India/Pakistan. Longest of the 5 rivers of the Punjab (1450 km; 900 miles), rising in Manasarowar Lake in SW Tibet and flowing WNW and then generally SW, crossing Himachal Pradesh and the plains of Punjab (India), entering Pakistan and finally joining the Chenab R. Chief tributary the Beas. Much used for irrigation: many dams, inc. the Bhakra Dam on the upper Sutlej, for irrigation and hydroelectric power.

Sutton England. London borough about 19 km (12 miles) SSW of central London, comprising the former municipal boroughs of Beddington and Wallington, Sutton and Cheam, and the urban district of Carshalton, all in Surrey. Pop. (1991) 170,300. Mainly residential.

Sutton Coldfield England. Town in West Midlands 11 km (7 miles) NE of Birmingham. Pop. (1991) 106,000. Largely residential.

Manufactures machinery and pharmaceutical products.

Sutton-in-Ashfield England. Town in Nottinghamshire 21 km (13 miles) NNW of Nottingham. Pop. (1990) 40,235.

Manufactures hosiery, metal containers. Industries inc. textiles and engineering.

Suva Fiji. Cap. and chief seaport on the SE coast of Viti Levu. Pop. (1986). 71,608 Extensive harbour.

Manufactures coconut oil and soap. Exports sugar, coconut oil and gold.

Proclaimed a city in 1953.

Suwannee River USA. River 400 km (250 miles) long, rising in the Okefenokee swamp (SE Georgia), following a winding course generally S, across N Florida and entering the Gulf of Mexico.

Suzdal Russia. Small town in the Vladimir region 32 km (20 miles) N of Vladimir. Founded in the 11th cent.; became an important religious centre with an ancient cathedral and monasteries.

Suzhou (Soochow) China. Town in S Jiangsu province on the Grand Canal 80 km (50 miles) W of Shanghai. Pop. (1990) 706,459.

Manufactures textiles (cotton and silk). Trade in rice.

It has many canals and is known as 'the Venice of China'. It is one of the most ancient of Chinese cities, probably founded in the 5th cent. BC Many gardens, temples and pagodas, inc. a nine-storey pagoda. A treaty port in 1896. Largely superseded as an industrial and commercial centre by Suzi (40 km; 25 miles NW).

Svalbard (Spitsbergen) Norway. Archipelago in the Arctic Ocean belonging to Norway and about 640 km (400 miles) N of that country, consisting of Spitsbergen (West Spitsbergen), North-east Land, Edge Island, Barents Island and several smaller islands, together with Bear Island to the S. Area 62,000 sq km (23,900 sq. miles). Pop. (1994) 2906 (1218 Norwegian, 1679 former USSR citizens and 9 Poles). The chief island, Spitsbergen (39,400 sq km; 15,200 sq. miles), is deeply indented with fiords and rises to 1718 m (5633 ft) in Mt Newton; its W coast is kept ice-free about April–Sept. by the North Atlantic Drift.

There are coalmines and 2 Norwegian and 2 Russian mining camps. Coal production from the Norwegian mines (1993) 266,734 tonnes. There are research and radio stations and an airport was opened in 1975 near Longyearbyen (Svalbard Lufthavn).

Used by whalers in the 17th cent.; awarded to Norway 1920 and formally incorporated by that country in 1925.

Svendborg Denmark. Cap. of Svendborg county in SE Fyn 40 km (25 miles) SSE of Odense. Pop. (1989) 40,871.

Seaport, yachting centre and industrial town. Shipbuilding and brewing. Manufactures textiles and machinery. Picturesque with many half-timbered houses.

Sverdlovsk ►YEKATERINBURG.

Svir River Russia. River 225 km (140 miles) long flowing WSW from L. Onega past the Svirstroi hydroelectric plant to L. Ladoga. Forms part of the Mariinsk canal system.

Svolvaer Norway. Chief town of the Lofoten Is. on the SE coast of Austvågöy. Pop. (1989) 4000.

Fishing port and centre of the Lofoten cod fisheries. Manufactures cod-liver oil and fertilizer.

Swabia (Ger. **Schwaben**) Germany. Region in the SW, approximating to the area now occupied by S Baden-Württemberg and SW Bavaria. The name derives from Suevi, the tribe once living here. A medieval duchy originating early in the 10th cent. Belonged to the house of Hohenstaufen from 1079 to 1268, when it was divided up.

Swadlincote England. Town in S Derbyshire 6 km (4 miles) SE of Burton-upon-Trent. Pop. (1991) 36,859.

Main industries gravel extraction and coal-mining. Manufactures earthenware and metal products.

Swakopmund Namibia. Town on the Atlantic coast 282 km (175 miles) W of Windhoek. Pop. (1990) 15,500. Chief port during the German administration; now closed, owing to the silting of the harbour. Railway terminus. Holiday resort. Saltpans to the N.

Swale River England. River 120 km (75 miles) long in North Yorkshire rising in the Pennines near the Cumbria border and flowing E past Richmond, then SSE through the Vale of York, joining the R. Ure to form the R. Ouse.

Swanage England. Town in Dorset on Swanage Bay (Isle of Purbeck) 11 km (7 miles) S of Poole. Pop. (1991) 9947. Holiday resort.

Swan Hill Australia. Town situated NNW of Melbourne, Victoria on the Murray R. Pop. (1989) 9600.

Processing centre for a sheep-farming, agricultural and fruit-growing area.

Swanland Australia. The SW and the most populous part of Western Australia; also its most fertile region, with a 'Mediterranean' climate, inc. a number of perennial rivers and considerable stretches of forest, mostly the hardwood eucalypts, jarrah and karri. Perth stands on the Swan R. and Fremantle at its mouth. Products inc. wheat, wool, timber, fruit, vines, tobacco and dairy produce.

Swansea Wales. County borough and sea-port in West Glamorgan at the mouth of the R. Tawe on Swansea Bay. Pop. (1994) 231,000.

Exports coal, tinplate and steel products. Imports tin ore, timber, petroleum products and petrochemicals. An important centre of tinplate manufacture. Foundries smelting zinc, copper, tin and nickel. Manufactures chemicals. Within its boundaries are the oil refinery of Llandarcy and the seaside resort of The Mumbles. Headquarters of the vehicle-licensing centre.

Seat of the University College of Swansea (1920), a constituent college of the University of Wales. Ruins of a 14th-cent. castle.

Swatow ►SHANTOU.

Swaziland. Kingdom in SE Africa bounded on the N, W and S by South Africa and on the E by Mozambique. Area 17,364 sq km (6704 sq. miles). Pop. (1995) 913,000 (urban 34 per cent). Life expectancy, 55 years male, 60 female. Administrative cap., Mbabane; royal and legislative cap., Lobamba. Other important city Manzini. Currency: Lilangeni = 100 cents. The country is divided into 3 regions extending N–S: the high veld over 1200 m (3936 ft) in the W, then the middle veld and finally the low veld at about 300 m (984 ft) in the E. The Komati and the Usutu, flowing W–E, are the main rivers. It has a temperate climate with two seasons: a wet

one November–March and cool dry for most of the rest of the year. Rainfall abundant on the high veld to the W but generally light on the low veld to the E. Land use: forested 6 per cent, meadows and pastures 60 per cent, agricultural and under permanent cultivation 12 per cent. About 77 per cent of the pop. is Christian and the majority of the remainder follow African indigenous and traditional beliefs. The ethnic composition, Swazi 84 per cent and Zulu 10 per cent. The official lang. are Swazi (siSwati) and English.

The chief economic activity is farming, inc. considerable cattle-ranching; crops inc. maize, rice, sugar, cotton and citrus fruits. Asbestos is found in the NW. Tourism is growing in importance. Manufactures inc. textiles, fertilizers, footwear and some engineering equipment.

The Swazi gained independence from the Zulus early in the 19th cent. and this independence was recognized by the British in 1881 and the Boers in 1884. In the Boer War the Swazi sided with the British and in 1906 their land was made a British protectorate under the High Commissioner for South Africa. In 1967 it gained internal self-government and in 1968 full independence. In 1973 the king assumed supreme power and abolished the Constitution in 1976. In 1996 the king announced plans for a new Constitution. There is also a traditional Swazi National Council headed by the king at which all Swazi men are entitled to be heard.

Sweden. Kingdom occupying the E part of the Scandinavian peninsula of N Europe. Bounded by Finland, the Gulf of Bothnia and the Baltic Sea to the E, The Sound, the Kattegat and the Skagerrak to the SW, and Norway to the W and NW. Area 449,964 sq km (173,732 sq. miles). Pop. (1995) 8,826,000 (83 per cent urban). Life expectancy, 75 years male, 81 female. Cap. Stockholm. Other cities Göteborg, Malmö, Uppsala, Linköping. Currency: Swedish krona = 100 ore. Mountains extend along most of the frontier with Norway, rising to their highest points (N) in Kebnekaise (2117 m, 6944 ft) and Sarektjåkko (2090 m, 6855 ft), and slope E down to a narrow coastal plain along the Gulf of Bothnia; mostly low-lying and level S of lat. 60°N. There are four main regions: Norrland, farthest N, occupies over half of the total area and is drained by many roughly parallel and swiftly flowing rivers which in their upper courses widen into long narrow lakes, e.g. the Torne, the Lule and the Ångerman; in summer, logs cut from the vast coniferous forests are floated down the rivers, which are also utilized for the development of hydroelectric power. Immediately S of Norrland are the central lowlands (Svealand), another region of numerous lakes; the largest are Väner, Vätter, Mälar and Hjälmar, linked with one another by rivers and canals. The Göta R. connects the Kattegat with L. Väner, which is linked with the Baltic Sea by the Göta Canal through L. Vätter. Götaland (S) is made up of two regions: the low plateau of Småland, rising to 377 m (1237 ft) and the fertile low-lying peninsula of Skåne (extreme S). Apart from Skåne, the coast of Sweden (like that of Norway) is fringed with innumerable small islands; the largest are Gotland and Öland (in the Baltic).

Sweden is almost 1600 km (1000 miles) long N–S; climatic conditions therefore vary considerably. In the far N winters are much colder and longer and summers much shorter and cooler than in the S; in general the climate is transitional between the relatively mild maritime type of Norway (W) and the continental type of Finland (E). The mean temperature for Feb. (the coldest month) is everywhere below freezing point; E coast ports are closed by ice for varying periods of the winter, but Göteborg (Gothenburg) (SW) is ice-free all the year. Annual rainfall is 35–65 cm (14–25 ins.) and increases generally N–S, with a much greater proportion of snow in the N. Land use: forested 68 per cent, meadows and pastures 1.4 per cent, agricultural and under permanent cultivation 7 per cent. Religion is predominantly evangelical Lutheran and the lang. is Swedish. Apart from a small number of Finns and 4000 Lapps (in the N) the people are almost entirely of Teutonic stock.

The forests and iron-ore deposits of

Sweden form some of the country's greatest natural assets and these resources have strongly influenced the external trade. Lumbering, woodworking, pulp-making and paper-milling are important occupations, esp. in Norrland. Timber, wood-pulp and paper represent about one quarter of the exports. Much of the timber is also manufactured into matches (at Jönköping) and furniture. Chief crops oats, barley, wheat, potatoes, sugar-beet and hay. Dairy-farming is also important. Iron ore of high grade is mined at Gällivare and Kiruna (in Lapland) and exported via Luleå on the Gulf of Bothnia in summer and via Narvik (in Norway) in winter. Also deposits of iron ore in Svealand, as well as copper, lead and zinc. The iron ore and imported coal are raw materials for the highly important steel and metallurgical industries, in the manufacture of certain products, e.g. electrical machinery, telecommunications equipment, ball-bearings, lighthouse apparatus, cream separators, in which Sweden specializes. Other industries inc. motor vehicles, ships, chemicals, food-processing and steel. Swedish glassware and porcelain are also world-famous. Because of few deposits of oil and coal, almost all the power required for industry and other purposes is derived from water; there are particularly important hydroelectric installations at Trollhättan on the Göta R. and Porjus on the Lule R., the former supplying power to most of S Sweden and the latter to the iron mines of Gällivare and to the Luleå–Narvik railway.

In early times Svealand was occupied by the Suiones (or Svear) and Götaland by the Götar; by the 7th cent. AD the two peoples had merged, with the Lapps inhabiting the N. The S part of Sweden was united under one king in the 12th cent. Christianity was firmly established and Finland conquered. By the Union of Kalmar (1397) Sweden, Norway and Denmark were united under a Danish dynasty, but with little support from the Swedes. Gustavus Vasa was elected king of Sweden in 1523 and as Gustavus I developed trade and military strength, and adopted the Lutheran religion; he is regarded as the founder of modern Sweden. Under Gustavus Adolphus (Gustavus II) Sweden attained its greatest power: Ingermanland, Karelia, most of Livonia, Pomerania and Bremen were acquired in the 17th cent. and the Danes driven from Skåne; Livonia was ceded to Sweden in 1660. After the death of Charles X Swedish power began to wane; there were military defeats and under the Peace of Nystad (1721) most continental possessions were lost. Gustavus III assumed absolute power, but a new constitution (the basis of the present monarchy) was adopted (1809) when Napoleon declared Marshal Bernadotte king of Sweden. Sweden was joined in 'personal union' with Norway in 1814 (unpopular with the Norwegians, this was ultimately dissolved in 1905). Bernadotte joined the last coalition against Napoleon, was confirmed as king in the post-Napoleonic settlement and founded the present dynasty, as Charles XIV (1818), in succession to the childless Charles XIII. The later 19th and early 20th cents. saw increasing industrialization, the rise of the Social Democratic party and the evolution of today's comprehensive system of social welfare. Throughout both world wars Sweden remained neutral.

Sweden is a constitutional monarchy and executive power is vested in the government, which is responsible to the 349-member unicameral Parliament (*Riksdag*). The king is head of state but has no participation in government since 1975. From 1971 the parliament consisted of 349 members elected for 3 years. Administratively divided into 24 counties (*län er*): Stockholm (city and county), Uppsala, Södermanland, Östergötland, Jönköping, Kronoberg, Kalmar, Gotland, Blekinge, Kristianstad, Malmöhus, Halland, Göteborg och Bohus, Älvsborg, Skaraborg, Värmland, Örebro, Västmanland, Kopparberg, Gävleborg, Västernorrland, Jämtland, Västerbotton, Norbotten.

Świdnica (Ger. **Schweidnitz**) Poland. Market town in the Walbrzych voivodeship 48 km (30 miles) SW of Wroclaw. Pop. (1991) 63,800.

Manufactures textiles, agricultural machinery, chemicals and furniture. Brewing and tanning.

Founded in the 13th cent. Temporarily cap. of an independent principality. Passed to Prussia 1742. Transferred to Poland after World War II.

Swift Current Canada. Town situated W of Regina on Swift Current Creek, Saskatchewan. Pop. (1989) 16,000.

Major distribution centre. Manufactures plastics, tempered glass, metal fasteners, hooks and agricultural equipment.

Swilly, Lough Ireland. Long narrow sea inlet into the N coast of Co. Donegal extending nearly 48 km (30 miles) inland from the entrance between Fanad Head and Dunaff Head.

Swindon England. Town and unitary authority 112 km (70 miles) W of London. Pop. (1991) 128,493.

Railway junction. Manufactures clothing, electronic equipment and car bodies. Many new industries established in recent years inc. financial services and book clubs.

Grew rapidly from a village with the establishment of the Great Western Railway locomotive and wagon works, now closed. Has an outstanding Railway Museum (opened 1962). Richard Jefferies, English novelist and naturalist (1848–87) was born at Coate Farm (2.4 km; 1½ miles SE).

Swinemünde ➤ŚWINOUJŚCIE.

Świnoujście (Ger. **Swinemünde**) Poland. Fishing port and seaside resort on the Baltic coast of Usedom Island in the Szczecin voivodeship 60 km (37 miles) NNW of Szczecin. Pop. (1991) 43,600. Formerly in Prussia, it was a German naval base in World War II, when it was largely destroyed. Ceded to Poland in 1945.

Swinton and Pendlebury England. Town in Greater Manchester 6 km (4 miles) NW of the city. Pop. (1991) 43,155.

Coalmining. Engineering. Manufactures cotton goods, electrical equipment (inc. batteries) and chemicals.

Switzerland (Ger. **Schweiz**, Fr. **Suisse**, Italian **Svizzera**). Inland republic in W. Europe. Bounded by Germany in the N, Austria and Liechtenstein in the E, Italy in the S and France in the W. Area 41,293 sq km (15,943 sq. miles). Pop. (1995) 7,039,000 (68 per cent urban). Life expectancy, 75 years male, 81 female. Cap. Bern. Other major cities Zürich, Basel, Geneva, Bern, Lausanne. Currency: Swiss franc = 100 centimes. There are 3 distinct regions, each running SW–NE: the Jura, the Central Plateau, the Alps. The Jura extend along the frontier with France, with several peaks exceeding 1500 m (4920 ft). On the Central Plateau, between the Jura and the Alps, the main industrial region, are the principal lakes: Constance, Zürich, Lucerne, Neuchâtel and Geneva. Over 50 per cent of Switzerland is occupied by the ranges of the Alps. N of the Rhône R. are the Bernese Alps, which contain the Finsteraarhorn (4280 m; 14,038 ft) and the Jungfrau (4164 m; 13,658 ft). S of the Rhône are the Pennine Alps, in which are the Matterhorn (4477 m; 14,688 ft) and the Dufourspitze of Monte Rosa (4634 m; 15,203 ft, the highest peak wholly in Switzerland). The mountains to the E are rather less lofty, though the Piz Bernina in the Bernina Alps (SE) rises to 4058 m (13,310 ft). There are hundreds of glaciers among the Alpine peaks. On the S frontier (where parts of L. Maggiore and L. Lugano lie in Switzerland) the beautiful Alpine zone with its snow-covered peaks changes to a region of almost subtropical vegetation. The Alps are cut W–E by the deep valleys of the upper Rhône and the Rhine; the Inn flows NE through the Engadine to the Danube and the Ticino flows S to the Po. The climate is largely dictated by relief and altitude and inc. continental and mountain types. Summers are generally warm, with quite considerable rainfall; winters are fine, with clear, cold air. In the Alpine region the danger from avalanches is increased by the warm dry wind called the föhn. Land use: forested 26 per cent, meadows and pastures 41 per cent, agricultural and under permanent cultivation 10 per cent. Protestants are 44 per cent of the pop.; Roman Catholics 47 per cent. Langs. are French, German, Italian and Romansch and the ethnolinguistic groupings are German 63 per cent, French 18 per cent and Italian 9 per cent.

Tourism is an extremely important part of the economy, attracting large numbers of tourists in both summer and winter and contributing 8 per cent of GDP. Among the many world-famous resorts are St Moritz, Davos, Zermatt, Gstaad, Interlaken and Arosa. Agriculture and forestry are important, as is watch-making, the main export industry. Financial services inc. banking and insurance which are internationally renowned. In summer the mountain pastures ('alps') high above the valley farms are used for grazing dairy cattle. Much of the cheese, butter and condensed milk is exported. Chief crops wheat, barley, potatoes. Wine is produced in most cantons. The country, however, is far from self-sufficient in foodstuffs esp. cereals. Principally an industrial country, even though minerals and other raw materials have to be imported; the Swiss have concentrated on the manufacture of goods of high value relative to their bulk. Leading exports machinery, scientific instruments, clocks and watches, chemicals and dyes, textiles, clothing and footwear.

Inhabited in early times by the Helvetii. Conquered by the Romans 58 BC. After the fall of the Roman Empire, it was overrun by the Burgundii and Alemanni in the 5th cent. AD, and in the 6th cent. passed to the Franks. Part of the Holy Roman Empire from 1033. The first movement towards political unity came in 1291, when the three forest cantons (Uri, Schwyz, Unterwalden) formed a defensive league against the Habsburg overlords. After a great victory at Morgarten (1315) they were joined by five others; further defeats of the Austrians followed (1386, 1388). Charles of Burgundy was vanquished in 1477; there were 13 cantons in the league by 1513. Largely through the activities of Calvin in Geneva and Zwingli in Zürich, Switzerland played a great part in the Reformation during the 16th cent. and suffered considerable religious discord. Neutrality was maintained in the Thirty Years War; Swiss independence of the Holy Roman Empire was recognized by the Peace of Westphalia (1648) which ended the war. The French Revolution brought an invasion by French troops (1798); the Swiss Confederation was dissolved and replaced by the French-dominated Helvetic Republic. The Confederation was restored in 1815 with 22 cantons and its present boundaries; the powers guaranteed its perpetual neutrality. Seven Catholic cantons concluded a separate alliance (with *Sonderbund*) and threatened to secede (1845) but were defeated. A new Constitution was adopted in 1848; this was superseded (1874) by the present Constitution which increased the powers of the central government and introduced the principle of the referendum. Swiss neutrality was preserved in both world wars. It was the headquarters of the League of Nations (from 1920) and is the headquarters of several international organizations, esp. at Geneva, e.g. the International Red Cross, the International Labour Organization (1919), the World Health Organization (1946).

Legislative authority is vested in a bicameral Parliament: the *Ständerat* (Council of States) with 46 members (two for each whole canton), and the *Nationalrat* (National Council), with 200 members directly elected for 4 years (in proportion to the pop. of the cantons). It is a confederation of 20 cantons and 6 half-cantons, making 26 in all, with year of establishment: Zurich (1351), Bern (1553), Luzern (1332), Uri (1291), Schwyz (1291), Unterwalden (Obwalden and Nidwalden; 1291), Glarus (1352), Zug (1352), Fribourg (1481), Solothurn (1481), Basel (Basel-Stadt and Basel-Land; 1501), Schaffhausen (1501), Appenzel (Ausser-Rhoden and Inner-Rhoden; 1513), St Gallen (1803), Graubunden (1803), Aargau (1803), Thurgau (1803), Ticino (1803), Vaud (1803), Valais (1815), Neuchâtel (1815), Geneva (1815), Jura (1979).

Sybaris Italy. Ancient Greek city of great wealth in the S on the Gulf of Tarentum (Taranto), founded *c.* 720 BC. Its inhabitants,

the Sybarites, were well known for their luxury and voluptuousness. Destroyed in a war with Crotona 510 BC.

Sydney Australia. Cap. of New South Wales, largest city and chief seaport in Australia, mainly on the S shore of Port Jackson. Pop. (1991) 3,538,749. Developed from an early settlement at Sydney Cove (1788). Its fine silt-free harbour has a depth of 12 m (39 ft) to wharves which extend along inlets of the drowned valley. Serves an extensive hinterland, handling a large volume of exports, esp. wheat and wool from the Murray basin, but also from the E coastlands. Lies on a great coal basin, with deep mines within the city limits. Iron and steel, tinplate and the products of heavy industries are obtainable from Newcastle or Port Kembla, and Sydney is able to provide consumer goods for its own growing pop. and also for its hinterland.

Metalworking, oil-refining, food-processing and brewing. Manufactures machinery, scientific apparatus, clothing, textiles, leather goods, furniture, paper, chemicals and bricks. Australia's chief wool-selling centre. Most of the industrial development is S of the harbour, the N side having remained largely residential; the two areas are connected by the harbour bridge (completed 1932), 1150 m (3772 ft) in total length. There are excellent beaches and resorts close to the city, mainly E, inc. the famous Bondi beach, and it is well provided with open spaces, such as Centennial Park, Moore Park and the botanical gardens. The Opera House, under construction for 14 years, was opened in 1973. Water comes from a complex system of reservoirs, large supplies being dammed back along the Nepean and other rivers. The metropolitan area now extends S to Botany Bay, with its 48 municipalities covering 1774 sq km (685 sq. miles).

Sydney Canada. Seaport and industrial town in Nova Scotia on the NE coast of Cape Breton Island. Pop. (1971) 33,230.

Exports coal. Imports iron ore and limestone from Newfoundland. Coalmining. Manufactures steel, chemicals and bricks.

Founded (1784) by United Empire Loyalists.

Sydney Mines Canada. Town situated NNW of Sydney on E coast of Cape Breton Island, Nova Scotia. Pop. (1988) 8001.

Industries inc. coal reclamation and processing of waste.

Syene ➤ASWAN.

Syktyvkar Russia. Cap. of the Komi Republic on the Vychegda R. 354 km (220 miles) NNE of Kirov. Pop. (1989) 233,000.

Mainly a centre of the timber trade. Sawmilling, boatbuilding and fur-processing. Manufactures wood-pulp and paper.

Sylhet Bangladesh. Chief town of the tea-producing district of Sylhet on the Surma R. 193 km (120 miles) NE of Dacca. Pop. (1991) 100,000. Formerly in Assam; transferred to Pakistan at the partition of India (1947), in Bangladesh from 1971.

Symond's Yat England. Viewpoint on the R. Wye where the river, flowing through a narrow gorge, describes a loop nearly 8 km (5 miles) long around Huntsham Hill, curving back to within 550 m (1804 ft) of its former course. The Yat, or Gate, is 10 km (6 miles) SSW of Ross in Herefordshire.

Syracuse (Italian **Siracusa**) Italy. Cap. of Siracusa province on the SE coast of Sicily. Pop. (1991) 125,444.

Seaport. Exports olive oil and wine. Fisheries, saltworks. Manufactures chemicals and cement.

On the small island of Ortygia, connected by bridge with the mainland, are the cathedral, the ruins of the Temple of Apollo, the fountain of Arethusa and the Maniace castle erected by the Emperor Frederick II. On the mainland are the famous Greek theatre, a Roman amphitheatre, the fortress of Euryalus, built by Dionysius and a cave with remarkable acoustic properties known as 'Dionysius' Ear'. Syracuse was founded on Ortygia by Greek colonists from Corinth in 734 BC. Became an important cultural centre under Hiero I (478–467 BC), with Aeschylus and Pindar at his court. Withstood a siege

from the Athenians (415–413 BC) and attained its greatest power under Dionysius I (406–367 BC). Besieged and taken by the Romans (214–212 BC); Archimedes was killed during the plunder of the city. Now it became a mere provincial city, and lost still more of its former glory when assaulted by the Saracens (AD 878).

Syracuse USA. Industrial town in New York at the S end of L. Onondaga 217 km (135 miles) E of Buffalo. Pop. (1990) 163,860.

Manufactures machinery, metal goods, typewriters and chemicals.

Salt production was the main industry in the early 19th cent. but declined after 1870.

Syr Darya. Ancient Jaxartes. River 2250 km (1400 miles) long in Central Asia, rising as the Naryn R. in Kyrgyzstan S of L. Issyk Kul. Flowing generally W and SW and cutting through wild gorges, it enters and irrigates the fertile Fergana valley in Uzbekistan. It then turns NW across SW Kazakhstan, where the Kyzyl Kum desert extends to its left bank and enters the Aral Sea (NE) by a delta.

Syria. Republic of SW Asia bounded by Turkey in the N, Iraq in the E, Jordan and Israel in the SW, Lebanon and the Mediterranean Sea in the W. Area 185,180 sq km (71,498 sq. miles). Pop. (1995) 14,313,000 (52 per cent urban). Life expectancy, 65 years male, 69 female. Cap. Damascus. Major cities Aleppo, Homs, Latakia and Hama. Currency: Syrian pound = 100 piastres. Essentially an agricultural and pastoral country, though much of its area consists of desert. In the W mountain ranges run more or less parallel to the coast, the highest being the Anti-Lebanon, on the Lebanon border, which rises to 2814 m (9230 ft) in Mt Hermon; in the SW, near the Jordan border, the Jebel ed Druz exceeds 1650 m (5412 ft). The plateau of the Syrian Desert, occupying most of the central area, descends E to the basin of the Euphrates, which flows NW–SE across the E region. Along the coast the climate is Mediterranean, but inland the temperatures become more extreme and the rainfall decreases from 75 cm (30 ins.) or more near the sea to less than 25 cm (10 ins.) annually, in the desert. Land use: forested 4 per cent, steppe and pasture 43 per cent, cultivable 30 per cent. The lang. is Arabic. About 90 per cent of the people are Muslims, mostly of the Sunni sect, with substantial minorities of Alawites and Druses (heretical Muslim sects), the latter dwelling in the Jebel ed Druz. Christians inc. Greek Orthodox and Greek Catholic, the Armenian Orthodox and Armenian Catholic, and the Syrian Orthodox.

Along the coast in the Euphrates valley and around Damascus, in the fertile and well-watered regions, wheat and barley are the principal food crops and vines, olives, tomatoes and apricots are widely cultivated. Cotton has become the leading cash crop, others are wool, cereals and tobacco. There is an increasing number of light engineering plants producing textiles, plastics, cement, vegetable oil, soap, copper and brass objects, and sugar. Oil is being exploited and there are 2 oil refineries, at Homs and Banias.

The region known historically as Syria inc. modern Syria, Lebanon, Israel and Jordan, i.e. all the lands along the Mediterranean coast; it was inhabited from very early times and occupied by many peoples. Here the Phoenicians established their trading posts along the coasts, mainly in present-day Lebanon. Its geographical position and the fertility of its coastlands made it an object of conquest and it was ruled by Assyria, Babylonia, Egypt, Persia, Macedonia and the Seleucidae; Antioch on the Orontes was founded and made cap. by Seleucus Nicator (301 BC) and became an important province of the Roman Empire, passing on the division of the latter to Byzantine rule. In the 7th cent. AD it was conquered by the Arabs (636) and was largely converted to the Muslim religion. Continued to prosper even through the Crusades, but never fully recovered from the fierce Mongol invasions of the 13th cent. It was a province of the Ottoman Empire 1516–1918. After World War I France was given a mandate over Syria and Lebanon (1920), but found it difficult to govern. Following a serious Druse rebellion (1925) the Lebanon was made a separate state (1926); the sanjak of Alexandretta was ceded to Turkey 1939. During World War II British and Free French troops ejected the Vichy French and Syria was proclaimed independent in 1941. The republic took part in the unsuccessful Arab war on Israel in 1948. Joined Egypt in the United Arab Republic in 1958, but the new regime rapidly became unpopular; after an army revolt it withdrew from the UAR in 1961. The President holds executive power and is elected for 5-year terms by universal adult suffrage. He appoints the Vice-Presidents and the Council of Ministers. Legislative authority lies with a 250-member unicameral People's Council elected for 4-year terms.

Syros (Gr. **Síros**) Greece. Island in the Cyclades in the Aegean Sea. Area 85 sq km (33 sq. miles). Pop. 19,000. Chief town and port Syros (Hermoupolis). Mainly mountainous; produces grain, fruits and wine.

Syzran Russia. Town in the Samara region on the right bank of the Volga R. Pop. (1992) 175,000.

Important river port, railway junction and industrial centre. Oil-refining. Manufactures machinery, building materials and clothing.

Founded (1684) as a fortress. Developed in the 19th cent. as a grain market and expanded rapidly with the oil industry in the 1930s.

Szczecin (Ger. **Stettin**) Poland. Cap. of the Szczecin voivodeship on the Oder R. 27 km (17 miles) above the mouth in Stettiner Haff. Pop. (1991) 414,200.

Important Baltic seaport and industrial centre. Exports coal and timber. Ship-building. Manufactures synthetic fibres, paper, fertilizers and cement.

A Wendish settlement as early as the 9th cent. Joined the Hanseatic League 1360. Passed to Prussia (1720), becoming cap. of the province of Pomerania and to Poland (1945). Birthplace of Catherine the Great of Russia (1729–96).

Szechwan ➤SICHUAN.

Szeged Hungary. Town in (but independent of) Csongrád county near the confluence of the Tisza and Maros rivers 160 km (100 miles) SSE of Budapest. Pop. (1991) 176,135.

Commercial and industrial centre in an agricultural region. Flour and paprika milling, brewing, sawmilling. Manufactures textiles, footwear and tobacco products.

Székesfehérvár Hungary. Ancient Alba Regia. Cap. of Fejér county 60 km (37 miles) SW of Budapest. Pop. (1991) 109,106.

Market town. Trade in wine, tobacco. Manufactures footwear and has aluminium works.

Coronation and burial place of Hungarian kings from the 11th to the 16th cent.

Székszard Hungary. Cap. of Tolna county.

Market town situated SSW of Budapest. Pop. (1989) 39,000.

Industries inc. making red wine, distilling alcohol and making bricks.

Szolnok Hungary. Cap. of Szolnok county at the confluence of the Tisza and Zagyva rivers 80 km (50 miles) ESE of Budapest. Pop. (1989) 82,000.

Railway junction. River port. Flour-milling, sawmilling and brickmaking.

Szombathely Hungary. Cap. of Vas county in the W near the Austrian frontier. Pop. (1989) 88,000.

Industrial town in a fertile fruit-growing region. Manufactures textiles, agricultural machinery. Flour-milling, sawmilling.

Built on the site of a Roman settlement.

T

Tabasco Mexico. State in the SE on the Gulf of Campeche, bordered on the SE by Guatemala. Area 25,267 sq km (9756 sq. miles). Pop. (1990) 1,501,744. Cap. Villahermosa. Mainly low-lying and covered by jungle; many swamps, lagoons and watercourses. Climate hot and humid. The forests provide dyewoods and other valuable timber.

Crops inc. rice, sugar-cane and bananas. Livestock-farming and fishing make important contributions to the economy. It has large reserves of oil.

Tabuaeran (Fanning Island) Kiribati. Atoll situated NW of Kiritimani in the Line Islands, Pacific Ocean. Area 34 sq km (13 sq. miles). Pop. (1990) 1309. Its main production is copra.

Table Mountain South Africa. Mountain 1086 m (3563 ft) high in Western Cape Province overlooking Table Bay and Cape Town; the N end of the range which terminates (S) in the Cape of Good Hope. Flat-topped; the summit is often cloud covered, esp. in summer, by a white cloud (called the 'Tablecloth') overhanging the precipitous N face. A cable railway (completed 1929) runs from Cape Town to the summit, where the view S inc. the whole of the Cape Peninsula; from one point the Atlantic Ocean and the Indian Ocean may both be seen.

Tabora Tanzania. Town 720 km (450 miles) WNW of Dar-es-Salaam at a height of 1170 m (3838 ft). Pop. (1985) 134,000. On the railway to Kigoma on L. Tanganyika, with a branch line to Mwanza on L. Victoria.

Agricultural market. Trade in cotton, millet and groundnuts.

Founded in the early 19th cent. and became a centre of the slave trade.

Tabriz Iran. Cap. of E Azerbaijan province

and Iran's fourth largest city 523 km (325 miles) NW of Tehrán at a height of 1300 m (4264 ft) just N of the volcanic Kuh-e-Sahand (3722 m; 12,208 ft). Pop. (1991) 1,088,985.

Important market town in a fertile agricultural region. Manufactures carpets, textiles, leather goods and soap. Trade in dried fruit and almonds.

Has the ruins of the famous 15th-cent. Blue Mosque and an old citadel of massive proportions. An ancient city, Tabriz was several times almost destroyed by earthquakes.

Táchira Venezuela. An inland state bordering on Colombia. Area 11,098 sq km (4285 sq. miles). Pop. (1990) 722,707. Mainly mountainous, traversed by the Sierra Nevada de Mérida; with the Maracaibo lowlands in the NW. It is the principal coffee-growing area of the country. Other crops inc. cereals, sugar, fruit, vegetables and tobacco. Cattle-raising and forestry are also important. There are deposits of gold, coal, petroleum, copper and sulphur. Cap. San Cristóbal.

Tacna Peru. Cap. of the Tacna department at 540 m (1771 ft) in the Andean foothills 48 km (30 miles) N of Arica (Chile), to which it is linked by railway. Pop. (1990) 150,200.

Serves an irrigated area where tobacco, cotton and sugar-cane are cultivated.

Held by Chile 1883–1929.

Tacoma USA. Seaport and industrial town in Washington on Commencement Bay in Puget Sound 40 km (25 miles) S of Seattle. Pop. (1990) 176,664.

Exports timber, grain, flour, phosphates and refined copper. Manufactures chemicals, clothing and food products. Copper-smelting, woodworking, flour-milling and boatbuilding.

Tadoussac Canada. Village in SE Quebec

on the Saguenay R. near the confluence with the St Lawrence R. Reputedly the site of the earliest European settlement in Canada: a house was built here in 1600 by Pierre Chauvin, French explorer and fur trader.

Taegu South Korea. Commercial town in the SE 88 km (55 miles) NNW of Pusan on the railway to Seoul. Pop. (1990) 2,229,040.

In an agricultural region producing grain, tobacco, fruits. It is the centre of the country's textile industry producing silk, cotton, wool and synthetic fabrics.

Taganrog Russia. Seaport in the Rostov region on the Gulf of Taganrog, an arm of the Sea of Azov. Pop. (1992) 293,000.

Exports grain and coal from its 3 harbours. More important now as an industrial centre. Manufactures iron and steel goods, inc. agricultural machinery, hydraulic presses, tools, boilers and aircraft.

Founded as a fortress by Peter the Great 1698. Twice lost to the Turks; finally annexed to Russia 1769. Birthplace of Anton Chekhov, Russian playwright (1860–1904).

Tagus (Portuguese **Tejo**, Sp. **Tajo**) **River** Spain/Portugal. River 909 km (565 miles) long rising in the Montes Universales of E Spain (Teruel), flowing first NW, then generally SW and W across the Meseta and past Toledo. In Estremadura it again passes through a mountainous region and is impeded by rapids, forms the boundary between Spain and Portugal for about 48 km (30 miles) and finally enters an extensive estuary on the N shore of which is Lisbon. Navigable to small vessels only as far upstream as Abrantes (Portugal). The bridge over the estuary, linking Lisbon with Almada, the Setúbal peninsula, and the S, was inaugurated in 1966.

Tahiti (French Polynesia) South Pacific Ocean. Largest and most important island of French Polynesia in the Windward Is. Area 1042 sq km (402 sq. miles). Pop. (1988) 115,800. Cap. Papeete, also cap of French Polynesia. Mountainous, the higher of its

two ancient volcanoes, Mt Orohena, reaching 2238 m (7341 ft).

Exports phosphates, copra and vanilla.

Discovered 1767. After an unsuccessful attempt at colonization by the Spaniards, was a French protectorate (1843–80) and was then ceded to France.

Tahoua Niger. Cap. of department in the SW situated NE of Niamey. Pop. (1988) 49,941.

Centre of agricultural and grazing area.

Taichung Taiwan. Market town 137 km (85 miles) SW of Taipei. Pop. (1992) 774,197.

In an agricultural region producing rice, sugar-cane and jute. Industries inc. sugar-refining, distilling and the manufacture of footwear and watches.

Taif Saudi Arabia. Town in the Hejaz in an oasis at a height of 1590 m (5215 ft) 64 km (40 miles) ESE of Mecca. Pop. (1986) 205,000. Summer resort.

Taimyr. 1. Peninsula on the Arctic coast of Siberia (Russia) between the Kara Sea and the Laptev Sea; the Byrranga Mountains extend across it and Cape Chelyuskin is at its N extremity. The Taimyr R. (530 km; 330 miles) flows NE and N through L. Taimyr to the N coast.

2. National Area in the N Krasnoyarsk Territory, Russia almost co-extensive with the Taimyr peninsula. Area 862,100 sq km (332,857 sq. miles). Pop. (1991) 54,000. Cap. Dudinka. Consists mainly of tundra. The inhabitants are chiefly nomadic Samoyeds.

Main occupations hunting, fishing, reindeer-breeding and mining at Norilsk.

Tainan Taiwan. Market town in the SW 40 km (25 miles) N of Kaohsiung. Pop. (1992) 689,541.

Industries inc. plastics, electrical goods, clothing, footwear, iron-working, rice and sugar milling. A cultural centre.

Formerly cap. of the island, replaced by Taipei.

Tainaron, Cape ➤MATAPAN, CAPE.

Taipa Islands Macao. Two islands situated

SSE of Macao peninsula. Taipa port is situated on the SW coast of the larger island. The main occupation is fishing.

Taipei Taiwan. Cap. of the island in the N on the Tanshi R. 24 km (15 miles) WSW of its port, Keelung. Pop. (1992) 2,717,992.

Commercial centre. Industries inc. engineering, textiles, food-procesing, printing and chemicals. Trade in rice and tea, processed here. Coalmining in the neighbourhood.

Replaced Tainan as cap. 1885. Developed under Japanese rule 1895–1945. Became useless as a seaport owing to silting of the harbour.

Taiwan (Formosa). The 'Republic of China' is situated on the island of Taiwan about 161 km (100 miles) off the coast of SE China, from which it is separated by the Formosa Strait. It also inc. the islands of Quemoy and Matsu close to mainland China. Area 35,975 sq km (13,890 sq. miles). Pop. (1995) 21,268,000, of whom 2 million are mainland Chinese, who came with the Nationalist government (75 per cent urban). Life expectancy, 72 years male, 78 female. Cap. Taipei. Major cities Kaohsiung, Taichung, Tainan and Chilung. Currency: New Taiwan dollar = 100 cents. A mountain range crosses it N–S, the slopes descending steeply to the nearer E coast and more gently to the W, with Yu Shan rising to 3952 m (12,963 ft) and several peaks exceeding 3000 m (9840 ft); the mountains are densely forested. The Tropic of Cancer passes through the island and the climate is tropical, with abundant rainfall received from the SW and NE monsoons with occasional typhoons. Land use: forested 55 per cent, agricultural 25 per cent. About 84 per cent of the pop. is Taiwanese and there are 345,523 aborigines. Religious affiliation: Buddhist 25 per cent, Daoist 16 per cent and Roman Catholics 14 per cent. The official lang. is Mandarin Chinese.

Taiwan is a major trading nation, in spite of its diplomatic isolation, and exports data-processing equipment, clothing, electronic and electrical equipment, plastic articles and sports equipment. Rice, sugar-cane, bananas, citrus fruits and pineapples are grown, but agriculture has declined in recent years. It has reserves of coal, gold, oil, natural gas and marble.

Taiwan was discovered by the Portuguese (1590). Chinese settlement began in the 17th cent. and it was ceded to Japan in 1895. It was returned to China in 1945 and became the last territory of the Chinese Nationalist government when Chiang Kai-shek (Jiang Jie Chi) withdrew there in 1950, the Chinese Communists dominating the mainland. The US broke off diplomatic relations in 1979 when it established diplomatic relations with the People's Republic of China; earlier Taiwan had lost its seat on the UN Security Council. There is a 161-member Legislative Yuan of which 125 members are directly elected.

Taiyuan China. Formerly Yanku. Cap. of Shanxi province on the Fen-he at a height of 790 m (2592 ft) 410 km (255 miles) SW of Beijing. Pop. (1990) 1,533,884.

Industrial centre in a coalmining district. Manufactures iron and steel, agricultural and textile machinery, textiles, cement and paper.

An ancient city, walled in the 14th cent. to protect it against Mongol attacks; many historical relics in the Shanxi provincial museum. Occupied by the Japanese 1937–45.

Taiz Yemen. Town situated NW of Aden. Pop. (1986) 178,043.

Centre of a coffee-growing area. Industries inc. cotton-weaving, tanning and the manufacture of jewellery.

Tajikistan. Republic in Central Asia bounded on the E by Xinjiang Uygur Autonomous Region of China and on the S by Afghanistan. Area 143,100 sq km (55,240 sq. miles). Pop. (1995) 5,832,000 (30 per cent urban). Life expectancy, 66 years male, 72 female. Cap. Dushanbe. Chief cities Khudzhand, Kulyab. Currency: Russian ruble = 100 kopecks. The Republic is in a lofty mountain and plateau region of the Pamir and Alai systems, with the country's highest peak Mount Garmo, formerly Peak Kommunizma (7495 m; 24,590 ft), the lowest valleys of the Pamirs being over 3300 m

(10,824 ft). The only true lowlands are its section of the Fergana Valley (N) and the valley of the Amu Darya (SW), which forms the S boundary with Afghanistan, inc. the Gorno-Badakhshan. About 62 per cent of the people are Tadzhiks, who are Sunni Muslims speaking a lang. similar to Persian; about 24 per cent are Uzbeks and most of the remainder are Russians, Tatars and Ukrainians.

The main occupations are agriculture and stock-rearing. Cotton is the most important crop; wheat, maize, fruits (inc. grapes) and vegetables are also grown. Large numbers of sheep and cattle are raised, the Gissar sheep in the S being noted for its meat and fat; karakul sheep are bred for their skins. Agricultural methods have been improved with the extension of irrigation and electric power. Mineral resources, particularly antimony, mercury and molybdenum, have been tapped and other industries inc. textiles and carpet-making.

The area was annexed by Russia between 1860 and 1868 and it became a constituent republic of the USSR in 1929. It declared its independence in 1991 which was recognized by the international community later that year. Civil war between former Communists and Muslim fundamentalists caused a state of emergency to be declared in 1993. There is a 230-member Supreme Soviet.

Tajo River ➤TAGUS RIVER.

Takamatsu Japan. Cap. of Kagawa prefecture on the N coast of Shikoku 137 km (85 miles) WSW of Osaka. Pop. (1992) 330,568.

Seaport and industrial centre. Exports tobacco and rice. Manufactures wood-pulp and paper, cotton goods, fans and parasols, lacquer ware. Famous for the landscape gardens in Ritsuri Park, a tourist attraction.

Takaoka Japan. Industrial town in Toyama prefecture W Honshu 40 km (25 miles) ENE of Kanazawa. Pop. (1992) 175,413.

Manufactures cotton goods and lacquer ware.

Takasaki Japan. Town in Gumma prefec-

ture, central Honshu 96 km (60 miles) NW of Tokyo. Pop. (1992) 238,043.

Manufactures textiles and machinery. Flour-milling.

Takatsuki Japan. Town in Osaka prefecture 21 km (13 miles) NNE of Osaka on the route to Kyoto. Pop. (1992) 360,748.

Manufactures textiles and pharmaceutical products.

Taklamakan China. Extensive sandy desert in the Xinjiang-Uygur Autonomous Region lying S of the Tien Shan and occupying the major part of the Tarim Basin, with the Tarim R. flowing along its N edge. Area 327,000 sq km (126,000 sq. miles). Uninhabited because of its shifting sand dunes. Principal oases around its margins are Yarkand (W) and Khotan (SW).

Takoradi Ghana. Chief seaport (a single municipality with Sekondi) on the Gulf of Guinea 185 km (115 miles) WSW of Accra. Pop. (with Sekondi) (1988) 103,653. Linked with the interior by the important railway to Kumasi.

The modern harbour (opened 1928) is protected by two breakwaters; has ample storage facilities for oil, timber and cacao. Exports cacao, diamonds, gold, manganese and timber. Handles most of the overseas trade. Cocoa-processing, sawmilling. Manufactures cigarettes.

Talara Peru. Seaport in the Piura department 88 km (55 miles) NW of Piura in the NW desert region. Pop. (1989) 44,500.

Centre of the Peruvian petroleum industry, linked by pipelines with the oilfields. Peru's second port by virtue of the oil exports. Oil-refining. Water is piped 40 km (25 miles) from the Chira R.

Talca Chile. Cap. of Talca province 249 km (155 miles) SSW of Santiago in the central valley. Pop. (1992) 171,467.

Important industrial centre in a wine-producing area. Manufactures matches, leather, footwear, paper and tobacco products. Flour-milling, distilling and tanning.

Founded 1692. Destroyed by earthquake

(1928) and since rebuilt. Chile's independence was proclaimed here (1818).

Talcahuano Chile. Seaport and naval station in Concepción province on Concepción Bay 13 km (8 miles) NNW of Concepción. Pop. (1992) 246,566.

Excellent harbour and dry docks. Exports timber, wool and hides. Imports iron ore for a modern steel plant. Fishing and fish-canning, flour-milling and oil-refining.

Tallahassee USA. State cap. of Florida in the NW 257 km (160 miles) W of Jacksonville. Pop. (1990) 124,773.

Commercial centre. Industries inc. tourism, high technology, woodworking and food products.

Settled by Spaniards in the 16th–17th cent.

Tallinn (Tallin) Estonia. Formerly Revel. Cap. and chief seaport on the S coast of the Gulf of Finland opposite Helsinki. Pop. (1992) 471,608.

Exports timber, paper and textiles. Industries inc. shipbuilding and heavy engineering. Manufactures cotton goods, paper and cement. The port is kept open for most of the winter by icebreakers.

Modern Tallinn surrounds the Lower Town, which is walled and largely medieval, and Toompea Hill which was fortified by the Danes. Old buildings have been restored and traditional events like the Song Festival preserved. The pop. however, has been much altered by Russian immigration and earlier German influences. An ancient fort, Tallinn became a trading town in the Middle Ages and a Hansa League trading port in 1285; it belonged to the Teutonic Knights from 1346, to Sweden from 1561 and to Russia from 1710 to 1918, when it became the cap. of an independent state. It was a Soviet Union Republic cap. 1940–91.

Tamale Ghana. Cap. of the Northern Region and the largest town on the Volta river basin 434 km (270 miles) NNW of Accra. Pop. (1988) 151,069.

Market town. Trade in groundnuts, rice and cotton. Cotton-milling, shea-nut processing.

Tamar River Australia. River in N Tasmania formed by the union of the N Esk and the S Esk rivers at Launceston, flowing generally NNW to Bass Strait and forming a navigable 64-km (40-mile) waterway; has a winding course, tidal throughout.

Tamar River England. River 96 km (60 miles) long flowing generally SSE and forming part of the boundary between Cornwall and Devon, entering Plymouth Sound by its estuary, the Hamoaze. A road suspension bridge across the river between Devonport (Devon) and Saltash (Cornwall), replacing the ferry, was opened in 1961.

Tamatave ➤TOAMASINA.

Tamaulipas Mexico. State in the NE, bordering N on the USA (across the Rio Grande) and E on the Gulf of Mexico. Area 79,384 sq km (30,650 sq. miles). Pop. (1990) 2,249,581. Cap. Ciudad Victoria. On the coast, where there are many lagoons, the climate is hot and humid; the W, in the Sierra Madre Oriental, is more temperate. Petroleum from the Tampico region is the main source of revenue. Crops inc. cotton, sugar-cane, sorghum and tobacco. Main industries are located in Tampico, Nuevo Laredo (in the NW 'panhandle'), Ciudad Victoria, Matamoros.

Tambov Russia. Cap. of the Tambov Region on the Tsna R. 257 km (160 miles) WSW of Penza. Pop. (1992) 311,000.

Railway junction. Industrial centre in a fertile black-earth agricultural region. Flour-milling, sugar-refining, distilling. Manufactures machinery, chemicals, synthetic rubber and textiles.

Founded (1636) as a fortified Muscovite outpost.

Tamil Nadu India. Formerly Madras. Constituent state of the Indian Union in the SE less than half its former area owing to the formation of Andhra Pradesh (1953) and various boundary adjustments. Area 130,058 sq km (50,804 sq. miles). Pop. (1991) 55,638,318 (mainly Tamil-speaking). With a coastal plain 80–240 km (50–150 miles) wide along the Coromandel Coast, facing the Bay of Bengal, it is mountainous in the W, rising to more than 2400 m (7872 ft) in the Nilgiri Hills and the Palni Hills. Nearly two-thirds of the people are engaged in agriculture.

Leading crops rice, millets, groundnuts, sugar-cane, pulses, oilseeds, chillies, tea, rubber, coffee and cotton. Industries inc. railway coach factory, textiles, oil refinery, petrochemicals, leather, sugar, fertilizers, heavy vehicles, paper and photographic films. Important minerals are limestone, lignite, bauxite, gypsum, quartz and felspar.

Chief towns Madras (cap.), Madurai, Combatore, Tiruchirapalli and Salem. The first trading post was established by the British in 1611; by 1801 they were in control of practically the whole area. In 1937 Madras was made an autonomous province and in 1950 a constituent state of the republic of India.

Tammerfors ➤TAMPERE.

Tampa USA. Seaport and city in Florida on an inlet in Tampa Bay on the W coast. Pop. (1990) 280,015.

Exports chiefly phosphates and canned grapefruit. Principal cigar-making centre in the USA. Also fruit-canning, shipbuilding, and meat-packing. A tourist resort.

Tampere (Tammerfors) Finland. Third largest city situated in the Häme province 160 km (100 miles) NNW of Helsinki. Pop. (1990) 172,580.

Principal industrial area of the country, deriving hydroelectric power from the Tammerkoski rapids, between Lakes Näsi and Phyä. Also a railway junction. Manufactures textiles, railway rolling-stock, wood-pulp and paper, footwear and plastics.

Tampico Mexico. Important seaport and oil-refining city in Tamaulipas state in the NE on the Pánuco R. Pop. (1990) 272,690.

Exports petroleum and petroleum products. Industries inc. oil-refining, boatbuilding, sawmilling, and it manufactures chemicals. Popular winter resort; famous for tarpon fishing.

Tamworth Australia. Market town and railway junction in New South Wales on the Peel R. 306 km (190 miles) N of Sydney. Pop. (1984) 34,000.

Flour-milling, sawmilling. Manufactures furniture.

Tamworth England. Market town in Staffordshire on the R. Tame 21 km (13 miles) NE of Birmingham. Pop. (1991) 68,440.

Manufactures cars, clothing, bricks and tiles.

Has a castle overlooking the confluence of the Tame and the Anker, a 14th-cent. church and 17th-cent. almshouses built by Thomas Guy, founder of Guy's Hospital, London.

Tana (Tsana), Lake Ethiopia. Ethiopia's largest lake 80 km (50 miles) long and up to 64 km (40 miles) wide S of Gondar at a height of 1830 m (6002 ft). Fed mainly by the Little Abbai R. (SW). Drained by the Blue Nile (SE). Site of a projected dam to control irrigation in Egypt and the Sudan.

Tananarive ➤ANTANANARIVO.

Tana River Kenya. River 708 km (440 miles) long rising in the Aberdare Mountains, flowing generally E and S and entering the Indian Ocean at Kipini. Navigable for small vessels in the lower course.

Tandil Argentina. Resort and market town in Buenos Aires province just N of the Sierra del Tandil 306 km (190 miles) SSW of Buenos Aires. Pop. (1985) 70,000.

In a dairy-farming region. Granite quarries in the neighbourhood.

Tanga Tanzania. Second seaport on the Indian Ocean 193 km (120 miles) N of Dar-es-Salaam. Pop. (1988) 187,634.

Exports sisal, copra and coffee. There are fertilizer plants. Terminus of the railway to Moshi (Kilimanjaro), Arusha.

Tanganyika ➤TANZANIA.

Tanganyika, Lake. Second largest lake in Africa and second deepest (1435 m; 4708 ft) in the world (after L. Baikal) 676 km (420 miles) long and 45–75 km (30–45 miles) wide in the Great Rift Valley at a height of 770 m (2565 ft). In all 32,900 sq km (13,860 sq. miles). Borders on Burundi (NE), Tanzania (E), Zambia (S) and Democratic Republic of the Congo (W). Around the lake the land rises abruptly in places to over 2400 m (7872 ft). The Ruzizi R. (N, outlet of L. Kivu) is the main feeder. The Lukuga R. (W, flowing to the Congo R. basin), the only outlet, often silts up and raises the surface level. Principal lake ports Kalemie (Democratic Republic of the Congo), Bujumbura (Burundi) and Kigoma (Tanzania). Discovered by Burton and Speke 1858. Later explored by Livingstone and Stanley, whose famous meeting (1871) took place at Ujiji, on the E shore.

Tangier (Tanger) Morocco. Seaport on the N coast at the W entrance to the Strait of Gibraltar. Pop. (1982) 266,346.

Commercial centre with minor industries, e.g. soap manufacture. Important tourist trade. Significance as a seaport has declined. Linked by rail with the main Casablanca–Tunis line through Morocco.

Held in turn by Romans, Vandals, Byzantines and Arabs. Taken by the Portuguese 1471. Then successively in Spanish, Portuguese and English hands; abandoned by the English in 1684. The International Zone of Tangier, providing for its neutrality and its government by an international commission, was established 1923. Occupied by Spain during World War II 1940–5. The international status was restored in 1945, but abolished when Morocco became independent (1956). It became the summer cap. 1961 and declared a free port in 1962.

Tangshan China. Industrial city in Hobei province 153 km (95 miles) ESE of Beijing. Pop. (1990) 1,044,194.

Coalmining centre; manufactures iron and steel, cement.

Devastated by earthquake 1976: more than 600,000 people were estimated to have been killed.

Tanintharyi ➤TENASSERIM.

Tanis Egypt. Ancient Egyptian city in the Nile delta (where the modern village of San el Hagar stands). Flourished in the 21st Dynasty. Abandoned when threatened with flooding from L. Manzala. Excavations by Flinders Petrie (and later P. Montel) have revealed tombs, statues and inscriptions.

Tannenberg (modern **Stebark**) Poland. Village in the Olsztyn voivodeship 40 km (25 miles) SW of Olsztyn (Allenstein). Scene of two famous battles: the Teutonic Knights were routed by the combined forces of Poland and Lithuania under King Jagiello (1410); the Russians were defeated by the Germans in World War I (1914) and 92,000 prisoners taken.

Tantâ Egypt. Cap. of the Gharbiya governorate 80 km (50 miles) NNW of Cairo in the Nile delta. Pop. (1991) 372,000.

Important railway junction and commercial centre. Cotton-ginning, cotton-seed oil extraction. Manufactures soap. Noted for its fairs and Muslim festivals.

Tanzania. Republic in East Africa bounded NE by Kenya, N by L. Victoria and Uganda, NW by Rwanda and Burundi, W by L. Tanganyika, SW by Zambia and Malawi and S by Mozambique. It also inc. the offshore islands of Zanzibar and Pemba. Area 942,799 sq km (364,017 sq. miles). Pop. (1995) 28,072,000 (24 per cent urban). Life expectancy, 41 years male, 45 female. Seat of government Dar es Salaam; future cap. seat of legislature, Dodoma. Other cities, Mwanza, Tanga and Zanzibar. Currency: Tanzanian shilling = 100 cents. From the narrow coastal plain the land rises gradually to a savannah plateau of an average height of 1050 m (3444 ft), dominated by the volcanic peaks of Kilimanjaro (5895 m; 19,340 ft), the highest peak in Africa and Meru (4565 m; 14,979 ft) in the NE and rising to 2961 m (9712 ft) in the Kipingere Mountains, N of L. Malawi. Climate tropical, with distinct rainy and dry seasons. Annual rainfall exceeds 150 cm (60 ins.) in the highlands, and is 75–100 cm (30–40 ins.) on much of the plateau. Land use: forested 46 per cent, meadows and pastures

39 per cent, agricultural and under permanent cultvation 4 per cent. Some 40 per cent are Christian, 33 per cent Sunni Muslim, but reaching 66 per cent in the coastal towns. Zanzibar is 96 per cent Muslim and 4 per cent Hindu. The official langs. are Swahili and English.

Subsistence crops grown by 80 per cent of the labour force inc. maize, millet and groundnuts, with rice along the coast. Large numbers of cattle, sheep and goats reared. Leading export crops are cotton, coffee and sisal. Chief minerals are diamonds and gold. Other industries inc. food-processing, textiles, oil-refining and cement.

In the 16th and 17th cent. the Portuguese exercised influence over the coastal towns, which later became the centres of Arab trade in ivory and slaves. In the 19th cent. Germany took an increasing interest in the territory; in 1885 it was declared a protectorate as German East Africa and the coastal strip was acquired from the Sultan of Zanzibar in 1890. After World War I (as Tanganyika Territory) it became a mandated territory administered by Britain, except for the NW region, which was made the Belgian mandated territory of Ruanda–Urundi. After World War II it became a UN Trust Territory, as Tanganyika, administered by Britain (1946) and achieved independence in 1961. In 1964 Zanzibar united with it and the new state was named Tanzania. Until 1992 Tanzania was a one-party state but multi-party democracy has been introduced, to be completed by 1995. There is a 255-member National Assembly of which 180 members are directly elected. Zanzibar has its own legislature.

Taormina Italy. Resort in Messina province on the E coast of Sicily 43 km (27 miles) SSW of Messina. Pop. (1990) 10,905. Famous for the large Greek theatre, rebuilt by the Romans; also has the Church of S Pancrazio, built into a temple of the 3rd cent. BC, and the 14th-cent. Palazzo Corvaia. Founded early in the 4th cent. BC.

Tapajós (Tapajóz) River Brazil. Tributary of the Amazon R. 1440 km (900 miles) long, formed by the union of the São Manuel and

Juruena rivers, flowing generally NNE past the Forlandia and the Belterra rubber plantations to join the Amazon at Santarém.

Tapti River India. River 697 km (436 miles) long rising in the Satpura Range in S Madhya Pradesh and flowing generally W past Burhanpur and Surat to the Gulf of Cambay. Lower course navigable only to small vessels.

Tara Ireland. Village in Co. Meath 10 km (6 miles) SSE of Navan (An Uaimh). The Hill of Tara (155 m; 508 ft) was the residence of the Irish High kings until c. 560. On the hill are 6 raths or earthworks, within the largest of which, the King's Rath, stands a pillar-stone, called the Lia Fáil (Stone of Destiny), on which the monarchs were crowned. According to another story the true Stone of Destiny was taken to Scone, Scotland and later to Westminster Abbey.

Taranaki New Zealand. Former provincial district in the W of North Island. Area (statistical area) 9713 sq km (3750 sq. miles). Pop. (1991) 107,222. Cap. and chief port New Plymouth. The pastoral region encircling Mt Egmont (Taranaki) has many dairy factories producing butter and cheese. Inland as far as the upper Wanganui R. is hill country where sheep are reared. There are petrochemical plants at Montunui where there are on- and off-shore oil and gas fields.

Taranaki, Mount ➤MOUNT EGMONT.

Taranto Italy. Ancient Tarentum. Cap. of Ionio province, Apulia 77 km (48 miles) SSE of Bari on the Gulf of Taranto. Pop. (1991) 244,033.

Important naval base with shipyards and arsenal; also a seaport. Exports wine, olive oil. Oysters and mussels cultivated. Manufactures furniture, glass and footwear. Excellent museum of antiquities.

Was a powerful city in Magna Graecia but declined in Roman times. Destroyed by the Saracens and rebuilt in the 10th cent. Gave its name to the dance, the tarantella. The largest integrated steelworks in Italy was inaugurated here in 1965.

Tarascon France. Town in the Bouches-du-Rhône department on the left bank of the Rhône R. opposite Beaucaire and 21 km (13 miles) SW of Avignon. Pop. (1982) 11,024.

Manufactures textiles, furniture. Trade in fruit and vegetables.

Has a 14th/15th-cent. castle and the Church of St Martha. Immortalized in Alphonse Daudet's satirical *Tartarin de Tarascon*.

Tarawa Kiribati. Atoll in the N Gilberts group consisting of a group of islets surrounding a lagoon in the W Central Pacific; Bairiki on Tarawa cap. of the republic. Pop. (1990) 28,802.

Exports copra, mother-of-pearl.

Occupied by the Japanese 1941; captured by US marines 1943.

Tarbes France. Prefecture of the Hautes-Pyrénées department on the Adour R. 120 km (75 miles) WSW of Toulouse. Pop. (1990) 55,000.

Tourist centre. Trade in horses, farm produce. Industries inc. tanning and sawmilling, and the manufacture of footwear, furniture and machinery.

Seat of a bishopric dating from the 5th cent.; has a partly 13th-cent. cathedral. Was cap. of the old countship of Bigorre.

Taree Australia. Town in E New South Wales on the Manning R. 137 km (85 miles) NE of Newcastle. Pop. (1989) 17,000. Dairy factories.

Târgu-Mureş ➤TÎRGU MUREŞ.

Tarifa Spain. Minor seaport in Cádiz province on the Strait of Gibraltar. Pop. (1991) 14,187. The most southerly town in Spain.

Fishing centre. Trade in oranges and cereals. Industries inc. tanning and fish-canning.

Moorish in appearance, with white houses and narrow, winding streets. Taken by the Moors 711. Recaptured by Sancho IV of Castile 1292.

Tarija Bolivia. Cap. of the Tarija department in the basin of the Guadalquivir R. 290 km (180 miles) SSE of Sucre at a height of 1900 m (6232 ft). Pop. (1992) 90,000.

Market town. Trade in local agricultural produce (cereals and potatoes).

Noteworthy cathedral. Founded by the Spanish 1574; one of the oldest settlements in Bolivia.

Tarim Basin China. Vast depression in the Xinjiang-Uygur Autonomous Region extending about 1450 km (900 miles) E–W and up to 480 km (300 miles) N–S, enclosed by the Tien Shan (N), the Altyn Tagh and Kunlun Shan (S) and the Pamirs (W), and largely occupied by the Takla Makan desert. The Tarim R. flows generally E about 1600 km (1000 miles) along the N margin of the desert and finally disappears in the Lop Nor basin. Khotan, Yarkand, Kashi and Aksu are important oases along the edge of the Tarim Basin.

Tarn France. Department in Languedoc on the edge of the Massif Central (E) and the basin of Aquitaine (W), reaching a height of 1261 m (4136 ft) in the Monts de Lacaune in the extreme SE. Area 5758 sq km (2232 sq. miles). Pop. (1992) 341,800. Prefecture Albi. Drained by the Tarn R. and its tributary the Agout. Cereals and vegetables cultivated. Cattle and sheep raised. Coal, zinc and iron are mined and there are varied industries. Chief towns Albi and Castres.

Tarn-et-Garonne France. Department in the SW, formed from parts of Guienne, Gascony and Languedoc. Area 3718 sq km (1435 sq. miles). Pop. (1992) 204,000. Prefecture Montauban. Drained by the Garonne, Tarn and Aveyron rivers. Generally fertile; produces cereals, vines and plums. Chief towns Montauban and Moissac.

Tarnów Poland. Cap. of the Tarnów voivodeship on the Biala R. 77 km (48 miles) E of Cracow. Pop. (1991) 121,900.

Industrial town and railway junction. Manufactures agricultural machinery and glass.

Gothic cathedral (15th-cent.); 14th-cent. town hall.

Tarn River France. River 377 km (234 miles) long, rising on Mont Lozère in the

Cévennes and flowing generally W through the limestone Causses, forming the picturesque Tarn gorge, past Millau, Albi and Montauban to join the Garonne R. below Moissac.

Tarquinia Italy. Formerly Corneto. Town in Viterbo province, Latium 72 km (45 miles) NW of Rome. Pop. (1971) 12,183. Impressively situated on a rocky height overlooking the Tyrrhenian Sea.

Manufactures cement and paper.

Has 12th/13th-cent. Romanesque-Gothic churches and the 15th-cent. Vitelleschi palace containing a museum with Etruscan antiquities. To the SE is the necropolis from the ancient Etruscan city of Tarquinii, which flourished in the 8th-6th cent. BC and was the leading city of Etruria.

Tarragona Spain. 1. Province in the NE, in Catalonia, bordering on the Mediterranean Sea. Area 6283 sq km (2426 sq. miles). Pop. (1991) 537,951. Mountainous inland. Coastal plain containing the delta of the Ebro R. Produces wine, olive oil, almonds and fruit. Chief towns Tarragona and Reus.

2. Ancient Tarraco. Cap. of Tarragona province, a Mediterranean seaport 80 km (50 miles) WSW of Barcelona. Pop. (1991) 110,003.

Exports large quantities of wine. Manufactures pharmaceutical products, electrical equipment, liqueurs and wines.

The old town stands on a steep hill overlooking the sea and is enclosed by ruined walls with a cyclopean lowest course of massive unhewn blocks surmounted by Roman masonry. Also has a Roman aqueduct and a 12th/13th-cent. cathedral. Taken by the Romans in the 3rd cent. BC; made cap. of the province of Hispania Tarraconensis by Augustus (26 BC).

Tarrasa Spain. Industrial town in Barcelona province, Catalonia 21 km (13 miles) NNW of Barcelona. Pop. (1991) 154,300.

Manufactures textiles, textile machinery, dyes and fertilizers, and trades in agricultural products, oil and wine.

Tarsus Turkey. Market town in Içel province (S) 35 km (22 miles) W of Adana. Pop. (1990) 187,508.

Trade in wheat, barley and fruits.

There are ruins of the ancient city, which flourished in Roman times and was famous as the birthplace of St Paul – who described himself as a 'citizen of no mean city'.

Tartu (Ger. **Dorpat**) Estonia. Formerly Yuryev. Industrial city, the second largest in Estonia on the Ema R. 160 km (100 miles) SE of Tallinn. Pop. (1992) 113,410.

Manufactures agricultural machinery, footwear, food products, textiles, cigars and cigarettes.

Cathedral (13th-cent., restored) on one of the city's two hills; Estonian National Museum. Founded in the 11th cent. as Yuryev. Held by Russians, Poles and Swedes. Took its present name on passing to Estonia (1918).

Tashkent (Toshkent) Uzbekistan. Cap. in an oasis irrigated by the Chirchik R., a tributary of the Syr Darya. Pop. (1991) 2,113,000.

Important route and industrial centre. Manufactures textiles (cotton), textile and agricultural machinery, leather goods and paper.

Also a leading educational centre, with a university (1920) and the Uzbek Academy of Sciences (1943) in the new Russian town; the old Oriental town to the SW has the ruins of ancient *madrassas* (Muslim seminaries). Coal is produced (Angren); hydroelectric plants in the district. Probably founded in the 7th cent. Taken by the Russians 1865. Expanded rapidly after being reached by the Trans-Caspian Railway (1898). Cap. of the former Turkestan Soviet Socialist Republic 1918–24 and of the Uzbek Soviet Socialist Republic from 1930 to 1991.

Tasman Glacier ➤SOUTHERN ALPS.

Tasmania Australia. Island and state of the Commonwealth, separated from the mainland by Bass Strait, 240 km (150 miles) wide. Area (inc. adjacent islands) 68,331 sq km (26,383 sq. miles). Pop. (1993) 471,500. Cap. Hobart. A compact island with a central plateau of hard old rocks, an extension of the E highlands of the mainland. The plateau (about 900 m; 2952 ft) with peaks rising above 1500 m (4920 ft) has shallow lakes. Rivers descend steeply from the plateau, the chief being the Derwent, flowing to a broad estuary in the SE, and the Tamar in the N; the coastal plains are narrow. Lying in a zone of prevailing westerlies and depressions, the W has a high rainfall, mostly over 200 cm (80 ins.) a year; the sheltered E is drier, averaging below 75 cm (30 ins.) except for the NE highlands. Mean monthly temperatures are about 7°–15°C (44°–59°F). Eucalypts cover much of the island, furnishing timber, wood-pulp and paper. The wetter, cooler parts have beech, pine and yew, and the SW supports a tangle of 'horizontal scrub' where the rare Tasmanian wolf still lives.

The chief agricultural regions are: the N coastal area, with mixed farming, dairying and cultivation of potatoes and vegetables; the central lowlands, with sheep-rearing; the SE, with sheep and cattle rearing; the Derwent and Huon valleys, with cultivation of apples, pears, berry fruits and hops. Large mineral deposits in the NE and NW, where coal occurs, enable Tasmania to produce more tin than any other state and also export zinc, copper, lead and silver. Large quantities of ores and concentrates are received for electrolytic refining, esp. zinc near Hobart and aluminium at Bell Bay. Many hydroelectric stations on and around the central plateau providing over 85 per cent of the state's electricity. Chief exports metals, wool, temperate fruits and vegetables, timber.

Discovered by Tasman 1642; named Van Diemen's Land. Visited by Capt. Cook 1777. Used as a penal colony 1803–53, and was then renamed Tasmania. Became a state of the Commonwealth 1901. The last of the Tasmanian aborigines died in 1876.

Tasman Sea Australia. Part of the Pacific Ocean between SE Australia and Tasmania (W) and New Zealand (E), lying in the Roaring Forties; to the N is the Coral Sea and to the SW the Indian Ocean.

Tatabánya Hungary. Cap. of Komárom county 48 km (30 miles) W of Budapest. Pop. (1993) 74,000.

Lignite-mining centre and manufactures bricks.

Tatarstan Republic Russia. Autonomous Republic occupying a region round the middle Volga and lower Kama rivers. Area 68,000 sq km (26,250 sq. miles). Pop. (1991) 3,679,000 (48 per cent Tatar, 42 per cent Russian). Cap. Kazan. Wheat, rye and oats cultivated. Petroleum and other minerals produced and other industries such as timber, textiles, food products and chemicals are expanding. Industry is concentrated in Kazan. The Tatars, Muslim by religion, are mainly descendants of Mongols and Bulgars.

Tatra Mountains Slovakia/Poland. The highest mountain group in the Carpathians, known as the High Tatra (Vysoké Tatry), on the border of Slovakia and Poland, rising to 2655 m (8708 ft) in Gerlachovka. Scenically beautiful, with many summer resorts and winter-sports centres. To the S is the Low Tatra (Nízké Tatry), a parallel range reaching 2043 m (6701 ft).

Tatung ➤ DATONG.

Ta'u Island American Samoa. Situated E of Tutuila. Area 44 sq km (17 sq. miles). Cone-shaped with steep forested slopes rising to 931 m (3056 ft) above sea level.

Taunton England. Market town in the picturesque vale of Taunton Dean in Somerset on the R. Tone 61 km (38 miles) SW of Bristol. Pop. (1991) 55,856.

Manufactures bedding, computer software, precast concrete, instruments, hydrographic charts, cider and engineering products.

Remains of the 12th-cent. castle; the Great Hall where Judge Jeffreys held his 'Bloody Assize' after the defeat of Monmouth's rebellion at Sedgemoor (1685).

Taunton USA. Industrial town in Massachusetts on the Taunton R. 50 km (31 miles) S of Boston. Pop. (1985) 45,000.

Manufactures textile machinery, plastics, jewellery and silverware.

Taunus Germany. Range of hills in Hessen extending 72 km (45 miles) ENE from the Rhine R., rising to 881 m (2890 ft) in the Grosser Feldberg. Wine produced on the S slopes (Rheingau). Mineral springs. Tourist area with well-known spas of Wiesbaden, Bad Homburg, Bad Nauheim.

Taupo, Lake New Zealand. Largest lake in the country 40 km (25 miles) long and up to 29 km (18 miles) wide in the centre of North Island. In a volcanic area with hot springs. Source of the Waikato R. On the NE shore is the small town of Taupo.

Tauranga New Zealand. Port in Tauranga Harbour, Bay of Plenty, North Island 160 km (100 miles) SE of Auckland. Pop. (1989) 62,000. The harbour lies behind the bar of Matakana Island and is approached through a tidal channel. Centre of a region noted for citrus fruits, esp. lemons, and kiwi fruit. Exports dairy produce, meat and timber.

Taurus Mountains Turkey. Mountain system in the S extending SE from L. Eğridir, then curving E and NE parallel to the Mediterranean coast, forming the S rim of the Anatolian plateau. Many peaks exceed 3000 m (9840 ft); Ala Dağ rises to 3734 m (12,248 ft) and the detached Erciyas Daği to 3770 m (12,366 ft). To the NE it is continued as the so-called Anti-Taurus.

Tavistock England. Market town in Devon on the R. Tavy 19 km (12 miles) N of Plymouth. Pop. (1991) 10,222.
Manufactures agricultural implements and chemicals.
Built round a 10th-cent. abbey. Formerly a tin-mining centre; one of the four stannary towns of Devon. Sir Francis Drake, English merchant and pirate (1542–96) was born nearby.

Tavoy (Dawei) Myanmar (Burma). 1. Port in Tenasserim at the head of the Tavoy R. estuary 282 km (175 miles) S of Moulmein. Pop. 40,000. Coastal trade. Rice-milling and sawmilling.
2. Island in the N Mergui Archipelago

105 km (65 miles) S of the town of Tavoy in the Andaman Sea.

Taw River England. River in Devon 80 km (50 miles) long, rising on Dartmoor and flowing generally N past Barnstaple to the estuary in Bideford Bay, Bristol Channel.

Tayport Scotland. Small seaside resort in Fife on the Firth of Tay 5 km (3 miles) ESE of Dundee. Pop. (1991) 3346.

Tay River Scotland. River in Perth and Kinross, the longest in Scotland (190 km; 118 miles) rising on Ben Lui on the Argyll and Bute border. Known as the Fillan from its source to Loch Dochart, and from here to Loch Tay (23 km; 14½ miles long) as the Dochart. Below Loch Tay it flows generally E and SE past Aberfeldy, Dunkeld and Perth, to enter its tidal estuary, the Firth of Tay (40 km, 25 miles long). At Dundee it is crossed by the Tay Bridge (railway), which replaces the one blown down with a train in 1879, and a new road bridge opened in 1966. Chief tributaries the Tummel and the Earn. Famous for its salmon.

Tayside Region Scotland. Former region of E Scotland, from 1975 to 1996.

Taza Morocco. Town ENE of Fès situated on a pass between the Rif Mountains in the N and the Middle Atlas S 549 m (1800 ft) above sea level. Pop. (1982) 77,216.
Manufactures inc. carpets, footwear and building materials.

Tbilisi (Russian **Tiflis**) Georgia. Cap. on the Kura R. Pop. (1991) 1,279,000.
Commercial, cultural and route centre on the Baku–Batumi trunk railway and at the S end of the famous Georgian Military Highway. Engineering, woodworking. Manufactures textiles, textile machinery, electrical equipment. Derives power from the great Zemo-Avchala hydroelectric station. Trade in carpets, textiles and dried fruits.
Sheltered by the Caucasus foothills and rising in terraces above the river valley; has an old Oriental section with narrow streets and a bazaar and a new Russian area of wide

roads and modern buildings. University (1918). The Sion cathedral dates from the 5th cent. and the Armenian cathedral of Van from the 15th cent. Founded in the 4th cent. Cap. of Georgia in the 5th cent. Destroyed and rebuilt several times before passing to Russia (1800). Became cap. of the Georgian Soviet Socialist Republic in 1936, when the name was officially changed from Tiflis to the Georgian Tbilisi.

Tczew Poland. Industrial town and railway junction in the Gdańsk voivodeship on the Vistula R. 32 km (20 miles) SSE of Gdańsk. Pop. (1991) 59,900.

Manufactures building materials, agricultural machinery. Railway engineering and sugar-refining.

Founded in the 13th cent. Passed to Prussia 1772. Returned to Poland 1919.

Tébessa Algeria. Ancient Theveste. Town at the E end of the Saharan Atlas Mountains 160 km (100 miles) SE of Constantine. Pop. (1987) 107,559.

Important mining centre for phosphates. Manufactures carpets. Trade in wool and esparto grass.

Notable Roman remains in the neighbourhood, inc. the 3rd-cent. arch of Caracalla.

Teddington England. Residential district in Twickenham in the London borough of Richmond-upon-Thames on the R. Thames 19 km (12 miles) WSW of London. Contains Bushy Park and the National Physical Laboratory. Teddington Lock, the largest on the Thames, marks the tidal limit of the river; above it river navigation is controlled by the Thames Water Authority; below it by the Port of London Authority.

Tees River England. River 113 km (70 miles) long rising on Cross Fell and flowing generally E forming the Durham–Cumbria and then the Durham–North Yorkshire boundary, passing Barnard Castle, Stockton-on-Tees, Thornaby-on-Tees and Middlesbrough to enter the estuary on the North Sea.

Teesside England. District in Cleveland, formed as a county borough in 1968 from the former country borough of Middlesbrough, the municipal boroughs of Redcar, Thornaby-on-Tees and Stockton-on-Tees, and the urban districts of Billingham and Eston. Manufactures steel.

Tegucigalpa Honduras. Cap. of the republic and of the Francisco Morazán department on the Choluteca R. at a height of 980 m (3214 ft). Pop. (1990) 608,100 inc. Comayagüela.

Industries inc. food-processing, brewing, distilling, chemicals and textile manufacture.

Founded (1578) as a gold and silver mining centre. Became cap. 1880.

Tehrán (Teheran) Iran. Cap., at the S foot of the Elburz Mountains at a height of 1160 m (3805 ft). Pop. (1986) 6,042,584. Iran's largest city and leading industrial and route centre at the intersection of railways N–S from the Caspian Sea to the Persian Gulf and E–W from Meshed to Tabriz.

Manufactures textiles, carpets, chemicals and glass. Industries inc. car assembly.

The city extends N up the lower slopes of the Elburz Mountains into the district of Shemran, a favourite residential area in the summer. Although the lower, S part is still typically Oriental, the central area was transformed after 1925 by Riza Shah: broad avenues, open squares and modern buildings were constructed. In the heart of the city is the large square known as the Maidan Sepah and S of this is the old royal palace with the famous Peacock Throne, brought by Nadir Shah from India. Became cap. of Persia 1788. Scene of the Tehrán Conference in 1943 between Stalin, Churchill and Roosevelt.

Tehuacán Mexico. Town in Puebla state 113 km (70 miles) SE of Puebla at a height of 1690 m (5543 ft). Pop. (1990) 139,450.

Health resort. Mineral springs, the water from which is bottled and widely distributed.

Tehuantepec, Isthmus of Mexico. Isthmus 209 km (130 miles) wide in E Veracruz and Oaxaca, between the Gulf of Campeche on the Gulf of Mexico (N) and the

Gulf of Tehuantepec on the Pacific Ocean (S). The N is swampy and jungle-covered; in the S are the foothills of the Sierra Madre. An inter-oceanic railway (completed 1907) links the ports of Salina Cruz (S) and Coatzacoalcos (N).

Teignmouth England. Seaside resort in Devon at the mouth of the R. Teign. Pop. (1991) 13,528. An important seaport in the Middle Ages.

Now a small fishing port. Granite and ball clay are exported.

Teign River England. River 48 km (30 miles) long, rising on Dartmoor and flowing SE past Newton Abbot to the English Channel at Teignmouth.

Tejo River ➤TAGUS RIVER.

Telanaipura Indonesia. Town in Jambi province, Sumatra on the Batang Hari R. Pop. (1980) 230,373.

A minor port trading in rubber, timber and rattan.

Tel Aviv-Jaffa Israel. Largest city and the chief industrial and commercial centre of Israel on the Mediterranean coast 56 km (35 miles) NW of Jerusalem. Pop. (1991) 346,800 (conurbation 1,131,700).

Manufactures textiles, metal goods, food products and chemicals.

The main centre of modern Israeli culture and seat of a university (1953); its appearance is entirely modern. Founded in 1906 and in 1949 absorbed the former Arab town of Jaffa.

Tel el Amarna Egypt. The collection of ruins and rock tombs on the E bank of the Nile 64 km (40 miles) NNW of Asyût. Site of the city of Akhetaton, built by Ikhnaton *c.* 1370 BC to replace Thebes as his cap.

Telford England. 'New town' and unitary authority 18 km (11 miles) ESE of Shrewsbury, developed from Dawley, Wellington and Oakengates, to accommodate people from Birmingham and the Black Country. Pop. (1991) 115,000.

Industries inc. metal and vehicle manufacture, electronics and plastics.

Tema Ghana. Seaport 27 km (17 miles) ENE of Accra. Pop. (1988) 109,975. The harbour was opened in 1962 and has since taken the traffic formerly handled by the 'surf' ports of Accra, Keta, Winneba and Cape Coast.

Industries inc. oil-refining, aluminium-smelting and fishing.

Témbi (Tempe) Gorge (Vale of Tempe) Greece. Gorge in Thessaly 8 km (5 miles) long, through which the Peneus (Piniós) R. flows, between Mt Ossa and Mt Olympus. Sacred to Apollo and an important route into Thessaly.

Temirtau Kazakhstan. Town in central Kazakhstan on the Nura R. Pop. (1995) 180,000.

Important steel-making centre and also manufactures synthetic rubber and has a large thermal power station.

Tempe USA. Town in Arizona on the Salt R. 13 km (8 miles) E of Phoenix. Pop. (1990) 141,865.

Commercial centre. Flour-milling.

Temple USA. Town in Texas 182 km (113 miles) S of Fort Worth. Pop. (1970) 33,431.

Commercial and industrial centre in an agricultural region. Manufactures furniture, footwear and cottonseed oil.

Temuco Chile. Cap. of Cautín province on the Cautín R. 611 km (380 miles) SSW of Santiago. Pop. (1992) 240,880.

Market town in an agricultural and forest region producing cereals, apples and timber. Tanning, flour-milling and sawmilling. A market for the Araucanian Indians.

A treaty with the Araucanians ending the Indian wars was signed here in 1881.

Tenasserim (Tanintharyi) Myanmar (Burma). Region in the S consisting of a coastal strip extending from Moulmein (N) to Victoria Point (S) on the Isthmus of Kra. Chief towns Moulmein, Tavoy and Mergui.

Main products rice, teak, tin and tungsten.

Tenasserim River Myanmar (Burma). River in Tenasserim 400 km (250 miles) long, flowing first S and then NW and entering the Andaman Sea near Mergui.

Tenby Wales. Seaside resort in Pembrokeshire 14 km (9 miles) E of Pembroke on a headland overlooking Carmarthen Bay, Bristol Channel. Pop. (1991) 5619. Has two sandy beaches and a harbour. Just NE are the ruins of the 12th/13th-cent. castle.

Tenerife Canary Islands. Largest of the islands, between Gomera (W) and Gran Canaria (E); part of the Spanish province of Santa Cruz de Tenerife. Area 2059 sq km (795 sq. miles). Pop. (1991) 727,326. Cap. Santa Cruz. Rises to 3712 m (12,172 ft) in the volcanic Pico de Teide. The mild climate makes it a popular resort. In the fertile valleys bananas, tomatoes, early fruits and vegetables are grown.

Tennessee USA. State in S central USA, bordered (W) along the Mississippi R. by Arkansas and Missouri. Area 109,152 sq km (42,144 sq. miles). Pop. (1990) 4,877,185. Cap. Nashville. In the E are the Unaka and Great Smoky Mountains of the Appalachian ranges; Clingmans Dome rises to 2026 m (6645 ft). Farther W is the Cumberland Plateau, at about 540 m (1771 ft). The land then slopes W to the Mississippi R. Largely drained by the Tennessee R. and its tributaries; the N is drained by the Cumberland R. (also a tributary of the Ohio). Short and mild winters, hot summers. Rainfall plentiful, about 125 cm (50 ins.) annually.

Agriculture important. Chief crops cotton, maize, tobacco and hay. Cattle, pigs and poultry extensively reared. Coal, zinc, pyrites and phosphates mined. E Tennessee is an industrial area and the most important industries are chemicals, synthetic resins, electrical goods, iron and steel, food-processing and sawmilling. Principal centres Memphis, Nashville, Chattanooga, Knoxville.

The Tennessee Valley Authority (TVA) established in 1933 as a multi-purpose project for developing the Tennessee R. valley in the interests of transport, flood control and hydroelectric power, which operates mainly in Tennessee but extends into neighbouring states. Associated with TVA was the large fertilizer plant at Muscle Shoals and 27 dams were built on the Tennessee R. and its tributaries. TVA has also been concerned with afforestation and soil conservation in the area.

The first permanent settlement in Tennessee was made by Virginians (1769). The region became part of the USA in 1783. In the American Civil War it was on the Confederate side. Admitted to the Union in 1796 as the 16th state.

Tennessse River USA. River 1049 km (652 miles) long, formed by the union of the Holston and the French Broad rivers near Knoxville in Tennessee, flowing generally SW past Knoxville and Chattanooga, turning WNW in N Alabama and re-entering Tennessee, and finally entering Kentucky to join the Onio R. at Paducah. The drainage basin occupies about 99,715 sq km (38,500 sq. miles); the area has been developed by the Tennessee Valley Authority.

Tenterden England. Market town in Kent 14 km (9 miles) SW of Ashford. Pop. (1991) 6803. In the 15th cent. it was made a member of the Cinque Port of Rye, for the sea was then only 3 km (2 miles) S.

Tepic Mexico. Cap. of Nayarit state at the foot of the extinct volcano Sangangüey 193 km (120 miles) NW of Guadalajara. Pop. (1990) 206,967.

Market town. Sugar-refining, rice-milling and cotton-ginning. Founded 1531.

Teplice (Ger. **Teplitz**) Czech Republic. Industrial town in NW Bohemia 16 km (10 miles) W of Ústi-nad-Labem. Pop. (1984) 54,000.

Manufactures glass, pottery, textiles and cement. Also the Czech Republic's oldest watering-place with thermal mineral springs.

Teramo Italy. Cap. of Teramo province in Abruzzi on the Tordino R. 48 km (30 miles) NW of Pescara. Pop. (1971) 47,866.

Market town. Manufactures textiles and pasta.

Romanesque-Gothic cathedral (14th-cent.).

Terek River Georgia. River 595 km (370 miles) long, rising in the Caucasus in glaciers on Mt Kazbek, flowing NNW through the Daryal Gorge past Ordzhonikidze, then E and NE, forming a swampy delta about 113 km (70 miles) wide on the Caspian Sea. Used for irrigation along the lower course and for hydroelectric power on its head-streams.

Terengganu Malaysia. State in West Malaysia on the E coast. Area 12,955 sq km (5002 sq. miles). Pop. (1991) 770,931. Cap. Kuala Trengganu. Consists of a narrow coastal plain rising inland to densely forested mountains reaching nearly 1500 m (4920 ft).
Chief products rice, rubber and copra.

Teresina Brazil. Cap. of Piauí state on the Parnaíba R. 320 km (200 miles) SE of São Luís to which it is linked by railway. Pop. (1991) 598,449.
Trade in cattle, hides and skins, rice and cotton. Sugar-refining. Manufactures textiles and soap.

Terni Italy. Ancient Interamna Nahars. Cap. of Terni province in Umbria on the Nera R. 74 km (46 miles) NNE of Rome. Pop. (1991) 109,809.
Railway junction. Industrial centre. Manufactures iron and steel, armaments, locomotives, turbines and chemicals.
Roman remains. Cathedral (13th-cent., restored in the 17th cent.). Nearby are the Cascata delle Marmore waterfalls, which supply hydroelectric power for the factories. Founded in the 7th cent. BC. Birthplace of Marcus Claudius Tacitus, Roman emperor AD 275–6.

Ternopol (Tarnopól) Ukraine. Cap. of the Ternopol Region on the Seret R. 120 km (75 miles) ESE of Lvov. Pop. (1991) 218,000.
Railway junction. Market town. Industries inc. sugar-refining and flour-milling. Manufactures agricultural machinery and cement.
Founded (1540) by Jan Tarnowski

(Polish). Taken by the Russians in World War I; returned to Poland 1919; ceded to the USSR 1945.

Terracina Italy. Town in Latina province, Latium on the Gulf of Gaeta 96 km (60 miles) SE of Rome. Pop. (1971) 33,526.
Port. Seaside resort. Fishing.
Roman remains inc. an amphitheatre and baths; the modern *piazza* was the Roman forum.

Terranova di Sicilia ➤GELA.

Terre Adélie (Adélie Land) Antarctica. Antarctic territory between long. 136°E and 142°E and S of lat. 60°S. Discovered by Dumont d'Urville 1840; explored by Sir Douglas Mawson 1912–13. Placed under French sovereignty 1938. From 1955 part of French Southern and Antarctic Territories. The staff of the permanent scientific stations, about 190, form the only pop.

Terre Haute USA. Town in Indiana on the Wabash R. 113 km (70 miles) WSW of Indianapolis. Pop. (1990) 57,483.
Manufactures bricks and tiles, chemicals, plastics and glass.

Terror, Mount ➤ROSS ISLAND.

Teruel Spain. 1. Province in Aragón. Area 14,804 sq km (5713 sq. miles). Pop. (1991) 143,305. Mountainous and largely barren, rising to over 1800 m (5904 ft) in the S and SW. Has few good roads or railways; one of the most sparsely populated provinces in Spain.
2. Cap. of Teruel province on the Turia R. 217 km (135 miles) E of Madrid. Pop. (1991) 28,400.
Market town. Manufactures soap and tiles.
The old walled town has narrow streets and a 16th-cent. cathedral.

Tessin ➤TICINO.

Teton Range USA. Range of the Rocky Mountains, mainly in the NW Wyoming, just S of Yellowstone National Park and now mainly in the Grand Teton National Park. Highest peak Grand Teton (4199 m;

13,772 ft). Noted for scenic beauty; much frequented by climbers, hikers and campers.

Tetuán Morocco. Cap. of Tetuán province, formerly cap. of Spanish Morocco, 32 km (20 miles) S of Ceuta and 10 km (6 miles) WSW of Río Martín (its port on the Mediterranean), to both of which it is linked by rail. Pop. (1982) 199,615.

Manufactures textiles, soap and leather goods.

The modern town was founded at the end of the 15th cent. by Jewish refugees from Portugal.

Tewkesbury England. Market town in Gloucestershire on the R. Severn at the confluence with the Warwickshire Avon. Pop. (1991) 9488.

There is light industry and tourism is important.

Has many timbered houses, but the principal feature is the fine Norman abbey church, consecrated 1123, with 14th-cent. additions. The Yorkist victory at the Battle of Tewkesbury (1471) brought the Wars of the Roses to an end.

Texarkana USA. Town partly in NE Texas and partly in SW Arkansas (hence the name). Pop. (1970) 52,179 (30,497 in Texas, 21,682 in Arkansas).

Manufactures wood products, cottonseed oil and textiles.

Texas USA. State in the S and SW, the second largest in the USA (after Alaska), bordered on the S along the Rio Grande by Mexico and on the SE by the Gulf of Mexico. Area 691,027 sq km (266,807 sq. miles). Pop. (1990) 18,031,000. Largely plains and flat tablelands. In the W is the Llano Estacado (Staked Plain), a rather dry, short-grass region at a height of 900–1200 m (2952–3936 ft); in the SW, between the Rio Grande and its tributary the Pecos, are the Sacramento Mountains, rising to 2669 m (8754 ft) in Guadalupe Mountain, the highest point in the state. The coast is fringed with many long narrow islands, lagoons and bays. Along the N border is the Red R. (a tributary of the Mississippi); rivers draining to the Gulf

of Mexico are the Rio Grande, the Colorado, the Brazos, the Trinity, the Sabine. The climate varies from humid subtropical on the coastal plain to dry continental (the NW 'panhandle'). An important agricultural state with 186,000 farms, but soil erosion is serious in some areas. Chief crop cotton, in which it leads the USA, as it does also in sorghum; also has the greatest number of cattle and sheep in the USA. Petroleum and natural gas (of which it is by far the leading producer) are the most important mineral products. Industries are mainly the processing of the agricultural and mineral products; leading centres Houston (chief seaport), Dallas, San Antonio, El Paso, Austin, Fort Worth, Arlington and Corpus Christi. The mixed pop. and stormy history make it one of the most colourful of the states. Once part of Mexico; won its independence in 1836 and in 1845 joined the Union as the 28th state.

Texas City USA. Industrial town and seaport in Texas on Galveston Bay 10 km (6 miles) NW of Galveston. Pop. (1970) 39,908.

Industries inc. tin-smelting and oil-refining. Manufactures chemicals. Exports petroleum products, chemicals and sulphur.

Thailand. Kingdom in SE Asia bounded W by Myanmar (Burma), N and E by Laos and SE by Cambodia. In the S it becomes a peninsula bounded W by the Indian Ocean, S by Malaysia and E by the Gulf of Thailand. Area 513,115 sq km (198,115 sq. miles). Pop. (1995) 58,791,000 (18 per cent urban). Life expectancy, 66 years male, 71 female. Cap. Bangkok. Other cities Nonthaburi, Nakhon, Ratchasima, Chiang Mai, Khon Kaen. Currency: Thai baht = 100 stangs. There are 4 main geographical regions. The N consists of a series of parallel hills rising to 2595 m (8514 ft) in Doi Inthanon (NW). Four of the principal valley streams join to form the Chao Phraya R. Teak is a valuable product of the highland forests. Central Thailand is a broad alluvial plain watered mainly by the Chao Phraya, the important rice-growing area. The E consists of a shallow basin surrounded by hills and drained to the Mekong on the E border, a thinly populated region of poor soils and inhospitable climate. S Thailand comprises a narrow strip of land along the W shores of the Gulf of Thailand, continuing S across the Isthmus of Kra into the N part of the Malay peninsula, a region of palm-fringed beaches and inland forests. Climate is tropical, with high temperatures and humidity. Over most of the country, 3 seasons may be recognized. The rainy season is June to Oct., the cool season from Nov. to Feb. and the hot season is March to May. Rainfall is generally heaviest in the S and lightest in the NE. Land use: forested 27 per cent, meadows and pastures 2 per cent, agricultural and under permanent cultivation 45 per cent. The religion is mainly Buddhist and the official lang. Thai.

About 60 per cent of the people are engaged in agriculture and fishing, and rice and fish are the staple foods; rice is also an important export. The main crop is rice, of which it normally produces a considerable surplus. Irrigation projects have considerably increased the area of cultivated land on the Central Plain. Other crops inc. rubber, sugarcane, cassava, maize and copra. Teak is floated from the forests of the NW down the Chao Phraya to Bangkok or down the Salween to Moulmein (Myanmar) for export. Tin and wolfram (tungsten), mined in the S. Bangkok, which handles most of the country's foreign trade, is linked by rail with Chiang Mai (N), with the Malaysian railway system (S) and with Laos and Cambodia at the respective frontiers. Away from the railways and rivers, buffalo and bullock carts are widely used for transport. Other industries inc. textiles, electrical and electronic equipment, food-processing and clothing.

The Thai people first occupied the country in the 13th cent., when they were driven out of SW China by Kublai Khan. About a cent. later (1350) Ayutthaya was made cap. and the first king of Siam (as Thailand was then called) was crowned. Then followed a long series of wars with neighbouring peoples, particularly the Burmese, who finally destroyed Ayutthaya (1767). In 1782 the present dynasty was founded by an army general and Bangkok became the new cap. During the 19th cent. Siam was brought increasingly into contact with French and British interests, and was compelled to cede Laos and parts of Cambodia to the former (1893–1907) and 4 Malay states to the latter (1909). After a *coup d'état*, constitutional government was introduced in 1932. During World War II Siam supported Japan and annexed parts of Laos, Cambodia, Malaya and Burma, all of which were returned in 1946. The country was virtually ruled by dictatorship from 1947, but the 1932 constitution was restored in 1951. Elections did not lead to political stability, the National Assembly was dissolved (1958) and an interim constitution was decreed (1959). Numerous *coups* have followed. In 1991 a military junta seized power, deposing the prime minister and appointing a general to the post. In 1992 there were massive anti-government demonstrations and the 360-member House of Representatives established that it should appoint prime ministers not the military. It is divided into 73 provinces for administrative purposes.

Thame England. Market town in SE Oxfordshire on the R. Thame 19 km (12 miles) E of Oxford. Pop. (1991) 10,806. Has a 16th-cent. grammar school which was attended by John Hampden, English parliamentarian (1594–1643).

Thame, River England. River 48 km (30 miles) long, flowing generally SW through Buckinghamshire and Oxfordshire past Thame to join the R. Thames near Dorchester, Oxfordshire.

Thames, Firth of ➤HAURAKI GULF.

Thames, River England. The chief (though not the longest) river, 346 km (215 miles) from Thames Head to the Nore, rising on the SE slope of the Cotswold Hills in 2 headstreams: the Thames (Isis), with its source at Thames Head 5 km (3 miles) SW of Cirencester; the Churn, with its source at Seven Springs 6 km (4 miles) SSE of Cheltenham. The Churn joins the Thames near Cricklade; the Coln and the Leach join it near Lechlade. Flowing generally ENE, the Thames receives the Windrush and turns SE past Oxford, receiving first the Cherwell and then the Thame (above and near Oxford the main stream is often called the Isis). Receiving the Kennet at Reading, it follows a winding course, generally E, past Windsor, Kingston-on-Thames, London, Tilbury and Southend-on-Sea and enters the North Sea by a wide estuary at the Nore. Below Reading the chief tributaries are the Colne, the Lea and the Roding on the left bank and the Wey, the Mole, the Darent and the Medway on the right. Joined by several canals; navigable for barges as far as Lechlade. Ships of 800 tonnes can reach London Bridge; the largest ocean-going vessels can dock at Tilbury. Tidal as far as Teddington; above this point navigation is controlled by the Thames Water Authority, and below it by the Port of London Authority. The stretch of water between London Bridge and Tower Bridge is called the Pool of London. Because of flooding on occasions at high water, an antiflood barrier was constructed in 1984 and this protects London. Above London the Thames has much attractive scenery and is noted for angling; it is also the chief boating river in England. Scene of the annual Henley Regatta and of the Oxford and Cambridge boat race (Putney–Mortlake).

Thana India. Town in Maharashtra 32 km (20 miles) NNE of Bombay. Pop. (1991) 803,400.

Trade in rice, sugar-cane. Manufactures textiles (cottons, woollens), matches, carbon paper, plastics, refined oil, oxygen, toiletries, chemicals and steel castings.

Thanet, Isle of England. Island forming the NE corner of Kent, from which it is separated by the two branches of the R. Stour. Contains the seaside resorts of Ramsgate, Broadstairs, Margate and West-gate. The N Foreland is at the NE extremity.

Thanjavur India. Formerly Tanjore. Industrial town in Tamil Nadu 290 km (180 miles) SSW of Madras. Pop. (1991) 202,000.

Rice-milling. Manufactures cotton and silk goods, jewellery and inlaid copperware.

The last cap. of the Hindu Chola dynasty, it has a large 11th-cent. temple and a 16th-cent. rajah's palace.

Thar (Great Indian) Desert India/Pakistan. Sandy desert mainly in NW Rajasthan (India) but extending into the adjoining areas of Pakistan. Rainfall irregular and generally less than 25 cm (10 ins.) annually. Sparsely populated. Chief town Bikaner.

Thásos Greece. Island in Kaválla *nome* in the N Aegean 24 km (15 miles) SE of Kaválla. Area 399 sq km (154 sq. miles). Rises to nearly 1200 m (3936 ft).

Produces olive oil and wine.

Colonized from Paros in the 8th cent. BC. Once famous for its goldmines. Fell to the Turks in 1455 and returned to Greece 1913.

Thebes Egypt. Ancient cap. of Upper Egypt on the banks of the Nile 499 km (310 miles) SSE of modern Cairo. The site is now occupied by Luxor, Karnak and Qurna. Referred to in Homer's *Iliad* as a city of '100 gates', probably because of its numerous temples (with gates). In the Eleventh dynasty it began to develop into an important city; from about 1600 BC it became the cap. of the Eighteenth, Nineteenth and Twentieth dynasties and the centre of the worship of Ammon. When the new Empire began to decay, Thebes lost much of its importance; it was destroyed by the Assyrians (668 BC) and by the Romans (29 BC) and a few years later had become merely a collection of villages. Many outstanding archaeological discoveries have been made in the ruins of Thebes, among them the tomb of Tutankhamun (1922); much of the material is now housed in the Cairo Museum. The modern Luxor, a winter resort, has a pop. of (1991) 142,000.

Thebes Greece. Important city in ancient Greece in Boeotia 56 km (35 miles) NW of Athens. Founded by Cadmus, after whom the citadel Cadmeia was named. In the 6th cent. BC it led the Boeotian League. Animosity towards Athens led the Thebans to support Sparta in the Peloponnesian War, but they turned against their allies and destroyed

Spartan power at Leuctra (371 BC) under the leadership of Epaminondas and Pelopidas. With the Athenians, they were defeated by Philip II of Macedon at Chaeronea (338 BC) and the city was destroyed by Alexander the Great. The modern town of Thívai was built on the site. Birthplace of the poet, Pindar (c. 518–438 BC).

Thermopylae Greece. Pass in E central Greece 16 km (10 miles) SE of Lamia, famous for the heroic defence by Leonidas and his 300 Spartans against the Persians under Xerxes (480 BC). Here, too, in 279 BC the Greeks checked the Gauls for several months, to be ultimately defeated.

Thesprotia Greece. A *nome* in N bounded by Albania and the Strait of Corfu. Area 1515 sq km (588 sq. miles). Cap. Egoumenitsa. Pop. (1991) 44,202. The principal rivers are Acheron and Thyamis. Mainly agricultural producing barley, corn, olive oil and almonds. Lumbering.

Thessaloníki (English **Salonika**) Greece.
1. *Nome* in Macedonia to the N of the Chalcidice peninsula. Area 3683 sq km (1422 sq. miles). Pop. (1991) 977,528. Cereals and vines cultivated.
2. Ancient Therma. Cap. of Macedonia and of the Thessaloníki *nome*. Pop. (1991) 377,951.

Seaport at the head of the Gulf of Salonika, with a free zone; second city of Greece and an industrial centre. Exports tobacco, hides, metallic ores. Manufactures textiles, metal goods, chemicals and cigarettes. Flour-milling and tanning. Also an important transportation centre.

Has several Byzantine churches, though much of the old city was destroyed in the disastrous fires of 1890 and 1917. The ancient town was so named because of neighbouring hot springs; it was refounded in the 4th cent. BC, as Thessalonica. It became important because of its position on the Roman Via Egnatia, the highway linking the Adriatic with Constantinople. St Paul, visiting the Christians here, addressed two epistles to the Thessalonians. Taken by the Turks 1430;

passed to Greece in 1912. In World War I it was the base for the Allied Salonika campaigns against the Bulgarians. Birthplace of Kemal Atatürk (1881–1938).

Thessaly (Gr. **Thessalía**) Greece. Regional division of E central Greece. Area 14,037 sq km (5419 sq. miles). Pop. (1991) 731,230. Consists of fertile lowlands in the centre drained by the Peneus (Piniós) R., surrounded by mountains. Divided administratively into the Kardítsa, Lárissa, Magnesia and Trikkala *nomes*.

Thetford England. Market town in Norfolk at the confluence of the Thet and Little Ouse rivers 45 km (28 miles) SW of Norwich. Pop. (1991) 19,901. Industrial estate for London overspill.

Light engineering and food-processing.

Originally the cap. of East Anglia, there are ruins of a Cluniac priory (founded 1104). In the 14th cent. it had 20 churches and 8 monasteries. Birthplace of Thomas Paine, the revolutionary philosopher and writer (1737–1809).

Thetford Mines Canada. Town in Quebec 80 km (50 miles) S of Quebec. Pop. (1986) 18,561.

An important centre of the asbestos industry; the world's largest asbestos deposits (discovered 1876) are in the neighbourhood, producing 30 per cent of the world's supply.

Thiès Senegal. Town 51 km (32 miles) ENE of Dakar. Pop. (1992) 201,350.

Railway junction. Market town. Trade in groundnuts, rice and fruit. Manufactures fertilizer from phosphates quarried in the neighbourhood.

Thimphu Bhutan. Cap. of Bhutan situated in the Himalayas. Pop. (1993) 30,340. Since 1962 the official seat of the royal government. Parois is the administrative cap. It stands at a height of 2370 m (7775 ft). One of the country's few roads links the cap. with Assam.

Thionville France. Town in the Moselle department in Lorraine on the Moselle R. 29 km (18 miles) N of Metz. Pop. (1990) 40,835.

Industrial centre. Manufactures iron and steel, metal goods and cement.

Thíra (Thera) Greece. Formerly Santorini. Volcanic island in the Cyclades in the S Aegean Sea 113 km (70 miles) N of Crete. Area 75 sq. km (29 sq. miles). Rises to 567 m (1860 ft).

Produces wine.

Thirlmere England. Lake 5 km (3 miles) long in the Lake District, Cumbria 6 km (4 miles) SSE of Keswick. Provides Manchester with part of its water supply.

Thirsk England. Market town in North Yorkshire 34 km (21 miles) NNW of York. Pop. (1991) 6860.

Flour-milling. Has a well-known racecourse.

Thiruvananthapuram (Trivandrum) India. Cap. of Kerala near the Malabar coast 209 km (130 miles) SW of Madurai. Pop. (1991) 604,200.

Manufactures electronics, textiles, coir ropes and mats, copra and soap. Centre of Malayalam culture; seat of Kerala University (1937). Has an old Hindu temple.

Thompson Canada. City situated N of Winnipeg, Manitoba, a northern regional service centre for other communities in N Manitoba and the Central Arctic of Canada. Pop. (1991) 14,977.

Industries inc. mining, milling, smelting and refining for nickel, cobalt, copper and some precious metals.

Thornaby-on-Tees England. Industrial town in Cleveland on the R. Tees 5 km (3 miles) WSW of Middlesbrough. From 1968 part of the county borough of Teesside.

Heavy engineering, iron-founding and flour-milling. Linked by bridge with Stockton-on-Tees.

Thornton Clevelys England. Town in W Lancashire comprising the market town of Thornton, 5 km (3 miles) S of Fleetwood, and the seaside resort of Clevelys, on the Irish Sea. Pop. (1991) 28,061.

Thousand Islands Canada/USA. Group of about 1700 small islands and islets in the St Lawrence R. near the E end of L. Ontario, mainly in Ontario (Canada) and the remainder in New York (USA). Popular resort area.

Thrace (Gr. **Thráki**) Greece. Region, with Macedonia East, in the extreme NE, bordering N on Bulgaria and E on Turkey, comprising the *nomes* of Cavalla, Drama, Evros, Thodope and Xánthi. Area 14,157 sq km (5466 sq. miles). Pop. (1991) 570,261. In ancient times it occupied a much larger area, extending N to the Danube R. and E to the Black Sea.

Three Rivers ➤TROIS RIVIÈRES.

Thun Switzerland. Town in the Bern canton on the Aar R. where the latter leaves L. Thun (NW). Pop. (1990) 32,124.

Manufactures metal goods, watches and clothing.

Has a 12th-cent. castle.

Thun, Lake (Ger. **Thunersee**) Switzerland. Lake in the Bern canton 18 km (11 miles) long and 3 km (2 miles) wide at a height of 560 m (1837 ft). Picturesque; popular with tourists. It is entered in the SE by the Aar R., connecting it with L. Brienz, and the river leaves it in the NW near Thun.

Thunder Bay Canada. Lake port in Ontario on the NW shore of L. Superior, formed 1970 by the amalgamation of the twin cities of Fort William and Port Arthur, the W terminus of the St Lawrence–Great Lakes Waterway. Pop. (1991) 113,946.

Important outlet for prairie grain and there are huge elevators along the waterfront. Industries inc. flour-milling, sawmilling, engineering and brewing. Manufactures wood-pulp and paper.

Founded by the French as a fur-trading post 1678; a fort was built in 1801 (Fort William).

Thurgau Switzerland. Canton in the NE bordering N on L. Constance. Area 991 sq km (383 sq. miles). Pop. (1992) 210,237 (German-speaking). Cap. Frautenfeld. Hilly but fertile, especially in the Thur R. valley.

Produces cereals, vines. Textile industry. Became a canton of the Swiss Confederation 1803.

Thuringia (Ger. **Thüringen**) Germany. *Land* reconstituted from former German Democratic territory in 1990, bounded by Saxony in the E, Bavaria in the S, Hessen in the W and Sachsen-Anhalt in the N. Area 16,251 sq km (6275 sq. miles). Pop. (1990) 2,572,100. Cap. Erfurt. Hilly and crossed NW–SE by the Thuringian Forest, it is drained by the Saale, Werra and White Elster rivers. It is fertile, producing cereals, sugar-beet and fruit. Important textile, glass and other industries. When the lands belonging to the Saxon house of Wettin were divided (1485), most of Thuringia went to the Ernestine branch, and later it was divided into a number of duchies, inc. Saxe-Coburg, Saxe-Gotha and Saxe-Meiningen. Thuringia became a state under the Weimar Republic in 1920, a *Land* of the German Democratic Republic in 1945 and of Germany from 1990.

Thuringian Forest (Ger. **Thüringerwald**) Germany. Wooded mountain range extending about 113 km (70 miles) NW–SE between the Werra R. and the Thuringian Saale, rising to 983 m (3224 ft) in Beerberg.

Thurles Ireland. Town in Co. Tipperary on the Suir R. 37 km (23 miles) NNW of Clonmel. Pop. (1991) 6687.

Hunting and fishing centre, with a beet-sugar refinery and a racecourse.

Has a 19th-cent. cathedral in Romanesque style and a ruined 12th-cent. castle; 6 km (4 miles) S is the famous ruined Holy Cross Abbey, dating from the 12th cent.

Thurrock England. Town and unitary authority on the N bank of the R. Thames, formed (1936) from the urban districts of Grays Thurrock, Purfleet and Tilbury, and other districts. Pop. (1994) 131,400.

Manufactures cement. Docks and passenger landing stage at Tilbury (Port of London). Oil refineries at Shell Haven and Coryton. A road tunnel (opened 1963) links Essex and Kent, from Purfleet to Dartford.

Thursday Island Australia. Small island in Queensland, in Torres Strait, 24 km (15 miles) NW of Cape York. Pop. (1971) 2216. Chief town Port Kennedy, a centre of pearl and trepang (*bêche-de-mer*) fishing.

Thurso Scotland. Market town in Highland on Thurso Bay at the mouth of the R. Thurso. Pop. (1991) 8488. Port. The most northerly town on the Scottish mainland. Ferries sail to Orkney.

Tianjin (Tientsin) China. City (municipality) in the N and the third largest city in China on the Grand Canal and on the Hei-he at the confluence with several tributaries 113 km (70 miles) SE of Beijing. Pop. (1990) 8,830,000 (metropolitan area), 5 million (city).

Important railway junction and industrial centre. Manufactures iron and steel, chemicals, textiles (cottons, woollens), leather goods, matches, glass. Food-processing, engineering. It is the port of Beijing, with outports 48 km (30 miles) downstream at the mouth of the Hei-he. Exports hog bristles, wool and skins.

Usually kept open for 2 months in winter by icebreakers. Tianjin had relatively little importance until it was occupied by British and French forces and opened to foreign trade (1858–61). After the Boxer Rebellion in 1900, during which it suffered severely, its ancient walls were pulled down and the city was reconstructed. It was occupied by the Japanese 1937–45.

Tiber (Italian **Tevere**) **River** Italy. Italy's most famous river, 405 km (252 miles) long, rising in the Tuscan Apennines and flowing generally S past Rome and Ostia to the Tyrrhenian Sea. Chief tributary the Nera. It has two mouths, the N mouth at Fiumicino being navigable for 34 km (21 miles) to Rome owing to canalization.

Tiberias Israel. Town in the NE on the W shore of the Sea of Galilee (L. Tiberias) 53 km (33 miles) E of Haifa at 207 m (679 ft) below sea level. Pop. 23,900. Health resort with medicinal springs.

Founded by Herod Antipas *c.* AD 21 and

named after the Emperor Tiberius, the town became a centre of Jewish learning; it became the seat of the Sanhedrin late in the 2nd cent. and the Talmud was completed here (*c.* 400). Taken by the Arabs 637.

Tiberias, Lake ➤GALILEE, SEA OF.

Tibesti Highlands Chad/Libya. Saharan mountain region of volcanic origin; mainly in N Chad but extending NE into Libya. Highest peak Emi Koussi (3415 m; 11,201 ft). Dates and cereals grown in scattered fertile oases. Camels, donkeys, sheep and goats raised. The people are mainly nomadic Tibbu and Arabs.

Tibet (Xizang) China. Autonomous Region in the SW, bounded on the S by India, Bhutan, Sikkim and Nepal, and on the W by Kashmir. Area 1,221,600 sq km (470,000 sq. miles). Pop. (1990) 2,196,010. Cap. Lhasa. The most extensive high plateau region in the world, with an average height of over 3600 m (11,808 ft) lying between the Kunlun Mountains (N) and the Himalayas (S). A number of still loftier mountain ranges with a general E–W trend cross the tableland. In the S, on the border with Nepal, is Everest 8848 m (29,028 ft), and there are several other peaks exceeding 6000 m (19,680 ft). Many salt lakes are scattered about the plateau, the largest being Nam Tso in the SE. Some of the great rivers of S and SE Asia have their source here: the Indus and Sutlej rise in the SW, the Salween in the E, while the Tsangpo (Brahmaputra) flows generally E across S Tibet (Xizang). The Mekong, Chang Jiang and Huang He rise in the extension of the Tibetan (Xizang) plateau in neighbouring Chinghai (Tsinghai) (NE). Climate unusually rigorous, with long, cold winters and short, hot summers and an annual rainfall which reaches 25–35 cm (10–14 ins.) in places but is elsewhere considerably less. Temperatures vary greatly with altitude and there are marked differences between day and night and between sun and shade temperatures. Much of the land, esp. in the N, is treeless and barren. A scanty grass is the most widespread type of natural vegetation

and there are considerable woodlands in the E.

Agriculture is possible in the more favoured parts of the S and E, where the rains of the summer monsoon can penetrate the river valleys, and barley, wheat, peas and beans are grown. The Tibetans, many of whom are nomadic, raise large numbers of yaks (which are invaluable beasts of burden on the steep highland tracks), ponies, donkeys and sheep; these animals provide wool, hides and yak hair for export. Principal minerals borax, soda and salt; alluvial gold is widely distributed. Leading towns Lhasa, Shigatse and Gyangtse, all in the S. Trade is mainly conducted by animal and sometimes by human transport over rough tracks and mountain passes, but a motor road has been constructed between Lhasa and Lanzhou on the Chinese railway system and an air service between Lhasa and Beijing was inaugurated in 1957.

The Tibetan (Xizang) people are of Mongoloid stock. Their religion is Lamaism, derived from the Mahayana form of Buddhism. Religion occupies a dominant place in their lives and about one-fifth of the male pop. are lamas, dwelling in hundreds of monasteries scattered throughout the country. From the mid 17th cent. until recent years Xizang was a theocracy, ruled by the Dalai Lama as head of the Lamaist religion, assisted by the Panchen Lama and a council of 4 ministers. Since the country was invaded (1950), effective government has been in the hands of the Chinese.

The known history of Tibet (Xizang) commences in the 7th cent. AD, when it was a powerful independent kingdom; in the following cent. it exacted tribute from China. Buddhism was introduced from India and an alphabet based on Sanskrit made possible the translation of the Buddhist scriptures into Tibetan. Various reforms were effected and in the 17th cent. the grand lama of Lhasa took the title of Dalai Lama, with the chief abbot of the Tashi Lumpo lamasery, the Panchen Lama, as second in command. From 1720, when a Chinese army invaded Xizang and took Lhasa, the country was ruled, at least

Tibet (Xizang)

909

nominally, by the Manchu dynasty. Various Jesuits, Capuchins and others entered Xizang, and in the late 18th cent. Britain made contact with the country from India. In the 19th cent. Europeans were systematically excluded and Lhasa became the 'forbidden city'. In 1904 the Younghusband expedition to Lhasa enforced the establishment of trading posts at Yatung, Gyangtse and Gartock, and Britain recognized Chinese sovereignty over Tibet (Xizang); when the Manchu dynasty came to an end, however, all Chinese officials and troops were expelled (1912). In 1918 the Chinese unsuccessfully attacked Xizang over the division of the country into Inner Tibet, under Chinese authority, and Outer Tibet; in 1920 Sir Charles Bell was invited by the Dalai Lama to Lhasa to assist in effecting a settlement. In 1922 Lhasa was linked by telegraph with India. Chinese Communist forces invaded Tibet (Xizang) in 1950; resistance to the Chinese developed into open rebellion, which was quickly suppressed (1959), and the Dalai Lama fled to India. It became an Autonomous Region of China in 1965.

Ticino (Ger. **Tessin**) Switzerland. Canton in the S. Area 2812 sq km (1086 sq. miles). Pop. (1992) 290,001 (Italian-speaking, Roman Catholic). Cap. Bellinzona. Mainly mountainous, with the Lepontine Alps in the N. Drained by the Ticino and Maggia rivers. Vines and tobacco grown in the valleys; the sheltered shores of L. Maggiore and L. Lugano enjoy a Mediterranean type of climate and have many resorts. Chief towns Bellinzona, Lugano, Locarno. The canton was formed and became a member of the Swiss Confederation in 1803.

Ticino River Switzerland. River 259 km (161 miles) long, rising in the Lepontine Alps and flowing generally S through Ticino canton and L. Maggiore into Italy to join the Po R. just below Pavia. Much used for irrigation in its lower course.

Tien Shan. Great mountain system in Central Asia extending about 2400 km (1500 miles) generally WSW–ENE from Kirgizia

through the Xinjiang Uygur Autonomous Region (China) to the Mongolian border. Highest peaks Pobedy (7439 m; 24,406 ft) and Khan Tengri (6995 m; 22,944 ft). In the W it divides into a number of different mountain ranges of which the most SW are by some considered part of the Pamir–Alai system.

Tientsin ►TIANJIN.

Tierra del Fuego Argentina/Chile. Archipelago at the S extremity of South America, separated from the mainland by the Strait of Magellan. Total area 73,700 sq km (28,450 sq. miles), the major W part in Chile (in Magallanes province) and the E part in Argentina (Tierra del Fuego province). The N of the main island (46,620 sq km; 18,000 sq. miles) is mainly flat, treeless tableland; in the S, Andean mountains run E, presenting sheer rock walls broken by fiords to the sea. Main occupations sheep-farming, lumbering and oil production. Chief towns Punta Arenas (Chile), Ushuaia (Argentina), the world's most southerly town. It was discovered by Ferdinand Magellan, the Portuguese explorer in 1530.

Tiflis ►TBILISI.

Tigris River. River in SW Asia 1850 km (1150 miles) long, rising in E Turkey and flowing generally SE past Diarbakir, where for a short distance it forms the border with Syria; it then continues SE through Iraq, more or less parallel to the Euphrates R., past Mosul and Baghdad. It is joined by the Euphrates near Al Qurna and the river, from this point known as the Shatt-al-Arab, enters the (Persian) Gulf. Liable to floods in the late spring when the snows in the Turkish mountains melt: reaches its highest level in April, its lowest in Sept.–Oct. Navigable by shallow-draught vessels to Baghdad. Together with the Euphrates, the Tigris embraces the land of Mesopotamia ('the Land between the Rivers') which they have irrigated from time immemorial. It is used extensively for irrigation.

Tijuana Mexico. Town in the NW of Baja

California on the Tijuana R. and on the US–Mexico frontier 19 km (12 miles) SE of San Diego (California). Pop. (1990) 698,752.

Tourist resort, catering largely for Americans; gambling casinos, racecourses and other amenities.

Tilburg Netherlands. Industrial town and railway junction in North Brabant 32 km (20 miles) WNW of Eindhoven. Pop. (1992) 160,618.

Important centre of textile manufacture. Other industries inc. dyeing, tanning and soap manufacture.

Tilbury ➤THURROCK.

Tillicoultry Scotland. Town in Clackmannanshire 5 km (3 miles) NE of Alloa at the S foot of the Ochil Hills. Pop. (1986) 4000.

Woollen and paper milling.

Timaru New Zealand. Seaport, railway junction and market town in South Island 153 km (95 miles) SW of Christchurch. Pop. (1985) 28,500.

In a sheep-rearing and grain-producing area. Exports wool, grain, chilled and frozen meat. Also a holiday resort.

Timbuktu (Tombouctou) Mali. Town 720 km (450 miles) NE of Bamako, 10 km (6 miles) N of the Niger R. Pop. (1985) 20,000.

For cents. a centre of caravan routes and a slave market, also trading in salt, cereals and livestock. Changed hands many times; then its prosperity declined with the abolition of the slave trade and again with the diminishing importance of the desert caravans. Seized by the French in 1893.

Timgad Algeria. Ancient Thamugas. Ruined city 29 km (18 miles) ESE of Batna on the lower N slopes of the Aurès Massif. Founded by Trajan AD 100. Destroyed by the Berber in the 7th cent. Excavations begun in 1881 revealed important Roman remains, inc. Trajan's triumphal arch, restored in 1900.

Timişoara (Hungarian **Temesvár**) Romania. Cap. of the Timiş district 418 km

(260 miles) WNW of Bucharest. Pop. (1992) 334,278.

Railway junction. Manufactures textiles, footwear, chemicals and machine-tools. Trade in grain.

It was a Roman settlement, became Hungarian in the 11th cent., was taken by the Turks (1552) and was annexed to Romania from Hungary after World War I.

Timmins Canada. Town in Ontario on the Mattagami R. 209 km (130 miles) N of Sudbury. Pop. (1986) 46,657.

A commercial centre for the Porcupine goldmining region. Founded in 1911 for workers in the Hollinger goldmine. Other minerals inc. silver, zinc and tin.

Timor Indonesia. Largest and most E of the Lesser Sunda Is. in the Malay Archipelago, formerly divided politically between Indonesia (W) and Portugal (E). Area 33,854 sq km (13,071 sq. miles). Mountainous, rising to 2920 m (9578 ft) in Ramelau (East Timor). Chief products copra, sandalwood and coffee.

1. East Timor: Area 14,847 sq km (5732 sq. miles). Pop. (1989) 714,847. Cap. and seaport Dili. Inc. also the enclave of Ocussi Ambeno on the NW coast of Timor.

2. West Timor: Area 14,874 sq km (5743 sq. miles). Pop. (1989) 3,383,490. With adjacent islands, inc. Roti and Savu, forms the province of E Nusa Tenggara, of which the island's chief town, Kupang, is cap. The island of Timor was divided between Portugal and the Netherlands by treaty (1859). The Dutch part passed to Indonesia 1950. After the withdrawal of Portuguese authority from East Timor and the ensuing civil war (1975–6), Indonesia effectively assumed control over the whole island.

Tintagel England. Village in Cornwall 27 km (17 miles) WNW of Launceston. The rugged promontory of Tintagel Head is nearby. Here are the remains of Tintagel Castle, the legendary birthplace of King Arthur. The ruins of an early Celtic monastery were also unearthed on the site.

Tintern Abbey Wales. Ruined abbey in

Monmouthshire beside the R. Wye 6 km (4 miles) N of Chepstow. Founded (1131) by Walter de Clare for Cistercian monks; it inspired Wordsworth's poem, *Lines Composed a Few Miles above Tintern Abbey*.

Tipperary Ireland. 1. Inland county in Munster. Area 4255 sq km (1643 sq. miles). Pop. (1991) 132,620. Now divided for administrative purposes into two areas, North and South. Tipperary (N): area 1996 sq km (771 sq. miles); pop. (1991) 57,829. Tipperary (S): area 2258 sq km (872 sq. miles); pop. (1991) 91,608. Mountainous in parts, with the Knockmealdown Mountains rising to 795 m (2608 ft) (S) and the Galty Mountains to 920 m (3018 ft) in Galtymore (SW). Along its W border are Lough Derg and the R. Shannon, and it is drained by the latter and the R. Suir and their tributaries. In the SW is part of the fertile Golden Vale, where dairy-farming is the main occupation; potatoes and sugar-beet are cultivated. There are minor industries in the main towns, which inc. Clonmel, Cashel, Tipperary, Carrick-on-Suir, Nenagh and Roscrea.

2. Market town in Co. Tipperary 34 km (21 miles) WNW of Clonmel. Pop. (1991) 5033.

In a dairy-farming region. Manufactures cheese, mineral waters, computers and condensed milk.

Tipton England. Industrial town in the West Midlands in the Black Country 6 km (4 miles) SSE of Wolverhampton, from 1966 part of the county borough of Dudley.

Iron-founding, engineering. Manufactures electrical equipment, metal goods and glass.

Tiranë (Tirana) Albania. Cap. 27 km (17 miles) E of Durrës (its port) on the Adriatic and linked with it by railway. Pop. (1990) 243,000. On the edge of a fertile plain.

A communication, service and trading centre; heavy industries expanded after 1951 with new hydroelectric power. Manufactures textiles, soap and tobacco products.

A Roman fortress of *c.* AD 520, the town developed at an important route junction. It grew rapidly under the Turks, esp. in the 17th cent., and was decreed national cap. in 1920 when the centre was redesigned on a grand scale under Italian influence.

Tiree Scotland. Low, windswept island in the Inner Hebrides in Argyll and Bute 23 km (14 miles) W of N Mull. Area 78 sq km (30 sq. miles). Pop. (1991) 768. Visited by many migratory birds.

Tîrgu Jiu Romania. Town situated NW of Bucharest on the Jiu R. in the Gorj district. Pop. (1989) 93,300.

Manufactures inc. furniture, textiles, wood products and bricks. Trades in lumber, livestock and cheese.

Tîrgu Mureş Romania. Cap. of the Mureş district on the Mureş R. 129 km (80 miles) NW of Brasov. Pop. (1992) 163,625.

Market town. Sugar-refining, brewing. Manufactures chemicals, textiles, fertilizers, furniture and soap, and there is some engineering. Trade in timber, grain, sugar and wine. It is the centre of the natural gas industry.

Has a 15th-cent. Gothic church.

Tirol (Tyrol) Austria. Federal state in the W bordering N on Germany and S on Italy. Area 12,648 sq km (4883 sq. miles). Cap. Innsbruck. Pop. (1991) 631,410. Almost entirely mountainous, with the Zillertal Alps, the Ötztal Alps (rising to 3797 m; 12,454 ft, in the Gross Glockner), and part of the Rhaetian Alps in the S, the Lechtal Alps in the NW. Drained SW–NE by the Inn R. The famous Brenner Pass (S), between the Zillertal and Ötztal Alps, links Innsbruck with Bolzano (Italy). Cereals cultivated; dairy cattle raised. The picturesque scenery attracts many tourists. After the unsuccessful rebellion of the peasants, led by Andreas Hofer, against Bavarian rule established by Napoleon (1805), the whole Tirol was restored to Austria in 1814. After World War I, however, S Tirol, inc. a mainly German-speaking area, was awarded to Italy by the Treaty of St Germain (1919), reducing its area by half, and this left E Tirol, with cap. Lienz, separated from the present province.

Tiruchirapalli (Trichinopoly) India. Industrial town and railway junction in Tamil Nadu on the Cauvery R. 306 km (190 miles) SW of Madras. Pop. (1991) 387,200.

Railway engineering. Manufactures textiles, cigars, power generation equipment, gold and silver ware. Other industries inc. steel.

In the town is the Rock of Trichinopoly, 83 m (272 ft) high, ascended by an ornamental stone staircase and surmounted by a temple.

Tirunelveli (Tinnevelly) India. Town in Tamil Nadu 145 km (90 miles) SSW of Madurai. Pop. (1991) 135,825.

Sugar-refining.

Here St Francis Xavier first preached in India and there are important mission stations.

Tisza (Ger. **Theiss**) **River** Ukraine/Hungary/Yugoslavia. River 1344 km (840 miles) long, rising in the NE Carpathians in the W Ukraine and flowing generally W and then S, crossing the Hungarian plain. Passing through Szeged, it joins the Danube below Novi Sad (Serbia). Important fisheries. In Serbia it is linked by canals with the Danube and with Timişoara (Romania). Navigable by ships to Szolnok (Hungary).

Titicaca, Lake Bolivia/Peru. Largest lake in South America (area 8340 sq km; 3220 sq. miles) and, at 3810 m (12,500 ft), the highest in the world, crossed by the boundary between Peru and Bolivia. Consists of the large NW lake Chucuito and the smaller SE lake Uinamarca joined by a narrow strait; drained S by the Desaguadero R. to L. Poopó. Terraces and old shorelines show that it was more extensive in the past. The great depth of the lake (304 m; 997 ft) keeps it at an even all-year temperature of 11°C (52°F), which modifies the climate and makes agriculture (barley, potatoes) possible on the surrounding land. Small steamships ply between Peru and Bolivia, forming an 80-km (50-mile) water link in a rail system from La Paz (Bolivia) to terminals in Peru (Mollendo, Matarani). The ships were built in Britain

and assembled from sections carried from the Peruvian coast.

Titograd ►PODGORICA.

Tiverton England. Market town in Devon on the R. Exe 19 km (12 miles) N of Exeter. Pop. (1991) 14,805. Formerly important in the woollen trade; in the 19th cent. it became famous for lace manufacture. Industries inc. textiles and engineering.

Remains of the 12th-cent. castle. Nearby is Blundell's school (founded 1604), described in *Lorna Doone*.

Tivoli Italy. Ancient Tibur. Town in Roma province, Latium on the Aniene R. 27 km (17 miles) ENE of Rome. Pop. (1990) 55,000.

Manufactures paper and footwear. It is esp. famous for the remains of Hadrian's Villa, the beautiful 16th-cent. Villa d'Este with terraced gardens and the waterfalls which now provide hydroelectric power. It was a favourite resort of wealthy patricians in the days of the Roman Empire and tourism is important today.

Tlaxcala Mexico. 1. The smallest state, in central Mexico. Area 4106 sq km (1551 sq. miles). Pop. (1990) 761,277. Mountainous. Mainly agricultural. Chief crops cereals and maguey (from which the liquor pulque is made).

2. Officially Tlaxcala de Xicohténcatl. Cap. of Tlaxcala state 96 km (60 miles) E of Mexico City on the central plateau at a height of 2255 m (7399 ft). Pop. (1985) 51,000.

The Church of San Francisco, founded (1521) by Cortés, is the oldest in the Americas. On a nearby hill is the famous Sanctuary of Ocotlán.

Tlemcen (Tilimsen) Algeria. Ancient Pomaria. Town in the Tell (NW) 113 km (70 miles) SW of Oran near the Morocco frontier. Pop. (1987) 107,632. Linked by rail with Oran and Oujda (Morocco). In a fertile region where olives, fruits and cereals are cultivated.

Large trade in agricultural produce, wool and sheep. Manufactures hosiery, footwear, furniture. Handicraft industries, e.g. carpets, rugs and brassware.

Architecturally one of the most famous of Arab towns, the mosques, minarets, dating from the Middle Ages. Flourished from the 13th to the 16th cent. Declined after capture by the Turks (1553). Occupied by the French 1842, but has remained a predominantly Muslim town.

Toamasina Madagascar. Seaport on the E coast (Indian Ocean) 225 km (140 miles) ENE of Antananarivo and connected with it by rail. Pop. (1990) 145,431. The deep-water harbour was completed in 1935.

Exports coffee, rice and sugar. Industries inc. meat-packing.

Tobago West Indies. Island NE of Trinidad. ►TRINIDAD AND TOBAGO.

Tobata ►KITAKYUSHU.

Tobermory Scotland. Small fishing port on the N coast of the island of Mull, Argyll and Bute. Pop. (1991) 825. Resort.

A Spanish galleon was sunk in the bay in 1588 and several attempts have been made to recover the supposed treasure.

Tobol River Russia. River 1290 km (800 miles) long, rising in the S Ural Mountains and flowing generally NNE past Kustanai and Kurgan to join the Irtysh R. at Tobolsk.

Tobolsk Russia. Town in the Tyumen region at the confluence of the Irtysh and Tobol rivers 193 km (120 miles) NE of Tyumen.

Sawmilling. Trade in fish and furs.

Founded in 1587, it has an old fortress of the reign of Peter the Great built in the style of the Moscow Kremlin. It was long the chief administrative and commercial centre of W Siberia, but it declined when the Trans-Siberian Railway was built.

Tobruk Libya. Small port in E Cyrenaica 362 km (225 miles) E of Benghazi on the coast road. Pop. (1986) 60,000. A supply port in World War II, changing hands 5 times; finally taken by the British 1942.

Tocantins River Brazil. River 2700 km (1680 miles) long rising in Goiás state on the

central plateau, flowing generally N to join the Pará R. 80 km (50 miles) WSW of Belém. Chief tributary the Araguaia R. Navigable by ocean-going ships for about 209 km (130 miles) to Tocuruí; from here a railway circumvents a series of rapids to Jatobá.

Tocopilla Chile. Port in Antofagasta province on the arid N coast 177 km (110 miles) N of Antofagasta. Pop. (1985) 22,600.

Exports nitrates and iodine from the caliche fields inland. Supplies electric power to the Chuquicamata coppermine, from which it takes copper ores for smelting and export. Fishing industry.

Todmorden England. Town in West Yorkshire on the R. Calder 11 km (7 miles) SE of Burnley. Pop. (1991) 11,969.

Manufactures cotton goods and textile machinery.

Togliatti Russia. Formerly Stavropol; renamed 1964 in honour of Palmiro Togliatti (1893–1964), the Italian Communist leader. River port near the S end of the Samara Reservoir (Volga R.) 64 km (40 miles) WNW of Samara. Pop. (1994) 689,000.

Industrial centre. Ship-repairing, engineering and food-processing. Manufactures chemicals, synthetic rubber and furniture.

Togo. Republic in W Africa on the Gulf of Guinea, bounded in the N by Burkina Faso, E by Benin and W by Ghana. Area 56,785 sq km (21,925 sq. miles). Pop. (1995) 4,138,000 (26 per cent urban). Life expectancy, 53 years male, 57 female. Cap. and chief seaport Lomé. Other cities Sokodé, Kpalimé. Currency: CFA franc = 100 centimes. Both the N and the S are lowlands; the N is savannah and the S is tropical rainforest, fringed by coastal lagoons. The central area is crossed SSW–NNE by mountains rising to nearly 900 m (2952 ft). Land use: forested 29 per cent, meadows and pastures 33 per cent, agricultural and under permanent cultivation 12 per cent. French is the official lang., but Ewe Kabra and other local lang. are spoken. Over 50 per cent have traditional beliefs, Christian 27 per cent, Muslim 12 per cent.

Cacao, palm kernels and copra are the main products in the S, and coffee is grown on the interior uplands and these are the main agricultural exports. Increasing quantities of phosphates have been mined in recent years and are now over 50 per cent of total exports. It has a tropical climate and subsistence crops inc. yams and millet. Industry is small-scale and inc. cement, textiles and food-processing. There is an oil refinery at Lomé.

Togoland was annexed by Germany in 1884, but the N frontiers of the protectorate were not fixed till 1899. After World War I it was divided and placed under British (W) and French (E) League of Nations mandate. British Togoland was administered as part of the Gold Coast (now Ghana) and joined Ghana when it became independent in 1956. The remainder became a UN Trust Territory administered by France and achieved independence as a republic in 1960. There has been great political instability and the government has been controlled by the military with a 79-member High Council of the Republic. In 1991 pressure was brought to establish a multi-party political system.

Tokaj (Tokay) Hungary. Town in Borsod-Abauj-Zemplen county at the confluence of the Tisza and Bodrog rivers. Pop. (1990) 5000. From the vineyards in the neighbourhood, on the slopes of the Hegyalja, comes Tokay wine, which has been produced for 700 years.

Tokat Turkey. Cap. of Tokat province 80 km (50 miles) NNW of Sivas. Pop. (1985) 73,008.

Manufactures copperware and leather goods.

Tokelau Islands S Pacific. Group of 3 atolls (Atafu, Nukunono, Fakaofo) 480 km (300 miles) N of Western Samoa. Area 10 sq km (4 sq. miles). Pop. (1991) 1577.

The soil is infertile and the economy is based on fishing, crops and livestock. It exports copra.

Formerly part of the Gilbert and Ellice Is.

Colony. Transferred to New Zealand 1926; became part of New Zealand 1949. In the late 1960s many of the inhabitants emigrated to New Zealand. The inhabitants are British subjects and New Zealand citizens.

Tokushima Japan. Cap. of Tokushima prefecture in NE Shikoku 113 km (70 miles) SW of Osaka. Pop. (1992) 264,503.

Seaport. Large market town. Manufactures chemicals, cotton goods and saké.

Tokyo Japan. Cap. of Japan virtually co-extensive with Tokyo prefecture, in central Honshu at the mouth of the Sumida R. on Tokyo Bay. Pop. (1992) 8,129,377.

Important seaport since the deepening of the harbour, handling mainly coastal shipping; its port amalgamated with Yokohama as Keihin in 1941. Also the leading Japanese business centre; has a great variety of industries, inc. shipbuilding, engineering, printing and publishing. Manufactures inc. textiles, chemicals, cars, electrical and electronic goods. All road distances in Japan are measured from the famous Nihnbashi, or Bridge of Japan, over the Sumida R.; the Shiba and Ueno are the most celebrated of the many parks.

Founded in the mid 15th cent. and known as Edo, it was not important until its castle was occupied by the first of the Tokugawa shoguns. In 1868, with the abolition of the shogunate, it replaced Kyoto as imperial cap. and was renamed Tokyo ('Eastern Capital'). In 1923 an earthquake and the ensuing fire destroyed much of the city and killed tens of thousands of its inhabitants. Reconstruction was largely designed to prevent a recurrence of the disaster and massive modern buildings arose, dwarfing the ancient temples.

Tolbukhin ▶DÓBRICH.

Toledo Spain. 1. Province in New Castile in central Spain. Area 15,368 sq km (5925 sq. miles). Pop. (1991) 377,152. Generally mountainous, with the Montes de Toledo (S) rising to over 1350 m (4428 ft). Watered by the Tagus (Tajo) R. and its tributaries.

Sheep and goats are raised. Wheat, barley cultivated.

2. Ancient Toletum. Cap. of Toledo province on the Tagus R. 64 km (40 miles) SSW of Madrid. Pop. (1991) 45,377.

Still famous for its swords, as it was 2000 years ago; also manufactures firearms and textiles.

Stands on a granite hill flanked on 3 sides by the Tagus, with narrow, winding streets. With its historic buildings and its many art treasures, one of Spain's outstanding cities. Its archbishop is the primate of Spain and the magnificent 13th-cent. cathedral is notable for stained-glass windows, tapestries and paintings (El Greco, Goya, Rubens). The house where El Greco (1542–1614) lived is now a museum; many fine churches and two Moorish bridges. Captured by the Romans in the 2nd cent. BC. Became cap. of the Visigothic kingdom. After being recaptured from the Moors (1085), cap. of Spain. Declined when Philip II moved the cap. to Madrid (1561).

Toledo USA. Important Great Lakes port in Ohio at the W end of L. Erie. Pop. (1990) 332,943.

Trade in coal, oil and agricultural produce. Also a railway, industrial and commercial centre. Industries inc. shipbuilding and the manufacture of vehicles, glass, machine-tools, machinery and electrical equipment.

Toliary Madagascar. Formerly Tulear. Cap. of province of same name and port situated SW of Antananarivo on the Mozambique Channel. Pop. (1990) 61,460.

Exports inc. agricultural products, mother-of-pearl, tortoise-shell and edible molluscs.

Tolpuddle England. Village in Dorset 11 km (7 miles) ENE of Dorchester. Made famous by the 'Tolpuddle Martyrs', agricultural labourers who were condemned to transportation in 1834 for forming a trade union.

Toluca (Toluca de Lerdo) Mexico. Cap. of Mexico state 64 km (40 miles) WSW of Mexico City at a height of 2640 m (8659 ft). Pop. (1990) 327,865.

Manufactures textiles, food products, pottery, cars and machinery. There is brewing and distilling. The Toluca valley breeds bulls for Mexican bullfights.

Tolyatti ►TOGLIATTI.

Tomaszów Mazowiecki Poland. Industrial town in the Piotrków Trybunalski voivodeship on the Pilica R. 48 km (30 miles) SE of Łódź. Pop. (1991) 69,900.

Manufactures textiles and bricks. Tanning and flour-milling.

Tombouctou ►TIMBUKTU.

Tomsk Russia. Cap. of the Tomsk region on the Tom R., a tributary of the Ob R., and on a branch of the Trans-Siberian Railway 193 km (120 miles) NE of Novosibirsk. Pop. (1992) 505,000.

Industrial centre. Manufactures machinery, electrical equipment, ball-bearings and matches. Also an educational centre, with a university (1888) and other academic institutions.

Founded 1604. Developed in the early 19th cent. when gold was discovered in the neighbourhood; became a leading commercial centre. Declined when bypassed by the Trans-Siberian Railway and revived again on being associated with the development of the Kuznetsk Basin.

Tonbridge England. Market town in Kent on the R. Medway 19 km (12 miles) SW of Maidstone. Pop. (1994) 34,260.

Manufactures cricket balls. Printing and sawmilling.

Tonga. Kingdom of 169 islands and islets situated SE of Fiji in the South Pacific Ocean. There are 3 main groups, Tongatabu in the S, Ha'apai in the centre and Vava'u in the N. Area 780 sq km (301 sq. miles). Pop. (1995) 100,400 (39 per cent urban). Life expectancy, 66 years male, 70 female. Cap. Nuku'alofa. Other towns Mu'a, Neiafu, Haveluloto. Currency: Pa'anga = 100 seniti. The islands are of coral and volcanic origin; 36 are inhabited. Kao, 1014 m (3326 ft), an

Toronto

extinct volcano, is the highest point. The climate is semi-tropical. Land use: forested 11 per cent, meadows and pastures 6 per cent, agricultural and under permanent cultivation 67 per cent. The government owns all land. Tongan and English are the official langs. The majority of Tongans are Christian and adherents of the Free Wesleyan Church.

The main industries are tourism and coconut-pressing. Exports inc. fish, copra, coconut oil, melons, taro, root crops, bananas and vanilla.

The islands were discovered by the Dutch in 1616 and were visited in 1773 by Capt. Cook, who named them the Friendly Is. English Methodist missionaries arrived in 1822 and the ruler King George I was converted to Christianity in 1831, to be followed by his people. In 1862 a constitutional monarchy was established, preparing the way for the present form of democratic government. The group came under British protection in 1900 achieving independence in 1970. Tonga is a constitutional monarchy and the Legislative Assembly is composed of 9 nobles, elected by their peers, 9 elected representatives of the people and 11 Privy Councillors. There are no political parties.

Tonlé Sap, Lake Cambodia. Lake in the central plains, linked with the Mekong R. by the Tonlé Sap R. Area (dry season) about 2600 sq km (1000 sq. miles). In the rainy season (July–Oct.) the Mekong R. discharges into the lake, which expands to 10,360 sq km (4000 sq. miles) or more and acts as a vast flood reservoir. The Tonlé Sap R. defies gravity and flows uphill for half the year. As the spring waters melting off the Himalayas, coupled with the regional monsoon-swollen tributaries, cause the Mekong to expand beyond its capacity, the waters are sent gushing backwards up the Tonlé Sap, to burst the banks of the lake. Water levels rise by up to 14 m (45 ft) and a third of the country's fertile land is flooded. In the dry season (Nov.–June) the lake discharges into the Mekong R. Fishing is important and there is considerable trade in live, dried and smoked fish.

Toowoomba Australia. Town in Queensland 113 km (70 miles) W of Brisbane. Pop. (1990) 82,438.

Market town for the Darling Downs. Butter, cheese and clothing factories, iron foundries, pecan-nut processing, saddlery and machine shops. Coalmines are in the neighbourhood.

Topeka USA. State cap. of Kansas on the Kansas R. 96 km (60 miles) W of Kansas City. Pop. (1990) 119,883.

Industrial and commercial centre in an agricultural region, and it manufactures tyres. There is railway engineering, flour-milling, meat-packing, printing and publishing.

Tor Bay England. Inlet in the S coast of Devon between the headlands of Hope's Nose and Berry Head. Torquay, Paignton and Brixham (together forming the county borough of Torbay) are on its shore.

Torbay England. Unitary authority in Devon formed from the former municipal borough of Torquay and the urban districts of Paignton and Brixham. Pop. (1991) 112,800.

Torfaen Wales. County Borough created 1996, formerly part of Gwent. Pop. (1994) 91,000.

Torino ➤TURIN.

Torne (Finnish **Tornio**) **River** Finland/Sweden. River 512 km (320 miles) long rising in N Sweden, passing through L. Torne, flowing generally SE to form part of the Swedish–Finnish border and entering the Gulf of Bothnia. The towns of Haparanda (Sweden) and Tornio (Finland) are at the mouth.

Toronto Canada. Cap. and largest city of Ontario, second largest city in Canada (after Montreal), at the mouth of the Humber R. on the N shore of L. Ontario. Pop. (1991) 635,395.

Important industrial, commercial and financial centre. Varied industries inc. aircraft, shipbuilding, railway engineering, printing and publishing, meat-packing, food-processing, and iron and steel. Manufactures agricultural machinery. Cheap electric power supplied from Niagara Falls. The finest natural harbour on the Great Lakes; handles an immense volume of freight, esp. wheat and other agricultural produce. Educational and cultural centre; the university was founded in 1827 (as King's College).

Anglican and Roman Catholic cathedrals and many churches. Lakeside bathing beaches. Numerous parks: High Park is the largest; Queen's Park contains the provincial parliament building; the annual Canadian National Exhibition is held in Exhibition Park. The name Toronto is derived from a Huron Indian expression probably meaning 'Meeting Place'. Fort Toronto, a French fur-trading post, was established in 1749; it was soon occupied by the British. Became cap. of Upper Canada (1793) as York, but when incorporated as a city (1834) the name Toronto was restored. It became cap. of Ontario in 1867.

Torquay England. Town in Devon on Tor Bay 29 km (18 miles) S of Exeter, from 1968 part of Torbay. Pop. (1991) 59,587. Popular seaside resort and yachting centre well known for its mild climate. It has Torre Abbey, founded in 1196 and within the borough are Babbacombe, a smaller resort, Cockington, with a forge and Kent's Cavern (stalactites), where prehistoric remains were discovered in the 19th cent.

Torrance USA. Industrial and residential town in California 24 km (15 miles) SSW of Los Angeles. Pop. (1990) 133,107.

Industries inc. oil-refining, railway engineering, computers, electronics and aerospace.

Torre Annunziata Italy. Seaport and industrial town in Napoli province, Campania, on the Bay of Naples. Pop. (1991) 58,000.

Manufactures pasta, firearms and iron.

Torre del Greco Italy. Seaport, resort and industrial town in Napoli province, Campania on the Bay of Naples 11 km (7 miles) SE of Naples. Pop. (1991) 102,647.

Coral-fishing and cameo and pasta manufacture.

Built on the 1631 lava stream from Vesuvius, it has often been damaged by earthquakes and eruptions.

Torremolinos ➤MÁLAGA.

Torreón Mexico. Town in Coahuila state 320 km (200 miles) W of Monterrey. Pop. (1990) 439,436.

In the cotton and wheat growing Laguna district. Silver, zinc and copper mines in the neighbourhood. Industries inc. textile and flour milling, brewing and chemicals.

Torres Strait Australasia. Channel between the S coast of New Guinea and the N coast of the Cape York Peninsula about 145 km (90 miles) wide, connecting the Arafura Sea (W) and the Coral Sea (E). Discovered (1606) by the Spanish navigator Luis Vacz de Torres.

Torridge River England. River 64 km (40 miles) long in Devon rising near the Cornish border and flowing ESE and then NNW past Great Torrington and Bideford to the R. Taw estuary on the N Devon coast.

Torrington (England) ➤GREAT TORRINGTON.

Torrington USA. Industrial town in Connecticut on the Naugatuck R. 35 km (22 miles) W of Hartford. Pop. (1989) 35,000.

Manufactures hardware, machinery, electrical appliances, anti-friction bearings, corrugated containers and brushes.

Birthplace of John Brown (1800–59), the American abolitionist.

Tortola British Virgin Islands. The main island of the group, situated between St John and Virgin Gorda. Area 54 sq km (21 sq. miles). Pop. (1991) 13,586. Rises to 543 m (1781 ft) above sea level in Mount Sage.

The main occupations are stock-rearing and the growing of sugar-cane, fruit and vegetables. Charcoal is also produced and exported.

Tortosa Spain. Ancient Dertosa. Port in Tarragona province on the Ebro R. 35 km (22 miles) above its mouth. Pop. (1991) 28,561.

Flour-milling. Manufactures soap and pottery.

Built largely of granite, the town has a 14th-cent. cathedral occupying the site of a 10th-cent. mosque. An important town under the Moors.

Tortuga Haiti. In Spanish 'Turtle'. Island off the NW of Haiti. Area 181 sq km (70 sq. miles). Haunt of English and French buccaneers in the 17th cent.

Toruń (Ger. **Thorn**) Poland. Cap. of the Toruń voivodeship on the Vistula R. 43 km (27 miles) ESE of Bydgoszcz. Pop. (1991) 202,000.

Industrial town and railway junction. Manufactures machinery, chemicals and textiles. Sawmilling. Trade in grain and timber.

University (1945). Founded by the Teutonic Order in the 13th cent. Became an important Hanseatic town, but declined after the Partitions of Poland. Was included (as Thorn) in Prussia 1815–1918. Birthplace of Nicolas Copernicus, astronomer (1473–1543).

Totnes England. Market town in Devon on the R. Dart 11 km (7 miles) WSW of Torquay. Pop. (1991) 6,929.

Industries inc. boatbuilding, sawmilling, brewing, country crafts and the production of bacon and cream.

Has the ruins of a Norman castle, a 15th-cent. church and a 16th–17th-cent. guildhall, as well as two of the four original town gates. Trout and salmon fishing in the river.

Tottenham England. Part of the London borough of Haringey. Largely residential, with some industry (furniture). The 16th/18th-cent. mansion Bruce Castle (in Bruce Castle Park) now houses a museum.

Tottori Japan. Cap. of Tottori prefecture in W Honshu on the Sea of Japan 148 km (92 miles) WNW of Kyoto. Pop. (1992) 141,161.

Seaport. Industrial centre. Manufactures textiles and paper.

Touggourt Algeria. Town and oasis 193 km (120 miles) S of Biskra, with which it is linked by railway. Pop. 26,000.

Commercial centre. Trade in dates. Vast numbers of date palms in the oasis. On the oil pipeline from Hassi Messaoud to Bougie.

Toulon France. Important naval base on the Mediterranean Sea in the Var department 47 km (29 miles) ESE of Marseille. Pop. (1990) 170,167. Has an excellent roadstead, sheltered by hills and a breakwater.

Industries, shared by La Seyne-sur-Mer (5 km; 3 miles SW), inc. shipbuilding and ship-repairing; manufactures armaments and chemicals.

The arsenal and fortifications were constructed by Vauban in the 17th cent. after Henry IV had encouraged its development as a naval base. In 1942 the French fleet was scuttled here to prevent it from falling into German hands.

Toulouse France. Ancient Tolosa. Prefecture of the Haute-Garonne department in Languedoc, on the Garonne R. and the Canal du Midi. Pop. (1990) 365,933.

Important commercial and industrial centre on the route to the Mediterranean through the Gate of Carcassonne. Trade in the agricultural produce of Aquitaine. Industries inc. flour-milling, tanning, publishing, printing, technological activities (data-processing, computer and robotics) and aerospace and aeronautics (Concorde and the European Airbus). Manufactures aircraft, chemicals, agricultural machinery electrical equipment, footwear and hosiery.

Seat of France's second oldest university (founded 1230). Has a magnificant 11th/13th-cent. Romanesque basilica, St Sernin; a 13th/16th-cent. Gothic cathedral, St Étienne; the 13th-cent. church of the Jacobins; the 18th-cent. Capitole (town hall); several outstanding Renaissance mansions. Was cap. of the Visigoths (419–507), of the kingdom of Aquitaine (781–848) and of the comté of Toulouse until it passed to the French crown (1271). Scene of many battles and massacres during the papal crusade against the Albigenses, whose headquarters it was. Continued to play an important political role in S France until the French Revolution (1790). Expanded rapidly with the development of roads and railways in the 19th cent.

Touquet, Le France. Seaside resort in the Pas-de-Calais department 24 km (15 miles) S of Boulogne. Pop. (1968) 4403. With adjoining Paris-Plage, it is often known as Le Touquet-Paris-Plage.

Touraine France. Former province corresponding approximately to the present department of Indre-et-Loire, with cap. Tours. Drained by the Loire R. and its tributaries, the Cher, Indre and Vienne. Known as the 'Garden of France'. Took its name from the Turones, the tribe inhabiting it when Caesar conquered Gaul. The famous châteaux were built when French monarchs and nobles came to live in the region.

Tourcoing France. Industrial town in the Nord department 13 km (8 miles) NNE of Lille. Pop. (1990) 94,425. With its twin town of Roubaix (just SSE), produces most of France's woollen goods. Also manufactures carpets, clothing, cotton goods and leather.

Tournai (Flemish **Doornik**) Belgium. Industrial town in the Hainaut province on the Scheldt R. 19 km (12 miles) ESE of Roubaix (France). Pop. (1993) 67,875.

Manufactures carpets, hosiery, cement and leather.

The famous cathedral, dating from the 11th cent., is part Romanesque and part Gothic.

Tours France. Ancient Caesarodunum. Prefecture of the Indre-et-Loire department on the strip of land between the Loire and the Cher rivers near the confluence 206 km (128 miles) SW of Paris. Pop. (1990) 133,403.

Manufactures agricultural machinery, fertilizers, cement, textiles, pottery and food products. Trade in wine and brandy. Popular tourist centre for the castles of the Loire valley.

Has a 12th/16th-cent. Gothic cathedral, a 17th/18th-cent. former archbishop's palace (now an art museum) and several 15th-cent.

houses. Fell to the Visigoths in the 5th cent. and to the Franks in the 6th. Charles Martel defeated the Moors about 48 km (30 miles) S of the town at the so-called Battle of Tours (732). A silk industry was established by Louis XI, but this declined after the revocation of the Edict of Nantes (1685) and the flight of the Huguenot weavers. Birthplace of Honoré de Balzac (1799–1850).

Towcester England. Market town in Northamptonshire 13 km (8 miles) SSW of Northampton. Pop. (rural district, 1971) 20,998. Site of a Roman station (on Watling Street). Claims to be the 'Eatanswill' of *Pickwick Papers*.

Tower Hamlets England. London borough, comprising the former metropolitan boroughs of Bethnal Green, Stepney and Poplar. The centre of London's 'East End'. Pop. (1994) 170,500.

Townsville Australia. Seaport in NE Queensland on the Cleveland Bay 1110 km (690 miles) NW of Brisbane. Pop. (1991) 101,398. The second port in the state serving a vast hinterland in the N.

Receives minerals from the Mt Isa–Cloncurry region and cattle from the E highlands and the Great Artesian Basin. Exports wool, frozen meat, sugar and minerals. It has meat works and a copper refinery.

Toyama Japan. Cap. of Toyama prefecture, Honshu on Toyama Bay 177 km (110 miles) N of Nagoya. Pop. (1992) 323,015.

Leading centre for the manufacture of patent medicines and drugs; also manufactures textiles, chemicals and machinery.

Toyohashi Japan. Industrial town in Aichi prefecture, Honshu 64 km (40 miles) SE of Nagoya. Pop. (1992) 346,741.

Food-processing and metalworking. Manufactures cotton goods.

Toyonaka Japan. Town situated N of Osaka in Honshu. Pop. (1992) 406,126.

Wheat, rice and flowers are grown.

Trabzon (Trebizond) Turkey. Cap. of Trabzon province on the Black Sea coast

169 km (105 miles) NW of Erzurum. Pop. (1990) 143,941.

Port, modernized since World War II. Exports tobacco, hazelnuts and flour. Food-processing.

A Greek colony of the 8th cent BC. Rose to greatness when it became the cap. of an empire, founded by Alexius Comnenus, which lasted from AD 1204 to 1461, when it was taken by the Turks.

Trafalgar, Cape Spain. Headland on the Atlantic coast of Cádiz province near the Strait of Gibraltar. Scene of the decisive naval victory of the British fleet which ended Napoleon's sea power and in which Nelson was mortally wounded (1805).

Trail Canada. Industrial town in SE British Columbia on the Columbia R. near the US frontier. Pop. (1986) 7948.

Smelting of lead, zinc, copper and silver. Manufactures chemicals.

Tralee Ireland. County town of Kerry on the R. Lee near Tralee Bay, with which it is connected by ship canal. Pop. (1991) 17,109.

Market and tourist town. Manufactures textiles and food products. Exports dairy produce.

The port of Fenit, birthplace of St Brendan (483–578), is 11 km (7 miles) W.

Trani Italy. Adriatic seaport in Bari province, Apulia 43 km (27 miles) WNW of Bari. Pop. (1985) 45,000. Produces wine.

Has a 12th/13th-cent. Romanesque cathedral and a 13th/16th-cent. castle. It framed the first of the medieval codes of maritime law (1063).

Transcaucasia. Territory lying S of the Caucasus separated from the rest of European Russia; comprising the republics of Georgia, Azerbaijan and Armenia.

Transkei South Africa. Former homeland given 'independence' in 1974. It became part of East Cape Province in 1994 with the end of apartheid.

Transvaal South Africa. Former province

in the NE between the Limpopo (N) and the Vaal (S) rivers.

Transylvania Romania. Former province, separated from Moldavia (E) by the Carpathians and from Walachia (S) by the Transylvanian Alps. Mainly plateau 300–500 m (984–1640 ft) high, rising in the Bihar Mountains (W) to 1800 m (5094 ft); crossed NE–SW by the Mureş R.

Largely forested. The mineral resources are as yet little exploited. Cereals, potatoes and vines cultivated in the fertile valleys. Chief towns Cluj, Braşov. Most of the people are Romanians, but there are considerable numbers of Hungarians and Germans. Part of the Roman province of Dacia from AD 103. Incorporated into Hungary early in the 11th cent. Virtually independent 1526–1699, then part of the Austro–Hungarian Empire. The Magyar element in the pop. worked continually for union with Hungary, ultimately gained in 1867. Ceded to Romania (1920) after World War I. Hitler awarded most of the area to Hungary (1940); it was returned to Romania 1947. Divided into Regions (inc. the predominantly Hungarian Magyar Autonomous Region) 1952; changed to Districts 1968.

Trapani Italy. Ancient Drepanum. Cap. of Trapani province in W Sicily. Pop. (1985) 73,300.

Seaport with tuna-fishing and it produces salt, wine and pasta.

An important Carthaginian naval base in the 1st Punic War.

Trasimeno (Perugia), **Lake** Italy. The largest lake in central Italy in Umbria 18 km (11 miles) W of Perugia. Area 128 sq km (49 sq. miles). Drained by an artificial tunnel to a tributary of the Tiber R. On its N shore Hannibal defeated the Romans under Flaminius (217 BC).

Trebizond ▶TRABZON.

Treblinka Poland. Extermination camp about 100 km (60 miles) NE of Warsaw, near the town of Malkinia. Used by the Nazis (1942–3) to exterminate some 800,000 people, mainly Jews and Polish partisans. In 1943 the Jews rose in revolt and burnt the camp down. Some 500 escaped but only 52 survived. Now a museum memorial.

Tredegar Wales. Town in Blaenau Gwent 26 km (16 miles) NW of Newport. Pop. (1991) 15,390. Industries inc. engineering.

Trelew Argentina. Town in Chubut province (Patagonia) 16 km (10 miles) WNW of Rawson. Pop. (1986) 90,000.

Market town serving agricultural settlements. Sawmilling, brewing.

Founded (1881) by Welshmen.

Trengganu ➤TERENGGANU.

Trentino-Alto Adige Italy. Mountainous region bordering on Switzerland and Austria and comprising the provinces of Trento and Bolzano, formerly part of Austria. Area 13,618 sq km (5258 sq. miles). Pop. (1991) 934,731.

Trento (Trent) Italy. Cap. of Trento province in Trentino-Alto Adige on the Adige R. and on the Brenner Pass route through the Alps. Pop. (1990) 102,124.

Electrical engineering. Manufactures chemicals and cement.

A picturesque town with a 13th/16th-cent. cathedral and the 16th-cent. Church of Santa Maria Maggiore where the Council of Trent met (1545–63). Passed to Austria 1803; restored to Italy 1919.

Trenton USA. State cap. of New Jersey at the head of navigation on the Delaware R. Pop.(1990) 88,675.

Industrial centre. Manufactures wire rope, cables, pottery, aircraft equipment, steam turbines and textiles.

First settled in 1679. At the Battle of Trenton (1776) Washington defeated the British in the American War of Independence.

Trent River England. Chief river in the Midlands 274 km (170 miles) long, rising on Biddulph Moor, N Staffordshire and flowing first SE past Stoke-on-Trent, then turning NE past Burton-on-Trent, Nottingham,

Newark and Gainsborough to join the R. Ouse 24 km (15 miles) W of Hull and form the Humber. Chief tributaries the Dove, Derwent, Soar and Devon. Linked with the Mersey by the Trent and Mersey Canal.

Tres Arroyos Argentina. Town in Buenos Aires province 185 km (115 miles) ENE of Bahía Blanca. Pop. (1985) 70,000.

Market town in a wheat-growing and stock-rearing area. Flour-milling. Manufactures furniture.

Tresco ➤ISLES OF SCILLY.

Trèves ➤TRIER.

Treviso Italy. Cap. of Treviso province in Veneto 27 km (17 miles) NNW of Venice. Pop. (1985) 85,800.

Manufactures agricultural machinery, paper and brushes, and lamps.

The cathedral (12th-cent., later restored) contains work by Titian and by Bordone (1500–71), who was born here.

Trichinopoly ➤TIRUCHIRAPALLI.

Trier (Fr. **Trèves**) Germany. Town in Rhineland-Palatinate on the Moselle R. 96 km (60 miles) SW of Coblenz. Pop. (1989) 94,119.

Centre of the Moselle wine trade. Manufactures textiles, leather goods.

Named after the Treveri, a tribe of the Belgae, it was important from Roman times and among its remains are the Porta Nigra (a fortified gate), a large amphitheatre and baths. The cathedral, built from a Roman basilica and extended in the 11th–13th cent., has a relic, the 'Holy Coat of Trier', said to be the seamless coat of Christ. Birthplace of Karl Marx (1818–83).

Trieste (Slovenian **Trst**) Italy. Seaport on the Gulf of Trieste on the NE coast of the Adriatic Sea 117 km (73 miles) ENE of Venice. Pop. (1991) 231,047.

Important transit port for Central Europe; also an industrial centre. Shipbuilding, oil-refining and steel. Manufactures marine engines, jute products and paper.

The narrow, winding streets of the old

town extend up Monte Giusto, on which are the cathedral and castle; near the sea is the Piazza dell' Unità. The white castle of Miramare, once the home of the Archduke Maximilian who became Emperor of Mexico, is 6 km (4 miles) NW. A port in Roman times. Passed to Austria in 1382 and (with brief interruptions) remained in Austrian hands till 1918. An imperial free port 1719–1891. Ceded to Italy after World War I. After World War II (1947) it was made cap. of the Free Territory of Trieste, which was divided into Zone A (Italian, occupied by US and UK forces), inc. the city of Trieste, and Zone B (Yugoslav) to the S, larger but less populous. Most of Zone A passed to Italy, and Trieste became cap. of Friuli-Venezia Giulia (1954).

Triglav, Mount Slovenia. Country's highest peak (2863 m; 9391 ft) in the Julian Alps 64 km (40 miles) NW of Ljubljana, near the Austrian and Italian frontiers.

Trikkala Greece. 1. *Nome* in Thessaly, bounded on the W by the Pindus Mountains. Area 3384 sq km (1307 sq. miles). Pop. (1991) 137,819.
Cereals and olives cultivated.
2. Cap. of Trikkala *nome*, 60 km (37 miles) WSW of Larissa. Pop. (1981) 45,160.
Market town. Trade in cereals and tobacco.
Seriously damaged by earthquake in 1954.

Trim Ireland. County town of Meath on the R. Boyne 42 km (26 miles) NW of Dublin. Pop. (1991) 1784.
Market town. Trade in cereals.
In the castle (founded in the 12th cent.) Henry of Lancaster, afterwards Henry IV, was imprisoned by Richard II. There are also two gates of the old town wall.

Trincomalee Sri Lanka. Seaport on the NE coast. Pop. (1981) 44,313. Has one of the world's outstanding natural harbours; formerly a British naval base. Was settled by Tamils from S India: their famous Temple of a Thousand Columns, standing on a height in the E of the town, was destroyed by the

Portuguese (1622) and the Dutch built a fortress on its site (1676).

Tring England. Town in W Hertfordshire 23 km (14 miles) WNW of St Albans. Pop. (1991) 11,282. Nearby is Tring Park with a zoological museum bequeathed (1938) by Lord Rothschild to the British Museum.

Trinidad and Tobago West Indies. Trinidad is an island in the Caribbean Sea 12 km (8 miles) off the NE coast of Venezuela, part of the state of Trinidad and Tobago. There are also several islets inc. Chacachacare, Huevos, Monos and Gaspar Grande. Tobago, the smaller island, lies 31 km (19 miles) further to the NE. Area 5128 sq km (1980 sq. miles) of which Tobago 300 sq km (116 sq. miles). Pop. (1995) 1,265,000, of which Tobago 50,282 (71 per cent urban). Life expectancy, 68 years male, 73 female. Cap. and chief seaport Port of Spain. Other towns inc. Chaguanas, San Fernando, Arima, Point Fortin, Scarborough. Currency: Trinidad and Tobago dollar = 100 cents. Trinidad is crossed by three ranges of hills E–W, the highest peaks just exceeding 900 m (2952 ft). The climate is tropical and humid. Land use: forested 43 per cent, meadows and pastures 2 per cent, agricultural and under permanent pasture 23 per cent. The lang. is English and the ethnic composition comprises black 43 per cent, East Indian 36 per cent, mixed 16 per cent, white 2 per cent, Chinese 1 per cent. The Christian church has about 70 per cent, Hindu 23 per cent and Muslim 6 per cent.
Petroleum and petroleum products are the chief exports. There are resources of asphalt and natural gas. Tourism is extremely important to the economy and it is the birthplace of the steel band and the calypso. Agricultural products inc. sugar, coconuts and citrus fruits.
Discovered in 1498 by Columbus, Trinidad was ceded to Britain 1802 and Tobago in 1814. Amalgamated with Tobago as a British Crown Colony 1888. The state opted out of the shortlived Federation of the West Indies (1958–62) and became independent in 1962. A republican constitution was adopted in 1976. Trinidad and Tobago is

a multiparty republic and has a bicameral Parliament; a 31-member Senate and a 36-member House of Representatives (2 members for Tobago). The Parliament elects the President.

Tripoli (Ar. **Tarabulus**) Lebanon. Seaport on the Mediterranean coast 72 km (45 miles) NNE of Beirut. Pop. (1988) 160,000.

Has an oil refinery, being a terminus of the pipeline from Iraq. Manufactures textiles, soap and cement. Exports citrus fruits and tobacco.

An ancient city, it became cap. of the Phoenician federation of Tyre, Sidon and Aradus, each with its own district in the town, and was extended and improved under the Seleucids and Romans. Taken by the Arabs 638. Destroyed by the Mamelukes 1289; rebuilt on its present site.

Tripoli (Ar. **Tarabulus**) Libya. Cap., seaport on the Mediterranean coast 640 km (400 miles) W of Benghazi. Pop. (1988) 591,062. Near a large oasis.

Exports esparto grass, hides, dates, salt, sponges. Manufactures tobacco products, soap, leather, rugs and carpets, and pottery. Sponge and tunny fishing.

Founded about the 7th cent. BC by Phoenicians from Tyre and subsequently occupied by Rome; some Roman walls survive. To the E is the ancient city of Leptis Magna (also founded by the Phoenicians) with the most extensive Roman ruins in N Africa. Ruled by Turkey, and a pirate stronghold, from the mid 16th cent. Occupied by the Italians 1911; became the cap. of the Italian colony of Libya. Taken by the British during World War II (1943).

Tripura India. State in the NE, bounded by Bangladesh (N, W and S) and Assam (E). Area 10,486 sq km (4096 sq. miles). Pop. (1991) 2,744,827. Cap. and chief commercial centre Agartala (pop. 157,636). Mainly hilly, with much jungle.

Chief products timber, rice, jute and cotton. Natural gas has been discovered in the state and gas-based power-generating units, industries are being established.

Formerly a princely state, it became a centrally administered area of the Indian Union in 1949 and a Union Territory in 1956.

Tristan da Cunha S Atlantic Ocean. Group of volcanic islands about halfway between South Africa and South America; since 1938 a dependency of St Helena. The largest island, Tristan, in the N (area 41 sq km; 16 sq. miles), has a central volcanic cone 2062 m (6763 ft) high and a circumference at the base of 34 km (21 miles), often snow-capped, with a crater lake.

Potatoes are grown and cattle, sheep and pigs are raised on the NW plateau, and there is fishing.

It was discovered (1506) by the Portuguese Tristão da Cunha. The first permanent settler was Thomas Currie (1810); others arriving from 1817 onwards; the pop. increased from 109 in 1880 to 313 in 1988, all living in the settlement of Edinburgh. In 1961 a volcanic eruption made it necessary to evacuate the inhabitants to Britain; two years later, after the cessation of danger, the majority elected to return to Tristan (1963). Other islands in the group are Gough, Inaccessible and Nightingale Islands, all uninhabited.

Trivandrum ➤THIRUVANANTHAPURAM.

Trnava Slovakia. Market town 43 km (27 miles) NE of Bratislava. Pop. (1990) 73,000.

In a fertile agricultural region. Sugar-refining, brewing. Manufactures fertilizers, textiles, washing-machines and food products.

Detached from Hungary 1920.

Trois Rivières (Three Rivers) Canada. Industrial town in Quebec on the St Lawrence R. at its confluence with the St Maurice R. 129 km (80 miles) NE of Montreal. Pop. (1990) 49,426.

A leading world centre of newsprint production. Iron-founding. Manufactures textiles, clothing and electrical equipment. Hydroelectric power is derived from the St Maurice R.

Trollhättan Sweden. Industrial town in Älvsborg county on the Göta R. 68 km

(42 miles) NNE of Göteborg. Pop. (1991) 51,217.

Manufactures machinery, chemicals and cellulose.

The river here descends 32 m (105 ft) in 6 falls, supplying power for an important hydroelectric plant, which in turn provides electricity for much of S Sweden as well as for the town's industries.

Tromsö Norway. Cap. of Troms county in the N on an island just off the coast. Pop. (1990) 51,218.

Industries inc. fishing, ship repairs, brewing, prefabricated houses, high technology and tourism.

Largest town N of the Arctic Circle and has an Arctic Museum.

Trondheim Norway. Formerly Nidaros, Trondhjem. Cap. of Sör Tröndelag county on Trondheim Fiord and at the mouth of the Nid R. Pop. (1993) 140,718.

Important seaport and fishing centre. Shipbuilding, fish-canning, metalworking are the main industries and it manufactures margarine and soap. Exports wood-pulp, paper, fish and metals.

The cathedral, dating from the 11th cent., is reputedly the finest church in Norway. Founded (996) as Nidaros and was the cap. until 1380. Renamed Trondhjem in the 16th cent., Nidaros (1930–1) and then Trondheim.

Troödos Mountains ➤CYPRUS.

Troon Scotland. Small town in South Ayrshire 10 km (6 miles) N of Ayr. Pop. (1991) 15,231.

Seaside resort. Industries inc. fishing, shipbuilding and breaking.

Trossachs Scotland. In Gaelic, 'the Bristly Country'. Picturesque wooded glen in Stirling, between Loch Achray and Loch Katrine, with Ben Venue (729 m; 2391 ft) to the SW. Described in Scott's *The Lady of the Lake* and *Rob Roy*.

Trouville France. Popular seaside resort and fishing port in the Calvados department at

the mouth of the Touques R. opposite Deauville. Pop. (1990) 6000.

Trowbridge England. Market town in Wiltshire 13 km (8 miles) ESE of Bath. Pop. (1991) 27,600.

Industries inc. brewing, food-processing, clothing, seed-processing and printing. Manufactures mattresses and heating and ventilating equipment.

George Crabbe, English poet (1754–1832), is buried in the parish church. Birthplace of Sir Isaac Pitman, English educationist and inventor of a shorthand system (1813–97).

Troy. Ancient Troja, Ilium. Ancient city in Asia Minor just SE of the entrance to the Dardanelles from the Aegean Sea in the region known as Troas. Excavations begun in 1872 revealed 9 successive cities on the site, of which the Homeric Troy (c. 1200 BC) was probably the 7th.

Troy USA. Industrial town in New York at the head of steamboat navigation on the Hudson R. 11 km (7 miles) NNE of Albany. Pop. (1990) 54,269.

Manufactures clothing (esp. shirts), fire hydrants and brushes.

Home of Samuel Wilson (1816–1906), reputedly the original of 'Uncle Sam'.

Troyes France. Prefecture of the Aube department on the Seine R. 145 km (90 miles) ESE of Paris. Pop. (1990) 60,775.

Road and railway junction. Industrial town. Manufactures knitwear, hosiery, paper, electrical goods and textile machinery. Dyeing and flour-milling.

Has a 13th/16th-cent. cathedral and many churches famous for their stained-glass windows, some of which were damaged in World War II. The bishopric was created in the 4th cent. Became cap. of Champagne and its medieval fairs were renowned – it gave its name to the standard troy weight; its trade suffered severely, however, from the revocation of the Edict of Nantes (1685).

Trucial States ➤UNITED ARAB EMIRATES.

Trujillo Peru. Cap. of La Libertad department in the NW on the coastal plain 13 km (8 miles) NNW of its port Salaverry on the Pan-American Highway. Pop. (1990) 532,000.

Important commercial and industrial centre in an irrigated region producing sugar-cane and rice. Manufactures soap, candles, cocaine, and there is food-processing, tanning and brewing.

Truk Islands ➤CHUUK.

Truro England. Market town in Cornwall on the Truro R. 13 km (8 miles) N of Falmouth. Pop. (1989) 17,000.

Manufactures pottery and biscuits.

The bishopric was established in 1876 and the cathedral was built in Early English style.

Trust Territory of the Pacific Islands ➤MARSHALL ISLANDS, BELAU, NORTH MARIANA ISLANDS, MICRONESIA.

Tsamkong (Chinghai) China. Seaport in Guangdong province on the NE coast of the Luichow peninsula. Pop. 170,000. Developed as a seaport 1954–7. A railway links it with Litang (Kwangi-chuang Autonomous Region) in the interior.

Tselinograd Kazakhstan. Formerly Akmolinsk. Cap. of the Tselinny (Virgin Land) Territory and the Tselinograd region on the Ishim R. 193 km (120 miles) NW of Karaganda. Pop. (1991) 286,000.

Important railway junction, industrial and commercial centre. Industries inc. meat-packing, flour-milling and tanning. Manufactures agricultural machinery.

Founded 1830.

Tshikapa Democratic Republic of the Congo. Town situated 580 km (360 miles) SE of Kinshasa. Pop. (1985) 100,000. Diamond industry centre.

Tsinan ➤JINAN.

Tsinghai ➤QINGHAI.

Tsingtao ➤QINGDAO.

Tsitsihar ➤QIQIUHAR.

Tskhinvali Georgia. Cap. of the South

Ossetian Autonomous Region 88 km (55 miles) NW of Tbilisi. Pop. (1990) 34,000. Fruit-canning.

Tsu Japan. Cap. of Mie prefecture 84 km (52 miles) E of Osaka. Pop. (1990) 161,436.

Industrial centre. Manufactures textiles. There are ancient temples.

Tsuen Wan Hong Kong. One of eight new towns founded in 1963 and the most populous, situated in the New Territories. Pop. (1987) 700,000. Tsuen Wan's container terminal at Kwai Chang is the largest in Asia and one of the largest in the world.

Tsukuba Japan. A 'science' city situated 60 km (37 miles) NE of Tokyo. Pop. (1985) 150,000. It comprises educational and research institutions relocated from the cap.

Tsushima Japan. Group of 5 islands in Nagasaki prefecture between Kyushu (Japan) and South Korea 129 km (80 miles) WNW of Kitakyushu. Area 702 sq km (271 sq. miles). Pop. (1989) 49,000. Chief town Izuhara.

Main occupation fishing.

During the Russo–Japanese War the Russian fleet was utterly defeated by the Japanese nearby (1905).

Tuam Ireland. Market town in Co. Galway 31 km (19 miles) NNE of Galway. Pop. (1991) 3448. Sugar-refining.

Has a Protestant cathedral (founded 1130) and a Roman Catholic cathedral.

Tuapse Russia. Seaport in the Krasnodar Territory on the Black Sea 105 km (65 miles) S of Krasnodar. Pop. (1970) 51,000.

Exports petroleum products. Oil-refining; terminus of pipelines from the Grozny and Maikop oilfields.

Tübingen Germany. Town in Baden-Württemberg on the Neckar R. 31 km (19 miles) SSW of Stuttgart. Pop. (1986) 76,200.

Printing and publishing. Manufactures textiles and precision instruments.

Has a 15th-cent. town hall and church and a 16th-cent. castle.

Tucson USA. Industrial and commercial town and popular health and holiday resort in Arizona 177 km (110 miles) SE of Phoenix at a height of 730 m (2394 ft). Pop. (1990) 405,390.

Railway engineering, flour-milling. Manufactures missile, aeronautical, computer and electronic equipment.

Tucumán, San Miguel de Argentina. Cap. of Tucumán province at the foot of the E Andes in the most populous region of the NW. Pop. (1989) 955,000.

Commercial and industrial centre in a region producing sugar-cane, maize and rice. Sugar-refining, flour-milling and distilling.

An attractive city (the 'garden of Argentina') with many colonial buildings. Cathedral. Founded 1565 and moved to its present site 1580.

Tugela River South Africa. River 480 km (300 miles) long in KwaZulu/Natal, rising on Mont-aux-Sources in the Drakensberg. It soon plunges over the escarpment in a series of falls, passing through a beautiful wooded gorge, then flowing generally E and emptying into the Indian Ocean 80 km (50 miles) NE of Durban. Various battles were fought in its upper basin during the Zulu War (1879).

Tula Russia. Cap. of the Tula region 169 km (105 miles) S of Moscow. Pop. (1992) 541,000.

Railway junction. Industrial centre. Manufactures pig iron, firearms, agricultural machinery and samovars, fuel being derived from the local Moscow—Tula lignite basin. Sugar-refining and flour-milling.

The 16th-cent. kremlin, in the centre of the city, was restored after World War II. Founded in the 12th cent. Became an important iron-working centre in the 17th cent., after Boris Godunov had established the first gun factory (1595). Industrial expansion was considerable in the 19th cent.

Tulcán Ecuador. Town NE of Quito situated in the Andes in Carchi. Pop. (1990) 37,069.

Industries inc. tanning, cattle-rearing and the manufacture of woollen goods and carpets. Trades in agricultural produce.

Tulcea Romania. Port situated ESE of Galați on Sfantu-Gheorghe R., Galați. Pop. (1989) 95,236.

Industries inc. flour-milling, woodworking, tobacco-processing and the manufacture of sulphuric acid and cordage. Trades in agricultural produce.

Tullamore Ireland. County town of Offaly on the Grand Canal 80 km (50 miles) W of Dublin. Pop. (1991) 8622.

Market town. Brewing, distilling and bacon-curing.

At Durrow Abbey (6 km; 4 miles N), founded by St Columba in the 6th cent., the 7th-cent. *Book of Durrow* (now in the Trinity College Library, Dublin) was written.

Tulle-sur-Mer France. Prefecture of Corrèze department 76 km (47 miles) SSE of Limoges. Pop. (1985) 20,700.

Market town. Manufactures firearms and textiles; gave its name to the fabric 'tulle', first produced here.

Has a 12th/14th-cent. cathedral.

Tulsa USA. Industrial town in Oklahoma on the Arkansas R. 169 km (105 miles) NE of Oklahoma City. Pop. (1990) 367,302.

A leading centre of the oil industry in a rich oil-producing region; sometimes called 'the oil cap. of the world'. Manufactures oilfield equipment, aircraft, machinery, metal goods and glass, and plastics.

Grew rapidly after the discovery of oil (1901).

Tumaco Colombia. Pacific port in the Nariño department on a small offshore island 306 km (190 miles) SW of Buenaventura in one of the world's rainiest areas. Pop. (1989) 100,000.

Exports coffee, tobacco and tagua nuts. Climate hot and humid.

Tummel River Scotland. River 88 km (55 miles) long in Perth and Kinross flowing generally E from Loch Rannoch through Loch Tummel, turning SE past Pitlochry to join the Tay R. near Ballinluig. Near Pitlochry it has been dammed as part of a hydroelectric scheme, creating the new Loch Faskally.

Tunbridge Wells England. Town in SW Kent 24 km (15 miles) SW of Maidstone. Pop. (1991) 60,272. A spa owing its popularity to a chalybeate spring, whose medicinal value was discovered by Lord North in 1606. Among subsequent notable visitors were Henrietta Maria, Charles II and Catherine of Braganza, Dr Johnson, David Garrick and Beau Nash, and it reached the height of its fame in the latter half of the 18th cent. Its outstanding feature, now as then, is the colonnaded, tree-lined promenade known as the Pantiles.

Manufactures biscuits, bricks and other light industry.

'Tunbridge ware', articles made in wood-mosaic, was well-known for three cents. Known as Royal Tunbridge Wells.

Tung Ting Lake ➤ DONGTING HU.

Tunis Tunisia. Cap. and chief seaport on a shallow lagoon, the Lake of Tunis (El Bahira), at the head of the Gulf of Tunis on the Mediterranean Sea. Pop. (1989) 620,149. Linked with its outport Halq el Oued (La Goulette) by a channel 10 km (6 miles) long through the lagoon. The E terminus of the main railway through Morocco and Algeria; also connected by rail (S) with Sousse, Sfax, Gabès and Gafsa. Favourably situated for Mediterranean trade: serves the Tell, the Medjerda valley, the plateau and the coastal lowlands.

Exports phosphates, iron ore. Mediterranean fruits, dates, olive oil, esparto grass. Tourist centre. The chief commercial and industrial centre. Food-processing, brewing. Manufactures soap, footwear and cement.

The ruins of ancient Carthage are 14 km (9 miles) NE.

Tunisia. Republic in NW Africa. Bounded by the Mediterranean Sea to the N and E, Libya to the SE and Algeria in the W. Area 164,150 sq km (63,378 sq. miles). Pop. (1995) 8,896,000 (53 per cent urban). Life expectancy, 70 years male, 69 female. Cap. and chief seaport Tunis. Other cities Sfax, Biz-

erta, Djerba, Gabès, Sousse and the Muslim holy city of Kaironan. Currency: Dinar = 1000 millimes. The main regions are the N highlands, an extension of the Tell Atlas, the highest point, Jabal ash-Shanabi 1544 m (5066 ft); the irrigated Medjerda valley growing wheat and barley; the Cape Bon peninsula cultivating citrus fruits, the Sahel (E lowlands) where olives are grown; the central plateau, with the E–W depression containing the shallow salt lakes of Chott Djerid, Gharsa Fedjedj; and the S Sahara, with oases growing dates. The climate ranges from warm temperate in the N to desert in the S. Land use: forested 4 per cent, meadows and pastures 22 per cent, agricultural and under permanent cultivation 30 per cent. The official lang. is Arabic but French is widely spoken. Islam (Sunni) is the religion of the majority and Arabs make up 98 per cent of the pop.

Chief mineral exports are phosphates and iron ore, petroleum and petroleum products, and lead. Chief agricultural exports olive oil, wine, wheat, barley. Other exports inc. clothing; tourism is important to the economy. Tunis is the E terminus of the trunk line through Morocco and Algeria.

For many years it was dominated by Carthage, becoming the Roman province of 'Africa' in the 2nd cent. BC and served as a granary for Rome. Taken in turn by Vandals in the 5th cent. AD, Byzantines in the 6th and Arabs in the 7th; became most powerful under the Berber Hafsid dynasty in the 13th–16th cent. Under Turkish suzerainty became a haunt of pirates; European powers intervened and France established a protectorate in 1881. It was the scene of much fighting during World War II and the Axis troops finally surrendered in 1943. The Nationalists forced France to grant internal autonomy in 1955 and independence in 1956. The monarchy was abolished and a republic established in 1957. Since 1988 multiparty politics have been established. There is a unicameral 141-seat Chamber of Deputies.

Tunja Colombia. Cap. of the Boyaca department at a height of 2820 m (9250 ft) in the E Cordillera 129 km (80 miles) NE of Bogotá. Pop. (1992) 112,400. Market town.

Founded by the Spanish (1539) on the site of one of the Chibcha caps. Much fine architecture of the early colonial period.

Tunstall ►STOKE-ON-TRENT.

Tupelo USA. Town in NE Mississippi. Pop. (1990) 30,685. Convention and route centre on the upper Tombigbee R.

Turfan China. 1. Formerly Lukchun. Depression in the Xinjiang-Uyghur Autonomous Region between the Tien Shan (N) and the Kuruk Tagh (Dry Mountains). Its lowest point is 300 m (984 ft) below sea level. Rain almost unknown. Fruits (esp. grapes), cotton and cereals cultivated by irrigation.

2. Chief town of the Turfan Depression, 45 km (90 miles) SE of Urumchi on the Lanzhou–Urumchi railway. Pop. 20,000. Manufactures cotton goods.

Turin (Italian **Torino**) Italy. Ancient Augusta Taurinorum. Cap. of Piedmont and of the Turin province, the fourth largest city in Italy at the confluence of the Po R. with the Dora Riparia. Pop. (1991) 991,870.

Important industrial and route centre. It has Italy's chief motor-car plants; also manufactures aircraft, textiles, clothing, leather goods, plastics, confectionery and paper, utilizing considerable hydroelectric power from the rivers.

Its wide, straight streets cutting one another at right-angles are a relic of Roman times. Among its noteworthy buildings are the 15th-cent. cathedral, with its façade of white marble and a chapel containing the shroud in which Christ's body was reputedly wrapped after the Crucifixion; the Palazzo Madama and Palazzo Carignano, both now housing museums; the 19th-cent. Mole Antonelliana, also used as a museum and said to be the highest brick-built edifice in Europe (166 m; 544 ft); and the university (founded 1404). Became a Roman colony under Augustus. Cap. of the kingdom of Sardinia 1720. Cap. of Italy 1861–4.

Turkana, Lake Ethiopia/Kenya. Formerly L. Rudolph. Lake in the Great Rift Valley 282 km (155 miles) long and up to 56 km (35 miles) wide, at a height of 375 m (1230 ft) mainly in Kenya, with the N tip in Ethiopia. Fed by the Omo and the Turkwell rivers. No visible outlet. Gradually diminishing and becoming increasingly saline owing to evaporation. It is well stocked with fish, inc. the large Nile Perch. Discovered (1888) by Count Teleki. Formerly named after the Crown Prince of Austria.

Turkestan. Region in Central Asia between Siberia (N) and Iran, Afghanistan and Tibet (S), and between the Caspian Sea (W) and Mongolia and the Gobi desert (E).

Turkey. Republic mainly in SW Asia with a small area in SE Europe. The major part, about 97 per cent of the total area, consists of Asia Minor which is bounded by the Black Sea to the N, Georgia, Armenia and Iran to the E, Iraq, Syria and the Mediterranean Sea to the S and the Aegean Sea to the W. This region is separated from Turkey in Europe by the Bosporus, the Sea of Marmara and the Dardanelles. The European part occupies Eastern Thrace, bounded by Bulgaria in the N and Greece in the W. Area 779,452 sq km (300,948 sq. miles) Pop. (1995) 62,526,000. (63 per cent urban). Life expectancy, 69 years male, 73 female. Cap. Ankara. Other cities Istanbul, Izmir, Adana, Bursa and Gaziantep. Currency: Turkish lira = 100 kurush. The Anatolian Plateau, which forms the greater part of Turkey in Asia, has an average height of about 900 m (2952 ft) and is bounded in the N by a series of ranges known as the Pontic Mountains and in the S by the Taurus Mountains, the former roughly parallel to the Black Sea coast and the latter to the Mediterranean coast. Towards the E the Taurus, the parallel Anti-Taurus and the Pontic Mountains converge and rise to the knot of the Armenian highlands, which contain the country's highest peak, Mt Ararat (5165 m, 16,945 ft), and its largest Lake, L. Van. The most important rivers, the Euphrates and the Tigris, flow generally S from East Anatolia to Syria and Iraq; the longest river entirely in Turkey is the Kizil Irmak, which enters the Black Sea. None of the Turkish rivers is navigable. On the plateau the climate is dry, with hot summers and cold winters, and only the limited plains along the W and S coasts enjoy a Mediterranean type of climate; rainfall is heaviest along the East Black Sea coast. Land use: forested 26 per cent, meadows and pastures 11 per cent, agricultural and under permanent cultivation 36 per cent. The largest minority in the pop. are the Kurds living mainly in the E provinces, and Sunni Muslims; they number about 12 million. Of the smaller minorities the most numerous are the Arabs, Circassians, Greeks, Armenians and Georgians. Turkish is the official lang. and about 20 per cent speak Kurdish. There are about 38 million Sunni Muslims and 17 million Shiites (Alevis).

Turkey is primarily an agricultural and pastoral country; where irrigation is practised the soil is fertile. Of the grain crops wheat and barley occupy by the far the greatest acreage. These and other cereals are grown mainly for domestic consumption and the country is better known for its export crops, the chief of which is cotton, cultivated particularly in the Adana district. Tobacco, grown largely in the Samsun district, and hazelnuts, from the NE coastal region, are also important exports, and grapes (partly for sultanas), olives, citrus fruits and figs are produced on the W and S coastal plains. In recent years considerable tracts of land have been distributed among peasants who were either landless or owned areas that were inadequate for subsistence. Large flocks of sheep and goats inc. the Angora goats, which yield mohair, are raised on the plateau. Turkey is one of the world's leading producers of chrome ore; coal, lignite, iron ore and petroleum are exploited, and the chemical and steel industries have grown in recent years. The textile industry accounts for 30 per cent of exports. The tourist industry has expanded recently and many Turks work abroad and foreign currency is remitted to Turkey.

Among the many early civilizations in Anatolia was the Hittite, which flourished in the 2nd millennium BC, and the ruins of such cities as Troy and Ephesus show the importance of the region. In the 11th cent. AD the conquerors were the Seljuk Turks, who spread W from the deserts of Turkestan and established a powerful empire, to be followed by the Ottoman or Osmanli Turks, themselves driven W by the Mongols. Osman I (Othman), leader of the Ottomans, took the title of Sultan, and thus founded the Ottoman Empire, which was to survive for more than 6 cent. until the end of World War I. The Ottomans invaded Europe, taking Constantinople (Istanbul) in 1453; by the mid 16th cent. they had conquered the Balkan Peninsula and most of Hungary, as well as Syria, Egypt, Arabia, Mesopotamia and Tripolitania. In 1683, however, they were defeated outside Vienna and the long period of decline began. Britain and France, seeking to curb the expansion of Russia fought with Turkey in the Crimean War (1854–6), but the Turks were gradually being forced back towards the Bosporus. The Greeks won their independence (1829) and by the Treaty of Berlin (1878), following revolts in the Balkans and another war with Russia, so also did Serbia, Romania and Bulgaria. Despite the efforts of the nationalistic Young Turks, the country suffered further humiliation when Tripolitania was seized by Italy (1911–12) and the army was driven out of Albania and Macedonia and utterly defeated in the Balkan War (1912–13). In World War I Turkey took sides with Germany; at the end Syria, Palestine, Mespotomia (Iraq) and Arabia were lost. The Turks now found an outstanding leader in Mustafa Kemal, later known as Kemal Atatürk; he became the first President of the Republic (1923) when the Sultanate was abolished, and with dictatorial powers he inaugurated a drastic policy of westernization. During World War II Turkey remained neutral. Since 1928 the Latin script has been in use and since 1929 the publication of books in Arabic characters has been forbidden. Legislative power is vested in the 450-member Grand National Assembly, elected by universal adult suffrage for five years. The President appoints the Prime Minister and a Cabinet. For administrative purposes the country is divided into 73 *ils* or provinces.

Turkish Republic of Northern Cyprus
➤CYPRUS.

Turkmenistan. Republic in Central Asia, bounded on the N by the Autonomous Kara-Kalpak Republic, a constituent of Uzbekistan, on the W by the Caspian Sea and on the S by Iran and Afghanistan. Area 488,100 sq km (188,460 sq. miles). Pop. (1995) 4,081,000 (45 per cent urban). Life expectancy, 63 years male, 70 female. Currency: Mamat. Cap. Ashkhabad. Other cities Chadzhou, Mary (Merv), Nebit-Dag, Krasnovdsk. It consists mainly of an arid lowland, almost 85 per cent of its area being occupied by the Kara-Kum desert, and the pop. is concentrated in oases along the Amu Darya, Murghab and Tedzhen rivers and in the foothills of the Kopet Dagh Mountains (S). Irrigation has been much improved, esp. with the construction of the Kara-Kum Canal from the Tedzhen oases to the Amu Darya. Land use: forested 35 per cent, meadows and pastures 62 per cent, agricultural and under permanent cultivation 2 per cent. Turkman is the official lang.; Russian, Uzbek and Kazakh are also used. Believers are mainly Sunni Muslims. About 72 per cent are Turkmen, 10 per cent Russian and 9 per cent Uzbek.

Cotton is the most important crop, maize the chief grain; sericulture and fruit and vegetable growing are important. Karakul and other sheep, goats and cattle and a special breed of Turkoman horses are raised. Fishing and fish-canning along the Caspian Sea coast. Considerable mineral resources; oil and natural gas are produced in the Nebit Dag district and sodium sulphate around the Kara Bogaz Gol. Other industries inc. engineering, textiles and metal-processing.

Until conquered by the Russians (1881), the Turkmen tribes were largely nomadic; their republic was founded 1924. It entered the Soviet Union as a Constituent Republic in 1925. Independence was declared in 1991. There is a transitional Constitution with unicameral 50-member *Majlis* (Parliament).

Turks and Caicos Islands West Indies. United Kingdom Overseas Territory comprising two groups of islands, geographically part of the Bahamas. The Turks Islands Passage, 35 km (22 miles) wide, separates the Turks Is. (E) from the Caicos Is. (W). There are about 30 islands, of which 6 are inhabited. Area 497 sq km (192 sq. miles). Pop. (1990) 11,696. Chief town Grand Turk, on Grand Turk Island. The currency in circulation is the US dollar. The largest island Grand Caicos is 40 km (25 miles) long and 19 km (12 miles) wide. The climate is equable as a result of regular trade winds but severe damage is caused from time to time by hurricanes.

Principal industry salt-panning. Main exports conch, crawfish and other fish, mainly to the US after processing in South Caicos. Tourism is important; 75 per cent of the visitors come from USA.

Discovered (1512) by Juan Ponce de León. First settled (1678) by Bermudians, who established the salt-panning industry. Placed under the Bahamas (1799), then under Jamaica (1873). Became a British Crown Colony when Jamaica became independent (1962).

Turku (Swedish **Åbo**) Finland. Cap. of Turku-Pori province, Finland's third largest city, on the Gulf of Bothnia 153 km (95 miles) WNW of Helsinki. Pop. (1993) 160,320.

Seaport with a harbour kept open throughout the winter. Industrial and cultural centre. Exports timber and butter. Industries inc. shipbuilding, sawmilling, sugar-refining and textiles.

Founded 1229. Cap. of Finland until 1812.

Turnhout Belgium. Industrial and market town in Antwerp province 40 km (25 miles) ENE of Antwerp. Pop. (1989) 37,000.

Manufactures paper, playing cards, textiles, agricultural implements, cement and bricks.

The town hall was once a palace of the dukes of Brabant.

Turnu Severin Romania. Ancient Drobeta, Turris Severi. Cap. of Mehedinţi district in Walachia on the Danube R. below the Iron Gate (Yugoslav frontier). Pop. (1989) 107,460.

River port. Shipbuilding, railway engineering. Trade in cereals and petroleum.

Nearby are the remains of Trajan's bridge (AD 103) over the Danube, parts of which are sometimes visible.

Turriff Scotland. Market town in Aberdeenshire 50 km (31 miles) NNW of Aberdeen. Pop. (1971) 2858.

Engineering.

Scene of the first engagement of the Civil War in Scotland, called 'Trot of Turriff' (1639).

Tuscaloosa USA. Industrial town in Alabama on the Black Warrior R. 80 km (50 miles) SW of Birmingham. Pop. (1990) 77,759.

Oil-refining. Manufactures cotton goods, paper and tyres.

State cap. 1826–46.

Tuscany (Italian **Toscana**) Italy. Region in central Italy bordering W on the Ligurian and Tyrrhenian Seas, corresponding roughly to the ancient Etruria and comprising the provinces of Apuania, Arezzo, Florence (Firenze), Grosseto, Leghorn (Livorno), Lucca, Pisa, Pistoia and Siena. Area 22,992 sq km (8876 sq. miles). Pop. (1991) 3,599,085. Cap. Florence. Mainly mountainous. Drained chiefly by the Arno R. and its tributaries.

Wheat, vines and olives cultivated. Most of Italy's iron ore (island of Elba) and mercury (Siena) are mined here.

Chief towns Florence, Leghorn, Pisa, Lucca and Siena. A grand duchy from 1567 almost continuously until 1860; it then joined the kingdom of Sardinia, and that of Italy in 1861.

Tuticorin India. Seaport in Tamil Nadu on the Gulf of Mannar 129 km (80 miles) S of Madurai. Pop. (1991) 199,900.

Exports cotton goods and coffee. Also a railway terminus. Manufactures cotton goods and petrochemicals. Saltworks.

Founded in the 16th cent. by the Portuguese; long held by the Dutch.

Tuttlingen Germany. Town in Baden-Württemberg on the Danube R. 93 km (58 miles) SSW of Stuttgart. Pop. (1986) 30,800.

Manufactures surgical instruments and footwear.

Tuva Republic Russia. Republic situated between the Sayan mountains (N) and the Tannu Ola Mountains (S) and bounded on the S by the Mongolian People's Republic. Area 170,500 sq km (65,810 sq. miles). Pop. (1991) 307,000. Cap. Kyzyl. Extensive pastures.

Main occupation cattle-rearing.

The Tuvans, who form about 60 per cent of the pop., are a Turkic people who were formerly ruled by tribal chiefs. Their region was a Chinese dependency, became a Russian protectorate (1914), gained independence as the Tannu Tuva People's Republic (1921) and was incorporated into the USSR (1944) as an Autonomous Region. Raised to the status of Autonomous Republic in 1961.

Tuvalu South West Pacific Ocean. Independent state, formerly called Lagoon Islands, then Ellice Islands, part of Gilbert and Ellice Islands. Area 24 sq km (9¼ sq. miles). Pop. (1995) 9400 (46 per cent urban). Life expectancy, 67 years male, 64 female. Cap. Fongafale on Funafuti atoll. Currency: Tuvalu dollar = 100 Tuvalu cents. Archipelago situated between the Fiji and Gilbert Is., consisting of 9 groups of atolls. There are no rivers and the highest point is 6 m (20 ft). There is plentiful rainfall and temperatures are uniformly high. Land use: agricultural and under permanent cultivation 75 per cent. Tuvaluan and English are the langs. and 91 per cent are Tuvaluan (Polynesian). About 98 per cent of believers are Congregationalists (Church of Tuvalu).

The main occupation is subsistence farming and copra, clothing and footwear are exported.

A British protectorate was established in 1892 and in 1915 the islands became part of the Gilbert and Ellice Islands. After a referendum in 1975 the island group separated from the Gilbert Islands and achieved independence in 1978. There is a 12-member House of Assembly.

Tuxtla Gutiérrez Mexico. Cap. of Chiapas state in the S 710 km (440 miles) ESE of Mexico City at a height of 530 m (1738 ft). Pop. (1990) 289,626.

Market town in an agricultural region producing coffee, sugar-cane, tobacco and bananas.

Tuz, Lake Turkey. Salt lake in central Turkey 105 km (65 miles) SSE of Ankara at a height of 870 m (2854 ft). Area 1620 sq km (625 sq. miles) in winter, much reduced in summer. Large quantities of salt produced.

Tuzla Bosnia-Hercegovina. Town W of the Majevica (mountain range) 80 km (50 miles) NNE of Sarajevo. Pop. (1991) 131,861. In a district producing salt, lignite and coal.

Tver Russia. Formerly Kalinin (1933–90). Cap. of the Tver Region at the confluence of the Volga and the Tversta rivers 169 km (105 miles) NW of Moscow. Pop. (1992) 456,000.

Industrial centre and river port. Manufactures railway rolling-stock, textiles, clothing, plastics and leather goods.

Founded in the 12th cent. as Tver, it was cap. of the independent principality of Tver from c. 1240 until nearly the end of the 15th cent.

Tweed River England/Scotland. River 156 km (97 miles) long rising in Tweed's Well 10 km (6 miles) N of Moffat flowing first NE. It turns E then NE forming part of the boundary between Scotland and England, and finally E again, to cross Northumberland for about 5 km (3 miles) and enters the North Sea at Berwick-on-Tweed. Chief tributaries the Ettrick Water, Teviot and Till. Cereals and root crops are grown in its lower valley, the Merse. Sheep are raised on the surrounding hills; several small towns on its banks have become woollen-manufacturing centres, esp. Peebles and Galashiels. The name 'tweed' for woollen cloth is believed to derive from a misreading of

'tweel' (Scottish for twill) by association with the river.

Twickenham England. Part of the London borough of Richmond-upon-Thames on the N bank of the R. Thames 18 km (11 miles) WSW of London. Mainly residential. Hampton, Hampton Wick and Teddington were added to the borough in 1937. Contains the English Rugby Football Union ground, Hampton Court Palace and Bushy Park.

Tyburn Brook England. Short stream in W London flowing S from Hampstead towards the R. Thames, now an underground sewer. Gave its name to Tyburn gallows (near the modern Marble Arch), used for public executions until 1783.

Tyler USA. Town in Texas 153 km (95 miles) ESE of Dallas. Pop. (1990) 75,450.

Famous chiefly for its rose-growing industry. Also oil-refining, iron-founding, food-processing. Manufactures cottonseed oil and clothing. Has an annual rose festival (Oct.); grows roses and ornamental shrubs.

Tyne and Wear England. Former metropolitan county around the lower R. Tyne and R. Wear and centred on Newcastle-upon-Tyne, inc. also the districts of Tynemouth, Gateshead, South Shields and Sunderland. Mainly industrial. Pop. (1991) 1,125,000. Since 1986 a geographic entity only. The functions of Tyne and Wear are now undertaken by other local authorities.

Tynemouth England. Residential and industrial town in Tyne and Wear at the mouth of the R. Tyne 11 km (7 miles) ENE of Newcastle-upon-Tyne. Pop. (1991) 17,422.

Seaside resort. Inc. North Shields, which is largely industrial: ship-repairing and engineering.

Ruins of an ancient priory and castle.

Tyne River England. River formed by the union of the N Tyne, which rises in the SW Cheviot Hills and flows 51 km (32 miles) SE, and the S Tyne, which rises near Cross Fell and flows 53 km (33 miles) N and E. The two rivers join 3 km (2 miles) above Hexham and the Tyne then flows 48 km (30 miles) E past Blaydon, Newcastle-upon-Tyne, Gateshead, Wallsend, Hebburn, Jarrow and South Shields to the North Sea at Tynemouth. The valleys of the two headstreams are picturesque, but the Tyne for the last 29 km (18 miles) of its course passes through a region of collieries, shipyards and factories.

Tyre (Ar. **Sur**) Lebanon. Ancient Phoenician city and seaport 72 km (45 miles) SSW of Beirut, now a small commercial town. Pop. (1988) 14,000.

Trade in cotton and tobacco.

Originally built on an island, but accumulation of sand has turned this into a peninsula. Probably founded in the 15th cent. BC. One of its kings, the biblical Hiram, traded with Solomon and built a causeway linking the island with the mainland. Its island fortress gave it a strong defence and in the 6th cent. BC it withstood siege by Nebuchadnezzar for 13 years. It was taken and destroyed by Alexander the Great, however, after 7 months' siege. Tyre quickly recovered and flourished again under the Seleucids and the Romans, acquiring fame for its silks and its Tyrian purple dye. It was taken by the Arabs in the 7th cent. AD and by the Crusaders (1124); in 1291 it was destroyed by the Muslims and never completely recovered.

Tyrol ➤TIROL.

Tyrone Northern Ireland. County W of Lough Neagh, bordered by Co. Donegal in the Republic of Ireland (W). Area 3266 sq km (1260 sq. miles). County town Omagh. Hilly; the Sperrin Mountains along the N boundary rise to 683 m (2240 ft) in Sawel. Oats and potatoes cultivated. Dairy cattle raised.

Tyumen Russia. Cap. of the Tyumen region on the Tura R. 290 km (180 miles) E of Sverdlovsk. Pop. (1992) 496,000.

Industrial centre. Linked by rail with Sverdlovsk and Omsk. Tanning, sawmilling and boatbuilding. Manufactures carpets and chemicals.

One of the oldest towns in Siberia (1585). For 3 cents. the gateway to Siberia, until superseded by Chelyabinsk with the building of the Trans-Siberian Railway. From 1964 the centre of a region producing oil and natural gas.

Tywyn Wales. Town situated on Cardigan Bay N of Aberystwyth, Gwynedd. Pop. (1991) 2864.

Holiday resort. Small industrial estate producing honey, puppets, printing, electronics and model engineering.

U

Uapon (Uapu) French Polynesia. Volcanic island in the Marquesas group rising to 1232 m (4043 ft). Area 66 sq km (25 sq. miles). Island group pop. (1988) 7538.

Ubangi River. River 1130 km (700 miles) long in Central Africa, formed by the union of the Mbomu and the Uèle rivers, flowing generally W along the frontier between the Democratic Republic of the Congo and the Central African Republic, turning S near Bangui, forming the frontier between the Democratic Republic of the Congo and the Republic of the Congo, and joining the Congo R. W of L. Tumba. Navigable in parts of the upper and lower courses.

Ube Japan. Town in Yamaguchi prefecture, Honshu on the Inland Sea 120 km (75 miles) WSW of Hiroshima. Pop. (1991) 175,355.

Coalmining and industrial centre. Manufactures chemicals and cement. Industries inc. railway engineering.

Úbeda Spain. Town in Jaén province, Andalusia, 45 km (28 miles) NE of Jaén. Pop. (1991) 30,268.

Manufactures olive oil and soap. Tanning, flour-milling and distilling.

Uberaba Brazil. Town in Minas Gerais state 420 km (260 miles) W of Belo Horizonte at a height of 690 m (2263 ft). Pop. (1990) 241,500.

Important rail and road junction; centre of a cattle-rearing and agricultural region. Industries inc. sugar-milling.

Ucayali River Peru. River 1600 km (1000 miles) long, formed in the E Peruvian *montaña* by the union of the Apurímac and the Urubamba rivers, flowing generally N to join the Marãnón R. and form the main course of the Amazon R. Navigable for 960 km (600 miles).

Udaipur India. Town in S Rajasthan at the S end of the Aravalli Hills 346 km (215 miles) SW of Jaipur. Pop. (1991) 308,600.

Trade in grain and cotton. Industries inc. zinc-smelting, timber, jewellery, silverware, dye-printing and handicrafts.

Standing at a height of 750 m (2460 ft) it is beautifully situated in the wooded hills, and on its W side is the picturesque L. Pichola, on whose two small islands there are palaces of the 17th and 18th cent. Cap. of the former princely state of Udaipur (Mewar) 1568–1948; has a 16th-cent. maharana's palace.

Uddevalla Sweden. Industrial town and railway junction in Göteborg och Bohus county, on Byfiord 71 km (44 miles) N of Göteborg. Pop. (1991) 47,668.

Manufactures textiles, paper and matches.

Udine Italy. Cap. of Friuli-Venezia Giulia and Udine province 100 km (62 miles) NE of Venice. Pop. (1990) 98,000.

Industrial centre. Manufactures textiles, paper, furniture, pharmaceutical products. Sugar-refining and tanning.

It has a 13th-cent Romanesque cathedral standing in an arcaded square, a 15th-cent. Gothic town hall and a 16th/18th-cent. archbishop's palace with frescoes by Tiepolo.

Udmurt Autonomous Republic Russia. Situated W of the Urals between the Vyatka and Kama rivers. Area 42,100 sq km (16,250 sq. miles). Pop. (1991) 1,628,000 (32 per cent Udmurts, 58 per cent Russians, 7 per cent Tatars). Cap. Izhevsk. Consists largely of forests, which provide timber.

Chief crop flax; rye, oats, potatoes also cultivated. Industries largely centred in Izhevsk and inc. the manufacture of locomotives, machine-tools, clothing, furniture, food and building materials.

The Udmurts, formerly known as Votyaks, were colonized by the Russians in the 16th cent. and the Votyak Autonomous Region was constituted in 1920. In 1932 the name was changed to Udmurt and in 1934 it was raised to the status of an Autonomous Republic.

Uèle River Democratic Republic of the Congo. River 1200 km (750 miles) long in Central Africa, rising NW of L. Albert near the frontier between the Democratic Republic of the Congo and Uganda as the Kibali R., flowing NW, then taking a meandering course W through an important cotton-growing region and joining the Mbomu R. at Yakoma to form the Ubangi R.

Ufa Russia. Cap. of the Bashkir Autonomous Republic at the confluence of the Ufa and Belaya rivers. Pop. (1991) 1,097,000.

Oil-refining centre, connected by pipeline with the Volga–Ural oilfield. Also a railway junction and industrial town. Engineering, sawmilling, food-processing. Manufactures chemicals, machinery, electrical equipment, paper and matches.

Founded in the 16th cent. and became a commercial centre on the route to Siberia.

Ufa River Russia. River 720 km (450 miles) long, rising in the S Urals, flowing NW and then SSW to join the Belaya R. at Ufa. Extensively used for floating timber.

Uganda. Republic in East Africa. Bounded by Sudan (N), Kenya (E), Tanzania and Rwanda (S) and the Democratic Republic of the Congo (W). The country is divided into four regions Central, Eastern, Northern and Western. Area 241,040 sq km (93,070 sq. miles) (35,430 sq km; 13,690 sq. miles is water and swamp, with part of Lakes Victoria, Albert and Edward and the whole of L. Kioga). Pop. (1991) 16,582,700. Life expectancy, 51 years male, 55 female. Cap. Kampala. Other towns Jinja and Mbale. Currency: Uganda shilling = 100 cents.

Uganda lies between the eastern and western arms of the Great Rift Valley and is part of the East African plateau, at a height of 900–1500 m (2952–4920 ft), with the Ruwenzori highlands (5109 m; 16,758 ft) near the frontier of the Democratic Republic of the Congo, Mt Elgon (4321 m; 14,173 ft) on the Kenya frontier and other peaks rise to 6094 m (20,000 ft). The Victoria Nile is the chief river and flows into L. Kioga and becomes the main course of the Nile. It has a tropical climate with annual rainfall 100–140 cm (40–55 ins.). There are two rainy seasons March–May and Sept.–Nov. Land use: forested 28 per cent, meadows and pasture 9 per cent, agricultural and under permanent cultivation 37 per cent. Nearly half the pop. is Bantu, the others are of Nilotic, Hamitic and Sudanese tribes. Official langs. are English and Swahili; 70 per cent of the pop. speak Bantu languages. Religion, Christian 78 per cent and Muslim 6 per cent.

Main exports coffee and cotton; others, tea and tobacco. Uganda possesses one of the largest fresh-water fisheries in the world and fish-farming is a growing industry. Food crops bananas, maize, millet. Chief minerals are copper, tungsten, phosphate, beryl, tin and cobalt. Manufactures inc. soap, sugar, cement, animal feed, footwear, textiles, cigarettes, beer and metal products.

The Englishman John Speke was the first European to explore the region (1862). Buganda came under the control of the Imperial British East Africa Company in 1890 and a British protectorate was proclaimed in 1894; adjoining territories were added in 1896. From 1948 the technical services (railways, mail and customs) were coordinated with those of Tanganyika (now Tanzania) and Kenya, under the East Africa High Commission, reorganized as the East African Common Services Organization in 1961. The Organization ceased to operate in 1977 and the main reasons were failure to agree a budget and because of animosity between the Presidents of Tanzania and Uganda. Uganda became independent in 1962 and became a republic in 1967. The Kabaka of Buganda, who had been President of all Uganda, was deposed in 1966 and fled the country; his office was taken over by the then Prime

Ukraine

Minister, Dr Milton Obote. In 1971 the latter was deposed in a military *coup* and a rapidly promoted General Idi Amin became head of state. His period of rule was characterized by widespread repression and the expulsion of Asian residents in 1972. In 1979 a force of the Tanzanian army and Ugandan exiles advanced from Uganda taking Kampala. Amin fled into exile. Obote was re-elected President in 1980 but again deposed in 1985. Since 1986 President Museveni has ruled the country as the head of the 298-member National Resistance Movement. The NRM has acted as the legislative body until a new Constitution is enacted.

Uist, North and South Scotland. Islands in the Outer Hebrides in the Western Isles, North Uist being 13 km (8 miles) SW of Harris across the Sound of Harris. North Uist, 27 km (17 miles) long and 21 km (13 miles) wide, is swampy and hilly, rising to 347 m (1138 ft) in Ben Eaval, in the E, and here are the sea lochs Maddy and Eport. Pop. (1991) 1404. Chief village Lochmaddy. Just S is the smaller island of Benbecula. S again is South Uist, 35 km (22 miles) long and 13 km (8 miles) wide, which rises to 620 m (2034 ft) in Ben More and has the sea lochs Eynort and Boisdale. Pop. (1991) 2106. Chief village Lochboisdale.

Main occupations on both islands crofting and fishing.

South Uist was the birthplace of Flora Macdonald (1722–90).

Uitenhage South Africa. Town in Eastern Cape Province, founded 1804, 29 km (18 miles) NW of Port Elizabeth. Pop. (1980) 70,000. Industries inc. railway engineering and the manufacture of textiles and tyres.

Ujda ►OUJDA.

Ujiji Tanzania. Small port on the E shore of L. Tanganyika. Once a centre of the Arab slave and ivory trade. The place where Livingstone was found by Stanley (1871).

Ujjain India. Town in Madhya Pradesh on the Sipra R. 56 km (35 miles) NNW of Indore. Pop. (1991) 362,600.

Trade in grain and cotton. Manufactures textiles, hosiery, tiles and chemicals.

A sacred city of the Hindus and a well-known place of pilgrimage. An ancient city, it was cap. of the former Gwalior state in the second half of the 18th cent.

Ujung (Ujang) Pandang Indonesia. Cap. of S Sulawesi province, on the W coast of Sulawesi peninsula. Pop. (1990) 709,038. Chief seaport and largest town of the island.

Exports coffee, gums, vegetable oil, teak, copra and spices.

Visited by the Portuguese in 1512 and settled by the Dutch in 1607.

UK ►UNITED KINGDOM.

Ukraine. Independent republic, bounded in the E by Russia, the N by Belorussia, the W by Poland, Slovakia, Hungary, Romania and Moldavia and the S by the Black Sea and the Sea of Azov. Area 603,700 sq km (233,100 sq. miles). Pop. (1991) 51,944,400. Life expectancy, 66 years male, 75 female. Cap. Kiev. Other important towns Kharkov, Donetsk, Odessa and Dnepropetrovsk. Currency: ruble = 100 kopecks.

Ukraine is very fertile and a densely populated republic. The Donets basin has important coalfields. Large deposits of iron ore are found at Krivoi Rog and of manganese at Nikopol. Principally lowland, with a section of the Carpathians in the extreme W in Zakarpatskaya (the Transcarpathian Region). Chief rivers the Dniester, the South Bug, the Dnieper and its tributaries, and the North Donets. Three main natural regions: the level and often marshy forests of the NW; the wooded steppes of the central area (inc. some of the rich black-earth soils); the true black-earth steppes of the S. Land use: forested 14 per cent, meadows and pastures 12 per cent, agricultural and under permanent cultivation 56 per cent. The pop. consists of Ukrainians 73 per cent, Russians 22 per cent. The official lang. is Ukrainian; believers are predominantly Ukrainian Orthodox and there is a Ukrainian Catholic minority.

Agriculture produces considerable quantities of grain (wheat, maize) and sugar-beet, as well as potatoes, sunflower seeds and dairy produce. Important manufactures are iron and steel, machinery, chemicals, food products, power generation and refining of natural gas and petroleum.

Part of the N and W of Ukraine formed part of Kievan Russia from the 9th cent. The area was devastated by the Tatar invasion of the 13th cent. Under Polish rule after the union of Lithuania and Poland (1569); many of the peasants fled to the Dnieper and beyond and set up rebel 'Cossack' communities and it was also known as 'Little Russia'. Russia annexed Kiev and the Ukraine E of the Dnieper in 1667, and the remainder by the Partititions of Poland (1793–5). The 19th-cent. Ukrainian nationalist movement favoured unity with Germany rather than Russia. The Ukrainian Soviet Socialist Republic, proclaimed in 1917, became part of the USSR on its creation in 1922. By the settlement after World War II, it now inc. North Bukovina, part of Bessarabia, the Transcarpathian Region and the SE of prewar Poland. The Moldavian Autonomous Soviet Socialist Republic was separated and became the Moldavian Soviet Socialist Republic in 1940. The Crimea was incorporated (formerly Russia) in 1954. It suffered severely in World War II and was occupied by the Germans 1941–4. In 1991 Ukraine unanimously repudiated the 1922 Treaty of Union and declared its independence. Ukraine was one of the founder members of the Commonwealth of Independent States. There is a 450-member Supreme Soviet.

Ulan Bator Mongolia. Cap. of the Mongolian People's Republic, which dates from the 17th cent., 450 km (280 miles) S of Ulan-Ude, Russia at a height of 1310 m (4297 ft). Pop. (1990) 575,000.

The chief industrial and commercial centre. Industries inc. the manufacture of woollen goods, saddles, footwear, meat-packing, flour-milling, textiles and building materials. Linked by rail with Ulan-Ude and the Trans-Siberian Railway, and with Beijing (China).

Ulan-Ude Russia. Cap. of the Buryat Autonomous Republic on the Selenga R. at the confluence with the Uda R. 217 km (135 miles) E of Irkutsk. Pop. (1991) 362,400.

Industrial centre. Railway engineering, sawmilling, meat-packing. Manufactures woollen goods and glass. Also an important route centre on the Trans-Siberian Railway; the railway and road to Ulan Bator (Mongolia) carry considerable trade.

Uleåborg ➤OULU.

Ulhasnagar India. Town situated 40 km (25 miles) NE of Bombay in Maharashtra. Pop. (1990) 369,100.

Industries inc. cosmetics, electronics, chemicals and plastics.

Ullswater England. The second largest lake in England 12 km (7½ miles) long and 0.8 km (½ mile) wide, situated E of Keswick, in the Lake District.

Ulm Germany. Industrial town and railway junction in Baden-Württemberg on the Danube R. 74 km (46 miles) SE of Stuttgart. Pop. (1991) 108,930.

Manufactures metal goods, textiles and cement. Brewing, tanning.

An ancient town; many of its historic buildings were damaged in World War II, but the dominating 14th-cent. cathedral was unscathed. Birthplace of Albert Einstein (1879–1955) creator of the theory of relativity.

Ulster Ireland. The NE province of ancient Ireland. Nine counties: Antrim, Armagh, Down, Fermanagh, Londonderry (Derry), Tyrone (6 in Northern Ireland); Cavan, Donegal, Monaghan (3 in Irish Republic). Area 22,160 sq km (8556 sq. miles).

Largely agricultural. Important shipbuilding, linen and other industries, centred chiefly on Belfast.

Throughout the 17th cent. most of the land was confiscated and distributed among English and Scottish settlers (the 'Plantation'). The Unionist Protestant party violently opposed the Home Rule movement 1885–1920; Ireland and Ulster were partitioned by the 1921 Government of Ireland Act, establishing 6 counties as Northern Ireland and the remaining 26 as the Irish Free State (since 1948 the Irish Republic). Ulster is also used by some citizens of Northern Ireland as the name for the province.

Ulverston England. Market town in Cumbria 13 km (8 miles) NE of Barrow-in-Furness. Pop. (1991) 11,866.

Engineering and tanning. Birthplace of Sir John Barrow (1764–1848), the explorer.

Ulyanovsk Russia. Now Simbirsk. Cap. of the Simbirsk region on a hill above the right bank of the Volga R. between this river and the Sviyaga R. 177 km (110 miles) NW of Samara Pop. (1991) 667,700.

River port. Railway junction. Industrial centre. Manufactures machinery, motor vehicles. Sawmilling, tanning, brewing, flour-milling.

Founded 1648. Renamed after Lenin (V. I. Ulyanov, 1870–1924), who was born here; also birthplace of the writer Ivan Goncharov (1812–91). ➤SIMBIRSK.

Umbria Italy. Region in central Italy in the Apennines, comprising the provinces of Perugia and Terni. Area 8456 sq km (3265 sq. miles). Pop. (1991) 822,972. Largely mountainous. Drained by the upper Tiber. Contains L. Trasimeno.

Produces cereals, wine, olive oil. Some industry at Terni.

The Umbrians allied themselves with Rome early in the 3rd cent. BC. The Umbrian school of painting of the 15th–16th cents. inc. Perugino and Raphael.

Umeå Sweden. Cap. of Västerbotten county at the mouth of the Ume R. 225 km (140 miles) NE of Sundsvall. Pop. (1990) 92,653. Port.

Industrial centre. Exports inc. timber and tar. Manufactures machinery, wood-pulp and furniture.

Umn Said Qatar. Oil terminal and industrial town situated 40 km (25 miles) S of Doha. Pop. (1985) 7000.

Industries also inc. fertilizers and petrochemicals.

Umtali ➤MUTARE.

Umtata South Africa. Former cap. of the Transkei, now in Eastern Cape Province, on the Umtata R. 185 km (115 miles) NNE of East London. Pop. (1980) 25,000. Terminus of the railway from East London.

Ungava Canada. District in N Quebec around Ungava Bay, inc. the Ungava Peninsula (W). Area 911,110 sq km (351,780 sq. miles). It has great mineral reserves and is sparsely inhabited. Annexed to Quebec in 1912.

Union City (Union Township) USA. Industrial town in New Jersey situated SW of New York City. Pop. (1990) 58,012.

Residential and business centre, it manufactures textiles, electrical equipment and pharmaceutical products.

Union of Soviet Socialist Republics (USSR, Soviet Union). Until 1917 the territory forming the former USSR, together with that of Finland, Poland and certain tracts ceded in 1918 to Turkey, but less the territories then forming part of the German, Austro–Hungarian and Japanese empires – East Prussia, East Galicia, Transcarpathia, Bukovina, East Sakhalin and Kurile Is. – which were acquired during and after World War II, was constituted as the Russian Empire. In 1917 a revolution broke out, a Provisional Government was appointed and in a few months a republic was proclaimed. Late in 1917 power was transferred to the second All-Russian Congress of Soviets. This elected a new government, the Council of People's Commissars, headed by Lenin. Early in 1918 the third All-Russian Congress of Soviets issued a Declaration of Rights of the Toiling and Exploited Masses, which proclaimed Russia a Republic of Soviets of Workers', Soldiers' and Peasants' Deputies; and in the middle of 1918 the fifth Congress adopted a Constitution for the Russian Socialist Federal Soviet Republic. In the course of the civil war other Soviet Republics were set up in the Ukraine, Belorussia and Transcaucasia. The constituent republics immediately before 1991 were: Russian Soviet Federal Socialist Republic, Ukraine, Uzbekistan, Kazakhstan, Belorussia, Azerbaijan, Georgia, Moldavia, Tadzhikistan, Kirgizia, Lithuania, Armenia, Turkmenistan, Latvia and Estonia.

Negotiations in 1990 and 1991 under the directions of President Gorbachev attempted to establish a 'renewed federation' and to conclude a new Union Treaty, but these failed and the Union was declared 'no longer in existence' in December 1991 and the Commonwealth of Independent States was formed.

United Arab Emirates. The UAE is a federation of 7 countries in E Arabia. Bounded on the N by the (Persian) Gulf and Oman, E by the Gulf of Oman and Oman, S and W by Saudi Arabia and NW by Qatar. Area 83,657 sq km (32,300 sq. miles). Pop. (1995) 2,195,000; pop. of the individual Emirates (1991), Abu Dhabi (798,000), Dubai (501,000), Sharjah (314,000), Ajman (76,000), Umm al Qiwain (27,000), Ras al Khaimah (130,000) and Fujairah (63,000). Life expectancy, 70 years male, 75 female. Provisional federal cap. Abu Dhabi. Other towns Dubai and Sharjah. Currency: UAE dirham = 100 fils. Ninety-seven per cent of the country is desert and rainfall is both limited and erratic. Land use: forested nil, meadows and pastures 2 per cent, agricultural or under permanent pasture 0.5 per cent. About 10 per cent are nomads and about 87 per cent are Arabs. The majority of the pop. is Muslim of which 80 per cent are of the Sunni sect.

Oil and gas provide about 50 per cent of the gross national product and in 1992 crude oil reserves stood at 98,000 million barrels. The traditional occupations are fishing and trading, but aluminium, cables, cement, fertilizers, steel, clothing and plastics are also manufactured.

The United Arab Emirates were known as the Trucial States until 1971 when British forces withdrew. A Treaty had been signed by the Rulers of the seven Trucial States in 1820 and as a result Britain had been responsible for defence and foreign policy, and this was replaced in 1971 by a treaty of friendship. The UAE was formed in 1971 and Ras al Khaimah joined in 1972. The small state of Kalba was merged with Sharjah in 1952.

The federation is headed by a Supreme Council of Rulers with an elected President. There is a federal 40-member National Council which may propose amendments to draft legislation, but has no executive power.

United Kingdom. The United Kingdom of Great Britain and Northern Ireland: i.e. England, Wales, Scotland and six of the nine counties of Ulster. Bounded S by the English Channel, E by the North Sea, N and W by the Atlantic Ocean and Ireland. Area 244,755 sq km (94,500 sq. miles). Pop. (1995) 58,586,000 (89 per cent urban). Life expectancy, 74 years male, 79 female. Cap. London. Other cities Cardiff (cap. of Wales), Edinburgh (cap. of Scotland), Belfast (cap. of Northern Ireland), Birmingham, Glasgow, Liverpool, Manchester, Sheffield, Leeds, Bristol, Coventry, Nottingham, Bradford, Wolverhampton, Derby, Hull, Leicester, Newcastle upon Tyne, Southampton, Stoke-on-Trent, Sunderland, Dundee, Aberdeen, Swansea and Portsmouth. Currency: Pound sterling (£) = 100 pence.

The mainland is low-lying in the SE rising to highland in the Pennine ridge which extends N to S up central England. Beyond it is broad lowland watered by the Dee and Severn Rs and rising again to mountains in N and central Wales and in NW England. At the N end of the Pennines the hills of the Scottish border slope down to a central Scottish lowland which rises (N) to mountains with Ben Nevis, 1343 m (4406 ft) above sea level, the highest peak. The NW coast is deeply indented with many offshore islands. Northern Ireland is fertile plain bounded NW, NE and SE by hills. NW England and NW Scotland have numerous lakes and sea-inlets. The main rivers are the Severn, Thames, Great Ouse, Nene, Welland, Trent,

Dee, Mersey, Aire, Swale, Tees, Tyne, Tweed, Clyde, Forth, Tay, Wye, Usk, Teifi and Bann. The industrial midlands of England have a canal network linking navigable rivers, but these are not used for transport as much as in the past. The climate is cool temperate oceanic, with mild conditions and rainfall evenly distributed over the year, though the weather is very changeable because of cyclonic influences. In general, temperatures are higher in the west and lower in the east in winter and rather the reverse in summer. Rainfall amounts are greatest in the west, where most of the high ground occurs. Land use: forested 10 per cent, meadows and pasture 46 per cent, agricultural and under permanent cultivation 25 per cent.

About 8,500,000 are active members of religious organizations of which 80 per cent are Christian (Roman Catholic 21 per cent, Anglican 20 per cent, Presbyterian 14 per cent, Methodist 5 per cent, Baptist 3 per cent), Muslim 11 per cent, Sikh 4 per cent, Hindu 2 per cent, Jewish 1 per cent. About 95 per cent are white, Asian Indian 1.5 per cent, Pakistani 1 per cent, West Indian 0.8 per cent, Chinese 0.3 per cent, Bangladeshi 0.2 per cent, Arab 0.12 per cent .

Chief crops are cereals, especially barley, wheat and oats, potatoes, sugar-beet and fodder crops. Dairying, beef-cattle and sheep-farming are important. Vegetable crops are grown extensively in E England and also in E Scotland. Manufacturing exists throughout the UK, but there is a great concentration in the Midlands, particularly vehicle production, and the N of England. The chief minerals are iron, coal, limestone, chalk, clays, salt, fluorspar, gypsum, barytes, lead and slate. There are submarine deposits of oil and natural gas in the North Sea. Coastal fisheries produce cod, haddock, whiting, coal-fish, hake, mackerel, sole, herring, plaice, halibut, turbot and shell-fish.

From 1801 to 1920 it was the United Kingdom of Great Britain and Ireland; 'Northern Ireland' replaced 'Ireland' after the creation of the Irish Free State by the Government of Ireland Act (1921). Legislative powers for the UK as a whole are vested in the Westminster Parliament. The United Kingdom does not inc. the Channel Islands or the Isle of Man which are direct dependencies of the Crown with their own legislature and taxation systems. England and Wales form an administrative entity, with some special arrangements for Wales. 'Great Britain' is the geographical name of the British Isles which comprises England, Scotland and Wales (so called to distinguish it from 'Little Britain' or Brittany). The supreme legislative power in the United Kingdom is vested in Parliament, which consists of the House of Commons and the House of Lords. The House of Commons comprises 651 members (524 from England, 38 for Wales, 72 for Scotland and 18 for Northern Ireland), elected by universal suffrage by persons over 18 years of age; the House of Lords is made up of hereditary and life peers and peeresses, archbishops, and bishops. A Bill was presented to Parliament in 1999 which aims to abolish the hereditary peerage. Executive authority, vested nominally in the Crown, in practice rests with a committee of Ministers known as the Cabinet, chosen from the majority party in the House of Commons; a system which has been in force since 1714. The United Kingdom joined the European Economic Community (now European Union) in 1972 and sends 87 members to the European Parliament. In 1999 elections took place to elect a Scottish Parliament and Welsh and Northern Ireland Assemblies.

United Kingdom Overseas Territories. Formerly British dependent territories consisted (1999) of Anguilla; Bermuda; British Antarctic Territory; British Indian Ocean Territory; British Virgin Islands; Cayman Islands; Falkland Islands; Gibraltar; Montserrat; Pitcairn, Henderson, Ducie and Oeno Islands; St Helena, Ascension and Tristan da Cunha; South Georgia and South Sandwich Islands; Turks and Caicos Islands.

United States of America. Federal republic in N America. The main part of the USA, i.e. excluding the states of Alaska and

Hawaii, occupies most of the S half of N America. Bounded by Canada (N), largely along the 49th parallel and the Great Lakes, and Mexico (S), partly along the Rio Grande, lying between the Atlantic (E), the Gulf of Mexico (SE) and the Pacific (W). Alaska lies NW of Canada on the N American mainland and Hawaii in the Pacific. It consists of the following 50 states and the District of Columbia (with dates of admission to the Union): *New England* (NE): Maine (1820), New Hampshire (1788), Vermont (1791), Massachusetts (1788), Rhode Island (1790), Connecticut (1788). *Middle Atlantic:* New York (1788), New Jersey (1787), Pennsylvania (1787). *E North Central:* Ohio (1803), Indiana (1816), Illinois (1818), Michigan (1837), Wisconsin (1848). *W North Central:* Minnesota (1858), Iowa (1846), Missouri (1821), North Dakota (1889), South Dakota (1889), Nebraska (1867), Kansas (1861). *S Atlantic:* Delaware (1787), Maryland (1788), District of Columbia (1791), Virginia (1788), West Virginia (1863), North Carolina (1789), South Carolina (1788), Georgia (1788), Florida (1845). *E South Central:* Kentucky (1792), Tennessee (1796), Alabama (1819), Mississippi (1817). *W South Central:* Arkansas (1836), Louisiana (1812), Oklahoma (1907), Texas (1845). *Mountain (W):* Montana (1889), Idaho (1890), Wyoming (1890), Colorado (1876), New Mexico (1912), Arizona (1912), Utah (1896), Nevada (1864). *Pacific:* Washington (1889), Oregon (1859), California (1850), Alaska (1959), Hawaii (1960). The District of Columbia is co-extensive with the cap., Washington DC. Outlying territories of the USA consist of Puerto Rico (1898), Virgin Islands of the USA (1917), American Samoa (1900), Guam (1898), Northern Marianas (1947), Palau (1947), Midway Islands (1867), Wake Island (1898), Johnston and Sand Islands (1858). Area 9,529,063 sq km (3,679,192 sq. miles). Pop. (1997) 267,636,061 (76 per cent urban). Life expectancy, white male 73 years, black and other male 69; white female 79 years, black and other female 76. Cap. Washington DC. Other major cities: New York, Los Angeles, Chicago, Houston, Philadelphia, San Diego, Detroit, Dallas, Phoenix and San Antonio. Currency: US dollar = 100 cents.

The Atlantic coastline is heavily indented, the largest inlet being Chesapeake Bay; at the SE corner is the long peninsula of Florida and then follows the Gulf coast, extending W to the mouth of the Rio Grande and containing Tampa Bay, the Mississippi delta and numerous coastal lagoons. Among the many offshore islands on the Atlantic are (N–S) Nantucket and Martha's Vineyard (Mass.), the island of Rhode Island (RI), Long Island and Staten Island (NY), the Sea Island and the Florida Keys. The Pacific coast is much less indented, though it contains Puget Sound (Wash.) and San Francisco Bay (Cal.); the only offshore islands of note are the Santa Barbara Islands (Cal.) and those in Puget Sound.

The USA is a country of great mountain ranges, vast plains and long rivers; its highest point is Mt McKinley, Alaska (6194 m; 20,320 ft) and its lowest point is in Death Valley, California, 84 m (276 ft) below sea level. It may be divided into 7 physical regions: the Atlantic coastal plain, continuing along the Gulf of Mexico as the Gulf coastal plain; the Appalachian Mountains; the central plains; the Rocky Mountains; the basins and plateaux W of the Rockies; the Coast Ranges and other mountains and valleys of the Pacific coastal region; finally, the Great Lakes region, an extension of the Laurentian Plateau of Canada. The Atlantic and Gulf coastal plain, with its many indentations and islands, slopes gradually down to the sea and continues as a broad continental shelf. To the W is the Piedmont, a transitional zone bordering W on the Appalachian Mountains, which extend NE–SW from the St Lawrence R. to the Gulf Plain; the highest peak in the Appalachians is Mt Mitchell (2037 m; 6681 ft). W of the Appalachian Plateau is the great lowland region of the central plains, at 150–300 m (492–994 ft), drained by the Missouri–Mississippi system, rising W to the Great Plains, which themselves rise to about 1650 m (5412 ft) in the foothills of the Western Cordillera. Here the Rocky Mountains stretch N–S across the USA from

Canada, continuing in Mexico as the Sierra Madre and reaching 4398 m (14,431 ft) in Mt Elbert. W of the Rockies is the region of basins and plateaux, with the Columbia Plateau (N) and the Colorado Plateau (S) and in the centre the vast area of interior drainage known as the Great Basin, containing the Great Salt Lake as well as Death Valley and other desert tracts. In the Pacific zone there are two N–S mountain belts: firstly, the Cascade Range, continued S by the Sierra Nevada, which has Mt Whitney (4418 m; 14,495 ft), the highest point in the USA outside Alaska; and secondly, farther W, the Coast Ranges, which in many parts slope steeply down to the ocean. Between the Sierra Nevada and the Coast Range is the elongated Central Valley of California.

Of the numerous rivers the greatest is the Mississippi, with its chief tributary the Missouri. It flows N–S from Minnesota to Louisiana and the Gulf of Mexico, thus nearly dividing the country into E and W sections; the Missouri–Mississippi, i.e. the Missouri R. together with the Mississippi from the confluence to the mouth, is about 6050 km (3760 miles), a length exceeded only by the Nile and the Amazon. Other great rivers inc. the Colorado in the SW, the Columbia in the NW and the Rio Grande in the S. The Great Lakes, which are partly in Canada, drain to the Atlantic via the St Lawrence R. Other notable lakes are the Great Salt Lake (Utah), L. Okeechobee (Florida) and L. Champlain (NY and Vermont).

Because of its great extent and varied topography the USA has a wide range of climate. In the E half, i.e. E of about the 100th meridian, three climatic zones may be distinguished according to latitude. The N section has a humid continental climate, with annual rainfall of 50–100 cm (20–40 ins.), generally increasing W–E, and cold winters; the zone to the S in general has a heavier rainfall and higher temperatures throughout the year; the most southerly zone has a humid subtropical climate, with a still more abundant rainfall (200 cm (80 ins.) annually along parts of the Gulf coast), warm summers and mild winters.

To the W of the 100th meridian the climate of the Great Plains is characterized by hot summers and relatively cold winters, with annual rainfall of only 25–50 cm (10–20 ins.). In the Rockies and other mountain ranges in the W the climate varies with altitude and exposure; the lowlands of the SW, shielded by the mountains from rain-bearing westerly winds, have a low rainfall, amounting to less than 25 cm (10 ins.) annually, and a high range of temperatures and in this area are to be found the deserts. The moisture-laden winds from the Pacific, on the other hand, deposit considerable rainfall on the windward slopes of the mountains and in the NW coastal region annual amounts vary from 100 cm (40 ins.) to more than 250 cm (100 ins.); the climate is mild and may be best described as maritime temperate. Much of S California enjoys a Mediterranean type of climate, with warm, dry summers and mild, rainy winters. Land use: forested 32 per cent, meadow and pasture 26 per cent, agricultural and under permanent cultivation 21 per cent.

The religion is Christian, of which Protestant 53 per cent and Roman Catholic 26 per cent. Lang. English. The Middle Atlantic and S New England states are the most densely populated areas. Blacks comprise about 12 per cent of the total pop. and are most numerous in the SE states (the 'deep south'). American Indians, descendants of the aboriginal inhabitants, numbered 1,959,234 in 1990; they are settled largely in Indian 'reservations' in the W states. The Chinese are mainly in San Francisco and other Pacific coast cities. Japanese, almost exclusively settled on the Pacific coast and in Hawaii, as are Filipinos. There are Mexican communities in the SW and Spanish-speaking Puerto Ricans in New York City; in Alaska there are some thousands of Eskimos and Aleuts. In Florida there is a large pop. of Cubans. Apart from such minorities, the people generally speak English.

Since World War II there have been considerable increases in production per acre and per farm animal. Among the contributory causes there have been conservation and irrigation policy, increased mechanization, effective control of pests, the use of fertilizers and better feeding of livestock. But during this period land included in farms decreased slowly, harvested crop land declined somewhat more rapidly, but the number of farms declined sharply. A hundred years ago 75 per cent of the US pop. was rural and practically all rural people lived on farms. In the early 1990s, 27 per cent of the pop. were rural and farm residents were 2 per cent.

The main crops are grain, cotton and tobacco. Maize is grown chiefly in the corn belt with Iowa the leading state; Kansas is the principal wheat-growing state (winter wheat), followed by North Dakota (spring wheat). Cotton is grown increasingly W of the Mississippi: Texas has the highest production, followed by Arizona, Louisiana and Mississippi. Tobacco is grown mainly in Kentucky and North Carolina, and Winston-Salem (NC) is the world's greatest tobacco market. Many other crops are grown on a large scale, e.g. soya beans, flax, sugarbeet, rice and potatoes. The Great Lakes region and the Atlantic coastal plain are noted for fruit and market-garden produce. California is famous for its grapes, citrus and other fruits. Hawaii grows sugar-cane and pineapples and the Gulf coast region sugarcane and rice. On the Great Plains and in Texas there are huge cattle ranches: in 61 years (1930–91) the number of cattle and calves has increased from 64 million to 99 million, but the number of sheep has fallen from 57 million to 11 million and the number of pigs has remained about the same at 56 million. Dairy-farming extends from the Middle Western states to New England and is especially important in Wisconsin. Agricultural output has been greatly increased through irrigation schemes, which often also inc. the provision of hydroelectric power, the Tennessee Valley Authority scheme being particularly noteworthy. At the same time the serious problem of soil erosion and soil depletion in certain areas, brought about largely by over-cropping, over-stocking and deforestation, is being dealt with by Federal and State governments. Forests cover almost a third of the entire land area of the country and about one half is classified as commercial timber. A large proportion of the softwoods produced come from the Pacific states, where the giant redwoods of California and the Douglas firs are outstanding. There are also extensive forests in the N – in Michigan, Wisconsin and Minnesota, whence come most the hardwoods; in the S and SE various species of pine provide most of the remaining softwoods.

The USA has considerable and varied mineral resources. It has long been the largest single producer of petroleum. Bituminous coal and anthracite are mined chiefly in the Appalachians and the central plains, Pennsylvania being especially noted for its anthracite. Petroleum and natural gas are produced mainly in Texas but also in California, Oklahoma, Louisiana. Of the metallic minerals, iron, copper, lead, zinc, gold and silver are the most important; iron ore comes chiefly from the L. Superior region (Minnesota, Michigan), and the non-ferrous metallic ores from the thinly populated mountain states of Arizona, Utah, Nevada, Montana and Idaho. Non-metallic minerals inc. phosphates (Florida) and sulphur (Louisiana). Nevertheless the USA has to import most of its supplies of industrial diamonds, tin and nickel and, to satisfy the demands of industry, part of its bauxite (aluminium) and other non-ferrous ores and even iron ore.

The chief industrial belt is in the NE, comprising New England, the Middle Atlantic states, and most of the Middle Western states. In this area are such leading industrial centres as Detroit (automobiles), Pittsburgh and Youngstown (steel), Chicago, New York, Boston, Philadelphia, Buffalo and many others, with an enormous range of manufactures. There are other industrial concentrations at St Louis, Kansas City, Omaha, New Orleans, Minneapolis, Los Angeles and San Francisco, to name only some of the major centres.

The main seaports are New York, Philadelphia, Baltimore, Boston (Atlantic coast); New Orleans and Houston (Gulf coast); Los Angeles, San Francisco, Portland, Seattle (Pacific). Of the inland waterways the most important are the Great Lakes and the St Lawrence Seaway (shared with Canada) and the Mississippi. The length of main track railways, densest in the E, is 232,000 km (144,000 miles), of roads, 6,243,163 km (3,879,322 miles) of which 58 per cent paved; there are 17,446 airports and landing facilities, 4014 heliports. Owing to the great E–W extent, there are four different time zones, Eastern, Central, Mountain and Pacific, between the two oceans, and three further time zones in Alaska.

The early history of the USA is the history of the discovery and colonization of the country by the leading maritime powers of Europe, of which three, Britain, Spain and France, played the chief parts. It proved to be the British who exercised the most enduring influence on the new nation in the vital period of its development, so that the US inherited the English language, English habits of thought and free speech, and to some extent English culture. Probably the first Europeans to land on the mainland were the Spaniards under Ponce de León, who landed on the coast of Florida in 1513; the first permanent white settlement was established in 1565 at St Augustine, Florida. By 1540 Florida was a subject province of the Spanish domain in Mexico, the Californian coast was surveyed and an expedition penetrated into the interior beyond the Grand Canyon of the Colorado R. – with plunder rather than settlement its main purpose. The French in their turn proved to be better explorers than colonizers: Samuel de Champlain reached Lakes Huron and Ontario (1615) and paved the way for later 17th-cent. French explorers, missionaries and fur traders who gradually traversed the vast area S of the Great Lakes to the Gulf of Mexico. In the 1680s Robert de la Salle explored the Great Lakes and the Mississippi R. and delta, taking possession of the region for France under the name of Louisiana. But French colonization was not very successful, and by 1700 there were only about 1000 French settlers throughout this great region. The English finally proved the most successful colonists; their first permanent settlement was at Jamestown, Virginia

(1607); the group of Puritans from England and Holland who landed at Plymouth, Mass., in 1620 (the famous 'Pilgrim Fathers') are widely regarded as the true founders of the US. In the 18th cent. large numbers of immigrants arrived from Germany and Ireland, but up to the end of the colonial period about four-fifths of the colonists were of English or Scottish origin. There were 13 colonies, which became the 13 original states of the Union after the American War of Independence (1775–83).

The new republic acquired all the territory E of the Mississippi which had passed from France to Britain in 1763. In 1803 came the next major acquisition of territory through the Louisiana Purchase, whereby the US gained the vast region known as Louisiana (area 2,141,900 sq km; 827,000 sq. miles) stretching from the Mississippi to the Rockies and N from the Gulf of Mexico; its boundaries were somewhat ill-defined at the time, but it was to prove a source of immense strength to the country. In 1819 Florida was purchased from Spain. In 1821 Mexico achieved independence and acquired much of the SW part of the present US from Spain; then in 1848, after the US–Mexican War (1846–8), the territory (1,370,100 sq km; 529,000 sq. miles) was ceded by Mexico to the US. Texas (1,010,100 sq km; 390,000 sq. miles) which had broken away from Mexico and established an independent republic (1836), was annexed in 1845. In the NW the region known as the Oregon Territory (738,150 sq km; 285,000 sq. miles) was occupied jointly by the US and Britain (1818–46), but was then ceded to the US. The E part of the boundary with Canada was settled in 1842 and the W part was fixed along the 49th parallel in 1846; the US–Mexico boundary was settled in 1853–4.

From c. 1850 events began to move towards the Civil War of 1861–5; the issue being national unity, which was threatened by a dispute between the N and S states over the question of slavery. The slaves were the Negro plantation workers, descendants of African slaves shipped to North America during the colonial period. Matters came to a head when Lincoln took office as president (1861), for the S states feared that he would try to abolish slavery. From the material standpoint the N was overwhelmingly stronger than the S and finally the S surrendered (9 April 1865). As a result of the Civil War the slaves were liberated, but not integrated into the general society, even in the N states.

The last 40 years of the 19th cent. saw an immense expansion of the railway system. In 1860 there were 48,000 km (30,000 miles) of railway, chiefly E of the Mississippi, but in 1900 there were nearly 320,000 km (200,000 miles). The first transcontinental railway was completed in 1869 and settlement of the W developed rapidly as communications improved. Between 1880 and 1900 the pop. increased from 50 million to 75 million and agricultural and industrial production was doubled. In 1867 Alaska was purchased from Russia and in 1898 Hawaii was annexed. As a result of the Spanish American War Puerto Rico and the Philippines were acquired (1898); the latter became independent in 1946.

Along with the tremendous burst of economic activity that followed the Civil War, the US began to play an increasing part in world affairs – though reluctantly at first, owing to the traditional isolationism of many Americans. However, it early (1823) asserted the principle of the Monroe Doctrine, that the Western hemisphere should not be a European sphere of influence except in existing colonies. It fought a war with Spain (1898) over Cuba, which became independent. The US intervened from time to time in such Latin American states as were in political turmoil. After initially proclaiming its neutrality the US entered World War I in 1916 and its help proved decisive; but it failed to support President Wilson's creation, the League of Nations.

In the succeeding years, the US was overtaken (1929) by an economic depression of great magnitude; conditions improved under the New Deal policies of Franklin D. Roosevelt, but unemployment was not entirely overcome until the US entered World War II, since when the country has experienced economic growth of immense proportions.

Since World War II the US has played a leading role in world politics – as a source of economic rehabilitation for Europe under the 'Marshall Plan', as a major partner in the 'Free World' and as the most powerful and dynamic of the world economies. In the defence of the 'Free World', the US took costly military action in Korea in the 1950s and in Vietnam in the 1960s. US involvement in the Vietnam War ended with the withdrawal of American troops and the final surrender of the South Vietnam government in Saigon (1975). Since the end of the Cold War and the collapse of the USSR the US has played an important part in UN peacekeeping in Iraq, the former Yugoslavia and Somalia.

The Federal government is based in Washington DC, where the President, elected every fourth year, resides and carries out his official functions and where Congress (Senate and House of Representatives) have their sittings. The senate consists of 2 members from each state, chosen by popular vote for 6 years, one-third retiring or seeking re-election every 2 years; the House of Representatives has 435 members, elected every second year, the number from each state being dependent on its pop. (e.g. California 43, New York 39, Idaho 2, Wyoming 1). The form of government is based on the constitution of 17 Sept. 1787, which gives the Federal government authority in taxation, foreign affairs, the armed forces, postal services, coins, weights and measures, patents, copyright and crimes against the US. It has sole legislative authority over the District of Columbia and overseas possessions and controls the National Parks and Indian Reservations. State legislatures, however, have power to deal with all matters not reserved for the Federal government, such as civil and criminal law, trade, transport, education, licensing and fisheries within state waters. Each state has an elected governor and cap. city, with the Capitol as the centre of administration.

University City USA. Residential suburb situated immediately NW of St Louis, Missouri. Pop. (1980) 42,600.

Unna Germany. Industrial town in North Rhine-Westphalia in the Ruhr region 16 km (10 miles) E of Dortmund. Pop. (1985) 58,000.

Coalmining centre. Manufactures metal goods.

Unterwalden Switzerland. Canton in central Switzerland S of L. Lucerne comprising the two half-cantons of Obwalden and Nidwalden. Area 973 sq km (415 sq. miles). Pop. (1991) 61,441 (German-speaking and Roman Catholic; about equally divided between the half-cantons). In 1291 Nidwalden formed the Everlasting League with Uri and Schwyz, to be joined later by Obwalden; with Lucerne they became the Forest Cantons.

Upington South Africa. Market town and railway junction in Northern Cape Province on the Orange R., founded as a mission station in 1875, 354 km (220 miles) W of Kimberley. Pop. (1989) 56,100.

Flour-milling, cotton-ginning. Also a tourist centre for the Aughrabies Falls (Orange R.).

Upolu Samoa. Volcanic island situated SE of Savaii in the South Pacific. Area 1119 sq km (432 sq. miles). Pop. (1986) 112,228. The second largest but most important island of W Samoa. The cap. Apia is on the N coast. It is mountainous, rising to 1100 m (3608 ft) in Vaaifetu. The lowlands are fertile, producing bananas, cacao, coconuts and rubber.

Upper Austria (Ger. **Oberösterreich**) Austria. Northern federal state, bordering W on Bavaria (Germany) and N on Czechoslovakia. Area 11,980 sq km (4626 sq. miles). Pop. (1991) 1,340,076. Cap. Linz. Generally hilly, becoming mountainous in the S. Drained by the Danube, Inn and Enns rivers.

Main occupations agriculture, forestry. Industries chiefly in Linz, Wels and Steyr.

With Lower Austria it formed the nucleus of the Austrian empire of the Habsburgs.

Upper Egypt ➤EGYPT.

Upper Nile Sudan. Province in central S bordered by Ethiopia. Area 238,792 sq km (92,198 sq. miles). Pop. (1983) 1,599,605. Cap. Malakal. Mainly grassland with forests in the S. The principal rivers are Bahr el Jebel and Sobat.

The most important occupation is stock-rearing, mainly cattle, sheep and goats. Peanuts, corns and durra are grown.

Upper Volta ➤BURKINA FASO.

Uppingham England. Market town in Leicestershire 32 km (20 miles) W of Peterborough, chiefly known for its public school (founded 1584). Pop. (1991) 3140.

Uppsala Sweden. Cap. of Uppsala county 64 km (40 miles) NNW of Stockholm. Pop. (1992) 170,743. Cultural centre, with Sweden's oldest university (founded 1477), which has a famous library containing a 6th-cent. *Codex Argenteus* and other manuscripts.

Industries inc. publishing, pharmaceuticals and engineering.

The cathedral (13th/15th-cent.), where Swedish kings were formerly crowned, has the tombs of Gustavus Vasa, Linnaeus and Swedenborg. Old Uppsala, about 3 km (2 miles) N, was a centre of pagan worship in the 9th cent.; after a destructive fire the new city grew up on its present site (13th cent.).

Uqsur ➤LUXOR.

Ur Iraq. Ancient city in Sumer, the biblical Ur of the Chaldees, on a site 169 km (105 miles) WNW of modern Basra near the Euphrates R. Dates between 6000 and 5000 BC, excavations having shown that it was a prosperous city *c.* 3500 BC; it was the reputed home of the Old Testament patriarch, Abraham. The outstanding ruin is the ziggurat or temple tower. After Ur had been destroyed, it was restored by Nebuchadnezzar in the 6th cent. BC; but soon afterwards it began to decline, possibly because the Euphrates, beside which it had grown up and flourished, had changed its course; before the end of the 4th cent. BC it was abandoned.

Ural Mountains Russia. Mountain system extending over 2250 km (1400 miles) N–S from the Arctic Ocean and forming part of the physical boundary between Europe and Asia. Of generally low elevation, the Urals reach their greatest height in Narodnaya (1894 m; 6212 ft) in the N section; there are few other peaks exceeding 1500 m (4920 ft). Well forested. The central section contains some of the country's richest mineral deposits (inc. iron, manganese, nickel, copper), which have contributed much to the development of such great industrial centres as Sverdlovsk and Chelyabinsk; the minerals were known to exist more than 1000 years ago but have been exploited on a large scale only since the 1930s.

Ural River Russia. River 2250 km (1400 miles) long rising in the S Ural Mountains and flowing S past Magnitogorsk and Orsk, W past Orenburg and Uralsk, then S again to enter the Caspian Sea near Guryev. It is navigable to Orenburg.

Uralsk Kazakhstan. Cap. of the Uralsk region, founded 1775, on the Ural R. 240 km (150 miles) SSE of Samara. Pop. (1991) 214,000.

Commercial centre in an agricultural region. Trade in cereals, livestock. Industries inc. meat-packing, tanning and flour-milling.

Uranium City Canada. Mining town in NW Saskatchewan, N of L. Athabaska. Pop. (1986) 2748. Developed in the 1950s for the production of uranium concentrates.

Urawa Japan. Cap. of Saitama prefecture 24 km (15 miles) NNW of Tokyo, of which it is a residential suburb. Pop. (1991) 427,690.

Urbana USA. Market town in Illinois 200 km (125 miles) SSW of Chicago. Pop. (1970) 32,800.

Manufactures scientific instruments and paints.

Urbino Italy. Tourist town in Pesaro e Urbino province, The Marches 110 km (70 miles) E of Florence. Pop. (1990) 15,500.

Manufactures textiles and majolica.

Standing on a hill, it is dominated by the 15th-cent. ducal palace; also has a cathedral. University (1506). Noted in the 15th–16th cent. for its majolica. Birthplace of the Italian painter, Raphael (1483–1520).

Ure River England. River in North Yorkshire 80 km (50 miles) long, rising in the Pennines and flowing E and SE past Ripon to join the R. Swale and form the R. Ouse. The upper part of the valley is known as Wensleydale.

Urfa Turkey. Cap. of Urfa province in the S 120 km (75 miles) E of Gaziantep. Pop. (1990) 276,528.

Market town. Trade in wheat, cotton.

Changed hands many times. Fell to the Muslims (638), the Crusaders (1097) and finally to the Turks (1637).

Uri Switzerland. Canton in central Switzerland. Area 1076 sq km (416 sq. miles). Pop. (1991) 33,650 (German-speaking and Roman Catholic). Cap. Altdorf. Inc. the upper Reuss valley, from which rise lofty peaks and glaciers, and in the N inc. part of L. Lucerne; on the S border is the St Gotthard Pass. Main industry is forestry. With Schwyz and Unterwalden it formed the Everlasting League (1291), which was the foundation of the Swiss confederation, and was one of the Forest Cantons.

Urmia, Lake Iran. The largest lake in the NW at a height of 1300 m (4264 ft). Area 3885 sq km (1500 sq. miles) (increasing at times to over 5960 sq km (2300 sq. miles)). Saline and shallow. Has no outlet.

Uruapán Mexico. Town in Michoacán state 306 km (190 miles) W of Mexico City at a height of 1620 m (5314 ft). Pop. (1990) 217,142.

Industries inc. articles made by local craftsmen: lacquer and glass ware, wooden and embroidered goods. Tourist centre for the volcano Paricutín.

Urubamba River Peru. River 720 km (450 miles) long, rising in the high Andes of the SE and flowing generally NNW through gorges to join the Apurímac R. and form the Ucayali R.

Uruguaiana Brazil. Town in Rio Grande do Sul state on the Uruguay R. and on the Argentine frontier 590 km (365 miles) W of Pôrto Alegre. Pop. (1985) 106,000.

Cattle centre. Meat-packing. Manufactures leather goods, candles and soap.

Uruguay (Replublíca Oriental del Uruguay). The smallest republic in South America is bounded NE by Brazil, on the SE by the Atlantic, on the S by the Río de la Plata and on the W by Argentina. It is divided into 19 departments. Area 178,215 sq km (68,037 sq. miles). Pop. (1992) 3,130,000. Life expectancy, 69 years male, 75 female. Cap. Montevideo. Other major cities: Salto, Paysandú, Las Piedras and Rivera. Currency: Uruguayan new peso = 100 centésimos.

The S is a gently undulating plain similar to the Argentine pampas; the N is more varied, with low hills extending S from the Brazilian border. Central Uruguay is crossed from the NE by the Río Negro, which joins the Uruguay R. In its middle course a dam creates a lake 140 km (87 miles) long and 29 km (18 miles) wide, with a hydroelectric power plant. Climate warm, temperate and healthy, with mild winters and warm summers, well suited to all-year sheep and cattle grazing. Rainfall moderate and well distributed, though occasionally serious droughts occur. Land use: forested 4 per cent, meadows and pastures 77 per cent, agriculture and under permanent pasture 8 per cent.

About 62 per cent are Christian, mainly Roman Catholic. The ethnic composition is mixed Spanish–Italian 86 per cent, mestizo 3 per cent, Italian 3 per cent, Jewish 2 per cent. The lang. is Spanish.

The country's wealth is derived almost enirely from agriculture (mainly pastoral). Nearly all the people are of European stock, chiefly Italian or Spanish, and a high degree of prosperity and literacy has been achieved. Except for forests along the valleys and plains in the S and E, the country remains largely natural grassland. Earlier exports were dried

and salted meat, hides and tallow, but refrigeration led to the large-scale shipment of chilled and frozen meat. Herefords and other European breeds of cattle were introduced, the production of meat and meat extracts began at Fray Bentos in the 19th cent. and continues there and at Montevideo. Sheep-rearing is extremely important, the flocks being mostly of British breeds (Corriedale, Lincoln, Romney Marsh) as well as merinos. Wool is the second leading export (after meat and meat products). Livestock are reared on enclosed grasslands, sheep being rather more numerous in the N, while the best cattle pastures, inc. those for dairy cattle, are mainly in the S. Many roads have parallel grassy tracks for flocks and herds, and the small towns are situated at crossroads to serve the widely spaced *estancias* or ranches. Most of the arable land lies within 80 km (50 miles) of the S coast; the principal crops are wheat, maize, flax (linseed), sunflowers and rice, and enough wine is produced for domestic consumption. There are few minerals and there is great dependency on hydroelectric power. Industries inc. meat-packing, oil-refining, cement, food-processing, transport equipment, chemicals and light engineering. Montevideo handles most of the country's trade and has a considerable proportion of its industries.

Uruguay was the last colony to be settled by Spain in the Americas. In 1776 it became part of the Spanish vice-royalty of La Plata and in 1820 a province of Brazil. Led by the national hero Artigas, the Uruguayans fought for and won independence in 1825, but for the remainder of the 19th cent. the country suffered from internal strife and corruption. An outstanding programme of social reform was introduced during the second administration of President Batille y Ordóñez in 1911, however, and in 1951 the individual presidency was abolished in favour of a two-party National Council of nine members. The presidential system was reintroduced in 1967. Marxist urban guerrillas aimed at violent revolution but were finally defeated by the army in 1972. Presidential elections were allowed by the military in 1984. There is a 31-member Senate and a 99-member Chamber of Representatives.

Uruguay River South America. River 1600 km (1000 miles) long rising in S Brazil only 64 km (40 miles) from the Atlantic coast (as the Pelotas), flowing W and then SW and S, marking the Brazil–Argentina and the Uruguay–Argentina frontiers, and joining the Paraná R. to form the Río de la Plata. Navigation is impeded by falls and rapids above Salto (Uruguay), but the river is navigable by ocean-going ships upstream to Paysandú (Uruguay), about 209 km (130 miles) from the mouth.

Urumchi ►URUMQI.

Urumqi (Urumchi) China. Cap. of Xinjiang Uygur (Sinkiang Uigur) Autonomous Region in a valley through the Tien Shan at a height of 2700 m (8856 ft). Pop. (1991) 1,160,000.

Commercial centre on the route between China (Lanchow) and Russia. Industries inc. flour-milling, tanning, iron and steel, and the manufacture of chemicals, textiles and cement.

USA ►UNITED STATES OF AMERICA.

Usedom (Uznam) Germany/Poland. Island between the Stettiner Haff and the Baltic Sea; since 1945 divided between Germany in the W and Poland in the E. Area 445 sq km (172 sq. miles). Pop. 45,000. Chief town Swinoujście (E). Part of the ancient Polish province of Pomorze (Pomerania). In E Prussia 1919–39.

Ushant (Fr. **Ouessant**) France. Island 8 km (5 miles) long and 3 km (2 miles) wide in the Finistère department off the W coast of Brittany 42 km (26 miles) WNW of Brest. Rocky coastline. Main occupation fishing. Two naval battles (1778, 1794) were fought nearby between the French and the English.

Ushuaia Argentina. Cap. of Tierra del Fuego province on Beagle Channel. Pop. (1985) 11,000. The most southerly town in the world.

Centre of a sheep-rearing, lumbering and fishing region.

Usk Wales. Town in Monmouthshire, on the R. Usk 14 km (9 miles) NNE of Newport. Pop. (1991) 2187. Has the remains of a 13th-cent. castle.

Usk River Wales. River 92 km (57 miles) long, rising 8 km (5 miles) SE of Llandovery and flowing E, SE and S past Brecon, Abergavenny, Usk and Caerleon to the Bristol Channel at Newport.

Uspallata Pass (La Cumbre) Argentina/Chile. Pass through the Andes at a height of 3840 m (12,595 ft) at the foot of Mt Aconcagua. The statue 'Christ of the Andes' in the pass, dedicated in 1904, commemorates the boundary settlement between Argentina and Chile. The railway tunnel beneath the pass links Mendoza (Argentina) and Valparaiso (Chile).

USSR ►UNION OF SOVIET SOCIALIST REPUBLICS.

Ussuri River Russia. River 870 km (540 miles) long rising in the S Sikhote Alin Range and flowing generally NNE, forming the border between the Primorye Territory, Russia and Heilongiang province (China), to join the Amur R.; linked with L. Khanka. Used for floating timber, but frozen Nov.–April.

Ussuriisk Russia. Formerly Nikolsk-Ussuriiski, then (1935–62) Voroshilov. Industrial town and railway centre at the junction of the Trans-Siberian and Chinese Eastern Railways in S Primorye Territory 48 km (30 miles) N of Vladivostok. Pop. (1991) 160,200.

Railway engineering, sawmilling, soya bean processing.

Developed rapidly after the completion of the Trans-Siberian Railway in 1905.

Ústi-nad-Labem Czech Republic. Cap. of the Severočeský region, Bohemia on the Elbe (Labe) R. 72 km (45 miles) NNW of Prague. Pop. (1990) 106,000.

Railway junction and river port. Industrial

centre with chemical works. It manufactures textiles, machinery and rubber products.

Ust-Kamenogorsk Kazakhstan. Industrial town on the Irtysh R. 177 km (110 miles) ESE of Semipalatinsk. Pop. (1991) 332,000.

In a mining district (zinc, lead, copper) and industries inc. metal refining and processing. Manufactures inc. food products, clothing and furniture.

Ust-Ordynsky Russia. National Area in S Siberia in the Irkutsk region. Area 22,400 sq km (8600 sq. miles). Pop. (1991) 138,300. Cap. Ust-Ordynsky (72 km (45 miles) NNE of Irkutsk). Largely wooded steppe. Cattle-rearing, dairy-farming.

Usulután El Salvador. Cap. of Usulatán department in the SE at the foot of the volcano Usulután. Pop. (1992) 62,976.

Market town trading in maize and tobacco, bananas.

Utah USA. State in the W. Area 219,887 sq km (84,899 sq. miles). Pop. (1990) 1,722,850 (87 per cent urban). Cap. Salt Lake City. Its average altitude is about 1800 m (5904 ft). The E consists of high plateau and the W forms part of the Great Basin; the central highlands, inc. the Wasatch Range, run roughly N–S through the state. In the NE the Uinta Mountains rise to 4112 m (13,523 ft) in Kings Peak. In the NW are the Great Salt Lake, the largest salt lake in the Americas, and the Great Salt Lake Desert. Climate dry continental, with a rainfall of less than 12.5 cm (5 ins.) annually in the W and an average for the state of 25–40 cm (10–15 ins.). Only about a quarter of the land area is classified as farm land and of the total surface area 9 per cent is severely eroded and only 9.4 per cent is free from erosion.

Chief crops wheat, hay, sugar-beet, potatoes. Minerals important, esp. copper, petroleum, coal and gold. Major industries inc. aeronautical research, machinery, transport equipment, electronic equipment and food-processing. Bryce Canyon and Zion National Parks and other scenic areas attract tourists. Leading towns Salt Lake City, Ogden.

About 70 per cent of all church members in the state are Latter-day Saints (Mormons). Utah was first settled (1847) by Mormons led by Brigham Young. Ceded to the USA by Mexico 1848, the Territory of Utah was formed in 1850. Admitted to the union in 1896 as the 45th state.

Utica USA. Town in New York on the Mohawk R. 77 km (48 miles) E of Syracuse. Pop. (1990) 68,637.

Manufactures cotton goods, knitwear, clothing and machinery. Industry centred on textiles since the mid 19th cent., has become more diversified in recent years.

Utrecht Netherlands. 1. The smallest province, bordering N on Ijsselmeer. Area 1331 sq km (513 sq. miles). Pop. (1990) 1,015,515. Heath and woodland in the E; vegetable and fruit-growing and dairy-farming in the SW. Industries centred on Utrecht and Amersfoort.

2. Cap. of Utrecht province on the Kromme Rijn (Crooked Rhine) where it divides into the Old Rhine and the Vecht 34 km (21 miles) SSE of Amsterdam. Pop. (1991) 231,231.

Important railway junction. Railway engineering. Manufactures machinery, radio sets, food and tobacco products, chemicals and clothing. Famous for its industrial fairs.

It has a university (founded 1636), several outstanding museums and a cathedral dating from the 13th cent. The Union of Utrecht (1579) laid the foundation of the Netherlands. The Treaty of Utrecht (1713) ended the War of the Spanish Succession.

Utrera Spain. Town in Seville province, Andalusia 29 km (18 miles) SE of Seville. Pop. (1970) 35,775.

Market town and railway junction. Manufactures olive oil. Industries inc. flour-milling and tanning. There are remains of a Moorish alcázar.

Utsunomiya Japan. Cap. of Tochigi prefecture 100 km (62 miles) N of Tokyo. Pop. (1991) 430,967. Railway junction and tourist centre, terminus of a branch line to the Nikko National Park.

Uttar Pradesh India. State in the N, bounded on the N by Tibet (China) and Nepal. Area 294,411 sq km (115,004 sq. miles). Pop. (1991) 139,031,130. Cap. Lucknow. In the NW are the Himalayas, rising to over 7500 m (24,600 ft) in Kamet and Nanda Devi, but the majority of the state lies in the Upper Ganges plain. Crossed by the three great tributaries, the Jumna, Gogra and Gumti, as well as the Ganges itself. About three-quarters of the pop. depend on agriculture.

Principal crops wheat, rice, pulses, sugarcane, oilseeds. Large numbers of cattle, used mainly as draught animals. Chief industrial centres Kanpur, Lucknow, Allahabad, Ghaziabad, Mirzapur, Agra (containing the Taj Mahal), Varanasi and Bareilly. Industries inc. leather, sugar, oil-refining, fertilizers, aluminium, electronics, diesel locomotives, aeronautical parts, glass, brewing, textiles and automotive tyres. A petrochemical complex is being established at Auraiya.

In 1877 the provinces of Agra and Oudh were united and in 1902 their name was changed to the United Provinces of Agra and Oudh. When India became independent the states of Rampur, Benares and Tehri-Garhwal were incorporated into the Uttar Pradesh (1949); present name adopted 1950.

Uttoxeter England. Market town in Staffordshire 19 km (12 miles) NW of Burton-on-Trent. Pop. (1991) 10,329.

Manufactures agricultural machinery and biscuits.

Uusimaa Finland. Province situated on the Gulf of Finland. Area 9898 sq km (3822 sq. miles). Cap. Helsinki. Pop. (1992) 1,262,752. Mainly low-level country drained by short streams.

Industries inc. lumbering, sawmilling, dairying, stock-rearing and metalworking.

Uxbridge England. Former municipal borough in Middlesex on the R. Colne 24 km (15 miles) WNW of London; from 1965 part of the Greater London borough of Hillingdon. A largely residential town.

Brickmaking, sawmilling and engineering.

The Old Treaty House was the scene of the abortive negotiations between Charles I and the Parliamentarians (1645).

Uzbekistan (Ozbekiston Respublikasy). Republic in Central Asia, bounded on the N by Kazakhstan, on the E by Kirghizia and Tajikistan, on the S by Afghanistan and on the W by Turkmenistan. The country is divided into the regions of Andizhan, Bukhara, Dzhizak, Ferghana, Kashkadar, Khorezm, Namangan, Samarkand, Surkhan-Darya, Syr-Darya, Tashkent and the Karakalpak Autonomous Republic. Area 447,400 sq km (172,741 sq. miles). Pop. (1990) 20,332,000 (41 per cent urban). Life expectancy, 66 years male, 73 female. Cap. Tashkent. Other major cities Samarkand, Namangan, Andhizan and Bukhara. Currency: Ruble = 100 kopuks.

The Kyzyl Kum desert occupies a large part of the republic, but it is watered by the Amu Darya and Syr Darya, and irrigation is highly developed. Climate dry continental, with hot summers; rainfall varies from less than 12.5 cm (5 ins.) annually in the desert in the N to 50–65 cm (20–25 ins.) in the foothills of the Pamirs and Tien Shan in the SE. With the help of irrigation agriculture flourishes, esp. in the fertile Ferghana Valley and the Tashkent, Khorezm and Zeravshan oases. Land use: forested 4 per cent, meadows and pastures 53 per cent, agricultural and under permanent cultivation 10 per cent.

Sunni Muslims make up the majority of the pop. and Uzbeks represent 71 per cent of the ethnic composition; Russian 8 per cent, Tajik 5 per cent, Kazakh 4 per cent, Tatar 2 per cent and Kara-Kalpak 2 per cent. The official lang. is Uzbek.

Uzbekistan, as a result of irrigation systems, has become a leading cotton producer. Rice and alfalfa are important crops and there are large numbers of sheep and cattle. Agriculture is highly mechanized. Principal minerals coal and oil.

The Uzbeks, or Uzbegs, derive their name

from the 14th-cent. Uzbeg Khan, a chief of the Golden Horde, who introduced Islam. They divided into separate khanates and were compelled to submit to the Russians between 1864 and 1873, though Khiva and Bukhara were nominally independent till 1917. The Uzbek Soviet Socialist Republic was formed in 1924 and it became a constituent republic in 1925. In 1990 a declaration of sovereignty was made and in 1991, following an unsuccessful *coup*, Uzbekistan declared itself independent which was confirmed by referendum. Later that year Uzbekistan became a member of the Commonwealth of Independent States. A new Constitution was adopted in 1993 which states that the country is a pluralist democracy. There is a 500-member Supreme Soviet.

V

Vaal River South Africa. River 1200 km (750 miles) long rising in the Drakensberg mountains, flowing generally WSW to join the Orange R. The reservoir behind the Vaal Dam, where the Vaal is joined by the Wilge 32 km (20 miles) SE of Vereeniging, supplies water to the Witwatersrand and irrigates 27,000 ha (66,000 acres) of land.

Vaasa (Swedish **Vasa**) Finland. Formerly (1852–1918) Nikolainkaupunki (or Niko-laistad). Cap. of the Vaasa province on the Gulf of Bothnia 370 km (230 miles) NNW of Helsinki. Pop. (1991) 53,764.

Seaport. Exports timber, tar, wood products. Ship-repairing, sawmilling, flour-milling and sugar-refining. Manufactures textiles.

Founded 1606. Destroyed by fire 1852; rebuilt nearer the sea and renamed.

Vadodara ➤BARODA.

Vaduz Liechtenstein. Cap. of the principality near the flood-plain of the Rhine R. and the Swiss frontier 37 km (23 miles) SSE of St Gallen (Switzerland). Pop. (1990) 4870. Vaduz is a small town dominated by the castle of the princes of Liechtenstein. It lies above the drainage canal which reclaimed its marshy surroundings in the 1930s. The economy depends on commerce and on tourism and its related services. Vaduz was the seat of a small independent ruler until it came to the princes of Liechtenstein in the early 18th cent. It served a rural area until 1945, since when tourism and industrialization have greatly increased.

Valais (Ger. **Wallis**) Switzerland. Canton in the S bordering S on Italy and W on France. Area 5226 sq km (2017 sq. miles). Pop. (1991) 253,882 (mostly French-speaking and Roman Catholic). Cap. Sion. Inc. the upper Rhône valley from the source to L. Geneva and many of the peaks of the Bernese (N) and Pennine (S) Alps – Finsteraarhorn, Matterhorn, Monte Rosa – and also the Great St Bernard and Simplon passes. Fine Alpine scenery. Lower mountain slopes forested. In the Rhône valley cereals and vines are culti-vated. Principal resort Zermatt. Valais was a French department (Simplon) 1810–13 and then joined the Swiss Confederation in 1815.

Valdai Hills Russia. Low ridges NW of Moscow rising at the highest point to 315 m (1033 ft) and forming the watershed to the Volga, W Dvina and other rivers.

Val-de-Marne France. Department just SE of Paris, formed in 1964 when the former Seine and Seine-et-Oise departments were reorganized. Area 245 sq km (95 sq. miles). Pop. (1991) 1,219,300. Prefecture Créteil.

Valdepeñas Spain. Town in Ciudad Real province, New Castile 158 km (98 miles) NE of Córdoba. Pop. (1991) 25,241.

Vine-growing centre, noted for its wines and *bodegas*. Also produces olive oil, vinegar and leather.

Valdez USA. Oil pipeline terminal at the head of Prince William Sound, Gulf of Alaska. Pop. (1991) 9900. It receives oil from the Beaufort Sea.

Valdivia Chile. Cap. of Valdivia province 740 km (460 miles) SSW of Santiago on the Valdivia R. 18 km (11 miles) from its port, Corral. Pop. (1991) 123,580.

Industrial and commercial centre, in a rich agricultural region noteworthy for the beauty of its scenery. Tanning, flour-milling, brewing. Manufactures food products, metal goods and paper.

Founded (1552) and much developed by German settlers in the 1850s.

Val-d'Oise France. Department just N and NW of Paris, formed in 1964 when the former Seine and Seine-et-Oise departments were reorganized. Area 1246 sq km (481 sq. miles). Pop. (1991) 1,064,900. Prefecture Pontoise.

Valdosta USA. Town in S Georgia 249 km (155 miles) SW of Savannah. Pop. (1970) 32,303.

Railway junction. In a region producing cotton, tobacco, timber. Manufactures textiles and wood products.

First settled 1859; named after the Italian Valle d'Aosta.

Valence France. Prefecture of the Drôme department on the Rhône R. 93 km (58 miles) S of Lyon. Pop. (1990) 65,026.

Market town. Trade in fruits, olives, wines and cereals. Industries inc. flour-milling and it manufactures rayon and silk goods and furniture.

It was important in Roman times and was the medieval cap. of the duchy of Valentinois. Romanesque cathedral (11th-cent., restored).

Valencia (Ireland) ➤VALENTIA.

Valencia Spain. 1. Autonomous community and former kingdom in the E on the Mediterranean Sea, comprising the modern provinces of Castellón de la Plana, Valencia and Alicante, formed from it in 1833. Regained from the Moors by the Cid (1094), it was taken by James I of Aragón (1238), but maintained its political identity until the 18th cent. Area 504,750 sq km (194,885 sq. miles). Pop. (1991) 3,831,197.

2. Province of the Valencia autonomous community. Area 10,763 sq km (4239 sq. miles). Pop. (1991) 2,117,927. Cap. Valencia. Mountainous in the interior and rising to over 1200 m (3936 ft) in the NW, with a narrow but extremely fertile coastal plain. The irrigation system derives much of its water from the Turia and Júcar rivers. Famous for its *huertas*, irrigated lands yielding more than one crop annually. Produces oranges and raisins.

3. Cap. of Valencia province and the third largest city in Spain on the Turia R. on the irrigated coastal plain. Pop. (1991) 752,909.

Industrial centre and seaport (harbour 3 km (2 miles) E). Exports oranges, raisins, vegetables, olive oil and wine. Shipbuilding, railway engineering. Manufactures textiles (silk, rayon, linen), chemicals, machinery and tiles. Tourism is important.

In one of the porches of the 13th/15th-cent. cathedral the 'water tribunal' has met every week since 1350 to discuss irrigation problems. The Lonja de Mercadero (medieval silk mart) is perhaps finer architecturally than the cathedral. The university dates from *c.* 1500. The art gallery is second only to the Prado (Madrid).

Valencia Venezuela. Cap. of Carabobo state just W of L. Valencia. Pop. (1990) 903,076.

Commercial and industrial centre in the leading agricultural region (sugar-cane, cotton). Tanning, sugar-refining, meatpacking. Manufactures textiles and leather goods. Linked by road and rail with its port Puerto Cabello 32 km (20 miles) N.

Founded 1555.

Valenciennes France. Town in the Nord department on the Escau (Scheldt) R. 47 km (29 miles) SE of Lille. Pop. (1990) 39,276.

Coalmining and industrial centre, manufacturing textiles and chemicals. Engineering and sugar-refining. Formerly famous for its lace.

Valentia (Valencia) Ireland. Island 11 km (7 miles) long and 3 km (2 miles) wide just off the coast of Co. Kerry. Terminal station of the original transatlantic cable, laid (1865) by the *Great Eastern.*

Farming, fishing. Slate, once important, is no longer quarried.

Vale of Glamorgan Wales. County Borough created in 1996, formerly part of South Glamorgan. Pop. (1994) 119,000.

Valetta ➤VALLETTA.

Valladolid (Mexico) ➤MORELIA.

Valladolid Spain. 1. Province in Old Castile. Area 8202 sq km (3158 sq. miles). Pop. (1991) 491,733. Situated on the Meseta. Drained by the Duero (Douro) R. and its tributaries. Fertile areas produce cereals and wine.

2. Cap. of Valladolid province at the confluence of the Pisuerga and the Esgueva rivers 160 km (100 miles) NW of Madrid at a height of 660 m (2165 ft). Pop. (1991) 328,365.

Railway junction. Industrial centre. Railway engineering, tanning, flour-milling and brewing. Manufactures textiles, chemicals and metal goods.

Cathedral (16th-cent.), several older churches, university (founded in the 13th cent.) and the home of Cervantes are noteworthy.

Valle d'Aosta Italy. Autonomous region (since 1948) in the NW, bordering N on Switzerland (Pennine Alps) and W on France (Graian Alps). Area 3262 sq km (1259 sq. miles). Pop. (1991) 117,208 (mainly French-speaking). Cap. Aosta. Comprises the upper basin of the Dora Baltea R. It is largely agricultural and there are many hydroelectric plants.

Vallejo USA. Port and industrial town in California on San Pablo Bay 32 km (20 miles) N of Oakland. Pop. (1990) 109,199.

Flour-milling, meat-packing. Naval station on Mare Island.

State cap. for a brief period 1852–3.

Vallenar Chile. Town in Atacama province in the irrigated Huasco valley 145 km (90 miles) SSW of Copiapó. Pop. (1989) 42,000. On the main N–S railway; also linked by rail with its port Huasco. Market town in a wine-producing district.

Valletta (Valetta) Malta. Cap., chief seaport, commercial and cultural centre, built at the end of a rocky peninsula, Mt Sceberras, on the E coast, lying between Grand and Marsamxett (Marsamuscetto) Harbours. Pop. (1991) 9199. The city lies on a promontory between its E and W harbours, which it overlooks from a height. The most important buildings are those surviving from the rule of the Knights of St John of Jerusalem; the former naval dockyard survives in commercial use.

The city is a trading centre and a tourist base as well as the centre of government; coastal and island shipping is important. There is light engineering and food-processing.

Built in 1565 by the Knights, Valletta fell to the French in 1798 and the British in 1800; it was a strategic naval base, suffering severe damage in World War II. The town became once more the cap. of an independent state in 1964.

Valleyfield (officially **Salaberry de Valleyfield**) Canada. Industrial town in Quebec on the St Lawrence R. at the E end of L. St Francis 53 km (33 miles) SW of Montreal. Pop. (1971) 30,173.

Manufactures textiles, paper and felt.

Valley Stream USA. Town in New York on the SW coast of Long Island. Pop. (1970) 40,413. Mainly residential; an outer suburb of New York City.

Valois France. Ancient district NE of Paris, now in the Oise and Aisne departments. A county, later a duchy, it was united to the crown in 1214 and again in 1498. Its cap. was Crépy-en-Valois.

Valona ►VLONË.

Valparaiso Chile. Cap. of Valparaiso province on a wide bay, sheltered naturally from the S and artificially from the N, 96 km (60 miles) WNW of Santiago. Pop. (1991) 295,594. The leading seaport of Chile and of the W coast of South America.

Important industrial centre. Industries inc. sugar-refining, and manufactures textiles, clothing, chemicals and leather goods.

Founded in 1536, it has suffered many earthquakes. Largely destroyed by that of 1906.

Valsad India. Town situated S of Surat on the Gulf of Cambay in Gujarat. Pop. (1981) 82,697.

Port exporting timber, cotton, silk fabrics, millet, wheat, molasses and tiles. Industries inc. coach-building, engineering; manufactures bricks and pottery.

Valtellina Italy. Valley of the upper Adda R. in Lombardy, extending from the Ortler mountain group to L. Como. Has many hydroelectric plants and tourist resorts. The chief town is Sondrio. Belonged to the Cisalpine Republic from 1797; passed to Austria (1815) and to Italy (1859).

Van, Lake Turkey. Salt lake in the E at a height of 1700 m (5575 ft), the largest in Turkey, with no outlet. Area 3763 sq km (1453 sq. miles). The small town of Van, cap. of Van province, stands near its E shore. Salt and soda are obtained from the lake water by evaporation.

Vancouver Canada. Largest city in British Columbia, the third largest in Canada and the country's chief Pacific seaport on Burrard Inlet of Georgia Strait. Pop. (1991) 471,844. Has an excellent natural harbour.

Handles cargoes of grain, fish, minerals and timber. Commercial, financial and industrial metropolis of W Canada. Industries inc. shipbuilding, fish-canning, oil-refining, sawmilling and the manufacture of wood-pulp and paper, steel goods, furniture and chemicals. Also the terminus of the transcontinental railways. International airport. Linked with the Alberta oilfields by a pipeline (completed 1953). It is a popular tourist centre.

Before World War II most of its inhabitants were of British extraction, but since 1945 it has become more cosmopolitan.

Vancouver USA. Port and commercial town in SW Washington, on the Columbia R. opposite Portland (Oregon), with which it is connected by bridge. Pop. (1990) 238,000 (metropolitan area).

Exports grain, timber. Manufactures aluminium, chemicals and paper. Also a military station.

Founded 1825.

Vancouver Island Canada. Largest island off the W coast of America in SW British Columbia. Area 32,135 sq km (12,405 sq. miles). Largely mountainous and densely for-ested; highest peak Golden Hinde (2202 m, 7223 ft) in Strathcona Provincial Park. No navigable rivers, but the indented coastline provides a number of good harbours. Esquimault, on the S coast, is the chief Canadian naval base in the Pacific. Climate mild and temperate.

Main occupations lumbering, fishing and fish-canning, dairy and fruit farming. Coal, gold and copper mined. Chief towns Victoria (cap. of British Columbia), Nanaimo.

The island became a Crown Colony 1849 and was united with British Columbia 1866.

Väner, Lake Sweden. The largest lake in Sweden in the SW. Area 5545 sq km (2141 sq. miles). Drained SW by the Gota R. to the Kattegat. Linked with L. Vätter and the Baltic Sea by the Gota Canal. Karlstad is on the N shore.

Vannes France. Prefecture of the Morbihan department in Brittany on the Gulf of Morbihan 96 km (60 miles) SW of Rennes. Pop. (1990) 48,450. Port.

Industries inc. boatbuilding, tanning and the manufacture of textiles.

Vanuatu. Republic in SW Pacific Ocean, consisting of a group of 80 islands about 800 km (500 miles) W of Fiji and 400 km (250 miles) NE of Caledonia. Area 12,190 sq km (4707 sq. miles). Pop. (1995) 168,000 (19 per cent urban). Life expectancy, 65 years male, 68 female. Cap. Vila (on Efate). Currency: Vatu. Most of the islands are volcanic and there are three active volcanoes. The largest island is Espiritu Santo and 67 are inhabited. The climate is tropical but moderated by oceanic influences. There is high humidity from time to time and cyclones are possible. The pop. is 98 per cent Ni-Vannatu and the official langs. are Bislama, French and English. About 77 per cent are Christians.

Chief product smoke-dried copra, cacao, coffee and frozen fish. The principal catch is tuna mainly exported to the USA. There are several food-processing plants and a beef industry is developing. Tourism and financial services are other important industries.

The islands were discovered in 1606 by the Portuguese, rediscovered by the French in 1768 and named the New Hebrides by Capt. Cook in 1774. The Anglo–French Condominium of the New Hebrides was established in 1906 and in 1960 it achieved independence and became the Republic of Vanuatu. There is a 46-member unicameral Parliament.

Var France. Department in Provence on the Mediterranean Sea. Area 5973 sq km (2306 sq. miles). Pop. (1991) 828,300. Prefecture Toulon. Contains part of the Alpes de Provence in the N and the Monts des Maures in the S; between them is the Argens R. valley. Vines, olives and mulberries cultivated. Extensive bauxite deposits (Brignoles). Chief towns Toulon, Draguignan; Hyères, St Tropez, Fréjus and St Raphael are resorts. On the transfer of the Grasse district to the Alpes-Maritimes department (1860) the river which gave it its name no longer remained within the department.

Varanasi India. Formerly Benares, then Benaras. Sacred Hindu city in SE Uttar Pradesh on the Ganges R. 113 km (70 miles) E of Allahabad. Pop. (1991) 932,400.

Industries inc. oilseed-milling and engineering. Manufactures hand-made textiles, brassware, jewellery, silk, carpets and locomotives.

For about 5 km (3 miles) along the Ganges the left bank is lined with ghats (flights of steps), where tens of thousands of pilgrims bathe annually in the sacred river; it is the ambition of every devout Hindu to have his sins thus washed away and at death to be cremated here and have his ashes scattered on the water. In the city there are about 1500 Hindu temples and several mosques, inc. the Golden Temple (1777) and the 17th-cent. mosque of Aurangzeb. For some centuries an important centre of Buddhism. Ceded to Britain 1775.

Varberg Sweden. Port and resort situated S of Göteborg on the Kattegat in Halland county. Pop. (1983) 45,367.

Industries inc. a nuclear power station, pulp mill and sawmill, and it manufactures bicycles, metal goods, shoes and linen.

Vardar River Greece/Macedonia. Chief river in Macedonia 338 km (210 miles) long, rising in the Šar Mountains and flowing NNE and then SSE, past Skoplje; it enters Greece, where it is known as the Axios and reaches the Aegean Sea near Thessaloníki (Salonika).

Varese Italy. Cap. of Varese province in Lombardy 48 km (30 miles) NW of Milan. Pop. (1990) 90,000.

Industrial centre, it manufactures machinery, textiles, footwear, vehicles and leather goods.

Has a 16th/17th-cent. basilica. L. Varese is 5 km (3 miles) W.

Varna Bulgaria. Seaport, railway terminus and resort on the Black Sea 370 km (230 miles) ENE of Sofia. Pop. (1991) 314,913. Also a commercial and industrial centre.

Trade in canned fish, grain, livestock. Tanning and food processing.

Founded by Greeks in the 6th cent BC. Taken from the Turks by the Russians and ceded to Bulgaria 1877.

Var River France. River 135 km (84 miles) long in the Alpes-Maritimes department, rising in the Maritime Alps and flowing generally SSE to the Mediterranean 6 km (4 miles) SW of Nice.

Vasa ➤VAASA.

Västerås Sweden. Cap. of Västmanland county on L. Mälar 88 km (55 miles) WNW of Stockholm. Pop. (1992) 120,354.

Important centre for the electrical industry; manufactures motors, generators, turbines, transformers, also steel and glass.

Several national Diets were held here, notably that of 1527 when the Reformation was introduced into Sweden by Gustavus Vasa.

Vatican City Italy. Sovereign papal state forming an enclave in the city of Rome. Area 0.44 sq km (⅕ sq. mile). Pop. (1993) 1000. Situated mainly on the W bank of the Tiber W of the Castel Sant'Angelo. Inc. the

Velbert

papal residence and church, and administrative buildings. In the SE is the great Piazza leading to St Peter's Basilica, immediately N and NW of which are the Vatican Palace and its gardens. Famous art collections; one of the world's greatest libraries. Also has extra-territorial rights over three great basilicas outside the City (St John Lateran, Santa Maria Maggiore and St Paul Outside the Walls), the palace of San Callisto and the papal summer residence of Castel Gandolfo. It has its own railway and radio and television stations, which broadcast in 34 languages; it issues its own stamps and coinage. Currency: Vatican City Lira = 100 centesimi, but Italian currency also used.

Created by the Lateran Treaty in 1929 between the Pope and the Italian government. It was embodied in the Constitution of the Italian Republic in 1947. A revised Concordat between the Italian Republic and The Holy See came into force in 1985. The Vatican City State is governed by a Commission appointed by the Pope.

Vatnajökull Iceland. Large icefield in the SE. Area 8133 sq km (3140 sq. miles). Inc. active volcanoes; rises to 2120 m (6954 ft) in Öraefajökull in the extreme S; in places it is 1000 m (3280 ft) thick.

Vättern, Lake Sweden. Second largest lake in Sweden SE of L. Väner. Area 1898 sq km (733 sq. miles). Linked to L. Väner by the Göta Canal (W) and to the Baltic Sea via the Motala R. (E). Jönköping is at the S end.

Vaucluse France. Department in Provence, bounded on the W by the Rhône R. and on the S by the Durance R. Area 3567 sq km (1377 sq. miles). Pop. (1991) 471,800. Prefecture Avignon. The W half is in the fertile, low-lying Rhône valley; the E half is crossed by ranges of the Alpes de Provence, rising to 1912 m (6271 ft) in Mont Ventoux. Noted for its wines (e.g. Châteauneuf-du-Pape) and fruits; olives, mulberries, cereals also cultivated. Chief towns Avignon, Orange, Cavaillon, Carpentras. Has an enclave, the canton of Valréas, in the Drôme department.

Vaud (Ger. **Waadt**) Switzerland. Canton in the W, extremely irregular in shape, bordering W on France and lying mainly between L. Neuchâtel and L. Geneva. Area 3219 sq km (1243 sq. miles). Pop. (1991) 583,625 (mainly French-speaking and Protestant). Cap. Lausanne. Mountainous in the SE but generally fertile; noted for its wines. Chief towns and resorts Lausanne, Montreux and Vevey on L. Geneva; Yverdon on L. Neuchâtel. Joined the Swiss Confederation 1803.

Vaupés Colombia. Department in SE bordering on Venezuela and Brazil. Area 90,625 sq km (34,990 sq. miles). Pop. (1992) 34,428. Cap. Mitú. Mainly forested lowland and largely undeveloped, producing rubber and balata gum.

Vauxhall England. District in the London borough of Lambeth on the S bank of the R. Thames. Named after Vauxhall Gardens (opened *c*. 1660), much frequented as a public garden from 1732 till its closure in 1859.

Växjö Sweden. Cap. of Kronoberg county 190 km (120 miles) SE of Göteborg. Pop. (1990) 70,704.

Manufactures paper, hosiery and matches. Other industries include engineering and timber.

Veenendaal Netherlands. Town situated ESE of Utrecht. Pop. (1992) 50,791.

It manufactures textiles and trades in agricultural products.

Veii Italy. Ancient city in Etruria in modern Latium 14 km (9 miles) NNW of Rome. An Etruscan stronghold, continually at war with Rome until captured by Camillus in 396 BC after a long siege. Etruscan and Roman remains have been discovered.

Vejle Denmark. Port and industrial town in E Jutland on Vejle Fiord. Pop. (1990) 51,263.

Manufactures hardware, machinery and textiles. Trade in dairy produce. Nearby is Billund, the home of Legoland.

Velbert Germany. Industrial town in North

Rhine-Westphalia in the Ruhr 13 km (8 miles) S of Essen. Pop. (1986) 88,600.

Manufactures locks, vehicle fittings and windows.

Velebit Mountains Croatia. Mountain range in the Dinaric Alps, extending about 160 km (100 miles) along the Adriatic Sea, rising to 1759 m (5770 ft) in Vaganjski Vrh.

Velebit Strait Croatia. Narrow channel about 130 km (80 miles) long parallel to the Velebit Mountains and separating the mainland from the neighbouring islands of Pag and Rab.

Vélez Málaga Spain. Town in Málaga province, Andalusia on the Vélez R. 29 km (18 miles) ENE of Málaga. Pop. (1991) 50,936.

Market town in a fertile region producing vines, citrus fruits, sugar-cane. Sugar-refining and tanning. Manufactures soap. Served by the nearby port of Torre del Mar.

Velletri Italy. Ancient Velitrae. Town in Roma province, Latium in the Alban Hills 35 km (22 miles) SE of Rome. Pop. (1985) 42,000.

Wine-making. Railway junction.

Vellore India. Town in Tamil Nadu on the Palar R. 129 km (80 miles) WSW of Madras. Pop. (1991) 172,467.

Trade in agricultural produce, sandalwood.

Famous for its fortress and a temple of Siva.

Velsen Netherlands. Industrial town in N Holland province 21 km (13 miles) WNW of Amsterdam, forming a municipality with the fishing port of Ijmuiden (Ymuiden) 3 km (2 miles) W on the North Sea Canal. Pop. (1992) 61,506.

Important centre of the steel industry; also manufactures chemicals, cement and paper.

Venda. Formerly a Bantu Homeland which was granted 'independence' by the Republic of South Africa in 1979, but now part of Northern Province, South Africa. Area 7460 sq km (2880 sq. miles). Pop. (1991) *de jure* 726,436, *de facto* 558,797. Cap. Thohoy-

andou. Most of the country is only useful for raising livestock. Industrial development is still at early stages. Tourism is being developed.

Vendée France. Department on the Bay of Biscay, formed (1790) from part of Poitou. Area 6720 sq km (2595 sq. miles). Pop. (1991) 512,000. Prefecture La Roche-sur-Yon. Hilly in the NE but generally low-lying. Drained by the Sèvre Nantaise, the Sèvre Niortaise and its tributary the Vendée. Mainly agricultural. Cattle-rearing. Produces wheat, fodder crops, fruit and wine. Tourism is important. Chief towns La Roche-sur-Yon, Les Sables d'Olonne. Scene of the Vendée royalist resistance to the French Revolution (1793–5).

Veneto Italy. Formerly Venezia Euganea. Region in the NE comprising the provinces of Belluno, Padova (Padua), Rovigo, Treviso, Venezia, Verona, Vicenza. Area 18,364 sq km (7090 sq. miles). Pop. (1991) 4,452,667. Cap. Venice. Mountainous in the N, inc. the Dolomites, the Asiago Plateau and part of the Carnic Alps. Extends to L. Garda in the SW and Austria in the NE. The fertile plain (S) is drained by the Po, Adige, Brenta, Piave and other rivers. Produces wheat, vines, sugar-beet and hemp. Chief towns Venice, Padua, Treviso, Vicenza, Verona. Lost the province of Udine after World War II (1946), when this became part of Friuli-Venezia Giulia.

Venezia Giulia Italy. Former region in the NE comprising the provinces of Carnaro, Gorizia, Istria, Trieste and Zara. After World War II most of the region was ceded to Yugoslavia, the remainder becoming part of Friuli-Venezia Giulia.

Venezuela. Republic in South America bounded on the N by the Caribbean, E by Guyana, S by Brazil and SW by Colombia. Area 912,050 sq km (352,143 sq. miles). Pop. (1995) 21,844,000 (84 per cent urban). Life expectancy, 70 years male, 76 female. Cap. Caracas. Other leading towns Maracaibo, Valencia, Barquisimeto,

Maracay and Petare. Currency: Bolívar = 100 centimos.

In the W the East Cordillera of the Andes trends NE as the high Cordillera de Mérida, then E, where lower highlands run parallel with the coast. W of L. Maracaibo is another spur of the East Cordillera, the Sierra de Perijá and to the NE are the Segovia Highlands. Inland the vast lowland plains or *llanos* of central Venezuela are traversed by meandering tributaries of the Orinoco R. In the SE the Guiana Highlands occupy almost half the country, rivers rising here cut deep valleys as they too flow to the Orinoco, whose C-shaped course follows the massif edge.

There are four main climatic zones (according to altitude): the *Tierra caliente* up to 900 m (2952 ft) with mean annual temperatures over 24°C (75°F), rainforest in wet locations, cacao, bananas and sugar-cane being cultivated; the *tierra templada*, 900–1800 m (2953–5904 ft), 18°–24°C (64°–75°F) coffee being the chief crop on forest-cleared slopes; the *tierra fria*, 1800–3000 m (5905–9840 ft), 13°–18°C (55°–64°F), with cultivation of cereals; the *páramos*, alpine meadows from 3000 m (9840 ft) to the snow-line at about 4650 m (15,252 ft). Differences in rainfall are considerable and affect vegetation and land use at all levels. In N Venezuela E to NE winds prevail, so that sometimes the E slopes bear rainforest while the W slopes have scrub savannah. Seasonal variations are most marked in the *llanos*, which are covered with tall-grass savannah, swamp grasses and low deciduous woodland; they are often flooded April–Oct., but are dry Nov.-March, when the green, swamp-like conditions of the hot, wet season change to a landscape of dry, brown grasses, leafless trees and cracked mudflats. The lower Orinoco and NE Guiana Highlands carry dense rainforest; the W Guiana Highlands have much deciduous forest and wooded savannah. Land use: forested 35 per cent, meadows and pastures 20 per cent, agricultural and under permanent cultivation 4 per cent. Religion, Roman Catholic 92 per cent of the pop. and the lang. is Spanish. About 69 per cent of the pop. are mestizos of Spanish–Indian stock, about 20 per cent are white, 9 per cent black and 2 per cent Indian.

A leading petroleum exporter and oil reserves are large. The industry was nationalized in 1976, but private and foreign investment has been allowed since 1992. Petroleum represents over 80 per cent of total exports. It is produced chiefly around L. Maracaibo, with other wells in the E *llanos*. Pipelines run from the oilfields to refineries on the shores of L. Maracaibo, on the Paraguaná peninsula and at Puerto la Cruz in the NE. A dredged channel (completed 1956) enables ocean-going vessels to enter L. Maracaibo and tankers transport oil to the Dutch Caribbean islands of Curaçao and Aruba. Resources of iron ore, manganese and bauxite are tapped on the northern edge of the Guiana Highlands, formerly yielding only gold and diamonds, and iron ore is a significant export; there is a steel works at Puerto Ordaz and a hydroelectric plant on the Caroní R. The revenue from oil aids the growth of secondary industries, though development has been very limited. Principal manufactures steel, paper, textiles, clothing, footwear, cement, tyres and petrochemicals. There is food-processing. Despite the country's mineral wealth, many of the people have a low living standard, particularly those engaged in agriculture. Coffee grown in the highlands is the principal commercial crop, cacao, sugar-cane, tobacco and cotton are grown, and cattle are raised; large areas of the *llanos* are either undeveloped or used for rough grazing.

The first settlements in Venezuela were established by the Spaniards at Cumaná (1521) and Coro (1527) on the N coast; Valencia was founded in 1555 and Caracas in 1567. They penetrated the highlands, seeking gold, but made no settlement in the Orinoco basin until the 18th cent. Resisting Spanish oppression and avarice, in 1811, Francisco de Miranda and Simón Bolívar declared a short-lived independence which was finally won after the Spanish defeat at Carabobo (1821). In 1830, however, Venezuela seceded from the newly-formed union of Gran Colombia. There followed more than a century of civil war, dictatorships and international disputes, though economic relief was gained with oilfield development, begun in 1918. In 1947 a constitution provided for presidential election by popular vote, which was followed by a military *coup d'état* (1948). The head of the junta government was assassinated, however, and the promulgation of a new constitution in 1961 did not save the country from further internal strife and there were two abortive military *coups* in 1992. The country is divided into 20 states, two federal territories, a federal district round the cap. and 72 federal dependencies. Parliament consists of a bicameral National Congress comprising a Senate of 44 elected members (plus 3 ex-Presidents) and a 201-member Chamber of Deputies.

Venice (Italian **Venezia**) Italy. Cap. of Veneto region and of the Venezia province at the head of the Adriatic Sea in the NW of the Gulf of Venice. Pop. (1991) 317,837. Seaport. Naval base.

Industrial centre. Industries inc. the manufacture of glassware, jewellery, textiles, furniture; there is oil-refining, petrochemicals, engineering, shipbuilding, printing and publishing. Most industries are located in the mainland suburbs of Porto Marghera and Mestre, where two-thirds of the pop. live.

The city is built on a cluster of more than 100 small islands; linked with the mainland by a railway and road bridge. The islands are divided into two groups by the Grand Canal, the main artery of traffic, winding NW–SE. About 170 smaller canals (crossed by 400 bridges) serve the Grand Canal; means of transport consist of steamers, launches and gondolas. Beside the canals are many Byzantine, Gothic and Renaissance palaces, erected on piles driven into the soft mud. At the centre is the famous St Mark's Square (Piazza San Marco) where are the great 11th/15th-cent. Basilica of St Mark, the 15th-cent. Clock Tower (Torre dell' Orologio), the Campanile, the Doge's Palace and the Bridge of Sighs (connecting the Palace with the state prison). Among the many other churches are those of SS. Giovanni e Paolo, San Salvatore and Santa Maria della Salute. The Academy of Fine Arts has the world's finest collection of Venetian paintings, with works by Bellini, Mantegna, Titian, Veronese, Tintoretto, Giorgione. 3 km (2 miles) SE, on a low island between the lagoon and the Gulf of Venice, is the fashionable seaside resort, Lido.

Founded by mainland refugees escaping from the barbarian invasions which began in the 5th cent. The first Doge was elected in 697. With its favourable position for trade between Europe and the East the city became a strong maritime and commercial power; Venetian rule extended over the E Mediterranean and the Aegean to the Black Sea. It was governed by a strict oligarchy. Defeated Genoa, its great rival, in 1380; attained the peak of prosperity in the 14th and early 15th cent. Began to decline after the discovery of the Cape route to India. Ceded to Austria by Napoleon 1797. Passed to the new kingdom of Italy 1866. There were devastating floods in 1966 and great efforts are being made to prevent Venice from sinking.

Venlo Netherlands. Industrial town and railway junction in Limburg province on the Maas R. near the German frontier. Pop. (1992) 64,890.

Brewing, distilling, tanning. Manufactures chemicals. Also a river port and market town, with a large trade in market-garden produce.

Ventimiglia Italy. Seaport in Imperial province, Liguria on the Gulf of Genoa 13 km (8 miles) W of San Remo. Pop. (1989) 27,003. Also a seaside resort (Italian Riviera) with an important flower market.

Cathedral (12th-cent., restored). The ruins of the ancient Album Intimilium lie 5 km (3 miles) E of the modern town.

Ventnor England. Seaside resort on the S coast of the Isle of Wight. Pop. (1991) 5710. Built on terraces above the sea, it has a mild climate and contains several hospitals and convalescent homes. To the E is Bonchurch, where Swinburne (1837–1909) is buried. To the N is St Boniface Down (240 m; 787 ft), the highest point in the Isle of Wight.

Veracruz Mexico. 1. State on the Gulf of Mexico and its arm, the Gulf of Campeche, inc. part of the Isthmus of Tehuantepec. Area 71,699 sq km (27,683 sq. miles). Pop. (1990) 6,215,142. Cap. Jalapa. Extends from the coastal plain into the Sierra Madre Oriental.

Mainly agricultural. Crops inc. cotton, sugar-cane, tobacco. Rubber, chicle and hardwoods obtained from the forests. There are oil wells along the Gulf coast. Chief towns Jalapa and Veracruz.

2. Leading seaport of Mexico on the Gulf of Mexico in Veracruz state. Pop. (1990) 327,522.

Exports coffee, chicle, vanilla and tobacco. Flour-milling. Manufactures textiles, chemicals and soap. Also a seaside resort.

Founded nearby in 1519 and moved to the present site in 1599.

Vercelli Italy. Ancient Vercellae. Cap. of Vercelli province in Piedmont on the Sesia R. 64 km (40 miles) ENE of Turin. Pop. (1988) 51,103.

Important trade in rice. Industries inc. rice and flour milling, sugar-refining and textile manufacture.

In the cathedral library is the Vercelli Book (*Codex Vercellensis*), an Anglo-Saxon MS. dating from the early 11th cent. Chief town of the ancient Ligurian tribe of Libici.

Verde, Cape Senegal. The westernmost point of Africa, a promontory 32 km (20 miles) long E–W. The W tip is Cape Almadies. Dakar is on the S coast.

Verdun France. Ancient Verodunum. Small industrial town in the Meuse department on the canalized Meuse R. 58 km (36 miles) W of Metz. Pop. (1985) 24,000.

Manufactures alcohol, clothing and furniture.

The ancient town was already important by the Roman conquest. By the famous Treaty of Verdun (843) the empire of Charlemagne was divided into three parts. It was one of the Three Bishoprics (with Toul and Metz) taken by France from the Holy Roman Empire (1552). In its strategic position at the E approach to the Paris Basin, Verdun became an important French fortress. During World War I it was the scene of a long and costly battle (1916), characterized by a powerful German offensive repulsed by an equally determined and courageous French resistance.

Vereeniging South Africa. Town in Gauteng on the Vaal R. 53 km (33 miles) S of Johannesburg at a height of 1450 m (4756 ft). Pop. (1985) 61,000.

Coalmining and industrial centre. Manufactures iron and steel, nuts and bolts, cables and wire, bricks and tiles.

The Boer War was ended by the Treaty of Vereeniging (1902).

Verkhoyansk Russia. Town in the Sakha Republic on the Yana R. 676 km (420 miles) NNE of Yakutsk, with which it is linked by air.

Fur-trading and mining centre. Situated near the so-called 'cold pole' of the earth, with a mean Jan. temperature of $-51°$ C ($-54°$ F) but a mean July temperature of $15°$ C ($59°$ F); here the lowest temperature then recorded on the earth's surface, $-68°$ C ($-82°$ F), was registered (1892) and the temperature has since reached almost $-73°$ C ($-90°$ F). Formerly used as a place of exile.

Verkhoyansk Range Russia. Range of mountains in the Sakha Republic, extending about 1600 km (1000 miles) W and N in an arc parallel to and E of the Lena R. Rises in the extreme SE to 2460 m (8069 ft).

Vermont USA. New England state in the NE, bordering N on Quebec (Canada). Area 24,900 sq km (9614 sq. miles). Pop. (1990) 570,000. Cap. Montpelier. Traversed N–S by the Green Mountains, which rise to 1340 m (4395 ft) in Mt Mansfield. Principal river the Connecticut, which forms the E boundary. Climate humid continental; average rainfall 90–110 cm (35–43 ins.) annually.

Mainly agricultural. Leading crops hay, maize, apples, potatoes; produces maple syrup and sugar. Granite and marble quarried. Flourishing tourist industry. Vermont has always been a mainly rural state; only Burlington has a pop. exceeding 30,000.

It was admitted to the Union (1791) as the 14th state.

Véroia (Verria) Greece. Cap. of Imathia *nome*, Macedonia, 64 km (40 miles) WSW of Thessaloniki (Salonika). Pop. (1971) 29,538.

Trade in cereals. Manufactures textiles.

Verona Italy. Cap. of Verona province in Veneto on the Adige R. 106 km (66 miles) W of Venice. Pop. (1991) 258,946. Hub of routes from N Italy (Milan, Venice) through the Brenner Pass.

Trade in cereals. Manufactures paper, plastics and rope. Printing.

Renowned for its buildings, among which are the 12th/17th-cent. Romanesque cathedral, the churches of S Zeno, S Anastasia and S Fermo Maggiore, the tombs of the della Scala family (Scaligeri) and the medieval Castel Vecchio, which houses the fine Museum of Art. Of the Roman remains the outstanding is the restored amphitheatre, seating about 25,000 people, where open-air performances are held during the summer. Powerful and prosperous under the Romans, it was still more important in medieval times, and at various periods was a leading centre of art. Under Austrian rule (1797–1866) it was one of the famous 'Quadrilateral' of fortresses (with Peschiera, Mantua and Legnago). Birthplace of the painter, Paolo Veronese (1528–88).

Versailles France. Prefecture of the Yvelines department, a residential suburb 18 km (11 miles) WSW of Paris. Pop. (1990) 91,029.

Also a tourist centre, chiefly famous for the magnificent palace. Varied industries. Louis XIII had a hunting lodge built near the village in 1624; the palace was designed in the late 17th cent. for Louis XIV by Le Vau and Mansart on a grand scale and at enormous cost. Among the outstanding features are the Hall of Mirrors, the Orangery and the gardens planned by Le Nôtre. Nearby are two smaller palaces the Grand Trianon and the Petit Trianon, the latter a favourite residence of Marie Antoinette. In the Hall of

Mirrors William I of Prussia was crowned Emperor of Germany (1871) and the Treaty of Versailles between the Allied powers and Germany was signed (1919) at the end of World War I.

Verviers Belgium. Industrial town in Liège province on the Vesdre R. 24 km (15 miles) ESE of Liège. Pop. (1992) 53,716.

Important woollen industry. Also manufactures textile machinery, leather goods, chemicals and chocolate.

Vesuvius (Italian **Vesuvio**) Italy. Active volcano in Campania near the E shore of the Bay of Naples 13 km (8 miles) ESE of Naples. The cone is half enclosed by a ridge, Monte Somma (1133 m; 3716 ft), which is the wall of a great prehistoric crater, and the slopes are marked by lava flows. On the W slope is a seismological observatory (established 1844). Vineyards on the fertile lower slopes produce grapes for the well-known Lacrima Christi wine. The first recorded eruption occurred in AD 79 and destroyed Pompeii, Herculaneum and Stabiae. For centuries Vesuvius was then much less active, but a severe eruption occurred in 1631, and further great convulsions in 1779, 1794, 1822, 1872, 1906, 1929 and 1944. These eruptions have continually altered its height, which is now 1277 m (4190 ft); that of 1944 destroyed the funicular railway and a chair lift now takes visitors almost to the edge of the crater.

Veszprém Hungary. Cap. of Veszprém county on the S slopes of the Bakony Hills 96 km (60 miles) SW of Budapest. Pop. (1989) 66,000.

Railway junction. Market town. Industries inc. electronics and engineering, and it manufactures textiles and wine.

Vevey Switzerland. Resort in Vaud canton on the NE shore of L. Geneva 18 km (11 miles) ESE of Lausanne. Pop. (1985) 15,000.

Manufactures chocolate and tobacco products.

Viana do Castelo Portugal. 1. District in N bordered by Spain and the Atlantic Ocean. Area 2255 sq km (871 sq. miles). Pop. (1991)

248,700. Mountains in E, the principal river is the Lima.

2. Cap. of district and port situated N of Oporto. Pop. (1991) 8780.

Manufactures inc. carpets, flour products and chocolate. It has an important trade in cod.

Viareggio Italy. Seaside resort in Lucca province, Tuscany, on the Ligurian Sea 21 km (13 miles) WNW of Lucca. Pop. (1985) 60,000. Sandy beaches sheltered by pine woods.

Manufactures hosiery.

The body of Shelley was cremated here after his death by drowning (1822).

Viborg Denmark. Cap. of Viborg county in Jutland 42 km (26 miles) W of Randers. Pop. (1985) 25,000.

Iron-founding and distilling. Manufactures textiles.

Vicenza Italy. Ancient Vicetia (Vicentia). Cap. of Vicenza province in Veneto 64 km (40 miles) WNW of Venice. Pop. (1991) 109,333.

Railway junction. Industrial centre. Manufactures iron and steel, machinery, furniture, glass and textiles, and has a food-processing industry.

Has a mainly 13th-cent. Gothic cathedral. Birthplace of Andrea Palladio (1518–80); has many of his most famous buildings (e.g. the Teatro Olimpico, the basilica and the Palazzo Chiericati).

Vichada Colombia. A department in E bordering on Venezuela. Area 98,970 sq km (38,212 sq. miles). Pop. (1992) 19,370. Cap. La Primavera. Mainly undeveloped. The principal rivers are Tomo and Vichada. Forest products inc. gums, resins and vanilla. Crops inc. corn and yucca and some cattle are reared.

Vichy France. Health resort and spa in the Allier department on the Allier R. 48 km (30 miles) NNE of Clermont-Ferrand. Pop. (1985) 64,000. Has many hotels, thermal establishments, recreational centres.

Vichy water, consumed for stomach and liver complaints, is bottled and exported. Manufactures pharmaceutical products.

Seat of the Pétain ('Vichy') government of France during World War II (1940–4).

Vicksburg USA. River port in Mississippi on the Mississippi R. near its confluence with the Yazoo R. Pop. (1990) 20,908.

Trade in cattle, cotton. Manufactures cottonseed oil, clothing and chemicals.

In the Civil War it was a confederate stronghold and was besieged for nearly 7 weeks before capitulating (1863). Just N is Vicksburg National Cemetery (established 1865) with over 16,000 soldiers' graves.

Victoria Australia. State in the SE bounded by New South Wales (N), the Tasman Sea, Bass Strait and Indian Ocean (S) and South Australia (W). Area 227,620 sq km (87,884 sq. miles). Pop. (1992) 4,452,200. Cap. Melbourne. The plains in the N and NW form part of the Murray Basin. S of these lies the extension of the Great Dividing Range, then there are fairly level lowlands, sometimes called the Great Valley and still farther S the coastal uplands. Port Phillip Bay is a drowned part of the Great Valley; into it flows the Yarra R., on which Melbourne stands. The driest area is the Murray Basin, but irrigation makes possible fruit orchards, vineyards and pastures. Extensive wheatlands and sheep country lie SW of the basin and on the inner mountain slopes. E of Melbourne there is dairy-farming, and fruit and vegetables are also grown in the S. Gold stimulated the early settlement of Victoria, with the rushes to Ballarat and Bendigo in the 1850s, but today the state produces little gold. Coal is mined in S Gippsland, and huge lignite deposits W of Melbourne supply power stations; hydroelectricity comes from dams on the Murray R. and its tributaries, and from the Snowy Mountains scheme. Many industries, esp. in Melbourne and at Geelong, Bendigo and Ballarat, and smaller towns; they inc. engineering, oil-refining and the manufacture of textiles, cars, aircraft, agricultural equipment, newsprint and chemicals. At inland towns and ports fruit is canned, preserved and dried. Pop. predominantly urban;

67 per cent of the state pop. live in the Melbourne metropolitan area. Exports inc. non-ferrous metals, fish, newsprint, refined aluminium, wool, wheat, textiles, dairy produce and canned fruit.

The first settlement was made at Portland in the SW in 1834 and in the following year Melbourne was founded. Victoria formed part of the New South Wales colony 1836–51 and was a separate colony 1851–1901. Became a state of the Commonwealth 1901, with Melbourne the Commonwealth cap. until 1927.

Victoria Canada. Cap. of British Columbia at the SE tip of Vancouver Island facing the Juan de Fuca Strait. Pop. (1991) 71,228.

Seaport and base for the fishing fleet. Exports fish, timber and cement. Industries inc. fish-canning and the manufacture of paper, computer software, electronic equipment and matches. Tourism is important.

Founded (1843) by the Hudson's Bay Company as a fur-trading post. Became cap. of British Columbia 1868.

Victoria (Hong Kong) ►HONG KONG.

Victoria (Malaysia) ►LABUAN.

Victoria (Malta) ►GOZO.

Victoria (Seychelles) ►SEYCHELLES.

Victoria USA. Industrial town in S Texas on the Guadalupe R. 193 km (120 miles) SW of Houston. Pop. (1990) 55,026.

Oil-refining. Manufactures cottonseed oil and chemicals.

Founded (1824) by Spanish settlers.

Victoria (Victoria Nyanza), Lake E Africa. The largest lake in Africa and the second largest freshwater lake in the world. Area 69,485 sq km (26,828 sq. miles). In the plateau basin between the E and W branches of the Great Rift Valley at a height of 1110 m (3641 ft). Fed by the Kagera R. (often regarded as the farthest headstream of the Nile), the Katonga R. and the Mara R. Drained N from Jinja (Uganda) by the Victoria Nile. Just below Jinja is the Owen Falls dam (completed 1954), which stores the headwaters of the Nile and has raised the lake level by 1 m (39 ins.). Many inlets in the shores, e.g. the Kavirondo Gulf (NE) and the Speke Gulf (SE). Many islands. Steamer services; main ports Jinja and Entebbe in Uganda, Bukoba and Mwanza in Tanzania, Kisumu in Kenya. Discovered (1858) by Speke; explored (1875) by Stanley. Originally Lake Ukerewe; renamed in honour of Queen Victoria.

Victoria de Durango Mexico. Cap. of Durango state in the Sierra Madre Occidental 209 km (130 miles) SW of Torreón at a height of 1925 m (6314 ft). Pop. (1990) 414,015.

Railway junction and mining town. Iron ore is mined on the famous hill Cerro del Mercado 3 km (2 miles) N. Iron-founding, sugar-refining. Manufactures textiles and glass.

Founded 1563.

Victoria Falls Zimbabwe/Zambia. Falls on the middle Zambezi R. on the frontier between Zambia and Zimbabwe. Greater in height and width than Niagara Falls; divided by islets into 3 main sections, the Eastern Cataract, the Rainbow Falls and the Main Falls. The Zambezi plunges into a great chasm over 1.6 km (1 mile) long at right-angles to its course, about 126 m (413 ft) deep at the centre. Less than 120 m (393 ft) from the edge of the falls, and at the same level, are the opposite cliffs. The river leaves the chasm through a narrow opening in the cliffs (the 'Boiling Pot') and enters a winding gorge crossed by a railway and road bridge. The Victoria Falls are an important tourist attraction, esp. June–Oct., immediately after the flood period. A hydroelectric plant serves Livingstone (Zambia).

Victoria Island Canada. Second largest island in the Canadian Arctic Archipelago in the SW Franklin District of the Northwest Territories, separated from the mainland by the Dolphin and Union Strait, Coronation Gulf and Queen Maud Gulf. Area 208,080 sq km (80,340 sq. miles). Discovered 1838.

Vienna (Ger. **Wien**) Austria. Cap., administratively a province, mainly on the right bank of the Danube R. and on the Danube Canal at the foot of wooded hills (the Wiener Wald) 32 km (20 miles) from the Slovakian border. Pop. (1991) 1,533,176.

Commercial, industrial and cultural centre, and the former seat of the Habsburg dynasty. Route centre. Inland port. Manufactures machinery, electrical equipment, textiles, pharmaceuticals, ceramics, chemicals, paper, furniture and leather goods.

The NE districts straddle the R. Danube and its parallel canal; to the SW the city rises in natural terraces into the Vienna Woods. The old city is inside the Ringstrasse, a boulevard which replaced the medieval walls and SW of the watercourses. Apart from great Gothic churches it principal buildings are baroque. The Ringstrasse is lined with parks, palaces and public buildings. Residential and industrial suburbs lie beyond the Ring and beyond the Danube. The woods to the W and some riverside woodland form a recreational greenbelt. Much of the pop. is employed in government, in state-owned cultural institutions, tourist or conference centres, services and trade. It is the headquarters of Opec and the UN International Atomic Agency. Traffic and trade on the river has increased following recent canal improvements.

After Celtic and Roman occupation the medieval town grew and received its charter in 1137. A river trading point and strategic fort, it became the Habsburgs' cap. in 1276. Vienna was a staging-post for the Crusades and profited greatly, but was also at risk from the E. The 13th-cent. walls withstood the last Turkish siege in 1683. Then there was peace, with much rebuilding and expansion. By 1850 most Viennese lived outside the original walls, which were flattened in the 1850s and replaced by the Ringstrasse. Workers' apartments went up on a massive scale at this time and again after 1918 in the first years of the republic.

Vienne France. Department in W central France, formed (1790) mainly from Poitou. Area 6990 sq km (2699 sq. miles). Pop. (1991) 380,900. Prefecture Poitiers. Drained chiefly by the Vienne R. Mainly agricultural (cereals, potatoes, wines, stock-rearing). Chief towns Poitiers and Châtellerault.

Vienne (Isère) France. Town in the Isère department on the left bank of the Rhône R. 27 km (17 miles) S of Lyon. Pop. (1968) 26,512.

Manufactures woollen and leather goods, and other industries inc. iron-founding and distilling.

Has noteworthy Roman remains (inc. the temple of Augustus and Livia) and the 11th/16th-cent. church (former cathedral) of St Maurice.

Originally cap. of the Allobroges; became an important city in Roman Gaul.

Vienne River France. River 354 km (220 miles) long, rising on the Plateau de Millevaches (N Corrèze) and flowing generally NNW past Limoges and Châtellerault to join the Loire R.

Vientiane Laos. Administrative cap. of Laos on the left bank of the Mekong R. where the latter forms the boundary with Thailand. Pop. (1985) 178,203.

River port. Commercial centre. Trades in timber, resins and gums, and textiles. Has the former royal palace and several pagodas.

It was cap. of the kingdom of Vientiane from 1707, but declined after being taken by the Thais (1827), to revive in the present cent. as cap. of all Laos.

Viersen Germany. Industrial town in North Rhine-Westphalia, on the Niers R. 6 km (4 miles) NNW of München-Gladbach. Pop. (1986) 78,160.

Manufactures textiles (velvet, cotton and linen) and paper.

Vierzon France. Town in the Cher department at the confluence of the Cher and Yèvre rivers 27 km (17 miles) NW of Bourges. Pop. (1982) 34,886.

Manufactures bricks and tiles, porcelain and agricultural machinery.

Vietnam. Republic of SE Asia bounded on the W by Cambodia and Laos, N by China and E and S by the South China Sea. Area

331,033 sq km (127,813 sq. miles). Pop. (1995) 74,545,000 (21 per cent urban). Life expectancy, 64 years male, 68 female. Cap. Hanoi. Other important cities Ho Chi Minh (Saigon), Haiphong, Da Nang. Currency: Dong = 10 hao = 100 xu.

Vietnam has a coastline of 2560 km (1600 miles) and occupies a narrow strip along the W shore of the South China Sea. It broadens out in the S at the Mekong R. delta and in the N along the valley of the Red R. The two river plains are separated by a narrow mountainous central zone. The humid monsoon climate gives tropical conditions in the S and subtropical conditions in the N, though real winter conditions can affect the N from time to time when polar air blows S over Asia. Land use: forested 30 per cent, pasture 1 per per cent, agricultural 20 per cent. Of the ethnic composition 87 per cent are Vietnamese, who are of Mongolian origin; there are minorities of Khmers and Chinese, and various aboriginal tribes such as the Moi and Miong are thinly scattered over the mountainous regions. About 55 per cent is Buddhist and 7 per cent Roman Catholic. Vietnamese is the official lang. but Chinese, French and English are also spoken.

Since unification, considerable efforts have been made to restore rail, air and road links. Manufacturing industry based on wood and rubber products, textiles, fertilizers, glass, paper, cement and light engineering is growing. Over 70 per cent of the pop. work in agriculture and rice is the most important crop and, having been an importer of rice for 20 years, in 1990 it started to export rice and is now the third largest exporter of rice in the world. Maize, beans, sugar, sorghum and sweet potatoes are grown for home consumption. Tea, coffee, tobacco are grown for export. Fishing and forestry are important industries. Minerals exploited inc. coal (which is an important export), iron, chrome manganese, phosphates, limestone and salt.

Conquered by the Chinese in 111 BC, Vietnam broke free from Chinese domination in AD 939, though at many subsequent periods it was a nominal Chinese vassal. European influence was not established till the mid-19th cent., when a French punitive expedition was sent to avenge the death of some missionaries and by 1884 Cochin-China was a French colony and Annam and Tonkin were French protectorates. There was considerable opposition to French rule, however, and this became active during the Japanese occupation of World War II, when the Vietminh League was founded by the Communists in 1941. In 1945 a Vietnamese republic was set up by the Vietminh, but the French objected to the inclusion of Cochin-China; hostilities broke out, the French were forced to withdraw and the country was partitioned approximately along the 17th parallel in 1954. At the same time South Vietnam left the French Union and attained full sovereignty. There was much disaffection over the dictatorial methods of the President of the Republic (South Vietnam), particularly in his persecution of the Buddhists (he was a Roman Catholic), and he was overthrown and shot in a military *coup* in 1963; meanwhile the Communist guerrillas or Vietcong, aided from North Vietnam, intensified their campaign and made steady progress. US economic and military aid to South Vietnam was increased rapidly 1964–6 to offset the growing strength of the Vietcong. Peace talks began in Paris in 1968. In South Vietnam political power changed hands or was seized several times. A cease-fire in the Vietnam War was agreed in 1973, but in 1975 the North Vietnamese forces launched an offensive, advanced steadily southwards and entered Saigon. Thousands of South Vietnamese and Americans were evacuated and a new (Communist) government was formed. US involvement in Vietnam came to an end. The country was reunified in 1976 and is divided administratively into 40 provinces. Under the 1992 Constitution the Communist Party of Vietnam retained its position as 'a leading force of the state and society', but it also legalized market-orientated reforms which have been under way since the mid-1980s. There is a 395-member National Assembly.

Vigevano Italy. Industrial town in Pavia

province, Lombardy near the Ticino R. 32 km (20 miles) SW of Milan. Pop. (1985) 66,000.

Manufactures footwear, textiles and plastics.

Has a 14th-cent. castle of the Sforza family.

Vigo Spain. Seaport, fishing port and resort in Pontevedra province, Galicia on the S shore of Vigo Bay (Ría de Vigo). Pop. (1991) 274,629. A port of call for transatlantic liners, with a fine natural harbour.

Fish-processing, boatbuilding, oil-refining, distilling. Manufactures chemicals, soap, cement and paper.

Attacked by Drake 1585 and 1589. A British and Dutch fleet destroyed a Spanish fleet in the bay (1702); some of the treasure of the latter is believed to be still lying there.

Viipuri ➤VYBORG.

Vijayawada India. Commercial town and railway junction in Andhra Pradesh on the Krishna R. 240 km (150 miles) ESE of Hyderabad. Pop. (1991) 701,800.

Industries inc. engineering, rice and oilseed milling. Manufactures inc. automobile bodies, handicrafts, toys, Kalam-kari textile prints. Also headquarters of the Krishna canal system for irrigation and navigation.

Vila ➤NEW HEBRIDES.

Vila Real Portugal. 1. District in N bordered by Spain. Area 4328 sq km (1671 sq. miles). Pop. (1991) 248,700. Mountainous in N. The principal rivers are Douro and Corgo. The main industry is viticulture.

2. Cap. of district of same name sit. ENE of Oporto on the Corgo R.

Manufactures inc. ceramics, cotton and flour products. It is the centre of the wine industry.

Villach Austria. Industrial town in Carinthia on the Drau (Drava) R. 35 km (22 miles) W of Klagenfurt. Pop. (1991) 55,165.

Manufactures lead products. Has a considerable tourist traffic; 3 km (2 miles) S of Warmbad Villach, with hot mineral springs.

Villahermosa Mexico. Cap. of Tabasco state on the Grijalva R. 386 km (240 miles) ESE of Veracruz. Pop. (1990) 390,161.

In recent years it has grown into a modern city, based on oil, and has two of the most interesting archaeological museums in the country. Industries inc. sugar-refining and distilling.

Villa María Argentina. Market town and railway junction in Córdoba province on the Tercero R. 145 km (90 miles) SE of Córdoba. Pop. (1985) 68,000.

Manufactures textiles. Flour-milling. Trade in grain, timber and dairy produce.

Villarrica Paraguay. Cap. of Guairá department 145 km (90 miles) ESE of Asunción in an agricultural region. Pop. (1985) 22,000.

Market town. Trade in yerba maté, tobacco, cotton and sugar-cane. Flour-milling and sugar-refining.

Villavicencio Colombia. Cap. of Meta department at the foot of the E Cordillera 72 km (45 miles) SE of Bogotá. Pop. (1985) 161,166.

Commercial centre for the *llanos*. Trade in cattle and hides. Rice-milling.

Vilnyus (Vilnius, Russian **Vilna,** Polish **Wilno)** Lithuania. Cap. on the Viliya R. in the SE. Pop. (1991) 597,700. Important railway junction and industrial centre. Saw-milling, food-processing. Manufactures agricultural implements, fertilizers and paper, engineering, electronics and processed food.

The old town covers hillsides rising above the confluence of the Neris and Vilnia rivers and is dominated by the ruined 14th-cent. castle. Newer districts, inc. the centre of government, were planned on a grid formation spreading out from the old city. The city became the national cap. in 1323; it grew in size and wealth despite a sequence of invasions and calamities. In 1920–39 it was part of Poland. The German invasion destroyed its important Jewish community; Soviet rule increased Russian settlement 1945–91, putting ethnic Lithuanians in the minority.

Vilvoorde Belgium. Industrial town in Brabant province 10 km (6 miles) NNE of Brussels. Pop. (1992) 32,997.

Industries inc. oil-refining and the manufacture of chemicals, electrical equipment and textiles.

Viña del Mar Chile. Residential suburb and seaside resort, one of the most popular in South America, just NE of Valparaiso. Pop. (1991) 312,306. Has many bathing beaches, parks and hotels, a casino and a racecourse. Also an industrial and commercial centre.

Sugar-refining. Manufactures textiles and paint. Trade in fruit, wine and vegetables.

Vincennes France. Suburb of E Paris in the Val-de-Marne department. Pop. (1985) 44,000.

Manufactures electrical equipment, chemicals, perfumes, rubber products.

Its famous castle on the N border of the Bois de Vincennes was begun in the 12th cent., later became a state prison.

Vindhya Range India. Range of mountains in central India about 960 km (600 miles) long, extending ENE roughly parallel to and N of the Narmada R. valley. Average height 450–750 m (1450–2460 ft). Separates the Ganges basin (N) from the Deccan (S).

Vinnitsa (Vinnytsya) Ukraine. Cap. of the Vinnitsa region on the S Bug R. 200 km (125 miles) SW of Kiev. Pop. (1991) 318,000.

Flour-milling and meat-packing. Manufactures machinery, fertilizers.

Ruled by Poland from 1569 and by Russia from 1793.

Vinnytsya ►VINNITSA.

Virginia USA. Middle Atlantic state, roughly triangular in shape and inc. the S end of the Delmarva peninsula across Chesapeake Bay. Area 102,558 sq km (39,598 sq. miles). Pop. (1990) 6,187,358. Cap. Richmond. Consists of three distinct regions: the low coastal plain, deeply indented with estuaries and inc. the marshy Dismal Swamp in the SE; to the W the gently undulating Piedmont plateau, rising from 90 m (295 ft) (E) to 360 m (1181 ft) (W); and still farther W the Blue Ridge, extending about 480 km (360 miles) NE–SW across the state and rising to 1745 m (5724 ft) in Mt Rogers, and the ridges and valleys of the Appalachians (inc. the famous Shenandoah Valley). Chief rivers the Potomac, James, Roanoke, Rappahannock. Most of the state has a humid subtropical climate, with an annual rainfall of 100–130 cm (40–50 ins.).

Leading commercial crop tobacco; maize, wheat, oats, peanuts also grown. Extensive fishing in Chesapeake Bay. Most important mineral coal. Chief industrial centres Norfolk, Richmond, Portsmouth and Newport News – the last two being ports on Hampton Roads. It manufactures tobacco products, rayon and ships.

Virginia was the first permanent English settlement in America made at Jamestown (1607) and the state produced such famous men as Washington, Jefferson, Monroe and Robert E. Lee. One of the original 13 states and the 10th to ratify the Constitution (1788). In the Civil War it espoused the Confederate cause and was re-admitted to the Union in 1870.

Virgin Islands West Indies. Archipelago lying E of Puerto Rico and geologically similar to the Greater Antilles, belonging partly to Britain (►BRITISH VIRGIN ISLANDS) and partly to the USA (►VIRGIN ISLANDS OF THE USA).

Virgin Islands of the USA West Indies. Group of about 50 islands and islets between Puerto Rico and the British Virgin Is. Area 344 sq km (133 sq. miles). Pop. (1990) 101,809. Cap. Charlotte Amalie on St Thomas (area 83 sq km; 32 sq. miles); the other two main islands are St Croix and St John (area 49 sq km; 19 sq. miles). The remaining islets are uninhabited.

Cattle-rearing, rum-distilling and the cultivation of vegetables are important; sugar has been abandoned as a commercial crop. Tourism is expanding and there are about 1.5 million visitors a year.

The islands were purchased by the USA from Denmark (1917) because of their strategic position on the route from the Atlantic to the Caribbean Sea and the Panama Canal.

Vis (Italian **Lissa**) Croatia. Island off the Dalmatian coast 53 km (33 miles) SSW of Split. Area 101 sq km (39 sq. miles). Pop. 7000. Chief town Vis.

Main occupations vine-growing, fishing.

The British defeated the French (1811) and the Austrians defeated the Italians (1866) in naval engagements off the island.

Visakhapatnam (Vizagapatam) India. Seaport and naval station in Andhra Pradesh on the Bay of Bengal 499 km (310 miles) ENE of Hyderabad. Pop. (1991) 752,000.

Exports manganese and oilseeds. Has a modern protected harbour, an oil refinery, a steel plant and a major shipyard. Manufactures inc. fertilizers, sugar, chemicals, petrochemicals, transformers, zinc, lead, electronic and agricultural equipment. The suburb of Waltair, a seaside resort, is the seat of Andhra University (1926).

Visby Sweden. Cap. of Gotland county on the W coast of Gotland island. Pop. (1985) 19,500.

Seaport. Resort. Sugar-refining, metal-working. Manufactures cement.

Has a medieval appearance; its walls and massive towers, the cathedral (12th/13th-cent., restored) and several other partly ruined churches all provide evidence of its former wealth. An early member of the Hanseatic League. It achieved its greatest prosperity from the 11th to the 14th cent. It changed hands between Sweden and Denmark, lost much of its trade, became Swedish again in 1645 and revived in the late 19th cent.

Vistula (Polish **Wisla**, Ger. **Weichsel**, Russian **Visla**) **River** Poland. River 1094 km (680 miles) long rising in the W Beskids (Carpathians) and flowing generally N and NW past Cracow, Warsaw and Toruń. Below Tczew it forms a delta, the Martwa Wisla ('Dead Vistula') and the Nogat being the main channels and reaches the Gulf of Gdańsk. Linked with the Neman, Oder and

Bug rivers by canals; thus of considerable value to Polish trade.

Vitebsk Belarus. Cap. of the Vitebsk region on the W Dvina R. 233 km (145 miles) NE of Minsk. Pop. (1991) 361,500.

Industrial centre. Manufactures agricultural machinery, electrical and electronic equipment, linen goods, footwear, glass, furniture and processed food.

The chief town of the Polotsk principality, it passed to Lithuania in the 14th cent., to Poland in the 16th cent. and was annexed to Russia in 1772.

Viterbo Italy. Cap. of Viterbo province in Latium 64 km (40 miles) NNW of Rome. Pop. (1990) 60,210. A tourist centre.

Manufactures furniture, pottery, olive oil and pasta.

Has a 12th-cent. cathedral; beautiful fountains. Here Pope Adrian IV (Nicholas Breakspear) enforced the homage of the emperor Frederick I.

Viti Levu ➤FIJI ISLANDS.

Vitim River Russia. River in S Siberia 1770 km (1100 miles) long, rising on the Vitim plateau E of L. Baikal and flowing S, NE, N and NW to join the Lena R. at Vitim. Bodaibo, on the river, is the centre of a goldmining industry.

Vitória Brazil. Cap. of Espirito Santo state on an island linked by bridge with the mainland 434 km (270 miles) NE of Rio de Janeiro. Pop. (1990) 276,170.

A seaport. Exports iron ore from the Itabira mines, also coffee and timber. Other industries inc. sugar-refining and the manufacture of textiles and cement.

Vitoria Spain. Cap. of Álava province 51 km (32 miles) SSE of Bilbao at a height of 530 m (1738 ft). Pop. (1991) 204,961.

Manufactures furniture. Industries inc. tanning and flour-milling. Trade in cereals, potatoes, wool and wine.

In the Peninsular War Wellington decisively defeated the French here (1813).

Vittoria Italy. Town in Ragusa province

SE Sicily 19 km (12 miles) WNW of Ragusa. Pop. (1985) 51,000.

Important wine trade. Manufactures alcohol and pasta.

Vittorio Veneto Italy. Town in Treviso province, Veneto 37 km (23 miles) N of Treviso. Pop. (1985) 31,500.

Manufactures textiles and is a tourist resort.

Vizcaya Spain. One of the Basque Provinces on the Bay of Biscay. Area 2217 sq km (858 sq. miles). Pop. (1990) 1,155,106. Cap. Bilbao.

Rich iron mines and an important iron and steel industry centred on Bilbao. Other town Guernica, Durango.

Vlaardingen Netherlands. Port and fishing centre in S Holland province on the New Maas R. 10 km (6 miles) W of Rotterdam. Pop. (1992) 73,893.

Fish-processing. Manufactures fertilizers, rope, sails and soap.

Has a 17th-cent. town hall.

Vladikavkaz Russia. Formerly Ordzhonikidze. Cap of North Ossetian Republic on the Terek R. where it issues from the Caucasus at a height of 715 m (2345 ft). Pop. (1991) 306,000. The N terminus of the Georgian Military Highway to Tbilisi (Tiflis), which was opened in 1864 and led to its expansion.

Important metallurgical plants for refining zinc, lead and silver from the Sadon mines. Also food-processing, chemicals, woodworking and glass manufacture.

Marked the farthest advance of German armies into Caucasus (1942).

Vladimir Russia. Cap. of the Vladimir region on the Klyazma R. 185 km (115 miles) ENE of Moscow. Pop. (1991) 355,600.

Industrial centre. Manufactures textiles, tractors, machine-tools and precision instruments.

The kremlin (citadel), situated on a hill, contains two 12th-cent. cathedrals (restored in the 19th cent.) and there are several 12th-cent. churches. Founded in the early 12th

cent., became cap. of the Vladimir principality and passed to Moscow in the 14th cent.

Vladivostok Russia. Cap. of the Primorye Territory on the Pacific coast between Amur Bay and the Golden Horn 610 km (380 miles) SSW of Khabarovsk. Pop. (1991) 648,000.

Chief seaport and naval base on this coast. Fishing, whaling. Exports soya-bean oil, oil-cake, coal, timber and fish. Also an industrial centre and terminus of the Trans-Siberian Railway. Shipbuilding, sawmilling, fish-canning and food-processing. Has a good natural harbour, kept open by ice-breakers in winter.

Seat of a university (1923, closed 1939–56). Founded 1860. Developed rapidly after the completion of the Chinese Eastern Railway (1904).

Vlissingen ➤FLUSHING.

Vlonë (Valona) Albania. Cap. of the Vlonë district in the SW 100 km (62 miles) SSW of Tiranë. Pop. (1988) 76,000.

Seaport. Market town. Exports petroleum. Linked by pipeline with the Qytet Stalin oilfield. Fishing, fish-canning, oil-refining. Manufactures olive oil, cement.

The independence of Albania was proclaimed here in 1912.

Vltava (Ger. **Moldau**) **River** Czech Republic. River 434 km (270 miles) long rising in the Bohemian Forest (Böhmerwald) and flowing SSE and then generally N past České Budějovice and Prague to join the Elbe (Labe) R. near Melnik. Important hydro-electric installations.

Vojvodina Serbia. Former autonomous province in N Serbia, bordering on Hungary (N) and Romania (E). Area 21,506 sq km (8303 sq. miles). Pop. (1991) 2,012,517 (inc. Serbs, Croats, Hungarians, Romanians and Slovaks). Cap. Novi Sad. Generally low-lying and fertile; drained chiefly by the Danube, Sava and Tisa (Tisza) rivers. Produces large quantities of cereals, fruit, vegetables. Chief towns Novi Sad, Subotica, Zrenjanin, Pančevo. Ceded by Hungary to Yugoslavia after World War I. It became an autonomous province after World War II, but in 1990 Serbia deprived it of its autonomy and Serbo-Croat was declared the only official lang.

Volcano Islands (Japanese **Kazan-retto**) W Pacific Ocean. Group of 3 volcanic islands 1200 km (750 miles) S of Tokyo, the largest being Iwo Jima. Total area 28 sq km (11 sq. miles). Pop. about 1000. Sugar plantations. Sulphur mines. Annexed by Japan 1887. Taken by US forces in World War II and afterwards administered by the US Navy. Returned to Japan in 1968.

Volga Heights (Volga Hills) Russia. Hills extending along the right bank of the Volga R. between Nizhny Novgorod and Volgograd, rising to about 300 m (984 ft).

Volga River Russia. River 3688 km (2290 miles) long, the longest in Europe and the most important in Russia, navigable for almost the entire course. Rising in the Valdai Hills, it flows generally E past Tver, Yaroslavl, Kostroma and Nizhny Novgorod to Kazan, turns S and flows past Samara (on a wide bend), Saratov, Volgograd and Astrakhan, entering the Caspian Sea by a broad delta. Chief tributaries the Oka (right bank) and the Kama (left bank). A vast scheme for the greater exploitation of the Volga, to provide hydroelectric power, irrigate the dry wheat-growing steppes E of the middle course and improve navigation, was undertaken in the 1930s. Between Tver and Nizhny Novgorod are the Volga Reservoir, the great Rybinsk Reservoir, the Kostroma Reservoir and the Gorky Reservoir. Below Nizhny Novgorod are the Cheboksary Reservoir and the Samara Reservoir (which extends up the Kama R.), the Saratov Reservoir and the Volgograd Reservoir. The Moscow–Volga Canal was opened in 1937 and the Volga–Don Canal in 1952; with the Mariinsk Canal System, these made the river and the cap. accessible to vessels from the White Sea, the Baltic, the Caspian, the Sea of Azov and the Black Sea. Closed by ice 3–5 months annually and impeded by shoals in late summer, but of paramount importance

to transportation in European Russia. Below the Volgograd Reservoir it receives no tributaries and forms a braided flood-plain below sea level. The many distributaries on the delta are rich in sturgeon and other fish.

Volgograd Russia. Formerly Tsaritsyn, Stalingrad. Cap. of the Volgograd region on the Volga R. near the junction with the Volga–Don Canal (opened 1952). Pop. (1991) 1,007,300.

Important river port and industrial centre. Manufactures iron and steel, tractors, machine-tools, oilfield machinery, railway equipment, cement, footwear, clothing. Sawmilling, oil-refining.

Founded (as Tsaritsyn) 1589. Became important in the 19th cent. chiefly because of its position on the Volga–Don route. Besieged by the White Army after the 1917 revolution; renamed (1925) after Stalin because of his part in the defence. Besieged by the Germans during World War II (1942–3) and seriously damaged. After a Soviet counter-attack the German army capitulated; the Battle of Stalingrad was the turning-point of the war on the Soviet front. Renamed 1961.

Volhynia ➤VOLYN.

Volkhov River Russia. River 225 km (140 miles) long, rising in L. Ilmen and flowing NNE past Novgorod and Volkhov to L. Ladoga; an important waterway. Volkhov is the site of a hydroelectric power station at the rapids and a large aluminium plant.

Völklingen Germany. Industrial town in Saarland on the Saar R. 11 km (7 miles) WNW of Saarbrücken. Pop. (1986) 43,100.

Coalmining. Manufactures steel, machinery, electrical equipment and cement.

Vologda Russia. Cap. of the Vologda region on the Vologda R. 177 km (110 miles) N of Yaroslavl. Pop. (1991) 289,200.

Industrial centre. Railway junction. Railway engineering. Manufactures agricultural machinery, textiles, glass and cement. Important trade in dairy produce from the surrounding area.

Cathedral (16th-cent.). Founded (1147) as a colony of Novgorod, it flourished as a commercial centre in the 16th cent., declined later and recovered with the construction of the railway to Archangel.

Vólos Greece. Cap. of Magnesia *nome*, Thessaly at the head of the Gulf of Vólos 160 km (100 miles) NNW of Athens. Pop. (1985) 107,000. Chief seaport Thessaly.

Manufactures textiles, chemicals and cement. Exports tobacco, olive oil.

A relatively modern city; severely damaged in earthquakes (1954, 1955) and rebuilt.

Volta Redonda Brazil. Town in Rio de Janeiro state on the Paraíba R. 96 km (60 miles) WNW of Rio de Janeiro on the main Rio–São Paulo railway. Pop. (1990) 230,530. Has the country's main steel plant, inaugurated in 1947. Well-known as a model industrial town, with the steel plant near the river and workers' homes built on the nearby wooded slopes.

Volta River Burkina Faso/Ghana. River 1125 km (700 miles) long formed by the union of the Black Volta and the White Volta 64 km (40 miles) NW of Yeji in Ghana and flowing generally SE and S to the Gulf of Guinea; the most important river in Ghana and the basin of the system covers nearly 75 per cent of the country. The Volta River Scheme inc. a dam, which impounds a lake (area 4920 sq km; 1900 sq. miles), and hydroelectric power station at Akosombo, and an aluminium smelter at Tema to develop Ghana's bauxite resources and improve navigation. The dam and power station were completed in 1966; the first aluminium was marketed in 1967.

Volyn (Volhynia, Wolyń) Ukraine. Region in the NW between the Bug and Dnieper rivers. Drained chiefly by right-bank tributaries of the Pripet R. Consists largely of marshy woodlands. The medieval Volhynia, more extensive than present-day Volyn, passed to Lithuania in the 14th cent., to Poland in the 16th cent. and to Russia in the Partitions of Poland (1795). The W part was returned to Poland in 1921, but was ceded to the USSR in 1945, as the Volyn region.

Volzhsky Russia. Town in the Volgograd region on the left bank of the Volga R. 24 km (15 miles) NE of Volgograd. Pop. (1991) 278,400.

Aluminium smelting; manufactures chemicals.

Voorburg Netherlands. Industrial town in S Holland province 5 km (3 miles) E of The Hague. Pop. (1993) 39,734.

Manufactures ball-bearings and machinery.

Vorarlberg Austria. Federal state bordering on W Germany (N), Switzerland (S and W) and Liechtenstein (SW). Area 2601 sq km (1004 sq. miles). Pop. (1991) 333,138. Cap. Bregenz. The Rhätikon Alps and part of the Silvretta massif (rising to over 3350 m; 10,988 ft) lie along the S boundary and part of the Lechtal Alps is in the NE; renowned for mountain scenery. Main occupations forestry, dairy-farming and tourism.

Voronezh Russia. Cap. of the Voronezh region on the Voronezh R. near its confluence with the Don R. Pop. (1991) 900,000.

A major industrial centre and chief town of the central black-earth (chernozem) area. Manufactures synthetic rubber tyres, machine-tools, excavators, radio and television sets.

A Russian fort was built here (1586) on the site of an 11th-cent. Khazar town and in 1695 Peter the Great made Voronezh a shipbuilding centre; later it traded in grain and wool. The town had to be rebuilt after disastrous fires (1703, 1748 and 1773).

Voroshilovgrad ►LUHANSK.

Vosges France. Department lying W of the Vosges Mountains, formed (1790) chiefly from Lorraine. Area 5874 sq km (2268 sq. miles). Pop. (1991) 385,200. Prefecture Épinal. Mainly uplands, with the Vosges Mountains forming a natural boundary in the E and the Monts Faucilles crossing the S. Drained by the Moselle, Meuse and Meurthe rivers. Agriculture (cereals, potatoes, hops) and forestry practised. There are several spas.

Vosges (Mountains) France. Range of mountains in the E extending about 240 km (150 miles) SSW–NNE structurally similar and roughly parallel to the Black Forest (Germany), from which it is separated by the rift valley of the Rhine R. The mountains slope steeply down to Alsace (E) and more gently to Lorraine (W), are well forested and rise to 1424 m (4671 ft) in the Ballon de Guebwiller. The Moselle, Meurthe and Sarre (Saar) rivers rise on their W slopes and the Ill on their E slopes.

Votkinsk Russia. Town in the Udmurt Republic 48 km (30 miles) ENE of Izhevsk. Pop. (1991) 104,500.

Railway engineering. Manufactures agricultural machinery, boilers and dredgers.

Founded 1759. Birthplace of P. I. Tchaikovsky (1840–93), the composer.

Vršac Yugoslavia. Town in Vojvodina near the Romanian frontier 76 km (47 miles) ENE of Belgrade. Pop. (1971) 34,231.

Flour-milling, distilling and meat-packing. Trade in wine and brandy.

Vyatka ➤KIROV.

Vyborg (Finnish **Viipuri**, Swedish **Viborg**) Russia. Seaport in the Leningrad region on Vyborg Bay, Gulf of Finland 113 km (70 miles) NW of Leningrad. Pop. (1989) 80,000.

Exports timber and wood products. There is a shipbuilding industry and it manufactures agricultural machinery, furniture and electrical equipment. Linked by canal with L. Saimaa.

It grew up round a 13th-cent. Swedish castle, became a Hanseatic port and was ceded to Russia in 1721. Passed to Finland 1812; regained by the USSR in 1945.

Vyrnwy, Lake Wales. Artificial lake (reservoir) 7 km (4½ miles) long and up to 0.8 km (½ mile) wide in N Powys. Formed by damming the R. Vyrnwy (1880–90) to provide a water supply for Liverpool.

Vyrnwy River Wales. River 56 km (35 miles) long rising 10 km (6 miles) S of Bala, flowing generally ESE through N Powys and joining the R. Severn 19 km (11 miles) WNW of Shrewsbury.

Vyshni Volochek Russia. Town in the Tver region 113 km (70 miles) NW of Tver. Pop. (1970) 74,000. On the Vyshnevolotsk canal system, originally constructed by Peter the Great in the early 18th cent. to link the Volga R. with the Baltic, and now of minor importance.

Industries inc. sawmilling and the manufacture of textiles and glass.

W

Waadt ➤VAUD.

Wabash River USA. River 764 km (475 miles) long rising in Grand Lake, W Ohio and flowing generally W and then S, forming the Indiana–Illinois boundary below Terre Haute and joining the Ohio R.

Waco USA. Town in Texas on the Brazos R. 142 km (88 miles) SSW of Dallas. Pop. (1990) 103,590.

Important trade in cotton. Railway and aeronautical engineering. Manufactures glass, tyres, textiles and cottonseed oil.

Wadi Halfa Sudan. Town in the N near the Egyptian frontier on the right bank of the Nile 386 km (240 miles) NNW of Atbara about 10 km (6 miles) below the Second Cataract. Pop. (1983) 11,000. Terminus of the railway from Khartoum and of ferry services from Shellal in Egypt. Important transfer point for Sudanese–Egyptian trade.

Wad Medani Sudan. Cap. of the Blue Nile province on the left bank of the Blue Nile on the railway from Khartoum (177 km (110 miles) NW). Pop. (1987) 147,000. Centre of the Gezira irrigation scheme.

Important cotton centre. Cotton-ginning. Also trade in cereals.

Wageningen Netherlands. Port situated W of Arnhem on the Lower Rhine R., Gelderland. Pop. (1992) 32,854.

Wagga Wagga Australia. Town in New South Wales on the Murrumbidgee R. 160 km (100 miles) W of Canberra. Pop. (1988) 51,480.

Railway junction and commercial centre for a wheat-growing and dairy-farming area.

Waikato River New Zealand. Longest river in the country rising in L. Taupo, North Island and flowing 354 km (220 miles) NW over a series of rapids and through gorges across a volcanic plateau. It enters the Tasman Sea 40 km (25 miles) SSE of the entrance to Manukau Harbour.

Many hydroelectric power stations, inc. Arapuni and Maraetai, on the upper course. The lower plains are noted for the raising of dairy cattle and fat lambs. Popular tourist attraction.

Wainganga River India. River 640 km (400 miles) long in Madhya Pradesh, rising in the Satpura Range and flowing generally S to join the Wardha R., forming the Pranhita R., a tributary of the Godavari R.

Waitaki River New Zealand. River 153 km (95 miles) long in South Island formed by the union of the Ahuriri and Tekapo rivers, the latter being fed from Lakes Ohau, Pukaki and Tekapo, flowing generally SE to the Pacific about 21 km (13 miles) NE of Oamaru. Hydroelectric power stations at Kurow and elsewhere.

Wakamatsu ➤KITAKYUSHU.

Wakatipu, Lake New Zealand. S-shaped lake in W Otago, South Island 80 km (50 miles) long and up to 5 km (3 miles) wide at a height of 310 m (1017 ft) in a glacial valley. Has an outlet via the Kawarau R. to the Clutha R. Queenstown, a major tourist centre, is on the N shore.

Wakayama Japan. Cap. of Wakayama prefecture, S Honshu on the Kii peninsula 56 km (35 miles) SSW of Osaka. Pop. (1991) 315,900.

Industrial centre. Manufactures iron and steel, textiles, chemicals and saké.

Wakefield England. Industrial city and unitary authority on the R. Calder 13 km (8 miles) S of Leeds. Pop. (1991) 73,955.

A centre of the woollen and worsted industry it also manufactures chemicals, machine-tools, mining machinery. Trade in agricultural produce.

Has a 14th-cent cathedral with a spire 75 m (246 ft) high, a 14th-cent. chantry chapel on one of its bridges and a 16th-cent. grammar school. Scene of a battle in the Wars of the Roses (1460), in which Richard Duke of York was defeated and killed by the Lancastrians. Birthplace of John Radcliffe, English physician (1650–1714) and George Gissing, English novelist (1857–1903).

Wake Island N Pacific Ocean. US Outlying Territory comprising three small islands 3700 km (2300 miles) W of Hawaii. Area 8 sq km (3 sq. miles). Pop. (1990) 300 service personnel. Discovered by Capt. Wake (British) 1796; claimed by the USA 1899; made an airline base on the route to the Philippines in 1935 and a naval and air base in 1939. After a stubborn defence by US marines it fell to the Japanese (1941); recaptured 1945.

Walachia (Wallachia) Romania. Region and former principality in S Romania bounded on the N by the Transylvanian Alps and on the W, S and E by the Danube R., which separates it from Serbia, Bulgaria and the Romanian Dobruja respectively. Area 76,599 sq km (29,575 sq. miles). Chief city Bucharest, cap. of Romania. Divided by the Olt R. into Muntenia or Greater Walachia (E) and Oltenia or Lesser Walachia. Main occupation agriculture (cereals, vines, fruit). Oil produced around Ploeşti. The principality of Walachia was founded (1290) by Radu Negru, a Transylvanian ruler, became independent in the 14th cent., then remained under Turkish rule almost continuously until the mid 19th cent. Its union with the principality of Moldavia (1859) laid the foundation of modern Romania.

Wałbrzych (Ger. **Waldenburg**) Poland. Cap. of the Wałbrzych voivodeship in the

Sudeten Mountains 68 km (42 miles) SW of Wrocław. Pop. (1992) 141,200.

Coalmining centre. Manufactures china, glass, linen goods.

Formerly in Germany (as Waldenburg); passed to Poland in 1945 after World War II.

Walchensee Germany. Lake in Bavaria in the Bavarian Alps 60 km (37 miles) SSW of Munich at a height of 800 m (2624 ft). Area 16 sq km (6 sq. miles). Has one of the country's most important hydroelectric plants.

Walcheren Netherlands. Island in Zeeland province in the estuary of the Scheldt R., linked with S Beveland island and the mainland by railway and road causeways. Area 212 sq km (82 sq. miles).

Fertile; produces potatoes, sugar-beet and vegetables. Chief towns Flushing and Middelburg.

During World War II it was liberated from the Germans after the dykes had been breached.

Waldech Germany. Former principality under Prussian administration from 1867. Cap. Arolsen. Chiefly agricultural; produces cereals, potatoes and fruit. From 1918 to 1929 it was a *Land* of the German Republic; it then became part of Hesse-Nassau, later (1945) of Hessen.

Wales. The Principality of Wales (*Cymru*) is a peninsula in the SW of Great Britain and is bounded by England in the E, the Bristol Channel in the S, St George's Channel to the W and the Irish Sea to the N. It inc. the island of Anglesey off the NW coast, separated from the mainland by the Menai Strait (crossed by railway and road bridges). The counties and county boroughs of Wales are: Blaenau Gwent (CB), Bridgend (CB), Caerphilly (CB), Cardiff (CB), Carmarthenshire, Ceredigion, Conwy (CB), Denbighshire, Flintshire, Gwynedd, Isle of Anglesey, Merthyr Tydfil (CB), Monmouthshire, Neath Port Talbot (CB), Newport (CB), Pembrokeshire, Powys; Rhondda, Cynon and Taff (CB), Swansea,

Wales

Torfaen (CB), Vale of Glamorgan (CB) and Wrexham (CB). Area 20,768 sq km (8019 sq. miles). Pop. (1991) 2,811,865. Cap. Cardiff. Other towns inc. Swansea, Mold, Carmarthen, Merthyr Tydfil, Newport, Caernarvon and Llandrindod Wells. The central mountainous counties are sparsely populated; the pop. is concentrated mainly in the industrial region of the S. Few economic ties between the N and S; each is less closely associated with the other than with the neighbouring parts of England. About 19 per cent of the people (1991) are Welsh-speaking. Interest in the Welsh lang. (which is Celtic in origin) was stimulated by the founding in 1893 of the University of Wales, which has constituent colleges at Aberystwyth, Cardiff, Bangor, Swansea and Lampeter, and is maintained by the National Eisteddfod (revived in the mid 19th cent. and held annually). In general the educational system is similar to that of England, but the Welsh lang. is widely taught in the schools. The strength of the Nonconformist sects in Wales is due to the Methodist movement of the 18th cent.; leading denominations are the Calvinistic Methodist (Presbyterian) Church of Wales, the Methodist (Wesleyan) Church, the Baptist Church and the Congregationalist Church. The Anglican Church of Wales was disestablished in 1914.

The farming is mainly pastoral; less than one-fifth of the land surface is arable and most of the remainder is rough grazing land and permanent pasture, in approximately equal areas. In the mountains sheep-rearing is the chief occupation; beef and dairy cattle are raised on the coastal plains of the Isle of Anglesey and in the Lleyn peninsula, Pembrokeshire, Carmarthenshire and Rhondda, Cynon, Taff and the Vale of Glamorgan. Oats, barley and root crops are cultivated, mainly for feeding to livestock. With the Industrial Revolution the almost uniformly agricultural economy changed radically, and people crowded into the coalmining valleys of the SE. Welsh steam coal and anthracite achieved a high reputation and the S Wales coalfield became the world's chief coal-exporting region. Largely through foreign

competition this overseas trade diminished to negligible proportions after World War I. Local supplies of iron ore assisted the development of a great steel industry; most of the ore is now imported. Tin-plate manufacture (an offshoot of the steel industry) and the smelting of zinc, copper, tin and nickel are concentrated in the Swansea–Llanelli area; there are important oil refineries at Milford Haven and Llandarcy. S Wales suffered severely from the economic depression of the 1930s; to relieve unemployment, new trading estates were established (e.g. Treforest), new industries were introduced (e.g. nylon manufacture at Pontypool) and the steel industry was modernized. The much less important industrial region centred on Wrexham is based on the smaller N Wales coalfield. The slate quarries in the N have lost markets but resorts along the N coast and the district around Snowdon attract holidaymakers and climbers. The three major industrial centres – Cardiff, Swansea and Newport – are all in the S and are all seaports.

The Romans conquered and occupied Wales but made little impression. The Anglo–Saxon invasion of England was at first of no serious consequence to Wales; later the defeats at Deorham (577) and Chester (613) separated the Welsh from their compatriots in the SW (Cornwall) and the NW (Cumberland), and confined them to the mountainous W peninsula. King Offa of Mercia constructed Offa's Dyke as a defence against the Welsh in the 8th cent. During this cent. the Welsh Church (established 200 years earlier) maintained regular contact with Rome. During the 9th–11th cents. the Welsh, divided among small tribal kingdoms, were raided along the coasts by Northmen and engaged on their landward border with the Mercians. Gruffyd ap Llewelyn (1039–63) defeated the Mercians and temporarily united the Welsh. They continued to resist after the Norman conquest, but Llewelyn ap Gruffyd was defeated (1282) by Edward I, who had his son (born 1284 in Caernarvon Castle) proclaimed Prince of Wales in 1301; the title has been held by the eldest son of the English monarch ever since. Owen

Glendower rebelled unsuccessfully in the early 15th cent. With the accession of Henry VII (part Welsh by birth) peace was established; Henry VIII incorporated Wales politically into England and gave it parliamentary representation by the Act of Union (1536); Welsh history thereafter was approximately that of England. The Reformation hardly reached Wales. In the early 7th cent. it was mainly Royalist, but Protestant ideas began to take root during the Cromwellian era. The 18th-cent. Methodist 'revival' movement had as great an impact on Welsh life as did the Industrial Revolution; partly religious, partly educational, it produced an outstanding leader in Griffith Jones, a Carmarthenshire rector, and culminated in the Methodist Secession (1811). More recently Wales has been a stronghold of trade unionism and socialism and there has also been a revival of Welsh nationalism. Wales has been politically linked to England since 1536, returning members to the House of Commons at Westminster; some legislation applies to Wales alone. A Cabinet Minister has been in charge of Welsh affairs since 1951. In 1997 a referendum was held to consider the institution of a Welsh Assembly; 50.3 per cent voted for an Assembly and 49.7 per cent against, a majority of 6,721 votes on a 50 per cent turnout.

Wallasey England. Town in Merseyside on the Wirral peninsula near the mouth of the R. Mersey opposite Liverpool. Pop. (1991) 60,895. Seaside resort and residential suburb of Liverpool, inc. New Brighton and Egremont.

Wallingford England. Market town in Oxfordshire on the R. Thames 19 km (12 miles) SSE of Oxford. Pop. (1991) 9315. Picturesque; important in medieval times. Has a much older history than its many Georgian buildings would suggest.

Wallingford USA. Town situated NNE of New Haven on Quinnipiac R., Connecticut. Pop. (1988) 41,710.
   Industries inc. the manufacture of silver-

ware, metal products, electrical goods, plastics, chemicals and clothing.

Wallis ➤VALAIS.

Wallis and Futuna Islands SW Pacific Ocean. Island group NE of Fiji, consisting of Uvéa and several uninhabited coral islets, with Futuna and Alofi to the S. Area 240 sq km (93 sq. miles). Pop. (1992) 14,100. Cap. Matautu (Uvéa). Formed the French protectorate of the Wallis and Futuna Is. from 1842, but in 1959 their inhabitants, almost entirely Polynesians, voted overwhelmingly to become an overseas territory of the French Community.

Wallsend England. Town in Tyne and Wear on the N bank of the R. Tyne. Pop. (1991) 45,280.
   Marine engineering and coalmining. The last ship to be built was launched in 1994. Manufactures chemicals and ropes. Stands at the E end of Hadrian's Wall – hence its name.

Walsall England. Town and unitary authority in the Black Country 13 km (8 miles) NNW of Birmingham. Pop. (1991) 255,953.
   Industrial town specializing in leather goods. Also manufactures hardware and machine-tools. Coalmining and limestone quarrying in the neighbourhood.

Walsingham England. Two villages in N Norfolk. Little Walsingham 40 km (25 miles) NW of Norwich. Pop. (1991) 871. Has the 11th-cent. shrine of Our Lady of Walsingham, an important centre of medieval pilgrimages; the ruins of the priory stand in the grounds of the modern abbey. Great Walsingham is 1.6 km (1 mile) NE. At Houghton St Giles, 1.6 km (1 mile) SSW is the Slipper Chapel where pilgrims (kings and commoners alike) had to leave their shoes before proceeding barefoot to the shrine.

Waltham USA. Industrial town in Massachusetts on the Charles R. 16 km (10 miles) W of Boston. Pop. (1990) 57,878.
   Famous for the manufacture of clocks and watches since the mid 19th cent. Also pro-

duces electronic equipment and precision instruments.

Seat of Brandeis University (1948).

Waltham Abbey (Waltham Holy Cross) England. Town in SW Essex on the R. Lea 13 km (8 miles) SW of Harlow. Pop. (1991) 15,629.

Manufactures plastics and tiles. Has a government explosive research establishment.

It had a great 11th-cent. Augustinian abbey, founded by King Harold, the nave of which is now used as the parish church; Harold was said to have been buried here after the Battle of Hastings.

Waltham Cross England. Town in Hertfordshire on the R. Lea opposite Waltham Abbey, part of the urban district of Cheshunt.

Manufactures insecticides.

So called because of its Eleanor Cross.

Waltham Forest England. London borough (1965) comprising the former municipal boroughs of Chingford, Leyton and Walthamstow, all in Essex. Pop. (1994) 221,800.

Waltham Holy Cross ➤WALTHAM ABBEY.

Walthamstow England. Borough in SW Essex, also a NE suburb. Part of the London borough of Waltham Forest. Mainly residential.

Engineering and brewing.

Has a 16th-cent. church. Large reservoirs. Birthplace of William Morris, poet, craftsman and socialist (1834–96).

Walton and Weybridge England. Town in N Surrey on the R. Thames inc. Walton-on-Thames, Weybridge (at the mouth of the R. Wey) and Hersham. Pop. (1991) 52,800. Mainly residential.

Manufactures electrical equipment, bricks and tiles, and has other light industry.

The first British motor-racing track (Brooklands) and first aerodrome were located here.

Walton-le-Dale England. Town in Lanca-

shire on the R. Ribble just SE of Preston. Pop. (1971) 26,841.

Engineering. Manufactures cotton goods.

Walton-le-Soken
➤WALTON-ON-THE-NAZE.

Walton-on-Thames ➤WALTON AND WEYBRIDGE.

Walton-on-the-Naze **(Walton-le-Soken)** England. Seaside resort in NE Essex on the North Sea 10 km (6 miles) S of Harwich, forming part of Frinton and Walton; just NE is the low headland of The Naze.

Walvis Bay Namibia. Chief seaport 265 km (165 miles) WSW of Windhoek. Pop. (1980) 25,000. Terminus of the railway system, by which it is linked with Swakopmund and Windhoek. With 969 sq km (374 sq. miles) of its hinterland it forms an exclave of South Africa, but was administered transitionally by Namibia and South Africa from 1982 and in 1994 it was transferred to Namibian administration.

Exports chilled meat. Industries inc. fishing, fish-canning, and manufactures fish oil and fish meal.

Annexed by Britain 1878.

Wandsworth England. Formerly the largest metropolitan borough of London on the S bank of the R. Thames, inc. Putney, Streatham, Balham, Tooting and part of Clapham; now a London borough comprising the former metropolitan borough (except the Clapham and Streatham areas – now inc. in the borough of Lambeth) and the former metropolitan borough of Battersea. Pop. (1991) 258,700.

Residential and industrial. Textile printing, dyeing and brewing.

Open spaces inc. Putney Heath, Tooting Common, Wandsworth Park and parts of Richmond Park and Wandsworth Common. Contains Wandsworth prison. Linked by Wandsworth Bridge with Fulham.

Wanganui New Zealand. Town and port on the SW coast of North Island 153 km (95 miles) NNE of Wellington near the mouth of the Wanganui R. Pop. (1989) 42,000.

Regional centre for dairy-farming and sheep-rearing districts. Meat works, woollen mills, clothing and soap factories.

Founded 1842.

Wanganui River New Zealand. River 225 km (140 miles) long in North Island, rising in the Rangitoto Range and flowing generally S to Cook Strait through broken hill country and forests and, on the lower plains, dairy-farming land.

Wangaratta Australia. Town in Victoria on the Ovens R. 200 km (125 miles) NE of Melbourne. Pop. (1971) 15,586.

Manufactures textiles (woollen, rayon). Trade in livestock.

Wanhsien ➤WANXIAN.

Wankie ➤HWANGE.

Wanks River ➤COCO RIVER.

Wanne-Eickel Germany. Industrial town in North Rhine-Westphalia in the Ruhr 5 km (3 miles) NNW of Bochum. Pop. (1980) 100,000. Port on the Rhine–Herne Canal.

Coalmining centre. Manufactures chemicals.

Wanstead and Woodford England. Part of the Greater London borough of Redbridge. Mainly residential. Contains Wanstead Park and most of Wanstead Flats.

Wantage England. Market town in S Oxfordshire 21 km (13 miles) SW of Oxford on the N edge of the Berkshire Downs. Pop. (1991) 9452. Has a 13th-cent. church and a large statue of Alfred the Great (849–900), who was born here.

Wanxian (Wanhsien) China. River port in Sichuan province on the left bank of the Yangtse R. 225 km (140 miles) NE of Chongqing. Pop. (1990) 156,823.

Trade in tung oil, hog bristles and tobacco.

Wapping England. District in the London borough of Tower Hamlets (E) between the London Docks and the R. Thames. Connected with Rotherhithe by the Thames Tunnel (1843). The newspaper industry has relocated here. Has the famous 'Prospect of Whitby' inn. Near the Tunnel Pier is the site of Execution Dock, where pirates were hanged.

Warangal India. Town in Andhra Pradesh 137 km (85 miles) NE of Hyderabad. Pop. (1991) 447,700.

Industries inc. cotton-milling, printing and it manufactures carpets. Trade in grain and hides.

Was cap. of a 12th-cent. Hindu kingdom; there are a fort and remains of a temple of that period.

Ware England. Town in Hertfordshire on the R. Lea 3 km (2 miles) ENE of Hertford. Pop. (1991) 17,069.

Brewing. Manufactures plastics.

The 'Great Bed of Ware', in Shakespeare's *Twelfth Night*, formerly at the Saracen's Head here, is now in the Victoria and Albert Museum, London.

Wareham England. Market town in Dorset on the R. Frome 10 km (6 miles) WSW of Poole. Pop. (1991) 2454. Inhabited since pre-Roman times and almost surrounded by Saxon earthworks. Has the restored Saxon Church of St Martin; in the ancient Church of St Mary is the marble coffin of Edward the Martyr.

Warley England. Town in West Midlands on the W outskirts of Birmingham, formed as a county borough in 1966 from the former county borough of Smethwick and the municipal boroughs of Oldbury and Rowley Regis. Pop. (1971) 163,388.

Warminster England. Market town in Wiltshire on the W edge of Salisbury Plain 31 km (19 miles) WNW of Salisbury. Pop. (1991) 16,800.

Manufactures gloves and food products. Military headquarters. Longleat, the beautiful Elizabethan mansion of the Marquis of Bath is 6 km (4 miles) WSW.

Warren USA. Industrial town in Ohio on

the Mahoning R. 23 km (14 miles) NW of Youngstown. Pop. (1990) 50,793.

Manufactures steel, machinery and electrical appliances.

Warrenpoint Northern Ireland. Town in Co. Down near the head of Carlingford Lough 10 km (6 miles) SE of Newry. Pop. (1991) 5408. Seaside resort and centre for the Mourne Mountains.

Warrington England. Industrial town and unitary authority on the R. Mersey 26 km (16 miles) E of Liverpool. Pop. (1991) 185,100.

Industries inc. high-tech, electronics and nuclear equipment, iron-founding, engineering, brewing and tanning. Manufactures soap, detergents, chemicals and wire.

An important town in Roman times; has a grammar school founded in the 16th cent.

Warrnambool Australia. Seaport with an artificial harbour in SW Victoria 233 km (145 miles) WSW of Melbourne. Pop. (1991) 23,950.

Also a commercial town and resort. Serves a rich dairy-farming and sheep-rearing region. Exports wool and butter. Manufactures butter and woollen goods.

Warsaw (Polish **Warszawa**) Poland. Cap. of Poland and of the Warszawa voivodeship (but independent of it) on both banks of the Vistula R. in N central Poland. Pop. (1992) 1,653,300.

Route, commercial and industrial centre. Metalworking, flour-milling, sugar-refining, brewing and distilling. Manufactures tractors, machine-tools, electrical equipment, chemicals, textiles, clothing, pharmaceuticals and food products.

Seat of a university (1818), of academies of arts and sciences and of a Roman Catholic archbishopric. At first the residence of the dukes of Mazovia; became cap. of Poland 1550. Taken by the Swedes (1702) and the Russians (1794). Passed to Prussia 1795. Became cap. of Napoleon's 'duchy of Warsaw' in 1807 and of the post-Napoleonic 'Congress Kingdom' in 1815, but in fact remained in Russian hands until the 1917 Bolshevik

Revolution. Became cap. of the re-created Polish republic after World War I (1919). Suffered very severely in World War II; occupied by the Germans from Aug. 1939. The Jews were enclosed in the ghetto which was wiped out (1943); the Warsaw Rising was suppressed and the city was virtually obliterated (1944). The older areas on the W bank of the embanked Vistula have been rebuilt in their original styles since 1945, but with a simpler, mainly rectangular, layout and new highways. The E bank district is broken up by the parks around the Dziesięciolecia Stadium and the zoo. There is also a Sports Park in the SW. The city is divided into seven districts covering an area of 29 km (18 miles) by 25.8 km (16 miles).

Warta (Ger. **Warthe**) **River** Poland. River 770 km (480 miles) long, rising 13 km (8 miles) SSE of Częstochowa and flowing generally N and W past Częstochowa and Poznań to join the Oder R. at Kostrzyn. Linked by its tributary the Noteć and the Bydgoszcz Canal with the Vistula R.

Warwick Australia. Town and tourist resort in Queensland situated SW of Brisbane on Condamine R. Pop. (1985) 10,000.

Railway centre serving an agricultural area producing wheat, sorghum, maize and fruit. Industries inc. food-processing and furniture manufacture.

Warwick England. Historic town in Warwickshire on the R. Avon 31 km (19 miles) SE of Birmingham. Pop. (1991) 22,476.

Engineering. Manufactures gelatine and furniture.

The magnificent 14th-cent. castle, standing on a rock above the river, is associated with several famous Earls of Warwick and has a fine collection of armour, furniture and pictures. It survived the disastrous fire of 1694, along with the 15th-cent. Beauchamp Chapel of St Mary's Church, the 16th-cent. Leycester Hospital and the E and W gates of the medieval town walls, with chapels. Birthplace of Walter Savage Landor, English writer (1775–1864).

Warwick USA. Industrial and residential

town in Rhode Island on Narragansett Bay 16 km (10 miles) S of Providence, inc. several villages within its limits. Pop. (1991) 118,200.

Industries inc. food-processing, carpets and tourism. Manufactures metal goods, machinery and boilers.

Warwickshire England. County in the Midlands. Area 1981 sq km (765 sq. miles). Pop. (1991) 489,900. It is divided into the districts of North Warwickshire, Nuneaton and Bedworth, Rugby, Stratford-upon-Avon and Warwick. Generally undulating, rising to 226 m (741 ft) in Edgehill in the extreme SE, it is crossed NE–SW by the R. Avon. A considerable part of the former county, inc. Birmingham, Coventry, Solihull and Sutton Coldfield and their surrounding districts, was transferred to West Midlands (1974). Rugby and Leamington (spa) stand near the Avon; Nuneaton is in the NE. Coal is mined chiefly in the NE. To the S of the R. Avon agriculture and fruit-farming are the main occupations. Warwick, Kenilworth and Stratford-upon-Avon are smaller but more picturesque and historically more interesting towns than the industrial centres to the N. Stratford-upon-Avon and the Forest of Arden are inevitably associated with the county's most distinguished son, William Shakespeare.

Wasatch Range USA. Range of the Rocky Mountains extending 320 km (200 miles) N–S through SE Idaho to central Utah and rising to 3662 m (12,011 ft) in Mt Timpanogos.

Wash, The England. Shallow bay of the North Sea into the coasts of Norfolk and Lincolnshire 35 km (20 miles) long and up to 24 km (15 miles) wide. There are two navigable deep-water channels: Boston Deeps, maintained by the Witham and Welland rivers, and Lynn Deeps, by the Nene and Great Ouse rivers, giving access to the small ports of Boston and King's Lynn respectively. The Wash has long been subject to silting and covers a much smaller area than formerly; at times parts of it have been reclaimed.

Washington England. Town in Tyne and Wear 10 km (6 miles) W of Sunderland. Pop. (1991) 56,848.

Manufactures electronics, electrical products, vehicles and components.

The home of George Washington's ancestors before their removal to Sulgrave Manor, Northamptonshire. Designated a 'new town' (1964), formed from most of Washington and parts of Houghton-le-Spring urban district and Chester-le-Street rural district: target pop. 80,000.

Washington USA. State in the extreme NW bounded on the N by British Columbia (Canada). Area 176,479 sq km (68,139 sq. miles). Pop. (1993) 5,255,000. Cap. Olympia. Its coast is heavily indented in the NW, with Puget Sound, connecting with Juan de Fuca Strait, extending 160 km (100 miles) N–S. Largely mountainous, it is divided into E and W parts by the Cascade Range, which rises to 4392 m (14,408 ft) in Mt Rainier, its highest point. The main river is the Columbia and such tributaries as the Snake and Spokane are also important. The climate to the E of the Cascades is dry continental and to the W maritime temperate. Forests cover more than 50 per cent of its area, and it was long the leading timber-producing state.

Fruit, vegetables and hops are widely grown, apples being one of the chief commercial crops. The fisheries are of great importance (salmon and halibut). Chief cities Seattle, which is also the leading seaport, Spokane and Tacoma. Hydroelectric development has assisted industrial progress, esp. through the Grand Coulee and Bonneville Dams on the Columbia R. Manufactures aircraft and aerospace equipment. Minerals inc. sand and gravel, stone, zinc, coal, lead, uranium, clay and peat.

The mountain and coastal scenery is noteworthy, many resorts have sprung up, and the Olympic and Mt Rainier National Parks are justly famous. Jointly occupied by the USA and Britain from 1818, then in 1846 the 49th parallel was fixed as the US–Canadian boundary and large-scale settlements began in the 1850s. Admitted to the Union in 1889 as the 42nd state.

Washington (District of Columbia) USA. Cap., on the left bank of the Potomac R. at the head of navigation and 160 km (100 miles) from its mouth. Pop. (1990) 606,900. The first modern city to be planned from the start as a seat of national government; regulations restrict the height of buildings and it has no skyscrapers. The site was designated by Act of Congress (1790) and was laid out by Andrew Ellicott from the plans of the French engineer Pierre l'Enfant commissioned by George Washington. Work began on the White House, the President's official residence, in 1792 and on the Capitol building in 1793. The Federal government moved to Washington in 1800 from Philadelphia but the city developed very slowly. The plan was centred upon the Capitol with broad, tree-lined avenues radiating from it like the spokes of a wheel; these, however, in practice have been interrupted, e.g. by parks, which are a noteworthy feature of the city (the Potomac Park: 300 ha (741 acres), inc. the Tidal Basin ringed with Japanese flowering cherry trees; Rock Creek Park: 729 ha (1800 acres); Anacostia Park: 445 ha (1099 acres); the National Zoological Park: 71 ha (175 acres)).

The Capitol, the central and dominating building, stands on a ridge 26 m (85 ft) above the level of the Potomac R. With the growth of legislative business it became necessary to add extensions to it (a Senate Chamber on the N and a House of Representatives Chamber on the S side, built 1851–9); at the top of the dome is a statue of Freedom. Down Pennsylvania Avenue from the Capitol is the White House. Both buildings were burned by the British in 1814 and the White House was afterwards painted white to disguise damage – the origin of its name. In the vicinity are the buildings of the Treasury, the State Department, the Supreme Court, the Pan-American Union and Ford's Theater, where Lincoln was assassinated (1865), now a museum. Among the many cultural and scientific institutions are the Smithsonian Institution, the Library of Congress and the National Gallery of Art. Of the monuments, the most striking is the Washington Monument, a white marble obelisk 169 m (554 ft) high, the city's most famous landmark; others are the Lincoln Memorial and the Thomas Jefferson National Memorial.

There is little industry except printing and publishing. In the main the residents are civil servants and employees of the US Government, foreign embassies or international organizations. Outside the District of Columbia proper there is a 'metropolitan area' in adjacent parts of Virginia and Maryland, and this area serves largely as residential suburbs, but also contains important scientific and medical research institutions, and the Pentagon, the largest single building in the world, headquarters of the US military forces.

Washington, Mount USA. Highest peak in the White Mountains, New Hampshire and in NE USA (1917 m; 6288 ft). Well-known for its scenery. Rack-and-pinion railway to the summit (opened 1869).

Wassenaar Netherlands. Residential town in South Holland province 10 km (6 miles) NE of The Hague. Pop. (1992) 26,065. Bulb-growing is the main occupation, but mainly residential.

Wast Water England. Lake in SW Cumbria in the Lake District 21 km (13 miles) W of Ambleside, 5 km (3 miles) long and 0.8 km (½ mile) wide, wild-looking and the deepest in England (78 m; 256 ft). About 3 km (2 miles) E of the N end of its valley, Wasdale is Scafell.

Watchet England. Small port in Somerset on Bridgwater Bay 24 km (15 miles) NW of Taunton. Pop. (1991) 3147. Seaside resort.

Waterbury USA. Industrial town in Connecticut on the Naugatuck R. 29 km (18 miles) NNW of New Haven. Pop. (1991) 108,961.

A leading centre of the brass industry. Also manufactures clocks and watches, hardware, machinery, plastics and clothing.

Watling Street

Incorporated 1686. The brass industry dates from *c.* 1800.

Waterford Ireland. 1. County in Munster in the SE, bounded on the S by the Atlantic Ocean. Area 1838 sq km (710 sq. miles). Pop. (1991) 51,296. Largely mountainous, with the Knockmealdown Mountains rising to 783 m (2568 ft) (NW); also the Comeragh Mountains (751 m; 2463 ft) and the Monavullagh Mountains (728 m; 2388 ft). Drained chiefly by the Blackwater and the Suir rivers. The coast has many indentations, esp. Waterford Harbour. Main occupations dairyfarming, cattle and pig rearing. Chief towns Waterford, Dungarvan and Lismore.

2. County town of Co. Waterford on the R. Suir near the mouth on Waterford harbour, an inlet formed by the estuaries of the Suir, Nore and Barrow. Pop. (1991) 40,328.

Seaport. Exports cattle and dairy produce. Bacon-curing, brewing and flour-milling.

Among its old buildings is Reginald's Tower (1003) and there are Roman Catholic and Protestant cathedrals, both dating from the 18th cent. An important Danish settlement until taken (1171) by Strongbow, who here married Eva, daughter of the king of Leinster. Withstood siege by Cromwell (1649) but fell to Ireton (1650). In the 18th cent. famous for glass manufacture; the trade had died out by the mid 19th cent. but has been revived and its glass factory is the largest in the world. Birthplace of Charles Kean (1811–68), the actor.

Waterloo Belgium. Small town in Brabant 19 km (12 miles) S of Brussels near which was fought the famous battle (1815) in which British and Prussian forces (with some Dutch and Belgians) under the Duke of Wellington and Blücher defeated the French under Napoleon.

Waterloo USA. Formerly Prairie Rapids. Town in Iowa on the Cedar Rapids. Pop. (1990) 66,467.

Has the annual National Dairy Cattle Congress. Manufactures agricultural machinery, cement mixers, leather goods, wood and food products.

First settled 1845; renamed 1851.

Waterton-Glacier International Peace Park Canada/USA. International park created (1932) by the amalgamation of two adjoining National Parks – Waterton Lakes National Park, Alberta (528 sq km; 204 sq. miles) and Glacier National Park, Montana (4040 sq km; 1560 sq. miles). Many glaciers and lakes. Highest peak Mt Cleveland (3185 m; 10,447 ft).

Watertown (Massachusetts) USA. Residential and industrial town on the Charles R. just W of Boston. Pop. (1985) 35,000.

Manufactures textiles, clothing and rubber products.

Founded and incorporated 1630.

Watertown (New York) USA. Town on the Black R. 105 km (65 miles) NNE of Syracuse. Pop. (1990) 29,429.

In a dairy-farming region. Manufactures paper, plumbing appliances and thermometers.

Founded 1800. F. W. Woolworth, originator of the famous stores, started business here (1878).

Waterville USA. City situated N of Augusta, Maine on the Kennebec R. at Ticonic Falls. Pop. (1985) 16,750.

Market for agricultural produce. Industries inc. timber products, metals, machinery, stone, clay, glass and concrete products, transport equipment and instruments.

Watford England. Town in SW Hertfordshire on the R. Colne 26 km (16 miles) NW of London. Pop. (1991) 83,376.

Industrial and residential centre. Printing, engineering and brewing. Manufactures paper, office equipment and electronic equipment. Also serves as a dormitory suburb of London.

Watling (Watlings) Island ➤SAN SALVADOR (BAHAMAS).

Watling Street England. Early English name for the Roman road linking London

985

(Londinium), through St Albans (Verula-mium), with Wroxeter (Viroconium) 6 km (4 miles) ESE of Shrewsbury. Much of it is still in use today. The name is also applied to parts of the main road from London to Dover (via Canterbury).

Wattenscheid Germany. Industrial town in North Rhine-Westphalia in the Ruhr 10 km (6 miles) E of Essen. Pop. (1985) 68,000.

Coalmining centre. Metalworking. Manufactures footwear and electrical equipment.

Waukegan USA. Industrial and residential town and lake port in Illinois on L. Michigan 60 km (37 miles) NNW of Chicago. Pop. (1990) 69,392.

Manufactures steel products, hardware, boilers and radiators, wire, outboard motors and footwear.

Waukesha USA. Town in Wisconsin on the Fox R. 26 km (16 miles) W of Milwaukee. Pop. (1990) 56,958.

Trade in dairy cattle. Manufactures metal and wood products. Other industries inc. food-processing and the bottling of mineral spring water.

Wausau USA. Town in Wisconsin on the Wisconsin R. 260 km (160 miles) NNW of Milwaukee. Pop. (1990) 37,060.

Brewing and granite-quarrying. Industries inc. the manufacture of electrical appliances, wood products, paper, plastics and chemicals.

Wauwatosa USA. Industrial town in SE Wisconsin just W of Milwaukee. Pop. (1990) 49,366.

Manufactures metal and concrete products and chemicals.

Waveney River England. River 80 km (50 miles) long rising 13 km (8 miles) SW of Diss and flowing generally NE past Diss, Bungay and Beccles, forming much of the boundary between Norfolk and Suffolk and entering the SW end of Breydon Water.

Waziristan Pakistan. Former mountainous tribal region at the N end of the Sulaiman Range, bounded on the W by Afghanistan.

Peopled mainly by Waziris, a Pathan tribe with an evil reputation for banditry. Many British military expeditions were needed to quell lawlessness in the latter half of the 19th cent.

Weald, The England. Region in SE England between the North and South Downs in Kent, Surrey and Sussex. Formerly forested, supplying charcoal for the iron industry, which flourished in the 16th and the 17th cent. but had practically died out by the early 19th cent.; now the region is more important for grazing and the cultivation of hops, fruit and vegetables. Remnants of the original woodlands exist in Ashdown, Tilgate and St Leonards forests.

Wear River England. River 105 km (65 miles) long rising in W Durham near the Cumbria border and flowing E and then NE, past Bishop Auckland, Durham and Chester-le-Street to the North Sea at Sunderland. Above Bishop Auckland its valley (Weardale) is picturesque. Navigable in the lower reaches.

Weaver River England. River 80 km (50 miles) long in Cheshire, rising 19 km (12 miles) SSW of Crewe and flowing N and then NW past Nantwich, Winsford and Northwich, to join the R. Mersey near Runcorn. Navigable below Winsford.

Weddell Sea Antarctica. Arm of the S Atlantic Ocean. Discovered by Capt. James Weddell (1787–1834) in 1823.

Wednesbury England. Industrial town in West Midlands 8 km (5 miles) SE of Wolverhampton in the Black Country.

Manufactures steel tubes and other metal goods. The Church of St Bartholomew is supposed to stand on the site of a temple of Woden (hence the name Wednesbury).

Wednesfield England. Industrial town in West Midlands (the Black Country) 3 km (2 miles) ENE of Wolverhampton.

Manufactures hardware, nuts and bolts and seamless steel tubes.

Scene of the defeat of the Danes by the

Wellingborough

Saxons (who named it 'Woden's Field') in 910.

Weert Netherlands. Industrial town in Limburg province 26 km (16 miles) SE of Eindhoven near the Belgian frontier. Pop. (1992) 40,695.
Manufactures metal goods and textiles.

Weiden Germany. Industrial town in Bavaria 53 km (33 miles) SE of Bayreuth. Pop. (1988) 41,750.
Manufactures china, glassware and textiles.

Weimar Germany. Industrial town in the Erfurt district on the Ilm R. 84 km (52 miles) WSW of Leipzig. Pop. (1991) 59,100.
Manufactures inc. textiles, machinery, electrical equipment.
Outstanding among its many famous buildings is the former grand-ducal palace (1789–1803); others inc. the houses of Goethe, Schiller and Liszt and the Stadtkirche (City Church). Became important from the mid 16th cent. as cap. of the duchy and then the grand duchy of Saxe-Weimar-Eisenach, later of the *Land* of Thuringia. J. S. Bach was court organist (1708–17) and in the late 18th and early 19th cent. Weimar was a leading cultural centre, esp. during the residence here of Goethe and Schiller; Franz Liszt was musical director (1848–59). At the end of World War I the constitution of the new German Republic (the 'Weimar Republic') was adopted here (1919) and lasted until 1933 when Adolf Hitler assumed power.

Weinhelm Germany. Town in Baden-Württemberg 13 km (8 miles) NE of Mannheim at the foot of the Odenwald. Pop. (1984) 41,200.
Industrial centre. Resort. Industries inc. tanning and the manufacture of soap.
Has a 16th-cent. Gothic town hall.

Weirton USA. Industrial town in West Virginia on the Ohio R. 51 km (32 miles) W of Pittsburgh. Pop. (1990) 22,124.
Important steelworks producing sheet steel, tinplate; cement and chemicals.

Weissenfels Germany. Industrial town in the Halle district on the Saale R. 32 km (20 miles) WSW of Leipzig. Pop. (1989) 39,000.
In a lignite-mining region. Manufactures footwear, paper and machinery.
The former 17th-cent. Augustusburg palace stands above the town.

Weisshorn Switzerland. One of the highest peaks (4509 m; 14,789 ft) in the Pennine Alps in the S 10 km (6 miles) NNW of Zermatt.

Welkom South Africa. Town in the Free State 137 km (85 miles) NNE of Bloemfontein at a height of 1350 m (4,428 ft). Pop. (1984) 228,000.
Residential and commercial centre serving the goldmining area.

Welland Canada. Town in S Ontario on the Welland R. and the Welland Ship Canal 60 km (37 miles) ESE of Hamilton. Pop. (1971) 44,397.
Industrial centre. Canal port. Manufactures steel, agricultural machinery and footwear.

Welland River England. River 113 km (70 miles) long rising near Market Harborough, forming much of the Leicestershire–Northamptonshire boundary and flowing generally NE across Lincolnshire and past Spalding to the Wash.

Welland Ship Canal Canada. Canal in S Ontario joining Lakes Erie and Ontario, bypassing the Niagara Falls; just over 44 km (27½ miles) long, part of its course being formed by the Welland R. Constructed 1913–32 to supersede the Old Welland Canal (built 1824–33). One of the world's busiest inland waterways and since 1973 carrying ships up to 221 m (725 ft) long and with up to 7.9 m (26 ft) draught.

Wellingborough England. Industrial town in Northamptonshire on the R. Nene at the confluence with the R. Ise 16 km (10 miles) ENE of Northampton. Pop. (1991) 67,789.
Tanning, iron-founding, footwear manufacture; also produces tanning chemicals and clothing.
Has a public school (founded 1595).

Wellington (Shropshire) England. Market town 16 km (10 miles) E of Shrewsbury. Pop. (1991) 18,494.

Manufactures automobile components and cranes.

The Wrekin (407 m; 1335 ft) is 3 km (2 miles) SW; 10 km (6 miles) WSW is Wroxeter.

Wellington (Somerset) England. Market town 10 km (6 miles) WSW of Taunton. Pop. (1991) 9621.

Manufactures woollen goods, made here since the reign of Elizabeth I.

On the Blackdown Hills to the S is a monument to the Duke of Wellington, who took his title from the town.

Wellington New Zealand. 1. Local Government Region in the SW of North Island. Pop. (1992) 404,300. Largely mountainous, esp. in the N; a fertile coastal region in the S and W, with dairy and sheep farms. Wellington (city) is in the SW.

2. Cap., on the SW shore of Port Nicholson, now Wellington Harbour, off Cook Strait. Pop. (stat. division) (1992) 150,100.

Important seaport with a large deep, sheltered harbour and the city has spread among the high encircling hills. Among its outstanding buildings are the Houses of Parliament, Victoria University (1897) and the National Museum and Art Gallery. In 1872 earth movements raised the shoreline so that Lambton Quay, with large commercial and administrative buildings, now lies inland of the waterfront.

Exports dairy produce, wool, meat and hides. The main industrial growth has been in the Hutt valley, just to the NE, where woollen mills, food-processing plants, engineering industries, vehicle assembly, rubber manufactures and oil refineries are located. Railways to the N follow the W coast and the Hutt valley, and there are regular inter-island links by sea to Picton and by air to Nelson. Founded 1840. Succeeded Auckland as cap. 1865.

Wells England. Cathedral city in Somerset 27 km (17 miles) S of Bristol at the S foot of the Mendip Hills. Pop. (1991) 9763.

Manufactures dairy products, inc. cheese, and electronic goods.

Within the borough is the ecclesiastical city, surrounded by medieval walls and containing the small but very beautiful 12th/13th-cent. cathedral, the moated bishop's palace. The W front of the cathedral, which is mainly Early English in style, has 300 finely carved figures, and is attributed to Bishop Jocelyn (1206–42). Just NW is the limestone cave of Wookey Hole.

Wells-next-the-Sea England. Small port and holiday resort in Norfolk 47 km (29 miles) NW of Norwich, well-known for its shellfish. Pop. (1991) 2400.

Wels Austria. Industrial town in Upper Austria 24 km (15 miles) SW of Linz on the Traun R. Pop. (1991) 52,594.

Manufactures machinery and food products, deriving fuel from natural-gas wells in the vicinity.

Has a 14th-cent. Gothic church and an imperial castle.

Welshpool Wales. Market town in Powys near the R. Severn 27 km (17 miles) WSW of Shrewsbury. Pop. (1991) 5724.

There is some light industry.

To the SW are Powys (Powis) Castle, seat of the earls of Powys and the picturesque Powys Park.

Welwyn Garden City England. Town in Hertfordshire 10 km (6 miles) NE of St Albans. Pop. (1991) 41,700.

Manufactures food products, chemicals and plastics.

Planned (1919) by Sir Ebenezer Howard as a residential and industrial centre.

Wembley England. Former municipal borough in Middlesex and NW suburb of London; from 1965 part of the London borough of Brent. Largely residential.

Electrical engineering. Manufactures food products and industrial gases.

Site of the British Empire Exhibition (1924–5), many of the buildings of which were converted into factories. Wembley Stadium is the venue of the Cup Finals of the Football Association and Rugby League and international football matches; the Olympic Games were held there in 1948.

Wenchow ➤WENZHOU.

Wendover England. Market town in Buckinghamshire in the Chiltern Hills 8 km (5 miles) SE of Aylesbury on the Upper Icknield Way. Pop. (1971) 8600. Coombe Hill (260 m; 853 ft) 2.4 km (1½ miles) WSW, presents magnificent views over the Vale of Aylesbury. Chequers, country residence of the British prime minister, is 4 km (2½ miles) SW. Birthplace of Roger de Wendover (d. 1237), an early English historian.

Wenlock England. District in Shropshire 18 km (11 miles) SE of Shrewsbury. Pop. (1971) 14,149. Comprises Much Wenlock, a market town with the ruins of a convent founded in the 7th cent., Little Wenlock, Ironbridge, with the first iron bridge built in England (1779), Broseley, Coalbrookdale and Madeley.

Manufactures pottery and tiles.

Wenlock Edge, a ridge rising to 264 m (866 ft), extends about 24 km (15 miles) to the SW.

Wensleydale England. The picturesque upper valley of the R. Ure in North Yorkshire, widening at its lower end into the Vale of York. Famous for its cheese.

Wenzhou (Wenchou/Wenchow) China. River port in SE Zhejiang province on the Wukiang 24 km (15 miles) from the sea and 260 km (160 miles) SSE of Hangzhou. Pop. (1990) 401,871.

Trade in tea, timber, bamboo, oranges. Manufactures leather goods, mats and umbrellas.

It was opened to European trade in 1877.

Wernigerode Germany. Tourist resort in the Magdeburg district 72 km (45 miles) SW of Magdeburg at the N foot of the Harz Mountains. Pop. (1989) 36,778.

Industries inc. paper, chemicals and engineering.

Wesel Germany. Town in North Rhine-Westphalia near the confluence of the Rhine and Lippe rivers 27 km (17 miles) NNW of Duisburg. Pop. (1986) 54,600.

Manufactures machinery.

Weser River Germany. River 499 km (310 miles) long, formed by the union of the Fulda and Werra rivers at Münden, flowing generally N past Minden and Bremen, entering the North Sea at Bremerhaven. Navigable throughout; connected by the Mittelland Canal system with the Rhine, Ems and Elbe rivers.

Wessex Britain. Kingdom of the West Saxons, probably founded by Cerdic around the R. Avon in Wiltshire towards the end of the 5th cent. and comprising in the first place the modern counties of Wiltshire, Hampshire and Berkshire; Dorset, Somerset and parts of Devon were added by the end of the 7th cent. Egbert (802–39) defeated Mercia and annexed Essex, Sussex and Kent; under Alfred (871–900) Wessex controlled all England not ruled by the Danes and its history then becomes that of England. The Wessex novels of Thomas Hardy refer mainly to Dorset.

West Allis USA. Industrial town in SE Wisconsin just W of Milwaukee. Pop. (1990) 69,221.

Manufactures lorries.

West Bank Israel. Area of Palestine W of the Jordan R. occupied by Israel since the 'Six Day' war in 1967. Area 5879 sq km (2270 sq. miles). Pop. (1992) 973,000; 97 per cent Palestinian Arabs. In 1993 agreement was reached between Israel and the Palestine Liberation Organization (PLO) for limited self-rule in Jericho.

West Bay ➤BRIDPORT.

West Bengal India. State in the NE created from Bengal 1947. Area 88,752 sq km (34,669 sq. miles). Pop. (1991) 67,982,732. Cap. Calcutta. Absorbed the former princely state of Cooch Behar 1950, Chandernagore 1954, parts of Bihar 1956.

Chief crops are rice, wheat, tobacco, jute,

tea and oilseeds. One of the major industrial states. Industries inc. the manufacture of automobiles, tyres, oil-refining, fertilizers, steel, alloy steel, graphite, jute, railway wagons, electric locomotives, glass, paper, textiles, shipbuilding, chemicals, pharmaceuticals, aluminium, brewing. Important minerals are coal and china clay. Darjeeling is a hill resort, a tourist centre. Murshidabad, Malda and Changannagar are places of historical interest.

West Bridgford England. Residential urban district of Nottinghamshire and a S suburb of Nottingham, with Trent Bridge cricket ground. Pop. (1971) 28,496.

West Bromwich England. Industrial town in West Midlands in the Black Country 8 km (5 miles) NW of Birmingham. Pop. (1991) 154,531.

Manufactures metal goods (springs, nails, safes, stoves, weighing machines); also chemicals and paint.

Westbury England. Market town in Wiltshire 18 km (11 miles) SE of Bath. Pop. (1991) 10,200.

Industries inc. cement and glove-making.

To the E is the White Horse of Westbury, cut (1873) in the chalk downs over an earlier figure.

West Covina USA. Town in California 31 km (19 miles) E of Los Angeles. Pop. (1990) 96,086. Almost entirely residential. Its working pop. commutes largely to Los Angeles.

West Drayton ➤YIEWSLEY AND WEST DRAYTON.

West End Bahamas. Town at the W tip of Grand Bahama Is. in the West Indies, situated E of the Florida coast.

Fishing port with fish-processing plant.

Westerham England. Market town in W Kent on the R. Darent 8 km (5 miles) W of Sevenoaks. Pop. 3162.

Industries inc. tourism and some manufacturing.

Birthplace of General Wolfe (1727–59),

who is commemorated in Quebec House. Just S is Chartwell, home (1922–65) of Sir Winston Churchill.

Western Australia Australia. Largest state in Australia, W of the meridian 129°E, which separates it from the Northern Territory and South Australia. Area 2,525,500 sq km (975,100 sq. miles). Pop. (1993) 1,672,500. Cap. Perth in the only fertile and populous area, Swanland (SW). There is a great diversity of landscape and land-use. In the NE the Kimberleys consist of broken blocks of high country, much eroded and cut by river gorges; here monsoon rains support grass and permit low-density cattle-rearing, with agricultural possibilities if rivers such as the Ord are utilized. To the SW are eroded plateaux such as the Hamersley Range. Summers are hot; the temperature in some parts has exceeded 38°C (100°F) on more than 100 consecutive days. The SW interior has granites and gneisses at the surface, and here the spinifex and dwarf acacia give way to closer mulga and dry grassland. The extreme SW is forested (largely with the hardwood eucalypts jarrah and karri), the climate being of 'Mediterranean' type.

Main occupations dairying, lumbering and the cultivation of citrus and other fruits and vines. Much of the inland area with a mean annual rainfall between 65 cm (25 ins.) and 25 cm (10 ins.) has been cleared for wheat and sheep farming. Irrigation has been established by the government along the SW coastal plain in the N. Chief mineral gold, occurring mostly in a wide belt in the SW interior inc. such centres as Kalgoorlie, Meekatharra, Wiluna; the gold rush of 1892 saw the beginnings of large-scale goldmining at and near Kalgoorlie. Iron is mined on islands in Yampi Sound in the NW, coal comes from Collie in the SW and asbestos from the Hamersley Range. Other minerals inc. nickel, bauxite, oil, mineral sands and salt. Chief commercial and administrative city Perth; at Fremantle, its port, and Kwinana, just S, industries are growing and inc. the manufacture of iron and steel, chemicals and textiles, food-processing, mining equipment and oil-refining. Exports inc. iron ore and concentrates, petroleum and petroleum products, gold bullion, textile fibres, wheat, wool, dairy produce and timber.

The first settlement was formed (1826) at Albany by convicts. In 1829 Capt. Fremantle took possession of the territory for Britain and Capt. Sterling founded the Swan River Settlement in the Perth–Fremantle area. The colony became a state of the Commonwealth of Australia in 1901.

Western Cape South Africa. Province created in 1994. Area 129,370 sq km (49,950 sq. miles). Pop. (1995) 3,721,200. Cap. Cape Town.

Western Desert Egypt. Ill-defined section of the Libyan Desert on the border of Cyrenaica, containing the Siwa, Bahariya and Farafra oases and the Qattara Depression (N). A railway runs along the coast from Alexandria through El Alamein to Matruh and then a coastal road to Sidi Barrani and Salum (all well known in World War II).

Western Isles Scotland. From 1975 the islands area comprising the Outer Hebrides.

Western Malaysia ➤PENINSULAR MALAYSIA.

Western Sahara. Formerly Spanish Sahara, a Spanish overseas province in W Africa. Area 265,940 sq km (102,680 sq. miles). Pop. (1993) 214,000. Cap.El Aaiún (97,000).

Mainly desert with several oases; considerable phosphate deposits, which form the chief export. All trade is controlled by the Moroccan authorities.

In 1975 Morocco and Mauritania agreed on the division of the region between them, on the withdrawal of the Spanish armed forces. In 1975 Morocco took over the Mauritanian sector. The Polisario liberation movement which had been challenging Spain's rule since 1973, supported by Algeria, continued an armed struggle to liberate their country. A ceasefire was agreed in 1988, but the lull in fighting ended in 1989.

Western Samoa ➤SAMOA.

Westfalen ➤WESTPHALIA.

Westfield (Massachusetts) USA. Town on the Westfield R. 11 km (7 miles) WNW of Springfield. Pop. (1970) 31,433.

Manufactures machinery, bicycles and paper.

Founded 1660 as a trading post.

Westfield (New Jersey) USA. Town 18 km (11 miles) SW of Newark. Pop. (1970) 33,720. Mainly residential. Some light industries.

West Flanders ➤FLANDERS.

West Glamorgan Wales. Former county on the Bristol Channel formed in 1974 from the W portion of Glamorganshire, inc. the districts around Swansea, Neath and Port Talbot. ➤SWANSEA AND NEATH PORT TALBOT.

West Ham England. Part of the London borough of Newham. Inc. Stratford, Forest Gate, Plaistow, Canning Town and Silvertown on the N bank of the R. Thames.

Industrial and residential. Railway engineering. Manufactures rubber and jute products, chemicals and soap.

West Hartford USA. Town in Connecticut 5 km (3 miles) W of Hartford. Pop. (1990) 60,110. Mainly residential. Birthplace of Noah Webster (1758–1843), the lexicographer.

West Hartlepool England. Industrial town in Cleveland on the S side of Hartlepool Bay 11 km (7 miles) N of Middlesbrough. Since 1967 part of Hartlepool.

Seaport. Shipbuilding. Manufactures machinery, paper, hosiery and cement. Includes seaside resort of Seaton Carew.

West Haven USA. Industrial town in Connecticut, just SW of New Haven. Pop. (1990) 54,021.

Manufactures textiles, aircraft parts and fertilizers.

Westhoughton England. Town in Greater Manchester 6 km (4 miles) WSW of Bolton. Pop. (1971) 17,729.

Manufactures cotton goods, chemicals and paint.

West Indies. Archipelago off Central America separating the Atlantic Ocean from the Caribbean Sea and extending in a wide arc about 4000 km (2500 miles) long from near the Florida coast to near the coast of Venezuela. Consists of 3 main groups, the Greater Antilles, the Lesser Antilles and the Bahamas. The Greater Antilles inc. Cuba (the westernmost and by far the largest island in the West Indies), Hispaniola, Puerto Rico and Jamaica; the Bahamas are the northernmost group, lying E of Florida; the Lesser Antilles inc. the Leeward Is., the Windward Is., Barbados, Trinidad and Tobago, Margarita and islands of the Netherlands Antilles (Curaçao, Aruba, Bonaire). All the islands have a wide measure of autonomy or are independent republics. Hispaniola is divided between Haiti (W) and the Dominican Republic (E) which, like Cuba, are independent. The USA possesses Puerto Rico and the Virgin Is. of the USA; France has Guadeloupe and Martinique; the Netherlands has the Netherlands Antilles; Venezuela has Margarita and some small adjacent islands. The remaining islands, inc. the Bahamas, are associated with Britain, either as independent members of the Commonwealth or as Crown Colonies. Most of the West Indies are of volcanic origin, being the peaks of a submerged range of mountains; some, notably the Bahamas, are of coral formation. No important rivers, but plentiful supplies of underground water. Some of the islands are mountainous: Hispaniola has peaks exceeding 3000 m (9840 ft); the Blue Mountains of Jamaica rise above 2100 m (6888 ft). Climate tropical but tempered by the NE Trade Winds; many islands experience hurricanes Aug.–Oct. Volcanic eruptions in modern times have been confined to Martinique and St Vincent. There are many fine natural harbours, inc. Havana (Cuba), Kingston (Jamaica), San Juan (Puerto Rico).

The fertile soil yields many varieties of tropical products. Main crop sugar-cane; others exported in quantity are tobacco, cacao, citrus fruits, bananas, coffee; sugar-refining is a major industry; rum and lime juice are prepared for export. Jamaica has large bauxite deposits and Trinidad produces asphalt from its Pitch Lake; Curaçao and Aruba have petroleum industries of great importance. Blacks form the bulk of the pop., being descendants of African slaves brought to work on the plantations; they predominate in most of the islands, though in Cuba and Puerto Rico whites of Spanish stock are in the majority. The aboriginal peoples, Arawaks and Caribs, have almost disappeared, but a few Caribs survive in Dominica.

The West Indies were discovered by Columbus, who made his first landfall in the Americas (1492) on San Salvador (Watling) Island in the Bahamas. As he believed that he had reached India by a westerly route, the islands were named 'West Indies'. Spaniards were the first Europeans to settle; in 1496 Santo Domingo, on Hispaniola, was founded as the first European town in the New World. The West Indies and the adjacent waters became the haunt of pirates and buccaneers, and continual struggles took place (esp. between the English, French and Dutch) for possession of the islands. Slave-trading began in the 1560s and grew apace in the 17th and 18th cent. Slavery was abolished in the British West Indies in 1834 and in the other islands later. During the 19th cent. the islands of the British West Indies were made Crown Colonies, and some, e.g. Trinidad and Tobago, were combined for administrative purposes. In 1958 the Federation of the British West Indies was formed, with the cap. at Port of Spain (Trinidad). In 1962, however, the Federation was dissolved because Jamaica and Trinidad opted out. The US has a number of naval and air bases outside its own territory – Guantánamo Bay in Cuba and the bases in the West Indies obtained in 1940–1 on a 99-year lease.

West Irian ➤NEW GUINEA.

West Lothian Scotland. Former county in the central lowlands bordering N on the Firth of Forth. Formerly Linlithgowshire. ➤EAST AND WEST LOTHIAN.

Westmeath Ireland. Inland county in Leinster. Area 1764 sq km (681 sq. miles). Pop.

(1991) 61,880. County town Mullingar. Generally low-lying, with a considerable area of bog; has many loughs, inc. Loughs Ree (on the R. Shannon), Sheelin, Derravaragh and Ennell, all noted for their trout. Main occupations cattle-rearing and dairy-farming. Chief towns Mullingar, Athlone.

West Memphis USA. City situated W of Memphis, Tennessee on the Mississippi R., Arkansas. Pop. (1990) 28,259.

Industries inc. sawmilling, distilling, cotton-milling and cottonseed-processing.

West Midlands England. Metropolitan county in the Midlands formed (1974) from parts of Staffordshire, Warwickshire and Worcestershire. Area 899 sq km (347 sq. miles). Pop. (1994) 2,627,800. It is divided into the boroughs of Birmingham, Coventry, Dudley, Sandwell, Solihull, Walsall and Wolverhampton. There is a wide variety of industry but dominated by the car and aircraft manufacture and their related trades. The last steel-making in the county was in 1990.

Westminster England. City and former metropolitan borough of London on the N bank of the R. Thames; London borough comprising the former Westminster and the metropolitan boroughs of Paddington and St Marylebone. Pop. (1991) 182,400. Contains many of the chief theatres, restaurants and shops (West End) and a large number of London's historic buildings and monuments, e.g. Buckingham Palace, St James's Palace. In front of the former, at the head of the Mall, is the Queen Victoria Memorial; nearby are the royal parks, Hyde Park and the much smaller St James's Park and Green Park. Westminster Abbey (officially the Collegiate Church of St Peter), stands on the site of a 7th-cent. abbey built by Sebert, king of the E Saxons, which was destroyed but rebuilt by Edward the Confessor in the 11th cent. Further rebuilding was begun in the 13th cent. Later additions inc. Henry VII's Chapel (16th-cent.) and the two W towers, designed by Wren (17th cent.) and completed 1740. Scene of the coronation of all English mon-

archs since William the Conqueror (except the uncrowned Edward V and Edward VIII); the burial-place of many of them, and of many other famous Englishmen, inc. some of the greatest poets (in 'Poets' Corner') and the Unknown Soldier. Westminster School (St Peter's College, originally attached to the Abbey and refounded by Elizabeth I in 1560) is one of the oldest public schools, with Ben Jonson, Dryden, Wren and Gibbon among its former scholars. Opposite the Abbey, in New Palace Yard, is Westminster Hall, completed in 1099, rebuilt 1394–1402, as part of the royal Palace of Westminster, which inc. courts of law; it has witnessed many historic events, e.g. the deposition of Richard II and the trials of Charles I and Warren Hastings (whose trial lasted 7 years). The adjoining Houses of Parliament, in imitated Perpendicular style (1840–67), are dominated by the Victoria Tower and the Clock Tower (which contains the celebrated hour bell Big Ben). The thoroughfare Whitehall, leading N from Parliament Square to Trafalgar Square, contains the Cenotaph war memorial and the principal government offices; close by is Downing Street, with the residences of the Prime Minister and the Chancellor of the Exchequer. In Trafalgar Square is Nelson's Column (1843) and on the N side the National Gallery (1838). From Westminster Bridge (crossing the Thames near the Houses of Parliament) the Victoria Embankment curves past the Cleopatra's Needle obelisk (brought from Egypt 1878) to Waterloo Bridge. From Trafalgar Square the Strand runs parallel to the river, with Somerset House, King's College (University of London), and the two 'island' churches, St Mary-le-Strand and St Clement Danes; just N, towards the E end of the Strand, is Covent Garden, with the Royal Opera House and, formerly, a fruit and vegetable market. The S side of Westminster is Pimlico, with Victoria Station and the Byzantine-style Roman Catholic cathedral (1895–1903); in the W are many embassies and institutions, the residential districts of Belgravia and Mayfair, and the Royal Albert Hall and the Albert Memorial; in the N is the less fashionable Soho (London's 'Latin quarter'). Piccadilly (running alongside Green Park in the N) is well-known for shops and also for Burlington House, seat of Royal Academy and learned societies. Many famous buildings (inc. the House of Commons, Westminster School and St Clement Danes Church) were severely damaged by bombing in World War II. The 13th-cent. Statutes of Westminster (1275, 1285) expressed basic principles in English law. Those of 1931 defined the relationship between Britain and the Dominions, within the Commonwealth. There have been many Synods of Westminster, esp. the Westminster Assembly (1643–9), which drew up a Confession of faith accepted by the Presbyterian churches.

Westmorland ►CUMBRIA.

West New York USA. Industrial town in NE New Jersey on the Hudson R. opposite Manhattan. Pop. (1970) 40,627.

Manufactures textiles, clothing, leather goods and toys.

Weston-super-Mare England. Town in North Somerset on the Bristol Channel 29 km (18 miles) WSW of Bristol. Pop. (1991) 69,372. Seaside resort, popular with holidaymakers from Bristol and the West Midlands.

West Orange USA. Town in New Jersey 8 km (5 miles) NW of Newark. Pop. (1970) 43,715.

Residential and industrial. Manufactures electrical equipment and machinery.

Home of Thomas A. Edison (1887–1931), the inventor of the electric light bulb.

West Palm Beach USA. Winter resort in SE Florida on the W shore of L. Worth opposite Palm Beach 105 km (65 miles) NNE of Miami. Pop. (1990) 67,643.

Manufactures air-conditioning equipment, prefabricated buildings, and develops aeronautics and electronic equipment. Has an important tourist trade.

Westphalia (Ger. **Westfalen**) Germany. Former province of Prussia; since 1946 part of the *Land* of North Rhine-Westphalia. In

the W is the Ruhr district, one of the most important industrial regions in Europe, based on the coalfield; among its many large manufacturing towns are Cologne, Essen, Düsseldorf, Dortmund. Westphalia was originally the W part of the old duchy of Saxony. Some of the area passed to the archbishops of Cologne (1180) as the duchy of Westphalia. In 1803 the Church lands were secularized and part of Westphalia went to Prussia. Napoleon created the kingdom of Westphalia (inc. territory never before associated with it) for his brother Jérôme (1807). The Prussian province (cap. Münster) formed in 1816 more or less coincided with the original region. The Treaty of Westphalia (1648), concluded at Münster and Osnabrück, brought the Thirty Years War to an end.

West Point USA. US military reservation, home of the US Military Academy, opened in 1802, on a plateau above the Hudson R. 13 km (8 miles) SSE of Newburgh in SE New York, inc. Constitution Island in the Hudson R.

Westport Ireland. Market town and fishing port in Co. Mayo on Westport Bay, an inlet of Clew Bay. Pop. (1991) 3688.

Manufactures hosiery.

Has the 18th-cent. Westport House, seat of the Marquess of Sligo.

West Sussex England. County in the S bounded on the S by the English Channel. Area 1989 sq km (768 sq. miles). Pop. (1991) 713,600. County town Chichester. It is divided into the districts of Adur, Arun, Chichester, Crawley, Horsham, Mid Sussex and Worthing. The South Downs extend W–E across the S half, roughly parallel to the coast, rising to 255 m (836 ft) drained by the R. Arun and its tributary the Rother. Cereals and root crops grown, cattle and sheep raised. There is light industry and electronic equipment manufacture. Several coastal resorts, e.g. Worthing, Bognor Regis; Crawley is the principal inland town.

West Virginia USA. State in E central USA. Area 62,758 sq km (24,232 sq. miles).

Pop. (1990) 1,820,000. Cap. Charleston. Has two narrow extensions, the N Panhandle between Ohio and Pennsylvania and the E Panhandle between Maryland and Virginia. The Allegheny Plateau covers two-thirds of its area. Highest point Spruce Knob (1482 m; 4861 ft). Chief rivers the Ohio and the Potomac, on the W and N borders respectively. Climate humid continental, with a mean annual rainfall of 100–125 cm (40–50 ins.). Most important occupation mining; 38 per cent of the state is underlain with mineable coal. Other minerals inc. petroleum, salt, sand, gravel, sandstone and limestone. Chief crops hay, maize. Large quantities of apples and peaches grown. Tourism is important, inc. ski resorts. Leading industrial centres Charleston, Huntington and Wheeling. Industries inc. fabricated metals, glass, chemicals, wood products, textiles and clothing, plastics, aerospace and machinery. Originally part of Virginia, the region resented domination by the E Virginians and at the outbreak of the Civil War sided with the Union (1861) and was admitted to the Union in 1863 as the 35th state.

Westward Ho! England. Village and small seaside resort in Devon in the urban district of Northam on Bideford Bay 3 km (2 miles) NW of Bideford. Named after Charles Kingsley's novel. The writer, Rudyard Kipling, was educated at the United Services College, which was formerly here.

West Yorkshire England. Former county in the N, formed 1974 from the former West Riding of Yorkshire and inc. the districts around Leeds, Bradford, Halifax, Huddersfield and Wakefield. Area 2039 sq km (787 sq. miles). Pop. (1995) 2,105,800. It was divided into the boroughs of Bradford, Calderdale, Kirklees, Leeds and Wakefield. Textile manufacture and some coalmining are important industries but efforts to attract light industry have been successful. On the edge of two national parks. In the W the Pennine Range is capped by rather bleak, wind-swept moors, penetrated by the Aire and Calder rivers.

Wetaskiwin Canada. Town situated S of Edmonton, Alberta. Pop. (1991) 10,634.
Railway junction for freight only serving a farming area. Industries inc. food-processing, cranes, plastics, furniture, transport and agricultural equipment.

Wetzlar Germany. Industrial town in Hessen on the Lahn R. 108 km (67 miles) ESE of Bonn. Pop. (1985) 50,000.
Iron-founding. Manufactures cameras, optical instruments and machine-tools.
Associated with Goethe's *Werther*.

Wexford Ireland. 1. County in Leinster in the extreme SE bounded on the E and S by St George's Channel. Area 2351 sq km (908 sq. miles). Pop. (1991) 102,045. In the main gently undulating; mountainous along the NW border, rising to 796 m (2611 ft) in Mt Leinster. Drained by the Slaney and Barrow (SW border) rivers. Cereals and potatoes cultivated. Dairy-farming. Cattle-rearing. The first Irish county to be colonized from England, the Anglo–Normans landing in 1169 at the invitation of Diarmid MacMurrough, overlord of Leinster.
2. County town of Co. Wexford on Wexford Harbour, formed by the estuary of the R. Slaney. Pop. (1991) 9544.
Fishing port. Manufactures agricultural implements. Iron-founding, bacon and ham curing, and tanning. Owing to the bar at the mouth of the estuary, Wexford declined as a seaport and was superseded by Rosslare.
A Danish settlement in the 9th cent. Lost its independence (1169) when Diarmid MacMurrough and his Anglo–Norman allies captured it. Birthplace of Sir Robert M'Clure (1807–73), who won fame in the discovery of the Northwest Passage.

Weybridge ➤WALTON AND WEYBRIDGE.

Weymouth USA. Industrial town in Massachusetts on Massachusetts Bay 18 km (11 miles) SSE of Boston. Pop. (1989) 58,226.
Manufactures footwear, machinery and fertilizers. A dormitory town for Boston.
First colonized 1622. A tannery was established in 1697.

Weymouth and Portland England. Seaside resort on the coast of Dorset at the mouth of the short R. Wey (10 km; 6 miles). Pop. (1991) 46,065. There are ferries for the Channel Is. There is some light engineering.

Popularized as a resort by George III, a frequent visitor. Just S is the Isle of Portland. Birthplace of T. L. Peacock, English poet and novelist (1785–1866).

Wey River England. River 56 km (35 miles) long formed from two streams, one rising near Alton (Hampshire) and the other near Haslemere (Surrey), flowing generally NE past Godalming and Guildford to join the R. Thames at Weybridge.

Whangarei New Zealand. Industrial town and port on the E coast of Auckland Peninsula, North Island 137 km (85 miles) NNW of Auckland. Pop. (1974) 36,320.

Harbour improved by dredging Exports coal, dairy produce and fruit. Manufactures glass and cement.

Wharfe River England. River 96 km (60 miles) long mainly in North Yorkshire, rising 5 km (3 miles) N of Pen-y-ghent and flowing generally ESE past Ilkley, Otley and Tadcaster to join the R. Ouse just above Cawood. Its upper valley, Wharfedale, is one of the most beautiful in England.

Wheat Ridge USA. City immediately W of Denver, Colorado. Pop. (1980) 30,293. Residential.

Wheeling USA. Town in West Virginia on the Ohio R. 72 km (45 miles) SW of Pittsburgh in the N Panhandle of the state. Pop. (1990) 38,882.

Large iron and steel industry. Manufactures tinplate, nails, glass and tiles.

Founded 1769. Site of the Wheeling Conventions (1861–2) which led to the separation of West Virginia from Virginia. State cap. 1863–70 and 1875–85.

Whipsnade England. Village in Bedfordshire 5 km (3 miles) S of Dunstable. Has a Zoological Park of 200 ha (494 acres) (opened 1931 by the London Zoological Society) where animals and birds are bred and exhibited in their natural state.

Whitby England. Seaside resort in North Yorkshire at the mouth of the R. Esk, which divides the town into the old and new parts. Pop. (1991) 13,640.

Fishing port. Boatbuilding and fish-curing. The manufacture of jet ornaments is still carried on. There is a potash mine nearby.

The ruins of the abbey, founded in the 7th cent., stand on the E cliff. Capt. Cook lived here and the ships for his voyages were built here. Birthplace of William Scoresby (1789–1857), the Arctic explorer.

Whitchurch England. Market town in Shropshire 29 km (18 miles) N of Shrewsbury. Pop. (1989) 7500. Has a 17th-cent. almshouse and several Georgian houses. Birthplace of Sir Edward German, English composer (1862–1936).

Whitechapel England. District in the London borough of Tower Hamlets (E). The Sunday morning market of 'Petticoat Lane' (Middlesex Street) is on its W boundary. Contains the Whitechapel Art Gallery.

Whitehaven England. Seaport in Cumbria on the Irish Sea 58 km (36 miles) SW of Carlisle. Pop. (1991) 26,542.

Seaport. Industries inc. printing. Manufactures textiles, food products, chemicals and detergents.

Whitehorse Canada. Cap. and largest town of the Yukon Territory on the Lewes (Upper Yukon) R. just below Whitehorse Rapids and 153 km (95 miles) N of Skagway (Alaska), with which it is connected by rail. Pop. (1991) 22,907.

Trading centre for a mining and fur-trapping region. Tourism is important.

White Horse, Vale of England. Valley of the R. Ock, which flows ENE across S Oxfordshire to join the R. Thames at Abingdon. Flat and well-wooded in contrast with the Berkshire Downs to the S. Called after White Horse Hill (261 m; 856 ft) in the Downs just S of the village of Uffington, which has the figure of a horse 114 m (274 ft) long, cut on its N slope by removing the turf and exposing the underlying chalk; on the summit is the earthwork known as Uffington Castle. The figure is supposed to commemorate the victory of Alfred the Great over the Danes at Ashdown (871). There are similar white horses elsewhere in England, notably near Westbury (Wilts).

White Mountains USA. 1. Range in N New Hampshire, part of the Appalachian Mountains. A favourite resort area owing to the fine scenery. Highest peak Mt Washington (1917 m; 6288 ft).

2. Range in E California and SW Nevada. Highest peak White Mountain (4344 m; 14,248 ft).

White Plains USA. Town in SE New York on the Bronx R. 40 km (25 miles) NNE of New York City. Pop. (1990) 48,718.

Residential and industrial. Manufactures clothing, plastics, food products, and is a corporate office and shopping centre.

During the American Revolution the provincial congress met here and approved the Declaration of Independence (1776) and a battle was fought between Washington and the British (1776).

White Russia ►BELARUS.

White Sea Russia. Inlet of the Barents Sea entered by a channel 50–150 km (30–90 miles) wide between the Kola and Kanin peninsulas. Area 95,000 sq km (36,680 sq. miles). Receives the Mezen, North Dvina and Onega rivers. Contains the Kandalaksha, Onega and Dvina gulfs. Principal port Archangel (Arkhangelsk). Usually frozen Oct.– May. Its commercial importance increased with the completion of the Baltic–White Sea Canal (1933).

Whitehorn Scotland. Market town in Dumfries and Galloway 14 km (9 miles) S of Wigtown. Pop. (1991) 750. Ruins of the 12th-cent. St Ninian's Priory, built for Preconstratensian monks. According to some authorities this was the site of the stone church called Candida Casa ('White House'),

built in 397 by St Ninian, the first Christian missionary to Scotland; others place the site at the coastal village known as Isle of Whithorn 5 km (3 miles) SE.

Whitley Bay England. Seaside resort in Tyne and Wear 13 km (8 miles) NE of Newcastle-upon-Tyne. Pop. (1991) 33,335.

Whitney, Mount USA. Highest peak in USA outside Alaska, rising to 4418 m (14,495 ft), situated about 280 km (175 miles) N of Los Angeles near the S end of the Sierra Nevada, California. Discovered (1864) by Josiah D. Whitney (1819–96), the geologist, and named after him.

Whitstable England. Town in Kent near the E entrance to the Swale 10 km (6 miles) NNW of Canterbury. Pop. (1985) 27,284. Seaside resort and small port, famous for at least 2000 years for its oyster beds. The Canterbury–Whitstable railway line (1830), one of the earliest in the country, was closed to passengers in 1930.

Whittier USA. Town in California 18 km (11 miles) SE of Los Angeles. Pop. (1990) 77,671.

Residential and industrial. Manufactures tools, gas and oil heaters, and photographic equipment.

Founded (1887) by Quakers.

Whittlesey England. Market town in Cambridgeshire 8 km (5 miles) ESE of Peterborough. Pop. (1991) 10,275.

Manufactures bricks and tiles. Market-gardening.

Whyalla Australia. Port on the NW shore of Spencer Gulf, South Australia 225 km (140 miles) NNW of Adelaide. Pop. (1994) 25,740. Created as an outlet for the iron-ore mines of the Middleback Range.

Manufactures iron and steel. Shipbuilding. Water is piped 354 km (220 miles) from the Murray R. A new steel plant was inaugurated in 1965.

Wichita USA. Largest town in Kansas on the Arkansas R. at the confluence with the

Little Arkansas R. 290 km (180 miles) SW of Kansas City. Pop. (1990) 304,011.

Commercial and industrial centre in a wheat-growing and oil-producing region. Large trade in grain and livestock. Industries inc. flour-milling, meat-packing and oil-refining. Manufactures aircraft and chemicals.

Wichita Falls USA. Town in Texas on the Wichita R. 160 km (100 miles) NW of Fort Worth in a region producing oil and grain. Pop. (1990) 96,259.

Oil-refining, flour-milling. Manufactures oilfield machinery, glass and cottonseed oil.

Wick Scotland. Town in Highland 129 km (80 miles) NE of Inverness. Pop. (1989) 8500.

Port. Fishing centre. Distilling. Manufactures hosiery and glass.

The harbour was built (1800) by Telford. On the cliff edge 5 km (3 miles) NNE stand the ruins of the 15th-cent. Castle Girnigoe.

Wicklow Ireland. 1. County in Leinster in the SE, bordering E on the Irish Sea. Area 2025 sq km (782 sq. miles). Pop. (1991) 97,293. Generally mountainous apart from a narrow coastal strip, rising to 926 m (3037 ft) in Lugnaquillia (Wicklow Mountains). Main rivers the Liffey and the Slaney. Among the beautiful glens are Glendalough, Glen of the Downs, Glenmalure and the Vale of Avoca – the river formed by the union of the Avonmore and the Avonbeg. In the NW, on the Liffey, are the Poulaphuca dam, hydroelectric power station and reservoir (1938), which serves as a water supply for Dublin. Chief towns Wicklow, Arklow and Bray, the last a seaside resort; the village of Shillelagh gave its name to the traditional Irish cudgel.

2. County town of Co. Wicklow at the mouth of the R. Vartry 43 km (27 miles) SSE of Dublin. Pop. (1991) 5847. Small seaport. Market town. Remains of the 12th-cent. Black Castle on cliffs to the S; 13th-cent. Franciscan friary.

Widecombe-in-the-Moor England. Village in Devon on the E edge of Dartmoor 27 km (17 miles) SW of Exeter. Has a 14th/ 16th-cent. church and a 15th-cent. church house. Immortalized in the song about its annual fair.

Widnes England. Town in Cheshire on the N bank of the R. Mersey opposite Runcorn, with which it is connected by railway and high-level bridges. Pop. (1991) 57,162.

Important centre of the chemical industry. Also manufactures soap, paint, metal products, fertilizers and metal castings.

Wien ➤VIENNA.

Wiener Neustadt Austria. Town in Lower Austria 45 km (28 miles) S of Vienna. Pop. (1991) 35,134.

Industrial centre. Manufactures locomotives, railway rolling-stock, vehicles, machinery, leather goods and textiles.

Has the 12th cent. Castle of Babenberg, converted in 1752 into a military academy and in 1919 into a school, but chiefly modern in appearance, having been largely rebuilt in 1834 after a disastrous fire.

Wiesbaden Germany. Cap. of Hessen at the S foot of the Taunus Hills 32 km (20 miles) W of Frankfurt. Pop. (1992) 264,022. One of the oldest and most famous wateringplaces in Germany, with warm springs and a mild climate.

Manufactures textiles, chemicals, plastics, cement, pottery and sparkling wine.

Was a well-known Roman spa and the wall known as the *Heidenmauer* was probably part of the fortifications erected under Diocletian (3rd cent.). By the 9th cent. it was known as Wisibada ('Meadow Bath'). Cap. of the duchy of Nassau 1815–66.

Wigan England. Town and unitary authority on the R. Douglas and the Leeds–Liverpool Canal 27 km (17 miles) NE of Liverpool. Pop. (1991) 85,819.

Formerly in a coalmining area, industries inc. engineering, food-processing and mail order. Manufactures cotton goods, metal goods, tools and plastics.

Wight, Isle of England. Island and administrative county (from 1995) in the S, separated from Hampshire by the Solent (NW) and

Spithead (NE) 35 km (22 miles) long E–W and 21 km (13 miles) wide N–S. Area 381 sq km (147 sq. miles). Pop. (1991) 126,600. It is divided into the districts of Medina and South Wight. Chief town Newport. A line of chalk hills runs E–W across the island, ending in the Needles, and there are further hills in the S. The R. Medina, on whose estuary Newport stands, flows S–N and practically bisects the island. Scenery and a mild climate have combined to make it popular with holidaymakers; among the resorts are Ryde, Sandown, Shanklin, Ventnor and Cowes (headquarters of English yachting).

Industries inc. tourism, electronics and the construction of hovercraft and boats. There are ferry services from Lymington, Portsmouth and Southampton.

Of the Roman remains the best known is the villa at Brading (discovered 1879). In Carisbrooke Castle Charles I was imprisoned before his trial and execution.

Wigston England. Town in Leicestershire 5 km (3 miles) SSE of Leicester. Pop. (1991) 32,864.

Manufactures footwear, textiles, food products, hosiery and other industries inc. foundries and engineering.

Wigtown Scotland. Market town in Dumfries and Galloway on the W shore of Wigtown Bay. Pop. (1991) 1117. Small port. In the churchyard are buried the Wigtown Martyrs, two women Covenanters who were drowned here (1685). The ancient circle known as the Standing Stones of Torhouse is 5 km (3 miles) WNW.

Wigtownshire Scotland. Former county in Dumfries and Galloway, separated from Northern Ireland by the North Channel.

Wilhelmshaven Germany. Port in Lower Saxony on the NW shore of the Jadebusen and at the E end of the Ems–Jade Canal 64 km (40 miles) NW of Bremen. Pop. (1988) 98,200.

Industrial centre. Oil-refining. Manufactures chemicals, agricultural machinery and refrigerators.

After the harbour was opened (1869) it became the chief German naval base on the North Sea.

Wilkes–Barre USA. Industrial town in Pennsylvania on the Susquehanna R. 26 km (16 miles) SW of Scranton. Pop. (1984) 50,677.

An important anthracite-mining centre in the Wyoming Valley. Manufactures locomotives, mining machinery, wire and electrical appliances.

Wilkes Land ➤AUSTRALIAN ANTARCTIC TERRITORY.

Willamette River USA. River 467 km (290 miles) long in W Oregon formed by the union of the Coast Fork and Middle Fork and flowing generally N to join the Columbia R. below Portland. Provides power for various hydroelectric installations.

Willemstad Netherlands Antilles. Cap., on the SW coast of Curaçao. Pop. (1985) 125,000. Has an excellent natural harbour. Important refining centre for Venezuelan oil, also an entrepôt for the SE Caribbean and a popular tourist resort. Has several 17th and 18th cent. Dutch buildings.

Willenhall England. Industrial town in West Midlands 5 km (3 miles) E of Wolverhampton.

Manufactures locks, tools, hardware and car radiators.

Willesden England. Part of the London borough of Brent. Largely residential.

Food-processing. Manufactures motorcar accessories.

Williamsburg USA. Historic town in Virginia 74 km (46 miles) ESE of Richmond, forming part of the Colonial National Historical Park. Pop. (1990) 11,530. Since 1926 500 buildings have been reconstructed in colonial form, among them the Governor's Palace (1720), Raleigh Tavern, the Capitol, largely through the generosity of John D. Rockefeller Jr. First settled in 1632 and called Middle Plantation; renamed on becoming state cap. (1699–1779).

Williamsport USA. Industrial town in

Pennsylvania on the W branch of the Susquehanna R. 113 km (70 miles) WSW of Scranton. Pop. (1985) 33,000.

Manufactures textiles, clothing, fire hydrants, aircraft parts and furniture.

A lumbering centre in the 19th cent. until the forests were depleted.

Wilmington England. Village in East Sussex 8 km (5 miles) NW of Eastbourne. Just S is Windover Hill on the slope of which is the Long Man of Wilmington, a figure about 72 m (236 ft) tall, of unknown age and origin, formed by removing the turf from the underlying chalk.

Wilmington (Delaware) USA. Largest town and chief industrial and commercial centre of Delaware on the Delaware R. 40 km (25 miles) SW of Philadelphia. Pop. (1990) 71,529.

Important chemical industry. Also shipbuilding, tanning, meat-packing. Manufactures textiles.

First settled (1638) by Swedish colonists, it has several historic buildings inc. Old Swedes Church (1698).

Wilmington (North Carolina) USA. Chief seaport in the state on the Cape Fear R. 185 km (115 miles) SSE of Raleigh. Pop. (1990) 55,530.

Exports tobacco, cotton, wood-pulp. Manufactures textiles, clothing and wood products.

Wilmslow England. Town in Cheshire 18 km (11 miles) S of Manchester. Pop. (1991) 28,604.

Manufactures cotton goods, clothing, pharmaceuticals, and there is engineering.

Wilno ►VILNYUS.

Wilson USA. Town in North Carolina 64 km (40 miles) E of Raleigh. Pop. (1970) 29,347.

Important trade in leaf tobacco. Tobacco-processing, meat-packing and flour-milling.

Wilson, Mount USA. Peak (1739 m; 5700 ft) in the San Gabriel Mountains, S California, just NE of Pasadena. Famous for the Mt Wilson Observatory (1904–5), administered jointly by the Carnegie and California Institutes of Technology.

Wilton England. Small town in Wiltshire at the confluence of the Wylye and Nadder rivers 5 km (3 miles) WNW of Salisbury. Pop. (1991) 3800.

Market town famous since the 16th cent. for carpet manufacture (esp. Wiltons and Axminsters) and long an important sheep market.

Wilton House nearby is associated esp. with Sir Philip Sidney, whose sister, the Countess of Pembroke, entertained many of the great Elizabethan poets here, and it has several portraits by Van Dyck. Wilton was the ancient cap. of Wessex and gave its name to the county.

Wiltshire England. Inland county in the S. Area 3484 sq km (1344 sq. miles). Pop. (1991) 564,471. It is divided into the districts of Kennet, North Wiltshire, Salisbury, Thamesdown and West Wiltshire. County town Salisbury. Largely chalk uplands, e.g. the Marlborough Downs (N) and Salisbury Plain (S; important as a military training-ground). Also has the fertile Vales of Pewsey and Wardour. Chief rivers the Kennet, Bristol Avon, Hampshire Avon and Wylye. Dairy-farming, bacon-curing. Principal crop wheat. Chief towns Swindon (the largest and the most industrialized), Salisbury, Chippenham, Trowbridge. Stonehenge and Avebury are famous prehistoric monuments.

Wimbledon England. Part of the London borough of Merton. Mainly residential. Headquarters of the All England Lawn Tennis Club since 1877. Wimbledon Common, a large open space adjoining Putney Heath, has ancient earthworks known as 'Caesar's Camp'.

Wimborne Minster (Wimborne) England. Market town in Dorset on the R. Stour 10 km (6 miles) N of Poole. Pop. (1971) 5000. Dominated by its minster, which contains the tomb of Ethelred I; also a chained library and a 14th-cent. astronomical clock.

Winburg South Africa. Market town 105 km (65 miles) NE of Bloemfontein. Pop. (1985) 7000. The oldest town in Free State, founded in 1836 by the Voortrekkers.

Winchelsea England. Town in East Sussex 11 km (7 miles) NE of Hastings. Pop. (1985) 1200. Once an important seaport and a member of the Cinque Port of Hastings. The old town was engulfed by the sea (1287) and the present town was laid out in the 14th cent. – an excellent example of early town planning. The remarkable Church of St Thomas à Becket was never completed.

Winchester England. Ancient Venta Belgarum. County town of Hampshire on the R. Itchen 19 km (12 miles) NNE of Southampton. Pop. (1991) 36,121. Cathedral city, route centre and market town. Tourism is important and there is some light industry.

The great cathedral, built by Bishop Walkelin (1079–98) to replace an earlier Saxon cathedral, is the longest in England and contains the mortuary chests of Saxon kings and the tombs of Isaak Walton, English writer (1593–1683) and Jane Austen, English novelist (1775–1817). All that remains of the Norman castle is the Great Hall, which has the so-called King Arthur's Round Table, dating possibly from the 13th cent. Also the ruins of Wolvesey Castle, a residence of the bishops. Two gates of the ancient city walls remain. The 12th-cent. Hospital of St Cross still provides a dole of bread and beer for wayfarers. An educational centre from very early times; Winchester College (founded by William of Wykeham in 1382) is the oldest English public school. Winchester was a Roman-British town, and is identified by some with Camelot. Became extremely important in Saxon times as the cap. of Wessex; it rivalled London, e.g. for the crowning and burial of kings. Under the Normans it was a leading commercial centre.

Windermere England. Market town in Cumbria above the E shore of L. Windermere. Pop. (1991) 6847. Resort. Inc. Bowness on the lakeside.

Windermere, Lake England. Picturesque lake in Cumbria in the SE of the Lake District, with wooded banks and several small islands; the largest lake in England, 17 km (10½ miles) long and rather less than 1.6 km (1 mile) wide. Fed by the Rothay, Brathay and Trout Beck. Drained by the R. Leven into Morecambe Bay. It has water sports and attracts thousands of tourists.

Windhoek Namibia. Cap. and chief commercial centre in the central area 1290 km (800 miles) N of Cape Town at a height of 1620 m (5314 ft). Pop. (1991) 144,558. Linked by rail with Walvis Bay and with the South African system.

Trade in karakul (Persian lamb) skins. Refrigerating plants. Meat-canning, brewing. Manufactures bone meal.

Called Windhuk when cap. of German Southwest Africa (1892–1915).

Windsor Canada. Major industrial city in S Ontario on the Detroit R. opposite Detroit (Michigan), with which it is linked by road and railway tunnels, a suspension bridge and ferry services. Pop. (1991) 191,435.

Chief industry motor-car manufacture. Also salt-refining; manufactures machinery, steel products and chemicals.

Windsor England. Residential town in the unitary authority of the Royal Borough of Windsor and Maidenhead on the R. Thames 37 km (23 miles) W of London and linked by bridge with Eton. Pop. (1991) 30,135. Official name New Windsor, to distinguish it from Old Windsor, 3 km (2 miles) SE. The town is dominated by the royal castle, which was founded by William the Conqueror on the site of an earlier stronghold, and has since remained the principal residence of English monarchs. Here, from the top of the 69-m (226-ft) Round Tower, parts of 12 counties may be seen. To the W of the Round Tower the Lower Ward contains St George's Chapel, an outstanding example of Perpendicular architecture, and the Albert Memorial Chapel; to the E the Upper Ward has the state apartments, with noteworthy paintings, furniture and the private and visitors' apartments. The Home Park, adjoining the castle, and the Great Park extend S to Virginia Water, an artificial lake. Also in Windsor is the 17th-cent. town hall built by Sir Christopher Wren, English architect (1632–1723), who was MP for the borough. Old Windsor, though of small importance today, has an older history than New Windsor, for in the time of Edward the Confessor it was a royal residence.

Windsor and Maidenhead, Royal Borough of England. Area 197 sq km (76 sq miles). Unitary authority created in 1998 from Berkshire. Pop. (1997) 138,000.

Windward Islands (Pacific) ➤SOCIETY ISLANDS.

Windward Islands West Indies. Island group of the Lesser Antilles, in the West Indies, extending 480 km (300 miles) S from the Leeward Is. Comprises the islands of (N–S): Dominica, Martinique, St Lucia, St Vincent, the Grenadines and Grenada. Area of the latter 2126 sq km (821 sq. miles). The islands are volcanic in origin and have an equable tropical climate with occasional hurricanes and earth tremors; they have a rich variety of tropical flora. So named because of their location in the path of the NE Trade Winds.

Winnipeg Canada. Cap. and largest city of Manitoba on the Red R. at the confluence with the Assiniboine R. Pop. (1991) 616,790.

The country's chief wheat market and financial and distribution centre of the Prairie Provinces, well named 'The Gateway to the West'. Has vast grain elevators, railway yards, stockyards, flour mills and meat-packing plants. Manufactures agricultural machinery, cereal foods, clothing, furniture, jute and fur products.

The first white settlement was made here by La Vérendrye (1738) and was called Fort Rouge. Winnipeg was incorporated under its present name in 1873 and developed rapidly as a railway centre, the Canadian Pacific Railway being completed in 1885.

Winnipeg, Lake Canada. Lake in S central Manitoba. Area 23,553 sq km (9094 sq.

miles). Receives the surplus waters of L. Manitoba. Area 23,553 sq km (9094 sq. miles). Receives the surplus waters of L. Manitoba, L. Winnipegosis and the Lake of the Woods, draining through the Nelson R. to Hudson Bay. Tributary rivers inc. the Red, Winnipeg and Saskatchewan.

Winnipegosis, Lake Canada. Lake in SW Manitoba. Area 5403 sq km (2086 sq. miles). Drains by the Waterhen R. to L. Manitoba and thence into L. Winnipeg.

Winnipeg River Canada. River 764 km (475 miles) long issuing from the N end of the Lake of the Woods and flowing generally NW to the SE corner of L. Winnipeg. Several rapids on its lower course, used for hydroelectric power for the industries of Winnipeg.

Winona USA. City situated SE of St Paul, Minnesota on bluffs overlooking Mississippi R. Pop. (1990) 25,400.

Industries inc. the manufacture of vehicle controls, plastics, knitwear, electronics, food and construction equipment.

Winsford England. Town in Cheshire on the R. Weaver 37 km (23 miles) SW of Manchester. Pop. (1991) 26,839.

Centre of the salt industry; chemical manufacture, silica and quartz-processing.

Winston-Salem USA. Industrial town in North Carolina 108 km (67 miles) NNE of Charlotte. Pop. (1990) 143,485. Formed (1913) by the union of the adjacent towns Winston and Salem.

Important tobacco centre; manufactures cigarettes and pipe tobacco, also nylon yarn, hosiery, furniture, telephone equipment, air conditioning and metal products.

Founded (1766) as the centre of a Moravian colony.

Winterswijk Netherlands. Town in Gelderland province 56 km (35 miles) E of Arnhem near the German frontier. Pop. (1992) 27,972.

Manufactures cotton goods and furniture.

Winterthur Switzerland. Industrial town

and railway junction in Zürich canton 18 km (11 miles) NE of Zürich. Pop. (1990) 86,143.

Manufactures electric locomotives, diesel engines, textiles and soap.

Wirksworth England. Market town in Derbyshire 18 km (11 miles) NNW of Derby. Pop. (1991) 4235.

Limestone-quarrying; lead mines, worked from Roman times, have been abandoned. Founded in 1175.

Wirral, The England. Unitary authority on a peninsula between the estuaries of the R. Mersey and the R. Dee. Low-lying, once a royal forest. In the NE are Birkenhead and Wallasey in Merseyside.

Wisbech England. Town in Cambridgeshire on the R. Nene 31 km (19 miles) ENE of Peterborough. Pop. (1991) 24,981.

Market town and river port; also centre of a region growing bulbs, fruit, vegetables and flowers. Fruit and vegetable canning, brewing and printing. Manufactures paper, cement.

Birthplace of Thomas Clarkson (1760–1846), the anti-slavery campaigner.

Wisconsin USA. A Great Lakes state, bounded on the N by L. Superior and on the E by L. Michigan. Area 171,496 sq km (66,215 sq. miles). Pop. (1990) 5,038,000. Cap. Madison. Much of it is low-lying, but the Superior Highlands (N) rise to 595 m (1952 ft) in Sugarbush Hill, the highest point in the state. Continental climate, with hot summers and cold winters and an annual rainfall of 75–90 cm (30–35 ins.).

Produces cheese, butter and milk that are widely sold outside the state. Chief crops maize, oats, hay, largely for the dairying industry. Iron ore mined in the Gogebic Range (N). There is much heavy industry in the Milwaukee area. Tourism is important.

Chief towns Milwaukee, Madison. Exploration of the region was begun by the French (1634). Ceded to Britain 1763 and to the USA 1783. In the Civil War it supported the Union. Admitted to the Union in 1848 as the 30th state.

Wishaw ➤MOTHERWELL.

Wisla River ➤VISTULA RIVER.

Wisley England. Village in NW Surrey 5 km (3 miles) E of Woking with the gardens of the Royal Horticultural Society.

Wismar Germany. Seaport and industrial town in the Rostock district 51 km (32 miles) E of Lübeck. Pop. (1991) 54,471.

Shipbuilding, sugar-refining. Manufactures railway rolling-stock and machinery.

A prosperous Hanse town in the 13th and 14th cent.

Witbank South Africa. Town situated 105 km (65 miles) E of Pretoria at a height of 1590 m (5215 ft). Pop. (1970) 41,950.

The chief coalmining centre. Manufactures chemicals. Thermal electric power station, fuelled by the local coalfield.

Witham England. Market town in Essex 13 km (8 miles) NE of Chelmsford. Pop. (1989) 26,264.

There is some light engineering and it manufactures metal windows, chemicals, fruit juices and fertilizers.

Witham River England. River 145 km (90 miles) long rising in E Leicestershire, flowing N into Lincolnshire, past Grantham, then E and SE past Lincoln and Boston to the Wash.

Witney England. Market town in Oxfordshire 16 km (10 miles) WNW of Oxford on the R. Windrush. Pop. (1991) 20,377.

Long famous for the manufacture of blankets and other woollen goods.

Has an old butter cross (1683) and a grammar school also dating from the 17th cent.

Witten Germany. Industrial town in North Rhine-Westphalia on the Ruhr R. 13 km (8 miles) SW of Dortmund. Pop. (1992) 105,242.

Manufactures steel, machinery, coal-tar products and glass.

Wittenberg Germany. Industrial town and river port in the Halle district on the Elbe

R. 92 km (57 miles) SW of Berlin. Pop. (1989) 56,600.

Manufactures paper, machinery, soap and food products.

Famous for its association with Martin Luther during the early years of the Reformation. In 1517 Luther nailed his Ninety-five Theses on the door of the Schlosskirche and in 1520 in the market place publicly burned the papal bull that condemned him.

Wittenberge Germany. Industrial town in the Schwerin district on the Elbe R. 129 km (80 miles) NW of Berlin. Pop. (1989) 30,200.

Railway engineering and metalworking. Manufactures woollen goods.

Witwatersrand South Africa. In Afrikaans, 'White Waters Ridge'; familiarly known as the Rand. Ridge 1500–1800 m (4920–5905 ft) high in the S of Gauteng Province, extending 240 km (150 miles) E–W, and centred on Johannesburg. The central part has a gold-bearing reef about 80 km (50 miles) long which produces one-half of the world's gold; here are the large towns (E–W) of Springs, Brakpan, Benoni, Boksburg, Germiston, Johannesburg, Roodepoort-Maraisburg, Krugersdorp, all linked by railway. Coal and manganese are also mined. Many industries. Gold was discovered in 1886 (when Johannesburg was founded).

Wloclawek Poland. Cap. of Wloclawek voivodeship on the Vistula R. 145 km (90 miles) WNW of Warsaw. Pop. (1992) 122,800.

Manufactures machinery, paper, fertilizers and dyes. Lignite deposits nearby.

Woburn England. Market town in SW Bedfordshire 19 km (12 miles) NW of Luton. Pop. (1971) 1062. Nearby Woburn Abbey, seat of the Duke of Bedford and occupying the site of a 12th-cent. Cistercian abbey, has a famous art collection.

Woburn USA. Town in Massachusetts 16 km (10 miles) NNW of Boston. Pop. (1970) 37,406.

Residential and industrial. Manufactures leather goods and food products.

Birthplace of Sir Benjamin Thompson (Count von Rumford) (1753–1814), the scientist.

Woking England. Residential town in Surrey on the R. Wey 37 km (23 miles) SW of London. Pop. (1991) 98,138, with Byfleet.

Mainly residential with light industry, inc. printing.

Has a Muslim mosque and a museum of Eastern antiquities. Brookwood Cemetery, with the first crematorium in England and an American military cemetery, is 6 km (4 miles) WSW.

Wokingham England. Market town and unitary authority 11 km (7 miles) ESE of Reading. Pop. (1991) 38,063.

Engineering. Manufactures electrical appliances.

Picturesque 17th-cent. almshouses. Wellington College, the public school (1853) is 6 km (4 miles) SSE.

Wokingham Unitary Authority was created in 1998.

Wolds, The England. Range of chalk hills in North Yorkshire, Humberside and Lincolnshire, running roughly parallel to the coast and rising to 242 m (794 ft) in the N. The N part, usually known as the Yorkshire Wolds, is separated from the S part (the Lincolnshire Wolds) by the Humber estuary.

Wolfenbüttel Germany. Town in Lower Saxony 11 km (7 miles) S of Brunswick on the Oker R. Pop. (1984) 49,200.

Manufactures agricultural machinery and soap.

Grew around an 11th-cent. castle. Cap. of the dukes of Brunswick-Wölfenbüttel 1671–1753.

Wolfsburg Germany. Industrial town in Lower Saxony 27 km (17 miles) NE of Brunswick on the Weser–Elbe Canal. Pop. (1992) 128,995.

Important centre of the motorcar industry (Volkswagen). Has grown rapidly with the expansion of this industry.

Founded 1938.

Wolin (Ger. **Wollin**) Poland. Island on the Baltic coast (NW) 45 km (28 miles) N of Szczecin, with Usedom (W) enclosing the Stettiner Haff. Area 246 sq km (95 sq. miles). Chief town Wolin, a fishing port on the SE coast (pop. 3000).

Fishing and tourism are important occupations.

Wollongong Australia. Residential and industrial town in New South Wales 64 km (40 miles) SSW of Sydney. Pop. (Greater Wollongong 1991) 235,966.

A coalmining centre. Manufactures sheet steel, wires and cables, machinery and chemicals, 8 km (5 miles) S is the heavy industrial centre and port, Port Kembla.

Wolverhampton England. Industrial town and unitary authority in the Black Country 21 km (13 miles) NW of Birmingham. Pop. (1991) 240,700.

Varied manufactures, inc. bicycles, bricks, brewing, tools, locks and keys, hardware, tyres, rayon and chemicals.

St Peter's Church was founded in the 10th cent. and restored in the 19th and there is a grammar school founded in the 16th cent. From the 14th to the 16th cent. it was important in the wool trade, but by mid 18th cent. it had transferred to metalworking; its principal manufacture was locks.

Wolverton England. Town in Buckinghamshire 27 km (17 miles) N of Aylesbury on the R. Ouse. Pop. (1991) 55,733.

Railway workshops. Engineering. Inc. Stony Stratford (W).

Wonsan North Korea. Cap. of S Pyongan province on the E coast 153 km (95 miles) E of Pyongyang. Pop. (1987) 274,500.

Seaport with a good natural harbour. Industries inc. fishing, railway-engineering and oil-refining.

Severely damaged in the Korean War (1950–1).

Woodbridge England. Market town in Suffolk on the R. Deben estuary 11 km (7 miles) ENE of Ipswich. Pop. (1991) 10,950.

Fruit and vegetable canning, boatbuilding.

A picturesque town, it has many fine Georgian houses. Bredfield House (3 km; 2 miles N) was the birthplace of Edward Fitzgerald (1809–83), translator of Omar Khayyam.

Wood Buffalo National Park Canada. Vast National Park in NE Alberta and S Mackenzie District, Northwest Territories. Area 44,807 sq km (17,300 sq. miles). Contains large herds of buffalo, also bear, caribou, moose and other animals. Established 1922.

Woodford ➤ WANSTEAD AND WOODFORD.

Wood Green England. Part of the London borough of Haringey. Mainly residential. Contains the former Alexandra Park racecourse, and Alexandra Palace, which was opened in 1873, burned and reopened in 1878, and where the first BBC television transmitter was established (1936).

Woodhall Spa England. Small town in Lincolnshire 23 km (14 miles) ESE of Lincoln. Pop. (1991) 3337. Spa: bromoiodine springs, discovered accidentally during a search for coal. Nearby is Kirkstead, with the ruins of a 13th-cent. Cistercian abbey.

Woods, Lake of the Canada/USA. Lake situated in Minnesota, USA and in Manitoba, Canada. Area 3846 sq km (1485 sq. miles). The main river entering the lake is Rainy, flowing from L. Rainy and the lake is drained by Winnipeg R. flowing into L. Winnipeg.

Woodstock England. Small town in Oxfordshire 13 km (8 miles) NNW of Oxford on the R. Glyme. Pop. (1991) 2898. Long known for the manufacture of gloves. Site of an old palace which was the scene of Henry II's courtship of the 'Fair Rosamond', of the birth of the Black Prince and of the imprisonment of Elizabeth I (1554), and a royal residence until the Civil War, when it was used as a royalist garrison; it was largely destroyed by Parliamentary forces later. The manor was bestowed on John Churchill, Duke of Marlborough, after his victory at Blenheim (1704) and Blenheim Palace, designed by Vanbrugh, was built for him.

The town is the scene of Scott's novel *Woodstock*.

Wookey Hole England. Village in Somerset 3 km (2 miles) NW of Wells, named after a large natural cave formed where the R. Axe emerges from the Mendip Hills. Objects shown in the museum demonstrate that the cave was occupied in prehistoric times. Also here are handmade paper mills dating from the 17th cent.

Wool England. Market town in Dorset 16 km (10 miles) WSW of Poole on the R. Frome. Pop. (1971) 2290. Has a 15th-cent. bridge; beside this is the manor house of Woolbridge, the 'Wellbridge House' of Hardy's *Tess of the D'Urbervilles*.

Woolwich England. Part of the London borough of Greenwich (but excluding the portions on the N bank). Contains the Royal Arsenal (1805), with barracks and warehouses. Became important as a dockyard and naval base in Henry VIII's reign, but the Royal Dockyard was closed and converted into a military stores department in 1869. The Royal Military Academy on Woolwich Common, known as 'the shop' (founded 1741) was transferred to Sandhurst (1946) on amalgamation with the Royal Military College. Within the borough are Plumstead, with Plumstead Marshes (E) and Eltham, with the former royal palace; Shooter's Hill (130 m; 426 ft) was crossed by the Roman Watling Street.

Woomera Australia. Town in South Australia, in semi-arid country 177 km (110 miles) NW of Port Augusta, from which water is piped. Pop. (1985) 4100. Since 1946 base of the Long Range Weapons Establishment, whose range extends about 2000 km (1250 miles) NW over desert land.

Woonsocket USA. Industrial town in Rhode Island on the Blackstone R. 21 km (13 miles) NNW of Providence. Pop. (1990) 45,914.

Textile centre, producing woollen, cotton and rayon goods; also clothing and rubber products.

Wootton Bassett England. Market town and railway junction in Wiltshire 8 km (5 miles) WSW of Swindon in a dairy-farming region. Pop. (1991) 10,800.

Worcester England. Cathedral city in Worcestershire on the R. Severn. Pop. (1991) 82,661.

Industrial centre, long famous for the manufacture of gloves, porcelain and 'Worcester sauce'. Also produces footwear and hardware.

Its beautiful cathedral is mainly 14th-cent., with a Norman crypt dating from the 11th cent., the outstanding feature being the Early English choir; the Three Choirs Festival is held here once every 3 years. There are several churches of the 12th–15th cent.; among other old buildings are the Commandery, founded (1085) as a hospital by St Wulstan and rebuilt in Tudor times and the 18th-cent. Guildhall. The King's School and the Royal Grammar School were both founded in the 16th cent. At the Battle of Worcester (1651) Cromwell finally defeated Charles II and the Scots. Birthplace of Sir Edward Elgar, the English composer (1857–1934) at Broadheath (3 km; 2 miles NW).

Worcester South Africa. Town in Western Cape Province 101 km (63 miles) ENE of Cape Town, with which it is linked by rail, and near the Hex River Mountains. Pop. (1970) 40,610.

In a fruit-growing region. Produces wine, brandy, jam, dried and canned fruit. Industries inc. tourism and food-processing, also textiles. Water supply from the Hex R. and the Stettynskloof Dam (1954).

Worcester USA. Industrial town in Massachusetts on the Blackstone R. 61 km (38 miles) WSW of Boston. Pop. (1990) 169,759.

Manufactures textiles, electrical appliances, machine-tools, paper and precision instruments.

Also an important cultural and educational centre, with Clark University (1887) and several colleges; noted for its annual musical festival. Its industries developed rapidly after the construction (1828) of the Blackstone Canal, linking it with Providence (Rhode Island).

Worcestershire England. County in W central. Area 1738 sq km (671 sq miles). Pop. (1998) 538,000. From 1974 to 1998 it was amalgamated with Herefordshire. In 1998 it consisted of the districts of Bromsgrove, Malvern Hills, Redditch, Worcester, Wychavon and Wyre Forest. It lies mainly in the valleys of the Severn and the Warwickshire Avon, but there are hills around its boundary: in the SW the Malvern Hills, in the N the Clent Hills and Lickey Hills and in the extreme SE the edge of the Cotswolds. The land is fertile and dairy farming and the cultivation of fruit, vegetables and hops are important: the Vale of Evesham along the R. Avon is esp. noted for plums. Salt is produced in the Droitwich area. Important towns are Worcester, Kidderminster and Redditch.

Workington England. Town and seaport in Cumbria at the mouth of the R. Derwent 48 km (30 miles) SW of Carlisle. Pop. (1991) 25,579.

Industries inc. steel railmaking, bus manufacture, packaging, heavy and light engineering.

Worksop England. Town in Nottinghamshire on the R. Ryton 18 km (11 miles) NNE of Mansfield. Pop. (1991) 32,247.

Industries inc. declining coalmining, sawmilling, food-processing, chemicals, glass, hosiery and light engineering. Flourmilling.

Remains of an early 12th-cent. Augustinian priory. The 19th-cent Worksop Manor was built on the site of an earlier mansion burned down in 1761.

Worms Germany. Ancient Borbetomagus. Town in Rhineland-Palatinate on the Rhine R. 19 km (12 miles) NNW of Mannheim. Pop. (1989) 73,000.

River port in a vine-growing and wine-producing region on the left bank of the R. Rhine. Manufactures machinery, chemicals, plastics, detergents, furniture and cereal products.

The 12th/14th cent. Romanesque cathedral was seriously damaged, along with many other buildings, in World War II. Often the seat of Imperial Diets, inc. the famous Diet of Worms (1521) at which Luther appeared in order to defend his doctrine before the emperor Charles V.

Worsley England. Town in Greater Manchester 10 km (6 miles) WNW of the city. Pop. (1971) 49,573.

Engineering. Manufactures cotton goods and clothing.

Worthing England. Seaside resort in West Sussex 16 km (10 miles) W of Brighton. Pop. (1991) 95,732.

Residential town. Has many glasshouses, producing tomatoes. Also manufactures pharmaceutical products and is the headquarters of several financial companies.

The prehistoric earthworks of Cissbury Ring are 5 km (3 miles) N on the South Downs; Roman remains have been found in the borough.

Wrangel Island Russia. Island in the Khabarovsk Territory in the Arctic Ocean about 130 km (80 miles) off the coast of NE Siberia. Area 4660 sq km (1800 sq. miles). Largely consists of tundra; rises to 760 m (2493 ft). First explored (1881) by Capt. Hooper of the US Navy. Claimed by the Russians 1924.

Wrath, Cape Scotland. Promontory in Highland at the NW extremity of the mainland.

Wrekin, The England. Isolated hill 407 m (1335 ft) high in central Shropshire 5 km (3 miles) SW of Wellington.

Wrexham Wales. County borough situated 18 km (11 miles) SSW of Chester. Pop. (1994) 123,000 county borough; (1991) 40,614 town.

Manufactures cables, chemicals, metal goods, computers, instruments, food products. Coal production has ceased.

The 14th/16th-cent. parish church has a 41-m (134-ft) tower and the tomb of Elihu

Yale (d. 1721), founder of Yale University, USA. Wrexham is the seat of the Roman Catholic bishopric of Menevia, which inc. all Wales except the former Glamorganshire. Formerly in Clwyd and became a county borough in 1996.

Wroclaw Poland. Formerly (Ger.) **Breslau.** Cap. of the Wroclaw voivodeship on the Oder (Odra) R. 306 km (190 miles) WSW of Warsaw. Pop. (1992) 643,600.

River port and important road, railway and industrial centre. Railway-engineering and food-processing. Manufactures machinery, machine-tools, chemicals, textiles and pottery.

Before 1945 it was cap. of the German province of Lower Silesia. Has a 13th/15th-cent. cathedral and a 13th/15th-cent. town hall; about two-thirds of the buildings were destroyed in World War II. The university, founded in 1702 and Polish since 1945, was transferred from the universities of Lwow (Lvov) and Wilno (Vilna), now Russian. Cap. of the duchy of Silesia in the 12th cent. Passed to the Habsburgs in the 16th cent. and to Prussia 1742.

Wroxeter England. Village in Shropshire on the R. Severn 6 km (4 miles) ESE of Shrewsbury. Nearby are remains of the Roman camp of Viroconium.

Wuchang ➤WUHAN.

Wuchow ➤WUZHOU.

Wuhan (Hankow) China. Cap. of Hubei province and the largest city in central China on the Chang Jiang R. at the confluence with the Han R. Pop. (1990) 3,284,229. Formed by the union of three cities, Hankow, Hanyang and Wuchang.

Important route centre at the point where the Beijing–Guangzhou (Canton) Railway crosses the Chang Jiang. Hankow is a river port, accessible to ocean-going vessels and the leading industrial and commercial centre of central China. Manufactures textiles, machinery, chemicals, cement. Flour-milling. Trade in tea, cotton and other agricultural produce. Its great development dates from

1858, when it was opened to foreign trade. Hanyang became the centre of an important iron and steel industry, using ore from the Tayeh iron deposits 96 km (60 miles) SE, having expanded considerably after the establishment of the first modern steel works in China (1891). The steel plant was dismantled and removed to Chongqing (1938); a new steel plant was established E of Wuchang in the 1950s. Wuchang, which faces the other two cities from the S bank of the Chang Jiang and is linked with them by a railroad bridge (1958), is an administrative and cultural centre and is the seat of Wuhan University (1913). Important concentration of manufacturing inc. iron and steel, textiles, cement and paper-making.

Wuhu China. River port in Anhui on the Chang Jiang R. 88 km (55 miles) SSW of Nanjing. Pop. (1990) 425,740.

Tanning, flour-milling. Manufactures textiles (cotton and silk). Important rice market; also trade in cotton.

Opened to foreign trade in 1877.

Wuppertal Germany. Industrial town in North Rhine-Westphalia on the Wupper R. 27 km (17 miles) E of Düsseldorf. Pop. (1992) 385,463.

Important centre of the textile industry (woollen, cotton, rayon), extending about 16 km (10 miles) along the Wupper valley; an overhead railway runs along the river. Also manufactures pharmaceutical products, paper, machinery, tools and rubber products. Other industries inc. brewing, printing and publishing.

Formed (1929) by the amalgamation of the two large towns of Elberfeld and Barmen and the smaller Cronenberg, Vohwinkel, Beyenburg. The purity of the Wupper water led to the establishment of bleaching here in the 16th cent.

Württemberg Germany. Former kingdom in the SW, after 1918 a republic, bounded on the E by Bavaria and on the S and W by Baden, with the partial enclave of Hohenzollern (Prussia) in the S. Area 19,508 sq km (7532 sq. miles). Cap. Stuttgart. Mountainous and undulating, crossed SW–NE by the Swabian Jura, with the Black Forest in the W. Drained by the Neckar R. Largely agricultural. Incorporated with the duchy of Swabia in the 9th cent. By the 13th cent. it was ruled by the counts of Württemberg. Became a duchy in 1495 and a kingdom in 1806. After World War II (1945) it was divided: the N part combined with N Baden to form Württemberg-Baden; the S part with Hohenzollern became Württemberg-Hohenzollern. In 1952 these two *Länder* were combined with Baden to form Baden-Württemberg.

Würzburg Germany. Historic town and railway junction in NW Bavaria on the Main R. 88 km (55 miles) WNW of Nuremberg. Pop. (1992) 128,512.

Centre of the wine trade. Brewing. Manufactures machine-tools, chemicals, furniture and tobacco products.

Romanesque cathedral (11th/12th-cent. with later additions); among other ancient buildings are the Marienberg fortress, residence of the bishops 1261–1720, the later Baroque episcopal palace, the 16th-cent. Julius hospital and the university (founded 1582). The town probably existed as early as the 7th cent.; the bishopric was founded *c.* 740.

Wusih ➤ WUXI.

Wuxi (Wuhsi/Wusih) China. Industrial town in S Jiangsu province on the Grand Canal and on the Shanghai–Nanjing Railway 105 km (65 miles) WNW of Shanghai. Pop. (1990) 826,833.

Manufactures textiles, machinery. There is rice and flour milling and trade in rice and wheat. It has superseded Suzhou as economic centre of the Tai Hu basin.

Wuzhou (Wuchou/Wuchow) China. Formerly (1913–46) Tsangwu. Town and river port in the Guanxhi Zhuang Autonomous Republic on the Si-kiang at the confluence with the Kewi R. 193 km (120 miles) WNW of Guangzhou (Canton). Pop. (1990) 210,452.

Manufactures textiles, chemicals. There is

food-processing and sugar-refining. Trade in grain, tung oil and bamboo.

Wyandotte USA. Industrial town in Michigan on the Detroit R. 16 km (10 miles) SSW of Detroit. Pop. (1985) 34,000.

Important chemical industry based on local salt deposits. Also manufactures gaskets, paint, vehicle parts, paper products and barrels.

Wyandotte Cave USA. Large limestone cave in S Indiana 39 km (24 miles) W of Louisville. Has many imposing chambers, passages and rock formations; one chamber is nearly 45 m (148 ft) long and 17 m (56 ft) wide and is surmounted by a great dome.

Wye River England. River 32 km (20 miles) long in Derbyshire, rising on the outskirts of Buxton and flowing generally SE through the beautiful Miller's Dale and Monsal Dale, past Bakewell and joining the R. Derwent.

Wye River Wales. River 210 km (130 miles) long, rising on the E slope of Plynlimmon near the source of the Severn (central Wales), flowing generally SE and then S, past Rhayader, Builth Wells, Hereford, Ross-on-Wye and Monmouth, and joining the Severn 3 km (2 miles) below Chepstow. Noted for beautiful scenery, esp. between Ross and Chepstow (inc. Symonds Yat).

Wymondham England. (Pronounced 'Windham'.) Market town in Norfolk 14 km (9 miles) SW of Norwich. Pop. (1991) 10,869. Has a 17th-cent. half-timbered market cross and a partly Norman church which was attached to a 12th-cent. Benedictine priory.

Wyoming USA. State in the W. Area 253,324 sq km (97,809 sq. miles). Pop. (1990) 470,000. Cap. Cheyenne. Largely mountainous, it lies within the region of the Rocky Mountains and the Great Plains. Gannett Peak (4202 m; 13,783 ft) in the Wind River Mountains (W) is the highest point; Grand Teton in the Teton Mountains rises to 4196 m (13,763 ft). In the E are the Great Plains, which have extensive stretches of grassland; in the NW is the Yellowstone

National Park (9026 sq km; 3485 sq. miles); in the centre and SW is the semi-desert Wyoming basin. Dry continental climate, with substantial snowfalls in winter, and a rainfall of 25–50 cm (10–20 ins.) annually. Sheep and cattle reared on a large scale, the ranches being located mainly in the Great Plains. Chief mineral petroleum, others inc. natural gas, coal and uranium. Tourism attracts about 7 million annually, mainly hunters and fishermen. Cheyenne and Casper are the only towns with more than 40,000 inhabitants. First explored in the early 19th cent. Formed part of the vast territory acquired from France by the Louisiana Purchase agreeent (1803). Became a territory 1869. Admitted to the Union in 1890 as the 44th state.

X

Xanthi Greece. 1. *Nome* in W Thrace, bounded on the N by Bulgaria (Rhodope Mountains) and on the S by the Aegean Sea. Area 1793 sq km (692 sq. miles). Pop. (1991) 90,450. Mainly agricultural. Produces tobacco and cereals.

2. Cap. of Xanthi *nome* on the railway 177 km (110 miles) ENE of Thessaloníki (Salonika). Pop. (1989) 33,000.

Important trade in tobacco.

Xauen (Chaouèn) Morocco. City situated 60 km (37 miles) S of Tetuán. Pop. (1985) 24,000. It was founded in the 15th cent. after the expulsion of the Moors from Granada. Non-Muslims were not freely admitted until 1922.

It manufactures carpets.

Xiamen (Amoy) China. Seaport in Fujian province on Xiamen Is. in the Formosa Strait opposite Taiwan. Pop. (1990) 368,786.

Exports sugar, tobacco and paper. Industrial and commercial centre and, since 1981, has been one of China's 'special economic zones'. Manufactures chemicals, electronic goods, food products, textiles, building materials and paper.

Hinterland restricted to SE Fujian until the building of the Yingtan–Amoy railway (1956). One of the first Chinese ports to trade with Europeans (1842); its once flourishing tea exports diminished in the late 19th cent. Unofficial trade with Taiwan flourishes.

Xian (Sian) China. Cap. of Shaanxi province, in the NW, 850 km (530 miles) SW of Beijing in the valley of the Wei-he. Pop. (1992) 2,790,000. Important route centre on the Lunghai railway (E–W trunk line).

Industrial and commercial centre. Flour-milling, tanning. Manufactures iron and steel, textiles, chemicals and cement. Trade in grain, tea and tobacco.

It is an ancient walled city, at various times cap. of China from the 3rd cent. BC and was visited by Marco Polo in the 13th cent AD. In the provincial museum is a Nestorian stone tablet with a lengthy inscription dating from the 8th cent. Here in 1936 Chiang Kai-shek was kidnapped by Chang Hsueh-Liang, an incident which resulted in the former combining with the Communists against the Japanese.

Xi Jiang (Si-kiang) China. The most southerly of the country's three great rivers, also known as the Pearl R., 2129 km (1323 miles) long, rising in E Yunnan, flowing generally E and then turning S to enter the South China Sea. Important waterway with Kwangchow (Canton), Hong Kong and Macao around the delta and mouth.

Xingu River Brazil. River 1930 km (1200 miles) long rising on the Mato Grosso plateau and flowing generally N to the Amazon delta. Has a series of rapids in the middle course.

Xining (Sining/Hsining) China. Cap. of Qinqhai province on the Xining R. at a height of 2250 m (7380 ft) 193 km (120 miles) WNW of Lanzhou. Pop. (1990) 551,776.

Commercial centre and trades in cereals, wool, salt and timber. Industries inc. textile and machinery manufacture, tanning, iron and steel and fertilizers.

Xinjiang Uygur (Sinkiang Uighur) China. Autonomous region in the NW bounded by Mongolia (NE), Tibet (Xizang) and Kashmir (S), and by Tajikistan and Kirgizia (W and NW). Area 1,646,900 sq km (635,900 sq. miles). Pop. (1990) 15,155,778. Cap. Urümqi. It corresponds roughly to the historic Chinese Turkestan and is divided by the Tien Shan into Zunggar (Dzungaria) (N) and the Tarim Basin (S). The latter, which is much the larger, is a region of internal drainage containing the great sandy Takla Makan desert and, in the NE, the Turfan depression. Rainfall is scanty throughout the region and temperatures are extreme.

Wheat, maize, cotton, rice and fruits are cultivated in the oases and mountain valleys, deriving water from the melting snows on the surrounding heights. Livestock raised by the nomads of Dzungaria.

The people are mainly Turkic Uighurs, with Kazakh and Chinese minorities. The principal oasis towns of the Tarim Basin are Kashi, Yarkand and Khotan in the SW. In the past the Chinese hold over the region was precarious, and in the economic sphere a greater influence was often exercised by the Russians; but with the takeover by the Communist regime in 1950 the Chinese undertook the planned development of the region, an initial step being the construction of the Lanzhou–Xinjiang railway. Oil, coal and metals are found in the area but to exploit them efficiently there is a need for improvements in the infrastructure of the region. Other industries inc. forestry, chemicals and textiles.

Xizang ►TIBET.

Xuzhou China. Town in Jiangsu province in E central China. Pop. (1990) 805,695.

An important railway junction on the lines from Tianjin to Shanghai and is a coalmining centre. Industries inc. flour-milling and the manufacture of textiles and machinery.

Y

Yablonovy (Yablonoi) Range Russia. Range of mountains in SE Siberia, E of L. Baikal, extending SW–NE for about 1130 km (700 miles) and forming part of the watershed between rivers flowing to the Arctic and Pacific Oceans. Average height 1200–1800 m (3936–5904 ft).

Yakima USA. Town in Washington on the Yakima R. 177 km (110 miles) SE of Seattle. Pop. (1990) 49,836. Situated in an irrigated agricultural region and noted for fruit packing, drying and canning. Flour-milling also important.

Yakut ►SAKHA REPUBLIC.

Yakutsk Russia. Cap. of the Sakha (formerly Yakut) Republic near the left bank of the Lena R. 1830 km (1140 miles) NE of Irkutsk. Pop. (1991) 193,300.
  Commercial centre. Trade in furs, mammoth ivory and hides. Tanning, sawmilling and brickmaking. Some of its trade is by river which is open to navigation June–Nov. and it is linked by road with the Trans-Siberian Railway and by air with Irkutsk.
  A fort was founded here in 1632.

Yalta Ukraine. Town on the S coast of the Crimea 51 km (32 miles) ESE of Sevastopol. Pop. (1990) 88,800.
  A leading resort enjoying a Mediterranean climate and set amid vineyards and orchards. It has many hotels, sanatoria and convalescent homes. Industries inc. wine-making and fish-canning.
  During World War II it was the scene of an important conference between Churchill, Roosevelt and Stalin (1945).

Yalu River China/North Korea. River 788 km (490 miles) long rising on the S slopes of the Changpai Shan and flowing first S then W and SW past Antung (China), forming much of the border between China and North Korea, and entering Korea Bay at Tatungkow. Navigable only near its mouth. Frozen Nov.–March. Several important hydroelectric power stations; also used for floating timber.

Yamagata Japan. Cap. of Yamagata prefecture in N Honshu 120 km (75 miles) ENE of Niigata. Pop. (1991) 249,615.
  Commercial centre in a region producing rice and silk. Manufactures metal goods.

Yamaguchi Japan. Cap. of Yamaguchi prefecture in SW Honshu 56 km (35 miles) ENE of Shimonoseki. Pop. (1991) 130,451. An ancient commercial centre dating from the 14th cent.

Yamalo–Nenets Russia. Republic in the N Tyumen region, inc. the Yamal Peninsula, between the Kara Sea and the Gulf of Ob. Area 750,000 sq km (289,700 sq. miles). Pop. (1991) 492,600. Cap. Salekhard. Main occupations fur-trapping, reindeer-breeding and fishing. Chief towns Salekhard and Novy Port, a port on the Gulf of Ob.

Yambol Bulgaria. Cap. of Yambol province on the Tundzha R. 80 km (50 miles) W of Burgas. Pop. (1990) 99,225.
  Manufactures textiles and metal goods. Industries inc. food-processing and tanning and it trades in grain.
  First mentioned in the 11th cent. Has the ruins of an ancient stone mosque.

Yamoussoukro Côte d'Ivoire. Replaced Abidjan as capital in 1963. Pop. (1990) 120,000.

Yampi Sound Australia. Inlet in the coast of Western Australia N of Derby. Hematite deposits on Cockatoo and other islands.

There are opencast workings, crushing plant and loading gear on Cockatoo, and the ore is carried by sea to iron and steel centres in New South Wales.

Yana River Russia. River 1130 km (700 miles) long in the N Sakha (Yakut) Republic, rising in the Verkhoyansk Range and flowing generally N to the Laptev Sea, which it enters by a broad delta. Navigable in the lower course June–Sept.

Yangôn (Rangoon) Myanmar (Burma). Cap. and chief seaport of Myanmar in the Yangôn region on the Yangôn R. 34 km (21 miles) from its mouth. Pop. (1983) 2,513,023.

It exports rice, cotton and teak. Industries inc. rice-milling, oil-refining (at Syriam), sawmilling and engineering. Manufactures matches and soap. Linked by rail with Prome and Mandalay, and by canal with the Irrawaddy and Sittang rivers. Important airport.

Dominated by the impressive and ornate, gold-covered Shwe Dagôn pagoda, 295 m (968 ft) high and standing on high ground; the pagoda contains relics of Buddha and is one of the country's principal shrines. There are many fine public buildings and it owed its development to its rebuilding by Alompra, founder of the last Burmese dynasty (1753). Taken by the British 1824 and again in 1852. Became cap. of all Burma in 1886. In recent times it has been a cosmopolitan rather than a purely Burmese city. It was severely damaged in World War II during the Japanese occupation (1942–5).

Yangtse-kiang ➤CHANG JIANG.

Yantai (Chefoo) China. Former Treaty port in Shandong on the N coast of the Shandong peninsula. Pop. (1990) 452,127.

Industries inc. tourism, fishing and the production of brandy. It exports soya beans, vegetable oil and fruits.

The original harbour at Chefoo silted up in the 19th cent. and the name is still applied to the new harbour at Yentai. Opened to foreign trade 1858. Trade increased when linked by rail with the main Tsingtao–Tsinan line 1955.

Yaoundé Cameroon. Cap. and terminus of the railway from Douala (200 km; 125 miles W), at a height of 750 m (2460 ft). Pop. (1991) 649,000.

Commercial centre. Handles much of the trade of the Central African Republic. Industries inc. oil-refining, tourism and the manufacture of soap and cigarettes.

Yap Islands Micronesia. Group of 4 main islands and over 100 smaller ones in the W Caroline Is., W Pacific Ocean, with cable and radio stations. Pop. (1990) 9000. The Micronesians produce copra and dried fish. Important Japanese naval and air base in World War II.

Yare River England. River 80 km (50 miles) long in Norfolk rising near East Dereham and flowing generally E past Norwich to Breydon Water, entering the North Sea at Great Yarmouth. Chief tributaries the Wensum, Waveney and Bure. It is thus connected with the Norfolk Broads.

Yarkand (Chinese **Sache**) China. Chief town of the Yarkand oasis in SW Xinjiang-Uygur Autonomous Republic 145 km (90 miles) SE of Kashi at a height of 1170 m (3838 ft). Pop. (1985) 60,000.

Commercial centre. Manufactures textiles and carpets. Cereals and fruit grown in the oasis.

The town stands on the W side of the Takla Makan desert and on the Yarkand (Sache) R., which irrigates the oasis, and is a centre of the caravan trade between China, Russia and Kashmir.

Yarmouth (Isle of Wight) England. Port and resort on the Solent 16 km (10 miles) WSW of Cowes. Pop. (1981) 900. Linked by ferry with Lymington in Hampshire.

Yarmouth (Norfolk) ➤GREAT YARMOUTH.

Yaroslavl Russia. Cap. of the Yaroslavl region on the Volga R. at the confluence with the Kotorosl R. 257 km (160 miles) NE of Moscow. Pop. (1990) 638,100.

River port. Industrial centre. Manufactures textiles, motor vehicles, tyres, synthetic rubber, leather goods, agricultural machinery and paints.

Founded in the 11th cent. by Prince Yaroslav I; became cap. of a principality but was annexed by Moscow in the 15th cent. Although much of the old city was destroyed during the revolution, several churches and monasteries remain.

Yarrow Water Scotland. River 39 km (24 miles) long in Scottish Borders, flowing generally ENE through St Mary's Loch and past the village of Yarrow to join Ettrick Water just above Selkirk. Its valley, noted for its beauty, was extolled by Wordsworth and Scott.

Yasnaya Polyana Russia. Village in the Tula region 11 km (7 miles) S of Tula. Birthplace and home of the writer, Leo Tolstoy (1828–1910), whose house is now a museum.

Yawata (Yahata) Japan. Chief industrial town in Kyushu in Fukuoka prefecture 40 km (25 miles) NE of Fukuoka.

Coalmining. Important centre of the steel industry; also manufactures chemicals and cement. Formerly a fishing port; grew rapidly with the steel and associated industries during the 20th cent.

Merged (1963) with Moji, Kokura, Tobata and Wakamatsu to form a new city. ➤KI-TAKYUSHU.

Yazd ➤YEZD.

Yekaterinburg Russia. Formerly Sverdlovsk. Cap. of the Yekaterinburg region in the E foothills of the central Ural Mountains. Pop. (1991) 1,375,400.

Important railway junction and industrial centre. It has large metallurgical plants. Manufactures steel, mining and heavy engineering equipment, ball-bearings, lathes, railway rolling-stock, aircraft, chemicals, clothing and furniture. Copper-smelting, gem-cutting and polishing. W terminus of the Trans-Siberian Railway; also links the other Ural industrial towns with W Siberia. Principal cultural centre of the Urals.

Founded (1721) as Yekaterinburg (after the Empress Catherine I). Tsar Nicholas II and his family were executed here (1918). Renamed Sverdlovsk in 1924. Its industrial importance began with the building of the first ironworks (1725). Expanded rapidly after the construction of the Trans-Siberian Railway (1895) and again with the development of the metallurgical industry during the 1930s and World War II.

Yelgava ➤JELGAVA.

Yellowhead Pass Canada. Pass at a height of 1110 m (3641 ft) between Alberta and British Columbia in the Rocky Mountains on the Canadian National Railway main line. The first recorded crossing was made in 1827.

Yellowknife Canada. Cap. of Northwest Territories from 1967 and goldmining town in S Mackenzie District on the N shore of the Great Slave Lake; also an RCMP station, with airport, school, hospital and radio and meteorological stations. Pop. (1990) 15,179, much augmented by civil servants. Founded in 1935 after the discovery of gold. Largely abandoned in the early 1940s, but developed again in 1944 on the discovery of a new goldmine.

Yellow River ➤HUANG-HE.

Yellow Sea (Chinese **Huang Hai**). Large inlet of the Pacific Ocean between Korea and the mainland of China, the main area being linked by the Strait of Bohai with the Gulfs of Bohai and Liaodong. The name is due to the yellow colour of the silt carried into it by various rivers. Among the rivers it receives are the Huang-he ('Yellow River'), Liaou and Yalu Jiang.

Yellowstone National Park USA. The country's oldest and largest National Park, established in 1872, mainly in NW Wyoming. Area 8991 sq km (3472 sq. miles). Consists of volcanic plateaux of the Rocky Mountains, averaging 2400 m (7872 ft) in altitude, surrounded by ranges rising to over 3300 m (10,824 ft). The chief river is the Yellowstone, with its Grand Canyon, 32 km (20 miles) long and spectacular waterfalls; it feeds Yellowstone Lake (area 360 sq km; 139 sq. miles), which has great scenic beauty.

Thousands of hot springs and about 200 geysers, the most notable being the geyser called 'Old Faithful', which erupts every 67 minutes. The protected wild life inc. bison, moose, deer, elk, antelopes, goats, bear and many species of birds.

Yemen. Republic in the SW of the Arabian peninsula, bounded by Saudi Arabia in the N, Oman in the E and the Red Sea in the W. Area 531,869 sq km (205,356 sq. miles). Pop. (1995) 13,058,000 (25 per cent urban). Life expectancy, 62 years male, 64 female. Cap. San'a. Other important towns Aden, Ta'iz and the port of Hodeida. Currrency: Yemeni dinar = 100 fils. It is the most fertile part of the peninsula, being substantially the Arabia Felix of the ancients, but nevertheless remains an isolated and underdeveloped country. A narrow coastal plain known as the Tihama, which is hot and dry, rises sharply inland to mountain and plateau exceeding 3000 m (9840 ft) in places, representing the uptilted edge of the Arabian tableland. A desert climate, but in the highlands there is a summer rainfall amounting to about 50 cm (20 ins.) Land use: forested 8 per cent, meadows and pastures 30 per cent, agricultural and under permanent cultivation 3 per cent. Religion Muslim and the lang. Arabic. The highland pop. belongs to the Zaidi sect of Shias, the remainder being mainly a mixture of Sunni and Shia Muslims. Most of the Jews (of whom there was an ancient and numerous community) emigrated to Israel after the Arab–Israeli war in 1948.

About 56 per cent of the labour force is engaged in agriculture and the main food crop is millet and sesame; wheat, fruit (esp. grapes), barley, *qat* (a narcotic shrub) are also grown. Cotton is grown in the coast belt in the Tihama. Fishing is a major industry. The only commercial mineral being exploited is salt. The first oilfield and pipeline came on stream in 1987. Further major oil and gas finds were made in 1991. There is little industry but textiles, plastics, aluminium, goods, paint and matches are produced.

The earliest known civilization of the region was that of the Minaean kingdom, which survived for more than 500 years until the mid 7th cent. BC, to be followed by the Sabaean, until the 2nd cent. BC and the Himyarite, until the 6th cent. AD. In the 7th cent. Yemen was converted to Islam, becoming a mere province of the Arab caliphate and about three centuries later came under the control of the Zaidi dynasty, which ruled until modern times; for two periods (1538–1630, 1849–1918) the country was occupied by the Turks. In 1958 North Yemen became part of the United Arab Republic together with Egypt and Syria, but this was dissolved in 1961. In 1962 the reigning king, Imam Ahmed, was deposed by a group of army officers and the Yemen Arab Republic (North Yemen) was proclaimed; fighting broke out between republican and royalist forces, the former being aided by Egypt and the latter by Saudi Arabia. Egyptian troops were withdrawn and peace was restored by the end of 1967. Aden was part of the Federation of South Arabia, which consisted of 17 states in 1963. There were repeated political disturbances in the 1960s; eventually the country was taken over by the National Liberation Front, British troops were withdrawn and the People's Democratic Republic of Yemen (Southern Yemen) was proclaimed in 1967, ending 129 years of British rule.

The present Republic of Yemen was established in 1990 by the unification of the Yemen Arab Republic and the People's Democratic Republic of Yemen. There is a transitional form of government, with a 301-member House of Representatives, which is a merger of the former northern and southern assemblies.

Yenakiyevo (Enakievo) Ukraine. Formerly Rykovo (1928–35), Orzhonikidze (1935–43). Industrial town in the Donbas 40 km (25 miles) NE of Donetsk. Pop. (1990) 120,000.

Important centre of the coalmining and iron and steel industries; also manufactures chemicals.

Yenisei River Russia. One of the longest rivers in Asiatic Russia (4090 km; 2556 miles) formed in the Tuva Republic by the union of two headstreams at Kyzyl, themselves rising in the extreme S near the Mongolian border. It flows W and then for most of its course generally N, through Siberia, past Krasnoyarsk and Igarka, to enter the Arctic Ocean by a long estuary. Its chief tributaries are the Angara (Upper Tunguska), the Stony Tunguska and the Lower Tunguska, all joining it by the right bank. Navigable throughout its length to Kyzyl, but the lower reaches are ice-free only July–Oct. Chiefly used for the transportation of timber and grain.

Yeovil England. Town in Somerset on the R. Yeo 32 km (20 miles) ESE of Taunton. Pop. (1990) 28,500.

Market town with a glove-making industry almost 400 years old; also manufactures cheese, helicopters, air-conditioning equipment, aircraft control systems, light engineering and electronics.

East Coker nearby was the birthplace of the English hydrographer, William Dampier (1652–1715).

Yerevan (Erevan, Erivan) Armenia. Cap. on the Zanga R. 177 km (110 miles) S of Tbilisi at a height of 1020 m (3346 ft). Pop. (1991) 1,283,000. Situated in a mountainous area, with Mt Ararat (5165m; 16,945 ft) 64 km (40 miles) SSW (in Turkey) usually visible.

Developed into a leading industrial centre. Important producer of chemicals, inc. synthetic rubber and plastics; also manufactures machinery, machine-tools, tyres, wine, brandy and textiles. Aluminium refining. Power derived from hydroelectric plants on the Zanga R. (the Sevan–Zanga Cascade) and natural gas received by pipeline from Karadag (Azerbaijan).

Its outstanding building is the mosque of Hasan Ali Khan (the Blue Mosque), and there are many old Turkish and Persian buildings. Founded in the 7th cent., it often changed hands between Turks and Persians; taken by the Russians 1827. The name was officially changed to Yerevan in 1936.

Yezd (Yazd) Iran. Town in Isfahan prov-ince at a height of 1170 m (3838 ft) 274 km (170 miles) ESE of Isfahan, with which it is connected by road. Pop. (1986) 230,483.

Manufactures textiles (inc. silks), carpets.

Has part of the old walls, dating from the 12th cent. and several noteworthy mosques. Its inhabitants inc. many Zoroastrians, whose ancestors fled here from the Arabs.

Yichang (Ichang) China. Town in Hubei province on the Yangtse R. just below its great gorges. Pop. (1990) 371,601.

An important point of transhipment between ocean-going vessels and those which can negotiate the gorges to Chungkiang. Trade in tung oil and grain.

Yingkou (Yingkow) China. Formerly Newchwang. Seaport in Liaoning province at the mouth of the Liao R. 177 km (110 miles) SW of Shenyang. Pop. (1990) 421,589.

Exports soya beans, grain, coal. Ice-bound for 3 or 4 months in winter.

Until 1907 a major commercial outlet for South Manchuria, but then largely superseded by Dairen. It now has only local trade. Manufactures soya-bean oil, textiles and matches.

Yingkow ►YINGKOU.

Yipin (Ipin) China. Formerly Suifu, Suchow. River port in Sichuan at the confluence of the Yangtse and Min rivers. Pop. (1990) 241,019. Commercial centre for Yunnan and Xizang (Tibet).

Ynys Môn ►ANGLESEY.

Yogyakarta ►JOGJAKARTA.

Yoho National Park Canada. National Park in SE British Columbia in the Rocky Mountains. Established 1886. Area 1313 sq km (507 sq. miles). Has some of the most spectacular scenery in the Canadian Rockies. A favourite region for mountaineers.

Yokkaichi Japan. Seaport, industrial and commercial town in Mie prefecture, Honshu 35 km (22 miles) SW of Nagoya. Pop. (1991) 277,502.

Exports cotton goods. Oil-refining.

Manufactures textiles, chemicals and porcelain.

Yokohama Japan. Cap. of Kanagawa prefecture, central Honshu on the W shore of Tokyo Bay 27 km (17 miles) S of Tokyo. Pop. (1991) 3,250,887. The second largest city and the leading seaport.

Main exports silk and rayon goods, canned fish. Manufactures steel, motor vehicles and chemicals. Shipbuilding and oil-refining.

It was only a small fishing village until 1859, when it became the first Japanese port to be opened to foreign trade. Almost destroyed by earthquake in 1923, thousands of its inhabitants being killed, but was quickly rebuilt.

Yokosuka Japan. Seaport and naval base in Kanagawa prefecture on the SW shore of Tokyo Bay. Pop. (1991) 434,957. Important shipbuilding industry.

Yonkers USA. Industrial and residential town in New York on the Hudson R. just NNE of New York City. Pop. (1990) 188,082.

Manufactures carpets and rugs, clothing, cables and elevators. Sugar-refining.

First settled (1646) by Adriaen van der Donck, a Dutch 'jonker' or young nobleman – from which the name Yonkers was evolved.

Yonne France. Department in central France formed from parts of Champagne, Burgundy and Orléanais. Area 7427 sq km (2868 sq. miles). Pop. (1991) 324,600. Prefecture Auxerre. Highest in the SE (Monts du Morvan), it slopes gently down to the Paris Basin and is drained S–N by the Yonne R. and its tributaries. Mainly agricultural. Produces wine, cereals and sugar-beet. Chief towns Auxerre, Chablis and Sens.

Yonne River France. River 290 km (180 miles) long rising in the Monts du Morvan and flowing generally NNW past Auxerre and Sens to join the Seine R. at Montereau.

York England. Cathedral city. Formerly in North Yorkshire, on the R. Ouse at the confluence with the Foss. From 1996 it became a unitary authority and inc. Ryedale, Selby and Harrogate. Area 278 sq km (105 sq. miles). Pop. (1995) 174,400 (unitary authority area).

Important railway junction. Industries inc. engineering, sugar-refining and brewing. Manufactures chocolate and confectionery, glass and furniture. Tourism is important and a science park is being developed.

The old city is enclosed by walls dating mainly from the 14th cent. which are penetrated by four main gates (Bars). The great Cathedral of St Peter (generally known as York Minister) was begun in 1154 on the site of the wooden church where King Edwin was baptized by Paulinus (627) and was continued for over 3 centuries. The world-famous stained glass was carefully preserved in the Civil War and in both world wars; the celebrated Five Sisters window was restored (1925) as a memorial to the women who died in World War I. In 1984 lightning caused damage to the medieval roof and the great rose window was cracked, both subsequently restored. Clifford's Tower (built in the 13th cent.) is the principal survival on the site of the castle erected by William the Conqueror. Among other notable buildings are the 14th/15th-cent. guest house of St Mary's Abbey (now a museum of Roman antiquities), St William's College (1453), the 14th-cent. Merchant Adventurers' Museum. As Roman Eboracum, it was the military cap. of Britain, where Constantine the Great was proclaimed Emperor (AD 306). There was a Bishop of York in the 4th cent. When Britain was divided into two archiepiscopal Provinces (7th cent.), it became cap. of the N Province and has remained so (though Scotland is now excluded); the Archbishop ranks second only to the Archbishop of Canterbury in the Church of England. It was one of the most famous educational centres in Europe in the 8th cent. Has had a Lord Mayor since 1389 and ranked as a county in 1396. Birthplace of John Flaxman (1755–1826), the sculptor.

York USA. Town in S Pennsylvania 35 km (22 miles) SSE of Harrisburg. Pop. (1980) 44,619.

Manufactures refrigerators, agricultural machinery, turbines and building materials.

Yorke Peninsula Australia. Peninsula between Spencer Gulf and Gulf St Vincent, South Australia.

Wheat-growing and sheep-rearing. Chief ports Port Pirie and Wallaroo.

Yorkshire ►HULL, EAST RIDING, EAST YORKSHIRE.

Yorkton Canada. Town situated ENE of Regina on Yorkton R. in Saskatchewan. Pop. (1991) 15,315.

Distribution and processing centre for E Saskatchewan. Manufactures inc. agricultural equipment, food-processing and concrete products.

Yorktown USA. Historic town in SE Virginia on the York R. 18 km (11 miles) ESE of Williamsburg. Pop. (1990) 400. Headquarters of the Colonial National Historical Park. Famous as the scene of the British surrender at the end of the Revolutionary War (1781).

Yosemite National Park USA. National Park in California on the W slopes of the Sierra Nevada. Area 3083 sq km (1190 sq. miles). Established 1890. An outstanding feature is the Yosemite Valley, a great canyon 11 km (7 miles) long, overlooked by many peaks exceeding 2100 m (6888 ft) in height. The highest peaks of all are Mt Lyell (3994 m; 13,100 ft) and Mt Dana (3982 m; 12,076 ft) near the E boundary. Yosemite is probably most famous for its waterfalls, inc. Ribbon Fall (492 m; 1614 ft), the second highest single cataract in the world and Upper Yosemite (436 m; 1430 ft); these falls are seen at their best in May and June, when swollen by melting snow. There are three groves of sequoia trees, Merced and Tuolumne (W) and Mariposa (S), the last-named inc. the famous Wawona or Tunnel tree, through which a road 3.4 m (11.2 ft) wide was driven.

Yoshkar-Ola (Ioshkar-Ola) Russia. Cap. of the Mari Republic 250 km (155 miles) ENE of Nizhny Novgorod. Pop. (1989) 242,000.

Industrial and commercial centre. Industries inc. pharmaceuticals, sawmilling, food-processing and agricultural machinery. Founded 1578.

Youghal Ireland. Fishing port and seaside resort in Co. Cork on the estuary of the R. Blackwater 43 km (27 miles) E of Cork. Pop. (1991) 5532.

Well-known for its lace. Manufactures carpets.

Has the 15th-cent. (restored) St Mary's Church, near which is Myrtle Grove, an Elizabethan house where Sir Walter Raleigh lived intermittently (1584–97) and introduced the potato and tobacco to Ireland. Also has remains of the 13th-cent. North Abbey and the 14th-cent. St John's Abbey.

Youngstown USA. Industrial town in Ohio on the Mahoning R. 92 km (57 miles) NNW of Pittsburgh. Pop. (1990) 95,732. First blast furnace built 1826.

Important iron and steel centre, manufacturing a wide variety of metal products, also electrical equipment, chemicals, plastics and clothing.

First settled 1796.

Youth, Isle of Cuba. Formerly Isle of Pines. A special municipality situated off the SW coast. Area 2398 sq km (926 sq. miles). Pop. (1990) 73,319. Cap. Nueva Gerona.

Ypres (Flemish **Ieper**) Belgium. Town in W Flanders province on the small canalized Yperlée R., a tributary of the User R. 64 km (40 miles) WSW of Ghent. Pop. (1990) 35,300.

Important centre of the textile industry since the Middle Ages. Three great battles were fought here in World War I (1914, 1915, 1917), and the town, inc. its famous 13th/14th-cent. Cloth Hall and the cathedral, was almost completely destroyed. It was later rebuilt and the Menin Gate was erected as a memorial to British soldiers killed here; to these troops the town was generally known as 'Wipers'.

Ysselmeer ►IJSSELMEER.

Yssel Rivers ►IJSSEL RIVERS.

Yucatán

Yucatán Mexico. State in the SE, forming the N part of the Yucatán peninsula. Area 38,402 sq km (14,827 sq. miles). Pop. (1990) 1,362,940. Cap. and largest city Mérida. Flat and low-lying. Climate tropical.

Chief product henequen (sisal), exported through Progreso. Sugar-cane, tobacco, maize are also grown. Other industries inc. tourism, brewing and textiles.

Yucatán Channel ➤MEXICO, GULF OF.

Yucatán Peninsula. Peninsula separating the Gulf of Mexico (W) from the Caribbean Sea (E), mainly in SE Mexico but also inc. Belize and Northern Guatemala. Area about 181,000 sq km (70,000 sq. miles). A low plateau of limestone, remarkable for the absence of surface rivers, which have underground courses in the limestone. The peasants raise the water by innumerable windmills. In the S there are dense tropical forests yielding mahogany, dyewoods. Savannah in the NW. A great centre of Mayan civilization in pre-Columbian times, as is evidenced by the ruins of Chichén Itzá and Uxmal (Yucatán, Mexico).

Yugoslavia. Republic in SE Europe. Federal Republic of Yugoslavia also known as 'Former Yugoslavia'. Bounded by Hungary in the N, Romania in the NE, Macedonia and Albania in the S, Adriatic Sea, Bosnia and Hercegovina, and Croatia in the W. A Federation of 2 republics: Serbia (with 2 former autonomous provinces within Serbia of Vojvodina and Kosovo-Metohija) and Montenegro. Area 102,173 sq km (39,449 sq. miles). Pop. (1996) 10,574,000 (51 per cent urban). Serbian (62 per cent), Albanian (17 per cent), Montenegrin (5 per cent), Croatian (1.1 per cent). Life expectancy, 70 years male, 75 female.Cap. Belgrade. Other major towns Novi Sad, Niš, Kragujevas, Podgorica (cap. of Montenegro), Subotica. Currency: New Dinar = 100 Paras. Southern Serbia and Montenegro are very mountainous and the N has the low-lying plains of the Danube. The Danube is the main river which flows from the N of Serbia. Others are the Sara which rises in the Julian Alps of

Slovenia and flows through Bosnia to join the Danube at Belgrade, the Drina which rises as the Tara and Piva in the mountains of Montenegro and flows N along the Bosnia–Serbia boundaries to meet the Sava W of Belgrade and the Morava which is another tributary of the Danube. Most parts have a central European type of climate with cold winters and hot summers. Land use: 64 per cent of agricultural land is arable, 22 per cent pasture, 13 per cent meadows.

Serbia has been traditionally Orthodox and the Serbian Orthodox Church has its seat at Belgrade. The Serbian Orthodox Church is the official church of Montenegro. Muslims are found in the S as a result of Turkish occupation. There are 9 communities of Jews. Serbo-Croat is the official lang. Serbs use the Cyrillic alphabet.

The economy in the early 1990s was stagnant and most factories were closed because of the trade sanctions and embargo. Self-sufficiency in agriculture has been a life-line and there was some evasion of the sanctions. Inflation reached 21,000 per cent a month in 1993.

After World War I (which began ostensibly because of the assassination in 1914 of the Austrian Archduke Francis Ferdinand at Sarajevo) the Kingdom of the Serbs, Croats and Slovenes was formed (1918) from Serbia, Montenegro and regions which had formerly belonged to the Austro-Hungarian Empire (Croatia, Slovenia, and Bosnia and Hercegovina). Internal dissension among the various Slav groups caused Alexander I to establish a dictatorship in 1929 (when the name of the state was changed to Yugoslavia); he was assassinated at Marseille in 1934 and was succeeded by his infant son, Peter II, with a regency government headed by Prince Paul. Their sympathies were with Nazi Germany; when they were ousted, Yugoslavia was invaded by German troops (1941) and soon overrun. Guerrilla forces maintained a heroic resistance in the mountains, their most successful leader being the communist Josip Broz (Tito). After the end of World War II the republic was proclaimed (1945) under Marshal Tito, who welded the heterogeneous nation together by encouraging rather than suppressing regional aspirations, granting a large measure of autonomy to the 6 constituent republics of Bosnia and Hercegovina, Montenegro, Croatia, Macedonia, Slovenia, Serbia (with Vojvodina and Kosovo-Metohija). From Italy, Yugoslavia received part of Venezia Giulia, the Dalmatian town of Zadar, and certain Adriatic islands (1947). Having drifted away from domination by the USSR, it was expelled from the Cominform (1948) and from then on pursued a policy of independence, preserving friendly relations with the West and, with the death of Stalin (1953), effecting a *rapprochement* with the USSR. With the death of Tito (1980) and the political changes in eastern Europe there was a rise in nationalism which led to the eventual secession of Slovenia, Croatia, Bosnia-Hercegovina and Macedonia from the federation. In 1992 Serbia and Montenegro announced the formation of a Federal Republic of Yugoslavia as the legal successors of the former Socialist Federal Republic of Yugoslavia. Serbia became involved in civil war in Croatia because the Serb minority would not accept Croatia's independence, which caused the UN to raise sanctions and the EU to impose a trade embargo. These sanctions were lifted in 1995 following agreement of the Dayton Peace Accord.

The constitution of 1945, when the Federal People's Republic was proclaimed, was on Soviet lines, but was modified by the new constitutions of 1953 and 1963. The constitution of 1974 replaced the 5-chamber Federal Assembly with one of 2 chambers. In 1996 the Chamber of the Republics had 40 members (20 Serb, 20 Montenegrin) and the Chamber of Citizens 138 (108 Serbian, 30 Montenegrin).

Yukon Canada. Territory in the NW bordered on the W by Alaska. Area 483,450 sq km (186,661 sq. miles). Pop. (1991) 27,797. Cap. and largest town Whitehorse. Largely mountainous: in the SW are the St Elias Mountains, with Mt Logan (6050 m; 19,849 ft), the highest peak in Canada; along much of the E border are the Mackenzie Mountains. Chief river the Yukon. Climate Arctic, with long cold winters and short summers. Mining is the basis of the economy; chief minerals silver, gold lead and zinc. Fur trade important.

Yukon River Canada/USA. River 3185 km (1980 miles) long in Yukon (Canada) and Alaska (USA), its furthest headwater being the source of the Nisutlin R. on the Yukon–British Columbia border. Flows N and NW through Yukon, past Whitehorse and Dawson, and follows a great westward curve through Alaska to empty into the Bering Sea. Navigable (June–Sept.) for 2859 km (1777 miles) to Whitehorse. Tributaries inc. the White, Stewart, Klondike, Porcupine and Tanana rivers.

Yunnan China. Province in the SW bordering W on Myanmar (Burma) and S on Laos and Vietnam. Area 436,200 sq km (168,420 sq. miles). Pop. (1990) 36,972,610. Cap. Kunming. In the NW and W there are high forested mountain ranges and the deep gorges of the Yangtse, Mekong and Salween. The remainder consists mainly of a plateau, cut in the SE by the valleys of the Red and Black rivers. In the valleys and on terraced hill slopes, rice, wheat, barley, tea and tobacco are grown. Tin, tungsten and other minerals obtained. Chief towns Kunming, Mengtsz, Szemao. Among the pop. are the many non-Chinese, inc. the Lolos and Shans. Scene of a Muslim rebellion (1855–72); still has a relatively high proportion of Muslims.

Yuzhno-Sakhalinsk Russia. Town situated S of Aleksandrovsk on the E coast railway in Siberia. Pop. (1991) 164,000.

Railway junction in an agricultural area. Industries inc. pulp and paper milling, sugar-refining, brewing and the manufacture of plastic goods.

Yvelines France. Department W of Paris formed in 1964 when the former Seine and Seine-et-Oise departments were reorganized. Area 2284 sq km (882 sq. miles). Pop. (1991) 1,320,000. Prefecture Versailles.

Yverdon-les-Bains Switzerland. Town in Vaud canton at the SW end of L. Neuchatel. Pop. (1990) 22,400.

Manufactures typewriters and cigars.

In the early 19th cent. its castle housed the school founded by Johann Heinrich Pestalozzi (1746–1827), the Swiss educationalist.

Z

Zaanstad Netherlands. Town situated 13 km (8 miles) NW of Amsterdam. Pop. (1992) 131,273.

Main occupations are food-processing, metal-forming and machinery manufacture.

Formed in 1974 by amalgamating Zaandam, Koog a/d Zaan, Zaandijk, Wormerveer, Krommenie, Westzaan and Assendelft.

Zabrze Poland. Industrial town in Katowice voivodeship 18 km (11 miles) WNW of Katowice. Pop. (1992) 205,500.

Coalmining. Manufactures iron and steel, machinery, chemicals and glass.

Founded in the 14th cent. Passed to Prussia 1742. Restored to Poland after World War II (1945).

Zacapa Guatemala. Cap. of the Zacapa department 105 km (65 miles) ENE of Guatemala City. Pop. (1989) 36,000.

Railway junction. Market town. Sulphur springs.

Zacatecas Mexico. 1. State on the central plateau, crossed NW–SE by the Sierra Madre Occidental. Area 73,252 sq km (28,283 sq. miles). Pop. (1990) 1,276,323. Cap. Zacatecas. Main resources minerals, esp. silver; also gold, zinc and lead. Chief towns Zacatecas and Fresnillo.

2. Cap. of Zacatecas state 600 km (375 miles) NW of Mexico City at a height of 2400 m (7872 ft) in a deep gulch in the central plateau. Pop. (1989) 188,000.

A silver-mining centre. Minor industries inc. the making of *serapes* (Mexican shawls).

Founded (1546) after the discovery of rich silver deposits.

Zacatecoluca El Salvador. Cap. of the La Paz department 43 km (27 miles) SE of San Salvador. Pop. (1992) 57,032.

Market town. Manufactures cotton goods and cigars.

Zadar (Italian **Zara**) Croatia. Seaport and seaside resort on the Adriatic Sea 116 km (72 miles) NW of Split. Pop. (1988) 116,200.

Noted for the manufacture of maraschino liqueur.

The 9th-cent. Church of St Donat, built over a Roman forum, is one of the oldest buildings in Dalmatia; there are other medieval churches and also Roman remains. Acquired by Venice 1409, it passed to Austria 1797 and became an Italian enclave in Yugoslavia 1920. It was ceded to Yugoslavia 1947.

Zagazig Egypt. Cap. of the Sharqiya governorate on the Nile delta 61 km (38 miles) NNE of Cairo. Pop. (1990) 255,000.

Railway and canal junction in a fertile region. Trade in cotton and grain. Cotton mills.

Zagorsk ➤SERGIYEV POSAD.

Zagreb Croatia. Cap. situated in central Croatia on the Sava R. 169 km (105 miles) ENE of Trieste. Pop. (1991) 930,753. The second largest city in Croatia and a road and railway junction on the route between Belgrade and Ljubljana.

Manufactures machinery, textiles, asbestos, pharmaceuticals, leather goods, paper, glass, furniture, chemicals and carpets.

The walled medieval settlements were joined and extended by new building in the 19th cent. Growth was rapid after 1860 and again after 1945. Zagreb has often been a centre of Croatian nationalism and became a national cap. in 1991.

Zagros Mountains Iran. Mountain system forming the SW edge of the plateau of Iran, extending NW–SE along the frontiers with

Turkey and Iraq, and across S Iran N of the Persian Gulf. Inc. several parallel ranges. Rises to 4548 m (14,918 ft) in Zard Kuh. Iran's main oilfields are located in the foothills of the central Zagros in Khuzistán.

Zāhedān Iran. Cap. situated ESE of Kerman in Báluchestán near the border with Afghanistan and Pakistan. Pop. (1986) 281,923. An important transport centre.

Zahlé Lebanon. Town situated ESE of Beirut on the Beirut–Damascus railway in the Bekaa valley at 945 m (3100 ft). Pop. (1988) 45,000. It is a summer resort in a vine-growing area.

Zaïre ➤DEMOCRATIC REPUBLIC OF THE CONGO.

Zaïre River ➤CONGO RIVER.

Zákinthos ➤ZANTE.

Zalaegerszeg Hungary. Cap. of Zala county, on the Zala R. 185 km (115 miles) WSW of Budapest. Pop. (1993) 63,000. Market town in a stock-rearing and cereal-growing region.

Zama (Zama Regia) Tunisia. Ancient village 21 km (13 miles) N of the modern town of Maktar (137 km; 85 miles SW of Tunis). Site of one of the decisive battles of world history, in which the Roman Scipio Africanus defeated the Carthaginian army under Hannibal (202 BC), thus ending the 2nd Punic War and the power of Carthage.

Zambezi River. Fourth longest river in Africa, 2650 km (1650 miles) long, rising in the extreme NW of Zambia near the frontiers of the Democratic Republic of the Congo and Angola, flowing generally SE in an immense S-curve and entering the Mozambique Channel 210 km (130 miles) NE of Beira. From the source, it flows S across E Angola and Lesotho, turns ESE to form the frontier between Zambia and the Caprivi Strip (Namibia), and continues E, between Kasungula and Zumbo forming the frontier between Zambia and Zimbabwe: in this section are the Victoria Falls and the Kariba hydroelectric scheme. It enters

Mozambique at Zumbo; below the Kebrabasa Rapids it turns SE past Tete (head of steamer navigation) and enters the sea by a marshy delta, only one channel of which (the Chinde) is navigable. River traffic declined with the opening of the railway bridge at Sena (1935) linking Malawi (then Nyasaland) with Beira. Elsewhere along the course it is seriously impeded by rapids and falls; only limited stretches are navigable. Chief tributaries the Lungwebungu, the Luanginga, the Chobe, the Shangani and the Sanyati on the right, and the Kafue, the Luangwa and the Shiré (outlet of L. Malawi) on the left.

Zambia. Republic in central Africa bounded by Tanzania and Malawi in the NE, Mozambique, Zimbabwe, Botswana and Namibia in the S, Angola in the W and the Democratic Republic of the Congo in the N. Area 752,614 sq km (290,586 sq. miles). Pop. (1995) 9,456,000 (42 per cent urban). Life expectancy, 45 years male, 46 female. Cap. Lusaka. Other major cities Kitwe, Ndola, Kabwe and Mufulira. Currency: Zambian kwacha = 100 ngwee. Zambia occupies a high rolling plateau at a height of 1200 m (3936 ft) rising to over 1500 m (4920 ft) in the Muchinga Mountains (E and NE). Drained principally by the Zambezi and its tributaries the Kafue and the Luangwa; the NW is drained by the Luapula, a headstream of the Congo R., rising in L. Bangweulu. The Tanzam Railway, 1770 km (1106 miles) links the Congolese Copperbelt with Dar-es-Salaam (Tanzania); 892 km (558 miles) of the route is in Zambia. Maramba (Livingstone) near the Victoria Falls and cap. until 1935, is a well-known tourist attraction. The climate is tropical, but has three seasons. The cool, dry one is from May to Aug., a hot, dry one follows until Nov., when the wet season commences. The natural vegetation is savannah but there is sufficient woodland in some areas for timber exploitation. Land use: forested 39 per cent, meadows and pastures 40 per cent, agricultural and under permanent cultivation 7 per cent. The majority of the pop. is Bantu and 67 per cent is Christian, the remainder follow traditional beliefs. English is the official lang. but there are many local lang. inc. Bemba, Njanja, Lozi and Tonga.

Agriculture consists mainly of the cultivation by Africans of subsistence crops, e.g. maize, cassava, millet, groundnuts. Cattle-rearing is restricted to uplands not infested by the tsetse fly. Minerals are the chief source of wealth, esp. from the Copperbelt (near the Democratic Republic of the Congo frontier), which provides about 85 per cent of exports; Zambia is a leading world producer of copper. The chief mines are at Kabwe (Broken Hill), Roan, Antelope, Nkana, Mufulira and Mchanga. Other minerals are cobalt, gold, lead, zinc, vanadium and silver. Industries also inc. vehicle assembly, food-processing, chemicals, textiles, clothing, sugar, oil-refining and brewing.

Zambia was explored and described by Livingstone 1851–5. It suffered from the activities of Arab slave traders in the 19th cent.; the slave trade was suppressed by the British 1891–4 and the two provinces of NE and NW Rhodesia were amalgamated (1911) as Northern Rhodesia. Administration transferred from the British South Africa Company, which had been in control since 1889, to the British government 1924. Proposals for a new constitution led to disturbances in 1961, but full independence was achieved without difficulty in 1964. The mineral wealth was nationalized, with moderate compensation to the British South Africa Company. There is a 150-member unicameral National Assembly and the Constitution of 1990 allows for multi-party elections.

Zamboanga Philippines. Cap. of Zamboanga province at the SW extremity of Mindanao on Basilan Strait. Pop. (1990) 444,000.

Seaport. Exports copra, timber, abacá and coconut oil.

Founded (1635) by the Spanish.

Zamora Spain. 1. Province in León in the NW, bordering W on Portugal. Area 10,559 sq km (4082 sq. miles). Pop. (1991) 213,668. Cap. Zamora. Mountainous in the NW, but chiefly plateau. Drained by the Douro R. and its tributaries. Main occupation agriculture (cereals, vines) and sheep-rearing.

2. Cap. of Zamora province on a steep hill above the Douro R. 88 km (55 miles) WSW of Valladolid. Pop. (1988) 60,000.

Trade in cereals and wine. Flour-milling. Manufactures textiles, cement, and soap.

Has a small but beautiful 12th-cent. Romanesque cathedral, other 12th-cent. churches and a 14th-cent bridge across the river.

Zanesville USA. Industrial town in central Ohio on the Muskingum R. at the confluence with the Licking R. 80 km (50 miles) E of Columbus. Pop. (1990) 26,788.

Manufactures iron and steel, tiles, pottery, glass and cement.

Zanjan ►ZENJAN.

Zante (Gr. **Zákinthos**) Greece. Ancient Zacynthus. 1. The most S of the main Ionian Islands 19 km (12 miles) from the NW coast of the Peloponnese, forming with some small islets the *nome* of Zante. Area 406 sq km (158 sq. miles). Pop. (1991) 32,746.

Produces currants, wine and olive oil. Its main industry is tourism.

Annexed by Rome 191 BC. Long a Venetian possession (1482–1797). Has often suffered from earthquakes, notably in 1811, 1820, 1840, 1893, 1953.

2. Cap. of Zante *nome* on the E coast. Pop. (1985) 9500.

Seaport. Exports currants and olive oil. Flour-milling. Manufactures soap.

Zanzibar Tanzania. 1. Coralline island in the Indian Ocean separated from the E coast of Africa by the 35-km (22-mile)-wide Zanzibar Channel. Area 1554 sq km (601 sq. miles). Pop. (1988) 1,450,848. The Portuguese occupied Zanzibar and Pemba early in the 16th cent., but were superseded by the Arabs (from Oman) in the 17th cent. The Sultan of Muscat made Zanzibar his cap. in 1832, and the link with Oman was broken; one of his sons later became Sultan of Zanzibar. The Sultan's island possessions were proclaimed a British protectorate (as Zanzibar) in 1890, but the N of his mainland possession was purchased by Italy and the S by Germany; the central 16-km (10-mile)-wide strip along the Kenya coast was leased by Britain (its administration passing to Kenya) and known after 1920 as the Kenya Protectorate. After a very brief period of independence within the British Commonwealth (1963–4) Zanzibar united with Tanganyika as Tanzania (1964).

2. Cap. of Zanzibar island and of Zanzibar and Pemba on the W coast of Zanzibar 72 km (45 miles) N of Dar-es-Salaam. Pop. (1988) 157,634.

Commercial centre, entrepôt for E African trade; the world's leading exporter of cloves.

Grew in importance after becoming the Omani cap. (instead of Muscat) but declined with the rise of Mombasa and Dar-es-Salaam.

Zaporozhye (Zaporizhzhya) Ukraine. Cap. of the Zaporozhye region on the Dnieper R. 64 km (40 miles) S of Dnepropetrovsk. Pop. (1991) 897,000.

Industrial centre which has expanded rapidly in recent years, largely owing to the Dneprostroi Dam and hydroelectric power station on the Dnieper R. It has developed a great metallurgical and engineering industry, manufacturing special steels and alloys, aluminium, machinery, machine-tools, wire, ball-bearings.

The present name, meaning 'Beyond the Rapids', refers to its position below the Dnieper falls which led to the Dneprostroi power station.

Zara ►ZADAR.

Zaragoza (Eng. **Saragossa**) Spain. Province in Aragón, in the NE. Area 17,194 sq km (6615 sq. miles). Pop. (1991) 837,327. Mountainous along the N, W and S borders; consists mainly of a barren plain crossed by the Ebro R. and its tributaries. Agriculture (sugar-beet, cereals) is impeded by extremes of temperature and low rainfall.

2. Ancient Caesarea Augusta or Caesaraugusta (of which the modern name is a corruption). Cap. of Zaragoza province, on the Ebro R. at the confluence with the

Huerva and Gállego rivers 257 km (160 miles) W of Barcelona. Pop. (1991) 586,219.

Important railway junction and commercial and industrial centre. Engineering, sugar-refining, flour-milling, wine-making. Manufactures chemicals, soap and cement.

Cap. of the kingdom of Aragón in the 12th–15th cent., but declined after the union with Castile. Goya, the painter (1746–1828), was born at the village of Fuendetodos near by.

Zárate Argentina. Formerly (1930–45) General José F. Uriburu. Industrial town on the Paraná R. 80 km (50 miles) NW of Buenos Aires. Pop. (1980) 65,504.

In an agricultural region, linked by ferry with Iticuy. Meat-packing. Manufactures paper.

Zaria Nigeria. Historic walled town in the N 137 km (85 miles) SW of Kano. Pop. (1992) 345,000. On the main railway from Lagos to Kano and Nguru (with a branch line to the NW with terminus at Kaura Namoda).

Market town in a cotton-growing region. Railway engineering, cotton-ginning, printing, tanning are important industries and it manufactures cigarettes, textiles, cosmetics and bicycles.

Founded in the 14th cent. and was the centre of the slave trade.

Zarka Jordan. Town situated NE of Amman on the Hejaz railway. Pop. (1990) 514,980. It is the site of a power plant and phosphate mines with yellow ochre nearby.

Zasieki ►FORST.

Zealand (Sjaelland) Denmark. Largest island, between the Kattegat and the Baltic Sea, separated from Sweden by The Sound and from Funen (Fyn) by the Great Belt, and connected by road and railway bridge with Falster. Area 7016 sq km (2709 sq. miles). Pop. (1990) 1,972,711. Low and slightly undulating.

Main occupations cereal cultivation, dairy-farming and cattle-rearing.

Chief towns Copenhagen and Roskilde.

Zeebrugge Belgium. Seaport in W Flanders

province 14 km (9 miles) N of Bruges at the N end of the Bruges–Zeebrugge canal.

Exports coke, chemicals (produced here).

Zeeland Netherlands. Province in the SW comprising a small area on the mainland bordering S on Belgium and islands in the Scheldt estuary inc. Walcheren, N and S Beveland. Area 1792 sq km (692 sq. miles). Pop. (1990) 355,937. Cap. Middelburg.

Mainly agricultural. Cereal cultivation, dairy-farming, cattle-rearing.

Chief towns Middelburg and Flushing (chief port).

Zeist Netherlands. Residential and industrial town in Utrecht province 8 km (5 miles) E of Utrecht. Pop. (1992) 59,211.

Manufactures pharmaceutical goods, toys and soap. Market-gardening in the neighbourhood.

A Moravian settlement was established here in the 18th cent.

Zeitz Germany. Industrial town in the Halle district of Saxony on the White Elster R. 40 km (25 miles) SSW of Leipzig. Pop. (1991) 59,357.

Industries inc. sugar-refining and it manufactures textiles, chemicals and pianos.

Cap. of the duchy of Saxe-Zeitz in the 17th and 18th cent. Passed to Prussia 1815.

Zenjan (Zanjan, Zinjan) Iran. Town in Gilan province 282 km (175 miles) WNW of Tehrán. Pop. (1986) 215,261.

Manufactures cotton goods, rugs and matches.

Zenta ➤SENTA.

Zeravshan River Tajikistan/Uzbekistan. River 736 km (460 miles) long, rising at the W end of the Alai Mountains, flowing generally W and watering the oases of Samarkand and Bukhara, petering out in the desert before reaching the Amu Darya.

Zermatt Switzerland. Village and climbing centre in Valais canton at a height of 1620 m (5315 ft) at the foot of the Matterhorn (8 km; 5 miles SW), with Monte Rosa also near by. Pop. (1989) 4200. There is a rack-and-pinion

railway to the summit of the Gornergrat (3138 m; 10,293 ft). It can only be reached by rail.

Zetland ➤SHETLAND ISLANDS.

Zhangjoukou China. City near the Great Wall 160 km (100 miles) NW of Beijing in Hubei province. Pop. (1984) 607,900.

Commercial and route centre, often termed the 'gateway to Mongolia', linked by road through Inner Mongolia with Ulan Bator (Mongolia). Trade in tea, sugar, cotton goods from China, and hides and wool from Mongolia. Industries inc. tanning and the manufacture of cotton goods.

Zhdanov ➤MARIUPOL.

Zhejiang (Chekiang) China. Maritime province on the E China Sea. Area 101,800 sq km (39,300 sq. miles). Pop. (1990) 30,048,224. Cap. Hangzhou. It is the smallest province, but one of the most densely populated. Largely mountainous and the climate varies from subtropical (S) to temperate (N). Chief crops tea, rice, cotton. It manufactures paper, machinery and chemicals. Principal towns Hangzhou, Ningbo and Wenzhou; all are seaports.

Zhengzhou (Chengcou/Chengchow) China. Cap. of Henan province in the N near the Huang-he. Pop. (1991) 1,159,679.

Important railway junction on the Beijing–Guangzhou (N–S) and Lienyun–Lanchow (E–W) lines and it is also a commercial centre. It trades in grain, hides and skins, and industries inc. flour-milling, vegetable oil processing and the manufacture of machinery and textiles.

Zhen Jiang China. Town in the Jiangsu province on the Chang Jiang at its junction with the Grand Canal. Pop. (1984) 899,500.

Flour-milling. Manufactures textiles and matches. Trade in rice, wheat and soya beans.

Opened to foreign trade in 1859. Lost importance later owing to competition from Shanghai and the decline of the Grand Canal as a significant waterway.

Zhitomir (Zhytomyr) Ukraine. Cap. of

the Zhitomir region situated on the Teterev R. 129 km (80 miles) WSW of Kiev. Pop. (1991) 298,000.

Road and railway junction. Industrial centre. Metalworking, brewing. Manufactures furniture and clothing.

Passed to Lithuania in the 14th cent., to Poland in the 16th cent. and was occupied by Russia in 1778.

Zhob River Pakistan. Rises near Kand Peak in the Toba-Kakar range, Baluchistan and flows c. 368 km (230 miles) E past Hindubagh then NE to enter the Gumal R. NNE of Fort Sandeman. Its flow is subject to wide seasonal variation.

Zhousan Archipelago China. Group of islands in the East China Sea off Hangzhou Bay on important fishing grounds but dangerous to navigate owing to fogs and strong currents. Largest island Zhousan (596 sq km; 230 sq. miles).

Zhu Jiang. River formed by the confluence of the Xi Jiang, Bei Jiang and the Dong Jiang Rs. It flows 176 km (110 miles) into a broad delta to enter the South China Sea near Macao. Also known as the Pearl R.

Zielona Góra (Ger. **Grünberg**) Poland. Cap. of the Zielona Góra voivodeship 117 km (73 miles) WSW of Poznań. Pop. (1992) 114,300.

Industrial centre with railway engineering and lignite-mining. It manufactures textiles and trades in wine.

Ziguinchor Senegal. Port on the estuary of the Casamance R. 270 km (170 miles) SSE of Dakar. Pop. (1992) 148,831.

Exports groundnuts.

Žilina Slovakia. Town situated on the Vah R. 169 km (105 miles) NE of Bratislava. Pop. (1990) 97,000.

Railway junction. Industrial centre. Railway engineering. Manufactures paper, matches and fertilizers.

Zimbabwe. Republic in southern Africa bounded in the N by Zambia, E by Mozambique, S by South Africa and W by Botswana.

Area 390,759 sq km (150,873 sq. miles). Pop. (1995) 11,261,000 (26 per cent urban). Life expectancy, 58 years male, 62 female. Cap. Harare. Other chief towns Bulawayo, Chitungwiza, Gweru and Mutare. Currency: Zimbabwe dollar = 100 cents. Zimbabwe consists of a broad ridge of the High Veld running SW–NE at a height of 1200–1800 m (3936–5904 ft), flanked by the Middle Veld at 900–1200 m (2952–3936 ft), with the Low Veld along the Limpopo and Zambezi rivers; the highest land, in the Inyanga Mountains near the Mozambique frontier, rises to over 2500 m (8200 ft). Though situated in the tropics, conditions are remarkably temperate throughout the year because of altitude and the inland position keeps humidity low. The warmest weather occurs in the three months before the main rainy season, which starts in Nov. and lasts until March. Land use: forested 49 per cent, meadows and pasture 13 per cent, agriculture and under permanent cultivation 7 per cent. About 72 per cent of the pop. is Christian and 27 per cent hold traditional beliefs. English is the official lang., Shona and Ndebele are also spoken. About 97 per cent are African, of which Shona-speaking Bantu 71 per cent.

The most important single food crop in Zimbabwe is maize, the staple food of a large proportion of the pop. The livestock industry is second to tobacco as regards its export potential. Dairying forms the foundation of many mixed farms. Fish-farming is being developed and large catches are taken from L. Kariba, where a fish-freezing plant was completed in 1964. Sugar is being produced in the Triangle and Hippo Valley estates.

The citrus estates of the British South Africa Company, the state-owned deciduous orchards at Nyanga and a scheme for large-scale citrus-growing at Hippo Valley form the basis of the citrus-fruit industry. However, many parts of the country between 769 m (2500 ft) and 1231 m (4000 ft) above sea level are suitable for citrus culture, and large numbers of deciduous fruit trees planted in the Chimanimani and Nyanga areas are coming into production. There are large tea plantations. Other crops grown in substantial quantities inc. small grains (sorghums and millet), rice, groundnuts, cassava. These crops form the basis of much subsistence farming undertaken by the African pop. Tobacco is the most important single product. Cotton and wheat are also important. Minerals inc. asbestos, gold, chrome ore, coal and copper. Metal products account for 20 per cent of industrial output. Other industries inc. food-processing, textiles, furniture and timber products.

The Matabele invaded the region and absorbed the Mashona tribe in the 19th cent. It was administered by the British South Africa Company 1889–1923 and became a self-governing colony, as Southern Rhodesia, in 1923. The Federation of Rhodesia and Nyasaland was formed in 1953, but the Federation broke up in 1962 and the other two states became fully independent in 1964; Northern Rhodesia as Zambia and Nyasaland as Malawi. Unilateral declaration of independence (UDI) was declared by the Rhodesian government in 1965. UN economic sanctions against Rhodesia were only partially successful and in 1970 the country was declared a republic. British efforts were designed to ensure greater African participation in government and eventual majority rule; this was also the aim of neighbouring states and spasmodic guerrilla activity took place, esp. along the Mozambique border. After years of negotiations a conference took place in London in 1979 and agreed the Constitution for an independent Zimbabwe, forms for the return to legality and a cease-fire. Elections took place in March 1980 and Southern Rhodesia became Zimbabwe. The Constitution provides for a unicameral parliament with a 150-member House of Assembly.

Zimbabwe National Park Zimbabwe. Site, discovered 1868, of a ruined town built by a Bantu people in the SE 24 km (15 miles) SE of Fort Victoria, consisting of dry granite walls which were apparently never roofed. The main ruins are the 'elliptical temple' (a stone kraal, not strictly elliptical); the 'acropolis' (a fortified citadel), on the summit of a granite hill; and the 'valley ruins' (small buildings which were probably dwellings). Relics from Zimbabwe (pottery, metal ornaments) are now in museums in Harare and Cape Town. The name Zimbabwe means literally 'stone houses'; originally considered a great mystery but now identified as a Shona chieftain's compound dating from the 13th to the 15th cent.

Zinder Niger. Town in the S 755 km (465 miles) E of Niamey. Pop. (1988) 120,892. Terminus of a Trans-Saharan motor route from N Algeria. Until 1926 it was cap. of the French colony of Niger.

A commercial centre trading in groundnuts, hides and skins, and local crafts inc. leather goods and blankets.

Zinjan ►ZENJAN.

Zion National Park USA. Reserve in SW Utah. Area 593 sq km (229 sq. miles). Established 1919. Chief feature Zion Canyon, a gorge containing beautifully coloured rocks and unusual rock formations.

Zipaquirá Colombia. Town in the Cundinamarca department at a height of 2650 m (8692 ft) in the E Cordillera 48 km (30 miles) N of Bogotá. Pop. (1989) 41,000.

In a cattle-rearing district. It has a mine containing immense quantities of rock salt, which provides raw material for the local chemical industry.

Zittau Germany. Industrial town and railway junction in the Dresden district of Saxony near the Czech Republic and Polish frontiers 80 km (50 miles) ESE of Dresden. Pop. (1989) 36,246.

Manufactures textiles, commercial vehicles and machinery.

First settled by Sorbs (Lusatian Serbs); a member of the Lusatian League (from 1346).

Zlatoust Russia. Industrial town in the Chelyabinsk region on the Ai R. 113 km (70 miles) W of Chelyabinsk. Pop. (1991) 210,700.

Important centre of the iron and steel industry, esp. producing special steels; manufactures agricultural machinery and cutlery.

Established in 1754 as a metallurgical centre.

Zlín Czech Republic. Formerly Gott-waldov. Town in Moravia 77 km (48 miles) E of Brno. Pop. (1990) 87,000. Owes its economic importance to the establishment of the great footwear industry by Tomas Bata in 1913. Also manufactures domestic wood products and machinery.

Zonguldak Turkey. Cap. of Zonguldak province on the Black Sea 177 km (110 miles) NNW of Ankara. Pop. (1990) 116,725.

Seaport. Exports coal mined in the district. Chief industry coal-processing.

Zoutpansberg South Africa. In Afrikaans, 'Salt Pan Mountain'. Mountain range S of the Limpopo R. in the Transvaal, extending 160 km (100 miles) E–W and rising to 1740 m (5707 ft). Chief town in the district Louis Trichardt.

Zrenjanin Yugoslavia (Serbia). Formerly Veliki Bečkerek (till the 1930s), then Petrovgrad (till 1947). Town in Vojvodina on the canalized Becej R. 45 km (28 miles) ENE of Novi Sad. Pop. (1991) 81,328.

River port. Manufactures agricultural machinery and food products.

Zug Switzerland. 1. The smallest undivided canton in N central Switzerland. Area 239 sq km (92 sq. miles). Pop. (1991) 84,908 (mainly German-speaking and Roman Catholic). It joined the Swiss Confederation 1352.

2. Cap. of Zug canton on the NE shore of L. Zug and 24 km (15 miles) S of Zürich. Pop. (1985) 23,500.

Printing, woodworking. Manufactures electrical equipment, metal goods.

Stands at the foot of the Zugerberg (995 m; 3264 ft). Has a 16th-cent. town hall.

Zug, Lake (Ger. **Zugersee**) Switzerland. Lake 14 km (9 miles) long and 4 km (2½ miles) wide N of L. Lucerne and mainly in Zug canton. On the NE shore is the town of Zug; to the S is the Rigi (1801 m; 5907 ft).

Zugspitze Germany. Country's highest peak (2968 m; 9735 ft) in the Bavarian Alps and on the Austrian frontier. Ascended from Garmisch-Partenkirchen (Germany) by rack-and-pinion and then cable railway, and from Ehrwald (Austria) by cable railway.

Zuider Zee Netherlands. Former gulf of the North Sea, probably once a lake, the coast being represented then by the line of the W Frisian Is. By the 14th cent. the sea had breached the coast and formed the shallow gulf. It now touches on five provinces of the Netherlands: Friesland, Gelderland, Overijssel, Utrecht and Noord Holland. Area 5180 sq km (c. 2000 sq. miles). Reclamation began in 1923 behind two barrages which cut off an interior lake for reclamation in four 'polders', surrounding a water area now called the Ijsselmeer. The exterior area beyond the barrages is called the Wadden Zee.

Zuid-Holland Netherlands. Province bounded W by the North Sea, S by Zeeland, N by Brabant. Area 2908 sq km (1123 sq. miles). Pop. (1990) 3,219,839. Cap. The Hague. Mainly below sea level and protected by dunes, drained by the R. Rhine delta.

Dairy-farming and horticulture are important in the rural districts, but the province is the most densely populated with industries centred on numerous manufacturing towns, chiefly Rotterdam, Schiedam, Ulaardingen, Delft, Leiden and Dordrecht.

Zululand ➤KWAZULU.

Zürich Switzerland. 1. Canton in the N. Area 1729 sq km (668 sq. miles). Pop. (1991) 1,150,546 (mainly German-speaking and Protestant). Contains a considerable area of forests. Cereals, fruit, vines cultivated. Industries concentrated chiefly in Zürich and Winterthur. It joined the Swiss Confederation in 1351.

2. Cap. of Zürich canton, the country's largest city on the Limmat R. where it leaves L. Zürich. Pop. (1991) 341,276.

The leading industrial, banking and insurance centre. Manufactures textiles, electrical machinery and is a centre for publishing and printing. Tourism is important. The cultural centre of German-speaking Switzerland, with a university (1833), the Federal Institute of Technology (1855), the National Museum, the Central Library and Art Gallery. Among famous buildings are the 11th/14th-cent. Grossmünster and the 13th/15th-cent. Fraumünster, both Protestant churches, and the 17th-cent. town hall.

First inhabited by prehistoric lake-dwellers, who were followed by the Helvetii and the Romans. Became a free Imperial city 1218. Joined the Swiss Confederation 1351. Played a leading part in the Reformation and the reformer Zwingli (1484–1531) became pastor at the Grossmünster in 1518; he was later killed whilst fighting with the Protestant forces. Birthplace of Pestalozzi (1746–1827), Gottfried Keller (1819–90), Conrad Meyer (1825–98).

Zürich, Lake Switzerland. Lake mainly in Zürich canton 40 km (25 miles) long and up to 4 km (2½ miles) wide at 406 m (1332 ft) above sea level, fed by the Linth R. and drained by the Limmat R. At its N end is Zürich. Crossed by a causeway carrying a road and a railway between Rapperswil (N) and Pfäffikon (S). Although lacking the spectacular Alpine scenery of some Swiss lakes, it is pleasantly situated amid vineyards and orchards.

Zutphen Netherlands. Industrial town in Gelderland province on the Ijssel R. 26 km (16 miles) NE of Arnhem. Pop. (1993) 31,117.

Manufactures bricks, clothing, paper, glue, footwear, leather and soap. Trade in grain and timber.

Has the remains of the ancient town walls and a 12th-cent. church. Sir Philip Sidney was mortally wounded here (1586).

Zvishavane (Shabani) Zimbabwe. Town

and rail terminus situated E of Bulawayo. Pop. (1982) 27,000. An asbestos-mining centre.

Zweibrücken Germany. Town in Rhineland-Palatinate near the Saarland border 37 km (23 miles) SW of Kaiserslautern. Pop. (1989) 42,000.

Manufactures leather goods and textiles.

Dates from the 12th cent. Belonged to France 1801–14, when it was called Deux-Ponts.

Zwickau Germany. Industrial town in Saxony on the Zwickauer Mulde R. 64 km (40 miles) S of Leipzig. Pop. (1991) 118,914.

Manufactures textiles (cotton, woollen, rayon), paper, machinery, tractors and chemicals.

Has the 15th/16th-cent. Gothic Church of St Mary and a 16th-cent. town hall. The Anabaptist movement was founded here *c.* 1521. Birthplace of Robert Schumann (1810–56).

Zwijndrecht Netherlands. Town situated NW of Dordrecht in Zuid-Holland on Old Maas R. Pop. (1992) 42,429.

Industries inc. shipbuilding, salt and rice processing, jute-spinning and the manufacture of chemicals and edible fats.

Zwolle Netherlands. Cap. of Overijssel province 34 km (21 miles) NNE of Apeldoorn on the Zwartewater. Pop. (1992) 97,131.

A canal and railway junction. Important cattle market. Manufactures chemicals, metal goods and dairy products.

Has a 14th/15th-cent. church. Thomas à Kempis, German religious writer (1380–1471), spent most of his life at the monastery on the nearby Agnietenberg. Birthplace of Gerard Terborch (1617–81), the painter.

'Terrific scenes . . . . disaster that was the
raid on Dieppe is grippingly rendered'
Observer

'A profound and moving novel; a tender and compassionate
meditation on love and God and duty and how to be good'
Guardian

'I love William Nicholson's simple, intense style. One to get lost in'
Red Magazine

'Nicholson tells his ambitious story with a moving eloquence'
Sunday Times

'Blends romance and adventure to intoxicating effect'
Good Housekeeping

'A screenwriter's instinct for dialogue'
Daily Express

'Writing of the highest calibre . . . a novel of empathy and
insight into the human mind and heart both a poignant, affecting
love story and a superb work of fiction'
Good Book Guide

'An involving and satisfying read'
Woman & Home

William Nicholson's plays include *Shadowlands* and *Life Story*, both of which won the BAFTA Best Television Drama award of their year. He co-wrote the script for the film *Gladiator*, and, more recently, he has scripted *Les Misérables* and *Mandela*. He is married to the writer Virginia Nicholson and they have three children. William Nicholson lives in East Sussex.

Also by William Nicholson

The Trial of True Love
The Society of Others
The Secret Intensity of Everyday Life
All the Hopeful Lovers
The Golden Hour

Books for children

The Wind Singer
Slaves of the Mastery
Firesong
Seeker
Jango
Noman

William
NICHOLSON
MOTHERLAND

Quercus

First published in Great Britain in year of 2013 by Quercus Editions Ltd
The paperback edition published in 2013 by Quercus Editions Ltd

Quercus
55 Baker Street
7th Floor, South Block
London W1U 8EW

A CIP catalogue record for this book is available
from the British Library

ISBN 978 1 78087 623 8
PB ISBN 978 1 78087 622 1

10 9 8 7 6 5 4 3 2 1

Printed and bound in Great Britain by Clays Ltd, St Ives plc

Typeset by Ellipsis Digital Limited, Glasgow

For Virginia

Our parents have loved before us, and their parents before them. For all we know we inherit our ways of loving along with the colour of our eyes. The joys we feel have been felt before; the mistakes we make have been made before. We carry within us the hopes and fears of the generations that have formed us. This is the unknown motherland from which we are always escaping, and to which we will always, helplessly, be true.

PROLOGUE

2012

Alice Dickinson sits in the back of the Peugeot, though she would prefer to sit in the front, watching the orchards of Normandy roll by. The driver, a heavy middle-aged man with sad eyes, was waiting at the ferry port holding a sign displaying her name. Her clumsy prep-school French was met with incomprehension. Now he sits stooped over the wheel, one finger tapping out some inner rhythm, brooding on some secret unhappiness. She has no idea of his role. He could be an employee, he could be a member of the family. He's driving her to the grandmother she has never met, whose name is Pamela Avenell, who didn't know she existed until ten days ago.

The car turns off the main road onto a smaller road that runs along the east bank of the Varenne. Now the streets of steep-roofed houses give way to stands of mature beech trees, their broad leaves dusty in the mid-August sun. The late hot summer disturbs Alice. This is the weather for lying in long grass beside your lover, not the season for ending an affair.

You lead the life you choose to lead. It should be simple but it's not. Her own mother's love life, for example. She was just the age Alice is now, twenty-three, when she had an affair with a man who didn't love her, or not enough to want her baby. 'Get an abortion,' he told her. 'I'll pay.'

My father, Guy Caulder, the bastard. And me, the not-abortion. The genuine bastard, to be precise.

The strange thing is she doesn't hate her father. For some time she thought she despised him, which is different. Guy is handsome, selfish, shameless. He has played no part in her life: not a secret, but not a real person, either. An idea, a few anecdotes, and a genetic legacy.

That's what hooks you in the end. That's what reels you in. One day you wake up thinking: half of me comes from him. What if I take after him after all? That's when you start to want to know more.

'Why are you such a bastard, Guy?'

She asks the question without rancour, and he takes no offence. He's buying her lunch in one of the restaurants in Charlotte Street he favours; this one is called Mennula, smart Sicilian.

'Usual reason,' he says. 'My mother didn't want me.'

Of course. Blame the mother. The father can fuck off and no one blinks, but the all-nurturing mother must never stop giving. Give birth, give suck, give unconditional love.

So back it goes, another generation.

Alice has seen so little of Guy in her life that she knows nothing at all about his family. Now she has started to want to know.

'Why didn't your mother want you?'

'Oh,' says Guy, as if the whole affair lost its interest long ago, 'my mother married the wrong man, the way people do. Probably because her mother married the wrong man. So you see, you come from a long line of mistakes.'

I come from a long line of mistakes. Thanks for that.

'Is she still alive?'

'God, yes. Very much so. She's only just seventy, not that you'd know it. Still a very good-looking woman. Still getting her own way. Mind you, I haven't actually seen her for years now.'

'Why not?'

'It works out better for both of us that way.'

More than this he will not say.

This story of a chain of unsuccessful marriages haunts Alice. She tells Guy she wants to meet this grandmother she's never known, who *gets her own way*.

Guy says, 'She has no idea you even exist.'

'Would you mind?'

He has to think about that one. But of course he has no real choice.

'All I've got is an address,' he says. 'In Normandy.'

The Peugeot has no air-conditioning, but the sad-eyed driver has his window fully open, and the speed-wind ruffles Alice's hair. She has dressed with care for this trip, wanting to appear smart but not over-eager to impress. She's wearing

3

fashionably tight jeans and an off-white linen jacket. Her modest luggage is a canvas tote bag printed with a Caillebotte painting of Paris on a rainy day. She has a notion that Pamela Avenell is stylish.

The beech trees screen the road on both sides now. They pass a road sign pointing to the right, to St-Hellier and Cressy. The driver half-turns towards her.

'Après Bellencombre nous plongeons dans la forêt.'

We plunge into the forest.

The beech trees are spaced well apart from each other, but they recede as far as the eye can see. The columns of light and shade form shifting avenues that appear and disappear as they pass. Why would anyone choose to live in a forest?

But now the trees are retreating, and the bright afternoon sunlight is flooding a wide roadside meadow. They turn off the road and bump over an unmade track that climbs a gentle rise. And there at the top, commanding an immense view of the forest, stands La Grande Heuze: a steep-roofed many-gabled manor house, with cream-coloured walls striped by close-set vertical beams of grey wood.

The Peugeot rolls to a stop by a front porch that is dense with overhanging clematis. The driver stays in his seat.

'Voilà,' he says. 'Vous trouverez Madame dedans.'

Alice gets out, and the car drives away round the back of the house. A golden retriever appears and gives a token sleepy bark. The door within the porch is open. There is no doorbell.

4

She knocks, then she calls.

'Hello? Mrs Avenell?'

Ahead she sees down a wide dark hall to a doorway that is bright with daylight. The only sign of life is the dog, which has crossed the hall and disappeared into the room beyond.

'Hello?' Alice calls again. 'Anyone in?'

Still no answer. She follows the path taken by the dog and enters a long room with two sets of French windows that look onto a garden. The windows stand open. The dog lies in the sun on the terrace outside.

Alice goes onto the terrace and sees, across an expanse of lawn, the beech trees of the forest begin again. Where is her grandmother? She has the uncomfortable sensation that she might be watching her, even now. With this comes a new thought: what if her grandmother doesn't like her? This hasn't occurred to Alice before. She realises that unconsciously she has supposed herself to be a surprise gift. *Look! A real live granddaughter!* But just as Guy never wanted a daughter, perhaps this grandmother who gets her own way never wanted a granddaughter.

She is not arriving unannounced. There has been an exchange of letters. But her grandmother's letter of invitation was not effusive. Curious to see her, certainly, but guarded, cool.

She crosses the lawn to look into the trees, as if there might be some secret there: a leftover impulse from childhood fairy tales. There is no wall or fence. The garden is a glade in the forest. A few years' neglect and the tall beeches would advance to the very steps of the old house itself, and press like bars on its windows and doors. And yet it doesn't make her afraid. This is not the tormented forest of night-mares. Beech alleys form spaces that are light-speckled, domesticated, a chain of rooms that go on for ever. You could go wild here, and be safe.

Turning back, she sees a figure standing in the open French windows. She's slim, with short-cropped silver hair and smooth lightly tanned skin. A long white blouse loose over jeans. Her arms raised in a gesture of welcome.

'You've come! How wonderful!'

Wide brown eyes watch Alice cross the grass towards her. Shining eyes that give full attention, that want to know everything. No holding back here.

'Darling one!' she says. 'What took you so long?'

Alice is flooded with an inexplicable wave of happiness. This silver-haired woman, this never-known grandmother, is simply beautiful. Alice, who has never been beautiful, sees in her at once herself as she could have been; herself as maybe one day she could be.

Pamela Avenell takes both Alice's hands in hers and studies her with rapt wondering attention. Alice feels infinitely precious under that gaze.

'You've got my eyes.'

'Have I?' says Alice.

'Of course you have. I saw it at once.'

'I can hardly believe it,' says Alice. 'You're so beautiful. How can you be my grandmother?'

'I'm sixty-nine, darling,' says Pamela. 'But don't tell a soul.'

'I just can't believe it,' says Alice again.

They stand there like fools, holding hands, grinning at each other, looking and looking. Alice doesn't know why this makes her so happy, nor does she ask herself.

'Come into the house,' says Pamela. 'Let's have a drink and tell each other everything. It's far too hot outside.'

In the house she calls out, 'Gustave!' and the driver appears from an inner room. She speaks to him rapidly in excellent French, touching him lightly on one arm before he departs to carry out her orders.

'Gustave is an angel,' she says. 'I simply don't know how I managed before he came.'

They're sitting down and her big brown eyes are fixed on Alice once more.

'So you're my granddaughter,' she says. 'How cruel and wicked of Guy to hide you away from me.'

'He hid me away from himself,' says Alice. 'He never wanted me. I was an accident.'

'He never wanted you.' Her gaze is penetrating ever deeper into Alice, past all her defences. 'Oh, my dear. I know all about that.'

'I'm not blaming him. My mother says it was all her own choice.'

'No, there's nothing to be gained by blaming people. But that doesn't stop us doing it.'

Gustave comes back into the room carrying a tray of drinks. He sets it down on the low table between them. There's a bottle of Noilly Prat, two glasses, a plate of biscuits.

7

'Chilled vermouth,' says Pamela, pouring golden liquid into the glasses. 'Just right for a hot day.'

She thanks Gustave with a quick smile, and he departs again. Alice takes her glass.

'To accidents,' says Pamela.

She's wearing no make-up, Alice thinks. Her hair isn't dyed. How can she be almost seventy, and so beautiful?

'I don't understand why Guy hasn't told me about you before,' Alice says. 'He should be so proud of you.'

'Ah, well. These things go back a long way. But I don't want to talk about me. I want to know all about you.'

Under her grandmother's intoxicating gaze, Alice tells her life so far. How sometimes a love affair ends for no reason except it's your first and you're too young and there's so much more you need to find out about yourself. How you drift apart and only know it's happened when the space between you has grown too wide, and you reach across and find you're no longer touching. How the old questions which you thought had gone away turn out to have been waiting all along, as unanswerable as ever. What do I really want? Who am I when it's just me? When I love again, will I love with all my heart?

She hears herself say, 'If I love only him, I'll be a smaller person than I know I can be.'

'How wise you are, my darling,' says Pamela. 'I wish I'd known that when I was your age. How old are you? Twenty-one?'

'Twenty-three.'

'When I was twenty-three I had a husband and a baby.'

The husband was Alice's grandfather. His name was Hugo Caulder. This much Alice knows. The baby was Guy. The baby is Guy.

'Guy said something about you marrying the wrong man.'

'Yes, I did. As a matter of fact, I've done it three times. You'd think I'd learn.'

'I want to learn,' says Alice.

'Not from me.' Pamela laughs. 'Unless you study everything I've ever done and do the opposite.'

'I want to learn about who I am. Some of me comes from Guy. And some of him comes from you.'

'Well, yes,' says Pamela. 'It's all rather devastating, isn't it? You see the patterns more clearly as you grow older.'

'Guy says I come from a long line of mistakes.'

'Does he, now? What a little beast he is. I bet he didn't tell you our one true love story.'

Our one true love story. Like the unicorn: beautiful, impossible, long sought but never found.

'Is it yours?'

'Mine? No, it's certainly not mine.' She refills their glasses with vermouth. 'It's my mother's story. Your great-grandmother's.'

She raises her glass, as she did before.

'To mothers,' she says.

'And grandmothers,' says Alice.

They both drink. Alice feels the vermouth warming her inside.

'I adored my mother,' says Pamela. 'You can't imagine how much I adored her. Then later, I envied her. I wanted

9

to be loved as she was loved. Don't you find the trouble with love stories is that they make you sad? You want to have a love story like it for your very own. You go on looking for it and looking for it. And you don't find it.'

'But your mother did.'

'Yes, she did.'

She gets up and takes a framed photograph off the wall. The frame is far too grand for the photograph, which is an old snapshot of three young people: a woman between two men. The woman is young and pretty, in the slightly artificial manner of the 1940s. The men gaze at the camera with that bold self-confidence that is somehow so heartbreaking to see today: boys who believe themselves to be men. One of them, the good-looking one, doesn't smile. The other smiles.

'That's my mother,' says Pamela. 'She was called Kitty. That's my father, Ed Avenell. And that's my father's best friend, Larry Cornford.'

'Your mother was very pretty,' says Alice.

'Your great-grandmother. And wasn't my father handsome?'

'Very.'

'He won the Victoria Cross.'

'How?'

'I'll tell you. And what do you think of Larry?'

Alice studies the friendly smiling face in the photograph.

'He looks nice,' she says.

'Nice. Poor dear Larry. How he'd hate that.'

PART ONE
WAR

1942—45

I

The staff cars are pulled up by the coastguard cottages, close to the cliff edge. A steady drizzle is falling and visibility is poor. A cluster of officers stand in glistening greatcoats, binoculars raised, tracking the movements on the beach below.

'Bloody mess as usual,' says the brigadier.

'Better than last time,' says Parrish. 'At least they found the beach.'

Seven assault landing craft are rolling in the grey water of the bay, as men of the Canadian Eighth Infantry Brigade flounder ashore. Each man wears an inflated Mae West and carries a rifle and a full battle pack. They move slowly through the water, blurred by rain, like dreamers who stride ever onward but never advance.

The watchers on the clifftop command a view that is almost parodic in its Englishness: a river winds through green meadows to a shingle beach, framed by a line of receding hump-backed white cliffs. They are known as the

Seven Sisters. Today barely two of the Seven Sisters are visible. The beach is defended by concrete anti-tank blocks, scaffolding tubes and long rolls of barbed wire. Small thunderflashes explode among the pebbles at random, and to no obvious purpose. The popping sounds rise up to the officers with the binoculars.

One of the landing craft has cut its engine out in deep water. The tiny figures of the men on board can be seen jumping one by one from the ramp. Parrish reads the craft's identifying number through his binoculars.

'ALC85. Why's it stopped?'

'It's sunk,' says Colonel Jevons, who devised the exercise. 'Further out than I intended. Still, they should all float.'

'A couple of six-inch howitzers up here,' says the brigadier, 'and not a man would make it ashore alive.'

'Ah, but the advance raiding party has cut your throats,' says Jevons.

'Let's hope,' says the brigadier.

Behind the staff officers the two ATS drivers are seeking shelter at the back of the Signals truck. The Signals sergeant, Bill Carrier, finds himself in the unfamiliar situation of being outnumbered by women. If a few other lads from his unit were with him he'd know how to banter with these English girls, but on his own like this, unsure of his ground, he's feeling shy.

'Look at it,' says the pretty one. 'June! You've got to admit it's a joke.'

She laughs and wriggles her whole body, as if the absurdity of the world has taken possession of her. She has curly

14

brown hair, almost touching her collar, and brown eyes with strong eyebrows, and a wide smiling mouth.

'Don't mind Kitty,' says the other one, who is blonde and what is called handsome, meaning her features are a little too prominent, her frame a little too large. She speaks through barely parted lips, in the amused tones of the upper classes. 'Kitty's perfectly mad.'

'Mad as a currant bun,' says Kitty.

The rain intensifies. The two drivers in their brown uniforms huddle under the shelter of the truck's raised back.

'Christ, I could murder a cup of tea,' says the blonde one. 'How much longer, O Lord?'

'Louisa was going to be a nun,' says Kitty. 'She's tremendously holy.'

'Like hell,' says Louisa.

'Sorry,' says the sergeant. 'We're still on action stations.'

'Only an exercise,' says Kitty.

'My whole life is only an exercise,' says Louisa. 'When do we get to the real thing?'

'I'm with you there,' says the sergeant. 'Me and the lads are going nuts.'

He answers Louisa but his eyes are on Kitty.

'All you Canucks want to do is fight,' says Kitty, smiling for him.

'That's what we come over for,' says the sergeant. 'Two bloody years ago now.'

'Ah, but you see,' says Kitty, pretending seriousness, trying not to laugh, 'that's not what Louisa's talking about at all. She's talking about getting married.'

'Kitty!' Louisa pummels her friend, making her crouch over, laughing. 'You are such a tell-tale.'

'Nothing wrong with wanting to get married,' says the sergeant. 'I want to get married myself.'

'There!' says Kitty to Louisa. 'You can marry the sergeant and go and live in Canada and have strings of healthy bouncing Canadian babies.'

'I've got a girl in Winnipeg,' says the sergeant. He thinks how he'd ditch her in a flash for Kitty, but not for Louisa.

'Anyway,' says Kitty, 'Louisa's tremendously posh and only allowed to marry people who went to Eton and have grouse moors. Did you go to Eton, Sergeant?'

'No,' says the sergeant.

'Do you have a grouse moor?'

'No.'

'Then your girl in Winnipeg is safe.'

'You really are quite mad,' says Louisa. 'Don't believe a single word she says, Sergeant. I'd be proud and honoured to marry a Canadian. I expect you have moose moors.'

'Sure,' says Bill Carrier, tolerantly playing along. 'We hunt moose all the time.'

'Isn't it meese?' says Kitty.

'They're not fussy what you call them,' says the sergeant.

'How sweet of them,' says Kitty. 'Dear meese.'

She gives the sergeant such an adorable smile, her eyes crinkling at the corners, that he wants to take her in his arms there and then.

'Stop it,' says Louisa, smacking Kitty on the arm. 'Put him down.'

A ship's horn sounds from the bay, a long mournful blare. This is the signal to the men on the beach to re-embark.

'There she blows,' says the sergeant.

The two ATS girls get up. The officers on the clifftop are on the move, talking as they go, huddled together in the rain.

'So what's your names anyway?' the sergeant says.

'I'm Lance-Corporal Teale,' says Kitty. 'And she's Lance-Corporal Cavendish.'

'I'm Bill,' says the sergeant. 'See you again, maybe.'

They part to their various vehicles. Kitty stands to attention by the passenger door of the brigadier's staff car.

'Ride with me, Johnny,' the brigadier says to Captain Parrish.

The officers get in. Kitty takes her place behind the wheel.

'Back to HQ,' says the brigadier.

Kitty Teale loves driving. Secretly she regards the big khaki Humber Super Snipe as her own property. She has learned how to nurse its grumbly engine to a smooth throb on cold early mornings, and takes pleasure in slipping into just the right gear for each section of road, so that the vehicle never has to strain. She carries out the simpler operations of car maintenance herself, watching over oil levels and tyre pressures with an almost maternal care. She also cleans the car, in the long hours waiting at HQ for the next duty call.

Today, driving home through the little towns of Seaford and Newhaven, she resents the drizzle because she knows it will leave a film of grime over every surface. At least she's not in convoy behind an army lorry, enduring the spatter of mud from high back wheels. Louisa, who is following behind her in the Ford, will be getting some of the spray from her wheels. But Louisa has no sense of loyalty to the car she drives. 'It's not a pet,' she says to Kitty. 'It's got no feelings.'

To Kitty, everything has feelings. People and animals, of course. But also machines, and even furniture. She's grateful to the chair on which she sits for bearing her weight, and to the knife in her hand for cutting her bread. It seems to her that they've done her a kindness out of a desire to make her happy. Her gratitude is the tribute she pays, as a pretty child grown accustomed to the kindness of strangers, afraid that she does too little to deserve it. She's been brought up to believe it's wrong to think herself attractive, and so is caught in a spiral of charm, in which those who seek to please her must be pleased by her in return. This gives rise to frequent misunderstandings. Unable to offend, she is forever encouraging false hopes. There's a young man in the navy who supposes her to be his girlfriend, after two meetings and a dance. It's true they kissed, but she's kissed other boys. Now he's written her a passionate letter asking her to meet him in London this Friday, when he has twenty-four hours' leave.

The officers in the back are talking about the coming big show.

'All I pray is the flyers do their job,' says the brigadier. 'I want those beaches bombed to buggery.'

'Do we have a forecast?' says Captain Parrish. 'This is no good to anyone.'

He indicates the rain blurring the car windows.

'Supposed to clear by tomorrow,' says the brigadier. 'Then we have to wait for the moon. We've got a few days. Not that anyone ever tells me anything. Bloody liaison officer knows more than I do.'

The Humber turns off the road up the long drive to Edenfield Place, where the battalion is based. The great Victorian Gothic mansion looms out of the drizzle. Kitty pulls the car to a gentle stop before the ornate porch, and the officers clamber out. Behind her, Louisa brings the Ford to a noisier halt on the gravel.

'Thank you, Corporal,' says the brigadier to Kitty. 'That's all for today.'

'Yes, sir. Thank you, sir.'

He signs her work docket.

'If you have a moment, be nice to our friend George. The boys have made a bit of a mess of his wine cellar and he's rather cut up.'

The rightful owner of Edenfield Place, George Holland, second Lord Edenfield, has opted to go on living in the house through this period of wartime requisition. In the sacrificial spirit of the times he has retained for himself a modest suite of three rooms that were formerly occupied by his father's butler. George is barely thirty years old; soft-spoken, shy, in poor health.

'Yes, sir,' says Kitty.

She drives the car round to the garage at the back, followed by Louisa in the Ford. They go together to hand in their work dockets at the Motor Transport Office.

'Fancy a drink at the Lamb?' says Louisa.

'I'll just give the car a wipe-down,' says Kitty. 'Meet you in the hall in half an hour.'

She takes a bucket and cloth and swabs the Humber's flanks, patting the metalwork as she goes. Then she fills the petrol tank back up, and finally immobilises the car by removing its rotor arm, as required by regulations.

Her route through the big house takes her down the cloister, across the galleried hall, past the organ room to the nursery stairs. The room she shares with Louisa is on the second floor, under the eaves, in what was once the night nursery. As she goes she ponders the best strategy to deal with Stephen and Friday. She could say she's run out of travel warrants, which she has, but she's always hitch-hiked before. And anyway, she'd like to see him. They could go to the 400 Club and dance and forget the war for the night. Surely there's no harm in that?

In the attic nursery Kitty sits on her bed and unrolls her regulation lisle stockings. She stretches out her bare legs, wiggling her toes, relishing the sensation of cool freedom. She possesses one pair of rayon stockings, but they won't last for ever, and she has no intention of wasting them on the crowd in the Lamb. Friday, maybe, if she does decide to go up to town.

She sighs as she touches up her lipstick. It's all very well having boys be sweet on you, but why must they all try to own you? Louisa says it's because she smiles too much, but what can she do about that? You're allowed to smile at someone without marrying them, aren't you?

At No.2 Motor Transport Training Centre in North Wales there'd been a girl her age who said she'd done it with four different men. She said it was ten times better than dancing. She said the trick was to pretend to be tipsy, then afterwards you say you don't remember a thing. She said if you were lucky and got a good one it was heaven, but you could never tell from the outside which ones would be good.

On the way back down the narrow carpetless stairs Kitty meets George himself, loitering on the first floor. Somehow since being billeted in Edenfield Place she has befriended its owner, rather in the way you take in a stray dog.

'Oh, hullo,' he says, blinking at her. He has poor eyesight, apparently. 'Are they still keeping you hard at work?'

'No, I'm off now,' says Kitty. Then remembering the brigadier's request, 'I'm really sorry about the wine.'

'Oh, the wine,' he says. 'All the '38 Meursault is gone. I'm told they drank it laced with gin.'

'That's terrible!' Kitty is more shocked by the gin than by the theft. 'They should be shot.'

'Well, not shot, perhaps. You know the Canadians are all volunteers? We should be grateful to them. And I am grateful.'

'Oh, George. You're allowed to be angry.'

'Am I?'

His unfocused eyes gaze at her with silent longing.

'I suppose they meant no real harm,' says Kitty. 'They're like children who don't know what damage they're doing. But even so. You'll get compensation, won't you?'

'I expect I'll be paid something.' Then with a sudden rush, 'The thing is, Kitty, I was hoping we could find a moment to talk.'

'Later, George,' she says. 'I'm late already.'

She touches his arm and gives him a smile to soften the implied rejection, and runs on down the main stairs. Louisa is waiting by the ornate fireplace in the great hall. She's wearing her now-obsolete FANY uniform, made for her by her father's tailor, with the lanyard on the left, yeomanry-style, in the FANY colours of pink and blue. Kitty raises her eyebrows.

'To hell with them all,' says Louisa cheerfully. 'If I have to wear uniform when I'm out in the evenings, I'll bloody well wear one that fits me.'

Kitty and Louisa both volunteered for the FANYs, so much more socially acceptable than the ATS, and met at the training camp in Strensall.

'I don't mind being bossed about by lesbians in trilbies,' says Louisa, 'so long as they're my own class.'

Two years ago the proud FANYs were merged with the ATS, which is not at all Louisa's class, and has the least fetching uniform of all the services.

Outside the rain has stopped at last. There's a crowd of Camerons by the pub, sprawled on the damp grass strip between the door and the road. From inside come cheers and waves of laughter.

'You don't want to go in there, darling,' one soldier calls out to them.

'I don't see any drinks out here,' responds Louisa.

They go into the saloon bar and find a mixed bunch of Camerons and Royals banging on the tables, roaring out encouragement. A trooper from the Fusiliers Mont-Royal is dancing on a table.

'Frenchie! Frenchie! Frenchie!' they chant. 'Off! Off! Off!'

The trooper, a gangling French-Canadian with a craggy stubble-dark face, is performing a mime striptease. Without removing a single actual garment he is managing to create the illusion that he's a sexy young woman peeling off layer after layer.

Kitty and Louisa watch, mesmerised.

'Bravo, Marco!' shout his comrades. '*Baisez-moi*, Marco! Allez Van Doo!'

The trooper writhes with seductive sinuousness, as little by little, with careful tugs, he eases invisible stockings down his legs. Now mock-naked but for brassiere and panties he plays at coyly covering his crotch with his hands, opening and closing his legs. Looking round the faces of the watching men, Kitty realises they're genuinely aroused.

'Show us what you've got, Frenchie!' they call out. 'Knickers down! Off, off, off!'

Teasing inch by teasing inch, down come the imaginary knickers, while the performer remains in full khaki battle-dress. Kitty catches Louisa's eye and sees there the same surprise. It's only a joke; but the male sexual hunger on display is all too real.

Now the knickers are off. The legs are tightly crossed. The ugly soldier who is also a gorgeous naked woman holds his audience spellbound with anticipation. Now at last he throws up his hands, parts his legs, thrusts out his crotch, and a great sigh of satisfaction fills the smoky air.

The show over, the young men packing the bar become suddenly aware that there are two actual females in their midst. Laughing, jostling, they compete to get close.

'Look who's here! Let me buy you a drink, gorgeous! This one's on me. Budge up, pal! Give a guy a chance.'

Kitty and Louisa find themselves pushed back and back until they're pressed to the wall. The friendly attentions of the excited soldiers become uncomfortable.

'Take it easy, boys,' says Kitty, smiling even as she tries to fend off reaching hands.

'Hey!' cries Louisa. 'Get off me! You're squashing me!'

None of the soldiers means to push, but the ones behind are surging forward, and the ones in front find themselves thrust against the girls. Kitty starts to feel frightened.

'Please,' she says. 'Please.'

A commanding voice rings out.

'Move! Get back! Out of my way!'

A tall soldier is forcing himself through the crush, taking men by the arm, pulling them aside.

'Idiots! Baboons! Get back!'

The crowding soldiers part before him, all at once sheepishly aware that things have got out of control. He reaches Kitty and Louisa and spreads his arms to create a clear space before them.

'Sorry about that. No harm done, I hope?'

'No,' says Kitty.

The man before her wears battledress with no insignia

of any kind. He's young, not much older than Kitty herself, and strikingly handsome. His face is narrow, with a strong nose over a full sensitive mouth. His blue eyes, beneath arching brows, are fixed on her with a look she's never encountered before. His look says, Yes, I can see you, but I have other more important concerns than you.

The soldiers he has displaced are now recovering their poise.

'Who do you think you are, buddy?'

The young man turns his faraway gaze on his accuser, and sees him raise a threatening hand.

'Touch me,' he says, 'and I'll break your neck.'

There's something about the way he says it that makes the soldier lower his hand. One of the others mutters, 'Leave him alone, mate. He's a fucking commando.'

After that the crowd disperses, leaving Kitty and Louisa with their rescuer.

'Thanks,' says Kitty. 'I don't think they meant any harm.'

'No, of course not. Just horsing around.'

He guides them to the bar.

'Got any brandy?' he says to the barman. 'These young ladies are suffering from shock.'

'Oh, no, I'm fine,' says Kitty.

'Yes, please,' says Louisa, treading on her foot.

The barman produces a bottle of cooking brandy from under the counter and furtively pours two small shots. The soldier hands them to Kitty and Louisa.

'For medicinal purposes,' he says.

Kitty takes her glass and sips at it. Louisa drinks more briskly.

'Cheers,' she says. 'I'm Louisa, and this is Kitty.'

'Where are you based?'

'The big house.' Louisa nods up the road.

'Secretaries?'

'Drivers.'

'Take care at night,' he says. 'More killed on the roads in the blackout than by enemy action.'

Kitty drinks her brandy without being aware she's doing so. She begins to feel swimmy.

'So who are you?' she says. 'I mean, what are you?'

'Special services,' he says.

'Oh.'

'Sorry. I don't mean to sound mysterious. But that really is all I can say.'

'Are you allowed to tell us your name?'

'Avenell,' he says, pushing back the sweep of dark hair that keeps falling into his eyes. 'Ed Avenell.'

'You're a knight in shining armour,' says Louisa. 'You came to the rescue of damsels in distress.'

'Damsels, are you?' Not a flicker on his pale face. 'If I'd known, I'm not sure I'd have bothered.'

'Don't you like damsels?' says Kitty.

'To tell you the truth,' he says, 'I'm not entirely clear what a damsel is. I think it may be a kind of fruit that bruises easily.'

'That's a damson,' says Kitty. 'Perhaps we're damsons in distress.'

'You can't distress a damson,' says Louisa.

'I don't know about that,' says Ed. 'It can't be much fun being made into jam.'

26

'I wouldn't mind,' says Louisa. 'You get squeezed until you're juicy, and then you get all licked up.'

'Louisa!' says Kitty.

'Sorry,' says Louisa. 'It's the brandy.'

'She's really very well brought up,' Kitty says to Ed. 'Her cousin is a duke.'

'My second cousin is a tenth duke,' says Louisa.

'And you still a mere corporal,' he says. 'It just isn't right.'

'Lance-corporal,' says Louisa, touching her single stripe.

The young man turns his steady gaze on Kitty.

'And what about you?'

'Oh, I'm not top-drawer at all,' says Kitty. 'We Teales are very middle-drawer. All vicars and doctors and that sort of thing.'

Suddenly she feels so wobbly she knows she must lie down. The brandy has come at the end of a long day.

'Sorry,' she says. 'We were up at four for the exercise.'

She starts for the door. Apparently she staggers a little, because before she knows it he's taking her arm.

'I'll walk you back,' he says.

'And me,' says Louisa. 'I was up at four too.'

So the gallant commando takes a lady on either arm, and they walk back up the road to the big house. The soldiers they pass on the way grin and say, 'Good work, chum!' and, 'Give a shout if you need help.'

They part by the porch.

'Corporal Kitty,' he says, saluting. 'Corporal Louisa.'

The girls return the salute.

'But we don't know your rank,' says Kitty.

'I think I'm a lieutenant or something,' he says. 'My firm isn't very big on ranks.'

'Can you really break people's necks?' says Louisa.

'Just like that,' he says, snapping his fingers.

Then he goes.

Kitty and Louisa enter the cloister and their eyes meet and they both burst out laughing.

'My God!' exclaims Louisa. 'He's a dream!'

'Squeezed until you're juicy? Honestly, Louisa!'

'Well, why not? There's a war on, isn't there? He's welcome to come round and lick me up any time he wants.'

'Louisa!'

'Don't sound so shocked. I saw you simpering away at him.'

'That's just how I am. I can't help myself.'

'Want to come into the mess?'

'No,' says Kitty. 'I really am bushed. I wasn't making it up.'

Alone in the attic nursery Kitty undresses slowly, thinking about the young commando officer. His grave amused face is printed clearly on her memory. Most of all she recalls the gaze of those wide-set blue eyes, that seemed to see her and not see her at the same time. For all his staring, she never felt he wanted something from her. There was no pleading there. Instead there was something else, something vulnerable but all his own, a kind of sadness. Those eyes say that he doesn't expect happiness to last. It's this, more than his good looks, that causes her to keep him in her thoughts right up to the moment she finally surrenders to sleep.

2

The rear wheel of the motorbike slews on the chalk slime of the farm track, making the engine race. Its rider swerves to regain traction and slows and leans in to the turn, swinging round the barn end into the farmyard. Chickens scatter, squawking, only to return as soon as the engine cuts out. This is the time that kitchen scraps are thrown out. There are crows waiting in the birches.

The rider pushes his goggles up and rubs at his eyes. The roads have been slick and dangerous all day, and he's thankful to be off his bike at last. Mary Funnell, the farmer's wife, opens the farmhouse door, one hand holding her apron hem, and calls to him, 'You've got a visitor.'

Larry Cornford pulls off his helmet to reveal a tumble of golden-brown curls. His broad friendly face looks round the yard, his eyes blinking. He sees an unfamiliar jeep.

'Thanks, Mary.'

The farmer's wife shakes out the contents of her apron and the chickens make a rush for the scraps. Larry pulls his satchel out of the motorbike's pannier and strides into the farmhouse kitchen, wondering who his visitor might be.

Rex Dickinson, the medic with whom he shares this billet, is sitting at the kitchen table, smoking his pipe and laughing uneasily. With his owl glasses and his long thin neck and his teetotalism Rex is always the butt of jokes, which he takes with patient good humour. Everyone likes Rex, if only because he wants so little for himself. He's so modest in his needs that he has to be reminded to use his own rations.

Facing Rex, dark against the bright rectangle of the kitchen window, is a lean figure Larry recognises at once.

'Eddy!'

Ed Avenell reaches out one lazy hand for Larry to grasp.

'This housemate of yours, Larry, has been putting me in the picture about divine providence.'

'Where in God's name have you sprung from?'

'Shanklin, Isle of Wight, since you ask.'

'This calls for a celebration! Mary, put out the cider.'

'Cider, eh?' says Ed.

'No, it's good. Home-made, with a kick like a mule.'

Larry stands beaming at his friend.

'This bastard,' he says to Rex, 'ruined the five best years of my life.'

'Oh, he's one of your lot, is he?' says Rex, meaning Catholics. He himself is the son of a Methodist minister. 'I should have guessed.'

'Don't put me in a box with him,' says Ed. 'Just because we went to the same school doesn't mean a thing. The monks never got to me.'

'Still protesting?' says Larry fondly. 'I swear, if Ed had been sent to a Marxist-atheist school, he'd be a monk himself by now.'

'You're the one who wanted to be a monk.'

This is true. Larry laughs to remember it. For a few heady months at the age of fifteen he had considered taking vows.

'Has Mary fed you? I'm starving. What are you doing here? What outfit are you in? What kind of uniform do you call that?'

The questions tumble out as Larry settles down to eat his delayed supper.

'I'm with 40 Royal Marine Commando,' says Ed.

'God, I bet you love that.'

'It gets me out of the army. I think I hate the army even more than I hated school.'

'It's still the army, though.'

'No. We do things our own way.'

'Same old Ed.'

'So how are you winning the war, Larry?'

'I'm liaison officer attached to First Division, Canadian Army, from Combined Operations headquarters.'

'Combined Ops? How did you get in with that mob?'

'My father knows Mountbatten. But I don't do anything interesting. I get a War Office-issue BSA M20 and a War Office-issue briefcase and I ride back and forth with top-secret papers telling the Canadians to carry out more exercises because basically there's sod all for them to do.'

'Tough job,' says Ed. 'You get any time to paint?'

'Some,' says Larry.

'First he wants to be a monk,' Ed says to Rex, 'then he wants to be an artist. He's always been a bit touched in the head.'

'No more than you,' protests Larry. 'What's this about joining the commandos? You want to die young?'

'Why not?'

'You're doing it because you want to give your life to the noblest cause you know.' Larry speaks firmly, pointing his fork at Ed, as if instructing a wayward child. 'And that's what monks do, and that's what artists do.'

'Seriously, Larry,' says Ed. 'You should have stuck with bananas.'

Larry bursts into laughter again; though in fact this is no joke. His father's firm imports bananas, with such success that it has achieved a virtual monopoly.

'So what are you doing here, you bandit?' he says.

'I've come to see you.'

'Is your journey really necessary?'

These days it takes real clout to wangle both a jeep and the petrol to run it.

'I've got an understanding CO,' says Ed.

'Will you bunk here tonight?'

'No, no. I'll be on the road back by ten. But listen here, Larry. I was trying to track you down, so I stopped at the pub in the village. And guess what happened?'

'He's been struck by a thunderbolt,' says Rex. 'Like St Paul on the road to Damascus. He was telling me.'

This is Rex's dry humour.

'I met this girl,' says Ed.

'Oh,' says Larry. 'A girl.'

'I have to see her again. If I don't, I'll die.'

'You want to die anyway.'

'I want to see her again first.'

'So who is she?'

'She says she's an ATS driver from the camp.'

'Those ATS girls get around.'

Arthur Funnell appears in the doorway, his shoulders slumped, his face wearing its habitual expression of doom.

'Any of you gents seen a weather forecast?' he says. 'If it's more rain, I don't want to know, because I've had enough and that's the truth.'

'Sunny tomorrow, Arthur,' says Larry. 'Back into the seventies.'

'For how long?'

'That I can't tell you.'

'I need a week's sunshine, you tell 'em, or the hay'll rot.'

'I'll tell them,' says Larry.

The farmer departs.

'He wants help bringing the hay in,' says Rex. 'He was telling me earlier.'

'He should get himself some Canucks,' says Larry. 'They're all farm boys. They're bored to death in the camp.'

'Who cares about the hay?' says Ed. 'What am I going to do about this girl?'

Larry pulls out a pack of cigarettes and offers one to Ed.

'Here. Canadian, but not bad.'

33

They're called Sweet Caporal. Rex lights up his pipe as Larry pulls gratefully on his after-dinner cigarette.

'I'm stuck in bloody Shanklin,' says Ed. 'There's no way I can get back over here till the weekend.'

'So see her at the weekend.'

'She could be married by then.'

'Hey!' exclaims Larry. 'She really has got to you, hasn't she?'

'How about you find her for me? Give her a message. You're the liaison officer. Do some bloody liaising.'

'I could try,' says Larry. 'What's her name?'

'Corporal Kitty. She's a staff driver.'

'What's the message?'

'Come to Sunday lunch. Here at your billet. You don't mind, do you? And the other girl can come too. The horsey one.'

'How's she horsey?'

'Looks like a horse.'

He stubs out the last of his cigarette. He's smoked it twice as fast as Larry.

'Quite decent,' he says.

'So who's laying on the lunch?' says Larry.

'You are,' says Ed. 'You're the one billeted on a farm. And Rex too. I'm issuing a general invitation.'

'Very big of you,' says Larry.

'I'll be out on Sunday,' says Rex.

'Sunday your big day, is it, Rex?' says Ed.

'I help out here and there,' says Rex.

'I'll do my best,' says Larry. 'How do I reach you?'

'You don't. I'll just show up here, noon Sunday. You produce Kitty. But no sticky fingers in the till. I saw her first.'

Next morning a pale sun rises as promised, and by eight o'clock a mist hangs over the water meadows. Larry rides his motorbike the short distance to the big house with his helmet off, wanting to enjoy the arrival of summer at last. Soldiers in the camp, stripped to the waist, are playing a raucous game of volleyball. The pale stone towers of Edenfield Place gleam in the sun.

On such a day before the war he would have tramped off alone up the Downs, carrying an easel and a fresh canvas, a box of paints and a picnic, and painted till dusk: precious empty days, few enough but intense in memory, when the world simplified before him to the play of light on form. Now like everyone else his time is filled with the tedium and pettiness of war. The cause may be great, but the life is diminished.

He leaves his bike in front of the house and goes through to the galleried hall. The first person he meets coming down the sweeping staircase, taking the steps two at a time, is Johnny Parrish.

'We're running late,' says Parrish. 'CO's morning briefing's now at 0830.'

'Not like Woody to run late.'

'Bobby Parks is joining us. He's one of your lot, isn't he?'

Parks is in Intelligence at Combined Ops. Larry has

not been told he's coming, but this is par for the course. Communication between the various branches of the organisation is erratic at best.

He checks his watch. He has a good fifteen minutes.

'I'll go and find the ATS drivers.'

'Motor Transport Office in A Block. Who are you after?'

'Corporal Kitty. I don't know the rest of her name.'

'Oh, Kitty.' Parrish raises his bushy eyebrows. 'We're all after her.'

'Just passing on a message for a friend.'

'Well, you can tell your friend,' says Parrish, 'that Kitty has a boyfriend in the navy, and if, God forbid, her sailor buys it one day, an orderly queue will form at her door, and your friend can go to the end.'

'Righto,' says Larry cheerfully.

Captain Parrish goes into the dining room where breakfast is laid out for senior staff. Larry makes his way down the passage past the organ room to the garden door. Outside there's a wide stone-paved terrace enclosed by a low stone balustrade. This terrace is raised above a second grass terrace, which in turn is raised above the extensive park. An avenue of lime trees crosses the park, leading to an ornamental lake. On either side of the avenue, laid out in grid formation between the lake and the house, lie row upon row of Nissen huts.

Larry pauses to admire the camp. The anonymous engineer who devised its plan has instinctively worked to counterpoise the neo-Gothic riot that is the big house. The camp is a modernist vision of order. Military discipline asserts control over the mess of life. What can be made straight is made straight.

He passes down the stone steps to camp level. A soldier heading for the ablutions huts gives him a grin and a wave. Larry is still new as liaison officer to the division, but the Royal Hamilton Light Infantry are a friendly crowd, and seem to have accepted him. Johnny Parrish calls him their 'native guide'.

The door to the transport office stands open. Inside, two ATS girls are drinking tea in their shirtsleeves. One is stocky and red-faced. The other is tall and blonde, with a long face that might be called 'horsey'.

Larry says, 'I'm looking for Kitty.'

'Who wants her?' says the horsey girl.

'Just delivering a message. Purely social. From a friend she met in the pub last night.'

'The commando?'

'Yes.'

The horsey girl's manner changes. She throws a glance at the red-faced girl.

'What did I say?' Then to Larry, 'She's in the lake house.'

'Thanks.'

He needs no directions to the lake house. It's a shingle-roofed hexagonal wooden structure built out over the water, linked to the shore by a jetty. The jetty is roped off, and a sign on the rope reads: *Out of bounds to all ranks*.

He steps over the rope and crosses the jetty to tap softly on the closed door. Getting no answer, he opens the door.

37

There, seated on the floor with a book resting in her lap, is a very pretty young woman in uniform.

'Are you Kitty?' he says.

'For God's sake shut the door,' she says. 'I'm hiding.'

He comes in and shuts the door.

'Down,' she says. 'They can see you.'

He drops down to sit on the floor, below the level of the windows. All he has to do now is pass on his message and leave. Instead, he finds himself taking in every detail of this moment. The moving patterns on the walls thrown by sunlight reflected from the surface of the lake. The folds of her brown uniform jacket, discarded on the floor. The pebbled leather of her shoes. The way her body is curled, legs tucked beneath her and to one side. Her hand resting on the book.

The book is *Middlemarch*.

'That's a wonderful book.'

She looks at him in surprise. He realises that what has felt to him like a slow passage of time, within which he has come to know her well, has in reality been no more than a second or two, and he doesn't know her at all.

'Who told you I was here?' she says.

'The girls in the office.'

'What do you want?'

'I'm just passing on a message. You met a friend of mine in the pub, yesterday evening.'

'The commando?'

'He wants to ask you to lunch on Sunday.'

'Oh.' She wrinkles her brow. He watches her, but all he

can think is how lovely she is. How he wants her to see him properly.

'Do you like it?' he says.

'What?'

'*Middlemarch.*'

'Yes,' she says. 'I didn't at first.'

'I suppose you find Dorothea a bit much.'

'Excuse me,' she says, 'but who exactly are you?'

'Larry Cornford. Liaison officer attached to Eighth Infantry.'

He holds out his hand. She shakes it, half-smiling at the formality. Smiling at the whole strange meeting.

'What on earth is she doing marrying Mr Casaubon?' she says. 'Anyone can see it's a really stupid idea.'

'Well, of course it is,' says Larry. 'But she's idealistic. She wants to do something noble and fine with her life.'

'She's a nincompoop,' says Kitty.

'Don't you want to do something noble and fine with your life?'

He can't help himself speaking as if they're on intimate terms. It just feels that way to him.

'Not particularly,' she says.

But her sweet face, those big brown eyes exploring him, puzzling over him, tell him otherwise.

'I don't expect you'll be an army driver for the rest of your life,' he says.

'Actually I love driving.' And then, briskly, aware that this is heading into uncharted waters, 'So what's this lunch?'

'Sunday. About twelve? The farm behind the church. It's

where I'm billeted. Ed says bring your friend too. The blonde one.'

He manages not to say the 'horsey one'.

'If it's a farm, does that mean real food?'

'Absolutely.'

'Then we accept.'

'Right. Message delivered.' He rises. 'I shall leave you with Dorothea.'

Striding briskly back across the camp to the big house, anxious not to be late for the CO's morning meeting, Larry is aware of a new sensation. He feels light of body, light of heart. It seems to him that nothing really matters very much at all. Not his senior officers, not the war, not the turning of the whole great world. He tells himself it's the morning sunshine after weeks of rain. He tells himself it's no more than natural animal spirits inspired by the smile of a pretty girl. But he can still see that smile before him in his mind's eye. She's sharing with him the oddity that two strangers should be crouched on the floor of a lake house in wartime, discussing a nineteenth-century novel. She's trying to make him out. That wrinkle between her eyebrows asks: what sort of person are you? Her smile so much more than a smile.

As is his habit, his mind reaches for comparisons in art. Renoir's smudgy pink-cheeked girl reading a book, smiling to herself. But Kitty's smile wasn't private; nor was it provocative, like a hundred faux-innocent Venuses. She smiles to lay a courteous veil over an active curiosity. There's a painting like it by Ingres, of Louise de Broglie, gazing, head a little tilted, one finger to her cheek, daring the viewer to know her.

'Buck up,' says Johnny Parrish.

Larry hurries into the library, which is already noisy with the chatter of officers. Brigadier Wills arrives and the meeting begins. Most of it concerns the lessons to be learned from yesterday's exercise. Larry, perched on a window shelf at the back, allows his mind to drift.

He thinks of the library in his father's house in Kensington; far smaller than this grand open-roofed hall, but sharing the magic of all libraries, which is that the books on their shelves open onto infinite space. He came every evening in the school holidays to join his father in prayers in the library, which gave it something of the mystery of a church. He has almost no memory of his mother, who is in heaven, and therefore inescapably confused with the Mother of God. It came as a shock to him to discover when he was sent away to school that the Blessed Virgin cared for other children as well.

Our Lady, hear my prayer. St Lawrence, hear my prayer.

St Lawrence is his own saint, the third-century martyr who was roasted to death on a grid-iron, saying apocryphally, 'Turn me over, I'm cooked on this side.' There was fun with that at school.

Larry prays often, from long habit, inattentively. It has become the manner in which he expresses his desires. This despite the fact that at Downside the subtle monks taught him a wiser notion of prayer. Its object is not to seek God's intervention in our favour, but to align ourselves with God's

41

will for us. Perhaps even – Larry has been especially drawn to this – to relieve us of self-will altogether. Dom Ambrose, the same monk who taught him to love George Eliot, was a devoted follower of Jean-Pierre de Caussade. The eighteenth-century Jesuit preached abandonment to the will of God within the sacrament of the present moment. Père de Caussade's prayer was 'Lord have pity on me. With you all things are possible.'

Lord have pity on me, prays Larry. Find me a girl like Kitty.

3

Ed Avenell shows up at River Farm early on Sunday morning, and by the time Larry gets up he finds Mary Funnell is eating out of his hands.

'Mary, sweet Mary,' he's saying to her, 'do you dance, Mary? Of course you do. I can always tell a girl who has dancing feet.'

He spins her round the kitchen table, bringing her back pink-faced and flustered to the draining board where she's been washing dishes.

'You'd dance the night away if you could.'

'What a terrible man your friend is,' Mary Funnell says to Larry. 'The things he says to me.'

'I'm buying your love, Mary,' says Ed. 'I'll say almost anything for a hard-boiled egg.'

Larry marvels to see Ed's charm operating at full throttle. The wonder of it is he tells nothing but the unvarnished truth, and yet he so manages it that the lonely and overworked farmer's wife feels he understands her and respects her.

The results are to be seen in the basket she is assembling for their lunch. Ed has decided it is to be a picnic. He now heads off to recce its location.

'You sort out the crockery, Larry. And don't forget glasses.'

By the time Kitty and Louisa come bicycling into the farmyard in their summer frocks, the war seems a thousand miles away. Ed reappears, and treats Kitty with an offhand friendliness, as if they have known each other for years.

'Larry, you take the basket. I'll take the box.'

'What am I to carry?' says Kitty.

'You can carry the rug if you like.'

Ed's plan is that they picnic in the copse above the nearby village of Glynde, on the flank of Mount Caburn. Kitty sits in the front of his jeep, with Larry and Louisa behind.

'You get your own jeep?' says Kitty.

'Not exactly,' says Ed. 'But in our outfit the idea is we use our initiative.'

'He's stolen it,' says Larry.

'What exactly is your outfit?' says Louisa.

'40 Royal Marine Commando,' says Ed.

'I've heard that name.' Kitty frowns, trying to recall where.

'Kitty drives the Brig,' says Louisa. 'She hears everything.'

'Is your CO called Phillips?'

'Joe Phillips, yes. How do you know that?'

'I must have had him in the back of the car. Does that mean your lot are part of the big show that's coming up?'

Ed laughs and glances back at Larry.

44

'What price security, eh?'

'Oh, save your breath,' says Louisa. 'Even the dumb Canucks know it's coming.'

Ed drives the jeep off the road up rising land into a wood, and stops on the far side. Here a small clearing in the trees opens out to the east, giving a wide view of the Sussex plain. The fields, not yet harvested, lie brown and gold in the midday sun. Here and there the faded red of tiled roofs reveal a village.

Larry spreads the rug over the ground, and Kitty and Louisa unpack the picnic, exclaiming at the discovery of each new delight.

'Tomatoes! Hard-boiled eggs! Oh my God, I'm in heaven! Is this home-made bread? Look, Louisa! Real butter!'

Ed opens the flagon of cider and pours them all a glass. He proposes a toast.

'To luck,' he says.

Larry keeps looking at Kitty, and each time he looks he sees that her eyes are on Ed. He makes an effort to take control of his own foolishness. This entire picnic has been got up, after all, to give Ed a clear run at Kitty. As Ed's friend his duty is to pay attention to Louisa.

'Do you believe in luck?' he says to her.

'Not really,' she says. 'I'm not sure what I believe in. Does everyone have to believe in something?'

'You don't have to,' says Larry, 'but I think you do, whether you realise it or not. Even Ed.'

Ed has taken out a scary-looking long-bladed knife and starts cutting slices off the loaf.

45

'I believe in luck,' he says. 'And I believe in impulse. And I believe in glory.'

'What does that mean?' says Kitty.

'It means you do what you feel like, when you feel it. No fear, no shame, no hesitation. Live your life like an arrow in flight. Strike hard, strike deep.'

He strikes the loaf hard and deep.

'Good heavens!' says Kitty. 'How thrillingly single-minded.'

Her words are teasing, but her eyes shine.

'That is classic Ed tommyrot,' says Larry. 'Who wants to be an arrow?'

Louisa gathers up the chunks of bread as they fall.

'Do you mind if I start eating?' she says. 'I feel like I haven't eaten for at least a year.'

They all set to, getting their fingers messy with butter and tomato pulp, forming their bread into thick ragged sandwiches. Kitty takes on the job of peeling the hard-boiled eggs. Larry watches her, seeing the care with which she manages to remove the shell in large sections.

'You look as if you've done that before,' Ed says.

'I like peeling eggs,' says Kitty. 'I hate it when people take the shells off roughly, just smashing them into tiny pieces. How would you like to be undressed like that?'

She looks up and sees Ed's eyes on her, silently amused. She blushes. Ed takes one of the unpeeled eggs and says, 'Can anyone make this stand on one end?'

'Oh, that's Columbus's trick,' says Louisa. 'You just bash its bottom in.'

'No,' says Ed. 'No bashing.'

He scoops a little hollow in the earth and stands the egg upright in it.

'That's cheating,' says Kitty. 'You have to make it stand on a flat surface.'

'Only according to your rules,' says Ed. 'There's nothing about a flat surface in my rules.'

'Anyone can win if they make up their own rules.'

'So there's the moral,' says Ed. 'Always play by your own rules.'

Now he's looking at Kitty in a way that makes her shiver.

'I think you must be quite a ruthless person,' she says.

'Don't tell him that,' says Larry. 'You're just feeding his fantasy. He'll go on about impulse and glory again. Ed's always been rotten with romanticism. I expect that's why he joined the commandos. The lone warrior who kills without a sound and cares nothing for his own life.'

Ed laughs, not offended.

'More like a bunch of oddballs who can't fit in with the rest of the army,' he says.

'But don't you have to be tremendously tough?' says Louisa.

'Not really,' says Ed. 'Just a little crazy.'

Kitty looks at Ed most of the time because most of the time he seems not to be looking at her. She sees the small impatient movements he makes, the jerk of his head with which he flicks back the dark hair out of his eyes, the opening and closing of his hands as if he's grasping the air, or perhaps letting it go. He has long, delicate, almost feminine fingers.

His complexion too is pale and girlish. And yet there's nothing soft about him, he feels as if he's made of taut wire; and every time those blue eyes turn on her his gaze hits her like a splash of cold water.

He says odd things in a straight way, his voice giving no clues. She can't tell when he's joking or serious. She feels out of her depth with him. She wants to touch the cool pale skin of his cheek. She wants to feel his arms pulling her towards him. She wants him to want her.

'That egg story,' Larry says. 'Columbus didn't make it up at all. Years before Columbus, Brunelleschi pulled the same trick, when asked to present a model for his design for the duomo in Florence. According to Vasari, at least.'

This is met by silence.

'Larry, as you can tell,' says Ed, 'was actually listening during class.'

Larry pulls a face to show he's a good sport, but in truth he's not having a good time. He's doing his best not to look at Kitty because every time he does so he's swept by a wave of longing. He watches Ed, so lean and debonair and at ease with himself, and he knows he has none of his effort-less style. He can only look on in awe at the careless charm with which he is all too visibly fascinating Kitty. His own freckled face gives him away at every turn, wrinkling with earnest eagerness when he talks, smoothing out when under-stood into a grateful smile.

'I've always wanted to see Florence,' says Kitty.

'Rather you than me,' says Louisa. 'Art gives me a headache.'

'Don't say that to Larry,' says Ed. 'He wants to be an artist when he grows up.'

'And what do you want to be?' says Louisa.

'Oh, I shan't ever grow up.'

'Ed will succeed at whatever he turns his hand to,' says Larry. 'He can't help it. He's loved by the gods.'

Ed grins and tosses a fragment of bread at him.

'Those whom the gods love,' he says, 'die young.'

After they've eaten and drunk, Louisa takes out her box Brownie and makes them pose for a photograph.

'Kitty, you in the middle.'

'I hate being photographed,' says Kitty.

'That's because you're vain,' says Louisa. 'Be like Ed. He doesn't care.'

Ed is sitting by Kitty's side, his arms round his knees, his blue eyes gazing unseeingly into the distance. His shoulder touches Kitty's arm, but he seems not to be aware of it. Larry places himself on Kitty's other side, cross-legged, his hands on the rug behind him.

'Smile, Larry,' says Louisa.

Larry smiles. The shutter clicks. Louisa winds the film on.

'Oh, bother. That's the last one.'

'But we have to get you too,' says Kitty.

'There's no film left.'

'We'll make a memory instead,' says Ed.

They all look at him in surprise.

'What do you mean?' says Kitty.

'Oh, I don't know,' says Ed. 'Stand on our heads. Howl at the moon.'

'Kitty could sing for us,' says Louisa. 'She's got an amazing voice. She used to sing solos in her church choir.'

Ed fixes Kitty with a sudden intent gaze.

'Yes,' he says. 'Kitty can sing for us.'

Kitty blushes.

'You don't want to hear me sing.'

Ed raises one hand, as if it's a vote. He's still got his eyes fixed on Kitty. Larry raises his hand. So does Louisa.

'It's unanimous,' says Ed. 'Now you have to.'

'There's no accompaniment,' protests Kitty. 'I can't sing unaccompanied.'

'Yes, you can,' says Louisa. 'I've heard you.'

'Well, I can't sing with you all staring at me.'

'We'll close our eyes,' says Larry.

'I won't,' says Ed.

'It's all right,' says Kitty. 'I'll close mine.'

So she gets to her feet and stands there for a moment, collecting herself. The others watch her in silence, suddenly aware that for Kitty this is a serious matter.

Then she closes her eyes and sings.

> The water is wide
> I cannot cross o'er
> And neither have I
> The wings to fly.
> Build me a boat
> That can carry two
> And both shall row,
> My true love and I.

Her voice is high and pure and true. Larry looks from her to Ed and sees on his friend's face a look he's never seen before. So that's it, he tells himself. Ed's in love.

A ship there is
And she sails the seas.
She's laden deep
As deep can be;
But not so deep
As the love I'm in,
And I know not if
I sink or swim.

Then like one waking from a dream Kitty opens her eyes and takes in Ed's watching gaze. He holds her eyes and says nothing. She lifts her shoulders in a shrug of apology.

'That's all I can remember.'

'I think perhaps you're an angel,' says Ed.

'I'd just as soon not be,' says Kitty.

Later they lie on their backs on the rug, partly in sun and partly in shade, and gaze up at the summer sky. Isolated clouds go by, like sailing ships scudding slowly in the breeze. A single aircraft, high above, whines towards London.

'I'm sick of this war,' says Louisa. 'The world was so beautiful before. Now everything's so ugly.'

'What were you doing before the war, Louisa?'

'Oh, nothing. I came out in '39, the way you do. It was all very silly, I suppose. At the time I didn't like it really, being dressed up like a parcel and made to smile at dull little men. But now it seems to me it was heaven.'

'I'm grateful for the war,' says Larry. 'It's saved me from a life in bananas.'

That makes them laugh.

'It's not over yet,' says Ed. 'The bananas may get you yet.'

Kitty wants to know about the bananas. Larry tells her how his grandfather, the Lawrence Cornford after whom he's named, built up Elders & Fyffes, and invented the blue label stuck on bananas, and was the first to advertise fruit, and was known as the 'banana king'.

'When the Great War came along we had sixteen ships, and my grandfather was called in by the First Sea Lord to help with the war effort. He said, "My fleet is at the disposal of my country." The First Sea Lord was Prince Louis of Battenberg, Mountbatten's father. Which is why I'm in Combined Ops now.'

'The long arm of the banana,' says Ed.

'I think it sounds like a wonderful business,' says Kitty.

'Well, everyone laughs when you say it's bananas,' says Larry, 'but actually places like Jamaica depend on the banana trade. And this blue label thing really was quite revolutionary in its day. No one believed you could brand fruit until my grandfather did it. It was a tremendous struggle finding the right sort of gum, and persuading the packers to stick the labels on. But my grandfather said, "Our bananas are the best, and when people realise that, they'll look for the blue label." And they did.'

'Now his dad runs the company,' says Ed. 'Guess who's next.'

'Unfortunately I'm a bit of a disappointment to my father,' says Larry.

'Isn't there a banana called Cavendish?' says Louisa.

'Absolutely,' says Larry. 'The Duke of Devonshire grew it in Paxton's conservatory at Chatsworth.'

'I'm a sort of cousin,' says Louisa.

'Then you should be very proud. My grandfather began the business shipping Cavendishes from the Canaries.'

'Why are you a disappointment to your father, Larry?' Kitty asks.

'Oh, because I want to be an artist. Dad was rather hoping I'd follow him into the firm. But mostly he's just afraid I won't be able to make a living.'

'Larry's good,' says Ed.

'You haven't seen anything of mine since school.'

'So? You were good then. I say follow your dream.'

'Impulse and glory, eh, Ed?'

'Strike hard, strike deep.'

His words hang lazily in the air above them, softened by the laconic tone.

Because Ed has been kind about his art, and because he's his best friend, and because it's going to happen anyway, Larry decides to be a good sport. Anything to put a stop to this ridiculous hankering feeling.

'Why don't you show Kitty Mount Caburn, Ed? Me and Louisa can stay here and talk about Cavendishes.'

'I've seen Mount Caburn,' says Kitty.

'You have to climb up to the top,' says Larry. 'Then you'll see a whole lot more.'

Ed gets up.

'Come on, then,' he says to Kitty. 'Ours not to reason why.'

Kitty gets up obediently.

'Well, all right,' she says. 'If I must.'

They set off together across the rising flank of the Downs.

'What was that all about?' says Louisa when they're out of earshot.

'Ed's stuck on her,' says Larry. 'He needs a shot at her on his own.'

'So kind Uncle Larry arranges it for him.'

Larry can tell from Louisa's voice that she understands precisely what he's done and why.

'I'd rather be kind Uncle Larry than sulk in a corner,' he says.

'Good for you,' says Louisa. 'I hope he realises.'

Larry sighs.

'Yes. He knows.'

They lie in silence for a while. Then Louisa sits up and wraps her arms round her knees and looks down at Larry.

'You seem a good sort,' she says.

'I am,' says Larry. 'Worse luck.'

'So I suppose you're in love with Kitty too.'

'Should I be?'

'It's just that everyone else is. I don't see why you should be any different.'

'Well, then.'

'She's a good sort too, actually. It's not as if she can help it. She told me she's had seven proposals. Seven!'

'And she still hasn't said yes.'

'Not so far.'

'I wonder what she's waiting for.'

'God knows. If you ask me she wants someone to make up her mind for her. You could just carry her off.'

Larry laughs at that.

'Ed would kill me,' he says. 'He did see her first.'

'Oh God, so what? All's fair and so on. But let's not talk about Kitty. She gets so much attention sometimes it makes me feel quite ill. And anyway, I've got a question to ask you.'

'Ask away.'

'How can I get George Holland to marry me?'

Larry bursts into laughter.

'Have you tried just asking him?'

'Girls can't do that.'

'Do you think he'd say yes if you did?'

'Put it this way. I think I'd make a jolly good wife for him, and he should be jolly grateful. But I don't think he knows it yet.'

'Well,' says Larry after a moment's thought, 'you could pretend to think he's proposed to you. Then you could accept. And by the time you've done accepting he'll think he must have proposed.'

Louisa gazes at Larry with a new respect.

'That,' she says, 'is brilliant advice.'

'Not my idea,' says Larry. 'Tolstoy's, in *War and Peace*.'

★

Kitty follows Ed up the long grassy slope, picking her way through the piles of sheep droppings. He strides ahead of her, not looking back, leaving her to follow at her own pace. She doesn't mind. Watching his lean powerful body climb the hill, she understands that his single-mindedness is in his nature, and nothing to do with her. He sees a hill to be climbed and he climbs it. This leaves her free, unburdened by her habitual impulse to please.

When he reaches the long flat approach to the top he stops and waits for her. Ahead the circular ridges of the old Iron Age fort ring the summit.

'Bit of a scramble here,' he says. 'You might need some help.'

He holds her hand as they descend into the wide grassy ditch, and supports her on the steep climb up the other side. His hand is warm and dry and very strong. As they reach the shallow dome of the summit he lets go of her and spreads his arms at the view.

'There!' he says, as if the view is his gift to her.

That makes her laugh.

Southward below them the river winds past the sprawling village of Edenfield to the distant sea. Kitty gazes down as if from an aeroplane. She sees the Canadian Army camp drawn up in its ranked rows in the park, and the shine of the lake, and the spikes and towers of Edenfield Place. Seen from this distance her little world seems to dwindle into nothingness. There's a wind up here on the top of the Downs, it flurries her hair and makes her eyes water.

'You see over there,' says Ed, 'where the river meets the sea. That's a haven.'

'Newhaven,' says Kitty.

She gazes at the harbour of the little port, and the long embracing arm of its pier.

'I like the idea of a haven,' says Ed. 'The river always running, running. And then at last it meets the sea, and can rest.'

'I've never thought of the sea as restful,' says Kitty. She's touched by his words. 'But haven does rather sound like heaven, doesn't it?'

She looks up. The sky above is big and bare and frightening.

'Heaven's too far away,' he says.

'It makes me feel like I don't matter at all,' she says.

She looks down again. He's gazing at her with that perpetual half-smile.

'You don't matter. None of us matter. So what?'

'I don't know.' His smile confuses her. 'You want to feel you're some use, don't you?'

He doesn't answer this. Instead he reaches out one hand and gently pushes the hair away from her face.

'You're a lovely angel, Kitty,' he says.

'Am I?'

'I'm not what you think I am.'

'What do I think you are?'

'Single-minded. Ruthless.'

She's flattered that he's remembered her words. At the time he seemed hardly to hear.

'So it's all just an act, is it?'

'No,' he says. 'It's true enough. It's just not everything.'

'So what else are you?'

'Restless,' he says. 'Alone.'

Kitty has a sensation of falling. She wants to reach out to him. She's overwhelmed by the simple desire to hold him in her arms.

'Stupid thing to say,' he says. 'I don't know why I said it.'

'It's a terrible thing to say.'

'Yes, it is terrible. There are times when I feel terror. Doesn't everyone?'

'I expect so,' says Kitty.

'But we don't talk about it, do we?'

'No,' she says.

'In case it wins.'

'Yes.'

'Will you kiss me?'

He means, if you kiss me the terror won't win. If you kiss me, we won't be alone any more.

'If you want,' she says.

He draws her into his arms and they kiss, wind-blown on the top of Mount Caburn, beneath the infinite emptiness of the sky.

4

Opposite Downing Street, across Whitehall, a short but grand street named Richmond Terrace runs down to the river. The entrance to 1A Richmond Terrace, a handsome doorway into a ponderous stone building, is neither identified nor guarded. This is the headquarters of Combined Operations, a warren of overcrowded offices that are always bustling with activity. Officers from all three services stride purposefully down basement corridors, past unmarked doors where unnamed teams are at work on secret schemes to win the war. Combined Operations was formed to develop amphibious assaults, bringing together sections of Army, Navy and Air Force. The ethos is non-hierarchical. The head of Intelligence, a one-time racing driver, was until recently managing the Curzon Cinema in Mayfair. Organisations have a way of reflecting the personality of their leaders, and this is supremely so in this case. Its chief, appointed by Churchill personally, is Vice-Admiral Lord Louis Mountbatten, known to all as Dickie. When Churchill offered him the job, Mountbatten initially declined, wishing to stay in the navy. 'Have you no sense of glory?' Churchill thundered.

Dickie Mountbatten has a sense of glory. Direct in all his dealings, handsome, charming, with a strong streak of the maverick, he has set about building an organisation that is free-thinking, innovative, and above all, informal. He has brought in friends, and friends of friends, who are known collectively as the Dickie Birds. Staff numbers have grown from twenty-three on his appointment to over four hundred.

A chance encounter between Lord Mountbatten and William Cornford at a club led to an invitation to Larry to present himself at Richmond Terrace in early March. There, as is the way of these things, Larry was greeted by someone who had been in his house at school, in the year above him: a beak-nosed, prematurely balding young man called Rupert Blundell.

'Cornford, isn't it? You thinking of joining us?'

'That seems to be the general idea.'

'You know what they call this place? HMS Wimbledon. All rackets and balls. But don't let that put you off.'

The interview with Lord Mountbatten, which Larry supposed would explore his own very limited war record, was entirely taken up with memories of his grandfather.

'Lawrence Cornford was a fine man,' said Mountbatten. 'My father thought highly of him. My father was First Sea Lord at the time, but when the war came, the Great War, they pushed him out because he had a German name. Disgraceful business. Even the King had to scuttle about and bodge himself up an English name. If my father was German, so was the entire royal family. It was Asquith behind it, he was a total shit. Though Winston comes out of it pretty poorly, too. He was at the Admiralty back then; he could have stopped that nonsense. I was a naval cadet at Osborne when it happened, fourteen years old. It was quite a blow, I can tell you. But anyway, your grandfather, the banana king, wrote a letter to *The Times* deploring the decision. "Have we so many great men," he wrote, "that we can afford to lose one because his name is not Smith or Jones? If Great Britain is to remain great, we need leaders of the stature of Prince Louis of Battenberg." My father appreciated that very much. So you're looking for a change of scenery, are you? Well, we're an odd bunch. The only lunatic asylum in the world run by its own inmates. But if I've got anything to do with it we should have some fun.'

This was the extent of it. Larry learned he was seconded to Combined Ops, and duly reported to Richmond Terrace. Rupert Blundell took him under his wing.

'Any idea what you're supposed to be doing?'

'None whatever,' said Larry.

'Something'll come up,' said Rupert. 'Inertia, crisis, panic, exhaustion. The four phases of military planning.'

He carried Larry off to a dungeon-like basement room which was fitted out as a canteen. Here over mugs of tea they swapped memories of schooldays.

'Of course I hated every minute of it,' said Rupert, the steam from his mug of tea misting his glasses. 'But as far as I can tell that's the point of school.'

'I rather liked it,' said Larry. 'It was more fun than life at home, I can tell you.'

'Fun?' Rupert shook his head, bemused. 'I expect it's me that's the problem. I've never been much of a one for fun.'

'You were a brainbox,' said Larry. 'We were all in awe of you.'

He could picture Rupert Blundell from those long-ago schooldays, moving rapidly down the long corridors, keeping close to the wall, books under one arm, murmuring to himself. Spindly, bespectacled, alone.

He found himself wondering what Rupert was doing in Combined Ops. He couldn't imagine this unworldly figure leading an amphibious assault.

'Oh, we're all cranks and Communists in COHQ,' Rupert told him. 'Solly Zuckerman roped me in to do what he calls thinking the unthinkable. I'm supposed to come up with wacky ideas that challenge the conventional military approach. Could it be done other ways? Is the price worth the cost? Keeping an eye on the bigger picture, and so forth.'

Larry's period of idleness did not last long. General Eisenhower arrived in London charged with planning the invasion of Europe, and began by calling for a probe of Nazi Europe's defences. No full-scale invasion could function without a port. A raid was planned that was designed to discover whether a major French port could be captured in working order.

At a meeting of the chiefs of staff Eisenhower emphasised the need to find the right commander for this 'reconnaissance in force'.

'I have heard,' he said, 'that Admiral Mountbatten is vigorous, intelligent and courageous. If the operation is to be staged with British forces predominating, I assume he could do the job.'

Mountbatten, who Eisenhower had not met before, was sitting across the table as he spoke. This was the beginning of an excellent working relationship. The planned raid was code-named Operation Rutter.

Mountbatten's intention was to use a combination of marines and commandos for Operation Rutter. However, the War Cabinet had become increasingly embarrassed over the Canadian troops stationed in England. For two years now an entire Canadian Army had been training and waiting. The Canadian press was agitating for their boys to be given some real fighting. So Mountbatten was ordered to expand the scale of Rutter, and make it a Canadian show.

The raid depended on absolute secrecy and surprise for its success. All information between Combined Ops in London and the Canadian forces encamped on the south coast had to be carried by hand. In this way, Larry found himself with a function.

On the last day of June 1942 Larry enters the main Ops Room as instructed, to find a heated discussion under way. The room is crowded, the key officers clustered round a table on which is spread a large map of the French coast. Rupert Blundell is making himself useful laying out a sequence of aerial photographs.

'I don't understand,' Mountbatten is saying. 'We asked for bomber strikes. Winston signed up for bomber strikes.'

'Scratched,' says the RAF man. 'Meeting of June the tenth. I've got the minutes somewhere.'

'Scratched?'

'Roberts didn't like it,' says the army man. 'Doesn't want bomb damage blocking the advance of his new tanks.'

'Leigh-Mallory said the target was too small,' says the RAF man.

Mountbatten looks disconcerted.

'Where was I when all this was decided?'

'You were in Washington, Dickie,' says Peter Murphy.

'How many battleships have we got? We have to soften them up somehow.'

'No battleships,' says the navy man. 'Dudley Pound vetoes battleships off the French coast in daylight. Says it's utter madness.'

'So what have we got?'

'Hunt-class destroyers.'

'Destroyers?'

'And,' says the army man, 'one hell of a lot of Canadians.'

Larry feels he shouldn't be hearing this. He moves forward just as Rupert Blundell moves back.

'I was told to pick up a packet for Div HQ,' he says in a whisper.

Blundell looks round his colleagues.

'Orders for Div HQ?' he says to no one in particular.

Bobby Casa Maury, Head of Intelligence, sees Larry by

the doorway and frowns. He speaks low to Mountbatten.
Mountbatten looks up and recognises Larry.

'One of ours,' he says. He returns to the map. 'What's
the story on air support?'

'Full pack there,' says the RAF man. 'Should be the biggest
show of the war.'

'Excellent,' says Mountbatten, cheering up. 'Control the
air and the battle's half won.'

Bobby Casa Maury catches Larry's eye and waves one
hand, palm downwards, fingers flicking forwards, in a
gesture that means go away. Larry withdraws.

In the hallway outside a Wren called Joyce Wedderburn
sits at a desk with a typewriter and two telephones, guarding
entrance to the chief. She gives Larry a friendly smile as he
sits himself down on one of the upright chairs that line the
long wall.

'Back to waiting?' she says. 'Want a cup of tea?'

'No, thanks,' says Larry. 'Shouldn't be long.'

He finds himself thinking how much better it would be
if there were pictures on the walls. So much of wartime
consists of sitting, waiting, staring at blank walls. Why not
get all the artists painting, and hang all their pictures on all
the walls? Even if you don't like a picture you can stare at
it and see everything that's wrong with it, which passes the
time. All it would take would be for someone like
Mountbatten to give the order, and all over the country
armies of artists would set to work doing watercolours of
sunsets, and army canteens and ministry corridors would

take on a new eccentric character. Put a picture on a wall and you cut a window into another world.

From this he falls to thinking of all the paintings he knows which represent actual windows, and the view beyond. Leonardo's *Madonna of the Carnation*, which he saw once in Munich, with its view of mountains framed by arched openings. Or Magritte's strange broken windows, where the fragments of glass carry the same sunset sky as the view beyond, but fractured and displaced. The effect of the frame within the frame is potent, almost magical. What is it about windows? The comfort and safety of the known world set beside the promise and excitement of a world beyond.

'There you go.'

It's Rupert Blundell with a big brown envelope. Larry jumps up and takes the packet, pushes it into his satchel.

'Wish the boys luck from us,' says Blundell.

5

A sharp rat-a-tat at the bedroom door summons Kitty and Louisa from a deep sleep. Hurriedly they wake, wash, dress. Downstairs the great hall is abuzz with activity. Colonel Jevons is standing in the Oak Room lobby with a sheet of paper on which are lists of names.

'You've just got time for a bite of breakfast,' he tells Kitty. 'Have the Brig's car outside for 0330.'

She follows the stream of half-asleep men clustering round the tea urn in the dining room. At this hour she can't eat. The others coming and going round her seem to be taking care to make as little noise as possible. Then she realises they're all wearing soft-soled boots.

Her section leader, Sergeant Sissons, is pacing the yard by the garages, using her torch to direct the troop transport trucks.

'Got your orders?'

'All set,' says Kitty.

She opens the garage doors and feels her way down the side of the Humber to the driver's door.

'Early for you, Hum,' she tells the car. 'Be a darling and start first time.'

As she reverses out into the yard she sees the lines of soldiers filing into the transport trucks. They move silently, shadows in the deeper shadow of the night. The headquarters building is alive with purposeful activity, but all of it muffled and cloaked in darkness. She drives slowly out of the yard and round the chapel, finding her way to the front porch by the slot of light from the car's blackout masks.

Jevons comes out and sees that she's in place. Other cars begin to arrive. She no longer feels in the least sleepy. She hears the throb of truck engines in the yard, the crackle of boots on the gravel, the drone of a plane passing overhead. Not yet dawn, but the world is up and about its work.

A mass of officers now appear from the house. They stand close together, torchlight flickering over papers held open between them. The heavy lorries start rumbling past, away down the drive. Then the doors of the Humber are being opened from the outside and officers are climbing in. Shortly Kitty hears the brigadier's voice from behind her head.

'Let's go,' he says.

'Where to, sir?' says Kitty.

That causes a soft laugh from the officers. So much secrecy, no one has thought to tell the driver.

'Newhaven,' says the brigadier. 'The harbour.'

Kitty eases the Humber down the drive, following behind a long line of troop transports, their tail lights glowing softly in the night. At the junction with the road she takes her

68

turn, waiting as vehicle after vehicle rolls past. A faint gleam is now appearing in the sky to the east. Behind her the voices of the officers murmur, and papers rustle. She hasn't been told what's going on, and knows better than to ask, but it doesn't take a genius to guess.

On the dark winding road now, and making for the coast. The light grows brighter on the horizon. The boys in the back of the truck ahead wave at her and grin. One of the officers behind lights up a cigarette, and the tang of smoke fills the car.

The harbour cranes come into view. The road runs along-side the railway. The column of trucks rolls into the port, and the Humber follows. The great marshalling yard by the quay is full of vehicles and disembarking men. Out on the water, lit now by the dawn, lies an immense fleet of craft of every size. Little boats are buzzing about, carrying men from craft to craft. A crane is hoisting an armoured vehicle onto a deck. The heavy throb of ship's engines fills the air.

'This'll do,' says the brigadier.

Kitty pulls up and the officers get out. Kitty too gets out, and stands by the car as she's been taught. No one pays her any attention. The brigadier strides away, trailed by his staff. All round, platoons of men are being marched across the concrete yard to the boarding ramps. They wear helmets and carry guns and kitbags. No one shouts or breaks into song, the way troops on the move usually do. The early morning is filled with a purposeful seriousness.

Kitty waits and watches, and the sun rises. The scale of

the operation slowly becomes visible. There are ships at sea all the way from the pier to the horizon. As each craft fills up with men and vehicles, it churns out of the harbour to join the waiting fleet.

A train pulls into the quayside and more streams of men get out. Among them Kitty sees a group moving differently to the rest. Instead of forming up in marching order, they slope along in a disorderly straggle, wearing wool hats in place of tin helmets. She hears one of the other drivers murmur, 'Commandos.' For the first time it occurs to her that Ed might be part of the operation.

She leaves her post and goes to one of the muster officers by the ramps.

'Is 40 Commando going?' she asks.

'Can't say,' he replies.

She tries to find Ed among the faces streaming by, but there are too many and it's still too dark. She returns to her post.

The endless flow of tramping men moves onto the boats. After a while Sergeant Sissons comes round, releasing the drivers.

'Return to HQ. Await orders.'

'Will it be long, Sarge?'

'Long enough.'

One by one the staff cars pull away from the quay. Kitty is reluctant to leave. She's still there, standing by her car, when the muster officer she approached comes over to her.

'Got a boyfriend in 40 RM, then?' he says.

She nods.

'They've embarked,' he says. 'Don't say I said so.'

He leaves her there, looking out to sea at the great fleet.

Got a boyfriend in 40 RM, then?

She hardly knows him. They've met twice, kissed once. And yet the memory of his pale face is before her, his mouth almost smiling, his blue eyes holding hers, his thoughts unreachable. She realises with a sudden ache that she wants more than anything to see him one more time. There's something she wants to say to him that he may not know. That she wants him to know.

We've only just begun. Don't leave me yet. I'm waiting for you, here on the harbour side at Newhaven. Where the river meets the sea.

She gets back into the Humber and starts the engine. The great yard is almost empty now. Day has begun. A ridge of low cloud has gathered to hide the sun. It's the second day of July, and still this strange summer is keeping everyone guessing.

The journey back, alone in the car, alone on the road, has none of the electric anticipation of the journey out. The big house and the camp are empty and silent. She returns the car to its garage and crosses the yard to the inner courtyard, entering the house by the servants' door. The long dining room with its three bay windows and its heavy fake-leather wallpaper has been cleared of all signs of the early breakfast. Hungry now, she seeks out the kitchen.

Here, sitting at the scrubbed deal table, she finds George Holland. He's eating a bowl of porridge by himself. From the scullery beyond comes the clatter of washing up.

'Ah, Kitty,' he says, visibly cheered by her appearance. 'It's the strangest thing. I got up this morning and found the house empty.'

'Yes,' says Kitty. 'There's a big show on.'

'So when will they be back?'

'I don't know.'

'The real thing this time, is it?'

'Yes,' says Kitty.

George eats some more of his porridge.

'I expect you think it's a bit rich, me sitting here eating while men are risking their lives.'

'Not at all,' says Kitty.

'It's different for you,' he says. 'You're a girl. A man should fight.'

'We can't all be fighting. Someone's got to keep the country going.'

'I do have various official duties,' he says, frowning down at his bowl. 'Local defence, magistrate, that sort of thing. But I can't fight. Eyesight, you know.'

'I'd better be going,' says Kitty.

'Don't go. There's something I want to say.'

He takes his bowl and spoon into the scullery and returns empty-handed, nervous, avoiding her eyes.

'Odd to have your own house full of strangers,' he says. 'Have you seen the library?'

'It's the officers' mess,' says Kitty.

He leads her across the hall and into the Oak Room, the lobby to the library. He points to the lettering on the doors.

'*Litera scripta manet, verba locuta volant.* "The written word

72

remains, the spoken word flies away." All very true, of course. But even so . . .'

His voice tails away. He leads her into the library itself.

The great arched window at the end floods the long room with light. Down the walls on both sides stand book-stacks numbered with Latin numerals, holding leather-bound volumes with gold titles. The floor is a pattern of inlaid marble, a tangle of leaves and flowers. Clusters of War Office-supply armchairs stand about on this shiny expanse. A table at the far end is crowded with bottles.

'It's not the way we had it before the war, of course,' says George, looking round. 'My father was a great traveller, you know. He collected maps and travel books. I do a bit in that way myself.'

'It's a beautiful room,' says Kitty. 'You must hate having your house messed up like this.'

'No, no. It's good to see it full of life. Houses need to be lived in.'

He crosses to the high window and stands looking out at the park and the distant rows of Nissen huts. Kitty understands that he's leading up to something.

'The world has changed so much, hasn't it?' he says.

'War does that,' says Kitty.

'People come and go. They live and die. You can't stand on ceremony any more. My father has left me a relatively wealthy man. That must be worth something, don't you think?'

'Oh, yes,' says Kitty.

'But this eyesight business isn't so good. Rather clips

my wings. Cramps my style. No point in complaining. There are pros and cons to every venture you undertake. Are you a reader?'

'Yes,' says Kitty. 'I love reading.'

'I'm not so much of a reader myself. I find it tires me. Anyway, the thing is this. What do you say about it? Is it something you could contemplate? Or do you recoil in horror?'

Kitty's about to say he's not made himself clear, when she stops herself. Of course he's made himself clear. She's known from the moment he finished his porridge in the kitchen. He doesn't deserve to be forced into the humiliation of speaking the plain words.

'Earlier this morning,' she says, 'I was at Newhaven watching the men go into the boats. Wherever they're going, they're going into danger. And you see, among them is the man I love.'

Strange to be saying these words to someone she barely knows; words she has not yet said to Ed.

'The man you love,' says George. 'Yes. Of course.'

'I shall be there on the quayside when he returns.'

'Quite right. Quite right.'

He moves away down the long empty room. His arms hang loosely by his sides, as if he's lost the use of them.

'I should report back to my section leader,' says Kitty.

'Yes, of course.'

He's standing before the carved stone mantelpiece, gazing at the framed photographs arrayed there.

'My mother,' he says, indicating one of the photographs.

'If you go into the chapel, there's a plaque on the south wall. It says, "In memory of a faithful wife and a loving mother." I could have said much more, but in the end that seemed to cover it. A faithful wife. A loving mother. What more can a man ask?'

Kitty leaves him with his photographs and his memories. She wants to be out of this house. It's too full of sadness.

She finds Louisa in the Motor Transport Office in A Block.

'Let's get out of here,' says Kitty. 'No one'll miss us.'

They ride their bikes down the Eastbourne road as the clouds gather and the sky darkens. They've just reached the Cricketers in Berwick when the rain starts to fall. There, wet and panting and pink-cheeked, they beg the bar girl for something – anything – to eat, and she brings them cold boiled potatoes. Two farm workers come in to escape the rain and stare at them.

'Don't know why we bother,' they grumble to each other. 'Could have done with this back in April.'

By silent agreement Kitty and Louisa don't talk about the great military operation now under way. Kitty tells Louisa about George Holland.

'I knew it,' says Louisa. 'I could tell from the way he watched you like a dog waiting for his dinner.'

'Poor George. He always looks so lost.'

'Not all that poor. He's a millionaire, and a lord. There's a limit to how sorry you can feel for him.'

'Anyway, I told him my heart was pledged to another.'

'Even though that's a whopping lie.'

'Actually it isn't,' says Kitty. 'It turns out I'm in love with Ed.'

'Kitty! When did this happen?'

'I don't quite know. I only realised it this morning, when I was watching the boys going away. I just want him to come home safe.'

'Oh, Kitty.' Louisa is touched by Kitty's trembling voice. 'Have you really fallen in love at last?'

'I think so. I'm not sure.'

The rain passes, blown away by strong south-westerly winds. They bicycle home down the empty road, side by side, with the wind on their backs.

'So what's going to happen to poor George?' says Louisa.

'He'll be fine,' says Kitty. 'Some strong-minded female will gobble him up.'

'You make him sound like a canapé.'

'He's rich and titled. Someone'll have him.'

'What about poor Stephen?'

'I'll write to him. Oh, God. Isn't it all difficult?'

'You know what,' says Louisa, 'now that you're out of the running with George, I might have a go myself.'

Kitty wobbles wildly on her bike and regains control.

'Are you serious? You know he's practically blind?'

'I haven't had a single proposal, Kitty. My people have no money to speak of. God has billeted me in the house of a young unmarried man with a title and a fortune. It would be ungrateful to the Almighty not to give it a shot.'

Kitty pedals on without further comment.

'I expect you despise me for seeing things this way,' Louisa says.

'No, not at all,' says Kitty. 'I just want you to be happy.'

'Don't you think I'd be happy with George?'

'If you loved him you would.'

'If he marries me,' says Louisa simply, 'I shall love him.'

They bicycle down the back lane into the camp. A small crowd has gathered round the front of the NAAFI to share such news as there is. Everyone is asking if this is the start of the second front.

Kitty sees Larry Cornford come out of the big house onto the west terrace. He gives her a wave, and they meet up in the lime avenue. They too talk about the big show.

'I saw them go,' says Kitty.

'I don't like this wind,' says Larry. 'They need calm seas for the crossing.'

'Do you know where they're going?'

'I know,' says Larry, 'but I can't say.'

'Has to be somewhere in France.'

'Nothing we can do now till they come back.'

Kitty says, 'I think Ed's with them.'

'It's quite likely.'

'Will you promise to come and tell me if you hear anything?'

'Yes, of course.'

They walk on in silence to the lake. The lake house stands empty before them.

'How are you getting along with *Middlemarch*?' says Larry.

'I can't read,' says Kitty. 'I can't do anything.'

'He'll come back,' says Larry.

'You don't know that. He may not.'

Larry says nothing to that.

'At least you've not gone,' she says. 'You, and George.'

Larry looks away over the wind-ruffled lake.

'I expect my turn will come,' he says.

That night the winds grow stronger, and rattle the casement in the nursery window. Kitty sleeps fitfully, tormented by half-dreams in which Ed is reaching for her from a distance she can't cross.

In the morning word spreads round the camp that the fleet is still standing offshore, and has not yet sailed. The forecast is that the weather will worsen. In the way of such things, half-understood terms are passed from mouth to mouth. 'They'll miss the tide.' 'The RAF won't fly in this.' 'You need air cover for a big op.'

The day passes slowly. In the late afternoon rain begins to fall again. Larry rides over to Divisional HQ and takes part in a meeting with the Acting CO. When he comes out he goes looking for Kitty and finds her cleaning the Humber in the garage.

'You could eat your dinner off that,' he says.

'What's the news?'

'The show's off. Don't say I told you.'

'It's off?'

'All troops to be disembarked.'

'He'll come back?'

'Yes.'

Kitty feels a surge of relief beyond her power to control. There in front of Larry's kind concerned gaze she bursts into tears.

'Honestly,' she says, dabbing at her eyes, 'what have I got to cry about now?'

Larry smiles and offers her a handkerchief.

'He's a lucky sod,' he says. 'I hope he knows it.'

'You won't tell him, will you?'

'Not if you don't want.'

'It's too silly, crying like that.'

'If I was Ed,' says Larry, 'I'd be proud to know you cried for me.'

Just after six in the evening the order comes through for all drivers to muster at Newhaven harbour. Kitty makes the short journey with a light heart. No one has been wounded. No one has died. But as she sees the men file off the ships, all their former swagger gone, she realises that for them this is a kind of failure. Standing by her car, she scans the hundreds of moving figures for the group that will contain Ed, but she doesn't find him. The trucks fill with men and grind past on the way back to the camp. Brigadier Wills comes stamping out to find her.

'Good girl. I'll be with you when I've seen to the navy chaps.'

So she waits on. She's used to it. A staff driver spends more time waiting than driving. This is usually when she reads, but recent events have unsettled her. So she stays beside the car, watching the slow dispersal of an army.

Soldiers go by laughing, grumbling.

'That was a fucking waste of time. I'd like to meet the genius dreamed that one up.'

One Canadian soldier mimics a British officer: 'I say, you chaps! The colonials are getting restless. Let's shut them in the hold for twenty-four hours and spray them with vomit, eh, what?'

Their laughter recedes into the distance.

'What's a nice girl like you doing in a dump like this?'

'Ed!'

She spins round, eyes glowing, and there he is. He's wearing rumpled battledress and carrying all sorts of bundles and his face is smeared with black. But underneath he's just the same. The same cool gaze in those blue eyes.

'Oh, Eddy!'

She throws her arms round him and kisses him. He holds her for a moment, and then gently eases her away.

'There's a welcome,' he says.

'I thought you'd never come back.'

'No chance of that,' he says. 'We never even went away.'

'Oh, Ed. I'm so happy.'

She can't disguise how she feels, and makes no attempt to. He smiles to see her happiness.

'Seeing you almost makes it worth it,' he says.

'Was it horrible?'

'I'll tell you,' he says, 'I'd rather parachute naked behind enemy lines than do that again.'

Kitty sees the brigadier heading across the yard towards the cars, accompanied by two of his staff.

'When can I see you, Ed?'

'Soon,' he says. 'I can't give you a day. Very soon.'

His eyes rest on her, suddenly gentle in that wild black-smeared face.

'My lovely angel,' he says.

Then he's gone.

The brigadier reaches the car.

'Well, that was Operation Rutter,' he says. 'Now you see it, now you don't.'

6

William Cornford is not an old man, but his bald head, together with a slight stoop in his posture, makes him appear more than his fifty or so years. He stands now in the doorway of the company offices at 95 Aldwych, feeling for his hat, watching as his son climbs off his motorbike. He hasn't seen him for many weeks. He looks on as he removes his helmet and gloves, noting every remembered detail of the boy who is all his family, his only child, the one he loves more than himself.

Then his son is before him, reaching out one hand, and the old formality returns.

'Spot on time,' Larry says. 'That's what the army's done to me.'

'Good to see you.' The father shakes the son's hand. 'Good to see you.'

'So what's the plan?'

'Lunch at Rules, I thought. Give us a chance to catch up.'

They walk round Aldwych and up Catherine Street, talking as they go. Larry asks about the company, knowing that this is what occupies his father's waking hours.

'Difficult times,' says William Cornford. 'Very difficult. But we've managed to keep all our people on so far.'

This is a major achievement in itself, as Larry knows. Since November 1940 bananas have been a prohibited food.

'No signs of a change of heart at the Ministry?'

'No,' says William Cornford. 'Woolton has told me himself the ban is for the duration. At least I've managed to convince him to do something for the growers in Jamaica.'

'The war can't go on for ever.'

'That's what I tell our people. In the meantime, we've become the vegetable distribution arm of the Ministry of Food. When the war's over, we'll just have to start again from scratch.'

'And how's Cookie?'

Miss Cookson is his father's housekeeper, at the family home in Kensington.

'Same as ever. Asks after you. Do look her up some day.'

Larry realises they've walked on past their turning.

'We should go down Tavistock Street, surely?'

'I thought we might take a turn past the old building,' says his father.

'Isn't that rather depressing?' says Larry.

'I find it has some value. *Lacrimae rerum*, you know.'

They walk up Bow Street to the place where the company headquarters building once stood. A direct hit in January last year destroyed the entire six-storey structure, leaving the tall side of the adjoining building standing, fireplaces exposed, doors agape. The site is still filled with rubble.

'Fifty years,' says William Cornford. 'Almost my entire life. This is where my father built the company up from nothing.'

Larry too remembers it well. The dark panelled room where his father worked. Where they had their one and only terrible quarrel.

'Why are we here?'

'Thirteen of our people died that night.'

'Yes, Dad. I know.'

'Eight company ships sunk since the start of hostilities. Over six hundred members of staff on active service. All still on the payroll.'

'Yes, Dad. I know.'

'This is the front line too, Larry. We're fighting this war too.'

Larry says nothing to this. He understands what his father would like to say, but will never say. How does his son serve his country any better by wearing a uniform and riding a motorbike?

William Cornford was and remains deeply hurt that his son has not chosen to enter the family firm. The company built by his father, the first Lawrence Cornford, and made great by himself in the second generation, should be passed on, its culture and traditions intact, to the third. But Larry dreams a different dream.

Father and son walk on to Rules. They take their usual table under the stairs.

'Not what it was, of course,' says William Cornford, glancing over the menu. 'But they've still got shepherd's pie.'

'So how's Bennett?' says Larry.

'At his desk every morning. You know he'll be seventy this year?'

'I don't believe he ever actually goes home.'

'He asks after you from time to time. Maybe you could stop by after lunch and give him five minutes.'

'Yes, of course.'

The long-serving employees of the company are Larry's greater family. Most of them still believe he'll take his proper place in the hierarchy in time.

William Cornford studies the wine list.

'Care to share a bottle of Côte Rôtie?'

Larry asks his father to tell him more about the trading conditions of the company, framing his questions to show he understands the current difficulties; aware there's no one else his father can speak to of his worries.

'The branch depots are actually all running at full capacity, believe it or not. But the truth is I've been turned into a sort of a civil servant. I have to take my orders from the Ministry, which goes against the grain a little. I've never been a man for committees.'

'My God! You must hate it.'

'I'm not as patient as perhaps I should be.'

He gives his son a quick shy smile.

'But I expect you have your frustrations too.'

'Soldiering is ninety-nine per cent frustration,' says Larry.

'And the other one per cent?'

'They say it's terror.'

'Ah, yes,' says William Cornford. 'Battle.'

He himself has never been a soldier. In the Great War he remained in the company, which was then the nation's sole importer of fruit. Larry fully understands his father's complex feelings about his son's war service. He represents the family on the sacrificial altar of war, even as he deserts the company in its hour of need.

'So is Mountbatten looking after you?' his father asks him.

'Oh, I'm just a glorified messenger boy.'

'Still, I don't want you to come to any harm.'

This is the war his father has arranged for him: if not safe in Fyffes, then safe in a headquarters building in London.

'As it happens,' Larry says, 'the division I'm attached to looks like it's going into action soon.'

He sees his father's face, and at once regrets his words. He feels ashamed of pretending to a coming military action that will give his father sleepless nights.

'Though I doubt if they'll be taking me along. I'm afraid I'm doomed to be a paper-pusher.'

The wine comes. His father thanks the waiter with his usual courtesy.

'An excellent Rhône,' he says. 'We shall drink to the liberation of France.'

'Do you have any news of the house?'

The family has a house in Normandy, in the Forêt d'Eawy.

'I believe it's been requisitioned by German officers,' says his father.

He meets his son's eyes over their raised glasses. They

share a love of France. For William Cornford it's the land of the great cathedrals: Amiens, Chartres, Albi, Beauvais. For Larry it's the land of Courbet and Cézanne.

'To France,' says Larry.

With the cancellation of Operation Rutter an uneasy calm settles over the Sussex countryside. The thousands of troops encamped on the Downs resume the training exercises designed more to occupy them than to raise their fighting form. More beer is drunk in the long evenings, and more brawls break out in the warm nights. The storms of early July pass, leaving overcast skies and a heavy sunless heat by day. No one believes the operation will be off for good. Everyone is waiting.

On a rare bright day Larry gathers up his paints and his portable easel and goes down to the water meadows by Glynde Reach. He sets up his easel on the hay-strewn ground and starts work preparing the board he's using as a canvas. He has in mind to paint a view of Mount Caburn.

As he works away, a figure appears from the direction of the farm. It turns out to be Ed.

'Thank God someone's around,' he says. 'I come all the way from the other side of the country to see Kitty and she's not bloody there.'

'Did you tell her you were coming?'

'How could I? I didn't know myself.'

He stands behind Larry, looking at the sketch forming on the board.

'I really admire you for this,' he says.

'Good Lord! Why?'

'Because it's something you love to do.' He kicks moodily at the hay on the ground. 'There's nothing I really want to do. I feel like a spectator.'

'You want to see Kitty.'

'That's different. Anyway, she won't be back till this evening. What do I do till then?'

'You could always help Arthur get his hay in.'

This is not a serious suggestion, but rather to Larry's surprise his friend seizes on it eagerly. He goes back to the farmhouse and reappears a little later pulling a light hay cart.

'Arthur says I'll make a mess of it,' he says, 'but it doesn't matter as it's ruined already.'

'Rather you than me,' says Larry.

Ed strips to the waist, takes a long-handled rake out of the cart, and proceeds to gather the lying hay into mounds. Larry looks round from his painting from time to time, expecting to see his friend leaning on his rake, but Ed never stops. His lean, tight-muscled body gleams with sweat as he works, keeping up a pace no overseer would ever demand. As he forms the hay into knee-high piles he drags the cart alongside and hoists the hay into it. With each lift he emits a short low grunt of effort.

Larry's attention is on the line of trees before him, and the rise of land that culminates in the round prominence that is Mount Caburn. His brush, moving rapidly, is reducing the scene to its essential elements, in which land and sky are masses of equal weight, the one cupped into the other. The flanks of the hill meet the dull sunlight at different angles, forming elongated triangles of different tones. He works with browns and reds and yellows, applying paint in rough dabs, hurrying to capture the ever-changing light.

When he next pays attention to his friend, he finds the hay cart is piled high.

'My God!' he exclaims. 'You must be exhausted. Give yourself a break, for heaven's sake.'

'Just getting into my stride,' says Ed, tossing another forkful of hay over the high hurdle side of the cart.

Larry watches him for a few moments, awed by his relentless self-discipline. For a man who wants to do nothing he has a remarkable capacity for work.

'You know what it's called, doing what you're doing?'

'What?' says Ed, never ceasing in his work.

'It's called doing penance. You're paying for your sins.'

'Not me,' says Ed. 'That's for you believers. I don't have to pay for my sins. They come free.'

Larry laughs at that and goes back to his painting.

At midday Rex Dickinson appears, carrying a basket.

'The good Mary has taken pity on you,' he says.

The three of them settle down in the shadow of the hay cart and eat bread and cheese and drink cider. Larry looks at Ed sitting sprawled on the hay-strewn earth, breathing slow deep breaths, chewing the thick home-made bread, sweat drying on his face and shoulders.

'You look like a handsome healthy animal,' he says.

'That's all I want to be,' says Ed.

Rex goes over to look at Larry's painting.

'Very Cézanne,' he says.

'I don't know why I bother,' says Larry. 'It's all been done before, and better.'

Rex looks round the silent landscape.

'You'd hardly know there's a war on.'

'I love war,' says Ed.

'That's because you're a romantic,' says Larry. 'Half in love with easeful death.'

'That's rather good.'

'Not me. Keats.'

'As far as I'm concerned,' says Ed, 'I'll be dead by Christmas. And that's just fine. Once you make up your mind to it, everything tastes and smells so much better.'

Larry frowns, unsure whether or not to believe him.

'But what about Kitty?' he says.

'What about her?'

'I thought you loved her.'

'Oh, Lord, I don't know.' Ed stretches himself out full length on the ground. 'What kind of future can I offer a girl?'

'Have you told her you're planning on being dead by Christmas?'

'She doesn't believe me. She says that if she loves me enough I won't be killed.'

'She's right,' says Larry. 'When you love someone, you can't believe they'll ever die.'

'I believe we're all going to die,' says Ed. 'I suppose that means I don't love anyone.'

'Kitty thinks you love her.'

'Well, I do.'

'You just say the first thing that comes into your head, don't you?'

Ed rolls over and shades his eyes with one hand so he can gaze at Larry.

'We've known each other a long time,' he says. 'We don't have to piss about saying polite nothings, do we? We can be pretty straight with each other, I'd say.'

'I go along with that.'

'The thing is, Larry, I think you genuinely are a good chap. One of the very few I know. But I'm not a good chap. I live in what you might call the outer darkness. I really do. I'm not proud of it. What I see when I look ahead is darkness. I know you think I'm just being selfish. But I do love Kitty, and I ask myself if it's fair to drag her into that dark place.'

Larry realises now what it is his friend wants from him. He loves him for it, even as he feels the sad weight of it fall upon him.

'What is this, Ed? You want some kind of blessing from me?'

'Maybe I do.'

'All you owe her is your love,' he says.

'What about the darkness?'

'It's not your private darkness.'

He speaks so softly that Ed doesn't hear him.

'What's that?'

'It's not your private darkness,' he says again, louder.

Ed stares at him.

'We all have to face it,' says Larry. 'Kitty too. She's not a child.'

Ed goes on staring at him.

'The war won't go on for ever,' says Rex.

Larry returns to his painting. His brush moves more quickly now, applying paint in bolder strokes. Above the hill the sun is burning through the layer of cloud, and in his painting the sky becomes charged with amber and gold.

Ed has had enough of haymaking. He puts one hand on Larry's shoulder, squeezing it.

'Thanks.'

'What for?'

'You know.'

Rex stays on after Ed has left them, mooching about the stream bank looking for butterflies.

'You should study butterflies, Larry. Their colouring is just like a work of modern art. See there, that's a Meadow Brown. A really common species. But on each brown wing there's a patch of yellow, and in each patch of yellow there's a black spot, like an eye.'

Larry goes on painting, but he's grateful for Rex's presence. He wants to talk.

'What do you think about Ed and Kitty?' he says.

'Nothing, really,' says Rex.

'Do you think he's right for her?'

'I wouldn't know. That's rather up to her, isn't it?'

Larry changes brushes, and mixes up a blob of blue with a touch of black. He wants the sky to be more dangerous.

'Don't you think he sounds odd about it all?'

'He's an odd fellow,' says Rex.

He's found another butterfly worthy of remark.

'That's a Chalkhill Blue. Isn't he a beauty?'

Larry continues to pursue his line of thought.

'You say it's up to Kitty,' he says, 'which it is, of course. But she can only go on what's on offer. And right now, that's Ed.'

'Oh, I get it,' says Rex. 'You want to make a bid.'

'Do you think that's wrong?'

'It's not morally wrong,' says Rex. 'I suppose it might be considered bad form.'

'Well, that's just it,' says Larry. 'If one chap announces he's interested in a girl, does that mean he has some kind of rights over her? Does it mean everyone else has to keep off?'

Rex thinks about that.

'I think the general idea is you back off while the first fellow takes his shot. Then if he misses, you take a pot.'

'That's what I thought,' says Larry. 'But listening to Ed today I started thinking maybe I'm being a bit feeble. As you say, it's all up to Kitty.'

'Look, Larry,' says Rex. 'If you want to drop a hint to Kitty, I should just do it. I don't see what harm it can do.'

'Really?'

Larry works away on his thunderous sky.

'What about you, Rex? Don't you ever wish you had a girl?'

'Oh,' says Rex, 'I'm not very good at that sort of thing.'

Louisa Cavendish receives orders assigning her to new duties in central London, effective from the start of September. This has the effect of concentrating her mind.

'I'm taking the afternoon off,' she announces.

She touches up her lipstick, brushes out her corn-coloured hair, tightens her belt, and heads for the private quarters of the big house.

'George,' she says, finding the lord of the manor in the kitchen as usual, 'it's a warm day, and you should be outside. It's no good to be indoors all the time.'

George Holland looks at her in surprise.

'You sound like my mother,' he says.

'Did you like your mother?'

'I adored her.'

'Come on, then. Out for a walk.'

Not knowing how to refuse, George rises and follows.

'I know we've met,' he says politely, as they make their way through the outer courtyard, 'but I seem to have forgotten your name.'

'I expect I never told you. I'm Louisa Cavendish. Same family as the Devonshires. I'm a friend of Kitty's.'

'Oh, very well, then.'

'Why don't you take your glasses off?'

'I shouldn't be able to see very much if I did,' he says.

'Don't worry, I'll make sure you don't bump into things. Here, take my hand.'

She removes his glasses and he takes her hand. They walk out past the chapel. Louisa does not want to be seen by the camp.

'I expect you could do this walk with your eyes shut,' she says. 'We'll go up onto Edenfield Hill.'

She turns him towards the cart track that runs up the flank of the Downs.

'It's strange without my glasses,' he says. 'The world feels very different.'

'Different good or different bad?'

'Less alarming, somehow.' He turns to her with a shy smile. 'Rather a good idea of yours.'

'And what do I look like?' says Louisa.

'Somewhat indefinite,' says George.

'Describe what you see.'

He stares at her.

'White face. Eyes. Mouth.'

'Ten out of ten so far.'

'Sorry. I'm being dim.'

'What impression does my face make?'

'Rather impressive. Rather fine.'

'Okay. That'll do.'

They walk on to the top of the hill. A steady warm wind is blowing in off the sea, bringing with it flocks of gulls with their harsh cries.

'Can you see the view with your glasses off?' she asks him.

'Not exactly. I get the feeling of it, though.'

'What feeling?'

'Spacious,' he says. 'Roomy.'

'Liberating?'

'Yes. That's the one.'

'You see, I was right,' says Louisa. 'You should get out more.'

They walk a little way along the ridge.

'Don't you hate the war?' says Louisa.

'Yes,' he says. 'I think I do.'

'Having to give up your house. Having all those ghastly huts in your park. Having all the servants leave.'

'Yes,' he says with a sigh. 'It was all so different in my father's day.' Then he adds after a moment's thought, 'But I'm not the man my father was, of course.'

'He was a great man, I hear.'

'He was a giant,' says George. 'He made his fortune from nothing, you know. People think it was luck, that he stumbled on this little pill that everyone wanted, and that was that. But it wasn't luck at all. My father was the sort of man who could make the world do his bidding.'

'I'm not sure I'd like to have a giant for a father,' says Louisa.

'No,' says George. 'He did rather frighten me.'

He comes to a stop and peers at Louisa in his half-blind way. Then all at once his face crumples. To her dismay she realises he's about to cry. Without his glasses his face looks soft and helpless.

'I've never said that before,' he says.

'What you need is a hug,' says Louisa.

He comes awkwardly into her arms and lets her embrace him. Then pressing his face to her shoulder he begins to sob. She strokes his back gently, not speaking, letting him cry himself out like a child.

He takes out a handkerchief at last, and dries his eyes and blows his nose.

'You've been left alone too much, haven't you?' she says.

7

The conference room was built as a ballroom for the great London house, in the days when it belonged to the Duke of Buccleuch. Now, its tall windows bandaged with tape and blinded by blackout curtains, it exists in the perpetual gloom of underpowered electric lights. Here the commanding officers of the Canadian forces in southern England have gathered for a briefing by the chief of Combined Operations. Mountbatten, flanked by his service heads, wears the uniform of a vice-admiral of the fleet.

'Gentlemen,' he announces. 'We have been given the go-ahead. Your boys, weather permitting, will see action this summer after all. Naturally I can't give you a precise date today. But my message to you is: stand by!'

This is met with murmurs of approbation.

'The relaunched operation goes under the code name of Jubilee. Detailed orders for each sector are now being drawn up. My staff will issue them within a matter of days.'

He then invites questions. General Ham Roberts speaks first.

'Is there any concern, sir,' he says, 'that the element of surprise has been lost?'

'Because of Rutter, you mean?' says Mountbatten, nodding encouragingly.

'Yes, sir. The Germans can hardly have failed to notice something was afoot last time.'

'You're perfectly right,' says Mountbatten. 'So what are the Germans thinking? They're thinking that we couldn't possibly be so stupid as to lay on the same operation again.'

He pauses, and looks at the assembled commanders with his infectious boyish smile.

'So that's precisely what we're going to do!'

The last half of the drive back takes place in silence. The brigadier evidently has much on his mind. Kitty concentrates on her route, watching the road for the potholes caused by the endless convoys of heavy army vehicles. For much of the way she has the road to herself, and is able to maintain a steady fifty miles an hour. The petrol tank is on the low side. She makes a note to herself to fill it up tomorrow.

As they weave their way round the outskirts of Brighton the brigadier becomes conversational.

'I've been meaning to ask you, Kitty,' he says. 'Where do you come from? What do you call home?'

'Wiltshire, sir.'

'Is that a fine part of the world?'

'Yes, sir. Hills and woods.'

'I miss my home,' he says. 'I miss it real bad. My boys'll be turning ten soon. I haven't seen them for two years. Do you know Canada at all?'

'No, sir.'

'Why would you? I grew up in a little place on the shores of Lake Huron called Grand Bend. Feels like a long way away now, I can tell you.'

He gazes out of the car window as they drive along the foothills of the Downs.

'This is pretty country,' he says, 'but it looks small to me.'

Kitty delivers the brigadier back to headquarters, and returns the Humber to its garage. She looks in on the Motor Transport Office to hand in her work docket and to request petrol for tomorrow. Louisa is there, and some of the other girls, and Sergeant Sissons.

'Don't forget the clocks go back on Saturday night,' says Sissons. 'End of double summer time.'

'Is that good or bad?'

'Another hour in bed, isn't it?'

'Anything on for this evening?' says Louisa.

'My night off,' says Kitty. 'I need it.'

'All right for some,' says Louisa.

She's looking at Kitty in an odd way.

'What?'

'Nothing,' says Louisa. 'Sweet dreams.'

Kitty climbs the terrace steps into the main house, suddenly feeling the strain of the long drive. She thinks maybe she'll just lie on her bed and read. She should be writing to Stephen, should have written to him days ago, it's not fair to leave him dangling. Except she never asked him to fall in love with her. How can you fall in love with someone you've only met twice? Then she thinks of Ed and blushes. But what can she say to Stephen? That she's met someone she likes better? Dear Stephen, I value your friendship but I don't want to tie you down. And so on.

She has no means of communicating with Ed, and no idea when she'll see him again, but she thinks about him all the time. Not in a making-plans sort of way: it's more that the idea of him is a permanent presence in her life now, which causes her to feel differently about everything. Because of him the immediate future has become unpredictable and exciting.

She can hear her mother's warning voice: Don't get in too deep. What are his prospects? How's he going to provide for you? But her secret dreams of Ed have nothing to do with marriage. It's not about living happily ever after.

I want to get in too deep, Mummy. I want to be swept off my feet, and not be able to do anything about it. I want adventure.

She climbs the dark and narrow nursery stairs to the corridor in the eaves. As she goes she begins the process of unbuckling her belt, then undoing the four brass buttons of her uniform jacket. She loosens her tie and undoes the top button of her shirt. She's tugging the tie out of her collar as she enters the nursery bedroom.

Ed is lying on her bed.

He puts a finger to his lips.

'Shut the door,' he says softly.

She shuts the door.

He lies there in his shirtsleeves, his hands behind his head, his shoes kicked off his feet. His eyes hold her with that mocking gaze.

'How did you know this was my room?'

'Louisa told me,' he says.

'I'm going to kill her.'

'That would be an overreaction,' he says.

She stands there gazing down at him, confused but excited. She's not sure what he expects her to do.

'How about saying hello?' he says.

He makes no move to get up. She goes nearer to the bed. His arms reach up and draw her down. They kiss, in a polite, almost formal way.

'Hello,' she says.

Then he pulls her onto the bed, and she finds herself lying half across him. Now he's kissing her properly. She feels his lips on her lips, his hands on her back, his body warm beneath hers, the rise and fall of his chest. She lets him overwhelm her, saying to herself, I have no choice. From the moment she entered the room and saw him lying on her bed she ceased to take responsibility for her own actions.

He shifts to the edge of the narrow bed and arranges her beside him, now kissing her forehead, her ears, her neck. She closes her eyes, wanting to feel his lips on her eyelids. His fingers move down her throat. He starts to unbutton her shirt. When he reaches the third button she holds his hand with hers.

'Wait,' she whispers.

The room has two dormer windows and a corner tower window. On this summer early evening it's filled with light. Kitty is ashamed to be seen in her army-issue underwear.

She leaves the bed and pulls the blackout curtains closed. The room is plunged into darkness, but for a faint thread of light coming under the door.

She feels her way back into his arms. Liberated by the darkness, she lets his hands go where they will. He takes her shirt off, and her brassiere. She feels the light touch of his fingers on her bare breasts. Her skin tingles. Her entire body begins to tremble. She wants his touch. She wants to feel his body against hers.

'Not fair,' she whispers. 'You're still dressed.'

He pulls off his shirt and they lie together naked from the waist up, kissing eagerly. The more he touches her the more her body awakens, and the closer she wants to be to him. She knows now what will happen, and knows that she wants it. She's been wanting it since he kissed her on Mount Caburn. Since he came back to her on the quay at Newhaven, not killed after all.

Kitty has never been naked like this with a man before. She has never made love. She's not ignorant, there are girls in her unit who give graphic descriptions of their nights out, but every moment is new to her. She has no words for what she's doing now other than the crude slang of toilet walls, the laughing exchanges in the training camp dorm. *You should have seen his equipment! I screamed like a stuck pig. Takes a big hammer to drive a big nail.*

She feels it now, swelling against her body, this mystery that is his desire for her. She pushes against it and feels it grow hard. He takes her hand and places it on the ridge it makes. She moves her hand gently up and down, learning its form by touch in the darkness. Then his fingers are unbuckling his belt and opening his trousers. Her hand slips inside to touch his naked body *there*. It's warm and soft and strong and hard all at once. She holds it and strokes it, not knowing how tightly she should grip, and feels it give little twitches of response. All her body is hot now, her skin is burning. She wants him, she wants all of him. She wants him so close that he drowns her thoughts in the smell and touch and feel of him.

Now his hands are tugging gently at her skirt. Of course, she must be as naked as he is, it's obvious. She moves quickly to unbutton her skirt, and unpop the clips on her stockings. As she does so she feels his hand between her legs, moving right up inside her knickers, and she becomes still. She wants his touch so much that she's holding her breath. He strokes her *there*, and she shivers with nervous intensity. His touch makes her body new for her, as if *there* has never been discovered before. He explores her unknown land, he inhabits her. She lets her legs part so that his hand can move more freely over her and into her.

I'm all yours, Eddy. All of me is yours.

Now she's undoing the hooks and eyes of her suspender belt and letting it fall away. His hands slip inside the waistband of her army knickers, blessedly invisible in the dark, and pull them down over her buttocks and thighs. She helps him with twists of her legs to get them off. Now all she's wearing are her lisle stockings.

His hand is back between her legs, stroking, probing, burrowing. She feels for his erection, and holds it between her palms. Her eyes have become more accustomed to the dark, and the single thread of light lets her see a little. She looks up to his face and thinks she sees him smiling at her.

'Ah!'

She gives a gasp of surprise. His fingers have found a place to touch that sends shocks of pleasure all through her body.

'Oh, Eddy! Oh, Eddy!'

He kisses her breasts, lingering over the nipples, tweaking them with his lips. Kitty feels as if she has never had a body before, as if his touch creates it. She wants to hold him so close, so close that she ceases to exist. She wants to give herself to him and lose herself in him.

'Darling,' she whispers. 'Darling, darling.'

He moves his body over hers and she parts her legs, making herself open for him, longing for him. She feels the push, the soft head nuzzling at her crotch, seeking the way in. She wriggles her hips and it finds its place, and rests there.

He lowers his face to hers to kiss her. As his lips touch hers, he gives a little push, and it's in. Just the tip, but it's begun.

Kitty feels her heart pounding, scrambling all rational thought. Somewhere far away there are things she should be concerned about, but she doesn't want to know. She wants to possess him. She wants all of him in all of her.

He moves again, and penetrates a little deeper. She can tell from his breathing that he's excited. Then she feels a spasm of pain, and makes a sound. He stops. For a brief moment of terror she thinks, He can't do it. I'm too small for him. But all the time she can feel herself opening up. And now he's moving again, and it hurts but she doesn't make a sound, and he's deeper in.

This is his desire. His desire is hot and hard. The deeper into me he goes, the more he wants me.

Now he's all the way in. She can feel the weight of his body on hers. He lies still, letting her grow accustomed to the sensation. For Kitty this is the time, when he's inside her but neither of them are moving, this is the time she remembers for the rest of her life. Their haven of love.

He's mine. We'll never be parted now.

'Darling,' she whispers. 'Darling.'

He starts to move, drawing almost all the way out, then pushing back all the way in. Kitty feels the pain again.

'Slowly,' she whispers.

He moves slowly after that, and when he's all the way in he pauses. Then out, then in. The sweet pause.

'Oh, God!' he cries.

'What is it?'

A shudder goes through his body. His hips convulse in a series of sharp jerks. She feels him twitch inside her. Then he lies still.

So it's happened. She thinks she can feel it, a liquid warmth, but maybe she imagines it. This is what they do it for. This is the prize.

'Was it good?' she whispers.

He grunts. She realises that whatever it is he has just experienced, it has half-stunned him. All his limbs have gone slack. His weight is heavy on her. She doesn't mind, she wraps her arms round him, holds him tight. His moment of helplessness touches her deeply. Then all at once she has the strangest thought.

He has died for me.

She pushes the thought away, ashamed to compare what they've just done to the real death that waits in this real war. But the two are tangled up, even so. Had she not stood on the quay at Newhaven and thought of him dying in France, would she be naked in his arms now?

He's shrinking inside her. She feels a cool trickle between her thighs. He gives a long groaning sigh. Then he rolls off her, and lying beside her, takes her in his arms.

For a while they lie together in the dark room in silence. She thinks he might be sleeping, but she can't tell. He has become infinitely precious to her, she doesn't want to disturb him, doesn't need to disturb him. What they have just done together changes everything. They're together now.

Kitty wonders at this, wonders that her girlfriends have so much to say about the act and so little about the closeness. Perhaps it's just too ordinary. It happens to all couples. Except it's extraordinary, it's beyond anything she believed possible, that two people can lie together and become one.

'Kitty?'

His soft voice interrupts her thoughts. He's looking at her, smiling.

'Will you marry me?'

'Yes.'

She feels no sense of surprise. Of course she'll marry him. They're married already. But the way he asks, with a slight hesitation in his voice, floods her with a tender joy. She draws him close, kissing him.

'Of course I'll marry you, Eddy darling.'

'We seem to have done things the wrong way round.'

'What difference does it make?'

'And I'm sorry . . .'

She understands he feels bad because it was all over so quickly, but doesn't know how to say so.

'It was wonderful, Eddy. It was perfect.'

'No,' he says. 'But it will be.'

He gazes at her and there's no mockery any more. No distance.

'I do love you, Kitty,' he says. 'I'll do my best for you.'

8

The library at Wakehurst Place is packed with officers assembled for the operational briefing by General Harry Crerar, commander of the 2nd Canadian Infantry Division. Larry Cornford stands near the back, his hands clasped behind his back, his gaze roaming the room. The Elizabethan library has an embossed ceiling and an elaborately carved fireplace. As he listens to the general's steady tones, he finds himself studying the figures in the niches on either side of the fireplace. A curiously shaped female, naked from the waist up, holds a large naked child horizontally across her midriff, like a roll of carpet. The child reaches one hand up to tweak her left nipple, and with the other hand pats the head of a second smaller child at its mother's knee; if mother it is. What can it all signify?

'The forces chosen for Operation Jubilee are as follows. The RHLI, the Essex Scottish, the South Saskatchewans, the Camerons, the Royals, and the Fusiliers Mont-Royal. The 14th Armored, the Calgary regiment, will be in action for the first time with the new Churchill tanks. Number 3 Commando, Number 4 Commando, and 40 Royal Marine Commando will carry out designated tasks, as will a small unit of US Rangers, and Free French forces. Operation Jubilee will be a reconnaissance in force. Its object is to seize and hold a seaport for twenty-four hours, and then to withdraw. It is not an invasion. It is not the opening of a second front. I can't tell you our destination, or our planned date. But I can tell you that it will be very soon now.'

A murmur of satisfaction runs round the room.

'This is pretty much a Canadian show, boys,' says the general. 'Ham Roberts will be in overall charge. I'm very proud that we're being given the first real smack at the Hun on his own ground. I know you won't let me down.'

There's nothing in the general's briefing that hasn't been rumoured for weeks now, but the official confirmation creates a buzz of excitement. As the meeting breaks up, Larry sees Brigadier Wills go into a huddle with Crerar and Roberts. A trolley of tea and coffee is wheeled clanking into the room by two members of the kitchen staff. Officers crowd round, jostling each other to be first in line. Dick Lowell, Larry's Canadian opposite number, joins him by the doorway.

'Bigger show than I expected,' he says. 'But my God, are they ready for it! What do you reckon? Boulogne? I say Le Touquet.'

Larry, who has known the target port for weeks, says nothing to this. He looks out through the high windows to the handsome grounds beyond.

'Quite a place, isn't it?'

'Famous, too,' says Dick Lowell. 'Culpeper the herbalist lived here.'

'Do you think I've got time for a wander round the grounds?'

'Christ, we'll be here all morning. There's still the supply and logistic meetings to go.'

'Do me a favour, Dick? If Woody comes looking for me, give me a shout.'

Larry leaves the library, and passes down the wood-panelled corridor and out through the south-east door to the gravelled forecourt. Here the rows of staff cars are pulled up, waiting to convey the top brass back to their bases. Beyond the line of cars, in a bend of the drive, stand two tall sequoia trees. The staff drivers have gathered in the shade of the trees to gossip, or just to doze.

Larry shields his eyes from the glare and scans the shadowed figures. He locates Kitty at last, sitting a little apart from the rest, reading a book.

He goes to her.

'Still on *Middlemarch*?'

She looks up with a pleased smile.

'Almost at the end now. Poor, poor Lydgate.'

'I've got another book for you.' He takes a book out of his shoulder bag. 'You may have read it already.'

It's *The Warden* by Trollope.

'No, I haven't,' she says. 'How sweet of you.'

'There are so few good men in books,' says Larry. 'In

good books, I mean. All the best characters are bad. But there's one in *The Warden*. It's the story of a good man.'

'That's just what I need,' says Kitty.

'Care for a walk in the park?'

She jumps up, slipping the books into her long-strap handbag.

'What if they come out?'

'We won't go far.'

They go round the house and down a path that runs south between unkempt lawns. The once-grand gardens are suffering from neglect. Yet another casualty of war.

'I think you must be a good man, Larry,' says Kitty.

'Why do you say that?'

'I don't know. Just a feeling I get.'

'Not half good enough,' says Larry. 'Sometimes I look at myself in the mirror and all I see is idleness and selfishness.'

'Oh, we all think that about ourselves. Me most of all.'

'So what's to be done?'

'We shall get better,' says Kitty.

'You're right. We shall get better.'

'I think loving people makes you a better person,' says Kitty. 'Don't you?'

'Yes, I do,' says Larry.

'But it has to not be selfish love. It has to be selfless love. And that's so hard.'

'That's because it's your self that does the loving,' says Larry.

'You love them for them, and then they love you back,

and that makes you happy. So maybe it's all selfishness in the end.'

The path leads to a circular terrace with a small stone monument at its centre. Round the stone base is a brass plaque on which lines of poetry are engraved.

> Give fools their gold and knaves their power
> Let fortune's bubbles rise and fall
> Who sows a field or trains a flower
> Or plants a tree is more than all.

'Do you think that's true?' says Kitty.

'Well, I've never sown a field,' says Larry. 'Or trained a flower, or planted a tree.'

'Nor have I.'

'So I think it's tosh.'

'I think it's tosh too.'

They stand by the curving stone balustrade and look down into an overgrown pond, and return to talk of love.

'The thing is,' says Kitty, 'I can only love with all of myself. And if that makes me happy, well, I just have to lump it, don't I?'

'There is another side to it, you know? You have to accept love as well as give it.'

'Yes, but that's not up to me. That's up to the other person.'

'Well, you do have to let yourself be loved.'

'What an odd notion,' says Kitty. 'Let myself be loved? I don't understand that at all. That's like saying let myself be warmed by the sun. The sun shines and it warms me, whether I choose to let it or not.'

'You could go into the shade.'

'Oh, well, yes.'

She frowns, becoming confused.

'What I mean,' says Larry, 'is that some people don't let themselves be loved. Maybe they're frightened. Maybe they don't feel worthy.'

'Oh, I see. But you don't feel that, do you?'

'Sometimes. A little. You can call it shyness, if you like. People can be afraid to ask for love, even though they may want it very much.'

'Yes, I can see that.'

'After all, not everyone feels they're bound to be lovable. Most of us wonder why anyone would ever be remotely interested.'

Kitty is silent for a moment.

'It's funny about people loving people,' she says. 'I don't really know what it is makes you love one person and not another. I know it's supposed to be about looks, but I don't think it is at all.'

'So what is it?' says Larry.

'It's something that gets inside you,' she says. 'Suddenly it's inside you, and you know it can't ever be taken out. Not without tearing you apart.'

'What makes that something get inside you?' says Larry.

Kitty gives him a quick frowning look, and for a moment her sweet face is filled with sadness.

'Standing on the quay at Newhaven harbour,' she says, 'and knowing he's going to die.'

Larry looks back towards the house. He feels far away from everyone and everything. He nods slowly, wanting to show he's heard her, not trusting himself to speak.

'We're going to get married,' Kitty says. 'Do you think I'm a terrible fool?'

'No,' he says. 'Of course not. That's wonderful news.'

He forces lightness into his voice.

'Congratulations, and so on. Lucky old Ed.'

'I do love him, Larry. I love him so much it hurts.'

They walk back down the path. Larry is filled with an aching emptiness. Following some instinct of self-preservation he says all the good things he can think of about Ed.

'He was my best friend at school. I know him better than anyone. He's incredibly intelligent, and ruthlessly honest. And though he likes to make out he sees through everything, it's not true. He cares too much, really. That's where the sadness comes from.'

'The sadness,' she says. 'I think that's almost what makes me love him the most.'

'He'll make a fine husband,' says Larry. 'If Ed says he'll do a thing, he does it. But look here' – he suddenly remembers the morning's briefing – 'you'd better get a move on if you're to get married. He could be posted overseas any day now.'

Kitty takes his hand and squeezes it.

'What's that for?'

'For being a darling.'

They return in silence to the side of the house where the cars and drivers wait.

'I'll see how much longer they're going to be,' says Larry.

He goes into the house. In the central hallway, by the dark oak staircase, he meets Brigadier Wills coming out of his meeting with General Roberts.

'All done,' says the brigadier. 'Let's get on the road.'

Larry walks back through the house with the brigadier.

'This op, sir,' he says. 'I know it's a Canadian show. But I was wondering if you could find a berth for me.'

'It won't be a picnic, Lieutenant.'

'My war too, sir.'

'So it is, so it is.'

They come out onto the forecourt. The drivers are now all standing by their cars, waiting for their officers.

'I can use you, Lieutenant. But you'll have to clear it with Combined Ops.'

'Thank you, sir.'

The brigadier finds his car. Kitty opens the passenger door for him.

'Back to base, Corporal.'

Larry watches the Humber drive away past the giant trees and out of sight. Then he makes his way slowly across to the stable block, where he has left his motorbike. He stands for a long time, motionless, his helmet held in his hands, before at last he raises it to his head.

In the car driving south the brigadier says to Kitty, 'You know Lieutenant Cornford, don't you?'

'Yes, sir.'

'He just asked me if he can ride along when we go into action.'

He shakes his head as he thinks about it.

'That's war for you. A man leaves his home and his loved ones and puts himself in the line of fire, all of his own free will. Don't tell me he does that because he wants to free the world from tyranny. Don't tell me he does that for his country. He does it for his buddies. That's what war's about. If your buddies are fighting and dying, you want to fight and die alongside them.'

'Yes, sir,' says Kitty.

Larry knows by now how the system works. Rather than putting his request through the official channels, he goes to Joyce Wedderburn.

'I just need two minutes,' he says.

'He's not here right now,' says Joyce. 'But if you don't mind waiting.'

'Of course not.'

'They also serve who only stand and wait,' she says, smiling.

'Bet you don't know where that comes from,' says Larry.

'I've no idea.'

'Milton. His poem on his blindness. "Who best bears his mild yoke, they serve him best." Meaning God, of course.'

'How clever of you to know that.'

Larry sighs as he settles down to wait.

'Over-educated and under-employed,' he says.

Mountbatten shows up fifteen minutes or so later, striding along in a great hurry with Harold Wernher at his side. He sees Larry waiting and stops at his office door.

'You want me?'

'A very quick request, sir.'

In the office, Mountbatten hears him out, and turns to Wernher.

'This is why we're going to win the war,' he says. Then to Larry, 'Your father won't thank me if I say yes.'

'My father will be proud of me, sir,' says Larry, 'if you tell him I've done my duty.'

Mountbatten smacks his hands together.

'By George, that's right!' he says. 'I wish to God I could do the same. But surely, you've not been trained for this sort of command?'

'Not a command, sir. I'll go in the ranks.'

Mountbatten gazes at him, evidently moved.

'Bless you, my boy,' he says. 'If that's what you want, I'll not stand in your way.'

9

The cellars at Edenfield Place are kept locked these days, and George Holland has the only key. He unlocks the cellar door and leads Larry down the steep steps, bending his head as he goes.

'Watch out here. Low arch.'

Light filters into the cool vaults through dusty cobwebbed slots. Bay after bay is filled with bottles.

'Mostly from my father's time,' says George.

'Seriously, you don't have to do this,' says Larry.

'Someone has to drink it,' says George. 'You're his friend, aren't you?'

He moves down the bays, peering at the labels.

'St Émilion '38,' he says. 'That should be good.'

He pulls out two bottles and gives them to Larry.

'You must join us, George,' says Larry.

'No, no. It's for the two of them.'

On an impulse he pulls out two more bottles.

'There. Tell Kitty congratulations from me.'

Larry carries the bottles in the pannier of his motorbike, wrapped in his pullover so they don't bang against each other. He transfers them to the kitchen table in the farm-house and wipes them down. They're standing on the table, glowing deep purple in the evening sunlight, when the outer door opens, and Ed enters.

'Can't keep away, can I?' he says.

He sees the wine.

'Grand Cru Bordeaux! Where in God's name did you get this?'

'It's for you,' says Larry. 'For you and Kitty, from the lord of the manor. He says congratulations. And so do I.'

'Word travels fast. I came here to tell you myself.'

'I saw Kitty at the corps briefing.'

'She still happy about it?'

'She's crazy about you, Eddy. You know that.'

'And I'm crazy about her.' He picks up one of the bottles. 'Why such generosity from the lord of the manor?'

'He has a soft spot for Kitty. Or had, I should say.'

Ed goes out into the yard to empty his bladder. Rex shows up, in a subdued mood.

'I just heard,' he says, 'they're fitting out warehouses by the docks as field hospitals.'

'Won't be long now,' says Larry.

Rex touches the bottles of wine, one by one, clearly unaware that he's doing so.

'You want to hear a funny story?' he says. 'There's this fellow in the RAMC who faints at the sight of blood.'

'He's in the wrong job, I'd say.'

119

'I don't faint,' says Rex. 'I'm fine with blood. But sometimes I think, what if I don't know what to do? What if I do the wrong thing?'

'Has to happen sometimes,' says Larry.

'If I do the wrong thing, someone dies.'

He takes off his glasses and looks at Larry, blinking.

'Rex,' Larry says, 'you can't think that way. You'll go nuts. You're a medic, you do your job. That's all.'

Ed comes back in and tells Rex his news. Rex offers his congratulations, glancing at Larry as he does so. Ed proposes they open one of George's bottles of wine.

'So we can drink to Kitty,' he says.

'Not for me,' says Rex. 'I'm not a wine drinker.'

'I know you're teetotal,' says Ed. 'But this is Grand Cru Bordeaux!'

'I just don't like the taste,' says Rex.

'You'll have some, Larry.'

'You bet.'

The wine is good.

'You don't know what you're missing, Rex,' says Ed. 'See the smile on my face? That should give you some idea.'

He refills Larry's glass, then his own.

'Two smiles are better than one.'

Ed decides to stay for dinner. They finish the bottle between them. Rex excuses himself.

'Early night for me.'

Left on their own, Ed fixes Larry with his cool blue eyes.

'Now comes the big question,' he says. 'Do we open bottle number two?'

'It may not be as good as number one,' says Larry.

'That is true. That is very true.'

'We could be gravely disappointed,' says Larry.

'We could,' says Ed.

'But we bear up under disappointment, don't we?'

'Always,' says Ed. 'The show must go on.'

'So let's risk it.'

Ed opens the second bottle, and fills Larry's glass.

'Still good,' Larry says, drinking.

'So far,' says Ed.

'We live in hope,' says Larry.

'The other reason I came over this evening,' says Ed, 'was to ask you to be my best man.'

'Honoured,' says Larry.

'Kitty wants a church wedding. Not a grand do or anything. But she wants the full vows.'

'Then she shall have them.'

'All right for you. But I don't go in for all that stuff.'

'So what? You can go through the motions, can't you?'

Ed sits back in the deep old chair in the corner and stares at the ceiling.

'Yes. I can go through the motions. But I'm marrying the girl I love. I want it to be real. I want to mean every word I say. I don't want to tell lies.'

'You're not lying. You're just saying words that have no meaning for you.'

'Would you do that at your wedding?'

Larry says nothing to that. Ed follows his own thoughts.

'Kitty believes in God. I asked her why, and she said she didn't know.'

'You can't ask why someone believes in God,' says Larry. 'It's not rational. It's just something you know.'

'So how come I don't know it?'

'I don't know. You must have believed once.'

'I can see a thousand reasons for saying there's no God, and no reasons for saying there is a God. But just about everyone in the world believes there is a God.'

'So who's out of step here?'

Ed jumps up, suddenly restless. He fills up their glasses once more, and starts to pace the room.

'I want to be wrong, Larry. Believe me, I want to be wrong. I want to be on Kitty's side. I want to be on your side. But I don't know how to get there. I only have to look out of the window and I see what a shit-filled world we live in.'

'Why call it a shit-filled world? What about all the beauty?'

'And all the misery, and all the cruelty. The human race has a lot to answer for. Just look at this bloody war.'

'Yes,' says Larry. 'There are bad men out there. But there are good men too. For every Hitler there's a Francis of Assisi.'

'I notice your good man is long dead and your bad man is very much with us.'

'Gandhi, then.'

'Oh, I don't know about Gandhi. I don't trust vegetarians.'

'He lives the life he preaches. Simplicity. Non-violence. Self-sacrifice.'

'So why doesn't God make us all like Gandhi?'

'Oh, come on,' says Larry. 'You know the drill as well as I do. God made us free. If he made us so we couldn't go against his will, we'd be slaves, or machines. You know all this.'

'What I don't understand is why he couldn't at least make us so we're more good than bad.'

'He does. I believe we are more good than bad. I do. I believe people's deepest instinct is to love each other, not to hurt each other.'

'Do you?' Ed stops pacing to stare at Larry, as if unsure he can really mean what he says. 'Do you?'

'Yes. I do.'

'Any day now,' says Ed, 'I'm going to be sent into some godforsaken corner of France to kill people who'll be doing their damnedest to kill me. Where's the love in that?'

'I'm coming too.'

'What!'

'I'm on loan to the RHLI. At my request.'

Ed seizes Larry by the shoulders and turns him so he can't avoid his gaze.

'What's going on?'

'I'm a soldier,' says Larry. 'Soldiers fight.'

Ed holds his gaze, his blue eyes searching for the truth Larry is withholding.

'Soldiers kill. Are you going to kill?'

'If I have to.'

'For your King and country?'

'Yes.'

Ed lets him go with a laugh.

'Well, there you are. Even you. What hope for humanity now?'

'If it's wrong for me to kill, it's wrong for you too.'

'Of course it's wrong! Everything's wrong!'

Larry is shaken by Ed's challenge. Will he kill? He can't imagine it. He's not going into action to kill, he's going into action to come under fire. It's all about self-respect. Or pride. Or Kitty.

'Anyway,' he says, 'war isn't the common human condition. Most of the time we're not trying to kill each other.'

'Fine!' says Ed. 'Forget war. Forget killing. How about plain old common-or-garden unhappiness? You can't deny that most people are unhappy most of the time. What's the point of that?'

Larry wants to say, Kitty loves you. You at least can be happy. He wants to say, What more do you want to be happy? But even as the thought forms in his mind he knows this talk of happiness is all beside the point.

'The fact is,' he says, 'you can't make sense of any of it if you believe this world is all there is. You have to see it in the light of eternity.'

'Ah, the light of eternity!'

'You think it all ends with death, as far as I can tell.'

'Yes. Lights out and that's it.'

'I see us as on a journey towards becoming gods.'

'Gods!' Ed laughs. 'We're to be gods!'

'That's the simplest way to put it.'

'All sitting on thrones together, up in the sky.'

'I'm doing my best here. You could at least try to take me seriously.'

'Yes. Yes, of course. You're right, my dear comrade-in-arms! What do you say to the third bottle?'

'That wine's for you and Kitty.'

'Mine is the greater need right now.'

He opens the third bottle.

'What we're going to do,' announces Ed as he extracts the cork, 'what we're going to do is we're going to go out in the cool night air, bringing this excellent bottle with us, and that way we'll stay sober, and you'll tell me why you and Kitty are right, and I'll take you seriously.'

They go out through the farmyard into the hay meadow beyond. They hand the bottle back and forth as they go, drinking from its neck. The night sky is clear, with a quarter moon low over the Downs.

'You know what, Ed,' says Larry. 'Neither of us knows the truth about this. All we've got is beliefs, and all our beliefs come from is our feelings. I can't imagine this life being all there is. I can't imagine death being extinction. There has to be more. And as it happens, Jesus says there is more. He says he came to give eternal life. He says he's the son of God. I don't understand what that means, but he says it, and he says that all that matters is love, and he says his kingdom is not of this earth. And all that just feels *likely* to me. I mean, what sort of a world would it be if I knew it all? It would be tiny. Existence has to be bigger than me. So the fact that I don't understand it doesn't make it unlikely, it makes it far more likely. I just know there has to be more than I know. More than you know, too. That's all you have to concede. Just accept that you don't know *everything*. Leave a bit of room in your philosophy for surprises. Leave a bit of room for hope.'

Larry becomes more and more expansive as he speaks, liberated by the wine and the darkness round him and the majesty of the star-filled sky.

'You know what,' says Ed laughing. 'I think I'd rather be you than me. All this love. All this hope. That's good stuff.'

He passes Larry the bottle. Reaching his arms out on either side he begins to make pirouettes over the grass. Larry puts the bottle to his lips and tips it back. The last of the wine runs down his throat and spills out over his chin. He tosses the bottle away with a fine disregard and it lands in the stream.

Ed comes spinning up to Larry and takes him by the hand.

'Come on, best man!' he says. 'If we're going to die, let's die together!'

They swoop about together, laughing out loud, until they lose their balance and tumble to the ground. There they lie, panting, smiling at the stars, still clasping hands.

On Saturday August 15th Ed and Kitty are married in the chapel of Edenfield Place. The wedding is small. Both bride and groom wear uniform. Kitty's parents, the Reverend

Michael Teale and his wife Molly, come from Malmesbury. Ed's parents, Harry and Gillian Avenell, come from Hatton in Derbyshire. Larry Cornford is best man. Others present are Louisa Cavendish, George Holland, Brigadier Wills, and Ed's commanding officer, Colonel Joe Picton-Phillips. After the ceremony there's a wedding breakfast in the mess, hosted by George Holland and Brigadier Wills.

Everyone is smiling and cheerful, most of all Kitty's parents, but it's not an easy occasion. The two families are meeting for the first time. Harry Avenell is a tall distinguished man, a director of a brewing company, but Kitty's pink-cheeked father has far more of the look of a brewer about him. Ed's mother teasingly reprimands Ed for not marrying in a Catholic church.

'Why would I do that, Mummy?' Ed says. 'You know I'm through with all of that.'

'Oh, so you say,' says Gillian Avenell.

Kitty likes the way he calls his mother 'Mummy' so unselfconsciously, but wonders a little at the way he behaves with both his parents. There are no embraces, no kisses. Harry Avenell takes part in the ceremony with an oddly detached manner, as if standing in for the father of the groom before the real man arrives.

Kitty's mother talks in a ceaseless stream.

'If only Harold could be here, but even if he could get leave it would be no good. He's in North Africa, you know, with the Eleventh Hussars, they call them the Cherry Pickers, they were in the Charge of the Light Brigade, but they drive armoured cars now. I remember when my mother got the news about Timmy, he was behind the lines at Passchendaele, but there was a shell and that was that. Of course it was happening to everybody, but even so. And now here's Harold out in the desert when he should be here with us, and I can't help thinking it's just all wrong.'

'Now then, Molly,' says her husband. 'This is Kitty's day.'

The newly-weds have booked a week's leave for their honeymoon, which they take in Brighton.

The Old Ship Hotel is one of the few on the seafront that hasn't been requisitioned for war personnel. The hotel is very rundown, its paintwork cracking and its wallpaper peeling. The only porter is old and sick. A girl called Milly offers to carry their bags up to their room, but Ed says he can manage. The stairs creak as they climb.

The room has a double bed, and a window that looks out over the promenade. Outside they can see the beach with its concrete anti-tank blocks and its undulations of rolled barbed wire.

'The beach will be mined,' Ed says. 'We won't be going swimming.'

The Palace Pier is deserted, its walkway broken in the middle so that it can't be used as a landing stage. The seafront is under curfew by the time they arrive. The sea gleams in the light of a golden summer evening, but there's nobody about.

'Maybe we should have gone to a B&B in the countryside,' says Ed.

'I don't care where we are,' says Kitty.

Ed is quiet, looking round the shabby room. He seems to be almost at a loss.

'What is it, Ed?'

'I wanted everything to be perfect for you,' he says.

'And for you too.'

'Oh, I don't mind. So long as I've got you.'

'Well, you have got me. You'd better think of something to do with me.'

He takes her in his arms. She leans her body against his.

'I love you so much, Kitty.'

'Just as well.'

'I love you so much I can't think or move or hardly even breathe.'

'That's too much,' Kitty says. 'You'd better love me less and breathe more.'

He kisses her.

Later they lie in bed together, and every time they move the bed makes a pinging noise. They try to stay still but it isn't easy. They start moving again and the pinging returns. They try lying in different places on the bed, and find one position, right on the edge, that almost silences the noisy bed-spring, but it's hard not to fall off.

Ed stops moving, holding Kitty close in his arms.

'We have a choice,' he says. 'We lie doggo, or we jangle.'

'Let's jangle,' she says.

On Sunday morning they walk along the seafront as far as the big Bofors gun outside the Grand Hotel. A crowd of

Canadian soldiers are playing football on the promenade, using kitbags for goalposts. Kitty holds Ed's arm and leans a little against him as they walk, and loves him so much it hurts. The sun shines on the sea, and on the patches of black tar on the pebbles under the barbed wire, and on the dull metal of the big gun. Ahead the West Pier has been severed like its sister. Across the water lies France.

I'm married, thinks Kitty. He belongs to me now. His body belongs to me.

She loves his body. She loves the feel of it pressed against hers all the way down. She wants to tell him so but there seem to be no words and she's shy. So instead she squeezes his arm and strokes the small of his back. They come to a stop by the Bofors gun and kiss. The soldiers playing soccer pause in their game to clap.

Later that Sunday afternoon all leave is cancelled and all personnel are recalled to their units. On Tuesday August 18th Admiral Lord Mountbatten, Commander-in-Chief Combined Operations, gives the order for Operation Jubilee, the largest military assault on mainland Europe since the disaster of Dunkirk.

It's a clear night, and the sea is calm. Larry is up on deck with Johnny Parrish to escape the thick fog of tobacco smoke below. He looks through a gap in the tarpaulin at the dark coast of England as it recedes. On either side of the troop-ship other craft reach as far as the eye can see, their low rumble filling the night. Bulbous transport ships carrying invasion barges; tank landing craft lying low in the water; the sleek forms of destroyers.

'Bloody big show,' says Johnny.

Over the lapping of the waves against the hull they hear the sound of a motorboat drawing alongside.

'That'll be the CO,' says Johnny. 'Better get below.'

The troop deck is packed and buzzing with excitement. Larry joins the crowd of officers by the companionway. Shortly after, the brigadier enters, with General Ham Roberts. Roberts wastes no time in preliminaries.

'We're on our way, men,' he says. 'You've been told this

is another training exercise. Well, it isn't. This is the real thing.'

A great shout goes up from the mass of soldiers, followed by hoots and cheers. The officers look at each other and grin.

'Our destination is Dieppe. We will land at dawn, hold the port for a maximum of twelve hours, and withdraw. This is not an invasion. This will be the very first reconnaissance in force of the enemy mainland. The port of Dieppe is well defended. This isn't going to be a picnic. But it's our first chance in this war to get a poke at the Hun. So let's see we give him a poke he won't forget.'

The men cheer again. Roberts departs, to repeat his short speech on the next ship in the great armada.

Larry retreats to the wardroom, where he and the crowd of other officers are joined shortly by Brigadier Wills. Orders are now opened and given out, complete with maps, schedules, and aerial photographs. Jevons talks them through the plan.

'RAF air cover will be in place by dawn. Naval bombardment of the beaches will begin at 0510 hours. At 0520 hours our landing craft will hit Red Beach, here. Our mission is to seize and hold the Casino, which is here.'

Larry listens attentively. The plan is so detailed, so specific, that it has an air of inevitability. But what is it all for? Why are they to attack this fortified port, and then go home again? All round him, beneath the grave faces and the air of businesslike concentration, he feels wild pulsing excitement. They're going into battle. No one asks to measure the risk against the reward. All they require is the assurance that the cause is just.

'Just point us at 'em,' the men say, 'and leave us to do the rest.'

Larry feels it too, but he doesn't yet understand it. All he knows is it's nothing to do with love of England, or hatred of Germany. He isn't on this mission because he wants to die for his country. He's here because his whole world is on the march, and it has become impossible to stand on the margins and watch the parade go by. He sees on the faces of the men around him the same conviction that possesses him: we're on our way at last.

Shortly after midnight the fleet enters a minefield. The order goes out for all men to inflate their lifejackets. The command ship, the Hunt-class destroyer HMS *Calpe*, enters the minefield first, following the channel cleared by navy sweepers. The convoy falls in behind, guided by the faint green lights of marker buoys.

Larry stands at the ship's rail on the open deck, now packed tight with silent men. All watch the white froth of the ship's wake as the engines drive them fast through the danger zone.

'The old man's gone through first,' says a voice. 'He's got guts, give him that.'

'They lay these magnetic mines,' says another. 'You don't have to hit them. They come and hit you.'

'Just like me and the girls.'

'Me, I'm old-fashioned. I like to hit the girls first.'

Subdued laughter ripples outwards in the night. The ship veers suddenly to starboard and the men fall silent. Then the ship veers again, to port. A light on the water ahead comes nearer, and then passes away into the darkness.

A bell jangles. Voices and laughter break out again. The troopship is safely through the minefield. The tension lifts. Brigadier Wills, doing the rounds, finds Larry still leaning on the rail.

'Try to get some sleep,' he says.

'Yes, sir, I will,' says Larry.

'Good to have you along. The boys appreciate it.'

Larry finds a space to lie down below deck, but he knows he won't sleep. He's in a state he's not experienced before, a strange combination of stillness and intense inner excitement. He takes out a cigarette and lights it, noticing now that all round him glow the tips of other cigarettes. He inhales deeply, and feels a tingling sensation pass through his body, followed by a deep powerful languor. Unthinkingly he gives a sigh of pleasure. His neighbour says out of the darkness, 'Always fresh,' and Larry follows up with a laugh, 'And truly mild.' The slogan of the Sweet Caps he smokes these days, to show his solidarity with the Canadian forces. As he exhales he can see the cigarette smoke shivering in the air above him, shaken back and forth by the vibrations of the ship's engines.

The river gunboat *Locust* emerges from the minefield in its turn, following the long line of troopships and landing craft. Three hundred and seventy officers and men of 40

Commando are crowded onto the narrow deck, either asleep or sitting still and breathing evenly to conserve energy. The commanding officer, Colonel Phillips, is reviewing the maps and photographs of White Beach, and familiarising himself with the layout of the town beyond.

'You know what Dieppe's famous for?' says Ed Avenell. 'Dirty weekends.'

'You should know, Ed,' says Abercrombie.

Ed smiles and says nothing.

Breakfast is served early, just before two in the morning. Beef stew, bread and butter and marmalade, and coffee. The officers eat in silence.

At fleet rendezvous point new orders are received from Operational Command. Phillips announces that 40 Commando is to be held in reserve. A groan goes up from the men.

'What are we, fucking nursemaids?'

'We're to wait for the Canadians to clear the main beach.'

4 Commando's job is demolition. By the time they're through, not one port facility will be left operational. Joe Phillips doesn't like the new orders any more than his men. Commandos are raiders, trained to move fast and light. They're not assault troops.

'Try to get some sleep,' he tells the men.

Ed Avenell remains on deck, leaning on the stern rail, watching the long line of the fleet behind them. Here Phillips finds him, as he does his rounds.

'Biggest naval operation of the war,' he says.

'Looks like it,' says Ed.

'You've not told the boys you got hitched.'

'No,' says Ed.

'You don't want any special treatment.'

'That's about it, sir.'

Titch Houghton joins them.

'Lovat and his boys will be ready to go in about now,' he says.

4 Commando are to make a night landing on Orange Beach to the west, while Durnford-Slater's 3 Commando makes for Yellow Beach and the big guns of Berneval.

'Has Lovat taken his bloody piper?' says Phillips.

'Of course,' says Titch Houghton.

'I don't like this reserve bullshit. It means we go in by daylight.'

At three in the morning, as required by the complex timetable of the operation, the men of the RHLI form up below decks in their platoons to prepare for the transfer to landing craft. They wear their netted tin hats. The inflated Mae Wests beneath their tunics give them all powerful chests. They carry Brens, Stens and rifles over their shoulders, hand grenades on their belts, knives at their hips. Larry Cornford, armed like the rest, takes his place in the line for Number 6 boat, and waits for the man in front of him to move.

This is what his entire life has become: waiting, moving, waiting again, always in lines, carried along by the great machine of which he is one tiny part. Now the lines begin to move up onto deck, where the night is still dark. Ahead men are climbing ladders into the slung barges, great black masses against the starlit sky. Larry follows in his turn, jumping down onto the benches that run the length of the craft. Men are ahead of him, and all the time more men are piling on after him, and soon he finds himself pushed towards the back of the starboard bench. A voice hisses at him, 'Sit crossways! Face forward!' Shortly he is wedged tight on the bench between the packs and weapons of other men.

The barge lurches and swings. The davit gear emits its high-pitched whine. The side of the ship rises above them. Then comes the slap of the water as the long steel craft settles, and the throb of the engine starting up.

A voice from above calls, 'You're on your own now, boys! Give 'em hell!'

The landing craft chugs away from the mother ship, taking its place in a line of other assault craft. The coast of France is still fifteen miles to the south-east, two hours and more away.

Larry gazes at the steersman in his armoured box over the bow, and hears the ping-ping of the engine-room telegraph. These are navy boys, their job is to ferry the assault troops, not to take part in the attack.

I'll be in the attack. I will fight.

This extraordinary fact has filled his being since he left England. Every single moment since then, however tedious, however uncomfortable, has been charged with intensity. All this time is *before*. Nothing has prepared him for the feelings he now experiences. It's not fear, not yet. The danger he faces has no reality yet. Nor is it that state he's heard talk of, called battle exultation. He feels sharp, as if all his being has been sharpened to a single point. Gone are all the usual little complications of life. He has no thoughts of his family or friends, no memories of his life gone by. Nothing but this landing craft, the pressure of the man behind him, the juddering of the engine, the twinge of cramp in his leg, the smell of spray on the air, the stars above, and *it* – the battle to which they sail.

After this nothing will ever be the same again. I am about to be transformed. Out there in the darkness there waits for me an *enemy*, men who wish me harm, who will try to hurt me, even though they know nothing about me. And will I try to hurt them? Of course. And because of this, nothing will ever be the same again.

He settles down at last into a doze. All along the benches men grunt and mutter in their sleep, as the craft maintains its course straight ahead. The flotilla, no longer in single file, is spread out over the surface of the night sea, seeming almost not to be moving.

Suddenly there comes a streak of bright light to the north-east, and a flare explodes in the sky. It drops slowly down, illuminating the water's surface.

'What the fuck was that?'

Men jerk out of sleep to watch.

Brilliant green streaks arc up into the sky, followed by red streaks, rising, cresting a curve, falling and fading to nothing. There follow bright white silent shell bursts, and shooting stars of gold, and more lazy leaping arcs of dazzling red.

'Tracer! Some bugger's hit trouble!'

The landing craft has neither slowed nor deviated from its course. Now the men on board hear the bark of ack-ack guns from the French coast.

'Sounds like Jerry's woken up.'

'That'll be fun for us.'

The men of 40 Commando are halfway through transferring from the *Locust* to their landing craft when the tracer battle lights up the sky. Colonel Phillips is on the bridge with the navy team, trying to make out what's happening.

'Not good,' he says. 'There goes our surprise.'

Wireless traffic between HMS *Calpe* and HMS *Berkeley* reveals that the easternmost craft in the fleet, Number 3 Commando's boats, have run into a German tanker and its escort. Orders are to continue according to plan.

Phillips leaves the gunboat last of his men, jumping down into the fourth landing craft. The *Locust* is to accompany them all the way, short of the beach itself.

'Don't worry about it, boys!' says Phillips, standing in the craft so all can see him. 'It's only 3 Commando screwing up.'

Soft laughter ripples through the boats.

'Let's go.'

The four barges set course for the coast of France, joining almost two hundred others now spread over a line eight miles wide. Ed Avenell is in 2 Boat commanded by Titch Houghton. The diminutive major stands up in the bow as they pick up speed.

'Plenty of time yet, boys,' he says. 'We're to get into position offshore, then we wait for the order to go in.'

As the glow of dawn appears to the east, the naval barrage opens up, according to plan. The eight destroyers pound the coastal defences for ten minutes, filling the air with the scream and glare of high explosive. At the same time there comes a distant singing in the sky as the squadrons of Spitfires arrive, escorting the Boston bombers. At 0530 hours the barrage ceases, and the main assault on the beaches begins.

Larry waits in his landing craft a little way off the beach, dazed by the bombardment, unable to see anything ahead other than his fellow soldiers. The barge heaves and lurches on the tide. All round, the darkness is fading into light. Bostons rumble low overhead, laying a trail of thick white smoke along the beach. Tank landing craft come surging past, first in line for the assault. He hears the boom of guns open up, followed by the rattle of light weapons. On either side other assault craft wait for the signal to advance. The men in his boat are tensed, ready to go. The sound of gunfire grows louder all the time, a ceaseless refrain now, but nothing can be seen through the smoke. Then comes the deep hollow boom of a big gun.

'Howitzer!' murmurs a voice. 'Six-incher.'

Tracer bullets flash across the sky ahead. Somewhere in the dawn shadows, in the white smoke, the battle has already begun. Then at last, in response to some unheard command, the engines pick up speed and the barge surges forward. A loud cheer goes up from the men. A sergeant in the bows starts up a progress report.

'Five hundred yards . . . I can see the beach . . . Three hundred . . . Smoke's lifting . . .'

The smoke is being swept away in long streamers by a westerly wind. In the dawn light the beach appears before them, with the town beyond. All along the shore, landing craft stand beached on the shingle. Beyond, between the sea-line and the town, a dozen or so box-like objects are spread out, crawling slowly. Between them the pale grey beach is in constant eruption, like the surface of a heated pan of porridge. Each bursting bubble emits its small puff of smoke, which arises and disperses on the wind.

'Brace, lads! Here we go!'

The landing craft smashes into the sandbar and every man lurches forward. The ramp falls and the lead men are out, floundering in shallow water. Larry sees only the men ahead, and he follows in his turn, possessed by one passionate desire, to move, to be in action.

He jumps, sinks in the water, hits the pebble ridge, scrambles to find a footing, feels the shingle skid beneath his weight. Round him men flounder and fall, thrashing the water with their arms. A spout of seawater rises up before him, and a shockwave hits him in the face, stinging his eyes. His boots won't grip the seabed, he struggles to advance, but with each downward kick he feels himself slipping back. Then a wave comes in and lurches him forward, and all at once he's climbing, he's up onto the beach proper, and he's tramping over the spreadeagled body of a man.

Shocked more by the touch than the sight he stops and looks round, bewildered, unable to make sense of what he sees. A man nearby throws himself over on one side. Ahead a man is crawling, groaning as he goes. Beyond there are figures to be seen scattered here and there over the beach, crouched or toppled. The sounds round him are deafening, irregular, inescapable. Men come heaving past him, loaded down with packs and weapons, firing as they go.

Who are they shooting at? There's no sign of the enemy. Only these puffs of smoke, these eruptions in the pebbles.

Ahead a tank is thrashing its tracks, struggling to make way over the slippery beach. A shrill whine, a violent bang, and the tank kicks over onto its side, ripped apart by an artillery shell. There are men running past Larry again, as the next wave of troops streams out of the landing craft. A mortar lands in their midst, hurling them to the ground. Larry too, unbalanced by the blast, falls forward onto his arms. Somewhere nearby a man is screaming.

'Buddy! I need a hand here! Buddy!'

The rattle of machine-gun fire comes and goes. Bullets ping on stones. Larry lies still, thinking. Their orders are to take the Casino. He can see the Casino from where he lies. Much of the fire that pins them down is coming from its windows. It would be suicidal madness to charge across the open beach into those guns.

Between himself and the promenade wall he counts seven disabled tanks. As for men, there are too many to count, and more are falling all the time. What is the purpose of this? Why have they been sent ashore unprotected into heavy enemy fire, to capture a heavily defended Casino for which they have no use?

The men around him who've not been hit are up again and struggling forward. Larry too staggers to his feet and lurches forward, not because there's any sense to it, but because this is what the others are doing. He finds that his progress is slow and flailing, as if he's still running in water. I must be in shock, he thinks. Then the beach erupts before him, and he feels the sting of a thousand tiny pebbles. His ears ring, his skin trickles with wetness. Ahead of him stands a man with blood shooting out of his neck and shoulder, pierced by shell splinters, toppling slowly forward into the crater formed by the mortar.

There are hundreds of men advancing up the beach, but Larry has the sensation of being alone. Gone are the orderly ranks and lines of army life. Here there is only howling space, sudden danger, and the deep rolling surge of the sea.

He drives himself on up the beach, flinching with every screaming shell or whining bullet that passes, and so reaches one of the abandoned Churchill tanks. It's shed its tracks in its desperate efforts to claw its way over the pebbles, and now stands sideways on to the promenade. Larry crawls up close and sinks to the ground, resting his back against its steel flank, taking cover from the machine guns that strafe the beach. From this position he can see the waves of men still spilling from the assault landing craft, still charging the beach into the withering enemy fire.

Now for the first time he understands that he is almost

paralysed by fear. Until this moment the shock of being under fire has driven out all other thoughts. Now in the comparative safety of his one-walled fortress he understands that he will certainly be injured, that he'll maybe die, and he feels his guts melt with terror. Fear turns out to be physical, a rebellion of the body, the refusal to do anything that will take him closer to danger. He would burrow himself into the ground if he could. He has become an animal who has nowhere left to run, and so has frozen into immobility.

Then after a little time the fear too passes. In its place comes a strange detachment. He watches the aircraft circling high above, like starlings turning to follow their leader. He sees the sun climb into the sky. He thinks how meaningless it all is, the explosions and the killing, the winning and losing. He thinks of his father, and how there's something he needs to tell him, but he can't remember what it is. He thinks of Kitty, and her sweet smile, and how he'd like to tell her how much he loves her. But it's too late now, because he's going to die. He finds he's not afraid of dying after all, it turns out just to be another thing that happens. You think you're in control of your life but really all you can do is accept what happens with a good grace.

I'm not fighting any more.

Not meaning fighting as a soldier, fighting in a war, God knows he's done little enough of that. He's no longer fighting for life. Whatever that instinct or passion is that chooses life at all costs has slipped away, overwhelmed by fatigue and fear. So the fear hasn't left him after all, it's merely taken this new form, of loss of will. Like a dog that accepts its master's blows in silence, hoping by lack of opposition to win reprieve.

I've surrendered, Larry thinks. Take me prisoner. Take me home. Let me sleep.

There comes a roar overhead and the shadow of low-flying bombers, and then the smoke rolls down the beach. Larry gazes at the veil of whiteness that curtains him in his refuge and pretends to himself that now he's safe after all.

General Roberts on the command ship HMS *Calpe* receives a steady stream of messages from the assault forces, many of which contradict each other. Some of the Calgary regiment's tanks are reported to have broken into the town itself. A platoon of the RHLI has fought its way up to the six-inch gun before the Casino. 4 Commando are back on their mother ship after successfully destroying the coastal battery behind Varengeville. The Royals have suffered heavy losses on Blue Beach, which remains exposed to the Berneval guns, but the RAF still have air supremacy, and the Essex Scottish, following the RHLI, are ashore in the centre. Reports are coming in that the beaches have been cleared. With all the information the commander has at his disposal it makes sense to commit his reserve forces. The objective remains the outright capture of the port. Fresh troops, sweeping past the units who have done so much to break the enemy's resistance, will tip the balance of the day.

'Send in the reserves now.'

The order is transmitted to the landing craft standing offshore, holding seven hundred men of the Fusiliers Mont-

Royal, and three hundred and seventy men of 40 Commando. The smokescreen hangs heavy over the sea and shore as the barges line up and make their approach.

On Ed Avenell's boat the order is received with a cheer.

'About fucking time!'

For three hours now they've sat helpless as shells from shore batteries have passed overhead, or into the water nearby, while from the distant beach has come the ceaseless chatter of gunfire. Now at last they can go about their business.

The four boats of the commando advance in line with each other, forming the last wave after the Fusiliers. They pass through the smokescreen and out into sunlight, and so get their first clear sight of the beach, barely a hundred yards ahead. They see the Fusiliers landing, scrambling onto the beach, falling, hit by the relentless crossfire. They see mortars plop down and blow men away like dolls. They see the shells of the big howitzers rip up the beach. And most of all they see the countless corpses that lie all the way from the water to the promenade.

Ed Avenell, rising to his feet, preparing to jump, sees all this and knows that he is participating in a cruel and bloody joke.

'This is fucking insane!'

Colonel Phillips understands that a terrible mistake has been made. He pulls on a pair of white gloves so that his signalling hands can be seen by the other boats, and standing tall in the bow he shouts and gestures the command to go back.

'Turn about! Turn about!'

As he signals his order a bullet strikes him in the forehead, killing him instantly. Number 2 Boat, running a little ahead, does not see the signal. The others turn back.

Titch Houghton, eyes on the beach, shouts to the men in Number 2 Boat, 'Stand by! This is it!'

The barge shudders to a stop and the commandos spring out, guns in firing position. Moving at speed they lope up the beach, spreading out as they go. Whatever plan there was has been overtaken by events. They're hunting enemy to kill.

Now there are silver Focke-Wulf 109s up in the sky as well as the Spitfires of the RAF. As the Spitfires run short on fuel and turn for home the Focke-Wulfs fly low, strafing the men on the beach. Ed Avenell, fuelled by a toxic mixture of frustration and rage, storms the promenade wall, firing from a Bren gun as he goes. The enemy are nowhere to be seen, but their shells and bullets are everywhere. Racing down an empty street, shooting as he goes, he shouts, 'Come on out, you bastards!' A sniper fires at him from a house, and catching a glimpse of him at an upper window, he swings back, spraying bullets.

The Fusiliers punch their way into the marketplace just as the RHLI finally capture the Casino. But the mortars keep on coming, and the big guns on the clifftop emplacements keep on booming. An empty building on the promenade has been taken over as an assembly point for the wounded and the dead. A large contingent of Camerons has formed a defensive line against enemy forces massing in the woods on the west side of the town. There is no objective any more, no overall strategy. Men run with great urgency in opposite directions, each following some imperative of his own. In the midst of this random violence the inhabitants of the town go about their business seemingly indifferent to the danger. One man leads four cows into the shelter of a barn, and then goes back out again to fetch in hay. Another, in hat and jacket but no shirt, bicycles down the street with a baguette in his basket. Small boys stare with big eyes at the soldiers running past. Some buildings are burning, but not fiercely, issuing thin trails of smoke into the clear sky.

The tide is far out now. Between the pebble beach with its litter of corpses and the sea where the armada waits, shrouded in smoke, there lies a wide strip of shining sand. The hour is past ten. On HMS *Calpe* General Roberts knows the assault has failed. He gives the order to retreat.

Ed Avenell's rage has only grown as he has taken in the scale of the disaster. He rages at the enemy who won't come out to fight. But most of all he rages at the sheer folly of it all. Why would any sane military planner send men to storm a heavily defended beach in broad daylight? But there are no sane military planners. The world is run by fools and the outcome is and always will be chaos. So together with his rage goes a fierce gladness that his deepest instincts should be proved so visibly right. This battle, that has no structure and no objective, that takes place merely to cause men to die to no purpose, is for Ed a perfect model of existence stripped bare. His anger flows from him in a right-eous stream, but he's laughing at himself even as he deals out his vengeance, because he knows his only true justification for killing is that he too is prepared to die.

By the time he gets the order to retreat he has entered an almost ecstatic state. He should have been hit countless times, but somehow the bullets have not found him, and the shell splinters have passed him by. Now he believes his luck is impregnable, and he takes no precautions at all. He has become invulnerable.

Larry remains crouched behind the abandoned tank as the retreat unfolds. He sees men running back down the beach towards the returning landing craft. He smells seaweed, and salt water, and blood. He has no desire to get up himself and go to the boats. The space between himself and the water is a killing zone, men fall repeatedly as they run, hit by the guns in the cliffs, or the strafing of planes, or the unending boom of the mortars. But Larry does not stay where he is because he's afraid of the danger on the open beach. He remains motionless because he has lost the will to act. He has become utterly resigned, even to his own destruction.

His dulled gaze is caught by a man who is striding down the beach with another man in his arms. Larry sees him deliver his burden to the group clustered round the landing craft. Then he returns, striding back up the beach, oblivious to the bullets flying all round him.

It's Ed Avenell. Larry watches him with a smile. He even

attempts to greet him, 'Eddy!', as if he's passing in a London street, but he makes no sound. Larry is pleased to have found a friend in this strange place. His eyes follow him.

He sees him pick up another wounded man and carry him down to the water's edge. Slowly it enters Larry's fuddled mind that the assault force is now withdrawing. He sees Ed return up the beach, still unharmed, and gather up a third wounded man.

It's the way he walks that strikes Larry. He walks with his head held high, in a straight line, briskly but with no sense of hurry. And he never stops. While others stream for the boats, and load them to the point of sinking in their desperation to escape that deadly beach, Ed simply delivers his load and walks back up again.

Well, then, thinks Larry. That's how it's done.

He stumbles to his feet, and looks down towards the waterline. Every hundred yards or so boats lie with their noses grounded in the sand. Beyond them dozens of boats are coming in or going out, some circling to pick up survivors in the water. The batteries on the cliffs maintain their relentless barrage, now directed at the landing craft, their shells sending up great showers of water as they land between the boats.

Better get going, thinks Larry.

He sets off down the beach, just as he has seen Ed do. A rattle of gunfire, the wind of passing bullets, and suddenly he's running. His boots feel heavy, he stumbles on the pebbles, wrenching one ankle. Careless of the pain, possessed by terror, he runs onto the strip of wet sand. Now he feels as if his boots don't even touch the ground, he's flying. He hears a man shout, it's a stretcher bearer standing there with a stretcher at his feet. His other stretcher bearer lies dead on the beach.

'Give me a hand here!'

Larry runs on, powerless to arrest his flight. He sees a landing craft ahead, its ramp raised for sailing. He runs into the water, feeling its sudden chill. He reaches the craft, clings to its side, pressing himself to the steel plates, sobbing. The craft moves, rocked by a wave, settles back onto the sand bar, and then rocks again. Larry crouches low in the water by its side, as if the bullets won't find him if they can't see him. He has hold of a rope dangling over the craft's side in a long loop. A young boy comes lurching through the water and grabs another loop of rope, but as he does so the boat swings away out to sea and the rope is jerked from his hand. He lowers his arms and stands still, waist deep in water, watching the craft move away.

Larry, clinging tight, is carried out into deep water. His hands are now numb with cold. He loops the rope round his arm so he won't be cast adrift. Others clinging to ropes like him now climb up the flat steel side and onto the deck. Larry tries to climb, but all he has is the rope, and he lacks the strength for the pull to the top. Then he feels his reaching hand clasped from above, and he begins to rise. At the same time a hand below locks onto one of his legs, and drags him down again. He kicks violently, and the hand lets him go. Up he rises again, and so at last is pulled floundering onto the deck.

He lies gasping, exhausted, his cheek pressed to the cold steel plates. He feels the juddering of the engine as the boat pulls away from the shore, away from the nightmare of the beach. His gaze takes in the hold below, which is packed tight with wounded men. They seem to be standing knee-deep in water. As he watches, the water rises, up to their waists. The water is red. And still the water rises.

Now he becomes aware of commotion all round him.

'Jump, lads! Jump in the water! Swim for it!'

The craft is sinking. The bow end of the boat is dipping lower and lower. The wounded men are scrambling out of the bloody water now filling the hold.

Larry jumps with the rest. Bobbing in the water, kept afloat by his Mae West, he looks towards the beach. It's barely yards away. He's still in the danger zone. A plop in the water nearby is followed by a gushing explosion that buries him in seawater, and leaves him choking. The men who had been bobbing on that spot are gone. Here and there tin hats float on the water.

Another landing craft is now circling towards the throng of men in the water. Larry paddles to its sides and takes his place in the crowd attempting to board. One by one they're hauled up onto the deck. When Larry's turn comes he hears a series of sharp pinging sounds and feels a sudden sting in his buttock. At the same time strong hands are hauling him up and over the side. Helpless to control his exhausted body he topples over the edge and slithers down into the hold seven feet below. He lands on men already packed there, and almost at once becomes himself a cushion for the next man to fall. The sharp pinging sounds continue above.

Voices are shouting. 'Lighten ship! We're too low in the water! Lighten ship!'

Men throw up their tin hats, out of the hold. They pull off boots, tunics, trousers. They throw out water bottles and webbing. The craft is under way now, its deck almost flush with the water.

Larry is in his underclothes, surrounded by men in their underclothes. Someone passes him a cigarette, but his fingers are numb, and he hasn't enough breath left to smoke it.

'You take it.' He passes it on. 'I'll have one later.'

Half a mile out from shore the landing craft is made fast to a big ship and the wounded are taken aboard. Larry is limping as he follows the others across the main deck. A tap on his shoulder and a voice says, 'Wardroom's down the companionway, Lieutenant.' His legs buckle as he descends the ladder, and he feels himself helped to a chair. A blanket is wrapped round him, and a glass of brandy thrust into his hands.

'Rough out there,' says the steward.

Larry nods, and sips his brandy.

'The MO'll take a look at you when he can.'

'Nothing serious,' says Larry. 'What ship am I on?'

'You're on the *Calpe*,' says the steward. 'You're on the command ship.'

Another wounded man calls out, 'Say, could you send down a jug or something?'

'Right away,' says the steward.

The wardroom is packed with wounded officers, some on the couches, some on the floor, some seated at the mess table, their heads resting on their arms. No one speaks. A sickbay attendant appears with a white enamel jug. The wounded man pees into it, making a bell-like ringing sound. After that the jug makes the rounds.

A naval officer comes down to tell them the MO will be with them as soon as he can, but there are so many emergency cases in the sickbay.

'How long before we're home?' one man asks.

'Once we get under way,' says the officer, 'we'll be back in two hours. But I don't think we'll be leaving until every man's off the beach.'

'So where are we now?'

'Dieppe,' comes the reply.

Here below decks the battle feels far away, but for the ceaseless sound of the big guns. They know the ship's under attack from the air because they hear the heavy-calibre ack-acks followed by the clatter of the Oerlikons and then the roar of the bombers passing overhead. Then the guns reverse order, the light rattle chasing the retreating planes, and the heavy pom-pom-pom of the 4.7 guns taking the long shots.

The steward brings food: ship's biscuits and tins of sardines. The medical officer comes at last, blinking with exhaustion. His head sways from side to side as he speaks.

'Hey, doc, you need a drink.'

'Yes, I expect I do.'

But he doesn't drink, he makes his round of the wounded

officers. When he gets to Larry, Larry says, 'Don't bother with me. It's nothing.' But he looks anyway.

'You've got a bullet in the bum,' he says. 'Can you cope for now?'

'Sure.'

'Go and get it sorted when you're home.'

Now that he's been told the wound is real, Larry becomes aware that it hurts. He tries to shift his position to ease the pain but only succeeds in making it worse. He accepts another glass of brandy in the hope that he might sleep.

HMS *Calpe* finally begins its journey home at three in the afternoon, the last ship to leave the scene. The return is slow, because there are heavily laden landing craft to escort. It's past midnight when the last of the fleet reaches Newhaven.

Larry files off the destroyer in his underwear, wrapped in a blanket. On the quayside there are hundreds of figures moving about with hurricane lamps, lighting up the ambulances, troop trucks and mobile canteens lined up along the dock. A soldier hands him a pack of cigarettes as he steps off the gangway. A nurse takes his arm and ask him questions.

'Can you walk? Do you need immediate assistance?'

'I'm okay for now. I could do with a cup of tea.'

She takes him directly to the canteen, and gets him a cup of tea.

'See to the others, Nurse,' Larry says. 'I'll be all right.'

He stands on the dark quay among the quiet bustle and drinks his tea. Now that he's out of danger the numb sensations of the last many hours are beginning to lift. Exhaustion and pain sweep through him in waves. And then at first in fragments, then in whole sequences like scenes from a film, he starts to recall his day under fire. He feels the pebbles slip under his boots. He sees the corpse-strewn beach. He tastes the memory of his fear. He sees the tall lean figure of his friend striding up and down the beach, saving the lives of others. And he sees himself, crouched under cover, thinking only of his own survival.

Where is Ed now?

As Larry sips the hot strong tea and feels strength return to his body, the shame in him grows and grows. He bows his head and starts to sob. He weeps for the horror and the weariness and the waste, but most of all for his own moral failure. He wants to ask forgiveness but doesn't know who to ask. He wants to be comforted but believes he doesn't deserve comfort.

'Larry?'

He looks up, face streaming with tears, and there's Kitty.

'Oh, Larry!' He sees the shock on her face. 'Are you wounded?'

'Nothing much,' he says.

He reaches up to rub the tears from his cheeks. His blanket slips. She holds it in place for him.

'Come on,' she says. 'There are beds right here.'

He lets her lead him to a nearby warehouse, which has been fitted out as a field hospital. She hands him over to the nurses. They take him in and get him into a bed. They examine his wound and dress it for the night and tell him he's going to be fine. Then Kitty comes back and sits by him and holds his hand.

'I saw Ed over there,' Larry says. 'He was a hero. A real hero.'

'He hasn't come back,' says Kitty.

'Why not?' Larry knows how stupid this is even as he speaks the words. Somehow it hasn't occurred to him that Ed wouldn't make it.

'Not accounted for,' says Kitty.

'But I saw him!'

Larry falls silent. He wants to say, Nothing can touch him. He was invulnerable. But as he forms the thought he realises the absurdity of it. The opposite is true. Ed took insane risks. How can he have survived?

'He hasn't come back,' says Kitty again, her voice shivering like glass about to break.

Larry closes his eyes and lets his head lie back on the pillow.

'A lot of men haven't come back,' says Kitty. 'But at least you have.'

'Amazing job! First class!'

Admiral Mountbatten paces up and down the room, flexing his upper arms, as if so moved by admiration that only his agitated limbs can express his feelings.

'I want to hear all about it.'

Larry Cornford is standing, using a walking stick to ease the weight on his right buttock, from which a bullet has been extracted. The only other person in the room with them is Rupert Blundell. Larry has no idea how to tell his supreme commander about the action at Dieppe. Two months and more have passed, but it feels like a hundred years.

'I don't really know what to say, sir.'

'I know, I know,' cries Mountbatten, turning on him his intent and seductive gaze. 'That's what we all say afterwards. When the *Kelly* sank under me, I thought, no one can ever know what this feels like. No one. But then I got talking to Noel, and you know what he's done? He's made a film of it! Bloody good film, too. I've seen it. It should be showing in a few weeks. Go and see it. I can fix tickets for you if you want.'

'Thank you, sir,' says Larry.

'You were on the beach at Dieppe, were you?'

'Yes, sir.'

'Good for you. That's what I want. The real unvarnished PBI view. They say the lessons we've learned from Jubilee are priceless. Shorten the war by years, they say. Plus the whole show finally lured the Luftwaffe out of their hidey-holes and let the RAF give them one hell of a spanking. I've had Winston patting me on the back, I've had Eisenhower like a kid in a candy store. But at the end of the day it's the Poor Bloody Infantry who did the job.'

Larry can think of nothing to say to this.

'Pretty bloody for real, eh?'

'Yes, sir.'

'That's war for you. You heard about Lovat's outfit? Copybook operation. So the Canadians did us proud, did they?'

'Yes, sir.'

'A hard, savage clash, as Winston says.'

'Yes, sir.'

'I shall tell your father when I next see him, Larry. You chose to go in the line of fire. You didn't have to be there. I don't forget things like that. Your name has been put forward.'

'No, sir.' Suddenly Larry becomes agitated. 'I did nothing,

sir. I landed, I was on the beach for two or three hours, and I got away. I don't deserve to be noticed above the others, sir. Above any of the others.'

Mountbatten continues to eye him keenly.

'I understand,' he says. 'Good man.'

'If you're putting names forward, sir, there's one you should add to the list. Lieutenant Ed Avenell of 40 Royal Marine Commando. I watched him carrying wounded men to the boats, while under constant fire himself. He must have saved ten lives at least.'

Mountbatten turns to Rupert Blundell.

'Make a note of that, Rupert.'

'Another one of ours, sir,' says Rupert.

Mountbatten turns back to Larry.

'What's become of him?'

'Missing in action, sir,' says Larry.

'Got that, Rupert?'

'Yes, sir.'

'And there's something else to note,' says Mountbatten, apparently still talking to Blundell, but with a nod towards Larry. 'Here's a man who volunteers for the front line, charges into the heart of battle, catches a bullet, and all he'll tell me is how some other fellow is the true hero. That's the sort of spirit that Noel understands.'

He turns to Larry and holds out his hand.

'It's an honour to have you on my staff.'

Rupert Blundell escorts Larry back down the corridor to the exit.

'He's not a complete chump,' he says. 'He knows it was

an almighty balls-up. He asked me if I thought he should resign.'

'What did you tell him?'

'I told him it all depended on the nature of his failure. Was it extrinsic or intrinsic? Did he think he could learn from it?'

'Christ, Rupert, you sound like his father confessor.'

'It is an odd relationship. But he's a very unusual man. He's vain and childish, but at the same time he's humble and genuinely serious. Of course, Edwina makes an enormous difference. He depends on her approval more than anything, and she holds him to very high standards.'

'Edwina Mountbatten?' says Larry. 'Isn't she supposed to be a playgirl?'

'People are always so much more complicated than one thinks, aren't they?'

At the door, bidding Larry goodbye, he adds, 'Did you mean that about Ed Avenell?'

'Every word.'

'I'll see that it gets looked into.'

The army camp in the park of Edenfield Place is now a ghost town. Twelve hundred men left from here to join the assault on Dieppe. A little over five hundred returned. This rump has now departed, to combine with other units of the Canadian forces, in new quarters. The NAAFI shelves have been cleared, the mess huts stripped of their tables and chairs, the Canadian flag struck from the flagpole in the parade ground.

Larry walks slowly up the camp's main street, limping a little, using his walking stick. He is back in Edenfield to collect his few belongings from his farmhouse billet, and is making this last visit as a kind of homage. Too many men have died.

He turns away from the camp and down the avenue of lime trees to the lake. There is the lake house, where he first set eyes on Kitty. That sunlit day now seems to him to have slipped away into the distant past. He's been trying not to think of Kitty, because that leads to thoughts of Ed, and the possibility that he was killed on the beach at Dieppe. Thinking this causes such turmoil within him that he shakes his head from side to side, as if by doing so he can drive out the shameful hope that follows.

He makes his way back up the avenue to the big house, wondering if George Holland is at home, when he sees a figure coming towards him.

'Kitty?'

The figure breaks into a run.

'Larry!'

She comes to him and hugs him, laughing out loud.

'I thought it must be you!'

'Careful! I'm still wobbly.'

'Oh, Larry! How wonderful to see you!'

Her eyes so bright, her lovely face so filled with happiness.

'I didn't think you'd still be here,' Larry says. 'Haven't your mob been posted somewhere else?'

'I'm out,' she says. 'Para eleven.'

One of the few ways of being released from service, and available only to women.

'Kitty! You're going to have a baby!'

She nods, smiling.

'And even better – Ed's alive! He's a prisoner of war.'

'Oh! Thank God!'

He speaks quietly, but he means it. A deep sensation of relief flows through him. It's as if in loving Kitty, in hoping to benefit from Ed's death, he has wanted to kill him. But Ed is not dead. As soon as he understands this Larry knows that it's the right way for things to be. Ed, so gallant, so genuinely courageous, deserves to live. He deserves to be loved by Kitty. He deserves to be the father of her child.

Kitty feels the silent intensity of his relief, and is moved.

'You really are good friends, aren't you?' she says.

'Ed's part of my life,' says Larry.

She slips her arm through his, and they walk back together to the house.

'I'm glad Ed has you,' she says. 'It shows he has good taste in friends.'

'In wives, too.'

This reminds Kitty of her other news.

'Guess what? George is going to marry Louisa!'

'Is he, now?'

'Are you surprised?'

'Not entirely. Though I'd like to know how George ever got round to popping the question.'

'I don't think he did. I think Louisa did the popping.'

Oddly enough, this news leaves Larry feeling a little sad.

Everyone round him is getting married. Life moves so fast in wartime.

'So where will you go to have the baby?'

'Back home. Mummy is going to look after me.'

'In deepest Wiltshire.'

'Malmesbury's the oldest borough in England, you know. We're very proud of that. Also the dullest. So you'll have to come and visit me.'

'And it.'

'Definitely. It must be visited.'

They enter the house through the garden porch.

'It's awful here now the Canadians have gone,' says Kitty. 'We all miss them frightfully. That whole Dieppe affair was pretty bad, wasn't it?'

'The rumour is seventy per cent casualties,' says Larry.

'I can't even imagine that. I know it's wrong, but all I can think is, Ed's alive, and you're alive.'

'It's not wrong. It's how we're made. There's only so many people we can care about.'

'You know what, Larry?' She clasps his hands and drops her voice, as if she's imparting a secret that's almost too precious to be spoken aloud. 'I shall love my baby so much.'

1 2

The first days of June bring rain and sunshine. The corn-flowers at the wild end of the garden glow bright blue in the slanting early-morning light. The bedroom has no blackout curtains. In these long summer days there's no need for lights going to bed.

Kitty is woken early, as she is every morning, by the baby's sudden cry. For some reason the little thing is incapable of waking gently. She comes out of sleep with a sharp call of alarm, as if frightened to find herself alone in her cot. Kitty is out of bed at once, and has her baby in her arms.

'There, darling. Don't cry, darling. Mummy's here.'

She settles down in the high-backed armchair in the bay window, and opens up her nightdress. The baby's eager searching mouth finds the breast, and settles down to contented sucking. Kitty holds her close, stroking her fine hair, feeling the heat of her tiny body against hers. Her baby is not quite four weeks old.

It's just after five and the house is still, and the town is still. The baby makes regular snuffling noises as she sucks, and Kitty holds her close and loves her more than she ever knew it was humanly possible to love.

'You're my baby, my baby, my only baby. Mummy'll love you for ever and ever.'

These early mornings have become precious to her. She knows the two of them will never be as close again. This is their time of utter absorption in each other, when she is everything to her child, food and drink, warmth and love and protection. In return this tiny creature takes up her every waking moment, and half of her dreams.

Her name is Pamela, after Kitty's grandmother. When it came time to fix on a name her mother said to her, 'What are the girls' names in Ed's family?', and Kitty realised she didn't know. There's so much she doesn't know.

'Daddy'll come home to us one day, darling. And won't you be his princess? Won't he just love you more than anyone in all the world?'

Little Pamela finishes feeding at last, and slips back into sleep. Kitty watches her sleeping in her arms, her eyelids blue-shadowed, her cheeks radiant as the morning, her perfect little lips twitching as she dreams. She kisses her, knowing it won't wake her, and lowers her back into her cot.

Hungry herself now she pads barefoot down to the kitchen, and draws back the heavy blackout curtains. Brilliant light streams into the familiar room, making the white tiles on the walls glitter, throwing a stripe of gold over the scrubbed-wood kitchen table. She gets the iron hook and lifts the plug out of the Rayburn hotplate, and shakes a handful of coke into the furnace. Then she opens up the air vent below to get a good heat going, and puts the kettle on to boil.

She explores the larder, before the war always so crowded with good things to eat, now given over to jars of pickled cabbage and apple chutney and potatoes still clotted with the earth from which they were dug. Her mother has become a grower of vegetables. 'Life would not be bearable without onions.' At such a time before the war Kitty would cut herself a slice of leftover veal pie, or feast on some of her mother's famously moist and chewy gingerbread. Now there is a thin end of a loaf left, and no butter until the new week's ration is fetched.

She puts a small pan of porridge on the hob, wishing she'd remembered to set the oats to soak last night. The kettle boils. She scoops a spoon of tea leaves into the pot, and adds the steaming hot water. There's milk in the cold safe in the larder, put aside for her exclusive consumption, because she's a nursing mother.

By the time the porridge is cooked, and she's eating it sweetened with a precious spoonful of pre-war home-made blackberry jam, she can hear her mother rising in her bedroom overhead. The water pipes gurgle as she runs the taps. Soon now she'll be down, and Kitty's time of quiet will be over.

Kitty misses her life in the service. She misses driving. She would almost say she misses the war, since here in this ancient little town nothing seems to have changed, except for the food shortages. The main roads still pass to the east or west of the town, and the canals and railways miss it altogether.

It's not been easy being home again. Once her pregnancy was confirmed, and the news came through that Ed was a prisoner of war, she understood that her life was to change. Her job now is to raise little Pamela, and wait for the end of the war to bring Ed home. Then they can have their own house together, the three of them, and she won't have to be grateful to her mother any more.

A little later Mrs Teale comes down and joins her in the kitchen, and the stream of well-meaning anxious chatter begins.

'How are you this morning, darling? I heard Pamela grizzling in the night and I almost got up to tell you to make sure to lie her on her tummy or she won't sleep. I see you've not had the last of the bread which I left specially for you. It'll be good for nobody by tomorrow. Such a beautiful morning, really you could almost put Pamela outside in the pram now, fresh air makes such a difference when they're tiny. Harold used to love it so, he cried when I brought him back inside.'

There's been no word of Harold for several weeks now. This awareness floats briefly past Mrs Teale's eyes, causing her to look to one side and wince as if stung.

'You were so different, you didn't like being in your pram at all, I never could work out why,' she resumes. 'Sometimes I wonder where they all come from, the ideas you get. I still have no idea why you refused the Reynolds boy, I should have thought he was perfect for you, and he adored you. Of course, he is in the church, and you're set against that, though I can't imagine why, you sing so beautifully in the abbey choir, and Robert Reynolds is just the kind to do well, everyone says so. You ask your father.'

'Mummy, I'm married.'

'Yes, darling, of course you are.' Though truth to tell, Mrs Teale has temporarily forgotten this fact. Kitty's husband has made such a fleeting appearance in their lives, and who knows what new sorrows this terrible war will bring before it's over? 'Robert Reynolds hasn't married yet, as it happens, which many people find very strange, but I always did think he was such a serious boy, not the kind to chop and change once his mind is made up.'

'I hope you don't mean his mind is made up to marry me.'

'No, of course not, though as it happens I'm not perfectly sure he knows that you're married. After all, the wedding wasn't really done in the way people might have expected, was it? I mean, not from home and in the Abbey as would have been so natural, and all in such a rush, so that there was no time to tell people, and Harold not there, and Michael so disappointed not to be asked to conduct the service.'

'Daddy didn't mind a rap. You know that very well.'

'He tells you that so as not to hurt your feelings, but of course he minded, it's only natural.'

Kitty gets up from the table.

'I'd better go and see to Pammy.'

As usual her mother has managed to put her out of temper. She meets her father in the hall as he comes downstairs, dressed for the day in clerical suit and dog collar. His round pink face lights up as he sees her.

'Kitty, my dear!' he says, embracing her. 'You have no idea how the sight of you lifts my spirits each morning.'

'You didn't mind not doing our wedding, did you, Daddy?'

'Not one bit. Why would I mind? I spend my life doing weddings. It was pure pleasure to have nothing to do but admire you.'

A rustling in the letterbox announces that the paperboy has delivered the morning *Times*. Michael Teale draws it out of the wire basket and points it unopened at Kitty.

'You give that beautiful child of yours a kiss from her grandpa.'

He goes on into the kitchen. When Kitty is halfway up the stairs she comes to a stop. Her father is speaking to her mother in a cold clear voice.

'I told you never to tell Kitty I minded about her wedding.'

'But Michael . . .' Her mother's voice wheedling, placatory.

'You're a fool. What are you?'

'A fool, Michael.'

Kitty continues up the stairs, not wanting to hear, not wanting to feel. Little Pamela senses her coming into the room and is lying awake, big eyes gazing up at her from her cot.

'Did you have a lovely sleep, sweetheart? Would you like to have a nice clean nappy? Then we'll go out for a walk by the river and see the swans.'

Mrs Teale, though in many respects a fool, has undeniable skills when it comes to household management in wartime. As soon as she knew of Kitty's pregnancy she set about preparing for the baby. In this way, when Kitty arrived in the house in Malmesbury, heavily pregnant, she was presented with four cotton baby gowns, four vests, three matinée jackets, three pairs of knitted woollen bootees, and two knitted shawls. Most magnificently of all her mother had tracked down a reconditioned pre-war Marmet perambulator, for which her father paid £10.

This is the pram in which Kitty takes her baby out for walks along the River Avon; attracting as she goes admiring and envious glances from other young mothers. There are large concrete blocks all along the riverbank to stop tanks, which people say are there to defend the secret factory at Cowbridge. No one knows what goes on at Cowbridge. The rumour is that rich people pay to send their sons there so they can get out of being called up.

Kitty no longer believes in the war. She never says so, that would be defeatism, but all she wants is for it to be over and Ed to come home. It's gone on too long and she no longer feels part of it. The world has become tired. She wants to start all over again.

The hardest part is that she's finding she can't remember Ed. Their time together was so brief. She remembers the feeling of him, the intense excitement she felt when he was with her; but his face has become hazy, little more than an expression, which is itself little more than a feeling. The way he looked at her, smiling with his mouth but not his eyes. That sense that he was always out of reach. She has his photograph, of course, but she has gazed at it for too long, and her gaze has drained it of life. His photograph no longer looks back at her.

She wheels the pram down the river path, and returns up the High Street. The queue outside Mallards is shorter than usual so she joins it, and smiles as the other women coo over her baby. One woman gives Kitty a shy smile and says, 'I was told your husband got the VC.'

'Yes,' says Kitty.

'You must be so proud.'

'Yes, I am.'

It's almost her turn now. She takes out her ration book and the baby's ration book.

'You make sure you get your share,' says the woman to little Pamela. 'Your dad's a hero.'

As Kitty arrives home again her mother is looking out for her.

'You've got a visitor,' she says.

Kitty gathers Pamela up from the pram, letting her mother take the shopping and the pram itself, which lives in the shed down the side path.

'Who is it?' she says.

'I didn't catch his name,' says Mrs Teale.

Kitty goes on into the house. The visitor is not in the parlour. She goes through to the kitchen, and finds the back door standing open. There's a man at the far end of the garden.

She goes out into the sunshine, Pamela wriggling in her arms. The visitor is in uniform. He hears her, and turns.

'Larry!'

A wave of joy passes through her. He too is grinning with delight as he comes towards her. He's taken his cap off and his curly hair is all golden in the sunlight, like a halo over his cherub face. A freckly cherub with a snub nose and a worried look, like a pug dog.

'Oh, Larry! How wonderful to see you!'

'Well, I promised I'd come and visit the little stranger, didn't I?'

He gazes intently at the baby. Unusually for her, Pamela stops wriggling and gazes just as steadily back.

'Hello,' he says softly. 'Aren't you a beauty.'

'You can hold her if you want.'

'Can I?'

She arranges the baby in his careful arms. He clasps her too tightly, like all men with babies, as if afraid she'll jump out. Then he paces back and forth over the small lawn, swaying slowly from side to side. It makes Kitty laugh to see him.

'Am I doing it wrong?'

'No, no. I think she's a bit surprised.'

Pamela starts to cry. Hastily, Larry gives her back.

'I'm afraid she does a lot of crying,' she says.

Once in Kitty's arms, the baby closes her eyes and goes to sleep.

'Luckily she does an awful lot of sleeping too,' Kitty says.

Larry beams at her.

'It really is good to see you, Kitty. I'd have come sooner. But you know how it is.'

'How's your wound?'

'Oh, that's all sorted. I get twinges, but as you see, I'm up on my pins. Desk jobs only, of course.'

'I'm glad.'

Kitty knows her mother will be looking out from the house, consumed with that strange greed for company that afflicts her; but she wants Larry to herself.

'Let's stay out here for a bit,' she says. 'It's such a beautiful day. Do you mind?'

They sit side by side on the iron bench by the wild garden and talk about the few short weeks when they were all together in Sussex.

'It seems like another life, doesn't it?' Kitty says. 'And one day it just ended.'

'Over three thousand men were killed or captured in that show,' says Larry. 'People don't talk about it much, but it was a pretty bloody mess.'

'Oh, Larry. Sometimes I think I just can't bear any more.'

He pulls a thin newspaper out of his satchel.

'I brought you this.'

It's a copy of the official publication, the *London Gazette*, that carries the citation for Ed's award. He's folded it open to the right page. Kitty reads it, only partly registering what she reads.

The King has been graciously pleased to approve the
award of the Victoria Cross to Lt Edward Avenell, 40
Commando Royal Marine. At Dieppe on August 19th
1942 Lt Avenell landed under heavy fire . . . During a
period of approximately five hours . . . carried wounded
personnel across the open beach under fire . . . utter
disregard for his personal safety . . . saved at least ten
lives . . . refused a final opportunity to leave the shore
. . . The calmness and courage of this heroic officer
will never be forgotten . . .

Larry says, 'You have to have at least three witnesses for
the VC. Ed had over twenty.'

She gives the *Gazette* back to him.

'No. It's for you. And for Pamela.'

Kitty looks at him with tears in her eyes.

'I know he's a hero, Larry. Everyone keeps telling me
so.'

She wants to ask the question that haunts her: why didn't
he get on that last boat and save himself?

'He'll come home,' says Larry, understanding what she
doesn't say. 'You'll have him back.'

'He's in a camp near a place called Eichstätt. I looked it
up on a map. It's north of Munich.'

'It could take another year. But he'll come home.'

'Another year,' she says, looking at her baby asleep in
her arms.

'So how's motherhood? You look well on it, I must say.'

'It's like nothing else in the world,' says Kitty. 'It's utterly,

utterly different. I keep on bursting into tears for no reason. My heart wants to explode with happiness. I feel like I'm a thousand years old. I want to scream with boredom. I long to be young and silly again. But if I lost her I'd die. It's as simple as that.'

'Very simple,' says Larry.

'Darling Larry. I'm so glad you came. How long can you stay?'

'I'll head back after lunch. I hitched a ride with a chap in MI who's visiting some facility near here.'

Kitty's face falls.

'So little time. Let's not talk about the war.'

'What do you want to talk about?'

'I finally got round to reading that book you gave me. *The Warden*.'

'How was it?'

'I wasn't all that gripped by it, to be honest. I think maybe I see enough of clergymen in ordinary life.'

'It's a bit plodding, I grant you. It's a sort of moral thriller, really. Everything hinges on the power of a good but weak man to find the courage to do the right thing.'

'Yes, I do see that,' says Kitty. 'I did read faster towards the end. But poor Mr Harding is so fearfully drippy, isn't he? And I do think Trollope could have done more in the way of punishing the archdeacon. I wanted to have him be publicly humiliated.'

'Ah, you're a harder judge than I am. I can find it in my heart to pity the archdeacon, with his secret drawer and his secret copy of Rabelais.'

'I do want to believe that goodness wins in the end,' says Kitty. 'But you have to admit, in real life it doesn't always seem that way.'

'That's why it's our duty to make it be that way,' says Larry.

'Oh, Larry.' She takes his hand with her free hand. 'I am so glad you came.'

Larry joins them for a simple lunch. Kitty's father returns from the abbey promptly at one. He too is all smiles to see that they have a guest, and better still, a male guest.

'What do you make of the bombing of Pantelleria, eh? I've been saying for weeks the invasion will begin in the Med. Sicily is the open door.'

Kitty shows her father the *London Gazette* with Ed's citation. Both he and her mother read it, taking in every word.

'If ever a man deserved a VC, that's the man,' says her father.

'Larry was there,' says Kitty. 'He saw him.'

'Oh, my Lord!' exclaims her father. 'The tales you must have to tell! And here I am, worrying myself to death over the repairs to the abbey.'

'The war will be over one day,' says Larry, 'and when it's over we'll still want to see the grand old churches, and the cornflowers in bloom.'

'Larry is such a romantic,' says Kitty, smiling across the table at him. 'He's an artist, really.'

'An artist!' exclaims her mother.

'I like to paint,' says Larry.

'You should paint Kitty,' says Mr Teale. 'I'm always telling her we should have her portrait done.'

'I'm afraid I don't dare attempt portraits,' says Larry. 'That requires skills I have yet to acquire.'

'Larry paints like Cézanne,' says Kitty. 'All blotchy and wrong colours.'

'A very accurate description,' says Larry.

When it's time for him to leave Kitty walks with him to the road junction, leaving Pamela in her mother's care.

'You know I'm not really so silly about your painting, Larry. I'm only teasing.'

'Yes, I know.'

'Thank you for being so sweet to Daddy.'

Larry glances at her as they walk.

'You find it hard, don't you?' he says. 'Ed being away.'

'Yes, I suppose so. Oh, Larry. I'm so afraid I'm forgetting him.'

She feels she's about to cry and knows she mustn't. But then he puts his arms round her and it's so good to be held in a man's arms that she does cry, just a little.

'This time will pass,' he says.

'I know. I know it will. I have to be strong, for Pamela.'

He kisses her gently on the cheek.

'That's from Ed,' he says. 'He's thinking of you right now. He loves you so much.'

'Darling Larry,' she says. 'Can I kiss him back?'

She kisses Larry on the cheek, as he kissed her. They stand still for a moment, saying nothing. Then they part, and walk on to the junction.

Larry's friend is waiting in his car. As he climbs in the back Kitty says to him, 'I heard from Louisa the other day. She's turned into a lady of the manor. She's practically taking soup to villagers.'

'Hurrah for Lady Edenfield!' says Larry.

Then the car is driving away, down the road to Swindon, and Kitty turns to walk slowly back.

13

After the Dieppe raid, a number of German soldiers are found dead, shot in the head, with their hands tied behind their backs. This is believed to be the work of commandos. In reprisal, the German High Command orders that all commandos held in prisoner-of-war camps are to be shackled until further notice.

A later commando raid on the island of Sark leaves more German soldiers dead, also with their hands tied. Hitler, enraged, issues a secret order known as the *Kommandobefehl*. Only twelve copies are made. The order states:

> For a long time now our opponents have been employing in their conduct of war, methods which contravene the International Convention of Geneva. The members of the so-called Commandos behave in a particularly brutal and underhand manner . . . I order therefore: from now on all men operating against German troops in so-called Commando raids . . . are to be annihilated . . .

The *Kommandobefehl* does not go unchallenged. Field Marshal Rommel refuses to issue the order to his troops, believing it to be a breach of the code of war. In prisoner-of-war camps its implementation varies with the character of individual commanders. In Oflag VII-B near Eichstätt captured members of commando units are shackled, but they are not handed over to the *Sicherheitsdienst*, the Security Service; more because of inter-service rivalry than out of any wish to save the men from execution.

However, when news reaches the camp authorities that Lieutenant Edward Avenell of 40 RM Commando has been awarded the Victoria Cross, there is a reaction of anger.

The prisoner is woken from his bunk in Block 5 before dawn by two camp orderlies who are themselves still half asleep. They march him out, handcuffed, into the parade ground. Here they order him to stand before the stony bank that rises to the Lagerstrasse and the kitchen block.

An *Obersturmführer* arrives from the *Kommandantur*. He opens a folder and shines a small electric torch on the typed order within. The light reflects off the paper onto his face as he reads the order aloud. Ed understands nothing of the German except that this is how the order for an execution is given. When the voice falls silent, the *Obersturmführer* draws a pistol and orders him to kneel. Not a firing squad, then.

Ed feels cold. His spirit is indifferent but his body cares. Dryness in his mouth and throat, a hot loosening in his bowels. He should close his eyes but they remain open, seeing nothing. There are rooks in the trees on the hillside across the parade ground, he hears their cries. Light seeping into the sky.

He's aware of the raw pain in his wrists from the handcuffs, and how any time now he's going to shit his pants. He'd kill for a cigarette, or at least die for one.

There comes a loud report. The pistol shot echoes down the valley. The rooks burst up in a swarm into the light of the coming day.

The pistol is lowered once more. The *Obersturmführer* departs. The orderlies march Ed back to his quarters.

'So what was that all about?' say the others in his block.

Ed has no answer.

The pantomime is repeated the next day. The pre-dawn summons, the reading of the order, the shot in the air. And then again the next day. The process of repetition brings no lessening of the fear. Each time the game could turn real. Each time his body betrays him. But the failure is secret. To outside eyes he remains indifferent, magnificent.

He understands that it's not his death they want, but his disintegration. Or perhaps it's all just a way for bored camp officers to pass the time. There's a rumour they're laying bets in the guardroom, so many days before he cracks, at such-and-such odds, paid out in cigarettes. You want your life to have value and your death to have meaning, but in the end it's all just a game.

The hero doesn't crack. At least not so you can see from the outside.

In December 1943, after he's been a prisoner for almost five hundred days, the handcuffs are removed.

In April 1945, after he's been a prisoner for almost a thousand days, the war stutters to its end.

The American Army is rumoured to be across the Rhine and advancing rapidly. The commandant of the camp calls an early-morning parade of all prisoners and announces that for their safety they will be moving east to Moosburg. The officer-prisoners are issued bulk rations and march out in good order down the road to Eichstätt. Five Thunderbolts of the US Air Force spot the marching column and mistaking them for German troops, dive-bomb the prisoners. For thirty minutes they strafe them with their cannon, oblivious to all the waving arms. Fourteen British officers are killed and forty-six are wounded. The survivors return to the camp.

Ed Avenell is among the party detailed to bury the dead.

'Fucking typical,' says one of his companions. 'Talk about giving your life for your country.'

Ed says nothing. He's been saying nothing for a long time now.

That night the column forms up again, and under cover of darkness they march south-east. At dawn they sleep in a barn. As dusk falls they resume their march. American planes can be heard high overhead day and night. A fine cold rain is falling as they march through Ernsgaden and Mainburg. The prisoners are growing weaker all the time. In the course of the next seven days and nights, four men die on the march. On the eighth day they reach Oflag V, the giant camp at Moosburg. Here over thirty thousand prisoners of all ranks and nationalities have been herded together. There are thunderstorms that evening, and rumours that Bavaria is suing for a separate peace. American guns can be heard. The Seventh Army is said to be as close as Ingolstadt. The prisoners are packed four hundred to a hut. Rations are pitifully low.

Next morning the commandant goes searching for an American officer of high enough rank to receive his surrender. By noon the camp is liberated. The liberators are C Company, 47th Tank Battalion, 14th Armored Division, 3rd Corps, Third US Army. They raise the US flag and tell the cheering prisoners they will be evacuated in Dakotas, taking twenty-five men at a time, starting as soon as a landing strip can be prepared.

Ed smiles when he hears this, and draws deeply on the American cigarette he's been given, and fixes his gaze on the far distance.

'We're not going anywhere in a hurry, boys,' he says.

On the first day of May snow falls over the camp. A rumour spreads that Hitler is dead. The men are too tired and hungry to care. All they want now is to go home.

On May 3rd they're transported in six-wheeler trucks to Landshut. The houses they pass on the way have white flags in their windows. At Landshut the former prisoners of war are billeted in empty flats, six to a room, and supplied with American K rations. Here the waiting begins again.

The snow turns to rain, and the winds are too strong for

planes to take off. The American POWs who arrived earlier take precedence; also a batch of seven hundred Indians. Two hundred planes are promised, flying back from Prague, but only seventy arrive.

On the morning of May 7th, which is being celebrated at home as VE Day, Ed takes his turn at the aerodrome, and by mid-afternoon he is boarding. The Dakota lands at St Omer in northern France, where he is cleaned up and deloused. Next day RAF Lancasters fly the British contingent to Duxford air base near Cambridge. It is now twenty-five days since they were marched out of the camp; and two years, eight months and twenty days since Ed left England.

He sends two telegrams, one to his parents and one to his wife. A repatriation orderly recognises his name on the manifest and tells the base commander, a young-looking squadron leader.

'I'm told you're a VC,' says the squadron leader.

'Yes,' says Ed. 'I've been told that too.'

'Honour to have you here. Anything I can do for you?'

'No, thank you, sir. I'm on my way first thing in the morning.'

'Good job,' says the squadron leader, shaking his hand. 'Damn good job.'

Kitty arrives early at King's Cross station, holding very tight to Pamela's hand. Pamela is just over two years old, and a sturdy walker, but the giant railway station overawes her. Kitty is wearing her prettiest pre-war frock beneath a dark grey wool coat. It's a chilly spring day.

'Daddy,' says Pamela, pointing to a man striding across the concourse.

'No, that's not Daddy,' says Kitty. 'I'll tell you when it's him.'

She's been training Pamela ever since the telegram came. She wants her to say, 'Hello, Daddy,' and give him a kiss.

There are other women waiting, staring anxiously down the long platforms. One holds a bunch of flowers. Kitty thinks Ed wouldn't want flowers, though the truth is she doesn't know. In her letters to him she's told him all her news, mostly about Pamela, and how pretty she is, and how forward. She's told Ed how they've left her parents' house and are now living in Edenfield Place, thanks to her friend Louisa. It's somewhere to be until he comes home, and they can set up house on their own.

Ed's letters from Germany have been strange. He writes about the absurdity of the life he leads, and the folly of human nature, but never about his own state of mind. Nor does he ask after his daughter. The letters always end, 'I love you.' But they have not brought him closer.

'You have to expect it,' Louisa says in their late-night talks. 'You had three weeks together, almost three years ago. It'll be like starting all over again.'

'I know you're right,' Kitty says. 'But he's the most important person in my life, apart from Pamela. The thought of him takes up almost all the space I have.'

'My advice is, don't get your hopes up.'

Kitty hardly knows what she feels as she waits at King's Cross. All she wants is for it to be over. She has longed for this moment for so long that now it's close, it frightens her.

'Hello, Daddy,' Pamela says to a young airman on the platform.

'No!' says Kitty a little too sharply. 'I'll tell you when it's Daddy.'

Pamela feels the rebuke. Her sweet face sets in a look Kitty knows well, eyes unfocused, lips pouting.

'Daddy,' she says, pointing to an elderly man sitting on a bench.

She calls out to a porter wheeling a trolley, 'Daddy! Daddy!'

A soldier appears, running, breathless.

'Hello, Daddy!' cries Pamela.

'Stop it!' says Kitty. 'Stop it!'

She controls an overwhelming urge to smack the child.

'Daddy,' says Pamela, very quietly now. 'Daddy, Daddy, Daddy.'

Only the arrival of the train silences her. The immense engine sighs slowly to a stop, thrilling her with its living breathing power. The carriage doors open and the passengers come streaming down the platform. Kitty looks without seeing, afraid he isn't on the train after all, afraid he isn't coming home, afraid he is coming home.

She remembers standing on the quay at Newhaven after the first aborted operation against Dieppe, and all the men filing off the boats in the night, and how she looked for him and couldn't see him. Then all at once he was there before her. Remembering that moment, her love for him bursts within her, and she wants so much, so much, to hold him in her arms again.

Pamela senses that she's lost her mother's attention. She tugs at the hand that holds hers, saying, 'Go home. Go home.'

The people from the train stream by, mostly men, mostly in uniform. There are too many, their faces hazy in the steamy air, the sound of boots tramping the platform dulling the nervous hugger-mugger of reunions.

Pamela starts to cry. She feels ignored and sorry for herself. At the same time she's intensely excited. As she maintains a steady low-level snivelling she holds tight to her mother's hand, knowing that she'll feel it in her mother's body when it happens, the mysterious and wonderful moment for which they've come.

Kitty catches her breath. He's there, she knows it, though she hasn't yet seen him. She searches the faces bobbing towards her, and finds him. He hasn't seen her yet. He looks so thin, so sad. He's bareheaded, wearing worn battle-dress, a kitbag over one shoulder. He looks like his photograph, except older, more real, wiser. There's a nobility about him she never knew he possessed.

Oh my darling, she says to herself. You've come back to me.

He sees her now, and a brightness lights up his face. He hurries faster towards her, one arm half raised, half waving. She lifts a timid hand in answer.

He comes to her and at once takes her in his arms. She holds him close, letting go of Pamela's hand to give all of herself to him. His body is so thin, she can feel all his bones. Then he kisses her, only lightly, as if he's afraid she's fragile, and she kisses him, nuzzling her face against his. Then he drops down onto his haunches to greet his unknown daughter.

'Hello,' he says.

Pamela gazes back at him in silence. Kitty strokes the top of her head.

'Say hello to Daddy, darling.'

Pamela still says nothing.

'Don't you say a word,' says Ed. 'Why should you?'

He reaches out one hand and lightly touches her cheek. Then he stands up.

'Let's go,' he says.

'I have it all planned,' says Kitty. 'We're going to take a taxi to Victoria.'

'A taxi! We must be rich.'

'Special occasion.'

Pamela trots along obediently by her mother's side, from time to time peeping up at the stranger. She has no notion of him being her father, and doesn't even know what that means. But from the very first moment she saw him take her mother in his arms, and felt her mother let go of her hand to embrace him, she surrendered to him. He has become in an instant the most powerful being in her universe. When he knelt before her, and fixed her with his grave blue eyes, she knew that all she desired in life from now on was the love and admiration of this magnificent stranger.

In the taxi Kitty stops trembling and becomes more talk-ative.

'You're so thin, my darling,' she says. 'I'm going to feed you and feed you.'

'I'm all for that.'

'I don't know what to ask you first. There's so much.'

'Let's not talk about it,' he says.

'Tell me what you want. Tell me what I should do.'

'Nothing at all,' he says. 'Just be my beautiful wife.'

Pamela leans across her mother and says to him in her clear high voice, 'Hello, Daddy.'

Louisa has scraped together a celebration dinner of some magnificence. There's an actual roast chicken and George contributes a bottle of Meursault, one of the few not consumed by the Canadians.

'We have to welcome home our hero,' Louisa says.

Ed retires to the rooms where Kitty and Pamela live, a bedroom, dressing room and bathroom above the dining room. He soaks in a deep warm bath, and then dresses in clothes lent him by his host. There is nothing here that belongs to him.

'I didn't know what else to do,' says Kitty.

'This is perfect,' says Ed. 'I shall be a new man.'

A bed is made up for Pamela in the dressing room. Kitty is surprised she accepts her expulsion from her mother's bedroom without protest. Ed comes and kisses her good night at her bedtime. He seems to expect nothing from her, which Pamela finds thrilling. After he's given her a kiss he touches her cheek with one forefinger, as he did when they met for the first time. As he does so, his gaze lingers on her, and he's almost smiling.

At dinner his homecoming is toasted with the mellow burgundy.

'There's some newspaperman wants to talk to you,' Kitty says. 'He wants the story of your VC.'

'Well, he won't get it,' says Ed mildly.

'But we're all so proud of you!' says Louisa.

'I'm afraid it's a lot of nonsense,' says Ed. 'Let's leave it at that, shall we?'

They eat by candlelight, in the dining room. The effects of the military occupation are everywhere in the house, but in the warm glow of the candles it's almost as if the war has never been. Ed, bathed and wearing a freshly laundered shirt that hangs loose on his spare frame, draws all their eyes. His face, hollowed out by his years in prison, has the austere beauty of a medieval saint. He seems to the others to be present only partly in their world. A part of him has gone on, to a place where they can't follow him.

That night he lies in Kitty's arms, but they don't make love.

'I need time,' he says.

'Of course you do, my darling. We have all the time in the world.'

In the night while Kitty is sleeping he gets out of their bed and lies down to sleep on the floor. In the morning, finding him there, Kitty asks him if he'd like a room of his own.

'Just for a night or two,' he says. 'It's been so long since I've been able to be alone.'

Kitty doesn't look at him as she answers, and she forces her voice to remain light.

'Of course,' she says.

After that Ed spends his nights in a bedroom across the passage. By day he goes for long solitary walks over the Downs.

Kitty has made plans for his return, for them to have a house of their own. The idea comes from Louisa, that they should rent one of the farmhouses on the estate. Since Arthur Funnell's death the land attached to River Farm has been worked by the tenant at the Home Farm, and the house is no longer occupied. The rent would be nominal. But for now she says nothing of this to Ed. It's as if he hasn't yet fully returned from the war.

When they're alone together, she tries to get him to talk about his time in the camps.

'What did they do to you over there, Ed?'

'Nothing much,' he says. 'Some of the other fellows had it far worse than me.'

Little by little she builds a picture of his time in captivity. He tells her about the hunger, and the cold, but not as if he was much troubled by either. He seems to have suffered most from restrictions on his movement.

'Do you mean being locked in a cell?'

'No, we weren't locked up. We were in blockhouses most of the time. But the handcuffs got me down rather.'

'Handcuffs?'

He shows her, holding out his wrists a foot or so apart.

'It's not like I was chained to a wall. But you'd be surprised how many things you can't do when you're cuffed. Makes it hard to sleep at night, too.'

'How long were you in handcuffs?'

'A little over a year.'

'A year!'

'Four hundred and eleven days.'

He delivers the number with a wry smile, as if ashamed to admit that he kept count.

'But handcuffs don't kill you,' he says.

One night Kitty is woken by a sudden cry. She knows it comes from Ed's room. She goes to him and finds him standing in the middle of the room, eyes staring, still half asleep. Her appearance wakes him fully.

'Sorry,' he says. 'God, I'm sorry.'

She sits him down on the bed and takes him in her arms. He huddles against her, trembling.

'Just a bad dream,' he says.

'Darling.' She kisses his damp cheek. 'Darling. You're safe home now.'

The more she learns of how much he's been hurt, the more she loves him. That cry in the night binds him to her more tightly than any words of love.

She watches him when he can't see her watching, wanting to be part of what's happening to him. There are so many stories these days about men coming home from war, and how difficult it is for them to adjust. Always the advice is the same: give them time. Kitty is willing to give him all the time in the world, so long as she can be sure he still loves her. Often when his faraway gaze falls upon her she sees his face light up with happiness. And once, kissing her before retiring to his solitary bed, he says, 'If it wasn't for you, I'd have let them kill me over there.'

One great consolation is that he loves Pamela, and she loves him. Often she'll sit on his lap for an hour at a time, clinging to him tightly, her face pressed to his chest. They never talk. They just sit like that, his arms round the child's little body, in one or other of the empty echoing rooms of the great house, and let the world go by.

PART TWO
ART

1945–47

14

In early November of 1945 the painter William Coldstream, finally released from the army, accepts an invitation to teach at the Camberwell College of Art. His friends Victor Pasmore, Claude Rogers and Lawrence Gowing are already on the staff; and altogether it's as if the pre-war Euston Road school has been reborn and moved south of the river.

Coldstream takes his first evening class wearing his dark blue demob suit, looking more like a bank clerk than an artist. His class of twenty students covers a range of ages, from the very young, fresh from the Downs School or a foundation course in a provincial town, to ex-service men and women in their late twenties. Among them is Larry Cornford. The class takes place in one of the Life Rooms in the shabby Victorian building on the Peckham Road, where the roar of passing lorries outside competes with the shriek of tram wheels. A life model waits, fully dressed, sitting on an upright chair to one side.

The teacher begins by reading from Ruskin's *Elements of Drawing*.

'I believe that the excellence of an artist depends wholly upon refinement of perception, and that it is this which a master or a school can teach.'

Larry watches his teacher intently as he speaks. He's seen some of his paintings and he admires them. The man himself is a surprise: his voice unassertive, his face almost expressionless as he speaks. He tells the class that they must learn to judge the distance of objects from the eye. He calls the life model to stand in front of the class. He faces her, one arm outreached, holding a pencil vertically in his hand.

'The eye notes the length of the head, crown to chin, on the pencil. The hand transfers the same distance to the pad, making marks accordingly. Now looking again, note the distance from eyebrows to mouth. Make the marks. You see how, little by little, you build up a precise set of relationships between the elements of the face.'

Larry does as he is told. The model is young and has a thick fringe. Her straight brown hair falls to her shoulders, framing a pale face with sleepy eyes. She seems not to mind being looked at.

Coldstream moves among the students as they work, peering at their sketch pads, saying nothing. Larry finds the process of measuring and making marks an awkward business, far removed from the rapid freehand sketching with which he has always begun before. The student beside him, a very young man, almost a boy, evidently feels this too, judging by the way he scowls and mutters as he works. When the teacher is by him he vents his frustration.

'It's like painting by numbers, isn't it?' he says.

'What would you rather do?' says Coldstream, unoffended.

'I'd rather paint what I feel.'

'That comes later,' says Coldstream. 'First you must see.'

As the students work, the girl model's gaze roams the room and comes to rest on Larry. Her eyes linger on him with disarming directness, as if she supposes he doesn't see her. Larry realises with a shock that this face he's been so obediently mapping is, if not exactly beautiful, certainly very striking. Her nose is too strong, her mouth too full, her eyes too startling; but the overall effect is undeniably attractive. She looks both very young and very sure of herself, almost imperious.

When the class ends some of the students gather round Coldstream, who is pulling on a beige officer's topcoat against the night chill. The others pack up their sketch pads and drift out down the bare-board corridor to the street.

'Poor old Bill,' says a voice behind Larry.

It's the young model. Larry is vaguely aware that Coldstream's first name is Bill.

'Do you know him?' he says.

'No, not at all. But you just have to look at him to see he's unhappy.'

'Oh, do you think so?'

It hasn't occurred to Larry to consider the personal happiness of his teacher.

'I'm Nell,' she says. 'Who are you?'

'Lawrence Cornford. Larry, I mean.'

'I like Lawrence better. How old are you, Lawrence?'

Her command of the situation so surprises him that he doesn't think to object to such a sudden personal question.

'Twenty-seven,' he says.

'I suppose you had a harrowing war and now you're mature beyond your years. All I've been doing is going quietly mad in Tunbridge Wells. It seems so unfair that just when I'm old enough to be harrowed they take the war away.'

'How old are you?'

'Nineteen. But if you count former lives, I'm about nine hundred.'

'Do you believe in former lives?'

'No, of course not,' she says. 'Do I look completely potty?' Then without waiting for an answer, 'So why are you here?'

'To learn,' says Larry. 'I want to be a better painter.'

By now they're out on the street. Coldstream and the group with him are walking down the road. Without thinking, Larry and Nell follow.

'So you have a private income, I suppose,' Nell says.

'My father is supporting me.' Larry blushes a little at the admission. 'But we have a strictly limited agreement. He's giving me a year.'

'To prove you're a genius?'

'To prove I'm in with a chance.'

'How do you prove that?'

'I'm to show my work. And we'll see if anyone buys anything.'

The group ahead turn into the pub on the corner, the Hermit's Rest.

'How about you buy me a drink?' says Nell.

They go into the pub, which is half full and noisy and smoky. The intense young student who was Larry's neighbour in the class leaves Coldstream's group and joins them.

'Old boys' reunion,' he says, nodding behind him. 'They were all at Euston Road. What do you make of all this Ruskin and taking measurements like a fucking tailor? I signed up to be inspired by an artist not trained by a draughtsman.'

'I suppose he could be both,' says Larry.

'Never!' The boy's eyes flash with contempt. 'An artist is an artist above everything. He may teach to earn his bread, but even when teaching he's an artist. Why should he care about us? We're impedimenta. I've seen his work. It's good. But there should be more of himself on the canvas. He should take more risks. There should be more danger.'

Having so delivered himself of this verdict, he departs.

'God, how the young bore me!' says Nell.

'You being so very old,' says Larry.

'Oh, I promise you, I bore myself. But I mean to grow older just as fast as I can.'

'Not too fast, I hope.'

'Why? Did you like being nineteen? Was it the best year of your life?'

'No,' says Larry.

'You know life models pose naked.'

'Yes.'

'Shall I tell you why I'm doing it?'

'If you want to.'

'No. I'm asking you if you want me to tell you.'

She fixes him with truth-demanding eyes. Confused by her nearness, Larry smiles and shakes his head.

'You don't want me to tell you?'

'Yes. Yes, I do.'

'Well, then,' she says. 'I've left home, and I'm not going back. I would have died if I'd stayed one day longer. I'm starting my whole life again, and this time I'm going to live it quite differently, among quite different people. I'm going to live a real life, not a show life. And I'm going to do it among people who live real lives. I know I'm not an artist myself, but I want to live among artists.'

'Sounds like you want danger, like that boy.'

'That's just silly play-acting. Who wants danger? I want truth.'

This is strong stuff, made all the stronger by her unrelenting gaze, and her pale sensual face. The more he looks at her the more fascinated he becomes.

'I think that's what I want too,' he says.

'Then shall we help each other find it? Shall we, Lawrence?'

'Why not?' he says.

'No, that's no good. We don't do things because we can't think of a reason not to. We do things we want to do. We act out of desire.'

She doesn't smile as she speaks, but nor is she as sure of herself as he first thought. Her intense gaze is asking for his support.

'Yes,' he says. 'Yes.'

'The rule is, we say what we want. We tell each other the truth.'

'Yes.'

'So I'll start. I want to be friends with you, Lawrence.' She holds out her hand. 'Do you want to be friends with me?'

'Yes. I do.'

He takes her hand and holds it, not shaking it. He feels her warmth.

'There,' she says. 'Now we're friends.'

'Golly, you were hard to find,' says Kitty, giving Larry a warm hug. 'You shouldn't just disappear and leave no forwarding address.'

'I thought I had.'

She ushers him out of Lewes station to a dark green Wolseley Hornet parked outside.

'George bought her in '32. Isn't she glorious?'

The December roads are icy. Driving slowly back to Edenfield, Kitty confides her worries.

'You'll find Ed's changed a lot.'

'I suppose it must be hard for him to adjust,' says Larry.

'See what you think when you meet him.'

Larry gazes out of the window at the familiar hump of the Downs.

'You remember that place where you were billeted?' Kitty says. 'George is offering it to us at a peppercorn rent.'

'Are you short of money?'

'We have no money at all. We're living off Ed's demob

payments. No, actually we're living off George and Louisa. Ed's looking round for some sort of job, but you wouldn't say his heart was in it.'

'He's a VC, for God's sake! Where's the nation's gratitude?'

'The nation awards VCs an annual sum of ten pounds. But only if you're non-commissioned. Officer class is assumed to have private means.'

She eases the car off the road and down the drive to Edenfield Place.

'Just wait till you see Pammy. She's turning into such a little madam.'

Louisa is there to greet Larry, and then George appears, nodding and blinking. Gareth, the indoor man, takes Larry's weekend bag and his satchel up to his allocated bedroom. There's tea laid out in the drawing room.

'All a bit more civilised than when I was last here,' Larry says.

'I rather miss the Canadians,' says George. 'They made such a jolly noise.'

'Where's Pammy?' says Kitty.

'Out somewhere with Ed,' says Louisa. 'They'll be back soon.'

Ed doesn't appear, so after they've had a cup of tea Larry and Kitty go in search of him.

'He'll be in the wood beyond the lake,' says Kitty. 'If he's not up on the Downs.'

As they stroll past the lake house in the gathering dusk Larry says lightly, 'That's where I first met you.'

'Reading *Middlemarch*.'

Ed comes into view on the far side of the lake. He has Pamela on his shoulders, and he holds her fast by her ankles.

'My God!' says Larry softly. 'He's so thin!'

Ed sees them and breaks into a careful bounding run. The little girl squeals with fear and delight.

Eyes shining, chest heaving, Ed reaches them and swings Pamela down to the ground.

'Larry! Good man!'

He takes his hand and pumps it.

'I would have come sooner,' says Larry, 'but I didn't know what sort of a state you were in. And look at you! You look like a ghost!'

'I am a ghost.' Then his eyes meet Kitty's and he smiles. 'No, I'm not. Not a ghost at all. And will you look at this! I have a daughter!'

Pamela is gazing curiously up at Larry. Her father's joy at his friend's arrival causes her to give him serious attention.

'Hello, Pamela,' says Larry.

'Hello,' says the little girl.

'Come along, then,' says Kitty. 'There's still some tea left.'

Ed puts one arm over Larry's shoulders. He's more animated than he's been for days.

'Oh, Larry, Larry, Larry. I am so glad to see you.'

He beats with one fist on Larry's shoulder as they walk back to the house.

'Me too, old chap. For a while I wasn't sure I'd ever see you again.'

'I hope you trusted you'd meet me in heaven. Or wasn't I to be allowed in?'

'They'll serenade you with trumpets, Ed. You're a genuine hero.'

'No, no. Don't say that.'

'I was on that beach.'

'I don't want to talk about that,' says Ed, withdrawing his arm. 'Tell me about you. Is it art, or is it bananas?'

'It's art for now. I've enrolled in a course at Camberwell College. I'm having a go at taking it seriously.'

'And frivolously too, I hope. Art should be fun too.'

'It's more than fun, Ed. It's what gives me my deepest happiness.'

Ed stops and gazes into his friend's eyes.

'There, you see,' he says. 'I'd give anything to have that.'

Alone in his bedroom, a fine large room over the organ room with a west-facing window, Larry changes slowly for dinner, and thinks about Kitty. It frightens him how much he longs to be in her company, and how happy he is when her lovely face is turned towards him. But his part is to play the role of faithful friend, both to her and to Ed; and play it he will.

Over dinner he has an opportunity to observe the curious relationship between George and Louisa. Louisa has got into the habit of talking about George in his presence as if he doesn't hear her.

'Is George doing something about the wine?' she says. 'Oh, isn't he hopeless! Sometimes I wonder that he manages to get out of bed in the morning. You never saw a person with less get up and go.'

'The wine is on the table, my dear.'

'He hasn't got his napkin on. You'll see, he'll spill the sauce all down his tie.'

Obediently, George tucks his napkin into his collar. His eyes peep at Larry through the thick lenses of his glasses.

'She's quite something, isn't she?' he says.

Ed hardly touches his food. Larry sees how Kitty watches his plate with anxious eyes. Louisa complains bitterly about the petrol rations.

'They say they've increased the ration, but four gallons a month! That won't get anyone very far.'

'I think the truth is we're broke,' says Larry. 'The country, I mean.'

'Do let's not complain,' says Kitty. 'Think how frightening it was, not knowing day by day if people were still alive even.'

When dinner is over Ed slips away, not saying where he's going. Louisa and George settle down to a game of Pelmanism, which it turns out is their customary evening relaxation. Louisa spreads out the cards face down on the long table in the library.

'George has a surprisingly good memory for cards,' she says. 'I think it must come from all that peering at maps.'

Kitty and Larry leave them to their game. They retreat to the smallest of the family rooms, the West Parlour. Here family portraits hang on chains against a pale eau-de-nil wallpaper, and the chintz-covered armchairs are deep and comfortable. For a few moments Kitty looks at Larry in silence, and he too remains silent, not wanting to break the sweet intimacy.

'Well?' she says at last.

'He's not in a good way, is he?'

'He won't see a doctor. He won't see anyone.'

'How is he with you?' says Larry.

'He's kind, and gentle, and loving. And you see how he is with Pammy. But most of the time he just wants to be alone.'

'What does he do when he's alone?'

'I don't know. Nothing, as far as I can tell. He just thinks. Or maybe he doesn't think. Maybe he wants to be alone so he can switch himself off, or something.'

'Sounds like some sort of breakdown.'

'He had a terrible time in the camps. He was kept hand-cuffed for four hundred and eleven days.'

'Jesus! Poor bastard.'

'I just don't know what to do.'

She's clasping her hands together as she speaks, working them against each other, as if trying to rub out some invisible stain.

'Will you help us, Larry?'

Her lovely face is looking at him in mute appeal, admitting the unhappiness she can't name.

'I'll try talking to him,' says Larry. 'But he may not want to talk to me.'

'He'll talk to you if he talks to anyone.'

'You say he's looking round for a job.'

'He isn't really. He knows he must find some kind of income. But the way he is at present, I don't see that he's employable.'

Larry nods, frowning, pondering what best to do.

'I love him so much, Larry,' Kitty says. 'But we're sleeping in separate bedrooms for now. It's what he wants.' There's the glisten of tears in her eyes as she speaks. 'I wish I knew why.'

'Oh, Kitty.'

'Do you think it's me?'

'No. It's not you.'

'We've been apart so long. You'd think at least he'd want that.'

'I'll try and talk to him,' Larry says.

'Now,' says Kitty. 'Go to him now.'

'Do you know where he is?'

'Yes, I know.' She looks down, suddenly ashamed. 'I follow him sometimes, just so I know where he goes. He'll be in the chapel.'

'The chapel!'

'We were married there, remember?'

'Of course I remember.'

'He goes and sits there by himself. Sometimes for hours.'

Larry gets up out of his armchair.

'I'll see what I can do.'

A first floor corridor leads past bedrooms to a bridge across the courtyard entrance. This is the family's private way to the chapel. The vaulted space is in darkness but for a single light over the altar. When Larry first enters, it appears to be empty.

'Anyone here?'

A voice answers from the darkness.

'Is that Larry?'

'Yes, it's me.'

Ed uncoils himself from where he's been lying, stretched out on a row of dark oak chairs. Larry walks down the aisle to him.

'I suppose Kitty sent you.'

'Yes.'

'Dear Kitty. She does her best with me.'

Larry is on the point of saying something noncommittal and sympathetic when he changes his mind.

'Why don't you just sort yourself out, Ed?'

Ed raises his eyebrows, smiling.

'There speaks the voice of reason.'

'Sorry. Stupid thing to say.'

'No, you're right. But the thing is, I'm not sure I can sort myself out. And even if I could, who'd sort out the world?'

'Oh, honestly,' says Larry.

'All the rottenness and mess.'

Larry thinks of Kitty gazing at him in the parlour with tears in her eyes.

'It won't do, Ed,' he says. 'What right do you have to indulge yourself in the luxury of despair? You have a wife. You have a child.'

'Well, well.' He's not smiling any more. 'Did Kitty ask you to tell me that?'

'This isn't from Kitty. This is from me. We've known each other for almost fifteen years. You're my best friend. You're the man I admire most in the world. Compared to you, I'm nothing.'

'Oh, don't talk such rot.'

'You think I don't mean it? I was on that beach, Ed. I was in such a total funk I couldn't move. I would have sat there on those bloody pebbles for all eternity. I was sick with fear, helpless with fear. And then I saw you.'

Only now does Larry realise he is here for his own reasons too. There's something he must say to his friend: a tribute and a confession.

'Don't do this, Larry,' says Ed.

But Larry can't be stopped now.

'It was like seeing an angel,' he says. 'I saw this man come walking up the beach where the bullets were flying and the shells were landing, like he was taking a stroll in the park. Up and down that beach he went, saving life after life, and every time he turned back from the boats he threw his own life away. And as I watched him, the fear went out of me. You were my angel, Ed. Because of you I got up and I walked to the boat, and I lived. I'll never forget that to the day I die. Mine was one of the lives you saved that day. By Christ, you earned that VC. You earned a hundred VCs. Do you have any idea what that means? God was with you that day, Ed. I know you don't believe in God, but I swear to you he was by your side on that beach. I'm supposed to be the believer, but God wasn't with me. God abandoned me the moment I stepped off the boat into that sea of dead men. But God was with you, Ed. Why? I'll tell you why. Because you gave yourself up to God and God knows his own. I didn't. I clung to my wretched little life. I thought only of myself. You walked with angels, and God saw you, and God loved you. And because God loved you and protected you, you have *lost the right to despair*. You have to love yourself, whether you want to or not. That's the choice you made on the beach at Dieppe. That's your life now. So wake up, and live it.'

He stands before his friend, pink in the cheeks, breathing fast, furiously pushing his hands through his curly hair. Ed looks back at him, his blue eyes bright.

'Quite a speech.'

'Have you heard a single word I've been saying?'

'I heard every word.'

'I'm right, aren't I? You know I'm right.'

Ed gets up and stretches, reaching his arms high up into the shadowed air. Then he starts to prowl, up as far as the altar and back.

'You say I've lost the right to despair,' he says. 'But you live in a different world to me. I'm somewhere else, far away, beyond despair.'

'Why should you live in a different world to me?'

'I don't know. Maybe we all live in different worlds. You have God in your world. You say God was with me on that beach. Why wasn't he with all the other poor bastards?'

'I told you. God knows his own.'

'You say I gave myself up to God. You have no idea. No idea at all.'

'Then tell me,' says Larry.

'Why?'

'Because I'm your friend.'

Ed doesn't speak for a few moments, pacing the aisle of the chapel like a ghost in the night.

'Well, then,' he says at last. 'I'll tell you how Lieutenant Ed Avenell of 40 Royal Marine Commando won his Victoria Cross.'

He comes to a stop in the aisle and stands facing the altar. His voice is quiet as a prayer.

'I'm in the landing craft. In the smoke. And there ahead of me is Red Beach. The Fusiliers have gone in just before us. I stand up in the boat and see bodies in the water, and bodies on the beach. I see shell craters and I hear the big guns booming out of the cliffs. And I know, beyond a shadow of a doubt, that it's all a colossal mistake. It's a stupidity. It's a joke. All these men are being sent to die for no reason. A bunch of fools in London have dreamed up this adventure without the first idea of the price to be paid. And here am I in the middle of it, and I'm going to die. The folly of it, the wickedness of it, just took my breath away. My CO saw it too, he's no fool. He gave the order to turn back, and then a bullet got him. A fine man went down, just like that, for no reason. That made me angry, I can tell you. Jesus, I was angry. I wasn't angry at the Germans, I was angry at Mountbatten, and the chiefs of staff. And then I got angry at all the world, this stupid wicked world that hurts people for no reason. So after that I went a little crazy. I thought, I've had enough, time to go. Time to say goodbye. So I waded ashore and the mortars were dropping in front of me and behind me and the bullets were humming over my head and nothing touched me. Not a blind thing. I wasn't being a hero, Larry. I was being a fool. I wanted to die. I was going up that beach shouting, Here I am! Come and get me! And nothing touched me. So I thought to myself, while I'm waiting for my number to come up, why don't I help some poor bastard lying on the beach? So I went from body to body and rolled them over until one moved, and I picked him up. Not his fault he was smashed up. He never asked for this. So I took him down to the boats, and went back up the beach, waiting for my turn. Here I am! Come and get me! You hear what I'm saying, Larry? It wasn't courage. It was rage. I didn't want to stick around to see the whole sick joke told to the end. I wanted to get out, all the way out, finished, dead. But nothing touched me. You say God was with me. God was nowhere on that beach. God was absent without leave. God knows the way the joke ends and he's gone off to get pissed and forget all about it. Why didn't any of those bullets get me? Luck, that's all. There's nothing unusual about that. Half the men who landed on that beach were killed or wounded. That leaves half the men who never got a scratch. I was one of those men, one among thousands. That's all. The only way I was maybe different to them is I wanted to die. So it wasn't an angel you saw, Larry. It was a dead man walking. I never saved your life. You did that yourself. And I'll tell you something for free. The guns didn't get me on Red Beach, but I died anyway. I don't belong in the world of the living any more.'

He puts his hands on Larry's shoulders and holds him with those bright eyes.

'Do you understand a single word of all that? Because I'm never going to say it again, and I'm never going to say it to anyone else.'

'Yes,' says Larry. 'I understand.'

'Then in the camps – did you ever hear of something called the Commando Order?'

'Yes,' says Larry. 'A lot of our best men were shot in captivity.'

'Well, I wasn't shot.' Ed laughs as if it's all a joke. 'They just pretended to shoot me. But it's not as different as you might think. When a German reads out an order and then puts a gun to your head, you think that's pretty much it.'

'Is that what they did to you?'

'Three times. Just their little game.'

'Jesus!'

'You know how you survive? You stop caring. You want to die. Anything to escape the long slow horror of life.'

'But you didn't die, Ed. You came home.'

'Home, yes. I come home and they give me a medal, and I'm supposed to be proud. These arrogant halfwits who play their war games with other men's lives think *they* can honour *me*? I don't want them anywhere near me. Let them go crawling up the beach at Dieppe and try to wash away the blood.'

'It was a terrible, terrible mistake,' says Larry.

'The world is a terrible mistake,' says Ed. 'Life is a terrible mistake.'

'But you're in it.'

'I wish to God I wasn't.'

'And you have a wife and child.'

Ed turns away abruptly, as if stung.

'Why do you think I go on? Don't you think I'd have got out before this if it wasn't for Kitty?'

'Just going on isn't enough, Ed.'

'Don't tell me that!' He's shouting suddenly, the tension breaking through. 'I'm doing all I can! What more do you want of me?'

'You know as well as I do.'

'You want me to pretend? You want me to smile and say I'm happy and isn't the world a beautiful place?'

'No,' says Larry. 'Just let her near you.'

'You want me to drag her down to the hell I live in?'

'She loves you, Ed. She can take it.'

'That's what you said to me before.' He points an accusing finger at Larry. 'You and me in that hayfield. It's not your private darkness, you said. That's why I went to her, Larry. Because of you.'

'You went to her because you loved her.'

'Yes. Yes, God knows I do love her.'

'Then why do you hide yourself away from her?'

'Because I must.'

Now he's pacing again. Away down the mosaic-floored aisle and back.

'You ask me to let her near me,' he says. 'You have no idea how much I long to do just that. To me, Kitty is the only pure good thing in a bad world. And Pammy, too.

Those two are all that's precious and holy to me. You can keep your Jesus and your Virgin Mary. The only gods I worship are my wife and child. I don't want the rottenness of the world to touch them. But here's the devil of it. I'm part of that rottenness. Of course I want to let her near me. Of course I want to touch her. I'm a man, aren't I?'

Larry begins to understand.

'Kitty says you sleep in your own room.'

'For her sake.'

'You leave her alone, letting her think you can't really love her, for her sake?'

'God damn it! What am I supposed to do? What do you want me to tell you, Larry? I'm not a good man, do you hear? Think of me as sick. Tell yourself poor old Ed's got leprosy or something. Kitty doesn't need my attentions, I can promise you that.'

'But she does.'

Ed shouts out of the darkness.

'You think she'd like it if I raped her?'

Larry is silent.

'Yes, she's my wife. A man can't rape his wife, can he? But what if he's a bad man? What if something happens inside him that makes him want to hurt and crush and destroy? Sex is a monster, Larry! I don't want Kitty to meet that monster.'

He swings away from him, all the way up to the altar.

'How long has it been like this?' says Larry.

'I don't know. Maybe it's what the war's done to me. Maybe I was always this way.'

'You could at least talk to Kitty about it.'

'How would she ever understand? You're a man, you know how it is.'

'Yes,' says Larry.

'Kitty's a girl. Girls have no idea at all. For them it's all a part of loving. How can I talk to her the way I talk to you?'

'I think you have to tell her something.'

'I know, I know.' The old despairing tone returns. 'Every day I think, I'll talk to her today. But the moment comes, and I let it pass. I don't want to lose her, you see. She's all I've got.'

'You think if she knew the truth about you she'd stop loving you?'

'Oh, yes! Without a doubt! Look at me!'

'I can't see a thing,' says Larry with a laugh.

'Just as well. Thank God for darkness. I wouldn't have been able to say any of this in daylight.'

Footsteps sound, approaching the chapel across the bridge.

'Time's up,' says Ed.

'Please talk to her,' says Larry.

'Oh, we'll muddle along somehow,' says Ed.

Louisa enters the chapel.

'Heavens, it's all dark! Are you in here, you bad-mannered men?'

'We're here,' says Ed.

'Everyone's on their way to bed. Are you proposing an all-night vigil?'

'No, we're coming too,' says Ed.

Kitty is in the library with George, helping him put away the cards. She looks up first at Ed as they enter, then at Larry.

'Had a good talk?' she says.

'Larry's been giving me a good wigging,' says Ed. 'I'm to stop being so bloody antisocial.'

Larry has changed into his pyjamas and washed and is ready for bed when there comes a tap on his bedroom door. It's Kitty, in her nightgown.

'Sorry,' she says. 'I just know I won't sleep.'

She comes in and closes the door behind her.

'Please tell me.'

She sits herself down in the single armchair and fixes him with her eyes.

'It's not easy to explain,' Larry says.

'But you'll try.'

He tells her about Ed's anger and how he wanted to die on the beach at Dieppe, and again in the camps. She nods as he speaks, doing her best to understand.

'What did he say about me?'

'He said he loves you more than anyone or anything.'

'So why does he keep away from me?'

Larry hesitates.

'It's still all very recent, Kitty. This nightmare he's been through.'

She shakes her head impatiently.

'Tell me, Larry.'

'The thing is, he almost worships you. He sees you as the only good there is in the world.'

'He worships me? He said that?'

'Yes.'

'Is that why . . . why he won't touch me?'

Larry doesn't answer.

'Don't protect me, please,' she says. 'I have to understand this or I shall go mad.'

Larry sits himself down on the side of the bed and fixes his gaze on the rug on the floor between them.

'I think,' he says slowly, 'Ed feels there's a part of him that's bad, and he doesn't want that to . . . to hurt you.'

'Because I'm good.'

'Yes.'

'You're talking about sex, aren't you?'

Larry keeps his eyes on the rug.

'Yes,' he says.

'Sorry, Larry, but I don't know any other way to get to the truth of this. You mustn't be afraid of upsetting me. Up to now I've been thinking he no longer finds me . . . he's stopped being attracted to me. Almost anything's better than that.'

'No, it's not that.'

'He feels that sex is bad, and I'm good.'

'Something like that.'

'But it's so silly, isn't it?'

Larry looks up and finds her attempting a smile. But she's trembling at the same time.

'Yes, it is.'

'Do lots of men think sex is bad? Do you?'

'No, not exactly. But there is a kind of sex that can feel bad.'

'What kind? Tell me about it.'

'Oh, Kitty. This isn't easy.'

'Just shut your eyes and pretend you're talking to a man. What's this bad kind of sex?'

Larry shuts his eyes.

'It's a feeling you get,' he says, 'that's quite aggressive, and urgent, and entirely selfish. You want a girl, any girl. Not to be sweet to, or to love. Just for the one thing. You don't want to ask, you just want to take. It's a kind of conquering, I suppose. It's very primitive. You don't like it about yourself. But it's there in you.'

'Yes,' says Kitty. 'Yes, I can understand that.'

'Does it disgust you?'

'No. Not at all. Now tell me more. This bad feeling, is it there all the time?'

'Oh, no.'

'So what's there the rest of the time? Is there a good feeling?'

'Yes, there is. There's real love, where you want to be loved back. The opposite of taking what you want, and conquering, and selfishness.'

'And this real love – is that part of sex too?'

'Yes. I think so.' He hesitates, and then gives up the effort of pretence. 'Actually, I don't know. I don't have enough experience.'

'Does Ed have experience? Apart from me, I mean?'

'I don't know. Not that I know of. Probably.'

'It doesn't matter. I don't mind about that, really I don't. I just want so much to understand what it is men are thinking and feeling. It's hard for us girls, you know. We're told such stories all the time. Then you come up against the reality, and nothing makes any sense.'

'It's the same for us. We don't really know anything about girls. I don't, at least.'

'You can forget about worshipping us, for a start.'

She gets up out of her chair.

'Now I'm going to let you get some sleep.'

She reaches out for him, and gives his hand a little squeeze.

'Thank you, Larry. You're a good friend.'

16

One afternoon Larry's class is set to work on a life drawing of a female nude. The model is Nell. She takes off her clothes without hesitation, and places herself as the teacher instructs her, sitting on an upright chair, one leg tucked a little back. She asks him how she should hold her head, and he tells her to make herself comfortable. She chooses to bend her head a little forward, gazing over her knees at the bare boards of the floor.

The students set to work on a pencil sketch, following the measuring technique Coldstream has taught them. The teacher moves among them, checking to see they are marking what he calls the 'fixed points'.

'It's all about touch,' he says. 'Your own feelings about what you see are unimportant. See accurately, and the touch will come.'

Larry doesn't fully understand this, but he works away as best he can, and a passable sketch begins to emerge. At the same time he can't deny the presence of other feelings.

Nell's naked body becomes more beautiful to him, and more desirable, as his pencil traces the curves of her thigh. He glances round the other students, almost all of them male, and sees them all intent on their work, and wonders if they're feeling the same.

When the class finishes Nell puts her clothes back on, and lingers in the Life Room as the students pack up their sketches. Larry, watching furtively, sees the effect she has on the others, how they stand up straighter when talking to her, and laugh more loudly. He hears her asking Leonard Fairlie if she can see his sketch, and hears Fairlie say, 'I'm useless at figures.'

'It's not figures,' Nell says. 'It's me.'

Fairlie laughs at that, his baby face going pink beneath his month-old beard. Larry wants Nell to come over and talk to him, but instead now she's talking to Tony Armitage, the wild boy who's become something of a friend. Larry can tell at once from Armitage's agitated arm movements that he's trying to impress Nell.

'What are you thinking when you're drawing?' she says.

'I don't think,' Armitage replies. 'Artists never think. I look.' He gives Nell a ferocious glare. 'I look.'

'And what do you see?'

'I see *you*,' says Armitage.

Then evidently aware that he can't improve on this, he sweeps himself out of the room, following the others.

Larry has lingered. Now he gets his reward.

'I think they're all shy,' Nell says to him.

'Well, they have been staring at you with no clothes on.'

225

'You wouldn't know it. No one's mentioned it.'

'What do you expect them to say?' says Larry.

'Oh, you know. Ooh, I can see your titties! Ooh, I can see your bum!'

Larry laughs. She slips one arm through his.

'Buy me a drink, Lawrence.'

The Hermit's Cave has survived the war unscathed, protected, say the locals, by the hermit himself, who gazes philosophically into the distance on the pub sign, wearing what seems to be a nightdress. Inside, beneath the smoke-grimed mustard-coloured ceilings, the students from the art college lunch on Scotch eggs and Murphy's stout and argue about art and politics and religion. Leonard Fairlie takes the orthodox Marxist line on Christianity.

'How else are the ruling classes to persuade the masses to be content with their pitiful share of the nation's wealth? Obviously you have to create a compensation mechanism for them. You have to tell them the less jam they have today, the more jam they'll have tomorrow.'

'So who are these people, Leonard? Who are these cynical liars who've fabricated this monstrous perversion for their own evil ends?'

Peter Prout is a big smiley young man who may or may not be homosexual.

'You want me to tell you who rules the country?' says Leonard.

'Somehow I don't think Churchill dreamed up Christianity,' says Peter. 'Or Attlee or Bevin, for that matter.'

'Beveridge, more like,' says Larry.

'Listen,' says Peter. 'I'm not saying any of it's *true*. I don't believe in Jesus being the son of God and all that. But it doesn't have to be a conspiracy. It's a folk myth. It's a kind of communal dream.'

Larry then says, almost apologetically, 'Actually I do believe Jesus was the son of God.'

This causes general amazement. Nell, sitting by Larry's side, grins to see the looks on their faces.

'You can't!' says Tony Armitage.

'And I believe in heaven and hell,' says Larry. 'And the Last Judgement. And I think I believe in the virgin birth. And I'm trying hard to believe in papal infallibility.'

'Oh, God!' says Leonard. 'You're a Catholic.'

'Born and bred,' says Larry.

'But Larry,' says Tony Armitage, 'you can't believe all that rubbish. You just can't.'

'I suppose it may be rubbish,' says Larry, 'some of it, anyway. But it's the rubbish I grew up with. And it does make a sort of sense, you know. You belong to a church because you believe the wisdom of an institution is greater than the wisdom of one man. We have rather overdone the cult of the individual, don't you think?'

'The cult of the individual!' Peter Prout mocks shock. 'Next you'll be doubting the romance of the lone artist!'

'But Larry!' exclaims Armitage. 'Virgin birth! Papal infallibility!'

'Well, to be honest,' says Larry, 'I don't really follow some of that. But then, why would I? I don't know everything. It's like falling in love. You don't go down a checklist of all the girl's opinions, making sure you agree with each one. You just love her, and you take what you get.'

'I can understand that,' says Nell.

'It's theatre,' says Peter Prout. 'The Catholic Church is all about theatre.'

'But where's the intellectual honesty?' says Leonard.

'Who needs intellectual honesty?' says Nell. 'Who needs intellectual anything? That's just another way for people to bully people. Larry grew up believing in a religion that really matters to him, and it's got power and beauty and so on to him, so why not let him get on with it?'

'But Nell,' says Armitage, 'we're not talking about art, or poetry. We're talking about so-called eternal truths.'

'It is art and poetry for me,' says Larry. 'It's just like that. Once you decide your brain is too small to know everything, you look at things differently. You say, all right, I might as well stick with my traditions until I run into a good reason not to. I'm not saying the Catholic Church has the only truth. It's just the faith I've grown up with. So for me, it's faith itself. It's the part of me that believes there's more than this life, and that goodness wins in the end, and that there's a purpose to existence. I expect if I'd been born in Cairo I'd get all that from being a Muslim, but I wasn't. I was taken to the Carmelite church in Kensington every Sunday, and I was sent to a school run by Benedictine monks, and so it's all just part of who I am.'

'You're allowed to grow up,' says Leonard. 'You're not obliged to stay a child for ever. You can break out on your own.'

'What did you grow up believing, Leonard?' says Nell.

'My parents have always been free-thinkers,' says Leonard. 'I've been allowed to grow up in my own way.'

'Do they believe in God?'

'Not at all.'

'So you've been raised by atheists,' says Nell, 'and you're an atheist. When do you break out on your own?'

The others laugh at that. Larry grins and holds out his hand. Nell shakes it.

Nell walks down Camberwell Grove with Larry later that afternoon, heading for the room Larry rents in McNeil Road.

'I love it that you're a Catholic,' she says. 'It's just so wacky and different. I've never known anyone who's a Catholic.'

'What are your family, then?'

'Oh, nothing, of course. You know, Anglican. They never talk about religion. I think it's supposed to be bad manners, like talking about sex.'

'God and sex. Big secrets. Not in front of the children.'

'What I like about you, Lawrence,' she goes on, 'is the way you're not afraid to be who you are. Actually I'm quite impressed that you know who you are at all. I've no idea who I am.'

'Well, I am older than you.'

'Yes, I like that too.'

When they get to the door of his digs she says, 'Are you going to ask me in?'

'Would you like to come in, Nell?'

'Yes, thank you, Lawrence. I would.'

His room has a bed, a table, a small high-backed armchair, and a washbasin. A gas fire has been crammed into the small fireplace. Larry lights the gas. Nell sits on the bed, crossing her legs.

'It's funny to think,' Nell says, 'that I was sitting naked in front of you and you were staring at me, and there were all the others there too, and now we're alone and I'm all dressed, and you can't even look at me.'

'Yes, it is funny,' says Larry.

'Is it because you'd rather I wasn't here?'

'No. No, not at all.'

'Do you think it's wrong for me to be a life model?'

'Of course I don't.'

'But you must think it's a bit strange. I mean, most people are shy about taking their clothes off.'

'Well, I'm glad you're not.'

'I am shy, really. But I make myself do it. I'm determined to get away.'

He understands what she means. This is her equivalent of his impulse to paint.

'You know we agreed we should always tell each other what we want?' says Nell.

'Yes.'

'I want to kiss you.'

'Oh,' says Larry, taken by surprise.

'Do you want to kiss me?'

'Yes.'

'Then come over here. That way we'll warm up quicker, too.'

Larry goes to sit beside her on the bed. She reaches up to cup one hand round his head.

'Do you think it's wrong for me to be so forward?'

'No,' he says.

He leans close and they kiss. Then she lies down full length on the bed and he lies down with her and they kiss holding each other in their arms. He feels her slight body warm against his, and her lips soft and secret on his, and he's overwhelmed by the sweet rush of desire.

She feels him growing hard against her.

'What's this?' she says.

'Sorry,' he says. 'Nothing I can do about it.'

'Of course there is,' she says.

She slips her hand down between them and strokes the ridge in his trousers.

'Does the Catholic Church say it's wrong for me to do this?' she says.

'No,' he whispers.

She feels for the buckle of his belt and undoes it. Then she unbuttons his flies. He lies still, grateful and amazed. She pushes her hands inside his pants and touches his cock, gently stroking it.

'How about this?' she says. 'Is this a sin?'

'No,' he whispers.

'Do you think maybe we should draw the curtains?'

'Yes,' he says.

He gets up off the bed and his trousers fall down. He stoops and pulls them up, but Nell says, 'Take them off, silly.' He goes to the window and pulls the thin curtains closed. Now the room is filled with a green shade, in the midst of which the gas fire glows orange.

Nell is sitting up on his bed pulling her dress over her head. Larry stands there in shirt and underpants and socks, shaking with confused excitement. Beneath the dress she wears a brassiere and knickers. She tosses the dress to the floor and unhooks the brassiere.

'It's not as if you haven't seen it all before,' she says.

Larry takes off his shirt and socks, but not his pants. His erection pushes out all too visibly. Nell poses for him on the bed, as she did in the life class.

'Remember?'

'Yes,' he says. 'Yes.'

'Come here, then.'

He goes into her arms, and holds her naked body close.

'My God, Nell,' he whispers. 'My God, you're lovely.'

'Have we started doing anything wrong yet?'

'No, not yet. But we're very close.'

'I want to do something wrong with you, Lawrence. I want you to want to do it with me.'

'I do. I do.'

Her hand is back feeling his cock, stroking it, making the desire in him go crazy. Then she takes his hand and puts it between her legs.

'Feel me there, Lawrence. I want you there.'

He feels the tickly mound of pubic hair, and the yielding

softness below. She moves her hips, pushing her crotch against his hand.

'All yours,' she says.

'Oh, God, Nell,' he says, feeling his blood race. The wonder of her touch wipes his mind clean of all other thoughts. He knows only that he is entirely possessed by his desire, and that she is wonderfully, generously, inexplicably granting it.

'God, you're beautiful,' he says.

She rubs her body against his, exciting him to near-frenzy.

'Are we going to do it, Lawrence?' she says. 'Are we?'

'I'm not prepared,' he says. 'I haven't got—'

'Don't worry about that,' she says. 'I've dealt with that.'

She has his cock in her hand now, and she's rubbing the tip against her slit. Larry feels tremors of dangerous delight run down his cock.

'So are we going to do it, Lawrence?'

'Yes,' he whispers. 'Yes.'

'Doesn't the Catholic Church say it's wrong?'

'Yes,' he says.

'Fucking me is wrong.'

'Yes.'

'But you want to fuck me even so, Lawrence.'

'Yes,' he groans, feeling the tip of his cock pushing into her a little way.

'If you fuck me, will God punish you, Lawrence?'

'I don't care,' he says.

'God won't punish you,' she says, 'if you love me.'

'I love you, Nell. I love you. I love you.'

233

He feels the intensity of his love for her with each repetition, along with the tingling in his cock, and the profound shock of joy with which he has heard each utterance by her of the word *fuck*. She seems to know how much this electrifies him. She moves her hips, pushing him deeper into her all the time, and as she does so she whispers, 'Fuck me now, Lawrence. Fuck me now.'

His cock is in her now, gripped by sweet warmth, and he knows he can't restrain himself any longer. His desire is in total control of his being, and it seeks its explosive release.

'I can't,' he says, 'I can't—'

'Do it, Lawrence,' she says. 'Do it. Do it.'

He thrusts deep into her, and pulls back, and thrusts again, and the moment comes, and he half-faints with the intense pleasure of it. He feels the pulsing release spread from his cock to every part of his body.

She strokes his back with warm hands.

'There,' she says. 'There.'

'Oh, Nell.'

'Was that nice?'

'Oh, God! It was heaven!'

'I'm glad,' she says. 'I wanted it to be nice for you.'

He lies over her, still helpless, his entire being disintegrated, his muscles powerless to move. Then his frantic heart begins to regain its usual rhythm, and his senses return. He kisses her eagerly, gratefully, adoringly.

'You're wonderful, you're amazing, you're perfect.'

'Darling Lawrence.'

'I've never known anything like that before.'

'That's because you're a good Catholic boy.'

'Not any more.'

'Yes, you are. It doesn't change anything. And anyway, all you have to do is go to confession.'

'But I want to do it again,' says Larry.

'Of course we'll do it again,' says Nell. 'This is only the beginning.'

She puts on his dressing gown and pads upstairs to the shared bathroom to clean herself up. Larry dresses slowly in the green light. Then she's back and he watches her lithe naked body as she too puts her clothes on.

'You've had boyfriends before, haven't you?' he says.

'Would you mind if I had?'

'No, not at all. It makes me feel proud.'

He feels no jealousy at all of her past. Only this gigantic gratitude that she grants him the same supreme privilege.

'I had a boyfriend when I was sixteen,' she says. 'Not a boy, a man. He taught me things. He liked me to say the dirty words. He was kind.'

'What happened to him?'

'The war,' says Nell. 'He died.'

Larry feels both shocked and elated. She's so young, it's cruel that she should have had to experience love and loss. But now she belongs entirely to him.

'I'm sorry,' he says.

'I was sorry then,' she says. 'But now there's you.'

'I don't understand,' says Larry. 'Why me? You're so beautiful you could have any man you wanted.'

'I'm not really beautiful,' she says. 'But it's true, if I want a man, I can have him. Men aren't that hard to get. But a good man – that's another matter. I think you may be a good man, Lawrence.'

'Because I'm a Catholic?'

'Because you're kind. Most people are mean. You're not mean.'

'You are beautiful, Nell.'

'You say that because I let you fuck me.'

'I love it the way you say that word.'

'That word.' She grins at him mischievously. 'What word would that be, Lawrence?'

'Fuck,' he says, blushing.

17

Harry Avenell's club is the Travellers in Pall Mall. Like so much in his life this is a second-best, but he has neither the connections nor the income to put up for White's. For all that, the Travellers, in its handsome Barry building, provides the civilised surroundings that he appreciates. By profession a director of Marston's Brewery, Burton-upon-Trent, by taste he is a country gentleman, the master of a small estate that overlooks the river Dove. The Queen Anne house is furnished with what might be called modest excellence. Every item, from the umbrella stand in the hall to the cutglass decanter on the dining-room sideboard, is the best of its kind. The high standards of Hatton House have always exceeded the actual income of the family, but only by so much as to make living correctly demand a life of austerity that comes naturally to both Harry and his wife. Harry's philosophy is declared by his tailoring. His suits are of the best cloth, made by Gieves & Hawkes of Savile Row, and are expected to last his lifetime. Gillian Avenell, by contrast, though always immaculately dressed, has no real care for her appearance at all. Where Harry is anxious about money, she is frugal, happier on her knees in prayer than before a dressing-table mirror. She is the devout Roman Catholic of the family. Her husband has no religion. He calls himself a stoic, meaning he is an admirer of Marcus Aurelius, and values self-mastery above all.

Harry Avenell has come to town to make some arrangements for his son. Ed has distinguished himself on the field of battle, he has a wife and child, but he has no employment and no income. By the age of twenty-eight a man needs to have fixed on a career, but Ed shows no signs of even so much as looking about him. Harry has therefore looked about him on his son's behalf. A business acquaintance, Jock Caulder, turns out to have a son also in need of a parental push into the world of work. Caulder is a wealthy man, and proposes to set his boy up with a business of his own, importing French wine. The boy is willing enough, but being only just twenty years old, he's understandably nervous at the prospect of being solely responsible for the enterprise. A partner is required. Harry Avenell has proposed his son, who is older, can be said to be battle-tested, and is looking for a career. It's true he knows nothing about wine, but that can be learned. And his Victoria Cross, without being flaunted in any vulgar way, will surely add prestige to the infant business.

Jock Caulder is minded to agree. His son Hugo declares himself willing to give it a go. It remains only to sound out the war hero himself.

Harry is ensconced on a blue sofa at the far end of the Outer Morning Room of his club, a pot of Earl Grey tea before him, when Ed comes in and greets him with a raised hand. Harry has only seen his son once since his return, when he came up to Hatton and stayed for a single night. He feels shy in his son's company.

He waves him to the sofa opposite and offers him tea.

'How's Kitty? How's our granddaughter?'

'Flourishing,' says Ed. 'Pamela turns out to be tremendously strong-minded.'

'You're still living in the big house?'

'For now, yes. How's Mummy?'

'Very well. Do drop her a line sometime. Or better still, pay us a visit. You know she'd never dream of asking anything for herself, but it would mean a lot to her.'

'Yes, of course,' says Ed, his gaze drifting to the trees in the Mall outside. 'So tell me the news of Hatton.'

'Life goes on in its quiet way,' says Harry. 'But now, here's what I want to talk to you about, Ed. Something's come up that might suit you.'

He lays out the proposal. Ed listens, his handsome face revealing nothing. When he's done, his father expects some questions about the partnership terms and the anticipated income. Instead Ed gives a slight shrug and looks away again, out of the window.

'I suppose I have to do something.'

'It's quite a chance, Ed,' his father says. 'You'd be going in as a full partner without having to invest a penny.'

'Yes, I suppose I would.'

'Obviously everything would depend on how you and Hugo hit it off.'

'I'm sure he's a decent enough chap.'

'Well, yes, he is. He went to Harrow. Not the university type, his father tells me. Clever in his way, but a bit inclined to rest on his oars.'

'Not like me, then.'

He meets his father's eyes and smiles, and for a brief second they share the secret of how far life falls short of dreams.

'I've no doubts about you, Ed. Once you make up your mind to do something, I know you'll do it with all your heart.'

'French wine,' says Ed. 'Well, after all, why not?'

Kitty waits until Pamela is well settled for her afternoon nap and then turns to Louisa for advice. She doesn't expect Louisa to know anything more than herself, but her friend has a knack of seeing the obvious that Kitty has learned to value. She passes on some of what Larry has told her, ending up with what has become for her the simplest expression of her dilemma.

'Ed thinks I'm good, and sex is bad.'

'Bloody Catholics,' says Louisa.

'No, Ed isn't a Catholic any more,' says Kitty. 'He lost all of that ages ago.'

'Like hell,' says Louisa. 'Honestly! What a heap of nonsense! You're his wife! What's bad about it?'

'I think it's just something men feel.'

'It's that damn Virgin Mary of theirs,' says Louisa. 'All the good women have to be virgins, which means they can only do it with whores.'

'From what Larry said to me,' Kitty says, 'it's such a strong thing for them that it almost frightens them.'

'Can't be that strong, darling.'

'That's what I don't understand. If it's so strong, what's he doing about it?'

'Don't ask.'

'Oh,' says Kitty, going red. 'Do you think so?'

'I'll tell you something I've never told anyone,' says Louisa. 'About five years ago I found out my father has affairs with other women. He visits those houses men go to. A friend told me, Oh yes, your father's famous for it. I went to my mother to tell me it wasn't true, but she said, Yes, it's all true. So then I wanted to know why and she sat me down and she said to me, Darling, do you know the facts of life? I said yes, I thought so. She said, You know how men have seed in them, that makes babies? I said, Yes. She said, Well, there's a lot of it, and it has to come out at least once a day, and that's not always convenient for me, so he goes elsewhere.'

'Louisa!'

'Yes, I know. Quite an eye-opener, I can tell you.'

'Once a day!'

'At least. Some men have to do it three times a day.'

'I had no idea,' says Kitty faintly.

'Once you know, it makes sense of a lot of things.'

'Doesn't your mother mind?'

'Well, yes, I think so. But the funny thing is, they seem to get on really well.'

Kitty ponders in silence.

'So what am I to do about Ed?' she says at last. 'I can't make him come to me if he doesn't want to.'

'Why don't you go to him?'

'I wouldn't know what to say.'

'Don't say anything,' says Louisa. 'Just do it.'

'I couldn't! Suppose he got angry? Suppose it made him think I was . . . I was . . .'

'What? You're his wife, Kitty.'

'Yes, but if he doesn't want me . . .'

'Of course he wants you! And anyway, how's he going to stop himself? Men can't. Crank the starter handle and they're off.'

Kitty starts to laugh, and that sets Louisa off laughing.

'What about George?'

'Well, no. Obviously not George.'

They both laugh until they have tears in their eyes.

'Oh, Lord, Louisa!' says Kitty. 'What a mess it all is.'

'Would you mind me giving you a little tip?' says Louisa.

'Tell me anything,' says Kitty. 'I'm done with blushing.'

'How long has it been?'

Kitty hangs her head and answers in a low voice.

'Not since he came home. Not since he went away. Three years.'

'So if you're going to go to him, it might be a good idea to go prepared.'

'Prepared?'

Louisa leaves the West Parlour where they've gone for their tête-à-tête and runs upstairs. She returns shortly with a small embroidered drawstring bag, which she gives to Kitty. Inside is a tin of Vaseline.

Ed comes back from town full of brittle nervous energy. When Pamela comes running to greet him he sweeps her up in his arms and tosses her into the air, again and again, until she's screaming with excitement.

'Your daddy's going to get a job!' he says to her. 'Your daddy's going to make money so you can have pretty frocks!'

'What is this, Ed?' says Kitty, laughing, watching the flying child anxiously.

'My father, my esteemed father,' says Ed, 'having sacrificed his life to a job in which he has no interest whatsoever, in order to earn enough money to keep us all in the style he believes to be our birthright, has done me the great kindness of finding me a sacrificial job all of my own.'

'What are you talking about? What job?'

'I'm to become a partner in a business that imports wine at low prices from France, and sells at high prices in England. Apparently a child of three could do it. Would you like to be a wine importer, Pammy? You could be a partner too.'

'I can do it!' squeals the little girl, wriggling in his arms.

'Is this serious, Ed?' says Kitty.

'I have to do something, darling. Would you mind very much?'

'Not if it's what you want to do.'

'Oh, that's asking too much! I don't *want* to do it. But I

243

dare say I'll get into the way of it. I like wine, and I like France. It's just the buying and selling that fails to excite me.'

Over dinner more details of the plan emerge. Ed explains about his father's rich friend, and the rich friend's son.

'So you see, I'm to be a species of babysitter. If he has tantrums I'm to give him my VC to play with.'

'Well, it all sounds grand to me,' says George. 'You can help me restock my white burgundy.'

'You haven't even met this boy yet,' says Kitty.

'My father's met his father. That's how this sort of thing's done, you know. Like an arranged marriage.'

'Ed, promise me,' says Kitty, 'you won't do this unless it really feels right. I don't want you sacrificing yourself for us.'

He reaches across the table and takes her hand.

'Darling Kitty,' he says, smiling. 'You mustn't pay any attention to all the rot I talk. There isn't any sacrifice. All I care about in the world is you and Pammy.'

That night Kitty goes to bed as usual, but she lies awake until she's sure that all the rest of the house is asleep. Then she leaves her bedroom and passes softly down the passage to the room where Ed is sleeping. She enters without knocking.

The window curtains are wide open, and the light of a full moon fills the room. The bed is empty. Ed is lying asleep on the floor beside the bed, covered by a sheet and a blanket. He lies on his side, one arm tucked beneath him, the other arm thrown out. He looks peaceful, and beautiful.

Kitty lies down on the floor beside him, making as little sound as possible, and he doesn't wake. Slowly she moves her body up against his, and still he doesn't wake. Then he stirs in his sleep, and straightens out his legs, and rolls onto his back.

Very gently, she draws the sheet and the blanket down, until they're no longer covering him. He lies in the moonlight, in his pyjamas, the pyjama top buttoned up, the trouser cord tied in a bow.

Kitty undoes the buttons one by one, and she loosens the bow and draws apart the cords. She folds back the flaps of his pyjama trousers, and lays her warm hand between his thighs. Very slowly, back and forth, she strokes his cock, and feels it start to grow. She looks up at his face, but his eyes are closed, and his breathing is steady. She goes on stroking until the cock has grown big and hard. She can feel her own heart beating, and wonders that he can sleep on.

'What?'

He starts out of sleep, raising his arms to defend himself.

'What are you doing?'

'Hush,' she says. 'Hush.'

She goes on stroking him, moving her hand faster now.

'No, Kitty!' he says.

'It's all right,' she says. 'Don't talk.'

She leans close and kisses him, her hand moving all the time up and down his cock. His arms reach round her, pull her close. She hears him groan.

Then his hands are tugging at her nightdress, pulling it up, and she moves to free it, wanting to be naked for him. His whole body begins to turn now, his hips thrust upwards, his head thrown back, his eyes closed. His hands pull her onto him. She lets him do as he wants, moving her hand away so that he can press her body to his.

Now she feels his hard cock against her belly, and his chest against her breasts, and he's groaning loudly as if in pain. Then with a rough and powerful movement he rolls her over and now he's on top of her and he's forcing her legs apart and his cock is pushing between her thighs. She lifts her hips, wanting it to be easy for him, and feels his cock drive into her.

'You want it? You want it?'

His voice harsh and distant.

'Yes,' she says. 'I want it.'

He starts to ram into her, making wordless sounds with each thrust.

'I want it,' she whispers. 'I want it!'

Then all at once she realises she does want it. Her body awakens, she wraps herself round him, pulling him deep into her, hungry for sensation, rubbing herself against him, rocking with his angry thrusts.

'Ah!' he cries. 'Ah! Ah!'

He hammers at her, shouts at her, a creature possessed. Then there comes a gasping moan, and she feels his convulsion and feels the pumping inside her. Now he's sinking down onto her, moving still, but slowly now. She feels his body come to rest, heavy on hers, and she lies still, holding him in her arms. She kisses the sweat on his brow.

For a long moment he doesn't move. Then she realises he's weeping.

'No, darling. No.'

She kisses the tears on his cheeks.

'Sorry,' he says. 'Sorry. Sorry.'

'No, darling,' she says, kissing him. 'I wanted you. I came to you because I wanted you.'

'Not like that.'

'Yes,' she says. 'Like that.'

They lie in each other's arms until they become cold. Then she moves him off her, and he climbs shakily to his feet.

'Lie down now, darling.'

He lies on the bed and she covers him with the bedclothes. He holds her hand, doesn't want her to go.

'Kitty, I'm sorry. I didn't want to be like that with you.'

'I'm yours,' she says. 'You can be anything you want with me.'

'I didn't know. I thought . . . I don't know what I thought.'

'You thought I was too good for you.'

'You are good.'

'I'm yours,' she says again.

'Is it going to be all right?' he says.

'Yes, my darling,' she says. 'It's going to be all right.'

★

247

The next day Ed moves back into Kitty's room. Pamela expresses her disapproval.

'That's not your room. That's Mummy's room.'

'I want to be with Mummy,' he says.

'So do I want to be with Mummy,' says Pamela. 'But we have to sleep in our own rooms.'

Kitty points out that George and Louisa share a bedroom. Pamela becomes puzzled.

'Who can I share with?' she says.

'When you're grown up, you can share with your husband.'

'My husband!'

This enchanting idea distracts her entirely.

'What's his name?'

'Augustus,' says Ed.

'Augustus? Yech!'

That night Kitty lies in Ed's arms, and it's both strange and familiar at the same time. She thinks she won't sleep but she does sleep, and when she wakes in the morning he's still there.

She gives him a kiss and he too wakes.

'Good morning,' she says.

18

Larry Cornford kneels beside his father in the Carmelite church on Kensington Church Street, murmuring the familiar Latin words. All round him he hears the soft voices of the others in the packed pews. Before him the priest stands, his back to them, green-robed at the altar.

'*Beato Michaeli Archangelo, beato Joanni Baptistae, Sanctis Apostolis Petro et Paulo, omnibus Sanctis et tibi, Pater . . .*'

The names are friends Larry has known all his life. At the appropriate moment in the prayer his hand forms a fist and taps his breast in the sign of contrition.

'*Mea culpa, mea culpa, mea maxima culpa.*'

He feels no sense of blame, only deep and comforting familiarity. The shape of the Mass never varies, its mystery has embraced him since childhood. The buildings may change, priests may come and go, but the ritual unfolds always in the same way. When the time comes for the consecration – '*Haec dona, haec munera, haec sancta sacrificia illibata*' – and the priest bends in holy secrecy over the altar, making the sign of the cross over the bread and wine – '*Benedixit, fregit, deditque discipulis suis dicens, Accipite et manducate ex hoc omnes, hoc est enim corpus meum*' – and kneels, and raises the host, and the altar boy tinkles the bell – at this time the wonder always returns, and he feels himself to be in the presence of the supernatural. The child who was taught to see in the Mass a true ever-repeated miracle, the real presence, the coming of God among them – that same child lives still in Larry today, as the priest elevates the host, and the smell of incense rolls over the pews.

Later he takes his place following his father in the line of communicants, and receives the papery biscuit on his tongue. He feels the living God melt in his mouth. He knows that by the letter of the law he has committed mortal sin and should not take communion, but his God and his Church are merciful. Larry is a very modern Catholic, taught by enlightened monks that God loves the generous heart and the truthful mind more than a petty conformity to rules. He returns to his place in the pews, and kneeling with his head in his hands he prays that he may learn to serve God with his chosen work.

After Mass he walks home with his father to the tall house on Camden Grove and shares a late breakfast with him. His father talks to him about the company and its present difficulties. He is to make a trip to Jamaica very shortly, to attend to problems on the ground.

'I'm afraid we're facing a serious supply shortage,' he says. 'Partly it's the hurricane season. But we also have a bad outbreak of leaf-spot disease.'

'I thought the *Tilapa* came into Avonmouth with a full cargo.'

'So she did, God bless her.' His father sips at his coffee and sighs. 'But there's not much more where that came from. We're looking seriously at the Cameroons. Also I think it's time now to come to a new arrangement with the Ministry.'

'Are you still managing the Ministry depots?'

'One hundred and twenty, all told. It's far too much, of course. But the truth is the Ministry is still operating on a wartime footing.'

'Will you see Joe Kiefer when you're in Kingston?'

'Joe's retired now. I'm glad you remember him, Larry. I shall tell him so.'

William Cornford gazes wistfully across the breakfast table at his son.

'You know we've got the house in Normandy habitable now,' he says. 'Why not join me there this summer? It should be a good place for your painting.'

'I'd like that,' says Larry.

'How's it coming along?' He wipes his mouth with his napkin. 'The painting and so forth.'

'I can't exactly say how I'm getting on,' says Larry, 'but I'm hard at work. I'm afraid I've no accounts to show you. No figures to prove my progress.'

'Of course not. But are you happy?'

'Yes, Dad. I'm very happy.'

His father smiles.

'Well, then. That's the point, isn't it?'

Larry tells his father he's happy because his father is subsidising him and he wishes to give some return on his investment. The truth is more complex. He is finding that the work he has chosen – he calls it 'work' following his teacher's example, shy of grander terms – causes him almost constant unease. Somehow, however steadily he applies himself, he always ends up dissatisfied with the end result. The process itself never fails to absorb him, even to obsess him. But he remains unconvinced of his talent.

He has chosen in recent weeks to limit himself to landscapes. Noticing that artists he admires have a way of repeating motifs in their work, or of working in defined geographical areas, he has decided to choose landscapes that feature a church. This is mostly a formal preference: the spire of the church, breaking the skyline like a knife, delivers a visual pivot for his composition. But it's also an emotional choice. The church acts as a lightning conductor, a conduit for the supernatural into his scene. This is not something he talks about with his fellow students. More and more of them are coming under the influence of Victor Pasmore, drawn towards pictorial geometry, if not full-blown abstract painting. Among the hold-outs is Tony Armitage, the farouche boy who is showing an extraordinary talent for portraiture.

'Geometry!' exclaims Armitage with disgust. 'It's pure funk. They can't face the world. They're running away from life.'

Larry is inclined to agree. The Pasmore school strikes him as a form of Puritanism.

'They're visual Calvinists,' he says. 'All this reduction to pure form.'

Nevertheless his own work is highly formal. He is painting a view of St Giles's church seen from an upper window of the college. The grey and white tower is built in three diminishing stages, two square, the last a hexagonal spire. On two sides of the tower project steep-pitched grey-tiled roofs. The church is the work of Gilbert Scott and has a window reputedly designed by Ruskin, but to Larry it has become a series of lines to be projected outward and upward as he forms his composition. He is painting both the actual church, and a diagram of sacred space. It's not something he fully understands, but as he works he knows very quickly which lines have significance and which are trivial. As he begins to overlay the lines with tones of grey and brown and white, he struggles to let the various colours convey the light he wants in the picture, the instinct he has that it's not stone walls he's painting so much as the space they enclose.

There are moments as he works when he feels so near to capturing this simple truth that all he needs to do is let his brush go free. The thing is there before him. Rather than painting it into existence he is uncovering it, his brush the instrument of exposure. At such times his excitement is so intense that he loses all awareness of time and place, and works on long into the evening.

'You know something,' says Armitage, pausing to look. 'That's not as bad as your usual stuff.'

Larry stands back to see for himself.

'No,' he says. 'It's not there yet.'

'Of course it's not *there*!' exclaims Armitage. 'It's never *there*! But it's not bad. And take it from me, not bad is as good as it gets.'

Larry has grown to like Tony Armitage very much, for all his startling outbursts and lack of personal hygiene. He has painted a head and shoulders of Nell that is to Larry's mind quite extraordinary. Somehow he has managed to capture both her directness and her evasiveness. Nell of course hates the portrait.

The more Larry now looks at his St Giles, the less he likes it. But at this point Bill Coldstream appears.

'Just the men I wanted to see,' he says.

He stands still for a moment, examining Larry's picture.

'Yes,' he says. 'Good. Do you know the Leicester Galleries?'

'Of course,' says Larry. 'I saw the John Piper show there.'

'They're putting together a summer show. Artists of Promise and so on. Phillips has asked me to suggest some of our people. I'd like to put you and Armitage up for it.'

Larry is speechless. Armitage takes it in his stride.

'How long have we got?'

'They want to open in early July,' says Coldstream. 'So the selection will have to be done by the end of April, I should think.'

With this he departs.

'That's one in the eye for Fairlie,' says Armitage.

'I had no idea,' says Larry.

He means he had no idea their teacher rated him so highly.

'I told you you were good.'

'No, you didn't. You said I wasn't bad.'

'What you need, Larry,' says Armitage, 'is faith in yourself.'

'Any idea where I'm to get it?'

'The great thing you have to keep in mind,' says Armitage, 'is that everyone else is clueless. They're all stumbling about in the dark. They've no idea what's good and what isn't. They're waiting to be told. So all you have to do is tell them, loudly and often.'

Larry sighs.

'Not my style, I'm afraid.'

Larry tells Nell the news that evening. She throws her arms round him and kisses him.

'I knew it! You're going to be famous!'

Nell no longer works as a life model at the school. She's got herself a job as receptionist to an art dealer in Cork Street. Julius Weingard, according to Nell, is both queer and crooked, but by her account so is everyone else. She tells Larry hair-raising stories of how Weingard cheats his clients. Everyone knows, she says, it's just how the art world works. No one believes in any artist's actual worth, only in reputation and the degree to which that can be converted into sales.

'I shall make Julius come to your show,' Nell says. 'Maybe he'll decide to take you on. He'll tell you to use brighter colours, darling. Everyone is tired of khaki.'

Nell continues to fascinate Larry, but their relationship

is not simple. They sleep together but they don't live together. Nell has her own digs, which Larry has never entered. She is often away, carrying out assignments for Weingard, or visiting friends about whom she tells him nothing. This other life, which she keeps from him with a teasing secrecy, should trouble him, and occasionally does. But the truth is that much of the time it suits him.

Larry's feelings for Nell are forever catching him by surprise. The volatility of their relationship both disturbs and excites him. When she's away he can build up a longing for her that almost paralyses him. But when she's been with him for a few days, he begins to withdraw into himself, and want to be alone.

'You're getting so middle-aged, Lawrence,' she tells him. 'You should let yourself go more.'

He knows she's right, and he loves her for being a true Bohemian, a free spirit, a wild creature. But then there are the moments when he catches a glimpse of the other side of this freedom, and sees in her a lost child. Her youth and her powerful attractiveness disguise this inner core of fear, but every now and again it breaks through. Once, after making love, she began to cry.

'Nell! What is it?'

'Doesn't matter. You don't want to know.'

'Yes, I do. Tell me.'

'You'll say I'm just being silly. I am being silly.'

'No, tell me.'

'Sometimes I think I'll never be married and have children.'

'Of course you will. We'll be married tomorrow if you like. We'll have hundreds of children.'

'Oh, Lawrence, you are sweet. Maybe one day. I'm still only twenty.'

Then just as he's beginning to think they should get a flat together somewhere, she'll disappear for days on end. On her return she gives him no real answers to his questions about where she's been. She holds fiercely to her right to live her own life in her own way.

'Don't try to tie me down, Lawrence. That's what my father did. It drives me crazy.'

And yet she can erupt with sudden explosions of jealousy. Once after a party where he talked with another girl, she turns on him in fury.

'Don't ever do that to me again! I don't care what you do and who you do it with, but don't do it while I'm in the same room.'

'What have I done?'

'And don't gape at me like you don't know exactly what I'm talking about. I'm not a complete idiot.'

'Nell, this is all some fantasy of yours.'

'I'm not asking for fidelity. I'm asking you to show me some respect in public.'

'All I was doing was talking to her. Am I not to talk to other girls?'

'Fine,' she says. 'Have it your own way. Call it what you like.'

'For God's sake, Nell. It's not as if you don't talk to other men. Do I ever ask you not to talk to other men?'

'If you don't want me to go out with other men, Lawrence, all you have to do is say so.'

'I don't want to lock you up. You know I don't.'

'So what do you want, Lawrence?'

'I want us to trust each other.'

He tells himself her behaviour has no consistency, but at a deeper unacknowledged level he knows well enough what she's asking of him. She wants unconditional love. She wants to be told that he will be her lover and her protector and her friend for ever, however badly she behaves. There are times when his own need is strong in him and he wants to make all the promises in the world; but an instinctive caution in him prevents him from saying the words. So long as she's wild and free and desired by other men she's all that he wants. But the closer they come to each other the more clearly he sees her fragility and neediness, and in self-protection he pulls back once more.

He tries to understand what's happening to him, and why he swings so wildly between extremes. Is it just sex? Is it as simple as that? She takes it for granted that he wants and needs sex, and makes herself readily available to him, and for this alone he adores her. But it's not just sex. After a few days without her what haunts him is not just her naked body and the gratifications it brings, but her teasing laughter, her unpredictable turns of phrase, the vitality with which she floods his life. It's Nell who takes him swimming at night in Hampstead pond, or who goes out on an impulse to get crumpets to toast on the gas fire. It's Nell who knows the all-night cab-drivers' hut by Albert

Bridge where a cup of tea can be had in the small hours. How can he not love her for the adventure she makes of his life? It seems to him then that this must be the fundamental shape of love, this cycle of craving and satiety and withdrawal.

Unless somewhere there's another kind of love, where you and your lover want never to be parted.

At such times he thinks of Kitty. He allows these thoughts with shame, knowing they're foolish. After all, what does he really know of Kitty? He's spent a few hours in her company, nothing more. It would be ridiculous to claim to be in love with her. Worse than ridiculous, it would condemn him to a life of loneliness. She's married to a man she loves, who is also his own best friend. Why then does it persist, this secret conviction? Sometimes, when he's alone, he feels a kind of terror at the thought of Kitty. What if it's given to every man to fall in love truly only once, and he has fallen for a girl he can never have?

'You know your trouble, Lawrence?' Nell tells him. 'You've got this thing about being good, but really you want to be bad.'

What does it mean, to be bad? It means to pursue your own desires at the expense of other people's. It means to live according to your own will, not the will of God. It means the pursuit of selfishness.

If I were to be bad, what would I do? I would paint, and I would love Kitty. That's all I want in life. And what value is that to others?

At such times he prays the prayer of Père de Caussade: 'Lord have pity on me. With you all things are possible.'

On the day of the private view Larry stands silent, smoking ceaselessly, white-faced, in the back of the room in which his three paintings hang. All three now seem to him to be lifeless and without merit. The guests move through the rooms exclaiming over the varied works, never pausing long over his paintings. No red spots appear beneath them to indicate a sale. Bill Coldstream is here, talking with his old Euston Road crowd. Leonard Fairlie is here, and while not being directly rude about Larry's work he makes it all too clear that he is unimpressed with the show.

'Of course it's a commercial show,' he says. 'One shouldn't be surprised. It's all about opening wallets. These days the kind of people who can afford to buy want to be reassured that the old world is with them still, in all its bourgeois glory. One has to expect to have one's mouth stuffed with bonbons.'

Tony Armitage is present, being one of the 'artists of promise'. He is as nervous as Larry, but shows it in a different way.

'Don't you hate the shits who come to these private views?' he growls. 'They wouldn't know real art if it was stuck up their bums with a poker.'

Despite this, Armitage's striking portraits are among the first to achieve the coveted red spot. Larry moves away, unable to bear the sight of his own unloved works. He sees Nell come in with her employer Julius Weingard, and another man who is small and prosperous and in his forties, if not older. He has his arm looped through Nell's in a proprietorial way, and is smiling at her as they go by. Two well-dressed middle-aged women pass near him, one saying to the other, 'Why are English artists so dreary compared to the French?'

This is hell, thinks Larry to himself. The glory of having been selected is all forgotten. He feels only the humiliation of looking on as his works are ignored. His distress is not wounded vanity. He has no conviction that his works deserve more attention. It's the gap between what he felt as he painted them and what he feels seeing them now that is so unbearable. These three all gave him such joy in the making. He can recall the heart-stopping excitement of realising the work was going to emerge at last, whole, living and harmonious, from the marks and daubs that went into their making. Impossible to describe to someone who hasn't attempted it. There's a magic to it, like being present at the birth of new life. And now these perfect creations, these gifts of wonder, are dying before his eyes. They hang on crowded walls, denied the love and attention which alone caused them to shine, revealed as commonplace efforts by a painter of no more than average ability.

'Larry!'

He looks round. There stands Kitty, her eyes bright, her pale face lit up by a smile.

'I'm so proud of you!'

She takes him in her arms for a warm hug.

'Kitty!' he exclaims. 'I didn't think you'd come.'

'Of course I've come. Your first exhibition! The others are still in front of your paintings, bathed in reflected glory. And I've come to find you.'

'Oh, Kitty. I just hate it here.'

'Do you, darling?'

Her eyes at once fill with sympathy, gazing at him intently, wanting to understand.

'It's all too much,' he says. 'Too many works. Too many people. I feel like an impostor. Any minute now someone's going to tap me on the shoulder and say, I'm afraid there's been a mistake, please take down your miserable daubs and leave.'

'Oh, Larry. How silly you are.'

But her eyes show she feels for him.

'No one will buy them, Kitty. I'm sure of that.'

'Louisa has George under orders to buy one,' says Kitty.

'Are George and Louisa here?'

'Of course. We want to take you out to dinner afterwards. Can you come? Or will you be going off with your smart art crowd?'

'I haven't got a smart art crowd. I'd far rather be with you.'

'Your paintings are wonderful, Larry. Really. I mean it.'

'Oh, Kitty.'

He doesn't care if she means it, he feels so grateful that she wants him to be happy. Now that she's here, before him, everything is transformed. He could stand in this corner for ever, gazing at her, filled with the sweet sensation of how much he loves her. It seems to him that she understands this, because she too stands there, saying nothing.

When he speaks again it's as if they've moved into a different and private space.

'How are you, Kitty?'

'Same as ever,' she says. 'Only older.'

'How is it with Ed?'

'Same as ever.'

Then he hears his name hallooed across the room, and Louisa is heading for him, with George in tow.

'Larry, you genius!' Louisa cries. 'We're all so excited! We know a real live famous artist!'

'Hello, Louisa.'

'We love your work. George loves your work. He's going to buy the big one with all the roofs. Go on, George. Go and tell them you're buying it.'

George shambles away to do as he's told. Ed now joins them.

'Larry, you old bastard,' he says.

His eyes glow with friendly warmth as he pumps Larry's hand. His face has grown even thinner.

'Hello, Ed,' says Larry.

'Next time you have a do, why don't you lay on some wine? You'll sell a whole lot more pictures. We're offering a very decent white right now. Between you and me it's made of peasants' pee, but only peasants who've drunk the best Grand Cru.'

Larry is taken unawares by just how pleased he is to be surrounded by his old friends.

'This is very decent of you all, I must say,' he says.

'Coming all this way.'

Nell comes over, bringing Julius Weingard. Larry makes introductions all round.

'Julius thinks he may have a buyer for you,' says Nell to Larry.

'No promises,' says Weingard. 'But this is a collector who likes to encourage new talent.'

'New talent is so much cheaper, isn't it?' says Louisa.

'That is so,' says Weingard with a smile.

'Lawrence darling,' says Nell, 'did you know you've sold one already?'

'That would be my husband,' says Louisa. 'He likes to encourage new talent too.'

Weingard at once produces his card.

'Send your husband to me,' he says. 'This is a circus.' He glances round in contempt. 'In Cork Street we are more civilised.'

He gives an old-fashioned bow and leaves the group of friends.

'What a repellent little man,' says Louisa.

'Louisa!' says Kitty, with a glance at Nell. 'Behave yourself.'

'He is a bit creepy,' says Nell, 'but he's terrifically good at what he does, and he knows everybody.'

Ed is looking at Nell with interest.

'So you're a friend of Larry's,' he says.

'A sort of a friend,' says Nell, glancing at Larry.

At once they all realise that she sleeps with Larry.

'Why don't you join us?' says Kitty. 'We're taking Larry

out to dinner to celebrate. We've booked a table at Wilton's.'

George has a car outside, but they can't all fit in. Larry says he'd rather walk anyway, and Kitty says she would too, so in the end they all walk.

Larry walks with Ed. They fall at once into the real conversation that's only possible between old friends.

'She's interesting,' Ed says. 'Is she a serious proposition?'

'Maybe,' says Larry. Then realising Nell is not far behind, walking with Kitty, he says, 'How's the wine trade coming along?'

'Slow,' says Ed. 'The English seem to think drinking wine is like committing adultery, something you do rarely and abroad. What I really like is all the driving down empty roads in France.'

'Haven't you had enough of being away from home?'

'I've had enough of just about everything, if you really want to know. Do you ever get that feeling that nothing tastes of anything any more? Nothing excites you. Nothing hurts you.'

'Not good, Ed.'

'Sometimes I think what I need is another war.'

Outside the restaurant Nell says she won't come in with them after all. She has made other arrangements. She gives Larry a quick almost shy kiss as she goes, saying, 'Nice friends.'

'Why wouldn't she join us?' says Ed.

'Nell's like that,' says Larry. 'She likes to go her own way.'

Dinner turns out to be rather grand.

'Have whatever you want,' Louisa says. 'George is paying.'

Kitty is intrigued by this notion that Nell goes her own way.

'But what does she do?' she keeps saying.

Larry does his best to explain, but in the telling even he has to admit that Nell's life sounds as if it's going nowhere in particular.

'I don't see why she has to go anywhere in particular,' says Ed.

'Because otherwise what's the point?' says Kitty. 'We all want to feel our life has some sort of point.'

'I don't understand this,' says Ed. 'A point for who? A point when? Right now we're celebrating Larry and his paintings. We're eating good food, surrounded by good friends. Doesn't that give our lives a point?'

'You're deliberately misunderstanding me,' says Kitty.

Larry, watching and listening, sees that Kitty is unhappy. He wonders a little at the edge in Ed's voice.

'Well, I think Larry's friend is rather wonderful,' says Louisa. 'And she is very young. I'm sure she'll find her way soon enough.'

'And I say Larry's a great artist,' says Ed. 'I say he's had the guts to stick to doing what he loves, and now it's paying off. Here's to you, Larry. You're a great man. I salute you.'

'Thank you, Ed,' says Larry. 'All I have to do now is sell more than one painting.'

19

'Look what I found,' Nell says to Larry.

Her bicycle basket holds six small empty clear-glass bottles, of the kind used for medicines.

'You know what you do with bottles?' she says. 'You put messages in them.'

'Of course you do,' says Larry.

'Come along, then,' she says.

Larry heaves his own bike out onto the street, and together they cycle up the Walworth Road, round the Elephant and Castle, past Waterloo station, to the wide expanse of the new Waterloo Bridge. Here Nell comes to a stop, more or less in the middle of the bridge, and leans her bike against the parapet. Larry does the same. It's a fine sunny day, and for a few moments he stands admiring the view. To the east, the dome of St Paul's stands clear of the bomb-damaged buildings of the City; to the south, round the bend in the river, the Houses of Parliament.

Nell has one of the bottles out, together with a pad of paper and a pencil.

'So what's our first message to be?' she says.

'We really are sending messages in bottles?'

'Of course. I'll do the first one.'

She writes on the pad, tears off the sheet of paper, shows it to Larry. She has written: *If you find this message you will have good luck for the rest of your life.*

'You don't think that's going to end in disappointment?' he says.

'Not at all. If you believe in your luck, it comes.'

She screws the cap on the little bottle and drops it from the parapet of the bridge into the river below. They see it hit the water and sink and then come bobbing up again, to swirl away downstream.

They cycle across to the north bank of the river, and along the Victoria Embankment to Westminster Bridge. Once again, Nell parks her bike in the middle of the bridge.

'We're on a bridge crawl,' says Larry.

'I want this to be a day you'll never forget,' says Nell.

She takes out the pad and pencil.

'Earth has not anything to show more fair,' says Larry.

'What?'

'Wordsworth's poem. "On Westminster Bridge".'

'Next message. Here. It's your turn.'

She hands him the pad. Larry is remembering the poem.

'The beauty of the morning, silent, bare,
Ships, towers, something something lie
Open unto the fields and to the sky,
All bright and glittering in the smokeless air.'

'No fields now,' says Nell.

'No smokeless air, either.' He looks at the Houses of Parliament on the riverbank. 'You think all this has been here for ever, but Wordsworth never saw this. This isn't even a hundred years old. There were other buildings here, that have just vanished.'

'Send the next message.'

Larry thinks for a moment and then writes: *If you find this message, look around you and enjoy what you see, because one day it will all be gone.*

'That's a bit glum, isn't it?' says Nell.

'It'll make them appreciate what they've got.'

He rolls up the paper and pushes it into the bottle. He gives the bottle to Nell but she says, 'Your message, your throw.' So he drops it from the bridge into the river below, and watches it bob away out of sight.

They mount their bikes once more and ride round Big Ben and down Millbank to Lambeth Bridge. The obelisks on either side have pineapples on top, according to Nell. Larry claims they're pinecones.

'Why would anyone carve a giant stone pinecone?' says Nell.

'Why pineapples?'

'Pineapples are thrilling. All hard and scratchy on the outside, and sweet and juicy on the inside.'

She's pushing her bike up onto the pavement, sunlight gleaming on her hair. Larry gazes at her in admiration.

'How did you ever get to be you, Nell?' he says.

'What do you mean?'

'You're so open, so uncorrupted, so . . . I don't know. You just go on surprising me.'

'Is that good?'

'It's very good.'

She writes her message and shows him.

If you find this message, go out and do the one thing you've been wanting to do all your life, but have been afraid to do.

'What if he wants to rob a bank?'

'Who says it'll be a he? It might be a girl. She might want to kiss the boy she's secretly in love with.'

She kisses Larry, there on Lambeth Bridge.

'Now it's not a secret any more,' says Larry.

He feels light-hearted, happy in a way he's not been happy for a long time. Nell's game makes everything good seem possible, and everything bad seem far away.

She drops her bottle into the water.

They ride on past the Tate, past Vauxhall Bridge – 'Too ugly' – along the embankment to Chelsea Bridge. Here on the guardian lamp-posts in place of pineapples or pinecones there are golden galleons. Across the river looms the immense block of Battersea Power Station. Two of its four chimneys are streaming black smoke into the summer sky.

Nell gives Larry the pad.

'Your turn.'

If you find this message, writes Larry, *believe that happiness exists, because I am happy now.*

'That's beautiful, Larry,' says Nell. 'I want you so much to be happy.'

He drops the bottle into the river on the downstream side and watches it swirl away under the railway bridge.

Nell has taken the pad back and is writing on it.

'Where next?' says Larry. 'Albert Bridge?'

'No more bridges.'

She puts her message into its bottle without showing it to Larry, pushing it deep inside.

'I have to go now, darling,' she says.

'Go? Where?'

'Just go.'

She gives him the little bottle.

'The last one's for you.'

She gives him a kiss, climbs onto her bike, and pedals away up Chelsea Bridge Road.

Larry unscrews the bottle cap and tries to get the roll of paper out, but the neck is too narrow. Baffled, mildly irritated, he gazes at the bottle, wondering what to do. The paper inside has partially unrolled itself, so even if he were able to grip it through the neck it would tear as he pulled it out. The only solution is to break the bottle.

He holds it by its neck and taps it against the kerb. Then he taps it more briskly. Finally he hits it a sharp blow, and it shatters. He picks the paper out from among the glittering fragments of glass, and unrolls it, and reads.

If you find this message please believe that I expect nothing from you and only want you to go on being happy. I am going to have a baby. I love you.

Larry stands up, blood draining from his face. His first instinct is to ride after Nell at once. But he realises he has

271

no idea where she's gone, and will never find her. So instead he wheels his bike slowly off the bridge, fighting a confusion of emotions.

Most of all, he feels frightened. It's not a specific fear, it's a kind of panic. Events are exploding beyond his control, unknown forces are bearing down upon him. Then through the panic, like a mist burned off by the sun, he feels a hot shining pride.

I'm going to be a father.

The thought is so immense it overwhelms him. It exhilarates him and fills him with dread at the same time. The responsibility is too great. It changes everything.

I'm to have a wife and child.

A wife! It's almost impossible to see Nell in this role. And yet of course they must marry.

So is this it? Is this my life already laid out before me?

He knows even as he forms the thought that this is not the life he meant to lead. But if not this, then what? What is this dream of a future that even now he sees being lost to him for ever?

Dazed, he mounts his bike and sets off pedalling up Chelsea Bridge Road, in the direction Nell took. He realises then that she must have planned it all to happen this way. She must have dreamed up her game with the messages in bottles as a way to give him time alone to form his response. He feels a sudden flood of love. What an extraordinary girl she is! Old beyond her years, she understands all he is now going through. She knows he'll have doubts about committing himself to a future with her. So she bicycles away. This touches him deeply. Adrift in the great world, she cares enough for him not to lay on him a greater burden than he can carry.

In this moment, pedalling behind a bus as it lumbers up Sloane Street, he feels only love for her, and gratitude. But as he swings left onto Knightsbridge and rides along the south side of the park, other concerns begin to present themselves. How is he to support a wife and child? Where are they to live? What will happen to his painting?

At this point he realises where he's going. This is the way home. Guided by instincts deeper than conscious thought, in this time of crisis he is returning to the house where he grew up. There's no purpose to this, he can't expect his father to resolve his dilemma for him. He is going home as to a refuge.

So he turns into Kensington Church Street and climbs the rise to Campden Grove. His father will be in his office now, of course, on the other side of town; but Larry has a key. He lets himself in, heaving the old bike after him, and stands it in the front hall. Miss Cookham, the house-keeper, comes up from the basement to see who it can be.

'Hello, Cookie,' says Larry. 'I thought I'd look in.'

'Mr Lawrence!' She actually goes pink with delight. 'There's a sight for sore eyes! Look at you! I hear you're a famous artist now.'

'Not so famous,' says Larry.

He's shocked at how much it pleases him to be welcomed in this way; and at how comforted he is by the gloomy house.

'Shall I get you a pot of tea, and maybe a slice of cake?'

'That would be wonderful. How are you, Cookie?'

'Quiet, as you might say. Your father won't be long now.'

Larry settles himself down in the third-floor back room that was once the nursery, and then became his study room. Here, home from school in the holidays, he would retreat to read or sketch or just gaze into the fire. Here he hid himself on the day his father told him his mother had gone to heaven. He was five years old.

Cookie knocks on the door, and comes in with a tray.

'It's only seed cake,' she says, 'and plainer than I'd like it, but you know how it is. You'd never guess we won the war.'

'Thank you, Cookie. You're an angel.'

She stands there, looking at him in his old armchair by the bookcase.

'It's a pleasure to have you home again, Mr Lawrence.'

Left alone, Larry drinks his tea and eats his cake and finds he can't persuade himself to address his situation. Each time he sets out to discover what he should do, his thoughts veer away to one side, and he finds himself remembering his schooldays. Ed Avenell, whose family lived in the north, would always stay with him here at the beginning and end of the holidays, as he travelled back and forth to school. He can see him now, hunched up on the floor in front of the fire, poking things into the coals, watching them burn. Ed was a great one for burning things, pencils, toy soldiers, matchboxes. He burned himself too, in an experimental sort of way, passing his hand through the flames until it was coated with soot.

He hears the shudder of the front door closing, and hears his father's voice in the hall. He hears Cookie's excited twitter. His father will be tired. He'll want to wash and change after his day in the office; and then to enjoy a whisky in the library while he glances over the evening paper.

Larry comes downstairs to greet him. He hasn't seen his father since his return from Jamaica.

'Larry! This is a happy surprise!'

His eyes show his real pleasure. As always on coming home, Larry is struck by how much he's still part of this world, which in his own mind he has left behind.

'Will you stay and eat with me?'

'I'd like a drink,' says Larry. 'And a chat. But then I'd better be back on my bike.'

'Ah, the artist's life!' says his father, smiling. 'Give me ten minutes.'

Larry goes into the library and picks up the evening paper his father has brought in. He reads a little about the Paris peace conference, then puts the paper down. This room is so filled with his father's presence that he feels like a child again. Here, every evening in the long school holidays, he sat in what was always his special chair, a low tub chair upholstered in deep red velvet, and his father read to him. They read *King Solomon's Mines*, and *The Lost World*, and *Treasure Island*, which his father was fond of saying was the best tale ever spun.

And am I to be a father too?

William Cornford joins him and pours them both a shot of Scotch. They talk for a little about Jamaica, and the

275

difficulties caused by the requisition of the fleet during the war.

'We've got the *Ariguani* and the *Bayano* back, but for now only the *Ariguani* is operating a regular schedule. We're badly short of capacity. I'm in negotiations to buy four ships from the Ministry. This government is doing all it can to increase non-dollar food imports. It's just going to take time. The great thing is we've managed to hold onto almost all our staff.'

'As far as I can see,' says Larry, 'no one ever leaves.'

'Not if I can help it,' says his father. 'People grow into jobs. They start off as little slips and they turn into oak trees.'

Larry knows he too should have been a little slip, should now be an oak tree in the family firm. His father, realising his words may be construed as a criticism, turns the conversation.

'So tell me,' he says, 'how is your art exhibition going?'

'Only two more days to go,' says Larry. 'Then I can have the dubious pleasure of reclaiming my works.'

'And what then?'

'That's something of a question.'

'Oh?' The single syllable spoken quietly, neutrally.

'There's been a new development. I'm not quite sure what to do.'

Until this moment Larry hasn't realised he wants his father's advice. He believes he knows what his father will say: his strong religious convictions give him very little choice. So why raise the matter?

Because whatever I do, Dad must approve.

This too is a surprise. Apparently, in order to feel that he has done the right thing he must obtain his father's blessing. This weary man sitting drinking Scotch, with his lined tanned face gazing so thoughtfully back at him, represents all that is just and right and good. This is what it is to be a father.

How can I ever live up to that?

'I've had a girlfriend for quite some time now,' he says. 'Her name's Nell. She works for an art dealer. She's a very unconventional sort of girl, very free-thinking, very independent.'

He pauses, and wonders whether his father can tell where this is going. As he speaks, he loses confidence. It seems to him that what he is about to say shows him to have been ridiculously irresponsible.

Why did I take no precautions to prevent this happening? Because Nell told me she had dealt with it. But I never asked more. I have no idea what method she used. I was too embarrassed, and too selfish, to pursue the question. Look at it rationally, as my father must look at it: my behaviour has been a kind of insanity.

'Anyway,' he says, 'I've run into a spot of difficulty with her. I expect you can guess.'

He finds he can't speak the actual words. He's too ashamed. And yet here he is, by his own choice, telling his father enough for him to draw his own conclusions.

'I see,' says his father.

'I know what I've done is wrong,' Larry says. 'I mean,

I know you'll tell me the Church will say I've sinned. And I have.'

'Do you love her?' his father says.

This is not what Larry has been braced for. He takes a moment before he answers.

'Yes,' he says.

'Do you want to marry her?'

'I think so,' says Larry. 'It's all so new. I'm confused about it all.'

'How old is she?'

'Twenty. Nearly twenty-one.'

'What have you told her?'

'Nothing. She gave me the news and then ran off. I think she wants me to have time to think about it before I make any decision. She's not the kind of girl who'd want me to marry her just for the sake of appearances.'

'She'd want to know you loved her?'

'Yes.'

'And you're not sure.'

He throws his father a quick glance. Is it so obvious?

'I don't know. I might be. I'm not sure I'm not sure, if you see what I mean.'

William Cornford nods. Yes, he sees what Larry means. He's watching his son closely.

'You're right about the Church,' he says. 'The Church's position is perfectly clear. What you've done is wrong. But it's done. And your duty now, as far as the Church is concerned, is also perfectly clear.'

'Yes,' says Larry. 'I realise that.'

'But marriage is for ever. It's till death.'

'Yes,' says Larry.

His father was married till death. Nine years, and then death. Those nine years have crystallised into a sacred monument. The perfect marriage.

'Can you do that, Larry?'

'I don't know,' says Larry. 'How do you know? Did you know?'

His father gives a slow emphatic nod. No words. He has never spoken about his dead wife. Never mentioned her name since her death, except in their prayers. *God bless Mummy and watch over us from heaven and keep us safe till we meet again.*

Watch over me now, Larry thinks, wanting to cry.

'I'm not your priest,' says his father. 'I'm your father. I want to say something the Church can't say to you. If you don't really love this girl, you would be doing a wicked thing if you married her. You would be condemning both of you, and your children, to a life of unhappiness. From what you tell me, she understands this very well. She doesn't want a husband who is merely doing his duty. Of course, whatever happens, you must support her. But if you marry, marry of your own free will. Marry for love.'

Larry is unable to speak. In every word his father utters, he feels the powerful force of his love for him. He may use the language of moral imperatives, but his underlying concern is for his son's happiness. This is what it is to be a father. He's willing to set aside even his most deeply cherished beliefs for the sake of his child.

'Don't ruin your life, Larry.'

'No,' says Larry. 'That is, if I haven't already.'

'But if you think you really can love her – well then.'

Larry meets his father's eyes. He wants so much to hug him, and feel his father's arms holding tight. But it's years since they hugged.

'There's the practical side of things,' he says. 'You say I must support her, and of course I must. But it's not so simple.'

'I take it,' says his father, 'that art has not proved to be remunerative so far.'

'Not so far.'

Now his father will tell him that this is just as he predicted in their one great row before the war. That he's wasted his youth on a foolish dream. That now he must face up to his responsibilities.

'But you love it?'

'I'm sorry?'

'Your painting. Your art. You love it.'

'Oh, yes.'

'You sound very certain about that.'

'You're asking me if I love to paint, Dad. I am certain of that. It's all I want to do. But I'm not certain about anything else. I'm not certain that I'm good enough. I'm not certain I'll ever be able to make my living at it.'

'But you love it.'

'Yes.'

'That's a rare thing, Larry. That's a gift from God.'

Abruptly he gets up from his chair and goes to the desk

where he keeps his private papers. For a few moments he fiddles about, consulting the pages of his ledgers.

'Here is what I propose,' he says. 'I will increase your allowance by an additional £100 a year. I will pay for the rental of an appropriate flat for this young lady. Whether you live there with her, and upon what terms, is entirely your own business. How will that do?'

'Oh, Dad!'

'I'm trying to be practical about this, Larry. It's not for me to judge you.'

'I thought you'd tell me to take a job in the company.'

'What, as a punishment? The company isn't a penal colony. If you ever join the company, it must be of your own free will.'

'Like marriage.'

'Yes. Very like.'

He holds out his hand. Larry takes it and grasps it.

'Let me know what you decide.'

Bicycling back across London, Larry finds himself once more tossed this way and that by conflicting emotions. His father's generosity awes him and leaves him floundering. Without realising it, he now knows he had gone home to receive instruction in his duty. Unable to take the decision himself, he looks to the institutions that frame his life, family, school, church, to force his hand. Instead he leaves his father's house freer and more empowered than when he arrived; and therefore more solitary and more burdened.

How is it that others make this decision so easily? Do

they feel absolute certainty? He thinks then of Ed and Kitty. They met twice – twice! – before deciding to marry. At the time he felt no surprise: why should love require more than an instant? And in wartime there was always too little time, and only a very uncertain future. But let peace break out, let the future stretch before you for its full span of years, and who can know for certain what they want?

So maybe, he thinks, it's this very demand for certainty that's the stumbling block. If certainty is impossible, then why expect it? Perhaps the decision to marry is a provisional one, made on best information at the time, and it takes years to grow into certainty. If this is the case, all that's needed to kick-start the process is some outside pressure. And what could be a more traditional outside pressure than a baby on the way? In some countries it's understood that no engagement takes place until the girl is pregnant; that, and not sex, being the purpose of marriage.

But what about love?

Still debating within himself, he turns into the road where he lives, and there's Nell, sitting on the steps, looking out for him. She jumps up, her face grinning from side to side.

'Guess what?' she says. 'I've been at Julius's. He says your pictures are all sold!'

'Sold! Who to?'

'Some anonymous buyer. Isn't that wonderful? You're being collected! Like a real artist!'

'I'm amazed.'

'It's good, isn't it?'

He feels a sudden exultation as the news sinks in. His

paintings are wanted. Money has been paid for them. There's no endorsement quite as gratifying as this. Words cost the speaker nothing. But no one pays out real money unless they mean it.

He props his bike against the wall and takes Nell in his arms. Her excitement is all for him. In this time of crisis for herself, she thinks only of him.

'I couldn't wait to tell you. I've been sitting on the steps hugging myself.'

'It's brilliant,' he says. 'I can't believe it.'

He kisses her, there on the steps.

'We have to celebrate,' she says.

'Yes, but what about your message?'

'Oh, that,' she says. 'Did you manage to get it out of the bottle without breaking it?'

'No. I had to smash it.'

'I thought you might.'

'You shouldn't have run away.'

'Shouldn't I?'

She's in his arms, and she's smiling up at him, and she's so funny and beautiful, and his paintings have sold and the sun is shining, and suddenly it seems easy.

'Marry me, Nell.'

She goes on smiling at him, but says nothing at all. This isn't how it's supposed to be.

'Nell? I asked you a question.'

'Oh, it was a question, was it?'

'I want you to marry me.'

'Maybe,' she says. 'I'll think about it.'

'Don't you want to?'

'Maybe,' she says. 'I'm not sure.'

'You're not sure!'

'Well, I am only twenty.'

'Almost twenty-one.'

'But I do love you, Lawrence.'

'There you are, then,' he says.

'I just don't know that I'd be good for you.'

'Of course you would!' Hearing her express her doubts frees him of his own. 'You're perfect for me. You're good to me, and you never stop surprising me, and you make me happy. How am I to live without you?'

She gives him such an odd look then, as if that secret part of herself is revealing itself to him for the first time, the fearful, vulnerable part of herself. Her look says to him: promise me you won't hurt me.

'You see,' she says, 'it's different for girls.'

'What do you mean?'

'You've got your painting, and being important in the world, and doing the things men do. But for us it's just the husband and the children. There isn't anything else. So we have to get it right.'

She sits back down on the step, and he sits down beside her and takes her hand in his.

'So let's get it right together,' he says.

'We don't have to decide anything today, do we?'

'Not if you don't want to,' he says.

'I don't really know what I want,' she says.

Larry is nonplussed.

'But I thought . . .'

He doesn't complete the thought. Suddenly it seems foolish.

'You thought all girls want to be married, and it's the men who have to be pushed.'

'You said you want to be married.'

'I do,' says Nell. 'But only in the right way.'

'What's the right way?'

'My parents are married,' she says. 'But they're not happy. Sometimes I think they hate each other. I don't want to end up like that.'

'But if two people love each other,' Larry says.

'I suppose they thought they loved each other. In the beginning. You never really know, it seems to me. Not for absolute sure.'

She's looking at him earnestly now, stroking his hand as she speaks. He feels as if the world is spinning round him. Her words and her touch contradict each other. Does she love him or not?

'But Nell,' he says helplessly. 'What about the baby?'

'You mean we should get married because of the baby?'

'Well, it's part of it, isn't it?'

'And if there hadn't been a baby, you wouldn't have wanted to?'

Larry is caught. He wants to answer her, 'I might not have asked you so soon, but I would have proposed later.' Is that true? He feels the blazing force of her honesty, and is ashamed.

'Darling Lawrence,' she says, squeezing his hand. 'I love

you so much. Let's not build ourselves any cages. I couldn't bear it if I thought you were trapped where you didn't want to be. Let's just love each other the way we do now, and let the days go by, and not ever have to lie to each other.'

In that moment he loves her more than he's ever done. This sweet child of truth, he thinks. Where does she come by such instinctive purity? An odd word to apply to a girl who gives her body freely to him, but he feels it deep in her, an innocence that is not a lack of experience, nor a childlikeness. Sometimes when she's looking at him with her solemn eyes he feels she's far older, certainly more mature, than he can ever be, for all his eight years longer in the world. Somehow Nell has been born true.

'If that's what you want,' he says.

'And if it's what you want,' she says softly.

20

Pamela makes her way slowly, deliberately, from rock pool to rock pool, in her ruched bathing costume and little wellington boots, carrying a plastic cup from a thermos flask. Her chubby three-year-old body moves gracefully. Reaching a miniature chasm between the rocks, she crouches and springs across to the other side, and in the same movement bends down to peer into the new pool. The tide is out, and the great expanse of shining rock and seaweed reaches almost to the horizon. She's exploring, seeking tiny crabs and transparent fishes, moving ever further from the narrow pebble beach beneath the cliffs. What if she were to fall?

'Don't go too far, darling,' Kitty calls, sitting at the bottom of the concrete steps.

Pamela pays her no attention as always. Silly to call out, really. This is a child who asserts her independent will so fiercely that she'll do the opposite of what she's told to do, just to make a point.

Hugo, who has gone hunting along the beach for treasure,

now returns to the steps. He's a sweet-faced youth, a boy really, though as he likes to tell her, there's only five years between them. He was called up, but it was near the end of the war, and he never saw active service.

'No chance of a VC for me,' he says.

He's pink-faced, bright-eyed, eager to learn. He admires Ed above all men, and without realising it, has picked up many of Ed's ways of thinking and talking.

'Look what I found,' he says. 'Jewels.'

He shows Kitty a handful of shiny translucent pebbles, dark green, milky white, amber, ruby red. Fragments of glass that were once bottles or jars, ground smooth by the action of the waves.

'Pammy'll love those,' says Kitty. And looking out at the distant figure of her daughter, 'Do you think she's gone too far?'

'She is quite a long way out.'

'She takes no notice of me when I call.'

'I'll go and get her, shall I?'

He lopes off over the rocks, eager to be of service. Kitty is well aware that Hugo likes her company more than he should, but she sees no harm in it. Somehow the division of labour in his partnership with Ed calls for Ed to be away, touring the humbler vineyards of France, while Hugo stays home and manages the delivery of the orders as they come in. The business is not yet established enough to have its own premises, so the barn beside their farmhouse is used for storage, stacked high with cases of wine. Hugo is forever building up or depleting the stacks as the shipments come and go. His Bedford van has become a familiar sight in the yard, and he himself almost another member of the family.

She watches him now, silhouetted against the bright horizon, as he reaches Pamela. He stands between the rock pools reasoning with her. Kitty sees how the little girl turns her back on him and hops further away from the shore; and how he circles round to block her venturing any further. Then come sharp cries of frustration, and she's hitting his legs. Finally he's bent down and picked her up by the waist, and he's carrying her back.

She kicks her feet and beats with her fists and screams at him, but he holds on tight. By the time he deposits her before Kitty, the little girl is scarlet in the face and seriously insulted.

'I hate you!' she says. 'I hate you!'

'You went too far,' says Kitty. 'What if you'd hurt yourself?'

Pamela kicks Hugo's shin hard with her little boots. He lets out an exclamation of pain.

'Pammy!' says Kitty. 'Stop that!'

'I hate you!' says the child.

With a mother's instinct, Kitty understands the source of her daughter's rage. It's the being picked up, the being rendered powerless. Nevertheless she can't be allowed to kick people.

'Pammy,' she says. 'You hurt Hugo. Look, he's crying.'

Hugo takes the hint, and starts to whimper.

'Poor Hugo,' says Kitty.

Pamela looks at Hugo suspiciously. Hugo is kneeling on the pebbles, rubbing his shin, crying.

'Kiss it better for him,' says Kitty.

Pamela crouches down and gives Hugo's knee a quick rough kiss.

'Thank you,' says Hugo in a small voice.

'There,' says Kitty, trusting the balance of power has been restored. 'Now say sorry.'

'Sorry,' says Pamela, scowling at the cliffs.

Kitty then shows her the jewels Hugo has found for her, and she becomes silent, absorbed in wonder. Kitty looks up to find Hugo gazing at her.

'You're amazing,' he says.

Kitty pretends she hasn't heard him. He's becoming more and more open in his manner with her, no longer even pretending to hide his admiration. Kitty treats it as a game, which allows him, in playing along, to say more than he should. One day soon, she thinks, she must have a quiet but firm word with him, before he does something he regrets. But in the meantime, with Ed away so much, she sees no harm in letting herself enjoy his company.

There was a time when Kitty found the attentions of men oppressive, with their furtive looks, their veiled suggestions, their endless importunities. But since marriage and motherhood it has all ceased, and she finds to her surprise that she sometimes misses it. So Hugo and his absurd puppy-love is not as unwelcome as she pretends.

The three of them climb the steep flight of concrete steps up the cliff. She holds Pamela's hand tight all the way, even though Pamela pulls crossly to be released. At the top of the steps a wide grass avenue, grazed close by rabbits, runs between banks of gorse over the brow of the hill. This is Hope Gap, a notch in the great chalk cliffs that lies between Seaford Head and the Cuckmere valley.

Pamela, let go at last, runs on ahead. Hugo carries the basket that contains the thermos flask and what's left of their cheese and apple sandwiches.

'She's going to be a heartbreaker, that one,' he says. 'Like her mother.'

'What does that mean, heartbreak?' says Kitty. 'I've never understood that. I don't see how anyone can be properly in love with someone unless they know they're loved back. And if they're loved back, nothing's broken.'

'You don't think it's possible to love all on your own?'

'I suppose in the very beginning. You can get excited, and build up your hopes, and so on. But if it all goes nowhere, then what's the point? You're just wasting your time.'

'You may not be able to help it,' says Hugo.

'Rubbish,' says Kitty firmly. Then seeing Pamela disappear out of sight, 'Don't go too far, Pammy!'

They reach the brow of the hill. From here they can see the coastline curving away for miles. Kitty looks as she always does for the long pier reaching out from Newhaven harbour. She remembers how she waited on the quayside for Ed to return, and how the first time he came back, and the second time he didn't.

When they reach the sheep barn by the road, Pamela has already climbed into the back of Kitty's ten-year-old Austin. She has the shiny pebbles in her open hands and is studying them intently.

'Put on a jersey, darling,' says Kitty. 'It'll be blowy driving home.'

Pamela shakes her head. Kitty gets into the driver's seat, with Hugo beside her.

'Feels strange being driven by a girl,' he says.

'I'm a trained driver,' says Kitty. 'And I'm not a girl any more.'

The shiny black open-topped Bantam is her car, and she maintains it in perfect condition. Now that Pamela is getting bigger Kitty is rediscovering the self that existed before motherhood. She recalls her days as an army driver wistfully, almost envying her past. Of course she's a wife as well as a mother, but Ed is away so much. The business is proving very slow to get up on its feet. The top end of the market is dominated by the old-established firms, and the bottom end, where Caulder & Avenell aim to carve their niche, is virtually non-existent. They are having to create the demand that they hope to serve.

So Ed works hard, seeking out bargain wines from remote vineyards, building up a stock of such value for money that even the wine-averse English might be tempted to try a bottle.

'Reliable quality plus a visible name,' Larry tells him, offering his knowledge of the banana business. 'What you need is little blue labels.'

'I'm not sticking little blue labels on our bottles,' says Ed. 'You don't stick little blue labels on your pictures.'

'I expect I should,' says Larry. 'Then maybe I'd sell more.'

Kitty finds Ed's trips abroad hard. When he's home, when

he's in her bed, in her arms, her life makes sense to her. But then he goes away again, and the bed is empty once more.

'You don't have to go so soon, do you, darling?'

'It'll only be like this for a year or so,' he says. 'Once we're properly up and running, I'll be able to be a gentleman of leisure.'

'I just miss you so,' she says.

'And I miss you, darling. But I'm doing it for you. And for Pammy. You know that.'

Pamela doesn't know it.

'Don't go, Daddy,' she says, clinging to him.

But he goes.

At the end of August Larry Cornford takes a train to Lewes and from there walks down the long and winding road to Edenfield. He carries a change of clothes and his paints and brushes in an old army kitbag. He keeps to the high grass verge, clear of the lorries rumbling to Newhaven. Once round the flank of the Downs he can see the village in the river valley below, and the church with its square tower, and the red roofs of the farmhouse behind it. He has not announced his coming and is not expected, but he has the sensation that the valley welcomes him back.

The farmyard looks much the same as when he was billeted here, except that the barn doors are open, and within he can make out stacks of wooden crates. A young man appears, carrying a crate out to the open back of a big van. Seeing Larry he gives a friendly nod and loads the crate into the van.

'Hello,' he says. 'Can I help?'

'I'm a friend of Ed's,' says Larry.

'Ed's away,' says the young man. 'Kitty's here.'

Larry turns to the house, and there in the doorway stands Kitty, looking towards him. For a moment as their eyes meet neither speaks. Then Pamela appears, pushing past her mother, and stares at Larry.

'Who's that?' she says.

'That's Larry,' says Kitty. 'He's Daddy's best friend. He came to see us when we lived in the big house. You said he was nice.'

'I don't remember,' says the little girl.

'He is nice,' says Kitty.

All this time her eyes hold Larry's, telling him how deeply quietly pleased she is to see him.

'Hello, Pamela,' says Larry.

'Hello,' says the little girl, looking from him to her mother and back.

'Did you walk from Lewes?' says Kitty.

'Yes,' says Larry. 'It's only an hour or so.'

'Come on in.'

She looks the same and different. A little older, a little wearier. She's wearing a cotton summer frock that makes her slight figure seem vulnerable. Her wide mouth unsmiling, her deep brown eyes steady beneath those strongly-defined eyebrows. A pale face framed in dark waves of hair. What is it that makes one face so much more beautiful than all others? Seeing her standing there in the farmhouse kitchen doorway, her little girl tugging at her skirt, Larry abandons what remains of his defences. He knows he will never love anyone as he loves her.

Hugo Caulder joins them over a pot of tea in the kitchen. He talks about the wine trade, and remote French vineyards still recovering from the war years where extraordinary deals are to be done, and his dream of having his own premises in London.

'In Bury Street, or maybe even in St James's Street. Then we'd start selling the fine wines as well.'

'When does Ed get back?' Larry asks.

'He'll be away at least another two weeks,' Kitty says.

Hugo returns to loading his van.

'So will you stay?' says Kitty.

'If I may,' says Larry. 'This is no weather for stewing in town.'

Hugo drives away in his loaded van. Kitty makes a potato omelette for their supper, and gives Larry a bottle of Vin de Pays d'Oc to open.

'Ed's best,' she says. 'To celebrate your visit.'

She waits until Pamela is asleep to ask the waiting questions.

'So how's Nell?'

'Nell's thriving. She's away right now. A buying trip, with her boss.'

'You can bring her down here any time, you know. She'd be very welcome.'

'Yes, of course. Thank you.'

He lets a silence fall between them. As always, these silences act as gear changes, moments in neutral before the shift to a slower speed.

'She's an unusual girl, Nell.' He wants very much to tell

Kitty about the baby, but something holds him back. 'She always had a thing about being independent. She has her job at the gallery, she earns far more money than I do. She knows I like to spend a lot of my time alone. So it works out quite well, really.'

'It sounds like you're leading separate lives.'

'No, not separate. We're very close.' He realises he sounds as if he's making excuses for her. 'It's hard to explain. She hates to make demands on me.'

He can see Kitty's lovely face puzzling over what he tells her, unable to make sense of it. He wants so much to touch her. But things are as they are, and he must make the best of it.

'She sounds a bit like Ed,' she says.

'You mustn't think I'm complaining,' he says. 'She's warm, and loving.'

'Maybe she's waiting for you to propose.'

'I've done that.'

'You've proposed!'

'She says she's thinking about it.'

'Well!' Now Kitty is awestruck. 'She must be a fool.'

But her tone of voice says otherwise. Her tone of voice shows Nell has risen sharply in her estimation.

'She's not a fool,' says Larry. 'She just doesn't want to compromise. Her parents have a bad marriage. She wants to be sure.'

'And she's not sure about you.'

'Apparently not.'

'How do you feel about that?'

'A bit odd, to be honest.'

'You're a good man, Larry. A rare man. What more does she want?'

'Who knows? It's not as if I'm such a terrific catch.'

'You know that's not true. But who am I to talk? We all play that game.'

'What game?' says Larry.

She gets up and starts clearing the table, speaking lightly as she works, to make out it's no more than idle chatter.

'Doing yourself down. Feeling you're not really worth very much at all. Thinking you haven't much to offer anybody. And there's the one person you're supposed to make happy, and you can't even do that.'

Larry understands then that she's telling him about herself.

'So what are we supposed to do about it?' he says.

'Try harder. Be more loving.' Stacking plates in the sink. 'Stop minding about our own happiness.'

So she's unhappy. He feels a sharp pang, both painful and sweet.

'He's away too much, isn't he?' he says.

'He works so hard.' Now she's standing still, her hands on the draining board, her head bent. 'He's doing it for us, so we don't have to live on George and Louisa's charity. So we can have a house of our own. He's thinking of Pammy and schools and all the things that need money. But I'd rather have him than the money.'

'Of course you would,' says Larry.

She looks up then, searching his face for clues.

'Why doesn't he know that?'

'That's how Ed is,' says Larry. 'He never does anything halfway. He's decided this is what he has to do, and he's doing it as well as he can.'

'What if it's because he doesn't love me any more?'

'No!' Larry's denial is immediate, urgent. Too urgent. 'Ed adores you. You know that.'

'Do I? I don't see why he should.'

'Kitty! What nonsense is this? Everyone adores you. You'd have to be blind not to see it.'

'Oh, that.' She passes one hand across her face, as if waving away a buzzing fly. 'That's just how you look. That's nothing.'

'But that's only the start of it! You're so much more than just a pretty girl.'

'I don't see how.'

She seems to mean it. There's a sadness in her voice that shocks him. How can she not know her own value?

'Ed loves you because you're beautiful and loyal and kind-hearted. He loves you because you're strong and don't weigh him down. He loves you because you understand things without having to be told them. He loves you because you don't ask him to be someone he isn't. Most of all, he loves you because you love him.'

He's looking at her as he speaks, and he can't help it, his eyes are giving him away. But what is there to give away? Kitty has known his feelings for her for a long time.

'Does he talk to you about me?' she says.

'Sometimes.'

'Does he say he loves me?'

'Many times.'

'All he says to me is that he doesn't deserve me.'

'Yes,' says Larry. 'He says that too.'

'You know what?' she says. 'I think it's because of that damned beach at Dieppe. That's where it all started.'

'Why do you say that?'

'I think that day did something to Ed. I don't know what. He won't talk about it. He hates it when anyone asks him about his VC. Why's he like that, Larry? So many people saw what he did on that beach. Why won't he talk about it? What happened to him there?'

'Something happened to all of us,' says Larry. 'It's hard to explain. You'd have to have been there. It was like the end of the world.'

'Is that what Ed thought? It was the end of the world?'

'It was all so stupid and pointless. Just a gigantic mistake, really. We all saw that. But Ed – he just went crazy. He was so angry he didn't care if he lived or died. He didn't even try to protect himself. He kept thinking it'd be his turn next, but his turn never came. He says it was just luck. And I think he feels he doesn't deserve his luck. I think some part of him feels he should have died on that beach.'

Kitty listens in silence. Larry is picking his words carefully, protecting her from the single most devastating cry that burst from Ed that night they talked in the chapel: *I wanted to die*. How can he say this to Kitty? Did he not want to live for her?

'Thank you,' Kitty says. 'That helps me.'

'But he should talk to you about all this himself.'

'People don't always talk about things.'

But you and I talk, Larry wants to say. You and I talk about everything and anything. There's nothing I can't say to you.

'It was different for me on that beach.' Suddenly he realises he's going to tell her what he's told nobody except Ed. 'I was a coward on that beach.'

'Oh, Larry. Everyone must have been terrified.'

'All I did was take cover. All I could think about was saving myself.'

'Anyone would've been the same.'

'No. There were a lot of brave men that day. I just wasn't one of them.'

She smiles at him.

'That damned beach,' she says.

Larry feels a weight roll off him, a weight he's been carrying for four years. He has told Kitty his shameful secret, and she doesn't mind. It seems to make no difference. He's flooded with love and gratitude; but this, unlike his shame, must remain unspoken.

There's something else he isn't telling Kitty, too. He isn't telling her about Nell and the baby.

Larry spends the next day painting. He sets up a board in the farmyard, using the split-chestnut rails as an easel. For a while Pamela watches him at work, saying nothing.

So long as he's absorbed in his painting he has no dreams and no regrets. This is the joy of it, the way it allows him to escape his own uncertain self, and live in another space.

There, within the frame of his chosen image, the complexities are limitless, the challenges insurmountable, but he himself almost ceases to exist.

Kitty comes out to tell him George and Louisa will join them for supper. She looks at the work in progress.

'Caburn again,' she says.

At supper Louisa is eager to hear news of the artist's model who poses naked.

'She doesn't do that any more,' says Larry.

'But is she still your girlfriend? Isn't it time you settled down? How old are you, Larry?'

'I'm twenty-eight.'

'Leave the poor man alone, Louisa,' says Kitty.

'Well, you know what they say,' says Louisa. 'You're not a man until you've planted a tree, had a son, and something else I forget.'

Louisa is desperate to have a baby, and makes no attempt to conceal it.

'A woman, a dog and a walnut tree,' says George, 'the more you beat them the better they be.'

'What on earth is he talking about?' says Louisa.

'Old English proverb,' says George.

'How extraordinary! The things he comes up with!'

Lying in bed that night, back in the room he occupied in the summer of '42, Larry thinks to himself of the baby waiting to be born, who might indeed be a son. It seems to him that Louisa is right. He isn't yet a man.

21

'So how were your friends in Sussex?' says Nell. 'Did you tell them about me?'

'We talked about you a bit,' says Larry. 'But I didn't give away any secrets.'

He means about the baby.

Nell has returned from her trip looking tired and behaving restlessly. Larry shows her the paintings he's been working on during his time away, but she only looks at them for a moment before moving on again. She makes funny little dance steps round the room, lights a cigarette, traces circles in the air with one hand.

'Don't you sometimes think there's too much art in the world?' she says.

'Far too much,' says Larry.

'So what *bit* did you talk about?'

'Oh, Louisa had a go at me for not settling down.'

'Like a Labrador.'

'Is that what Labradors do?'

'My parents have one. He goes round and round in his basket, pawing at his blanket, and then he settles down.'

She acts it out, with such vivid mimicry that Larry laughs.

'I can't see myself doing that,' he says.

'So what excuse did you give?'

'Oh, you know those sorts of dinner conversations. No one expects a serious answer.'

'No, I suppose not.'

She stops pirouetting and stands looking out of the window, her back to Larry.

'But you have more serious conversations with Kitty, I expect.'

'Sometimes,' says Larry.

'What do you talk about?'

'Ed, mostly.'

'You talk to Kitty about Ed?'

'Yes,' says Larry. Nell's voice has gone quiet and she's become very still, as if she doesn't want to miss a sound. 'I've known Ed for ever. He can be a strange chap sometimes.'

'What sort of strange?'

'He goes off on walks by himself. Spends a lot of time away. He's a bit of a brooder.'

'He seemed rather interesting to me.'

'He is. He's remarkable, actually.'

'I suppose all that going on walks by himself is hard for Kitty,' says Nell.

'Yes, it is a bit.'

'And you talk to her about that.'

Larry goes and stands behind her, taking her in his arms.

'What's all this about?' he says. 'You're not jealous of Kitty, are you?'

'Should I be?' says Nell.

'No. Of course not.'

'Why of course not? She's very pretty. Beautiful, really.'

'Because she's married to my best friend.'

Nell holds herself stiff and upright, not yielding to his embrace.

'I'm not blind, Larry,' she says. 'I saw how you looked at her.'

'For God's sake!' He moves away. 'What's that supposed to mean? You do talk nonsense sometimes, Nell.'

'There, you see,' she says, as if he's proved her point.

'No, I don't see. What am I supposed to see? That I enjoy looking at Kitty? Why wouldn't I? She's an old friend. What am I supposed to do? Glower at her?'

'Why are you getting so worked up about this?'

'Because it's ridiculous! Because it annoys me that you even raise such silliness. You of all people! I thought you'd escaped all that conventional claptrap. You go off with Julius for two weeks and I don't cross-question you about who you've been looking at or who you've been talking to.'

'You can if you want.'

'I don't want. What I love about us is that we trust each other. You said it yourself. We don't put each other in cages.'

Nell says nothing. Larry feels he's proved his point, and is demonstrably right, while at the same time knowing he's

304

in the wrong. As a result he's far more disturbed than he cares to admit.

Nell moves away and lights another cigarette. She stands by the window, smoking, looking out.

'Good old fags,' she says. 'Something to do while we're not talking.'

'Oh, Nell,' says Larry.

'Do you feel hurt?' she says. 'Do you think I'm being unfair to you?'

'Yes, I do,' says Larry.

'You know how I am,' she says. 'I've been the same from the start, haven't I? All I've ever said to you is, don't lie to me.'

'How am I lying to you?'

'I've never asked for promises. I've never tried to tie you down. We're with each other because we love each other. There's no other reason. If you don't want to be with me all you have to do is say so.'

'But I do want to be with you.'

'More than you want to be with Kitty?'

'Yes!' Larry feels helpless rage growing within him. 'Why do you keep going on about Kitty? She's my friend, just like Ed's my friend. Am I not to have friends now? Nothing has ever happened between me and Kitty. First she was Ed's girl, and now she's Ed's wife. That's all there is to it.'

'Why do you keep going on about Kitty, Larry?'

'Me!' He waves his hands in the air with frustration. 'Me! It's you who's been going on about Kitty, not me.'

'Can you guess why?'

'Of course I can guess why. You're jealous of her. But I keep telling you there is nothing between me and Kitty.'

'Still all about Kitty,' says Nell.

'All right! Forget Kitty! No more Kitty! She's not important.'

His chest feels tight. He wants to hit something.

'So what's important, Larry?'

He gets it then, the thing that's driving him wild. It's the soft relentless tone, as if he's a child who's been set a puzzle, and she's the teacher who wants to get him to work out the answer for himself. This has the perverse effect of making him not want to give the approved answer. He's supposed to say, 'You and me, that's what's important.' But it won't come out.

Instead he says, 'It doesn't matter. I've had enough of this conversation. I don't think it's getting us anywhere.'

'So what do you want to do instead?' she says.

'I don't know. Relax. Enjoy being with you. I haven't seen you for two weeks.'

'You want to go to bed?'

'No, I don't mean that. Well, yes, I do. But I mean just relax. Feel good together.'

'I want that too,' says Nell.

'Come over here, then. Give me a kiss.'

She comes to him and they kiss, but he can feel her holding back from him. This, and the kiss, and having her in his arms, fills him with a sudden rush of desire.

'We could go to bed,' he says.

'Would you mind if we didn't?' she says.

306

'No, of course not.'

But his body minds. The more he knows he can't have her, the more he wants her. The code of good manners sustains him. You don't grab. You wait to be served.

'I'm supposed to be having dinner with somebody,' she says.

'Who?'

'A friend of Julius's called Peter Beaumont. He came to your private view. He's rich.'

'Oh, well then. You'd better have dinner with him.'

'Why don't you come too?'

'Me!'

'I bet you could do with a square meal. I know I could.'

Suddenly it all seems too ridiculous for words. Larry feels the tension melting away.

'You just want the dinner?'

'Of course. He's bound to take us somewhere swish.'

'But he won't want me.'

'If I tell him to, he will.'

Peter Beaumont greets Larry with a soft handshake, a sweet sad smile.

'Nell's told me all about you. I did so admire your work. It's a pleasure to meet you.'

'I do hope you don't mind me tagging along,' says Larry.

'Of course he doesn't mind,' says Nell. 'I've told him you're a starving artist and it's the duty of the wealthy man to support the arts.'

Peter takes them to the Savoy Grill. It's immediately clear

that he's a familiar figure here. Larry feels under-dressed and out of place. Nell behaves as though she owns the restaurant.

'I want heaps and heaps of red meat,' she says.

Peter is all too obviously smitten with Nell. From time to time he meets Larry's eyes with a look that says, Isn't she extraordinary! It doesn't seem to occur to him that Larry might be a rival. He orders two bottles of excellent wine, and Larry, not really knowing what's going on, decides to drink as much as possible.

'Lawrence is a genius,' Nell tells Peter. 'You must buy his paintings.'

'Perhaps I could visit your studio,' Peter says to Larry, as if seeking a rare favour.

'I'm afraid Nell is too kind,' says Larry.

She's certainly kind to Peter. She smiles at him, and reaches across the table to touch his hand when wanting to hold his attention, and takes care to turn the conversation towards his concerns.

'Peter has this terrible wife,' she says. 'She treats him in the most vile manner. If he ever touches her, even by accident, she shudders.'

Peter gives Larry his sad smile.

'One of those mistakes one makes,' he says.

'Poor Peter,' says Nell, stroking his hand.

Larry is lost. He has only joined them because it seemed Nell wanted him to be there, to witness that her evening with this male friend is innocent. And yet here she is, acting as if they're lovers.

'Isn't Nell amazing?' Peter says to Larry. 'I tell her she's like a princess in a fairy tale.'

'I'm the prize you get after all that nasty questing,' says Nell.

By the end of the evening Peter is holding Nell's hand in his and Larry is thoroughly miserable.

'Now you must come back to my place for a nightcap,' says Peter.

Even Larry knows when the time has come to go.

'I'll be on my way,' he says. 'Excellent dinner. Do me good to walk it off.'

Nell barely notices that he's leaving.

The walk back to Camberwell through night streets takes a good hour, long enough in the cool air to sober Larry up and leave him hurt and angry. He has no idea what Nell was thinking of when she included him in the dinner, and he has no idea what her relationship is with Peter Beaumont. All he knows is that he has been made to look like a fool.

He half expects Nell to show up at his door later that night, but she never comes. Nor does she make contact the following day. His hurt and anger, feeding on itself, turns into a crazy obsession which stops him from working or thinking about anything else. Then in the evening, there she is.

'Nell! Where have you been?'

'That's not much of a welcome,' she replies.

'I've been going insane!'

'Why? Am I supposed to report to you daily?'

309

Her blank pretence of not understanding him drives Larry into open rage. He shouts at her, there on the doorstep.

'I don't know what the hell you're doing! I don't know what you want of me! I don't know why you treat me like this! But I'm sick of it. I don't want any more!'

She lets him shout, looking away down the street until he's finished. Then she turns back to him as if everything he's just said is an embarrassing body noise to be overlooked.

'May I come in?'

In his room she turns on him with cold anger.

'Never do that again. Never shout at me in public. What right have you to talk to me like that? You don't own me.'

'Oh, for God's sake, Nell!'

'If you have something to say to me, say it right now.'

'You know I have.'

'I only know what you tell me, Lawrence. I'm not a mind reader.'

'Last night,' says Larry. 'That was humiliating.'

'Humiliating? You ate a very good dinner, if I recall. Peter was extremely pleasant to you. Why was it humiliating?'

'You went off with him at the end.'

'Did you stop me?'

'No, of course not.'

'Why not? Apparently you minded.'

'Of course I minded!' he cries.

'Then why didn't you say so?'

'Oh, come on, Nell. I have my dignity. I'm not going to throw my weight about when a man has just bought me an expensive dinner.'

310

'So I'm the one who's supposed to throw his generosity back in his face, am I? I'm supposed to say, Sorry, Peter, I'm going home with Lawrence because he's sulking.'

'Why did you ask me last night? What was the point of that? Anybody can see he's in love with you. Why rub my face in that?'

'Maybe I wanted to show you you don't own me.'

'Of course I don't bloody own you!'

'Then what's all this fuss about, Lawrence?'

She's staring at him with those big truth-demanding eyes, and he knows now he's going to have to say something he really means.

'You're going to have my baby,' he says.

'Ah,' she says. 'So that's it.'

'Of course that's it. That's everything.'

She takes out her cigarettes and offers him one, but he shakes his head. Her hands are steady as he lights her cigarette, but his are shaking. She draws the smoke in deep and exhales, turning her face away.

'So if there wasn't a baby, you wouldn't mind about any of it?'

'I don't know,' he says. 'Yes, I'd mind.'

'Do you know something I've realised about you, Lawrence? You never take the physical initiative. You never touch me unless I touch you.'

Larry feels the tightness in his chest returning. Somehow he's got caught in a trap from which there's no escape. Perhaps she means him to touch her now. He feels paralysed.

'Do you realise that?' she says.

'That doesn't matter,' he says. 'That's not the point.'

'Oh,' she says, 'is there a point? Do tell.'

'The point is the baby.'

'What baby?' she says.

'The baby you're going to have. Our baby.'

'There is no baby,' she says. 'Not any more.'

She goes on smoking, barely looking at him.

'What?' he says.

'I had a miscarriage,' says Nell. 'I wasn't going to tell you yet.'

He stares at her, unable to take in what he's just heard.

'You weren't going to tell me?'

'But I have now.'

He struggles to make sense of what's happening.

'Why not tell me?'

'I thought if I didn't tell you,' she says simply, devastatingly, 'you'd go on loving me.'

He gives a sudden gasp.

'Oh, Nell!'

He takes her in his arms and holds her close, tears rising to his eyes.

'Oh, Nell!'

He's overwhelmed by pity and relief and guilt. Once again the future has changed before him, swinging abruptly to send him off in a new direction. Nell reaches out from within his embrace to stub out her cigarette.

'I'm so sorry, Nell. I'm so, so sorry.'

'Are you, darling?'

Her gentle voice is back.

'What happened? When did it happen?'

'Almost two weeks ago now.'

'What about your trip?'

'There wasn't any trip. Don't keep asking me questions, darling. It's been beastly, but I just tell myself it's over now.'

'You poor, poor sweetheart. And there I've been, making it all worse. You should have told me.'

'Well, I've told you now.'

They retreat to the bed, not for sex, but for mutual comfort. They lie there, curled in each other's arms, like babes in the wood. The child that existed for so short a time seems to lie in their arms with them like a ghost, uniting them.

'We can have another,' says Larry, whispering.

'Do you want to?'

'Of course I want to,' he says. 'Don't you?'

'I'm not sure I'm ready yet,' she says. 'Do you mind?'

'No, I don't mind.'

She's wiser than him. When he talks of another baby it's no more than his way of consoling her, and showing her he loves her. For him 'another baby' is an idea, not a reality. But she is the one whose body will carry the child. For her it's more than an emotional gesture.

'I want you so much to be free,' she tells him.

It amazes him how instinctively she understands his workings. Of course the baby placed him under a certain obligation. Hadn't he asked her to marry him? But she knew better than him that this was not a free choice. Now she gives him back his freedom. Her truthfulness and her generosity humble him.

Then he remembers the way she reached across the table at the Savoy Grill to stroke Peter Beaumont's hand, and confusion overtakes him once more. He feels he's being manipulated, but has no idea to what end.

'Sometimes I don't understand what's happening to us,' he says to her.

'It doesn't need to be understood,' she says. 'People either love each other or they don't.'

'I do love you, Nell. I'm sure of that.'

In this moment, lying with her in his arms, released by her promise of freedom, he can say the simple words.

'And I do love you, darling,' she replies.

For a while they stay like this, warmed by each other, silent. The immensity of the information they have exchanged has exhausted them. Then Nell pulls herself up into a sitting position and straightens her clothes.

'I'm going to go now,' she says.

'When will I see you again?'

She gets up off the bed and stretches like a cat. Then she turns to him with a smile.

'Darling Lawrence,' she says. 'You can see me any time you want. But do you know what I think? You're not to be cross with me. I think what you need to do now is have a real, truthful talk with your friend Kitty. Tell her whatever it is you've got to tell her, and hear what she has to say to you. Because until you've done that, I don't think you're really going to be able to love anyone else, not with all of your heart.'

'That's not true,' protests Larry, going pink. 'No, that's wrong. That's not how it is at all. And anyway, even if it was, what's the point? She's married to Ed.'

'Is she happy with Ed?'

Larry stares at Nell in consternation. It's like hearing his own secret thoughts out loud.

'I can't do that, Nell.'

'You're quite a one for not doing things, aren't you, Lawrence? But if you want something, you have to do something about it. It's no good just waiting for it to fall in your lap. If you want Kitty, tell her so, and see what happens. And if it doesn't work out, and you decide it's me you want after all, tell me so, and see what happens.'

She gives him a soft lingering kiss on the mouth before she leaves.

'Don't be such a scaredy-cat, darling. Those that don't ask don't get.'

22

Towards the end of January 1947 snow begins to fall over south-east England, and it continues to fall until the land is thickly blanketed. Within two days the roads and railways have become impassable. Larry, visiting River Farm for the weekend, finds himself obliged to stay longer than he intended.

On that first weekend they go out sledging. Heavily wrapped in warm clothes, they cross the silent main road and climb the long diagonal track to the top of Mount Caburn. Ed carries the sledge. Larry holds Pamela's hand, so that he can swing her up out of the deep drifts. Kitty follows behind, only her nose and eyes visible in the bundle of scarves and woolly hats.

The sky is clear as ice. From the top of the ridge they look out over a white world. Their breath makes clouds as they stand, panting from the climb through shin-deep snow, marvelling at the view.

'It's like the whole world is starting again,' says Kitty. 'All young and unwrinkled.'

'Are we to go right to the top?' says Ed. 'I have a tremendous urge to ride the sledge down the front of Caburn.'

'You'll do no such thing,' says Kitty.

The south face of Caburn drops steeply down to the valley, too steep for the shepherds and their sheep to climb. The tracks are all up the gentler sides of the Down.

'Want to sledge!' cries Pammy. 'Want to sledge!'

Even here the slope is of some concern.

'It'll be all right if we run sideways,' says Ed, volunteering to test the ground.

He lays the sledge on the snow and sits on it. He rocks his upper body back and forth, and away he goes. For a few minutes he proceeds sedately across the hillside. Then the sledge tips on a snow-covered ridge and he topples off to one side. The onlookers cheer.

Ed comes trudging back, caked with snow, dragging the sledge. Kitty brushes snow off his hair and eyebrows.

'Why aren't you wearing a hat, you foolish man?'

'Me, me, me!' cries Pammy.

The little girl has her turn, squealing with excitement, Ed loping along beside the sledge on the downhill side, holding the rope. When she in her turn tumbles off he scoops her up out of the snow and sits her back on the sledge and tows it up to the others. The collar of her coat is thick with snow, and there's snow all down her neck, but she's jumping with the excitement of it.

'Your turn, Larry,' says Ed, giving him the rope.

'Me, me, me!' cries Pammy.

'I'll share,' says Larry.

He sits on the sledge, and Pammy sits between his knees, little arms gripping his thighs. Ed gives them a push off. All the way down Pammy carols with joy, and Larry tries with outstretched gloved hands to control their direction and speed. The cold wind on his face stings his cheeks and makes his eyes water. The eager child wriggles and shouts between his legs. The sledge lurches and sways, steadily gathering speed. There are no brakes, no way of stopping, other than tumbling off into the snow.

Then Pammy isn't shouting any more and he realises they're going too fast. The sledge is plunging directly down the slope. The speed is thrilling and frightening. The child's arms cling ever tighter to his thighs. The hill stretches far below, to the snow-covered roofs of the village of Glynde and the carpet of farmland beyond. Larry knows he must bring the sledge ride to a stop, but he lets them ride on for a few moments longer, captivated by the sensation of being out of control. Pammy twists her head round then and he sees the same look in her bright eyes: her first taste of the addictive drug that is danger.

Then he holds her thin body in his arms and tips them both off to one side, to tumble over and over in the deep snow. They come to a stop, dazed and snow-covered but unhurt. He brushes her face clear, and she does the same to him. The sledge too has turned over onto its side and lies just below them.

'You all right, Pammy?'

'More!' she says. 'More!'

He fetches the sledge and they climb back up the hill.

'Don't do that again, Larry,' says Kitty, brushing snow off Pamela. 'You scared me half to death.'

'No, no!' cries the child. 'I want more!'

'You wild man,' says Ed to Larry.

Pamela is allowed to go on the sledge again, but this time with her mother, very slowly, and escorted by Ed and Larry.

'Faster!' she cries. 'I want to go faster!'

This time there's no tumbling off. Descending in a series of hairpin bends they make their way back down to the valley. Once on the road again they walk, and Ed tows the sledge behind him.

Larry walks with Pamela, holding hands.

'Mummy is married to Daddy,' says Pamela. 'So I can be married to you.'

'All right,' says Larry.

'So we can do more fast sledging,' says Pamela.

'Of course.'

'An excellent basis for marriage,' says Ed from behind them.

That night the temperature drops again, and more snow falls. The next day Larry and Ed take shovels and dig a path from the house to the road, hard labour which takes them the whole morning. A tractor has been down the Newhaven road driving a snowplough, but there are no cars or lorries to be seen.

'If this goes on we're going to have to stock up with coal,' says Ed.

The hours shovelling snow warm them and give them

an appetite. They head back down the path they've cleared, the shovels shouldered.

'So how's Nell?' says Ed. 'Is she still on the scene?'

'In a way,' says Larry. 'It's been a bit up and down lately. I was supposed to be seeing her when I got back today.'

'This weather's messed up everyone's plans.'

'The annoying thing is she's not on the phone. I suppose I could always ring the gallery.'

'I shouldn't worry. Everything's in chaos. She'll understand.'

'I wish I did,' says Larry.

'Oh,' says Ed with a smile. 'It's like that?'

'Not so long ago I was asking her to marry me. Now I'm not even sure if I'm ever going to see her again.'

'Why wouldn't you see her again?'

'I hardly even know myself,' says Larry. 'She's not like anyone else I've ever known. She lives entirely by her own truth. And that's what she wants me to do.'

'Whatever that means,' says Ed.

'It should be so simple. Say only what you mean. Do only what you want. No games, no pretence, no polite little lies. But what if you don't know what you want?'

'You can't tell people the truth,' says Ed. 'Being civilised is all about covering that stuff up.'

'Do you really think that?' says Larry.

'Don't you?'

'I suppose I think that if you really love someone, and they really love you, you can tell them everything.'

'That's because deep down you believe that people are good.'

'And you believe people are bad.'

'Not exactly,' says Ed. 'I believe we're alone.'

He gives a laugh, and punches Larry on the arm.

'Here you are, my oldest friend, and I'm telling you I'm alone. What an ungrateful dog of a fellow I must be.'

'You may be right even so,' says Larry quietly.

'Your Nell sounds to me like she's a bit of a handful.'

'But Ed,' says Larry, pursuing his own thoughts, 'you don't feel alone with Kitty, do you?'

'Now there's a question.'

'Sorry. Forget I said it.'

'No,' says Ed. 'It's a fair question. She's my wife, and I love her.'

He thinks it over as they come to a stop in the snowy farmyard.

'There are moments when I'm with Kitty, when I'm holding her in my arms, or when I'm watching her sleeping, when I go quiet. Very still moments. I don't feel alone then.'

Larry kicks the snow, making furrows in the virgin whiteness.

'But they don't last.'

'No. They don't last.'

'You shouldn't be away so much, Ed. It's hard on Kitty. And on Pammy.'

'I know.' He speaks humbly, accepting the rebuke. 'Unlikely as it may seem, I do my best.'

'Well,' says Larry, 'there'll be no trips to France in this.'

They go into the house, stamping the snow off their boots. Kitty and Pamela are making lunch.

'Daddy's back,' says Kitty. 'We can eat.'

'And Larry,' says Pamela. 'He's back too.'

The early excitement of the snow soon wears off, as the bitter cold grips the land. The electricity cuts out for hours at a time, without warning, plunging the house into a blackout as complete as any in wartime. For three nights running they eat their supper and go to bed by candlelight. Then the water pipes freeze, and it's no longer possible to wash, or go to the lavatory. They take to using potties, which Ed removes and empties in some secret place onto the hard snow. The wireless news tells them of the crisis that has overtaken the nation. Railway wagons can't move. Ships can't bring in supplies. Food rations are cut lower even than the worst years of the war. In early February the government announces there will be five hours of planned electricity cuts a day, three in the morning and two in the afternoon.

When the farmhouse supply of both coal and firewood runs out, Kitty turns for help to Louisa. Ed and Larry plot various ways of moving loads of fuel across the village, but in the end come up with a simpler solution. They move themselves. Edenfield Place is well stocked with coal, and by shutting up two-thirds of the house George reckons they can last a good six weeks. This terrible weather can't possibly go on to the end of March.

So Ed and Kitty return to the room in Edenfield Place

in which they began their married life, and Pamela to her little bed in the adjoining dressing room, and Larry to the guest room down the corridor. Fires are kept burning in the Oak Room and the morning room, while the far larger drawing room and library are left to the winter cold. The butler's pantry, the domain of Mr Lott the butler, and the kitchen, the domain of his wife, Mrs Lott the cook, are also kept warm. Three of the four great boilers are switched off. Oil lamps stand in readiness for the hours when the electricity cuts out.

Due to the more modern heating system of the house, the water pipes are still running in the family quarters, and three lavatories are usable. Ed's potty-emptying duties are suspended.

'I'm rather sorry, really,' he says. 'I was looking forward to the day the snow melts, and all round the houses there'd be revealed the waste matter of the mid-twentieth century.'

The hard winter locks them all in the big house on top of one another, and Larry finds no opportunity to talk to Kitty alone. He originally expected to visit for a weekend only, and so has not brought his paints and brushes. Now as his stay enters its third week and there's no sign of a thaw, he passes much of his time huddled by the Oak Room fire, rereading *War and Peace*. When he finishes the first volume, Kitty picks it up, and begins to read behind him. This reignites their old conversation about good characters in books, and whether they can ever be attractive. The character in question is Pierre Bezukhov.

'But he's so fat,' says Kitty, 'and he's so clumsy, and he's so naïve.' She's especially outraged by his marriage to the beautiful but cold Helene. 'All because of her bosom. It's ridiculous.'

'I promise you he gets better,' says Larry. 'You'll learn to love him.'

'I love Prince André.'

'Of course you do.'

'And you love Natasha.'

'I adore Natasha. From the moment she runs into the grown-ups' party and can't stop laughing. But do you know an odd thing? Tolstoy quite clearly tells us that she's not specially pretty. But when I imagine her, she's tremendously attractive.'

'Of course she's pretty!'

'Look.' He takes the volume from her and finds the page in question. '"This black-eyed, wide-mouthed girl, *not pretty* but full of life".'

'Oh, but she's still only a child,' says Kitty. 'She's only thirteen. She grows up to be beautiful.'

February is half gone, and the wireless news is that the miners in South Wales are to work full shifts even on Sundays. Ships have finally been able to dock with cargoes of coal. There are no signs of a thaw, but the trains are running once more, and everyone is telling everyone else that the thaw must come soon.

Kitty and Larry find themselves alone on either side of the Oak Room fire. Larry puts his bookmark in his place, closes his book, and lays it down.

'I shall go back to London tomorrow,' he says. 'I've been gone too long.'

'But we haven't had a chance to talk,' Kitty says. 'Not properly.'

She too lays down her book.

'I like having you here so much, Larry,' she says. 'I shall hate it when you go.'

'You know I'll always come back.'

'Will you? Always?'

'That's what friends do.'

Kitty looks at him, only half smiling.

'It's not much of a word, is it?' she says. '*Friend*. There should be a better word. *Friend* sounds so unimportant, someone you chat to at parties. You're more than that for me.'

'You too,' says Larry.

'I shan't like it when you marry, you know. Whoever it is. But of course you must. I'm not so selfish as not to see that.'

'The trouble is,' says Larry, 'I can't help comparing every girl I meet to you.'

'Oh, well. That shouldn't be too much of a problem. There are so many girls who are far more thrilling than me.'

'I have yet to meet one.'

She holds his gaze, not pretending she doesn't understand.

'Just tell me you're happy,' he says.

'Why ask me that? You know I'm not happy.'

'Can't anything be done?'

'No,' she says. 'I've thought about it so much. I've decided this is my task in life. Yes, I know how terrible that sounds, like some grim duty. I don't mean it that way. Do you remember saying to me once, Don't you want to do something noble and fine with your life? Well, I do. I love Ed, I'll never hurt him or be disloyal to him. This is just the thing I have to do. Being happy or unhappy doesn't matter any more.'

'Oh, Kitty.'

'Please don't pity me. I can't bear it.'

'It's not pity. I don't know what it is. Regret. Anger. It's all such a waste. You don't deserve this.'

'Why should I get a happier life than anyone else?'

'It could have been so different. That's what I can't bear.'

'Why think that way?' she says gently. 'I made my choice. I chose Ed. I chose him knowing there was a sadness in him. Maybe I chose him because of that. And I do love him.'

'Isn't there room in our lives to love more than one person?'

'Of course. But why think that way? There's nothing to be done.'

'Kitty—'

'No, please. Don't make me say anything more. I mustn't be selfish and greedy. You're more than a friend to me, Larry. But I mustn't hold on to you. What I want more than anything is for you to find someone who makes you happy. Then all I ask is that she lets you go on being my friend. I couldn't bear to lose you altogether. Promise me you'll always be my friend.'

'Even though it's not much of a word.'

'Even though.'

'Do friends love each other, Kitty?'

'Yes,' she says, her eyes on him. 'They love each other very much.'

'Then I promise.'

That same day Kitty sings to them, accompanying herself on the piano in the morning room. She sings 'The Ash Grove' and 'Drink To Me Only With Thine Eyes'.

> The thirst that from the soul doth rise
> Doth ask a drink divine . . .

Larry's eyes never leave her face as she sings. She plays by ear, and sings from memory, a slight frown of concentration on her face.

Then at Ed's request she sings 'The Water is Wide'.

> A ship there is
> And she sails the seas.
> She's laden deep
> As deep can be;
> But not so deep
> As the love I'm in,
> And I know not if
> I sink or swim.

Little Pamela is unimpressed by the sad songs and agitates for 'Little Brown Jug'.

> Ha ha ha!
> You and me
> Little brown jug
> Don't I love thee!

The following morning Larry walks the snowy road into Lewes, her sweet voice still sounding in his memory, her bright eyes reaching towards him across the piano.

23

London is quiet and mostly empty, the snow that lines the streets now a dirty shade of grey-brown. Occasional taxis clatter by over the lumps of ice. People passing on the pavements, heavily wrapped in overcoats, hats pulled low over their ears, keep their heads down to avoid stumbling on the ridged snow. All business seems to have closed down. Every day now like a Sunday in winter.

Larry returns to his room in Camberwell and lights the gas fire. It burns at low pressure, taking a long time to warm the chill air. Everything is cold to his touch, the covers on his bed, his books, his paints. He looks at the canvas he had begun before going to Sussex, and sees at once that it has no life in it. His room too, despite his return, has no life in it.

Suddenly he wants very much to see Nell.

He phones Weingard's gallery and a female voice answers. The gallery is closed. No, she doesn't know where Nell is. He writes a note to her, telling her he's back, and walks up the road to the post office on Church Street to send it. From there he goes on to the pub on the corner. It's a Monday and early for the evening crowd. The Hermit's Rest is eerily quiet. He sits at a table close to the meagre fire and works away slowly at a pint of stout. He thinks about Nell.

Ever since his last talk with Kitty he's been thinking new thoughts about his future. His feelings haven't changed. But he sees more clearly now that he must take active steps to make a life without Kitty, or he'll doom himself to live a life alone. Once again he marvels at Nell's insight. It seems she knows him better than he knows himself. She accuses him of never taking the initiative, and she's right. For too long he's allowed events outside his control to determine his course. The time has come to take charge of his own life.

He interrogates himself, sitting alone in the pub. Do I want to marry Nell? He recalls her elusiveness, her moodiness, her unpredictability, and he trembles. What sort of life would that be? But then he thinks of never seeing her again and he almost cries out loud, 'No! Don't leave me!' so powerful is the longing to hold her in his arms.

What is the gravest charge he has to bring against her? That she spends time with other men. That she leads them on to love her. In other words, that he does not possess her exclusive love. But what right has he to her exclusive love, when he makes no promise on his side? See it from her point of view: she has made herself over to him, body and soul, while he has kept much of himself apart.

But I asked her to marry me.

Ah, she saw through that. She knows me better than I know myself. She saw that I was doing my duty because of the baby. She puts no trust in duty. She requires true love.

Thinking this makes him admire her, and admiring her he feels he does love her after all. It's just a matter of letting go whatever last inhibition holds him back. Offer her all the love of which he's capable and she'll give him back love fourfold, and his fears will melt away.

What a rare creature she is! A child of truth. With her in his life there'll be no complacency, and no idling. His days will be vivid and his nights will be warm. He can see her naked body now, rosy in the gaslight, and feels his body's gratitude to her tingling in his veins. Is this such a small thing? Some would say it's the basis of everything. Find happiness with each other in bed and love will never die.

His beer finished, his spirits excited by his train of thought, he feels the need of companionship. With luck Nell will get his note tomorrow and be with him by the end of the day. He has much to say to her. But between now and then he does not want to be alone. He could walk into Kensington and call on his father. Then he has a better idea. He will call on Tony Armitage.

Armitage has a studio in Valmar Road, on the other side of Denmark Hill. There's a fair chance he'll be in. Larry buttons his overcoat up to his chin and sets out into the snowy streets once more. Valmar Road isn't far, but it's an awkward place to find. A distant church clock is chiming seven as he rings the top bell at the street door.

A window opens above. Armitage's head pokes out.

'Who's that?'

'Larry,' says Larry.

'Bloody hell!' exclaims Armitage. Then, 'I'll come down.'

He lets Larry in the front door.

'I've not been outside for a week,' he says. 'Too bloody cold.'

Larry follows him up several flights of bare stairs to the rooms in the roof.

'I've got nothing to eat,' says Armitage. 'There may be some brandy left.'

His living quarters consist of one sizeable room with a big north-facing window, which is his studio, his kitchen, and his washroom, a single butler sink serving all these purposes; beyond, a closed door leads to a small bedroom. The electric light bulb that illuminates the studio is either very low-powered or the electricity is weak. In its grudging light Larry sees a chaotic array of paintings, most of them unfinished.

'I lose heart,' says Armitage. 'I know exactly what it is I mean to do, and then I see what I've actually done, and I lose heart.'

He doesn't ask Larry why he's come. He offers him brandy in a teacup. Larry looks round the canvases.

'But your work is so good,' he says.

He means it. Even in this poor light he can see that his friend's paintings are exploding with life. As he admires

332

them, he feels with deep shock the contrast with his own work. Somehow this has never been as apparent to him before. Over the last two years his work has become accomplished, but looking at Armitage's pictures, he knows with a terrible certainty that he will never be a true artist. He has enough understanding of technique to see how Armitage achieves his effects, while at the same time knowing that this is so much more than technique. In his portraits particularly, he has the gift of expressing the fine complexity of life itself.

'This is so good,' he says again. 'You're good, Tony.'

'I'm better than good,' says Armitage. 'I'm the real thing. Which is why I drive myself crazy. All this' – he gestures round the studio – 'this is nothing. One day I'll show you what I can do.'

Larry comes upon two quite small sketches of Nell.

'There's Nell,' he says. In one of them she's looking towards the artist but past him, playing her unreachable game. 'That's so Nell.'

He realises now why he's come. He wants to talk to someone about Nell.

'She never sits still for long enough,' says Armitage. 'Also her skin's too smooth. I like wrinkles.'

'I think I might be in love with her,' says Larry.

'Oh, everyone's in love with Nell,' says Armitage. 'That's her function in life. She's a muse.'

'I don't think she wants to be a muse.'

'Of course she does. Why else does she hang around artists? You get girls like that.'

333

Larry laughs. Tony Armitage, barely twenty-one years old, his wild curls serving only to emphasise his boyish face, makes an unconvincing bohemian roué.

'How on earth do you know? You've only just left school.'

'It's nothing to do with age. I was seven when I found out I had talent. I was fifteen when I knew I would be one of the greats. Oh, don't get me wrong. I know all this is poor prentice work. But give me five more years, and you won't be laughing.'

'I'm not laughing at your work, Tony,' Larry says. 'I'm in awe of your work. But I'm not sure I'm quite ready to see you as a fount of wisdom on the opposite sex.'

'Oh, girls.' He speaks dismissively, evidently not very interested.

'Don't you care for girls?'

'Yes, in their way. Up to a point. One has to eat and so forth.'

Larry can't help laughing again. But he's impressed by the young man's invincible conviction of his own worth. It could be the groundless arrogance of youth, but on the whole Larry is inclined to take it at face value; all too aware that he lacks such self-belief himself.

'I'm afraid I get myself into much more of a mess with girls than you seem to,' he says. 'With Nell, anyway.' Then on an impulse he reveals more. 'Did she tell you I asked her to marry me?'

'No.' He seems surprised. 'Why?'

'Because I wanted to marry her. And also because she was pregnant.'

'Nell told you she was pregnant?'

'She isn't any more. She had a miscarriage. I expect I shouldn't be telling you this. But she's fine now.'

'Nell told you she had a miscarriage?'

'Yes.'

It strikes Larry now that Armitage is looking at him in an odd way.

'And you believed her?' he says.

'Yes,' says Larry. 'I know Nell's got her own strange ways, but the one thing she'd never do is tell a lie. She's got an obsession with truthfulness.'

Armitage stares at Larry. Then he lets out a harsh cackle of laughter. Larry frowns, annoyed.

'Nell never tell a lie!' says Armitage. 'She does nothing but lie.'

'I'm sorry,' says Larry. 'I don't think you know her as I do.'

'But Larry,' says Armitage. 'Telling you she's pregnant! It's the oldest trick in the book.'

He falls to laughing again.

'A trick to achieve what, precisely?'

Larry's voice has gone cold.

'To get you to marry her, of course.'

'I offered. She declined.'

This seems to Larry to be conclusive proof of Nell's integrity. To his surprise Armitage takes it in his stride.

'Oh, she's not stupid, our Nell. She must've picked up that you weren't a solid enough bet.'

'I'm sorry, Tony. I don't see things your way, that's all. I shouldn't have spoken about private matters.'

'Private? She tried the pregnancy trick on Peter Beaumont too, you know?'

Now it's Larry's turn to stare.

'Peter fell for it hook, line and sinker. But she decided to keep him in reserve. For a rainy day, as she puts it.'

'I don't understand.'

Larry's voice has become quiet. Armitage realises for the first time that this is no laughing matter.

'Didn't you know?' he says.

'Apparently not.'

'She's not a bad girl. She's a wonderful girl, really. But she's penniless. She has to look out for herself.'

'She told Peter Beaumont it was his baby?'

'Well, yes.'

Larry feels tired and confused. He passes one hand over his brow. He finds he's sweating.

'So whose baby was it?'

Armitage pours Larry the last of the brandy, and presses the teacup on him.

'There was no baby, Larry.'

'No baby?'

'No pregnancy. No miscarriage.'

'Are you sure?'

'Well, no one can ever be sure of anything with Nell. But I'm pretty sure. She tried it on me, but I just laughed.'

'You?'

Larry drinks the brandy, draining the cup.

'Look, old man,' says Armitage, 'I can see this has all rather hit you for six. Were you really serious about Nell?'

'Yes,' says Larry. 'I think I was.'

'I begin to see I've struck a bit of a wrong note.'

Larry can't reply. He's experiencing hot flushes of shame, beneath which far deeper griefs are waiting their turn.

'I'm very fond of Nell too,' says Armitage, trying clumsily to make amends. 'I suppose I don't mind her looking out for herself, because I do it too. We're all getting by as best we can.'

'But to lie to me.' Larry is still scarcely able to believe it. 'The first thing she ever said to me was, We tell each other the truth. She was always going on about the truth.'

'That's how it works, isn't it?' says Armitage. 'Thieves lock up their valuables. Cheats tell you the rules of the game.'

'Dear God,' says Larry. 'I feel so stupid.'

'Did you have a good time with her?'

'Yes,' says Larry with a sigh.

'Nothing stupid about that.'

Larry shakes his head, and looks round the room. There are all Armitage's works. There are the two sketches of Nell.

'You see more clearly than me, Tony,' he says. 'That's why you're a better artist.'

'Oh, come on. Don't start doing yourself down.'

'No, it's true. People talk about talent as if it's a gift of the gods, like being beautiful. But I think it's just as much to do with character. You've got the right character, Tony, and I haven't. You see clearly, and you believe in yourself. You're right, you will be one of the greats.'

337

'And you too, Larry. Why not?'

Larry turns from the power of the paintings to the boy who has painted them.

'You've seen my work,' he says. 'You know I'll never be like you.'

'Why shouldn't you be?' says Armitage. But Larry sees it in his eyes. He's not Nell. He can't look you in the face and lie.

'Thanks for the brandy,' Larry says. 'And thanks for the home truths. Not much fun, but I needed to know. Now I'm going to go off and sort myself out.'

Armitage sees him down to the street. Outside the street lights have gone off, and the only light on the icy pavements is the soft spill from curtained windows. Larry walks back to his room, oblivious to the cold. He's ashamed, and hurt, and angry, and lost.

When he gets back to his room he collects up all his paintings and bundles them in a blanket from his bed. There are over thirty works, mostly quite small, but one or two are an awkward size. He carries the bundle out into the street, and up the Grove to Church Street. He has some dim notion of walking all the way to the river, but a cab passes, and he hails it. The cab drops him at the southern end of Waterloo Bridge. He carries his bundle to the middle of the bridge, and unwraps it by the railings. Then one by one he throws his paintings into the river, and watches them slowly carried away downstream.

24

Larry lies awake in bed, cold even beneath all the blankets he possesses, and both his outer coats. He expects to pass the long night without sleep, dulled by dread, not wanting the new day to come, bringing with it the empty failure that is now his life. But in the small hours his body surrenders, and when he next opens his eyes there is light at his curtains.

Curtains he drew closed on that first afternoon Nell came to his room and undressed for him and lay in his arms. Light that has fallen on canvases that have held him breathless with concentration for hours on end. All this now gone: all this a stupidity, a vanity, a mistake. How is it possible to lose so much and still go on? Go on where?

At such times Larry has only one recourse. Just as he prayed when his mother died; just as he prayed when some small crisis at boarding school, great to him, left him friendless and alone; so now he turns to the familiar God of his childhood for kindness, and the comfort that lies in the prospect of eternity.

God, my God, God of my fathers, he prays. Show me what it is you want of me. Tell me where I'm to go, and what I'm to do. I have no will of my own any more. Your will be done, if only I can know it. Save me from myself. Teach me how to forget myself. I will serve only you.

How little, how ridiculous, his own existence now seems to him. Like a spoiled child he has strutted about, imagining that all eyes are on him, that the world has been made to gratify his desires. And all the time he has been a little squeaking nothing.

Driven from his bitter room by the need to escape himself and the memory of himself, he walks the dirty snow of London's streets, on and on, wanting only to wear himself out. In this way he trudges down the bombed canyon of Victoria Street to Westminster Cathedral. He has been here before, of course, with his father, to see the new mosaics in the Lady Chapel, and once, when he was ten, to Easter midnight Mass. He remembers the immensity of the nave, and its darkness. It's this darkness he now seeks, where he can become invisible, and his shame be forgotten.

On this winter Tuesday, approaching midday, the cathedral is virtually empty. Candles burn before the high altar, on the votive rack, but the electric lights are turned off. The massive walls of bare brick, one day to be made glorious with golden mosaic, reach up into the vaulted darkness on either side, as stern as a prison. He remains near the back of the nave, feeling neither the wish nor the right to approach the high altar. When some others enter from the street he

340

withdraws into a side chapel, preferring not to be seen even by strangers.

In the side chapel he kneels, and rests his elbows on the chairback in front, and stares unseeingly at the small chapel altar and the decorated panel above it. Two saints gaze back at him, both unsmilingly secure in the truth they have to offer. One is a pope, signified by the triple golden crown; the other a monk, with tonsure and humble robe. Like generals of a victorious army, they admit no doubt in the justice of their war. The pope has one hand raised, one finger pointing skyward, invoking the Almighty God he represents, whose power and authority flow through him.

Such massive certainty. And yet popes and saints must have known what he, Larry, now knows. How little we are, how ridiculous, how lost, in the eye of eternity.

To his irritation the strangers now follow him into the side chapel. A man of his own age and a younger woman. The woman is slender, dressed simply but elegantly. Looking up he catches a glimpse of her face, and it seems to him he's seen it before: the pure line of the cheek, the mouth that curves without smiling, the blue-grey eyes. They stand before the altar, speaking in whispers so as not to disturb him in his prayers.

'There he is,' says the man. 'That's Gregory the Great.'

Larry realises then that the pope in the altarpiece is the same St Gregory who presides over Downside Abbey and School; and that the tall balding man in the chapel is his old schoolfellow Rupert Blundell.

'Rupert, is that you?'

The man turns round and peers at him over his bony nose.

'Good God! Larry!'

Larry rises and they shake hands. Rupert introduces the girl, who turns out to be his sister Geraldine. Looking at her directly now, Larry remembers where he has seen her before. She has a little of the look of Primavera, the goddess of spring, in the Botticelli painting.

'Larry and I were at Downside together,' Rupert tells her, 'and then we were both in Combined Ops.' To Larry he says, 'We've been on a buying spree at the army and navy stores. Fancy bumping into you here. Though I suppose it's not so odd, given that we're both Old Gregorians.'

'That's enough, Rupert,' says Geraldine. 'Can't you see we're interrupting your friend's prayers?'

'Oh, I'm done,' says Larry. 'If prayers can ever be said to be done.'

'Do you make a habit of this?' says Rupert, gesturing round the chapel.

'Not at all,' says Larry. 'I've not been in here for years.'

'Me neither,' says Rupert. 'It's hideous, isn't it? Of course I know it's not finished. But it seems all wrong to me, building a cathedral out of red brick.'

'And all stripy, like a cake,' says Larry.

Geraldine smiles at that.

'To be fair, I think it's supposed to be Byzantine,' says Rupert. 'Do you approve of it, as an artist?'

'Oh, are you an artist?' says Geraldine, opening her eyes wide.

'I was,' says Larry. 'Not any more.'

Rupert is surprised to hear this.

'I'd got the idea you were pretty set on it.'

'You know how it goes,' says Larry. 'Time goes by. You move on.'

'So what line are you in now?' says Rupert.

'Just looking about,' says Larry.

'Nothing fixed?'

'Not as yet.'

They walk out of the chapel and across the nave to the exit. The light beyond the doors is a bright pearl-grey.

'Guess where I'm off to,' says Rupert. 'India.'

'Oh?' says Larry politely, not interested.

'I'm back with Dickie Mountbatten. He's been given the viceroy job. He's being sent out there to wind up the Empire.'

'At least it'll get you away from this winter,' says Larry.

'You know Dickie thinks the world of you,' says Rupert. 'Ever since you volunteered for the Dieppe show.'

'Not very bright of me, as it turned out.'

'Look here, Larry. Why don't you come with us?'

He's come to a standstill in the narthex. The cold air from the outer doors ruffles their coats. He's looking at Larry as if he's serious.

'To India?'

'Yes. Dickie's been told he can hire all the staff he likes. Alan Campbell-Johnson's coming, and Ronnie Brockman, and George Nicholls. There'll be a lot of the old crowd there.'

'But why would he want me? What would I do?'

343

'Oh, it's going to be a devil of a posting, don't you worry about that. More work than any of us can handle. The great thing is, Dickie says, to surround yourself with good men. And you know what, Larry? We'll see history in the making. It may not be what you call glorious, but it'll be unforgettable.'

The proposal is so far-fetched that Larry wants to laugh. But at the same time the prospect Rupert conjures up fills him with excitement. To go far away, to a new world, with new concerns. To learn fast and work hard and forget the past. To leave behind in the endless winter that is England the fool who thought he was an artist, and thought he was loved by Nell. To start again, and be someone new.

'Do you really think Dickie would have me?'

'Yes, I do. It's chaos, to be honest, the whole shooting match. We're scheduled to go east in a month, and they're still arguing over the timetable for independence, or even if it's to be called independence. Winston and the Tories won't hear of anything with that name, and of course the nationalist leaders out there won't accept anything less.'

'I'm getting cold, Rupert,' says Geraldine.

'Yes, right, we're on our way.' To Larry, 'Do you want me to put in a word?'

'How long would it be for?'

'Six months minimum. Current target is to get us out by June next year.'

'Sounds like it would be quite an experience.'

'Good for you. Let me have your number, and stand by for a call.'

They exchange phone numbers, and Rupert and Geraldine hurry out into the street. Larry lingers for a little while in the big dark church, so that he can say thank you. It seems to him his prayer has been answered.

Two days later Larry presents himself in his only good suit at Brook House on Park Lane, the mansion that became Mountbatten's London base on his marriage to the heiress Edwina Ashley. Rupert Blundell is waiting for him in the immense lobby.

'Looking good,' he says. 'He's got someone with him, but he says you're to hang on.'

He leads Larry up the wide curving staircase to a first-floor reception room.

'Do you mind if I abandon you? We've got a sort of staff pow-wow coming up. The old man knows you're here.'

'No, no. Off you go.'

Left to himself, Larry feels out of place in the grandeur and the aura of power of his surroundings. He goes to the wide window and stands gazing out at the bare trees and grey snow of Hyde Park. He tries to imagine India, a muddle of images from Kipling's stories and models of the Taj Mahal and newsreels of Gandhi in his loincloth. Strange to think that this little frozen island should govern a faraway continent where the hot sun is, presumably, shining even now.

Rapid footsteps outside and in bursts Mountbatten, bringing with him a wave of energy and goodwill.

'Cornford!' he cries. 'This is marvellous news! Will you join us?'

345

'If you'll have me, sir.'

'I need all the good men I can find. It's going to be what they call a challenge.'

He sits Larry down before him and pins him with his handsome boyish gaze.

'Probably best to get you back into uniform,' he says. 'They go for that sort of thing out there. What rank did you end on?'

'Captain, sir.'

'Pity it has to be army. There, the terrible snobbery of a navy man. You'll just have to forgive me.'

He runs through the team he's assembling, and the nature of the challenges they face, speaking briskly, even bluntly.

'Our job is to get us out without it looking like a scuttle, and without leaving too unholy a mess behind. Not a pretty job, when you look at it in the cold light of day. Not a job I wanted at all, to be honest. But one does one's duty. And I think both Edwina and I need to get out of London.'

At this point Lady Mountbatten herself looks into the room.

'Just on my way out, darling,' she says.

Mountbatten introduces Larry.

'His grandfather was the banana king,' he says. 'Larry was in Combined Ops with me.'

Edwina Mountbatten gives Larry a sharp appraising look, and a quick smile.

'That was a shambles, as far as I can tell.'

She goes again.

'The most remarkable woman in the world,' says

346

Mountbatten. 'I'll tell you what. Let me show you something.'

He strides out of the room and up the stairs. Larry hurries to keep up.

'My wife knows all I've ever really wanted is to be at sea. I worship the navy. You can keep all this viceroy nonsense. Just give me command of a capital ship and I'm a happy man.'

He leads Larry through a door into a suite at the back of the fourth floor. The walls and ceilings are white enamel, criss-crossed by pipes and cables. At one end is a ship's bunk, with a brass rail. On one side there are three portholes. The entire illusion is that they have entered the captain's cabin on a man-of-war.

Mountbatten looks happily at Larry's amazed face.

'Edwina had this made for me.'

On one side there stands a dressmaker's dummy wearing an admiral's uniform, complete with decorations.

'My father's uniform,' says Mountbatten. 'Prince Louis, who your grandfather wrote to *The Times* about. So you see, I don't forget.'

As they descend the stairs again he says, 'Speaking of not forgetting, and of what my wife calls a shambles, I've not forgotten Dieppe. I don't expect you have, either.'

'I'll never forget that day, sir.'

'Nor I. We did all we could, but I shall always have it on my conscience. What's done is done. All any of us can do is try to do better next time.'

At the bottom of the stairs an anxious group of staff members wait for him.

347

'Oh, Lord,' says Mountbatten. 'Is it time already?'

He turns and shakes Larry's hand.

'Welcome aboard,' he says. And with that he strides away, followed by his staff.

In the short period between his interview with Mountbatten and his departure for India, Larry sees no one. He writes his father a short letter to say he's leaving, implying that his trip to India is a chance opportunity too good to be missed. He says nothing about his abandoned ambition to be an artist. His father's support and generosity are now a reproach to him. He writes a second short letter, similarly reticent, to Ed and Kitty. He has heard nothing from Nell. He presumes that by now she's been alerted by Tony Armitage, and is keeping out of his way. He makes no attempt to contact her.

25

'It's like being back in the bloody Oflag,' says Ed, staring out at the falling snow. 'This winter's gone on longer than the bloody war.'

Kitty, still in bed, does not reply. She doesn't want to get up because the bedroom is so cold. She doesn't reply because she knows there's no point. These days Ed is always in a foul mood until he's got some breakfast inside him. Until he's got a drink or two inside him, to be precise.

Pamela comes in and scampers across the cold floor to jump into bed beside her mother.

'You're frozen!' exclaims Kitty, hugging her close.

'Snowing again,' says Pamela. 'Let's stay in bed.'

'See you downstairs,' says Ed, and off he goes.

Kitty lies in bed with her child in her arms, struggling with feelings of hurt and anger. At night in bed he can be so loving, but each day, when morning comes, it's as if she loses him all over again. Why must life be so hard for him? Can't he at least greet his own daughter? Why does he say it's like being in the prisoner-of-war camp when he's got her and Pammy with him? The winter has been endless, but it's the same for all of them. He behaves as if he's been specially singled out by fate.

By the time she and Pamela are downstairs he's outside, fetching in firewood from the stack by the gun room. There's no need for him to do this, old John Hunter is kept on for jobs like this, or one of the outside men can do it. But Ed needs reasons to be up and out. He needs reasons to be away.

This is what hurts Kitty most. Yes, this is a hard time, but it's also a time when they're together. This could be such a precious time. And the worst of it is, it feels like it must be her fault. She's not making him happy.

'What are we going to do today, Mummy?' says Pamela.

'I don't know, darling. Shall we do some more reading?'

'I hate reading.'

She's not yet four years old, there's no hurry. And you can't really call it lessons. All Kitty has been doing is reading her *The Tale of Tom Kitten*, following the words on the page with her finger. And however much Pamela pretends not to like it, she has clearly been listening. The other day Kitty heard her say to Mrs Lott the cook, 'I am affronted,' just like Mrs Tabitha Twitchit in the book.

Pamela is an outdoors creature, like her father. But outdoors has become such hard work. So many clothes to put on, and just walking to the lake is such a labour in the snow, and the lake itself is frozen over and dangerous. Pamela wants to go on it because it looks just like the rest of the park now, all flat and smooth and white. She refuses to believe there's ice under the snow, and water under the ice, and she might fall through and freeze and drown. Or maybe she does believe it but still wants to go on the ice, because she sees how it frightens and angers her mother. Why is she like that?

Louisa comes down, blinking and yawning.

'Why is Ed doing the logs?' she says. 'That's John Hunter's job.'

'I've no idea,' says Kitty. 'I suppose he just wants to keep busy.'

'George has decided to rearrange all the books in the library,' says Louisa. 'Maybe Ed could help him with that.'

'Daddy hates reading,' says Pamela.

'That's nonsense, darling,' says Kitty.

'I wouldn't say George exactly *reads* his books,' says Louisa. 'But he loves collecting them. And he loves rearranging them.'

Later Ed takes Pamela out into the park and they draw patterns in the snow with sticks, and the falling snow obliterates them, along with the prints of their footsteps.

At lunch Ed calls for beer.

'A good bracing bitter,' he says.

Mr Lott taps the barrel in the cellar. Ed drinks all of a pint tankard and calls for more, and then retreats to the billiard room.

'I wish he wouldn't drink so much,' says Kitty. 'Can't you tell Lott not to serve him?'

'Awkward,' says George. 'One doesn't want to appear to be telling a fellow how to live his life.'

'You have to do it, Kitty,' says Louisa.

The problem is that Ed's drinking is in its way quite controlled. He never becomes loud and abusive. He just becomes more remote. By the end of the evening, when he's moved on to Scotch, it's as if he isn't there at all. He goes about slowly, and looks without seeing. At such times Kitty is possessed by a frightening rage that makes her want to hit him, and hurt him, so that he cries out in pain. Anything to make him see her.

Pamela has gone out with Betsy the scullery maid to search for eggs. The hens have taken to laying in odd places, in the storerooms and the workshop, which being close to the boilers share some of their heat. Pamela likes Betsy and always does whatever Betsy tells her, which puzzled Kitty until she asked about it.

'Why are you so good with Betsy?'

'Because I don't have to be,' said Pamela.

Sometimes she frightens Kitty, she seems so grown-up. How can a four-year-old be so self-possessed?

Kitty goes to the billiard room to talk to Ed. The room is unheated, with a handsome west-facing window opposite the great but empty fireplace, and dormer windows in the high beamed roof. Ed is leaning over the billiard table, his cue reached out to attempt a tricky shot. A half-empty glass of Scotch stands on the shelf beside the scoreboard.

'You should have a fire if you're going to be in here,' Kitty says.

'Waste of fuel,' says Ed, not turning to look at her.

He takes his shot and misses.

'Damn.'

She watches him shamble round the billiard table, eyes on the balls, and realises he's already very drunk.

'I wish you wouldn't, Ed,' she says softly.

'Wouldn't what?'

'Drink so much.'

'No harm in it,' he says. 'Keeps me quiet.'

'I don't want you to be quiet,' she says. 'Not like this.'

'Well, I'm very sorry to hear that,' he says, speaking slowly and heavily. 'But there's not much I can do about it.'

He lines up his next shot.

'Of course there is.' She can feel herself digging her fingernails into the palms of her hands. 'You could if you tried.'

'Ah, if I tried. Yes, I could do anything if I tried.'

This is what maddens her when he's drunk. This slow hazy way he has of not taking anything in.

'Please, Eddy.' She's aware her voice has risen. 'For me.'

He takes his shot. The billiard balls crack sharply in the chill air.

'Please will you do it for me,' she says again.

He straightens himself up and turns to look at her.

'I'd do anything for you,' he says. 'What is it I'm to do?'

'I just want you not to drink so much.'

'Right, then,' he says. 'That's easy. I won't drink so much. What else?'

'That's all.'

'You wouldn't like me to be a better husband? A better father? A better human being?'

'No—'

But something has come over him that she's never seen before: a darkness contorts his face, and all at once he's raising his voice, speaking sharply.

'I am what I am, Kitty. I can't change. It's no good. I always knew it would be no good.'

'But Ed, what are you talking about? What's no good?'

'I can't be what you want me to be. I can't do it.'

He's shaking, almost shouting, but not at her. She watches him in terror. He's acting as if some invisible force is binding him, and he's fighting to set himself free.

'I don't want you to be anything,' she says. 'Truly, truly.'

She tries to touch him, to soothe him, but he throws her off with a violent gesture that shocks her.

'No! Get off! Get away from me!'

'Eddy! Please!'

She feels the tears rising to her eyes. But the worst of it is, she still feels angry with him. Why is he behaving like this? Why has it somehow become her fault?

He picks up his half-full glass of Scotch and drinks it, gulping it down. Then he holds out the empty glass for her to see.

'You want to know why I drink too much? Because it's better for you if I'm drunk.'

'No!' she says. 'No! It isn't better for me!'

Suddenly her anger comes flooding out.

'I hate the way you tell me you're doing it for me. You're not doing it for me. You're doing it for yourself. You're doing it to run away. That's just taking the coward's way out. You've no right to do that. Why should you run away and leave the rest of us to clean up the mess? It's not fair. It's not right. We're all worn out by this vile winter, it's not just you. Stop being so sorry for yourself, for God's sake! Make a bit of an effort for once, can't you?'

He stares at her in silence. Kitty feels the anger drain away.

'Please,' she says in a gentler voice.

'Right,' he says. 'You know what I need? I need some fresh air.'

With that, he walks briskly out of the room.

Kitty sits down in the armchair in the corner and wraps her arms round her body and shakes. This is where Pamela finds her.

'Look,' she says, holding out her basket. 'Four eggs.' Then aware of the masculine nature of the room, 'Where's Daddy?'

'He's gone out.'

'But it's still snowing.'

'I don't think Daddy minds the snow.'

Ed returns later, and makes himself busy building a fire in the big drawing room, one of the rooms that has been closed off to save heat. He says nothing to Kitty about their argument. He comes and goes with the manner of one who has too many tasks to do to stop and talk. Kitty feels sick and miserable and doesn't know what to do.

Louisa comes to her as she sits by the fire in the Oak Room.

'What on earth is Ed up to?' she says. 'He's pushing the furniture about in the drawing room.'

'I've no idea,' says Kitty. 'We had a bit of a row earlier.'

'Oh, I'm always having rows with George,' says Louisa. 'You're allowed to have rows when you're married.'

'I don't like it,' says Kitty. 'It frightens me.'

Then Ed himself appears.

'I've got something to show you,' he says to Kitty.

She follows him across the hall and through the ante-room to the drawing room. Here a cheerful fire is blazing, and there are candles glowing on all the side tables, throwing their soft light onto the red damask walls. He has moved the sofas and chairs to one end, and rolled up the carpet. A gramophone stands ready on the table by the door.

'What's this, Ed?' says Kitty, looking round. The shutters are open on the tall windows, and outside the white light of afternoon makes a strange contrast with the amber light of the fire and the candles within.

'Our ballroom,' says Ed.

He pulls the lever on the gramophone that starts the turntable spinning, and lowers the arm with the needle onto the disc. The sound of a dance band fills the room.

'Would you care to dance?' he says, holding out his hand.

Kitty takes his hand, and he draws her into his arms. The high clear voice of the singer begins, and Ed and Kitty dance together, holding each other close.

If I didn't care
More than words can say
If I didn't care
Would I feel this way?

They dance in a slow wide circle over the bared floor, from the windows to the fire. Kitty rests her head on his shoulder and feels his breath on her cheek and wants to cry.

If this isn't love
Then why do I thrill?
And what makes my head go round and
round
While my heart stands still?

He lowers his head to hers and they kiss as they dance. When she looks up again she sees Louisa standing smiling in the doorway, with Pamela beside her.

If I didn't care
Would it be the same?
Would my every prayer
Begin and end with just your name?
And would I be sure
That this is love beyond compare?
Would all this be true
If I didn't care
For you?

When the song finishes they come to a stop and stand by the fire in each other's arms.

'My Ink Spots record,' says Louisa. 'I love that.'

'Why are you dancing?' says Pamela.

'Because Daddy wanted to,' says Kitty.

'I want to dance,' says Pamela.

So Ed puts the song on again and dances with Pamela while Kitty and Louisa watch. The little girl frowns with concentration as they dance, trying to make sure she moves in time. Ed dances with his daughter, one arm on her shoulder, one hand holding her hand, looking down to make sure he's not treading on her toes, handling her with grave gentleness. Kitty feels almost more full of love watching him dance with Pamela than when she was in his arms herself. He has said nothing about their row, and nothing needs to be said.

The heaviest snowfall of that long hard winter comes near the end, on the first Tuesday of March. The blizzard rages all that day and night, and into Wednesday. Once again the men of the village set out with their tractors and shovels to clear the roads, grumbling to each other that the bad weather will never end. But as the next week begins, suddenly the thaw sets in. The air turns mild, and the snow that has lain so stubbornly for so long over the land starts at last to melt.

Ed travels up to London as soon as the trains are able to run again after the blizzard. There is still snow on the Downs as he leaves. Then comes several days of heavy rain, and the last of the snow disappears, leaving the land grey and waterlogged.

The postman returns to his rounds, bringing a letter from Larry.

I've accepted a place on Mountbatten's staff and am off to India! By the time you get this I'll be gone. I'm not at all sure what I'm to do, but it feels like a good time to be out of England. I'll write and tell you all about it when I'm settled in. I hope you've all survived this foul winter and when we meet again there'll be sun over Sussex.

PART THREE
INDEPENDENCE

1947–48

26

Two York aircraft carry the viceroy-designate and his team to India. The second plane containing chief-of-staff Lord Ismay and most of the new appointments, including Larry Cornford, takes a slower route, stopping overnight at Malta, Fayid and Karachi. On the way Ismay and Eric Miéville, the chief diplomat on the mission, speak openly of the difficulties ahead.

'Dickie doesn't want to go,' Pug Ismay says. 'The Indians don't want him. And we'll probably all get shot.' Then seeing that this isn't going down so well, he adds, 'Don't worry. Dickie's one of those chaps who was born with luck on his side. I like working for lucky men.'

The three-day journey to Karachi leaves them exhausted.

'Beginning to wish you hadn't come?' says Rupert Blundell to Larry as they emerge into the heat of RAF Mauripur.

'Not at all,' says Larry. 'I'm excited.'

Alan Campbell-Johnson, the press attaché, overhears him.

'This is my seventh flight between England and India,' he says. 'Believe me, the thrill wears off.'

They bunk for the night in the club house on the airfield, Larry doubling with Rupert. The ceiling fan makes little impact on the humid night air. They lie on top of the sheets, stripped to their underpants, sweating, unable to sleep.

'Apparently one adjusts,' says Rupert.

'God, I hope so,' says Larry.

'I fixed up for my sister to come out and join us. I'm beginning to think that was a mistake.'

'When's she due to come?'

'Three weeks' time. There's a flight laid on for family members.'

Larry is cheered by this news. He likes the idea of meeting Rupert's sister again.

'Is she coming on the staff?'

'No, no. More of a jolly, really. But I'm sure she'll be given something to do.' He drops his voice in the darkness. 'Between you and me, she's been let down rather badly by a chap. Bit of a case of broken heart and so on. Nothing like a change of scene.'

'There's been a bit of that for me too,' says Larry.

'Sorry to hear it. Rather goes with the human condition, I fear.'

'Except for you, Rupert. I refuse to believe you've ever done anything as worldly as allow your heart to be broken.'

'You think I'm too high-minded for love?' says Rupert.

Larry realises how foolish this sounds.

'No,' he says. 'Of course not. It's just that you've always

struck me as being' – he reaches for the right word – 'self-contained.'

'Yes,' says Rupert. 'I accept that. I've become selfish, I suppose. I value what I choose to call my freedom.' Then, after a slight pause, 'There was a moment, once. Right at the end of the war. But it didn't work out.'

He falls silent. Larry doesn't press him. He's learning to respect this awkward subtle man, who is so easy to mock, and yet who, for all his absurdity, seems to remain untouched by the world.

'What happened to your friend Ed Avenell? The one who got the VC.'

'He's married. Working in the wine trade.'

'I think of him from time to time. I remember him from school, of course. I bet he's married a pretty girl.'

'Very pretty.'

'I suppose I think of him because he's the opposite of me in every way. Good-looking, confident, gets the girls. I'd give a lot to have his life for just one day.'

'Ed's got his troubles too.'

After that they fall silent, lying in the hot darkness, listening to the clicking of the fan overhead.

The next day the party boards the York for the final leg of the journey, over the deserts of Sindh and Rajputana to Delhi.

'When you see how much of the world is desert,' says Alan Campbell-Johnson, 'it makes you appreciate our green little island a bit more.'

They land at Palam airfield on schedule. The heat and

glare on coming out of the plane hit Larry like a blow, punishing his travel-weary body. A convoy of viceregal cars waits on the runway to drive them into the city. He follows the others across the cracking tarmac, breathing air that smells of petrol and burns his throat.

The drive into Delhi carries them in a short half hour across a desert, through a teeming shanty-town, and into the ghostly grandeur of imperial New Delhi. Alan Campbell-Johnson is watching Larry's face as their destination comes into view at the end of Kingsway, the broad ceremonial avenue that links India Gate to the Viceroy's House. Larry is duly astounded. The official home of the ruler of India is absurdly immense, a long, columned façade topped by a giant dome, with a flagpole from which the Union flag is flying. The flight of steps leading up to the main entrance is so wide that the sentries standing on either side look like toy soldiers.

'My God!' Larry exclaims.

'It's the biggest residence of any chief of state in the world,' says Alan. 'The house has three hundred and forty rooms. There are more than seven thousand people on the state payroll.'

'*Sic transit gloria mundi*,' says Rupert.

'When I was here before, in '43,' says Alan, 'we had all the high command of Congress locked up in prison. Now we're about to hand over the country to them.'

The cars pull up, and the new arrivals are escorted up the giant steps and into the cool of the building. The outgoing viceroy, Lord Wavell, is there to greet them, along with his staff. Mountbatten himself is due to arrive later in the afternoon. Everyone seems to be greeting everyone else as old friends. Larry feels both worn out and exhilarated.

As he stands gazing round the great entrance hall he is approached by a young Indian in the uniform of a naval officer. He holds a typed list of names.

'Captain Cornford?'

'Yes, that's me.'

Lieutenant Syed Tarkhan is himself a recent appointment to the incoming viceroy's staff. He has a handsome intelligent face, and the slightly stiff bearing of a well-trained navy man.

'We've all been asked to muck in,' he says. 'Show the new team around. Viceroy's House is quite a maze.'

He offers to guide Larry to his allocated room so that he can wash and rest after his journey. As they go down the long corridors Larry tells him of his time under Mountbatten at Combined Operations, and Tarkhan tells of his time under Mountbatten when he was in charge of South East Asia Command.

'He's a great man,' says Tarkhan. 'But I'm afraid that's not how he's seen here. They think he's a playboy who knows nothing about India, and is bringing in a staff who know nothing about India.'

'Some truth in that,' says Larry. 'Not the playboy bit. But I know nothing about India.'

'If I may tell you the truth, Captain,' says Tarkhan, 'the less you know the better. India will make you weep.'

367

They come to a stop outside a door. Tarkhan checks the number on the door against the list in his hand.

'You're to bunk here,' he says. 'If you need anything just shout for your *khidmutgar*, your servant.'

'I'm to have a servant? I thought I was the servant.'

'We all serve,' says Tarkhan with a smile, 'and we are all served. I'm afraid there's no air cooling in this wing. Your luggage will arrive shortly. Do you think you can find your way back? The new viceroy is due to arrive at three forty-five p.m.'

With that, Larry is left alone in his new quarters. The room is small, high-ceilinged, with a recessed window. The shutters are closed, leaving the room in semi-darkness. He goes to the window and opens the shutters onto blinding light, and a wave of heat. Outside across a broad empty courtyard are more grand buildings, or perhaps a further wing of this same unending house. A servant in a turban is slowly sweeping the courtyard with a broom of sticks, making a mournful scritch-scritch sound. A heavy early afternoon stillness hangs over the scene. Larry feels briefly dizzy. He lies down on the narrow bed to rest.

What am I doing here? He thinks. And back comes the answer, I'm here to start again. I'm here to become someone else.

He oversleeps. When his *khidmutgar* wakes him it's past five.

'Why didn't you wake me before?'

'You did not so order me, Captain Sahib.'

He splashes water onto his face, brushes his hair,

straightens the uniform that he has slept in, and hurries back through the great house. There seem to be more turns in the corridors than he remembers, and no clear indication of which way to go. All he can think to do is keep walking until he finds someone to ask.

He's hurrying down a broader corridor than the others when a door opens and a voice says, 'Could you help?'

It's Lady Mountbatten, thin, elegant, careworn.

'It's my little dog,' she says. 'He's done his business on the floor here, and my *khidmutgar* says he won't touch it. I don't want to step on it myself. So I wonder if you could hunt me out a servant of low enough caste to deal with it?'

Larry can't help smiling, and seeing him smile Lady Mountbatten smiles too.

'Yes, I know,' she says. 'It's all too ridiculous for words.'

'Why don't I deal with it,' says Larry.

He takes some lavatory paper from the viceregal bathroom and picks up the dog mess and flushes it away.

'Now you bad boy,' says Lady Mountbatten to her little Sealyham. 'You are so kind,' she says to Larry. 'Who are you?'

Larry introduces himself.

'Oh, yes. Dickie did tell me. Something about bananas.'

'Is there anything else I can do, your ladyship?'

'You can get me out of here. I can't bear this house. It's a mausoleum. I feel like a corpse. Don't you? I know it's supposed to be Lutyens's masterpiece, but I can't imagine what he thought he was doing, putting up such a monstrosity.'

'Intimidating the natives, I think,' says Larry.

Lady Mountbatten gives Larry a sharp look of surprise. 'Just so,' she says.

The next two days are taken up with organising the swearing-in ceremony of the new viceroy. Alan Campbell-Johnson has discovered that the press were badly handled at the airfield when the Mountbattens arrived, and are making complaints. The Sunday edition of *Dawn* shows a photograph of Ronnie Brockman and Elizabeth Ward described as 'Lord and Lady Louis arriving'. Campbell-Johnson asks for an extra pair of hands in the press room, and is given Larry. He takes him into the Durbar Hall. A high platform is being built in the dome.

'The idea is we put the newsreel boys and the cameramen up there,' says Alan. 'There's going to be twenty-two of them. I want you to get them up there, and then down again.'

'Is it safe?' says Larry, gazing up.

'God knows,' says Alan. 'It's Dickie's idea. They won't like it, I can tell you now.'

Larry is kept too busy in Viceroy's House to venture into the old city, but reports come through of a riot in the main shopping street of Chandni Chowk. Apparently a meeting of Muslims at the great mosque of Jama Masjid has been attacked by lorry-loads of Sikhs brandishing kirpans, and several people are dead. Syed Tarkhan tells Larry over a hurried lunch, 'You see, this is why we must have Pakistan. We must have a homeland.'

When the time for the ceremony arrives, Larry shepherds his flock of cameramen. They grumble openly about being made to go on the high platform, but once up there they realise the advantage of the viewpoint. Larry takes up a place on the platform also. The hall below fills with Indian princes arrayed in jewelled robes, and English gentlemen in tailcoats, and politicians of the Hindu nationalist Congress party proudly wearing homespun kurtas, in the tradition of Gandhi. Two red and gold thrones stand beneath the scarlet-draped canopy, illuminated by concealed lights.

'It's like a bloody movie set!' exclaims an American newsreel cameraman.

The ceremony begins with a startlingly loud fanfare from trumpeters placed in the roof. Then the ADCs in their dress uniforms come stalking slowly down the centre aisle, between the crush of dignitaries. After them, side by side, come Lord and Lady Mountbatten, both in white. Mountbatten wears a mass of medals and decorations, a ceremonial sword at his side. Lady Mountbatten wears an ivory brocade dress of inspired simplicity, and long white gloves above the elbow, and a dark blue sash. The cameramen go crazy, popping their flashbulbs at the grandeur of the moment. Larry, looking on, is more struck by how plainly Lady Mountbatten presents herself. No tiara, no necklace, just the grave dignity of her slender figure.

The Lord Chief Justice of India, Sir Patrick Spens, administers the oath of office. The new viceroy then makes a short address. Up on the platform Larry is unable to hear his words; and he sees from their postures that the politicians below are straining to hear. Later, when the short ceremony is over, Alan thrusts a number of stencilled copies into Larry's hands, saying, 'Make sure they all get this. No one heard a bloody word.'

It turns out Mountbatten has asked India to help him in the difficult task ahead. This seems natural enough to Larry, but from the reaction of the press it's unprecedented. Eric Britter of *The Times* says it's as good as admitting the British have made mistakes in India, and if so, it'll win Mountbatten a lot of friends.

Rupert Blundell and Larry escape the marbled halls of Viceroy's House that afternoon, and Larry gets his first taste of the real India. They drive into old Delhi, which is now under curfew following the riot. There are no signs of the recent violence. The alleyways and bazaars are bursting with life and noise and colour. Everywhere Larry looks he sees, with his painter's eye, thrilling and jarring juxtapositions of scarlets and ambers and deep greens. The air smells rich with perfume and tobacco, dung and sweat. On foot now, moving through the bazaar, the crowd surges past them on either side, parting before them without touching them. Larry remembers Lady Mountbatten saying, 'I feel like a corpse.' It seems to him then that his people, the British, are dead, and only the Indian people are alive.

'What are we doing here?' he says to Rupert. 'I mean here, ruling India.'

'Not for much longer,' says Rupert.

'This isn't our country. This is another world.'

'Does it frighten you?'

'Frighten me?' Larry hasn't thought of it this way, but now that Rupert says it he realises it's true. 'Yes, in a way.'

'We English set such a high value on moderation. It strikes me that India is not moderate.'

An ox-cart passes, its driver shouting at the crowds in his way. Several voices shout back, hands raised in the air. The cart is piled high with manure and clouded with flies. There are children everywhere, their big solemn eyes tracking the Englishmen as they go by.

'The sooner we get out the better,' says Larry.

'If only it were as simple as that,' says Rupert. 'I'm part of the policy planning group. Our options are very limited. You could say the pot is boiling, and we're the lid.'

Over the next week the leaders of India take their turns in talks with Mountbatten. Larry, officially appointed assistant press attaché, is initiated into the complexities of the independence process. Syed Tarkhan shows him on the map of India how the Muslims are concentrated in what is called the 'ears of the elephant', Punjab in the north-west and Bengal in the north-east.

'This will be Pakistan,' he says. 'Jinnah will accept nothing less. There must be partition. We Muslims cannot live in a Hindu-controlled nation.'

'But you've lived in a British-controlled nation.'

'That is different.'

The difficulty with partition is that the 'ears' are not exclusively Muslim, and the rest of the elephant far from exclusively Hindu. What is to happen to the many who will find themselves in a fearful minority? Syed Tarkhan shakes his head over this.

'Nothing good,' he says.

'What does Gandhi say?' Larry asks.

'Ah, Gandhi. He of course wants a united India.'

'I've always had the idea that Gandhi is one of the few men alive who truly believes in the power of goodness.'

'The power of goodness?' says Tarkhan, raising his eyebrows. 'The mahatma is a very holy man. But whether goodness will prove to be powerful enough in the end, who is to say?'

Larry gets his own chance to see the mahatma when he makes a call at last on the new viceroy. A large gathering of newspapermen assembles to report on the meeting. Larry is on duty with Alan to attempt to control the story.

'You have to remember,' Alan tells Larry, 'that although Gandhi is the father of the nation and so forth, he's a Hindu, not a Muslim. So Jinnah and his lot are naturally suspicious of us getting too close to him.'

The press gather in the Mughal Gardens outside Mountbatten's study, where the meeting takes place. While they wait the *Times* man tells Larry, 'This little old fellow's the only one that can stop the violence. They listen to him.'

When at last the French windows open, and Gandhi comes out with Mountbatten to face the photographers, Larry is unexpectedly moved by the sight. Gandhi is so small and frail, with his bare legs and bald brown head and white khaddar robe and little round glasses. It seems inconceivable that such a tiny figure can have held the mighty British

Empire to ransom, without the backing of an army, without the threat of violence, solely through the moral force of his character.

It's plain that he doesn't enjoy being photographed, but he puts up with it with smiling good grace. Lady Mountbatten joins them, and more photographs are taken. Then as they turn to go back into the house, Gandhi rests one hand on Lady Mountbatten's shoulder for support. Max Desfor, the AP man, still has his camera out, and at once he takes a shot.

'That's the one,' he says.

After Gandhi has departed, Mountbatten calls Alan and Larry into the staff meeting to discuss the communiqué that is to be issued to the press. This turns out to be far from straightforward. Gandhi has proposed a radical solution to avoid partition, with all of the bloodshed that it's feared will follow.

'He proposes,' says Mountbatten, reading from the notes he dictated after the meeting, 'that the Congress cabinet be dismissed, and Jinnah invited to form an all-Muslim administration.'

This causes consternation in the room.

'Out of the question,' says Miéville. 'Nehru won't stand for it.'

'His reasoning is,' says Mountbatten, 'that with a Muslim leadership of a united India, the Muslims need not fear Hindu persecution. The alternative, he believes, that is to say, partition, will lead to a bloodbath.'

'He's senile,' says George Abell.

'It's a trick,' says Syed Tarkhan. 'It's a trap to catch Jinnah out.'

'Oh, I think he's sincere,' says Mountbatten. 'But I'm not sure he's realistic.'

'He tried this on Wavell before,' says Miéville. 'He tried it on Willingdon. It's the only shot he's got in his locker. Claim the moral high ground through self-sacrifice. That sort of stunt works on us British because we know we don't belong here. But just you try it on the Hindus.'

A communiqué of sorts is fudged for the press that leaves all options open. Mountbatten sighs and rubs his forehead.

'I'm beginning to think this is one of those cock-ups where there just isn't a way out,' he says.

After dinner Larry finds himself beside Lady Mountbatten. She has been friendly to him ever since the episode of the dog mess.

'What do you make of Gandhi?' Larry asks her.

'I worship at his feet,' says Lady Mountbatten. 'The man is a saint. But the one who's going to save India is Nehru.'

Larry writes a letter to Kitty and Ed, wanting the chance to get his unruly crowd of new experiences into some sort of order.

I feel as if I've tumbled into a different world, where all the rules no longer function. Nothing is simple. Whatever we do leaving India we will be blamed and hated. There is no great act of statesmanship that will resolve the crisis. Poor Mountbatten just looks done in. We've already said we're quitting India. The only thing left seems to be to go, but then there will be civil war. Gandhi says we must go anyway and 'accept the bloodbath'. So in the midst of all this you can imagine how unimportant my personal cares appear. I didn't tell you before I left that Nell and I have parted. Also that I'm no longer thinking that my future lies in art. Today there has been a story in the paper of riots in Calcutta and Bombay. Stabbings, bombings, throwing of acid. A car ambushed and set alight, four passengers burned alive, screaming for mercy. How can I even consider my own troubles worth one second's attention in the face of such suffering? Ed will read this and say, Where is your loving God now? But you, Kitty, will back me up when I say that there is good in us as well as evil, and we must believe in its power, and work for its victory. Otherwise what are our lives for?

27

The letter is addressed to Edenfield Place, but by the time it arrives Kitty and Pamela are back at River Farm. Louisa walks over to bring Kitty the letter and they read it together, sitting in the April sunshine on the seat in the yard.

'Heavens!' says Louisa. 'What dramas!'

Kitty realises with a shock that the news of Larry's parting from Nell pleases her more than it should.

'I wasn't ever sure that girl was right for him,' she says.

'Of course she wasn't,' says Louisa. 'Larry's far too good for her.'

'Doesn't it seem odd to think of him all the way over there and us still here?'

Still here. Kitty doesn't say so, but nothing has got any easier. The long hard winter is over, and her life is back in its usual pattern. Her days pass making modest meals, tidying up the old house so that Mrs Willis can clean it, repairing Pamela's torn clothing, helping out at the village church, driving into the shops in Lewes, listening to the wireless, reading to Pamela, reading to herself. There always seems to be just a little more to do than there's time to do it, and yet she has the feeling that she does nothing at all. She envies Larry his Indian adventure.

Louisa has her own reasons for being dissatisfied with her life. She's been trying for a long time now to get pregnant.

'Did I tell you,' she says, 'I'm going to see a quack? Mummy's persuaded me to go. George has to see him too.'

'Well, I suppose there's no harm,' says Kitty.

'I expect he'll tell me to eat raw eggs and lay off the booze or something. Just so long as he doesn't tell me to rest. Nothing gets me quite so worked up as being told to rest.'

'Maybe you should go up to town for a few weeks,' says Kitty.

'I don't see how that would get me a baby,' says Louisa. 'Unless, of course . . .' She gives Kitty a wicked look, like the old Louisa. 'Remember the girls who used to stand outside the barracks at night shouting "Para Eleven"?'

'Oh, God!' says Kitty, giggling. 'I do miss the war.'

'All we wanted at the time was for it to be over.'

Kitty sighs as she remembers.

'All I wanted was my own house, and my own husband, and my own little baby. I used to daydream about making curtains, and baking bread, and waking up in a sunny bedroom in my very own little home.'

'I don't see why it all had to be so little,' says Louisa.

'I think I was playing at dolls' houses,' says Kitty. 'Now it's real, and I'm turning into my mother.'

She doesn't tell Louisa the worst of it, which is that some-times she sits in a chair for an hour or more, seized by a strange heavy torpor, doing nothing. She feels tired all the time these days. Her mind goes blank, and she can't think what she's meant to be doing. Then Pamela will appear, demanding to be fed or entertained, and so she'll stir herself; but even as she boils an egg, and toasts a slice of bread, she has this numb feeling that it's all pointless and going nowhere.

She can't share this with Louisa because Louisa believes having a baby will solve all her problems. She can't tell her that there are times when Pamela makes her want to scream. Of course she adores her daughter and would die for her if need be, but what's proving harder is the enterprise of living for her. It turns out a child is not enough. But not enough for what?

She wishes Larry were here. She could talk to Larry about all this. That's what's so good about people with faith, even if you don't share their faith. They know what you mean when you talk about meaning. They understand that there has to be some sort of greater purpose. She's never forgotten how he said to her, the very first time they met, 'Don't you want to do something noble and fine with your life?'

Sometimes, sitting doing nothing in the kitchen chair, Kitty thinks ahead to the time when Pamela will be grown-up, and will no longer need her. She asks herself, What will I do then?

I'll have Ed, of course.

Then her mind slides away from these thoughts, not liking

where they lead her, and her head fills with grey vapour like a cloud.

Hugo comes, more than is justified by the demands of the business. He sits with her, and plays with Pammy, and acts the part of the dear old family friend, except for the looks he gives her. She reprimands him, always in light, easy terms, as if he's an over-eager child.

'That's enough, Hugo. Stop it.'

Then when she's expecting him one day and he doesn't come, she finds she misses his attentions. That frightens her.

She has a dream. In her dream she's wearing a bathing costume and all the boys are looking at her. She feels youthful and desirable. She's on a beach, and the waves that come rolling in are frothing and churning on the shore. The ocean beyond is infinitely big. She starts to run, and runs over the sand and the pebbles towards the sea. She runs faster and faster, filled with gladness, because she knows she's going to hurl herself into those great crashing waves. The waves are going to embrace her and sweep her away.

She wakes before she reaches the water, but her heart is thundering, and her whole body is glowing. It's not a death dream at all, this isn't a desire to drown. It's a longing to use all of herself, to hold nothing back, to experience an overwhelming desire. And instead of the explosive urgency of her dream, all she feels in her waking life is fatigue.

'You know what I think we should do for Easter?' she tells Pamela. 'I think we should go and visit Grandma and Grandpa.'

Pamela thinks about this.

'I am affronted,' she says.

Kitty's parents always make a great fuss of Pamela, and there's nothing the little girl appreciates as much as attention. As for Kitty herself, she's aware that she doesn't visit her parents nearly as much as they'd like. Her mother has a way of getting on the wrong side of her, and so Kitty always ends up behaving badly, and being what her mother calls 'moody'. Still, they didn't visit at Christmas time, and tired and restless as she is, Kitty would rather go than stay.

'Hello, little stranger,' says Mrs Teale to Pamela. 'I expect you've entirely forgotten who I am.'

'You're Grandma,' says Pamela.

'Guess what I've got for the most beautiful little girl in the world?'

'A present,' says Pamela.

'I wonder whether you want it now, or whether you'd rather keep it for Easter Day?'

'Now,' says Pamela.

Kitty follows this exchange with helpless irritation. It's been a long slow journey and all she wants is a comfortable chair and a cup of tea. Why must her mother go in for this ludicrous arch teasing tone of voice, as if she and Pamela are engaged in some conspiracy?

The present is a small chocolate egg, wrapped in silver paper. Pamela unwraps it at once and puts it whole into her mouth.

'Who's a hungry girl?' says Mrs Teale.

'Say thank you, Pammy,' says Kitty.

'Thank you,' says the child, her mouth full.

Mrs Teale turns to her daughter.

'No handsome young husband, then?'

Kitty wants to scream. She's been in the house five minutes and already her mother has managed to enrage her.

'I told you, Mummy. Ed's in France.'

'Well, I don't know, darling. No one ever tells me anything. It would just be nice if he visited us once in a while. Michael was saying only the other day that he's never heard the story of how he got his Victoria Cross.'

'You know Ed doesn't like to talk about that.'

'I can't think why not. You'd think he'd be proud. Did I tell you Robert Reynolds has been made a canon of Wells? He still asks after you, you know?'

'I thought he was married.'

'Is he?' says Mrs Teale vaguely. 'Maybe he is. I can't keep up these days. We all thought Harold would marry the Stanley girl, but he says it's off, and there was never anything in it in the first place. I don't understand young people. It seems you can go about together and it all means nothing at all. Pamela is looking a bit peaky, isn't she? We'll do our best to feed her up and give her lots of good country air.'

'We live in the country too, Mummy.'

'Somehow I never think of Sussex as being the real country. I suppose because it's on the way to France.'

Kitty's father's return puts a stop to the stream of barbed prattle that issues from her mother's mouth. In his presence she becomes timid, clumsy, awkward. Michael Teale, by contrast, is all smiles and hugs.

'My two best girls!' he cries. 'My word, Pamela! You smell chocolatey enough to eat.' And turning to Kitty, 'Guess who's been filling my ear with your praises? Jonathan Saxon!'

'Dear Mr Saxon,' says Kitty. 'Is he still bossing the poor little choirboys about?'

'He asked me to ask you if you'd sing in the abbey on Sunday. You know he always says you were the best soprano he ever had.'

Kitty hasn't sung in public for years, and she was never properly trained. But this request pleases her more than she would have expected.

'Oh, I couldn't,' she says. 'I'm far too rusty.'

'Well, you tell Jonathan yourself. All I can say is, he seems dead set on it.'

When Mrs Teale hears of the proposal she manages to turn it around and make it a source of disappointment.

'Oh, do sing, darling. It's such a waste, the way you do nothing with your beautiful voice.'

'I've no intention of making a fool of myself in front of a full congregation,' says Kitty sharply.

'You could sing "Little Brown Jug",' says Pamela.

Mr Saxon calls round to make his request in person. Charmed by the sweet old gentleman's pink smiling face and flattered by his praise, Kitty agrees to sing, on condition that they can go through the piece at least once beforehand. He wants her to sing César Franck's *Panis Angelicus*.

Pamela's greatest pleasure on these visits is playing with the dolls her own mother played with when she was little. This notion, that her mother was a little girl once, both puzzles and fascinates her. She wants to know the names of every doll, and which ones were her mother's special favourites, and what they all did together. Then once told she repeats the pattern as faithfully as she can.

'Rosie, you're the birthday girl today. You can sit on the birthday chair. And Ethel, you're Rosie's best friend. Droopy, you can be by Rosie's feet. Oh, Rosie, I forgot your flower hat. You have to wear the flower hat on your birthday.'

Kitty watches her child's grave re-creation of her past with a smile. But along with the fond memories comes another more shadowed picture. She sees her daughter growing up and having a daughter of her own, and that little child playing the same game. And is this all? whispers a voice in her head. Are we never to leave the nursery?

Her father brings out the sherry before dinner, in Kitty's honour, and her mother drinks her entire glassful. It's clear from Michael Teale's frown that this is not what he wants, though having poured his wife the sherry it seems odd that she should not be supposed to drink it. However, he says nothing.

His smiles are all for his daughter.

'So have you had any trouble with these terrible floods?' he says.

'The river burst its banks,' says Kitty, 'but our house has never been in danger. I'm just so happy not to be freezing any more.'

'What a winter it's been! Here's Easter at last, the feast of the Resurrection, and I'm telling everyone the worst is over.'

'But Michael,' says Mrs Teale, 'winter will come round again.'

'Yes, yes,' he says, his eyes still on Kitty. 'So how's that famous husband of yours getting along?'

'He's in France,' says Kitty. 'He works so hard.'

'Jesus rises from the dead on Easter Day,' says Mrs Teale, her cheeks now a little flushed. 'And the year goes round, and then he's crucified all over again.'

'Be quiet!' says Mr Teale. 'You're a fool.'

Silence falls over the table. This is the first time Kitty has known her father reprimand her mother in the presence of others. It frightens her. She looks down at her plate. But her father resumes the conversation as if nothing has happened.

'I respect a man who works hard,' he says.

'It does mean he's away from home a great deal,' says Kitty, avoiding looking at her mother.

'We all have to make sacrifices,' says her father. 'When I was a young man I had a great dream. I was going to go round the world, working my passage on cargo ships. Then the war came along, of course, and that was that.'

Kitty has never heard of this dream before.

'Maybe you could go now,' she says.

'Impossible.' He beams at her, as if this impossibility somehow suits him. 'Here I am, nearly sixty years old. And there's your mother. No, I shall stick by the old abbey now, and be buried beside it. The abbey and I will crumble away together.'

She sees then, for the merest instant, a flicker of horror

in his eyes, not at the coming of death but at the losing of life; at the life he might have lived, and knows he never will.

Lying awake that night in the bed she slept in as a child, Kitty tells herself her life will be different, that it is already different. She will not grow old in a loveless angry marriage. And yet her mother could never have anticipated such a fate. How is it to be avoided? The years go by, and the shadows lengthen. For a while you live for your children, and then the children leave home, and what do you do then? Turn slowly sour, like undrunk milk.

On Easter Day, at the big mid-morning service, Kitty sings *Panis Angelicus*. The abbey is full. Her father stands robed and beaming at the altar behind her. Her mother sits with Pamela in the front pew before her. Old Mr Saxon plays the gently falling chords of the introduction on the big organ. And the melody rises up from within her like the sweet breath of life itself.

> *Panis Angelicus, fit panis hominum*
> *Dat panis coelicus figuris terminum . . .*

She has sung it many times in her younger years, and the words flow effortlessly. She has no nervousness before the congregation: she hardly sees them. She is surrendering herself to the music, her body an instrument beyond her own control. She hears the throbbing hum of the organ notes as if the same keys and pedals press the clear high song from her throat, and she need do nothing. As she sings she can hear herself make mistakes, but somehow even her wrong notes sound right. So, self-forgetting, she reaches out for the high note, and gets it and loses it, and comes stepping down the melody, singing with a purity and a whole-heartedness she has rediscovered from her youth.

Pamela watches and hears with her lips parted, enraptured. It's not only the voice that astonishes her this Easter morning, a voice she never knew her mother had. It's the shining eyes of all the others round her, eyes fixed in admiration on her mother. From this moment the child knows that this is what she wants for herself: to be the object of such looks of love.

There's no applause as Kitty finishes. This is a religious service. But a kind of collective sigh goes up from the pews. Afterwards there are many old friends and neighbours pressing forward with their congratulations, and Kitty smiles and thanks them for their kind words, and Pamela clings tight to one arm wherever she goes so that everyone knows it's her mother who is the star of Easter Day. But inside herself Kitty has gone far away, and wishes she could be alone, because something big has happened. She's found a place where she can give all of herself. She has entered the wave.

Then comes the reaction, a sudden exhaustion so powerful she can no longer stand, accompanied by a bad taste in her mouth. Her mother sees her stumble, and coming to her side, takes her away from the crowd.

'You're worn out, darling. Go and lie down. Pammy, you stay here with me. Just go, darling. I'll explain.'

Kitty throws her a grateful look and runs upstairs to her room. There she lies full length on the bed and hears the buzz of voices below and attempts to find again the extraordinary joy she felt while singing. She can do no more than catch a faint echo; and even that is slipping fast away from her.

For a while she rests, half-sleeping. Then, wanting not to lose the precious moment for ever, she gets up and goes to her old desk. She will write it down, in a letter. There's only one person to whom she can send such confused thoughts. She writes to Larry.

I do so envy you your great adventure. Here life goes on the same old way, and sometimes I find myself wondering how it will be in a few years' time, when Pamela no longer needs me. I expect I shall turn into one of those good women who do good works, and then you, who believe in goodness, can come and praise me. I shall be duly grateful, I assure you, but I can't promise that it will be enough. I may grow restless and bad-tempered, and what is far worse, disappointed. I don't think you'll praise me for that.

Today has turned out to be a special day. It's Easter Day, but that's not what's special. As my mother says, it comes round every year. What happened is this. When I was younger I used to sing in the choir, I sang the soprano solos, and the very same choirmaster is still here. He begged me to sing in the abbey and I did, and Larry, for three or four minutes I was what

389

Ed called me once, I was an angel in heaven. Actually I've no idea what it's like to be an angel or what heaven is like but I was let go – I don't know how else to write it – I escaped and got away and I was so happy. Is this what happens to you when you paint? You say you're not thinking of art any more, but how can that be? If it's the same for you with art as it is for me when I sing, at least as I sang today, then you can't give it up. It would be to give up the only time when you're fully alive. Do you feel that? How most of the time we're only half alive, or even half asleep? I've been so tired lately, I don't know why, it's not as if I have to do such hard work. I think people need something more than just food and shelter, they need a mission in life, and without a mission they go slower and slower until they can hardly move at all. I think Ed feels this most strongly of all of us, and that's why he drives himself so hard. I don't feel as if I want to drive myself, it's more that I want to jump, or fall, or fly away. I wish you had been here to hear me sing. You would have been so proud. I do miss you a lot. When things happen to me it's you I want to tell. Come home soon, please.

She folds the letter up and puts it in her suitcase to send when she gets home. Then as she straightens up again she feels a tightness in her chest, and a tingling of the skin of her breasts. All at once it comes to her.

I'm pregnant.

This simple immense fact drops into her mind like a key into a lock. Suddenly everything makes sense. The constant fatigue, the mild nausea, the metallic taste in her mouth.

I'm going to have another baby.

Of course there'll be doctors to visit, tests to endure, but she knows it beyond any possibility of a doubt. Her body is telling her. And as for all her questions about the future, they are already melting away. There is no future. She is to have another baby. With a baby there is only today, and today, and today.

28

The camp followers, as Pug Ismay calls them, arrive in the viceregal aeroplane in early May, just as the temperature in Delhi is rising to unbearable levels. A crowd of exhausted children come tumbling down the steps: three Brockman girls, a Nicholls boy, two little Campbell-Johnsons shepherded by Alan's wife Fay. Ismay's grown-up daughters Susan and Sarah follow, with Rupert Blundell's sister Geraldine.

That evening Larry is invited to join the Campbell-Johnsons and Rupert and his sister for a drink at the Imperial Hotel in honour of the new arrivals.

They sit in the gardens, in low basket chairs, drinking gin and lemonade. After sundown the air is cool and pleasant. The perfectly kept lawns are lit by soft lamps. The tinkling of tonga bells sounds from the street beyond the walls. Turbaned servants stand discreetly by the open doors to the hotel, waiting to fulfil the guests' needs.

'Rupert, this is heavenly,' says Geraldine. 'And to think you've been making such a fuss.'

'I got cold feet about her coming out,' Rupert says to the others.

'This isn't the real India, I'm afraid,' says Alan.

'I suppose you mean it isn't the India of the poor,' says Geraldine. 'But at home I don't live in the England of the poor either. Perhaps I'm simply not real.'

She speaks with a smile in her voice, and they laugh as if she has made a joke, but Larry senses from the first that, like Rupert, she's someone who knows her own mind. To look at she's delicate, even fragile, with her pale perfect skin and her slender figure. The way she moves her head or her small hands is economical and precise, performing just enough of an action to achieve her object. She seems to be quite unaware how pretty she is, and entirely lacks the little tricks of flirtation that others take for granted. Modest, then, but also proud.

The men smoke, but both the ladies decline. Geraldine barely touches her drink. Alan catches sight of Colin Reid of the London *Daily Telegraph*, and beckons him over to join them.

'Colin's a real expert,' he says. 'He's studied Muslim culture in the Middle East. He's even read the Koran in Arabic. Am I right, Colin?'

'More than once,' says Colin. 'Don't quote me on this, but I know my Koran rather better than Muhammad Ali Jinnah.'

'Which one's Jinnah?' says Geraldine.

'He's the leader of the Muslim League,' says Larry.

'So tell us,' says Alan to the *Telegraph* man. 'Is this

Muslim–Hindu division really about religion, or is it something else?'

'That's rather a broad question,' says Colin Reid.

'Religion is always something else, surely,' says Rupert. 'I mean, religion is not just about what you do on the holy days. It's how you see your life.'

'I should explain,' says Alan. 'We're surrounded by believers. Rupert and Larry both went to the same Catholic school. I expect Geraldine is one of them too.'

'Certainly,' says Geraldine with a pretty smile. 'Like all the best people.'

'But Rupert's perfectly right,' says Colin Reid. 'Religion is more about identity and community than creed. And I'm afraid the different communities here are moving further apart every day.'

He and Alan and Rupert then get into a discussion about the nationalist leaders and whether they can ever find common ground. Geraldine, who is sitting near Larry, turns to him and asks him in a low voice, 'Did Rupert always know best at school?'

'I'm sure he did,' says Larry, smiling. 'But I didn't really know him. He pretty much kept himself to himself. He was in my house, but in the year above me.'

'I expect you've lost your faith too.'

'No, not yet. Is that what I'm supposed to do?'

'I rather got the impression that Downside has that effect,' says Geraldine. 'You either come out a monk or an atheist.'

'No, I'm still a muddled but willing believer.'

'Me too. I expect it's very dull of me, but I like there being

394

rules. Fish on Friday. Mass on Sunday. Prayers at bedtime.'

'It's because it's what we're used to,' says Larry.

'No,' says Geraldine. 'It's what Rupert said. It's about how you see your life. Once you decide there's a right way to live your life, then that's what you want to do.' She stops, putting one hand to her pretty mouth, as if suddenly afraid she's said the wrong thing. 'I'm so sorry. I'm being serious. How bad-mannered of me.'

At the same time her eyes are laughing.

'I led you on,' says Larry. 'We're equally guilty.'

'It's because those rude men are talking Indian politics. Fay,' she says, turning to Alan Campbell-Johnson's wife, who is all too visibly falling asleep, 'Where have you hidden the children?'

'The children?' says Fay, blinking back to wakefulness. 'I'm taking them up to Simla, to get away from the heat.'

'They're such darlings,' Geraldine says to Larry. 'They were so good in that beastly plane. Fay, you need to be in bed. And so do I, to tell the truth.'

Larry is charmed by the graceful way Geraldine handles herself. He realises how much he misses feminine company; and in particular this way of speaking lightly while touching on serious matters. There's something else, too. He has the sense that Geraldine likes him.

As the party breaks up she says to him, 'I'm so glad you're out here. Rupert simply refuses to go to Mass any more. He's supposed to be a philosopher, but as far as I can tell he believes in nothing at all.'

That Sunday Larry accompanies Geraldine to the Sacred Heart on Connaught Place, a curious Italian-style church built only a few years before the war. Inside, with its rounded arches and long nave, its smell of burning candles and wood polish, it could be any Catholic church in the world. Geraldine kneels beside him, her face partly obscured by a black lace mantilla, and murmurs the responses in that absent but familiar way that is common to all Catholics. The words they speak are after all in Latin, and essentially meaningless incantations. And yet to Larry this itself is comforting. The Mass in Delhi is identical to the Mass at home. The raised hands of the robed celebrant, the tang of incense in the air, the tinkle of the consecration bell: he could be in the Carmelite church in Kensington, or Downside Abbey, or St Martin in Bellencombre, and it would all be the same.

After Mass they find their driver waiting in the hot sun, and drive back along the broad new roads of the imperial capital. New Delhi has the look of a city built for giants who have not yet got around to moving in.

'Or perhaps,' Larry says, elaborating his thought, 'they built it and then abandoned it, like Fatehpur Sikri.'

Geraldine hasn't heard of Fatehpur Sikri.

'It was the first Mughal city, built by Akbar the Great. But it turned out there wasn't enough water there, so they abandoned it after only fourteen years. It took fifteen years to build. It's been left to the sun and the wind for almost four hundred years now.'

'Is it still there?'

'Oh, yes, it's still there. There's no one living there, but people visit.'

'I'd like to go there.'

'I think it's quite a drive.'

Geraldine looks out of the open car windows at the bleak grandeur of the new city.

'I expect this took fifteen years to build,' she says.

'More or less,' says Larry. 'And here we are, getting ready to abandon it.'

'At least it won't be deserted when we leave.'

'Not at all. It'll come to life.'

They drive in silence for a few moments. Then Geraldine says, 'Why did you come out here, Larry?'

'Oh, you know how it is,' says Larry. 'Life has these turning points, doesn't it? I suppose it was just chance, bumping into Rupert when I did.'

'You think it was chance?'

'Why, don't you believe in chance?'

'I don't know that I do,' she says. 'After all—' She breaks off, not out of nervousness, but with a kind of old-fashioned courtesy, to say, 'Do you mind if I talk about God?'

'Not at all,' he says. 'It is Sunday.'

'Well,' she says, 'if you believe God has a plan for you, then nothing happens by chance. Even the bad things have their purpose, however hard it is to see what that might be at the time.'

'Yes,' says Larry, wondering how far he agrees with this. 'But that doesn't mean we never have to make any decisions for ourselves, does it?'

'I think our duty is to do the right thing, as far as we know it. And beyond that, to submit to the will of God. If that means we are to suffer, then so be it.'

She speaks in a low voice that makes it all too plain she speaks from recent personal experience.

'I'm sorry if you've suffered,' says Larry.

She looks round, meeting his eyes with a searching gaze. Her look says to him, Don't play with me.

'I've been unhappy,' she says. 'I can't claim any more than that.'

The car pulls up by the north entrance to Viceroy's House, and they go inside. Larry hears Geraldine pausing to thank their driver. Breakfast is still being served in the staff mess.

'Here they are!' cries Rupert Blundell, halfway through eating a soft-boiled egg. 'Are you suitably shriven?'

'You will go to hell,' says Geraldine calmly. 'Pour me some coffee.'

Freddie Burnaby-Atkins, one of the ADCs, points a butter knife at Geraldine.

'Why only Rupert?' he complains. 'I've not been to church either.'

'You're one of the innocents, Freddie,' says Geraldine. 'You'll go to limbo. But Rupert knows better, so he goes to hell.'

There are several single young men on the staff, and Geraldine's arrival among them has created something of a flutter. As Rupert predicted, she is soon put to work assisting the hard-pressed team. She has no training in shorthand or typing, but she has a natural talent for organisation. Within a few days she has taken charge of the circulation of notes. Mountbatten has instituted a system where each hour of meetings is followed by fifteen minutes of dictation, in which he makes a résumé of the discussion. The resulting notes are then typed, stencilled, and distributed. Geraldine draws up a chart with the names of all key members of staff, and the date and issue number of each note, and ticks them off as they are sent out.

The workload grows heavier as the temperature of the capital rises. The thermometer in the entrance hall is now reading 110° in the shade. Mountbatten has been closeted in Simla with Nehru, and in London with Attlee and Churchill. Jinnah has made his demand for a 'corridor' between the two parts of what will become Pakistan. Baldev Singh has issued ominous warnings about the Sikhs, who will be the biggest losers in partition. The Indian states representatives have met and failed to agree. Lord and Lady Mountbatten are rumoured to be barely on speaking terms. No one has the least idea what Gandhi thinks.

In this atmosphere of confusion and mistrust, the viceroy calls a meeting of the five leaders: Nehru and Patel for the Congress party, Jinnah and Liaquat Ali Khan for the Muslim League, and Baldev Singh for the Sikhs. Nehru asks that Acharya Kripalani be included, as Congress President. Jinnah counters with a demand that Rab Nishtar be included for the League. So the five becomes seven.

Larry is on duty controlling the press photographers. When it emerges that no photographs are to be permitted, he finds himself with a rebellion on his hands. Max Desfor leads a walkout by the foreign press men, saying as he goes, 'You'll get a signed protest on this one, Larry. You tell your people, this is no way to get yourselves a good press.'

Larry does his best.

'The viceroy wants as little distraction as possible. We'll get you in there later, I promise you.'

The purpose of the meeting is to win all the leaders' consent to a carefully drafted plan for the transfer of power. Because different aspects of the plan are unacceptable to each one of the leaders, this is no easy task. Mountbatten's object is to make them realise that poor though the plan is, every alternative is worse. If the British are to quit India, somebody must take over the running of the country. If Jinnah will not work with Congress, there must be partition. If there is to be partition, there must be boundaries, and many people will find themselves on the wrong side of whatever lines are drawn.

Mountbatten explains carefully that he understands he cannot expect to win *agreement*. Instead he asks for *acceptance*, which means that the leaders believe the plan to be a fair and sincere attempt to solve the problems, for the good of all. He asks for their goodwill in the attempt to make the plan work. Nehru, for Congress, says he is willing on balance to accept the plan. Jinnah says he must consult further with his working committee.

The meeting then breaks up, to be resumed next day. Mountbatten calls a staff meeting to report progress.

'Bloody Jinnah,' he says wearily. 'I shall have to see him alone.'

The other hold-out is Gandhi, who is due at Viceroy's House shortly.

'He's never going to buy partition,' says V.P. Menon.

'He doesn't have to buy it,' says Mountbatten. 'Just so long as he doesn't speak against it.'

Gandhi comes, and says nothing at all. It turns out that he is observing one of his periodic days of silence. Instead of speaking he scribbles notes on scraps of paper.

I know you don't want me to break my silence. Have I said one word against you during my speeches?

No one knows what this means. Mountbatten, incurably optimistic, deeply relieved not to have run into the stone wall that is Gandhi's conscience, says, 'He's letting out rope. He's giving me some space to try to pull it off.'

Jinnah then returns for his private session. He continues to insist that he can make no decision on his own.

'Delay now,' Mountbatten tells him, 'and Congress will withhold their acceptance of the plan too. Chaos will follow, and you'll lose your Pakistan.'

'What must be, must be,' says Jinnah.

Mountbatten gazes into Jinnah's implacable eyes.

'Mr Jinnah,' he says, 'this is what I'm going to do. Tomorrow, when we all meet again, I will ask the others formally if they accept the plan. They will say yes. I will then turn to you. I will say that I am satisfied with the assurances you have given me. I require you to say nothing. By that means, if your council so requires, you can deny later that you gave your acceptance. However, I have one condition. When I say, "Mr Jinnah has given me assurances which I have accepted and which satisfy me," you will not contradict me, and when I look towards you, you will nod your head.'

Jinnah gives this a moment of careful thought, then he nods his head.

The next day the conference resumes. The frustrated press photographers are allowed in, to record the historic meeting. The room is then cleared, and Mountbatten asks for formal acceptance of the plan. One by one the leaders accept. Jinnah gives his agreed nod of the head. Mountbatten then produces a thirty-four-page staff paper, raises it high above his head, and bangs it down on the table.

'This paper,' he says, 'is headed "The Administrative Consequences of Partition". You will find when you read it that time is of the essence. The longer we delay, the more the uncertainty will translate into unrest. I have therefore determined that the transfer of power will take place on August the fifteenth of this year. In ten weeks' time.'

The leaders are silent with shock.

Immediately after this bombshell the press staff go into battle stations, to distribute the right texts to the right people at the right time, and to avoid news leaking out in a manner that might provoke riots on the streets. Larry goes with Alan, accompanying Mountbatten in the viceregal Rolls-Royce, to All-India Radio. A group of orange-capped sadhus shout out slogans as they enter the building, protesting against any possible betrayal of the Hindu cause. Larry sees to the newsreel men while Alan attends Mountbatten in his broadcast. When the speech is done, Mountbatten comes through to the studio to repeat it for the cameras. A recording of the radio broadcast is played, and Mountbatten moves his lips to fit the words as the cameras run.

As the filming is completed, Nehru begins his own radio address. They stop to listen.

'We are little men serving great causes,' says Nehru. 'But because the cause is great, something of that greatness falls upon us also.'

Returning in the Rolls, Mountbatten, utterly exhausted, says, 'I never want to go through all that again.' Then he adds, 'I do truly believe that Pandit Nehru is a very great man.'

After the shock announcement of the date for Indian independence, Mountbatten has calendars printed and distributed to all staff. On each day is printed a number indicating the days left to transfer of power. The viceroy and his senior staff, including Alan Campbell-Johnson, then fly to London for consultations while the India Independence Bill passes through Parliament.

For those left behind, the pressure of work eases. Geraldine Blundell announces her intention to do some sightseeing, and reminds Larry of his promise to show her Fatehpur Sikri. Syed Tarkhan, hearing them speaking, reveals that he is knowledgeable on Mughal history, and would be happy to show them the sights. Rupert Blundell agrees to join them, but when he learns the trip involves four hours in a car each way, with no facilities for guests at the destination, he changes his mind.

'Too damn hot,' he says. 'You'll regret it.'

But Geraldine is smilingly stubborn.

'I want to see the deserted city,' she says. 'I may not get another chance.'

On Tarkhan's advice they set off early, leaving Delhi at seven in the morning. They take with them a picnic lunch, a canteen of water, and a bottle of Lebanese wine. Tarkhan, in his capacity as guide and leader, sits in the front beside the driver. Larry and Geraldine sit in the back.

In anticipation of the great heat, Geraldine wears a light cotton dress that leaves her arms and her lower legs bare. Larry, sitting beside her, is acutely aware of the nearness of her golden skin. He finds himself remembering Nell, naked in the Life Room at Camberwell, and later naked in his arms in the green light of his digs. Geraldine looks out of the window as they drive, and asks Tarkhan constant questions about what she sees, but Larry has the feeling that she senses the physicality of his thoughts. There's something in the way she moves her hands, from time to time smoothing her dress over her knees, that seems to be a response to his nearness.

'Those women with baskets on their heads,' she says to Tarkhan, 'how far will they walk?'

'For miles,' says Tarkhan. 'Perhaps all day. They're taking fruit to sell. They go on until they sell it.'

At one point a young man on a bicycle dashes out from behind a house right into the road before them, and the car hits him, sending him flying. The driver stops at once and jumps out.

'The poor boy!' says Geraldine. 'Is he all right?'

They see the driver haul the bike rider off the road and proceed to cuff him sharply about the head.

'No!' cries Geraldine.

'Don't interfere,' says Tarkhan.

The driver returns, shaking his head.

'Bloody fool should look where he's going,' he says. 'My apologies, Sahibs.'

'But is the boy hurt?' says Geraldine as they drive on.

They see him climbing back on his bicycle.

'This is India,' says Tarkhan.

Geraldine says nothing for a while. When she speaks at last it's clear she's been pondering the meaning of this minor accident.

'I wonder if we've really been all that good for India,' she says. 'I wonder what sort of a country it would be now if we'd never come.'

'That is a question we can never answer,' says Tarkhan from the front seat.

'You think we should be quitting India, don't you, Syed?' says Larry.

'Without a doubt,' says Tarkhan. 'But you know, for many of us it will also be a sad day. I am a navy man. I've been raised in a family that has deep respect for the motherland. It's not so easy to throw off such things overnight. Then again, when I hear the British saying they are graciously giving us our freedom, I want to say, Excuse me, sir, by what right did you take our freedom in the first place?'

'There was never any right,' says Larry. 'Only power.'

They are driving now between sunburned fields of brown earth, broken here and there by clusters of small green trees. The temperature has risen, and the air that rushes in at the open window is dusty and hot.

'I don't understand about power,' says Geraldine. 'I don't understand about war, either. Isn't there enough suffering in the world already?'

'You will see, when we get to Fatehpur Sikri,' says Tarkhan, 'there's a saying of Jesus inscribed on the victory arch: "The world is a bridge. Pass over it, but build no houses on it."'

'Where does Jesus say that?' says Geraldine.

'I thought Akbar the Great was a Muslim,' says Larry.

'So he was.'

He says no more. Geraldine falls into a doze, and as the car lurches on over the rough road her bare right arm comes to rest against Larry's left side. He feels its slight pressure there, and from time to time glances at Geraldine's face. Her eyes are closed, her lips very slightly parted. Somehow even in the heat of the car she manages to look fresh and lovely.

The last part of the journey is over a road that is cracked and fissured by the sun. The sharp jolting of the car wakes Geraldine.

'Almost there,' says Larry.

The car comes to a stop in the shade of a sheltering ashoka tree. Tarkhan, Larry and Geraldine step out into the burning noon. Geraldine puts on her straw hat and sunglasses and looks like a film star. Before them the track leads on to a gap in a ruined wall. An elderly man in a faded khaki shirt comes hobbling towards them and speaks with Tarkhan, bobbing his head repeatedly. Then he goes again.

'We're the only ones here,' says Tarkhan. 'We're the brave ones, he says.'

He leads them up the rising track through the gap in the wall, and there before them, quite suddenly, is the abandoned city. Its palaces are built of the same red sandstone on which it stands, and stripped of all life as they are, seem to be sculpted from the land. Domes and turrets reach skywards on spindly pillars, atop vast structures that are themselves so pierced and open to the sky that they seem to be light and insubstantial.

Tarkhan sees with gratification the astonishment on the faces of his guests.

'In its day the city was bigger than London,' he says, 'and far more magnificent. Akbar the Great ruled over a hundred million subjects, at a time when your Queen Elizabeth had barely three million.'

He leads them across the dusty square, in the centre of which is a paved cross, made of panels of red stone between bands of cream.

'This is a pachisi court,' he says. 'You know the game? It's like what you call Ludo. In Akbar's day it was played with people serving as the playing pieces.'

'This is extraordinary, Syed,' says Larry. 'How can it all still be here?'

'The dryness, I suppose. That building there is the Diwan-i-Am, the Hall of Public Audience. The five-storey structure is the Panch Mahal, where the ladies of the court lived.'

'How big is the city?'

'About four square miles. But come over here. This is what I want to show you.'

He leads them to a square building with four turrets on its corners, each one holding, on four slender pillars, an ornate dome.

'Come inside, into the shade.'

Each side of the building is pierced by a wide central door. Within, there is a single space, dominated by an immense and intricately carved central pillar.

'This is the Diwan-i-Khas,' says Tarkhan. 'The Hall of Private Audience. This is where Akbar held his meetings.'

Larry is studying the complex carvings at the top of the pillar. It branches out into four stone overhead walkways sustained by a cluster of snakelike brackets.

'Remarkable,' he murmurs.

'I must now confess to an ulterior motive in bringing you here,' says Tarkhan. 'As you know, my country faces a great crisis, caused by the fears Muslims and Hindus have of each other. The terrible communal violence shows that the different faiths cannot live together. This is why there must be Pakistan. And yet, look more closely at this pillar.'

He guides their eyes with his hands.

'The designs at the base are Muslim. A little higher, and we have Hindu symbols. The third tier is Christian. And here at the top, the designs are Buddhist. And if you look higher up still, you will see the secret place behind the pierced screen where Akbar would sit, every Thursday evening, and listen to the discussions below. Hindus, Buddhists, Roman

Catholics, atheists, he invited them all to come here and talk to each other.'

'Roman Catholics came here too?' says Geraldine.

'From Portugal, I believe,' says Tarkhan. 'Akbar wanted to formulate what he called the Din-i-Ilahi, the ultimate faith that would bring all religions together. According to the Din-i-Ilahi, there were to be no sacred scriptures or rituals, but all would take an oath to do good to all. And in his day, and for many years after, there was no hatred between the faiths.'

'And then the British came,' says Larry, 'and all the toleration came to an end.'

'No,' says Tarkhan gently. 'That would be too harsh. Though as you know, there are those who believe you kept control of your great empire by the policy of divide and rule. For whatever reason, now to our shame and suffering, we are divided.'

'How difficult it all is,' murmurs Geraldine.

'Did you know,' says Tarkhan, 'that Tennyson wrote a poem about Akbar the Great? It's called "Akbar's Dream". It's rather long, but I remember two lines he gave to Akbar. "I can but lift the torch of reason, In the dusty cave of life."'

The three walk the deserted courts of the ghost city, made thoughtful by all that Tarkhan has said. Round them rise the skeletons of past glory, as if to mock the pretensions of the present imperial race. Larry thinks of the cold grey bankrupt homeland he has left behind.

'You say you were raised to respect the motherland,' he says to Tarkhan. 'How can we pretend to be the mother of any other peoples?'

'Perhaps we all have many mothers,' says Tarkhan.

They return to the car and take their picnic in the shade of the tree. The heat and the walking have wearied them. The Lebanese wine makes them sleepy.

'I think it would be good to return soon,' says Tarkhan.

On the drive back Geraldine abandons formality and falls asleep with her head in Larry's lap. Larry himself does not sleep. His head is buzzing with new thoughts. He thinks about the claims of the different religions to ultimate truth. He watches Geraldine's lips as they tremble with her sleep breaths. He asks himself why his own faith, that Jesus is the son of God, that His resurrection gives us promise of eternal life, should be the one true faith, and the others pale copies, or downright superstitious falsehoods. His gaze lingers on Geraldine's soft blond hair where the curls lie on her pale brow. Jesus said, 'I am the way, the truth, and the life.' So what of other ways, and other truths? Geraldine believes as he believes, she knelt beside him at Mass, her cheek shadowed by her lace mantilla. He would like to kiss her now, on the temple, just where the locks of hair fall away. He looks towards Tarkhan, dozing in the front seat, and thinks how much he likes him. How courteously he delivered his history lesson in the abandoned city, and yet how devastating its implications. You suppose yourself to be a modern man, free of the baseless prejudices of earlier generations, and then quite unexpectedly you catch a glimpse of your true self, and find it rests on an ocean of unexamined assumptions: that as an Englishman you inherit the civilised values that others will in time acquire; that as a Christian you possess the eternal truths that others will in time acknowledge. And all the time this slender girl lies trustful in your lap, and you long to kiss her, to slip off her dress, to enjoy her naked body.

Am I such a self-deceiver? Have I grown a mask that clings so tight I no longer know my own face? For whose benefit have I done so?

For the ones who look at me. For the ones who judge me.

So many masks. The mask of the gentleman. The mask of the man of culture. The mask of the good man. All worn for the onlookers, the judges, to appease them, to win their approval. But what is it that the maskless self wants? Who am I when no one is looking? Why do I care so much for goodness?

Fear, comes the answer. Fear, and love.

I'm afraid that if I'm not good, I won't be loved. And I want more than everything else, more than eternal life, to be loved.

This thought enters his mind in a flash, with the force of revelation. Can it be true? He thinks back to his time of terror on Dieppe beach. That was true fear, fear of extinction. That was an animal instinct that overrode any other demands he could make upon himself. But what of the shame that followed, which he has lived with ever since? That's a different kind of fear.

I'm afraid that I don't deserve to be loved.

If this is true, is this all it is? All man's achievements, all acts of heroism, all acts of creation, no more than a plea to be counted worthy of love? Loved by whom?

Geraldine moves in his lap with the motion of the car, but she doesn't wake. There's something about her that's so contained, so quietly sure of herself, that makes her approval desirable and hard to win. And yet there was a man she loved, Rupert said, who broke her heart.

The driver honks loudly on his horn to disperse a flock of goats on the road ahead. Geraldine wakes, and sits up.

'Have I been lying on you? I'm so sorry. I do hope you don't mind.'

'No trouble at all,' says Larry.

He can see from the way she looks at him that she knows he liked it.

'You're very tolerant.'

The journey still has an hour or more to go. Tarkhan sleeps in the front. This time will not come again.

'You asked me why I came here,' Larry says. 'I came out to India because the girl I was in love with went off with another man. It seemed to be the end of the world then. Now it seems of no importance at all.'

'Why do you tell me that?' she says.

'I don't know, really.'

'It was the same for me,' she says. 'There was a man I loved very much. I thought we were going to be married. Then he told me he was going away. He never said why.'

'He's the loser,' says Larry.

'No,' says Geraldine simply. 'I was the loser.'

Tarkhan now wakes, and looks at the road, and then checks his watch.

'We'll be back in good time for dinner,' he says.

29

Ed Avenell descends the flank of Edenfield Hill, steadily tramping down the sheep path that cuts a diagonal into the valley. The evening sun, low in the sky, casts deep shadows over the bowls and billows of the Downs. As he goes the lines of the song run in his head, round and round.

> *If I didn't care*
> *More than words can say*
> *If I didn't care*
> *Would I feel this way?*

Sometimes he walks the Downs for hours looking and not seeing, wanting only to stop caring, to stop feeling. There's a state he can sometimes reach if he walks long and far enough that is very like intoxication, a state in which he loses all sense of himself. Rabbits scuttle into the gorse as he passes; sheep lumber away. He envies them their lives. You only have to look at a sheep to know it has no idea at all that it's a sheep, or even that it has an existence. It does what it needs to do, eats, sleeps, flees from danger, tends its young, all from instinct. People talk of animals as being innocent, and incapable of sin. Even when they see a fox eat a rabbit alive, they say it's obeying its nature. But animals aren't innocent, they're merely moral blanks. There's no more evil in a fox than in an earthquake. And no more good, either. This is what Ed envies. They have sidestepped the judgement. They know nothing of the speeding car that will crush them on the road, or the slaughterhouse at the end of the country lane.

Not to care. Not to feel. That's the trick. Then to return home as empty as a discarded wine bottle, and to see, beyond the opening door, her questioning eyes. How is he this time? Is he drunk or sober? Does he love me or does he not?

All it takes is a few simple words, but the words don't come. What paralysis is it that has him in its grip? If she could hear the crying in his head she would be reassured, but also dismayed. *I love you, I love you, I love you*, constant as the west wind. And relentless as the wind from the east comes the other cry. *All for nothing, all for nothing*.

The path leads him down to America Cottage, which has been unlived-in for many years now. The way to the coach road runs between the cottage and the collection of barns beside it, where the tenant of Home Farm stores his hay. Ed is passing round the end of the long barn when he hears voices, and comes to a stop to listen. There are two voices, a man's and a woman's. From where he stands he can't see into the barn, but the voices come clearly through the thin board walls.

The man's voice says, 'Baby wants cuddles.'

The woman's voice says, 'Bad baby wants spanky-spank.'

There follows a scuffling sound, mingled with gasping and laughter. Then the man's voice says, 'Bare botty! Bare botty! Spanky-spank!' More scuffling and panting. Then the woman, 'What's Georgy got here? What's this then? Where's this come from?'

Ed is frozen to the spot, afraid of drawing attention to himself. If he walks on to the coach road he'll pass the open front of the barn and they'll see him. His only option is to retrace his steps as quietly as possible. Instead, he moves a little closer to the barn wall, where there's a gap in the boards. He doesn't mean to spy, and doesn't think of himself as spying, but he is compelled by a powerful impulse to understand.

'Baby wants cuddles,' the man is saying, more urgently now.

'Bad baby,' says the woman. 'Bad baby with his trousers down.'

Ed can see now, through the gap in the boards, through a fringe of hay, a large pink thigh, a rucked-up dress, a writhing half-undressed form beyond.

'Baby wants cuddles,' says the man, his voice choking.

'Bad baby,' says the woman, soothing, chanting, spreading her legs. 'Bad baby.'

After this there are no more words, only the gasping sounds of the man and the creaking and scratching of the hay that is their bed. Ed moves quietly away.

He knows both of them. The man is George Holland, Lord Edenfield. The woman is Gwen Willis, who comes twice a week to the farmhouse to clean and do the ironing. Ed knows her as a simple kindly woman in her mid-forties.

He reaches the sunken coach road and moves out of sight behind its fringe of trees. Here for no reason he comes to a stop. There's a fallen tree that offers its trunk as a bench, shaded by the canopy of the other trees. Ed sits himself down and waits.

What am I waiting for?

Not to shame poor George, that he's sure of. And yet he is waiting for George. He wants to touch and be touched by that simple urgent delight that he spied on in the barn. He wants to know that it's real. For all its absurdity, Ed senses that he has been a witness to a powerful force, one strong enough to override all convention, all good sense, and every instinct of self-preservation. George is riding the life force itself.

In time he hears voices again, then footsteps. Mrs Willis appears in the coach road, walking fast, alone. She throws him a startled look, and hurries past without a word. Some moments pass. Then George appears, strolling with an aimless air.

He too jumps when he sees Ed.

'Oh!' he says.

'Hello, George,' says Ed. 'Lovely evening for a walk.'

'Yes,' says George, going bright red.

Ed gets up off his tree trunk and joins George, ambling slowly down the track.

'Look, Ed,' says George at last. 'I don't know what to say.'

'You don't need to say anything, old chap,' says Ed. 'Nor do I.'

'Really?'

'None of my business.'

This evidently gives George much-needed relief.

'I appreciate that,' he says.

They walk on. Ahead through the trees loom the roofs and pinnacles of Edenfield Place.

'I say, Ed,' says George.

'Yes, George?' says Ed.

'It's not the way it looks, you know.'

'If you say so, George.'

'Look, stop for a moment, will you?'

They stop. George peers earnestly at Ed through his glasses, then looks equally earnestly at the stones of the track.

'This is nothing whatsoever to do with Louisa,' he says.

'I wouldn't dream of saying a word,' says Ed.

'No, I mean it really is nothing to do with her. I love her dearly. George Holland will always be a good and faithful husband to her. Always.'

'Right,' says Ed.

'But you see, there's someone else. There's Georgy.'

It's clear from the earnestness with which he speaks that George needs him to understand what he's confessing to him.

'Georgy's quite different. Georgy likes to play games.

Georgy isn't shy or afraid of making a fool of himself, not with his Doll. Georgy is happy, Ed.'

'Right,' says Ed.

'Happier than I've ever been. And Georgy can do things I can't do. There's no real harm in that, is there? If Georgy can do it with Doll, then you never know. Maybe . . .'

'Why not?' says Ed.

'I expect I seem a bit of a joke to you. I'm a bit of a joke to most people.'

'No,' says Ed. 'Right now I'm thinking you're a bit of a genius.'

'A genius? I don't think I'm that, you know.'

'Tell me, George. When you go back to the house, now. When you meet Louisa. Will you be thinking about what you've just been doing? Will you be afraid Louisa might guess?'

'No,' says George. 'You see, I've not been doing anything. That was Georgy.'

'Yes, of course. Silly of me.'

They part outside the big house. Ed's opinion of George has undergone a reappraisal. He's impressed by the radical simplicity of his solution. Faced with irreconcilable demands upon him, by the world in which he lives and by his own needs, he has split himself into two people. Who knows through what accident he discovered this other self, the Georgy who finds his erotic fulfilment in the nursery? But having encountered him he has embraced him, made room for him in his life, and not judged him. This seems to Ed to be an act of great maturity.

Georgy is happy.

What greater achievement is there in any man's life?

Ed walks back across the park to the farmhouse, his thoughts occupied with this revelation. He too is pulled in opposite directions, by his love for Kitty and by his need to be alone. What if he were to split himself in two as George has done? One self could be the loving husband, while the other self remains untouched and untouchable.

He has never considered such a solution before, because he has assumed that there's a fundamental dishonesty to it. According to his own sense of integrity, his duty to Kitty is to tell her the truth about himself. Only then, surely, can he know that she truly loves him. But it strikes him now that this is selfish. This need to know that it's the real him who is loved: what is it but the child's fierce grip on the mother?

Baby wants cuddles.

Look at it from Kitty's point of view. What she wants is to know that he loves her. So why not construct, for Kitty's benefit, out of all the real love he has for her, a part-self, an Ed who can give her all she needs? This wouldn't be a falsehood, just an incomplete version. He imagines doing this, playing the part of an Ed who loves her and has no darker fears. To his amazement he finds at once he's released. He can say the words she so longs to hear.

But she'll see through his act, surely. She knows him too well. He considers what he'll say if challenged. He'll say, Yes, it's an act, but this loving Ed is real too. What will she say then? Will she say, Only all of you is enough for me?

There's Pammy too. And a new baby coming. This half-Ed can be a good father, in fact has been a good father for some time. The self he brings to his daughter is exactly that, a partial, edited self, suitable for children.

Think of it as a good Ed and a bad Ed. The bad Ed is weak or sick or mad. He drinks too much to numb all sensation, because the world to him is a dark and purpose-less place. The bad Ed withdraws from contact with other people, most of all those he loves, because he knows his unhappiness is contagious. The good Ed is funny and brave and loving. The good Ed is the one Kitty fell in love with, the one who talks late into the night with Larry, the one who dances in the fields by moonlight. The good Ed has a shot at happiness.

He gets home, and pushing open the farmhouse door, calls out cheerfully, 'I'm back.'

Good Ed is back.

The kitchen is empty. He hears the sloshing of water upstairs. Bath time. He climbs the stairs to the bathroom. There's Kitty on her knees by the bath, and Pamela, pink and naked, squirming in the bath.

'Here you are,' he says. 'My two lovely girls.'

Kitty looks round in surprise.

'This is an honour,' she says.

'Do my story, Daddy,' says Pamela.

'I will,' says Ed, 'as soon as you're washed and dressed. But first I want to kiss my wife, because I love her.'

'Yuck!' says Pamela, impressed.

Ed kisses Kitty.

'What's brought this on?' says Kitty.

'Oh, nothing,' says Ed. 'I've been doing a bit of thinking.'

Pamela splashes in the bathwater, wanting attention.

'Not about *you*,' says Ed. 'I never think about *you*.'

'You do! You do think about me!' shrieks the little girl, eyes bright.

'Well, whatever it is, it's much appreciated,' says Kitty, fetching a towel to lift Pamela out of the bath. 'Nice to have a husband who comes home and wants to kiss his wife.'

The good Ed is a great success. It turns out Kitty has noticed nothing amiss after all.

30

The Maharaj Rana of Dholpur drinks his tea with modest sips, then puts down the cup and sighs.

'I can't tell you that I like what is happening, Captain Cornford. This new India is a very recent invention. Dholpur's Paramountcy Treaty with Britain goes back to 1756.'

He's a small scholarly man, who wears a pink turban. In '21, during George V's tour of India, he and Dickie Mountbatten were ADCs together. Now, prince and ruler of his own state, history is about to brush him aside.

'Do me a favour,' Mountbatten told Larry earlier. 'Look after Dholpur while he's in Delhi. He's a decent man.'

'I suppose these days,' Larry says to the maharaj, 'it's harder to justify imperial rule by a far-off country.'

'Ah, these days.' Dholpur sighs again. 'That is the modern mind in action. The assumption that fundamental truths must change with time. Are you a religious man, Captain Cornford?'

'Yes,' says Larry. 'Catholic.'

'Catholic?' The maharaj brightens. 'Like the Stuart kings of England. Then perhaps you will understand when I tell you that I believe most profoundly in the divine right of kings. The so-called Glorious Revolution of 1688, that drove James II into exile, was in my opinion both a disaster and an outrage. All the suffering that has followed springs from the false notion that the people can choose their own rulers. How are they to choose? What do the people know? Let God choose, and let the people be humbly thankful.'

'I see you're no believer in democracy,' says Larry.

'Democracy!' The maharaj gives him a look that combines melancholy with contempt. 'You think the people of India are choosing their rulers? You think when the British are gone the people of India will be free? Just wait a little, my friend. Wait, and watch, and weep.'

In these last days before the transfer of power the viceroy's staff work ever longer hours. They're planning the two days of ceremonial that will see the creation of two new sovereign nations. Sir Cyril Radcliffe, who has been shut away for weeks in a bungalow on the viceregal estate, has almost completed the award of the Boundary Commission. Everyone knows that once the details of the award are made public, the trouble will begin. Punjab and Bengal have now been partitioned; only Sylhet in Assam remains. Mountbatten makes it known that a late delivery on August 13th would be acceptable, fully aware that on that day he flies to Karachi for Pakistan's independence ceremony on

August 14th. The following day, August 15th, India's Independence Day, is to be a national holiday, and the printing presses will be closed. In this way the precise details of the two new nations will not be made public until the celebrations are over.

The viceroy's staff spend the day of August 14th clearing their desks and contemplating the historic moment they are about to witness. The general feeling is that the British are making a dignified job of winding up the Empire, thanks in no small part to the charm, energy, and informality of the Mountbattens.

'He's an amazing chap,' Rupert Blundell says to Larry, as they break for a much-needed drink. 'He loves dressing up and prancing about with his medals, but actually he's the least stuffy man I've ever met. He's a member of the royal family, his nephew's marrying our future queen, but he's all for the Labour government. You know, in some strange way I think he sees himself as an outsider.'

'She's the one who amazes me,' says Larry. By this he means Edwina. 'They all adore her.' By this he means the Indian leaders.

'You know she and Dickie fight like cats,' says Rupert. 'But you're right. He adores her too.'

With the coming of independence, Mountbatten will cease to be viceroy, but will stay on as Governor-General of India. Viceroy's House is to become Government House. Some staff will remain, but many will go. Syed Tarkhan, a Muslim, plans to leave for Karachi, where he is to be an ADC to Jinnah. Rupert Blundell has decided to stay on for two more weeks, to assist in the transition, and then he and Geraldine will go home.

'What will you do then?' Larry asks him.

'Back to academia, I think. Charlie Broad says he'll have me at Trinity. How about you?'

'God knows,' says Larry.

On that same day, Independence eve, as the monsoon rains stream down over the Mughal Gardens, he has a conversation with Geraldine Blundell that focuses his thoughts. She's been talking to Rupert, and is curious to know about the banana connection. Unlike most others, she doesn't seem to think this is comical.

'So Fyffes is your family firm, is it?'

'In a way,' says Larry. 'We're actually a wholly owned subsidiary of the United Fruit Company. But they leave the UK operation to us.'

'Is it a big firm?'

'Before the war we employed over four thousand people. The war hit us hard. But we're building the business back up again.'

Hearing himself speak he's struck by his use of the possessive pronoun 'we'. Somehow here on the other side of the world his sense of separation from the family firm has diminished.

'And your father runs it?'

'Yes, that's right. My grandfather started it, in 1892. My father took over in '29.'

'And you'll take over from him?'

'Oh, no, I don't think so. I've not really ever been part of the firm.'

Geraldine's eyes open wide in astonishment.

'Why not?'

'I had other ideas. You know how when you're young you want to go your own way.'

'Yes, but don't you have a duty?' She looks at him so earnestly that he feels ashamed of his youthful dreams. 'You're born into privilege. You have to accept the responsibility that goes with it, don't you?'

'All I can tell you,' says Larry, feeling uncomfortable, 'is that it didn't feel that way.'

'So what was it you wanted to do?'

Larry shrugs, aware how inadequate his answer will sound to her; indeed, in this moment it sounds inadequate to his own ears.

'I wanted to be an artist.'

'An artist! You mean someone who paints pictures?'

'Yes.'

'I think that's wonderful, Larry. But it's not a job.'

Geraldine sees everything in a simple clear light, not distorted by vanity or illusion. She's strongly pragmatic, concerned to deal only with the realities of life, but she's also idealistic in her way. She believes in the grace of God.

She becomes more beautiful to him every day. Larry loves to look at her going about her work, unaware of his gaze. He has begun to think he would like to be more to her than a friend and colleague, but he hesitates to make

426

any move. He's afraid of finding his overtures rejected. After all, what has he to offer?

He steals a moment to write to Kitty and Ed, which really means to Kitty.

> All is chaos and monsoon rain here as we prepare for Independence Day. There's much talk of England, the benign mother, looking on proudly as the child she has raised now comes of age. I do think this is perfect nonsense. The Indians have been civilised far longer than us. And speaking personally, when I'm in the presence of men like Nehru and Patel, and of course Gandhi, I'm the one who feels like a child.
>
> I've been puzzling mightily these last days over my own future. When am I to win my independence? I expect that sounds odd to you, after all I'm almost thirty, but since I've been out here I've been having many new thoughts. What sort of life do I want to lead? Does what I want even matter all that much? I do so feel with you, Kitty, when you write that you want to be fully alive. I want that too. But at the same time I have this growing idea that chasing after what I want is not the answer. Perhaps I should think more of my responsibilities. A man my age, in my position, should do a useful job, and marry, and have children. Isn't that so? If I'm to remain unmarried, and without an occupation, then what use am I? This is what you call a mission in life, I think.

Anyway, I feel the world changing about me, in this historic moment, so maybe I'll change too. I think of coming home soon. To what? At least I can look forward to long talks with you and Ed, and Ed can tell me it's all luck and chance, and you can tell me I must learn to fly, and I'll sit there smiling and nodding, just happy to be back with you again.

After he's finished his letter it strikes him that he hasn't mentioned Geraldine, though she has never once left the forefront of his mind. Time enough to tell about her should there ever be anything to tell.

So the hour of midnight arrives, and with the dawn that follows the rains cease and the city is given over to parades and rejoicing. The national flag hangs at every window; saffron, white and green bunting festoons the trees. A huge crowd converges on Princes Park, where an arena has been built. In the centre of Princes Park stands a pagoda housing a giant statue of King George V; in a wide circle round it stand the palaces of the Nizam of Hyderabad, the Gaekwar of Baroda, and the Maharajas of Patiala, Bikaner and Jaipur. Today their windows gaze on a temporary dais and flag-pole, where the flag of the new nation will be raised, and will thus eclipse the symbols of past power.

Larry sets off on foot to watch the grand moment, in a group that includes Rupert and Geraldine Blundell, Marjorie Brockman and Fay Campbell-Johnson. It becomes very obvious very soon that the crowd is far bigger than has been anticipated. The entire length of Kingsway, all the way to India Gate, is packed solid with cheering, laughing, flag-waving people, all eager to reach Princes Park. The group from Government House presses on, showing their tickets to beaming officials, but by the time they get to the parade ground all semblance of order has collapsed. The crowd has swarmed over the reserved stands and taken possession of the chairs, standing on the seats and arms and backs.

'Make way for the memsahibs!' call out happy voices, as Larry and Rupert attempt to squeeze their companions through the throng. They get within sight of the flagpole and then can go no further. The crush is so intense that women hold their babies over their heads. Nehru himself can be seen struggling to get through to the central dais. Unable to make progress he climbs onto a man's shoulders and walks in his sandals on the heads of the crowd.

There comes a great cheer. All heads twist round. Larry catches a glimpse of the ADCs in white, followed by the fluttering lance-pennants of the bodyguard, and then the state carriage itself, carrying the new governor-general. Mountbatten is in his white dress uniform, with Lady Mountbatten, also in white, by his side in the open landau.

Nehru, now standing on the central dais, waves his arms and calls for the crowd to let the procession pass through, but no one heeds him. Larry glances at Geraldine, held in the crush beside him, and sees that she has her eyes closed.

'Are you all right?' he says.

She doesn't answer.

The carriage and its escort come to a stop, some way

from the flagpole. It's all too obvious that they can go no further. Mountbatten rises to his feet in the carriage, and gestures to Nehru to proceed. Nehru gives the signal, and the Indian tricolour rises up the flagpole. The crowd bursts into a giant roar. Mountbatten, trapped in the landau, takes the salute. A light rain begins to fall. The crowd discovers a rainbow in the sky: saffron, white and green. The cheering is redoubled.

In the midst of all the noise, Geraldine begins to utter low screams. She has her eyes tight shut, her hands over her ears, and she shakes her head from side to side.

'It's all right,' says Larry, putting his right arm round her. 'It's all right. I'll get you out.'

Holding her tight and close, he forces his way back through the cheering crowd, using his left shoulder to open up a space between the packed bodies. He feels Geraldine shaking, and hears her low screams, as he pulls her after him. At first their progress is slow, but as he works his way to the back of the crowd he finds they can move more easily. And so at last they emerge into a side street, where there is open space.

He holds her in his arms and lets her sob.

'There,' he says, soothing her. 'There, all safe now.'

The sobbing ceases. She remains in his arms, her face pressed to his chest. He feels the jerky shuddering of her chest as her breaths come slower and slower. Then she turns away, to dab the tears from her eyes.

'I'm so sorry,' she says. 'What a little fool you must think me.'

'Of course I don't,' says Larry.

'I don't know what happened. Suddenly I started to feel trapped. I couldn't bear it.'

'You were trapped. That's quite a crowd.'

'But you got me out.'

The light rain is still falling, bringing welcome refreshment on this burning day.

'Come on. Let's walk back.'

The next day Mountbatten hands Radcliffe's award to Nehru, and cables it to Jinnah in Karachi. Within hours, the Punjab is in flames. Ten million people are on the move, seeking safety on either side of the new borders. Three hundred thousand Hindus and Sikhs flee Lahore. In Amritsar Muslim women are stripped naked, paraded through the streets, and raped. Sikh fighting mobs, armed with machine guns and grenades, descend on Muslim villages and slaughter the inhabitants. Muslims at Ferozepur attack a train carrying Sikh refugees, and kill all they can reach. What begins as hysterical fear mutates into hysterical rage.

Hindu refugees begin to arrive in Delhi, bringing with them hunger, disease, and a poisonous lust for revenge. Within days the riots and the killings have taken over the capital. The main railway station, packed with Muslims trying to flee, is bombed by Hindus. In the subsequent riot police fire into the crowd. Looters smash Muslim shops in Connaught Circus. Muslim tonga drivers are dragged from their tongas and hacked to death. Arson attacks start fires across the city.

All flights in and out of Delhi are cancelled. Syed Tarkhan is unable to make his transfer to Karachi. Rupert and Geraldine Blundell, due to fly home on September 8th, are obliged to remain in Government House, one of the few islands of security. Lady Mountbatten learns that hospitals are being attacked, and the wounded massacred in their beds. She requests that the troops protecting Government House, who are the governor-general's bodyguard reinforced by the 5/6th Gurkhas, should add to their duties the protection of hospitals. She asks Larry and Syed Tarkhan to coordinate the allocation of guards.

'No need to go into the city yourselves,' she says. 'Just make sure we do the best we can with the men we have.'

Syed Tarkhan is deeply distressed by the violence.

'It's only what you said would happen,' says Larry.

Tarkhan shakes his head.

'I feel ashamed,' he says. 'I feel to blame.'

So many staff have left that there is a shortage of both cars and drivers. Government House rents three Buick Eights, and one is made available to transport hospital guards. Larry learns that Tarkhan proposes to drive the car himself.

'I'll come with you.'

'No, Larry,' says Tarkhan. 'There's no need.'

He means there's no need for Larry to put himself in danger. This is no longer Larry's country. But Larry too feels shame and blame.

'Think of it as a last hurrah for the motherland,' he says.

'Ah, I see.' Tarkhan smiles at that. 'A noble gesture.'

They pack into the Buick: a Gurkha lieutenant, three of

432

his men, and Larry. Tarkhan takes the wheel. They drive across the city to Old Delhi. They encounter no trouble on the way, but here and there they see burned-out shops and overturned trucks.

At the Victoria Zenana Hospital the Gurkhas take up their post, and Larry receives a report on the latest casualties from the nurse in charge.

'Not so terrible.'

'The mobs will be out after dark,' says Tarkhan.

They drive back through the deserted streets of the Paharganj area as the light fades in the sky. Crossing the overbridge by New Delhi station they hear shouts. Then comes a burst of gunfire, and the windscreen explodes into fragments. Tarkhan gives a grunt and tips over to one side, then with a convulsive movement rights himself.

'Syed!'

The car lurches out of control, heading for the parapet of the bridge. Tarkhan struggles with the wheel, panting loudly. The car shudders to a stop. Tarkhan slumps forward, blood pouring from his right shoulder. The engine cuts out.

'Syed!'

Before Larry can make a move to help him, an army lorry comes screeching up, and eight or nine armed men jump out.

'Out of the way! Out of the way!' They point their guns through the shattered windscreen. 'This is for the Muslim scum!'

Larry can hear from their voices that they're beyond

433

reason. They've come out hunting to kill, and they no longer care. The gun barrels jab at him.

'Out of the way!'

Half paralysed by terror, he realises dimly that he himself is not in danger. He is an Englishman. Their war is no longer with the likes of him. All he has to do is move aside and let the fratricidal rage take its course. These thoughts pass through his mind at lightning speed, even as his eyes fall on Tarkhan's hands, which still grip the steering wheel. He hears the wounded man groan. He sees the fingers of one hand open and close. This simple human gesture is all it takes.

'No!' he cries.

He throws himself across Tarkhan, embracing him, as if his arms have the power to shield him from gunfire.

'Muslim scum!' shout the armed men. 'We shoot Muslim dogs! You will die too!'

Larry pulls Tarkhan even more tightly into his arms, so that the blood from his wound runs down his own chest. He hears Tarkhan's choking voice.

'Go, Larry. Leave me.'

The men with the guns tug at his sleeves, shouting. He closes his eyes and rocks his friend in his arms and waits to die.

Now the shouting is loud and close. A gun fires, a single shot echoing in the night. He smells the smell of fresh blood. He hears Syed Tarkhan's low groans. Then he hears another sound: the growl of the army lorry driving away.

He draws a long deep breath. He becomes aware of the

drumming sound in his ears, and knows it's his own pulsing blood. Have they killed his friend in his arms?

'Syed?'

Tarkhan turns to him, groaning. He can see no fresh wound.

'I'm taking you to the hospital.'

He drags the wounded man into the passenger seat, and wedges him between the seat and the door. He starts the engine. Hand trembling on the gear stick, he reverses onto the road, and turns to drive back the way they came.

At the Victoria Zenana Hospital the nurses stretcher Tarkhan into a ward and tear the blood-soaked clothing from his upper body. Larry stays by his side.

'How badly is he hurt?'

'He'll live,' they tell him. 'How about you?'

'I'm not hurt.'

Tarkhan has lost consciousness. A doctor comes and examines the single gunshot wound.

'Smashed the collarbone,' he says. 'Lucky not to have got the main artery.'

So that second gunshot missed its target. How could they miss, at point-blank range? Reliving its sound now in memory, it seems to Larry that the second shot was fired into the air. Why?

He drives the Buick back to Government House alone, careless of any further danger. The warm night air streams through the smashed windscreen, bathing his face. A strange lightness of spirit has taken possession of him. He feels as if he has died and risen again and is now immortal.

Entering Government House through the north door, he makes his way down the corridor, past the startled looks of servants, to the small office where Geraldine keeps her charts. He finds her there alone. She stares at him, mute with shock.

'It's all right,' he says. 'It's not my blood.'

He opens his arms. Responding instinctively to his gesture, she comes into his embrace.

He holds her tight, feels her trembling in his arms. He bends his head towards her, and understanding, she turns her face to his. He kisses her, clumsily at first. Then he feels her lips respond, and her body soften in his arms.

When they part, there are bloodstains on her dress, and she is looking at him wonderingly.

'Larry,' she says.

Suddenly it's all so clear. He could have died back there on the overbridge, but he didn't die. That second gunshot was a command that said: live. Time is so short, death comes so soon. While we have this precious gift of life we must cherish it. We must love each other.

'I have so much love to give you,' he says.

'Do you, Larry?'

'Will you let me love you?'

He doesn't ask for her love. That's for her to give. This isn't about his own needs or fears. This is about the life force within him, that's pouring from him in a ceaseless stream.

'Yes,' she says. 'Yes.'

Larry goes back to the Victoria Zenana Hospital the next day to find Syed Tarkhan sitting up in bed and drinking tea.

'Larry,' he says. 'My brother.'

'So you're going to pull through, are you?'

'I'm leaving, my brother. This afternoon I leave for Karachi.' He holds out his hand. His eyes have never left Larry from the moment he entered the ward. 'I will never forget you.'

His limpid gaze speaks to Larry, saying, There are no words.

'So you're off to build a brand-new country,' says Larry.

'If God wills.'

'I'll miss you.'

Tarkhan holds his hand tight, and nods and shakes his head at the same time, all the while looking into his eyes with his tender loving gaze.

'It truly was a noble gesture, Larry,' he says.

'Married?' says William Cornford.

'Well, we're not married yet,' says Larry. 'But we're going to get married.'

'Well, well, well,' says his father, nodding his head. 'This is very good news. Very good news. Cookie will be so excited. As am I. So who is she?'

'Her name is Geraldine Blundell. Her brother was at Downside a year above me. So she's a good Catholic, you'll be pleased to hear.'

'All I need to please me is to know that you're happy.'

'I'm very happy, Dad. You wait till you meet her. She's very lovely, and very special. She's been in India with her brother.'

'So we have poor India to thank, do we? I don't expect when you took yourself off there you thought you'd come back with a wife.'

'It was the last thing on my mind.'

'Well, my boy, I think this calls for a drink.'

William Cornford fusses about in his library, searching through his bottles for something suitably celebratory. He settles on a single-malt whisky.

'Now I know it's none of my business,' he says, his attention on the glasses, 'but have you given any thought to what you're going to live on?'

'Yes, Dad,' says Larry. 'I do realise I need a job.'

'I rather think you do.'

'I was wondering if you had anything going?'

William Cornford continues pouring whisky, but now his hands are trembling. He hands Larry his glass. Not trusting himself to speak, he raises his glass in a silent toast.

They drink.

'Welcome to the company,' he says at last, his voice throaty with emotion.

The Blundells live in Arundel. The marriage is to take place in the church of St Philip. Mrs Blundell has hopes that the Duke of Norfolk will attend, in his capacity as Earl of Arundel and head of the premier Catholic family in the land.

'You know he's also the first peer of the realm,' she tells Larry. 'As hereditary earl marshal he organised the coronation of the king. Not that Hartley and I care for titles as such. Really it's the sheer weight of *history* that we find so moving.'

Geraldine has warned Larry about her mother.

'She's one of those people who doesn't really believe in failure. She sees it as a lack of moral fibre, I think. I can hear her now, saying to us children, "Do it properly or don't do it at all."'

'She sounds terrifying,' says Larry.

But Barbara Blundell takes to Larry from the beginning.

'If you don't mind my saying so,' she tells him, 'you come as something of a relief after the last one. Geraldine is my special pet. You'll forgive my partiality, but I think you'd have to look far and wide to find her combination of beauty without and beauty within. She deserves a husband of true faith and ample fortune. And since Bernard Howard has sired only daughters . . .'

She gives a shrill high laugh, to show that this is a joke. Bernard Howard is the Duke of Norfolk. Larry is a little alarmed by the 'ample fortune' part, which seems not to be a joke. Geraldine tells him not to worry.

'Mummy knows you're only starting out. But she's tremendously reassured to know it's the family firm. Also I told her you have a best friend who's a lord.'

'Do you mean George?' Larry is surprised to find George in the role of asset. 'His grandfather sold patent medicine.'

'A lord is a lord,' says Geraldine placidly.

England has enjoyed a blazing summer, which extends into a warm dry autumn. The outlook is good for the wedding, now fixed for Saturday, October 25th.

'After all, we don't want to compete with the royal wedding, do we?' says Barbara Blundell with her high laugh. Princess Elizabeth is to be married on November 20th. This turns out to be the reason why the Duke of Norfolk can't come to Geraldine's big day. 'I am a little disappointed, but

I suppose someone has to organise the wedding of our future queen.'

The honeymoon is to be in the Cornford house in Normandy, which has been fully refurbished after its wartime occupation. Louisa offers their house as a staging post for the Channel crossing.

'They're to stay the night of the wedding with the Edenfields at Edenfield Place,' Barbara Blundell tells her friends. 'Then they go on to the family estate of La Grande Heuze.' She lingers on the words *place*, *estate*, *grande*, with a light but pointed emphasis.

Larry bears all this with a good spirit. He sees Geraldine now in her element, quietly countermanding her mother's extravagances, making sure that the correct information passes down the chain of family, priests, guests and trades-people who each have their part to play in the wedding. Her grasp of details astonishes him, as does her confidence in her own judgement in all matters of taste. She will wear her mother's wedding dress, the seamstress will adjust it to fit her. Larry will wear morning dress. There will be four bridesmaids, of descending size, and two very small page-boys. She suggests that George would make a suitable best man, but here Larry holds out. He makes it clear that he wants Ed Avenell.

'You've never met George,' he says. 'Ed is far more dashing.'

While Geraldine busies herself with plans for the wedding, Larry is given a crash course on the family company, Elders

& Fyffes, in all its current aspects. The London headquarters has recently moved from the Aldwych to 15 Stratton Street in Piccadilly. The rooms are unfamiliar to Larry, but the faces are all the same. Everywhere he goes he meets a general smiling delight that he is to join the firm at last.

'You know why they're so happy?' his father asks him. 'It's not because of your pretty face. It's because they expect you to take over after me, and that means things will go on being run in the same way.'

'So they shall,' says Larry, 'if I have anything to do with it.'

'Subject, of course, to our ultimate masters in New Orleans.'

This means the mighty United Fruit Company.

'I thought they pretty much left us alone to run the show,' says Larry.

'They do. That was the understanding, back in '02, when the company nearly went under, and my father turned to them for help. Andrew Preston was running United then, and he was a man of his word. But Preston is long gone. There's a fellow called Zemurray in charge now. Very different kettle of fish.'

'Zemurray?'

'I think he began as Zmurri. Russian, I believe.'

'And you don't trust him.'

'I wouldn't want to get on the wrong side of him. But so long as we make money for him, I think he'll leave us alone.'

As part of his familiarisation process, Larry makes a tour of the main company facilities. He walks the quays of the purpose-built docks at Avonmouth, and at Liverpool. He inspects the purpose-built temperature-controlled railway wagons, and several of the huge depots where the fruit is kept in chilled storerooms until ready for delivery. He goes on board *Zent III*, the company's most recently acquired vessel, originally built in Norway and operated by Harald Schuldt, a German importer, before being seized as a war prize. The Fyffes fleet numbers fourteen ships, down from the twenty-one before the war, but more than enough for the current depressed level of trade. He studies figures that show the problems the company faces, due to shortages in Jamaica and government restrictions.

'We believe the answer may be to go back to the Canaries,' says William Cornford, 'which is of course where the company started.'

'The cargo side seems to be very modest,' says Larry.

'More trouble than it's worth,' says his father. 'Our ships are built as specialised bulk carriers.'

'Even so,' says Larry, 'we should take a look at it.'

The talk of tonnages and leaf-spot disease is familiar to Larry from his father's mealtime conversation. He finds that he slips into the company surprisingly easily, soon comfortable in the Stratton Street offices. He begins to understand how the company has become his father's family.

His father, noting this with some complacency, says to him, 'You see it now? You were born for this.'

The sun shines on the day of the wedding. George shows up in a grand old Rolls-Royce, accompanied by Ed and Kitty and Pamela.

'Where on earth did you get that?' exclaims Larry.

'It was my father's,' says George. 'I only get it out on special occasions. It uses far too much petrol.'

Barbara Blundell is thrilled.

'I do like the aristocracy to put on a show,' she says.

Louisa has stayed at home, feeling unwell. Kitty whispers the details to Larry.

'It's very early days, but she thinks she may actually be pregnant!'

Kitty herself is very pregnant.

'That's wonderful.'

'If it's true, it's a miracle,' says Kitty. Then taking his arm for support, she walks away to a spot where they can speak in private. 'I'm just so happy for you, darling. You deserve a family of your own. Is Geraldine as wonderful as I want her to be?'

'If I tell you she's the opposite of Nell in every way,' says Larry, 'that should give you some idea.'

'But I did like Nell's honesty. She had a way of saying just what she thought.'

'Oh, Geraldine's honest. But she's also moral, which Nell never was. You'll see when you meet her. She has high standards.'

'And she makes you happy?'

'I adore her,' says Larry. 'The more I know her, the more perfect she turns out to be.'

'She couldn't be too perfect for you,' says Kitty. 'You deserve the best.'

Ed in tailcoat and grey waistcoat and white tie looks as

handsome as Larry has promised. Geraldine's father, older, shorter and plumper, looks almost decrepit by his side. 'Stand up straight, Hartley,' his wife says. 'You're not to sag.'

'Another one on the way, then,' Larry says to Ed.

'Mid-December, they tell me,' says Ed. 'An early Christmas present.' He looks round all the bustle of last-minute arrangements. 'Doing it in style, I see.'

'That's Geraldine,' says Larry. 'Or perhaps I should say her mother.'

Rupert Blundell wanders about looking uncomfortable in a morning suit, smiling but not fraternising.

'You look bewildered, Rupert. Is it really that bad?'

'Do I? I don't mean to. A great occasion.' His eyes are on Ed. 'That's Ed Avenell, isn't it?'

'Yes, of course. Come and say hello.'

Larry takes Rupert over to Ed and they shake hands and say yes, they remember each other, but it's clear Ed has no idea who Rupert is.

'Rupert was with Mountbatten,' Larry says.

'Good work on the VC,' says Rupert.

Rupert's father joins them, seeking the quiet haven of masculine company.

'What a lot of fuss,' he says with a sigh. 'Makes me wish I was a Quaker.'

'Look at you three!' Larry exclaims. 'Anyone would think you were all waiting to see the dentist.'

'Sorry,' says Hartley Blundell, straightening his posture. 'Attention! Ready for the salute!'

Ed smiles at that. Courage under fire.

'I really appreciate this,' Larry murmurs to Ed when he gets the chance. 'It's your idea of a nightmare, isn't it?'

'I'm not all that fond of people in crowds,' says Ed. 'But I'm rather fond of you.'

They move on in due course to the church in a convoy of cars. Larry's father travels with the bride's mother, and so gets the benefit of her close knowledge of the Duke of Norfolk.

'When he plays in the town cricket team, his butler is the umpire, and when he's bowled out, which he always is in no time at all, the butler raises his hand and announces, "His Grace is not in."'

William Cornford smiles polite appreciation.

'Class distinction means nothing to me,' Barbara Blundell confides. 'I take as I find. But I do love the quirky traditions you get in the great houses. They add colour to life.'

The church of St Philip, like Westminster Cathedral, like the Sacred Heart in New Delhi, is a new building conceived in an old style; in this instance French Gothic. As Larry stands at the altar rail waiting for the bride to arrive he finds himself thinking about English Catholics and their churches, and how odd it is that a faith that defines itself as rooted in tradition should have to function in new buildings. Of course in France, in Italy, all this is different. There the evocations of the saints ring out in pillared aisles once walked by the saints themselves. He thinks of his father's love of the great French cathedrals. Then, for no reason, he thinks how odd it is to be getting married.

Why am I doing this?

He asks the question not because he has any doubts, but because he's suddenly aware he doesn't know the answer. From the moment he took Geraldine in his arms, and stained her white dress with blood, he has known that this is what must happen. It has never presented itself to him as a decision. From the start it has been for him a solution to his puzzles about the future: puzzles of love, and sex, and status, and identity, and no doubt many more, all resolved by this one act. He is becoming a husband. He is forming a clearer picture of that misty realm that reaches before him, his grown-up life.

The organ booms out the wedding march. Geraldine enters the church in her mother's dress, on her father's arm. She looks fragile, and grave, and beautiful. The nuptial Mass begins.

The newly married couple pass that night at Edenfield Place. Louisa appears only briefly, white-faced, to apologise for her absence, and then retreats to her room. George, now proud, now fearful at her condition, makes an abstracted host. Bride and groom retire early to the principal guest bedroom.

Both are exhausted. The bed that awaits them has ornate barley-sugar posts holding a high carved wooden canopy, and curtains in a pink and blue floral fabric. The immense wardrobe has a mirrored central panel in which they see themselves reflected, smiling, uncertain.

'I'll go and use the bathroom first, shall I?' says Larry. 'I'll get into my pyjamas there.'

He understands that Geraldine is shy of undressing in front of him. He takes his time in the bathroom. When he returns, he finds Geraldine standing where he left her, but now in a white silk nightdress. The silk clings to the curves of her body.

'You look ravishing,' he says.

She smiles, and goes on tiptoe to the bathroom. He turns out the bedroom centre light, leaving on a bedside lamp. He gets into bed. The linen sheets are chilly.

Geraldine returns, and stands, hesitating, in the middle of the room.

'Would you rather have the light out?' says Larry.

'Maybe,' she says. 'Let's try.'

He turns out the bedside lamp. The room is plunged into total darkness. He hears her approach the bed, and pat her way up it to the head. She creeps under the bedclothes, barely disturbing them, and lies beside him without touching him. He hears her breathing.

'Tired?' he says.

'A little,' she says.

He reaches out his right hand towards her, and encounters her silk-clad hip. She gives a start.

'Hello,' he says.

'Hello.'

'Cold?'

'A little,' she says.

'Why don't I warm you?'

He shuffles alongside her and with some awkwardness takes her in his arms. She curls her body so that she's lying

448

on her side, her head in the crook of his shoulder, her knees against his thighs. He strokes her back softly, to soothe the tension of her muscles.

'All a bit new, isn't it?' he says.

'Yes,' she whispers.

He kisses her, and she responds at once, in the manner of one who is determined to show willing. His caressing hands reach down her silk-clad back to the curve of her bottom. She moves a little, to release one hand, and finds his shoulder, and the back of his neck. In silence, in darkness, they touch each other lightly in safe places.

Then his left hand comes up her back to her neck and cheek, and down over her throat, over the lace ties of her nightdress, to her breast. He draws his fingers very lightly over her breast, feeling the nub of the nipple beneath the silk. While he does this she stops her own caresses entirely.

'Do you mind?' he says.

'No,' she whispers. 'You must do whatever you want.'

He runs his hand down her body to her curled-up knees, and softly presses them, making her straighten out her legs. She offers no resistance, but he feels her nervousness. For a little while longer he does no more than stroke her, from her cheek, down over her breast, to her hip. As he does so, discovering by touch alone the lines of her slender body, he becomes aroused.

Now he lets his caressing hand roam lower down her leg. His fingers tug at the fabric of her nightdress, drawing it up, until he can touch the bare skin of her thigh beneath.

'There,' he says. 'That's the real you.'

She lies still, trembling a little. He eases her nightdress up higher.

'Why don't you take it off?' he whispers.

Obediently she sits up and draws her nightdress over her head. As soon as it's off she wriggles back down under the bedclothes. He takes her in his arms again, kisses her. Each stage is an experiment for him, its outcome unknown. Excited, he now realises she will indeed cooperate with his wishes.

But he understands he must proceed slowly.

'Shall I take mine off too?'

'If you want,' she says, her voice muffled beneath the sheet.

He sits up in his turn, and pulls off his pyjama top. Then he unties the cord of his pyjama trousers and pushes them down his body, kicking them off at the bottom of the bed. Now as naked as she is he draws her back into his arms, and feels her skin against his skin. He shifts the position of his hips so that his erection lies touching her body.

She stiffens with shock. For the first time he wonders how much she knows, and what she's expecting.

'It's all right,' he murmurs. 'It's all right.'

Slowly her body softens against him. He strokes her with long slow passes, all down her body, and timidly, she begins to caress him too.

He takes her hand and places it on his erection, wanting her to know that part of him and not be frightened. He moves her hand up and down, and she allows herself to excite him in this simple way. But when he takes his hand away, her hand stops moving.

He strokes her thighs, and runs his hand over the furry mound where her thighs meet.

'Do you know what it is we do?' he whispers.

'A little,' she says.

From the way she says it he realises that she doesn't know. He goes on stroking her, thinking now how brave she is to submit to this unknown ordeal. He kisses her.

'It's all right,' she says. 'You must do what you want.'

So this is her sacrifice, in her love for him. But once the unknown becomes known it will cease to be a sacrifice. It will become their shared delight.

Her naked body against his is having its natural effect. He wants very much to be closer still. But he wants her to know what's going to happen. So he runs his hand between her thighs and, easing them a little apart, he feels for the place where he will enter her.

As soon as his fingers began to probe, she stiffens once more. He withdraws his hand, and taking her hand again, causes it to move up and down his erection.

'When we make love,' he says, 'this has a special way of being close to you.' He takes her hand and places it between her thighs. 'In here. Inside you.'

She says nothing for a moment. Then, very low, she says, 'How?'

'It just does. It goes in.'

'Is that what you want?'

'It's just how it works,' he says. 'It's how love works.'

'Is that what love is?' she says.

'Oh, my darling. Your mother told you nothing?'

'She told me I must do whatever you asked of me. She said my wedding present to you was the gift of my body.'

'It is. It is. And mine to you.'

'Then you must do it, my love,' she whispers. 'You have only to tell me what it is you want of me. I belong to you now.'

Her submission touches him deeply. It also excites him. The idea that he can command her to pleasure him as he wills excites him.

He moves his body so that he's lying over her, and easing himself into position, begins to press to enter her. She opens her legs, now understanding his intent, but at the same time she holds her breath. He nuzzles against her, meaning to make no harsh move, aware that to start with she could feel some pain. But he makes no progress at all.

He pushes a little harder. From his lovemaking with Nell, he's familiar with the sensation of yielding and opening up, but this time there's no giving way. Her body is soft and exciting, almost too exciting, but offers him no right of entrance.

'Is there something I must do?' she says.

'Don't be afraid,' he says.

He wants to say, Open yourself to me, welcome me, love me. But he understands how frightening it must be to her, and that he must be patient. At the same time the desire is mounting in him, the simple hunger for satisfaction, and he wants to force himself into her before it's too late. He pushes more eagerly, and hears her utter a low gasp. Then comes a wave of guilt.

What right have I to put my own pleasure before hers? We have a whole lifetime ahead of us. I can surely afford to wait one more day.

He eases himself off her body, and lies on his back beside her.

'Have you done it?' she says.

He can't contain a short laugh.

'No, my darling,' he says. 'But it doesn't matter. We're both tired. There'll be other nights.'

She lies beside him in the darkness, in silence. After a while he thinks perhaps she's gone to sleep. But when at last she speaks he realises she's been crying soundlessly.

'I'm sorry,' she says.

'Darling, darling, sweetheart. It's not your fault.'

'I'm so stupid and ignorant,' she says. 'But I'll get better, I promise you. I'll be a good wife.'

'You are a good wife, my darling. The best in the world. You'll see. It'll all come right soon. It's my fault, I shouldn't be in so much of a hurry. But if I am, it's because I love you and want you so much.'

'And I do love you so much too,' says Geraldine.

After that they kiss, and put their night clothes back on, and settle down to sleep. Larry lies awake far into the night. Geraldine lies still and quiet beside him, and he's not sure if she sleeps or not.

Late October in Normandy is golden with sunlight. Geraldine, enchantingly pretty, stays close by Larry's side, smiling for him, touching him, leaning her soft head against his shoulder. The French staff of La Grande Heuze all fall in love with the young couple, and wait on them with tender care. Geraldine does her best with the servants, laughing at her own poor French, thanking them with smiling bobs of her pretty head. 'Qu'elle est charmante,' they say to each other. 'Vraiment bien élevée, cette petite Madame Cornford.'

At night, progress of a sort is made. Geraldine now understands fully what is required of her, and professes herself willing to do all that her husband wants; but her body is not under the command of her will. By the third night it seems to Larry that he is being too cautious, and that what is needed is a more powerful attack. He explains this to Geraldine and she accepts his analysis, saying as ever, 'If that's what you think is for the best.' However, when the theory is put into practice she suffers a violent reaction. She starts breathing in short rapid jerks, and almost faints. Alarmed, full of self-reproach, Larry abandons his attack at once, and spends the rest of the night cradling her in his arms. When they are found to be sleeping in late the following morning the servants smile at each other and whisper, 'Qu'il est doux, l'amour des jeunes.'

For the remaining days of their honeymoon Larry treats his young bride with great gentleness, and she shows him even more physical affection than before. They speak about the matter openly only once.

'It will be all right, won't it, darling?' she says.

'Of course it will,' he replies. 'It's just a matter of giving it time.'

'You aren't too horribly disappointed in me?'

'How could I be?'

He reaches his hand across the breakfast table and she takes it in hers. They smile into each other's eyes.

'I do love you so much, darling,' she says. 'I'm so proud and happy to be married to you. I promise you I'll make you happy too.'

'You make me happy already,' he says.

In so many ways she's so perfect. And of course, she's still young, only twenty-two. Easy to forget in view of the formidable efficiency with which she manages herself and those around her. If her body is young and fearful, that should be no surprise. All will come right in time.

32

Kitty's new baby is a good baby right from the start. She feeds well and sleeps well, and seems to be happy wherever she's put. Her name is Elizabeth. Her arrival changes everything for Kitty. Her life is now filled from morning to night with tending to the baby's simple and immediate needs. All other concerns withdraw to that shadowy space on the edge of consciousness. At the centre, pink-cheeked, smelling of warm milk, chirruping with contentment, lies little Elizabeth.

Pamela is less delighted.

'She looks like a monkey,' she says.

'But she's a dear little monkey, isn't she?'

'I suppose so,' says Pamela.

Somehow this name clings on, and the baby comes to be called the Monkey, which is later shortened to the Monk. Pamela, who has recently passed her fifth birthday, becomes aware that the Monk is often compared favourably to herself as a baby. Apparently she cried a lot, and wouldn't eat what she was given, and threw her toys out of the pram. The Monk's placidity is much remarked upon, always in highly approving terms.

'She was born with a good nature,' they say, gazing fondly on her as she sleeps.

'She might be dead,' says Pamela.

She takes to poking the baby surreptitiously, to make her cry.

Louisa comes calling most days. Her own pregnancy is now well advanced. The early sickness has passed, but she continues to give her doctors cause for concern.

'It's so unfair,' she complains to Kitty. 'I should be dancing for joy, but instead I feel like a cow with a hangover.'

George fusses round her, and tells her to sit down all the time. To Kitty's surprise, Louisa shows no irritation at this. She leans on his arm for support, and pats him, like a horse.

'George says if it's a boy he's to be William, after his father.'

'I think it will be a boy,' says George.

'Oh, you don't want a boy,' Ed says. 'Boys are always shouting and fighting.'

Ed is so much sweeter these days. Kitty knows very well that deep down he's not happy, but at least he's making a real effort to be friendly. She even has hopes that he's overcome his habit of drinking too much. Then one day Mrs Willis finds a stash of empty bottles while cleaning the small parlour. This is the room Ed calls his 'office', to which he often retires. The empty bottles were in a cupboard.

'Why hide empty bottles, Ed?'

'I wasn't hiding them. I was storing them. We reuse glass bottles, you know? Every bottle costs tuppence. That soon adds up.'

She can tell by the way his voice goes up in pitch that he's ashamed and defensive, so she lets the matter drop. But from now on, when he seems more silent and sleepy-eyed than usual, she suspects him of having been drinking. She knows she should talk to him about it, but the baby occupies all her time and care, and truth to tell she's afraid of raising the issue.

In May, when the hawthorn blossom is white in the hedges and the young leaves are bright on the trees, Larry and Geraldine come down for the weekend. This visit has been long promised, and at last a time has arrived when Ed is home, and Larry's business can spare him. The Cornfords motor down from London in a new Riley saloon, a shiny dark-red car with cream sides. This is only the first sign of Larry's new prosperity. He gets out to reveal he's wearing a tailored tweed suit, and a tie that looks suspiciously like an old school tie.

Kitty bursts into laughter.

'Larry, what's happened to you! You've turned into landed gentry!'

'That's Geraldine,' says Larry. 'She's taken me in hand.'

Geraldine is wearing a tight-fitting red wool coat with a long full skirt of a kind Kitty has never seen before. On Geraldine's slim and elegant figure the effect is stunning.

'Lord, I feel so dowdy and provincial,' Kitty exclaims.

'You mustn't be too disappointed by the way we live.'

'How could we be?' says Geraldine, looking round with the smile of one who has come determined to be pleased. 'It's bliss to be out of London. Just look at all this!' She means the trees, the Downs, the sky. 'It makes Kensington Gardens feel very poky, I assure you.'

Geraldine has perfect manners. She goes into raptures over baby Elizabeth, now almost five months old. She has a present for Pamela, a doll that isn't a baby at all but a lady, with clothes you can take off and another set of clothes to change her into. Pamela is mute with pleasure.

'Say thank you, Pammy.'

The little girl looks up at the beautiful lady and can't speak. Her eyes shine with gratitude.

'That's so clever of you,' says Kitty. 'You couldn't have got her anything she'd like more.'

There are presents for Kitty too, or as Geraldine puts it, 'for the house.' A box of chocolates from Fortnum & Mason and a bottle of Dom Pérignon.

'How in God's name did you get that?' says Ed, examining the label.

'From Larry's cellar,' says Geraldine. She and Larry have set up house in Campden Grove, along with Larry's father. 'It's a '37, which I'm told was a very good year. I hope you don't think I'm bringing coals to Newcastle.'

Over lunch Larry tells them about the source of his new-found prosperity, which is the family firm.

'The whole thing has been a revelation to me,' he says. 'You know how I was so dead set against going into the business, or any business, for that matter. And I'm sure you think the only reason I'm doing it now is for the big car and so forth. But the truth is, I've become almost passionate about the job.'

'Passionate about bananas, Larry?' says Ed, smiling as he watches him.

'Passionate about bananas if you like,' says Larry. 'But it's the firm itself I love. I'm so proud of what my grandfather and my father have built. Do you know we're just about the only company that provides retirement pensions for our employees? We've been doing it since '22. It's called the Staff Provident Fund. The company pays an extra ten per cent of salary every year into a special benefit account for each employee. Then they get a lump sum on retirement, and if it's not enough we top it up.'

Geraldine reaches out to touch his arm, stopping him in mid-flow.

'But I shouldn't go on like this about business. We're not in the office now.'

'No, do go on,' says Kitty. 'I love it that you love what you do.'

'The thing is,' says Larry, catching fire again, 'our people love the company. No one ever leaves. We have company sports grounds. In New Malden for the London-based staff, and in Avonmouth, and in Liverpool. We have an annual cricket match, Fyffes versus the MCC. Some of our men are county players.'

'I take it all back,' says Ed. 'This is more than bananas.'

'Well, of course the banana trade creates the wealth of

the company,' says Larry. 'But the wealth of the company is spread round all our people, just as if every worker was a member of the family. Though of course' – he blushes as he realises he has perhaps gone a little too far – 'my father and I get a greater share of the wealth than most.'

'I'm impressed with wealth in any form,' says Ed. 'I know what damned hard work it is getting it.'

'Ed's doing so well,' says Kitty. 'He and Hugo now have crowds of people working for them.'

'If three counts as a crowd,' says Ed. 'But once all the restrictions are lifted I think we should make a decent go of it.'

'Don't talk about restrictions!' says Geraldine with a light laugh. 'I'm so tired of restrictions.'

Kitty wants to like Geraldine and tries to like her, but the truth is she does not like her. She's ashamed of this, suspecting that it springs from simple jealousy. Larry has always been her special friend, as she puts it to herself, choosing not to investigate further. She should be happy to see him settled at last, but she doesn't much care for the way he's changing. She doesn't like the tweed suit or the big car. She wants her old shabby Larry back, with his friendly puzzled face and his paint-stained fingers. She wants to have him to herself again, to talk about characters in books and how hard it is to make good people interesting.

Geraldine asks after the neighbours, which turns out after a little confusion to mean George and Louisa.

'Sometimes if it's not a bore I'd love to see Edenfield Place again,' she says. 'It is rather extraordinary.'

'Rather hideous is the word,' says Ed. 'It's the sort of monster that can only be created when money is no object. They say in his day George's father was the richest man in England.'

'We can walk over after lunch if you like,' says Kitty.

'I'd love that,' says Geraldine. 'Larry has such fond memories of being billeted in the big house.'

'No, darling,' says Larry. 'I was billeted here, in the farmhouse. Kitty was billeted in the big house.'

'Then how did you become so pally with Lord Edenfield?'

'Because of Kitty. George had a soft spot for Kitty. Kitty fell for Ed. Ed is my best friend.'

'Oh,' says Geraldine. 'I don't quite follow. But never mind.'

They walk across the park to the big house, Kitty pushing the Monk in her pram, with Pamela on one side and Geraldine on the other. Geraldine asks her about motherhood and babies. Kitty can't rid herself of the sensation that Geraldine has no personal interest in the topic, but chooses it out of politeness, supposing it to be Kitty's current central concern. In this she is correct, but that doesn't remove the faint polishy smell of good manners.

'And you manage it all without help!' says Geraldine.

'I do have someone to clean,' says Kitty. 'Two or three days a week.'

'Have you had any time at all away from her, since she was born?'

'No, not so far.'

'She doesn't do anything,' says Pamela from the far side of the pram. 'She can't talk or play or anything.'

'Oh, well,' says Geraldine with a smile, 'perhaps we'd better send her back.'

'Yes, that's what I think,' says Pamela.

'No, you don't, darling,' chides Kitty. 'She's your little baby sister. You love her.'

Larry walks ahead with Ed.

'Marriage seems to suit you,' Ed says to him.

'Yes, I suppose it does,' says Larry.

'I've always thought you were husband material. Unlike me.'

'Why aren't you?'

'You'll have to ask Kitty that. She's very patient with me, but I can be a bit much, you know? Or maybe I mean not enough.'

'Ed, Kitty adores you.'

'Yes, well.' He looks away, towards the steep rise of Edenfield Hill beyond the big house. 'It's a funny thing you going and getting married when you did. Just as well, I expect.'

'I've no idea what you're talking about,' says Larry.

'Nothing,' says Ed. 'Pay no attention to a word I say.'

They go into the house by the terrace door, Kitty calling as they enter.

'Louisa! George! It's only us!'

They find George on his own. Louisa has gone up to town to be examined yet again by her doctors. George is welcoming, but it's clear they've woken him from an afternoon nap. He keeps taking his spectacles off and rubbing them with an enormous pocket handkerchief, as if this will clear his fuddled thoughts.

'I'm so sorry Louisa's not here. We're very quiet when she's away. So this is your wife, Larry! I must congratulate you.'

'You were at the wedding, George,' says Kitty.

'Yes, I was. You're perfectly right.'

The butler appears, in response to a bell George has rung.

'Lott,' George says, 'we have guests. What are we to give them?'

'We don't need anything,' says Kitty. 'We've only come to let Geraldine have a peep at the house.'

'Our last visit was so rushed,' says Geraldine. 'I hardly saw a thing.'

'Maybe Mrs Lott could keep an eye on Elizabeth,' says Kitty.

The butler goes in search of his wife. The baby is sleeping contentedly. George becomes more animated at the prospect of showing off the house. He has done this many times, and finds himself on familiar ground. Ed and Larry opt out of the tour, and Pamela, who also knows the house well, runs off to the billiard room to play with the electric scoreboard. This leaves Kitty and Geraldine to follow in George's wake.

'The short tour please, George,' says Kitty. 'We don't want to bore Geraldine.'

'Oh, you won't bore me!' exclaims Geraldine. 'I adore old houses.'

'We'll start in the hall,' says George. 'You have to look up. The roof is the big thing here. The ridge beam is forty feet above us. All English oak. The architect was John

464

Norton, who was a friend of Pugin. He built Elveden Hall in Suffolk, too. And this portrait here, this is my father, painted by Lorimer. He's wearing the uniform he served in, in South Africa. I've never been in uniform myself. I rather regret that.'

Meanwhile Ed and Larry settle down in the library.

'You've never told me about India,' Ed says. 'Was it fun?'

'You obviously don't know what's happening over there,' says Larry. 'Don't you read the newspapers?'

'Never,' says Ed. 'What's the point? I don't need a daily list of horrors to tell me what sort of world we live in.'

'Well, India's joined the horrors,' says Larry. 'God knows how many have died since independence. Hundreds of thousands.'

'Another glorious triumph for Mountbatten, then.'

'Actually I don't blame Dickie,' says Larry. 'It had all gone too far long before he got out there. But my God! The savagery. The hatred. It makes our war look like a gentlemanly scrap.'

'And your God looks on like a fat nanny, too lazy to get up off the park bench.'

'They've got their own gods. They don't need ours.'

'And here you are, still convinced of the essential goodness of the human race. I take my hat off to you, Larry. The triumph of hope over experience.'

'That's Dr Johnson on marriage.'

'The great doctor,' says Ed.

He's smiling at Larry, but his eyes are sad.

'I've had my own little brush with experience,' says Larry.

'As a matter of fact, it's one of the reasons I've ended up married. I was in a car with a friend of mine, a Muslim, when it was attacked by a Hindu mob. They wanted to murder my friend, just because he was a Muslim. They shot him and wounded him, but when they tried to finish him off I leaned over him and got in the way.'

'You saved his life.'

'I suppose so. I wasn't hurt at all. And afterwards – I don't know how to put it – I felt like I was floating on air. I got myself back, and went looking for Geraldine, and – well, here we are.'

'The intoxication of self-sacrifice,' says Ed. 'Strong medicine.'

'Don't laugh at me, Ed. That day on the beach in Dieppe left me thinking I wasn't worth all that much. Those few minutes in the car, holding Syed in my arms . . .'

He doesn't say any more. Ed is gazing at him now with nothing but affection in his eyes.

'You're a fine man, Larry,' he says. 'You always have been. I admire you. Did you know that? I wish I could be you.'

'You're the one with the VC.'

'Oh, that dammed VC! Can't you see you're worth a hundred of me?'

'What are you talking about? You were just telling me how your business is about to take off. You've got a beautiful new baby girl. Kitty loves you.'

'Has Kitty told you about my secret vice?'

'No.'

'She will. No need to look so alarmed, it's only good old booze. Not very original, I admit. Naturally I struggle against it. Naturally I lose.'

Larry gazes at his friend in sorrow.

'Why, Ed?'

'The horror,' says Ed. 'As told in the newspapers. Which I don't read.'

On their tour of the house, George and Kitty and Geraldine have reached the bedroom floor.

'You said you were billeted here in the war,' Geraldine says to Kitty. 'Did you have one of the grand rooms, like me and Larry on our wedding night?'

'Oh, no,' says Kitty with a laugh. 'Louisa and I were up in the attics.' She indicates a narrow servants' staircase. 'Up there.'

'You were in the nursery, weren't you, Kitty?' says George.

'Yes,' says Kitty. She remembers how she came back one evening to find Ed lying on her bed. 'We were in the nursery.'

'I haven't been up there for years,' says George. 'I've no idea what state it's in. Do you want to take a look, for old times' sake?'

'Why not?' says Kitty.

George leads them up the narrow stairs. They go along the passage, with its steep sloping ceiling and its peeling walls. Kitty remembers it all.

The nursery door is closed. George opens it and goes in.

'I used to sleep here when I was a little boy,' he says. Then he falls silent, staring at the room.

It's bright and clean. The beds are made with fresh linen. On one bed sits a smiling doll, on the other a teddy bear. Four tiny cotton hand-embroidered nightdresses hang from a rail. Four pairs of knitted bootees are lined up below them. A baby's basket, lined with rosebud-printed fabric, sits on the old rocking chair. A book lies open, face down, on the floor beside it. It's *The Common Book of Baby and Child Care.*

'How extraordinary,' says George. 'I had no idea.'

He moves round the room as if in a dream.

'Odd place to put the nursery,' he says. 'Up among the servants' bedrooms. But I was very fond of it. You see here, it has a tower window in one corner. I used to go in there and draw the curtains. I think I believed when I was in there no one could find me.'

'Such a pretty room,' says Geraldine.

'Yes,' says George. 'How extraordinary.'

'It's not so very extraordinary, George,' says Kitty. 'You are going to have a baby, after all.'

'The odd thing is,' says George, 'you don't quite realise it at first. I suppose he'll have this room, just as I did.'

'Isn't it more of a servant's room?' says Geraldine.

'No,' George insists. 'This is the nursery. I'm glad Louisa understands that.'

As they descend the main staircase they hear the sound of the gramophone coming from the drawing room. They go through the anteroom into the great room. Its red damask walls are brightly lit by the spring sunlight streaming in through the three tall south-facing windows. There on the red carpet between the sofas Ed is dancing with Pamela to the singing of the Ink Spots.

He looks round and smiles as they come to a stop in the doorway.

'Pammy found it,' he says. 'She insisted on a dance.'

Kitty watches them as they dance, Pamela gravely concentrating, looking up from time to time at her handsome father. Ed seems carefree, happy in a way that is all too rare these days.

'That is such a charming sight,' says Geraldine. 'Where have you hidden my husband?'

'I'm here,' says Larry, speaking from behind them.

'We should dance,' says Geraldine. Her dancing is generally admired.

'No,' says Larry. 'This is Pammy's dance.'

Kitty throws him a quick grateful look.

'Last time we played this song,' Kitty tells Geraldine, 'there was a foot of snow outside and we could hardly get out of the house.'

'Oh, that terrible winter,' says Geraldine, watching the dancers. 'Ed is a graceful mover, I must say.'

'Unlike me, she means,' says Larry.

'Not at all! You're a very good dance partner, darling. But Ed looks so relaxed, while at the same time being so very much in charge. He's the pure English type of hero, isn't he?' This is for Kitty. 'Going into battle as if he's taking a stroll in the park.'

Kitty doesn't answer. She's watching Ed and feeling how much she loves him, and how much it hurts.

PART FOUR

A GOOD MAN

1950

33

Early May in London, and the last of the day's sunshine lingers over the city. Larry leaves the office early and walks home, as he often does, through the park. Past the Serpentine and the Round Pond where he sailed his boat as a child, just as other children are doing today; and so to the streets of Kensington.

There is a conversation waiting to be had, about which he is not thinking.

As he enters the house, Geraldine appears from the garden to greet him with a kiss, in the usual way, but he has learned to read the small signs. When under stress she retreats into efficiency, doing whatever is to be done with extra care and precision. This spring afternoon she has been weeding the rose beds in their town garden. She wears an apron, and carries a shallow basket to collect the weeds, and a small two-pronged fork.

'Do you mind if I carry on? I'm almost finished.'

'No, of course not,' says Larry.

He follows her out down the back steps, and settles himself on the garden bench. Geraldine kneels down on a rubber mat and digs away with her little fork, neither hurrying nor lingering over the task. She says nothing: waiting for him to begin.

'So how was the doctor?' says Larry.

'He was extremely thorough,' she replies. 'A very professional man.'

Larry waits for her to say more, but she seems intent on her weeding.

'Was he able to help?'

'Yes, I think so,' says Geraldine. 'He was able to reassure me on some points. There's no physical problem, he tells me. No' – her voice trembles for a moment – 'no physical defect.'

'Good,' says Larry. 'Good.'

'He told me that my situation is not unique. Far from it.'

She tugs out the weeds from the loosened soil and lays them carefully in her basket.

'And did he suggest that something can be done?'

'Time, he said. Time.'

'I see.'

Geraldine stops weeding. She rises to her feet and stands with her back to him, her head bowed. This is how she asks for affection. For a brief moment Larry rebels. He feels a pulse of anger go through him, that she should claim the role of the victim. Then he sees the way her basket shakes on her arm, and his anger melts into pity.

474

He gets up and goes to her, folding her in his arms. At once she turns round and presses herself to him.

'Oh, Larry. It was so horrible.'

She puts her basket on the ground and drops the gardening fork into the bed of weeds and begins to cry in soft gulps.

He holds her close, kissing her cheek, soothing her.

'All over now,' he says.

'I know he's a doctor, I know he does it all the time, but it was so horrible. I had to undress. I had to . . . I don't want to say it, I don't want to remember it.'

'But he told you there's nothing wrong, that's the important thing. It's good that we know that.'

She clings to him, sobbing.

'Nothing physical,' she says. 'Not physical.'

'Did he have some other suggestion?'

'He said if I wanted I could see . . . see a psychiatrist. He said it might help. He couldn't promise. He said some people benefit from talking . . . talking about it. Not everyone. Not most, even, he thought. He said sometimes these things just have to be accepted.'

'I see,' says Larry.

'Darling, I'm sorry, but I couldn't bear to talk about it with some strange man. I just couldn't. It would kill me.'

'Then you shan't,' says Larry.

'Oh, darling, darling.' She kisses him gratefully. 'I'll make it up to you in other ways. You'll see. I'll do everything for you. I'll be such a good wife to you.'

'You're that already, my love,' says Larry.

But his heart is heavy.

She wants to talk. She wants him to understand.

'I've been thinking about it so much since I got home. At first I was desperate, I kept telling myself how terrible it was, I couldn't see any way to carry on. So I did the only thing I could. I prayed about it. And while I was praying, I don't know why, I remembered what that Indian friend of yours told us, when we went to the abandoned city. Do you remember? He said it was the words of Jesus, carved on an arch. "The world is a bridge, pass over it, but build no houses on it." I don't really think they're the words of Jesus at all, but I think they're beautiful, and true. This is only a bridge, darling. What really matters is the world to come, on the other side. And when I thought that, I became calmer. I said to myself, this is the burden we're asked to carry in this life. This is our cross. But we still love each other. We're still married. We can still make each other happy. I'm right, aren't I, darling? So long as we've got each other, we're rich in love. Then I saw that there's a kind of vanity, or maybe it's greed, in expecting to have everything. Think how many cripples there are in the world, how many starving people. This is our cross, darling. Not so heavy a cross, once you get used to it. I know you want children. I know I do too. But if Almighty God is asking us to offer up to him that dearest hope of our hearts, then let's do it gladly! Let's not go about with sad faces, as if we've lost the one thing that makes life worth living. You at least understand, darling, and I so thank God you do, that this life isn't everything. This world is only a bridge. Eternity, my love. We must fix our eyes on eternity!'

Her beautiful eyes shine with a kind of ecstasy as she speaks, and she draws him into a kiss more passionate than any she has given him before.

After this Larry asks her no more. He is aware that she is more conscientious than usual, anticipating his wishes and deferring to his preferences, even when he hasn't expressed them. Having noticed the wordless tussle that takes place over *The Times* each breakfast between Larry and his father, she orders a second copy to be delivered: a simple solution that had not occurred to either of them. She discovers the date of Cookie's birthday and makes her a small present in Larry's name, and forewarns Larry so that he's prepared for Cookie's touching gratitude. She memorises the names of the humblest people in the Fyffes head office – the doorman, the cleaners, the junior secretaries – and makes a point of using them, knowing this will please Larry. She can tell almost before he knows it himself when his war wound starts to hurt him, and makes sure there are painkillers available. She's sensitive to his moods, and takes care to leave him alone when he wants to write letters, or read a book. She never criticises him, or interrupts him, or makes those sharp little jokes with which married couples sometimes pinch each other. And always, without exception, she looks lovely.

Larry's father thinks the world of her. His colleagues at head office are all half in love with her. Larry is universally said to be a lucky man. But Larry himself struggles with darker feelings.

He can't blame Geraldine, and yet he does. He knows

that the physical side of love is not the most important, but he can't stop regretting it. He tells himself that this is his lower nature, his animal nature, and that he should rise above it. He reminds himself of all the priests of the Church, and the monks at Downside, who have taken vows of chastity the better to serve God. His mind admires them and wishes to emulate them, but his body aches with unsatisfied desire.

He can't blame Geraldine, and yet he does. Every time he's told how lucky he is to have such a perfect wife he flinches, stung by guilt that he doesn't appreciate her more. But what can he do? Somewhere buried deep within him, beyond the reach of faith or reason, lies the stubborn belief that she could love him better, with her body as well as her soul, but does not choose to. The matter appears to be closed as far as she's concerned.

'Let's not talk about it, darling. It makes me so miserable. We just have to be brave.'

The worst of it for Larry is that for all her concern for him, he doesn't believe she knows the price he has to pay. The few times they've talked about his 'sacrifice' it's always been in terms of the children they'll never have. Perhaps she doesn't mention the pleasures of sex because she's shy of the words she'd have to use. But what if she's never known or even guessed at such pleasures? How could she consider it a significant loss? Of course she will have heard that men keep mistresses and frequent houses of ill repute, but men have other pursuits that aren't shared by women. They play cricket and smoke cigars. A man may not wish to give up smoking, but if his wife's health requires that he do so, he'll surely surrender the modestly pleasurable habit with a good grace.

If this is so, if Geraldine is unaware of the strain she subjects him to, then that makes her all the more innocent and deserving of his love. But at the same time, in that deep secret place within him, it adds to the growing store of his anger. This anger frightens him, and shames him. The sweeter she is to him, the more he punishes himself for his ingratitude and his selfishness. The more he chastises himself, the more he longs to chastise her. And so, swept by fantasies of violence, he begins to fear himself.

He remembers Ed in the dark chapel at Edenfield shouting at him, 'Sex is a monster, Larry!' He remembers Nell, naked in his arms, saying, 'If you fuck me will God punish you, Lawrence?' He remembers the electric thrill of hearing her say the word *fuck*. He had no fear then of God's punishment, he knows sex is part of God's creation. But perhaps he's being punished now.

The longing is too strong. It must be controlled. All men know this instinctively, that if released to do as they wish they would run amok, they would *fuck* and *fuck* and *fuck*. There's little love in this, only appetite. It's the dark side of love, perhaps it's not love at all, perhaps it's the absence of love. Which means that Geraldine is right, sex isn't what really matters. The good life can be lived without it.

So why does this capitulation feel like weakness? Because it does. Larry has felt the tug all his life of opposing forces: he wishes to be good, and he wishes to be a man. He wishes, in short, to be a good man. But when he's good he senses that he's weak, and a true man is strong. He has known himself to be weak countless times, most of all on the beach at Dieppe. He has been a good man just the once, in the midst of the Indian partition riots, when he held his wounded friend in his arms. In his exultation and relief he went, blood still wet on his clothing, to offer his newly purified love to a woman who wanted his goodness, but not his manhood.

When he thinks this way it half drives him mad. He wants to stamp and shout out, I'm a man! How does a man behave under these circumstances? He demands his rights. He satisfies his desires.

You think she'd like it if I raped her?

Ed's voice echoing out of the past.

No, she wouldn't like it. Nor would I. And anyway I could never do it. I'm too good, and too weak.

He begins to spend longer hours in the office. He studies the history of the business, and tries to understand the key factors that contribute to the good years and the bad years. Like all newcomers to a long-established business, he believes he can see better ways of ordering matters. He dreams of the day he'll be in charge of the company, and able to lead it into a new era of security and prosperity.

He talks over his ideas with his father.

'What's the biggest problem we have in the banana business? Uncertainty of supply. We have years when we just don't have the fruit to fill the ships, but we still have to maintain the fleet. These are the fixed costs that kill us. We *must* maintain the supply. So it all comes down to the producers on the ground. If they keep ahead of disease, if they replant rapidly after hurricane damage, if they manage the picking and packing as efficiently as possible, if they care as much as we do about the quality of the fruit – well, that's going to deliver a more reliable stream, isn't it? So it makes sound economic sense to get them to regard the company as *their* company. How do we do that? How do we make them understand we're all working together for the same goal? We extend to Jamaica and the Canaries and the Cameroons the benefits and the bonuses we give our people here at home.'

William Cornford nods his head in his slow way, that does not signify agreement.

'What you suggest costs money.'

'Of course. But my way, the company makes *more* money. If everyone on the payroll wants the company to succeed, then they work harder, they're more vigilant, they use their local knowledge and ingenuity to do the job better, they don't get into labour disputes, they don't fall sick, they see the fruits of their labour, and we all make money!'

His father nods his head again and frowns and sighs.

'We are a subsidiary of a larger company,' he says.

He goes to his shelves and takes down a book called *The Banana Empire*, by Kepner and Soothill, and opens it to a page he has previously marked.

'This is an investigation into the United Fruit Company,' he says. 'It was written and published before the war, in '35. In all fairness to the company I should tell you that the authors have been accused of making Communist propaganda.'

He reads from the book in his slow grave voice.

'This powerful company has throttled competitors, dominated governments, manacled railroads, ruined planters, choked cooperatives, domineered over workers, fought organised labour, and exploited consumers. Such usage of power by a corporation of a strongly industrialised nation in relatively weak foreign countries constitutes a variety of economic imperialism.'

Larry hears this in silence.

'I should also add,' says his father, 'that such practices have not been the norm in Jamaica, which has the great benefit of being part of the British Empire.'

Larry gives a short laugh.

'One empire pitched against another.'

He reaches out one hand for the book.

'I'd better read it, hadn't I?'

'You'll only find one mention of our company, on page 181. I know it by heart. They write, "Elders & Fyffes from then on" – that is, from 1902 – "became the European arm of the United Fruit Company." That is not so.' His voice has risen. His face is flushed. 'Fyffes is an independent company, in spirit if not in fact.'

Larry stays up late that night reading the book. The next morning he speaks to his father over breakfast.

'I believe it even more strongly now. There is a better way of doing business.'

He has the book before him. He reads out his own chosen extract.

'If the United Fruit Company had been more concerned

with the improvement of human relations and social welfare than with the mere obtaining of profits, it could have rendered extraordinary service to the Americas.'

William Cornford gazes at his son across his copy of *The Times* and says nothing.

'Just give me a chance to prove it,' says Larry.

'What is it you want to prove, darling?' says Geraldine, joining them at the breakfast table.

'That we can run our business for the benefit of all,' says Larry.

'All who?' says Geraldine.

Larry is watching his father. He answers Geraldine impatiently.

'All the employees.'

'But of course the business benefits the employees,' says Geraldine. 'It gives them jobs.'

'What do you say, Dad?'

'I'll tell you what I think you should do,' says his father. 'I think you should take a trip to Jamaica.'

Larry leaps up in excitement and strides up and down the breakfast room.

'The very idea I had myself! Of course I must go to Jamaica. I must see for myself. I must learn everything for myself. Of course I must go to Jamaica. I'm convinced we can produce and sell double the tonnage we're bringing in.'

'I've no doubt you're right,' says his father, smiling.

'When would you go?' says Geraldine. 'How long would you be gone?'

'You don't mind, do you?' Larry turns to her, his face bright at the new prospect.

'Of course not,' says Geraldine with composure. 'You are the breadwinner. Your work must always come first.'

The day before he sails, Larry receives a letter addressed to him as Lawrence Cornford, care of Fyffes head office. It's been opened by the office staff, who must have thought it was intended for his long-dead grandfather. The letter is from Nell.

> Darling, we're going to live in France, but I can't
> leave without writing to you. I expect you hate me
> but you shouldn't, if you had given me the chance
> I'd have explained. Darling I did it for you, and I
> was right, wasn't I? You were never sure about me. I
> told that story to see what you'd say and I was
> watching your face and saw how you were frightened
> and then a gentleman doing his duty so that was that
> really. I expect you were hurt and angry etc etc but
> I'm quite sure you've got over all that now and
> forgiven me. Tony Armitage and I are married, I
> expect you heard, I don't really know why he's such
> a pig most of the time and all this fame has gone to
> his head. He stamps and rants and calls everyone
> fools and how he can't bear fakes and posers, so we're
> going to live in France though I don't see why there
> shouldn't be fakes and posers in France too. I do love
> you darling and you mustn't mind about the story

but come and visit us in France, it's called Houlgate just down the coast from Deauville and I'm going to be so bored I expect I'll kill him. He won't care, all he cares about is himself and his painting which is actually quite restful for me. If I don't kill him we should get on all right. Remember we said we'd be friends so we have to go on being friends it's much better than being lovers. The other thing makes men so cross really I'm bored with it. Please write to me at the address above and tell me you forgive me.

34

After a day of driving down long straight empty roads, Ed reaches Narbonne, in the region of France called the Aude. He puts up in a modest inn, and eats a solitary supper of veal, accompanied by the excellent local red wine. Then as is his habit he questions his host about the vineyards of the region. He learns that the best wines are made in the land to the south, in the corner between the Pyrenees and the sea. He is advised to seek out the domaines round the village of Treilles; in particular the domaine de Montgaillard.

The next morning he drives south. On either side of the dusty white road lie shallow valleys planted with vines, sheltered by belts of almond and cypress trees. Low hills rise up beyond, the pink land studded with the grey of olive trees. Umbrella pines grow on the ridges, slanting under the pressure of the prevailing wind. The houses he passes are pink as the land, made of the same stone. He sees no one. The clusters of houses and barns have an air of abandonment.

He reaches a village at last, and stops by the church. A small bar seems to be open. In its dark interior, he finds a somnolent woman, who gives him directions to the chateau.

He follows the road, which becomes a rising track. He notes vines in their neat rows on either side. Then there at the end of the track appears the chateau, which is in fact little more than a fortified farm.

The house is big and square, with a single tower attached as if by some afterthought at one end. Two very old cars are pulled up in front of the wide door, which stands open. Ed knocks, and getting no response, calls out. After a while a girl of about ten appears, and stares at him, and runs away. After another while Ed hears a slow heavy tread, and a large elderly man presents himself. He has grey hair and grey skin that falls down his face in folds. He stoops, as tall men often do, which gives him a sad and defeated air.

Ed introduces himself and explains his business. His host, whose name is Monsieur de Nabant, is astonished to learn that an Englishman has arrived with a view to buying his wine. He keeps shaking his head, and rubbing at his cheeks. Then he invites his visitor into his house.

The interior seems to consist of one very large room, where all the affairs of the family are conducted at once. The shutters are closed against the heat, so the room is cool and dark. In the beamed and shadowy spaces Ed makes out a daybed, on which reclines an elderly lady; a kitchen table, round which sit several children; an immense fireplace, holding an iron cooking range; a grand piano; and some item of agricultural machinery on the floor, in the process of being mended by a young man. Assorted dogs gather round him to sniff at his legs.

Ed is shown to an upholstered chair in the part of the hall that might be called the sitting room. In a matching chair facing him there sits a second elderly man, small as a dwarf, with an entirely bald head, a smooth almost blank face, and remarkable grey curled moustaches. This person, who is not introduced to Ed, gazes at him with unsmiling intensity; exactly as if he supposes himself to be invisible.

M. de Nabant issues a stream of orders, and the children jump up and rush out. A middle-aged woman in an apron then comes in, makes a little bob of respect to Ed, and goes out again.

'Vous mangerez chez nous,' says M. de Nabant.

Ed thanks him.

Food arrives, carried in by the children. A bowl of olives, a *saucisson*, a block of pâté, a slab of *pain de campagne*, a cake of butter.

'Pour boire, il faut manger,' says M. de Nabant.

The wine arrives in unlabelled bottles. Ed and his host and his host's luxuriantly moustached friend eat and drink. The rest of the household and the dogs look on from the shadows. The wine is unusual, very ripe and gamy. M. de Nabant watches Ed as he drinks and notes his response with satisfaction.

'Notre premier vendange depuis la guerre.'

Ed asks what combination of grape varieties he uses.

'Carignan, Mourvèdre, Grenache Noir.'

Another bottle is opened.

'Seulement Mourvèdre,' says M. de Nabant.

Between the three of them they drink a bottle and a half of the wine. The woman comes and goes with the dishes. The boy on the floor grunts and mutters over his spanners. The children, no longer excited by the newcomer, return to giggling round the table. The dogs roll over and go back to sleep.

After they've eaten M. de Nabant rises, and with the same air he has projected throughout, that this is the way everything must be, he says to Ed, 'Maintenant nous allons visiter le vignoble.'

His moustached friend does not accompany them on their tour of the vineyard. Ed learns that his name is Vivier, that he is a scholar and a historian, and that he studied long ago at Oxford University.

The vines on closer inspection turn out to be extremely well maintained. The tiny green berries are just beginning to form. In all, the domaine extends to a little under five hectares, and produces ten thousand bottles a year.

Ed discusses quantities and prices and means of transport. He proposes an initial purchase from last year's bottling of ten cases, to test the market. The price is so low he finds himself suggesting a higher figure, which M. de Nabant accepts without comment.

On their return to the house, Ed is left by his host in the company of his silent friend while he searches out his account books.

'I understand you studied at Oxford,' Ed says in English.

The old man nods, and suddenly smiles a sweet smile that makes the ends of his moustache quiver.

'Is our local wine to your liking?'

He speaks softly and distinctly, with a charming accent.

'Very much,' says Ed.

'You are a long way from home.'

'I go where my business takes me,' says Ed.

M. Vivier studies him with an intent gaze.

'You have no need to travel so far to find good wine,' he says. 'The English are usually content to stop at Bordeaux.'

'Your prices are lower,' says Ed.

M. Vivier nods. Then after a pause he says, 'Are you aware that you are in the land of the *bons hommes*?'

'No,' says Ed. 'Who are the *bons hommes*?'

'Also called the Cathars.'

'Yes, of course,' says Ed.

Here in the Aude, as he knows very well, he's deep in what was once Cathar country: Carcassonne, Montségur, Albi. They say twenty thousand heretics were massacred in the siege of Béziers. But this is all ancient history.

'I haven't heard Cathars called *bons hommes* before,' Ed says.

'It was their own name for themselves,' says M. Vivier. 'They are a much misunderstood sect.'

M. de Nabant re-enters with his account book.

'They held heretical beliefs, I seem to remember,' Ed says. 'The pope launched a crusade against them.'

'That is so. May I ask, do you subscribe to a faith yourself?'

'I was raised a Catholic,' says Ed. 'But I've rather fallen away, I'm afraid.'

'Fallen away? You no longer believe?'

'I no longer believe.'

M. de Nabant, unable to follow the conversation in English, speaks rapidly to his friend in the local dialect. His friend replies, also in dialect. Then he turns to Ed.

'He tells me you have come to buy wine,' he says. 'I am not to bore you with dangerous nonsense from the past.'

After the wine and the music and the sunny tour of the vines, Ed finds himself in a mellow state of mind.

'What is this dangerous nonsense?'

'It is the creed of the *bons hommes*,' says M. Vivier. 'My own special area of study.'

M. de Nabant throws up his hands, as if giving up on his attempt to control his friend. He lays down his account book and reaches down to stroke his dogs.

'May I presume to ask,' says M. Vivier to Ed, 'why you no longer believe? Is it perhaps because you question how a good God could make an evil world?'

'Something like that,' says Ed.

'But you don't enquire further. You don't take the next step, obvious though it is.'

'I'm sorry,' says Ed. 'I seem to have missed it.'

'That this evil world was made by an evil God.'

Ed smiles, amused by what could indeed be called an obvious step.

'Ah, yes. That would follow.'

'Many things follow, once you open your mind. This

world is a prison. In our hearts we know this is not where we belong. We seek freedom, sir. You seek freedom.'

'I'd gladly seek freedom,' says Ed, 'if I knew where to find it.'

'You do know. You have in you the divine spark. There is only freedom in the spirit.'

'It seems you know more about me than I know about myself.'

M. Vivier takes this as a rebuke.

'Forgive me. As my friend will tell you, I can forget my good manners once launched on this subject. The English care greatly about good manners.'

'Not me,' says Ed. 'I'm much more interested in this evil God.'

The little man is gratified.

'You are not shocked?'

'Not at all.'

'Then allow me to go further. All men have a natural instinct to look for meaning in their lives. We crave meaning, and love, and order. You too, perhaps?'

'Me too, perhaps,' says Ed.

'And do you find meaning, and love, and order?'

'No.'

'Of course not. You live in an evil world, made by an evil God. You are a *bon homme* in a *mauvais monde*.'

M. de Nabant utters a low groan and rolls his eyes. Evidently he has witnessed this performance by his friend before.

'I'm a good man?' says Ed. 'I'm a Cathar?'

'Names are unimportant,' says the old man. 'Only the truth is important.'

'And that truth is, that this world is evil?'

'This world is created and ruled by the power the *bons hommes* call Rex Mundi. The king of the world.'

'And this king of the world is evil?'

'We know it,' says the old man, 'by his works. This world is evil. All matter is evil. Our bodies are evil. But our spirit seeks the good, which is love. It is this suffering of the spirit, trapped in the prison of the body, which causes mankind so much unhappiness.'

Ridiculous though this should be, Ed finds himself taking the little man's words seriously. Partly it's the absolute confidence with which that soft earnest voice speaks. Partly it's because he seems to see into Ed's own heart with such uncanny accuracy.

'Do I understand,' says Ed, 'that you yourself follow this Cathar creed?'

'No. I follow no creed. I am a historian. I study the beliefs of those who are long gone. But my mind is open.'

'Did the Cathars have an answer? How did they seek to escape this trap?'

'The *bons hommes* taught that we must renounce this world, and set our spirits free.'

'How?'

'Must I tell you how? If the body is the prison of the spirit, how is the spirit to go free?'

'By death,' says Ed.

'The death of the body,' says the old man. 'The death of this world.'

'And after death?'

'After death is life.'

'How do we know that?'

'We know it because we have the divine spark in us. That is the source of our unhappiness. It is also our proof of eternal life.'

Ed is more struck by this than he cares to admit. For the first time he is being offered a version of existence that matches his own experience. The terror he feels, that he calls 'the darkness', is nothing more nor less than the world he lives in. The God who made it, in whom he could never believe, is an evil God. This he can believe all too readily. The pain he lives with every day is the longing to escape.

And yet surely this is all nonsense. Yet more superstition, cobbled together to meet man's bottomless hunger for meaning in a meaningless world.

'Why did the pope call the Cathars heretics?' he says. 'Why did they have to be exterminated?'

'Why does power hate freedom? Need you even ask?'

'Why did they call themselves *bons hommes*?'

'They believed themselves to be the true Christians. They believed the Roman Catholic Church had become an abomination, and they were returning to the pure faith as preached by Jesus Christ. They sought no power, no glory. No hierarchy, no great churches. They wanted something that is very simple and very challenging. They wanted to be good.'

Driving away from Montgaillard, tracing his route back through Treilles and Narbonne and so on to Carcassonne, Ed laughs at himself for his partial surrender. There was a moment in which he almost thought he had stumbled on a truth that could set him free. And what does it turn out to be? Some warmed-up version of a long-dead heresy.

In Carcassonne he visits a library and finds a book about the Cathars. He learns that they were willing to die for their faith in their thousands. At the siege of Béziers their attacker, Simon de Montfort, mutilated a column of prisoners, sent them back into the town with their eyes gouged out, their lips and noses cut off, led by a one-eyed man, to frighten them into surrender. They all chose to die. At its height whole congregations converted en masse to the heresy, whole chapters of cathedrals, so compelling was the Cathar teaching. All Languedoc was infected, the highest born, the best educated, the most intelligent leading the way. It took the pope and the mercenary armies of northern France twenty-one years to crush the heretics. They never recanted. They had to be killed, by hanging or burning at the stake. Whatever else you might say of them, the *bons hommes* were brave and sincere.

Of course, he thinks; and laughs at the simplicity of it. Why should they fear death? Through death they found freedom.

35

Larry sails from Avonmouth on the company's newest purpose-built ship, the TSS *Golfito*. In the course of the two-week crossing he questions the captain on all aspects of the business, in particular the issue of how much cargo they carry on the westbound run. Larry finds it hard to believe the hold space can't be more valuably used.

'Everyone thinks that,' says the captain, 'but once you start running about here, there and everywhere, picking up a little of this and little of that, you've ended up paying out more than you're getting in. We carry bulk bananas. That's what our ships are built for.'

The *Golfito* has cabins for ninety-four passengers, sandwiched in the middle of the ship, between the giant refrigerated holds. It will make the return voyage with 1,750 tons of bananas.

One of the passengers, a colonial civil servant called Jenkins, takes it upon himself to dispel any illusions that Larry might have about the Jamaicans.

'Delightful people,' he says, 'friendly, happy, excellent company and all that. Just don't ever ask them to hurry up. They won't hurry up. I'm not saying they're slow-witted. Not at all. They're more what you might call easy. They like to take life easy.'

'But we don't. We take life hard.'

'That's one way of looking at it. We work hard. We get things done. We build railways, and shipping lines. So we end up in charge. But I'll tell you one thing, Cornford. If I'd grown up in Jamaica I'd be all for taking life easy. It's a very pleasant climate most of the time. I'm a subscriber to the climate theory of empire. Cold weather makes you active. So it's the nippy northerners who end up ruling the sleepy southerners.'

'Not in India any more.'

'True, but look what happens as soon as we leave. They all start massacring each other.'

'You don't think that's something to do with us?'

'How could it be?' says Jenkins, to whom this thought has obviously never occurred. 'They lived together happily enough under our rule for two hundred years.'

Larry decides not to tell Jenkins that he was in India at the time of partition. He still hasn't worked out in his own mind what he thinks about what happened.

'The killing of Gandhi,' he says. 'I was shocked by that.'

'That fellow lived in cloud-cuckoo-land,' says Jenkins. 'Did you know he drank his own urine? Mind you, it's coming here too. God alone knows how the place will run without us.'

By the end of the crossing Larry has had the opportunity to speak to many of the other passengers. They all tell him the same thing.

'You should have seen Jamaica before the war. It was a paradise. All over now, of course.'

When he tries to discover why, he learns that it's not just a matter of the damage the war years have done to the island's economy.

'The people aren't the same any more. What with the trade unions and the strikes, and Bustamante and Manley working them up to feel aggrieved about everything. The sugar strike in '38, that was the day old Jamaica died.'

They're all on deck as the ship sails round Port Royal and into Kingston harbour. The air is heavy and warm. The Fyffes manager, Cecil Owen, is waiting at the quayside. He's a red-faced comfortably built man in his fifties, who seems to know everyone he passes. He greets Larry with great warmth.

'Knew you as soon as I set eyes on you,' he says. 'Just like your dad, only with hair. How was the crossing?'

'Excellent. Very smooth.'

'She's a beauty, isn't she?'

He runs his eyes with satisfaction over the handsome new ship, then turns back to Larry.

'You'll stay with me, of course.'

'I don't want to cause you any trouble.'

'No trouble. I'm a bachelor. Glad of the company. Watch out, here it comes!'

A sudden downpour sends everyone on the dockside scurrying for cover. The warm rain dances on the paving stones, and the air fills with a rich sweet smell. Black dockworkers, careless of the rain, get on with unloading the passengers' trunks from the newly arrived ship. Cars roll by, splashing in the sudden puddles, rain overwhelming their windscreen wipers. Cecil and Larry stand under the cover of the long customs shed, waiting for the cloudburst to pass.

'Should be a driver somewhere,' says Cecil. 'He'll have seen the ship coming. He'll find us.'

That evening Larry finds himself sitting with Cecil on the wide porch of his house, drinking rum and fresh lime juice, gazing out over the dark blue waters of Hunt's Bay. The afternoon rain has left the roofs of the town below sparkling in the evening sunlight.

'They told me on the ship that Jamaica was a paradise once,' Larry says, 'but now it's all over.'

'All over, is it?' says Cecil. 'Who told you that?'

'A fellow called Jenkins. He thinks the people here aren't up to running things.'

'Johnny Jenkins? He's an idiot. I've lived here for thirty years and I love the place, but you have to look at it from their point of view. We bring them over from Africa as slaves. Then we set them free and tell them we're the mother country and they're our children, and they're to be grateful to us. Then we make a lot of money getting them to grow bananas for us. Then we get ourselves into a war and tell them we don't want their bananas after all. After all that, you'd want to run your own show, wouldn't you? But the difficulty is, if you spend three hundred years telling people they're children, they become afraid to go out alone. They need us, and they don't want to need us. So you see,' he concludes with a chuckle, 'what we've ended up with is an island full of angry children.'

Larry thinks of India, and the complicated mix of admiration and resentment he found there.

'Does everyone think the way you do, Cecil?'

'Good God, no! By everyone you mean the white men, of course.'

'Yes, I suppose I do.'

'No, no. Your average planter here thinks the Jamaicans are idle, ungrateful, and incapable of taking a piss without someone to unbutton their trousers. Happy children of nature and all that balls.'

'Children again.'

'There's the British Empire for you. Make the darkies work for you for nothing, then tell them you're all one big family.'

'There are other kinds of empire,' says Larry. 'What's your view of our American owners?'

'Gangsters, the lot of them!'

'So are we gangsters too?'

'Not in the United class. They wrote the book. You have to hand it to those boys. Did you hear about how Zemurray got Bonilla in as President of Honduras? One yacht, a case of rifles, three thousand rounds of ammunition, and a bruiser called Machine Gun Maloney. Those were the days.'

Larry relaxes in the warm evening air, tired after the long voyage, made dreamy by rum. A brown lizard scurries across the porch before him, to disappear over the side. The bougainvillea is in brilliant bloom on the slopes below the house. Then as he watches, a hummingbird passes, hanging briefly in the air before him.

'There,' says Cecil. 'That's a real Jamaican welcome.'

The bird has a tiny bright green body and a long red bill. As Larry watches, it jumps back and forth in the air before him, and then flits away into the purple blossoms.

'This is paradise, Cecil.'

Larry realises sitting on that porch that he is at ease in a way he hasn't been for many months. He chooses not to explore this realisation. Enough to enjoy it while it lasts.

Cecil takes him on a tour of the plantations. Many have been hit by Panama disease, a fungus that attacks the roots of the banana plants. He finds a vigorous programme under way of rooting out the diseased Gros Michel plants, and replacing them with the Panama-resistant Lacatan variety. He watches the plantation workers cutting the heavy stems of green bananas, and carrying them long distances to the collection points. He talks to them about the work, but can get very little out of them.

'They think you'll sack them if they complain,' says Cecil.

'I won't sack you,' says Larry.

'Sacking is nothing,' says Cecil. 'In Guatemala the United people shoot them if they complain.'

They laugh at that.

'I won't shoot you either, I promise. But I do want to know if you think the company's treating you fairly.'

They shrug and look down at the hard earth.

'It's a job,' says one.

The others nod in agreement.

'Could you get a better job?'

'Not today.'

'But maybe one day?'

They all give cautious nods, watching to see if he minds.

'One day Jamaica will be independent,' Larry says. 'Will everything be better then?'

They shrug and remain silent.

'Come on, Joseph,' says Cecil. 'You don't usually sit on your tongue.'

'Well, sir,' says Joseph. He strokes the fruit on the stem of bananas beside him. 'I don't see no one like me getting rich.'

'So when independence comes,' says Larry, 'you'll ask us to go.'

A great shaking of heads greets the suggestion.

'Fyffes leave Jamaica? Never!'

Rumbling across the island's rutted roads in Cecil's company jeep, the warm wind in his hair, Larry tries out the idea that has been forming in his mind for weeks now. He describes his vision of a company where every employee feels valued.

'Won't make a blind bit of difference,' Cecil says. 'They'll carry on just the same as ever.'

'But why? If we improve their pay, their benefits?'

'Whatever you give them they'll take gladly, but they've got people telling them every day that we get rich on their backs. They're comfortable being dissatisfied. They wouldn't know how to be content with their lot.'

'Why should they be so different to us?'

'Who says they're different to us? Hell, I'm dissatisfied. Improve my pay and my benefits if you want.'

Larry likes Cecil. He strikes him as a man who is at ease with himself. Sharing the evening meal with him, watching the pleasure he takes in his food, he returns to the subject of his dream company.

'There just has to be a way for people to work together in a business the way they work together in a regiment, or in a football team. Where every success is a success for all. Why does there have to be this feeling that one man's gain is another man's loss?'

'Because one man's richer than another.'

'I don't agree. I think everyone understands about differentials in pay. They don't expect everyone to get the same. They know some people are cleverer, or harder working, or more burdened with responsibility than others. Not everyone wants to be the boss. What everyone does want is to feel respected and valued in their work. They want to be proud of their company, and know that their company is proud of them. They want to be known as individuals, not bought and sold like cattle. They want their work to give meaning to their life.'

Cecil gazes across the table at Larry with a puzzled but affectionate look.

'I think you really mean it,' he says.

'Why shouldn't I?'

'Well, you're up against human nature, aren't you? Deep down, people are shits.'

'Are you a shit? Because I assure you I'm not.'

'You're a good man, Larry Cornford. Like your father before you. God bless you. I pray you don't get too hurt.'

Larry bids farewell to Cecil Owen and sails from Kingston to New Orleans, on a ship of the Great White fleet. New Orleans is now the headquarters of the United Fruit Company. Given Larry's position in Fyffes, inexperienced but marked for leadership, his father has thought it necessary for him to meet the president of the parent company, the legendary Sam Zemurray. However when Larry presents himself at United's handsome headquarters on St Charles Avenue, he finds he is scheduled to meet a vice-president of the company called James D. Brunstetter.

'Call me Jimmy. Great to meet you, Larry. We have a high regard for your father, as I'm sure you know. He doesn't go for the quick buck, but a slow buck is still a buck, right?'

He's a small man in his sixties who chain-smokes and talks fast.

'So you've been in Jamaica. Did you meet Jack Cranston, our main man there? You'd like Jack, everyone likes Jack. So how old are you, Larry?'

'I'm thirty-two, sir.'

'Well now, I wasn't around when your grandfather did the deal with Andy Preston, but as I understand it, the deal went like this. Back us, leave us alone, and we'll make you money. Is that how you understand it?'

'Exactly how I understand it.'

'Then we'll get along just fine. There's only one rule in business. Just keep making money. That way no one's going to bother you. Now what can I do for you? You want to check out our operation here? You want to take a look at our docks?'

'I'd like that very much.'

'I'll take a stroll with you myself. The Thalia Street wharf is only a hop and skip away. Grab your hat, young man.'

Jimmy Brunstetter walks as fast as he talks. By the time they reach the wharf Larry is sweating freely in the humid heat.

The United wharf is three times the size of the Fyffes' wharf at Avonmouth. Lines of men walk one behind the other, each with a stem of bananas on their shoulder, forming a ceaseless stream from ship to store. Two ships are docked, each one being unloaded by specialist cranes.

'You know how many stems we bring in each year?' says Brunstetter. 'Twenty-three million. You heard of Miss Chiquita Banana? Sure you have. We're labelling the fruit now, every hand, with the Chiquita brand.'

'My grandfather did the same with the Fyffes blue label, in '29.'

'Okay! So you got there ahead of us. Good for you.'

They enter the welcome cool of the transit shed. All down the long aisles stems of green bananas hang from racks as far as the eye can see.

'There it is,' says Brunstetter. 'That's where the money comes from. You want to know the secret of our success?

Control. Ask Sam, he'll tell you the same thing every time. Control. Control every stage in the process. Planting, growing, transporting, shipping, marketing. And how do you get control? Ownership. Own the plantations, own the railroads, own the ships, own the docks.'

'Own the countries,' says Larry.

Brunstetter gives a hoot of laughter.

'You got it! Own the countries. Damn right! Only we don't do it the way you guys do it, with your empire. We don't put our name over the door. That way everyone hates you. No, we leave the local boys to run the show. All we ask is that they run it our way.'

'So I hear,' says Larry.

Before he sails for home Larry writes two letters, to Ed and Kitty and to Geraldine, even though he knows they'll reach England only a few days ahead of his own return.

> This trip has taught me so much about this strange
> business I'm in, and a lot of it's not very edifying.
> The general idea seems to be that if it makes money
> it's good. There is a kind of logic to this, we all need
> money to live, so making it is good however you go
> about it. But the more I think this through, the more
> it seems to me that the world of business is missing
> the bigger picture. Man does not live by bread alone.
> I can hear Ed utter a groan. But you don't need to
> bring in God for this. Surely it's obvious. We need
> bread to stay alive, but bread is not *what we live for*.

And so it is with money. It's not an end, it's a means. The goal we're all after is the good life. So you see, Kitty, all our talks about goodness turn out to be important after all. Even in the hard world of business, goodness matters. It's the heart of the good life. To be honest I'm not sure what I mean by this, I'm working it out as I write. What has goodness to do with the good life? I suppose what I call the good life means life that is both happy and valued. We all want to feel our existence has some purpose. And I don't see how we can feel that if we live in such a way that all our comforts come from the suffering of others. So we need to believe that we're fundamentally good, on the side of the angels as we say, in order to lead a good life. And yes, we need money too. So the business of business must be to *make good money*. As soon as businesses introduce a split between their profits and their morality they lose the point of the whole enterprise. You can say, like St Augustine, 'I'll be wicked for twenty years and then when I've got enough money I'll be good.' But in those twenty years you've poisoned your world and lost your soul. Yes, Ed, I know you haven't got a soul. But you've got a heart, you live among people you love. Kitty, you tell him. Love is goodness. Love is people being good to each other.

Maybe I'm missing something here. It's hot as hell and I sweat like a pig. Do pigs sweat? Better say I sweat like a horse. So my brain may be softening.

But here's my confession. I'm excited. I can see a way to use something as mundane as selling bananas to create the good life for several thousand people. I'm sure the company will grow over the coming years. What if it were to be a force for good? We're so accustomed to think of making money as the devil's work. I want to reclaim it for God. I expect by now you're both smiling tolerantly. Poor old Larry, he can't cross a road without looking for a greater purpose. It's true, I admit it. I want meaning in my life. But so do you in yours. So does everybody. And that's what we want our work to give us, more than money, more than status. We're hungry for meaning.

There, I've rambled on for too long. I shall be home in two weeks and four days. I miss you both and long to see you again. Give Pammy and the Monk a kiss each from me, of equal size. We never seem to have enough time together. Why don't you and the girls join us this summer in our house in Normandy? Seriously, do think about it. We plan to be there all of August.

To Geraldine he writes:

My dear darling. Only two weeks or so before I'm with you again, and by the time you're reading this it will be only a few days. New Orleans is beautiful and lush and dirty and hot and half-mad, I think. The whole city feels like an over-ripe fruit about to

burst. I've met our parent company, but I think
they're not very good parents. All they tell me is,
Make money. Oddly enough this place reminds me
of India. The same brightness and energy and noise,
but underneath, the savagery. I trust you got my
second letter from Kingston. I've heard nothing from
you since Kingston, so I expect your last few letters
will follow me home. I've had an idea to ask Ed and
Kitty and their girls to La Grande Heuze this August.
It would be jolly to have children running about,
don't you think? I can't wait to be home again, and
to hold you in my arms again. I feel as if I've been
away half my life, and when I get home everyone
will be wrinkled and stooped and ninety years old,
all except you, darling, who are ageless and whose
beauty never fades.

36

Pamela falls in love with La Grande Heuze at first sight. Larry watches her running from room to room, and out into the garden where the great forest begins, and sees in her wide excited eyes the same wonder that possessed him twenty-five years ago and more, when he first came here. That was the summer before his mother died. He was five years old, two years younger than Pamela is now. He has clear memories of his mother sitting in the shade of a giant parasol on the terrace, and walking rather too slowly down the long straight *allées* that cut through the endless world of the forest.

'Is it your house?' Pamela says. 'Do you really live here?'

'When I'm on holiday,' Larry says, smiling down at her.

'I love it!' she cries. 'It's so beautiful. It's a secret house in a forest. Can I come and live here with you?'

'You are living here with me.'

'No, I mean for ever and ever.'

'I'm not sure your mother would approve of that.'

'She could come too. But not the Monkey. She wouldn't understand.'

In this way Pamela appropriates the house and its garden and its surrounding forest as her rightful domain. She announces that its name, La Grande Heuze, is a reference to herself.

'It's *hers*, you see, Mummy. That means it's mine.'

'Well, darling,' says Kitty, 'you'll have to fight it out with Larry and Geraldine. I rather think they think it's theirs.'

'Geraldine!' Pammy is indignant. 'It's Larry's house, not Geraldine's house.'

Geraldine is looking lovelier than ever. In her light cotton dresses, her sunglasses perched on her blond curls, she looks like summer itself. Under her management, the old house is filled with softly coloured light. She makes sure there are fresh flowers in the rooms every day, and fruit in shallow blue and white bowls, and a large glass jug of lemonade on a table on the terrace.

She asks Ed and Kitty for news of their neighbours in the big house at Edenfield.

'We haven't seen them in such a long time. How's the new baby?'

'Not a baby any more,' says Kitty. 'He's walking now. But Louisa still isn't right. I do worry about her. You remember how she was always so jolly? These days she seems much quieter. I don't think she's as strong as she should be.'

'Why does everyone want babies so much?' says Pamela,

511

scowling at her little sister. 'I don't see the point of them.'

'You were a baby once,' says Ed.

'*One* baby is all right.'

She jumps up and goes over to Elizabeth, who is toddling out through the open garden doors.

'No, Monk. Don't go outside.'

'Leave her alone, darling,' says Kitty.

'That forest out there,' says Ed. 'How far does it go?'

'A long way,' says Larry. 'You can walk for miles and see nothing but trees.'

'It frightens me,' says Geraldine. 'I've been telling Larry we should sell this house and buy somewhere on the coast. Étretat, maybe, or Honfleur. I love to look out over the sea.'

Pamela stares at Geraldine in astonishment.

'It's not mine to sell,' says Larry lightly. 'Not for many years yet, I hope.'

Their guests have hardly been installed for a day before Ed finds his way into one of the forest paths. He's gone for hours.

'Don't worry about him,' says Kitty. 'He'll be back for dinner.'

Geraldine takes pride in her dinners; not just the food laid on the table, but every detail of the table settings. She speaks poor French and has difficulty communicating with Albert and Véronique, the young couple recently hired by Larry's father to cook and clean and tend the garden. This produces many moments of frustration.

'Larry, could you tell Albert not to put out bowls for

coffee in the morning. Why do the French drink coffee from a bowl? When it's hot you can't pick it up, and before you know it the coffee's stone cold.'

And, 'When will Véronique get it into her head that I want the vegetables served at the same time as the meat? I told her, I said, "Toutes ensembles," but she just gaped at me.'

The standard of service at La Grande Heuze, under Geraldine's watchful eye, is in fact very high. The bread, crusty and fresh, arrives on a bicycle each morning from the *boulangerie* in Bellencombre. The coffee, made in a glass retort as if in a science lab, is dark and smooth and strong. The plain unsalted butter comes in a large cake, white and creamy, too good to need jam.

'You have no idea what a luxury this is for me,' says Kitty to Geraldine. 'It's simply heaven.'

'My mother always says guests are like horses. You have to keep them warm and watered and well fed.'

'I'm a very happy horse. You think of everything.'

'It's all about putting yourself in other people's place, isn't it?' says Geraldine. 'I think that's all that good manners comes down to.'

In the evenings the Monk is fed early, in the kitchen, where she is much fussed over by Véronique. Pamela is allowed to stay up to dinner with the grown-ups.

Larry can tell that this agitates Geraldine.

'Shall I say we'd rather the children both ate in the kitchen?'

'No, no,' says Geraldine, giving him a quick guilty look.

'If that's what Kitty wants. I'm just worried she'll find the food a bit much for her. Do you think I can serve *moules*?'

Pamela is aware that this privilege is also a test, and is undaunted by the *moules*.

'I like this,' she says. 'I expect I shall ask for more.'

'Oh, it's too bad!' exclaims Geraldine, taking her napkin out of its ring. 'I told Albert the napkins must be clean each evening. What am I to do, Larry? They don't pay any attention to a single thing I say.'

'I'll make sure they understand,' says Larry.

Geraldine smiles at Ed and Kitty, and smooths the offending napkin on her lap.

'I know it doesn't really matter, but one might as well get things right. Otherwise why don't we all sit on the ground and eat with our fingers?'

'Like the Monk,' says Pamela.

Kitty wants to know what's happened to Larry's painting.

'I don't have the time any more,' says Larry.

She looks at him with a puzzled smile, trying to guess what he really feels. Returning her gaze, lingering on her long-loved features, he realises that there's no one else who knows what this renunciation has cost him. Since that day he threw his canvases into the Thames, he has resolutely turned his back on his artist-self. He tells himself this is honesty, this is realism. But seeing Kitty's troubled look, he remembers the pain of it.

'To tell you the truth,' he says, 'I realised I just wasn't good enough.'

'But you sold your paintings! You told me so.'

'To George, because Louisa made him.'

'No. The others too.'

'Yes, there was a genuine buyer. I never knew who. That was my moment of glory.'

Kitty appeals to Ed.

'He was so good. Wasn't he, Ed?'

'I've believed in Larry since school,' says Ed. 'But we all have to live.'

'Don't you love his paintings?'

Kitty says this to Geraldine, innocently confident of support.

'I've never seen them,' says Geraldine.

'What?'

Kitty's bewilderment is devastating. Geraldine blushes, and turns to Larry.

'Why haven't I seen them, darling?'

'Because there are none to see,' says Larry. 'I threw them all away.'

He speaks flatly, meaning to remove any emotional weight from his words. Instead he communicates to all of them how much he cares.

A silence follows. Véronique comes in to clear the plates. The clatter of crockery releases them.

'Have you ever heard of a painter called Anthony Armitage?' says Larry, his voice now bright again, conversational. 'He's younger than me, but he's become quite a legend already. I knew him at art college, before he was famous.'

It's clear from their faces that none of the others have heard of him.

'It was my bad luck,' Larry goes on, 'to come up against a true talent. I looked at Armitage's work, and I looked at mine, and I knew I was fooling myself.'

'Oh, Larry.' Kitty soft with compassion.

'It's not all bad luck,' says Geraldine. 'That's one of the reasons why Larry came out to India.'

'That's quite true,' says Larry, smiling at her.

'This Armitage,' says Ed. 'Is he really so wonderful?'

'You can see for yourself if you want,' says Larry. 'He lives not very far away. A little place on the coast called Houlgate.'

'You never told me that,' says Geraldine, caught by surprise.

Nor has Larry told her that Armitage lives there with Nell. There has seemed to be no point. But now he finds he wants to see Nell again, and Armitage, though for very different reasons.

'And guess who he's married?' he says to Kitty. 'Nell.'

'Nell! Your Nell?'

'Not mine for a long time.'

'Oh, do let's go and visit them!'

That night going to bed Geraldine is silent in the way she goes when she feels ill-treated. This annoys Larry, but he also knows she's right.

'Look, I'm sorry,' he says.

'Oh, you're sorry. I wonder what for.'

'I shouldn't have sprung all that on you.'

'So we're going to go and visit them, are we? Your ex-girlfriend who you asked to marry you, and her famous artist?'

516

Larry knows he should say that Nell means nothing to him, that of course they won't go if she doesn't want them to. Then she'll cry a little and say she only wants him to be happy. But a stubbornness takes hold of him.

'I think it would be fun,' he says. 'And Kitty wants to.'

'Oh, well then, we must go.'

They lie down on the bed side by side, not touching, in silence. After some time, neither of them asleep, Geraldine wriggles close and kisses his shoulder.

'Sorry,' she says. 'I'm being silly. Of course we can go.'

The Monk is happy to stay behind and help Véronique cook. The rest of the house party set off, squeezed into the sand-coloured Renault 4CV usually driven by Albert. They drive through Rouen and Pont-Audemer, passing war-damaged buildings all the way. Larry tells the others how La Grande Heuze was occupied in the war first by German officers, then by Americans as the front advanced, and finally by former prisoners-of-war en route home.

'There's supposed to be compensation for all the damage,' he says, 'but I don't expect we'll ever see it.'

They look out for the sea all the way from the outskirts of Houlgate, but it remains out of sight until they're winding their way through the little town itself. Then all at once there it is, at the far end of the narrow street, trapped between the grey shuttered houses: a band of dull gold, a band of blue. They turn onto the Rue des Bains and drive slowly past the half-timbered houses, with the wide sands and sea stretching out to their left.

'Oh, I do so love the sea,' says Geraldine. 'Why do we have to be shut up in a forest? Don't you feel when you can see all the way to the horizon that anything is possible?'

'Mere illusion,' says Ed. 'Very few things are possible. Most of the time we do as we must, not as we would.'

'Pay no attention to him, Geraldine,' says Kitty. 'He's a terrible Eeyore.'

The Armitages live on Rue Henri Dobert. Larry pulls up and asks a man pushing a bicycle for directions. Driving on, he finds the road and crawls along it hunting for the house.

'Good God! I think that must be it!'

The house is high and narrow, stuccoed, with brick edging round the windows and ivy climbing to the second storey.

'That's not an artist's house,' says Ed. 'That's a bank manager's house.'

They drive onto the forecourt. On closer inspection the house can be seen to be run down, with weeds fringing the paving stones and the paintwork on the door crazed and flaking.

'They are expecting us?' says Geraldine.

'Possibly,' says Larry. 'If the post works.'

Larry doesn't show it, but he too is nervous. They get out and kick their legs, stiff after the long drive.

'What'll be for lunch?' says Pamela.

'Hush, darling,' says Kitty. 'It's rude to ask.'

'Why?' says Pamela. 'Why can't I ask?'

Those that don't ask don't get. Larry's mind echoes with the last words Nell ever spoke to him.

The door opens before they can knock, and there's Nell.

'You beautiful people!' she cries, bounding out. 'I'm going to kiss every one of you!'

She's just the same as Larry remembers, perhaps a little plumper, her hair longer, pulled back and held under an Alice band. She's wearing a bright check blouse and trousers. The same ease with her body, the same uncompromising meeting of eyes, the same lack of restraint.

'So you're Geraldine! Oh, you're perfect! What did Lawrence do to deserve you?'

Larry sees Geraldine flinch in her embrace. Then it's his turn.

'Darling Larry. Don't you look prosperous! My God, Camberwell feels like it was a million years ago. Come in and meet the monster.'

She ushers them in to a cluttered hall, and on to a big room at the rear of the house. Here windows open startlingly onto the sun-dazzled sea.

'There!' says Nell. 'The house is hideous, but you could hardly get closer to the sea, could you?'

She turns and yells, 'Tony, you mannerless shit! Come and greet your guests!'

She gives a laugh as she throws open the windows.

'He's completely unshameable. Now that he's an officially proclaimed genius he behaves as if none of the usual rules apply to him.'

She loops her arm through Larry's and leads him out into the bright sunshine.

'Come on, darling. We have some catching up to do.'

They walk arm in arm down a path that runs beside the beach.

'So are we still friends, Lawrence?'

'Yes,' says Larry, marvelling at the ease he feels in her company. 'Of course.'

'I know I'm a bad girl.'

'It doesn't matter. All in the past.'

'The thing you have to understand,' she says, 'is that when people say things to each other they aren't always saying what they're saying. They're saying something else, that's harder to say.'

'Like, Do you really love me?'

'Exactly.' She gives his arm a squeeze. 'You are such a sweetie-pie, Lawrence.'

'So how are things with Tony?'

'Oh, Tony! He'll do for now. How are things with Geraldine?'

'Very good.'

'Liar, liar, pants on fire.'

Back in the house the others, abandoned, look at each other, unsure what to do.

'Speaking purely personally, I need a drink,' says Ed. 'Do you think we forage for ourselves?'

'I want to go out on the beach too,' says Pamela.

At this point the artist himself appears, looking as if he's only just got up.

'Who the hell are you?' he says.

'Friends of Nell's,' says Kitty. 'She's out on the beach with Larry.'

'Oh, Larry.' He rubs his eyes. 'So what am I supposed to do with you?'

'You're supposed to greet us in a friendly manner,' says Geraldine, 'and make us feel at home, and offer us a drink.'

She utters this advice with a charming smile. Armitage is unnerved by the direct assault.

'Am I?' he says, looking about him as if seeking a way out. 'A drink, you say?'

Abruptly he withdraws to some other part of the house. Ed and Kitty both applaud Geraldine with softly clapping hands.

'Bravo, Geraldine!'

'Well, really!' says Geraldine, going pink.

Armitage reappears with a bottle of pastis, a bottle of water, and three glasses.

'Couldn't find any more glasses,' he says. 'Not clean ones.'

'You can even pour it if you want,' says Geraldine. 'But not for me, thanks.'

'Nor me,' says Kitty.

'I'll do it,' says Ed.

He mixes the pastis half-and-half with water and drinks it down. Armitage leans out of the window.

'Nell, you great cow! Get back here!'

The guests act as if they haven't heard him.

Nell returns, with Larry in tow.

'You behave yourself,' she says to Armitage, 'or no jiggery-pokery for a week.'

'What have I done?' says Armitage in an aggrieved voice. 'Hello, Larry. What's wrong with you?'

'I don't know. What is wrong with me?'

'You look all shiny. Have you been varnished?'

'I told you,' says Nell. 'He got rich.'

It turns out there is lunch of a kind waiting for them. Nell has planned a picnic on the beach. She's filled a big basket with bread, tomatoes, and pork *rillettes*. To drink, there's a flagon of the local cider.

'The whole idea of living here is that we have the beach on our doorstep. Tony spends hours staring at the sea. I can't see what there is to look at, myself. It's just a lot of nothing.'

'You're an empty-headed fool,' says Armitage.

'I think he stares at the sea to clear his mind,' says Nell as if he hasn't spoken. 'Like preparing a canvas.'

'That is perfectly true,' says Armitage.

He goes to her and kisses her in front of them all.

They sit in a ring on the sand in the shade of a large beach umbrella, and make themselves sandwiches by tearing the baguettes apart. Pammy loves it.

'We're sitting on the ground and eating things with our fingers,' she says.

Armitage stares at Kitty as he eats.

'Don't mind him,' Nell says. 'It just means he wants to paint you.'

'Yes, I do,' says Armitage. 'You have an interesting face.'

'So where do you paint?' says Larry.

'Over there,' says Armitage.

'He's got a studio in the house,' says Nell. 'No more crouching in bed-sitting rooms. But it was fun in those days, wasn't it?' She turns to Geraldine, wanting to include her. 'Larry and Tony and me used to walk along the river in the small hours of the morning and drink hot sweet tea from the cabbies' café by Albert Bridge.'

'More cider?' says Ed, pouring from the flagon.

An extended family goes trudging by, grandparents, parents, children, dog, carrying baskets, rugs, umbrellas. A steamer crosses the horizon, moving without seeming to move. From time to time Nell strokes Armitage's arm, as if to reassure him she's still there.

Then they have a sudden violent row. It's about letting their visitors see his studio.

'I'm not a zoo animal,' he says.

'You *exhibit*, don't you?' demands Nell. 'You're an *exhibitionist*, aren't you?'

'I don't care if no one ever sees my work.'

'That is such shit! You hypocrite!'

'Cow!'

'You're afraid, aren't you? Bloody hell!' she appeals to the others. 'He sells everything he does. He's got famous people begging him to paint them. He gets compared to Titian. And all along he's wetting himself with fear.'

'Bitch!'

'Oh, yes! Very effective! That'll shut me up, won't it? That's a really conclusive argument!'

Armitage gets up and stalks away down the beach.

'Go on!' Nell shouts after him. 'Run away! Coward!' Then in a suddenly normal voice to the others, 'Don't worry. I'll take you to see his studio.'

'But if he doesn't want it,' says Geraldine.

'Why should he be the one who gets what he wants? What about what I want?'

They gather up the picnic and brush the sand off their bottoms and troop back to the house. Armitage is nowhere to be seen. Nell leads them up the stairs to the back room on the first floor. Here what was once a large light bedroom has been transformed into an artist's studio. Canvases lean against the walls and stack up on a long paint-spattered table. Two easels, both bearing works in progress, stand by the window. An armchair draped with a multicoloured shawl occupies the middle of the room. The portraits taking shape on the easels are of an old man and a stout middle-aged woman.

Larry and the others look round the studio in silence, examining the paintings.

'I hate to say it,' Larry says, 'but the bastard's got even better.'

'Why are they all so sad?' says Kitty.

'Tony would say he just paints what he sees,' Nell says. 'The way he sees it, most people are disappointed by their lives.'

'Do you think he's right?'

'Probably,' says Nell.

'I think that's ungrateful,' says Geraldine.

'Ungrateful to who?' says Nell.

'To God, actually.'

Nell gives her an incredulous look.

'We're supposed to be grateful to God?' she says. 'What for?'

'For being our Creator,' says Geraldine. 'I know it means nothing if you don't have faith.'

'Take it from me,' says Nell, 'I know about creators. It's all vanity. It's all look at me, aren't I wonderful? As far as I'm concerned God is just another immature egotistical artist whining on about how no one appreciates him.'

Driving back to Bellencombre, Kitty says, 'You've got to admit they're not dull.'

Geraldine says, 'I thought they were pitiful.'

In their bedroom that night she says to Larry, 'I don't understand how you could ever have loved her. I just don't understand.'

'I was young,' says Larry.

'It's only five years ago. You weren't a child. She's just so . . . so crude. So loud. So coarse.'

'She's fun as well. You must see that.'

'Fun! Is that your idea of fun? All that childish swearing?'

Larry feels the stirrings of anger.

'It's late,' he says. 'That was a long drive.'

'No, Larry. I want to know. Did you really love her?'

'I thought I did. For a time.'

'Was it just because of . . . you know?'

This is the closest she can come to talk of sex.

'Maybe it was,' says Larry.

'I could understand that,' says Geraldine. 'I know that makes perfectly sensible men do really stupid things.'

'Not really stupid,' says Larry. 'Don't say it was really stupid to love Nell. Don't say that.'

'Well, what am I supposed to say? Why else would you give a creature like that more than a glance?'

'A creature like that.' He feels his heart pounding. 'What do you know?' His voice is rising. 'Who are you to criticise her? Who are you to tell me why I do what I do? You think you do everything so bloody perfectly. Well take it from me, you don't!'

Geraldine lies perfectly still beneath the bedclothes.

'Please don't swear at me,' she whispers.

'I'll bloody well swear at you if I want!' shouts Larry.

'Hush!' she says. 'Keep your voice down.'

'No! I won't! And don't shush me! I'm not a child.'

'Then I don't know what to say.'

'Then don't say anything at all. If all you can do is insult my friends I'd rather you said nothing. Why should everyone be like you? What makes you so right about everything?'

Geraldine says nothing.

'And in case you haven't noticed, we're not in Arundel any more. We're in France. They do things the French way in France. And why the hell shouldn't they?'

He feels her shudder, but still she says nothing.

'Well?' he demands.

'I was told not to speak,' she whispers.

'Oh, for God's sake, Geraldine!'

Robbed of opposition, his anger trickles out of him. They lie side by side in a wretched silence, both feeling sorry for themselves. After some time, wanting to go to sleep, Larry attempts a half-hearted resolution.

'Sorry,' he mumbles.

'It doesn't matter,' she says. 'I just didn't know.'

'Didn't know what?'

'That you don't love me at all.'

'Oh, please.'

'It's all right. It's not the first time.'

'Geraldine, you're taking this far too seriously. It's just a row. People have rows. It's not the end of the world.'

'I'm not blaming you. I know it's my fault. I try so hard, but somehow I'm never good enough.'

'No, darling, no.' He feels only a heavy weariness now. 'You know that's not true.'

'I've always known I'm not good enough, deep down.' She goes on whispering to herself, hearing nothing he says. 'I've never felt anyone's really loved me. Not Mummy or Daddy. Not even God.'

'Oh, darling.'

'There's something wrong with me. I don't know what it is. I try so hard. It's nothing physical. Not physical. I say to myself, I must just try harder. I must do better. And I will. I promise you. I'll be a good wife.'

'Of course you will. You are.'

But as he lies beside her in the night Larry is overwhelmed with desolation.

'This life is such a hard journey,' she whispers. 'All I ask is that from time to time you hold my hand. So I know you're still there.'

He reaches out under the bedclothes and holds her hand.

'Thank you,' she says, her voice almost inaudible.

Next day Geraldine appears as charming and elegant as ever. She's especially attentive to Kitty, teasingly aligning herself with her against the boorishness of the men.

'What are we to do with them, Kitty? Sometimes I think men have no manners at all. You see how Larry leans on the table, and reaches for whatever he wants, as if he's the only person at breakfast?'

'You should pity me,' says Larry, smiling. 'I had no mother to teach me manners.'

'Ed has a mother,' says Kitty, 'but he might as well have been raised in the jungle.'

'I've no idea what you're talking about,' says Ed, deep in the morning edition of *Le Figaro*. 'You may like to know that Princess Elizabeth has had a baby girl. The princess is naturally radiant, and naturally she repeated the words she uttered on her marriage, and on the birth of her son. "Nous sommes tellement chanceux, Philip et moi." Odd that she said it in French.'

'You see what a beast he is,' Kitty says to Geraldine. 'He makes fun of all good news.'

'I'm so impressed he understands French,' says Geraldine.

'Oh, he practically lives in France these days.'

'I'll tell you what,' says Larry. 'Why don't we beasts clear off for the day?'

'Clear off where?'

'I thought Dieppe.'

Ed looks up from his newspaper.

'Why on earth do you want to go there?'

'I don't know. Lay the odd ghost.'

'I think you should, Ed,' says Kitty.

'All right,' says Ed abruptly. 'We'll go.'

They park in front of one of the hotels, and walk down the concrete pathway between strips of grass where boys are playing soccer, to the broader strip of concrete that is the promenade. They stand here gazing over pebbles to the sea. It's a sunny August afternoon, and the long flat beach is dotted with families stretched out on towels, and children flying kites.

'Do you dream about it?' says Larry.

'Sometimes.'

'Once I woke from a dream of it, and I'd wet myself.'

Ed shakes his head.

'What a fuck-up that was,' he says. 'What an utter God-awful fuck-up.'

They reach the shiny strip of pebbles, washed by the waves as they roll in and roll out. Here they turn round. Now they're looking up the beach to the promenade and the town, just as they looked when they came off the landing craft eight years ago.

'Am I supposed to be feeling something?' says Ed. 'Because I'm not.'

'Remembering,' says Larry.

'I'd rather forget.'

'This is where you won your VC, Ed. Right here.'

Ed scans the beach, with its scampering children and its barefoot bathers picking their way over the pebbles.

'I should have died here,' he says.

'Maybe you did,' says Larry. 'Maybe I did.'

He walks up the beach a little way, fancying that he follows the path he took eight years ago.

'There was a wrecked tank round about here,' he says. 'I sat down against it and prayed it would protect me.'

'You prayed?'

'No, you're right. I don't remember praying. I just remember the dead feeling of terror. You never felt that, Ed. I saw you. You weren't afraid.'

'I've always been afraid,' says Ed. 'I've been running away all my life. I'm still running.'

'But why? Why are we so afraid? What is it we're afraid of?'

No need to tell Ed he's not talking about sniper bullets and mortar shells.

'God knows,' says Ed. Then he laughs. 'Afraid of God, I expect. The God we've constructed so that we're bound to fail in the end.'

'Who says it has to be in the end?' says Larry. 'Some of us are failing right now.'

Ed turns on him, almost angry.

'Don't you talk like that! You're the one who's got it right. I need to know at least someone's come through.'

'You've got eyes, Ed.'

'Geraldine?'

'Yes.'

They walk on up to the promenade and sit down on the concrete wall. Below them bewildered farm boys from

Alberta and Ontario died in their hundreds, on that day that happened somewhere else, long ago and far away.

'Geraldine isn't great on the physical side of things,' says Larry.

'Maybe she just needs time.'

'Ed, it's nearly three years.'

'How bad is it?'

'There is no physical side of things.'

'Bloody hell,' says Ed softly.

'She tries, but she can't.'

'Bloody hell,' says Ed again.

'It's not going to change. I know that now.'

'So what do you do?' says Ed.

'What do you think? I don't have a whole lot of choice.'

'Are we talking tarts or wanking?'

'Good old Ed. The latter.'

Ed gazes out over the sea to the horizon.

'Remember the smoke?' he says. 'Bloody smoke over everything, so you didn't know you were coming off the boats into the end of the world.'

'I remember the smoke,' says Larry.

'You're going to have to get out of this, my friend. Time to beat a retreat. Back to the boats and sail away.'

'I can't.'

'Why not? Oh yes, your dumb religion.'

'And yours.'

'It's a fairy story, chum. Don't let them bully you.'

'It still means something to me,' says Larry. 'It's just too deep in me.'

'Do you still go to confession?'

'From time to time. I like it.'

'Do you tell the priest about the wanking?'

Larry laughs.

'No, not any more. It got too boring. And I knew I wasn't going to stop.'

'There's faith for you. You know it's nonsense but you let it ruin your life. Sometimes I swear to you I think the human race has a built-in need to suffer. When there aren't enough plagues or earthquakes we have wars. When we run out of wars we turn our daily lives into misery.'

'So what do you advise me to do?' says Larry.

'How would I know?' says Ed. 'I drink. But I don't recommend it.'

Larry sighs.

'Remember sitting in the library at school, with our feet up on the table, and you reading out the dirty bits from your illicit copy of *Lady Chatterley's Lover*?'

'Sex in the gamekeeper's hut. As far as I can remember she had no underclothes, and slept through the whole thing.'

'It was still exciting.'

'That's the trouble with sex. It's never as good as when you're sixteen years old and haven't had it yet.'

'So what do we do, Ed?'

'We stumble on, chum. Stumble on in the smoke until that one merciful bullet finds us at last.'

3 7

Louisa is back home and a lot better, but one look at her and Kitty knows she's not yet her old self. Little Billy hangs about her, clinging to her skirts, but she makes no objection when his nurse comes and carries him off for his tea.

'I'm all right really,' she tells Kitty, 'but everything's so tiring. I want to have Billy all the time, but I can't manage it. Aren't I hopeless?'

She gives Kitty one of her old mischievous smiles, but ends with a grimace.

'Oh, Kitty. Were your babies such hard work?'

'Of course,' says Kitty loyally. 'Having babies is hell.'

'It's like being disembowelled, isn't it? But I should be over it by now.'

'What do your doctors say?'

'They can't find anything wrong with me, which should be cheering but somehow isn't. If only I could cough blood or something. At least then I'd know it wasn't my own fault.'

'Of course it's not your own fault.'

Louisa is sitting on a sofa in the big drawing room with cushions all round her and a little table by her side. Mrs Lott brings through a pot of tea and some home-made scones. Kitty offers to pour the tea.

'Still, it's good to be home,' says Louisa.

Then she shakes her head and bites her lip and says, 'No, it isn't.'

Suddenly she sounds like a frightened child.

'I've become so useless.' She's on the point of tears. 'In the nursing home I sit about all day, doing nothing, and it's restful. Here I sit about all day, not doing things I should be doing, and I feel terrible. What's gone wrong with me, Kitty?'

'It'll pass,' says Kitty. 'You'll get better.'

'Darling Kitty. Do you mind if I tell you a secret?'

'You say anything you want,' says Kitty.

'I'm so afraid I might never get better.'

'Oh, rubbish!' exclaims Kitty.

'There is a good side to it, though. I've become much nicer to George. He turns out to be such a lovely man. And of course, he adores little Billy.'

'You're just feeling tired,' says Kitty firmly. 'People don't just not get better for no reason.'

'Well, I've thought about that,' says Louisa. 'Really, most things happen for no reason. We die for no reason. It's not a punishment or anything. It's like in the war. It's all just chance. Remember Ed saying how he believed in luck?'

'Yes,' says Kitty.

'We've had good times along the way, though, haven't we?'

'Yes,' says Kitty.

George comes in to join them, and it's marvellous to Kitty to see how his presence cheers Louisa. He sits by her side on the sofa and fusses over her.

'Have another scone. You're to be stuffed like a goose, doctor's orders. She's so much better, isn't she, Kitty? Getting her colour back.'

'She's going to be just fine,' says Kitty.

'In the spring we're going to go to the South of France,' he tells Louisa. 'To Menton. You and me and Billy. We'll sit in the sunshine and watch the boats in the harbour and get lazy and fat, all three of us.'

'Will we, George? I shall like that.'

Kitty collects Elizabeth from the kitchen, where she always goes when they visit the big house, and they walk back home across the park. Kitty is filled with troubled thoughts. Louisa has always been the one who laughs away such moments, the living proof that even as life lets you down there are good times to be had. Now the good times seem to be receding into the past.

I'm thirty years old, Kitty thinks. Don't tell me it's over.

They stop at the kissing gate out of the park and Elizabeth puts up her face to be kissed.

'I do love you so much, darling,' says Kitty.

When they get back to the farmhouse, there's Hugo's van in the yard, and Hugo himself in the kitchen. His presence is not welcome. Kitty is feeling too fragile to deal with his boyish flirtations.

'What are you doing here, Hugo? You know Ed's away.'

'That's why I'm here,' he says. 'To talk about Ed.'

'I don't want to talk about Ed.'

'I want tea,' says Elizabeth.

Kitty looks round a little distractedly, glancing at the clock, trying to calculate how long it will be before Pamela gets home from school. She likes to have her tea ready on the table.

'Soon, darling.'

Elizabeth runs off. Kitty puts the kettle on to boil.

'You know it and I know it,' says Hugo. 'We've just never said it aloud.'

'Know what?'

'Ed's drinking too much.'

'Oh, God.'

Kitty knows she should sound surprised, even angry, but she can no longer summon up the energy to defend Ed.

'He's not really capable of doing the job any more,' says Hugo.

She turns to look at Hugo, so serious, so earnest; the boy become a man.

'I didn't know it had got that bad,' she says.

'I'm getting calls from producers saying he's showed up hours late, or not at all. The orders he places have to be rechecked by someone else, we've had so many errors. Last week we received a shipment of a hundred cases of rosé we've never stocked before. Ed couldn't even remember placing the order.'

Kitty stares at him hopelessly.

'Why are you telling me this, Hugo?'

'As chairman of the firm,' he says. 'I'm going to have to ask him to take a leave of absence.'

Chairman of the firm. Leave of absence. And he's still in his twenties.

'Is that a nice way of saying you want him to go?'

'That depends on whether he can sort himself out,' says Hugo.

Kitty says nothing. The kettle boils. She takes it off the stove, but she stays standing there, one hand resting on its handle, as the steam dissipates into the air.

'Look, Kitty, I like Ed. And I'm grateful to him. He's worked like a Trojan building up the business. We probably have more contacts in provincial French vineyards than any other importer. But his heart just isn't in it any more. I can't let him damage the reputation of the firm.' He pauses, looks down, gives a quick shake of his head. 'And I hate seeing him hurt you.'

'Hurt me?'

'Come on. I'm not blind. He's killing you, Kitty.'

'Killing me?'

She repeats his words like a fool to play for time. Nothing Hugo says comes as a surprise, except for the fact that it's Hugo who says it. If anything it's a relief to hear it spoken aloud.

'He's stealing your life away from you. You're so lovely

and so kind-hearted and so . . . so full of light. And now, it's as if he's dimmed you. He's letting your light fade. He gives you nothing, Kitty. You must see that. He's stealing your spirit, because he has none of his own left.'

Kitty bites her lower lip to hold back the tears. This is so exactly what she feels that it frightens her.

'But I love him,' she whispers.

'But he's no good for you. You must see that.'

Tears brim in her eyes. Hugo jumps up and takes her in his arms.

'You know how I feel about you,' he says. 'You've known from the beginning.'

'No, Hugo—'

'Why not? Aren't you at least allowed to live?'

It's too much for Kitty. The tears flow, and as she weeps he kisses her: at first as if to brush away the tears, and then on the mouth. She doesn't push him away. She has no resistance left. And it's good to be wanted, and held in a man's arms, if only for a moment.

A clatter at the door. She looks round. There's Pamela, frozen on the threshold, staring at her.

She backs away from Hugo and wipes her eyes.

'And I haven't even got the children's tea on the table,' she says.

'Hello, Pammy,' says Hugo.

Pamela says nothing. Elizabeth comes pushing into the kitchen from behind her.

'I'm so hungry,' she says, 'I'm going to die.'

'You shut up, Monkey,' says Pamela, her eyes still on her mother.

'I won't shut up!' says Elizabeth. 'And don't call me Monkey!'

Kitty is now in motion, putting out bread and butter and honey, milk and biscuits.

'Monkey, Monkey, Monkey,' says Pamela.

'Now, Pamela,' says Hugo.

'You're not my father,' says Pamela.

'Tell her not to call me Monkey,' Elizabeth cries, tugging at her mother's skirt.

'You know she doesn't like it, Pammy,' says Kitty.

'Why do you side with her always?' Pamela is suddenly furious. 'Why is it always me who's wrong? Why do you hate me?'

'I don't hate you, darling.'

Kitty is overwhelmed. It's all too much. She wants to sit down and cry until she can cry no more.

'You know I don't like Rich Tea biscuits, so why do you get them?' Pamela senses her mother's weakness, and attacks with all the cruelty of a self-righteous seven-year-old. 'I don't know why I even come home. The food's always dull or horrid. We never have cakes with icing, like Jean has, or chocolate milk. I wish I lived in Jean's house and Jean's mummy was my mummy.'

'Pamela!' says Hugo sharply. 'That's enough.'

Pamela turns her burning eyes on him.

'Oh, yes,' she says. 'It's enough.'

539

She goes back out into the hall and can be heard running up the stairs.

Kitty proceeds with the automatic tasks of slicing and buttering bread, and pouring milk into glasses.

'You'd better go, Hugo,' she says. 'I'll talk to Ed.'

'Are you sure?' says Hugo. 'You don't want me to go to Pamela?'

'No. It'll only make things worse.'

She puts out the tea for Elizabeth.

'Here you are, darling. Do you want me to spread the honey for you?'

'I'll do it,' says Elizabeth happily. Then as she spoons out unwarranted amounts of honey, 'I don't want to live in Jean's house. I want to live here.'

Kitty meets Larry off the train at Lewes. Driving back, she asks after Geraldine, who is spending a week in Arundel with her parents.

'Geraldine's fine,' says Larry.

Pamela and Elizabeth greet Larry with cries of joy, and fight over who's to sit on his lap. Kitty looks on with a smile.

'Sometimes I think they see more of you than they do of Ed.'

'Pure cupboard love,' says Larry, searching his weekend bag. 'Now what have I got here?'

He takes out two small packets of sweet buttery biscuits from Normandy.

'And the bananas!' cries Elizabeth.

'Bananas?' says Larry. 'What bananas?'

His gifts are always much anticipated, always the same. He takes a bunch of ripe bananas from his bag and hands them over. The girls retire to gorge.

'How are bananas?' says Kitty, meaning his work.

'Challenging,' says Larry. 'My father has just decided to retire. Which puts me in the driving seat.'

'But that's wonderful, isn't it?'

'As I say, challenging. After all these years of having the market pretty much to ourselves, it looks like we're about to get some serious competition. A Dutch firm called Geest.'

'Geesed? As in goosed?'

'Almost.'

'You've been wanting to take over for ages, Larry. Now you can do all those things you've been dreaming of doing.'

'Yes, that's the exciting part.' He looks round. 'I take it Ed's away.'

'As usual. I want to talk to you about that. Later, when the girls are in bed. Oh, Larry, I'm so glad you've come.'

The guest bedroom above the kitchen is known as 'Larry's room', because whenever he comes, with or without Geraldine, this is where he sleeps. He's in the room, hanging up the modest changes of clothes he's brought for the weekend, when he hears a soft tap-tap on the door.

'Come in!' he calls.

No one comes in. He opens the door himself. There stands Pamela, looking unsure whether she wants to come in or run away.

'Pamela?'

She twists about on her toes and turns her head this way and that, but says not a word.

'You want to talk to me?'

She nods, not meeting his eyes.

'Come on in, then.'

She comes in. He closes the door. Realising she might find it easier to speak if he isn't looking at her, he continues with hanging up his clothes.

'Larry,' she says after a while, 'do you think Mummy would ever leave us?'

'Leave you?' says Larry. 'No, never. Why would you ever think such a thing?'

'Do mothers ever leave their children?'

'No, they don't, sweetheart. Hardly ever.'

'Judy Garland got divorced. She's got a little girl.'

'But she didn't leave her daughter, did she? And anyway, film stars aren't like us.'

'So Mummy wouldn't ever go off with another man?'

'No, Pamela, never.' She has his full attention now. 'Why are you asking me this?'

'I can't tell you.'

'Then tell your mother. You can tell her.'

'No!' says Pamela. 'I could never tell her!'

'Pammy, this must be some silly muddle you've got your-self into.'

'It's not a silly muddle! You don't know. But I jolly well do know.'

Larry can see that she wants to tell him, but holds back for fear of the consequences.

'How about I promise not to tell anyone else, if you tell me?'

'No one else at all?'

'No one in all the world.'

'Not Mummy or Daddy?'

'No one. Cross my heart and hope to die.'

'You have to do it,' Pamela says.

'What?'

'Cross your heart.'

Larry makes the sign of the cross.

'No, not like that!' Pamela demonstrates, describing an X across her skinny chest. 'Like that.'

Larry complies. There follows a silence. Then Pamela bursts into tears, and mumbles some indistinct words that Larry fails to catch.

'Come here, sweetheart,' he says gently, opening his arms. 'Whisper it in my ear.'

She presses her lips to his ear and whispers.

'I saw Mummy kissing Hugo.'

He moves her round so he can look her in the face.

'Hugo?'

She nods, snuffling.

'You're sure?'

Another nod.

'Where?'

'In the kitchen. When I came back from school.'

'They were probably having a friendly hug.'

'No! It was mouth kissing!'

Larry says nothing. He's not sure what to think. He's not sure what he feels.

'You don't believe me.'

'Yes,' he says. 'I believe you.'

'So you see. It's not a silly muddle I've got myself into.'

'No,' says Larry, 'but it may be a silly muddle all the same.'

All through the remainder of that Saturday Pamela's revelation fills Larry's mind. He knows he must talk to Kitty about it, but doesn't know how. His promise to Pamela seems to him to be overruled by the seriousness of the situation. Kitty is clearly in trouble. Apart from Louisa, who's not at all well, he's her best friend. Who else can she confide in?

All day long his thoughts bounce back and forth, from Kitty to Ed to Hugo and back, missing out only himself and his own feelings for Kitty. So long controlled if not denied, he dares not unlock the secret room in which he has hidden away his love for her. Kitty is married to his best friend. He himself has a wife. Things are as they are, and must be lived with.

But Hugo?

It makes no sense at all. Behind the locked door waits the secret cry: if Hugo, why not me? Except he knows why it can't be him.

But Hugo!

One case reported by a child, one kiss that may never have happened, has rocked the fragile equilibrium with which he's been living for so long. The old self-accusation rises up to taunt him.

I've been too weak. I've been too afraid. If I'd spoken out long ago. If I'd made demands. If I'd been a man.

If you don't ask, you don't get.

Evening comes. The girls are tucked up in bed, presumed asleep. Kitty talks freely now, telling him about Ed and his absences and his drinking. All the time she's talking, Larry looks on her lovely face and asks himself, Is it possible she has sought consolation elsewhere?

'Hugo was here the other day,' she says. 'He told me he wants Ed to take leave of absence from the firm. That's how bad it's got.'

Hugo was here the other day.

'What will you say to him? To Ed, I mean.'

'I don't know, Larry. I don't know what to do with Ed. He knows I hate his drinking. So now of course he does it in secret. But there's something I hate more than the drinking. Why is he so unhappy? Have I failed him? What have I done wrong? He's got me, he's got the girls. I've never asked him to do anything he doesn't want. I don't ask him for smart cars or fur coats. I'm a good wife to him, aren't I? He knows I love him. And I do, I do love him. Sometimes he can be so sweet and I think I've got him back, the old Ed. But then it's like a door closes, and I'm on one side, and he's on the other, with his unhappiness.'

She speaks rapidly but calmly, long past the stage of incoherence and tears. Larry understands that what he's hearing is the cycle of thoughts that go round and round in her head.

'Of course I blame myself, how can I not blame myself? But I'm so tired of it all, Larry, it wears me out. And there's something worse. I get angry, too. Angry with Ed. Why is he doing this to us? Why can't he see how good his life could be? Why can't he see how unhappy he's making me?'

'I think he knows that,' says Larry.

'Then why doesn't he do something about it?'

'I don't know,' says Larry. 'But I'm sure of one thing. It's not your fault. I know he'd say that too. It's something in him.'

'What?' she says, searching his face as if to find it there. 'What in him? Why?'

'I think he'd call it the darkness,' says Larry. 'I don't understand it. But it's been there as long as I've known him.'

'Even at school?'

'Oh, yes.'

'If only he'd talk to me about it.'

'I think the problem there,' says Larry slowly, 'is that he feels he's already let you down. He feels so much guilt about you, he doesn't want to burden you with even more. He loves you so much, it must be torture to him, knowing he's making you unhappy too. I think he's trying to keep it away from you, his unhappiness. Like a contagious disease, you know? He's quarantining himself.'

'Then what am I to do?'

'I don't know,' says Larry. 'I suppose you could seek consolation elsewhere.'

'Elsewhere? Where?'

'Hugo, maybe.'

'Hugo?' She laughs at the sheer absurdity of it. 'Why Hugo of all people?' Then she guesses. 'Pamela told you.'

She sees from his face that she's right.

'Oh, God! I should have talked to her. I just couldn't think how to explain. Poor Hugo has had this idea he's in love with me for ages and ages, and when he was telling me about Ed and how he had to stop work I got upset and cried a little, and he kissed me. Pamela had just got back from school and she saw. What did she tell you? Is she terribly upset? Oh, what fools we all are.'

'She thought you might leave her to go off with Hugo.'

'Go off with Hugo? He's a child! It's all a fantasy of his. No, I'd never go off with Hugo.'

'That's what I told her.'

Even so, the sweet relief is running through his veins, making his skin tingle. He hadn't realised how afraid he had become of that kiss.

'Anyway, I never kissed Hugo. He kissed me.'

'What does he think of it all now?'

'Oh, he's fine. We're still good friends. I just told him to stop being silly. He's so used to his little game of unreciprocated love that I think he was almost relieved to go back to the way things were.'

His little game of unreciprocated love. There's more than one of those.

He sees that she follows his thoughts. How could she not? It's been so many years now.

'How's Geraldine?' she says; even though she asked in the car, and he replied then, 'Geraldine's fine.'

'Geraldine and I,' he says this time, 'are as unhappy together as you and Ed. Different couple, different problems, same misery.'

Kitty's face shows sympathy but not surprise.

'I did think, in France.'

'We keep up appearances. But we more or less lead separate lives now.'

Kitty reaches across the table and takes his hand.

'How do you cope with it?' she says.

'I work. Work can take up all your time, if you want it to.'

'Like Ed.'

'Ed's angry with himself. The worst of my situation is I'm angry with Geraldine. I know I shouldn't be. I half understand why she is the way she is. I'm sorry for her. But more than everything else I'm angry with her. She won't do the one simple thing that makes marriages possible. She won't love me.'

'Does that mean what I think it means?'

'We sleep in separate rooms.'

'Oh, Larry.'

'I'm ashamed of myself for minding so much. But I do.'

'Oh, Larry.'

'So one way or another, we've both made a bit of a botch of our lives, haven't we?'

She goes on stroking his hand, gazing into his eyes.

'You were the one I wanted,' he says.

It seems so easy to say it now.

'I know,' she says.

'Have you always known?'

'Yes,' she says. 'I think so.'

'But you love Ed. Even though he doesn't know how to be happy.'

'Sometimes I think that's why I love him.'

'So if I'd just been a bit more miserable, might you have gone for me instead?'

'Probably,' she says, smiling.

'I could start now.'

He pulls a sad face.

'Darling Larry.'

'Don't be too nice to me. I don't think I can take it.'

'I could have been happy with you,' she says.

'Well, there it is,' he says. 'What might have been.'

She goes on looking at him, and he sees so much love there that he doesn't want either of them to say any more. This moment is so sweet to him that he'd ask for nothing else in life if only it would go on for ever.

Then she says, 'If Hugo can kiss me, I don't see why you can't. I've known you far longer.'

He gets up from his side of the table and goes round to hers. She stands, and puts her face up to his, timid but willing, like a young girl. He kisses her very gently at first. Then he draws her into his arms and they kiss as he has longed to kiss her ever since the first moment he set eyes on her, ten years ago.

And so they part at last.

'I can't help it,' he says. 'I've always loved you, and I always will.'

'Dearest darling Larry. Don't ask me to say it. I'll never do anything to hurt Ed. You know that.'

'Of course I do.'

'But this' – she strokes his arms, smiling at him, meaning the acknowledgement of his love – 'this makes it easier.'

'For me too.'

And it does. Nothing can change. Their circumstances make anything more between them impossible. But everything has changed. Larry feels filled with a joyful lightness. Now, and to the day either he or Kitty dies, he will never be alone.

'That was it,' she says. But she looks so much happier. 'That was what might have been. Now back to what is.'

38

'What system of budgetary controls do you operate, Mr Cornford?'

'I'm sorry,' says Larry. 'I don't follow you.'

Donohue, the young man leading the McKinsey team, frowns and leans back in his chair. He exchanges glances with Neill and Hollis, his colleagues. All three wear dark suits and white shirts with dark ties. All three are younger than Larry.

'Purchasing, transport, stock management, maintenance contracts – every part of the running of the company incurs costs, and these costs have to be managed. But of course you know that.' Donohue smiles suddenly and brightly. Larry waits to be told something he doesn't know. 'I'm simply asking what systems you have in place, as managing director, to ensure that your costs are kept as low as possible.'

The question annoys Larry. Donohue annoys Larry. The team from McKinsey & Co, brought in by the parent company in New Orleans, annoys Larry.

'I don't assume,' he answers carefully, 'that the lowest costs will always deliver the greatest benefit.'

'But you must have some system for monitoring costs,' says Donohue.

'It's called my staff,' says Larry. 'Each purchase is made by a member of staff who knows his business and has the best interests of the company at heart.'

'I see,' says Donohue, making a note. 'Would it be correct to say that your staff are only lightly supervised?'

'You could say that,' says Larry. 'Or you could say our staff are greatly trusted.'

'And what if it were to turn out that your trust had been abused? Indeed, has it ever so turned out?'

'We all fall short of the glory of God, Mr Donohue,' says Larry. 'The question is, what are we to do about it? We can set up what you call a monitoring system, which tells people what they should be doing, and detects when they're failing to do it, and presumably punishes them in some way. Or we can give them an area of responsibility, and ask them to work out how best to operate for themselves, and rely on their pride in their work and their loyalty to the company to deliver the best possible results.'

'And if they're incompetent, or idle, or corrupt?'

'Then the failure is mine. I've failed to make them see that the company's good is also their good. Perhaps we need a system for monitoring me.'

Donohue exchanges looks with Neill and Hollis.

'I think you're talking about the ethos of the small family firm, Mr Cornford,' he says. 'What you might call the paternalistic model. But Fyffes is neither family owned, nor' – he checks his notes – 'small. You have over three thousand employees.'

'Yes,' says Larry with a sigh. 'You're quite right. And of course if you and your team can show us ways to operate more efficiently, we'll gladly implement them.'

'That's what we're here for,' says Donohue.

'One question, Mr Donohue. In all your calculations, do you have a column for the life satisfaction of the staff of the company?'

There follows a pause.

'I understand you, of course,' says Donohue at last. 'But firstly, there's no easy way to measure it. And secondly, without profits there is no company, and without a company, there is no life satisfaction for its staff. Or, to put it plainly, you all sink or float together.' He rises, and Neal and Hollis rise with him. 'With your permission, we'll get to work.'

At home after dinner that evening, Larry paces the library and vents his frustration on his father.

'What do they know about our business? They've never run a business. All they can do is add up numbers and spread insecurity. God only knows how much they get paid! And what revelation will come out at the end? That we'd be advised to make a profit rather than a loss.'

'We've been through this sort of thing before,' says his father. 'In our business there are lean years and fat years. Once we're back paying a healthy dividend all this nonsense will go away.'

'I hope you're right. The Geest operation changes things.'

'Geest came into the market because we've not been able to meet the demand,' says William Cornford. 'We'll lose market share, that's inevitable. But there's enough out there for both of us.'

'Of course there is! And of course we'll diversify. And of course we'll modernise the distribution network. I don't need consultants to tell me that.'

His father smiles to hear him.

'It makes me very happy to know you're with us, Larry. I could never have stepped down for anyone else.'

'Don't worry, Dad. I won't let them rape the old firm.'

'I think I always knew you'd come back to us.'

Geraldine looks in at the library door.

'I'm going up, darling,' she says. 'Good night, William.'

Larry gives her a kiss on the cheek.

'Don't stay up too late,' she says.

Alone again, William Cornford watches his son return to his agitated pacing.

'Larry, I've been meaning to ask you,' he says. 'Wouldn't it be easier for you and Geraldine if I were to get myself a place of my own somewhere?'

'But this is your house. We can't turn you out of your own house.'

'I would make the house over to you.'

'No, Dad. I don't want you to go.'

'How about Geraldine?'

'She's very fond of you. You know that.'

'She's very good to me,' says William Cornford. 'She's

554

always charming, and considerate. I'm not sure I know that she actually likes me.'

'Of course she does! Why wouldn't she?'

'I don't know. I'm sure it's all nothing. Forget I mentioned it.'

Larry is silent. He has stopped pacing. Some private train of thought leads him to ask a question he's long meant to ask.

'Dad, why did you never marry again?'

'Oh, Lord,' exclaims his father. 'What a question.'

'All I mean is, was it by choice?'

'These things are mostly a matter of chance, aren't they? You don't meet the right person. You work hard. You grow to like the life you have.'

'So it's not because you found your marriage was . . . was not what you'd hoped?'

'No, not at all. Your mother and I got along better than most. Her death was the most terrible shock. When something like that happens, you remember only the good times. I suppose it all depends what you expect marriage to be. It can't be everything, you know.'

He says this gently, sensing his son's reasons for raising the topic.

'No, of course not,' says Larry.

'Your mother never really understood why the company took up so much of my time. I expect Geraldine finds that, too.'

'No, I don't think so,' says Larry.

'Well, then. You're doing better than I did.'

'No,' says Larry flatly. 'I'm not.'

His father says no more.

'The truth is, Dad,' says Larry after a long moment, 'my marriage isn't working out at all.'

'I'm very sorry to hear that.'

'Perhaps I should get the McKinsey men in.' He gives a bitter laugh. 'They could install a monitoring system to make my marriage more efficient.'

'Are you quite sure you wouldn't rather have me out of your hair?'

'No, Dad. It wouldn't help. Things have gone too far.'

He looks up at the clock on the mantelpiece.

'I should be going on up.'

He turns and sees his father's familiar face, loving as always, puzzled as to what to say or do. It strikes him then how his father has been there all his life, the constant presence that has watched over him and protected him. There was a time when all he wanted was not to turn into his father, not to lead his life. There seemed to him, in his youthful arrogance, so little to show for it. What did the world care if a few more bananas were sold, or a few fewer? What sort of enterprise was that for a life? But now he sees matters differently. Not just because he's joined the company. It seems to him that every sphere of life can offer meaning, if lived properly. That there is as much nobility in living rightly among bananas as in an artist's studio. And that his father has lived rightly.

'Good night, then, son,' says William Cornford, lightly clasping Larry's shoulder with one hand.

Larry thinks then he would like to hug his father, but he doesn't make the move. He thinks he'd like to say something to him, along the lines of, 'I admire you so much, Dad. Any good there is in me I owe to you.' But the two of them are not accustomed to such exchanges, and the words don't come.

'Good night, Dad,' he says.

The report on Fyffes by McKinsey & Co recommends the closure of the current seventy-four store branches and their replacement with nine new strategically placed large modern facilities. It proposes that the current thirteen departments be rationalised to five, and that a unified budgetary control system be rigidly enforced across the company. Overall the report identifies potential savings of a remarkable 39% on current operating costs, largely by what it calls a 'shakeout of excess personnel'.

Larry presents the report to his board in Stratton Street.

'I calculate,' says Larry, 'that if we were to accept this report as it stands we would have to terminate over one thousand of our people. That is not the Fyffes way. I will not do it.'

The board applauds him. He invites his colleagues to work with him in the creation of a new report.

'If costs are too high we can bring them down. If there is over-manning in some departments, we can reallocate staff. But you know and I know this is a cyclical business, and it would be madness to lose experienced staff, staff we will dearly need later, just because we're at a low point in the cycle. There is another aspect to this also. These employees who we're advised to sack are men who have given their working lives to the company, men who've made it successful. They have families. We all know them. They're our friends. I measure the success of Fyffes not just by the profits we make, which vary year on year, but in the well-being of the families that our company supports. They have trusted us. I will not let them down.'

The board applauds again.

Larry is invited to present his response to the parent company's management in New Orleans.

Jimmy Brunstetter greets him as an old friend.

'Too long, Larry, too long. I'm going to take you out tonight and give you a dinner that will knock your socks off. Now you go and freshen up, and do what you have to do, because I have to run.'

Larry has brought his report, and holds it in his hand.

'Maybe you'd like to take a look at this.'

'Sure, sure I would. Only right now I'm late for the meeting I cancelled another meeting for on account of being late for that one, if you get my drift.'

And away he trots, head bobbing, smoking as he hurries to the elevator. His assistant takes over.

'Mr Brunstetter has booked a table at Broussard's for seven p.m., Mr Cornford. Is there anything more I can do for you now?'

Broussard's, in the heart of the Vieux Carré, is very grand. Ornate gold-framed mirrors line the walls. A statue of Napoleon holds pride of place.

'I got us a table in the courtyard,' says Jimmy Brunstetter, arriving fifteen minutes late. 'They looking after you okay?'

'Excellently, thank you,' says Larry.

The courtyard is wisteria-covered, mild in the evening air, and grandly relaxed. Brunstetter seems to know everybody, most notably the proprietor-chef Joe Broussard.

'So, Papa,' Brunstetter tells him, 'I got a VIP guest from England, and we're going to do him proud, right?'

'You said it,' beams the chef.

Brunstetter takes personal charge of Larry's menu choices.

'Fried oysters. You ever had fried oysters? You have not lived. So you'll have Oysters Broussard, you will die and go to heaven. Then, let's see, oh sure, Creole Ribeye, that's the one. You ever had Creole cooking? You have not lived. So what are you drinking? Tell you what, my friend. You order a Brandy Napoleon here, you know what they do? They bring it out and all the waiters sing the 'Marseillaise'. Gives you one hell of a kick the first time, but after that it's a pain in the ass, to be frank with you. But if you'd like? No? That's good for me.'

'So what's the Napoleon connection?' says Larry politely.

Brunstetter looks at him as if he's mad.

'This joint is French,' he says. 'Joe Broussard is French. Napoleon was French, right?'

'Yes,' says Larry. 'I believe he was.'

The food is superb. Two courses come and go and no mention is made of the reason for Larry's trip.

'So you heard Sam retired?' says Brunstetter.

'Yes,' says Larry. 'What's the new man like? I hope to meet him.'

'A good man. A good man. But Sam was something else. Big shoes to fill.'

'So is there a meeting planned for tomorrow? They didn't seem to know in your office.'

'Meetings? Don't tell me about meetings! My life is meetings. But we're here to enjoy ourselves, right? How about the brandy without the singing waiters?'

'I left a copy of my report with your assistant,' says Larry. 'Can I be sure he'll get it to the president?'

'Don't you worry about that. Don't you worry about anything. This is the VIP treatment. You're having a good time, right? Have a cigarette. You like something sweet? They got crêpes here, they roll 'em round cream cheese and brandy pecan stuffing, they float 'em in strawberry sauce, and all you have to do is open your mouth. You will die and go to heaven.'

The next day is a frustrating one for Larry. He waits in his hotel but no message comes. He calls Brunstetter's office, only to learn he's out of town for the day. He calls the president's office to confirm that they received his report, and is assured the matter is being attended to. Left to his own devices, reluctant to walk the streets in the sultry heat, he stays in his hotel room and thinks about Kitty. He thinks about how he kissed her and how he told her he loved her, and the petty annoyances of the day fade into nothing. Something so big has come so right that now all he can do is rest silent, grateful, in its presence.

In the end, because thoughts of Kitty so fill his mind, he writes her a letter. All his letters to her have been love letters, but this is the first time he has written openly about his love.

I don't know how to begin this letter. Whatever I write will sound either too faint to express what I feel or too presumptuous. What am I to you? One who has loved you for ten years and only kissed you once. One who wants only to spend the rest of his life with you and knows it's impossible. What a mess it is. What a wonderful ridiculous joyful mess! Everything is wrong but all I feel is happiness. I suppose from now on we're to lead lives of guilt and subterfuge but I don't care. It turns out I don't care about anything or anyone but you. I suppose this is how crimes of passion come about. As you see from the letter paper I'm in a grand hotel in New Orleans. They give me grand dinners, and a car and driver to take me wherever I want. And all I want is you. I long to say to my driver, Take me to Kitty. Then an immense American car would come swishing down the track to your house, and you'd get in the back seat with me, which is deep and soft and long, and . . .

He doesn't finish the letter. Nor does he send it. He knows he can't involve Kitty in a secret life she has to hide from Ed. But he keeps the letter, just in case the time should ever come when he can show it to her.

The next day a message comes from Jimmy Brunstetter. He would like to meet Larry at ten a.m.

Larry finds Brunstetter has the McKinsey report on his desk, but sees no sign of his own report. There's another man in the room who is only introduced as 'Walter'. This time Jimmy Brunstetter gets straight down to business.

'So the McKinsey boys did a fine job, right? We were pretty pleased with what they turned up. There's your company future right there, Larry. You seen the latest figures? We didn't see Geest coming, did we?'

'No, we didn't,' says Larry. 'But the market's potentially big enough for both of us.'

'Potentially.' Brunstetter glances at Walter. 'We like *actually*.' He taps the McKinsey report. 'This is *actually*.'

Larry made up his mind before leaving London to show no signs of his real feelings about the McKinsey report. After all, United have paid for it.

'The report is excellent in its analysis of costs,' he says. 'But it doesn't take account of company culture. You'll find in my report that there's another approach.'

'That's good, that's good,' says Brunstetter. Once more he taps the McKinsey report. 'The president and the board have signed off on this.'

'Signed off? I don't understand.'

'The recommendations of this report will now be implemented.'

'Implemented? I'm sorry, Jimmy, there's some misunderstanding here. I don't accept the McKinsey findings, and nor does my board.'

'I don't think you mean that, Larry.'

Walter is taking notes.

'Give me a year,' says Larry. 'You'll see in my report how I plan to tackle the issues the McKinsey report raises.'

'You'll make the redundancies?'

'I'll do all that's necessary.'

'Come on, Larry. We're old friends, we don't need to bull around. Fyffes needs to lose at least half its people. You know that. I know that. Are you going to do it?'

'I don't accept that cuts on that scale are needed,' says Larry. 'The company's in good health. In a year we'll be back in profit.'

Brunstetter turns to Walter.

'What do you reckon, Walter?'

'The question is very simple,' says Walter. As soon as he starts talking Larry knows he's a lawyer. 'The board of the parent company requires the report here to be implemented in full. Is Mr Cornford willing to do that or not?'

'Of course I'm not,' says Larry. 'I'm here to talk about the report. I'm here to talk about the best way forward for Fyffes. After all, I was born into this company. My grandfather created it. My father made it successful. I think I can claim to know more about how Fyffes works than either McKinsey or your board.'

'Well, there you have the problem,' says Brunstetter. 'You just put your finger right on the button, Larry. You were born into the company. Maybe the time has come for fresh blood.'

'Fresh blood?'

'The question is very simple,' says Walter. 'Will you or will you not implement the recommendations of this report?'

'Why should I?' He can't help himself. 'It's narrowly based, error-riddled, ill-conceived, and concerned with nothing but the bottom line.'

'We are concerned with the bottom line, Larry,' says Brunstetter.

'The company is greater than its profits.'

The two Americans greet this with silence.

'The question is very simple,' says Walter doggedly.

'No! It is not!' Larry is angry now. 'It's complex, and there are many ways forward. I will not accept this corner shop chiselling as any way to run a company.'

Another silence follows.

'Are we to understand,' says Walter, 'that you are offering your resignation?'

That's when Larry gets it at last. They want him out.

'No,' he says. 'Fyffes is my family. How do you resign from your family?'

He looks from one to the other. He realises now that it's Walter who's the power in the room.

'Are you telling me that if I don't agree to implement this report, I'm out?'

'Are we to understand,' says Walter, 'that you're offering your resignation?'

'Can I have time to think about this?'

'No, sir,' says Walter.

'No time? You ask me to choose between the jobs of a thousand employees of my company, and my own job?'

They give no answer to that.

Larry gives a laugh.

'It seems the question is very simple after all,' he says. 'You've already made up your minds. Half the staff are to go. The only remaining question is whether I go too.'

He turns and looks out of the window, seeing nothing of the street below, not wanting to see their faces.

'I believe this strategy to be profoundly mistaken,' he says. 'I can't run the company on this basis. If so many lives are to be destroyed by the shortsightedness and greed of you gentlemen in the United Fruit Company, then let mine be destroyed too. You're choosing to sink a fine company. As captain, I choose to go down with the ship.'

'Are we to understand,' says Walter, 'that you are offering your resignation?'

'Yes,' says Larry. 'You are.'

39

On landing at Heathrow, Larry finds his driver is not there to meet him. Exhausted by the flight, he considers taking a taxi home, but chooses instead to ask the cabbie to take him to Piccadilly. The company is in crisis and he feels an urgent need to be with his colleagues; almost as urgently, he does not want to have to explain to Geraldine how everything will now have to change.

London looks drab and poor after New Orleans. A smattering of rain brings out the black umbrellas on the pavements. Larry sits in the jolting cab, eyes closed, preparing himself for the shock he is about to deliver. He remains sure he has done the right thing, and is ready to pay the price. But so many others will pay too.

It's just past three in the afternoon when the taxi pulls up outside 15 Stratton Street. Larry hauls his suitcase through the heavy door into the dark lobby where Stanley the doorman has his cubbyhole.

'Mr Lawrence, sir!'

'Hello, Stanley. Sorry if I look like a tramp, I've come straight from the airport. I'll leave this with you.'

He drops his suitcase and makes for the stairs.

'Sir!' cries Stanley. 'Sir! I'm sorry, Mr Lawrence!'

Larry turns round.

'What is it, Stanley?'

'I'm not to admit you, sir.'

'Not admit me?'

'Your things have all been sent to the house, sir. Mr Angelotti is in your office now.'

'Mr Angelotti?'

'The new boss, sir.' Stanley can't meet Larry's eyes. 'He came Thursday.'

'Thursday!'

'And sir. Mr Lawrence, sir. We was all so sad to hear about Mr William, sir.' Now he looks up at Larry, and his eyes are blurry. 'They're saying it's all over for us, sir.'

Larry struggles to keep a grip on what he's hearing. As gently as possible he responds to the doorman.

'Nothing's over,' he says. 'Now tell me what's happened to my father?'

'Your father, sir? Didn't no one tell you? He passed away, sir. We heard this morning. I'm sorry, sir. He was a gentleman.'

Larry returns to the house in Campden Grove to find the situation entirely under control. Geraldine is superb in a crisis. Undertakers have been called. The library has been turned into a lying-in room. All the necessary people have been informed.

567

'I tried to reach you,' she says.

Larry is almost mute with shock and grief. Coming on top of the stress induced by his resignation, and the long flight home, this news comes close to breaking him.

'When? How?'

'Yesterday evening. They phoned with the news from the office. We were in the middle of dinner. Cookie called him to the phone. He spoke on the phone, then he came back to the dining room and said, "They've brought in an American to run the company." Then he put his hands forward on the table, as if to steady himself. Then he fell to the floor.'

'Dear Lord!' groans Larry.

'The doctor says it was a single big stroke. They say it must have been instantaneous.'

'Oh, Dad,' says Larry. 'Oh, Dad.'

'I'm so sorry, Larry. What can I do? Just tell me how I can help you.'

'You've been wonderful. You've done everything. I don't know. I can't think.'

Timidly she says, 'There'll have to be a funeral.'

'Yes. Yes, of course.'

'I can arrange it if you like.'

'Please. Arrange everything.'

He goes into the library, where the curtains are closed, and two candles burn on either side of an open coffin. His father lies in the coffin, looking like a poorly executed dummy. Larry kneels and prays, briefly. But his father is not here.

He climbs the stairs to the suite of rooms on the second floor his father has used for the whole of his life. The small sitting room opens onto a bedroom, a bathroom, a dressing room. Everything here is neat and tidy, as his father liked it. Larry came into this suite of rooms from time to time as a child, but has not been through the doors for twenty years or more. He closes the door onto the stairwell behind him, wanting to be alone in his father's presence. Almost delirious with exhaustion, he walks about the rooms, touching the items his father touched every day: his quilted dark-red bathrobe, his badger-hair shaving brush, the pomade with which he added a discreet shine to his greying hair. On the bedside table lie his rosary and his breviary, its silk marker in yesterday's place. He read Compline to himself every evening, Matins every morning. How can he be dead?

His father kept a prie-dieu in the little sitting room, though Larry never saw him kneeling at it. He must have done so in the night, the kneeler cushion is deeply indented.

Larry kneels, resting his elbows on the armrest, letting his head sink into his hands.

'Lord Jesus Christ,' he prays, 'take my beloved father into your loving arms. Let him know the peace and rest he deserves. Tell him I admired him so much. Tell him he was the only truly good man I've ever known. Tell him I loved him all my life. Tell him . . . tell him . . . Dad . . . don't leave me now. Don't leave me. Dad, I need you so.'

Then he lets himself cry, wetting his jacket sleeves with his tears.

In time the tears pass. He looks up and sees, through the open dressing-room door, on the wall above the chest of drawers, a blur of colour. He blinks and dabs at his eyes. He rises from the prie-dieu and goes into the dressing room. There, close beside the rail of suits his father wore that still carry his familiar smell, hang two small pictures on the wall. Two views of Mount Caburn, with Edenfield church in the foreground. Two pictures painted by a son who had disappointed his father. Bought from the Leicester Galleries five years ago, by a father who wanted only that his son should be happy.

Requiem aeternam dona eis Domine.

The Carmelite church is packed for the funeral. Looking around the pews Larry sees board members, directors, managers, storemen, porters, maintenance workers; ships' captains and crew men; company representatives from Jamaica, Honduras, the Canaries, Cameroon. These are the people his father served. These are the people he too has served in his turn. And now it's all over.

This is not how it should have been. His father's death should have been celebrated as the end of a good life, his achievements recognised and perpetuated. He built a company that he meant to outlast him. And when he took his leave, honourably, asking for nothing for himself, looters and wreckers rose up to destroy his heritage.

Who are these mighty masters of the world, these presidents of a far-off empire who look with their cold eyes on balance sheets and turn them into shrouds? Zemurray and Brunstetter and McKinsey and the rest, what God do they worship? In the name of what grand design do they exploit their workers and corrupt their governments?

Dies irae!

'Oh what fear man's bosom rendeth, when from heaven the Judge descendeth, on whose sentence all dependeth!'

So while others mourn, Larry rages. His anger is directed against himself, too. His father entrusted the company to him, and he promised to keep the company safe, and he failed.

I have killed my father.

Libera me, domine.

'Deliver me O Lord from eternal death on that awful day when the heavens and the earth shall be moved, when Thou shalt come to judge the world by fire.'

Sitting in the car following the hearse, with Geraldine by his side elegant in black, leading a convoy of cars from Kensington to Kensal Green, he feels entirely alone. Standing by the grave-side, watching the priest sprinkle the coffin with holy water, he wants to laugh at the absurdity of the whole charade.

My father isn't here.

'May his soul and the souls of all the faithful departed through the mercy of God rest in peace.'

What mercy? The good men are broken and the hard men endure. Here lies a man abandoned by God. He built a business, and that business was the well-being of others. They told him a slow buck is still a buck. But they lied.

No, don't rest in peace, Dad. Stand up before that heavenly throne and rage. Waken the anger of the Lord of Hosts. The time has come to judge the world by fire.

'What I don't understand,' says Geraldine, her voice soft and insistent, 'is why you resigned?'

'Hardly a resignation,' says Larry. 'Even while I was in that meeting, back in London they were clearing my office.'

'But you said you resigned.'

It's true. Larry clings to this version of events to salvage something of his honour. When asked to preside over the butchery of his father's company, he declined.

'I had no choice,' he says wearily.

The funeral is over. The guests are gone. The tall dark house is left to Geraldine and him.

'I'm sure you're right, darling,' says Geraldine, 'but I wish I could understand. Why couldn't you have stayed on, and done your best to make it not be so bad? I don't see what you meant to achieve by resigning.'

'Why should I keep my job and my comforts when the rest lose theirs? Because that would be all I'd be left with. The title, the salary, the car. Do you think I'd have been able to look my colleagues in the eye, as they cleared their desks and crept away?'

'Yes, I do see that, darling. But how are things any better this way? I don't see how it helps them having you out of a job too.'

Larry contemplates his wife. She seems to him to be

living in another universe, far away. Nothing touches her. She remains perfectly groomed.

'You miss the title, and the salary, and the car?'

'Am I wrong to worry?' she says. 'What will we live on? Do we even own this house?'

'Yes, Geraldine,' says Larry. 'We own this house. And the house in France. We have some shares in the company. We won't starve. And anyway, we're young still. We can work.'

'What will you do?'

'I don't know.'

Then he realises he does know; or at least a part of it. With this knowledge comes a release of kindness for his wife.

'Geraldine. Please. Let's not pretend any more.'

'Pretend what?'

But she's frightened. She knows too.

'Our marriage hasn't worked. It doesn't work. We don't make each other happy.'

She looks away. She's trembling.

'I've done my best,' she says in a whisper. 'I've tried and tried.'

'I know you have. It's not your fault. It's just who we are.'

'But Larry, we're still married. Nothing can change that.'

'We can divorce.'

She gasps, as if he's struck her.

'Divorce! No!'

'Then you can find someone you can really love. You're young. You're beautiful. You don't want to spend the rest of your life here, with me. You know you don't.'

'But Larry. The sacrament. We can't break it.'

'It's only words.'

Again that quick sharp gasp.

'Only words! And is the Church only words? Is the love of God only words? Are we all to do as we please, and think only of our own pleasure, and live and die like animals?'

'But Geraldine—'

The words pour out of her in a fervent stream, overwhelming him.

'What does it matter if you and I aren't as happy as we'd like to be? We can bear it. We know how to do our duty. We're married. For better, for worse, till death us do part. You swore it, and so did I. That's real, Larry. That's the rock on which we stand. Nothing can ever change that.'

She clasps his hands, willing him to join her.

'We're bound for eternity, Larry.'

'It's too late,' he says.

'Too late? How can it be too late?'

'I've gone too far. I'm sorry. I just can't go on any more.'

She lets go of his hands. Her voice changes, becomes bitter.

'It's Kitty, isn't it?'

'No—'

'You can never have her! She's another man's wife. I know you love her, I've always known, do you think I'm blind and deaf?' Now in her pain and anger her face contorts, becomes ugly. 'What do you think it's been like for me, seeing you dangling around her, playing your childish little games? But have I ever said a word? Not one word! How do you think I feel, knowing my husband loves another woman? But have I ever told you not to insult me with her presence in my house? Never! Not once! I am your wife. I know my duty. But do you know your duty? Because believe me, at the peril of your immortal soul, you must do your duty! You can't have her, Larry. Would you lose your immortal soul, would you burn in hell for ever, for one silly little woman?'

'Yes,' says Larry.

'Oh!' She buries her face in her hands. 'What's happened to you? What have you become?'

'You're right,' says Larry. 'I can't have Kitty. Even by losing my immortal soul. But this isn't about Kitty. It's about me, and you.'

She waits, her face in her hands. He no longer has any doubts. Somehow his father's death, the loss of the company, have set him free.

'You and I must part. For my sake, and for yours. I'll share all I have with you. I'll give you this house. You'll not be poor. We must each make new lives for ourselves.'

Geraldine begins to weep.

'I'm sorry that I'm not the man you thought I was,' says Larry. 'I'm sorry to let you down. I've let many people down. I'll try to do better in future.'

'Please, Larry.' The ecstasy gone now, and the bitterness. 'Please promise me one thing. Talk to a priest.'

'About my marriage? What does a priest know of marriage?'

'A priest knows the mind of God.'

'No one knows the mind of God,' says Larry. 'Not priests. Not the pope. Not even God. God has no mind. God is just our word for everything that is, and our hope that it has some meaning. But that's all it is. A hope.'

'You know you don't believe that.'

'Do I? Maybe I do, maybe I don't. Who knows what I believe any more? Everything's changing.'

She says nothing. He's not been looking at her, ashamed and afraid to meet her eyes. His whole body feels knotted and hard.

'Larry?'

'Yes?'

'I'm frightened.'

He looks at her then. She stands with her hands clasped before her, her head bowed, like a child come for punishment.

'There's no need,' he says sadly. 'No need.'

'What is it that's wrong with me? Why does no one love me?'

'That's not true. Not true.'

'Why am I all alone? What have I done to deserve such a punishment? Please tell me. I'll try not to do it again.'

'There's nothing, sweetheart. There's nothing.'

No offence. No remedy. The gentleness forced out of him by pity. But it changes nothing.

'Sometimes things don't work out. That's all.'

40

Kitty goes ahead of the others, with the girls running ahead of her.

'Is it here?' shouts Pamela. 'Is it here?'

Ed and Larry come behind, carrying the baskets with the food and the rugs. The car is parked in the lane in Glynde below. They are hunting out the place where they picnicked ten years ago.

'No,' calls Kitty. 'Further on. In the trees.'

It's a golden October day, and on all sides the tawny Downs reach rolling down to the patchwork of russet fields. Kitty is happy, because Larry has come, and because Ed is light-hearted. She looks back down the hill to see them climbing slowly after her, laughing together; just as it was all those years ago.

'Here!' cries Elizabeth. 'I've found it!'

The little girl stands on one side of the copse.

'It's all nettles!' says Pamela. 'Yuck!'

'A little further,' calls Kitty.

She remembers the place exactly. Nothing has changed. The trees rise up from the sloping land, their leaves more faded than they were then, but that was June and summer had just begun. She catches up with the girls and confirms the spot.

'I found it!' says Pamela.

'You did not!' says Elizabeth.

But the girls aren't really quarrelling. They're happy too, excited by the prospect of the picnic, and their father's company, and Larry's too.

The men join them, and lay out the tartan rug. Elizabeth at once sits down, right in the middle. The food comes out of the basket to whoops of delight.

'Treacle sandwiches! Meat!'

'It's cold lamb, darling.'

'Can I have cider, Mummy?'

'No, Pamela. There's orange squash.'

'Are you sure this is where we came?' says Larry.

'Totally sure. You were over there. I was here, with Louisa here.'

'Poor Louisa. It doesn't seem fair.'

'It isn't fair,' says Ed. 'When will you get it into your head that life isn't fair?'

Larry grins at Ed.

'What was it?' he says. 'Impulse and glory?'

'Something about an arrow in flight,' says Kitty.

'Dear God!' exclaims Ed. 'Did I really talk like that?'

Larry pours them all drinks and stands to make a toast.

'My dear friends,' he says. 'My dear friends' children.'

Pamela smiles up at him.

'You are funny, Larry.'

'You see me now, a poor bare forked animal—'

'You're not bare,' says Pamela. 'You've got your clothes on.'

'Be quiet. That's King Lear upon the heath. He's lost everything, just like me. No job. No father. No wife.'

'Did King Lear have a wife?' says Ed. 'I suppose there must have been a Queen Lear to produce those daughters. You don't hear much about her.'

'For heaven's sake!' complains Larry. 'Here I am baring my soul, and you keep interrupting.'

'Go on, Larry,' says Kitty.

'I am the thing itself,' says Larry, waving his mug of cider in the air. 'Unaccommodated man. Off, off, you lendings.' He looks down at the girls. 'In the play he actually does take off all his clothes at this point. I'll spare you that. My toast. Raise your glasses!'

They all do so.

'My toast is – to freedom!'

'To freedom!' they cry.

Then they settle down to eat their picnic.

'But Larry,' says Kitty, 'it's terrible about your job. You loved it so.'

'Gone,' says Larry, his mouth full of hard-boiled egg. 'Gone with the wind.'

'He's demob happy,' says Ed. 'It's because he's got away from Geraldine.'

'Eddy!' says Kitty.

'You know we couldn't stand her,' says Ed, unashamed.

'Geraldine was,' says Larry, waving a fork in the air. 'Geraldine is. Geraldine will be.'

Kitty bursts into laughter.

'So much for Geraldine.'

'So what are you going to do now?' says Ed. 'Live the life of the idle rich?'

'Not at all,' says Larry, indignant. 'I'm not idle enough. And actually, I'm not rich enough. I shall find work. I shall offer the sweat of my brow.'

'Yuck!' says Elizabeth, looking at Pamela to check she's got it right.

'Well, here's an idea,' says Ed. 'Kitty may have told you that my labours in the wine trade appear to have reached their natural end. So why don't you take over? You could buy me out of the partnership. I'd have money, you'd have a job.'

'When did you dream this up, Ed?' says Kitty, surprised.

'When Larry told us he'd been sacked.'

'I don't know anything about wine,' says Larry.

'Much like bananas,' says Ed. 'Except it grows in France, and ripens more slowly.'

'Well, I suppose it's worth a thought,' says Larry. 'But what will you do?'

'Oh, I'll find something.'

'Larry,' says Pamela, climbing onto his lap. 'Is it true you're not married to Geraldine any more?'

'I won't be soon,' says Larry.

'Does that mean you can marry me? When I'm older, of course.'

'I suppose it does.'

'You have to wait till I'm sixteen. That's only nine years.'

'But sweetheart, won't I be too horribly old by then?'

'Maybe,' says Pamela. 'We can decide then.'

'Yes, I think that's probably wise.'

'What about me?' says Elizabeth. 'Who can I marry?'

'You can marry Hugo,' says Ed.

'No,' says Pamela, 'I want Hugo as well.'

Everyone laughs except for Elizabeth.

'She always does that,' she says. 'She always takes everything for herself.'

When they've had all they want of the picnic they lie on their backs on the rug and gaze up at the passing clouds. Kitty lies between Ed and Larry, with Elizabeth half on top of her.

'We should go to the top of Caburn,' she says.

'You and Ed go,' says Larry. 'Like last time.'

'Would you like that?' Kitty says, turning her head to smile at Ed.

'Of course,' says Ed.

'I'm coming too,' says Pamela.

'Me too!' cries Elizabeth.

'No,' says Larry, 'I want all those who are going to marry me to stay here and practise.'

'Practise what?' says Pamela dubiously.

'Being married,' says Larry. 'I tell you to do things, and you don't do them.'

This goes down well. Both girls stay with Larry. Ed and Kitty climb the hill. As they go they hear the game begin.

'I go first,' says Larry. 'Pamela, make me a cup of tea.'

'Shan't!' cries Pamela joyfully.

They climb on, out of earshot.

'That's a good friend you have there, Ed,' says Kitty.

'I know it,' says Ed.

They walk to the end of the long ridge, and down the steep side of the ditch at the top, and up the other side to come out onto the summit. Here they stand, side by side, holding hands, looking over the immense view towards the sea.

'Remember how the park was full of huts,' says Kitty.

'And the harbour full of ships,' says Ed.

'I've never forgotten what you said.'

'What did I say?'

She looks at the looping river, and Newhaven beyond.

'You said the river's always running, until it meets the sea and can rest.'

'Well, I suppose that's true enough in its way.'

They gaze over the great sweep of Downs and sea in silence. Both are thinking how they kissed for the first time, standing here in the warm wind.

'I'm sorry you've not been happy,' Kitty says.

'Not your fault,' says Ed. 'Just how I'm made.'

'It feels like my fault.'

He takes her in his arms and smiles for her, just like the old Eddy did.

'You're my lovely angel,' he says. 'I love you so much.'

'And I love you, my darling.'

'I want you to be happy more than I want anything.'

'That doesn't matter,' she says. 'And anyway, I am happy now.'

'Will you kiss me?'

'Of course I will,' she says.

He kisses her. For a long time after the kiss has ended he holds her close, his head bent over her shoulder, his eyes closed.

Back at the farmhouse, the car unloaded, Ed wheels out his old bike.

'Just going for a spin,' he says.

He follows the road to Newhaven and through sleepy Seaford, down the long hill to Cuckmere Haven and up the other side, heaving on the pedals, to the high ridge over Friston. Then down again into the forest, and up again, tired now. He gets off halfway and pushes the bike. At the summit he climbs onto the saddle again and pedals down the road to Birling Gap. It's a long ride, the sun dropping slowly in the sky behind him, throwing his shadow before him. From Birling Gap the track runs unmade along the clifftop to Beachy Head. Here he dismounts and wheels the bicycle over the close-cropped turf. He lays the bicycle down, and takes off his jacket, and bundling it up, pushes it into the bicycle basket. In the breast pocket of his jacket there are two letters.

He stands looking round. Behind him the soft roll of Downland; before him the sea, ruffled by the wind, brownish-yellow near the land, grey-blue further out. There's a low brick structure by the cliff edge, the remains of a Lloyd's shipping watchtower, now converted into a viewing platform. Wooden benches are set inside its octagonal walls. On the outer wall there's a new metal plaque.

On this headland and the surrounding Downs in the years of the Second World War between 1939 and 1945, the men and women of the Allied Forces helped defend their country.

The plaque is in honour of the Royal Observer Corps, the RAF, the WAAF, the Home Guard, the Anti-Aircraft Defences.

This plaque also commemorates the epic Dieppe Raid in 1942, which was partly controlled from the radar station on this headland. Beachy Head is once more in peace. But the devotion and patriotism of those who operated on this stretch of Downland in Britain's greatest time of suffering will not be forgotten.

The plaque is dated October 16th 1949.
He reads, and gives a small wry smile, and moves on. He follows the cliff edge to a point where the chalkland forms a jagged projection. He stands here for a moment looking down at the red and white lighthouse. The breakers splash softly at its concrete base. The tide is in, the sea pushing against the foot of the great white cliffs five hundred feet below. He looks up, over the sea to the hazy horizon. Somewhere over there is Dieppe, and the beach where he thought he would die, but did not die.

Beachy Head is once more in peace.

He has been happy today for the first time in months; perhaps years. That's something.

There's a light wind blowing off the sea. He breathes in the salt air. He feels young again, and strong. The late afternoon sunlight gleams on the water, forming a bright broken road to the horizon.

Live like an arrow in flight. How he must be laughing, Rex Mundi, the king of the world. Only a few short steps to freedom.

He walks briskly towards the edge and jumps. As he falls, accelerating all the time, his arms reach out as if to slow his descent. Halfway down his body strikes the cliff, lacerating his side, tumbling him over. Near the bottom his flailing body hits the cliff again. So he hurtles on down to meet the yielding water and the unyielding rocks.

The letter to Larry reads:

> Dear Larry. I'm sorry but I can't do it any more. I've done all I can to provide for Kitty and the girls. Believe me, I've worked like a very devil. The business is in good shape. I don't expect most people will understand, but I think you might. You've known me long enough. The simple truth is life has long been a torment to me. I don't know why this should be so. The darkness is always there, waiting for me. I try to keep away from other people. I know my unhappiness is a burden and a sadness to them. In the

end, this is the only way I know to keep away for ever. And dear old friend, don't be angry with me for writing what I'm about to write. I want you to believe that I'm doing the little I can to make amends. I know you love Kitty, and have loved her from the first. I believe she loves you, without lessening her love for me. I've always known you could make her happy, and that I never will. In my selfishness I held on for too long. But now I know you're free to be with her, I must go. Don't pity me. Be happy for me. You have no idea how many times I've dreamed of this. Thank you, my friend, for your endless kindness to me. You're a good man, and a braver man than I can ever be. Love Kitty and my girls for me. You'll make a better job of it than I've ever done. Goodbye, dear friend. I'm not afraid of the darkness any more. Rest at last.

The letter to Kitty reads:

My only darling. Loving you has been the one good thing I've done in my life. Being loved by you has been a miracle to me. But we each have to live our own lives. I won't drag you down with me any more. Don't believe that your duty is to save me. I know how much I've hurt you. There's no remedy for that. So now I've decided to go. My dearest darling, you're so beautiful, so young, you have so much of your life ahead. Why should you live in the

darkness with me? I don't do this for you, I do it for
me, to be free at last. But now you will be free too.
My dearest, I know you love me. I've known it from
the start. But I know you love Larry too. No shame
in that. Who could not love Larry? Now that he too
is free, I can go. Love Larry, darling, he deserves
your love, and remember me, and love me too, and
know that I've found rest at last. Don't hate me for
leaving you. Don't be angry. Just say he did his best,
and when he could do no more he laid himself down
to sleep. Kiss the girls from me. Tell them if there's a
heaven after all, I'll be waiting for them. Tell them I
go with my head held high, still storming the fatal
beach, still the war hero. Tell them I'll love them for
eternity. As I'll love you. If we meet again it'll be in
a place where all things are known, and you'll
forgive me. Good night, my darling. I shall fall asleep
in your arms, and the hurting will be over.

41

Larry stays on at River Farm, taking charge of all the necessary arrangements. Ed's body is recovered by the coast-guards. After a short service in Edenfield church, through-out which Kitty remains silent and dry-eyed, the body is buried in the churchyard. The obituary notice in *The Times* is entirely taken up by the events of one day in August eight years ago that won Edward Avenell the Victoria Cross.

Pamela cries in her mother's arms, but Kitty hardly cries at all. Grief has paralysed her. At the same time she finds she can't forgive Ed for what he's done to them. She's angry that he believed what he was doing was best for her. Alone in bed at night she speaks to him, not shouting, bitter in her insistence.

'What gave you the right to walk away? What makes your suffering so much greater than everyone else's? How can you not see the damage you've done? You have oblivion. What about us? We have a sorrow that won't end. We have our failure to love you enough. We have your example before us for the rest of our lives, that unhappiness wins in the end.'

Larry makes no attempt to console Kitty, nor she him. He concentrates his energies on securing the family's finances, and helping Hugo with the wine import business. By the time Hugo asks him to become a legal partner in the firm he has already made himself indispensable.

'So now Ed's got what he wanted,' says Kitty. 'You're obliged to look after us, whether you want to or not.'

She doesn't refer to Ed's other bequest to them. Kitty feels numbed, trapped by Ed's final act, rendered powerless. The thought of profiting from his death is repugnant to her. Such a hurtful wasteful denial of life can have no good consequences.

Elizabeth, three years old, placid and good-tempered, cries for a while and then returns to her daily concerns. Her father had always been away for such long periods that little in the daily routine changes. Pamela moves on from grief to incomprehension. Neither of the girls has been told the truth about their father's death. He was out walking, they've been told, and he had an accident, perhaps a heart attack, and fell to his death.

'How is it an accident?' says Pamela. 'Why was he so close to the edge? I don't understand.'

There are no answers.

'We just don't know,' Larry tells her. 'It's a terrible thing to have happened. All we can do is help each other.'

'How?' says Pamela. 'How are we to help each other?'

'By loving each other,' says Larry.

'Will you love me and Elizabeth? Will you love Mummy?'

'Yes,' says Larry.

'Will you marry Mummy?'

'I don't know,' says Larry.

'I don't want you to,' says Pamela. 'I'm waiting till I'm grown up, then you can marry me.'

'All right,' says Larry.

Larry makes a pilgrimage of sorts to Beachy Head. He goes on his own. He has no way of knowing where Ed stood in that last moment of his life, but this seems to be the closest he can get to him now.

There are other walkers out on the bald grass. They throw him furtive looks. He knows what they're thinking. Is he a jumper? Will it happen now, the unstoppable unforgivable act of self-termination?

I could do it. They could do it. That's what grips the imagination. Just a few steps, and then a few more, and the story ends.

But for us the story hasn't ended.

My best and oldest friend. I dream of running after you, of arriving here on the cliff top just in time. There you stand, the deed not yet done, and I shout out to you, 'Wait!' You turn and see me, and you wait for me. I take you by one arm, I hold you tight, I say, 'Come home.' You smile that half smile of yours and step away from the cliff edge and we walk home together, you pushing your bike. There are two letters in your jacket pocket that will never be delivered.

I've loved you for so long. How could you leave me?

Larry has a visit from Rupert Blundell. He seems uncomfortable, which is to be expected, since they haven't met since the break-up of Larry's marriage to Geraldine. It turns out he's seen Ed's obituary.

'I was so shocked,' he says. 'I don't quite know why, but he always seemed to me to be immortal.'

'I sometimes felt that too.'

'He was' – Rupert reaches for the right word – 'debonair.'

'Some of the time,' says Larry.

'I suppose he meant to do it.'

'Yes.'

'Dear God. The poor boy.'

There seems to be nothing more to say.

'How's Geraldine?' asks Larry.

'Geraldine?' Rupert takes his glasses off and cleans them with one end of his tie. 'She's as you'd expect. Miserable. Angry.'

'I'm sorry.'

'She says there's another woman in the case.'

'Yes.'

Rupert puts his glasses back on and looks up at Larry.

'She feels what you've done is breaking one of the fundamental laws of the Church,' he says.

'I don't want to duck my share of the blame,' says Larry.

'But if you go by the laws of the Church you could say I have grounds for annulment.'

'Right.' Rupert passes one hand across his eyes. 'There was something of that sort before.'

'So I gather.'

'Just to be clear,' Rupert says after a pause. 'You're saying the marriage was never consummated.'

'Yes,' says Larry.

Rupert bows his head as if in prayer.

''Tis a consummation,' he murmurs, 'devoutly to be wished.'

He shakes his head. 'Hamlet's talking about death, of course. Ed Avenell, of all people.'

He looks up and meets Larry's puzzled gaze.

'People always turn out to be so much more complicated than we imagine.'

He rises.

'Well, I'd better be off.'

Larry walks with him to his car.

'One question. I ask because it rather obsesses my sister. What's become of your faith?'

'It seems to have fallen off the back of the truck,' says Larry. 'It's been a bumpy ride.'

Larry tells Kitty about Rupert Blundell's visit, and how Geraldine said there was another woman in the case. For the first time since Ed's death she bursts into laughter.

'Another woman in the case? Meaning me?'

'Who else?'

'Oh, Larry. I've never been the other woman before.'

'I've no idea where Geraldine got the idea from. I never said a thing to her.'

'Things don't need to be said.'

'Yes, they do,' says Larry.

Kitty smiles for him, and he knows then that the sadness will pass.

'I love you,' he says. 'All I want is to be with you. I want to go to sleep with you at night, and I want to wake up with you in the morning.'

She takes his hand and raises it to her lips and kisses it. Such an odd old-fashioned gesture, that speaks of her humility, her sadness, her gratitude.

'Here I am,' she says.

He folds her into his arms and they kiss, a true lovers' kiss that doesn't have to end, the kiss that has been waiting for so long. Then she remains warm and close in his arms, and lets herself cry. It's the first time she's cried since Ed died.

'I really did love him,' she says.

'So did I,' says Larry.

EPILOGUE

2012

Alice comes down on the morning of her last day to find the house silent, bathed in sunlight. Breakfast is laid on the terrace. Gustave appears with coffee and fresh bread. Alice eats and drinks alone. She wonders where her grandmother is.

When she's had her breakfast she gets up and walks across the grass to the trees, as she did on her first day at La Grande Heuze. Ahead of her stretches the forest, as far as the eye can see. There are no paths, or many paths. She walks a little way between the smooth trunks over the crunching ground. Her mind is lost in the past, haunted by ghosts.

Alone now among the trees, seeing only the same patterns of light and shade in every direction, it seems to her that with her new deeper past has come a deeper future. Her life extends infinitely backwards, but also forwards. The story her grandmother has told has shown her, as if from a great height, her own place in time. This immensity is consoling. One life can contain so much.

She returns to the house, and finds Pamela taking her breakfast on the terrace. She joins her, and drinks another cup of coffee.

'I was thinking,' her grandmother says, 'before you go home maybe we should visit the graves.'

'The graves?'

'They're buried here, in Bellencombre. My mother, and Larry. Larry made it to eighty-four, not such a bad age. I was with him when he died.'

'Here?'

'Yes, here. This was his house. This is where they lived in their later years.'

Somehow this comes as a surprise. After the long story of the distant past, it brings them shockingly close. I could have met them, Alice thinks. I could have known them.

'I adored Larry,' says Pamela. 'Really he was the one I wanted to marry.'

'But you married Hugo.'

'Yes. Poor Hugo. All frightfully Freudian, I suppose. Except I can't help thinking Freud got it all wrong. I was never in competition with my mother. I loved her far too much for that. No, it was all the other way about. I wanted to *be* my mother.'

They drive in to Bellencombre and visit the graveyard by the side of the church of St Martin. Here Kitty and Larry lie buried in the same grave. The headstone, looking disconcertingly new, bears only their names and dates. Kitty is named as Katherine Avenell.

'They were together for just over fifty years,' says Pamela.

'Were they happy together?' says Alice.

'Yes, they were very happy.'

'They deserved to be happy.'

'Why do you say that? Because Larry had waited for so long?'

'I suppose so,' says Alice.

'He wasn't just a sweet patient man waiting in the wings, you know. His love was the biggest thing in all our lives. It was like a blazing fire in the room. Love can be so ruthless, can't it?'

They walk back between the headstones to the waiting car. Alice is silent, thinking.

'Has any of that helped you?'

'In a way,' says Alice.

Why should love end? Once you start loving someone the love continues to grow and change for the rest of your life. But we're all so afraid, so unsure we're lovable, so fragile. We want love never to change.

I'm growing stronger now. I want a life of my own. I want adventures of my own. If one day I marry and have children, I want to be able to make that commitment as a woman who knows she deserves to be loved.

I come from a long line of mistakes. And one true love story.

AUTHOR'S NOTE

The historical background to the events in *Motherland* is as accurate as I have been able to make it. The account of the Dieppe raid is based on several first-hand reports, in particular by the war journalists A.B. Austin, Quentin Reynolds, and Wallace Reyburn.

My knowledge of the events surrounding Indian independence began when I was asked to write a screenplay based on Alex von Tunzelmann's excellent *Indian Summer*. For the details I have relied heavily on Alan Campbell-Johnson's diary of that time, published in 1951 as *Mission with Mountbatten*.

For background on William Coldstream and Camberwell College of Art in the post-war period I have been greatly helped by the first-hand memories of my mother-in-law, Anne Olivier Bell.

For the tale of Fyffes and the banana business I am indebted to my old friend David Stockley, whose father, grandfather and great-grandfather managed Elders & Fyffes for so many successful years. The business details are accurate; the character details of the fictional Cornford family are of course invented. I have relied also on A.H. Stockley's privately printed autobiography *Consciousness of Effort: The Romance of the Banana*, 1937; *The Banana Empire* by Charles Kepner and Jay Soothill, 1935; and *Fyffes and the Banana* by Peter N. Davies, 1990.

In matters of historical fact and tone of voice I have relied throughout on my wife, the social historian Virginia Nicholson, whose own books, particularly *Millions Like Us*, her account of the lives of women in the Second World War and after, have been an inspiration to me.

Readers may be interested to trace the links between the characters in *Motherland* and characters in my other Sussex-based novels. Alice Dickinson appears at the age of eleven in *The Secret Intensity of Everyday Life*, and again aged nineteen in *All the Hopeful Lovers*. Her father Guy Caulder also plays a part in both novels. George Holland's curious love life is discovered long after his death in *Secret Intensity*, where a very old Gwen Willis makes an appearance. Louisa, George Holland's wife, dies in 1955, after *Motherland* has ended and many years before *Secret Intensity* begins, but her son Billy has a large part to play in the later book. Anthony Armitage, the artist, appears as an angry old man in *All the Hopeful Lovers*. Rex Dickinson, briefly encountered in *Motherland*, is the absent husband of Mrs Dickinson, who appears in *Secret Intensity* and *The Golden Hour*. The farmhouse where Larry and Rex are billeted, and where Kitty and Ed later live, appears in all three earlier novels as the home of the Broad family. Edenfield Place appears in all four novels, at different stages of its existence. This great Victorian Gothic house is based on Tyntesfield, the Gibbs family mansion near Bristol, now owned by the National Trust.

Read on for an extract of
William Nicholson's
next novel . . .

RECKLESS

PRELUDE

Tea at Cliveden, September 1943

Rupert Blundell did not want to go to tea with the princess. He was unsure how to address her, and he was shy with girls at the best of times. Lord Mountbatten, his commanding officer, brushed aside his murmurs of dissent.

'Nancy wants some young people,' he said. 'You're a young person, and you're available.'

Rupert was twenty-six, which felt to himself both young and old. Princess Elizabeth was of course much younger, but being heir to the throne she was unlikely to be short of savoir-faire.

'And anyway,' said Mountbatten, 'you'll like Cliveden. They still have a pastry cook there, and it has one of the best views in England.'

So Rupert put on his rarely worn No.2 dress uniform, which fitted poorly round the crotch, and reported to COHQ in Richmond Terrace. A car was to pick him up from here and drive him to Cliveden, Lady Astor's country house.

'Very smart, Rupert,' said Joyce Wedderburn, passing through on her way back to her office.

'I'm under orders,' said Rupert glumly.

'Aren't the trousers a bit small for you?'

'In parts.'

'Well, I think you look very dashing.'

She gave him one of her half-smiles that he could never interpret, that suggested she meant something other than what she seemed to be saying. But Rupert liked Joyce. He could talk to her more freely than to the other girls. There was no nonsense about her, and she had a fiancé in the Navy, in minesweepers.

The car arrived: a Humber Imperial Landaulette, driven by one of Lady Astor's chauffeurs. Its rear hood was down, and sitting in the wide back seat was an American officer of about Rupert's own age. He introduced himself as Captain McGeorge Bundy, an aide attached to Admiral Alan R. Kirk, commander of the Allied amphibious forces.

'Call me Mac,' he said.

He revealed to Rupert that they were to represent the wartime allies at this tea party. There was to be a Russian too. All this in a crisp monotone, as if to impart the information in the most efficient way possible.

The Russian was news to Rupert.

'I've no idea what we're supposed to do,' he said. 'Have you?'

'I think the idea is the princess wants to meet people nearer to her own age,' said Bundy.

'What for?'

'Maybe it's a blind date.' Bundy smiled, but with his mouth only. 'How'd you like to marry your future queen?'

'God preserve me,' said Rupert.

Mac Bundy was trim and sleek, with sand-coloured hair brushed back smoothly over his high forehead. He wore wire-rimmed glasses. His navy-blue uniform had every appearance of being excellently cut. Looking at him, Rupert felt as he did with so many Americans that they were the physically perfected version of the model, while he himself was a poor first draft.

He shifted on the car seat to ease the itching in his trousers. The landaulette drove through Hyde Park, past the Serpentine. From where he was sitting he could see himself reflected in the driver's mirror: his long face, his thick-rimmed spectacles, his protruding ears. He looked away, out of long habit.

'So who got you into this?' said Bundy.

'Mountbatten. He's a friend of Lady Astor's.'

'Kirk fingered me,' said Bundy, adding in a lower tone, with a glance at the driver, 'His actual order was, "Go and humour the old bat."'

They exchanged details of their postings. Bundy confessed he owed his staff job to family connections.

'I wanted a combat posting. My mother had other ideas.'

His father, Harvey Bundy, was currently a senior adviser in the US War Department under Henry Stimson.

'So this princess,' he said. 'I hear she's all there.'

'All there?' said Rupert.

Bundy curved one hand before his chest.

'Oh, right,' said Rupert. 'I wouldn't know.'

He had never thought of the seventeen-year-old Princess Elizabeth as a sexual being.

'Don't worry,' said Bundy. 'I'm not going to wolf-whistle.'

Rupert looked at the passing shopfronts and was silent. Wartime was supposed to change things, break down the barriers. But even when the barriers were down, you had to do it yourself. No one was going to do it for you. There was no one you could talk to about these things. No one in all the world. About feeling ashamed. About wanting it so much.

The car emerged onto the Bayswater Road.

'I asked round for tips on meeting royalty,' said Bundy. 'Apparently you call her ma'am, and you don't sit until she sits.'

'Ma'am? The poor girl's only seventeen.'

'So what are you going to call her? Liz?'

'In the family she's called Lilibet.'

'How'd you know that?'

'Mountbatten told me.'

'Okay. Lilibet it is. Have another slice of pie, Lilibet. Want to take a walk in the shrubbery, Lilibet?'

Rupert glanced nervously at the back of the chauffeur's head, but he showed no signs that he was listening.

'Is that what you do with girls?' said Rupert. 'Take them into the shrubbery?'

'I'll be honest with you,' said Bundy. 'I'm no expert.' He leaned closer and spoke low. 'When I was twelve years old we went to Paris, and my mother took me to the Folies-Bergère. The way she tells it, I got bored by the naked girls and went outside to read a book.'

'And did you?'

'That's her story.'

The car was now turning into Kensington Palace Gardens. There on the pavement outside the Soviet embassy was a young Russian officer, standing stiffly, almost at attention.

'Our noble ally,' said Bundy.

The Russian had a square, serious face and heavy eyebrows. He gazed inscrutably on the open-backed car as it pulled up beside him.

'You are the party for Lady Astor?'

He sounded exactly like an American.

'That's us,' said Bundy. 'Jump in.'

He squeezed onto the seat beside them, and the car set off down Notting Hill Gate to Holland Park. His name was Oleg Troyanovsky. His father had been the Soviet Ambassador in Washington before the war, and he had been sent to school at Sidwell Friends. Within minutes he and Bundy had discovered mutual acquaintances.

'Of course I know the Hayes boys,' said the Russian. 'I was on the tennis team with Oliver Hayes.'

'So what are you doing in London?'

'Joint committee on psych warfare.' The wrinkles between his eyebrows deepened as he spoke. 'My father arranged it, to keep me away from the eastern front.'

'Check,' said Bundy. 'Privilege knows no boundaries.'

'And here we are, going to tea with a princess.'

They grinned at each other, bound together by a shared awareness of the absurdity of their situation. The car picked up speed coming out of Hammersmith and onto the Great West Road. The wind blew away their words, and conversation languished. They looked out at the endless line of suburban villas rolling by, and thought their own thoughts.

The war had gone on too long. It was no longer a crisis, with the excitement that crisis brings with it, and the promise of change. It had become an intermission. The phrase most often heard was 'for the duration'. Shops were closed 'for the duration'. Trains ran a restricted service 'for the duration'. Life had paused, for the duration.

Meanwhile, thought Rupert, my youth is slipping away.

Last month Mountbatten had accepted a new appointment, as Commander-in-Chief, South East Asia.

'You'll come with me, won't you, Rupert? I must have my old team round me.'

Rupert was more than willing to go. A brighter sun, a bluer sky. Maybe even a new dawn.

The landaulette turned off the main road at last and made its way up a wooded hill, through the pretty red-brick village of Taplow, and so to the great gates of Cliveden. A long drive wound through a wilderness of untended woodland, until quite suddenly there appeared before them a fountain, in which winged and naked figures sported round a giant shell. No water flowed, and the angels, or goddesses, wore an embarrassed air, as if sensing that their nakedness was no longer appropriate. The car made a sharp left turn. Ahead lay a broad beech-lined avenue, at the end of which stood a cream-coloured palace.

'Ah!' sighed Troyanovsky. 'What it is to be rich!'

'Not rich,' said Bundy. 'Very rich. They don't come richer than the Astors.'

The house grew as they approached it, revealing on either

side of the central block two curving wings, reaching out as if to embrace the awed visitor. To the right there rose an ornate water tower, faced with a clock that had perhaps once been gold, but was now a tarnished brown. The grass of the flanking lawns grew long round ancient mulberry trees.

The chauffeur drew the car to a stop before the porte cochère, and a butler emerged from the house to greet them.

'Her ladyship and her Royal Highness will join you shortly, gentlemen.'

They followed the butler into an immense oak-panelled hall, hung with faded tapestries. At one end, before a carved stone fireplace, tea had been laid out on two small tables. To the left of the fireplace hung a full-size portrait of a young woman in a gauzy pale-blue dress, her hands clasped behind her back, her head turned coquettishly to the viewer.

'That is Nancy Astor,' said Bundy with crisp authority.

'But she's beautiful!' exclaimed Troyanovsky. He stood back to appreciate her, evidently as a woman rather than as a work of art.

'She was younger then, of course.'

Rupert was puzzled by the painting. The pose was unusual: a slight forward tilt from the waist, as if she was on the point of running away.

Bundy examined the waiting tea. There was fruitcake topped with marzipan. A silver dish with a lid stood warming on a spirit lamp. He lifted the lid to discover a nest of small scones.

'What do we have to do to deserve this?'

'We could link arms and perform a dance,' said Troyanovsky gravely. It took the others a moment to realise he was making fun. 'Or perhaps we could sing together, to represent the harmony of the Alliance.'

They grinned at that.

'And youth,' said Rupert. 'We're here to represent youth.'

'I'm not young,' said Bundy. 'Who wants to be young? I want to be a grown man, in charge of my own destiny.'

'Only an American could say that,' said Troyanovsky. 'We who come from older civilisations know that we will never be in charge of our own destinies.'

He looked to Rupert as he spoke, his heavy brow wrinkling. Rupert nodded to be friendly, unsure whether or not he agreed.

'But you know what?' said Bundy. 'I'm all for this idea of us singing together.'

He started to croon the current hit by the Andrews Sisters, making small hand movements before him in the air.

> 'There were three little sisters
> Three little sisters
> And each one only in her teens—'

A door opened, and he fell silent. In swept a small tornado of a woman, followed a few paces behind by a young girl.

'Oh my God! They're here already! Make yourselves at home, boys! Which one of you is Bundy?'

Mac Bundy presented himself.

'I knew your father, I knew your mother, I warned them

607

not to marry, and if they had to marry, not to produce any children. Bound to be morons. Are you a moron?'

'No, Lady Astor,' said Bundy, smoothly unperturbed. 'I don't believe I am.'

'Humph. We'll see about that.'

She was in her mid-sixties, her face now bony, but her bright blue eyes as brilliant as in the portrait. She held her head high, and moved in hops and starts, as if unable to contain the energy within her. Her voice was thin and crackly, half American, half English.

'This is just an informal get-together. No need to stand on ceremony.'

The three young officers were introduced to the young girl, who turned out to be Princess Elizabeth. She was even smaller than Lady Astor, and had wavy dark-brown hair, and very white skin. Her modest knee-length white dress, patterned with pink flowers, could not disguise the fact that she was, as Bundy had put it, 'all there'.

'Come along, Lilibet,' said Lady Astor. 'You sit here. You know no one can sit down until you've sat down. God, what a country! How I've stood it all these years I'll never know.'

They sat down. Their hostess poured out tea, talking as she did so.

'I've told Lilibet that family of hers keeps her far too shut away, she never meets anyone at all, so I promised her some young men, and here you are. You must help your-selves to the scones. It was Lilibet's idea to invite our allies, and a very good idea if I may say so. You three' – teapot in mid-air, piercing blue eyes fixed on the young men – 'you are the future of the world. You must make a better job of it than we have.'

'With Her Royal Highness's help,' said Bundy, leaning his upper body forward as if attempting a bow while sitting down.

'Oh, the royals can't do a thing,' said Lady Astor. 'No one pays the slightest attention to a word they say. Of course, everyone loves them, but only in the way you love a family pet.' She reached out one hand to pat the shy young princess. 'Do you mind me going on like this, darling? Are you shocked?'

'Not at all,' said the princess in a small clear voice. 'But I'd like to hear what the gentlemen have to say.'

So she wasn't such a little girl after all.

'That's telling me,' said Lady Astor. 'What have you got to say, boys?'

There followed a brief silence.

'Well, ma'am,' said Bundy. 'I think we all agree that this war will be over sometime next year.'

'Oh, I do hope so,' said the princess. 'That's what the officers at Windsor tell me too.'

Rupert was looking at the princess's hands. Her hands were so delicate, the nails varnished a very pale pink. She was interlacing her fingers in her lap, nervously squeezing them.

'I'm so bored by the war,' said Lady Astor. 'Can't we talk about something else?'

'I'm not sure I would say I was bored exactly,' said the princess.

Her enunciation was so clear that everything she said sounded carefully considered. Her earnest gaze fell on Rupert, as if inviting him to complete her thought.

'It's a hard feeling to describe,' said Rupert. 'One feels bored and frightened at the same time. And then beneath it all there's this feeling that one's real life is waiting to begin.'

The princess looked at him in surprise.

'Yes,' she said.

Then she smiled. Rupert realised for the first time that she was pretty.

'It's all right for you young people,' said Lady Astor with a grunt. 'Some of us are waiting for our life to end.'

'Not for many years yet, I hope,' said Bundy.

'Look at that!' She pointed at the portrait hanging by the fireplace. 'I have that staring at me every day, reminding me how old I am.'

'But it's a wonderful portrait,' said Troyanovsky. 'I have been admiring it.'

'Don't you think I'm standing in an odd way? It's because Sargent had this idea of painting me with my little boy on my back.' She stood up and assumed the same pose as in the painting, hands clasped behind her back. 'But Bill was only one year old at the time, and he just wouldn't keep still, so Sargent painted him out.'

'It is a very fine portrait,' said the princess, gazing at it.

'I can't look at it any more,' said Lady Astor. 'Don't grow old, my dear. It's too tiresome.'

'I would like to be a little older,' said the princess.

As she spoke she glanced at Rupert. This gave him an odd feeling. It was as if some secret understanding had sprung up between the two of them.

The princess turned to Troyanovsky.

'Tell me about Russia,' she said. 'I know so little about your country.'

'Well, ma'am,' said Troyanovsky, 'if I'm to tell you about my country I must speak about the war. We have been fighting a life and death battle.'

'Yes, I know,' said the princess. 'We all so admire Mr Stalin.'

'Humph!' said Lady Astor. 'I met Joe Stalin.'

'Did you?' said Troyanovsky, much surprised. 'When was that?'

'1931. I went to Russia with George Bernard Shaw. We were both introduced to Uncle Joe. Shaw was all over him, of course. When it came to my turn, I said, "Mr Stalin, why have you slaughtered so many of your own people?"'

The Russian's teacup froze halfway to his lips.

'What did he reply?'

'Some nonsense about defending the revolution. What could he say? The man's a mass murderer.'

Troyanovsky was silent. The groove deepened between his eyebrows.

'The Russians are fighting like lions,' said Bundy. 'We owe them a great debt.'

'The revolution is still young,' Troyanovsky said.

'I hope,' said the princess, speaking earnestly, 'that after the war we can all go on being friends.'

'I believe our nations can and must be friends, ma'am,' said Bundy. 'I think we've all had our fill of hatred. We may not always see things the same way, but I believe we can agree to disagree.'

'I expect you'll think I'm very naive,' said the princess, 'but I do so much want this to be the last war we ever have to fight.'

'There will always be war,' declared Troyanovsky.

'But why?'

'Human nature, ma'am.'

'I disagree,' said Bundy. 'I believe we have the power to control our impulses.' Quite suddenly he became vehement. 'There's evil in all of us, no doubt about that, but we must grow up, and accept it, and manage it. We have to live with our imperfections. You people' – this was to the Russian – 'you're perfectionists. You believe you're creating the perfect society. I think that's dangerous. It permits your leaders to take extreme measures.'

'War is an extreme measure, I think.' The Russian nodded his big head, frowning. 'In the West, you are pragmatists. We are idealists. But you know, in spite of this, we want much the same as you. To eat. To sleep safe in our beds. To go dancing. To talk late into the night about the wrongs of the world.'

'So after the war,' said the princess, 'when we who are young now are old enough to influence the affairs of the world, let's agree that we'll have no more wars.'

'Hear, hear!' said the young officers, raising their teacups.

Rupert was touched by the young princess's gentle

diplomacy. He sensed that it was more than good manners, that she was genuinely distressed by conflict. What a curious mixture she was, he thought. Scrupulous in the performance of her duty; her face so serious, but still lit by the lingering innocence of childhood.

Lady Astor now rose. This was the cue for the gentlemen to rise.

'I must show our guests the view from the terrace,' she said.

The princess rose, smoothing her dress down as she did so. Lady Astor led the way across the adjoining library and out through French windows.

Rupert found the princess was by his side.

'So you feel your real life is waiting to begin,' she said to him, speaking softly.

'I do, ma'am,' he said.

'And what will it be, this real life?'

'I wish I could tell you it'll be a life of honourable service to my country,' said Rupert. 'But I'm afraid all I mean is love.'

'Ah, love.'

They came out onto the terrace.

'There it is,' said Lady Astor with a sweep of one arm. 'England. The land we're fighting for.'

The view was indeed spectacular. Below the terrace stretched a long formal lawn, laid out in two parterres. To the east rose a wooded hill. The river flowed round the foot of this hill, concealed by trees, here and there glinting into view. Beyond the river the land stretched for miles to the south, to Maidenhead and beyond. Above it all rose a peaceful late-afternoon sky.

'Did you know,' said Lady Astor, 'that the first ever performance of "Rule Britannia" took place right here? Two hundred years ago, at a big party down there, given by the Prince of Wales.'

She pointed at the long lawn below them.

'So beautiful, so untouched by war,' said Troyanovsky. 'Hitler could have marched his armies up this valley. Instead he turned them on my homeland.'

They strolled slowly down the length of the terrace. Once again Rupert found himself by the princess's side.

'So you're not married, Captain Blundell?'

'No, ma'am.'

'That is a happiness still to come.'

A conventional enough remark, but there was a wistfulness to her tone.

'I hope so, ma'am.'

She then turned to make conversation with Bundy, and Rupert was left with his thoughts.

'There's someone for everyone, Rupert,' his mother used to tell him. But all you had to do was look around you to know this was not true. Add together the solitary young, the unmarried, the divorced, the widowed and the solitary old, and it was hard not to conclude that loneliness was the natural condition of humanity.

It was now time for the princess to return to Windsor Castle. Her detective appeared as if by magic.

'I'm ready, Mr Giles,' she said.

She shook hands with each of the young officers.

'Remember,' she said. 'No more wars.'

Lady Astor accompanied the princess to her car. Left alone, the young men relaxed. They stood looking out over the great view, reluctant to leave.

'So where do you go next, Rupert?' said Bundy.

'India. Mountbatten's taking command out there.'

'Me, I'm in London until the second front.'

'Pray it may come soon,' said the Russian.

'My dad says one more year,' said Bundy, 'and it'll all be over.'

Troyanovsky took out a pack of cigarettes and offered them to the others. They both declined. He lit up, and inhaled deeply.

'Your princess,' he said to Rupert, 'she is charming.'

'I agree,' said Rupert. 'I thought she was lovely.'

'No life for a girl, though,' said Bundy. 'She should be out every night dancing, not fretting over the future of the world.'

'Leave that to Lady Astor,' said Rupert.

They laughed at that. Then the Russian shook his head.

'What she said to Stalin, that I find it hard to believe.'

'But she's right,' said Bundy.

Troyanovsky puffed on his cigarette, frowning.

'The day will come,' he said slowly, 'when you will ask yourself not what is right, but what is possible.'

'Who's the pragmatist now?' said Bundy.

'I think I can claim that honour,' said Rupert, peace-making. 'We British have a long history of calling a spade a spade, and then getting some other fellow to do the digging.'

Bundy smiled his smile at that.

'But your princess,' said Troyanovsky, 'what she said to us, that was good. No more wars.'

'We're all with you there,' said Bundy.

'So we must make it be so,' said the Russian. 'We three.'

He put out one large hand. Rupert understood his meaning, and clasped it. After a moment Bundy put his hand on top of theirs.

A solitary plane appeared in the far distance and buzzed slowly across the sky. The sun dropped below the clouds and threw shafts of golden light over the landscape. Rupert felt a sudden rush of fellow feeling for the other two. Partly it was this odd triple hand-clasp that they seemed unable to break, and partly the conviction that such a moment would never come again. There really was a symbolic power to their presence, joined together on the long terrace, looking out over England.

'No more wars,' said Rupert. 'Wouldn't that just be something?'